KEY TO WORLD MAP PAGES

- Large scale maps
  (> 1:2 500 000)
- Medium scale maps
  (1:2 800 000–1:9 000 000)
- Small scale maps
  (< 1:10 000 000)

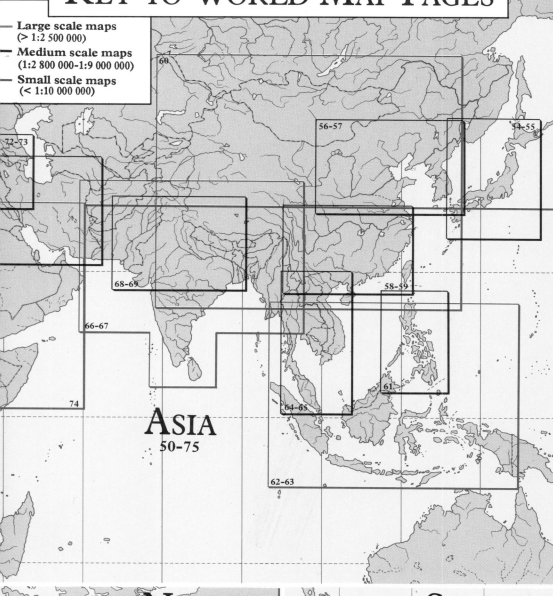

ASIA
50–75

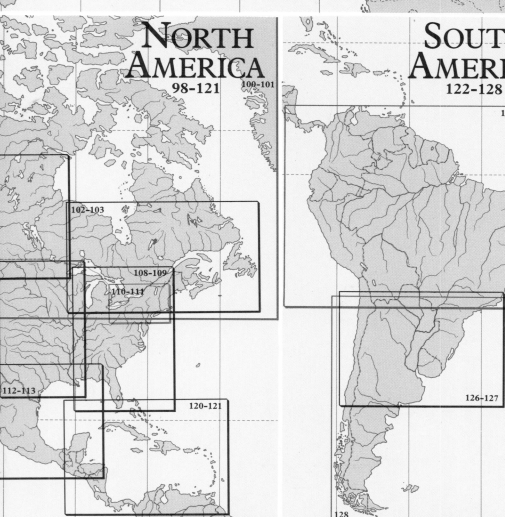

NORTH AMERICA
98–121

SOUTH AMERICA
122–128

COUNTRY INDEX

Country	Page	Country	Page
Afghanistan	66	Kuwait	70–71
Albania	40	Kyrgyzstan	50
Algeria	78		
Angola	84–85	Laos	64
Argentina	126, 128	Latvia	46
Armenia	73	Lebanon	75
Australia	92–95	Lesotho	88–89
Austria	26–27	Liberia	82
Azerbaijan	73	Libya	79
		Lithuania	46
Bahamas	120–121	Luxembourg	17
Bahrain	71		
Bangladesh	67	Macedonia	40
Barbados	121	Madagascar	89
Belarus	46–47	Malawi	87
Belgium	17	Malaysia	62–63
Belize	120	Mali	78, 82–83
Benin	83	Malta	36
Bhutan	67	Mauritania	78, 82
Bolivia	124	Mauritius	77
Bosnia-Herzegovina	29, 40	Mexico	118–119
Botswana	88–89	Moldova	43
Brazil	124–127	Mongolia	60
Brunei	78	Morocco	78
Bulgaria	40–41	Mozambique	85, 87
Burkina Faso	82–83		
Burma	67	Namibia	88
Burundi	86	Nepal	69
		Netherlands	17
Cambodia	64–65	New Zealand	91
Cameroon	84	Nicaragua	120
Canada	100–101	Niger	83
Central African Republic	84	Nigeria	83
Chad	79	Northern Ireland	15
Chile	124, 128	Norway	8–9
China	56–60		
Colombia	124	Oman	74
Congo	84		
Congo, Dem. Rep. of the	84–85	Pakistan	68
Costa Rica	120	Panama	120
Croatia	29, 42	Papua New Guinea	90
Cuba	120–121	Paraguay	126–127
Cyprus	36	Peru	124
Czech Republic	26–27	Philippines	61
		Poland	44–45
Denmark	11	Portugal	34–35
Djibouti	74	Puerto Rico	121
Dominican Republic	121	Qatar	71
		Romania	42–43
Ecuador	124	Russia	50–51
Egypt	80	Rwanda	86
El Salvador	120		
England	12–13	Saudi Arabia	74
Equatorial Guinea	84	Scotland	14
Eritrea	80–81	Senegal	82
Estonia	46	Sierra Leone	82
Ethiopia	74, 81	Singapore	65
		Slovak Republic	27
Fiji	91	Slovenia	29
Finland	8–9	Somali Republic	74
France	18–21	South Africa	88–89
French Guiana	125	Spain	32–35, 37
		Sri Lanka	66
Gabon	84	Sudan	79, 81
Gambia	82	Surinam	124–125
Georgia	73	Swaziland	89
Germany	24–25	Sweden	8–9
Ghana	82–83	Switzerland	25
Greece	38–41	Syria	72–73
Greenland	4		
Guatemala	120	Taiwan	59
Guinea	82	Tajikistan	50
Guinea-Bissau	82	Tanzania	86–87
Guyana	124	Thailand	64–65
		Togo	83
Haiti	121	Trinidad and Tobago	121
Honduras	120	Tunisia	78–79
Hungary	42	Turkey	72–73
		Turkmenistan	50
Iceland	8		
India	66–69	Uganda	86
Indonesia	62–63	Ukraine	47
Iran	70–71	United Arab Emirates	71
Iraq	70–71	United Kingdom	
Irish Republic	15	USA	
Israel	75	Uruguay	
Italy	28–31	Uzbekistan	
Ivory Coast	82		
		Venezuela	
Jamaica	120	Vietnam	
Japan	54–55		
Jordan	75	Wales	
Kazakstan	50	Yemen	
Kenya	86	Yugoslavia	
Korea, North	57		
Korea, South	57	Zambia	8
		Zimbabwe	

PHILIP'S

CONCISE WORLD ATLAS

TENTH EDITION

IN ASSOCIATION WITH
THE ROYAL GEOGRAPHICAL SOCIETY
WITH THE INSTITUTE OF BRITISH GEOGRAPHERS

THE EARTH IN SPACE
Cartography by Philip's

Text
Keith Lye

Illustrations
Stefan Chabluk

Star Charts
John Cox
Richard Monkhouse

PICTURE ACKNOWLEDGEMENTS
Robert Harding Picture Library /PHOTRI 13, /Bill Ross 41, /Adam Woolfitt 43
Hutchison Library /Melanie Friend 47, /John Hatt 46
Image Bank /Peter Hendrie 20, /Daniel Hummel 34, /Image Makers 8 top, /Pete Turner 39
Images Colour Library Limited 15
Japan National Tourist Organisation 45
NASA/Galaxy Picture Library 8 bottom left
NPA Group, Edenbridge, UK /EROS 48
Panos Pictures /Howard Davies 35
Chris Rayner 19 top
Rex Features /SIPA Press /Scott Andrews 12
Science Photo Library /Martin Bond 14, /CNES, 1992 Distribution Spot Image 27 top, /Luke Dodd 3, 6, /Earth Satellite Corporation 25 bottom, /NASA 9 centre right, 9 top, 22, 23, 24, /David Parker 26, /Peter Ryan 27 below, /Jerry Schad 4, /Space Telescope Science Institute /NASA 9 centre left, 9 bottom right, /US Geological Survey 8 centre right
Space Telescope Science Institute /R. Williams /NASA 2
Starland Picture Library /NASA 8 centre left
Still Pictures /Francois Pierrel 28, /Heine Pedersen 31, 40
Tony Stone Images 33, /Glen Allison 38, /James Balog 16, /John Beatty 21, /Neil Beer 30, /Kristin Finnegan 11, /Jeremy Horner 42, /Gary Norman 36, /Frank Oberle 25 top, /Dennis Oda 17, /Nigel Press 37, /Donovan Reese 18, 19, /Hugh Sitton 32, /Richard Surman 44, /Michael Townsend 29, /World Perspectives 10
Telegraph Colour Library /Space Frontiers 9 bottom left

Published in Great Britain in 2000
by George Philip Limited,
a division of Octopus Publishing Group Limited,
2–4 Heron Quays, London E14 4JP

Copyright © 2000 George Philip Limited

Cartography by Philip's

ISBN 0–540–07892–1

A CIP catalogue record for this book is available from the British Library.

Printed in China

Details of other Philip's titles and services can be found on our website at:
www.philips-maps.co.uk

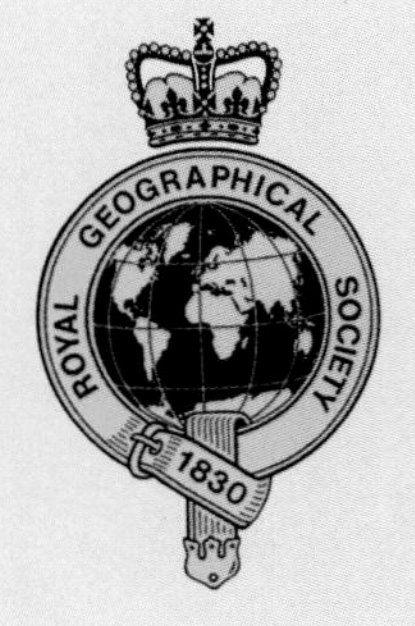

Philip's is proud to announce that its World Atlases are now published in association with The Royal Geographical Society (with The Institute of British Geographers).

The Society was founded in 1830 and given a Royal Charter in 1859 for 'the advancement of geographical science'. It holds historical collections of national and international importance, many of which relate to the Society's association with and support for scientific exploration and research from the 19th century onwards. It was pivotal in establishing geography as a teaching and research discipline in British universities close to the turn of the century, and has played a key role in geographical and environmental education ever since.

Today the Society is a leading world centre for geographical learning – supporting education, teaching, research and expeditions, and promoting public understanding of the subject.

The Society welcomes those interested in geography as members. For further information, please visit the website at: www.rgs.org

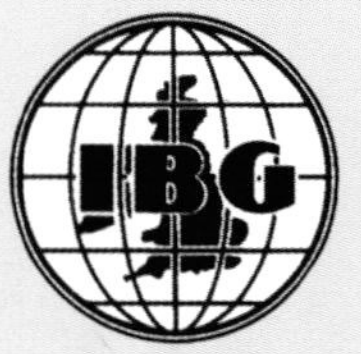

Philip's World Maps

The reference maps which form the main body of this atlas have been prepared in accordance with the highest standards of international cartography to provide an accurate and detailed representation of the Earth. The scales and projections used have been carefully chosen to give balanced coverage of the world, while emphasizing the most densely populated and economically significant regions. A hallmark of Philip's mapping is the use of hill shading and relief colouring to create a graphic impression of landforms: this makes the maps exceptionally easy to read. However, knowledge of the key features employed in the construction and presentation of the maps will enable the reader to derive the fullest benefit from the atlas.

MAP SEQUENCE

The atlas covers the Earth continent by continent: first Europe; then its land neighbour Asia (mapped north before south, in a clockwise sequence), then Africa, Australia and Oceania, North America and South America. This is the classic arrangement adopted by most cartographers since the 16th century. For each continent, there are maps at a variety of scales. First, physical relief and political maps of the whole continent; then a series of larger-scale maps

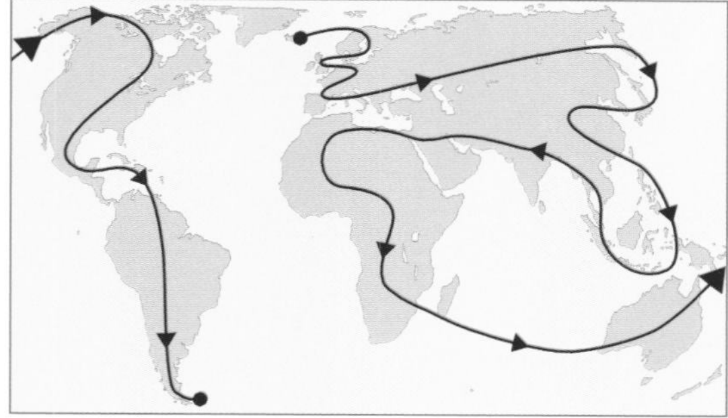

of the regions within the continent, each followed, where required, by still larger-scale maps of the most important or densely populated areas. The governing principle is that by turning the pages of the atlas, the reader moves steadily from north to south through each continent, with each map overlapping its neighbours. A key map showing this sequence, and the area covered by each map, can be found on the endpapers of the atlas.

MAP PRESENTATION

With very few exceptions (e.g. for the Arctic and Antarctic), the maps are drawn with north at the top, regardless of whether they are presented upright or sideways on the page. In the borders will be found the map title; a locator diagram showing the area covered and the page numbers for maps of adjacent areas; the scale; the projection used; the degrees of latitude and longitude; and the letters and figures used in the index for locating place names and geographical features. Physical relief maps also have a height reference panel identifying the colours used for each layer of contouring.

MAP SYMBOLS

Each map contains a vast amount of detail which can only be conveyed clearly and accurately by the use of symbols. Points and circles of varying sizes locate and identify the relative importance of towns and cities; different styles of type are employed for administrative, geographical and regional place names to aid identification. A variety of pictorial symbols denote landscape features such as glaciers, marshes and coral reefs, and man-made structures including roads, railways, airports, canals and dams. International borders are shown by red lines. Where neighbouring countries are in dispute, for example in parts of the Middle East, the maps show the *de facto* boundary between nations, regardless of the legal or historical situation. The symbols are explained on the first page of the World Maps section of the atlas.

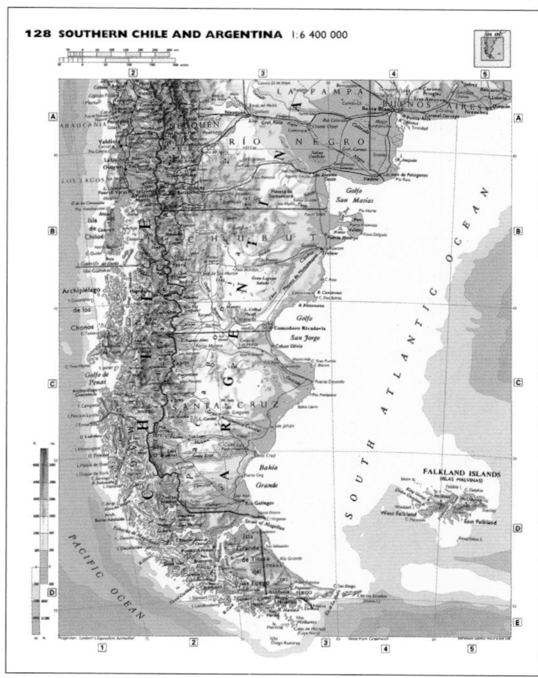

MAP SCALES

1:16 000 000
1 inch = 252 statute miles

The scale of each map is given in the numerical form known as the 'representative fraction'. The first figure is always one, signifying one unit of distance on the map; the second figure, usually in millions, is the number by which the map unit must be multiplied to give the equivalent distance on the Earth's surface. Calculations can easily be made in centimetres and kilometres, by dividing the Earth units figure by 100 000 (i.e. deleting the last five 0s). Thus 1:1 000 000 means 1 cm = 10 km. The calculation for inches and miles is more laborious, but 1 000 000 divided by 63 360 (the number of inches in a mile) shows that 1:1 000 000 means approximately 1 inch = 16 miles. The table below provides distance equivalents for scales down to 1:50 000 000.

LARGE SCALE		
1:1 000 000	1 cm = 10 km	1 inch = 16 miles
1:2 500 000	1 cm = 25 km	1 inch = 39.5 miles
1:5 000 000	1 cm = 50 km	1 inch = 79 miles
1:6 000 000	1 cm = 60 km	1 inch = 95 miles
1:8 000 000	1 cm = 80 km	1 inch = 126 miles
1:10 000 000	1 cm = 100 km	1 inch = 158 miles
1:15 000 000	1 cm = 150 km	1 inch = 237 miles
1:20 000 000	1 cm = 200 km	1 inch = 316 miles
1:50 000 000	1 cm = 500 km	1 inch = 790 miles
SMALL SCALE		

MEASURING DISTANCES

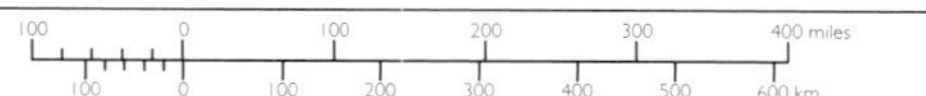

Although each map is accompanied by a scale bar, distances cannot always be measured with confidence because of the distortions involved in portraying the curved surface of the Earth on a flat page. As a general rule, the larger the map scale (i.e. the lower the number of Earth units in the representative fraction), the more accurate and reliable will be the distance measured. On small-scale maps such as those of the world and of entire continents, measurement may only

be accurate along the 'standard parallels', or central axes, and should not be attempted without considering the map projection.

MAP PROJECTIONS

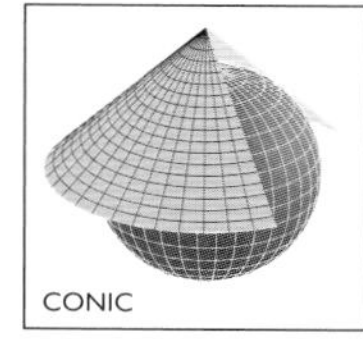

Unlike a globe, no flat map can give a true scale representation of the world in terms of area, shape and position of every region. Each of the numerous systems that have been devised for projecting the curved surface of the Earth on to a flat page involves the sacrifice of accuracy in one or more of these elements. The variations in shape and position of landmasses such as Alaska, Greenland and Australia, for example, can be quite dramatic when different projections are compared.

For this atlas, the guiding principle has been to select projections that involve the least distortion of size and distance. The projection used for each map is noted in the border. Most fall into one of three categories – conic, cylindrical or azimuthal – whose basic concepts are shown above. Each involves plotting the forms of the Earth's surface on a grid of latitude and longitude lines, which may be shown as parallels, curves or radiating spokes.

LATITUDE AND LONGITUDE

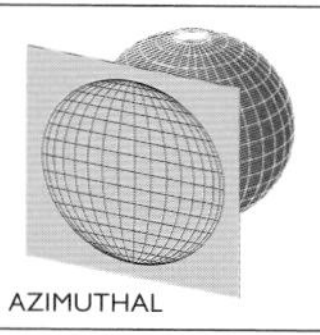

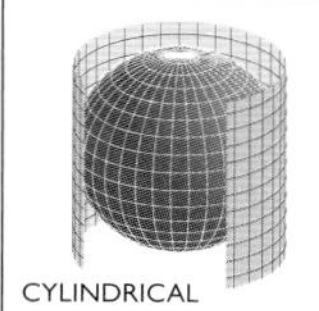

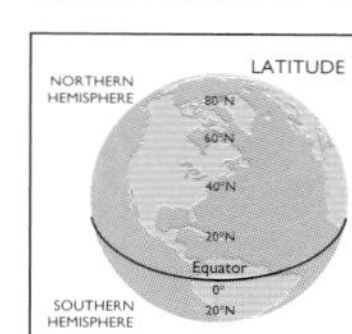

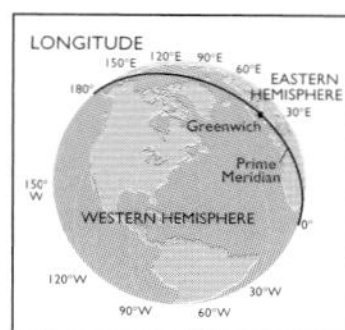

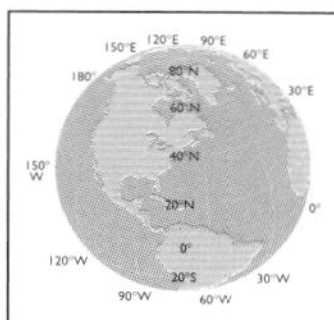

Accurate positioning of individual points on the Earth's surface is made possible by reference to the geometrical system of latitude and longitude. Latitude *parallels* are drawn west–east around the Earth and numbered by degrees north and south of the Equator, which is designated 0° of latitude. Longitude *meridians* are drawn north–south and numbered by degrees east and west of the *prime meridian*, 0° of longitude, which passes through Greenwich in England. By referring to these co-ordinates and their subdivisions of minutes (1/60th of a degree) and seconds (1/60th of a minute), any place on Earth can be located to within a few hundred yards. Latitude and longitude are indicated by blue lines on the maps; they are straight or curved according to the projection employed. Reference to these lines is the easiest way of determining the relative positions of places on different maps, and for plotting compass directions.

NAME FORMS

For ease of reference, both English and local name forms appear in the atlas. Oceans, seas and countries are shown in English throughout the atlas; country names may be abbreviated to their commonly accepted form (e.g. Germany, not The Federal Republic of Germany). Conventional English forms are also used for place names on the smaller-scale maps of the continents. However, local name forms are used on all large-scale and regional maps, with the English form given in brackets only for important cities – the large-scale map of Russia and Central Asia thus shows Moskva (Moscow). For countries which do not use a Roman script, place names have been transcribed according to the systems adopted by the British and US Geographic Names Authorities. For China, the Pin Yin system has been used, with some more widely known forms appearing in brackets, as with Beijing (Peking). Both English and local names appear in the index, the English form being cross-referenced to the local form.

Contents

World Statistics

Countries	x
Cities	xi
Climate	xii
Physical Dimensions	xiv
Regions in the News	xvi

The Earth In Space

The Universe	2–3
Star Charts and Constellations	4–7
The Solar System	8–9
The Earth: Time and Motion	10–11
The Earth From Space	12–13
The Dynamic Earth	14–15
Earthquakes and Volcanoes	16–17
Forces of Nature	18–19
Oceans and Ice	20–21
The Earth's Atmosphere	22–23
Climate and Weather	24–25
Water and Land Use	26–27
The Natural World	28–29
The Human World	30–31
Languages and Religions	32–33
International Organizations	34–35
Agriculture	36–37
Energy and Minerals	38–39
World Economies	40–41
Trade and Commerce	42–43
Travel and Communications	44–45
The World Today	46–47

World Maps

Map Symbols	**1**
The World: Political 1:71 100 000	**2–3**
Arctic Ocean 1:31 100 000	**4**
Antarctica 1:31 100 000	**5**

Europe

Europe: Physical
1:17 800 000
6

Europe: Political
1:17 800 000
7

Scandinavia
1:4 400 000

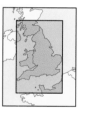

8–9

Denmark and Southern Sweden
1:2 200 000

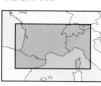

10–11

England and Wales
1:1 800 000

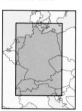

12–13

Scotland
1:1 800 000

14

Ireland
1:1 800 000

15

British Isles
1:4 400 000

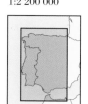

16

Netherlands, Belgium and Luxembourg
1:2 200 000

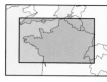

17

Northern France
1:2 200 000

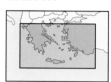

18–19

Southern France
1:2 200 000

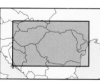

20–21

Middle Europe
1:4 400 000

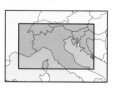

22–23

Germany and Switzerland
1:2 200 000

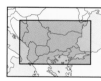

24–25

**Austria, Czech Republic
and Slovak Republic**
1:2 200 000

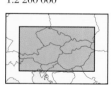

26–27

Northern Italy, Slovenia and Croatia
1:2 200 000

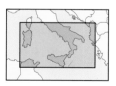

28–29

Southern Italy
1:2 200 000

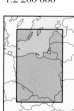

30–31

Eastern Spain
1:2 200 000

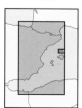

32–33

Western Spain and Portugal
1:2 200 000

34–35

Malta, Crete, Corfu, Rhodes and Cyprus
1:900 000 / 1:1 200 000

36

The Balearics, the Canaries and Madeira
1:900 000 / 1:1 800 000

37

Southern Greece and Western Turkey
1:2 200 000

38–39

Northern Greece, Bulgaria and Yugoslavia
1:2 200 000

40–41

Hungary, Romania and the Lower Danube
1:2 200 000

42–43

Poland and the Southern Baltic
1:2 200 000

44–45

Baltic States, Belarus and Ukraine
1:4 400 000

46–47

The Volga Basin and the Caucasus
1:4 400 000

48–49

Asia

Russia and Central Asia
1:17 800 000

50–51

Asia: Physical
1:44 400 000

52

Asia: Political
1:44 400 000

53

Japan
1:4 400 000

54–55

Northern China and Korea
1:5 300 000

56–57

Southern China
1:5 300 000

58–59

China
1:17 800 000

60

The Philippines
1:6 700 000

61

Indonesia and the Philippines
1:11 100 000

62–63

Mainland South-east Asia
1:5 300 000

64–65

South Asia
1:8 900 000

66–67

The Indo-Gangetic Plain
1:5 300 000

68–69

The Middle East
1:6 200 000

70–71

Turkey and Transcaucasia
1:4 400 000

72–73

Arabia and the Horn of Africa
1:13 300 000

74

The Near East
1:2 200 000

75

Africa

Africa: Physical
1:37 300 000

76

Africa: Political
1: 37 300 000

77

Northern Africa
1:13 300 000

78–79

The Nile Valley and the Nile Delta
1:7 100 000 / 1:3 600 000

80–81

West Africa
1:7 100 000

82–83

Central and Southern Africa
1:13 300 000

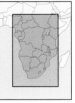

84–85

East Africa
1:7 100 000

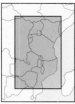

86–87

Southern Africa
1:7 100 000 / 1:7 100 000

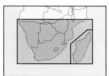

88–89

Australia and Oceania

Australia and Oceania:
 Physical and Political
1:44 400 000   90

New Zealand and Samoa, Fiji and Tonga
1:5 300 000 / 1:10 700 000

91

Western Australia
1:7 100 000

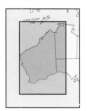

92–93

Eastern Australia
1:7 100 000

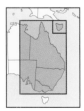

94–95

Pacific Ocean
1:48 000 000   96–97

North America

North America: Physical
1:31 100 000   98

North America: Political
1:31 100 000   99

Canada and Alaska
1:13 300 000 / 1:26 700 000

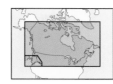

100–101

Eastern Canada
1:6 200 000

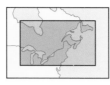

102–103

Western Canada
1:6 200 000

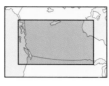

104–105

United States and Hawaii
1:10 700 000 / 1:8 900 000

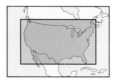

106–107

Eastern United States
1:5 300 000

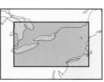

108–109

North-eastern United States
1:2 200 000

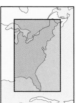

110–111

Middle United States
1:5 300 000

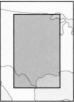

112–113

Western United States
1:5 300 000

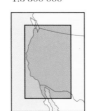

114–115

Central and Southern California
 and Western Washington
1:2 200 000

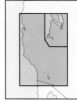

116–117

Mexico
1:7 100 000

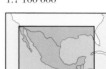

118–119

Central America and the West Indies
1:7 100 000

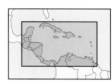

120–121

South America

South America: Physical
1:31 100 000   122

South America: Political
1:31 100 000   123

South America – North
1:14 200 000

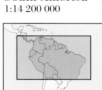

124–125

Central South America
1:7 100 000

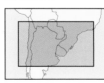

126–127

South America – South
1:14 200 000

128

Index to World Maps

129–224

World Statistics: Countries

This alphabetical list includes all the countries and territories of the world. If a territory is not completely independent, then the country it is associated with is named. The area figures give the total area of land, inland water and ice. Units for areas and populations are thousands. The population figures are 2000 estimates. The annual income is the Gross National Product per capita in US dollars. The figures are the latest available, usually 1998.

Country/Territory	Area km² Thousands	Area miles² Thousands	Population Thousands	Capital	Annual Income US $
Afghanistan	652	252	26,511	Kabul	800
Albania	28.8	11.1	3,795	Tirana	810
Algeria	2,382	920	32,904	Algiers	1,550
American Samoa (US)	0.20	0.08	39	Pago Pago	2,600
Andorra	0.45	0.17	49	Andorra La Vella	18,000
Angola	1,247	481	13,295	Luanda	340
Anguilla (UK)	0.1	0.04	8	The Valley	6,800
Antigua & Barbuda	0.44	0.17	79	St John's	8,300
Argentina	2,767	1,068	36,238	Buenos Aires	8,970
Armenia	29.8	11.5	3,968	Yerevan	480
Aruba (Netherlands)	0.19	0.07	58	Oranjestad	22,000
Australia	7,687	2,968	18,855	Canberra	20,300
Austria	83.9	32.4	7,613	Vienna	26,850
Azerbaijan	86.6	33.4	8,324	Baku	490
Azores (Portugal)	2.2	0.87	238	Ponta Delgada	–
Bahamas	13.9	5.4	295	Nassau	20,100
Bahrain	0.68	0.26	683	Manama	7,660
Bangladesh	144	56	150,589	Dhaka	350
Barbados	0.43	0.17	265	Bridgetown	7,890
Belarus	207.6	80.1	10,697	Minsk	2,200
Belgium	30.5	11.8	9,832	Brussels	25,380
Belize	23	8.9	230	Belmopan	2,610
Benin	113	43	6,369	Porto-Novo	380
Bermuda (UK)	0.05	0.02	62	Hamilton	34,000
Bhutan	47	18.1	1,906	Thimphu	1,000
Bolivia	1,099	424	9,724	La Paz/Sucre	1,000
Bosnia-Herzegovina	51	20	4,601	Sarajevo	1,720
Botswana	582	225	1,822	Gaborone	3,600
Brazil	8,512	3,286	179,487	Brasília	4,570
Brunei	5.8	2.2	333	Bandar Seri Begawan	24,000
Bulgaria	111	43	9,071	Sofia	1,230
Burkina Faso	274	106	12,092	Ouagadougou	240
Burma (= Myanmar)	677	261	51,129	Rangoon	1,200
Burundi	27.8	10.7	7,358	Bujumbura	140
Cambodia	181	70	10,046	Phnom Penh	280
Cameroon	475	184	16,701	Yaoundé	610
Canada	9,976	3,852	28,488	Ottawa	20,020
Canary Is. (Spain)	7.3	2.8	1,494	Las Palmas/Santa Cruz	–
Cape Verde Is.	4	1.6	515	Praia	1,060
Cayman Is. (UK)	0.26	0.10	35	George Town	20,000
Central African Republic	623	241	4,074	Bangui	300
Chad	1,284	496	7,337	Ndjaména	230
Chile	757	292	15,272	Santiago	4,810
China	9,597	3,705	1,299,180	Beijing	750
Colombia	1,139	440	39,397	Bogotá	2,600
Comoros	2.2	0.86	670	Moroni	370
Congo	342	132	3,167	Brazzaville	690
Congo (Dem. Rep. of the)	2,345	905	49,190	Kinshasa	110
Cook Is. (NZ)	0.24	0.09	17	Avarua	900
Costa Rica	51.1	19.7	3,711	San José	2,780
Croatia	56.5	21.8	4,960	Zagreb	4,520
Cuba	111	43	11,504	Havana	1,560
Cyprus	9.3	3.6	762	Nicosia	13,000
Czech Republic	78.9	30.4	10,500	Prague	5,040
Denmark	43.1	16.6	5,153	Copenhagen	33,260
Djibouti	23.2	9	552	Djibouti	1,200
Dominica	0.75	0.29	87	Roseau	3,010
Dominican Republic	48.7	18.8	8,621	Santo Domingo	1,770
Ecuador	284	109	13,319	Quito	1,530
Egypt	1,001	387	64,210	Cairo	1,290
El Salvador	21	8.1	6,739	San Salvador	1,850
Equatorial Guinea	28.1	10.8	455	Malabo	1,500
Eritrea	94	36	4,523	Asmara	200
Estonia	44.7	17.3	1,647	Tallinn	3,390
Ethiopia	1,128	436	61,841	Addis Ababa	100
Faroe Is. (Denmark)	1.4	0.54	49	Tórshavn	16,000
Fiji	18.3	7.1	883	Suva	2,110
Finland	338	131	5,077	Helsinki	24,110
France	552	213	58,145	Paris	24,940
French Guiana (France)	90	34.7	130	Cayenne	6,000
French Polynesia (France)	4	1.5	268	Papeete	10,800
Gabon	268	103	1,612	Libreville	3,950
Gambia, The	11.3	4.4	1,119	Banjul	340
Georgia	69.7	26.9	5,777	Tbilisi	930
Germany	357	138	76,962	Berlin	25,850
Ghana	239	92	20,564	Accra	390
Gibraltar (UK)	0.007	0.003	32	Gibraltar Town	5,000
Greece	132	51	10,193	Athens	11,650
Greenland (Denmark)	2,176	840	60	Nuuk (Godthåb)	16,100
Grenada	0.34	0.13	83	St George's	3,170
Guadeloupe (France)	1.7	0.66	365	Basse-Terre	9,200
Guam (US)	0.55	0.21	128	Agana	19,000
Guatemala	109	42	12,222	Guatemala City	1,640
Guinea	246	95	7,830	Conakry	540
Guinea-Bissau	36.1	13.9	1,197	Bissau	160
Guyana	215	83	891	Georgetown	770
Haiti	27.8	10.7	8,003	Port-au-Prince	410
Honduras	112	43	6,846	Tegucigalpa	730
Hong Kong (China)	1.1	0.40	6,336	–	23,670
Hungary	93	35.9	10,531	Budapest	4,510
Iceland	103	40	274	Reykjavik	28,010
India	3,288	1,269	1,041,543	New Delhi	430
Indonesia	1,905	735	218,661	Jakarta	680
Iran	1,648	636	68,759	Tehran	1,770
Iraq	438	169	26,339	Baghdad	2,400
Ireland	70.3	27.1	4,086	Dublin	18,340
Israel	27	10.3	5,321	Jerusalem	15,940
Italy	301	116	57,195	Rome	20,250
Ivory Coast (Côte d'Ivoire)	322	125	17,600	Yamoussoukro	700
Jamaica	11	4.2	2,735	Kingston	1,680
Japan	378	146	128,470	Tokyo	32,380
Jordan	89.2	34.4	5,558	Amman	1,520
Kazakstan	2,717	1,049	19,006	Astana	1,310
Kenya	580	224	35,060	Nairobi	330
Kiribati	0.72	0.28	72	Tarawa	1,180
Korea, North	121	47	26,117	Pyŏngyang	1,000
Korea, South	99	38.2	46,403	Seoul	7,970
Kuwait	17.8	6.9	2,639	Kuwait City	22,700
Kyrgyzstan	198.5	76.6	5,403	Bishkek	350
Laos	237	91	5,463	Vientiane	330
Latvia	65	25	2,768	Riga	2,430
Lebanon	10.4	4	3,327	Beirut	3,360
Lesotho	30.4	11.7	2,370	Maseru	570
Liberia	111	43	3,575	Monrovia	1,000
Libya	1,760	679	6,500	Tripoli	6,700
Liechtenstein	0.16	0.06	28	Vaduz	50,000
Lithuania	65.2	25.2	3,935	Vilnius	2,440
Luxembourg	2.6	1	377	Luxembourg	43,570
Macau (China)	0.02	0.006	656	Macau	16,000
Macedonia	25.7	9.9	2,157	Skopje	1,290
Madagascar	587	227	16,627	Antananarivo	260
Madeira (Portugal)	0.81	0.31	253	Funchal	–
Malawi	118	46	12,458	Lilongwe	200
Malaysia	330	127	21,983	Kuala Lumpur	3,600
Maldives	0.30	0.12	283	Malé	1,230
Mali	1,240	479	12,685	Bamako	250
Malta	0.32	0.12	366	Valletta	9,440
Marshall Is.	0.18	0.07	70	Dalap-Uliga-Darrit	1,540
Martinique (France)	1.1	0.42	362	Fort-de-France	10,700
Mauritania	1,030	412	2,702	Nouakchott	410
Mauritius	2.0	0.72	1,201	Port Louis	3,700
Mayotte (France)	0.37	0.14	141	Mamoundzou	1,430
Mexico	1,958	756	107,233	Mexico City	3,970
Micronesia, Fed. States of	0.70	0.27	110	Palikir	1,800
Moldova	33.7	13	4,707	Chişinău	410
Monaco	0.002	0.0001	30	Monaco	25,000
Mongolia	1,567	605	2,847	Ulan Bator	400
Montserrat (UK)	0.10	0.04	13	Plymouth	4,500
Morocco	447	172	31,559	Rabat	1,250
Mozambique	802	309	20,493	Maputo	210
Namibia	825	318	2,437	Windhoek	1,940
Nauru	0.02	0.008	10	Yaren District	10,000
Nepal	141	54	24,084	Katmandu	210
Netherlands	41.5	16	15,829	Amsterdam/The Hague	24,760
Netherlands Antilles (Neths)	0.99	0.38	203	Willemstad	11,500
New Caledonia (France)	18.6	7.2	195	Nouméa	11,400
New Zealand	269	104	3,662	Wellington	14,700
Nicaragua	130	50	5,261	Managua	390
Niger	1,267	489	10,752	Niamey	190
Nigeria	924	357	105,000	Abuja	300
Northern Mariana Is. (US)	0.48	0.18	50	Saipan	11,500
Norway	324	125	4,331	Oslo	34,330
Oman	212	82	2,176	Muscat	7,900
Pakistan	796	307	162,409	Islamabad	480
Palau	0.46	0.18	18	Koror	5,000
Panama	77.1	29.8	2,893	Panama City	3,080
Papua New Guinea	463	179	4,845	Port Moresby	890
Paraguay	407	157	5,538	Asunción	1,760
Peru	1,285	496	26,276	Lima	2,460
Philippines	300	116	77,473	Manila	1,050
Poland	313	121	40,366	Warsaw	3,900
Portugal	92.4	35.7	10,587	Lisbon	10,690
Puerto Rico (US)	9	3.5	3,836	San Juan	9,000
Qatar	11	4.2	499	Doha	17,100
Réunion (France)	2.5	0.97	692	Saint-Denis	4,800
Romania	238	92	24,000	Bucharest	1,390
Russia	17,075	6,592	155,096	Moscow	2,300
Rwanda	26.3	10.2	10,200	Kigali	230
St Kitts & Nevis	0.36	0.14	44	Basseterre	6,130
St Lucia	0.62	0.24	177	Castries	3,410
St Vincent & Grenadines	0.39	0.15	128	Kingstown	2,420
San Marino	0.06	0.02	25	San Marino	20,000
São Tomé & Príncipe	0.96	0.37	151	São Tomé	280
Saudi Arabia	2,150	830	20,697	Riyadh	9,000
Senegal	197	76	8,716	Dakar	530
Seychelles	0.46	0.18	75	Victoria	6,450
Sierra Leone	71.7	27.7	5,437	Freetown	140
Singapore	0.62	0.24	3,000	Singapore	30,060
Slovak Republic	49	18.9	5,500	Bratislava	3,700
Slovenia	20.3	7.8	2,055	Ljubljana	9,760
Solomon Is.	28.9	11.2	429	Honiara	750
Somalia	638	246	9,736	Mogadishu	600
South Africa	1,220	471	43,666	C. Town/Pretoria/Bloem.	2,880
Spain	505	195	40,667	Madrid	14,080
Sri Lanka	65.6	25.3	19,416	Colombo	810
Sudan	2,506	967	33,625	Khartoum	290
Surinam	163	63	497	Paramaribo	1,660
Swaziland	17.4	6.7	1121	Mbabane	1,400
Sweden	450	174	8,560	Stockholm	25,620
Switzerland	41.3	15.9	6,762	Bern	40,080
Syria	185	71	17,826	Damascus	1,020
Taiwan	36	13.9	22,000	Taipei	12,400
Tajikistan	143.1	55.2	7,041	Dushanbe	350
Tanzania	945	365	39,639	Dodoma	210
Thailand	513	198	63,670	Bangkok	2,200
Togo	56.8	21.9	4,861	Lomé	330
Tonga	0.75	0.29	92	Nuku'alofa	1,690
Trinidad & Tobago	5.1	2	1,484	Port of Spain	4,430
Tunisia	164	63	9,924	Tunis	2,050
Turkey	779	301	66,789	Ankara	3,160
Turkmenistan	488.1	188.5	4,585	Ashkhabad	1,630
Turks & Caicos Is. (UK)	0.43	0.17	12	Cockburn Town	5,000
Tuvalu	0.03	0.01	11	Fongafale	600
Uganda	236	91	26,958	Kampala	320
Ukraine	603.7	233.1	52,558	Kiev	850
United Arab Emirates	83.6	32.3	1,951	Abu Dhabi	18,220
United Kingdom	243.3	94	58,393	London	21,400
United States of America	9,373	3,619	266,096	Washington, DC	29,340
Uruguay	177	68	3,274	Montevideo	6,1820
Uzbekistan	447.4	172.7	26,044	Tashkent	870
Vanuatu	12.2	4.7	206	Port-Vila	1,270
Venezuela	912	352	24,715	Caracas	350
Vietnam	332	127	82,427	Hanoi	330
Virgin Is. (UK)	0.15	0.06	15	Road Town	–
Virgin Is. (US)	0.34	0.13	135	Charlotte Amalie	12,500
Wallis & Futuna Is. (France)	0.20	0.08	26	Mata-Utu	–
Western Sahara	266	103	228	El Aaiún	300
Western Samoa	2.8	1.1	171	Apia	1,020
Yemen	528	204	13,219	Sana	300
Yugoslavia	102.3	39.5	10,761	Belgrade	2,300
Zambia	753	291	12,267	Lusaka	330
Zimbabwe	391	151	13,123	Harare	610

World Statistics: Cities

This list shows the principal cities with more than 500,000 inhabitants (for Brazil, China and India only cities with more than 1 million inhabitants are included). The figures are taken from the most recent census or population estimate available, and as far as possible are the population of the metropolitan area, e.g. greater New York, Mexico or Paris. All the figures are in thousands. Local name forms have been used for the smaller cities (e.g. Kraków).

AFGHANISTAN
Kabul 1,565
ALGERIA
Algiers 2,168
Oran 916
ANGOLA
Luanda 2,418
ARGENTINA
Buenos Aires 11,256
Córdoba 1,208
Rosario 1,118
Mendoza 773
La Plata 642
San Miguel de Tucumán 622
Mar del Plata 512
ARMENIA
Yerevan 1,248
AUSTRALIA
Sydney 3,770
Melbourne 3,217
Brisbane 1,489
Perth 1,262
Adelaide 1,080
AUSTRIA
Vienna 1,595
AZERBAIJAN
Baku 1,720
BANGLADESH
Dhaka 6,105
Chittagong 2,041
Khulna 877
Rajshahi 517
BELARUS
Minsk 1,700
Homyel 512
BELGIUM
Brussels 948
BENIN
Cotonou 537
BOLIVIA
La Paz 1,126
Santa Cruz 767
BOSNIA-HERZEGOVINA
Sarajevo 526
BRAZIL
São Paulo 16,417
Rio de Janeiro 9,888
Salvador 2,211
Belo Horizonte 2,091
Fortaleza 1,965
Brasília 1,821
Curitiba 1,476
Recife 1,346
Pôrto Alegre 1,288
Manaus 1,157
Belém 1,144
Goiânia 1,004
BULGARIA
Sofia 1,116
BURKINA FASO
Ouagadougou 690
BURMA (MYANMAR)
Rangoon 2,513
Mandalay 533
CAMBODIA
Phnom Penh 920
CAMEROON
Douala 1,200
Yaoundé 800
CANADA
Toronto 4,344
Montréal 3,337
Vancouver 1,831
Ottawa–Hull 1,022
Edmonton 885
Calgary 831
Québec 693
Winnipeg 677
Hamilton 643
CENTRAL AFRICAN REP.
Bangui 553
CHAD
Ndjaména 530
CHILE
Santiago 5,067
CHINA
Shanghai 15,082
Beijing 12,362
Tianjin 10,687
Hong Kong (SAR)* 6,502
Chongqing 3,870
Shenyang 3,860
Wuhan 3,520
Guangzhou 3,114
Harbin 2,505
Nanjing 2,211
Xi'an 2,115
Chengdu 1,933
Dalian 1,855
Changchun 1,810
Jinan 1,660
Taiyuan 1,642
Qingdao 1,584
Fuzhou, Fujian 1,380
Zibo 1,346
Zhengzhou 1,324

Lanzhou 1,296
Anshan 1,252
Fushun 1,246
Kunming 1,242
Changsha 1,198
Hangzhou 1,185
Nanchang 1,169
Shijiazhuang 1,159
Guiyang 1,131
Ürümqi 1,130
Jilin 1,118
Tangshan 1,110
Qiqihar 1,104
Baotou 1,033
Hefei 1,000
COLOMBIA
Bogotá 6,004
Cali 1,985
Medellín 1,970
Barranquilla 1,157
Cartagena 812
CONGO
Brazzaville 937
Pointe-Noire 576
CONGO (DEM. REP.)
Kinshasa 1,655
Lubumbashi 851
Mbuji-Mayi 806
COSTA RICA
San José 1,220
CROATIA
Zagreb 931
CUBA
Havana 2,241
CZECH REPUBLIC
Prague 1,209
DENMARK
Copenhagen 1,362
DOMINICAN REPUBLIC
Santo Domingo 2,135
Santiago 691
ECUADOR
Guayaquil 1,973
Quito 1,487
EGYPT
Cairo 9,900
Alexandria 3,431
El Gîza 2,144
Shubra el Kheima 834
EL SALVADOR
San Salvador 1,522
ETHIOPIA
Addis Ababa 2,112
FINLAND
Helsinki 532
FRANCE
Paris 9,319
Lyon 1,262
Marseille 1,087
Lille 959
Bordeaux 696
Toulouse 650
Nice 516
GEORGIA
Tbilisi 1,300
GERMANY
Berlin 3,470
Hamburg 1,706
Munich 1,240
Cologne 964
Frankfurt 651
Essen 616
Dortmund 600
Stuttgart 587
Düsseldorf 571
Bremen 549
Duisburg 535
Hanover 524
GHANA
Accra 949
GREECE
Athens 3,097
GUATEMALA
Guatemala 1,167
GUINEA
Conakry 1,508
HAITI
Port-au-Prince 1,255
HONDURAS
Tegucigalpa 813
HUNGARY
Budapest 1,885
INDIA
Bombay (Mumbai) 12,572
Calcutta (Kolkata) 10,916
Delhi 7,207
Madras (Chennai) 5,361
Hyderabad 4,280
Bangalore 4,087
Ahmadabad 3,298
Pune 2,485
Kanpur 2,111
Nagpur 1,661
Lucknow 1,642
Surat 1,517
Jaipur 1,514

Coimbatore 1,136
Vadodara 1,115
Indore 1,104
Patna 1,099
Madurai 1,094
Bhopal 1,064
Vishakhapatnam 1,052
Varanasi 1,026
Ludhiana 1,012
INDONESIA
Jakarta 11,500
Surabaya 2,701
Bandung 2,368
Medan 1,910
Semarang 1,366
Palembang 1,352
Tangerang 1,198
Ujung Pandang 1,092
Bandar Lampung 832
Malang 763
Padang 721
Pakanbaru 558
Samarinda 536
Banjarmasin 535
Surakarta 516
IRAN
Tehran 6,750
Mashhad 1,964
Esfahan 1,221
Tabriz 1,166
Shiraz 1,043
Ahvaz 828
Qom 780
Bakhtaran 666
Karaj 588
IRAQ
Baghdad 3,841
Diyala 961
As Sulaymaniyah 952
Arbil 770
Al Mawsil 664
Kadhimain 521
IRELAND
Dublin 952
ISRAEL
Tel Aviv-Yafo 1,502
Jerusalem 591
ITALY
Rome 2,775
Milan 1,369
Naples 1,067
Turin 962
Palermo 698
Genoa 678
IVORY COAST
Abidjan 2,500
JAMAICA
Kingston 644
JAPAN
Tokyo–Yokohama 26,836
Osaka 10,601
Nagoya 2,152
Sapporo 1,757
Kyoto 1,464
Kobe 1,424
Fukuoka 1,285
Kawasaki 1,203
Hiroshima 1,109
Kitakyushu 1,020
Sendai 971
Chiba 857
Sakai 803
Kumamoto 650
Okayama 616
Sagamihara 571
Hamamatsu 562
Kagoshima 546
Funabashi 541
Higashiosaka 517
Hachioji 503
JORDAN
Amman 1,300
Az-Zarqa 609
KAZAKSTAN
Almaty 1,150
Qaraghandy 573
KENYA
Nairobi 2,000
Mombasa 600
KOREA, NORTH
Pyŏngyang 2,639
Hamhung 775
Chŏngjin 754
Chinnampo 691
Sinŭiju 500
KOREA, SOUTH
Seoul 11,641
Pusan 3,814
Taegu 2,449
Inchon 2,308
Taejŏn 1,272
Kwangju 1,258
Ulsan 967
Sŏngnam 869
Puch'on 779
Suwŏn 756

Anyang 590
Chŏnju 563
Chŏngju 531
Ansan 510
P'ohang 509
KYRGYZSTAN
Bishkek 584
LATVIA
Riga 846
LEBANON
Beirut 1,900
Tripoli 500
LIBYA
Tripoli 1,083
LITHUANIA
Vilnius 580
MACEDONIA
Skopje 541
MADAGASCAR
Antananarivo 1,053
MALAYSIA
Kuala Lumpur 1,145
MALI
Bamako 800
MAURITANIA
Nouakchott 735
MEXICO
Mexico City 15,048
Guadalajara 2,847
Monterrey 2,522
Puebla 1,055
León 872
Ciudad Juárez 798
Tijuana 743
Culiacán Rosales 602
Mexicali 602
Acapulco de Juárez 592
Mérida 557
Chihuahua 530
San Luis Potosí 526
Aguascalientés 506
MOLDOVA
Chişinău 700
MONGOLIA
Ulan Bator 627
MOROCCO
Casablanca 3,079
Rabat-Salé 1,344
Fès 735
Marrakesh 621
MOZAMBIQUE
Maputo 2,000
NEPAL
Katmandu 535
NETHERLANDS
Amsterdam 1,101
Rotterdam 1,076
The Hague 694
Utrecht 548
NEW ZEALAND
Auckland 997
NICARAGUA
Managua 864
NIGERIA
Lagos 10,287
Ibadan 1,365
Ogbomosho 712
Kano 657
NORWAY
Oslo 714
PAKISTAN
Karachi 9,863
Lahore 5,085
Faisalabad 1,875
Peshawar 1,676
Gujranwala 1,663
Rawalpindi 1,290
Multan 1,257
Hyderabad 1,107
PARAGUAY
Asunción 945
PERU
Lima–Callao 6,601
Callao 638
Arequipa 620
Trujillo 509
PHILIPPINES
Manila 9,280
Quezon City 1,989
Davao 1,191
Caloocan 1,023
Cebu 662
Zamboanga 511
POLAND
Warsaw 1,638
Łódź 825
Kraków 745
Wrocław 642
Poznań 581
PORTUGAL
Lisbon 2,561
Oporto 1,174
ROMANIA
Bucharest 2,060
RUSSIA
Moscow 9,233

Petersburg 4,883
Nizhniy Novgorod 1,425
Novosibirsk 1,400
Yekaterinburg 1,300
Samara 1,200
Omsk 1,200
Chelyabinsk 1,100
Kazan 1,100
Ufa 1,100
Volgograd 1,003
Perm 1,000
Rostov 1,000
Voronezh 908
Saratov 895
Krasnoyarsk 869
Togliatti 689
Simbirsk 678
Izhevsk 654
Krasnodar 645
Vladivostok 632
Yaroslavl 629
Khabarovsk 618
Barnaul 596
Irkutsk 585
Novokuznetsk 572
Ryazan 536
Penza 534
Orenburg 532
Tula 532
Naberezhnyye-Chelny 526
Kemerovo 503
SAUDI ARABIA
Riyadh 1,800
Jedda 1,500
Mecca 630
SENEGAL
Dakar 1,571
SIERRA LEONE
Freetown 505
SINGAPORE
Singapore 3,104
SOMALIA
Mogadishu 1,000
SOUTH AFRICA
Cape Town 2,350
East Rand 1,379
Johannesburg 1,196
Durban 1,137
Pretoria 1,080
West Rand 870
Port Elizabeth 853
Vanderbijlpark–Vereeniging 774
Soweto 597
Sasolburg 540
SPAIN
Madrid 3,029
Barcelona 1,614
Valencia 763
Sevilla 719
Zaragoza 607
Málaga 532
SRI LANKA
Colombo 1,863
SUDAN
Omdurman 1,267
Khartoum 925
Khartoum North 879
SWEDEN
Stockholm 1,744
Göteborg 775
SWITZERLAND
Zürich 1,175
Bern 942
SYRIA
Aleppo 1,591
Damascus 1,549
Homs 644
TAIWAN
Taipei 2,653
Kaohsiung 1,405
Taichung 817
Tainan 700
Panchiao 544
TAJIKISTAN
Dushanbe 524
TANZANIA
Dar-es-Salaam 1,361
THAILAND
Bangkok 5,572
TOGO
Lomé 590
TUNISIA
Tunis 1,827
TURKEY
Istanbul 7,490
Ankara 3,028
Izmir 2,333
Adana 1,472
Bursa 1,317
Konya 1,040
Gaziantep 930
Icel 908
Antalya 734
Diyarbakir 677
Kocaeli 661
Urfa 649

Kayseri 648
Manisa 641
Hatay 561
Samsun 557
Eskisehir 508
Balikesir 501
TURKMENISTAN
Ashkhabad 536
UGANDA
Kampala 773
UKRAINE
Kiev 2,630
Kharkiv 1,555
Dnipropetrovsk 1,147
Donetsk 1,088
Odesa 1,046
Zaporizhzhya 887
Lviv 802
Kryvyy Rih 720
Mariupol 510
Mykolayiv 508
UNITED KINGDOM
London 8,089
Birmingham 2,373
Manchester 2,353
Liverpool 852
Glasgow 832
Sheffield 661
Nottingham 649
Newcastle 617
Bristol 552
Leeds 529
UNITED STATES
New York 16,329
Los Angeles 12,410
Chicago 7,668
Philadelphia 4,949
Washington, DC 4,466
Detroit 4,307
Houston 3,653
Atlanta 3,331
Boston 3,240
Dallas 2,898
Minneapolis–St Paul 2,688
San Diego 2,632
St Louis 2,536
Phoenix 2,473
Baltimore 2,458
Pittsburgh 2,402
Cleveland 2,222
San Francisco 2,182
Seattle 2,180
Tampa 2,157
Miami 2,025
Newark 1,934
Denver 1,796
Portland (Or.) 1,676
Kansas City (Mo.) 1,647
Cincinnati 1,581
San Jose 1,557
Norfolk 1,529
Indianapolis 1,462
Milwaukee 1,456
Sacramento 1,441
San Antonio 1,437
Columbus (Oh.) 1,423
New Orleans 1,309
Charlotte 1,260
Buffalo 1,189
Salt Lake City 1,178
Hartford 1,151
Oklahoma 1,007
Jacksonville (Fl.) 665
Omaha 663
Memphis 614
El Paso 579
Austin 514
Nashville 505
URUGUAY
Montevideo 1,378
UZBEKISTAN
Tashkent 2,107
VENEZUELA
Caracas 2,784
Maracaibo 1,364
Valencia 1,032
Maracay 800
Barquisimeto 745
Ciudad Guayana 524
VIETNAM
Ho Chi Minh City 4,322
Hanoi 3,056
Haiphong 783
YEMEN
Sana 972
Aden 562
YUGOSLAVIA
Belgrade 1,137
ZAMBIA
Lusaka 982
ZIMBABWE
Harare 1,189
Bulawayo 622

* SAR = Special Administrative Region of China

World Statistics: Climate

Rainfall and temperature figures are provided for more than 70 cities around the world. As climate is affected by altitude, the height of each city is shown in metres beneath its name. For each location, the top row of figures shows the total rainfall or snow in millimetres, and the bottom row the average temperature in degrees Celsius; the average annual temperature and total annual rainfall are at the end of the rows. The map opposite shows the city locations.

CITY	JAN.	FEB.	MAR.	APR.	MAY	JUNE	JULY	AUG.	SEPT.	OCT.	NOV.	DEC.	YEAR
EUROPE													
Athens, Greece	62	37	37	23	23	14	6	7	15	51	56	71	402
107 m	10	10	12	16	20	25	28	28	24	20	15	11	18
Berlin, Germany	46	40	33	42	49	65	73	69	48	49	46	43	603
55 m	−1	0	4	9	14	17	19	18	15	9	5	1	9
Istanbul, Turkey	109	92	72	46	38	34	34	30	58	81	103	119	816
14 m	5	6	7	11	16	20	23	23	20	16	12	8	14
Lisbon, Portugal	111	76	109	54	44	16	3	4	33	62	93	103	708
77 m	11	12	14	16	17	20	22	23	21	18	14	12	17
London, UK	54	40	37	37	46	45	57	59	49	57	64	48	593
5 m	4	5	7	9	12	16	18	17	15	11	8	5	11
Málaga, Spain	61	51	62	46	26	5	1	3	29	64	64	62	474
33 m	12	13	16	17	19	29	25	26	23	20	16	13	18
Moscow, Russia	39	38	36	37	53	58	88	71	58	45	47	54	624
156 m	−13	−10	−4	6	13	16	18	17	12	6	−1	−7	4
Odesa, Ukraine	57	62	30	21	34	34	42	37	37	13	35	71	473
64 m	−3	−1	2	9	15	20	22	22	18	12	9	1	10
Paris, France	56	46	35	42	57	54	59	64	55	50	51	50	619
75 m	3	4	8	11	15	18	20	19	17	12	7	4	12
Rome, Italy	71	62	57	51	46	37	15	21	63	99	129	93	744
17 m	8	9	11	14	18	22	25	25	22	17	13	10	16
Shannon, Ireland	94	67	56	53	61	57	77	79	86	86	96	117	929
2 m	5	5	7	9	12	14	16	16	14	11	8	6	10
Stockholm, Sweden	43	30	25	31	34	45	61	76	60	48	53	48	554
44 m	−3	−3	−1	5	10	15	18	17	12	7	3	0	7
ASIA													
Bahrain	8	18	13	8	<3	0	0	0	0	0	18	18	81
5 m	17	18	21	25	29	32	33	34	31	28	24	19	26
Bangkok, Thailand	8	20	36	58	198	160	160	175	305	206	66	5	1,397
2 m	26	28	29	30	29	29	28	28	28	28	26	25	28
Beirut, Lebanon	191	158	94	53	18	3	<3	<3	5	51	132	185	892
34 m	14	14	16	18	22	24	27	28	26	24	19	16	21
Bombay (Mumbai), India	3	3	3	<3	18	485	617	340	264	64	13	3	1,809
11 m	24	24	26	28	30	29	27	27	27	28	27	26	27
Calcutta, India	10	31	36	43	140	297	325	328	252	114	20	5	1,600
6 m	20	22	27	30	30	30	29	29	29	28	23	19	26
Colombo, Sri Lanka	89	69	147	231	371	224	135	109	160	348	315	147	2,365
7 m	26	26	27	28	28	27	27	27	27	27	26	26	27
Harbin, China	6	5	10	23	43	94	112	104	46	33	8	5	488
160 m	−18	−15	−5	6	13	19	22	21	14	4	−6	−16	3

CITY	JAN.	FEB.	MAR.	APR.	MAY	JUNE	JULY	AUG.	SEPT.	OCT.	NOV.	DEC.	YEAR
ASIA (continued)													
Ho Chi Minh, Vietnam	15	3	13	43	221	330	315	269	335	269	114	56	1,984
9 m	26	27	29	30	29	28	28	28	27	27	27	26	28
Hong Kong, China	33	46	74	137	292	394	381	361	257	114	43	31	2,162
33 m	16	15	18	22	26	28	28	28	27	25	21	18	23
Jakarta, Indonesia	300	300	211	147	114	97	64	43	66	112	142	203	1,798
8 m	26	26	27	27	27	27	27	27	27	27	27	26	27
Kabul, Afghanistan	31	36	94	102	20	5	3	3	<3	15	20	10	338
1,815 m	−3	−1	6	13	18	22	25	24	20	14	7	3	12
Karachi, Pakistan	13	10	8	3	3	18	81	41	13	<3	3	5	196
4 m	19	20	24	28	30	31	30	29	28	28	24	20	26
Kazalinsk, Kazakstan	10	10	13	13	15	5	5	8	8	10	13	15	125
63 m	−12	−11	−3	6	18	23	25	23	16	8	−1	−7	7
New Delhi, India	23	18	13	8	13	74	180	172	117	10	3	10	640
218 m	14	17	23	28	33	34	31	30	29	26	20	15	25
Omsk, Russia	15	8	8	13	31	51	51	51	28	25	18	20	318
85 m	−22	−19	−12	−1	10	16	18	16	10	1	−11	−18	−1
Shanghai, China	48	58	84	94	94	180	147	142	130	71	51	36	1,135
7 m	4	5	9	14	20	24	28	28	23	19	12	7	16
Singapore	252	173	193	188	173	173	170	196	178	208	254	257	2,413
10 m	26	27	28	28	28	28	28	27	27	27	27	27	27
Tehran, Iran	46	38	46	36	13	3	3	3	3	8	20	31	246
1,220 m	2	5	9	16	21	26	30	29	25	18	12	6	17
Tokyo, Japan	48	74	107	135	147	165	142	152	234	208	97	56	1,565
6 m	3	4	7	13	17	21	25	26	23	17	11	6	14
Ulan Bator, Mongolia	<3	<3	3	5	10	28	76	51	23	5	5	3	208
1,325 m	−26	−21	−13	−1	6	14	16	14	8	−1	−13	−22	−3
Verkhoyansk, Russia	5	5	3	5	8	23	28	25	13	8	8	5	134
100 m	−50	−45	−32	−15	0	12	14	9	2	−15	−38	−48	−17
AFRICA													
Addis Ababa, Ethiopia	<3	3	25	135	213	201	206	239	102	28	<3	0	1,151
2,450 m	19	20	20	20	19	18	18	19	21	22	21	20	20
Antananarivo, Madag.	300	279	178	53	18	8	8	10	18	61	135	287	1,356
1,372 m	21	21	21	19	18	15	14	15	17	19	21	21	19
Cairo, Egypt	5	5	5	3	3	<3	0	0	<3	<3	3	5	28
116 m	13	15	18	21	25	28	28	28	26	24	20	15	22
Cape Town, S. Africa	15	8	18	48	79	84	89	66	43	31	18	10	508
17 m	21	21	20	17	14	13	12	13	14	16	18	19	17
Jo'burg, S. Africa	114	109	89	38	25	8	8	8	23	56	107	125	709
1,665 m	20	20	18	16	13	10	11	13	16	18	19	20	16

CITY	JAN.	FEB.	MAR.	APR.	MAY	JUNE	JULY	AUG.	SEPT.	OCT.	NOV.	DEC.	YEAR
AFRICA (continued)													
Khartoum, Sudan	<3	<3	<3	<3	3	8	53	71	18	5	<3	0	158
390 m	24	25	28	31	33	34	32	31	32	32	28	25	29
Kinshasa, Congo (D.R.)	135	145	196	196	158	8	3	3	31	119	221	142	1,354
325 m	26	26	27	27	26	24	23	24	25	26	26	26	25
Lagos, Nigeria	28	46	102	150	269	460	279	64	140	206	69	25	1,836
3 m	27	28	29	28	28	26	26	25	26	26	28	28	27
Lusaka, Zambia	231	191	142	18	3	<3	<3	0	<3	10	91	150	836
1,277 m	21	22	21	21	19	16	16	18	22	24	23	22	21
Monrovia, Liberia	31	56	97	216	516	973	996	373	744	772	236	130	5,138
23 m	26	26	27	27	26	25	24	25	25	25	26	26	26
Nairobi, Kenya	38	64	125	211	158	46	15	23	31	53	109	86	958
820 m	19	19	19	19	18	16	16	16	18	19	18	18	18
Timbuktu, Mali	<3	<3	3	<3	5	23	79	81	38	3	<3	<3	231
301 m	22	24	28	32	34	35	32	30	32	31	28	23	29
Tunis, Tunisia	64	51	41	36	18	8	3	8	33	51	48	61	419
66 m	10	11	13	16	19	23	26	27	25	20	16	11	18
Walvis Bay, Namibia	<3	5	8	3	3	<3	<3	3	<3	<3	<3	<3	23
7 m	19	19	19	18	17	16	15	14	14	15	17	18	18
AUSTRALIA, NEW ZEALAND AND ANTARCTICA													
Alice Springs, Aust.	43	33	28	10	15	13	8	8	8	18	31	38	252
579 m	29	28	25	20	15	12	12	14	18	23	26	28	21
Christchurch, N.Z.	56	43	48	48	66	66	69	48	46	43	48	56	638
10 m	16	16	14	12	9	6	6	7	9	12	14	16	11
Darwin, Australia	386	312	254	97	15	3	<3	3	13	51	119	239	1,491
30 m	29	29	29	29	28	26	25	26	28	29	30	29	28
Mawson, Antarctica	11	30	20	10	44	180	4	40	3	20	0	0	362
14 m	0	−5	−10	−14	−15	−16	−18	−18	−19	−13	−5	−1	−11
Perth, Australia	8	10	20	43	130	180	170	149	86	56	20	13	881
60 m	23	23	22	19	16	14	13	13	15	16	19	22	18
Sydney, Australia	89	102	127	135	127	117	117	76	73	71	73	73	1,181
42 m	22	22	21	18	15	13	12	13	15	18	19	21	17
NORTH AMERICA													
Anchorage, USA	20	18	15	10	13	18	41	66	66	56	25	23	371
40 m	−11	−8	−5	2	7	12	14	13	9	2	−5	−11	2
Chicago, USA	51	51	66	71	86	89	84	81	79	66	61	51	836
251 m	−4	−3	2	9	14	20	23	22	19	12	5	−1	10
Churchill, Canada	15	13	18	23	32	44	46	58	51	43	39	21	402
13 m	−28	−26	−20	−10	−2	6	12	11	5	−2	−12	−22	−7
Edmonton, Canada	25	19	19	22	43	77	89	78	39	17	16	25	466
676 m	−15	−10	−5	4	11	15	17	16	11	6	−4	−10	3
Honolulu, USA	104	66	79	48	25	18	23	28	36	48	64	104	643
12 m	23	18	19	20	22	24	25	26	26	24	22	19	22
Houston, USA	89	76	84	91	119	117	99	99	104	94	89	109	1,171
12 m	12	13	17	21	24	27	28	29	26	22	16	12	21

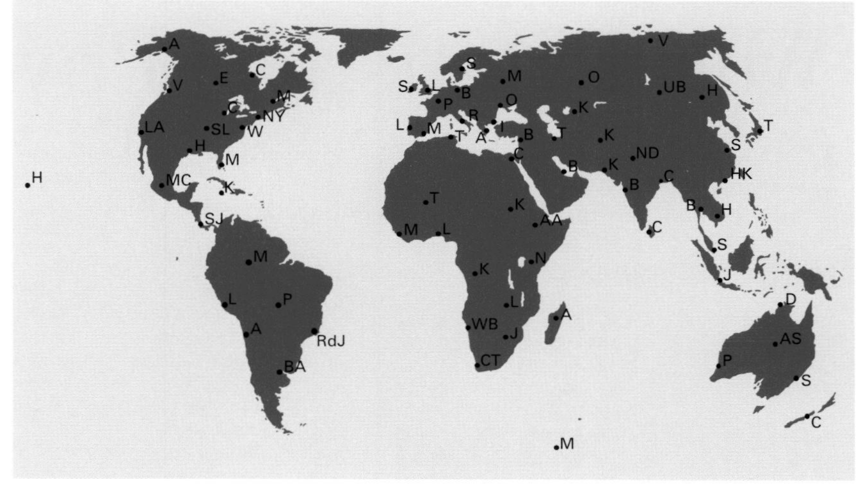

CITY	JAN.	FEB.	MAR.	APR.	MAY	JUNE	JULY	AUG.	SEPT.	OCT.	NOV.	DEC.	YEAR
NORTH AMERICA (continued)													
Kingston, Jamaica	23	15	23	31	102	89	38	91	99	180	74	36	800
34 m	25	25	25	26	26	28	28	28	27	27	26	26	26
Los Angeles, USA	79	76	71	25	10	3	<3	<3	5	15	31	66	381
95 m	13	14	14	16	17	19	21	22	21	18	16	14	17
Mexico City, Mexico	13	5	10	20	53	119	170	152	130	51	18	8	747
2,309 m	12	13	16	18	19	19	17	18	18	16	14	13	16
Miami, USA	71	53	64	81	173	178	155	160	203	234	71	51	1,516
8 m	20	20	22	23	25	27	28	28	27	25	22	21	24
Montréal, Canada	72	65	74	74	66	82	90	92	88	76	81	87	946
57 m	−10	−9	−3	−6	13	18	21	20	15	9	2	−7	6
New York City, USA	94	97	91	81	81	84	107	109	86	89	76	91	1,092
96 m	−1	−1	3	10	16	20	23	23	21	15	7	2	11
St Louis, USA	58	64	89	97	114	114	89	86	81	74	71	64	1,001
173 m	0	1	7	13	19	24	26	26	22	15	8	2	14
San José, Costa Rica	15	5	20	46	229	241	211	241	305	300	145	41	1,798
1,146 m	19	19	21	21	22	21	21	21	21	20	20	19	20
Vancouver, Canada	154	115	101	60	52	45	32	41	67	114	150	182	1,113
14 m	3	5	6	9	12	15	17	17	14	10	6	4	10
Washington, DC, USA	86	76	91	84	94	99	112	109	94	74	66	79	1,064
22 m	1	2	7	12	18	23	25	24	20	14	8	3	13
SOUTH AMERICA													
Antofagasta, Chile	0	0	0	<3	<3	3	5	3	<3	3	<3	0	13
94 m	21	21	20	18	16	15	14	14	15	16	18	19	17
Buenos Aires, Arg.	79	71	109	89	76	61	56	61	79	86	84	99	950
27 m	23	23	21	17	13	9	10	11	13	15	19	22	16
Lima, Peru	3	<3	<3	<3	5	5	8	8	8	3	3	<3	41
120 m	23	24	24	22	19	17	17	16	17	18	19	21	20
Manaus, Brazil	249	231	262	221	170	84	58	38	46	107	142	203	1,811
44 m	28	28	28	27	28	28	28	28	29	29	29	28	28
Paraná, Brazil	287	236	239	102	13	<3	3	5	28	127	231	310	1,582
260 m	23	23	23	23	23	21	21	22	24	24	24	23	23
Rio de Janeiro, Brazil	125	122	130	107	79	53	41	43	66	79	104	137	1,082
61 m	26	26	25	24	22	21	21	21	22	23	23	25	23

World Statistics: Physical Dimensions

Each topic list is divided into continents and within a continent the items are listed in order of size. The order of the continents is as in the atlas, Europe through to South America. The lists down to this mark > are complete; below they are selective. The world top ten are shown in square brackets; in the case of mountains this has not been done because the world top 30 are all in Asia. The figures are rounded as appropriate.

WORLD, CONTINENTS, OCEANS

THE WORLD

	km²	miles²	%
The World	509,450,000	196,672,000	–
Land	149,450,000	57,688,000	29.3
Water	360,000,000	138,984,000	70.7
Asia	44,500,000	17,177,000	29.8
Africa	30,302,000	11,697,000	20.3
North America	24,241,000	9,357,000	16.2
South America	17,793,000	6,868,000	11.9
Antarctica	14,100,000	5,443,000	9.4
Europe	9,957,000	3,843,000	6.7
Australia & Oceania	8,557,000	3,303,000	5.7
Pacific Ocean	179,679,000	69,356,000	49.9
Atlantic Ocean	92,373,000	35,657,000	25.7
Indian Ocean	73,917,000	28,532,000	20.5
Arctic Ocean	14,090,000	5,439,000	3.9

SEAS

South China Sea	2,974,600	1,148,500
Bering Sea	2,268,000	875,000
Sea of Okhotsk	1,528,000	590,000
East China & Yellow	1,249,000	482,000
Sea of Japan	1,008,000	389,000
Gulf of California	162,000	62,500
Bass Strait	75,000	29,000

ATLANTIC

	km²	miles²
Caribbean Sea	2,766,000	1,068,000
Mediterranean Sea	2,516,000	971,000
Gulf of Mexico	1,543,000	596,000
Hudson Bay	1,232,000	476,000
North Sea	575,000	223,000
Black Sea	462,000	178,000
Baltic Sea	422,170	163,000
Gulf of St Lawrence	238,000	92,000

INDIAN

	km²	miles²
Red Sea	438,000	169,000
The Gulf	239,000	92,000

MOUNTAINS

EUROPE

		m	ft
Elbrus	Russia	5,642	18,510
Mont Blanc	France/Italy	4,807	15,771
Monte Rosa	Italy/Switzerland	4,634	15,203
Dom	Switzerland	4,545	14,911
Liskamm	Switzerland	4,527	14,852
Weisshorn	Switzerland	4,505	14,780
Taschorn	Switzerland	4,490	14,730
Matterhorn/Cervino	Italy/Switz.	4,478	14,691
Mont Maudit	France/Italy	4,465	14,649
Dent Blanche	Switzerland	4,356	14,291
Nadelhorn	Switzerland	4,327	14,196
> Grandes Jorasses	France/Italy	4,208	13,806
Jungfrau	Switzerland	4,158	13,642
Barre des Ecrins	France	4,103	13,461
Gran Paradiso	Italy	4,061	13,323
Piz Bernina	Italy/Switzerland	4,049	13,284
Eiger	Switzerland	3,970	13,025
Monte Viso	Italy	3,841	12,602
Grossglockner	Austria	3,797	12,457
Wildspitze	Austria	3,772	12,382
Monte Disgrazia	Italy	3,678	12,066
Mulhacén	Spain	3,478	11,411
Pico de Aneto	Spain	3,404	11,168
Marmolada	Italy	3,342	10,964
Etna	Italy	3,340	10,958
Zugspitze	Germany	2,962	9,718
Musala	Bulgaria	2,925	9,596
Olympus	Greece	2,917	9,570
Triglav	Slovenia	2,863	9,393
Monte Cinto	France (Corsica)	2,710	8,891
Gerlachovka	Slovak Republic	2,655	8,711
Galdhøpiggen	Norway	2,468	8,100
Hvannadalshnúkur	Iceland	2,119	6,952
Ben Nevis	UK	1,343	4,406

ASIA

		m	ft
Everest	China/Nepal	8,850	29,035
K2 (Godwin Austen)	China/Kashmir	8,611	28,251
Kanchenjunga	India/Nepal	8,598	28,208
Lhotse	China/Nepal	8,516	27,939
Makalu	China/Nepal	8,481	27,824
Cho Oyu	China/Nepal	8,201	26,906
Dhaulagiri	Nepal	8,172	26,811
Manaslu	Nepal	8,156	26,758
Nanga Parbat	Kashmir	8,126	26,660
Annapurna	Nepal	8,078	26,502
Gasherbrum	China/Kashmir	8,068	26,469
Broad Peak	China/Kashmir	8,051	26,414
Xixabangma	China	8,012	26,286
Kangbachen	India/Nepal	7,902	25,925
Jannu	India/Nepal	7,902	25,925
Gayachung Kang	Nepal	7,897	25,909
Himalchuli	Nepal	7,893	25,896
Disteghil Sar	Kashmir	7,885	25,869
Nuptse	Nepal	7,879	25,849
Khunyang Chhish	Kashmir	7,852	25,761
Masherbrum	Kashmir	7,821	25,659
Nanda Devi	India	7,817	25,646
Rakaposhi	Kashmir	7,788	25,551
Batura	Kashmir	7,785	25,541
Namche Barwa	China	7,756	25,446
Kamet	India	7,756	25,446
Soltoro Kangri	Kashmir	7,742	25,400
Gurla Mandhata	China	7,728	25,354
Trivor	Pakistan	7,720	25,328
> Kongur Shan	China	7,719	25,324
Tirich Mir	Pakistan	7,690	25,229
K'ula Shan	Bhutan/China	7,543	24,747
Pik Kommunizma	Tajikistan	7,495	24,590
Demavend	Iran	5,604	18,386
Ararat	Turkey	5,165	16,945
Gunong Kinabalu	Malaysia (Borneo)	4,101	13,455
Yu Shan	Taiwan	3,997	13,113
Fuji-San	Japan	3,776	12,388

AFRICA

		m	ft
Kilimanjaro	Tanzania	5,895	19,340
Mt Kenya	Kenya	5,199	17,057
Ruwenzori (Margherita)	Uganda/Congo (D.R.)	5,109	16,762
Ras Dashan	Ethiopia	4,620	15,157
Meru	Tanzania	4,565	14,977
Karisimbi	Rwanda/Congo (D.R.)	4,507	14,787
Mt Elgon	Kenya/Uganda	4,321	14,176
Batu	Ethiopia	4,307	14,130
Guna	Ethiopia	4,231	13,882
Toubkal	Morocco	4,165	13,665
Irhil Mgoun	Morocco	4,071	13,356
Mt Cameroon	Cameroon	4,070	13,353
Amba Ferit	Ethiopia	3,875	13,042
Pico del Teide	Spain (Tenerife)	3,718	12,198
Thabana Ntlenyana	Lesotho	3,482	11,424
Emi Koussi	Chad	3,415	11,204
> Mt aux Sources	Lesotho/S. Africa	3,282	10,768
Mt Piton	Réunion	3,069	10,069

OCEANIA

		m	ft
Puncak Jaya	Indonesia	5,029	16,499
Puncak Trikora	Indonesia	4,750	15,584
Puncak Mandala	Indonesia	4,702	15,427
Mt Wilhelm	Papua NG	4,508	14,790
> Mauna Kea	USA (Hawaii)	4,205	13,796
Mauna Loa	USA (Hawaii)	4,169	13,681
Mt Cook (Aoraki)	New Zealand	3,753	12,313
Mt Balbi	Solomon Is.	2,439	8,002
Orohena	Tahiti	2,241	7,352
Mt Kosciuszko	Australia	2,237	7,339

NORTH AMERICA

		m	ft
Mt McKinley (Denali)	USA (Alaska)	6,194	20,321
Mt Logan	Canada	5,959	19,551
Citlaltepetl	Mexico	5,700	18,701
Mt St Elias	USA/Canada	5,489	18,008
Popocatepetl	Mexico	5,452	17,887

NORTH AMERICA (continued)

		m	ft
Mt Foraker	USA (Alaska)	5,304	17,401
Ixtaccihuatl	Mexico	5,286	17,342
Lucania	Canada	5,227	17,149
Mt Steele	Canada	5,073	16,644
Mt Bona	USA (Alaska)	5,005	16,420
Mt Blackburn	USA (Alaska)	4,996	16,391
Mt Sanford	USA (Alaska)	4,940	16,207
Mt Wood	Canada	4,848	15,905
Nevado de Toluca	Mexico	4,670	15,321
Mt Fairweather	USA (Alaska)	4,663	15,298
Mt Hunter	USA (Alaska)	4,442	14,573
Mt Whitney	USA	4,418	14,495
Mt Elbert	USA	4,399	14,432
Mt Harvard	USA	4,395	14,419
Mt Rainier	USA	4,392	14,409
> Blanca Peak	USA	4,372	14,344
Longs Peak	USA	4,345	14,255
Tajumulco	Guatemala	4,220	13,845
Grand Teton	USA	4,197	13,770
Mt Waddington	Canada	3,994	13,104
Mt Robson	Canada	3,954	12,972
Chirripó Grande	Costa Rica	3,837	12,589
Pico Duarte	Dominican Rep.	3,175	10,417

SOUTH AMERICA

		m	ft
Aconcagua	Argentina	6,960	22,834
Bonete	Argentina	6,872	22,546
Ojos del Salado	Argentina/Chile	6,863	22,516
Pissis	Argentina	6,779	22,241
Mercedario	Argentina/Chile	6,770	22,211
Huascaran	Peru	6,768	22,204
Llullaillaco	Argentina/Chile	6,723	22,057
Nudo de Cachi	Argentina	6,720	22,047
Yerupaja	Peru	6,632	21,758
N. de Tres Cruces	Argentina/Chile	6,620	21,719
Incahuasi	Argentina/Chile	6,601	21,654
Cerro Galan	Argentina	6,600	21,654
Tupungato	Argentina/Chile	6,570	21,555
> Sajama	Bolivia	6,542	21,463
Illimani	Bolivia	6,485	21,276
Coropuna	Peru	6,425	21,079
Ausangate	Peru	6,384	20,945
Cerro del Toro	Argentina	6,380	20,932
Siula Grande	Peru	6,356	20,853
Chimborazo	Ecuador	6,267	20,561
Alpamayo	Peru	5,947	19,511
Cotapaxi	Ecuador	5,896	19,344
Pico Colon	Colombia	5,800	19,029
Pico Bolivar	Venezuela	5,007	16,427

ANTARCTICA

	m	ft
Vinson Massif	4,897	16,066
Mt Kirkpatrick	4,528	14,855
Mt Markham	4,349	14,268

OCEAN DEPTHS

ATLANTIC OCEAN

	m	ft	
Puerto Rico (Milwaukee) Deep	9,220	30,249	[7]
Cayman Trench	7,680	25,197	[10]
Gulf of Mexico	5,203	17,070	
Mediterranean Sea	5,121	16,801	
Black Sea	2,211	7,254	
North Sea	660	2,165	
Baltic Sea	463	1,519	
Hudson Bay	258	846	

INDIAN OCEAN

	m	ft
Java Trench	7,450	24,442
Red Sea	2,635	8,454
Persian Gulf	73	239

PACIFIC OCEAN

	m	ft	
Mariana Trench	11,022	36,161	[1]
Tonga Trench	10,882	35,702	[2]
Japan Trench	10,554	34,626	[3]
Kuril Trench	10,542	34,587	[4]
Mindanao Trench	10,497	34,439	[5]
Kermadec Trench	10,047	32,962	[6]

PACIFIC OCEAN (continued)

	m	ft	
Peru–Chile Trench	8,050	26,410	[8]
Aleutian Trench	7,822	25,662	[9]

ARCTIC OCEAN

	m	ft
Molloy Deep	5,608	18,399

LAND LOWS

		m	ft
Dead Sea	Asia	−403	−1,322
Lake Assal	Africa	−156	−512
Death Valley	N. America	−86	−282
Valdés Peninsula	S. America	−40	−131
Caspian Sea	Europe	−28	−92
Lake Eyre North	Oceania	−16	−52

RIVERS

EUROPE

		km	miles	
Volga	Caspian Sea	3,700	2,300	
Danube	Black Sea	2,850	1,770	
Ural	Caspian Sea	2,535	1,575	
Dnepr (Dnipro)	Black Sea	2,285	1,420	
Kama	Volga	2,030	1,260	
Don	Black Sea	1,990	1,240	
Petchora	Arctic Ocean	1,790	1,110	
Oka	Volga	1,480	920	
Belaya	Kama	1,420	880	
Dnister (Dniester)	Black Sea	1,400	870	
Vyatka	Kama	1,370	850	
Rhine	North Sea	1,320	820	
N. Dvina	Arctic Ocean	1,290	800	
Desna	Dnepr (Dnipro)	1,190	740	
Elbe	North Sea	1,145	710	
Wisla	Baltic Sea	1,090	675	
Loire	Atlantic Ocean	1,020	635	

ASIA

		km	miles	
Yangtze	Pacific Ocean	6,380	3,960	[3]
Yenisey–Angara	Arctic Ocean	5,550	3,445	[5]
Huang He	Pacific Ocean	5,464	3,395	[6]
Ob–Irtysh	Arctic Ocean	5,410	3,360	[7]
Mekong	Pacific Ocean	4,500	2,795	[9]
Amur	Pacific Ocean	4,400	2,730	[10]
Lena	Arctic Ocean	4,400	2,730	
Irtysh	Ob	4,250	2,640	
Yenisey	Arctic Ocean	4,090	2,540	
Ob	Arctic Ocean	3,680	2,285	
Indus	Indian Ocean	3,100	1,925	
Brahmaputra	Indian Ocean	2,900	1,800	
Syrdarya	Aral Sea	2,860	1,775	
Salween	Indian Ocean	2,800	1,740	
Euphrates	Indian Ocean	2,700	1,675	
Vilyuy	Lena	2,650	1,645	
Kolyma	Arctic Ocean	2,600	1,615	
Amudarya	Aral Sea	2,540	1,575	
Ural	Caspian Sea	2,535	1,575	
Ganges	Indian Ocean	2,510	1,560	
Si Kiang	Pacific Ocean	2,100	1,305	
Irrawaddy	Indian Ocean	2,010	1,250	
Tarim–Yarkand	Lop Nor	2,000	1,240	
Tigris	Indian Ocean	1,900	1,180	

AFRICA

		km	miles	
Nile	Mediterranean	6,670	4,140	[1]
Congo	Atlantic Ocean	4,670	2,900	[8]
Niger	Atlantic Ocean	4,180	2,595	
Zambezi	Indian Ocean	3,540	2,200	
Oubangi/Uele	Congo (D.R.)	2,250	1,400	
Kasai	Congo (D.R.)	1,950	1,210	
Shaballe	Indian Ocean	1,930	1,200	
Orange	Atlantic Ocean	1,860	1,155	
Cubango	Okavango Swamps	1,800	1,120	
Limpopo	Indian Ocean	1,600	995	
Senegal	Atlantic Ocean	1,600	995	
Volta	Atlantic Ocean	1,500	930	

AUSTRALIA

		km	miles
Murray–Darling	Indian Ocean	3,750	2,330
Darling	Murray	3,070	1,905
Murray	Indian Ocean	2,575	1,600
Murrumbidgee	Murray	1,690	1,050

NORTH AMERICA

		km	miles	
Mississippi–Missouri	Gulf of Mexico	6,020	3,740	[4]
Mackenzie	Arctic Ocean	4,240	2,630	
Mississippi	Gulf of Mexico	3,780	2,350	
Missouri	Mississippi	3,780	2,350	
Yukon	Pacific Ocean	3,185	1,980	
Rio Grande	Gulf of Mexico	3,030	1,880	

NORTH AMERICA (continued)

		km	miles
Arkansas	Mississippi	2,340	1,450
Colorado	Pacific Ocean	2,330	1,445
Red	Mississippi	2,040	1,270
Columbia	Pacific Ocean	1,950	1,210
Saskatchewan	Lake Winnipeg	1,940	1,205
Snake	Columbia	1,670	1,040
Churchill	Hudson Bay	1,600	990
Ohio	Mississippi	1,580	980
Brazos	Gulf of Mexico	1,400	870
St Lawrence	Atlantic Ocean	1,170	730

SOUTH AMERICA

		km	miles	
Amazon	Atlantic Ocean	6,450	4,010	[2]
Paraná–Plate	Atlantic Ocean	4,500	2,800	
Purus	Amazon	3,350	2,080	
Madeira	Amazon	3,200	1,990	
São Francisco	Atlantic Ocean	2,900	1,800	
Paraná	Plate	2,800	1,740	
Tocantins	Atlantic Ocean	2,750	1,710	
Paraguay	Paraná	2,550	1,580	
Orinoco	Atlantic Ocean	2,500	1,550	
Pilcomayo	Paraná	2,500	1,550	
Araguaia	Tocantins	2,250	1,400	
Juruá	Amazon	2,000	1,240	
Xingu	Amazon	1,980	1,230	
Ucayali	Amazon	1,900	1,180	
Marañón	Amazon	1,600	990	
Uruguay	Plate	1,600	990	

LAKES

EUROPE

		km²	miles²
Lake Ladoga	Russia	17,700	6,800
Lake Onega	Russia	9,700	3,700
Saimaa system	Finland	8,000	3,100
Vänern	Sweden	5,500	2,100
Rybinskoye Res.	Russia	4,700	1,800

ASIA

		km²	miles²	
Caspian Sea	Asia	371,800	143,550	[1]
Lake Baykal	Russia	30,500	11,780	[8]
Aral Sea	Kazakstan/Uzbekistan	28,687	11,086	[10]
Tonlé Sap	Cambodia	20,000	7,700	
Lake Balqash	Kazakstan	18,500	7,100	
Lake Dongting	China	12,000	4,600	
Lake Ysyk	Kyrgyzstan	6,200	2,400	
Lake Orumiyeh	Iran	5,900	2,300	
Lake Koko	China	5,700	2,200	
Lake Poyang	China	5,000	1,900	
Lake Khanka	China/Russia	4,400	1,700	
Lake Van	Turkey	3,500	1,400	

AFRICA

		km²	miles²	
Lake Victoria	E. Africa	68,000	26,000	[3]
Lake Tanganyika	C. Africa	33,000	13,000	[6]
Lake Malawi/Nyasa	E. Africa	29,600	11,430	[9]
Lake Chad	C. Africa	25,000	9,700	
Lake Turkana	Ethiopia/Kenya	8,500	3,300	
Lake Volta	Ghana	8,500	3,300	
Lake Bangweulu	Zambia	8,000	3,100	
Lake Rukwa	Tanzania	7,000	2,700	
Lake Mai-Ndombe	Congo (D.R.)	6,500	2,500	
Lake Kariba	Zambia/Zimbabwe	5,300	2,000	
Lake Albert	Uganda/Congo (D.R.)	5,300	2,000	
Lake Nasser	Egypt/Sudan	5,200	2,000	
Lake Mweru	Zambia/Congo (D.R.)	4,900	1,900	
Lake Cabora Bassa	Mozambique	4,500	1,700	
Lake Kyoga	Uganda	4,400	1,700	
Lake Tana	Ethiopia	3,630	1,400	

AUSTRALIA

		km²	miles²
Lake Eyre	Australia	8,900	3,400
Lake Torrens	Australia	5,800	2,200
Lake Gairdner	Australia	4,800	1,900

NORTH AMERICA

		km²	miles²	
Lake Superior	Canada/USA	82,350	31,800	[2]
Lake Huron	Canada/USA	59,600	23,010	[4]
Lake Michigan	USA	58,000	22,400	[5]
Great Bear Lake	Canada	31,800	12,280	[7]
Great Slave Lake	Canada	28,500	11,000	
Lake Erie	Canada/USA	25,700	9,900	
Lake Winnipeg	Canada	24,400	9,400	
Lake Ontario	Canada/USA	19,500	7,500	
Lake Nicaragua	Nicaragua	8,200	3,200	
Lake Athabasca	Canada	8,100	3,100	
Smallwood Reservoir	Canada	6,530	2,520	
Reindeer Lake	Canada	6,400	2,500	
Nettilling Lake	Canada	5,500	2,100	
Lake Winnipegosis	Canada	5,400	2,100	

SOUTH AMERICA

		km²	miles²
Lake Titicaca	Bolivia/Peru	8,300	3,200
Lake Poopo	Peru	2,800	1,100

ISLANDS

EUROPE

		km²	miles²	
Great Britain	UK	229,880	88,700	[8]
Iceland	Atlantic Ocean	103,000	39,800	
Ireland	Ireland/UK	84,400	32,600	
Novaya Zemlya (N.)	Russia	48,200	18,600	
W. Spitzbergen	Norway	39,000	15,100	
Novaya Zemlya (S.)	Russia	33,200	12,800	
Sicily	Italy	25,500	9,800	
Sardinia	Italy	24,000	9,300	
N.E. Spitzbergen	Norway	15,000	5,600	
Corsica	France	8,700	3,400	
Crete	Greece	8,350	3,200	
Zealand	Denmark	6,850	2,600	

ASIA

		km²	miles²	
Borneo	S. E. Asia	744,360	287,400	[3]
Sumatra	Indonesia	473,600	182,860	[6]
Honshu	Japan	230,500	88,980	[7]
Sulawesi (Celebes)	Indonesia	189,000	73,000	
Java	Indonesia	126,700	48,900	
Luzon	Philippines	104,700	40,400	
Mindanao	Philippines	101,500	39,200	
Hokkaido	Japan	78,400	30,300	
Sakhalin	Russia	74,060	28,600	
Sri Lanka	Indian Ocean	65,600	25,300	
Taiwan	Pacific Ocean	36,000	13,900	
Kyushu	Japan	35,700	13,800	
Hainan	China	34,000	13,100	
Timor	Indonesia	33,600	13,000	
Shikoku	Japan	18,800	7,300	
Halmahera	Indonesia	18,000	6,900	
Ceram	Indonesia	17,150	6,600	
Sumbawa	Indonesia	15,450	6,000	
Flores	Indonesia	15,200	5,900	
Samar	Philippines	13,100	5,100	
Negros	Philippines	12,700	4,900	
Bangka	Indonesia	12,000	4,600	
Palawan	Philippines	12,000	4,600	
Panay	Philippines	11,500	4,400	
Sumba	Indonesia	11,100	4,300	
Mindoro	Philippines	9,750	3,800	

AFRICA

		km²	miles²	
Madagascar	Indian Ocean	587,040	226,660	[4]
Socotra	Indian Ocean	3,600	1,400	
Réunion	Indian Ocean	2,500	965	
Tenerife	Atlantic Ocean	2,350	900	
Mauritius	Indian Ocean	1,865	720	

OCEANIA

		km²	miles²	
New Guinea	Indon./Papua NG	821,030	317,000	[2]
New Zealand (S.)	Pacific Ocean	150,500	58,100	
New Zealand (N.)	Pacific Ocean	114,700	44,300	
Tasmania	Australia	67,800	26,200	
New Britain	Papua NG	37,800	14,600	
New Caledonia	Pacific Ocean	19,100	7,400	
Viti Levu	Fiji	10,500	4,100	
Hawaii	Pacific Ocean	10,450	4,000	
Bougainville	Papua NG	9,600	3,700	
Guadalcanal	Solomon Is.	6,500	2,500	
Vanua Levu	Fiji	5,550	2,100	
New Ireland	Papua NG	3,200	1,200	

NORTH AMERICA

		km²	miles²	
Greenland	Atlantic Ocean	2,175,600	839,800	[1]
Baffin Is.	Canada	508,000	196,100	[5]
Victoria Is.	Canada	212,200	81,900	[9]
Ellesmere Is.	Canada	212,000	81,800	[10]
Cuba	Caribbean Sea	110,860	42,800	
Newfoundland	Canada	110,680	42,700	
Hispaniola	Dom. Rep./Haiti	76,200	29,400	
Banks Is.	Canada	67,000	25,900	
Devon Is.	Canada	54,500	21,000	
Melville Is.	Canada	42,400	16,400	
Vancouver Is.	Canada	32,150	12,400	
Somerset Is.	Canada	24,300	9,400	
Jamaica	Caribbean Sea	11,400	4,400	
Puerto Rico	Atlantic Ocean	8,900	3,400	
Cape Breton Is.	Canada	4,000	1,500	

SOUTH AMERICA

		km²	miles²	
Tierra del Fuego	Argentina/Chile	47,000	18,100	
Falkland Is. (East)	Atlantic Ocean	6,800	2,600	
South Georgia	Atlantic Ocean	4,200	1,600	
Galapagos (Isabela)	Pacific Ocean	2,250	870	

World: Regions in the News

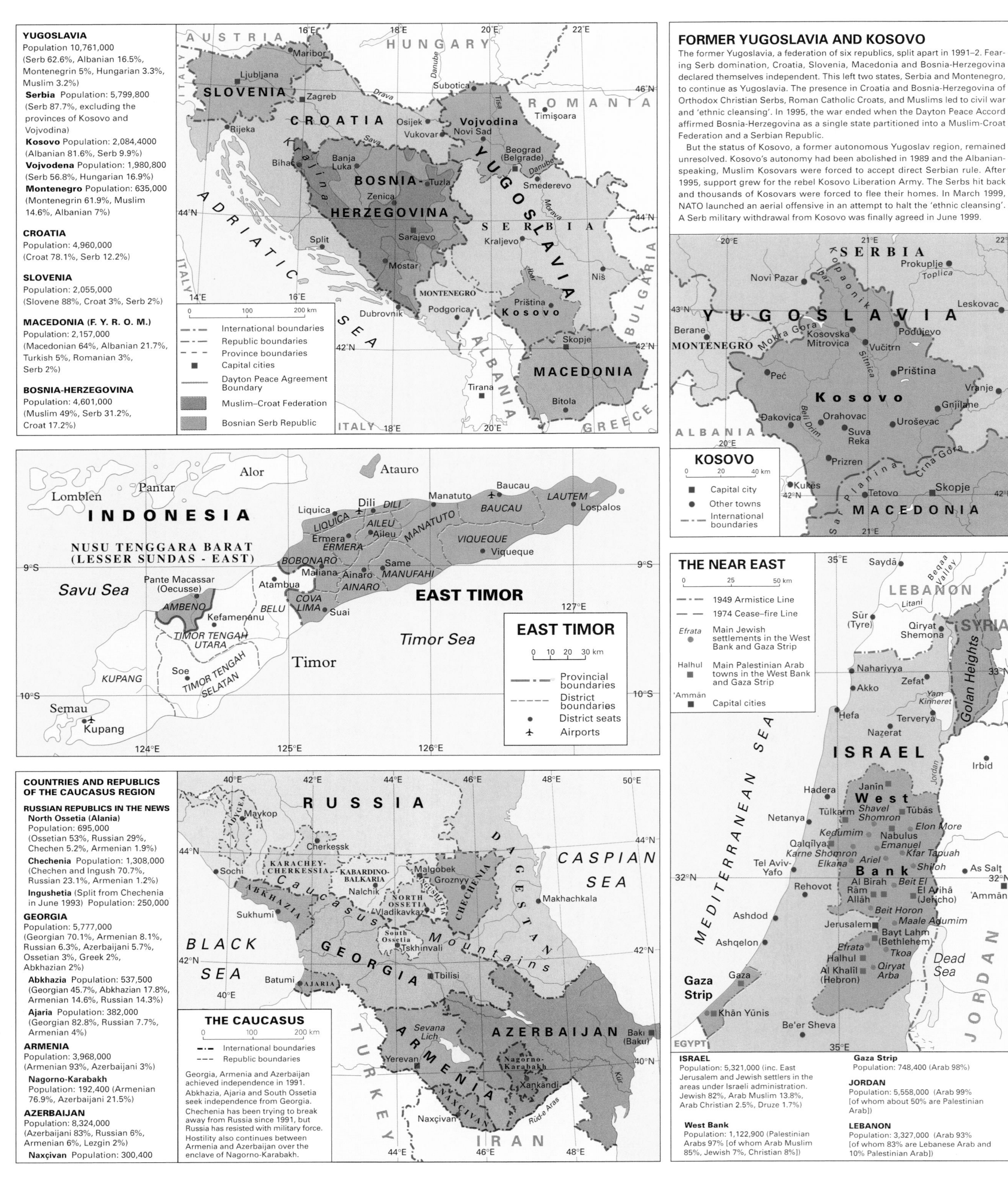

YUGOSLAVIA
Population 10,761,000
(Serb 62.6%, Albanian 16.5%, Montenegrin 5%, Hungarian 3.3%, Muslim 3.2%)
Serbia Population: 5,799,800 (Serb 87.7%, excluding the provinces of Kosovo and Vojvodina)
Kosovo Population: 2,084,4000 (Albanian 81.6%, Serb 9.9%)
Vojvodena Population: 1,980,800 (Serb 56.8%, Hungarian 16.9%)
Montenegro Population: 635,000 (Montenegrin 61.9%, Muslim 14.6%, Albanian 7%)
CROATIA
Population: 4,960,000
(Croat 78.1%, Serb 12.2%)
SLOVENIA
Population: 2,055,000
(Slovene 88%, Croat 3%, Serb 2%)
MACEDONIA (F. Y. R. O. M.)
Population: 2,157,000
(Macedonian 64%, Albanian 21.7%, Turkish 5%, Romanian 3%, Serb 2%)
BOSNIA-HERZEGOVINA
Population: 4,601,000
(Muslim 49%, Serb 31.2%, Croat 17.2%)
International boundaries
Republic boundaries
Province boundaries
Capital cities
Dayton Peace Agreement Boundary
Muslim–Croat Federation
Bosnian Serb Republic
FORMER YUGOSLAVIA AND KOSOVO
The former Yugoslavia, a federation of six republics, split apart in 1991–2. Fearing Serb domination, Croatia, Slovenia, Macedonia and Bosnia-Herzegovina declared themselves independent. This left two states, Serbia and Montenegro, to continue as Yugoslavia. The presence in Croatia and Bosnia-Herzegovina of Orthodox Christian Serbs, Roman Catholic Croats, and Muslims led to civil war and 'ethnic cleansing'. In 1995, the war ended when the Dayton Peace Accord affirmed Bosnia-Herzegovina as a single state partitioned into a Muslim-Croat Federation and a Serbian Republic.
But the status of Kosovo, a former autonomous Yugoslav region, remained unresolved. Kosovo's autonomy had been abolished in 1989 and the Albanian-speaking, Muslim Kosovars were forced to accept direct Serbian rule. After 1995, support grew for the rebel Kosovo Liberation Army. The Serbs hit back and thousands of Kosovars were forced to flee their homes. In March 1999, NATO launched an aerial offensive in an attempt to halt the 'ethnic cleansing'. A Serb military withdrawal from Kosovo was finally agreed in June 1999.
KOSOVO
Capital city
Other towns
International boundaries
EAST TIMOR
Provincial boundaries
District boundaries
District seats
Airports
INDONESIA
NUSU TENGGARA BARAT (LESSER SUNDAS - EAST)
Savu Sea
Timor Sea
Timor
THE NEAR EAST
1949 Armistice Line
1974 Cease-fire Line
Main Jewish settlements in the West Bank and Gaza Strip
Main Palestinian Arab towns in the West Bank and Gaza Strip
Capital cities
ISRAEL
Population: 5,321,000 (inc. East Jerusalem and Jewish settlers in the areas under Israeli administration. Jewish 82%, Arab Muslim 13.8%, Arab Christian 2.5%, Druze 1.7%)
West Bank
Population: 1,122,900 (Palestinian Arabs 97% [of whom Arab Muslim 85%, Jewish 7%, Christian 8%])
Gaza Strip
Population: 748,400 (Arab 98%)
JORDAN
Population: 5,558,000 (Arab 99% [of whom about 50% are Palestinian Arab])
LEBANON
Population: 3,327,000 (Arab 93% [of whom 83% are Lebanese Arab and 10% Palestinian Arab])
COUNTRIES AND REPUBLICS OF THE CAUCASUS REGION
RUSSIAN REPUBLICS IN THE NEWS
North Ossetia (Alania)
Population: 695,000
(Ossetian 53%, Russian 29%, Chechen 5.2%, Armenian 1.9%)
Chechenia Population: 1,308,000 (Chechen and Ingush 70.7%, Russian 23.1%, Armenian 1.2%)
Ingushetia (Split from Chechenia in June 1993) Population: 250,000
GEORGIA
Population: 5,777,000
(Georgian 70.1%, Armenian 8.1%, Russian 6.3%, Azerbaijani 5.7%, Ossetian 3%, Greek 2%, Abkhazian 2%)
Abkhazia Population: 537,500 (Georgian 45.7%, Abkhazian 17.8%, Armenian 14.6%, Russian 14.3%)
Ajaria Population: 382,000 (Georgian 82.8%, Russian 7.7%, Armenian 4%)
ARMENIA
Population: 3,968,000
(Armenian 93%, Azerbaijani 3%)
Nagorno-Karabakh Population: 192,400 (Armenian 76.9%, Azerbaijani 21.5%)
AZERBAIJAN
Population: 8,324,000
(Azerbaijani 83%, Russian 6%, Armenian 6%, Lezgin 2%)
Naxçivan Population: 300,400
THE CAUCASUS
International boundaries
Republic boundaries
Georgia, Armenia and Azerbaijan achieved independence in 1991. Abkhazia, Ajaria and South Ossetia seek independence from Georgia. Chechenia has been trying to break away from Russia since 1991, but Russia has resisted with military force. Hostility also continues between Armenia and Azerbaijan over the enclave of Nagorno-Karabakh.

The Earth in Space

The Universe 2

Star Charts and Constellations 4

The Solar System 8

The Earth: Time and Motion 10

The Earth from Space 12

The Dynamic Earth 14

Earthquakes and Volcanoes 16

Forces of Nature 18

Oceans and Ice 20

The Earth's Atmosphere 22

Climate and Weather 24

Water and Land Use 26

The Natural World 28

The Human World 30

Languages and Religions 32

International Organizations 34

Agriculture 36

Energy and Minerals 38

World Economies 40

Trade and Commerce 42

Travel and Communications 44

The World Today 46

The Universe

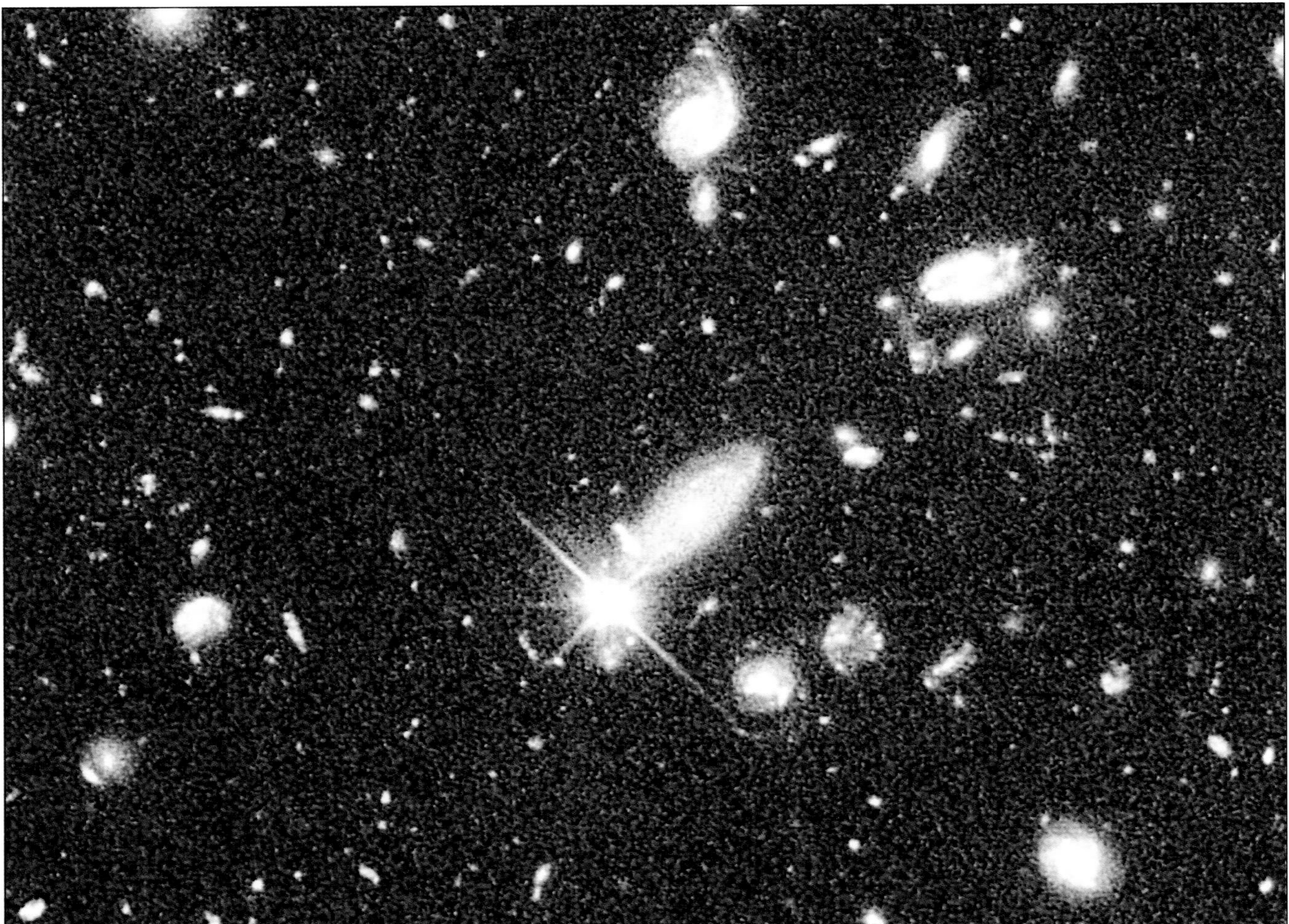

The depths of the Universe
This photograph shows some of the 1,500 or more galaxies that were recorded in the montage of photographs taken by the Hubble Space Telescope in 1995.

Just before Christmas 1995, the Hubble Space Telescope, which is in orbit about 580 km [360 miles] above the Earth, focused on a tiny area in distant space. Over a ten-day period, photographs taken by the telescope revealed unknown galaxies billions of times fainter than the human eye can see.

Because the light from these distant objects has taken so long to reach us, the photographs transmitted from the telescope and released to the media were the deepest look into space that astronomers have ever seen. The features they revealed were in existence when the Universe was less than a billion years old.

The Hubble Space Telescope is operated by the Space Telescope Science Institute in America and was launched in April 1990. The photographs it took of the Hubble Deep Field have been described by NASA as the biggest advance in astronomy since the work of the Italian scientist Galileo in the early 17th century. US scientists have graphically described the astonishing photographs received from the Telescope as 'postcards from the edge of space and time'.

THE BIG BANG

According to the latest theories, the Universe was created, and 'time' began, about 15,000 million (or 15 billion) years ago, though other estimates range from 8 to 24 billion years. Following a colossal explosion, called the 'Big Bang', the Universe expanded in the first millionth of a

The End of the Universe
The diagram shows two theories concerning the fate of the Universe. One theory, top, suggests that the Universe will expand indefinitely, moving into an immense dark graveyard. Another theory, bottom, suggests that the galaxies will fall back until everything is again concentrated in one point in a so-called 'Big Crunch'. This might then be followed by a new 'Big Bang'.

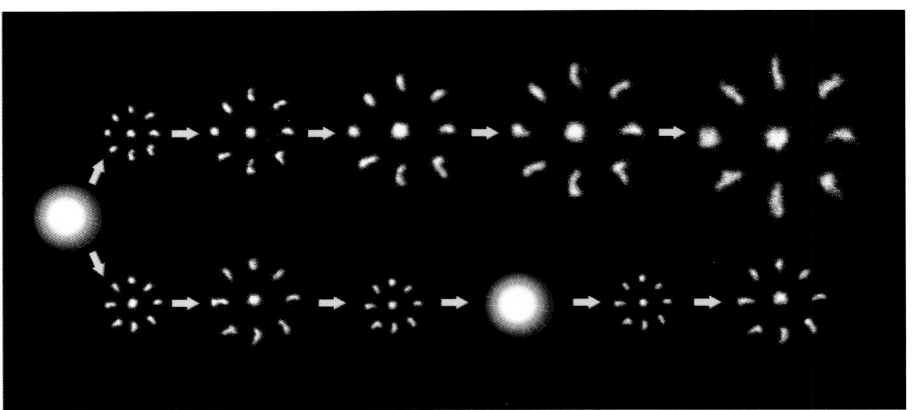

second of its existence from a dimensionless point of infinite mass and density into a fireball, about 30 billion km [19 billion miles] across. The Universe has been expanding ever since, as demonstrated in the 1920s by Edwin Hubble, the American astronomer after whom the Hubble Space Telescope was named.

The temperature at the end of the first second was perhaps 10 billion degrees – far too hot for composite atomic nuclei to exist. As a result, the fireball consisted mainly of radiation mixed with microscopic particles of matter. Almost a million years passed before the Universe was cool enough for atoms to form.

A few billion years later, atoms in regions where matter was relatively dense began, under the influence of gravity, to move together to form proto-galaxies – masses of gas separated by empty space. The proto-galaxies were dark, because the Universe had cooled. But a few billion years later, stars began to form within the proto-galaxies as particles were drawn together. The internal pressure produced as matter condensed created the high temperatures required to cause nuclear fusion. Stars were born and later destroyed. Each generation of stars fed on the debris of extinct ones. Each generation produced larger atoms, increasing the number of different chemical elements.

The Home Galaxy

This schematic plan shows that our Solar System is located in one of the spiral arms of the Milky Way galaxy, a little less than 30,000 light-years from its centre. The centre of the Milky Way galaxy is not visible from Earth. Instead, it is masked by light-absorbing clouds of interstellar dust.

THE GALAXIES

At least a billion galaxies are scattered through the Universe, though the discoveries made by the Hubble Space Telescope suggest that there may be far more than once thought, and some estimates are as high as 100 billion. The largest galaxies contain trillions of stars, while small ones contain less than a billion.

Galaxies tend to occur in groups or clusters, while some clusters appear to be grouped in vast superclusters. Our Local Cluster includes the spiral Milky Way galaxy, whose diameter is about 100,000 light-years; one light-year, the distance that light travels in one year, measures about 9,500 billion km [5,900 billion miles]. The Milky Way is a huge galaxy, shaped like a disk with a bulge at the centre. It is larger, brighter and more massive than many other known galaxies. It contains about 100 billion stars which rotate around the centre of the galaxy in the same direction as the Sun does.

One medium-sized star in the Milky Way galaxy is the Sun. After its formation, about 5 billion years ago, there was enough leftover matter around it to create the planets, asteroids,

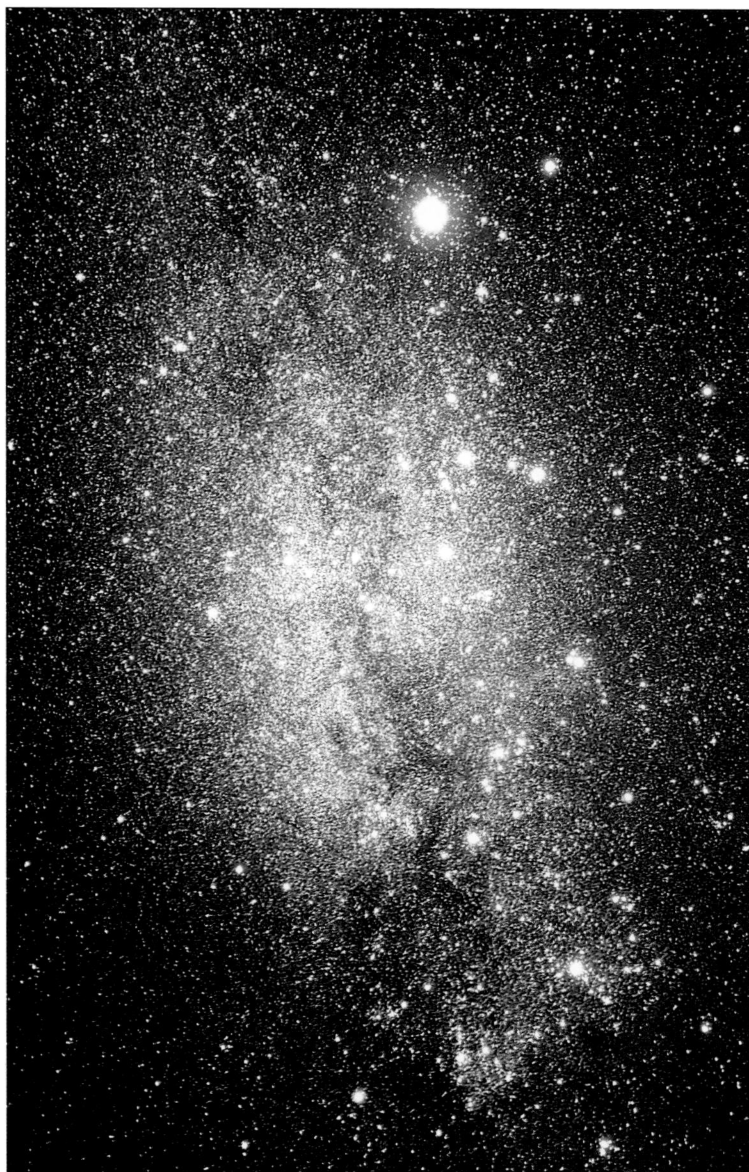

The Milky Way

This section of the Milky Way is dominated by Sirius, the Dog Star, top centre, in the constellation of Canis Major. Sirius is the brightest star in the sky.

moons and other bodies that together form our Solar System. The Solar System rotates around the centre of the Milky Way galaxy approximately every 225 million years.

Recent discoveries suggest that other stars similar to our Sun have planets orbiting around them, while evidence from the Hubble Space Telescope suggests that the raw materials from which planets are formed is common in dusty disks around many stars. This provokes one of the most intriguing of all the questions that has ever faced humanity. If there are other planets in the Universe, then do living organisms exist elsewhere?

Before the time of Galileo, people thought that the Earth lay at the centre of the Universe. But we now know that our Solar System and even the Milky Way galaxy are tiny specks in the Universe as a whole. Perhaps our planet is also not unique in being the only one to support intelligent life.

Star Charts and Constellations

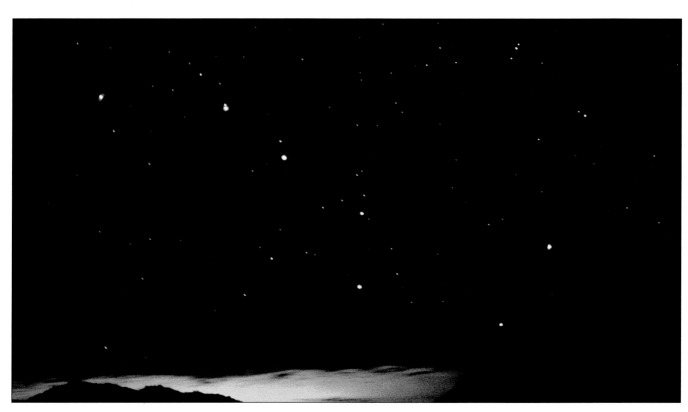

THE BRIGHTEST STARS

The 15 brightest stars visible from northern Europe. Magnitudes are given to the nearest tenth.

Sirius	−1.5
Arcturus	0.0
Vega	0.0
Capella	0.1
Rigel	0.1
Procyon	0.4
Betelgeuse	0.4
Altair	0.8
Aldebaran	0.8
Antares	1.0
Spica	1.0
Pollux	1.1
Fomalhaut	1.2
Deneb	1.2
Regulus	1.3

The Plough

The Plough, or Big Dipper, above glowing yellow clouds lit by city lights. It is part of a larger group called Ursa Major one of the best-known constellations of the northern hemisphere. The two bright stars to the lower right of the photograph (Merak and Dubhe) are known as the Pointers because they show the way to the Pole Star.

On a clear night, under the best conditions and far away from the glare of city lights, a person in northern Europe can look up and see about 2,500 stars. In a town, however, light pollution can reduce visibility to 200 stars or less. Over the whole celestial sphere it is possible to see about 8,500 stars with the naked eye and it is only when you look through a telescope that you begin to realize that the number of stars is countless.

SMALL AND LARGE STARS

Stars come in several sizes. Some, called neutron stars, are compact, with the same mass as the Sun but with diameters of only about 20 km [12 miles]. Larger than neutron stars are the small white dwarfs. Our Sun is a medium-sized star, but many visible stars in the night sky are giants with diameters between 10 and 100 times that of the Sun, or supergiants with diameters over 100 times that of the Sun.

Two bright stars in the constellation Orion are Betelgeuse (also known as Alpha Orionis) and Rigel (or Beta Orionis). Betelgeuse is an orange-red supergiant, whose diameter is about 400 times that of the Sun. Rigel is also a supergiant. Its diameter is about 50 times that of the Sun, but its luminosity is estimated to be over 100,000 times that of the Sun.

The stars we see in the night sky all belong to our home galaxy, the Milky Way. This name is also used for the faint, silvery band that arches across the sky. This band, a slice through our

THE CONSTELLATIONS

The constellations and their English names. Constellations visible from both hemispheres are listed.

Andromeda	Andromeda	Delphinus	Dolphin	Perseus	Perseus
Antlia	Air Pump	Dorado	Swordfish	Phoenix	Phoenix
Apus	Bird of Paradise	Draco	Dragon	Pictor	Easel
Aquarius	Water Carrier	Equuleus	Little Horse	Pisces	Fishes
Aquila	Eagle	Eridanus	River Eridanus	Piscis Austrinus	Southern Fish
Ara	Altar	Fornax	Furnace	Puppis	Ship's Stern
Aries	Ram	Gemini	Twins	Pyxis	Mariner's Compass
Auriga	Charioteer	Grus	Crane	Reticulum	Net
Boötes	Herdsman	Hercules	Hercules	Sagitta	Arrow
Caelum	Chisel	Horologium	Clock	Sagittarius	Archer
Camelopardalis	Giraffe	Hydra	Water Snake	Scorpius	Scorpion
Cancer	Crab	Hydrus	Sea Serpent	Sculptor	Sculptor
Canes Venatici	Hunting Dogs	Indus	Indian	Scutum	Shield
Canis Major	Great Dog	Lacerta	Lizard	Serpens*	Serpent
Canis Minor	Little Dog	Leo	Lion	Sextans	Sextant
Capricornus	Sea Goat	Leo Minor	Little Lion	Taurus	Bull
Carina	Ship's Keel	Lepus	Hare	Telescopium	Telescope
Cassiopeia	Cassiopeia	Libra	Scales	Triangulum	Triangle
Centaurus	Centaur	Lupus	Wolf	Triangulum Australe	
Cepheus	Cepheus	Lynx	Lynx		Southern Triangle
Cetus	Whale	Lyra	Lyre	Tucana	Toucan
Chamaeleon	Chameleon	Mensa	Table	Ursa Major	Great Bear
Circinus	Compasses	Microscopium	Microscope	Ursa Minor	Little Bear
Columba	Dove	Monoceros	Unicorn	Vela	Ship's Sails
Coma Berenices	Berenice's Hair	Musca	Fly	Virgo	Virgin
Corona Australis	Southern Crown	Norma	Level	Volans	Flying Fish
Corona Borealis	Northern Crown	Octans	Octant	Vulpecula	Fox
Corvus	Crow	Ophiuchus	Serpent Bearer		
Crater	Cup	Orion	Hunter		
Crux	Southern Cross	Pavo	Peacock	** In two halves: Serpens Caput, the*	
Cygnus	Swan	Pegasus	Winged Horse	*head, and Serpens Cauda, the tail.*	

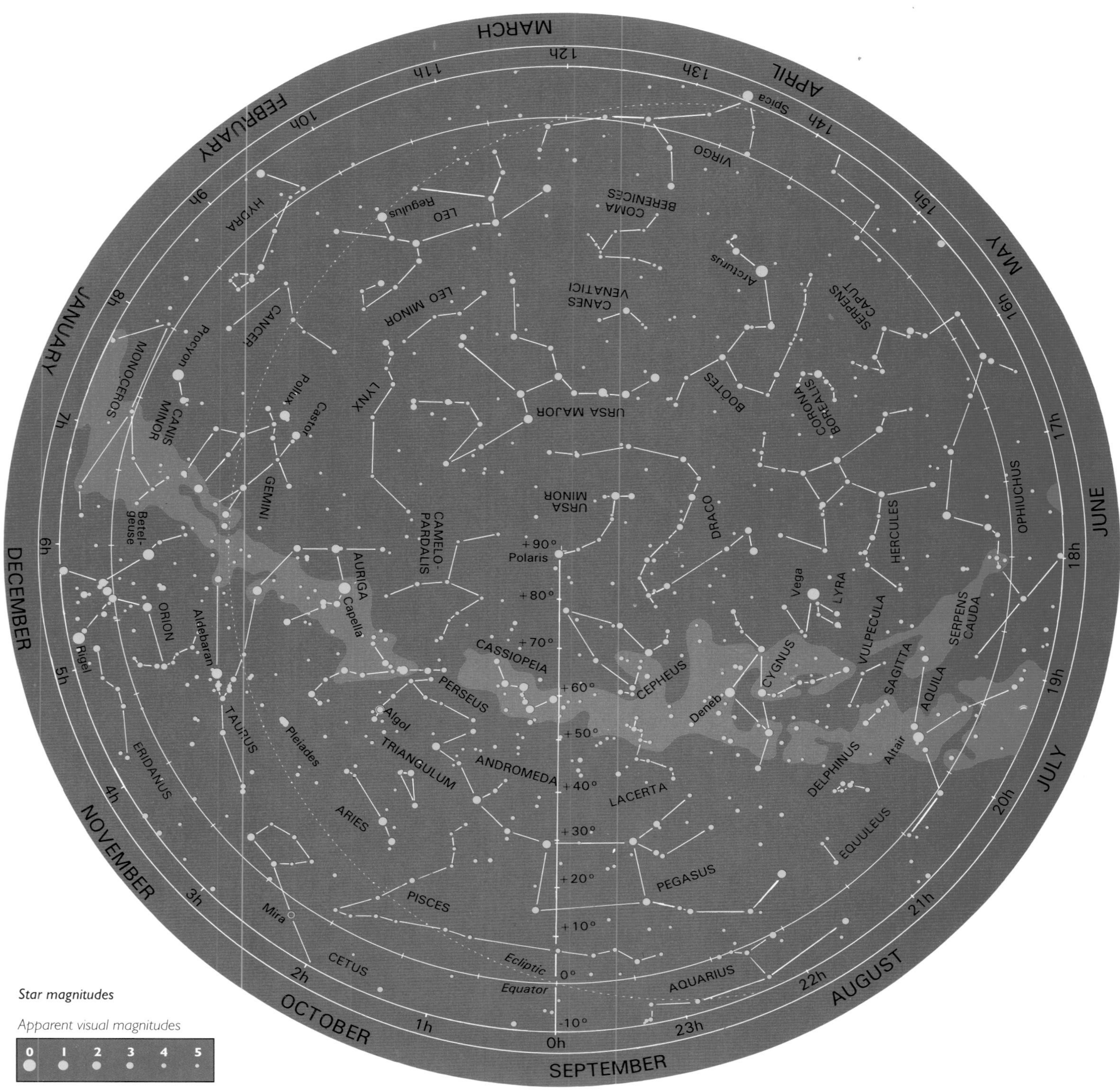

Star magnitudes

Apparent visual magnitudes

0	1	2	3	4	5
●	●	●	●	•	·

The Milky Way is shown in light blue on the above chart.

galaxy, contains an enormous number of stars. The nucleus of the Milky Way galaxy cannot be seen from Earth. Lying in the direction of the constellation Sagittarius in the southern hemisphere, it is masked by clouds of dust.

THE BRIGHTNESS OF STARS
Astronomers use a scale of magnitudes to measure the brightness of stars. The brightest visible to the naked eye were originally known as first-magnitude stars, ones not so bright were second-magnitude, down to the faintest visible, which were rated as sixth-magnitude. The brighter the star, the lower the magnitude. With the advent of telescopes and the development of accurate instruments for measuring brightnesses, the magnitude scale has been refined and extended.

Star chart of the northern hemisphere

When you look into the sky, the stars seem to be on the inside of a huge dome. This gives astronomers a way of mapping them. This chart shows the sky as it would appear from the North Pole. To use the star chart above, an observer in the northern hemisphere should face south and turn the chart so that the current month appears at the bottom. The chart will then show the constellations on view at approximately 11pm Greenwich Mean Time. The map should be rotated clockwise 15° for each hour before 11pm and anticlockwise for each hour after 11pm.

Very bright bodies such as Sirius, Venus and the Sun have negative magnitudes. The nearest star is Proxima Centauri, part of a multiple star system, which is 4.2 light-years away. Proxima Centauri is very faint and has a magnitude of 11.3. Alpha Centauri A, one of the two brighter members of the system, is the nearest visible star to Earth. It has a magnitude of 1.7.

These magnitudes are known as apparent magnitudes – measures of the brightnesses of the stars as they appear to us. These are the magnitudes shown on the charts on these pages. But the stars are at very different distances. The star Deneb, in the constellation Cygnus, for example, is over 1,200 light-years away. So astronomers also use absolute magnitudes – measures of how bright the stars really are. A star's absolute magnitude is the apparent magnitude it would have if it could be placed 32.6 light-years away. So Deneb, with an apparent magnitude of 1.2, has an absolute magnitude of –7.2.

The brightest star in the night sky is Sirius, the Dog Star, with a magnitude of –1.5. This medium-sized star is 8.64 light-years distant but it gives out about 20 times as much light as the Sun. After the Sun and the Moon, the brightest objects in the sky are the planets Venus, Mars and Jupiter. For example, Venus has a magnitude of up to –4. The planets have no light of their own however, and shine only because they reflect the Sun's rays. But whilst stars have fixed positions, the planets shift nightly in relation to the constellations, following a path called

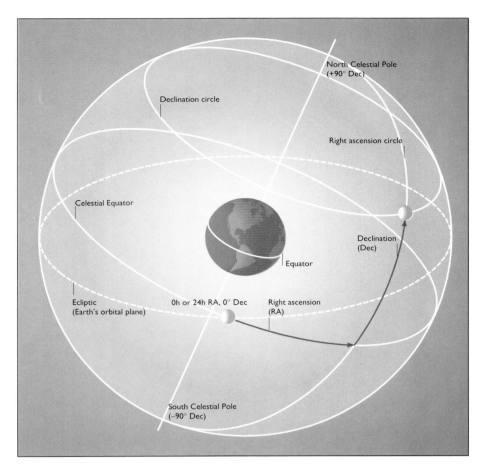

Celestial sphere
The diagram shows the imaginary surface on which astronomical positions are measured. The celestial sphere appears to rotate about the celestial poles, as though an extension of the Earth's own axis. The Earth's axis points towards the celestial poles.

the Ecliptic (shown on the star charts). As they follow their orbits around the Sun, their distances from the Earth vary, and therefore so also do their magnitudes.

While atlas maps record the details of the Earth's surface, star charts are a guide to the heavens. An observer at the Equator can see the entire sky at some time during the year, but an observer at the poles can see only the stars in a single hemisphere. As a result, star charts of both hemispheres are produced. The northern hemisphere chart is centred on the North Celestial Pole, while the southern hemisphere chart is centred on the South Celestial Pole.

In the northern hemisphere, the North Pole is marked by the star Polaris, or North Star. Polaris lies within a degree of the point where an extension of the Earth's axis meets the sky. Polaris appears to be stationary and navigators throughout history have used it as a guide. Unfortunately, the South Pole has no convenient reference point.

Star charts of the two hemispheres are bounded by the Celestial Equator, an imaginary line in the sky directly above the terrestrial Equator. Astronomical co-ordinates, which give the location of stars, are normally stated in terms of right ascension (the equivalent of longitude) and declination (the equivalent of latitude). Because the stars appear to rotate around the Earth every 24 hours, right ascension is measured eastwards in hours and minutes. Declination is measured in degrees north or south of the Celestial Equator.

The Southern Cross
The Southern Cross, or Crux, in the southern hemisphere, was classified as a constellation in the 17th century. It is as familiar to Australians and New Zealanders as the Plough is to people in the northern hemisphere. The vertical axis of the Southern Cross points towards the South Celestial Pole.

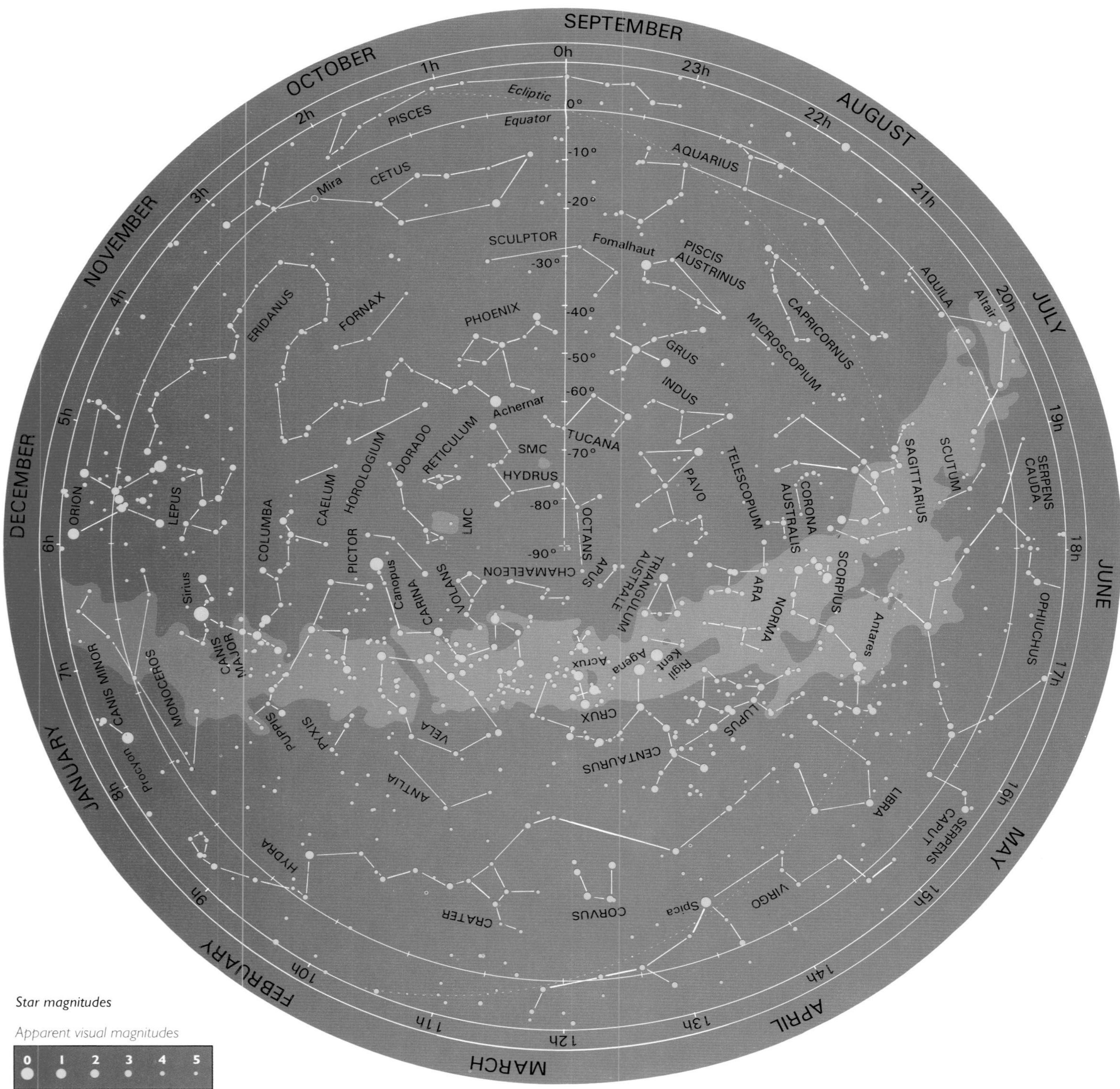

Star magnitudes

Apparent visual magnitudes

| 0 | 1 | 2 | 3 | 4 | 5 |

The Milky Way is shown in light blue on the above chart.

Star chart of the southern hemisphere

Many constellations in the southern hemisphere were named not by the ancients but by later astronomers. Some, including Antila (Air Pump) and Microscopium (Microscope), have modern names. The Large and Small Magellanic Clouds (LMC, SMC) are small 'satellite' galaxies of the Milky Way. To use the chart, an observer in the southern hemisphere should face north and turn the chart so that the current month appears at the bottom. The map will then show the constellations on view at approximately 11pm Greenwich Mean Time. The chart should be rotated clockwise 15° for each hour before 11pm and anticlockwise for each hour after 11pm.

CONSTELLATIONS

Every star is identifiable as a member of a constellation. The night sky contains 88 constellations, many of which were named by the ancient Greeks, Romans and other early peoples after animals and mythological characters, such as Orion and Perseus. More recently, astronomers invented names for constellations seen in the southern hemisphere, in areas not visible around the Mediterranean Sea.

Some groups of easily recognizable stars form parts of a constellation. For example, seven stars form the shape of the Plough or Big Dipper within the constellation Ursa Major. Such groups are called asterisms.

The stars in constellations lie in the same direction in space, but normally at vastly differ-

ent distances. Hence, there is no real connection between them. The positions of stars seem fixed, but in fact the shapes of the constellations are changing slowly over very long periods of time. This is because the stars have their own 'proper motions', which because of the huge distances involved are imperceptible to the naked eye.

The Solar System

Although the origins of the Solar System are still a matter of debate, many scientists believe that it was formed from a cloud of gas and dust, the debris from some long-lost, exploded star. Around 5 billion years ago, material was drawn towards the hub of the rotating disk of gas and dust, where it was compressed to thermonuclear fusion temperatures. A new star, the Sun, was born, containing 99.8% of the mass of the Solar System. The remaining material was later drawn together to form the planets and the other bodies in the Solar System. Spacecraft, manned and unmanned, have greatly increased our knowledge of the Solar System since the start of the Space Age in 1957, when the Soviet Union launched the satellite Sputnik I.

The Planets

Mercury is the closest planet to the Sun and the fastest moving. Space probes have revealed that its surface is covered by craters, and looks much like our Moon. Mercury is a hostile place, with no significant atmosphere and temperatures ranging between 400°C [750°F] by day and −170°C [−275°F] by night. It seems unlikely that anyone will ever want to visit this planet.

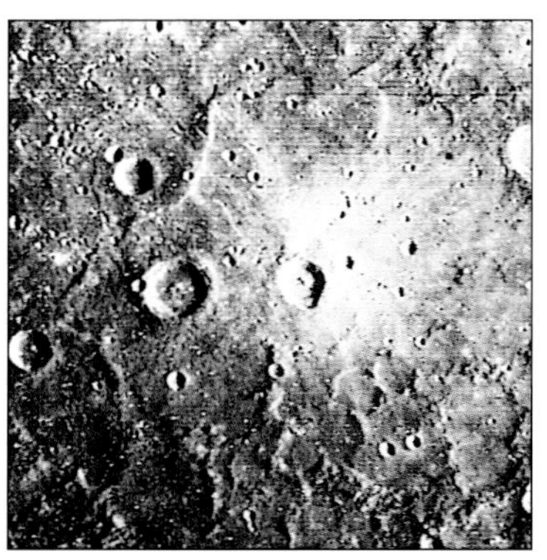

Venus is much the same size as Earth, but it is the hottest of the planets, with temperatures reaching 475°C [885°F], even at night. The reason for this scorching heat is the atmosphere, which consists mainly of carbon dioxide, a gas that traps heat thus creating a greenhouse effect. The density of the atmosphere is about 90 times that of Earth and dense clouds permanently mask the surface. Active volcanic regions discharging sulphur dioxide may account for the haze of sulphuric acid droplets in the upper atmosphere.

From planet Earth, Venus is brighter than any other star or planet and is easy to spot. It is often the first object to be seen in the evening sky and the last to be seen in the morning sky. It can even be seen in daylight.

Earth, seen from space, looks blue (because of the oceans which cover more than 70% of the planet) and white (a result of clouds in the atmosphere). The atmosphere and water make Earth the only planet known to support life. The Earth's hard outer layers, including the crust and the top of the mantle, are divided into rigid plates. Forces inside the Earth move the plates, modifying the landscape and causing earthquakes and volcanic activity. Weathering and erosion also change the surface.

Mars has many features in common with Earth, including an atmosphere with clouds and polar caps that partly melt in summer. Scientists once considered that it was the most likely planet on which other life might exist, but the two Viking space probes that went there in the 1970s found only a barren rocky surface with no trace of water. But Mars did have flowing water at one time and there are many dry channels – but these are not the fictitious 'canals'. There are also giant, dormant volcanoes.

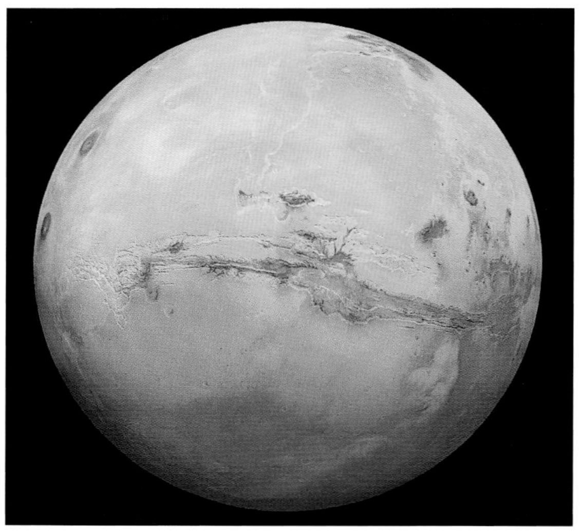

PLANETARY DATA

Planet	Mean distance from Sun (million km)	Mass (Earth=1)	Period of orbit (Earth yrs)	Period of rotation (Earth days)	Equatorial diameter (km)	Average density (water=1)	Surface gravity (Earth=1)	Number of known satellites
Sun	–	333,000	–	25.4	1,391,000	1.41	28	–
Mercury	57.9	0.055	0.2406	58.67	4,880	5.43	0.38	0
Venus	108.2	0.815	0.6152	243.0	12,104	5.20	0.90	0
Earth	149.6	1.0	1.00	1.00	12,756	5.52	1.00	1
Mars	227.9	0.107	1.88	1.028	6,792	3.91	0.38	2
Jupiter	778.3	317.8	11.86	0.411	142,800	1.33	2.69	16
Saturn	1,426.8	95.2	29.46	0.427	120,000	0.69	1.19	18
Uranus	2,869.4	14.53	84.01	0.748	51,118	1.29	0.79	20
Neptune	4,496.3	17.14	164.8	0.710	49,528	1.64	0.98	8
Pluto	5,900.1	0.002	2447.7	6.39	2,320	2.00	0.03	1

Asteroids are small, rocky bodies. Most of them orbit the Sun between Mars and Jupiter, but some small ones can approach the Earth. The largest is Ceres, 913 km [567 miles] in diameter. There may be around a million asteroids bigger than 1 km [0.6 miles].

Jupiter, the giant planet, lies beyond Mars and the asteroid belt. Its mass is almost three times as much as all the other planets combined and, because of its size, it shines more brightly than any other planet apart from Venus and, occasionally, Mars. The four largest moons of Jupiter were discovered by Galileo. Jupiter is made up mostly of hydrogen and helium, covered by a layer of clouds. Its Great Red Spot is a high-pressure storm. Jupiter made headline news when it was struck by fragments of Comet Shoemaker–Levy 9 in July 1994. This was the greatest collision ever seen by scientists between a planet and another heavenly body. The fragments of the comet that crashed into Jupiter created huge fireballs that caused scars on the planet that remained visible for months after the event.

Saturn is structurally similar to Jupiter but it is best known for its rings. The rings measure about 270,000 km [170,000 miles] across, yet they are no more than a few hundred metres thick. Seen from Earth, the rings seem divided into three main bands of varying brightness, but photographs sent back by the *Voyager* space probes in 1980 and 1981 showed that they are broken up into thousands of thin ringlets composed of ice particles ranging in size from a snowball to an iceberg. The origin of the rings is still a matter of debate.

Uranus was discovered in 1781 by William Herschel who first thought it was a comet. It is broadly similar to Jupiter and Saturn in composition, though its distance from the Sun makes its surface even colder. Uranus is circled by thin rings which were discovered in 1977. Unlike the rings of Saturn, the rings of Uranus are black, which explains why they cannot be seen from Earth.

Neptune, named after the mythological sea god, was discovered in 1846 as the result of mathematical predictions made by astronomers to explain irregularities in the orbit of Uranus, its near twin. Little was known about this distant body until *Voyager 2* came close to it in 1989. Neptune has thin rings, like those of Uranus. Among its blue-green clouds is a prominent dark spot, which rotates anticlockwise every 18 hours or so.

Pluto is the smallest planet in the Solar System, even smaller than our Moon. The American astronomer Clyde Tombaugh discovered Pluto in 1930. Its orbit is odd and it sometimes comes closer to the Sun than Neptune. The nature of Pluto, a gloomy planet appropriately named after the Greek and Roman god of the underworld, is uncertain. At Pluto's distance and beyond are many small, asteroid-like bodies the first of which was found in 1992.

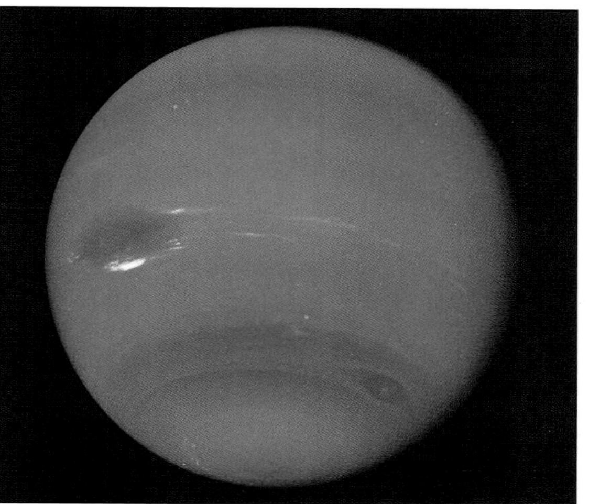

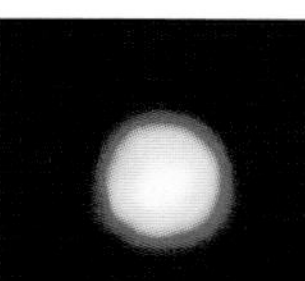

Comets are small icy bodies that orbit the Sun in highly elliptical orbits. When a comet swings in towards the Sun some of its ice evaporates, and the comet brightens and may become visible from Earth. The best known is Halley's Comet, which takes 76 years to orbit the Sun.

The Earth: Time and Motion

The Earth is constantly moving through space like a huge, self-sufficient spaceship. First, with the rest of the Solar System, it moves around the centre of the Milky Way galaxy. Second, it rotates around the Sun at a speed of more than 100,000 km/h [more than 60,000 mph], covering a distance of nearly 1,000 million km [600 million miles] in a little over 365 days. The Earth also spins on its axis, an imaginary line joining the North and South Poles, via the centre of the Earth, completing one turn in a day. The Earth's movements around the Sun determine our calendar, though accurate observations of

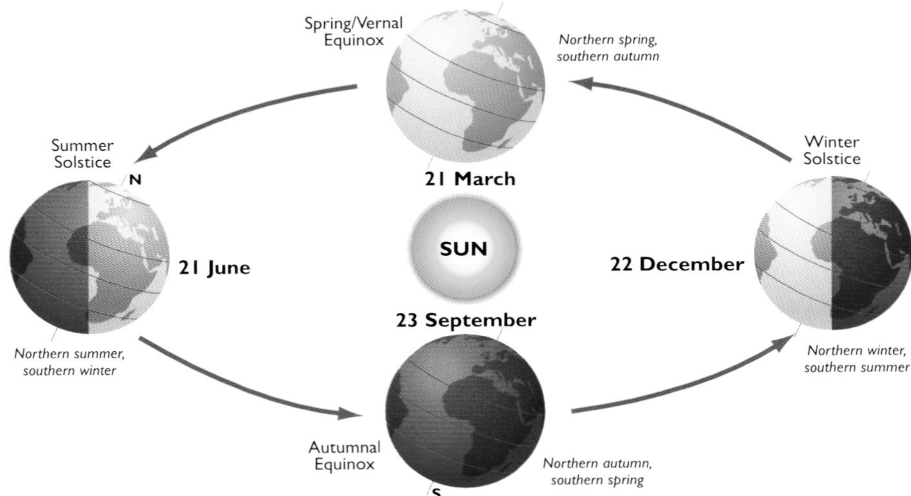

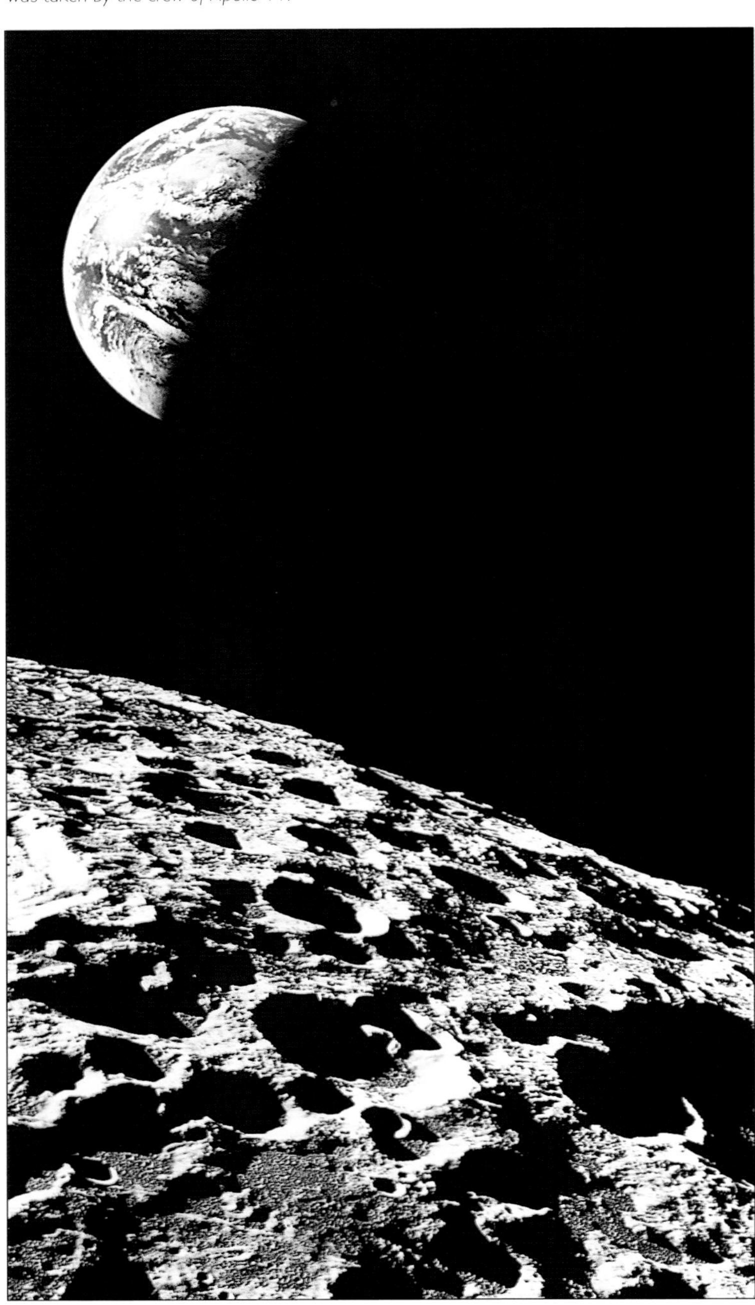

The Earth from the Moon

In 1969, Neil Armstrong and Edwin 'Buzz' Aldrin Junior were the first people to set foot on the Moon. This superb view of the Earth was taken by the crew of Apollo 11.

the stars made by astronomers help to keep our clocks in step with the rotation of the Earth around the Sun.

THE CHANGING YEAR

The Earth takes 365 days, 6 hours, 9 minutes and 9.54 seconds to complete one orbit around the Sun. We have a calendar year of 365 days, so allowance has to be made for the extra time over and above the 365 days. This is allowed for by introducing leap years of 366 days. Leap years are generally those, such as 1992 and 1996, which are divisible by four. Century years, however, are not leap years unless they are divisible by 400. Hence, 1700, 1800 and 1900 were not leap years, but the year 2000 was one. Leap years help to make the calendar conform with the solar year.

Because the Earth's axis is tilted by 23½°, the middle latitudes enjoy four distinct seasons. On 21 March, the vernal or spring equinox in the northern hemisphere, the Sun is directly overhead at the Equator and everywhere on Earth has about 12 hours of daylight and 12 hours of darkness. But as the Earth continues on its journey around the Sun, the northern hemisphere tilts more and more towards the Sun. Finally, on 21 June, the Sun is overhead at the Tropic of Cancer (latitude 23½° North). This is

The Seasons

The 23½° tilt of the Earth's axis remains constant as the Earth orbits around the Sun. As a result, first the northern and then the southern hemispheres lean towards the Sun. Annual variations in the amount of sunlight received in turn by each hemisphere are responsible for the four seasons experienced in the middle latitudes.

Tides

The daily rises and falls of the ocean's waters are caused by the gravitational pull of the Moon and the Sun. The effect is greatest on the hemisphere facing the Moon, causing a 'tidal bulge'. The diagram below shows that the Sun, Moon and Earth are in line when the spring tides occur. This causes the greatest tidal ranges. On the other hand, the neap tides occur when the pull of the Moon and the Sun are opposed. Neap tides, when tidal ranges are at their lowest, occur near the Moon's first and third quarters.

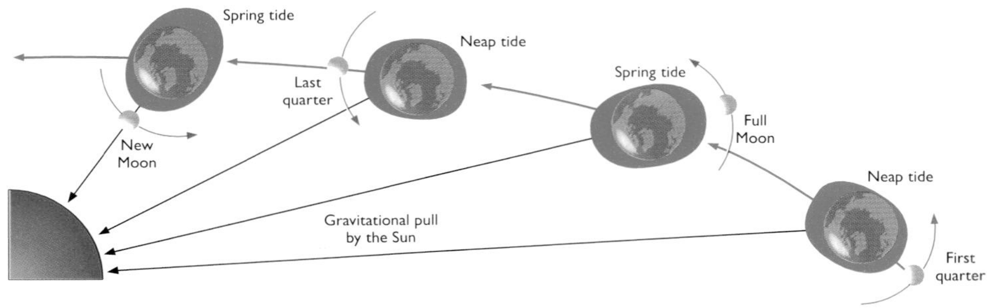

SUN DATA

DIAMETER	1.391 × 10⁶ km
VOLUME	1.412 × 10¹⁸ km³
VOLUME (EARTH=1)	1.303 × 10⁶
MASS	1.989 × 10³⁰ kg
MASS (EARTH=1)	3.329 × 10⁵
MEAN DENSITY (WATER=1)	1.409
ROTATION PERIOD	
AT EQUATOR	25.4 days
AT POLES	about 35 days
SURFACE GRAVITY (EARTH=1)	28
MAGNITUDE	
APPARENT	−26.9
ABSOLUTE	+4.71
TEMPERATURE	
AT SURFACE	5,400°C [5,700 K]
AT CORE	15 × 10⁶ K

MOON DATA

DIAMETER	3,476 km
MASS (EARTH=1)	0.0123
DENSITY (WATER=1)	3.34
MEAN DISTANCE FROM EARTH	384,402 km
MAXIMUM DISTANCE (APOGEE)	406,740 km
MINIMUM DISTANCE (PERIGEE)	356,410 km
SIDERIAL ROTATION AND REVOLUTION PERIOD	27.322 days
SYNODIC MONTH (NEW MOON TO NEW MOON)	29.531 days
SURFACE GRAVITY (EARTH=1)	0.165
MAXIMUM SURFACE TEMPERATURE	+130°C [403 K]
MINIMUM SURFACE TEMPERATURE	−158°C [115 K]

Phases of the Moon

The Moon rotates more slowly than the Earth, making one complete turn on its axis in just over 27 days. This corresponds to its period of revolution around the Earth and, hence, the same hemisphere always faces us. The interval between one full Moon and the next (and also between new Moons) is about 29½ days, or one lunar month. The apparent changes in the appearance of the Moon are caused by its changing position in relation to Earth. Like the planets, the Moon produces no light of its own. It shines by reflecting the Sun's rays, varying from a slim crescent to a full circle and back again.

the summer solstice in the northern hemisphere.

The overhead Sun then moves south again until on 23 September, the autumn equinox in the northern hemisphere, the Sun is again overhead at the Equator. The overhead Sun then moves south until, on around 22 December, it is overhead at the Tropic of Capricorn. This is the winter solstice in the northern hemisphere, and the summer solstice in the southern, where the seasons are reversed.

At the poles, there are two seasons. During half of the year, one of the poles leans towards the Sun and has continuous sunlight. For the other six months, the pole leans away from the Sun and is in continuous darkness.

Regions around the Equator do not have marked seasons. Because the Sun is high in the sky throughout the year, it is always hot or warm. When people talk of seasons in the tropics, they are usually referring to other factors, such as rainy and dry periods.

DAY, NIGHT AND TIDES

As the Earth rotates on its axis every 24 hours, first one side of the planet and then the other faces the Sun and enjoys daylight, while the opposite side is in darkness.

The length of daylight varies throughout the year. The longest day in the northern hemisphere falls on the summer solstice, 21 June, while the longest day in the southern hemisphere is on 22 December. At 40° latitude, the length of daylight on the longest day is 14 hours, 30 minutes. At 60° latitude, daylight on that day lasts 18 hours, 30 minutes. On the shortest day, 22 December in the northern hemisphere and 21 June in the southern, daylight hours at 40° latitude total 9 hours and 9 minutes. At latitude 60°, daylight lasts only 5 hours, 30 minutes in the 24-hour period.

Tides are caused by the gravitational pull of the Moon and, to a lesser extent, the Sun on the waters in the world's oceans. Tides occur twice every 24 hours, 50 minutes – one complete orbit

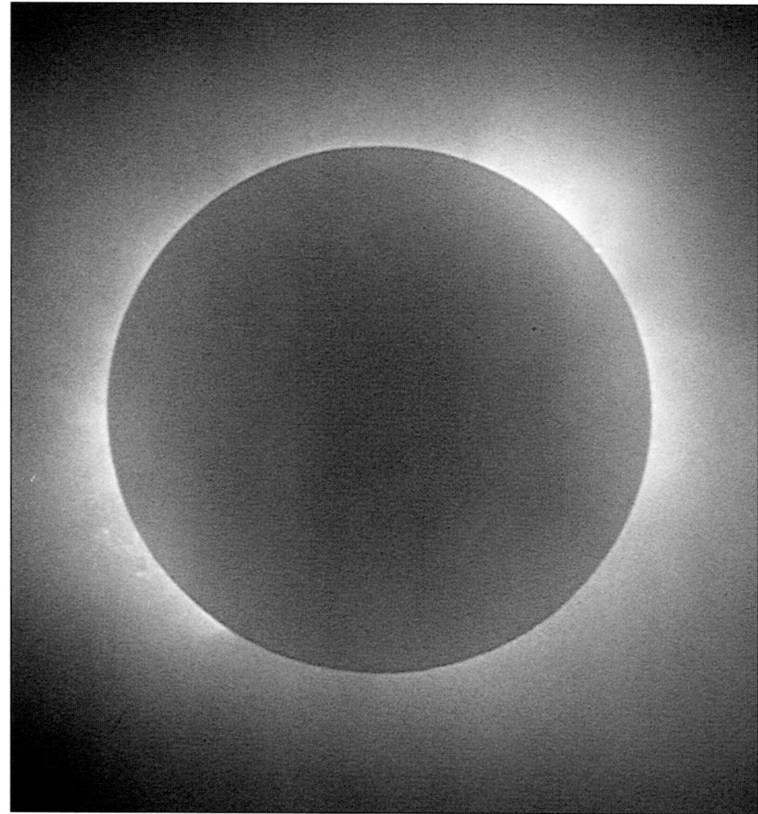

Total eclipse of the Sun

A total eclipse is caused when the Moon passes between the Sun and the Earth. With the Sun's bright disk completely obscured, the Sun's corona, or outer atmosphere, can be viewed.

of the Moon around the Earth.

The highest tides, the spring tides, occur when the Earth, Moon and Sun are in a straight line, so that the gravitational pulls of the Moon and Sun are combined. The lowest, or neap, tides occur when the Moon, Earth and Sun form a right angle. The gravitational pull of the Moon is then opposed by the gravitational pull of the Sun. The greatest tidal ranges occur in the Bay of Fundy in North America. The greatest mean spring range is 14.5 m [47.5 ft].

The speed at which the Earth is spinning on its axis is gradually slowing down, because of the movement of tides. As a result, experts have calculated that, in about 200 million years, the day will be 25 hours long.

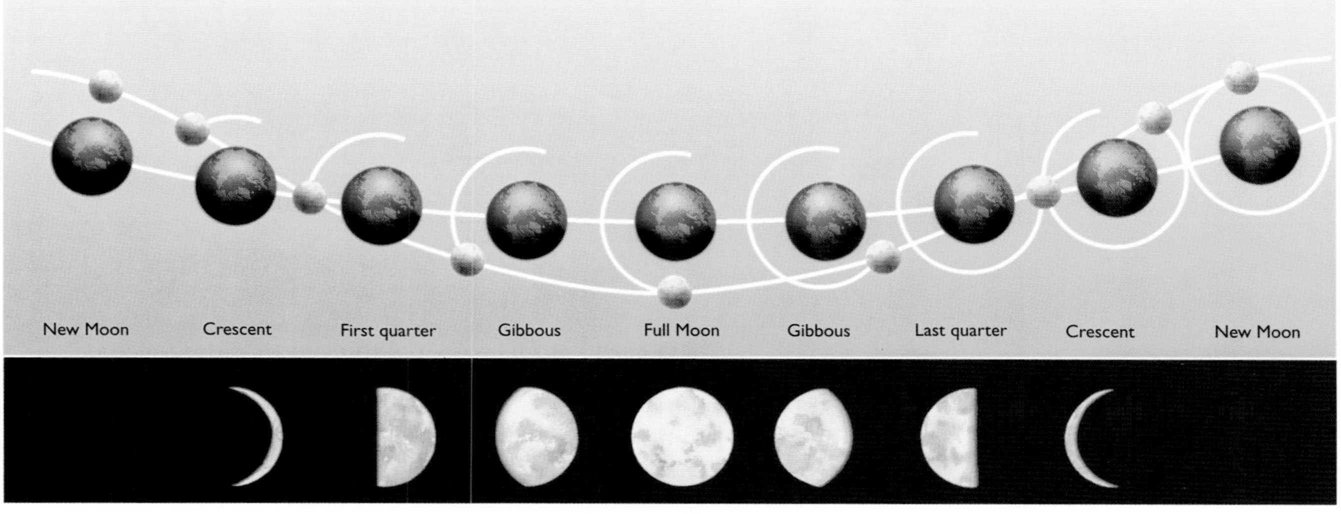

New Moon	Crescent	First quarter	Gibbous	Full Moon	Gibbous	Last quarter	Crescent	New Moon

The Earth from Space

Any last doubts about whether the Earth was round or flat were finally resolved by the appearance of the first photographs of our planet taken at the start of the Space Age. Satellite images also confirmed that map- and globe-makers had correctly worked out the shapes of the continents and the oceans.

More importantly, images of our beautiful, blue, white and brown planet from space impressed on many people that the Earth and its resources are finite. They made people realize that if we allow our planet to be damaged by such factors as overpopulation, pollution and irresponsible over-use of resources, then its future and the survival of all the living things upon it may be threatened.

Views from Above

The first aerial photographs were taken from balloons in the mid-19th century and their importance in military reconnaissance was recognized as early as the 1860s during the American Civil War.

Launch of the Space Shuttle Atlantis
Space Shuttles transport astronauts and equipment into orbit around the Earth. The American Space Shuttle Atlantis, *shown below, launched the Magellan probe, which undertook a radar mapping programme of the surface of Venus in the early 1990s.*

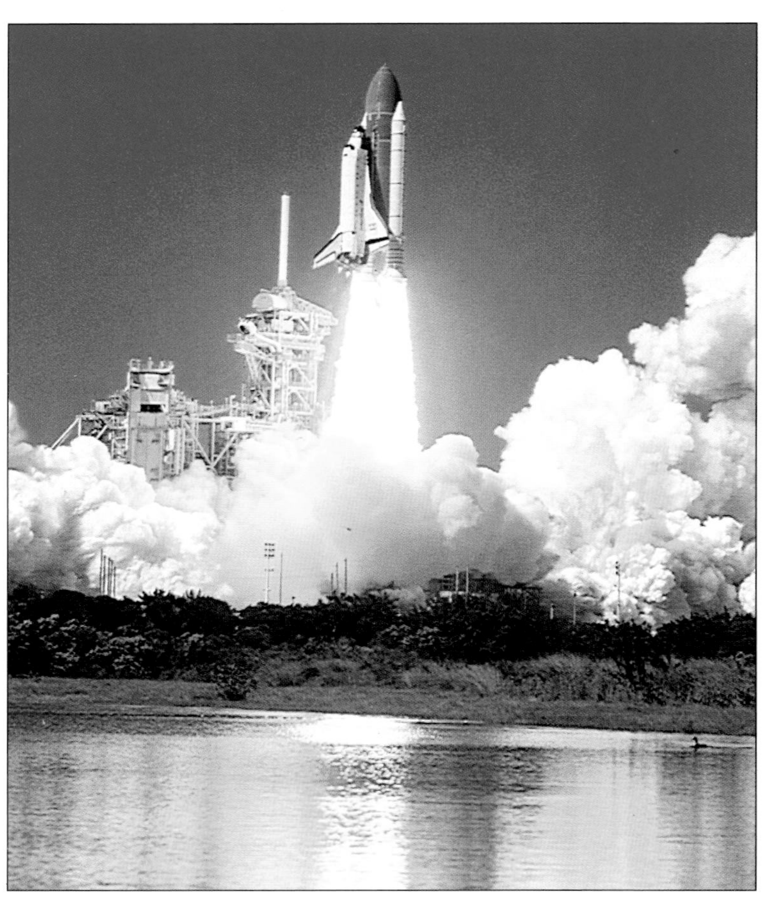

Since the end of World War II, photographs taken by aircraft have been widely used in map-making. The use of air photographs has greatly speeded up the laborious process of mapping land details and they have enabled cartographers to produce maps of the most remote parts of the world.

Aerial photographs have also proved useful because they reveal features that are not visible at ground level. For example, circles that appear on many air photographs do not correspond to visible features on the ground. Many of these mysterious shapes have turned out to be the sites of ancient settlements previously unknown to archaeologists.

Images from Space

Space probes equipped with cameras and a variety of remote sensing instruments have sent back images of distant planets and moons. From these images, detailed maps have been produced, rapidly expanding our knowledge of the Solar System.

Photographs from space are also proving invaluable in the study of the Earth. One of the best known uses of space imagery is the study of the atmosphere. Polar-orbiting weather satellites that circle the Earth, together with geostationary satellites, whose motion is synchronized with the Earth's rotation, now regularly transmit images showing the changing patterns of weather systems from above. Forecasters use these images to track the development and the paths taken by hurricanes, enabling them to issue storm warnings to endangered areas, saving lives and reducing damage to property.

Remote sensing devices are now monitoring changes in temperatures over the land and sea, while photographs indicate the melting of ice sheets. Such evidence is vital in the study of global warming. Other devices reveal polluted areas, patterns of vegetation growth, and areas suffering deforestation.

In recent years, remote sensing devices have been used to monitor the damage being done to the ozone layer in the stratosphere, which prevents most of the Sun's harmful ultraviolet radiation from reaching the surface. The discovery of 'ozone holes', where the protective layer of ozone is being thinned by chlorofluorocarbons (CFCs), chemicals used in the manufacture of such things as air conditioners and refrigerators, has enabled governments to take concerted action to save our planet from imminent danger.

EARTH DATA

MAXIMUM DISTANCE FROM SUN (APHELION)
152,007,016 km

MINIMUM DISTANCE FROM SUN (PERIHELION)
147,000,830 km

LENGTH OF YEAR – SOLAR TROPICAL (EQUINOX TO EQUINOX)
365.24 days

LENGTH OF YEAR – SIDEREAL (FIXED STAR TO FIXED STAR)
365.26 days

LENGTH OF DAY – MEAN SOLAR DAY
24 hours, 03 minutes, 56 seconds

LENGTH OF DAY – MEAN SIDEREAL DAY
23 hours, 56 minutes, 4 seconds

SUPERFICIAL AREA
510,000,000 km²

LAND SURFACE
149,000,000 km² (29.3%)

WATER SURFACE
361,000,000 km² (70.7%)

EQUATORIAL CIRCUMFERENCE
40,077 km

POLAR CIRCUMFERENCE
40,009 km

EQUATORIAL DIAMETER
12,756.8 km

POLAR DIAMETER
12,713.8 km

EQUATORIAL RADIUS
6,378.4 km

POLAR RADIUS
6,356.9 km

VOLUME OF THE EARTH
1,083,230 × 10⁶ km³

MASS OF THE EARTH
5.9 × 10²¹ tonnes

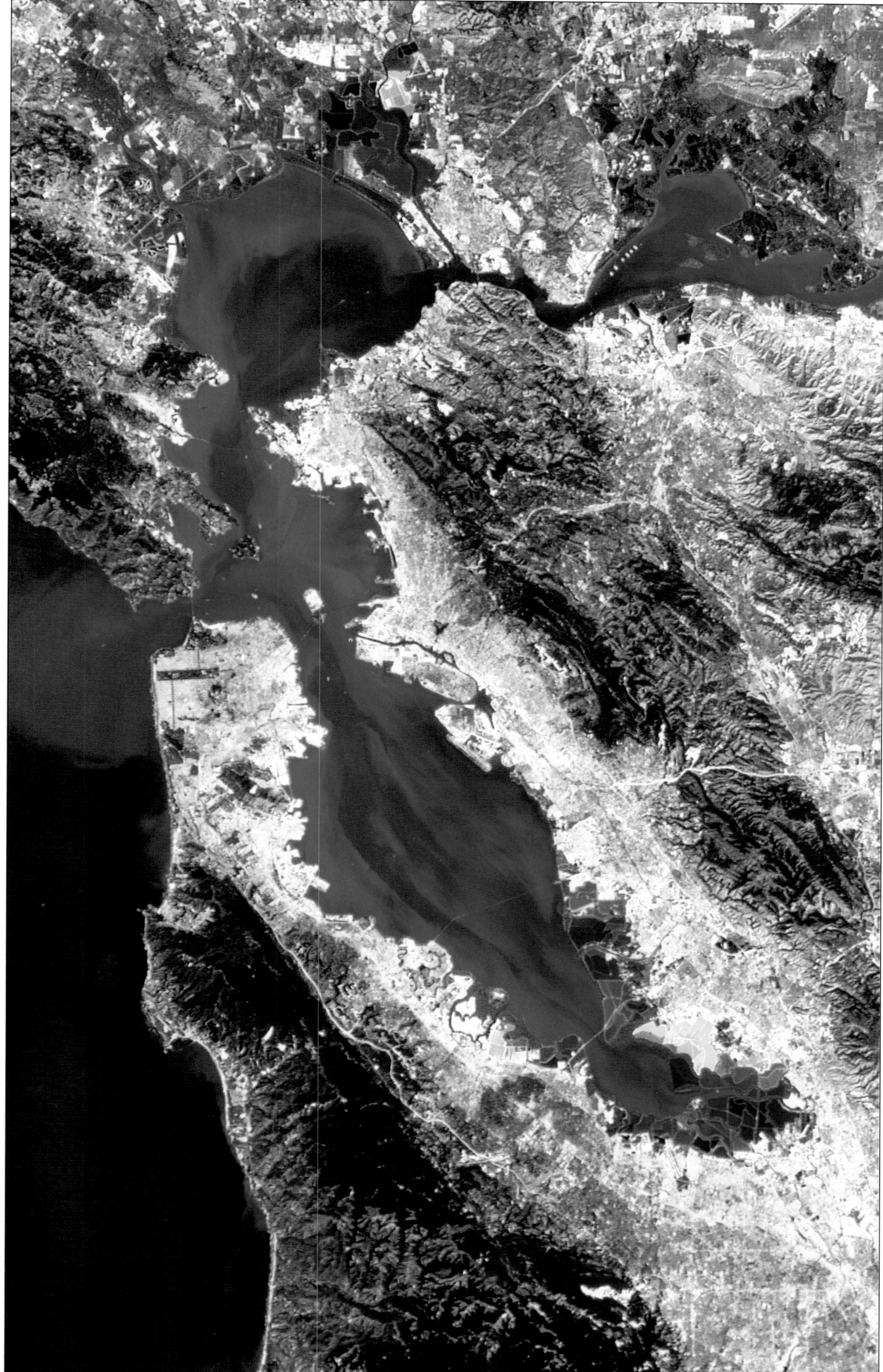

Satellite image of San Francisco Bay

Unmanned scientific satellites called ERTS *(Earth Resources Technology Satellites), or* Landsats, *were designed to collect information about the Earth's resources. The satellites transmitted images of the land using different wavelengths of light in order to identify, in false colours, such subtle features as areas that contain minerals or areas covered with growing crops, that are not identifiable on simple photographs using the visible range of the spectrum. They were also equipped to monitor conditions in the atmosphere and oceans, and also to detect pollution levels. This Landsat image of San Francisco Bay covers an area of great interest to geologists because it lies in an earthquake zone in the path of the San Andreas fault.*

The Dynamic Earth

The Earth was formed about 4.6 billion years ago from the ring of gas and dust left over after the formation of the Sun. As the Earth took shape, lighter elements, such as silicon, rose to the surface, while heavy elements, notably iron, sank towards the centre.

Gradually, the outer layers cooled to form a hard crust. The crust enclosed the dense mantle which, in turn, surrounded the even denser liquid outer and solid inner core. Around the Earth was an atmosphere, which contained abundant water

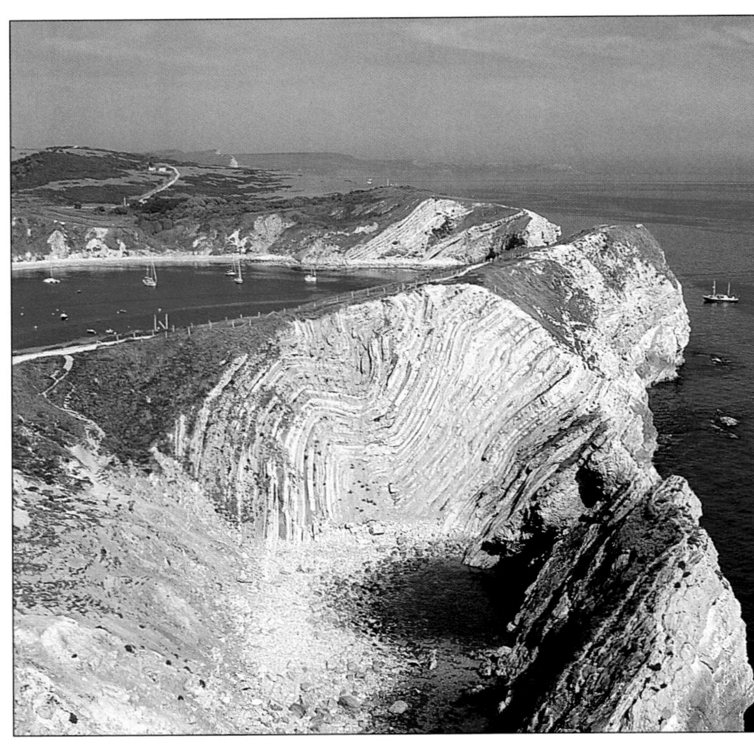

Lulworth Cove, southern England
When undisturbed by earth movements, sedimentary rock strata are generally horizontal. But lateral pressure has squeezed the Jurassic strata at Lulworth Cove into complex folds.

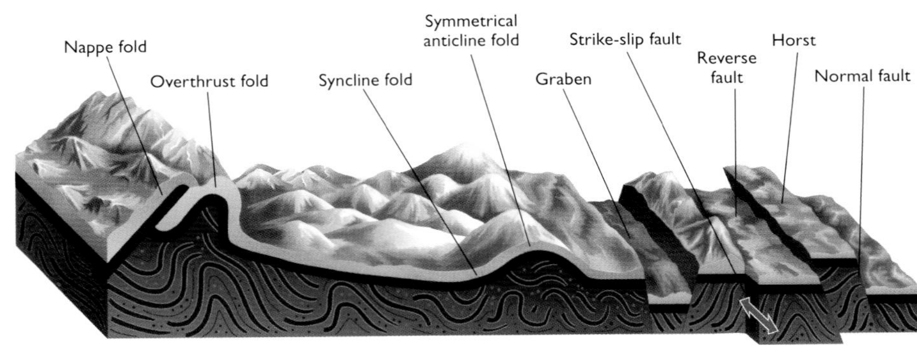

vapour. When the surface cooled, rainwater began to fill hollows, forming the first lakes and seas. Since that time, our planet has been subject to constant change – the result of powerful internal and external forces that still operate today.

THE HISTORY OF THE EARTH

From their study of rocks, geologists have pieced together the history of our planet and the life forms that evolved upon it. They have dated the oldest known crystals, composed of the mineral zircon, at 4.2 billion years. But the oldest rocks are younger, less than 4 billion years old. This is because older rocks have been weathered away by natural processes.

The oldest rocks that contain fossils, which are

evidence of once-living organisms, are around 3.5 billion years old. But fossils are rare in rocks formed in the first 4 billion years of Earth history. This vast expanse of time is called the Precambrian. This is because it precedes the Cambrian period, at the start of which, about 590 million years ago, life was abundant in the seas.

The Cambrian is the first period in the Paleozoic (or ancient life) era. The Paleozoic era is followed by the Mesozoic (middle life) era, which witnessed the spectacular rise and fall of the dinosaurs, and the Cenozoic (recent life) era, which was dominated by the evolution of mammals. Each of the eras is divided into periods, and the periods in the Cenozoic era, covering the last 65 million years, are further divided into epochs.

THE EARTH'S CHANGING FACE

While life was gradually evolving, the face of the Earth was constantly changing. By piecing together evidence of rock structures and fossils, geologists have demonstrated that around 250 million years ago, all the world's land areas were grouped together in one huge landmass called Pangaea. Around 180 million years ago, the supercontinent Pangaea, began to break up. New oceans opened up as the continents began to move towards their present positions.

Evidence of how continents drift came from studies of the ocean floor in the 1950s and 1960s. Scientists discovered that the oceans are young features. By contrast with the continents, no part of the ocean floor is more than 200 million years old. The floors of oceans older than 200 million years have completely vanished.

Studies of long undersea ranges, called ocean ridges, revealed that the youngest rocks occur along their centres, which are the edges of huge plates – rigid blocks of the Earth's lithosphere, which is made up of the crust and the solid upper layer of the mantle. The Earth's lithosphere is split into six large and several smaller

Mountain building
Lateral pressure, which occurs when plates collide, squeezes and compresses rocks into folds. Simple symmetrical upfolds are called anticlines, while downfolds are synclines. As the pressure builds up, strata become asymmetrical and they may be tilted over to form recumbent folds. The rocks often crack under the intense pressure and the folds are sheared away and pushed forward over other rocks. These features are called overthrust folds or nappes. Plate movements also create faults along which rocks move upwards, downwards and sideways. The diagram shows a downfaulted graben, or rift valley, and an uplifted horst, or block mountain.

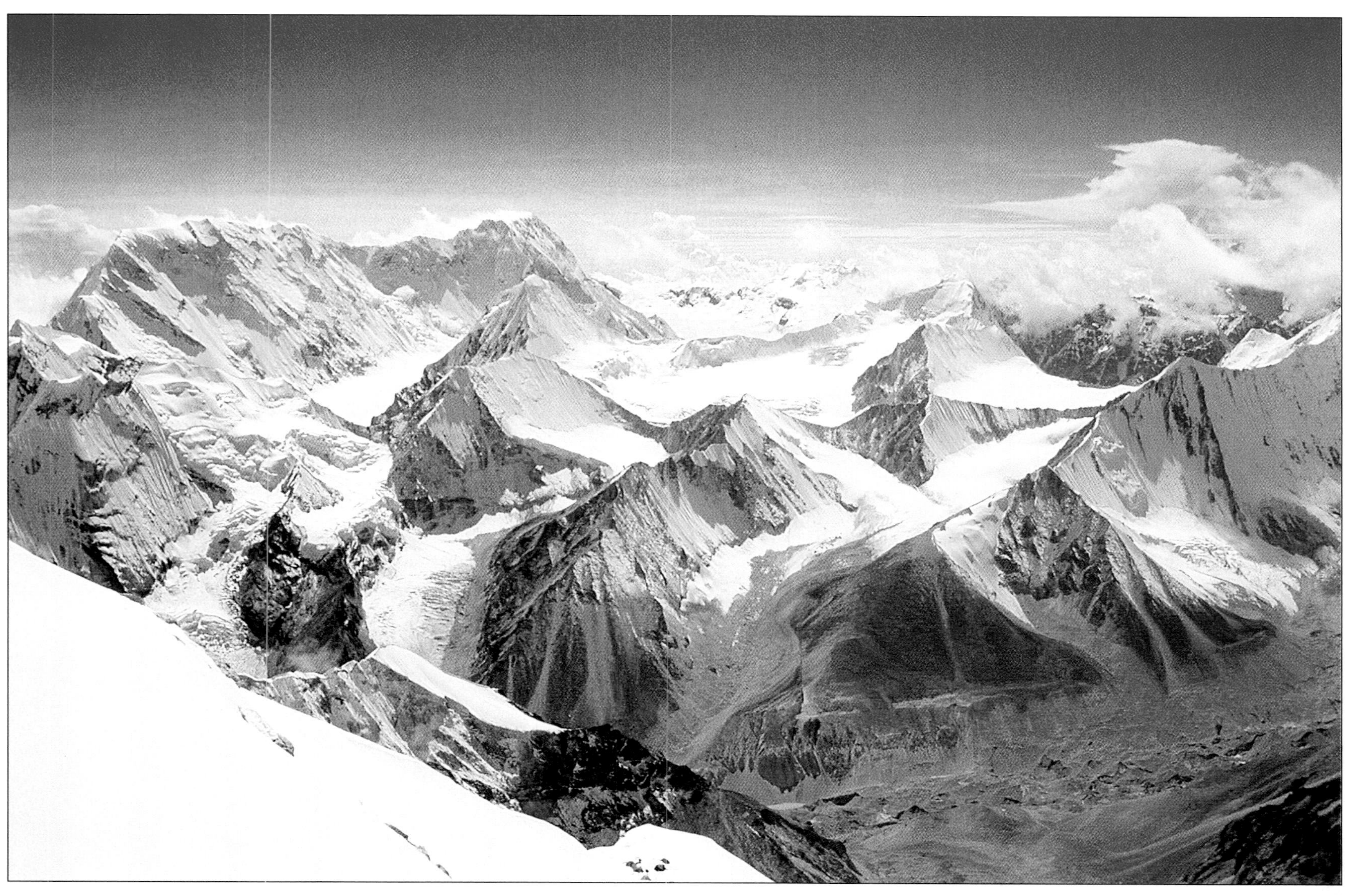

The Himalayas seen from Nepal
The Himalayas are a young fold mountain range formed by a collision between two plates. The earthquakes felt in the region testify that the plate movements are still continuing.

plates. The ocean ridges are 'constructive' plate margins, because new crustal rock is being formed there from magma that wells up from the mantle as the plates gradually move apart. By contrast, the deep ocean trenches are 'destructive' plate edges. Here, two plates are pushing against each other and one plate is descending beneath the other into the mantle where it is melted and destroyed. Geologists call these areas subduction zones.

A third type of plate edge is called a transform fault. Here two plates are moving alongside each other. The best known of these plate edges is the San Andreas fault in California, which separates the Pacific plate from the North American plate.

Slow-moving currents in the partly molten asthenosphere, which underlies the solid lithosphere, are responsible for moving the plates, a process called plate tectonics.

Geological time scale
The geological time scale was first constructed by a study of the stratigraphic, or relative, ages of layers of rock. But the absolute ages of rock strata could not be fixed until the discovery of radioactivity in the early 20th century. Some names of periods, such as Cambrian (Latin for Wales), come from places where the rocks were first studied. Others, such as Carboniferous, refer to the nature of the rocks formed during the period. For example, coal seams (containing carbon) were formed from decayed plant matter during the Carboniferous period.

MOUNTAIN BUILDING

The study of plate tectonics has helped geologists to understand the mechanisms that are responsible for the creation of mountains. Many of the world's greatest ranges were created by the collision of two plates and the bending of the intervening strata into huge loops, or folds. For example, the Himalayas began to rise around 50 million years ago, when a plate supporting India collided with the huge Eurasian plate. Rocks on the floor of the intervening and long-vanished Tethys Sea were squeezed up to form the Himalayan Mountain Range.

Plate movements also create tension that cracks rocks, producing long faults along which rocks move upwards, downwards or sideways. Block mountains are formed when blocks of rock are pushed upwards along faults. Steep-sided rift valleys are formed when blocks of land sink down between faults. For example, the basin and range region of the south-western United States has both block mountains and down-faulted basins, such as Death Valley.

Pre-Cambrian	Lower			Paleozoic (Primary)		Upper		Mesozoic (Secondary)			Cenozoic (Tertiary, Quaternary)		Era
Pre-Cambrian	Cambrian	Ordovician	Silurian	Devonian	Carboniferous	Permian	Triassic	Jurassic	Cretaceous	Paleocene / Eocene / Oligocene / Miocene / Pliocene / Quaternary		System
			CALEDONIAN FOLDING		HERCYNIAN FOLDING					LARAMIDE FOLDING	ALPINE FOLDING	Orogeny
600	550	500	450	400	350	300	250	200	150	100	50	

Millions of years before present

Earthquakes and Volcanoes

On 20 September 1999, the north-west counties of Taiwan were struck by a large earthquake. The death toll was put at 2,400, with more than 8,700 people injured and 600,000 left homeless. Only a month earlier, in the Izmit region of western Turkey, over 17,000 people were killed, 50,000 injured and thousands went missing when a slightly less severe earthquake struck.

THE RESTLESS EARTH

Earthquakes can occur anywhere, whenever rocks move along faults. But the most severe and most numerous earthquakes occur near the edges of the plates that make up the Earth's lithosphere. Japan, for example, lies in a

San Andreas Fault, United States
Geologists call the San Andreas fault in south-western California a transform, or strike-slip, fault. Sudden movements along it cause earthquakes. In 1906, shifts of about 4.5 metres [15 ft] occurred near San Francisco, causing a massive earthquake.

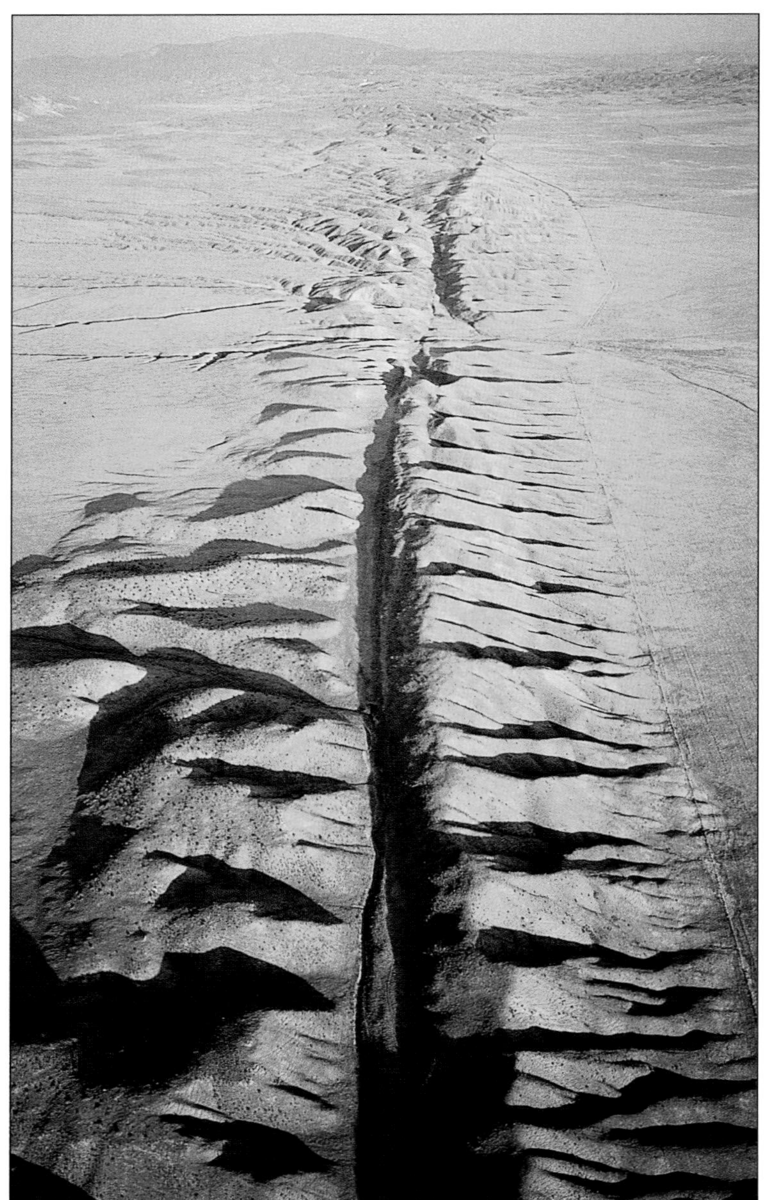

particularly unstable region above subduction zones, where plates are descending into the Earth's mantle. It lies in a zone encircling the Pacific Ocean, called the 'Pacific ring of fire'.

Plates do not move smoothly. Their edges are jagged and for most of the time they are locked together. However, pressure gradually builds up until the rocks break and the plates lurch forwards, setting off vibrations ranging from tremors that are recorded only by sensitive instruments to terrifying earthquakes. The greater the pressure released, the more destructive the earthquake.

Earthquakes are also common along the ocean trenches where plates are moving apart, but they mostly occur so far from land that they do little damage. Far more destructive are the earthquakes that occur where plates are moving alongside each other. For example, the earthquakes that periodically rock south-western California are caused by movements along the San Andreas Fault.

The spot where an earthquake originates is called the focus, while the point on the Earth's surface directly above the focus is called the epicentre. Two kinds of waves, P-waves or compressional waves and S-waves or shear waves, travel from the focus to the surface where they make the ground shake. P-waves travel faster than S-waves and the time difference between their arrival at recording stations enables scientists to calculate the distance from a station to the epicentre.

Earthquakes are measured on the Richter scale, which indicates the magnitude of the shock. The most destructive earthquakes are shallow-focus, that is, the focus is within 60 km [37 miles] of the surface. A magnitude of 7.0 is a major earthquake, but earthquakes with a somewhat lower magnitude can cause tremendous damage if their epicentres are on or close to densely populated areas.

NOTABLE
EARTHQUAKES
(since 1900)

Year	Location	Mag.
1906	San Francisco, USA	8.3
1906	Valparaiso, Chile	8.6
1908	Messina, Italy	7.5
1915	Avezzano, Italy	7.5
1920	Gansu, China	8.6
1923	Yokohama, Japan	8.3
1927	Nan Shan, China	8.3
1932	Gansu, China	7.6
1934	Bihar, India/Nepal	8.4
1935	Quetta, India†	7.5
1939	Chillan, Chile	8.3
1939	Erzincan, Turkey	7.9
1964	Anchorage, Alaska	8.4
1968	N. E. Iran	7.4
1970	N. Peru	7.7
1976	Guatemala	7.5
1976	Tangshan, China	8.2
1978	Tabas, Iran	7.7
1980	El Asnam, Algeria	7.3
1980	S. Italy	7.2
1985	Mexico City, Mexico	8.1
1988	N. W. Armenia	6.8
1990	N. Iran	7.7
1993	Maharashtra, India	6.4
1994	Los Angeles, USA	6.6
1995	Kobe, Japan	7.2
1995	Sakhalin Is., Russia	7.5
1996	Yunnan, China	7.0
1997	N. E. Iran	7.1
1998	N. Afghanistan	6.1
1998	N. E. Afghanistan	7.0
1999	Izmit, Turkey	7.4
1999	Taipei, Taiwan	7.6

† *now Pakistan*

Earthquakes in subduction zones
Along subduction zones, one plate is descending beneath another. The plates are locked together until the rocks break and the descending plate lurches forwards. From the point where the plate moves – the origin – seismic waves spread through the lithosphere, making the ground shake. The earthquake in Mexico City in 1985 occurred in this way.

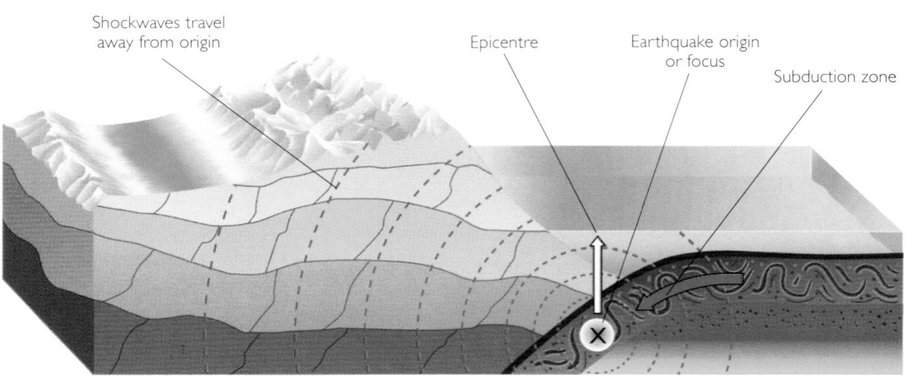

Shockwaves travel away from origin
Epicentre
Earthquake origin or focus
Subduction zone

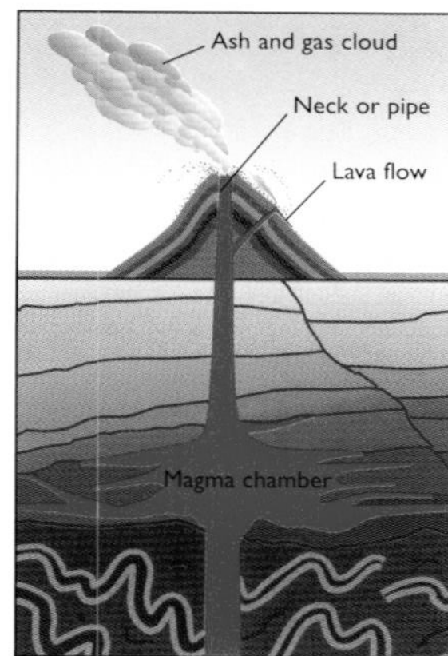

Cross-section of a volcano
Volcanoes are vents in the ground, through which magma reaches the surface. The term volcano is also used for the mountains formed from volcanic rocks. Beneath volcanoes are pockets of magma derived from the semi-molten asthenosphere in the mantle. The magma rises under pressure through the overlying rocks until it reaches the surface. There it emerges through vents as pyroclasts, ranging in size from large lumps of magma, called volcanic bombs, to fine volcanic ash and dust. In quiet eruptions, streams of liquid lava run down the side of the mountain. Side vents sometimes appear on the flanks of existing volcanoes.

Scientists have been working for years to find effective ways of forecasting earthquakes but with very limited success. Following the Kobe earthquake in 1995, many experts argued that they would be better employed developing techniques of reducing the damage caused by earthquakes, rather than pursuing an apparently vain attempt to predict them.

VOLCANIC ERUPTIONS

Most active volcanoes also occur on or near plate edges. Many undersea volcanoes along the ocean ridges are formed from magma that wells up from the asthenosphere to fill the gaps created as the plates, on the opposite sides of the ridges, move apart. Some of these volcanoes reach the surface to form islands. Iceland is a country which straddles the Mid-Atlantic Ocean Ridge. It is gradually becoming wider as magma rises to the surface through faults and vents. Other volcanoes lie alongside subduction zones. The magma that fuels them comes from the melted edges of the descending plates.

A few volcanoes lie far from plate edges. For example, Mauna Loa and Kilauea on Hawaii are situated near the centre of the huge Pacific plate. The molten magma that reaches the surface is created by a source of heat, called a 'hot spot', in the Earth's mantle.

Magma is molten rock at temperatures of about 1,100°C to 1,200°C [2,012°F to 2,192°F]. It contains gases and superheated steam. The chemical composition of magma varies. Viscous magma is rich in silica and superheated steam, while runny magma contains less silica and steam. The chemical composition of the magma affects the nature of volcanic eruptions.

Explosive volcanoes contain thick, viscous magma. When they erupt, they usually hurl clouds of ash (shattered fragments of cooled magma) into the air. By contrast, quiet volcanoes emit long streams of runny magma, or lava. However, many volcanoes are intermediate in type, sometimes erupting explosively and sometimes emitting streams of fluid lava. Explosive and intermediate volcanoes usually have a conical shape, while quiet volcanoes are flattened, resembling upturned saucers. They are often called shield volcanoes.

One dangerous type of eruption is called a *nuée ardente*, or 'glowing cloud'. It occurs when a cloud of intensely hot volcanic gases and dust particles and superheated steam are exploded from a volcano. They move rapidly downhill, burning everything in their path and choking animals and people. The blast that creates the *nuée ardente* may release the pressure inside the volcano, resulting in a tremendous explosion that hurls tall columns of ash into the air.

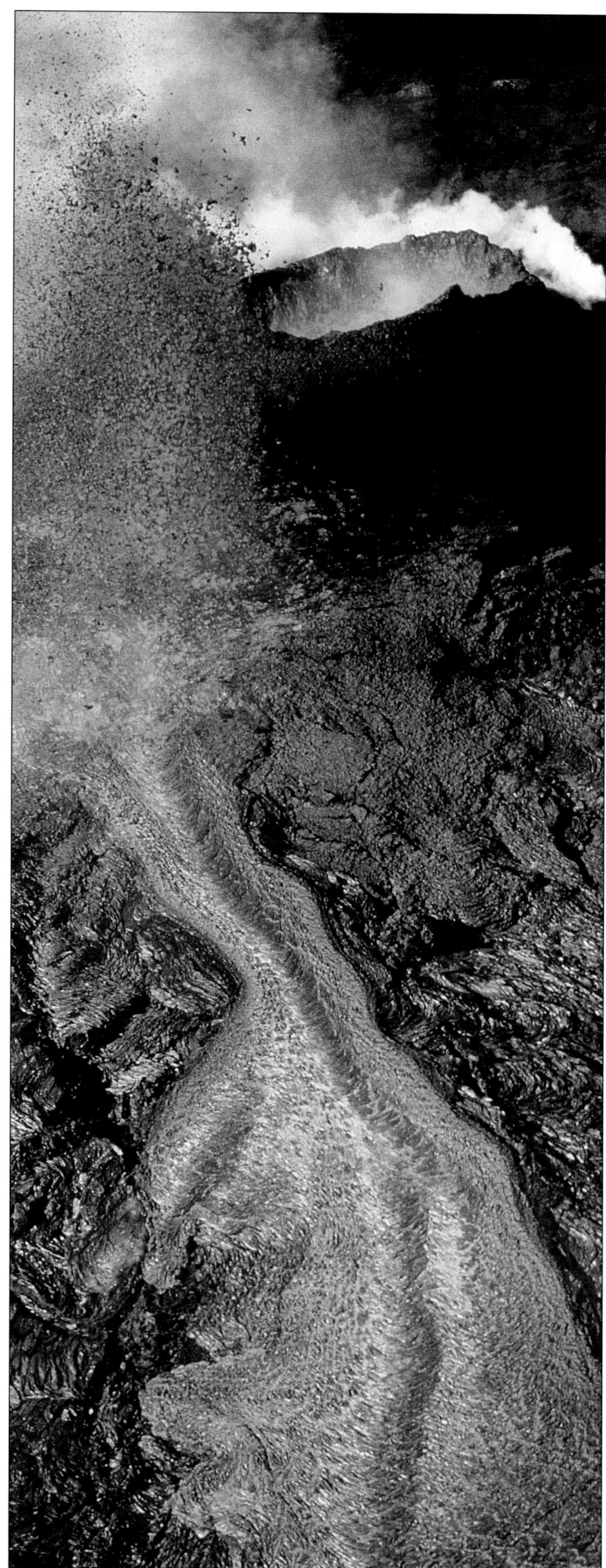

Kilauea Volcano, Hawaii
The volcanic Hawaiian islands in the North Pacific Ocean were formed as the Pacific plate moved over a 'hot spot' in the Earth's mantle. Kilauea on Hawaii emits blazing streams of liquid lava.

Forces of Nature

When the volcano Mount Pinatubo erupted in the Philippines in 1991, large areas around the mountain were covered by ash. Later, rainwater mixed with the loose ash on sloping land, created lahars, or mudflows, which swept down river valleys burying many areas. Such incidents are not only reminders of the great forces that operate inside our planet but also of those natural forces operating on the surface, which can have dramatic effects on the land.

The chief forces acting on the surface of the Earth are weathering, running water, ice and winds. The forces of erosion seem to act slowly. One estimate suggests that an average of only 3.5 cm [1.4 in] of land is removed by natural processes every 1,000 years. This may not sound much, but over millions of years, it can reduce mountains to almost flat surfaces.

WEATHERING

Weathering occurs in all parts of the world, but the most effective type of weathering in any area depends on the climate and the nature of the rocks. For example, in cold mountain areas,

Grand Canyon, Arizona, at dusk
The Grand Canyon in the United States is one of the world's natural wonders. Eroded by the Colorado River and its tributaries, it is up to 1.6 km [1 mile] deep and 29 km [18 miles] wide.

RATES OF EROSION

	SLOW	WEATHERING RATE	FAST
Mineral solubility	low (e.g. quartz)	moderate (e.g. feldspar)	high (e.g. calcite)
Rainfall	low	moderate	heavy
Temperature	cold	temperate	hot
Vegetation	sparse	moderate	lush
Soil cover	bare rock	thin to moderate soil	thick soil

Weathering is the breakdown and decay of rocks in situ. It may be mechanical (physical), chemical or biological.

when water freezes in cracks in rocks, the ice occupies 9% more space than the water. This exerts a force which, when repeated over and over again, can split boulders apart. By contrast, in hot deserts, intense heating by day and cooling by night causes the outer layers of rocks to expand and contract until they break up and peel away like layers of an onion. These are examples of what is called mechanical weathering.

Other kinds of weathering include chemical reactions usually involving water. Rainwater containing carbon dioxide dissolved from the air or the soil is a weak acid which reacts with limestone, wearing out pits, tunnels and networks of caves in layers of limestone rock. Water also combines with some minerals, such as the feldspars in granite, to create kaolin, a white

Rates of erosion
The chart shows that the rates at which weathering takes place depend on the chemistry and hardness of rocks, climatic factors, especially rainfall and temperature, the vegetation and the nature of the soil cover in any area. The effects of weathering are increased by human action, particularly the removal of vegetation and the exposure of soils to the rain and wind.

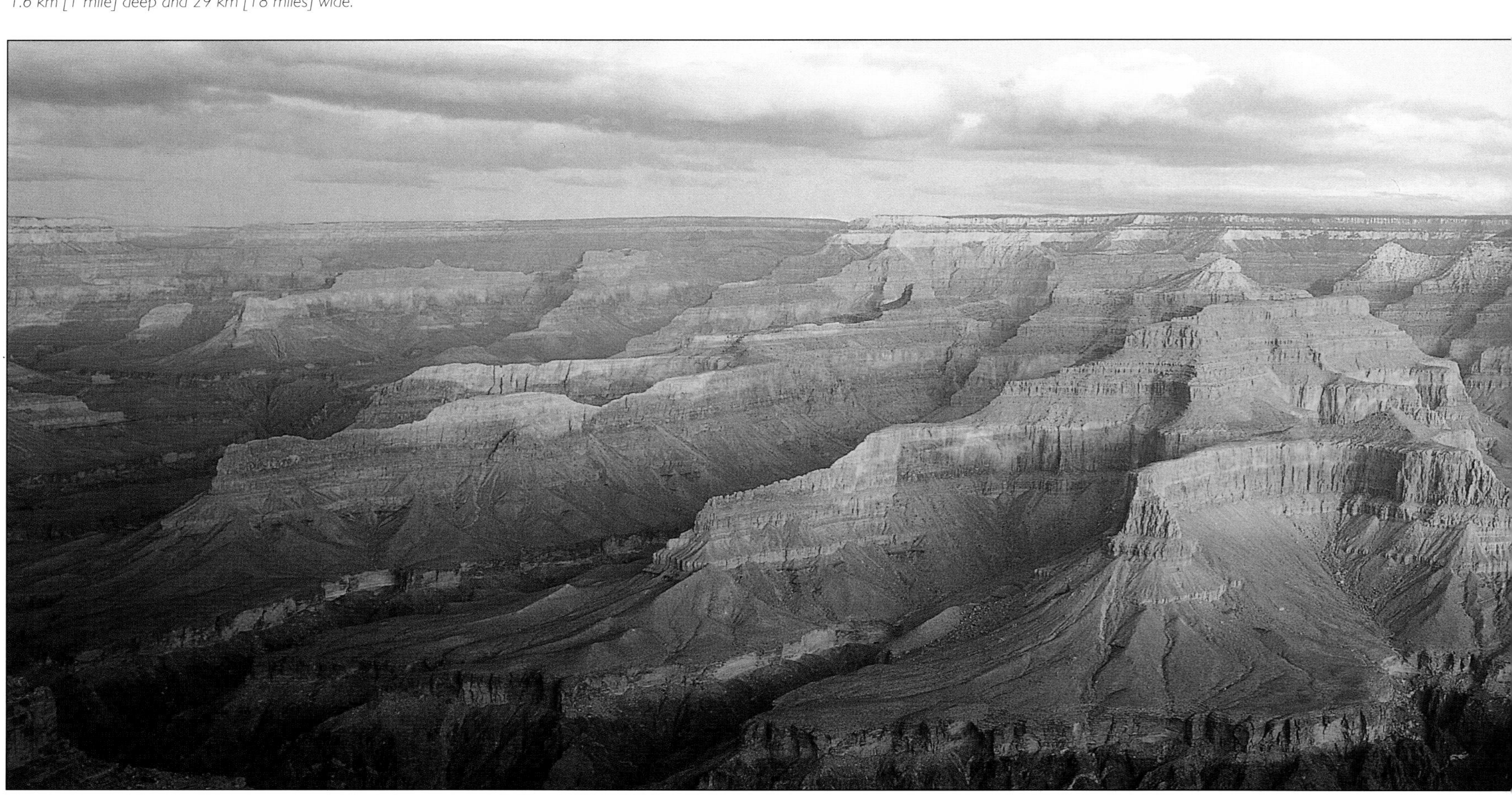

clay. These are examples of chemical weathering which constantly wears away rock.

RUNNING WATER, ICE AND WIND

In moist regions, rivers are effective in shaping the land. They transport material worn away by weathering and erode the land. They wear out V-shaped valleys in upland regions, while vigorous meanders widen their middle courses. The work of rivers is at its most spectacular when earth movements lift up flat areas and rejuvenate the rivers, giving them a new erosive power capable of wearing out such features as the Grand Canyon. Rivers also have a constructive role. Some of the world's most fertile regions are deltas and flood plains composed of sediments

Glaciers

During Ice Ages, ice spreads over large areas and the effect of glacial erosion on landscapes is enormous. However, during warm periods, the world's ice sheets and glaciers retreat. The chart shows that in recent years, the volumes of many glaciers around the world have been decreasing, possibly as a result of global warming.

ANNUAL FLUCTUATIONS FOR SELECTED GLACIERS

| Glacier name and location | Changes in the annual mass balance † | | Cumulative total |
	1970–1	1990–1	1970–90
Alfotbreen, Norway	+940	+790	+12,110
Wolverine, USA	+770	–410	+2,320
Storglaciaren, Sweden	–190	+170	–120
Djankuat, Russia	–230	–310	–1,890
Grasubreen, Norway	+470	–520	–2,530
Ürümqi, China	+102	–706	–3,828
Golubin, Kyrgyzstan	–90	–722	–7,105
Hintereisferner, Austria	–600	–1,325	–9,081
Gries, Switzerland	–970	–1,480	–10,600
Careser, Italy	–650	–1,730	–11,610
Abramov, Tajikistan	–890	–420	–13,700
Sarennes, France	–1,100	–1,360	–15,020
Place, Canada	–343	–990	–15,175

† *The annual mass balance is defined as the difference between glacier accumulation and ablation (melting) averaged over the whole glacier. Balances are expressed as water equivalent in millimetres. A plus indicates an increase in the depth or length of the glacier; a minus indicates a reduction.*

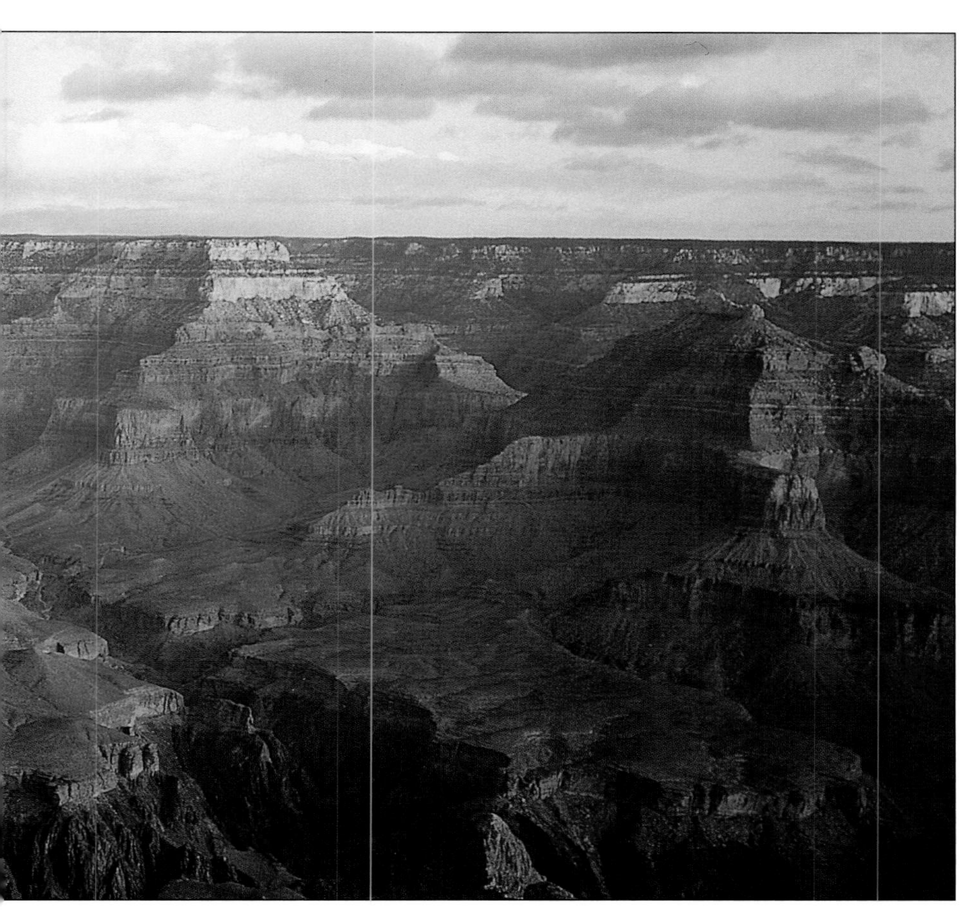

Juneau Glacier, Alaska

Like huge conveyor belts, glaciers transport weathered debris from mountain regions. Rocks frozen in the ice give the glaciers teeth, enabling them to wear out typical glaciated land features.

periodically dumped there by such rivers as the Ganges, Mississippi and Nile.

Running water in the form of sea waves and currents shapes coastlines, wearing out caves, natural arches, and stacks. The sea also transports and deposits worn material to form such features as spits and bars.

Glaciers in cold mountain regions flow downhill, gradually deepening valleys and shaping dramatic landscapes. They erode steep-sided U-shaped valleys, into which rivers often plunge in large waterfalls. Other features include cirques, armchair-shaped basins bounded by knife-edged ridges called *arêtes*. When several glacial cirques erode to form radial *arêtes*, pyramidal peaks like the Matterhorn are created. Deposits of moraine, rock material dumped by the glacier, are further evidence that ice once covered large areas. The work of glaciers, like other agents of erosion, varies with the climate. In recent years, global warming has been making glaciers retreat in many areas, while several of the ice shelves in Antarctica have been breaking up.

Many land features in deserts were formed by running water at a time when the climate was much rainier than it is today. Water erosion also occurs when flash floods are caused by rare thunderstorms. But the chief agent of erosion in dry areas is wind-blown sand, which can strip the paint from cars, and undercut boulders to create mushroom-shaped rocks.

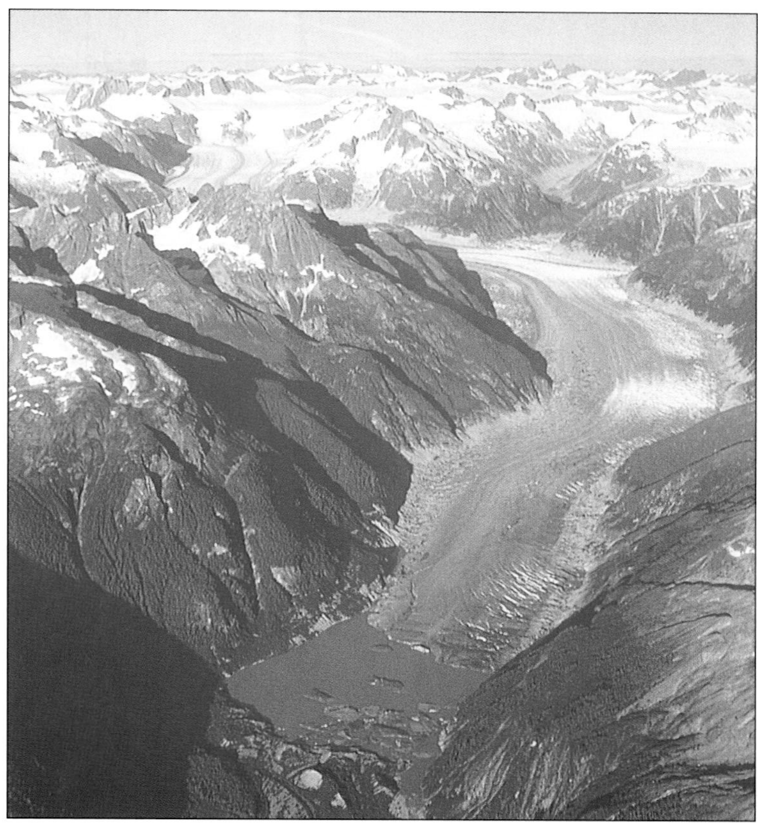

Oceans and Ice

Since the 1970s, oceanographers have found numerous hot vents on the ocean ridges. Called black smokers, the vents emit dark, mineral-rich water reaching 350°C [662°F]. Around the vents are chimney-like structures formed from minerals deposited from the hot water. The discovery of black smokers did not surprise scientists who already knew that the ridges were plate edges, where new crustal rock was being formed as molten magma welled up to the surface. But what was astonishing was that the hot water contained vast numbers of bacteria, which provided the base of a food chain that included many strange creatures, such as giant worms, eyeless shrimps and white clams. Many species were unknown to science.

Little was known about the dark world beneath the waves until about 50 years ago. But through the use of modern technology such as echo-sounders, magnetometers, research ships equipped with huge drills, submersibles that can carry scientists down to the ocean floor, and satellites, the secrets of the oceans have been gradually revealed.

The study of the ocean floor led to the discovery that the oceans are geologically young features – no more than 200 million years old. It also revealed evidence as to how oceans form and continents drift because of the action of plate tectonics.

THE BLUE PLANET

Water covers almost 71% of the Earth, which makes it look blue when viewed from space. Although the oceans are interconnected, geographers divide them into four main areas: the Pacific, Atlantic, Indian and Arctic oceans. The average depth of the oceans is 3,370 m [12,238 ft], but they are divided into several zones.

Around most continents are gently sloping continental shelves, which are flooded parts of the continents. The shelves end at the continental slope, at a depth of about 200 m [656 ft]. This slope leads steeply down to the abyss. The deepest parts of the oceans are the trenches, which reach a maximum depth of 11,033 m [36,198 ft] in the Mariana Trench in the western Pacific.

Most marine life is found in the top 200 m [656 ft], where there is sufficient sunlight for plants, called phytoplankton, to grow. Below this zone, life becomes more and more scarce, though no part of the ocean, even at the bottom of the deepest trenches, is completely without living things.

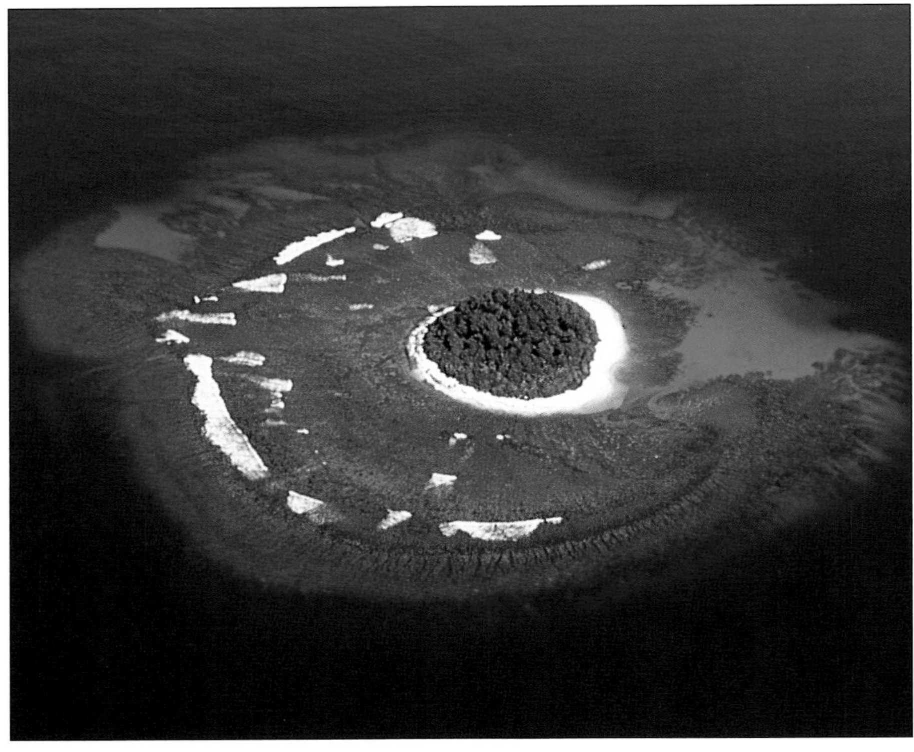

Vava'u Island, Tonga
This small coral atoll in northern Tonga consists of a central island covered by rainforest. Low coral reefs washed by the waves surround a shallow central lagoon.

Continental islands, such as the British Isles, are high parts of the continental shelves. For example, until about 7,500 years ago, when the ice sheets formed during the Ice Ages were melting, raising the sea level and filling the North Sea and the Strait of Dover, Britain was linked to mainland Europe.

By contrast, oceanic islands, such as the Hawaiian chain in the North Pacific Ocean, rise from the ocean floor. All oceanic islands are of volcanic origin, although many of them in warm parts of the oceans have sunk and are capped by layers of coral to form ring- or horseshoe-shaped atolls and coral reefs.

OCEAN WATER

The oceans contain about 97% of the world's water. Seawater contains more than 70 dissolved elements, but chloride and sodium make up 85% of the total. Sodium chloride is common salt and it makes seawater salty. The salinity of the oceans is mostly between 3.3–3.7%. Ocean water fed by icebergs or large rivers is less saline than shallow seas in the tropics, where the evaporation rate is high. Seawater is a source of salt but the water is useless for agriculture or drinking unless it is desalinated. However, land

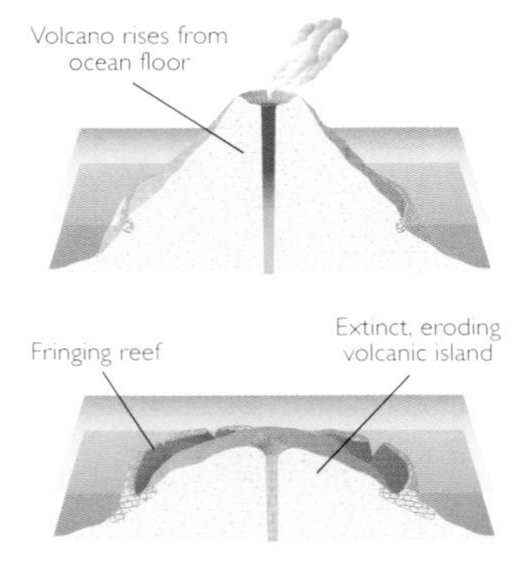
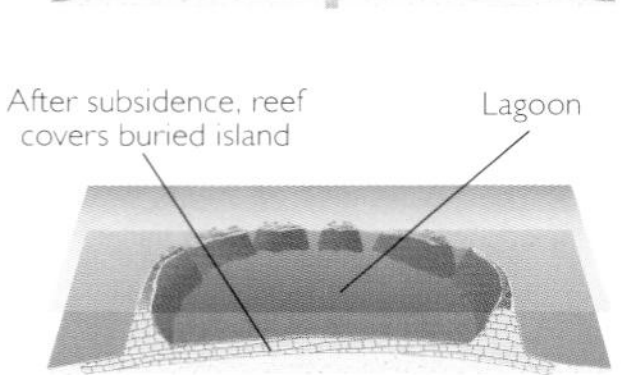

Development of an atoll
Some of the volcanoes that rise from the ocean floor reach the surface to form islands. Some of these islands subside and become submerged. As an island sinks, coral starts to grow around the rim of the volcano, building up layer upon layer of limestone deposits to form fringing reefs. Sometimes coral grows on the tip of a central cone to form an island in the middle of the atoll.

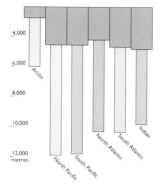

The ocean depths

The diagram shows the average depths (in dark blue) and the greatest depths in the four oceans. The North Pacific Ocean contains the world's deepest trenches, including the Mariana Trench, where the deepest manned descent was made by the bathyscaphe Trieste in 1960. It reached a depth of 10,916 metres [35,813 ft].

Relative sizes of the world's oceans:

PACIFIC   49%   ATLANTIC   26%
INDIAN   21%   ARCTIC   4%

Some geographers distinguish a fifth ocean, the Southern or Antarctic Ocean, but most authorities regard these waters as the southern extension of the Pacific, Atlantic and Indian oceans.

areas get a regular supply of fresh water through the hydrological cycle (see page 26).

The density of seawater depends on its salinity and temperature. Temperatures vary from –2°C [28°F], the freezing point of seawater at the poles, to around 30°C [86°F] in parts of the tropics. Density differences help to maintain the circulation of the world's oceans, especially deep-sea currents. But the main cause of currents within 350 m [1,148 ft] of the surface is the wind. Because of the Earth's rotation, currents are deflected, creating huge circular motions of surface water – clockwise in the northern hemisphere and anticlockwise in the southern hemisphere.

Ocean currents transport heat from the tropics to the polar regions and thus form part of the heat engine that drives the Earth's climates. Ocean currents have an especially marked effect on coastal climates, such as north-western Europe. In the mid-1990s, scientists warned that global warming may be weakening currents, including the warm Gulf Stream which is responsible for the mild winters experienced in north-western Europe.

ICE SHEETS, ICE CAPS AND GLACIERS
Global warming is also a threat to the world's ice sheets, ice caps and glaciers that together account for about 2% of the world's water. There are two ice sheets in the world, the largest covers most of Antarctica. With the ice reaching maximum depths of 4,800 m [15,748 ft], the Antarctic ice sheet contains about 70% of the world's fresh water, with a total volume about nine times greater than the Greenland ice sheet. Smaller bodies of ice include ice caps in northern Canada, Iceland and Scandinavia. Also throughout the world in high ranges are many valley glaciers, which help to shape dramatic mountain scenery.

Only about 11,000 years ago, during the final phase of the Pleistocene Ice Age, ice covered much of the northern hemisphere. The Ice Age, which began about 1.8 million years ago, was not a continuous period of cold. Instead, it consisted of glacial periods when the ice advanced and warmer interglacial periods when temperatures rose and the ice retreated.

Some scientists believe that we are now living in an inter-glacial period, and that glacial conditions will recur in the future. Others fear that global warming, caused mainly by pollution, may melt the world's ice, raising sea levels by up to 55 m [180 ft]. Many fertile and densely populated coastal plains, islands and cities would vanish from the map.

Weddell Sea, Antarctica

Antarctica contains two huge bays, occupied by the Ross and Weddell seas. Ice shelves extend from the ice sheet across parts of these seas. Researchers fear that warmer weather is melting Antarctica's ice sheets at a dangerous rate, after large chunks of the Larsen ice shelf and the Ronne ice shelf broke away in 1997 and 1998, respectively.

The Earth's Atmosphere

Since the discovery in 1985 of a thinning of the ozone layer, creating a so-called 'ozone hole', over Antarctica, many governments have worked to reduce the emissions of ozone-eating substances, notably the chlorofluorocarbons (CFCs) used in aerosols, refrigeration, air conditioning and dry cleaning.

Following forecasts that the ozone layer would rapidly repair itself as a result of controls on these emissions, scientists were surprised in early 1996 when a marked thinning of the ozone layer occurred over the Arctic, northern Europe, Russia and Canada. The damage, which was recorded as far south as southern Britain, was due to pollution combined with intense cold in the stratosphere. It was another sharp reminder of the dangers humanity faces when it interferes with and harms the environment.

The ozone layer in the stratosphere blocks out most of the dangerous ultraviolet B radiation in the Sun's rays. This radiation causes skin cancer and cataracts, as well as harming plants on the land and plankton in the oceans. The ozone layer is only one way in which the atmosphere protects life on Earth. The atmosphere also

provides the air we breathe and the carbon dioxide required by plants. It is also a shield against meteors and it acts as a blanket to prevent heat radiated from the Earth escaping into space.

LAYERS OF AIR
The atmosphere is divided into four main layers. The troposphere at the bottom contains about 85% of the atmosphere's total mass, where most weather conditions occur. The troposphere is about 15 km [9 miles] thick over the Equator and 8 km [5 miles] thick at the poles. Temperatures decrease with height by approximately 1°C [2°F] for every 100 m [328 ft]. At the top of the troposphere is a level called the tropopause where temperatures are stable at around –55°C [–67°F]. Above the tropopause is the stratosphere, which contains the ozone layer. Here, at about 50 km [31 miles] above the Earth's surface, temperatures rise to about 0°C [32°F].

The ionosphere extends from the stratopause to about 600 km [373 miles] above the surface. Here temperatures fall up to about 80 km

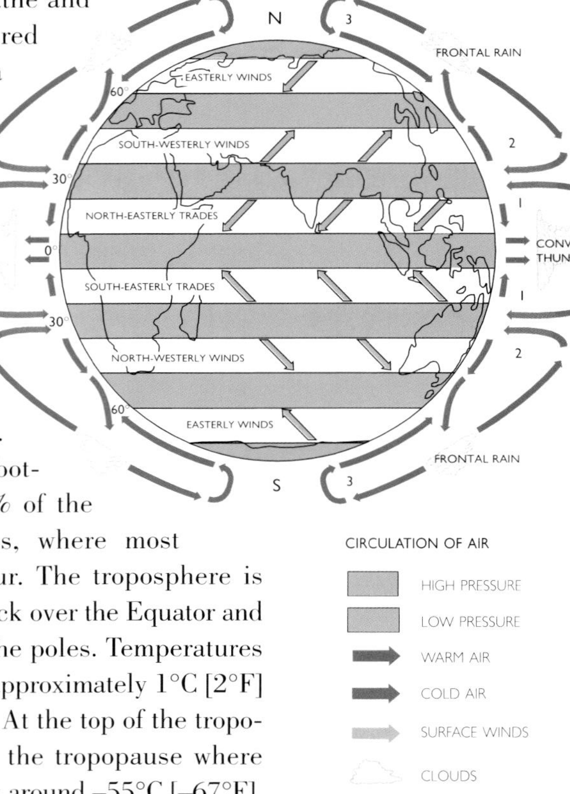

CIRCULATION OF AIR

▨	HIGH PRESSURE
▨	LOW PRESSURE
➔	WARM AIR
➔	COLD AIR
➔	SURFACE WINDS
☁	CLOUDS

The circulation of the atmosphere can be divided into three rotating but interconnected air systems, or cells. The Hadley cell (figure 1 on the above diagram) is in the tropics; the Ferrel cell (2) lies between the subtropics and the mid-latitudes, and the Polar cell (3) is in the high latitudes.

Moonrise seen from orbit
This photograph taken by an orbiting Shuttle shows the crescent of the Moon. Silhouetted at the horizon is a dense cloud layer. The reddish-brown band is the tropopause, which separates the blue-white stratosphere from the yellow troposphere.

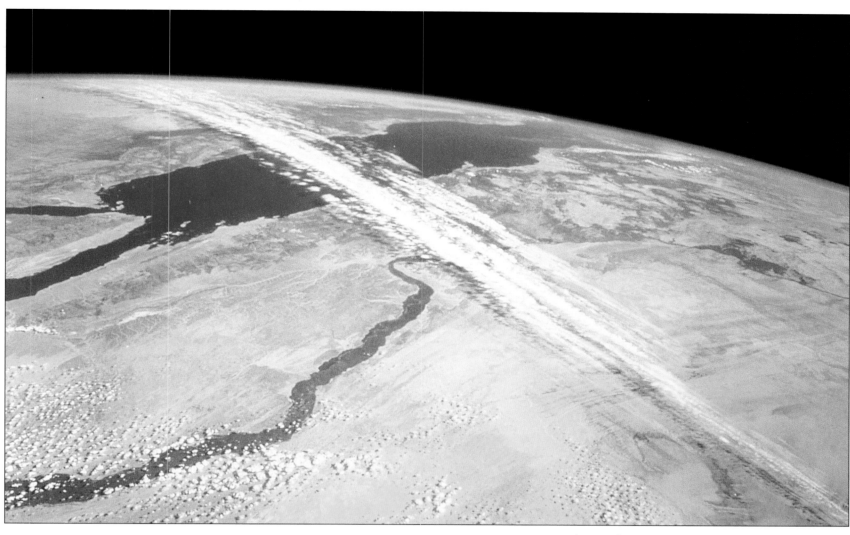

Jetstream from space

Jetstreams are strong winds that normally blow near the tropopause. Cirrus clouds mark the route of the jet stream in this photograph, which shows the Red Sea, North Africa and the Nile valley, which appears as a dark band crossing the desert.

[50 miles], but then rise. The aurorae, which occur in the ionosphere when charged particles from the Sun interact with the Earth's magnetic field, are strongest near the poles. In the exosphere, the outermost layer, the atmosphere merges into space.

CIRCULATION OF THE ATMOSPHERE

The heating of the Earth is most intense around the Equator where the Sun is high in the sky. Here warm, moist air rises in strong currents, creating a zone of low air pressure: the doldrums. The rising air eventually cools and spreads out north and south until it sinks back

to the ground around latitudes 30° North and 30° South. This forms two zones of high air pressure called the horse latitudes.

From the horse latitudes, trade winds blow back across the surface towards the Equator, while westerly winds blow towards the poles. The warm westerlies finally meet the polar easterlies (cold dense air flowing from the poles). The line along which the warm and cold air streams meet is called the polar front. Depressions (or cyclones) are low air pressure frontal systems that form along the polar front.

COMPOSITION OF THE ATMOSPHERE

The air in the troposphere is made up mainly of nitrogen (78%) and oxygen (21%). Argon makes up more than 0.9% and there are also minute amounts of carbon dioxide, helium, hydrogen, krypton, methane, ozone and xenon. The atmosphere also contains water vapour, the gaseous form of water, which, when it condenses around minute specks of dust and salt, forms tiny water droplets or ice crystals. Large masses of water droplets or ice crystals form clouds.

Classification of clouds

Clouds are classified broadly into cumuliform, or 'heap' clouds, and stratiform, or 'layer' clouds. Both types occur at all levels. The highest clouds, composed of ice crystals, are cirrus, cirrostratus and cirrocumulus. Medium-height clouds include altostratus, a grey cloud that often indicates the approach of a depression, and altocumulus, a thicker and fluffier version of cirrocumulus. Low clouds include stratus, which forms dull, overcast skies; nimbostratus, a dark grey layer cloud which brings almost continuous rain and snow; cumulus, a brilliant white heap cloud; and stratocumulus, a layer cloud arranged in globular masses or rolls. Cumulonimbus, a cloud associated with thunderstorms, lightning and heavy rain, often extends from low to medium altitudes. It has a flat base, a fluffy outline and often an anvil-shaped top.

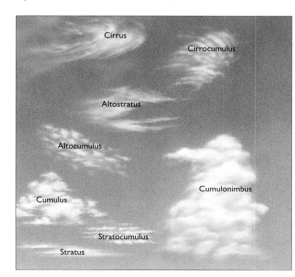

Cirrus

Cirrocumulus

Altostratus

Altocumulus

Cumulus

Cumulonimbus

Stratocumulus

Stratus

Climate and Weather

In 1992, Hurricane Andrew struck the Bahamas, Florida and Louisiana, causing record damage estimated at $30 billion. In September 1998, following heavy monsoon rains, floods submerged two-thirds of Bangladesh. The same month, in Central America, more than 7,000 people died in floods and mudslides caused by Hurricane Mitch. The economy of Honduras, already crippled by debt, was thought to have been put back by 15 to 20 years. On 3 May 1999, devastating tornadoes caused $1 billion of damage in central Oklahoma.

Every year, exceptional weather conditions cause disasters around the world. Modern forecasting techniques now give people warning of advancing storms, but the toll of human deaths continues as people are powerless in the face of the awesome forces of nature.

Weather is the day-to-day condition of the atmosphere. In some places, the weather is normally stable, but in other areas, especially the middle latitudes, it is highly variable, changing with the passing of a depression. By contrast, climate is the average weather of a place, based on data obtained over a long period.

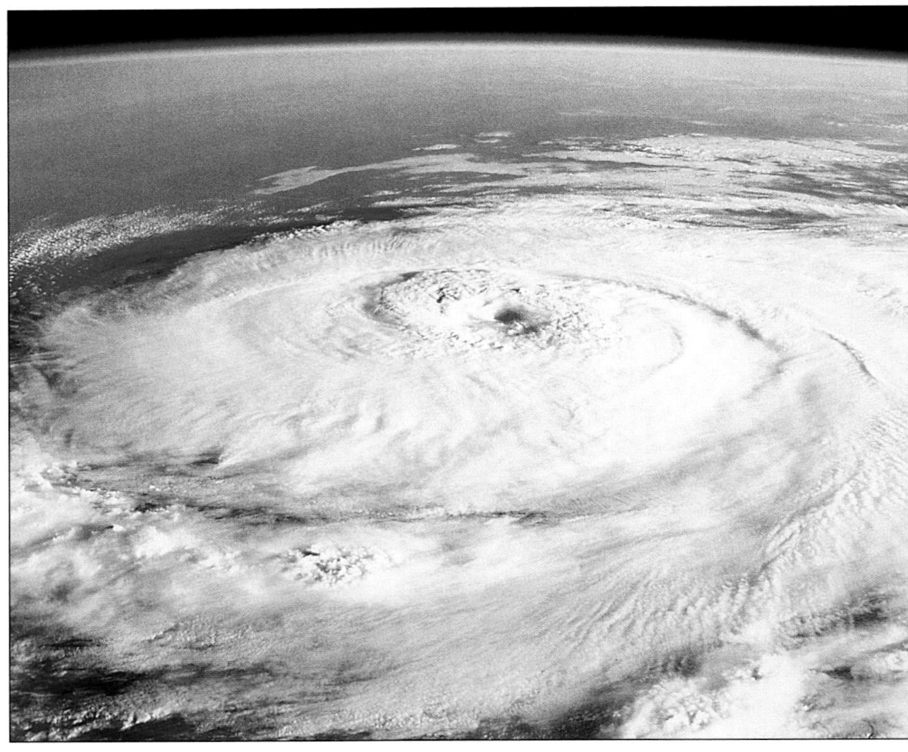

Hurricane Elena, 1995
Hurricanes form over warm oceans north and south of the Equator. Their movements are tracked by satellites, enabling forecasters to issue storm warnings as they approach land. In North America, forecasters identify them with boys' and girls' names.

CLIMATIC FACTORS

Climate depends basically on the unequal heating of the Sun between the Equator and the poles. But ocean currents and terrain also affect climate. For example, despite their northerly positions, Norway's ports remain ice-free in winter. This is because of the warming effect of the North Atlantic Drift, an extension of the Gulf Stream which flows across the Atlantic Ocean from the Gulf of Mexico.

By contrast, the cold Benguela current which flows up the coast of south-western Africa cools the coast and causes arid conditions. This is because the cold onshore winds are warmed as they pass over the land. The warm air can hold more water vapour than cold air, giving the winds a drying effect.

The terrain affects climate in several ways. Because temperatures fall with altitude, highlands are cooler than lowlands in the same

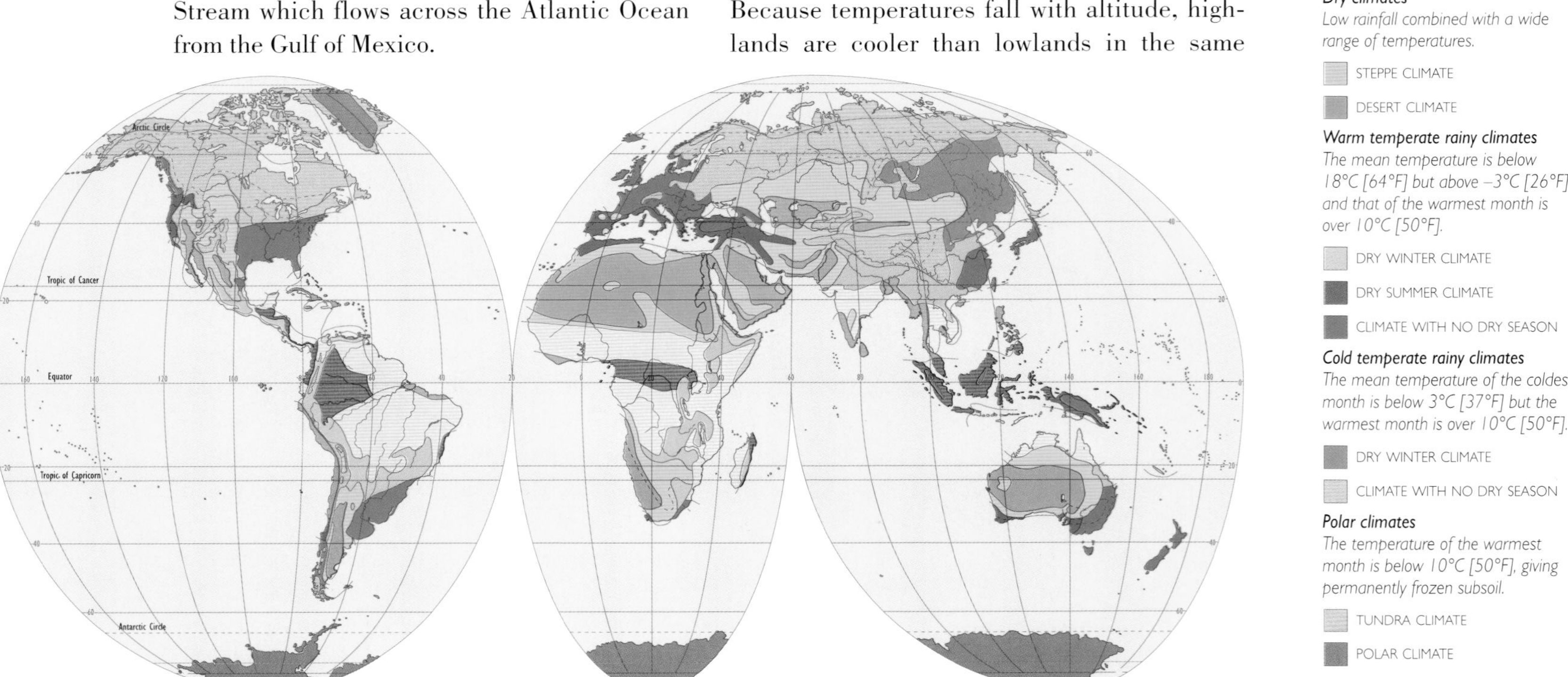

CLIMATIC REGIONS

Tropical rainy climates
All mean monthly temperatures above 18°C [64°F].

⬛ RAINFOREST CLIMATE

⬛ MONSOON CLIMATE

⬜ SAVANNA CLIMATE

Dry climates
Low rainfall combined with a wide range of temperatures.

⬜ STEPPE CLIMATE

⬛ DESERT CLIMATE

Warm temperate rainy climates
The mean temperature is below 18°C [64°F] but above −3°C [26°F] and that of the warmest month is over 10°C [50°F].

⬜ DRY WINTER CLIMATE

⬛ DRY SUMMER CLIMATE

⬛ CLIMATE WITH NO DRY SEASON

Cold temperate rainy climates
The mean temperature of the coldest month is below 3°C [37°F] but the warmest month is over 10°C [50°F].

⬛ DRY WINTER CLIMATE

⬜ CLIMATE WITH NO DRY SEASON

Polar climates
The temperature of the warmest month is below 10°C [50°F], giving permanently frozen subsoil.

⬜ TUNDRA CLIMATE

⬛ POLAR CLIMATE

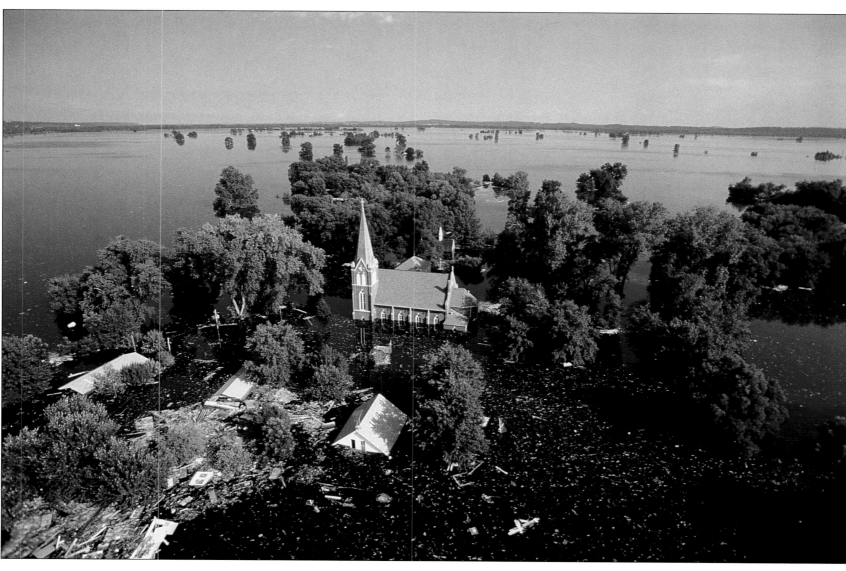

Floods in St Louis, United States
The satellite image, right, shows the extent of the floods at St Louis at the confluence of the Mississippi and the Missouri rivers in June and July 1993. The floods occurred when very heavy rainfall raised river levels by up to 14 m [46 ft]. The floods reached their greatest extent between Minneapolis in the north and a point approximately 150 km [93 miles] south of St Louis. In places, the width of the Mississippi increased to nearly 11 km [7 miles], while the Missouri reached widths of 32 km [20 miles]. In all, more than 28,000 sq km [10,800 sq miles] were inundated and hundreds of towns and cities were flooded. Damage to crops was estimated at $8 billion. The USA was hit again by flooding in early 1997, when heavy rainfall in North Dakota and Minnesota caused the Red River to flood. The flooding had a catastrophic effect on the city of Grand Forks, which was inundated for months.

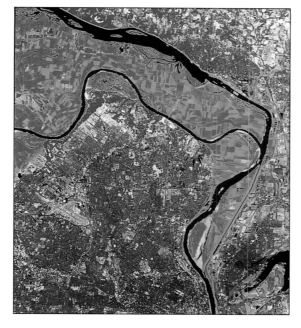

Flood damage in the United States
In June and July 1993, the Mississippi River basin suffered record floods. The photograph shows a sunken church in Illinois. The flooding along the Mississippi, Missouri and other rivers caused great damage, amounting to about $12 billion. At least 48 people died in the floods.

latitude. Terrain also affects rainfall. When moist onshore winds pass over mountain ranges, they are chilled as they are forced to rise and the water vapour they contain condenses to form clouds which bring rain and snow. After the winds have crossed the mountains, the air descends and is warmed. These warm, dry winds create rain shadow (arid) regions on the lee side of the mountains.

CLIMATIC REGIONS

The two major factors that affect climate are temperature and precipitation, including rain and snow. In addition, seasonal variations and other climatic features are also taken into account. Climatic classifications vary because of the weighting given to various features. Yet most classifications are based on five main climatic types: tropical rainy climates; dry climates; warm temperate rainy climates; cold temperate rainy climates; and very cold polar climates. Some classifications also allow for the effect of altitude. The main climatic regions are subdivided according to seasonal variations and also to the kind of vegetation associated with the climatic conditions. Thus, the rainforest climate, with rain throughout the year, differs from monsoon and savanna climates, which have marked dry seasons. Similarly, parched desert climates differ from steppe climates which have enough moisture for grasses to grow.

Water and Land Use

All life on land depends on fresh water. Yet about 80 countries now face acute water shortages. The world demand for fresh water is increasing by about 2.3% a year and this demand will double every 21 years. About a billion people, mainly in developing countries, do not have access to clean drinking water and around 10 million die every year from drinking dirty water. This problem is made worse in many countries by the pollution of rivers and lakes.

In 1995, a World Bank report suggested that wars will be fought over water in the 21st century. Relations between several countries are

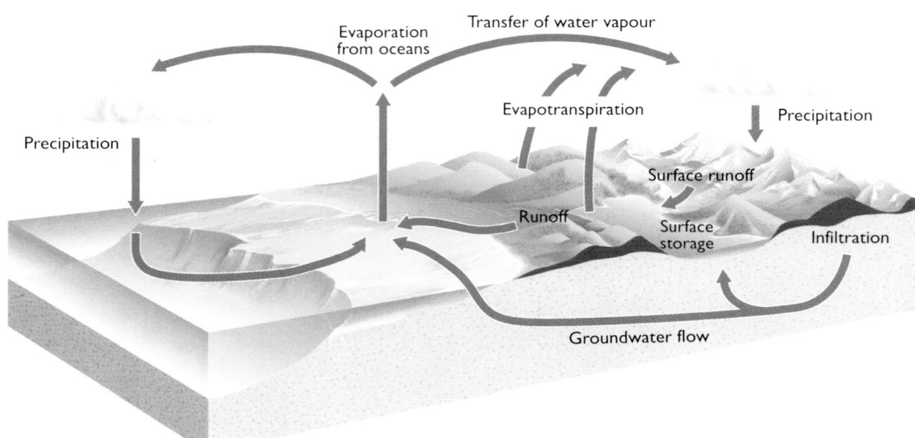

Hoover Dam, United States
The Hoover Dam in Arizona controls the Colorado River's flood waters. Its reservoir supplies domestic and irrigation water to the south-west, while a hydroelectric plant produces electricity.

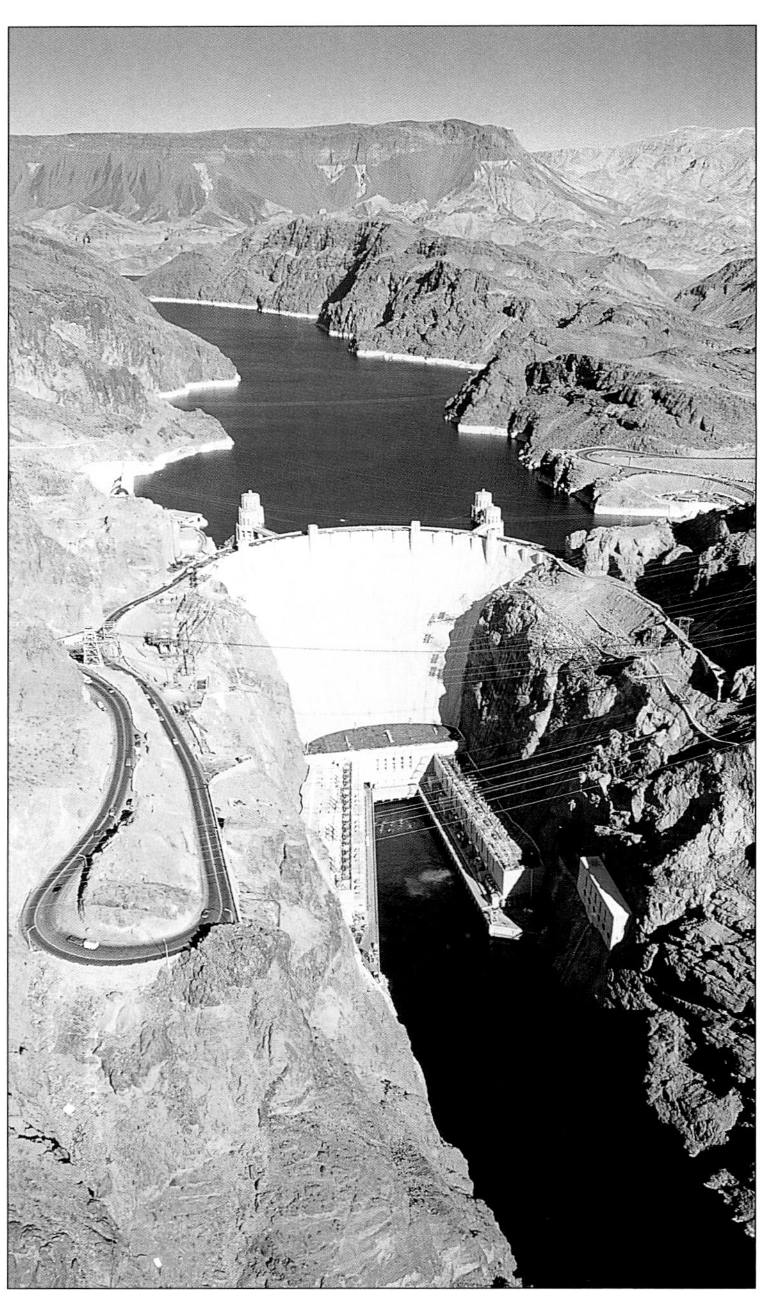

already soured by disputes over water resources. Egypt fears that Sudan and Ethiopia will appropriate the waters of the Nile, while Syria and Iraq are concerned that Turkish dams will hold back the waters of the Euphrates.

However, experts stress that while individual countries face water crises, there is no global crisis. The chief global problems are the uneven distribution of water and its inefficient and wasteful use.

THE WORLD'S WATER SUPPLY

Of the world's total water supply, 99.4% is in the oceans or frozen in bodies of ice. Most of the rest circulates through the rocks beneath our feet as ground water. Water in rivers and lakes, in the soil and in the atmosphere together make up only 0.013% of the world's water.

The freshwater supply on land is dependent on the hydrological, or water cycle which is driven by the Sun's heat. Water is evaporated from the oceans and carried into the air as invisible water vapour. Although this vapour averages less than 2% of the total mass of the atmosphere, it is the chief component from the standpoint of weather.

When air rises, water vapour condenses into visible water droplets or ice crystals, which eventually fall to earth as rain, snow, sleet, hail or frost. Some of the precipitation that reaches the ground returns directly to the atmosphere through evaporation or transpiration via plants. Much of the rest of the water flows into the rocks to become ground water or across the surface into rivers and, eventually, back to the oceans, so completing the hydrological cycle.

WATER AND AGRICULTURE

Only about a third of the world's land area is used for growing crops, while another third

The hydrological cycle
The hydrological cycle is responsible for the continuous circulation of water around the planet. Water vapour contains and transports latent heat, or latent energy. When the water vapour condenses back into water (and falls as rain, hail or snow), the heat is released. When condensation takes place on cold nights, the cooling effect associated with nightfall is offset by the liberation of latent heat.

WATER DISTRIBUTION
The distribution of planetary water, by percentage.

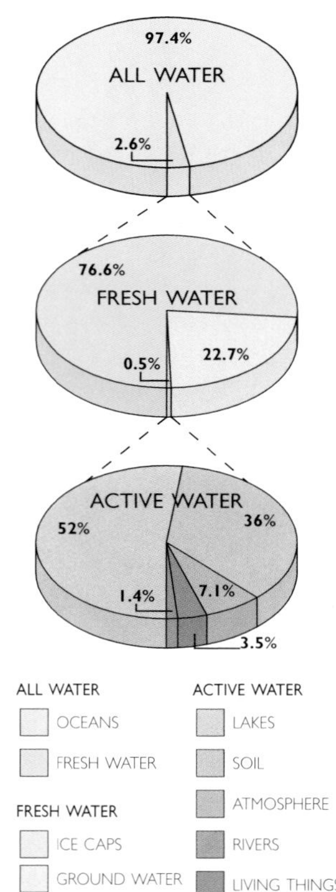

ALL WATER	ACTIVE WATER
☐ OCEANS	☐ LAKES
☐ FRESH WATER	☐ SOIL
	☐ ATMOSPHERE
FRESH WATER	
☐ ICE CAPS	☐ RIVERS
☐ GROUND WATER	☐ LIVING THINGS
☐ ACTIVE WATER	

Irrigation in Saudi Arabia

Irrigation in Saudi Arabia

Saudi Arabia is a desert country which gets its water from oases, which tap ground water supplies, and desalination plants. The sale of oil has enabled the arid countries of south-western Asia to develop their agriculture. In the above satellite image, vegetation appears brown and red.

Irrigation boom

The photograph shows a pivotal irrigation boom used to sprinkle water over a wheat field in Saudi Arabia. Irrigation in hot countries often takes place at night so that water loss through evaporation is reduced. Irrigation techniques vary from place to place. In monsoon areas with abundant water, the fields are often flooded, or the water is led to the crops along straight furrows. Sprinkler irrigation has become important since the 1940s. In other types of irrigation, the water is led through pipes which are on or under the ground. Underground pipes supply water directly to the plant roots and, as a result, water loss through evaporation is minimized.

consists of meadows and pasture. The rest of the world is unsuitable for farming, being too dry, too cold, too mountainous, or covered by dense forests. Although the demand for food increases every year, problems arise when attempts are made to increase the existing area of farmland. For example, the soils and climates of tropical forest and semi-arid regions of Africa and South America are not ideal for farming. Attempts to work such areas usually end in failure. To increase the world's food supply, scientists now concentrate on making existing farmland more productive rather than farming marginal land.

To grow crops, farmers need fertile, workable land, an equable climate, including a frost-free growing period, and an adequate supply of fresh water. In some areas, the water falls directly as rain. But many other regions depend on irrigation.

Irrigation involves water conservation through the building of dams which hold back storage reservoirs. In some areas, irrigation water comes from underground aquifers, layers of permeable and porous rocks through which ground water percolates. But in many cases, the water in the aquifers has been there for thousands of years, having accumulated at a time when the rainfall was much greater than it is today. As a result, these aquifers are not being renewed and will, one day, dry up.

Other sources of irrigation water are desalination plants, which remove salt from seawater and pump it to farms. This is a highly expensive process and is employed in areas where water supplies are extremely low, such as the island of Malta, or in the oil-rich desert countries around the Gulf, which can afford to build huge desalination plants.

LAND USE BY CONTINENT

	Forest	Permanent pasture	Permanent crops	Arable	Non-productive
North America	32.2%	17.3%	0.3%	12.6%	37.6%
South America	51.8%	26.7%	1.5%	6.6%	13.4%
Europe	33.4%	17.5%	3.0%	26.8%	19.3%
Africa	23.2%	26.6%	0.6%	5.6%	44.0%
Asia	20.2%	25.0%	1.2%	16.0%	37.8%
Oceania	23.5%	52.2%	0.1%	5.7%	18.5%

The Natural World

In 1995, a United Nations Environment Programme report stated that 11% of all mammal species, 18% of birds and 5% of fish are now threatened with extinction. Furthermore, it predicted that half of all bird and mammal species will become extinct within 300 years, or sooner if current trends continue. This will greatly reduce the biodiversity of our planet, causing the disappearance of unique combinations of genes that could be vital in improving food yields on farms or in the production of drugs to combat diseases.

Extinctions of species have occurred throughout Earth history, but today the extinction rate is estimated to be about 10,000 times the natural average. Some scientists have even compared it with the mass extinction that wiped out the dinosaurs 65 million years ago. However, the main cause of today's high extinction rate is not some natural disaster, such as the impact of an asteroid a few kilometres across, but it is the result of human actions, most notably the destruction of natural habitats for farming and other purposes. In some densely populated areas, such as Western Europe, the natural

Rainforest in Rwanda

Rainforests are the most threatened of the world's biomes. Effective conservation policies must demonstrate to poor local people that they can benefit from the survival of the forests.

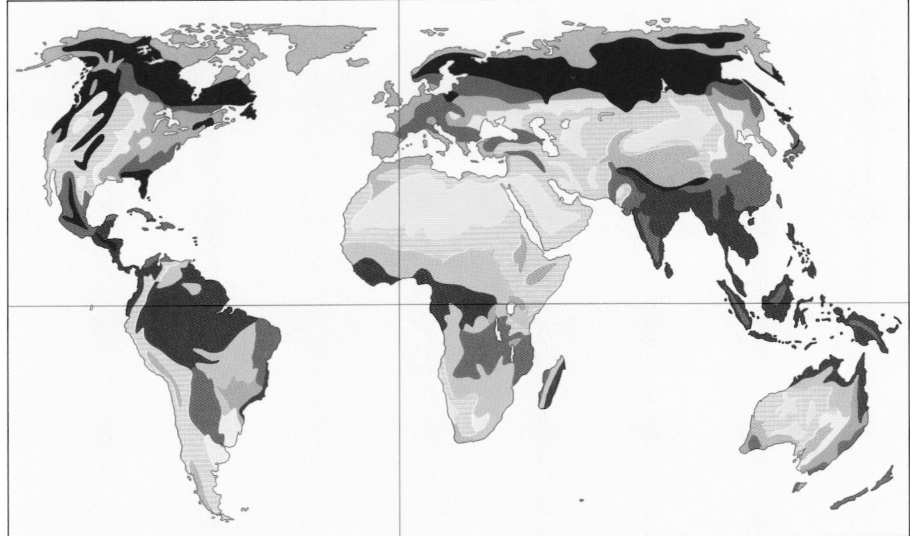

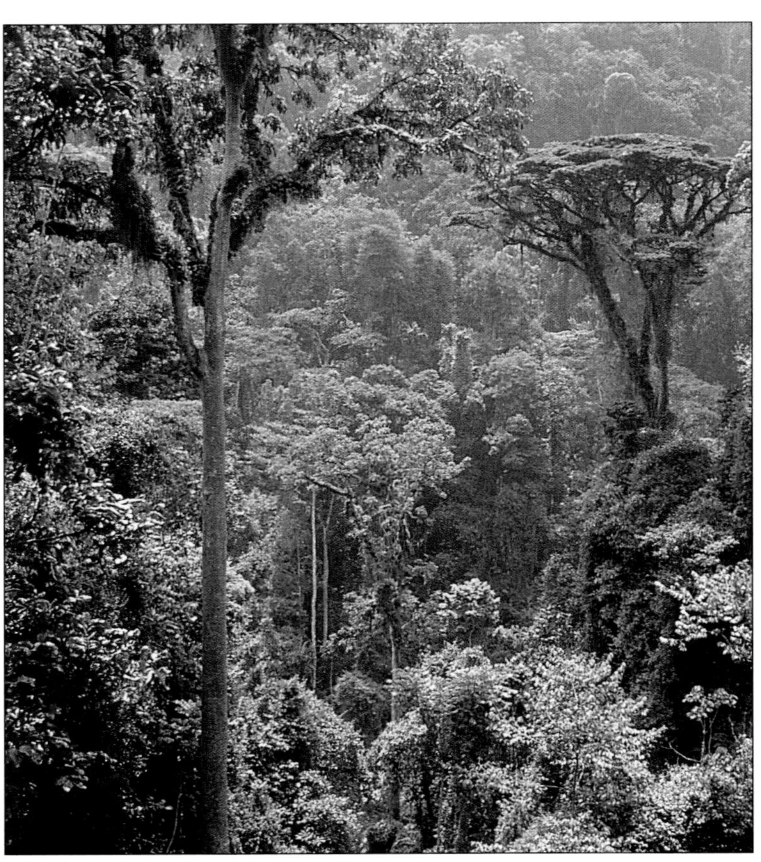

habitats were destroyed long ago. Today, the greatest damage is occurring in tropical rainforests, which contain more than half of the world's known species.

Modern technology has enabled people to live comfortably almost anywhere on Earth. But most plants and many animals are adapted to particular climatic conditions, and they live in association with and dependent on each other. Plant and animal communities that cover large areas are called biomes.

THE WORLD'S BIOMES

The world's biomes are defined mainly by climate and vegetation. They range from the tundra, in polar regions and high mountain regions, to the lush equatorial rainforests.

The Arctic tundra covers large areas in the polar regions of the northern hemisphere. Snow covers the land for more than half of the year and the subsoil, called permafrost, is permanently frozen. Comparatively few species can survive in this harsh, treeless environment. The main plants are hardy mosses, lichens, grasses, sedges and low shrubs. However, in summer, the tundra plays an important part in world animal geography, when its growing plants and swarms of insects provide food for migrating animals and birds that arrive from the south.

The tundra of the northern hemisphere merges in the south into a vast region of needleleaf evergreen forest, called the boreal forest or taiga. Such trees as fir, larch, pine and spruce are adapted to survive the long, bitterly cold winters of this region, but the number of plant and animal species is again small. South of the boreal forests is a zone of mixed needleleaf evergreens and broadleaf deciduous trees, which

NATURAL VEGETATION

- TUNDRA & MOUNTAIN VEGETATION
- NEEDLELEAF EVERGREEN FOREST
- MIXED NEEDLELEAF EVERGREEN & BROADLEAF DECIDUOUS TREES
- BROADLEAF DECIDUOUS WOODLAND
- MID-LATITUDE GRASSLAND
- EVERGREEN BROADLEAF & DECIDUOUS TREES & SHRUBS
- SEMI-DESERT SCRUB
- DESERT
- TROPICAL GRASSLAND (SAVANNA)
- TROPICAL BROADLEAF RAINFOREST & MONSOON FOREST
- SUBTROPICAL BROADLEAF & NEEDLELEAF FOREST

The map shows the world's main biomes. The classification is based on the natural 'climax' vegetation of regions, a result of the climate and the terrain. But human activities have greatly modified this basic division. For example, the original deciduous forests of Western Europe and the eastern United States have largely disappeared. In recent times, human development of some semi-arid areas has turned former dry grasslands into barren desert.

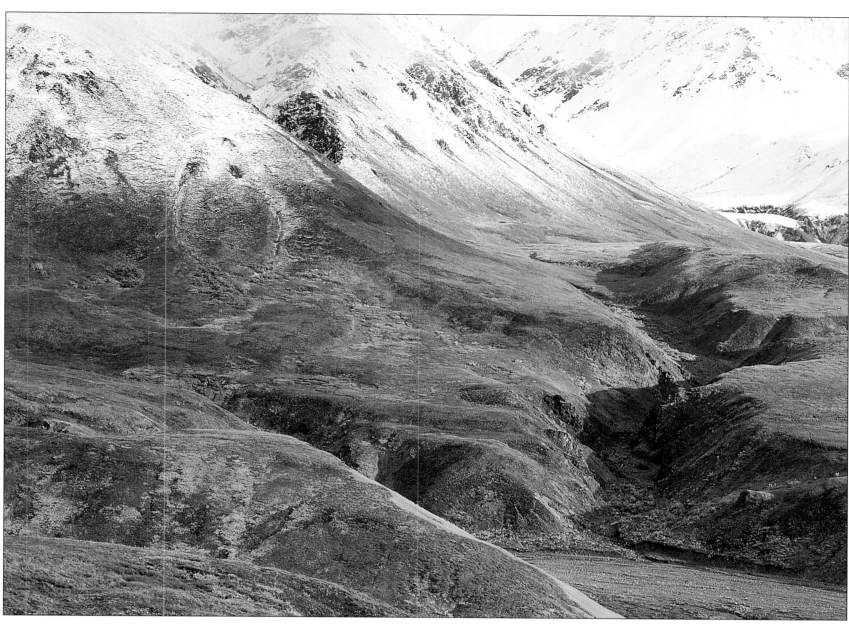

Tundra in subarctic Alaska
The Denali National Park, Alaska, contains magnificent mountain scenery and tundra vegetation which flourishes during the brief summer. The park is open between 1 June and 15 September.

shed their leaves in winter. In warmer areas, this mixed forest merges into broadleaf deciduous forest, where the number and diversity of plant species is much greater.

Deciduous forests are adapted to temperate, humid regions. Evergreen broadleaf and deciduous trees grow in Mediterranean regions, with their hot, dry summers. But much of the original deciduous forest has been cut down and has given way to scrub and heathland. Grasslands occupy large areas in the middle latitudes, where the rainfall is insufficient to support forest

growth. The moister grasslands are often called prairies, while drier areas are called steppe.

The tropics also contain vast dry areas of semi-desert scrub which merges into desert, as well as large areas of savanna, which is grassland with scattered trees. Savanna regions, with their marked dry season, support a wide range of mammals.

Tropical and subtropical regions contain three types of forest biomes. The tropical rainforest, the world's richest biome measured by its plant and animal species, experiences rain and high temperatures throughout the year. Similar forests occur in monsoon regions, which have a season of very heavy rainfall. They, too, are rich in plant species, though less so than the tropical rainforest. A third type of forest is the subtropical broadleaf and needleleaf forest, found in such places as south-eastern China, south-central Africa and eastern Brazil.

NET PRIMARY PRODUCTION OF EIGHT
MAJOR BIOMES

- ■ TROPICAL RAINFORESTS
- ■ DECIDUOUS FORESTS
- ▦ TROPICAL GRASSLANDS
- ■ CONIFEROUS FORESTS
- ▦ MEDITERRANEAN
- ▦ TEMPERATE GRASSLANDS
- □ TUNDRA
- □ DESERTS

The net primary production of eight major biomes is expressed in grams of dry organic matter per square metre per year. The tropical rainforests produce the greatest amount of organic material. The tundra and deserts produce the least.

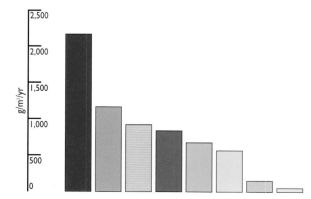

The Human World

Every minute, the world's population increases by between 160 and 170. While forecasts of future growth are difficult to make, most demographers are in agreement that the world's population, which passed the 6 billion mark in October 1999, would reach 8.9 billion by 2050. It was not expected to level out until 2200, when it would peak at around 11 billion. After 2200, it is expected to level out or even decline a little. The fastest rates of increase will take place in the developing countries of Africa, Asia and Latin America – the places least able to afford the enormous costs incurred by such a rapidly expanding population.

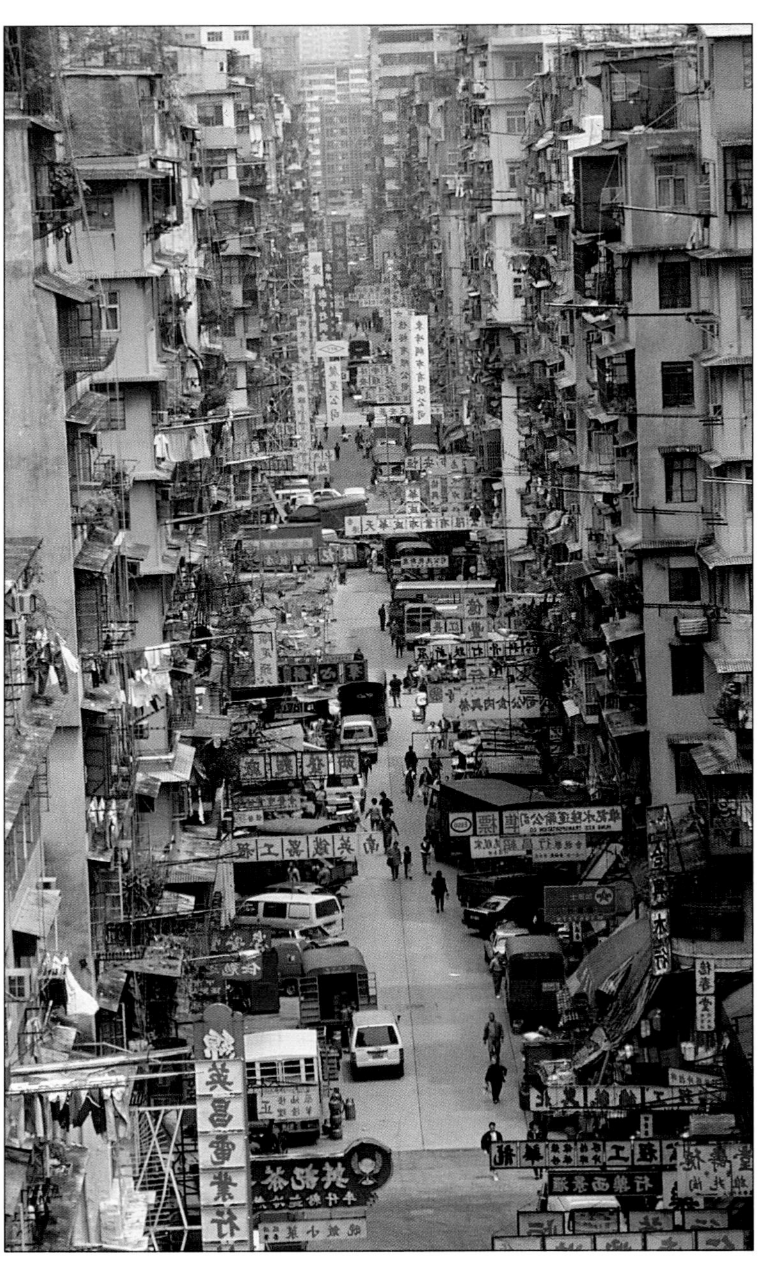

Elevated view of Ki Lung Street, Hong Kong
Urban areas of Hong Kong, a Special Administrative Region on the southern coast of China, contain busy streets overlooked by crowded apartments.

Average world population growth rates have declined from about 2% a year in the early 1960s to 1.3% in 1997. This was partly due to a decline in fertility rates – that is, the number of births to the number of women of child-bearing age – especially in developed countries where, as income has risen, the average size of families has fallen.

Declining fertility rates were also evident in many developing countries. Even Africa shows signs of such change, though its population is expected to triple before it begins to fall. Population growth is also dependent on death rates, which are affected by such factors as famine, disease and the quality of medical care.

THE POPULATION EXPLOSION

The world's population has grown steadily throughout most of human history, though certain events triggered periods of population growth. The invention of agriculture around 10,000 years ago, led to great changes in human society. Before then, most people had obtained food by hunting animals and gathering plants. Average life expectancies were probably no more than 20 years and life was hard. However, when farmers began to produce food surpluses, people began to live settled lives. This major milestone in human history led to the development of the first cities and early civilizations.

From an estimated 8 million in 8000 BC, the world population rose to about 300 million by AD 1000. Between 1000 and 1750, the rate of world population increase was around 0.1% per year, but another period of major economic and social change – the Industrial Revolution – began in the late 18th century. The Industrial Revolution led to improvements in farm technology and increases in food production. The world population began to increase quickly as industrialization spread across Europe and into North America. By 1850, it had reached 1.2 billion. The 2 billion mark was passed in the 1920s, and then the population rapidly doubled to 4 billion by the 1970s.

POPULATION FEATURES

Population growth affects the structure of societies. In developing countries with high annual rates of population increase, the large majority of the people are young and soon to become parents themselves. For example, in Kenya, which had until recently an annual rate of population growth of around 4%, just over half

LARGEST CITIES

Within 10 years, for the first time ever, the majority of the world's population will live in urban areas. Almost all the urban growth will be in developing countries. Below is a list of cities with their estimated populations in the year 2015, in millions.

1	Tokyo	28.7
2	Bombay (Mumbai)	27.4
3	Lagos	24.1
4	Shanghai	23.2
5	Jakarta	21.5
6	São Paulo	21.0
7	Karachi	20.6
8	Beijing	19.6
9	Dhaka	19.2
10	Mexico City	19.1
11	Calcutta (Kolkata)	17.6
12	Delhi	17.5
13	New York City	17.4
14	Tianjin	17.1
15	Metro Manila	14.9
16	Cairo	14.7
17	Los Angeles	14.5
18	Seoul	13.1
19	Buenos Aires	12.5
20	Istanbul	12.1

These city populations are based on figures for urban agglomerations rather than actual city limits.

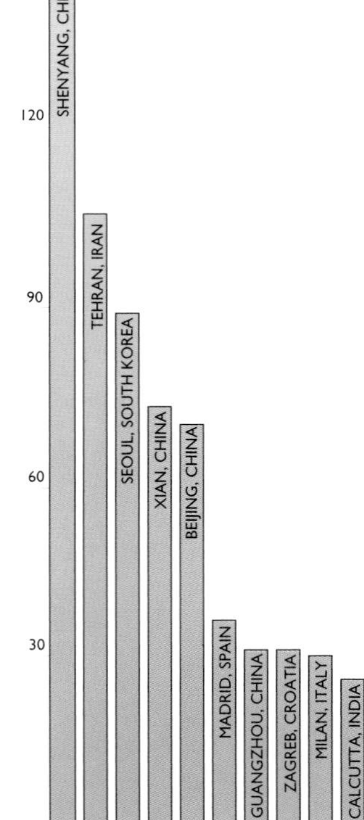

Urban air pollution
This diagram of the world's most polluted cities indicates the number of days per year when sulphur dioxide levels exceed the WHO threshhold of 150 micrograms per cubic metre.

Hong Kong's business district
By contrast with the picturesque old streets of Hong Kong, the business district of Hong Kong City, on the northern shore of Hong Kong Island, is a cluster of modern high-rise buildings. The glittering skyscrapers reflect the success of this tiny region, which has one of the strongest economies in Asia.

POPULATION CHANGE 1990–2000
The estimated population change for the years 1990–2000.

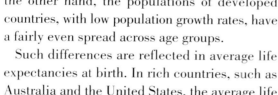

- OVER 40% POPULATION GAIN
- 30–40% POPULATION GAIN
- 20–30% POPULATION GAIN
- 10–20% POPULATION GAIN
- 0–10% POPULATION GAIN
- NO CHANGE OR LOSS

TOP 5 COUNTRIES

Kuwait	+75.0%
Namibia	+62.5%
Afghanistan	+60.1%
Mali	+55.5%
Tanzania	+54.6%

BOTTOM 5 COUNTRIES

Belgium	–0.1%
Hungary	–0.2%
Grenada	–2.4%
Germany	–3.2%
Tonga	–3.2%

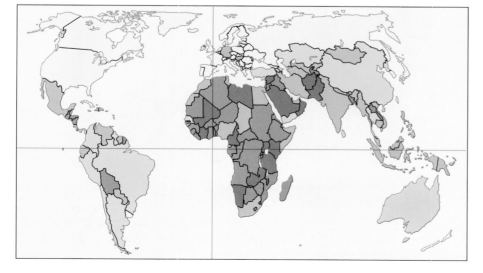

of the population is under 15 years of age. On the other hand, the populations of developed countries, with low population growth rates, have a fairly even spread across age groups.

Such differences are reflected in average life expectancies at birth. In rich countries, such as Australia and the United States, the average life expectancy is 77 years (74 years for men and 80 for women; women live longer, on average, than their male counterparts). As a result, an increasing proportion of the people are elderly and retired, contributing little to the economy. The reverse applies in many of the poorer countries, where average life expectancies are below 60 years. In more than a dozen countries in Africa, the average life expectancy is less than 50.

Paralleling the population explosion has been a rapid growth in the number and size of cities and towns, which contained nearly half of the world's people by the 1990s. This proportion is expected to rise to nearly two-thirds by 2025.

Urbanization occurred first in areas undergoing the industrialization of their economies, but today it is also a feature of the developing world. In developing countries, people are leaving impoverished rural areas hoping to gain access to the education, health and other services available in cities. But many cities are unable to provide the housing and other facilities necessitated by rapid population growth. As a result, slums grow up around the cities. Pollution, crime and disease become features of everyday life.

The population explosion poses another probem for the entire world. No one knows how many people the world can support or how consumer demand will damage the fragile environments on our planet. The British economist Thomas Malthus argued in the late 18th century that overpopulation would lead to famine and war. But an increase in farm technology in the 19th and 20th centuries, combined with a green revolution, in which scientists developed high-yield crop varieties, has greatly increased food production since Malthus' time.

However, some modern scientists argue that overpopulation may become a problem in the 21st century. They argue that food shortages leading to disastrous famines will result unless population growth can be halted. Such people argue in favour of birth control programmes. China, the only country with more than a billion people, has introduced a one-child family policy. Their action has slowed the growth of China's huge population, though rising living standards seem to be the most effective brakes on rapid population growth.

Languages and Religions

In 1995, 90-year-old Edna Guerro died in northern California. She was the last person able to speak Northern Pomo, one of about 50 Native American languages spoken in the state. Her death marked the extinction of one of the world's languages.

This event is not an isolated incident. Language experts regularly report the disappearance of languages and some of them predict that between 20 to 50% of the world's languages will no longer exist by the end of the 21st century. Improved transport and communications are partly to blame, because they bring people from various cultures into closer and closer contact. Many children no longer speak the language of their parents, preferring instead to learn the language used at their schools. The pressures on

children to speak dominant rather than minority languages are often great. In the first part of the 20th century, Native American children were punished if they spoke their native language.

The disappearance of a language represents the extinction of a way of thinking, a unique expression of the experiences and knowledge of a group of people. Language and religion together give people an identity and a sense of belonging. However, there are others who argue that the disappearance of minority languages is a step towards international understanding and economic efficiency.

THE WORLD'S LANGUAGES

Definitions of what is a language or a dialect vary and, hence, estimates of the number of languages spoken around the world range from about 3,000 to 6,000. But whatever the figure, it is clear that the number of languages far exceeds the number of countries.

RELIGIOUS ADHERENTS	
The number of adherents to the world's major religions, in millions.	
Christian	1,667
Roman Catholic	952
Protestant	337
Orthodox	162
Anglican	70
Other Christian	148
Muslim	881
Sunni	841
Shia	40
Hindu	663
Buddhist	312
Chinese Folk	172
Tribal	92
Jewish	18
Sikhs	17

Buddhist monks in Katmandu, Nepal

Hinduism is Nepal's official religion, but the Nepalese observe the festivals of both Hinduism and Buddhism. They also regard Buddhist shrines and Hindu temples as equally sacred.

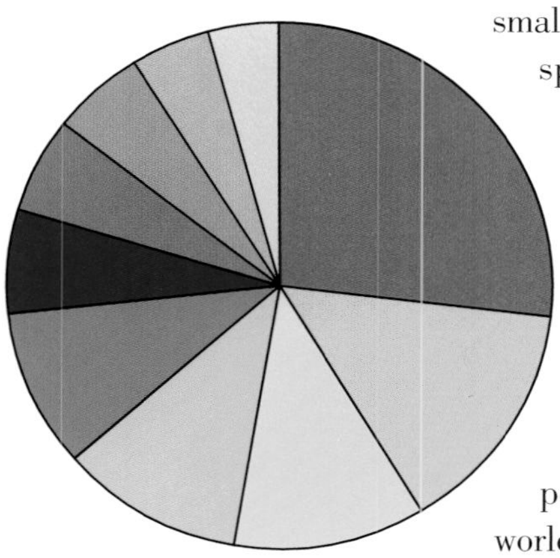

Countries with only one language tend to be small. For example, in Liechtenstein, everyone speaks German. By contrast, more than 860 languages have been identified in Papua New Guinea, whose population is only about 4.3 million people. Hence, many of its languages are spoken by only small groups of people. In fact, scientists have estimated that about a third of the world's languages are now spoken by less than 1,000 people. By contrast, more than half of the world's population speak just seven languages.

The world's languages are grouped into families. The Indo-European family consists of languages spoken between Europe and the Indian subcontinent. The growth of European empires over the last 300 years led several Indo-European languages, most notably English, French, Portuguese and Spanish, to spread throughout much of North and South America, Africa, Australia and New Zealand.

English has become the official language in many countries which together contain more than a quarter of the world's population. It is now a major international language, surpassing in importance Mandarin Chinese, a member of the Sino-Tibetan family, which is the world's leading first language. Without a knowledge of English, businessmen face many problems when conducting international trade, especially with the United States or other English-speaking countries. But proposals that English, French, Russian or some other language should become a world language seem unlikely to be acceptable to a majority of the world's peoples.

WORLD RELIGIONS

Religion is another fundamental aspect of human culture. It has inspired much of the world's finest architecture, literature, music and painting. It has also helped to shape human cultures since prehistoric times and is responsible for the codes of ethics by which most people live.

The world's major religions were all founded in Asia. Judaism, one of the first faiths to teach that there is only one god, is one of the world's oldest. Founded in south-western Asia, it influenced the more recent Christianity and Islam, two other monotheistic religions which

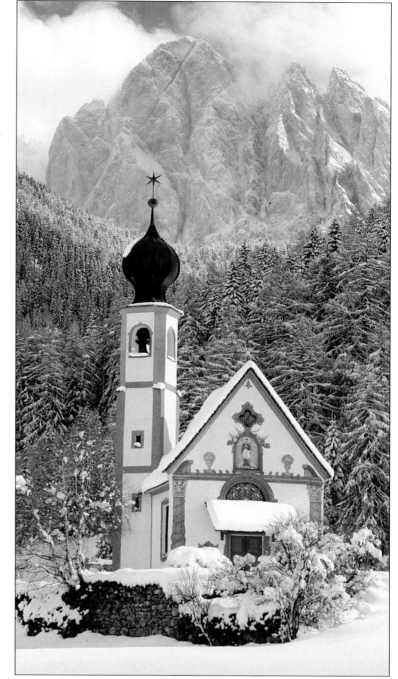

The Church of San Giovanni, Dolomites, Italy
Christianity has done much to shape Western civilization. Christian churches were built as places of worship, but many of them are among the finest achievements of world architecture.

now have the greatest number of followers. Hinduism, the third leading faith in terms of the numbers of followers, originated in the Indian subcontinent and most Hindus are now found in India. Another major religion, Buddhism, was founded in the subcontinent partly as a reaction to certain aspects of Hinduism. But unlike Hinduism, it has spread from India throughout much of eastern Asia.

Religion and language are powerful creative forces. They are also essential features of nationalism, which gives people a sense of belonging and pride. But nationalism is often also a cause of rivalry and tension. Cultural differences have led to racial hatred, the persecution of minorities, and to war between national groups.

MOTHER TONGUES
Native speakers of the major languages, in millions (1990).

- MANDARIN CHINESE 834M
- ENGLISH 443M
- HINDI 352M
- SPANISH 341M
- RUSSIAN 293M
- ARABIC 197M
- BENGALI 184M
- PORTUGUESE 173M
- MALAY 142M
- JAPANESE 125M

OFFICIAL LANGUAGES: % OF WORLD POPULATION

English	27.0%
Chinese	19.0%
Hindi	13.5%
Spanish	5.4%
Russian	5.2%
French	4.2%
Arabic	3.3%
Portuguese	3.0%
Malay	3.0%
Bengali	2.9%
Japanese	2.3%

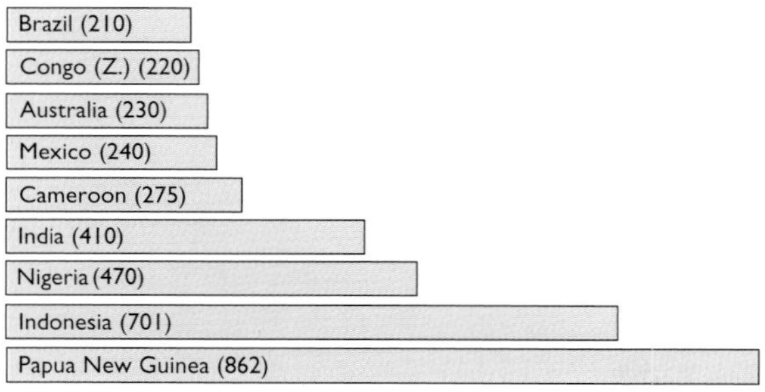

Polyglot nations
The graph, right, shows countries of the world with more than 200 languages. Although it has only about 4.3 million people, Papua New Guinea holds the record for the number of languages spoken.

Brazil (210)
Congo (Z.) (220)
Australia (230)
Mexico (240)
Cameroon (275)
India (410)
Nigeria (470)
Indonesia (701)
Papua New Guinea (862)

International Organizations

Twelve days before the surrender of Germany and four months before the final end of World War II, representatives of 50 nations met in San Francisco to create a plan to set up a peace-keeping organization, the United Nations. Since its birth on 24 October 1945, its membership has grown from 51 to 188.

Its first 50 years have been marked by failures as well as successes. While it has helped to prevent some disputes from flaring up into full-scale wars, the Blue Berets, as the UN troops are called, have been forced, because of their policy of neutrality, to stand by when atrocities are committed by rival warring groups.

THE WORK OF THE UN

The United Nations has six main organs. They include the General Assembly, where member states meet to discuss issues concerned with peace, security and development. The Security Council, containing 15 members, is concerned with maintaining world peace. The Secretariat, under the Secretary-General, helps the other organs to do their jobs effectively, while the Economic and Social Council works with spe-cialized agencies to implement policies con-cerned with such matters as development, education and health. The International Court of Justice, or World Court, helps to settle disputes between member nations. The sixth organ of the UN, the Trusteeship Council, was designed to bring 11 UN trust territories to independence. Its task has now been completed.

The specialized agencies do much important

work. For example, UNICEF (United Nations International Children's Fund) has provided health care and aid for children in many parts of the world. The ILO (International Labour Organization) has improved working conditions in many areas, while the FAO (Food and Agri-cultural Organization) has worked to improve the production and distribution of food. Among the other agencies are organizations to help refugees, to further human rights and to control the environment. The latest agency, set up in 1995, is the WTO (World Trade Organization), which took over the work of GATT (General Agreement on Tariffs and Trade).

OTHER ORGANIZATIONS

In a world in which nations have become increasingly interdependent, many other organiz-ations have been set up to deal with a variety of problems. Some, such as NATO (the North Atlantic Treaty Organization), are defence alli-ances. In the early 1990s, the end of the Cold War suggested that NATO's role might be fin-ished, but the civil war in the former Yugoslavia showed that it still has a role in maintaining peace and security.

Other organizations encourage social and economic co-operation in various regions. Some are NGOs (non-governmental organizations), such as the Red Cross and its Muslim equiva-lent, the Red Crescent. Other NGOs raise funds to provide aid to countries facing major crises, such as famine.

Some major international organizations aim at economic co-operation and the removal of trade barriers. The best known of these organizations is the European Union, which has 15 members. Its

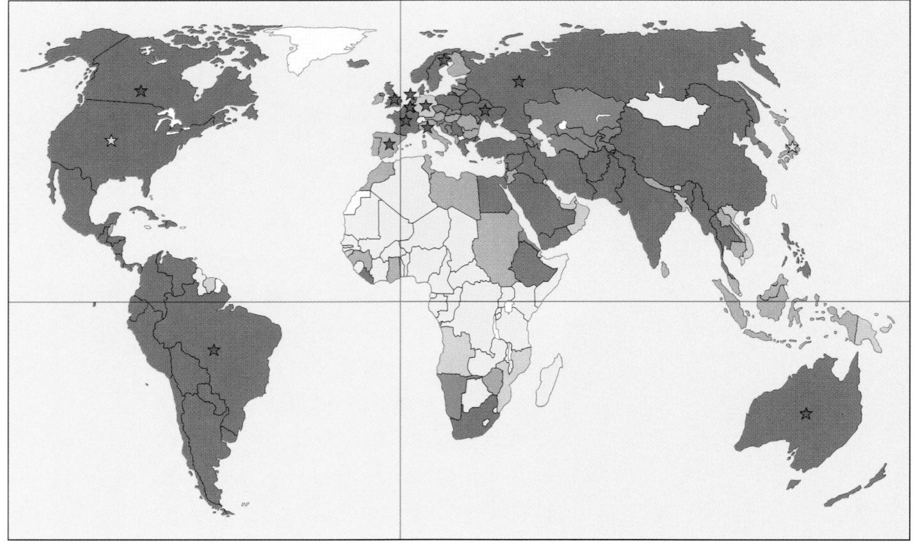

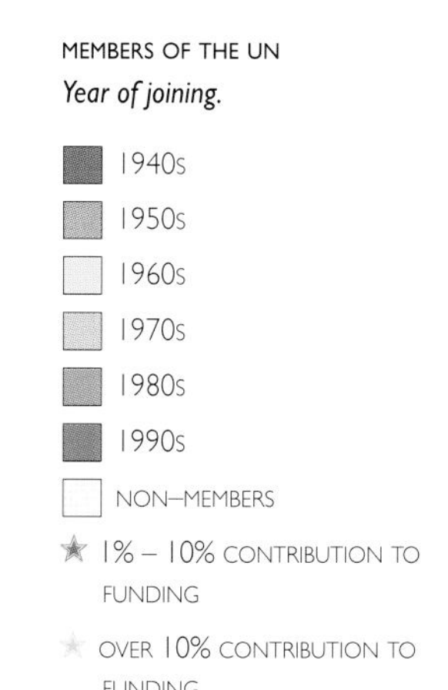

MEMBERS OF THE UN
Year of joining.

- 1940s
- 1950s
- 1960s
- 1970s
- 1980s
- 1990s
- NON–MEMBERS
- ★ 1% – 10% CONTRIBUTION TO FUNDING
- ★ OVER 10% CONTRIBUTION TO FUNDING

Food aid
International organizations supply aid to people living in areas suffering from war or famine. In Bosnia-Herzegovina, the UN Protection Force supervised the movements of food aid, as did NATO on the borders of Kosovo a few years later.

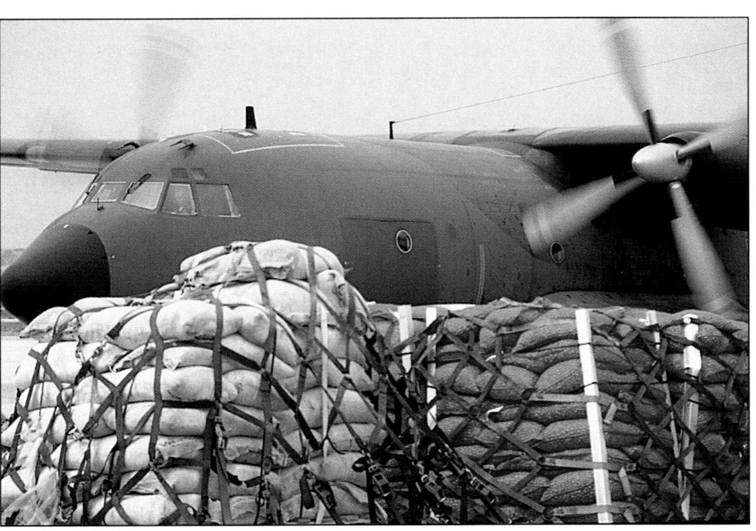

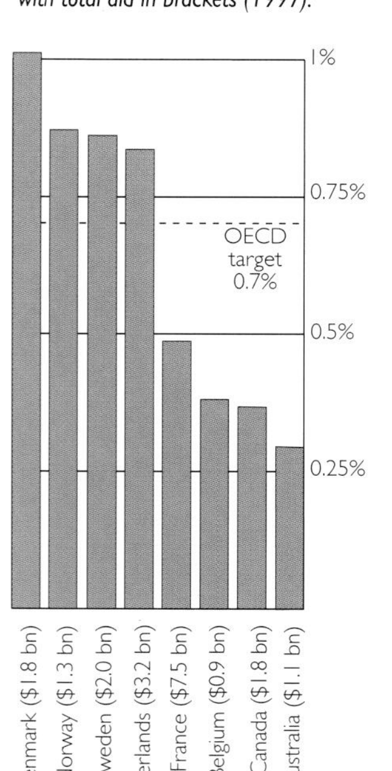

INTERNATIONAL AID AND GNP
Aid provided as a percentage of GNP, with total aid in brackets (1997).

1%

0.75%

OECD target 0.7%

0.5%

0.25%

Denmark ($1.8 bn)
Norway ($1.3 bn)
Sweden ($2.0 bn)
Netherlands ($3.2 bn)
France ($7.5 bn)
Belgium ($0.9 bn)
Canada ($1.8 bn)
Australia ($1.1 bn)

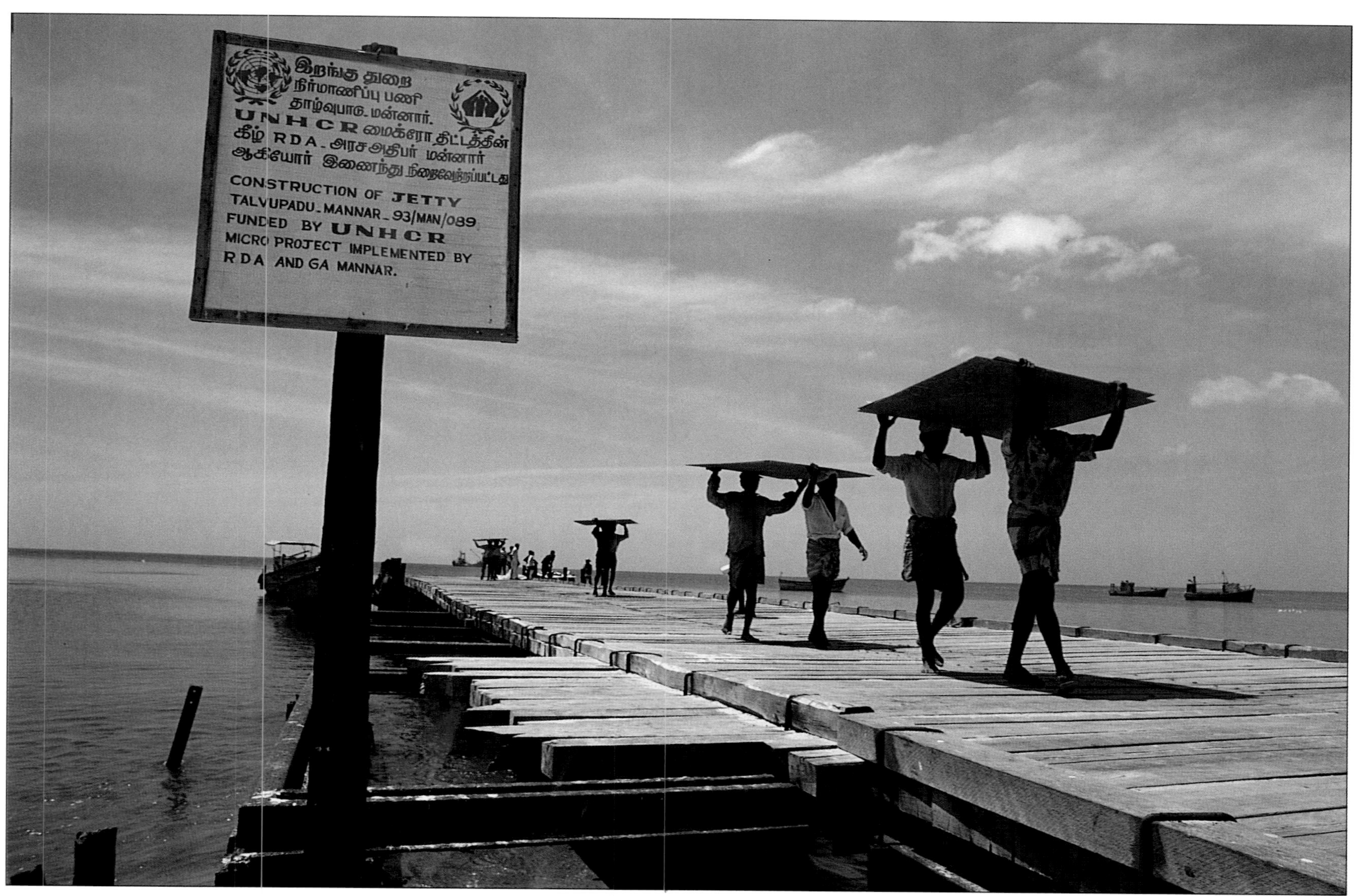

UNHCR-funded jetty, Sri Lanka

In 1994, the UN High Commission for Refugees was responsible for 23 million people. Sometimes, it has to provide transport facilities, such as this jetty, to get aid to the refugees.

economic success has led some people to support the idea of setting up a federal Europe. Others oppose such developments, they fear that a 'United States of Europe' would lead to a loss of national identity among the member states.

Other groupings include ASEAN (the Association of South-east Asian Nations) which aims to reduce trade barriers between its members (Brunei, Burma [Myanmar], Cambodia, Indonesia, Laos, Malaysia, the Philippines, Singapore, Thailand and Vietnam). APEC (the Asia-Pacific Co-operation Group), founded in 1989, aims to create a free trade zone between the countries of eastern Asia, North America, Australia and New Zealand by 2020. Meanwhile, Canada, Mexico and the United States have formed NAFTA (the North American Free Trade Agreement), while other economic groupings link most of the countries in Latin America. Another grouping with a more limited but important objective is OPEC (the Organization of Oil-Exporting Countries). OPEC works to unify policies concerning trade in oil on the world markets.

Some organizations exist to discuss matters of common interest between groups of nations. The Commonwealth of Nations, for example, grew out of links created by the British Empire. In North and South America, the OAS (Organization of American States) aims to increase understanding in the Western hemisphere. The OAU (Organization of African Unity) has a similar role in Africa, while the Arab League represents the Arab nations of North Africa and the Middle East.

COUNTRIES OF THE EUROPEAN UNION

	Total land area (sq km)	Total population (2000 est.)	GNP per capita, US$ (1998)	Unemployment rate, % (1996)	Year of accession to the EU	Seats in EU parliament (1998)
Austria	83,850	7,613,000	26,850	7%	1995	21
Belgium	30,510	9,832,000	25,380	12.7%	1958	25
Denmark	43,070	5,153,000	33,260	8.7%	1973	16
Finland	338,130	5,077,000	24,110	16.3%	1995	16
France	551,500	58,145,000	24,940	12.3%	1958	87
Germany	356,910	76,962,000	25,850	10.4%	1958	99
Greece	131,990	10,193,000	11,650	10.3%	1981	25
Ireland	70,280	4,086,000	18,340	11.9%	1973	15
Italy	301,270	57,195,000	20,250	12.1%	1958	87
Luxembourg	2,590	377,000	43,570	3.3%	1958	6
Netherlands	41,526	15,829,000	24,760	6.6%	1958	31
Portugal	92,390	10,587,000	10,690	7.3%	1986	24
Spain	504,780	40,667,000	14,080	22.2%	1986	64
Sweden	449,960	8,560,000	25,620	8.1%	1995	22
United Kingdom	243,368	58,393,000	21,400	7.6%	1973	87

Agriculture

In 1995, the world production of grains was lower than average – the result mainly of a wet spring in the United States, and bad weather combined with economic turmoil in the former Soviet Union. Downward trends in world food production in the 1990s reopened an old debate – whether food production will be able to keep pace with a rapidly rising world population in the 21st century.

Some experts argue that the lower than expected production figures in the 1990s heralded a period of relative scarcity and high prices of food, which will be felt most in the poorer developing countries. Others are more optimistic. They point to the successes of the 'green revolution' which, through the use of new crop varieties produced by scientists, irrigation and the extensive use of fertilizers and pesticides,

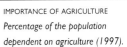

IMPORTANCE OF AGRICULTURE
Percentage of the population dependent on agriculture (1997).

OVER 75% DEPENDENT

50–75% DEPENDENT

25–50% DEPENDENT

10–25% DEPENDENT

UNDER 10% DEPENDENT

Rice harvest, Bali, Indonesia

More than half of the world's people eat rice as their basic food. Rice grows well in tropical and subtropical regions, such as in Indonesia, India and south-eastern China.

has revolutionized food production since the 1950s and 1960s.

The green revolution has led to a great expansion in the production of many crops, including such basic foods as rice, maize and wheat. In India, its effects have been spectacular. Between 1955 and 1995, grain production trebled, giving the country sufficient food reserves to prevent famine in years when droughts or floods reduce the harvest. While once India had to import food, it is now self-sufficient.

FOOD PRODUCTION

Agriculture, which supplies most of our food, together with materials to make clothes and other products, is the world's most important economic activity. But its relative importance has declined in comparison with manufacturing and service industries. As a result, the end of the 20th century marked the first time for 10,000 years when the vast majority of the people no longer had to depend for their living on growing crops and herding animals.

However, agriculture remains the dominant economic activity in many developing countries in Africa and Asia. For example, in the late 1990s, 90% or more of the people of Bhutan, Burundi, Nepal and Rwanda depended on farming for their living.

Many people in developing countries eke out the barest of livings by nomadic herding or shifting cultivation, combined with hunting, fishing and gathering plant foods. A large proportion of farmers live at subsistence level, producing little more than they require to provide the basic needs of their families.

The world's largest food producer and exporter is the United States, although agriculture employs

	Food	Population
AUSTRALASIA	1.2%	0.4%
EUROPE	27.6%	15.5%
ASIA	44.5%	58.3%
SOUTH AMERICA	6.5%	6.7%
NORTH AMERICA	13.8%	7.1%
AFRICA	6.7%	12.0%

A comparison of world food production and population by continent.

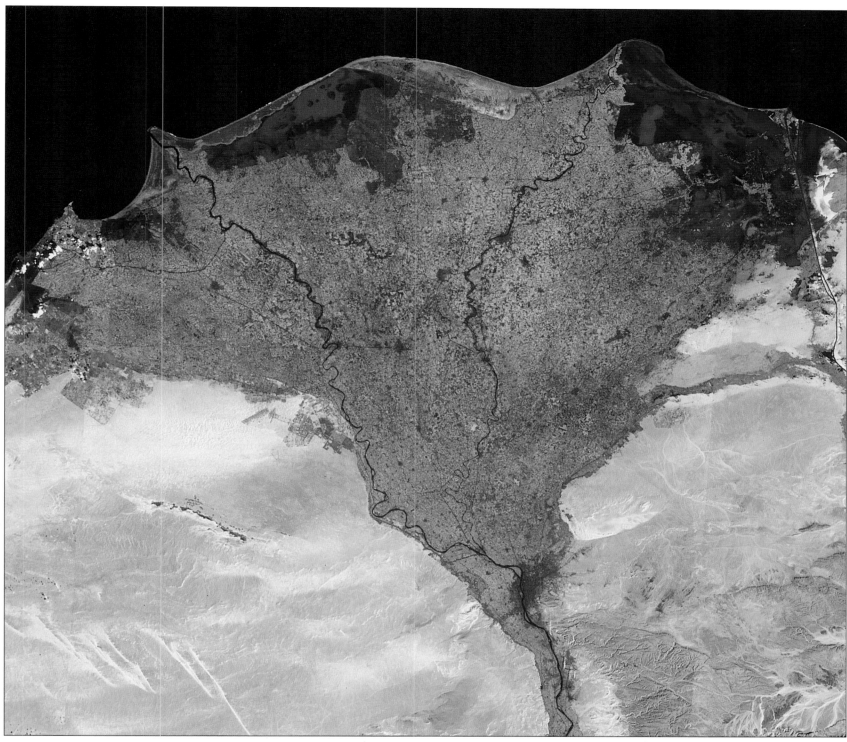

Landsat *image of the Nile delta, Egypt*

Most Egyptians live in the Nile valley and on its delta. Because much of the silt carried by the Nile now ends up on the floor of Lake Nasser, upstream of the Aswan Dam, the delta is now retreating and seawater is seeping inland. This eventuality was not foreseen when the Aswan High Dam was built in the 1960s.

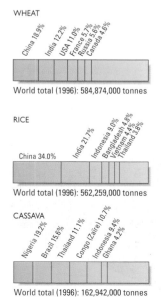

WHEAT

China 18.9% India 12.2% USA 11.0% France 5.7% Russia 5.6% Canada 4.6%

World total (1996): 584,874,000 tonnes

RICE

China 34.0% India 21.7% Indonesia 9.0% Bangladesh 4.8% Vietnam 4.4% Thailand 3.8%

World total (1996): 562,259,000 tonnes

CASSAVA

Nigeria 19.2% Brazil 15.6% Thailand 11.1% Congo (Zaire) 10.7% Indonesia 9.4% Ghana 4.2%

World total (1996): 162,942,000 tonnes

around 3% of its total workforce. The high production of the United States is explained by its use of scientific methods and mechanization, which are features of agriculture throughout the developed world.

INTENSIVE OR ORGANIC FARMING

By the late 20th century, some people were beginning to question the dependence of farmers on chemical fertilizers and pesticides. Many people became concerned that the widespread use of chemicals was seriously polluting and damaging the environment.

Others objected to the intensive farming of animals to raise production and lower prices. For example, the suggestion in Britain in 1996 that BSE, or 'mad cow disease', might be passed on to people causing CJD (Creuzfeldt-Jakob Disease) caused widespread alarm.

Such problems have led some farmers to return to organic farming, which is based on animal-welfare principles and the banning of chemical fertilizers and pesticides. The costs of organic foods are certainly higher than those produced by intensive farming, but an increasing number of consumers in the Western world are beginning to demand organic products from their retailers.

Energy and Minerals

In March 1996, floods in Ukraine carried radioactive waste dumped near Chernobyl hundreds of kilometres downstream. This was the latest chapter in the disaster caused by the explosion at the Chernobyl nuclear power station in 1986, the worst nuclear accident in history. Nuclear power now provides about 17% of the world's electricity and experts once thought that it would eventually supply much of the world's energy supply. But concern about safety and worries about the high costs involved make this seem unlikely. Several developed countries have already abandoned their nuclear programmes.

FOSSIL FUELS

Huge amounts of energy are needed for heating, generating electricity and for transport. In the early years of the Industrial Revolution, coal

Wind farms in California, United States
Wind farms using giant turbines can produce electricity at a lower cost than conventional power stations. But in many areas, winds are too light or too strong for wind farms to be effective.

formed from organic matter buried beneath the Earth's surface, was the leading source of energy. It remains important as a raw material in the manufacture of drugs and other products and also as a fuel, despite the fact that burning coal causes air pollution and gives off carbon dioxide, an important greenhouse gas.

However, oil and natural gas, which came into wide use in the 20th century, are cheaper to produce and easier to handle than coal, while, kilogram for kilogram, they give out more heat. Oil is especially important in moving transport, supplying about 97% of the fuel required.

In 1995, proven reserves of oil were sufficient to supply the world, at current rates of production, for 43 years, while supplies of natural gas stood at about 66 years. Coal reserves are more abundant and known reserves would last 200 years at present rates of use. Although these figures must be regarded with caution, because they do not allow for future discoveries, it is clear that fossil fuel reserves will one day run out.

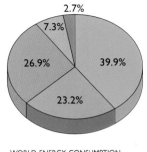

2.7%
7.3%
26.9%
39.9%
23.2%

WORLD ENERGY CONSUMPTION
- OIL
- GAS
- COAL
- NUCLEAR
- HYDRO

The diagram shows the proportion of world energy consumption in 1997 by form. Total energy consumption was 8,509.2 million tonnes of oil equivalent. Such fuels as wood, peat and animal wastes, together with renewable forms of energy, such as wind and geothermal power, are not included, although they are important in some areas.

SELECTED MINERAL PRODUCTION STATISTICS (1995)

Bauxite		Diamonds	
Australia	38%	Australia	38%
Guinea	13%	Congo (Zaïre)	18%
Jamaica	10%	Botswana	16%
Brazil	9%	Russia	12%
China	6%	South Africa	8%

Gold		Iron ore	
South Africa	23%	China	15%
USA	14%	Brazil	12%
Australia	11%	Australia	9%
Canada	7%	Russia	4%
Russia	6%	India	4%

Potash		Zinc	
Canada	37%	China	12%
Germany	13%	Canada	8%
Belarus	11%	Japan	8%
Russia	11%	USA	7%
USA	6%	Germany	5%

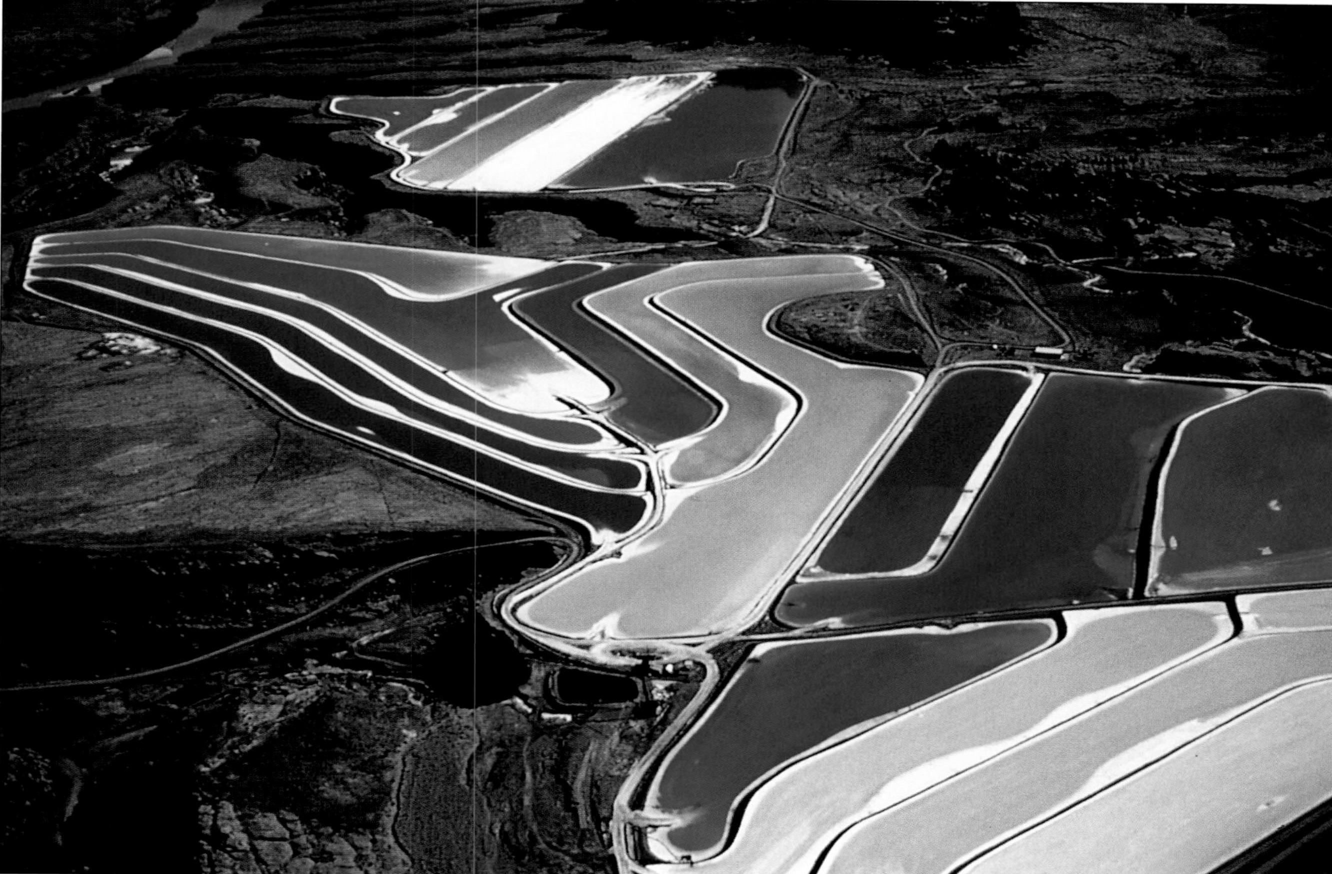

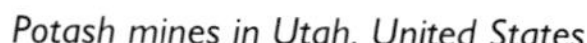

Potash mines in Utah, United States

Potash is a mineral used mainly to make fertilizers. Much of it comes from mines where deposits formed when ancient seas dried up are exploited. Potash is also extracted from salt lakes.

MINERAL DISTRIBUTION

Location of the principal mines and deposits.

IRON & FERRO-ALLOYS
- IRON
- CHROME
- MANGANESE
- NICKEL

PRECIOUS METALS
- GOLD
- SILVER

PRECIOUS STONES
- DIAMONDS

LIGHT METALS
- BAUXITE

BASE METALS
- COPPER
- LEAD
- MERCURY
- TIN
- ZINC

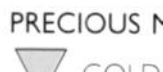

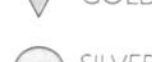

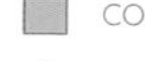

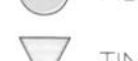

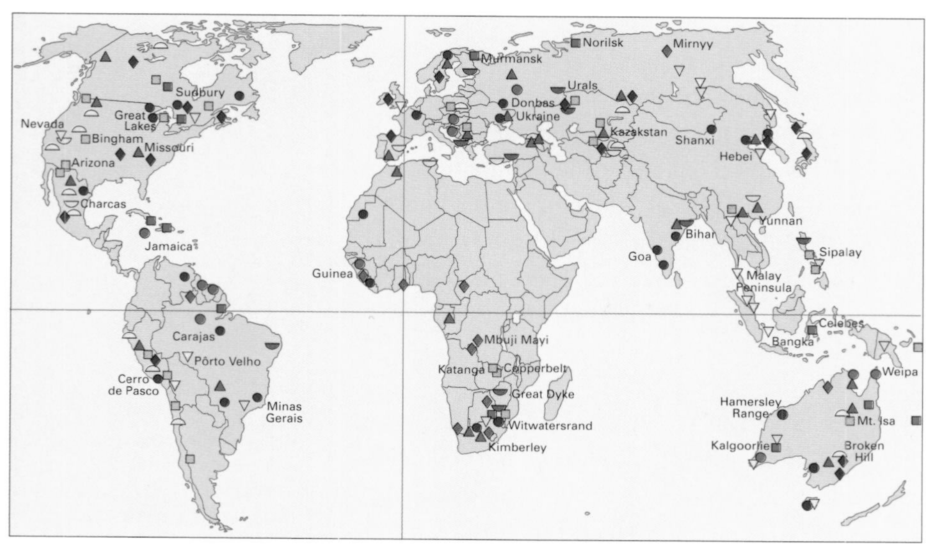

ALTERNATIVE ENERGY

Other sources of energy are therefore required. Besides nuclear energy, the main alternative to fossil fuels is water power. The costs of building dams and hydroelectric power stations is high, though hydroelectric production is comparatively cheap and it does not cause pollution. But the creation of reservoirs uproots people and, in tropical rainforests, it destroys natural habitats. Hydroelectricity is also suitable only in areas with plenty of rivers and steep slopes, such as Norway, while it is unsuitable in flat areas, such as the Netherlands.

In Brazil, alcohol made from sugar has been used to fuel cars. Initially, this government-backed policy met with great success, but it has proved to be extremely expensive. Battery-run, electric cars have also been developed in the United States, but they appear to have limited use, because of the problems involved in regular and time-consuming recharging.

Other forms of energy, which are renewable and cleaner than fossil fuels, are winds, sea waves, the rise and fall of tides, and geothermal power. These forms of energy are already used to some extent. However, their contribution in global terms seems likely to remain small in the immediate future.

MINERALS FOR INDUSTRY

In addition to energy, manufacturing industries need raw materials, including minerals, and these natural resources, like fossil fuels, are being used in such huge quantities that some experts have predicted shortages of some of them before long.

Manufacturers depend on supplies of about 80 minerals. Some, such as bauxite (aluminium ore) and iron, are abundant, but others are scarce or are found only in deposits that are uneconomical to mine. Many experts advocate a policy of recycling scrap metal, including aluminium, chromium, copper, lead, nickel and zinc. This practice would reduce pollution and conserve the energy required for extracting and refining mineral ores.

World Economies

In 1998, Tanzania had a per capita GNP (Gross National Product) of US$210, as compared with Switzerland, whose per capita GNP stood at $44,080. These figures indicate the vast gap between the economies and standards of living of the two countries.

The GNP includes the GDP (Gross Domestic Product), which consists of the total output of goods and services in a country in a given year, plus net exports – that is, the value of goods and services sold abroad less the value of foreign goods and services used in the country in the same year. The GNP divided by the population gives a country's GNP per capita. In low-income developing countries, agriculture makes a high contribution to the GNP. For example, in Tanzania, 56% of the GDP in 1995 came from

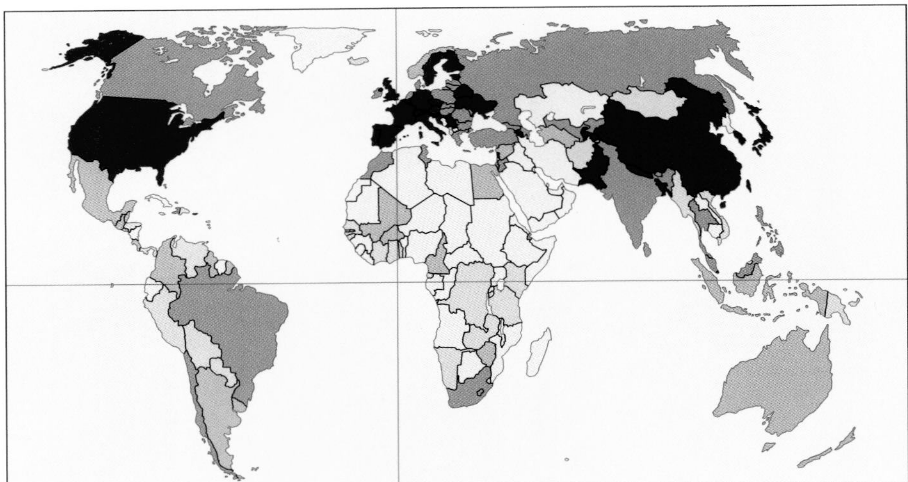

Microchip production, Taiwan

Despite its lack of resources, Taiwan is one of eastern Asia's 'tiger' economies. Its high-tech industries have helped it to achieve fast economic growth and to compete on the world market.

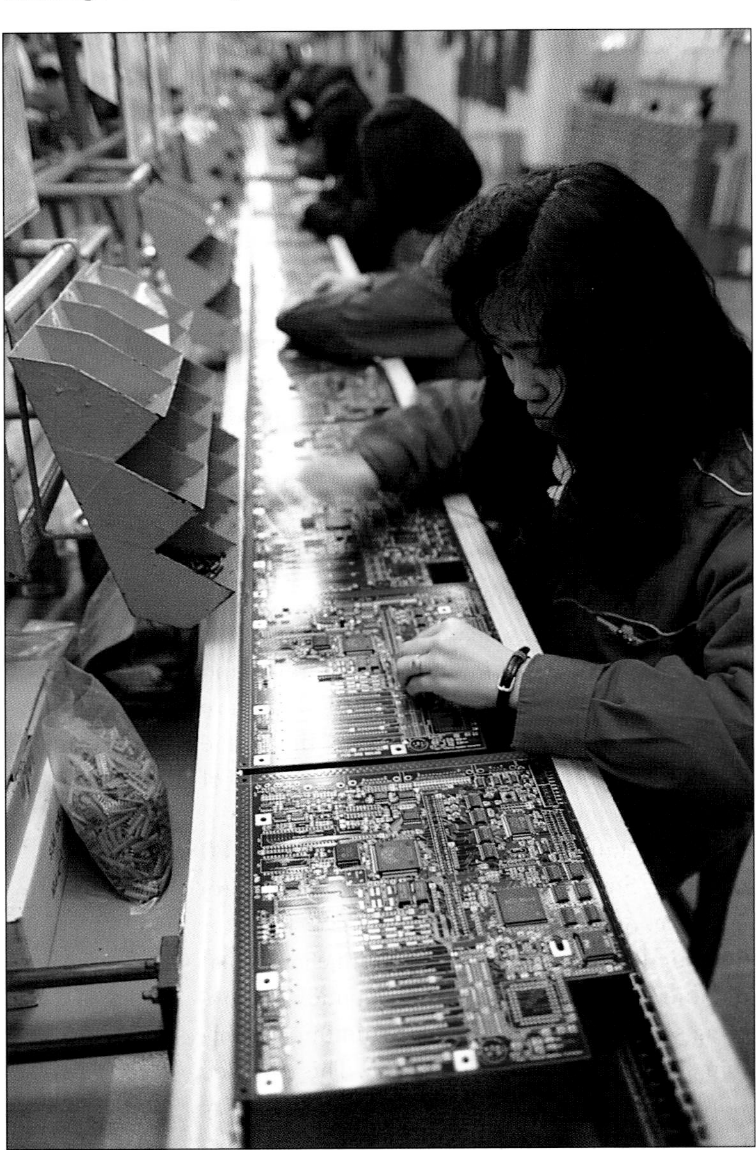

agriculture. On the other hand, manufacturing was small-scale and contributed only 5% of the GDP. By comparison, in high-income economies, the percentage contribution of manufacturing far exceeds that of agriculture.

INDUSTRIALIZATION

The Industrial Revolution began in Britain in the late 18th century. Before that time, most people worked on farms. But with the Industrial Revolution came factories, using machines that could manufacture goods much faster and more cheaply than those made by cottage industries which already existed.

The Industrial Revolution soon spread to several countries in mainland Europe and the United States and, by the late 19th century, it had reached Canada, Japan and Russia. At first, industrial development was based on such areas as coalfields or ironfields. But in the 20th century, the use of oil, which is easy to transport along pipelines, made it possible for industries to be set up anywhere.

Some nations, such as Switzerland, became industrialized even though they lacked natural resources. They depended instead on the specialized skills of their workers. This same pattern applies today. Some countries with rich natural resources, such as Mexico (with a per capita GNP in 1998 of $3,970), lag far behind Japan ($32,380) and Taiwan ($12,400), which lack resources and have to import many of the materials they need for their manufacturing industries.

SERVICE INDUSTRIES

Experts often refer to high-income countries as industrial economies. But manufacturing employs only one in six workers in the United

INDUSTRY AND TRADE

Manufactured goods (including machinery and transport) as a percentage of total exports.

- ■ OVER 75%
- ■ 50–75%
- ■ 25–50%
- ■ 10–25%
- □ UNDER 10%

Eastern Asia, including Japan (98.3%), Taiwan (92.7%) and Hong Kong (93.0%), contains countries whose exports are most dominated by manufactures. But some countries in Europe, such as Slovenia (92.5%), are also heavily dependent on manufacturing.

GROSS NATIONAL PRODUCT PER CAPITA US$ (1998)

1	Liechtenstein	50,000
2	Luxembourg	43,570
3	Switzerland	40,080
4	Norway	34,330
5	Bermuda	34,000
6	Denmark	33,260
7	Japan	32,380
8	Singapore	30,060
9	USA	29,340
10	Iceland	28,070
11	Austria	26,850
12	Germany	25,850
13	Sweden	25,620
14	Belgium	25,380
15	Monaco	25,000
16	France	24,940
17	Netherlands	24,760
18	Finland	24,110
19	Brunei	24,000
20	Hong Kong	23,670

New cars awaiting transportation, Los Angeles, United States
Cars are the most important single manufactured item in world trade, followed by vehicle parts and engines. The world's leading car producers are Japan, the United States, Germany and France.

States, one in five in Britain, and one in three in Germany and Japan.

In most developed economies, the percentage of manufacturing jobs has fallen in recent years, while jobs in service industries have risen. For example, in Britain, the proportion of jobs in manufacturing fell from 37% in 1970 to 21% in 1995, while jobs in the service sector rose from just under 50% to 66%. While change in Britain was especially rapid, similar changes were taking place in most industrial economies. By 1995, service industries accounted for well over half the jobs in the generally prosperous countries that made up the OECD (Organization for Economic Co-operation and Development). Instead of being called the 'industrial' economies, these countries might be better named the 'service' economies.

Service industries offer a wide range of jobs and many of them require high educational qualifications. These include finance, insurance and high-tech industries, such as computer programming, entertainment and telecommunications. Service industries also include marketing and advertising, which are essential if the cars and television sets made by manufacturers are to be sold. Another valuable service industry is tourism; in some countries, such as the Gambia, it is the major foreign exchange earner. Trade in services now plays an important part in world economics. The share of services in world trade rose from 17% in 1980 to 22% in 1992.

THE WORKFORCE
Percentage of men and women between 15 and 64 years old in employment, selected countries (latest available year).

MEN
WOMEN

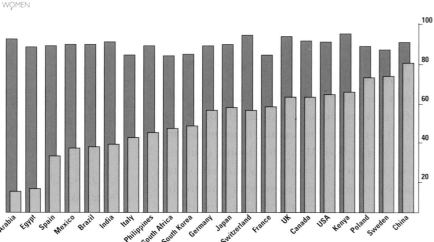

Trade and Commerce

The establishment of the WTO (World Trade Organization) on 1 January 1995 was the latest step in the long history of world trade. The WTO was set up by the eighth round of negotiations, popularly called the 'Uruguay round', conducted by the General Agreement on Tariffs and Trade (GATT). This treaty was signed by representatives of 125 governments in April 1994 after many difficulties. There are now 135 members.

GATT was first established in 1948. Its initial aim was to produce a charter to create a body called the International Trade Organization. This body never came into being. Instead, GATT, acting as an *ad hoc* agency, pioneered a series of agreements aimed at liberalizing world trade by reducing tariffs on imports and other obstacles to free trade.

GATT's objectives were based on the belief

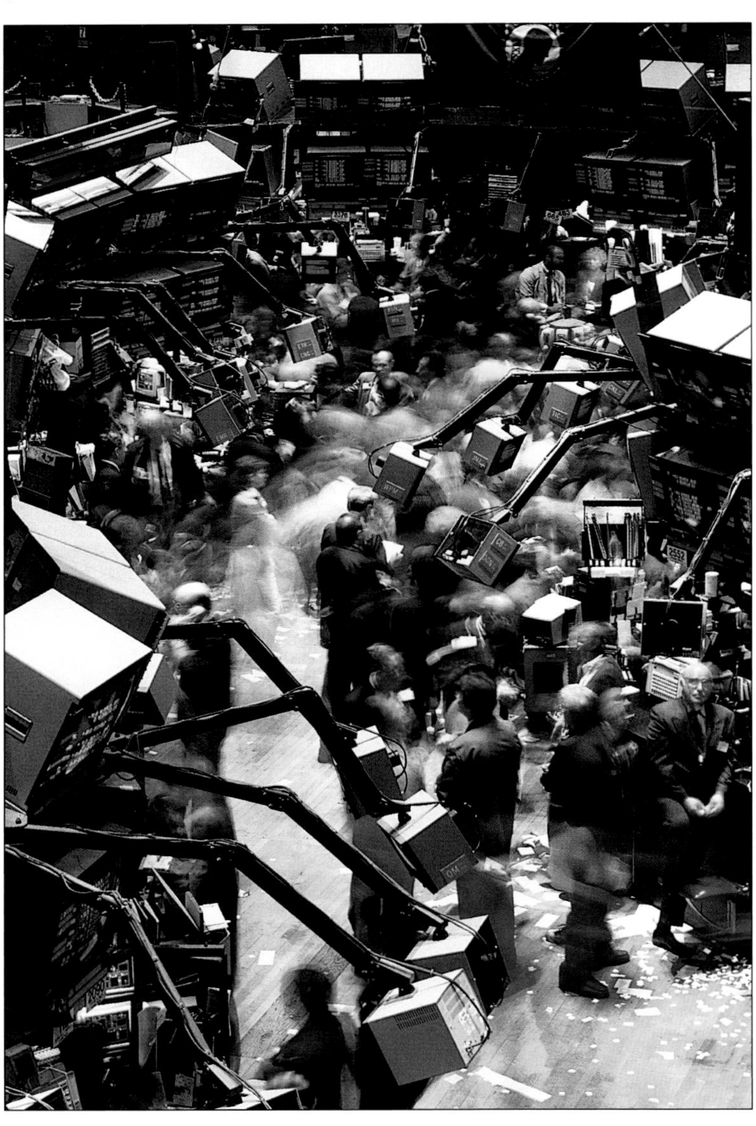

New York City Stock Exchange, United States
Stock exchanges, where stocks and shares are sold and bought, are important in channelling savings and investments to companies and governments. The world's largest stock exchange is in Tokyo, Japan.

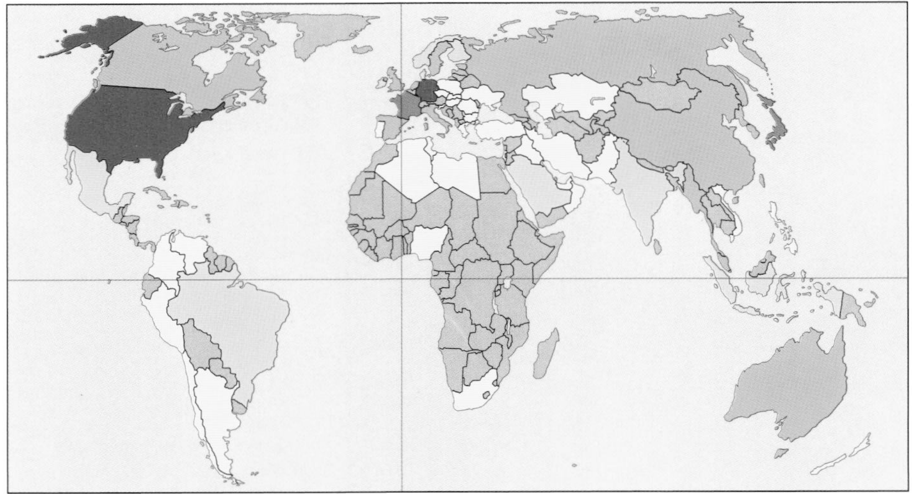

that international trade creates wealth. Trade occurs because the world's resources are not distributed evenly between countries, and, in theory, free trade means that every country should concentrate on what it can do best and purchase from others goods and services that they can supply more cheaply. In practice, however, free trade may cause unemployment when imported goods are cheaper than those produced within the country.

Trade is sometimes an important factor in world politics, especially when trade sanctions are applied against countries whose actions incur the disapproval of the international community. For example, in the 1990s, worldwide trade sanctions were imposed on Serbia because of its involvement in the civil war in Bosnia-Herzegovina.

CHANGING TRADE PATTERNS

The early 16th century, when Europeans began to divide the world into huge empires, opened up a new era in international trade. By the 19th century, the colonial powers, who were among the first industrial powers, promoted trade with their colonies, from which they obtained unprocessed raw materials, such as food, natural fibres, minerals and timber. In return, they shipped clothes, shoes and other cheap items to the colonies.

From the late 19th century until the early 1950s, primary products dominated world trade, with oil becoming the leading item in the later part of this period. Many developing countries still depend heavily on the export of one or two primary products, such as coffee or iron ore, but overall the proportion of primary products in world trade has fallen since the 1950s. Today the most important elements in world trade are

WORLD TRADE
Percentage share of total world exports by value (1996).

- ■ OVER 10% OF WORLD TRADE
- ■ 5–10% OF WORLD TRADE
- ▨ 1–5% OF WORLD TRADE
- □ 0.5–1% OF WORLD TRADE
- □ 0.1–0.5% OF WORLD TRADE
- ▨ UNDER 0.1% OF WORLD TRADE

The world's leading trading nations, according to the combined value of their exports and imports, are the United States, Germany, Japan, France and the United Kingdom.

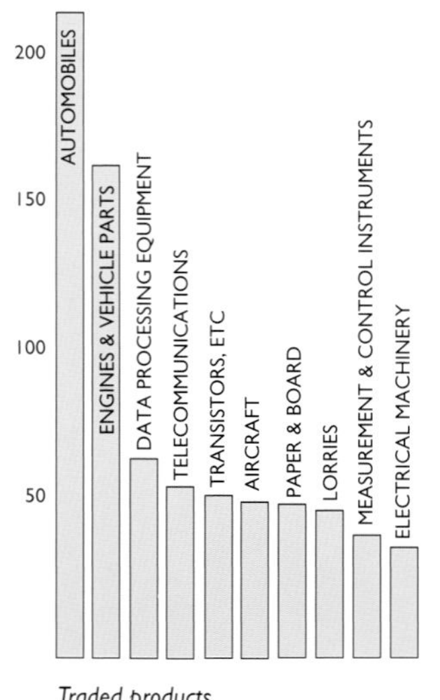

Traded products
Top ten manufactures traded by value in billions of US$ (latest available year).

Rotterdam, Netherlands

World trade depends on transport. Rotterdam, the world's largest port, serves not only the Netherlands, but also industrial areas in parts of Germany, France and Switzerland.

manufactures and semi-manufactures, exchanged mainly between the industrialized nations.

THE WORLD'S MARKETS

Private companies conduct most of world trade, but government policies affect it. Governments which believe that certain industries are strategic, or essential for the country's future, may impose tariffs on imports, or import quotas to limit the volume of imports, if they are thought to be undercutting the domestic industries.

For example, the United States has argued that Japan has greater access to its markets than the United States has to Japan's. This might have led the United States to resort to protectionism, but instead the United States remains committed to free trade.

Other problems in international trade occur when governments give subsidies to its producers, who can then export products at low prices. Another difficulty, called 'dumping', occurs when products are sold at below the market price in order to gain a market share. One of the aims of the newly-created WTO is the phasing out of government subsidies for agricultural products, though the world's poorest countries will be exempt from many of the WTO's most severe regulations.

Governments are also concerned about the volume of imports and exports and most countries keep records of international transactions. When the total value of goods and services imported exceeds the value of goods and services exported, then the country has a deficit in its balance of payments. Large deficits can weaken a country's economy.

DEPENDENCE ON TRADE

Value of exports as a percentage of GDP (Gross Domestic Product) 1997.

- OVER 50% GDP FROM EXPORTS
- 40–50% GDP FROM EXPORTS
- 30–40% GDP FROM EXPORTS
- 20–30% GDP FROM EXPORTS
- 10–20% GDP FROM EXPORTS
- UNDER 10% GDP FROM EXPORTS
- ○ MOST DEPENDENT ON INDUSTRIAL EXPORTS (OVER 75% OF TOTAL)
- ● MOST DEPENDENT ON FUEL EXPORTS (OVER 75% OF TOTAL)
- ● MOST DEPENDENT ON METAL & MINERAL EXPORTS (OVER 75% OF TOTAL)

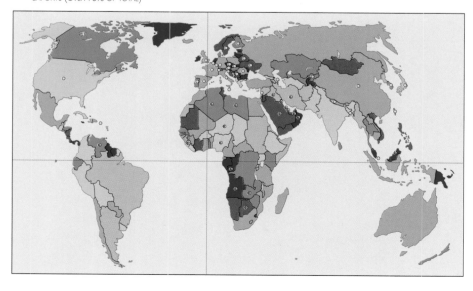

Travel and Communications

In the 1990s, millions of people became linked into an 'information superhighway' called the Internet. Equipped with a personal computer, an electricity supply, a telephone and a modem, people are able to communicate with others all over the world. People can now send messages by e-mail (electronic mail), they can engage in electronic discussions, contacting people with similar interests, and engage in 'chat lines', which are the latest equivalent of telephone conferences.

These new developments are likely to affect the working lives of people everywhere, enabling them to work at home whilst having many of the facilities that are available in an office. The Internet is part of an ongoing and astonishingly rapid evolution in the fields of communications and transport.

TRANSPORT

Around 200 years ago, most people never travelled far from their birthplace, but today we are much more mobile. Cars and buses now provide convenient forms of transport for many millions of people, huge ships transport massive cargoes around the world, and jet airliners, some travelling faster than the speed of sound, can transport high-value goods as well as holiday-makers to almost any part of the world.

Land transport of freight has developed greatly

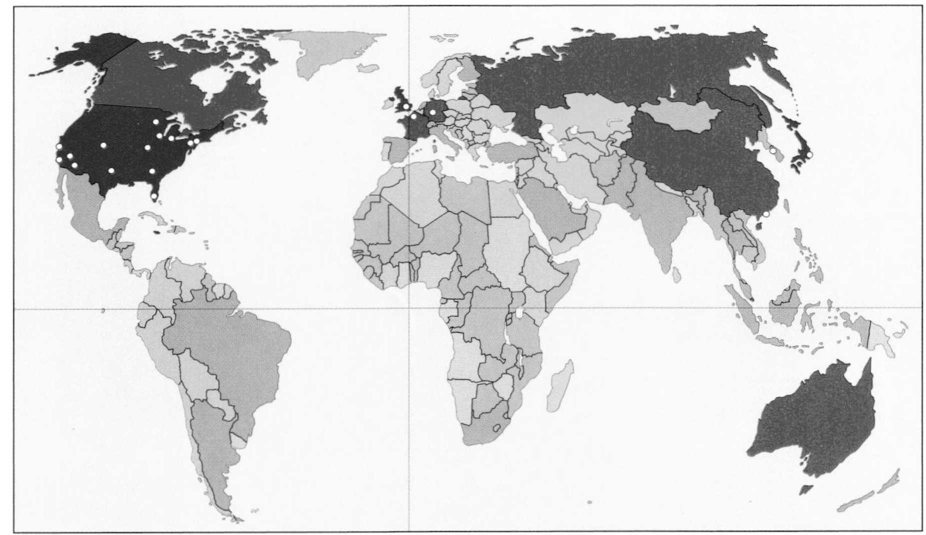

AIR TRAVEL – PASSENGER KILOMETRES* FLOWN *(1996)*.

- ■ OVER 100,000 MILLION
- ■ 50,000–100,000 MILLION
- 10,000–50,000 MILLION
- 1,000–10,000 MILLION
- 500–1,000 MILLION
- UNDER 500 MILLION
- ○ MAJOR AIRPORTS (HANDLING OVER 25 MILLION PASSENGERS IN 1996)

* Passenger kilometres are the number of passengers (both international and domestic) multiplied by the distance flown by each passenger from the airport of origin.

since the start of the Industrial Revolution. Canals, which became important in the 18th century, could not compete with rail transport in the 19th century. Rail transport remains important, but, during the 20th century, it suffered from competition with road transport, which is cheaper and has the advantage of carrying materials and goods from door to door.

Road transport causes pollution and the burning of fuels creates greenhouse gases that contribute to global warming. Yet privately owned cars are now the leading form of passenger traffic in developed nations, especially for journeys of less than around 400 km [250 miles]. Car owners do not have to suffer the inconvenience of waiting for public transport, such as buses, though they often have to endure traffic jams at peak travel times.

Ocean passenger traffic is now modest, but ships carry the bulk of international trade. Huge oil tankers and bulk grain carriers now ply the oceans with their cargoes, while container ships

Jodrell Bank Observatory, Cheshire, England
The world's first giant radio telescope began operations at Jodrell Bank in 1957. Radio telescopes can explore the Universe as far as 16 billion light-years away.

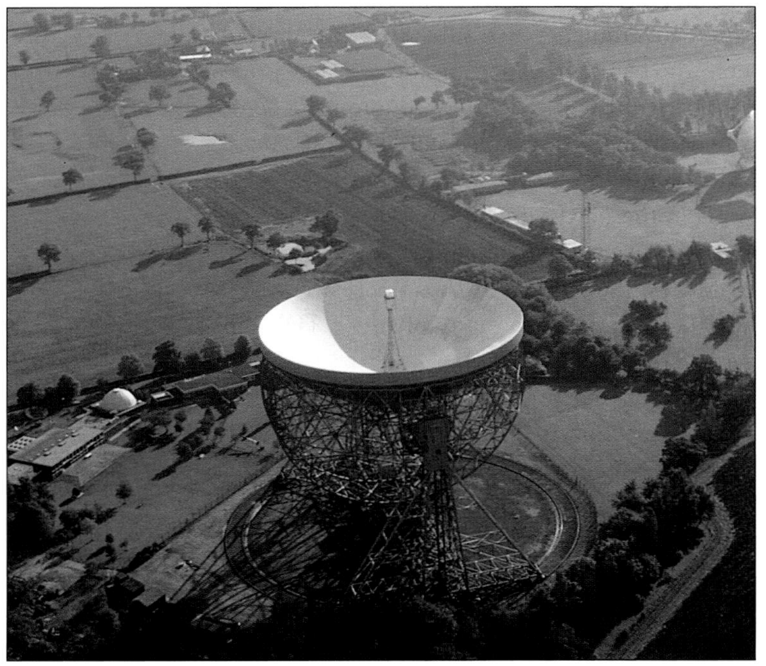

SELECTED NEWSPAPER CIRCULATION FIGURES (1995)

France			**Russia**		
Le Monde		357,362	*Pravda*		1,373,795
Le Figaro		350,000	*Ivestia*		700,000
Germany			**Spain**		
Bild		4,500,000	*El Pais*		407,629
Süddeutsche Zeitung		402,866			
			United Kingdom		
Italy			*The Sun*		4,061,253
Corriera Della Sella		676,904	*Daily Mirror*		2,525,000
La Republica		655,321	*Daily Express*		1,270,642
La Stampa		436,047	*The Times*		672,802
			The Guardian		402,214
Japan					
Yomiuri Shimbun	(a.m. edition)	9,800,000	**United States**		
	(p.m. edition)	4,400,000	*New York Times*		1,724,705
Manichi Shimbun	(a.m. edition)	3,200,000	*Chicago Tribune*		1,110,552
	(p.m. edition)	1,900,000	*Houston Chronicle*		605,343

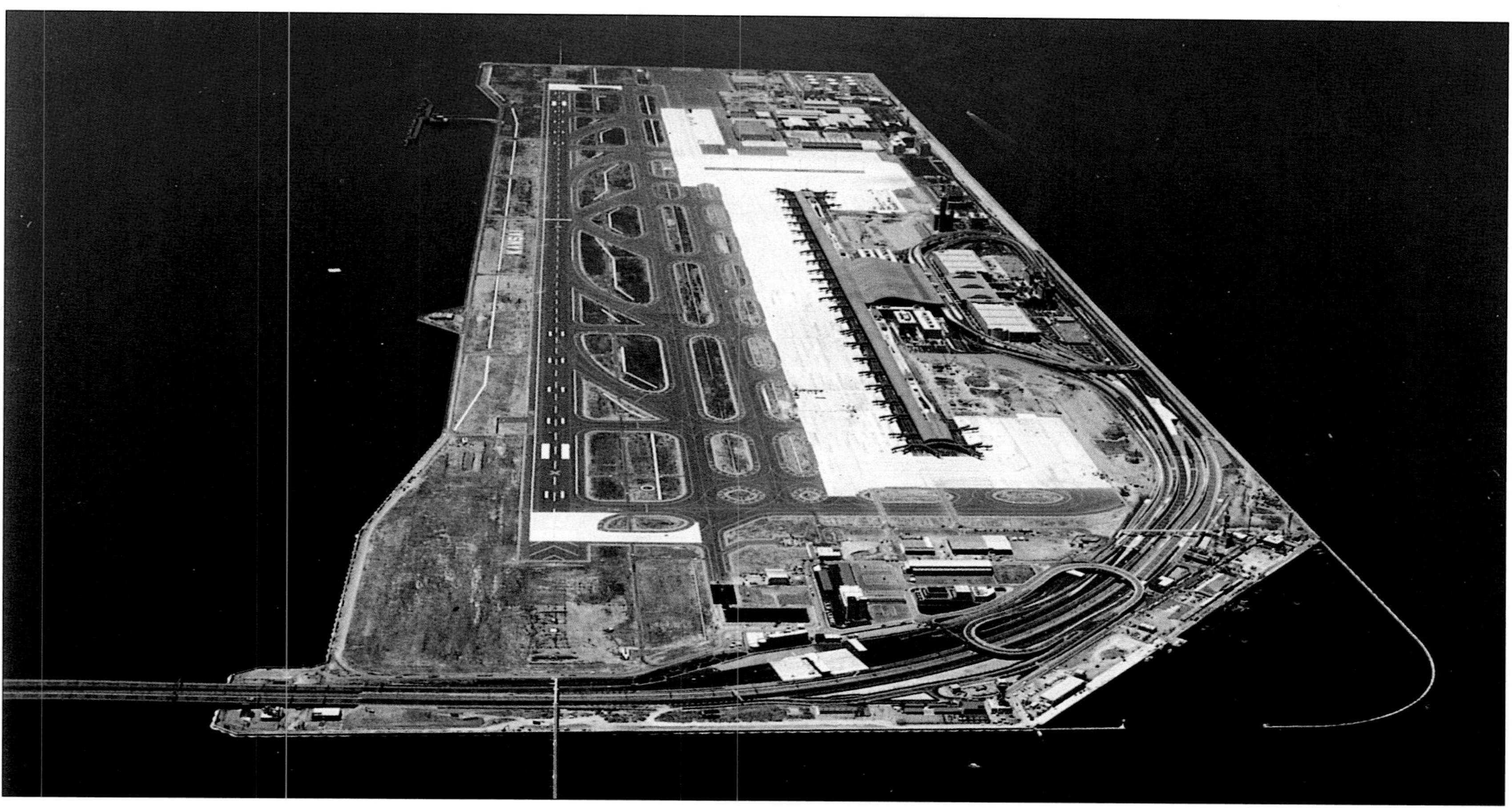

Kansai International Airport, Japan
The new airport, opened in September 1994, is built on an artificial island in Osaka Bay. The island holds the world's biggest airport terminal at nearly 2 km [1.2 miles] long.

carry mixed cargoes. Containers are boxes built to international standards that contain cargo. Containers are easy to handle, and so they reduce shipping costs, speed up deliveries and cut losses caused by breakages. Most large ports now have the facilities to handle containers.

Air transport is suitable for carrying goods that are expensive, light and compact, or perishable. However, because of the high costs of air freight, it is most suitable for carrying passengers along long-distance routes around the world. Through air travel, international tourism, with people sometimes flying considerable distances, has become a major and rapidly expanding industry.

COMMUNICATIONS

After humans first began to communicate by using the spoken word, the next great stage in the development of communications was the invention of writing around 5,500 years ago.

The invention of movable type in the mid 15th century led to the mass production of books and, in the early 17th century, the first newspapers. Newspapers now play an important part in the mass communication of information, although today radio and, even more important, television have led to a decline in the circulation of newspapers in many parts of the world.

The most recent developments have occurred in the field of electronics. Artificial communications satellites now circle the planet, relaying radio, television, telegraph and telephone signals. This enables people to watch events on the far side of the globe as they are happening. Electronic equipment is also used in many other ways, such as in navigation systems used in air, sea and space, and also in modern weaponry, as shown vividly in the television coverage of the 1991 Gulf War.

THE AGE OF COMPUTERS

One of the most remarkable applications of electronics is in the field of computers. Computers are now making a huge contribution to communications. They are able to process data at incredibly high speeds and can store vast quantities of information. For example, the work of weather forecasters has been greatly improved now that computers can process the enormous amount of data required for a single weather forecast. They also have many other applications in such fields as business, government, science and medicine.

Through the Internet, computers provide a free interchange of news and views around the world. But the dangers of misuse, such as the exchange of pornographic images, have led to calls for censorship. Censorship, however, is a blunt weapon, which can be used by authoritarian governments to suppress the free exchange of information that the new information superhighway makes possible.

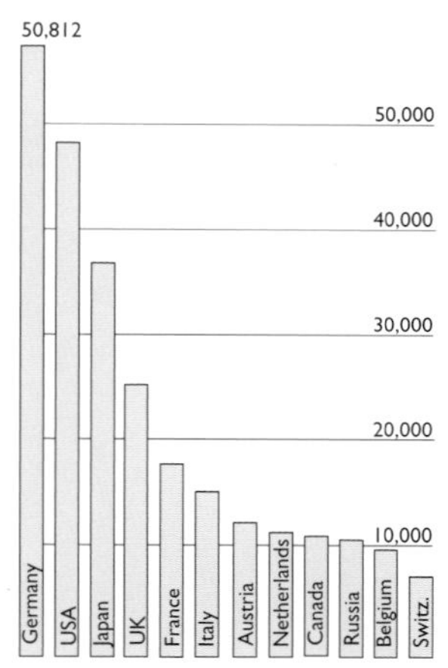

Spending on tourism
Countries spending the most on overseas tourism, US$ million (1996).

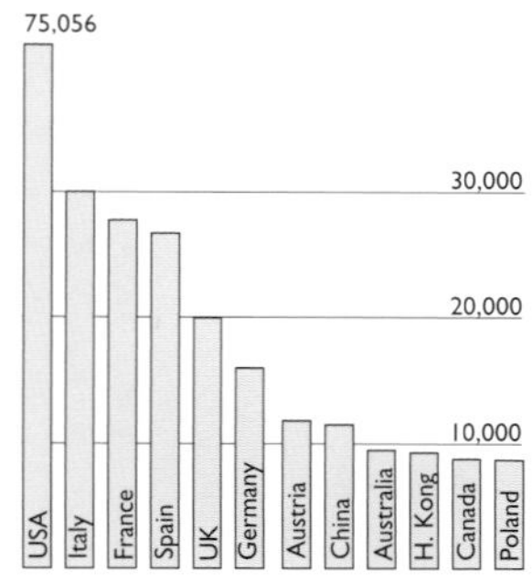

Receipts from tourism
Countries receiving the most from overseas tourism, US$ million (1996).

The World Today

The early years of the 20th century witnessed the exploration of Antarctica, the last uncharted continent. Today, less than 100 years later, tourists are able to take cruises to the icy southern continent, while almost no part of the globe is inaccessible to the determined traveller. Improved transport and images from space have made our world seem smaller.

A DIVIDED WORLD

Between the end of World War II in 1945 and the late 1980s, the world was divided, politically and economically, into three main groups: the developed countries or Western democracies, with their free enterprise or mixed economies; the centrally planned or Communist countries; and the developing countries or Third World.

This division became obsolete when the former Soviet Union and its old European allies, together with the 'special economic zones' in eastern China, began the transition from centrally planned to free enterprise economies. This left the world divided into two broad camps: the prosperous developed countries and the poorer developing countries. The simplest way of distinguishing between the groups is with reference to their per capita Gross National Products (per capita GNPs).

The World Bank divides the developing countries into three main groups. At the bottom are the low-income economies, which include China, India and most of sub-Saharan Africa. This group contains about 56% of the world's population but

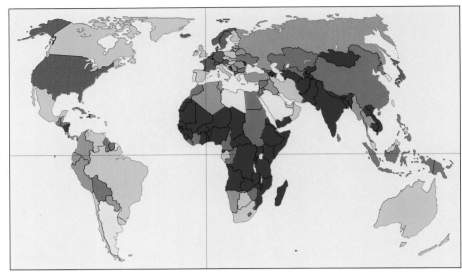

its average per capita GNP in 1994 was only US$390. The other two groups are the lower-middle-income economies with an average GNP per capita of $1,650, and the upper-middle-income economies, with an average GNP per capita of $4,640. By contrast, the high-income economies, also called the developed countries, contain less than 15% of the world's population but have the high (and rising) average GNP per capita of $24,170.

ECONOMIC AND SOCIAL CONTRASTS

Economic differences are coupled with other factors, such as rates of population growth. For example, in 1980–93, the low-income economies had a high rate of population growth of 2% per year, while the populations of the middle-income economies were increasing by 1.7%. By contrast, the populations of countries in the high-income category were increasing by only 0.6%.

Stark contrasts exist worldwide in the quality

GROSS NATIONAL PRODUCT PER CAPITA
The value of total production divided by the population (1997).

- OVER 400% OF WORLD AVERAGE
- 200–400% OF WORLD AVERAGE
- 100–200% OF WORLD AVERAGE

[WORLD AVERAGE WEALTH PER PERSON US$6,316]

- 50–100% OF WORLD AVERAGE
- 25–50% OF WORLD AVERAGE
- 10–25% OF WORLD AVERAGE
- UNDER 10% OF WORLD AVERAGE

RICHEST COUNTRIES

Liechtenstein	$50,000
Luxembourg	$45,570
Switzerland	$40,080
Norway	$34,330
Bermuda	$34,000

POOREST COUNTRIES

Ethiopia	$100
Congo (Dem. Rep.)	$110
Burundi	$140
Sierra Leone	$140
Guinea-Bissau	$160

Porters carrying luggage for tourists, Selous Park, Tanzania
Improved and cheaper transport has led to a boom in tourism in many developing countries. Tourism provides jobs and foreign exchange, though it can undermine local cultures.

Birth control poster, China

China is the only country with more than a billion people. Central to its economic development policies is population control. Posters exhort the advantages of one-child families.

of life. Generally, the people in Western Europe and North America are better fed, healthier and have more cars and better homes than the people in low- and middle-income economies.

The average life expectancy at birth in low-income economies in 1993 was 62 years, 15 years less than in the high-income economies. Illiteracy in countries in the low-income category is high, at 42% in 1992, while for women, who get fewer opportunities, the percentage of those who could not read and write stood at 54%. By contrast, illiteracy is relatively rare in the high-income economies.

FUTURE DEVELOPMENT

In the last 50 years, despite all the aid supplied to developing countries, much of the world still suffers from poverty and economic backwardness. Some countries are even poorer now than they were a generation ago while others have become substantially richer.

The most remarkable success has been achieved in eastern Asia. Japan and the 'tiger economies' of Hong Kong, Indonesia, Malaysia, Singapore, South Korea, Thailand and Taiwan had an average annual economic growth rate of 5.5% between 1965 and 1993, while their share in the exports of manufactured goods more than doubled in the same period. In 1997, however,

an Asian market crash temporarily halted this dramatic economic expansion.

Reasons advanced to explain the success of the eastern Asian countries include low wage scales, strong family structures, low state expenditure on welfare and large investment in education for both sexes. Some of the arguments are contradictory. For example, while some argue that the success of Hong Kong is due to free enterprise, the governments of Japan and South Korea have intervened substantially in the development of their economies.

Eastern Asia's economic growth has been exceptional and probably cannot be regarded as a model for the developing world. But several factors suggest that poor countries may find progress easier in the 21st century. For example, technology is now more readily transferable between countries, while improved transport and communications make it easier for countries to take part in the world economy. But industrial development and rising living standards could lead to an increase in global pollution. Hence, any strategy for global economic expansion must also take account of environmental factors.

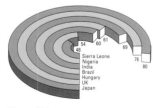

Years of life expectancy at birth, selected countries (1997).

The chart shows the contrasting range of average life expectancies at birth for a range of countries, including both low-income and high-income economies. Generally, improved health services are raising life expectancies. On average, women live longer than men, even in the poorer developing countries.

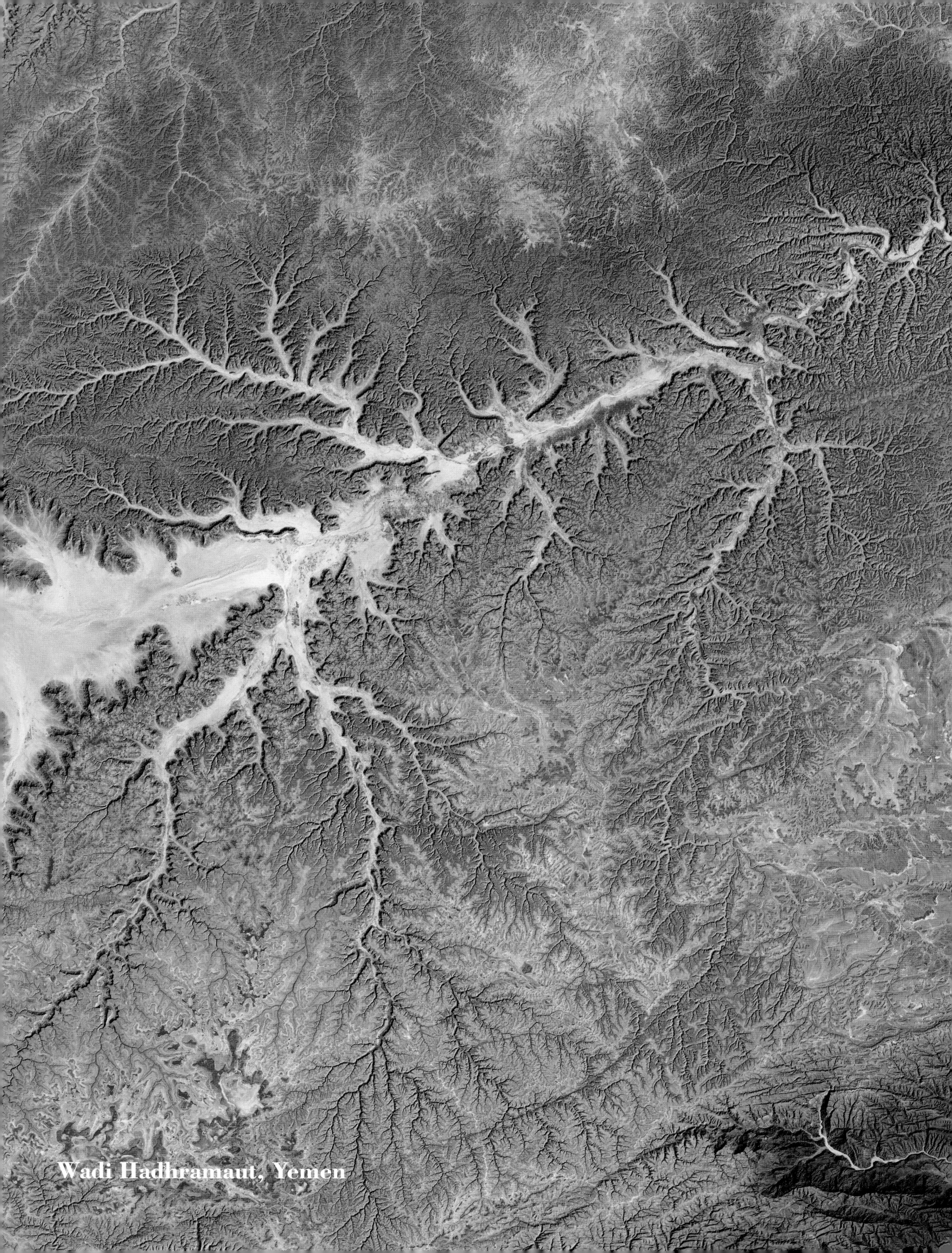

Wadi Hadhramaut, Yemen

WORLD MAPS

SETTLEMENTS

■ PARIS   ■ Berne   ◉ Livorno   ◎ Brugge   ⊚ Algeciras   ○ Frejus   ○ Oberammergau   ○ Thira

Settlement symbols and type styles vary according to the scale of each map and indicate the importance
of towns on the map rather than specific population figures

∴   Ruins or Archæological Sites   Wells in Desert

ADMINISTRATION

——— International Boundaries

– – – – International Boundaries
(Undefined or Disputed)

·········· Internal Boundaries

National Parks

Country Names
NICARAGUA

Administrative
Area Names

KENT
CALABRIA

International boundaries show the *de facto* situation where there are rival claims to territory

COMMUNICATIONS

——— Principal Roads

——— Other Roads

+–··+ Road Tunnels

≍ Passes

⊕ Airfields

——— Principal Railways

– ‿ – Railways
Under Construction

‿ Other Railways

+–··+ Railway Tunnels

·········· Principal Canals

PHYSICAL FEATURES

‿‿ Perennial Streams

– ‿ – Intermittent Streams

⬭ Perennial Lakes

⬭ Intermittent Lakes

⬭ Swamps and Marshes

⬭ Permanent Ice
and Glaciers

▲ 8848 Elevations in metres

▼ 8500 Sea Depths in metres

1134 Height of Lake Surface
Above Sea Level in metres

ELEVATION AND DEPTH TINTS

Height of Land above Sea Level   Land Below Sea Level   Depth of Sea

in metres	6000	4000	3000	2000	1500	1000	400	200	0						
in feet	18 000	12 000	9000	6000	4500	3000	1200	600		6000	12 000	15 000	18 000	24 000	in feet
									0	200	2000	4000	5000	6000	8000	in metres

Some of the maps have different contours to highlight and clarify the principal relief features

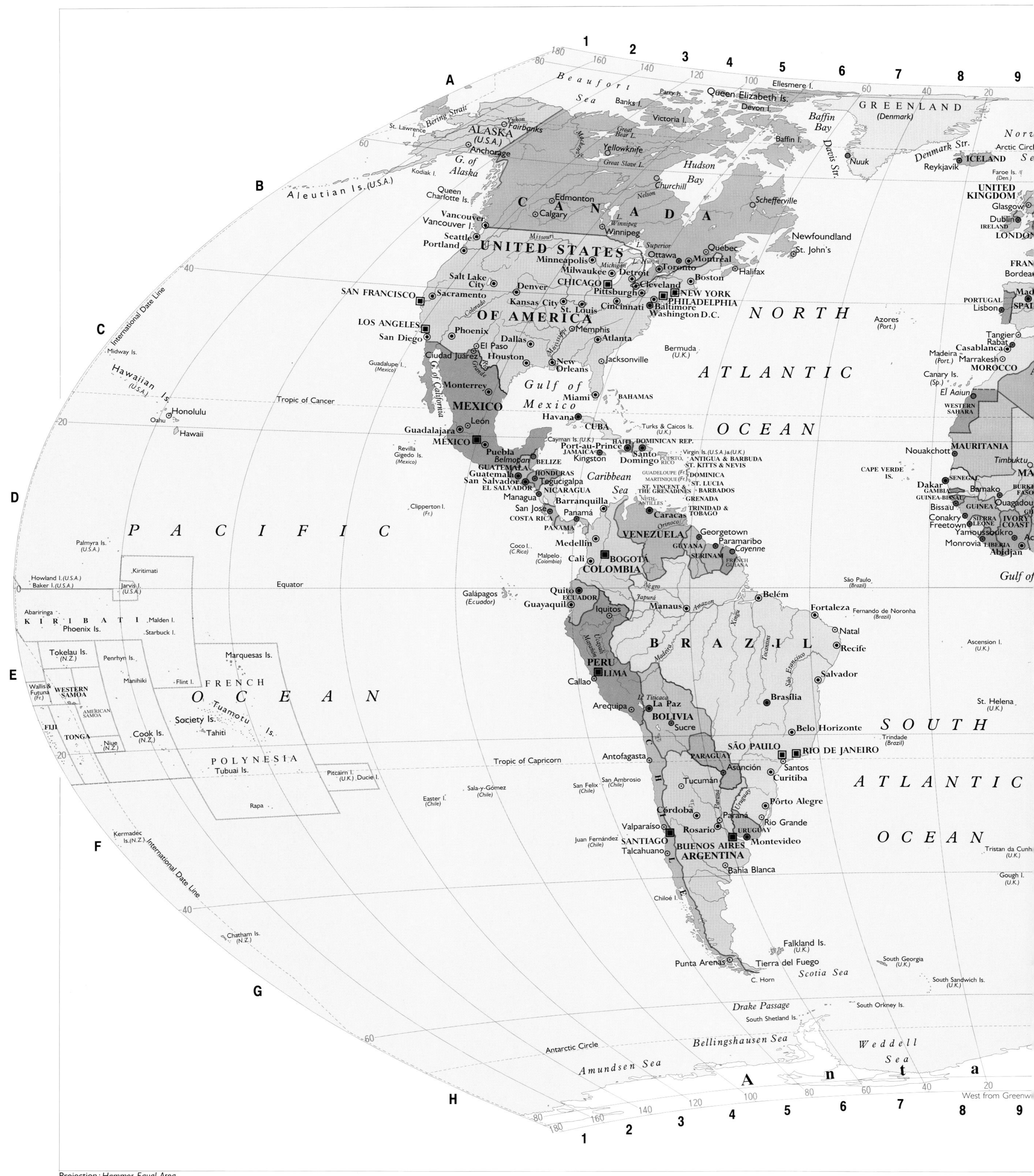

Beaufort Sea
Bering Strait
St. Lawrence I.
ALASKA (U.S.A.)
Fairbanks
Anchorage
G. of Alaska
Kodiak I.
Aleutian Is. (U.S.A.)
Banks I.
Victoria I.
Parry Is.
Queen Elizabeth Is.
Ellesmere I.
Devon I.
Baffin Bay
Baffin I.
Davis Str.
GREENLAND (Denmark)
Nuuk
Denmark Str.
Reykjavík
ICELAND
Arctic Circle
Faroe Is. (Den.)
UNITED KINGDOM
Glasgow
Dublin
IRELAND
LONDON
Yellowknife
Great Bear L.
Great Slave L.
Hudson Bay
Churchill
Nelson
Schefferville
CANADA
Edmonton
Calgary
L. Winnipeg
Winnipeg
Queen Charlotte Is.
Vancouver
Vancouver I.
Seattle
Portland
Missouri
Newfoundland
St. John's
Quebec
Montreal
Ottawa
Toronto
Halifax
Boston
L. Superior
L. Huron
Michigan
UNITED STATES OF AMERICA
Minneapolis
Milwaukee
Detroit
CHICAGO
Cleveland
Pittsburgh
NEW YORK
PHILADELPHIA
Baltimore
Washington D.C.
Salt Lake City
Denver
Kansas City
St. Louis
Cincinnati
SAN FRANCISCO
Sacramento
LOS ANGELES
San Diego
Phoenix
Colorado
Dallas
Memphis
Atlanta
El Paso
Ciudad Juárez
Rio Grande
Houston
New Orleans
Jacksonville
Mississippi
Bermuda (U.K.)
NORTH ATLANTIC OCEAN
Azores (Port.)
PORTUGAL
Lisbon
SPAIN
Tangier
Rabat
Casablanca
Madeira (Port.)
Marrakesh
MOROCCO
Canary Is. (Sp.)
El Aaiun
WESTERN SAHARA
Guadalupe I. (Mexico)
G. of California
Monterrey
MEXICO
León
Guadalajara
MÉXICO
Puebla
Revilla Gigedo Is. (Mexico)
Gulf of Mexico
Miami
BAHAMAS
Havana
CUBA
Turks & Caicos Is. (U.K.)
Cayman Is. (U.K.)
Port-au-Prince
HAITI
DOMINICAN REP.
JAMAICA
Kingston
Santo Domingo
PUERTO RICO
Virgin Is. (U.S.A.) & (U.K.)
ANTIGUA & BARBUDA
ST. KITTS & NEVIS
GUADELOUPE (Fr.)
DOMINICA
MARTINIQUE (Fr.)
ST. LUCIA
ST. VINCENT & THE GRENADINES
BARBADOS
NETH. ANTILLES
GRENADA
TRINIDAD & TOBAGO
Caribbean Sea
Belmopan
BELIZE
GUATEMALA
Guatemala
HONDURAS
Tegucigalpa
San Salvador
EL SALVADOR
NICARAGUA
Managua
San José
COSTA RICA
Panamá
PANAMA
Barranquilla
Caracas
VENEZUELA
Orinoco
Georgetown
GUYANA
Paramaribo
SURINAM
Cayenne
FRENCH GUIANA
Clipperton I. (Fr.)
Medellín
Cali
BOGOTÁ
COLOMBIA
Coco I. (C.Rica)
Malpelo (Colombia)
Galápagos (Ecuador)
Quito
ECUADOR
Guayaquil
Iquitos
Negro
Japurá
Manaus
Amazon
Belém
Xingu
Fortaleza
Fernando de Noronha (Brazil)
Natal
Recife
BRAZIL
Madeira
Tocantins
São Francisco
Salvador
Brasília
PERU
LIMA
Callao
Marañón
Ucayali
L. Titicaca
La Paz
BOLIVIA
Sucre
Arequipa
Belo Horizonte
SÃO PAULO
RIO DE JANEIRO
Santos
Curitiba
PARAGUAY
Asunción
Antofagasta
Tucumán
CHILE
Paraná
Uruguay
Pôrto Alegre
Rio Grande
Córdoba
Rosario
URUGUAY
Montevideo
BUENOS AIRES
ARGENTINA
Valparaíso
SANTIAGO
Talcahuano
Bahía Blanca
Chiloé I.
Falkland Is. (U.K.)
Punta Arenas
Tierra del Fuego
C. Horn
Scotia Sea
Drake Passage
South Shetland Is.
South Georgia (U.K.)
South Sandwich Is. (U.K.)
South Orkney Is.
SOUTH ATLANTIC OCEAN
São Paulo (Brazil)
Ascension I. (U.K.)
St. Helena (U.K.)
Trindade (Brazil)
Tristan da Cunha (U.K.)
Gough I. (U.K.)
Nouakchott
MAURITANIA
Timbuktu
CAPE VERDE IS.
Dakar
SENEGAL
GAMBIA
GUINEA-BISSAU
Bissau
Bamako
BURKINA FASO
Ouagadougou
GUINEA
Conakry
SIERRA LEONE
Freetown
IVORY COAST
Yamoussoukro
LIBERIA
Monrovia
Abidjan
Gulf of
San Felix (Chile)
San Ambrosio (Chile)
Juan Fernández (Chile)
Easter I. (Chile)
Sala-y-Gómez (Chile)
Tropic of Capricorn
Tropic of Cancer
Equator
International Date Line
Midway Is.
Hawaiian Is. (U.S.A.)
Honolulu
Oahu
Hawaii
PACIFIC OCEAN
Palmyra Is. (U.S.A.)
Kiritimati
Howland I. (U.S.A.)
Baker I. (U.S.A.)
Jarvis I. (U.S.A.)
Abariringa
KIRIBATI
Phoenix Is.
Malden I.
Starbuck I.
Tokelau Is. (N.Z.)
Penrhyn Is.
Marquesas Is.
Manihiki
Flint I.
FRENCH POLYNESIA
Wallis & Futuna (Fr.)
WESTERN SAMOA
AMERICAN SAMOA
FIJI
TONGA
Niue (N.Z.)
Cook Is. (N.Z.)
Society Is.
Tahiti
Tuamotu Is.
Tubuai Is.
Pitcairn I. (U.K.)
Ducie I.
Rapa
Kermadec Is. (N.Z.)
Chatham Is. (N.Z.)
Antarctic Circle
Amundsen Sea
Bellingshausen Sea
Weddell Sea
Antarctica
West from Greenwich

Projection: *Hammer Equal Area*

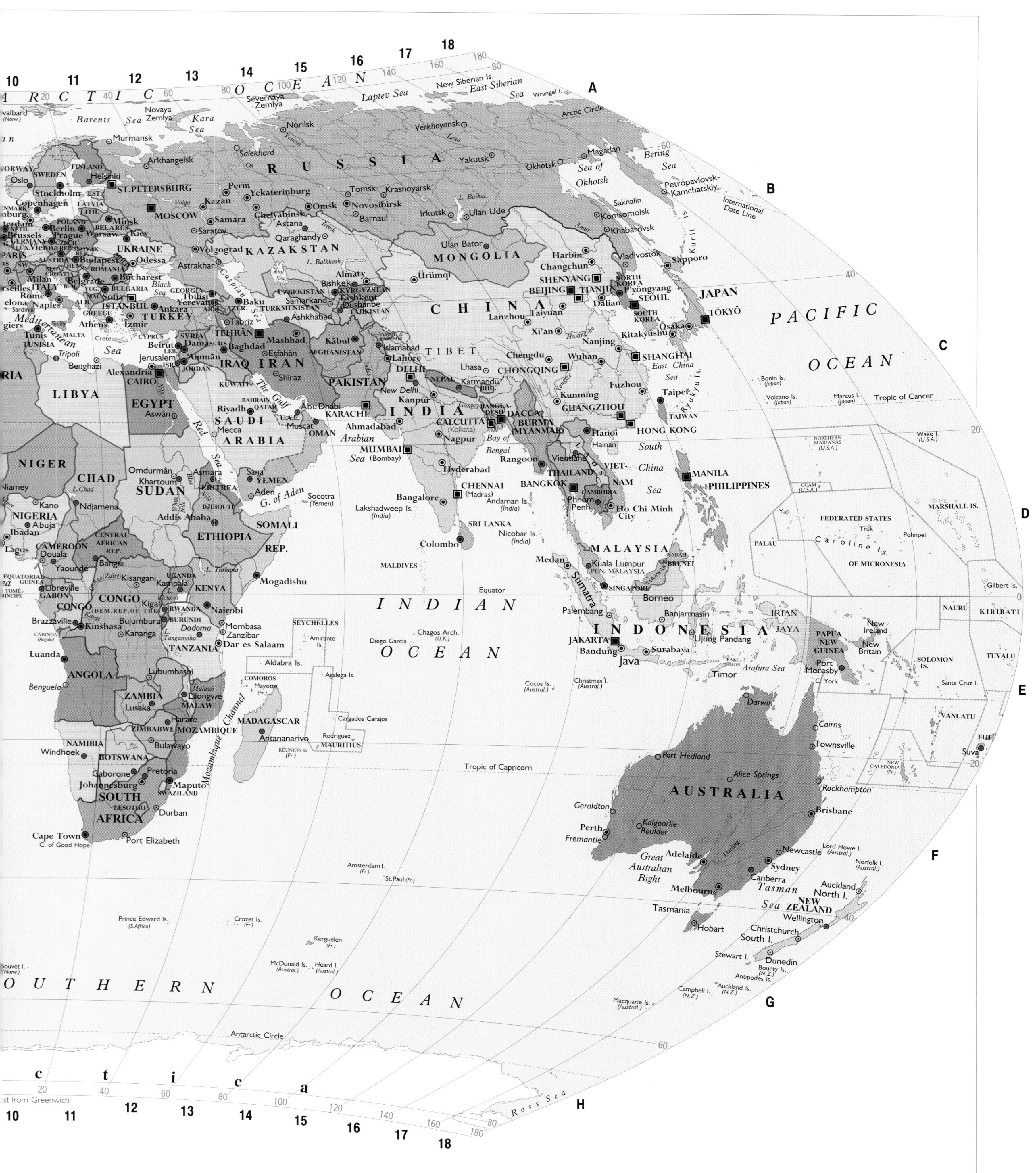

ARCTIC OCEAN

Barents
Sea
Kara
Sea
Novaya
Zemlya
Severnaya
Zemlya
New Siberian Is.
Laptev Sea
East Siberian
Sea
Wrangel I.
Arctic Circle

Murmansk
Salekhard
Norilsk
Yenisey
Verkhoyansk
Lena
Yakutsk
Okhotsk
Magadan
Sea of
Okhotsk
Bering
Sea

R U S S I A

Arkhangelsk
Ob

Sea of
Okhotsk
Petropavlovsk-
Kamchatskiy

St.PETERSBURG
Helsinki
FINLAND
SWEDEN
NORWAY
Oslo
Stockholm
EST.

Perm
Yekaterinburg
Tomsk
Krasnoyarsk

Sakhalin

International
Date Line

Copenhagen
DENMARK
LATVIA
LITH.
MOSCOW
Kazan
Volga
Samara
Omsk
Novosibirsk
Irkutsk
Ulan Ude
Komsomolsk
Khabarovsk
Kuril Is.

terdam
burg
Berlin
POLAND
BELARUS
Minsk
Saratov
Chelyabinsk
Astana
Barnaul

Sapporo

GERMANY
NETH.
Brussels
Prague
CZECH
Warsaw
Kiev
UKRAINE
Volgograd
Qaraghandy
Ulan Bator
Harbin
Changchun
Vladivostok

PARIS
LUX.
Vienna
AUSTRIA
SLOVAK.
Budapest
HUNG.
ROMANIA
Odessa
Astrakhan
KAZAKSTAN
L. Balkhash
MONGOLIA
SHENYANG
Pyongyang
NORTH
KOREA
JAPAN

sseilles
Milan
SLOV.
CRO.
Belgrade
Bucharest
Black Sea
Aral
Sea
Almaty
Bishkek
Ürümqi
BEIJING
TIANJIN
Dalian
SEOUL
SOUTH
KOREA
TŌKYŌ
PACIFIC

Rome
ITALY
BOS.
Sofia
BULGARIA
GEORGIA
Tbilisi
UZBEKISTAN
KYRGYZSTAN
Tashkent
Lanzhou
Taiyuan
Xi'an
Hwang Ho
Kitakyūshū
Ōsaka

elona
Sardinia
Naples
ALB.
GREECE
ISTANBUL
Ankara
Yerevan
AZER.
Baku
Samarkand
TAJIKISTAN
Dushanbe
C H I N A
Nanjing
SHANGHAI
East China
Sea

giers
TUNISIA
Sicily
Athens
Izmir
TURKEY
ARM.
TURKMENISTAN
Ashkhabad
Chengdu
Wuhan
CHONGQING
Ryukyu Is.

Tunis
MALTA
Crete
CYPRUS
SYRIA
Damascus
Mashhad
Kābul
Islamabad
TIBET
Lhasa
Kunming
Fuzhou
Taipei
OCEAN

Tripoli
Benghazi
Mediterranean
Sea
LEB.
Beirut
Damascus
Baghdad
Esfahān
AFGHANISTAN
Lahore
DELHI
NEPAL
Katmandu
BHU.
GUANGZHOU
TAIWAN

Alexandria
CAIRO
ISRAEL
Jerusalem
JORDAN
Ammān
IRAQ
I R A N
TEHRĀN
Shīrāz
PAKISTAN
New Delhi
Kanpur
Ganges
BANGLA-
DESH
DACCA
CALCUTTA
(Kolkata)
HONG KONG

LIBYA
EGYPT
Aswān
KUWAIT
The Gulf
BAHRAIN
QATAR
Riyadh
Abu Dhabi
U.A.E.
Muscat
OMAN
Karachi
I N D I A
Nagpur
BURMA
MYANMAR
Hanoi
Hainan
South

RIA
NIGER
CHAD
SUDAN
Khartoum
Omdurmân
Red Sea
Mecca
SAUDI
ARABIA
Arabian
Sea
Ahmadabad
MUMBAI
(Bombay)
Bay of
Bengal
Rangoon
Vientiane
China

Niamey
Kano
L.Chad
Ndjamena
Asmara
ERITREA
Sana
YEMEN
Aden
G. of Aden
Socotra
(Yemen)
Hyderabad
THAILAND
VIET-
NAM
Sea
MANILA

NIGERIA
Abuja
Ibadan
Addis Ababa
Bangalore
CHENNAI
(Madras)
Andaman Is.
(India)
BANGKOK
CAMBODIA
Phnom
Penh
Ho Chi Minh
City
PHILIPPINES

Lagos
CAMEROON
Douala
CENTRAL
AFRICAN
REP.
DJIBOUTI
SOMALI
REP.
Lakshadweep Is.
(India)
SRI LANKA
Nicobar Is.
(India)

EQUATORIAL
GUINEA
Yaounde
Bangui
ETHIOPIA
Colombo
MALDIVES
MALAYSIA
Medan
Kuala Lumpur
PEN. MALAYSIA
SABAH
BRUNEI
FEDERATED STATES
OF MICRONESIA

TOMÉ
Libreville
GABON
Kisangani
Zaire
UGANDA
Kampala
KENYA
Nairobi
Victoria
L. Turkana
Equator
INDIAN
SINGAPORE
Borneo
IRIAN
JAYA

CONGO
DEM.REP.OF THE
CONGO
RWANDA
Kigali
BURUNDI
Bujumbura
Kananga
Dodoma
Mombasa
Zanzibar
TANZANIA
SEYCHELLES
Amirante
Is.
OCEAN
Palembang
Sumatra
Banjarmasin
I N D O N E S I A
PAPUA
NEW
GUINEA

Brazzaville
Kinshasa
CABINDA
(Angola)
Kananga
L. Tanganyika
Dar es Salaam
Diego Garcia
Chagos Arch.
(U.K.)
JAKARTA
Bandung
Java
Surabaya
Ujung Pandang
Port
Moresby

Luanda
ANGOLA
Lubumbashi
MALAWI
Lilongwe
COMOROS
Mayotte
(Fr.)
Cargados Carajos
Timor
EAST
TIMOR
Arafura Sea

Benguela
ZAMBIA
Lusaka
Malawi
ZIMBABWE
MOZAMBIQUE
MADAGASCAR
Antananarivo
Rodriguez
(Fr.)
MAURITIUS
Darwin

NAMIBIA
Windhoek
BOTSWANA
Harare
Bulawayo
Mozambique Channel
RÉUNION
(Fr.)
Tropic of Capricorn
Port Hedland
Alice Springs
Cairns
Townsville

Gaborone
Pretoria
Johannesburg
SWAZILAND
Maputo
Amsterdam I.
(Fr.)
AUSTRALIA
Rockhampton
Brisbane

SOUTH
AFRICA
LESOTHO
Durban
St.Paul (Fr.)
Geraldton
Kalgoorlie-
Boulder
Great
Australian
Bight
Adelaide
Darling
Newcastle
Sydney
Canberra

Cape Town
C. of Good Hope
Port Elizabeth
Perth
Fremantle
Melbourne
Tasman
Sea

Prince Edward Is.
(S.Africa)
Crozet Is.
(Fr.)
Kerguelen
(Fr.)
McDonald Is.
(Austral.)
Heard I.
(Austral.)
Tasmania
NEW
ZEALAND
Wellington

SOUTHERN   OCEAN

Antarctic Circle

A n t a r c t i c a

Hanoi ● Capital Cities

ARCTIC OCEAN 1:31 100 000

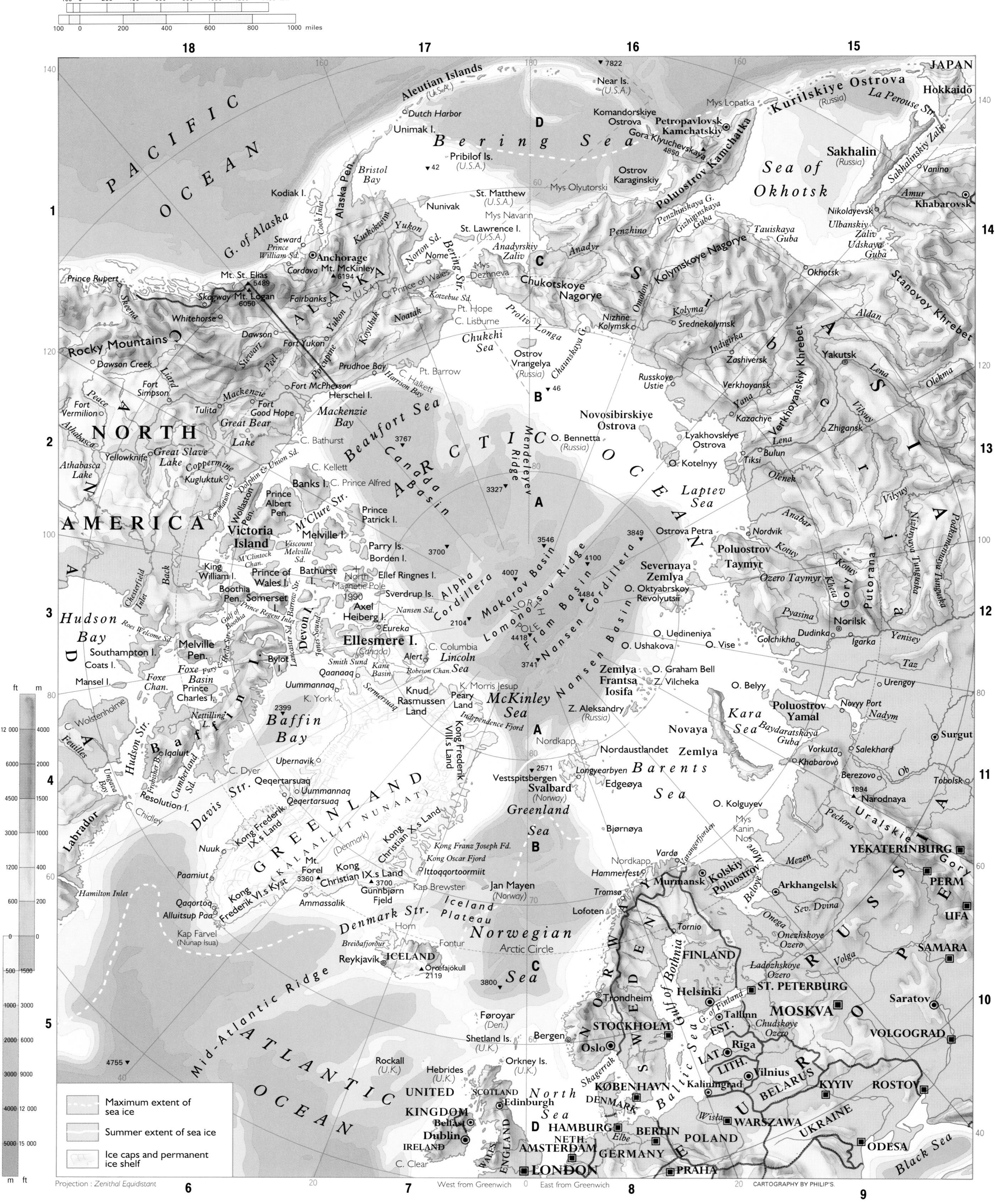

100 0 200 400 600 800 1000 1200 1400 km
100 0 200 400 600 800 1000 miles
PACIFIC OCEAN
Aleutian Islands (U.S.A.)
Near Is. (U.S.A.)
7822
Dutch Harbor
Unimak I.
Bering Sea
Komandorskiye Ostrova
Petropavlovsk Kamchatskiy
Gora Klyuchevskaya 4850
Poluostrov Kamchatka
Mys Lopatka
Kurilskiye Ostrova (Russia)
JAPAN
Hokkaidō
La Perouse Str.
Sakhalin (Russia)
Sakhalinskiy Zaliv
Vanino
Sea of Okhotsk
Amur
Khabarovsk
Nikolayevsk
Ulbanskiy Zaliv
Udskaya Guba
Okhotsk
Stanovoy Khrebet
Aldan
Tauiskaya Guba
Penzhinskaya G.
Gizhiginskaya Guba
Penzhino
Ostrov Karaginskiy
Mys Olyutorski
Pribilof Is. (U.S.A.)
42
Bristol Bay
Kodiak I.
Alaska Pen.
Cook Inlet
St. Matthew (U.S.A.)
Nunivak
Mys Navarin
St. Lawrence I. (U.S.A.)
Anadyrskiy Zaliv
Anadyr
Kuskokwim
Yukon
Norton Sd.
Nome
Bering Str.
Mys Dezhneva
Chukotskoye Nagorye
Kolymskoye Nagorye
Omolon
Kolyma
Srednekolymsk
Nizhne Kolymsk
G. of Alaska
Seward
Prince William Sd.
Anchorage
Cordova
Mt. McKinley 6194
ALASKA (U.S.A.)
Prince Rupert
Mt. St. Elias 5489
Skagway
Mt. Logan 6050
Fairbanks
C. Prince of Wales
Kotzebue Sd.
Pt. Hope
C. Lisburne
Proliv Longa
Noatak
Koyukuk
Skeena
Whitehorse
Dawson
Fort Yukon
Porcupine
Stewart
Peel
Chukchi Sea
Ostrov Vrangelya (Russia)
Chaunskaya G.
Rocky Mountains
Dawson Creek
Prudhoe Bay
Harrison Bay
Pt. Barrow
C. Halkett
Fort McPherson
Herschel I.
Fort Simpson
Liard
Mackenzie
Peace
Fort Vermilion
Tulita
Fort Good Hope
Mackenzie Bay
Beaufort Sea
Great Bear Lake
NORTH AMERICA
CANADA
Athabasca
C. Bathurst
Yellowknife
Great Slave Lake
Coppermine
Athabasca Lake
Dolphin & Union Sd.
Kugluktuk
C. Kellett
Banks I.
C. Prince Alfred
Prince Albert Pen.
Wollaston Pen.
Coronation G.
Victoria Island
M'Clure Str.
Prince Patrick I.
Melville I.
Viscount Melville Sd.
M'Clintock Chan.
Parry Is.
Borden I.
King William I.
Back
Chesterfield Inlet
Prince of Wales I.
Bathurst I.
North Magnetic Pole 1990
Ellef Ringnes I.
Boothia Pen.
Somerset I.
Sverdrup Is.
Gulf of Boothia
Prince Regent Inlet
Barrow Str.
Lancaster Sd.
Devon I.
Jones Sound
Axel Heiberg I.
Nansen Sd.
Eureka
Hudson Bay
Roes Welcome Sd.
Melville Pen.
Hecla & Fury Str.
Southampton I.
Coats I.
Foxe Chan.
Foxe Basin
Prince Charles I.
Mansel I.
Ellesmere I. (Canada)
C. Columbia
Smith Sund
Qaanaaq
Kane Basin
Alert
Robeson Chan.
Lincoln Sea
Bylot I.
Uummannaq
K. York
Sermersuaq
Knud Rasmussen Land
K. Morris Jesup
Peary Land
Independence Fjord
Kong Frederik VIII.s Land
2399
Baffin Bay
Nettilling L.
Baffin I.
C. Wolstenholme
Hudson Str.
Feuilles
Iqaluit
Frobisher B.
Cumberland Sd.
Ungava Bay
Resolution I.
C. Chidley
Labrador
C. Dyer
Upernavik
Qeqertarsuaq
Uummannaq
Qeqertarsuaq
Davis Str.
GREENLAND (KALAALLIT NUNAAT) (Denmark)
Kong Frederik IX.s Land
Kong Christian X.s Land
Kong Franz Joseph Fd.
Kong Oscar Fjord
Ittoqqortoormiit
Nuuk
Mt. Forel 3360
Kong Christian IX.s Land
3700
Gunnbjørn Fjeld
Kap Brewster
Paamiut
Kong Frederik VI.s Kyst
Ammassalik
Hamilton Inlet
Qaqortoq
Alluitsup Paa
Kap Farvel (Nunap Isua)
Denmark Str.
Horn
Breiðafjörður
Fontur
ICELAND
Reykjavík
Öræfajökull 2119
Iceland Plateau
Jan Mayen (Norway)
Norwegian Sea
Arctic Circle
3800
Mid-Atlantic Ridge
ATLANTIC OCEAN
4755
Rockall (U.K.)
Hebrides (U.K.)
Føroyar (Den.)
Shetland Is. (U.K.)
Orkney Is. (U.K.)
UNITED KINGDOM
SCOTLAND
Edinburgh
Belfast
Dublin
IRELAND
C. Clear
WALES
ENGLAND
LONDON
North Sea
AMSTERDAM
NETH.
HAMBURG
Elbe
BERLIN
GERMANY
PRAHA
POLAND
WARSZAWA
Wisła
DENMARK
KØBENHAVN
Skagerrak
Bergen
Oslo
STOCKHOLM
SWEDEN
NORWAY
Trondheim
Lofoten
Tromsø
Hammerfest
Nordkapp
Vardø
Varangerfjorden
Murmansk
Kolskiy Poluostrov
Tornio
Gulf of Bothnia
FINLAND
Helsinki
G. of Finland
Tallinn
EST.
Riga
LAT.
LITH.
Vilnius
Kaliningrad
Baltic Sea
BELARUS
KYYIV
UKRAINE
ODESA
Black Sea
ROSTOV
ST. PETERBURG
Ladozhskoye Ozero
Onezhskoye Ozero
Chudskoye Ozero
MOSKVA
Volga
VOLGOGRAD
Saratov
SAMARA
UFA
PERM
YEKATERINBURG
Uralskie Gory
Arkhangelsk
Sev. Dvina
Onega
Mezen
Beloye More
Mys Kanin Nos
O. Kolguyev
Pechora
Narodnaya 1894
Tobolsk
Berezovo
Ob
Khabarovo
Vorkuta
Salekhard
Baydaratskaya Guba
Poluostrov Yamal
Novyy Port
Nadym
Surgut
Urengoy
Taz
Kara Sea
Novaya Zemlya
Barents Sea
Edgeøya
Longyearbyen
Vestspitsbergen
Svalbard (Norway)
2571
Nordaustlandet
Nordkapp
Bjørnøya
Greenland Sea
Z. Aleksandry (Russia)
Zemlya Frantsa Iosifa
O. Graham Bell
Z. Vilcheka
O. Belyy
McKinley Sea
Nansen Basin
Nansen Cordillera
Fram Basin
NORTH POLE
4418
3741
Lomonosov Ridge
Makarov Basin
Alpha Cordillera
2104
4007
4484
4100
3546
3849
3700
3327
3767
Canada Basin
ARCTIC OCEAN
Mendeleyev Ridge
O. Bennetta (Russia)
46
Novosibirskiye Ostrova
Lyakhovskiye Ostrova
O. Kotelnyy
Laptev Sea
Ostrova Petra
Severnaya Zemlya
O. Oktyabrskoy Revolyutsii
O. Uedineniya
O. Ushakova
O. Vise
Poluostrov Taymyr
Ozero Taymyr
Nordvik
Anabar
Kotuy
Kheta
Pyasina
Dudinka
Norilsk
Gory Putorana
Golchikha
Igarka
Yenisey
Nizhnyaya Tunguska
Podkamennaya Tunguska
Vilyuy
Olenek
Tiksi
Bulun
Lena
Zhigansk
Kazachye
Yana
Verkhoyansk
Verkhoyanskiy Khrebet
Russkoye Ustie
Indigirka
Zashiversk
Yakutsk
Olekma
Siberia
ASIA
RUSSIA
Maximum extent of sea ice
Summer extent of sea ice
Ice caps and permanent ice shelf
ft m
12 000 4000
6000 2000
4500 1500
3000 1000
1200 400
600 200
0 0
500 1500
1000 3000
2000 6000
3000 9000
4000 12 000
5000 15 000
m ft
Projection : Zenithal Equidistant
West from Greenwich
East from Greenwich
CARTOGRAPHY BY PHILIP'S.

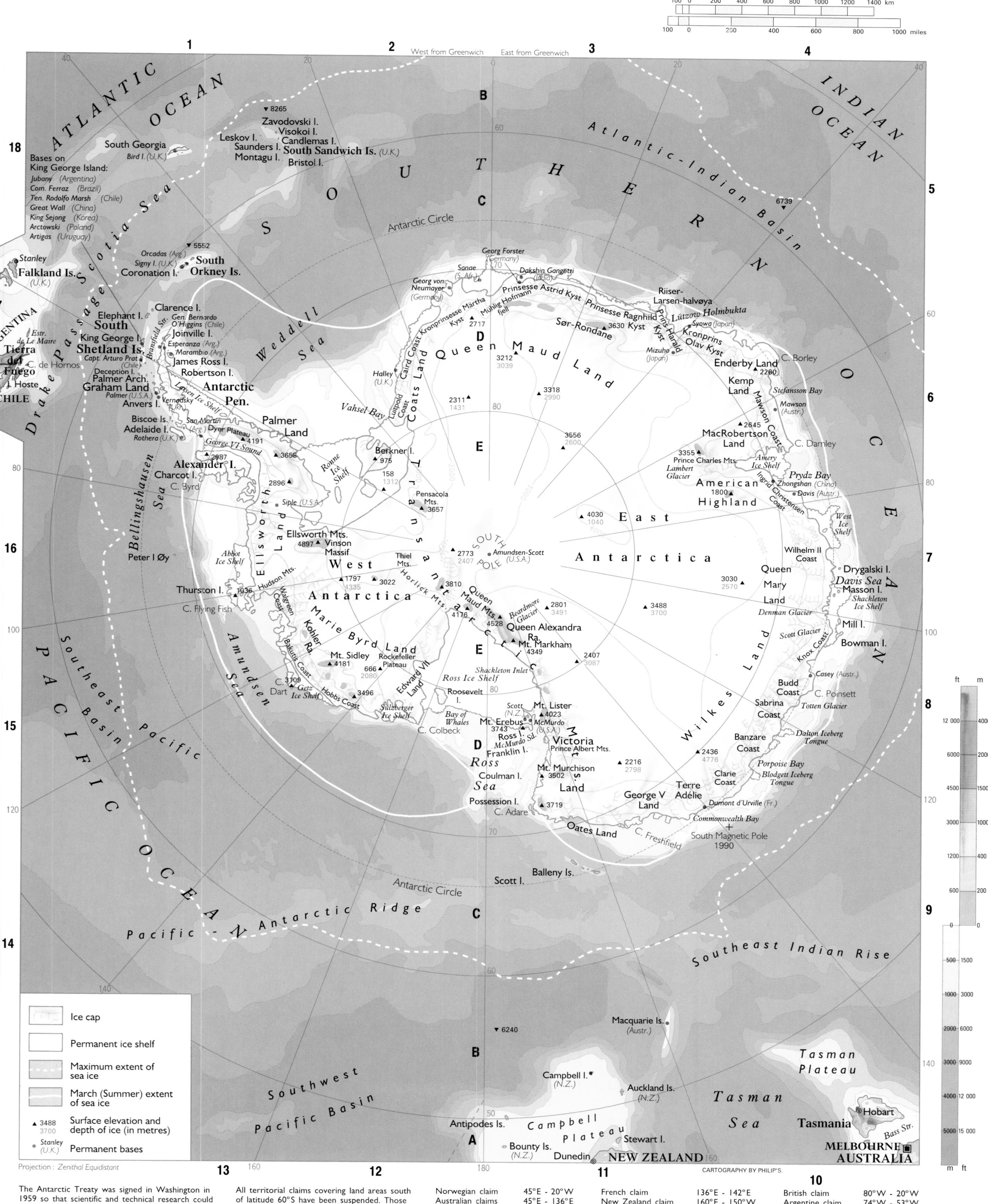

100 0   200   400   600   800   1000 1200 1400 km

100 0   200   400   600   800   1000 miles

ATLANTIC **OCEAN**

1 2 West from Greenwich East from Greenwich 3 4

INDIAN
OCEAN

18

▼ 8265

Zavodovski I.
Leskov I. Visokoi I.
Saunders I. Candlemas I.
Montagu I. **South Sandwich Is.** (U.K.)
Bristol I.

South Georgia
Bird I. (U.K.)

**Bases on
King George Island:**
Jubany (Argentina)
Com. Ferraz (Brazil)
Ten. Rodolfo Marsh (Chile)
Great Wall (China)
King Sejong (Korea)
Arctowski (Poland)
Artigas (Uruguay)

S
O
U
T
H

E
R
N

Atlantic-Indian Basin

B

C

▼ 5552
Orcadas (Arg.)
Signy I. (U.K.) **South**
Coronation I. **Orkney Is.**

Antarctic Circle

Georg Forster
(Germany)
Sanae
(S. Afr.) Dakshin Gangotri
(India)
Georg von
Neumayer
(Germany)

Prinsesse Astrid Kyst
Prinsesse Ragnhild Kyst

Riiser-
Larsen-halvøya
Lützow Holmbukta

6739

5

Falkland Is.
(U.K.)
Stanley

Scotia Sea

Weddell Sea

Kronprinsesse Martha Kyst
Mühlig Hofmann
fjell
2717

Queen Maud Land

3630
Sør-Rondane
Prins Harald Kyst
Kronprins
Olav Kyst
Syowa (Japan)
Mizuho (Japan)

Enderby Land
2260

C. Borley

60

ARGENTINA
Estr.
de Le Maire
South
Elephant I.
Clarence I.
King George I.
Shetland Is.

Gen. Bernardo
O'Higgins (Chile)
Joinville I.
Esperanza (Arg.)
Marambio (Arg.)

3212
Halley
(U.K.)

2311
1431

3318
2990

3656
2600

Kemp
Land
Stefansson Bay
Mawson
(Austr.)

6

Tierra
del
Fuego
I. Hoste
C. de Hornos
CHILE

Capt. Arturo Prat (Chile)
Deception I.
Palmer Arch.
Graham Land Palmer (U.S.A.)
Anvers I.
Vernadsky (U.K.)

Coats Land
Caird Coast
Luitpold Coast
Vahsel Bay

Berkner I.
975

E

D

2645
MacRobertson
Land
3355
Prince Charles Mts.
Lambert
Glacier
Amery
Ice Shelf
Zhongshan (China)
Davis (Austr.)
Ingrid Christensen Coast
Prydz Bay
C. Darnley

Antarctic
Pen.
Robertson I.
James Ross I.

Biscoe Is.
Adelaide I.
Rothera (U.K.)
San Martin
(Arg.)
Dyer Plateau
4191

Ronne
Ice
Shelf

158
1312

Pensacola
Mts.
3657

3656

3656

American
Highland
1800
1040

East

7

16

Alexander I.
2987
Charcot I.
C. Byrd

2896

Siple (U.S.A.)

Ellsworth Mts.
4897 ▲ Vinson
Massif
Thiel
Mts.

4030
1040

Wilhelm II
Coast

West Ice Shelf

80

Bellingshausen
Sea

Peter I Øy

1797
4335
3022

3810
4176

2773
2407
**SOUTH
POLE**
Amundsen-Scott
(U.S.A.)

Antarctica

3030
2570

Queen
Mary
Land

Drygalski I.
Davis Sea
Masson I.
Shackleton
Ice Shelf
Mill I.

Thurston I.
1936
Hudson Mts.
C. Flying Fish

West
Antarctica

Horlick Mts.

Queen
Maud Mts.
4528
Beardmore
Glacier
2801
3491

3488
3700

Scott Glacier
Knox Coast
Bowman I.

Casey (Austr.)

100

Marie Byrd Land

Kohler Ra.
Bakutis Coast
Mt. Sidley
4181
Rockefeller
Plateau

666
2080

Queen Alexandra
Ra.
Mt. Markham
4349

2407
3087

Wilkes

Budd
Coast
Sabrina
Coast

Totten Glacier
C. Poinsett

Dalton Iceberg
Tongue

8

15

C. 3109
Dart
Getz
Ice Shelf
Hobbs Coast
3496
Edward VII
Land
Sulzberger
Ice Shelf
C. Colbeck

Roosevelt I.

Shackleton Inlet
Ross Ice Shelf

80

Scott
(N.Z.)
Mt. Lister
4023
McMurdo
(U.S.A.)

Land

Banzare
Coast

Clarie
Coast
2436
4776

Porpoise Bay
Blodgett Iceberg
Tongue

Amundsen
Sea

Bay of
Whales
Mt. Erebus
3743
Ross I.
McMurdo Sd.
Franklin I.

Victoria
Prince Albert Mts.

2216
2798

Terre
Adélie
Dumont d'Urville (Fr.)
Commonwealth Bay

120

14

Pacific

Ross
Sea

Coulman I.
Possession I.
C. Adare

Mt. Murchison
3502

Land

3719

George V
Land
South Magnetic Pole
1990

C. Freshfield
Oates Land

Pacific-
Antarctic Ridge

Antarctic Circle

70
60

Scott I.
Balleny Is.

50

Southeast Indian Rise

9

	Ice cap
	Permanent ice shelf
	Maximum extent of sea ice
	March (Summer) extent of sea ice
▲ 3488 / 3700	Surface elevation and depth of ice (in metres)
• Stanley (U.K.)	Permanent bases

▼ 6240

Macquarie Is.
(Austr.)

Tasman
Plateau

B

Southwest
Pacific Basin

Campbell I.
(N.Z.)
Auckland Is.
(N.Z.)

Tasman
Sea Tasmania
Hobart
Bass Str.

140

Projection: Zenithal Equidistant

13

Antipodes Is.
A Bounty Is.
(N.Z.)
Campbell
Plateau
Stewart I.
Dunedin **NEW ZEALAND**
12 180 11

CARTOGRAPHY BY PHILIP'S.

MELBOURNE
AUSTRALIA

10

ft m
12 000 4000
6000 2000
4500 1500
3000 1000
1200 400
600 200
0 0
500 1500
2000 6000
3000 9000
4000 12 000
5000 15 000
m ft

The Antarctic Treaty was signed in Washington in
1959 so that scientific and technical research could
continue unhampered by international politics.

All territorial claims covering land areas south
of latitude 60°S have been suspended. Those
claims were:

Norwegian claim	45°E – 20°W
Australian claims	45°E – 136°E
	142°E – 160°E
French claim	136°E – 142°E
New Zealand claim	160°E – 150°W
Chilean claim	90°W – 53°W
British claim	80°W – 20°W
Argentine claim	74°W – 53°W

EUROPE : Physical 1:17 800 000

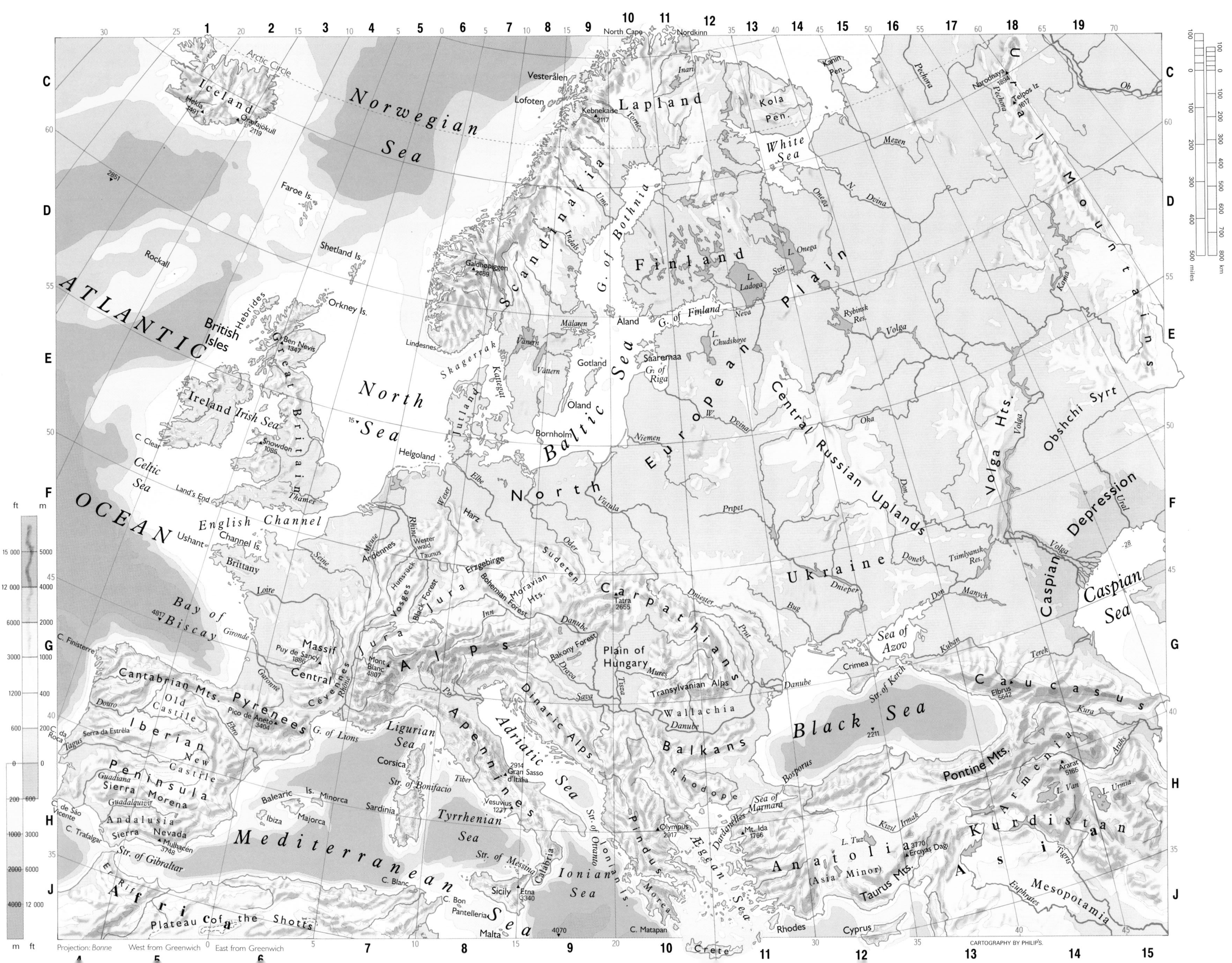

100 0 100 200 300 400 500 600 700 800 km
100 0 100 200 300 400 500 miles
Norwegian Sea
North Sea
ATLANTIC OCEAN
Bay of Biscay
English Channel
Celtic Sea
Irish Sea
Baltic Sea
G. of Bothnia
G. of Finland
G. of Riga
White Sea
Black Sea
Sea of Azov
Caspian Sea
Caspian Depression
Mediterranean Sea
Tyrrhenian Sea
Adriatic Sea
Ionian Sea
Ægean Sea
Ligurian Sea
Sea of Marmara
Str. of Gibraltar
Str. of Otranto
Str. of Messina
Str. of Bonifacio
Str. of Kerch
G. of Lions
Skagerrak
Kattegat
Arctic Circle
Iceland
Hekla 1491
Öræfajökull 2119
Faroe Is.
Shetland Is.
Orkney Is.
Hebrides
British Isles
Great Britain
Ireland
Ben Nevis 1347
Snowdon 1085
Channel Is.
Brittany
Land's End
Ushant
C. Clear
Rockall
Thames
Loire
Seine
Garonne
Gironde
Ebro
Douro
Tagus
Guadiana
Guadalquivir
Rhône
Rhine
Meuse
Weser
Elbe
Oder
Vistula
Danube
Tisza
Drava
Sava
Mureş
Prut
Dniester
Bug
Dnieper
Pripet
Donets
Don
Volga
Oka
Kama
Ural
Pechora
Mezen
N. Dvina
W. Dvina
Niemen
Onega
Neva
Svir
Ob
Iberian Peninsula
Cantabrian Mts.
Old Castile
New Castile
Sierra Morena
Sierra Nevada
Mulhacén 3748
Andalusia
Pyrenees
Pico de Aneto 3404
Massif Central
Puy de Sancy 1886
Cevennes
C. Finisterre
C. da Roca
Serra da Estrêla
C. de São Vicente
C. Trafalgar
Balearic Is.
Majorca
Minorca
Ibiza
Corsica
Sardinia
Sicily
Etna 3340
Malta
Pantelleria
C. Bon
C. Blanc
Plateau of the Shotts
Africa
Er Rif
Alps
Mont Blanc 4807
Jura
Vosges
Black Forest
Hunsrück
Taunus
Westerwald
Ardennes
Harz
Erzgebirge
Bohemian Forest
Moravian Hts.
Sudeten
Bakony Forest
Inn
Po
Tiber
Apennines
Gran Sasso d'Italia 2914
Vesuvius 1277
Calabria
Dinaric Alps
Carpathians
Tatra 2655
Transylvanian Alps
Plain of Hungary
Wallachia
Balkans
Rhodope
Pindus
Olympus 2917
Morea
C. Matapan
Ionian Is.
Crete
Rhodes
Dardanelles
Bosporus
Mt. Ida 1766
Anatolia (Asia Minor)
L. Tuz
Kizil Irmak
Taurus Mts.
Erciyas Daği 3770
Cyprus
Asia
Pontine Mts.
Armenia
Ararat 5165
L. Van
L. Urmia
Kurdistan
Mesopotamia
Tigris
Euphrates
Araks
Kura
Terek
Kuban
Manych
Caucasus
Elbrus 5642
Crimea
Ukraine
Central Russian Uplands
Volga Hts.
Obshchi Syrt
Ural Mountains
Narodnaya 1894
Telpos Iz 1617
Tsimlyansk Res.
Rybinsk Res.
L. Ladoga
L. Onega
L. Chudskoye
North European Plain
Finland
Lapland
Scandinavia
Kola Pen.
Kanin Pen.
Inari
Nordkinn
North Cape
Kebnekaise 2117
Lofoten
Vesterålen
Torne
Ume
Indals
Galdhøpiggen 2469
Lindesnes
Jutland
Vänern
Vättern
Mälaren
Gotland
Öland
Bornholm
Åland
Saaremaa
Helgoland
Projection: Bonne
West from Greenwich 0 East from Greenwich
CARTOGRAPHY BY PHILIP'S.
ft m
15 000 5000
12 000 4000
6000 2000
3000 1000
1200 400
600 200
0 0
200 600
1000 3000
2000 6000
4000 12 000
m ft

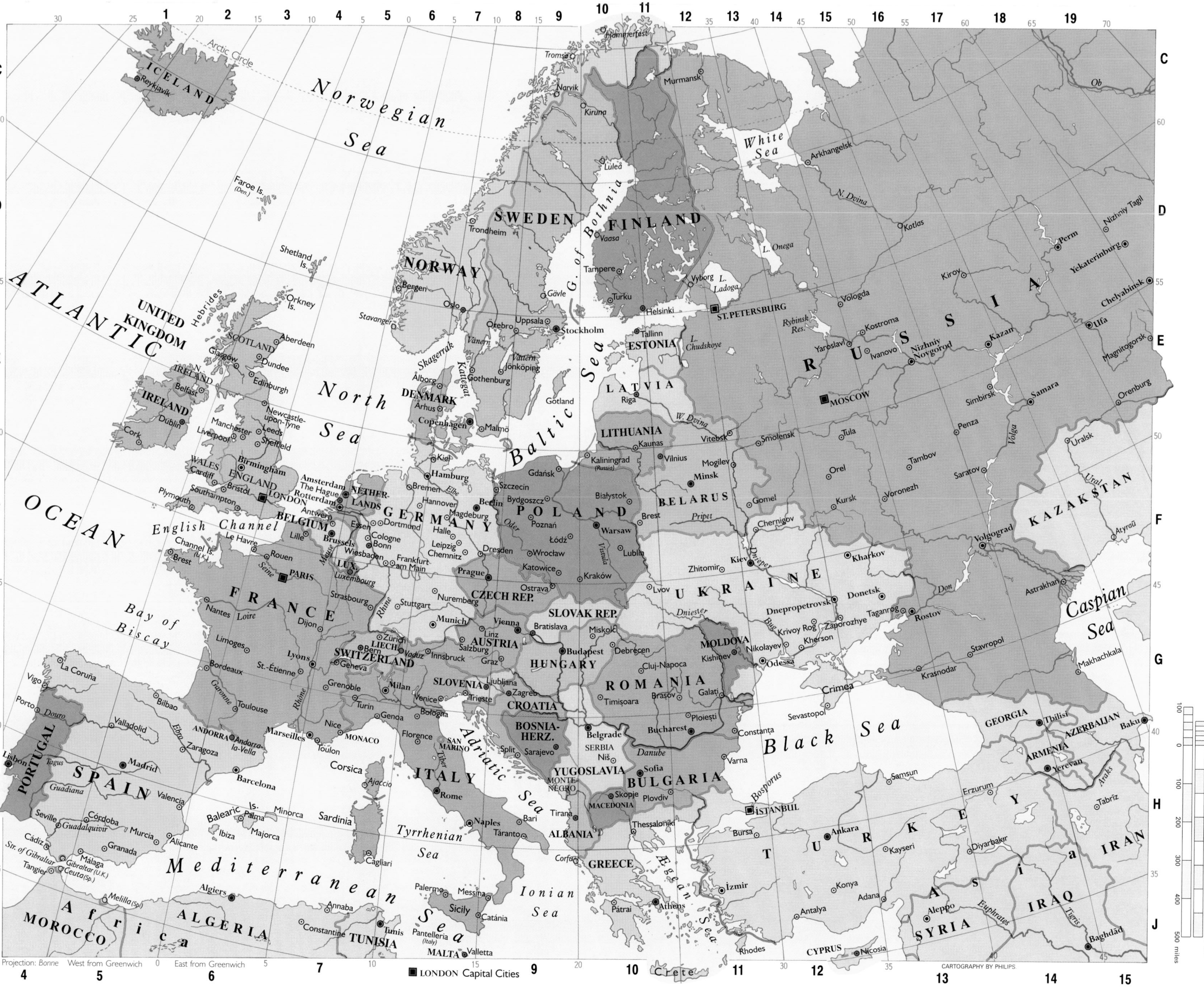
100 0 100 200 300 400 500 600 700 800 km
100 0 100 200 300 400 500 miles
ATLANTIC OCEAN
Norwegian Sea
North Sea
Baltic Sea
G. of Bothnia
White Sea
English Channel
Bay of Biscay
Mediterranean Sea
Tyrrhenian Sea
Adriatic Sea
Ionian Sea
Ægean Sea
Black Sea
Caspian Sea
Africa
ICELAND
UNITED KINGDOM
IRELAND
NORWAY
SWEDEN
FINLAND
DENMARK
ESTONIA
LATVIA
LITHUANIA
BELARUS
RUSSIA
POLAND
GERMANY
NETHERLANDS
BELGIUM
LUX.
FRANCE
SWITZERLAND
LIECH.
AUSTRIA
CZECH REP.
SLOVAK REP.
HUNGARY
SLOVENIA
CROATIA
BOSNIA-HERZ.
YUGOSLAVIA
SERBIA
MONTENEGRO
MACEDONIA
ALBANIA
GREECE
BULGARIA
ROMANIA
MOLDOVA
UKRAINE
KAZAKSTAN
GEORGIA
AZERBAIJAN
ARMENIA
TURKEY
SYRIA
IRAQ
IRAN
CYPRUS
ITALY
SAN MARINO
MALTA
MONACO
ANDORRA
SPAIN
PORTUGAL
MOROCCO
ALGERIA
TUNISIA
LONDON
PARIS
MOSCOW
ST. PETERSBURG
LONDON Capital Cities
Projection: Bonne
West from Greenwich
East from Greenwich
Arctic Circle
CARTOGRAPHY BY PHILIPS

SCANDINAVIA 1:4 400 000

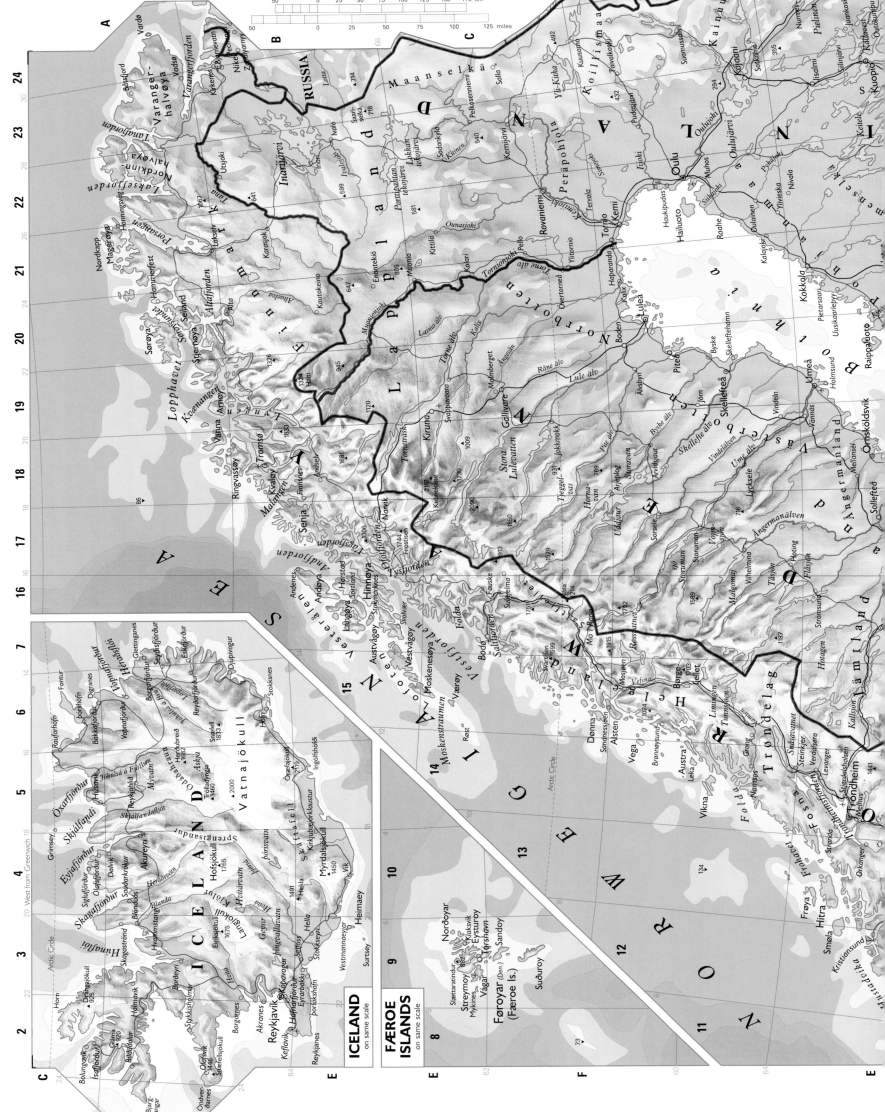

ICELAND
on same scale

FÆROE
ISLANDS
on same scale

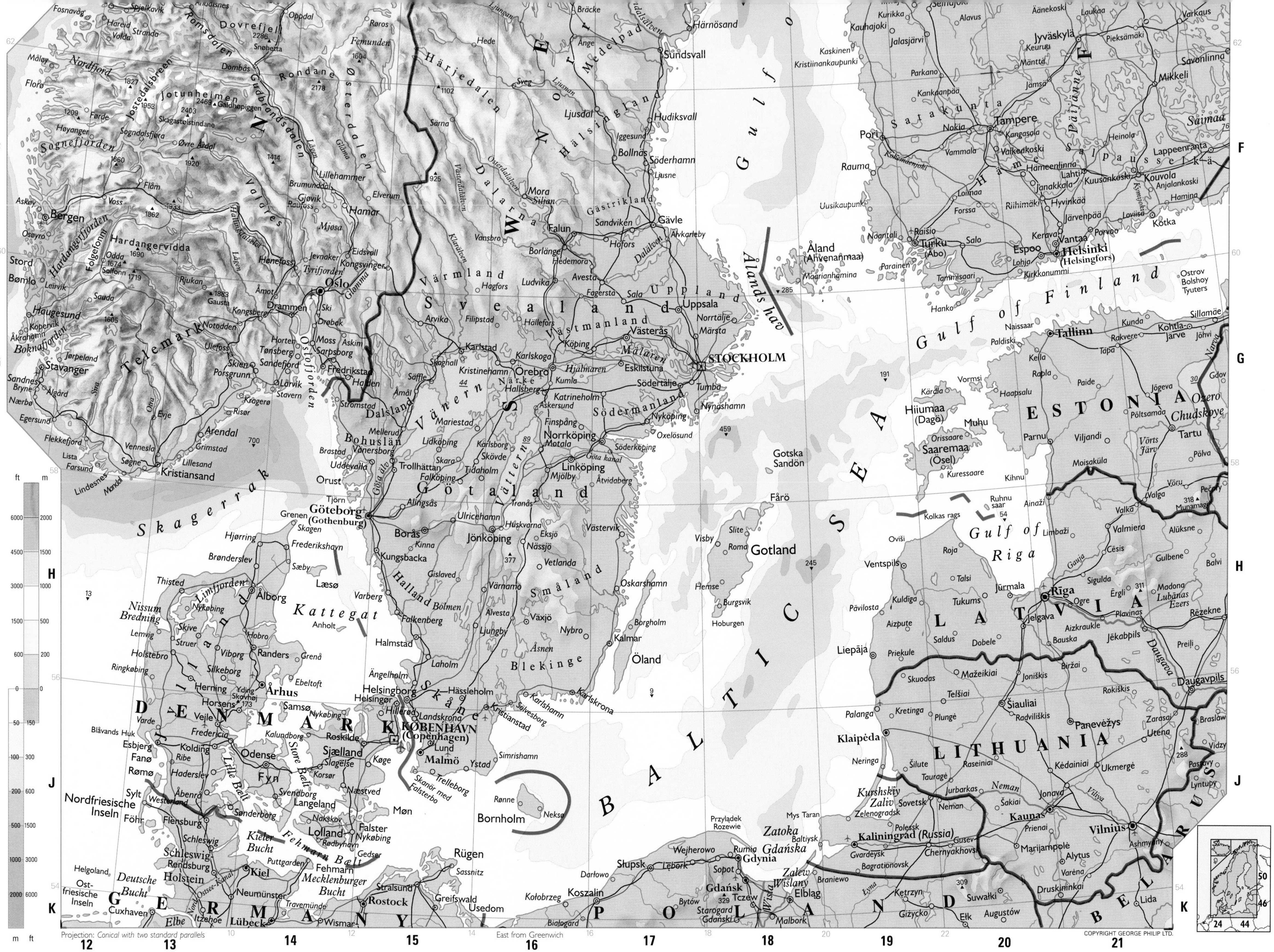

Countries and regions: FINLAND, ESTONIA, LATVIA, LITHUANIA, RUSSIA, SWEDEN, NORWAY, DENMARK, GERMANY, POLAND

Seas and gulfs: Gulf of Finland, Gulf of Riga, BALTIC SEA, Ålands hav, Skagerrak, Kattegat

Major cities: Helsinki (Helsingfors), Tallinn, Tartu, Riga, Vilnius, Kaunas, Kaliningrad (Russia), Stockholm, Uppsala, Göteborg (Gothenburg), Oslo, Bergen, Stavanger, København (Copenhagen), Malmö, Gdańsk, Gdynia, Lübeck, Kiel, Rostock

Islands: Åland (Ahvenanmaa), Gotland, Öland, Saaremaa (Ösel), Hiiumaa (Dagö), Bornholm, Rügen, Fyn, Sjælland, Lolland, Falster, Fehmarn

COPYRIGHT GEORGE PHILIP LTD.

East from Greenwich

Projection: Conical with two standard parallels

ft — m
6000 / 2000
4500 / 1500
3000 / 1000
1500 / 600
600 / 200
0
0
150 / 50
300 / 100
600 / 200
1500 / 500
3000 / 1000
6000 / 2000
ft — m

10 0 10 20 30 40 50 60 70 80 90 km
10 0 10 20 30 40 50 60 miles

Gulf of Bothnia

VÄSTER-NORRLANDS LÄN

Östersund

Storsjön

JÄMTLANDS LÄN

NOREG

Härjedalen

SÖR-TRØNDELAG

Trondheim

Dovrefjell

Rondane

Jotunheimen

OPPLAND

MØRE OG ROMSDAL

Medelpad

Sundsvall

Indalsälven

Ljungan

Hälsingland

GÄVLEBORGS LÄN

Bollnäs

KOPPARBERGS LÄN

DALARNA LÄN

Falun

Borlänge

Siljan

Mora

HEDMARK

Österdalen

Gudbrandsdalen

Lillehammer

Hamar

Mjøsa

Gävle

UPPSALA LÄN

Uppsala

STOCKHOLMS LÄN

STOCKHOLM

VÄSTMANLANDS LÄN

Västerås

SÖDERMANLANDS LÄN

Eskilstuna

Södertälje

Örebro

ÖREBRO LÄN

Närke

VÄRMLANDS LÄN

Karlstad

Klarälven

Västerdalälven

Söderhamn

Hudiksvall

Härnösand

VÄRMLAND

AKERSHUS

Oslo

Drammen

BUSKERUD

VESTFOLD

ØSTFOLD

Fredrikstad

Sarpsborg

Moss

TELEMARK

Kongsberg

Hønefoss

Gjøvik

Glomma

Kongsvinger

Hallingdal

Numedal

Valdres

m 2000 1500 1000 500 200 50 0
ft 6000 4500 3000 1500 600 200 0

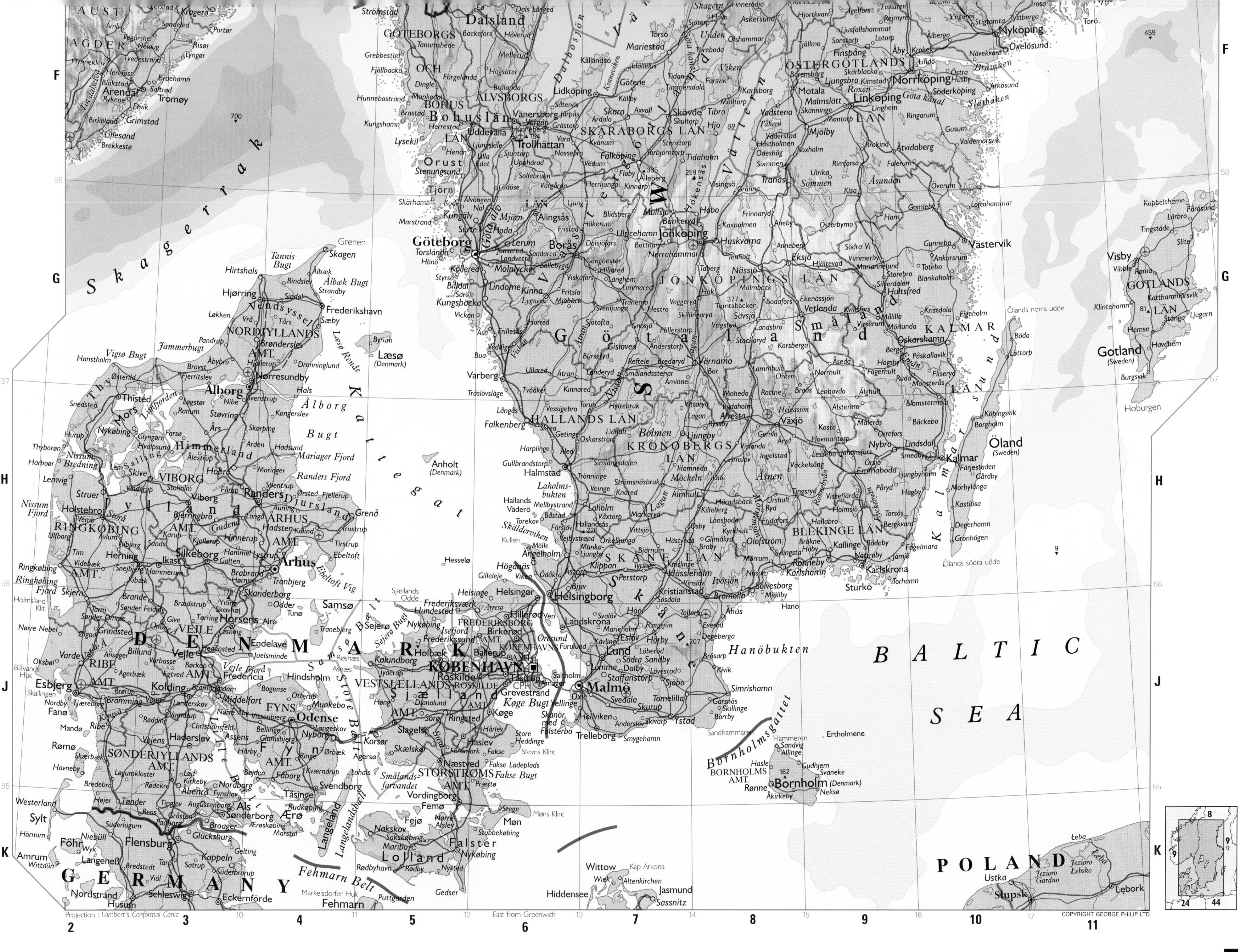

Skagerrak
Kattegat
BALTIC SEA
DENMARK
GERMANY
POLAND
Götaland
Småland
Skåne
Jylland
Sjælland
Fyn
Lolland
Falster
Bornholm (Denmark)
Öland (Sweden)
Gotland (Sweden)
Læsø (Denmark)
Anholt (Denmark)
Göteborg
Malmö
KØBENHAVN
Helsingborg
Jönköping
Norrköping
Linköping
Borås
Kalmar
Karlskrona
Växjö
Halmstad
Ålborg
Århus
Odense
Esbjerg
Flensburg
Visby
Västervik
Vättern
Hanöbukten
Kalmarsund
Fehmarn Belt
Store Bælt
Lille Bælt
Øresund
Bornholmsgattet
Projection : Lambert's Conformal Conic
East from Greenwich
COPYRIGHT GEORGE PHILIP LTD.

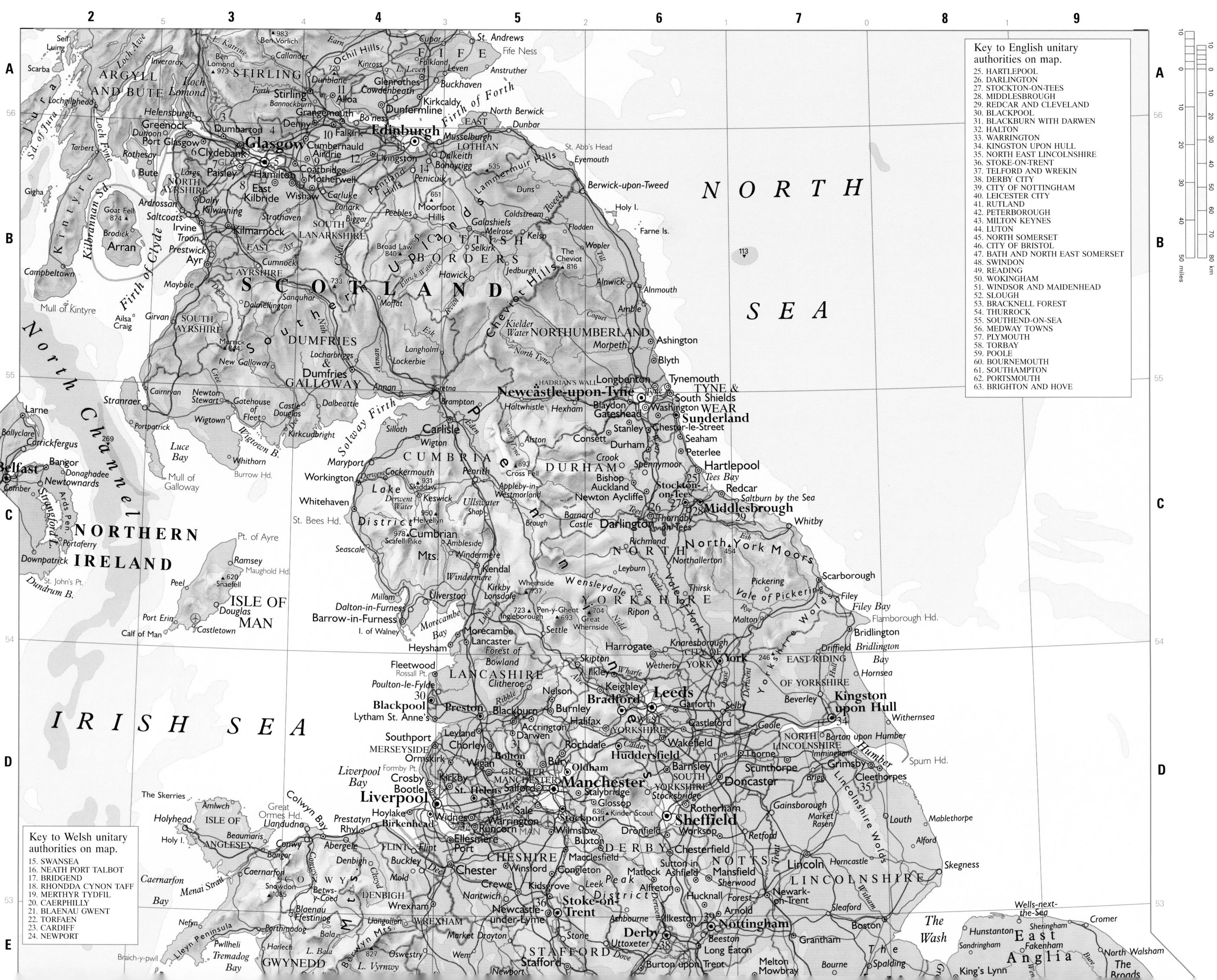

Key to English unitary authorities on map.

25. HARTLEPOOL
26. DARLINGTON
27. STOCKTON-ON-TEES
28. MIDDLESBROUGH
29. REDCAR AND CLEVELAND
30. BLACKPOOL
31. BLACKBURN WITH DARWEN
32. HALTON
33. WARRINGTON
34. KINGSTON UPON HULL
35. NORTH EAST LINCOLNSHIRE
36. STOKE-ON-TRENT
37. TELFORD AND WREKIN
38. DERBY CITY
39. CITY OF NOTTINGHAM
40. LEICESTER CITY
41. RUTLAND
42. PETERBOROUGH
43. MILTON KEYNES
44. LUTON
45. NORTH SOMERSET
46. CITY OF BRISTOL
47. BATH AND NORTH EAST SOMERSET
48. SWINDON
49. READING
50. WOKINGHAM
51. WINDSOR AND MAIDENHEAD
52. SLOUGH
53. BRACKNELL FOREST
54. THURROCK
55. SOUTHEND-ON-SEA
56. MEDWAY TOWNS
57. PLYMOUTH
58. TORBAY
59. POOLE
60. BOURNEMOUTH
61. SOUTHAMPTON
62. PORTSMOUTH
63. BRIGHTON AND HOVE

Key to Welsh unitary authorities on map.

15. SWANSEA
16. NEATH PORT TALBOT
17. BRIDGEND
18. RHONDDA CYNON TAFF
19. MERTHYR TYDFIL
20. CAERPHILLY
21. BLAENAU GWENT
22. TORFAEN
23. CARDIFF
24. NEWPORT

ENGLAND

WALES

FRANCE

NORMANDIE

HAUTE-NORMANDIE

SEINE-MARITIME

CALVADOS

MANCHE

ENGLISH CHANNEL

Bristol Channel

Cardigan Bay

Strait of Dover

Thames Estuary

Baie de la Seine

Baie de la Somme

CHANNEL ISLANDS (U.K.)

Isles of Scilly — On same scale

Projection: Lambert's Conformal Conic

COPYRIGHT GEORGE PHILIP LTD.

East from Greenwich • West from Greenwich

Selected place names:

London, Birmingham, Bristol, Cardiff, Southampton, Portsmouth, Brighton, Bournemouth, Plymouth, Exeter, Oxford, Cambridge, Ipswich, Colchester, Chelmsford, Canterbury, Dover, Folkestone, Hastings, Eastbourne, Worthing, Guildford, Reading, Swindon, Gloucester, Cheltenham, Hereford, Worcester, Coventry, Northampton, Bedford, Luton, Watford, Swansea, Newport, Merthyr Tydfil, Aberystwyth, Penzance, Truro, Newquay, Falmouth, Torquay, Taunton, Bath, Salisbury, Winchester, Weymouth

Calais, Boulogne-sur-Mer, Le Touquet-Paris-Plage, Berck, Dieppe, Fécamp, Le Havre, Rouen, Caen, Cherbourg, Évreux, Lisieux, Bayeux, St-Lô, Coutances, Granville, St-Malo

Jersey, Guernsey, Alderney, Sark, Herm, St. Helier, St. Peter Port

Isle of Wight, Isles of Scilly, Lundy

ft / m elevation legend: 3000 / 1000, 1500 / 500, 600 / 200, 300 / 100, 0, -150, -300, -600

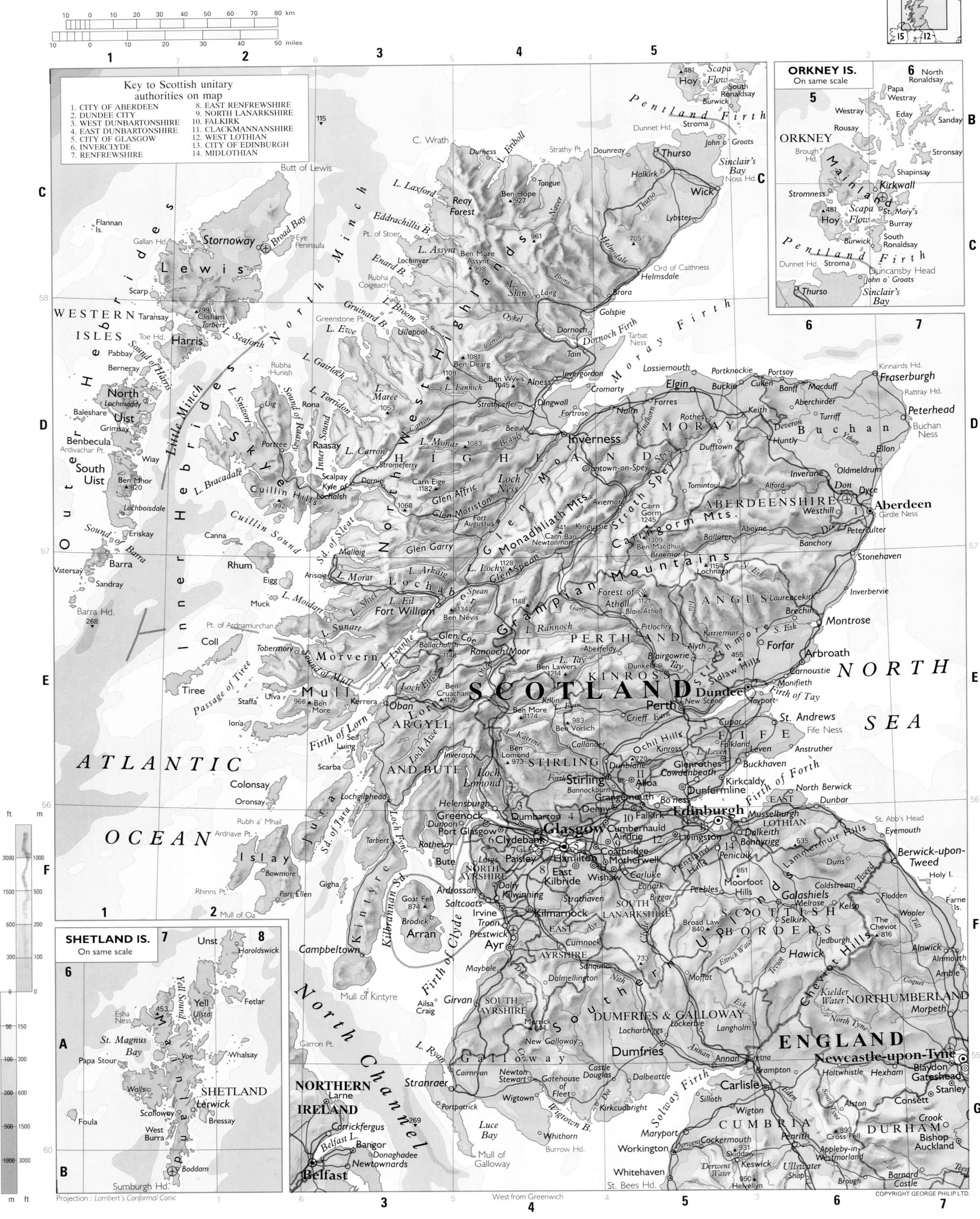

Key to Scottish unitary authorities on map
1. CITY OF ABERDEEN
2. DUNDEE CITY
3. WEST DUNBARTONSHIRE
4. EAST DUNBARTONSHIRE
5. CITY OF GLASGOW
6. INVERCLYDE
7. RENFREWSHIRE
8. EAST RENFREWSHIRE
9. NORTH LANARKSHIRE
10. FALKIRK
11. CLACKMANNANSHIRE
12. WEST LOTHIAN
13. CITY OF EDINBURGH
14. MIDLOTHIAN
ORKNEY IS.
On same scale
SHETLAND IS.
On same scale
SCOTLAND
ENGLAND
NORTHERN IRELAND
NORTH SEA
ATLANTIC OCEAN
North Channel
Moray Firth
Pentland Firth
Firth of Forth
Firth of Clyde
Solway Firth
The Minch
Little Minch
Outer Hebrides
Inner Hebrides
WESTERN ISLES
HIGHLAND
North West Highlands
Grampian Mountains
Cairngorm Mts.
Monadhliath Mts.
Southern Uplands
Glen Mor
MORAY
ABERDEENSHIRE
ANGUS
PERTH AND KINROSS
FIFE
STIRLING
ARGYLL AND BUTE
LOTHIAN
SCOTTISH BORDERS
DUMFRIES & GALLOWAY
SOUTH LANARKSHIRE
NORTH AYRSHIRE
EAST AYRSHIRE
SOUTH AYRSHIRE
NORTHUMBERLAND
CUMBRIA
DURHAM
Lewis
Harris
North Uist
South Uist
Barra
Skye
Mull
Islay
Jura
Arran
Stornoway
Inverness
Aberdeen
Dundee
Perth
Edinburgh
Glasgow
Stirling
Fort William
Oban
Thurso
Wick
Kirkwall
Lerwick
Ayr
Dumfries
Carlisle
Newcastle-upon-Tyne
Belfast
Ben Nevis
Projection : Lambert's Conformal Conic
West from Greenwich

10 0 10 20 30 40 50 60 70 80 km
10 0 10 20 30 40 50 miles

OCEAN

A

Mull of Oa
Kintyre
Campbeltown
Brodick
Arran
Firth of Clyde
Mull of Kintyre
Ailsa
Craig

Tory I.
Horn Hd.
Malin Hd.
Fanad Hd.
Malin Pen.
Carndonagh
Giants
Causeway
Rathlin I.
Portstewart Portrush
Ballycastle
Fair Hd.
Garron Pt.
Rathlin Hd.
North Channel
Cairnryan
Stranraer
Portpatrick

55

Sheep Haven
Mulroy B.
Lough Swilly
Inishowen Pen.
Moville
Buncrana
Portstewart
Coleraine
Limavady
Ballymoney
554
Trostan
Larne

Bloody Foreland
Inishfree B.
Aran I.
Gweedore
Errigal 752
The Rosses
Derryveagh Mts.
683
Letterkenny
Rathmelton
L. Foyle
LONDONDERRY
Londonderry
Roe
Mts. of Antrim
Ballymena
Carrickfergus
269

Crohy Hd.
Gweebarra B.
Dawros Hd.
Loughros More B.
Rossan Pt.
Glenties
Lavagh More 676
DONEGAL
Finn
Lifford Strabane
Sion Mills
Newtownstewart
Sawel Mt. 683
Sperrin Mts.
Magherafelt
Randalstown Ballyclare
Antrim
NORTHERN
Newtownabbey
Belfast
Bangor
Newtownards

B

Killybegs
Donegal
St. John's Pt.
Donegal Bay
Ballyshannon
Bundoran
Erne
Lower L. Erne
Enniskillen
FERMANAGH
Upper Erne
TYRONE
Omagh
Dromore
Irvinestown
Dungannon
Cookstown
Coalisland
Lough Neagh
Aughnacloy
Monaghan
ARMAGH
Armagh
Middletown
Keady
IRELAND
Lisburn
Saintfield
Craigavon
Lurgan
Portadown
Banbridge
Tandragee
DOWN
Comber
Strangford L.
Ards Pen.
Downpatrick
Ballynahinch
Dundrum
Ballyquintin Pt.
Portaferry

Broad Haven
Erris Hd.
Mullet Pen.
Belmullet
Inishkea North
Inishkea South
Blacksod Bay
Achill Hd.
Achill I.
Killala B.
Killala
Ballina
MAYO
544
Dromore West
Sligo Bay
SLIGO
Sligo
Slieve Gamph
Collooney
Ballymote
L. Arrow
LEITRIM
Leitrim
L. Allen
Belturbet
Clones
MONAGHAN
Castleblaney
Cootehill
Annalee
Keady
Newry
Mourne Mts.
Slieve Gullion
Warrenpoint
Kilkeel
Dundrum B.
St. John's Pt.
Newcastle
852
Slieve Donard

54

St. John's Pt.
L. Conn 806
Nephin
Corraun Pen.
Clare I.
Clew Bay
Westport
Newport
Castlebar
Swinford
Charlestown
Boyle
Carrick-on-Shannon
CAVAN
Cavan
L. Gowna
L. Sheelin
Kingscourt
Carrickmacross
LOUTH
Ardee
Dundalk
577
Greenore
Carlingford L.
Dundalk Bay

Inishturk
Inishbofin
Inishshark
Slyne Hd.
Connemara
Clifden
Killary Harbour
Croagh Patrick 765
Mweelrea 819
Ballyhaunis
Knock
Claremorris
Ballinrobe
Lough Mask
Glennamaddy
ROSCOMMON
Castlerea
Ballaghaderreen
Roscommon
Castlepollard
Granard
Longford
LONGFORD
Oldcastle
Ceanannus Mor (Kells)
Blackwater
MEATH
Clogher Hd.
Dunleer
Drogheda

C

Oughterard
Lough Corrib
Tuam
Lough Ree
IRELAND
Athlone
Mullingar
WESTMEATH
Leinster
Trim
An Uaimh (Navan)
Boyne
Athboy
Moate
Royal Canal
Maynooth
Swords
DUB
Rush
Lambay I.
Balbriggan

GALWAY
Galway
Athenry
Ballinasloe
Loughrea
Black Hd.
Clara
Edenderry
Daingean
KILDARE
Kildare
Naas
Clondalkin
DUBLIN
Dublin
Dun Laoghaire
Howth Hd.
Malahide

Galway Bay
Aran Is.
Inishmore
Inishmaan
Inisheer
Gort
368
Slieve Aughty
Portumna
Shannon
Birr
Mountmellick
Portarlington
Tullamore
Bog of Allen
Grand Canal
Monasterevan
Port Laoise
Kildare
Poulaphouca Res.
Bray
Greystones

53

Hags Hd.
Liscannor Bay
Ennistimon
Tulla
Lough Derg
Nenagh
Roscrea
Slieve Bloom
Arderin 528
Mountrath
LAOIS
Athy
Carlow
WICKLOW
Lugnaquilla 926
Wicklow Mts.
Wicklow
Rathdrum
Wicklow Hd.

Mal Bay
Mutton I.
CLARE
Ennis
Sixmilebridge
Killaloe
694 Keeper Hill
Templemore
Thurles
Durrow
CARLOW
Carlow
Muine Bheag
Tullow
Shillelagh
Gorey
Arklow
Mizen Hd.

D

Loop Hd.
Kilrush
Shannon Airport
Foynes
LIMERICK
Limerick
TIPPERARY
Golden Vale
Tipperary
Cashel
KILKENNY
Kilkenny
Callan
796 Mt. Leinster
Bunclody
Enniscorthy
WEXFORD
Cahore Pt.

Kerry Hd.
Tralee B.
Smerwick Harbour
Brandon B.
Brandon Mt. 953
Dingle
Slieve Mish 863
Rathkeale
Newcastle West
Kilfinnane
Galtymore 920
Galty Mts.
Caher
Slievenamon 722
Clonmel
Carrick-on-Suir
New Ross
Wexford
Rosslare
Wexford Harbour
Greenore Pt.
Carnsore Pt.

Brandon Hd.
Great Blasket I.
Inishvickillane
Dingle Bay
Anascaul
KERRY
Killorglin
Killarney
Newmarket
Kanturk
Mitchelstown
Buttevant
Fermoy
Knockmealdown Mts. 795
Comeragh Mts. 792
WATERFORD
Tramore
Waterford
Dungarvan
Hook Hd.
Saltee Is.
Tramore Harbour
St. David's Hd.
St. David's

52

Valencia I.
Puffin I.
Great Skellig
Cahersiveen
Macgillycuddy's Reeks
Carrauntoohill 1041
L. Leane
Kenmare
Macroom
Lee
Blackwater
Mallow
Blarney
CORK
646
Boggeragh Mts.
Cork
Midleton
Youghal
Lismore
Dungarvan
Youghal B.
Dungarvan Harbour
St. Brides Bay

Ballinskelligs B.
Great Skellig
Scariff I.
Kenmare River
Caha Mts.
635
Glengarriff
Bantry
Dunmanway
Bandon
Kinsale
Passage West
Cobh
Crosshaven
Cork Harbour
Old Head of Kinsale

E

Dursey I.
Crow Hd.
Bear I.
Castletown Bearhaven
Bantry Bay
Dunmanus B.
Skull
Mizen Hd.
Long I.
Baltimore
Sherkin I.
C. Clear Clear I.
Clonakilty
Skibbereen
Clonakilty B.
Galley Hd.

CELTIC SEA

ATLANTIC

IRISH SEA

St. George's Channel

Projection : Lambert's Conformal Conic
West from Greenwich
COPYRIGHT GEORGE PHILIP LTD.

ft m
1500 500
600 200
300 100
0 0
50 150
100 300
200 600
500 1500
1000 3000
2000 6000
m ft

50 0 25 50 75 100 125 150 175 km
50 0 25 50 75 100 125 miles

1 2 3 4 5 6 7 8 9

A

ATLANTIC OCEAN

Shetland Is.

Yell Unst
Fetlar
Foula Mainland
Lerwick

Askay
Bergen

NORWAY
Haugesund
Kopervik
Åkrahamn
Bømlo
Stord
Stavanger
Sandn
Bryn
Nærb

Fair Isle

B

316

Orkney Is.
Westray Sanday
Stronsay
Mainland Kirkwall
Hoy South Ronaldsay

Pentland Firth

C. Wrath
Thurso Wick
Helmsdale

Lewis Stornoway
Outer Hebrides
Harris
St. Kilda
789
North Minch
North Uist
Benbecula
South Uist

North West Highlands
Ullapool
Lairg Golspie
Tain
Invergordon
Dingwall
L. Ness Inverness
Nairn Elgin Buckie Banff Fraserburgh
1182 Aviemore Huntly Peterhead
Inverurie

Moray Firth

238

NORTH SEA

C

Inner Hebrides
Skye
Mallaig Rhum Eigg
Barra
Coll
Tobermory
Tiree
Mull
Oban

SCOTLAND
Grampian Mts
Ben Nevis 1342
Fort William
1214
Perth
L. Lomond
973

1311 Dee Ballater Aberdeen
Stonehaven
Montrose
Forfar Arbroath
Dundee
St. Andrews

Colonsay
Jura
Islay
Campbeltown

Greenock Paisley
East Kilbride
Irvine
Arran Kilmarnock
Ayr

Stirling
Glenrothes
Kirkcaldy
Dunfermline
Dunbar
Glasgow Edinburgh
Hamilton Berwick-upon-Tweed
Southern Uplands
Galashiels
840 Jedburgh 816
Hawick Cheviot Hills
Alnwick

D

Malin Hd.
Aran I. Buncrana
Letterkenny Coleraine
Donegal Lifford
Londonderry
Ballymena Larne
NORTHERN IRELAND Antrim Bangor
Omagh Lough Neagh Belfast
Enniskillen Portadown Lisburn Lurgan
Lower L. Erne Clones Armagh Newry
Cavan

North Channel
Firth of Clyde

Stranraer
Kirkcudbright
Mull of Galloway

Dumfries
Annan
Carlisle
Hexham
Gateshead
Durham
Darlington

Newcastle-upon-Tyne
South Shields
Sunderland
Hartlepool
Redcar
Middlesbrough
Stockton-on-Tees
Scarborough

893

16

Achill
Ballina
L. Conn Castlebar
Sligo Leitrim
Lough Gill
Ballaghaderreen
Roscommon Longford
Lough Mask Westport
Connemara Lough Carrib
Galway B. Galway Ballinasloe Athlone
Aran Is. Ennis

UNITED
KINGDOM
IRISH SEA

Douglas
I. of Man
Barrow-in-Furness
Lancaster
978
Blackpool Burnley Keighley
Preston Blackburn
Whitehaven
Workington
Cumbrian Mts.
Pennines
Harrogate York
Bridlington
Beverley
Kingston upon Hull

E

IRELAND

Lough Derg
Lough Ree
Mullingar
Athy Carlow
Portlaoise
Tullamore
Birr
Nenagh
Thurles

Dublin
Dun Laoghaire
Bray
Wicklow Mts
926
Arklow

Holyhead
Anglesey
Bangor
Snowdon
1085
Pwllheli

Liverpool
Warrington Stockport
Chester Crewe
Wrexham
Stoke-on-Trent
Derby
Stafford
Telford
ENGLAND

Manchester
Bolton Oldham
636
Sheffield
Chesterfield
Mansfield
Nottingham
Grantham

Bradford Leeds
Huddersfield Barnsley
Halifax Doncaster
Rotherham
Lincoln
Louth
Skegness
Boston The Wash
Cromer

F

Limerick
Tipperary
953
Dingle
Carrantoohill
1041
Tralee Listowel
Valencia I. Killarney
Mallow
Macgillycuddy's Reeks
Bantry
Kinsale
C. Clear

Shannon
Clonmel
Carrick-on-Suir
Waterford
Dungarvan
Youghal
Cork Cobh
Bandon

Wexford
Rosslare

St. George's Channel

Fishguard
Milford Haven
Haverfordwest
Pembroke

Cardigan Bay
Aberystwyth
Cambrian Mts

WALES

Carmarthen
Merthyr Tydfil 886
Neath
Llanelli
Swansea Rhondda
Port Talbot
Newport
Barry Cardiff

Shrewsbury
Welshpool

Wolverhampton
BIRMINGHAM
Redditch
Worcester
Hereford
Cheltenham
Gloucester
Cotswold Hills

Leicester
Nuneaton
Coventry
Rugby
Leamington Spa
Royal
Northampton
Corby
Peterborough
Rugby

Bristol
Bath
Bristol Channel
Weston-super-Mare

99

CELTIC SEA

Barnstaple
Exmoor
Taunton
Bude
Newquay
618 Dartmoor
Exeter
Exmouth

Swindon
Newbury
Reading
Basingstoke
Salisbury
Winchester
Southampton
Fareham
Bournemouth
Poole
Weymouth Newport
Isle of Wight
Portsmouth
Worthing

Ely
Cambridge
Bedford
Milton Keynes
Stevenage
Luton Harlow
Hemel
Hempstead
High Wycombe
Oxford
Watford
Slough
LONDON
Thames
Guildford
Crawley
Hastings
Brighton
Eastbourne

Norwich
Great Yarmouth
Lowestoft
Thetford
Bury St. Edmunds
Ipswich
Colchester
Harwich
Felixstowe
Chelmsford
Basildon
Southend-on-Sea
Margate
Canterbury
Rochester Dover
Chatham
Maidstone
Ashford Folkestone
Reigate

36

G

Torbay
Plymouth
Truro
St. Austell
Falmouth
Land's End
Penzance
Isles of Scilly

ENGLISH CHANNEL

Str. of Dover
C. Gris Nez
Boulogne-sur-Mer
Le Touquet-Paris-Plage 33

Portsmouth

NETHERLANDS
's-Gravenhage (Den Haag)
Hoek van Holland
ROTTERDAM
Dordre
Haarle
Den Hel
Alkm

Vlissingen
Zeebrugge
Oostende
Brugge
Gent
BELGIUM
BRUSSELS (Bruxelles)
Antwerp
Mechelen

Dunkerque
Calais
St-Omer
Béthune
Bruay-la-Buissière
Lens Lille
Villeneuve-d'Ascq
Valenciennes
Cambrai

Le Tréport
Dieppe
Abbeville
Amiens
FRANCE
Picardie
St-Quentin

C. de la Hague
Alderney
Pte. de Barfleur
Guernsey St. Peter Port
Channel Is. (U.K.)
Sark
St. Helier Jersey

Cotentin
Cherbourg
Valognes
Bayeux
Trouville-sur-Mer
Lisieux
Caen
Le Havre
Bolbec
Rouen
Elbeuf
Seine
Fécamp
Pays de Caux
Pte. de la Hague

ft m
3000 1000
1500 500
600 200
0
50 150
100 300
200 600
500 1500
1000 3000
2000 6000
m ft

NORTH SEA

UNITED KINGDOM

NETHERLANDS

BELGIUM

FRANCE

GERMANY

LUXEMBOURG

NORD-RHEIN

WESTFALEN

RHEINLAND-

PFALZ

RHEINHESSEN-PFALZ

SAARLAND

LORRAINE

PAS-DE-CALAIS

PICARDIE

SOMME

ARDENNES

ZEELAND

NOORD BRABANT

FRIESLAND

DRENTHE

GRONINGEN

OVERIJSSEL

GELDERLAND

LIMBURG

WESER-EMS

Waddeneilanden

Ostfriesische Inseln

Amsterdam · Rotterdam · 's-Gravenhage (Den Haag) · Utrecht · Haarlem · Groningen · Leeuwarden · Arnhem · Nijmegen · Eindhoven · Tilburg · Breda · Dordrecht · Antwerpen · Brussel (Bruxelles) · Gent (Gand) · Brugge · Oostende · Charleroi · Namur · Liège · Luxembourg · Paris · Reims · Nancy · Strasbourg · Düsseldorf · Köln · Bonn · Essen · Dortmund · Bochum · Duisburg · Münster · Bremerhaven · Oldenburg · Lille · Calais · Dunkerque · Boulogne-sur-Mer · Amiens · St-Quentin · Charleville-Mézières · Metz · Thionville · Verdun · Maastricht · Aachen · Mainz · Wiesbaden · Koblenz · Kaiserslautern · Saarbrücken

Projection : Lambert's Conformal Conic

East from Greenwich

COPYRIGHT GEORGE PHILIP LTD.

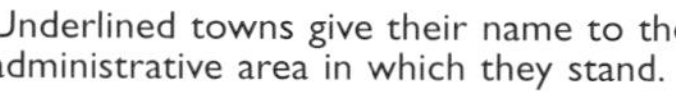

Underlined towns give their name to the administrative area in which they stand.

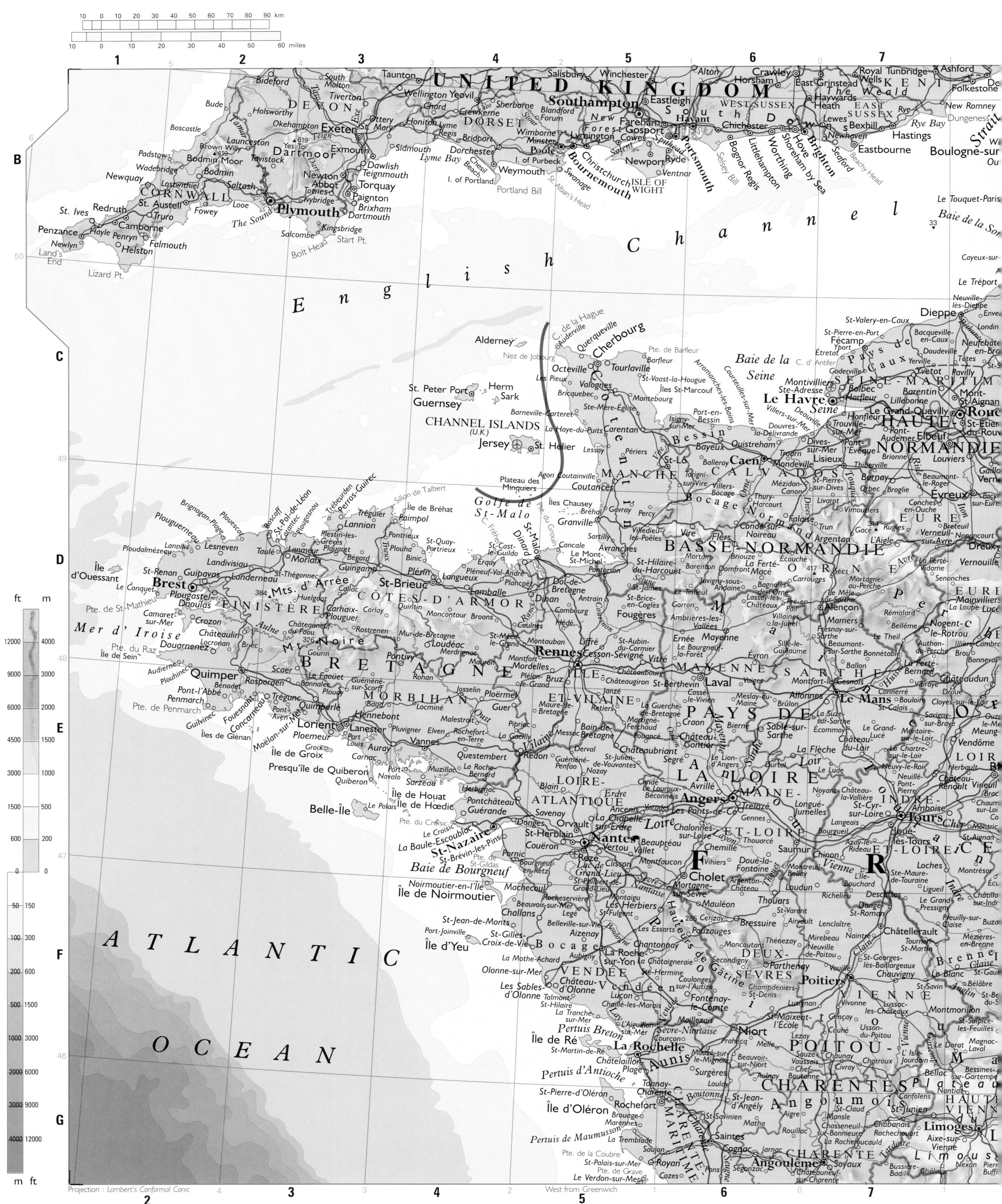

DÉPARTEMENTS IN THE PARIS AREA
1. Ville de Paris 3. Val-de-Marne
2. Seine-St-Denis 4. Hauts-de-Seine

Underlined towns give their name to the
administrative area in which they stand.

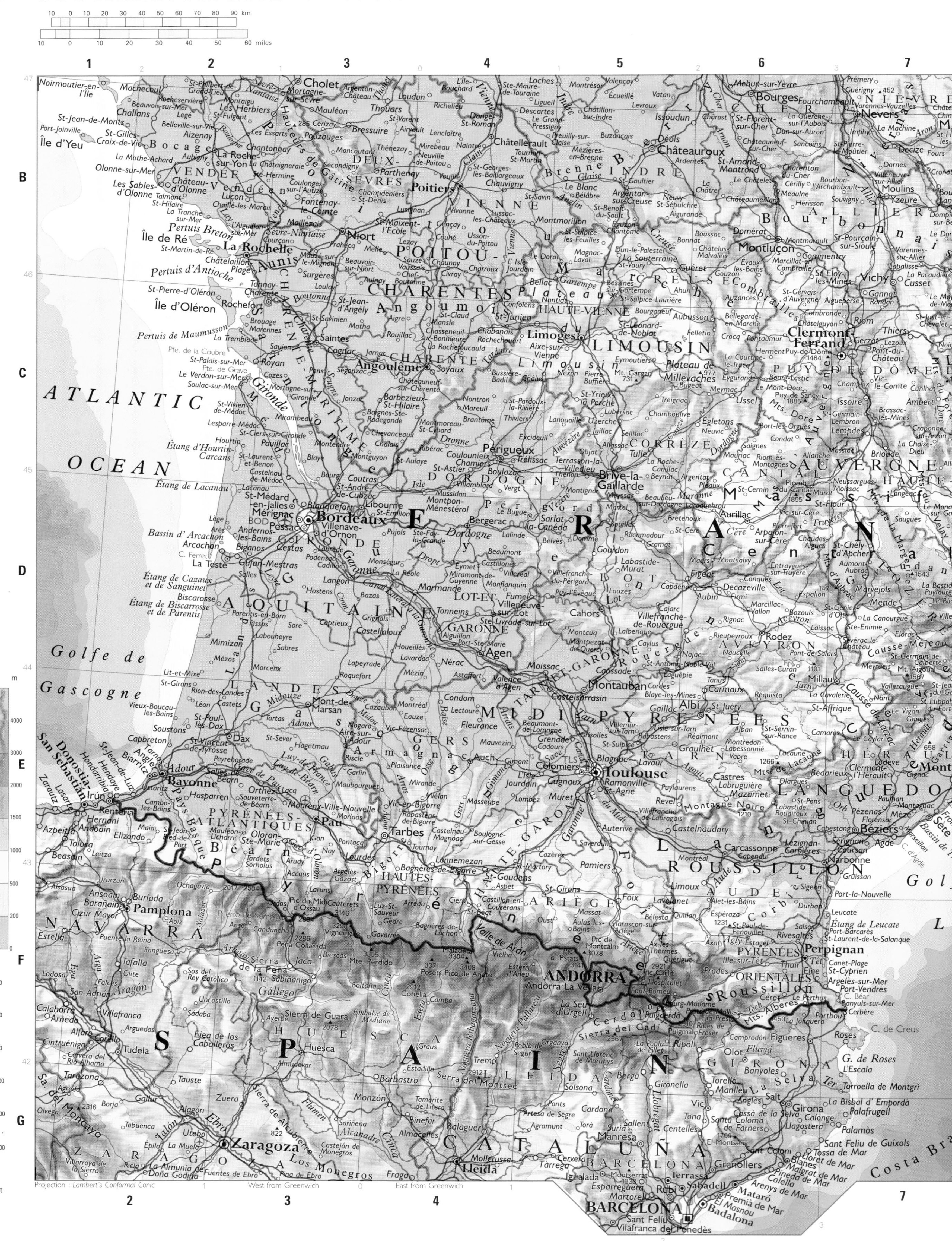

ATLANTIC OCEAN
Golfe de Gascogne
FRANCE
SPAIN
ANDORRA
Bordeaux
Toulouse
Limoges
Clermont-Ferrand
Poitiers
La Rochelle
Angoulême
Périgueux
Agen
Montauban
Pau
Tarbes
Bayonne
Perpignan
Béziers
Carcassonne
Zaragoza
Pamplona
Huesca
Lleida
BARCELONA
AQUITAINE
LIMOUSIN
AUVERGNE
LANGUEDOC
MIDI-PYRÉNÉES
POITOU-CHARENTES
CATALUÑA
NAVARRA
Projection : Lambert's Conformal Conic
West from Greenwich
East from Greenwich

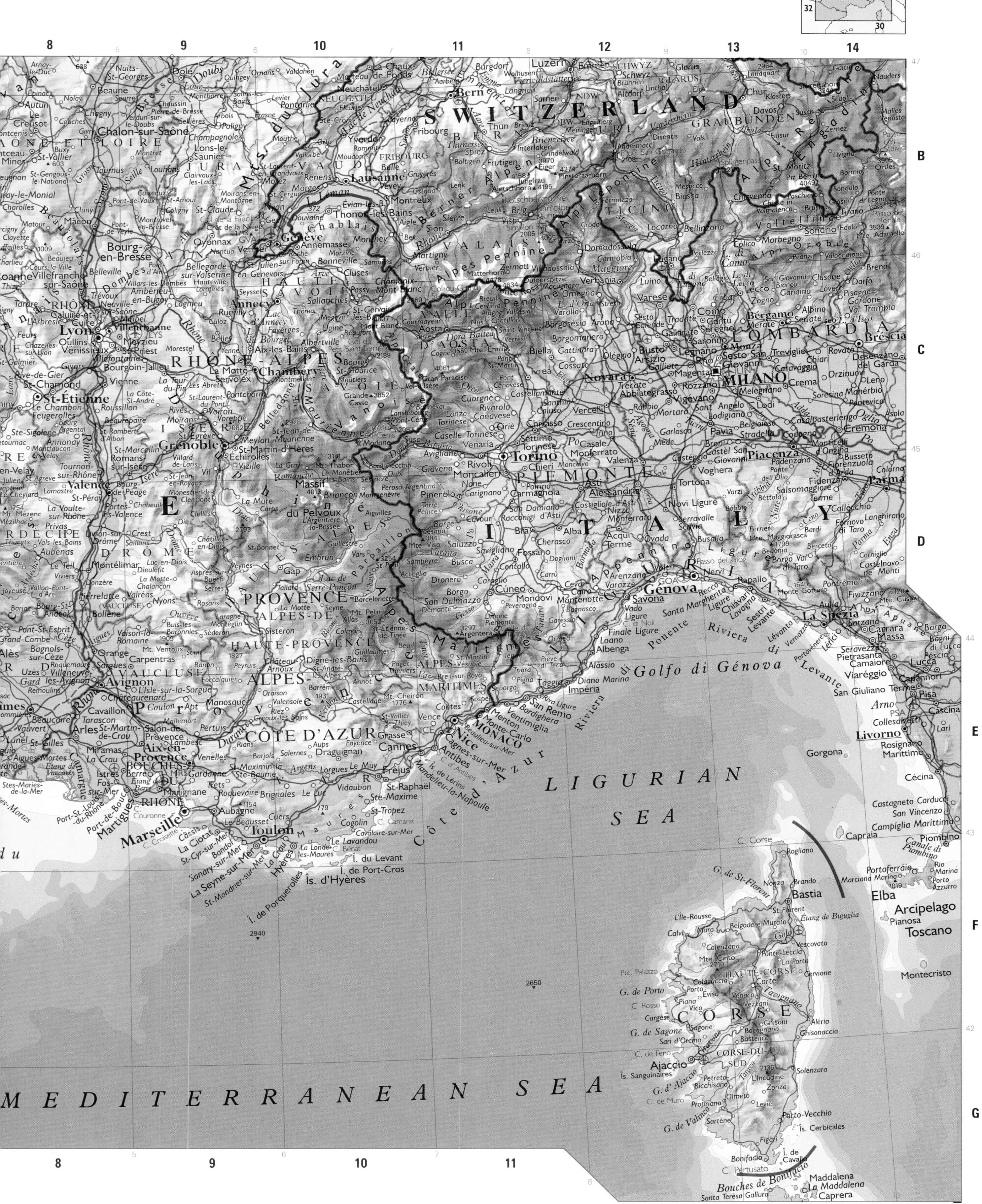

MEDITERRANEAN SEA

LIGURIAN SEA

Golfo di Génova

SWITZERLAND

ITALY

LOMBARDIA

PIEMONTE

RHÔNE-ALPES

PROVENCE

CÔTE D'AZUR

CORSE

Toscano

Arcipelago

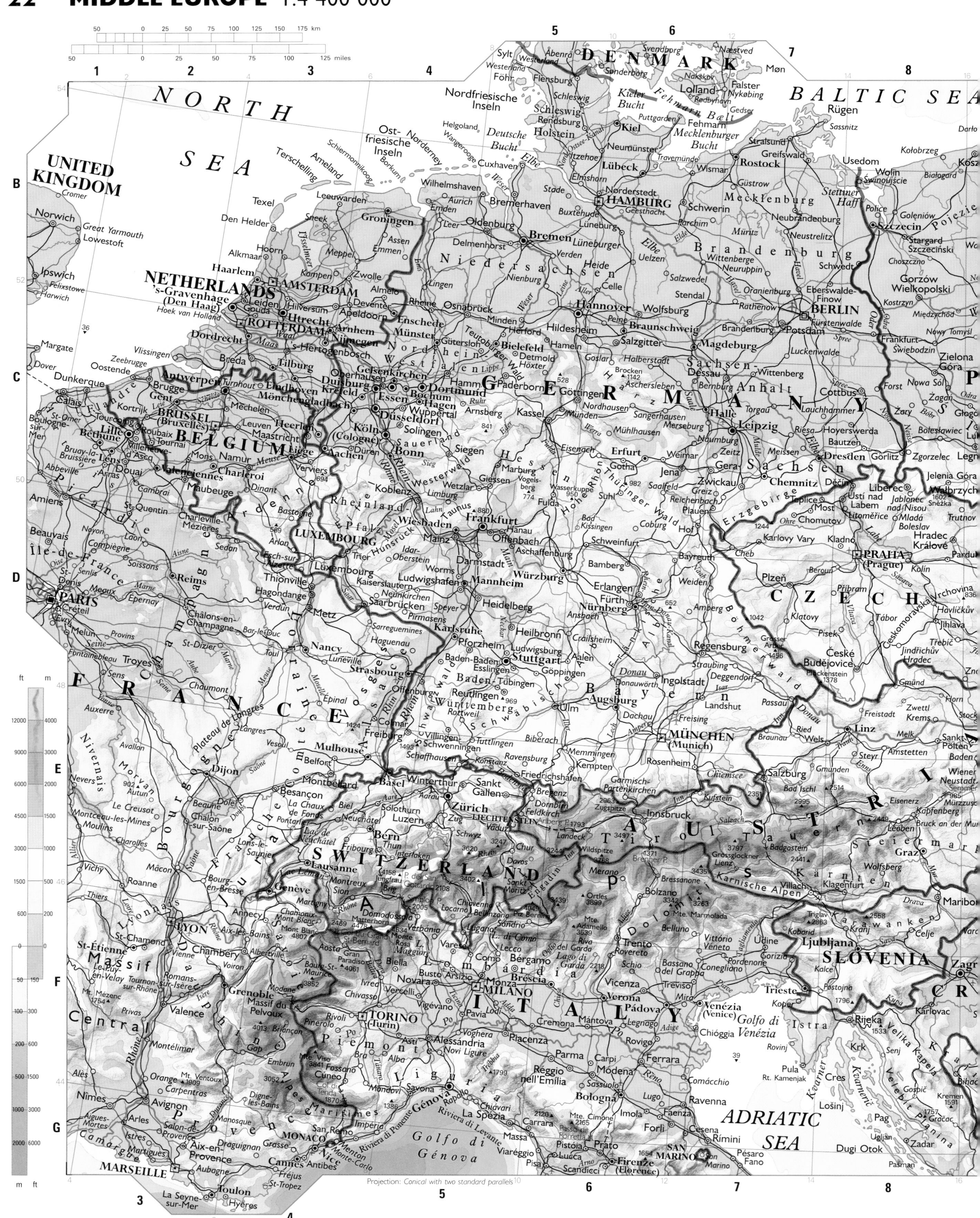

Projection: Conical with two standard parallels

9
46
16
18
48
20
40
41

9 10 11 12 13 14 15 16

Zatoka Gdańska
Baltiysk
Kaliningrad (Russia)
Gdynia
Wejherowo
Rumia
Sopot
Gdańsk
Tczew
Elbląg
Zalew Wiślany
Gvardeysk
Chernyakhovsk
Gusev
Bagrationovsk
Braniewo
Polessk
Prienai
Marijampolė
Vilnius
LITHUANIA
Varėna
Druskininkai
Ashmyany
Smarhon
Vileyka
Maladzyechna
Zhodzina
Barysaw
Krupki
Shklow
Mstsislaw
Mahilyow
Krychaw
MINSK
Cherven
Valozhyn
Lida
Hrodna
Navahrudak
Dzyarzhynsk
Stowbtsy
Nyasvizh
Hrodzyanka
Asipovichy
Babruysk
Bykhaw
Slawharad
Cherykaw
Rahachow
Zhlobin
Homyel
Dobrush
B E L A R U S
Pojezierze Mazurskie
Malbork
Kwidzyn
Olsztyn
Ostróda
Iława
Ełk
Giżycko
Suwałki
Augustów
Kętrzyn
Szczytno
Sokółka
Białystok
Grudziądz
Brodnica
Działdowo
Łomża
Starogard Gdański
Chojnice
Świecie
Chełmno
Bydgoszcz
Toruń
Rypin
Mława
Ciechanów
Ostrołęka
Ostrów Mazowiecka
Hajnówka
Bielsk Podlaski
Inowrocław
Włocławek
Płock
Pułtusk
Sokołów Podlaski
Gniezno
Września
Poznań
Legionowo
WARSZAWA (Warsaw)
Mińsk Mazowiecki
Siedlce
Biała Podlaska
Brest
Zhabinka
Kobryn
Pruzhany
Bereza
Dragichyn
Ivanava
Pinsk
Luninyets
Tsyelyakhany
Baranavichy
Slonim
Vawkavysk
Svislach
Masty
Dzyatlava
Lyakhavichy
Hantsavichy
Ivatsevichy
Klyetsk
Slutsk
Salihorsk
Glusk
Svyetlahorsk
Aktsyabrski
Rechytsa
Kalinkavichy
Vasilevichi
Mazyr
Khoyniki
Loyew
Yelsk
Davyd Haradok
Stolin
Pripet Marshes
Pruszków
Otwock
Łowicz
Żyrardów
Skierniewice
Kutno
Konin
Koło
Łęczyca
Kalisz
Łódź
Pabianice
Zduńska Wola
Sieradz
Ostrów Wielkopolski
Krotoszyn
Tomaszów Mazowiecki
Grójec
Radom
Puławy
Lublin
Łuków
Międzyrzec Podlaski
Włodawa
Chełm
Świdnik
Kraśnik
Piotrków Trybunalski
Końskie
Skarżysko-Kamienna
Starachowice
Ostrowiec-Świętokrzyski
Kielce
Radomsko
Częstochowa
Wieluń
Oleśnica
Wrocław
Oława
Opole
Kluczbork
Sandomierz
Stalowa Wola
Zamość
Tarnobrzeg
Mielec
Rzeszów
Jarosław
Przemyśl
Dębica
Tarnów
Kraków
Bochnia
Oświęcim
Katowice
Sosnowiec
Bytom
Zabrze
Gliwice
Chorzów
Tychy
Racibórz
Tarnowskie Góry
Myszków
Zawiercie
Jędrzejów
Pińczów
Nysa
Opava
Ostrava
Karviná
Havířov
Frýdek-Místek
Bielsko-Biała
Cieszyn
Żywiec
Nowy Sącz
Nowy Targ
Zakopane
Jasło
Krosno
Sanok
Dukelský Průsmyk
Vychodné Beskydy
Západné Beskydy
Carpathians
Malaryta
Kamin-Kashyrskyy
Dubrovytsya
Ovruch
Chornobyl
Olevsk
Belokorovichi
Korosten
Malyn
Kovel
Lyuboml
Staryy Chartoriysk
Kostopil
Kivertsi
Rozhyshche
Volodymyr-Volynskyy
Lutsk
Rivne
Zdolbuniv
Korets
Novohrad-Volynskyy
Radomyshl
KYYIV (Kiev)
Irpin
Oster
Kyyivske Vdskh.
Dymer
Novovolynsk
Sokal
Chervonohrad
Horokhiv
Dubno
Ostroh
Slavuta
Shepetivka
Polonne
Zhytomyr
Pershotravensk
Korostyshev
Vasylkiv
Fastiv
Berdychiv
Bila Tserkva
Radekhiv
Berestechko
Kremenets
Izyaslav
Rava-Ruska
Kamyanka-Buzka
Brody
Nesterov
Yavoriv
Mostyska
Horodok
Lviv (Lvov)
Zolochiv
Zbarazh
Starokonstyantyniv
Khmelnyk
Khmelnytskyy
Vinnytsya
U K R A I N E
Kozyatyn
Skvyra
Tarashcha
Tetiyev
Lipovets
Zhashkiv
Sambir
Drohobych
Boryslav
Truskavets
Stryy
Skole
Kalush
Khodoriv
Rogatyn
Berezhany
Ternopil
Terebovlya
Skalat
Hrymayliv
Kopychyntsi
Chortkiv
Buchach
Horodok
Podilska Vysochyna
Bar
Zhmerynka
Haysyn
Uman
Tulchyn
Buh
Hayvoron
Vapnyarka
Bershad
Balta
Bolekhiv
Ivano-Frankivsk
Horodenka
Zalishchyky
Skala-Podilska
Kamyanets-Podilskyy
Kolomyya
Snyatyn
Khotyn
Mohyliv-Podilskyy
Nadvirna
Pechenizhyn
Yaremcha
Chernivtsi
Novoselytsya
Lipcani
Ocnița
Yampil
Drochia
Soroca
Edineț
Florești
Rîbnița
Ananyiv
Kotovsk
Bălți
Făleşti
Dubăsari Vdkhr.
Dubăsari
Cornești
Orhei
Chișinău
Tiraspol
Ungheni
Tighina
Rozdilna
Nistru
Dnister
Cimișlia
Leova
Comrat
Basarabeasca
Bilhorod-Dnistrovskyy
Artsyz
Ceadâr-Lunga
Cahul
Tatarbunary
Vulcanești
Bolhrad
Izmayil
Kiliya
Vylkove
Reni
Ozero Sasyk
M O L D O V A
Bessarabia
Šumperk
Olomouc
Přerov
Zlín
Považská Bystrica
Žilina
Martin
Ružomberok
Poprad
Bardejov
Prešov
Humenné
Michalovce
Košice
Uzhhorod
Chop
Mukacheve
Berehove
Khust
Tyachiv
Vynohradiv
Volovets
Rakhiv
Yasinya
Storozhynets
Hlyboka
Dorohoi
Siret
Botoșani
Rădăuți
Suceava
Fălticeni
Pașcani
Iași
Prut
Huși
Vaslui
Bârlad
Roman
Piatra Neamț
Bacău
Onești
Tecuci
Focșani
Galați
Brăila
Tulcea
Babadag
Lacul Razelm
Sulina
Trenčín
Prievidza
Banská Bystrica
Nízke Tatry
Slovenské Rudohorie
S L O V A K R E P.
Biele Karpaty
Malé Karpaty
Trnava
Topoľčany
Zvolen
Lučenec
Nitra
Levice
Bratislava
Nové Zámky
Komárno
Sátoraljaújhely
Ózd
Miskolc
Salgótarján
Vác
Gyöngyös
Eger
Mezőkövesd
Hajdúböszörmény
Nyíregyháza
Satu Mare
Carei
Baia Mare
Sighetu Marmației
Borșa
Vatra Dornei
Pietrosul
Bistrița
Dej
Zalău
Oradea
Debrecen
Karcag
Jászberény
Hatvan
Dunakeszi
Esztergom
Győr
Tatabánya
Mosonmagyaróvár
Sopron
Pápa
Érd
BUDAPEST
Székesfehérvár
Cegléd
Szolnok
Mezőtúr
Veszprém
Szombathely
Ajka
Bakony
Balaton
Siófok
Dunaújváros
Nagykőrös
Kecskemét
Kiskunfélegyháza
Csongrád
Szentes
Békéscsaba
Gyula
Orosháza
Hódmezővásárhely
Makó
Szeged
Kiskőrös
Kiskunhalas
Kalocsa
Szekszárd
Baja
Nagykanizsa
Kaposvár
Pécs
Mohács
Zalaegerszeg
H U N G A R Y
Cluj-Napoca
Salonta
Turda
Reghin
Târgu Mureș
Mureș
Odorheiu Secuiesc
Miercurea Ciuc
Munții Bihor
Abrud
Aiud
Târnăveni
Sighișoara
Mediaș
Alba-Iulia
Brad
Arad
Sânnicolau Mare
Deva
Simeria
Hunedoara
Sibiu
Făgăraș
Brașov
Săcele
Sfântu Gheorghe
Transilvania
Timișoara
Lugoj
Caransebeș
Reșița
Vf. Peleaga
Vulcan
Petroșani
Parângul Mare
Carpații Meridionali
Moldoveanu
Vf. Omul
Câmpulung
Câmpina
Curtea de Argeș
Târgoviște
Ploiești
Buzău
Râmnicu Sărat
Râmnicu Vâlcea
Târgu-Jiu
Pitești
Slobozia
Fetești
Dunărea (Danube)
Porta Orientalis
Bela Crkva
Portile de Fier
Orșova
Drobeta-Turnu-Severin
Drăgășani
Slatina
BUCUREȘTI (Bucharest)
Călărași
Oltenița
Craiova
Roșiori-de-Vede
Alexandria
Băilești
Caracal
Turnu Măgurele
Zimnicea
Giurgiu
Ruse
Razgrad
Tutrakan
Silistra
Medgidia
Constanța
Năvodari
Mangalia
Dobrich
Balchik
Nos Kaliakra
Varna
Dobrogea
Wallachia
R O M A N I A
Calafat
Vidin
Lom
Oryakhova
B U L G A R I A
Subotica
Sombor
Senta
Kikinda
Bečej
Vojvodina
Novi Sad
Zrenjanin
Vršac
Petrovaradin
Sremska Mitrovica
Pančevo
Šabac
Zemun
BEOGRAD (Belgrade)
Smederevo
Požarevac
Negotin
Bor
Zaječar
Valjevo
Kragujevac
Jagodina
Čačak
Kraljevo
Užice
Y U G O S L A V I A
Osijek
Vukovar
Vinkovci
Slavonski Brod
Virovitica
Našice
Bosanska Gradiška
Banja Luka
Brčko
Doboj
Bijeljina
Tuzla
Zenica
Travnik
Zepče
Sarajevo
Srebrenica
Han Pijesak
Višegrad
Cincar
BOSNIA-HERZEGOVINA
Drava
Sava
Dunav
Tisza
Duna
Dunaj
Wisła (Vistula)
Bug
Narew
Pilica
Warta
Prosna
Wieprz
San
Dniester
Pripet
Nyoman
Sluch
Teterev
Uzh
Desna
Dnipro
Byarezina
Prut
Siret
Olt
Jiu
Argeș
Ialomița
Mureș
Someș
Criș
Timok
Morava
Drina
Bosna
Vrbas
Una

B C D E F G

East from Greenwich
18 20 22 24 26 28 30

9 10 11 12 13 14 15

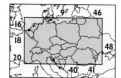

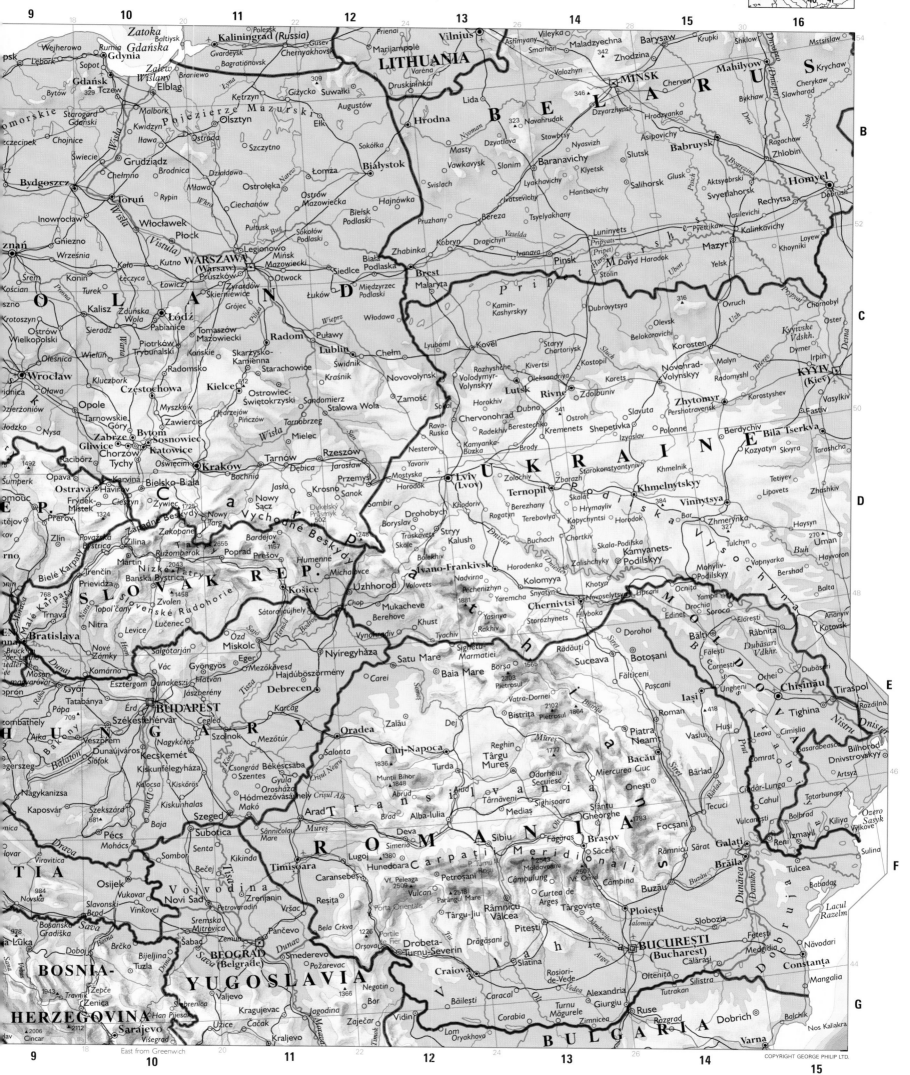

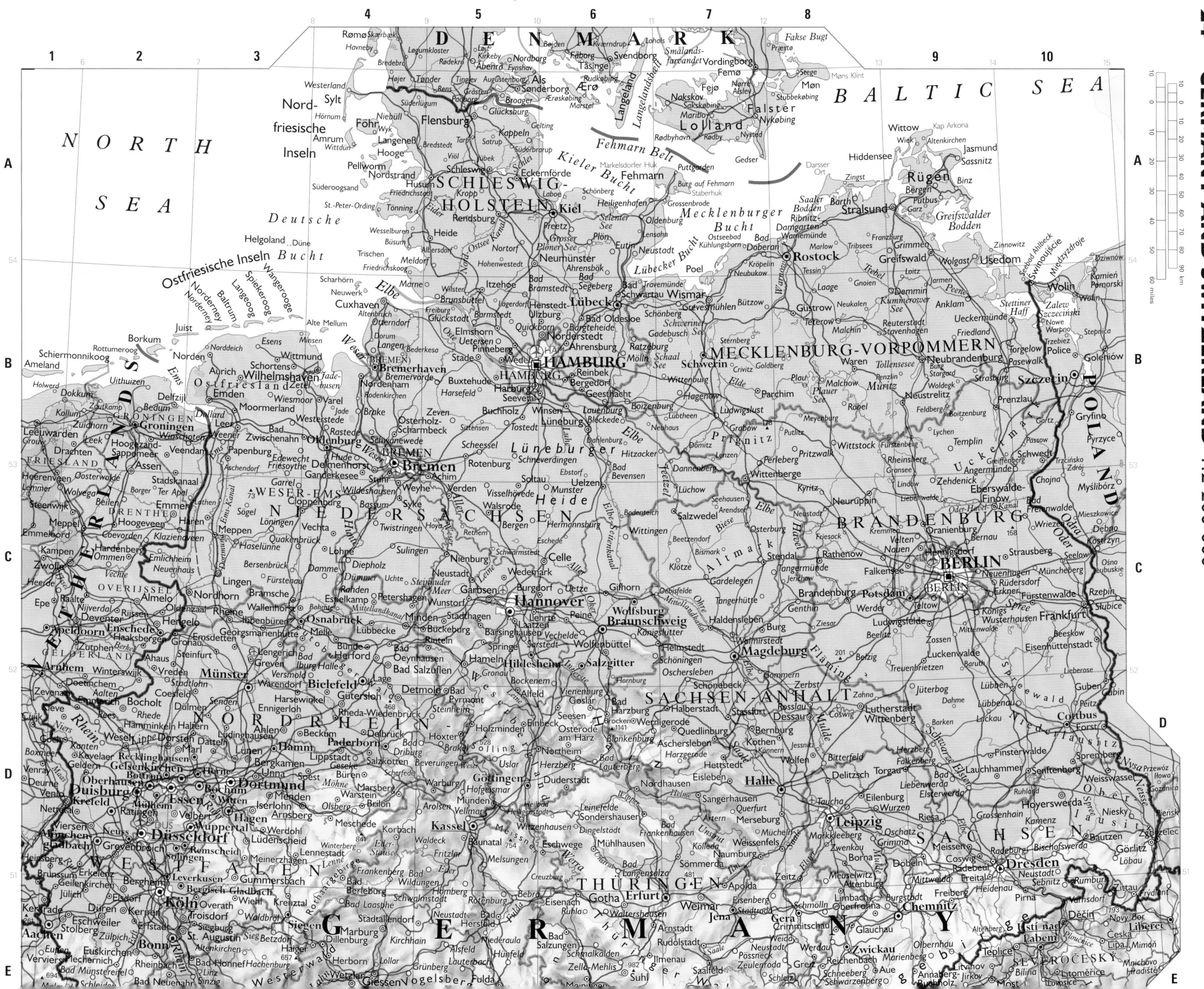
10 0 10 20 30 40 50 60 70 80 90 km
10 0 10 20 30 40 50 60 miles
NORTH SEA
BALTIC SEA
DENMARK
POLAND
NETHERLANDS
GERMANY
SCHLESWIG-HOLSTEIN
MECKLENBURG-VORPOMMERN
BRANDENBURG
BERLIN
HAMBURG
BREMEN
NIEDERSACHSEN
SACHSEN-ANHALT
SACHSEN
THÜRINGEN
NORDRHEIN-WESTFALEN
Nordfriesische Inseln
Ostfriesische Inseln
Deutsche Bucht
Mecklenburger Bucht
Kieler Bucht
Fehmarn Belt
Lübecker Bucht
Lüneburger Heide
Altmark
Rügen
Lolland
Falster
Møn
Fehmarn
Elbe
Weser
Ems
Rhein
Oder
Hannover
Bremen
Kiel
Rostock
Magdeburg
Leipzig
Dresden
Halle
Erfurt
Dortmund
Düsseldorf
Köln
Bonn
Münster
Bielefeld
Kassel
Braunschweig
Chemnitz
Groningen
Szczecin

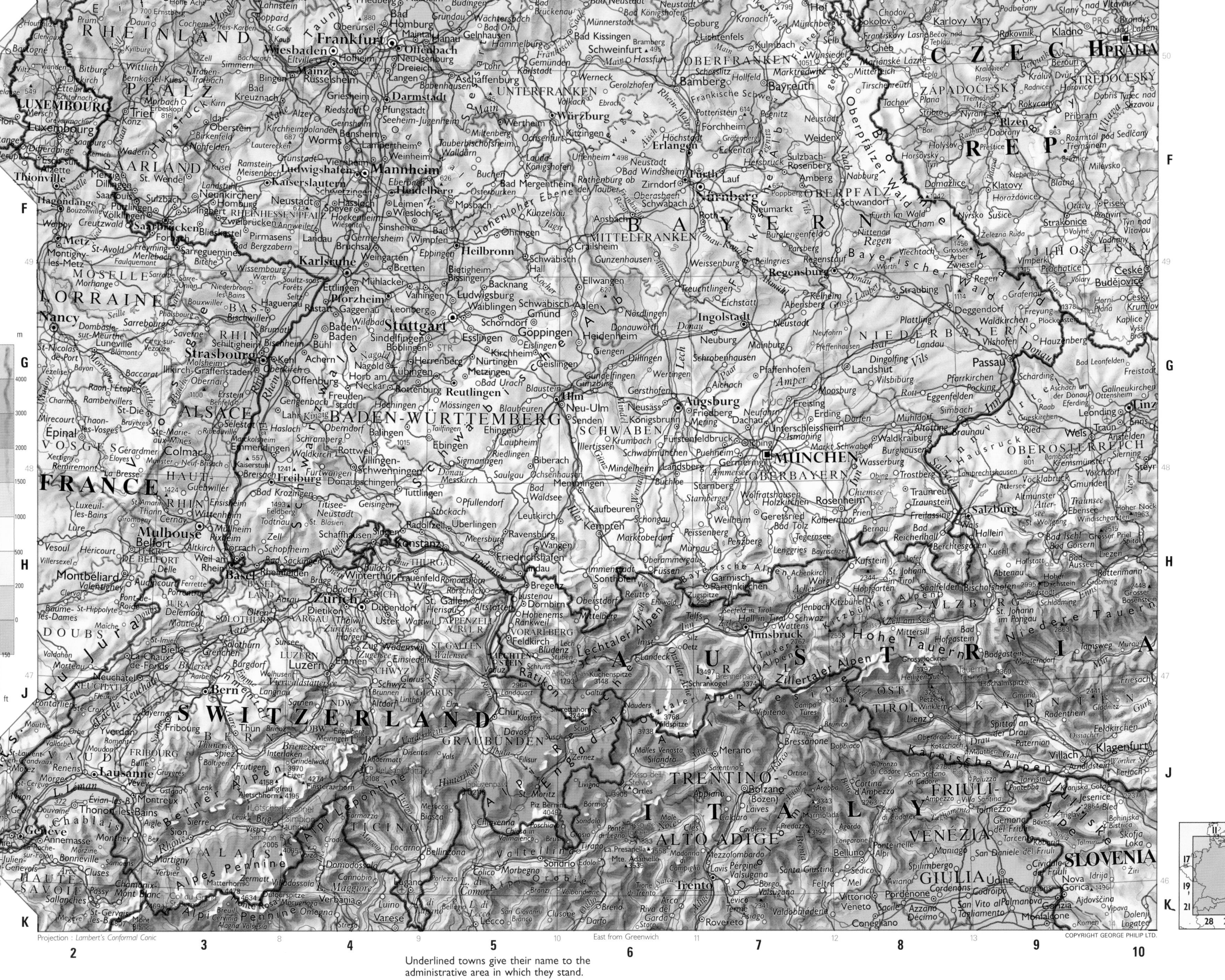

Underlined towns give their name to the administrative area in which they stand.

Projection: *Lambert's Conformal Conic*

East from Greenwich

COPYRIGHT GEORGE PHILIP LTD.

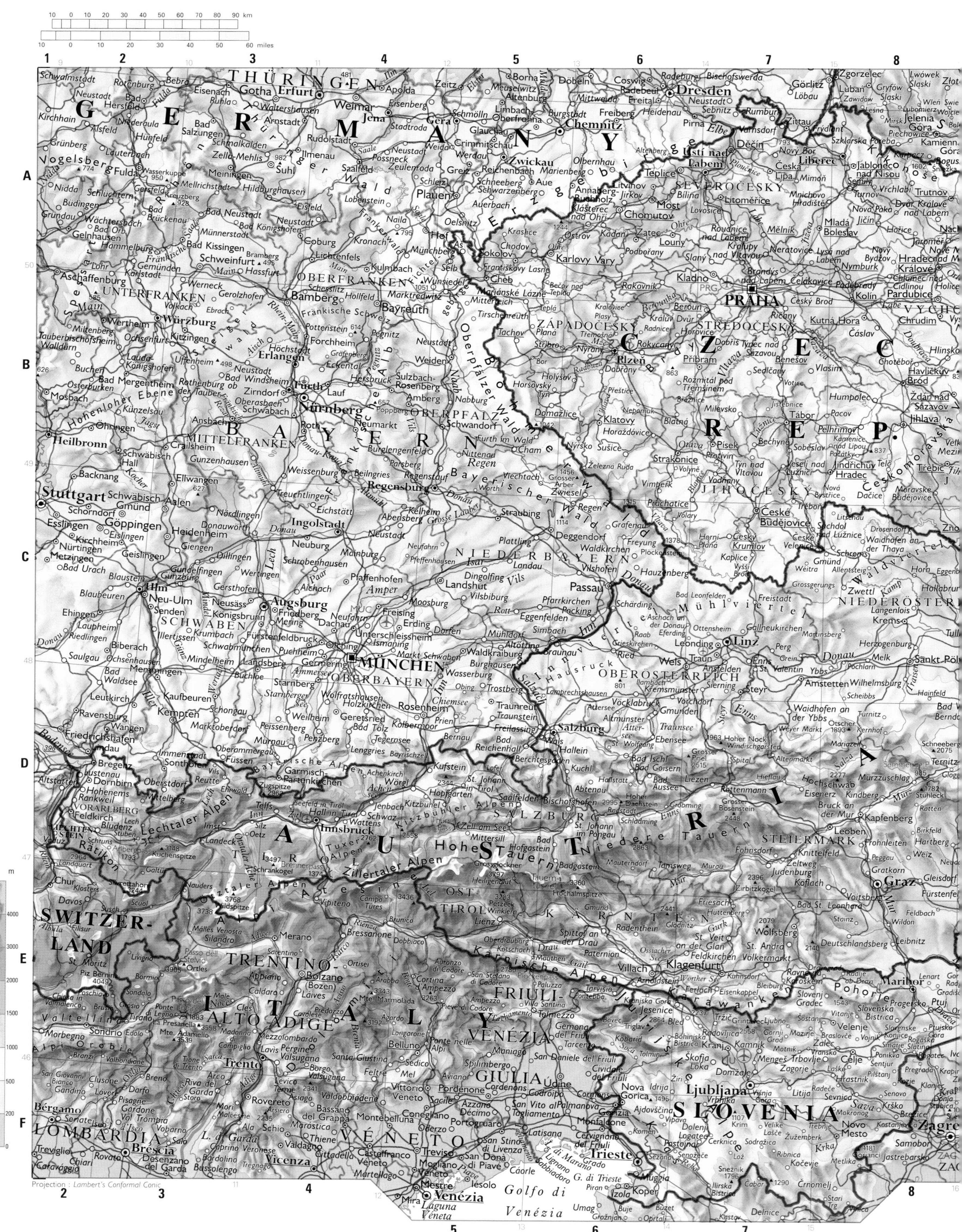
GERMANY
CZECH REP.
AUSTRIA
ITALY
SWITZERLAND
SLOVENIA
THÜRINGEN
BAYERN
OBERFRANKEN
UNTERFRANKEN
MITTELFRANKEN
OBERPFALZ
NIEDERBAYERN
SCHWABEN
OBERBAYERN
ZÁPADOČESKÝ
STŘEDOČESKÝ
SEVEROČESKÝ
JIHOČESKÝ
VÝCHOČESKÝ
NIEDERÖSTERREICH
OBERÖSTERREICH
SALZBURG
STEIERMARK
KÄRNTEN
OST-TIROL
TIROL
VORARLBERG
TRENTINO-ALTO ADIGE
FRIULI-VENEZIA GIULIA
VENETO
LOMBARDIA
PRAHA
MÜNCHEN
Dresden
Chemnitz
Erfurt
Nürnberg
Würzburg
Augsburg
Stuttgart
Regensburg
Ingolstadt
Salzburg
Linz
Innsbruck
Graz
Klagenfurt
Ljubljana
Maribor
Trieste
Venézia
Plzeň
České Budějovice
Bolzano
Trento
Vicenza
Brescia
Passau
Golfo di Venézia
Hohe Tauern
Niedere Tauern
Zillertaler Alpen
Lechtaler Alpen
Karnische Alpen
Böhmerwald
Bayerischer Wald
Oberpfälzer Wald
Erzgebirge
Thüringer Wald
Donau
Projection : Lambert's Conformal Conic

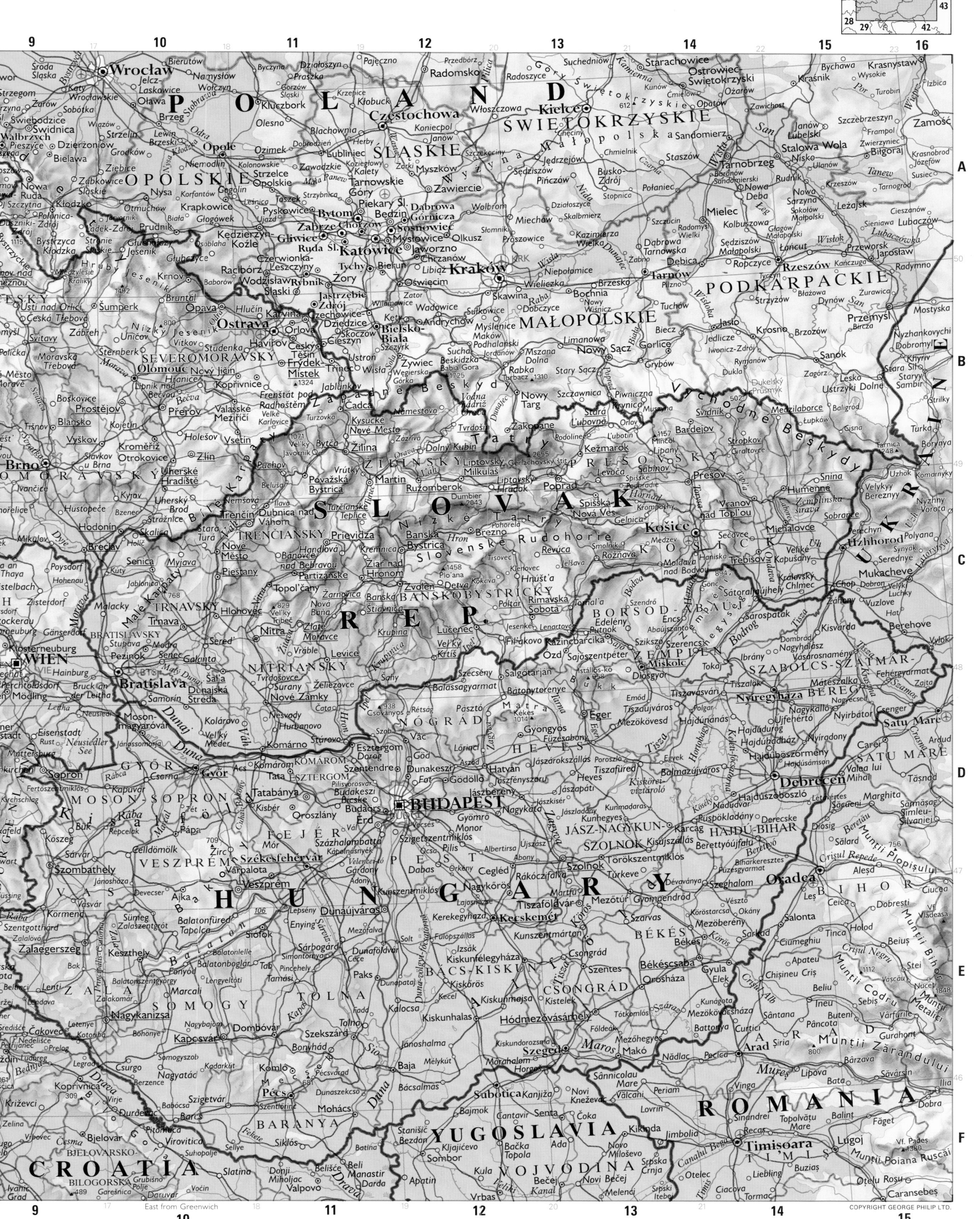

Underlined towns give their name to the
administrative area in which they stand.

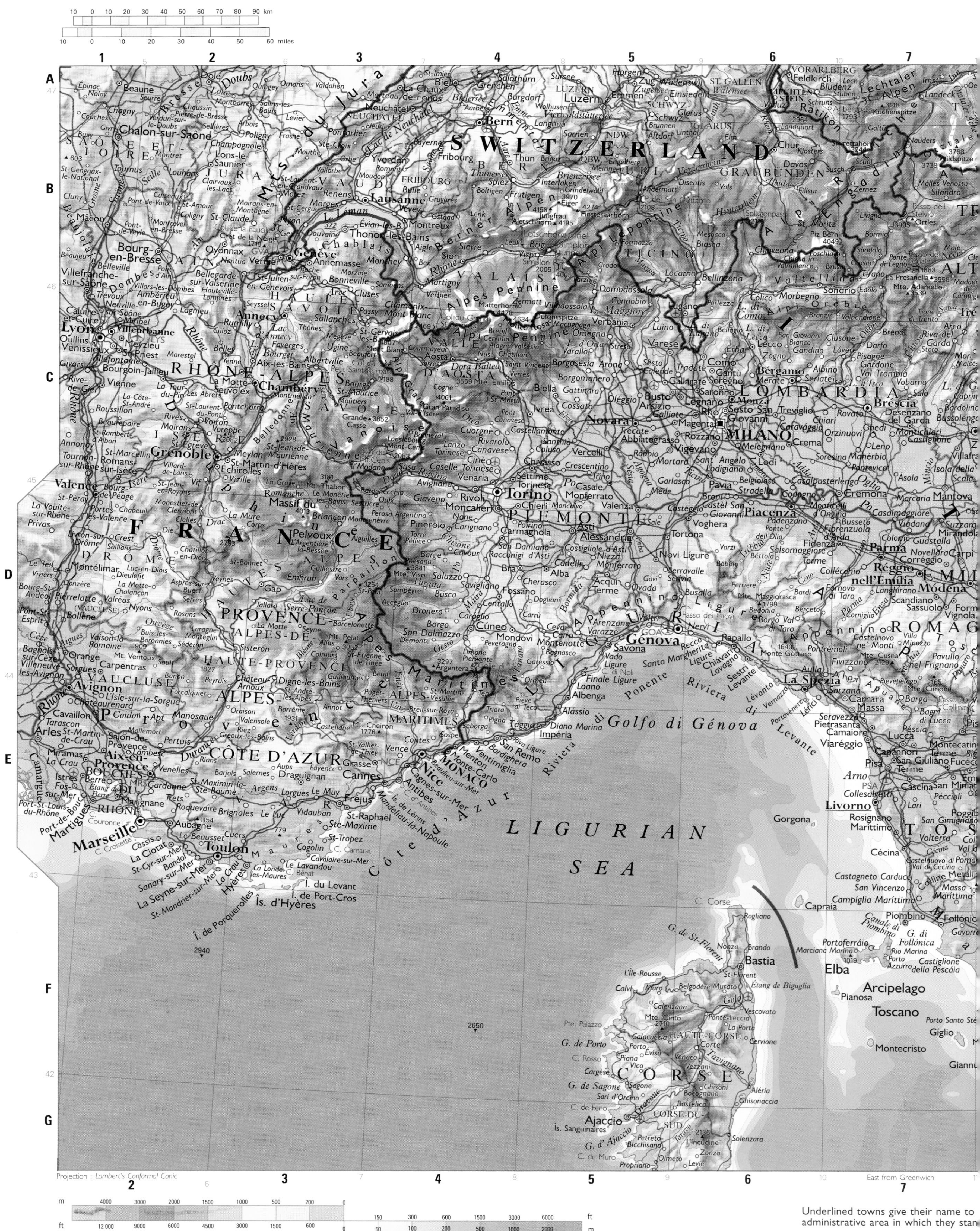

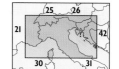

Administrative divisions in Croatia:

odsko-Posavska   4. Medimurska   8. Virovitičko-Podravska

oprivničko-Križevačka   6. Požeško-Slavonska   IO. Zagrebačka

rapinsko-Zagorska   7. Varaždinska

Inter-entity boundaries as agreed
at the 1995 Dayton Peace Agreement.

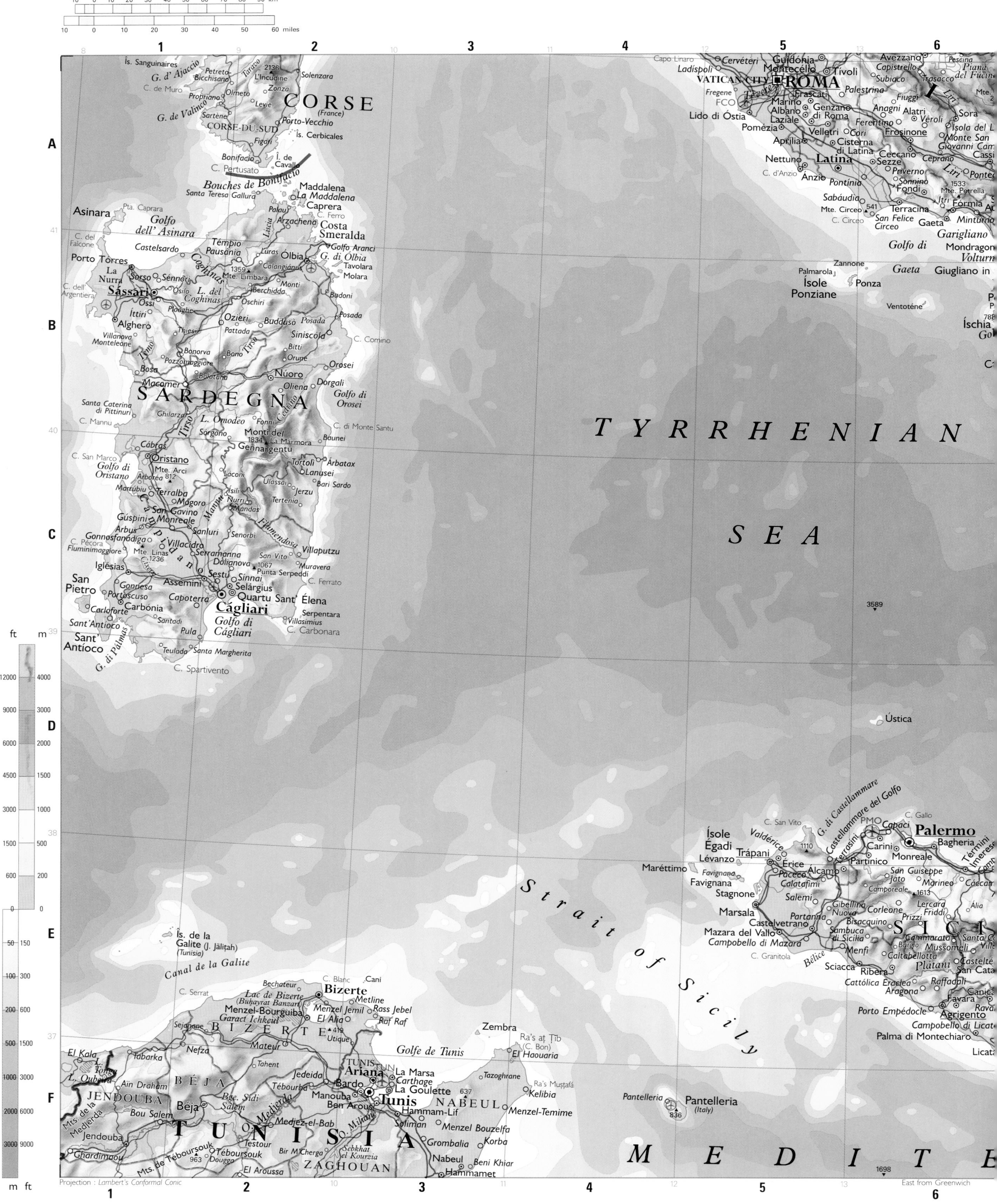

CORSE
(France)
CORSE-DU-SUD
Ajaccio
Sartène
Porto-Vecchio
Bonifacio
Bouches de Bonifacio
Maddalena
La Maddalena
Caprera
Asinara
Golfo dell' Asinara
Costa Smeralda
Porto Torres
Castelsardo
Tèmpio Pausània
Òlbia
G. di Òlbia
Tavolara
Molara
Sássari
Alghero
Ozieri
Siniscola
C. Comino
Macomer
Bosa
SARDEGNA
Núoro
Oliena
Dorgali
Golfo di Orosei
Orosei
L. Omodeo
Monti del Gennargentu
La Màrmora
Oristano
Golfo di Oristano
Arbatax
Tortolì
Lanusei
Bari Sardo
Terralba
San Gavino Monreale
Sanluri
Guspini
Villacidro
Iglésias
Villaputzu
Muravera
San Pietro
Carloforte
Carbónia
Assemini
Sestu
Selàrgius
Quartu Sant' Élena
Cágliari
Golfo di Cágliari
Sant'Antíoco
G. di Palmas
Teulada
C. Spartivento
C. Carbonara
Villasimius
Serpentara
Cerveteri
Ladispoli
Guidonia-Montecelio
Tívoli
VATICAN CITY
ROMA
Frascati
Fiumicino
Lido di Óstia
Pomezia
Marino
Albano Laziale
Genzano di Roma
Velletri
Aprilia
Cisterna di Latina
Latina
Nettuno
Ánzio
C. d'Anzio
Pontínia
Sabáudia
Mte. Circeo
C. Circeo
San Felice Circeo
Terracina
Fondi
Formia
Gaeta
Golfo di Gaeta
Frosinone
Anagni
Avezzano
Sora
Palmarola
Zannone
Ísole Ponziane
Ponza
Ventotène
Íschia
T Y R R H E N I A N
S E A
3589
Ústica
Ísole Égadi
Lévanzo
Marèttimo
Favignana
Trápani
Érice
Paceco
Alcamo
Castellammare del Golfo
G. di Castellammare
C. San Vito
C. Gallo
Capaci
Palermo
Bagheria
Carini
Monreale
Partinico
Marsala
Stagnone
Salemi
Castelvetrano
Mazara del Vallo
Campobello di Mazara
C. Granitola
Sciacca
Ribera
Menfi
Porto Empédocle
Agrigento
Palma di Montechiaro
Licata
Strait of Sicily
Pantelleria
(Italy)
836
Ís. de la Galite (J. Jāliṭah) (Tunisia)
Canal de la Galite
C. Serrat
C. Blanc
Cani
Bizerte
Lac de Bizerte (Buḩayrat Banzart)
Menzel-Bourguiba
Menzel Jemil
Metline
Rass Jebel
Raf Raf
El Alia
Utique
BIZERTE
Zembra
Ra's aṭ Ṭib (C. Bon)
El Haouaria
Golfe de Tunis
El Kala
Tabarka
Nefza
Mateur
Ariana
La Marsa
Carthage
La Goulette
Bardo
Tunis
Manouba
Ben Arous
Hammam-Lif
Soliman
NABEUL
Kelibia
Menzel-Temime
Menzel Bouzelfa
Korba
Grombalia
Nabeul
Beni Khiar
Hammamet
JENDOUBA
BÉJA
Béja
Jendouba
Ghardimaou
Medjez-el-Bab
TUNISIA
Testour
Téboursouk
El Aroussa
ZAGHOUAN
Mts. de Teboursouk
M E D I T E
1698
Projection : Lambert's Conformal Conic
East from Greenwich

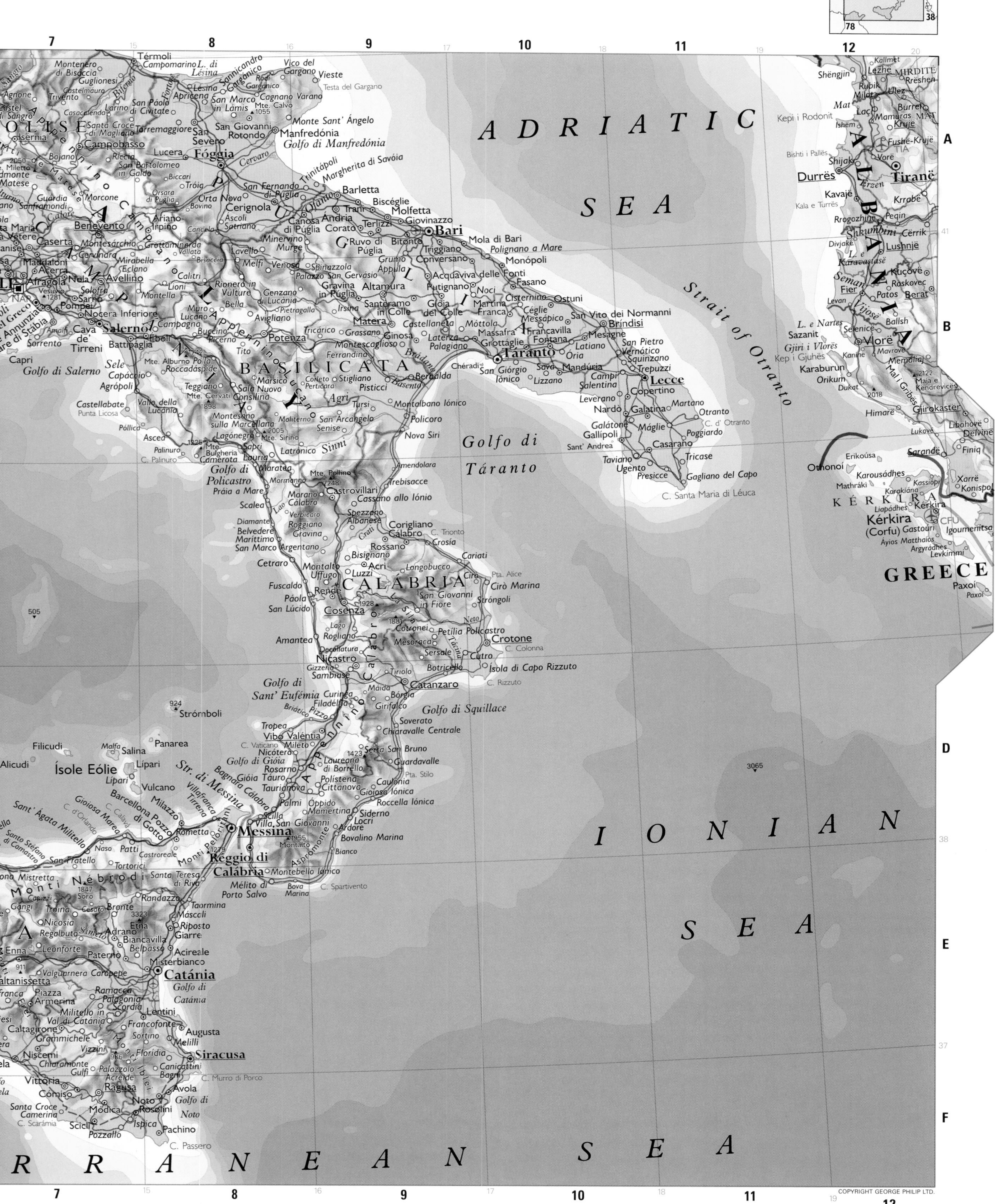

ADRIATIC

SEA

ALBANIA

GREECE

Strait of Otranto

Golfo di
Táranto

IONIAN

SEA

RRANEAN SEA

BASILICATA

CALÀBRIA

KÉRKIRA

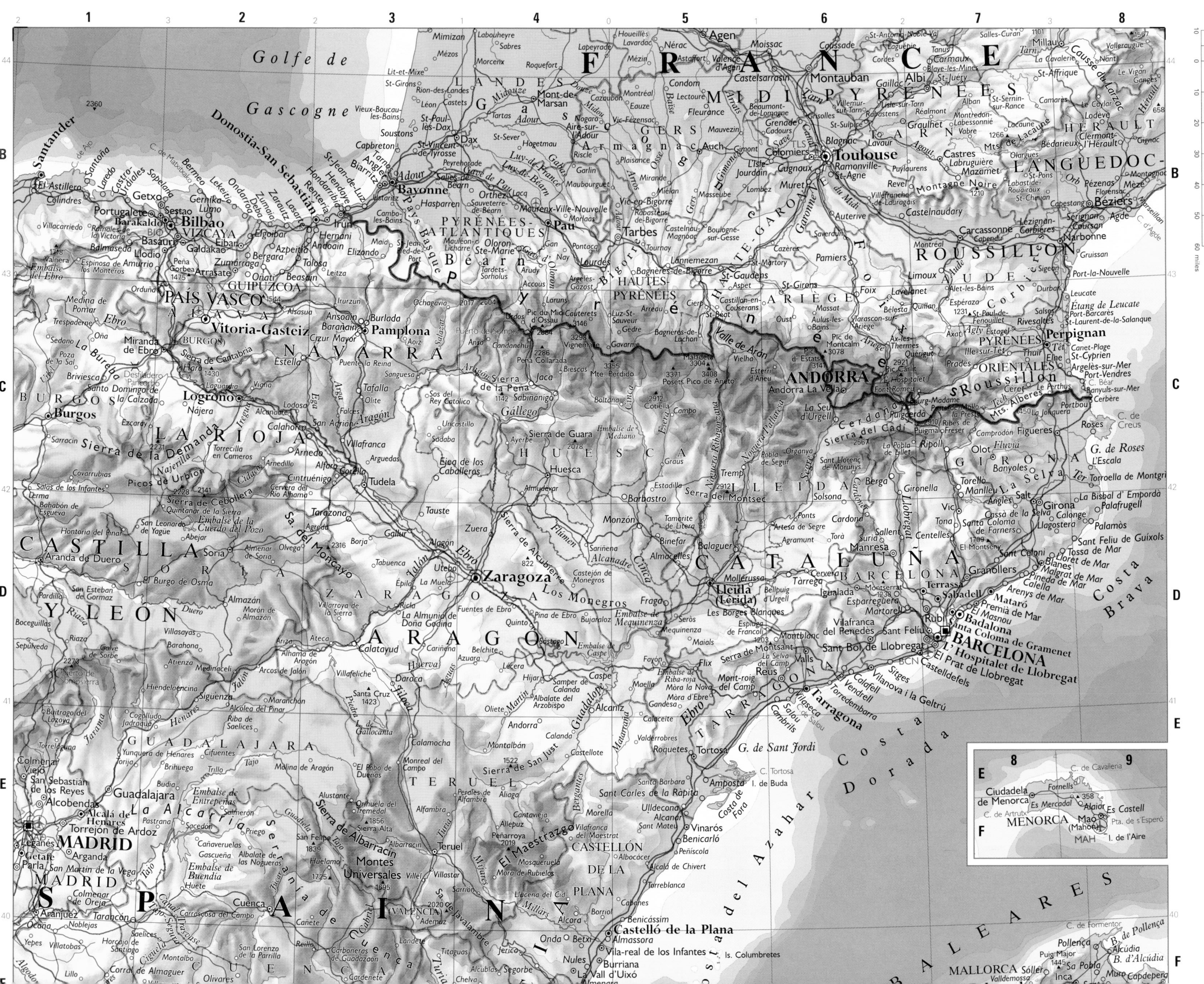

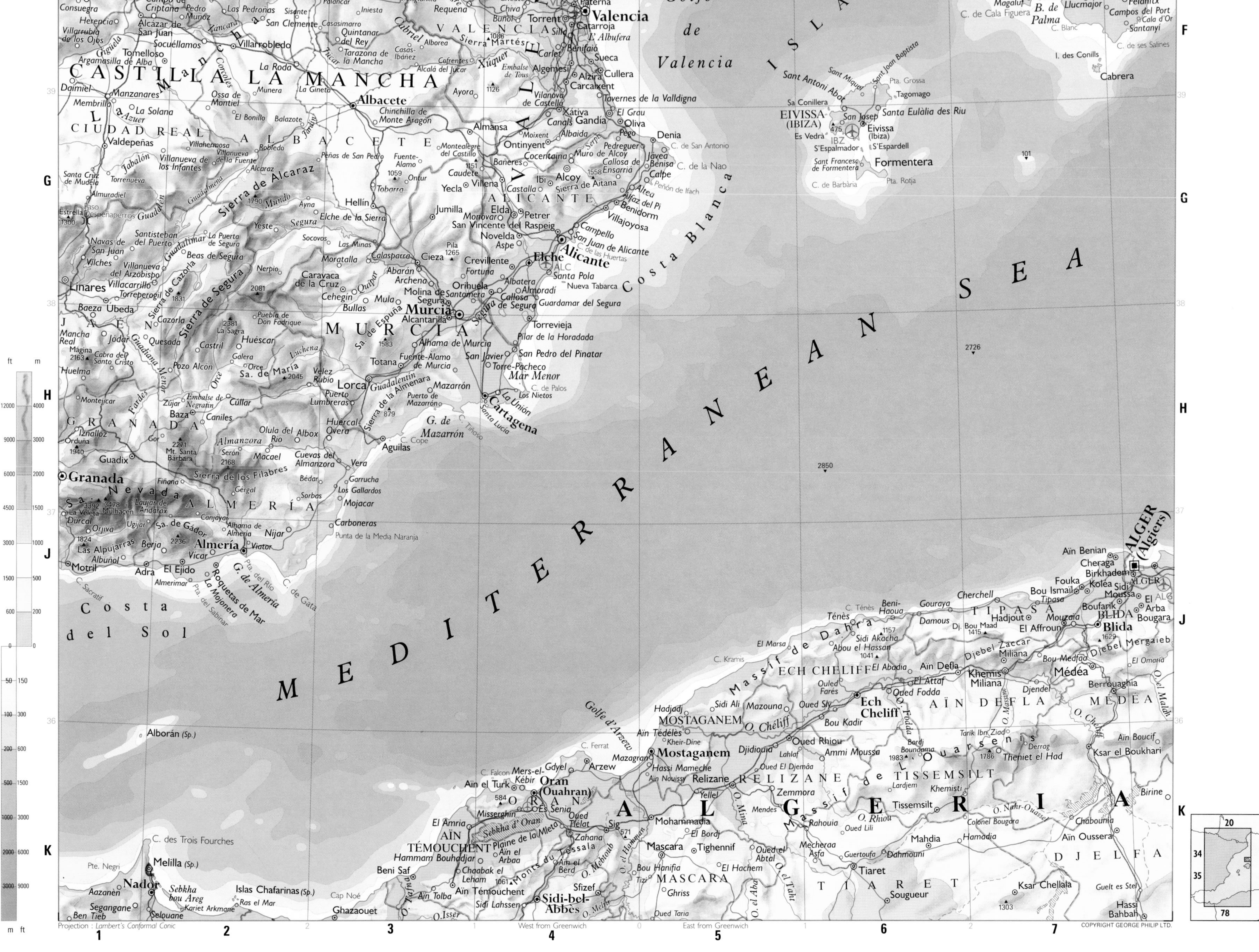

MEDITERRANEAN SEA
Golfo de Valencia
ISLAS
CASTILLA LA MANCHA
CIUDAD REAL
ALBACETE
VALENCIA
ALICANTE
MURCIA
GRANADA
ALMERÍA
JAÉN
Costa Blanca
Costa del Sol
Valencia
Albacete
Alicante
Elche
Murcia
Cartagena
Lorca
Granada
Almería
Motril
Adra
Aguilas
Mar Menor
G. de Mazarrón
G. de Almería
Sierra de Segura
Sierra de Alcaraz
Sa. Nevada
Sierra de los Filabres
EIVISSA (IBIZA)
Eivissa (Ibiza)
Formentera
Cabrera
Palma
B. de Palma
Alborán (Sp.)
Melilla (Sp.)
Nador
Islas Chafarinas (Sp.)
C. des Trois Fourches
ALGER (Algiers)
Blida
Médéa
Ech Cheliff
Mostaganem
Oran (Ouahran)
Sidi-bel-Abbès
Mascara
Relizane
Tiaret
Ghazaouet
Golfe d'Arzew
A L G E R I A
TIPASA
BLIDA
MÉDÉA
AÏN DEFLA
ECH CHELIFF
MOSTAGANEM
RELIZANE
TISSEMSILT
ORAN
AÏN TÉMOUCHENT
MASCARA
TIARET
DJELFA
Ouarsenis
Massif de Dahra
Projection : Lambert's Conformal Conic
West from Greenwich
East from Greenwich
COPYRIGHT GEORGE PHILIP LTD.

WESTERN SPAIN AND PORTUGAL 1:2 200 000

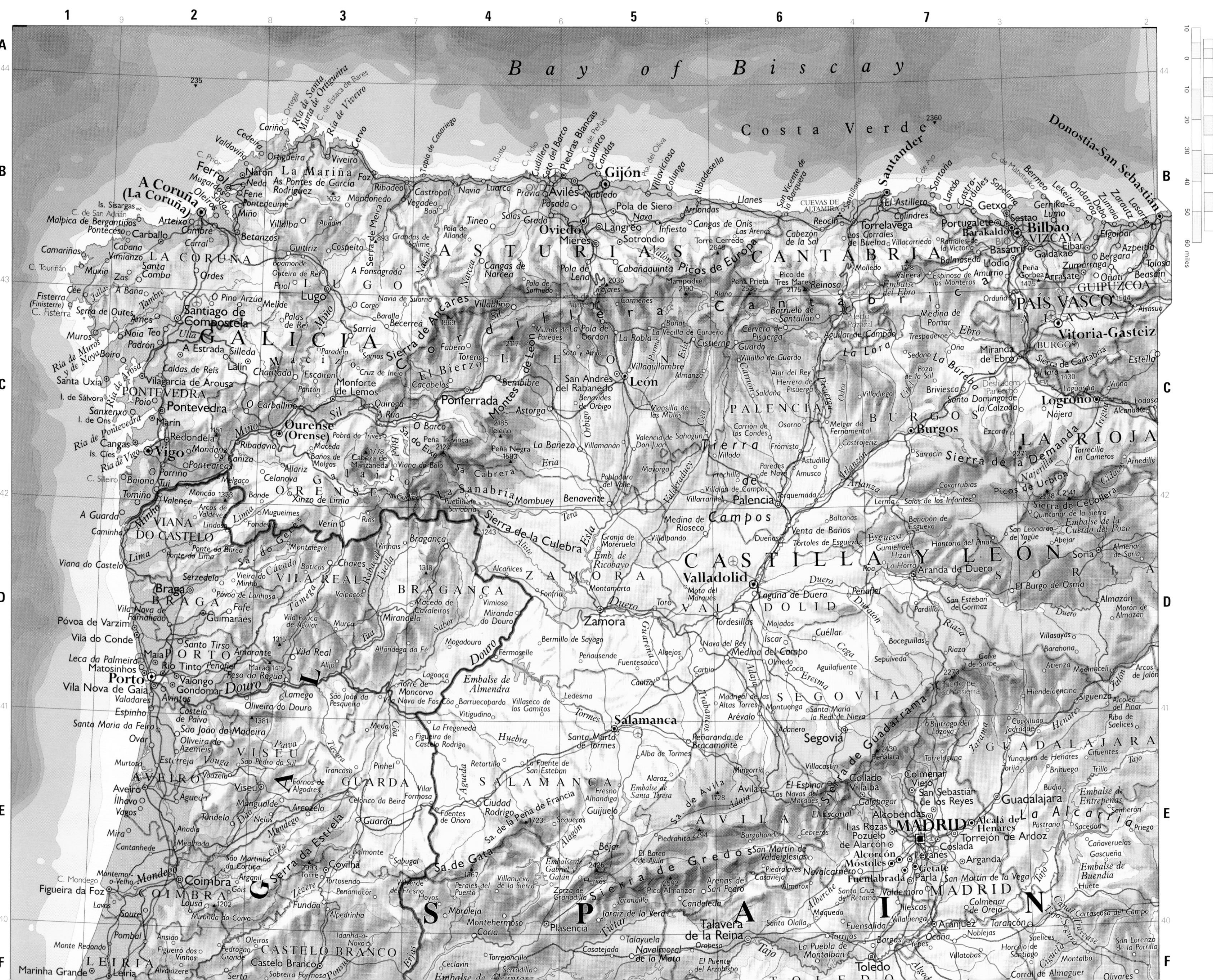

10 0 10 20 30 40 50 60 70 80 90 km
10 0 10 20 30 40 50 60 miles
Bay of Biscay
Costa Verde
Donostia-San Sebastián
Santander
Gijón
Oviedo
Avilés
A Coruña (La Coruña)
Ferrol
Santiago de Compostela
Lugo
Pontevedra
Vigo
Ourense (Orense)
Ponferrada
León
Burgos
Bilbao
Vitoria-Gasteiz
Logroño
Palencia
Valladolid
Zamora
Salamanca
Segovia
Ávila
Soria
Guadalajara
MADRID
Toledo
Talavera de la Reina
Plasencia
Braga
Porto
Vila Nova de Gaia
Coimbra
Aveiro
Viseu
Guarda
Bragança
Vila Real
Castelo Branco
Figueira da Foz
Marinha Grande
GALICIA
ASTURIAS
CANTABRIA
PAÍS VASCO
LA RIOJA
CASTILLA Y LEÓN
MADRID
Cordillera Cantábrica
Picos de Europa
Sierra de Guadarrama
Sierra de Gredos
Serra da Estrela
Montes de León
Sierra de la Culebra
Sierra de la Demanda
Picos de Urbión
Campos
Tierra de Campos
Douro
Duero
Ebro
Tajo
Miño
Sil
Esla
Pisuerga
Tormes
Eresma
Adaja
Côa
Tâmega
Vouga
Mondego
Zêzere
Alagón
Tiétar
Alberche
Henares
Jarama
Jalón
VIANA DO CASTELO
BRAGA
PORTO
AVEIRO
VISEU
GUARDA
COIMBRA
LEIRIA
CASTELO BRANCO
LA CORUÑA
LUGO
ORENSE
PONTEVEDRA
LEÓN
PALENCIA
BURGOS
SORIA
ZAMORA
VALLADOLID
SEGOVIA
SALAMANCA
ÁVILA
GUADALAJARA
CÁCERES
S P A I N
P O R T U G A L

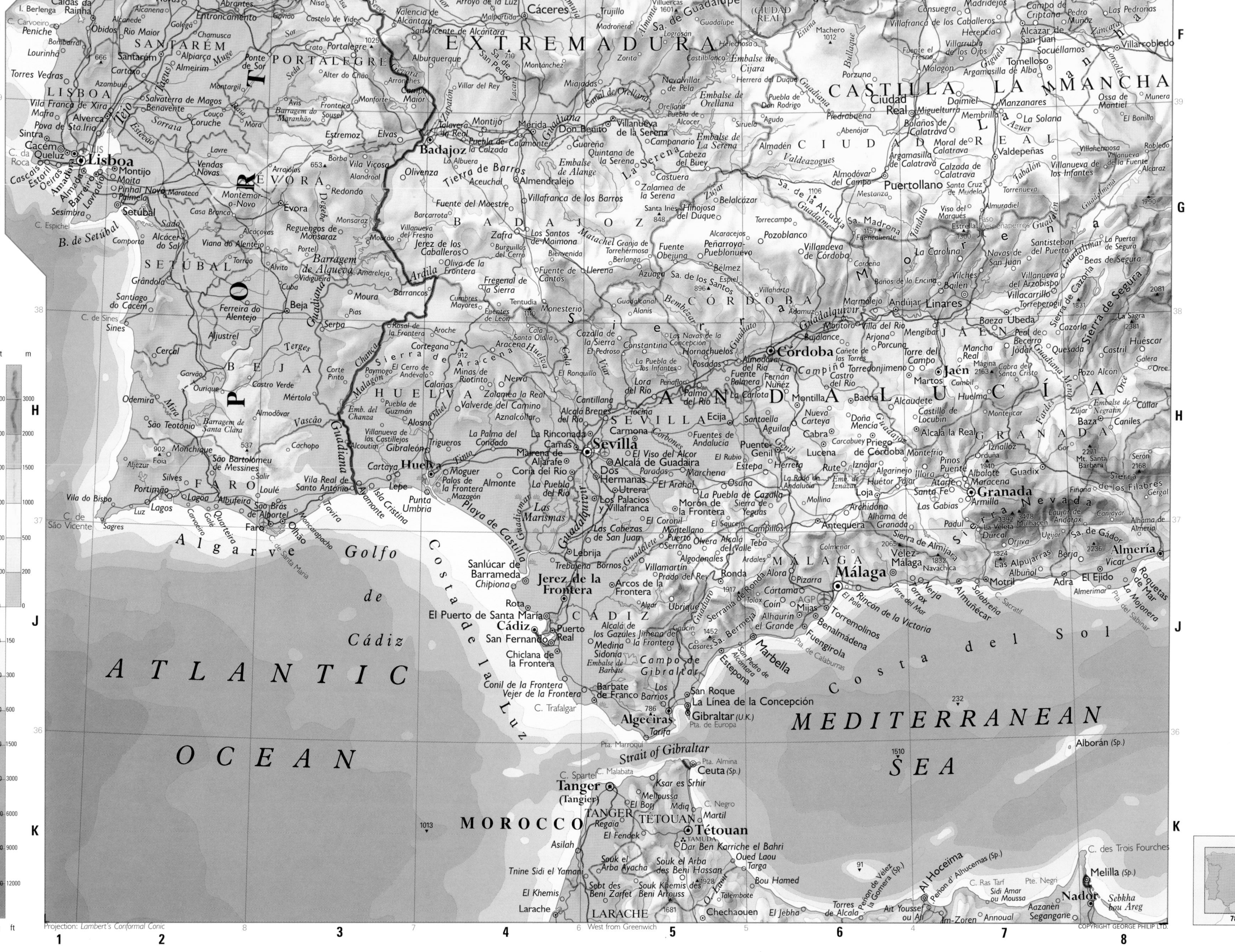
ATLANTIC OCEAN
MEDITERRANEAN SEA
Golfo de Cádiz
Costa de la Luz
Costa del Sol
Strait of Gibraltar
MOROCCO
PORTUGAL
EXTREMADURA
CASTILLA-LA MANCHA
ANDALUCÍA
Sierra Morena
Sierra Nevada
LISBOA
SANTARÉM
PORTALEGRE
ÉVORA
SETÚBAL
BEJA
FARO
BADAJOZ
CIUDAD REAL
CÓRDOBA
JAÉN
SEVILLA
HUELVA
CÁDIZ
MÁLAGA
GRANADA
TANGER
TETOUAN
LARACHE
Lisboa
Setúbal
Évora
Beja
Faro
Badajoz
Cáceres
Mérida
Ciudad Real
Puertollano
Córdoba
Jaén
Linares
Granada
Sevilla
Huelva
Cádiz
Jerez de la Frontera
Algeciras
Gibraltar (U.K.)
Málaga
Marbella
Almería
Motril
Ceuta (Sp.)
Melilla (Sp.)
Tanger (Tangier)
Tétouan
Larache
Nador
Alborán (Sp.)
Guadiana
Guadalquivir
Algarve
Playa de Castilla
Projection: Lambert's Conformal Conic
West from Greenwich
COPYRIGHT GEORGE PHILIP LTD.
ft
m
9000
6000
4500
3000
1500
600
3000
2000
1500
1000
500
200
0
50
100
200
500
1000
2000
3000
4000
150
300
600
1500
3000
6000
9000
12000

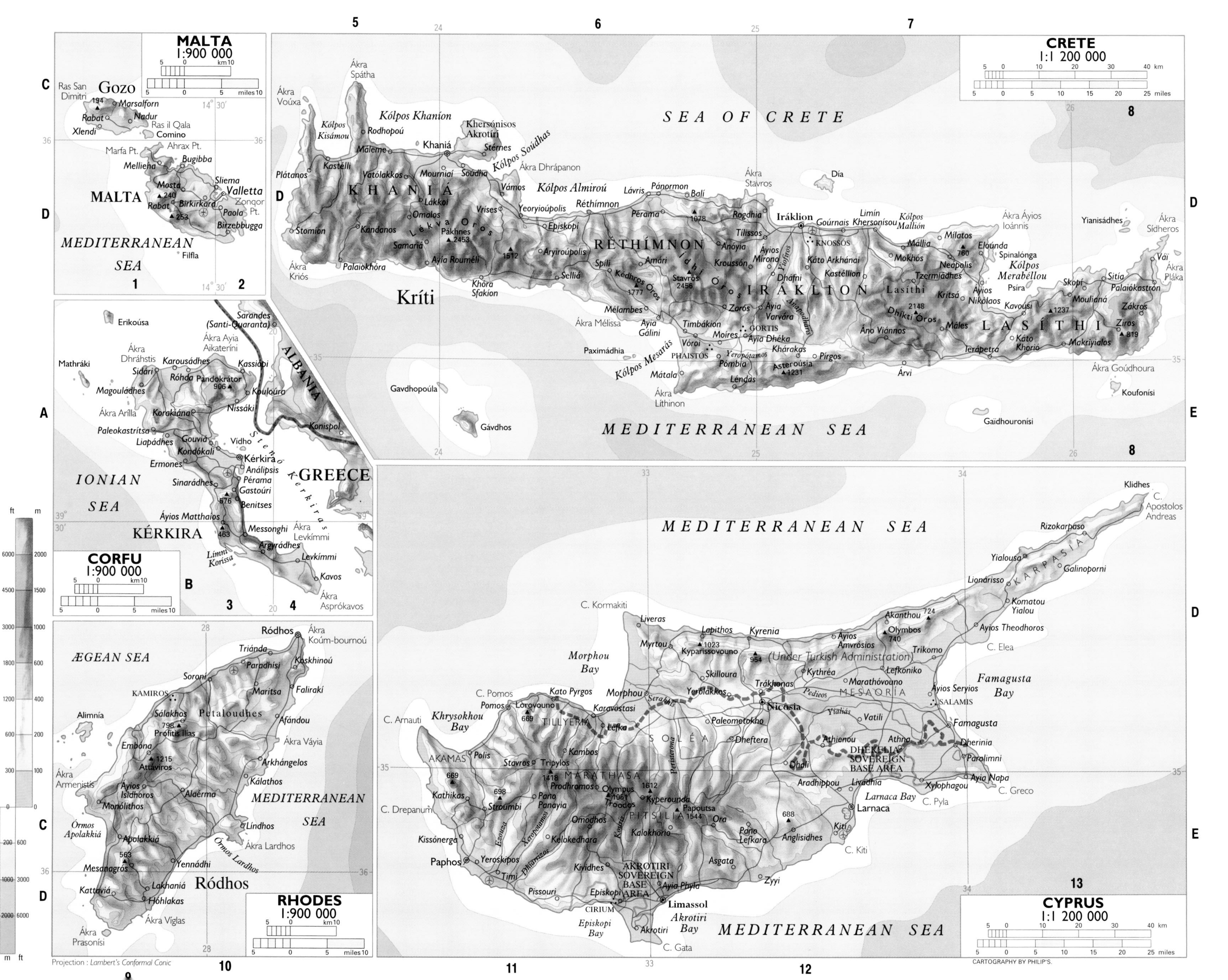

CRETE
1:1 200 000

MALTA
1:900 000

CORFU
1:900 000

RHODES
1:900 000

CYPRUS
1:1 200 000

CARTOGRAPHY BY PHILIP'S

Projection: Lambert's Conformal Conic

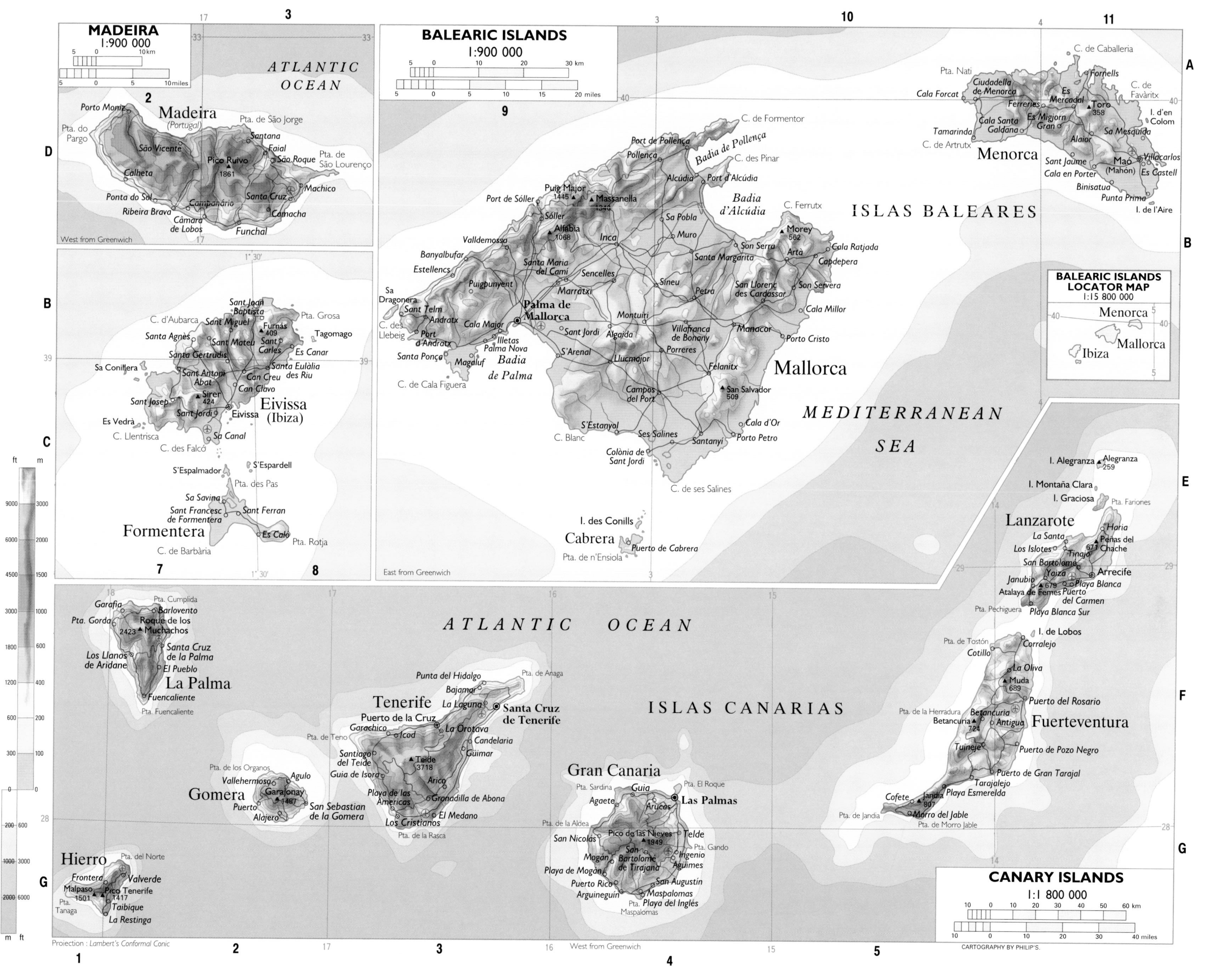
MADEIRA
1:900 000
ATLANTIC OCEAN
Madeira (Portugal)
Funchal
West from Greenwich
BALEARIC ISLANDS
1:900 000
ISLAS BALEARES
Mallorca
Palma de Mallorca
Badia de Palma
Badia d'Alcúdia
Badia de Pollença
Menorca
Cabrera
Eivissa (Ibiza)
Formentera
BALEARIC ISLANDS LOCATOR MAP
1:15 800 000
Menorca
Mallorca
Ibiza
MEDITERRANEAN SEA
East from Greenwich
ATLANTIC OCEAN
ISLAS CANARIAS
Lanzarote
Fuerteventura
Gran Canaria
Las Palmas
Tenerife
Santa Cruz de Tenerife
Gomera
La Palma
Hierro
CANARY ISLANDS
1:1 800 000
Projection : Lambert's Conformal Conic
West from Greenwich
CARTOGRAPHY BY PHILIP'S

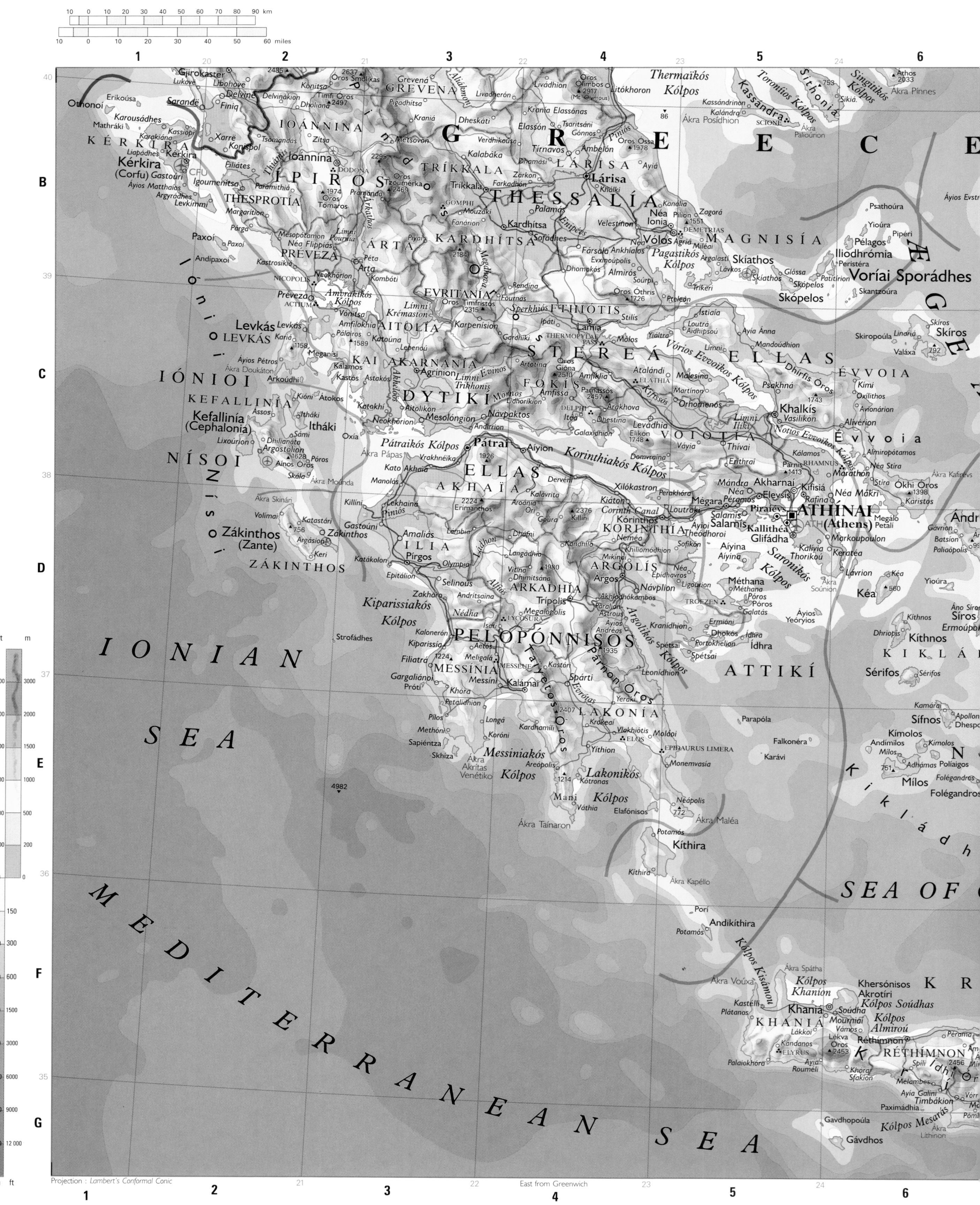

IONIAN SEA
MEDITERRANEAN SEA
SEA OF
GREECE
PELOPÓNNISOS
ATHÍNAI (Athens)
Pátrai
Lárisa
Vólos
Kérkira (Corfu)
Kefallinía (Cephalonia)
Zákinthos (Zante)
Ionioi Nísoi
Vóriai Sporádhes
Kíthira
Khaniá
Projection : Lambert's Conformal Conic
East from Greenwich

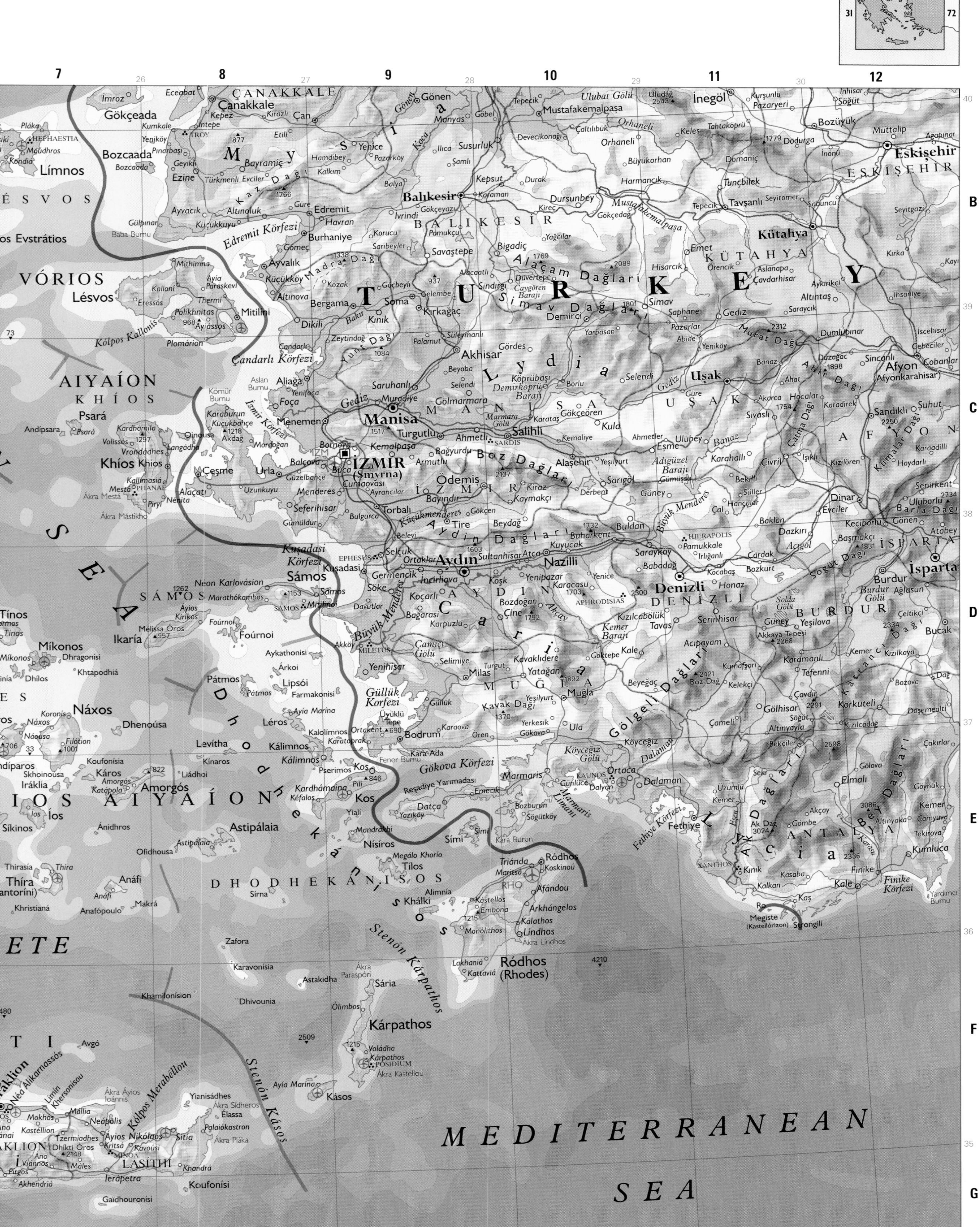
TURKEY
MEDITERRANEAN SEA
İzmir (Smyrna)
Manisa
Aydın
Denizli
Kütahya
Eskişehir
Balıkesir
Uşak
Afyon (Afyonkarahisar)
Isparta
Burdur
Muğla
Çanakkale
Rodhos (Rhodes)
Kárpathos
Sámos
Khíos
Lésvos
Límnos
Náxos
Kos
Bodrum
Fethiye
Nazilli
Salihli
Akhisar
Bergama
Edremit
Simav
Gediz
Lycia
Lydia
Caria
Mysia
DHODHEKÁNISOS
AIYAÍON
Stenón Kárpathos
Stenón Kásos
Gökova Körfezi
Edremit Körfezi
Kuşadası Körfezi
Çandarlı Körfezi
Güllük Körfezi
Fethiye Körfezi
Finike Körfezi
Büyük Menderes
Küçükmenderes
Gediz
Boz Dağları
Aydın Dağları
Simav Dağları
Alaçam Dağları
Murat Dağı
Gölgeli Dağları
Ak Dağları
Bey Dağları
COPYRIGHT GEORGE PHILIP LTD.

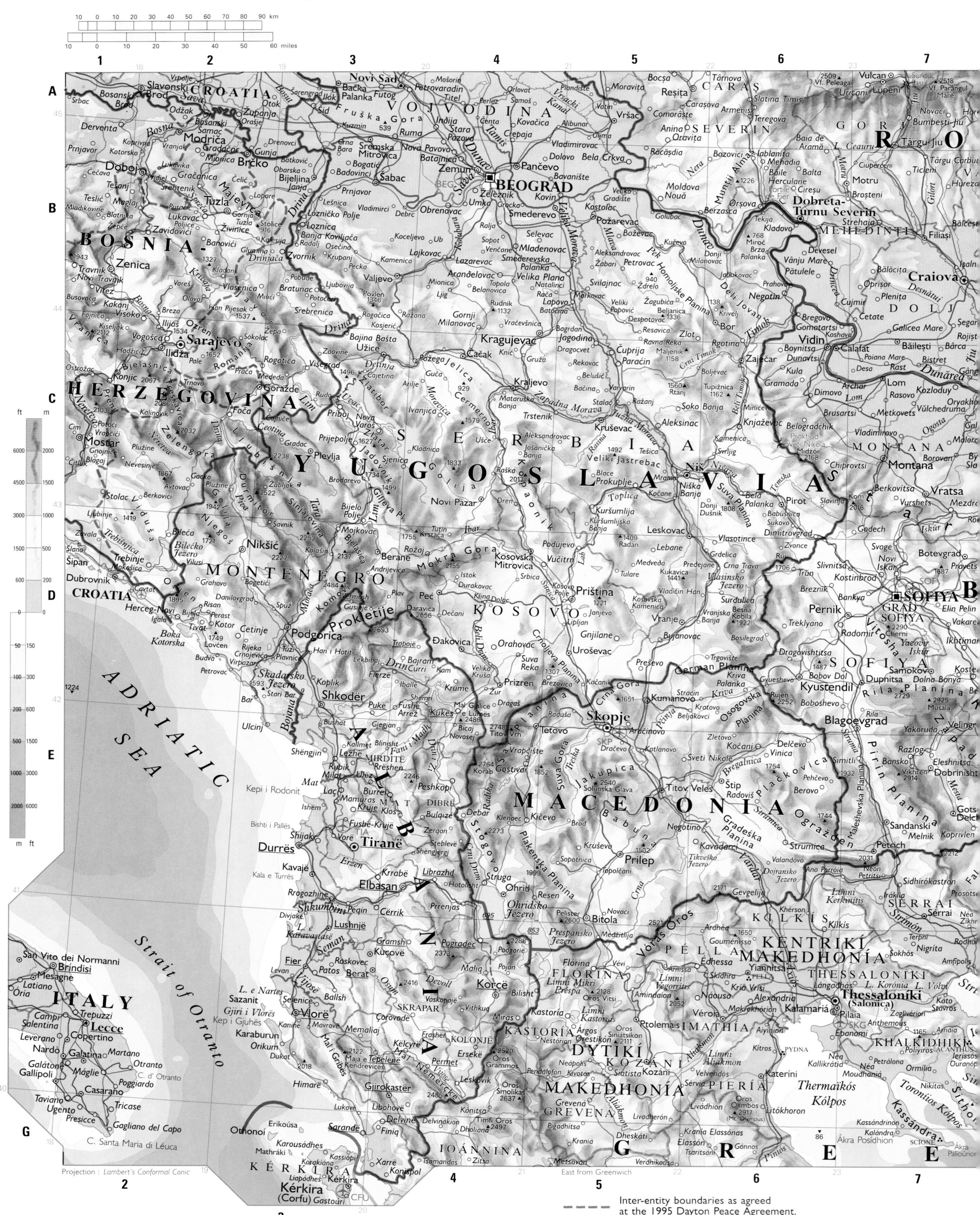

Projection : Lambert's Conformal Conic

East from Greenwich

Inter-entity boundaries as agreed
at the 1995 Dayton Peace Agreement.

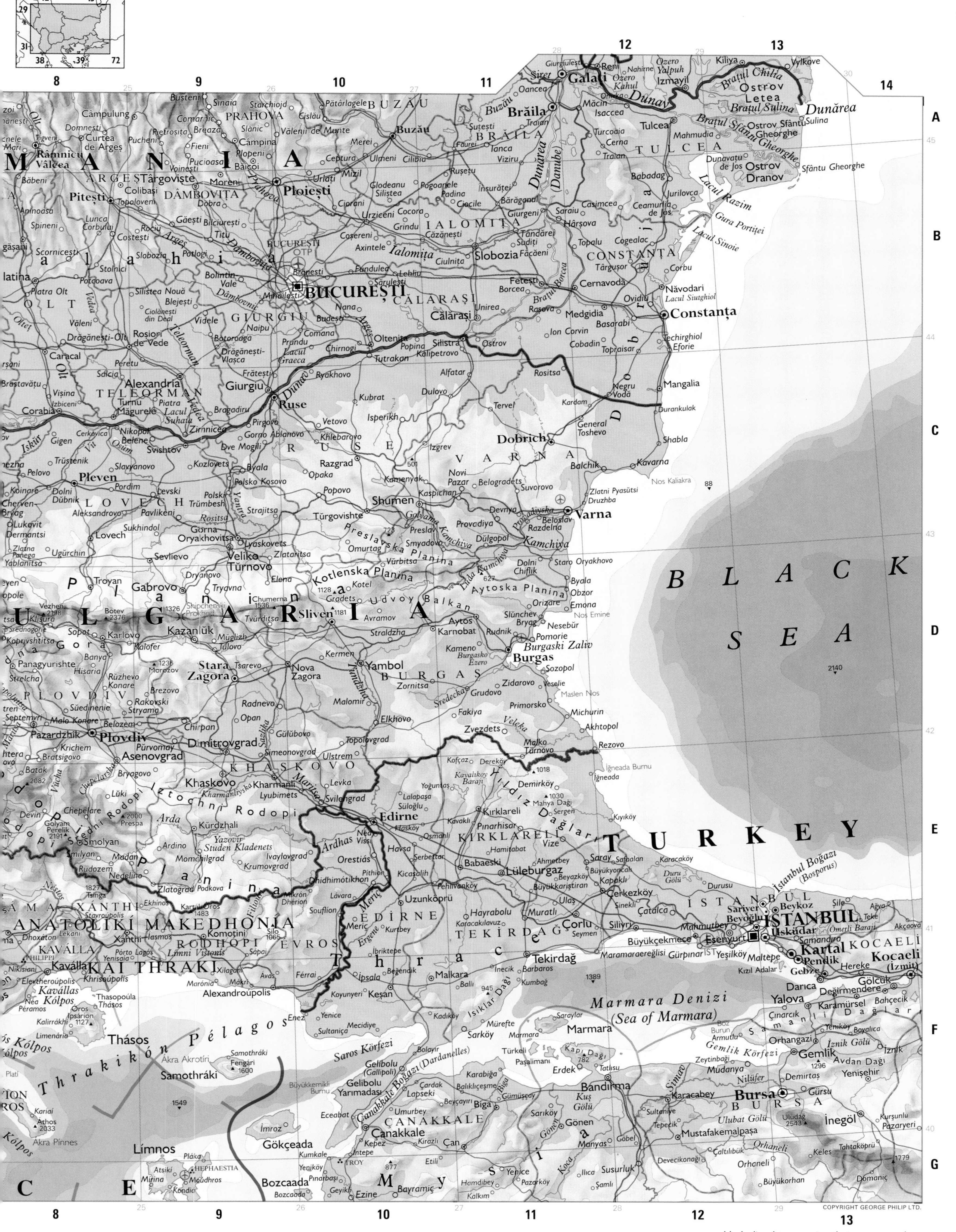

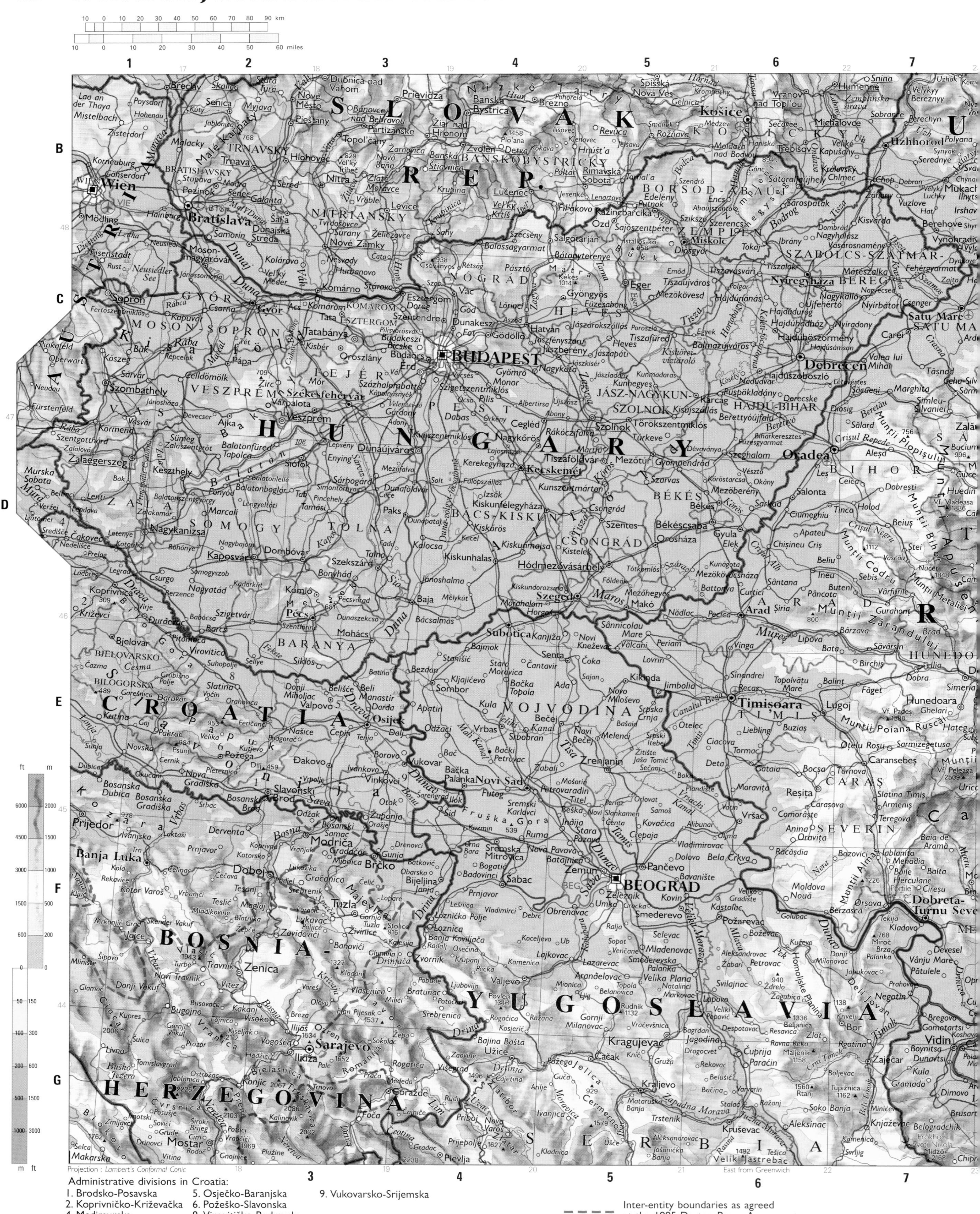

Projection : Lambert's Conformal Conic

East from Greenwich

Administrative divisions in Croatia:
1. Brodsko-Posavska   5. Osječko-Baranjska   9. Vukovarsko-Srijemska
2. Koprivničko-Križevačka 6. Požeško-Slavonska
4. Medimurska   8. Virovitičko-Podravska

Inter-entity boundaries as agreed
at the 1995 Dayton Peace Agreement.

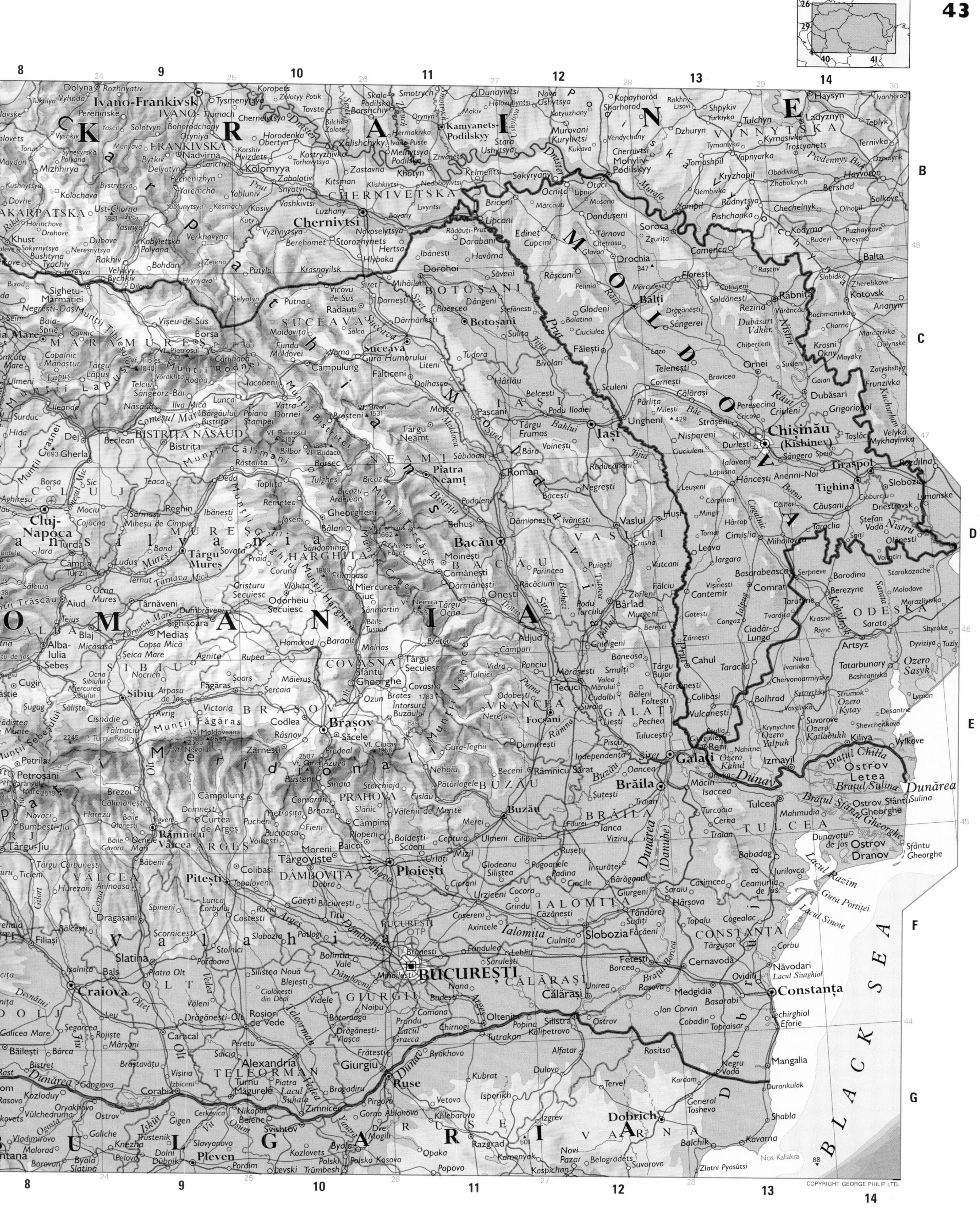

Underlined towns give their name to the
administrative area in which they stand.

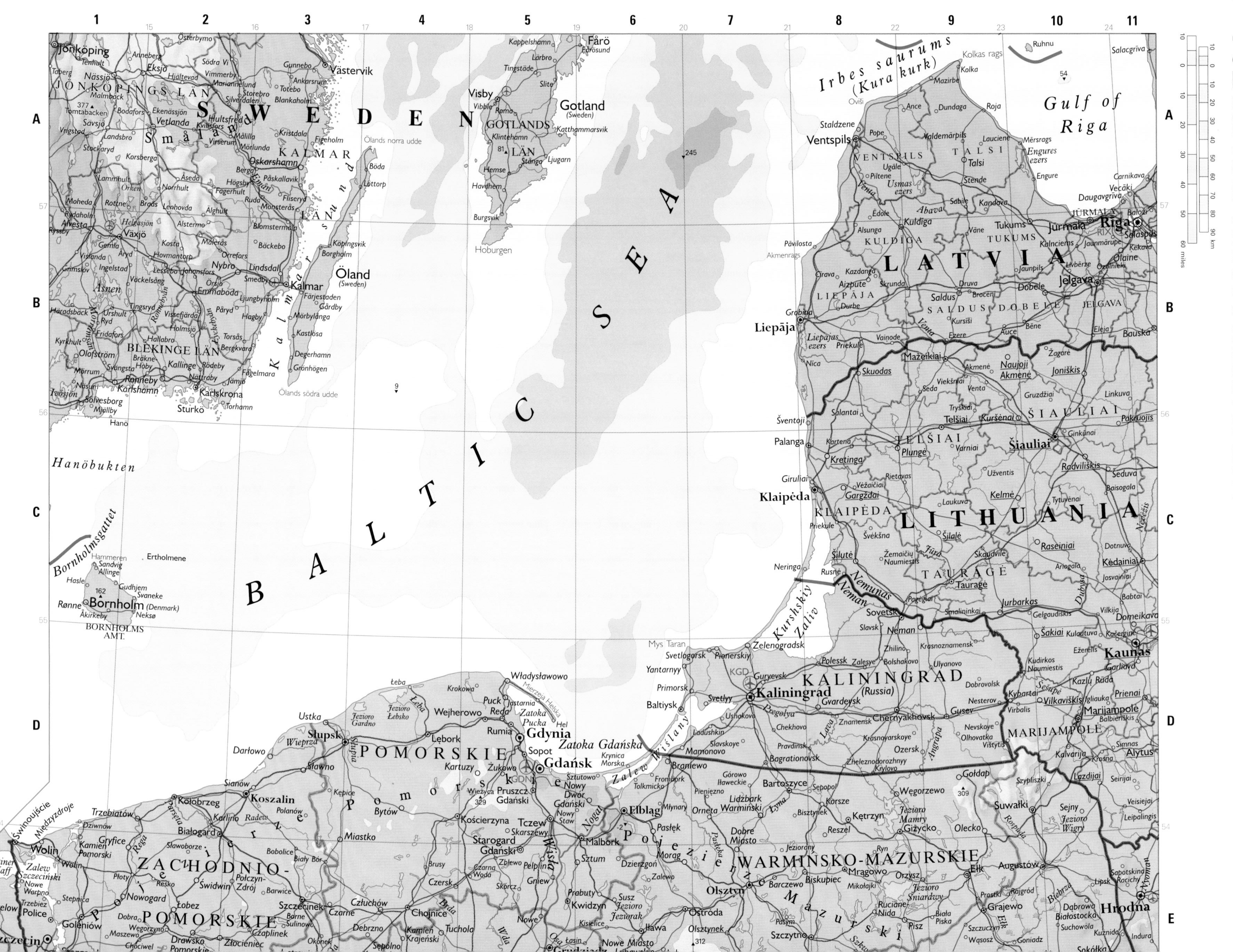
10 0 10 20 30 40 50 60 70 80 90 km
10 0 10 20 30 40 50 60 miles
BALTIC SEA
Gulf of Riga
Irbes šaurums (Kura kurk)
LATVIA
LITHUANIA
SWEDEN
Riga
Jūrmala
Jelgava
Ventspils
Liepāja
Klaipėda
Šiauliai
Kaunas
Marijampolė
Hrodna
Kaliningrad
(Russia)
KALININGRAD
Sovetsk
Neman
Baltiysk
Gdańsk
Gdynia
Sopot
Zatoka Gdańska
Elbląg
Olsztyn
Suwałki
Augustów
Ełk
WARMIŃSKO-MAZURSKIE
POMORSKIE
ZACHODNIO-POMORSKIE
Koszalin
Słupsk
Szczecin
Świnoujście
Bornholm
(Denmark)
BORNHOLMS AMT.
Rønne
Gotland
(Sweden)
Visby
GOTLANDS LÄN
Öland
(Sweden)
Kalmar
KALMAR LÄN
Karlskrona
BLEKINGE LÄN
Växjö
Jönköping
JÖNKÖPINGS LÄN
Västervik
Småland
Hanöbukten
Kalmarsund
Kurshskiy Zaliv
Wisła
Nemunas
Mazurskie
Pojezierze

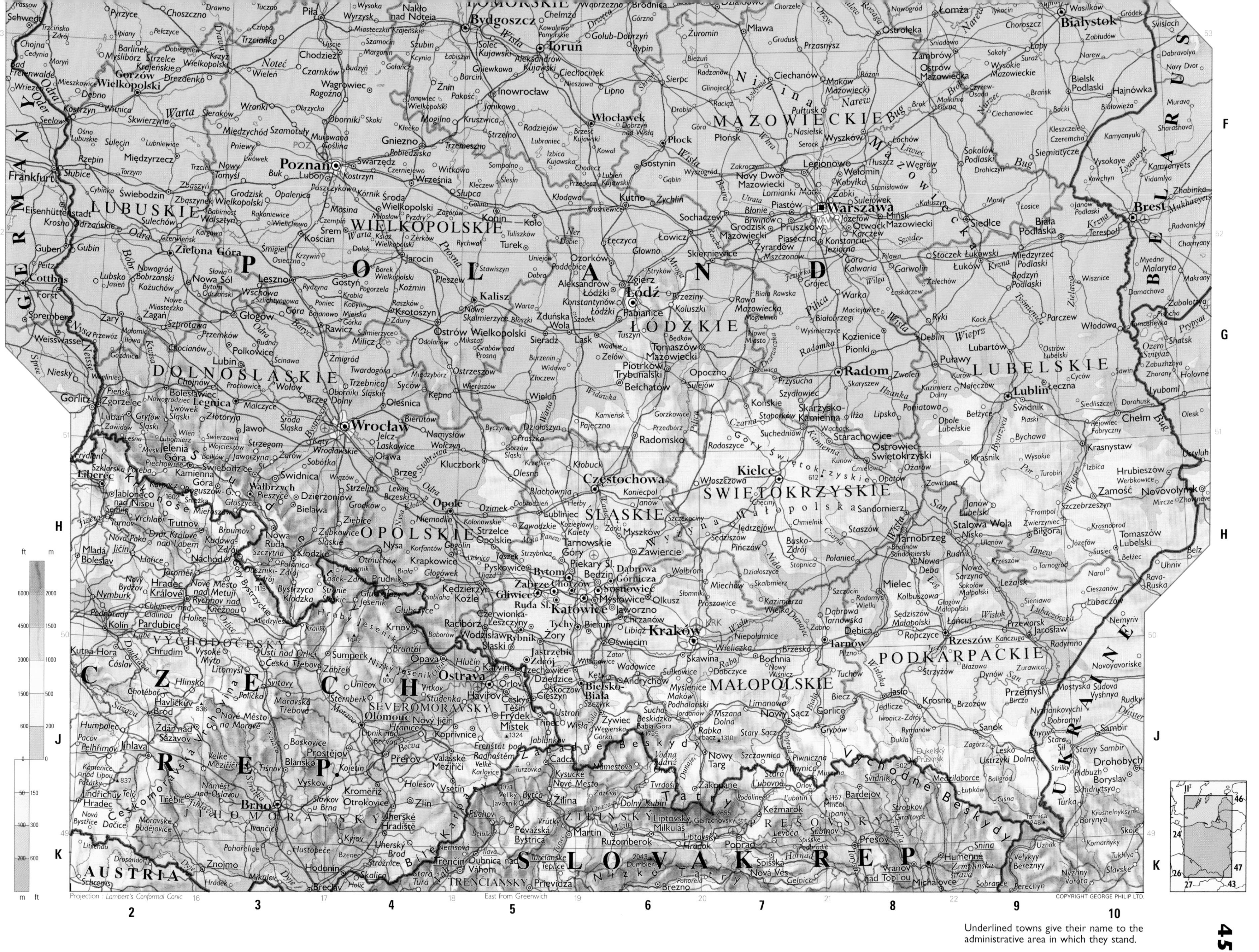

Underlined towns give their name to the
administrative area in which they stand.

East from Greenwich

Projection: Lambert's Conformal Conic

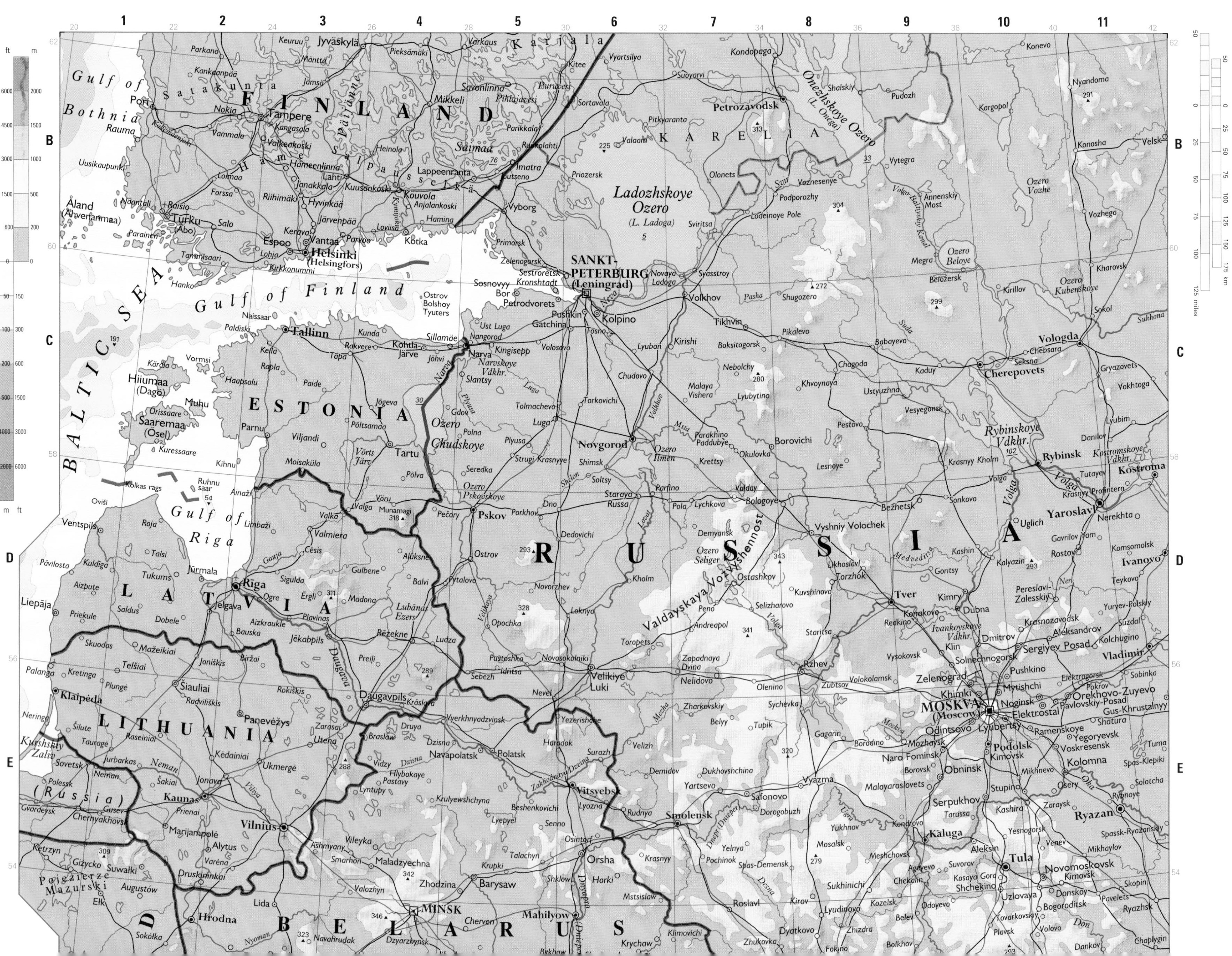
50 0 25 50 75 100 125 150 175 km
50 0 25 50 75 100 125 miles
FINLAND
ESTONIA
LATVIA
LITHUANIA
BELARUS
RUSSIA
KARELIA
BALTIC SEA
Gulf of Finland
Gulf of Riga
Gulf of Bothnia
Ladozhskoye Ozero (L. Ladoga)
Onezhskoye Ozero (L. Onega)
Ozero Chudskoye
Ozero Pskovskoye
Rybinskoye Vdkhr.
Valdayskaya Vozvyshennost
SANKT-PETERBURG (Leningrad)
MOSKVA (Moscow)
MINSK
Helsinki (Helsingfors)
Tallinn
Riga
Vilnius
Kaunas
Klaipėda
Daugavpils
Tartu
Pskov
Novgorod
Tver
Smolensk
Vitsyebsk
Orsha
Mahilyow
Hrodna
Vologda
Cherepovets
Yaroslavl
Kostroma
Ivanovo
Vladimir
Ryazan
Tula
Kaluga
Petrozavodsk
Vyborg
Turku (Åbo)
Tampere
Saaremaa (Ösel)
Hiiumaa (Dagö)
Åland (Ahvenanmaa)
Daugava
Volga
Dnyapro (Dnieper)
m ft
2000 1500 1000 500 200 0
6000 4500 3000 1500 600 0
50 150 100 300 200 600 500 1500 1000 3000 2000 6000

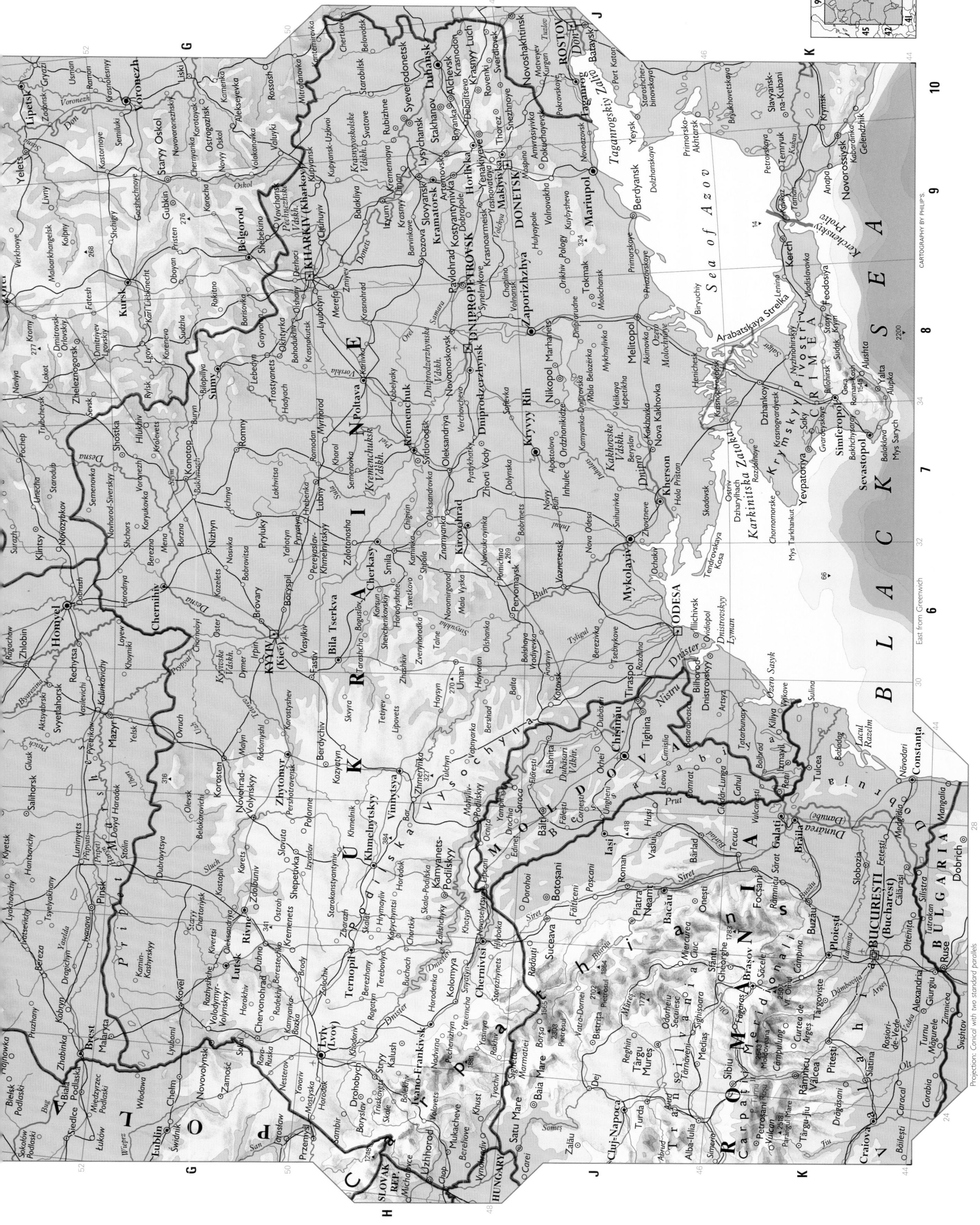

Map: Ukraine, Moldova, Romania and surrounding regions

Countries / regions: RUSSIA, UKRAINE, BELORUSSIA, POLAND, SLOVAK REP., HUNGARY, ROMANIA, MOLDOVA, BULGARIA, CRIMEA, Podolia, Volhynia, Transylvania, Dobrudja, Bessarabia

Seas: Sea of Azov, BLACK SEA, Taganrogskiy Zaliv, Karkinitska Zatoka, Kerchenskiy Proliv, Pivostrov Krymskyy

Major cities: KHARKIV (Kharkov), KYIV (Kiev), DONETSK, DNIPROPETROVSK, ROSTOV, ODESA, BUCUREŞTI (Bucharest), Chişinău, Zaporizhzhya, Mariupol, Mykolayiv, Kherson, Kryvyy Rih, Poltava, Sumy, Chernihiv, Homyel, Kursk, Belgorod, Voronezh, Lipetsk, Yelets, Staryy Oskol, Luhansk, Simferopol, Sevastopol, Yalta, Feodosiya, Kerch, Novorossiysk, Constanţa, Galaţi, Braşov, Iaşi, Cluj-Napoca, Sibiu, Ploieşti, Ruse, Dobrich

Other towns (selection): Lviv (Lvov), Lutsk, Rivne, Ternopil, Ivano-Frankivsk, Chernivtsi, Khmelnytskyy, Vinnytsya, Zhytomyr, Cherkasy, Kremenchuk, Kirovohrad, Uman, Bila Tserkva, Fastiv, Nizhyn, Konotop, Hlukhiv, Shostka, Kremenchuk Vdskh., Kakhovske Vdskh., Dnipro, Nikopol, Melitopol, Berdyansk, Tokmak, Pology, Orikhiv, Pavlohrad, Kramatorsk, Slovyansk, Lysychansk, Sverdlovsk, Stakhanov, Alchevsk, Antratsit, Horlivka, Makiyivka, Yenakiyeve, Thorez, Snizhne, Azov, Bataysk, Novoshakhtinsk, Taganrog, Yeysk, Anapa, Gelendzhik

Rivers: Don, Donets, Dnieper, Dnister, Prut, Siret, Buh, Desna, Prypyat, Oskol, Psël, Vorskla

ROMANIA — Carpathian Mountains (Carpaţii Meridionali), Transilvania

MOLDOVA

CARTOGRAPHY BY PHILIP'S

East from Greenwich

Projection: Conical with two standard parallels

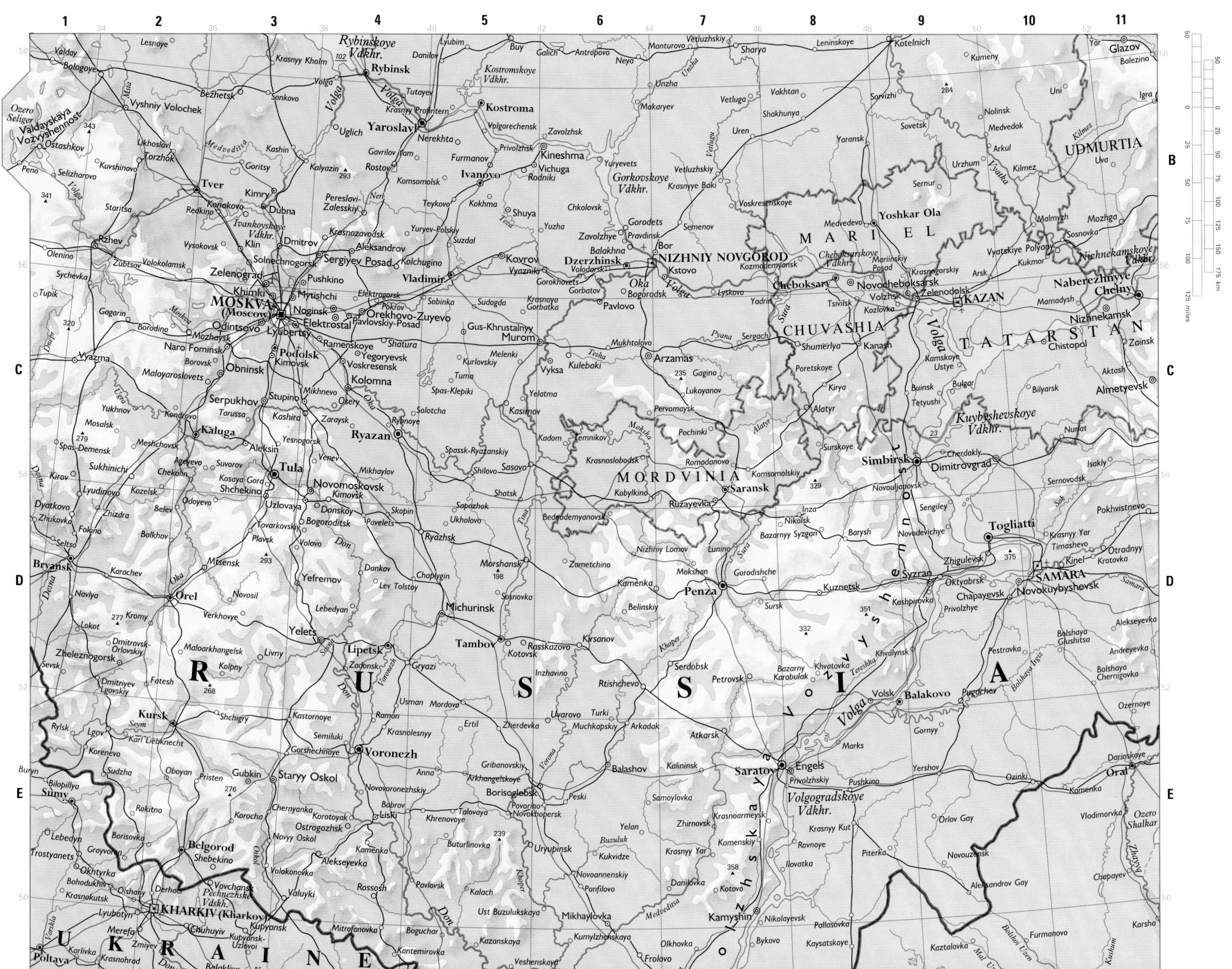
50 0 25 50 75 100 125 150 175 km
50 0 25 50 75 100 125 miles
1
2
3
4
5
6
7
8
9
10
11
B
C
D
E
UDMURTIA
MARI EL
TATARSTAN
CHUVASHIA
MORDVINIA
RUSSIA
UKRAINE
Volzhskaya Vozvyshennost
Valdayskaya Vozvyshennost
NIZHNIY NOVGOROD
MOSKVA (Moscow)
KAZAN
SAMARA
KHARKIV (Kharkov)
Volga
Oka
Don
Sura
Moksha
Khoper
Rybinskoye Vdkhr.
Kostromskoye Vdkhr.
Gorkovskoye Vdkhr.
Cheboksarskoye Vdkhr.
Nizhnekamskoye Vdkhr.
Kuybyshevskoye Vdkhr.
Volgogradskoye Vdkhr.
Ivankovskoye Vdkhr.
Glazov
Kotelnich
Rybinsk
Kostroma
Yaroslavl
Tver
Ivanovo
Kineshma
Vladimir
Kovrov
Dzerzhinsk
Murom
Arzamas
Cheboksary
Novocheboksarsk
Yoshkar Ola
Naberezhnyye Chelny
Nizhnekamsk
Almetyevsk
Chistopol
Simbirsk
Dimitrovgrad
Togliatti
Syzran
Novokuybyshevsk
Saransk
Penza
Kuznetsk
Saratov
Engels
Balakovo
Volsk
Kamyshin
Oral
Balashov
Tambov
Michurinsk
Lipetsk
Voronezh
Yelets
Ryazan
Tula
Novomoskovsk
Kaluga
Obninsk
Serpukhov
Kolomna
Podolsk
Zelenograd
Orel
Kursk
Belgorod
Staryy Oskol
Bryansk
Sumy
Poltava

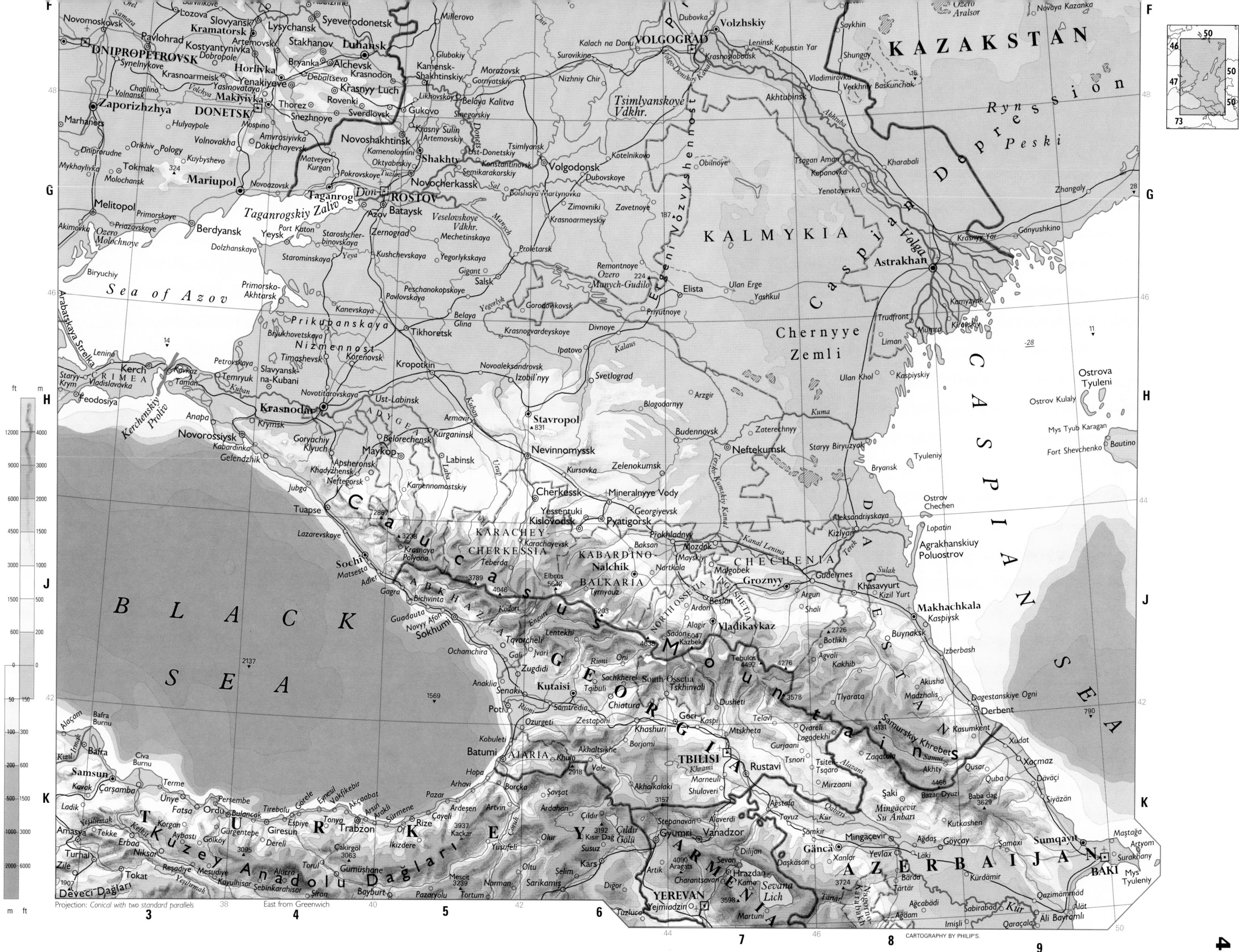
KAZAKSTAN
Caspian Depression
Ryn Peski
CASPIAN SEA
BLACK SEA
Sea of Azov
Taganrogskiy Zaliv
KALMYKIA
Chernyye Zemli
Prikubanskaya Nizmennost
Yergeni Vozvyshennost
DAGESTAN
CHECHENIA
INGUSHETIA
NORTH OSSETIA
KABARDINO-BALKARIA
KARACHEY-CHERKESSIA
ADYGEA
ABKHAZIA
AJARIA
South Ossetia
GEORGIA
ARMENIA
AZERBAIJAN
Nagorno-Karabakh
TURKEY
CRIMEA
Caucasus Mountains
Samurskiy Khrebet
Kuzey Anadolu Dağları
Dëveci Dağları
Volga
Don
Kuban
Kerchenskiy Proliv
Tsimlyanskoye Vdkhr.
Mingəçevir Su Anbarı
Sevana Lich
Astrakhan
VOLGOGRAD
Volzhskiy
ROSTOV
Taganrog
Krasnodar
Stavropol
Elista
Makhachkala
Groznyy
Vladikavkaz
Nalchik
Sochi
Novorossiysk
TBILISI
YEREVAN
BAKI
Sumqayıt
Gəncə
Kutaisi
Batumi
Sokhumi
Trabzon
Samsun
DONETSK
Luhansk
Mariupol
Zaporizhzhya
DNIPROPETROVSK
Kerch
Feodosiya
Melitopol
Berdyansk
Derbent
Pyatigorsk
Kislovodsk
Maykop
Tuapse
Anapa
Poti
Rustavi
Gyumri
Kars
Projection: Conical with two standard parallels
East from Greenwich
CARTOGRAPHY BY PHILIP'S

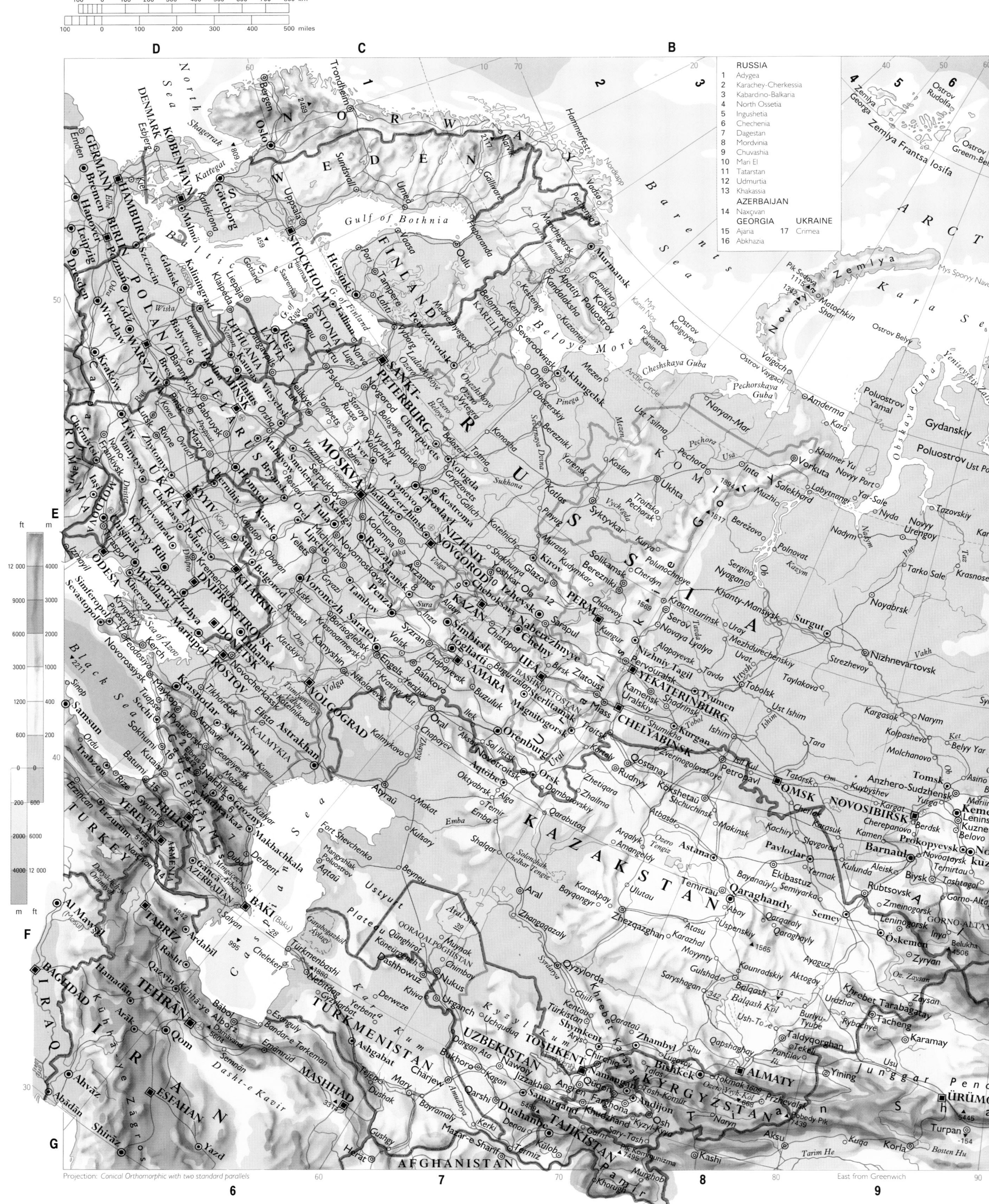

100 0 100 200 300 400 500 600 700 800 km
100 0 100 200 300 400 500 miles
RUSSIA
1 Adygea
2 Karachey-Cherkessia
3 Kabardino-Balkaria
4 North Ossetia
5 Ingushetia
6 Chechenia
7 Dagestan
8 Mordvinia
9 Chuvashia
10 Mari El
11 Tatarstan
12 Udmurtia
13 Khakassia
AZERBAIJAN
14 Naxçivan
GEORGIA
15 Ajaria
16 Abkhazia
UKRAINE
17 Crimea
Projection: Conical Orthomorphic with two standard parallels
East from Greenwich
RUSSIA
KAZAKSTAN
UZBEKISTAN
TURKMENISTAN
KYRGYZSTAN
TAJIKISTAN
AFGHANISTAN
IRAN
IRAQ
TURKEY
UKRAINE
BELARUS
POLAND
FINLAND
SWEDEN
NORWAY
MOSKVA
SANKT-PETERBURG
Barents Sea
Kara Sea
Black Sea
Caspian Sea
Aral Sea

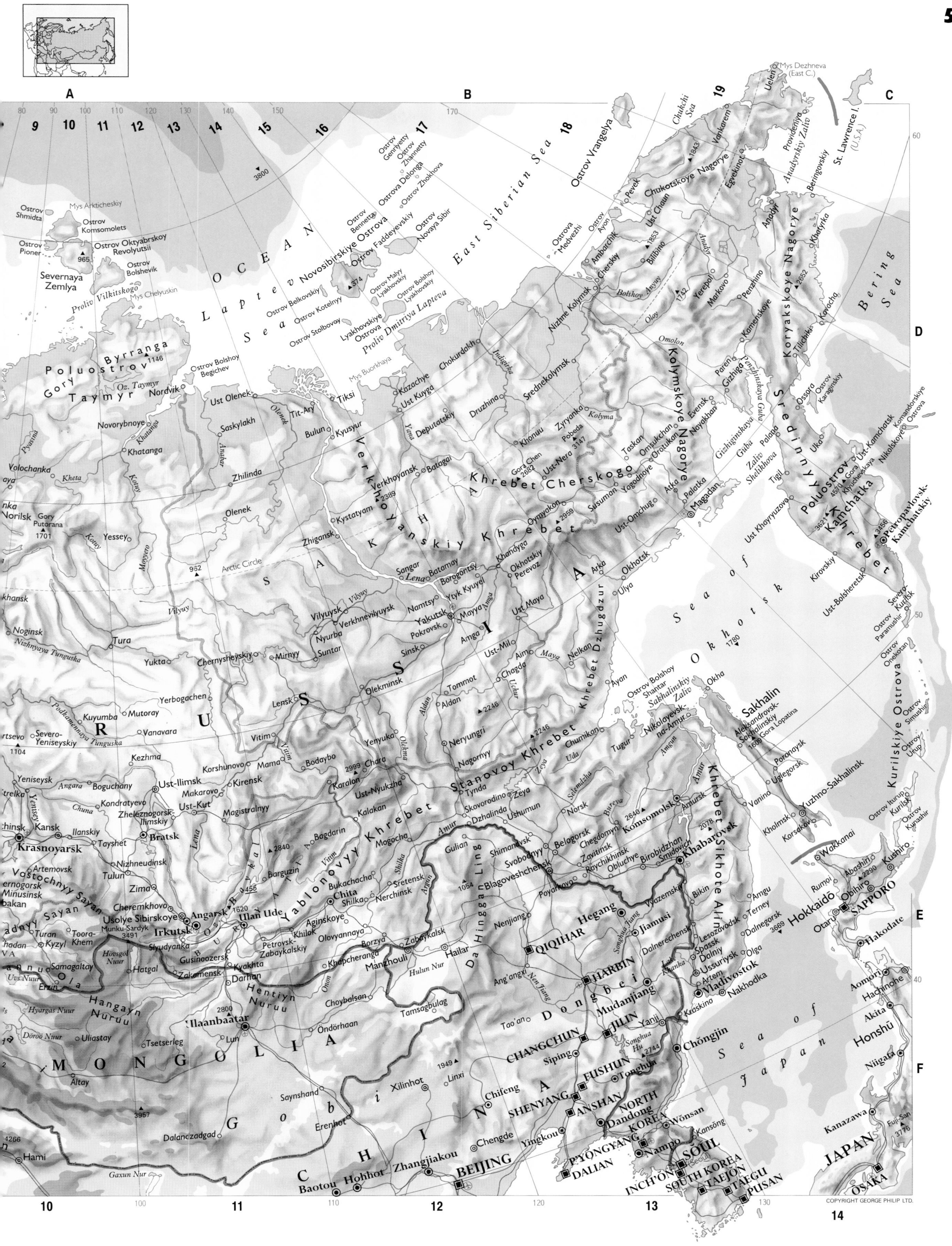

OCEAN

Laptev Sea

East Siberian Sea

Bering Sea

Severnaya Zemlya

Poluostrov Gory Byrranga Taymyr

RUSSIA

Arctic Circle

Verkhoyanskiy Khrebet

Khrebet Cherskogo

Kolymskoye Nagorye

Koryakskoye Nagorye

Poluostrov Kamchatka

Sredinnyy Khrebet

Petropavlovsk-Kamchatskiy

SAKHA

Yakutsk

Sea of Okhotsk

Stanovoy Khrebet

Yablonovyy Khrebet

Krasnoyarsk

Bratsk

Irkutsk

Ulan Ude

MONGOLIA

Ulaanbaatar

Hangayn Nuruu

Hentiyn Nuruu

Gobi

CHINA

BEIJING

Baotou · Hohhot · Zhangjiakou

Chengde

Yingkou

Chifeng

SHENYANG

ANSHAN

FUSHUN

CHANGCHUN

JILIN

QIQIHAR

HARBIN

Jiamusi

Hegang

Mudanjiang

Dongbei

Khabarovsk

Khrebet Sikhote Alin

Komsomolsk

Vladivostok

Nakhodka

Sakhalin

Yuzhno-Sakhalinsk

Kurilskiye Ostrova

Hokkaidō

SAPPORO

Hakodate

Honshū

JAPAN

OSAKA

Sea of Japan

NORTH KOREA

PYONGYANG

Nampo

DALIAN

SOUTH KOREA

SOUL

INCH'ON

TAEJON

TAEGU

PUSAN

COPYRIGHT GEORGE PHILIP LTD.

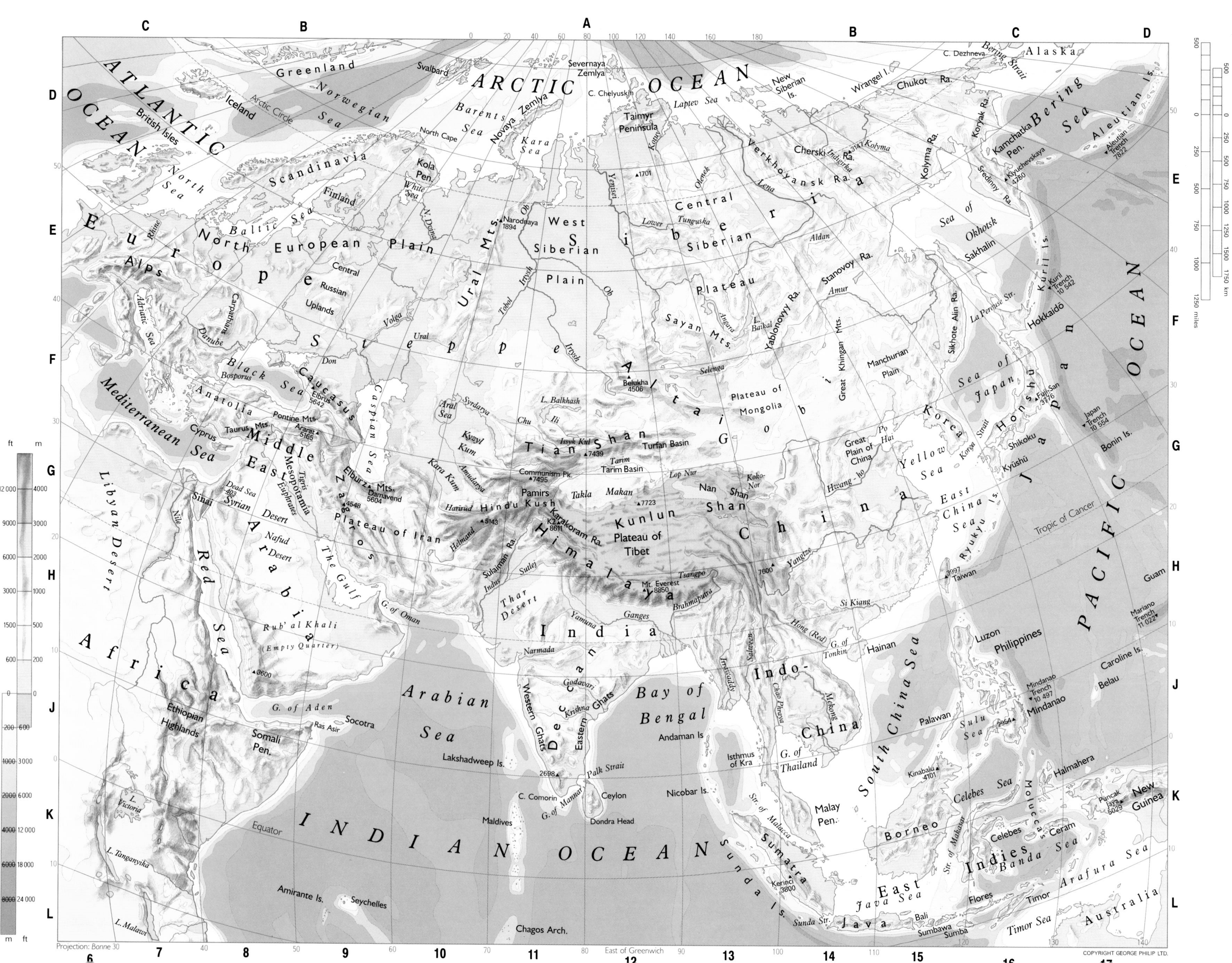
500 0 250 500 750 1000 1250 1500 1750 km
500 0 250 500 750 1000 1250 miles
ARCTIC OCEAN
ATLANTIC OCEAN
PACIFIC OCEAN
INDIAN OCEAN
Greenland
Svalbard
Severnaya Zemlya
C. Chelyuskin
Laptev Sea
New Siberian Is.
Wrangel I.
Chukot Ra.
C. Dezhneva
Bering Strait
Alaska
Iceland
Arctic Circle
Norwegian Sea
Barents Sea
Novaya Zemlya
Kara Sea
North Cape
Taimyr Peninsula
British Isles
North Sea
Scandinavia
Finland
Kola Pen.
White Sea
Baltic Sea
North European Plain
Central Russian Uplands
Europe
Alps
Adriatic Sea
Carpathians
Danube
Rhine
Ural Mts.
Narodnaya 1894
West Siberian Plain
Siberia
Central Siberian Plateau
Verkhoyansk Ra.
Cherski Ra.
Kolyma Ra.
Koryak Ra.
Kamchatka Pen.
Bering Sea
Aleutian Is.
Aleutian Trench 7822
Klyuchevskaya 4750
Sredinny Ra.
Sea of Okhotsk
Sakhalin
Kuril Is.
Kuril Trench 10 542
Hokkaido
La Perouse Str.
Sikhote Alin Ra.
Stanovoy Ra.
Yablonovyy Ra.
L. Baikal
Sayan Mts.
Steppe
Altai
Belukha 4506
Black Sea
Bosporus
Caucasus
Elbrus 5642
Caspian Sea
Anatolia
Pontine Mts.
Taurus Mts.
Ararat 5165
Cyprus
Mediterranean Sea
Middle East
Mesopotamia
Tigris
Euphrates
Dead Sea -403
Sinai
Syrian Desert
Nafud Desert
Arabia
Rub' al Khali (Empty Quarter)
The Gulf
G. of Oman
Elburz Mts.
Damavend 5604
Zagros
Plateau of Iran
Aral Sea
Syrdarya
Amudarya
Kyzyl Kum
Kara Kum
L. Balkhash
Tian Shan
Issyk Kul
Communism Pk. 7495
Pamirs
Hindu Kush
Karakoram Ra.
K2 8611
Tarim Basin
Turfan Basin
Takla Makan
Lop Nur
Nan Shan
Koko Nor
Kunlun Shan
Plateau of Tibet
Himalaya
Mt. Everest 8850
Tsangpo
Brahmaputra
Thar Desert
Indus
Sulaiman Ra.
Sutlej
Ganges
Yamuna
Narmada
Godavari
Krishna
India
Deccan
Western Ghats
Eastern Ghats
Palk Strait
Ceylon
C. Comorin
G. of Mannar
Dondra Head
Lakshadweep Is.
Maldives
Chagos Arch.
Gobi
Plateau of Mongolia
Great Khingan Mts.
Manchurian Plain
Amur
Selenga
Angara
Lena
Olenek
Yenisei
Ob
Irtysh
Tobol
Volga
Ural
Don
Nile
China
Great Plain of China
Hwang-ho
Yangtze
Si Kiang
Korea
Yellow Sea
East China Sea
Sea of Japan
Japan
Honshu
Shikoku
Kyushu
Fuji-San 3776
Korea Strait
Japan Trench 10 554
Bonin Is.
Ryukyu Is.
Taiwan
Tropic of Cancer
Guam
Mariano Trench 11 022
Hainan
G. of Tonkin
Hong (Red)
Indo-China
Mekong
Chao Phraya
Salween
Irrawaddy
G. of Thailand
Isthmus of Kra
Malay Pen.
Str. of Malacca
Sumatra
Kerinci 3800
Sunda Is.
Sunda Str.
Java
Java Sea
Bali
Sumbawa
Sumba
Flores
Timor
Timor Sea
Arafura Sea
Australia
Borneo
Kinabalu 4101
South China Sea
Luzon
Philippines
Palawan
Sulu Sea
Mindanao
Mindanao Trench 10 497
Caroline Is.
Belau
Celebes Sea
Celebes
Str. of Makasar
Moluccas
Ceram
Halmahera
Banda Sea
East Indies
New Guinea
Puncak Jaya 5029
Bay of Bengal
Andaman Is.
Nicobar Is.
Arabian Sea
G. of Aden
Socotra
Ras Asir
Somali Pen.
Ethiopian Highlands
Red Sea
Africa
Libyan Desert
L. Victoria
L. Tanganyika
L. Malawi
Equator
Amirante Is.
Seychelles
Projection: Bonne
East of Greenwich
COPYRIGHT GEORGE PHILIP LTD.

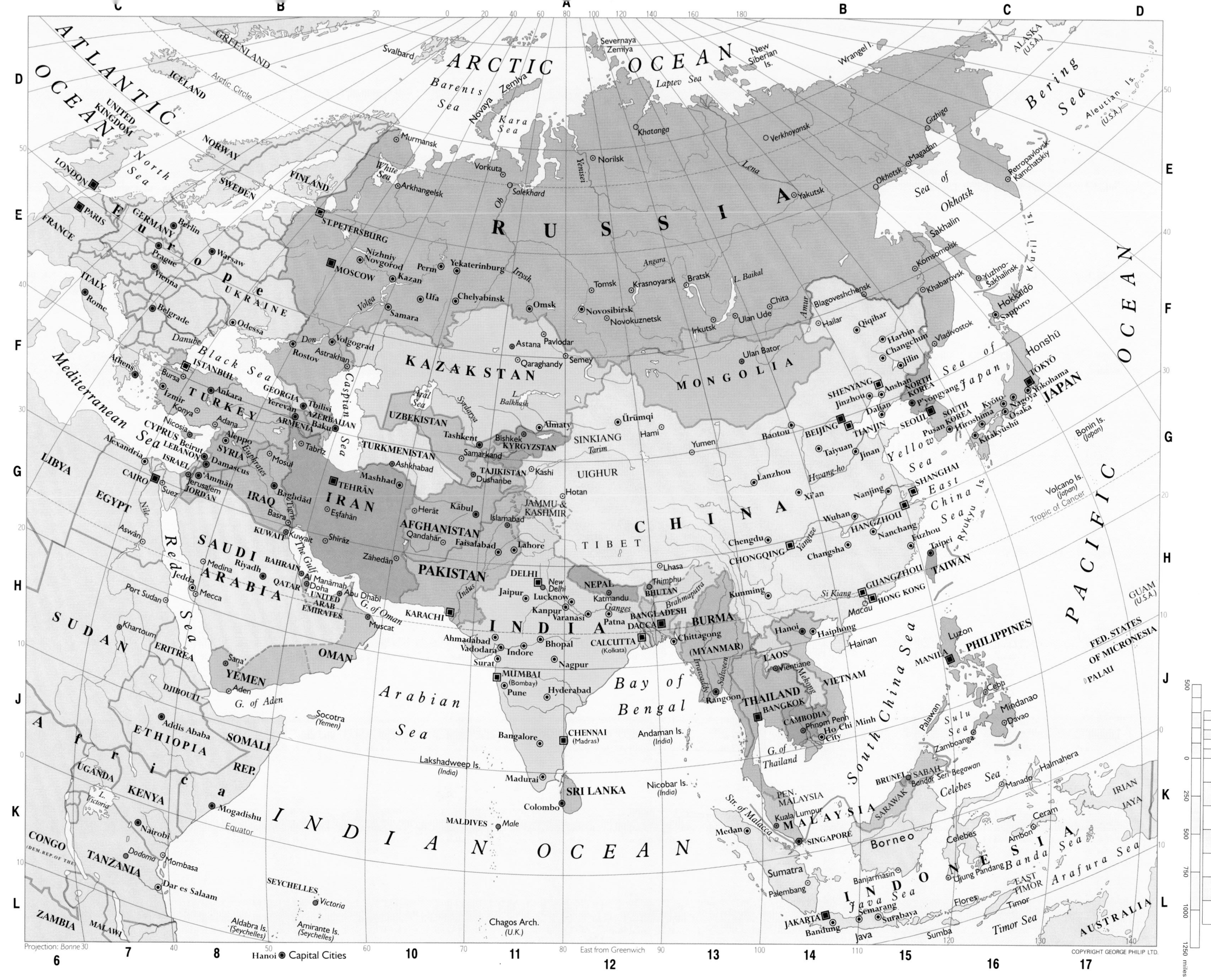

500   0   250   500   750 1000 1250 1500 1750 km
500   0   250   500   750   1000 1250 miles

JAPAN 1:4 400 000

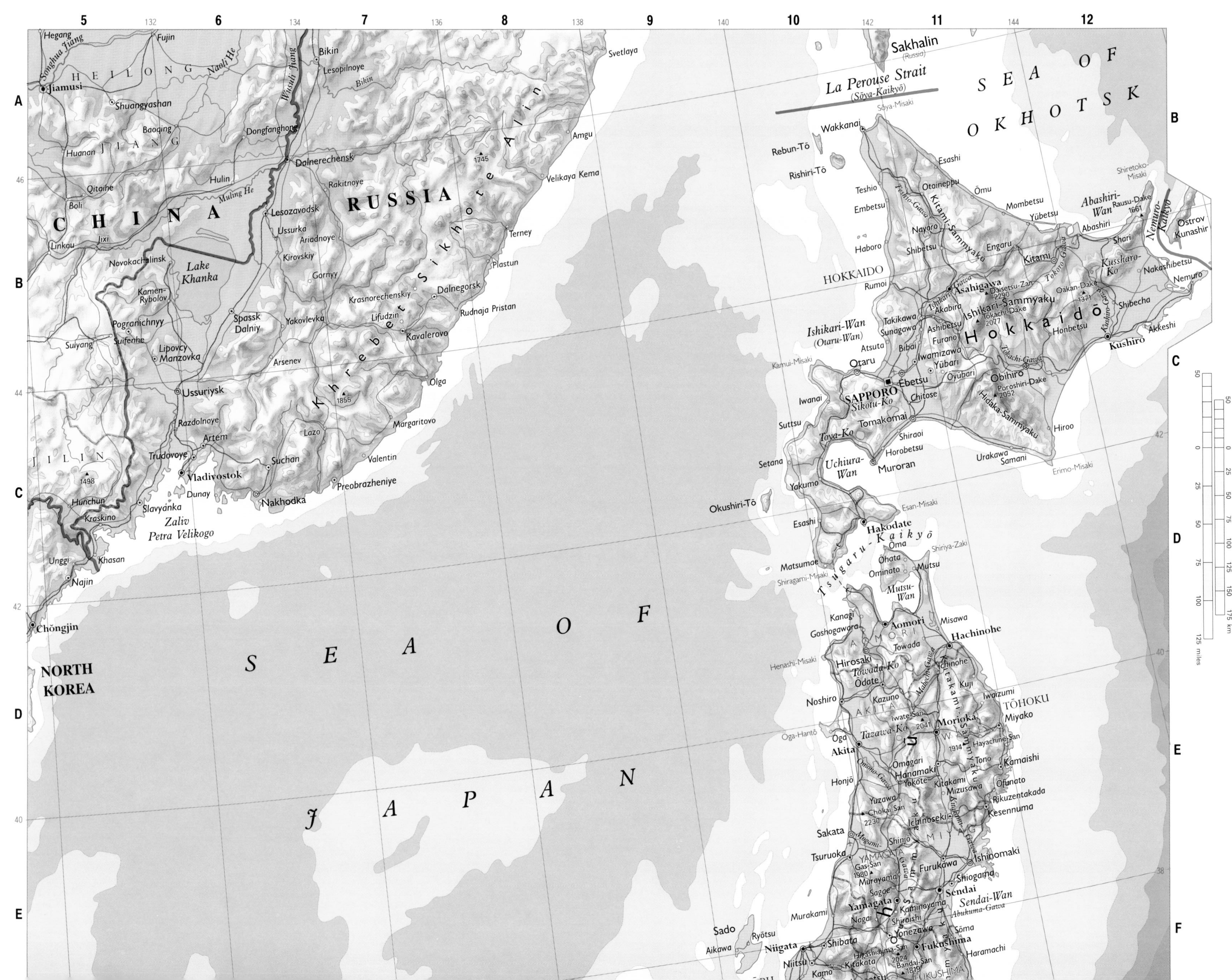

50 25 0 25 50 75 100 125 150 175 km
50 0 25 50 75 100 125 miles

SEA OF OKHOTSK

Ostrov Kunashir
Nemuro-Kaikyō
Shiretoko-Misaki
Rausu-Dake 1661
Abashiri-Wan
Abashiri
Shari
Nakashibetsu
Shibecha
Nemuro
Akkeshi
Kushiro
Kussharo-Ko
Kushiro-Gawa

Sakhalin
(Aossa)
La Perouse Strait
(Sōya-Kaikyō)
Sōya-Misaki

HOKKAIDO

Mombetsu
Yūbetsu
Engaru
Kitami
Kitami-Sammyaku
Asahigawa
Daisetsu-Zan
Asahi-Dake 2290
Tokoro-Gawa
Teshio-Gawa
Okan-Dake 1372
Takikawa-Dake
Obihiro
Poroshiri-Dake 2052
Hidaka-Sammyaku
Urakawa
Samani
Hiroo
Erimo-Misaki

Ōtoneppu
Ōmu
Esashi

Rebun-Tō
Rishiri-Tō
Wakkanai

Teshio
Embetsu
Haboro
Rumoi

Nayoro
Shibetsu
Furano
Yūbari
Iwamizawa
Bibai
Sunagawa
Takikawa

Ishikari-Sammyaku
SAPPORO
Ebetsu
Chitose
Oyama
Shiraoi
Tomakomai

Ishikari-Wan
(Otaru-Wan)
Otaru
Shikotsu-Ko
Toya-Ko
Uchiura-Wan

Kamui-Misaki
Iwanai
Suttsu
Atsuta
Yokuno
Horobetsu
Muroran

Setana
Esashi
Matsumae
Shiragami-Misaki
Shiriya-Zaki

Okushiri-Tō

Esan-Misaki
Hakodate
Tsugaru-Kaikyō
Ōma
Ōhata
Mutsu
Mutsu-Wan
Ominato

SEA OF JAPAN

RUSSIA

Svetlaya
Amgu
Velikaya Kema
Terney
Plastun
Rudnaja Pristan
Dalnegorsk

Sikhote
Alin
1745
Kavalerovo
Olga
Margaritovo
Valentin
Preobrazheniye

Bikin
Lesopilnoye
Bikin
Rakitnoye
Dalnerechensk
Ussurka
Aradnoye
Gornyy
Krasnorechenskiy
Lifudzin
Yakovlevka
1855
Lazo
Suchan

Khor

CHINA
HEILONGJIANG
Hegang
Songhua Jiang
Jiamusi
Shuangyashan
Qitaihe
Boli
Linkou
Baoqing
Fujin

Wusuli Jiang
Ussuri

Spassk
Dalniy
Nakhodka

Mishan
Hulin
Muling He
Mudan Jiang
Sulyang

Lake Khanka
Kamen-Rybolov
Pogranichnyy
Kirovskiy
Ussuriysk
Razdolnoye
Artem
Vladivostok
Dunay
Zaliv Petra Velikogo

Novokachalinsk
Suifenhe

JILIN
1498
Hunchun
Kraskino
Khasan
Najin
Unggi
Chŏngjin

NORTH KOREA

TŌHOKU
Hachinohe
Misawa
Towada
Aomori
Noheji
Mutsu-Wan

Kitakami
Kuji
Iwaizumi
Miyako
Morioka
Kamaishi
Ōfunato
Rikuzentakada
Kesennuma
Ishinomaki
Oshika-Hantō
Sendai
Sendai-Wan
Shiogama

Kanagi
Goshogawara
Hirosaki
Ōdate
Noshiro
Oga-Hantō
Oga
Akita
Honjō
Sakata
Tsuruoka
Murakami
Niitsu
Niigata
Sado
Ryōtsu
Akkawa

AKITA
YAMAGATA
Yamagata
Yonezawa
Shinjō
Furukawa

Sado

51
57

SOUTH KOREA

JAPAN

PACIFIC OCEAN

Korea Strait

Pohang
Yŏngdŏk
Ullŭng-do (S. Korea)
Tok-do
Tsushima
Oki-Shotō
Iki
Gotō-Rettō
Fukue-Shima
Nakadōri-Shima
Hirado
Katsumoto
Gō-no-ura
FUKUOKA
KITAKYŪSHŪ
Shimonoseki
Nōgata
Iizuka
Yukuhashi
Buzen
Bungotakada
Kitsuki
Beppu
Ōita
Usuki
Saiki
Karatsu
Imari
Matsuura
Saga
Tosu
Kurume
Yame
Yanagawa
Ōmuta
Sasebo
Takeo
Ōmura
Isahaya
Nagasaki
Shimabara
Kuchinotsu
Kumamoto
Yatsushiro
Hondo
Amakusa-Shotō
Ushibuka
Minamata
Hitoyoshi
Nobeoka
Hyūga
Takachiho
Taketa
Kujū-San 1787
Miyazaki
Kobayashi
Miyakonojō
Nichinan
Kushima
Sendai
Kagoshima
Kushikino
Koshiki-Rettō
Makurazaki
Ibusuki
Kanoya
Tarumizu
Shibushi
KYŪSHŪ
KAGOSHIMA
KUMAMOTO
MIYAZAKI
Ōsumi-Kaikyō
Ōsumi-Shotō
Sata-Misaki
Take-Shima
Iō-Jima
Kuro-Shima
Uji-Guntō
Tane-ga-Shima
Nishino'omote
Yaku-Shima
Miyanoura-Dake 1935
Kuchino-eruba-Jima
Kuchino-Shima
Nakano-Shima
Suwanose-Jima
Akuseki-Shima
Tokara-Rettō
Satsunan-Shotō

CHŪGOKU
Hagi
Nagato
Mine
Onoda
Ube
Hōfu
Yamaguchi
Tokuyama
Iwakuni
HIROSHIMA
Kure
Ōtake
Mihara
Masuda
Hamada
Gōtsu
Ōda
Izumo
Matsue
Sakaiminato
Yonago
Kurayoshi
Daisen 1712
Tottori
Tsuyama
Okayama
Kurashiki
Fukuyama
Onomichi
Fuchū
Kake
Miyoshi
Niimi
Tamano
Bizen
Himeji
Kakogawa
Akashi
KOBE
Nishinomiya
Amagasaki
OSAKA
Sakai
Kishiwada
Izumi-sano
Higashiosaka
Takatsuki
KYŌTO
Ōtsu
Fukuchiyama
Ayabe
Maizuru
Toyooka
Kasumi
Obama
Wakasa-Wan
Tsuruga
Fukui
Takefu
Echizen-Misaki
Kyō-ga-Saki
Komatsu
Kanazawa
Matsutō
Takaoka
Toyama
Toyama-Wan
Himi
Nanao
Hakui
Wajima
Shirakawa
Takayama
Hakusan 2702
Gero
Gifu
Ōgaki
Ichinomiya
NAGOYA
Seto
Toyota
Okazaki
Kariya
Handa
Toyohashi
Gamagōri
Hamamatsu
Tsu
Ise
Ise-Wan
Toba
Matsusaka
Yokkaichi
Suzuka
Kuwana
Nara
Hikone
Nagahama
Biwa-Ko
Wakayama
Gobō
Arida
Tanabe
Shingū
Kushimoto
Owase
Shio-no-Misaki
Daiō-Misaki
KINKI
Kii-Suidō
Awaji-Shima
Tokushima
Naruto
Anan
Takamatsu
Sakaide
Marugame
Kan'onji
Kawanoe
Niihama
Saijō
Imabari
Matsuyama
Ishizuchi-San 1981
Tsurugi-San 1955
Ikeda
Kōchi
Nankoku
Tosa-Wan
Susaki
Kubokawa
Nakamura
Sukumo
Tosa-shimizu
Ashizuri-Zaki
Uwajima
Yawatahama
Muroto
Muroto-Misaki
Mugi
SHIKOKU
Bungo-Suidō

Nagano
Matsumoto
Ueda
Komoro
Hodaka-Dake 3190
Ontake-San 3063
Kita-Dake 3192
Kōfu
Fuji
Fuji-yoshida
Fuji-San 3776
Fujinomiya
Shimizu
Shizuoka
Shimada
Iwata
Numazu
Mishima
Atami
Itō
Odawara
Hiratsuka
Suruga-Wan
Omae-Zaki
Irō-Zaki
Takasaki
Maebashi
Kumagaya
Chichibu
Kawagoe
Ōmiya
Urawa
Kawaguchi
TOKYO
Hachiōji
KAWASAKI
YOKOHAMA
Fujisawa
Yokosuka
Chiba
Funabashi
Ichikawa
Ichihara
Kisarazu
Tateyama
Nojima-Zaki
Katsuura
Chōshi
Narita
Tōgane
Sawara
Noda
Koga
Oyama
Tochigi
Utsunomiya
Ashikaga
Kiryū
Numata
Nikkō
Mito
Hitachi
Takahagi
Kitaibaraki
Nakaminato
Ishioka
Tsuchiura
KANTŌ
Kanto Sanchi
Ō-Shima
Nii-Jima
Miyake-Jima
Izu-Shotō
Hachijō-Jima
Aoga-Shima
Nanpō-Shotō
Tōri-Shima
Sōfu-Gan
8412
9076
6365
7214

RYUKYU ISLANDS

on same scale

EAST CHINA SEA

PACIFIC OCEAN

Nansei-Shotō (Ryukyu Is.)
Amami-Ō-Shima
Kakeroma-Jima
Kikaiga-Shima
Uke-Shima
Tokuno-Shima
KAGOSHIMA
Okino-erabu-Shima
Yoron-Jima
Amami-Guntō
Okinawa-Guntō
Iheya-Shima
Izena-Shima
Ii-Shima
Kume-Shima
OKINAWA
Okinawa-Jima
Naha
Koza
Kerama-Rettō
Tokashiki-Shima
Senkaku-Shotō
Uotsuri-Shima
Kobi-Sho
Sakishima-Guntō
Yonaguni-Jima
Iriomote-Jima
Hateruma-Shima
Yaeyama-Rettō
Kuro-Shima
Ishigaki-Shima
Tarama-Jima
Irabu-Jima
Miyako-Jima
Miyako-Rettō

East from Greenwich

Projection: Conical with two standard parallels

m | ft
9000 | 3000
6000 | 2000
4500 | 1500
3000 | 1000
1200 | 400
600 | 200
0 | 0
200 | 600
2000 | 6000
4000 | 12 000
6000 | 18 000
8000 | 24 000

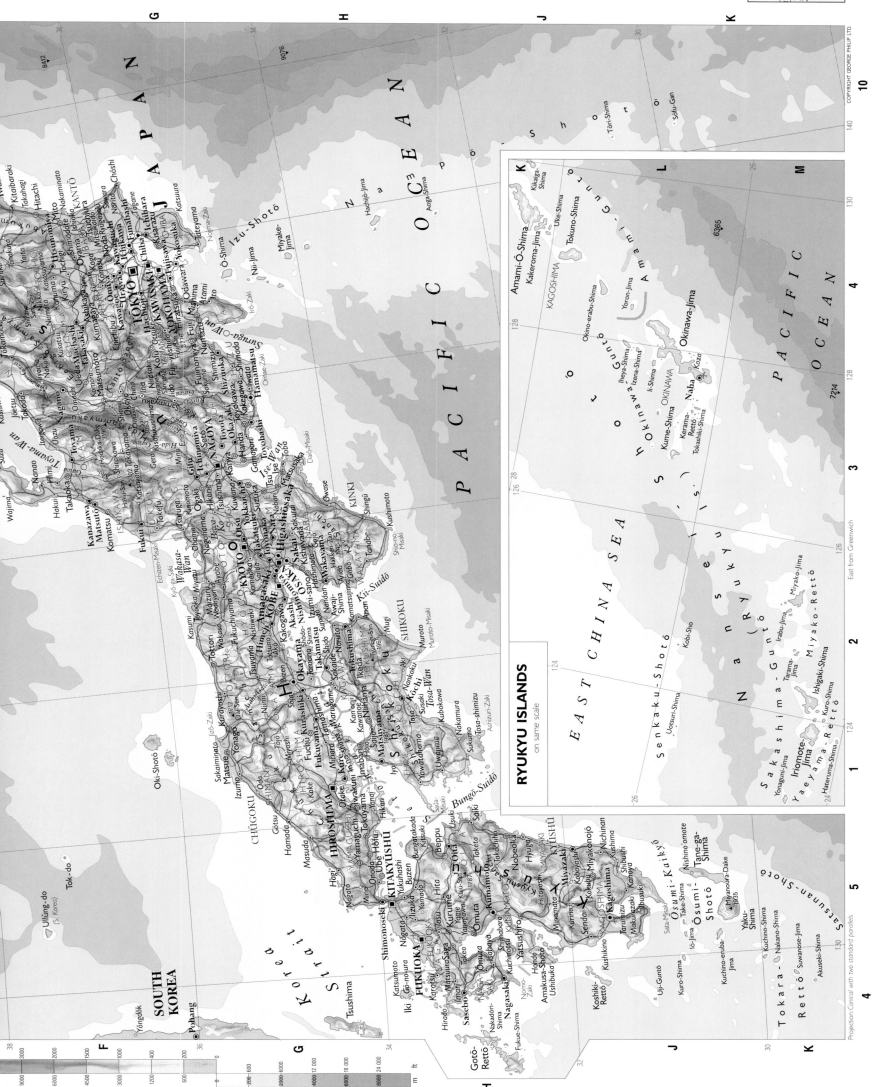

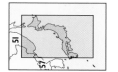

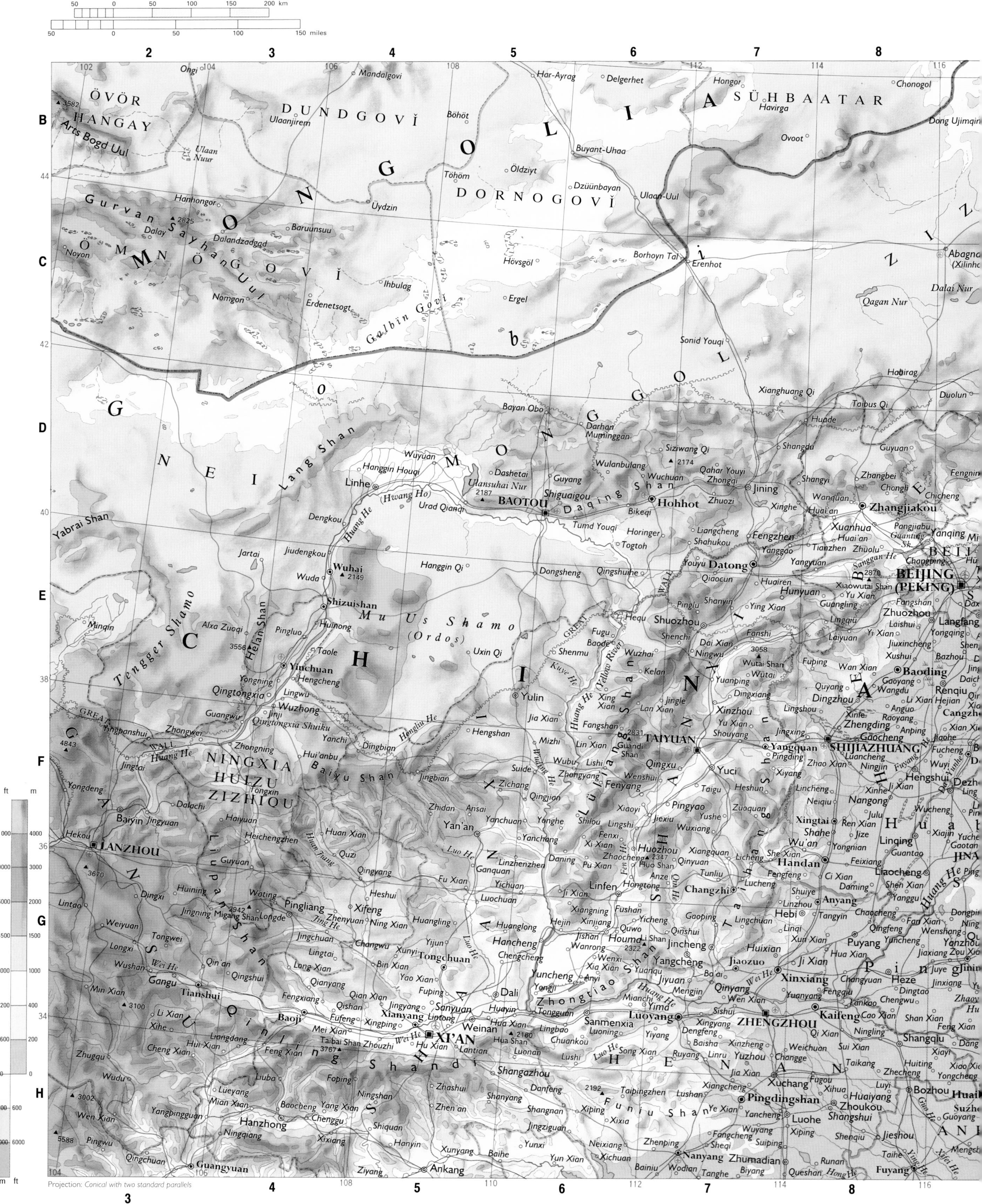

Projection: Conical with two standard parallels

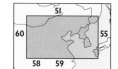

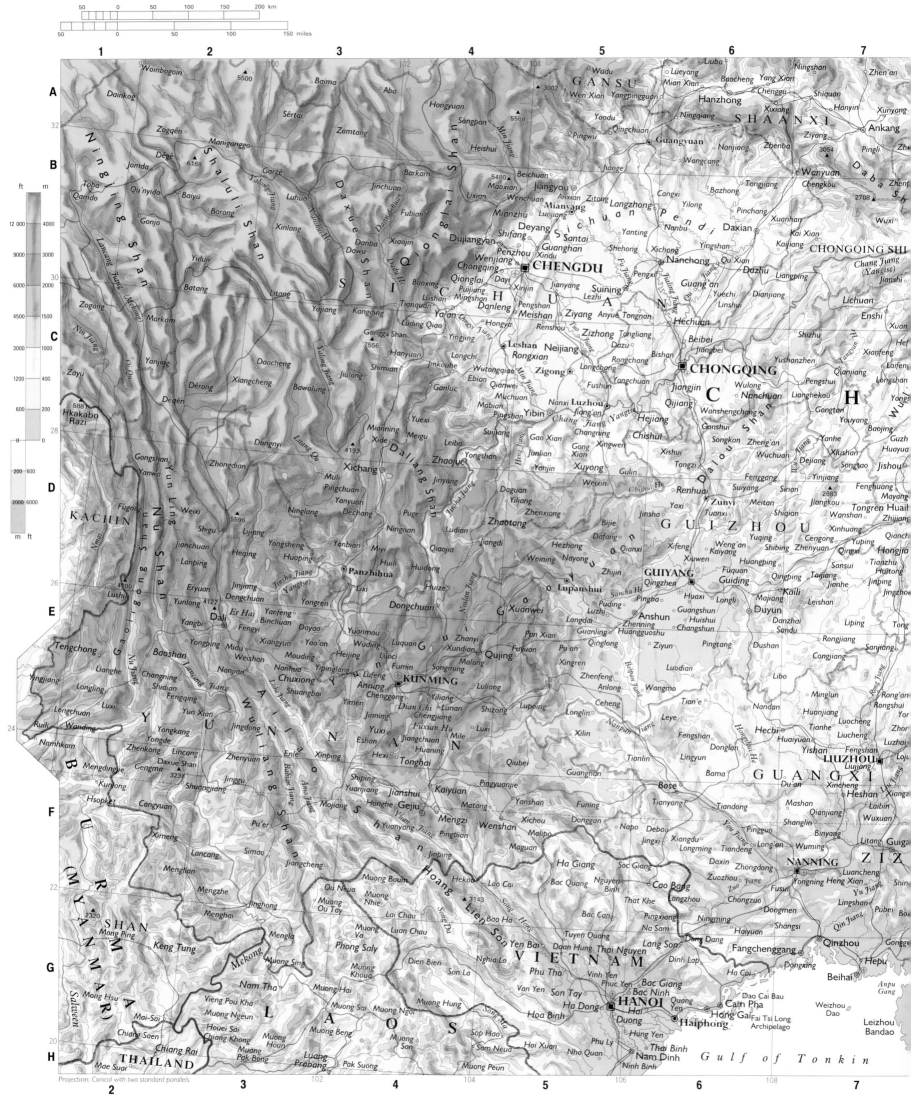

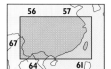

SOUTH CHINA SEA

East from Greenwich

COPYRIGHT GEORGE PHILIP LTD.

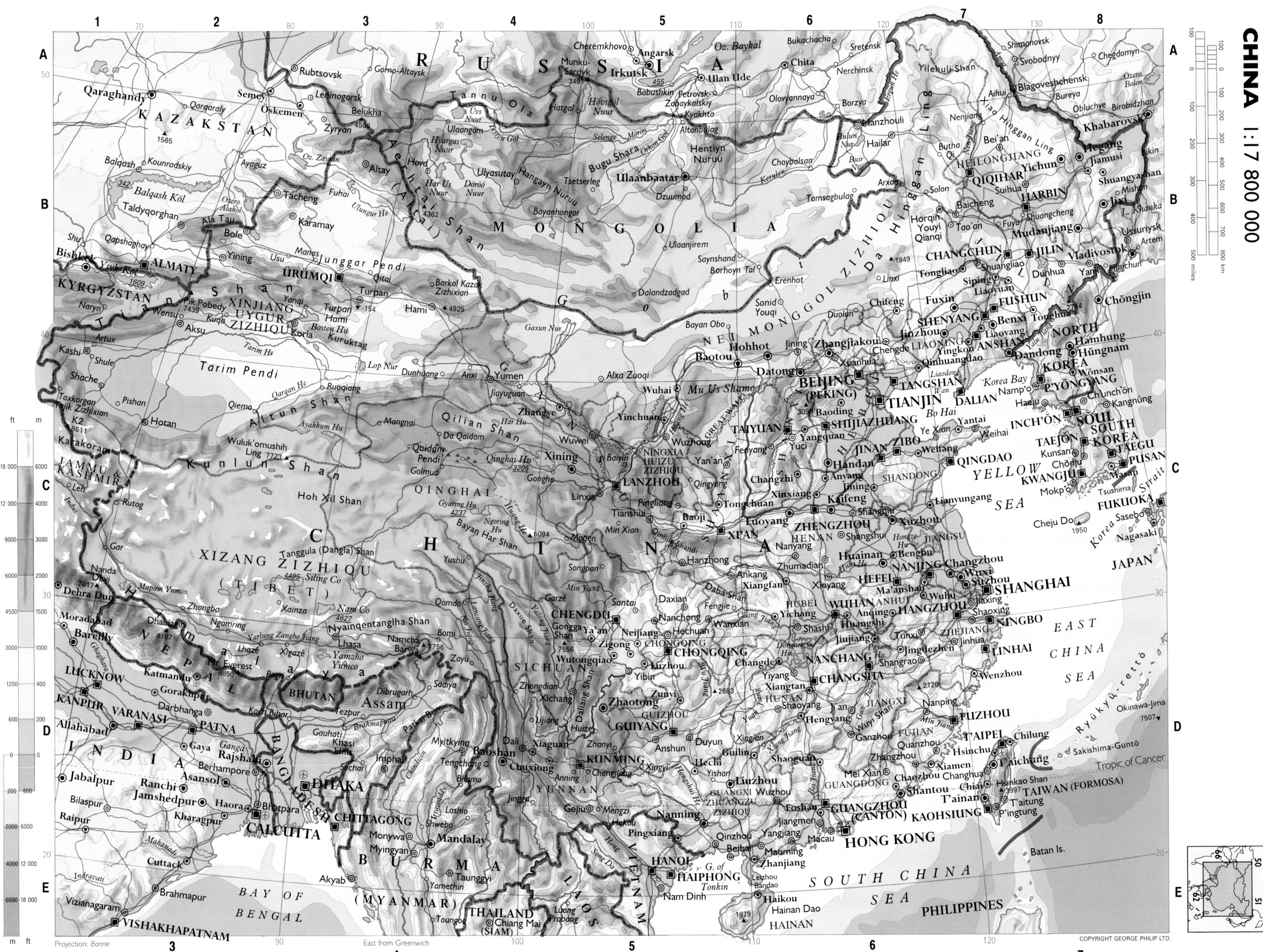

100 0 100 200 300 400 500 600 700 800 km
100 0 100 200 300 400 500 miles
RUSSIA
KAZAKSTAN
MONGOLIA
KYRGYZSTAN
CHINA
XINJIANG UYGUR ZIZHIQU
XIZANG ZIZHIQU (TIBET)
NEI MONGGOL ZIZHIQU
QINGHAI
SICHUAN
YUNNAN
BEIJING (PEKING)
TIANJIN
SHANGHAI
HONG KONG
GUANGZHOU (CANTON)
TAIWAN (FORMOSA)
NORTH KOREA
SOUTH KOREA
JAPAN
INDIA
NEPAL
BHUTAN
BANGLADESH
BURMA (MYANMAR)
THAILAND (SIAM)
LAOS
VIETNAM
PHILIPPINES
YELLOW SEA
EAST CHINA SEA
SOUTH CHINA SEA
BAY OF BENGAL
Tarim Pendi
Junggar Pendi
Kunlun Shan
Tian Shan
Tropic of Cancer
Projection: Bonne
East from Greenwich
COPYRIGHT GEORGE PHILIP LTD.

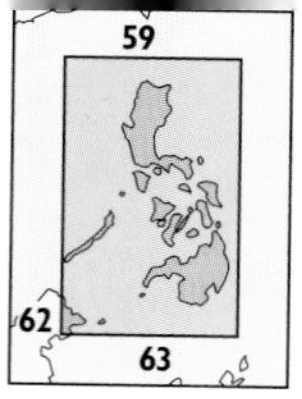

59
62 63

50 0 100 150 200 250 300 km
50 0 50 100 150 200 miles

THE PHILIPPINES

PACIFIC

OCEAN

PHILIPPINES

Itbayat I.
Batanes Is.
Batan I.

Balintang Channel

Calayan I.
Dalupiri I. Babuyan
Islands Camiguin I.
Fuga I.

Mayraira Pt. *Babuyan Channel*

Bacarra Claveria
San Nicolas Bangui Aparri Santa Ana
Batac Laoag Kabugao Gonzaga
Cabugao Gattaran
Vigan Bangued Tuao Tuguegarao
Santa Tuao Mt. Cresta
Maria 2360 1689
Candon Bontoc
Tagudin San Mateo Ilagan Palanan Pt.
Balaoan Roxas Santiago Palanan
San Fernando Cordon
Lingayen Gulf Mt. Pulog Solano
Bolinao Baguio 2928 Bayombong
Alaminos Mt. Anacuao C. San Ildefonso
Lingayen Dagupan 1852
San Carlos San Manuel
Santa Cruz Bayambang San Jose Baler Bay
Masinloc Moncada Cuyapo Bale
Camiling Victoria Baler

Luzon

Iba Tarlac La Cabanatuan
Concepcion 2037 Paz Gapan Dingalan
Mt. Pinatubo Angeles San Fernando
San Antonio 1780 Polillo Str.
Olongapo Orani Malabon Patnanongan I.
Bataan Manila **Caloocan** Jomalig I.
Cavite Bay **Quezon City** Polillo Is.
Dasmariñas **MANILA** Paracale
Nasugbu Tagaytay **Pasay** Santa Cruz Lobo
Balayan Lipa L. de Bay Lucban Daet Pandan
Lubang Lemery Batangas Lucena Calauag Viga
Is. Lobo Lopez Naga Catanduanes
C. Calavite Verde I. Pass Tayabas Bay Catanauan Iriga San Andres
Calapan Boac Marin- Nabua 2421 Virac
Mindoro Victoria duque Legazpi Mayon Vol. Rapu Rapu I.
Sablayan Mt. Baco Pinamalayan Burias I. Donsol Sorsogon
2487 SIBUYAN Magallanes Gubat
Bongabong Bulan San Bernardino Str.
Roxas Tablas I. Romblon Ticao I. Irosin Laoang
San Jose Odiongan Sibuyan I. Aroroy Allen Mondragon
Busuanga I. Ili I. SEA Masbate Milagros Catarman Gamay
Culion I. Calamian Pandan Mandaon Arteche
Group Masbate Catbalogan **Samar** Oras
Linapacan Str. Kalibo Placer Paranas Taft
Linapacan I. Dao Roxas VISAYAN Bilinan I. Calbiga Santa
Palawan Tibiao 2117 SEA Calubian Basey Rita
Taytay Cuyo Is. Ajuy Calbayog General MacArthur
Cuyo West Pass Bugasong Passi **Panay** Cadiz Corigara Palompon **Leyte** Tacloban Guiuan
Cuyo East Pass Cuyo Pototan Iloilo Silay Sagay Jubuan Ormoc Homonhon I.
San Jose Bacolod Victorias Danao Leyte Gulf
Dumaran I. Guimaras Jordan San Carlos Camotes Baybay
Irahuon 1593 Hinigaran Carlota Mandaue Camotes Sea Bato San Juan Dinagat I.
Honda Bay Binalbagan 2450 Cebu Maasin Dinagat
Puerto Princesa Himamaylan Guihulngan Carcar Panaon I. Siargao I. 10 497
Kabankalan Argao Bohol I. Surigao Placer
Sipalay Bais Oslob Tagbilaran Bucas Grande I.
Cagayan Is. Hinoba-an Tanjay Dumaguete BOHOL Cabadbaran Carrascal
Negros Bayawan Siaton Siquijor I. SEA Mainit Lanuza
Mt. Mantalingajan Zamboanguita Camiguin I. 2012 Tandag
2085 Talisayan Butuan Tago
C. Buliluyan Bugsuk I. Dapitan Nasipit Bayugan Marihatag
Balabac I. Dipolog SEA Balingasag Lianga
Balabac Strait Manukan Esperanza Talacogan Hinatuan
Balambangan Bangai Labason Iligan Opol Alubijid Malaybalay Bislig
Kudat Senaja Jembongan Sindangan Bay Cagayan de Oro
Langkon Suba Talon Loay Ozamiz Iligan 2938 Marawi City Bunawan Cateel
Tenghilan Kota Belud Telok Kabasalan Pagadian L. Lanao Baganga
Kota G. Kinabalu Labuk Siocon Kabasalan Mindanao Tagum
Kinabalu 4101 Sandakan Margosatubig 2815 Panabo Pantukan Manay
Papar SABAH Turtle Is. Sibuca Parang Panabo Mt. Apo Davao Mati
Kuamut Pangutaran Basilan Malabang Midsayap 2954 Digos Davao
MALAYSIA Group Illana Cotabato Pikit Koronadal Gulf San Isidro
Pilas Bay Datu Piang Malita
Borneo Isabela Talayan
Teluk Darvel Basilan I. Kalamansig Lebak 2083 General C. San Agustin
Lamitan Palimbang Santos
Jolo Samales Kiamba Sarangani Is.
Parang Group Tinaca Pt.
Talipao Pata I.
Siasi I.
Tapul
Group CELEBES
Tawi-tawi Sulu Archipela-go SEA
Group INDONESIA Kep. Talaud
Sibutu
Group

SOUTH CHINA SEA

SULU SEA

MORO GULF

Mindanao Trench

East from Greenwich

Projection: Lambert's Conformal Conic

ft m
9000 3000
6000 2000
4500 1500
3000 1000
1200 400
600 200
0
200 600
4000 12 000
8000 24 000
m ft

COPYRIGHT, GEORGE PHILIP LTD.

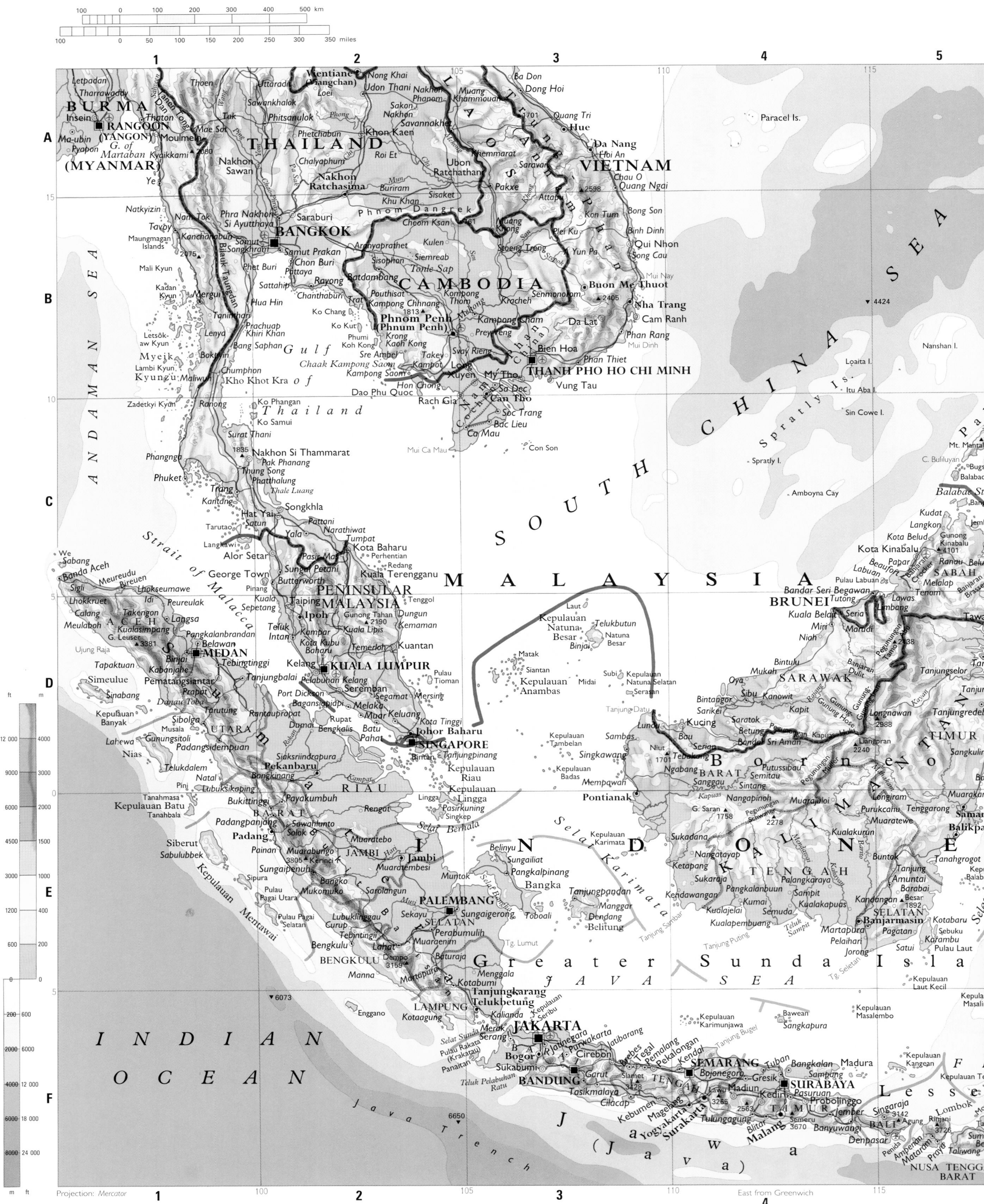

BURMA
(MYANMAR)

THAILAND

LAOS

VIETNAM

CAMBODIA

A N D A M A N   S E A

Gulf of Thailand

S O U T H   C H I N A   S E A

MALAYSIA

PENINSULAR MALAYSIA

Strait of Malacca

BRUNEI

SARAWAK

SABAH

KUALA LUMPUR

SINGAPORE

MEDAN

B o r n e o

KALIMANTAN

I   N   D   O   N   E

PALEMBANG

PONTIANAK

Java Sea

Greater Sunda Isla

BANJARMASIN

JAKARTA

SEMARANG

SURABAYA

BANDUNG

I   N   D   I   A   N   O   C   E   A   N

J   a   v   a

BALI

NUSA TENGG
BARAT

Lesse

Java Trench

Projection: Mercator

East from Greenwich

1   2   3   4

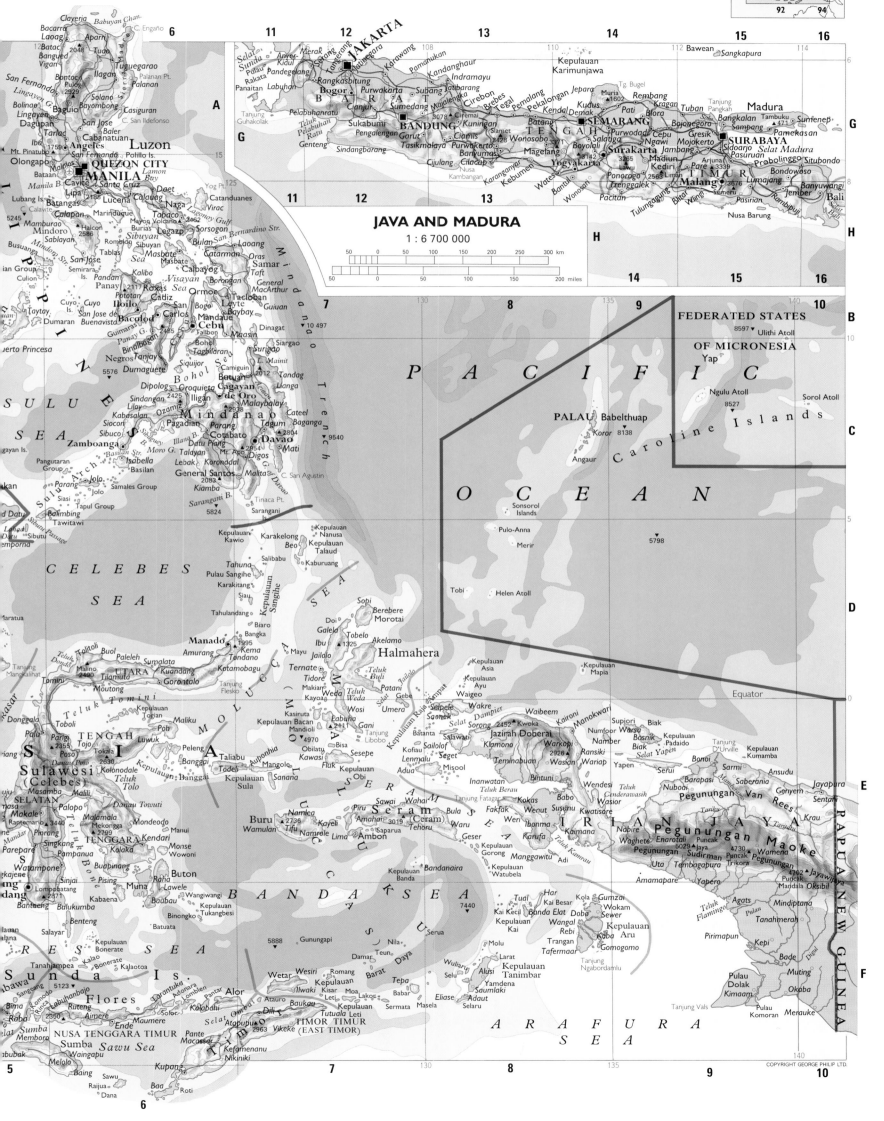
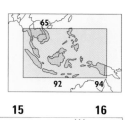

JAVA AND MADURA

1 : 6 700 000

50 0 50 100 150 200 250 300 km

50 0 50 100 150 200 miles

FEDERATED STATES

OF MICRONESIA

P A C I F I C

O C E A N

Caroline Islands

C E L E B E S

S E A

M O L U C C A   S E A

B A N D A   S E A

A R A F U R A

S E A

Sawu Sea

Flores Sea

COPYRIGHT GEORGE PHILIP LTD.

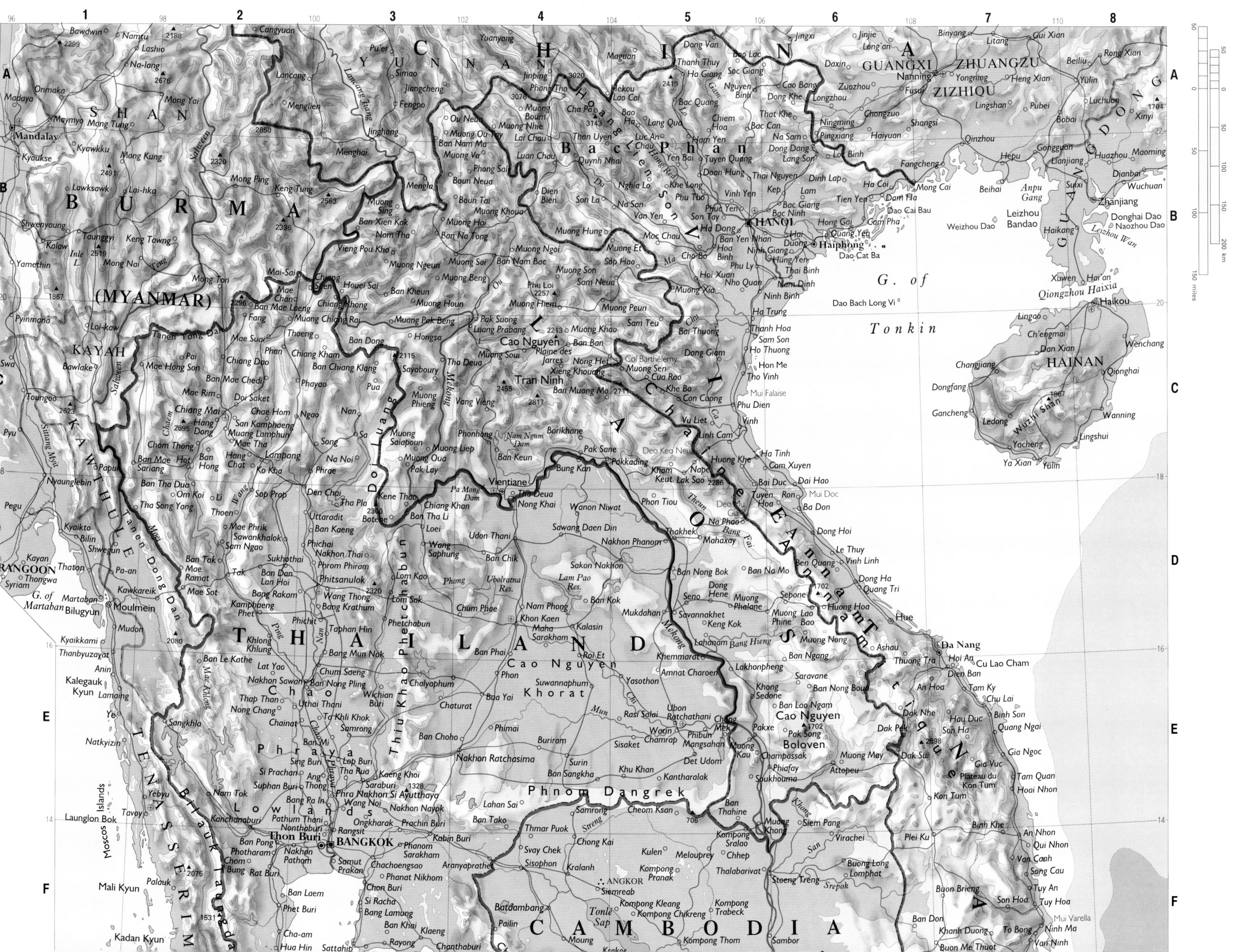
50 0 50 100 150 200 km
50 0 50 100 150 miles
BURMA (MYANMAR)
THAILAND
CAMBODIA
LAOS
VIETNAM
YUNNAN
GUANGXI ZHUANGZU ZIZHIQU
GUANGDONG
HAINAN
G. of Tonkin
Mekong
BANGKOK
RANGOON
Vientiane
HANOI
Mandalay
Moulmein
Haikou
Da Nang
Hue
Haiphong
Vinh
Tran Ninh
Cao Nguyen Khorat
Phnom Dangrek
KAWTHULE
KAYAH
SHAN
Tenasserim
G. of Martaban
Moscos Islands
Tonle Sap
ANGKOR

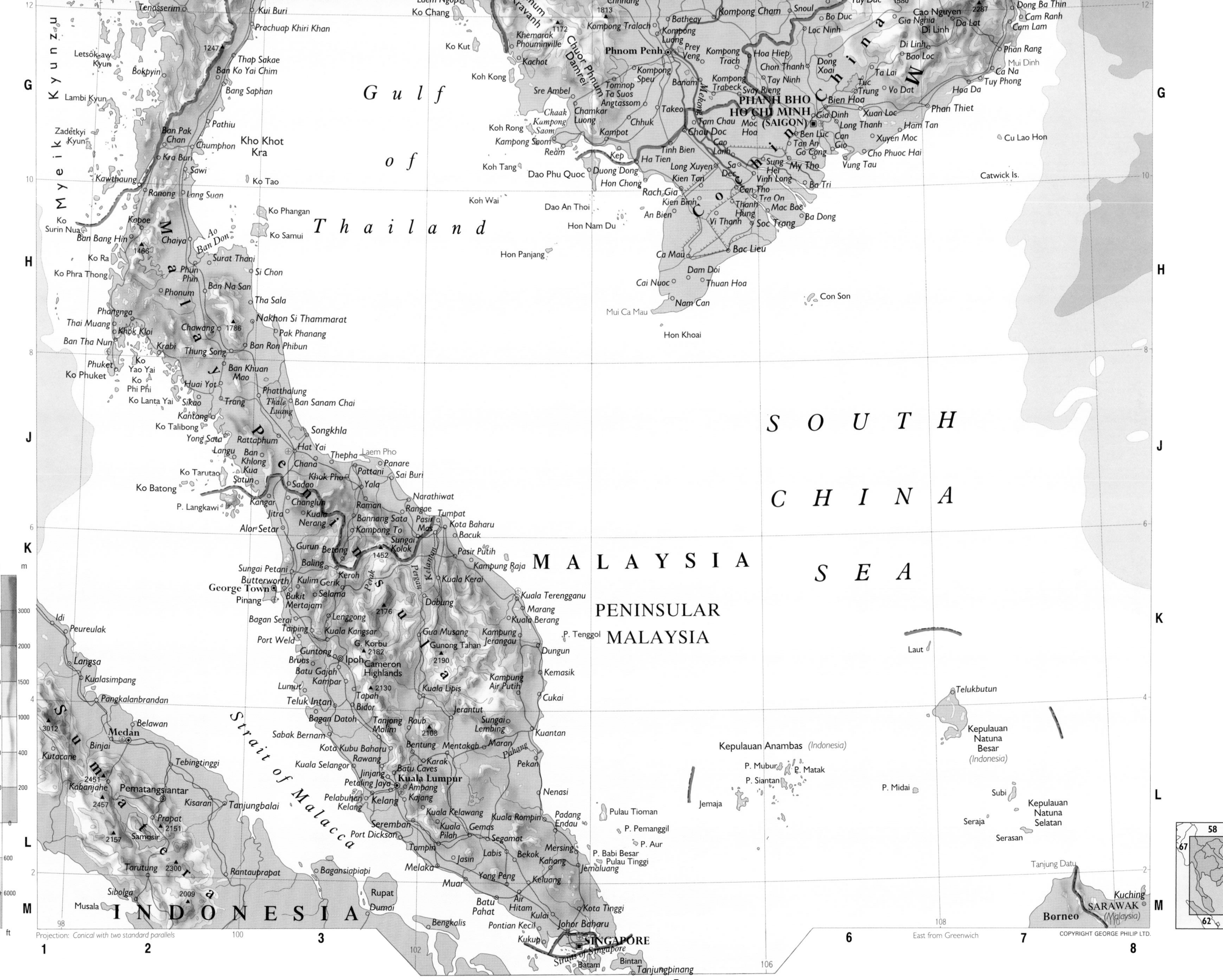

SOUTH

CHINA

SEA

MALAYSIA

PENINSULAR
MALAYSIA

Gulf

of

Thailand

Strait of Malacca

INDONESIA

Borneo

SARAWAK
(Malaysia)

Kuching

Kepulauan Anambas (Indonesia)

Kepulauan
Natuna
Selatan

Kepulauan
Natuna
Besar
(Indonesia)

PHNOM BHO
HOCHI MINH
HO CHI MINH
(SAIGON)

Phnom Penh

Mekong

Chuor Phnum
Damrei

SINGAPORE

Sumatera

East from Greenwich

Projection: Conical with two standard parallels

m   ft

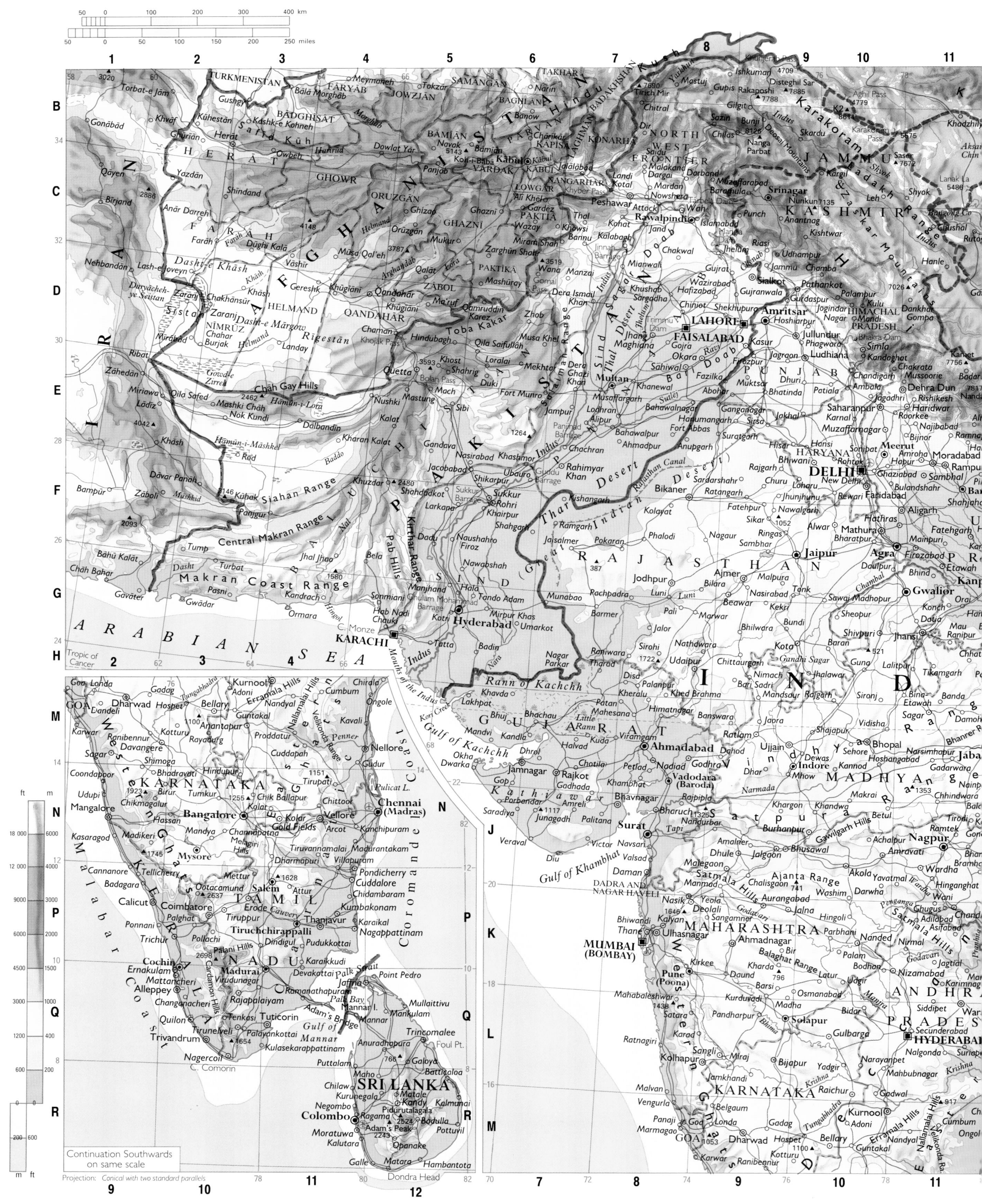

50 0 100 200 300 400 km
50 0 50 100 150 200 250 miles
ARABIAN SEA
IRAN
AFGHANISTAN
PAKISTAN
INDIA
TURKMENISTAN
SRI LANKA
JAMMU & KASHMIR
NORTH WEST FRONTIER
BALUCHISTAN
SIND
PUNJAB
RAJASTHAN
GUJARAT
MADHYA PRADESH
MAHARASHTRA
KARNATAKA
TAMIL NADU
KERALA
GOA
HARYANA
HIMACHAL PRADESH
ANDHRA PRADESH
DADRA AND NAGAR HAVELI
Kabul
Herat
Qandahar
Ghazni
Jalalabad
Islamabad
Rawalpindi
Peshawar
Quetta
LAHORE
FAISALABAD
Multan
Hyderabad
KARACHI
Srinagar
Amritsar
DELHI
New Delhi
Agra
Jaipur
Ahmadabad
Surat
MUMBAI (BOMBAY)
Pune (Poona)
Nagpur
HYDERABAD
Bangalore
Chennai (Madras)
Mysore
Madurai
Colombo
Kandy
Jaffna
Trincomalee
Hindu Kush
Karakoram
Thar Desert
Great Indian Desert
Rann of Kachchh
Gulf of Kachchh
Gulf of Khambhat
Western Ghats
Eastern Ghats
Malabar Coast
Coromandel Coast
Gulf of Mannar
Palk Strait
Adam's Bridge
Tropic of Cancer
Makran Coast Range
Central Makran Range
Siahan Range
Kirthar Range
Sulaiman Range
Satpura Range
Vindhya Range
Indus
Dashte Margow
Registan
Dasht-e Khash
K2 8611
Nanga Parbat 8126
Tirich Mir 7690
Adam's Peak 2243
C. Comorin
Dondra Head
Continuation Southwards on same scale
Projection: Conical with two standard parallels

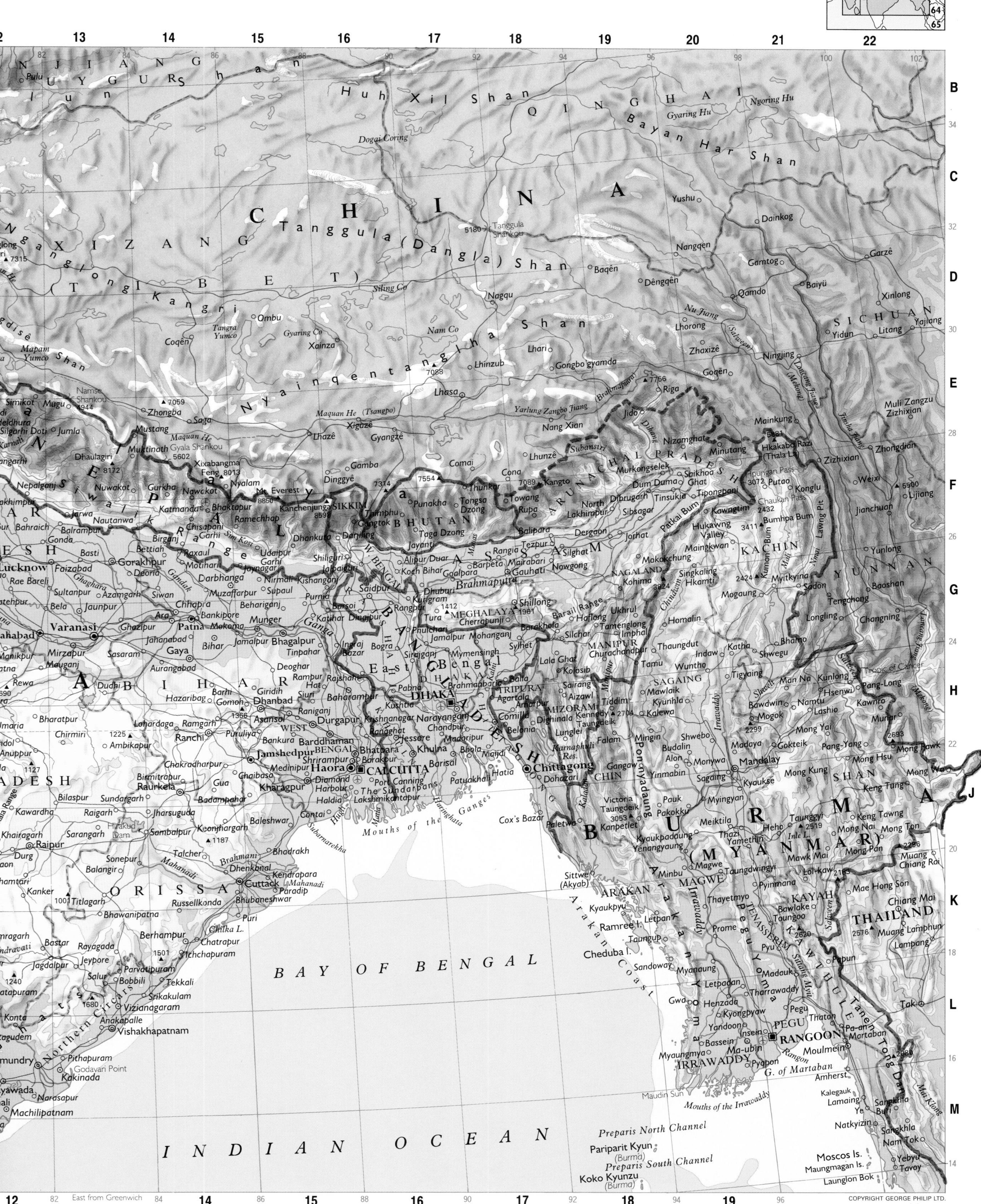
C H I N A
X I Z A N G
(T I B E T)
Q I N G H A I
Huh Xil Shan
Bayan Har Shan
Tanggula (Dangla) Shan
Nyainqentanglha Shan
Ngangla Kangri
Gangdisê Shan
Dogai Coring
Gyaring Hu
Ngoring Hu
Yushu
Dainkog
Nangqen
Garzê
Baqên
Dêngqên
Gamtog
Baiyü
Qamdo
Xinlong
Siling Co
Nagqu
Nu Jiang
Lhorong
S I C H U A N
Yidun
Litang
Yajiang
Tangra Yumco
Ombu
Gyaring Co
Nam Co
Xainza
Coqên
Mapam Yumco
Lhari
Zhaxizê
Gongbo'gyamda
Lhünzhub
Goqên
Ningjing
Lhasa
Riga
Maquan He (Tsangpo)
Yarlung Zangbo Jiang
Brahmaputra
Xigazê
Gyangzê
Nang Xian
Lhazê
Zhongba
Saga
Mustang
Muktinath
Gamba
Comai
Lhünzê
Nizamghat
Minutang
Mainkung
Hkakabo Razi (Thala La)
Zizhixian
Zhongdian
Muli Zangzu Zizhixian
Weixi
Lijiang
Jianchuan
Xixabangma Feng 8013
Nyalam
Dinggyê
Thunkar
Cona
Kangto
Mt. Everest 8850
Kanchenjunga 8598
SIKKIM
Thimphu
Punakha
Tongsa Dzong
B H U T A N
Taga Dzong
Towang
Rupa
ARUNACHAL PRADESH
Murkongselek
Dum Duma
Saikhoa Ghat
Putao
Konglu
Dibrugarh
Tinsukia
Tipongpani
North Lakhimpur
Sibsagar
Kawngtim
Bumhpa Bum
Patkai Bum
Hukawng Valley
Jorhat
Dergaon
Balipara
Tezpur
Rangia
Silghat
Nowgong
A S S A M
Maingkwan
K A C H I N
Yunlong
Y U N N A N
Mokokchung
NAGALAND
Kohima
Singkaling Hkamti
Myitkyina
Sadon
Baoshan
Tengchong
Mogaung
Longling
Changning
N E P A L
Siwalik Range
Simikot
Mugu
Jumla
Dhaulagiri 8172
Dhaulagiri
Nepalganj
Nuwakot
Gurkha
Nawakot
Katmandu
Bhaktapur
Ramechhap
Jarwa
Nautanwa
Bahraich
Balrampur
Gonda
Basti
Lucknow
Faizabad
Gorakhpur
Rae Bareli
Sultanpur
Azamgarh
Bettiah
Raxaul
Motihari
Birganj
Chisapani Garhi
Dhankuta
Darjiling
Jayanti
Shiliguri
Jalpaiguri
Alipur Duar
Koch Bihar
Goalpara
Dhubri
Barpeta
Mairabari
Gauhati
Brahmaputra
Shillong
MEGHALAYA
Cherrapunji
Tura
Darbhanga
Muzaffarpur
Nirmali
Kishanganj
Purnia
Saidpur
Rangpur
Kurigram
Barail Range
Haflong
Ukhrul
Tamenglong
Imphal
MANIPUR
Churachandpur
Silchar
Homalin
Thaungdut
Indaw
Katha
Bhamo
Shwegu
Varanasi
Ghazipur
Chhapra
Siwan
Ara
Patna
Mokama
Bihar
Munger
Bhagalpur
Ganga
Katihar
Dinajpur
Phulchari
Jamalpur
Mohanganj
Sylhet
Barakhola
Gaya
Jahanabad
Sasaram
Mirzapur
Tinpahar
Bogra
Mymensingh
Lala Ghat
Kolasib
Tamu
Wuntho
Tigyaing
Man Na
Kunlong
Hsenwi
Pang-Long
Tropic of Cancer
B I H A R
Deoghar
Rampur Hat
Siuri
Rajshahi
Pabna
Kushtia
East Bengal
DHAKA
TRIPURA
Agartala
Brahmanbaria
Sairang
Aizawl
MIZORAM
Tiddim
SAGAING
Mawlaik
Kyunhla
Kalewa
Bawdwin
Namtu
Lashio
Kawnto
Giridih
Dhanbad
Hazaribag
Gomoh
Asansol
Raniganj
Durgapur
Baharampur
Krishnanagar
Narayanganj
Comilla
Belonia
Dighinala
Kennedy
Taungdeik
Lunglei
Mogok
Madaya
Gokteik
Mong Yai
Pang-Yang
Mong Hsu
Ranchi
Purulia
Bankura
Barddhaman
Jessore
Khulna
Chandpur
Madaripur
Bhola
Maijdi
Hatia
Karnaphuli Res.
Falam
Mingin
Shwebo
Budalin
Alon
Monywa
Mandalay
Jamshedpur
Shrirampur
Barakpur
Bhatpara
Haora
CALCUTTA
Barisal
Patuakhali
Chittagong
Dohazari
CHIN
Gangaw
Yinmabin
Sagaing
Kyaukse
Mong Kung
S H A N
Chaibasa
Kharagpur
Medinipur
Diamond Harbour
Port Canning
The Sundarbans
Haldia
Lakshmikantapur
Contai
Mouths of the Ganges
Cox's Bazar
Paletwa
Victoria
Kanpetlet
Pauk
Pakokku
Myingyan
Meiktila
Thazi
Yamethin
Heho
Taunggyi
Inle L.
B U R M A
(M Y A N M A R)
Keng Tung
Keng Tawng
Mong Nai
Mong Ton
Mong Pan
Mawk Mai
Muang Chiang Rai
Mong Hawk
Mong Wa
Raurkela
Bilaspur
Sundargarh
Raigarh
Jharsuguda
Hirakud Dam
Sambalpur
Baleshwar
Bhadrakh
Kyaukpadaung
Yenangyaung
Minbu
Magwe
MAGWE
Taungdwingyi
Pyinmana
Loi-kaw
KAYAH
Mae Hong Son
Chiang Mai
Raipur
Durg
Balangir
Sonepur
Talcher
Brahmani
Dhenkanal
Mahanadi
Kendrapara
Cuttack
Paradip
Bhubaneshwar
Russellkonda
O R I S S A
Sittwe (Akyab)
ARAKAN
Kyaukpyu
Ramree I.
Letpan
Taungup
Thayetmyo
Prome
Bawlake
Toungoo
THAILAND
Muang Lamphun
Lampang
Kanker
Titlagarh
Bhawanipatna
Puri
Chilka L.
Berhampur
Chatrapur
Ichchapuram
Bastar
Rayagada
Jeypore
Parvatipuram
Jagdalpur
Salur
Bobbili
Tekkali
Srikakulam
Vizianagaram
Anakapalle
Vishakhapatnam
Northern Circars
Pithapuram
Godavari Point
Kakinada
Narasapur
Machilipatnam
B A Y   O F   B E N G A L
Cheduba I.
Sandoway
Arakan Coast
Arakan Yoma
Irrawaddy
Pegu Yoma
Sittang Myit
Myanaung
Letpadan
Henzada
Tharrawaddy
Madauk
Pyu
TENASSERIM
Papun
Tak
Gwa
Kyongpyaw
Pegu
PEGU
Yandoon
Insein
Bassein
RANGOON
Thaton
Pa-an
Martaban
Moulmein
Ma-ubin
Myaungmya
IRRAWADDY
Pyapon
Rangoon
G. of Martaban
Amherst
Mouths of the Irrawaddy
Maudin Sun
Kalegauk
Lamaing
Ye
Natkyizin
Sangkhla Buri
Mai Klong
Nam Tok
Yebyu
Tavoy
Moscos Is.
Maungmagan Is.
Launglon Bok
Preparis North Channel
Pariparit Kyun (Burma)
Preparis South Channel
Koko Kyunzu (Burma)
I N D I A N   O C E A N
East from Greenwich

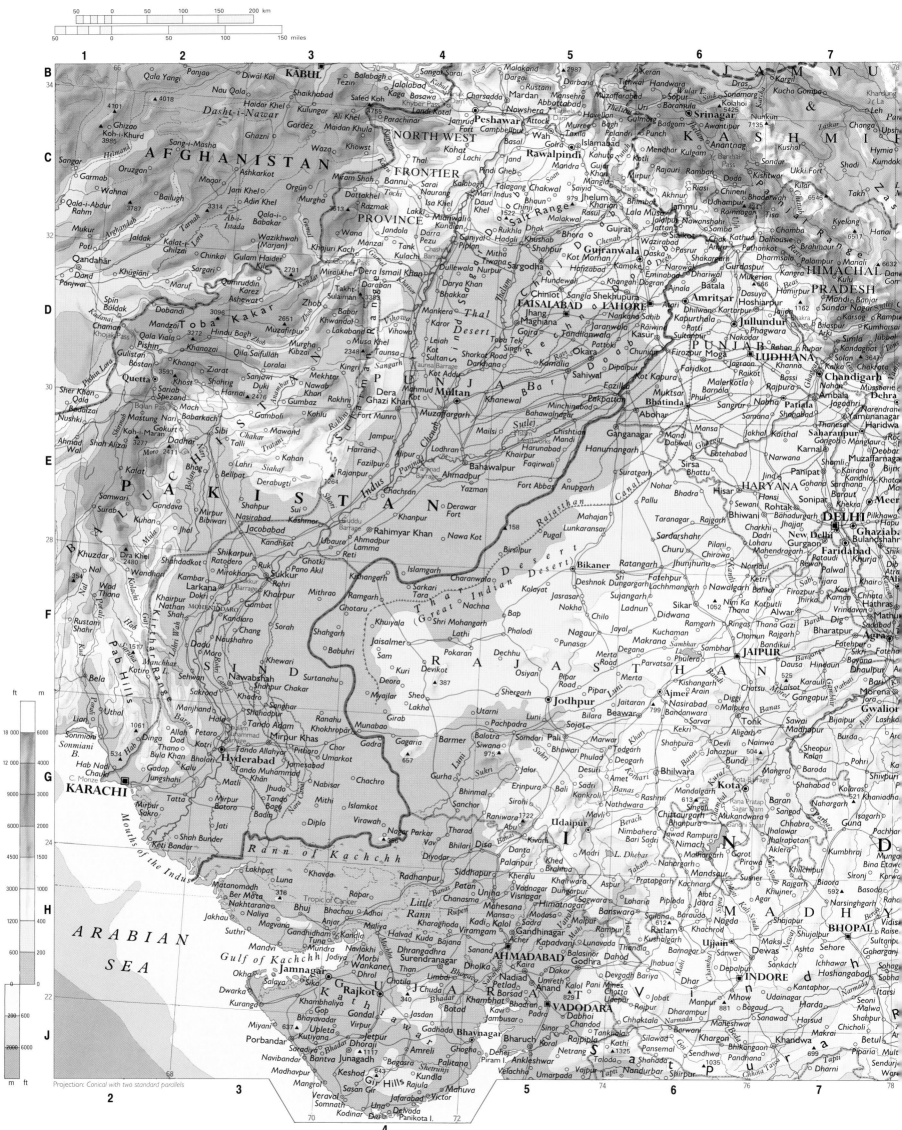

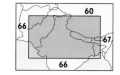

JAMMU AND KASHMIR
On same scale as Main Map

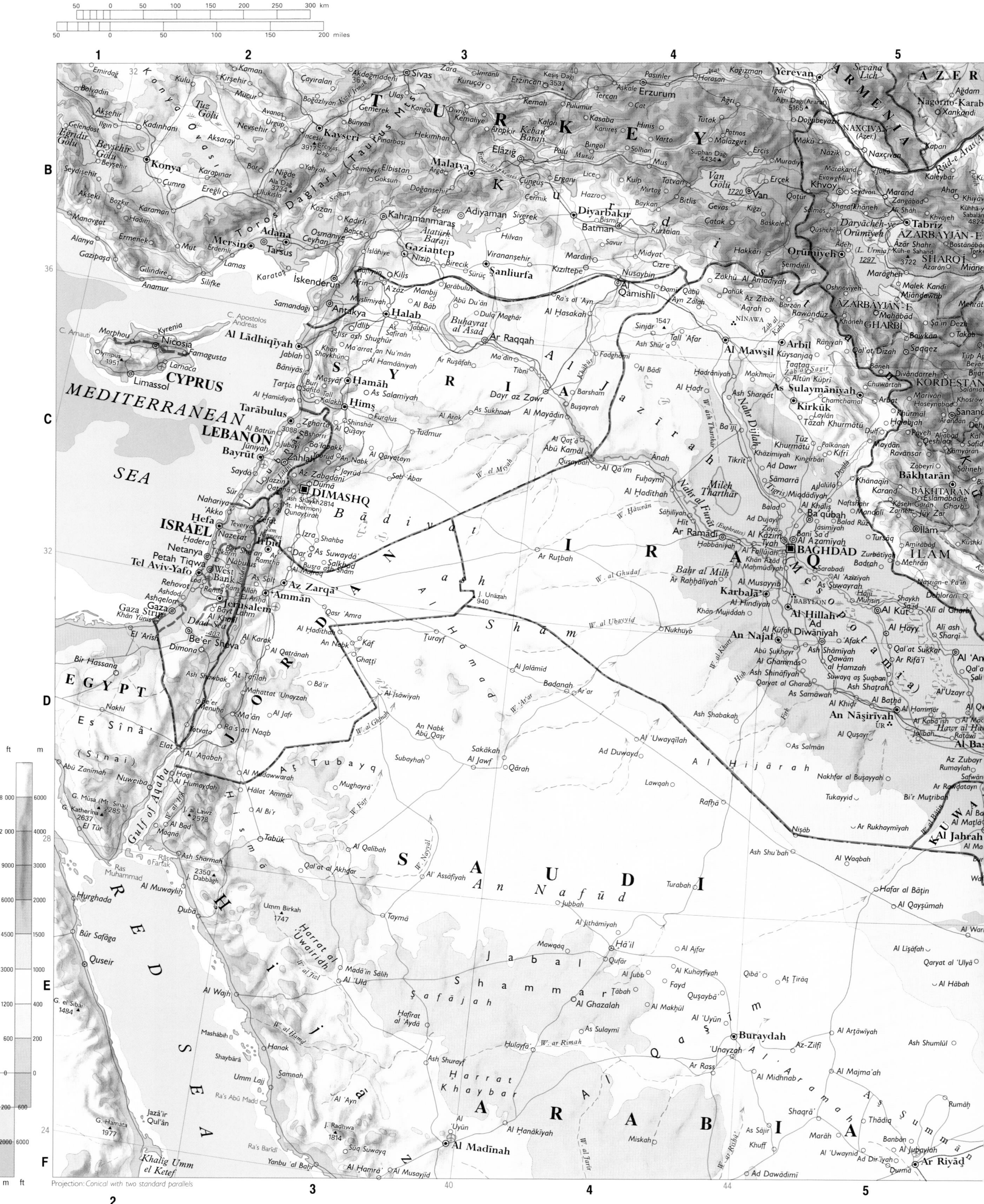

TURKEY
SYRIA
LEBANON
ISRAEL
JORDAN
IRAQ
CYPRUS
EGYPT
SAUDI ARABIA
ARMENIA
MEDITERRANEAN SEA
RED SEA
Gulf of Aqaba
Es Sînâ' (Sinai)
An Nafūd
Jabal Shammar
Bādiyat ash Shām
Al Jazīrah
Al Ḥijārah
Harrat Khaybar
Toros Dağları (Taurus Mts)
Mesopotamia
Dimashq
Baghdād
Bayrūt
'Ammān
Jerusalem
Tel Aviv-Yafo
Nicosia
Ḥalab
Ḥimṣ
Ḥamāh
Al Mawṣil
Arbīl
Kirkūk
Karbalā'
An Najaf
Al Madīnah
Ar Riyāḍ
Ḥā'il
Buraydah
Tabūk
Konya
Adana
Kayseri
Malatya
Erzurum
Diyarbakır
Sivas
Yerevan
Tabrīz
Van Gölü
Dead Sea
Projection: Conical with two standard parallels

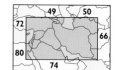

AR JAN · **BAKÏ**

Qazimämmäd
Älät
Neftçala
Qızılağaç Körfäzi
Kür Dili
Länkäran
Ostrov Ogurchinskiy
Chelekën Yarymadasy
26 Bakinskikh Komissarov
Nebitdag
Khrebet Bolshoy Balkhan 1880
T U R K M E N I S T A N
Chärjew
Amudarya
995

Qazvïn
Ardabïl
Tälesh
Äsärä
GÏLÄN
Rasht
Lähïjän
Rüd Sar
Rämsar
Tonekabon
Now Shahr
Bandar-e Torkeman
Gorgan
Ko**p**e**t** **D**a**g**h

Ashgabat
Mary
Bayramaly
Yoloten

C A S P I A N S E A

-28

Reshteh-ye Kühhä-ye Alborz

Kajan · **Tehrân**
Karaj
Tajrïsh
Eslamshahr
Rey
Damavand 5604

MARKAZÏ
Garmsär

I R A N

Qom
Daryächeh-ye Namak

Dasht-e Kavïr

SEMNÄN

KHORÄSÄN

HERÄT
Herat

AFGHANISTAN

FARÄH

ESFAHÄN
Esfahän

YAZD
Yazd

Da**s**h**t**-**e** **L**ü**t**

KERMÄN
Kerman

FARS
Shïräz

BÜSHEHR
Büshehr

PAKISTAN
Zähedän

SÏSTÄN VA BALÚCHESTÄN

KHUZESTÄN
Ahväz
Äbädän

HORMOZGÄN
Bandar 'Abbäs

THE GULF

BAHRAIN
Manämah
QATAR
Ad Dawhah
Ad Dammäm

Qeshm
Sïr of Hormuz
Ra's Masandam (Oman)

Dubayy
Ash Shäriqah
Umm al Qaywayn
Abü Zäby
U N I T E D   A R A B   E M I R A T E S

G u l f   o f   O m a n

O M A N

Al 'Ayn

East from Greenwich

COPYRIGHT GEORGE PHILIP LTD.

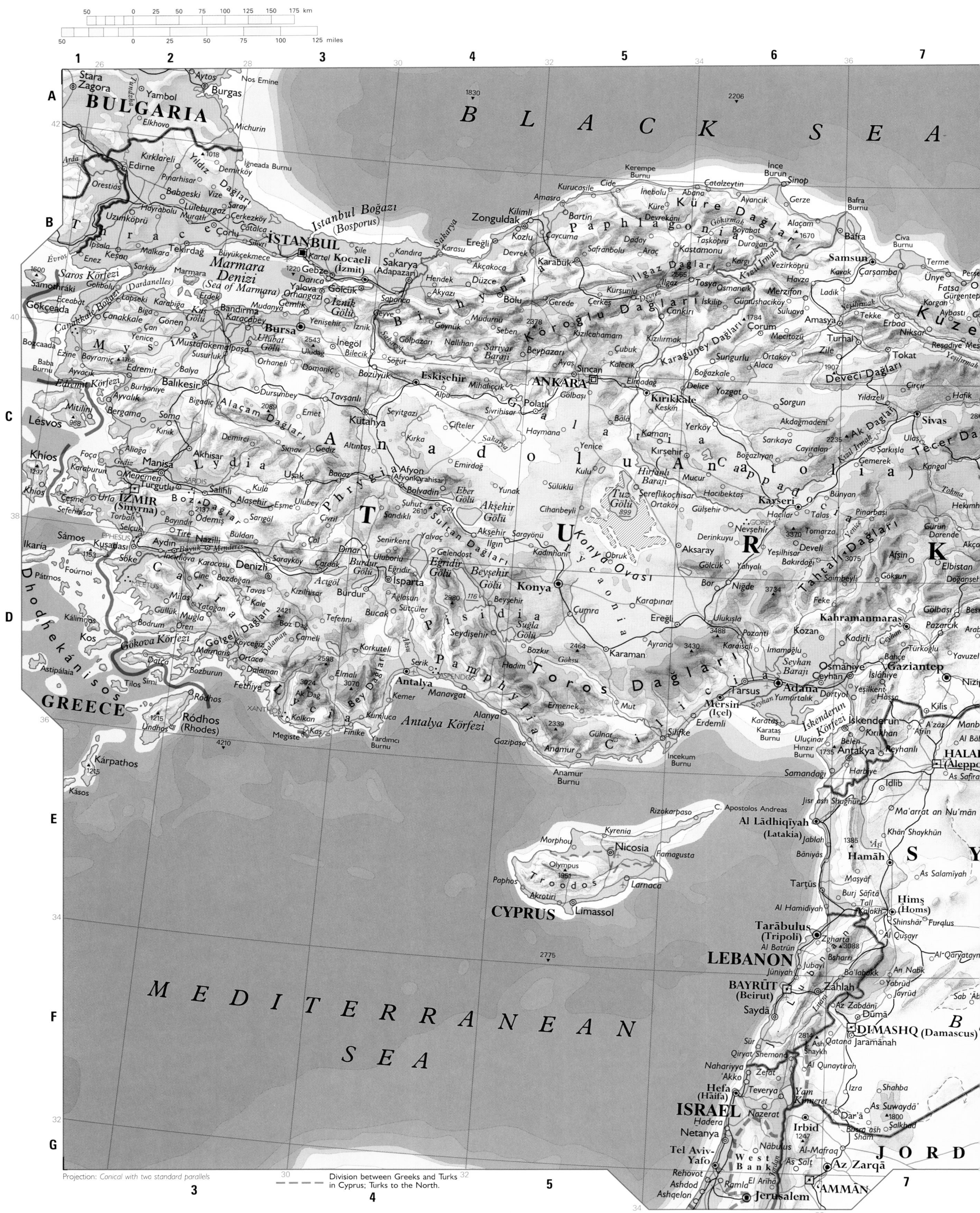

Division between Greeks and Turks
in Cyprus; Turks to the North.

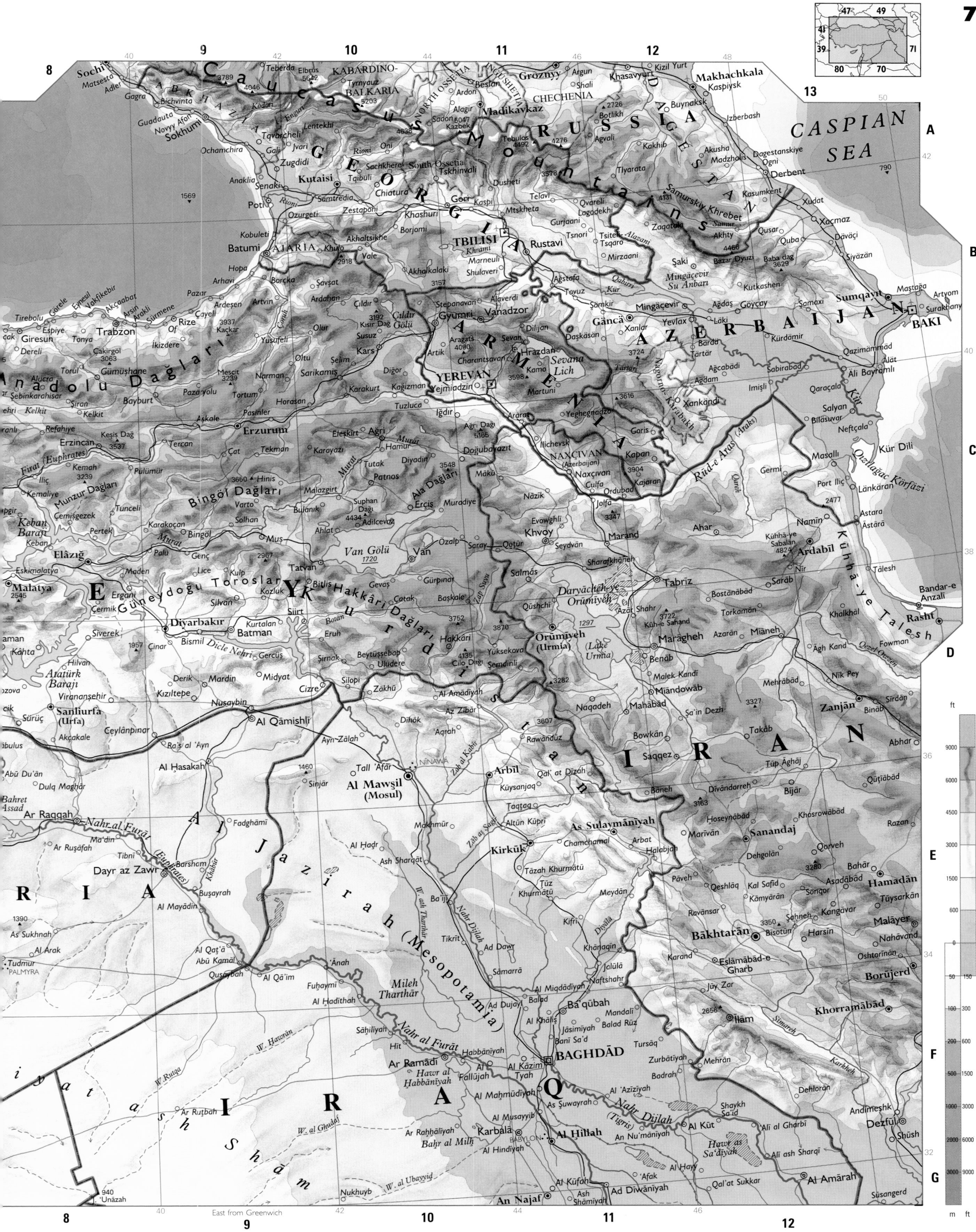

CASPIAN SEA

RUSSIA

GEORGIA

AZERBAIJAN

ARMENIA

TURKEY

IRAN

IRAQ

SYRIA

Caucasus Mountains

KABARDINO-BALKARIA
NORTH OSSETIA
CHECHENIA
INGUSHETIA
DAGESTAN
ABKHAZIA
AJARIA
South Ossetia
NAXÇIVAN (Azerbaijan)

Sochi · Matsesta · Adler · Gagra · Bichvinta · Novyy Afon · Sokhum · Guadauta · Ochamchira · Gali · Zugdidi · Anaklia · Senaki · Poti · Ozurgeti · Kobuleti · Batumi · Hopa · Borçka · Ardeşen · Rize · Çayeli · Pazar

Teberda · Elbrus 5642 · 3789 · 4046 · 5203 · Tyrnyauz · Kodori · Engur · Lentekhi · Tavorcheli · Jvari · Oni · Rioni · Sachkhere · Chiatura · Kutaisi · Tqibuli · Samtredia · Zestaponi · Khashuri · Gori · Kaspi · Borjomi · Akhaltsikhe · Akhalkalaki · Vale · Khulo · 2918 · 3157

Vladikavkaz · Beslan · Ardon · Sadon 6047 · Tskhinvali · 3578 · Dusheti · Mtskheta · **TBILISI** · Khrami · Rustavi · Marneuli · Shulaveri · Telavi · Gurjaani · Logadekhi · Tsnori · Tsiteli-Tsqaro · Mirzaani

Groznyy · Argun · Shali · Khasavyurt · Kizil Yurt · **Makhachkala** · Kaspiysk · Buynaksk · Izberbash · Botlikh 2726 · 4492 · 4276 · Agvali · Tlyarata · Kakhib · Akusha · Madzholis · Ogni · Derbent · 790 · Kasumkent · Samur · Xudat · Xaçmaz · Qusar · Quba · Däväçi · Siyäzän · Baba dag 3629 · Bazar Dyuzi

Qvareli · Zaqatala · Şaki · Mingäçevir Su Anbarı · Kutkashen · Göyçay · Ağdaş · Yevlax · Läki · Goranboy

Çıldır · Çıldır Gölü · Stepanavan · Alaverdi · Tovuz · Şämkir · Gänçä · Xanlar · Mingäçevir · Şamaxı · Sumqayıt · Maştağa · **BAKI** · Artyom · Suraxanı

Ardahan · Artvin · Şavşat · Olur · 3192 Kısır Dağı · Gyumri · Vanadzor · Dilijan · Sevan · Daşkäsän · Kürdämir · Salyan · 3724 · Qazımämmäd · Äli Bayramlı · Ağcabädi · Sabirabad · Imişli

Kaçkar 3937 · Yusufeli · Susuz · Kars · Aragats 4090 · Artik · Sevana Lich · Hrazdan · Kamo · 3598 · **YEREVAN** · Ejmiadzin · Martuni · Yeghegnadzor · 3616 · Xankändi · Ağdam · Bärdä · Tärtär

Trabzon · Of · İkizdere · Gümüşhane · Bayburt · Kelkit · Kelkit · Erzurum · Askale · Pasinler · Horasan · Tortum · Oltu · Narman · Sarıkamış · Şelim · Digor · Karakurt · Kağızman · Tuzluca · Iğdır · Ararat · Doğubayazıt · Ağrı Dağı 5166 · Maku · İlıçevsk

Giresun · Espiye · Tirebolu · Görele · Vakfıkebir · Akçaabat · Sürmene · Araklı

Anadolu Dağları · Şebinkarahisar · Alucra · Torul · Refahiye · Kemah · İliç · Kemaliye · Pülümür · Tercan · Çat · Tekman · Eleşkirt · Ağrı · Tutak · Muş · Patnos · Ala Dağları 3548 · Diyadin · Hamur · Karayazı · Malazgirt · Bulanık · Erciş · Muradiye · Adilcevaz · Ahlat · Van · Özalp · Saray · Qotur

Erzincan 3537 · 3239 · Refahiye · Kemah · Munzur Dağları · Çemişgezek · Tunceli · Karakoçan · Bingöl · Genç · Muş · Solhan · Varto · Bingöl Dağları 3660 · Hınıs · Suphan Dağı 4434 · Van Gölü 1720

Eskimalatya · Malatya 2545 · Elâzığ · Keban Barajı · Keban · Maden · Palu · Kulp · Tatvan · Gevaş · Bitlis · Kozluk · Siirt · Gürpınar · Başkale · Khvoy · Marand · Seydvan · Salmas

Kâhta · Ergani · Çermik · Siverek · Diyarbakır · Silvan · Kurtalan · Batman · Bismil · Lice · Çatak · Hakkâri 3752 · Şemdinli · 3870 · Tabriz · Kuh-e Sahand 3722 · Azar Shahr · Qushchi · Daryācheh-ye Orūmīyeh

Güneydoğu Toroslar · Hakkâri Dağları · Cilo Dağı 4135 · Yüksekova · Rawānduz · Orūmīyeh (Urmia) · Lake Urmia 1297

Viranşehir · Kızıltepe · Derik · Mardin · Midyat · Cizre · Silopi · Zākhū · Al 'Amādīyah · Az Zibār · 'Aqrah · 3282 · Naqadeh · Mahābād

Şanlıurfa (Urfa) · Akçakale · Ceylanpınar · Ra's al 'Ayn · Nusaybin · Al Qāmishlī · Dīhōk · 3607 · Arbīl · Küysanjaq · Sa'in Dezh · Bowkān · Saqqez · Takāb · Zanjān · Abhar

Bahret Assad · Ar Raqqah · Ayn Zālah · Tall 'Afar · Sinjār 1460 · NINAWA · Al Mawşil (Mosul) · Qal'at Dīzah · Bāneh · Mariwān · Sanandaj · Dīvāndarreh · Bījār · Qūṭīābād

Abū Du'ān · Dulq Maghār · Al Hasakah · Fadghāmī · 1957 Çınar · Ba'shīqah · Qayyarah · Makhmūr · Altūn Küprī · As Sulaymānīyah · Chamchamal · Arbat · 3163 · Hoseynābād · Khosrowābād · Razan

Nahr al Furāt (Euphrates) · Ma'dan · Tibnī · Barsham · Ar Ruşāfah · Al Hadr · Ash Sharqāt · Kirkūk · Tāzah Khurmātū · Tūz Khurmātū · Halabjah · Pāveh · Mariwān · Ravānsar · Kāmyārān · Qeshlāq · 3280 · Asadābād · Hamadān

Dayr az Zawr · Al Mayādīn · Būşayrah · Tikrīt · Ad Dawr · Kifrī · Khānaqīn · Maydān · Sanandaj · Sorqor · Şehneh · Kangāvar · Tūysarkān · Nahāvand

Al Qāt'ā · Abū Kamāl · Al Qā'im · 'Ānah · Sāmarrā' · Al Miqdādīyah · Jalūlā' · 3350 · Bākhtarān · Bisotūn · Harsin · Malāyer · Oshtorīnān · Borūjerd

Tudmur · PALMYRA · Al Arak · As Sukhnah · 1390 · Hīt · Ar Ramādī · Habbānīyah · Al Kāzim · Balad · Bā'qūbah · Balad Rūz · Mandalī · 2656 · Īlām · Khorramābād · Dehlorān

Mileh Tharthār · W. ath Tharthār · Nahr Dijlah · Al Hadīthah · Fuhaymī · Al Kufah · **BAGHDĀD** · Al Mahmūdīyah · Al 'Azīzīyah · Zurbātīyah · Mehrān · Badrah

Ar Ruţbah · W. Rutga · W. Hawrān · W. al Ghadaf · Nukhayb · Al Kūfah · An Najaf · Karbalā' · BABYLON · Al Hillah · Al Hindīyah · Al Musayyib · Ash Shāmīyah · Ad Dīwānīyah · Afak · Nukhayb

Bahr al Milh · Bahr al Milh · Al Hayy · Al Kūt · Al Gharbī · Hawr as Sa'dīyah · Shaykh Sa'd · Qal'at Sukkar · Al 'Amārah · Sūsangerd · Dehloran · Andimeshk · Dezfūl · Shūsh · Karkheh

Naftshahr · Qaşr-e Shīrīn · Jalūlā' · Naft Khāneh · Jāsimīyah · Banī Sa'd · Tursāq

East from Greenwich

ft — m
9000 — 3000
6000 — 2000
4500 — 1500
3000 — 1000
1500 — 500
600 — 200
0 — 0
150 — 50
300 — 100
600 — 200
1500 — 500
3000 — 1000
6000 — 2000
9000 — 3000
m — ft

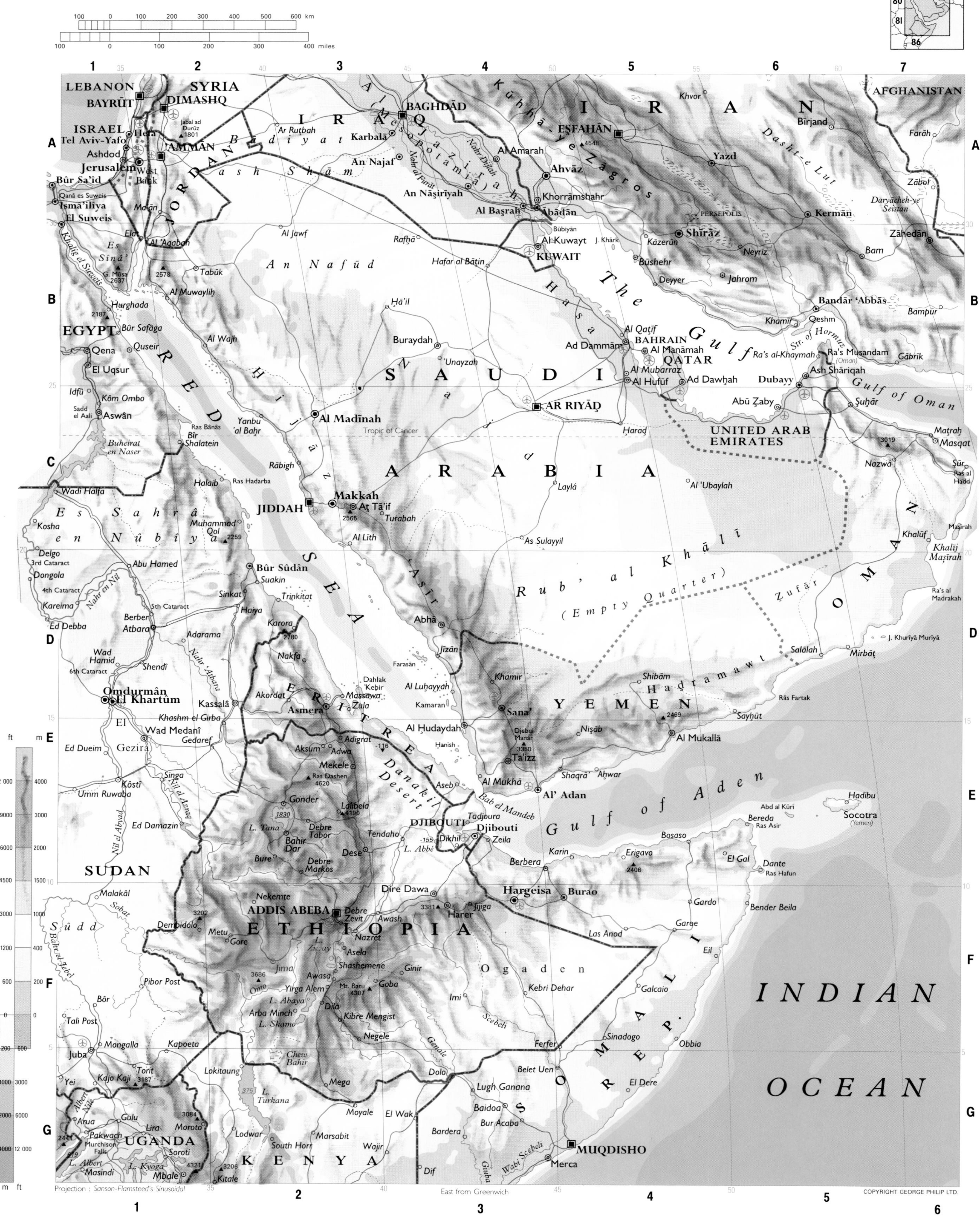

100 0 100 200 300 400 500 600 km
100 0 100 200 300 400 miles

1   2   3   4   5   6   7

LEBANON   SYRIA
BAYRŪT   DIMASHQ
ISRAEL
Tel Aviv-Yafo   Hefa
Ashdod   'AMMĀN
Jerusalem   West Bank
Bûr Sa'îd   Qanâ es Suweis
Isma'îliya
El Suweis   Es Sina'   El 'Aqaba   Jabal ad
Durūz   1801
2637

IRAQ   BAGHDAD   Al Qāsim   ĪRĀN   AFGHANISTAN
Ar Ruṭbah   Karbalā'   An Najaf   Khvor   Birjand   Farāh
Ash Shām   An Nāṣirīyah   Al Amarah   4548   Yazd   Zābol
Ahvāz   ESFAHĀN   Daryācheh-ye
Khorramshahr   Seistan
Al Baṣrah   Ābādān   Shīrāz   Kermān   Zāhedān
Al Kuwayt   Kāzerūn   Neyrīz   Bam
KUWAIT   Būshehr   Jahrom   Bandar 'Abbās   Bampūr
Deyyer   Khamīr   Ra's Musandam
Ad Dammām   BAHRAIN   Ra's al-Khaymah   Gābrīk
QATAR   Dubayy   Ash Shāriqah
Al Hufūf   Ad Dawḥah   Abū Ẓaby   Ṣuḥār   Maṭraḥ   Masqaṭ
AR RIYĀD   UNITED ARAB   3019   Nazwā   Ṣūr
EMIRATES   Khalūf   Ra's al Hadd

EGYPT
Hurghada   2187
Bûr Safâga
Qena   Quseir
El Uqsur
Idfû
Kôm Ombo
Aswân
Sadd el Aali
Buheirat en Naser

An Nafūd   Al Jawf   Rafḥā   Hafar al Bāṭin   Būbiyān   J. Khārk   PERSEPOLIS
Tabūk   Ḥā'il   Burayḍah   'Unayzah   Al Qaṭīf   Al Manāmah
Al Muwayliḥ   Al Wajh   SAUDI   Al Mubarraz   Ḥaraḍ
Yanbu 'al Baḥr   Al Madīnah   ARABIA   Laylā   Al 'Ubaylah
Tropic of Cancer   As Sulayyil
Rābigh   Ras Bānās   Bîr Shalatein   Makkah   Aṭ Ṭā'if   2565   Turabah
JIDDAH   Al Līth   Rub' al Khālī   Zufār
Halaib   Ras Hadarba   (Empty Quarter)   Salālah   Mirbāṭ
Muhammad Qol   2259   Abhā   J. Khurīyā Murīyā
Es   Sahrâ   Wadi Halfa   Jīzān   Khamīr   Shibām   Rās Fartak   Khalīj   Maṣīrah
en   Nûbiya   Farasān   Hadramawt   Ra's al
3rd Cataract   Kosha   Abu Hamed   Bûr Sûdân   Dahlak Kebir   Al Luḥayyah   Sayhūt
Delgo   Suakin   Massawa   Sana   YEMEN   2469
Dongola   4th Cataract   Trinkitat   Kamaran   Al Mukallā
Kareima   Sinkat   Al Ḥudaydah   Niṣāb   Ras Fartak
Ed Debba   5th Cataract   Haiya   Karora   Djebel Manar   OMAN
Berber   Adarama   2780   3350   Shaqrā   Ahwar
Wad   Atbara   Nakfa   Ta'izz   Abd al Kūrī
Hamid   6th Cataract   ERITREA   Al Mukhā   Hadibu
Omdurmân   Kassalā   Akordat   Aseb   Al' Adan   Socotra   (Yemen)
El Khartûm   Khashm el Girba   Asmera   Zula   Bab el Mandeb   Gulf of Aden
El   Wad Medanî   Adigrat   Danakil   DJIBOUTI   Bereda   Ras Asir
Ed Dueim   Gedaref   Aksum   -116   Desert   Tadjoura   Djibouti   Bosaso
Umm Ruwaba   Adwa   Mekele   Aseb   Zeila   Karin   Erigavo   El-Gal   Dante
Gezira   Ras Dashen   4620   Berbera   2406   Ras Hafun
Ed Damazin   Gonder   Lalibela   Dikhil   Hargeisa   Burao
SUDAN   1830   4190   -155   Dire Dawa   Gardo   Bender Beila
Malakâl   L. Tana   Debre Tabor   L. Abbé   Jijiga   Garoe   Eil
Sobat   Bahir   Dese   Harer   Las Anod
Sûdd   Dar   Debre   3381   SOMALI REP.
Bahr-el-Jebel   Bure   Markos   ADDIS ABEBA   Debre   Awash   Galcaio
Nekemte   Zevit   Kebri Dehar
Dembidolo   ETHIOPIA   Ogaden   Eil
Metu   3202   Nazret   Sinadogo   Obbia
Gore   L. Ziway   Imi
Bôr   3686   Asela   Ginir   Scebeli   Ferfer
Jima   Shashemene   Goba   Garge
Tali Post   Awasa   Mt. Batu   4307   Kibre Mengist
Yirga Alem   Dila   Negele   Belet Uen
Mongalla   L. Abaya   Galcaio   Lugh Ganana   El Dere
Kapoeta   Arba Minch   Dolo   Baidoa
L. Shamo   Mega   Bur Acaba
Juba   Chew   Moyale   El Wak   MUQDISHO
Yei   Bahir   375   Bardera   Merca
Lokitaung   L. Turkana   Dif   Giuba   Wabi Scebeli
UGANDA   3084   South Horn   Lodwar   Marsabit   Wajir
Gulu   Lira   Moroto   INDIAN
Pakwach   Soroti   4321   3206   OCEAN
Murchison   KENYA
Falls   L. Kyoga   Kitale
L. Albert   Masindi   Mbale

East from Greenwich   COPYRIGHT GEORGE PHILIP LTD.

Projection : Sanson-Flamsteed's Sinusoidal

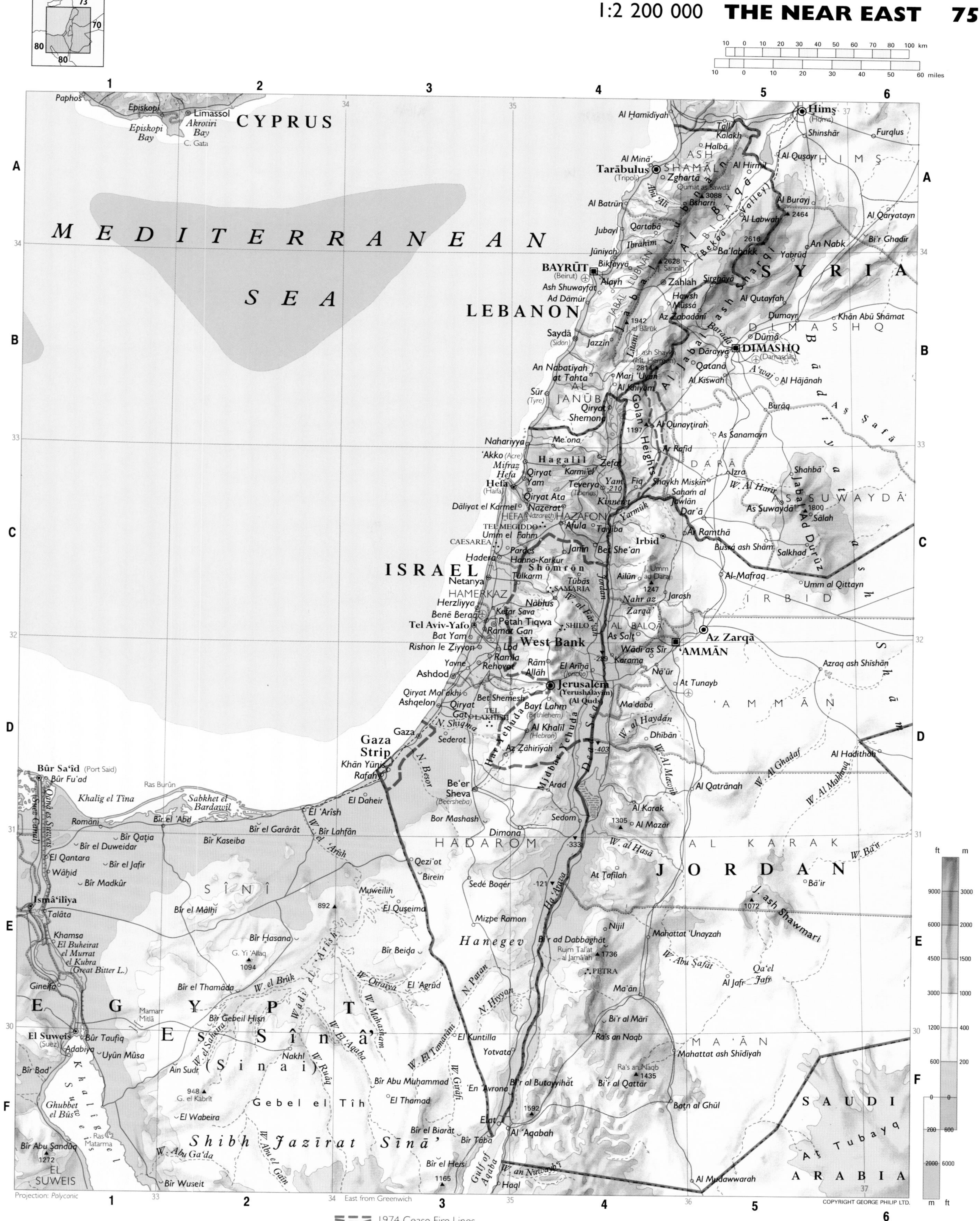

100 km

60 miles

CYPRUS

Paphos
Episkopi
Episkopi Bay
Limassol
Akrotiri Bay
C. Gata

M E D I T E R R A N E A N

S E A

Al Ḥamīdīyah
Tall Kalakh
Shinshār
Furqlus
◉ **Hims**
(Homs)

ASH
SHAMĀL
Al Minā'
Tarābulus ◉
(Tripoli)
Zgharta
Halbā
Al Hirmil
Al Quṣayr
Al Qaryatayn
Al Batrūn
Qurnat as Sawdā
3088
Bsharri
Al Labwah
2464
Al Burayj
Bi'r Ghadīr
Jubayl
Qartaba
Ba'labakk
2616
Yabrūd
An Nabk
Ibrāhīm
Jūniyah
Bikfayyā
2628
Sannin

LEBANON

BAYRŪT ◉
(Beirut)
'Alayh
Ash Shuwayfāt
Ad Dāmūr
Zahlah
Hawsh
Mussá
Al Qutayfah
Dumayr
Khān Abū Shāmat
1942
al Bārūk
Az Zabadānī
Saydā
(Sidon)
Jazzin
Dūmā
DIMASHQ
(Damascus)

SYRIA

DIMASHQ
Dārayyā
A'waj
Al Hājānah
An Nabaṭīyah
at Tahta
2814
Marj 'Uyūn
Al Khiyām
Qaṭana
Al Kiswah
AL
JANŪB
Sūr
(Tyre)
Qiryat Shemona
Golan Heights
1197
Al Qunayṭirah
Buraq
Burāq
As Sanamayn
Nahariyya
'Akko (Acre)
Mifraz Hefa
Zefat
Ar Rafid
As Ṣafā
Hagalil
Karmi'el
Fiq
Shaykh Miskin
Shahbā'
DARĀ
Izra
Jabal
Qiryat Yam
Teverya
(Tiberias)
Hefa
(Haifa)
Qiryat Ata
Yam -210
Kinneret
Saham al Jawlān
Dar'ā
As Suwaydā
1800
Ṣālah
AS SUWAYDĀ
Ad Durūz
Dāliyat el Karmel
Nazerat
(Nazareth)
'Afula
Tanība
Yarmūk
HAZAFON
TEL MEGIDDO
Umm el Fahm
Bet She'an
Irbid
Al Ramthā
Buṣrá ash Shām
Salkhad
Umm al Qittayn
CAESAREA
Janin
Ailūn
Dar'ā
IRBID
Hadera
Pardes
Hanna-Karkur
Ṭulkarm
Shōmrōn
Tūbās
1247
Umm ad Daraj
Jarash
ISRAEL
Netanya
SAMARIA
Nahr az Zarqā'
Al-Mafraq
HAMERKAZ
Nāblus
W. al Far'a
Herzliyya
Benē Beraq
Kefar Sava
Petah Tiqwa
Ramat Gan
SHILO
AL BALQĀ'
As Salt
Az Zarqā' ◉
Tel Aviv-Yafo
Bat Yam
Rishon le Ziyyon
Lod
Ramla
Rām Allāh
Wādī as Sīr
Karama
'AMMĀN
Azraq ash Shīshān
Yavne
Rehovot
El Arīhā
(Jericho)
-289
Na'ūr
At Tunayb
'AMMĀN
Ashdod
Qiryat Mal'akhi
Bet Shemesh
Jerusalem
(Yerushalayim)
(Al Quds)
Ma'dabā
Ashqelon
Qiryat Gat
TEL LAKHISH
Bayt Lahm
(Bethlehem)
403
Dhībān
Sederot
Gaza
N. Shiqma
Al Khalīl
(Hebron)
W. al Haydān
Gaza Strip
Khān Yūnis
Rafah
N. Besor
Az Zāhirīyah
W. al Mūjib
Al Karak
Bûr Sa'îd (Port Said)
Bûr Fu'ad
Ras Burūn
Be'er Sheva
(Beersheba)
Arad
Al Mazār
1305
Khalîg el Tîna
Sabkhet el Bardawîl
Bîr el 'Abd
El Daheir
Bîr Lahfân
Bor Mashash
Sedom
AL KARAK
Români
Bîr el Garârât
W. al Hasā
W. al Bâr
Bîr Qaṭia
Bîr el Duweidar
Bîr Kaseiba
W. 'Arîsh
HADAROM
-333
Dimona
JORDAN
El Qantara
Bîr el Jafir
El 'Arîsh
At Ṭafilah
Bā'ir
Wâhid
Bîr Madkûr
S Î N Î
Qezi'ot
Sedé Boqér
-121
Ismâ'iliya
Talâta
Birein
J. ash Shawmari
1072
Khamsa
El Buheirat
el Murrat
el Kubra
(Great Bitter L.)
Bîr Hasana
892
Muweilih
El Quseima
Mizpe Ramon
Nijil
Mahaṭṭat 'Unayzah
Qa'el Jafi
Gineifa
G. Yi'Allaq
1094
Bîr Beida
Hanegev
Bîr ad Dabbāghāt
Rujm Ṭal'at
al Jamā'ah
1736
W. Abū Ṣafāt
Al Jafr
Jafi
E G Y P T
Bîr el Thamâda
W. el Brûk
El 'Agrûd
N. Paran
PETRA
Ma'ān
Mamarr
Mitlā
Sahara Hisn
N. Hiyyon
MA'ĀN
El Suweis (Suez)
Bûr Taufiq
Adabiya
Uyûn Mûsa
E S S î n â'
(S i n a i)
Ain Sudr
Nakhl
El Kuntilla
Yotvata
Ra's an Naqb
Mahaṭṭat ash Shīdīyah
Bîr Bad'
W. el Aqaba
El Thamad
Bîr Abu Muhammad
'En 'Avrona
Bîr al Māri
Bîr al Butayyihāt
Baṭn al Ghūl
SAUDI
948
G. el Kabrît
Ghubbet
el Bûs
Gebel el Tîh
El Wabeira
Ra's an Naqb
1435
El Suweis
1272
Bîr Abu Sanduq
Shibh Jazîrat Sinâ'
Bîr al Biarât
1592
Elat
Al 'Aqabah
At Tubayq
ARABIA
Bîr el Hersi
1165
Bîr Tâba
Gulf of Aqaba
W. an Nuwaybi'
Al Mudawwarah
Haql

▬ ▬ ▬ 1974 Cease Fire Lines

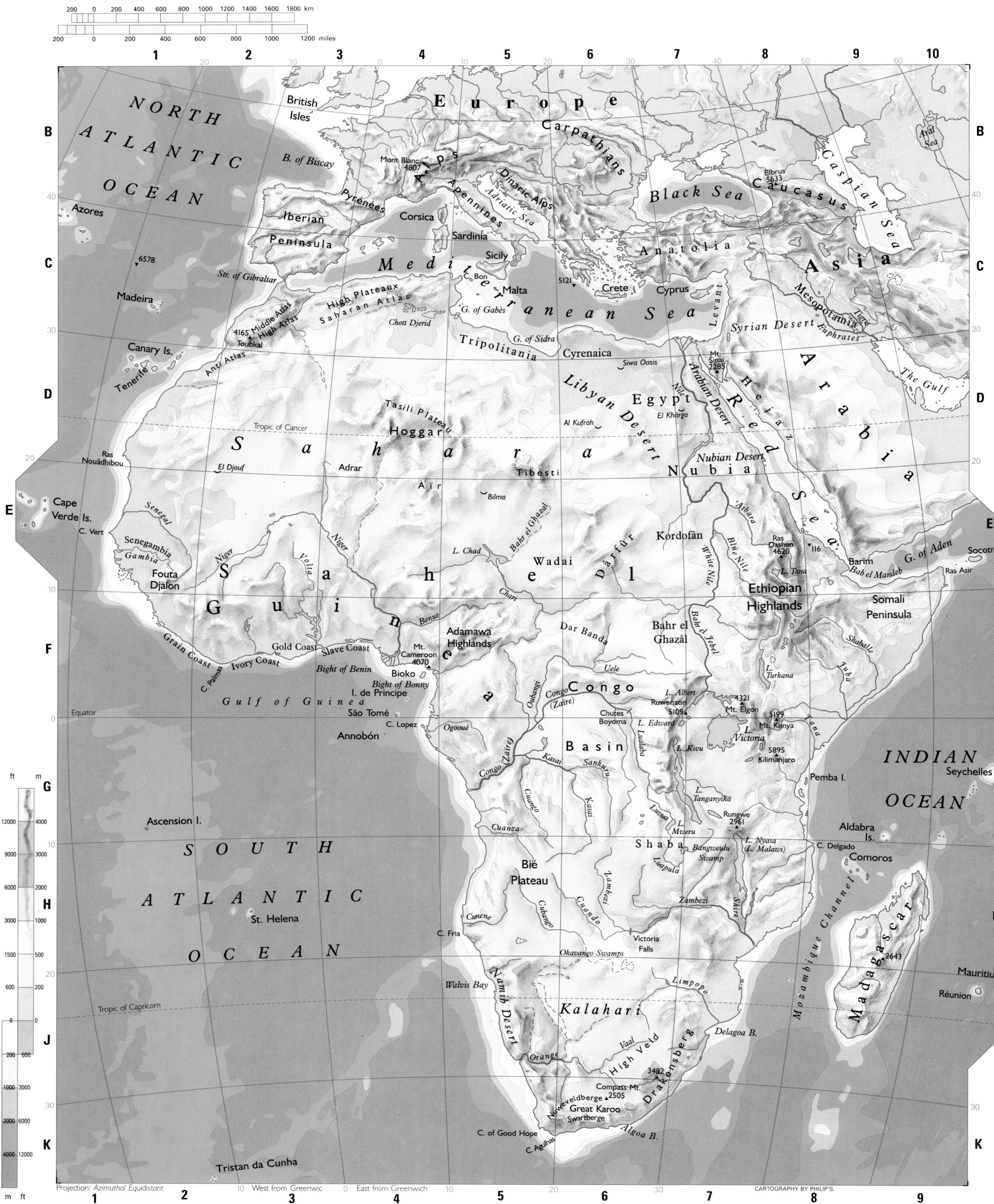
NORTH ATLANTIC OCEAN
Europe
British Isles
B. of Biscay
Carpathians
Alps
Mont Blanc 4807
Pyrénées
Dinaric Alps
Apennines
Adriatic Sea
Black Sea
Caucasus
Elbrus 5633
Caspian Sea
Aral Sea
Azores
Iberian Peninsula
Corsica
Sardinia
Sicily
Mediterranean Sea
Anatolia
Asia
Str. of Gibraltar
C. Bon
Malta
Crete
Cyprus
Levant
Mesopotamia
Tigris
Euphrates
Madeira
High Plateaux
Saharan Atlas
Middle Atlas
High Atlas
Toubkal
G. of Gabès
Chott Djerid
G. of Sidra
Syrian Desert
Canary Is.
Tenerife
Anti Atlas
Tripolitania
Cyrenaica
Siwa Oasis
Mt. Sinai 2285
Arabia
The Gulf
Libyan Desert
Egypt
Nile
El Kharga
Arabian Desert
Red Sea
Hejaz
Tasili Plateau
Hoggar
Tropic of Cancer
Al Kufrah
Sahara
Ras Nouâdhibou
El Djouf
Adrar
Tibesti
Nubia
Nubian Desert
Aïr
Bilma
Cape Verde Is.
C. Vert
Senegal
Niger
Atbara
Senegambia
Gambia
Fouta Djalon
Volta
L. Chad
Bahr el Ghazal
Wadai
Dârfûr
Kordofân
White Nile
Blue Nile
Ras Dashen 4620
L. Tana
Barim
Bab el Mandeb
G. of Aden
Socotra
Ras Asir
Sahel
Ethiopian Highlands
Somali Peninsula
Guinea
Chari
Benue
Adamawa Highlands
Dar Banda
Bahr el Ghazâl
Bahr el Jebel
Shaballe
Grain Coast
Ivory Coast
Gold Coast
Slave Coast
Mt. Cameroon 4070
Bight of Benin
Bioko
Bight of Bonny
I. de Principe
C. Palmas
Gulf of Guinea
São Tomé
Annobón
C. Lopez
Equator
Uele
Oubangi
Congo (Zaïre)
Congo Basin
L. Albert
Ruwenzori 5109
Mt. Elgon 4321
L. Turkana
Juba
Chutes Boyoma
L. Edward
Ogooué
Lualaba
L. Kivu
L. Victoria
Mt. Kenya 5199
Tana
Kilimanjaro 5895
INDIAN OCEAN
Seychelles
Pemba I.
Kasai
Sankuru
Cuango
L. Tanganyika
Ascension I.
Cuanza
Luvua
L. Mweru
Rungwe 2961
Aldabra Is.
C. Delgado
Comoros
SOUTH ATLANTIC OCEAN
Shaba
Bangweulu Swamp
L. Nyasa (L. Malawi)
Luapula
Bié Plateau
Zambezi
Shire
Mozambique Channel
Madagascar 2643
St. Helena
Cunene
Cubango
Cuando
C. Fria
Victoria Falls
Okavango Swamps
Walvis Bay
Namib Desert
Limpopo
Mauritius
Réunion
Tropic of Capricorn
Kalahari
Delagoa B.
Vaal
High Veld
Drakensberg 3482
Orange
Compass Mt. 2505
Nuweveldberge
Great Karoo
Swartberge
C. of Good Hope
C. Agulhas
Algoa B.
Tristan da Cunha
Projection: Azimuthal Equidistant
West from Greenwich
East from Greenwich
CARTOGRAPHY BY PHILIP'S

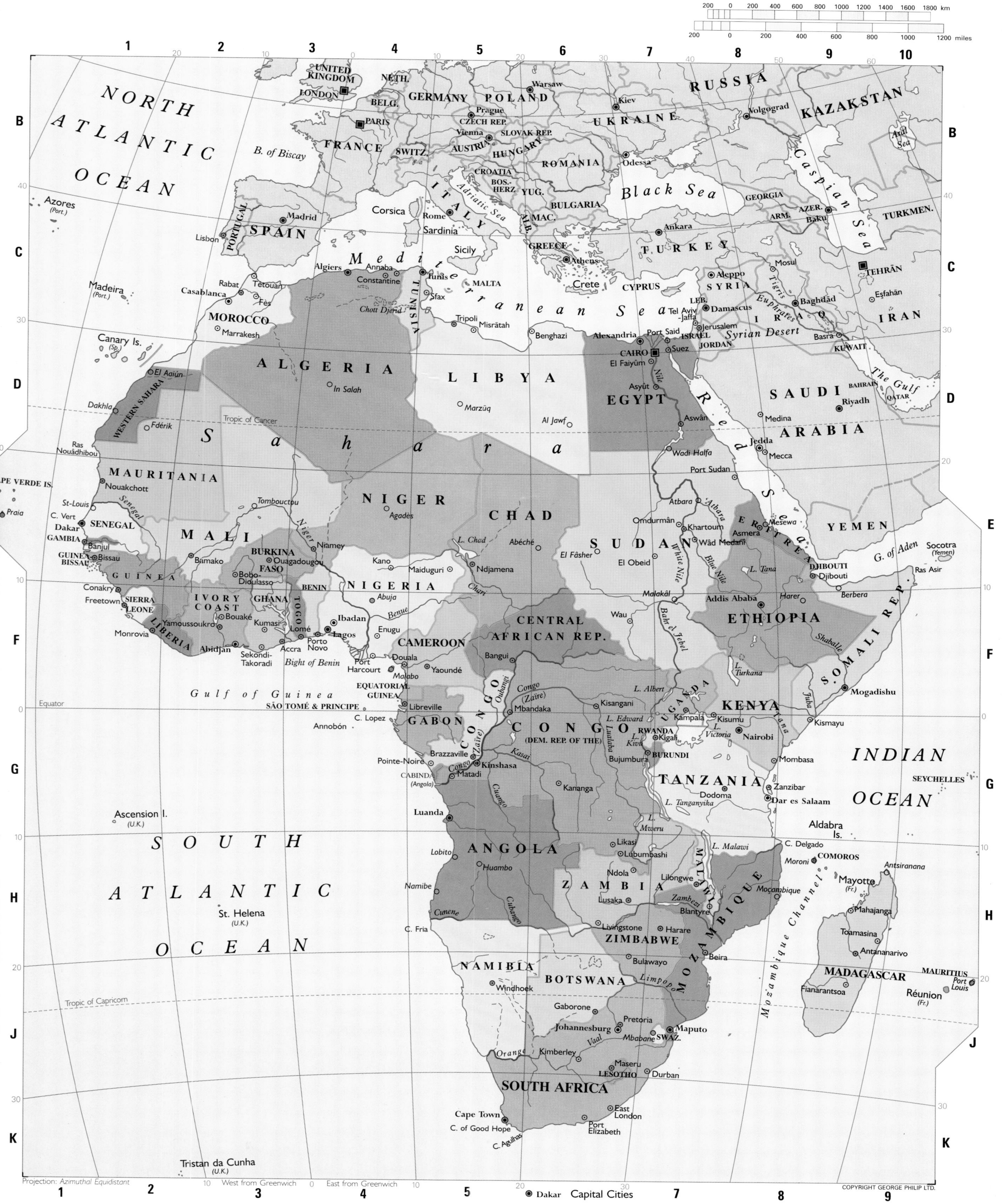

200 0 200 400 600 800 1000 1200 1400 1600 1800 km
200 0 200 400 600 800 1000 1200 miles

NORTH ATLANTIC OCEAN

UNITED KINGDOM
LONDON
NETH.
BELG.
PARIS
GERMANY POLAND Warsaw
CZECH REP.
Prague
Vienna SLOVAK REP.
FRANCE SWITZ. AUSTRIA HUNGARY
CROATIA BOS. HERZ. YUG. ROMANIA
Kiev
UKRAINE
RUSSIA
Volgograd
KAZAKSTAN
Aral Sea

B. of Biscay

Azores (Port.)

Madeira (Port.)
Lisbon PORTUGAL
Madrid
SPAIN
Corsica
Rome
Sardinia
ITALY
Adriatic Sea
ALB.
MAC.
BULGARIA
GREECE
Athens
Crete
CYPRUS
Odessa
Black Sea
Ankara
TURKEY
GEORGIA
ARM. AZER.
Baku
Caspian Sea
TURKMEN.
Mosul
SYRIA
Aleppo
LEB.
Damascus
Tel Aviv-Jaffa
ISRAEL
Jerusalem
JORDAN
Baghdad
Euphrates
Tigris
IRAQ
TEHRĀN
Eşfahān
IRAN
Basra
KUWAIT

Algiers
Annaba
Constantine
Tunis
TUNISIA
MALTA
Sfax
Tripoli
Misrātah
Benghazi
Mediterranean Sea
Alexandria
Port Said
CAIRO
Suez
El Faiyûm

Casablanca
Rabat
Tétouan
Fès
MOROCCO
Marrakesh
Chott Djerid

Canary Is. (Sp.)

El Aaiún
Dakhla
WESTERN SAHARA
Ras Nouâdhibou
Fdérik

ALGERIA
In Salah
LIBYA
Marzûq
Al Jawf
EGYPT
Asyût
Aswân
Nile
Wadi Halfa
Port Sudan
SAUDI ARABIA
Medina
Riyadh
Jedda
Mecca
BAHRAIN
QATAR
The Gulf

Tropic of Cancer

Sahara

MAURITANIA
Nouakchott

PE VERDE IS.
C. Vert
Praia

St-Louis
Senegal
Dakar
SENEGAL
GAMBIA
Banjul
GUINEA BISSAU
Bissau
Conakry
GUINEA
Freetown
SIERRA LEONE
Monrovia
LIBERIA

Tombouctou
MALI
Niger
BURKINA FASO
Bamako
Ouagadougou
Bobo-Dioulasso
Yamoussoukro
IVORY COAST
Bouaké
GHANA
Kumasi
Sekondi-Takoradi
Accra
TOGO
BENIN
Lomé
Porto Novo
Abidjan

Agadès
NIGER
L. Chad
Niamey
Kano
NIGERIA
Maiduguri
Abuja
Ibadan
Lagos
Enugu
Benue
Port Harcourt
Bight of Benin

CHAD
Abéché
Ndjamena
Chari

SUDAN
El Fâsher
El Obeid
Wâd Medani
Khartoum
Omdurmân
Atbara
Atbara
ERITREA
Asmera
Massawa
Nîle
White Nile
Blue Nile
L. Tana
DJIBOUTI
Djibouti
G. of Aden
Berbera
Ras Asir
Socotra (Yemen)
YEMEN

Malakâl
Wau
Bahr el Jebel
Addis Ababa
ETHIOPIA
Harer
SOMALI REP.

CAMEROON
Douala
Malabo
Yaoundé
EQUATORIAL GUINEA
SÃO TOMÉ & PRINCIPE
Libreville
GABON
C. Lopez
Annobón

CENTRAL AFRICAN REP.
Bangui
Congo (Zaïre)
Oubangui
Mbandaka
Kisangani
CONGO
CONGO (DEM. REP. OF THE)
UGANDA
Kampala
L. Albert
L. Edward
L. Kivu
RWANDA
Kigali
BURUNDI
Bujumbura
L. Turkana
KENYA
Kisumu
L. Victoria
Nairobi
Mogadishu
Kismayu
Juba

Gulf of Guinea
Equator

Brazzaville
Pointe-Noire
CABINDA (Angola)
Kinshasa
Matadi
Congo
Kasai
Kananga

Luanda

SOUTH ATLANTIC OCEAN

Ascension I. (U.K.)

St. Helena (U.K.)

Lobito
Benguela
ANGOLA
Huambo
Namibe
Cunene
Cubango

Likasi
Lubumbashi
Ndola
ZAMBIA
Lusaka
L. Mweru
L. Malawi
MALAWI
Lilongwe
Zambezi
Blantyre
L. Tanganyika
TANZANIA
Dodoma
Dar es Salaam
Zanzibar
Mombasa
INDIAN OCEAN
SEYCHELLES
Aldabra Is.
C. Delgado
COMOROS
Moroni
Mayotte (Fr.)
Antsiranana

Livingstone
Harare
Beira
ZIMBABWE
Bulawayo
MOZAMBIQUE
Moçambique
Mahajanga
Toamasina
Antananarivo
MADAGASCAR
MAURITIUS
Port Louis
Réunion (Fr.)

Tropic of Capricorn

NAMIBIA
Windhoek
BOTSWANA
Gaborone
Limpopo
Orange
Vaal
Johannesburg
Kimberley
Pretoria
Mbabane
SWAZ.
Maputo
Maseru
LESOTHO
Durban
SOUTH AFRICA
Cape Town
C. of Good Hope
C. Agulhas
East London
Port Elizabeth
Fianarantsoa

West from Greenwich
East from Greenwich

Dakar Capital Cities

COPYRIGHT GEORGE PHILIP LTD.

Tristan da Cunha (U.K.)

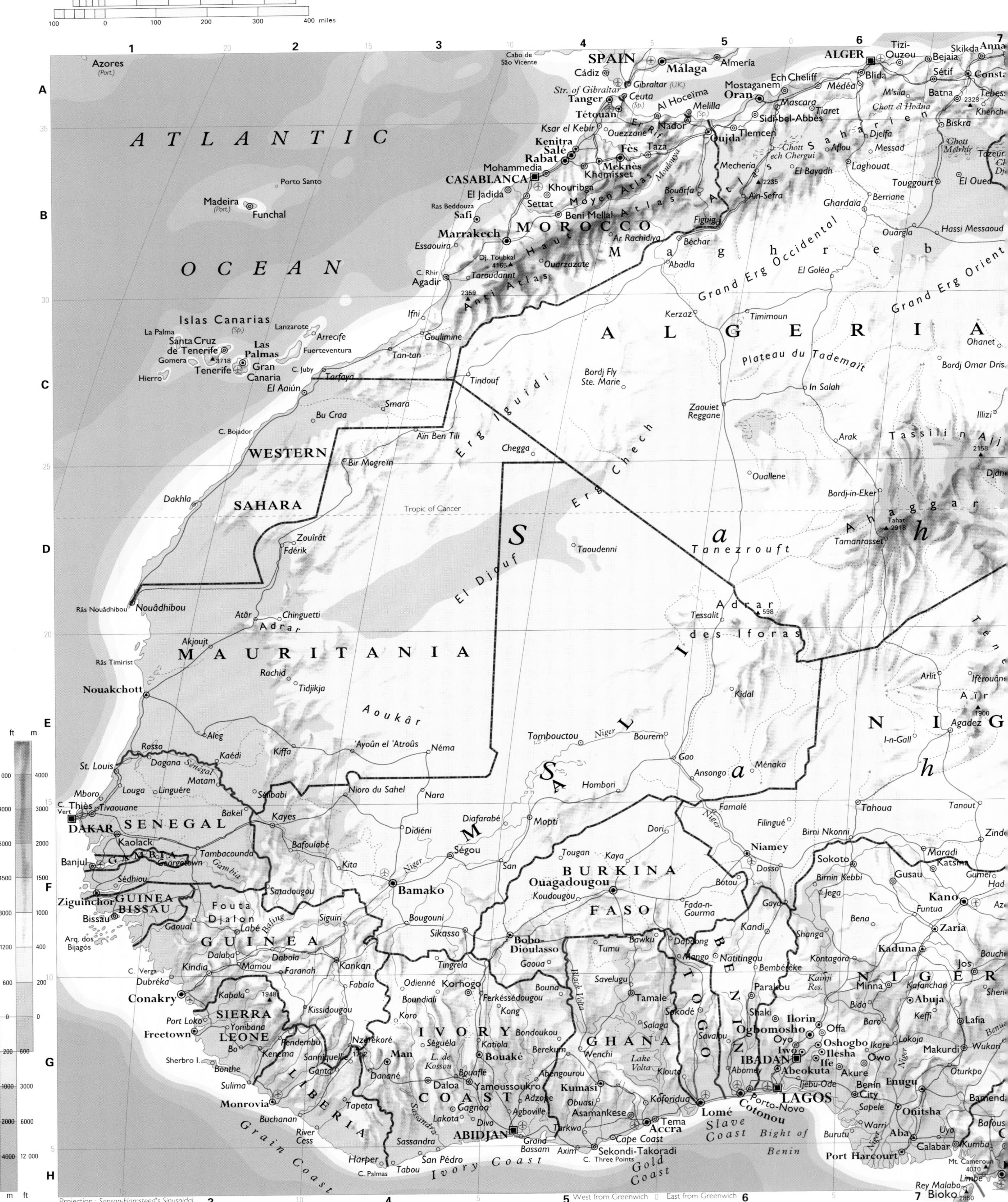

Projection: Sanson-Flamsteed's Sinusoidal

West from Greenwich 0 East from Greenwich

74
84
86

8
9
10
11
12
13
14
Bizerte
Ariana
CARTHAGE
TUNIS
Béja
Nabeul
Sousse
Mahdia
Sfax
Golfe de Gabès
Gabès
Île de Djerba
Zarzis
Médenine
Zuwārah
Tarābulus
Az Zāwiyah
Al Khums
Misrātah
Gharyān
968
Mizdah
Dehibat
Tripolitania
Daraj
Ghudāmis
Sicilia
MALTA
Valletta
MEDITERRANEAN SEA
GREECE
Iráklion
Kríti
Ródhos
Antalya
TURKEY
ADANA
CYPRUS
Nicosia
Antakya
HALAB
Al Lādhiqīyah
Nahr al Furāt
SYRIA
Tarābulus
Hims
LEBANON
BAYRŪT
DIMASHQ
IRAQ
Jabal ad Durūz
1801
ISRAEL
Haifa
Tel Aviv-Yafo
Ashdod
Jerusalem
West Bank
'AMMĀN
JORDAN
Ar Rutbah
Bādiyat ash Shām
Zāwiyat al Baydā
Darnah
Banghāzī
Al Marj
Tubruq
Bardīyah
Salūm
Suluq
Khalīj Surt
Surt
Ajdābiyah
Cyrenaica
EL ISKANDARÎYA
El Mahalla el Kubra
Damanhûr
Dumyât
Bûr Sa'îd
El Mansûra
Tanta
Zagazig
Qanâ es Suweis
Ismâ'iliya
Marsâ Matrûh
El Alamein
EL GÎZA
EL QÂHIRA
Helwân
El Suweis
Ma'ān
Elat
Al 'Aqabah
Al Jawf
Al Jaghbūb
-133
Munkhafed el Qattâra
Sîwa
El Faiyûm
Beni Suef
Maghâgha
El Minyâ
Mallawi
Manfalût
Asyût
Es Sina'
G. Mûsa 2637
2578
Tabūk
SAUDI ARABIA
Al Muwaylih
Hūn
Awjilah
Zillah
Idehan Awbārī
Brach
LIBYA
Sahrâ' Lîbîya
EGYPT
Es Sahrâ Esh Sharqîya
Khalîg el Suweis
Nahr en Nîl
Hurghada
2187
Bûr Safâga
Sabhah
Awbārī
1200
Qasr Farâfra
Tahta
Sohâg
Girga
Qena
Quseir
THEBES
KARNAK
El Uqsur
Al Wajh
Marzūq
Fezzan
Wāw al Kabīr
El Wâhât el-Dakhla
Mût
El Khârga
El Wâhât el-Khârga
RED SEA
Hijaz
Ghat
Al Qatrūn
Sahrâ' Rebiana
Al Kufrah
Al Jawf
Idfû
Kom Ombo
Sadd el Aali
Aswân
Yanbu 'al Bahr
Ras Bânâs
Buheirat en Naser
Bîr Shalatein
ABU SIMBEL
1082
Rābigh
J. Uweinat 1893
Wadi Halfa
Halaib
Ras Hadarba
Tummo
Madama
Aozou
Bardai
Pic Toussidé 3265
3150 Tarso Emissi
Tibesti
Zouar
Chirfa
Emi Koussi 3415
Ma'tan as Sarra
El Wâhât el Selîma
Es Sahrâ en Nûbîya
Kosha
Muhammad Qol
2259
Delgo
3rd Cataract
Dongola
Abu Hamed
Bûr Sûdân
Suakin
Ouinianga Sérir
Bilma
Grand Erg du Bilma
Borkou
Dépression du Mourdi
Bir 'Atrun
Kareima
4th Cataract
5th Cataract
Sinkat
Trinkitat
Haiya
Fachi
Faya-Largeau
Ed Debba
Nahr en Nil
Berber
Atbara
Karora
2780
Fada
Ennedi
1310
Adarama
Nakfa
Erg du Djourab
Zagaoua
Wad Hamid
6th Cataract
Shendi
Nahr 'Atbara
ERITREA
Oum Chalouba
SUDAN
Omdurmân
El Khartûm
Kassalâ
Akordat
CHAD
Malha
El Wuz
Biltine
1954
Khashm el Girba
Nguigmi
Zigey
Bahr el Ghazal
Kutum
Sodiri
El Gezira
Wad Medanî
Gedaref
Mao
Lac Tchad
Moussoro
Abéché
Al Junaynah
Umm Keddada
Ed Dueim
Bosso
Ati
El Fâsher
El Obeid
Gashua
Geidam
Massakory
Oum Hadjer
Djebel Marra 3088
Zalingei
Singa
Kôstî
Umm Ruwaba
Nil el Azraq
Gonder
Maiduguri
Ndjamena
Kousseri
Bokoro
Mongo
Goz Beïda
Nyâlâ
Dârfûr
En Nahud
Er Rahad
Potiskum
Bama
Massenya
Abou-Deïa
El Odaiya
Abu Zabad
Kordofân
Ed Damazin
Nil el Abyad
1830
L. Tana
Bajoga
Biu
Maroua
Chari
Bongor
Am-Timan
1325
Kâdugli
Bahir Dar
Kumo
Mubi
Guider
Bure
Birao
Bahr el Arab
Debre Markos
Numan
Garoua
Yola
Logone
Pala
Laï
Sarh
Songo
1226
Malakâl
Sobat
Bahr el Ghazal
Jur
Nekemte
Moundou
Kouma
Doba
Ndélé
Sa'id Bundas
Bahr el Ghazâl
Raga
Sudd
Bahr el Jebel
3202
Dembidolo
ETHIOPIA
Metu
Gore
Baibokoum
Gashaka
Ngaoundéré
Banyo
Paoua
Kaga Bandoro
Gogriâl
Wâw
Tonj
Jima
Bossangoa
CENTRAL AFRICAN REPUBLIC
Rumbêk
Pibor Post
3686
Omo
Tibati
Foumban
Bétaré Oya
Bouar
Bozoum
Yalinga
Toinya
Bôr
L. Abaya
Arba Minch
L. Shamo
Sibut
Bambari
Ippy
Bakouma
Amadi
Tali Post
Yoko
Carnot
Bossembélé
Obo
El Istiwa'iya
CAMEROON
Sanaga
Bertoua
Batouri
Bangassou
Bomu
Yambiô
Juba
Mongalla
Kapoeta
Chew Bahir
Nanga-Eboko
Abong-Mbang
Berbérati
Bangui
Zongo
Bosobolo
Mobaye
Mobayi
Oubangi
Torit
3187
Lokitaung
Kajo Kaji
Yei
Yaoundé
Mbaïki
Libenge
Bondo
Uele
Ango
Dungu
Faradje
L. Turkana
375
A
B
C
D
E
F
G
H
8
9
10
11
12
13

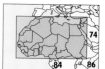

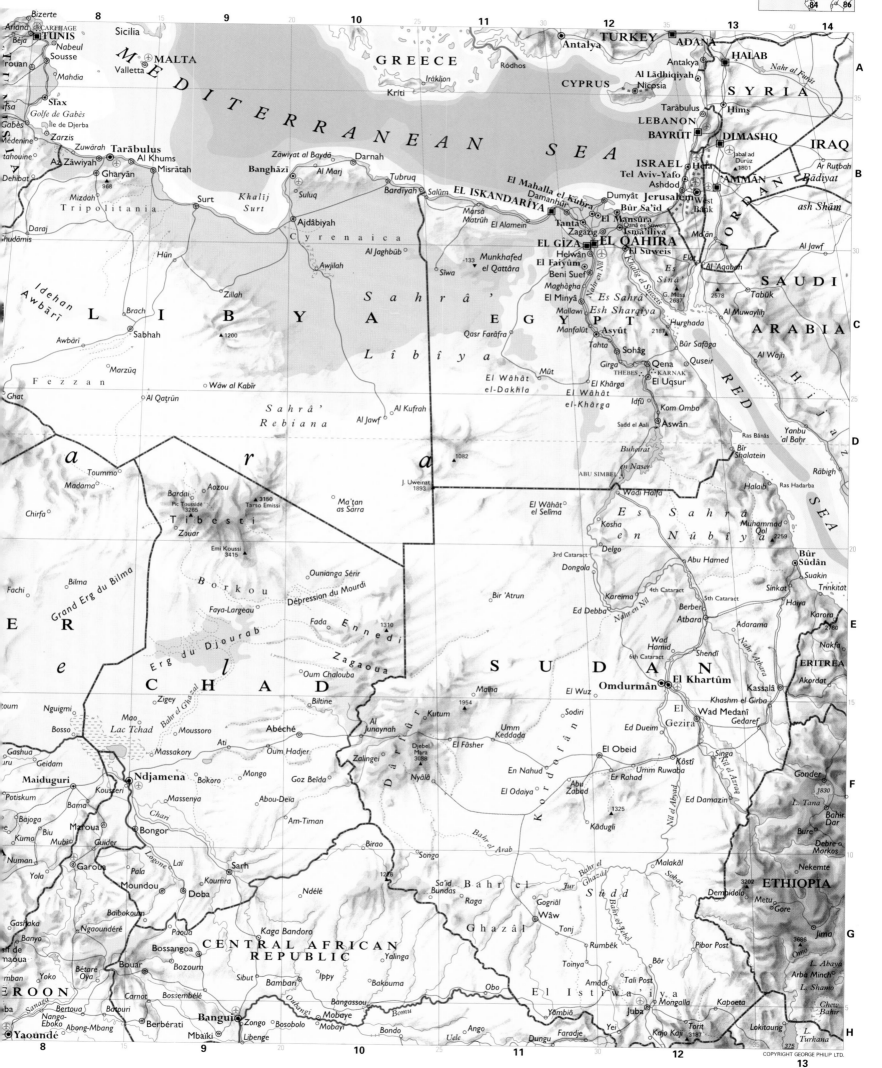

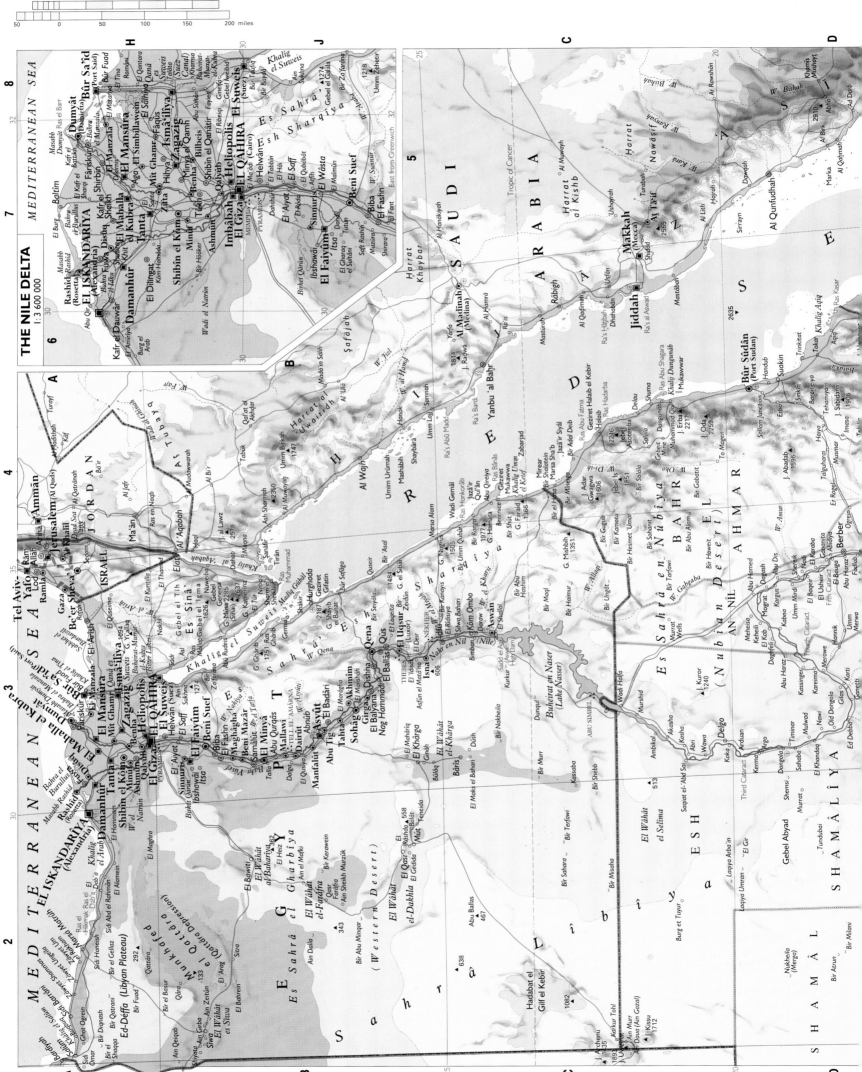

THE NILE DELTA
1:3 600 000

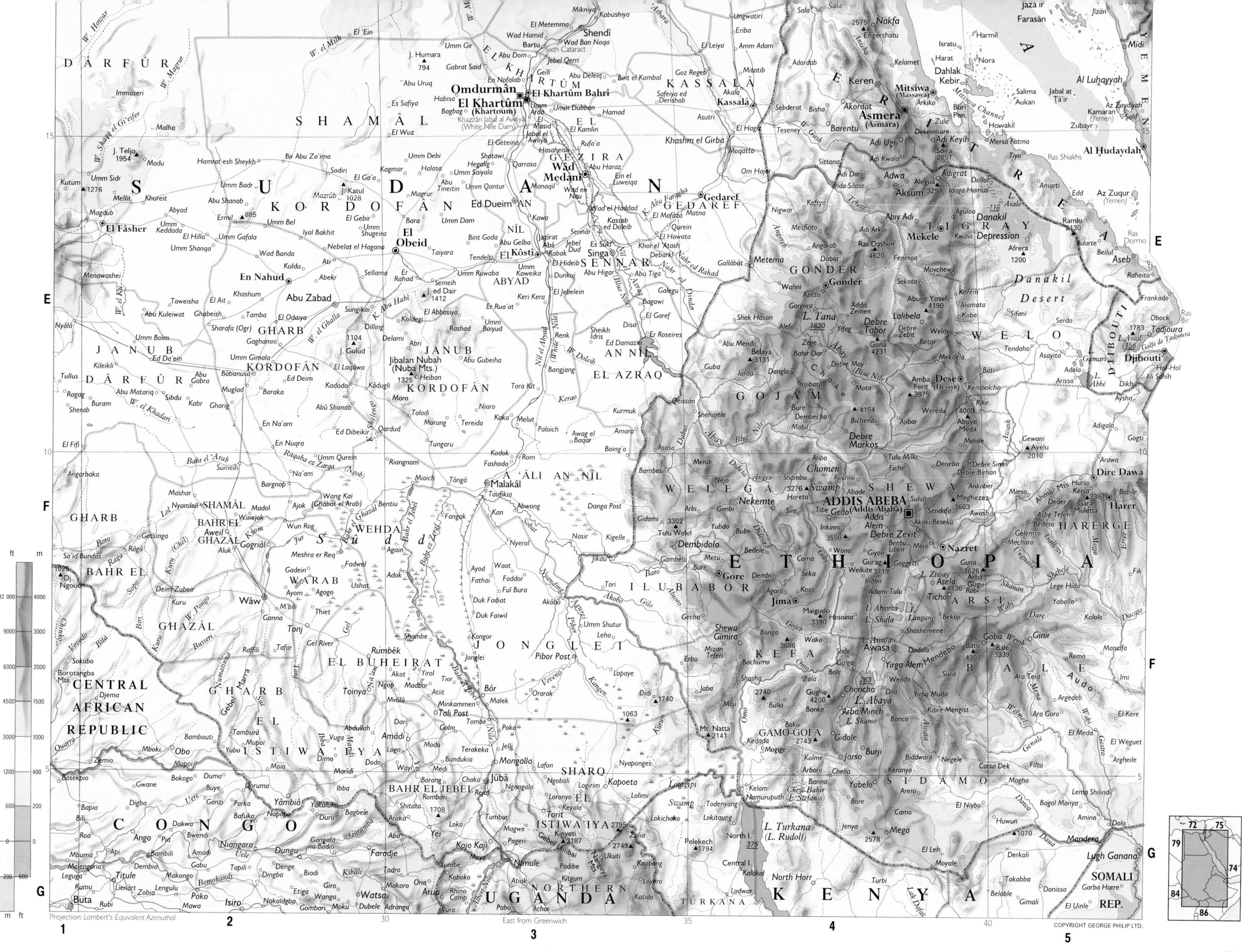

SUDAN
ETHIOPIA
ERITREA
DJIBOUTI
KENYA
UGANDA
CONGO
CENTRAL AFRICAN REPUBLIC
SOMALI REP.
YEMEN
DÂRFÛR
SHAMÂL
KORDOFÂN
KASSALÂ
GEZIRA
GEDAREF
SENNAR
JANUB KORDOFÂN
GHARB KORDOFÂN
JANUB DÂRFÛR
A'ÂLI AN NÎL
EL AZRAQ
JONGLEI
EL BUHEIRAT
WARAB
WEHDA
BAHR EL JEBEL
SHARQ EL ISTIWA'IYA
GHARB EL ISTIWA'IYA
GONDER
GOJAM
WELO
TIGRAY
SHEWA
WELEGA
ILUBABOR
KEFA
ARSI
BALE
HARERGE
SIDAMO
GAMO-GOFA
Omdurmân
El Khartûm (Khartoum)
El Khartûm Bahrî
Wad Medanî
El Obeid
Kassalâ
Gedaref
Asmera (Asmara)
Mitsiwa (Massawa)
Aseb
Djibouti
ADDIS ABEBA (Addis Ababa)
Dire Dawa
Harer
Gonder
Dese (Dessye)
Jima
Nazret
Awasa
Malakâl
Jûbâ
Wâw
El Fâsher
En Nahud
Abu Zabad
Kôsti
Al Hudaydah
Lugh Ganana
L. Tana
L. Turkana (L. Rudolf)
Danakil Depression
Danakil Desert
Projection: Lambert's Equivalent Azimuthal
East from Greenwich
COPYRIGHT GEORGE PHILIP LTD.

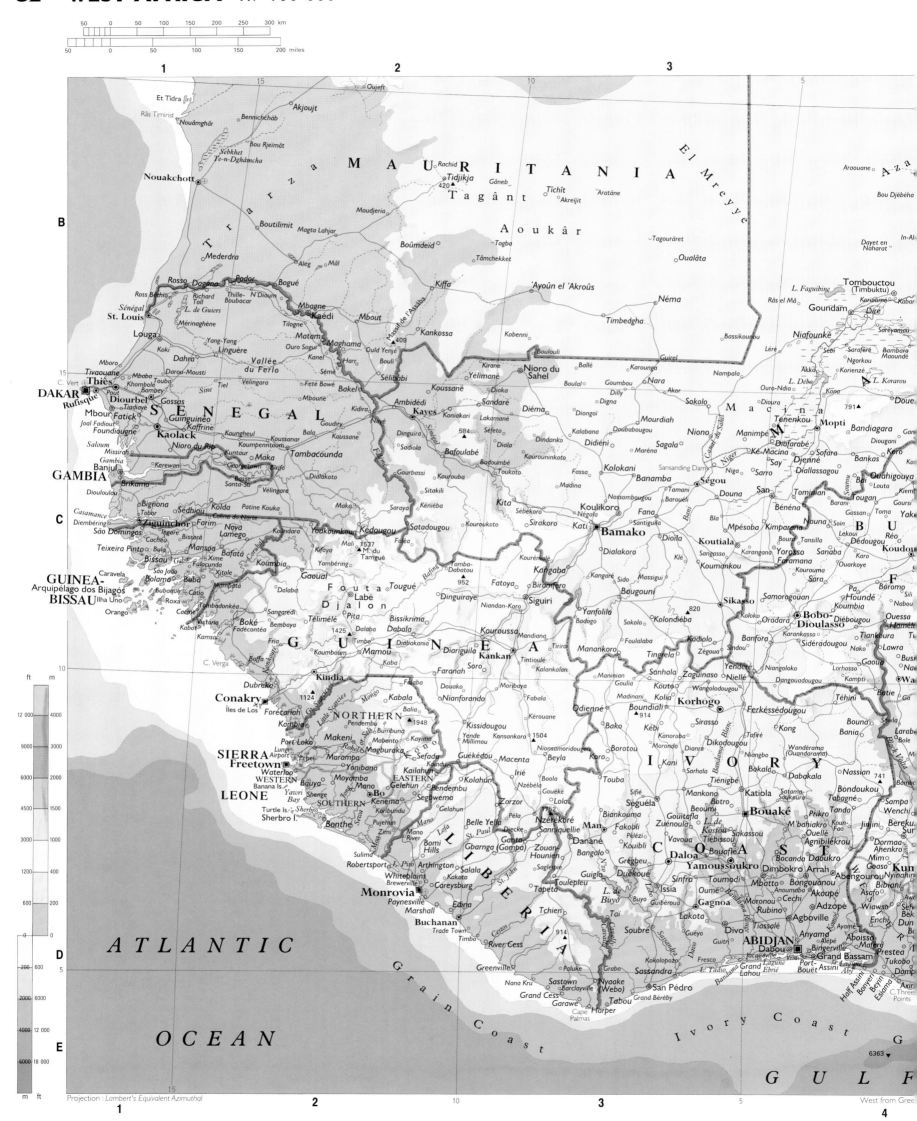

Projection : Lambert's Equivalent Azimuthal

West from Gree

78
79
84
84

ALGERIA

NIGER

NIGERIA

BENIN

TOGO

GHANA

BURKINA

CAMEROON

CHAD

EQUATORIAL GUINEA

GULF OF GUINEA

Bight of Benin

Bight of Bonny

Slave Coast

Niger Delta

Adrar des Iforas

Aïr (Azbine)

Ténéré

Talak

Agadez

Tahoua

Tillabéri

Manga

Niamey

Ouagadougou

Accra

Lomé

Cotonou

Porto-Novo

Lagos

Ibadan

Abuja

Kano

Kaduna

Zaria

Sokoto

Maiduguri

Port Harcourt

Calabar

Douala

Yaoundé

Lake Volta

Lac Tchad

N.E. NIGERIA
on same scale
as general map

East from Greenwich

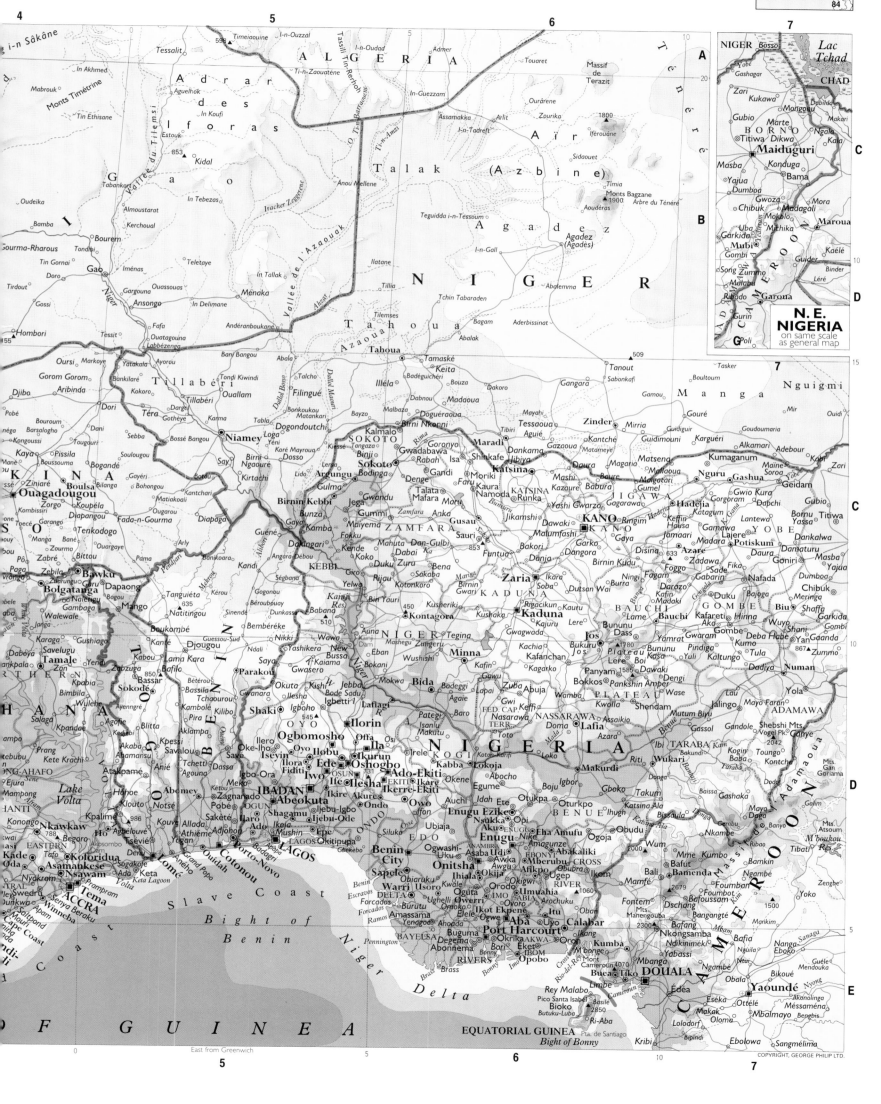

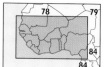

CENTRAL AND SOUTHERN AFRICA 1:13 300 000

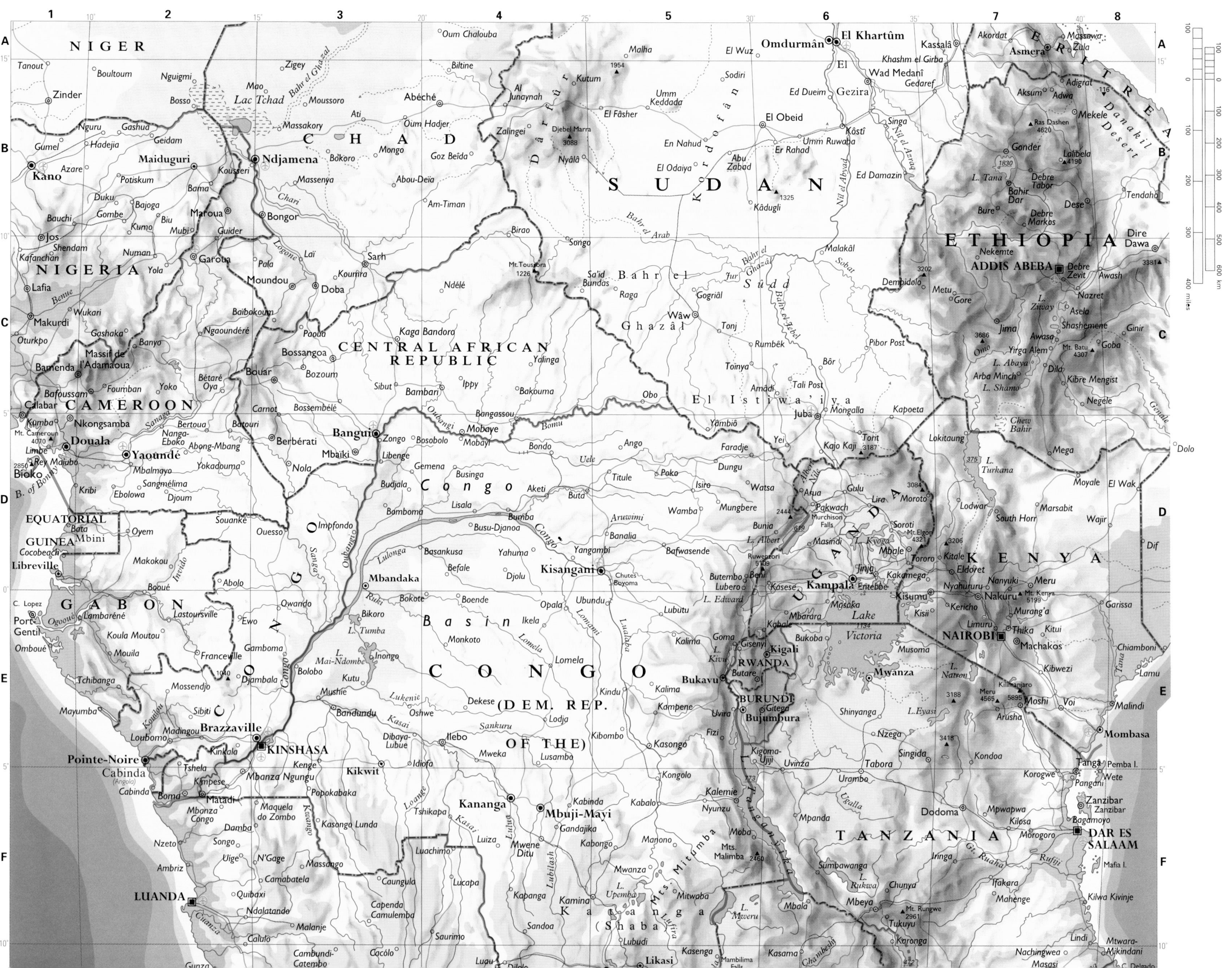
100 0 100 200 300 400 500 600 km
100 0 100 200 300 400 miles
NIGER
CHAD
Ndjamena
SUDAN
El Khartûm
Omdurmân
ERITREA
Asmera
Danakil Desert
ETHIOPIA
ADDIS ABEBA
NIGERIA
Kano
CAMEROON
Douala
Yaoundé
CENTRAL AFRICAN REPUBLIC
Bangui
EQUATORIAL GUINEA
Libreville
GABON
CONGO
Brazzaville
KINSHASA
Congo Basin
CONGO (DEM. REP. OF THE)
Kisangani
Kananga
Mbuji-Mayi
UGANDA
Kampala
KENYA
NAIROBI
Mombasa
Lake Victoria
RWANDA
Kigali
BURUNDI
Bujumbura
TANZANIA
DAR ES SALAAM
Zanzibar
Pointe-Noire
Cabinda
LUANDA
Katanga (Shaba)
Lac Tchad

78
79
74
89

ATLANTIC OCEAN
INDIAN OCEAN
NAMIBIA
BOTSWANA
ZAMBIA
ZIMBABWE
MOZAMBIQUE
MALAWI
SOUTH AFRICA
LESOTHO
SWAZILAND
Kalahari
Namib Desert
Namaland
Damaraland
Ovamboland
Barotseland
Mashonaland
Matabeleland
Transvaal
Free State
Natal
Cape Province
Great Karoo
Caprivi Strip
Tropic of Capricorn
CAPE TOWN
Table Mt. 1087
Cape of Good Hope
Cape Agulhas
Port Elizabeth
East London
DURBAN
Pietermaritzburg
Bloemfontein
Kimberley
JOHANNESBURG
Soweto
PRETORIA
Vereeniging
MAPUTO
HARARE
Chitungwiza
Bulawayo
Lusaka
Lilongwe
Blantyre
Beira
Windhoek
Walvis Bay
Swakopmund
Lüderitz
Gaborone
Francistown
Livingstone
Victoria Falls
Lake Kariba
Okavango Swamps
Makgadikgadi Salt Pans
Namibe
Lubango
Benguela
Huambo
Kitwe
Ndola
Nampula
Quelimane
INDIAN OCEAN
Bassas da India (Réunion)
Île Europa (Réunion)
I. do Bazaruto
Is. Glorieuses (Réunion)
Mayotte (Fr)
Antananarivo
Ankaratra 2643
Mahajanga
Toamasina
Fianarantsoa
Pic Boby 2658
Toliara
Antsiranana
Tsaratanana 2876
Taolanaro
MADAGASCAR
On same scale as General Map
Projection : Sanson-Flamsteed's Sinusoidal
East from Greenwich
ft m
12 000 4000
9000 3000
6000 2000
4500 1500
3000 1000
1200 400
600 200
0 0
200 600
1000 3000
2000 6000
4000 12 000
m ft

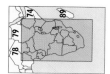

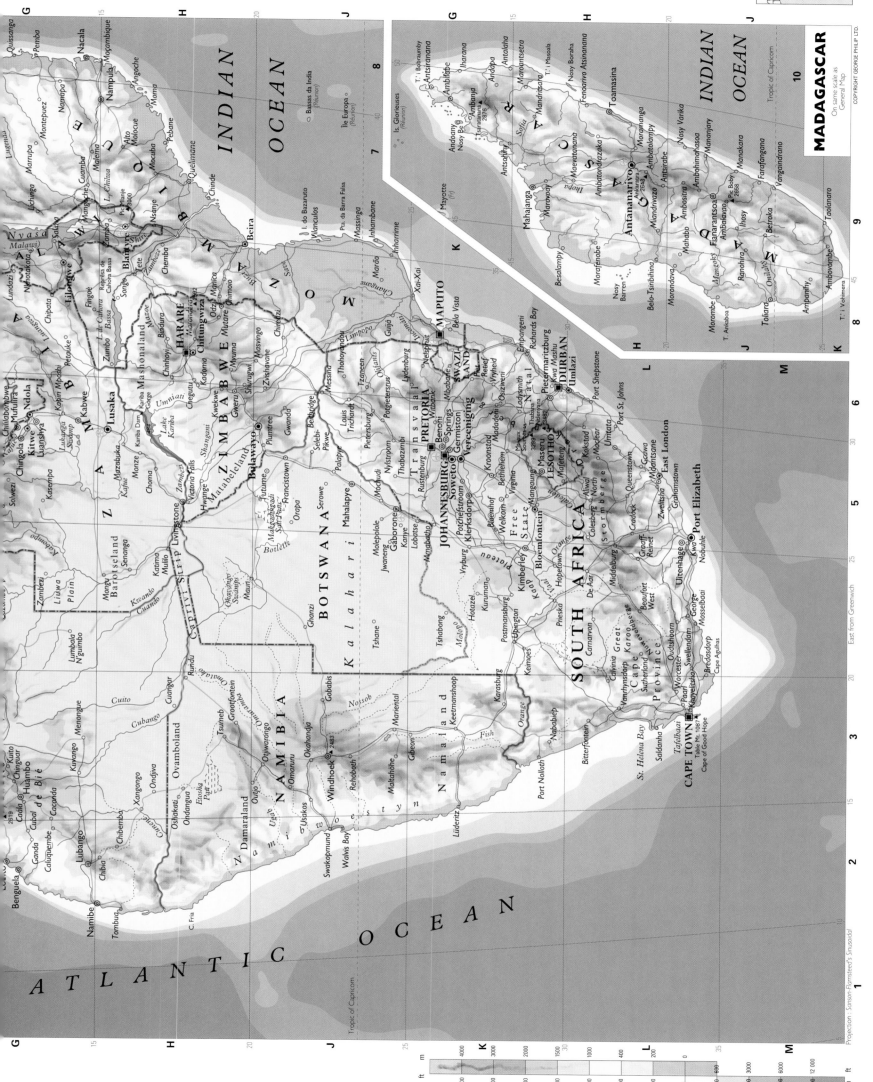

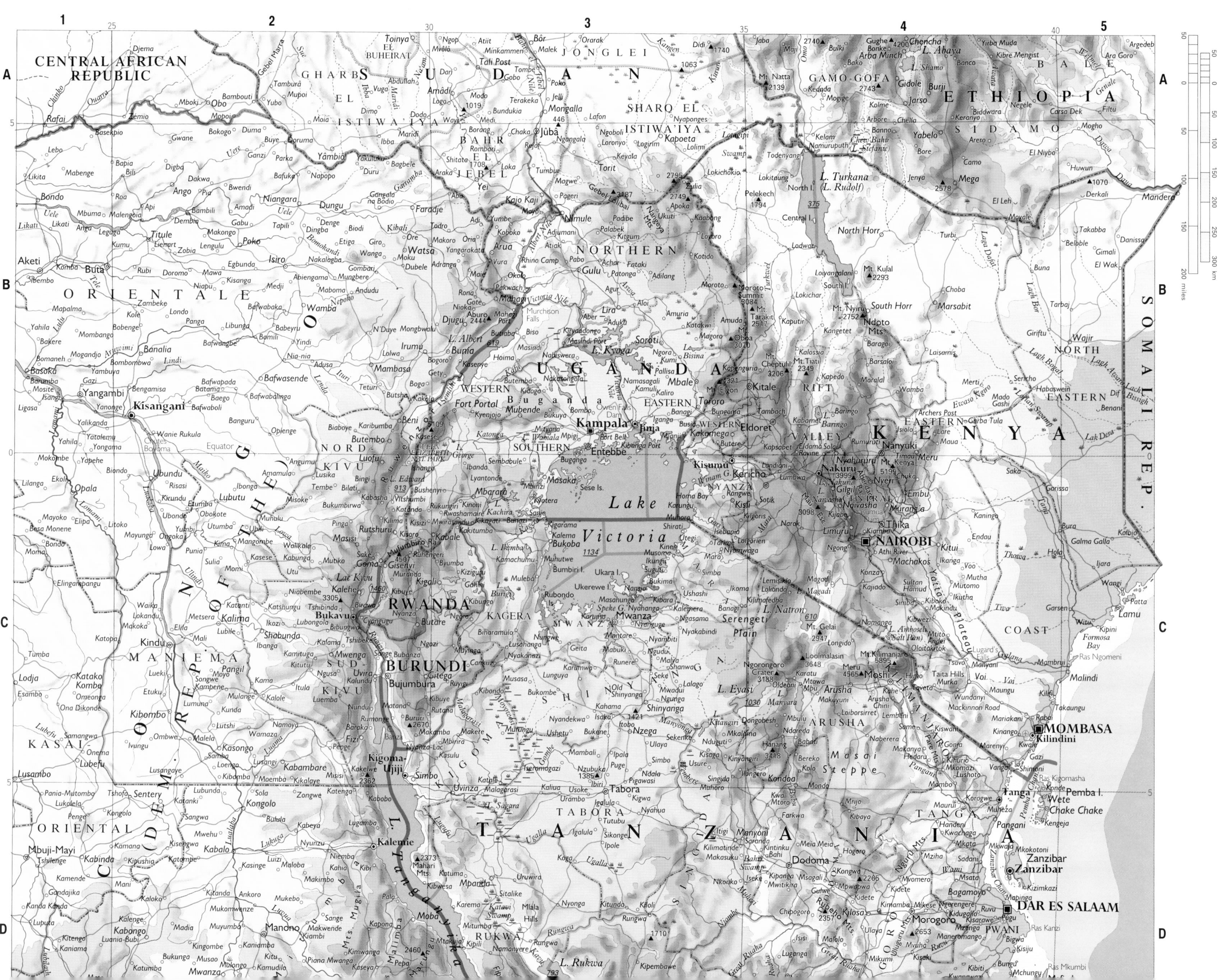

50 0 50 100 150 200 250 300 km
50 0 50 100 150 200 miles
CENTRAL AFRICAN REPUBLIC
SUDAN
ETHIOPIA
SOMALI REP.
KENYA
UGANDA
RWANDA
BURUNDI
TANZANIA
Lake Victoria
L. Turkana (L. Rudolf)
L. Albert
L. Edward
Lac Kivu
L. Tanganyika
L. Rukwa
L. Natron
L. Eyasi
NAIROBI
MOMBASA
DAR ES SALAAM
Zanzibar
Pemba I.
Kampala
Entebbe
Jinja
Kigali
Bujumbura
Dodoma
Kisangani
Juba
Arusha
Moshi
Mwanza
Tabora
Kigoma-Ujiji
Nakuru
Eldoret
Kisumu
Gulu
Tanga
Serengeti Plain
Masai Steppe
Yatta Plateau
Equator

74
89
81
84
85
88
89

Projection: Lambert's Equivalent Azimuthal

East from Greenwich

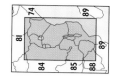

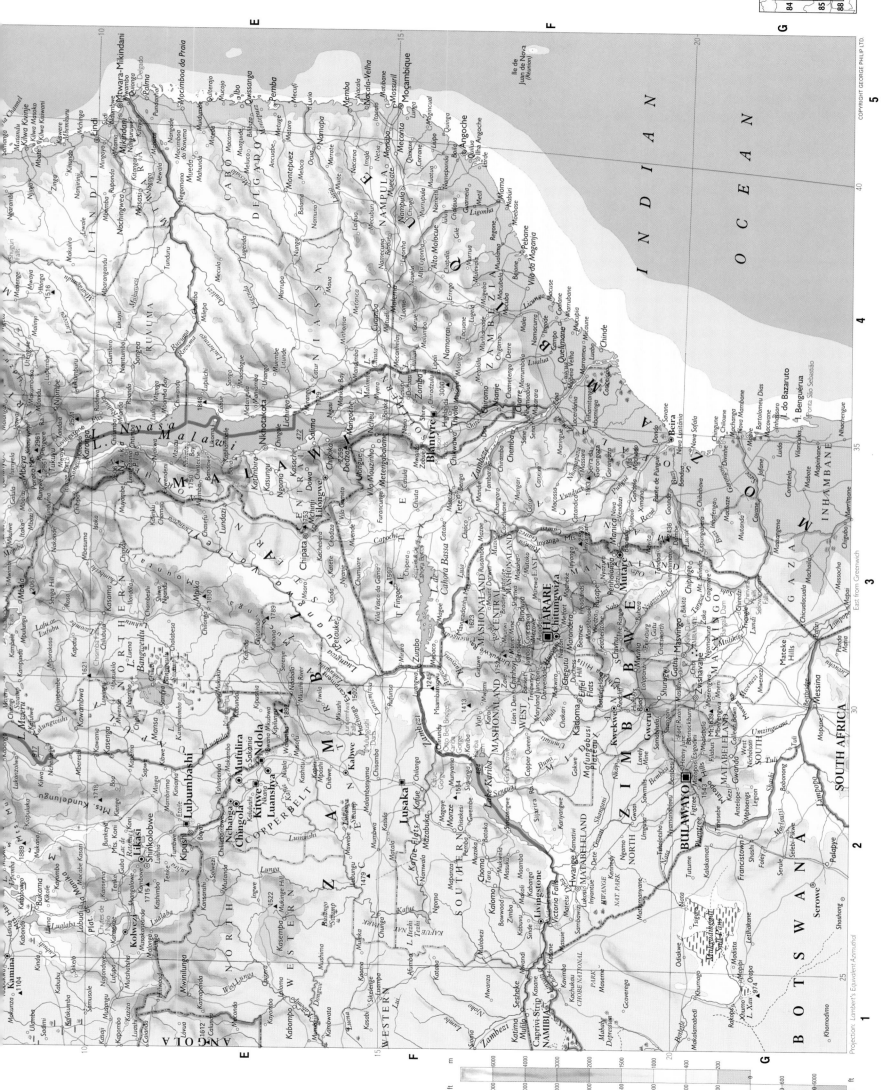

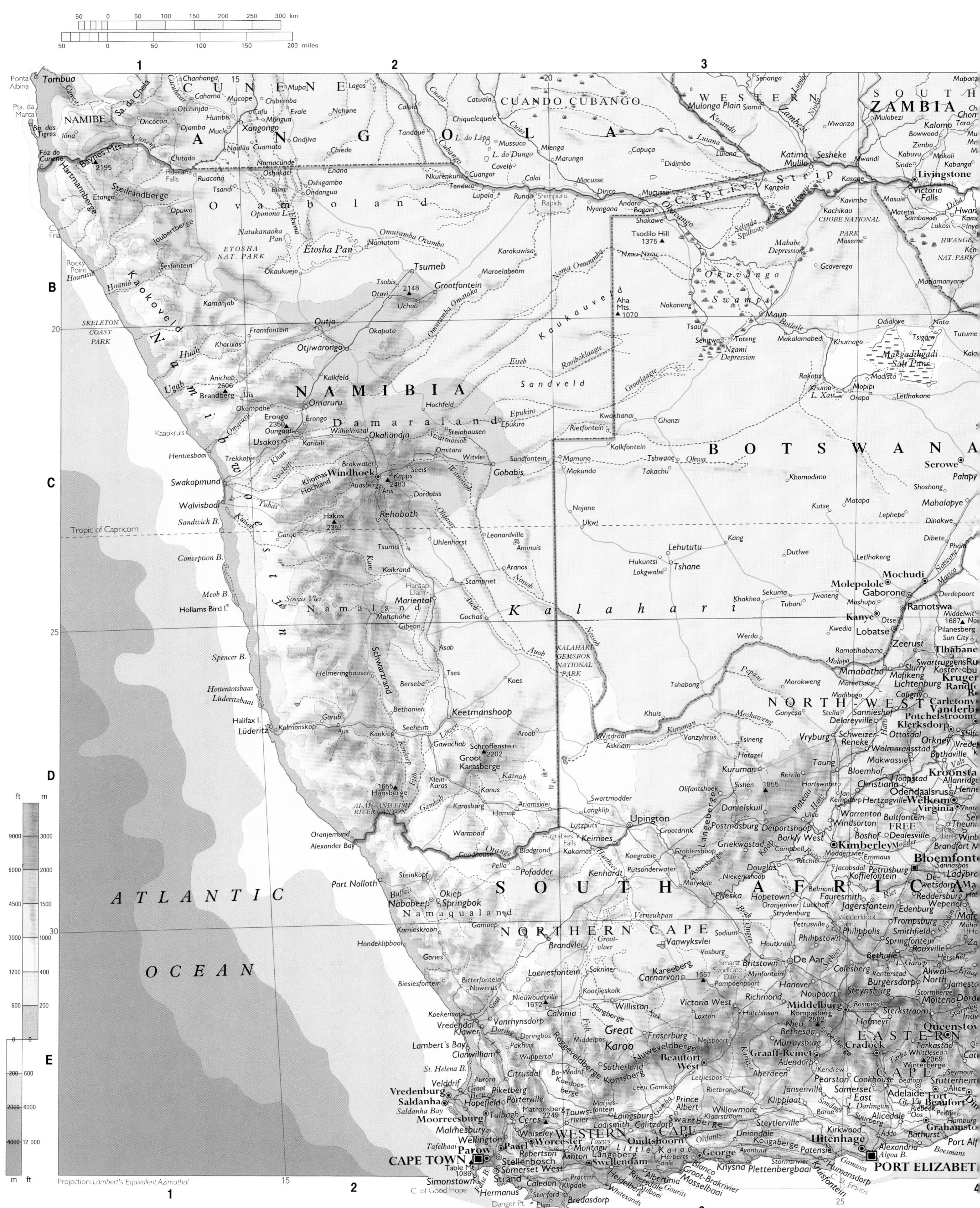
50 0 50 100 150 200 250 300 km
50 0 50 100 150 200 miles
ANGOLA
CUNENE
CUANDO CUBANGO
ZAMBIA
NAMIBIA
BOTSWANA
SOUTH AFRICA
NORTH-WEST
NORTHERN CAPE
WESTERN CAPE
EASTERN CAPE
FREE
ATLANTIC
OCEAN
Ovamboland
Damaraland
Namaland
Namaqualand
Kaokoveld
Namib Desert
Kalahari
Sandveld
Kaukauveld
Caprivi Strip
Okavango Swamps
Great Karoo
Little Karoo
Etosha Pan
Makgadikgadi Salt Pans
Ngami Depression
SKELETON COAST PARK
ETOSHA NAT. PARK
KALAHARI GEMSBOK NATIONAL PARK
CHOBE NATIONAL PARK
Tropic of Capricorn
Windhoek
Walvisbaai
Swakopmund
Lüderitz
Keetmanshoop
Rehoboth
Mariental
Okahandja
Otjiwarongo
Tsumeb
Grootfontein
Gobabis
Maun
Gaborone
Lobatse
Kanye
Molepolole
Mochudi
Serowe
Livingstone
Victoria Falls
Kimberley
Bloemfontein
Upington
Kuruman
Vryburg
Mafikeng
Welkom
De Aar
Beaufort West
Graaff-Reinet
Oudtshoorn
George
Knysna
Plettenbergbaai
Uitenhage
PORT ELIZABETH
CAPE TOWN
Paarl
Stellenbosch
Worcester
Swellendam
Simonstown
C. of Good Hope
C. Agulhas
Saldanha
Vredenburg
Springbok
Port Nolloth
Calvinia
Carnarvon
Orange
Okavango
Kunene
Zambezi
Schwarzrand
Tsodilo Hill 1375
Baynes Mts. 2195
Brandberg 2606
Hochland
Projection: Lambert's Equivalent Azimuthal
ft m
9000 3000
6000 2000
4500 1500
3000 1000
1200 400
600 200
0 0
200 600
2000 6000
4000 12 000
m ft

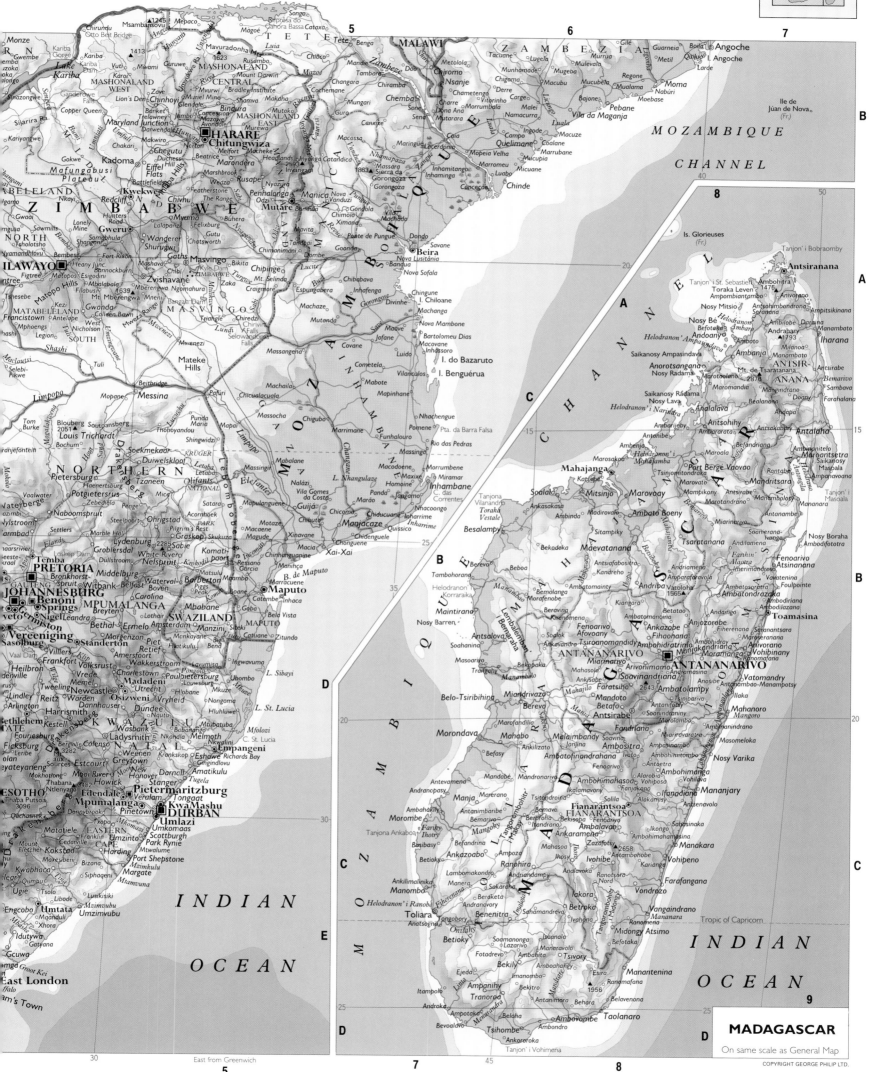

MADAGASCAR

On same scale as General Map

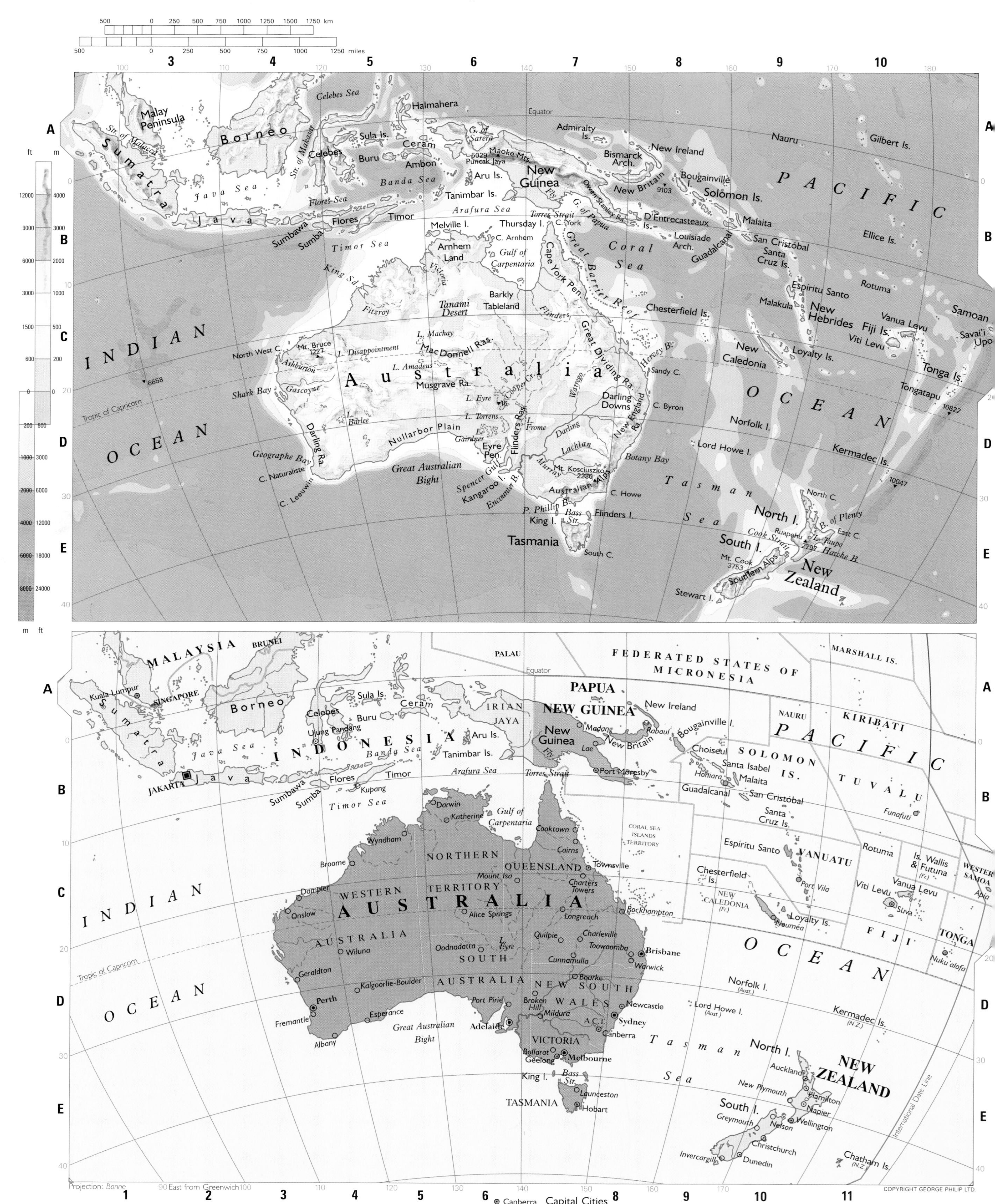
INDIAN OCEAN
PACIFIC OCEAN
Australia
New Guinea
New Zealand
Tasmania
Coral Sea
Tasman Sea
Arafura Sea
Timor Sea
Java Sea
Banda Sea
Great Australian Bight
Great Dividing Ra.
Great Barrier Reef
Gulf of Carpentaria
Cape York Pen.
Nullarbor Plain
MacDonnell Ras.
Tanami Desert
Tropic of Capricorn
Equator
INDONESIA
PAPUA NEW GUINEA
SOLOMON IS.
VANUATU
FIJI
TONGA
TUVALU
KIRIBATI
NAURU
MALAYSIA
BRUNEI
FEDERATED STATES OF MICRONESIA
MARSHALL IS.
WESTERN AUSTRALIA
NORTHERN TERRITORY
QUEENSLAND
SOUTH AUSTRALIA
NEW SOUTH WALES
VICTORIA
TASMANIA
A.C.T.
NEW ZEALAND
Canberra
Sydney
Melbourne
Brisbane
Adelaide
Perth
Hobart
Darwin
Alice Springs
Wellington
Auckland
Christchurch
JAKARTA
Port Moresby
Projection: Bonne
East from Greenwich
Canberra Capital Cities
International Date Line

50 0 50 100 150 200 km
50 0 50 100 150 miles

PACIFIC OCEAN

C. Reinga
C. Maria van Diemen
North C.
Houhora Heads
Rangaunu B.
Doubtless B.
Ahipara B.
Mangonui
Whangaroa Harb.
Kaitaia
Tauroa Pt.
Okaihau
Kaikohe
B. of Islands
Opua
C. Brett
Raweni
Hikurangi
Hokianga Harbour
Whangarei
Whangarei Harb.
Donnelly's Crossing
Bream Hd.
Dargaville
Waipu
Bream B.
Little Barrier I.
Great Barrier I.
Warkworth
C. Rodney
Kaipara Harbour
C. Colville
Cuvier I.
Helensville
Coromandel
Takapuna
Devonport
Whitianga
AUCKLAND
Manukau
Papakura
Thames
Waiuku
Pukekohe
Mercer
Waihi
Mayor I.
Waikato
Paeroa
Te Aroha
White I.
C. Runaway

North Island

Huntly
Morrinsville
Mount Maunganui
Bay of Plenty
Hamilton
Tauranga
Tauranga Harb.
Raglan
Cambridge
Whakatane
Te Awamutu
Rotorua
Kawerau
Raukumara Ra.
Mt. Hikurangi 1753
Kawhia Harbour
Putaruru
Taratvera L.
Taneatua
Opotiki
Motu
Waipiro
Otorohanga
Tokoroa
Te Kuiti
Mokau
Kinleith
Kaingaroa
Waimana Mts.
Tolaga Bay
North Taranaki Bight
Mokau
Mokai
Waikakopu
Forest
Murupara
Ormond
Te Taupo
Ongarue L.
Taupo
Gisborne
New Plymouth
Waitara
Whangamomona
Turangi
Kaimanawa Mts.
Tarawera
Nuhaka
Poverty Bay
Inglewood
Ruapehu 2797
Waikaremoana L.
Mt. Egmont 2518
Stratford
Ohakune
Mahia Pen.
Opunake
Eltham
Raetihi
Waiouru
Wairoa
Kapuni
Taihape
Bay View
Hawke Bay
Hawera
Waverley
Mangaweka
Rangitikei Ra.
Napier
South Taranaki Bight
Patea
Morton
Hunterville
C. Kidnappers
Wanganui
Halcombe
Feilding
Waipawa
Hastings
Bulls
Woodville
Waipukurau
Palmerston North
Foxton
Shannon
Dannevirke
Pahiatua
Levin
Eketahuna
Otaki
C. Turnagain
Paraparaumu
Kapiti I.
Featherston
Masterton
Upper Hutt
Carterton
Greytown
Petone
Martinborough
WELLINGTON
Lower Hutt
Eastbourne
Wairarapa L.

TASMAN SEA

C. Farewell
Collingwood
Golden B.
D'Urville I.
Takaka
Tasman B.
Tasman Mts.
Motueka
Karamea
Nelson
Havelock
Pelorus Sd.
Karamea Bight
Richmond
Picton
Seddonville
Wakefield
Blenheim
Cook Str.
Granity
Seddon
Lyell
Westport
Murchison
Ward
Inangahua Jn.
Rotoroa L.
2885 Mt. Tapuaenuku
Reefton
Mt. Travers 2338
Spenser Mts.
Kaikoura
Blackball
Lewis Pass
Hanmer Springs
Runanga
Clarence R.
Greymouth
Stillwater
Waiau
Kumara
L. Brunner
Culverden
Hokitika
Jacksons
Amberley
Ross
Waikari
Hurunui R.
Oxford
Pegasus Bay
Coleridge L.
Rangiora
Kaiapoi
Abut Hd.
Springfield
New Brighton
Whitecliffs
Christchurch
Riccarton
Lincoln
Lyttelton
Banks Pen.
Rolleston
Little River
Methven
Staveley
Akaroa
Jackson B.
Southbridge
Okuru R.
Fairlie
Rakaia R.
Mt. Cook 3753
Tekapo L.
Rangitata R.
Ashburton Bight
Mt. Aspiring 3027
Pukaki L.
Temuka
Southern Alps
Ohau L.
Timaru
Mt. Earnslaw 2818
Hawea L.
St. Andrews
Milford Sd.
Wanaka L.
Wanaka
Waimate
Bligh Sound
Arrowtown
Kurow
George Sound
Cromwell
Ngapara
Tokarahi
South Island
Queenstown
Clyde
Naseby
Oamaru
Secretary I.
Wakatipu L.
Alexandra
Kakanui Mts.
Maheno
Doubtful Sd.
Garvie Mts.
Roxburgh
Hampden
Breaksea Sd.
Te Anau L.
Kingston
Dunback
Palmerston
Resolution I.
Manapouri
Lumsden
Waikouaiti
Dusky Sd.
Messburn
Clutha R.
Port Chalmers
Otago Harbour
Mararoa
Ohai
Edievale
Saunders C.
Chalky Inlet
Clifden
Balclutha
Lawrence
Dunedin
Preservation Inlet
Tuatapere
Nightcaps
Winton
Kelso
Tapanui
Mataura
Clinton
Milton
Hedgehope
Te Waewae B.
Orepuki
Gore
Kaitangata
Riverton
Balfour
Wyndham
Nugget Pt.
Invercargill
Southland
Owaka
Tahakopa
Bluff Invercargill
Takaroa
Foveaux Str.
Ruapuke I.
Southwest C.
Halfmoon Bay
Stewart I.
Port Pegasus

SAMOA ISLANDS
1:10 700 000

WESTERN SAMOA
AMERICAN SAMOA
Savai'i
Apia
Upolu
Pago Pago
Tutuila
West from Greenwich

FIJI AND TONGA ISLANDS
1:10 700 000

Futuna
Wallis & Futuna (Fr.)
Niuafo'ou (Tonga)
Thikombia
Lambasa
Yasawa Group
Vanua Levu
FIJI
Taveuni
Koro
Vanua Mbalavu
Lautoka
1323
Levuka
Nandi
Viti Levu
Ovalau
Koro Sea
Lakemba
Lau Group
TONGA (Friendly Is.)
Suva
Gau
Moala
Vava'u
Kandavu
Vatoa
Tofua
Tongatapu
Nuku'alofa
East from Greenwich
West from Greenwich

ft m
9000 3000
6000 2000
3000 1000
1200 400
600 200
0 0
200 600
2000 6000
4000 12 000
6000 18 000
m ft

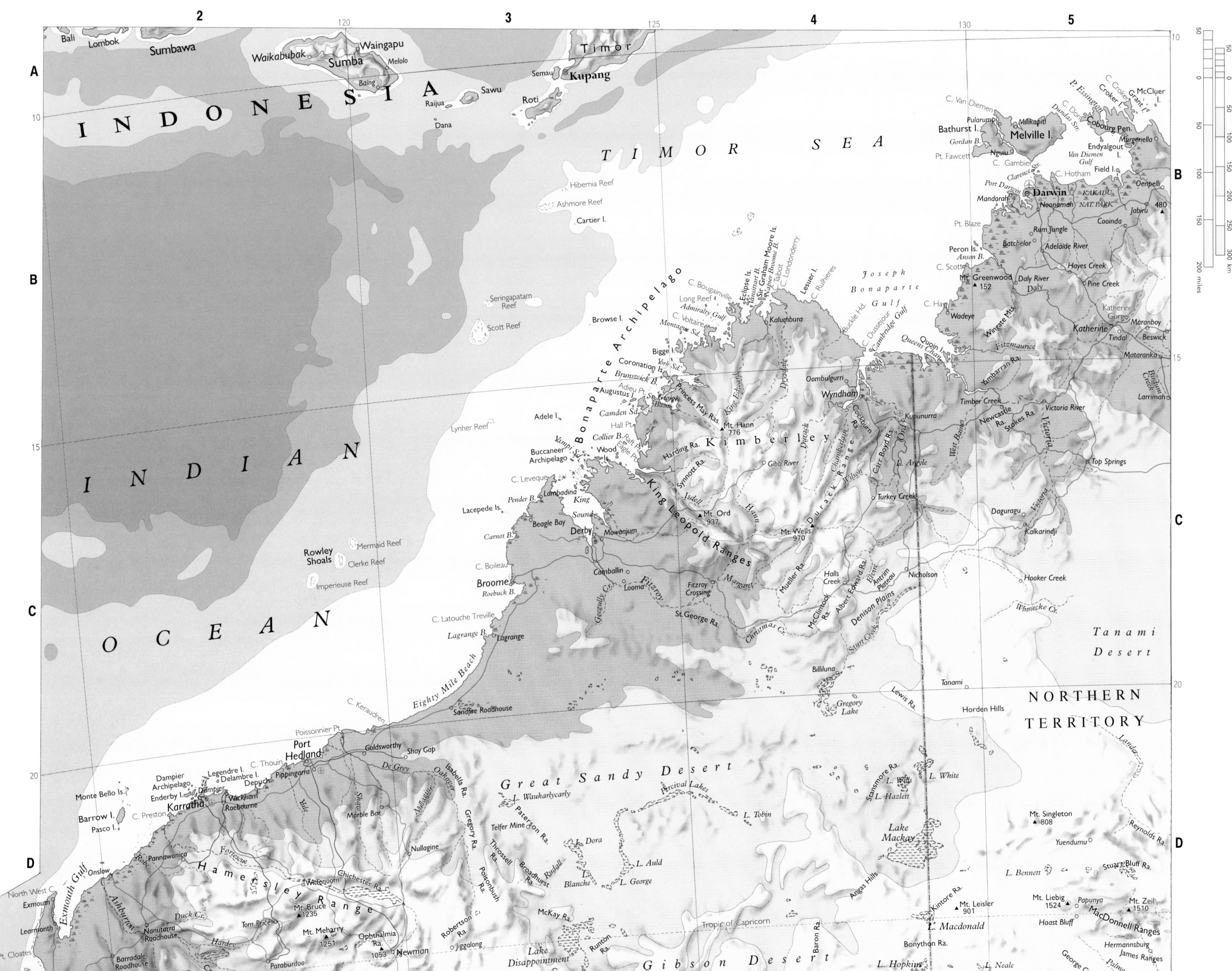
50 0 50 100 150 200 250 300 km
50 0 50 100 150 200 miles
A
B
C
D
2
3
4
5
10
15
20
120
125
130
I N D O N E S I A
T I M O R S E A
I N D I A N
O C E A N
N O R T H E R N
T E R R I T O R Y
Tanami Desert
Great Sandy Desert
Gibson Desert
Kimberley
King Leopold Ranges
Hamersley Range
Bonaparte Archipelago
Joseph Bonaparte Gulf
Bali
Lombok
Sumbawa
Sumba
Waikabubak
Waingapu
Melolo
Baing
Sawu
Raijua
Dana
Roti
Semau
Kupang
Timor
Hibernia Reef
Ashmore Reef
Cartier I.
Seringapatam Reef
Scott Reef
Browse I.
Adele I.
Lynher Reef
Rowley Shoals
Mermaid Reef
Clerke Reef
Imperieuse Reef
Lacepede Is.
Buccaneer Archipelago
Yampi Sd.
King Sound
Derby
Broome
Roebuck B.
Lagrange B.
Lagrange
C. Latouche Treville
Eighty Mile Beach
Sandfire Roadhouse
Port Hedland
Goldsworthy
Shay Gap
C. Keraudren
Poissonnier Pt.
Karratha
Dampier
Roebourne
Wickham
Dampier Archipelago
Legendre I.
Delambre I.
Depuch I.
Enderby I.
C. Preston
Monte Bello Is.
Barrow I.
Pasco I.
Onslow
Exmouth Gulf
Exmouth
North West C.
Learmonth
Pt. Cloates
Ashburton
Pannawonica
Nanutarra Roadhouse
Barradale Roadhouse
Duck Cr.
Fortescue
Tom Price
Paraburdoo
Mt. Bruce 1235
Mt. Meharry 1251
Wittenoom
Newman
Ophthalmia Ra.
Chichester Ra.
Marble Bar
Nullagine
De Grey
Yule
Shaw
Isabella Ra.
Gregory Ra.
Paterson Ra.
Telfer Mine
Throssell Ra.
Poisonbush Ra.
Broadhurst Ra.
Robertson Ra.
Jiggalong
Lake Disappointment
McKay Ra.
L. Blanche
L. Dora
L. Waukarlycarly
Percival Lakes
L. Auld
L. George
Runton Ra.
L. Tobin
Tropic of Capricorn
Baron Ra.
Fitzroy
Fitzroy Crossing
Camballin
Looma
Mowanjum
St. George Ra.
Margaret
Christmas Cr.
Mt. Ord 937
Isdell
Mt. Hann 776
Gibb River
Mt. Wells 970
Halls Creek
Billiluna
Gregory Lake
McClintock Ra.
Mueller Ra.
Albert Edward Ra.
Denison Plains
Sturt Creek
Nicholson
Turkey Creek
Kununurra
Ord
L. Argyle
Carr Boyd Ra.
Wyndham
Cockburn Ra.
Durack Range
Oombulgurri
Kalumburu
C. Londonderry
Drysdale
Lesueur I.
C. Rulhieres
C. Bougainville
Admiralty Gulf
C. Voltaire
Montague Sd.
Long Reef
Princess May Ras.
Harding Ra.
Synnot Ra.
Coronation Is.
Brunswick B.
Augustus I.
Camden Sd.
Collier B.
Hall Pt.
Cambridge Gulf
C. Dussejour
Queens Channel
Quoin I.
Wadeye
Mt. Greenwood 152
Peron Is.
Anson B.
C. Scott
Pt. Blaze
Bathurst I.
Melville I.
C. Van Diemen
Pt. Fawcett
Darwin
Dundas Str.
Cobourg Pen.
Croker I.
Grant I.
C. Croker
Van Diemen Gulf
Field I.
Kakadu Nat. Park
Jabiru
Oenpelli
Katherine
Mataranka
Larrimah
Tindal
Pine Creek
Hayes Creek
Adelaide River
Rum Jungle
Batchelor
Daly River
Victoria River
Victoria
Timber Creek
Top Springs
Kalkaringi
Daguragu
Hooker Creek
Tanami
Horden Hills
Lewis Ra.
L. White
Stansmore Ra.
L. Hazlett
Lake Mackay
Mt. Singleton 808
Yuendumu
L. Bennett
Mt. Liebig 1524
Papunya
MacDonnell Ranges
Mt. Zeil 1510
Hermannsburg
James Ranges
Haast Bluff
Mt. Leisler 901
Kintore Ra.
L. Macdonald
Bonython Ra.
Angas Hills
L. Hopkins
L. Neale
Reynolds Ra.

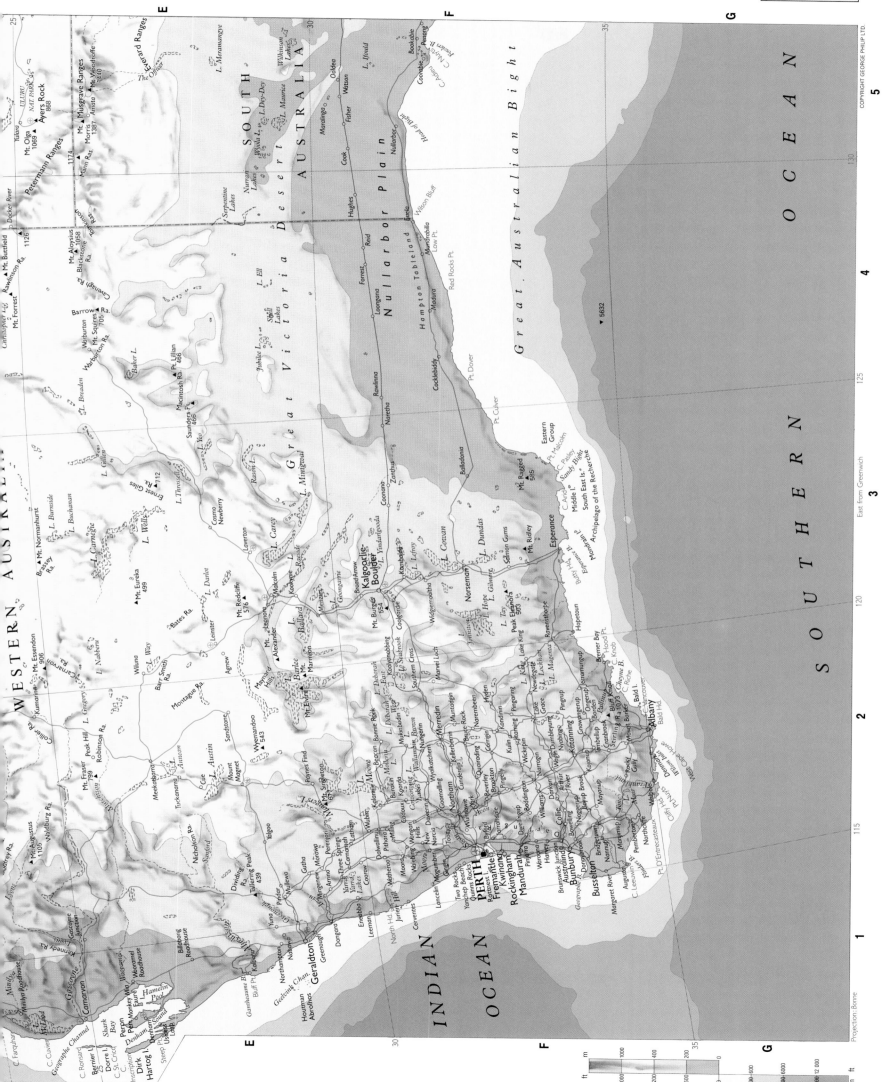

WESTERN AUSTRALIA

SOUTH AUSTRALIA

Great Victoria Desert

Nullarbor Plain

Great Australian Bight

INDIAN OCEAN

SOUTHERN OCEAN

PERTH

Kalgoorlie-Boulder

Geraldton

Carnarvon

Albany

Esperance

Bunbury

Busselton

Mandurah

Rockingham

Fremantle

Kwinana

ULURU NAT. PARK
Ayers Rock 868

Mt. Olga 1069
Mt. Musgrave Ranges
Morris 1387
Amata
Mann Ra.

Petermann Ranges 1174

Everard Ranges

Mt. Woodroffe 1440

COPYRIGHT GEORGE PHILIP LTD.

Projection: Borne

East from Greenwich

m
3000
1200
600
0
200
600

ft
12 000
6000
2000
1000
400
200
0

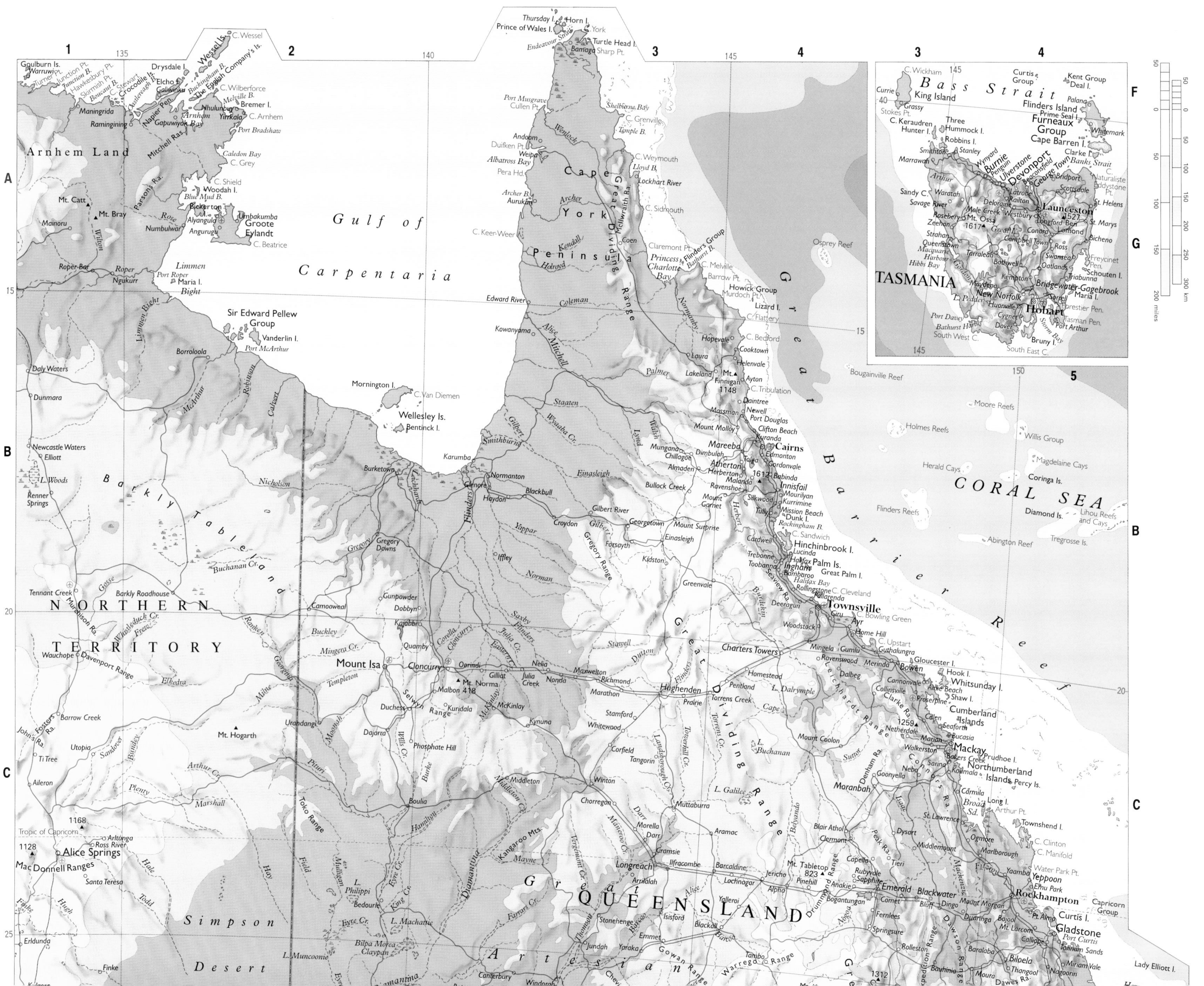

50 0 50 100 150 200 250 300 km
50 0 50 100 150 200 miles
TASMANIA
Bass Strait
King Island
Flinders Island
Furneaux Group
Cape Barren I.
Launceston
Devonport
Burnie
Hobart
New Norfolk
Bruny I.
Gulf of Carpentaria
Arnhem Land
Groote Eylandt
Sir Edward Pellew Group
Mornington I.
Wellesley Is.
Cape York Peninsula
Great Dividing Range
Great Barrier Reef
CORAL SEA
Thursday I.
Prince of Wales I.
Cairns
Townsville
Hinchinbrook I.
Charters Towers
Bowen
Whitsunday I.
Cumberland Islands
Mackay
Northumberland Islands
Rockhampton
Gladstone
Mount Isa
Cloncurry
Longreach
Emerald
NORTHERN TERRITORY
Barkly Tableland
Tennant Creek
Alice Springs
MacDonnell Ranges
Tropic of Capricorn
Simpson Desert
QUEENSLAND
Gregory Range
Selwyn Range
Toko Range
Davenport Range

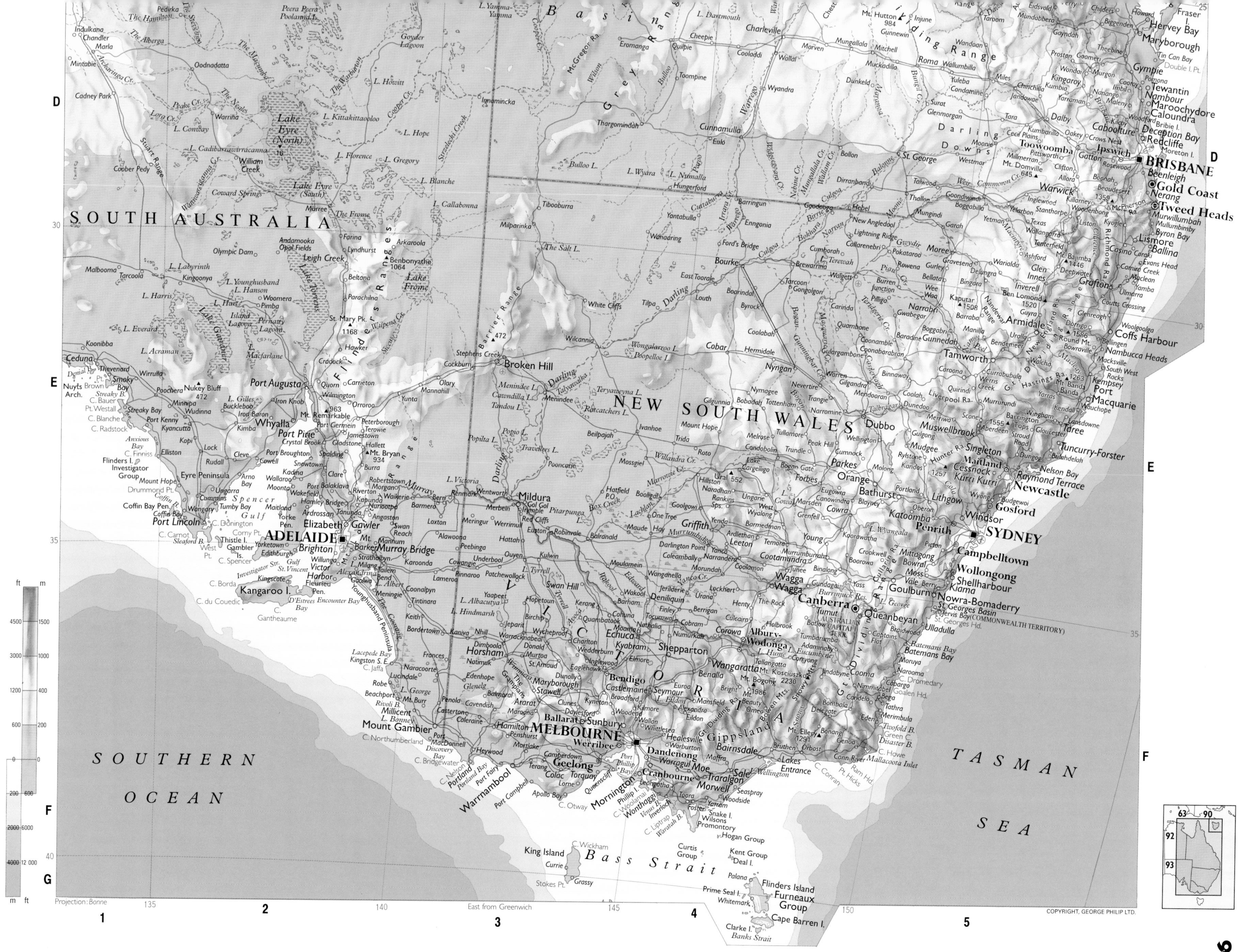

SOUTHERN OCEAN

TASMAN SEA

SOUTH AUSTRALIA

NEW SOUTH WALES

VICTORIA

Bass Strait

BRISBANE

SYDNEY

Canberra

MELBOURNE

ADELAIDE

Newcastle

Wollongong

Geelong

King Island

Flinders Island

Kangaroo I.

Furneaux Group

Great Dividing Range

Darling Downs

Murray R.

Darling R.

Lake Eyre

Lake Torrens

Lake Gairdner

Lake Frome

Eyre Peninsula

Yorke Peninsula

Spencer Gulf

Gulf St. Vincent

Broken Hill

Mildura

Mount Gambier

Warrnambool

Dubbo

Tamworth

Armidale

Coffs Harbour

Grafton

Port Macquarie

Gold Coast

Tweed Heads

Lismore

Toowoomba

Gympie

Maryborough

Hervey Bay

Fraser I.

Projection: Bonne

East from Greenwich

COPYRIGHT, GEORGE PHILIP LTD.

RUSSIA

MOSKVA Yekaterinburg Tomsk
Volga Astana (Aqmola) Novosibirsk Irkutsk *Oz. Baykal* Chita Blagoveshchensk *Amur* Sea of Okhotsk Okhotsk *Poluostrov Kamchatka* Komandorskiye Ostrova (Russia) Near Is. (U.S.A.)
KAZAKSTAN Semey Ulaanbaatar Khabarovsk Sakhalin Petropavlovsk-Kamchatskiy *Aleutian Trench*
Aral Sea *Balqash Köl* MONGOLIA Harbin *La Pérouse Str.* *Kurilskiye Ostrova (Russia)*
Almaty Ürümqi Changchun Vladivostok Hakodate *Kuril Trench* ▼10,542 *Emperor Seamount Chain*
Toshkent KYRGYZSTAN SHENYANG Sapporo *Sea of Japan*
TAJIKISTAN BEIJING Taiyuan Dalian SOUL Sendai Midway Is. (U.S.A.)
AFGHANISTAN *Altai* TIANJIN NORTH KOREA SOUTH KOREA Nagoya TOKYO Fuji-San 3776 Yokohama
Kabul Srinagar *Huang He* Qingdao Kyoto Osaka JAPAN
PAKISTAN CHINA Lanzhou Xi'an Kitakyushu Shikoku *Japan Trench*
Lahore *Kunlun Shan* XIZANG Nanjing *Yellow Sea* Kyūshū ▼10,554
DELHI *Himalaya* Lhasa Wuhan CHONGQING SHANGHAI *Ogasawara Gunto (Japan)*
Kanpur *Ganga* Mt. Everest 8850 *Chang J.* Changsha HANGZHOU *East China Sea* Minami-Tori-Shima (Japan) Lisianski I. (U.S.A.)
NEPAL *Brahmaputra* Kunming Fuzhou Kazan-Rettō (Japan)
INDIA BANGLADESH DHAKA Mandalay GUANGZHOU Taipei *Ryukyu-retto (Japan)*
CALCUTTA BURMA *Salween* Macau HONG KONG TAIWAN
Hyderabad *Irrawaddy* Hanoi *Marcus Necker Ridge* Wake I. (U.S.A.)
Bay of Bengal Rangoon *Mekong* Hainan C. Engano NORTHERN MARIANAS (U.S.A.) Saipan MARSHALL IS. **P**
CHENNAI (Madras) THAILAND BANGKOK Luzon GUAM (U.S.A.) 11,022 Enewetak Atoll Bikini Atoll
Andaman Is. (India) CAMBODIA Paracel Is. MANILA *Mariana Trench* *Micronesia*
SRI LANKA Phnom Penh Mindoro PHILIPPINES Samar Yap Caroline Is. Truk *Dalap-Uliga-Darrit*
Colombo Nicobar Is. (India) *G. of Thailand* Phanh Bho Ho Chi Minh *South China Sea* Palawan 10,497 Koror Pohnpei Jaluit I.
Sulu Sea Mindanao PALAU FEDERATED STATES Butaritari
MALAYSIA Kuala Lumpur BRUNEI SABAH *Celebes Sea* 4101 *Mindanao Trench* OF MICRONESIA Tarawa Gilbert Is. Howland
PENINSULAR MALAYSIA *SARAWAK* *Maluku* NAURU Banaba Baker
SINGAPORE Borneo Sulawesi Halmahera Seram PAPUA NEW GUINEA *Melanesia* Phoenix Is. Abarir Enderb
Sumatera Palembang Ujung Pandang Buru Puncak Jaya 5029 IRIAN JAYA Admiralty Is. Bismarck Arch. New Ireland
INDONESIA *Java Sea* *Banda Sea* 7440 New Guinea Rabaul *KI*
JAKARTA *Flores Sea* Flores Lae New Britain Bougainville SOLOMON IS. *Fongafale* TUVALU Toke
Jawa Surabaya Bali Sumbawa Sumba Timor *Arafura Sea* Port Moresby Honiara Guadalcanal Rotuma Is. Wallis & Futuna (Fr.) WES SAM
Java Trench Christmas I. (Austral.) *Torres Strait* C. York Santa Cruz I. 9165 Vanua Levu
Cocos Is. (Austral.) Darwin C. Arnhem Louisiade Arch. Espiritu Santo VANUATU Viti Levu FIJI
INDIAN *Gulf of Carpentaria* *Coral Sea* Is. Chesterfield Port Vila Suva
OCEAN Broome Cairns 7570 NEW CALEDONIA (Fr.) Is. Loyauté *Nuku'alofa* TON
North West C. Mount Isa Townsville 10,822 Tong Tren
AUSTRALIA Alice Springs Rockhampton Nouméa
Geraldton *L. Eyre* *Great Dividing Ra.* Brisbane Norfolk I. (Austral.) Kermadec (N.Z.)
Darling Lord Howe I. (Austral.) Kermadec Trench 10,047
Perth *Great Australian Bight* Sydney NEW ZEALAND
Albany *Murray* Canberra Mt. Kosciuszko 2237 *Tasman Sea* Auckland
Nouvelle Amsterdam (Fr.) Adelaide Melbourne *Cook Strait*
I. St. Paul (Fr.) *Bass Str.* Aoraki Mt. Cook 3753 Wellington Chat
Tasmania Hobart Christchurch
Is. Crozet (Fr.) Dunedin
Kerguelen (Fr.) Invercargill Bounty Is. (N.Z.)
Mid Indian Ridge Auckland Is. (N.Z.) Antipodes Is. (N.Z.)
Heard I. (Austral.) Macquarie Is. (Austral.) Campbell I. (N.Z.)

ft m
12 000 4000
9000 3000
6000 2000
3000 1000
1500 500
600 200
0 0
200 600
1000 3000
2000 6000
4000 12 000
6000 18 000
8000 24 000
m ft

Projection: Mollweide's Homolographic East from Greenwich

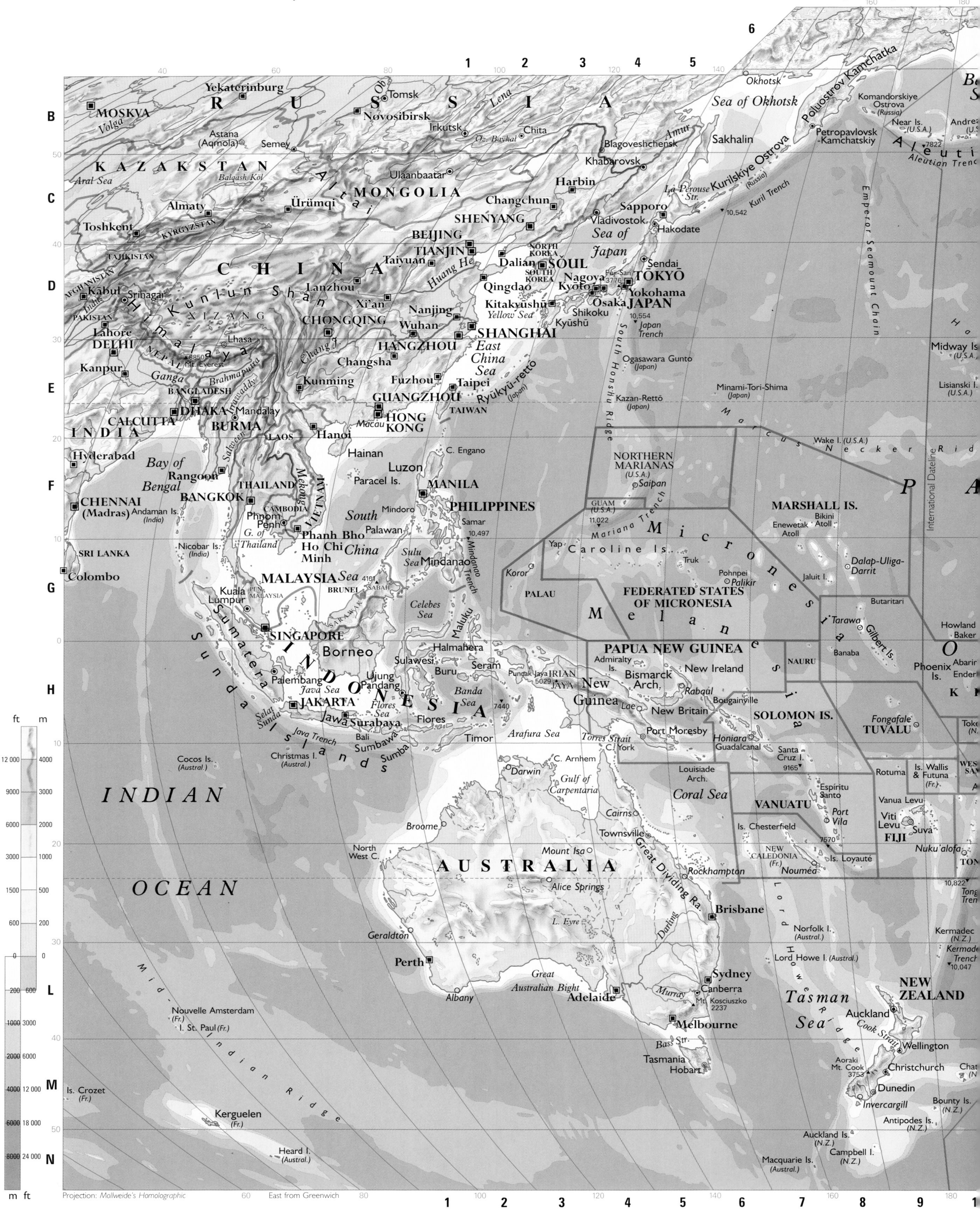

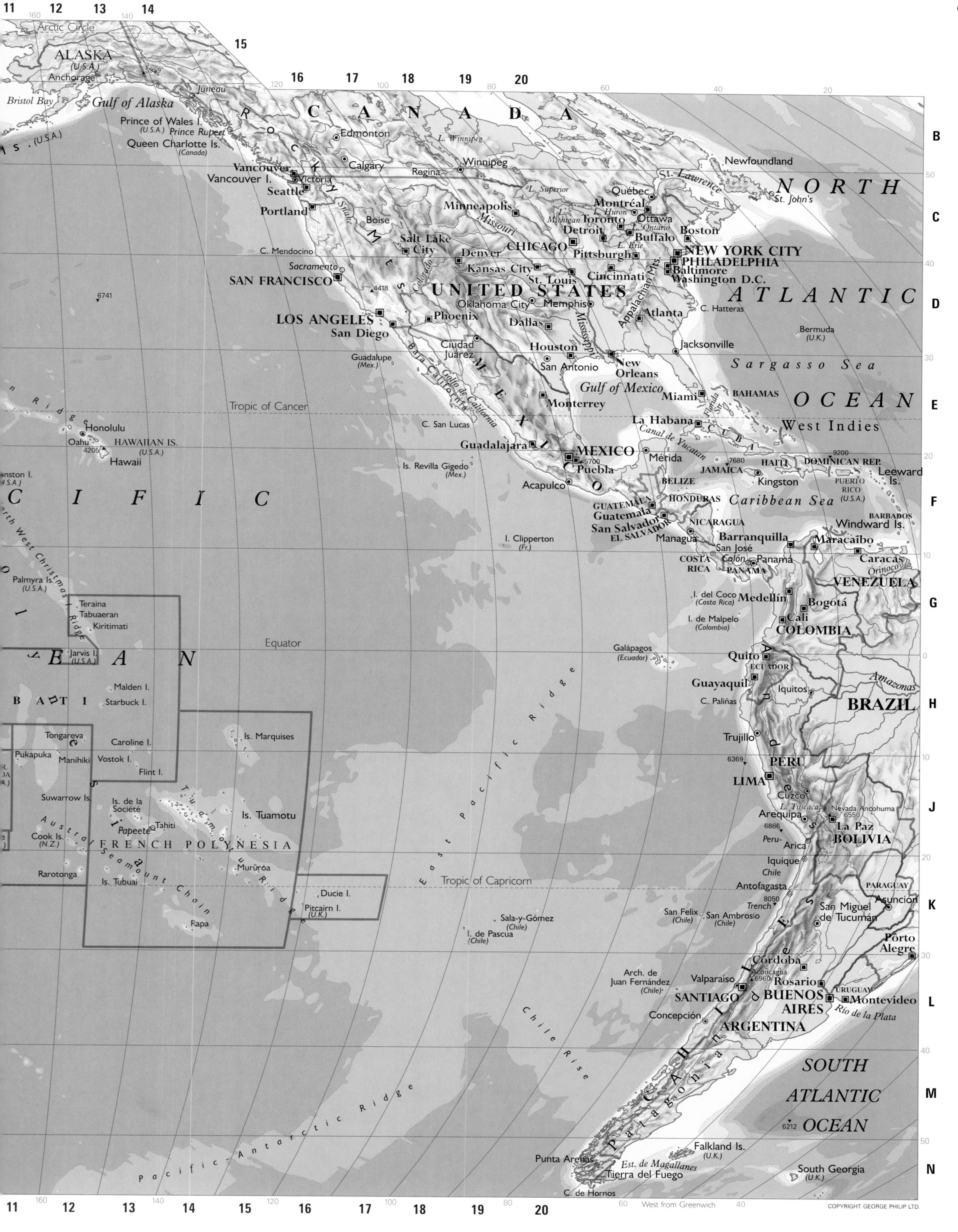
ALASKA (U.S.A.)
Anchorage
Arctic Circle
Gulf of Alaska
Bristol Bay
Juneau
Prince of Wales I. (U.S.A.)
Prince Rupert
Queen Charlotte Is. (Canada)
CANADA
ROCKY MTS
Edmonton
Calgary
Regina
Winnipeg
L. Winnipeg
Vancouver
Vancouver I.
Victoria
Seattle
Portland
Boise
Snake
Salt Lake City
Denver
Minneapolis
Missouri
L. Superior
Québec
Montréal
Ottawa
Toronto
Detroit
Buffalo
Boston
Newfoundland
St. Lawrence
St. John's
NORTH ATLANTIC OCEAN
CHICAGO
Pittsburgh
NEW YORK CITY
PHILADELPHIA
Baltimore
Washington D.C.
Cincinnati
St. Louis
Kansas City
C. Mendocino
Sacramento
SAN FRANCISCO
UNITED STATES
Oklahoma City
Memphis
Atlanta
C. Hatteras
Appalachian Mts.
Mississippi
LOS ANGELES
San Diego
Phoenix
Dallas
Bermuda (U.K.)
Ciudad Juárez
Houston
San Antonio
New Orleans
Jacksonville
Guadalupe (Mex.)
Sargasso Sea
Gulf of Mexico
Miami
BAHAMAS
Monterrey
MEXICO
Tropic of Cancer
C. San Lucas
La Habana
CUBA
West Indies
Honolulu
Oahu
HAWAIIAN IS. (U.S.A.)
Hawaii
Guadalajara
Mérida
HAITI
DOMINICAN REP.
JAMAICA
Kingston
PUERTO RICO (U.S.A.)
Leeward Is.
Is. Revilla Gigedo (Mex.)
Puebla
Acapulco
BELIZE
HONDURAS
Caribbean Sea
PACIFIC OCEAN
GUATEMALA
Guatemala
San Salvador
EL SALVADOR
NICARAGUA
Managua
BARBADOS
Windward Is.
I. Clipperton (Fr.)
Barranquilla
Maracaibo
Caracas
Orinoco
San José
COSTA RICA
Colón
Panamá
PANAMA
VENEZUELA
Palmyra Is. (U.S.A.)
I. del Coco (Costa Rica)
Medellín
Bogotá
Cali
COLOMBIA
I. de Malpelo (Colombia)
Teraina
Tabuaeran
Kiritimati
Equator
Jarvis I. (U.S.A.)
Galápagos (Ecuador)
Quito
ECUADOR
Guayaquil
C. Paliñas
Iquitos
Amazonas
BRAZIL
Malden I.
Starbuck I.
Is. Marquises
Tongareva
Caroline I.
Pukapuka
Manihiki
Vostok I.
Flint I.
Trujillo
PERU
LIMA
Cuzco
L. Titicaca
Nevada Ancohuma
La Paz
BOLIVIA
Arequipa
Suwarrow Is.
Is. de la Société
Tahiti
Papeete
Is. Tuamotu
Cook Is. (N.Z.)
FRENCH POLYNESIA
Peru-Chile Trench
Arica
Iquique
Antofagasta
Rarotonga
Is. Tubuai
Mururoa
Tropic of Capricorn
Ducie I.
Pitcairn I. (U.K.)
PARAGUAY
Asunción
Sala-y-Gómez (Chile)
I. de Pascua (Chile)
San Felix (Chile)
San Ambrosio (Chile)
San Miguel de Tucumán
Porto Alegre
Rapa
East Pacific Ridge
Austral Seamount Chain
Tuamotu Ridge
Córdoba
Aconcagua
Rosario
Arch. de Juan Fernández (Chile)
Valparaíso
SANTIAGO
BUENOS AIRES
URUGUAY
Montevideo
Río de la Plata
Concepción
ARGENTINA
Chile Rise
ANDES
PATAGONIA
SOUTH ATLANTIC OCEAN
Pacific-Antarctic Ridge
Falkland Is. (U.K.)
Punta Arenas
Est. de Magallanes
Tierra del Fuego
C. de Hornos
South Georgia (U.K.)
West from Greenwich

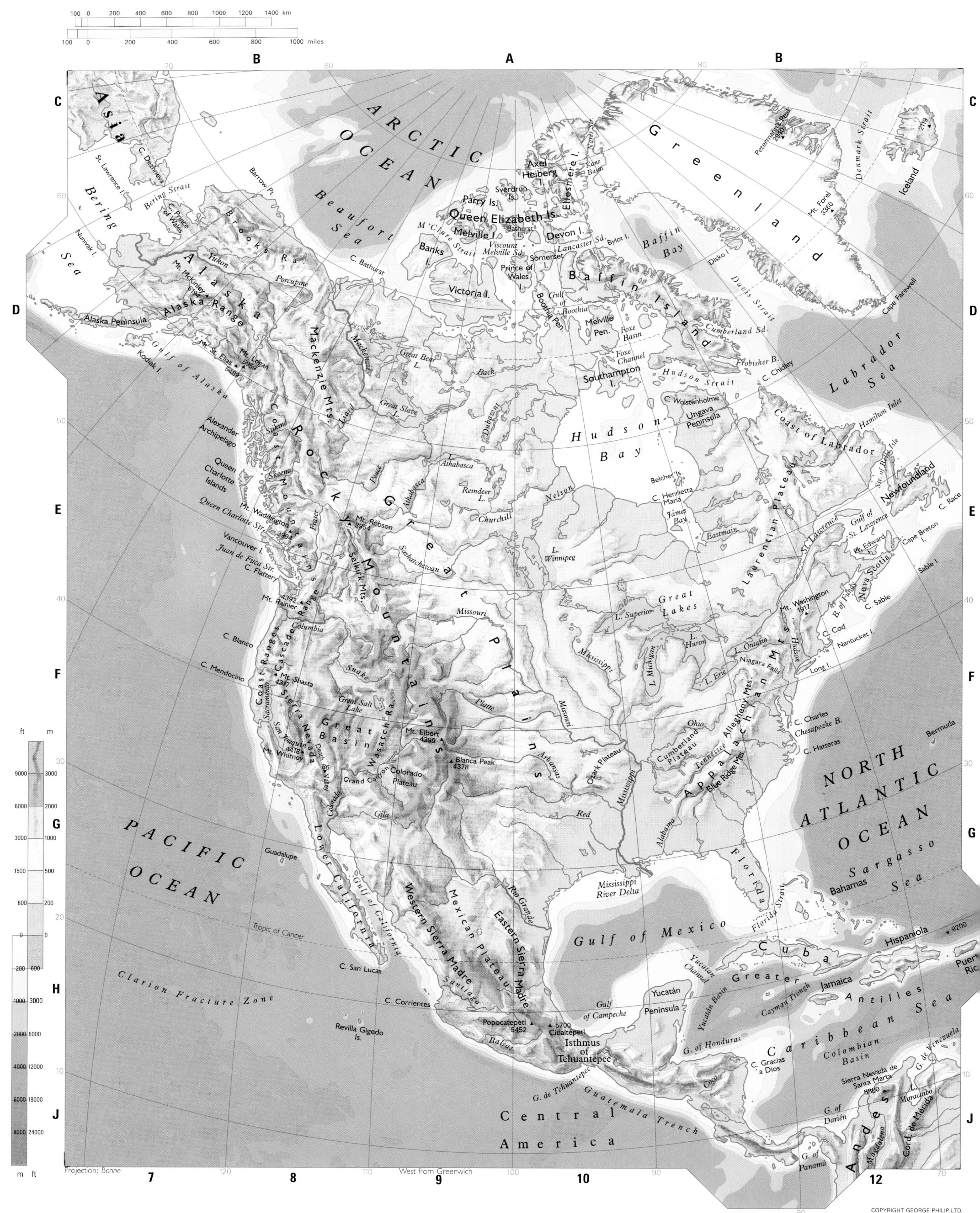
ARCTIC OCEAN
Beaufort Sea
Greenland
Baffin Bay
Queen Elizabeth Is.
Ellesmere I.
Axel Heiberg I.
Melville I.
Banks I.
Victoria I.
Baffin Island
Hudson Bay
Hudson Strait
Labrador Sea
Coast of Labrador
Newfoundland
Iceland
Denmark Strait
Davis Strait
Bering Sea
Bering Strait
Asia
Alaska
Alaska Range
Alaska Peninsula
Brooks Ra.
Mt. McKinley 6194
Mt. Logan 5959
Mt. St. Elias 5489
Gulf of Alaska
Kodiak I.
Mackenzie Mts.
Rocky Mountains
Coast Mountains
Great Plains
Mt. Robson 3954
Mt. Waddington 3994
Vancouver I.
Queen Charlotte Islands
Alexander Archipelago
Great Slave L.
Great Bear L.
L. Athabasca
Reindeer L.
L. Winnipeg
Great Lakes
L. Superior
L. Michigan
L. Huron
L. Erie
L. Ontario
Laurentian Plateau
Ungava Peninsula
James Bay
Gulf of St. Lawrence
Nova Scotia
Appalachian Mts.
Mt. Washington 1917
Cascade Range
Mt. Rainier 4392
Mt. Shasta 4317
Sierra Nevada
Mt. Whitney 4418
Great Basin
Great Salt Lake
Wasatch Ra.
Colorado Plateau
Grand Canyon
Mt. Elbert 4399
Blanca Peak 4378
Ozark Plateau
Cumberland Plateau
Mississippi
Missouri
Mississippi River Delta
Florida
NORTH ATLANTIC OCEAN
Sargasso Sea
Bermuda
Bahamas
PACIFIC OCEAN
Gulf of Mexico
Gulf of California
Lower California
Western Sierra Madre
Mexican Plateau
Eastern Sierra Madre
Popocatepetl 5452
Citlaltepetl 5700
Isthmus of Tehuantepec
Yucatán Peninsula
Cuba
Hispaniola
Jamaica
Greater Antilles
Caribbean Sea
Central America
Guatemala Trench
Clarion Fracture Zone
Tropic of Cancer
Andes
Projection: Bonne
West from Greenwich

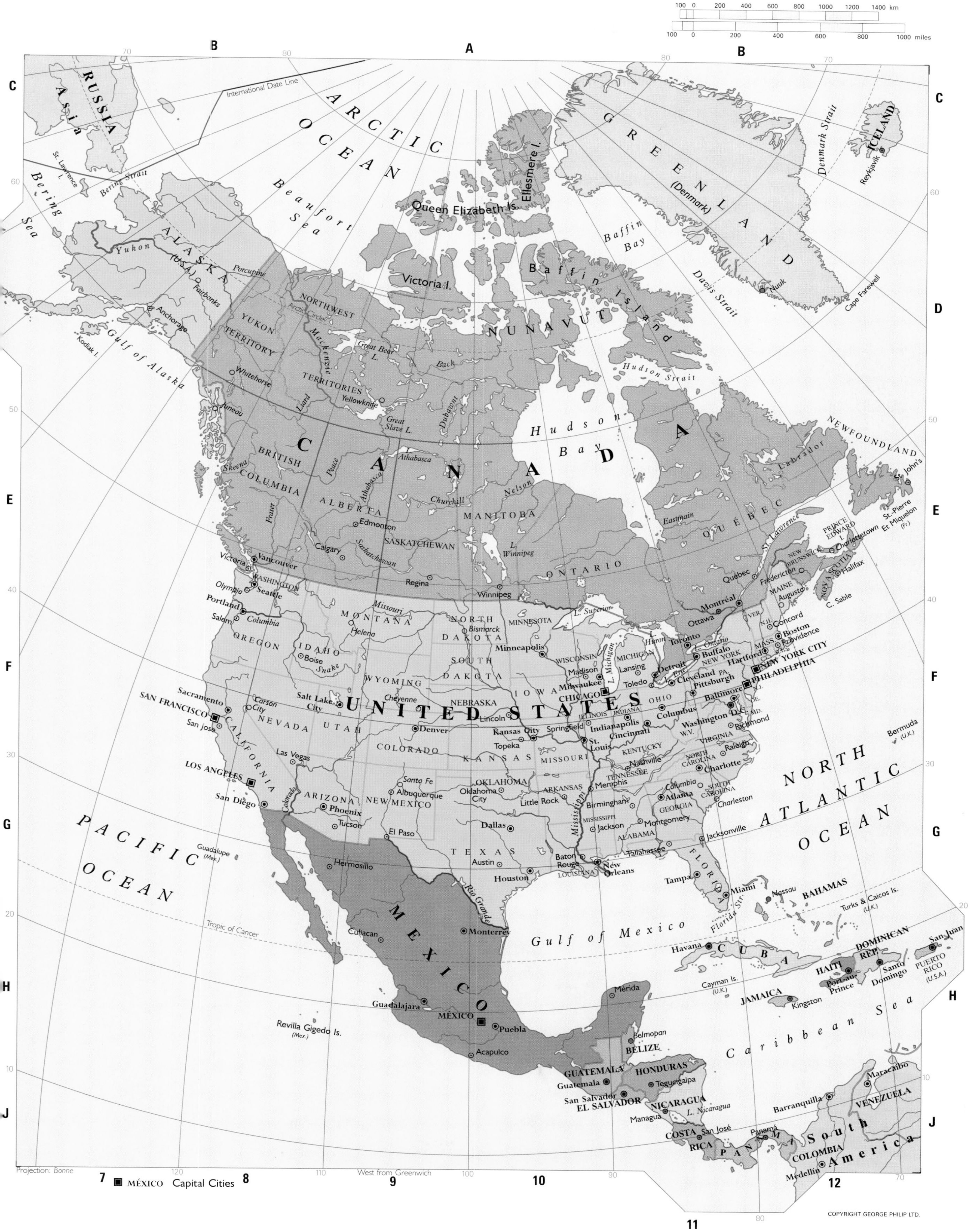

100 0   200   400   600   800   1000 1200 1400 km
100 0   200   400   600   800   1000 miles

Projection: Bonne

7 ■ MÉXICO Capital Cities 8

West from Greenwich

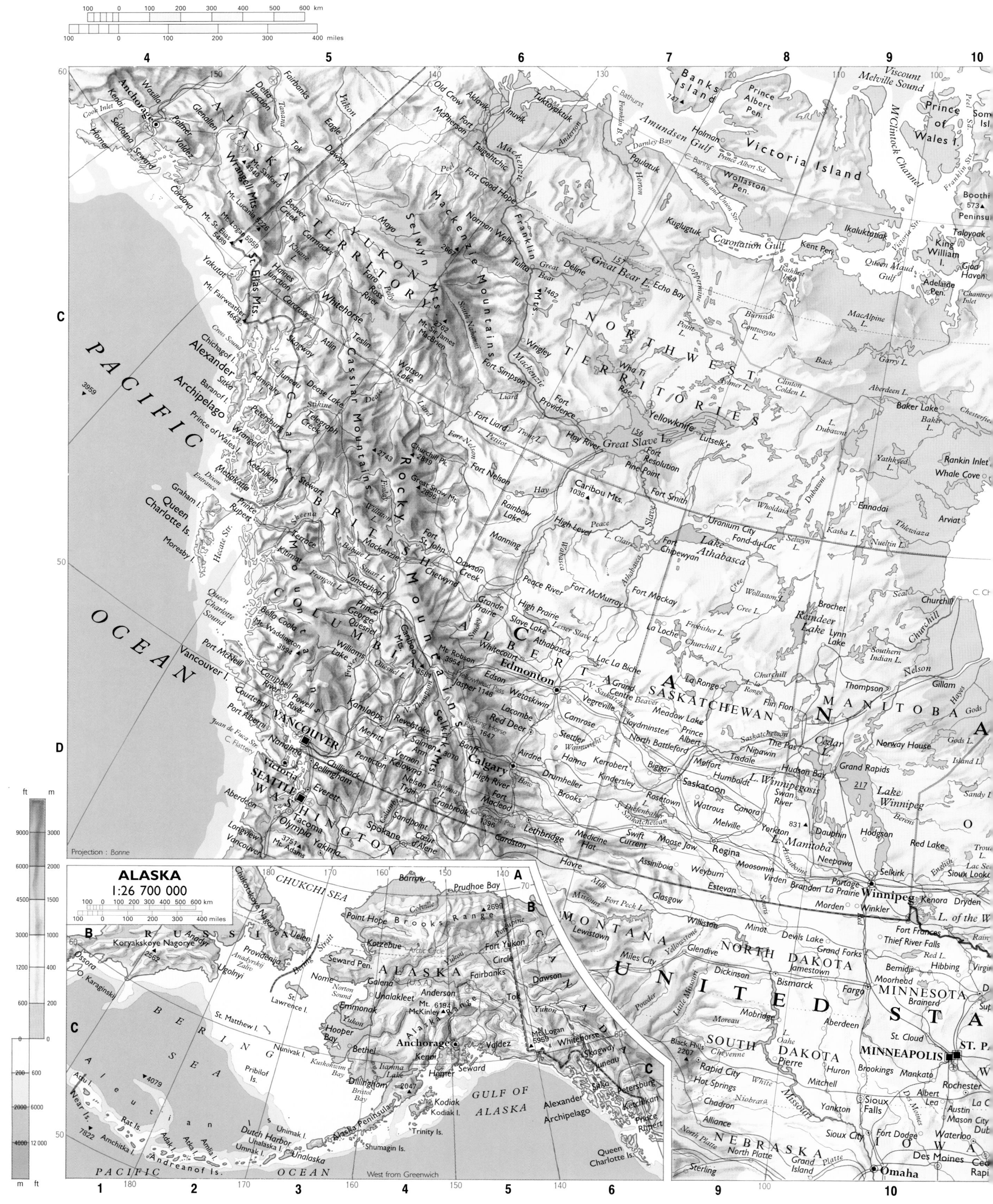

PACIFIC OCEAN
ALASKA
YUKON TERRITORY
NORTHWEST TERRITORIES
BRITISH COLUMBIA
ALBERTA
SASKATCHEWAN
MANITOBA
MONTANA
NORTH DAKOTA
SOUTH DAKOTA
NEBRASKA
MINNESOTA
IOWA
WASHINGTON
UNITED STATES
Anchorage
Fairbanks
Dawson
Whitehorse
Inuvik
Tuktoyaktuk
Yellowknife
Great Slave L.
Great Bear L.
Victoria Island
Banks Island
Prince of Wales I.
Amundsen Gulf
Coronation Gulf
Queen Maud Gulf
Viscount Melville Sound
M'Clintock Channel
King William I.
Rocky Mountains
Mackenzie Mountains
Selwyn Mts.
Cassiar Mountains
Coast Mountains
Columbia Mountains
Selkirk Mts.
Wrangell Mts.
St. Elias Mts.
Mt. Logan 5959
Mt. St. Elias 5489
Mt. Fairweather 4663
Alexander Archipelago
Queen Charlotte Is.
Vancouver I.
VANCOUVER
Victoria
SEATTLE
Edmonton
Calgary
Lake Athabasca
Reindeer Lake
Lake Winnipeg
L. Winnipegosis
L. Manitoba
Winnipeg
Regina
Saskatoon
Churchill
MINNEAPOLIS
ST. PAUL
Omaha
Projection : Bonne
ALASKA
1:26 700 000
CHUKCHI SEA
BERING SEA
GULF OF ALASKA
Brooks Range
Alaska Range
Mt. McKinley 6194
Aleutian Is.
Kodiak I.
Alaska Peninsula
West from Greenwich

106
107

GREENLAND (KALAALLIT NUNAAT) (Denmark)
Baffin Bay
Davis Strait
Labrador Sea
ATLANTIC OCEAN
Baffin Island
NUNAVUT
Foxe Basin
Hudson Strait
Hudson Bay
James Bay
Péninsule d'Ungava
Ungava Bay
NEWFOUNDLAND
Labrador
QUÉBEC
Gulf of St. Lawrence
NEW BRUNSWICK
NOVA SCOTIA
PR. EDWARD I.
MAINE
VERMONT
NEW HAMPSHIRE
NEW YORK
MONTRÉAL
Québec
Ottawa
TORONTO
BOSTON
NEW YORK
CHICAGO
DETROIT
CLEVELAND
BUFFALO
HARTFORD
Halifax
St. John's
West from Greenwich

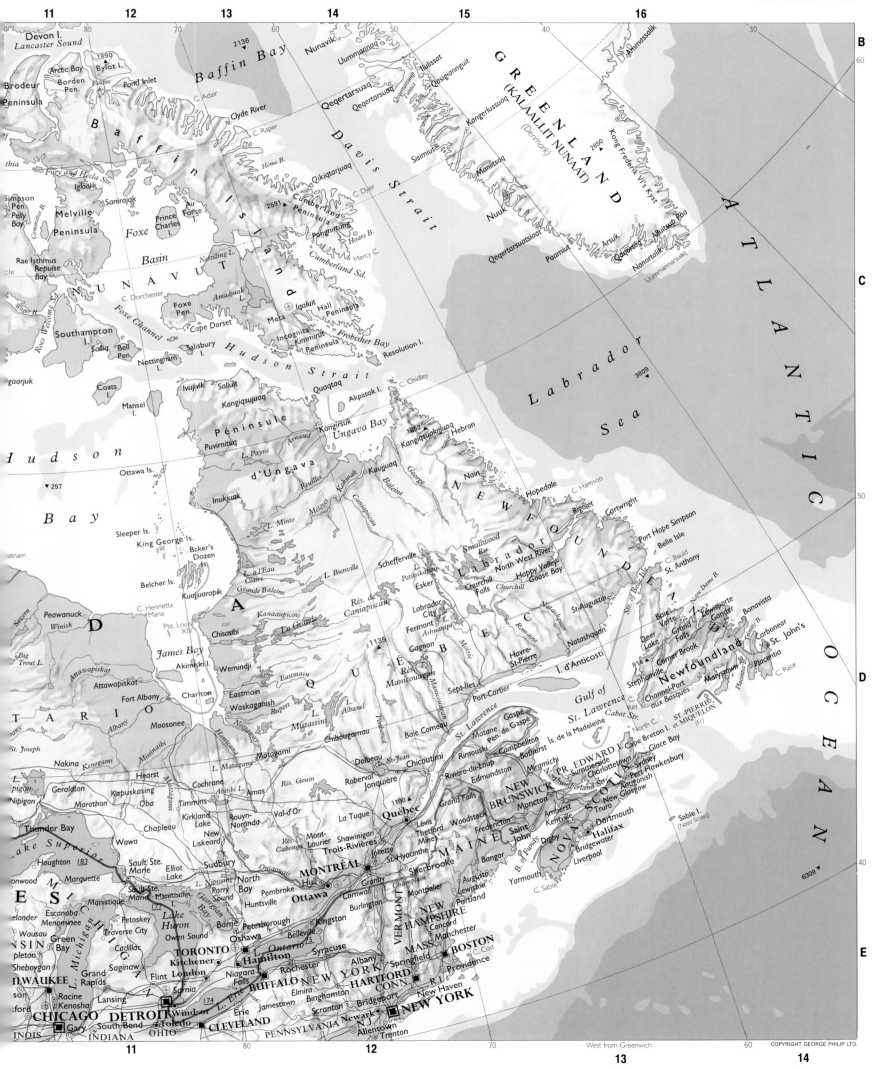

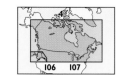

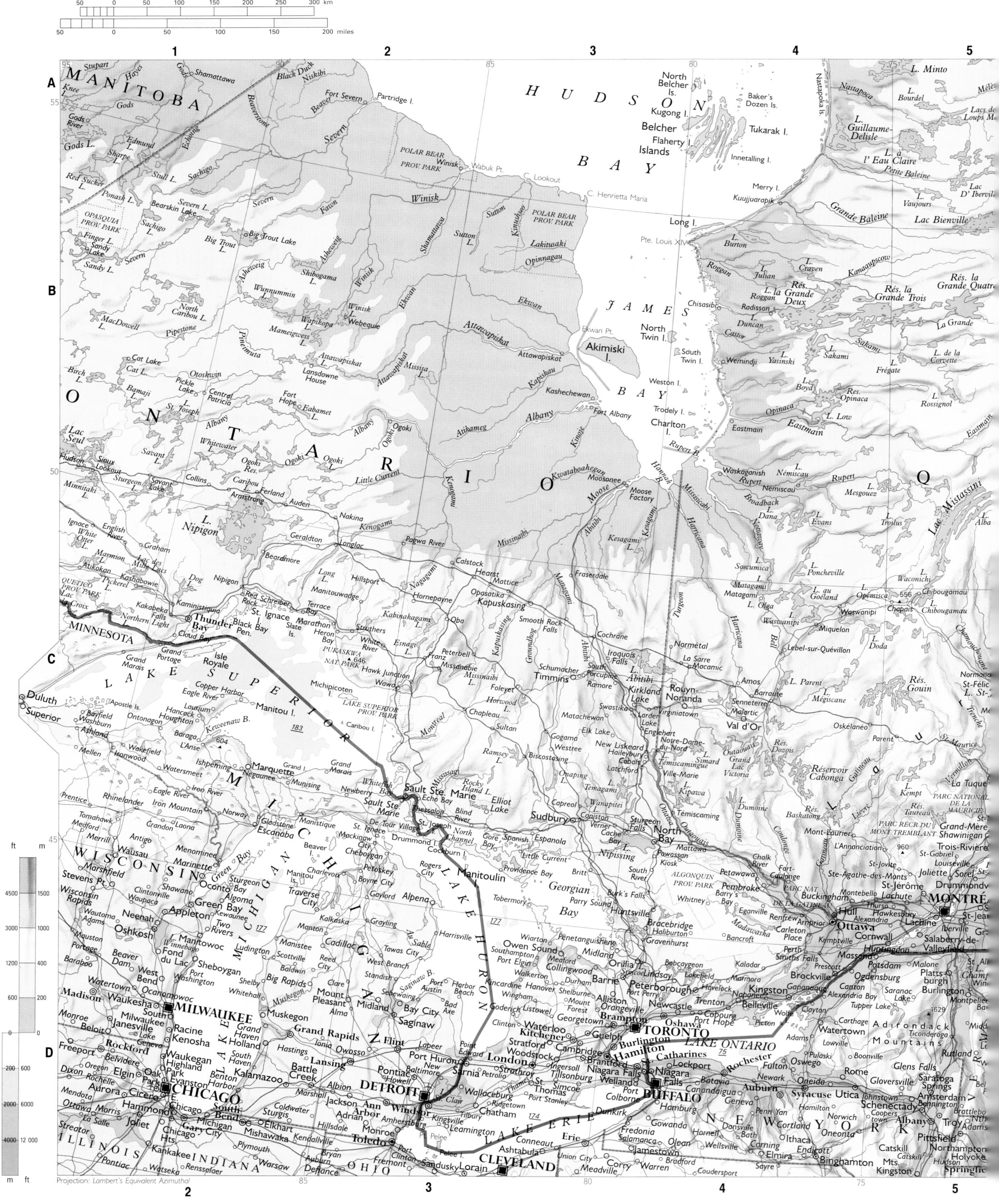
50 0 50 100 150 200 250 300 km
50 0 50 100 150 200 miles
1 2 3 4 5
A B C D
MANITOBA
ONTARIO
HUDSON BAY
JAMES BAY
MINNESOTA
WISCONSIN
MICHIGAN
ILLINOIS
INDIANA
OHIO
NEW YORK
LAKE SUPERIOR
LAKE MICHIGAN
LAKE HURON
LAKE ONTARIO
LAKE ERIE
Georgian Bay
Belcher Islands
Akimiski I.
North Twin I.
South Twin I.
Charlton I.
Lac Mistassini
Réservoir Cabonga
Rés. la Grande Deux
Rés. la Grande Trois
Lac Bienville
Polar Bear Prov. Park
Opasquia Prov. Park
Quetico Prov. Park
Lake Superior Prov. Park
Pukaskwa Nat. Park
Algonquin Prov. Park
Manitoulin
Isle Royale
L. Nipigon
Lac Seul
Big Trout Lake
Moosonee
Moose Factory
Fort Albany
Attawapiskat
Kashechewan
Winisk
Eastmain
Chisasibi
Radisson
Matagami
Chibougamau
Val d'Or
Amos
Rouyn-Noranda
Kirkland Lake
Timmins
Cochrane
Kapuskasing
Hearst
Geraldton
Thunder Bay
Nipigon
Marathon
Wawa
Chapleau
Sault Ste. Marie
Elliot Lake
Sudbury
North Bay
New Liskeard
Parry Sound
Huntsville
Bracebridge
Orillia
Barrie
Owen Sound
Peterborough
Kingston
Belleville
Brockville
Pembroke
Ottawa
Hull
MONTRÉAL
Trois-Rivières
Cornwall
TORONTO
Oshawa
Brampton
Hamilton
Burlington
St. Catharines
Niagara Falls
Kitchener
Waterloo
Guelph
Cambridge
Brantford
Woodstock
Stratford
London
Sarnia
Chatham
Windsor
DETROIT
Toledo
CLEVELAND
BUFFALO
Rochester
Syracuse
Utica
Schenectady
Albany
Binghamton
Erie
CHICAGO
MILWAUKEE
Madison
Green Bay
Duluth
Superior
Marquette
Escanaba
Flint
Saginaw
Lansing
Grand Rapids
Kalamazoo
South Bend
Gary
Projection: Lambert's Equivalent Azimuthal

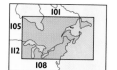

LABRADOR

SEA

A

B

N E W F O U N D

Labrador

Q U É B E C

Smallwood Reservoir

Labrador City
Fermont
Wabush

Î. d'Anticosti

Newfoundland

Long Range Mts.

Corner Brook

50

C

GULF OF
ST. LAWRENCE

Gaspé
Pen. de Gaspé

St. Lawrence

Cabot Strait

St-Pierre
et Miquelon
(France)

Sept-Îles

Baie Comeau

St. John's

NEW
BRUNSWICK

PRINCE EDWARD
ISLAND

Charlottetown

Cape Breton
Island

Sydney

45

Fredericton
Saint John

NOVA SCOTIA

Moncton

Halifax
Dartmouth

Bay of Fundy

ATLANTIC

Sable I.
(Nova Scotia)

MAINE

Bangor

Augusta

Portland

O C E A N

D

UNITED

STATES

BOSTON

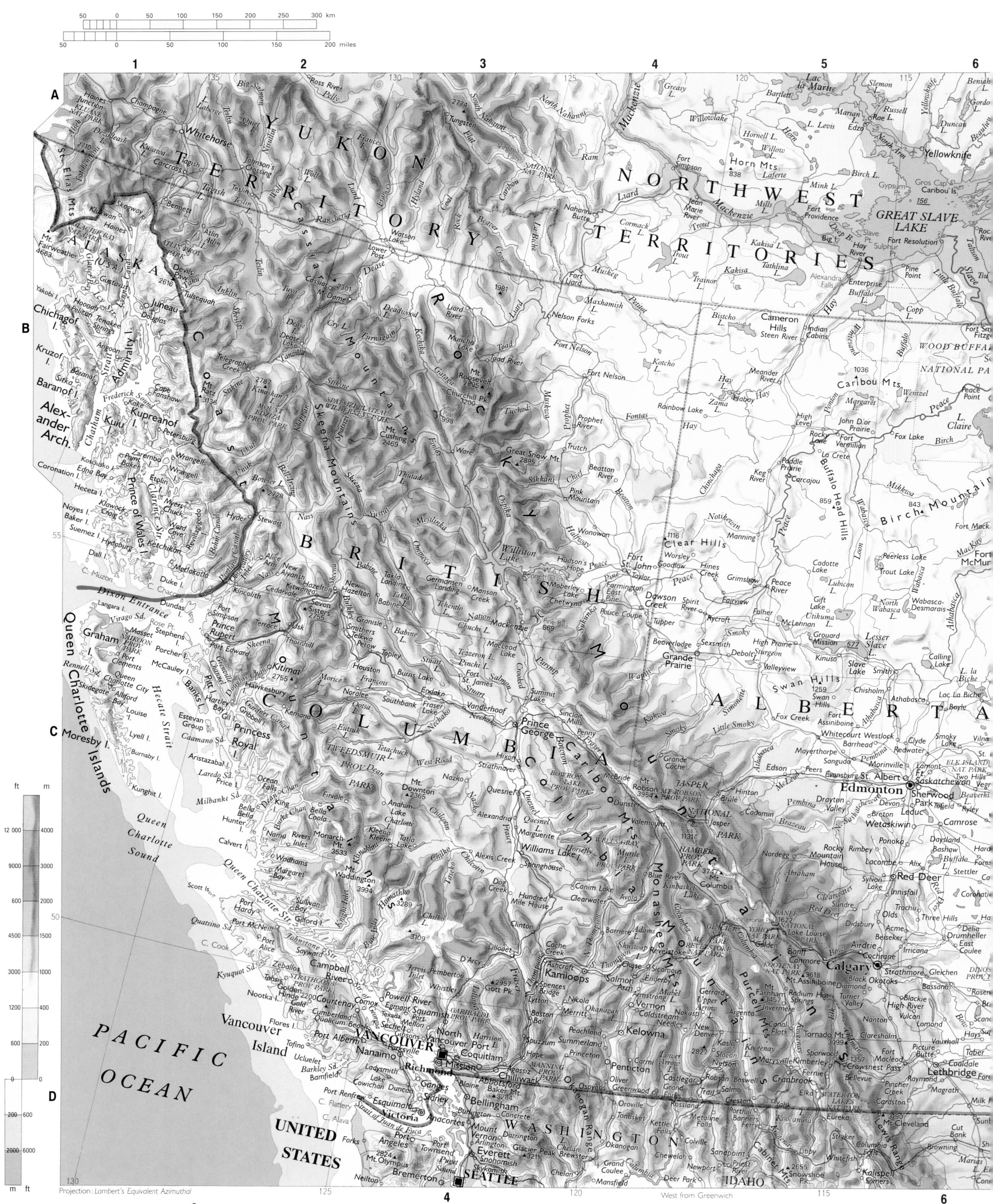

50 0 50 100 150 200 250 300 km
50 0 50 100 150 200 miles
YUKON TERRITORY
NORTHWEST TERRITORIES
BRITISH COLUMBIA
ALBERTA
ALASKA (U.S.A.)
WASHINGTON
IDAHO
UNITED STATES
PACIFIC OCEAN
GREAT SLAVE LAKE
Coast Mountains
Rocky Mountains
Cassiar Mountains
Skeena Mountains
Cariboo Mts.
Columbia Mts.
Monashee Mts.
Purcell Mts.
Selkirk Mts.
Caribou Mts.
Birch Mountains
Swan Hills
Clear Hills
Horn Mts.
Cameron Hills
Buffalo Head Hills
Queen Charlotte Islands
Queen Charlotte Sound
Hecate Strait
Dixon Entrance
Vancouver Island
Alexander Arch.
Chichagof I.
Baranof I.
Kupreanof I.
Prince of Wales I.
Graham I.
Moresby I.
Princess Royal I.
Whitehorse
Yellowknife
Fort Simpson
Fort Providence
Hay River
Fort Resolution
Fort Nelson
Fort St. John
Dawson Creek
Grande Prairie
Peace River
Prince Rupert
Prince George
Kitimat
Quesnel
Williams Lake
Kamloops
Kelowna
Penticton
Vernon
Edmonton
St. Albert
Red Deer
Calgary
Lethbridge
Medicine Hat
Juneau
Ketchikan
Sitka
Skagway
Campbell River
Nanaimo
VANCOUVER
Richmond
Victoria
Bellingham
SEATTLE
Everett
Jasper
Banff
Mt. Robson 3954
Mt. Columbia 3747
Mt. Waddington 3994
Mt. Fairweather 4663
Mackenzie
Liard
Peace
Fraser
Skeena
Stikine
Athabasca
Columbia
Projection: Lambert's Equivalent Azimuthal
West from Greenwich

100
102
114
112

7 8 9 10 11

A
B
C
D

NUNAVUT

HUDSON BAY

MANITOBA

SASKATCHEWAN

ONTARIO

MINNESOTA

NORTH DAKOTA

MONTANA

LAKE WINNIPEG

Lake Athabasca

7 8 9 10

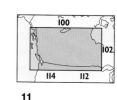

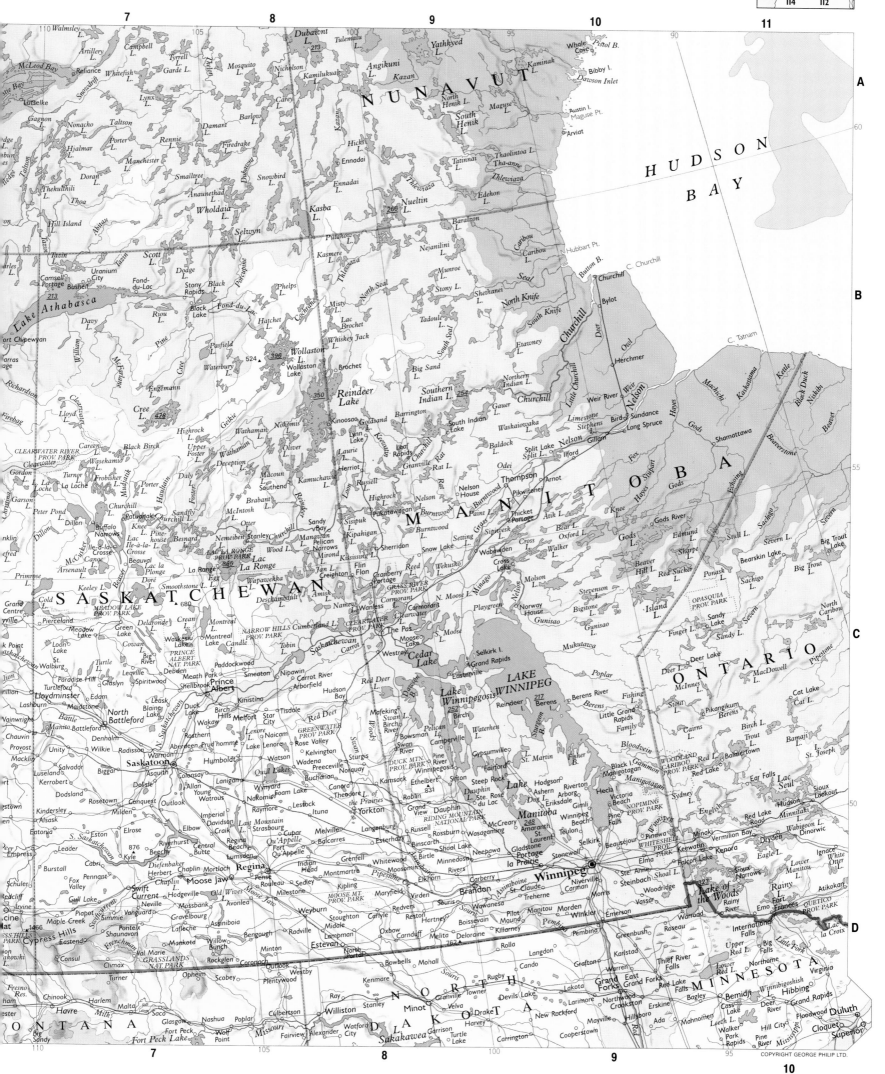

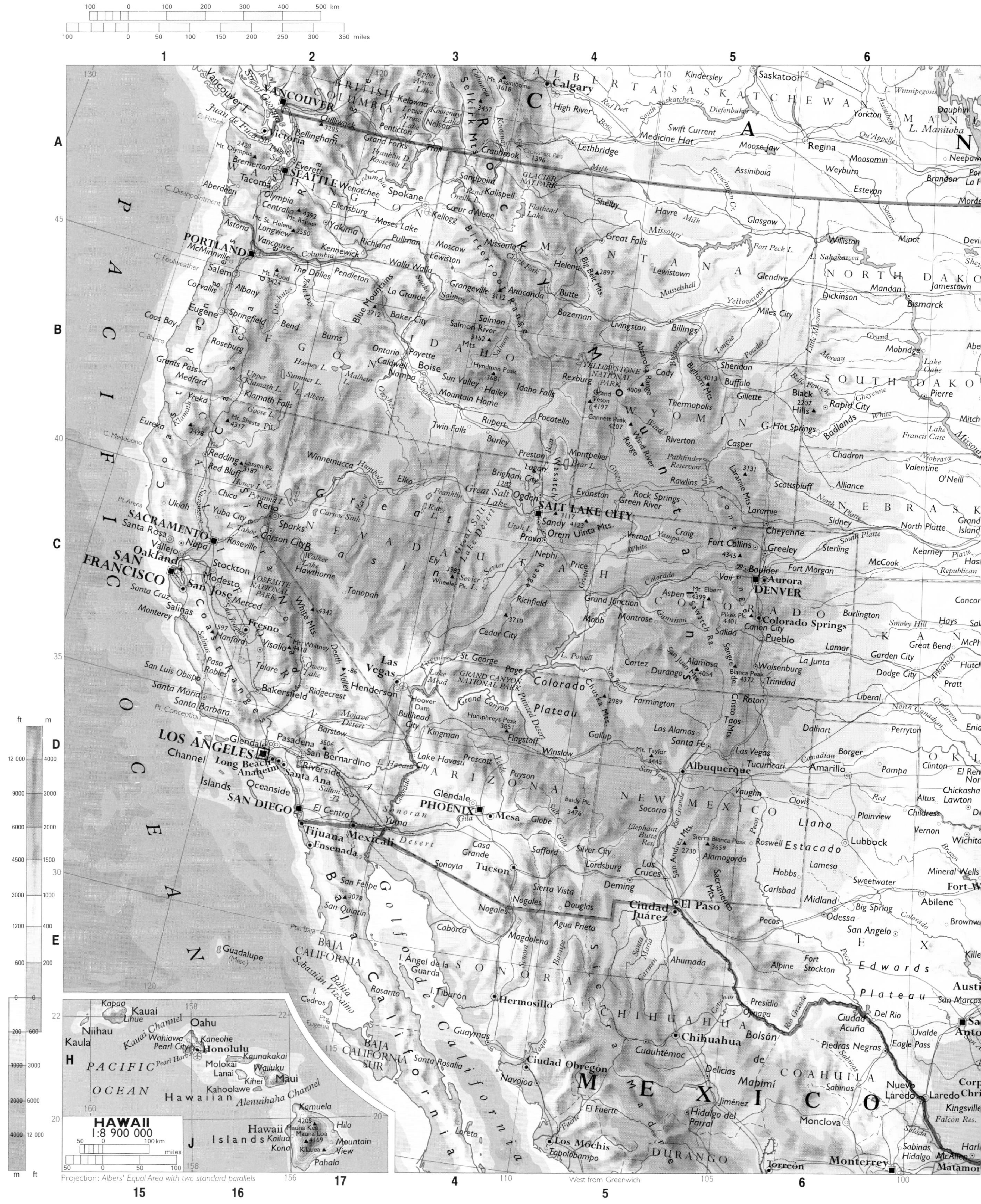

HAWAII
1:8 900 000

Projection: Albers' Equal Area with two standard parallels

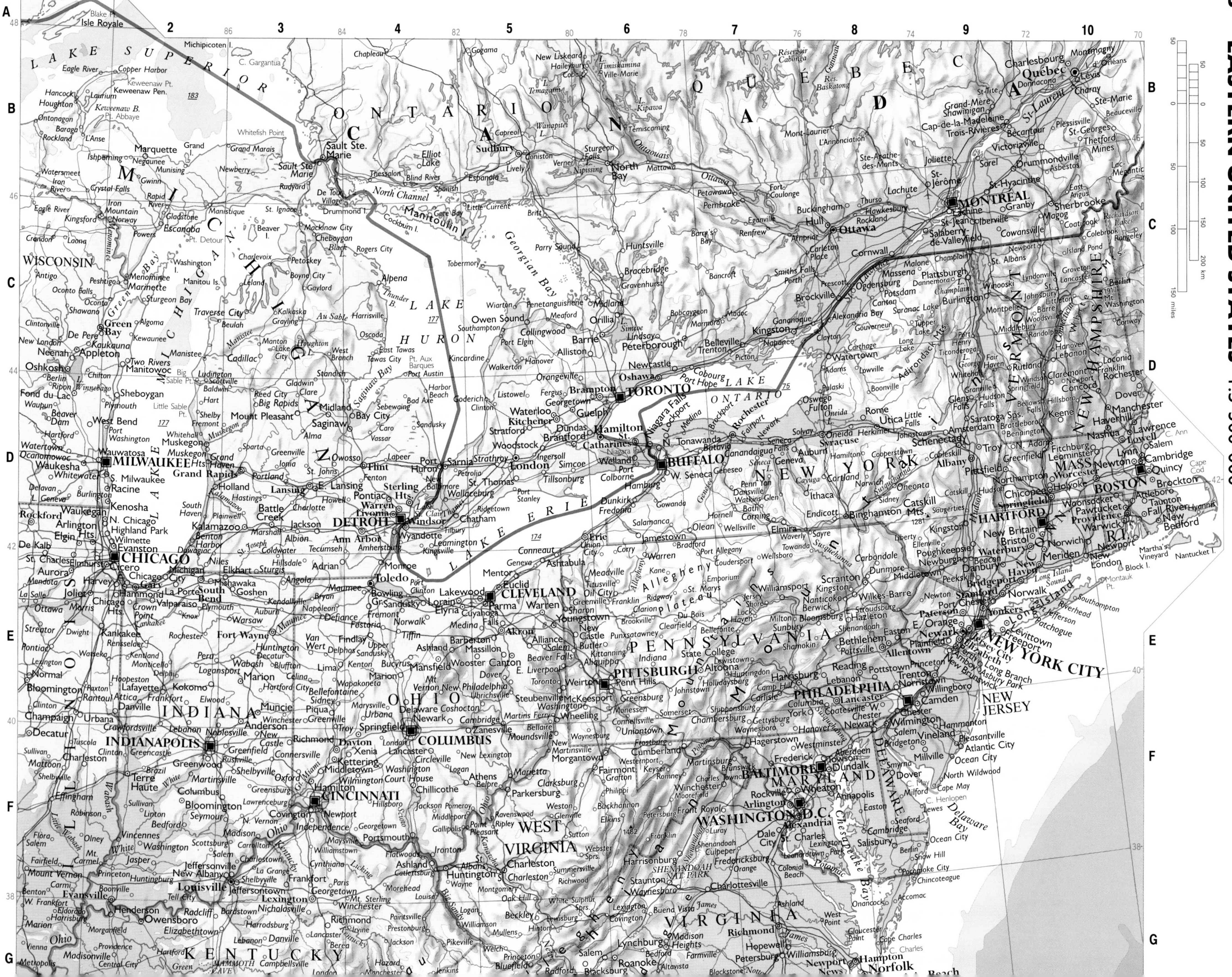

ATLANTIC OCEAN

GULF OF MEXICO

BAHAMAS

TENNESSEE

NORTH CAROLINA

SOUTH CAROLINA

GEORGIA

ALABAMA

MISSISSIPPI

FLORIDA

MAINE

NEW HAMPSHIRE

Continuation Eastwards On same scale.

Projection: Albers' Equal Area with two standard parallels

West from Greenwich

COPYRIGHT GEORGE PHILIP LTD.

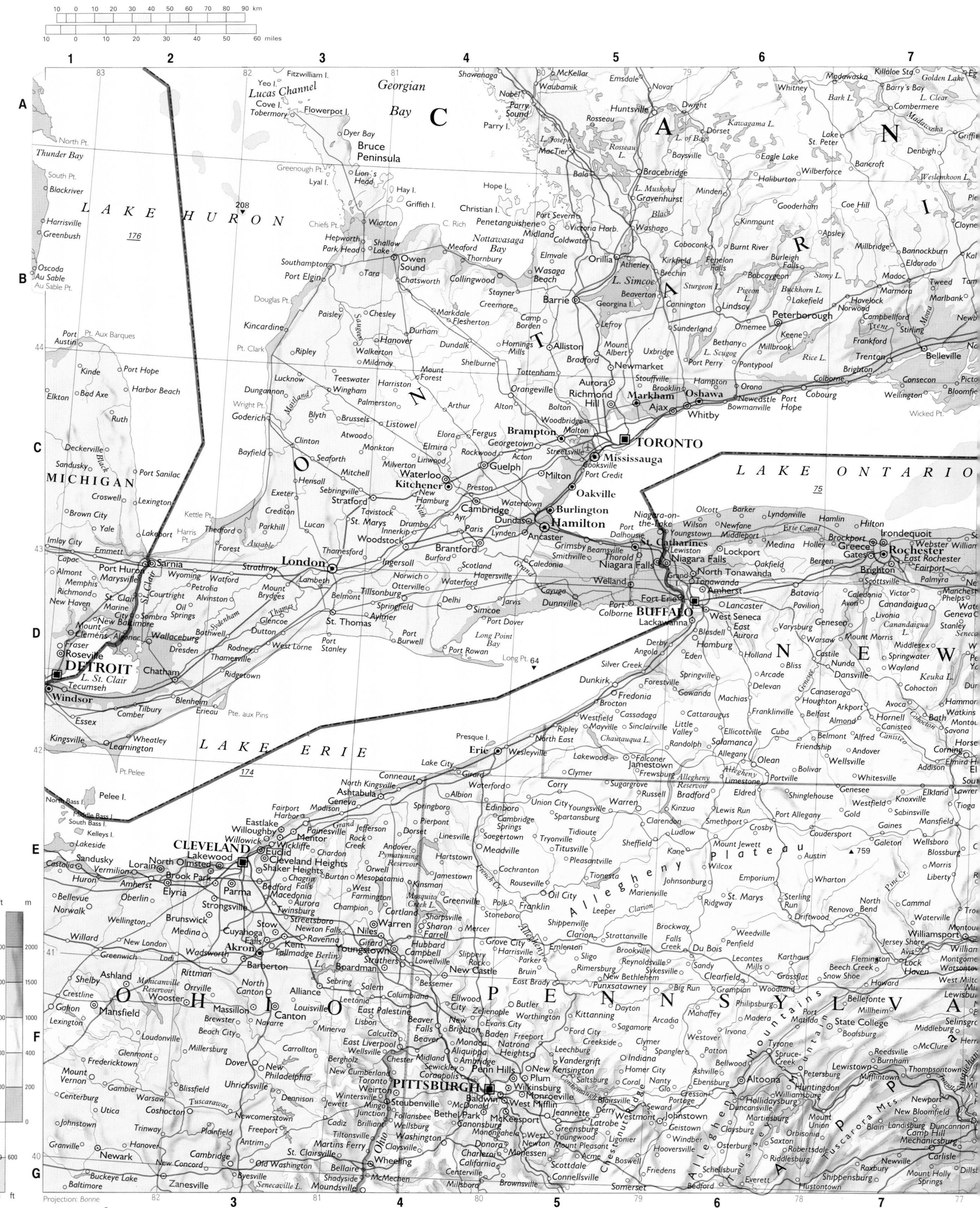

LAKE HURON
Georgian Bay
Bruce Peninsula
LAKE ERIE
LAKE ONTARIO
MICHIGAN
OHIO
PENNSYLVANIA
NEW
ONTARIO
CANADA
Allegheny Plateau
Allegheny Mountains
Tussey Mountains
Tuscarora Mts.
APPALACHIAN
TORONTO
Mississauga
Hamilton
St. Catharines
Niagara Falls
BUFFALO
Rochester
DETROIT
Windsor
London
Kitchener
Waterloo
Guelph
Brampton
Oakville
Burlington
Barrie
Oshawa
Peterborough
Belleville
Sarnia
Port Huron
CLEVELAND
Akron
Canton
Youngstown
Erie
PITTSBURGH
Altoona
State College
Williamsport
Lake Erie
Projection: Bonne

102
108
108
8
9
10
11
12
13
14
A
B
C
D
E
F
G
MONTREAL
Ottawa
QUÉBEC
VERMONT
NEW HAMPSHIRE
MAINE
MASSACHUSETTS
CONNECTICUT
RHODE ISLAND
NEW JERSEY
NEW YORK
HARTFORD
BOSTON
PHILADELPHIA
Providence
Albany
Syracuse
Springfield
Worcester
Sherbrooke
Burlington
Concord
Manchester
Binghamton
Allentown
Newark
Jersey City
Yonkers
Bridgeport
New Haven
Long Island
Long Island Sound
Block Island Sound
Martha's Vineyard
Adirondack Mountains
Green Mountains
White Mountains
Catskill Mts.
Kittatinny Mts.
Blue Mountains
L. Champlain
L. St-François
Mt. Washington
1917
Mt. Marcy
1629
Mt. Mansfield
1339
ATLANTIC OCEAN
West from Greenwich
76
74
73
72
71
45
44
43
41
40

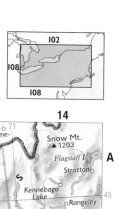

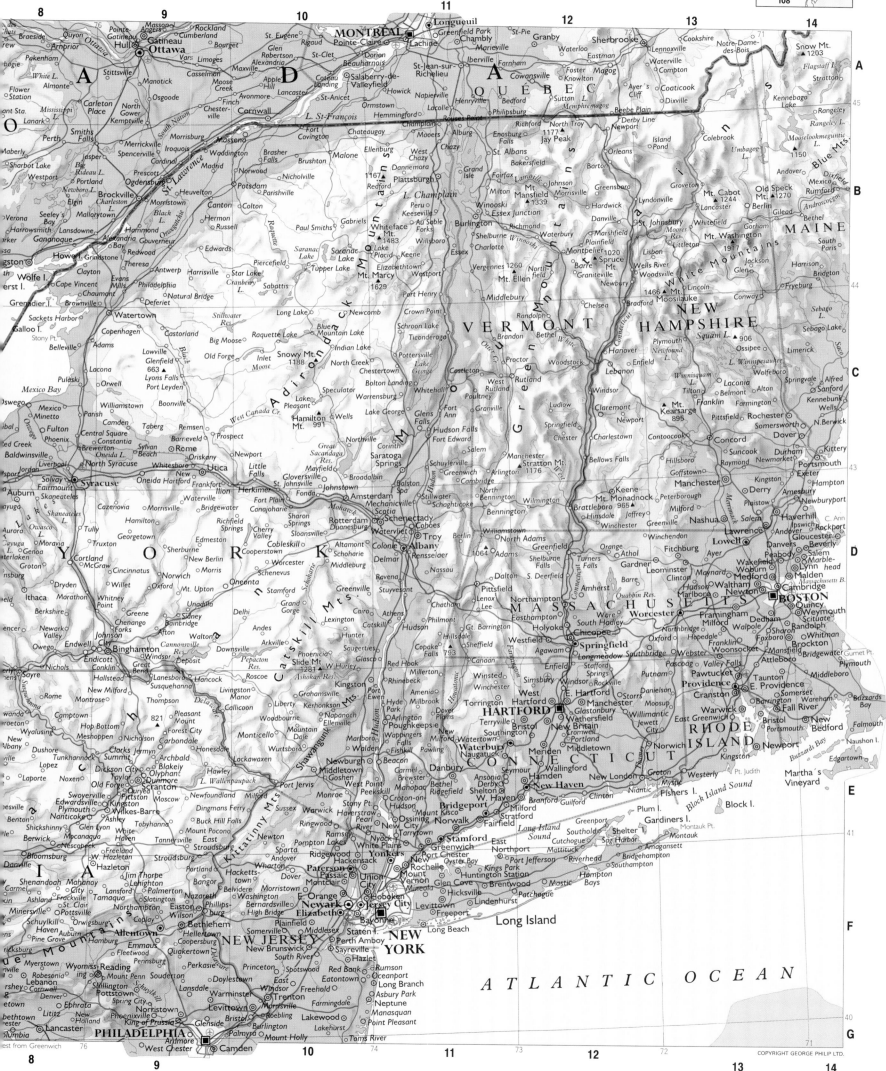

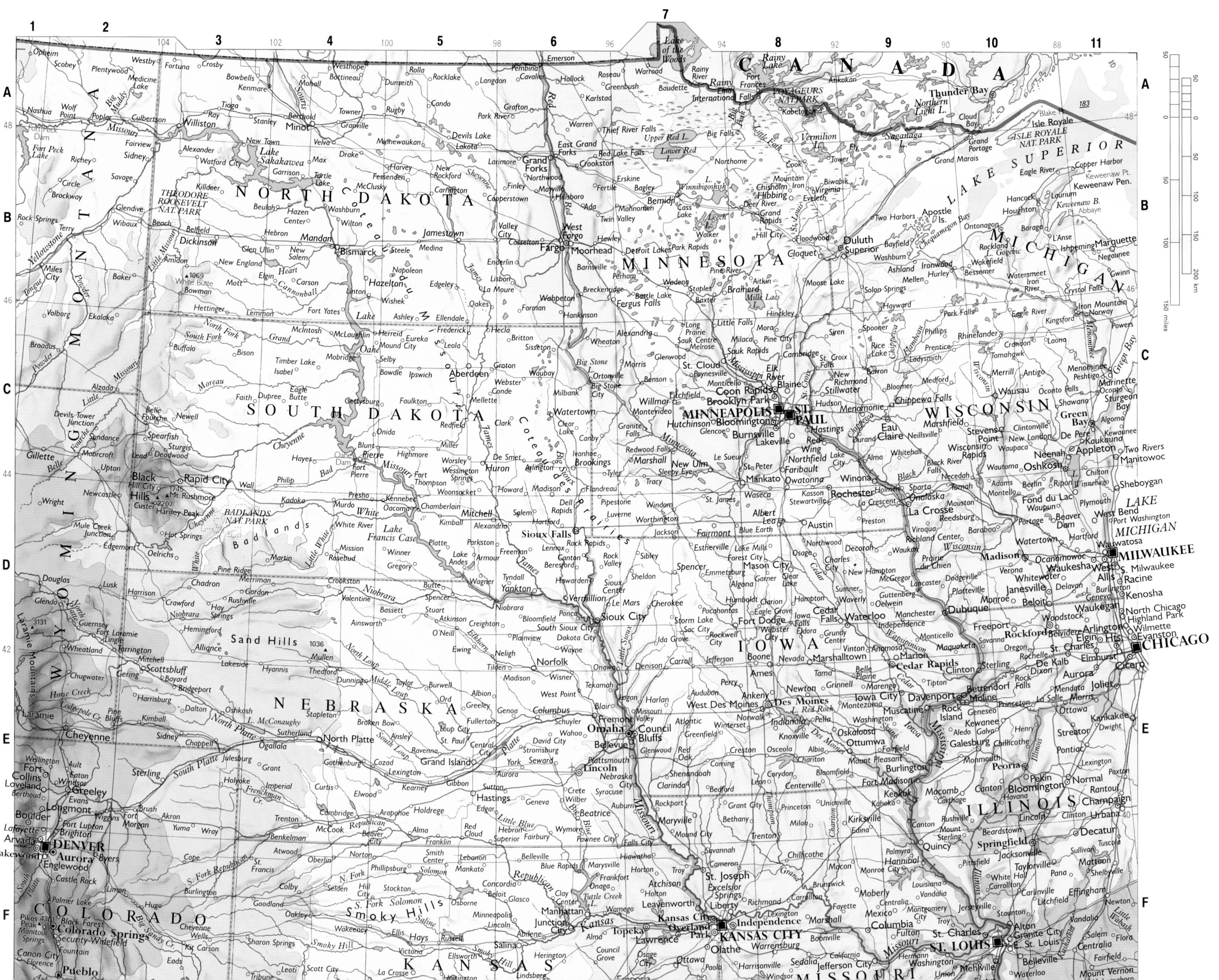

50 0 50 100 150 200 km
50 0 50 100 150 miles
C A N A D A
LAKE SUPERIOR
LAKE MICHIGAN
MINNESOTA
WISCONSIN
IOWA
ILLINOIS
MISSOURI
NORTH DAKOTA
SOUTH DAKOTA
NEBRASKA
KANSAS
COLORADO
WYOMING
MONTANA
MILWAUKEE
CHICAGO
MINNEAPOLIS
ST. PAUL
KANSAS CITY
ST. LOUIS
DENVER

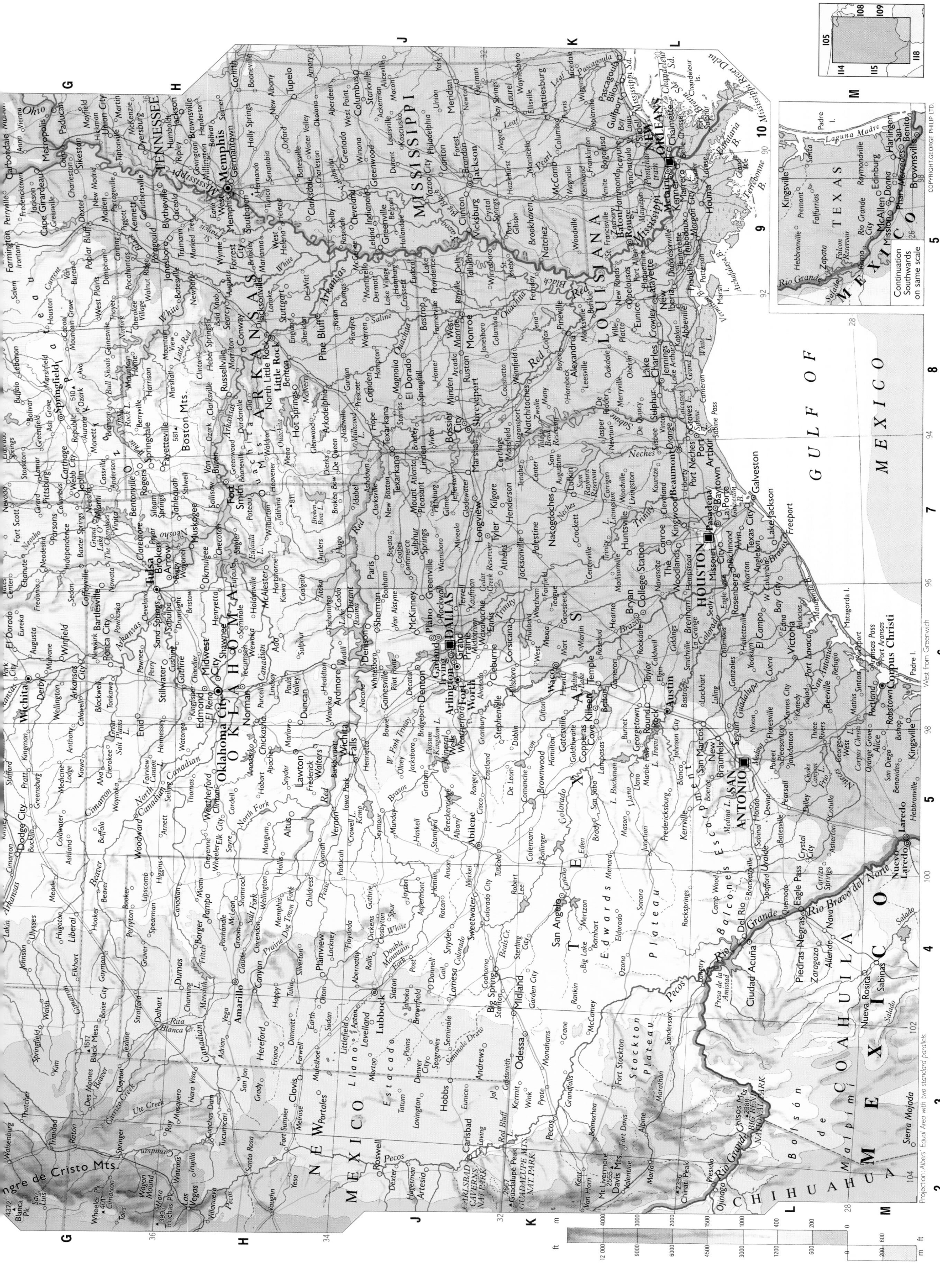

TENNESSEE

MISSISSIPPI

ARKANSAS

LOUISIANA

OKLAHOMA

NEW MEXICO

TEXAS

GULF OF MEXICO

MEXICO

COAHUILA

CHIHUAHUA

Memphis

New Orleans

Dallas

Fort Worth

Houston

San Antonio

Austin

Corpus Christi

Oklahoma City

Tulsa

Wichita

Little Rock

Baton Rouge

Brownsville

Laredo

Nuevo Laredo

Projection: Albers' Equal Area with two standard parallels

50 0 50 100 150 200 km
50 0 50 100 150 miles

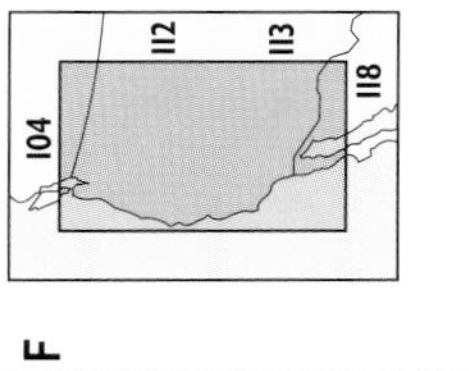

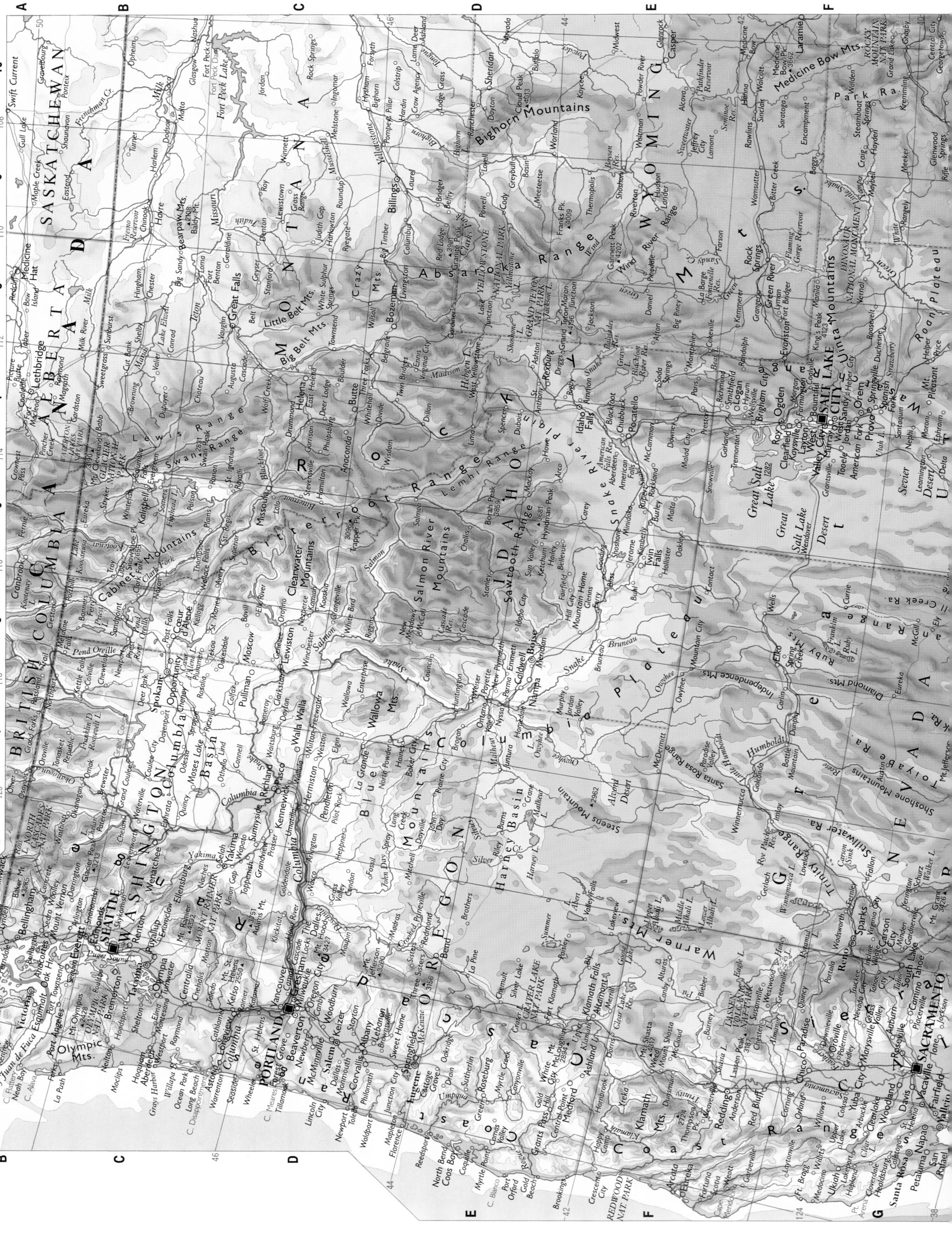

SASKATCHEWAN

ALBERTA

BRITISH COLUMBIA

MONTANA

WYOMING

IDAHO

OREGON

NEVADA

WASHINGTON

ROCKY MOUNTAINS

Bighorn Mountains

Medicine Bow Mts.

Park Ra.

Absaroka Range

YELLOWSTONE NATIONAL PARK

GRAND TETON NAT. PARK

Lewis Range

Swan Range

Cabinet Mountains

Bitterroot Mountains

Clearwater Mountains

Salmon River Mountains

Sawtooth Range

Lemhi Range

Great Salt Lake

Great Salt Lake Desert

Uinta Mountains

Columbia Basin

Blue Mountains

Wallowa Mts.

Harney Basin

Columbia Plateau

Steens Mountain

Santa Rosa Range

Shoshone Mountains

Toiyabe Ra.

Stillwater Ra.

Warner Mts.

Trinity Range

Ruby Mts.

Independence Mts.

Cascade Range

Coast Range

Olympic Mts.

NORTH CASCADES NAT. PARK

MOUNT RAINIER NAT. PARK

CRATER LAKE NAT. PARK

LASSEN VOLCANIC NAT. PARK

REDWOOD NAT. PARK

VANCOUVER

SEATTLE

PORTLAND

SALT LAKE CITY

SACRAMENTO

Spokane

Billings

Great Falls

Helena

Butte

Boise

Ogden

Provo

Reno

Vancouver Island

Strait of Juan de Fuca

Puget Sound

Snake River

Columbia River

Missouri River

Yellowstone River

Bighorn Mts.

Big Belt Mts.

Little Belt Mts.

Crazy Mts.

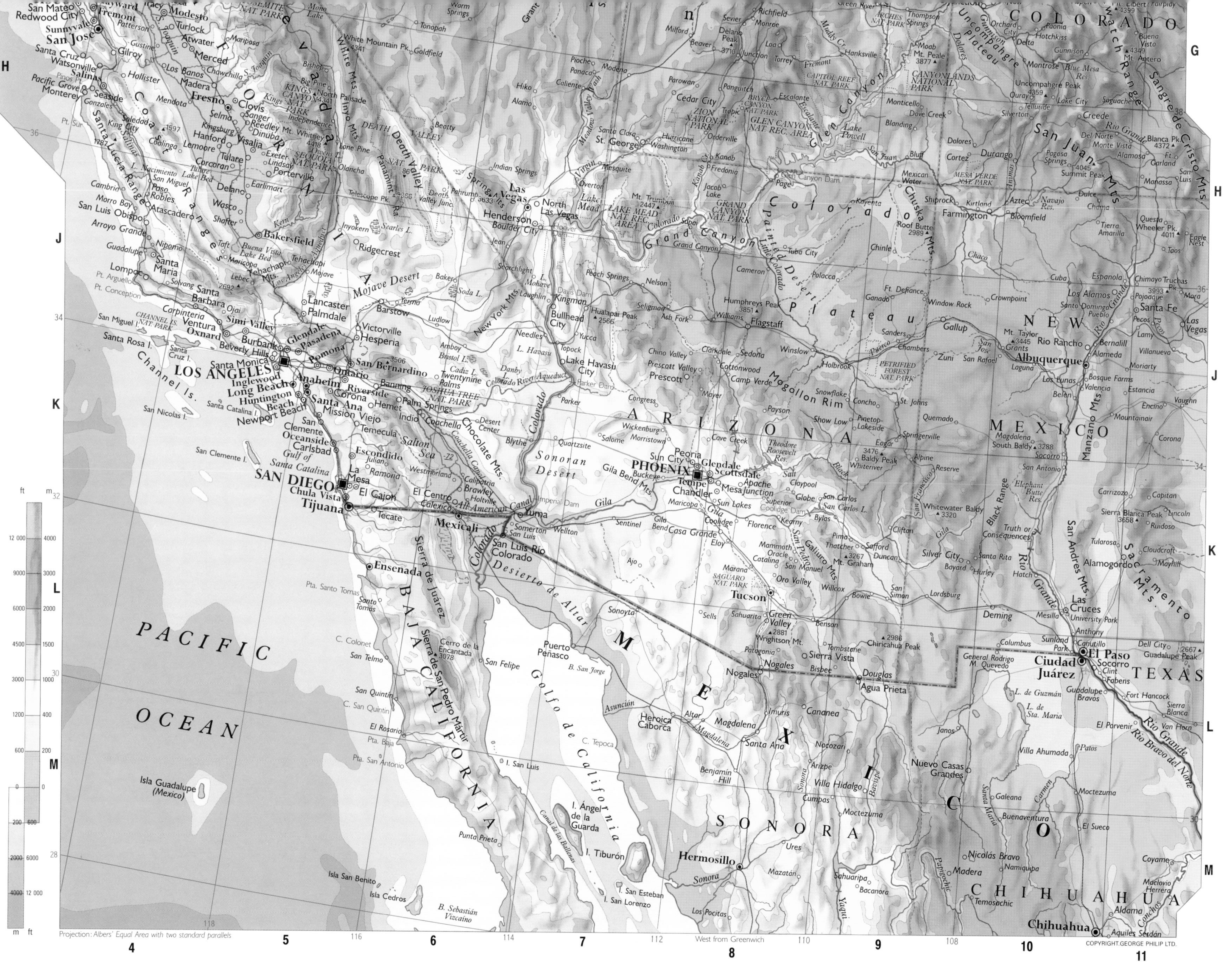
COLORADO
NEW MEXICO
ARIZONA
TEXAS
CHIHUAHUA
SONORA
MEXICO
BAJA CALIFORNIA
PACIFIC OCEAN
Golfo de California
Colorado Plateau
Sangre de Cristo Mts.
San Juan Mts.
Sacramento Mts.
Manzano Mts.
San Andres Mts.
Black Range
Mogollon Rim
Painted Desert
Sonoran Desert
Mojave Desert
Death Valley
Desierto de Altar
Sierra de Juárez
Sierra de San Pedro Mártir
Chocolate Mts.
Rio Grande
Rio Bravo del Norte
Colorado
Gila
Grand Canyon
Santa Fe
Albuquerque
Rio Rancho
Las Cruces
El Paso
Ciudad Juárez
Chihuahua
Tucson
PHOENIX
Flagstaff
Prescott
Yuma
Las Vegas
Henderson
LOS ANGELES
SAN DIEGO
Tijuana
Mexicali
Ensenada
Hermosillo
Nogales
Fresno
Bakersfield
San Jose
Salinas
Monterey
Farmington
Gallup
Durango
Kingman
Lake Havasu City
St. George
Cedar City
Isla Guadalupe (Mexico)
Channel Is.
Isla Cedros
I. Tiburón
I. Ángel de la Guarda
Projection: Albers' Equal Area with two standard parallels
West from Greenwich
COPYRIGHT GEORGE PHILIP LTD.
m
ft

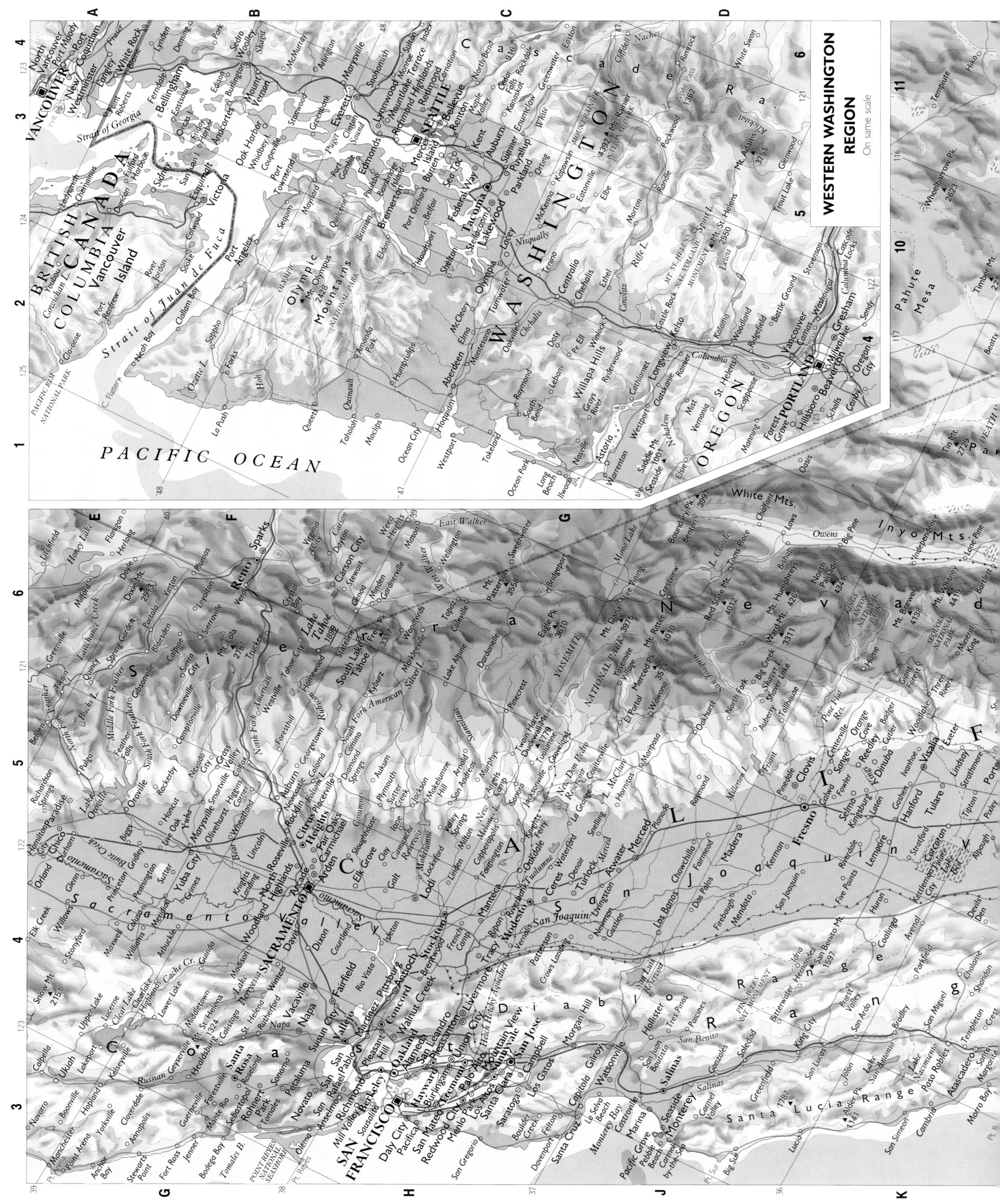

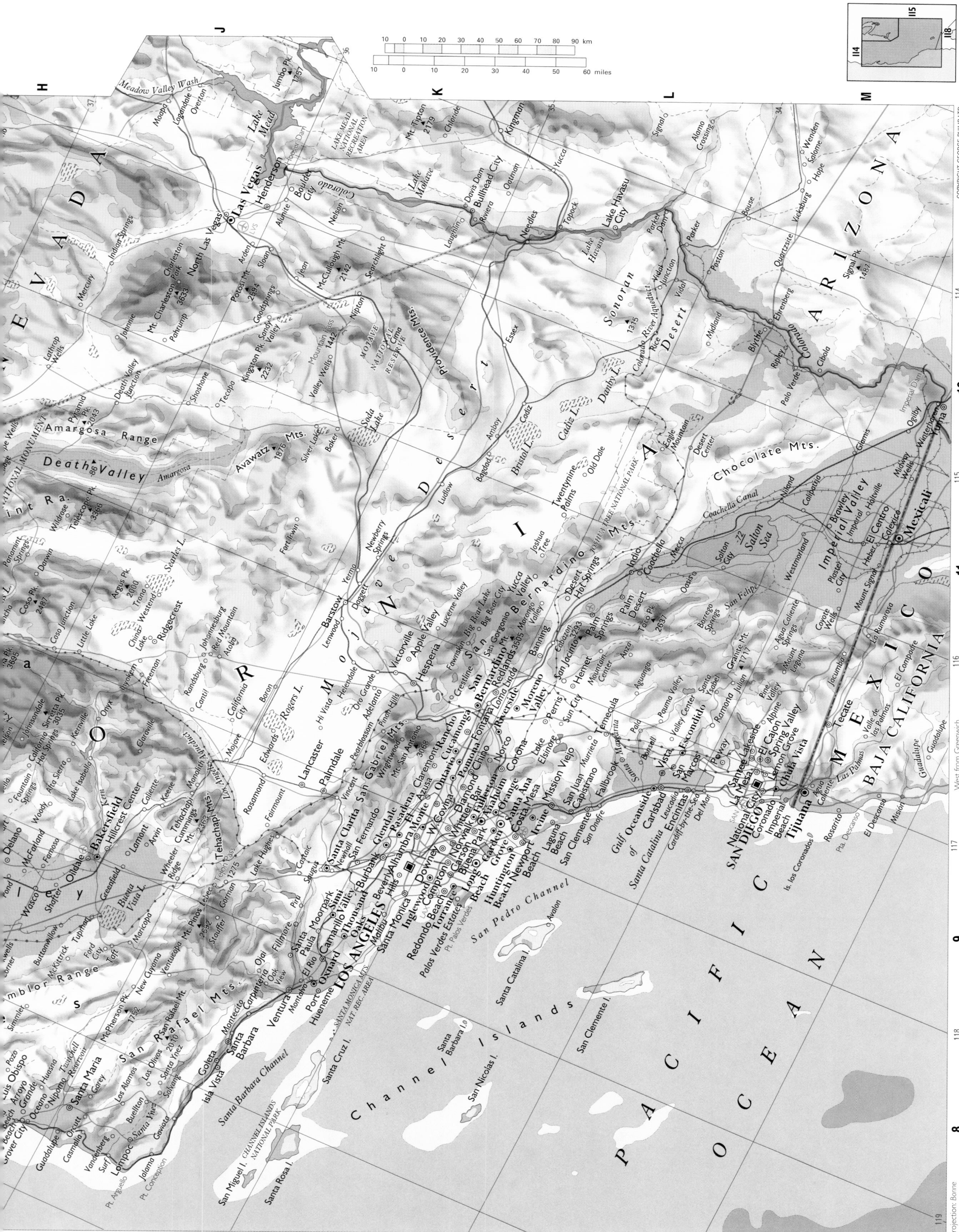

114 118

COPYRIGHT GEORGE PHILIP LTD.

J H K L M

10 0 10 20 30 40 50 60 70 80 90 km
10 0 10 20 30 40 50 60 miles

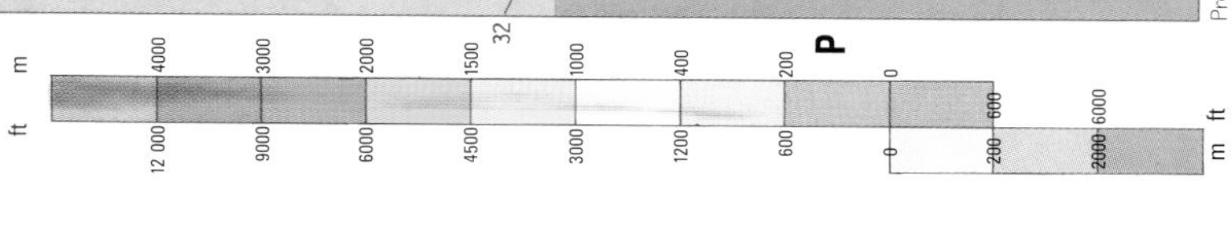

13

NEVADA

Meadow Valley Wash
Moapa
Logandale
Overton
Lake Mead
Jumbo Pk. 1757
Indian Springs
Lathrop Wells
Las Vegas
North Las Vegas
Henderson
Boulder City
Hoover Dam
LAKE MEAD NATIONAL RECREATION AREA
Lake Mohave
Mt. Tipton 2179
Chloride
Kingman
Arden
Sloan
Jean
McCullough Mt. 2142
Searchlight
Nelson
Davis Dam
Bullhead City
Oatman
Riviera
Topock
Hucca
Yucca
Goodsprings
Pahrump
Mt. Charleston Pk. 3633
Potosi Mt. 2064
Signal
Alamo Crossing
Wenden
Hope
Salome
Charleston Park
Mercury
Johnnie

ARIZONA

Lake Havasu
Lake Havasu City
Parker Dam
Parker
Vidal Junction
Earp
Bouse
Vicksburg
Quartzsite
Ehrenberg
Blythe
Ripley
Palo Verde
Cibola
Signal Pk. 1487

12

Sonoran Desert
Colorado River Aqueduct
Rice
Midland
Desert Center
Eagle Mountain
Chocolate Mts.
Coachella Canal
Glamis
Imperial Dam
Ogilby
Winterhaven
Yuma

Death Valley
NATIONAL MONUMENT
Pyramid Pk. 2043
Telescope Pk. 3366
Amargosa Range
Amargosa
int Ra.
Wildrose
Shoshone
Tecopa
Silver Lake
Soda Lake
Baker
Avawatz Mts.
Silurian 1676
Pahrump
Panamint Springs
Darwin
Coso Pk. 2487
Argus Range 2004
Trona
Searles L.
Ridgecrest
Randsburg
Johannesburg
Red Mountain
Atolia
Kramer
Boron
Rogers L.
Edwards
Mojave
Rosamond
Lancaster
Palmdale
Victorville
Adelanto
Hesperia
Apple Valley
Lucerne Valley
Newberry Springs
Ludlow
Amboy
Bagdad
Bristol L.
Cadiz L.
Danby L.
Essex
Cadiz
Chambless
Goffs
Needles
Twentynine Palms
JOSHUA TREE NATIONAL PARK
Joshua Tree
Old Dale

M O J A V E   D E S E R T

MOJAVE NATIONAL PRESERVE
Providence Mts.
Mountain Pass 1442
Nipton
Valley Wells
Kelso
Cima 1315

Barstow
Daggett
Lenwood
Hinkley
Hi Vista
California City
Helendale
Oro Grande
Phelan
Wrightwood
San Gabriel Mts.
Mt. San Antonio 3068
Mt. San Gorgonio 3506
San Bernardino Mts.
Big Bear Lake
Big Bear City
Crestline
Lake Arrowhead
Yucca Valley
Morongo Valley
Desert Hot Springs
Palm Springs
Cathedral City
Coachella
Indio
Mecca
Salton Sea
Salton City
Westmorland
Brawley
Calipatria
Niland
Oasis
Imperial Valley
Imperial
El Centro
Calexico
Mexicali
Plaster City
Mount Signal
Coyote Wells

11

a

Coso Junction
Little Lake
Inyokern
China Lake
Kernville
Lake Isabella
Onyx
Weldon
Sierra Pk. 3605
Sinetta Pk. 3035
Woody
Glennville
Alta Sierra

Bakersfield
Hillcrest Center
Lamont
Arvin
Caliente
Keene
Tehachapi
Cummings
Mt. San Antonio
Wheeler Ridge
Maricopa
Tehachapi Mts. 2356
Tejon Pass 1275
Gorman
Lebec
Frazier Park
Mt. Pinos 2692
New Cuyama
Ventucopa
Pine Mtn.
San Rafael Mt. 2010
San Rafael Mts.
Los Olivos
Santa Ynez
Solvang
Buellton
Los Alamos
Santa Ynez
Lompoc
Vandenberg
Jalama
Pt. Arguello
Pt. Concepcion

Santa Clarita
Newhall
San Fernando
Santa Paula
Fillmore
Moorpark
Simi Valley
Thousand Oaks
Santa Monica Mts.
Agoura
Calabasas
Malibu
Oxnard
Port Hueneme
Camarillo
El Rio
Ventura
Carpinteria
Montecito
Santa Barbara
Goleta
Isla Vista

LOS ANGELES
Pasadena
Glendale
Burbank
Alhambra
El Monte
W. Covina
Pomona
Ontario
Chino
Rancho Cucamonga
Fontana
San Bernardino
Redlands
Loma Linda
Riverside
Moreno Valley
Perris
Sun City
Hemet
San Jacinto
Banning
Beaumont
Mt. San Jacinto 3293
Idyllwild
Palm Desert
La Quinta
Anza
Aguanga
Temecula
Murrieta
Lake Elsinore
Corona
Norco
Chino
Diamond Bar
Whittier
Norwalk
Downey
Compton
Inglewood
Torrance
Redondo Beach
Palos Verdes Estates
Pt. Palos Verdes
Santa Monica
Beverly Hills
Culver City
Fullerton
Buena Park
Anaheim
Garden Grove
Santa Ana
Costa Mesa
Orange
Long Beach
Huntington Beach
Newport Beach
Irvine
Mission Viejo
San Juan Capistrano
San Clemente
San Onofre
Fallbrook
Bonsall
Vista
San Marcos
Escondido
Valley Center
Ramona
Julian
Warner Springs
Santa Ysabel
Pine Valley
Alpine
El Cajon
La Mesa
Lemon Grove
Spring Valley
Poway
Santee
Lakeside
Chula Vista
National City
Coronado
Imperial Beach
Tijuana
Tecate
Rosarito
La Rumorosa

SAN DIEGO

Oceanside
Carlsbad
Encinitas
Leucadia
Cardiff-by-the-Sea
Del Mar
La Jolla
Solana Beach

P A C I F I C   O C E A N

San Pedro Channel
Avalon
Santa Catalina I.
San Clemente I.
San Nicolas I.
Santa Barbara I.
Channel Islands
CHANNEL ISLANDS NATIONAL PARK
San Miguel I.
Santa Rosa I.
Santa Cruz I.
Anacapa I.
Santa Barbara Channel

Gulf of Santa Catalina

BAJA CALIFORNIA
MEXICO
Agua Caliente
Tecate
Guadalupe
El Cóndor
El Compadre
Valle de los Palmas

West from Greenwich

9 8

Projection: Bonne

L M N P

m ft
12 000 4000
9000 3000
6000 2000
4500 1500
3000 1000
1200 400
600 200
0 0
200 600
2000 6000
ft m

10 11 12 13

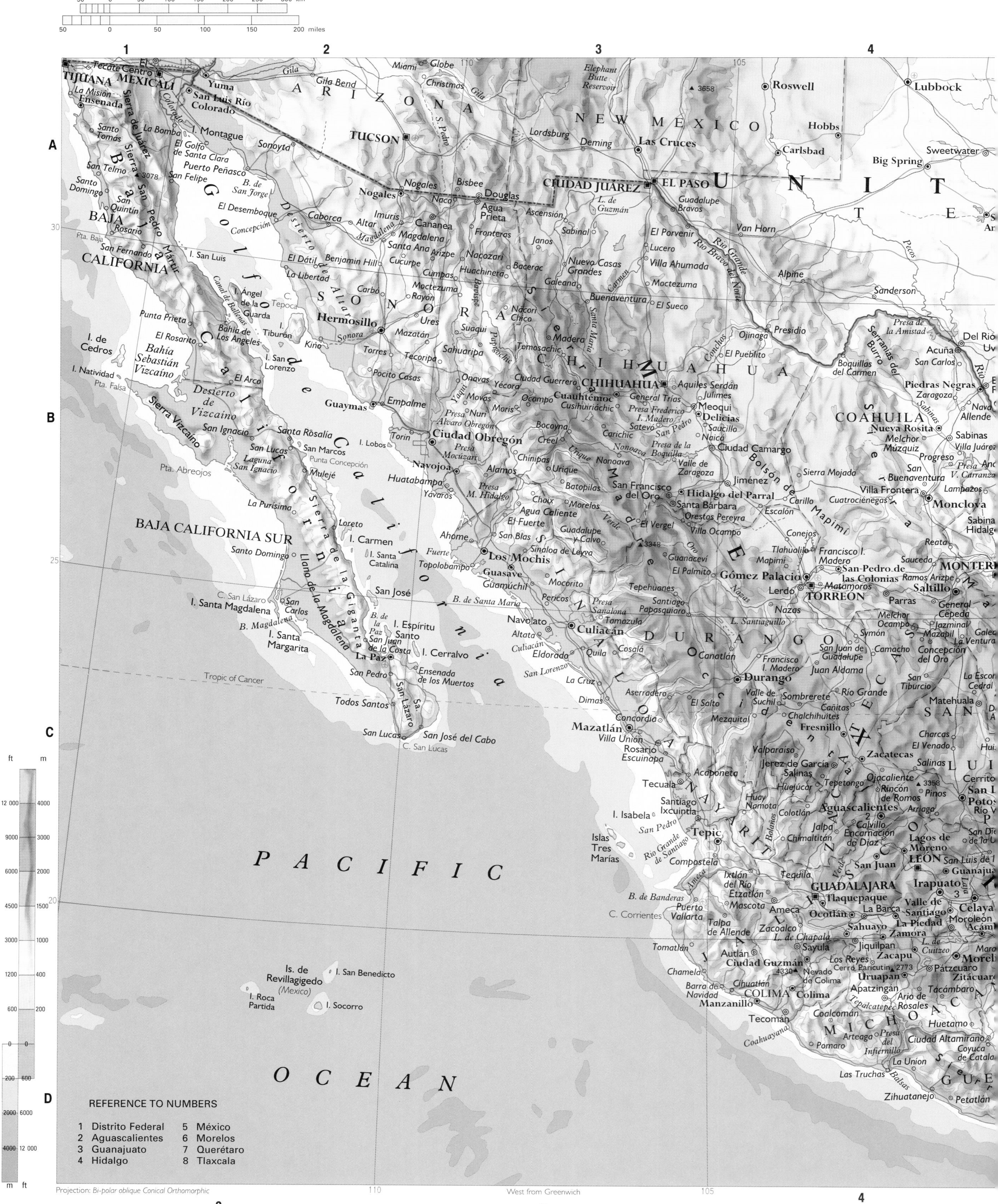

50 0 50 100 150 200 250 300 km
50 0 50 100 150 200 miles

1 2 3 4

A

B

C

D

Tijuana Tecate Mexicali
La Misión Centro El
Ensenada San Luis Río
Santo Tomás Colorado
San Telmo La Bomba
Santo Domingo San Felipe
El Golfo de Santa Clara
Puerto Peñasco

ARIZONA

Yuma
Gila Bend
Globe
Miami
Christmas
Gila

Roswell
Lubbock

Elephant
Butte
Reservoir
3658

NEW MEXICO

Lordsburg
Deming
Las Cruces
Hobbs
Carlsbad
Big Spring
Sweetwater

CIUDAD JUÁREZ EL PASO
UNITE

Nogales Nogales Bisbee
Naco Douglas
Agua Prieta

Tucson
Sonoyta
Sásabe
S. Pedro

BAJA
CALIFORNIA

San Quintín
San Fernando
Rosario
Pta. Baja

Sierra de Juárez
3078
Sierra San Pedro Martir

Caborca
Altar
Imuris
Magdalena
Cananea
Fronteras
Janos
Sabinal

Nuevo Casas
Grandes
Villa Ahumada
L. de Guzmán
El Porvenir
Lucero
Moctezuma

Van Horn
Alpine
Sanderson

Ascensión

Pecos
Río Bravo del Norte

Galeana
Buenaventura El Sueco

Presidio
Del Río
Uv

El Desemboque
Benjamin Hill
Santa Ana Arizpe
Moctezuma
Rayón
Carbó
Cumpas
Huachineta
Bacerac

Ojinaga
El Pueblito

Presa de
la Amistad
Acuña
San Carlos

GOLFO DE

I. Ángel
de la
Guarda

I. Tiburón
Kino

Hermosillo
Ures
Mazatán
Suaqui
Ónavas
Tecoripa
Sahuaripa
Nácori
Chico

CHIHUAHUA

Madera
Temósachic

Conchos
Serranías del Burro

Piedras Negras
Zaragoza

SONORA

Guaymas
Empalme
Torin
I. Lobos

Torres
Sonora
Pocito Casas

Presa
Álvaro Obregón

 Yaqui
Movas
Yécora
Ciudad Guerrero
Ocampo
CHIHUAHUA

Cuauhtémoc
General Trías
Cusihuiriáchic
Julimes
Aquiles Serdán
Meoqui
Delicias
Satevó
San Pedro
Saucillo

Nacozari

COAHUILA

Nueva Rosita
Melchor Múzquiz
Progreso
Sabinas
Villa Allende

Ciudad Obregón
Navojoa
Presa
Mocúzari

Creel
Bocoyna
Chinipas
Úrique
Nonoava
Carichic
Naica
Ciudad Camargo

Presa de la
Boquilla

Sierra Mojada
San Buenaventura
Villa Frontera
V. Carranza
Lampazos

Monclova
Sabinas
Hidalgo

BAJA CALIFORNIA SUR

I. de Cedros
I. Natividad
Pta. Falsa

El Rosarito
Punta Prieta
El Arco

Bahía de
Los Angeles
I. San Lorenzo

Santa Rosalía
San Ignacio
Mulegé
Loreto

La Paz
San Pedro
Todos Santos
San Lucas
San José del Cabo
C. San Lucas

Huatabampa
Yavaros
Ahome
Los Mochis
Guasave
Guamúchil

Álamos
El Fuerte
San Blas
Agua Caliente
Morelos
Sinaloa de Leyva
Batopilas
Choix

San Francisco
del Oro
Guadalupe
y Calvo
3348
El Vergel
Orestos Pereyra
Villa Ocampo
Escalón
Conejos

Hidalgo del Parral
Santa Bárbara

Guanaceví
El Palmito
Tepehuanes
Santiago
Papasquiaro

Mapimí
Tlahualilo
Francisco I.
Madero
San Pedro de
las Colonias
Matamoros
Gómez Palacio
Lerdo
TORREÓN
Parras

Bolsón de Mapimí

Cuatrociénegas
Reata
Sabinas
Monclova

MONTER
Saltillo
Ramos Arizpe
General
Cepeda

PACIFIC

Navolato
Culiacán
Eldorado
Quila
Cosalá

DURANGO

Santiaguillo
Canatlán
Durango
El Salto
Aserradero

San Juan de
Guadalupe
Juan Aldama
Símón
Camacho
Concepción
del Oro
La Ventura

Melchor
Ocampo
San
Tiburcio
Matehuala

SAN

Topolobampo
Pericos
Guamúchil
B. de Santa Maria
Altata
San Lorenzo
La Cruz
Dimas

Valle de
Suchil
Sombrerete
Río Grande
Chalchihuites
Cañitas
Mezquital

Fresnillo
Charcas
El Venado
Cedral

Mazatlán
Villa Unión
Rosario
Escuinapa
Concordia

Valparaiso
Jerez de García
Salinas
Zacatecas
Salinas

ZACATECAS

Cerrito
San
San Potosí

Tecuala
Santiago
Ixcuintla

Huajicori
Acaponeta

Ojocaliente
Huejúcar
Tepetongo
Colotlán
Rincón
de Romos
Pinos
3350
Arriaga

Aguascalientes
Calvillo
Encarnación
de Díaz
Chimaltitán

NAYARIT

I. Isabela
Islas
Tres
Marías
San Pedro
Río Grande
de Santiago

Tepic
Jalpa
Balanos

Lagos de
Moreno
LEÓN
Guanajuato
San Luis de
San Di
San

I. Isabela

Ixtlán
del Río
Etzatlán
Mascota
Ameca

Jalisco
San Juan
Tequila
GUADALAJARA
Tlaquepaque
Valle de
Irapuato
3

PACIFIC

B. de Banderas
Puerto
Vallarta
C. Corrientes

Talpa
de Allende
Zacoalco
Ocotlán
La Barca
La Piedad
Sahuayo
Zamora

Celaya
Moroleón
Acám

Is. de
Revillagigedo
(Mexico)
I. San Benedicto
I. Roca
Partida
I. Socorro

Tomatlán
Autlán
Ciudad Guzmán
Sayula
4330
Nevado
de Colima

Jiquilpan
L. de Chapala
Los Reyes
Zacapu
L. de
Cuitzeo

Zamora
Morel
Pátzcuaro
Zitácuaro
Tacámbaro

Chamela
Barra de
Navidad
Cihuatlán
Manzanillo
COLIMA Colima

Cerro Paricutín 2773
Uruapan
Apatzingán
Ario de
Rosales

Tecomán
Coalcomán

MICHOACÁN

Coahuayana
Artéago
Pómaro

Coalcomán
Coyuca
de Catalán
La Unión

Ciudad Altamirano
Huetamo
La Union

O C E A N

Las Truchas
Zihuatanejo
Balsas
Petatlán

Tropic of Cancer

30
25
20

110
105

110 105

ft m

12 000 4000
9000 3000
6000 2000
4500 1500
3000 1000
1200 400
600 200
0 0
200 600
2000 6000
4000 12 000
m ft

REFERENCE TO NUMBERS

1 Distrito Federal
2 Aguascalientes
3 Guanajuato
4 Hidalgo
5 México
6 Morelos
7 Querétaro
8 Tlaxcala

106
107
120

5 6 7 8

A B C D E

UNITED STATES
TEXAS
ARKANSAS
MISSISSIPPI
ALABAMA
GEORGIA
LOUISIANA
FLORIDA

Wichita Falls
Denison
Sherman
Paris
Hope
Camden
Texarkana
El Dorado
Greenville
Tuscaloosa
Opelika
Columbus
McRae
Denton
Greenville
Phenix City
Possum Kingdom Res.
FORT WORTH
DALLAS
Marshall
Monroe
Vicksburg
Meridian
Selma
Montgomery
Americus
Cordele
Abilene
Ranger
Cleburne
Longview
Tyler
Shreveport
Tallulah
Jackson
Troy
Albany
Tifton
Waycross
Hillsboro
Corsicana
Palestine
Toledo Bend Res.
Nacogdoches
Natchez
Laurel
Hattiesburg
Dothan
Jim Woodruff Res.
Valdosta
Brownwood
Waco
Lufkin
Sam Rayburn Reservoir
Alexandria
McComb
Flomaton
Chattahoochee
Tallahassee
Jewett
Temple
Huntsville
Bryan
Baton Rouge
Hammond
Bogalusa
Biloxi
MOBILE
Pensacola
Panama City
Lake City
Gulfport
Apalachee Bay
Austin
Navasota
Lake Charles
Lafayette
L. Pontchartrain
NEW ORLEANS
Mobile Bay
C. San Blas
Beaumont
HOUSTON
Port Arthur
Breton Sd.
Suwannee
Rosenberg
Galveston
Atchafalaya Bay
Terrebonne Bay
Mississippi River Delta
Clearwater
SAN ANTONIO
Victoria
Guadalupe
Dilley
Nueces
Alice
Corpus Christi
Laredo
Kingsville
Nuevo Laredo
Zapata
Laguna Madre
Camargo
McAllen
Harlingen
Brownsville
Reynosa
Presa M.R. Gomez
China
Matamoros
Valle Hermoso
Santa Teresa
Laguna Madre
Montemorelos
Mendez
Conchos
Linares
San Fernando
Villagrán
Hidalgo
Santander Jiménez
Zaragoza
La Pesca
Soto la Marina
Ciudad Victoria
Sierra de Tamaulipas
Llera
Aldama
Calles
Pta. Jerez
Ocampo
Ciudad Mante
TAMAULIPAS
Altamira
Ciudad Madero
Tampico
Ciudad de Valles
Cárdenas
Pánuco
L. de Tamiahua
Ozuluama
Tempoal
Magozal
C. Rojo
Tantoyuca
Tamazunchale
Chicontepec
Tuxpan
Zimapán
Zacualtipán
Poza Rica
Papantla
Nautla
Misantla
Huichapan
Pachuca
Huauchinango
Tulancingo
Teziutlán
Jalapa Enríquez
Zumpango
Tula
MÉXICO
Apizaco
Tlaxcala
Amecameca
PUEBLA
Coatepec
Veracruz
Citlaltépetl 5700
Popocatépetl 5452
4282
Córdoba
Orizaba
Alvarado
Tlacotalpan
Cuernavaca
Tehuacán
Cosamaloapan
San Andrés Tuxtla
Izúcar de Matamoros
Chilac
Ajalpan
Tres Valles
1879
Coatzacoalcos
Iguala
Acatlán
Huautla de Jiménez
Presa Miguel Alemán
Acayucan
Minatitlán
Cárdenas
Villahermosa
TABASCO
VERACRUZ
Huajuapan de León
Asunción Nochixtlán
San Juan Bautista Valle Nacional
Istmo de Tehuantepec
Jesús Carranza
Presa Netzahualcóyotl
Raudales de Malpaso
Teapa
Chilapa
Chilpancingo
Silacayoapan
Tlaxiaco
Oaxaca
Tlacolula
Sierra Madre del Sur
Tierra Colorada
Ayutla
Ometepec
Acapulco
OAXACA
Ocotlán
Ejutla
San Jerónimo Taviche
Ixtepec
Matías Romero
Tuxtla Gutiérrez
Chiapa de Corzo
San Cristóbal de las Casas
Copainalá
Simojovel
Ocosingo
La Independencia
Comitán
Lacantún
CHIAPAS
Pinotepa Nacional
Jamiltepec
Tututepec
Miahuatlán
3139
Tehuantepec
Juchitán
Arriaga
Tonalá
Sierra Madre
La Concordia
Punta Maldonado
Papagayo
Verde
San Pedro Mixtepec
Puerto Escondido
Pochutla
Puerto Ángel
Salina Cruz
Mar Muerto
Puerto Arista
Pijijiapan
Mapastepec
Golfo de Tehuantepec
Motozintla
Huixtla
Tapachula
Coatepeque
Retalhuleu
Cuilco
3993
4220
San Marcos
Mazatenango
Totonicapán
Sololá
Antigua
GUATEMALA
Amatitlán
Jalapa
Chiquimula
Zacapa
Gualán
Huehuetenango
Cobán
Sierra de los Cuchumatanes
Sierra de las Minas
L. de Izabal
Sebol
Livingston
Puerto Barrios
Santa Bárbara
Santa Rosa de Copán
Esperanza
La Paz
Comayagua
Tegucigalpa
Yuscarán
Danlí
Juticalpa
Catacamas
Patuca
Yoro
Sulaco
Olanchito
Arenal
El Progreso
San Pedro Sula
Tela
Balfate
Savá
Trujillo
HONDURAS
Puerto Castilla
Iriona
Roatán
Is. de la Bahía
Golfo de Honduras
Monkey River
San Antonio
Punta Gorda
Maya Mts.
Dangriga
Belmopan
Benque Viejo
San Ignacio
Belize City
BELIZE
Turneffe Is.
Ambergris Cay
Flores
La Libertad
L. Petén Itzá
Uaxactún
San Luis
Salinas
Usumacinta
Tenosique
Balancán
Macuspana
Palizada
Frontera
Paraíso
Comalcalco
Ciudad del Carmen
L. de Términos
CAMPECHE
Concepción
Matamoros
Orange Walk
Hondo
Corozal
Chetumal
B. de Chetumal
Bacalar
Banco Chinchorro
QUINTANA ROO
Felipe Carrillo Puerto
B. del Espíritu Santo
B. de la Ascensión
Vigía Chico
Chenkán
Champotón
Campeche
Hopelchén
Bolonchenticul
Tenabo
Tekax
Ticul
Peto
Maxcanú
Sotuta
Valladolid
Mérida
YUCATÁN
Progreso
Dzilam de Bravo
Motul
Temax
Izamal
Espita
Tizimín
El Cuyo
Río Lagartos
Pta. Yalkubul
Cozumel
Isla Cozumel
Puerto Morelos
Cancún
Puerto Juárez
C. Catoche
Canal de Yucatán
C. San Antonio
C. Corrientes
La Esperanza
CUBA
Guane
La Fé
I. Desterrada
I. Pérez (Mexico)
Tropic of Cancer
Golfo de Campeche
GULF OF MEXICO

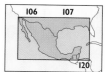

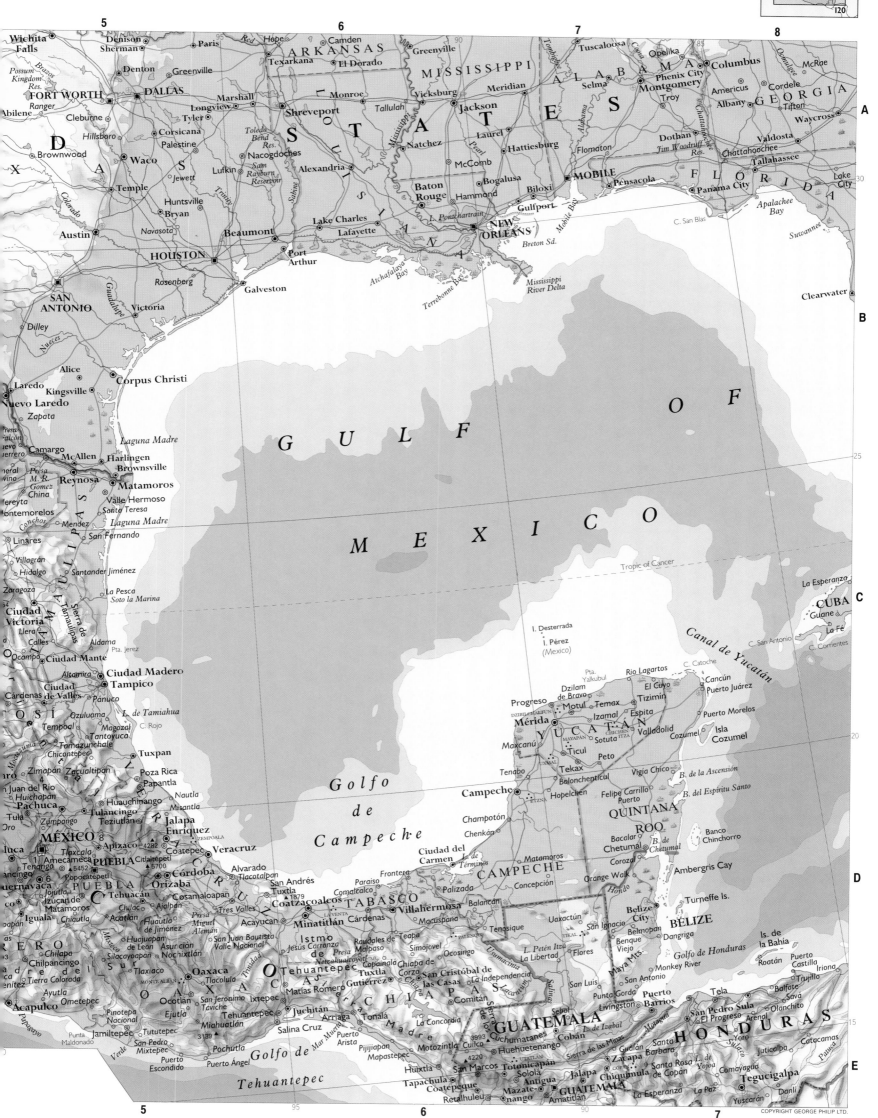

1:7 100 000

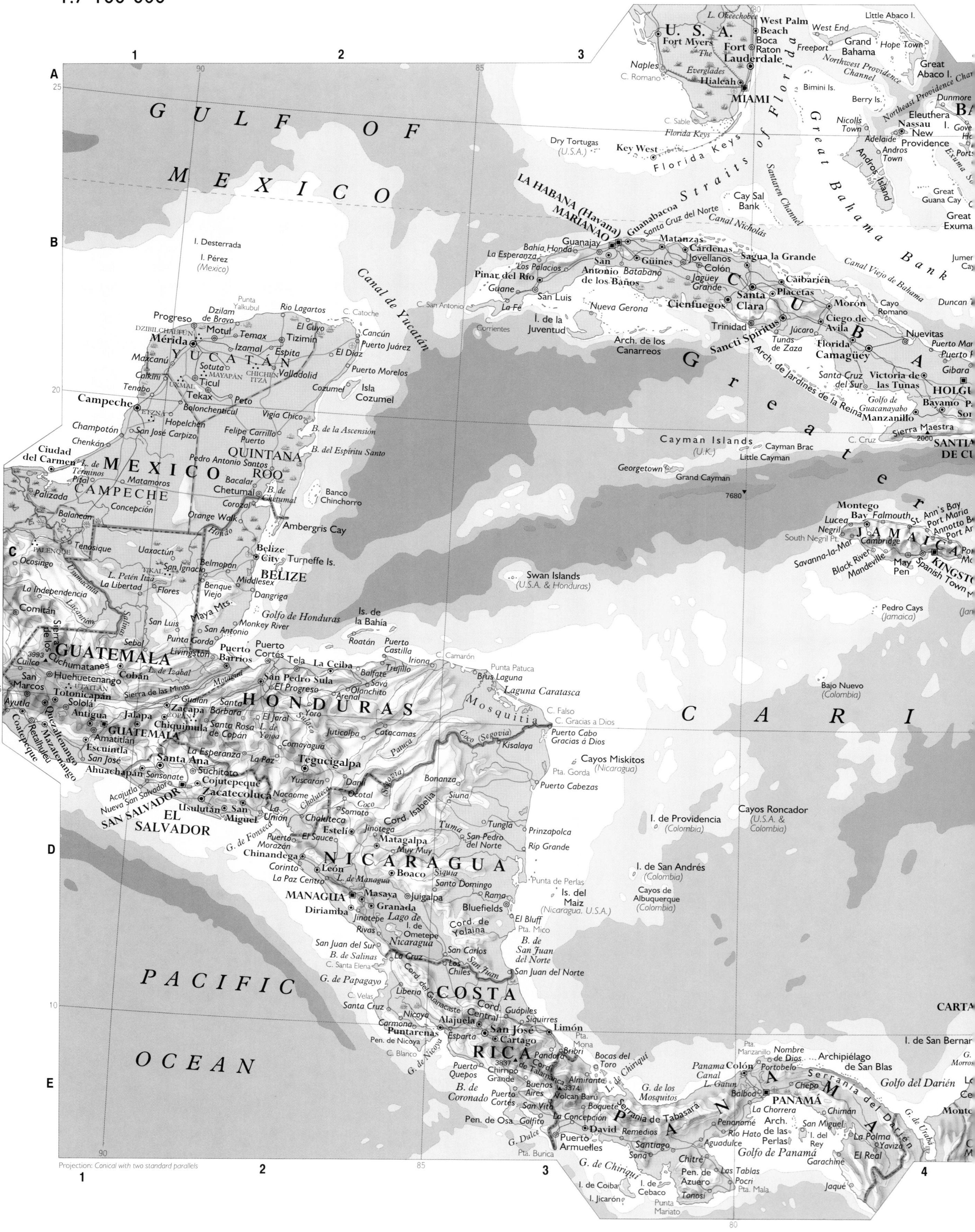

GULF OF MEXICO

PACIFIC OCEAN

CARIBBEAN (CARI...)

U.S.A.
Fort Myers · West Palm Beach · Little Abaco I. · West End · Hope Town · Grand Bahama · Great Abaco I.
Naples · Boca Raton · Fort Lauderdale · Freeport · Northwest Providence Channel
C. Romano · The Everglades · Miami · Hialeah · Bimini Is. · Berry Is. · Eleuthera · Nassau · Adelaide · New Providence · Andros Town · Great Guana Cay · Great Exuma
C. Sable · Dry Tortugas (U.S.A.) · Key West · Florida Keys · Straits of Florida · Nicolls Town · Andros Island · Northeast Providence Channel · Dunmore

LA HABANA (Havana) · MARIANAO · Guanabacoa · Santa Cruz del Norte · Canal Nicholás · Cay Sal Bank · Great Bahama Bank
Bahía Honda · Guanajay · Matanzas · Cárdenas · Jovellanos · Sagua la Grande · Caibarién · Canal Viejo de Bahama
La Esperanza · Los Palacios · San Antonio · Batabanó · Güines · Colón · Jagüey Grande · Santa Placetas · Morón · Cayo Romano · Duncan
Pinar del Río · Guane · San Luis · de los Baños · Grande · **C U B A** · Clara · Ciego de Ávila · Nuevitas
La Fé · Corrientes · Nueva Gerona · Cienfuegos · Santa Clara · Trinidad · Sancti Spíritus · Júcaro · Florida · Camagüey · Puerto P.
I. de la Juventud · Arch. de los Canarreos · Sancti Spíritus · Tunas de Zaza · Santa Cruz del Sur · Victoria de las Tunas · Gibara · HOLG
Arch. de Jardines de la Reina · Golfo de Guacanayabo · Bayamo · Manzanillo · Sierra Maestra · SANTI... DE CU...
Cayman Islands (U.K.) · Cayman Brac · Little Cayman · C. Cruz · 2000
Georgetown · Grand Cayman · 7680

JAMAICA · Montego Bay · Falmouth · St. Ann's Bay · Port Maria · Annotto B... · Lucea · Negril · Port An...
South Negril Pt. · Cambridge · May Pen · Spanish Town · KINGSTO...
Savanna-la-Mar · Black River · Mandeville · Pen
Pedro Cays (Jamaica)
Bajo Nuevo (Colombia)

Progreso · Dzilam de Bravo · Río Lagartos · C. Catoche · Punta Yalkubul
Mérida · Motul · Temax · Tizimín · Cancún · Puerto Juárez
Izamal · Espita · El Díaz · Cozumel · Isla Cozumel
Maxcanú · Sotuta · Valladolid · Puerto Morelos
Campeche · Tekax · Peto · Vigía Chico
Champotón · Hopelchén · Felipe Carrillo Puerto · B. de la Ascensión
Chenkán · San José Carpizo · Bacalar · B. del Espíritu Santo
Ciudad del Carmen · I. de Términos · **MEXICO** · Chetumal · Banco Chinchorro
Palizada · Balancán · Concepción · Orange Walk · Corozal · B. de Chetumal
CAMPECHE · Tenosique · Uaxactún · Ambergris Cay
PALENQUE · Tumbalá · Belmopan · Belize City · Turneffe Is.
Ocosingo · San Ignacio · **BELIZE** · Middlesex
La Independencia · L. Petén Itzá · La Libertad · Benque Viejo · Dangriga
Comitán · Flores · Maya Mts. · Monkey River
Sierra de los... · San Luis · San Antonio
3993 · GUATEMALA · Cuilco · Cuchumatanes · Punta Gorda · Puerto Barrios · Livingston · Puerto Cortés
San Marcos · Huehuetenango · Cobán · L. de Izabal · Tela · La Ceiba · Roatán · Puerto Castilla · Iriona
Totonicapán · Sololá · Sierra de las Minas · San Pedro Sula · El Progreso · Olanchito · Savá · Trujillo · Punta Patuca
Ayutla · Antigua · Jalapa · Santa Bárbara · **HONDURAS** · Yoro · Sulaco · Balfate · Brus Laguna
Quetzaltenango · Chiquimula · Santa Rosa de Copán · L. de Yojoa · Juticalpa · Catacamas · C. Camarón
Mazatenango · Amatitlán · La Esperanza · Comayagua · Coco (Segovia) · Laguna Caratasca
Escuintla · GUATEMALA · La Paz · Tegucigalpa · Yuscarán · Danlí · Mosquitia · C. Falso
Retalhuleu · Santa Ana · Suchitoto · Nacaome · Ocotal · Bonanza · C. Gracias á Dios
San José · Ahuachapán · Sonsonate · Cojutepeque · Choluteca · Somoto · Cord. Isabelia · Siuna · Puerto Cabo Gracias á Dios
Acajutla · Nueva San Salvador · Zacatecoluca · La Unión · Estelí · Jinotega · Tuma · Kisalaya
SAN SALVADOR · Usulután · San Miguel · Jalteva · El Sauce · Matagalpa · Muy Muy · Tungla · Cayos Miskitos (Nicaragua)
EL SALVADOR · G. de Fonseca · Puerto Morazán · León · **NICARAGUA** · San Pedro del Norte · Puerto Cabezas · Pta. Gorda
Chinandega · Corinto · La Paz Centro · Boaco · Siquia · Río Grande · Prinzapolca
MANAGUA · Masaya · Juigalpa · Santo Domingo · Rama · Cayos Roncador (U.S.A. & Colombia)
Diriamba · Granada · Lago de · Bluefields · I. de Providencia (Colombia)
Jinotepe · Rivas · I. de Ometepe · Cord. de Yolaina · El Bluff · Pta. Mico · I. de San Andrés (Colombia)
San Juan del Sur · B. de Salinas · La Cruz · San Carlos · B. de San Juan · Cayos de Albuquerque (Colombia)
C. Santa Elena · Los Chiles · San Juan del Norte · Is. del Maíz (Nicaragua, U.S.A.)
G. de Papagayo · Liberia · Cord. de Guanacaste · Punta de Perlas
Santa Cruz · Nicoya · **COSTA RICA** · Cord. Central · Guápiles · Siquirres · Limón
Carmona · Alajuela · **San José** · Cartago · Pta. Mona · CARTA...
Puntarenas · Espartsa · Bribri · Bocas del Toro · Laguna de Chiriquí · I. de San Bernar...
Pen. de Nicoya · C. Blanco · Chirripó · Pandora · Nombre de Dios · Archipiélago de San Blas
Puerto Quepos · 3837 · Cord. de Talamanca · Almirante · Panama Canal · Colón · Portobelo · Serranía del Darién · Golfo del Darién
B. de Coronado · Puerto Cortés · Buenos Aires · 3374 · Volcán Barú · L. de Gatún · Balboa · Chepo · G. Morros...
San Vito · Boquete · La Chorrera · **PANAMÁ** · San Miguel · Yaviza
La Concepción · David · **PANAMA** · Penonomé · Río Hato · Arch. de las Perlas · I. del Rey · La Palma · El Real
Puerto Armuelles · Pta. Burica · Remedios · Aguadulce · Chimán · Garachine · Jaqué
Santiago · Soná · Chitré · Pen. de Azuero · Las Tablas · Pocrí · Golfo de Panamá
G. de Chiriquí · I. de Coiba · I. de Cebaco · Tonosí · Punta Mariato · I. Jicarón

Swan Islands (U.S.A. & Honduras)

Golfo de Honduras · Is. de la Bahía

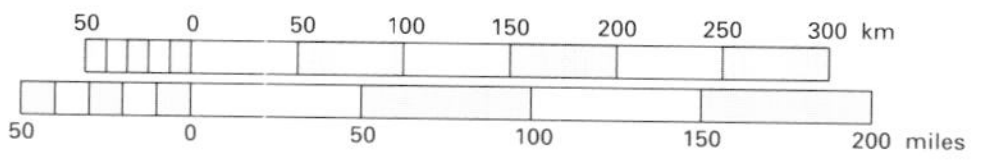

50 0 50 100 150 200 250 300 km
50 0 50 100 150 200 miles

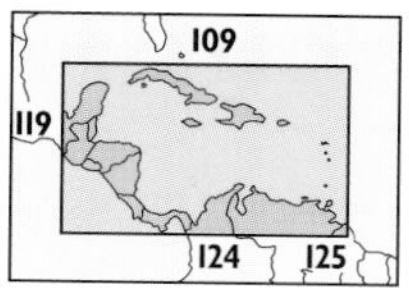

109
119
124 125

5 **6** **7** **8**

75 70 65 60

A
25

AMAS

A T L A N T I C

Arthur's Town
The Bight
Cat I.
San Salvador I.
Conception I.
Rum Cay
Long I.
Clarence Town
Samana Cay
Albert Town
Snug Corner
Mayaguana I.
Crooked I.
Plana Cays
Acklins I.
Mira por vos Cay
Cay Verde

O C E A N

B

Tropic of Cancer

ay Santa
omingo
Moa
anes
tilla
Mayari

Lake Rosa
Great
Inagua I.
Matthew
Town
Little Inagua I.
Hogsty Reef

Turks & Caicos
(U.K.)
Caicos Is.
Turks Is.

20

Baracoa
Pta. de
Maisi
Maisi
uantanamo
Paso de los Vientos
(Windward Passage)
Cap-
Haïtien
Monte
Cristi
LA ISABELA
Santiago de los Cabelleros

Puerto Rico Trench

Milwaukee
Deep
9200

C

Jean Rabel
Cap-à-
Foux
Port-de-
Paix
Fort Liberté
Gonaïves
Puerto
Plata
La Vega
Nagua
San Francisco de Macorís
Samana
Sánchez

Bayamón
SAN JUAN
Carolina

Anegada
Virgin Is.
Tortola
(U.K.)
Sombrero (U.K.)

G. de la
Gonâve
St-Marc
Hinche
Cord.
Central
3175

Sabana de la Mar

Arecibo
Aguadilla
St. Thomas
(U.S.A.)
Virgin Gorda
Road Town
Anguilla (U.K.)

HAITI
DOMINICAN
REP.
Jérémie
Î. de la Gonâve
PORT-
AU-PRINCE
San Pedro
de Macorís
San Juan
L. Enriquillo
Hato Mayor
Higüey
C. Engaño

Ponce
1338
Caguas
Charlotte-Amalie
St.-Martin
(Neth.)
St.-Barthélemy (Fr.)

Fajardo
Virgin Is.
(U.S.A.)
Saba (Neth.)
St. Maarten
Barbuda

vassa I.
(U.S.A.)
C. Carcasse
Dame
Massif de la Hotte
Petit
Goâve
2280
Jacmel
SANTO
DOMINGO
Agua de
Compostela
Bani
San Cristóbal
La Romana
B. de
Yuma

PUERTO
RICO
(U.S.A.)
Guayama
Christiansted
(Neth.)
St. Croix
Frederiksted
St. Eustatius
(Neth.)
Basseterre
Nevis
ST. KITTS
& NEVIS
ANTIGUA
& BARBUDA
St. John's
Antigua

Les Cayes
Aquin
Î. à Vache
Pointe-à- Gravois
Barahona
Pedernales
Isla
Mona
(U.S.A.)
Redonda
Montserrat
(U.K.)

H i s p a n i o l a
Î. Beata
C. Beata

A n t i l l e s
L e s s e r

Guadeloupe Passage
Ste.-Rose
Le Moule
La Désirade
GUADELOUPE
(Fr.)
Pointe-à-Pitre
Marie-Galante (Fr.)
Basse-Terre
Grand-Bourg
I. des Saintes
Dominica Passage
Portsmouth
DOMINICA
Roseau

Leeward Islands

I. de Aves
(Venezuela)

15

B E A N

S E A

Mt. Pelée
1397
Ste.-Marie
Le François
Rivière-Pilote
Fort-de-
France
MARTINIQUE
(Fr.)
St. Lucia Channel
Castries
ST. LUCIA
Soufrière

Windward Islands
Lesser Antilles

St. Vincent Passage
La Soufrière 1234
ST. VINCENT
Speightstown
Bridgetown
BARBADOS
Kingstown
Grenadines
& THE
GRENADINES

L e s s e r
A n t i l l e s

Hillsborough

St. George's
GRENADA

60

D

Aruba
(Neth.)
Curaçao
Bonaire
NETH.
ANTILLES
Willemstad

Pta. Gallinas
C. San Román
Pen. de
Paraguaná

Is. Las Aves
(Ven.)
Is. Los Roques
(Ven.)
I. Orchila
(Ven.)

I. Blanquilla (Ven.)
Is. Los Hermanos
(Ven.)
Is. Los Testigos
(Ven.)
Tobago
Scarborough

SANTA
MARTA
Ríohacha
Uribia
Pen. de la
Guajira
Pta.
Espada
Punto Fijo
Punta
Cardón
Puerto
Cumarebo
Coro
La Vela de Coro
Maiquetía
La Guaira
I. La Tortuga
(Ven.)
NUEVA
ESPARTA
I. de Margarita
La Asunción
Porlamar
Port of
Spain
Galera
Point
Trinidad
Arima
Rio Claro

RRAN-
UILLA
aranoa
ÁNTICO
Soledad
Ciénaga
GUAJIRA
San
Rafael
Sierra Nevada de
Santa Marta
9800
Golfo de
Venezuela
Mene de Mauroa
FALCÓN
Tucacas
Puerto
Cabello
Maracay
CARACAS
DISTRITO FEDERAL
C. Codera
Higuerote
Río Chico
Puerto
La Cruz
Cumaná
Cariaco
Carúpano
G. de Paria
Caribe
Güiria
Pen. de Paria
SUCRE
Caripito
TRINIDAD
& TOBAGO
San Fernando

Sabanalarga
MARACAIBO
La Concepción
Santa Rita
Cabimas
Baragua
Tocuyo
San Felipe
YARACUY
CARABOBO
Valencia
MIRANDA
Los Teques
ARAGUA
Ocumare del Tuy
Barcelona
Caicara
Maturín

Fundación
Calamar
Agustín
Codazzi
Ciudad
Ojeda
Mene Grande
LARA
BARQUISIMETO
Yaritagua de
los Morros
Villa
de Cura
San Juan
de los Morros de Orituco
Altagracia
de Orituco
Anaco
Aragua de
Barcelona
MONAGAS
DELTA
Tucupita

armen
arm
BA
laneta
ÁNTICO
Plato
Zambrano
Valledupar
CÉSAR
Lago de
Maracaibo
Machiques
Trujillo
TRUJILLO
Valera
El Tocuyo
San Carlos
COJEDES
El Baúl
Calabozo
Valle de
la Pascua
El Sombrero
GUÁRICO
Santa María
de Ipire
El Tigre
ANZOÁTEGUI
AMACURO
Los Barrancos

ince
Sahagún
artos
 laneta
ica
Corozal
El Banco
Mompós
ZULIA
Betijoque
Acarigua
PORTUGUESA
Guanare
Portuguesa
El Pao
Ciudad Guayana
Sierra Imataca

Sincé
Magangué
San Carlos
del Zulia
Encontrados
San
Rafael del
Rosario
MÉRIDA
MÉRIDA
Barinas
Libertad
Guárico
Soledad
Ciudad Bolívar
Upata

Ayapel
Majagual
NORTE
DE
Ocaña
Ciudad
Bolivia
BARINAS
Puerto de Nutrias
Mapire
Sierra Imataca

arto
Caucasia
Simití
SANTANDER
TÁCHIRA
Cúcuta
San
Bárbara
V E N E Z U E L A
Bruzual
Achaguas
San Fernando
de Apure
Apure
Caicara
Orinoco
Embalse de Guri
Guasipati
El Callao
Tumeremo

E
10

West from Greenwich
COPYRIGHT GEORGE PHILIP LTD

5 **6** **7**

75 70 65

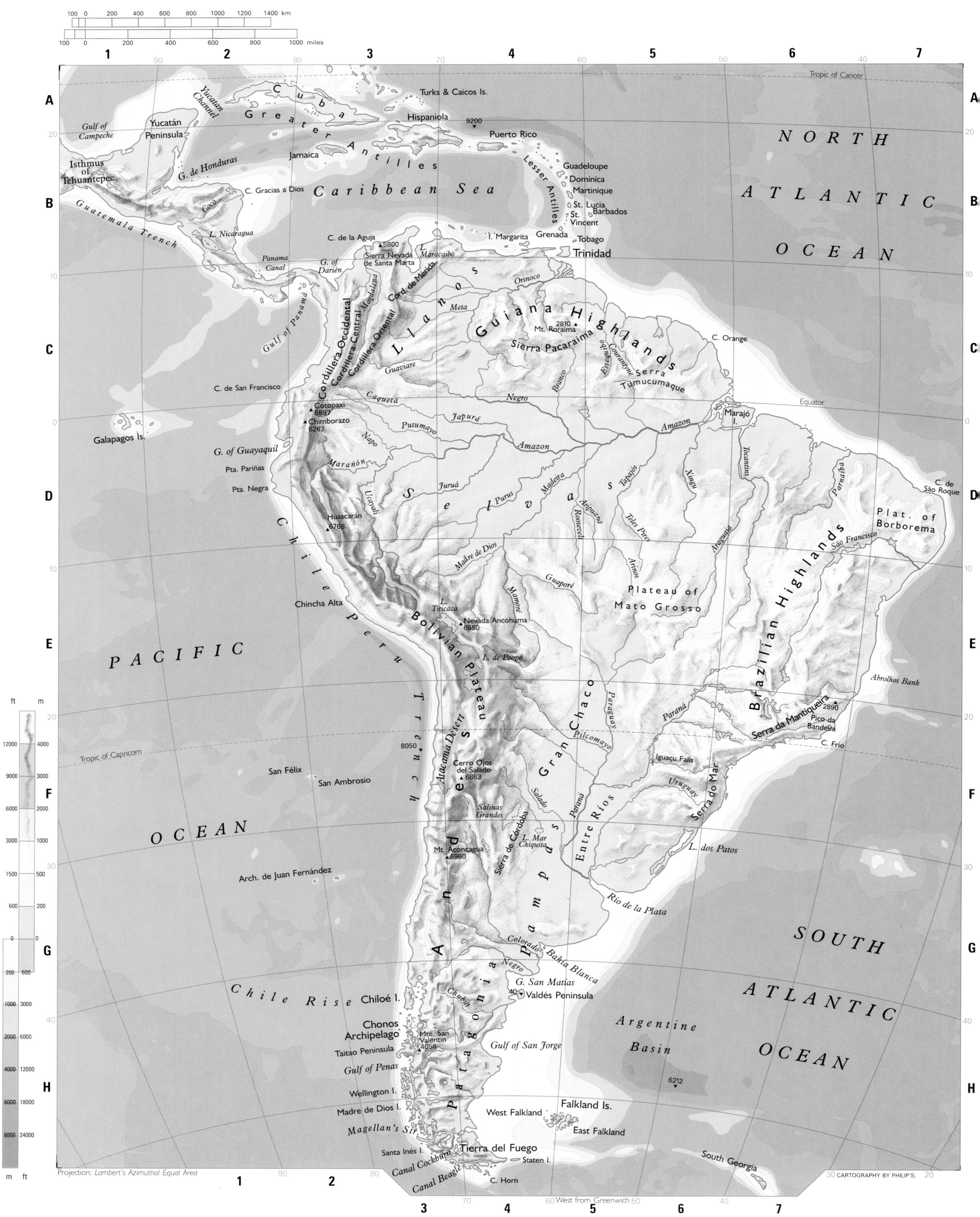

NORTH ATLANTIC OCEAN
SOUTH ATLANTIC OCEAN
PACIFIC OCEAN
Caribbean Sea
Greater Antilles
Lesser Antilles
Cuba
Hispaniola
Puerto Rico
Jamaica
Turks & Caicos Is.
Yucatán Peninsula
Yucatan Channel
Gulf of Campeche
Isthmus of Tehuantepec
G. de Honduras
C. Gracias a Dios
Guatemala Trench
L. Nicaragua
Panama Canal
G. of Darién
Gulf of Panamá
Guadeloupe
Dominica
Martinique
St. Lucia
St. Vincent
Barbados
Grenada
Tobago
Trinidad
I. Margarita
C. de la Aguja
Sierra Nevada de Santa Marta
L. Maracaibo
Cord. de Mérida
Cordillera Occidental
Cordillera Central
Cordillera Oriental
Magdalena
Llanos
Orinoco
Meta
Guiana Highlands
Mt. Roraima
Sierra Pacaraima
Serra Tumucumaque
C. Orange
Guaviare
Branco
Negro
C. de San Francisco
Cotopaxi
Chimborazo
Galapagos Is.
G. of Guayaquil
Pta. Pariñas
Pta. Negra
Caquetá
Japurá
Putumayo
Napo
Marañón
Amazon
Marajó I.
Equator
Tocantins
Xingu
Tapajós
Madeira
Purus
Juruá
Ucayali
Selvas
Huascarán
Aripuanã
Roosevelt
Teles Pires
Araguaia
Parnaíba
C. de São Roque
Plat. of Borborema
São Francisco
Brazilian Highlands
Arinos
Guaporé
Mamoré
Madre de Dios
Plateau of Mato Grosso
Chile Peru Trench
Chincha Alta
L. Titicaca
Nevada Ancohuma
Bolivian Plateau
L. de Poopó
Abrolhos Bank
Gran Chaco
Paraguay
Paraná
Pilcomayo
Serra da Mantiqueira
Pico da Bandeira
C. Frio
Tropic of Capricorn
San Félix
San Ambrosio
Atacama Desert
Cerro Ojos del Salado
Andes
Iguaçu Falls
Uruguay
Serra do Mar
Salado
Salinas Grandes
Entre Ríos
Sierra de Córdoba
L. Mar Chiquita
Mt. Aconcagua
L. dos Patos
Arch. de Juan Fernández
Pampas
Río de la Plata
Colorado
Bahía Blanca
Negro
G. San Matías
Valdés Peninsula
Chubut
Patagonia
Chile Rise
Chiloé I.
Chonos Archipelago
Mte. San Valentin
Taitao Peninsula
Gulf of Penas
Gulf of San Jorge
Argentine Basin
Wellington I.
Madre de Dios I.
Magellan's Str.
West Falkland
Falkland Is.
East Falkland
Santa Inés I.
Tierra del Fuego
Canal Cockburn
Canal Beagle
Staten I.
C. Horn
South Georgia
Tropic of Cancer
Projection: Lambert's Azimuthal Equal Area
West from Greenwich
CARTOGRAPHY BY PHILIP'S.

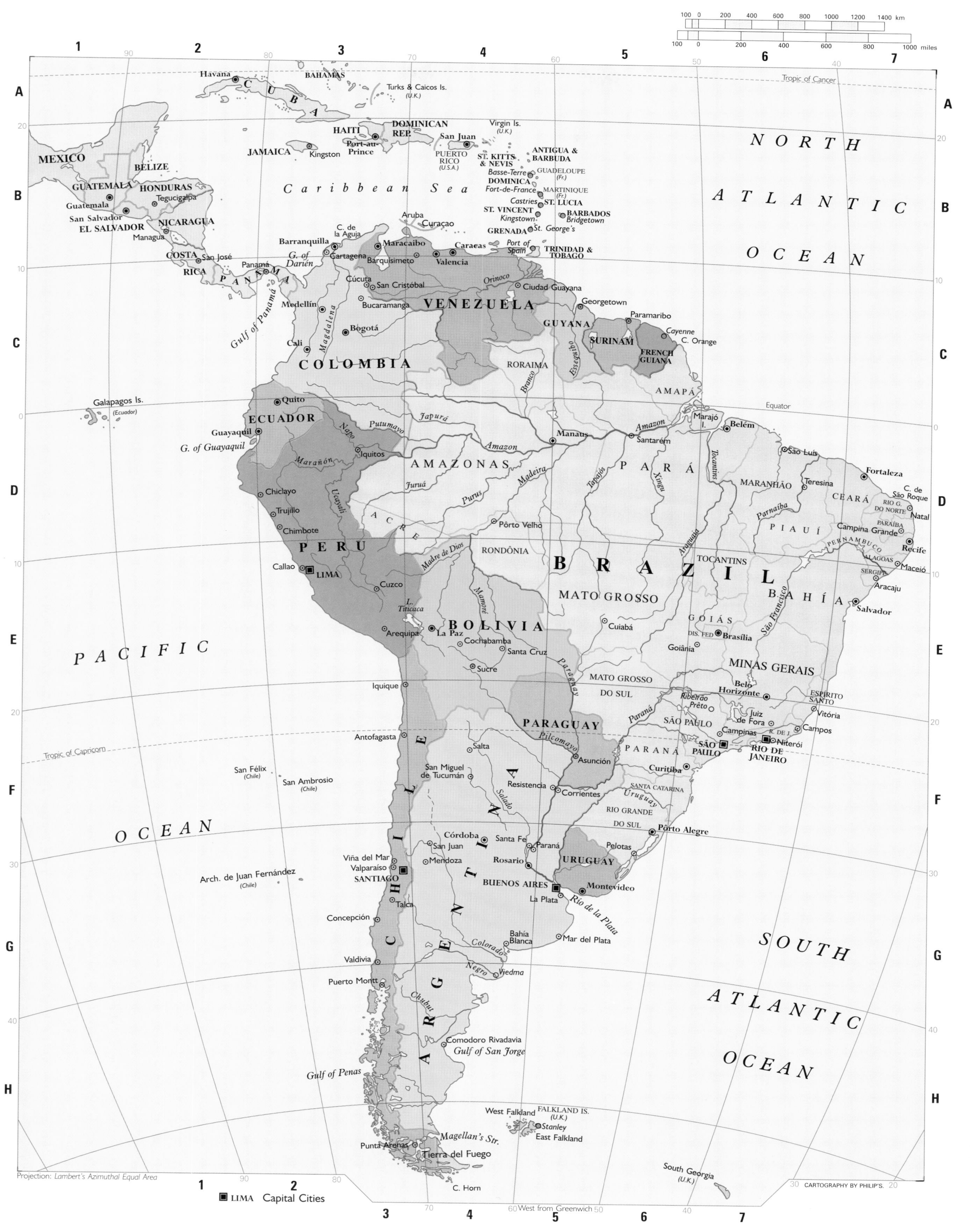

100 0 200 400 600 800 1000 1200 1400 km
100 0 200 400 600 800 1000 miles

Tropic of Cancer

A

Havana *CUBA* BAHAMAS Turks & Caicos Is. (U.K.)

NORTH

MEXICO

HAITI DOMINICAN REP. Virgin Is. (U.K.)

San Juan ANTIGUA & BARBUDA

JAMAICA Kingston Port-au-Prince PUERTO RICO (U.S.A.) ST. KITTS & NEVIS Basse-Terre GUADELOUPE (Fr.) DOMINICA

GUATEMALA **HONDURAS** Tegucigalpa Fort-de-France MARTINIQUE (Fr.)

ATLANTIC

B

Guatemala San Salvador **NICARAGUA** Caribbean Sea Castries ST. LUCIA ST. VINCENT BARBADOS

EL SALVADOR Kingstown Bridgetown

Managua GRENADA St. George's

COSTA San José Aruba Curaçao Port of Spain TRINIDAD & TOBAGO

OCEAN

RICA Panamá *PANAMA* Barranquilla C. de la Aguja

Maracaibo Caracas

G. of Darién Cartagena Barquisimeto Valencia

Cúcuta San Cristóbal Orinoco Ciudad Guayana

C

Medellín Bucaramanga **VENEZUELA** Georgetown

Gulf of Panamá Bogotá **GUYANA** Paramaribo

Cali **SURINAM** Cayenne C. Orange

COLOMBIA RORAIMA Esequibo **FRENCH GUIANA**

Galapagos Is. (Ecuador) Quito **AMAPÁ**

Equator

D

Guayaquil **ECUADOR** Napo Marajó I. Belém

G. of Guayaquil Iquitos Japurá Amazon Santarém São Luís

Marañón **AMAZONAS** Amazon Manaus *PARÁ* **MARANHÃO** Teresina Fortaleza

Chiclayo Juruá Purus Madeira Tapajós Xingu Tocantins **CEARÁ** C. de São Roque

Trujillo *ACRE* Pôrto Velho **PIAUÍ** RIO G. DO NORTE Natal

Chimbote Madre de Dios RONDÔNIA **BRAZIL** PARAÍBA Campina Grande

E

PERU Callao LIMA Cuzco L. Titicaca **MATO GROSSO** TOCANTINS PERNAMBUCO Recife

Mamoré Cuiabá GOIÁS **BAHÍA** ALAGOAS Maceió

Arequipa La Paz **BOLIVIA** Brasília SERGIPE Aracaju

Cochabamba DIS. FED. São Francisco Salvador

Santa Cruz Goiânia **MINAS GERAIS**

Iquique Sucre **MATO GROSSO DO SUL** Belo Horizonte

PACIFIC Paraguay Paraná ESPÍRITO SANTO

F

Antofagasta **PARAGUAY** Pilcomayo Ribeirão Prêto Vitória

Campinas SÃO PAULO R. DE J. Campos

Salta Asunción **PARANA** **SÃO PAULO** Niterói RIO DE JANEIRO

San Félix (Chile) San Miguel de Tucumán Resistencia Curitiba

San Ambrosio (Chile) Salado Corrientes SANTA CATARINA

OCEAN *CHILE* Uruguay Uruguay RIO GRANDE DO SUL Pôrto Alegre

G

Córdoba Santa Fe Paraná Pelotas

Viña del Mar San Juan Mendoza Rosario **URUGUAY**

Valparaíso Montevideo

Arch. de Juan Fernández (Chile) SANTIAGO *ARGENTINA* BUENOS AIRES

Talca La Plata Rio de la Plata

Concepción Bahía Blanca Mar del Plata

SOUTH

Valdivia Negro Viedma

Puerto Montt Colorado

ATLANTIC

H

Chubut

Comodoro Rivadavia Gulf of San Jorge

Gulf of Penas *OCEAN*

West Falkland FALKLAND IS. (U.K.)

Magellan's Str. Stanley

Punta Arenas East Falkland

Tierra del Fuego South Georgia (U.K.)

C. Horn

Projection: Lambert's Azimuthal Equal Area

■ LIMA Capital Cities

West from Greenwich

CARTOGRAPHY BY PHILIP'S

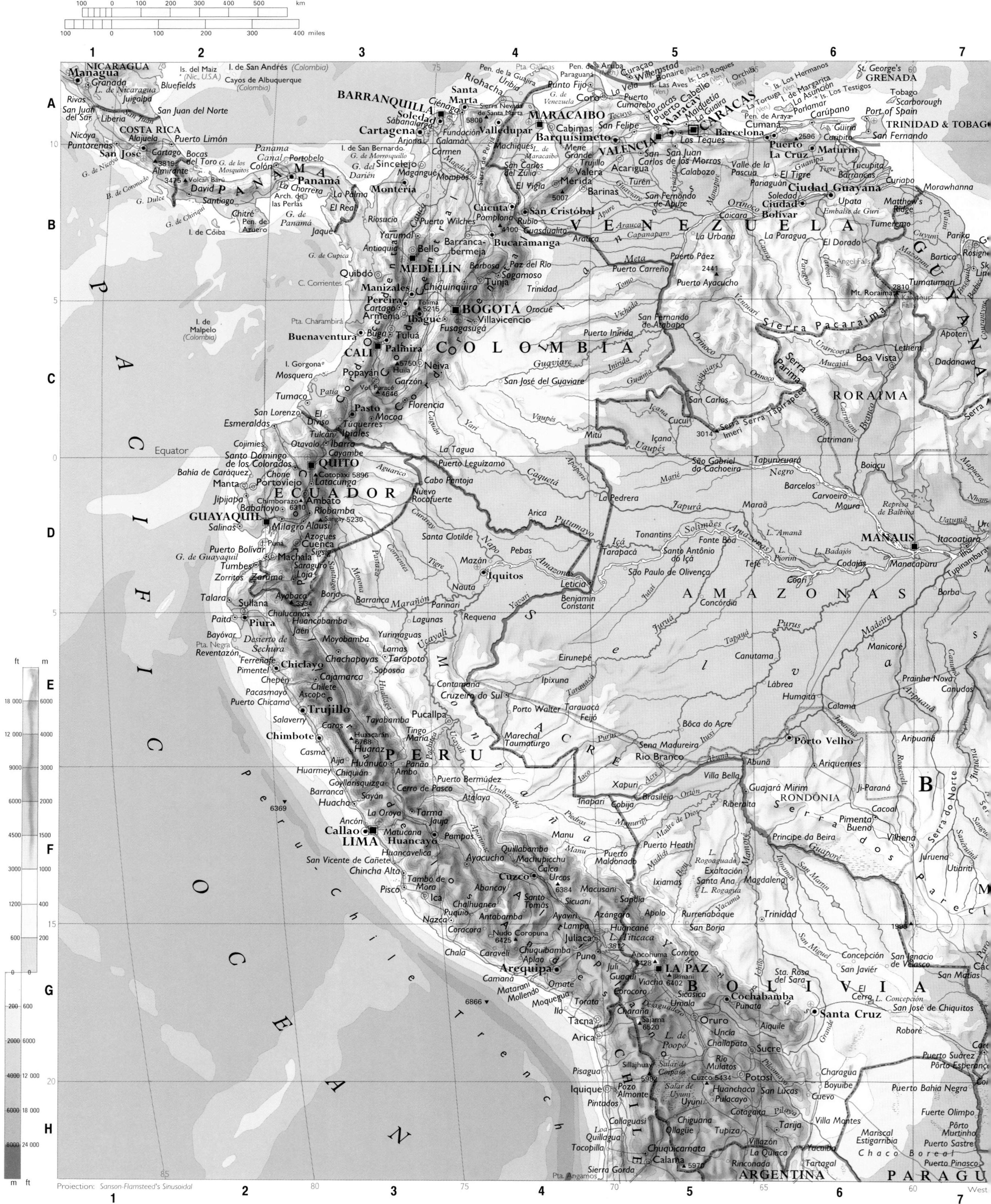
100 0 100 200 300 400 500 km
100 0 100 200 300 400 miles
NICARAGUA
Managua
Granada
L. de Nicaragua
Bluefields
I. de San Andrés (Colombia)
Cayos de Albuquerque (Colombia)
San Juan del Norte
COSTA RICA
San José
Puerto Limón
Panama Canal
Colón
Panamá
PANAMA
G. de Panamá
I. de Coiba
Pen. de Azuero
David
BARRANQUILLA
Cartagena
Santa Marta
Riohacha
Pen. de la Guajira
MARACAIBO
Barquisimeto
Valledupar
Punto Fijo
Coro
Curaçao
Willemstad
Aruba
Bonaire
Puerto Cabello
Maracay
La Guaira
CARACAS
VALENCIA
Barcelona
Cumaná
Carúpano
Port of Spain
TRINIDAD & TOBAGO
St. George's
GRENADA
Tobago
Scarborough
San Fernando
Maturín
Ciudad Guayana
Ciudad Bolívar
Sincelejo
Montería
Mérida
San Cristóbal
Cúcuta
Barinas
Bucaramanga
VENEZUELA
Orinoco
Puerto Carreño
Puerto Ayacucho
Angel Falls
Mt. Roraima 2810
Sierra Pacaraima
GUYANA
Lethem
Boa Vista
RORAIMA
Medellín
Bello
Quibdó
Manizales
Pereira
Armenia
Ibagué
BOGOTÁ
Villavicencio
Tunja
Buenaventura
CALI
Palmira
Tuluá
Neiva
Popayán
Pasto
Florencia
COLOMBIA
Guaviare
San José del Guaviare
Mitú
Tumaco
Esmeraldas
Equator
Ibarra
QUITO
Cotopaxi 5896
Chimborazo 6310
Ambato
Riobamba
Manta
Portoviejo
ECUADOR
GUAYAQUIL
Cuenca
Machala
Loja
G. de Guayaquil
Tumbes
Talara
Sullana
Piura
Chiclayo
Cajamarca
Trujillo
Chimbote
Huascarán 6768
Huaraz
Huánuco
Cerro de Pasco
Callao
LIMA
Huancayo
Pucallpa
Iquitos
Leticia
Marañón
Amazonas
Ucayali
PERU
Cuzco
Ayacucho
Abancay
Ica
Nazca
Arequipa
Juliaca
Puno
L. Titicaca
LA PAZ
Cochabamba
Oruro
Sucre
Potosí
Santa Cruz
BOLIVIA
Trinidad
Tacna
Arica
Iquique
Calama
CHILE
ARGENTINA
PARAGUAY
Manaus
AMAZONAS
Purus
Juruá
Madeira
Pôrto Velho
Rio Branco
ACRE
RONDÔNIA
Guajará Mirim
Sena Madureira
Cruzeiro do Sul
Tefé
Coari
Humaitá
Manicoré
PACIFIC OCEAN
Peru-Chile Trench
Projection: Sanson-Flamsteed's Sinusoidal
West

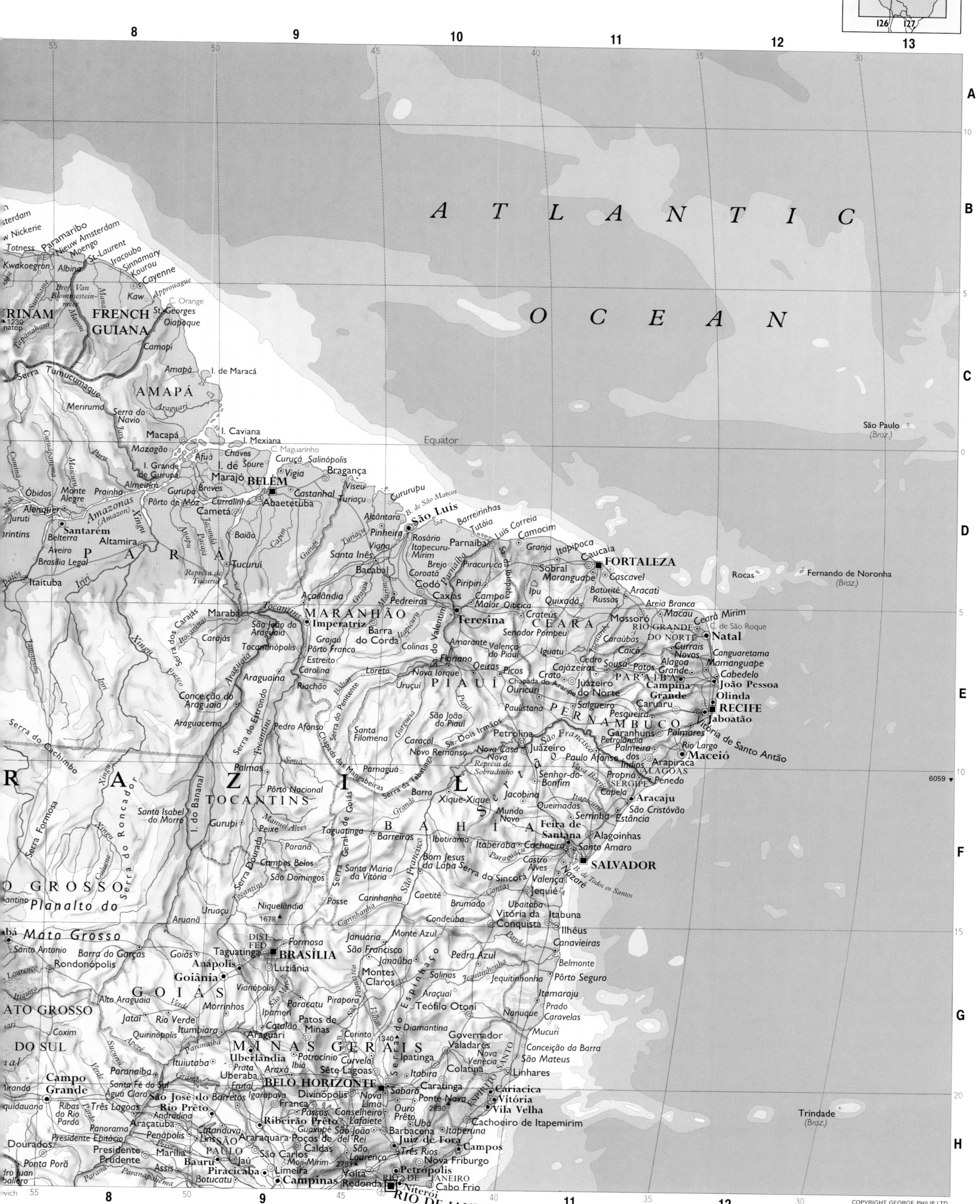

119
120
121
126
127
8
9
10
11
12
13
A
B
C
D
E
F
G
H
A T L A N T I C
O C E A N
Equator
FRENCH GUIANA
Paramaribo
Nieuw Amsterdam
Moengo
St-Laurent
Iracoubo
Sinnamary
Kourou
Cayenne
Kaw
C. Orange
St-Georges
Oiapoque
Camopi
Serra Tumucumaque
AMAPÁ
Amapá
I. de Maracá
Serra do Navio
Macapá
Mazagão
I. Caviana
I. Mexiana
C. Maguarinho
I. Grande de Gurupá
I. de Marajó
Chaves
Soure
Afuá
Breves
Curuçá
Salinópolis
Vigia
Bragança
BELÉM
Castanhal
Abaetetuba
Cametá
Almeirim
Óbidos
Monte Alegre
Prainha
Alenquer
Santarém
Belterra
Aveiro
Brasília Legal
Itaituba
Altamira
Tucuruí
Marabá
Carajás
Serra dos Carajás
Baião
Pôrto de Moz
Gurupá
Amazonas
Xingu
Tocantins
P A R Á
São Luís
Alcântara
Pinheiro
Viana
Rosário
Itapecuru-Mirim
Santa Inês
Bacabal
Coroatá
Codó
Caxias
Pedreiras
Açailândia
Imperatriz
Barra do Corda
Grajaú
Pôrto Franco
Estreito
Carolina
Colinas
Balsas
Riachão
Loreto
M A R A N H Ã O
São João do Araguaia
Tocantinópolis
Araguaína
Conceição do Araguaia
Araguacema
Pedro Afonso
Palmas
Pôrto Nacional
Gurupi
Peixe
T O C A N T I N S
I. do Bananal
Santa Isabel do Morro
Serra Formosa
Serra do Cachimbo
B R A Z I L
Parnaíba
Tutóia
Barreirinhas
Luís Correia
Camocim
Granja
Itapipoca
Caucaia
FORTALEZA
Maranguape
Sobral
Cascavel
Aracati
Baturité
Russas
Quixadá
Ipu
Crateús
Piripiri
Campo Maior
Oiticica
Teresina
Valença do Piauí
Floriano
Oeiras
Picos
Nova Iorque
Uruçuí
P I A U Í
São João do Piauí
Santa Filomena
Caracol
Novo Remanso
Paulistana
Ouricuri
Crato
Juazeiro do Norte
Iguatu
Senador Pompeu
C E A R Á
Mossoró
Macau
Areia Branca
Ceará Mirim
C. de São Roque
Natal
RIO GRANDE DO NORTE
Caraúbas
Caicó
Currais Novos
Alagoa Grande
Canguaretama
Mamanguape
Cabedelo
João Pessoa
Campina Grande
Sousa
Patos
Cajàzeiras
P A R A Í B A
Caruaru
RECIFE
Olinda
Jaboatão
Vitória de Santo Antão
Palmares
Garanhuns
Pesqueira
Salgueiro
Petrolina
Juàzeiro
P E R N A M B U C O
Petrolândia
Palmeira dos Índios
Maceió
Rio Largo
Arapiraca
ALAGOAS
Penedo
SERGIPE
Propriá
Capela
Aracaju
São Cristóvão
Estância
Paulo Afonso
Senhor-do-Bonfim
Jacobina
Xique-Xique
Barra
Mundo Novo
Queimadas
Serrinha
Feira de Santana
Alagoinhas
Santo Amaro
Cachoeira
SALVADOR
Castro Alves
Valença
Nazaré
Jequié
Ibotirama
Itaberaba
Bom Jesus da Lapa
Barreiras
Taguatinga
B A H I A
Serra do Sincorá
Caetité
Brumado
Ubaitaba
Vitória da Conquista
Itabuna
Ilhéus
Canavieiras
Belmonte
Pôrto Seguro
Jequitinhonha
Itamaraju
Prado
Caravelas
Nanuque
Mucuri
Rocas
Fernando de Noronha (Braz.)
São Paulo (Braz.)
Trindade (Braz.)
6059
Campos Belos
São Domingos
Posse
Carinhanha
Niquelândia
1678
Uruaçu
Aruanã
Condeúba
Januária
Monte Azul
São Francisco
Januúba
Montes Claros
Salinas
Pedra Azul
Araçuaí
Teófilo Otoni
Pirapora
Paracatu
Patos de Minas
Diamantina
Governador Valadares
Conceição da Barra
São Mateus
Linhares
Colatina
Nova Venécia
Itabira
Ipatinga
Caratinga
Cariacica
Vitória
Vila Velha
Cachoeiro de Itapemirim
Campos
Nova Friburgo
Petrópolis
Niterói
Cabo Frio
RIO DE JANEIRO
Volta Redonda
Juiz de Fora
Barbacena
Três Rios
Itaperuna
Ouro Prêto
Sabará
BELO HORIZONTE
Sete Lagoas
Curvelo
Divinópolis
Conselheiro Lafaiete
São João del Rei
Lavras
Varginha
Poços de Caldas
M I N A S G E R A I S
Uberlândia
Uberaba
Araxá
Patrocínio
Ibiá
Araguari
Catalão
Ituiutaba
Frutal
Franca
Ribeirão Prêto
Araraquara
São Carlos
Limeira
Campinas
Piracicaba
Jaú
Bauru
Marília
Assis
Botucatu
SÃO PAULO
Catanduva
São José do Rio Prêto
Araçatuba
Penápolis
Andradina
Presidente Prudente
Presidente Epitácio
Dourados
Ponta Porã
Campo Grande
Três Lagoas
Paranaíba
Santa Fé do Sul
Água Clara
Ribas do Rio Pardo
Coxim
MATO GROSSO DO SUL
MATO GROSSO
Planalto do Mato Grosso
Rondonópolis
Barra do Garças
Goiás
Anápolis
Goiânia
Taguatinga
BRASÍLIA
DIST. FED.
Formosa
Luziânia
Vianópolis
Morrinhos
Itumbiara
Quirinópolis
Jataí
Rio Verde
Alto Araguaia
G O I Á S
Ipameri
2890
2787
1340
55
50
45
40
35
30
10
5
0
15
20

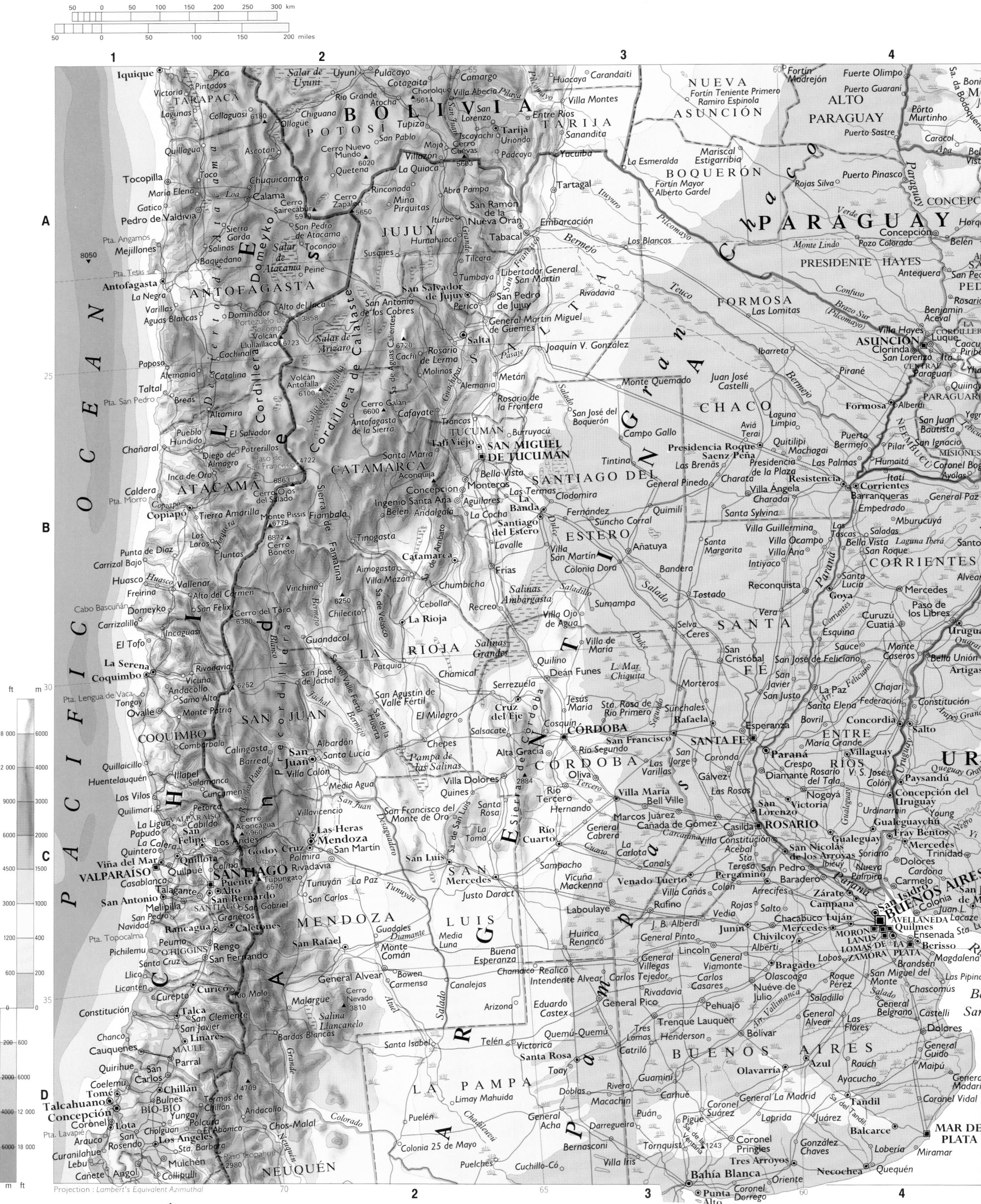
50 0 50 100 150 200 250 300 km
50 0 50 100 150 200 miles
PACIFIC OCEAN
BOLIVIA
PARAGUAY
ARGENTINA
CHILE
Gran Chaco
Cordillera Domeyko
Cordillera de Calalaste
Precordillera
Pampas
TARAPACÁ
ANTOFAGASTA
ATACAMA
COQUIMBO
VALPARAÍSO
SANTIAGO
O'HIGGINS
MAULE
BIO-BIO
POTOSÍ
TARIJA
NUEVA ASUNCIÓN
BOQUERÓN
ALTO PARAGUAY
PRESIDENTE HAYES
JUJUY
SALTA
FORMOSA
CHACO
TUCUMÁN
CATAMARCA
SANTIAGO DEL ESTERO
CORRIENTES
LA RIOJA
SAN JUAN
SANTA FÉ
ENTRE RÍOS
CÓRDOBA
MENDOZA
SAN LUIS
LA PAMPA
BUENOS AIRES
NEUQUÉN
Iquique
Antofagasta
Calama
Copiapó
La Serena
Coquimbo
VALPARAÍSO
SANTIAGO
Talca
Concepción
Talcahuano
Chillán
Los Angeles
Tarija
ASUNCIÓN
Salta
San Salvador de Jujuy
SAN MIGUEL DE TUCUMÁN
Santiago del Estero
Catamarca
La Rioja
San Juan
Mendoza
San Luis
CÓRDOBA
SANTA FE
Paraná
ROSARIO
Corrientes
Resistencia
Formosa
BUENOS AIRES
LA PLATA
MAR DE PLATA
Bahía Blanca
Santa Rosa
Río Cuarto
Projection : Lambert's Equivalent Azimuthal

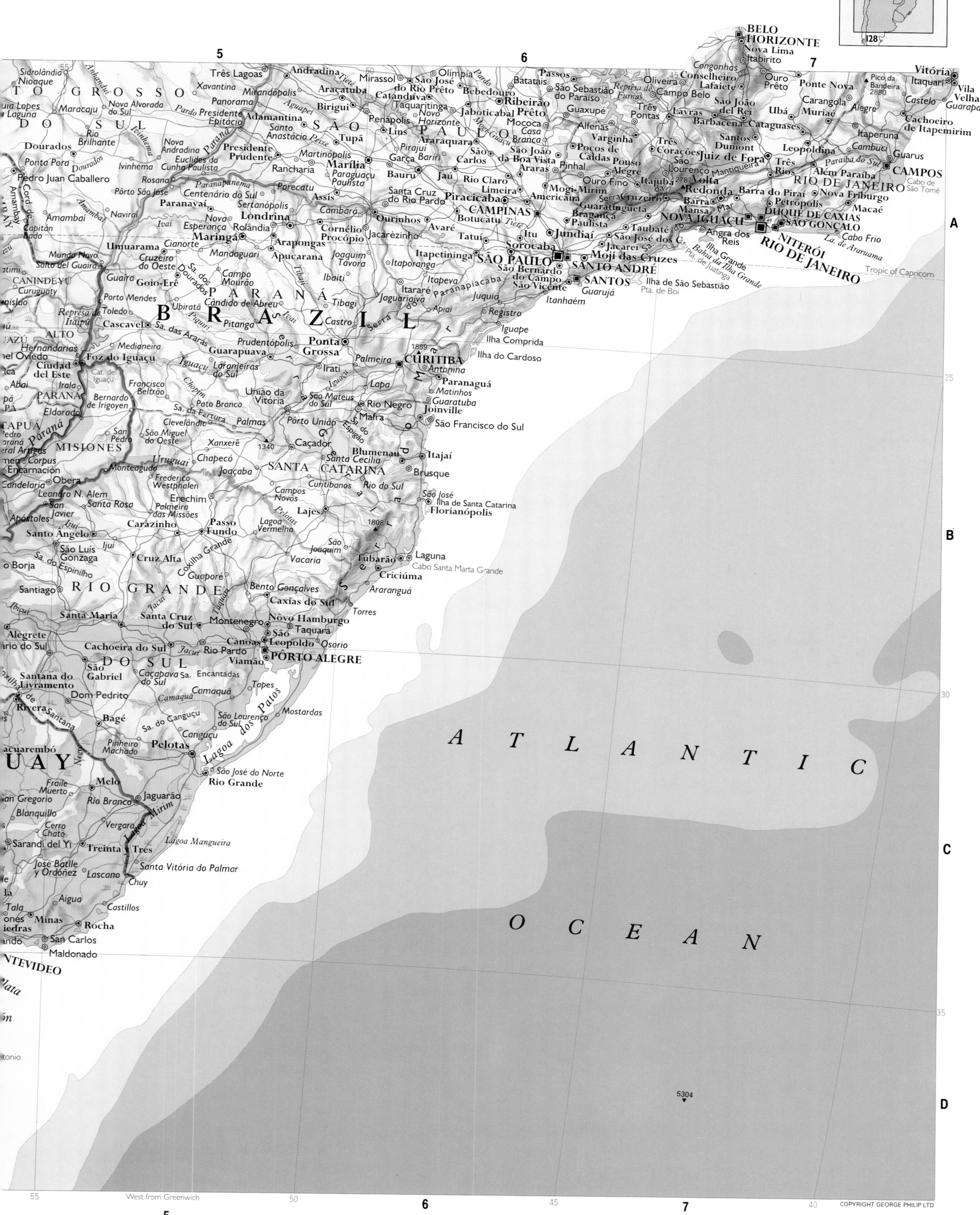
124
125
128
BELO HORIZONTE
Nova Lima
Itabirito
Vitória
Vila Velha
Guarapari
Pico da Bandeira 2890
Três Lagoas
Andradina
Mirassol
São José do Rio Prêto
Olímpia
Passos
Batatais
Ribeirão Prêto
Bebedouro
Araçatuba
Birigui
Catanduva
Taquaritinga
Jaboticabal
Mococa
Franca
São Sebastião do Paraiso
Oliveira
Conselheiro Lafaiete
Ouro Prêto
Ponte Nova
Campo Belo
São João del Rei
Barbacena
Ubá
Muriaé
Carangola
Alegre
Castelo
Cachoeiro de Itapemirim
Itaperuna
Cataguases
Leopoldina
Juiz de Fora
Três Rios
Guarus
CAMPOS
Cabo de São Tomé
Além Paraíba
RIO DE JANEIRO
Nova Friburgo
Petrópolis
Macaé
DUQUE DE CAXIAS
SÃO GONÇALO
NOVA IGUAÇU
NITERÓI
RIO DE JANEIRO
Cabo Frio
La. de Araruama
Tropic of Capricorn
Volta Redonda
Barra Mansa
Barra do Piraí
Angra dos Reis
Ilha Grande
Baía da Ilha Grande
Taubaté
São José dos Campos
Jacareí
Moji das Cruzes
SÃO PAULO
SANTO ANDRÉ
São Bernardo do Campo
São Vicente
SANTOS
Guarujá
Ilha de São Sebastião
Pta. de Boi
Itanhaém
Jundiaí
CAMPINAS
Piracicaba
Limeira
Americana
Rio Claro
Araraquara
São Carlos
Bauru
Jaú
Marília
Presidente Prudente
Presidente Epitácio
Adamantina
Tupã
Lins
Assis
Ourinhos
Botucatu
Sorocaba
Itu
Tatuí
Itapetininga
Itapeva
Itararé
Registro
Iguape
Ilha Comprida
Ilha do Cardoso
CURITIBA
Paranaguá
Antonina
Ponta Grossa
Guarapuava
Castro
Londrina
Maringá
Apucarana
Arapongas
Umuarama
Cascavel
Foz do Iguaçu
Ciudad del Este
Encarnación
Posadas
Posadas
Joinville
São Francisco do Sul
Blumenau
Itajaí
Brusque
Florianópolis
Ilha de Santa Catarina
Lajes
Tubarão
Laguna
Cabo Santa Marta Grande
Criciúma
Araranguá
Torres
Caxias do Sul
Nôvo Hamburgo
São Leopoldo
Canoas
PÔRTO ALEGRE
Viamão
Osorio
Santa Maria
Santa Cruz do Sul
Passo Fundo
Erechim
Chapecó
Cruz Alta
Santo Angelo
Alegrete
Uruguaiana
Bagé
Pelotas
Rio Grande
Lagoa dos Patos
Lagoa Mirim
Lagoa Mangueira
Jaguarão
Melo
Treinta y Tres
Santa Vitória do Palmar
Chuy
Rocha
Maldonado
San Carlos
MONTEVIDEO
B R A Z I L
SÃO PAULO
PARANÁ
SANTA CATARINA
RIO GRANDE DO SUL
MATO GROSSO DO SUL
MISIONES
URUGUAY
A T L A N T I C
O C E A N
5304
West from Greenwich
A
B
C
D
5
6
7
25
30
35
40
45
50
55

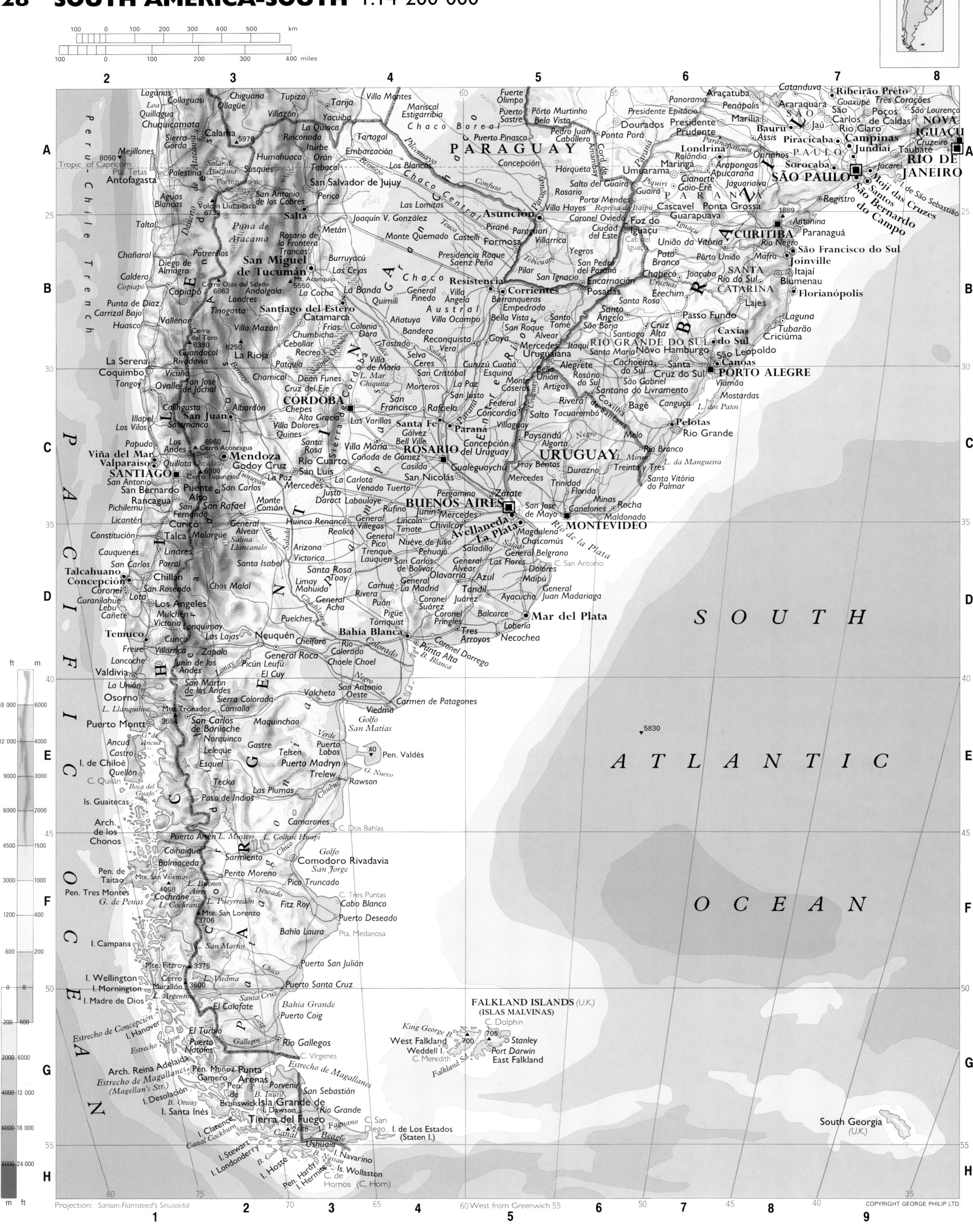
PACIFIC OCEAN
SOUTH ATLANTIC OCEAN
PARAGUAY
URUGUAY
BRAZIL
ARGENTINA
CHILE
FALKLAND ISLANDS (U.K.)
(ISLAS MALVINAS)
South Georgia (U.K.)
Peru-Chile Trench
Tropic of Capricorn
BUENOS AIRES
MONTEVIDEO
SANTIAGO
SÃO PAULO
RIO DE JANEIRO
PORTO ALEGRE
Asunción
CÓRDOBA
ROSARIO
Mendoza
Antofagasta
Tierra del Fuego
Estrecho de Magallanes
Projection: Sanson-Flamsteed's Sinusoidal
West from Greenwich
COPYRIGHT GEORGE PHILIP LTD.

INDEX

The index contains the names of all the principal places and features shown on the World Maps. Each name is followed by an additional entry in italics giving the country or region within which it is located. The alphabetical order of names composed of two or more words is governed primarily by the first word and then by the second. This is an example of the rule:

Mīr Kūh, *Iran* **71** **E8**
Mīr Shahdād, *Iran* **71** **E8**
Mira, *Italy* **29** **C9**
Mira por vos Cay, *Bahamas* . . **121** **B5**
Miraj, *India* **66** **L9**

Physical features composed of a proper name (Erie) and a description (Lake) are positioned alphabetically by the proper name. The description is positioned after the proper name and is usually abbreviated:

Erie, L., *N. Amer.* **110** **D4**

Where a description forms part of a settlement or administrative name however, it is always written in full and put in its true alphabetic position:

Mount Morris, *U.S.A.* **110** **D7**

Names beginning with M' and Mc are indexed as if they were spelled Mac. Names beginning St. are alphabetised under Saint, but Sankt, Sint, Sant', Santa and San are all spelt in full and are alphabetised accordingly. If the same place name occurs two or more times in the index and all are in the same country, each is followed by the name of the administrative subdivision in which it is located. The names are placed in the alphabetical order of the subdivisions. For example:

Jackson, *Ky., U.S.A.* **108** **G4**
Jackson, *Mich., U.S.A.* **108** **D3**
Jackson, *Minn., U.S.A.* **112** **D7**

The number in bold type which follows each name in the index refers to the number of the map page where that feature or place will be found. This is usually the largest scale at which the place or feature appears.

The letter and figure which are in bold type immediately after the page number give the grid square on the map page, within which the feature is situated. The letter represents the latitude and the figure the longitude.

In some cases the feature itself may fall within the specified square, while the name is outside. This is usually the case only with features which are larger than a grid square.

Rivers are indexed to their mouths or confluences, and carry the symbol → after their names. A solid square ■ follows the name of a country, while an open square □ refers to a first order administrative area.

ABBREVIATIONS USED IN THE INDEX

A.C.T. – Australian Capital Territory
Afghan. – Afghanistan
Ala. – Alabama
Alta. – Alberta
Amer. – America(n)
Arch. – Archipelago
Ariz. – Arizona
Ark. – Arkansas
Atl. Oc. – Atlantic Ocean
B. – Baie, Bahía, Bay, Bucht, Bugt
B.C. – British Columbia
Bangla. – Bangladesh
Barr. – Barrage
Bos.-H. – Bosnia-Herzegovina
C. – Cabo, Cap, Cape, Coast
C.A.R. – Central African Republic
C. Prov. – Cape Province
Calif. – California
Cent. – Central
Chan. – Channel
Colo. – Colorado
Conn. – Connecticut
Cord. – Cordillera
Cr. – Creek
Czech. – Czech Republic
D.C. – District of Columbia
Del. – Delaware
Dep. – Dependency
Des. – Desert
Dist. – District
Dj. – Djebel
Domin. – Dominica
Dom. Rep. – Dominican Republic
E. – East

E. Salv. – El Salvador
Eq. Guin. – Equatorial Guinea
Fla. – Florida
Falk. Is. – Falkland Is.
G. – Golfe, Golfo, Gulf, Guba, Gebel
Ga. – Georgia
Gt. – Great, Greater
Guinea-Biss. – Guinea-Bissau
H.K. – Hong Kong
H.P. – Himachal Pradesh
Hants. – Hampshire
Harb. – Harbor, Harbour
Hd. – Head
Hts. – Heights
I.(s). – Île, Ilha, Insel, Isla, Island, Isle
Ill. – Illinois
Ind. – Indiana
Ind. Oc. – Indian Ocean
Ivory C. – Ivory Coast
J. – Jabal, Jebel, Jazira
Junc. – Junction
K. – Kap, Kapp
Kans. – Kansas
Kep. – Kepulauan
Ky. – Kentucky
L. – Lac, Lacul, Lago, Lagoa, Lake, Limni, Loch, Lough
La. – Louisiana
Liech. – Liechtenstein
Lux. – Luxembourg
Mad. P. – Madhya Pradesh
Madag. – Madagascar
Man. – Manitoba
Mass. – Massachusetts

Md. – Maryland
Me. – Maine
Medit. S. – Mediterranean Sea
Mich. – Michigan
Minn. – Minnesota
Miss. – Mississippi
Mo. – Missouri
Mont. – Montana
Mozam. – Mozambique
Mt.(e) – Mont, Monte, Monti, Montaña, Mountain
N. – Nord, Norte, North, Northern, Nouveau
N.B. – New Brunswick
N.C. – North Carolina
N. Cal. – New Caledonia
N. Dak. – North Dakota
N.H. – New Hampshire
N.I. – North Island
N.J. – New Jersey
N. Mex. – New Mexico
N.S. – Nova Scotia
N.S.W. – New South Wales
N.W.T. – North West Territory
N.Y. – New York
N.Z. – New Zealand
Nebr. – Nebraska
Neths. – Netherlands
Nev. – Nevada
Nfld. – Newfoundland
Nic. – Nicaragua
O. – Oued, Ouadi
Occ. – Occidentale
Okla. – Oklahoma
Ont. – Ontario
Or. – Orientale

Oreg. – Oregon
Os. – Ostrov
Oz. – Ozero
P. – Pass, Passo, Pasul, Pulau
P.E.I. – Prince Edward Island
Pa. – Pennsylvania
Pac. Oc. – Pacific Ocean
Papua N.G. – Papua New Guinea
Pass. – Passage
Pen. – Peninsula, Péninsule
Phil. – Philippines
Pk. – Park, Peak
Plat. – Plateau
Prov. – Province, Provincial
Pt. – Point
Pta. – Ponta, Punta
Pte. – Pointe
Qué. – Québec
Queens. – Queensland
R. – Rio, River
R.I. – Rhode Island
Ra.(s). – Range(s)
Raj. – Rajasthan
Reg. – Region
Rep. – Republic
Res. – Reserve, Reservoir
S. – San, South, Sea
Si. Arabia – Saudi Arabia
S.C. – South Carolina
S. Dak. – South Dakota
S.I. – South Island
S. Leone – Sierra Leone
Sa. – Serra, Sierra
Sask. – Saskatchewan
Scot. – Scotland
Sd. – Sound

Sev. – Severnaya
Sib. – Siberia
Sprs. – Springs
St. – Saint
Sta. – Santa, Station
Ste. – Sainte
Sto. – Santo
Str. – Strait, Stretto
Switz. – Switzerland
Tas. – Tasmania
Tenn. – Tennessee
Tex. – Texas
Tg. – Tanjung
Trin. & Tob. – Trinidad & Tobago
U.A.E. – United Arab Emirates
U.K. – United Kingdom
U.S.A. – United States of America
Ut. P. – Uttar Pradesh
Va. – Virginia
Vdkhr. – Vodokhranilishche
Vf. – Vîrful
Vic. – Victoria
Vol. – Volcano
Vt. – Vermont
W. – Wadi, West
W. Va. – West Virginia
Wash. – Washington
Wis. – Wisconsin
Wlkp. – Wielkopolski
Wyo. – Wyoming
Yorks. – Yorkshire
Yug. – Yugoslavia

A Baña

A

A Baña, *Spain* 34 C2
A Cañiza, *Spain* 34 C2
A Coruña, *Spain* 34 B2
A Estrada, *Spain* 34 C2
A Fonsagrada, *Spain* 34 B3
A Guarda, *Spain* 34 D2
A Gudiña, *Spain* 34 C3
A Rúa, *Spain* 34 C3
Aachen, *Germany* 24 E2
Aalborg = Ålborg, *Denmark* 11 G3
Aalen, *Germany* 25 G6
A'âli an Nîl □, *Sudan* 81 F3
Aalst, *Belgium* 17 D4
Aalten, *Neths.* 17 C6
Aalter, *Belgium* 17 C3
Äänekoski, *Finland* 9 E21
Aarau, *Switz.* 25 H4
Aarberg, *Switz.* 25 H3
Aare →, *Switz.* 25 H4
Aargau □, *Switz.* 25 H4
Aarhus = Århus, *Denmark* 11 H4
Aarschot, *Belgium* 17 D4
Aba, *China* 58 A3
Aba,
Dem. Rep. of the Congo 86 B3
Aba, *Nigeria* 83 D6
Âbâ, Jazîrat, *Sudan* 81 E3
Abadab, J., *Sudan* 80 D4
Ābādān, *Iran* 71 D6
Abade, *Ethiopia* 81 F4
Ābādeh, *Iran* 71 D7
Abadin, *Spain* 34 B3
Abadla, *Algeria* 78 B5
Abaetetuba, *Brazil* 125 D9
Abagnar Qi, *China* 56 C9
Abai, *Paraguay* 127 B4
Abak, *Nigeria* 83 E6
Abakaliki, *Nigeria* 83 D6
Abakan, *Russia* 51 D10
Abala, *Niger* 83 C5
Abalak, *Niger* 83 B6
Abalemma, *Niger* 83 B6
Abana, *Turkey* 72 B6
Abancay, *Peru* 124 F4
Abano Terme, *Italy* 29 C8
Abarán, *Spain* 33 G3
Abariringa, *Kiribati* 96 H10
Abarqū, *Iran* 71 D7
Abashiri, *Japan* 54 C12
Abashiri-Wan, *Japan* 54 C12
Abaújszántó, *Hungary* 42 B6
Abava →, *Latvia* 44 A8
Ābay = Nîl el Azraq →,
Sudan 81 D3
Abay, *Kazakstan* 50 E8
Abaya, L., *Ethiopia* 81 F4
Abaza, *Russia* 50 D10
Abbadia San Salvatore, *Italy* 29 F8
'Abbāsābād, *Iran* 71 C8
Abbay = Nîl el Azraq →,
Sudan 81 D3
Abbaye, Pt., *U.S.A.* 108 B1
Abbé, L., *Ethiopia* 81 E5
Abbeville, *France* 19 B8
Abbeville, *Ala., U.S.A.* 109 K3
Abbeville, *La., U.S.A.* 113 L8
Abbeville, *S.C., U.S.A.* 109 H4
Abbiategrasso, *Italy* 28 C5
Abbot Ice Shelf, *Antarctica* 5 D16
Abbottabad, *Pakistan* 68 B5
Abd al Kūrī, *Ind. Oc.* 74 E5
Ābdar, *Iran* 71 D7
'Abdolābād, *Iran* 71 C8
Abdulpur, *Bangla.* 69 G13
Abéché, *Chad* 79 F10
Abejar, *Spain* 32 D2
Abekr, *Sudan* 81 E2
Abengourou, *Ivory C.* 82 D4
Abenójar, *Spain* 35 G6
Åbenrå, *Denmark* 11 J3
Abensberg, *Germany* 25 G7
Abeokuta, *Nigeria* 83 D5
Aber, *Uganda* 86 B3
Aberaeron, *U.K.* 13 E3
Aberayron = Aberaeron,
U.K. 13 E3
Aberchirder, *U.K.* 14 D6
Abercorn = Mbala, *Zambia* 87 D3
Abercorn, *Australia* 95 D5
Aberdare, *U.K.* 13 F4
Aberdare Ra., *Kenya* 86 C4
Aberdeen, *Australia* 95 E5
Aberdeen, *Canada* 105 C7
Aberdeen, *S. Africa* 88 E3
Aberdeen, *U.K.* 14 D6
Aberdeen, *Ala., U.S.A.* 109 J1
Aberdeen, *Idaho, U.S.A.* 114 E7
Aberdeen, *Md., U.S.A.* 108 F7
Aberdeen, *S. Dak., U.S.A.* 112 C5
Aberdeen, *Wash., U.S.A.* 116 D3
Aberdeen, City of □, *U.K.* 14 D6
Aberdeenshire □, *U.K.* 14 D6
Aberdovey = Aberdyfi,
U.K. 13 E3
Aberdyfi, *U.K.* 13 E3
Aberfeldy, *U.K.* 14 E5
Abergavenny, *U.K.* 13 F4
Abergele, *U.K.* 12 D4
Abernathy, *U.S.A.* 113 J4
Abert, L., *U.S.A.* 114 E3
Aberystwyth, *U.K.* 13 E3
Abhā, *Si. Arabia* 74 D3
Abhar, *Iran* 71 B6
Abhayapuri, *India* 69 F14
Abia □, *Nigeria* 83 D6
Abide, *Turkey* 39 C11
Abidiya, *Sudan* 80 D3
Abidjan, *Ivory C.* 82 D4
Abilene, *Kans., U.S.A.* 112 F6
Abilene, *Tex., U.S.A.* 113 J5
Abingdon, *U.K.* 13 F6
Abingdon, *U.S.A.* 109 G5
Abington Reef, *Australia* 94 B4
Abitau →, *Canada* 105 B7
Abitibi →, *Canada* 102 B3
Abitibi, L., *Canada* 102 C4
Abiy Adi, *Ethiopia* 81 E4
Abkhaz Republic =
Abkhazia □, *Georgia* 49 J5
Abkhazia □, *Georgia* 49 J5
Abminga, *Australia* 95 D1
Abnûb, *Egypt* 80 B3
Åbo = Turku, *Finland* 9 F20
Abocho, *Nigeria* 83 D6
Abohar, *India* 68 D6
Aboisso, *Ivory C.* 82 D4
Abomey, *Benin* 83 D5
Abong-Mbang, *Cameroon* 84 D2
Abonnema, *Nigeria* 83 E6
Abony, *Hungary* 42 C5
Aboso, *Ghana* 82 D4
Abou-Deïa, *Chad* 79 F9
Aboyne, *U.K.* 14 D6
Abra Pampa, *Argentina* 126 A2
Abraham L., *Canada* 104 C5
Abrantes, *Portugal* 35 F2
Abreojos, Pta., *Mexico* 118 B2
Abri, *Esh Shamâliya, Sudan* 80 C3
Abri, *Janub Kordofân,*
Sudan 81 E3
Abrud, *Romania* 42 D8
Abruzzo □, *Italy* 29 F10
Absaroka Range, *U.S.A.* 114 D9
Abtenau, *Austria* 26 D6
Abu, *India* 68 G5
Abū al Abyad, *U.A.E.* 71 E7
Abū al Khaṣīb, *Iraq* 71 D6
Abū 'Alī, *Si. Arabia* 71 E6
Abū 'Alī →, *Lebanon* 75 A4
Abu Ballas, *Egypt* 80 C2
Abu Deleiq, *Sudan* 81 D3
Abu Dhabi = Abū Ẓāby,
U.A.E. 71 E7
Abu Dis, *Sudan* 80 D3
Abu Dom, *Sudan* 81 D3
Abū Du'ān, *Syria* 70 B3
Abu el Gairi, W. →, *Egypt* 75 F2
Abu Fatma, Ras, *Sudan* 80 C4
Abu Gabra, *Sudan* 81 E2
Abu Ga'da, W. →, *Egypt* 75 F1
Abu Gelba, *Sudan* 81 E3
Abu Gubeiha, *Sudan* 81 E3
Abu Habl, Khawr →, *Sudan* 81 E3
Abū Ḥadrīyah, *Si. Arabia* 71 E6
Abu Hamed, *Sudan* 80 D3
Abu Haraz, *An Nîl el Azraq,*
Sudan 80 D3
Abu Haraz, *El Gezira,*
Sudan 81 E3
Abu Haraz, *Esh Shamâliya,*
Sudan 80 D3
Abu Higar, *Sudan* 81 E3
Abū Kamāl, *Syria* 70 C4
Abu Kuleiwat, *Sudan* 81 E2
Abū Madd, Ra's, *Si. Arabia* 70 E3
Abu Matariq, *Sudan* 81 E2
Abu Mendi, *Ethiopia* 81 E4
Abū Mūsā, *U.A.E.* 71 E7
Abu Qir, *Egypt* 80 H7
Abu Qireiya, *Egypt* 80 C4
Abu Qurqâs, *Egypt* 80 B3
Abu Ṣafāt, W. →, *Jordan* 75 E5
Abu Shagara, Ras, *Sudan* 80 C4
Abu Shanab, *Sudan* 81 E2
Abu Simbel, *Egypt* 80 C3
Abū Şukhayr, *Iraq* 70 D5
Abu Sultân, *Egypt* 80 H8
Abu Tabari, *Sudan* 80 D2
Abu Tig, *Egypt* 80 B3
Abu Tiga, *Sudan* 81 E3
Abu Tineitin, *Sudan* 81 E3
Abu Uruq, *Sudan* 81 D3
Abu Zabad, *Sudan* 81 E2
Abū Ẓāby, *U.A.E.* 71 E7
Abū Zeydābād, *Iran* 71 C6
Abuja, *Nigeria* 83 D6
Abukuma-Gawa →, *Japan* 54 E10
Abukuma-Sammyaku, *Japan* 54 F10
Abunã, *Brazil* 124 E5
Abunã →, *Brazil* 124 E5
Abune Yosef, *Ethiopia* 81 E4
Aburo,
Dem. Rep. of the Congo 86 B3
Abut Hd., *N.Z.* 91 K3
Abuye Meda, *Ethiopia* 81 E4
Abwong, *Sudan* 81 F3
Åby, *Sweden* 11 F10
Aby, Lagune, *Ivory C.* 82 D4
Abyad, *Sudan* 81 E2
Åbybro, *Denmark* 11 G3
Acadia National Park,
U.S.A. 109 C11
Açailândia, *Brazil* 125 D9
Acajutla, *El Salv.* 120 D2
Acámbaro, *Mexico* 118 D4
Acanthus, *Greece* 40 F7
Acaponeta, *Mexico* 118 C3
Acapulco, *Mexico* 119 D5
Acarai, Serra, *Brazil* 124 C7
Acarigua, *Venezuela* 124 B5
Acatlán, *Mexico* 119 D5
Acayucan, *Mexico* 119 D6
Accéglio, *Italy* 28 D4
Accomac, *U.S.A.* 108 G8
Accous, *France* 20 E3
Accra, *Ghana* 83 D4
Accrington, *U.K.* 12 D5
Acebal, *Argentina* 126 C3
Aceh □, *Indonesia* 62 D1
Acerra, *Italy* 31 B7
Aceuchal, *Spain* 35 G4
Achalpur, *India* 66 J10
Acheng, *China* 57 B14
Achenkirch, *Austria* 26 D4
Achensee, *Austria* 26 D4
Acher, *India* 68 H5
Achern, *Germany* 25 G4
Achill Hd., *Ireland* 15 C1
Achill I., *Ireland* 15 C1
Achim, *Germany* 24 B5
Achinsk, *Russia* 51 D10
Acıgöl, *Turkey* 39 D11
Acıpayam, *Turkey* 39 D11
Acireale, *Italy* 31 E8
Ackerman, *U.S.A.* 113 J10
Acklins I., *Bahamas* 121 B5
Acme, *Canada* 104 C6
Acme, *U.S.A.* 110 F5
Aconcagua, Cerro, *Argentina* 126 C2
Aconquija, Mt., *Argentina* 126 B2
Açores, Is. dos = Azores,
Atl. Oc. 78 A1
Acornhoek, *S. Africa* 89 C5
Acquapendente, *Italy* 29 F8
Acquasanta Terme, *Italy* 29 F10
Acquasparta, *Italy* 29 F9
Acquaviva delle Fonti, *Italy* 31 B9
Ácqui Terme, *Italy* 28 D5
Acraman, L., *Australia* 95 E2
Acre = 'Akko, *Israel* 75 C4
Acre □, *Brazil* 124 E4
Acre →, *Brazil* 124 E5
Acri, *Italy* 31 C9
Acs, *Hungary* 42 C3
Actium, *Greece* 38 C2
Acton, *Canada* 110 C4
Acuña, *Mexico* 118 B4
Ad Dammām, *Si. Arabia* 71 E6
Ad Dāmūr, *Lebanon* 75 B4
Ad Dawādimī, *Si. Arabia* 70 E5
Ad Dawḥah, *Qatar* 71 E6
Ad Dawr, *Iraq* 70 C4
Ad Dir'īyah, *Si. Arabia* 70 E5
Ad Dīwānīyah, *Iraq* 70 D5
Ad Dujayl, *Iraq* 70 C5
Ad Duwayd, *Si. Arabia* 70 D4
Ada, *Ghana* 83 D5
Ada, *Serbia, Yug.* 42 E5
Ada, *Minn., U.S.A.* 112 B6
Ada, *Okla., U.S.A.* 113 H6
Adabiya, *Egypt* 75 F1
Adair, C., *Canada* 101 A12
Adaja →, *Spain* 34 D6
Adak I., *U.S.A.* 100 C2
Adamaoua, Massif de l',
Cameroon 83 D7
Adamawa □, *Nigeria* 83 D7
Adamawa Highlands =
Adamaoua, Massif de l',
Cameroon 83 D7
Adamello, Mte., *Italy* 28 B7
Adami Tulu, *Ethiopia* 81 F4
Adaminaby, *Australia* 95 F4
Adams, *Mass., U.S.A.* 111 D11
Adams, *N.Y., U.S.A.* 111 C8
Adams, *Wis., U.S.A.* 112 D10
Adam's Bridge, *Sri Lanka* 66 Q11
Adams L., *Canada* 104 C5
Adams Mt., *U.S.A.* 116 D5
Adam's Peak, *Sri Lanka* 66 R12
Adamuz, *Spain* 35 G6
Adana, *Turkey* 70 B2
Adanero, *Spain* 34 E6
Adapazarı = Sakarya,
Turkey 72 B4
Adar Gwagwa, J., *Sudan* 80 C4
Adarama, *Sudan* 81 D3
Adare, C., *Antarctica* 5 D11
Adarte, *Eritrea* 81 E5
Adaut, *Indonesia* 63 F8
Adavale, *Australia* 95 D3
Adda →, *Italy* 28 C6
Addis Ababa = Addis
Abeba, *Ethiopia* 81 F4
Addis Abeba, *Ethiopia* 81 F4
Addis Alem, *Ethiopia* 81 F4
Addis Zemen, *Ethiopia* 81 E4
Addison, *U.S.A.* 110 D7
Addo, *S. Africa* 88 E4
Adebour, *Niger* 83 C7
Ādeh, *Iran* 70 B5
Adel, *U.S.A.* 109 K4
Adelaide, *Australia* 95 E2
Adelaide, *Bahamas* 120 A4
Adelaide, *S. Africa* 88 E4
Adelaide I., *Antarctica* 5 C17
Adelaide Pen., *Canada* 100 B10
Adelaide River, *Australia* 92 B5
Adelanto, *U.S.A.* 117 L9
Adele I., *Australia* 92 C3
Adélie, Terre, *Antarctica* 5 C10
Adélie Land = Adélie,
Terre, *Antarctica* 5 C10
Ademuz, *Spain* 32 E3
Aden = Al 'Adan, *Yemen* 74 E4
Aden, G. of, *Asia* 74 E4
Adendorp, *S. Africa* 88 E3
Aderbissinat, *Niger* 83 B6
Adh Dhayd, *U.A.E.* 71 E7
Adhoi, *India* 68 H4
Adi, *Indonesia* 63 E8
Adi Arkai, *Ethiopia* 81 E4
Adi Daro, *Ethiopia* 81 E4
Adi Keyih, *Eritrea* 81 E4
Adi Kwala, *Eritrea* 81 E4
Adi Ugri, *Eritrea* 81 E4
Adieu, C., *Australia* 93 F5
Adieu Pt., *Australia* 92 C3
Adigala, *Ethiopia* 81 E5
Adige →, *Italy* 29 C9
Adigrat, *Ethiopia* 81 E4
Adıgüzel Barajı, *Turkey* 39 C11
Adilabad, *India* 66 K11
Adilcevaz, *Turkey* 73 C10
Adin Khel, *Afghan.* 66 C6
Adirondack Mts., *U.S.A.* 111 C10
Adıyaman, *Turkey* 73 D8
Adjohon, *Benin* 83 D5
Adjud, *Romania* 43 D12
Adjumani, *Uganda* 86 B3
Adlavik Is., *Canada* 103 A8
Adler, *Russia* 49 J4
Admer, *Algeria* 83 A6
Admiralty G., *Australia* 92 B4
Admiralty I., *U.S.A.* 104 B2
Admiralty Is., *Papua N. G.* 96 H6
Ado, *Nigeria* 83 D5
Ado-Ekiti, *Nigeria* 83 D6
Adok, *Sudan* 81 F3
Adola, *Ethiopia* 81 E5
Adonara, *Indonesia* 63 F6
Adoni, *India* 66 M10
Adony, *Hungary* 42 C3
Adour →, *France* 20 E2
Adra, *India* 69 H12
Adra, *Spain* 35 J7
Adrano, *Italy* 31 E7
Adrar, *Mauritania* 78 D3
Adrar des Iforas, *Algeria* 76 D4
Ádria, *Italy* 29 C9
Adrian, *Mich., U.S.A.* 108 E3
Adrian, *Tex., U.S.A.* 113 H3
Adriatic Sea, *Medit. S.* 6 G9
Adua, *Indonesia* 63 E7
Adwa, *Ethiopia* 81 E4
Adygea □, *Russia* 49 H5
Adzhar Republic =
Ajaria □, *Georgia* 49 K6
Adzopé, *Ivory C.* 82 D4
Ægean Sea, *Medit. S.* 39 C7
Aerhtai Shan, *Mongolia* 60 B4
Ærø, *Denmark* 11 K4
Ærøskøbing, *Denmark* 11 K4
Aëtós, *Greece* 38 D3
'Afak, *Iraq* 70 C5
Afándou, *Greece* 36 C10
Afghanistan ■, *Asia* 66 C4
Afikpo, *Nigeria* 83 D6
Aflou, *Algeria* 78 B6
Afragóla, *Italy* 31 B7
Afram →, *Ghana* 83 D4
Afrera, *Ethiopia* 81 E5
Africa 76 E6
'Afrīn, *Syria* 70 B3
Afşin, *Turkey* 72 C7
Afton, *N.Y., U.S.A.* 111 D9
Afton, *Wyo., U.S.A.* 114 E8
Afuá, *Brazil* 125 D8
'Afula, *Israel* 75 C4
Afyon, *Turkey* 39 C12
Afyon □, *Turkey* 39 C12
Afyonkarahisar = Afyon,
Turkey 39 C12
Aga, *Egypt* 80 H7
Agadès = Agadez, *Niger* 83 B6
Agadez, *Niger* 83 B6
Agadir, *Morocco* 78 B4
Agaete, *Canary Is.* 37 F4
Agaie, *Nigeria* 83 D6
Again, *Sudan* 81 F2
Ağapınar, *Turkey* 39 B12
Agar, *India* 68 H7
Agaro, *Ethiopia* 81 F4
Agartala, *India* 67 H17
Agăş, *Romania* 43 D11
Agassiz, *Canada* 104 D4
Agats, *Indonesia* 63 F9
Agawam, *U.S.A.* 111 D12
Agbélouvé, *Togo* 83 D5
Agboville, *Ivory C.* 82 D4
Ağcabädi, *Azerbaijan* 49 K8
Ağdam, *Azerbaijan* 49 L8
Ağdaş, *Azerbaijan* 49 K8
Agde, *France* 20 E7
Agde, C. d', *France* 20 E7
Agdzhabedi = Ağcabädi,
Azerbaijan 49 K8
Agen, *France* 20 D4
Agerbæk, *Denmark* 11 J2
Agersø, *Denmark* 11 J5
Ageyevo, *Russia* 46 E9
Āgh Kand, *Iran* 71 B6
Aghireşu, *Romania* 43 D8
Aginskoye, *Russia* 51 D12
Ağlasun, *Turkey* 39 D12
Agly →, *France* 20 F7
Agnew, *Australia* 93 E3
Agnibilékrou, *Ivory C.* 82 D4
Agnita, *Romania* 43 E9
Agnone, *Italy* 29 G11
Agofie, *Ghana* 83 D5
Agogna →, *Italy* 28 C5
Agogo, *Sudan* 81 F2
Agön, *Sweden* 10 C11
Agon Coutainville, *France* 18 C5
Agordo, *Italy* 29 B9
Agori, *India* 69 G10
Agouna, *Benin* 83 D5
Agout →, *France* 20 E5
Agra, *India* 68 F7
Agrakhanskiuy Poluostrov,
Russia 49 J8
Agramunt, *Spain* 32 D6
Agreda, *Spain* 32 D3
Ağri, *Turkey* 73 C10
Agri →, *Italy* 31 B9
Ağrı Dağı, *Turkey* 70 B5
Agriá, *Greece* 38 B5
Agrigento, *Italy* 30 E6
Agrínion, *Greece* 38 C3
Agrópoli, *Italy* 31 B7
Ağstafa, *Azerbaijan* 49 K7
Agua Caliente, *Baja Calif.,*
Mexico 117 N10
Agua Caliente, *Sinaloa,*
Mexico 118 B3
Agua Caliente Springs,
U.S.A. 117 N10
Água Clara, *Brazil* 125 H8
Agua Hechicero, *Mexico* 117 N10
Agua Prieta, *Mexico* 118 A3
Aguadilla, *Puerto Rico* 121 C6
Aguadulce, *Panama* 120 E3
Aguanga, *U.S.A.* 117 M10
Aguanish, *Canada* 103 B7
Aguanus →, *Canada* 103 B7
Aguapey →, *Argentina* 126 B4
Aguaray Guazú →,
Paraguay 126 A4
Aguarico →, *Ecuador* 124 D3
Aguas →, *Spain* 32 D4
Aguas Blancas, *Chile* 126 A2
Aguas Calientes, Sierra de,
Argentina 126 B2
Aguascalientes, *Mexico* 118 C4
Aguascalientes □, *Mexico* 118 C4
Agudo, *Spain* 35 G6
Águeda, *Portugal* 34 E2
Agueda →, *Spain* 34 D4
Aguelhok, *Mali* 83 B5
Aguié, *Niger* 83 C6
Aguilafuente, *Spain* 34 D6
Aguilar, *Spain* 35 H6
Aguilar de Campóo, *Spain* 34 C6
Aguilares, *Argentina* 126 B2
Águilas, *Spain* 33 H3
Agüimes, *Canary Is.* 37 G4
Aguja, C. de la, *Colombia* 122 B3
Agulaa, *Ethiopia* 81 E4
Agulhas, C., *S. Africa* 88 E3
Agulo, *Canary Is.* 37 F2
Agung, *Indonesia* 62 F5
Agur, *Uganda* 86 B3
Agusan →, *Phil.* 61 G6
Ağva, *Turkey* 41 E13
Agvali, *Russia* 49 J8
Aha Mts., *Botswana* 88 B3
Ahaggar, *Algeria* 78 D7
Ahamansu, *Ghana* 83 D5
Ahar, *Iran* 70 B5
Ahat, *Turkey* 39 C11
Ahaus, *Germany* 24 C2
Ahipara B., *N.Z.* 91 F4
Ahir Dağı, *Turkey* 39 C12
Ahiri, *India* 66 K12
Ahlat, *Turkey* 73 C10
Ahlen, *Germany* 24 D3
Ahmad Wal, *Pakistan* 68 E1
Ahmadabad, *India* 68 H5
Aḥmadābād, *Khorāsān, Iran* 71 C9
Aḥmadābād, *Khorāsān, Iran* 71 C8
Aḥmadī, *Iran* 71 E8
Ahmadnagar, *India* 66 K9
Ahmadpur, *Pakistan* 68 E4
Ahmadpur Lamma, *Pakistan* 68 E4
Ahmar, *Ethiopia* 81 F5
Ahmedabad = Ahmadabad,
India 68 H5
Ahmednagar =
Ahmadnagar, *India* 66 K9
Ahmetbey, *Turkey* 41 E11
Ahmetler, *Turkey* 39 C11
Ahmetli, *Turkey* 39 C9
Ahoada, *Nigeria* 83 D6
Ahome, *Mexico* 118 B3
Ahoskie, *U.S.A.* 109 G7
Ahr →, *Germany* 24 E3
Ahram, *Iran* 71 D6
Ahrax Pt., *Malta* 36 D1
Ahrensbök, *Germany* 24 A6
Ahrensburg, *Germany* 24 B6
Āhū, *Iran* 71 C6
Ahuachapán, *El Salv.* 120 D2
Ahun, *France* 19 F9
Åhus, *Sweden* 11 J8
Ahvāz, *Iran* 71 D6
Ahvenanmaa = Åland,
Finland 9 F19
Aḥwar, *Yemen* 74 E4
Ahzar →, *Mali* 83 B5
Ai →, *India* 69 F14
Ai-Ais, *Namibia* 88 D2
Aichach, *Germany* 25 G7
Aichi □, *Japan* 55 G8
Aigle, *Switz.* 25 J2
Aignay-le-Duc, *France* 19 E11
Aigoual, Mt., *France* 20 D7
Aigre, *France* 20 C4
Aigua, *Uruguay* 127 C5
Aigueperse, *France* 19 F10
Aigues →, *France* 21 D8
Aigues-Mortes, *France* 21 E8
Aigues-Mortes, G. d', *France* 21 E8
Aiguilles, *France* 21 D10
Aiguillon, *France* 20 D4
Aigurande, *France* 19 F8
Aihui, *China* 60 A7
Aija, *Peru* 124 E3
Aikawa, *Japan* 54 E9
Aiken, *U.S.A.* 109 J5
Ailao Shan, *China* 58 F3
Aileron, *Australia* 94 C1
Aillant-sur-Tholon, *France* 19 E10
Aillik, *Canada* 103 A8
Ailsa Craig, *U.K.* 14 F3
'Ailūn, *Jordan* 75 C4
Aim, *Russia* 51 D14
Aimere, *Indonesia* 63 F6
Aimogasta, *Argentina* 126 B2
Ain □, *France* 19 F12
Ain →, *France* 21 C9
Aïn Ben Tili, *Mauritania* 78 C4

Aleutian Trench

Ain Dalla, *Egypt* 80 B2
Ain el Mafki, *Egypt* 80 B2
Ain Girba, *Egypt* 80 B2
Ain Murr, *Sudan* 80 C2
Ain Qeiqab, *Egypt* 80 B1
Aïn-Sefra, *Algeria* 78 B5
Ain Sheikh Murzûk, *Egypt* 80 B2
Ain Sudr, *Egypt* 75 F2
Ain Sukhna, *Egypt* 80 J8
Ain Zeitûn, *Egypt* 80 B2
Ainaži, *Latvia* 9 H21
Aínos Óros, *Greece* 38 C2
Ainsworth, *U.S.A.* 112 D5
Aiquile, *Bolivia* 124 G5
Aïr, *Niger* 83 B6
Air Force I., *Canada* 101 B12
Air Hitam, *Malaysia* 65 M4
Airaines, *France* 19 C8
Airdrie, *Canada* 104 C6
Airdrie, *U.K.* 14 F5
Aire →, *France* 19 C11
Aire →, *U.K.* 12 D7
Aire, I. de l', *Spain* 37 B11
Aire-sur-la-Lys, *France* 19 B9
Aire-sur-l'Adour, *France* 20 E3
Airlie Beach, *Australia* 94 C4
Airvault, *France* 18 F6
Aisch →, *Germany* 25 F6
Aisne □, *France* 19 C10
Aisne →, *France* 19 C9
Ait, *India* 69 G8
Aitana, Sierra de, *Spain* 33 G4
Aitkin, *U.S.A.* 112 B8
Aitolía Kai Akarnanía □, *Greece* 38 C3
Aitolikón, *Greece* 38 C3
Aiud, *Romania* 43 D8
Aix-en-Provence, *France* 21 E9
Aix-la-Chapelle = Aachen, *Germany* 24 E2
Aix-les-Bains, *France* 21 C9
Aixe-sur-Vienne, *France* 20 C5
Áíyina, *Greece* 38 D5
Aiyínion, *Greece* 40 F6
Aíyion, *Greece* 38 C4
Aizawl, *India* 67 H18
Aizenay, *France* 18 F5
Aizkraukle, *Latvia* 9 H21
Aizpute, *Latvia* 9 H19
Aizuwakamatsu, *Japan* 54 F9
Ajaccio, *France* 21 G12
Ajaccio, G. d', *France* 21 G12
Ajaigarh, *India* 69 G9
Ajalpan, *Mexico* 119 D5
Ajanta Ra., *India* 66 J9
Ajari Rep. = Ajaria □, *Georgia* 49 K6
Ajaria □, *Georgia* 49 K6
Ajax, *Canada* 110 C5
Ajdâbiyah, *Libya* 79 B10
Ajdovščina, *Slovenia* 29 C10
Ajibar, *Ethiopia* 81 E4
Ajka, *Hungary* 42 C2
'Ajmān, *U.A.E.* 71 E7
Ajmer, *India* 68 F6
Ajnala, *India* 68 D6
Ajo, *U.S.A.* 115 K7
Ajo, C. de, *Spain* 34 B7
Ajok, *Sudan* 81 F2
Ajuy, *Phil.* 61 F5
Ak Dağ, *Turkey* 39 E11
Ak Dağları, *Muğla, Turkey* 39 E11
Ak Dağları, *Sivas, Turkey* 72 C7
Akaba, *Togo* 83 D5
Akabira, *Japan* 54 C11
Akaki Beseka, *Ethiopia* 81 F4
Akala, *Sudan* 81 D4
Akamas □, *Cyprus* 36 D11
Akanthou, *Cyprus* 36 D12
Akarca, *Turkey* 39 C11
Akaroa, *N.Z.* 91 K4
Akasha, *Sudan* 80 C3
Akashi, *Japan* 55 G7
Akbarpur, *Bihar, India* 69 G10
Akbarpur, *Ut. P., India* 69 F10
Akçaabat, *Turkey* 73 B8
Akçadağ, *Turkey* 72 C7
Akçakale, *Turkey* 73 D8
Akçakoca, *Turkey* 72 B4
Akçaova, *Turkey* 41 E13
Akçay, *Turkey* 39 E11
Akçay →, *Turkey* 39 D10
Akdağ, *Turkey* 39 C8
Akdağmadeni, *Turkey* 72 C6
Akelamo, *Indonesia* 63 D7
Åkers styckebruk, *Sweden* 10 E11
Åkersberga, *Sweden* 10 E12
Aketi, *Dem. Rep. of the Congo* 84 D4
Akhaïa □, *Greece* 38 C3
Akhalkalaki, *Georgia* 49 K6
Akhaltsikhe, *Georgia* 49 K6
Akharnaí, *Greece* 38 C5
Akhelóös →, *Greece* 38 C3
Akhendriá, *Greece* 39 G7
Akhisar, *Turkey* 39 C9
Akhladhókambos, *Greece* 38 D4
Akhmîm, *Egypt* 80 B3
Akhnur, *India* 69 C6
Akhtopol, *Bulgaria* 41 D11
Akhtuba →, *Russia* 49 G8
Akhtubinsk, *Russia* 49 F8
Akhty, *Russia* 49 K8
Akhtyrka = Okhtyrka, *Ukraine* 47 G8
Aki, *Japan* 55 H6
Akimiski I., *Canada* 102 B3
Akimovka, *Ukraine* 47 J8
Åkirkeby, *Denmark* 11 J8
Akita, *Japan* 54 E10
Akita □, *Japan* 54 E10
Akjoujt, *Mauritania* 82 B2
Akka, *Mali* 82 B4
Akkaya Tepesi, *Turkey* 39 D11
Akkeshi, *Japan* 54 C12
'Akko, *Israel* 75 C4
Akköy, *Turkey* 39 D9
Aklampa, *Benin* 83 D5
Aklavik, *Canada* 100 B6
Aklera, *India* 68 G7
Akmenė, *Lithuania* 44 B9
Akmenrags, *Latvia* 44 B8
Akmolinsk = Astana, *Kazakstan* 50 D8
Akmonte = Almonte, *Spain* 35 H4
Akō, *Japan* 55 G7
Ako, *Nigeria* 83 C7
Akôbô, *Sudan* 81 F3
Akobo →, *Ethiopia* 81 F3
Akola, *India* 66 J10
Akonolinga, *Cameroon* 83 E7
Akor, *Mali* 82 C3
Akordat, *Eritrea* 81 D4
Akosombo Dam, *Ghana* 83 D5
Akot, *Sudan* 81 F3
Akoupé, *Ivory C.* 82 D4
Akpatok I., *Canada* 101 B13
Åkrahamn, *Norway* 9 G11
Akranes, *Iceland* 8 D2
Akreïjit, *Mauritania* 82 B3
Akrítas Venétiko, Ákra, *Greece* 38 E3
Akron, *Colo., U.S.A.* 112 E3
Akron, *Ohio, U.S.A.* 110 E3
Akrotiri, *Cyprus* 36 E11
Akrotíri, Ákra, *Greece* 41 F9
Akrotiri Bay, *Cyprus* 36 E12
Aksai Chin, *India* 69 B8
Aksaray, *Turkey* 70 B2
Aksay, *Kazakstan* 50 D6
Akşehir, *Turkey* 70 B1
Akşehir Gölü, *Turkey* 72 C4
Akstafa = Ağstafa, *Azerbaijan* 49 K7
Aksu, *China* 60 B3
Aksu →, *Turkey* 72 D4
Aksum, *Ethiopia* 81 E4
Aktash, *Russia* 48 C11
Aktogay, *Kazakstan* 50 E8
Aktsyabrski, *Belarus* 47 F5
Aktyubinsk = Aqtöbe, *Kazakstan* 50 D6
Aku, *Nigeria* 83 D6
Akure, *Nigeria* 83 D6
Akureyri, *Iceland* 8 D4
Akuseki-Shima, *Japan* 55 K4
Akusha, *Russia* 49 J8
Akwa-Ibom □, *Nigeria* 83 E6
Akyab = Sittwe, *Burma* 67 J18
Akyazı, *Turkey* 72 B4
Al 'Adan, *Yemen* 74 E4
Al Aḩsā = Hasa □, *Si. Arabia* 71 E6
Al Ajfar, *Si. Arabia* 70 E4
Al Amādīyah, *Iraq* 70 B4
Al 'Amārah, *Iraq* 70 D5
Al 'Aqabah, *Jordan* 75 F4
Al Arak, *Syria* 70 C3
Al 'Aramah, *Si. Arabia* 70 E5
Al Arṭāwīyah, *Si. Arabia* 70 E5
Al 'Āṣimah = 'Ammān □, *Jordan* 75 D5
Al 'Assāfīyah, *Si. Arabia* 70 D3
Al 'Ayn, *Oman* 71 E7
Al 'Ayn, *Si. Arabia* 70 E3
Al 'Aẓamīyah, *Iraq* 70 C5
Al 'Azīzīyah, *Iraq* 70 C5
Al Bāb, *Syria* 70 B3
Al Bad', *Si. Arabia* 70 D2
Al Bādī, *Iraq* 70 C4
Al Baḩrah, *Kuwait* 70 D5
Al Baḩral Mayyit = Dead Sea, *Asia* 75 D4
Al Balqā' □, *Jordan* 75 C4
Al Bārūk, J., *Lebanon* 75 B4
Al Başrah, *Iraq* 70 D5
Al Baṭḩā, *Iraq* 70 D5
Al Batrūn, *Lebanon* 75 A4
Al Bayḑā, *Libya* 79 B10
Al Biqā, *Lebanon* 75 A5
Al Bi'r, *Si. Arabia* 70 D3
Al Burayj, *Syria* 75 A5
Al Faḑilī, *Si. Arabia* 71 E6
Al Fallūjah, *Iraq* 70 C4
Al Fāw, *Iraq* 71 D6
Al Fujayrah, *U.A.E.* 71 E8
Al Ghadaf, W. →, *Jordan* 75 D5
Al Ghammās, *Iraq* 70 D5
Al Ghazālah, *Si. Arabia* 70 E4
Al Ḩābah, *Si. Arabia* 70 E5
Al Ḩadīthah, *Iraq* 70 C4
Al Ḩadīthah, *Si. Arabia* 75 D6
Al Ḩaḑr, *Iraq* 70 C4
Al Ḩājānah, *Syria* 75 B5
Al Hajar al Gharbi, *Oman* 71 E8
Al Hāmad, *Si. Arabia* 70 D3
Al Hamdānīyah, *Syria* 70 C3
Al Ḩamīdīyah, *Syria* 75 A4
Al Ḩammār, *Iraq* 70 D5
Al Ḩamrā', *Si. Arabia* 70 E3
Al Ḩanākīyah, *Si. Arabia* 70 E4
Al Harīr, W. →, *Syria* 75 C4
Al Ḩasā, W. →, *Jordan* 75 D4
Al Ḩasakah, *Syria* 70 B4
Al Haydān, W. →, *Jordan* 75 D4
Al Ḩayy, *Iraq* 70 C5
Al Ḩijarah, *Asia* 70 D4
Al Ḩillah, *Iraq* 70 C5
Al Hindīyah, *Iraq* 70 C5
Al Hirmil, *Lebanon* 75 A5
Al Hoceïma, *Morocco* 78 A5
Al Ḩudaydah, *Yemen* 74 E3
Al Hufūf, *Si. Arabia* 71 E6
Al Ḩumayḑah, *Si. Arabia* 70 D2
Al Ḩunayy, *Si. Arabia* 71 E6
Al Īsāwīyah, *Si. Arabia* 70 D3
Al Jafr, *Jordan* 75 E5
Al Jāfūrah, *Si. Arabia* 71 E7
Al Jaghbūb, *Libya* 79 C10
Al Jahrah, *Kuwait* 70 D5
Al Jalāmīd, *Si. Arabia* 70 D3
Al Jamalīyah, *Qatar* 71 E6
Al Janūb □, *Lebanon* 75 B4
Al Jawf, *Libya* 79 D10
Al Jawf, *Si. Arabia* 70 D3
Al Jazirah, *Iraq* 70 C5
Al Jithāmīyah, *Si. Arabia* 70 E4
Al Jubayl, *Si. Arabia* 71 E6
Al Jubaylah, *Si. Arabia* 70 E5
Al Jubb, *Si. Arabia* 70 E4
Al Junaynah, *Sudan* 79 F10
Al Kabā'ish, *Iraq* 70 D5
Al Karak, *Jordan* 75 D4
Al Karak □, *Jordan* 75 E5
Al Kāẓim Tyah, *Iraq* 70 C5
Al Khābūra, *Oman* 71 F8
Al Khafji, *Si. Arabia* 71 E6
Al Khalīl, *West Bank* 75 D4
Al Khāliş, *Iraq* 70 C5
Al Kharsānīyah, *Si. Arabia* 71 E6
Al Khaşab, *Oman* 71 E8
Al Khawr, *Qatar* 71 E6
Al Khiḑr, *Iraq* 70 D5
Al Khiyām, *Lebanon* 75 B4
Al Khums, *Libya* 79 B8
Al Kiswah, *Syria* 75 B5
Al Kūfah, *Iraq* 70 C5
Al Kufrah, *Libya* 79 D10
Al Kuhayfīyah, *Si. Arabia* 70 E4
Al Kūt, *Iraq* 70 C5
Al Kuwayt, *Kuwait* 70 D5
Al Labwah, *Lebanon* 75 A5
Al Lādhiqīyah, *Syria* 70 C2
Al Līth, *Si. Arabia* 74 C3
Al Liwā', *Oman* 71 E8
Al Luḩayyah, *Yemen* 74 D3
Al Madīnah, *Iraq* 70 D5
Al Madīnah, *Si. Arabia* 70 E3
Al Mafraq, *Jordan* 75 C5
Al Maḩmūdīyah, *Iraq* 70 C5
Al Majma'ah, *Si. Arabia* 70 E5
Al Makhruq, W. →, *Jordan* 75 D6
Al Makḩūl, *Si. Arabia* 70 E4
Al Manāmah, *Bahrain* 71 E6
Al Maqwa', *Kuwait* 70 D5
Al Marj, *Libya* 79 B10
Al Maţlā, *Kuwait* 70 D5
Al Mawjib, W. →, *Jordan* 75 D4
Al Mawşil, *Iraq* 70 B4
Al Mayādin, *Syria* 70 C4
Al Mazār, *Jordan* 75 D4
Al Midhnab, *Si. Arabia* 70 E5
Al Minā', *Lebanon* 75 A4
Al Miqdādīyah, *Iraq* 70 C5
Al Mubarraz, *Si. Arabia* 71 E6
Al Mudawwarah, *Jordan* 75 F5
Al Mughayrā', *U.A.E.* 71 E7
Al Muḩarraq, *Bahrain* 71 E6
Al Mukallā, *Yemen* 74 E4
Al Mukhā, *Yemen* 74 E3
Al Musayjīd, *Si. Arabia* 70 E3
Al Musayyib, *Iraq* 70 C5
Al Muwayh, *Si. Arabia* 80 C5
Al Muwayliḩ, *Si. Arabia* 70 E2
Al Owuho = Otukpa, *Nigeria* 83 D6
Al Qā'im, *Iraq* 70 C4
Al Qalībah, *Si. Arabia* 70 D3
Al Qāmishlī, *Syria* 70 B4
Al Qaryatayn, *Syria* 75 A6
Al Qaşīm, *Si. Arabia* 70 E4
Al Qaṭ'ā, *Syria* 70 C4
Al Qaṭīf, *Si. Arabia* 71 E6
Al Qaṭrānah, *Jordan* 75 D5
Al Qaṭrūn, *Libya* 79 D9
Al Qayşūmah, *Si. Arabia* 70 D5
Al Quds = Jerusalem, *Israel* 75 D4
Al Qunayṭirah, *Syria* 75 C4
Al Qunfudhah, *Si. Arabia* 80 D5
Al Qurnah, *Iraq* 70 D5
Al Quşayr, *Iraq* 70 D5
Al Quşayr, *Syria* 75 A5
Al Qutayfah, *Syria* 75 B5
Al 'Ubaylah, *Si. Arabia* 74 C5
Al 'Uḑaylīyah, *Si. Arabia* 71 E6
Al 'Ulā, *Si. Arabia* 70 E3
Al 'Uqayr, *Si. Arabia* 71 E6
Al 'Uthmānīyah, *Si. Arabia* 71 E6
Al 'Uwaynid, *Si. Arabia* 70 E5
Al 'Uwayqīlah, *Si. Arabia* 70 D4
Al 'Uyūn, *Ḩijāz, Si. Arabia* 70 E3
Al 'Uyūn, *Najd, Si. Arabia* 70 E4
Al 'Uzayr, *Iraq* 70 D5
Al Wajh, *Si. Arabia* 70 E3
Al Wakrah, *Qatar* 71 E6
Al Wannān, *Si. Arabia* 71 E6
Al Waqbah, *Si. Arabia* 70 D5
Al Wari'āh, *Si. Arabia* 70 E5
Al Wusayl, *Qatar* 71 E6
Ala, *Italy* 28 C8
Ala Dağ, *Turkey* 70 B2
Ala Dağları, *Turkey* 73 C10
Alabama □, *U.S.A.* 109 J2
Alabama →, *U.S.A.* 109 K2
Alabaster, *U.S.A.* 109 J2
Alaca, *Turkey* 72 B6
Alacaatlı, *Turkey* 39 B10
Alaçam, *Turkey* 72 B6
Alaçam Dağları, *Turkey* 39 B10
Alaçatı, *Turkey* 39 C8
Alachua, *U.S.A.* 109 L4
Alaejos, *Spain* 34 D5
Alaérma, *Greece* 36 C9
Alagir, *Russia* 49 J7
Alagna Valsésia, *Italy* 28 C4
Alagoa Grande, *Brazil* 125 E11
Alagoas □, *Brazil* 125 E11
Alagoinhas, *Brazil* 125 F11
Alagón, *Spain* 32 D3
Alagón →, *Spain* 34 F4
Alaior, *Spain* 37 B11
Alajero, *Canary Is.* 37 F2
Alajuela, *Costa Rica* 120 D3
Alakamisy, *Madag.* 89 C8
Alaknanda →, *India* 69 D8
Alamarvdasht, *Iran* 71 E7
Alamata, *Ethiopia* 81 E4
Alameda, *Calif., U.S.A.* 116 H4
Alameda, *N. Mex., U.S.A.* 115 J10
Alaminos, *Phil.* 61 C3
Alamo, *U.S.A.* 117 J11
Alamo Crossing, *U.S.A.* 117 L13
Alamogordo, *U.S.A.* 115 K11
Alamos, *Mexico* 118 B3
Alamosa, *U.S.A.* 115 H11
Åland, *Finland* 9 F19
Alandroal, *Portugal* 35 G3
Ålands hav, *Sweden* 9 F18
Alandur, *India* 66 N12
Alange, Presa de, *Spain* 35 G4
Alania = North Ossetia □, *Russia* 49 J7
Alanís, *Spain* 35 G5
Alanya, *Turkey* 70 B1
Alaotra, Farihin', *Madag.* 89 B8
Alapayevsk, *Russia* 50 D7
Alar del Rey, *Spain* 34 C6
Alaraz, *Spain* 34 E5
Alarcón, Embalse de, *Spain* 32 F2
Alarobia-Vohiposa, *Madag.* 89 C8
Alaşehir, *Turkey* 39 C10
Alaska □, *U.S.A.* 100 B5
Alaska, G. of, *Pac. Oc.* 100 C5
Alaska Peninsula, *U.S.A.* 100 C4
Alaska Range, *U.S.A.* 100 B4
Alássio, *Italy* 28 E5
Älät, *Azerbaijan* 49 L9
Alatri, *Italy* 29 G10
Alatyr, *Russia* 48 C8
Alatyr →, *Russia* 48 C8
Alausi, *Ecuador* 124 D3
Álava □, *Spain* 32 C2
Alava, C., *U.S.A.* 114 B1
Alaverdi, *Armenia* 49 K7
Alavus, *Finland* 9 E20
Alawoona, *Australia* 95 E3
'Alayh, *Lebanon* 75 B4
Alazani →, *Azerbaijan* 49 K8
Alba, *Italy* 28 D5
Alba □, *Romania* 43 D8
Alba Adriática, *Italy* 29 F10
Alba de Tormes, *Spain* 34 E5
Alba-Iulia, *Romania* 43 D8
Albac, *Romania* 42 D7
Albacete, *Spain* 33 F3
Albacete □, *Spain* 33 G3
Albacutya, L., *Australia* 95 F3
Ålbæk, *Denmark* 11 G4
Ålbæk Bugt, *Denmark* 11 G4
Albaida, *Spain* 33 G4
Albalate de las Nogueras, *Spain* 32 E2
Albalate del Arzobispo, *Spain* 32 D4
Alban, *France* 20 E6
Albanel, L., *Canada* 102 B5
Albania ■, *Europe* 40 E4
Albano Laziale, *Italy* 29 G9
Albany, *Australia* 93 G2
Albany, *Ga., U.S.A.* 109 K3
Albany, *N.Y., U.S.A.* 111 D11
Albany, *Oreg., U.S.A.* 114 D2
Albany, *Tex., U.S.A.* 113 J5
Albany →, *Canada* 102 B3
Albardón, *Argentina* 126 C2
Albarracín, *Spain* 32 E3
Albarracín, Sierra de, *Spain* 32 E3
Albatera, *Spain* 33 G4
Albatross B., *Australia* 94 A3
Albegna →, *Italy* 29 F8
Albemarle, *U.S.A.* 109 H5
Albemarle Sd., *U.S.A.* 109 H7
Albenga, *Italy* 28 D5
Alberche →, *Spain* 34 F6
Alberdi, *Paraguay* 126 B4
Alberes, Mts., *France* 20 F6
Ålberga, *Sweden* 11 F10
Albersdorf, *Germany* 24 A5
Albert, *France* 19 C9
Albert, L., *Australia* 95 F2
Albert Edward Ra., *Australia* 92 C4
Albert L., *Africa* 86 B3
Albert Lea, *U.S.A.* 112 D8
Albert Nile →, *Uganda* 86 B3
Albert Town, *Bahamas* 121 B5
Alberta □, *Canada* 104 C6
Alberti, *Argentina* 126 D3
Albertinia, *S. Africa* 88 E3
Albertirsa, *Hungary* 42 C4
Alberton, *Canada* 103 C7
Albertville = Kalemie, *Dem. Rep. of the Congo* 86 D2
Albertville, *France* 21 C10
Albertville, *U.S.A.* 109 H2
Albi, *France* 20 E6
Albia, *U.S.A.* 112 E8
Albina, *Surinam* 125 B8
Albina, Ponta, *Angola* 88 B1
Albino, *Italy* 28 C6
Albion, *Mich., U.S.A.* 108 D3
Albion, *Nebr., U.S.A.* 112 E6
Albion, *Pa., U.S.A.* 110 E4
Albocácer, *Spain* 32 E5
Albolote, *Spain* 35 H7
Alborán, *Medit. S.* 35 K7
Alborea, *Spain* 33 F3
Ålborg, *Denmark* 11 G3
Ålborg Bugt, *Denmark* 11 H4
Alborz, Reshteh-ye Kūhhā-ye, *Iran* 71 C7
Albox, *Spain* 33 H2
Albufeira, *Portugal* 35 H2
Albula →, *Switz.* 25 J5
Albuñol, *Spain* 35 J7
Albuquerque, *U.S.A.* 115 J10
Albuquerque, Cayos de, *Caribbean* 120 D3
Alburg, *U.S.A.* 111 B11
Alburno, Mte., *Italy* 31 B8
Alburquerque, *Spain* 35 F4
Albury-Wodonga, *Australia* 95 F4
Alcácer do Sal, *Portugal* 35 G2
Alcáçovas, *Portugal* 35 G2
Alcalá de Chivert, *Spain* 32 E5
Alcalá de Guadaira, *Spain* 35 H5
Alcalá de Henares, *Spain* 34 E7
Alcalá de los Gazules, *Spain* 35 J5
Alcalá del Júcar, *Spain* 33 F3
Alcalá del Río, *Spain* 35 H5
Alcalá del Valle, *Spain* 35 J5
Alcalá la Real, *Spain* 35 H7
Álcamo, *Italy* 30 E5
Alcanadre, *Spain* 32 C2
Alcanadre →, *Spain* 32 D4
Alcanar, *Spain* 32 E5
Alcanede, *Portugal* 35 F2
Alcanena, *Portugal* 35 F2
Alcañices, *Spain* 34 D4
Alcañiz, *Spain* 32 D4
Alcântara, *Brazil* 125 D10
Alcántara, *Spain* 34 F4
Alcántara, Embalse de, *Spain* 34 F4
Alcantarilla, *Spain* 33 H3
Alcaracejos, *Spain* 35 G6
Alcaraz, *Spain* 33 G2
Alcaraz, Sierra de, *Spain* 33 G2
Alcaudete, *Spain* 35 H6
Alcázar de San Juan, *Spain* 35 F7
Alchevsk, *Ukraine* 47 H10
Alcira = Alzira, *Spain* 33 F4
Alcobaça, *Portugal* 35 F2
Alcobendas, *Spain* 34 E7
Alcolea del Pinar, *Spain* 32 D2
Alcora, *Spain* 32 E4
Alcorcón, *Spain* 34 E7
Alcoutim, *Portugal* 35 H3
Alcova, *U.S.A.* 114 E10
Alcoy, *Spain* 33 G4
Alcubierre, Sierra de, *Spain* 32 D4
Alcublas, *Spain* 32 F4
Alcúdia, *Spain* 37 B10
Alcúdia, B. d', *Spain* 37 B10
Alcudia, Sierra de la, *Spain* 35 G6
Aldabra Is., *Seychelles* 77 G8
Aldama, *Mexico* 119 C5
Aldan, *Russia* 51 D13
Aldan →, *Russia* 51 C13
Aldea, Pta. de la, *Canary Is.* 37 G4
Aldeburgh, *U.K.* 13 E9
Alder Pk., *U.S.A.* 116 K5
Alderney, *U.K.* 13 H5
Aldershot, *U.K.* 13 F7
Åled, *Sweden* 11 H6
Aledo, *U.S.A.* 112 E9
Alefa, *Ethiopia* 81 E4
Aleg, *Mauritania* 82 B2
Alegranza, *Canary Is.* 37 E6
Alegranza, I., *Canary Is.* 37 E6
Alegre, *Brazil* 127 A7
Alegrete, *Brazil* 127 B4
Aleisk, *Russia* 50 D9
Aleksandriya = Oleksandriya, *Kirovohrad, Ukraine* 47 H7
Aleksandriya = Oleksandriya, *Rivne, Ukraine* 47 G4
Aleksandriyskaya, *Russia* 49 J8
Aleksandrov, *Russia* 46 D10
Aleksandrov Gay, *Russia* 48 E9
Aleksandrovac, *Serbia, Yug.* 40 C5
Aleksandrovac, *Serbia, Yug.* 40 B5
Aleksandrovka = Oleksandrovka, *Ukraine* 47 H7
Aleksandrovo, *Bulgaria* 41 C8
Aleksandrovsk-Sakhalinskiy, *Russia* 51 D15
Aleksandrów Kujawski, *Poland* 45 F5
Aleksandrów Łódźki, *Poland* 45 G6
Alekseyevka, *Samara, Russia* 48 D10
Alekseyevka, *Voronezh, Russia* 47 G10
Aleksin, *Russia* 46 E9
Aleksinac, *Serbia, Yug.* 40 C5
Além Paraíba, *Brazil* 127 A7
Alemania, *Argentina* 126 B2
Alemania, *Chile* 126 B2
Alençon, *France* 18 D7
Alenquer, *Brazil* 125 D8
Alenuihaha Channel, *U.S.A.* 106 H17
Alépé, *Ivory C.* 82 D4
Aleppo = Ḩalab, *Syria* 70 B3
Aléria, *France* 21 F13
Alès, *France* 21 D8
Aleşd, *Romania* 42 C7
Alessándria, *Italy* 28 D5
Ålestrup, *Denmark* 11 H3
Ålesund, *Norway* 9 E12
Alet-les-Bains, *France* 20 F6
Aletschhorn, *Switz.* 25 J4
Aleutian Is., *Pac. Oc.* 100 C2
Aleutian Trench, *Pac. Oc.* 96 C10

Alexander, *U.S.A.* 112 B3
Alexander, Mt., *Australia* 93 E3
Alexander Arch., *U.S.A.* 100 C6
Alexander Bay, *S. Africa* 88 D2
Alexander City, *U.S.A.* 109 J3
Alexander I., *Antarctica* 5 C17
Alexandra, *Australia* 95 F4
Alexandra, *N.Z.* 91 L2
Alexandra Falls, *Canada* 104 A5
Alexandria = El Iskandarîya, *Egypt* 80 H7
Alexandria, *B.C., Canada* 104 C4
Alexandria, *Ont., Canada* 102 C5
Alexandria, *Romania* 43 G10
Alexandria, *S. Africa* 88 E4
Alexandria, *U.K.* 14 F4
Alexandria, *La., U.S.A.* 113 K8
Alexandria, *Minn., U.S.A.* 112 C7
Alexandria, *S. Dak., U.S.A.* 112 D6
Alexandria, *Va., U.S.A.* 108 F7
Alexandria Bay, *U.S.A.* 111 B9
Alexandrina, L., *Australia* 95 F2
Alexandroúpolis, *Greece* 41 F9
Alexis →, *Canada* 103 B8
Alexis Creek, *Canada* 104 C4
Alfabia, *Spain* 37 B9
Alfambra, *Spain* 32 E3
Alfândega da Fé, *Portugal* 34 D4
Alfaro, *Spain* 32 C3
Alfatar, *Bulgaria* 41 C11
Alfaz del Pi, *Spain* 33 G4
Alfeld, *Germany* 24 D5
Alfenas, *Brazil* 127 A6
Alfiós →, *Greece* 38 D3
Alföld, *Hungary* 42 D5
Alfonsine, *Italy* 29 D9
Alford, *Aberds., U.K.* 14 D6
Alford, *Lincs., U.K.* 12 D8
Alfred, *Maine, U.S.A.* 111 C14
Alfred, *N.Y., U.S.A.* 110 D7
Alfreton, *U.K.* 12 D6
Alfta, *Sweden* 10 C10
Alga, *Kazakstan* 50 E6
Algaida, *Spain* 37 B9
Algar, *Spain* 35 J5
Ålgård, *Norway* 9 G11
Algarinejo, *Spain* 35 H6
Algarve, *Portugal* 35 J2
Algeciras, *Spain* 35 J5
Algemesí, *Spain* 33 F4
Alger, *Algeria* 78 A6
Algeria ■, *Africa* 78 C6
Alghero, *Italy* 30 B1
Älghult, *Sweden* 11 G9
Algiers = Alger, *Algeria* 78 A6
Algoa B., *S. Africa* 88 E4
Algodonales, *Spain* 35 J5
Algodor →, *Spain* 34 F7
Algoma, *U.S.A.* 108 C2
Algona, *U.S.A.* 112 D7
Algonac, *U.S.A.* 110 D2
Algonquin Prov. Park, *Canada* 102 C4
Algorta, *Uruguay* 128 C5
Alhama de Almería, *Spain* 35 J8
Alhama de Aragón, *Spain* 32 D3
Alhama de Granada, *Spain* 35 H7
Alhama de Murcia, *Spain* 33 H3
Alhambra, *U.S.A.* 117 L8
Alhaurín el Grande, *Spain* 35 J6
Alhucemas = Al Hoceïma, *Morocco* 78 A5
'Alī al Gharbī, *Iraq* 70 C5
'Alī ash Sharqī, *Iraq* 70 C5
Äli Bayramlı, *Azerbaijan* 49 L9
'Alī Khēl, *Afghan.* 68 C3
Ali Sahîh, *Djibouti* 81 E5
Alī Shāh, *Iran* 70 B5
Ália, *Italy* 30 E6
'Alīābād, *Khorāsān, Iran* 71 C8
'Alīābād, *Kordestān, Iran* 70 C5
'Alīābād, *Yazd, Iran* 71 D7
Aliaga, *Spain* 32 E4
Aliağa, *Turkey* 39 C8
Aliákmon →, *Greece* 40 F6
Alibo, *Ethiopia* 81 F4
Alibori →, *Benin* 83 C5
Alibunar, *Serbia, Yug.* 42 E5
Alicante, *Spain* 33 G4
Alicante □, *Spain* 33 G4
Alice, *S. Africa* 88 E4
Alice, *U.S.A.* 113 M5
Alice →, *Queens., Australia* 94 C3
Alice →, *Queens., Australia* 94 B3
Alice, Punta, *Italy* 31 C10
Alice Arm, *Canada* 104 B3
Alice Springs, *Australia* 94 C1
Alicedale, *S. Africa* 88 E4
Aliceville, *U.S.A.* 109 J1
Alicudi, *Italy* 31 D7
Aliganj, *India* 69 F8
Aligarh, *Raj., India* 68 G7
Aligarh, *Ut. P., India* 68 F8
Alīgūdarz, *Iran* 71 C6
Alijó, *Portugal* 34 D3
Alimnía, *Greece* 36 C9
Alingsås, *Sweden* 11 G6
Alipur, *Pakistan* 68 E4
Alipur Duar, *India* 67 F16
Aliquippa, *U.S.A.* 110 F4
Alishan, *Taiwan* 59 F13
Aliste →, *Spain* 34 D5
Alitus = Alytus, *Lithuania* 9 J21
Alivérion, *Greece* 38 C6
Aliwal North, *S. Africa* 88 E4
Alix, *Canada* 104 C6
Aljezur, *Portugal* 35 H2
Aljustrel, *Portugal* 35 H2
Alkamari, *Niger* 83 C7
Alkmaar, *Neths.* 17 B4
All American Canal, *U.S.A.* 115 K6
Allada, *Benin* 83 D5
Allagash →, *U.S.A.* 109 B11
Allah Dad, *Pakistan* 68 G2
Allahabad, *India* 69 G9
Allan, *Canada* 105 C7
Allanche, *France* 20 C6
Allanmyo, *Burma* 67 K19
Allanridge, *S. Africa* 88 D4
Allaqi, Wadi →, *Egypt* 80 C3
Allariz, *Spain* 34 C3
Allassac, *France* 20 C5
Ålleberg, *Sweden* 11 F7
Allegany, *U.S.A.* 110 D6
Allegheny →, *U.S.A.* 110 F5
Allegheny Mts., *U.S.A.* 108 G6
Allegheny Reservoir, *U.S.A.* 110 E6
Allègre, *France* 20 C7
Allen, Bog of, *Ireland* 15 C5
Allen, L., *Ireland* 15 B3
Allendale, *U.S.A.* 109 J5
Allende, *Mexico* 118 B4
Allentown, *U.S.A.* 111 F9
Allentsteig, *Austria* 26 C8
Alleppey, *India* 66 Q10
Allepuz, *Spain* 32 E4
Aller →, *Germany* 24 C5
Alliance, *Nebr., U.S.A.* 112 D3
Alliance, *Ohio, U.S.A.* 110 F3
Allier □, *France* 19 F9
Allier →, *France* 19 F10
Alliford Bay, *Canada* 104 C2
Allinge, *Denmark* 11 J8
Alliston, *Canada* 102 D4
Alloa, *U.K.* 14 E5
Allones, *France* 18 D8
Allora, *Australia* 95 D5
Allos, *France* 21 D10
Alluitsup Paa, *Greenland* 4 C5
Alma, *Canada* 103 C5
Alma, *Ga., U.S.A.* 109 K4
Alma, *Kans., U.S.A.* 112 F6
Alma, *Mich., U.S.A.* 108 D3
Alma, *Nebr., U.S.A.* 112 E5
Alma Ata = Almaty, *Kazakstan* 50 E8
Almacelles, *Spain* 32 D5
Almada, *Portugal* 35 G1
Almaden, *Australia* 94 B3
Almadén, *Spain* 35 G6
Almanor, L., *U.S.A.* 114 F3
Almansa, *Spain* 33 G3
Almanza, *Spain* 34 C5
Almanzor, Pico, *Spain* 34 E5
Almanzora →, *Spain* 33 H3
Almaş, Munţii, *Romania* 42 F7
Almassora, *Spain* 32 F4
Almaty, *Kazakstan* 50 E8
Almazán, *Spain* 32 D2
Almeirim, *Brazil* 125 D8
Almeirim, *Portugal* 35 F2
Almelo, *Neths.* 17 B6
Almenar de Soria, *Spain* 32 D2
Almenara, *Spain* 32 F4
Almenara, Sierra de la, *Spain* 33 H3
Almendra, Embalse de, *Spain* 34 D4
Almendralejo, *Spain* 35 G4
Almere-Stad, *Neths.* 17 B5
Almería, *Spain* 35 J8
Almería □, *Spain* 33 H2
Almería, G. de, *Spain* 33 J2
Almetyevsk, *Russia* 48 C11
Älmhult, *Sweden* 11 H8
Almirante, *Panama* 120 E3
Almiropótamos, *Greece* 38 C6
Almirós, *Greece* 38 B4
Almiroú, Kólpos, *Greece* 36 D6
Almodôvar, *Portugal* 35 H2
Almodóvar del Campo, *Spain* 35 G6
Almodóvar del Río, *Spain* 35 H5
Almond, *U.S.A.* 110 D7
Almont, *U.S.A.* 110 D1
Almonte, *Canada* 111 A8
Almonte, *Spain* 35 H4
Almora, *India* 69 E8
Almoradí, *Spain* 33 G4
Almorox, *Spain* 34 E6
Almoustarat, *Mali* 83 B5
Älmsta, *Sweden* 10 E12
Almudévar, *Spain* 32 C4
Almuñécar, *Spain* 35 J7
Almunge, *Sweden* 10 E12
Almuradiel, *Spain* 35 G7
Alness, *U.K.* 14 D4
Alnmouth, *U.K.* 12 B6
Alnwick, *U.K.* 12 B6
Aloi, *Uganda* 86 B3
Alon, *Burma* 67 H19
Alor, *Indonesia* 63 F6
Alor Setar, *Malaysia* 65 J3
Álora, *Spain* 35 J6
Alosno, *Spain* 35 H3
Alot, *India* 68 H6
Aloysius, Mt., *Australia* 93 E4
Alpaugh, *U.S.A.* 116 K7
Alpedrinha, *Portugal* 34 E3
Alpena, *U.S.A.* 108 C4
Alpes-de-Haute-Provence □, *France* 21 D10
Alpes-Maritimes □, *France* 21 E11
Alpha, *Australia* 94 C4
Alphen aan den Rijn, *Neths.* 17 B4
Alpiarça, *Portugal* 35 F2
Alpine, *Ariz., U.S.A.* 115 K9
Alpine, *Calif., U.S.A.* 117 N10
Alpine, *Tex., U.S.A.* 113 K3
Alps, *Europe* 6 F7
Alpu, *Turkey* 72 C4
Alqueta, Barragem do, *Portugal* 35 G3
Alrø, *Denmark* 11 J4
Als, *Denmark* 11 K3
Alsace, *France* 19 D14
Alsask, *Canada* 105 C7
Alsasua, *Spain* 32 C2
Alsek →, *U.S.A.* 104 B1
Alsfeld, *Germany* 24 E5
Alsten, *Norway* 8 D15
Alstermo, *Sweden* 11 H9
Alston, *U.K.* 12 C5
Alta, *Norway* 8 B20
Alta, Sierra, *Spain* 32 E3
Alta Gracia, *Argentina* 126 C3
Alta Sierra, *U.S.A.* 117 K8
Altaelva →, *Norway* 8 B20
Altafjorden, *Norway* 8 A20
Altai = Aerhtai Shan, *Mongolia* 60 B4
Altamaha →, *U.S.A.* 109 K5
Altamira, *Brazil* 125 D8
Altamira, *Chile* 126 B2
Altamira, *Mexico* 119 C5
Altamira, Cuevas de, *Spain* 34 B6
Altamont, *U.S.A.* 111 D10
Altamura, *Italy* 31 B9
Altanbulag, *Mongolia* 60 A5
Altar, *Mexico* 118 A2
Altar, Desierto de, *Mexico* 118 B2
Altata, *Mexico* 118 C3
Altavista, *U.S.A.* 108 G6
Altay, *China* 60 B3
Altdorf, *Switz.* 25 J4
Alte Mellum, *Germany* 24 B4
Altea, *Spain* 33 G4
Altenberg, *Germany* 24 E9
Altenbruch, *Germany* 24 B4
Altenburg, *Germany* 24 E8
Altenkirchen, *Mecklenburg-Vorpommern, Germany* 24 A9
Altenkirchen, *Rhld-Pfz., Germany* 24 E3
Altenmarkt, *Austria* 26 D7
Alter do Chão, *Portugal* 35 F3
Altınoluk, *Turkey* 39 B8
Altınova, *Turkey* 39 B8
Altıntaş, *Turkey* 39 B12
Altınyaka, *Turkey* 39 E12
Altınyayla, *Turkey* 39 D11
Altiplano = Bolivian Plateau, *S. Amer.* 122 E4
Altkirch, *France* 19 E14
Altmark, *Germany* 24 C7
Altmühl →, *Germany* 25 G7
Altmunster, *Austria* 26 D6
Alto Adige = Trentino-Alto Adige □, *Italy* 29 B8
Alto Araguaia, *Brazil* 125 G8
Alto Cuchumatanes = Cuchumatanes, Sierra de los, *Guatemala* 120 C1
Alto del Carmen, *Chile* 126 B1
Alto del Inca, *Chile* 126 A2
Alto Ligonha, *Mozam.* 87 F4
Alto Molocue, *Mozam.* 87 F4
Alto Paraguay □, *Paraguay* 126 A4
Alto Paraná □, *Paraguay* 127 B5
Alton, *Canada* 110 C4
Alton, *U.K.* 13 F7
Alton, *Ill., U.S.A.* 112 F9
Alton, *N.H., U.S.A.* 111 C13
Altoona, *U.S.A.* 110 F6
Altötting, *Germany* 25 G8
Altstätten, *Switz.* 25 H5
Altūn Kūprī, *Iraq* 70 C5
Altun Shan, *China* 60 C3
Alturas, *U.S.A.* 114 F3
Altus, *U.S.A.* 113 H5
Alubijid, *Phil.* 61 G6
Alucra, *Turkey* 73 B8
Aluk, *Sudan* 81 F2
Alūksne, *Latvia* 9 H22
Alunda, *Sweden* 10 D12
Alunite, *U.S.A.* 117 K12
Aluoro →, *Ethiopia* 81 F3
Alupka, *Ukraine* 47 K8
Alushta, *Ukraine* 47 K8
Alusi, *Indonesia* 63 F8
Alustante, *Spain* 32 E3
Alva, *U.S.A.* 113 G5
Alvaiázere, *Portugal* 34 F2
Älvängen, *Sweden* 11 G6
Alvarado, *Mexico* 119 D5
Alvarado, *U.S.A.* 113 J6
Alvaro Obregón, Presa, *Mexico* 118 B3
Älvdalen, *Sweden* 10 C8
Alvear, *Argentina* 126 B4
Alverca, *Portugal* 35 G1
Alvesta, *Sweden* 11 H8
Alvin, *U.S.A.* 113 L7
Alvinston, *Canada* 110 D3
Alvito, *Portugal* 35 G3
Älvkarleby, *Sweden* 10 D11
Alvord Desert, *U.S.A.* 114 E4
Älvros, *Sweden* 10 B8
Älvsborgs län □, *Sweden* 11 F6
Älvsbyn, *Sweden* 8 D19
Alwar, *India* 68 F7
Alxa Zuoqi, *China* 56 E3
Alyangula, *Australia* 94 A2
Alyata = Älät, *Azerbaijan* 49 L9
Alyth, *U.K.* 14 E5
Alytus, *Lithuania* 9 J21
Alzada, *U.S.A.* 112 C2
Alzey, *Germany* 25 F4
Alzira, *Spain* 33 F4
Am-Timan, *Chad* 79 F10
Amadeus, L., *Australia* 93 D5
Amadi, *Dem. Rep. of the Congo* 86 B2
Amâdi, *Sudan* 81 F3
Amadjuak L., *Canada* 101 B12
Amadora, *Portugal* 35 G1
Amagansett, *U.S.A.* 111 F12
Amagasaki, *Japan* 55 G7
Amager, *Denmark* 11 J6
Amagunze, *Nigeria* 83 D6
Amahai, *Indonesia* 63 E7
Amakusa-Shotō, *Japan* 55 H5
Åmål, *Sweden* 10 E6
Amalfi, *Italy* 31 B7
Amaliás, *Greece* 38 D3
Amalner, *India* 66 J9
Amamapare, *Indonesia* 63 E9
Amambaí, *Brazil* 127 A4
Amambaí →, *Brazil* 127 A5
Amambay □, *Paraguay* 127 A4
Amambay, Cordillera de, *S. Amer.* 127 A4
Amami-Guntō, *Japan* 55 L4
Amami-Ō-Shima, *Japan* 55 L4
Amaná, L., *Brazil* 124 D6
Amanat →, *India* 69 G11
Amanda Park, *U.S.A.* 116 C3
Amangeldy, *Kazakstan* 50 D7
Amantea, *Italy* 31 C9
Amapá, *Brazil* 125 C8
Amapá □, *Brazil* 125 C8
Amara, *Sudan* 81 E3
Amarante, *Brazil* 125 E10
Amarante, *Portugal* 34 D2
Amaranth, *Canada* 105 C9
Amareleja, *Portugal* 35 G3
Amargosa →, *U.S.A.* 117 J10
Amargosa Range, *U.S.A.* 117 J10
Amári, *Greece* 36 D6
Amarillo, *U.S.A.* 113 H4
Amarkantak, *India* 69 H9
Amârna, Tell el', *Sudan* 80 B3
Amaro, Mte., *Italy* 29 F11
Amarpur, *India* 69 G12
Amarti, *Eritrea* 81 E5
Amarwara, *India* 69 H8
Amasra, *Turkey* 72 B5
Amassama, *Nigeria* 83 D6
Amasya, *Turkey* 72 B6
Amata, *Australia* 93 E5
Amatikulu, *S. Africa* 89 D5
Amatitlán, *Guatemala* 120 D1
Amatrice, *Italy* 29 F10
Amay, *Belgium* 17 D5
Amazon = Amazonas →, *S. Amer.* 122 D5
Amazonas □, *Brazil* 124 E6
Amazonas →, *S. Amer.* 122 D5
Amba Ferit, *Ethiopia* 81 E4
Ambah, *India* 68 F8
Ambahakily, *Madag.* 89 C7
Ambahita, *Madag.* 89 C8
Ambala, *India* 68 D7
Ambalavao, *Madag.* 89 C8
Ambanja, *Madag.* 89 A8
Ambararata, *Madag.* 89 B8
Ambarchik, *Russia* 51 C17
Ambarijeby, *Madag.* 89 A8
Ambaro, Helodranon', *Madag.* 89 A8
Ambato, *Ecuador* 124 D3
Ambato, *Madag.* 89 A8
Ambato, Sierra de, *Argentina* 126 B2
Ambato Boeny, *Madag.* 89 B8
Ambatofinandrahana, *Madag.* 89 C8
Ambatolampy, *Madag.* 89 B8
Ambatomainty, *Madag.* 89 B8
Ambatomanoina, *Madag.* 89 B8
Ambatondrazaka, *Madag.* 89 B8
Ambatosoratra, *Madag.* 89 B8
Ambelón, *Greece* 38 B4
Ambenja, *Madag.* 89 B8
Amberg, *Germany* 25 F7
Ambergris Cay, *Belize* 119 D7
Ambérieu-en-Bugey, *France* 21 C9
Amberley, *N.Z.* 91 K4
Ambert, *France* 20 C7
Ambidédi, *Mali* 82 C2
Ambikapur, *India* 69 H10
Ambikol, *Sudan* 80 C3
Ambilobé, *Madag.* 89 A8
Ambinanindrano, *Madag.* 89 C8
Ambinanitelo, *Madag.* 89 B8
Ambinda, *Madag.* 89 B8
Amble, *U.K.* 12 B6
Ambleside, *U.K.* 12 C5
Ambo, *Peru* 124 F3
Amboahangy, *Madag.* 89 C8
Ambodifototra, *Madag.* 89 B8
Ambodilazana, *Madag.* 89 B8
Ambodiriana, *Madag.* 89 B8
Ambohidratrimo, *Madag.* 89 B8
Ambohidray, *Madag.* 89 B8
Ambohimahamasina, *Madag.* 89 C8
Ambohimahasoa, *Madag.* 89 C8
Ambohimanga, *Madag.* 89 C8
Ambohimitombo, *Madag.* 89 C8
Ambohitra, *Madag.* 89 A8
Amboise, *France* 18 E8
Ambon, *Indonesia* 63 E7
Ambondro, *Madag.* 89 D8
Amboseli, L., *Kenya* 86 C4
Ambositra, *Madag.* 89 C8
Ambovombe, *Madag.* 89 D8
Amboy, *U.S.A.* 117 L11
Amboyna Cay, *S. China Sea* 62 C4
Ambridge, *U.S.A.* 110 F4
Ambriz, *Angola* 84 F2
Amchitka I., *U.S.A.* 100 C1
Amderma, *Russia* 50 C7
Amdhi, *India* 69 H9
Ameca, *Mexico* 118 C4
Ameca →, *Mexico* 118 C3
Amecameca, *Mexico* 119 D5
Ameland, *Neths.* 17 A5
Amélia, *Italy* 29 F9
Amendolara, *Italy* 31 C9
Amenia, *U.S.A.* 111 E11
American Falls, *U.S.A.* 114 E7
American Falls Reservoir, *U.S.A.* 114 E7
American Fork, *U.S.A.* 114 F8
American Highland, *Antarctica* 5 D6
American Samoa ■, *Pac. Oc.* 91 B13
Americana, *Brazil* 127 A6
Americus, *U.S.A.* 109 K3
Amersfoort, *Neths.* 17 B5
Amersfoort, *S. Africa* 89 D4
Amery Ice Shelf, *Antarctica* 5 C6
Ames, *Spain* 34 C2
Ames, *U.S.A.* 112 E8
Amesbury, *U.S.A.* 111 D14
Amet, *India* 68 G5
Amfíklia, *Greece* 38 C4
Amfilokhía, *Greece* 38 C3
Amfípolis, *Greece* 40 F7
Ámfissa, *Greece* 38 C4
Amga, *Russia* 51 C14
Amga →, *Russia* 51 C14
Amgu, *Russia* 51 E14
Amgun →, *Russia* 51 D14
Amherst, *Burma* 67 L20
Amherst, *Canada* 103 C7
Amherst, *Mass., U.S.A.* 111 D12
Amherst, *N.Y., U.S.A.* 110 D6
Amherst, *Ohio, U.S.A.* 110 E2
Amherst I., *Canada* 111 B8
Amherstburg, *Canada* 102 D3
Amiata, Mte., *Italy* 29 F8
Amidon, *U.S.A.* 112 B3
Amiens, *France* 19 C9
Amindaion, *Greece* 40 F5
Åminne, *Sweden* 11 G7
Amino, *Ethiopia* 81 G5
Aminuis, *Namibia* 88 C2
Amīrābād, *Iran* 70 C5
Amirante Is., *Seychelles* 52 K9
Amisk L., *Canada* 105 C8
Amistad, Presa de la, *Mexico* 118 B4
Amite, *U.S.A.* 113 K9
Amla, *India* 68 J8
Amlia I., *U.S.A.* 100 C2
Amlwch, *U.K.* 12 D3
Amm Adam, *Sudan* 81 D4
'Ammān, *Jordan* 75 D4
'Ammān □, *Jordan* 75 D5
Ammanford, *U.K.* 13 F4
Ammassalik = Tasiilaq, *Greenland* 4 C6
Ammerån →, *Sweden* 10 A10
Ammersee, *Germany* 25 G7
Ammon, *U.S.A.* 114 E8
Amnat Charoen, *Thailand* 64 E5
Amnura, *Bangla.* 69 G13
Amo Jiang →, *China* 58 F3
Āmol, *Iran* 71 B7
Amorgós, *Greece* 39 E7
Amory, *U.S.A.* 109 J1
Amos, *Canada* 102 C4
Åmot, *Norway* 9 G13
Åmotfors, *Sweden* 10 E6
Amoy = Xiamen, *China* 59 E12
Ampanavoana, *Madag.* 89 B9
Ampang, *Malaysia* 65 L3
Ampangalana, Lakandranon', *Madag.* 89 C8
Ampanihy, *Madag.* 89 C7
Amparafaravola, *Madag.* 89 B8
Ampasinambo, *Madag.* 89 C8
Ampasindava, Helodranon', *Madag.* 89 A8
Ampasindava, Saikanosy, *Madag.* 89 A8
Ampenan, *Indonesia* 62 F5
Amper, *Nigeria* 83 D6
Amper →, *Germany* 25 G7
Ampezzo, *Italy* 29 B9
Ampitsikinana, *Réunion* 89 A8
Ampombiantambo, *Madag.* 89 A8
Amposta, *Spain* 32 E5
Ampotaka, *Madag.* 89 D7
Ampoza, *Madag.* 89 C7
Amqui, *Canada* 103 C6
Amravati, *India* 66 J10
Amreli, *India* 68 J4
Amritsar, *India* 68 D6
Amroha, *India* 69 E8
Amrum, *Germany* 24 A4
Amsterdam, *Neths.* 17 B4
Amsterdam, *U.S.A.* 111 D10
Amsterdam, I. = Nouvelle-Amsterdam, I., *Ind. Oc.* 3 F13
Amstetten, *Austria* 26 C7
Amudarya →, *Uzbekistan* 50 E6
Amundsen Gulf, *Canada* 100 A7
Amundsen Sea, *Antarctica* 5 D15
Amungen, *Sweden* 10 C9
Amuntai, *Indonesia* 62 E5
Amur →, *Russia* 51 D15
Amur, W. →, *Sudan* 80 D3
Amurang, *Indonesia* 63 D6
Amuri Pass, *N.Z.* 91 K4
Amurrio, *Spain* 32 B1
Amursk, *Russia* 51 D14
Amusco, *Spain* 34 C6
Amvrakikós Kólpos, *Greece* 38 C2
Amvrosiyivka, *Ukraine* 47 J10
Amyderya = Amudarya →, *Uzbekistan* 50 E6

An Bien, Vietnam 65 H5
An Hoa, Vietnam 64 E7
An Nabatīyah at Tahta, Lebanon 75 B4
An Nabk, Si. Arabia 70 D3
An Nabk, Syria 75 A5
An Nabk Abū Qaşr, Si. Arabia 70 D3
An Nafūd, Si. Arabia 70 D4
An Najaf, Iraq 70 C5
An Nāşirīyah, Iraq 70 D5
An Nhon, Vietnam 64 F7
An Nîl □, Sudan 80 D3
An Nîl el Abyad □, Sudan 81 E3
An Nîl el Azraq □, Sudan 81 E3
An Nu'ayrīyah, Si. Arabia 71 E6
An Nu'mānīyah, Iraq 73 F11
An Nuwayb'ī, W. →, Si. Arabia 75 F3
An Thoi, Dao, Vietnam 65 H4
An Uaimh, Ireland 15 C5
Anabar →, Russia 51 B12
'Anabtā, West Bank 75 C4
Anaconda, U.S.A. 114 C7
Anacortes, U.S.A. 116 B4
Anacuao, Mt., Phil. 61 C4
Anadarko, U.S.A. 113 H5
Anadia, Portugal 34 E2
Anadolu, Turkey 72 C5
Anadyr, Russia 51 C18
Anadyr →, Russia 51 C18
Anadyrskiy Zaliv, Russia 51 C19
Anáfi, Greece 39 E7
Anafópoulo, Greece 39 E7
Anaga, Pta. de, Canary Is. 37 F3
Anagni, Italy 29 G10
'Ānah, Iraq 70 C4
Anaheim, U.S.A. 117 M9
Anahim Lake, Canada 104 C3
Anáhuac, Mexico 118 B4
Anakapalle, India 67 L13
Anakie, Australia 94 C4
Anaklia, Georgia 49 J5
Analalava, Madag. 89 A8
Analavoka, Madag. 89 C8
Análipsis, Greece 36 A3
Anambar →, Pakistan 68 D3
Anambas, Kepulauan, Indonesia 65 L6
Anambas Is. = Anambas, Kepulauan, Indonesia 65 L6
Anambra □, Nigeria 83 D6
Anamosa, U.S.A. 112 D9
Anamur, Turkey 70 B2
Anamur Burnu, Turkey 72 D5
Anan, Japan 55 H7
Anand, India 68 H5
Anánes, Greece 38 E6
Anantnag, India 69 C6
Ananyiv, Ukraine 47 J5
Anapa, Russia 47 K9
Anapodháris →, Greece 36 E7
Anápolis, Brazil 125 G9
Anapu →, Brazil 125 D8
Anār, Iran 71 D7
Anārak, Iran 71 C7
Anarisfjällen, Sweden 10 A7
Anas →, India 68 H5
Anatolia = Anadolu, Turkey 72 C5
Anatsogno, Madag. 89 C7
Añatuya, Argentina 126 B3
Anaunethad L., Canada 105 A8
Anbyŏn, N. Korea 57 E14
Ancares, Sierra de, Spain 34 C4
Ancaster, Canada 110 C5
Ancenis, France 18 E5
Anchor Bay, U.S.A. 116 G3
Anchorage, U.S.A. 100 B5
Anci, China 56 E9
Ancohuma, Nevada, Bolivia 122 E4
Ancón, Peru 124 F3
Ancona, Italy 29 E10
Ancud, Chile 128 E2
Ancud, G. de, Chile 128 E2
Ancy-le-Franc, France 19 E11
Andacollo, Argentina 126 D1
Andacollo, Chile 126 C1
Andaingo, Madag. 89 B8
Andalgalá, Argentina 126 B2
Åndalsnes, Norway 9 E12
Andalucía □, Spain 35 H6
Andalusia = Andalucía □, Spain 35 H6
Andalusia, U.S.A. 109 K2
Andaman Is., Ind. Oc. 52 H13
Andaman Sea, Ind. Oc. 62 B1
Andamooka Opal Fields, Australia 95 E2
Andapa, Madag. 89 A8
Andara, Namibia 88 B3
Andelot-Blancheville, France 19 D12
Andenes, Norway 8 B17
Andenne, Belgium 17 D5
Andéranboukane, Mali 83 B5
Andermatt, Switz. 25 J4
Andernach, Germany 24 E3
Andernos-les-Bains, France 20 D2
Anderslöv, Sweden 11 J7
Anderson, Alaska, U.S.A. 100 B5
Anderson, Calif., U.S.A. 114 F2
Anderson, Ind., U.S.A. 108 E3
Anderson, Mo., U.S.A. 113 G7
Anderson, S.C., U.S.A. 109 H4
Anderson →, Canada 100 B7
Anderstorp, Sweden 11 G7
Andes, U.S.A. 111 D10
Andes, Cord. de los, S. Amer. 122 F4
Andfjorden, Norway 8 B17
Andhra Pradesh □, India 66 L11
Andijon, Uzbekistan 50 E8
Andikíthira, Greece 38 F5
Andilamena, Madag. 89 B8
Andīmeshk, Iran 71 C6
Andímilos, Greece 38 E6
Andíparos, Greece 39 D7
Andípaxoi, Greece 38 B2
Andípsara, Greece 39 C7
Andírrion, Greece 38 C3
Andizhan = Andijon, Uzbekistan 50 E8
Andoain, Spain 32 B2
Andoany, Madag. 89 A8
Andong, S. Korea 57 F15
Andongwei, China 57 G10
Andoom, Australia 94 A3
Andorra, Spain 32 E4
Andorra ■, Europe 20 F5
Andorra La Vella, Andorra 20 F5
Andover, U.K. 13 F6
Andover, Maine, U.S.A. 111 B14
Andover, Mass., U.S.A. 111 D13
Andover, N.J., U.S.A. 111 F10
Andover, N.Y., U.S.A. 110 D7
Andover, Ohio, U.S.A. 110 E4
Andøya, Norway 8 B16
Andradina, Brazil 125 H8
Andrahary, Mt., Madag. 89 A8
Andramasina, Madag. 89 B8
Andranopasy, Madag. 89 C7
Andranovory, Madag. 89 C7
Andratx, Spain 37 B9
Andreanof Is., U.S.A. 100 C2
Andreapol, Russia 46 D7
Andrews, S.C., U.S.A. 109 J6
Andrews, Tex., U.S.A. 113 J3
Andreyevka, Russia 48 D10
Ándria, Italy 31 A9
Andriamena, Madag. 89 B8
Andriandampy, Madag. 89 C8
Andriba, Madag. 89 B8
Andrijevica, Montenegro, Yug. 40 D3
Andrítsaina, Greece 38 D3
Androka, Madag. 89 C7
Andropov = Rybinsk, Russia 46 C10
Ándros, Greece 38 D6
Andros I., Bahamas 120 B4
Andros Town, Bahamas 120 B4
Androscoggin →, U.S.A. 111 C14
Andrychów, Poland 45 J6
Andselv, Norway 8 B18
Andújar, Spain 35 G6
Andulo, Angola 84 G3
Aneby, Sweden 11 G8
Anegada I., Virgin Is. 121 C7
Anegada Passage, W. Indies 121 C7
Aného, Togo 83 D5
Anenni-Noi, Moldova 43 D14
Aneto, Pico de, Spain 32 C5
Anfu, China 59 D10
Ang Thong, Thailand 64 E3
Angamos, Punta, Chile 126 A1
Angara →, Russia 51 D10
Angara-Débou, Benin 83 C5
Angarab, Ethiopia 81 E4
Angarbaka, Sudan 81 F1
Angarsk, Russia 51 D11
Angas Hills, Australia 92 D4
Angaston, Australia 95 E2
Angaur I., Pac. Oc. 63 C8
Ånge, Sweden 10 B9
Ángel, Salto = Angel Falls, Venezuela 124 B6
Ángel de la Guarda, I., Mexico 118 B2
Angel Falls, Venezuela 124 B6
Angeles, Phil. 61 D4
Ängelholm, Sweden 11 H6
Angels Camp, U.S.A. 116 G6
Ängelsberg, Sweden 10 E10
Anger →, Ethiopia 81 F4
Angereb →, Ethiopia 81 E4
Ångermanälven →, Sweden 10 B11
Ångermanland, Sweden 8 E18
Angermünde, Germany 24 B9
Angers, Canada 111 A9
Angers, France 18 E6
Angerville, France 19 D9
Ängesån →, Sweden 8 C20
Angikuni L., Canada 105 A9
Angkor, Cambodia 64 F4
Anglès, Spain 32 D7
Anglesey, Isle of □, U.K. 12 D3
Anglet, France 20 E2
Angleton, U.S.A. 113 L7
Anglin →, France 20 B4
Anglisidhes, Cyprus 36 E12
Anglure, France 19 D10
Angmagssalik = Tasiilaq, Greenland 4 C6
Ango, Dem. Rep. of the Congo 86 B2
Angoche, Mozam. 87 F4
Angoche, I., Mozam. 87 F4
Angol, Chile 126 D1
Angola, Ind., U.S.A. 108 E3
Angola, N.Y., U.S.A. 110 D5
Angola ■, Africa 85 G3
Angoulême, France 20 C4
Angoumois, France 20 C4
Angra dos Reis, Brazil 127 A7
Angren, Uzbekistan 50 E8
Angtassom, Cambodia 65 G5
Angu, Dem. Rep. of the Congo 86 B1
Anguang, China 57 B12
Anguilla ■, W. Indies 121 C7
Anguo, China 56 E8
Angurugu, Australia 94 A2
Angus □, U.K. 14 E6
Angwa →, Zimbabwe 89 B5
Anhanduí →, Brazil 127 A5
Anholt, Denmark 11 H5
Anhua, China 59 C8
Anhui □, China 59 B11
Anhwei = Anhui □, China 59 B11
Anichab, Namibia 88 C1
Ánidhros, Greece 39 E7
Anié, Togo 83 D5
Animas →, U.S.A. 115 H9
Anina, Romania 42 E6
Aninoasa, Romania 43 F9
Anivorano, Madag. 89 B8
Anjalankoski, Finland 9 F22
Anjar, India 68 H4
Anji, China 59 B12
Anjidiv I., India 66 M9
Anjou, France 18 E6
Anjozorobe, Madag. 89 B8
Anju, N. Korea 57 E13
Anka, Nigeria 83 C6
Ankaboa, Tanjona, Madag. 89 C7
Ankang, China 56 H5
Ankara, Turkey 72 C5
Ankaramena, Madag. 89 C8
Ankaratra, Madag. 85 H9
Ankarsrum, Sweden 11 G10
Ankasakasa, Madag. 89 B7
Ankavandra, Madag. 89 B8
Ankazoabo, Madag. 89 C7
Ankazobe, Madag. 89 B8
Ankeny, U.S.A. 112 E8
Ankilimalinika, Madag. 89 C7
Ankilizato, Madag. 89 C8
Ankisabe, Madag. 89 B8
Anklam, Germany 24 B9
Ankober, Ethiopia 81 F4
Ankoro, Dem. Rep. of the Congo 86 D2
Ankororoka, Madag. 89 D8
Anlong, China 58 E5
Anlu, China 59 B9
Anmyŏn-do, S. Korea 57 F14
Ånn, Sweden 10 A6
Ann, C., U.S.A. 111 D14
Ann Arbor, U.S.A. 108 D4
Anna, Russia 48 E5
Anna, U.S.A. 113 G10
Annaba, Algeria 78 A7
Annaberg-Buchholz, Germany 24 E9
Annalee →, Ireland 15 B4
Annam, Vietnam 64 E7
Annamitique, Chaîne, Asia 64 D6
Annan, U.K. 14 G5
Annan →, U.K. 14 G5
Annapolis, U.S.A. 108 F7
Annapolis Royal, Canada 103 D6
Annapurna, Nepal 69 E10
Annean, L., Australia 93 E2
Anneberg, Sweden 11 G8
Annecy, France 21 C10
Annecy, Lac d', France 21 C10
Annemasse, France 19 F13
Annenskiy Most, Russia 46 B9
Anning, China 58 E4
Anniston, U.S.A. 109 J3
Annobón, Atl. Oc. 77 G4
Annonay, France 21 C8
Annot, France 21 E10
Annotto Bay, Jamaica 120 C4
Ånnsjön, Sweden 10 A6
Annville, U.S.A. 111 F8
Annweiler, Germany 25 F3
Áno Arkhánai, Greece 39 F7
Áno Porróia, Greece 40 E7
Áno Síros, Greece 38 D6
Áno Viánnos, Greece 36 D7
Anorotsangana, Madag. 89 A8
Anosibe, Madag. 89 B8
Anou Mellene, Mali 83 B5
Anoumaba, Ivory C. 82 D4
Anóyia, Greece 36 D6
Anping, Hebei, China 56 E8
Anping, Liaoning, China 57 D12
Anpu Gang, China 58 G7
Anqing, China 59 B11
Anqiu, China 57 F10
Anren, China 59 D9
Ansager, Denmark 11 J2
Ansai, China 56 F5
Ansbach, Germany 25 F6
Anseba →, Eritrea 81 D4
Ansfelden, Austria 26 C7
Anshan, China 57 D12
Anshun, China 58 D5
Ansião, Portugal 34 F2
Ansley, U.S.A. 112 E5
Ansó, Spain 32 C4
Ansoain, Spain 32 C3
Anson, U.S.A. 113 J5
Anson B., Australia 92 B5
Ansongo, Mali 83 B5
Ansonia, U.S.A. 111 E11
Anstruther, U.K. 14 E6
Ansudu, Indonesia 63 E9
Antabamba, Peru 124 F4
Antakya, Turkey 70 B3
Antalaha, Madag. 89 A9
Antalya, Turkey 72 D4
Antalya □, Turkey 39 E12
Antalya Körfezi, Turkey 72 D4
Antambohobe, Madag. 89 C8
Antanambao-Manampotsy, Madag. 89 B8
Antanambe, Madag. 89 B8
Antananarivo, Madag. 89 B8
Antananarivo □, Madag. 89 B8
Antanifotsy, Madag. 89 B8
Antanimbaribe, Madag. 89 C7
Antanimora, Madag. 89 C8
Antarctic Pen., Antarctica 5 C18
Antarctica 5 E3
Antelope, Zimbabwe 87 G2
Antequera, Paraguay 126 A4
Antequera, Spain 35 H6
Antero, Mt., U.S.A. 115 G10
Antevamena, Madag. 89 C7
Anthemoús, Greece 40 F7
Anthony, Kans., U.S.A. 113 G5
Anthony, N. Mex., U.S.A. 115 K10
Anti Atlas, Morocco 78 C4
Anti-Lebanon = Ash Sharqi, Al Jabal, Lebanon 75 B5
Antibes, France 21 E11
Antibes, C. d', France 21 E11
Anticosti, Î. d', Canada 103 C7
Antifer, C. d', France 18 C7
Antigo, U.S.A. 112 C10
Antigonish, Canada 103 C7
Antigua, Canary Is. 37 F5
Antigua, W. Indies 121 C7
Antigua & Barbuda ■, W. Indies 121 C7
Antigua Guatemala, Guatemala 120 D1
Antilla, Cuba 120 B4
Antilles = West Indies, Cent. Amer. 121 D7
Antioch, U.S.A. 116 G5
Antioche, Pertuis d', France 20 B2
Antioquia, Colombia 124 B3
Antipodes Is., Pac. Oc. 96 M9
Antlers, U.S.A. 113 H7
Antoetra, Madag. 89 C8
Antofagasta, Chile 126 A1
Antofagasta □, Chile 126 A2
Antofagasta de la Sierra, Argentina 126 B2
Antofalla, Argentina 126 B2
Antofalla, Salar de, Argentina 126 B2
Anton, U.S.A. 113 J3
Antongila, Helodrano, Madag. 89 B8
Antonibé, Madag. 89 B8
Antonibé, Presqu'île d', Madag. 89 A8
Antonina, Brazil 127 B6
Antrain, France 18 D5
Antrim, U.K. 15 B5
Antrim, U.S.A. 110 F3
Antrim □, U.K. 15 B5
Antrim, Mts. of, U.K. 15 A5
Antrim Plateau, Australia 92 C4
Antrodoco, Italy 29 F10
Antropovo, Russia 48 A6
Antsakabary, Madag. 89 B8
Antsalova, Madag. 89 B7
Antsenavolo, Madag. 89 C8
Antsiafabositra, Madag. 89 B8
Antsirabe, Antanarivo, Madag. 89 B8
Antsirabe, Antsiranana, Madag. 89 A8
Antsirabe, Mahajanga, Madag. 89 B8
Antsiranana, Madag. 89 A8
Antsiranana □, Madag. 89 A8
Antsohihy, Madag. 89 A8
Antsohimbondrona Seranana, Madag. 89 A8
Antu, China 57 C15
Antwerp = Antwerpen, Belgium 17 C4
Antwerp, U.S.A. 111 B9
Antwerpen, Belgium 17 C4
Antwerpen □, Belgium 17 C4
Anupgarh, India 68 E5
Anuppur, India 69 H9
Anuradhapura, Sri Lanka 66 Q12
Anveh, Iran 71 E7
Anvers = Antwerpen, Belgium 17 C4
Anvers I., Antarctica 5 C17
Anwen, China 59 C13
Anxi, Fujian, China 59 E12
Anxi, Gansu, China 60 B4
Anxian, China 58 B5
Anxiang, China 59 C9
Anxious B., Australia 95 E1
Anyama, Ivory C. 82 D4
Anyang, China 56 F8
Anyer-Kidul, Indonesia 63 G11
Anyi, Jiangxi, China 59 C10
Anyi, Shanxi, China 56 G6
Anyuan, China 59 E10
Anyue, China 58 B5
Anza, U.S.A. 117 M10
Anze, China 56 F7
Anzhero-Sudzhensk, Russia 50 D9
Ánzio, Italy 30 A5
Aoga-Shima, Japan 55 H9
Aoiz, Spain 32 C3
Aomen = Macau, Asia 59 F9
Aomori, Japan 54 D10
Aomori □, Japan 54 D10
Aonla, India 69 E8
Aosta, Italy 28 C4
Aoudéras, Niger 83 B6
Aoukâr, Mauritania 82 B3
Aozou, Chad 79 D9
Apa →, S. Amer. 126 A4
Apache, U.S.A. 113 H5
Apache Junction, U.S.A. 115 K8
Apalachee B., U.S.A. 109 L4
Apalachicola, U.S.A. 109 L3
Apalachicola →, U.S.A. 109 L3
Apam, Ghana 83 D4
Apapa, Nigeria 83 D5
Apaporis →, Colombia 124 D5
Aparri, Phil. 61 B4
Apateu, Romania 42 D6
Apatin, Serbia, Yug. 42 E4
Apatity, Russia 50 C4
Apatzingán, Mexico 118 D4
Apeldoorn, Neths. 17 B5
Apen, Germany 24 B3
Apennines = Appennini, Italy 28 E7
Aphrodisias, Turkey 39 D10
Apia, W. Samoa 91 A13
Apiacás, Serra dos, Brazil 124 E7
Apies →, S. Africa 89 D4
Apizaco, Mexico 119 D5
Aplao, Peru 124 G4
Apo, Mt., Phil. 63 C7
Apolakkiá, Greece 36 C9
Apolakkiá, Órmos, Greece 36 C9
Apolda, Germany 24 D7
Apollo Bay, Australia 95 F3
Apollonia, Greece 38 E6
Apolo, Bolivia 124 F5
Aporé →, Brazil 125 G8
Apostle Is., U.S.A. 112 B9
Apóstoles, Argentina 127 B4
Apostolos Andreas, C., Cyprus 36 D13
Apostolovo, Ukraine 47 J7
Apoteri, Guyana 124 C7
Appalachian Mts., U.S.A. 108 G6
Äppelbo, Sweden 10 D8
Appennini, Italy 28 E7
Appennino Ligure, Italy 28 D6
Appenzell-Ausser Rhoden □, Switz. 25 H5
Appenzell-Inner Rhoden □, Switz. 25 H5
Appiano, Italy 29 B8
Apple Hill, Canada 111 A10
Apple Valley, U.S.A. 117 L9
Appleby-in-Westmorland, U.K. 12 C5
Appleton, U.S.A. 108 C1
Approuague →, Fr. Guiana 125 C8
Apricena, Italy 29 G12
Aprília, Italy 30 A5
Apsheronsk, Russia 49 H4
Apsley, Canada 110 B6
Apt, France 21 E9
Apuane, Alpi, Italy 28 D7
Apucarana, Brazil 127 A5
Apulia = Púglia □, Italy 31 A9
Apure →, Venezuela 124 B5
Apurimac →, Peru 124 F4
Apuseni, Munţii, Romania 42 D7
Āqā Jarī, Iran 71 D6
Aqaba = Al 'Aqabah, Jordan 75 F4
Aqaba, G. of, Red Sea 70 D2
'Aqabah, Khalīj al = Aqaba, G. of, Red Sea 70 D2
'Aqdā, Iran 71 C7
Aqîq, Sudan 80 D4
Aqîq, Khalîg, Sudan 80 D4
Aqmola = Astana, Kazakstan 50 D8
Aqrah, Iraq 70 B4
Aqtaū, Kazakstan 50 E6
Aqtöbe, Kazakstan 50 D6
Aquidauana, Brazil 125 H7
Aquiles Serdán, Mexico 118 B3
Aquin, Haiti 121 C5
Aquitaine □, France 20 D3
Ar Rachidiya, Morocco 78 B5
Ar Rafīd, Syria 75 C4
Ar Raḩḩālīyah, Iraq 70 C4
Ar Ramādī, Iraq 70 C4
Ar Ramthā, Jordan 75 C5
Ar Raqqah, Syria 70 C3
Ar Rass, Si. Arabia 70 E4
Ar Rawshān, Si. Arabia 80 C5
Ar Rifā'ī, Iraq 70 D5
Ar Riyāḑ, Si. Arabia 70 E5
Ar Ru'ays, Qatar 71 E6
Ar Rukhaymīyah, Iraq 70 D5
Ar Ruqayyidah, Si. Arabia 71 E6
Ar Ruşāfah, Syria 70 C3
Ar Ruţbah, Iraq 70 C4
Ara, India 69 G11
Ara Goro, Ethiopia 81 F5
Ara Tera, Ethiopia 81 F5
Arab, U.S.A. 109 H2
'Arab, Bahr el →, Sudan 81 F2
Arab, Khalîg el, Egypt 80 A2
'Araba, W. →, Egypt 80 J8
'Arabābād, Iran 71 C8
Araban, Turkey 72 D7
Arabatskaya Strelka, Ukraine 47 K8
Arabba, Italy 29 B8
Arabia, Asia 52 G8
Arabian Desert = Es Sahrâ' Esh Sharqîya, Egypt 80 B3
Arabian Gulf = Gulf, The, Asia 71 E6
Arabian Sea, Ind. Oc. 52 H10
Araç, Turkey 72 B5
Aracaju, Brazil 125 F11
Aracati, Brazil 125 D11
Araçatuba, Brazil 127 A5
Aracena, Spain 35 H4
Aracena, Sierra de, Spain 35 H4
Aračinovo, Macedonia 40 D5
Araçuaí, Brazil 125 G10
'Arad, Israel 75 D4
Arad, Romania 42 D6
Arad □, Romania 42 D6
Arādān, Iran 71 C7
Aradhippou, Cyprus 36 E12
Arafura Sea, E. Indies 52 K17
Aragats, Armenia 49 K7
Aragón □, Spain 32 D4
Aragón →, Spain 32 C3
Aragona, Italy 30 E6

Araguacema, Brazil 125 E9
Araguaia →, Brazil 122 D6
Araguaína, Brazil 125 E9
Araguari, Brazil 125 G9
Araguari →, Brazil 125 C9
Arain, India 68 F6
Arak, Algeria 78 C6
Arāk, Iran 71 C6
Araka, Sudan 81 G3
Arakan Coast, Burma 67 K19
Arakan Yoma, Burma 67 K19
Arákhova, Greece 38 C4
Arakli, Turkey 73 B8
Araks = Aras, Rūd-e →, Azerbaijan 49 K9
Aral, Kazakstan 50 E7
Aral Sea, Asia 50 E7
Aral Tengizi = Aral Sea, Asia 50 E7
Aralsk = Aral, Kazakstan 50 E7
Aralskoye More = Aral Sea, Asia 50 E7
Aralsor, Ozero, Kazakstan 49 F9
Aramac, Australia 94 C4
Aran I., Ireland 15 A3
Aran Is., Ireland 15 C2
Aranda de Duero, Spain 34 D7
Arandān, Iran 70 C5
Aranđelovac, Serbia, Yug. 40 B4
Aranjuez, Spain 34 E7
Aranos, Namibia 88 C2
Aransas Pass, U.S.A. 113 M6
Aranyaprathet, Thailand 64 F4
Araouane, Mali 82 B4
Arapahoe, U.S.A. 112 E5
Arapey Grande →, Uruguay 126 C4
Arapgir, Turkey 70 B3
Arapiraca, Brazil 125 E11
Arapongas, Brazil 127 A5
Ar'ar, Si. Arabia 70 D4
Araranguá, Brazil 127 B6
Araraquara, Brazil 125 H9
Ararás, Serra das, Brazil 127 B5
Ararat, Armenia 73 C11
Ararat, Australia 95 F3
Ararat, Mt. = Ağrı Dağı, Turkey 70 B5
Araria, India 69 F12
Araripe, Chapada do, Brazil 125 E11
Araruama, L. de, Brazil 127 A7
Aras, Rūd-e →, Azerbaijan 49 K9
Aratāne, Mauritania 82 B3
Arauca, Colombia 124 B4
Arauca →, Venezuela 124 B5
Arauco, Chile 126 D1
Arawa, Ethiopia 81 F5
Araxá, Brazil 125 G9
Araya, Pen. de, Venezuela 124 A6
Arba Gugu, Ethiopia 81 F5
Arba Minch, Ethiopia 81 F4
Arbat, Iraq 70 C5
Árbatax, Italy 30 C2
Arbi, Ethiopia 81 F4
Arbīl, Iraq 70 B5
Arboga, Sweden 10 E9
Arbois, France 19 F12
Arbore, Ethiopia 81 F4
Arboréa, Italy 30 C1
Arborfield, Canada 105 C8
Arborg, Canada 105 C9
Arbre du Ténéré, Niger 83 B7
Arbroath, U.K. 14 E6
Arbuckle, U.S.A. 116 F4
Arbus, Italy 30 C1
Arc →, France 21 C10
Arc-lès-Gray, France 19 E12
Arcachon, France 20 D2
Arcachon, Bassin d', France 20 D2
Arcade, Calif., U.S.A. 117 L8
Arcade, N.Y., U.S.A. 110 D6
Arcadia, Fla., U.S.A. 109 M5
Arcadia, La., U.S.A. 113 J8
Arcadia, Pa., U.S.A. 110 F6
Arcata, U.S.A. 114 F1
Arcévia, Italy 29 E9
Archangel = Arkhangelsk, Russia 50 C5
Archar, Bulgaria 40 C6
Archbald, U.S.A. 111 E9
Archena, Spain 33 G3
Archer →, Australia 94 A3
Archer B., Australia 94 A3
Archers Post, Kenya 86 B4
Arches National Park, U.S.A. 115 G9
Archidona, Spain 35 H6
Arci, Mte., Italy 30 C1
Arcidosso, Italy 29 F8
Arcis-sur-Aube, France 19 D11
Arckaringa Cr. →, Australia 95 D2
Arco, Italy 28 C7
Arco, U.S.A. 114 E7
Arcos = Arcos de Jalón, Spain 32 D2
Arcos de Jalón, Spain 32 D2
Arcos de la Frontera, Spain 35 J5
Arcos de Valdevez, Portugal 34 D2
Arcot, India 66 N11
Arcozelo, Portugal 34 E3
Arctic Bay, Canada 101 A11
Arctic Ocean, Arctic 4 B18
Arctic Red River = Tsiigehtchic, Canada 100 B6
Arda →, Bulgaria 41 E10
Arda →, Italy 28 C7
Ardabīl, Iran 71 B6
Ardahan, Turkey 73 B10
Ardakān = Sepīdān, Iran 71 D7
Ardakān, Iran 71 C7
Ardala, Sweden 11 F7
Ardales, Spain 35 J6
Ardèche □, France 21 D8
Ardèche →, France 21 D8
Ardee, Ireland 15 C5
Arden, Canada 110 B8
Arden, Denmark 11 H3
Arden, Calif., U.S.A. 116 G5
Arden, Nev., U.S.A. 117 J11
Ardenne, Belgium 6 F7
Ardennes = Ardenne, Belgium 6 F7
Ardennes □, France 19 C11
Ardentes, France 19 F8
Arderin, Ireland 15 C4
Ardeşen, Turkey 73 B9
Ardestān, Iran 71 C7
Árdhas →, Greece 41 E10
Ardhéa, Greece 40 F6
Ardila →, Portugal 35 G3
Ardino, Bulgaria 41 E9
Ardivachar Pt., U.K. 14 D1
Ardlethan, Australia 95 E4
Ardmore, Okla., U.S.A. 113 H6
Ardmore, Pa., U.S.A. 111 G9
Ardnamurchan, Pt. of, U.K. 14 E2
Ardnave Pt., U.K. 14 F2
Ardon, Russia 49 J7
Ardore, Italy 31 D9
Ardres, France 19 B8
Ardrossan, Australia 95 E2
Ardrossan, U.K. 14 F4
Ards Pen., U.K. 15 B6
Arduan, Sudan 80 D3
Ardud, Romania 42 C7
Åre, Sweden 10 A7
Arecibo, Puerto Rico 121 C6
Areia Branca, Brazil 125 E11
Arena, Pt., U.S.A. 116 G3
Arenal, Honduras 120 C2
Arenas = Las Arenas, Spain 34 B6
Arenas de San Pedro, Spain 34 E5
Arendal, Norway 9 G13
Arendsee, Germany 24 C7
Arenys de Mar, Spain 32 D7
Arenzano, Italy 28 D5
Areópolis, Greece 38 E4
Arequipa, Peru 124 G4
Arero, Ethiopia 81 G4
Arès, France 20 D2
Arévalo, Spain 34 D6
Arezzo, Italy 29 E8
Arga, Turkey 70 B3
Arga →, Spain 32 C3
Argalastí, Greece 38 B5
Argamasilla de Alba, Spain 35 F7
Argamasilla de Calatrava, Spain 35 G6
Arganda, Spain 34 E7
Arganil, Portugal 34 E2
Argedeb, Ethiopia 81 F5
Argelès-Gazost, France 20 E3
Argelès-sur-Mer, France 20 F7
Argens →, France 21 E10
Argent-sur-Sauldre, France 19 E9
Argenta, Canada 104 C5
Argenta, Italy 29 D8
Argentan, France 18 D6
Argentário, Mte., Italy 29 F8
Argentat, France 20 C5
Argentera, Italy 28 D4
Argenteuil, France 19 D9
Argentia, Canada 103 C9
Argentiera, C. dell', Italy 30 B1
Argentina ■, S. Amer. 128 D3
Argentina Is., Antarctica 5 C17
Argentino, L., Argentina 128 G2
Argenton-Château, France 18 F6
Argenton-sur-Creuse, France 19 F8
Argeş □, Romania 43 F9
Argeş →, Romania 43 F11
Arghandab →, Afghan. 68 D1
Argheile, Ethiopia 81 F5
Argo, Sudan 80 D3
Argolikós Kólpos, Greece 38 D4
Argolís □, Greece 38 D4
Argonne, France 19 C12
Árgos, Greece 38 D4
Árgos Orestikón, Greece 40 F5
Argostólion, Greece 38 C2
Arguedas, Spain 32 C3
Arguello, Pt., U.S.A. 117 L6
Arguineguín, Canary Is. 37 G4
Argun, Russia 49 J7
Argun →, Russia 51 D13
Argungu, Nigeria 83 C5
Argus Pk., U.S.A. 117 K9
Argyle, L., Australia 92 C4
Argyll & Bute □, U.K. 14 E3
Arhavi, Turkey 73 B9
Århus, Denmark 11 H4
Århus Amtskommune □, Denmark 11 H4
Ariadnoye, Russia 54 B7
Ariamsvlei, Namibia 88 D2
Ariana, Tunisia 79 A7
Ariano Irpino, Italy 31 A8
Aribinda, Burkina Faso 83 C4
Arica, Chile 124 G4
Arica, Colombia 124 D4
Arico, Canary Is. 37 F3
Arid, C., Australia 93 F3
Arida, Japan 55 G7
Ariège □, France 20 F5
Ariège →, France 20 E5
Arieş →, Romania 43 D8
Arihā, Israel 80 A4
Arilje, Serbia, Yug. 40 C4
Arílla, Ákra, Greece 36 A3
Arima, Trin. & Tob. 121 D7
Arinos →, Brazil 122 E5
Ario de Rosales, Mexico 118 D4
Ariogala, Lithuania 44 C10
Aripuanã, Brazil 124 E6
Aripuanã →, Brazil 122 D4
Ariquemes, Brazil 124 E6
Arisaig, U.K. 14 E3
Arîsh, W. el →, Egypt 80 A3
Arissa, Ethiopia 81 E5
Aristazabal I., Canada 104 C3
Arivonimamo, Madag. 89 B8
Ariza, Spain 32 D2
Arizaro, Salar de, Argentina 126 A2
Arizona, Argentina 126 D2
Arizona □, U.S.A. 115 J8
Arizpe, Mexico 118 A2
Årjäng, Sweden 10 E6
Arjeplog, Sweden 8 D18
Arjona, Colombia 124 A3
Arjona, Spain 35 H6
Arjuna, Indonesia 63 G15
Arka, Russia 51 C15
Arkadak, Russia 48 E6
Arkadelphia, U.S.A. 113 H8
Arkadhía □, Greece 38 D4
Arkaig, L., U.K. 14 E3
Arkalyk = Arqalyk, Kazakstan 50 D7
Arkansas □, U.S.A. 113 H8
Arkansas →, U.S.A. 113 J9
Arkansas City, U.S.A. 113 G6
Arkaroola, Australia 95 E2
Árkathos →, Greece 38 B3
Arkhángelos, Greece 36 C10
Arkhangelsk, Russia 50 C5
Arkhangelskoye, Russia 48 E5
Arki, India 68 D7
Arkiko, Eritrea 81 D4
Arklow, Ireland 15 D5
Árkoi, Greece 39 D8
Arkona, Kap, Germany 24 A9
Arkösund, Sweden 11 F10
Arkoúdhi, Greece 38 C2
Arkport, U.S.A. 110 D7
Arkticheskiy, Mys, Russia 51 A10
Arkul, Russia 48 B10
Arkville, U.S.A. 111 D10
Ärla, Sweden 10 E10
Arlanza →, Spain 34 C6
Arlanzón →, Spain 34 C6
Arlbergpass, Austria 26 D3
Arles, France 21 E8
Arlington, S. Africa 89 D4
Arlington, N.Y., U.S.A. 111 E11
Arlington, Oreg., U.S.A. 114 D3
Arlington, S. Dak., U.S.A. 112 C6
Arlington, Tex., U.S.A. 113 J6
Arlington, Va., U.S.A. 108 F7
Arlington, Vt., U.S.A. 111 C11
Arlington, Wash., U.S.A. 116 B4
Arlington Heights, U.S.A. 108 D2
Arlit, Niger 78 E7
Arlon, Belgium 17 E5
Arltunga, Australia 94 C1
Arly, Burkina Faso 83 C5
Armagh, U.K. 15 B5
Armagh □, U.K. 15 B5
Armagnac, France 20 E4
Armançon →, France 19 E10
Armavir, Russia 49 H5
Armenia, Colombia 124 C3
Armenia ■, Asia 49 K7
Armeniş, Romania 42 E7
Armenistís, Ákra, Greece 36 C9
Armentières, France 19 B9
Armidale, Australia 95 E5
Armilla, Spain 35 H7
Armour, U.S.A. 112 D5
Armstrong, B.C., Canada 104 C5
Armstrong, Ont., Canada 102 B2
Armutlu, Bursa, Turkey 41 F12
Armutlu, Izmir, Turkey 39 C9
Arnaía, Greece 40 F7
Arnarfjörður, Iceland 8 D2
Arnaud →, Canada 101 B12
Arnauti, C., Cyprus 36 D11
Arnay-le-Duc, France 19 E11
Arnedillo, Spain 32 C2
Arnedo, Spain 32 C2
Arnett, U.S.A. 113 G5
Arnhem, Neths. 17 C5
Arnhem, C., Australia 94 A2
Arnhem B., Australia 94 A2
Arnhem Land, Australia 94 A1
Árnissa, Greece 40 F5
Arno →, Italy 28 E7
Arno Bay, Australia 95 E2
Arnold, U.K. 12 D6
Arnold, U.S.A. 116 G6
Arnoldstein, Austria 26 E6
Arnon →, France 19 E9
Arnot, Canada 105 B9
Arnøy, Norway 8 A19
Arnprior, Canada 102 C4
Arnsberg, Germany 24 D4
Arnstadt, Germany 24 E6
Aroab, Namibia 88 D2
Aroánia Óri, Greece 38 D4
Aroche, Spain 35 H4
Arochuku, Nigeria 83 D6
Arolsen, Germany 24 D5
Aron, India 68 G6
Aron →, France 19 F10
Arona, Italy 28 C5
Aroroy, Phil. 61 E5
Arosa, Ría de, Spain 34 C2
Arpajon, France 19 D9
Arpajon-sur-Cère, France 20 D6
Arpaşu de Jos, Romania 43 E9
Arqalyk, Kazakstan 50 D7
Arrah = Ara, India 69 G11
Arrah, Ivory C. 82 D4
Arraiolos, Portugal 35 G3
Arran, U.K. 14 F3
Arras, France 19 B9
Arrasate, Spain 32 B2
Arrats →, France 20 D4
Arreau, France 20 F4
Arrecife, Canary Is. 37 F6
Arrecifes, Argentina 126 C3
Arrée, Mts. d', France 18 D3
Arresø, Denmark 11 J6
Arriaga, Chiapas, Mexico 119 D6
Arriaga, San Luis Potosí, Mexico 118 C4
Arrilalah, Australia 94 C3
Arrino, Australia 93 E2
Arriondas, Spain 34 B5
Arromanches-les-Bains, France 18 C6
Arronches, Portugal 35 F3
Arros →, France 20 E3
Arrow, L., Ireland 15 B3
Arrowhead, L., U.S.A. 117 L9
Arrowtown, N.Z. 91 L2
Arroyo de la Luz, Spain 35 F4
Arroyo Grande, U.S.A. 117 K6
Ârs, Denmark 11 H3
Ars, Iran 70 B5
Ars-sur-Moselle, France 19 C13
Arsenault L., Canada 105 B7
Arsenev, Russia 54 B6
Arsi □, Ethiopia 81 F4
Arsiero, Italy 29 C8
Arsin, Turkey 73 B8
Arsk, Russia 48 B9
Årsunda, Sweden 10 D10
Árta, Greece 38 B3
Artà, Spain 37 B10
Árta □, Greece 38 B3
Arteaga, Mexico 118 D4
Arteche, Phil. 61 E6
Arteijo = Arteixo, Spain 34 B2
Arteixo, Spain 34 B2
Artem = Artyom, Azerbaijan 49 K10
Artem, Russia 54 C6
Artemovsk, Russia 51 D10
Artemovsk, Ukraine 47 H9
Artemovskiy, Russia 49 G5
Artenay, France 19 D8
Artern, Germany 24 D7
Artesa de Segre, Spain 32 D6
Artesia = Mosomane, Botswana 88 C4
Artesia, U.S.A. 113 J2
Arthington, Liberia 82 D2
Arthur, Canada 110 C4
Arthur →, Australia 94 G3
Arthur Cr. →, Australia 94 C2
Arthur Pt., Australia 94 C5
Arthur River, Australia 93 F2
Arthur's Pass, N.Z. 91 K3
Arthur's Town, Bahamas 121 B4
Artigas, Uruguay 126 C4
Artik, Armenia 49 K6
Artillery L., Canada 105 A7
Artois, France 19 B9
Artotína, Greece 38 C4
Artrutx, C. de, Spain 37 B10
Artsyz, Ukraine 47 J5
Artvin, Turkey 73 B9
Artyom, Azerbaijan 49 K10
Aru, Kepulauan, Indonesia 63 F8
Aru Is. = Aru, Kepulauan, Indonesia 63 F8
Arua, Uganda 86 B3
Aruanã, Brazil 125 F8
Aruba ■, W. Indies 121 D6
Arucas, Canary Is. 37 F4
Arudy, France 20 E3
Arun →, Nepal 69 F12
Arun →, U.K. 13 G7
Arunachal Pradesh □, India 67 F19
Arusha, Tanzania 86 C4
Arusha □, Tanzania 86 C4
Arusha Chini, Tanzania 86 C4
Aruwimi →, Dem. Rep. of the Congo 86 B1
Arvada, Colo., U.S.A. 112 F2
Arvada, Wyo., U.S.A. 114 D10
Arve →, France 19 F13
Arvi, Greece 36 E7
Arviat, Canada 105 A10
Arvidsjaur, Sweden 8 D18
Arvika, Sweden 10 E6
Arvin, U.S.A. 117 K8
Arwal, India 69 G11
Arxan, China 60 B6
Åryd, Sweden 11 H8
Aryirádhes, Greece 36 B3
Aryiroúpolis, Greece 36 D6
Arys, Kazakstan 50 E7
Arzachena, Italy 30 A2
Arzamas, Russia 48 C6
Arzgir, Russia 49 H7
Arzignano, Italy 29 C8
Arzúa, Spain 34 C2
Aš, Czech Rep. 26 A5
Ås, Sweden 10 A8
As Pontes de García Rodríquez, Spain 34 B3
Aş Şadr, U.A.E. 71 E7
Aş Şafā, Syria 75 B6
As Saffānīyah, Si. Arabia 71 E6
As Safīrah, Syria 70 B3
Aş Şahm, Oman 71 E8
As Sājir, Si. Arabia 70 E5
As Salamīyah, Syria 70 C3
As Salmān, Iraq 70 D5
As Salţ, Jordan 75 C4
As Sal'w'a, Qatar 71 E6
As Samāwah, Iraq 70 D5
As Sanamayn, Syria 75 B5
As Sohar = Şuḩār, Oman 71 E8
As Sukhnah, Syria 70 C3
As Sulaymānīyah, Iraq 70 C5
As Sulaymī, Si. Arabia 70 E4
As Sulayyil, Si. Arabia 74 C4
As Summān, Si. Arabia 70 E5
As Suwaydā', Syria 75 C5
As Suwaydā' □, Syria 75 C5
As Suwayq, Oman 71 F8
As Şuwayrah, Iraq 70 C5
Åsa, Sweden 11 G6
Asab, Namibia 88 D2
Asaba, Nigeria 83 D6
Asad, Buḩayrat al, Syria 70 C3
Asadābād, Iran 73 E13
Asafo, Ghana 82 D4
Asahi-Gawa →, Japan 55 G6
Asahigawa, Japan 54 C11
Asale, L., Ethiopia 81 E5
Asamankese, Ghana 83 D4
Asan →, India 69 F8
Asansol, India 69 H12
Åsarna, Sweden 10 B8
Asayita, Ethiopia 81 E5
Asbe Teferi, Ethiopia 81 F5
Asbesberge, S. Africa 88 D3
Asbestos, Canada 103 C5
Asbury Park, U.S.A. 111 F10
Ascea, Italy 31 B8
Ascensión, Mexico 118 A3
Ascensión, B. de la, Mexico 119 D7
Ascension I., Atl. Oc. 77 G2
Aschach an der Donau, Austria 26 C7
Aschaffenburg, Germany 25 F5
Aschendorf, Germany 24 B3
Aschersleben, Germany 24 D7
Asciano, Italy 29 E8
Áscoli Piceno, Italy 29 F10
Áscoli Satriano, Italy 31 A8
Ascope, Peru 124 E3
Ascotán, Chile 126 A2
Aseb, Eritrea 81 E5
Åseda, Sweden 11 G9
Asela, Ethiopia 81 F4
Åsen, Sweden 10 C7
Asenovgrad, Bulgaria 41 D8
Aserradero, Mexico 118 C3
Asfeld, France 19 C11
Asfûn el Matâ'na, Egypt 80 B3
Asgata, Cyprus 36 E12
Ash Fork, U.S.A. 115 J7
Ash Grove, U.S.A. 113 G8
Ash Shabakah, Iraq 70 D4
Ash Shamāl □, Lebanon 75 A5
Ash Shāmīyah, Iraq 70 D5
Ash Shāriqah, U.A.E. 71 E7
Ash Sharmah, Si. Arabia 70 D2
Ash Sharqāt, Iraq 70 C4
Ash Sharqi, Al Jabal, Lebanon 75 B5
Ash Shaţrah, Iraq 70 D5
Ash Shawbak, Jordan 70 D2
Ash Shawmari, J., Jordan 75 E5
Ash Shināfīyah, Iraq 70 D5
Ash Shu'bah, Si. Arabia 70 D5
Ash Shumlūl, Si. Arabia 70 E5
Ash Shūr'a, Iraq 70 C4
Ash Shurayf, Si. Arabia 70 E3
Ash Shuwayfāt, Lebanon 75 B4
Ashanti □, Ghana 83 D4
Ashau, Vietnam 64 D6
Ashbourne, U.K. 12 D6
Ashburn, U.S.A. 109 K4
Ashburton, N.Z. 91 K3
Ashburton →, Australia 92 D1
Ashcroft, Canada 104 C4
Ashdod, Israel 75 D3
Ashdown, U.S.A. 113 J7
Asheboro, U.S.A. 109 H6
Ashern, Canada 105 C9
Asherton, U.S.A. 113 L5
Asheville, U.S.A. 109 H4
Ashewat, Pakistan 68 D3
Asheweig →, Canada 102 B2
Ashford, Australia 95 D5
Ashford, U.K. 13 F8
Ashgabat, Turkmenistan 50 F6
Ashibetsu, Japan 54 C11
Ashikaga, Japan 55 F9
Ashington, U.K. 12 B6
Ashizuri-Zaki, Japan 55 H6
Ashkarkot, Afghan. 68 C2
Ashkhabad = Ashgabat, Turkmenistan 50 F6
Āshkhāneh, Iran 71 B8
Ashland, Kans., U.S.A. 113 G5
Ashland, Ky., U.S.A. 108 F4
Ashland, Mont., U.S.A. 114 D10
Ashland, Ohio, U.S.A. 110 F2
Ashland, Oreg., U.S.A. 114 E2
Ashland, Pa., U.S.A. 111 F8
Ashland, Va., U.S.A. 108 G7
Ashland, Wis., U.S.A. 112 B9
Ashley, N. Dak., U.S.A. 112 B5
Ashley, Pa., U.S.A. 111 E9
Ashmore Reef, Australia 92 B3
Ashmûn, Egypt 80 H7
Ashmyany, Belarus 9 J21
Ashokan Reservoir, U.S.A. 111 E10
Ashqelon, Israel 75 D3
Ashta, India 68 H7
Ashtabula, U.S.A. 110 E4
Ashton, S. Africa 88 E3
Ashton, U.S.A. 114 D8
Ashuanipi, L., Canada 103 B6
Ashville, U.S.A. 110 F6
'Āṣī →, Asia 72 D6
Asia 52 E11
Asia, Kepulauan, Indonesia 63 D8
Āsīā Bak, Iran 71 C6
Asiago, Italy 29 C8

Asifabad, India 66 K11
Asinara, Italy 30 A1
Asinara, G. dell', Italy 30 A1
Asino, Russia 50 D9
Asipovichy, Belarus 46 F5
'Asīr □, Si. Arabia 74 D3
Asir, Ras, Somali Rep. 74 E5
Aşkale, Turkey 73 C9
Askersund, Sweden 11 F8
Askham, S. Africa 88 D3
Askim, Norway 9 G14
Askja, Iceland 8 D5
Askøy, Norway 9 F11
Asl, Egypt 80 B3
Aslan Burnu, Turkey 39 C8
Aslanapa, Turkey 39 B11
Asmara = Asmera, Eritrea 81 D4
Asmera, Eritrea 81 D4
Asnæs, Denmark 11 J4
Åsnen, Sweden 11 H8
Asola, Italy 28 C7
Asosa, Ethiopia 81 E3
Asoteriba, Jebel, Sudan 80 C4
Aspe, Spain 33 G4
Aspen, U.S.A. 115 G10
Aspendos, Turkey 72 D4
Aspermont, U.S.A. 113 J4
Aspet, France 20 E4
Aspiring, Mt., N.Z. 91 L2
Aspres-sur-Buëch, France 21 D9
Asprókavos, Ákra, Greece 36 B4
Aspromonte, Italy 31 D9
Aspur, India 68 H6
Asquith, Canada 105 C7
Assâba, Massif de l', Mauritania 82 B2
Assaikio, Nigeria 83 D6
Assal, L., Djibouti 81 E5
Assam □, India 67 G18
Assamakka, Niger 83 B6
Asse, Belgium 17 D4
Assémini, Italy 30 C1
Assen, Neths. 17 A6
Assens, Denmark 11 J3
Assini, Ivory C. 82 D4
Assiniboia, Canada 105 D7
Assiniboine →, Canada 105 D9
Assiniboine, Mt., Canada 104 C5
Assis, Brazil 127 A5
Assisi, Italy 29 E9
Ássos, Greece 38 C2
Assynt, L., U.K. 14 C3
Astaffort, France 20 D4
Astakidha, Greece 39 F8
Astakós, Greece 38 C3
Astana, Kazakstan 50 D8
Āstāneh, Iran 71 B6
Astara, Azerbaijan 71 B6
Āstārā, Iran 73 C13
Asteroúsia, Greece 36 E7
Asti, Italy 28 D5
Astipálaia, Greece 39 E8
Astorga, Spain 34 C4
Astoria, U.S.A. 116 D3
Åstorp, Sweden 11 H6
Astrakhan, Russia 49 G9
Astudillo, Spain 34 C6
Asturias □, Spain 34 B5
Asunción, Paraguay 126 B4
Asunción Nochixtlán, Mexico 119 D5
Åsunden, Sweden 11 F9
Asutri, Sudan 81 D4
Aswa →, Uganda 86 B3
Aswad, Ra's al, Si. Arabia 80 C4
Aswân, Egypt 80 C3
Aswân High Dam = Sadd el Aali, Egypt 80 C3
Asyût, Egypt 80 B3
Asyûti, Wadi →, Egypt 80 B3
Aszód, Hungary 42 C4
At Ţafīlah, Jordan 75 E4
Aţ Tā'if, Si. Arabia 74 C3
Aţ Ţirāq, Si. Arabia 70 E5
Aţ Tubayq, Si. Arabia 70 D3
Atabey, Turkey 39 D12
Atacama □, Chile 126 B2
Atacama, Desierto de, Chile 126 A2
Atacama, Salar de, Chile 126 A2
Atakpamé, Togo 83 D5
Atalándi, Greece 38 C4
Atalaya, Peru 124 F4
Atalaya de Femes, Canary Is. 37 F6
Atami, Japan 55 G9
Atapupu, Indonesia 63 F6
Atâr, Mauritania 78 D3
Atarfe, Spain 35 H7
Atari, Pakistan 68 D6
Atascadero, U.S.A. 116 K6
Atasu, Kazakstan 50 E8
Atatürk Barajı, Turkey 73 D8
Atauro, Indonesia 63 F7
Atbara, Sudan 80 D3
'Atbara →, Sudan 80 D3
Atbasar, Kazakstan 50 D7
Atça, Turkey 39 D10
Atchafalaya B., U.S.A. 113 L9
Atchison, U.S.A. 112 F7
Atebubu, Ghana 83 D4
Ateca, Spain 32 D3
Aterno →, Italy 29 F10
Āteshān, Iran 71 C7
Atesine, Alpi, Italy 29 B8
Atessa, Italy 29 F11
Atfîh, Egypt 80 J7
Ath, Belgium 17 D3
Athabasca, Canada 104 C6
Athabasca →, Canada 105 B6
Athabasca, L., Canada 105 B7
Athboy, Ireland 15 C5
Athenry, Ireland 15 C3
Athens = Athínai, Greece 38 D5
Athens, Ala., U.S.A. 109 H2
Athens, Ga., U.S.A. 109 J4
Athens, N.Y., U.S.A. 111 D11
Athens, Ohio, U.S.A. 108 F4
Athens, Pa., U.S.A. 111 E8
Athens, Tenn., U.S.A. 109 H3
Athens, Tex., U.S.A. 113 J7
Atherley, Canada 110 B5
Atherton, Australia 94 B4
Athiéme, Benin 83 D5
Athienou, Cyprus 36 D12
Athínai, Greece 38 D5
Athlone, Ireland 15 C4
Athna, Cyprus 36 D12
Athol, U.S.A. 111 D12
Atholl, Forest of, U.K. 14 E5
Atholville, Canada 103 C6
Áthos, Greece 41 F8
Athy, Ireland 15 C5
Ati, Chad 79 F9
Ati, Sudan 81 E2
Atiak, Uganda 86 B3
Atienza, Spain 32 D2
Atiit, Sudan 81 F3
Atik L., Canada 105 B9
Atikameg →, Canada 102 B3
Atikokan, Canada 102 C1
Atikonak L., Canada 103 B7
Atimonan, Phil. 61 E4
Atka, Russia 51 C16
Atka I., U.S.A. 100 C2
Atkarsk, Russia 48 E7
Atkinson, U.S.A. 112 D5
Atlanta, Ga., U.S.A. 109 J3
Atlanta, Tex., U.S.A. 113 J7
Atlantic, U.S.A. 112 E7
Atlantic City, U.S.A. 108 F8
Atlantic Ocean 2 E9
Atlas Mts. = Haut Atlas, Morocco 78 B4
Atlin, Canada 104 B2
Atlin, L., Canada 104 B2
Atlin Prov. Park, Canada 104 B2
Atmore, U.S.A. 109 K2
Atoka, U.S.A. 113 H6
Átokos, Greece 38 C2
Atolia, U.S.A. 117 K9
Atrai →, Bangla. 69 G13
Atrak = Atrek →, Turkmenistan 71 B8
Ätran, Sweden 11 G6
Ätran →, Sweden 11 H6
Atrauli, India 68 E8
Atrek →, Turkmenistan 71 B8
Atri, Italy 29 F10
Atsikí, Greece 39 B7
Atsoum, Mts., Cameroon 83 D7
Atsuta, Japan 54 C10
Attalla, U.S.A. 109 H2
Attapu, Laos 64 E6
Attáviros, Greece 36 C9
Attawapiskat, Canada 102 B3
Attawapiskat →, Canada 102 B3
Attawapiskat L., Canada 102 B2
Attersee, Austria 26 D6
Attica, Ind., U.S.A. 108 E2
Attica, Ohio, U.S.A. 110 E2
Attichy, France 19 C10
Attigny, France 19 C11
Attikamagen L., Canada 103 B6
Attikí □, Greece 38 D5
Attleboro, U.S.A. 111 E13
Attock, Pakistan 68 C5
Attopeu = Attapu, Laos 64 E6
Attu I., U.S.A. 100 C1
Attur, India 66 P11
Atuel →, Argentina 126 D2
Åtvidaberg, Sweden 11 F10
Atwater, U.S.A. 116 H6
Atwood, Canada 110 C3
Atwood, U.S.A. 112 F4
Atyraū, Kazakstan 50 E6
Au Sable, U.S.A. 110 B1
Au Sable →, U.S.A. 108 C4
Au Sable Forks, U.S.A. 111 B11
Au Sable Pt., U.S.A. 110 B1
Aubagne, France 21 E9
Aubarca, C. d', Spain 37 B7
Aube □, France 19 D11
Aube →, France 19 D10
Aubenas, France 21 D8
Aubenton, France 19 C11
Auberry, U.S.A. 116 H7
Aubigny-sur-Nère, France 19 E9
Aubin, France 20 D6
Aubrac, Mts. d', France 20 D7
Auburn, Ala., U.S.A. 109 J3
Auburn, Calif., U.S.A. 116 G5
Auburn, Ind., U.S.A. 108 E3
Auburn, Maine, U.S.A. 109 C10
Auburn, N.Y., U.S.A. 111 D8
Auburn, Nebr., U.S.A. 112 E7
Auburn, Pa., U.S.A. 111 F8
Auburn, Wash., U.S.A. 116 C4
Auburn Ra., Australia 95 D5
Aubusson, France 20 C6
Auce, Latvia 44 B9
Auch, France 20 E4
Auchi, Nigeria 83 D6
Auckland, N.Z. 91 G5
Auckland Is., Pac. Oc. 96 N8
Aude □, France 20 E6
Aude →, France 20 E7
Auden, Canada 102 B2
Auderville, France 18 C5
Audierne, France 18 D2
Audincourt, France 19 E13
Audo, Ethiopia 81 F5
Audubon, U.S.A. 112 E7
Aue, Germany 24 E8
Auerbach, Germany 24 E8
Augathella, Australia 95 D4
Aughnacloy, U.K. 15 B5
Augrabies Falls, S. Africa 88 D3
Augsburg, Germany 25 G6
Augusta, Australia 93 F2
Augusta, Italy 31 E8
Augusta, Ark., U.S.A. 113 H9
Augusta, Ga., U.S.A. 109 J5
Augusta, Kans., U.S.A. 113 G6
Augusta, Maine, U.S.A. 101 D13
Augusta, Mont., U.S.A. 114 C7
Augustenborg, Denmark 11 K3
Augustów, Poland 44 E9
Augustus, Mt., Australia 93 D2
Augustus I., Australia 92 C3
Aukan, Eritrea 81 D5
Aukum, U.S.A. 116 G6
Auld, L., Australia 92 D3
Aulla, Italy 28 D6
Aulnay, France 20 B3
Aulne →, France 18 D2
Aulnoye-Aymeries, France 19 B10
Ault, France 18 B8
Ault, U.S.A. 112 E2
Aulus-les-Bains, France 20 F5
Aumale, France 19 C8
Aumont-Aubrac, France 20 D7
Auna, Nigeria 83 C5
Auning, Denmark 11 H4
Aunis, France 20 B3
Auponhia, Indonesia 63 E7
Aups, France 21 E10
Aur, Pulau, Malaysia 65 L5
Auraiya, India 69 F8
Aurangabad, Bihar, India 69 G11
Aurangabad, Maharashtra, India 66 K9
Auray, France 18 E4
Aurich, Germany 24 B3
Aurillac, France 20 D6
Auronzo di Cadore, Italy 29 B9
Aurora, Canada 110 C5
Aurora, S. Africa 88 E2
Aurora, Colo., U.S.A. 112 F2
Aurora, Ill., U.S.A. 108 E1
Aurora, Mo., U.S.A. 113 G8
Aurora, N.Y., U.S.A. 111 D8
Aurora, Nebr., U.S.A. 112 E6
Aurora, Ohio, U.S.A. 110 E3
Aurukun, Australia 94 A3
Aus, Namibia 88 D2
Ausable →, Canada 110 C3
Auschwitz = Oświęcim, Poland 45 H6
Austerlitz = Slavkov u Brna, Czech Rep. 27 B9
Austin, Minn., U.S.A. 112 D8
Austin, Nev., U.S.A. 114 G5
Austin, Pa., U.S.A. 110 E6
Austin, Tex., U.S.A. 113 K6
Austin, L., Australia 93 E2
Austin I., Canada 105 A10
Austra, Norway 8 D14
Austral Is. = Tubuai Is., Pac. Oc. 97 K13
Austral Seamount Chain, Pac. Oc. 97 K13
Australia ■, Oceania 96 K5
Australian Capital Territory □, Australia 95 F4
Australind, Australia 93 F2
Austria ■, Europe 26 E7
Austvågøy, Norway 8 B16
Auterive, France 20 E5
Authie →, France 19 B8
Authon-du-Perche, France 18 D7
Autlán, Mexico 118 D4
Autun, France 19 F11
Auvergne, France 20 C7
Auvergne, Mts. d', France 20 C6
Auvézère →, France 20 C4
Auxerre, France 19 E10
Auxi-le-Château, France 19 B9
Auxonne, France 19 E12
Auzances, France 19 F9
Ava, U.S.A. 113 G8
Avallon, France 19 E10
Avalon, U.S.A. 117 M8
Avalon Pen., Canada 103 C9
Avanos, Turkey 70 B2
Avaré, Brazil 127 A6
Ávas, Greece 41 F9
Avawatz Mts., U.S.A. 117 K10
Avdan Dağı, Turkey 41 F13
Aveiro, Brazil 125 D7
Aveiro, Portugal 34 E2
Aveiro □, Portugal 34 E2
Āvej, Iran 71 C6
Avellaneda, Argentina 126 C4
Avellino, Italy 31 B7
Avenal, U.S.A. 116 K6
Aversa, Italy 31 B7
Avery, U.S.A. 114 C6
Aves, Is. las, Venezuela 121 D6
Avesnes-sur-Helpe, France 19 B10
Avesta, Sweden 10 D10
Aveyron □, France 20 D6
Aveyron →, France 20 D5
Avezzano, Italy 29 F10
Avgó, Greece 39 F7
Aviá Terai, Argentina 126 B3
Aviano, Italy 29 B9
Aviemore, U.K. 14 D5
Avigliana, Italy 28 C4
Avigliano, Italy 31 B8
Avignon, France 21 E8
Ávila, Spain 34 E6
Ávila □, Spain 34 E6
Ávila, Sierra de, Spain 34 E5
Avila Beach, U.S.A. 117 K6
Avilés, Spain 34 B5
Avintes, Portugal 34 D2
Avionárion, Greece 38 C6
Avis, Portugal 35 F3
Avis, U.S.A. 110 E7
Avísio →, Italy 28 B8
Aviz = Avis, Portugal 35 F3
Avize, France 19 D11
Avlum, Denmark 11 H2
Avoca, U.S.A. 110 D7
Avoca →, Australia 95 F3
Avoca →, Ireland 15 D5
Avola, Canada 104 C5
Avola, Italy 31 F8
Avon, U.S.A. 110 D7
Avon →, Australia 93 F2
Avon →, Bristol, U.K. 13 F5
Avon →, Dorset, U.K. 13 G6
Avon →, Warks., U.K. 13 E5
Avon Park, U.S.A. 109 M5
Avondale, Zimbabwe 87 F3
Avonlea, Canada 105 D8
Avonmore, Canada 111 A10
Avramov, Bulgaria 41 D10
Avranches, France 18 D5
Avre →, France 18 D8
Avrig, Romania 43 E9
Avrillé, France 18 E6
Avtovac, Bos.-H. 40 C2
Awag el Baqar, Sudan 81 E3
A'waj →, Syria 75 B5
Awaji-Shima, Japan 55 G7
'Awālī, Bahrain 71 E6
Awantipur, India 69 C6
Awasa, Ethiopia 81 F4
Awasa, L., Ethiopia 81 F4
Awash, Ethiopia 81 F5
Awash →, Ethiopia 81 E5
Awaso, Ghana 82 D4
Awatere →, N.Z. 91 J5
Awbārī, Libya 79 C8
Awe, L., U.K. 14 E3
Aweil, Sudan 81 F2
Awgu, Nigeria 83 D6
Awjilah, Libya 79 C10
Awka, Nigeria 83 D6
Ax-les-Thermes, France 20 F5
Axat, France 20 F6
Axe →, U.K. 13 F5
Axel Heiberg I., Canada 4 B3
Axim, Ghana 82 E4
Axintele, Romania 43 F11
Axiós →, Greece 40 F6
Axminster, U.K. 13 G4
Axvall, Sweden 11 F7
Ay, France 19 C11
Ayabaca, Peru 124 D3
Ayabe, Japan 55 G7
Ayacucho, Argentina 126 D4
Ayacucho, Peru 124 F4
Ayaguz, Kazakstan 50 E9
Ayamé, Ivory C. 82 D4
Ayamonte, Spain 35 H3
Ayan, Russia 51 D14
Ayancık, Turkey 72 B6
Ayas, Turkey 72 B5
Ayaviri, Peru 124 F4
Aybastı, Turkey 72 B7
Aydın, Turkey 72 D2
Aydin □, Turkey 39 D9
Aydın Dağları, Turkey 39 D10
Ayelu, Ethiopia 81 E5
Ayenngré, Togo 83 D5
Ayer, U.S.A. 111 D13
Ayerbe, Spain 32 C4
Ayer's Cliff, Canada 111 A12
Ayers Rock, Australia 93 E5
Ayiá, Greece 38 B4
Ayia Aikateríni, Ákra, Greece 36 A3
Ayía Ánna, Greece 38 C5
Ayia Dhéka, Greece 36 D6
Ayia Gálini, Greece 36 D6
Ayía Marína, Kásos, Greece 39 F8
Ayía Marína, Léros, Greece 39 D8
Ayia Napa, Cyprus 36 E13
Ayía Paraskeví, Greece 39 B8
Ayia Phyla, Cyprus 36 E12
Ayía Rouméli, Greece 38 F5
Ayia Varvára, Greece 36 D7
Ayiássos, Greece 39 B8
Áyioi Theódhoroi, Greece 38 D5
Áyion Óros □, Greece 41 F8
Áyios Amvrósios, Cyprus 36 D12
Áyios Andréas, Greece 38 D4
Áyios Evstrátios, Greece 38 B6
Áyios Ioánnis, Ákra, Greece 36 D7
Áyios Isidhoros, Greece 36 C9
Áyios Kiríkos, Greece 39 D8
Áyios Matthaíos, Greece 36 B3
Áyios Mírono, Greece 39 F7
Áyios Nikólaos, Greece 36 D7
Áyios Pétros, Greece 38 C2
Áyios Seryios, Cyprus 36 D12
Áyios Theodhoros, Cyprus 36 D13
Áyios Yeóryios, Greece 38 D5
Aykathonisi, Greece 39 D8
Aykirikçi, Turkey 39 B12
Aylesbury, U.K. 13 F7
Aylmer, Canada 110 D4
Aylmer, L., Canada 100 B8
'Ayn, Wādī al, Oman 71 F7
Ayn Dār, Si. Arabia 71 E7
Ayn Zālah, Iraq 70 B4
Ayna, Spain 33 G2
Ayod, Sudan 81 F3
Ayolas, Paraguay 126 B4
Ayom, Sudan 81 F2
Ayon, Ostrov, Russia 51 C17
Ayora, Spain 33 F3
Ayorou, Niger 83 C5
'Ayoûn el 'Atroûs, Mauritania 82 B3
Ayr, Australia 94 B4
Ayr, Canada 110 C4
Ayr, U.K. 14 F4
Ayr →, U.K. 14 F4
Ayrancı, Turkey 72 D5
Ayrancılar, Turkey 39 C9
Ayre, Pt. of, U.K. 12 C3
Aysha, Ethiopia 81 E5
Ayton, Australia 94 B4
Aytos, Bulgaria 41 D11
Aytoska Planina, Bulgaria 41 D11
Ayu, Kepulauan, Indonesia 63 D8
Ayutla, Guatemala 120 D1
Ayutla, Mexico 119 D5
Ayvacık, Turkey 72 C2
Ayvalık, Turkey 39 B8
Az Zabadānī, Syria 75 B5
Az Zāhirīyah, West Bank 75 D3
Az Zahrān, Si. Arabia 71 E6
Az Zarqā, Jordan 75 C5
Az Zarqā', U.A.E. 71 E7
Az Zāwiyah, Libya 79 B8
Az Zībār, Iraq 70 B5
Az Zilfī, Si. Arabia 70 E5
Az Zubayr, Iraq 70 D5
Az Zuqur, Yemen 81 E5
Azambuja, Portugal 35 F2
Azamgarh, India 69 F10
Azangaro, Peru 124 F4
Azaoua, Niger 83 B5
Azaouad, Mali 82 B4
Azaouak, Vallée de l', Mali 83 B5
Āzār Shahr, Iran 70 B5
Azara, Nigeria 83 D6
Azarān, Iran 70 B5
Azärbayjan = Azerbaijan ■, Asia 49 K9
Āzarbāyjān-e Gharbī □, Iran 70 B5
Āzarbāyjān-e Sharqī □, Iran 70 B5
Azare, Nigeria 83 C7
Azay-le-Rideau, France 18 E7
A'zāz, Syria 70 B3
Azbine = Aïr, Niger 83 B6
Azerbaijan ■, Asia 49 K9
Azerbaijchan = Azerbaijan ■, Asia 49 K9
Azezo, Ethiopia 81 E4
Azimganj, India 69 G13
Aznalcóllar, Spain 35 H4
Azogues, Ecuador 124 D3
Azores, Atl. Oc. 78 A1
Azov, Russia 47 J10
Azov, Sea of, Europe 47 J9
Azovskoye More = Azov, Sea of, Europe 47 J9
Azpeitia, Spain 32 B2
Azraq ash Shīshān, Jordan 75 D5
Aztec, U.S.A. 115 H10
Azúa de Compostela, Dom. Rep. 121 C5
Azuaga, Spain 35 G5
Azuara, Spain 32 D4
Azuer →, Spain 35 F7
Azuero, Pen. de, Panama 120 E3
Azuga, Romania 43 E10
Azul, Argentina 126 D4
Azusa, U.S.A. 117 L9
Azzano Décimo, Italy 29 C9

B

Ba Don, Vietnam 64 D6
Ba Dong, Vietnam 65 H6
Ba Ngoi = Cam Lam, Vietnam 65 G7
Ba Tri, Vietnam 65 G6
Ba Xian = Bazhou, China 56 E9
Baa, Indonesia 63 F6
Baamonde, Spain 34 B3
Baarle-Nassau, Belgium 17 C4
Bab el Mandeb, Red Sea 74 E3
Baba, Bulgaria 40 D7
Baba Burnu, Turkey 39 B8
Baba dag, Azerbaijan 49 K9
Bābā Kalū, Iran 71 D6
Babadag, Romania 43 F13
Babadağ, Turkey 39 D10
Babadayhan, Turkmenistan 50 F7
Babaeski, Turkey 41 E11
Babahoyo, Ecuador 124 D3
Babai = Sarju →, India 69 F9
Babana, Nigeria 83 C5
Babanusa, Sudan 81 E2
Babar, Indonesia 63 F7
Babar, Pakistan 68 D3
Babarkach, Pakistan 68 E3
Babayevo, Russia 46 C8
Babb, U.S.A. 114 B7
Babelthuap, Pac. Oc. 63 C8
Babenhausen, Germany 25 F4
Băbeni, Romania 43 F9
Baberu, India 69 G9
Babi Besar, Pulau, Malaysia 65 L4
Babia Gora, Europe 45 J6
Babian Jiang →, China 58 F3
Babile, Ethiopia 81 F5
Babimost, Poland 45 F2
Babinda, Australia 94 B4
Babine, Canada 104 B3
Babine →, Canada 104 B3
Babine L., Canada 104 C3
Babo, Indonesia 63 E8
Babócsa, Hungary 42 D2
Bābol, Iran 71 B7
Bābol Sar, Iran 71 B7
Baborów, Poland 45 H5

Babruysk, *Belarus* 47 F5
Babuhri, *India* 68 F3
Babuna, *Macedonia* 40 E5
Babura, *Nigeria* 83 C6
Babusar Pass, *Pakistan* 69 B5
Babušnica, *Serbia, Yug.* 40 C6
Babuyan Chan., *Phil.* 61 B4
Babylon, *Iraq* 70 C5
Bač, *Serbia, Yug.* 42 E4
Bâc →, *Moldova* 43 D14
Bac Can, *Vietnam* 58 F5
Bac Giang, *Vietnam* 58 G6
Bac Lieu, *Vietnam* 65 H5
Bac Ninh, *Vietnam* 58 G6
Bac Phan, *Vietnam* 64 B5
Bac Quang, *Vietnam* 58 F5
Bacabal, *Brazil* 125 D10
Bacalar, *Mexico* 119 D7
Bacan, Kepulauan, *Indonesia* 63 E7
Bacarra, *Phil.* 61 B4
Bacău, *Romania* 43 D11
Bacău □, *Romania* 43 D11
Baccarat, *France* 19 D13
Bacerac, *Mexico* 118 A3
Băceşti, *Romania* 43 D12
Bach Long Vi, Dao, *Vietnam* 64 B6
Bacharach, *Germany* 25 E3
Bachelina, *Russia* 50 D7
Bachhwara, *India* 69 G11
Bachuma, *Ethiopia* 81 F4
Bačina, *Serbia, Yug.* 40 C5
Back →, *Canada* 100 B9
Bačka Palanka, *Serbia, Yug.* 42 E4
Bačka Topola, *Serbia, Yug.* 42 E4
Bäckebo, *Sweden* 11 H10
Bäckefors, *Sweden* 11 F6
Bäckhammar, *Sweden* 10 E8
Bački Petrovac, *Serbia, Yug.* 42 E4
Backnang, *Germany* 25 G5
Baco, Mt., *Phil.* 61 E4
Bacolod, *Phil.* 61 F5
Bacqueville-en-Caux, *France* 18 C8
Bács-Kiskun □, *Hungary* 42 D4
Bácsalmás, *Hungary* 42 D4
Bacuag = Placer, *Phil.* 61 G6
Bacuk, *Malaysia* 65 J4
Bād, *Iran* 71 C7
Bad →, *U.S.A.* 112 C4
Bad Aussee, *Austria* 26 D6
Bad Axe, *U.S.A.* 110 C2
Bad Bergzabern, *Germany* 25 F3
Bad Berleburg, *Germany* 24 D4
Bad Bevensen, *Germany* 24 B6
Bad Bramstedt, *Germany* 24 B5
Bad Brückenau, *Germany* 25 E5
Bad Doberan, *Germany* 24 A7
Bad Driburg, *Germany* 24 D5
Bad Ems, *Germany* 25 E3
Bad Frankenhausen, *Germany* 24 D7
Bad Freienwalde, *Germany* 24 C10
Bad Goisern, *Austria* 26 D6
Bad Harzburg, *Germany* 24 D6
Bad Hersfeld, *Germany* 24 E5
Bad Hofgastein, *Austria* 26 D6
Bad Homburg, *Germany* 25 E4
Bad Honnef, *Germany* 24 E3
Bad Iburg, *Germany* 24 C4
Bad Ischl, *Austria* 26 D6
Bad Kissingen, *Germany* 25 E6
Bad Königshofen, *Germany* 25 E6
Bad Kreuznach, *Germany* 25 F3
Bad Krozingen, *Germany* 25 H3
Bad Laasphe, *Germany* 24 E4
Bad Lands, *U.S.A.* 112 D3
Bad Langensalza, *Germany* 24 D6
Bad Lauterberg, *Germany* 24 D6
Bad Leonfelden, *Austria* 26 C7
Bad Liebenwerda, *Germany* 24 D9
Bad Mergentheim, *Germany* 25 F5
Bad Münstereifel, *Germany* 24 E2
Bad Nauheim, *Germany* 25 E4
Bad Neuenahr-Ahrweiler, *Germany* 24 E3
Bad Neustadt, *Germany* 25 E6
Bad Oeynhausen, *Germany* 24 C4
Bad Oldesloe, *Germany* 24 B6
Bad Orb, *Germany* 25 E5
Bad Pyrmont, *Germany* 24 D5
Bad Reichenhall, *Germany* 25 H8
Bad Säckingen, *Germany* 25 H3
Bad Salzuflen, *Germany* 24 C4
Bad Salzungen, *Germany* 24 E6
Bad Schwartau, *Germany* 24 B6
Bad Segeberg, *Germany* 24 B6
Bad St. Leonhard, *Austria* 26 E7
Bad Tölz, *Germany* 25 H7
Bad Urach, *Germany* 25 G5
Bad Vöslau, *Austria* 27 D9
Bad Waldsee, *Germany* 25 H5
Bad Wildungen, *Germany* 24 D5
Bad Wimpfen, *Germany* 25 F5
Bad Windsheim, *Germany* 25 F6
Bad Zwischenahn, *Germany* 24 B4
Bada Barabil, *India* 69 H11
Badagara, *India* 66 P9
Badagri, *Nigeria* 83 D5
Badajós, L., *Brazil* 124 D6
Badajoz, *Spain* 35 G4
Badajoz □, *Spain* 35 G4
Badalona, *Spain* 32 D7
Badalzai, *Afghan.* 68 E1
Badampahar, *India* 67 H15
Badanah, *Si. Arabia* 70 D4
Badarinath, *India* 69 D8
Badas, Kepulauan, *Indonesia* 62 D3
Baddo →, *Pakistan* 66 F4
Bade, *Indonesia* 63 F9
Badeggi, *Nigeria* 83 D6
Badéguichéri, *Niger* 83 C6
Baden, *Austria* 27 C9
Baden, *Switz.* 25 H4
Baden, *U.S.A.* 110 F4
Baden-Baden, *Germany* 25 G4
Baden-Württemberg □, *Germany* 25 G4
Badgastein, *Austria* 26 D6
Badger, *Canada* 103 C8
Badger, *U.S.A.* 116 J7
Bādghīsāt □, *Afghan.* 66 B3
Badgom, *India* 69 B6
Badia Polésine, *Italy* 29 C8
Badin, *Pakistan* 68 G3
Badlands National Park, *U.S.A.* 112 D3
Badogo, *Mali* 82 C3
Badoumbé, *Mali* 82 C2
Badrah, *Iraq* 70 C5
Badrinath, *India* 69 D8
Badulla, *Sri Lanka* 66 R12
Baena, *Spain* 35 H6
Baeza, *Spain* 35 H7
Bafang, *Cameroon* 83 D7
Bafatá, *Guinea-Biss.* 82 C2
Baffin B., *Canada* 4 B4
Baffin I., *Canada* 101 B12
Bafia, *Cameroon* 83 E7
Bafilo, *Togo* 83 D5
Bafing →, *Mali* 82 C2
Bafliyūn, *Syria* 70 B3
Bafoulabé, *Mali* 82 C2
Bafoussam, *Cameroon* 83 D7
Bāfq, *Iran* 71 D7
Bafra, *Turkey* 72 B6
Bafra Burnu, *Turkey* 72 B7
Bāft, *Iran* 71 D8
Bafut, *Cameroon* 83 D7
Bafwasende, *Dem. Rep. of the Congo* 86 B2
Bagam, *Niger* 83 B6
Bagamoyo, *Tanzania* 86 D4
Bagan Datoh, *Malaysia* 65 L3
Bagan Serai, *Malaysia* 65 K3
Baganga, *Phil.* 61 H7
Bagani, *Namibia* 88 B3
Bagansiapiapi, *Indonesia* 62 D2
Bagasra, *India* 68 J4
Bagaud, *India* 68 H6
Bagawi, *Sudan* 81 E3
Bagbag, *Sudan* 81 D3
Bagdad, *U.S.A.* 117 L11
Bagdarin, *Russia* 51 D12
Bagé, *Brazil* 127 C5
Bagenalstown = Muine Bheag, *Ireland* 15 D5
Baggs, *U.S.A.* 114 F10
Bagh, *Pakistan* 69 C5
Baghain →, *India* 69 G9
Baghdād, *Iraq* 70 C5
Bagheria, *Italy* 30 D6
Baghlān, *Afghan.* 66 A6
Bagley, *U.S.A.* 112 B7
Bagnara Cálabra, *Italy* 31 D8
Bagnasco, *Italy* 28 D5
Bagnères-de-Bigorre, *France* 20 E4
Bagnères-de-Luchon, *France* 20 F4
Bagni di Lucca, *Italy* 28 D7
Bagno di Romagna, *Italy* 29 E8
Bagnoles-de-l'Orne, *France* 18 D6
Bagnols-sur-Cèze, *France* 21 D8
Bagnorégio, *Italy* 29 F9
Bago = Pegu, *Burma* 67 L20
Bagodar, *India* 69 G11
Bagrationovsk, *Russia* 9 J19
Bagrdan, *Serbia, Yug.* 40 B5
Baguio, *Phil.* 61 C4
Bağyurdu, *Turkey* 39 C9
Bagzane, Monts, *Niger* 83 B6
Bah, *India* 69 F8
Bahabón de Esgueva, *Spain* 34 D7
Bahadurganj, *India* 69 F12
Bahadurgarh, *India* 68 E7
Bahama, Canal Viejo de, *W. Indies* 120 B4
Bahamas ■, *N. Amer.* 121 B5
Bahār, *Iran* 73 E13
Baharampur, *India* 69 G13
Baharîya, El Wâhât al, *Egypt* 80 B2
Bahawalnagar, *Pakistan* 68 E5
Bahawalpur, *Pakistan* 68 E4
Bahçe, *Turkey* 72 D7
Bahçecik, *Turkey* 41 F13
Baheri, *India* 69 E8
Bahgul →, *India* 69 F8
Bahi, *Tanzania* 86 D4
Bahi Swamp, *Tanzania* 86 D4
Bahía = Salvador, *Brazil* 125 F11
Bahía □, *Brazil* 125 F10
Bahía, Is. de la, *Honduras* 120 C2
Bahía Blanca, *Argentina* 126 D3
Bahía de Caráquez, *Ecuador* 124 D2
Bahía Honda, *Cuba* 120 B3
Bahía Laura, *Argentina* 128 F3
Bahía Negra, *Paraguay* 124 H7
Bahir Dar, *Ethiopia* 81 E4
Bahmanzād, *Iran* 71 D6
Bahr el Ahmar □, *Sudan* 80 D4
Bahr el Ghazâl □, *Sudan* 81 F2
Bahr el Jabal □, *Sudan* 81 G3
Bahr Yûsef →, *Egypt* 80 B3
Bahraich, *India* 69 F9
Bahrain ■, *Asia* 71 E6
Bahror, *India* 68 F7
Bāhū Kalāt, *Iran* 71 E9
Bai, *Mali* 82 C4
Bai Bung, Mui = Ca Mau, Mui, *Vietnam* 65 H5
Bai Duc, *Vietnam* 64 C5
Bai Thuong, *Vietnam* 64 C5
Baia de Aramă, *Romania* 42 E7
Baia Mare, *Romania* 43 C8
Baia-Sprie, *Romania* 43 C8
Baião, *Brazil* 125 D9
Baïbokoum, *Chad* 79 G9
Baicheng, *China* 57 B12
Băicoi, *Romania* 43 E10
Baidoa, *Somali Rep.* 74 G3
Baie Comeau, *Canada* 103 C6
Baie-St-Paul, *Canada* 103 C5
Baie Trinité, *Canada* 103 C6
Baie Verte, *Canada* 103 C8
Baignes-Ste-Radegonde, *France* 20 C3
Baigneux-les-Juifs, *France* 19 E11
Baihar, *India* 69 H9
Baihe, *China* 56 H6
Ba'ījī, *Iraq* 70 C4
Baijnath, *India* 69 E8
Baikal, L. = Baykal, Oz., *Russia* 51 D11
Baikunthpur, *India* 69 H10
Baile Atha Cliath = Dublin, *Ireland* 15 C5
Băile Govora, *Romania* 43 E9
Băile Herculane, *Romania* 42 F7
Băile Olăneşti, *Romania* 43 E9
Băile Tuşnad, *Romania* 43 D10
Bailén, *Spain* 35 G7
Băileşti, *Romania* 43 F8
Baima, *China* 58 A3
Bain-de-Bretagne, *France* 18 E5
Bainbridge, *Ga., U.S.A.* 109 K3
Bainbridge, *N.Y., U.S.A.* 111 D9
Baing, *Indonesia* 63 F6
Bainiu, *China* 56 H7
Baiona, *Spain* 34 C2
Bā'ir, *Jordan* 75 E5
Bairin Youqi, *China* 57 C10
Bairin Zuoqi, *China* 57 C10
Bairnsdale, *Australia* 95 F4
Bais, *Phil.* 61 G5
Baisha, *China* 56 G7
Baissa, *Nigeria* 83 D7
Baitadi, *Nepal* 69 E9
Baiyin, *China* 56 F3
Baiyü, *China* 58 B2
Baiyu Shan, *China* 56 F4
Baiyuda, *Sudan* 80 D3
Baj Baj, *India* 69 H13
Baja, *Hungary* 42 D3
Baja, Pta., *Mexico* 118 B1
Baja California, *Mexico* 118 A1
Baja California □, *Mexico* 118 B2
Baja California Sur □, *Mexico* 118 B2
Bajag, *India* 69 H9
Bajamar, *Canary Is.* 37 F3
Bajana, *India* 68 H4
Bājgīrān, *Iran* 71 B8
Bajimba, Mt., *Australia* 95 D5
Bajina Bašta, *Serbia, Yug.* 40 C3
Bajmok, *Serbia, Yug.* 42 E4
Bajo Nuevo, *Caribbean* 120 C4
Bajoga, *Nigeria* 83 C7
Bajool, *Australia* 94 C5
Bak, *Hungary* 42 D1
Bakar, *Croatia* 29 C11
Bakel, *Senegal* 82 C2
Baker, *Calif., U.S.A.* 117 K10
Baker, *Mont., U.S.A.* 112 B2
Baker, L., *Canada* 100 B10
Baker City, *U.S.A.* 114 D5
Baker I., *Pac. Oc.* 96 G10
Baker I., *U.S.A.* 104 B2
Baker L., *Australia* 93 E4
Baker Lake, *Canada* 100 B10
Baker Mt., *U.S.A.* 114 B3
Bakers Creek, *Australia* 94 C4
Baker's Dozen Is., *Canada* 102 A4
Bakersfield, *Calif., U.S.A.* 117 K8
Bakersfield, *Vt., U.S.A.* 111 B12
Bakhchysaray, *Ukraine* 47 K7
Bakhmach, *Ukraine* 47 G7
Bākhtarān, *Iran* 70 C5
Bākhtarān □, *Iran* 70 C5
Bakı, *Azerbaijan* 49 K9
Bakır →, *Turkey* 39 C9
Bakırdağı, *Turkey* 72 C6
Bakkafjörður, *Iceland* 8 C6
Baklan, *Turkey* 39 C11
Bako, *Ethiopia* 81 F4
Bako, *Ivory C.* 82 D3
Bakony, *Hungary* 42 C2
Bakony Forest = Bakony, *Hungary* 42 C2
Bakori, *Nigeria* 83 C6
Bakouma, *C.A.R.* 84 C4
Baksan, *Russia* 49 J6
Bakswaho, *India* 69 G8
Baku = Bakı, *Azerbaijan* 49 K9
Bakundi, *Nigeria* 83 D7
Bakutis Coast, *Antarctica* 5 D15
Baky = Bakı, *Azerbaijan* 49 K9
Bala, *Canada* 110 A5
Bala, *Senegal* 82 C2
Bâlâ, *Turkey* 72 C5
Bala, *U.K.* 12 E4
Bala, L., *U.K.* 12 E4
Balabac I., *Phil.* 62 C5
Balabac Str., *E. Indies* 62 C5
Balabagh, *Afghan.* 68 B4
Ba'labakk, *Lebanon* 75 B5
Balabalangan, Kepulauan, *Indonesia* 62 E5
Bălăciţa, *Romania* 43 F8
Balad, *Iraq* 70 C5
Balad Rūz, *Iraq* 70 C5
Bālādeh, *Fārs, Iran* 71 D6
Bālādeh, *Māzandaran, Iran* 71 B6
Balaghat, *India* 66 J12
Balaghat Ra., *India* 66 K10
Balaguer, *Spain* 32 D5
Balakhna, *Russia* 48 B6
Balaklava, *Ukraine* 47 K7
Balakliya, *Ukraine* 47 H9
Balakovo, *Russia* 48 D8
Balamau, *India* 69 F9
Bălan, *Romania* 43 D10
Balancán, *Mexico* 119 D6
Balashov, *Russia* 48 E6
Balasinor, *India* 68 H5
Balasore = Baleshwar, *India* 67 J15
Balassagyarmat, *Hungary* 42 B4
Balât, *Egypt* 80 B2
Balaton, *Hungary* 42 D2
Balatonboglár, *Hungary* 42 D2
Balatonfüred, *Hungary* 42 D2
Balatonszentgyörgy, *Hungary* 42 D2
Balayan, *Phil.* 61 E4
Balazote, *Spain* 33 G2
Balbieriškis, *Lithuania* 44 D10
Balbigny, *France* 21 C8
Balbina, Reprêsa de, *Brazil* 124 D7
Balboa, *Panama* 120 E4
Balbriggan, *Ireland* 15 C5
Balcarce, *Argentina* 126 D4
Balcarres, *Canada* 105 C8
Bălceşti, *Romania* 43 F8
Balchik, *Bulgaria* 41 C12
Balclutha, *N.Z.* 91 M2
Balcones Escarpment, *U.S.A.* 113 L5
Balçova, *Turkey* 39 C9
Bald Hd., *Australia* 93 G2
Bald I., *Australia* 93 F2
Bald Knob, *U.S.A.* 113 H9
Baldock L., *Canada* 105 B9
Baldwin, *Mich., U.S.A.* 108 D3
Baldwin, *Pa., U.S.A.* 110 F5
Baldwinsville, *U.S.A.* 111 C8
Baldy Mt., *U.S.A.* 114 B9
Baldy Peak, *U.S.A.* 115 K9
Bale, *Croatia* 29 C10
Bale, *Ethiopia* 81 F5
Bale □, *Ethiopia* 81 F5
Baleares, Is., *Spain* 37 B10
Balearic Is. = Baleares, Is., *Spain* 37 B10
Baleine = Whale →, *Canada* 103 A6
Băleni, *Romania* 43 E12
Baler, *Phil.* 61 D4
Baler Bay, *Phil.* 61 D4
Baleshare, *U.K.* 14 D1
Baleshwar, *India* 67 J15
Balezino, *Russia* 48 B11
Balfate, *Honduras* 120 C2
Bali, *Cameroon* 83 D7
Balí, *Greece* 36 D6
Bali, *India* 68 G5
Bali □, *Indonesia* 62 F5
Bali, Selat, *Indonesia* 63 H16
Balia, *S. Leone* 82 D2
Baliapal, *India* 69 J12
Baligród, *Poland* 45 J9
Balikeşir, *Turkey* 39 B9
Balikeşir □, *Turkey* 39 B9
Balıklıçeşme, *Turkey* 41 F11
Balikpapan, *Indonesia* 62 E5
Balimbing, *Phil.* 63 C5
Baling, *Malaysia* 65 K3
Balingen, *Germany* 25 G4
Balinţ, *Romania* 42 E6
Balintang Channel, *Phil.* 61 B4
Balipara, *India* 67 F18
Balkan Mts. = Stara Planina, *Bulgaria* 40 C7
Balkhash = Balqash, *Kazakstan* 50 E8
Balkhash, Ozero = Balqash Köl, *Kazakstan* 50 E8
Balla, *Bangla.* 67 G17
Ballachulish, *U.K.* 14 E3
Balladonia, *Australia* 93 F3
Ballaghaderreen, *Ireland* 15 C3
Ballarat, *Australia* 95 F3
Ballard, L., *Australia* 93 E3
Ballater, *U.K.* 14 D5
Ballé, *Mali* 82 B3
Ballenas, Canal de, *Mexico* 118 B2
Balleny Is., *Antarctica* 5 C11
Balleroy, *France* 18 C6
Ballerup, *Denmark* 11 J6
Ballı, *Turkey* 41 F11
Ballia, *India* 69 G11
Ballina, *Australia* 95 D5
Ballina, *Ireland* 15 B2
Ballinasloe, *Ireland* 15 C3
Ballinger, *U.S.A.* 113 K5
Ballinrobe, *Ireland* 15 C2
Ballinskelligs B., *Ireland* 15 E1
Ballon, *France* 18 D7
Ballsh, *Albania* 40 F3
Ballston Spa, *U.S.A.* 111 D11
Ballycastle, *U.K.* 15 A5
Ballyclare, *U.K.* 15 B5
Ballyhaunis, *Ireland* 15 C3
Ballymena, *U.K.* 15 B5
Ballymoney, *U.K.* 15 A5
Ballymote, *Ireland* 15 B3
Ballynahinch, *U.K.* 15 B6
Ballyquintin Pt., *U.K.* 15 B6
Ballyshannon, *Ireland* 15 B3
Balmaceda, *Chile* 128 F2
Balmaseda, *Spain* 32 B1
Balmazújváros, *Hungary* 42 C6
Balmertown, *Canada* 105 C10
Balmoral, *Australia* 95 F3
Balmorhea, *U.S.A.* 113 K3
Balonne →, *Australia* 95 D4
Balotra, *India* 68 G5
Balqash, *Kazakstan* 50 E8
Balqash Köl, *Kazakstan* 50 E8
Balrampur, *India* 69 F10
Balranald, *Australia* 95 E3
Balş, *Romania* 43 F9
Balsas, *Mexico* 119 D5
Balsas →, *Brazil* 125 E9
Balsas →, *Mexico* 118 D4
Bålsta, *Sweden* 10 E11
Balston Spa, *U.S.A.* 111 D11
Balta, *Romania* 42 F7
Balta, *Ukraine* 47 H5
Baltanás, *Spain* 34 D6
Bălţi, *Moldova* 43 C12
Baltic Sea, *Europe* 9 H18
Baltîm, *Egypt* 80 H7
Baltimore, *Ireland* 15 E2
Baltimore, *Md., U.S.A.* 108 F7
Baltimore, *Ohio, U.S.A.* 110 G2
Baltit, *Pakistan* 69 A6
Baltiysk, *Russia* 9 J18
Baltrum, *Germany* 24 B3
Baluchistan □, *Pakistan* 66 F4
Balurghat, *India* 69 G13
Balvi, *Latvia* 9 H22
Balya, *Turkey* 39 B9
Bam, *Iran* 71 D8
Bama, *China* 58 E6
Bama, *Nigeria* 83 C7
Bamaga, *Australia* 94 A3
Bamaji L., *Canada* 102 B1
Bamako, *Mali* 82 C3
Bamba, *Mali* 83 B4
Bambara Maoundé, *Mali* 82 B4
Bambari, *C.A.R.* 84 C4
Bambaroo, *Australia* 94 B4
Bambaya, *Guinea* 82 D2
Bamberg, *Germany* 25 F6
Bamberg, *U.S.A.* 109 J5
Bambesi, *Ethiopia* 81 F3
Bambey, *Senegal* 82 C1
Bambey, *Senegal* 82 C1
Bambili, *Dem. Rep. of the Congo* 86 B2
Bamboi, *Ghana* 82 D4
Bamenda, *Cameroon* 83 D7
Bamfield, *Canada* 104 D3
Bāmīān □, *Afghan.* 66 B5
Bamiancheng, *China* 57 C13
Bamkin, *Cameroon* 83 D7
Bampūr, *Iran* 71 E9
Ban, *Burkina Faso* 82 C4
Ban Ban, *Laos* 64 C4
Ban Bang Hin, *Thailand* 65 H2
Ban Chiang Klang, *Thailand* 64 C3
Ban Chik, *Laos* 64 D4
Ban Choho, *Thailand* 64 E4
Ban Dan Lan Hoi, *Thailand* 64 D2
Ban Don = Surat Thani, *Thailand* 65 H2
Ban Don, *Vietnam* 64 F6
Ban Don, Ao →, *Thailand* 65 H2
Ban Dong, *Thailand* 64 C3
Ban Hong, *Thailand* 64 C2
Ban Kaeng, *Thailand* 64 D3
Ban Kantang, *Thailand* 65 J2
Ban Keun, *Laos* 64 C4
Ban Khai, *Thailand* 64 F3
Ban Kheun, *Laos* 64 B3
Ban Khlong Kua, *Thailand* 65 J3
Ban Khuan Mao, *Thailand* 65 J2
Ban Ko Yai Chim, *Thailand* 65 G2
Ban Kok, *Thailand* 64 D4
Ban Laem, *Thailand* 64 F2
Ban Lao Ngam, *Laos* 64 E6
Ban Le Kathe, *Thailand* 64 E2
Ban Mae Chedi, *Thailand* 64 C2
Ban Mae Laeng, *Thailand* 64 B2
Ban Mae Sariang, *Thailand* 64 C1
Ban Mê Thuôt = Buon Ma Thuot, *Vietnam* 64 F7
Ban Mi, *Thailand* 64 E3
Ban Muong Mo, *Laos* 64 C4
Ban Na Mo, *Laos* 64 D5
Ban Na San, *Thailand* 65 H2
Ban Na Tong, *Laos* 64 B3
Ban Nam Bac, *Laos* 64 B4
Ban Nam Ma, *Laos* 64 A3
Ban Ngang, *Laos* 64 E6
Ban Nong Bok, *Laos* 64 D5
Ban Nong Boua, *Laos* 64 E6
Ban Nong Pling, *Thailand* 64 E3
Ban Pak Chan, *Thailand* 65 G2
Ban Phai, *Thailand* 64 D4
Ban Pong, *Thailand* 64 F2
Ban Ron Phibun, *Thailand* 65 H2
Ban Sanam Chai, *Thailand* 65 J3
Ban Sangkha, *Thailand* 64 E4
Ban Tak, *Thailand* 64 D2
Ban Tako, *Thailand* 64 E4
Ban Tha Dua, *Thailand* 64 D2
Ban Tha Li, *Thailand* 64 D3
Ban Tha Nun, *Thailand* 65 H2
Ban Thahine, *Laos* 64 E5
Ban Xien Kok, *Laos* 64 B3
Ban Yen Nhan, *Vietnam* 64 B6
Banaba, *Kiribati* 96 H8
Banalia, *Dem. Rep. of the Congo* 86 B2
Banam, *Cambodia* 65 G5
Banamba, *Mali* 82 C3
Banana Is., *S. Leone* 82 D2
Bananal, I. do, *Brazil* 125 F8
Banaras = Varanasi, *India* 69 G10
Banas →, *Gujarat, India* 68 H4
Banas →, *Mad. P., India* 69 G9
Bânâs, Ras, *Egypt* 80 C4
Banaz, *Turkey* 39 C11
Banaz →, *Turkey* 39 C11
Banbān, *Si. Arabia* 70 E5
Banbridge, *U.K.* 15 B5
Banbury, *U.K.* 13 E6
Banchory, *U.K.* 14 D6
Banco, *Ethiopia* 81 F4

Bancroft, *Canada* 102 C4
Band, *Romania* 43 D9
Band Bonī, *Iran* 71 E8
Band Qīr, *Iran* 71 D6
Banda, *Mad. P., India* 69 G8
Banda, *Ut. P., India* 69 G9
Banda, Kepulauan, *Indonesia* 63 E7
Banda Aceh, *Indonesia* 62 C1
Banda Banda, Mt., *Australia* 95 E5
Banda Elat, *Indonesia* 63 F8
Banda Is. = Banda, Kepulauan, *Indonesia* 63 E7
Banda Sea, *Indonesia* 63 F7
Bandai-San, *Japan* 54 F10
Bandama →, *Ivory C.* 82 D3
Bandama Blanc →, *Ivory C.* 82 D3
Bandama Rouge →, *Ivory C.* 82 D4
Bandān, *Iran* 71 D9
Bandanaira, *Indonesia* 63 E7
Bandanwara, *India* 68 F6
Bandar = Machilipatnam, *India* 67 L12
Bandār 'Abbās, *Iran* 71 E8
Bandar-e Anzalī, *Iran* 71 B6
Bandar-e Bushehr = Būshehr, *Iran* 71 D6
Bandar-e Chārak, *Iran* 71 E7
Bandar-e Deylam, *Iran* 71 D6
Bandar-e Khomeynı, *Iran* 71 D6
Bandar-e Lengeh, *Iran* 71 E7
Bandar-e Maqām, *Iran* 71 E7
Bandar-e Ma'shur, *Iran* 71 D6
Bandar-e Nakhīlū, *Iran* 71 E7
Bandar-e Rīg, *Iran* 71 D6
Bandar-e Torkeman, *Iran* 71 B7
Bandar Maharani = Muar, *Malaysia* 65 L4
Bandar Penggaram = Batu Pahat, *Malaysia* 65 M4
Bandar Seri Begawan, *Brunei* 62 C4
Bandar Sri Aman, *Malaysia* 62 D4
Bandawe, *Malawi* 87 E3
Bande, *Spain* 34 C3
Bandeira, Pico da, *Brazil* 127 A7
Bandera, *Argentina* 126 B3
Banderas, B. de, *Mexico* 118 C3
Bandhogarh, *India* 69 H9
Bandi →, *India* 68 F6
Bandiagara, *Mali* 82 C4
Bandikui, *India* 68 F7
Bandırma, *Turkey* 41 F11
Bandol, *France* 21 E9
Bandon, *Ireland* 15 E3
Bandon →, *Ireland* 15 E3
Bandula, *Mozam.* 87 F3
Bandundu, *Dem. Rep. of the Congo* 84 E3
Bandung, *Indonesia* 63 G12
Bané, *Burkina Faso* 83 C4
Băneasa, *Romania* 43 E12
Bāneh, *Iran* 70 C5
Bañeres, *Spain* 33 G4
Banes, *Cuba* 121 B4
Banff, *Canada* 104 C5
Banff, *U.K.* 14 D6
Banff Nat. Park, *Canada* 104 C5
Banfora, *Burkina Faso* 82 C4
Bang Fai →, *Laos* 64 D5
Bang Hieng →, *Laos* 64 D5
Bang Krathum, *Thailand* 64 D3
Bang Lamung, *Thailand* 64 F3
Bang Mun Nak, *Thailand* 64 D3
Bang Pa In, *Thailand* 64 E3
Bang Rakam, *Thailand* 64 D3
Bang Saphan, *Thailand* 65 G2
Bangaduni I., *India* 69 J13
Bangala Dam, *Zimbabwe* 87 G3
Bangalore, *India* 66 N10
Banganga →, *India* 68 F6
Bangangté, *Cameroon* 83 D7
Bangaon, *India* 69 H13
Bangassou, *C.A.R.* 84 D4
Banggai, *Indonesia* 63 E6
Banggai, Kepulauan, *Indonesia* 63 E6
Banggai Arch. = Banggai, Kepulauan, *Indonesia* 63 E6
Banggi, *Malaysia* 62 C5
Banghāzī, *Libya* 79 B10
Bangjang, *Sudan* 81 E3
Bangka, *Sulawesi, Indonesia* 63 D7
Bangka, *Sumatera, Indonesia* 62 E3
Bangka, Selat, *Indonesia* 62 E3
Bangkalan, *Indonesia* 63 G15
Bangkinang, *Indonesia* 62 D2
Bangko, *Indonesia* 62 E2
Bangkok, *Thailand* 64 F3
Bangladesh ■, *Asia* 67 H17
Bangolo, *Ivory C.* 82 D3
Bangong Co, *India* 69 B8
Bangor, *Down, U.K.* 15 B6
Bangor, *Gwynedd, U.K.* 12 D3
Bangor, *Maine, U.S.A.* 101 D13
Bangor, *Pa., U.S.A.* 111 F9
Bangued, *Phil.* 61 C4
Bangui, *C.A.R.* 84 D3
Bangui, *Phil.* 61 B4
Banguru, *Dem. Rep. of the Congo* 86 B2
Bangweulu, L., *Zambia* 87 E3
Bangweulu Swamp, *Zambia* 87 E3
Bani, *Dom. Rep.* 121 C5
Bani →, *Mali* 82 C4
Bani Bangou, *Niger* 83 B5
Banī Sa'd, *Iraq* 70 C5
Bania, *Ivory C.* 82 D4
Banihal Pass, *India* 69 C6
Banikoara, *Benin* 83 C5
Bāniyās, *Syria* 70 C3
Banja Luka, *Bos.-H.* 42 F2
Banjar, *India* 68 D7
Banjar →, *India* 69 H9
Banjarmasin, *Indonesia* 62 E4
Banjul, *Gambia* 82 C1
Banka, *India* 69 G12
Bankas, *Mali* 82 C4
Bankeryd, *Sweden* 11 G8
Banket, *Zimbabwe* 87 F3
Bankilaré, *Niger* 83 C5
Bankipore, *India* 67 G14
Banks I., *B.C., Canada* 104 C3
Banks I., *N.W.T., Canada* 100 A7
Banks Pen., *N.Z.* 91 K4
Banks Str., *Australia* 94 G4
Bankura, *India* 69 H12
Bankya, *Bulgaria* 40 D7
Banmankhi, *India* 69 G12
Bann →, *Arm., U.K.* 15 B5
Bann →, *L'derry., U.K.* 15 A5
Bannalec, *France* 18 E3
Bannang Sata, *Thailand* 65 J3
Banning, *U.S.A.* 117 M10
Banningville = Bandundu, *Dem. Rep. of the Congo* 84 E3
Banno, *Ethiopia* 81 G4
Bannockburn, *Canada* 110 B7
Bannockburn, *U.K.* 14 E5
Bannockburn, *Zimbabwe* 87 G2
Bannu, *Pakistan* 66 C7
Bano, *India* 69 H11
Bañolas = Banyoles, *Spain* 32 C7
Banon, *France* 21 D9
Baños de la Encina, *Spain* 35 G7
Baños de Molgas, *Spain* 34 C3
Bánovce nad Bebravou, *Slovak Rep.* 27 C11
Banovići, *Bos.-H.* 42 F3
Bansgaon, *India* 69 F10
Banská Bystrica, *Slovak Rep.* 27 C12
Banská Štiavnica, *Slovak Rep.* 27 C11
Bansko, *Bulgaria* 40 E7
Banskobystrický □, *Slovak Rep.* 27 C12
Banswara, *India* 68 H6
Bantaeng, *Indonesia* 63 F5
Bantaji, *Nigeria* 83 D7
Bantayan, *Phil.* 61 F5
Bantry, *Ireland* 15 E2
Bantry B., *Ireland* 15 E2
Bantul, *Indonesia* 63 G14
Bantva, *India* 68 J4
Banu, *Afghan.* 66 B6
Banya, *Bulgaria* 41 D8
Banyak, Kepulauan, *Indonesia* 62 D1
Banyalbufar, *Spain* 37 B9
Banyo, *Cameroon* 83 D7
Banyoles, *Spain* 32 C7
Banyuls-sur-Mer, *France* 20 F7
Banyumas, *Indonesia* 63 G13
Banyuwangi, *Indonesia* 63 H16
Banzare Coast, *Antarctica* 5 C9
Banzyville = Mobayi, *Dem. Rep. of the Congo* 84 D4
Bao Ha, *Vietnam* 58 F5
Bao Lac, *Vietnam* 64 A5
Bao Loc, *Vietnam* 65 G6
Bao'an = Shenzhen, *China* 59 F10
Baocheng, *China* 56 H4
Baode, *China* 56 E6
Baodi, *China* 57 E9
Baoding, *China* 56 E8
Baoji, *China* 56 G4
Baojing, *China* 58 C7
Baokang, *China* 59 B8
Baoshan, *Shanghai, China* 59 B13
Baoshan, *Yunnan, China* 58 E2
Baotou, *China* 56 D6
Baoxing, *China* 58 B4
Baoying, *China* 57 H10
Bap, *India* 68 F5
Bapatla, *India* 67 M12
Bapaume, *France* 19 B9
Bāqerābād, *Iran* 71 C6
Ba'qūbah, *Iraq* 70 C5
Baquedano, *Chile* 126 A2
Bar, *Montenegro, Yug.* 40 D3
Bar, *Ukraine* 47 H4
Bar Bigha, *India* 69 G11
Bar Harbor, *U.S.A.* 109 C11
Bar-le-Duc, *France* 19 D12
Bar-sur-Aube, *France* 19 D11
Bar-sur-Seine, *France* 19 D11
Bara, *India* 69 G9
Bâra, *Romania* 43 C12
Bara Banki, *India* 69 F9
Barabai, *Indonesia* 62 E5
Baraboo, *U.S.A.* 112 D10
Baracoa, *Cuba* 121 B5
Baradā →, *Syria* 75 B5
Baradero, *Argentina* 126 C4
Baradine, *Australia* 95 E4
Baraga, *U.S.A.* 112 B10
Bărăganul, *Romania* 43 F12
Barah →, *India* 68 F6
Barahona, *Dom. Rep.* 121 C5
Barahona, *Spain* 32 D2
Barail Range, *India* 67 G18
Baraka, *Sudan* 81 E2
Baraka →, *Sudan* 80 D4
Barakaldo, *Spain* 32 B2
Barakar →, *India* 69 G12
Barakhola, *India* 67 G18
Barakot, *India* 69 J11
Barakpur, *India* 69 H13
Baralaba, *Australia* 94 C4
Baralla, *Spain* 34 C3
Baralzon L., *Canada* 105 B9
Barameiya, *Sudan* 80 D4
Baramula, *India* 69 B6
Baran, *India* 68 G7
Baran →, *Pakistan* 68 G3
Barañain, *Spain* 32 C3
Baranavichy, *Belarus* 47 F4
Barani, *Burkina Faso* 82 C4
Baranof, *U.S.A.* 104 B2
Baranof I., *U.S.A.* 100 C6
Baranów Sandomierski, *Poland* 45 H8
Baranya □, *Hungary* 42 E3
Baraolt, *Romania* 43 D10
Barapasi, *Indonesia* 63 E9
Barasat, *India* 69 H13
Barat Daya, Kepulauan, *Indonesia* 63 F7
Barataria B., *U.S.A.* 113 L10
Barauda, *India* 68 H6
Baraut, *India* 68 E7
Barbacena, *Brazil* 127 A7
Barbados ■, *W. Indies* 121 D8
Barban, *Croatia* 29 C11
Barbària, C. de, *Spain* 37 C7
Barbaros, *Turkey* 41 F11
Barbastro, *Spain* 32 C5
Barbate = Barbate de Franco, *Spain* 35 J5
Barbate de Franco, *Spain* 35 J5
Barberino di Mugello, *Italy* 29 E8
Barberton, *S. Africa* 89 D5
Barberton, *U.S.A.* 110 E3
Barbezieux-St-Hilaire, *France* 20 C3
Barbosa, *Colombia* 124 B4
Barbourville, *U.S.A.* 109 G4
Barbuda, *W. Indies* 121 C7
Bârca, *Romania* 43 G8
Barcaldine, *Australia* 94 C4
Barcarrota, *Spain* 35 G4
Barcellona Pozzo di Gotto, *Italy* 31 D8
Barcelona, *Spain* 32 D7
Barcelona, *Venezuela* 124 A6
Barcelona □, *Spain* 32 D7
Barcelonette, *France* 21 D10
Barcelos, *Brazil* 124 D6
Barcin, *Poland* 45 F4
Barclayville, *Liberia* 82 E3
Barcoo →, *Australia* 94 D3
Barcs, *Hungary* 42 E2
Barczewo, *Poland* 44 E7
Bärdä, *Azerbaijan* 49 K8
Bardaï, *Chad* 79 D9
Bardas Blancas, *Argentina* 126 D2
Barddhaman, *India* 69 H12
Bardejov, *Slovak Rep.* 27 B14
Bardera, *Somali Rep.* 74 G3
Bardi, *Italy* 28 D6
Bardīyah, *Libya* 79 B10
Bardolino, *Italy* 28 C7
Bardonécchia, *Italy* 28 C3
Bardsey I., *U.K.* 12 E3
Bardstown, *U.S.A.* 108 G3
Bareilly, *India* 69 E8
Barela, *India* 69 H9
Barentin, *France* 18 C7
Barenton, *France* 18 D6
Barents Sea, *Arctic* 4 B9
Barentu, *Eritrea* 81 D4
Barfleur, *France* 18 C5
Barfleur, Pte. de, *France* 18 C5
Barga, *Italy* 28 D7
Bargara, *Australia* 94 C5
Bargas, *Spain* 34 F6
Bârgăului Bistriţa, *Romania* 43 C9
Barge, *Italy* 28 D4
Bargnop, *Sudan* 81 F2
Bargteheide, *Germany* 24 B6
Barguzin, *Russia* 51 D11
Barh, *India* 69 G11
Barhaj, *India* 69 F10
Barham, *Australia* 95 F3
Barharwa, *India* 69 G12
Barhi, *India* 69 G11
Bari, *India* 68 F7
Bari, *Italy* 31 A9
Bari Doab, *Pakistan* 68 D5
Bari Sadri, *India* 68 G6
Bari Sardo, *Italy* 30 C2
Barīdī, Ra's, *Si. Arabia* 70 E3
Barīm, *Yemen* 76 E8
Barinas, *Venezuela* 124 B4
Baring, C., *Canada* 100 B8
Baringo, *Kenya* 86 B4
Baringo, L., *Kenya* 86 B4
Bârîs, *Egypt* 80 C3
Barisal, *Bangla.* 67 H17
Barisan, Bukit, *Indonesia* 62 E2
Barito →, *Indonesia* 62 E4
Barjac, *France* 21 D8
Barjols, *France* 21 E10
Bark L., *Canada* 110 A7
Barka = Baraka →, *Sudan* 80 D4
Barkakana, *India* 69 H11
Barkam, *China* 58 B4
Barker, *U.S.A.* 110 C6
Barkley, L., *U.S.A.* 109 G2
Barkley Sound, *Canada* 104 D3
Barkly East, *S. Africa* 88 E4
Barkly Roadhouse, *Australia* 94 B2
Barkly Tableland, *Australia* 94 B2
Barkly West, *S. Africa* 88 D3
Barkol, Wadi →, *Sudan* 80 D3
Barla Dağı, *Turkey* 39 C12
Bârlad, *Romania* 43 D12
Bârlad →, *Romania* 43 E12
Barlee, L., *Australia* 93 E2
Barlee, Mt., *Australia* 93 D4
Barletta, *Italy* 31 A9
Barlinek, *Poland* 45 F2
Barlovento, *Canary Is.* 37 F2
Barlow L., *Canada* 105 A8
Barmedman, *Australia* 95 E4
Barmer, *India* 68 G4
Barmera, *Australia* 95 E3
Barmouth, *U.K.* 12 E3
Barmstedt, *Germany* 24 B5
Barna →, *India* 69 G10
Barnagar, *India* 68 H6
Barnala, *India* 68 D6
Barnard Castle, *U.K.* 12 C6
Barnaul, *Russia* 50 D9
Barnesville, *U.S.A.* 109 J3
Barnet, *U.K.* 13 F7
Barneveld, *Neths.* 17 B5
Barneveld, *U.S.A.* 111 C9
Barneville-Cartevert, *France* 18 C5
Barnhart, *U.S.A.* 113 K4
Barnsley, *U.K.* 12 D6
Barnstaple, *U.K.* 13 F3
Barnstaple Bay = Bideford Bay, *U.K.* 13 F3
Barnsville, *U.S.A.* 112 B6
Barnwell, *U.S.A.* 109 J5
Baro, *Nigeria* 83 D6
Baro →, *Ethiopia* 81 F3
Baroda = Vadodara, *India* 68 H5
Baroda, *India* 68 G7
Baroe, *S. Africa* 88 E3
Baron Ra., *Australia* 92 D4
Barong, *China* 58 B2
Barotseland, *Zambia* 85 H4
Barouéli, *Mali* 82 C3
Barpeta, *India* 67 F17
Barques, Pt. Aux, *U.S.A.* 110 B2
Barquísimeto, *Venezuela* 124 A5
Barr, Ras el, *Egypt* 80 H7
Barr Smith Range, *Australia* 93 E3
Barra, *Brazil* 125 F10
Barra, *U.K.* 14 E1
Barra, Sd. of, *U.K.* 14 D1
Barra de Navidad, *Mexico* 118 D4
Barra do Corda, *Brazil* 125 E9
Barra do Piraí, *Brazil* 127 A7
Barra Falsa, Pta. da, *Mozam.* 89 C6
Barra Hd., *U.K.* 14 E1
Barra Mansa, *Brazil* 127 A7
Barraba, *Australia* 95 E5
Barrackpur = Barakpur, *India* 69 H13
Barradale Roadhouse, *Australia* 92 D1
Barrafranca, *Italy* 31 E7
Barraigh = Barra, *U.K.* 14 E1
Barranca, *Lima, Peru* 124 F3
Barranca, *Loreto, Peru* 124 D3
Barrancabermeja, *Colombia* 124 B4
Barrancas, *Venezuela* 124 B6
Barrancos, *Portugal* 35 G4
Barranqueras, *Argentina* 126 B4
Barranquilla, *Colombia* 124 A4
Barraute, *Canada* 102 C4
Barre, *Mass., U.S.A.* 111 D12
Barre, *Vt., U.S.A.* 111 B12
Barreal, *Argentina* 126 C2
Barreiras, *Brazil* 125 F10
Barreirinhas, *Brazil* 125 D10
Barreiro, *Portugal* 35 G1
Barrême, *France* 21 E10
Barren, Nosy, *Madag.* 89 B7
Barretos, *Brazil* 125 H9
Barrhead, *Canada* 104 C6
Barrie, *Canada* 102 D4
Barrier Ra., *Australia* 95 E3
Barrière, *Canada* 104 C4
Barrington, *U.S.A.* 111 E13
Barrington L., *Canada* 105 B8
Barrington Tops, *Australia* 95 E5
Barringun, *Australia* 95 D4
Barro do Garças, *Brazil* 125 G8
Barron, *U.S.A.* 112 C9
Barrow, *U.S.A.* 100 A4
Barrow →, *Ireland* 15 D5
Barrow Creek, *Australia* 94 C1
Barrow I., *Australia* 92 D2
Barrow-in-Furness, *U.K.* 12 C4
Barrow Pt., *Australia* 94 A3
Barrow Pt., *U.S.A.* 98 B4
Barrow Ra., *Australia* 93 E4
Barrow Str., *Canada* 4 B3
Barruecopardo, *Spain* 34 D4
Barruelo de Santullán, *Spain* 34 C6
Barry, *U.K.* 13 F4
Barry's Bay, *Canada* 102 C4
Barsalogho, *Burkina Faso* 83 C4
Barsat, *Pakistan* 69 A5
Barsham, *Syria* 70 C4
Barsi, *India* 66 K9
Barsinghausen, *Germany* 24 C5
Barsoi, *India* 67 G15
Barstow, *U.S.A.* 117 L9
Barth, *Germany* 24 A8
Barthélemy, Col, *Vietnam* 64 C5
Bartica, *Guyana* 124 B7
Bartin, *Turkey* 72 B5
Bartlesville, *U.S.A.* 113 G7
Bartlett, *U.S.A.* 116 J8
Bartlett, L., *Canada* 104 A5
Bartolomeu Dias, *Mozam.* 87 G4
Barton, *U.S.A.* 111 B12
Barton upon Humber, *U.K.* 12 D7
Bartoszyce, *Poland* 44 D7
Bartow, *U.S.A.* 109 M5
Barú, Volcan, *Panama* 120 E3
Barumba, *Dem. Rep. of the Congo* 86 B1
Baruth, *Germany* 24 C9
Baruunsuu, *Mongolia* 56 C3
Barvinkove, *Ukraine* 47 H9
Barwani, *India* 68 H6
Barwice, *Poland* 44 E3
Barycz →, *Poland* 45 G3
Barysaw, *Belarus* 46 E5
Barysh, *Russia* 48 D8
Barzān, *Iraq* 70 B5
Bârzava, *Romania* 42 D6
Bas-Rhin □, *France* 19 D14
Bašaid, *Serbia, Yug.* 42 E5
Bāsa'īdū, *Iran* 71 E7
Basal, *Pakistan* 68 C5
Basankusa, *Dem. Rep. of the Congo* 84 D3
Basarabeasca, *Moldova* 43 D13
Basarabi, *Romania* 43 F13
Basauri, *Spain* 32 B2
Basawa, *Afghan.* 68 B4
Bascuñán, C., *Chile* 126 B1
Basel, *Switz.* 25 H3
Basel-Landschaft □, *Switz.* 25 H3
Basento →, *Italy* 31 B9
Bashākerd, Kūhhā-ye, *Iran* 71 E8
Bashaw, *Canada* 104 C6
Bāshī, *Iran* 71 D6
Bashkir Republic = Bashkortostan □, *Russia* 50 D6
Bashkortostan □, *Russia* 50 D6
Basibasy, *Madag.* 89 C7
Basilan I., *Phil.* 61 H5
Basilan Str., *Phil.* 61 H5
Basildon, *U.K.* 13 F8
Basilé, *Eq. Guin.* 83 E6
Basilicata □, *Italy* 31 B9
Basim = Washim, *India* 66 J10
Basin, *U.S.A.* 114 D9
Basingstoke, *U.K.* 13 F6
Baška, *Croatia* 29 D11
Başkale, *Turkey* 73 C10
Baskatong, Rés., *Canada* 102 C4
Basle = Basel, *Switz.* 25 H3
Başmakçı, *Turkey* 39 D12
Basoda, *India* 68 H7
Basoka, *Dem. Rep. of the Congo* 86 B1
Basque, Pays, *France* 20 E2
Basque Provinces = País Vasco □, *Spain* 32 C2
Basra = Al Başrah, *Iraq* 70 D5
Bass Str., *Australia* 94 F4
Bassano, *Canada* 104 C6
Bassano del Grappa, *Italy* 29 C8
Bassar, *Togo* 83 D5
Bassas da India, *Ind. Oc.* 85 J7
Basse-Normandie □, *France* 18 D6
Basse Santa-Su, *Gambia* 82 C2
Basse-Terre, *Guadeloupe* 121 C7
Bassein, *Burma* 67 L19
Basseterre, *St. Kitts & Nevis* 121 C7
Bassett, *U.S.A.* 112 D5
Bassi, *India* 68 D7
Bassigny, *France* 19 E12
Bassikounou, *Mauritania* 82 B3
Bassila, *Benin* 83 D5
Bassum, *Germany* 24 C4
Båstad, *Sweden* 11 H6
Bastak, *Iran* 71 E7
Baştām, *Iran* 71 B7
Bastar, *India* 67 K12
Bastelica, *France* 21 F13
Basti, *India* 69 F10
Bastia, *France* 21 F13
Bastogne, *Belgium* 17 D5
Bastrop, *La., U.S.A.* 113 J9
Bastrop, *Tex., U.S.A.* 113 K6
Bat Yam, *Israel* 75 C3
Bata, *Eq. Guin.* 84 D1
Bata, *Romania* 42 D7
Bataan □, *Phil.* 61 D4
Batabanó, *Cuba* 120 B3
Batabanó, G. de, *Cuba* 120 B3
Batac, *Phil.* 61 B4
Batagai, *Russia* 51 C14
Batajnica, *Serbia, Yug.* 40 B4
Batak, *Bulgaria* 41 E8
Batala, *India* 68 D6
Batalha, *Portugal* 34 F2
Batama, *Dem. Rep. of the Congo* 86 B2
Batamay, *Russia* 51 C13
Batang, *China* 58 B2
Batang, *Indonesia* 63 G13
Batangas, *Phil.* 61 E4
Batanta, *Indonesia* 63 E8
Batatais, *Brazil* 127 A6
Batavia, *U.S.A.* 110 D6
Bataysk, *Russia* 47 J10
Batchelor, *Australia* 92 B5
Batdambang, *Cambodia* 64 F4
Bateman's B., *Australia* 95 F5
Batemans Bay, *Australia* 95 F5
Bates Ra., *Australia* 93 E3
Batesburg, *U.S.A.* 109 J5
Batesville, *Ark., U.S.A.* 113 H9
Batesville, *Miss., U.S.A.* 113 H10
Batesville, *Tex., U.S.A.* 113 L5
Bath, *Canada* 111 B8
Bath, *U.K.* 13 F5
Bath, *Maine, U.S.A.* 109 D11
Bath, *N.Y., U.S.A.* 110 D7
Bath & North East Somerset □, *U.K.* 13 F5
Batheay, *Cambodia* 65 G5
Bathurst = Banjul, *Gambia* 82 C1
Bathurst, *Australia* 95 E4
Bathurst, *Canada* 103 C6
Bathurst, *S. Africa* 88 E4
Bathurst, C., *Canada* 100 A7
Bathurst B., *Australia* 94 A3
Bathurst Harb., *Australia* 94 G4
Bathurst I., *Australia* 92 B5
Bathurst I., *Canada* 4 B2
Bathurst Inlet, *Canada* 100 B9
Bati, *Ethiopia* 81 E5
Batie, *Burkina Faso* 82 D4

Batlow, *Australia* 95 F4
Batman, *Turkey* 70 B4
Baṭn al Ghūl, *Jordan* 75 F4
Batna, *Algeria* 78 A7
Batobato = San Isidro, *Phil.* 61 H7
Batočina, *Serbia, Yug.* 40 B5
Batoka, *Zambia* 87 F2
Baton Rouge, *U.S.A.* 113 K9
Batong, Ko, *Thailand* 65 J2
Bátonyterenye, *Hungary* 42 C4
Batopilas, *Mexico* 118 B3
Batouri, *Cameroon* 84 D2
Båtsfjord, *Norway* 8 A23
Battambang = Batdambang, *Cambodia* 64 F4
Batticaloa, *Sri Lanka* 66 R12
Battipáglia, *Italy* 31 B7
Battle, *U.K.* 13 G8
Battle →, *Canada* 105 C7
Battle Creek, *U.S.A.* 108 D3
Battle Ground, *U.S.A.* 116 E4
Battle Harbour, *Canada* 103 B8
Battle Lake, *U.S.A.* 112 B7
Battle Mountain, *U.S.A.* 114 F5
Battlefields, *Zimbabwe* 87 F2
Battleford, *Canada* 105 C7
Battonya, *Hungary* 42 D6
Batu, *Ethiopia* 81 F4
Batu, Kepulauan, *Indonesia* 62 E1
Batu Caves, *Malaysia* 65 L3
Batu Gajah, *Malaysia* 65 K3
Batu Is. = Batu, Kepulauan, *Indonesia* 62 E1
Batu Pahat, *Malaysia* 65 M4
Batuata, *Indonesia* 63 F6
Batumi, *Georgia* 49 K5
Baturaja, *Indonesia* 62 E2
Baturité, *Brazil* 125 D11
Bau, *Malaysia* 62 D4
Baubau, *Indonesia* 63 F6
Bauchi, *Nigeria* 83 C6
Bauchi □, *Nigeria* 83 C7
Baud, *France* 18 E3
Baudette, *U.S.A.* 112 A7
Bauer, C., *Australia* 95 E1
Bauhinia, *Australia* 94 C4
Baukau, *Indonesia* 63 F7
Bauld, C., *Canada* 101 C14
Baume-les-Dames, *France* 19 E13
Baunatal, *Germany* 24 D5
Baunei, *Italy* 30 B2
Baure, *Nigeria* 83 C6
Bauru, *Brazil* 127 A6
Bausi, *India* 69 G12
Bauska, *Latvia* 9 H21
Bautino, *Kazakstan* 49 H10
Bautzen, *Germany* 24 D10
Bauya, *S. Leone* 82 D2
Bavānāt, *Iran* 71 D7
Bavanište, *Serbia, Yug.* 42 F5
Bavaria = Bayern □, *Germany* 25 G7
Båven, *Sweden* 10 E10
Bavispe →, *Mexico* 118 B3
Bawdwin, *Burma* 67 H20
Bawean, *Indonesia* 62 F4
Bawku, *Ghana* 83 C4
Bawlake, *Burma* 67 K20
Bawolung, *China* 58 C3
Baxley, *U.S.A.* 109 K4
Baxoi, *China* 58 B1
Baxter, *U.S.A.* 112 B7
Baxter Springs, *U.S.A.* 113 G7
Bay, L. de, *Phil.* 61 D4
Bay City, *Mich., U.S.A.* 108 D4
Bay City, *Tex., U.S.A.* 113 L7
Bay Minette, *U.S.A.* 109 K2
Bay Roberts, *Canada* 103 C9
Bay St. Louis, *U.S.A.* 113 K10
Bay Springs, *U.S.A.* 113 K10
Bay View, *N.Z.* 91 H6
Baya, *Dem. Rep. of the Congo* 87 E2
Bayamo, *Cuba* 120 B4
Bayamón, *Puerto Rico* 121 C6
Bayan Har Shan, *China* 60 C4
Bayan Hot = Alxa Zuoqi, *China* 56 E3
Bayan Obo, *China* 56 D5
Bayan-Ovoo = Erdenetsogt, *Mongolia* 56 C4
Bayana, *India* 68 F7
Bayanaūyl, *Kazakstan* 50 D8
Bayandalay, *Mongolia* 56 C2
Bayanhongor, *Mongolia* 60 B5
Bayard, *N. Mex., U.S.A.* 115 K9
Bayard, *Nebr., U.S.A.* 112 E3
Bayawan, *Phil.* 61 G5
Baybay, *Phil.* 61 F6
Bayburt, *Turkey* 73 B9
Bayelsa □, *Nigeria* 83 E6
Bayerische Alpen, *Germany* 25 H7
Bayerischer Wald, *Germany* 25 G8
Bayern □, *Germany* 25 G7
Bayeux, *France* 18 C6
Bayfield, *Canada* 110 C3
Bayfield, *U.S.A.* 112 B9
Bayındır, *Turkey* 39 C9
Baykal, Oz., *Russia* 51 D11
Baykan, *Turkey* 70 B4
Baykonur = Bayqongyr, *Kazakstan* 50 E7
Baynes Mts., *Namibia* 88 B1
Bayombong, *Phil.* 61 C4
Bayon, *France* 19 D13
Bayona = Baiona, *Spain* 34 C2
Bayonne, *France* 20 E2
Bayonne, *U.S.A.* 111 F10
Bayovar, *Peru* 124 E2
Bayqongyr, *Kazakstan* 50 E7
Bayram-Ali = Bayramaly, *Turkmenistan* 50 F7
Bayramaly, *Turkmenistan* 50 F7
Bayramiç, *Turkey* 39 B8
Bayreuth, *Germany* 25 F7
Bayrischzell, *Germany* 25 H8
Bayrūt, *Lebanon* 75 B4
Bays, L. of, *Canada* 110 A5
Baysville, *Canada* 110 A5
Bayt Lahm, *West Bank* 75 D4
Baytown, *U.S.A.* 113 L7
Bayzo, *Niger* 83 C5
Baza, *Spain* 35 H8
Bazar Dyuzi, *Russia* 49 K8
Bazardüzü = Bazar Dyuzi, *Russia* 49 K8
Bazarny Karabulak, *Russia* 48 D8
Bazarnyy Syzgan, *Russia* 48 D8
Bazaruto, I. do, *Mozam.* 89 C6
Bazas, *France* 20 D3
Bazhong, *China* 58 B6
Bazhou, *China* 56 E9
Bazmān, Kūh-e, *Iran* 71 D9
Beach, *U.S.A.* 112 B3
Beach City, *U.S.A.* 110 F3
Beachport, *Australia* 95 F3
Beachy Hd., *U.K.* 13 G8
Beacon, *Australia* 93 F2
Beacon, *U.S.A.* 111 E11
Beaconsfield, *Australia* 94 G4
Beagle, Canal, *S. Amer.* 122 J4
Beagle Bay, *Australia* 92 C3
Bealanana, *Madag.* 89 A8
Beals Cr. →, *U.S.A.* 113 J4
Beamsville, *Canada* 110 C5
Bear →, *Calif., U.S.A.* 116 G5
Bear →, *Utah, U.S.A.* 106 B4
Béar, C., *France* 20 F7
Bear I., *Ireland* 15 E2
Bear L., *Canada* 105 B9
Bear L., *U.S.A.* 114 F8
Beardmore, *Canada* 102 C2
Beardmore Glacier, *Antarctica* 5 E11
Beardstown, *U.S.A.* 112 F9
Bearma →, *India* 69 G8
Béarn, *France* 20 E3
Bearpaw Mts., *U.S.A.* 114 B9
Bearskin Lake, *Canada* 102 B1
Beas →, *India* 68 D6
Beas de Segura, *Spain* 35 G8
Beasain, *Spain* 32 B2
Beata, C., *Dom. Rep.* 121 C5
Beata, I., *Dom. Rep.* 121 C5
Beatrice, *U.S.A.* 112 E6
Beatrice, *Zimbabwe* 87 F3
Beatrice, C., *Australia* 94 A2
Beatton →, *Canada* 104 B4
Beatton River, *Canada* 104 B4
Beatty, *U.S.A.* 116 J10
Beaucaire, *France* 21 E8
Beauce, Plaine de la, *France* 19 D8
Beauceville, *Canada* 103 C5
Beaudesert, *Australia* 95 D5
Beaufort, *France* 21 C10
Beaufort, *Malaysia* 62 C5
Beaufort, *N.C., U.S.A.* 109 H7
Beaufort, *S.C., U.S.A.* 109 J5
Beaufort Sea, *Arctic* 4 B1
Beaufort West, *S. Africa* 88 E3
Beaugency, *France* 19 E8
Beauharnois, *Canada* 111 A11
Beaujeu, *France* 19 F11
Beaujolais, *France* 19 F11
Beaulieu →, *Canada* 104 A6
Beaulieu-sur-Dordogne, *France* 20 D5
Beaulieu-sur-Mer, *France* 21 E11
Beauly, *U.K.* 14 D4
Beauly →, *U.K.* 14 D4
Beaumaris, *U.K.* 12 D3
Beaumont, *Belgium* 17 D4
Beaumont, *France* 20 D4
Beaumont, *U.S.A.* 113 K7
Beaumont-de-Lomagne, *France* 20 E5
Beaumont-le-Roger, *France* 18 C7
Beaumont-sur-Sarthe, *France* 18 D7
Beaune, *France* 19 E11
Beaune-la-Rolande, *France* 19 D9
Beaupré, *Canada* 103 C5
Beaupréau, *France* 18 E6
Beauraing, *Belgium* 17 D4
Beaurepaire, *France* 21 C9
Beauséjour, *Canada* 105 C9
Beauvais, *France* 19 C9
Beauval, *Canada* 105 B7
Beauvoir-sur-Mer, *France* 18 F4
Beauvoir-sur-Niort, *France* 20 B3
Beaver, *Okla., U.S.A.* 113 G4
Beaver, *Pa., U.S.A.* 110 F4
Beaver, *Utah, U.S.A.* 115 G7
Beaver →, *B.C., Canada* 104 B4
Beaver →, *Ont., Canada* 102 A2
Beaver →, *Sask., Canada* 105 B7
Beaver →, *U.S.A.* 113 G5
Beaver City, *U.S.A.* 112 E5
Beaver Creek, *Canada* 100 B5
Beaver Dam, *U.S.A.* 112 D10
Beaver Falls, *U.S.A.* 110 F4
Beaver Hill L., *Canada* 105 C10
Beaver I., *U.S.A.* 108 C3
Beaverhill L., *Canada* 104 C6
Beaverlodge, *Canada* 104 B5
Beaverstone →, *Canada* 102 B2
Beaverton, *Canada* 110 B5
Beaverton, *U.S.A.* 116 E4
Beawar, *India* 68 F6
Bebedouro, *Brazil* 127 A6
Beboa, *Madag.* 89 B7
Bebra, *Germany* 24 E5
Beccles, *U.K.* 13 E9
Bečej, *Serbia, Yug.* 42 E5
Beceni, *Romania* 43 E11
Becerreá, *Spain* 34 C3
Béchar, *Algeria* 78 B5
Bechyně, *Czech Rep.* 26 B7
Beckley, *U.S.A.* 108 G5
Beckum, *Germany* 24 D4
Beclean, *Romania* 43 C9
Bečov nad Teplou, *Czech Rep.* 26 A5
Bečva →, *Czech Rep.* 27 B10
Bédar, *Spain* 33 H3
Bédarieux, *France* 20 E7
Beddouza, Ras, *Morocco* 78 B4
Bedele, *Ethiopia* 81 F4
Bederkesa, *Germany* 24 B4
Bedeso, *Ethiopia* 81 F5
Bedford, *Canada* 111 A12
Bedford, *S. Africa* 88 E4
Bedford, *U.K.* 13 E7
Bedford, *Ind., U.S.A.* 108 F2
Bedford, *Iowa, U.S.A.* 112 E7
Bedford, *Ohio, U.S.A.* 110 E3
Bedford, *Pa., U.S.A.* 110 F6
Bedford, *Va., U.S.A.* 108 G6
Bedford, C., *Australia* 94 B4
Bedfordshire □, *U.K.* 13 E7
Będków, *Poland* 45 G6
Bednja →, *Croatia* 29 B13
Bednodemyanovsk, *Russia* 48 D6
Bedónia, *Italy* 28 D6
Bedourie, *Australia* 94 C2
Bedum, *Neths.* 17 A6
Będzin, *Poland* 45 H6
Beebe Plain, *Canada* 111 A12
Beech Creek, *U.S.A.* 110 E7
Beelitz, *Germany* 24 C8
Beenleigh, *Australia* 95 D5
Be'er Menuḥa, *Israel* 70 D2
Be'er Sheva, *Israel* 75 D3
Beersheba = Be'er Sheva, *Israel* 75 D3
Beeskow, *Germany* 24 C10
Beestekraal, *S. Africa* 89 D4
Beeston, *U.K.* 12 E6
Beetzendorf, *Germany* 24 C7
Beeville, *U.S.A.* 113 L6
Befale, *Dem. Rep. of the Congo* 84 D4
Befandriana, *Mahajanga, Madag.* 89 B8
Befandriana, *Toliara, Madag.* 89 C7
Befasy, *Madag.* 89 C7
Béfotaka, *Antsiranana, Madag.* 89 A8
Befotaka, *Fianarantsoa, Madag.* 89 C8
Bega, *Australia* 95 F4
Bega, Canalul, *Romania* 42 E5
Bégard, *France* 18 D3
Beğendik, *Turkey* 41 F10
Begoro, *Ghana* 83 D4
Begusarai, *India* 69 G12
Behābād, *Iran* 71 C8
Behala, *India* 69 H13
Behara, *Madag.* 89 C8
Behbehān, *Iran* 71 D6
Behm Canal, *U.S.A.* 104 B2
Behshahr, *Iran* 71 B7
Bei Jiang →, *China* 59 F9
Bei'an, *China* 60 B7
Beibei, *China* 58 C6
Beichuan, *China* 58 B5
Beihai, *China* 58 G7
Beijing, *China* 56 E9
Beijing □, *China* 56 E9
Beilen, *Neths.* 17 B6
Beiliu, *China* 59 F8
Beilngries, *Germany* 25 F7
Beilpajah, *Australia* 95 E3
Beilul, *Eritrea* 81 E5
Beinn na Faoghla = Benbecula, *U.K.* 14 D1
Beipan Jiang, *China* 58 E5
Beipiao, *China* 57 D11
Beira, *Mozam.* 87 F3
Beirut = Bayrūt, *Lebanon* 75 B4
Beiseker, *Canada* 104 C6
Beitaolaizhao, *China* 57 B13
Beitbridge, *Zimbabwe* 87 G3
Beiuş, *Romania* 42 D7
Beizhen = Binzhou, *China* 57 F10
Beizhen, *China* 57 D11
Beizhengzhen, *China* 57 B12
Beja, *Portugal* 35 G3
Béja, *Tunisia* 79 A7
Beja □, *Portugal* 35 H3
Bejaia, *Algeria* 78 A7
Béjar, *Spain* 34 E5
Bejestān, *Iran* 71 C8
Bekçiler, *Turkey* 39 E11
Békés, *Hungary* 42 D6
Békés □, *Hungary* 42 D6
Békéscsaba, *Hungary* 42 D6
Bekilli, *Turkey* 39 C11
Bekily, *Madag.* 89 C8
Bekisopa, *Madag.* 89 C8
Bekitro, *Madag.* 89 C8
Bekodoka, *Madag.* 89 B8
Bekoji, *Ethiopia* 81 F4
Bekok, *Malaysia* 65 L4
Bekopaka, *Madag.* 89 B7
Bekwai, *Ghana* 83 D4
Bela, *India* 69 G10
Bela, *Pakistan* 68 F2
Bela Crkva, *Serbia, Yug.* 42 F6
Bela Palanka, *Serbia, Yug.* 40 C6
Bela Vista, *Brazil* 126 A4
Bela Vista, *Mozam.* 89 D5
Bélâbre, *France* 20 B5
Belalcázar, *Spain* 35 G5
Belan →, *India* 69 G9
Belanovica, *Serbia, Yug.* 40 B4
Belarus ■, *Europe* 46 F4
Belau = Palau ■, *Pac. Oc.* 52 J17
Belavenona, *Madag.* 89 C8
Belawan, *Indonesia* 62 D1
Belaya, *Ethiopia* 81 E4
Belaya Glina, *Russia* 49 G5
Belaya Kalitva, *Russia* 49 F5
Belaya Tserkov = Bila Tserkva, *Ukraine* 47 H6
Belceşti, *Romania* 43 C12
Bełchatów, *Poland* 45 G6
Belcher Is., *Canada* 102 A3
Belchite, *Spain* 32 D4
Belden, *U.S.A.* 116 E5
Belém, *Brazil* 125 D9
Belén, *Argentina* 126 B2
Belén, *Paraguay* 126 A4
Belen, *U.S.A.* 115 J10
Belene, *Bulgaria* 41 C9
Beleni, *Turkey* 72 D7
Bélesta, *France* 20 F5
Belet Uen, *Somali Rep.* 74 G4
Belev, *Russia* 46 F9
Belevi, *Turkey* 39 C9
Belfair, *U.S.A.* 116 C4
Belfast, *S. Africa* 89 D5
Belfast, *U.K.* 15 B6
Belfast, *Maine, U.S.A.* 109 C11
Belfast, *N.Y., U.S.A.* 110 D6
Belfast L., *U.K.* 15 B6
Belfield, *U.S.A.* 112 B3
Belfort, *France* 19 E13
Belfort, Territoire de □, *France* 19 E13
Belfry, *U.S.A.* 114 D9
Belgaum, *India* 66 M9
Belgioioso, *Italy* 28 C6
Belgium ■, *Europe* 17 D4
Belgodère, *France* 21 F13
Belgorod, *Russia* 47 G9
Belgorod-Dnestrovskiy = Bilhorod-Dnistrovskyy, *Ukraine* 47 J6
Belgrade = Beograd, *Serbia, Yug.* 40 B4
Belgrade, *U.S.A.* 114 D8
Belhaven, *U.S.A.* 109 H7
Beli Drim →, *Europe* 40 D4
Beli Manastir, *Croatia* 42 E3
Beli Timok →, *Serbia, Yug.* 40 C6
Bélice →, *Italy* 30 E5
Belinskiy, *Russia* 48 D6
Belinyu, *Indonesia* 62 E3
Beliton Is. = Belitung, *Indonesia* 62 E3
Belitung, *Indonesia* 62 E3
Beliu, *Romania* 42 D6
Belize ■, *Cent. Amer.* 119 D7
Belize City, *Belize* 119 D7
Beljakovci, *Macedonia* 40 D5
Beljanica, *Serbia, Yug.* 40 B5
Belkovskiy, Ostrov, *Russia* 51 B14
Bell →, *Canada* 102 C4
Bell I., *Canada* 103 B8
Bell-Irving →, *Canada* 104 B3
Bell Peninsula, *Canada* 101 B11
Bell Ville, *Argentina* 126 C3
Bella, *Italy* 31 B8
Bella Bella, *Canada* 104 C3
Bella Coola, *Canada* 104 C3
Bella Unión, *Uruguay* 126 C4
Bella Vista, *Corrientes, Argentina* 126 B4
Bella Vista, *Tucuman, Argentina* 126 B2
Bellac, *France* 20 B5
Bellágio, *Italy* 28 C6
Bellaire, *U.S.A.* 110 F4
Bellária, *Italy* 29 D9
Bellary, *India* 66 M10
Bellata, *Australia* 95 D4
Belle-Chasse, *U.S.A.* 113 L10
Belle Fourche, *U.S.A.* 112 C3
Belle Fourche →, *U.S.A.* 112 C3
Belle Glade, *U.S.A.* 109 M5
Belle-Île, *France* 18 E3
Belle Isle, *Canada* 103 B8
Belle Isle, Str. of, *Canada* 103 B8
Belle Plaine, *U.S.A.* 112 E8
Belle Yella, *Liberia* 82 D3
Belledonne, *France* 21 C10
Bellefontaine, *U.S.A.* 108 E4
Bellefonte, *U.S.A.* 110 F7
Bellegarde, *France* 19 E9
Bellegarde-en-Marche, *France* 20 C6
Bellegarde-sur-Valserine, *France* 19 F12
Bellême, *France* 18 D7
Belleoram, *Canada* 103 C8
Belleville, *Canada* 102 D4
Belleville, *France* 19 F11
Belleville, *Ill., U.S.A.* 112 F10
Belleville, *Kans., U.S.A.* 112 F6
Belleville, *N.Y., U.S.A.* 111 C8
Belleville-sur-Vie, *France* 18 F5
Bellevue, *Canada* 104 D6
Bellevue, *Idaho, U.S.A.* 114 E6
Bellevue, *Nebr., U.S.A.* 112 E7
Bellevue, *Ohio, U.S.A.* 110 E2
Bellevue, *Wash., U.S.A.* 116 C4
Belley, *France* 21 C9
Bellin = Kangirsuk, *Canada* 101 B13
Bellinge, *Denmark* 11 J4
Bellingen, *Australia* 95 E5
Bellingham, *U.S.A.* 100 D7
Bellingshausen Sea, *Antarctica* 5 C17
Bellinzona, *Switz.* 25 J5
Bello, *Colombia* 124 B3
Bellows Falls, *U.S.A.* 111 C12
Bellpat, *Pakistan* 68 E3
Bellpuig d'Urgell, *Spain* 32 D6
Belluno, *Italy* 29 B9
Bellwood, *U.S.A.* 110 F6
Bélmez, *Spain* 35 G5
Belmont, *Canada* 110 D3
Belmont, *S. Africa* 88 D3
Belmont, *U.S.A.* 110 D6
Belmonte, *Brazil* 125 G11
Belmonte, *Portugal* 34 E3
Belmonte, *Spain* 33 F2
Belmopan, *Belize* 119 D7
Belmullet, *Ireland* 15 B2
Belo Horizonte, *Brazil* 125 G10
Belo-sur-Mer, *Madag.* 89 C7
Belo-Tsiribihina, *Madag.* 89 B7
Belogorsk = Bilohirsk, *Ukraine* 47 K8
Belogorsk, *Russia* 51 D13
Belogradchik, *Bulgaria* 40 C6
Belogradets, *Bulgaria* 41 C11
Beloha, *Madag.* 89 D8
Beloit, *Kans., U.S.A.* 112 F5
Beloit, *Wis., U.S.A.* 112 D10
Belokorovichi, *Ukraine* 47 G5
Belomorsk, *Russia* 50 C4
Belonia, *India* 67 H17
Belopolye = Bilopillya, *Ukraine* 47 G8
Belorechensk, *Russia* 49 H4
Belorussia = Belarus ■, *Europe* 46 F4
Beloslav, *Bulgaria* 41 C11
Belovo, *Bulgaria* 41 D8
Belovo, *Russia* 50 D9
Belovodsk, *Ukraine* 47 H10
Beloye, Ozero, *Russia* 46 B9
Beloye More, *Russia* 50 C4
Belozem, *Bulgaria* 41 D9
Belozersk, *Russia* 46 B9
Belpasso, *Italy* 31 E7
Belpre, *U.S.A.* 108 F5
Belrain, *India* 69 E9
Belt, *U.S.A.* 114 C8
Beltana, *Australia* 95 E2
Belterra, *Brazil* 125 D8
Beltinci, *Slovenia* 29 B13
Belton, *U.S.A.* 113 K6
Belton L., *U.S.A.* 113 K6
Beltsy = Bălţi, *Moldova* 43 C12
Belturbet, *Ireland* 15 B4
Belukha, *Russia* 50 E9
Beluran, *Malaysia* 62 C5
Beluša, *Slovak Rep.* 27 B11
Belušić, *Serbia, Yug.* 40 C5
Belvedere Maríttimo, *Italy* 31 C8
Belvès, *France* 20 D5
Belvidere, *Ill., U.S.A.* 112 D10
Belvidere, *N.J., U.S.A.* 111 F9
Belvis de la Jara, *Spain* 34 F6
Belyando →, *Australia* 94 C4
Belyy, *Russia* 46 E7
Belyy, Ostrov, *Russia* 50 B8
Belyy Yar, *Russia* 50 D9
Bełżec, *Poland* 45 H10
Belzig, *Germany* 24 C8
Belzoni, *U.S.A.* 113 J9
Bełżyce, *Poland* 45 G9
Bemaraha, Lembalemban' i, *Madag.* 89 B7
Bemarivo, *Madag.* 89 C7
Bemarivo →, *Antsiranana, Madag.* 89 A9
Bemarivo →, *Mahajanga, Madag.* 89 B8
Bemavo, *Madag.* 89 C8
Bembéréke, *Benin* 83 C5
Bembesi, *Zimbabwe* 87 G2
Bembesi →, *Zimbabwe* 87 F2
Bembézar →, *Spain* 35 H5
Bembibre, *Spain* 34 C4
Bemetara, *India* 69 J9
Bemidji, *U.S.A.* 112 B7
Bemolanga, *Madag.* 89 B8
Ben, *Iran* 71 C6
Ben Cruachan, *U.K.* 14 E3
Ben Dearg, *U.K.* 14 D4
Ben Hope, *U.K.* 14 C4
Ben Lawers, *U.K.* 14 E4
Ben Lomond, *N.S.W., Australia* 95 E5
Ben Lomond, *Tas., Australia* 94 G4
Ben Lomond, *U.K.* 14 E4
Ben Luc, *Vietnam* 65 G6
Ben Macdhui, *U.K.* 14 D5
Ben Mhor, *U.K.* 14 D1
Ben More, *Arg. & Bute, U.K.* 14 E2
Ben More, *Stirl., U.K.* 14 E4
Ben More Assynt, *U.K.* 14 C4
Ben Nevis, *U.K.* 14 E3
Ben Quang, *Vietnam* 64 D6
Ben Vorlich, *U.K.* 14 E4
Ben Wyvis, *U.K.* 14 D4
Bena, *Nigeria* 83 C6
Benāb, *Iran* 73 D12
Benalla, *Australia* 95 F4
Benalmádena, *Spain* 35 J6
Benares = Varanasi, *India* 69 G10
Bénat, C., *France* 21 E10
Benavente, *Portugal* 35 G2
Benavente, *Spain* 34 C5
Benavides, *U.S.A.* 113 M5
Benavides de Órbigo, *Spain* 34 C5
Benbecula, *U.K.* 14 D1
Benbonyathe, *Australia* 95 E2

Bend, *U.S.A.* 114 D3
Bendemeer, *Australia* 95 E5
Bender Beila, *Somali Rep.* 74 F5
Bendery = Tighina, *Moldova* 43 D14
Bendigo, *Australia* 95 F3
Bendorf, *Germany* 24 E3
Benē Beraq, *Israel* 75 C3
Bénéna, *Mali* 82 C4
Benenitra, *Madag.* 89 C8
Benešov, *Czech Rep.* 26 B7
Benevento, *Italy* 31 A7
Benfeld, *France* 19 D14
Benga, *Mozam.* 87 F3
Bengal, Bay of, *Ind. Oc.* 67 M17
Bengbis, *Cameroon* 83 E7
Bengbu, *China* 57 H9
Benghazi = Banghāzī, *Libya* 79 B10
Bengkalis, *Indonesia* 62 D2
Bengkulu, *Indonesia* 62 E2
Bengkulu □, *Indonesia* 62 E2
Bengough, *Canada* 105 D7
Bengtsfors, *Sweden* 10 E6
Benguela, *Angola* 85 G2
Benguérua, I., *Mozam.* 89 C6
Benha, *Egypt* 80 H7
Beni, *Dem. Rep. of the Congo* 86 B2
Beni →, *Bolivia* 124 F5
Beni Mazâr, *Egypt* 80 B3
Beni Mellal, *Morocco* 78 B4
Beni Suef, *Egypt* 80 J7
Beniah L., *Canada* 104 A6
Benicarló, *Spain* 32 E5
Benicássim, *Spain* 32 E5
Benicia, *U.S.A.* 116 G4
Benidorm, *Spain* 33 G4
Benin ■, *Africa* 83 D5
Benin →, *Nigeria* 83 D6
Benin, Bight of, *W. Afr.* 83 E5
Benin City, *Nigeria* 83 D6
Benisa, *Spain* 33 G5
Benitses, *Greece* 36 A3
Benjamin Aceval, *Paraguay* 126 A4
Benjamin Constant, *Brazil* 124 D4
Benjamin Hill, *Mexico* 118 A2
Benkelman, *U.S.A.* 112 E4
Benkovac, *Croatia* 29 D12
Bennett, *Canada* 104 B2
Bennett, L., *Australia* 92 D5
Bennetta, Ostrov, *Russia* 51 B15
Bennettsville, *U.S.A.* 109 H6
Bennichchāb, *Mauritania* 82 B1
Bennington, *N.H., U.S.A.* 111 D11
Bennington, *Vt., U.S.A.* 111 D11
Bénodet, *France* 18 E2
Benoni, *S. Africa* 89 D4
Benque Viejo, *Belize* 119 D7
Bensheim, *Germany* 25 F4
Benson, *Ariz., U.S.A.* 115 L8
Benson, *Minn., U.S.A.* 112 C7
Bent, *Iran* 71 E8
Benteng, *Indonesia* 63 F6
Bentinck I., *Australia* 94 B2
Bentiu, *Sudan* 81 F2
Bento Gonçalves, *Brazil* 127 B5
Benton, *Ark., U.S.A.* 113 H8
Benton, *Calif., U.S.A.* 116 H8
Benton, *Ill., U.S.A.* 112 G10
Benton, *Pa., U.S.A.* 111 E8
Benton Harbor, *U.S.A.* 108 D2
Bentonville, *U.S.A.* 113 G7
Bentu Liben, *Ethiopia* 81 F4
Bentung, *Malaysia* 65 L3
Benue □, *Nigeria* 83 D6
Benue →, *Nigeria* 83 D6
Benxi, *China* 57 D12
Beo, *Indonesia* 63 D7
Beograd, *Serbia, Yug.* 40 B4
Beoumi, *Ivory C.* 82 D3
Bepan Jiang →, *China* 58 E6
Beppu, *Japan* 55 H5
Beqaa Valley = Al Biqā, *Lebanon* 75 A5
Ber Mota, *India* 68 H3
Berach →, *India* 68 G6
Beraketa, *Madag.* 89 C7
Berane, *Montenegro, Yug.* 40 D3
Berati, *Albania* 40 F3
Berau, Teluk, *Indonesia* 63 E8
Beravina, *Madag.* 89 B8
Berber, *Sudan* 80 D3
Berbera, *Somali Rep.* 74 E4
Berbérati, *C.A.R.* 84 D3
Berbice →, *Guyana* 124 B7
Berceto, *Italy* 28 D6
Berchidda, *Italy* 30 B2
Berchtesgaden, *Germany* 25 H8
Berck, *France* 19 B8
Berdichev = Berdychiv, *Ukraine* 47 H5
Berdsk, *Russia* 50 D9
Berdyansk, *Ukraine* 47 J9
Berdychiv, *Ukraine* 47 H5
Berea, *U.S.A.* 108 G3
Berebere, *Indonesia* 63 D7
Bereda, *Somali Rep.* 74 E5
Berehove, *Ukraine* 47 H2
Berekum, *Ghana* 82 D4
Berenice, *Egypt* 80 C4
Berens →, *Canada* 105 C9
Berens I., *Canada* 105 C9
Berens River, *Canada* 105 C9
Beresford, *U.S.A.* 112 D6
Berestechko, *Ukraine* 47 G3
Bereşti, *Romania* 43 D12
Beretău →, *Romania* 42 C6
Berettyó →, *Hungary* 42 D6
Berettyóújfalu, *Hungary* 42 C6
Berevo, *Mahajanga, Madag.* 89 B7
Berevo, *Toliara, Madag.* 89 B7
Bereza, *Belarus* 47 F3
Berezhany, *Ukraine* 47 H3
Berezina = Byarezina →, *Belarus* 47 F6
Berezivka, *Ukraine* 47 J6
Berezna, *Ukraine* 47 G6
Berezniki, *Russia* 50 C5
Berezniki, *Russia* 50 D6
Berezovo, *Russia* 50 C7
Berga, *Spain* 32 C6
Berga, *Sweden* 11 G10
Bergama, *Turkey* 39 B9
Bérgamo, *Italy* 28 C6
Bergara, *Spain* 32 B2
Bergby, *Sweden* 10 D11
Bergedorf, *Germany* 24 B6
Bergeforsen, *Sweden* 10 B11
Bergen, *Mecklenburg-Vorpommern, Germany* 24 A9
Bergen, *Niedersachsen, Germany* 24 C5
Bergen, *Neths.* 17 B4
Bergen, *Norway* 9 F11
Bergen, *U.S.A.* 110 C7
Bergen op Zoom, *Neths.* 17 C4
Bergerac, *France* 20 D4
Bergheim, *Germany* 24 E2
Bergholz, *U.S.A.* 110 F4
Bergisch Gladbach, *Germany* 17 D7
Bergkamen, *Germany* 24 D3
Bergkvara, *Sweden* 11 H10
Bergshamra, *Sweden* 10 E12
Bergsjö, *Sweden* 10 C11
Bergues, *France* 19 B9
Bergviken, *Sweden* 10 C10
Bergville, *S. Africa* 89 D4
Berhala, Selat, *Indonesia* 62 E2
Berhampore = Baharampur, *India* 69 G13
Berhampur = Brahmapur, *India* 67 K14
Berheci →, *Romania* 43 E12
Bering Sea, *Pac. Oc.* 100 C1
Bering Strait, *Pac. Oc.* 100 B3
Beringovskiy, *Russia* 51 C18
Berisso, *Argentina* 126 C4
Berja, *Spain* 35 J8
Berkeley, *U.S.A.* 116 H4
Berkner I., *Antarctica* 5 D18
Berkovitsa, *Bulgaria* 40 C7
Berkshire, *U.S.A.* 111 D8
Berkshire Downs, *U.K.* 13 F6
Berlanga, *Spain* 35 G5
Berlenga, I., *Portugal* 35 F1
Berlin, *Germany* 24 C9
Berlin, *Md., U.S.A.* 108 F8
Berlin, *N.H., U.S.A.* 111 B13
Berlin, *N.Y., U.S.A.* 111 D11
Berlin, *Wis., U.S.A.* 108 D1
Berlin □, *Germany* 24 C9
Berlin L., *U.S.A.* 110 E4
Bermeja, Sierra, *Spain* 35 J5
Bermejo →, *Formosa, Argentina* 126 B4
Bermejo →, *San Juan, Argentina* 126 C2
Bermen, L., *Canada* 103 B6
Bermeo, *Spain* 32 B2
Bermillo de Sayago, *Spain* 34 D4
Bermuda ■, *Atl. Oc.* 98 F13
Bern, *Switz.* 25 J3
Bern □, *Switz.* 25 J3
Bernalda, *Italy* 31 B9
Bernalillo, *U.S.A.* 115 J10
Bernardo de Irigoyen, *Argentina* 127 B5
Bernardo O'Higgins □, *Chile* 126 C1
Bernardsville, *U.S.A.* 111 F10
Bernasconi, *Argentina* 126 D3
Bernau, *Bayern, Germany* 25 H8
Bernau, *Brandenburg, Germany* 24 C9
Bernay, *France* 18 C7
Bernburg, *Germany* 24 D7
Berndorf, *Austria* 26 D9
Berne = Bern, *Switz.* 25 J3
Berne = Bern □, *Switz.* 25 J3
Berner Alpen, *Switz.* 25 J3
Berneray, *U.K.* 14 D1
Bernier I., *Australia* 93 D1
Bernina, Piz, *Switz.* 25 J5
Bernkastel-Kues, *Germany* 25 F3
Beroroha, *Madag.* 89 C8
Béroubouay, *Benin* 83 C5
Beroun, *Czech Rep.* 26 B7
Berounka →, *Czech Rep.* 26 B7
Berovo, *Macedonia* 40 E6
Berre, Étang de, *France* 21 E9
Berre-l'Étang, *France* 21 E9
Berri, *Australia* 95 E3
Berriane, *Algeria* 78 B6
Berrigan, *Australia* 95 F4
Berry, *Australia* 95 E5
Berry, *France* 19 F8
Berry Is., *Bahamas* 120 A4
Berryessa L., *U.S.A.* 116 G4
Berryville, *U.S.A.* 113 G8
Berseba, *Namibia* 88 D2
Bersenbrück, *Germany* 24 C3
Bershad, *Ukraine* 47 H5
Berthold, *U.S.A.* 112 A4
Berthoud, *U.S.A.* 112 E2
Bertincourt, *France* 19 B9
Bertoua, *Cameroon* 84 D2
Bertraghboy B., *Ireland* 15 C2
Berwick, *U.S.A.* 111 E8
Berwick-upon-Tweed, *U.K.* 12 B6
Berwyn Mts., *U.K.* 12 E4
Beryslav, *Ukraine* 47 J7
Berzasca, *Romania* 42 F6
Berzence, *Hungary* 42 D2
Besal, *Pakistan* 69 B5
Besalampy, *Madag.* 89 B7
Besançon, *France* 19 E13
Besar, *Indonesia* 62 E5
Beshenkovichi, *Belarus* 46 E5
Beška, *Serbia, Yug.* 42 E5
Beslan, *Russia* 49 J7
Besna Kobila, *Serbia, Yug.* 40 D6
Besnard L., *Canada* 105 B7
Besni, *Turkey* 70 B3
Besor, N. →, *Egypt* 75 D3
Bessarabiya, *Moldova* 47 J5
Bessarabka = Basarabeasca, *Moldova* 43 D13
Bessèges, *France* 21 D8
Bessemer, *Ala., U.S.A.* 109 J2
Bessemer, *Mich., U.S.A.* 112 B9
Bessemer, *Pa., U.S.A.* 110 F4
Bessin, *France* 18 C6
Bessines-sur-Gartempe, *France* 20 B5
Beswick, *Australia* 92 B5
Bet She'an, *Israel* 75 C4
Bet Shemesh, *Israel* 75 D4
Betafo, *Madag.* 89 B8
Betancuria, *Canary Is.* 37 F5
Betanzos, *Spain* 34 B2
Bétaré Oya, *Cameroon* 84 C2
Betatao, *Madag.* 89 B8
Bétera, *Spain* 33 F4
Bétérou, *Benin* 83 D5
Bethal, *S. Africa* 89 D4
Bethanien, *Namibia* 88 D2
Bethany, *Canada* 110 B6
Bethany, *U.S.A.* 112 E7
Bethel, *Alaska, U.S.A.* 100 B3
Bethel, *Conn., U.S.A.* 111 E11
Bethel, *Maine, U.S.A.* 111 B14
Bethel, *Vt., U.S.A.* 111 C12
Bethel Park, *U.S.A.* 110 F4
Béthenville, *France* 19 C11
Bethlehem = Bayt Lahm, *West Bank* 75 D4
Bethlehem, *S. Africa* 89 D4
Bethlehem, *U.S.A.* 111 F9
Bethulie, *S. Africa* 88 E4
Béthune, *France* 19 B9
Béthune →, *France* 18 C8
Betioky, *Madag.* 89 C7
Betong, *Thailand* 65 K3
Betoota, *Australia* 94 D3
Betor, *Ethiopia* 81 E4
Betroka, *Madag.* 89 C8
Betsiamites, *Canada* 103 C6
Betsiamites →, *Canada* 103 C6
Betsiboka →, *Madag.* 89 B8
Bettendorf, *U.S.A.* 112 E9
Bettiah, *India* 69 F11
Bettna, *Sweden* 11 F10
Béttola, *Italy* 28 D6
Betul, *India* 66 J10
Betung, *Malaysia* 62 D4
Betws-y-Coed, *U.K.* 12 D4
Betxi, *Spain* 32 F4
Betzdorf, *Germany* 24 E3
Beuil, *France* 21 D10
Beulah, *Mich., U.S.A.* 108 C2
Beulah, *N. Dak., U.S.A.* 112 B4
Beuvron →, *France* 18 E8
Beveren, *Belgium* 17 C4
Beverley, *Australia* 93 F2
Beverley, *U.K.* 12 D7
Beverley Hills, *U.S.A.* 109 L4
Beverly, *U.S.A.* 111 D14
Beverly Hills, *U.S.A.* 117 L8
Beverungen, *Germany* 24 D5
Bevoalavo, *Madag.* 89 D7
Bewas →, *India* 69 H8
Bex, *Switz.* 25 J3
Bexhill, *U.K.* 13 G8
Bey Dağları, *Turkey* 39 E12
Beyānlū, *Iran* 70 C5
Beyazköy, *Turkey* 41 E11
Beyçayırı, *Turkey* 41 F10
Beydağ, *Turkey* 39 C10
Beyeğaç, *Turkey* 39 D10
Beyin, *Ghana* 82 D4
Beykoz, *Turkey* 41 E13
Beyla, *Guinea* 82 D3
Beynat, *France* 20 C5
Beyneu, *Kazakstan* 50 E6
Beyoba, *Turkey* 39 C9
Beyoğlu, *Turkey* 41 E12
Beypazarı, *Turkey* 72 B4
Beyşehir, *Turkey* 72 D4
Beyşehir Gölü, *Turkey* 70 B1
Beytüşşebap, *Turkey* 73 D10
Bezdan, *Serbia, Yug.* 42 E3
Bezhetsk, *Russia* 46 D9
Béziers, *France* 20 E7
Bezwada = Vijayawada, *India* 67 L12
Bhabua, *India* 69 G10
Bhachau, *India* 66 H7
Bhadar →, *Gujarat, India* 68 H5
Bhadar →, *Gujarat, India* 68 J3
Bhadarwah, *India* 69 C6
Bhadohi, *India* 69 G10
Bhadra, *India* 68 E6
Bhadrakh, *India* 67 J15
Bhadran, *India* 68 H5
Bhadravati, *India* 66 N9
Bhag, *Pakistan* 68 E2
Bhagalpur, *India* 69 G12
Bhagirathi →, *Ut. P., India* 69 D8
Bhagirathi →, *W. Bengal, India* 69 H13
Bhakkar, *Pakistan* 68 D4
Bhakra Dam, *India* 68 D7
Bhamo, *Burma* 67 G20
Bhandara, *India* 66 J11
Bhanpura, *India* 68 G6
Bhanrer Ra., *India* 69 H8
Bhaptiahi, *India* 69 F12
Bharat = India ■, *Asia* 66 K11
Bharatpur, *Mad. P., India* 69 H9
Bharatpur, *Raj., India* 68 F7
Bharno, *India* 69 H11
Bhatinda, *India* 68 D6
Bhatpara, *India* 69 H13
Bhattu, *India* 68 E6
Bhaun, *Pakistan* 68 C5
Bhaunagar = Bhavnagar, *India* 66 J8
Bhavnagar, *India* 66 J8
Bhawanipatna, *India* 67 K12
Bhawari, *India* 68 G5
Bhayavadar, *India* 68 J4
Bhera, *Pakistan* 68 C5
Bhikangaon, *India* 68 J6
Bhilsa = Vidisha, *India* 68 H7
Bhilwara, *India* 68 G6
Bhima →, *India* 66 L10
Bhimavaram, *India* 67 L12
Bhimbar, *Pakistan* 69 C6
Bhind, *India* 69 F8
Bhinga, *India* 69 F9
Bhinmal, *India* 68 G5
Bhiwandi, *India* 66 K8
Bhiwani, *India* 68 E7
Bhogava →, *India* 68 H5
Bhola, *Bangla.* 67 H17
Bholari, *Pakistan* 68 G3
Bhopal, *India* 68 H7
Bhubaneshwar, *India* 67 J14
Bhuj, *India* 68 H3
Bhusaval, *India* 66 J9
Bhutan ■, *Asia* 67 F17
Biafra, B. of = Bonny, Bight of, *Africa* 83 E6
Biak, *Indonesia* 63 E9
Biała, *Poland* 45 H4
Biała →, *Poland* 45 H7
Biała Piska, *Poland* 44 E9
Biała Podlaska, *Poland* 45 F10
Biała Rawska, *Poland* 45 G7
Białobrzegi, *Poland* 45 G7
Białogard, *Poland* 44 D2
Białowieża, *Poland* 45 F10
Biały Bór, *Poland* 44 E3
Białystok, *Poland* 45 E10
Biancavilla, *Italy* 31 E7
Bianco, *Italy* 31 D9
Biankouma, *Ivory C.* 82 D3
Biaora, *India* 68 H7
Bīārjmand, *Iran* 71 B7
Biaro, *Indonesia* 63 D7
Biarritz, *France* 20 E2
Biasca, *Switz.* 25 J4
Biba, *Egypt* 80 J7
Bibai, *Japan* 54 C10
Bibbiena, *Italy* 29 E8
Bibby I., *Canada* 105 A10
Bibel →, *Spain* 34 C3
Biberach, *Germany* 25 G5
Bibiani, *Ghana* 82 D4
Bibungwa, *Dem. Rep. of the Congo* 86 C2
Bic, *Canada* 103 C6
Bicaj, *Albania* 40 E4
Bicaz, *Romania* 43 D11
Bicazu Ardelean, *Romania* 43 D10
Bíccari, *Italy* 31 A8
Bicester, *U.K.* 13 F6
Bichena, *Ethiopia* 81 E4
Bicheno, *Australia* 94 G4
Bichia, *India* 69 H9
Bichvinta, *Georgia* 49 J5
Bickerton I., *Australia* 94 A2
Bicske, *Hungary* 42 C3
Bida, *Nigeria* 83 D6
Bidar, *India* 66 L10
Biddeford, *U.S.A.* 109 D10
Biddwara, *Ethiopia* 81 F4
Bideford, *U.K.* 13 F3
Bideford Bay, *U.K.* 13 F3
Bidhuna, *India* 69 F8
Bidor, *Malaysia* 65 K3
Bie, *Sweden* 10 E10
Bié, Planalto de, *Angola* 85 G3
Bieber, *U.S.A.* 114 F3
Biebrza →, *Poland* 45 E9
Biecz, *Poland* 45 J8
Biel, *Switz.* 25 H3
Bielawa, *Poland* 45 H3
Bielefeld, *Germany* 24 C4
Bielersee, *Switz.* 25 H3
Biella, *Italy* 28 C5
Bielsk Podlaski, *Poland* 45 F10
Bielsko-Biała, *Poland* 45 J6
Bien Hoa, *Vietnam* 65 G6
Bienne = Biel, *Switz.* 25 H3
Bienvenida, *Spain* 35 G4
Bienville, L., *Canada* 102 A5
Bierné, *France* 18 E6
Bierun, *Poland* 45 H6
Bierutów, *Poland* 45 G4
Biescas, *Spain* 32 C4
Biese →, *Germany* 24 C7
Biesiesfontein, *S. Africa* 88 E2
Bietigheim-Bissingen, *Germany* 25 G5
Bieżuń, *Poland* 45 F6
Biferno →, *Italy* 29 G12
Big →, *Canada* 103 B8
Big B., *Canada* 103 A7
Big Bear City, *U.S.A.* 117 L10
Big Bear Lake, *U.S.A.* 117 L10
Big Belt Mts., *U.S.A.* 114 C8
Big Bend, *Swaziland* 89 D5
Big Bend National Park, *U.S.A.* 113 L3
Big Black →, *U.S.A.* 113 K9
Big Blue →, *U.S.A.* 112 F6
Big Creek, *U.S.A.* 116 H7
Big Cypress National Preserve, *U.S.A.* 109 M5
Big Cypress Swamp, *U.S.A.* 109 M5
Big Falls, *U.S.A.* 112 A8
Big Fork →, *U.S.A.* 112 A8
Big Horn Mts. = Bighorn Mts., *U.S.A.* 114 D10
Big I., *Canada* 104 A5
Big Lake, *U.S.A.* 113 K4
Big Moose, *U.S.A.* 111 C10
Big Muddy Cr. →, *U.S.A.* 112 A2
Big Pine, *U.S.A.* 116 H8
Big Piney, *U.S.A.* 114 E8
Big Rapids, *U.S.A.* 108 D3
Big Rideau L., *Canada* 111 B8
Big River, *Canada* 105 C7
Big Run, *U.S.A.* 110 F6
Big Sable Pt., *U.S.A.* 108 C2
Big Salmon →, *Canada* 104 A2
Big Sand L., *Canada* 105 B9
Big Sandy, *U.S.A.* 114 B8
Big Sandy →, *U.S.A.* 108 F4
Big Sandy Cr. →, *U.S.A.* 112 F3
Big Sioux →, *U.S.A.* 112 D6
Big Spring, *U.S.A.* 113 J4
Big Stone City, *U.S.A.* 112 C6
Big Stone Gap, *U.S.A.* 109 G4
Big Stone L., *U.S.A.* 112 C6
Big Sur, *U.S.A.* 116 J5
Big Timber, *U.S.A.* 114 D9
Big Trout L., *Canada* 102 B2
Big Trout Lake, *Canada* 102 B2
Biğa, *Turkey* 41 F11
Biga →, *Turkey* 41 F11
Bigadiç, *Turkey* 39 B10
Biganos, *France* 20 D3
Biggar, *Canada* 105 C7
Biggar, *U.K.* 14 F5
Bigge I., *Australia* 92 B4
Biggenden, *Australia* 95 D5
Biggleswade, *U.K.* 13 E7
Biggs, *U.S.A.* 116 F5
Bighorn, *U.S.A.* 114 C10
Bighorn →, *U.S.A.* 114 C10
Bighorn L., *U.S.A.* 114 D9
Bighorn Mts., *U.S.A.* 114 D10
Bignona, *Senegal* 82 C1
Bigorre, *France* 20 E4
Bigstone L., *Canada* 105 C9
Biguglia, Étang de, *France* 21 F13
Bigwa, *Tanzania* 86 D4
Bihać, *Bos.-H.* 29 D12
Bihar, *India* 69 G11
Bihar □, *India* 69 G12
Biharamulo, *Tanzania* 86 C3
Bihariganj, *India* 69 G12
Biharkeresztes, *Hungary* 42 C6
Bihor □, *Romania* 42 D7
Bihor, Munţii, *Romania* 42 D7
Bijagós, Arquipélago dos, *Guinea-Biss.* 82 C1
Bijaipur, *India* 68 F7
Bijapur, *Karnataka, India* 66 L9
Bijapur, *Mad. P., India* 67 K12
Bījār, *Iran* 70 C5
Bijawar, *India* 69 G8
Bijeljina, *Bos.-H.* 42 F4
Bijelo Polje, *Montenegro, Yug.* 40 C3
Bijie, *China* 58 D5
Bijnor, *India* 68 E8
Bikaner, *India* 68 E5
Bikapur, *India* 69 F10
Bikeqi, *China* 56 D6
Bikfayyā, *Lebanon* 75 B4
Bikin, *Russia* 51 E14
Bikin →, *Russia* 54 A7
Bikini Atoll, *Marshall Is.* 96 F8
Bikita, *Zimbabwe* 89 C5
Bikoué, *Cameroon* 83 E7
Bila Tserkva, *Ukraine* 47 H6
Bilanga, *Burkina Faso* 83 C4
Bilara, *India* 68 F5
Bilaspur, *Mad. P., India* 69 H10
Bilaspur, *Punjab, India* 68 D7
Biläsuvar, *Azerbaijan* 73 C13
Bilauk Taungdan, *Thailand* 64 F2
Bilbao, *Spain* 32 B2
Bilbeis, *Egypt* 80 H7
Bilbo = Bilbao, *Spain* 32 B2
Bilbor, *Romania* 43 C10
Bilciureşti, *Romania* 43 F10
Bíldudalur, *Iceland* 8 D2
Bílé Karpaty, *Europe* 27 B11
Bileća, *Bos.-H.* 40 D2
Bilecik, *Turkey* 72 B4
Biłgoraj, *Poland* 45 H9
Bilgram, *India* 69 F9
Bilhaur, *India* 69 F9
Bilhorod-Dnistrovskyy, *Ukraine* 47 J6
Bilibino, *Russia* 51 C17
Bilibiza, *Mozam.* 87 E5
Bilishti, *Albania* 40 F5
Billabalong Roadhouse, *Australia* 93 E2
Billdal, *Sweden* 11 G5
Billiluna, *Australia* 92 C4
Billings, *U.S.A.* 114 D9
Billiton Is. = Belitung, *Indonesia* 62 E3
Billsta, *Sweden* 10 A12
Billund, *Denmark* 11 J3
Bilma, *Niger* 79 E8
Bilo Gora, *Croatia* 42 E2
Biloela, *Australia* 94 C5
Bilohirsk, *Ukraine* 47 K8
Bilopillya, *Ukraine* 47 G8

Biloxi, *U.S.A.* 113 K10
Bilpa Morea Claypan, *Australia* 94 D3
Biltine, *Chad* 79 F10
Bilyarsk, *Russia* 48 C10
Bima, *Indonesia* 63 F5
Bimban, *Egypt* 80 C3
Bimbila, *Ghana* 83 D5
Bimini Is., *Bahamas* 120 A4
Bin Xian, *Heilongjiang, China* 57 B14
Bin Xian, *Shaanxi, China* 56 G5
Bin Yauri, *Nigeria* 83 C5
Bina-Etawah, *India* 68 G8
Bināb, *Iran* 71 B6
Binalbagan, *Phil.* 61 F5
Binalong, *Australia* 95 E4
Bīnālūd, Kūh-e, *Iran* 71 B8
Binatang = Bintangor, *Malaysia* 62 D4
Binche, *Belgium* 17 D4
Binchuan, *China* 58 E3
Binder, *Chad* 83 D7
Bindki, *India* 69 F9
Bindslev, *Denmark* 11 G4
Bindura, *Zimbabwe* 87 F3
Binefar, *Spain* 32 D5
Bingara, *Australia* 95 D5
Bingen, *Germany* 25 F3
Bingerville, *Ivory C.* 82 D4
Bingham, *U.S.A.* 109 C11
Binghamton, *U.S.A.* 111 D9
Bingöl, *Turkey* 70 B4
Bingöl Dağları, *Turkey* 73 C9
Bingsjö, *Sweden* 10 C9
Binh Dinh = An Nhon, *Vietnam* 64 F7
Binh Khe, *Vietnam* 64 F7
Binh Son, *Vietnam* 64 E7
Binhai, *China* 57 G10
Binic, *France* 18 D4
Binisatua, *Spain* 37 B11
Binjai, *Indonesia* 62 D3
Binji, *Nigeria* 83 C5
Binnaway, *Australia* 95 E4
Binongko, *Indonesia* 63 F6
Binscarth, *Canada* 105 C8
Bint Goda, *Sudan* 81 E3
Bintan, *Indonesia* 62 D2
Bintangor, *Malaysia* 62 D4
Bintulu, *Malaysia* 62 D4
Bintuni, *Indonesia* 63 E8
Binyang, *China* 58 F7
Binz, *Germany* 24 A9
Binzert = Bizerte, *Tunisia* 79 A7
Binzhou, *China* 57 F10
Bío Bío □, *Chile* 126 D1
Biograd na Moru, *Croatia* 29 E12
Bioko, *Eq. Guin.* 83 E6
Biokovo, *Croatia* 29 E14
Bipindi, *Cameroon* 83 E7
Bir, *India* 66 K9
Bir, Ras, *Djibouti* 81 E5
Bîr Abu Hashim, *Egypt* 80 C3
Bîr Abu Minqar, *Egypt* 80 B2
Bîr Abu Muḥammad, *Egypt* 75 F3
Bi'r ad Dabbāghāt, *Jordan* 75 E4
Bîr Adal Deib, *Sudan* 80 C4
Bi'r al Butayyihāt, *Jordan* 75 F4
Bi'r al Mārī, *Jordan* 75 E4
Bi'r al Qattār, *Jordan* 75 F4
Bir 'Asal, *Egypt* 80 B3
Bîr Atrun, *Sudan* 80 D2
Bîr Beiḍa, *Egypt* 75 E3
Bîr Diqnash, *Egypt* 80 A2
Bîr el 'Abd, *Egypt* 75 D2
Bîr el Basur, *Egypt* 80 B2
Bîr el Biarât, *Egypt* 75 F3
Bîr el Duweidar, *Egypt* 75 E1
Bîr el Garârât, *Egypt* 75 D2
Bîr el Gellaz, *Egypt* 80 A2
Bîr el Heisi, *Egypt* 75 F3
Bîr el Jafir, *Egypt* 75 E1
Bîr el Mâlḥi, *Egypt* 75 E2
Bîr el Shaqqa, *Egypt* 80 A2
Bîr el Thamâda, *Egypt* 75 E2
Bîr Fuad, *Egypt* 80 A2
Bîr Gebeil Ḥiṣn, *Egypt* 75 E2
Bi'r Ghadīr, *Syria* 75 A6
Bîr Haimur, *Egypt* 80 C3
Bîr Ḥasana, *Egypt* 75 E2
Bîr Hôôker, *Egypt* 80 H7
Bîr Kanayis, *Egypt* 80 C3
Bîr Kaseiba, *Egypt* 75 E2
Bîr Kerawein, *Egypt* 80 B2
Bîr Lahfân, *Egypt* 75 E2
Bîr Madkûr, *Egypt* 75 E1
Bîr Maql, *Egypt* 80 C3
Bîr Mîneiga, *Sudan* 80 C4
Bîr Misaha, *Egypt* 80 C2
Bîr Mogreïn, *Mauritania* 78 C3
Bîr Murr, *Egypt* 80 C3
Bi'r Muṭribah, *Kuwait* 70 D5
Bîr Nakheila, *Egypt* 80 C3
Bîr Qaṭia, *Egypt* 75 E1
Bîr Qatrani, *Egypt* 80 A2
Bîr Ranga, *Egypt* 80 C4
Bîr Sahara, *Egypt* 80 C2
Bîr Seiyâla, *Egypt* 80 B3
Bîr Shalatein, *Egypt* 80 C4
Bîr Shebb, *Egypt* 80 C2
Bîr Shût, *Egypt* 80 C4
Bîr Terfawi, *Egypt* 80 C2
Bîr Umm Qubûr, *Egypt* 80 C3
Bîr Ungât, *Egypt* 80 C3
Bîr Za'farâna, *Egypt* 80 J8
Bîr Zeidûn, *Egypt* 80 B3
Biramféro, *Guinea* 82 C3
Biratnagar, *Nepal* 69 F12
Birawa, *Dem. Rep. of the Congo* 86 C2
Birch →, *Canada* 104 B6
Birch Hills, *Canada* 105 C7
Birch I., *Canada* 105 C9
Birch L., *N.W.T., Canada* 104 A5
Birch L., *Ont., Canada* 102 B1
Birch Mts., *Canada* 104 B6
Birch River, *Canada* 105 C8
Birchip, *Australia* 95 F3
Birchiş, *Romania* 42 E7
Bird, *Canada* 105 B10
Bird I. = Las Aves, Is., *W. Indies* 121 C7
Birdsville, *Australia* 94 D2
Birdum Cr., *Australia* 92 C5
Birecik, *Turkey* 70 B3
Birein, *Israel* 75 E3
Bireuen, *Indonesia* 62 C1
Biri →, *Sudan* 81 F2
Birifo, *Gambia* 82 C2
Birigui, *Brazil* 127 A5
Birjand, *Iran* 71 C8
Birkenfeld, *Germany* 25 F3
Birkenhead, *U.K.* 12 D4
Birkerød, *Denmark* 11 J6
Birket Qârûn, *Egypt* 80 J7
Birkfeld, *Austria* 26 D8
Bîrlad = Bârlad, *Romania* 43 D12
Birmingham, *U.K.* 13 E6
Birmingham, *U.S.A.* 109 J2
Birmitrapur, *India* 67 H14
Birni Ngaouré, *Niger* 83 C5
Birni Nkonni, *Niger* 83 C6
Birnin Gwari, *Nigeria* 83 C6
Birnin Kebbi, *Nigeria* 83 C5
Birnin Kudu, *Nigeria* 83 C6
Birobidzhan, *Russia* 51 E14
Birr, *Ireland* 15 C4
Birrie →, *Australia* 95 D4
Birsilpur, *India* 68 E5
Birsk, *Russia* 50 D6
Birštonas, *Lithuania* 44 D11
Birtle, *Canada* 105 C8
Birur, *India* 66 N9
Biryuchiy, *Ukraine* 47 J8
Biržai, *Lithuania* 9 H21
Birzebbugga, *Malta* 36 D2
Bisa, *Indonesia* 63 E7
Bisáccia, *Italy* 31 A8
Bisacquino, *Italy* 30 E6
Bisalpur, *India* 69 E8
Bisbee, *U.S.A.* 115 L9
Biscarosse, *France* 20 D2
Biscarrosse et de Parentis, Étang de, *France* 20 D2
Biscay, B. of, *Atl. Oc.* 6 F5
Biscayne B., *U.S.A.* 109 N5
Biscéglie, *Italy* 31 A9
Bischheim, *France* 19 D14
Bischofshofen, *Austria* 26 D6
Bischofswerda, *Germany* 24 D10
Bischwiller, *France* 19 D14
Biscoe Bay, *Antarctica* 5 D13
Biscoe Is., *Antarctica* 5 C17
Biscostasing, *Canada* 102 C3
Biševo, *Croatia* 29 F13
Bisha, *Eritrea* 81 D4
Bishah, W. →, *Si. Arabia* 80 C5
Bishan, *China* 58 C6
Bishkek, *Kyrgyzstan* 50 E8
Bishnupur, *India* 69 H12
Bisho, *S. Africa* 89 E4
Bishop, *Calif., U.S.A.* 116 H8
Bishop, *Tex., U.S.A.* 113 M6
Bishop Auckland, *U.K.* 12 C6
Bishop's Falls, *Canada* 103 C8
Bishop's Stortford, *U.K.* 13 F8
Bisignano, *Italy* 31 C9
Bisina, L., *Uganda* 86 B3
Biskra, *Algeria* 78 B7
Biskupiec, *Poland* 44 E7
Bismarck, *U.S.A.* 112 B4
Bismarck Arch., *Papua N. G.* 96 H7
Bismark, *Germany* 24 C7
Bismil, *Turkey* 73 D9
Biso, *Uganda* 86 B3
Bison, *U.S.A.* 112 C3
Bīsotūn, *Iran* 70 C5
Bispgården, *Sweden* 10 A10
Bissagos = Bijagós, Arquipélago dos, *Guinea-Biss.* 82 C1
Bissau, *Guinea-Biss.* 82 C1
Bissaula, *Nigeria* 83 D7
Bissikrima, *Guinea* 82 C2
Bissorã, *Guinea-Biss.* 82 C1
Bistcho L., *Canada* 104 B5
Bistreţ, *Romania* 43 G8
Bistrica = Ilirska-Bistrica, *Slovenia* 29 C11
Bistriţa, *Romania* 43 C9
Bistriţa →, *Romania* 43 D11
Bistriţa Năsăud □, *Romania* 43 C9
Bistriţei, Munţii, *Romania* 43 C10
Biswan, *India* 69 F9
Bisztynek, *Poland* 44 D7
Bitburg, *Germany* 25 F2
Bitche, *France* 19 C14
Bithynia, *Turkey* 72 B4
Bitlis, *Turkey* 70 B4
Bitola, *Macedonia* 40 E5
Bitolj = Bitola, *Macedonia* 40 E5
Bitonto, *Italy* 31 A9
Bitter Creek, *U.S.A.* 114 F9
Bitter L. = Buheirat-Murrat-el-Kubra, *Egypt* 80 H8
Bitterfeld, *Germany* 24 D8
Bitterfontein, *S. Africa* 88 E2
Bitterroot →, *U.S.A.* 114 C6
Bitterroot Range, *U.S.A.* 114 D6
Bitterwater, *U.S.A.* 116 J6
Bitti, *Italy* 30 B2
Bittou, *Burkina Faso* 83 C4
Biu, *Nigeria* 83 C7
Bivolari, *Romania* 43 C12
Bivolu, Vf., *Romania* 43 C10
Biwa-Ko, *Japan* 55 G8
Biwabik, *U.S.A.* 112 B8
Bixad, *Romania* 43 C8
Bixby, *U.S.A.* 113 H7
Biyang, *China* 56 H7
Biysk, *Russia* 50 D9
Bizana, *S. Africa* 89 E4
Bizen, *Japan* 55 G7
Bizerte, *Tunisia* 79 A7
Bjargtangar, *Iceland* 8 D1
Bjärnum, *Sweden* 11 H7
Bjästa, *Sweden* 10 A12
Bjelasica, *Montenegro, Yug.* 40 D3
Bjelašnica, *Bos.-H.* 42 G3
Bjelovar, *Croatia* 29 C13
Bjerringbro, *Denmark* 11 H3
Björbo, *Sweden* 10 D8
Björklinge, *Sweden* 10 D11
Björneborg, *Sweden* 10 E8
Bjørnevatn, *Norway* 8 B23
Bjørnøya, *Arctic* 4 B8
Bjursås, *Sweden* 10 D9
Bjuv, *Sweden* 11 H6
Bla, *Mali* 82 C3
Blace, *Serbia, Yug.* 40 C5
Blachownia, *Poland* 45 H5
Black = Da →, *Vietnam* 58 G5
Black →, *Canada* 110 B5
Black →, *Ariz., U.S.A.* 115 K8
Black →, *Ark., U.S.A.* 113 H9
Black →, *Mich., U.S.A.* 110 D2
Black →, *N.Y., U.S.A.* 111 C8
Black →, *Wis., U.S.A.* 112 D9
Black Bay Pen., *Canada* 102 C2
Black Birch L., *Canada* 105 B7
Black Diamond, *Canada* 104 C6
Black Duck →, *Canada* 102 A2
Black Forest = Schwarzwald, *Germany* 25 G4
Black Forest, *U.S.A.* 112 F2
Black Hd., *Ireland* 15 C2
Black Hills, *U.S.A.* 112 D3
Black I., *Canada* 105 C9
Black L., *Canada* 105 B7
Black L., *Mich., U.S.A.* 108 C3
Black L., *N.Y., U.S.A.* 111 B9
Black Lake, *Canada* 105 B7
Black Mesa, *U.S.A.* 113 G3
Black Mt. = Mynydd Du, *U.K.* 13 F4
Black Mts., *U.K.* 13 F4
Black Range, *U.S.A.* 115 K10
Black River, *Jamaica* 120 C4
Black River Falls, *U.S.A.* 112 C9
Black Sea, *Eurasia* 6 G12
Black Tickle, *Canada* 103 B8
Black Volta →, *Africa* 82 D4
Black Warrior →, *U.S.A.* 109 J2
Blackall, *Australia* 94 C4
Blackball, *N.Z.* 91 K3
Blackbull, *Australia* 94 B3
Blackburn, *U.K.* 12 D5
Blackburn with Darwen □, *U.K.* 12 D5
Blackfoot, *U.S.A.* 114 E7
Blackfoot →, *U.S.A.* 114 C7
Blackfoot River Reservoir, *U.S.A.* 114 E8
Blackie, *Canada* 104 C6
Blackpool, *U.K.* 12 D4
Blackpool □, *U.K.* 12 D4
Blackriver, *U.S.A.* 110 B1
Blacks Harbour, *Canada* 103 C6
Blacksburg, *U.S.A.* 108 G5
Blacksod B., *Ireland* 15 B1
Blackstone, *U.S.A.* 108 G7
Blackstone Ra., *Australia* 93 E4
Blackwater, *Australia* 94 C4
Blackwater →, *Meath, Ireland* 15 C4
Blackwater →, *Waterford, Ireland* 15 D4
Blackwater →, *U.K.* 15 B5
Blackwell, *U.S.A.* 113 G6
Blackwells Corner, *U.S.A.* 117 K7
Blaenau Ffestiniog, *U.K.* 12 E4
Blaenau Gwent □, *U.K.* 13 F4
Blagaj, *Bos.-H.* 40 C1
Blagnac, *France* 20 E5
Blagodarnoye = Blagodarnyy, *Russia* 49 H6
Blagodarnyy, *Russia* 49 H6
Blagoevgrad, *Bulgaria* 40 D7
Blagoveshchensk, *Russia* 51 D13
Blain, *France* 18 E5
Blain, *U.S.A.* 110 F7
Blaine, *Minn., U.S.A.* 112 C8
Blaine, *Wash., U.S.A.* 116 B4
Blaine Lake, *Canada* 105 C7
Blair, *U.S.A.* 112 E6
Blair Athol, *Australia* 94 C4
Blair Atholl, *U.K.* 14 E5
Blairgowrie, *U.K.* 14 E5
Blairsden, *U.S.A.* 116 F6
Blairsville, *U.S.A.* 110 F5
Blaj, *Romania* 43 D8
Blake Pt., *U.S.A.* 112 A10
Blakely, *Ga., U.S.A.* 109 K3
Blakely, *Pa., U.S.A.* 111 E9
Blâmont, *France* 19 D13
Blanc, C., *Spain* 37 B9
Blanc, Mont, *Alps* 21 C10
Blanc-Sablon, *Canada* 103 B8
Blanca, B., *Argentina* 122 G4
Blanca Peak, *U.S.A.* 115 H11
Blanche, C., *Australia* 95 E1
Blanche, L., *S. Austral., Australia* 95 D2
Blanche, L., *W. Austral., Australia* 92 D3
Blanco, *S. Africa* 88 E3
Blanco, *U.S.A.* 113 K5
Blanco →, *Argentina* 126 C2
Blanco, C., *Costa Rica* 120 E2
Blanco, C., *U.S.A.* 114 E1
Blanda →, *Iceland* 8 D3
Blandford Forum, *U.K.* 13 G5
Blanding, *U.S.A.* 115 H9
Blanes, *Spain* 32 D7
Blangy-sur-Bresle, *France* 19 C8
Blanice →, *Czech Rep.* 26 B7
Blankaholm, *Sweden* 11 G10
Blankenberge, *Belgium* 17 C3
Blankenburg, *Germany* 24 D6
Blanquefort, *France* 20 D3
Blanquilla, I., *Venezuela* 121 D7
Blanquillo, *Uruguay* 127 C4
Blansko, *Czech Rep.* 27 B9
Blantyre, *Malawi* 87 F4
Blarney, *Ireland* 15 E3
Blasdell, *U.S.A.* 110 D6
Błaszki, *Poland* 45 G5
Blatná, *Czech Rep.* 26 B6
Blato, *Croatia* 29 F13
Blaubeuren, *Germany* 25 G5
Blaustein, *Germany* 25 G5
Blåvands Huk, *Denmark* 11 J2
Blaydon, *U.K.* 12 C6
Blaye, *France* 20 C3
Blaye-les-Mines, *France* 20 D6
Blayney, *Australia* 95 E4
Blaze, Pt., *Australia* 92 B5
Błażowa, *Poland* 45 J9
Bleckede, *Germany* 24 B6
Bled, *Slovenia* 29 B11
Bleiburg, *Austria* 26 E7
Blejeşti, *Romania* 43 F10
Blekinge, *Sweden* 9 H16
Blekinge län □, *Sweden* 11 H9
Blenheim, *Canada* 110 D3
Blenheim, *N.Z.* 91 J4
Bléone →, *France* 21 D10
Blérancourt, *France* 19 C10
Bletchley, *U.K.* 13 F7
Blida, *Algeria* 78 A6
Blidö, *Sweden* 10 E12
Blidsberg, *Sweden* 11 G7
Blieskastel, *Germany* 25 F3
Bligh Sound, *N.Z.* 91 L1
Blind River, *Canada* 102 C3
Blinishti, *Albania* 40 E3
Bliss, *Idaho, U.S.A.* 114 E6
Bliss, *N.Y., U.S.A.* 110 D6
Blissfield, *U.S.A.* 110 F3
Blitar, *Indonesia* 63 H15
Blitta, *Togo* 83 D5
Block I., *U.S.A.* 111 E13
Block Island Sd., *U.S.A.* 111 E13
Blodgett Iceberg Tongue, *Antarctica* 5 C9
Bloemfontein, *S. Africa* 88 D4
Bloemhof, *S. Africa* 88 D4
Blois, *France* 18 E8
Blomskog, *Sweden* 10 E6
Blomstermåla, *Sweden* 11 H10
Blönduós, *Iceland* 8 D3
Błonie, *Poland* 45 F7
Bloodvein →, *Canada* 105 C9
Bloody Foreland, *Ireland* 15 A3
Bloomer, *U.S.A.* 112 C9
Bloomfield, *Canada* 110 C7
Bloomfield, *Iowa, U.S.A.* 112 E8
Bloomfield, *N. Mex., U.S.A.* 115 H10
Bloomfield, *Nebr., U.S.A.* 112 D6
Bloomington, *Ill., U.S.A.* 112 E10
Bloomington, *Ind., U.S.A.* 108 F2
Bloomington, *Minn., U.S.A.* 112 C8
Bloomsburg, *U.S.A.* 111 F8
Blora, *Indonesia* 63 G14
Blossburg, *U.S.A.* 110 E7
Blouberg, *S. Africa* 89 C4
Blountstown, *U.S.A.* 109 K3
Bludenz, *Austria* 26 D2
Blue Earth, *U.S.A.* 112 D8
Blue Mesa Reservoir, *U.S.A.* 115 G10
Blue Mountain Lake, *U.S.A.* 111 C10
Blue Mts., *Maine, U.S.A.* 111 B14
Blue Mts., *Oreg., U.S.A.* 114 D4
Blue Mts., *Pa., U.S.A.* 111 F8
Blue Mud B., *Australia* 94 A2
Blue Nile = Nîl el Azraq →, *Sudan* 81 D3
Blue Rapids, *U.S.A.* 112 F6
Blue Ridge Mts., *U.S.A.* 109 G5
Blue River, *Canada* 104 C5
Bluefield, *U.S.A.* 108 G5
Bluefields, *Nic.* 120 D3
Bluff, *Australia* 94 C4
Bluff, *N.Z.* 91 M2
Bluff, *U.S.A.* 115 H9
Bluff Knoll, *Australia* 93 F2
Bluff Pt., *Australia* 93 E1
Bluffton, *U.S.A.* 108 E3
Blumenau, *Brazil* 127 B6
Blunt, *U.S.A.* 112 C5
Bly, *U.S.A.* 114 E3
Blyth, *Canada* 110 C3
Blyth, *U.K.* 12 B6
Blythe, *U.S.A.* 117 M12
Blytheville, *U.S.A.* 113 H10
Bo, *S. Leone* 82 D2
Bo Duc, *Vietnam* 65 G6
Bo Hai, *China* 57 E10
Bo Xian = Bozhou, *China* 56 H8
Boa Vista, *Brazil* 124 C6
Boac, *Phil.* 61 E4
Boaco, *Nic.* 120 D2
Bo'ai, *China* 56 G7
Boal, *Spain* 34 B4
Boalsburg, *U.S.A.* 110 F7
Boane, *Mozam.* 89 D5
Boardman, *U.S.A.* 110 E4
Bobadah, *Australia* 95 E4
Bobai, *China* 58 F7
Bobbili, *India* 67 K13
Bóbbio, *Italy* 28 D6
Bobcaygeon, *Canada* 102 D4
Böblingen, *Germany* 25 G5
Bobo-Dioulasso, *Burkina Faso* 82 C4
Bobolice, *Poland* 44 E3
Boboshevo, *Bulgaria* 40 D7
Bobov Dol, *Bulgaria* 40 D6
Bóbr →, *Poland* 45 F2
Bobraomby, Tanjon' i, *Madag.* 89 A8
Bobrinets, *Ukraine* 47 H7
Bobrov, *Russia* 48 E5
Bobrovitsa, *Ukraine* 47 G6
Bobruysk = Babruysk, *Belarus* 47 F5
Boby, Pic, *Madag.* 85 J9
Bôca do Acre, *Brazil* 124 E5
Boca Raton, *U.S.A.* 109 M5
Bocanda, *Ivory C.* 82 D4
Bocas del Toro, *Panama* 120 E3
Boceguillas, *Spain* 34 D7
Bochnia, *Poland* 45 J7
Bocholt, *Germany* 24 D2
Bochum, *Germany* 24 D3
Bockenem, *Germany* 24 C6
Boćki, *Poland* 45 F10
Bocognano, *France* 21 F13
Bocoyna, *Mexico* 118 B3
Bocşa, *Romania* 42 E6
Böda, *Kalmar, Sweden* 11 G11
Boda, *Kopparberg, Sweden* 10 C9
Boda, *Västernorrland, Sweden* 10 B10
Bodafors, *Sweden* 11 G8
Bodaybo, *Russia* 51 D12
Boddam, *U.K.* 14 B7
Boddington, *Australia* 93 F2
Bode Sadu, *Nigeria* 83 D5
Bodega Bay, *U.S.A.* 116 G3
Boden, *Sweden* 8 D19
Bodensee, *Europe* 25 H5
Bodenteich, *Germany* 24 C6
Bodhan, *India* 66 K10
Bodinga, *Nigeria* 83 C6
Bodmin, *U.K.* 13 G3
Bodmin Moor, *U.K.* 13 G3
Bodø, *Norway* 8 C16
Bodrog →, *Hungary* 42 B6
Bodrum, *Turkey* 39 D9
Bódva →, *Hungary* 42 B5
Boën, *France* 21 C8
Boende, *Dem. Rep. of the Congo* 84 E4
Boerne, *U.S.A.* 113 L5
Boesmans →, *S. Africa* 88 E4
Boffa, *Guinea* 82 C2
Bogalusa, *U.S.A.* 113 K10
Bogan →, *Australia* 95 D4
Bogan Gate, *Australia* 95 E4
Bogandé, *Burkina Faso* 83 C4
Bogantungan, *Australia* 94 C4
Bogata, *U.S.A.* 113 J7
Bogatić, *Serbia, Yug.* 40 B3
Boğazkale, *Turkey* 72 B6
Boğazlıyan, *Turkey* 72 C6
Bogen, *Sweden* 10 D6
Bogense, *Denmark* 11 J4
Bogetići, *Montenegro, Yug.* 40 D2
Boggabilla, *Australia* 95 D5
Boggabri, *Australia* 95 E5
Boggeragh Mts., *Ireland* 15 D3
Boglan = Solhan, *Turkey* 70 B4
Bognor Regis, *U.K.* 13 G7
Bogo, *Phil.* 61 F6
Bogodukhov = Bohodukhiv, *Ukraine* 47 G8
Bogol Manya, *Ethiopia* 81 G5
Bogong, Mt., *Australia* 95 F4
Bogor, *Indonesia* 63 G12
Bogoroditsk, *Russia* 46 F10
Bogorodsk, *Russia* 48 B6
Bogoso, *Ghana* 82 D4
Bogotá, *Colombia* 124 C4
Bogotol, *Russia* 50 D9
Bogou, *Togo* 83 C5
Bogra, *Bangla.* 67 G16
Boguchany, *Russia* 51 D10
Boguchar, *Russia* 48 F5
Bogué, *Mauritania* 82 B2
Boguslav, *Ukraine* 47 H6
Boguszów-Gorce, *Poland* 45 H3
Bohain-en-Vermandois, *France* 19 C10
Bohemian Forest = Böhmerwald, *Germany* 25 F9
Bohinjska Bistrica, *Slovenia* 29 B11
Böhmerwald, *Germany* 25 F9
Bohmte, *Germany* 24 C4
Bohodukhiv, *Ukraine* 47 G8
Bohol □, *Phil.* 61 G6
Bohol Sea, *Phil.* 63 C6
Bohongou, *Burkina Faso* 83 C5
Böhönye, *Hungary* 42 D2
Bohuslän, *Sweden* 11 F5
Boi, *Nigeria* 83 D6
Boi, Pta. de, *Brazil* 127 A6
Boiaçu, *Brazil* 124 D6
Boileau, C., *Australia* 92 C3
Boing'o, *Sudan* 81 F3
Boiro, *Spain* 34 C2
Boise, *U.S.A.* 114 E5
Boise City, *U.S.A.* 113 G3

Boissevain, *Canada* 105 D8
Bóite →, *Italy* 29 B9
Boitzenburg, *Germany* 24 B9
Boizenburg, *Germany* 24 B6
Bojador C., *W. Sahara* 78 C3
Bojana →, *Albania* 40 E3
Bojano, *Italy* 31 A7
Bojanowo, *Poland* 45 G3
Bøjden, *Denmark* 11 J4
Bojnürd, *Iran* 71 B8
Bojonegoro, *Indonesia* 63 G14
Boju, *Nigeria* 83 D6
Boka, *Serbia, Yug.* 42 E5
Boka Kotorska,
   Montenegro, Yug. 40 D2
Bokala, *Ivory C.* 82 D4
Bokani, *Nigeria* 83 D6
Bokaro, *India* 69 H11
Boké, *Guinea* 82 C2
Bokhara →, *Australia* 95 D4
Bokkos, *Nigeria* 83 D6
Boknafjorden, *Norway* 9 G11
Bokoro, *Chad* 79 F9
Bokpyin, *Burma* 65 G2
Boksitogorsk, *Russia* 46 C7
Bol, *Croatia* 29 E13
Bolama, *Guinea-Biss.* 82 C1
Bolan →, *Pakistan* 68 E2
Bolan Pass, *Pakistan* 66 E5
Bolaños →, *Mexico* 118 C4
Bolaños de Calatrava, *Spain* 35 G7
Bolayır, *Turkey* 41 F10
Bolbec, *France* 18 C7
Boldājī, *Iran* 71 D6
Boldeşti-Scăeni, *Romania* . 43 E11
Bole, *China* 60 B3
Bole, *Ethiopia* 81 F4
Bole, *Ghana* 82 D4
Bolekhiv, *Ukraine* 47 H2
Bolesławiec, *Poland* 45 G2
Bolgatanga, *Ghana* 83 C4
Bolgrad = Bolhrad, *Ukraine* 47 K5
Bolhrad, *Ukraine* 47 K5
Bolinao, *Phil.* 61 C3
Bolintin-Vale, *Romania* ... 43 F10
Bolívar, *Argentina* 126 D3
Bolivar, *Mo., U.S.A.* 113 G8
Bolivar, *N.Y., U.S.A.* 110 D6
Bolivar, *Tenn., U.S.A.* ... 113 H10
Bolivia ■, *S. Amer.* 124 G6
Bolivian Plateau, *S. Amer.* . 122 E4
Boljevac, *Serbia, Yug.* 40 C5
Bolkhov, *Russia* 46 F9
Bolków, *Poland* 45 H3
Bollebygd, *Sweden* 11 G6
Bollène, *France* 21 D8
Bollnäs, *Sweden* 10 C10
Bollon, *Australia* 95 D4
Bollstabruk, *Sweden* 10 B11
Bolmen, *Sweden* 11 H7
Bolobo,
   Dem. Rep. of the Congo . 84 E3
Bologna, *Italy* 29 D8
Bologoye, *Russia* 46 D8
Bolonchenticul, *Mexico* .. 119 D7
Bolótana, *Italy* 30 B1
Boloven, Cao Nguyen, *Laos* 64 E6
Bolpur, *India* 69 H12
Bolsena, *Italy* 29 F8
Bolsena, L. di, *Italy* 29 F8
Bolshaya Chernigovka,
   Russia 48 D10
Bolshaya Glushitsa, *Russia* . 48 D10
Bolshaya Martynovka, *Russia* 49 G5
Bolshaya Vradiyevka,
   Ukraine 47 J6
Bolshevik, Ostrov, *Russia* . 51 B11
Bolshoi Kavkas = Caucasus
   Mountains, *Eurasia* 49 J7
Bolshoy Anyuy →, *Russia* . 51 C17
Bolshoy Begichev, Ostrov,
   Russia 51 B12
Bolshoy Lyakhovskiy,
   Ostrov, *Russia* 51 B15
Bolshoy Tokmak = Tokmak,
   Ukraine 47 J8
Bolshoy Tyuters, Ostrov,
   Russia 9 G22
Bolsward, *Neths.* 17 A5
Bolt Head, *U.K.* 13 G4
Boltaña, *Spain* 32 C5
Boltigen, *Switz.* 25 J3
Bolton, *Canada* 110 C5
Bolton, *U.K.* 12 D5
Bolton Landing, *U.S.A.* ... 111 C11
Bolu, *Turkey* 72 B4
Bolungavík, *Iceland* 8 C2
Boluo, *China* 59 F10
Bolvadin, *Turkey* 70 B1
Bolzano, *Italy* 29 B8
Bom Jesus da Lapa, *Brazil* . 125 F10
Boma,
   Dem. Rep. of the Congo . 84 F2
Bombala, *Australia* 95 F4
Bombarral, *Portugal* 35 F1
Bombay = Mumbai, *India* . 66 K8
Bomboma,
   Dem. Rep. of the Congo . 84 D3
Bombombwa,
   Dem. Rep. of the Congo . 86 B2
Bomi Hills, *Liberia* 82 D2
Bomili,
   Dem. Rep. of the Congo . 86 B2
Bømlo, *Norway* 9 G11
Bomokandi →,
   Dem. Rep. of the Congo . 86 B2
Bomu →, *C.A.R.* 84 D4
Bon, C., *Tunisia* 76 C5
Bon Sar Pa, *Vietnam* 64 F6
Bonaigarh, *India* 69 J11
Bonaire, *Neth. Ant.* 121 D6

Bonang, *Australia* 95 F4
Bonanza, *Nic.* 120 D3
Bonaparte Arch., *Australia* . 92 B3
Boñar, *Spain* 34 C5
Bonaventure, *Canada* 103 C6
Bonavista, *Canada* 103 C9
Bonavista, C., *Canada* ... 103 C9
Bonavista B., *Canada* 103 C9
Bondeno, *Italy* 29 D8
Bondo,
   Dem. Rep. of the Congo . 86 B1
Bondoukou, *Ivory C.* 82 D4
Bondowoso, *Indonesia* ... 63 G15
Bone, Teluk, *Indonesia* ... 63 E6
Bonerate, *Indonesia* 63 F6
Bonerate, Kepulauan,
   Indonesia 63 F6
Bo'ness, *U.K.* 14 E5
Bonete, Cerro, *Argentina* . 126 B2
Bong Son = Hoai Nhon,
   Vietnam 64 E7
Bonga, *Ethiopia* 81 F4
Bongabong, *Phil.* 61 E4
Bongor, *Chad* 79 F9
Bongouanou, *Ivory C.* 82 D4
Bonham, *U.S.A.* 113 J6
Boni, *Mali* 82 B4
Bonifacio, *France* 21 G13
Bonifacio, Bouches de,
   Medit. S. 30 A2
Bonin Is. = Ogasawara
   Gunto, *Pac. Oc.* 52 G18
Bonke, *Ethiopia* 81 F4
Bonkoukou, *Niger* 83 C5
Bonn, *Germany* 24 E3
Bonnat, *France* 19 F8
Bonne Terre, *U.S.A.* 113 G9
Bonners Ferry, *U.S.A.* ... 114 B5
Bonnétable, *France* 18 D7
Bonneval, *Eure-et-Loir,*
   France 18 D8
Bonneval, *Savoie, France* . 21 C11
Bonneville, *France* 19 F13
Bonney, L., *Australia* 95 F3
Bonnie Rock, *Australia* ... 93 F2
Bonny, *Nigeria* 83 E6
Bonny →, *Nigeria* 83 E6
Bonny, Bight of, *Africa* ... 83 E6
Bonny-sur-Loire, *France* .. 19 E9
Bonnyrigg, *U.K.* 14 F5
Bonnyville, *Canada* 105 C6
Bono, *Italy* 30 B2
Bonoi, *Indonesia* 63 E9
Bonorva, *Italy* 30 B1
Bonsall, *U.S.A.* 117 M9
Bontang, *Indonesia* 62 D5
Bonthe, *S. Leone* 82 D2
Bontoc, *Phil.* 61 C4
Bonyeri, *Ghana* 82 D4
Bonyhád, *Hungary* 42 D3
Bonython Ra., *Australia* .. 92 D4
Bookabie, *Australia* 93 F5
Booker, *U.S.A.* 113 G4
Boola, *Guinea* 82 D3
Booligal, *Australia* 95 E3
Boonah, *Australia* 95 D5
Boone, *Iowa, U.S.A.* 112 D8
Boone, *N.C., U.S.A.* 109 G5
Booneville, *Ark., U.S.A.* . 113 H8
Booneville, *Miss., U.S.A.* . 109 H1
Boonville, *Calif., U.S.A.* . 116 F3
Boonville, *Ind., U.S.A.* .. 108 F2
Boonville, *Mo., U.S.A.* ... 112 F8
Boonville, *N.Y., U.S.A.* .. 111 C9
Boorindal, *Australia* 95 E4
Boorowa, *Australia* 95 E4
Boothia, Gulf of, *Canada* . 101 A11
Boothia Pen., *Canada* ... 100 A10
Bootle, *U.K.* 12 D4
Booué, *Gabon* 84 E2
Boppard, *Germany* 25 E3
Boquete, *Panama* 120 E3
Boquilla, Presa de la, *Mexico* 118 B3
Boquillas del Carmen,
   Mexico 118 B4
Bor, *Czech Rep.* 26 B5
Bor, *Russia* 48 B7
Bor, *Serbia, Yug.* 40 B6
Bôr, *Sudan* 81 F3
Bor, *Sweden* 11 G8
Bor, *Turkey* 72 D6
Bor Mashash, *Israel* 75 D3
Borah Peak, *U.S.A.* 114 D7
Borang, *Sudan* 81 G3
Borås, *Sweden* 11 G6
Borāzjān, *Iran* 71 D6
Borba, *Brazil* 124 D7
Borba, *Portugal* 35 G3
Borborema, Planalto da,
   Brazil 122 D7
Borcea, *Romania* 43 F12
Borçka, *Turkey* 73 B9
Bord Khūn-e Now, *Iran* .. 71 D6
Borda, C., *Australia* 95 F2
Bordeaux, *France* 20 D3
Borden, *Australia* 93 F2
Borden, *Canada* 103 C7
Borden I., *Canada* 4 B2
Borden Pen., *Canada* ... 101 A11
Borders = Scottish
   Borders □, *U.K.* 14 F6
Bordertown, *Australia* ... 95 F3
Borðeyri, *Iceland* 8 D3
Bordighera, *Italy* 28 E4
Bordj Fly Ste. Marie, *Algeria* 78 C5
Bordj-in-Eker, *Algeria* ... 78 D7
Bordj Omar Driss, *Algeria* . 78 C7
Bore, *Ethiopia* 81 G4
Borehamwood, *U.K.* ... 13 F7
Borek Wielkopolski, *Poland* 45 G4
Borensberg, *Sweden* 11 F9

Borgå = Porvoo, *Finland* .. 9 F21
Borgarfjörður, *Iceland* 8 D7
Borgarnes, *Iceland* 8 D3
Børgefjellet, *Norway* 8 D15
Borger, *Neths.* 17 B6
Borger, *U.S.A.* 113 H4
Borgholm, *Sweden* 11 H10
Bórgia, *Italy* 31 D9
Borgo San Dalmazzo, *Italy* . 28 D4
Borgo San Lorenzo, *Italy* . 29 E8
Borgo Val di Taro, *Italy* ... 28 D6
Borgo Valsugana, *Italy* ... 29 B8
Borgomanero, *Italy* 28 C5
Borgorose, *Italy* 29 F10
Borgosésia, *Italy* 28 C5
Borhoyn Tal, *Mongolia* ... 56 C6
Bori, *Nigeria* 83 E6
Borikhane, *Laos* 64 C4
Borisoglebsk, *Russia* 48 E6
Borisov = Barysaw, *Belarus* 46 E5
Borisovka, *Russia* 47 G9
Borja, *Peru* 124 D3
Borja, *Spain* 32 D3
Borjas Blancas = Les Borges
   Blanques, *Spain* 32 D5
Borjomi, *Georgia* 49 K6
Borken, *Germany* 24 D9
Børkop, *Denmark* 11 J3
Borkou, *Chad* 79 E9
Borkum, *Germany* 24 B2
Borlänge, *Sweden* 10 D9
Borley, C., *Antarctica* 5 C5
Borlu, *Turkey* 39 C10
Bormida →, *Italy* 28 D5
Bórmio, *Italy* 28 B7
Borna, *Germany* 24 D8
Borne Sulinowo, *Poland* .. 44 E3
Borneo, *E. Indies* 62 D5
Bornholm, *Denmark* 11 J8
Bornholms
   Amtskommune □,
   Denmark 11 J8
Bornholmsgattet, *Europe* . 11 J8
Borno □, *Nigeria* 83 C7
Bornos, *Spain* 35 J5
Bornova, *Turkey* 39 C9
Bornu Yassa, *Nigeria* 83 C7
Boro →, *Sudan* 81 F2
Borodino, *Russia* 46 E8
Borogontsy, *Russia* 51 C14
Boromo, *Burkina Faso* ... 82 C4
Boron, *U.S.A.* 117 L9
Borongan, *Phil.* 61 F6
Borotangba Mts., *C.A.R.* .. 81 F2
Borotou, *Ivory C.* 82 D3
Borovan, *Bulgaria* 40 C7
Borovichi, *Russia* 46 C7
Borovsk, *Russia* 46 E9
Borrby, *Sweden* 11 J8
Borrego Springs, *U.S.A.* . 117 M10
Borriol, *Spain* 32 E4
Borroloola, *Australia* 94 B2
Borşa, *Cluj, Romania* 43 D8
Borşa, *Maramureş, Romania* 43 C9
Borsad, *India* 68 H5
Borsec, *Romania* 43 D10
Borsod-Abaúj-Zemplén □,
   Hungary 42 B6
Bort-les-Orgues, *France* ... 20 C6
Borth, *U.K.* 13 E3
Börtnan, *Sweden* 10 B7
Borüjerd, *Iran* 71 C6
Boryslav, *Ukraine* 47 H2
Boryspil, *Ukraine* 47 G6
Borzhomi = Borjomi,
   Georgia 49 K6
Borzna, *Ukraine* 47 G7
Borzya, *Russia* 51 D12
Bosa, *Italy* 30 B1
Bosanska Dubica, *Bos.-H.* . 29 C13
Bosanska Gradiška, *Bos.-H.* 42 E2
Bosanska Kostajnica,
   Bos.-H. 29 C13
Bosanska Krupa, *Bos.-H.* . 29 D13
Bosanski Brod, *Bos.-H.* .. 42 E2
Bosanski Novi, *Bos.-H.* .. 29 C13
Bosanski Petrovac, *Bos.-H.* 29 D13
Bosanski Šamac, *Bos.-H.* . 42 E2
Bosansko Grahovo, *Bos.-H.* 29 D13
Bosaso, *Somali Rep.* 74 E4
Boscastle, *U.K.* 13 G3
Bose, *China* 58 F6
Boshan, *China* 57 F9
Boshof, *S. Africa* 88 D4
Boshrūyeh, *Iran* 71 C8
Bosilegrad, *Serbia, Yug.* .. 40 D6
Boskovice, *Czech Rep.* ... 27 B9
Bosna →, *Bos.-H.* 42 E3
Bosna i Hercegovina =
   Bosnia-Herzegovina ■,
   Europe 42 G2
Bosnia-Herzegovina ■,
   Europe 42 G2
Bosnik, *Indonesia* 63 E9
Bosobolo,
   Dem. Rep. of the Congo . 84 D3
Bosporus = İstanbul Boğazı,
   Turkey 41 E13
Bosque Farms, *U.S.A.* ... 115 J10
Bossangoa, *C.A.R.* 84 C3
Bossé Bangou, *Niger* 83 C5
Bossier City, *U.S.A.* 113 J8
Bosso, *Niger* 83 C7
Bosso, Dallol →, *Niger* ... 83 C5
Bostan, *Pakistan* 68 D2
Bostānābād, *Iran* 70 B5
Bosten Hu, *China* 60 B3
Boston, *U.K.* 12 E7
Boston, *U.S.A.* 111 D13
Boston Bar, *Canada* 104 D4

Boston Mts., *U.S.A.* 113 H8
Bosut →, *Croatia* 42 E3
Boswell, *Canada* 104 D5
Boswell, *U.S.A.* 110 F5
Botad, *India* 68 H4
Botan →, *Turkey* 73 D10
Botene, *Laos* 64 D3
Botev, *Bulgaria* 41 D8
Botevgrad, *Bulgaria* 40 D7
Bothaville, *S. Africa* 88 D4
Bothnia, G. of, *Europe* ... 8 E19
Bothwell, *Australia* 94 G4
Bothwell, *Canada* 110 D3
Boticas, *Portugal* 34 D3
Botletle →, *Botswana* ... 88 C3
Botlikh, *Russia* 49 J8
Botna →, *Moldova* 43 D14
Botoroaga, *Romania* 43 F10
Botoşani, *Romania* 43 C11
Botoşani □, *Romania* ... 43 C11
Botou, *Burkina Faso* 83 C5
Botricello, *Italy* 31 D9
Botro, *Ivory C.* 82 D3
Botswana ■, *Africa* 88 C3
Bottineau, *U.S.A.* 112 A4
Bottnaryd, *Sweden* 11 G7
Bottrop, *Germany* 17 C6
Botucatu, *Brazil* 127 A6
Botwood, *Canada* 103 C8
Bou Djébéha, *Mali* 82 B4
Bou Izakarn, *Morocco* ... 78 C4
Bou Rjeïmât, *Mauritania* . 82 B1
Bouaflé, *Ivory C.* 82 D3
Bouaké, *Ivory C.* 82 D3
Bouar, *C.A.R.* 84 C3
Bouârfa, *Morocco* 78 B5
Boucaut B., *Australia* 94 A1
Bouches-du-Rhône □,
   France 21 E9
Bougainville, C., *Australia* . 92 B4
Bougainville I., *Papua N. G.* 96 H7
Bougainville Reef, *Australia* 94 B4
Bougie = Bejaia, *Algeria* .. 78 A7
Bougouni, *Mali* 82 C3
Bouillon, *Belgium* 17 E5
Boukombé, *Benin* 83 C5
Boulal, *Mali* 82 B3
Boulazac, *France* 20 C4
Boulder, *Colo., U.S.A.* ... 112 E2
Boulder, *Mont., U.S.A.* .. 114 C7
Boulder City, *U.S.A.* 117 K12
Boulder Creek, *U.S.A.* ... 116 H4
Boulder Dam = Hoover
   Dam, *U.S.A.* 117 K12
Bouli, *Mauritania* 82 B2
Boulia, *Australia* 94 C2
Bouligny, *France* 19 C12
Boulogne →, *France* 18 E5
Boulogne-sur-Gesse, *France* 20 E4
Boulogne-sur-Mer, *France* . 19 B8
Bouloire, *France* 18 E7
Boulouli, *Mali* 82 B3
Boulsa, *Burkina Faso* 83 C4
Boultoum, *Niger* 83 C7
Boûmdeïd, *Mauritania* .. 82 B2
Boun Neua, *Laos* 64 B3
Boun Tai, *Laos* 64 B3
Bouna, *Ivory C.* 82 D4
Boundary Peak, *U.S.A.* .. 116 H8
Boundiali, *Ivory C.* 82 D3
Bountiful, *U.S.A.* 114 F8
Bounty Is., *Pac. Oc.* 96 M9
Boura, *Mali* 82 C4
Bourbon-Lancy, *France* .. 19 F10
Bourbon-l'Archambault,
   France 19 F10
Bourbonnais, *France* 19 F10
Bourbonne-les-Bains, *France* 19 E12
Bourbourg, *France* 19 B9
Bourdel L., *Canada* 102 A5
Bourg, *France* 20 C3
Bourg-Argental, *France* .. 21 C8
Bourg-de-Péage, *France* . 21 C9
Bourg-en-Bresse, *France* . 19 F12
Bourg-Lastic, *France* 20 C6
Bourg-Madame, *France* . 20 F5
Bourg-St-Andéol, *France* . 21 D8
Bourg-St-Maurice, *France* . 21 C10
Bourganeuf, *France* 20 C5
Bourges, *France* 19 E9
Bourget, *Canada* 111 A9
Bourget, Lac du, *France* .. 21 C9
Bourgneuf, B. de, *France* . 18 E4
Bourgneuf-en-Retz, *France* . 18 E5
Bourgogne, *France* 19 F11
Bourgoin-Jallieu, *France* . 21 C9
Bourgueil, *France* 18 E7
Bourke, *Australia* 95 E4
Bourne, *U.K.* 12 E7
Bournemouth, *U.K.* 13 G6
Bournemouth □, *U.K.* .. 13 G6
Bourou, *Burkina Faso* ... 83 C4
Bouse, *U.S.A.* 117 M13
Boussac, *France* 19 F9
Boussé, *Burkina Faso* 83 C4
Boussouma, *Burkina Faso* . 83 C4
Boutilimit, *Mauritania* ... 82 B2
Boutonne →, *France* 20 C3
Bouvet I. = Bouvetøya,
   Antarctica 3 G10
Bouvetøya, *Antarctica* ... 3 G10
Bouxwiller, *France* 19 D14
Bouza, *Niger* 83 C6
Bouzonville, *France* 19 C13
Bova Marina, *Italy* 31 E8
Bovalino Marina, *Italy* ... 31 D9
Bovec, *Slovenia* 29 B10
Bovill, *U.S.A.* 114 C5
Bovino, *Italy* 31 A8
Bovril, *Argentina* 126 C4

Bow →, *Canada* 104 C6
Bow Island, *Canada* 104 D6
Bowbells, *U.S.A.* 112 A3
Bowdle, *U.S.A.* 112 C5
Bowelling, *Australia* 93 F2
Bowen, *Argentina* 126 D2
Bowen, *Australia* 94 C4
Bowen Mts., *Australia* ... 95 F4
Bowie, *Ariz., U.S.A.* 115 K9
Bowie, *Tex., U.S.A.* 113 J6
Bowkān, *Iran* 70 B5
Bowland, Forest of, *U.K.* .. 12 D5
Bowling Green, *Ky., U.S.A.* 108 G2
Bowling Green, *Ohio,*
   U.S.A. 108 E4
Bowling Green, C., *Australia* 94 B4
Bowman, *U.S.A.* 112 B3
Bowman I., *Antarctica* ... 5 C8
Bowmanville, *Canada* ... 110 C6
Bowmore, *U.K.* 14 F2
Bowral, *Australia* 95 E5
Bowraville, *Australia* 95 E5
Bowron →, *Canada* 104 C4
Bowron Lake Prov. Park,
   Canada 104 C4
Bowser L., *Canada* 104 B3
Bowsman, *Canada* 105 C8
Bowwood, *Zambia* 87 F2
Box Cr. →, *Australia* 95 E3
Boxholm, *Sweden* 11 F9
Boxmeer, *Neths.* 17 C5
Boxtel, *Neths.* 17 C5
Boyabat, *Turkey* 72 B6
Boyalıca, *Turkey* 41 F13
Boyang, *China* 59 C11
Boyce, *U.S.A.* 113 K8
Boyd L., *Canada* 102 B4
Boyle, *Canada* 104 C6
Boyle, *Ireland* 15 C3
Boyne →, *Ireland* 15 C5
Boyne City, *U.S.A.* 108 C3
Boynitsa, *Bulgaria* 40 C6
Boynton Beach, *U.S.A.* .. 109 M5
Boyolali, *Indonesia* 63 G14
Boyoma, Chutes,
   Dem. Rep. of the Congo . 86 B2
Boysen Reservoir, *U.S.A.* . 114 E9
Boyuibe, *Bolivia* 124 G6
Boyup Brook, *Australia* .. 93 F2
Boz Burun, *Turkey* 41 F12
Boz Dağ, *Turkey* 39 D11
Boz Dağları, *Turkey* 39 C10
Bozburun, *Turkey* 39 E10
Bozcaada, *Turkey* 72 C2
Bozdoğan, *Turkey* 39 D10
Bozeman, *U.S.A.* 114 D8
Bozen = Bolzano, *Italy* ... 29 B8
Boževac, *Serbia, Yug.* ... 40 B5
Bozhou, *China* 56 H8
Bozkır, *Turkey* 72 D5
Bozkurt, *Turkey* 39 D11
Bozouls, *France* 20 D6
Bozoum, *C.A.R.* 84 C3
Bozova, *Antalya, Turkey* . 39 D12
Bozova, *Sanliurfa, Turkey* . 73 D8
Bozovici, *Romania* 42 F7
Bozüyük, *Turkey* 39 B12
Bra, *Italy* 28 D4
Bråås, *Sweden* 11 G9
Brabant □, *Belgium* 17 D4
Brabant L., *Canada* 105 B8
Brabrand, *Denmark* 11 H4
Brač, *Croatia* 29 E13
Bracadale, L., *U.K.* 14 D2
Bracciano, *Italy* 29 F9
Bracciano, L. di, *Italy* 29 F9
Bracebridge, *Canada* 102 C4
Brach, *Libya* 79 C8
Bracieux, *France* 18 E8
Bräcke, *Sweden* 10 B9
Brackettville, *U.S.A.* 113 L4
Brački Kanal, *Croatia* 29 E13
Bracknell, *U.K.* 13 F7
Bracknell Forest □, *U.K.* . 13 F7
Brad, *Romania* 42 D7
Brádano →, *Italy* 31 B9
Bradenton, *U.S.A.* 109 M4
Bradford, *Canada* 110 B5
Bradford, *U.K.* 12 D6
Bradford, *Pa., U.S.A.* 110 E6
Bradford, *Vt., U.S.A.* 111 C12
Bradley, *Ark., U.S.A.* 113 J8
Bradley, *Calif., U.S.A.* ... 116 K6
Bradley Institute, *Zimbabwe* 87 F3
Brady, *U.S.A.* 113 K5
Brædstrup, *Denmark* ... 11 J3
Braemar, *U.K.* 14 D5
Braeside, *Canada* 111 A8
Braga, *Portugal* 34 D2
Braga □, *Portugal* 34 D2
Bragadiru, *Romania* 43 G10
Bragado, *Argentina* 126 D3
Bragança, *Brazil* 125 D9
Bragança, *Portugal* 34 D4
Bragança □, *Portugal* ... 34 D4
Bragança Paulista, *Brazil* . 127 A6
Brahmanbaria, *Bangla.* .. 67 H17
Brahmani →, *India* 67 J15
Brahmapur, *India* 67 K14
Brahmaputra →, *India* ... 69 H13
Braich-y-pwll, *U.K.* 12 E3
Braidwood, *Australia* 95 F4
Brăila, *Romania* 43 E12
Brăila □, *Romania* 43 E12
Brainerd, *U.S.A.* 112 B7
Braintree, *U.K.* 13 F8
Braintree, *U.S.A.* 111 D14
Brak →, *S. Africa* 88 D3
Brake, *Germany* 24 B4
Brakel, *Germany* 24 D5

Bräkne-Hoby, *Sweden* 11 H9
Brakwater, *Namibia* 88 C2
Brålanda, *Sweden* 11 F6
Bramberg, *Germany* 25 E6
Bramdrupdam, *Denmark* 11 J3
Bramming, *Denmark* 11 J2
Brämön, *Sweden* 10 B11
Brampton, *Canada* 102 D4
Brampton, *U.K.* 12 C5
Bramsche, *Germany* 24 C3
Branco →, *Brazil* 122 D4
Brandberg, *Namibia* 88 B2
Brande, *Denmark* 11 J3
Brandenburg = Neubrandenburg, *Germany* 24 B9
Brandenburg, *Germany* 24 C8
Brandenburg □, *Germany* 24 C9
Brandfort, *S. Africa* 88 D4
Brando, *France* 21 F13
Brandon, *Canada* 105 D9
Brandon, *U.S.A.* 111 C11
Brandon B., *Ireland* 15 D1
Brandon Mt., *Ireland* 15 D1
Brandsen, *Argentina* 126 D4
Brandvlei, *S. Africa* 88 E3
Brandýs nad Labem, *Czech Rep.* 26 A7
Brăneşti, *Romania* 43 F11
Branford, *U.S.A.* 111 E12
Braniewo, *Poland* 44 D6
Bransfield Str., *Antarctica* 5 C18
Brańsk, *Poland* 45 F9
Branson, *U.S.A.* 113 G8
Brantford, *Canada* 102 D3
Brantôme, *France* 20 C4
Branzi, *Italy* 28 B6
Bras d'Or L., *Canada* 103 C7
Brasher Falls, *U.S.A.* 111 B10
Brasil, Planalto, *Brazil* 122 E6
Brasiléia, *Brazil* 124 F5
Brasília, *Brazil* 125 G9
Brasília Legal, *Brazil* 125 D7
Braslaw, *Belarus* 9 J22
Braslovče, *Slovenia* 29 B12
Braşov, *Romania* 43 E10
Braşov □, *Romania* 43 E10
Brass, *Nigeria* 83 E6
Brass →, *Nigeria* 83 E6
Brassac-les-Mines, *France* 20 C7
Brasschaat, *Belgium* 17 C4
Brassey, Banjaran, *Malaysia* 62 D5
Brassey Ra., *Australia* 93 E3
Brasstown Bald, *U.S.A.* 109 H4
Brastad, *Sweden* 11 F5
Brastavățu, *Romania* 43 G9
Bratan = Morozov, *Bulgaria* 41 D9
Brateş, *Romania* 43 E11
Bratislava, *Slovak Rep.* 27 C10
Bratislavský □, *Slovak Rep.* 27 C10
Bratsigovo, *Bulgaria* 41 D8
Bratsk, *Russia* 51 D11
Brattleboro, *U.S.A.* 111 D12
Bratunac, *Bos.-H.* 42 F4
Braunau, *Austria* 26 C6
Braunschweig, *Germany* 24 C6
Braunton, *U.K.* 13 F3
Bravicea, *Moldova* 43 C13
Bråviken, *Sweden* 11 F10
Bravo del Norte, Rio = Grande, Rio →, *U.S.A.* 113 N6
Brawley, *U.S.A.* 117 N11
Bray, *Ireland* 15 C5
Bray, Mt., *Australia* 94 A1
Bray-sur-Seine, *France* 19 D10
Brazeau →, *Canada* 104 C5
Brazil, *U.S.A.* 108 F2
Brazil ■, *S. Amer.* 125 F9
Brazilian Highlands = Brasil, Planalto, *Brazil* 122 E6
Brazo Sur →, *S. Amer.* 126 B4
Brazos →, *U.S.A.* 113 L7
Brazzaville, *Congo* 84 E3
Brčko, *Bos.-H.* 42 F3
Brda →, *Poland* 45 E5
Brdy, *Czech Rep.* 26 B6
Breaden, L., *Australia* 93 E4
Breaksea Sd., *N.Z.* 91 L1
Bream B., *N.Z.* 91 F5
Bream Hd., *N.Z.* 91 F5
Breas, *Chile* 126 B1
Breaza, *Romania* 43 E10
Brebes, *Indonesia* 63 G13
Brechin, *Canada* 110 B5
Brechin, *U.K.* 14 E6
Brecht, *Belgium* 17 C4
Breckenridge, *Colo., U.S.A.* 114 G10
Breckenridge, *Minn., U.S.A.* 112 B6
Breckenridge, *Tex., U.S.A.* 113 J5
Breckland, *U.K.* 13 E8
Břeclav, *Czech Rep.* 27 C9
Brecon, *U.K.* 13 F4
Brecon Beacons, *U.K.* 13 F4
Breda, *Neths.* 17 C4
Bredaryd, *Sweden* 11 G7
Bredasdorp, *S. Africa* 88 E3
Bredebro, *Denmark* 11 J2
Bredstedt, *Germany* 24 A4
Bree, *Belgium* 17 C5
Bregalnica →, *Macedonia* 40 E6
Bregenz, *Austria* 26 D2
Bregovo, *Bulgaria* 40 B6
Bréhal, *France* 18 D5
Bréhat, Î. de, *France* 18 D4
Breiðafjörður, *Iceland* 8 D2
Breil-sur-Roya, *France* 21 E11
Breisach, *Germany* 25 G3
Brejo, *Brazil* 125 D10
Bremen, *Germany* 24 B4
Bremen □, *Germany* 24 B4
Bremer Bay, *Australia* 93 F2
Bremer I., *Australia* 94 A2
Bremerhaven, *Germany* 24 B4
Bremerton, *U.S.A.* 116 C4
Bremervörde, *Germany* 24 B5
Brenes, *Spain* 35 H5
Brenham, *U.S.A.* 113 K6
Brenne, *France* 20 B5
Brennerpass, *Austria* 26 D4
Breno, *Italy* 28 C7
Brent, *U.S.A.* 109 J2
Brenta →, *Italy* 29 C9
Brentwood, *U.K.* 13 F8
Brentwood, *Calif., U.S.A.* 116 H5
Brentwood, *N.Y., U.S.A.* 111 F11
Bréscia, *Italy* 28 C7
Breskens, *Neths.* 17 C3
Breslau = Wrocław, *Poland* 45 G4
Bresle →, *France* 18 B8
Bressanone, *Italy* 29 B8
Bressay, *U.K.* 14 A7
Bresse, *France* 19 F12
Bressuire, *France* 18 F6
Brest, *Belarus* 47 F2
Brest, *France* 18 D2
Brest-Litovsk = Brest, *Belarus* 47 F2
Bretagne, *France* 18 D3
Bretçu, *Romania* 43 D11
Bretenoux, *France* 20 D5
Breteuil, *Eure, France* 18 D7
Breteuil, *Oise, France* 19 C9
Breton, *Canada* 104 C6
Breton, Pertuis, *France* 20 B2
Breton Sd., *U.S.A.* 113 L10
Brett, C., *N.Z.* 91 F5
Bretten, *Germany* 25 F4
Breuil-Cervínia, *Italy* 28 C4
Brevard, *U.S.A.* 109 H4
Breves, *Brazil* 125 D8
Brewarrina, *Australia* 95 E4
Brewer, *U.S.A.* 109 C11
Brewer, Mt., *U.S.A.* 116 J8
Brewerville, *Liberia* 82 D2
Brewster, *N.Y., U.S.A.* 111 E11
Brewster, *Ohio, U.S.A.* 110 F3
Brewster, *Wash., U.S.A.* 114 B4
Brewster, Kap = Kangikajik, *Greenland* 4 B6
Brewton, *U.S.A.* 109 K2
Breyten, *S. Africa* 89 D5
Breza, *Bos.-H.* 42 F3
Brezhnev = Naberezhnyye Chelny, *Russia* 48 C11
Brežice, *Slovenia* 29 C12
Březnice, *Czech Rep.* 26 B6
Breznik, *Bulgaria* 40 D6
Brezno, *Slovak Rep.* 27 C12
Brezoi, *Romania* 43 E9
Brezovica, *Kosovo, Yug.* 40 D5
Brezovo, *Bulgaria* 41 D9
Briançon, *France* 21 D10
Briare, *France* 19 E9
Briático, *Italy* 31 D9
Bribie I., *Australia* 95 D5
Bribri, *Costa Rica* 120 E3
Briceni, *Moldova* 43 B12
Bricquebec, *France* 18 C5
Bridgehampton, *U.S.A.* 111 F12
Bridgend, *U.K.* 13 F4
Bridgend □, *U.K.* 13 F4
Bridgeport, *Calif., U.S.A.* 116 G7
Bridgeport, *Conn., U.S.A.* 111 E11
Bridgeport, *Nebr., U.S.A.* 112 E3
Bridgeport, *Tex., U.S.A.* 113 J6
Bridger, *U.S.A.* 114 D9
Bridgeton, *U.S.A.* 108 F8
Bridgetown, *Australia* 93 F2
Bridgetown, *Barbados* 121 D8
Bridgetown, *Canada* 103 D6
Bridgewater, *Canada* 103 D7
Bridgewater, *Mass., U.S.A.* 111 E14
Bridgewater, *N.Y., U.S.A.* 111 D9
Bridgewater, C., *Australia* 95 F3
Bridgewater-Gagebrook, *Australia* 94 G4
Bridgnorth, *U.K.* 13 E5
Bridgton, *U.S.A.* 111 B14
Bridgwater, *U.K.* 13 F5
Bridgwater B., *U.K.* 13 F4
Bridlington, *U.K.* 12 C7
Bridlington B., *U.K.* 12 C7
Bridport, *Australia* 94 G4
Bridport, *U.K.* 13 G5
Briec, *France* 18 D2
Brienne-le-Château, *France* 19 D11
Brienon-sur-Armançon, *France* 19 E10
Brienz, *Switz.* 25 J4
Brienzersee, *Switz.* 25 J3
Brig, *Switz.* 25 J3
Brigg, *U.K.* 12 D7
Brigham City, *U.S.A.* 114 F7
Bright, *Australia* 95 F4
Brighton, *Australia* 95 F2
Brighton, *Canada* 110 B7
Brighton, *U.K.* 13 G7
Brighton, *Colo., U.S.A.* 112 F2
Brighton, *N.Y., U.S.A.* 110 C7
Brignogan-Plage, *France* 18 D2
Brignoles, *France* 21 E10
Brihuega, *Spain* 32 E2
Brikama, *Gambia* 82 C1
Brilliant, *U.S.A.* 110 F4
Brilon, *Germany* 24 D4
Bríndisi, *Italy* 31 B10
Brinje, *Croatia* 29 D12
Brinkley, *U.S.A.* 113 H9
Brinnon, *U.S.A.* 116 C4
Brion, I., *Canada* 103 C7
Brionne, *France* 18 C7
Brionski, *Croatia* 29 D10
Brioude, *France* 20 C7
Briouze, *France* 18 D6
Brisbane, *Australia* 95 D5
Brisbane →, *Australia* 95 D5
Brisighella, *Italy* 29 D8
Bristol, *U.K.* 13 F5
Bristol, *Conn., U.S.A.* 111 E12
Bristol, *Pa., U.S.A.* 111 F10
Bristol, *R.I., U.S.A.* 111 E13
Bristol, *Tenn., U.S.A.* 109 G4
Bristol, City of □, *U.K.* 13 F5
Bristol B., *U.S.A.* 100 C4
Bristol Channel, *U.K.* 13 F3
Bristol I., *Antarctica* 5 B1
Bristol L., *U.S.A.* 115 J5
Bristow, *U.S.A.* 113 H6
Britain = Great Britain, *Europe* 6 E5
British Columbia □, *Canada* 104 C3
British Indian Ocean Terr. = Chagos Arch., *Ind. Oc.* 52 K11
British Isles, *Europe* 6 E5
Brits, *S. Africa* 89 D4
Britstown, *S. Africa* 88 E3
Britt, *Canada* 102 C3
Brittany = Bretagne, *France* 18 D3
Britton, *U.S.A.* 112 C6
Brive-la-Gaillarde, *France* 20 C5
Briviesca, *Spain* 34 C7
Brixen = Bressanone, *Italy* 29 B8
Brixham, *U.K.* 13 G4
Brnaze, *Croatia* 29 E13
Brno, *Czech Rep.* 27 B9
Broad →, *U.S.A.* 109 J5
Broad Arrow, *Australia* 93 F3
Broad B., *U.K.* 14 C2
Broad Haven, *Ireland* 15 B2
Broad Law, *U.K.* 14 F5
Broad Sd., *Australia* 94 C4
Broadalbin, *U.S.A.* 111 C10
Broadback →, *Canada* 102 B4
Broadford, *Australia* 95 F4
Broadhurst Ra., *Australia* 92 D3
Broads, The, *U.K.* 12 E9
Broadus, *U.S.A.* 112 C2
Broager, *Denmark* 11 K3
Broby, *Sweden* 11 H8
Broceni, *Latvia* 44 B9
Brochet, *Canada* 105 B8
Brochet, L., *Canada* 105 B8
Brocken, *Germany* 24 D6
Brockport, *U.S.A.* 110 C7
Brockton, *U.S.A.* 111 D13
Brockville, *Canada* 102 D4
Brockway, *Mont., U.S.A.* 112 B2
Brockway, *Pa., U.S.A.* 110 E6
Brocton, *U.S.A.* 110 D5
Brod, *Macedonia* 40 E5
Brodarevo, *Serbia, Yug.* 40 C3
Brodeur Pen., *Canada* 101 A11
Brodhead, Mt., *U.S.A.* 110 E7
Brodick, *U.K.* 14 F3
Brodnica, *Poland* 45 E6
Brody, *Ukraine* 47 G3
Brogan, *U.S.A.* 114 D5
Broglie, *France* 18 C7
Brok, *Poland* 45 F8
Broken Arrow, *U.S.A.* 113 G7
Broken Bow, *Nebr., U.S.A.* 112 E5
Broken Bow, *Okla., U.S.A.* 113 H7
Broken Bow Lake, *U.S.A.* 113 H7
Broken Hill = Kabwe, *Zambia* 87 E2
Broken Hill, *Australia* 95 E3
Brokind, *Sweden* 11 F9
Bromley, *U.K.* 13 F8
Bromölla, *Sweden* 11 H8
Bromsgrove, *U.K.* 13 E5
Brønderslev, *Denmark* 11 G3
Brong-Ahafo □, *Ghana* 82 D4
Broni, *Italy* 28 C6
Bronkhorstspruit, *S. Africa* 89 D4
Brønnøysund, *Norway* 8 D15
Bronte, *Italy* 31 E7
Brook Park, *U.S.A.* 110 E4
Brookhaven, *U.S.A.* 113 K9
Brookings, *Oreg., U.S.A.* 114 E1
Brookings, *S. Dak., U.S.A.* 112 C6
Brooklin, *Canada* 110 C6
Brooklyn Park, *U.S.A.* 112 C8
Brooks, *Canada* 104 C6
Brooks Range, *U.S.A.* 100 B5
Brooksville, *U.S.A.* 109 L4
Brookton, *Australia* 93 F2
Brookville, *U.S.A.* 110 E5
Broom, L., *U.K.* 14 D3
Broome, *Australia* 92 C3
Broons, *France* 18 D4
Brora, *U.K.* 14 C5
Brora →, *U.K.* 14 C5
Brørup, *Denmark* 11 J2
Brösarp, *Sweden* 11 J8
Brosna →, *Ireland* 15 C4
Broşteni, *Mehedinţi, Romania* 42 F7
Broşteni, *Suceava, Romania* 43 C10
Brothers, *U.S.A.* 114 E3
Brou, *France* 18 D8
Brouage, *France* 20 C2
Brough, *U.K.* 12 C5
Brough Hd., *U.K.* 14 B5
Broughton Island = Qikiqtarjuaq, *Canada* 101 B13
Broumov, *Czech Rep.* 27 A9
Brovary, *Ukraine* 47 G6
Brovst, *Denmark* 11 G3
Brown, L., *Australia* 93 F2
Brown, Pt., *Australia* 95 E1
Brown City, *U.S.A.* 110 C2
Brown Willy, *U.K.* 13 G3
Brownfield, *U.S.A.* 113 J3
Browning, *U.S.A.* 114 B7
Brownsville, *Oreg., U.S.A.* 114 D2
Brownsville, *Pa., U.S.A.* 110 F5
Brownsville, *Tenn., U.S.A.* 113 H10
Brownsville, *Tex., U.S.A.* 113 N6
Brownville, *U.S.A.* 111 C9
Brownwood, *U.S.A.* 113 K5
Browse I., *Australia* 92 B3
Bruas, *Malaysia* 65 K3
Bruay-la-Buissière, *France* 19 B9
Bruce, Mt., *Australia* 92 D2
Bruce Pen., *Canada* 110 B3
Bruce Rock, *Australia* 93 F2
Bruche →, *France* 19 D14
Bruchsal, *Germany* 25 F4
Bruck an der Leitha, *Austria* 27 C9
Bruck an der Mur, *Austria* 26 D8
Brue →, *U.K.* 13 F5
Bruges = Brugge, *Belgium* 17 C3
Brugg, *Switz.* 25 H4
Brugge, *Belgium* 17 C3
Bruin, *U.S.A.* 110 E5
Brûlé, *Canada* 104 C5
Brûlon, *France* 18 E6
Brumado, *Brazil* 125 F10
Brumath, *France* 19 D14
Brumunddal, *Norway* 9 F14
Bruneau, *U.S.A.* 114 E6
Bruneau →, *U.S.A.* 114 E6
Bruneck = Brunico, *Italy* 29 B8
Brunei = Bandar Seri Begawan, *Brunei* 62 C4
Brunei ■, *Asia* 62 D4
Brunflo, *Sweden* 10 A8
Brunico, *Italy* 29 B8
Brunna, *Sweden* 10 E11
Brunnen, *Switz.* 25 J4
Brunner, L., *N.Z.* 91 K3
Brunsbüttel, *Germany* 24 B5
Brunssum, *Neths.* 17 D5
Brunswick = Braunschweig, *Germany* 24 C6
Brunswick, *Ga., U.S.A.* 109 K5
Brunswick, *Maine, U.S.A.* 109 D11
Brunswick, *Md., U.S.A.* 108 F7
Brunswick, *Mo., U.S.A.* 112 F8
Brunswick, *Ohio, U.S.A.* 110 E3
Brunswick, Pen. de, *Chile* 128 G2
Brunswick B., *Australia* 92 C3
Brunswick Junction, *Australia* 93 F2
Bruntál, *Czech Rep.* 27 B10
Bruny I., *Australia* 94 G4
Brus Laguna, *Honduras* 120 C3
Brusartsi, *Bulgaria* 40 C7
Brush, *U.S.A.* 112 E3
Brushton, *U.S.A.* 111 B10
Brusio, *Switz.* 25 J6
Brusque, *Brazil* 127 B6
Brussel, *Belgium* 17 D4
Brussels = Brussel, *Belgium* 17 D4
Brussels, *Canada* 110 C3
Brusy, *Poland* 44 E4
Bruthen, *Australia* 95 F4
Bruxelles = Brussel, *Belgium* 17 D4
Bruyères, *France* 19 D13
Bruz, *France* 18 D5
Brwinów, *Poland* 45 F7
Bryagovo, *Bulgaria* 41 E9
Bryan, *Ohio, U.S.A.* 108 E3
Bryan, *Tex., U.S.A.* 113 K6
Bryan, Mt., *Australia* 95 E2
Bryanka, *Ukraine* 47 H10
Bryansk, *Bryansk, Russia* 47 F8
Bryansk, *Dagestan, Russia* 49 H8
Bryanskoye = Bryansk, *Russia* 49 H8
Bryce Canyon National Park, *U.S.A.* 115 H7
Bryne, *Norway* 9 G11
Bryson City, *U.S.A.* 109 H4
Bryukhovetskaya, *Russia* 47 K10
Brza Palanka, *Serbia, Yug.* 40 B6
Brzeg, *Poland* 45 H4
Brzeg Dolny, *Poland* 45 G3
Brześć Kujawski, *Poland* 45 F5
Brzesko, *Poland* 45 J7
Brzeziny, *Poland* 45 G6
Brzozów, *Poland* 45 J9
Bsharri, *Lebanon* 75 A5
Bū Baqarah, *U.A.E.* 71 E8
Bu Craa, *W. Sahara* 78 C3
Bū Ḥasā, *U.A.E.* 71 F7
Bua, *Sweden* 11 G6
Bua Yai, *Thailand* 64 E4
Buapinang, *Indonesia* 63 E6
Buba, *Guinea-Biss.* 82 C2
Bubanza, *Burundi* 86 C2
Bubaque, *Guinea-Biss.* 82 C1
Bube, *Ethiopia* 81 F4
Būbiyān, *Kuwait* 71 D6
Buca, *Turkey* 39 C9
Bucak, *Turkey* 39 D12
Bucaramanga, *Colombia* 124 B4
Bucas Grande I., *Phil.* 61 G6
Bucasia, *Australia* 94 C4
Buccaneer Arch., *Australia* 92 C3
Buccino, *Italy* 31 B8
Bucecea, *Romania* 43 C11
Buchach, *Ukraine* 47 H3
Buchan, *U.K.* 14 D6
Buchan Ness, *U.K.* 14 D7
Buchanan, *Canada* 105 C8
Buchanan, *Liberia* 82 D2
Buchanan, L., *Queens., Australia* 94 C4
Buchanan, L., *W. Austral., Australia* 93 E3
Buchanan, L., *U.S.A.* 113 K5
Buchanan Cr. →, *Australia* 94 B2
Buchans, *Canada* 103 C8
Bucharest = Bucureşti, *Romania* 43 F11
Buchen, *Germany* 25 F5
Buchholz, *Germany* 24 B5
Buchloe, *Germany* 25 G6
Buchon, Pt., *U.S.A.* 116 K6
Buciumi, *Romania* 42 C8
Buck Hill Falls, *U.S.A.* 111 E9
Bückeburg, *Germany* 24 C5
Buckeye, *U.S.A.* 115 K7
Buckeye Lake, *U.S.A.* 110 G2
Buckhannon, *U.S.A.* 108 F5
Buckhaven, *U.K.* 14 E5
Buckhorn L., *Canada* 110 B6
Buckie, *U.K.* 14 D6
Buckingham, *Canada* 102 C4
Buckingham, *U.K.* 13 F7
Buckingham B., *Australia* 94 A2
Buckinghamshire □, *U.K.* 13 F7
Buckle Hd., *Australia* 92 B4
Buckleboo, *Australia* 95 E2
Buckley, *U.K.* 12 D4
Buckley →, *Australia* 94 C2
Bucklin, *U.S.A.* 113 G5
Bucks L., *U.S.A.* 116 F5
Bucquoy, *France* 19 B9
Buctouche, *Canada* 103 C7
Bucureşti, *Romania* 43 F11
Bucyrus, *U.S.A.* 108 E4
Budacu, Vf., *Romania* 43 C10
Budalin, *Burma* 67 H19
Budaörs, *Hungary* 42 C3
Budapest, *Hungary* 42 C4
Budapest □, *Hungary* 42 C4
Budaun, *India* 69 E8
Budd Coast, *Antarctica* 5 C8
Buddusò, *Italy* 30 B2
Bude, *U.K.* 13 G3
Budennovsk, *Russia* 49 H7
Budeşti, *Romania* 43 F11
Budge Budge = Baj Baj, *India* 69 H13
Budgewoi, *Australia* 95 E5
Budia, *Spain* 32 E2
Büdingen, *Germany* 25 E5
Budjala, *Dem. Rep. of the Congo* 84 D3
Budoni, *Italy* 30 B2
Búdrio, *Italy* 29 D8
Budva, *Montenegro, Yug.* 40 D2
Budzyń, *Poland* 45 F3
Buea, *Cameroon* 83 E6
Buellton, *U.S.A.* 117 L6
Buena Esperanza, *Argentina* 126 C2
Buena Park, *U.S.A.* 117 M9
Buena Vista, *Colo., U.S.A.* 115 G10
Buena Vista, *Va., U.S.A.* 108 G6
Buena Vista Lake Bed, *U.S.A.* 117 K7
Buenaventura, *Colombia* 124 C3
Buenaventura, *Mexico* 118 B3
Buendía, Embalse de, *Spain* 32 E2
Buenos Aires, *Argentina* 126 C4
Buenos Aires, *Costa Rica* 120 E3
Buenos Aires □, *Argentina* 126 D4
Buenos Aires, L., *Chile* 128 F2
Buffalo, *Mo., U.S.A.* 113 G8
Buffalo, *N.Y., U.S.A.* 110 D6
Buffalo, *Okla., U.S.A.* 113 G5
Buffalo, *S. Dak., U.S.A.* 112 C3
Buffalo, *Wyo., U.S.A.* 114 D10
Buffalo →, *Canada* 104 A5
Buffalo →, *S. Africa* 89 D5
Buffalo Head Hills, *Canada* 104 B5
Buffalo L., *Alta., Canada* 104 C6
Buffalo L., *N.W.T., Canada* 104 A5
Buffalo Narrows, *Canada* 105 B7
Buffels →, *S. Africa* 88 D2
Buford, *U.S.A.* 109 H4
Bug = Buh →, *Ukraine* 47 J6
Bug →, *Poland* 45 F8
Buga, *Colombia* 124 C3
Buganda, *Uganda* 86 C3
Buganga, *Uganda* 86 C3
Bugasong, *Phil.* 61 F5
Bugeat, *France* 20 C5
Bugel, Tanjung, *Indonesia* 63 G14
Bugibba, *Malta* 36 D1
Bugojno, *Bos.-H.* 42 F2
Bugsuk, *Phil.* 62 C5
Buguma, *Nigeria* 83 E6
Bugun Shara, *Mongolia* 60 B5
Buguruslan, *Russia* 50 D6
Buh →, *Ukraine* 47 J6
Buharkent, *Turkey* 39 D10
Buheirat-Murrat-el-Kubra, *Egypt* 80 H8
Buhera, *Zimbabwe* 89 B5
Bühl, *Germany* 25 G4
Buhl, *U.S.A.* 114 E6
Buhuşi, *Romania* 43 D11
Builth Wells, *U.K.* 13 E4
Buinsk, *Russia* 48 C9
Buir Nur, *Mongolia* 60 B6
Buis-les-Baronnies, *France* 21 D9
Buitrago = Buitrago del Lozoya, *Spain* 34 E7
Buitrago del Lozoya, *Spain* 34 E7
Bujalance, *Spain* 35 H6
Bujanovac, *Serbia, Yug.* 40 D5
Bujaraloz, *Spain* 32 D4
Buje, *Croatia* 29 C10
Bujumbura, *Burundi* 86 C2
Bük, *Hungary* 42 C1
Buk, *Poland* 45 F3
Bukachacha, *Russia* 51 D12
Bukama, *Dem. Rep. of the Congo* 87 D2

Calhoun

Bukavu, Dem. Rep. of the Congo 86 C2
Bukene, Tanzania 86 C3
Bukhara = Bukhoro, Uzbekistan 50 F7
Bukhoro, Uzbekistan 50 F7
Bukima, Tanzania 86 C3
Bukit Mertajam, Malaysia 65 K3
Bukittinggi, Indonesia 62 E2
Bükk, Hungary 42 B5
Bukoba, Tanzania 86 C3
Bukuru, Nigeria 83 D6
Bukuya, Uganda 86 B3
Būl, Kuh-e, Iran 71 D7
Bula, Guinea-Biss. 82 C1
Bula, Indonesia 63 E8
Bülach, Switz. 25 H4
Bulahdelah, Australia 95 E5
Bulan, Phil. 61 E5
Bulancak, Turkey 73 B8
Bulandshahr, India 68 E7
Bulanık, Turkey 73 C10
Bûlâq, Egypt 80 B3
Bulawayo, Zimbabwe 87 G2
Buldan, Turkey 39 C10
Bulgar, Russia 48 C9
Bulgaria ■, Europe 41 D9
Bulgheria, Monte, Italy 31 B8
Bulgurca, Turkey 39 C9
Buli, Teluk, Indonesia 63 D7
Buliluyan, C., Phil. 61 G2
Bulki, Ethiopia 81 F4
Bulkley →, Canada 104 B3
Bull Shoals L., U.S.A. 113 G8
Bullaque →, Spain 35 G6
Bullas, Spain 33 G3
Bulle, Switz. 25 J3
Bullhead City, U.S.A. 117 K12
Büllingen, Belgium 17 D6
Bullock Creek, Australia 94 B3
Bulloo →, Australia 95 D3
Bulloo L., Australia 95 D3
Bulls, N.Z. 91 J5
Bully-les-Mines, France 19 B9
Bulnes, Chile 126 D1
Bulqiza, Albania 40 E4
Bulsar = Valsad, India 66 J8
Bultfontein, S. Africa 88 D4
Bulukumba, Indonesia 63 F6
Bulun, Russia 51 B13
Bumba, Dem. Rep. of the Congo 84 D4
Bumbeşti-Jiu, Romania 43 E8
Bumbiri I., Tanzania 86 C3
Bumbuna, S. Leone 82 D2
Bumhpa Bum, Burma 67 F20
Bumi →, Zimbabwe 87 F2
Buna, Kenya 86 B4
Bunawan, Phil. 61 G6
Bunazi, Tanzania 86 C3
Bunbury, Australia 93 F2
Bunclody, Ireland 15 D5
Buncrana, Ireland 15 A4
Bundaberg, Australia 95 C5
Bünde, Germany 24 C4
Bundey →, Australia 94 C2
Bundi, India 68 G6
Bundoran, Ireland 15 B3
Bundukia, Sudan 81 F3
Bung Kan, Thailand 64 C4
Bunga →, Nigeria 83 C6
Bungatakada, Japan 55 H5
Bungay, U.K. 13 E9
Bungil Cr. →, Australia 95 D4
Bungo-Suidō, Japan 55 H6
Bungoma, Kenya 86 B3
Bungu, Tanzania 86 D4
Bunia, Dem. Rep. of the Congo 86 B3
Bunji, Pakistan 69 B6
Bunkie, U.S.A. 113 K8
Buñol, Spain 33 F4
Bunsuru, Nigeria 83 C5
Buntok, Indonesia 62 E4
Bununu Dass, Nigeria 83 C6
Bununu Kasa, Nigeria 83 D6
Bünyan, Turkey 72 C6
Bunyu, Indonesia 62 D5
Bunza, Nigeria 83 C5
Buol, Indonesia 63 D6
Buon Brieng, Vietnam 64 F7
Buon Ma Thuot, Vietnam 64 F7
Buong Long, Cambodia 64 F6
Buorkhaya, Mys, Russia 51 B14
Buqayq, Si. Arabia 71 E6
Buqbuq, Egypt 80 A2
Bur Acaba, Somali Rep. 74 G3
Bûr Fuad, Egypt 80 H8
Bûr Safâga, Egypt 70 E2
Bûr Sa'îd, Egypt 80 H8
Bûr Sûdân, Sudan 80 D4
Bûr Taufiq, Egypt 80 J8
Bura, Kenya 86 C4
Burakin, Australia 93 F2
Buram, Sudan 81 E2
Burao, Somali Rep. 74 F4
Burāq, Syria 75 B5
Buraydah, Si. Arabia 70 E5
Burbank, U.S.A. 117 L8
Burda, India 68 G6
Burdekin →, Australia 94 B4
Burdur, Turkey 39 D12
Burdur □, Turkey 39 D12
Burdur Gölü, Turkey 39 D12
Burdwan = Barddhaman, India 69 H12
Bure, Gojam, Ethiopia 81 E4
Bure, Ilubabor, Ethiopia 81 F4
Bure →, U.K. 12 E9
Büren, Germany 24 D4
Bureya →, Russia 51 E13
Burford, Canada 110 C4
Burg, Germany 24 C7
Burg auf Fehmarn, Germany 24 A7
Burg el Arab, Egypt 80 H6
Burg et Tuyur, Sudan 80 C2
Burg Stargard, Germany 24 B9
Burgas, Bulgaria 41 D11
Burgas □, Bulgaria 41 D10
Burgaski Zaliv, Bulgaria 41 D11
Burgdorf, Germany 24 C6
Burgdorf, Switz. 25 H3
Burgenland □, Austria 27 D9
Burgeo, Canada 103 C8
Burgersdorp, S. Africa 88 E4
Burges, Mt., Australia 93 F3
Burghausen, Germany 25 G8
Búrgio, Italy 30 E6
Burglengenfeld, Germany 25 F8
Burgohondo, Spain 34 E6
Burgos, Spain 34 C7
Burgos □, Spain 34 C7
Burgstädt, Germany 24 E8
Burgsvik, Sweden 11 G12
Burguillos del Cerro, Spain 35 G4
Burgundy = Bourgogne, France 19 F11
Burhaniye, Turkey 39 B8
Burhanpur, India 66 J10
Burhi Gandak →, India 69 G12
Burhner →, India 69 H9
Buri Pen., Eritrea 81 D4
Burias I., Phil. 61 E5
Burica, Pta., Costa Rica 120 E3
Burien, U.S.A. 116 C4
Burigi, L., Tanzania 86 C3
Burin, Canada 103 C8
Buriram, Thailand 64 E4
Burj Sāfitā, Syria 70 C3
Burji, Ethiopia 81 F4
Burkburnett, U.S.A. 113 H5
Burke →, Australia 94 C2
Burke Chan., Canada 104 C3
Burketown, Australia 94 B2
Burkina Faso ■, Africa 82 C4
Burk's Falls, Canada 102 C4
Burlada, Spain 32 C3
Burleigh Falls, Canada 110 B6
Burley, U.S.A. 114 E7
Burlingame, U.S.A. 116 H4
Burlington, Canada 102 D4
Burlington, Colo., U.S.A. 112 F3
Burlington, Iowa, U.S.A. 112 E9
Burlington, Kans., U.S.A. 112 F7
Burlington, N.C., U.S.A. 109 G6
Burlington, N.J., U.S.A. 111 F10
Burlington, Vt., U.S.A. 111 B11
Burlington, Wash., U.S.A. 116 B4
Burlington, Wis., U.S.A. 108 D1
Burlyu-Tyube, Kazakstan 50 E8
Burma ■, Asia 67 J20
Burnaby I., Canada 104 C2
Burnet, U.S.A. 113 K5
Burney, U.S.A. 114 F3
Burnham, U.S.A. 110 F7
Burnham-on-Sea, U.K. 13 F5
Burnie, Australia 94 G4
Burnley, U.K. 12 D5
Burns, U.S.A. 114 E4
Burns Lake, Canada 104 C3
Burnside →, Canada 100 B9
Burnside, L., Australia 93 E3
Burnsville, U.S.A. 112 C8
Burnt L., Canada 103 B7
Burnt River, Canada 110 B6
Burntwood →, Canada 105 B9
Burntwood L., Canada 105 B8
Burqān, Kuwait 70 D5
Burra, Australia 95 E2
Burra, Nigeria 83 C6
Burray, U.K. 14 C6
Burreli, Albania 40 E4
Burren Junction, Australia 95 E4
Burriana, Spain 32 F4
Burrinjuck Res., Australia 95 F4
Burro, Serranías del, Mexico 118 B4
Burrow Hd., U.K. 14 G4
Burruyacú, Argentina 126 B3
Burry Port, U.K. 13 F3
Bursa, Turkey 41 F13
Burseryd, Sweden 11 G7
Burstall, Canada 105 C7
Burton, Ohio, U.S.A. 110 E3
Burton, S.C., U.S.A. 109 J5
Burton, L., Canada 102 B4
Burton upon Trent, U.K. 12 E6
Buru, Indonesia 63 E7
Burullus, Bahra el, Egypt 80 H7
Burûn, Râs, Egypt 75 D2
Burundi ■, Africa 86 C3
Bururi, Burundi 86 C2
Burutu, Nigeria 83 D6
Burwell, U.S.A. 112 E5
Burwick, U.K. 14 C5
Bury, U.K. 12 D5
Bury St. Edmunds, U.K. 13 E8
Buryatia □, Russia 51 D11
Buryn, Ukraine 47 G7
Burzenin, Poland 45 G5
Busalla, Italy 28 D5
Busango Swamp, Zambia 87 E2
Buşayrah, Syria 70 C4
Busca, Italy 28 D4
Bushati, Albania 40 E3
Būshehr, Iran 71 D6
Būshehr □, Iran 71 D6
Bushell, Canada 105 B7
Bushenyi, Uganda 86 C3
Bushire = Būshehr, Iran 71 D6
Busie, Ghana 82 C4
Businga, Dem. Rep. of the Congo 84 D4
Busko-Zdrój, Poland 45 H7
Busovača, Bos.-H. 42 F2
Buşra ash Shām, Syria 75 C5
Busselton, Australia 93 F2
Busseri →, Sudan 81 F2
Busseto, Italy 28 D7
Bussière-Badil, France 20 C4
Bussolengo, Italy 28 C7
Bussum, Neths. 17 B5
Buşteni, Romania 43 E10
Busto, C., Spain 34 B4
Busto Arsízio, Italy 28 C5
Busu-Djanoa, Dem. Rep. of the Congo 84 D4
Busuanga I., Phil. 61 E3
Büsum, Germany 24 A4
Buta, Dem. Rep. of the Congo 86 B1
Butare, Rwanda 86 C2
Butaritari, Kiribati 96 G9
Bute, U.K. 14 F3
Bute Inlet, Canada 104 C4
Butemba, Uganda 86 B3
Butembo, Dem. Rep. of the Congo 86 B2
Buteni, Romania 42 D7
Butera, Italy 31 E7
Butha Qi, China 60 B7
Butiaba, Uganda 86 B3
Butler, Mo., U.S.A. 112 F7
Butler, Pa., U.S.A. 110 F5
Buton, Indonesia 63 E6
Butte, Mont., U.S.A. 114 C7
Butte, Nebr., U.S.A. 112 D5
Butte Creek →, U.S.A. 116 F5
Butterworth = Gcuwa, S. Africa 89 E4
Butterworth, Malaysia 65 K3
Buttevant, Ireland 15 D3
Buttfield, Mt., Australia 93 D4
Button B., Canada 105 B10
Buttonwillow, U.S.A. 117 K7
Butty Hd., Australia 93 F3
Butuan, Phil. 61 G6
Butuku-Luba, Eq. Guin. 83 E6
Butung = Buton, Indonesia 63 E6
Buturlinovka, Russia 48 E5
Butzbach, Germany 25 E4
Bützow, Germany 24 B7
Buxa Duar, India 69 F13
Buxar, India 69 G10
Buxtehude, Germany 24 B5
Buxton, U.K. 12 D6
Buxy, France 19 F11
Buy, Russia 48 A5
Buynaksk, Russia 49 J8
Buyo, Ivory C. 82 D3
Buyo, L. de, Ivory C. 82 D3
Büyük Menderes →, Turkey 39 D9
Büyükçekmece, Turkey 41 E12
Büyükkariştiran, Turkey 41 E11
Büyükkemikli Burnu, Turkey 41 F10
Büyükorhan, Turkey 39 B10
Büyükyoncalı, Turkey 41 E11
Buzançais, France 18 F8
Buzău, Romania 43 E11
Buzău □, Romania 43 E11
Buzău →, Romania 43 E12
Buzău, Pasul, Romania 43 E11
Buzen, Japan 55 H5
Buzet, Croatia 29 C10
Buzi →, Mozam. 87 F3
Buziaş, Romania 42 E6
Buzuluk, Russia 50 D6
Buzuluk →, Russia 48 E6
Buzzards B., U.S.A. 111 E14
Buzzards Bay, U.S.A. 111 E14
Bwana Mkubwe, Dem. Rep. of the Congo 87 E2
Byala, Ruse, Bulgaria 41 C9
Byala, Varna, Bulgaria 41 D11
Byala Slatina, Bulgaria 40 C7
Byarezina →, Belarus 47 F6
Bychawa, Poland 45 G9
Byczyna, Poland 45 G5
Bydgoszcz, Poland 45 E5
Byelarus = Belarus ■, Europe 46 F4
Byelorussia = Belarus ■, Europe 46 F4
Byers, U.S.A. 112 F2
Byesville, U.S.A. 110 G3
Byford, Australia 93 F2
Bykhaw, Belarus 46 F6
Bykhov = Bykhaw, Belarus 46 F6
Bykovo, Russia 48 F7
Bylas, U.S.A. 115 K8
Bylot, Canada 105 B10
Bylot I., Canada 101 A12
Byrd, C., Antarctica 5 C17
Byrock, Australia 95 E4
Byron Bay, Australia 95 D5
Byrranga, Gory, Russia 51 B11
Byrranga Mts. = Byrranga, Gory, Russia 51 B11
Byrum, Denmark 11 G5
Byske, Sweden 8 D19
Byske älv →, Sweden 8 D19
Bystrzyca →, Dolnośląskie, Poland 45 G3
Bystrzyca →, Lubelskie, Poland 45 G9
Bystrzyca Kłodzka, Poland 45 H3
Bytča, Slovak Rep. 27 B11
Bytom, Poland 45 H5
Bytom Odrzański, Poland 45 G2
Bytów, Poland 44 D4
Byumba, Rwanda 86 C3
Bzenec, Czech Rep. 27 C10
Bzura →, Poland 45 F7

C

Ca →, Vietnam 64 C5
Ca Mau, Vietnam 65 H5
Ca Mau, Mui, Vietnam 65 H5
Ca Na, Vietnam 65 G7
Caacupé, Paraguay 126 B4
Caála, Angola 85 G3
Caamano Sd., Canada 104 C3
Caazapá, Paraguay 126 B4
Caazapá □, Paraguay 127 B4
Cabadbaran, Phil. 61 G6
Cabalian = San Juan, Phil. 61 F6
Cabana, Spain 34 B2
Cabañaquinta, Spain 34 B5
Cabanatuan, Phil. 61 D4
Cabanes, Spain 32 E5
Cabano, Canada 103 C6
Čabar, Croatia 29 C11
Cabazon, U.S.A. 117 M10
Cabedelo, Brazil 125 E12
Cabeza del Buey, Spain 35 G5
Cabezón de la Sal, Spain 34 B6
Cabildo, Chile 126 C1
Cabimas, Venezuela 124 A4
Cabinda, Angola 84 F2
Cabinda □, Angola 84 F2
Cabinet Mts., U.S.A. 114 C6
Cabo Blanco, Argentina 128 F3
Cabo Frio, Brazil 127 A7
Cabo Pantoja, Peru 124 D3
Cabonga, Réservoir, Canada 102 C4
Cabool, U.S.A. 113 G8
Caboolture, Australia 95 D5
Cabora Bassa Dam = Cahora Bassa, Représa de, Mozam. 87 F3
Caborca, Mexico 118 A2
Cabot, Mt., U.S.A. 111 B13
Cabot Hd., Canada 110 A3
Cabot Str., Canada 103 C8
Cabra, Spain 35 H6
Cabra del Santo Cristo, Spain 35 H7
Cábras, Italy 30 C1
Cabrera, Spain 37 B9
Cabrera, Sierra, Spain 34 C4
Cabri, Canada 105 C7
Cabriel →, Spain 33 F3
Cabugao, Phil. 61 C4
Cacabelos, Spain 34 C4
Caçador, Brazil 127 B5
Čačak, Serbia, Yug. 40 C4
Caçapava do Sul, Brazil 127 C5
Cáccamo, Italy 30 E6
Cacém, Portugal 35 G1
Cáceres, Brazil 124 G7
Cáceres, Spain 35 F4
Cáceres □, Spain 34 F5
Cache Bay, Canada 102 C4
Cache Cr. →, U.S.A. 116 G5
Cache Creek, Canada 104 C4
Cacheu, Guinea-Biss. 82 C1
Cachi, Argentina 126 B2
Cachimbo, Serra do, Brazil 125 E7
Cachinal de la Sierra, Chile 126 A2
Cachoeira, Brazil 125 F11
Cachoeira de Itapemirim, Brazil 127 A7
Cachoeira do Sul, Brazil 127 C5
Cachopo, Portugal 35 H3
Cacine, Guinea-Biss. 82 C1
Cacoal, Brazil 124 F6
Cacólo, Angola 84 G3
Caconda, Angola 85 G3
Čadca, Slovak Rep. 27 B11
Caddo, U.S.A. 113 H6
Cader Idris, U.K. 13 E4
Cadereyta, Mexico 118 B5
Cadí, Sierra del, Spain 32 C6
Cadibarrawirracanna, L., Australia 95 D2
Cadillac, France 20 D3
Cadillac, U.S.A. 108 C3
Cadiz, Phil. 61 F5
Cádiz, Spain 35 J4
Cadiz, Calif., U.S.A. 117 L11
Cadiz, Ohio, U.S.A. 110 F4
Cádiz □, Spain 35 J5
Cádiz, G. de, Spain 35 J3
Cadiz L., U.S.A. 115 J6
Cadney Park, Australia 95 D1
Cadomin, Canada 104 C5
Cadotte Lake, Canada 104 B5
Cadours, France 20 E5
Cadoux, Australia 93 F2
Caen, France 18 C6
Caernarfon, U.K. 12 D3
Caernarfon B., U.K. 12 D3
Caernarvon = Caernarfon, U.K. 12 D3
Caerphilly, U.K. 13 F4
Caerphilly □, U.K. 13 F4
Caesarea, Israel 75 C3
Caetité, Brazil 125 F10
Cafayate, Argentina 126 B2
Cafu, Angola 88 B2
Cagayan →, Phil. 61 B4
Cagayan de Oro, Phil. 61 G6
Cagayan Is., Phil. 61 G4
Cagayan Sulu I., Phil. 61 H3
Cagli, Italy 29 E9
Cágliari, Italy 30 C2
Cágliari, G. di, Italy 30 C2
Cagnano Varano, Italy 29 G12
Cagnes-sur-Mer, France 21 E11
Caguán →, Colombia 124 D4
Caguas, Puerto Rico 121 C6
Caha Mts., Ireland 15 E2
Cahama, Angola 88 B1
Caher, Ireland 15 D4
Caherciveen, Ireland 15 E1
Cahora Bassa, Représa de, Mozam. 87 F3
Cahore Pt., Ireland 15 D5
Cahors, France 20 D5
Cahul, Moldova 43 E13
Cai Bau, Dao, Vietnam 58 G6
Cai Nuoc, Vietnam 65 H5
Caia, Mozam. 87 F4
Caianda, Angola 87 E1
Caibarién, Cuba 120 B4
Caibiran, Phil. 61 F6
Caicara, Venezuela 124 B5
Caicó, Brazil 125 E11
Caicos Is., W. Indies 121 B5
Caicos Passage, W. Indies 121 B5
Caidian, China 59 B10
Căinari, Moldova 43 D14
Caird Coast, Antarctica 5 D1
Cairn Gorm, U.K. 14 D5
Cairngorm Mts., U.K. 14 D5
Cairnryan, U.K. 14 G3
Cairns, Australia 94 B4
Cairns L., Canada 105 C10
Cairo = El Qâhira, Egypt 80 H7
Cairo, Ga., U.S.A. 109 K3
Cairo, Ill., U.S.A. 113 G10
Cairo, N.Y., U.S.A. 111 D11
Cairo Montenotte, Italy 28 D5
Caithness, Ord of, U.K. 14 C5
Cajamarca, Peru 124 E3
Cajarc, France 20 D5
Cajàzeiras, Brazil 125 E11
Čajetina, Serbia, Yug. 40 C3
Çakirgol, Turkey 73 B8
Çakırlar, Turkey 39 E12
Čakovec, Croatia 29 B13
Çal, Turkey 39 C11
Cala, Spain 35 H4
Cala →, Spain 35 H4
Cala Cadolar, Punta de = Rotja, Pta., Spain 33 G6
Cala d'Or, Spain 37 B10
Cala en Porter, Spain 37 B11
Cala Figuera, C. de, Spain 37 B9
Cala Forcat, Spain 37 B10
Cala Major, Spain 37 B9
Cala Mezquida = Sa Mesquida, Spain 37 B11
Cala Millor, Spain 37 B10
Cala Ratjada, Spain 37 B10
Cala Santa Galdana, Spain 37 B10
Calabanga, Phil. 61 E5
Calabar, Nigeria 83 E6
Calabogie, Canada 111 A8
Calabozo, Venezuela 124 B5
Calàbria □, Italy 31 C9
Calaburras, Pta. de, Spain 35 J6
Calaceite, Spain 32 D5
Calacuccia, France 21 F13
Calafat, Romania 42 G7
Calafate, Argentina 128 G2
Calafell, Spain 32 D6
Calahorra, Spain 32 C3
Calais, France 19 B8
Calais, U.S.A. 109 C12
Calalaste, Cord. de, Argentina 126 B2
Calama, Brazil 124 E6
Calama, Chile 126 A2
Calamar, Colombia 124 A4
Calamian Group, Phil. 61 F3
Calamocha, Spain 32 E3
Calamonte, Spain 35 G4
Călan, Romania 42 E7
Calañas, Spain 35 H4
Calanda, Spain 32 E4
Calang, Indonesia 62 D1
Calangiánus, Italy 30 B2
Calapan, Phil. 61 E4
Călărasi, Moldova 43 C13
Călăraşi, Romania 43 F12
Călăraşi □, Romania 43 F12
Calasparra, Spain 33 G3
Calatafimi, Italy 30 E5
Calatayud, Spain 32 D3
Călăţele, Romania 42 D8
Calato = Kálathos, Greece 39 E10
Calauag, Phil. 61 E5
Calavà, C., Italy 31 D7
Calavite, C., Phil. 61 E4
Calayan, Phil. 61 B4
Calbayog, Phil. 61 E6
Calca, Peru 124 F4
Calcasieu L., U.S.A. 113 L8
Calcutta, India 69 H13
Calcutta, U.S.A. 110 F4
Caldaro, Italy 29 B8
Caldas da Rainha, Portugal 35 F1
Caldas de Reis, Spain 34 C2
Calder →, U.K. 12 D6
Caldera, Chile 126 B1
Caldwell, Idaho, U.S.A. 114 E5
Caldwell, Kans., U.S.A. 113 G6
Caldwell, Tex., U.S.A. 113 K6
Caledon, S. Africa 88 E2
Caledon →, S. Africa 88 E4
Caledon B., Australia 94 A2
Caledonia, Canada 110 C5
Caledonia, U.S.A. 110 D7
Calella, Spain 32 D7
Calemba, Angola 88 B2
Calen, Australia 94 C4
Calenzana, France 21 F12
Caletones, Chile 126 C1
Calexico, U.S.A. 117 N11
Calf of Man, U.K. 12 C3
Calgary, Canada 104 C6
Calheta, Madeira 37 D2
Calhoun, U.S.A. 109 H3

Cali, Colombia 124 C3
Calicut, India 66 P9
Caliente, U.S.A. 115 H6
California, Mo., U.S.A. 112 F8
California, Pa., U.S.A. 110 F5
California □, U.S.A. 116 H7
California, Baja, Mexico 118 A1
California, Baja, T.N. = Baja California □, Mexico 118 B2
California, Baja, T.S. = Baja California Sur □, Mexico 118 B2
California, G. de, Mexico 118 B2
California City, U.S.A. 117 K9
California Hot Springs, U.S.A. 117 K8
Călimănești, Romania 43 E9
Călimani, Munții, Romania 43 C10
Calingasta, Argentina 126 C2
Calipatria, U.S.A. 117 M11
Calistoga, U.S.A. 116 G4
Calitri, Italy 31 B8
Calitzdorp, S. Africa 88 E3
Callabonna, L., Australia 95 D3
Callac, France 18 D3
Callan, Ireland 15 D4
Callander, U.K. 14 E4
Callao, Peru 124 F3
Calles, Mexico 119 C5
Callicoon, U.S.A. 111 E9
Calling Lake, Canada 104 B6
Calliope, Australia 94 C5
Callosa de Ensarriá, Spain 33 G4
Callosa de Segura, Spain 33 G4
Calne, U.K. 13 F6
Calola, Angola 88 B2
Calolbon = San Andres, Phil. 61 E6
Calonge, Spain 32 D8
Caloocan, Phil. 61 D4
Calore →, Italy 31 A7
Caloundra, Australia 95 D5
Calpe, Spain 33 G5
Calpella, U.S.A. 116 F3
Calpine, U.S.A. 116 F6
Calstock, Canada 102 C3
Caltabellotta, Italy 30 E6
Caltagirone, Italy 31 E7
Caltanissetta, Italy 31 E7
Çaltılıbük, Turkey 41 G12
Caluire-et-Cuire, France 19 G11
Calulo, Angola 84 G2
Caluso, Italy 28 C4
Calvados □, France 18 C6
Calvert →, Australia 94 B2
Calvert I., Canada 104 C3
Calvert Ra., Australia 92 D3
Calvi, France 21 F12
Calviá, Spain 33 F7
Calvillo, Mexico 118 C4
Calvinia, S. Africa 88 E2
Calvo = Calvo, Mte., Italy 29 G12
Calvo, Mte., Italy 29 G12
Calwa, U.S.A. 116 J7
Calzada Almuradiel = Almuradiel, Spain 35 G7
Calzada de Calatrava, Spain 35 G7
Cam →, U.K. 13 E8
Cam Lam, Vietnam 65 G7
Cam Pha, Vietnam 58 G6
Cam Ranh, Vietnam 65 G7
Cam Xuyen, Vietnam 64 C6
Camabatela, Angola 84 F3
Camacha, Madeira 37 D3
Camacho, Mexico 118 C4
Camacupa, Angola 85 G3
Camagüey, Cuba 120 B4
Camaiore, Italy 28 E7
Camaná, Peru 124 G4
Camanche Reservoir, U.S.A. 116 G6
Camaquã, Brazil 127 C5
Camaquã →, Brazil 127 C5
Câmara de Lobos, Madeira 37 D3
Camarat, C., France 21 E10
Camarès, France 20 E6
Camaret-sur-Mer, France 18 D2
Camargo, Mexico 119 B5
Camargue, France 21 E8
Camarillo, U.S.A. 117 L7
Camariñas, Spain 34 B1
Camarón, C., Honduras 120 C2
Camarones, Argentina 128 E3
Camas, Spain 35 H4
Camas, U.S.A. 116 E4
Camas Valley, U.S.A. 114 E2
Camballin, Australia 92 C3
Cambará, Brazil 127 A5
Cambay = Khambhat, India 68 H5
Cambay, G. of = Khambhat, G. of, India 66 J8
Cambil, Spain 35 H7
Cambo-les-Bains, France 20 E2
Cambodia ■, Asia 64 F5
Camborne, U.K. 13 G2
Cambrai, France 19 B10
Cambre, Spain 34 B2
Cambria, U.S.A. 116 K5
Cambrian Mts., U.K. 13 E4
Cambridge, Canada 102 D3
Cambridge, Jamaica 120 C4
Cambridge, N.Z. 91 G5
Cambridge, U.K. 13 E8
Cambridge, Mass., U.S.A. 111 D13
Cambridge, Minn., U.S.A. 112 C8
Cambridge, N.Y., U.S.A. 111 C11
Cambridge, Nebr., U.S.A. 112 E4
Cambridge, Ohio, U.S.A. 110 F3
Cambridge Bay = Ikaluktutiak, Canada 100 B9
Cambridge G., Australia 92 B4
Cambridge Springs, U.S.A. 110 E4
Cambridgeshire □, U.K. 13 E7
Cambrils, Spain 32 D6
Cambuci, Brazil 127 A7
Cambundi-Catembo, Angola 84 G3
Camden, Ala., U.S.A. 109 K2
Camden, Ark., U.S.A. 113 J8
Camden, Maine, U.S.A. 109 C11
Camden, N.J., U.S.A. 111 G9
Camden, N.Y., U.S.A. 111 C9
Camden, S.C., U.S.A. 109 H5
Camden Sd., Australia 92 C3
Camdenton, U.S.A. 113 F8
Çameli, Turkey 39 D11
Camenca, Moldova 43 B13
Camerino, Italy 29 E10
Cameron, Ariz., U.S.A. 115 J8
Cameron, La., U.S.A. 113 L8
Cameron, Mo., U.S.A. 112 F7
Cameron, Tex., U.S.A. 113 K6
Cameron Highlands, Malaysia 65 K3
Cameron Hills, Canada 104 B5
Cameroon ■, Africa 84 C2
Camerota, Italy 31 B8
Cameroun →, Cameroon 83 E6
Cameroun, Mt., Cameroon 83 E6
Cametá, Brazil 125 D9
Çamiçi Gölü, Turkey 39 D9
Camiguin □, Phil. 61 G6
Camiguin I., Phil. 61 B4
Camiling, Phil. 61 D4
Camilla, U.S.A. 109 K3
Caminha, Portugal 34 D2
Camino, U.S.A. 116 G6
Camira Creek, Australia 95 D5
Cammal, U.S.A. 110 E7
Cammarata, Italy 30 E6
Camocim, Brazil 125 D10
Camooweal, Australia 94 B2
Camopi, Fr. Guiana 125 C8
Camotes Is., Phil. 61 F6
Camotes Sea, Phil. 61 F6
Camp Borden, Canada 110 B5
Camp Hill, U.S.A. 110 F8
Camp Nelson, U.S.A. 117 J8
Camp Pendleton, U.S.A. 117 M9
Camp Verde, U.S.A. 115 J8
Camp Wood, U.S.A. 113 L5
Campagna, Italy 31 B8
Campana, Argentina 126 C4
Campana, I., Chile 128 F1
Campanário, Madeira 37 D2
Campanario, Spain 35 G5
Campânia □, Italy 31 B7
Campbell, S. Africa 88 D3
Campbell, Calif., U.S.A. 116 H5
Campbell, Ohio, U.S.A. 110 E4
Campbell I., Pac. Oc. 96 N8
Campbell L., Canada 105 A7
Campbell River, Canada 104 C3
Campbell Town, Australia 94 G4
Campbellford, Canada 110 B7
Campbellpur, Pakistan 68 C5
Campbellsville, U.S.A. 108 G3
Campbellton, Canada 103 C6
Campbelltown, Australia 95 E5
Campbeltown, U.K. 14 F3
Campeche, Mexico 119 D6
Campeche □, Mexico 119 D6
Campeche, Golfo de, Mexico 119 D6
Campello, Spain 33 G4
Câmpeni, Romania 42 D8
Camperdown, Australia 95 F3
Camperville, Canada 105 C8
Campi Salentina, Italy 31 B11
Câmpia Turzii, Romania 43 D8
Campidano, Italy 30 C1
Campíglia Maríttima, Italy 28 E7
Campillo de Altobuey, Spain 33 F3
Campillos, Spain 35 H6
Câmpina, Romania 43 E10
Campina Grande, Brazil 125 E11
Campinas, Brazil 127 A6
Campli, Italy 29 F10
Campo, Spain 32 C5
Campo de Criptana, Spain 35 F7
Campo de Gibraltar, Spain 35 J5
Campo Grande, Brazil 125 H8
Campo Maíor, Brazil 125 D10
Campo Maior, Portugal 35 F3
Campo Mourão, Brazil 127 A5
Campo Túres, Italy 29 B8
Campobasso, Italy 31 A7
Campobello di Licata, Italy 30 E6
Campobello di Mazara, Italy 30 E5
Campofelice di Roccella, Italy 30 E6
Campomarino, Italy 29 G12
Camporeale, Italy 30 E6
Camporrobles, Spain 32 F3
Campos, Brazil 127 A7
Campos Belos, Brazil 125 F9
Campos del Puerto, Spain 37 B10
Campos Novos, Brazil 127 B5
Camprodón, Spain 32 C7
Camptonville, U.S.A. 116 F5
Camptown, U.S.A. 111 E8
Câmpulung, Argeș, Romania 43 E10
Câmpulung, Suceava, Romania 43 C10
Câmpuri, Romania 43 D11
Camrose, Canada 104 C6
Camsell Portage, Canada 105 B7
Çamyuva, Turkey 39 E12
Çan, Turkey 41 F11
Can Clavo, Spain 37 C7
Can Creu, Spain 37 C7
Can Gio, Vietnam 65 G6
Can Tho, Vietnam 65 G5
Canaan, U.S.A. 111 D11
Canada ■, N. Amer. 100 C10
Cañada de Gómez, Argentina 126 C3
Canadian, U.S.A. 113 H4
Canadian →, U.S.A. 113 H7
Canajoharie, U.S.A. 111 D10
Çanakkale, Turkey 41 F10
Çanakkale □, Turkey 41 F10
Çanakkale Boğazı, Turkey 41 F10
Canal Flats, Canada 104 C5
Canalejas, Argentina 126 D2
Canals, Argentina 126 C3
Canals, Spain 33 G4
Canandaigua, U.S.A. 110 D7
Canandaigua L., U.S.A. 110 D7
Cananea, Mexico 118 A2
Canarias, Is., Atl. Oc. 37 F4
Canarreos, Arch. de los, Cuba 120 B3
Canary Is. = Canarias, Is., Atl. Oc. 37 F4
Canaseraga, U.S.A. 110 D7
Canatlán, Mexico 118 C4
Canaveral, C., U.S.A. 109 L5
Cañaveruelas, Spain 32 E2
Canavieiras, Brazil 125 G11
Canberra, Australia 95 F4
Canby, Calif., U.S.A. 114 F3
Canby, Minn., U.S.A. 112 C6
Canby, Oreg., U.S.A. 116 E4
Cancale, France 18 D5
Canche →, France 19 B8
Cancún, Mexico 119 C7
Candanchu, Spain 32 C4
Çandarlı, Turkey 39 C8
Çandarlı Körfezi, Turkey 39 C8
Candas, Spain 34 B5
Candé, France 18 E5
Candela, Italy 31 A8
Candelaria, Argentina 127 B4
Candelaria, Canary Is. 37 F3
Candeleda, Spain 34 E5
Candelo, Australia 95 F4
Candia = Iráklion, Greece 36 D7
Candia, Sea of = Crete, Sea of, Greece 39 E7
Candle L., Canada 105 C7
Candlemas I., Antarctica 5 B1
Cando, U.S.A. 112 A5
Candon, Phil. 61 C4
Canea = Khaniá, Greece 36 D6
Canelli, Italy 28 D5
Canelones, Uruguay 127 C4
Canet-Plage, France 20 F7
Cañete, Chile 126 D1
Cañete, Peru 124 F3
Cañete, Spain 32 E3
Cañete de las Torres, Spain 35 H6
Cangas, Spain 34 C2
Cangas de Narcea, Spain 34 B4
Cangas de Onís, Spain 34 B5
Cangnan, China 59 D13
Canguaretama, Brazil 125 E11
Canguçu, Brazil 127 C5
Canguçu, Serra do, Brazil 127 C5
Cangwu, China 59 F8
Cangxi, China 58 B5
Cangyuan, China 58 F2
Cangzhou, China 56 E9
Caniapiscau →, Canada 103 A6
Caniapiscau Rés. de, Canada 103 B6
Canicattì, Italy 30 E6
Canicattini Bagni, Italy 31 E8
Caniles, Spain 35 H8
Canim Lake, Canada 104 C4
Canindeyu □, Paraguay 127 A5
Canino, Italy 29 F8
Canisteo, U.S.A. 110 D7
Canisteo →, U.S.A. 110 D7
Cañitas, Mexico 118 C4
Cañizal, Spain 34 D5
Canjáyar, Spain 35 H8
Çankırı, Turkey 72 B5
Cankuzo, Burundi 86 C3
Canmore, Canada 104 C5
Cann River, Australia 95 F4
Canna, U.K. 14 D2
Cannanore, India 66 P9
Cannes, France 21 E11
Canning Town = Port Canning, India 69 H13
Cannington, Canada 110 B5
Cannóbio, Italy 28 B5
Cannock, U.K. 13 E5
Cannon Ball →, U.S.A. 112 B4
Cannondale Mt., Australia 94 D4
Cannonsville Reservoir, U.S.A. 111 D9
Cannonvale, Australia 94 C4
Canoas, Brazil 127 B5
Canoe L., Canada 105 B7
Canon City, U.S.A. 112 F2
Canora, Canada 105 C8
Canosa di Púglia, Italy 31 A9
Canowindra, Australia 95 E4
Canso, Canada 103 C7
Cantabria □, Spain 34 B7
Cantabria, Sierra de, Spain 32 C2
Cantabrian Mts. = Cantábrica, Cordillera, Spain 34 C5
Cantábrica, Cordillera, Spain 34 C5
Cantal □, France 20 C6
Cantal, Plomb du, France 20 C6
Cantanhede, Portugal 34 E2
Cantavieja, Spain 32 E4
Čantavir, Serbia, Yug. 42 E4
Cantemir, Moldova 43 D13
Canterbury, Australia 94 D3
Canterbury, U.K. 13 F9
Canterbury □, N.Z. 91 K3
Canterbury Bight, N.Z. 91 L3
Canterbury Plains, N.Z. 91 K3
Cantil, U.S.A. 117 K9
Cantillana, Spain 35 H5
Canton = Guangzhou, China 59 F9
Canton, Ga., U.S.A. 109 H3
Canton, Ill., U.S.A. 112 E9
Canton, Miss., U.S.A. 113 J9
Canton, Mo., U.S.A. 112 E9
Canton, N.Y., U.S.A. 111 B9
Canton, Ohio, U.S.A. 110 F3
Canton, Pa., U.S.A. 110 E8
Canton, S. Dak., U.S.A. 112 D6
Canton L., U.S.A. 113 G5
Cantù, Italy 28 C6
Canudos, Brazil 124 E7
Canumã →, Brazil 124 D7
Canutama, Brazil 124 E6
Canutillo, U.S.A. 115 L10
Canvey, U.K. 13 F8
Canyon, U.S.A. 113 H4
Canyonlands National Park, U.S.A. 115 G9
Canyonville, U.S.A. 114 E2
Cao Bang, Vietnam 58 F6
Cao He →, China 57 D13
Cao Lanh, Vietnam 65 G5
Cao Xian, China 56 G8
Cáorle, Italy 29 C9
Cap-aux-Meules, Canada 103 C7
Cap-Chat, Canada 103 C6
Cap-de-la-Madeleine, Canada 102 C5
Cap-Haïtien, Haiti 121 C5
Capac, U.S.A. 110 C2
Capáccio, Italy 31 B8
Capaci, Italy 30 D6
Capanaparo →, Venezuela 124 B5
Capánnori, Italy 28 E7
Capbreton, France 20 E2
Capdenac, France 20 D6
Capdepera, Spain 32 F8
Cape →, Australia 94 C4
Cape Barren I., Australia 94 G4
Cape Breton Highlands Nat. Park, Canada 103 C7
Cape Breton I., Canada 103 C7
Cape Charles, U.S.A. 108 G8
Cape Coast, Ghana 83 D4
Cape Coral, U.S.A. 109 M5
Cape Dorset, Canada 101 B12
Cape Fear →, U.S.A. 109 H6
Cape Girardeau, U.S.A. 113 G10
Cape May, U.S.A. 108 F8
Cape May Point, U.S.A. 108 F8
Cape Province, S. Africa 85 L3
Cape Tormentine, Canada 103 C7
Cape Town, S. Africa 88 E2
Cape Verde Is. ■, Atl. Oc. 77 E1
Cape Vincent, U.S.A. 111 B8
Cape York Peninsula, Australia 94 A3
Capela, Brazil 125 F11
Capella, Australia 94 C4
Capendu, France 20 E6
Capestang, France 20 E7
Capim →, Brazil 125 D9
Capistrello, Italy 29 G10
Capitan, U.S.A. 115 K11
Capitol Reef National Park, U.S.A. 115 G8
Capitola, U.S.A. 116 J5
Capizzi, Italy 31 E7
Capoche →, Mozam. 87 F3
Capoterra, Italy 30 C1
Cappadocia, Turkey 72 C6
Capraia, Italy 28 E6
Caprara, Pta., Italy 30 A1
Caprarola, Italy 29 F9
Capreol, Canada 102 C3
Caprera, Italy 30 A2
Capri, Italy 31 B7
Capricorn Group, Australia 94 C5
Capricorn Ra., Australia 92 D2
Caprino Veronese, Italy 28 C7
Caprivi Strip, Namibia 88 B3
Captain's Flat, Australia 95 F4
Captieux, France 20 D3
Caquetá →, Colombia 122 D4
Caracal, Romania 43 F9
Caracas, Venezuela 124 A5
Caracol, Mato Grosso do Sul, Brazil 126 A4
Caracol, Piauí, Brazil 125 E10
Caráglio, Italy 28 D4
Carajas, Brazil 125 E8
Carajás, Serra dos, Brazil 125 E8
Carangola, Brazil 127 A7
Caransebeș, Romania 42 E7
Carantec, France 18 D3
Caraquet, Canada 103 C6
Caras, Peru 124 E3
Caraș Severin □, Romania 42 E7
Carașova, Romania 42 E6
Caratasca, L., Honduras 120 C3
Caratinga, Brazil 125 G10
Caraúbas, Brazil 125 E11
Caravaca = Caravaca de la Cruz, Spain 33 G3
Caravaca de la Cruz, Spain 33 G3
Caravággio, Italy 28 C6
Caravela, Guinea-Biss. 82 C1
Caravelas, Brazil 125 G11
Caraveli, Peru 124 G4
Caràzinho, Brazil 127 B5
Carballino = O Carballiño, Spain 34 C2
Carballo, Spain 34 B2
Carberry, Canada 105 D9
Carbó, Mexico 118 B2
Carbonara, C., Italy 30 C2
Carbondale, Colo., U.S.A. 114 G10
Carbondale, Ill., U.S.A. 113 G10
Carbondale, Pa., U.S.A. 111 E9
Carbonear, Canada 103 C9
Carboneras, Spain 33 J3
Carboneras de Guadazaón, Spain 32 F3
Carbónia, Italy 30 C1
Carcabuey, Spain 35 H6
Carcagente = Carcaixent, Spain 33 F4
Carcaixent, Spain 33 F4
Carcajou, Canada 104 B5
Carcar, Phil. 61 F5
Carcarana →, Argentina 126 C3
Carcasse, C., Haiti 121 C5
Carcassonne, France 20 E6
Carcross, Canada 104 A2
Çardak, Çanakkale, Turkey 41 F10
Çardak, Denizli, Turkey 39 D11
Cardamon Hills, India 66 Q10
Cardeña, Spain 35 G6
Cárdenas, Cuba 120 B3
Cárdenas, San Luis Potosí, Mexico 119 C5
Cárdenas, Tabasco, Mexico 119 D6
Cardenete, Spain 32 F3
Cardiff, U.K. 13 F4
Cardiff □, U.K. 13 F4
Cardiff-by-the-Sea, U.S.A. 117 M9
Cardigan, U.K. 13 E3
Cardigan B., U.K. 13 E3
Cardinal, Canada 111 B9
Cardona, Spain 32 D6
Cardona, Uruguay 126 C4
Cardoner →, Spain 32 D6
Cardoso, Ilha do, Brazil 127 B5
Cardston, Canada 104 D6
Cardwell, Australia 94 B4
Careen L., Canada 105 B7
Carei, Romania 42 C7
Careme = Ciremai, Indonesia 63 G13
Carentan, France 18 C5
Carey, U.S.A. 114 E7
Carey, L., Australia 93 E3
Carey L., Canada 105 A8
Careysburg, Liberia 82 D2
Cargèse, France 21 F12
Carhaix-Plouguer, France 18 D3
Carhué, Argentina 126 D3
Caria, Turkey 39 D10
Cariacica, Brazil 125 H10
Cariati, Italy 31 C9
Caribbean Sea, W. Indies 121 D5
Cariboo Mts., Canada 104 C4
Caribou, U.S.A. 109 B12
Caribou →, Man., Canada 105 B10
Caribou →, N.W.T., Canada 104 A3
Caribou I., Canada 102 C2
Caribou Is., Canada 104 A6
Caribou L., Man., Canada 105 B9
Caribou L., Ont., Canada 102 B2
Caribou Mts., Canada 104 B5
Carichic, Mexico 118 B3
Carigara, Phil. 61 F6
Carignan, France 19 C12
Carignano, Italy 28 D4
Carillo, Mexico 118 B4
Carinda, Australia 95 E4
Cariñena, Spain 32 D3
Carinhanha, Brazil 125 F10
Carinhanha →, Brazil 125 F10
Carini, Italy 30 D6
Cariño, Spain 34 B3
Carínola, Italy 30 A6
Carinthia = Kärnten □, Austria 26 E6
Caripito, Venezuela 124 A6
Carlbrod = Dimitrovgrad, Serbia, Yug. 40 C6
Carlet, Spain 33 F4
Carleton, Mt., Canada 103 C6
Carleton Place, Canada 102 C4
Carletonville, S. Africa 88 D4
Cârlibaba, Romania 43 C10
Carlin, U.S.A. 114 F5
Carlingford L., U.K. 15 B5
Carlinville, U.S.A. 112 F10
Carlisle, U.K. 12 C5
Carlisle, U.S.A. 110 F7
Carlit, Pic, France 20 F5
Carloforte, Italy 30 C1
Carlos Casares, Argentina 126 D3
Carlos Tejedor, Argentina 126 D3
Carlow, Ireland 15 D5
Carlow □, Ireland 15 D5
Carlsbad, Calif., U.S.A. 117 M9
Carlsbad, N. Mex., U.S.A. 113 J2
Carlsbad Caverns National Park, U.S.A. 113 J2
Carluke, U.K. 14 F5
Carlyle, Canada 105 D8
Carmacks, Canada 100 B6
Carmagnola, Italy 28 D4
Carman, Canada 105 D9
Carmarthen, U.K. 13 F3
Carmarthen B., U.K. 13 F3
Carmarthenshire □, U.K. 13 F3
Carmaux, France 20 D6
Carmel, U.S.A. 111 E11
Carmel-by-the-Sea, U.S.A. 116 J5
Carmel Valley, U.S.A. 116 J5
Carmelo, Uruguay 126 C4
Carmen, Colombia 124 B3
Carmen, Paraguay 127 B4
Carmen →, Mexico 118 A3
Carmen, I., Mexico 118 B2
Carmen de Patagones, Argentina 128 E4
Cármenes, Spain 34 C5
Carmensa, Argentina 126 D2

Carmi, *Canada* 104 D5
Carmi, *U.S.A.* 108 F1
Carmichael, *U.S.A.* 116 G5
Carmila, *Australia* 94 C4
Carmona, *Costa Rica* 120 E2
Carmona, *Spain* 35 H5
Carn Ban, *U.K.* 14 D4
Carn Eige, *U.K.* 14 D3
Carnamah, *Australia* 93 E2
Carnarvon, *Australia* 93 D1
Carnarvon, *S. Africa* 88 E3
Carnarvon Ra., *Queens., Australia* 94 D4
Carnarvon Ra., *W. Austral., Australia* 93 E3
Carnation, *U.S.A.* 116 C5
Carndonagh, *Ireland* 15 A4
Carnduff, *Canada* 105 D8
Carnegie, *U.S.A.* 110 F4
Carnegie, L., *Australia* 93 E3
Carnic Alps = Karnische Alpen, *Europe* 26 E6
Carniche Alpi = Karnische Alpen, *Europe* 26 E6
Carnot, *C.A.R.* 84 D3
Carnot, C., *Australia* 95 E2
Carnot B., *Australia* 92 C3
Carnoustie, *U.K.* 14 E6
Carnsore Pt., *Ireland* 15 D5
Caro, *U.S.A.* 108 D4
Carol City, *U.S.A.* 109 N5
Carolina, *Brazil* 125 E9
Carolina, *Puerto Rico* 121 C6
Carolina, *S. Africa* 89 D5
Caroline I., *Kiribati* 97 H12
Caroline Is., *Micronesia* 52 J17
Caroni →, *Venezuela* 124 B6
Caroníe = Nébrodi, Monti, *Italy* 31 E7
Caroona, *Australia* 95 E5
Carpathians, *Europe* 6 F10
Carpații Meridionali, *Romania* 43 E9
Carpentaria, G. of, *Australia* 94 A2
Carpentras, *France* 21 D9
Carpi, *Italy* 28 D7
Cărpineni, *Moldova* 43 D13
Carpinteria, *U.S.A.* 117 L7
Carpio, *Spain* 34 D5
Carr Boyd Ra., *Australia* 92 C4
Carrabelle, *U.S.A.* 109 L3
Carral, *Spain* 34 B2
Carranza, Presa V., *Mexico* 118 B4
Carrara, *Italy* 28 D7
Carrascal, *Phil.* 61 G6
Carrascosa del Campo, *Spain* 32 E2
Carrauntoohill, *Ireland* 15 D2
Carrick-on-Shannon, *Ireland* 15 C3
Carrick-on-Suir, *Ireland* 15 D4
Carrickfergus, *U.K.* 15 B6
Carrickmacross, *Ireland* 15 C5
Carrieton, *Australia* 95 E2
Carrington, *U.S.A.* 112 B5
Carrión →, *Spain* 34 D6
Carrión de los Condes, *Spain* 34 C6
Carrizal Bajo, *Chile* 126 B1
Carrizalillo, *Chile* 126 B1
Carrizo Cr. →, *U.S.A.* 113 G3
Carrizo Springs, *U.S.A.* 113 L5
Carrizozo, *U.S.A.* 115 K11
Carroll, *U.S.A.* 112 D7
Carrollton, *Ga., U.S.A.* 109 J3
Carrollton, *Ill., U.S.A.* 112 F9
Carrollton, *Ky., U.S.A.* 108 F3
Carrollton, *Mo., U.S.A.* 112 F8
Carrollton, *Ohio, U.S.A.* 110 F3
Carron →, *U.K.* 14 D4
Carron, L., *U.K.* 14 D3
Carrot →, *Canada* 105 C8
Carrot River, *Canada* 105 C8
Carrouges, *France* 18 D6
Carrù, *Italy* 28 D4
Carruthers, *Canada* 105 C7
Carsa Dek, *Ethiopia* 81 F4
Çarşamba, *Turkey* 72 B7
Carsòli, *Italy* 29 F10
Carson, *Calif., U.S.A.* 117 M8
Carson, *N. Dak., U.S.A.* 112 B4
Carson →, *U.S.A.* 116 F8
Carson City, *U.S.A.* 116 F7
Carson Sink, *U.S.A.* 114 G4
Cartagena, *Colombia* 124 A3
Cartagena, *Spain* 33 H4
Cartago, *Colombia* 124 C3
Cartago, *Costa Rica* 120 E3
Cártama, *Spain* 35 J6
Cartaxo, *Portugal* 35 F2
Cartaya, *Spain* 35 H3
Cartersville, *U.S.A.* 109 H3
Carterton, *N.Z.* 91 J5
Carthage, *Tunisia* 30 F3
Carthage, *Ill., U.S.A.* 112 E9
Carthage, *Mo., U.S.A.* 113 G7
Carthage, *N.Y., U.S.A.* 108 D8
Carthage, *Tex., U.S.A.* 113 J7
Cartier I., *Australia* 92 B3
Cartwright, *Canada* 103 B8
Caruaru, *Brazil* 125 E11
Carúpano, *Venezuela* 124 A6
Caruthersville, *U.S.A.* 113 G10
Carvin, *France* 19 B9
Carvoeiro, *Brazil* 124 D6
Carvoeiro, C., *Portugal* 35 F1
Cary, *U.S.A.* 109 H6
Casa Branca, *Portugal* 35 G2
Casa Grande, *U.S.A.* 115 K8
Casablanca, *Chile* 126 C1
Casablanca, *Morocco* 78 B4
Casacalenda, *Italy* 29 G11
Casalbordino, *Italy* 29 F11
Casale Monferrato, *Italy* 28 C5
Casalmaggiore, *Italy* 28 D7
Casalpusterlengo, *Italy* 28 C6
Casamance →, *Senegal* 82 C1
Casarano, *Italy* 31 B11
Casares, *Spain* 35 J5
Casas Ibáñez, *Spain* 33 F3
Casasimarro, *Spain* 33 F2
Casatejada, *Spain* 34 F5
Casavieja, *Spain* 34 E6
Cascade, *Idaho, U.S.A.* 114 D5
Cascade, *Mont., U.S.A.* 114 C8
Cascade Locks, *U.S.A.* 116 E5
Cascade Ra., *U.S.A.* 116 D5
Cascade Reservoir, *U.S.A.* 114 D5
Cascais, *Portugal* 35 G1
Cascavel, *Brazil* 127 A5
Cáscina, *Italy* 28 E7
Casco B., *U.S.A.* 109 D10
Caselle Torinese, *Italy* 28 C4
Caserta, *Italy* 31 A7
Cashel, *Ireland* 15 D4
Casiguran, *Phil.* 61 C5
Casilda, *Argentina* 126 C3
Casimcea, *Romania* 43 F13
Casino, *Australia* 95 D5
Casiquiare →, *Venezuela* 124 C5
Čáslav, *Czech Rep.* 26 B8
Casma, *Peru* 124 E3
Casmalia, *U.S.A.* 117 L6
Cásola Valsénio, *Italy* 29 D8
Cásoli, *Italy* 29 F11
Caspe, *Spain* 32 D4
Casper, *U.S.A.* 114 E10
Caspian Depression, *Eurasia* 49 G9
Caspian Sea, *Eurasia* 50 E6
Cass Lake, *U.S.A.* 112 B7
Cassà de la Selva, *Spain* 32 D7
Cassadaga, *U.S.A.* 110 D5
Cassano allo Iónio, *Italy* 31 C9
Casse, Grande, *France* 21 C10
Cassel, *France* 19 B9
Casselman, *Canada* 111 A9
Casselton, *U.S.A.* 112 B6
Cassiar, *Canada* 104 B3
Cassiar Mts., *Canada* 104 B2
Cassino, *Italy* 30 A6
Cassis, *France* 21 E9
Cassville, *U.S.A.* 113 G8
Castagneto Carducci, *Italy* 28 E7
Castaic, *U.S.A.* 117 L8
Castalia, *U.S.A.* 110 E2
Castanhal, *Brazil* 125 D9
Castéggio, *Italy* 28 C6
Castejón de Monegros, *Spain* 32 D4
Castèl di Sangro, *Italy* 29 G11
Castèl San Giovanni, *Italy* 28 C6
Castèl San Pietro Terme, *Italy* 29 D8
Castelbuono, *Italy* 31 E7
Castelfidardo, *Italy* 29 E10
Castelfiorentino, *Italy* 28 E7
Castelfranco Emília, *Italy* 28 D8
Castelfranco Véneto, *Italy* 29 C8
Casteljaloux, *France* 20 D4
Castellabate, *Italy* 31 B7
Castellammare, G. di, *Italy* 30 D5
Castellammare del Golfo, *Italy* 30 D5
Castellammare di Stábia, *Italy* 31 B7
Castellamonte, *Italy* 28 C4
Castellane, *France* 21 E10
Castellaneta, *Italy* 31 B9
Castelli, *Argentina* 126 D4
Castelló de la Plana, *Spain* 32 F4
Castellón de la Plana □, *Spain* 32 E4
Castellote, *Spain* 32 E4
Castelmáuro, *Italy* 29 G11
Castelnau-de-Médoc, *France* 20 C3
Castelnau-Magnoac, *France* 20 E4
Castelnaudary, *France* 20 E5
Castelnovo ne' Monti, *Italy* 28 D7
Castelnuovo di Val di Cécina, *Italy* 28 E7
Castelo, *Brazil* 127 A7
Castelo Branco, *Portugal* 34 F3
Castelo Branco □, *Portugal* 34 F3
Castelo de Paiva, *Portugal* 34 D2
Castelo de Vide, *Portugal* 35 F3
Castelsardo, *Italy* 30 B1
Castelsarrasin, *France* 20 D5
Casteltérmini, *Italy* 30 E6
Castelvetrano, *Italy* 30 E5
Casterton, *Australia* 95 F3
Castets, *France* 20 E2
Castiglion Fiorentino, *Italy* 29 E8
Castiglione del Lago, *Italy* 29 E9
Castiglione della Pescáia, *Italy* 28 F7
Castiglione delle Stiviere, *Italy* 28 C7
Castilblanco, *Spain* 35 F5
Castile, *U.S.A.* 110 D6
Castilla, Playa de, *Spain* 35 J4
Castilla-La Mancha □, *Spain* 6 H5
Castilla y Leon □, *Spain* 34 D6
Castillo de Locubín, *Spain* 35 H7
Castillon-en-Couserans, *France* 20 F5
Castillonès, *France* 20 D4
Castillos, *Uruguay* 127 C5
Castle Dale, *U.S.A.* 114 G8
Castle Douglas, *U.K.* 14 G5
Castle Rock, *Colo., U.S.A.* 112 F2
Castle Rock, *Wash., U.S.A.* 116 D4
Castlebar, *Ireland* 15 C2
Castleblaney, *Ireland* 15 B5
Castlederg, *U.K.* 15 B4
Castleford, *U.K.* 12 D6
Castlegar, *Canada* 104 D5
Castlemaine, *Australia* 95 F3
Castlepollard, *Ireland* 15 C4
Castlerea, *Ireland* 15 C3
Castlereagh →, *Australia* 95 E4
Castlereagh B., *Australia* 94 A2
Castleton, *U.S.A.* 111 C11
Castletown, *U.K.* 12 C3
Castletown Bearhaven, *Ireland* 15 E2
Castor, *Canada* 104 C6
Castor →, *Canada* 102 B4
Castorland, *U.S.A.* 111 C9
Castres, *France* 20 E6
Castricum, *Neths.* 17 B4
Castries, *St. Lucia* 121 D7
Castril, *Spain* 35 H8
Castro, *Brazil* 127 A6
Castro, *Chile* 128 E2
Castro Alves, *Brazil* 125 F11
Castro del Río, *Spain* 35 H6
Castro-Urdiales, *Spain* 34 B7
Castro Verde, *Portugal* 35 H2
Castrojeriz, *Spain* 34 C6
Castropol, *Spain* 34 B4
Castroreale, *Italy* 31 D8
Castrovíllari, *Italy* 31 C9
Castroville, *U.S.A.* 116 J5
Castuera, *Spain* 35 G5
Çat, *Turkey* 73 C9
Cat Ba, Dao, *Vietnam* 64 B6
Cat I., *Bahamas* 121 B4
Cat L., *Canada* 102 B1
Cat Lake, *Canada* 102 B1
Čata, *Slovak Rep.* 27 D11
Catacamas, *Honduras* 120 D2
Cataguases, *Brazil* 127 A7
Çatak, *Turkey* 73 C10
Catalão, *Brazil* 125 G9
Çatalca, *Turkey* 41 E12
Catalina, *Canada* 103 C9
Catalina, *Chile* 126 B2
Catalina, *U.S.A.* 115 K8
Catalonia = Cataluña □, *Spain* 32 D6
Cataluña □, *Spain* 32 D6
Çatalzeytin, *Turkey* 72 B6
Catamarca, *Argentina* 126 B2
Catamarca □, *Argentina* 126 B2
Catanauan, *Phil.* 61 E5
Catanduanes □, *Phil.* 61 E6
Catanduva, *Brazil* 127 A6
Catánia, *Italy* 31 E8
Catánia, G. di, *Italy* 31 E8
Catanzaro, *Italy* 31 D9
Catarman, *Phil.* 61 E6
Catbalogan, *Phil.* 61 F6
Cateel, *Phil.* 61 H7
Catembe, *Mozam.* 89 D5
Caterham, *U.K.* 13 F7
Cathcart, *S. Africa* 88 E4
Cathlamet, *U.S.A.* 116 D3
Catio, *Guinea-Biss.* 82 C1
Catlettsburg, *U.S.A.* 108 F4
Çatma Dağı, *Turkey* 39 C11
Catoche, C., *Mexico* 119 C7
Cátria, Mte., *Italy* 29 E9
Catriló, *Argentina* 126 D3
Catrimani, *Brazil* 124 C6
Catrimani →, *Brazil* 124 C6
Catskill, *U.S.A.* 111 D11
Catskill Mts., *U.S.A.* 111 D10
Catt, Mt., *Australia* 94 A1
Cattaraugus, *U.S.A.* 110 D6
Cattólica, *Italy* 29 E9
Cattólica Eraclea, *Italy* 30 E6
Catuala, *Angola* 88 B2
Catuane, *Mozam.* 89 D5
Catur, *Mozam.* 87 E4
Catwick Is., *Vietnam* 65 G7
Cauca →, *Colombia* 124 B4
Caucaia, *Brazil* 125 D11
Caucasus Mountains, *Eurasia* 49 J7
Caudete, *Spain* 33 G3
Caudry, *France* 19 B10
Caulnes, *France* 18 D4
Caulónia, *Italy* 31 D9
Caungula, *Angola* 84 F3
Cauquenes, *Chile* 126 D1
Caura →, *Venezuela* 124 B6
Cauresi →, *Mozam.* 87 F3
Căuşani, *Moldova* 43 D14
Causapscal, *Canada* 103 C6
Caussade, *France* 20 D5
Causse-Méjean, *France* 20 D7
Cauterets, *France* 20 F3
Cauvery →, *India* 66 P11
Caux, Pays de, *France* 18 C7
Cava de' Tirreni, *Italy* 31 B7
Cávado →, *Portugal* 34 D2
Cavaillon, *France* 21 E9
Cavalaire-sur-Mer, *France* 21 E10
Cavalese, *Italy* 29 B8
Cavalier, *U.S.A.* 112 A6
Cavalla = Cavally →, *Africa* 82 E3
Cavalleria, C. de, *Spain* 37 A11
Cavallo, I. de, *France* 21 G13
Cavally →, *Africa* 82 E3
Cavan, *Ireland* 15 B4
Cavan □, *Ireland* 15 C4
Cavárzere, *Italy* 29 C9
Çavdarhisar, *Turkey* 39 B11
Çavdır, *Turkey* 39 D11
Cave Creek, *U.S.A.* 115 K7
Cavenagh Ra., *Australia* 93 E4
Cavendish, *Australia* 95 F3
Caviana, I., *Brazil* 125 C8
Cavite, *Phil.* 61 D4
Cavnic, *Romania* 43 C8
Cavour, *Italy* 28 D4
Cavtat, *Croatia* 40 D2
Cawndilla L., *Australia* 95 E3
Cawnpore = Kanpur, *India* 69 F9
Caxias, *Brazil* 125 D10
Caxias do Sul, *Brazil* 127 B5
Çay, *Turkey* 72 C4
Cay Sal Bank, *Bahamas* 120 B4
Cayambe, *Ecuador* 124 C3
Çaycuma, *Turkey* 72 B5
Çayeli, *Turkey* 73 B9
Cayenne, *Fr. Guiana* 125 B8
Caygören Barajı, *Turkey* 39 B10
Cayiralan, *Turkey* 72 C6
Caylus, *France* 20 D5
Cayman Brac, *Cayman Is.* 120 C4
Cayman Is. ■, *W. Indies* 120 C3
Cayo Romano, *Cuba* 120 B4
Cayres, *France* 20 D7
Cayuga, *Canada* 110 D5
Cayuga, *U.S.A.* 111 D8
Cayuga L., *U.S.A.* 111 D8
Cazalla de la Sierra, *Spain* 35 H5
Căzăneşti, *Romania* 43 F12
Cazaubon, *France* 20 E3
Cazaux et de Sanguinet, Étang de, *France* 20 D2
Cazenovia, *U.S.A.* 111 D9
Cazères, *France* 20 E5
Cazin, *Bos.-H.* 29 D12
Čazma, *Croatia* 29 C13
Cazombo, *Angola* 85 G4
Cazorla, *Spain* 35 H7
Cazorla, Sierra de, *Spain* 35 G8
Cea →, *Spain* 34 C5
Ceamurlia de Jos, *Romania* 43 F13
Ceanannus Mor, *Ireland* 15 C5
Ceará = Fortaleza, *Brazil* 125 D11
Ceará □, *Brazil* 125 E11
Ceará Mirim, *Brazil* 125 E11
Ceauru, L., *Romania* 43 F8
Cebaco, I. de, *Panama* 120 E3
Cebollar, *Argentina* 126 B2
Cebollera, Sierra de, *Spain* 32 D2
Cebreros, *Spain* 34 E6
Cebu, *Phil.* 61 F5
Čečava, *Bos.-H.* 42 F2
Ceccano, *Italy* 30 A6
Cece, *Hungary* 42 D3
Cechi, *Ivory C.* 82 D4
Cecil Plains, *Australia* 95 D5
Cécina, *Italy* 28 E7
Cécina →, *Italy* 28 E7
Ceclavín, *Spain* 34 F4
Cedar →, *U.S.A.* 112 E9
Cedar City, *U.S.A.* 115 H7
Cedar Creek Reservoir, *U.S.A.* 113 J6
Cedar Falls, *Iowa, U.S.A.* 112 D8
Cedar Falls, *Wash., U.S.A.* 116 C5
Cedar L., *Canada* 105 C9
Cedar Rapids, *U.S.A.* 112 E9
Cedartown, *U.S.A.* 109 H3
Cedarvale, *Canada* 104 B3
Cedarville, *S. Africa* 89 E4
Cedeira, *Spain* 34 B2
Cedral, *Mexico* 118 C4
Cedrino →, *Italy* 30 B2
Cedro, *Brazil* 125 E11
Cedros, I. de, *Mexico* 118 B1
Ceduna, *Australia* 95 E1
Cedynia, *Poland* 45 F1
Cée, *Spain* 34 C1
Cefalù, *Italy* 31 D7
Cega →, *Spain* 34 D6
Cegléd, *Hungary* 42 C4
Céglie Messápico, *Italy* 31 B10
Cehegín, *Spain* 33 G3
Ceheng, *China* 58 E5
Cehu-Silvaniei, *Romania* 43 C8
Ceica, *Romania* 42 D7
Ceira →, *Portugal* 34 E2
Čelákovice, *Czech Rep.* 26 A7
Celano, *Italy* 29 F10
Celanova, *Spain* 34 C3
Celaya, *Mexico* 118 C4
Celebes Sea, *Indonesia* 63 D6
Čelić, *Bos.-H.* 42 F3
Celina, *U.S.A.* 108 E3
Celinac, *Bos.-H.* 42 F2
Celje, *Slovenia* 29 B12
Celldömölk, *Hungary* 42 C2
Celle, *Germany* 24 C6
Celorico da Beira, *Portugal* 34 E3
Çeltikçi, *Turkey* 39 D12
Çemişgezek, *Turkey* 73 C8
Cenderwasih, Teluk, *Indonesia* 63 E9
Cengong, *China* 58 D7
Ceno →, *Italy* 28 D7
Centallo, *Italy* 28 D4
Centelles, *Spain* 32 D7
Center, *N. Dak., U.S.A.* 112 B4
Center, *Tex., U.S.A.* 113 K7
Centerburg, *U.S.A.* 110 F2
Centerville, *Calif., U.S.A.* 116 J7
Centerville, *Iowa, U.S.A.* 112 E8
Centerville, *Pa., U.S.A.* 110 F5
Centerville, *Tenn., U.S.A.* 109 H2
Centerville, *Tex., U.S.A.* 113 K7
Cento, *Italy* 29 D8
Central □, *Ghana* 83 D4
Central □, *Kenya* 86 C4
Central □, *Malawi* 87 E3
Central □, *Zambia* 87 E2
Central, Cordillera, *Colombia* 122 C3
Central, Cordillera, *Costa Rica* 120 D3
Central, Cordillera, *Dom. Rep.* 121 C5
Central, Cordillera, *Phil.* 61 C4
Central African Rep. ■, *Africa* 84 C4
Central America, *America* 98 H11
Central Butte, *Canada* 105 C7
Central City, *Colo., U.S.A.* 114 G11
Central City, *Ky., U.S.A.* 108 G2
Central City, *Nebr., U.S.A.* 112 E6
Central I., *Kenya* 86 B4
Central Makran Range, *Pakistan* 66 F4
Central Patricia, *Canada* 102 B1
Central Point, *U.S.A.* 114 E2
Central Russian Uplands, *Europe* 6 E13
Central Siberian Plateau, *Russia* 52 C14
Central Square, *U.S.A.* 111 C8
Centralia, *Ill., U.S.A.* 112 F10
Centralia, *Mo., U.S.A.* 112 F8
Centralia, *Wash., U.S.A.* 116 D4
Cenxi, *China* 59 F8
Čeotina →, *Bos.-H.* 40 C2
Cephalonia = Kefallinía, *Greece* 38 C2
Čepin, *Croatia* 42 E3
Ceprano, *Italy* 30 A6
Ceptura, *Romania* 43 E11
Cepu, *Indonesia* 63 G14
Ceram = Seram, *Indonesia* 63 E7
Ceram Sea = Seram Sea, *Indonesia* 63 E7
Cerbère, *France* 20 F7
Cerbicales, Is., *France* 21 G13
Cercal, *Portugal* 35 H2
Cerdaña, *Spain* 32 C6
Cère →, *France* 20 D5
Cerea, *Italy* 29 C8
Ceredigion □, *U.K.* 13 E3
Ceres, *Argentina* 126 B3
Ceres, *S. Africa* 88 E2
Ceres, *U.S.A.* 116 H6
Céret, *France* 20 F6
Cergy, *France* 19 C9
Cerignola, *Italy* 31 A8
Cerigo = Kíthira, *Greece* 38 E5
Cérilly, *France* 19 F9
Cerisiers, *France* 19 D10
Cerizay, *France* 18 F6
Çerkeş, *Turkey* 72 B5
Çerkezköy, *Turkey* 41 E12
Cerknica, *Slovenia* 29 C11
Cerkovica, *Bulgaria* 41 C8
Cermerno, *Serbia, Yug.* 40 C4
Çermik, *Turkey* 73 C8
Cerna, *Romania* 43 E13
Cerna →, *Romania* 43 F8
Cernavodă, *Romania* 43 F13
Cernay, *France* 19 E14
Cernik, *Croatia* 42 E2
Cerralvo, I., *Mexico* 118 C3
Cërrik, *Albania* 40 E3
Cerritos, *Mexico* 118 C4
Cerro Chato, *Uruguay* 127 C4
Certaldo, *Italy* 28 E8
Cervaro →, *Italy* 31 A8
Cervati, Monte, *Italy* 31 B8
Cerventes, *Australia* 93 F2
Cervera, *Spain* 32 D6
Cervera de Pisuerga, *Spain* 34 C6
Cervera del Río Alhama, *Spain* 32 C3
Cervéteri, *Italy* 29 F9
Cérvia, *Italy* 29 D9
Cervignano del Friuli, *Italy* 29 C10
Cervinara, *Italy* 31 A7
Cervione, *France* 21 F13
Cervo, *Spain* 34 B3
Cesarò, *Italy* 31 E7
Cesena, *Italy* 29 D9
Cesenático, *Italy* 29 D9
Cēsis, *Latvia* 9 H21
Česká Lípa, *Czech Rep.* 26 A7
Česká Třebová, *Czech Rep.* 27 B9
České Budějovice, *Czech Rep.* 26 C7
České Velenice, *Czech Rep.* 26 C7
Českomoravská Vrchovina, *Czech Rep.* 26 B8
Český Brod, *Czech Rep.* 26 A7
Český Krumlov, *Czech Rep.* 26 C7
Český Těšín, *Czech Rep.* 27 B11
Česma →, *Croatia* 29 C13
Çeşme, *Turkey* 39 C8
Cessnock, *Australia* 95 E5
Cesson-Sévigné, *France* 18 D5
Cestas, *France* 20 D3
Cestos →, *Liberia* 82 D3
Cetate, *Romania* 42 F8
Cetin Grad, *Croatia* 29 C12
Cetina →, *Croatia* 29 E13
Cetinje, *Montenegro, Yug.* 40 D2
Cetraro, *Italy* 31 C8
Ceuta, *N. Afr.* 78 A4
Ceva, *Italy* 28 D5
Cévennes, *France* 20 D7
Ceyhan, *Turkey* 70 B2
Ceyhan →, *Turkey* 72 D6
Ceylânpınar, *Turkey* 73 D9
Ceylon = Sri Lanka ■, *Asia* 66 R12
Cèze →, *France* 21 D8
Cha-am, *Thailand* 64 F2
Cha Pa, *Vietnam* 64 A4
Chabanais, *France* 20 C4
Chabeuil, *France* 21 D9
Chablais, *France* 19 F13
Chablis, *France* 19 E10
Chacabuco, *Argentina* 126 C3
Chachapoyas, *Peru* 124 E3
Chachoengsao, *Thailand* 64 F3
Chachran, *Pakistan* 66 E7
Chachro, *Pakistan* 68 G4
Chaco □, *Argentina* 126 B3
Chaco □, *Paraguay* 126 B4

Chaco →, *U.S.A.* 115 H9
Chaco Austral, *S. Amer.* 128 B4
Chaco Boreal, *S. Amer.* 124 H6
Chaco Central, *S. Amer.* 128 A4
Chacon, C., *U.S.A.* 104 C2
Chad ■, *Africa* 79 E9
Chad, L. = Tchad, L., *Chad* 79 F8
Chadan, *Russia* 51 D10
Chadileuvú →, *Argentina* 126 D2
Chadiza, *Zambia* 87 E3
Chadron, *U.S.A.* 112 D3
Chadyr-Lunga = Ciadâr-Lunga, *Moldova* 43 D13
Chae Hom, *Thailand* 64 C2
Chaem →, *Thailand* 64 C2
Chaeryŏng, *N. Korea* 57 E13
Chagai Hills, *Afghan.* 66 E3
Chagda, *Russia* 51 D14
Chagny, *France* 19 F11
Chagoda, *Russia* 46 C8
Chagos Arch., *Ind. Oc.* 52 K11
Chagrin Falls, *U.S.A.* 110 E3
Chāh Ākhvor, *Iran* 71 C8
Chāh Bahār, *Iran* 71 E9
Chāh-e Kavīr, *Iran* 71 C8
Chahar Burjak, *Afghan.* 66 D3
Chahār Mahāll va Bakhtīarī □, *Iran* 71 C6
Chaibasa, *India* 67 H14
Chaillé-les-Marais, *France* 20 B2
Chainat, *Thailand* 64 E3
Chaiya, *Thailand* 65 H2
Chaj Doab, *Pakistan* 68 C5
Chajari, *Argentina* 126 C4
Chak Amru, *Pakistan* 68 C6
Chaka, *Sudan* 81 G3
Chakar →, *Pakistan* 68 E3
Chakari, *Zimbabwe* 89 B4
Chake Chake, *Tanzania* 86 D4
Chakhānsūr, *Afghan.* 66 D3
Chakonipau, L., *Canada* 103 A6
Chakradharpur, *India* 69 H11
Chakrata, *India* 68 D7
Chakwal, *Pakistan* 68 C5
Chala, *Peru* 124 G4
Chalais, *France* 20 C4
Chalchihuites, *Mexico* 118 C4
Chalcis = Khalkís, *Greece* 38 C5
Châlette-sur-Loing, *France* 19 D9
Chaleur B., *Canada* 103 C6
Chalfant, *U.S.A.* 116 H8
Chalhuanca, *Peru* 124 F4
Chalindrey, *France* 19 E12
Chaling, *China* 59 D9
Chalisgaon, *India* 66 J9
Chalk River, *Canada* 102 C4
Chalky Inlet, *N.Z.* 91 M1
Challans, *France* 18 F5
Challapata, *Bolivia* 124 G5
Challis, *U.S.A.* 114 D6
Chalmette, *U.S.A.* 113 L10
Chalon-sur-Saône, *France* 19 F11
Chalonnes-sur-Loire, *France* 18 E6
Châlons-en-Champagne, *France* 19 D11
Châlus, *France* 20 C4
Chalyaphum, *Thailand* 64 E4
Cham, *Germany* 25 F8
Cham, Cu Lao, *Vietnam* 64 E7
Chama, *U.S.A.* 115 H10
Chamaicó, *Argentina* 126 D3
Chaman, *Pakistan* 66 D5
Chamba, *India* 68 C7
Chamba, *Tanzania* 87 E4
Chambal →, *India* 69 F8
Chamberlain, *U.S.A.* 112 D5
Chamberlain →, *Australia* 92 C4
Chamberlain L., *U.S.A.* 109 B11
Chambers, *U.S.A.* 115 J9
Chambersburg, *U.S.A.* 108 F7
Chambéry, *France* 21 C9
Chambeshi →, *Zambia* 84 G6
Chambly, *Canada* 111 A11
Chambord, *Canada* 103 C5
Chamboulive, *France* 20 C5
Chamchamal, *Iraq* 70 C5
Chamela, *Mexico* 118 D3
Chamical, *Argentina* 126 C2
Chamkar Luong, *Cambodia* 65 G4
Chamoli, *India* 69 D8
Chamonix-Mont Blanc, *France* 21 C10
Chamouchouane →, *Canada* 102 C5
Champa, *India* 69 H10
Champagne, *Canada* 104 A1
Champagne, *France* 19 D11
Champagnole, *France* 19 F12
Champaign, *U.S.A.* 108 E1
Champassak, *Laos* 64 E5
Champaubert, *France* 19 D10
Champawat, *India* 69 E9
Champdeniers-St-Denis, *France* 20 B3
Champdoré, L., *Canada* 103 A6
Champeix, *France* 20 C7
Champion, *U.S.A.* 110 E4
Champlain, *U.S.A.* 111 B11
Champlain, L., *U.S.A.* 111 B11
Champlitte, *France* 19 E12
Champotón, *Mexico* 119 D6
Champua, *India* 69 H11
Chamusca, *Portugal* 35 F2
Chana, *Thailand* 65 J3
Chañaral, *Chile* 126 B1
Chanārān, *Iran* 71 B8
Chanasma, *India* 68 H5
Chanco, *Chile* 126 D1
Chand, *India* 69 J8
Chandan, *India* 69 G12
Chandan Chauki, *India* 69 E9
Chandannagar, *India* 69 H13
Chandausi, *India* 69 E8
Chandeleur Is., *U.S.A.* 113 L10
Chandeleur Sd., *U.S.A.* 113 L10
Chandigarh, *India* 68 D7
Chandil, *India* 69 H12
Chandler, *Australia* 95 D1
Chandler, *Canada* 103 C7
Chandler, *Ariz., U.S.A.* 115 K8
Chandler, *Okla., U.S.A.* 113 H6
Chandod, *India* 68 J5
Chandpur, *Bangla.* 67 H17
Chandrapur, *India* 66 K11
Chānf, *Iran* 71 E9
Chang, *Pakistan* 68 F3
Chang, Ko, *Thailand* 65 F4
Ch'ang Chiang = Chang Jiang →, *China* 59 B13
Chang Jiang →, *China* 59 B13
Changa, *India* 69 C7
Changanacheri, *India* 66 Q10
Changane →, *Mozam.* 89 C5
Changbai, *China* 57 D15
Changbai Shan, *China* 57 C15
Changchiak'ou = Zhangjiakou, *China* 56 D8
Ch'angchou = Changzhou, *China* 59 B12
Changchun, *China* 57 C13
Changchunling, *China* 57 B13
Changde, *China* 59 C8
Changdo-ri, *N. Korea* 57 E14
Changfeng, *China* 59 A11
Changhai = Shanghai, *China* 59 B13
Changhua, *China* 59 B12
Changhua, *Taiwan* 59 E13
Changhŭng, *S. Korea* 57 G14
Changhŭngni, *N. Korea* 57 D15
Changjiang, *China* 64 C7
Changjin, *N. Korea* 57 D14
Changjin-chŏsuji, *N. Korea* 57 D14
Changle, *China* 59 E12
Changli, *China* 57 E10
Changling, *China* 57 B12
Changlun, *Malaysia* 65 J3
Changning, *Hunan, China* 59 D9
Changning, *Sichuan, China* 58 C5
Changning, *Yunnan, China* 58 E2
Changping, *China* 56 D9
Changsha, *China* 59 C9
Changshan, *China* 59 C12
Changshu, *China* 59 B13
Changshun, *China* 58 D6
Changtai, *China* 59 E11
Changting, *China* 59 E11
Changwu, *China* 56 G4
Changxing, *China* 59 B12
Changyang, *China* 59 B8
Changyi, *China* 57 F10
Changyŏn, *N. Korea* 57 E13
Changyuan, *China* 56 G8
Changzhi, *China* 56 F7
Changzhou, *China* 59 B12
Chanhanga, *Angola* 88 B1
Chanlar = Xanlar, *Azerbaijan* 49 K8
Channapatna, *India* 66 N10
Channel Is., *U.K.* 13 H5
Channel Is., *U.S.A.* 117 M7
Channel Islands National Park, *U.S.A.* 117 M8
Channel-Port aux Basques, *Canada* 103 C8
Channel Tunnel, *Europe* 13 F9
Channing, *U.S.A.* 113 H3
Chantada, *Spain* 34 C3
Chanthaburi, *Thailand* 64 F4
Chantilly, *France* 19 C9
Chantonnay, *France* 18 F5
Chantrey Inlet, *Canada* 100 B10
Chanute, *U.S.A.* 113 G7
Chanza →, *Spain* 35 H3
Chao Hu, *China* 59 B11
Chao Phraya →, *Thailand* 64 F3
Chao Phraya Lowlands, *Thailand* 64 E3
Chaocheng, *China* 56 F8
Chaohu, *China* 59 B11
Chaoyang, *Guangdong, China* 59 F11
Chaoyang, *Liaoning, China* 57 D11
Chaozhou, *China* 59 F11
Chapais, *Canada* 102 C5
Chapala, *Mozam.* 87 F4
Chapala, L. de, *Mexico* 118 C4
Chapayev, *Kazakstan* 48 E10
Chapayevsk, *Russia* 48 D9
Chapecó, *Brazil* 127 B5
Chapel Hill, *U.S.A.* 109 H6
Chapleau, *Canada* 102 C3
Chaplin, *Canada* 105 C7
Chaplin L., *Canada* 105 C7
Chaplino, *Ukraine* 47 H9
Chaplygin, *Russia* 46 F11
Chappell, *U.S.A.* 112 E3
Chapra = Chhapra, *India* 69 G11
Chara, *Russia* 51 D12
Charadai, *Argentina* 126 B4
Charagua, *Bolivia* 124 G6
Charambirá, Punta, *Colombia* 124 C3
Charaña, *Bolivia* 124 G5
Charantsavan, *Armenia* 49 K7
Charanwala, *India* 68 F5
Charata, *Argentina* 126 B3
Charcas, *Mexico* 118 C4
Chard, *U.K.* 13 G5
Chardon, *U.S.A.* 110 E3
Chardzhou = Chärjew, *Turkmenistan* 50 F7
Charente □, *France* 20 C4
Charente →, *France* 20 C2
Charente-Maritime □, *France* 20 C3
Charenton-du-Cher, *France* 19 F9
Chari →, *Chad* 79 F8
Chārīkār, *Afghan.* 66 B6
Chariton →, *U.S.A.* 112 F8
Chärjew, *Turkmenistan* 50 F7
Charkhari, *India* 69 G8
Charkhi Dadri, *India* 68 E7
Charleroi, *Belgium* 17 D4
Charleroi, *U.S.A.* 110 F5
Charles, C., *U.S.A.* 108 G8
Charles City, *U.S.A.* 112 D8
Charles L., *Canada* 105 B6
Charles Town, *U.S.A.* 108 F7
Charleston, *Ill., U.S.A.* 108 F1
Charleston, *Miss., U.S.A.* 113 H9
Charleston, *Mo., U.S.A.* 113 G10
Charleston, *S.C., U.S.A.* 109 J6
Charleston, *W. Va., U.S.A.* 108 F5
Charleston L., *Canada* 111 B9
Charleston Peak, *U.S.A.* 117 J11
Charlestown, *Ireland* 15 C3
Charlestown, *S. Africa* 89 D4
Charlestown, *Ind., U.S.A.* 108 F3
Charlestown, *N.H., U.S.A.* 111 C12
Charleville = Rath Luirc, *Ireland* 15 D3
Charleville, *Australia* 95 D4
Charleville-Mézières, *France* 19 C11
Charlevoix, *U.S.A.* 108 C3
Charlieu, *France* 19 F11
Charlotte, *Mich., U.S.A.* 108 D3
Charlotte, *N.C., U.S.A.* 109 H5
Charlotte, *Vt., U.S.A.* 111 B11
Charlotte Amalie, *Virgin Is.* 121 C7
Charlotte Harbor, *U.S.A.* 109 M4
Charlotte L., *Canada* 104 C3
Charlottenberg, *Sweden* 10 E6
Charlottesville, *U.S.A.* 108 F6
Charlottetown, *Nfld., Canada* 103 B8
Charlottetown, *P.E.I., Canada* 103 C7
Charlton, *Australia* 95 F3
Charlton, *U.S.A.* 112 E8
Charlton I., *Canada* 102 B4
Charmes, *France* 19 D13
Charny, *Canada* 103 C5
Charolles, *France* 19 F11
Chârost, *France* 19 F9
Charre, *Mozam.* 87 F4
Charroux, *France* 20 B4
Charsadda, *Pakistan* 68 B4
Charters Towers, *Australia* 94 C4
Chartres, *France* 18 D8
Chascomús, *Argentina* 126 D4
Chasefu, *Zambia* 87 E3
Chashma Barrage, *Pakistan* 68 C4
Chasseneuil-sur-Bonnieure, *France* 20 C4
Chāt, *Iran* 71 B7
Chatal Balkan = Udvoy Balkan, *Bulgaria* 41 D10
Château-Arnoux, *France* 21 D10
Château-Chinon, *France* 19 E10
Château-d'Olonne, *France* 20 B2
Château-du-Loir, *France* 18 E7
Château-Gontier, *France* 18 E6
Château-la-Vallière, *France* 18 E7
Château-Landon, *France* 19 D9
Château-Renault, *France* 18 E7
Château-Salins, *France* 19 D13
Château-Thierry, *France* 19 C10
Châteaubourg, *France* 18 D5
Châteaubriant, *France* 18 E5
Châteaudun, *France* 18 D8
Chateaugay, *U.S.A.* 111 B10
Châteaugiron, *France* 18 D5
Châteauguay, L., *Canada* 103 A5
Châteaulin, *France* 18 D2
Châteaumeillant, *France* 19 F9
Châteauneuf-du-Faou, *France* 18 D3
Châteauneuf-sur-Charente, *France* 20 C3
Châteauneuf-sur-Cher, *France* 19 F9
Châteauneuf-sur-Loire, *France* 19 E9
Châteaurenard, *Bouches-du-Rhône, France* 21 E8
Châteaurenard, *Loiret, France* 19 E9
Châteauroux, *France* 19 F8
Châteauvillain, *France* 19 D11
Châtelaillon-Plage, *France* 20 B2
Châtelguyon, *France* 20 C7
Châtellerault, *France* 18 F7
Châtelus-Malvaleix, *France* 19 F9
Chatham = Miramichi, *Canada* 103 C6
Chatham, *Canada* 102 D3
Chatham, *U.K.* 13 F8
Chatham, *U.S.A.* 111 D11
Chatham Is., *Pac. Oc.* 96 M10
Châtillon, *Italy* 28 C4
Châtillon-Coligny, *France* 19 E9
Châtillon-en-Diois, *France* 21 D9
Châtillon-sur-Indre, *France* 18 F8
Châtillon-sur-Loire, *France* 19 E9
Châtillon-sur-Seine, *France* 19 E11
Chatmohar, *Bangla.* 69 G13
Chatra, *India* 69 G11
Chatrapur, *India* 67 K14
Chats, L. des, *Canada* 111 A8
Chatsu, *India* 68 F6
Chatsworth, *Canada* 110 B4
Chatsworth, *Zimbabwe* 87 F3
Chattahoochee, *U.S.A.* 109 K3
Chattahoochee →, *U.S.A.* 109 K3
Chattanooga, *U.S.A.* 109 H3
Chatteris, *U.K.* 13 E8
Chaturat, *Thailand* 64 E3
Chau Doc, *Vietnam* 65 G5
Chaudes-Aigues, *France* 20 D7
Chauffailles, *France* 19 F11
Chauk, *Burma* 67 J19
Chaukan La, *Burma* 67 F20
Chaumont, *France* 19 D12
Chaumont, *U.S.A.* 111 B8
Chaumont-en-Vexin, *France* 19 C8
Chaumont-sur-Loire, *France* 18 E8
Chaunay, *France* 20 B4
Chauny, *France* 19 C10
Chausey, Îs., *France* 18 D5
Chaussin, *France* 19 F12
Chautauqua L., *U.S.A.* 110 D5
Chauvigny, *France* 18 F7
Chauvin, *Canada* 105 C6
Chavanges, *France* 19 D11
Chaves, *Brazil* 125 D9
Chaves, *Portugal* 34 D3
Chawang, *Thailand* 65 H2
Chazelles-sur-Lyon, *France* 21 C8
Chazy, *U.S.A.* 111 B11
Cheb, *Czech Rep.* 26 A5
Cheboksarskoye Vdkhr., *Russia* 48 B8
Cheboksary, *Russia* 48 B8
Cheboygan, *U.S.A.* 108 C3
Chebsara, *Russia* 46 C10
Chech, Erg, *Africa* 78 D5
Chechen, Ostrov, *Russia* 49 H8
Chechenia □, *Russia* 49 J7
Checheno-Ingush Republic = Chechenia □, *Russia* 49 J7
Chechnya = Chechenia □, *Russia* 49 J7
Chech'ŏn, *S. Korea* 57 F15
Chęciny, *Poland* 45 H7
Checotah, *U.S.A.* 113 H7
Chedabucto B., *Canada* 103 C7
Cheduba I., *Burma* 67 K18
Cheepie, *Australia* 95 D4
Chef-Boutonne, *France* 20 B3
Chegdomyn, *Russia* 51 D14
Chegga, *Mauritania* 78 C4
Chegutu, *Zimbabwe* 87 F3
Chehalis, *U.S.A.* 116 D4
Chehalis →, *U.S.A.* 116 D3
Cheiron, Mt., *France* 21 E10
Cheju do, *S. Korea* 57 H14
Chekalin, *Russia* 46 E9
Chekiang = Zhejiang □, *China* 59 C13
Chel = Kuru, Bahr el →, *Sudan* 81 F2
Chela, Sa. da, *Angola* 88 B1
Chelan, *U.S.A.* 114 C4
Chelan, L., *U.S.A.* 114 B3
Cheleken, *Turkmenistan* 50 F6
Cheleken Yarymadasy, *Turkmenistan* 71 B7
Chelforó, *Argentina* 128 D3
Chelkar = Shalqar, *Kazakstan* 50 E6
Chelkar Tengiz, Solonchak, *Kazakstan* 50 E7
Chella, *Ethiopia* 81 F4
Chelles, *France* 19 D9
Chełm, *Poland* 45 G10
Chełmno, *Poland* 45 E5
Chelmsford, *U.K.* 13 F8
Chełmża, *Poland* 45 E5
Chelsea, *U.S.A.* 111 C12
Cheltenham, *U.K.* 13 F5
Chelva, *Spain* 32 F4
Chelyabinsk, *Russia* 50 D7
Chelyuskin, C., *Russia* 52 B14
Chemainus, *Canada* 116 B3
Chemba, *Mozam.* 85 H6
Chembar = Belinskiy, *Russia* 48 D6
Chemillé, *France* 18 E6
Chemnitz, *Germany* 24 E8
Chemult, *U.S.A.* 114 E3
Chen, Gora, *Russia* 51 C15
Chenab →, *Pakistan* 68 D4
Chenango Forks, *U.S.A.* 111 D9
Chencha, *Ethiopia* 81 F4
Chenchiang = Zhenjiang, *China* 59 A12
Cheney, *U.S.A.* 114 C5
Cheng Xian, *China* 56 H3
Chengbu, *China* 59 D8
Chengcheng, *China* 56 G5
Chengchou = Zhengzhou, *China* 56 G7
Chengde, *China* 57 D9
Chengdong Hu, *China* 59 A11
Chengdu, *China* 58 B5
Chenggong, *China* 58 E4
Chenggu, *China* 56 H4
Chenghai, *China* 59 F11
Chengjiang, *China* 58 E4
Chengkou, *China* 58 B7
Ch'engmai, *China* 64 C7
Ch'engtu = Chengdu, *China* 58 B5
Chengwu, *China* 56 G8
Chengxi Hu, *China* 59 A11
Chengyang, *China* 57 F11
Chenjiagang, *China* 57 G10
Chenkán, *Mexico* 119 D6
Chennai, *India* 66 N12
Chenôve, *France* 19 E12
Chenxi, *China* 59 C8
Chenzhou, *China* 59 E9
Cheo Reo, *Vietnam* 62 B3
Cheom Ksan, *Cambodia* 64 E5
Chepelare, *Bulgaria* 41 E8
Chepén, *Peru* 124 E3
Chepes, *Argentina* 126 C2
Chepo, *Panama* 120 E4
Chepstow, *U.K.* 13 F5
Cheptulil, Mt., *Kenya* 86 B4
Chequamegon B., *U.S.A.* 112 B9
Cher □, *France* 19 E9
Cher →, *France* 18 E7
Chéradi, *Italy* 31 B10
Cherasco, *Italy* 28 D4
Cheraw, *U.S.A.* 109 H6
Cherbourg, *France* 18 C5
Cherdakly, *Russia* 48 C9
Cherdyn, *Russia* 50 C6
Cheremkhovo, *Russia* 51 D11
Cherepanovo, *Russia* 50 D9
Cherepovets, *Russia* 46 C9
Chergui, Chott ech, *Algeria* 78 B6
Cherikov = Cherykaw, *Belarus* 46 F6
Cherkasy, *Ukraine* 47 H7
Cherkessk, *Russia* 49 H6
Cherlak, *Russia* 50 D8
Chernaya, *Russia* 51 B9
Cherni, *Bulgaria* 40 D7
Chernigov = Chernihiv, *Ukraine* 47 G6
Chernihiv, *Ukraine* 47 G6
Chernivtsi, *Ukraine* 47 H3
Chernobyl = Chornobyl, *Ukraine* 47 G6
Chernogorsk, *Russia* 51 D10
Chernomorskoye = Chornomorske, *Ukraine* 47 K7
Chernovtsy = Chernivtsi, *Ukraine* 47 H3
Chernyakhovsk, *Russia* 9 J19
Chernyanka, *Russia* 47 G9
Chernysheyskiy, *Russia* 51 C12
Chernyye Zemli, *Russia* 49 H8
Cherokee, *Iowa, U.S.A.* 112 D7
Cherokee, *Okla., U.S.A.* 113 G5
Cherokee Village, *U.S.A.* 113 G9
Cherokees, Grand Lake O' The, *U.S.A.* 113 G7
Cherrapunji, *India* 67 G17
Cherry Valley, *Calif., U.S.A.* 117 M10
Cherry Valley, *N.Y., U.S.A.* 111 D10
Cherskiy, *Russia* 51 C17
Cherskogo Khrebet, *Russia* 51 C15
Chertkovo, *Russia* 47 H11
Cherven, *Belarus* 46 F5
Cherven-Bryag, *Bulgaria* 41 C8
Chervonohrad, *Ukraine* 47 G3
Cherwell →, *U.K.* 13 F6
Cherykaw, *Belarus* 46 F6
Chesapeake, *U.S.A.* 108 G7
Chesapeake B., *U.S.A.* 108 G7
Cheshire □, *U.K.* 12 D5
Cheshskaya Guba, *Russia* 50 C5
Cheshunt, *U.K.* 13 F7
Chesil Beach, *U.K.* 13 G5
Chesley, *Canada* 110 B3
Cheste, *Spain* 33 F4
Chester, *U.K.* 12 D5
Chester, *Calif., U.S.A.* 114 F3
Chester, *Ill., U.S.A.* 113 G10
Chester, *Mont., U.S.A.* 114 B8
Chester, *Pa., U.S.A.* 108 F8
Chester, *S.C., U.S.A.* 109 H5
Chester, *Vt., U.S.A.* 111 C12
Chester, *W. Va., U.S.A.* 110 F4
Chester-le-Street, *U.K.* 12 C6
Chesterfield, *U.K.* 12 D6
Chesterfield, Is., *N. Cal.* 96 J7
Chesterfield Inlet, *Canada* 100 B10
Chesterton Ra., *Australia* 95 D4
Chestertown, *U.S.A.* 111 C11
Chesterville, *Canada* 111 A9
Chestnut Ridge, *U.S.A.* 110 F5
Chesuncook L., *U.S.A.* 109 C11
Chéticamp, *Canada* 103 C7
Chetrosu, *Moldova* 43 B12
Chetumal, *Mexico* 119 D7
Chetumal, B. de, *Mexico* 119 D7
Chetwynd, *Canada* 104 B4
Chevanceaux, *France* 20 C3
Cheviot, The, *U.K.* 12 B5
Cheviot Hills, *U.K.* 12 B5
Cheviot Ra., *Australia* 94 D3
Chew Bahir, *Ethiopia* 81 G4
Chewelah, *U.S.A.* 114 B5
Cheyenne, *Okla., U.S.A.* 113 H5
Cheyenne, *Wyo., U.S.A.* 112 E2
Cheyenne →, *U.S.A.* 112 C4
Cheyenne Wells, *U.S.A.* 112 F3
Cheyne B., *Australia* 93 F2
Chhabra, *India* 68 G7
Chhaktala, *India* 68 H6
Chhapra, *India* 69 G11
Chhata, *India* 68 F7
Chhatarpur, *Bihar, India* 69 G11
Chhatarpur, *Mad. P., India* 69 G8
Chhep, *Cambodia* 64 F5
Chhindwara, *Mad. P., India* 69 H8
Chhindwara, *Mad. P., India* 69 H8
Chhlong, *Cambodia* 65 F5
Chhota Tawa →, *India* 68 H7
Chhoti Kali Sindh →, *India* 68 G6
Chhuikhadan, *India* 69 J9
Chhuk, *Cambodia* 65 G5
Chi →, *Thailand* 64 E5
Chiai, *Taiwan* 59 F13
Chiali, *Taiwan* 59 F13
Chiamboni, *Somali Rep.* 84 E8
Chiamussu = Jiamusi, *China* 60 B8
Chianciano Terme, *Italy* 29 E8
Chiang Dao, *Thailand* 64 C2
Chiang Kham, *Thailand* 64 C3
Chiang Khan, *Thailand* 64 D3
Chiang Khong, *Thailand* 58 G3
Chiang Mai, *Thailand* 64 C2
Chiang Rai, *Thailand* 58 H2

Chiang Saen, Thailand 58 G3
Chiapa →, Mexico 119 D6
Chiapa de Corzo, Mexico 119 D6
Chiapas □, Mexico 119 D6
Chiaramonte Gulfi, Italy 31 E7
Chiaravalle, Italy 29 E10
Chiaravalle Centrale, Italy 31 D9
Chiari, Italy 28 C6
Chiatura, Georgia 49 J6
Chiautla, Mexico 119 D5
Chiávari, Italy 28 D6
Chiavenna, Italy 28 B6
Chiba, Japan 55 G10
Chiba □, Japan 55 G10
Chibabava, Mozam. 89 C5
Chibemba, Cunene, Angola 85 H2
Chibemba, Huila, Angola 88 B2
Chibi, Zimbabwe 89 C5
Chibia, Angola 85 H2
Chibougamau, Canada 102 C5
Chibougamau, L., Canada 102 C5
Chibuk, Nigeria 83 C7
Chibuto, Mozam. 89 C5
Chic-Chocs, Mts., Canada 103 C6
Chicacole = Srikakulam, India 67 K13
Chicago, U.S.A. 108 E2
Chicago Heights, U.S.A. 108 E2
Chichagof I., U.S.A. 100 C6
Chichén-Itzá, Mexico 119 C7
Chicheng, China 56 D8
Chichester, U.K. 13 G7
Chichester Ra., Australia 92 D2
Chichibu, Japan 55 F9
Ch'ich'ihaerh = Qiqihar, China 51 E13
Chicholi, India 68 H8
Chickasha, U.S.A. 113 H6
Chiclana de la Frontera, Spain 35 J4
Chiclayo, Peru 124 E3
Chico, U.S.A. 116 F5
Chico →, Chubut, Argentina 128 E3
Chico →, Santa Cruz, Argentina 128 G3
Chicomo, Mozam. 89 C5
Chicontepec, Mexico 119 C5
Chicopee, U.S.A. 111 D12
Chicoutimi, Canada 103 C5
Chicualacuala, Mozam. 89 C5
Chidambaram, India 66 P11
Chidenguele, Mozam. 89 C5
Chidley, C., Canada 101 B13
Chiducuane, Mozam. 89 C5
Chiede, Angola 88 B2
Chiefs Pt., Canada 110 B3
Chiem Hoa, Vietnam 64 A5
Chiemsee, Germany 25 H8
Chiengi, Zambia 87 D2
Chiengmai = Chiang Mai, Thailand 64 C2
Chienti →, Italy 29 E10
Chieri, Italy 28 C4
Chiers →, France 19 C11
Chiesa in Valmalenco, Italy 28 B6
Chiese →, Italy 28 C7
Chieti, Italy 29 F11
Chifeng, China 57 C10
Chigirin, Ukraine 47 H7
Chignecto B., Canada 103 C7
Chiguana, Bolivia 126 A2
Chigwell, U.K. 13 F8
Chiha-ri, N. Korea 57 E14
Chihli, G. of = Bo Hai, China 57 E10
Chihuahua, Mexico 118 B3
Chihuahua □, Mexico 118 B3
Chiili, Kazakstan 50 E7
Chik Bollapur, India 66 N10
Chikmagalur, India 66 N9
Chikwawa, Malawi 87 F3
Chilac, Mexico 119 D5
Chilam Chavki, Pakistan 69 B6
Chilanga, Zambia 87 F2
Chilapa, Mexico 119 D5
Chilas, Pakistan 69 B6
Chilaw, Sri Lanka 66 R11
Chilcotin →, Canada 104 C4
Childers, Australia 95 D5
Childress, U.S.A. 113 H4
Chile ■, S. Amer. 128 D2
Chile Rise, Pac. Oc. 97 L18
Chilecito, Argentina 126 B2
Chilete, Peru 124 E3
Chilia, Braţul →, Romania 43 E14
Chililabombwe, Zambia 87 E2
Chilin = Jilin, China 57 C14
Chilka L., India 67 K14
Chilko →, Canada 104 C4
Chilko L., Canada 104 C4
Chillagoe, Australia 94 B3
Chillán, Chile 126 D1
Chillicothe, Ill., U.S.A. 112 E10
Chillicothe, Mo., U.S.A. 112 F8
Chillicothe, Ohio, U.S.A. 108 F4
Chilliwack, Canada 104 D4
Chilo, India 68 F5
Chiloane, I., Mozam. 89 C5
Chiloé, I. de, Chile 122 H3
Chilpancingo, Mexico 119 D5
Chiltern Hills, U.K. 13 F7
Chilton, U.S.A. 108 C1
Chilubi, Zambia 87 E2
Chilubula, Zambia 87 E3
Chilumba, Malawi 87 E3
Chilung, Taiwan 59 E13
Chilwa, L., Malawi 87 F4
Chimaltitán, Mexico 118 C4
Chimán, Panama 120 E4
Chimanimani, Zimbabwe 89 B5
Chimay, Belgium 17 D4
Chimayo, U.S.A. 115 H11
Chimbay, Uzbekistan 50 E6
Chimborazo, Ecuador 122 D3
Chimbote, Peru 124 E3
Chimkent = Shymkent, Kazakstan 50 E7
Chimoio, Mozam. 87 F3
Chimpembe, Zambia 87 D2
Chin □, Burma 67 J18
Chin Ling Shan = Qinling Shandi, China 56 H5
China, Mexico 119 B5
China ■, Asia 60 D6
China Lake, U.S.A. 117 K9
Chinan = Jinan, China 56 F9
Chinandega, Nic. 120 D2
Chinati Peak, U.S.A. 113 L2
Chincha Alta, Peru 122 E3
Chinchaga →, Canada 104 B5
Chinchilla, Australia 95 D5
Chinchilla de Monte Aragón, Spain 33 G3
Chinchorro, Banco, Mexico 119 D7
Chinchou = Jinzhou, China 57 D11
Chincoteague, U.S.A. 108 G8
Chinde, Mozam. 87 F4
Chindo, S. Korea 57 G14
Chindwin →, Burma 67 J19
Chineni, India 69 C6
Chinga, Mozam. 87 F4
Chingola, Zambia 87 E2
Chingole, Malawi 87 E3
Ch'ingtao = Qingdao, China 57 F11
Chinguetti, Mauritania 78 D3
Chingune, Mozam. 89 C5
Chinhae, S. Korea 57 G15
Chinhanguanine, Mozam. 89 D5
Chinhoyi, Zimbabwe 87 F3
Chini, India 68 D8
Chiniot, Pakistan 68 D5
Chínipas, Mexico 118 B3
Chinji, Pakistan 68 C5
Chinju, S. Korea 57 G15
Chinle, U.S.A. 115 H9
Chinmen, Taiwan 59 E13
Chinmen Tao, Taiwan 59 E12
Chinnampo = Namp'o, N. Korea 57 E13
Chino, Japan 55 G9
Chino, U.S.A. 117 L9
Chino Valley, U.S.A. 115 J7
Chinon, France 18 E7
Chinook, U.S.A. 114 B9
Chinsali, Zambia 87 E3
Chióggia, Italy 29 C9
Chíos = Khíos, Greece 39 C8
Chipata, Zambia 87 E3
Chiperceni, Moldova 43 C13
Chipinge, Zimbabwe 87 G3
Chipiona, Spain 35 J4
Chipley, U.S.A. 109 K3
Chipman, Canada 103 C6
Chipoka, Malawi 87 E3
Chippenham, U.K. 13 F5
Chippewa →, U.S.A. 112 C8
Chippewa Falls, U.S.A. 112 C9
Chipping Norton, U.K. 13 F6
Chiprovtsi, Bulgaria 40 C6
Chiputneticook Lakes, U.S.A. 109 C11
Chiquián, Peru 124 F3
Chiquimula, Guatemala 120 D2
Chiquinquira, Colombia 124 B4
Chir →, Russia 49 F6
Chirala, India 66 M12
Chiramba, Mozam. 87 F3
Chirawa, India 68 E6
Chirchiq, Uzbekistan 50 E7
Chiredzi, Zimbabwe 89 C5
Chirfa, Niger 79 D8
Chiricahua Peak, U.S.A. 115 L9
Chiriquí, G. de, Panama 120 E3
Chiriquí, L. de, Panama 120 E3
Chirivira Falls, Zimbabwe 87 G3
Chirmiri, India 67 H13
Chirnogi, Romania 43 F11
Chirpan, Bulgaria 41 D9
Chirripó Grande, Cerro, Costa Rica 120 E3
Chirundu, Zimbabwe 89 B4
Chisamba, Zambia 87 E2
Chisapani Garhi, Nepal 67 F14
Chisasibi, Canada 102 B4
Ch'ishan, Taiwan 59 F13
Chisholm, Canada 104 C6
Chisholm, U.S.A. 112 B8
Chishtian Mandi, Pakistan 68 E5
Chishui, China 58 C5
Chishui He →, China 58 C5
Chisimaio, Somali Rep. 77 G8
Chisimba Falls, Zambia 87 E3
Chişinău, Moldova 43 C13
Chişineu Criş, Romania 42 D6
Chisone →, Italy 28 D4
Chisos Mts., U.S.A. 113 L3
Chistopol, Russia 48 C10
Chita, Russia 51 D12
Chitipa, Malawi 87 D3
Chitose, Japan 54 C10
Chitral, Pakistan 66 B7
Chitré, Panama 120 E3
Chittagong, Bangla. 67 H17
Chittagong □, Bangla. 67 G17
Chittaurgarh, India 68 G6
Chittoor, India 66 N11
Chitungwiza, Zimbabwe 87 F3
Chiusi, Italy 29 E8
Chiva, Spain 33 F4
Chivasso, Italy 28 C4
Chivhu, Zimbabwe 87 F3
Chivilcoy, Argentina 126 C4
Chiwanda, Tanzania 87 E3
Chixi, China 59 G9
Chizera, Zambia 87 E2
Chkalov = Orenburg, Russia 50 D6
Chkolovsk, Russia 48 B6
Chloride, U.S.A. 117 K12
Chlumec nad Cidlinou, Czech Rep. 26 A8
Chmielnik, Poland 45 H7
Cho Bo, Vietnam 58 G5
Cho-do, N. Korea 57 E13
Cho Phuoc Hai, Vietnam 65 G6
Choba, Kenya 86 B4
Chobe National Park, Botswana 88 B4
Choch'iwŏn, S. Korea 57 F14
Chocianów, Poland 45 G2
Chociwel, Poland 44 E2
Chocolate Mts., U.S.A. 117 M11
Choctawatchee →, U.S.A. 109 K3
Chodecz, Poland 45 F6
Chodov, Czech Rep. 26 A5
Chodziez, Poland 45 F3
Choele Choel, Argentina 128 D3
Choix, Mexico 118 B3
Chojna, Poland 45 F1
Chojnice, Poland 44 E4
Chojnów, Poland 45 G2
Chōkai-San, Japan 54 E10
Choke, Ethiopia 81 E4
Choke Canyon L., U.S.A. 113 L5
Chokurdakh, Russia 51 B15
Cholame, U.S.A. 116 K6
Cholet, France 18 E6
Cholguan, Chile 126 D1
Choluteca, Honduras 120 D2
Choluteca →, Honduras 120 D2
Chom Bung, Thailand 64 F2
Chom Thong, Thailand 64 C2
Choma, Zambia 87 F2
Chomen Swamp, Ethiopia 81 F4
Chomun, India 68 F6
Chomutov, Czech Rep. 26 A6
Chon Buri, Thailand 64 F3
Chon Thanh, Vietnam 65 G6
Ch'onan, S. Korea 57 F14
Chone, Ecuador 124 D3
Chong Kai, Cambodia 64 F4
Chong Mek, Thailand 64 E5
Chongde, China 59 B13
Chŏngdo, S. Korea 57 G15
Chŏngha, S. Korea 57 F15
Chŏngjin, N. Korea 57 D15
Chŏngjiu, S. Korea 57 F14
Chŏngju, N. Korea 57 E13
Chongli, China 56 D8
Chongming, China 59 B13
Chongming Dao, China 59 B13
Chongqing, Chongqing, China 58 C6
Chongqing, Sichuan, China 58 B4
Chongqing □, China 60 C5
Chongqing Shi □, China 58 C6
Chongren, China 59 D11
Chonguene, Mozam. 89 C5
Chŏngŭp, S. Korea 57 G14
Chongyi, China 59 E10
Chongzuo, China 58 F6
Chŏnju, S. Korea 57 G14
Chonos, Arch. de los, Chile 122 H3
Chop, Ukraine 47 H2
Chopim →, Brazil 127 B5
Chor, Pakistan 68 G3
Chorbat La, India 69 B7
Chorley, U.K. 12 D5
Chornobyl, Ukraine 47 G6
Chornomorske, Ukraine 47 K7
Chorolque, Cerro, Bolivia 126 A2
Choroszcz, Poland 45 E9
Chorregon, Australia 94 C3
Chortkiv, Ukraine 47 H3
Ch'ŏrwon, S. Korea 57 E14
Chorzele, Poland 45 E7
Chorzów, Poland 45 H5
Chos-Malal, Argentina 126 D1
Ch'osan, N. Korea 57 D13
Choszczno, Poland 45 E2
Choteau, U.S.A. 114 C7
Chotěboř, Czech Rep. 26 B8
Chotila, India 68 H4
Chotta Udepur, India 68 H6
Chowchilla, U.S.A. 116 H6
Choybalsan, Mongolia 60 B6
Christchurch, N.Z. 91 K4
Christchurch, U.K. 13 G6
Christian I., Canada 110 B4
Christiana, S. Africa 88 D4
Christiansfeld, Denmark 11 J3
Christiansted, Virgin Is. 121 C7
Christie B., Canada 105 A6
Christina →, Canada 105 B6
Christmas Cr. →, Australia 92 C4
Christmas I. = Kiritimati, Kiribati 97 G12
Christmas I., Ind. Oc. 96 J2
Christopher L., Australia 93 D4
Chrudim, Czech Rep. 26 B8
Chrzanów, Poland 45 H6
Chtimba, Malawi 87 E3
Chu = Shu, Kazakstan 50 E8
Chu = Shu →, Kazakstan 52 E10
Chu →, Vietnam 64 C5
Chu Lai, Vietnam 64 E7
Ch'uanchou = Quanzhou, China 59 E12
Chuankou, China 56 G6
Chubbuck, U.S.A. 114 E7
Chūbu □, Japan 55 F8
Chubut →, Argentina 122 H4
Chuchi L., Canada 104 B4
Chuda, India 68 H4
Chudovo, Russia 46 C6
Chudskoye, Ozero, Russia 9 G22
Chūgoku □, Japan 55 G6
Chūgoku-Sanchi, Japan 55 G6
Chuguyev = Chuhuyiv, Ukraine 47 H9
Chugwater, U.S.A. 112 E2
Chuhuyiv, Ukraine 47 H9
Chukchi Sea, Russia 51 C19
Chukotskoye Nagorye, Russia 51 C18
Chula Vista, U.S.A. 117 N9
Chulucanas, Peru 124 E2
Chulym →, Russia 50 D9
Chum Phae, Thailand 64 D4
Chum Saeng, Thailand 64 E3
Chumar, India 69 C8
Chumbicha, Argentina 126 B2
Chumerna, Bulgaria 41 D9
Chumikan, Russia 51 D14
Chumphon, Thailand 65 G2
Chumuare, Mozam. 87 E3
Chumunjin, S. Korea 57 F15
Chuna →, Russia 51 D10
Chun'an, China 59 C12
Ch'unch'ŏn, S. Korea 57 F14
Chunchura, India 69 H13
Chunga, Zambia 87 F2
Chunggang-ŭp, N. Korea 57 D14
Chunghwa, N. Korea 57 E13
Ch'ungju, S. Korea 57 F14
Chungking = Chongqing, China 58 C6
Chungli, Taiwan 59 E13
Ch'ungmu, S. Korea 57 G15
Chungt'iaoshan = Zhongtiao Shan, China 56 G6
Chungyang Shanmo, Taiwan 59 F13
Chunian, Pakistan 68 D6
Chunya, Tanzania 87 D3
Chunyang, China 57 C15
Chuquibamba, Peru 124 G4
Chuquicamata, Chile 126 A2
Chur, Switz. 25 J5
Churachandpur, India 67 G18
Churchill, Canada 105 B10
Churchill →, Man., Canada 105 B10
Churchill →, Nfld., Canada 103 B7
Churchill, C., Canada 105 B10
Churchill Falls, Canada 103 B7
Churchill L., Canada 105 B7
Churchill Pk., Canada 104 B3
Churki, India 69 H10
Churu, India 68 E6
Churún Merú = Angel Falls, Venezuela 124 B6
Chushal, India 69 C8
Chuska Mts., U.S.A. 115 H9
Chusovoy, Russia 50 D6
Chute-aux-Outardes, Canada 103 C6
Chuuronjang, N. Korea 57 D15
Chuvash Republic = Chuvashia □, Russia 48 C8
Chuvashia □, Russia 48 C8
Chuwārtah, Iraq 70 C5
Chuxiong, China 58 E3
Chuy, Uruguay 127 C5
Chuzhou, China 59 A12
Ci Xian, China 56 F8
Ciacova, Romania 42 E6
Ciadâr-Lunga, Moldova 43 D13
Ciamis, Indonesia 63 G13
Cianjur, Indonesia 63 G12
Cianorte, Brazil 127 A5
Cibola, U.S.A. 117 M12
Cicero, U.S.A. 108 E2
Cidacos →, Spain 32 C3
Cide, Turkey 72 B5
Ciechanów, Poland 45 F7
Ciechanowiec, Poland 45 F9
Ciechocinek, Poland 45 F5
Ciego de Avila, Cuba 120 B4
Ciénaga, Colombia 124 A4
Cienfuegos, Cuba 120 B3
Cierp, France 20 F4
Cíes, Is., Spain 34 C2
Cieszanów, Poland 45 H10
Cieszyn, Poland 45 J5
Cieza, Spain 33 G3
Çifteler, Turkey 72 C4
Cifuentes, Spain 32 E2
Cihanbeyli, Turkey 72 C5
Cihuatlán, Mexico 118 D4
Cijara, Embalse de, Spain 35 F6
Cijulang, Indonesia 63 G13
Cilacap, Indonesia 63 G13
Çıldır, Turkey 73 B10
Çıldır Gölü, Turkey 73 B10
Cili, China 59 C8
Cilibia, Romania 43 E12
Cilicia, Turkey 72 D5
Cill Chainnigh = Kilkenny, Ireland 15 D4
Cilo Dağı, Turkey 73 D10
Cima, U.S.A. 117 K11
Cimarron, Kans., U.S.A. 113 G4
Cimarron, N. Mex., U.S.A. 113 G2
Cimarron →, U.S.A. 113 G6
Cimişlia, Moldova 43 D13
Cimone, Mte., Italy 28 D7
Çinar, Turkey 73 D9
Çınarcık, Turkey 41 F13
Cinca →, Spain 32 D5
Cincar, Bos.-H. 42 G2
Cincinnati, U.S.A. 108 F3
Cincinnatus, U.S.A. 111 D9
Çine, Turkey 39 D10
Ciney, Belgium 17 D5
Cíngoli, Italy 29 E10
Cinigiano, Italy 29 F8
Cinto, Mte., France 21 F12
Cintruénigo, Spain 32 C3
Ciocile, Romania 43 F12
Ciolăneşti din Deal, Romania 43 F10
Ciorani, Romania 43 F11
Čiovo, Croatia 29 E13
Circeo, Mte., Italy 30 A6
Çirçir, Turkey 72 C7
Circle, Alaska, U.S.A. 100 B5
Circle, Mont., U.S.A. 112 B2
Circleville, U.S.A. 108 F4
Cirebon, Indonesia 63 G13
Ciremai, Indonesia 63 G13
Cirencester, U.K. 13 F6
Cireşu, Romania 42 F7
Cirey-sur-Vezouze, France 19 D13
Ciriè, Italy 28 C4
Cirium, Cyprus 36 E11
Cirò, Italy 31 C10
Cirò Marina, Italy 31 C10
Ciron →, France 20 D3
Cisco, U.S.A. 113 J5
Cislău, Romania 43 E11
Cisna, Poland 45 J9
Cisnădie, Romania 43 E9
Cisterna di Latina, Italy 30 A5
Cisternino, Italy 31 B10
Cistierna, Spain 34 C5
Citeli-Ckaro = Tsiteli-Tsqaro, Georgia 49 K8
Citlaltépetl, Mexico 119 D5
Citrus Heights, U.S.A. 116 G5
Citrusdal, S. Africa 88 E2
Città della Pieve, Italy 29 F9
Città di Castello, Italy 29 E9
Città Sant' Angelo, Italy 29 F11
Cittadella, Italy 29 C8
Cittaducale, Italy 29 F9
Cittanova, Italy 31 D9
Ciuc, Munţii, Romania 43 D11
Ciucaş, Vf., Romania 43 E10
Ciucea, Romania 42 D7
Ciuciulea, Moldova 43 C12
Ciuciuleni, Moldova 43 C13
Ciudad Altamirano, Mexico 118 D4
Ciudad Bolívar, Venezuela 124 B6
Ciudad Camargo, Mexico 118 B3
Ciudad de Valles, Mexico 119 C5
Ciudad del Carmen, Mexico 119 D6
Ciudad del Este, Paraguay 127 B5
Ciudad Delicias = Delicias, Mexico 118 B3
Ciudad Guayana, Venezuela 124 B6
Ciudad Guerrero, Mexico 118 B3
Ciudad Guzmán, Mexico 118 D4
Ciudad Juárez, Mexico 118 A3
Ciudad Madero, Mexico 119 C5
Ciudad Mante, Mexico 119 C5
Ciudad Obregón, Mexico 118 B3
Ciudad Real, Spain 35 G7
Ciudad Real □, Spain 35 G7
Ciudad Rodrigo, Spain 34 E4
Ciudad Trujillo = Santo Domingo, Dom. Rep. 121 C6
Ciudad Victoria, Mexico 119 C5
Ciudadela, Spain 37 B10
Ciulniţa, Romania 43 F12
Ciumeghiu, Romania 42 D6
Ciuperceni, Romania 42 F8
Civa Burnu, Turkey 72 B7
Cividale del Friuli, Italy 29 B10
Cívita Castellana, Italy 29 F9
Civitanova Marche, Italy 29 E10
Civitavécchia, Italy 29 F8
Civray, France 20 B4
Çivril, Turkey 39 C11
Cixerri →, Italy 30 C1
Cixi, China 59 B13
Cizre, Turkey 70 B4
Cizur Mayor, Spain 32 C3
Clackmannanshire □, U.K. 14 E5
Clacton-on-Sea, U.K. 13 F9
Clain →, France 18 F7
Claire, L., Canada 104 B6
Clairton, U.S.A. 110 F5
Clairvaux-les-Lacs, France 19 F12
Claise →, France 20 B5
Clallam Bay, U.S.A. 116 B2
Clamecy, France 19 E10
Clanton, U.S.A. 109 J2
Clanwilliam, S. Africa 88 E2
Clara, Ireland 15 C4
Claraville, U.S.A. 117 K8
Clare, Australia 95 E2
Clare, U.S.A. 108 D3
Clare □, Ireland 15 D3
Clare →, Ireland 15 C2
Clare I., Ireland 15 C1
Claremont, Calif., U.S.A. 117 L9
Claremont, N.H., U.S.A. 111 C12
Claremont Pt., Australia 94 A3
Claremore, U.S.A. 113 G7
Claremorris, Ireland 15 C3
Clarence →, Australia 95 D5
Clarence →, N.Z. 91 K4
Clarence, I., Chile 128 G2
Clarence I., Antarctica 5 C18
Clarence Str., Australia 92 B5
Clarence Town, Bahamas 121 B5
Clarendon, Pa., U.S.A. 110 E5
Clarendon, Tex., U.S.A. 113 H4
Clarenville, Canada 103 C9
Claresholm, Canada 104 D6
Clarie Coast, Antarctica 5 C9
Clarinda, U.S.A. 112 E7
Clarion, Iowa, U.S.A. 112 D8
Clarion, Pa., U.S.A. 110 E5
Clarion →, U.S.A. 110 E5
Clark, U.S.A. 112 C6
Clark, Pt., Canada 110 B3
Clark Fork, U.S.A. 114 B5
Clark Fork →, U.S.A. 114 B5

Clark Hill L., *U.S.A.* 109 J4
Clarkdale, *U.S.A.* 115 J7
Clarke City, *Canada* 103 B6
Clarke I., *Australia* 94 G4
Clarke Ra., *Australia* 94 C4
Clark's Fork →, *U.S.A.* 114 D9
Clark's Harbour, *Canada* 103 D6
Clarks Summit, *U.S.A.* 111 E9
Clarksburg, *U.S.A.* 108 F5
Clarksdale, *U.S.A.* 113 H9
Clarksville, *Ark., U.S.A.* 113 H8
Clarksville, *Tenn., U.S.A.* 109 G2
Clarksville, *Tex., U.S.A.* 113 J7
Clatskanie, *U.S.A.* 116 D3
Claude, *U.S.A.* 113 H4
Claveria, *Phil.* 61 B4
Clay, *U.S.A.* 116 G5
Clay Center, *U.S.A.* 112 F6
Claypool, *U.S.A.* 115 K8
Claysburg, *U.S.A.* 110 F6
Claysville, *U.S.A.* 110 F4
Clayton, *N. Mex., U.S.A.* 113 G3
Clayton, *N.Y., U.S.A.* 111 B8
Clear, C., *Ireland* 15 E2
Clear, L., *Canada* 110 A7
Clear Hills, *Canada* 104 B5
Clear I., *Ireland* 15 E2
Clear L., *U.S.A.* 116 F4
Clear Lake, *Iowa, U.S.A.* 112 D8
Clear Lake, *S. Dak., U.S.A.* 112 C6
Clear Lake Reservoir, *U.S.A.* 114 F3
Clearfield, *Pa., U.S.A.* 110 E6
Clearfield, *Utah, U.S.A.* 114 F8
Clearlake, *U.S.A.* 114 G2
Clearlake Highlands, *U.S.A.* 116 G4
Clearwater, *Canada* 104 C4
Clearwater, *U.S.A.* 109 M4
Clearwater →, *Alta., Canada* 104 C6
Clearwater →, *Alta., Canada* 105 B6
Clearwater L., *Canada* 105 C9
Clearwater Mts., *U.S.A.* 114 C6
Clearwater Prov. Park, *Canada* 105 C8
Clearwater River Prov. Park, *Canada* 105 B7
Cleburne, *U.S.A.* 113 J6
Clee Hills, *U.K.* 13 E5
Cleethorpes, *U.K.* 12 D7
Cleeve Cloud, *U.K.* 13 F6
Clelles, *France* 21 D9
Clemson, *U.S.A.* 109 H4
Clerke Reef, *Australia* 92 C2
Clermont, *Australia* 94 C4
Clermont, *France* 19 C9
Clermont, *U.S.A.* 109 L5
Clermont-en-Argonne, *France* 19 C12
Clermont-Ferrand, *France* 20 C7
Clermont-l'Hérault, *France* 20 E7
Clerval, *France* 19 E13
Clervaux, *Lux.* 17 D6
Cles, *Italy* 28 B8
Cleve, *Australia* 95 E2
Clevedon, *U.K.* 13 F5
Cleveland, *Miss., U.S.A.* 113 J9
Cleveland, *Ohio, U.S.A.* 110 E3
Cleveland, *Okla., U.S.A.* 113 G6
Cleveland, *Tenn., U.S.A.* 109 H3
Cleveland, *Tex., U.S.A.* 113 K7
Cleveland, C., *Australia* 94 B4
Cleveland, Mt., *U.S.A.* 114 B7
Cleveland Heights, *U.S.A.* 110 E3
Clevelândia, *Brazil* 127 B5
Clew B., *Ireland* 15 C2
Clewiston, *U.S.A.* 109 M5
Clifden, *Ireland* 15 C1
Clifden, *N.Z.* 91 M1
Cliffdell, *U.S.A.* 116 D5
Cliffy Hd., *Australia* 93 G2
Clifton, *Australia* 95 D5
Clifton, *Ariz., U.S.A.* 115 K9
Clifton, *Colo., U.S.A.* 115 G9
Clifton, *Tex., U.S.A.* 113 K6
Clifton Beach, *Australia* 94 B4
Climax, *Canada* 105 D7
Clinch →, *U.S.A.* 109 H3
Clingmans Dome, *U.S.A.* 109 H4
Clint, *U.S.A.* 115 L10
Clinton, *B.C., Canada* 104 C4
Clinton, *Ont., Canada* 102 D3
Clinton, *N.Z.* 91 M2
Clinton, *Ark., U.S.A.* 113 H8
Clinton, *Conn., U.S.A.* 111 E12
Clinton, *Ill., U.S.A.* 112 E10
Clinton, *Ind., U.S.A.* 108 F2
Clinton, *Iowa, U.S.A.* 112 E9
Clinton, *Mass., U.S.A.* 111 D13
Clinton, *Miss., U.S.A.* 113 J9
Clinton, *Mo., U.S.A.* 112 F8
Clinton, *N.C., U.S.A.* 109 H6
Clinton, *Okla., U.S.A.* 113 H5
Clinton, *S.C., U.S.A.* 109 H5
Clinton, *Tenn., U.S.A.* 109 G3
Clinton, *Wash., U.S.A.* 116 C4
Clinton C., *Australia* 94 C5
Clinton Colden L., *Canada* 100 B9
Clintonville, *U.S.A.* 112 C10
Clipperton, I., *Pac. Oc.* 97 F17
Clisham, *U.K.* 14 D2
Clisson, *France* 18 E5
Clitheroe, *U.K.* 12 D5
Clo-oose, *Canada* 116 B2
Cloates, Pt., *Australia* 92 D1
Clocolan, *S. Africa* 89 D4
Clodomira, *Argentina* 126 B3
Clogher Hd., *Ireland* 15 C5
Clonakilty, *Ireland* 15 E3
Clonakilty B., *Ireland* 15 E3
Cloncurry, *Australia* 94 C3
Cloncurry →, *Australia* 94 B3
Clondalkin, *Ireland* 15 C5
Clones, *Ireland* 15 B4
Clonmel, *Ireland* 15 D4
Cloppenburg, *Germany* 24 C4
Cloquet, *U.S.A.* 112 B8
Clorinda, *Argentina* 126 B4
Cloud Bay, *Canada* 102 C2
Cloud Peak, *U.S.A.* 114 D10
Cloudcroft, *U.S.A.* 115 K11
Cloverdale, *U.S.A.* 116 G4
Clovis, *Calif., U.S.A.* 116 J7
Clovis, *N. Mex., U.S.A.* 113 H3
Cloyes-sur-le-Loir, *France* 18 E8
Cloyne, *Canada* 110 B7
Cluj □, *Romania* 43 D8
Cluj-Napoca, *Romania* 43 D8
Clunes, *Australia* 95 F3
Cluny, *France* 19 F11
Cluses, *France* 19 F13
Clusone, *Italy* 28 C6
Clutha →, *N.Z.* 91 M2
Clwyd →, *U.K.* 12 D4
Clyde, *Canada* 104 C6
Clyde, *N.Z.* 91 L2
Clyde, *U.S.A.* 110 C8
Clyde →, *U.K.* 14 F4
Clyde, Firth of, *U.K.* 14 F3
Clyde River, *Canada* 101 A13
Clydebank, *U.K.* 14 F4
Clymer, *N.Y., U.S.A.* 110 D5
Clymer, *Pa., U.S.A.* 110 D5
Ćmielów, *Poland* 45 H8
Côa →, *Portugal* 34 D3
Coachella, *U.S.A.* 117 M10
Coachella Canal, *U.S.A.* 117 N12
Coahoma, *U.S.A.* 113 J4
Coahuayana →, *Mexico* 118 D4
Coahuila □, *Mexico* 118 B4
Coal →, *Canada* 104 B3
Coalane, *Mozam.* 87 F4
Coalcomán, *Mexico* 118 D4
Coaldale, *Canada* 104 D6
Coalgate, *U.S.A.* 113 H6
Coalinga, *U.S.A.* 116 J6
Coalisland, *U.K.* 15 B5
Coalville, *U.K.* 12 E6
Coalville, *U.S.A.* 114 F8
Coari, *Brazil* 124 D6
Coast □, *Kenya* 86 C4
Coast Mts., *Canada* 104 C3
Coast Ranges, *U.S.A.* 116 G4
Coatbridge, *U.K.* 14 F4
Coatepec, *Mexico* 119 D5
Coatepeque, *Guatemala* 120 D1
Coatesville, *U.S.A.* 108 F8
Coaticook, *Canada* 103 C5
Coats I., *Canada* 101 B11
Coats Land, *Antarctica* 5 D1
Coatzacoalcos, *Mexico* 119 D6
Cobadin, *Romania* 43 F13
Cobalt, *Canada* 102 C4
Cobán, *Guatemala* 120 C1
Çobanlar, *Turkey* 39 C12
Cobar, *Australia* 95 E4
Cobargo, *Australia* 95 F4
Cóbh, *Ireland* 15 E3
Cobija, *Bolivia* 124 F5
Cobleskill, *U.S.A.* 111 D10
Coboconk, *Canada* 110 B6
Cobourg, *Canada* 102 D4
Cobourg Pen., *Australia* 92 B5
Cobram, *Australia* 95 F4
Cóbué, *Mozam.* 87 E3
Coburg, *Germany* 25 E6
Coca, *Spain* 34 D6
Cocanada = Kakinada, *India* 67 L13
Cocentaina, *Spain* 33 G4
Cochabamba, *Bolivia* 124 G5
Cochem, *Germany* 25 E3
Cochemane, *Mozam.* 87 F3
Cochin, *India* 66 Q10
Cochin China, *Vietnam* 65 G6
Cochran, *U.S.A.* 109 J4
Cochrane, *Alta., Canada* 104 C6
Cochrane, *Ont., Canada* 102 C3
Cochrane, *Chile* 128 F2
Cochrane →, *Canada* 105 B8
Cochrane, L., *Chile* 128 F2
Cochranton, *U.S.A.* 110 E4
Cockburn, *Australia* 95 E3
Cockburn, Canal, *Chile* 122 J3
Cockburn I., *Canada* 102 C3
Cockburn Ra., *Australia* 92 C4
Cockermouth, *U.K.* 12 C4
Cocklebiddy, *Australia* 93 F4
Coco →, *Cent. Amer.* 120 D3
Coco, I. del, *Pac. Oc.* 97 G19
Cocoa, *U.S.A.* 109 L5
Cocobeach, *Gabon* 84 D1
Cocora, *Romania* 43 F12
Cocos Is., *Ind. Oc.* 96 J1
Cod, C., *U.S.A.* 108 D10
Codajás, *Brazil* 124 D6
Codigoro, *Italy* 29 D9
Codlea, *Romania* 43 E10
Codó, *Brazil* 125 D10
Codogno, *Italy* 28 C6
Codróipo, *Italy* 29 C10
Codru, Munții, *Romania* 42 D7
Cody, *U.S.A.* 114 D9
Coe Hill, *Canada* 110 B7
Coelemu, *Chile* 126 D1
Coen, *Australia* 94 A3
Coesfeld, *Germany* 24 D3
Cœur d'Alene, *U.S.A.* 114 C5
Cœur d'Alene L., *U.S.A.* 114 C5
Coevorden, *Neths.* 17 B6
Cofete, *Canary Is.* 37 F5
Coffeyville, *U.S.A.* 113 G7
Coffin B., *Australia* 95 E2
Coffin Bay, *Australia* 95 E2
Coffin Bay Peninsula, *Australia* 95 E2
Coffs Harbour, *Australia* 95 E5
Cofrentes, *Spain* 33 F3
Cogalnic →, *Moldova* 43 E14
Cogealac, *Romania* 43 F13
Coghinas →, *Italy* 30 B1
Coghinas, L. del, *Italy* 30 B2
Cognac, *France* 20 C3
Cogne, *Italy* 28 C4
Cogolin, *France* 21 E10
Cogolludo, *Spain* 32 E1
Cohocton, *U.S.A.* 110 D7
Cohocton →, *U.S.A.* 110 D7
Cohoes, *U.S.A.* 111 D11
Cohuna, *Australia* 95 F3
Coiba, I., *Panama* 120 E3
Coig →, *Argentina* 128 G3
Coigeach, Rubha, *U.K.* 14 C3
Coihaique, *Chile* 128 F2
Coimbatore, *India* 66 P10
Coimbra, *Brazil* 124 G7
Coimbra, *Portugal* 34 E2
Coimbra □, *Portugal* 34 E2
Coín, *Spain* 35 J6
Coipasa, Salar de, *Bolivia* 124 G5
Cojimies, *Ecuador* 124 C3
Cojocna, *Romania* 43 D8
Cojutepequé, *El Salv.* 120 D2
Čoka, *Serbia, Yug.* 42 E5
Cokeville, *U.S.A.* 114 E8
Colac, *Australia* 95 F3
Colatina, *Brazil* 125 G10
Colbeck, C., *Antarctica* 5 D13
Colborne, *Canada* 110 C7
Colby, *U.S.A.* 112 F4
Colchester, *U.K.* 13 F8
Cold L., *Canada* 105 C7
Coldstream, *Canada* 104 C5
Coldstream, *U.K.* 14 F6
Coldwater, *Canada* 110 B5
Coldwater, *Kans., U.S.A.* 113 G5
Coldwater, *Mich., U.S.A.* 108 E3
Coleambally, *Australia* 95 E4
Colebrook, *U.S.A.* 111 B13
Coleman, *U.S.A.* 113 K5
Coleman →, *Australia* 94 B3
Colenso, *S. Africa* 89 D4
Coleraine, *Australia* 95 F3
Coleraine, *U.K.* 15 A5
Coleridge, L., *N.Z.* 91 K3
Colesberg, *S. Africa* 88 E4
Coleville, *U.S.A.* 116 G7
Colfax, *Calif., U.S.A.* 116 F6
Colfax, *La., U.S.A.* 113 K8
Colfax, *Wash., U.S.A.* 114 C5
Colhué Huapi, L., *Argentina* 128 F3
Colibaşi, *Moldova* 43 E13
Colibaşi, *Romania* 43 F9
Cólico, *Italy* 28 B6
Coligny, *France* 19 F12
Coligny, *S. Africa* 89 D4
Colima, *Mexico* 118 D4
Colima □, *Mexico* 118 D4
Colima, Nevado de, *Mexico* 118 D4
Colina, *Chile* 126 C1
Colina do Norte, *Guinea-Biss.* 82 C2
Colinas, *Brazil* 125 E10
Colindres, *Spain* 34 B7
Coll, *U.K.* 14 E2
Collaguasi, *Chile* 126 A2
Collarada, Peña, *Spain* 32 C4
Collarenebri, *Australia* 95 D4
Colle di Val d'Elsa, *Italy* 28 E8
Collécchio, *Italy* 28 D7
Colleen Bawn, *Zimbabwe* 87 G2
College Park, *U.S.A.* 109 J3
College Station, *U.S.A.* 113 K6
Collesalvetti, *Italy* 28 E7
Collie, *Australia* 93 F2
Collier B., *Australia* 92 C3
Collier Ra., *Australia* 93 D2
Collina, Passo di, *Italy* 28 D7
Collingwood, *Canada* 102 D3
Collingwood, *N.Z.* 91 J4
Collins, *Canada* 102 B2
Collinsville, *Australia* 94 C4
Collipulli, *Chile* 126 D1
Collooney, *Ireland* 15 B3
Colmar, *France* 19 D14
Colmars, *France* 21 D10
Colmenar, *Spain* 35 J6
Colmenar de Oreja, *Spain* 34 E7
Colmenar Viejo, *Spain* 34 E7
Colo →, *Australia* 95 E5
Cologne = Köln, *Germany* 24 E2
Colom, I. d'en, *Spain* 37 B11
Coloma, *U.S.A.* 116 G6
Colomb-Béchar = Béchar, *Algeria* 78 B5
Colombey-les-Belles, *France* 19 D12
Colombey-les-Deux-Églises, *France* 19 D11
Colombia ■, *S. Amer.* 124 C4
Colombian Basin, *S. Amer.* 98 H12
Colombo, *Sri Lanka* 66 R11
Colomiers, *France* 20 E5
Colón, *Buenos Aires, Argentina* 126 C3
Colón, *Entre Ríos, Argentina* 126 C4
Colón, *Cuba* 120 B3
Colón, *Panama* 120 E4
Colonia de Sant Jordi, *Spain* 37 B9
Colonia del Sacramento, *Uruguay* 126 C4
Colonia Dora, *Argentina* 126 B3
Colonial Beach, *U.S.A.* 108 F7
Colonie, *U.S.A.* 111 D11
Colonna, C., *Italy* 31 C10
Colonsay, *Canada* 105 C7
Colonsay, *U.K.* 14 E2
Colorado □, *U.S.A.* 115 G10
Colorado →, *Argentina* 128 D4
Colorado →, *N. Amer.* 115 L6
Colorado →, *U.S.A.* 113 L7
Colorado City, *U.S.A.* 113 J4
Colorado Plateau, *U.S.A.* 115 H8
Colorado River Aqueduct, *U.S.A.* 117 L12
Colorado Springs, *U.S.A.* 112 F2
Colorno, *Italy* 28 D7
Colotlán, *Mexico* 118 C4
Colstrip, *U.S.A.* 114 D10
Colton, *U.S.A.* 111 B10
Columbia, *Ky., U.S.A.* 108 G3
Columbia, *La., U.S.A.* 113 J8
Columbia, *Miss., U.S.A.* 113 K10
Columbia, *Mo., U.S.A.* 112 F8
Columbia, *Pa., U.S.A.* 111 F8
Columbia, *S.C., U.S.A.* 109 J5
Columbia, *Tenn., U.S.A.* 109 H2
Columbia →, *N. Amer.* 116 D2
Columbia, C., *Canada* 4 A4
Columbia, District of □, *U.S.A.* 108 F7
Columbia, Mt., *Canada* 104 C5
Columbia Basin, *U.S.A.* 114 C4
Columbia Falls, *U.S.A.* 114 B6
Columbia Mts., *Canada* 104 C5
Columbia Plateau, *U.S.A.* 114 D5
Columbiana, *U.S.A.* 110 F4
Columbretes, Is., *Spain* 32 F5
Columbus, *Ga., U.S.A.* 109 J3
Columbus, *Ind., U.S.A.* 108 F3
Columbus, *Kans., U.S.A.* 113 G7
Columbus, *Miss., U.S.A.* 109 J1
Columbus, *Mont., U.S.A.* 114 D9
Columbus, *N. Mex., U.S.A.* 115 L10
Columbus, *Nebr., U.S.A.* 112 E6
Columbus, *Ohio, U.S.A.* 108 F4
Columbus, *Tex., U.S.A.* 113 L6
Colunga, *Spain* 34 B5
Colusa, *U.S.A.* 116 F4
Colville, *U.S.A.* 114 B5
Colville →, *U.S.A.* 100 A4
Colville, C., *N.Z.* 91 G5
Colwood, *Canada* 116 B3
Colwyn Bay, *U.K.* 12 D4
Coma, *Ethiopia* 81 F4
Comácchio, *Italy* 29 D9
Comalcalco, *Mexico* 119 D6
Comallo, *Argentina* 128 E2
Comana, *Romania* 43 F11
Comanche, *U.S.A.* 113 K5
Comăneşti, *Romania* 43 D11
Comarnic, *Romania* 43 E10
Comayagua, *Honduras* 120 D2
Combahee →, *U.S.A.* 109 J5
Combarbalá, *Chile* 126 C1
Combeaufontaine, *France* 19 E12
Comber, *Canada* 110 D2
Comber, *U.K.* 15 B6
Combermere, *Canada* 110 A7
Comblain-au-Pont, *Belgium* 17 D5
Combourg, *France* 18 D5
Combrailles, *France* 19 F9
Combronde, *France* 20 C7
Comeragh Mts., *Ireland* 15 D4
Comet, *Australia* 94 C4
Comilla, *Bangla.* 67 H17
Comino, *Malta* 36 C1
Comino, C., *Italy* 30 B2
Cómiso, *Italy* 31 F7
Comitán, *Mexico* 119 D6
Commentry, *France* 19 F9
Commerce, *Ga., U.S.A.* 109 H4
Commerce, *Tex., U.S.A.* 113 J7
Commercy, *France* 19 D12
Committee B., *Canada* 101 B11
Commonwealth B., *Antarctica* 5 C10
Commoron Cr. →, *Australia* 95 D5
Communism Pk. = Kommunizma, Pik, *Tajikistan* 50 F8
Como, *Italy* 28 C6
Como, Lago di, *Italy* 28 B6
Comodoro Rivadavia, *Argentina* 128 F3
Comorâşte, *Romania* 42 E6
Comorin, C., *India* 66 Q10
Comoro Is. = Comoros ■, *Ind. Oc.* 77 H8
Comoros ■, *Ind. Oc.* 77 H8
Comox, *Canada* 104 D4
Compiègne, *France* 19 C9
Comporta, *Portugal* 35 G2
Compostela, *Mexico* 118 C4
Comprida, I., *Brazil* 127 A6
Compton, *Canada* 111 A13
Compton, *U.S.A.* 117 M8
Comrat, *Moldova* 43 D13
Con Cuong, *Vietnam* 64 C5
Con Son, *Vietnam* 65 H6
Conakry, *Guinea* 82 D2
Conara, *Australia* 94 G4
Concarneau, *France* 18 E3
Conceição, *Mozam.* 87 F4
Conceição da Barra, *Brazil* 125 G11
Conceição do Araguaia, *Brazil* 125 E9
Concepción, *Argentina* 126 B2
Concepción, *Bolivia* 124 G6
Concepción, *Chile* 126 D1
Concepción, *Mexico* 119 D6
Concepción, *Paraguay* 126 A4
Concepción □, *Chile* 126 D1
Concepción →, *Mexico* 118 A2
Concepción, Est. de, *Chile* 128 G2
Concepción, L., *Bolivia* 124 G6
Concepción, Punta, *Mexico* 118 B2
Concepción del Oro, *Mexico* 118 C4
Concepción del Uruguay, *Argentina* 126 C4
Conception, Pt., *U.S.A.* 117 L6
Conception B., *Canada* 103 C9
Conception B., *Namibia* 88 C1
Conception I., *Bahamas* 121 B4
Concession, *Zimbabwe* 87 F3
Conchas Dam, *U.S.A.* 113 H2
Conches-en-Ouche, *France* 18 D7
Concho, *U.S.A.* 115 J9
Concho →, *U.S.A.* 113 K5
Conchos →, *Chihuahua, Mexico* 118 B4
Conchos →, *Tamaulipas, Mexico* 119 B5
Concord, *Calif., U.S.A.* 116 H4
Concord, *N.C., U.S.A.* 109 H5
Concord, *N.H., U.S.A.* 111 C13
Concordia, *Argentina* 126 C4
Concórdia, *Brazil* 124 D5
Concordia, *Mexico* 118 C3
Concordia, *U.S.A.* 112 F6
Concrete, *U.S.A.* 114 B3
Condamine, *Australia* 95 D5
Condat, *France* 20 C6
Conde, *U.S.A.* 112 C5
Condé-sur-Noireau, *France* 18 D6
Condeúba, *Brazil* 125 F10
Condobolin, *Australia* 95 E4
Condom, *France* 20 E4
Condon, *U.S.A.* 114 D3
Conegliano, *Italy* 29 C9
Conejera, I. = Conills, I. des, *Spain* 37 B9
Conejos, *Mexico* 118 B4
Confolens, *France* 20 B4
Confuso →, *Paraguay* 126 B4
Congaz, *Moldova* 43 D13
Conghua, *China* 59 F9
Congjiang, *China* 58 E7
Congleton, *U.K.* 12 D5
Congo (Kinshasa) = Congo, Dem. Rep. of the ■, *Africa* 84 E4
Congo ■, *Africa* 84 E3
Congo →, *Africa* 84 F2
Congo, Dem. Rep. of the ■, *Africa* 84 E4
Congo Basin, *Africa* 84 E4
Congonhas, *Brazil* 127 A7
Congress, *U.S.A.* 115 J7
Conil = Conil de la Frontera, *Spain* 35 J4
Conil de la Frontera, *Spain* 35 J4
Conills, I. des, *Spain* 37 B9
Coniston, *Canada* 102 C3
Conjeeveram = Kanchipuram, *India* 66 N11
Conklin, *Canada* 105 B6
Conklin, *U.S.A.* 111 D9
Conn, L., *Ireland* 15 B2
Connacht □, *Ireland* 15 C2
Conneaut, *U.S.A.* 110 E4
Connecticut □, *U.S.A.* 111 E12
Connecticut →, *U.S.A.* 111 E12
Connell, *U.S.A.* 114 C4
Connellsville, *U.S.A.* 110 F5
Connemara, *Ireland* 15 C2
Connemaugh →, *U.S.A.* 110 F5
Connerré, *France* 18 D7
Connersville, *U.S.A.* 108 F3
Connors Ra., *Australia* 94 C4
Conques, *France* 20 D6
Conquest, *Canada* 105 C7
Conrad, *U.S.A.* 114 B8
Conran, C., *Australia* 95 F4
Conroe, *U.S.A.* 113 K7
Consecon, *Canada* 110 C7
Conselheiro Lafaiete, *Brazil* 127 A7
Conselve, *Italy* 29 C8
Consett, *U.K.* 12 C6
Consort, *Canada* 105 C6
Constance = Konstanz, *Germany* 25 H5
Constance, L. = Bodensee, *Europe* 25 H5
Constanţa, *Romania* 43 F13
Constanţa □, *Romania* 43 F13
Constantia, *U.S.A.* 111 C8
Constantina, *Spain* 35 H5
Constantine, *Algeria* 78 A7
Constitución, *Chile* 126 D1
Constitución, *Uruguay* 126 C4
Consuegra, *Spain* 35 F7
Consul, *Canada* 105 D7
Contact, *U.S.A.* 114 F6
Contai, *India* 69 J12
Contamana, *Peru* 124 E4
Contarina, *Italy* 29 C9
Contas →, *Brazil* 125 F11
Contes, *France* 21 E11
Contoocook, *U.S.A.* 111 C13
Contra Costa, *Mozam.* 89 D5
Contres, *France* 18 E8
Contrexéville, *France* 19 D12
Contwoyto L., *Canada* 100 B8
Conversano, *Italy* 31 B10
Conway = Conwy, *U.K.* 12 D4
Conway = Conwy →, *U.K.* 12 D4
Conway, *Ark., U.S.A.* 113 H8
Conway, *N.H., U.S.A.* 111 C13
Conway, *S.C., U.S.A.* 109 J6
Conway, L., *Australia* 95 D2
Conwy, *U.K.* 12 D4
Conwy □, *U.K.* 12 D4
Conwy →, *U.K.* 12 D4
Coober Pedy, *Australia* 95 D1

Cooch Behar = Koch Bihar, *India* 67 F16
Cooinda, *Australia* 92 B5
Cook, *Australia* 93 F5
Cook, *U.S.A.* 112 B8
Cook, B., *Chile* 128 H3
Cook, C., *Canada* 104 C3
Cook, Mt., *N.Z.* 91 K3
Cook Inlet, *U.S.A.* 100 C4
Cook Is., *Pac. Oc.* 97 J12
Cook Strait, *N.Z.* 91 J5
Cookeville, *U.S.A.* 109 G3
Cookhouse, *S. Africa* 88 E4
Cookshire, *Canada* 111 A13
Cookstown, *U.K.* 15 B5
Cooksville, *Canada* 110 C5
Cooktown, *Australia* 94 B4
Coolabah, *Australia* 95 E4
Cooladdi, *Australia* 95 D4
Coolah, *Australia* 95 E4
Coolamon, *Australia* 95 E4
Coolgardie, *Australia* 93 F3
Coolidge, *U.S.A.* 115 K8
Coolidge Dam, *U.S.A.* 115 K8
Cooma, *Australia* 95 F4
Coon Rapids, *U.S.A.* 112 C8
Coonabarabran, *Australia* 95 E4
Coonalpyn, *Australia* 95 F2
Coonamble, *Australia* 95 E4
Coonana, *Australia* 93 F3
Coondapoor, *India* 66 N9
Cooninie, L., *Australia* 95 D2
Cooper, *U.S.A.* 113 J7
Cooper Cr. →, *Australia* 95 D2
Cooperstown, *N. Dak., U.S.A.* 112 B5
Cooperstown, *N.Y., U.S.A.* 111 D10
Coorabie, *Australia* 93 F5
Coorow, *Australia* 93 E2
Cooroy, *Australia* 95 D5
Coos Bay, *U.S.A.* 114 E1
Coosa →, *U.S.A.* 109 J2
Cootamundra, *Australia* 95 E4
Cootehill, *Ireland* 15 B4
Copahue Paso, *Argentina* 126 D1
Copainalá, *Mexico* 119 D6
Copake Falls, *U.S.A.* 111 D11
Copalnic Mănăştur, *Romania* 43 C8
Copán, *Honduras* 120 D2
Cope, *U.S.A.* 112 F3
Cope, C., *Spain* 33 H3
Copenhagen = København, *Denmark* 11 J6
Copenhagen, *U.S.A.* 111 C9
Copertino, *Italy* 31 B11
Copiapó, *Chile* 126 B1
Copiapó →, *Chile* 126 B1
Coplay, *U.S.A.* 111 F9
Copp L., *Canada* 104 A6
Copparo, *Italy* 29 D8
Coppename →, *Surinam* 125 B7
Copper Harbor, *U.S.A.* 108 B2
Copper Queen, *Zimbabwe* 87 F2
Copperas Cove, *U.S.A.* 113 K6
Copperbelt □, *Zambia* 87 E2
Coppermine = Kugluktuk, *Canada* 100 B8
Coppermine →, *Canada* 100 B8
Copperopolis, *U.S.A.* 116 H6
Copşa Mică, *Romania* 43 D9
Coquet →, *U.K.* 12 B6
Coquilhatville = Mbandaka, *Dem. Rep. of the Congo* 84 D3
Coquille, *U.S.A.* 114 E1
Coquimbo, *Chile* 126 C1
Coquimbo □, *Chile* 126 C1
Corabia, *Romania* 43 G9
Coracora, *Peru* 124 G4
Coraki, *Australia* 95 D5
Coral, *U.S.A.* 110 F5
Coral Gables, *U.S.A.* 109 N5
Coral Harbour = Salliq, *Canada* 101 B11
Coral Sea, *Pac. Oc.* 96 J7
Coral Springs, *U.S.A.* 109 M5
Coraopolis, *U.S.A.* 110 F4
Corato, *Italy* 31 A9
Corbeil-Essonnes, *France* 19 D9
Corbie, *France* 19 C9
Corbières, *France* 20 F6
Corbigny, *France* 19 E10
Corbin, *U.S.A.* 108 G3
Corbones →, *Spain* 35 H5
Corbu, *Romania* 43 F13
Corby, *U.K.* 13 E7
Corcaigh = Cork, *Ireland* 15 E3
Corcoran, *U.S.A.* 116 J7
Cordele, *U.S.A.* 109 K4
Cordell, *U.S.A.* 113 H5
Cordenòns, *Italy* 29 C9
Cordes, *France* 20 D5
Córdoba, *Argentina* 126 C3
Córdoba, *Mexico* 119 D5
Córdoba, *Spain* 35 H6
Córdoba □, *Argentina* 126 C3
Córdoba □, *Spain* 35 G6
Córdoba, Sierra de, *Argentina* 126 C3
Cordon, *Phil.* 61 C4
Cordova, *U.S.A.* 100 B5
Corella, *Spain* 32 C3
Corella →, *Australia* 94 B3
Corfield, *Australia* 94 C3
Corfu = Kérkira, *Greece* 36 A3
Corfu, Str. of, *Greece* 36 A4
Corgo = O Corgo, *Spain* 34 C3
Cori, *Italy* 30 A5
Coria, *Spain* 34 F4
Coria del Río, *Spain* 35 H4
Corigliano Cálabro, *Italy* 31 C9
Coringa Is., *Australia* 94 B4
Corinth = Kórinthos, *Greece* 38 D4
Corinth, *Miss., U.S.A.* 109 H1
Corinth, *N.Y., U.S.A.* 111 C11
Corinth, *N.Y., U.S.A.* 111 C11
Corinth, G. of = Korinthiakós Kólpos, *Greece* 38 C4
Corinth Canal, *Greece* 38 D4
Corinto, *Brazil* 125 G10
Corinto, *Nic.* 120 D2
Cork, *Ireland* 15 E3
Cork □, *Ireland* 15 E3
Cork Harbour, *Ireland* 15 E3
Corlay, *France* 18 D3
Corleone, *Italy* 30 E6
Corleto Perticara, *Italy* 31 B9
Çorlu, *Turkey* 41 E11
Cormack L., *Canada* 104 A4
Cormòns, *Italy* 29 C10
Cormorant, *Canada* 105 C8
Cormorant L., *Canada* 105 C8
Corn Is. = Maíz, Is. del, *Nic.* 120 D3
Cornélio Procópio, *Brazil* 127 A5
Corner Brook, *Canada* 103 C8
Corneşti, *Moldova* 43 C13
Corníglio, *Italy* 28 D7
Corning, *Ark., U.S.A.* 113 G9
Corning, *Calif., U.S.A.* 114 G2
Corning, *Iowa, U.S.A.* 112 E7
Corning, *N.Y., U.S.A.* 110 D7
Corno Grande, *Italy* 29 F10
Cornwall, *Canada* 102 C5
Cornwall, *U.S.A.* 111 F8
Cornwall □, *U.K.* 13 G3
Corny Pt., *Australia* 95 E2
Coro, *Venezuela* 124 A5
Coroatá, *Brazil* 125 D10
Corocoro, *Bolivia* 124 G5
Coroico, *Bolivia* 124 G5
Coromandel, *N.Z.* 91 G5
Coromandel Coast, *India* 66 N12
Corona, *Calif., U.S.A.* 117 M9
Corona, *N. Mex., U.S.A.* 115 J11
Coronach, *Canada* 105 D7
Coronado, *U.S.A.* 117 N9
Coronado, B. de, *Costa Rica* 120 E3
Coronados, Is. los, *U.S.A.* 117 N9
Coronation, *Canada* 104 C6
Coronation Gulf, *Canada* 100 B8
Coronation I., *Antarctica* 5 C18
Coronation Is., *Australia* 92 B3
Coronda, *Argentina* 126 C3
Coronel, *Chile* 126 D1
Coronel Bogado, *Paraguay* 126 B4
Coronel Dorrego, *Argentina* 126 D3
Coronel Oviedo, *Paraguay* 126 B4
Coronel Pringles, *Argentina* 126 D3
Coronel Suárez, *Argentina* 126 D3
Coronel Vidal, *Argentina* 126 D4
Coropuna, Nevado, *Peru* 124 G4
Çorovoda, *Albania* 40 F4
Corowa, *Australia* 95 F4
Corozal, *Belize* 119 D7
Corps, *France* 21 D9
Corpus, *Argentina* 127 B4
Corpus Christi, *U.S.A.* 113 M6
Corpus Christi, L., *U.S.A.* 113 L6
Corral de Almaguer, *Spain* 34 F7
Corralejo, *Canary Is.* 37 F6
Corraun Pen., *Ireland* 15 C2
Corréggio, *Italy* 28 D7
Correntes, C. das, *Mozam.* 89 C6
Corrèze □, *France* 20 C5
Corrèze →, *France* 20 C5
Corrib, L., *Ireland* 15 C2
Corridónia, *Italy* 29 E10
Corrientes, *Argentina* 126 B4
Corrientes □, *Argentina* 126 B4
Corrientes →, *Argentina* 126 C4
Corrientes →, *Peru* 124 D4
Corrientes, C., *Colombia* 124 B3
Corrientes, C., *Cuba* 120 B3
Corrientes, C., *Mexico* 118 C3
Corrigan, *U.S.A.* 113 K7
Corrigin, *Australia* 93 F2
Corry, *U.S.A.* 110 E5
Corryong, *Australia* 95 F4
Corse, *France* 21 G13
Corse, C., *France* 21 E13
Corse-du-Sud □, *France* 21 G13
Corsica = Corse, *France* 21 G13
Corsicana, *U.S.A.* 113 J6
Corte, *France* 21 F13
Corte Pinto, *Portugal* 35 H3
Cortegana, *Spain* 35 H4
Cortez, *U.S.A.* 115 H9
Cortina d'Ampezzo, *Italy* 29 B9
Cortland, *N.Y., U.S.A.* 111 D8
Cortland, *Ohio, U.S.A.* 110 E4
Cortona, *Italy* 29 E8
Corubal →, *Guinea-Biss.* 82 C2
Coruche, *Portugal* 35 G2
Çoruh →, *Turkey* 49 K5
Çorum, *Turkey* 72 B6
Corumbá, *Brazil* 124 G7
Corund, *Romania* 43 D10
Corunna = A Coruña, *Spain* 34 B2
Corvallis, *U.S.A.* 114 D2
Corvette, L. de la, *Canada* 102 B5
Corydon, *U.S.A.* 112 E8
Cosalá, *Mexico* 118 C3
Cosamaloapan, *Mexico* 119 D5
Cosenza, *Italy* 31 C9
Coşereni, *Romania* 43 F11
Coshocton, *U.S.A.* 110 F3
Cosmo Newberry, *Australia* 93 E3
Cosne-Cours-sur-Loire, *France* 19 E9
Coso Junction, *U.S.A.* 117 J9
Coso Pk., *U.S.A.* 117 J9
Cospeito, *Spain* 34 B3
Cosquín, *Argentina* 126 C3
Cossato, *Italy* 28 C5
Cossé-le-Vivien, *France* 18 E6
Cosson →, *France* 18 E8
Costa Blanca, *Spain* 33 G4
Costa Brava, *Spain* 32 D8
Costa del Sol, *Spain* 35 J6
Costa Dorada, *Spain* 32 D6
Costa Mesa, *U.S.A.* 117 M9
Costa Rica ■, *Cent. Amer.* 120 E3
Costa Smeralda, *Italy* 30 A2
Costeşti, *Romania* 43 F9
Costigliole d'Asti, *Italy* 28 D5
Cosumnes →, *U.S.A.* 116 G5
Coswig, *Sachsen, Germany* 24 D9
Coswig, *Sachsen-Anhalt, Germany* 24 D8
Cotabato, *Phil.* 61 H6
Cotagaita, *Bolivia* 126 A2
Côte d'Azur, *France* 21 E11
Côte-d'Ivoire = Ivory Coast ■, *Africa* 82 D4
Côte d'Or, *France* 19 E11
Côte-d'Or □, *France* 19 E11
Coteau des Prairies, *U.S.A.* 112 C6
Coteau du Missouri, *U.S.A.* 112 B4
Coteau Landing, *Canada* 111 A10
Cotentin, *France* 18 C5
Côtes-d'Armor □, *France* 18 D4
Côtes de Meuse, *France* 19 C12
Côtes-du-Nord = Côtes-d'Armor □, *France* 18 D4
Cotiella, *Spain* 32 C5
Cotillo, *Canary Is.* 37 F5
Cotiujeni, *Moldova* 43 C13
Cotonou, *Benin* 83 D5
Cotopaxi, *Ecuador* 122 D3
Cotronei, *Italy* 31 C9
Cotswold Hills, *U.K.* 13 F5
Cottage Grove, *U.S.A.* 114 E2
Cottbus, *Germany* 24 D10
Cottonwood, *U.S.A.* 115 J7
Cotulla, *U.S.A.* 113 L5
Coubre, Pte. de la, *France* 20 C2
Couches, *France* 19 F11
Couço, *Portugal* 35 G2
Coudersport, *U.S.A.* 110 E6
Couedic, C. du, *Australia* 95 F2
Couëron, *France* 18 E5
Couesnon →, *France* 18 D5
Couhé, *France* 20 B4
Coulanges-sur-Yonne, *France* 19 E10
Coulee City, *U.S.A.* 114 C4
Coulman I., *Antarctica* 5 D11
Coulommiers, *France* 19 D10
Coulon →, *France* 21 E9
Coulonge →, *Canada* 102 C4
Coulonges-sur-l'Autize, *France* 20 B3
Coulounieix-Chamiers, *France* 20 C4
Coulterville, *U.S.A.* 116 H6
Council, *U.S.A.* 114 D5
Council Bluffs, *U.S.A.* 112 E7
Council Grove, *U.S.A.* 112 F6
Coupeville, *U.S.A.* 116 B4
Courantyne →, *S. Amer.* 122 C5
Courcelles, *Belgium* 17 D4
Courçon, *France* 20 B3
Courmayeur, *Italy* 28 C3
Couronne, C., *France* 21 E9
Cours-la-Ville, *France* 19 F11
Coursan, *France* 20 E7
Courseulles-sur-Mer, *France* 18 C6
Courtenay, *Canada* 104 D4
Courtenay, *France* 19 D10
Courtland, *U.S.A.* 116 G5
Courtrai = Kortrijk, *Belgium* 17 D3
Courtright, *Canada* 110 D2
Coushatta, *U.S.A.* 113 J8
Coutances, *France* 18 C5
Coutras, *France* 20 C3
Coutts Crossing, *Australia* 95 D5
Couvin, *Belgium* 17 D4
Covarrubias, *Spain* 34 C7
Covasna, *Romania* 43 E11
Covasna □, *Romania* 43 E10
Cove I., *Canada* 110 A3
Coventry, *U.K.* 13 E6
Covilhã, *Portugal* 34 E3
Covington, *Ga., U.S.A.* 109 J4
Covington, *Ky., U.S.A.* 108 F3
Covington, *Okla., U.S.A.* 113 G6
Covington, *Tenn., U.S.A.* 113 H10
Covington, *Va., U.S.A.* 108 G5
Cowal, L., *Australia* 95 E4
Cowan, L., *Australia* 93 F3
Cowan L., *Canada* 105 C7
Cowangie, *Australia* 95 F3
Cowansville, *Canada* 102 C5
Coward Springs, *Australia* 95 D2
Cowcowing Lakes, *Australia* 93 F2
Cowdenbeath, *U.K.* 14 E5
Cowell, *Australia* 95 E2
Cowes, *U.K.* 13 G6
Cowichan L., *Canada* 116 B2
Cowlitz →, *U.S.A.* 116 D4
Cowra, *Australia* 95 E4
Cox, *Spain* 33 G4
Coxilha Grande, *Brazil* 127 B5
Coxim, *Brazil* 125 G8
Cox's Bazar, *Bangla.* 67 J17
Coyote Wells, *U.S.A.* 117 N11
Coyuca de Benítez, *Mexico* 119 D4
Coyuca de Catalan, *Mexico* 118 D4
Cozad, *U.S.A.* 112 E5
Cozes, *France* 20 C3
Cozumel, *Mexico* 119 C7
Cozumel, Isla, *Mexico* 119 C7
Cracow = Kraków, *Poland* 45 H6
Cracow, *Australia* 95 D5
Cradock, *Australia* 95 E2
Cradock, *S. Africa* 88 E4
Craig, *U.S.A.* 114 F10
Craigavon, *U.K.* 15 B5
Craigmore, *Zimbabwe* 87 G3
Craik, *Canada* 105 C7
Crailsheim, *Germany* 25 F6
Craiova, *Romania* 43 F8
Cramsie, *Australia* 94 C3
Cranberry L., *U.S.A.* 111 B10
Cranberry Portage, *Canada* 105 C8
Cranbrook, *Australia* 93 F2
Cranbrook, *Canada* 104 D5
Crandon, *U.S.A.* 112 C10
Crane, *Oreg., U.S.A.* 114 E4
Crane, *Tex., U.S.A.* 113 K3
Cranston, *U.S.A.* 111 E13
Craon, *France* 18 E6
Craonne, *France* 19 C10
Craponne-sur-Arzon, *France* 20 C7
Crasna, *Romania* 43 D12
Crasna →, *Romania* 42 C7
Crasnei, Munţii, *Romania* 43 C8
Crater L., *U.S.A.* 114 E2
Crater Lake National Park, *U.S.A.* 114 E2
Crateús, *Brazil* 125 E10
Crati →, *Italy* 31 C9
Crato, *Brazil* 125 E11
Crato, *Portugal* 35 F3
Craven, L., *Canada* 102 B4
Crawford, *U.S.A.* 112 D3
Crawfordsville, *U.S.A.* 108 E2
Crawley, *U.K.* 13 F7
Crazy Mts., *U.S.A.* 114 C8
Crean L., *Canada* 105 C7
Crécy-en-Ponthieu, *France* 19 B8
Crediton, *Canada* 110 C3
Cree →, *Canada* 105 B7
Cree →, *U.K.* 14 G4
Cree L., *Canada* 105 B7
Creede, *U.S.A.* 115 H10
Creekside, *U.S.A.* 110 F5
Creel, *Mexico* 118 B3
Creemore, *Canada* 110 B4
Creighton, *Canada* 105 C8
Creighton, *U.S.A.* 112 D6
Creil, *France* 19 C9
Crema, *Italy* 28 C6
Cremona, *Italy* 28 C7
Crepaja, *Serbia, Yug.* 42 E5
Crépy, *France* 19 C10
Crépy-en-Valois, *France* 19 C9
Cres, *Croatia* 29 D11
Crescent City, *U.S.A.* 114 F1
Crescentino, *Italy* 28 C5
Crespo, *Argentina* 126 C3
Cresson, *U.S.A.* 110 F6
Crest, *France* 21 D9
Cresta, Mt., *Phil.* 61 C5
Crestline, *Calif., U.S.A.* 117 L9
Crestline, *Ohio, U.S.A.* 110 F2
Creston, *Canada* 104 D5
Creston, *Calif., U.S.A.* 116 K6
Creston, *Iowa, U.S.A.* 112 E7
Crestview, *Calif., U.S.A.* 116 H8
Crestview, *Fla., U.S.A.* 109 K2
Crêt de la Neige, *France* 19 F12
Crete = Kríti, *Greece* 36 D7
Crete, *U.S.A.* 112 E6
Crete, Sea of, *Greece* 39 E7
Créteil, *France* 19 D9
Creus, C. de, *Spain* 32 C8
Creuse □, *France* 19 F9
Creuse →, *France* 20 B4
Creutzwald, *France* 19 C13
Creuzburg, *Germany* 24 D6
Crèvecœur-le-Grand, *France* 19 C9
Crevillente, *Spain* 33 G4
Crewe, *U.K.* 12 D5
Crewkerne, *U.K.* 13 G5
Criciúma, *Brazil* 127 B6
Cricova, *Moldova* 43 C13
Crieff, *U.K.* 14 E5
Crikvenica, *Croatia* 29 C11
Crimea □, *Ukraine* 47 K8
Crimean Pen. = Krymskyy Pivostriv, *Ukraine* 47 K8
Crimmitschau, *Germany* 24 E8
Cristuru Secuiesc, *Romania* 43 D10
Crişul Alb →, *Romania* 42 D6
Crişul Negru →, *Romania* 42 D6
Crişul Repede →, *Romania* 42 D5
Criuleni, *Moldova* 43 C14
Crivitz, *Germany* 24 B7
Crna →, *Macedonia* 40 E5
Crna Gora = Montenegro □, *Yugoslavia* 40 D3
Crna Gora, *Macedonia* 40 D5
Crna Reka = Crna →, *Macedonia* 40 E5
Crna Trava, *Serbia, Yug.* 40 D6
Crni Drim →, *Macedonia* 40 E4
Crni Timok →, *Serbia, Yug.* 40 C6
Crnoljeva Planina, *Kosovo, Yug.* 40 D5
Črnomelj, *Slovenia* 29 C12
Croagh Patrick, *Ireland* 15 C2
Croatia ■, *Europe* 29 C13
Crocker, Banjaran, *Malaysia* 62 C5
Crockett, *U.S.A.* 113 K7
Crocodile = Krokodil →, *Mozam.* 89 D5
Crocodile Is., *Australia* 94 A1
Crocq, *France* 20 C6
Crodo, *Italy* 28 B5
Crohy Hd., *Ireland* 15 B3
Croisette, C., *France* 21 E9
Croisic, Pte. du, *France* 18 E4
Croix, L. La, *Canada* 102 C1
Croker, C., *Australia* 92 B5
Croker, C., *Canada* 110 B4
Croker I., *Australia* 92 B5
Cromarty, *U.K.* 14 D4
Cromer, *U.K.* 12 E9
Cromwell, *N.Z.* 91 L2
Cromwell, *U.S.A.* 111 E12
Cronat, *France* 19 F10
Crook, *U.K.* 12 C6
Crooked →, *Canada* 104 C4
Crooked →, *U.S.A.* 114 D3
Crooked I., *Bahamas* 121 B5
Crooked Island Passage, *Bahamas* 121 B5
Crookston, *Minn., U.S.A.* 112 B6
Crookston, *Nebr., U.S.A.* 112 D4
Crookwell, *Australia* 95 E4
Crosby, *U.K.* 12 D4
Crosby, *N. Dak., U.S.A.* 112 A3
Crosby, *Pa., U.S.A.* 110 E6
Crosbyton, *U.S.A.* 113 J4
Crosía, *Italy* 31 C9
Cross →, *Nigeria* 83 E6
Cross City, *U.S.A.* 109 L4
Cross Fell, *U.K.* 12 C5
Cross L., *Canada* 105 C9
Cross Lake, *Canada* 105 C9
Cross River □, *Nigeria* 83 D6
Cross Sound, *U.S.A.* 100 C6
Crossett, *U.S.A.* 113 J9
Crosshaven, *Ireland* 15 E3
Crossville, *U.S.A.* 109 G3
Croswell, *U.S.A.* 110 C2
Croton-on-Hudson, *U.S.A.* 111 E11
Crotone, *Italy* 31 C10
Crow →, *Canada* 104 B4
Crow Agency, *U.S.A.* 114 D10
Crow Hd., *Ireland* 15 E1
Crowell, *U.S.A.* 113 J5
Crowley, *U.S.A.* 113 K8
Crowley, L., *U.S.A.* 116 H8
Crown Point, *Ind., U.S.A.* 108 E2
Crown Point, *N.Y., U.S.A.* 111 C11
Crownpoint, *U.S.A.* 115 J9
Crows Landing, *U.S.A.* 116 H5
Crows Nest, *Australia* 95 D5
Crowsnest Pass, *Canada* 104 D6
Croydon, *Australia* 94 B3
Croydon, *U.K.* 13 F7
Crozet, Is., *Ind. Oc.* 3 G12
Crozon, *France* 18 D2
Cruz, C., *Cuba* 120 C4
Cruz Alta, *Brazil* 127 B5
Cruz de Incio, *Spain* 34 C3
Cruz del Eje, *Argentina* 126 C3
Cruzeiro, *Brazil* 127 A7
Cruzeiro do Oeste, *Brazil* 127 A5
Cruzeiro do Sul, *Brazil* 124 E4
Cry L., *Canada* 104 B3
Crystal Bay, *U.S.A.* 116 F7
Crystal Brook, *Australia* 95 E2
Crystal City, *U.S.A.* 113 L5
Crystal Falls, *U.S.A.* 108 B1
Crystal River, *U.S.A.* 109 L4
Crystal Springs, *U.S.A.* 113 K9
Csenger, *Hungary* 42 C7
Csongrád, *Hungary* 42 D5
Csongrád □, *Hungary* 42 D5
Csorna, *Hungary* 42 C2
Csurgo, *Hungary* 42 D2
Cu Lao Hon, *Vietnam* 65 G7
Cua Rao, *Vietnam* 64 C5
Cuácua →, *Mozam.* 87 F4
Cuamato, *Angola* 88 B2
Cuamba, *Mozam.* 87 E4
Cuando →, *Angola* 85 H4
Cuando Cubango □, *Angola* 88 B3
Cuangar, *Angola* 88 B2
Cuanza →, *Angola* 76 G5
Cuarto →, *Argentina* 126 C3
Cuatrociénegas, *Mexico* 118 B4
Cuauhtémoc, *Mexico* 118 B3
Cuba, *Portugal* 35 G3
Cuba, *N. Mex., U.S.A.* 115 J10
Cuba, *N.Y., U.S.A.* 110 D6
Cuba ■, *W. Indies* 120 B4
Cubango →, *Africa* 88 B3
Çubuk, *Turkey* 72 B5
Cuchumatanes, Sierra de los, *Guatemala* 120 C1
Cuckfield, *U.K.* 13 F7
Cucuí, *Brazil* 124 C5
Cucurpe, *Mexico* 118 A2
Cúcuta, *Colombia* 124 B4
Cudalbi, *Romania* 43 E12
Cuddalore, *India* 66 P11
Cuddapah, *India* 66 M11
Cuddapan, L., *Australia* 94 D3
Cudillero, *Spain* 34 B4
Cue, *Australia* 93 E2
Cuéllar, *Spain* 34 D6
Cuenca, *Ecuador* 124 D3
Cuenca, *Spain* 32 E2
Cuenca □, *Spain* 32 F3
Cuenca, Serranía de, *Spain* 32 F3
Cuerdo del Pozo, Embalse de la, *Spain* 32 D2
Cuernavaca, *Mexico* 119 D5
Cuero, *U.S.A.* 113 L6
Cuers, *France* 21 E10
Cuevas del Almanzora, *Spain* 33 H3
Cuevo, *Bolivia* 124 H6
Cugir, *Romania* 43 E8
Cugnaux, *France* 20 E5
Cuhai-Bakony →, *Hungary* 42 C2
Cuiabá, *Brazil* 125 G7
Cuiabá →, *Brazil* 125 G7
Cuijk, *Neths.* 17 C5
Cuilco, *Guatemala* 120 C1
Cuillin Hills, *U.K.* 14 D2
Cuillin Sd., *U.K.* 14 D2

Cuiseaux, *France* 19 F12
Cuito →, *Angola* 88 B3
Cuitzeo, L. de, *Mexico* 118 D4
Cujmir, *Romania* 42 F7
Cukai, *Malaysia* 65 K4
Culbertson, *U.S.A.* 112 A2
Culcairn, *Australia* 95 F4
Culebra, Sierra de la, *Spain* 34 D4
Culfa, *Azerbaijan* 73 C11
Culgoa →, *Australia* 95 D4
Culiacán, *Mexico* 118 C3
Culiacán →, *Mexico* 118 C3
Culion, *Phil.* 61 F4
Cúllar, *Spain* 35 H8
Cullarin Ra., *Australia* 95 E4
Cullen, *U.K.* 14 D6
Cullen Pt., *Australia* 94 A3
Cullera, *Spain* 33 F4
Cullman, *U.S.A.* 109 H2
Culoz, *France* 21 C9
Culpeper, *U.S.A.* 108 F7
Culuene →, *Brazil* 125 F8
Culver, Pt., *Australia* 93 F3
Culverden, *N.Z.* 91 K4
Cumaná, *Venezuela* 124 A6
Cumaovası, *Turkey* 39 C9
Cumberland, *B.C., Canada* 104 D4
Cumberland, *Ont., Canada* 111 A9
Cumberland, *U.S.A.* 108 F6
Cumberland →, *U.S.A.* 109 G2
Cumberland, L., *U.S.A.* 109 G3
Cumberland I., *U.S.A.* 109 K5
Cumberland Is., *Australia* 94 C4
Cumberland L., *Canada* 105 C8
Cumberland Pen., *Canada* 101 B13
Cumberland Plateau, *U.S.A.* 109 H3
Cumberland Sd., *Canada* 101 B13
Cumbernauld, *U.K.* 14 F5
Cumborah, *Australia* 95 D4
Cumbres Mayores, *Spain* 35 G4
Cumbria □, *U.K.* 12 C5
Cumbrian Mts., *U.K.* 12 C5
Cumbum, *India* 66 M11
Cuminá →, *Brazil* 125 D7
Cummings Mt., *U.S.A.* 117 K8
Cummins, *Australia* 95 E2
Cumnock, *Australia* 95 E4
Cumnock, *U.K.* 14 F4
Cumpas, *Mexico* 118 B3
Cumplida, Pta., *Canary Is.* 37 F2
Çumra, *Turkey* 72 D5
Cunco, *Chile* 128 D2
Cuncumén, *Chile* 126 C1
Cunderdin, *Australia* 93 F2
Cunene →, *Angola* 88 B1
Cúneo, *Italy* 28 D4
Çüngüş, *Turkey* 70 B3
Cunillera, I. = Sa Conillera, *Spain* 37 C7
Cunlhat, *France* 20 C7
Cunnamulla, *Australia* 95 D4
Cuorgnè, *Italy* 28 C4
Cupar, *Canada* 105 C8
Cupar, *U.K.* 14 E5
Cupcini, *Moldova* 43 B12
Cupica, G. de, *Colombia* 124 B3
Ćuprija, *Serbia, Yug.* 40 C5
Curaçao, *Neth. Ant.* 121 D6
Curanilahue, *Chile* 126 D1
Curaray →, *Peru* 124 D4
Cure →, *France* 19 E10
Curepto, *Chile* 126 D1
Curiapo, *Venezuela* 124 B6
Curicó, *Chile* 126 C1
Curinga, *Italy* 31 D9
Curitiba, *Brazil* 127 B6
Curitibanos, *Brazil* 127 B5
Currabubula, *Australia* 95 E5
Currais Novos, *Brazil* 125 E11
Curralinho, *Brazil* 125 D9
Currant, *U.S.A.* 114 G6
Current →, *U.S.A.* 113 G9
Currie, *Australia* 94 F3
Currie, *U.S.A.* 114 F6
Curtea de Argeş, *Romania* 43 E9
Curtici, *Romania* 42 D6
Curtis, *U.S.A.* 112 E4
Curtis Group, *Australia* 94 F4
Curtis I., *Australia* 94 C5
Curuápanema →, *Brazil* 125 D7
Curuçá, *Brazil* 125 D9
Curuguaty, *Paraguay* 127 A4
Curup, *Indonesia* 62 E2
Cururupu, *Brazil* 125 D10
Curuzú Cuatiá, *Argentina* 126 B4
Curvelo, *Brazil* 125 G10
Cushing, *U.S.A.* 113 H6
Cushing, Mt., *Canada* 104 B3
Cusihuiriáchic, *Mexico* 118 B3
Cusna, Mte., *Italy* 28 D7
Cusset, *France* 19 F10
Custer, *U.S.A.* 112 D3
Cut Bank, *U.S.A.* 114 B7
Cutchogue, *U.S.A.* 111 E12
Cuthbert, *U.S.A.* 109 K3
Cutler, *U.S.A.* 116 J7
Cutro, *Italy* 31 C9
Cuttaburra →, *Australia* 95 D3
Cuttack, *India* 67 J14
Cuvier, C., *Australia* 93 D1
Cuvier I., *N.Z.* 91 G5
Cuxhaven, *Germany* 24 B4
Cuyahoga Falls, *U.S.A.* 110 E3
Cuyapo, *Phil.* 61 D4
Cuyo, *Phil.* 61 F4
Cuyo East Pass, *Phil.* 61 F4
Cuyo West Pass, *Phil.* 61 F4
Cuyuni →, *Guyana* 124 B7
Cuzco, *Bolivia* 124 H5
Cuzco, *Peru* 124 F4
Čvrsnica, *Bos.-H.* 42 G2
Cwmbran, *U.K.* 13 F4
Cyangugu, *Rwanda* 86 C2
Cybinka, *Poland* 45 F1
Cyclades = Kikládhes, *Greece* 38 E6
Cygnet, *Australia* 94 G4
Cynthiana, *U.S.A.* 108 F3
Cypress Hills, *Canada* 105 D7
Cypress Hills Prov. Park, *Canada* 105 D7
Cyprus ■, *Asia* 36 E12
Cyrenaica, *Libya* 79 C10
Czaplinek, *Poland* 44 E3
Czar, *Canada* 105 C6
Czarna →, *Łódzkie, Poland* 45 G6
Czarna →, *Świętokrzyskie, Poland* 45 H8
Czarna Białostocka, *Poland* 45 E10
Czarna Woda, *Poland* 44 E5
Czarne, *Poland* 44 E3
Czarnków, *Poland* 45 F3
Czech Rep. ■, *Europe* 26 B8
Czechowice-Dziedzice, *Poland* 45 J5
Czempiń, *Poland* 45 F3
Czeremcha, *Poland* 45 F10
Czerniejewo, *Poland* 45 F4
Czersk, *Poland* 44 E4
Czerwieńsk, *Poland* 45 F2
Czerwionka-Leszczyny, *Poland* 45 H5
Częstochowa, *Poland* 45 H6
Człopa, *Poland* 45 E3
Człuchów, *Poland* 44 E4
Czyżew-Osada, *Poland* 45 F9

D

Da →, *Vietnam* 58 G5
Da Hinggan Ling, *China* 60 B7
Da Lat, *Vietnam* 65 G7
Da Nang, *Vietnam* 64 D7
Da Qaidam, *China* 60 C4
Da Yunhe →, *China* 57 G11
Da'an, *China* 57 B13
Dab'a, Ras el, *Egypt* 80 H6
Daba Shan, *China* 58 B7
Dabai, *Nigeria* 83 C6
Dabakala, *Ivory C.* 82 D4
Dabas, *Hungary* 42 C4
Dabat, *Ethiopia* 81 E4
Dabbagh, Jabal, *Si. Arabia* 70 E2
Dabhoi, *India* 68 H5
Dąbie, *Poland* 45 F5
Dabie Shan, *China* 59 B10
Dabilda, *Cameroon* 83 C7
Dabnou, *Niger* 83 C6
Dabo = Pasirkuning, *Indonesia* 62 E2
Dabola, *Guinea* 82 C2
Dabou, *Ivory C.* 82 D4
Daboya, *Ghana* 83 D4
Dąbrowa Białostocka, *Poland* 44 E10
Dąbrowa Górnicza, *Poland* 45 H6
Dąbrowa Tarnowska, *Poland* 45 H7
Dabu, *China* 59 E11
Dabung, *Malaysia* 65 K4
Dabus →, *Ethiopia* 81 E4
Dacato →, *Ethiopia* 81 F5
Dacca = Dhaka, *Bangla.* 69 H14
Dacca = Dhaka □, *Bangla.* 69 G14
Dachau, *Germany* 25 G7
Dachstein, Hoher, *Austria* 26 D6
Dačice, *Czech Rep.* 26 B8
Dadanawa, *Guyana* 124 C7
Daday, *Turkey* 72 B5
Dade City, *U.S.A.* 109 L4
Dadhar, *Pakistan* 68 E2
Dadiya, *Nigeria* 83 D7
Dadra & Nagar Haveli □, *India* 66 J8
Dadri = Charkhi Dadri, *India* 68 E7
Dadu, *Pakistan* 68 F2
Dadu He →, *China* 58 C4
Daet, *Phil.* 61 D5
Dafang, *China* 58 D5
Dağ, *Turkey* 39 D12
Dagana, *Senegal* 82 B1
Dagash, *Sudan* 80 D3
Dagestan □, *Russia* 49 J8
Dagestanskiye Ogni, *Russia* 49 J9
Daggett, *U.S.A.* 117 L10
Daghestan Republic = Dagestan □, *Russia* 49 J8
Daghfeli, *Sudan* 80 D3
Dağlıq Qarabağ = Nagorno-Karabakh, *Azerbaijan* 70 B5
Dagö = Hiiumaa, *Estonia* 9 G20
Dagu, *China* 57 E9
Daguan, *China* 58 D4
Dagupan, *Phil.* 61 C4
Daguragu, *Australia* 92 C5
Dahab, *Egypt* 80 B3
Dahlak Kebir, *Eritrea* 81 D5
Dahlenburg, *Germany* 24 B6
Dahlonega, *U.S.A.* 109 H4
Dahme, *Germany* 24 D9
Dahod, *India* 68 H6
Dahomey = Benin ■, *Africa* 83 D5
Dahong Shan, *China* 59 B9
Dahra, *Senegal* 82 B1
Dahshûr, *Egypt* 80 J7
Dahūk, *Iraq* 70 B3
Dai Hao, *Vietnam* 64 C6
Dai-Sen, *Japan* 55 G6
Dai Shan, *China* 59 B14
Dai Xian, *China* 56 E7
Daicheng, *China* 56 E9
Daimiel, *Spain* 35 F7
Daingean, *Ireland* 15 C4
Dainkog, *China* 58 A1
Daintree, *Australia* 94 B4
Daiō-Misaki, *Japan* 55 G8
Dair, J. ed, *Sudan* 81 E3
Dairût, *Egypt* 80 B3
Daisetsu-Zan, *Japan* 54 C11
Dajarra, *Australia* 94 C2
Dajin Chuan →, *China* 58 B3
Dak Dam, *Cambodia* 64 F6
Dak Nhe, *Vietnam* 64 E6
Dak Pek, *Vietnam* 64 E6
Dak Song, *Vietnam* 65 F6
Dak Sui, *Vietnam* 64 E6
Dakar, *Senegal* 82 C1
Dakhla, *W. Sahara* 78 D2
Dakhla, El Wâhât el-, *Egypt* 80 B2
Dakingari, *Nigeria* 83 C5
Dakor, *India* 68 H5
Dakoro, *Niger* 83 C6
Dakota City, *U.S.A.* 112 D6
Đakovica, *Kosovo, Yug.* 40 D4
Đakovo, *Croatia* 42 E3
Dalaba, *Guinea* 82 C2
Dalachi, *China* 56 F3
Dalai Nur, *China* 56 C9
Dālakī, *Iran* 71 D6
Dalälven, *Sweden* 10 D10
Dalaman, *Turkey* 39 E10
Dalaman →, *Turkey* 39 E10
Dalandzadgad, *Mongolia* 56 C3
Dalap-Uliga-Darrit, *Marshall Is.* 96 G9
Dalarna, *Sweden* 10 D8
Dālbandīn, *Pakistan* 66 E4
Dalbeattie, *U.K.* 14 G5
Dalbeg, *Australia* 94 C4
Dalbosjön, *Sweden* 11 F6
Dalby, *Australia* 95 D5
Dalby, *Sweden* 11 J7
Dale City, *U.S.A.* 108 F7
Dale Hollow L., *U.S.A.* 109 G3
Dalga, *Egypt* 80 B3
Dalgān, *Iran* 71 E8
Dalhart, *U.S.A.* 113 G3
Dalhousie, *Canada* 103 C6
Dalhousie, *India* 68 C6
Dali, *Shaanxi, China* 56 G5
Dali, *Yunnan, China* 58 E3
Dalian, *China* 57 E11
Daliang Shan, *China* 58 D4
Daling He →, *China* 57 D11
Dāliyat el Karmel, *Israel* 75 C4
Dalj, *Croatia* 42 E3
Dalkeith, *U.K.* 14 F5
Dallas, *Oreg., U.S.A.* 114 D2
Dallas, *Tex., U.S.A.* 113 J6
Dallol, *Ethiopia* 81 E5
Dalmā, *U.A.E.* 71 E7
Dalmacija, *Croatia* 29 E13
Dalmas, L., *Canada* 103 B5
Dalmatia = Dalmacija, *Croatia* 29 E13
Dalmau, *India* 69 F9
Dalmellington, *U.K.* 14 F4
Dalnegorsk, *Russia* 51 E14
Dalnerechensk, *Russia* 51 E14
Daloa, *Ivory C.* 82 D3
Dalou Shan, *China* 58 C6
Dalry, *U.K.* 14 F4
Dalrymple, L., *Australia* 94 C4
Dals Långed, *Sweden* 11 F6
Dalsjöfors, *Sweden* 11 G7
Dalsland, *Sweden* 11 F6
Daltenganj, *India* 69 H11
Dalton, *Ga., U.S.A.* 109 H3
Dalton, *Mass., U.S.A.* 111 D11
Dalton, *Nebr., U.S.A.* 112 E3
Dalton Iceberg Tongue, *Antarctica* 5 C9
Dalton-in-Furness, *U.K.* 12 C4
Dalupiri I., *Phil.* 61 B4
Dalvík, *Iceland* 8 D4
Dalwallinu, *Australia* 93 F2
Daly →, *Australia* 92 B5
Daly City, *U.S.A.* 116 H4
Daly L., *Canada* 105 B7
Daly River, *Australia* 92 B5
Daly Waters, *Australia* 94 B1
Dalyan, *Turkey* 39 E10
Dam Doi, *Vietnam* 65 H5
Dam Ha, *Vietnam* 64 B6
Daman, *India* 66 J8
Dāmaneh, *Iran* 71 C6
Damanhûr, *Egypt* 80 H7
Damant L., *Canada* 105 A7
Damanzhuang, *China* 56 E9
Damar, *Indonesia* 63 F7
Damaraland, *Namibia* 88 C2
Damascus = Dimashq, *Syria* 75 B5
Damaturu, *Nigeria* 83 C7
Damāvand, *Iran* 71 C7
Damāvand, Qolleh-ye, *Iran* 71 C7
Damba, *Angola* 84 F3
Dâmboviţa □, *Romania* 43 F10
Dâmboviţa →, *Romania* 43 F11
Dâmbovnic →, *Romania* 43 F10
Dame Marie, *Haiti* 121 C5
Dāmghān, *Iran* 71 B7
Dămienesti, *Romania* 43 D11
Damietta = Dumyât, *Egypt* 80 H7
Daming, *China* 56 F8
Damīr Qābū, *Syria* 70 B4
Dammam = Ad Dammām, *Si. Arabia* 71 E6
Dammarie-les-Lys, *France* 19 D9
Dammartin-en-Goële, *France* 19 C9
Damme, *Germany* 24 C4
Damodar →, *India* 69 H12
Damoh, *India* 69 H8
Dampier, *Australia* 92 D2
Dampier, Selat, *Indonesia* 63 E8
Dampier Arch., *Australia* 92 D2
Damrei, Chuor Phnum, *Cambodia* 65 G4
Damvillers, *France* 19 C12
Dan-Gulbi, *Nigeria* 83 C6
Dan Xian, *China* 64 C7
Dana, *Indonesia* 63 F6
Dana, L., *Canada* 102 B4
Dana, Mt., *U.S.A.* 116 H7
Danakil Depression, *Ethiopia* 81 E5
Danakil Desert, *Ethiopia* 81 E5
Danané, *Ivory C.* 82 D3
Danao, *Phil.* 61 F6
Danau Poso, *Indonesia* 63 E6
Danba, *China* 58 B3
Danbury, *U.S.A.* 111 E11
Danby L., *U.S.A.* 115 J6
Dand, *Afghan.* 68 D1
Dandeldhura, *Nepal* 69 E9
Dandeli, *India* 66 M9
Dandenong, *Australia* 95 F4
Dandīl, *Egypt* 80 J7
Dandong, *China* 57 D13
Danfeng, *China* 56 H6
Dangan Liedao, *China* 59 F10
Dangé-St-Roman, *France* 20 B4
Dângeni, *Romania* 43 C11
Danger Is. = Pukapuka, *Cook Is.* 97 J11
Danger Pt., *S. Africa* 88 E2
Dangla, *Ethiopia* 81 E4
Dangla Shan = Tanggula Shan, *China* 60 C4
Dangora, *Nigeria* 83 C6
Dangouadougou, *Burkina Faso* 82 D4
Dangrek, Phnom, *Thailand* 64 E5
Dangriga, *Belize* 119 D7
Dangshan, *China* 56 G9
Dangtu, *China* 59 B12
Dangyang, *China* 59 B8
Dani, *Burkina Faso* 83 C4
Daniel, *U.S.A.* 114 E8
Daniel's Harbour, *Canada* 103 B8
Danielskuil, *S. Africa* 88 D3
Danielson, *U.S.A.* 111 E13
Danilov, *Russia* 46 C11
Danilovgrad, *Montenegro, Yug.* 40 D3
Danilovka, *Russia* 48 E7
Daning, *China* 56 F6
Danissa, *Kenya* 86 B5
Danja, *Nigeria* 83 C6
Danjiangkou, *China* 59 A8
Danjiangkou Shuiku, *China* 59 A8
Dank, *Oman* 71 F8
Dankalwa, *Nigeria* 83 C7
Dankama, *Nigeria* 83 C6
Dankhar Gompa, *India* 66 C11
Dankov, *Russia* 46 F10
Danleng, *China* 58 B4
Danlí, *Honduras* 120 D2
Dannemora, *U.S.A.* 111 B11
Dannenberg, *Germany* 24 B7
Dannevirke, *N.Z.* 91 J6
Dannhauser, *S. Africa* 89 D5
Dansville, *U.S.A.* 110 D7
Danta, *India* 68 G5
Dantan, *India* 69 J12
Dante, *Somali Rep.* 74 E5
Danube = Dunărea →, *Europe* 43 E14
Danvers, *U.S.A.* 111 D14
Danville, *Ill., U.S.A.* 108 E2
Danville, *Ky., U.S.A.* 108 G3
Danville, *Pa., U.S.A.* 111 F8
Danville, *Va., U.S.A.* 109 G6
Danville, *Vt., U.S.A.* 111 B12
Danyang, *China* 59 B12
Danzhai, *China* 58 D6
Danzig = Gdańsk, *Poland* 44 D5
Dão →, *Portugal* 34 E2
Dao Xian, *China* 59 E8
Daocheng, *China* 58 C3
Daoukro, *Ivory C.* 82 D4
Dapaong, *Togo* 83 C5
Dapchi, *Nigeria* 83 C7
Dapitan, *Phil.* 61 G5
Daqing Shan, *China* 56 D6
Daqu Shan, *China* 59 B14
Dar Banda, *Africa* 76 F6
Dar el Beida = Casablanca, *Morocco* 78 B4
Dar es Salaam, *Tanzania* 86 D4
Dar Mazār, *Iran* 71 D8
Dar'ā, *Syria* 75 C5
Dar'ā □, *Syria* 75 C5
Dārāb, *Iran* 71 D7
Daraban, *Pakistan* 68 D4
Darabani, *Romania* 43 B11
Daraina, *Madag.* 89 A8
Daraj, *Libya* 79 B8
Dārān, *Iran* 71 C6
Daravica, *Kosovo, Yug.* 40 D4
Daraw, *Egypt* 80 C3
Dārayyā, *Syria* 75 B5
Darazo, *Nigeria* 83 C7
Darband, *Pakistan* 68 B5
Darband, Kūh-e, *Iran* 71 D8
Darbhanga, *India* 69 F11
D'Arcy, *Canada* 104 C4
Darda, *Croatia* 42 E3
Dardanelle, *Ark., U.S.A.* 113 H8
Dardanelle, *Calif., U.S.A.* 116 G7
Dardanelles = Çanakkale Boğazı, *Turkey* 41 F10
Dare →, *Ethiopia* 81 F5
Darende, *Turkey* 72 C7
Dārestān, *Iran* 71 D8
Darfo, *Italy* 28 C7
Dârfûr, *Sudan* 79 F10
Dargai, *Pakistan* 68 B4
Dargan Ata, *Uzbekistan* 50 E7
Dargaville, *N.Z.* 91 F4
Dargol, *Niger* 83 C5
Darhan Muminggan Lianheqi, *China* 56 D6
Dari, *Sudan* 81 F3
Darıca, *Turkey* 72 B3
Darién, G. del, *Colombia* 122 C3
Dariganga = Ovoot, *Mongolia* 56 B7
Darinskoye, *Kazakstan* 48 E10
Darjeeling = Darjiling, *India* 69 F13
Darjiling, *India* 69 F13
Darkan, *Australia* 93 F2
Darkhana, *Pakistan* 68 D5
Darkhazīneh, *Iran* 71 D6
Darkot Pass, *Pakistan* 69 A5
Darling →, *Australia* 95 E3
Darling Downs, *Australia* 95 D5
Darling Ra., *Australia* 93 F2
Darlington, *U.K.* 12 C6
Darlington, *U.S.A.* 109 H6
Darlington □, *U.K.* 12 C6
Darlington, L., *S. Africa* 88 E4
Darlington Point, *Australia* 95 E4
Darlot, L., *Australia* 93 E3
Darłowo, *Poland* 44 D3
Dărmăneşti, *Bacău, Romania* 43 D11
Dărmăneşti, *Suceava, Romania* 43 C11
Darmstadt, *Germany* 25 F4
Darnah, *Libya* 79 B10
Darnall, *S. Africa* 89 D5
Darney, *France* 19 D13
Darnley, C., *Antarctica* 5 C6
Darnley B., *Canada* 100 B7
Daroca, *Spain* 32 D3
Darou-Mousti, *Senegal* 82 B1
Darr →, *Australia* 94 C3
Darra Pezu, *Pakistan* 68 C4
Darrequeira, *Argentina* 126 D3
Darrington, *U.S.A.* 114 B3
Darsser Ort, *Germany* 24 A8
Dart →, *U.K.* 13 G4
Dart, C., *Antarctica* 5 D14
Dartford, *U.K.* 13 F8
Dartmoor, *U.K.* 13 G4
Dartmouth, *Canada* 103 D7
Dartmouth, *U.K.* 13 G4
Dartmouth, L., *Australia* 95 D4
Dartuch, C. = Artrutx, C. de, *Spain* 37 B10
Daruvar, *Croatia* 42 E2
Darvaza, *Turkmenistan* 50 E6
Darvel, Teluk = Lahad Datu, Teluk, *Malaysia* 63 D5
Darwen, *U.K.* 12 D5
Darwendale, *Zimbabwe* 89 B5
Darwha, *India* 66 J10
Darwin, *Australia* 92 B5
Darwin, *U.S.A.* 117 J9
Darya Khan, *Pakistan* 68 D4
Daryoi Amu = Amudarya →, *Uzbekistan* 50 E6
Dās, *U.A.E.* 71 E7
Dashen, Ras, *Ethiopia* 81 E4
Dashetai, *China* 56 D5
Dashhowuz, *Turkmenistan* 50 E6
Dashkesan = Daşkäsän, *Azerbaijan* 49 K7
Dashköpri, *Turkmenistan* 71 B9
Dasht, *Iran* 71 B8
Dasht →, *Pakistan* 66 G2
Daska, *Pakistan* 68 C6
Daşkäsän, *Azerbaijan* 49 K7
Dassa, *Benin* 83 D5
Dasuya, *India* 68 D6
Datça, *Turkey* 39 E9
Datia, *India* 69 G8
Datian, *China* 59 E11
Datong, *Anhui, China* 59 B11
Datong, *Shanxi, China* 56 D7
Dattakhel, *Pakistan* 68 C3
Datteln, *Germany* 24 D3
Datu, Tanjung, *Indonesia* 62 D3
Datu Piang, *Phil.* 61 H6
Daud Khel, *Pakistan* 68 C4
Daudnagar, *India* 69 G11
Daugava →, *Latvia* 9 H21
Daugavpils, *Latvia* 9 J22
Daulpur, *India* 68 F7
Daun, *Germany* 25 E2
Dauphin, *Canada* 105 C8
Dauphin, *U.S.A.* 110 F8
Dauphin L., *Canada* 105 C9
Dauphiné, *France* 21 C9
Daura, *Borno, Nigeria* 83 C7
Daura, *Katsina, Nigeria* 83 C6
Dausa, *India* 68 F7
Däväçi, *Azerbaijan* 49 K9
Davangere, *India* 66 M9
Davao, *Phil.* 61 H6
Davao G., *Phil.* 61 H6
Dāvar Panāh, *Iran* 71 E9
Davenport, *Calif., U.S.A.* 116 H4
Davenport, *Iowa, U.S.A.* 112 E9
Davenport, *Wash., U.S.A.* 114 C4
Davenport Ra., *Australia* 94 C1
Daventry, *U.K.* 13 E6
David, *Panama* 120 E3
David City, *U.S.A.* 112 E6
David Gorodok = Davyd Haradok, *Belarus* 47 F4
Davidson, *Canada* 105 C7
Davis, *U.S.A.* 116 G5
Davis Dam, *U.S.A.* 117 K12

Davis Inlet, Canada 103 A7
Davis Mts., U.S.A. 113 K2
Davis Sea, Antarctica 5 C7
Davis Str., N. Amer. 101 B14
Davo →, Ivory C. 82 D3
Davos, Switz. 25 J5
Davutlar, Turkey 39 D9
Davy L., Canada 105 B7
Davyd Haradok, Belarus 47 F4
Dawa →, Ethiopia 81 G5
Dawaki, Bauchi, Nigeria 83 D6
Dawaki, Kano, Nigeria 83 C6
Dawei, Burma 64 E2
Dawes Ra., Australia 94 C5
Dawlish, U.K. 13 G4
Dawros Hd., Ireland 15 B3
Dawson, Canada 100 B6
Dawson, U.S.A. 109 K3
Dawson, I., Chile 128 G2
Dawson B., Canada 105 C8
Dawson Creek, Canada 104 B4
Dawson Inlet, Canada 105 A10
Dawson Ra., Australia 94 C4
Dawu, Hubei, China 59 B9
Dawu, Sichuan, China 58 B3
Dax, France 20 E2
Daxian, China 58 B6
Daxin, China 58 F6
Daxindian, China 57 F11
Daxinggou, China 57 C15
Daxue Shan, Sichuan, China 58 B3
Daxue Shan, Yunnan, China 58 F2
Dayao, China 58 E3
Daye, China 59 B10
Dayet en Naharat, Mali 82 B4
Dayi, China 58 B4
Daylesford, Australia 95 F3
Dayong, China 59 C8
Dayr az Zawr, Syria 70 C4
Daysland, Canada 104 C6
Dayton, Nev., U.S.A. 116 F7
Dayton, Ohio, U.S.A. 108 F3
Dayton, Pa., U.S.A. 110 F5
Dayton, Tenn., U.S.A. 109 H3
Dayton, Wash., U.S.A. 114 C4
Dayton, Wyo., U.S.A. 114 D10
Daytona Beach, U.S.A. 109 L5
Dayu, China 59 E10
Dayville, U.S.A. 114 D4
Dazhu, China 58 B6
Dazkırı, Turkey 39 D11
Dazu, China 58 C5
De Aar, S. Africa 88 E3
De Funiak Springs, U.S.A. 109 K2
De Grey →, Australia 92 D2
De Haan, Belgium 17 C3
De Kalb, U.S.A. 112 E10
De Land, U.S.A. 109 L5
De Leon, U.S.A. 113 J5
De Panne, Belgium 17 C2
De Pere, U.S.A. 108 C1
De Queen, U.S.A. 113 H7
De Quincy, U.S.A. 113 K8
De Ridder, U.S.A. 113 K8
De Smet, U.S.A. 112 C6
De Soto, U.S.A. 112 F9
De Tour Village, U.S.A. 108 C4
De Witt, U.S.A. 113 H9
Dead Sea, Asia 75 D4
Deadwood, U.S.A. 112 C3
Deadwood L., Canada 104 B3
Deal, U.K. 13 F9
Deal I., Australia 94 F4
Dealesville, S. Africa 88 D4
De'an, China 59 C10
Dean →, Canada 104 C3
Dean, Forest of, U.K. 13 F5
Dean Chan., Canada 104 C3
Deán Funes, Argentina 126 C3
Dease →, Canada 104 B3
Dease L., Canada 104 B2
Dease Lake, Canada 104 B2
Death Valley, U.S.A. 117 J10
Death Valley Junction, U.S.A. 117 J10
Death Valley National Park, U.S.A. 117 J10
Deauville, France 18 C7
Deba, Spain 32 B2
Deba Habe, Nigeria 83 C7
Debaltsevo, Ukraine 47 H10
Debao, China 58 F6
Debar, Macedonia 40 E4
Debden, Canada 105 C7
Dębica, Poland 45 H8
Dęblin, Poland 45 G8
Dębno, Poland 45 F1
Débo, L., Mali 82 B4
Debolt, Canada 104 B5
Deborah East, L., Australia 93 F2
Deborah West, L., Australia 93 F2
Debrc, Serbia, Yug. 40 B3
Debre Birhan, Ethiopia 81 F4
Debre Markos, Ethiopia 81 E4
Debre May, Ethiopia 81 E4
Debre Sina, Ethiopia 81 F4
Debre Tabor, Ethiopia 81 E4
Debre Zevit, Ethiopia 81 F4
Debre Zeyit, Ethiopia 81 E4
Debrecen, Hungary 42 C6
Debrzno, Poland 44 E4
Dečani, Kosovo, Yug. 40 D4
Decatur, Ala., U.S.A. 109 H2
Decatur, Ga., U.S.A. 109 J3
Decatur, Ill., U.S.A. 112 F10
Decatur, Ind., U.S.A. 108 E3
Decatur, Tex., U.S.A. 113 J6
Decazeville, France 20 D6
Deccan, India 66 L11
Deception Bay, Australia 95 D5
Deception L., Canada 105 B8
Dechang, China 58 D4
Dechhu, India 68 F5
Děčín, Czech Rep. 26 A7
Decize, France 19 F10
Deckerville, U.S.A. 110 C2
Decollatura, Italy 31 C9
Decorah, U.S.A. 112 D9
Deda, Romania 43 D9
Dedéagach = Alexandroúpolis, Greece 41 F9
Deder, Ethiopia 81 F5
Dedham, U.S.A. 111 D13
Dédougou, Burkina Faso 82 C4
Dedovichi, Russia 46 D5
Dedza, Malawi 87 E3
Dee →, Aberds., U.K. 14 D6
Dee →, Dumf. & Gall., U.K. 14 G4
Dee →, Wales, U.K. 12 D4
Deep B., Canada 104 A5
Deepwater, Australia 95 D5
Deer →, Canada 105 B10
Deer L., Canada 105 C10
Deer Lake, Nfld., Canada 103 C8
Deer Lake, Ont., Canada 105 C10
Deer Lodge, U.S.A. 114 C7
Deer Park, U.S.A. 114 C5
Deer River, U.S.A. 112 B8
Deeragun, Australia 94 B4
Deerdepoort, S. Africa 88 C4
Deferiet, U.S.A. 111 B9
Defiance, U.S.A. 108 E3
Degana, India 68 F6
Dêgê, China 58 B2
Degebe →, Portugal 35 G3
Degeberga, Sweden 11 J8
Dégelis, Canada 103 C6
Degema, Nigeria 83 E6
Degerfors, Sweden 10 E8
Degerhamn, Sweden 11 H10
Deggendorf, Germany 25 G8
Degh →, Pakistan 68 D5
Değirmendere, Turkey 41 F13
Deh Bīd, Iran 71 D7
Deh-e Shīr, Iran 71 D7
Dehaj, Iran 71 D7
Dehak, Iran 71 E9
Dehdez, Iran 71 D6
Dehej, India 68 J5
Dehestān, Iran 71 D7
Dehgolān, Iran 70 C5
Dehi Titan, Afghan. 66 C3
Dehibat, Tunisia 79 B8
Dehlorān, Iran 70 C5
Dehnow-e Kūhestān, Iran 71 E8
Dehra Dun, India 68 D8
Dehri, India 69 G11
Dehua, China 59 E12
Dehui, China 57 B13
Deim Zubeir, Sudan 81 F2
Deinze, Belgium 17 D3
Dej, Romania 43 C8
Deje, Sweden 10 E7
Dejiang, China 58 C7
Deka →, S. Africa 88 B4
Dekemhare, Eritrea 81 D4
Dekese, Dem. Rep. of the Congo 84 E4
Del Mar, U.S.A. 117 N9
Del Norte, U.S.A. 115 H10
Del Rio, U.S.A. 113 L4
Delai, Sudan 80 D4
Delambre I., Australia 92 D2
Delami, Sudan 81 E3
Delano, U.S.A. 117 K7
Delano Peak, U.S.A. 115 G7
Delareyville, S. Africa 88 D4
Delaronde L., Canada 105 C7
Delavan, U.S.A. 112 D10
Delaware, U.S.A. 108 E4
Delaware □, U.S.A. 108 F8
Delaware →, U.S.A. 111 G9
Delaware B., U.S.A. 108 F8
Delay →, Canada 103 A5
Delbrück, Germany 24 D4
Delčevo, Macedonia 40 E6
Delegate, Australia 95 F4
Delémont, Switz. 25 H3
Delevan, U.S.A. 110 D6
Delft, Neths. 17 B4
Delfzijl, Neths. 17 A6
Delgado, C., Mozam. 87 E5
Delgerhet, Mongolia 56 B6
Delgo, Sudan 80 C3
Delhi, Canada 110 D4
Delhi, India 68 E7
Delhi, La., U.S.A. 113 J9
Delhi, N.Y., U.S.A. 111 D10
Deli Jovan, Serbia, Yug. 40 B6
Delia, Canada 104 C6
Delice, Turkey 72 C6
Delicias, Mexico 118 B3
Delījān, Iran 71 C6
Déline, Canada 100 B7
Delisle, Canada 105 C7
Delitzsch, Germany 24 D8
Dell City, U.S.A. 115 L11
Dell Rapids, U.S.A. 112 D6
Delle, France 19 E14
Delmar, U.S.A. 111 D11
Delmenhorst, Germany 24 B4
Delnice, Croatia 29 C11
Delong, Ostrova, Russia 51 B15
Deloraine, Australia 94 G4
Deloraine, Canada 105 D8
Delphi, Greece 38 C4
Delphi, U.S.A. 108 E2
Delphos, U.S.A. 108 E3
Delportshoop, S. Africa 88 D3
Delray Beach, U.S.A. 109 M5
Delsbo, Sweden 10 C10
Delta, Colo., U.S.A. 115 G9
Delta, Utah, U.S.A. 114 G7
Delta □, Nigeria 83 D6
Delta Junction, U.S.A. 100 B5
Deltona, U.S.A. 109 L5
Delungra, Australia 95 D5
Delvada, India 68 J4
Delvinákion, Greece 38 B2
Delvinë, Albania 40 G4
Demak, Indonesia 63 G14
Demanda, Sierra de la, Spain 32 C2
Demavand = Damāvand, Iran 71 C7
Dembecha, Ethiopia 81 E4
Dembi, Ethiopia 81 F4
Dembia, Dem. Rep. of the Congo 86 B2
Dembidolo, Ethiopia 81 F3
Demchok, India 69 C8
Demer →, Belgium 17 D4
Demetrias, Greece 38 B5
Demidov, Russia 46 E6
Deming, N. Mex., U.S.A. 115 K10
Deming, Wash., U.S.A. 116 B4
Demini →, Brazil 124 D6
Demirci, Turkey 39 B10
Demirköprü Barajı, Turkey 39 C10
Demirköy, Turkey 41 E11
Demmin, Germany 24 B9
Demonte, Italy 28 D4
Demopolis, U.S.A. 109 J2
Dempo, Indonesia 62 E2
Demyansk, Russia 46 D7
Den Burg, Neths. 17 A4
Den Chai, Thailand 64 D3
Den Haag = 's-Gravenhage, Neths. 17 B4
Den Helder, Neths. 17 B4
Den Oever, Neths. 17 B5
Denain, France 19 B10
Denair, U.S.A. 116 H6
Denau, Uzbekistan 50 F7
Denbigh, Canada 110 A7
Denbigh, U.K. 12 D4
Denbighshire □, U.K. 12 D4
Dendang, Indonesia 62 E3
Dendermonde, Belgium 17 C4
Deneba, Ethiopia 81 F4
Dengchuan, China 58 E3
Denge, Nigeria 83 C6
Dengfeng, China 56 G7
Dengi, Nigeria 83 D6
Dengkou, China 56 D4
Dengzhou, China 59 A9
Denham, Australia 93 E1
Denham Ra., Australia 94 C4
Denham Sd., Australia 93 E1
Denholm, Canada 105 C7
Denia, Spain 33 G5
Denial B., Australia 95 E1
Deniliquin, Australia 95 F3
Denison, Iowa, U.S.A. 112 E7
Denison, Tex., U.S.A. 113 J6
Denison Plains, Australia 92 C4
Denizli, Turkey 39 D11
Denizli □, Turkey 39 D11
Denman Glacier, Antarctica 5 C7
Denmark, Australia 93 F2
Denmark ■, Europe 11 J3
Denmark Str., Atl. Oc. 4 C6
Dennison, U.S.A. 110 F3
Denny, U.K. 14 E5
Denpasar, Indonesia 62 F5
Denton, Mont., U.S.A. 114 C9
Denton, Tex., U.S.A. 113 J6
D'Entrecasteaux, Pt., Australia 93 F2
Denu, Ghana 83 D5
Denver, Colo., U.S.A. 112 F2
Denver, Pa., U.S.A. 111 F8
Denver City, U.S.A. 113 J3
Deoband, India 68 E7
Deogarh, India 68 G5
Deoghar, India 69 G12
Deolali, India 66 K8
Deoli = Devli, India 68 G6
Déols, France 19 F8
Deora, India 68 F4
Deori, India 69 H8
Deoria, India 69 F10
Deosai Mts., Pakistan 69 B6
Deosri, India 69 F14
Depalpur, India 68 H6
Deping, China 57 F9
Deposit, U.S.A. 111 D9
Depuch I., Australia 92 D2
Deputatskiy, Russia 51 C14
Dêqên, China 58 C2
Deqing, China 59 F8
Dera Ghazi Khan, Pakistan 68 D4
Dera Ismail Khan, Pakistan 68 D4
Derabugti, Pakistan 68 E3
Derawar Fort, Pakistan 68 E4
Derbent, Russia 49 J9
Derbent, Turkey 39 C10
Derby, Australia 92 C3
Derby, U.K. 12 E6
Derby, Conn., U.S.A. 111 E11
Derby, Kans., U.S.A. 113 G6
Derby, N.Y., U.S.A. 110 D6
Derby City □, U.K. 12 E6
Derby Line, U.S.A. 111 B12
Derbyshire □, U.K. 12 D6
Derecske, Hungary 42 C6
Dereköy, Turkey 41 E11
Dereli, Turkey 73 B8
Derg →, U.K. 15 B4
Derg, L., Ireland 15 D3
Dergachi = Derhaci, Ukraine 47 G9
Dergaon, India 67 F19
Derhaci, Ukraine 47 G9
Derik, Turkey 73 D9
Derinkuyu, Turkey 72 C6
Dermantsi, Bulgaria 41 C8
Dermott, U.S.A. 113 J9
Dêrong, China 58 C2
Derry = Londonderry, U.K. 15 B4
Derry = Londonderry □, U.K. 15 B4
Derry, N.H., U.S.A. 111 D13
Derry, Pa., U.S.A. 110 F5
Derryveagh Mts., Ireland 15 B3
Derudub, Sudan 80 D4
Derval, France 18 E5
Dervéni, Greece 38 C4
Derventa, Bos.-H. 42 F2
Derwent →, Cumb., U.K. 12 C4
Derwent →, Derby, U.K. 12 E6
Derwent →, N. Yorks., U.K. 12 D7
Derwent Water, U.K. 12 C4
Des Moines, Iowa, U.S.A. 112 E8
Des Moines, N. Mex., U.S.A. 113 G3
Des Moines →, U.S.A. 112 E9
Desa, Romania 42 G8
Desaguadero →, Argentina 126 C2
Desaguadero →, Bolivia 124 G5
Descanso, Pta., Mexico 117 N9
Descartes, France 20 B4
Deschaillons, Canada 103 C5
Deschambault L., Canada 105 C8
Deschutes →, U.S.A. 114 D3
Dese, Ethiopia 81 E4
Deseado →, Argentina 128 F3
Desenzano del Garda, Italy 28 C7
Desert Center, U.S.A. 117 M11
Desert Hot Springs, U.S.A. 117 M10
Deshnok, India 68 F5
Desna →, Ukraine 47 G6
Desnătui →, Romania 43 G8
Desolación, I., Chile 128 G2
Despeñaperros, Paso, Spain 35 G7
Despotovac, Serbia, Yug. 40 B5
Dessau, Germany 24 D8
Dessye = Dese, Ethiopia 81 E4
D'Estrees B., Australia 95 F2
Desuri, India 68 G5
Desvres, France 19 B8
Det Udom, Thailand 64 E5
Deta, Romania 42 E6
Dete, S. Africa 88 B4
Dete, Zimbabwe 87 F2
Đetinja →, Serbia, Yug. 40 C4
Detmold, Germany 24 D4
Detour, Pt., U.S.A. 108 C2
Detroit, U.S.A. 110 D1
Detroit Lakes, U.S.A. 112 B7
Detva, Slovak Rep. 27 C12
Deurne, Neths. 17 C5
Deutsche Bucht, Germany 24 A4
Deutschlandsberg, Austria 26 E8
Deux-Sèvres □, France 18 F6
Deva, Romania 42 E7
Devakottai, India 66 Q11
Devaprayag, India 69 D8
Dévaványa, Hungary 42 C5
Deveci Dağları, Turkey 72 B7
Devecikonağı, Turkey 41 G12
Devecser, Hungary 42 C2
Develi, Turkey 72 C6
Deventer, Neths. 17 B6
Deveron →, U.K. 14 D6
Devesel, Romania 42 F7
Devgadh Bariya, India 68 H5
Devikot, India 68 F4
Devils Den, U.S.A. 116 K7
Devils Lake, U.S.A. 112 A5
Devils Paw, Canada 104 B2
Devils Tower Junction, U.S.A. 112 C2
Devin, Bulgaria 41 E8
Devine, U.S.A. 113 L5
Devizes, U.K. 13 F6
Devli, India 68 G6
Devnya, Bulgaria 41 C11
Devolii →, Albania 40 F4
Devon, Canada 104 C6
Devon □, U.K. 13 G4
Devon I., Canada 4 B3
Devonport, Australia 94 G4
Devonport, N.Z. 91 G5
Devrek, Turkey 72 B4
Devrekâni, Turkey 72 B5
Devrez →, Turkey 72 B6
Dewas, India 68 H7
Dewetsdorp, S. Africa 88 D4
Dexing, China 59 C11
Dexter, Maine, U.S.A. 109 C11
Dexter, Mo., U.S.A. 113 G10
Dexter, N. Mex., U.S.A. 113 J2
Dey-Dey, L., Australia 93 E5
Deyang, China 58 B5
Deyhūk, Iran 71 C8
Deyyer, Iran 71 E6
Dezadeash L., Canada 104 A1
Dezfūl, Iran 71 C6
Dezhneva, Mys, Russia 51 C19
Dezhou, China 56 F9
Dhadhar →, India 69 G11
Dháfni, Kríti, Greece 36 D7
Dháfni, Pelóponnisos, Greece 38 D4
Dhahabān, Si. Arabia 80 C4
Dhahiriya = Az̧ Z̧āhirīyah, West Bank 75 D3
Dhahran = Az̧ Z̧ahrān, Si. Arabia 71 E6
Dhak, Pakistan 68 C5
Dhaka, Bangla. 69 H14
Dhaka □, Bangla. 69 G14
Dhali, Cyprus 36 D12
Dhamási, Greece 38 B4
Dhampur, India 69 E8
Dhamtari, India 67 J12
Dhanbad, India 69 H12
Dhangarhi, Nepal 67 E12
Dhankuta, Nepal 69 F12
Dhar, India 68 H6
Dharampur, India 68 H6
Dharamsala = Dharmsala, India 68 C7
Dhariwal, India 68 D6
Dharla →, Bangla. 69 G13
Dharmapuri, India 66 N11
Dharmjaygarh, India 69 H10
Dharmsala, India 68 C7
Dharni, India 68 J7
Dhasan →, India 69 G8
Dhaulagiri, Nepal 69 E10
Dhebar, L., India 68 G6
Dheftera, Cyprus 36 D12
Dhenkanal, India 67 J14
Dhenoúsa, Greece 39 D7
Dherinia, Cyprus 36 D12
Dheskáti, Greece 40 G5
Dhespotikó, Greece 38 E6
Dhestina, Greece 38 C4
Dhiarrizos →, Cyprus 36 E11
Dhībān, Jordan 75 D4
Dhidhimótikhon, Greece 41 E10
Dhíkti Óros, Greece 36 D7
Dhilianáta, Greece 38 C2
Dhílos, Greece 39 D7
Dhilwan, India 68 D6
Dhimarkhera, India 69 H9
Dhimitsána, Greece 38 D4
Dhírfis = Dhírfis Óros, Greece 38 C5
Dhírfis Óros, Greece 38 C5
Dhodhekánisos, Greece 39 E8
Dhodhekánisos □, Greece 39 E8
Dhokós, Greece 38 D5
Dholiana, Greece 38 B2
Dholka, India 68 H5
Dhomokós, Greece 38 B4
Dhoraji, India 68 J4
Dhoxáton, Greece 41 E8
Dhragonísi, Greece 39 D7
Dhráhstis, Ákra, Greece 36 A3
Dhrangadhra, India 68 H4
Dhrápanon, Ákra, Greece 36 D6
Dhriopís, Greece 38 D6
Dhrol, India 68 H4
Dhuburi, India 67 F16
Dhule, India 66 J9
Di-ib, W. →, Sudan 80 C4
Di Linh, Vietnam 65 G7
Di Linh, Cao Nguyen, Vietnam 65 G7
Día, Greece 36 D7
Diabakania, Guinea 82 C2
Diablo, Mt., U.S.A. 116 H5
Diablo Range, U.S.A. 116 J5
Diafarabé, Mali 82 C4
Diala, Mali 82 C3
Dialakoro, Mali 82 C3
Dialakoto, Senegal 82 C2
Diallassagou, Mali 82 C4
Diamante, Argentina 126 C3
Diamante, Italy 31 C8
Diamante →, Argentina 126 C2
Diamantina, Brazil 125 G10
Diamantina →, Australia 95 D2
Diamantino, Brazil 125 F7
Diamond Bar, U.S.A. 117 L9
Diamond Harbour, India 69 H13
Diamond Is., Australia 94 B5
Diamond Mts., U.S.A. 114 G6
Diamond Springs, U.S.A. 116 G6
Dian Chi, China 58 E4
Dianalund, Denmark 11 J5
Dianbai, China 59 G8
Diancheng, China 59 G8
Dianjiang, China 58 B6
Diano Marina, Italy 28 E5
Dianra, Ivory C. 82 D3
Diapaga, Burkina Faso 83 C5
Diapangou, Burkina Faso 83 C5
Diariguila, Guinea 82 C2
Dībā, Oman 71 E8
Dibai, India 68 E8
Dibaya-Lubue, Dem. Rep. of the Congo 84 E3
Dibete, Botswana 88 C4
Dibrugarh, India 67 F19
Dickens, U.S.A. 113 J4
Dickinson, U.S.A. 112 B3
Dickson = Dikson, Russia 50 B9
Dickson, U.S.A. 109 G2
Dickson City, U.S.A. 111 E9
Dicle Nehri →, Turkey 73 D9
Dicomano, Italy 29 E8
Didesa, W. →, Ethiopia 81 E4
Didi, Sudan 81 F3
Didiéni, Mali 82 C3
Didsbury, Canada 104 C6
Didwana, India 68 F6
Die, France 21 D9
Diébougou, Burkina Faso 82 C4
Diecke, Guinea 82 D3
Diefenbaker, L., Canada 105 C7
Diego de Almagro, Chile 126 B1
Diego Garcia, Ind. Oc. 3 E13
Diekirch, Lux. 17 E6
Diéma, Mali 82 C3
Diembéring, Senegal 82 C1
Dien Ban, Vietnam 64 E7
Dien Bien, Vietnam 58 G4
Dien Khanh, Vietnam 65 F7
Diepholz, Germany 24 C4
Dieppe, France 18 C8
Dierks, U.S.A. 113 H8
Diest, Belgium 17 D5

Dietikon, *Switz.* 25 H4
Dieulefit, *France* 21 D9
Dieuze, *France* 19 D13
Dif, *Somali Rep.* 74 G3
Differdange, *Lux.* 17 E5
Dig, *India* 68 F7
Digba, *Dem. Rep. of the Congo* 86 B2
Digby, *Canada* 103 D6
Diggi, *India* 68 F6
Dighinala, *Bangla.* 67 H18
Dighton, *U.S.A.* 112 F4
Digna, *Mali* 82 C3
Digne-les-Bains, *France* 21 D10
Digoin, *France* 19 F11
Digor, *Turkey* 73 B10
Digos, *Phil.* 61 H6
Digranes, *Iceland* 8 C6
Digul →, *Indonesia* 63 F9
Dihang →, *India* 67 F19
Dijlah, Nahr →, *Asia* 70 D5
Dijon, *France* 19 E12
Dikhil, *Djibouti* 81 E5
Dikili, *Turkey* 39 B8
Dikirnis, *Egypt* 80 H7
Dikkil = Dikhil, *Djibouti* 81 E5
Dikodougou, *Ivory C.* 82 D3
Diksmuide, *Belgium* 17 C2
Dikson, *Russia* 50 B9
Dikwa, *Nigeria* 83 C7
Dila, *Ethiopia* 81 F4
Dili, *Indonesia* 63 F7
Dilijan, *Armenia* 49 K7
Dilizhan = Dilijan, *Armenia* 49 K7
Dilj, *Croatia* 42 E3
Dillenburg, *Germany* 24 E4
Dilley, *U.S.A.* 113 L5
Dilling, *Sudan* 81 E2
Dillingen, *Bayern, Germany* 25 G6
Dillingen, *Saarland, Germany* 25 F2
Dillingham, *U.S.A.* 100 C4
Dillon, *Canada* 105 B7
Dillon, *Mont., U.S.A.* 114 D7
Dillon, *S.C., U.S.A.* 109 H6
Dillon →, *Canada* 105 B7
Dillsburg, *U.S.A.* 110 F7
Dilly, *Mali* 82 C3
Dilolo, *Dem. Rep. of the Congo* 84 G4
Dimas, *Mexico* 118 C3
Dimashq, *Syria* 75 B5
Dimashq □, *Syria* 75 B5
Dimbaza, *S. Africa* 89 E4
Dimbokro, *Ivory C.* 82 D4
Dimboola, *Australia* 95 F3
Dîmboviţa = Dâmboviţa →, *Romania* 43 F11
Dimbulah, *Australia* 94 B4
Dimitrovgrad, *Bulgaria* 41 D9
Dimitrovgrad, *Russia* 48 C9
Dimitrovgrad, *Serbia, Yug.* 40 C6
Dimitrovo = Pernik, *Bulgaria* 40 D7
Dimmitt, *U.S.A.* 113 H3
Dimo, *Sudan* 81 F2
Dimona, *Israel* 75 D4
Dimovo, *Bulgaria* 40 C6
Dinagat, *Phil.* 61 F6
Dinajpur, *Bangla.* 67 G16
Dinan, *France* 18 D4
Dīnān Āb, *Iran* 71 C8
Dinant, *Belgium* 17 D4
Dinapur, *India* 69 G11
Dinar, *Turkey* 39 C12
Dīnār, Kūh-e, *Iran* 71 D6
Dinara Planina, *Croatia* 29 D13
Dinard, *France* 18 D4
Dinaric Alps = Dinara Planina, *Croatia* 29 D13
Dindanko, *Mali* 82 C3
Dinder, Nahr ed →, *Sudan* 81 E3
Dindigul, *India* 66 P11
Dindori, *India* 69 H9
Ding Xian = Dingzhou, *China* 56 E8
Dinga, *Pakistan* 68 G2
Dingalan, *Phil.* 61 D4
Dingbian, *China* 56 F4
Dingelstädt, *Germany* 24 D6
Dingle, *Ireland* 15 D1
Dingle, *Sweden* 11 F5
Dingle B., *Ireland* 15 D1
Dingmans Ferry, *U.S.A.* 111 E10
Dingnan, *China* 59 E10
Dingo, *Australia* 94 C4
Dingolfing, *Germany* 25 G8
Dingtao, *China* 56 G8
Dinguira, *Mali* 82 C2
Dinguiraye, *Guinea* 82 C2
Dingwall, *U.K.* 14 D4
Dingxi, *China* 56 G3
Dingxiang, *China* 56 E7
Dingyuan, *China* 59 A11
Dingzhou, *China* 56 E8
Dinh, Mui, *Vietnam* 65 G7
Dinh Lap, *Vietnam* 58 G6
Dinokwe, *Botswana* 88 C4
Dinorwic, *Canada* 105 D10
Dinosaur National Monument, *U.S.A.* 114 F9
Dinosaur Prov. Park, *Canada* 104 C6
Dinuba, *U.S.A.* 116 J7
Diö, *Sweden* 11 H8
Dioïla, *Mali* 82 C3
Dioka, *Mali* 82 C2
Diongoï, *Mali* 82 C3
Diósgyör, *Hungary* 42 B5
Diosig, *Romania* 42 C7
Diougani, *Mali* 82 C4
Diouloulou, *Senegal* 82 C1
Dioura, *Mali* 82 C3
Diourbel, *Senegal* 82 C1
Dipalpur, *Pakistan* 68 D5
Diplo, *Pakistan* 68 G3
Dipolog, *Phil.* 61 G5
Dir, *Pakistan* 66 B7
Diré, *Mali* 82 B4
Dire Dawa, *Ethiopia* 81 F5
Diriamba, *Nic.* 120 D2
Dirk Hartog I., *Australia* 93 E1
Dirranbandi, *Australia* 95 D4
Disa, *India* 68 G5
Disa, *Sudan* 81 E3
Disappointment, C., *U.S.A.* 114 C2
Disappointment, L., *Australia* 92 D3
Disaster B., *Australia* 95 F4
Discovery B., *Australia* 95 F3
Disentis Muster, *Switz.* 25 J4
Dishna, *Egypt* 80 B3
Disina, *Nigeria* 83 C6
Disko = Qeqertarsuaq, *Greenland* 4 C5
Disko Bugt, *Greenland* 4 C5
Disna = Dzisna →, *Belarus* 46 E5
Diss, *U.K.* 13 E9
Disteghil Sar, *Pakistan* 69 A6
Distrito Federal □, *Brazil* 125 G9
Distrito Federal □, *Mexico* 119 D5
Disūq, *Egypt* 80 H7
Diu, *India* 68 J4
Dīvāndarreh, *Iran* 70 C5
Dives →, *France* 18 C6
Dives-sur-Mer, *France* 18 C6
Divichi = Däväçi, *Azerbaijan* 49 K9
Divide, *U.S.A.* 114 D7
Dividing Ra., *Australia* 93 E2
Divinópolis, *Brazil* 125 H10
Divjake, *Albania* 40 F3
Divnoye, *Russia* 49 H6
Divo, *Ivory C.* 82 D3
Divriği, *Turkey* 73 C8
Dīwāl Kol, *Afghan.* 68 B2
Dixie Mt., *U.S.A.* 116 F6
Dixon, *Calif., U.S.A.* 116 G5
Dixon, *Ill., U.S.A.* 112 E10
Dixon Entrance, *U.S.A.* 100 C6
Dixville, *Canada* 111 A13
Diyadin, *Turkey* 73 C10
Diyālā →, *Iraq* 70 C5
Diyarbakır, *Turkey* 70 B4
Diyodar, *India* 68 G4
Djakarta = Jakarta, *Indonesia* 63 G12
Djamba, *Angola* 88 B1
Djambala, *Congo* 84 E2
Djanet, *Algeria* 78 D7
Djawa = Jawa, *Indonesia* 63 G14
Djelfa, *Algeria* 78 B6
Djema, *C.A.R.* 86 A2
Djenné, *Mali* 82 C4
Djerba, I. de, *Tunisia* 79 B8
Djerid, Chott, *Tunisia* 78 B7
Djibo, *Burkina Faso* 83 C4
Djibouti, *Djibouti* 81 E5
Djibouti ■, *Africa* 81 E5
Djolu, *Dem. Rep. of the Congo* 84 D4
Djougou, *Benin* 83 D5
Djoum, *Cameroon* 84 D2
Djourab, Erg du, *Chad* 79 E9
Djugu, *Dem. Rep. of the Congo* 86 B3
Djúpivogur, *Iceland* 8 D6
Djurås, *Sweden* 10 D9
Djursland, *Denmark* 11 H4
Dmitriya Lapteva, Proliv, *Russia* 51 B15
Dmitriyev Lgovskiy, *Russia* 47 F8
Dmitrov, *Russia* 46 D9
Dmitrovsk-Orlovskiy, *Russia* 47 F8
Dnepr → = Dnipro →, *Ukraine* 47 J7
Dneprodzerzhinsk = Dniprodzerzhynsk, *Ukraine* 47 H8
Dneprodzerzhinskoye Vdkhr. = Dniprodzerzhynske Vdskh., *Ukraine* 47 H8
Dnepropetrovsk = Dnipropetrovsk, *Ukraine* 47 H8
Dneprorudnoye = Dniprorudne, *Ukraine* 47 J8
Dnestr → = Dnister →, *Europe* 47 J6
Dnestrovski = Belgorod, *Russia* 47 G9
Dnieper = Dnipro →, *Ukraine* 47 J7
Dniester = Dnister →, *Europe* 47 J6
Dnipro →, *Ukraine* 47 J7
Dniprodzerzhynsk, *Ukraine* 47 H8
Dniprodzerzhynske Vdskh., *Ukraine* 47 H8
Dnipropetrovsk, *Ukraine* 47 H8
Dniprorudne, *Ukraine* 47 J8
Dnister →, *Europe* 47 J6
Dnistrovskyy Lyman, *Ukraine* 47 J6
Dno, *Russia* 46 D5
Dnyapro = Dnipro →, *Ukraine* 47 J7
Doaktown, *Canada* 103 C6
Doan Hung, *Vietnam* 58 G5
Doany, *Madag.* 89 A8
Doba, *Chad* 79 G9
Dobandi, *Pakistan* 68 D2
Dobbiaco, *Italy* 29 B9
Dobbyn, *Australia* 94 B3
Dobczyce, *Poland* 45 J7
Dobele, *Latvia* 9 H20
Dobele □, *Latvia* 44 B10
Döbeln, *Germany* 24 D9
Doberai, Jazirah, *Indonesia* 63 E8
Dobiegniew, *Poland* 45 F2
Doblas, *Argentina* 126 D3
Dobo, *Indonesia* 63 F8
Doboj, *Bos.-H.* 42 F3
Dobra, *Wielkopolskie, Poland* 45 G5
Dobra, *Zachodnio-Pomorskie, Poland* 44 E2
Dobra, *Dîmboviţa, Romania* 43 F10
Dobra, *Hunedoara, Romania* 42 E7
Dobre Miasto, *Poland* 44 E7
Dobreşti, *Romania* 42 D7
Dobreta-Turnu Severin, *Romania* 42 F7
Dobrich, *Bulgaria* 41 C11
Dobrinishta, *Bulgaria* 40 E7
Dobříš, *Czech Rep.* 26 B7
Dobrodzień, *Poland* 45 H5
Dobropole, *Ukraine* 47 H9
Dobruja, *Europe* 43 F13
Dobrush, *Belarus* 47 F6
Dobrzany, *Poland* 44 E2
Dobrzyń nad Wisłą, *Poland* 45 F6
Doc, Mui, *Vietnam* 64 D6
Docker River, *Australia* 93 D4
Docksta, *Sweden* 10 A12
Doctor Arroyo, *Mexico* 118 C4
Doda, *India* 69 C6
Doda, L., *Canada* 102 C4
Dodecanese = Dhodhekánisos, *Greece* 39 E8
Dodge City, *U.S.A.* 113 G5
Dodge L., *Canada* 105 B7
Dodgeville, *U.S.A.* 112 D9
Dodo, *Cameroon* 83 D7
Dodo, *Sudan* 81 F2
Dodola, *Ethiopia* 81 F4
Dodoma, *Tanzania* 86 D4
Dodoma □, *Tanzania* 86 D4
Dodona, *Greece* 38 B2
Dodsland, *Canada* 105 C7
Dodson, *U.S.A.* 114 B9
Dodurga, *Turkey* 39 B11
Doesburg, *Neths.* 17 B6
Doetinchem, *Neths.* 17 C6
Dog Creek, *Canada* 104 C4
Dog L., *Man., Canada* 105 C9
Dog L., *Ont., Canada* 102 C2
Doğanşehir, *Turkey* 72 C7
Dogi, *Afghan.* 66 C3
Dogliani, *Italy* 28 D4
Dogondoutchi, *Niger* 83 C5
Dogran, *Pakistan* 68 D5
Doğubayazıt, *Turkey* 70 B5
Doguéraoua, *Niger* 83 C6
Doha = Ad Dawḩah, *Qatar* 71 E6
Dohazari, *Bangla.* 67 H18
Dohrighat, *India* 69 F10
Doi, *Indonesia* 63 D7
Doi Luang, *Thailand* 64 C3
Doi Saket, *Thailand* 64 C2
Dois Irmãos, Sa., *Brazil* 125 E10
Dojransko Jezero, *Macedonia* 40 E6
Dokkum, *Neths.* 17 A5
Dokri, *Pakistan* 68 F3
Dokuchayevsk, *Ukraine* 47 J9
Dol-de-Bretagne, *France* 18 D5
Dolac, *Kosovo, Yug.* 40 D4
Dolak, Pulau, *Indonesia* 63 F9
Dolbeau, *Canada* 103 C5
Dole, *France* 19 E12
Doleib, Wadi →, *Sudan* 81 E3
Dolenji Logatec, *Slovenia* 29 C11
Dolgellau, *U.K.* 12 E4
Dolgelley = Dolgellau, *U.K.* 12 E4
Dolhasca, *Romania* 43 C11
Dolianova, *Italy* 30 C2
Dolinskaya = Dolynska, *Ukraine* 47 H7
Dolj □, *Romania* 43 F8
Dollard, *Neths.* 17 A7
Dolna Banya, *Bulgaria* 40 D7
Dolni Chiflik, *Bulgaria* 41 D11
Dolni Dŭbnik, *Bulgaria* 41 C8
Dolnośląskie □, *Poland* 45 G3
Dolný Kubín, *Slovak Rep.* 27 B12
Dolo, *Ethiopia* 81 G5
Dolo, *Italy* 29 C9
Dolomites = Dolomiti, *Italy* 29 B8
Dolomiti, *Italy* 29 B8
Dolores, *Argentina* 126 D4
Dolores, *Uruguay* 126 C4
Dolores, *U.S.A.* 115 H9
Dolores →, *U.S.A.* 115 G9
Dolovo, *Serbia, Yug.* 42 F5
Dolphin, C., *Falk. Is.* 128 G5
Dolphin and Union Str., *Canada* 100 B8
Dolsk, *Poland* 45 G4
Dolynska, *Ukraine* 47 H7
Dolzhanskaya, *Russia* 47 J9
Dom Pedrito, *Brazil* 127 C5
Doma, *Nigeria* 83 D6
Domaniç, *Turkey* 39 B11
Domariaganj →, *India* 69 F10
Domasi, *Malawi* 87 F4
Domažlice, *Czech Rep.* 26 B5
Dombarovskiy, *Russia* 50 D6
Dombås, *Norway* 9 E13
Dombasle-sur-Meurthe, *France* 19 D13
Dombes, *France* 21 C9
Dombóvár, *Hungary* 42 D3
Dombrád, *Hungary* 42 B6
Domel I. = Letsôk-aw Kyun, *Burma* 65 G2
Domérat, *France* 19 F9
Domeyko, *Chile* 126 B1
Domeyko, Cordillera, *Chile* 126 A2
Domfront, *France* 18 D6
Dominador, *Chile* 126 A2
Dominica ■, *W. Indies* 121 C7
Dominica Passage, *W. Indies* 121 C7
Dominican Rep. ■, *W. Indies* 121 C5
Dömitz, *Germany* 24 B7
Domme, *France* 20 D5
Domneşti, *Romania* 43 E9
Domodóssola, *Italy* 28 B5
Dompaire, *France* 19 D13
Dompierre-sur-Besbre, *France* 19 F10
Dompim, *Ghana* 82 D4
Domrémy-la-Pucelle, *France* 19 D12
Domville, Mt., *Australia* 95 D5
Domvraína, *Greece* 38 C4
Domžale, *Slovenia* 29 B11
Don →, *Russia* 47 J10
Don →, *Aberds., U.K.* 14 D6
Don →, *S. Yorks., U.K.* 12 D7
Don, C., *Australia* 92 B5
Don Benito, *Spain* 35 G5
Dona Ana = Nhamaabué, *Mozam.* 87 F4
Doña Mencía, *Spain* 35 H6
Donaghadee, *U.K.* 15 B6
Donald, *Australia* 95 F3
Donaldsonville, *U.S.A.* 113 K9
Donalsonville, *U.S.A.* 109 K3
Donau = Dunărea →, *Europe* 43 E14
Donau →, *Austria* 17 D3
Donaueschingen, *Germany* 25 H4
Donauwörth, *Germany* 25 G6
Doncaster, *U.K.* 12 D6
Dondo, *Mozam.* 87 F3
Dondo, Teluk, *Indonesia* 63 D6
Dondra Head, *Sri Lanka* 66 S12
Donduşeni, *Moldova* 43 B12
Donegal, *Ireland* 15 B3
Donegal □, *Ireland* 15 B4
Donegal B., *Ireland* 15 B3
Donets →, *Russia* 49 G5
Donetsk, *Ukraine* 47 J9
Dong Ba Thin, *Vietnam* 65 F7
Dong Dang, *Vietnam* 58 G6
Dong Giam, *Vietnam* 64 C5
Dong Ha, *Vietnam* 64 D6
Dong Hene, *Laos* 64 D5
Dong Hoi, *Vietnam* 64 D6
Dong Jiang →, *China* 59 F10
Dong Khe, *Vietnam* 64 A6
Dong Ujimqin Qi, *China* 56 B9
Dong Van, *Vietnam* 64 A5
Dong Xoai, *Vietnam* 65 G6
Donga, *Nigeria* 83 D7
Donga →, *Nigeria* 83 D7
Dong'an, *China* 59 D8
Dongara, *Australia* 93 E1
Dongbei, *China* 57 D13
Dongchuan, *China* 58 D4
Donges, *France* 18 E4
Dongfang, *China* 64 C7
Dongfeng, *China* 57 C13
Donggala, *Indonesia* 63 E5
Donggan, *China* 58 F5
Donggou, *China* 57 E13
Dongguan, *China* 59 F9
Dongguang, *China* 56 F9
Donghai Dao, *China* 59 G8
Dongjingcheng, *China* 57 B15
Dongkou, *China* 59 D8
Donglan, *China* 58 E6
Dongliu, *China* 59 B11
Dongmen, *China* 58 F6
Dongning, *China* 57 B16
Dongnyi, *China* 58 C3
Dongola, *Sudan* 80 D3
Dongping, *China* 56 G9
Dongshan, *China* 59 F11
Dongsheng, *China* 56 E6
Dongtai, *China* 57 H11
Dongting Hu, *China* 59 C9
Dongtou, *China* 59 D13
Dongxiang, *China* 59 C11
Dongxing, *China* 58 G7
Dongyang, *China* 59 C13
Dongzhi, *China* 59 B11
Donington, C., *Australia* 95 E2
Doniphan, *U.S.A.* 113 G9
Donja Stubica, *Croatia* 29 C12
Donji Dušnik, *Serbia, Yug.* 40 C6
Donji Miholjac, *Croatia* 42 E3
Donji Milanovac, *Serbia, Yug.* 40 B6
Donji Vakuf, *Bos.-H.* 42 F2
Dønna, *Norway* 8 C15
Donna, *U.S.A.* 113 M5
Donnaconna, *Canada* 103 C5
Donnelly's Crossing, *N.Z.* 91 F4
Donnybrook, *Australia* 93 F2
Donnybrook, *S. Africa* 89 D4
Donora, *U.S.A.* 110 F5
Donostia = Donostia-San Sebastián, *Spain* 32 B3
Donostia-San Sebastián, *Spain* 32 B3
Donskoy, *Russia* 46 F10
Donsol, *Phil.* 61 E5
Donzère, *France* 21 D8
Donzy, *France* 19 E10
Doon →, *U.K.* 14 F4
Dora, L., *Australia* 92 D3
Dora Báltea →, *Italy* 28 C5
Dora Ripária →, *Italy* 28 C4
Doran L., *Canada* 105 A7
Dorchester, *U.K.* 13 G5
Dorchester, C., *Canada* 101 B12
Dordabis, *Namibia* 88 C2
Dordogne □, *France* 20 C4
Dordogne →, *France* 20 C3
Dordrecht, *Neths.* 17 C4
Dordrecht, *S. Africa* 88 E4
Dore →, *France* 20 C7
Dore, Mts., *France* 20 C6
Doré L., *Canada* 105 C7
Doré Lake, *Canada* 105 C7
Dorfen, *Germany* 25 G8
Dorgali, *Italy* 30 B2
Dori, *Burkina Faso* 83 C4
Doring →, *S. Africa* 88 E2
Doringbos, *S. Africa* 88 E2
Dorion, *Canada* 111 A10
Dormaa-Ahenkro, *Ghana* 82 D4
Dormans, *France* 19 C10
Dormo, Ras, *Eritrea* 81 E5
Dornbirn, *Austria* 26 D2
Dornes, *France* 19 F10
Dorneşti, *Romania* 43 C11
Dornie, *U.K.* 14 D3
Dornoch, *U.K.* 14 D4
Dornoch Firth, *U.K.* 14 D4
Dornogovĭ □, *Mongolia* 56 C6
Doro, *Mali* 83 B4
Dorog, *Hungary* 42 C3
Dorogobuzh, *Russia* 46 E7
Dorohoi, *Romania* 43 C11
Döröö Nuur, *Mongolia* 60 B4
Dorr, *Iran* 71 C6
Dorre I., *Australia* 93 E1
Dorrigo, *Australia* 95 E5
Dorris, *U.S.A.* 114 F3
Dorset, *Canada* 110 A6
Dorset, *U.S.A.* 110 E4
Dorset □, *U.K.* 13 G5
Dorsten, *Germany* 24 D2
Dortmund, *Germany* 24 D3
Dortmund-Ems-Kanal →, *Germany* 24 D3
Dörtyol, *Turkey* 72 D7
Dorum, *Germany* 24 B4
Doruma, *Dem. Rep. of the Congo* 86 B2
Dorūneh, *Iran* 71 C8
Dos Bahías, C., *Argentina* 128 E3
Dos Hermanas, *Spain* 35 H5
Dos Palos, *U.S.A.* 116 J6
Döşemealtı, *Turkey* 39 D12
Dosso, *Niger* 83 C5
Dothan, *U.S.A.* 109 K3
Doty, *U.S.A.* 116 D3
Douai, *France* 19 B10
Douako, *Guinea* 82 D2
Douala, *Cameroon* 83 E6
Douarnenez, *France* 18 D2
Doubabougou, *Mali* 82 C3
Double Island Pt., *Australia* 95 D5
Double Mountain Fork →, *U.S.A.* 113 J4
Doubrava →, *Czech Rep.* 26 A8
Doubs □, *France* 19 E13
Doubs →, *France* 19 F12
Doubtful Sd., *N.Z.* 91 L1
Doubtless B., *N.Z.* 91 F4
Doudeville, *France* 18 C7
Doué-la-Fontaine, *France* 18 E6
Douentza, *Mali* 82 C4
Douglas, *S. Africa* 88 D3
Douglas, *U.K.* 12 C3
Douglas, *Ariz., U.S.A.* 115 L9
Douglas, *Ga., U.S.A.* 109 K4
Douglas, *Wyo., U.S.A.* 112 D2
Douglas Chan., *Canada* 104 C3
Douglas Pt., *Canada* 110 B3
Douglasville, *U.S.A.* 109 J3
Doukáton, Ákra, *Greece* 38 C2
Doulevant-le-Château, *France* 19 D11
Doullens, *France* 19 B9
Doumen, *China* 59 F9
Douna, *Mali* 82 C3
Douna, *Mali* 83 C4
Dounreay, *U.K.* 14 C5
Dourada, Serra, *Brazil* 125 F9
Dourados, *Brazil* 127 A5
Dourados →, *Brazil* 127 A5
Dourados, Serra dos, *Brazil* 127 A5
Dourdan, *France* 19 D9
Douro →, *Europe* 34 D2
Douvaine, *France* 19 F13
Douvres-la-Délivrande, *France* 18 C6
Douze →, *France* 20 E3
Dove →, *U.K.* 12 E6
Dove Creek, *U.S.A.* 115 H9
Dover, *Australia* 94 G4
Dover, *U.K.* 13 F9
Dover, *Del., U.S.A.* 108 F8
Dover, *N.H., U.S.A.* 111 C14
Dover, *N.J., U.S.A.* 111 F10
Dover, *Ohio, U.S.A.* 110 F3
Dover, Pt., *Australia* 93 F4
Dover, Str. of, *Europe* 13 G9
Dover-Foxcroft, *U.S.A.* 109 C11
Dover Plains, *U.S.A.* 111 E11
Dovey = Dyfi →, *U.K.* 13 E3
Dovrefjell, *Norway* 9 E13
Dow Rūd, *Iran* 71 C6
Dowa, *Malawi* 87 E3
Dowagiac, *U.S.A.* 108 E2
Dowerin, *Australia* 93 F2
Dowgha'i, *Iran* 71 B8
Dowlatābād, *Iran* 71 D8
Down □, *U.K.* 15 B5
Downey, *Calif., U.S.A.* 117 M8
Downey, *Idaho, U.S.A.* 114 E7

Downham Market, U.K. 13 E8
Downieville, U.S.A. 116 F6
Downpatrick, U.K. 15 B6
Downpatrick Hd., Ireland 15 B2
Downsville, U.S.A. 111 D10
Downton, Mt., Canada 104 C4
Dowsārī, Iran 71 D8
Doyle, U.S.A. 116 E6
Doylestown, U.S.A. 111 F9
Dozois, Rés., Canada 102 C4
Dra Khel, Pakistan 68 F2
Drac →, France 21 C9
Dračevo, Macedonia 40 E5
Drachten, Neths. 17 A6
Drăgăneşti, Moldova 43 C13
Drăgăneşti-Olt, Romania 43 F9
Drăgăneşti-Vlaşca, Romania 43 F10
Dragaš, Kosovo, Yug. 40 D4
Drăgăşani, Romania 43 F9
Dragichyn, Belarus 47 F3
Dragocvet, Serbia, Yug. 40 C5
Dragovishtitsa, Bulgaria 40 D6
Draguignan, France 21 E10
Drain, U.S.A. 114 E2
Drake, U.S.A. 112 B4
Drake Passage, S. Ocean 5 B17
Drakensberg, S. Africa 89 D4
Dráma, Greece 41 E8
Dráma □, Greece 41 E8
Drammen, Norway 9 G14
Drangajökull, Iceland 8 C2
Dranov, Ostrov, Romania 43 F14
Dras, India 69 B6
Drau = Drava →, Croatia 42 E3
Drava →, Croatia 42 E3
Dravograd, Slovenia 29 B12
Drawa →, Poland 45 F2
Drawno, Poland 45 E2
Drawsko Pomorskie, Poland 44 E2
Drayton Valley, Canada 104 C6
Dreieich, Germany 25 E4
Dren, Kosovo, Yug. 40 C4
Drenthe □, Neths. 17 B6
Drepanum, C., Cyprus 36 E11
Dresden, Canada 110 D2
Dresden, Germany 24 D9
Dreux, France 18 D8
Drezdenko, Poland 45 F2
Driffield, U.K. 12 C7
Driftwood, U.S.A. 110 E6
Driggs, U.S.A. 114 E8
Drin i Zi →, Albania 40 E4
Drina →, Bos.-H. 40 B3
Drincea →, Romania 42 F7
Drini →, Albania 40 D3
Drinjača →, Bos.-H. 42 F4
Drissa = Vyerkhnyadzvinsk, Belarus 46 E4
Drniš, Croatia 29 E13
Drøbak, Norway 9 G14
Drobin, Poland 45 F6
Drochia, Moldova 43 B12
Drogheda, Ireland 15 C5
Drogichin = Dragichyn, Belarus 47 F3
Drogobych = Drohobych, Ukraine 47 H2
Drohiczyn, Poland 45 F9
Drohobych, Ukraine 47 H2
Droichead Atha = Drogheda, Ireland 15 C5
Droichead Nua, Ireland 15 C5
Droitwich, U.K. 13 E5
Drôme □, France 21 D9
Drôme →, France 21 D8
Dromedary, C., Australia 95 F5
Dromore, U.K. 15 B4
Dromore West, Ireland 15 B3
Dronero, Italy 28 D4
Dronfield, U.K. 12 D6
Dronne →, France 20 C3
Dronninglund, Denmark 11 G4
Dronten, Neths. 17 B5
Dropt →, France 20 D3
Drosendorf, Austria 26 C8
Droué, France 18 D8
Drumbo, Canada 110 C4
Drumheller, Canada 104 C6
Drummond, U.S.A. 114 C7
Drummond I., U.S.A. 108 C4
Drummond Pt., Australia 95 E2
Drummond Ra., Australia 94 C4
Drummondville, Canada 102 C5
Drumright, U.S.A. 113 H6
Druskininkai, Lithuania 9 J20
Drut →, Belarus 47 F6
Druya, Belarus 46 E4
Druzhba, Bulgaria 41 C12
Druzhina, Russia 51 C15
Drvar, Bos.-H. 29 D13
Drvenik, Croatia 29 E13
Drwęca →, Poland 45 E5
Dry Tortugas, U.S.A. 120 B3
Dryanovo, Bulgaria 41 D9
Dryden, Canada 105 D10
Dryden, U.S.A. 111 D8
Drygalski I., Antarctica 5 C7
Drysdale →, Australia 92 B4
Drysdale I., Australia 94 A2
Drzewica, Poland 45 G7
Drzewiczka →, Poland 45 G7
Dschang, Cameroon 83 D7
Du Bois, U.S.A. 110 E6
Du Gué →, Canada 102 A5
Du He, China 59 A8
Du Quoin, U.S.A. 112 G10
Du'an, China 58 F7
Duanesburg, U.S.A. 111 D10
Duaringa, Australia 94 C4
Ḑubā, Si. Arabia 70 E2
Dubai = Dubayy, U.A.E. 71 E7
Dubăsari, Moldova 43 C14
Dubăsari Vdkhr., Moldova 43 C13
Dubawnt →, Canada 105 A8
Dubawnt, L., Canada 105 A8
Dubayy, U.A.E. 71 E7
Dubbo, Australia 95 E4
Dubele, Dem. Rep. of the Congo 86 B2
Dübendorf, Switz. 25 H4
Dubica, Croatia 29 C13
Dublin, Ireland 15 C5
Dublin, Ga., U.S.A. 109 J4
Dublin, Tex., U.S.A. 113 J5
Dublin □, Ireland 15 C5
Dubna, Russia 46 D9
Dubnica nad Váhom, Slovak Rep. 27 C11
Dubno, Ukraine 47 G3
Dubois, U.S.A. 114 D7
Dubossary = Dubăsari, Moldova 43 C14
Dubossary Vdkhr. = Dubăsari Vdkhr., Moldova 43 C13
Dubovka, Russia 49 F7
Dubovskoye, Russia 49 G6
Dubrajpur, India 69 H12
Dubréka, Guinea 82 D2
Dubrovitsa = Dubrovytsya, Ukraine 47 G4
Dubrovnik, Croatia 40 D2
Dubrovytsya, Ukraine 47 G4
Dubuque, U.S.A. 112 D9
Dubysa →, Lithuania 44 C10
Duchang, China 59 C11
Duchesne, U.S.A. 114 F8
Duchess, Australia 94 C2
Ducie I., Pac. Oc. 97 K15
Duck →, U.S.A. 109 G2
Duck Cr. →, Australia 92 D2
Duck Lake, Canada 105 C7
Duck Mountain Prov. Park, Canada 105 C8
Duckwall, Mt., U.S.A. 116 H6
Duderstadt, Germany 24 D6
Dudhi, India 67 G13
Dudinka, Russia 51 C9
Dudley, U.K. 13 E5
Dudwa, India 69 E9
Duékoué, Ivory C. 82 D3
Dueñas, Spain 34 D6
Duero = Douro →, Europe 34 D2
Dufftown, U.K. 14 D5
Dufourspitz, Switz. 25 K3
Dugi Otok, Croatia 29 D11
Dugo Selo, Croatia 29 C13
Duifken Pt., Australia 94 A3
Duisburg, Germany 24 D2
Duiwelskloof, S. Africa 89 C5
Dujiangyan, China 58 B4
Duk Fadiat, Sudan 81 F3
Duk Faiwil, Sudan 81 F3
Dukati, Albania 40 F3
Dūkdamīn, Iran 71 C8
Dukelský Průsmyk, Slovak Rep. 27 B14
Dukhān, Qatar 71 E6
Dukhovshchina, Russia 46 E7
Duki, Pakistan 66 D6
Dukla, Poland 45 J8
Duku, Bauchi, Nigeria 83 C7
Duku, Sokoto, Nigeria 83 C5
Dulag, Phil. 61 F6
Dulce, U.S.A. 115 H10
Dulce →, Argentina 126 C3
Dulce, G., Costa Rica 120 E3
Dulf, Iraq 70 C5
Dŭlgopol, Bulgaria 41 C11
Dulit, Banjaran, Malaysia 62 D4
Duliu, China 56 E9
Dullewala, Pakistan 68 D4
Dullstroom, S. Africa 89 D5
Dülmen, Germany 24 D3
Dulovo, Bulgaria 41 C11
Dulq Maghār, Syria 70 B3
Duluth, U.S.A. 112 B8
Dum Dum, India 69 H13
Dum Duma, India 67 F19
Dūmā, Syria 75 B5
Dumaguete, Phil. 61 G5
Dumai, Indonesia 62 D2
Dumaran, Phil. 61 F3
Dumas, Ark., U.S.A. 113 J9
Dumas, Tex., U.S.A. 113 H4
Ḑumayr, Syria 75 B5
Dumbarton, U.K. 14 F4
Ďumbier, Slovak Rep. 27 C12
Dumbleyung, Australia 93 F2
Dumboa, Nigeria 83 C7
Dumbrăveni, Romania 43 D9
Dumfries, U.K. 14 F5
Dumfries & Galloway □, U.K. 14 F5
Dumitreşti, Romania 43 E11
Dumka, India 69 G12
Dumlupınar, Turkey 39 C12
Dümmer, Germany 24 C4
Dumoine →, Canada 102 C4
Dumoine, L., Canada 102 C4
Dumraon, India 69 G11
Dumyât, Egypt 80 H7
Dumyât, Masabb, Egypt 80 H7
Dún Dealgan = Dundalk, Ireland 15 B5
Dun Laoghaire, Ireland 15 C5
Dun-le-Palestel, France 19 F8
Dun-sur-Auron, France 19 F9
Dun-sur-Meuse, France 19 C12
Duna = Dunărea →, Europe 43 E14
Duna →, Hungary 42 E3
Duna-völgyi-főcsatorna, Hungary 42 D4
Dunaföldvár, Hungary 42 D3
Dunagiri, India 69 D8
Dunaj = Dunărea →, Europe 43 E14
Dunaj →, Slovak Rep. 27 D11
Dunajec →, Poland 45 H7
Dunajská Streda, Slovak Rep. 27 C10
Dunakeszi, Hungary 42 C4
Dunapataj, Hungary 42 D4
Dunărea →, Europe 43 E14
Dunaszekcső, Hungary 42 D3
Dunaújváros, Hungary 42 D3
Dunav = Dunărea →, Europe 43 E14
Dunavațu de Jos, Romania 43 F14
Dunavtsi, Bulgaria 40 C6
Dunay, Russia 54 C6
Dunback, N.Z. 91 L3
Dunbar, U.K. 14 E6
Dunblane, U.K. 14 E5
Duncan, Canada 104 D4
Duncan, Ariz., U.S.A. 115 K9
Duncan, Okla., U.S.A. 113 H6
Duncan, L., Canada 102 B4
Duncan L., Canada 104 A6
Duncan Town, Bahamas 120 B4
Duncannon, U.S.A. 110 F7
Duncansby Head, U.K. 14 C5
Duncansville, U.S.A. 110 F6
Dundaga, Latvia 44 A9
Dundalk, Canada 110 B4
Dundalk, Ireland 15 B5
Dundalk, U.S.A. 108 F7
Dundalk Bay, Ireland 15 C5
Dundas, Canada 110 C5
Dundas, L., Australia 93 F3
Dundas I., Canada 104 C2
Dundas Str., Australia 92 B5
Dundee, S. Africa 89 D5
Dundee, U.K. 14 E6
Dundee, U.S.A. 110 D8
Dundee City □, U.K. 14 E6
Dundgovĭ □, Mongolia 56 B4
Dundrum, U.K. 15 B6
Dundrum B., U.K. 15 B6
Dunedin, N.Z. 91 L3
Dunedin, U.S.A. 109 L4
Dunedoo, Australia 95 E4
Dunfermline, U.K. 14 E5
Dungannon, Canada 110 C3
Dungannon, U.K. 15 B5
Dungarpur, India 68 H5
Dungarvan, Ireland 15 D4
Dungarvan Harbour, Ireland 15 D4
Dungeness, U.K. 13 G8
Dungo, L. do, Angola 88 B2
Dungog, Australia 95 E5
Dungu, Dem. Rep. of the Congo 86 B2
Dungun, Malaysia 65 K4
Dungunâb, Sudan 80 C4
Dungunâb, Khalij, Sudan 80 C4
Dunhua, China 57 C15
Dunhuang, China 60 B4
Dunk I., Australia 94 B4
Dunkassa, Benin 83 C5
Dunkeld, Australia 95 E4
Dunkeld, U.K. 14 E5
Dunkerque, France 19 A9
Dunkery Beacon, U.K. 13 F4
Dunkirk = Dunkerque, France 19 A9
Dunkirk, U.S.A. 110 D5
Dunkuj, Sudan 81 E3
Dunkwa, Central, Ghana 82 D4
Dunkwa, Central, Ghana 83 D4
Dún Laoghaire = Dun Laoghaire, Ireland 15 C5
Dunleer, Ireland 15 C5
Dunmanus B., Ireland 15 E2
Dunmanway, Ireland 15 E2
Dunmara, Australia 94 B1
Dunmore, U.S.A. 111 E9
Dunmore Hd., Ireland 15 D1
Dunmore Town, Bahamas 120 A4
Dunn, U.S.A. 109 H6
Dunnet Hd., U.K. 14 C5
Dunning, U.S.A. 112 E4
Dunnville, Canada 110 D5
Dunolly, Australia 95 F3
Dunoon, U.K. 14 F4
Dunphy, U.S.A. 114 F5
Dunqul, Egypt 80 C3
Duns, U.K. 14 F6
Dunseith, U.S.A. 112 A4
Dunsmuir, U.S.A. 114 F2
Dunstable, U.K. 13 F7
Dunstan Mts., N.Z. 91 L2
Dunster, Canada 104 C5
Dunvegan L., Canada 105 A7
Duolun, China 56 C9
Duong Dong, Vietnam 65 G4
Dupree, U.S.A. 112 C4
Dupuyer, U.S.A. 114 B7
Duque de Caxias, Brazil 127 A7
Durack →, Australia 92 C4
Durack Ra., Australia 92 C4
Durağan, Turkey 72 B6
Durak, Turkey 39 B10
Đurakovac, Kosovo, Yug. 40 D4
Durance →, France 21 E8
Durand, U.S.A. 112 C9
Durango, Mexico 118 C4
Durango, U.S.A. 115 H10
Durango □, Mexico 118 C4
Durankulak, Bulgaria 41 C12
Durant, Miss., U.S.A. 113 J10
Durant, Okla., U.S.A. 113 J6
Duratón →, Spain 34 D6
Durazno, Uruguay 126 C4
Durazzo = Durrësi, Albania 40 E3
Durban, France 20 F6
Durban, S. Africa 89 D5
Durbuy, Belgium 17 D5
Dúrcal, Spain 35 J7
Đurđevac, Croatia 42 D2
Düren, Germany 24 E2
Durg, India 67 J12
Durgapur, India 69 H12
Durham, Canada 102 D3
Durham, U.K. 12 C6
Durham, Calif., U.S.A. 116 F5
Durham, N.C., U.S.A. 109 H6
Durham, N.H., U.S.A. 111 C14
Durham □, U.K. 12 C6
Durleşti, Moldova 43 C13
Ḑurmā, Si. Arabia 70 E5
Durmitor, Montenegro, Yug. 40 C2
Durness, U.K. 14 C4
Durrësi, Albania 40 E3
Durrow, Ireland 15 D4
Dursey I., Ireland 15 E1
Dursunbey, Turkey 39 B10
Durtal, France 18 E6
Duru, Dem. Rep. of the Congo 86 B2
Duru Gölü, Turkey 41 E12
Durusu, Turkey 41 E12
Durūz, Jabal ad, Jordan 75 C5
D'Urville, Tanjung, Indonesia 63 E9
D'Urville I., N.Z. 91 J4
Duryea, U.S.A. 111 E9
Dûsh, Egypt 80 C3
Dushak, Turkmenistan 50 F7
Dushan, China 58 E6
Dushanbe, Tajikistan 50 F7
Dusheti, Georgia 49 J7
Dushore, U.S.A. 111 E8
Dusky Sd., N.Z. 91 L1
Dussejour, C., Australia 92 B4
Düsseldorf, Germany 24 D2
Duszniki-Zdrój, Poland 45 H3
Dutch Harbor, U.S.A. 100 C3
Dutlwe, Botswana 88 C3
Dutsan Wai, Nigeria 83 C6
Dutton, Canada 110 D3
Dutton →, Australia 94 C3
Duved, Sweden 10 A6
Düvertepe, Turkey 39 B10
Duwayhin, Khawr, U.A.E. 71 E6
Duyun, China 58 D6
Düzağac, Turkey 39 C12
Düzce, Turkey 72 B4
Duzdab = Zāhedān, Iran 71 D9
Dve Mogili, Bulgaria 41 C9
Dvina, Severnaya →, Russia 50 C5
Dvinsk = Daugavpils, Latvia 9 J22
Dvor, Croatia 29 C13
Dvůr Králové nad Labem, Czech Rep. 26 A8
Dwarka, India 68 H3
Dwellingup, Australia 93 F2
Dwight, Canada 110 A5
Dwight, U.S.A. 108 E1
Dyatkovo, Russia 46 F8
Dyatlovo = Dzyatlava, Belarus 46 F3
Dyce, U.K. 14 D6
Dyer, C., Canada 101 B13
Dyer Bay, Canada 110 A3
Dyer Plateau, Antarctica 5 D17
Dyersburg, U.S.A. 113 G10
Dyfi →, U.K. 13 E3
Dyje →, Czech Rep. 27 C9
Dymer, Ukraine 47 G6
Dynów, Poland 45 J9
Dysart, Australia 94 C4
Dzamin Üüd = Borhoyn Tal, Mongolia 56 C6
Dzerzhinsk, Russia 48 B6
Dzhalinda, Russia 51 D13
Dzhambul = Zhambyl, Kazakstan 50 E8
Dzhankoy, Ukraine 47 K8
Dzhanybek, Kazakstan 48 F8
Dzharylhach, Ostriv, Ukraine 47 J7
Dzhezkazgan = Zhezqazghan, Kazakstan 50 E7
Dzhizak = Jizzakh, Uzbekistan 50 E7
Dzhugdzur, Khrebet, Russia 51 D14
Dzhvari = Jvari, Georgia 49 J6
Działdowo, Poland 45 E7
Działoszyce, Poland 45 H7
Działoszyn, Poland 45 G5
Dzibilchaltun, Mexico 119 C7
Dzierzgoń, Poland 44 E6
Dzierżoniów, Poland 45 H3
Dzilam de Bravo, Mexico 119 C7
Dzisna, Belarus 46 E5
Dzisna →, Belarus 46 E5
Dziwnów, Poland 44 D1
Dzungaria = Junggar Pendi, China 60 B3
Dzuumod, Mongolia 60 B5
Dzyarzhynsk, Belarus 46 F4
Dzyatlava, Belarus 46 F3

E

Eabamet L., Canada 102 B2
Eads, U.S.A. 112 F3
Eagar, U.S.A. 115 J9
Eagle, Alaska, U.S.A. 100 B5
Eagle, Colo., U.S.A. 114 G10
Eagle →, Canada 103 B8
Eagle Butte, U.S.A. 112 C4
Eagle Grove, U.S.A. 112 D8
Eagle L., Canada 105 D10
Eagle L., Calif., U.S.A. 114 F3
Eagle L., Maine, U.S.A. 109 B11
Eagle Lake, Canada 110 A6
Eagle Lake, Maine, U.S.A. 109 B11
Eagle Lake, Tex., U.S.A. 113 L6
Eagle Mountain, U.S.A. 117 M11
Eagle Nest, U.S.A. 115 H11
Eagle Pass, U.S.A. 113 L4
Eagle Pk., U.S.A. 116 G7
Eagle Pt., Australia 92 C3
Eagle River, Mich., U.S.A. 108 B1
Eagle River, Wis., U.S.A. 112 C10
Eaglehawk, Australia 95 F3
Eagles Mere, U.S.A. 111 E8
Ealing, U.K. 13 F7
Ear Falls, Canada 105 C10
Earle, U.S.A. 113 H9
Earlimart, U.S.A. 117 K7
Earn →, U.K. 14 E5
Earn, L., U.K. 14 E4
Earnslaw, Mt., N.Z. 91 L2
Earth, U.S.A. 113 H3
Easley, U.S.A. 109 H4
East Anglia, U.K. 12 E9
East Angus, Canada 103 C5
East Aurora, U.S.A. 110 D6
East Ayrshire □, U.K. 14 F4
East Bengal, Bangla. 67 H17
East Beskids = Vychodné Beskydy, Europe 27 B15
East Brady, U.S.A. 110 F5
East C., N.Z. 91 G7
East Chicago, U.S.A. 108 E2
East China Sea, Asia 60 C7
East Coulee, Canada 104 C6
East Dereham, U.K. 13 E8
East Dunbartonshire □, U.K. 14 F4
East Falkland, Falk. Is. 122 J5
East Grand Forks, U.S.A. 112 B6
East Greenwich, U.S.A. 111 E13
East Grinstead, U.K. 13 F8
East Hartford, U.S.A. 111 E12
East Helena, U.S.A. 114 C8
East Indies, Asia 52 K15
East Kilbride, U.K. 14 F4
East Lansing, U.S.A. 108 D3
East Liverpool, U.S.A. 110 F4
East London, S. Africa 89 E4
East Lothian □, U.K. 14 F6
East Main = Eastmain, Canada 102 B4
East Northport, U.S.A. 111 F11
East Orange, U.S.A. 111 F10
East Pacific Ridge, Pac. Oc. 97 J17
East Palestine, U.S.A. 110 F4
East Pine, Canada 104 B4
East Point, U.S.A. 109 J3
East Providence, U.S.A. 111 E13
East Pt., Canada 103 C7
East Renfrewshire □, U.K. 14 F4
East Retford = Retford, U.K. 12 D7
East Riding of Yorkshire □, U.K. 12 D7
East Rochester, U.S.A. 110 C7
East St. Louis, U.S.A. 112 F9
East Schelde = Oosterschelde →, Neths. 17 C4
East Siberian Sea, Russia 51 B17
East Stroudsburg, U.S.A. 111 E9
East Sussex □, U.K. 13 G8
East Tawas, U.S.A. 108 C4
East Timor = Timor Timur □, Indonesia 63 F7
East Toorale, Australia 95 E4
East Walker →, U.S.A. 116 G7
East Windsor, U.S.A. 111 F10
Eastbourne, N.Z. 91 J5
Eastbourne, U.K. 13 G8
Eastend, Canada 105 D7
Easter I. = Pascua, I. de, Pac. Oc. 97 K17
Eastern □, Ghana 83 D4
Eastern □, Kenya 86 C4
Eastern □, Uganda 86 B3
Eastern Cape □, S. Africa 88 E4
Eastern Cr. →, Australia 94 C3
Eastern Ghats, India 66 N11
Eastern Group = Lau Group, Fiji 91 C9
Eastern Group, Australia 93 F3
Eastern Province □, S. Leone 82 D2
Eastern Transvaal = Mpumalanga □, S. Africa 89 B5
Easterville, Canada 105 C9
Easthampton, U.S.A. 111 D12
Eastlake, U.S.A. 110 E3
Eastland, U.S.A. 113 J5
Eastleigh, U.K. 13 G6
Eastmain, Canada 102 B4
Eastmain →, Canada 102 B4
Eastman, Canada 111 A12
Eastman, U.S.A. 109 J4
Easton, Md., U.S.A. 108 F7
Easton, Pa., U.S.A. 111 F9
Easton, Wash., U.S.A. 116 C5
Eastpointe, U.S.A. 110 D2
Eastport, U.S.A. 109 C12
Eastsound, U.S.A. 116 B4
Eaton, U.S.A. 112 E2
Eatonia, Canada 105 C7
Eatonton, U.S.A. 109 J4
Eatontown, U.S.A. 111 F10
Eatonville, U.S.A. 116 D4
Eau Claire, U.S.A. 112 C9
Eau Claire, L. à l', Canada 102 A5
Eauze, France 20 E4

Eban, *Nigeria* 83 D5
Ebbw Vale, *U.K.* 13 F4
Ebeltoft, *Denmark* 11 H4
Ebeltoft Vig, *Denmark* . . 11 H4
Ebensburg, *U.S.A.* 110 F6
Ebensee, *Austria* 26 D6
Eber Gölü, *Turkey* 72 C4
Eberbach, *Germany* 25 F4
Eberswalde-Finow, *Germany* 24 C9
Ebetsu, *Japan* 54 C10
Ebian, *China* 58 C4
Ebingen, *Germany* 25 G5
Éboli, *Italy* 31 B8
Ebolowa, *Cameroon* 83 E7
Ebonyi □, *Nigeria* 83 D6
Ebrach, *Germany* 25 F6
Ébrié, Lagune, *Ivory C.* . . . 82 D4
Ebro →, *Spain* 32 E5
Ebro, Embalse del, *Spain* . . 34 C7
Ebstorf, *Germany* 24 B6
Eceabat, *Turkey* 41 F10
Ech Cheliff, *Algeria* 78 A6
Echigo-Sammyaku, *Japan* . . 55 F9
Échirolles, *France* 21 C9
Echizen-Misaki, *Japan* 55 G7
Echmiadzin = Yejmiadzin,
   Armenia 49 K7
Echo Bay, *N.W.T., Canada* 100 B8
Echo Bay, *Ont., Canada* . . 102 C3
Echoing →, *Canada* 102 B1
Echternach, *Lux.* 17 E6
Echuca, *Australia* 95 F3
Ecija, *Spain* 35 H5
Eckental, *Germany* 25 F7
Eckernförde, *Germany* . . . 24 A5
Eclipse Is., *Australia* 92 B4
Eclipse Sd., *Canada* 101 A11
Écommoy, *France* 18 E7
Écouché, *France* 18 D6
Ecuador ■, *S. Amer.* 124 D3
Écueillé, *France* 18 E8
Ed, *Sweden* 11 F5
Ed Dabbura, *Sudan* 80 D3
Ed Da'ein, *Sudan* 81 E2
Ed Damazin, *Sudan* 79 F12
Ed Dâmer, *Sudan* 80 D3
Ed Debba, *Sudan* 80 D3
Ed-Déffa, *Egypt* 80 A2
Ed Deim, *Sudan* 81 E2
Ed Dueim, *Sudan* 81 E3
Edam, *Canada* 105 C7
Edam, *Neths.* 17 B5
Edane, *Sweden* 10 E6
Eday, *U.K.* 14 B6
Edd, *Eritrea* 81 E5
Eddrachillis B., *U.K.* 14 C3
Eddystone Pt., *Australia* . . . 94 G4
Ede, *Neths.* 17 B5
Ede, *Nigeria* 83 D5
Edéa, *Cameroon* 83 E7
Edebäck, *Sweden* 10 D7
Edehon L., *Canada* 105 A9
Edelény, *Hungary* 42 B5
Eden, *Australia* 95 F4
Eden, *N.C., U.S.A.* 109 G6
Eden, *N.Y., U.S.A.* 110 D6
Eden, *Tex., U.S.A.* 113 K5
Eden →, *U.K.* 12 C4
Edenburg, *S. Africa* 88 D4
Edendale, *S. Africa* 89 D5
Edenderry, *Ireland* 15 C4
Edenhope, *Australia* 95 F3
Edenton, *U.S.A.* 109 G7
Edenville, *S. Africa* 89 D4
Eder →, *Germany* 24 D5
Eder-Stausee, *Germany* . . 24 D4
Edewecht, *Germany* 24 B3
Edgar, *U.S.A.* 112 E6
Edgartown, *U.S.A.* 111 E14
Edge Hill, *U.K.* 13 E6
Edgefield, *U.S.A.* 109 J5
Edgeley, *U.S.A.* 112 B5
Edgemont, *U.S.A.* 112 D3
Edgeøya, *Svalbard* 4 B9
Édhessa, *Greece* 40 F6
Edievale, *N.Z.* 91 L2
Edina, *Liberia* 82 D2
Edina, *U.S.A.* 112 E8
Edinboro, *U.S.A.* 110 E4
Edinburg, *U.S.A.* 113 M5
Edinburgh, *U.K.* 14 F5
Edinburgh, City of □, *U.K.* 14 F5
Edineţ, *Moldova* 43 B12
Edirne, *Turkey* 41 E10
Edirne □, *Turkey* 41 E10
Edison, *U.S.A.* 116 B4
Edithburgh, *Australia* 95 F2
Edmond, *U.S.A.* 113 H6
Edmonds, *U.S.A.* 116 C4
Edmonton, *Australia* 94 B4
Edmonton, *Canada* 104 C6
Edmund L., *Canada* 102 B1
Edmundston, *Canada* 103 C6
Edna, *U.S.A.* 113 L6
Edo □, *Nigeria* 83 D6
Edolo, *Italy* 28 B7
Edremit, *Turkey* 39 B9
Edremit Körfezi, *Turkey* . . 39 B8
Edsbro, *Sweden* 10 E12
Edsbyn, *Sweden* 10 C9
Edson, *Canada* 104 C5
Eduardo Castex, *Argentina* 126 D3
Edward →, *Australia* 95 F3
Edward, L., *Africa* 86 C2
Edward River, *Australia* . . . 94 A3
Edward VII Land, *Antarctica* 5 E13
Edwards, *Calif., U.S.A.* . . 117 L9
Edwards, *N.Y., U.S.A.* . . . 111 B9
Edwards Air Force Base,
   U.S.A. 117 L9

Edwards Plateau, *U.S.A.* . . 113 K4
Edwardsville, *U.S.A.* 111 E9
Edzo, *Canada* 104 A5
Eeklo, *Belgium* 17 C3
Eferding, *Austria* 26 C7
Effingham, *U.S.A.* 108 F1
Eforie, *Romania* 43 F13
Ega →, *Spain* 32 C3
Égadi, Ísole, *Italy* 30 E5
Egan Range, *U.S.A.* 114 G6
Eganville, *Canada* 102 C4
Eger = Cheb, *Czech Rep.* . . 26 A5
Eger, *Hungary* 42 C5
Eger →, *Hungary* 42 C5
Egersund, *Norway* 9 G12
Egg L., *Canada* 105 B7
Eggenburg, *Austria* 26 C8
Eggenfelden, *Germany* . . . 25 G8
Éghezée, *Belgium* 17 D4
Égletons, *France* 20 C6
Egmont, *Canada* 104 D4
Egmont, C., *N.Z.* 91 H4
Egmont, Mt., *N.Z.* 91 H5
Egra, *India* 69 J12
Eğridir, *Turkey* 72 D4
Eğridir Gölü, *Turkey* 70 B1
Egtved, *Denmark* 11 J3
Egume, *Nigeria* 83 D6
Éguzon-Chantôme, *France* . . 19 F8
Egvekinot, *Russia* 51 C19
Egyek, *Hungary* 42 C5
Egypt ■, *Africa* 80 B3
Eha Amufu, *Nigeria* 83 D6
Ehime □, *Japan* 55 H6
Ehingen, *Germany* 25 G5
Ehrenberg, *U.S.A.* 117 M12
Ehrwald, *Austria* 26 D3
Eibar, *Spain* 32 B2
Eichstätt, *Germany* 25 G7
Eider →, *Germany* 24 A4
Eidsvold, *Australia* 95 D5
Eidsvoll, *Norway* 9 F14
Eifel, *Germany* 25 E2
Eiffel Flats, *Zimbabwe* . . . 87 F3
Eiger, *Switz.* 28 B5
Eigg, *U.K.* 14 E2
Eighty Mile Beach, *Australia* 92 C3
Eil, *Somali Rep.* 74 F4
Eil, L., *U.K.* 14 E3
Eildon, *Australia* 95 F4
Eildon, L., *Australia* 95 F4
Eilenburg, *Germany* 24 D8
Ein el Luweiqa, *Sudan* . . . 81 E3
Einasleigh, *Australia* 94 B3
Einasleigh →, *Australia* . . . 94 B3
Einbeck, *Germany* 24 D5
Eindhoven, *Neths.* 17 C5
Einsiedeln, *Switz.* 25 H4
Eire = Ireland ■, *Europe* . . 15 C4
Eiríksjökull, *Iceland* 8 D3
Eirunepé, *Brazil* 124 E5
Eiseb →, *Namibia* 88 C2
Eisenach, *Germany* 24 E6
Eisenberg, *Germany* 24 E7
Eisenerz, *Austria* 26 D7
Eisenhüttenstadt, *Germany* 24 C10
Eisenkappel, *Austria* 26 E7
Eisenstadt, *Austria* 27 D9
Eisfeld, *Germany* 24 E6
Eisleben, *Germany* 24 D7
Eislingen, *Germany* 25 G5
Eivissa, *Spain* 37 C7
Eixe, Serra do, *Spain* 34 C4
Ejea de los Caballeros, *Spain* 32 C3
Ejeda, *Madag.* 89 C7
Ejura, *Ghana* 83 D4
Ejutla, *Mexico* 119 D5
Ekalaka, *U.S.A.* 112 C2
Ekenässjön, *Sweden* 11 G9
Ekerö, *Sweden* 10 E11
Eket, *Nigeria* 83 E6
Eketahuna, *N.Z.* 91 J5
Ekhínos, *Greece* 41 E9
Ekibastuz, *Kazakstan* 50 D8
Ekiti □, *Nigeria* 83 D6
Ekoli,
   Dem. Rep. of the Congo . 86 C1
Ekoln, *Sweden* 10 E11
Ekshärad, *Sweden* 10 D7
Eksjö, *Sweden* 11 G8
Ekuma →, *Namibia* 88 B2
Ekwan →, *Canada* 102 B3
Ekwan Pt., *Canada* 102 B3
El Aaiún, *W. Sahara* 78 C3
El Abanico, *Chile* 126 D1
El Abbasiya, *Sudan* 81 E3
El 'Agrûd, *Egypt* 75 E3
El Ait, *Sudan* 81 E2
El 'Aiyat, *Egypt* 80 J7
El Alamein, *Egypt* 80 A2
El 'Aqaba, W. →, *Egypt* . . 75 E2
El 'Arag, *Egypt* 80 B2
El Arahal, *Spain* 35 H5
El Arīḥā, *West Bank* 75 D4
El 'Arîsh, *Egypt* 75 D2
El 'Arîsh, W. →, *Egypt* . . . 75 D2
El Asnam = Ech Cheliff,
   Algeria 78 A6
El Astillero, *Spain* 34 B7
El Badâri, *Egypt* 80 B3
El Bahrein, *Egypt* 80 B2
El Ballâs, *Egypt* 80 B3
El Balyana, *Egypt* 80 B3
El Baqeir, *Sudan* 80 D3
El Barco de Ávila, *Spain* . . 34 E5
El Barco de Valdeorras = O
   Barco, *Spain* 34 C4
El Bauga, *Sudan* 80 D3
El Bawiti, *Egypt* 80 B2
El Bayadh, *Algeria* 78 B6
El Bierzo, *Spain* 34 C4

El Bluff, *Nic.* 120 D3
El Bonillo, *Spain* 33 G2
El Brûk, W. →, *Egypt* 75 E2
El Buheirat □, *Sudan* 81 F3
El Burgo de Osma, *Spain* . . 32 D1
El Cajon, *U.S.A.* 117 N10
El Campo, *U.S.A.* 113 L6
El Centro, *U.S.A.* 117 N11
El Cerro, *Bolivia* 124 G7
El Cerro de Andévalo, *Spain* 35 H4
El Compadre, *Mexico* . . . 117 N10
El Coronil, *Spain* 35 H5
El Cuy, *Argentina* 128 D3
El Cuyo, *Mexico* 119 C7
El Dab'a, *Egypt* 80 H6
El Daheir, *Egypt* 75 D3
El Dátil, *Mexico* 118 B2
El Deir, *Egypt* 80 B3
El Dere, *Somali Rep.* 74 G4
El Descanso, *Mexico* . . . 117 N10
El Desemboque, *Mexico* . . 118 A2
El Dilingat, *Egypt* 80 H7
El Diviso, *Colombia* 124 C3
El Djouf, *Mauritania* 78 D4
El Dorado, *Ark., U.S.A.* . . 113 J8
El Dorado, *Kans., U.S.A.* . . 113 G6
El Dorado, *Venezuela* . . . 124 B6
El 'Ein, *Sudan* 81 D2
El Ejido, *Spain* 35 J8
El Escorial, *Spain* 34 E6
El Espinar, *Spain* 34 D6
El Faiyûm, *Egypt* 80 J7
El Fâsher, *Sudan* 81 E2
El Fashn, *Egypt* 80 J7
El Ferrol = Ferrol, *Spain* . . 34 B2
El Fifi, *Sudan* 81 E2
El Fuerte, *Mexico* 118 B3
El Ga'a, *Sudan* 81 E2
El Gal, *Somali Rep.* 74 E5
El Garef, *Sudan* 81 E3
El Gebir, *Sudan* 81 E2
El Gedida, *Egypt* 80 B2
El Geneina = Al Junaynah,
   Sudan 79 F10
El Geteina, *Sudan* 81 E3
El Gezira □, *Sudan* 81 E3
El Gir, *Sudan* 80 D2
El Gîza, *Egypt* 80 J7
El Goléa, *Algeria* 78 B6
El Grau, *Spain* 33 G4
El Hagiz, *Sudan* 81 D4
El Hâi, *Egypt* 80 J7
El Hammam, *Egypt* 80 A2
El Hawata, *Sudan* 81 E3
El Heiz, *Egypt* 80 B2
El Hideib, *Sudan* 81 E3
El Hilla, *Sudan* 81 E2
El 'Idisât, *Egypt* 80 B3
El Iskandarîya, *Egypt* 80 H7
El Istiwa'iya, *Sudan* 79 G11
El Jadida, *Morocco* 78 B4
El Jardal, *Honduras* 120 D2
El Jebelein, *Sudan* 81 E3
El Kab, *Sudan* 80 D3
El Kabrît, G., *Egypt* 75 F2
El Kafr el Sharqi, *Egypt* . . 80 H7
El Kamlin, *Sudan* 81 D3
El Karaba, *Sudan* 80 D3
El Kere, *Ethiopia* 81 F5
El Khandaq, *Sudan* 80 D3
El Khârga, *Egypt* 80 B3
El Khartûm, *Sudan* 81 D3
El Khartûm □, *Sudan* 81 D3
El Khartûm Bahrî, *Sudan* . . 81 D3
El Kuntilla, *Egypt* 75 E3
El Laqâwa, *Sudan* 81 E2
El Laqeita, *Egypt* 80 B3
El Leh, *Ethiopia* 81 G4
El Leiya, *Sudan* 81 D4
El Maestrazgo, *Spain* 32 E4
El Mafâza, *Sudan* 81 E3
El Maghra, *Egypt* 80 A2
El Mahalla el Kubra, *Egypt* 80 H7
El Mahârîq, *Egypt* 80 B3
El Maîmûn, *Egypt* 80 J7
El Maks el Bahari, *Egypt* . . 80 C3
El Manshâh, *Egypt* 80 B3
El Mansûra, *Egypt* 80 H7
El Manzala, *Egypt* 80 H7
El Marâgha, *Egypt* 80 B3
El Masid, *Sudan* 81 D3
El Masnou, *Spain* 32 D7
El Matariya, *Egypt* 80 H8
El Meda, *Ethiopia* 81 F5
El Medano, *Canary Is.* 37 F3
El Metemma, *Sudan* 81 D3
El Milagro, *Argentina* . . . 126 C2
El Minyâ, *Egypt* 80 B3
El Monte, *U.S.A.* 117 L8
El Montseny, *Spain* 32 D7
El Mreyye, *Mauritania* . . . 82 B3
El Niybo, *Ethiopia* 81 G4
El Obeid, *Sudan* 81 E3
El Odaiya, *Sudan* 81 E2
El Oro, *Mexico* 119 D4
El Oued, *Algeria* 78 B7
El Palmito, Presa, *Mexico* . . 118 B3
El Paso, *U.S.A.* 115 L10
El Paso Robles, *U.S.A.* . . 116 K6
El Pedernoso, *Spain* 33 F2
El Pedroso, *Spain* 35 H5
El Pobo de Dueñas, *Spain* . . 32 E3
El Portal, *U.S.A.* 116 H7
El Porvenir, *Mexico* 118 A3
El Prat de Llobregat, *Spain* 32 D7
El Progreso, *Honduras* . . . 120 C2
El Pueblito, *Mexico* 118 B3
El Pueblo, *Canary Is.* 37 F2
El Puente del Arzobispo,
   Spain 34 F5

El Puerto de Santa María,
   Spain 35 J4
El Qâhira, *Egypt* 80 H7
El Qantara, *Egypt* 75 E1
El Qasr, *Egypt* 80 B2
El Qubâbât, *Egypt* 80 J7
El Queseima, *Egypt* 75 E3
El Qusîya, *Egypt* 80 B3
El Râshda, *Egypt* 80 B2
El Real, *Panama* 124 B3
El Reno, *U.S.A.* 113 H6
El Rîdisiya, *Egypt* 80 C3
El Rio, *U.S.A.* 117 L7
El Ronquillo, *Spain* 35 H4
El Roque, Pta., *Canary Is.* . . 37 F4
El Rosarito, *Mexico* 118 B2
El Rubio, *Spain* 35 H5
El Saff, *Egypt* 80 J7
El Saheira, W. →, *Egypt* . . 75 E2
El Salto, *Mexico* 118 C3
El Salvador ■, *Cent. Amer.* 120 D2
El Sauce, *Nic.* 120 D2
El Saucejo, *Spain* 35 H5
El Shallal, *Egypt* 80 C3
El Simbillawein, *Egypt* . . . 80 H7
El Sueco, *Mexico* 118 B3
El Suweis, *Egypt* 80 J8
El Tabbin, *Egypt* 80 J7
El Tamarâni, W. →, *Egypt* . . 75 E3
El Thamad, *Egypt* 75 F3
El Tigre, *Venezuela* 124 B6
El Tîh, Gebal, *Egypt* 75 F2
El Tîna, *Egypt* 80 H8
El Tîna, Khalîg, *Egypt* 75 D1
El Tofo, *Chile* 126 B1
El Tránsito, *Chile* 126 B1
El Tûr, *Egypt* 70 D2
El Turbio, *Argentina* 128 G2
El Uqsur, *Egypt* 80 B3
El Venado, *Mexico* 118 C4
El Vendrell, *Spain* 32 D6
El Vergel, *Mexico* 118 B3
El Vigía, *Venezuela* 124 B4
El Viso del Alcor, *Spain* . . 35 H5
El Wabeira, *Egypt* 75 F2
El Wak, *Kenya* 86 B5
El Waqf, *Egypt* 80 B3
El Weguet, *Ethiopia* 81 F5
El Wuz, *Sudan* 81 D3
Elafónisos, *Greece* 38 E4
Élancourt, *France* 19 D8
Élassa, *Greece* 39 F8
Elassón, *Greece* 38 B4
Elat, *Israel* 75 F3
Eláthia, *Greece* 38 C4
Eláziğ, *Turkey* 70 B3
Elba, *Italy* 28 F7
Elba, *U.S.A.* 109 K2
Elbasani, *Albania* 40 E4
Elbe →, *Europe* 24 B4
Elbe-Seitenkanal, *Germany* 24 C6
Elbert, Mt., *U.S.A.* 115 G10
Elberton, *U.S.A.* 109 H4
Elbeuf, *France* 18 C8
Elbidtan, *Turkey* 70 B3
Elbing = Elbląg, *Poland* . . 44 D6
Elbistan, *Turkey* 72 C7
Elbląg, *Poland* 44 D6
Elbow, *Canada* 105 C7
Elbrus, *Asia* 49 J6
Elburz Mts. = Alborz,
   Reshteh-ye Kūhhā-ye, *Iran* 71 C7
Elche, *Spain* 33 G4
Elche de la Sierra, *Spain* . . 33 G2
Elcho I., *Australia* 94 A2
Elda, *Spain* 33 G4
Elde →, *Germany* 24 B7
Eldon, *Mo., U.S.A.* 112 F8
Eldon, *Wash., U.S.A.* 116 C3
Eldora, *U.S.A.* 112 D8
Eldorado, *Argentina* 127 B5
Eldorado, *Canada* 110 B7
Eldorado, *Mexico* 118 C3
Eldorado, *Ill., U.S.A.* 108 G1
Eldorado, *Tex., U.S.A.* . . . 113 K4
Eldorado Springs, *U.S.A.* . . 113 G8
Eldoret, *Kenya* 86 B4
Eldred, *U.S.A.* 110 E6
Elea, C., *Cyprus* 36 D13
Eleanora, Pk., *Australia* . . . 93 F3
Elefantes →, *Mozam.* 89 C5
Elektrogorsk, *Russia* 46 E10
Elektrostal, *Russia* 46 E10
Elele, *Nigeria* 83 D6
Elena, *Bulgaria* 41 D9
Elephant Butte Reservoir,
   U.S.A. 115 K10
Elephant I., *Antarctica* . . . 5 C18
Eleshnitsa, *Bulgaria* 40 E7
Eleşkirt, *Turkey* 73 C10
Eleuthera, *Bahamas* 120 B4
Elevsís, *Greece* 38 C5
Elevtheroúpolis, *Greece* . . 41 F8
Elgin, *Canada* 111 B8
Elgin, *U.K.* 14 D5
Elgin, *Ill., U.S.A.* 108 D1
Elgin, *N. Dak., U.S.A.* . . . 112 B4
Elgin, *Oreg., U.S.A.* 114 D5
Elgin, *Tex., U.S.A.* 113 K6
Elgoibar, *Spain* 32 B2
Elgon, Mt., *Africa* 86 B3
Eliase, *Indonesia* 63 F8
Elikón, *Greece* 38 C4
Elim, *Namibia* 88 B2
Elim, *S. Africa* 88 E2
Elin Pelin, *Bulgaria* 40 D7
Elisabethville =
   Lubumbashi,
   Dem. Rep. of the Congo . 87 E2
Elista, *Russia* 49 G7

Elizabeth, *Australia* 95 E2
Elizabeth, *N.J., U.S.A.* . . . 111 F10
Elizabeth, *N.J., U.S.A.* . . . 111 F10
Elizabeth City, *U.S.A.* . . . 109 G7
Elizabethton, *U.S.A.* 109 G4
Elizabethtown, *Ky., U.S.A.* 108 G3
Elizabethtown, *N.Y., U.S.A.* 111 B11
Elizabethtown, *Pa., U.S.A.* 111 F8
Elizondo, *Spain* 32 B3
Ełk, *Poland* 44 E9
Elk →, *Canada* 104 C5
Ełk →, *Poland* 44 E9
Elk →, *U.S.A.* 109 H2
Elk City, *U.S.A.* 113 H5
Elk Creek, *U.S.A.* 116 F4
Elk Grove, *U.S.A.* 116 G5
Elk Island Nat. Park,
   Canada 104 C6
Elk Lake, *Canada* 102 C3
Elk Point, *Canada* 105 C6
Elk River, *Idaho, U.S.A.* . . 114 C5
Elk River, *Minn., U.S.A.* . . 112 C8
Elkedra →, *Australia* 94 C2
Elkhart, *Ind., U.S.A.* 108 E3
Elkhart, *Kans., U.S.A.* . . . 113 G4
Elkhorn, *Canada* 105 D8
Elkhorn →, *U.S.A.* 112 E6
Elkhovo, *Bulgaria* 41 D10
Elkin, *U.S.A.* 109 G5
Elkins, *U.S.A.* 108 F6
Elkland, *U.S.A.* 110 E7
Elko, *Canada* 104 D5
Elko, *U.S.A.* 114 F6
Elkton, *U.S.A.* 110 C1
Ell, L., *Australia* 93 E4
Ellef Ringnes I., *Canada* . . . 4 B2
Ellen, Mt., *U.S.A.* 111 B12
Ellenburg, *U.S.A.* 111 B11
Ellendale, *U.S.A.* 112 B5
Ellensburg, *U.S.A.* 114 C3
Ellenville, *U.S.A.* 111 E10
Ellery, Mt., *Australia* 95 F4
Ellesmere, L., *N.Z.* 91 M4
Ellesmere I., *Canada* 4 B4
Ellesmere Port, *U.K.* 12 D5
Ellice Is. = Tuvalu ■,
   Pac. Oc. 96 H9
Ellicottville, *U.S.A.* 110 D6
Elliot, *Australia* 94 B1
Elliot, *S. Africa* 89 E4
Elliot Lake, *Canada* 102 C3
Elliotdale = Xhora, *S. Africa* 89 E4
Ellis, *U.S.A.* 112 F5
Elliston, *Australia* 95 E1
Ellisville, *U.S.A.* 113 K10
Ellon, *U.K.* 14 D6
Ellore = Eluru, *India* 67 L12
Ellsworth, *Kans., U.S.A.* . . 112 F5
Ellsworth, *Maine, U.S.A.* . . 109 C11
Ellsworth Land, *Antarctica* . . 5 D16
Ellsworth Mts., *Antarctica* . . 5 D16
Ellwangen, *Germany* 25 G6
Ellwood City, *U.S.A.* 110 F4
Elm, *Switz.* 25 J5
Elma, *Canada* 105 D9
Elma, *U.S.A.* 116 D3
Elmadağ, *Turkey* 72 C5
Elmalı, *Turkey* 39 E11
Elmhurst, *U.S.A.* 108 E2
Elmina, *Ghana* 83 D4
Elmira, *Canada* 110 C4
Elmira, *U.S.A.* 110 D8
Elmira Heights, *U.S.A.* . . . 110 D8
Elmore, *Australia* 95 F3
Elmore, *U.S.A.* 117 M11
Elmshorn, *Germany* 24 B5
Elmvale, *Canada* 110 B5
Elne, *France* 20 F6
Elora, *Canada* 110 C4
Elos, *Greece* 38 E4
Eloúnda, *Greece* 36 D7
Eloy, *U.S.A.* 115 K8
Éloyes, *France* 19 D13
Elrose, *Canada* 105 C7
Elsdorf, *Germany* 24 E2
Elsie, *U.S.A.* 116 E3
Elsinore = Helsingør,
   Denmark 11 H6
Elster →, *Germany* 24 D7
Elsterwerda, *Germany* . . . 24 D9
Eltham, *N.Z.* 91 H5
Elton, *Russia* 49 F8
Elton, Ozero, *Russia* 49 F8
Eltville, *Germany* 25 E4
Eluru, *India* 67 L12
Elvas, *Portugal* 35 G3
Elven, *France* 18 E4
Elverum, *Norway* 9 F14
Elvire →, *Australia* 92 C4
Elvire, Mt., *Australia* 93 E2
Elvo →, *Italy* 28 C5
Elwell, L., *U.S.A.* 114 B8
Elwood, *Ind., U.S.A.* 108 E3
Elwood, *Nebr., U.S.A.* . . . 112 E5
Elx = Elche, *Spain* 33 G4
Ely, *U.K.* 13 E8
Ely, *Minn., U.S.A.* 112 B9
Ely, *Nev., U.S.A.* 114 G6
Elyria, *U.S.A.* 110 E2
Elyrus, *Greece* 38 F5
Elz →, *Germany* 25 G3
Emådalen, *Sweden* 10 C8
Emãmrûd, *Iran* 71 B7
Emãn →, *Sweden* 11 G10
Emba, *Kazakstan* 50 E6
Emba →, *Kazakstan* 50 E6
Embarcación, *Argentina* . . 126 A3
Embarras Portage, *Canada* . 105 B6
Embetsu, *Japan* 54 B10
Embi = Emba, *Kazakstan* . . 50 E6

Embi = Emba →, Kazakstan 50 E6
Embóna, Greece 36 C9
Embrun, France 21 D10
Embu, Kenya 86 C4
Emden, Germany 24 B3
Emecik, Turkey 39 E9
Emerald, Australia 94 C4
Emerson, Canada 105 D9
Emet, Turkey 39 B11
Emi Koussi, Chad 79 E9
Emília-Romagna □, Italy 28 D8
Emilius, Mte., Italy 28 C4
Eminabad, Pakistan 68 C6
Emine, Nos, Bulgaria 41 D11
Emirdağ, Turkey 72 C4
Emlenton, U.S.A. 110 E5
Emlichheim, Germany 24 C2
Emmaboda, Sweden 11 H9
Emmaus, S. Africa 88 D4
Emmaus, U.S.A. 111 F9
Emme →, Switz. 25 H3
Emmeloord, Neths. 17 B5
Emmen, Neths. 17 B6
Emmen, Switz. 25 H4
Emmendingen, Germany 25 G3
Emmental, Switz. 25 J3
Emmerich, Germany 24 D2
Emmet, Australia 94 C3
Emmetsburg, U.S.A. 112 D7
Emmett, Idaho, U.S.A. 114 E5
Emmett, Mich., U.S.A. 110 D2
Emmonak, U.S.A. 100 B3
Emo, Canada 105 D10
Emőd, Hungary 42 C5
Emona, Bulgaria 41 D11
Empalme, Mexico 118 B2
Empangeni, S. Africa 89 D5
Empedrado, Argentina 126 B4
Emperor Seamount Chain, Pac. Oc. 96 D9
Empoli, Italy 28 E7
Emporia, Kans., U.S.A. 112 F6
Emporia, Va., U.S.A. 109 G7
Emporium, U.S.A. 110 E6
Empress, Canada 105 C7
Empty Quarter = Rub' al Khālī, Si. Arabia 74 D4
Ems →, Germany 24 B3
Emsdale, Canada 110 A5
Emsdetten, Germany 24 C3
Emu, China 57 C15
Emu Park, Australia 94 C5
'En 'Avrona, Israel 75 F4
En Nahud, Sudan 81 E2
En Nofalab, Sudan 81 D3
Ena, Japan 55 G8
Enana, Namibia 88 B2
Enånger, Sweden 10 C11
Enaratoli, Indonesia 63 E9
Enard B., U.K. 14 C3
Enare = Inarijärvi, Finland 8 B22
Encampment, U.S.A. 114 F10
Encantadas, Serra, Brazil 127 C5
Encarnación, Paraguay 127 B4
Encarnación de Diaz, Mexico 118 C4
Enchi, Ghana 82 D4
Encinitas, U.S.A. 117 M9
Encino, U.S.A. 115 J11
Encounter B., Australia 95 F2
Encs, Hungary 42 B6
Endako, Canada 104 C3
Ende, Indonesia 63 F6
Endeavour Str., Australia 94 A3
Endelave, Denmark 11 J4
Enderbury I., Kiribati 96 H10
Enderby, Canada 104 C5
Enderby I., Australia 92 D2
Enderby Land, Antarctica 5 C5
Enderlin, U.S.A. 112 B6
Endicott, U.S.A. 111 D8
Endwell, U.S.A. 111 D8
Endyalgout I., Australia 92 B5
Eneabba, Australia 93 E2
Enewetak Atoll, Marshall Is. 96 F8
Enez, Turkey 41 F10
Enfield, Canada 103 D7
Enfield, Conn., U.S.A. 111 E12
Enfield, N.H., U.S.A. 111 C12
Engadin, Switz. 25 J6
Engaño, C., Dom. Rep. 121 C6
Engaño, C., Phil. 63 A6
Engaru, Japan 54 B11
Engcobo, S. Africa 89 E4
Engelberg, Switz. 25 J4
Engels, Russia 48 E8
Engemann L., Canada 105 B7
Engershatu, Eritrea 81 D4
Enggano, Indonesia 62 F2
England, U.S.A. 113 H9
England □, U.K. 12 D7
Englee, Canada 103 B8
Englehart, Canada 102 C4
Englewood, U.S.A. 112 F2
English →, Canada 105 C10
English Bazar = Ingraj Bazar, India 69 G13
English Channel, Europe 13 G6
English River, Canada 102 C1
Engures ezers, Latvia 44 A10
Enguri →, Georgia 49 J5
Enid, U.S.A. 113 G6
Enipévs →, Greece 38 B4
Enkhuizen, Neths. 17 B5
Enköping, Sweden 10 E11
Enle, China 58 F3
Enna, Italy 31 E7
Ennadai, Canada 105 A8
Ennadai L., Canada 105 A8
Ennedi, Chad 79 E10
Enngonia, Australia 95 D4
Ennigerloh, Germany 24 D4
Ennis, Ireland 15 D3
Ennis, Mont., U.S.A. 114 D8
Ennis, Tex., U.S.A. 113 J6
Enniscorthy, Ireland 15 D5
Enniskillen, U.K. 15 B4
Ennistimon, Ireland 15 D2
Enns, Austria 26 C7
Enns →, Austria 26 C7
Enontekiö, Finland 8 B20
Enosburg Falls, U.S.A. 111 B12
Enping, China 59 F9
Enriquillo, L., Dom. Rep. 121 C5
Enschede, Neths. 17 B6
Ensenada, Argentina 126 C4
Ensenada, Mexico 118 A1
Ensenada de los Muertos, Mexico 118 C2
Enshi, China 58 B7
Ensiola, Pta. de n', Spain 37 B9
Ensisheim, France 19 E14
Entebbe, Uganda 86 B3
Enterprise, Canada 104 A5
Enterprise, Ala., U.S.A. 109 K3
Enterprise, Oreg., U.S.A. 114 D5
Entraygues-sur-Truyère, France 20 D6
Entre Ríos, Bolivia 126 A3
Entre Ríos □, Argentina 126 C4
Entrepeñas, Embalse de, Spain 32 E2
Entroncamento, Portugal 35 F2
Enugu, Nigeria 83 D6
Enugu □, Nigeria 83 D6
Enugu Ezike, Nigeria 83 D6
Enumclaw, U.S.A. 116 C5
Envermeu, France 18 C8
Enviken, Sweden 10 D9
Enying, Hungary 42 D3
Enza →, Italy 28 D7
Eólie, Ís., Italy 31 D7
Epanomí, Greece 40 F6
Epe, Neths. 17 B5
Epe, Nigeria 83 D5
Épernay, France 19 C10
Épernon, France 19 D8
Ephesus, Turkey 39 D9
Ephraim, U.S.A. 114 G8
Ephrata, Pa., U.S.A. 111 F8
Ephrata, Wash., U.S.A. 114 C4
Epidaurus Limera, Greece 38 E5
Épila, Spain 32 D3
Épinac, France 19 F11
Épinal, France 19 D13
Episkopi, Cyprus 36 E11
Episkopí, Greece 36 D6
Episkopi Bay, Cyprus 36 E11
Epitálion, Greece 38 D3
Eppan = Appiano, Italy 29 B8
Eppingen, Germany 25 F4
Epsom, U.K. 13 F7
Epukiro, Namibia 88 C2
Equatorial Guinea ■, Africa 84 D1
Er Hai, China 58 E3
Er Rahad, Sudan 81 E3
Er Rif, Morocco 78 A5
Er Rogel, Sudan 80 D4
Er Roseires, Sudan 81 E3
Er Rua'at, Sudan 81 E3
Eraclea, Italy 29 C9
Erāwadī Myit = Irrawaddy →, Burma 67 M19
Erba, Italy 28 C6
Erba, Sudan 80 D4
Erba, J., Sudan 80 C4
Erbaa, Turkey 72 B7
Erbeskopf, Germany 25 F3
Erbil = Arbīl, Iraq 70 B5
Erbu, Ethiopia 81 E3
Erçek, Turkey 70 B4
Erçiş, Turkey 73 C10
Erciyaş Dağı, Turkey 70 B2
Érd, Hungary 42 C3
Erdao Jiang →, China 57 C14
Erdek, Turkey 41 F11
Erdemli, Turkey 72 D6
Erdene = Ulaan-Uul, Mongolia 56 B6
Erdenetsogt, Mongolia 56 C4
Erding, Germany 25 G7
Erdre →, France 18 E5
Erebus, Mt., Antarctica 5 D11
Erechim, Brazil 127 B5
Ereğli, Konya, Turkey 70 B2
Ereğli, Zonguldak, Turkey 72 B4
Erei, Monti, Italy 31 E7
Erenhot, China 56 C7
Eresma →, Spain 34 D6
Eressós, Greece 39 B7
Erewadi Myitwanya, Burma 67 M19
Erfenisdam, S. Africa 88 D4
Erfstadt, Germany 24 E2
Erft →, Germany 24 D2
Erfurt, Germany 24 E7
Erg Iguidi, Africa 78 C4
Ergani, Turkey 70 B3
Ergel, Mongolia 56 C5
Ergene →, Turkey 41 E10
Ergeni Vozvyshennost, Russia 49 G7
Ērgli, Latvia 9 H21
Erhlin, Taiwan 59 F13
Eria →, Spain 34 C5
Eriba, Sudan 81 D4
Eriboll, L., U.K. 14 C4
Érice, Italy 30 D5
Erie, U.S.A. 110 D4
Erie, L., N. Amer. 110 D4
Erie Canal, U.S.A. 110 C7
Erieau, Canada 110 D3
Erigavo, Somali Rep. 74 E4
Erikoúsa, Greece 36 A3
Eriksdale, Canada 105 C9
Erímanthos, Greece 38 D3
Erimo-misaki, Japan 54 D11
Erinpura, India 68 G5
Eriskay, U.K. 14 D1
Erithraí, Greece 38 C5
Eritrea ■, Africa 81 E4
Erjas →, Portugal 34 F3
Erkelenz, Germany 24 D2
Erkner, Germany 24 C9
Erlangen, Germany 25 F6
Erldunda, Australia 94 D1
Ermelo, Neths. 17 B5
Ermelo, S. Africa 89 D4
Ermenek, Turkey 70 B2
Ermil, Sudan 81 E2
Ermióni, Greece 38 D5
Ermones, Greece 36 A3
Ermoúpolis = Síros, Greece 38 D6
Ernakulam = Cochin, India 66 Q10
Erne →, Ireland 15 B3
Erne, Lower L., U.K. 15 B4
Erne, Upper L., U.K. 15 B4
Ernée, France 18 D6
Ernest Giles Ra., Australia 93 E3
Ernstberg, Germany 25 E2
Erode, India 66 P10
Eromanga, Australia 95 D3
Erongo, Namibia 88 C2
Erquy, France 18 D4
Erramala Hills, India 66 M11
Errer →, Ethiopia 81 F5
Errigal, Ireland 15 A3
Erris Hd., Ireland 15 B1
Erseka, Albania 40 F4
Erskine, U.S.A. 112 B7
Erstein, France 19 D14
Ertholmene, Denmark 11 J9
Ertil, Russia 48 E5
Ertis = Irtysh →, Russia 50 C7
Eruh, Turkey 73 D10
Eruwa, Nigeria 83 D5
Ervy-le-Châtel, France 19 D10
Erwin, U.S.A. 109 G4
Eryuan, China 58 D2
Erzgebirge, Germany 24 E8
Erzin, Russia 51 D10
Erzincan, Turkey 70 B3
Erzurum, Turkey 70 B4
Es Caló, Spain 37 C8
Es Canar, Spain 37 B8
Es Mercadal, Spain 37 B11
Es Migjorn Gran, Spain 37 B11
Es Safiya, Sudan 81 D3
Es Sahrâ' Esh Sharqîya, Egypt 80 B3
Es Sînâ', Egypt 75 F3
Es Sûkî, Sudan 81 E3
Es Vedrà, Spain 37 C7
Esambo, Dem. Rep. of the Congo 86 C1
Esan-Misaki, Japan 54 D10
Esashi, Hokkaidō, Japan 54 B11
Esashi, Hokkaidō, Japan 54 D10
Esbjerg, Denmark 11 J2
Escalante, U.S.A. 115 H8
Escalante →, U.S.A. 115 H8
Escalón, Mexico 118 B4
Escambia →, U.S.A. 109 K2
Escanaba, U.S.A. 108 C2
Esch-sur-Alzette, Lux. 17 E6
Eschede, Germany 24 C6
Eschwege, Germany 24 D6
Eschweiler, Germany 24 E2
Escondido, U.S.A. 117 M9
Escravos →, Nigeria 83 D6
Escuinapa, Mexico 118 C3
Escuintla, Guatemala 120 D1
Eséka, Cameroon 83 E7
Eşen →, Turkey 39 E11
Esenguly, Turkmenistan 50 F6
Esens, Germany 24 B3
Esenyurt, Turkey 41 E12
Esera →, Spain 32 C5
Eşfahān, Iran 71 C6
Eşfahān □, Iran 71 C6
Esfarāyen, Iran 71 B8
Esfīdeh, Iran 71 C8
Esgueva →, Spain 34 D6
Esh Sham = Dimashq, Syria 75 B5
Esh Shamâlîya □, Sudan 80 D2
Esha Ness, U.K. 14 A7
Eshan, China 58 E4
Esher, U.K. 13 F7
Eshowe, S. Africa 89 D5
Esiama, Ghana 82 E4
Esigodini, Zimbabwe 89 C4
Esil = Ishim →, Russia 50 D8
Esino →, Italy 29 E10
Esira, Madag. 89 C8
Esk →, Cumb., U.K. 14 G5
Esk →, N. Yorks., U.K. 12 C7
Eskān, Iran 71 E9
Esker, Canada 103 B6
Eskifjörður, Iceland 8 D7
Eskilsäter, Sweden 11 F7
Eskilstuna, Sweden 10 E10
Eskimalatya, Turkey 73 C8
Eskimo Pt., Canada 100 B10
Eskişehir, Turkey 39 B12
Eskişehir □, Turkey 39 B12
Esla →, Spain 34 D4
Eslāmābād-e Gharb, Iran 70 C5
Eslāmshahr, Iran 71 C6
Eslöv, Sweden 11 J7
Eşme, Turkey 39 C10
Esmeraldas, Ecuador 124 C3
Esnagi L., Canada 102 C3
Espalion, France 20 D6
Espanola, Canada 102 C3
Espanola, U.S.A. 115 H10
Esparreguera, Spain 32 D6
Esparta, Costa Rica 120 E3
Espelkamp, Germany 24 C4
Esperance, Australia 93 F3
Esperance B., Australia 93 F3
Esperanza, Argentina 126 C3
Esperanza, Phil. 61 G6
Espéraza, France 20 F6
Espichel, C., Portugal 35 G1
Espiel, Spain 35 G5
Espigão, Serra do, Brazil 127 B5
Espinazo, Sierra del = Espinhaço, Serra do, Brazil 125 G10
Espinhaço, Serra do, Brazil 125 G10
Espinho, Portugal 34 D2
Espinilho, Serra do, Brazil 127 B5
Espinosa de los Monteros, Spain 34 B7
Espírito Santo □, Brazil 125 H10
Espíritu Santo, Vanuatu 96 J8
Espíritu Santo, B. del, Mexico 119 D7
Espíritu Santo, I., Mexico 118 C2
Espita, Mexico 119 C7
Espiye, Turkey 73 B8
Espluga de Francolí, Spain 32 D6
Espoo, Finland 9 F21
Espuña, Sierra de, Spain 33 H3
Espungabera, Mozam. 89 C5
Esquel, Argentina 128 E2
Esquimalt, Canada 104 D4
Esquina, Argentina 126 C4
Essaouira, Morocco 78 B4
Essebie, Dem. Rep. of the Congo 86 B3
Essen, Belgium 17 C4
Essen, Germany 24 D3
Essendon, Mt., Australia 93 E3
Essequibo →, Guyana 122 C5
Essex, Canada 110 D2
Essex, Calif., U.S.A. 117 L11
Essex, N.Y., U.S.A. 111 B11
Essex □, U.K. 13 F8
Essex Junction, U.S.A. 111 B11
Esslingen, Germany 25 G5
Essonne □, France 19 D9
Estaca de Bares, C. de, Spain 34 B3
Estadilla, Spain 32 C5
Estados, I. de Los, Argentina 122 J4
Estagel, France 20 F6
Eşţahbānāt, Iran 71 D7
Estância, Brazil 125 F11
Estancia, U.S.A. 115 J10
Estārm, Iran 71 D8
Estarreja, Portugal 34 E2
Estats, Pic d', Spain 32 C6
Estcourt, S. Africa 89 D4
Este, Italy 29 C8
Estelí, Nic. 120 D2
Estella, Spain 32 C2
Estellencs, Spain 37 B9
Estena →, Spain 35 F6
Estepa, Spain 35 H6
Estepona, Spain 35 J5
Esterhazy, Canada 105 C8
Esternay, France 19 D10
Esterri d'Aneu, Spain 32 C6
Estevan, Canada 105 D8
Estevan Group, Canada 104 C3
Estherville, U.S.A. 112 D7
Estissac, France 19 D10
Eston, Canada 105 C7
Estonia ■, Europe 9 G21
Estoril, Portugal 35 G1
Estouk, Mali 83 B5
Estreito, Brazil 125 E9
Estrela, Serra da, Portugal 34 E3
Estrella, Spain 35 G7
Estremoz, Portugal 35 G3
Estrondo, Serra do, Brazil 125 E9
Esztergom, Hungary 42 C3
Et Tîdra, Mauritania 82 B1
Etah, India 69 F8
Étain, France 19 C12
Étampes, France 19 D9
Etanga, Namibia 88 B1
Étaples, France 19 B8
Etawah, India 69 F8
Etawney L., Canada 105 B9
Ete, Nigeria 83 D6
Ethel, U.S.A. 116 D4
Ethelbert, Canada 105 C8
Ethiopia ■, Africa 74 F3
Ethiopian Highlands, Ethiopia 52 J7
Etili, Turkey 41 G10
Etive, L., U.K. 14 E3
Etna, Italy 31 E7
Etoile, Dem. Rep. of the Congo 87 E2
Etosha Nat. Park, Namibia 88 B2
Etosha Pan, Namibia 88 B2
Etowah, U.S.A. 109 H3
Étréchy, France 19 D9
Étrépagny, France 19 C8
Étretat, France 18 C7
Etropole, Bulgaria 41 D8
Ettelbruck, Lux. 17 E6
Ettlingen, Germany 25 G4
Ettrick Water →, U.K. 14 F6
Etuku, Dem. Rep. of the Congo 86 C2
Etulia, Moldova 43 E13
Etzatlán, Mexico 118 C4
Etzná, Mexico 119 D6
Eu, France 18 B8
Euboea = Évvoia, Greece 38 C6
Eucla, Australia 93 F4
Euclid, U.S.A. 110 E3
Eucumbene, L., Australia 95 F4
Eudora, U.S.A. 113 J9
Eufaula, Ala., U.S.A. 109 K3
Eufaula, Okla., U.S.A. 113 H7
Eufaula L., U.S.A. 113 H7
Eugene, U.S.A. 114 E2
Eugowra, Australia 95 E4
Eulo, Australia 95 D4
Eunice, La., U.S.A. 113 K8
Eunice, N. Mex., U.S.A. 113 J3
Eupen, Belgium 17 D6
Euphrates = Furāt, Nahr al →, Asia 70 D5
Eure □, France 18 C8
Eure →, France 18 C8
Eure-et-Loir □, France 18 D8
Eureka, Canada 4 B3
Eureka, Calif., U.S.A. 114 F1
Eureka, Kans., U.S.A. 113 G6
Eureka, Mont., U.S.A. 114 B6
Eureka, Nev., U.S.A. 114 G5
Eureka, S. Dak., U.S.A. 112 C5
Eureka, Mt., Australia 93 E3
Euroa, Australia 95 F4
Europa, Île, Ind. Oc. 85 J8
Europa, Picos de, Spain 34 B6
Europa, Pta. de, Gib. 35 J5
Europe 6 E10
Europoort, Neths. 17 C4
Euskirchen, Germany 24 E2
Eustis, U.S.A. 109 L5
Euston, Australia 95 E3
Eutin, Germany 24 A6
Eutsuk L., Canada 104 C3
Evale, Angola 88 B2
Evans, U.S.A. 112 E2
Evans, L., Canada 102 B4
Evans City, U.S.A. 110 F4
Evans Head, Australia 95 D5
Evans Mills, U.S.A. 111 B9
Evansburg, Canada 104 C5
Evanston, Ill., U.S.A. 108 E2
Evanston, Wyo., U.S.A. 114 F8
Evansville, U.S.A. 108 G2
Évaux-les-Bains, France 19 F9
Evaz, Iran 71 E7
Evciler, Afyon, Turkey 39 C11
Evciler, Çanakkale, Turkey 39 B8
Eveleth, U.S.A. 112 B8
Evensk, Russia 51 C16
Everard, L., Australia 95 E2
Everard Ranges, Australia 93 E5
Everest, Mt., Nepal 69 E12
Everett, Pa., U.S.A. 110 F6
Everett, Wash., U.S.A. 116 C4
Everglades, The, U.S.A. 109 N5
Everglades National Park, U.S.A. 109 N5
Evergreen, Ala., U.S.A. 109 K2
Evergreen, Mont., U.S.A. 114 B6
Everöd, Sweden 11 J8
Evertsberg, Sweden 10 C7
Evesham, U.K. 13 E6
Évian-les-Bains, France 19 F13
Évinos →, Greece 38 C3
Évisa, France 21 F12
Evje, Norway 9 G12
Évora, Portugal 35 G3
Évora □, Portugal 35 G3
Evowghlī, Iran 70 B5
Évreux, France 18 C8
Evritanía □, Greece 38 B3
Évron, France 18 D6
Évros □, Greece 41 E10
Évros →, Bulgaria 72 B2
Evrótas →, Greece 38 E4
Évry, France 19 D9
Évvoia, Greece 38 C6
Évvoia □, Greece 38 C5
Evxinoúpolis, Greece 38 B4
Ewe, L., U.K. 14 D3
Ewing, U.S.A. 112 D5
Ewo, Congo 84 E2
Exaltación, Bolivia 124 F5
Excelsior Springs, U.S.A. 112 F7
Excideuil, France 20 C5
Exe →, U.K. 13 G4
Exeter, Canada 110 C3
Exeter, U.K. 13 G4
Exeter, Calif., U.S.A. 116 J7
Exeter, N.H., U.S.A. 111 D14
Exmoor, U.K. 13 F4
Exmouth, Australia 92 D1
Exmouth, U.K. 13 G4
Exmouth G., Australia 92 D1
Expedition Ra., Australia 94 C4
Extremadura □, Spain 35 F4
Exuma Sound, Bahamas 120 B4
Eyasi, L., Tanzania 86 C4
Eye Pen., U.K. 14 C2
Eyemouth, U.K. 14 F6
Eygurande, France 19 G9
Eyjafjörður, Iceland 8 C4
Eymet, France 20 D4
Eymoutiers, France 20 C5
Eynesil, Turkey 73 B8
Eyre (North), L., Australia 95 D2
Eyre (South), L., Australia 95 D2
Eyre Mts., N.Z. 91 L2
Eyre Pen., Australia 95 E2
Eysturoy, Færoe Is. 8 E9
Eyvānkī, Iran 71 C6
Ez Zeidab, Sudan 80 D3
Ezcaray, Spain 32 C1
Ežerėlis, Lithuania 44 D10
Ezhou, China 59 B10
Ezine, Turkey 39 B8
Ezouza →, Cyprus 36 E11

F.Y.R.O.M.

F

F.Y.R.O.M. = Macedonia ■, *Europe* 40 E5
Fabala, *Guinea* 82 D3
Fabens, *U.S.A.* 115 L10
Fabero, *Spain* 34 C4
Fåborg, *Denmark* 11 J4
Fabriano, *Italy* 29 E9
Făcăeni, *Romania* 43 F12
Fachi, *Niger* 79 E8
Fada, *Chad* 79 E10
Fada-n-Gourma, *Burkina Faso* 83 C5
Fadd, *Hungary* 42 D3
Faddeyevskiy, Ostrov, *Russia* 51 B15
Faddor, *Sudan* 81 F3
Fadghāmī, *Syria* 70 C4
Fadlab, *Sudan* 80 D3
Faenza, *Italy* 29 D8
Færoe Is. = Føroyar, *Atl. Oc.* 8 F9
Fafa, *Mali* 83 B5
Fafe, *Portugal* 34 D2
Fagam, *Nigeria* 83 C7
Făgăras, *Romania* 43 E9
Făgăras, Munţii, *Romania* 43 E9
Fågelmara, *Sweden* 11 H9
Fagerhult, *Sweden* 11 G9
Fagersta, *Sweden* 10 D9
Făget, *Romania* 42 E7
Făget, Munţii, *Romania* 43 C8
Fagnano, L., *Argentina* 128 G3
Fagnières, *France* 19 D11
Faguibine, L., *Mali* 82 B4
Fahlīān, *Iran* 71 D6
Fahraj, *Kermān, Iran* 71 D8
Fahraj, *Yazd, Iran* 71 D7
Fai Tsi Long Archipelago, *Vietnam* 58 G6
Faial, *Madeira* 37 D3
Fair Haven, *U.S.A.* 108 D9
Fair Hd., *U.K.* 15 A5
Fair Oaks, *U.S.A.* 116 G5
Fairbanks, *U.S.A.* 100 B5
Fairbury, *U.S.A.* 112 E6
Fairfax, *U.S.A.* 111 B11
Fairfield, *Ala., U.S.A.* 109 J2
Fairfield, *Calif., U.S.A.* 116 G4
Fairfield, *Conn., U.S.A.* 111 E11
Fairfield, *Idaho, U.S.A.* 114 E6
Fairfield, *Ill., U.S.A.* 108 F1
Fairfield, *Iowa, U.S.A.* 112 E9
Fairfield, *Tex., U.S.A.* 113 K7
Fairford, *Canada* 105 C9
Fairhope, *U.S.A.* 109 K2
Fairlie, *N.Z.* 91 L3
Fairmead, *U.S.A.* 116 H6
Fairmont, *Minn., U.S.A.* 112 D7
Fairmont, *W. Va., U.S.A.* 108 F5
Fairmount, *Calif., U.S.A.* 117 L8
Fairmount, *N.Y., U.S.A.* 111 C8
Fairplay, *U.S.A.* 115 G11
Fairport, *U.S.A.* 110 C7
Fairport Harbor, *U.S.A.* 110 E3
Fairview, *Canada* 104 B5
Fairview, *Mont., U.S.A.* 112 B2
Fairview, *Okla., U.S.A.* 113 G5
Fairweather, Mt., *U.S.A.* 104 B1
Faisalabad, *Pakistan* 68 D5
Faith, *U.S.A.* 112 C3
Faizabad, *India* 69 F10
Fajardo, *Puerto Rico* 121 C6
Fajr, W. →, *Si. Arabia* 70 D3
Fakenham, *U.K.* 12 E8
Fåker, *Sweden* 10 A8
Fakfak, *Indonesia* 63 E8
Fakiya, *Bulgaria* 41 D11
Fakobli, *Ivory C.* 82 D3
Fakse, *Denmark* 11 J6
Fakse Bugt, *Denmark* 11 J6
Fakse Ladeplads, *Denmark* 11 J6
Faku, *China* 57 C12
Falaba, *S. Leone* 82 D2
Falaise, *France* 18 D6
Falaise, Mui, *Vietnam* 64 C5
Falakrón Óros, *Greece* 40 E7
Falam, *Burma* 67 H18
Falces, *Spain* 32 C3
Fălciu, *Romania* 43 D13
Falcó, C. des, *Spain* 37 C7
Falcón, Presa, *Mexico* 119 B5
Falcon Lake, *Canada* 105 D9
Falcon Reservoir, *U.S.A.* 113 M5
Falconara Marittima, *Italy* 29 E10
Falcone, C. del, *Italy* 30 B1
Falconer, *U.S.A.* 110 D5
Faléa, *Mali* 82 C2
Falémé →, *Senegal* 82 C2
Falerum, *Sweden* 11 F10
Faleshty = Făleşti, *Moldova* 43 C12
Făleşti, *Moldova* 43 C12
Falfurrias, *U.S.A.* 113 M5
Falher, *Canada* 104 B5
Falirakí, *Greece* 36 C10
Falkenberg, *Germany* 24 D9
Falkenberg, *Sweden* 11 H6
Falkensee, *Germany* 24 C9
Falkirk, *U.K.* 14 F5
Falkirk □, *U.K.* 14 F5
Falkland, *U.K.* 14 E5
Falkland Is. □, *Atl. Oc.* 128 G5
Falkland Sd., *Falk. Is.* 128 G5
Falkonéra, *Greece* 38 E5
Falköping, *Sweden* 11 F7
Fall River, *U.S.A.* 111 E13
Fallbrook, *U.S.A.* 117 M9
Fallon, *U.S.A.* 114 G4
Falls City, *U.S.A.* 112 E7
Falls Creek, *U.S.A.* 110 E6
Falmouth, *Jamaica* 120 C4
Falmouth, *U.K.* 13 G2
Falmouth, *U.S.A.* 111 E14
Falsa, Pta., *Mexico* 118 B1
False B., *S. Africa* 88 E2
Falso, C., *Honduras* 120 C3
Falster, *Denmark* 11 K5
Falsterbo, *Sweden* 9 J15
Fălticeni, *Romania* 43 C11
Falun, *Sweden* 10 D9
Famagusta, *Cyprus* 36 D12
Famagusta Bay, *Cyprus* 36 D13
Famalé, *Niger* 78 F6
Famatina, Sierra de, *Argentina* 126 B2
Family L., *Canada* 105 C9
Famoso, *U.S.A.* 117 K7
Fan Xian, *China* 56 G8
Fana, *Mali* 82 C3
Fanad Hd., *Ireland* 15 A4
Fanárion, *Greece* 38 B3
Fandriana, *Madag.* 89 C8
Fang, *Thailand* 58 H2
Fang Xian, *China* 59 A8
Fangaga, *Sudan* 80 D4
Fangak, *Sudan* 81 F3
Fangchang, *China* 59 B12
Fangcheng, *China* 56 H7
Fangchenggang, *China* 58 G7
Fangliao, *Taiwan* 59 F13
Fangshan, *China* 56 E6
Fangzi, *China* 57 F10
Fani i Madh →, *Albania* 40 E4
Fanjakana, *Madag.* 89 C8
Fanjiatun, *China* 57 C13
Fannich, L., *U.K.* 14 D4
Fannūj, *Iran* 71 E8
Fanø, *Denmark* 11 J2
Fano, *Italy* 29 E10
Fanshi, *China* 56 E7
Fao = Al Fāw, *Iraq* 71 D6
Faqirwali, *Pakistan* 68 E5
Fâqûs, *Egypt* 80 H7
Fara in Sabina, *Italy* 29 F9
Faradje, *Dem. Rep. of the Congo* 86 B2
Farafangana, *Madag.* 89 C8
Farâfra, El Wâhât el-, *Egypt* 80 B2
Farāh, *Afghan.* 66 C3
Farāh □, *Afghan.* 66 C3
Farahalana, *Madag.* 89 A9
Faraid, Gebel, *Egypt* 80 C4
Farako, *Ivory C.* 82 D4
Faramana, *Burkina Faso* 82 C4
Faranah, *Guinea* 82 C2
Farasān, Jazā'ir, *Si. Arabia* 74 D3
Farasan Is. = Farasān, Jazā'ir, *Si. Arabia* 74 D3
Faratsiho, *Madag.* 89 B8
Fardes →, *Spain* 35 H7
Fareham, *U.K.* 13 G6
Farewell, C., *N.Z.* 91 J4
Farewell C. = Nunap Isua, *Greenland* 4 D5
Färgelanda, *Sweden* 11 F5
Farghona, *Uzbekistan* 50 E8
Fargo, *U.S.A.* 112 B6
Fār'iah, W. al →, *West Bank* 75 C4
Faribault, *U.S.A.* 112 C8
Faridabad, *India* 68 E6
Faridkot, *India* 68 D6
Faridpur, *Bangla.* 69 H13
Faridpur, *India* 69 E8
Färila, *Sweden* 10 C9
Farim, *Guinea-Biss.* 82 C1
Farīmān, *Iran* 71 C8
Farina, *Australia* 95 E2
Fariones, Pta., *Canary Is.* 37 E6
Fâriskûr, *Egypt* 80 H7
Färjestaden, *Sweden* 11 H10
Farkadhón, *Greece* 38 B4
Farmakonisi, *Greece* 39 D9
Farmerville, *U.S.A.* 113 J8
Farmingdale, *U.S.A.* 111 F10
Farmington, *Canada* 104 B4
Farmington, *Calif., U.S.A.* 116 H6
Farmington, *Maine, U.S.A.* 109 C10
Farmington, *Mo., U.S.A.* 113 G9
Farmington, *N.H., U.S.A.* 111 C13
Farmington, *N. Mex., U.S.A.* 115 H9
Farmington, *Utah, U.S.A.* 114 F8
Farmington →, *U.S.A.* 111 E12
Farmville, *U.S.A.* 108 G6
Färnäs, *Sweden* 10 D8
Farne Is., *U.K.* 12 B6
Farnham, *Canada* 111 A12
Farnham, Mt., *Canada* 104 C5
Faro, *Brazil* 125 D7
Faro, *Canada* 100 B6
Faro, *Portugal* 35 H3
Fårö, *Sweden* 9 H18
Faro □, *Portugal* 35 H2
Fårösund, *Sweden* 11 G13
Farquhar, C., *Australia* 93 D1
Farrars Cr. →, *Australia* 94 D3
Farrāshband, *Iran* 71 D7
Farrell, *U.S.A.* 110 E4
Farrokhī, *Iran* 71 C8
Farruch, C. = Ferrutx, C., *Spain* 37 B10
Farrukhabad-cum-Fatehgarh, *India* 66 F11
Fārs □, *Iran* 71 D7
Fársala, *Greece* 38 B4
Farsø, *Denmark* 11 H3
Farson, *U.S.A.* 114 E9
Farsund, *Norway* 9 G12
Fartak, Râs, *Si. Arabia* 70 D2
Fartak, Ra's, *Yemen* 74 D5
Fârţăneşti, *Romania* 43 E12
Fartura, Serra da, *Brazil* 127 B5
Faru, *Nigeria* 83 C6
Fārūj, *Iran* 71 B8
Fårup, *Denmark* 11 H3
Farvel, Kap = Nunap Isua, *Greenland* 4 D5
Farwell, *U.S.A.* 113 H3
Fasā, *Iran* 71 D7
Fasano, *Italy* 31 B10
Fashoda, *Sudan* 81 F3
Fassa, *Mali* 82 C3
Fastiv, *Ukraine* 47 G5
Fastov = Fastiv, *Ukraine* 47 G5
Fatagar, Tanjung, *Indonesia* 63 E8
Fatehabad, *Haryana, India* 68 E6
Fatehabad, *Ut. P., India* 68 F8
Fatehgarh, *India* 69 F8
Fatehpur, *Bihar, India* 69 G11
Fatehpur, *Raj., India* 68 F6
Fatehpur, *Ut. P., India* 69 G9
Fatehpur, *Ut. P., India* 69 F9
Fatehpur Sikri, *India* 68 F6
Fatesh, *Russia* 47 F8
Fathai, *Sudan* 81 F3
Fatick, *Senegal* 82 C1
Fatima, *Canada* 103 C7
Fátima, *Portugal* 35 F2
Fatoya, *Guinea* 82 C3
Fatsa, *Turkey* 72 B7
Faucille, Col de la, *France* 19 F13
Faulkton, *U.S.A.* 112 C5
Faulquemont, *France* 19 C13
Faure I., *Australia* 93 E1
Făurei, *Romania* 43 E12
Fauresmith, *S. Africa* 88 D4
Fauske, *Norway* 8 C16
Favara, *Italy* 30 E6
Faváritx, C. de, *Spain* 37 B11
Faverges, *France* 21 C10
Favignana, *Italy* 30 E5
Favignana, I., *Italy* 30 E5
Fawcett, Pt., *Australia* 92 B5
Fawn →, *Canada* 102 A2
Fawnskin, *U.S.A.* 117 L10
Faxaflói, *Iceland* 8 D2
Faxälven →, *Sweden* 10 A10
Faya-Largeau, *Chad* 79 E9
Fayd, *Si. Arabia* 70 E4
Fayence, *France* 21 E10
Fayette, *Ala., U.S.A.* 109 J2
Fayette, *Mo., U.S.A.* 112 F8
Fayetteville, *Ark., U.S.A.* 113 G7
Fayetteville, *N.C., U.S.A.* 109 H6
Fayetteville, *Tenn., U.S.A.* 109 H2
Fayied, *Egypt* 80 H8
Fayón, *Spain* 32 D5
Fazilka, *India* 68 D6
Fazilpur, *Pakistan* 68 E4
Fdérik, *Mauritania* 78 D3
Feale →, *Ireland* 15 D2
Fear, C., *U.S.A.* 109 J7
Feather →, *U.S.A.* 114 G3
Feather Falls, *U.S.A.* 116 F5
Featherston, *N.Z.* 91 J5
Featherstone, *Zimbabwe* 87 F3
Fécamp, *France* 18 C7
Fedala = Mohammedia, *Morocco* 78 B4
Federación, *Argentina* 126 C4
Féderal, *Argentina* 128 C5
Federal Capital Terr. □, *Nigeria* 83 D6
Federal Way, *U.S.A.* 116 C4
Fedeshkūh, *Iran* 71 D7
Fehérgyarmat, *Hungary* 42 C7
Fehmarn, *Germany* 24 A7
Fehmarn Bælt, *Europe* 11 K5
Fehmarn Belt = Fehmarn Bælt, *Europe* 11 K5
Fei Xian, *China* 57 G9
Feijó, *Brazil* 124 E4
Feilding, *N.Z.* 91 J5
Feira de Santana, *Brazil* 125 F11
Feixi, *China* 59 B11
Feixiang, *China* 56 F8
Fejér □, *Hungary* 42 C3
Fejø, *Denmark* 11 K5
Feke, *Turkey* 72 D6
Fekete →, *Hungary* 42 E3
Felanitx, *Spain* 37 B10
Feldbach, *Austria* 26 E8
Feldberg, *Baden-W., Germany* 25 H3
Feldberg, *Mecklenburg-Vorpommern, Germany* 24 B9
Feldkirch, *Austria* 26 D2
Feldkirchen, *Austria* 26 E7
Felipe Carrillo Puerto, *Mexico* 119 D7
Felixburg, *Zimbabwe* 89 B5
Felixstowe, *U.K.* 13 F9
Felletin, *France* 20 C6
Fellingsbro, *Sweden* 10 E9
Felton, *U.S.A.* 116 H4
Feltre, *Italy* 29 B8
Femer Bælt = Fehmarn Bælt, *Europe* 11 K5
Femø, *Denmark* 11 K5
Femunden, *Norway* 9 E14
Fen He →, *China* 56 G6
Fene, *Spain* 34 B2
Fenelon Falls, *Canada* 110 B6
Fener Burnu, *Turkey* 39 E9
Feneroa, *Ethiopia* 81 E4
Feng Xian, *Jiangsu, China* 56 G9
Feng Xian, *Shaanxi, China* 56 H4
Fengári, *Greece* 41 F9
Fengcheng, *Jiangxi, China* 59 C10
Fengcheng, *Liaoning, China* 57 D13
Fengfeng, *China* 56 F8
Fenggang, *China* 58 D6
Fenghua, *China* 59 C13
Fenghuang, *China* 58 D7
Fengkai, *China* 59 F8
Fengkang, *Taiwan* 59 F13
Fengle, *China* 59 B9
Fenglin, *Taiwan* 59 F13
Fengning, *China* 56 D9
Fengqing, *China* 58 E2
Fengqiu, *China* 56 G8
Fengrun, *China* 57 E10
Fengshan, *Guangxi Zhuangzu, China* 58 E7
Fengshan, *Guangxi Zhuangzu, China* 58 E6
Fengshan, *Taiwan* 59 F13
Fengshun, *China* 59 F11
Fengtai, *Anhui, China* 59 A11
Fengtai, *Beijing, China* 56 E9
Fengxian, *China* 59 B13
Fengxiang, *China* 56 G4
Fengxin, *China* 59 C10
Fengyang, *China* 57 H9
Fengyi, *China* 58 E3
Fengyüan, *Taiwan* 59 E13
Fengzhen, *China* 56 D7
Feno, C. de, *France* 21 G12
Fenoarivo, *Fianarantsoa, Madag.* 89 C8
Fenoarivo, *Fianarantsoa, Madag.* 89 C8
Fenoarivo Afovoany, *Madag.* 89 B8
Fenoarivo Atsinanana, *Madag.* 89 B8
Fens, The, *U.K.* 12 E7
Fensmark, *Denmark* 11 J5
Fenton, *U.S.A.* 108 D4
Fenxi, *China* 56 F6
Fenyang, *China* 56 F6
Fenyi, *China* 59 D10
Feodosiya, *Ukraine* 47 K8
Ferdows, *Iran* 71 C8
Fère-Champenoise, *France* 19 D10
Fère-en-Tardenois, *France* 19 C10
Ferentino, *Italy* 29 G10
Ferfer, *Somali Rep.* 74 F4
Fergana = Farghona, *Uzbekistan* 50 E8
Fergus, *Canada* 110 C4
Fergus Falls, *U.S.A.* 112 B6
Feričanci, *Croatia* 42 E2
Ferkéssédougou, *Ivory C.* 82 D3
Ferlach, *Austria* 26 E7
Ferland, *Canada* 102 B2
Ferlo, Vallée du, *Senegal* 82 B2
Fermanagh □, *U.K.* 15 B4
Fermo, *Italy* 29 E10
Fermont, *Canada* 103 B6
Fermoselle, *Spain* 34 D4
Fermoy, *Ireland* 15 D3
Fernán Nuñéz, *Spain* 35 H6
Fernández, *Argentina* 126 B3
Fernandina Beach, *U.S.A.* 109 K5
Fernando de Noronha, *Brazil* 125 D12
Fernando Póo = Bioko, *Eq. Guin.* 83 E6
Ferndale, *U.S.A.* 116 B4
Fernie, *Canada* 104 D5
Fernlees, *Australia* 94 C4
Fernley, *U.S.A.* 114 G4
Ferozepore = Firozpur, *India* 68 D6
Férrai, *Greece* 41 F10
Ferrandina, *Italy* 31 B9
Ferrara, *Italy* 29 D8
Ferrato, C., *Italy* 30 C2
Ferreira do Alentejo, *Portugal* 35 G2
Ferreñafe, *Peru* 124 E3
Ferrerías, *Spain* 37 B11
Ferret, C., *France* 20 D2
Ferrette, *France* 19 E14
Ferriday, *U.S.A.* 113 K9
Ferriere, *Italy* 28 D6
Ferrières, *France* 19 D9
Ferro, Capo, *Italy* 30 A2
Ferrol, *Spain* 34 B2
Ferron, *U.S.A.* 115 G8
Ferrutx, C., *Spain* 37 B10
Ferryland, *Canada* 103 C9
Fertile, *U.S.A.* 112 B6
Fertőszentmiklós, *Hungary* 42 C1
Fès, *Morocco* 78 B5
Fessenden, *U.S.A.* 112 B5
Festus, *U.S.A.* 112 F9
Feté Bowé, *Senegal* 82 C2
Feteşti, *Romania* 43 F12
Fethiye, *Turkey* 39 E11
Fethiye Körfezi, *Turkey* 39 E10
Fetlar, *U.K.* 14 A8
Feuilles →, *Canada* 101 C12
Feurs, *France* 21 C8
Fez = Fès, *Morocco* 78 B5
Fezzan, *Libya* 79 C8
Fiambalá, *Argentina* 126 B2
Fianarantsoa, *Madag.* 89 C8
Fianarantsoa □, *Madag.* 89 B8
Fiche, *Ethiopia* 81 F4
Fichtelgebirge, *Germany* 25 E7
Ficksburg, *S. Africa* 89 D4
Fidenza, *Italy* 28 D7
Fiditi, *Nigeria* 83 D5
Field →, *Australia* 94 C2
Field I., *Australia* 92 B5
Fieni, *Romania* 43 E10
Fieri, *Albania* 40 F3
Fierzë, *Albania* 40 D4
Fife □, *U.K.* 14 E5
Fife Ness, *U.K.* 14 E6
Fifth Cataract, *Sudan* 80 D3
Figari, *France* 21 G13
Figeac, *France* 20 D6
Figeholm, *Sweden* 11 G10
Figline Valdarno, *Italy* 29 E8
Figtree, *Zimbabwe* 87 G2
Figueira Castelo Rodrigo, *Portugal* 34 E4
Figueira da Foz, *Portugal* 34 E2
Figueiró dos Vinhos, *Portugal* 34 F2
Figueres, *Spain* 32 C7
Figuig, *Morocco* 78 B5
Fihaonana, *Madag.* 89 B8
Fiherenana, *Madag.* 89 B8
Fiherenana →, *Madag.* 89 C7
Fiji ■, *Pac. Oc.* 91 C8
Fik, *Ethiopia* 81 F5
Fika, *Nigeria* 83 C7
Filabres, Sierra de los, *Spain* 35 H8
Filabusi, *Zimbabwe* 89 C4
Filadélfia, *Italy* 31 D9
Fil'akovo, *Slovak Rep.* 27 C12
Filey, *U.K.* 12 C7
Filey B., *U.K.* 12 C7
Filfla, *Malta* 36 D1
Filiaşi, *Romania* 43 F8
Filiátes, *Greece* 38 B2
Filiatrá, *Greece* 38 D3
Filicudi, *Italy* 31 D7
Filingué, *Niger* 83 C5
Filiourí →, *Greece* 41 E9
Filipstad, *Sweden* 10 E8
Filisur, *Switz.* 25 J5
Fillmore, *Calif., U.S.A.* 117 L8
Fillmore, *Utah, U.S.A.* 115 G7
Filótion, *Greece* 39 D7
Filottrano, *Italy* 29 E10
Filtu, *Ethiopia* 81 F5
Finale Emília, *Italy* 29 D8
Finale Lígure, *Italy* 28 D5
Fiñana, *Spain* 35 H8
Finch, *Canada* 111 A9
Findhorn →, *U.K.* 14 D5
Findlay, *U.S.A.* 108 E4
Finger L., *Canada* 102 B1
Finger Lakes, *U.S.A.* 111 D8
Fíngoè, *Mozam.* 87 E3
Finike, *Turkey* 39 E12
Finike Körfezi, *Turkey* 39 E12
Finiq, *Albania* 40 G4
Finistère □, *France* 18 D3
Finisterre = Fisterra, *Spain* 34 C1
Finisterre, C. = Fisterra, C., *Spain* 34 C1
Finke, *Australia* 94 D1
Finland ■, *Europe* 8 E22
Finland, G. of, *Europe* 9 G21
Finlay →, *Canada* 104 B3
Finley, *Australia* 95 F4
Finley, *U.S.A.* 112 B6
Finn →, *Ireland* 15 B4
Finnerödja, *Sweden* 11 F8
Finnigan, Mt., *Australia* 94 B4
Finniss, C., *Australia* 95 E1
Finnmark, *Norway* 8 B20
Finnsnes, *Norway* 8 B18
Finspång, *Sweden* 11 F9
Finsteraarhorn, *Switz.* 25 J4
Finsterwalde, *Germany* 24 D9
Fiora →, *Italy* 29 F8
Fiorenzuola d'Arda, *Italy* 28 D6
Fiq, *Syria* 75 C4
Firat = Furāt, Nahr al →, *Asia* 70 D5
Firebag →, *Canada* 105 B6
Firebaugh, *U.S.A.* 116 J6
Firedrake L., *Canada* 105 A8
Firenze, *Italy* 29 E8
Firenzuola, *Italy* 29 D8
Firk →, *Iraq* 70 D5
Firmi, *France* 20 D6
Firminy, *France* 21 C8
Firozabad, *India* 69 F8
Firozpur, *India* 68 D6
Firozpur-Jhirka, *India* 68 F7
Fīrūzābād, *Iran* 71 D7
Fīrūzkūh, *Iran* 71 C7
Firvale, *Canada* 104 C3
Fish →, *Namibia* 88 D2
Fish →, *S. Africa* 88 E3
Fish River Canyon, *Namibia* 88 D2
Fisher, *Australia* 93 F5
Fisher B., *Canada* 105 C9
Fishers I., *U.S.A.* 111 E13
Fishguard, *U.K.* 13 E3
Fishing L., *Canada* 105 C9
Fishkill, *U.S.A.* 111 E11
Fismes, *France* 19 C10
Fisterra, *Spain* 34 C1
Fisterra, C., *Spain* 34 C1
Fitchburg, *U.S.A.* 111 D13
Fitz Roy, *Argentina* 128 F3
Fitzgerald, *Canada* 104 B6
Fitzgerald, *U.S.A.* 109 K4
Fitzmaurice →, *Australia* 92 B5
Fitzroy →, *Queens., Australia* 94 C5
Fitzroy →, *W. Austral., Australia* 92 C3
Fitzroy, Mte., *Argentina* 128 F2
Fitzroy Crossing, *Australia* 92 C4
Fitzwilliam I., *Canada* 110 A3
Fiuggi, *Italy* 29 G10
Fiume = Rijeka, *Croatia* 29 C11
Five Points, *U.S.A.* 116 J6
Fivizzano, *Italy* 28 D7
Fizi, *Dem. Rep. of the Congo* 86 C2
Fjällbacka, *Sweden* 11 F5
Fjärdhundra, *Sweden* 10 E10
Fjellerup, *Denmark* 11 H4
Fjerritslev, *Denmark* 11 G3

Fjugesta, *Sweden* 10 E8
Flagstaff, *U.S.A.* 115 J8
Flagstaff L., *U.S.A.* 109 C10
Flaherty I., *Canada* 102 A4
Flåm, *Norway* 9 F12
Flambeau →, *U.S.A.* 112 C9
Flamborough Hd., *U.K.* 12 C7
Fläming, *Germany* 24 C8
Flaming Gorge Reservoir, *U.S.A.* 114 F9
Flamingo, Teluk, *Indonesia* 63 F9
Flanders = Flandre, *Europe* 19 B9
Flandre, *Europe* 19 B9
Flandre Occidentale = West-Vlaanderen □, *Belgium* 17 D2
Flandre Orientale = Oost-Vlaanderen □, *Belgium* 17 C3
Flandreau, *U.S.A.* 112 C6
Flanigan, *U.S.A.* 116 E7
Flannan Is., *U.K.* 14 C1
Flåsjön, *Sweden* 8 D16
Flat →, *Canada* 104 A3
Flathead L., *U.S.A.* 114 C7
Flattery, C., *Australia* 94 A4
Flattery, C., *U.S.A.* 116 B2
Flatwoods, *U.S.A.* 108 F4
Fleetwood, *U.K.* 12 D4
Fleetwood, *U.S.A.* 111 F9
Flekkefjord, *Norway* 9 G12
Flemington, *U.S.A.* 110 E7
Flen, *Sweden* 10 E10
Flensburg, *Germany* 24 A5
Flers, *France* 18 D6
Flesherton, *Canada* 110 B4
Flesko, Tanjung, *Indonesia* 63 D6
Fleurance, *France* 20 E4
Fleurier, *Switz.* 25 J2
Fleurieu Pen., *Australia* 95 F2
Flevoland □, *Neths.* 17 B5
Flin Flon, *Canada* 105 C8
Flinders →, *Australia* 94 B3
Flinders B., *Australia* 93 F2
Flinders Group, *Australia* 94 A3
Flinders I., *S. Austral., Australia* 95 E1
Flinders I., *Tas., Australia* 94 G4
Flinders Ranges, *Australia* 95 E2
Flinders Reefs, *Australia* 94 B4
Flint, *U.K.* 12 D4
Flint, *U.S.A.* 108 D4
Flint →, *U.S.A.* 109 K3
Flint I., *Kiribati* 97 J12
Flintshire □, *U.K.* 12 D4
Fliseryd, *Sweden* 11 G10
Flix, *Spain* 32 D5
Flixecourt, *France* 19 B9
Floby, *Sweden* 11 F7
Floda, *Sweden* 11 G6
Flodden, *U.K.* 12 B5
Flogny-la-Chapelle, *France* 19 E10
Floodwood, *U.S.A.* 112 B8
Flora, *U.S.A.* 108 F1
Florac, *France* 20 D7
Florala, *U.S.A.* 109 K2
Florence = Firenze, *Italy* 29 E8
Florence, *Ala., U.S.A.* 109 H2
Florence, *Ariz., U.S.A.* 115 K8
Florence, *Colo., U.S.A.* 112 F2
Florence, *Oreg., U.S.A.* 114 E1
Florence, *S.C., U.S.A.* 109 H6
Florence, L., *Australia* 95 D2
Florencia, *Colombia* 124
Florennes, *Belgium* 17 D4
Florensac, *France* 20 E7
Florenville, *Belgium* 17 E5
Flores, *Guatemala* 120 C2
Flores, *Indonesia* 63 F6
Flores I., *Canada* 104 D3
Flores Sea, *Indonesia* 63 F6
Florești, *Moldova* 43 C13
Floresville, *U.S.A.* 113 L5
Floriano, *Brazil* 125 E10
Florianópolis, *Brazil* 127 B6
Florida, *Cuba* 120 B4
Florida, *Uruguay* 127 C4
Florida □, *U.S.A.* 109 L5
Florida, Straits of, *U.S.A.* 120 B4
Florida B., *U.S.A.* 120 B3
Florida Keys, *U.S.A.* 109 N5
Florídia, *Italy* 31 E8
Flórina, *Greece* 40 F5
Flórina □, *Greece* 40 F5
Florø, *Norway* 9 F11
Flower Station, *Canada* 111 A8
Flowerpot I., *Canada* 110 A3
Floydada, *U.S.A.* 113 J4
Fluk, *Indonesia* 63 E7
Flúmen →, *Spain* 32 D4
Flumendosa →, *Italy* 30 C2
Fluminimaggiore, *Italy* 30 C1
Flushing = Vlissingen, *Neths.* 17 C3
Fluviá →, *Spain* 32 C8
Flying Fish, C., *Antarctica* 5 D15
Foam Lake, *Canada* 105 C8
Foča, *Bos.-H.* 40 C2
Foça, *Turkey* 39 C8
Focșani, *Romania* 43 E12
Fodécontéa, *Guinea* 82 C2
Fogang, *China* 59 F9
Fóggia, *Italy* 31 A8
Foggo, *Nigeria* 83 C6
Foglia →, *Italy* 29 E9
Fogo, *Canada* 103 C9
Fogo I., *Canada* 103 C9
Fohnsdorf, *Austria* 26 D7
Föhr, *Germany* 24 A4
Foia, *Portugal* 35 H2
Foix, *France* 20 E5
Fojnica, *Bos.-H.* 42 G2
Fokino, *Russia* 46 F8
Fokís □, *Greece* 38 C4
Fokku, *Nigeria* 83 C5
Folda, *Nord-Trøndelag, Norway* 8 D14
Folda, *Nordland, Norway* 8 C16
Főldeák, *Hungary* 42 D5
Folégandros, *Greece* 38 E6
Foley, *Botswana* 88 C4
Foley, *U.S.A.* 109 K2
Foleyet, *Canada* 102 C3
Folgefonni, *Norway* 9 F12
Foligno, *Italy* 29 F9
Folkestone, *U.K.* 13 F9
Folkston, *U.S.A.* 109 K5
Follansbee, *U.S.A.* 110 F4
Follónica, *Italy* 28 F7
Follónica, G. di, *Italy* 28 F7
Folsom L., *U.S.A.* 116 G5
Foltești, *Romania* 43 E13
Fond-du-Lac, *Canada* 105 B7
Fond du Lac, *U.S.A.* 112 D10
Fond-du-Lac →, *Canada* 105 B7
Fonda, *U.S.A.* 111 D10
Fondi, *Italy* 30 A6
Fonfría, *Spain* 34 D4
Fongafale, *Tuvalu* 96 H9
Fonni, *Italy* 30 B2
Fonsagrada = A Fonsagrada, *Spain* 34 B3
Fonseca, G. de, *Cent. Amer.* 120 D2
Font-Romeu, *France* 20 F5
Fontaine-Française, *France* 19 E12
Fontainebleau, *France* 19 D9
Fontana, *U.S.A.* 117 L9
Fontas →, *Canada* 104 B4
Fonte Boa, *Brazil* 124 D5
Fontem, *Cameroon* 83 D6
Fontenay-le-Comte, *France* 20 B3
Fontenelle Reservoir, *U.S.A.* 114 E8
Fontur, *Iceland* 8 C6
Fonyód, *Hungary* 42 D2
Foochow = Fuzhou, *China* 59 D12
Foping, *China* 56 H5
Forbach, *France* 19 C13
Forbes, *Australia* 95 E4
Forbesganj, *India* 69 F12
Forcados, *Nigeria* 83 D6
Forcados →, *Nigeria* 83 D6
Forcalquier, *France* 21 E9
Forchheim, *Germany* 25 F7
Ford City, *Calif., U.S.A.* 117 K7
Ford City, *Pa., U.S.A.* 110 F5
Førde, *Norway* 9 F11
Ford's Bridge, *Australia* 95 D4
Fordyce, *U.S.A.* 113 J8
Forécariah, *Guinea* 82 D2
Forel, Mt., *Greenland* 4 C6
Foremost, *Canada* 104 D6
Forest, *Canada* 110 C3
Forest, *U.S.A.* 113 J10
Forest City, *Iowa, U.S.A.* 112 D8
Forest City, *N.C., U.S.A.* 109 H5
Forest City, *Pa., U.S.A.* 111 E9
Forest Grove, *U.S.A.* 116 E3
Forestburg, *Canada* 104 C6
Foresthill, *U.S.A.* 116 F6
Forestier Pen., *Australia* 94 G4
Forestville, *Canada* 103 C6
Forestville, *Calif., U.S.A.* 116 G4
Forestville, *N.Y., U.S.A.* 110 D5
Forez, Mts. du, *France* 20 C7
Forfar, *U.K.* 14 E6
Forks, *U.S.A.* 116 C2
Forksville, *U.S.A.* 111 E8
Forlì, *Italy* 29 D9
Forman, *U.S.A.* 112 B6
Formazza, *Italy* 28 B5
Formby Pt., *U.K.* 12 D4
Formentera, *Spain* 37 C7
Formentor, C. de, *Spain* 37 B10
Former Yugoslav Republic of Macedonia = Macedonia ■, *Europe* 40 E5
Fórmia, *Italy* 30 A6
Formígine, *Italy* 28 D7
Formosa = Taiwan ■, *Asia* 59 F13
Formosa, *Argentina* 126 B4
Formosa, *Brazil* 125 G9
Formosa □, *Argentina* 126 B4
Formosa, Serra, *Brazil* 125 F8
Formosa Bay, *Kenya* 86 C5
Formosa Strait = Taiwan Strait, *Asia* 59 E12
Fornells, *Spain* 37 A11
Fornos de Algodres, *Portugal* 34 E3
Fornovo di Taro, *Italy* 28 D7
Føroyar, *Atl. Oc.* 8 F9
Forres, *U.K.* 14 D5
Forrest, *Australia* 93 F4
Forrest, Mt., *Australia* 93 D4
Forrest City, *U.S.A.* 113 H9
Fors, *Sweden* 10 D10
Forsayth, *Australia* 94 B3
Forshaga, *Sweden* 10 E7
Förslöv, *Sweden* 11 H6
Forsmo, *Sweden* 10 A11
Forssa, *Finland* 9 F20
Forst, *Germany* 24 D10
Forsvik, *Sweden* 11 F8
Forsyth, *U.S.A.* 114 C10
Fort Abbas, *Pakistan* 68 E5
Fort Albany, *Canada* 102 B3
Fort Ann, *U.S.A.* 111 C11
Fort Assiniboine, *Canada* 104 C6
Fort Augustus, *U.K.* 14 D4
Fort Beaufort, *S. Africa* 88 E4
Fort Benton, *U.S.A.* 114 C8
Fort Bragg, *U.S.A.* 114 G2
Fort Bridger, *U.S.A.* 114 F8
Fort Chipewyan, *Canada* 105 B6
Fort Collins, *U.S.A.* 112 E2
Fort-Coulonge, *Canada* 102 C4
Fort Covington, *U.S.A.* 111 B10
Fort Davis, *U.S.A.* 113 K3
Fort-de-France, *Martinique* 121 D7
Fort Defiance, *U.S.A.* 115 J9
Fort Dodge, *U.S.A.* 112 D7
Fort Edward, *U.S.A.* 111 C11
Fort Erie, *Canada* 110 D6
Fort Fairfield, *U.S.A.* 109 B12
Fort Frances, *Canada* 105 D10
Fort Garland, *U.S.A.* 115 H11
Fort George = Chisasibi, *Canada* 102 B4
Fort Good-Hope, *Canada* 100 B7
Fort Hancock, *U.S.A.* 115 L11
Fort Hertz = Putao, *Burma* 67 F20
Fort Hope, *Canada* 102 B2
Fort Irwin, *U.S.A.* 117 K10
Fort Jameson = Chipata, *Zambia* 87 E3
Fort Kent, *U.S.A.* 109 B11
Fort Klamath, *U.S.A.* 114 E3
Fort-Lamy = Ndjamena, *Chad* 79 F8
Fort Laramie, *U.S.A.* 112 D2
Fort Lauderdale, *U.S.A.* 109 M5
Fort Liard, *Canada* 104 A4
Fort Liberté, *Haiti* 121 C5
Fort Lupton, *U.S.A.* 112 E2
Fort Mackay, *Canada* 104 B6
Fort Macleod, *Canada* 104 D6
Fort McMurray, *Canada* 104 B6
Fort McPherson, *Canada* 100 B6
Fort Madison, *U.S.A.* 112 E9
Fort Meade, *U.S.A.* 109 M5
Fort Morgan, *U.S.A.* 112 E3
Fort Munro, *Pakistan* 68 E3
Fort Myers, *U.S.A.* 109 M5
Fort Nelson, *Canada* 104 B4
Fort Nelson →, *Canada* 104 B4
Fort Norman = Tulita, *Canada* 100 B7
Fort Payne, *U.S.A.* 109 H3
Fort Peck, *U.S.A.* 114 B10
Fort Peck Dam, *U.S.A.* 114 C10
Fort Peck L., *U.S.A.* 114 C10
Fort Pierce, *U.S.A.* 109 M5
Fort Pierre, *U.S.A.* 112 C4
Fort Plain, *U.S.A.* 111 D10
Fort Portal, *Uganda* 86 B3
Fort Providence, *Canada* 104 A5
Fort Qu'Appelle, *Canada* 105 C8
Fort Resolution, *Canada* 104 A6
Fort Rixon, *Zimbabwe* 87 G2
Fort Rosebery = Mansa, *Zambia* 87 E2
Fort Ross, *U.S.A.* 116 G3
Fort Rupert = Waskaganish, *Canada* 102 B4
Fort St. James, *Canada* 104 C4
Fort St. John, *Canada* 104 B4
Fort Sandeman = Zhob, *Pakistan* 68 D3
Fort Saskatchewan, *Canada* 104 C6
Fort Scott, *U.S.A.* 113 G7
Fort Severn, *Canada* 102 A2
Fort Shevchenko, *Kazakstan* 49 H10
Fort Simpson, *Canada* 104 A4
Fort Smith, *Canada* 104 B6
Fort Smith, *U.S.A.* 113 H7
Fort Stockton, *U.S.A.* 113 K3
Fort Sumner, *U.S.A.* 113 H2
Fort Thompson, *U.S.A.* 112 C5
Fort Trinquet = Bir Mogreïn, *Mauritania* 78 C3
Fort Valley, *U.S.A.* 109 J4
Fort Vermilion, *Canada* 104 B5
Fort Walton Beach, *U.S.A.* 109 K2
Fort Wayne, *U.S.A.* 108 E3
Fort William, *U.K.* 14 E3
Fort Worth, *U.S.A.* 113 J6
Fort Yates, *U.S.A.* 112 B4
Fort Yukon, *U.S.A.* 100 B5
Fortaleza, *Brazil* 125 D11
Forteau, *Canada* 103 B8
Fortescue →, *Australia* 92 D2
Forth →, *U.K.* 14 E5
Forth, Firth of, *U.K.* 14 E6
Fortore →, *Italy* 29 G12
Fortrose, *U.K.* 14 D4
Fortuna, *Spain* 33 G3
Fortuna, *Calif., U.S.A.* 114 F1
Fortuna, *N. Dak., U.S.A.* 112 A3
Fortune, *Canada* 103 C8
Fortune B., *Canada* 103 C8
Forūr, *Iran* 71 E7
Fos-sur-Mer, *France* 21 E8
Foshan, *China* 59 F9
Fosna, *Norway* 8 E14
Fosnavåg, *Norway* 9 E11
Foso, *Ghana* 83 D4
Fossano, *Italy* 28 D4
Fossil, *U.S.A.* 114 D3
Fossombrone, *Italy* 29 E9
Foster, *Australia* 95 F4
Foster, *Canada* 111 A12
Foster →, *Canada* 105 B7
Fosters Ra., *Australia* 94 C1
Fostoria, *U.S.A.* 108 E4
Fotadrevo, *Madag.* 89 C8
Fouesnant, *France* 18 E2
Fougères, *France* 18 D5
Foul Pt., *Sri Lanka* 66 Q12
Foula, *U.K.* 14 A6
Foulalaba, *Mali* 82 C3
Foulness I., *U.K.* 13 F8
Foulpointe, *Madag.* 89 B8
Foulweather, C., *U.S.A.* 106 B2
Foumban, *Cameroon* 83 D7
Foumbot, *Cameroon* 83 D7
Foundiougne, *Senegal* 82 C1
Fountain, *U.S.A.* 112 F2
Fountain Springs, *U.S.A.* 117 K8
Fourchambault, *France* 19 E10
Fouriesburg, *S. Africa* 88 D4
Fourmies, *France* 19 B11
Fournás, *Greece* 38 B3
Foúrnoi, *Greece* 39 D8
Fours, *France* 19 F10
Fourth Cataract, *Sudan* 80 D3
Fouta Djalon, *Guinea* 82 C2
Foux, Cap-à-, *Haiti* 121 C5
Foveaux Str., *N.Z.* 91 M2
Fowey, *U.K.* 13 G3
Fowler, *Calif., U.S.A.* 116 J7
Fowler, *Colo., U.S.A.* 112 F3
Fowlers B., *Australia* 93 F5
Fowman, *Iran* 71 B6
Fox →, *Canada* 105 B10
Fox Creek, *Canada* 104 C5
Fox Lake, *Canada* 104 B6
Fox Valley, *Canada* 105 C7
Foxboro, *U.S.A.* 111 D13
Foxe Basin, *Canada* 101 B12
Foxe Chan., *Canada* 101 B11
Foxe Pen., *Canada* 101 B12
Foxen, *Sweden* 10 E5
Foxton, *N.Z.* 91 J5
Foyle, Lough, *U.K.* 15 A4
Foynes, *Ireland* 15 D2
Foz, *Spain* 34 B3
Fóz do Cunene, *Angola* 88 B1
Foz do Iguaçu, *Brazil* 127 B5
Frackville, *U.S.A.* 111 F8
Fraga, *Spain* 32 D5
Fraile Muerto, *Uruguay* 127 C5
Framingham, *U.S.A.* 111 D13
Frampol, *Poland* 45 H9
Franca, *Brazil* 125 H9
Francavilla al Mare, *Italy* 29 F11
Francavilla Fontana, *Italy* 31 B10
France ■, *Europe* 7 F6
Frances, *Australia* 95 F3
Frances →, *Canada* 104 A3
Frances L., *Canada* 104 A3
Franceville, *Gabon* 84 E2
Franche-Comté, *France* 19 F12
Francis Case, L., *U.S.A.* 112 D5
Francisco Beltrão, *Brazil* 127 B5
Francisco I. Madero, *Coahuila, Mexico* 118 B4
Francisco I. Madero, *Durango, Mexico* 118 C4
Francistown, *Botswana* 89 C4
Francofonte, *Italy* 31 E7
François, *Canada* 103 C8
François L., *Canada* 104 C3
Franeker, *Neths.* 17 A5
Frankado, *Djibouti* 81 E5
Frankenberg, *Germany* 24 D4
Frankenwald, *Germany* 25 E7
Frankford, *Canada* 110 B7
Frankfort, *S. Africa* 89 D4
Frankfort, *Ind., U.S.A.* 108 E2
Frankfort, *Kans., U.S.A.* 112 F6
Frankfort, *Ky., U.S.A.* 108 F3
Frankfort, *N.Y., U.S.A.* 111 C9
Frankfurt, *Brandenburg, Germany* 24 C10
Frankfurt, *Hessen, Germany* 25 E4
Fränkische Alb, *Germany* 25 F7
Fränkische Rezat →, *Germany* 25 F7
Fränkische Saale →, *Germany* 25 E5
Fränkische Schweiz, *Germany* 25 F7
Frankland →, *Australia* 93 G2
Franklin, *Ky., U.S.A.* 109 G2
Franklin, *La., U.S.A.* 113 L9
Franklin, *Mass., U.S.A.* 111 D13
Franklin, *N.H., U.S.A.* 111 C13
Franklin, *Nebr., U.S.A.* 112 E5
Franklin, *Pa., U.S.A.* 110 E5
Franklin, *Va., U.S.A.* 109 G7
Franklin, *W. Va., U.S.A.* 108 F6
Franklin B., *Canada* 100 B7
Franklin D. Roosevelt L., *U.S.A.* 114 B4
Franklin I., *Antarctica* 5 D11
Franklin L., *U.S.A.* 114 F6
Franklin Mts., *Canada* 100 B7
Franklin Str., *Canada* 100 A10
Franklinton, *U.S.A.* 113 K9
Franklinville, *U.S.A.* 110 D6
Franks Pk., *U.S.A.* 114 E9
Frankston, *Australia* 95 F4
Frånö, *Sweden* 10 B11
Fransfontein, *Namibia* 88 C2
Fränsta, *Sweden* 10 B10
Frantsa Iosifa, Zemlya, *Russia* 50 A6
Franz, *Canada* 102 C3
Franz Josef Land = Frantsa Iosifa, Zemlya, *Russia* 50 A6
Franzburg, *Germany* 24 A8
Frascati, *Italy* 29 G9
Fraser, *U.S.A.* 110 D2
Fraser →, *B.C., Canada* 104 D4
Fraser →, *Nfld., Canada* 103 A7
Fraser, Mt., *Australia* 93 E2
Fraser I., *Australia* 95 D5
Fraser Lake, *Canada* 104 C4
Fraserburg, *S. Africa* 88 E3
Fraserburgh, *U.K.* 14 D6
Fraserdale, *Canada* 102 C3
Frashëri, *Albania* 40 F4
Frasne, *France* 19 F13
Frătești, *Romania* 43 G10
Frauenfeld, *Switz.* 25 H4
Fray Bentos, *Uruguay* 126 C4
Frechilla, *Spain* 34 C6
Fredericia, *Denmark* 11 J3
Frederick, *Md., U.S.A.* 108 F7
Frederick, *Okla., U.S.A.* 113 H5
Frederick, *S. Dak., U.S.A.* 112 C5
Fredericksburg, *Pa., U.S.A.* 111 F8
Fredericksburg, *Tex., U.S.A.* 113 K5
Fredericksburg, *Va., U.S.A.* 108 F7
Fredericktown, *Mo., U.S.A.* 113 G9
Fredericktown, *Ohio, U.S.A.* 110 F2
Frederico I. Madero, Presa, *Mexico* 118 B3
Frederico Westphalen, *Brazil* 127 B5
Fredericton, *Canada* 103 C6
Fredericton Junction, *Canada* 103 C6
Frederiksborg Amtskommune □, *Denmark* 11 J6
Frederikshåb = Paamiut, *Greenland* 4 C5
Frederikshavn, *Denmark* 11 G4
Frederikssund, *Denmark* 11 J6
Frederiksted, *Virgin Is.* 121 C7
Frederiksværk, *Denmark* 11 J6
Fredonia, *Ariz., U.S.A.* 115 H7
Fredonia, *Kans., U.S.A.* 113 G7
Fredonia, *N.Y., U.S.A.* 110 D5
Fredriksberg, *Sweden* 10 D8
Fredrikstad, *Norway* 9 G14
Free State □, *S. Africa* 88 D4
Freehold, *U.S.A.* 111 F10
Freel Peak, *U.S.A.* 116 G7
Freeland, *U.S.A.* 111 E9
Freels, C., *Canada* 103 C9
Freeman, *Calif., U.S.A.* 117 K9
Freeman, *S. Dak., U.S.A.* 112 D6
Freeport, *Bahamas* 120 A4
Freeport, *Ill., U.S.A.* 112 D10
Freeport, *N.Y., U.S.A.* 111 F11
Freeport, *Ohio, U.S.A.* 110 F3
Freeport, *Pa., U.S.A.* 110 F5
Freeport, *Tex., U.S.A.* 113 L7
Freetown, *S. Leone* 82 D2
Frégate, L., *Canada* 102 B5
Fregenal de la Sierra, *Spain* 35 G4
Fregene, *Italy* 29 G9
Fréhel, C., *France* 18 D4
Freiberg, *Germany* 24 E9
Freibourg = Fribourg, *Switz.* 25 J3
Freiburg, *Baden-W., Germany* 25 H3
Freiburg, *Niedersachsen, Germany* 24 B5
Freilassing, *Germany* 25 H8
Freire, *Chile* 128 D2
Freirina, *Chile* 126 B1
Freising, *Germany* 25 G7
Freistadt, *Austria* 26 C7
Freital, *Germany* 24 D9
Fréjus, *France* 21 E10
Fremantle, *Australia* 93 F2
Fremont, *Calif., U.S.A.* 116 H4
Fremont, *Mich., U.S.A.* 108 D3
Fremont, *Nebr., U.S.A.* 112 E6
Fremont, *Ohio, U.S.A.* 108 E4
Fremont →, *U.S.A.* 115 G8
French Camp, *U.S.A.* 116 H5
French Creek →, *U.S.A.* 110 E5
French Guiana ■, *S. Amer.* 125 C8
French Pass, *N.Z.* 91 J4
French Polynesia ■, *Pac. Oc.* 97 K13
Frenchman Cr. →, *N. Amer.* 114 B10
Frenchman Cr. →, *U.S.A.* 112 E4
Frenštát pod Radhoštěm, *Czech Rep.* 27 B11
Fresco, *Ivory C.* 82 D3
Fresco →, *Brazil* 125 E8
Freshfield, C., *Antarctica* 5 C10
Fresnay-sur-Sarthe, *France* 18 D7
Fresnillo, *Mexico* 118 C4
Fresno, *U.S.A.* 116 J7
Fresno Alhandiga, *Spain* 34 E5
Fresno Reservoir, *U.S.A.* 114 B9
Freudenstadt, *Germany* 25 G4
Frévent, *France* 19 B9
Frew →, *Australia* 94 C2
Frewsburg, *U.S.A.* 110 D5
Freycinet Pen., *Australia* 94 G4
Freyming-Merlebach, *France* 19 C13
Freyung, *Germany* 25 G9
Fria, *Guinea* 82 C2
Fria, C., *Namibia* 88 B1
Friant, *U.S.A.* 116 J7
Frías, *Argentina* 126 B2
Fribourg, *Switz.* 25 J3
Fribourg □, *Switz.* 25 J3
Fridafors, *Sweden* 11 H8
Friday Harbor, *U.S.A.* 116 B3
Friedberg, *Bayern, Germany* 25 G6
Friedberg, *Hessen, Germany* 25 E4
Friedens, *U.S.A.* 110 F6
Friedland, *Germany* 24 B9
Friedrichshafen, *Germany* 25 H5
Friedrichskoog, *Germany* 24 A4
Friedrichstadt, *Germany* 24 A5
Friendly Is. = Tonga ■, *Pac. Oc.* 91 D11
Friendship, *U.S.A.* 110 D6
Friesach, *Austria* 26 E7
Friesack, *Germany* 24 C8
Friesland □, *Neths.* 17 A5
Friesoythe, *Germany* 24 B3
Friggesund, *Sweden* 10 C10
Frillesås, *Sweden* 11 G6
Frinnaryd, *Sweden* 11 G8
Frio →, *U.S.A.* 113 L5
Frio, C., *Brazil* 122 F6
Friol, *Spain* 34 B3
Friona, *U.S.A.* 113 H3
Fristad, *Sweden* 11 G6
Fritch, *U.S.A.* 113 H4

Fritsla, *Sweden* 11 G6
Fritzlar, *Germany* 24 D5
Friuli-Venézia Giulia □, *Italy* 29 B9
Frobisher B., *Canada* 101 B13
Frobisher Bay = Iqaluit, *Canada* 101 B13
Frobisher L., *Canada* 105 B7
Frohavet, *Norway* 8 E13
Frohnleiten, *Austria* 26 D8
Frolovo, *Russia* 48 F6
Frombork, *Poland* 44 D6
Frome, *U.K.* 13 F5
Frome →, *U.K.* 13 G5
Frome, L., *Australia* 95 E2
Frómista, *Spain* 34 C6
Front Range, *U.S.A.* 106 C5
Front Royal, *U.S.A.* 108 F6
Fronteira, *Portugal* 35 F3
Frontera, *Canary Is.* 37 G2
Frontera, *Mexico* 119 D6
Fronteras, *Mexico* 118 A3
Frontignan, *France* 20 E7
Frosinone, *Italy* 30 A6
Frostburg, *U.S.A.* 108 F6
Frostisen, *Norway* 8 B17
Frouard, *France* 19 D13
Frövi, *Sweden* 10 E9
Frøya, *Norway* 8 E13
Frumoasa, *Romania* 43 D10
Frunze = Bishkek, *Kyrgyzstan* 50 E8
Fruška Gora, *Serbia, Yug.* 42 E4
Frutal, *Brazil* 125 H9
Frutigen, *Switz.* 25 J3
Frýdek-Místek, *Czech Rep.* 27 B11
Frýdlant, *Czech Rep.* 26 A8
Fryeburg, *U.S.A.* 111 B14
Fryvaldov = Jeseník, *Czech Rep.* 27 A10
Fthiótis □, *Greece* 38 C4
Fu Jiang →, *China* 58 C6
Fu Xian = Wafangdian, *China* 57 E11
Fu Xian, *China* 56 G5
Fu'an, *China* 59 D12
Fubian, *China* 58 B4
Fucécchio, *Italy* 28 E7
Fucheng, *China* 56 F9
Fuchou = Fuzhou, *China* 59 D12
Fuchū, *Japan* 55 G6
Fuchuan, *China* 59 E8
Fuchun Jiang →, *China* 59 B13
Fúcino, Piana del, *Italy* 29 F10
Fuding, *China* 59 D13
Fuencaliente, *Canary Is.* 37 F2
Fuencaliente, *Spain* 35 G6
Fuencaliente, Pta., *Canary Is.* 37 F2
Fuengirola, *Spain* 35 J6
Fuenlabrada, *Spain* 34 E7
Fuensalida, *Spain* 34 E6
Fuente-Álamo, *Spain* 33 G3
Fuente-Álamo de Murcia, *Spain* 33 H3
Fuente de Cantos, *Spain* 35 G4
Fuente del Maestre, *Spain* 35 G4
Fuente el Fresno, *Spain* 35 F7
Fuente Obejuna, *Spain* 35 G5
Fuente Palmera, *Spain* 35 H5
Fuentes de Andalucía, *Spain* 35 H5
Fuentes de Ebro, *Spain* 32 D4
Fuentes de León, *Spain* 35 G4
Fuentes de Oñoro, *Spain* 34 E4
Fuentesaúco, *Spain* 34 D5
Fuerte →, *Mexico* 118 B3
Fuerte Olimpo, *Paraguay* 126 A4
Fuerteventura, *Canary Is.* 37 F6
Fufeng, *China* 56 G5
Fuga I., *Phil.* 61 B4
Fugong, *China* 58 D2
Fugou, *China* 56 G8
Fugu, *China* 56 E6
Fuhai, *China* 60 B3
Fuḩaymī, *Iraq* 70 C4
Fuji, *Japan* 55 G9
Fuji-San, *Japan* 55 G9
Fuji-yoshida, *Japan* 55 G9
Fujian □, *China* 59 E12
Fujinomiya, *Japan* 55 G9
Fujisawa, *Japan* 55 G9
Fujiyama, Mt. = Fuji-San, *Japan* 55 G9
Fukien = Fujian □, *China* 59 E12
Fukuchiyama, *Japan* 55 G7
Fukue-Shima, *Japan* 55 H4
Fukui, *Japan* 55 F8
Fukui □, *Japan* 55 G8
Fukuoka, *Japan* 55 H5
Fukuoka □, *Japan* 55 H5
Fukushima, *Japan* 54 F10
Fukushima □, *Japan* 54 F10
Fukuyama, *Japan* 55 G6
Fulacunda, *Guinea-Biss.* 82 C1
Fulda, *Germany* 24 E5
Fulda →, *Germany* 24 D5
Fulford Harbour, *Canada* 116 B3
Fuliang, *China* 59 C11
Fullerton, *Calif., U.S.A.* 117 M9
Fullerton, *Nebr., U.S.A.* 112 E6
Fulongquan, *China* 57 B13
Fülöpszállás, *Hungary* 42 D4
Fulton, *Mo., U.S.A.* 112 F9
Fulton, *N.Y., U.S.A.* 111 C8
Fuluälven →, *Sweden* 10 C7
Fulufjället, *Sweden* 10 C6
Fumay, *France* 19 C11
Fumel, *France* 20 D4
Fumin, *China* 58 E4
Funabashi, *Japan* 55 G10
Funäsdalen, *Sweden* 10 B6
Funchal, *Madeira* 37 D3
Fundación, *Colombia* 124 A4
Fundão, *Portugal* 34 E3
Fundu Moldovei, *Romania* 43 C10
Fundulea, *Romania* 43 F11
Fundy, B. of, *Canada* 103 D6
Funhalouro, *Mozam.* 89 C5
Funing, *Hebei, China* 57 E10
Funing, *Jiangsu, China* 57 H10
Funing, *Yunnan, China* 58 F5
Funiu Shan, *China* 56 H7
Funsi, *Ghana* 82 C4
Funtua, *Nigeria* 83 C6
Fuping, *Hebei, China* 56 E8
Fuping, *Shaanxi, China* 56 G5
Fuqing, *China* 59 E12
Fuquan, *China* 58 D6
Furano, *Japan* 54 C11
Furāt, Nahr al →, *Asia* 70 D5
Fürg, *Iran* 71 D7
Furmanov, *Russia* 48 B5
Furmanovo, *Kazakstan* 48 F9
Furnás, *Spain* 37 B8
Furnas, Reprêsa de, *Brazil* 127 A6
Furneaux Group, *Australia* 94 G4
Furqlus, *Syria* 75 A6
Fürstenau, *Germany* 24 C3
Fürstenberg, *Germany* 24 B9
Fürstenfeld, *Austria* 26 D9
Fürstenfeldbruck, *Germany* 25 G7
Fürstenwalde, *Germany* 24 C10
Fürth, *Germany* 25 F6
Furth im Wald, *Germany* 25 F8
Furtwangen, *Germany* 25 G4
Furudal, *Sweden* 10 C9
Furukawa, *Japan* 54 E10
Furulund, *Sweden* 11 J7
Fury and Hecla Str., *Canada* 101 B11
Fusagasuga, *Colombia* 124 C4
Fuscaldo, *Italy* 31 C9
Fushan, *Shandong, China* 57 F11
Fushan, *Shanxi, China* 56 G6
Fushë Arrëzi, *Albania* 40 D4
Fushë-Krujë, *Albania* 40 E3
Fushun, *Liaoning, China* 57 D12
Fushun, *Sichuan, China* 58 C5
Fusong, *China* 57 C14
Füssen, *Germany* 25 H6
Fusui, *China* 58 F6
Futog, *Yugoslavia* 42 E4
Futuna, *Wall. & F. Is.* 91 B8
Fuwa, *Egypt* 80 H7
Fuxian Hu, *China* 58 E4
Fuxin, *China* 57 C11
Fuyang, *Anhui, China* 56 H8
Fuyang, *Zhejiang, China* 59 B12
Fuyang He →, *China* 56 E9
Fuying Dao, *China* 59 D13
Fuyu, *China* 57 B13
Fuyuan, *China* 58 E5
Füzesgyarmat, *Hungary* 42 C6
Fuzhou, *China* 59 D12
Fylde, *U.K.* 12 D5
Fyn, *Denmark* 11 J4
Fyne, L., *U.K.* 14 F3
Fyns Amtskommune □, *Denmark* 11 J4
Fynshav, *Denmark* 11 K3

G

Ga, *Ghana* 82 D4
Gaanda, *Nigeria* 83 C7
Gabarin, *Nigeria* 83 C7
Gabas →, *France* 20 E3
Gabela, *Angola* 84 G2
Gabès, *Tunisia* 79 B8
Gabès, G. de, *Tunisia* 79 B8
Gabgaba, W. →, *Egypt* 80 C3
Gąbin, *Poland* 45 F6
Gabon ■, *Africa* 84 E2
Gaborone, *Botswana* 88 C4
Gabriels, *U.S.A.* 111 B10
Gābrīk, *Iran* 71 E8
Gabrovo, *Bulgaria* 41 D9
Gacé, *France* 18 D7
Gāch Sār, *Iran* 71 B6
Gachsārān, *Iran* 71 D6
Gacko, *Bos.-H.* 40 C2
Gadag, *India* 66 M9
Gadamai, *Sudan* 81 D4
Gadap, *Pakistan* 68 G2
Gadarwara, *India* 69 H8
Gadebusch, *Germany* 24 B7
Gadein, *Sudan* 81 F2
Gadhada, *India* 68 J4
Gádor, Sierra de, *Spain* 35 J8
Gadra, *Pakistan* 68 G4
Gadsden, *U.S.A.* 109 H3
Gadwal, *India* 66 L10
Gadyach = Hadyach, *Ukraine* 47 G8
Găeşti, *Romania* 43 F10
Gaeta, *Italy* 30 A6
Gaeta, G. di, *Italy* 30 A6
Gaffney, *U.S.A.* 109 H5
Gafsa, *Tunisia* 78 B7
Gagarawa, *Nigeria* 83 C6
Gagaria, *India* 68 G4
Gagarin, *Russia* 46 E8
Gaggenau, *Germany* 25 G4
Gaghamni, *Sudan* 81 E2
Gagino, *Russia* 48 C7
Gagliano del Capo, *Italy* 31 C11
Gagnef, *Sweden* 10 D9
Gagnoa, *Ivory C.* 82 D3
Gagnon, *Canada* 103 B6
Gagnon, L., *Canada* 105 A6
Gagra, *Georgia* 49 J5
Gahini, *Rwanda* 86 C3
Gahmar, *India* 69 G10
Gai Xian = Gaizhou, *China* 57 D12
Gaïdhouronísi, *Greece* 36 E7
Gail, *U.S.A.* 113 J4
Gail →, *Austria* 26 E6
Gaillac, *France* 20 E5
Gaillimh = Galway, *Ireland* 15 C2
Gaillon, *France* 18 C8
Gaines, *U.S.A.* 110 E7
Gainesville, *Fla., U.S.A.* 109 L4
Gainesville, *Ga., U.S.A.* 109 H4
Gainesville, *Mo., U.S.A.* 113 G8
Gainesville, *Tex., U.S.A.* 113 J6
Gainsborough, *U.K.* 12 D7
Gairdner, L., *Australia* 95 E2
Gairloch, L., *U.K.* 14 D3
Gaizhou, *China* 57 D12
Gaj, *Croatia* 42 E2
Gaj →, *Pakistan* 68 F2
Gakuch, *Pakistan* 69 A5
Galala, Gebel el, *Egypt* 80 J8
Galán, Cerro, *Argentina* 126 B2
Galana →, *Kenya* 86 C5
Galanta, *Slovak Rep.* 27 C10
Galapagar, *Spain* 34 E7
Galápagos, *Pac. Oc.* 122 D1
Galashiels, *U.K.* 14 F6
Galatás, *Greece* 38 D5
Galaţi, *Romania* 43 E13
Galaţi □, *Romania* 43 E12
Galatia, *Turkey* 72 C5
Galatina, *Italy* 31 B11
Galátone, *Italy* 31 B11
Galax, *U.S.A.* 109 G5
Galaxídhion, *Greece* 38 C4
Galcaio, *Somali Rep.* 74 F4
Galdhøpiggen, *Norway* 9 F12
Galeana, *Chihuahua, Mexico* 118 A3
Galeana, *Nuevo León, Mexico* 118 A3
Galegu, *Sudan* 81 E4
Galela, *Indonesia* 63 D7
Galena, *U.S.A.* 100 B4
Galera, *Spain* 33 H2
Galera Point, *Trin. & Tob.* 121 D7
Galesburg, *U.S.A.* 112 E9
Galeton, *U.S.A.* 110 E7
Galga, *Ethiopia* 81 F4
Gali, *Georgia* 49 J5
Galicea Mare, *Romania* 43 F8
Galich, *Russia* 48 A6
Galiche, *Bulgaria* 40 C7
Galicia □, *Spain* 34 C3
Galilee = Hagalil, *Israel* 75 C4
Galilee, L., *Australia* 94 C4
Galilee, Sea of = Yam Kinneret, *Israel* 75 C4
Galim, *Cameroon* 83 D7
Galinoporni, *Cyprus* 36 D13
Galion, *U.S.A.* 110 F2
Galiuro Mts., *U.S.A.* 115 K8
Galiwinku, *Australia* 94 A2
Gallabat, *Sudan* 81 E4
Gallan Hd., *U.K.* 14 C1
Gallarate, *Italy* 28 C5
Gallatin, *U.S.A.* 109 G2
Galle, *Sri Lanka* 66 R12
Gállego →, *Spain* 32 D4
Gallegos →, *Argentina* 128 G3
Galletti →, *Ethiopia* 81 F5
Galley Hd., *Ireland* 15 E3
Galliate, *Italy* 28 C5
Gallinas, Pta., *Colombia* 124 A4
Gallipoli = Gelibolu, *Turkey* 41 F10
Gallípoli, *Italy* 31 B10
Gallipolis, *U.S.A.* 108 F4
Gällivare, *Sweden* 8 C19
Gallneukirchen, *Austria* 26 C7
Gällö, *Sweden* 10 B9
Gallo, C., *Italy* 30 D6
Gallocanta, L. de, *Spain* 32 E3
Galloo I., *U.S.A.* 111 C8
Galloway, *U.K.* 14 F4
Galloway, Mull of, *U.K.* 14 G4
Gallup, *U.S.A.* 115 J9
Gallur, *Spain* 32 D3
Galoya, *Sri Lanka* 66 Q12
Galt, *U.S.A.* 116 G5
Galten, *Denmark* 11 H3
Galtür, *Austria* 26 E3
Galty Mts., *Ireland* 15 D3
Galtymore, *Ireland* 15 D3
Galva, *U.S.A.* 112 E9
Galve de Sorbe, *Spain* 32 D1
Galveston, *U.S.A.* 113 L7
Galveston B., *U.S.A.* 113 L7
Gálvez, *Argentina* 126 C3
Galway, *Ireland* 15 C2
Galway □, *Ireland* 15 C2
Galway B., *Ireland* 15 C2
Gam →, *Vietnam* 64 B5
Gamagori, *Japan* 55 G8
Gamari, L., *Ethiopia* 81 E5
Gamawa, *Nigeria* 83 C7
Gamay, *Phil.* 61 E6
Gambaga, *Ghana* 83 C4
Gambat, *Pakistan* 68 F3
Gambela, *Ethiopia* 81 F3
Gambhir →, *India* 68 F6
Gambia ■, *W. Afr.* 82 C1
Gambia →, *W. Afr.* 82 C1
Gambier, *U.S.A.* 110 F2
Gambier, C., *Australia* 92 B5
Gambier Is., *Australia* 95 F2
Gambo, *Canada* 103 C9
Gamboli, *Pakistan* 68 E3
Gamboma, *Congo* 84 E3
Gamka →, *S. Africa* 88 E3
Gamkab →, *Namibia* 88 D2
Gamla Uppsala, *Sweden* 10 E11
Gamlakarleby = Kokkola, *Finland* 8 E20
Gamleby, *Sweden* 11 G10
Gammon →, *Canada* 105 C9
Gamo-Gofa □, *Ethiopia* 81 F4
Gamou, *Niger* 83 C6
Gamtoos →, *S. Africa* 88 E4
Gan, *France* 20 E3
Gan Goriama, Mts., *Cameroon* 83 D7
Gan Jiang →, *China* 59 C11
Ganado, *U.S.A.* 115 J9
Gananita, *Sudan* 80 D3
Gananoque, *Canada* 102 D4
Ganāveh, *Iran* 71 D6
Gäncä, *Azerbaijan* 49 K8
Gancheng, *China* 64 C7
Gand = Gent, *Belgium* 17 C3
Ganda, *Angola* 85 G2
Gandajika, *Dem. Rep. of the Congo* 84 F4
Gandak →, *India* 69 G11
Gandava, *Pakistan* 68 E2
Gander, *Canada* 103 C9
Gander L., *Canada* 103 C9
Ganderkesee, *Germany* 24 B4
Ganderowe Falls, *Zimbabwe* 87 F2
Gandesa, *Spain* 32 D5
Gandhi Sagar, *India* 68 G6
Gandhinagar, *India* 68 H5
Gandi, *Nigeria* 83 C6
Gandía, *Spain* 33 G4
Gandino, *Italy* 28 C6
Gando, Pta., *Canary Is.* 37 G4
Gandole, *Nigeria* 83 D7
Gâneb, *Mauritania* 82 B2
Ganedidalem = Gani, *Indonesia* 63 E7
Ganetti, *Sudan* 80 D3
Ganga →, *India* 69 H14
Ganga Sagar, *India* 69 J13
Gangafani, *Mali* 82 C4
Gangan →, *India* 69 E8
Ganganagar, *India* 68 E5
Gangapur, *India* 68 F7
Gangara, *Niger* 83 C6
Gangaw, *Burma* 67 H19
Gangdisê Shan, *China* 67 D12
Ganges = Ganga →, *India* 69 H14
Ganges, *Canada* 104 D4
Ganges, *France* 20 E7
Ganges, Mouths of the, *India* 69 J14
Gånghester, *Sweden* 11 G7
Gangi, *Italy* 31 E7
Gângiova, *Romania* 43 G8
Gangoh, *India* 68 E7
Gangroti, *India* 69 D8
Gangtok, *India* 67 F16
Gangu, *China* 56 G3
Gangyao, *China* 57 B14
Gani, *Indonesia* 63 E7
Ganj, *India* 69 F8
Ganluc, *China* 58 C4
Gannat, *France* 19 F10
Gannett Peak, *U.S.A.* 114 E9
Ganquan, *China* 56 F5
Gänserdorf, *Austria* 27 C9
Ganshui, *China* 58 C6
Gansu □, *China* 56 G3
Ganta, *Liberia* 82 D3
Gantheaume, C., *Australia* 95 F2
Gantheaume B., *Australia* 93 E1
Gantsevichi = Hantsavichy, *Belarus* 47 F4
Ganye, *Nigeria* 83 D7
Ganyem = Genyem, *Indonesia* 63 E10
Ganyu, *China* 57 G10
Ganyushkino, *Kazakstan* 49 G9
Ganzhou, *China* 59 E10
Gao, *Mali* 83 B4
Gao, *Mali* 83 B5
Gao Xian, *China* 58 C5
Gao'an, *China* 59 C10
Gaochun, *China* 59 B12
Gaohe, *China* 59 F9
Gaohebu, *China* 59 B11
Gaokeng, *China* 59 D9
Gaolan Dao, *China* 59 G9
Gaoligong Shan, *China* 58 E2
Gaomi, *China* 57 F10
Gaoming, *China* 59 F9
Gaoping, *China* 56 G7
Gaotang, *China* 56 F9
Gaoua, *Burkina Faso* 82 C4
Gaoual, *Guinea* 82 C2
Gaoxiong = Kaohsiung, *Taiwan* 59 F13
Gaoyang, *China* 56 E8
Gaoyao, *China* 59 F9
Gaoyou, *China* 59 A12
Gaoyou Hu, *China* 57 H10
Gaoyuan, *China* 57 F9
Gaozhou, *China* 59 G8
Gap, *France* 21 D10
Gapan, *Phil.* 61 D4
Gapat →, *India* 69 G10
Gapuwiyak, *Australia* 94 A2
Gar, *China* 60 C2
Garabogazköl Aylagy, *Turkmenistan* 50 E6
Garachico, *Canary Is.* 37 F3
Garachiné, *Panama* 120 E4
Garafia, *Canary Is.* 37 F2
Garah, *Australia* 95 D4
Garajonay, *Canary Is.* 37 F2
Garango, *Burkina Faso* 83 C4
Garanhuns, *Brazil* 125 E11
Garautha, *India* 69 G8
Garawe, *Liberia* 82 E3
Garba Tula, *Kenya* 86 B4
Garberville, *U.S.A.* 114 F2
Garbiyang, *India* 69 D9
Garbsen, *Germany* 24 C5
Gard □, *France* 21 D8
Gard →, *France* 21 E8
Garda, L. di, *Italy* 28 C7
Gardanne, *France* 21 E9
Gårdby, *Sweden* 11 H10
Garde L., *Canada* 105 A7
Gardelegen, *Germany* 24 C7
Garden City, *Ga., U.S.A.* 109 J5
Garden City, *Kans., U.S.A.* 113 G4
Garden City, *Tex., U.S.A.* 113 K4
Garden Grove, *U.S.A.* 117 M9
Gardēz, *Afghan.* 68 C3
Gardhíki, *Greece* 38 C3
Gardiner, *Maine, U.S.A.* 109 C11
Gardiner, *Mont., U.S.A.* 114 D8
Gardiners I., *U.S.A.* 111 E12
Gardner, *U.S.A.* 111 D13
Gardner Canal, *Canada* 104 C3
Gardnerville, *U.S.A.* 116 G7
Gardno, Jezioro, *Poland* 44 D4
Gardo, *Somali Rep.* 74 F4
Gardone Val Trómpia, *Italy* 28 C7
Gárdony, *Hungary* 42 C3
Garešnica, *Croatia* 29 C13
Garéssio, *Italy* 28 D5
Garey, *U.S.A.* 117 L6
Garfield, *U.S.A.* 114 C5
Garforth, *U.K.* 12 D6
Gargaliánoi, *Greece* 38 D3
Gargan, Mt., *France* 20 C5
Gargouna, *Mali* 83 B5
Gargždai, *Lithuania* 44 C8
Garibaldi Prov. Park, *Canada* 104 D4
Gariep, L., *S. Africa* 88 E4
Garies, *S. Africa* 88 E2
Garigliano →, *Italy* 30 A6
Garissa, *Kenya* 86 C4
Garkida, *Nigeria* 83 C7
Garko, *Nigeria* 83 C6
Garland, *Tex., U.S.A.* 113 J6
Garland, *Utah, U.S.A.* 114 F7
Garlasco, *Italy* 28 C5
Garliava, *Lithuania* 44 D10
Garlin, *France* 20 E3
Garm, *Tajikistan* 50 F8
Garmāb, *Iran* 71 C8
Garmisch-Partenkirchen, *Germany* 25 H7
Garmsār, *Iran* 71 C7
Garner, *U.S.A.* 112 D8
Garnett, *U.S.A.* 112 F7
Garo Hills, *India* 69 G14
Garoe, *Somali Rep.* 74 F4
Garonne →, *France* 20 C3
Garonne, Canal Latéral à la, *France* 20 D4
Garot, *India* 68 G6
Garoua, *Cameroon* 83 D7
Garpenberg, *Sweden* 10 D10
Garphyttan, *Sweden* 10 E8
Garrauli, *India* 69 G8
Garrel, *Germany* 24 C4
Garrigue = Garrigues, *France* 20 E7
Garrigues, *France* 20 E7
Garrison, *Mont., U.S.A.* 114 C7
Garrison, *N. Dak., U.S.A.* 112 B4
Garrison Res. = Sakakawea, L., *U.S.A.* 112 B4
Garron Pt., *U.K.* 15 A6
Garrovillas, *Spain* 35 F4
Garrucha, *Spain* 33 H3
Garry →, *U.K.* 14 E5
Garry, L., *Canada* 100 B9
Garsen, *Kenya* 86 C5
Gärsnäs, *Sweden* 11 J8
Garson L., *Canada* 105 B6
Gartempe →, *France* 20 B4
Gartz, *Germany* 24 B10
Garu, *Ghana* 83 C4
Garu, *India* 69 H11
Garub, *Namibia* 88 D2
Garut, *Indonesia* 63 G12
Garvão, *Portugal* 35 H2
Garvie Mts., *N.Z.* 91 L2
Garwa = Garoua, *Cameroon* 83 D7
Garwa, *India* 69 G10
Garwolin, *Poland* 45 G8
Gary, *U.S.A.* 108 E2
Garz, *Germany* 24 A9
Garzê, *China* 58 B3
Garzón, *Colombia* 124 C3
Gas-San, *Japan* 54 E10
Gasan Kuli = Esenguly, *Turkmenistan* 50 F6
Gascogne, *France* 20 E4
Gascogne, G. de, *Europe* 20 E2
Gascony = Gascogne, *France* 20 E4
Gascoyne →, *Australia* 93 D1
Gascoyne Junction, *Australia* 93 E2
Gascueña, *Spain* 32 E2
Gash, Wadi →, *Ethiopia* 81 D4
Gashagar, *Nigeria* 83 C7
Gashaka, *Nigeria* 83 D7
Gasherbrum, *Pakistan* 69 B7
Gashua, *Nigeria* 83 C7
Gaspé, *Canada* 103 C7
Gaspé, C. de, *Canada* 103 C7
Gaspé, Pén. de, *Canada* 103 C6
Gaspésie, Parc de Conservation de la, *Canada* 103 C6
Gassan, *Burkina Faso* 82 C4
Gassol, *Nigeria* 83 D7
Gasteiz = Vitoria-Gasteiz, *Spain* 32 C2
Gastonia, *U.S.A.* 109 H5

Gastoúni, *Greece* 38 D3
Gastoúri, *Greece* 38 B1
Gastre, *Argentina* 128 E3
Gästrikland, *Sweden* 10 D10
Gata, C., *Cyprus* 36 E12
Gata, C. de, *Spain* 33 J2
Gata, Sierra de, *Spain* 34 E4
Gataga →, *Canada* 104 B3
Gătaia, *Romania* 42 E6
Gatchina, *Russia* 46 C6
Gatehouse of Fleet, *U.K.* 14 G4
Gates, *U.S.A.* 110 C7
Gateshead, *U.K.* 12 C6
Gatesville, *U.S.A.* 113 K6
Gaths, *Zimbabwe* 87 G3
Gatico, *Chile* 126 A1
Gâtinais, *France* 19 D9
Gâtine, Hauteurs de, *France* 20 B3
Gatineau, *Canada* 111 A9
Gatineau →, *Canada* 102 C4
Gatineau, Parc Nat. de la, *Canada* 102 C4
Gattaran, *Phil.* 61 B4
Gattinara, *Italy* 28 C5
Gatton, *Australia* 95 D5
Gatun, L., *Panama* 120 E4
Gatyana, *S. Africa* 89 E4
Gau, *Fiji* 91 D8
Gaucín, *Spain* 35 J5
Gauer L., *Canada* 105 B9
Gauhati, *India* 67 F17
Gauja →, *Latvia* 9 H21
Gaula →, *Norway* 8 E14
Gauri Phanta, *India* 69 E9
Gausta, *Norway* 9 G13
Gauteng □, *S. Africa* 89 D4
Gāv Koshī, *Iran* 71 D8
Gāvakān, *Iran* 71 D7
Gavarnie, *France* 20 F3
Gavāter, *Iran* 71 E9
Gāvbandī, *Iran* 71 E7
Gavdhopoúla, *Greece* 36 E6
Gávdhos, *Greece* 36 E6
Gavi, *Italy* 28 D5
Gavião, *Portugal* 35 F3
Gaviota, *U.S.A.* 117 L6
Gāvkhūnī, Bāţlāq-e, *Iran* 71 C7
Gävle, *Sweden* 10 D11
Gävleborgs län □, *Sweden* 10 C10
Gävlebukten, *Sweden* 10 D11
Gavorrano, *Italy* 28 F7
Gavray, *France* 18 D5
Gavrilov Yam, *Russia* 46 D10
Gávrion, *Greece* 38 D6
Gawachab, *Namibia* 88 D2
Gawilgarh Hills, *India* 66 J10
Gawler, *Australia* 95 E2
Gawu, *Nigeria* 83 D6
Gaxun Nur, *China* 60 B5
Gaya, *India* 69 G11
Gaya, *Niger* 83 C5
Gaya, *Nigeria* 83 C6
Gayéri, *Burkina Faso* 83 C5
Gaylord, *U.S.A.* 108 C3
Gayndah, *Australia* 95 D5
Gaysin = Haysyn, *Ukraine* 47 H5
Gayvoron = Hayvoron, *Ukraine* 47 H5
Gaza, *Gaza Strip* 75 D3
Gaza □, *Mozam.* 89 C5
Gaza Strip □, *Asia* 75 D3
Gazanjyk, *Turkmenistan* 71 B7
Gazaoua, *Niger* 83 C6
Gāzbor, *Iran* 71 D8
Gazi, *Dem. Rep. of the Congo* 86 B1
Gaziantep, *Turkey* 70 B3
Gazipaşa, *Turkey* 72 D5
Gbarnga, *Liberia* 82 D3
Gbekebo, *Nigeria* 83 D5
Gboko, *Nigeria* 83 D6
Gbongan, *Nigeria* 83 D5
Gcoverega, *Botswana* 88 B3
Gcuwa, *S. Africa* 89 E4
Gdańsk, *Poland* 44 D5
Gdańska, Zatoka, *Poland* 44 D6
Gdov, *Russia* 9 G22
Gdynia, *Poland* 44 D5
Geba →, *Guinea-Biss.* 82 C1
Gebe, *Indonesia* 63 D7
Gebeciler, *Turkey* 39 C12
Gebeit Mine, *Sudan* 80 C4
Gebel Abyad, *Sudan* 80 D2
Gebel Iweibid, *Egypt* 80 H8
Gebze, *Turkey* 41 F13
Gecha, *Ethiopia* 81 F4
Gedaref, *Sudan* 81 E4
Gedaref □, *Sudan* 81 E4
Gediz, *Turkey* 39 B11
Gediz →, *Turkey* 39 C8
Gedo, *Ethiopia* 81 F4
Gèdre, *France* 20 F4
Gedser, *Denmark* 11 K5
Geegully Cr. →, *Australia* 92 C3
Geel, *Belgium* 17 C4
Geelong, *Australia* 95 F3
Geelvink B. = Cenderwasih, Teluk, *Indonesia* 63 E9
Geelvink Chan., *Australia* 93 E1
Geesthacht, *Germany* 24 B6
Geidam, *Nigeria* 83 C7
Geikie →, *Canada* 105 B8
Geilenkirchen, *Germany* 24 E2
Geili, *Sudan* 81 D3
Geisingen, *Germany* 25 H4
Geislingen, *Germany* 25 G5
Geistown, *U.S.A.* 110 F6
Geita, *Tanzania* 86 C3
Gejiu, *China* 58 F4
Gel →, *Sudan* 81 F2
Gel, Meydān-e, *Iran* 71 D7
Gel River, *Sudan* 81 F2
Gela, *Italy* 31 E7
Gela, G. di, *Italy* 31 F7
Gelahun, *Liberia* 82 D2
Gelderland □, *Neths.* 17 B6
Geldern, *Germany* 24 D2
Geldrop, *Neths.* 17 C5
Geleen, *Neths.* 17 D5
Gelehun, *S. Leone* 82 D2
Gelembe, *Turkey* 39 B9
Gelemso, *Ethiopia* 81 F5
Gelendost, *Turkey* 72 C4
Gelendzhik, *Russia* 47 K10
Gelibolu, *Turkey* 41 F10
Gelibolu Yarımadası, *Turkey* 41 F10
Gelidonya Burnu, *Turkey* 72 D4
Gelnhausen, *Germany* 25 E5
Gelnica, *Slovak Rep.* 27 C13
Gelsenkirchen, *Germany* 24 D3
Gelting, *Germany* 24 A5
Gemas, *Malaysia* 65 L4
Gembloux, *Belgium* 17 D4
Gembu, *Nigeria* 83 D7
Gemena, *Dem. Rep. of the Congo* 84 D3
Gemerek, *Turkey* 70 B3
Gemla, *Sweden* 11 H8
Gemlik, *Turkey* 41 F13
Gemlik Körfezi, *Turkey* 41 F12
Gemona del Friuli, *Italy* 29 B10
Gemsa, *Egypt* 80 B3
Gemünden, *Germany* 25 E5
Genale →, *Ethiopia* 81 F4
Genç, *Turkey* 73 C9
Gençay, *France* 20 B4
Geneina, Gebel, *Egypt* 80 B3
General Acha, *Argentina* 126 D3
General Alvear, *Buenos Aires, Argentina* 126 D4
General Alvear, *Mendoza, Argentina* 126 D2
General Artigas, *Paraguay* 126 B4
General Belgrano, *Argentina* 126 D4
General Cabrera, *Argentina* 126 C3
General Cepeda, *Mexico* 118 B4
General Guido, *Argentina* 126 D4
General Juan Madariaga, *Argentina* 126 D4
General La Madrid, *Argentina* 126 D3
General MacArthur, *Phil.* 61 F6
General Martin Miguel de Güemes, *Argentina* 126 A3
General Paz, *Argentina* 126 B4
General Pico, *Argentina* 126 D3
General Pinedo, *Argentina* 126 B3
General Pinto, *Argentina* 126 C3
General Roca, *Argentina* 128 D3
General Santos, *Phil.* 61 H6
General Toshevo, *Bulgaria* 41 C12
General Trevino, *Mexico* 119 B5
General Trías, *Mexico* 118 B3
General Viamonte, *Argentina* 126 D3
General Villegas, *Argentina* 126 D3
Genesee, *Idaho, U.S.A.* 114 C5
Genesee, *Pa., U.S.A.* 110 E7
Genesee →, *U.S.A.* 110 C7
Geneseo, *Ill., U.S.A.* 112 E9
Geneseo, *N.Y., U.S.A.* 110 D7
Geneva = Genève, *Switz.* 25 J2
Geneva, *Ala., U.S.A.* 109 K3
Geneva, *N.Y., U.S.A.* 110 D8
Geneva, *Nebr., U.S.A.* 112 E6
Geneva, *Ohio, U.S.A.* 110 E4
Geneva, L. = Léman, L., *Europe* 19 F13
Geneva, L., *U.S.A.* 108 D1
Genève, *Switz.* 25 J2
Gengenbach, *Germany* 25 G4
Gengma, *China* 58 F2
Genichesk = Henichesk, *Ukraine* 47 J8
Genil →, *Spain* 35 H5
Genk, *Belgium* 17 D5
Genlis, *France* 19 E12
Gennargentu, Mti. del, *Italy* 30 B2
Gennes, *France* 18 E6
Genoa = Génova, *Italy* 28 D5
Genoa, *Australia* 95 F4
Genoa, *N.Y., U.S.A.* 111 D8
Genoa, *Nebr., U.S.A.* 112 E6
Genoa, *Nev., U.S.A.* 116 F7
Génova, *Italy* 28 D5
Génova, G. di, *Italy* 28 E6
Genriyetty, Ostrov, *Russia* 51 B16
Gent, *Belgium* 17 C3
Genteng, *Indonesia* 63 G12
Genthin, *Germany* 24 C8
Genyem, *Indonesia* 63 E10
Genzano di Lucánia, *Italy* 31 B9
Genzano di Roma, *Italy* 29 G9
Geoagiu, *Romania* 43 E8
Geographe B., *Australia* 93 F2
Geographe Chan., *Australia* 93 D1
Geokchay = Göyçay, *Azerbaijan* 49 K8
Georga, Zemlya, *Russia* 50 A5
George, *S. Africa* 88 E3
George →, *Canada* 103 A6
George, L., *N.S.W., Australia* 95 F4
George, L., *S. Austral., Australia* 95 F3
George, L., *W. Austral., Australia* 92 D3
George, L., *Uganda* 86 B3
George, L., *Fla., U.S.A.* 109 L5
George, L., *N.Y., U.S.A.* 111 C11
George Gill Ra., *Australia* 92 D5
George River = Kangiqsualujjuaq, *Canada* 101 C13
George Sound, *N.Z.* 91 L1
George Town, *Australia* 94 G4
George Town, *Bahamas* 120 B4
George Town, *Malaysia* 65 K3
George V Land, *Antarctica* 5 C10
George VI Sound, *Antarctica* 5 D17
George West, *U.S.A.* 113 L5
Georgetown, *Australia* 94 B3
Georgetown, *Ont., Canada* 102 D4
Georgetown, *P.E.I., Canada* 103 C7
Georgetown, *Cayman Is.* 120 C3
Georgetown, *Gambia* 82 C2
Georgetown, *Guyana* 124 B7
Georgetown, *Calif., U.S.A.* 116 G6
Georgetown, *Colo., U.S.A.* 114 G11
Georgetown, *Ky., U.S.A.* 108 F3
Georgetown, *N.Y., U.S.A.* 111 D9
Georgetown, *Ohio, U.S.A.* 108 F4
Georgetown, *S.C., U.S.A.* 109 J6
Georgetown, *Tex., U.S.A.* 113 K6
Georgia □, *U.S.A.* 109 K5
Georgia ■, *Asia* 49 J6
Georgia, Str. of, *Canada* 104 D4
Georgian B., *Canada* 102 C3
Georgina →, *Australia* 94 C2
Georgina I., *Canada* 110 B5
Georgiu-Dezh = Liski, *Russia* 47 G10
Georgiyevsk, *Russia* 49 H6
Georgsmarienhütte, *Germany* 24 C4
Gera, *Germany* 24 E8
Geraardsbergen, *Belgium* 17 D3
Geral, Serra, *Brazil* 127 B6
Geral de Goiás, Serra, *Brazil* 125 F9
Geraldine, *U.S.A.* 114 C8
Geraldton, *Australia* 93 E1
Geraldton, *Canada* 102 C2
Gérardmer, *France* 19 D13
Gercüş, *Turkey* 73 D9
Gerede, *Turkey* 72 B5
Gerês, Sierra do, *Portugal* 34 D3
Gereshk, *Afghan.* 66 D4
Geretsried, *Germany* 25 H7
Gérgal, *Spain* 33 H2
Gerik, *Malaysia* 65 K3
Gering, *U.S.A.* 112 E3
Gerlach, *U.S.A.* 114 F4
Gerlachovský štít, *Slovak Rep.* 27 B13
German Planina, *Macedonia* 40 D6
Germansen Landing, *Canada* 104 B4
Germantown, *U.S.A.* 113 M10
Germany ■, *Europe* 24 E6
Germencik, *Turkey* 39 D9
Germering, *Germany* 25 G7
Germersheim, *Germany* 25 F4
Germī, *Iran* 71 B6
Germiston, *S. Africa* 89 D4
Gernika-Lumo, *Spain* 32 B2
Gernsheim, *Germany* 25 F4
Gero, *Japan* 55 G8
Gerolzhofen, *Germany* 25 F6
Gerona = Girona, *Spain* 32 D7
Gerrard, *Canada* 104 C5
Gers □, *France* 20 E4
Gers →, *France* 20 D4
Gersfeld, *Germany* 24 E5
Gersthofen, *Germany* 25 G6
Gerzat, *France* 20 C7
Gerze, *Turkey* 72 B6
Geseke, *Germany* 24 D4
Geser, *Indonesia* 63 E8
Gesso →, *Italy* 28 D4
Gestro, Wabi →, *Ethiopia* 81 G5
Getafe, *Spain* 34 E7
Getinge, *Sweden* 11 H6
Gettysburg, *Pa., U.S.A.* 108 F7
Gettysburg, *S. Dak., U.S.A.* 112 C5
Getxo, *Spain* 32 B2
Getz Ice Shelf, *Antarctica* 5 D14
Gevaş, *Turkey* 73 C10
Gévaudan, *France* 20 D7
Gevgelija, *Macedonia* 40 E6
Gévora →, *Spain* 35 G4
Gewani, *Ethiopia* 81 E5
Gex, *France* 19 F13
Geyikli, *Turkey* 39 B8
Geyser, *U.S.A.* 114 C8
Geyserville, *U.S.A.* 116 G4
Geyve, *Turkey* 72 B4
Ghâbat el Arab = Wang Kai, *Sudan* 81 F2
Ghabeish, *Sudan* 81 E2
Ghaggar →, *India* 68 E6
Ghaghara →, *India* 69 G11
Ghaghat →, *Bangla.* 69 G13
Ghagra, *India* 69 H11
Ghagra →, *India* 69 F9
Ghalla, Wadi el →, *Sudan* 81 E2
Ghana ■, *W. Afr.* 83 D4
Ghansor, *India* 69 H9
Ghanzi, *Botswana* 88 C3
Gharb el Istiwa'iya □, *Sudan* 81 G3
Gharb Kordofân, *Sudan* 81 E2
Gharbîya, Es Sahrâ el, *Egypt* 80 B2
Ghardaïa, *Algeria* 78 B6
Ghârib, G., *Egypt* 80 B3
Gharig, *Sudan* 81 E2
Gharyān, *Libya* 79 B8
Ghat, *Libya* 79 D8
Ghatal, *India* 69 H12
Ghatampur, *India* 69 F9
Ghatsila, *India* 69 H12
Ghaţţī, *Si. Arabia* 70 D3
Ghawdex = Gozo, *Malta* 36 C1
Ghazal, Bahr el →, *Chad* 79 F9
Ghazâl, Bahr el →, *Sudan* 81 F3
Ghaziabad, *India* 68 E7
Ghazipur, *India* 69 G10
Ghaznī, *Afghan.* 68 C3
Ghaznī □, *Afghan.* 66 C6
Ghedi, *Italy* 28 C7
Ghelari, *Romania* 42 E7
Ghent = Gent, *Belgium* 17 C3
Gheorghe Gheorghiu-Dej = Oneşti, *Romania* 43 D11
Gheorgheni, *Romania* 43 D10
Gherla, *Romania* 43 C8
Ghidigeni, *Romania* 43 D12
Ghilarza, *Italy* 30 B1
Ghimeş-Făget, *Romania* 43 D11
Ghīnah, Wādī al, *Si. Arabia* 70 D3
Ghīnah, Wādī al →, *Si. Arabia* 80 B4
Ghisonaccia, *France* 21 F13
Ghisoni, *France* 21 F13
Ghizao, *Afghan.* 68 C1
Ghizar →, *Pakistan* 69 A5
Ghot Ogrein, *Egypt* 80 A2
Ghotaru, *India* 68 F4
Ghotki, *Pakistan* 68 E3
Ghowr □, *Afghan.* 66 C4
Ghudaf, W. al →, *Iraq* 70 C4
Ghudāmis, *Libya* 79 B7
Ghughri, *India* 69 H9
Ghugus, *India* 66 K11
Ghulam Mohammad Barrage, *Pakistan* 68 G3
Ghūrīān, *Afghan.* 66 B2
Gia Dinh, *Vietnam* 65 G6
Gia Lai = Plei Ku, *Vietnam* 64 F7
Gia Nghia, *Vietnam* 65 G6
Gia Ngoc, *Vietnam* 64 E7
Gia Vuc, *Vietnam* 64 E7
Giannutri, *Italy* 28 F8
Giant Forest, *U.S.A.* 116 J8
Giant Mts. = Krkonoše, *Czech Rep.* 26 A8
Giants Causeway, *U.K.* 15 A5
Giarabub = Al Jaghbūb, *Libya* 79 C10
Giarre, *Italy* 31 E8
Giaveno, *Italy* 28 C4
Gibara, *Cuba* 120 B4
Gibb River, *Australia* 92 C4
Gibbon, *U.S.A.* 112 E5
Gibe →, *Ethiopia* 81 F4
Gibellina Nuova, *Italy* 30 E5
Gibeon, *Namibia* 88 D2
Gibraleón, *Spain* 35 H4
Gibraltar ■, *Europe* 35 J5
Gibraltar, Str. of, *Medit. S.* 35 K5
Gibson Desert, *Australia* 92 D4
Gibsons, *Canada* 104 D4
Gibsonville, *U.S.A.* 116 F6
Giddings, *U.S.A.* 113 K6
Gidole, *Ethiopia* 81 F4
Gien, *France* 19 E9
Giengen, *Germany* 25 G6
Giessen, *Germany* 24 E4
Gīfān, *Iran* 71 B8
Gifatin, Geziret, *Egypt* 80 B3
Gifhorn, *Germany* 24 C6
Gift Lake, *Canada* 104 B5
Gifu, *Japan* 55 G8
Gifu □, *Japan* 55 G8
Gigant, *Russia* 49 G5
Giganta, Sa. de la, *Mexico* 118 B2
Gigen, *Bulgaria* 41 C8
Gigha, *U.K.* 14 F3
Gíglio, *Italy* 28 F7
Gignac, *France* 20 E7
Gigüela →, *Spain* 35 F7
Gijón, *Spain* 34 B5
Gil I., *Canada* 104 C3
Gila →, *U.S.A.* 115 K6
Gila Bend, *U.S.A.* 115 K7
Gila Bend Mts., *U.S.A.* 115 K7
Gīlān □, *Iran* 71 B6
Gilău, *Romania* 43 D8
Gilbert →, *Australia* 94 B3
Gilbert Is., *Kiribati* 96 G9
Gilbert River, *Australia* 94 B3
Gilead, *U.S.A.* 111 B14
Gilf el Kebîr, Hadabat el, *Egypt* 80 C2
Gilford I., *Canada* 104 C3
Gilgandra, *Australia* 95 E4
Gilgil, *Kenya* 86 C4
Gilgit, *India* 69 B6
Gilgit →, *Pakistan* 69 B6
Gilgunnia, *Australia* 95 E4
Giljeva Planina, *Serbia, Yug.* 40 C3
Gillam, *Canada* 105 B10
Gilleleje, *Denmark* 11 H6
Gillen, L., *Australia* 93 E3
Gilles, L., *Australia* 95 E2
Gillette, *U.S.A.* 112 C2
Gilliat, *Australia* 94 C3
Gillingham, *U.K.* 13 F8
Gilmer, *U.S.A.* 113 J7
Gilmore, L., *Australia* 93 F3
Gilo →, *Ethiopia* 81 F3
Gilort →, *Romania* 43 F8
Gilroy, *U.S.A.* 116 H5
Gimbi, *Ethiopia* 81 F4
Gimli, *Canada* 105 C9
Gimo, *Sweden* 10 D12
Gimone →, *France* 20 E5
Gimont, *France* 20 E4
Gin Gin, *Australia* 95 D5
Ginâh, *Egypt* 80 B3
Gineifa, *Egypt* 80 H8
Gingin, *Australia* 93 F2
Gingindlovu, *S. Africa* 89 D5
Ginir, *Ethiopia* 81 F5
Ginosa, *Italy* 31 B9
Ginzo de Limia = Xinzo de Limia, *Spain* 34 C3
Gióia, G. di, *Italy* 31 D8
Gióia del Colle, *Italy* 31 B9
Gióia Táuro, *Italy* 31 D8
Gioiosa Iónica, *Italy* 31 D9
Gioiosa Marea, *Italy* 31 D7
Gióna, Óros, *Greece* 38 C4
Giovi, Passo dei, *Italy* 28 D5
Giovinazzo, *Italy* 31 A9
Gippsland, *Australia* 95 F4
Gir Hills, *India* 68 J4
Girab, *India* 68 F4
Girâfi, W. →, *Egypt* 75 F3
Giraltovce, *Slovak Rep.* 27 B14
Girard, *Kans., U.S.A.* 113 G7
Girard, *Ohio, U.S.A.* 110 E4
Girard, *Pa., U.S.A.* 110 D4
Girard, *Pa., U.S.A.* 110 E4
Girdle Ness, *U.K.* 14 D6
Giresun, *Turkey* 73 B8
Girga, *Egypt* 80 B3
Giri →, *India* 68 D7
Giridih, *India* 69 G12
Girifalco, *Italy* 31 D9
Girne = Kyrenia, *Cyprus* 36 D12
Giro, *Nigeria* 83 C5
Giromagny, *France* 19 E13
Girona, *Spain* 32 D7
Girona □, *Spain* 32 C7
Gironde □, *France* 20 D3
Gironde →, *France* 20 C2
Gironella, *Spain* 32 C6
Giru, *Australia* 94 B4
Girvan, *U.K.* 14 F4
Gisborne, *N.Z.* 91 H7
Gisenyi, *Rwanda* 86 C2
Gislaved, *Sweden* 11 G7
Gisors, *France* 19 C8
Gitega, *Burundi* 86 C2
Giuba →, *Somali Rep.* 74 G3
Giugliano in Campania, *Italy* 31 B7
Giulianova, *Italy* 29 F10
Giurgeni, *Romania* 43 F12
Giurgiu, *Romania* 43 G10
Giurgiu □, *Romania* 43 F10
Giurgiuleşti, *Moldova* 43 E13
Give, *Denmark* 11 J3
Givet, *France* 19 B11
Givors, *France* 21 C8
Givry, *France* 19 F11
Giyon, *Ethiopia* 81 F4
Giza = El Gîza, *Egypt* 80 J7
Gizhiga, *Russia* 51 C17
Gizhiginskaya Guba, *Russia* 51 C16
Giżycko, *Poland* 44 D8
Gizzeria, *Italy* 31 D9
Gjalicës e Lumës, Mal, *Albania* 40 D4
Gjegjani, *Albania* 40 E4
Gjirokastra, *Albania* 40 F4
Gjoa Haven, *Canada* 100 B10
Gjøvik, *Norway* 9 F14
Gjuhës, Kep i, *Albania* 40 F3
Glace Bay, *Canada* 103 C8
Glacier Bay National Park and Preserve, *U.S.A.* 104 B1
Glacier National Park, *Canada* 104 C5
Glacier National Park, *U.S.A.* 114 B7
Glacier Peak, *U.S.A.* 114 B3
Gladewater, *U.S.A.* 113 J7
Gladstone, *Queens., Australia* 94 C5
Gladstone, *S. Austral., Australia* 95 E2
Gladstone, *Canada* 105 C9
Gladstone, *U.S.A.* 108 C2
Gladwin, *U.S.A.* 108 D3
Glafsfjorden, *Sweden* 10 E6
Głagów Małapolski, *Poland* 45 H8
Glåma = Glomma →, *Norway* 9 G14
Gláma, *Iceland* 8 D2
Glamis, *U.S.A.* 117 N11
Glamoč, *Bos.-H.* 29 D13
Glamsbjerg, *Denmark* 11 J4
Glarus, *Switz.* 25 H5
Glarus □, *Switz.* 25 J5
Glasco, *Kans., U.S.A.* 112 F6
Glasco, *N.Y., U.S.A.* 111 D11
Glasgow, *U.K.* 14 F4
Glasgow, *Ky., U.S.A.* 108 G3
Glasgow, *Mont., U.S.A.* 114 B10
Glasgow, City of □, *U.K.* 14 F4
Glaslyn, *Canada* 105 C7
Glastonbury, *U.K.* 13 F5
Glastonbury, *U.S.A.* 111 E12
Glauchau, *Germany* 24 E8
Glava, *Sweden* 10 E6
Glavice, *Croatia* 29 E13
Glazov, *Russia* 48 A11
Gleichen, *Canada* 104 C6
Gleisdorf, *Austria* 26 D8
Gleiwitz = Gliwice, *Poland* 45 H5
Glen, *U.S.A.* 111 B13
Glen Affric, *U.K.* 14 D3
Glen Canyon, *U.S.A.* 115 H8
Glen Canyon Dam, *U.S.A.* 115 H8
Glen Canyon National Recreation Area, *U.S.A.* 115 H8
Glen Coe, *U.K.* 14 E3
Glen Cove, *U.S.A.* 111 F11
Glen Garry, *U.K.* 14 D3
Glen Innes, *Australia* 95 D5
Glen Lyon, *U.S.A.* 111 E8
Glen Mor, *U.K.* 14 D4
Glen Moriston, *U.K.* 14 D4
Glen Robertson, *Canada* 111 A10
Glen Spean, *U.K.* 14 E4
Glen Ullin, *U.S.A.* 112 B4
Glénan, Îs. de, *France* 18 E3

Glencoe, Canada 110 D3
Glencoe, S. Africa 89 D5
Glencoe, U.S.A. 112 C7
Glendale, Ariz., U.S.A. 115 K7
Glendale, Calif., U.S.A. 117 L8
Glendale, Zimbabwe 87 F3
Glendive, U.S.A. 112 B2
Glendo, U.S.A. 112 D2
Glenelg →, Australia 95 F3
Glenfield, U.S.A. 111 C9
Glengarriff, Ireland 15 E2
Glenmont, U.S.A. 110 F2
Glenmorgan, Australia 95 D4
Glenn, U.S.A. 116 F4
Glennallen, U.S.A. 100 B5
Glennamaddy, Ireland 15 C3
Glenns Ferry, U.S.A. 114 E6
Glenore, Australia 94 B3
Glenreagh, Australia 95 E5
Glenrock, U.S.A. 114 E11
Glenrothes, U.K. 14 E5
Glens Falls, U.S.A. 111 C11
Glenside, U.S.A. 111 F9
Glenties, Ireland 15 B3
Glenville, U.S.A. 108 F5
Glenwood, Canada 103 C9
Glenwood, Ark., U.S.A. 113 H8
Glenwood, Hawaii, U.S.A. 106 J17
Glenwood, Iowa, U.S.A. 112 E7
Glenwood, Minn., U.S.A. 112 C7
Glenwood, Wash., U.S.A. 116 D5
Glenwood Springs, U.S.A. 114 G10
Glettinganes, Iceland 8 D7
Glifádha, Greece 38 D5
Glimåkra, Sweden 11 H8
Glina, Croatia 29 C13
Glinojeck, Poland 45 F7
Gliwice, Poland 45 H5
Globe, U.S.A. 115 K8
Glodeanu Siliştea, Romania 43 F11
Glodeni, Moldova 43 C12
Glödnitz, Austria 26 E7
Gloggnitz, Austria 26 D8
Głogów, Poland 45 G3
Głogówek, Poland 45 H4
Glomma →, Norway 9 G14
Glorieuses, Is., Ind. Oc. 89 A8
Glóssa, Greece 38 B5
Glossop, U.K. 12 D6
Gloucester, Australia 95 E5
Gloucester, U.K. 13 F5
Gloucester, U.S.A. 111 D14
Gloucester I., Australia 94 C4
Gloucester Point, U.S.A. 108 G7
Gloucestershire □, U.K. 13 F5
Gloversville, U.S.A. 111 C10
Glovertown, Canada 103 C9
Głowno, Poland 45 G6
Głubczyce, Poland 45 H4
Glubokiy, Russia 49 F5
Glubokoye = Hlybokaye, Belarus 46 E4
Głuchołazy, Poland 45 H4
Glücksburg, Germany 24 A5
Glückstadt, Germany 24 B5
Glukhov = Hlukhiv, Ukraine 47 G7
Glusk, Belarus 47 F5
Głuszyca, Poland 45 H3
Glyngøre, Denmark 11 H2
Gmünd, Kärnten, Austria 26 E6
Gmünd, Niederösterreich, Austria 26 C8
Gmunden, Austria 26 D6
Gnarp, Sweden 10 B11
Gnesta, Sweden 10 E11
Gniew, Poland 44 E5
Gniewkowo, Poland 45 F5
Gniezno, Poland 45 F4
Gnjilane, Kosovo, Yug. 40 D5
Gnoien, Germany 24 B8
Gnosjö, Sweden 11 G7
Gnowangerup, Australia 93 F2
Go Cong, Vietnam 65 G6
Gō-no-ura, Japan 55 H4
Goa, India 66 M8
Goa □, India 66 M8
Goalen Hd., Australia 95 F5
Goalpara, India 67 F17
Goaltor, India 69 H12
Goalundo Ghat, Bangla. 69 H13
Goaso, Ghana 82 D4
Goat Fell, U.K. 14 F3
Goba, Ethiopia 81 F4
Goba, Mozam. 89 D5
Gobabis, Namibia 88 C2
Göbel, Turkey 41 F12
Gobi, Asia 56 C6
Gobō, Japan 55 H7
Gobo, Sudan 81 F3
Göçbeyli, Turkey 39 B9
Goch, Germany 24 D2
Gochas, Namibia 88 C2
Godavari →, India 67 L13
Godavari Pt., India 67 L13
Godbout, Canada 103 C6
Godda, India 69 G12
Godech, Bulgaria 40 C7
Goderich, Canada 102 D3
Goderville, France 18 C7
Godfrey Ra., Australia 93 D2
Godhavn = Qeqertarsuaq, Greenland 4 C5
Godhra, India 68 H5
Gödöllő, Hungary 42 C4
Godoy Cruz, Argentina 126 C2
Gods →, Canada 102 A1
Gods L., Canada 102 B1
Gods River, Canada 105 C10
Godthåb = Nuuk, Greenland 101 B14
Godwin Austen = K2, Pakistan 69 B7
Goeie Hoop, Kaap die = Good Hope, C. of, S. Africa 88 E2
Goéland, L. au, Canada 102 C4
Goeree, Neths. 17 C3
Goes, Neths. 17 C3
Goffstown, U.S.A. 111 C13
Gogama, Canada 102 C3
Gogebic, L., U.S.A. 112 B10
Goggetti, Ethiopia 81 F4
Gogolin, Poland 45 H5
Gogonou, Benin 83 C5
Gogra = Ghaghara →, India 69 G11
Gogriâl, Sudan 81 F2
Gogti, Ethiopia 81 E5
Gohana, India 68 E7
Goharganj, India 68 H7
Goi →, India 68 H6
Goiânia, Brazil 125 G9
Goiás, Brazil 125 G8
Goiás □, Brazil 125 F9
Goio-Ere, Brazil 127 A5
Góis, Portugal 34 E2
Gojam □, Ethiopia 81 E4
Gojeb, Wabi →, Ethiopia 81 F4
Gojō, Japan 55 G7
Gojra, Pakistan 68 D5
Gökçeada, Turkey 41 F9
Gökçedağ, Turkey 39 B10
Gökçen, Turkey 39 C9
Gökçeören, Turkey 39 C10
Gökçeyazı, Turkey 39 B9
Gökırmak →, Turkey 72 B6
Gökova, Turkey 39 D10
Gökova Körfezi, Turkey 39 E9
Göksu →, Turkey 72 D6
Göksun, Turkey 72 C7
Gokteik, Burma 67 H20
Göktepe, Turkey 39 D10
Gokurt, Pakistan 68 E2
Gokwe, Zimbabwe 89 B4
Gol Gol, Australia 95 E3
Gola, India 69 E9
Golakganj, India 69 F13
Golan Heights = Hagolan, Syria 75 C4
Gołańcz, Poland 45 F4
Golāshkerd, Iran 71 E8
Golaya Pristen = Hola Pristan, Ukraine 47 J7
Gölbaşı, Adiyaman, Turkey 72 D7
Gölbaşı, Ankara, Turkey 72 C5
Golchikha, Russia 4 B12
Golconda, U.S.A. 114 F5
Gölcük, Kocaeli, Turkey 41 F13
Gölcük, Niğde, Turkey 72 C6
Gold, U.S.A. 110 E7
Gold Beach, U.S.A. 114 E1
Gold Coast, W. Afr. 83 E4
Gold Hill, U.S.A. 114 E2
Gold River, Canada 104 D3
Goldap, Poland 44 D9
Goldberg, Germany 24 B8
Golden, Canada 104 C5
Golden B., N.Z. 91 J4
Golden Gate, U.S.A. 114 H2
Golden Hinde, Canada 104 D3
Golden Lake, Canada 110 A7
Golden Vale, Ireland 15 D3
Goldendale, U.S.A. 114 D3
Goldfield, U.S.A. 115 H5
Goldsand L., Canada 105 B8
Goldsboro, U.S.A. 109 H7
Goldsmith, U.S.A. 113 K3
Goldsworthy, Australia 92 D2
Goldthwaite, U.S.A. 113 K5
Golegã, Portugal 35 F2
Goleniów, Poland 44 E1
Golestānak, Iran 71 D7
Goleta, U.S.A. 117 L7
Golfito, Costa Rica 120 E3
Golfo Aranci, Italy 30 B2
Gölgeli Dağları, Turkey 39 D10
Gölhisar, Turkey 39 D11
Goliad, U.S.A. 113 L6
Golija, Montenegro, Yug. 40 C2
Golija, Serbia, Yug. 40 C4
Golina, Poland 45 F5
Gölköy, Turkey 72 B7
Göllersdorf, Austria 26 C9
Gölmarmara, Turkey 39 C9
Golo →, France 21 F13
Gölova, Turkey 39 E12
Golpāyegān, Iran 71 C6
Gölpazarı, Turkey 72 B4
Golra, Pakistan 68 C5
Golspie, U.K. 14 D5
Golub-Dobrzyń, Poland 45 E6
Golubac, Serbia, Yug. 40 B5
Golyam Perelik, Bulgaria 41 E8
Golyama Kamchiya →, Bulgaria 41 C11
Goma, Dem. Rep. of the Congo 86 C2
Gomal Pass, Pakistan 68 D3
Gomati →, India 69 G10
Gombari, Dem. Rep. of the Congo 86 B2
Gombe, Nigeria 83 C7
Gömbe, Turkey 39 E11
Gombe □, Nigeria 83 C7
Gombe →, Tanzania 86 C3
Gombi, Nigeria 83 C7
Gomel = Homyel, Belarus 47 F6
Gomera, Canary Is. 37 F2
Gómez Palacio, Mexico 118 B4
Gomīshān, Iran 71 B7
Gommern, Germany 24 C7
Gomogomo, Indonesia 63 F8
Gomoh, India 67 H15
Gomotartsi, Bulgaria 40 B6
Gompa = Ganta, Liberia 82 D3
Gomphi, Greece 38 B3
Gonābād, Iran 71 C8
Gonaïves, Haiti 121 C5
Gonâve, G. de la, Haiti 121 C5
Gonâve, I. de la, Haiti 121 C5
Gonbad-e Kāvūs, Iran 71 B7
Gönc, Hungary 42 B6
Gonda, India 69 F9
Gondal, India 68 J4
Gonder, Ethiopia 81 E4
Gonder □, Ethiopia 81 E4
Gondia, India 66 J12
Gondola, Mozam. 87 F3
Gondomar, Portugal 34 D2
Gondrecourt-le-Château, France 19 D12
Gönen, Balıkesir, Turkey 41 F11
Gönen, Isparta, Turkey 39 D12
Gönen →, Turkey 41 F11
Gong Xian, China 58 C5
Gong'an, China 59 B9
Gongcheng, China 59 E8
Gongga Shan, China 58 C3
Gongguan, China 58 G7
Gonghe, China 60 C5
Gongola →, Nigeria 83 D7
Gongolgon, Australia 95 E4
Gongshan, China 58 D2
Gongtan, China 58 C7
Gongzhuling, China 57 C13
Goniadz, Poland 44 E9
Goniri, Nigeria 83 C7
Gonjo, China 58 B2
Gonnesa, Italy 30 C1
Gónnos, Greece 38 B4
Gonnosfanádiga, Italy 30 C1
Gonzaga, Phil. 61 B5
Gonzales, Calif., U.S.A. 116 J5
Gonzales, Tex., U.S.A. 113 L6
González Chaves, Argentina 126 D3
Good Hope, C. of, S. Africa 88 E2
Gooderham, Canada 110 B6
Goodhouse, S. Africa 88 D2
Gooding, U.S.A. 114 E6
Goodland, U.S.A. 112 F4
Goodlow, Canada 104 B4
Goodooga, Australia 95 D4
Goodsprings, U.S.A. 117 K11
Goole, U.K. 12 D7
Goolgowi, Australia 95 E4
Goolwa, Australia 95 F2
Goomalling, Australia 93 F2
Goomeri, Australia 95 D5
Goonda, Mozam. 87 F3
Goondiwindi, Australia 95 D5
Goongarrie, L., Australia 93 F3
Goonyella, Australia 94 C4
Goose →, Canada 103 B7
Goose Creek, U.S.A. 109 J5
Goose L., U.S.A. 114 F3
Gop, India 66 H6
Gopalganj, India 69 F11
Göppingen, Germany 25 G5
Gor, Spain 35 H8
Góra, Dolnośląskie, Poland 45 G3
Góra, Mazowieckie, Poland 45 F7
Góra Kalwaria, Poland 45 G8
Gorakhpur, India 69 F10
Goražde, Bos.-H. 42 G3
Gorbatov, Russia 48 B6
Gorbea, Peña, Spain 32 B2
Gorda, U.S.A. 116 K5
Gorda, Pta., Canary Is. 37 F2
Gorda, Pta., Nic. 120 D3
Gordan B., Australia 92 B5
Gördes, Turkey 39 C10
Gordon, U.S.A. 112 D3
Gordon →, Australia 94 G4
Gordon L., Alta., Canada 105 B6
Gordon L., N.W.T., Canada 104 A6
Gordonvale, Australia 94 B4
Gore, Ethiopia 81 F4
Gore, N.Z. 91 M2
Gore Bay, Canada 102 C3
Görele, Turkey 73 B8
Goreme, Turkey 72 C6
Gorey, Ireland 15 D5
Gorg, Iran 71 D8
Gorgān, Iran 71 B7
Gorgona, Italy 28 E6
Gorgona, I., Colombia 124 C3
Gorgora, Ethiopia 81 E4
Gorgoram, Nigeria 83 C7
Gorham, U.S.A. 111 B13
Gori, Georgia 49 J7
Goriganga →, India 69 E9
Gorinchem, Neths. 17 C4
Goris, Armenia 73 C12
Goritsy, Russia 46 D9
Gorízia, Italy 29 C10
Gorj □, Romania 43 E8
Gorki = Horki, Belarus 46 E6
Gorki = Nizhniy Novgorod, Russia 48 B7
Gorkiy = Nizhniy Novgorod, Russia 48 B7
Gorkovskoye Vdkhr., Russia 48 B6
Gorlice, Poland 45 J8
Görlitz, Germany 24 D10
Gorlovka = Horlivka, Ukraine 47 H10
Gorman, U.S.A. 117 L8
Gorna Dzhumayo = Blagoevgrad, Bulgaria 40 D7
Gorna Oryakhovitsa, Bulgaria 41 C9
Gornja Radgona, Slovenia 29 B13
Gornja Tuzla, Bos.-H. 42 F3
Gornji Grad, Slovenia 29 B11
Gornji Milanovac, Serbia, Yug. 40 B4
Gornji Vakuf, Bos.-H. 42 G2
Gorno Ablanovo, Bulgaria 41 C9
Gorno-Altay □, Russia 50 D9
Gorno-Altaysk, Russia 50 D9
Gornyatskiy, Russia 49 F5
Gornyy, Saratov, Russia 48 E9
Gornyy, Sib., Russia 54 B6
Gorodenka = Horodenka, Ukraine 47 H3
Gorodets, Russia 48 B6
Gorodishche = Horodyshche, Ukraine 47 H6
Gorodishche, Russia 48 D7
Gorodnya = Horodnya, Ukraine 47 G6
Gorodok = Haradok, Belarus 46 E6
Gorodok = Horodok, Ukraine 47 H2
Gorodovikovsk, Russia 49 G5
Gorokhov = Horokhiv, Ukraine 47 G3
Gorokhovets, Russia 48 B6
Gorom Gorom, Burkina Faso 83 C4
Goromonzi, Zimbabwe 87 F3
Gorong, Kepulauan, Indonesia 63 E8
Gorongose →, Mozam. 89 C5
Gorongoza, Mozam. 87 F3
Gorongoza, Sa. da, Mozam. 87 F3
Gorontalo, Indonesia 63 D6
Goronyo, Nigeria 83 C6
Górowo Iławeckie, Poland 44 D7
Gorron, France 18 D6
Gorshechnoye, Russia 47 G10
Gort, Ireland 15 C3
Gortis, Greece 36 D6
Góry Bystrzyckie, Poland 45 H3
Goryachiy Klyuch, Russia 49 H4
Gorzkowice, Poland 45 G6
Górzno, Poland 45 E6
Gorzów Śląski, Poland 45 G5
Gorzów Wielkopolski, Poland 45 F2
Gosford, Australia 95 E5
Goshen, Calif., U.S.A. 116 J7
Goshen, Ind., U.S.A. 108 E3
Goshen, N.Y., U.S.A. 111 E10
Goshogawara, Japan 54 D10
Goslar, Germany 24 D6
Gospič, Croatia 29 D12
Gosport, U.K. 13 G6
Gossas, Senegal 82 C1
Gosse →, Australia 94 B1
Gossi, Mali 83 B4
Gossinga, Sudan 81 F2
Gostivar, Macedonia 40 E4
Gostyń, Poland 45 G4
Gostynin, Poland 45 F6
Göta älv →, Sweden 11 G5
Göta kanal, Sweden 11 F9
Götaland, Sweden 11 G8
Göteborg, Sweden 11 G5
Göteborgs och Bohus län □, Sweden 11 F5
Götene, Sweden 11 F7
Goteşti, Moldova 43 D13
Gotha, Germany 24 E6
Gothenburg = Göteborg, Sweden 11 G5
Gothenburg, U.S.A. 112 E4
Gothèye, Niger 83 C5
Gotland, Sweden 11 G12
Gotlands län □, Sweden 11 G12
Gotō-Rettō, Japan 55 H4
Gotse Delchev, Bulgaria 40 E7
Gotska Sandön, Sweden 9 G18
Gōtsu, Japan 55 G6
Gott Pk., Canada 104 C4
Góttero, Monte, Italy 28 D6
Göttingen, Germany 24 D5
Gottwald = Zmiyev, Ukraine 47 H9
Gottwaldov = Zlín, Czech Rep. 27 B10
Goubangzi, China 57 D11
Gouda, Neths. 17 B4
Goúdhoura, Ákra, Greece 36 E8
Goudiry, Senegal 82 C2
Goudoumaria, Niger 83 C7
Gouéké, Guinea 82 D3
Gough I., Atl. Oc. 2 G9
Gouin, Rés., Canada 102 C5
Gouitafla, Ivory C. 82 D3
Goulburn, Australia 95 E4
Goulburn Is., Australia 94 A1
Goulia, Ivory C. 82 C3
Goulimine, Morocco 78 C3
Goumbou, Mali 82 B3
Gouménissa, Greece 40 F6
Goundam, Mali 82 B4
Goúra, Greece 38 D4
Gourbassi, Mali 82 C2
Gourdon, France 20 D5
Gouré, Niger 83 C7
Gourin, France 18 D3
Gourits →, S. Africa 88 E3
Gourma-Rharous, Mali 83 B4
Goúrnais, Greece 36 D7
Gournay-en-Bray, France 19 C8
Goursi, Burkina Faso 82 C4
Gouverneur, U.S.A. 111 B9
Gouviá, Greece 36 A3
Gouzon, France 19 F9
Governador Valadares, Brazil 125 G10
Governor's Harbour, Bahamas 120 A4
Govindgarh, India 69 G9
Gowan Ra., Australia 94 D4
Gowanda, U.S.A. 110 D6
Gowd-e Zirreh, Afghan. 66 E3
Gower, U.K. 13 F3
Gowna, L., Ireland 15 C4
Goya, Argentina 126 B4
Göyçay, Azerbaijan 49 K8
Goyder Lagoon, Australia 95 D2
Goyllarisquisga, Peru 124 F3
Göynük, Antalya, Turkey 39 E12
Göynük, Bolu, Turkey 72 B4
Goz Beîda, Chad 79 F10
Goz Regeb, Sudan 81 D4
Gozdnica, Poland 45 G2
Gozo, Malta 36 C1
Graaff-Reinet, S. Africa 88 E3
Grabo, Ivory C. 82 D3
Grabow, Germany 24 B7
Grabów nad Prosną, Poland 45 G5
Gračac, Croatia 29 D12
Gračanica, Bos.-H. 42 F3
Graçay, France 19 E8
Gracias a Dios, C., Honduras 120 D3
Graciosa, I., Canary Is. 37 E6
Grad Sofiya □, Bulgaria 40 D7
Gradac, Montenegro, Yug. 40 C3
Gradačac, Bos.-H. 42 F3
Gradeška Planina, Macedonia 40 E6
Gradets, Bulgaria 41 D10
Gradišče, Slovenia 29 B12
Grădiştea de Munte, Romania 43 E8
Grado, Italy 29 C10
Grado, Spain 34 B4
Grady, U.S.A. 113 H3
Graeca, Lacul, Romania 43 F11
Grafenau, Germany 25 G9
Gräfenberg, Germany 25 F7
Grafham Water, U.K. 13 E7
Grafton, Australia 95 D5
Grafton, N. Dak., U.S.A. 112 A6
Grafton, W. Va., U.S.A. 108 F5
Graham, Canada 102 C1
Graham, U.S.A. 113 J5
Graham, Mt., U.S.A. 115 K9
Graham Bell, Ostrov = Greem-Bell, Ostrov, Russia 50 A7
Graham I., B.C., Canada 104 C2
Graham I., N.W.T., Canada 100 C6
Graham Land, Antarctica 5 C17
Grahamstown, S. Africa 88 E4
Grahamsville, U.S.A. 111 E10
Grahovo, Montenegro, Yug. 40 D2
Graie, Alpi, Europe 21 C11
Grain Coast, W. Afr. 82 E3
Grajaú, Brazil 125 E9
Grajaú →, Brazil 125 D10
Grajewo, Poland 44 E9
Gramada, Bulgaria 40 C6
Gramat, France 20 D5
Grammichele, Italy 31 E7
Grámmos, Óros, Greece 40 F4
Grampian, U.S.A. 110 F6
Grampian Highlands = Grampian Mts., U.K. 14 E5
Grampian Mts., U.K. 14 E5
Grampians, The, Australia 95 F3
Gramsh, Albania 40 F4
Gran Canaria, Canary Is. 37 G4
Gran Chaco, S. Amer. 126 B3
Gran Paradiso, Italy 28 C4
Gran Sasso d'Itália, Italy 29 F10
Granada, Nic. 120 D2
Granada, Spain 35 H7
Granada, U.S.A. 113 F3
Granada □, Spain 35 H7
Granadilla de Abona, Canary Is. 37 F3
Granard, Ireland 15 C4
Granbury, U.S.A. 113 J6
Granby, Canada 102 C5
Granby, U.S.A. 114 F11
Grand →, Canada 110 D5
Grand →, Mo., U.S.A. 112 F8
Grand →, S. Dak., U.S.A. 112 C4
Grand Bahama, Bahamas 120 A4
Grand Bank, Canada 103 C8
Grand Bassam, Ivory C. 82 D4
Grand Béréby, Ivory C. 82 E3
Grand-Bourg, Guadeloupe 121 C7
Grand Canal = Yun Ho →, China 57 E9
Grand Canyon, U.S.A. 115 H7
Grand Canyon National Park, U.S.A. 115 H7
Grand Cayman, Cayman Is. 120 C3
Grand Centre, Canada 105 C6
Grand Cess, Liberia 82 E3
Grand Coulee, U.S.A. 114 C4
Grand Coulee Dam, U.S.A. 114 C4
Grand Erg du Bilma, Niger 79 E8
Grand Erg Occidental, Algeria 78 B6
Grand Erg Oriental, Algeria 78 B7
Grand Falls, Canada 103 C6
Grand Falls-Windsor, Canada 103 C8
Grand Forks, Canada 104 D5
Grand Forks, U.S.A. 112 B6
Grand Gorge, U.S.A. 111 D10
Grand Haven, U.S.A. 108 D2
Grand I., Mich., U.S.A. 108 B2
Grand I., N.Y., U.S.A. 110 D6
Grand Island, U.S.A. 112 E5
Grand Isle, La., U.S.A. 113 L9
Grand Isle, Vt., U.S.A. 111 B11
Grand Junction, U.S.A. 115 G9
Grand L., N.B., Canada 103 C6

Grand L., Nfld., Canada . . . 103 C8
Grand L., Nfld., Canada . . . 103 B7
Grand L., U.S.A. 113 L8
Grand Lahou, Ivory C. 82 D3
Grand Lake, U.S.A. 114 F11
Grand-Lieu, L. de, France . 18 E5
Grand Manan I., Canada . . 103 D6
Grand Marais, Canada 112 B9
Grand Marais, U.S.A. 108 B3
Grand-Mère, Canada 102 C5
Grand Popo, Benin 83 D5
Grand Portage, U.S.A. 112 B10
Grand Prairie, U.S.A. 113 J6
Grand Rapids, Canada 105 C9
Grand Rapids, Mich., U.S.A. 108 D2
Grand Rapids, Minn., U.S.A. 112 B8
Grand St-Bernard, Col du, Europe 25 K3
Grand Teton, U.S.A. 114 E8
Grand Teton National Park, U.S.A. 114 D8
Grand Union Canal, U.K. . . 13 E7
Grand View, Canada 105 C8
Grandas de Salime, Spain . . 34 B4
Grande →, Jujuy, Argentina 126 A2
Grande →, Mendoza, Argentina 126 D2
Grande →, Bolivia 124 G6
Grande →, Bahia, Brazil . . 125 F10
Grande →, Minas Gerais, Brazil 125 H8
Grande, B., Argentina 128 G3
Grande, Rio →, U.S.A. . . . 113 N6
Grande Baleine, R. de la →, Canada 102 A4
Grande Cache, Canada 104 C5
Grande-Entrée, Canada 103 C7
Grande Prairie, Canada 104 B5
Grande-Rivière, Canada . . . 103 C7
Grande-Vallée, Canada 103 C6
Grandfalls, U.S.A. 113 K3
Grândola, Portugal 35 G2
Grandpré, France 19 C11
Grandview, U.S.A. 114 C4
Grandvilliers, France 19 C8
Graneros, Chile 126 C1
Grangemouth, U.K. 14 E5
Granger, U.S.A. 114 F9
Grängesberg, Sweden 10 D9
Grangeville, U.S.A. 114 D5
Granisle, Canada 104 C3
Granite City, U.S.A. 112 F9
Granite Falls, U.S.A. 112 C7
Granite L., Canada 103 C8
Granite Mt., U.S.A. 117 M10
Granite Pk., U.S.A. 114 D9
Graniteville, U.S.A. 111 B12
Granitola, C., Italy 30 E5
Granity, N.Z. 91 J3
Granja, Brazil 125 D10
Granja de Moreruela, Spain 34 D5
Granja de Torrehermosa, Spain 35 G5
Gränna, Sweden 11 F8
Granollers, Spain 32 D7
Gransee, Germany 24 B9
Grant, U.S.A. 112 E4
Grant, Mt., U.S.A. 114 G4
Grant City, U.S.A. 112 E7
Grant I., Australia 92 B5
Grant Range, U.S.A. 115 G6
Grantham, U.K. 12 E7
Grantown-on-Spey, U.K. . . 14 D5
Grants, U.S.A. 115 J10
Grants Pass, U.S.A. 114 E2
Grantsville, U.S.A. 114 F7
Granville, France 18 D5
Granville, N. Dak., U.S.A. . 112 A4
Granville, N.Y., U.S.A. . . . 111 C11
Granville, Ohio, U.S.A. . . . 110 F2
Granville L., Canada 105 B8
Graskop, S. Africa 89 C5
Gräsö, Sweden 10 D12
Grass →, Canada 105 B9
Grass Range, U.S.A. 114 C9
Grass River Prov. Park, Canada 105 C8
Grass Valley, Calif., U.S.A. 116 F6
Grass Valley, Oreg., U.S.A. 114 D3
Grassano, Italy 31 B9
Grasse, France 21 E10
Grassflat, U.S.A. 110 F6
Grasslands Nat. Park, Canada 105 D7
Grassy, Australia 94 G3
Gråsten, Denmark 11 K3
Grästorp, Sweden 11 F6
Gratkorn, Austria 26 D8
Graubünden □, Switz. 25 J5
Graulhet, France 20 E5
Graus, Spain 32 C5
Grave, Pte. de, France 20 C2
Gravelbourg, Canada 105 D7
Gravelines, France 19 A9
's-Gravenhage, Neths. 17 B4
Gravenhurst, Canada 102 D4
Gravesend, Australia 95 D5
Gravesend, U.K. 13 F8
Gravina in Púglia, Italy . . . 31 B9
Gravois, Pointe-à-, Haiti . . 121 C5
Gravone →, France 21 G12
Gray, France 19 E12
Grayling, U.S.A. 108 C3
Grays Harbor, U.S.A. 114 C1
Grays L., U.S.A. 114 E8
Grays River, U.S.A. 116 D3
Grayvoron, Russia 47 G8
Graz, Austria 26 D8
Grdelica, Serbia, Yug. 40 D6
Greasy L., Canada 104 A4
Great Abaco I., Bahamas . . 120 A4
Great Artesian Basin, Australia 94 C3
Great Australian Bight, Australia 93 F5
Great Bahama Bank, Bahamas 120 B4
Great Barrier I., N.Z. 91 G5
Great Barrier Reef, Australia 94 B4
Great Barrington, U.S.A. . . 111 D11
Great Basin, U.S.A. 114 G5
Great Basin Nat. Park, U.S.A. 114 G6
Great Bear →, Canada 100 B7
Great Bear L., Canada 100 B7
Great Belt = Store Bælt, Denmark 11 J4
Great Bend, Kans., U.S.A. . 112 F5
Great Bend, Pa., U.S.A. . . . 111 E9
Great Blasket I., Ireland . . . 15 D1
Great Britain, Europe 6 E5
Great Codroy, Canada 103 C8
Great Dividing Ra., Australia 94 C4
Great Driffield = Driffield, U.K. 12 C7
Great Exuma I., Bahamas . 120 B4
Great Falls, U.S.A. 114 C8
Great Fish = Groot Vis →, S. Africa 88 E4
Great Guana Cay, Bahamas 120 B4
Great Inagua I., Bahamas . . 121 B5
Great Indian Desert = Thar Desert, India 68 F5
Great Karoo, S. Africa 88 E3
Great Lake, Australia 94 G4
Great Lakes, N. Amer. 98 E11
Great Malvern, U.K. 13 E5
Great Miami →, U.S.A. . . . 108 F3
Great Ormes Head, U.K. . . 12 D4
Great Ouse →, U.K. 12 E8
Great Palm I., Australia . . . 94 B4
Great Plains, N. Amer. 106 A6
Great Ruaha →, Tanzania . 86 D4
Great Sacandaga Res., U.S.A. 111 C10
Great Saint Bernard Pass = Grand St-Bernard, Col du, Europe 25 K3
Great Salt L., U.S.A. 114 F7
Great Salt Lake Desert, U.S.A. 114 F7
Great Salt Plains L., U.S.A. 113 G5
Great Sandy Desert, Australia 92 D3
Great Sangi = Sangihe, Pulau, Indonesia 63 D7
Great Scarcies →, S. Leone 82 D2
Great Skellig, Ireland 15 E1
Great Slave L., Canada 104 A5
Great Smoky Mts. Nat. Park, U.S.A. 109 H4
Great Snow Mt., Canada . . 104 B4
Great Stour = Stour →, U.K. 13 F9
Great Victoria Desert, Australia 93 E4
Great Wall, China 56 E5
Great Whernside, U.K. 12 C6
Great Yarmouth, U.K. 13 E9
Greater Antilles, W. Indies . 121 C5
Greater London □, U.K. . . . 13 F7
Greater Manchester □, U.K. 12 D5
Greater Sunda Is., Indonesia 62 F4
Grebbestad, Sweden 11 F5
Grebenka = Hrebenka, Ukraine 47 G7
Greco, C., Cyprus 36 E13
Greco, Mte., Italy 29 G10
Gredos, Sierra de, Spain . . . 34 E6
Greece, U.S.A. 110 C7
Greece ■, Europe 38 B3
Greeley, Colo., U.S.A. 112 E2
Greeley, Nebr., U.S.A. 112 E5
Greem-Bell, Ostrov, Russia 50 A7
Green, U.S.A. 114 E2
Green →, Ky., U.S.A. 108 G2
Green →, Utah, U.S.A. . . . 115 G9
Green B., U.S.A. 108 C2
Green Bay, U.S.A. 108 C2
Green C., Australia 95 F5
Green Cove Springs, U.S.A. 109 L5
Green Lake, Canada 105 C7
Green Mts., U.S.A. 111 C12
Green River, Utah, U.S.A. . 115 G8
Green River, Wyo., U.S.A. . 114 F9
Green Valley, U.S.A. 115 L8
Greenbank, U.S.A. 116 B4
Greenbush, Mich., U.S.A. . . 110 B1
Greenbush, Minn., U.S.A. . . 112 A6
Greencastle, U.S.A. 108 F2
Greene, U.S.A. 111 D9
Greenfield, Calif., U.S.A. . . 116 J5
Greenfield, Calif., U.S.A. . . 117 K8
Greenfield, Ind., U.S.A. . . . 108 F3
Greenfield, Iowa, U.S.A. . . 112 E7
Greenfield, Mass., U.S.A. . . 111 D12
Greenfield, Mo., U.S.A. . . . 113 G8
Greenfield Park, Canada . . . 111 A11
Greenland ■, N. Amer. 4 C5
Greenland Sea, Arctic 4 B7
Greenock, U.K. 14 F4
Greenore, Ireland 15 B5
Greenore Pt., Ireland 15 D5
Greenough, Australia 93 E1
Greenough →, Australia . . . 93 E1
Greenough Pt., Canada 110 B3
Greenport, U.S.A. 111 E12
Greensboro, Ga., U.S.A. . . . 109 J4
Greensboro, N.C., U.S.A. . . 109 G6
Greensboro, Vt., U.S.A. . . . 111 B12
Greensburg, Ind., U.S.A. . . 108 F3
Greensburg, Kans., U.S.A. . 113 G5
Greensburg, Pa., U.S.A. . . . 110 F5
Greenstone Pt., U.K. 14 D3
Greenvale, Australia 94 B4
Greenville, Liberia 82 D3
Greenville, Ala., U.S.A. . . . 109 K2
Greenville, Calif., U.S.A. . . 116 E6
Greenville, Maine, U.S.A. . 109 C11
Greenville, Mich., U.S.A. . . 108 D3
Greenville, Miss., U.S.A. . . 113 J9
Greenville, Mo., U.S.A. . . . 113 G9
Greenville, N.C., U.S.A. . . . 109 H7
Greenville, N.H., U.S.A. . . . 111 D13
Greenville, N.Y., U.S.A. . . . 111 D10
Greenville, Ohio, U.S.A. . . . 108 E3
Greenville, Pa., U.S.A. 110 E4
Greenville, S.C., U.S.A. . . . 109 H4
Greenville, Tenn., U.S.A. . . 109 G4
Greenville, Tex., U.S.A. . . . 113 J6
Greenwater Lake Prov. Park, Canada 105 C8
Greenwich, U.K. 13 F8
Greenwich, Conn., U.S.A. . . 111 E11
Greenwich, N.Y., U.S.A. . . 111 C11
Greenwich, Ohio, U.S.A. . . . 110 E2
Greenwood, Canada 104 D5
Greenwood, Ark., U.S.A. . . 113 H7
Greenwood, Ind., U.S.A. . . . 108 F2
Greenwood, Miss., U.S.A. . . 113 J9
Greenwood, S.C., U.S.A. . . 109 H4
Greenwood, Mt., Australia . 92 B5
Gregbe, Ivory C. 82 D3
Gregory, U.S.A. 112 D5
Gregory →, Australia 94 B2
Gregory, L., S. Austral., Australia 95 D2
Gregory, L., W. Austral., Australia 93 E2
Gregory Downs, Australia . . 94 B2
Gregory L., Australia 92 D4
Gregory Ra., Queens., Australia 94 B3
Gregory Ra., W. Austral., Australia 92 D3
Greiffenberg, Germany 24 B9
Greifswald, Germany 24 A9
Greifswalder Bodden, Germany 24 A9
Grein, Austria 26 C7
Greiz, Germany 24 E8
Gremikha, Russia 50 C4
Grenå, Denmark 11 H4
Grenada, U.S.A. 113 J10
Grenada ■, W. Indies 121 D7
Grenade, France 20 E5
Grenadier I., U.S.A. 111 B8
Grenadines, W. Indies 121 D7
Grenchen, Switz. 25 H3
Grenen, Denmark 11 G4
Grenfell, Australia 95 E4
Grenfell, Canada 105 C8
Grenoble, France 21 C9
Grenville, C., Australia 94 A3
Grenville Chan., Canada . . . 104 C3
Gréoux-les-Bains, France . . 21 E9
Gresham, U.S.A. 116 E4
Gresik, Indonesia 63 G15
Gretna, U.K. 14 F5
Greven, Germany 24 C3
Grevená, Greece 40 F5
Grevená □, Greece 40 F5
Grevenbroich, Germany . . . 24 D2
Grevenmacher, Lux. 17 E6
Grevesmühlen, Germany . . . 24 B7
Grevestrand, Denmark 11 J6
Grey →, Canada 103 C8
Grey →, N.Z. 91 K3
Grey, C., Australia 94 A2
Grey Ra., Australia 95 D3
Greybull, U.S.A. 114 D9
Greymouth, N.Z. 91 K3
Greystones, Ireland 15 C5
Greytown, N.Z. 91 J5
Greytown, S. Africa 89 D5
Gribanovskiy, Russia 48 E5
Gribbell I., Canada 104 C3
Gribës, Mal i, Albania 40 F3
Gridley, U.S.A. 116 F5
Griekwastad, S. Africa 88 D3
Griesheim, Germany 25 F4
Grieskirchen, Austria 26 C6
Griffin, U.S.A. 109 J3
Griffith, Australia 95 E4
Griffith, Canada 110 A7
Griffith I., Canada 110 B4
Grignols, France 20 D3
Grigoriopol, Moldova 43 C14
Grimaylov = Hrymayliv, Ukraine 47 H4
Grimes, U.S.A. 116 F5
Grimma, Germany 24 D8
Grimmen, Germany 24 A9
Grimsay, U.K. 14 D1
Grimsby, Canada 110 C5
Grimsby, U.K. 12 D7
Grímsey, Iceland 8 C5
Grimshaw, Canada 104 B5
Grimslöv, Sweden 11 H8
Grimstad, Norway 9 G13
Grindelwald, Switz. 25 J4
Grindsted, Denmark 11 J2
Grindstone I., Canada 111 B8
Grindu, Romania 43 F11
Grinnell, U.S.A. 112 E8
Grintavec, Slovenia 29 B11
Gris-Nez, C., France 19 B8
Grisolles, France 20 E5
Grisons = Graubünden □, Switz. 25 J5
Grisslehamn, Sweden 10 D12
Grmeč Planina, Bos.-H. . . . 29 D13
Groais I., Canada 103 B8
Grobiņa, Latvia 44 B8
Groblersdal, S. Africa 89 D4
Grobming, Austria 26 D6
Grocka, Serbia, Yug. 40 B4
Gródek, Poland 45 E10
Grodków, Poland 45 H4
Grodno = Hrodna, Belarus . 46 F2
Grodzisk Mazowiecki, Poland 45 F7
Grodzisk Wielkopolski, Poland 45 F3
Grodzyanka = Hrodzyanka, Belarus 46 F5
Groesbeck, U.S.A. 113 K6
Groix, France 18 E3
Groix, Î. de, France 18 E3
Grójec, Poland 45 G7
Gronau, Niedersachsen, Germany 24 C5
Gronau, Nordrhein-Westfalen, Germany 24 C3
Grong, Norway 8 D15
Grönhögen, Sweden 11 H10
Groningen, Neths. 17 A6
Groningen □, Neths. 17 A6
Groom, U.S.A. 113 H4
Groot →, S. Africa 88 E3
Groot Berg →, S. Africa . . . 88 E2
Groot-Brakrivier, S. Africa . 88 E3
Groot Karasberge, Namibia . 88 D2
Groot-Kei →, S. Africa 89 E4
Groot Vis →, S. Africa 88 E4
Grootdrink, S. Africa 88 D3
Groote Eylandt, Australia . . . 94 A2
Grootfontein, Namibia 88 B2
Grootlaagte →, Africa 88 C3
Grootvloer →, S. Africa . . . 88 E3
Gros C., Canada 104 A6
Gros Morne Nat. Park, Canada 103 C8
Grósio, Italy 28 B7
Grosne →, France 19 F11
Grossa, Pta., Spain 37 B8
Grossenbrode, Germany 24 A7
Grossenhain, Germany 24 D9
Grosser Arber, Germany 25 F9
Grosser Plöner See, Germany 24 A6
Grosseto, Italy 29 F8
Grossgerungs, Austria 26 C7
Grossglockner, Austria 26 D5
Groswater B., Canada 103 B8
Groton, Conn., U.S.A. 111 E12
Groton, N.Y., U.S.A. 111 D8
Groton, S. Dak., U.S.A. 112 C5
Grottáglie, Italy 31 B10
Grottaminarda, Italy 31 A8
Grottammare, Italy 29 F10
Grouard Mission, Canada . . . 104 B5
Grouin, Pte. du, France 18 D5
Groundhog →, Canada 102 C3
Grouw, Neths. 17 A5
Grove City, U.S.A. 110 E4
Grove Hill, U.S.A. 109 K2
Groveland, U.S.A. 116 H6
Grover City, U.S.A. 117 K6
Groves, U.S.A. 113 L8
Groveton, U.S.A. 111 B13
Grožnjan, Croatia 29 C10
Groznyy, Russia 49 J7
Grubišno Polje, Croatia 42 E2
Grudovo, Bulgaria 41 D11
Grudusk, Poland 45 E7
Grudziądz, Poland 44 E5
Gruinard B., U.K. 14 D3
Gruissan, France 20 E7
Grumo Áppula, Italy 31 A9
Grums, Sweden 10 E7
Grünberg, Germany 24 E4
Gründau, Germany 25 E5
Grundy Center, U.S.A. 112 D8
Grünstadt, Germany 25 F4
Gruvberget, Sweden 10 C10
Gruver, U.S.A. 113 G4
Gruyères, Switz. 25 J3
Gruža, Serbia, Yug. 40 C4
Gryazi, Russia 47 F10
Gryazovets, Russia 46 C11
Grybów, Poland 45 J7
Grycksbo, Sweden 10 D9
Gryfice, Poland 44 E2
Gryfino, Poland 45 E1
Gryfów Śląski, Poland 45 G2
Grythyttan, Sweden 10 E8
Gstaad, Switz. 25 J3
Gua, India 67 H14
Gua Musang, Malaysia 65 K3
Guacanayabo, G. de, Cuba . . 120 B4
Guachípas →, Argentina . . . 126 B2
Guadajoz →, Spain 35 H6
Guadalajara, Mexico 118 C4
Guadalajara, Spain 32 E1
Guadalajara □, Spain 32 E2
Guadalcanal, Solomon Is. . . 96 H8
Guadalcanal, Spain 35 G5
Guadalén →, Spain 35 G7
Guadales, Argentina 126 C2
Guadalete →, Spain 35 J4
Guadalimar →, Spain 35 G7
Guadalmena →, Spain 35 G8
Guadalmez →, Spain 35 G5
Guadalope →, Spain 32 D4
Guadalquivir →, Spain 35 J4
Guadalupe = Guadeloupe ■, W. Indies 121 C7
Guadalupe, Mexico 117 N10
Guadalupe, Spain 35 F5
Guadalupe, U.S.A. 117 L6
Guadalupe →, Mexico 117 N10
Guadalupe →, U.S.A. 113 L6
Guadalupe, Sierra de, Spain 35 F5
Guadalupe Bravos, Mexico . 118 A3
Guadalupe I., Pac. Oc. 98 G8
Guadalupe Mts. Nat. Park, U.S.A. 113 K2
Guadalupe Peak, U.S.A. . . . 113 K2
Guadalupe y Calvo, Mexico 118 B3
Guadarrama, Sierra de, Spain 34 E7
Guadauta, Georgia 49 J5
Guadeloupe ■, W. Indies . . 121 C7
Guadeloupe Passage, W. Indies 121 C7
Guadiamar →, Spain 35 J4
Guadiana →, Portugal 35 H3
Guadiana Menor →, Spain . 35 H7
Guadiaro →, Spain 35 J5
Guadiato →, Spain 35 H5
Guadiela →, Spain 32 E2
Guadix, Spain 35 H7
Guafo, Boca del, Chile 128 E2
Guainía →, Colombia 124 C5
Guaíra, Brazil 127 A5
Guaíra □, Paraguay 126 B4
Guaitecas, Is., Chile 128 E2
Guajará-Mirim, Brazil 124 F5
Guajira, Pen. de la, Colombia 124 A4
Gualán, Guatemala 120 C2
Gualdo Tadino, Italy 29 E9
Gualeguay, Argentina 126 C4
Gualeguaychú, Argentina . . . 126 C4
Gualequay →, Argentina . . . 126 C4
Guam ■, Pac. Oc. 96 F6
Guaminí, Argentina 126 D3
Guamúchil, Mexico 118 B3
Guanabacoa, Cuba 120 B3
Guanacaste, Cordillera del, Costa Rica 120 D2
Guanaceví, Mexico 118 B3
Guanahani = San Salvador I., Bahamas 121 B5
Guanajay, Cuba 120 B3
Guanajuato, Mexico 118 C4
Guanajuato □, Mexico 118 C4
Guandacol, Argentina 126 B2
Guane, Cuba 120 B3
Guang'an, China 58 B6
Guangchang, China 59 D11
Guangde, China 59 B12
Guangdong □, China 59 F9
Guangfeng, China 59 C12
Guanghan, China 58 B5
Guangling, China 56 E8
Guangnan, China 58 E5
Guangning, China 59 F9
Guangrao, China 57 F10
Guangshui, China 59 B9
Guangshun, China 58 D6
Guangwu, China 56 F3
Guangxi Zhuangzu Zizhiqu □, China 58 F7
Guangyuan, China 58 A5
Guangze, China 59 D11
Guangzhou, China 59 F9
Guanipa →, Venezuela 124 B6
Guanling, China 58 E5
Guannan, China 57 G10
Guantánamo, Cuba 121 B4
Guantao, China 56 F8
Guanyang, China 59 E8
Guanyun, China 57 G10
Guápiles, Costa Rica 120 D3
Guaporé, Brazil 127 B5
Guaporé →, Brazil 122 E4
Guaqui, Bolivia 124 G5
Guara, Sierra de, Spain 32 C4
Guarapari, Brazil 127 A7
Guarapuava, Brazil 127 B5
Guaratinguetá, Brazil 127 A6
Guaratuba, Brazil 127 B6
Guarda, Portugal 34 E3
Guarda □, Portugal 34 E3
Guardafui, C. = Asir, Ras, Somali Rep. 74 E5
Guardamar del Segura, Spain 33 G4
Guardavalle, Italy 31 D9
Guárdia Sanframondi, Italy . 31 A7
Guardiagrele, Italy 29 F11
Guardo, Spain 34 C6
Guareña, Spain 35 G4
Guareña →, Spain 34 D5
Guárico □, Venezuela 124 B5
Guarujá, Brazil 127 A6
Guarus, Brazil 127 A7
Guasave, Mexico 118 B3
Guasdualito, Venezuela 124 B4
Guastalla, Italy 28 D7
Guatemala, Guatemala 120 D1
Guatemala ■, Cent. Amer. . . 120 C1
Guaviare →, Colombia 122 C4
Guaxupé, Brazil 127 A6
Guayama, Puerto Rico 121 C6
Guayaquil, Ecuador 124 D3
Guayaquil, G. de, Ecuador . . 122 D2
Guaymas, Mexico 118 B2
Guazhou, China 59 A12
Guba, Dem. Rep. of the Congo . 87 E2
Guba, Ethiopia 81 E4
Gûbâl, Madîq, Egypt 80 B3
Gubat, Phil. 61 E6
Gúbbio, Italy 29 E9
Guben, Germany 24 D10
Gubin, Poland 45 G1
Gubio, Nigeria 83 C7
Gubkin, Russia 47 G9
Guča, Serbia, Yug. 40 C4

Gucheng, *China* 59 A8
Gudata = Guadauta, *Georgia* 49 J5
Gudbrandsdalen, *Norway* 9 F14
Guddu Barrage, *Pakistan* 66 E6
Gudenå →, *Denmark* 11 H4
Gudermes, *Russia* 49 J8
Gudhjem, *Denmark* 11 J8
Gudivada, *India* 67 L12
Gudur, *India* 66 M11
Guebwiller, *France* 19 E14
Guecho = Getxo, *Spain* 32 B2
Guékédou, *Guinea* 82 D2
Guéle Mendouka, *Cameroon* 83 E7
Guelph, *Canada* 102 D3
Guéméné-Penfao, *France* 18 E5
Guéméné-sur-Scorff, *France* 18 D3
Guéné, *Benin* 83 C5
Guer, *France* 18 E4
Guérande, *France* 18 E4
Guéret, *France* 19 F8
Guérigny, *France* 19 E10
Guerneville, *U.S.A.* 116 G4
Guernica = Gernika-Lumo, *Spain* 32 B2
Guernsey, *U.K.* 13 H5
Guernsey, *U.S.A.* 112 D2
Guerrero □, *Mexico* 119 D5
Guessou-Sud, *Benin* 83 C5
Gueugnon, *France* 19 F11
Guéyo, *Ivory C.* 82 D3
Gughe, *Ethiopia* 81 F4
Gügher, *Iran* 71 D8
Guglionesi, *Italy* 29 G11
Guhakolak, Tanjung, *Indonesia* 63 G11
Gui Jiang →, *China* 59 F8
Guia, *Canary Is.* 37 F4
Guia de Isora, *Canary Is.* 37 F3
Guia Lopes da Laguna, *Brazil* 127 A4
Guiana, *S. Amer.* 122 C4
Guibéroua, *Ivory C.* 82 D3
Guichi, *China* 59 B11
Guider, *Cameroon* 83 D7
Guidiguir, *Niger* 83 C6
Guidimouni, *Niger* 83 C6
Guiding, *China* 58 D6
Guidong, *China* 59 D9
Guidónia-Montecélio, *Italy* 29 F9
Guiers, L. de, *Senegal* 82 B1
Guigang, *China* 58 F7
Guiglo, *Ivory C.* 82 D3
Guihulñgan, *Phil.* 61 F5
Guijá, *Mozam.* 89 C5
Guijuelo, *Spain* 34 E5
Guildford, *U.K.* 13 F7
Guilford, *U.S.A.* 111 E12
Guilin, *China* 59 E8
Guillaume-Delisle L., *Canada* 102 A4
Guillaumes, *France* 21 D10
Guillestre, *France* 21 D10
Guilvinec, *France* 18 E2
Güimar, *Canary Is.* 37 F3
Guimarães, *Portugal* 34 D2
Guimaras □, *Phil.* 61 F5
Guinda, *U.S.A.* 116 G4
Guinea, *Africa* 76 F4
Guinea ■, *W. Afr.* 82 C2
Guinea, Gulf of, *Atl. Oc.* 83 E5
Guinea-Bissau ■, *Africa* 82 C2
Güines, *Cuba* 120 B3
Guingamp, *France* 18 D3
Guinguinéo, *Senegal* 82 C1
Guipavas, *France* 18 D2
Guiping, *China* 59 F8
Guipúzcoa □, *Spain* 32 B2
Guir, *Mali* 82 B4
Guirel, *Mauritania* 82 B3
Güiria, *Venezuela* 124 A6
Guiscard, *France* 19 C10
Guise, *France* 19 C10
Guitiriz, *Spain* 34 B3
Guitri, *Ivory C.* 82 D3
Guiuan, *Phil.* 61 F6
Guixi, *China* 59 C11
Guiyang, *Guizhou, China* 58 D6
Guiyang, *Hunan, China* 59 E9
Guizhou □, *China* 58 D6
Gujan-Mestras, *France* 20 D2
Gujar Khan, *Pakistan* 68 C5
Gujarat □, *India* 68 H4
Gujiang, *China* 59 D10
Gujranwala, *Pakistan* 68 C6
Gujrat, *Pakistan* 68 C6
Gukovo, *Russia* 49 F5
Gulargambone, *Australia* 95 E4
Gulbarga, *India* 66 L10
Gulbene, *Latvia* 9 H22
Gulf, The, *Asia* 71 E6
Gulfport, *U.S.A.* 113 K10
Gulgong, *Australia* 95 E4
Gulin, *China* 58 C5
Gulistan, *Pakistan* 68 D2
Gull Lake, *Canada* 105 C7
Gullbrandstorp, *Sweden* 11 H6
Gullspång, *Sweden* 11 F8
Güllük, *Turkey* 39 D9
Güllük Korfezi, *Turkey* 39 D9
Gulma, *Nigeria* 83 C5
Gulmarg, *India* 69 B6
Gülnar, *Turkey* 72 D5
Gülpınar, *Turkey* 39 B8
Gülşehir, *Turkey* 72 C6
Gulshad, *Kazakstan* 50 E8
Gulu, *Uganda* 86 B3
Gülübovo, *Bulgaria* 41 D9
Gulud, J., *Sudan* 81 E2
Gulwe, *Tanzania* 86 D4
Gulyaypole = Hulyaypole, *Ukraine* 47 J9
Gumal →, *Pakistan* 68 D4
Gumbaz, *Pakistan* 68 D3
Gumel, *Nigeria* 83 C6
Gumiel de Hizán, *Spain* 34 D7
Gumla, *India* 69 H11
Gumlu, *Australia* 94 B4
Gumma □, *Japan* 55 F9
Gummersbach, *Germany* 24 D3
Gummi, *Nigeria* 83 C6
Gümüldür, *Turkey* 39 C9
Gümüşçay, *Turkey* 41 F11
Gümüşhaciköy, *Turkey* 72 B6
Gümüşhane, *Turkey* 73 B8
Gümüşsu, *Turkey* 39 C11
Gumzai, *Indonesia* 63 F8
Guna, *Ethiopia* 81 F4
Guna, *India* 68 G7
Gundelfingen, *Germany* 25 G6
Güney, *Burdur, Turkey* 39 D11
Güney, *Denizli, Turkey* 39 C11
Güneydoğu Toroslar, *Turkey* 73 C9
Gunisao →, *Canada* 105 C9
Gunisao L., *Canada* 105 C9
Gunjyal, *Pakistan* 68 C4
Günlüce, *Turkey* 39 E10
Gunnarskog, *Sweden* 10 E6
Gunnbjørn Fjeld, *Greenland* 4 C6
Gunnebo, *Sweden* 11 G10
Gunnedah, *Australia* 95 E5
Gunnewin, *Australia* 95 D4
Gunningbar Cr. →, *Australia* 95 E4
Gunnison, *Colo., U.S.A.* 115 G10
Gunnison, *Utah, U.S.A.* 114 G8
Gunnison →, *U.S.A.* 115 G9
Gunpowder, *Australia* 94 B2
Guntakal, *India* 66 M10
Guntersville, *U.S.A.* 109 H2
Guntong, *Malaysia* 65 K3
Guntur, *India* 67 L12
Gunungapi, *Indonesia* 63 F7
Gunungsitoli, *Indonesia* 62 D1
Günz →, *Germany* 25 G6
Gunza, *Angola* 84 G2
Günzburg, *Germany* 25 G6
Gunzenhausen, *Germany* 25 F6
Guo He →, *China* 57 H9
Guoyang, *China* 56 H9
Gupis, *Pakistan* 69 A5
Gura Humorului, *Romania* 43 C10
Gura-Teghii, *Romania* 43 E11
Gurag, *Ethiopia* 81 F4
Gurahonț, *Romania* 42 D7
Gurdaspur, *India* 68 C6
Gurdon, *U.S.A.* 113 J8
Güre, *Balıkesir, Turkey* 39 B8
Güre, *Uşak, Turkey* 39 C11
Gurgaon, *India* 68 E7
Gürgentepe, *Turkey* 72 B7
Gurghiu, Munții, *Romania* 43 D10
Gurgueia →, *Brazil* 125 E10
Gurha, *India* 68 G4
Guri, Embalse de, *Venezuela* 124 B6
Gurin, *Nigeria* 83 D7
Gurjaani, *Georgia* 49 K7
Gurk →, *Austria* 26 E7
Gurkha, *Nepal* 69 E11
Gurley, *Australia* 95 D4
Gurnet Point, *U.S.A.* 111 D14
Gürpınar, *Ist., Turkey* 41 F12
Gürpınar, *Van, Turkey* 73 C10
Gürsu, *Turkey* 41 F13
Gurué, *Mozam.* 87 F4
Gurun, *Malaysia* 65 K3
Gürün, *Turkey* 72 C7
Gurupá, *Brazil* 125 D8
Gurupá, I. Grande de, *Brazil* 125 D8
Gurupi, *Brazil* 125 F9
Gurupi →, *Brazil* 125 D9
Guruwe, *Zimbabwe* 89 B5
Guryev = Atyraū, *Kazakstan* 50 E6
Gus-Khrustalnyy, *Russia* 48 C5
Gusau, *Nigeria* 83 C6
Gusev, *Russia* 9 J20
Gushan, *China* 57 E12
Gushgy, *Turkmenistan* 50 F7
Gushi, *China* 59 A10
Gushiago, *Ghana* 83 D4
Gusinje, *Montenegro, Yug.* 40 D3
Gusinoozersk, *Russia* 51 D11
Gúspini, *Italy* 30 C1
Güssing, *Austria* 27 D9
Gustavsberg, *Sweden* 10 E12
Gustavus, *U.S.A.* 104 B1
Gustine, *U.S.A.* 116 H6
Güstrow, *Germany* 24 B8
Gusum, *Sweden* 11 F10
Guta = Kolárovo, *Slovak Rep.* 27 D10
Gütersloh, *Germany* 24 D4
Gutha, *Australia* 93 E2
Guthalungra, *Australia* 94 B4
Guthrie, *Okla., U.S.A.* 113 H6
Guthrie, *Tex., U.S.A.* 113 J4
Gutian, *China* 59 D12
Guttenberg, *U.S.A.* 112 D9
Gutu, *Zimbabwe* 89 B5
Guyana ■, *S. Amer.* 124 C7
Guyane française = French Guiana ■, *S. Amer.* 125 C8
Guyang, *China* 56 D6
Guyenne, *France* 20 D4
Guymon, *U.S.A.* 113 G4
Guyra, *Australia* 95 E5
Guyuan, *Hebei, China* 56 D8
Guyuan, *Ningxia Huizu, China* 56 G4
Güzelbahçe, *Turkey* 39 C8
Guzhang, *China* 58 C7
Guzhen, *China* 57 H9
Guzmán, L. de, *Mexico* 118 A3
Gvardeysk, *Russia* 9 J19
Gvardeyskoye, *Ukraine* 47 K8
Gwa, *Burma* 67 L19
Gwaai, *Zimbabwe* 87 F2
Gwabegar, *Australia* 95 E4
Gwadabawa, *Nigeria* 83 C6
Gwādar, *Pakistan* 66 G3
Gwagwada, *Nigeria* 83 C6
Gwalior, *India* 68 F8
Gwanara, *Nigeria* 83 D5
Gwanda, *Zimbabwe* 87 G2
Gwandu, *Nigeria* 83 C5
Gwane, *Dem. Rep. of the Congo* 86 B2
Gwaram, *Nigeria* 83 C7
Gwarzo, *Nigeria* 83 C6
Gwasero, *Nigeria* 83 D5
Gwda →, *Poland* 45 E3
Gweebarra B., *Ireland* 15 B3
Gweedore, *Ireland* 15 A3
Gweru, *Zimbabwe* 87 F2
Gwi, *Nigeria* 83 D6
Gwinn, *U.S.A.* 108 B2
Gwio Kura, *Nigeria* 83 C7
Gwoza, *Nigeria* 83 C7
Gwydir →, *Australia* 95 D4
Gwynedd □, *U.K.* 12 E3
Gyandzha = Gäncä, *Azerbaijan* 49 K8
Gyaring Hu, *China* 60 C4
Gydanskiy Poluostrov, *Russia* 50 C8
Gympie, *Australia* 95 D5
Gyomaendrőd, *Hungary* 42 D5
Gyöngyös, *Hungary* 42 C4
Győr, *Hungary* 42 C2
Győr-Moson-Sopron □, *Hungary* 42 C2
Gypsum Pt., *Canada* 104 A6
Gypsumville, *Canada* 105 C9
Gyueshevo, *Bulgaria* 40 D6
Gyula, *Hungary* 42 D6
Gyumri, *Armenia* 49 K6
Gyzylarbat, *Turkmenistan* 50 F6
Gyzyletrek, *Turkmenistan* 71 B7
Gzhatsk = Gagarin, *Russia* 46 E8

H

Ha 'Arava →, *Israel* 75 E4
Ha Coi, *Vietnam* 58 G6
Ha Dong, *Vietnam* 58 G5
Ha Giang, *Vietnam* 58 F5
Ha Tien, *Vietnam* 65 G5
Ha Tinh, *Vietnam* 64 C5
Ha Trung, *Vietnam* 64 C5
Haaksbergen, *Neths.* 17 B6
Haapsalu, *Estonia* 9 G20
Haarlem, *Neths.* 17 B4
Haast →, *N.Z.* 91 K2
Haast Bluff, *Australia* 92 D5
Hab →, *Pakistan* 68 G3
Hab Nadi Chauki, *Pakistan* 68 G2
Habaswein, *Kenya* 86 B4
Habay, *Canada* 104 B5
Ḩabbānīyah, *Iraq* 70 C4
Ḩabbānīyah, Hawr al, *Iraq* 73 F10
Habo, *Sweden* 11 G8
Haboro, *Japan* 54 B10
Ḩabshān, *U.A.E.* 71 F7
Hachenburg, *Germany* 24 E3
Hachijō-Jima, *Japan* 55 H9
Hachinohe, *Japan* 54 D10
Hachiōji, *Japan* 55 G9
Hachŏn, *N. Korea* 57 D15
Hacıbektaş, *Turkey* 72 C6
Hacılar, *Turkey* 72 C6
Hackås, *Sweden* 10 B8
Hackensack, *U.S.A.* 111 F10
Hackettstown, *U.S.A.* 111 F10
Hadali, *Pakistan* 68 C5
Hadarba, Ras, *Sudan* 80 C4
Hadarom □, *Israel* 75 E4
Hadd, Ra's al, *Oman* 74 C6
Hadejia, *Nigeria* 83 C7
Hadejia →, *Nigeria* 83 C7
H̱adera, *Israel* 75 C3
H̱adera, N. →, *Israel* 75 C3
Haderslev, *Denmark* 11 J3
Hadhramaut = Ḩaḑramawt, *Yemen* 74 D4
Hadibu, *Yemen* 74 E5
Hadım, *Turkey* 72 D5
Hadong, *S. Korea* 57 G14
Ḩaḑramawt, *Yemen* 74 D4
Ḩadrānīyah, *Iraq* 70 C4
Hadrian's Wall, *U.K.* 12 B5
Hadsten, *Denmark* 11 H4
Hadsund, *Denmark* 11 H4
Hadyach, *Ukraine* 47 G8
Haeju, *N. Korea* 57 E13
Haenam, *S. Korea* 57 G14
Haenertsburg, *S. Africa* 89 C4
Haerhpin = Harbin, *China* 57 B14
Hafar al Bāţin, *Si. Arabia* 70 D5
Hafik, *Turkey* 72 C7
Ḩafirat al 'Aydā, *Si. Arabia* 70 E3
Ḩafit, *Oman* 71 F7
Ḩafit, Jabal, *Oman* 71 E7
Hafizabad, *Pakistan* 68 C5
Haflong, *India* 67 G18
Hafnarfjörður, *Iceland* 8 D3
Haft Gel, *Iran* 71 D6
Hafun, Ras, *Somali Rep.* 74 E5
Hagalil, *Israel* 75 C4
Hagby, *Sweden* 11 H10
Hagen, *Germany* 24 D3
Hagenow, *Germany* 24 B7
Hagerman, *U.S.A.* 113 J2
Hagerstown, *U.S.A.* 108 F7
Hagersville, *Canada* 110 D4
Hagetmau, *France* 20 E3
Hagfors, *Sweden* 10 D7
Hagi, *Japan* 55 G5
Hagolan, *Syria* 75 C4
Hagondange, *France* 19 C13
Hags Hd., *Ireland* 15 D2
Hague, C. de la, *France* 18 C5
Hague, The = 's-Gravenhage, *Neths.* 17 B4
Haguenau, *France* 19 D14
Hai Duong, *Vietnam* 58 G6
Hai'an, *Guangdong, China* 59 G8
Hai'an, *Jiangsu, China* 59 A13
Haicheng, *Fujian, China* 59 E11
Haicheng, *Liaoning, China* 57 D12
Haidar Khel, *Afghan.* 68 C3
Haidargarh, *India* 69 F9
Haifa = H̱efa, *Israel* 75 C4
Haifeng, *China* 59 F10
Haiger, *Germany* 24 E4
Haikou, *China* 60 D6
Ḩā'il, *Si. Arabia* 70 E4
Hailar, *China* 60 B6
Hailey, *U.S.A.* 114 E6
Haileybury, *Canada* 102 C4
Hailin, *China* 57 B15
Hailing Dao, *China* 59 G8
Hailong, *China* 57 C13
Hailuoto, *Finland* 8 D21
Haimen, *Guangdong, China* 59 F11
Haimen, *Jiangsu, China* 59 B13
Hainan □, *China* 60 E5
Hainaut □, *Belgium* 17 D4
Hainburg, *Austria* 27 C9
Haines, *Alaska, U.S.A.* 104 B1
Haines, *Oreg., U.S.A.* 114 D5
Haines City, *U.S.A.* 109 L5
Haines Junction, *Canada* 104 A1
Hainfeld, *Austria* 26 C8
Haining, *China* 59 B13
Haiphong, *Vietnam* 58 G6
Haitan Dao, *China* 59 E12
Haiti ■, *W. Indies* 121 C5
Haiya, *Sudan* 80 D4
Haiyan, *China* 59 B13
Haiyang, *China* 57 F11
Haiyuan, *Guangxi Zhuangzu, China* 58 F6
Haiyuan, *Ningxia Huizu, China* 56 F3
Haizhou, *China* 57 G10
Haizhou Wan, *China* 57 G10
Hajdú-Bihar □, *Hungary* 42 C6
Hajdúböszörmény, *Hungary* 42 C6
Hajdúdurog, *Hungary* 42 C6
Hajdúhadház, *Hungary* 42 C6
Hajdúnánás, *Hungary* 42 C6
Hajdúsámson, *Hungary* 42 C6
Hajdúszoboszló, *Hungary* 42 C6
Hajipur, *India* 69 G11
Ḩājjī Muḩsin, *Iraq* 70 C5
Ḩājjīābād, *Iran* 71 D7
Ḩājjīābād-e Zarrīn, *Iran* 71 C7
Hajnówka, *Poland* 45 F10
Hakansson, Mts., *Dem. Rep. of the Congo* 87 D2
Hakkâri, *Turkey* 70 B4
Hakkâri Dağları, *Turkey* 73 C10
Hakken-Zan, *Japan* 55 G7
Hakodate, *Japan* 54 D10
Hakos, *Namibia* 88 C2
Håksberg, *Sweden* 10 D9
Haku-San, *Japan* 55 F8
Hakui, *Japan* 55 F8
Hala, *Pakistan* 66 G6
Ḩalab, *Syria* 70 B3
Ḩalabjah, *Iraq* 70 C5
Halaib, *Sudan* 80 C4
Halasa, *Sudan* 81 E3
Hālat 'Ammār, *Si. Arabia* 70 D3
Halbā, *Lebanon* 75 A5
Halberstadt, *Germany* 24 D7
Halcombe, *N.Z.* 91 J5
Halcon, *Phil.* 63 B6
Halden, *Norway* 9 G14
Haldensleben, *Germany* 24 C7
Haldia, *India* 67 H16
Haldwani, *India* 69 E8
Hale →, *Australia* 94 C2
Haleakala Crater, *U.S.A.* 106 H16
Halesowen, *U.K.* 13 E5
Haleyville, *U.S.A.* 109 H2
Half Assini, *Ghana* 82 D4
Halfway →, *Canada* 104 B4
Halia, *India* 69 G10
Haliburton, *Canada* 102 C4
Halifax, *Australia* 94 B4
Halifax, *Canada* 103 D7
Halifax, *U.K.* 12 D6
Halifax, *U.S.A.* 110 F8
Halifax B., *Australia* 94 B4
Halifax I., *Namibia* 88 D2
Halīl →, *Iran* 71 E8
Halkirk, *U.K.* 14 C5
Hall Beach = Sanirajak, *Canada* 101 B11
Hall in Tirol, *Austria* 26 D4
Hall Pen., *Canada* 101 B13
Hall Pt., *Australia* 92 C3
Hallabro, *Sweden* 11 H9
Halland, *Sweden* 9 H15
Hallands län □, *Sweden* 11 H6
Hallands Väderö, *Sweden* 11 H6
Hallandsås, *Sweden* 11 H7
Hällbybrunn, *Sweden* 10 E10
Halle, *Belgium* 17 D4
Halle, *Nordrhein-Westfalen, Germany* 24 C4
Halle, *Sachsen-Anhalt, Germany* 24 D7
Hällefors, *Sweden* 10 E8
Hälleforsnäs, *Sweden* 10 E10
Hallein, *Austria* 26 D6
Hällekis, *Sweden* 11 F7
Hallen, *Sweden* 10 A8
Hallett, *Australia* 95 E2
Hallettsville, *U.S.A.* 113 L6
Hallim, *S. Korea* 57 H14
Hallingdalselvi →, *Norway* 9 F13
Hallock, *U.S.A.* 112 A6
Halls Creek, *Australia* 92 C4
Hallsberg, *Sweden* 10 E9
Hallstahammar, *Sweden* 10 E10
Hallstatt, *Austria* 26 D6
Hallstavik, *Sweden* 10 D12
Hallstead, *U.S.A.* 111 E9
Halmahera, *Indonesia* 63 D7
Halmeu, *Romania* 42 C8
Halmstad, *Sweden* 11 H6
Hals, *Denmark* 11 H4
Hälsingborg = Helsingborg, *Sweden* 11 H6
Hälsingland, *Sweden* 10 C10
Halstead, *U.K.* 13 F8
Haltern, *Germany* 24 D3
Halti, *Finland* 8 B19
Halton □, *U.K.* 12 D5
Haltwhistle, *U.K.* 12 C5
Halul, *Qatar* 71 E7
Halvad, *India* 68 H4
Ḩalvān, *Iran* 71 C8
Ham, *France* 19 C10
Ham Tan, *Vietnam* 65 G6
Ham Yen, *Vietnam* 64 A5
Hamab, *Namibia* 88 D2
Hamad, *Sudan* 81 D3
Hamada, *Japan* 55 G6
Hamadān, *Iran* 71 C6
Hamadān □, *Iran* 71 C6
Ḩamāh, *Syria* 70 C3
Hamamatsu, *Japan* 55 G8
Hamar, *Norway* 9 F14
Hamâta, Gebel, *Egypt* 70 E2
Hambantota, *Sri Lanka* 66 R12
Hamber Prov. Park, *Canada* 104 C5
Hamburg, *Germany* 24 B5
Hamburg, *Ark., U.S.A.* 113 J9
Hamburg, *N.Y., U.S.A.* 110 D6
Hamburg, *Pa., U.S.A.* 111 F9
Hamburg □, *Germany* 24 B5
Ḩamḑ, W. al →, *Si. Arabia* 70 E3
Hamden, *U.S.A.* 111 E12
Hamdibey, *Turkey* 39 B9
Häme, *Finland* 9 F20
Hämeenlinna, *Finland* 9 F21
Hamélé, *Ghana* 82 C4
Hamelin Pool, *Australia* 93 E1
Hameln, *Germany* 24 C5
Hamerkaz □, *Israel* 75 C3
Hamersley Ra., *Australia* 92 D2
Hamhung, *N. Korea* 57 E14
Hami, *China* 60 B4
Hamilton, *Australia* 95 F3
Hamilton, *Canada* 102 D4
Hamilton, *N.Z.* 91 G5
Hamilton, *U.K.* 14 F4
Hamilton, *Ala., U.S.A.* 109 H1
Hamilton, *Mont., U.S.A.* 114 C6
Hamilton, *N.Y., U.S.A.* 111 D9
Hamilton, *Ohio, U.S.A.* 108 F3
Hamilton, *Tex., U.S.A.* 113 K5
Hamilton →, *Australia* 94 C2
Hamilton City, *U.S.A.* 116 F4
Hamilton Inlet, *Canada* 103 B8
Hamilton Mt., *U.S.A.* 111 C10
Hamina, *Finland* 9 F22
Hamirpur, *H.P., India* 68 D7
Hamirpur, *Ut. P., India* 69 G9
Hamitabat, *Turkey* 41 E11
Hamlet, *U.S.A.* 109 H6
Hamley Bridge, *Australia* 95 E2
Hamlin = Hameln, *Germany* 24 C5
Hamlin, *N.Y., U.S.A.* 110 C7
Hamlin, *Tex., U.S.A.* 113 J4
Hamm, *Germany* 24 D3
Ḩammār, Hawr al, *Iraq* 70 D5
Hammarstrand, *Sweden* 10 A10
Hammelburg, *Germany* 25 E5
Hammeren, *Denmark* 11 J8
Hammerfest, *Norway* 8 A20
Hammerum, *Denmark* 11 H3
Hamminkeln, *Germany* 24 D2
Hammond, *Ind., U.S.A.* 108 E2
Hammond, *La., U.S.A.* 113 K9
Hammond, *N.Y., U.S.A.* 111 B9
Hammondsport, *U.S.A.* 110 D7
Hammonton, *U.S.A.* 108 F8
Hamneda, *Sweden* 11 H7
Hamoyet, Jebel, *Sudan* 80 D4
Hampden, *N.Z.* 91 L3
Hampshire □, *U.K.* 13 F6
Hampshire Downs, *U.K.* 13 F6
Hampton, *N.B., Canada* 103 C6
Hampton, *Ont., Canada* 110 C6
Hampton, *Ark., U.S.A.* 113 J8
Hampton, *Iowa, U.S.A.* 112 D8
Hampton, *N.H., U.S.A.* 111 D14
Hampton, *S.C., U.S.A.* 109 J5
Hampton, *Va., U.S.A.* 108 G7
Hampton Bays, *U.S.A.* 111 F12
Hampton Tableland, *Australia* 93 F4
Hamra, *Sweden* 10 C8
Hamrat esh Sheykh, *Sudan* 81 E2
Hamur, *Turkey* 73 C10
Hamyang, *S. Korea* 57 G14
Han Jiang →, *China* 59 F11

Han Shui, China 58 A7
Han Shui →, China 59 B10
Hana, U.S.A. 106 H17
Hanak, Si. Arabia 70 E3
Hanamaki, Japan 54 E10
Hanang, Tanzania 86 C4
Hanau, Germany 25 E4
Hanbogd = Ihbulag, Mongolia 56 C4
Hançalar, Turkey 39 C11
Hâncești, Moldova 43 D13
Hancheng, China 56 G6
Hanchuan, China 59 B9
Hancock, Mich., U.S.A. 112 B10
Hancock, N.Y., U.S.A. 111 E9
Handa, Japan 55 G8
Handan, China 56 F8
Handeni, Tanzania 86 D4
Handlová, Slovak Rep. 27 C11
Handub, Sudan 80 D4
Handwara, India 69 B6
Hanegev, Israel 75 E4
Hanford, U.S.A. 116 J7
Hang Chat, Thailand 64 C2
Hang Dong, Thailand 64 C2
Hangang →, S. Korea 57 F14
Hangayn Nuruu, Mongolia 60 B4
Hangchou = Hangzhou, China 59 B13
Hanggin Houqi, China 56 D4
Hanggin Qi, China 56 E5
Hangu, China 57 E9
Hangzhou, China 59 B13
Hangzhou Wan, China 59 B13
Hanhongor, Mongolia 56 C3
Ḥanīdh, Si. Arabia 71 E6
Ḥanīsh, Yemen 74 E3
Haniska, Slovak Rep. 27 C14
Hanjiang, China 59 E12
Hankinson, U.S.A. 112 B6
Hanko, Finland 9 G20
Hankou, China 59 B10
Hanksville, U.S.A. 115 G8
Hanle, India 69 C8
Hanmer Springs, N.Z. 91 K4
Hann →, Australia 92 C4
Hann, Mt., Australia 92 C4
Hanna, Canada 104 C6
Hanna, U.S.A. 114 F10
Hannah B., Canada 102 B4
Hannibal, Mo., U.S.A. 112 F9
Hannibal, N.Y., U.S.A. 111 C8
Hannik, Sudan 80 D3
Hannover, Germany 24 C5
Hanö, Sweden 11 H8
Hanöbukten, Sweden 11 J8
Hanoi, Vietnam 58 G5
Hanover = Hannover, Germany 24 C5
Hanover, Canada 102 D3
Hanover, S. Africa 88 E3
Hanover, N.H., U.S.A. 111 C12
Hanover, Ohio, U.S.A. 110 F2
Hanover, Pa., U.S.A. 108 F7
Hanover, I., Chile 128 G2
Hansdiha, India 69 G12
Hanshou, China 59 C8
Hansi, India 68 E6
Hanson, L., Australia 95 E2
Hanstholm, Denmark 11 G2
Hantsavichy, Belarus 47 F4
Hanumangarh, India 68 E6
Hanyin, China 58 A7
Hanyuan, China 58 C4
Hanzhong, China 56 H4
Hanzhuang, China 57 G9
Haora, India 69 H13
Haoxue, China 59 B9
Haparanda, Sweden 8 D21
Happy, U.S.A. 113 H4
Happy Camp, U.S.A. 114 F2
Happy Valley-Goose Bay, Canada 103 B7
Hapsu, N. Korea 57 D15
Hapur, India 68 E7
Ḥaql, Si. Arabia 75 F3
Har, Indonesia 63 F8
Har-Ayrag, Mongolia 56 B5
Har Hu, China 60 C4
Har Us Nuur, Mongolia 60 B4
Har Yehuda, Israel 75 D3
Ḥaraḍ, Si. Arabia 74 C4
Haradok, Belarus 46 E6
Häradsbäck, Sweden 11 H8
Haranomachi, Japan 54 F10
Harare, Zimbabwe 87 F3
Harat, Eritrea 81 D4
Harbin, China 57 B14
Harbiye, Turkey 72 D7
Harbo, Sweden 10 D11
Harboør, Denmark 11 H2
Harbor Beach, U.S.A. 110 C2
Harbour Breton, Canada 103 C8
Harbour Deep, Canada 103 B8
Harburg, Germany 24 B5
Hårby, Denmark 11 J4
Harda, India 68 H7
Hardangerfjorden, Norway 9 F12
Hardangervidda, Norway 9 F12
Hardap Dam, Namibia 88 C2
Hardenberg, Neths. 17 B6
Harderwijk, Neths. 17 B5
Hardey →, Australia 92 D2
Hardin, U.S.A. 114 D10
Harding, S. Africa 89 E4
Harding Ra., Australia 92 C3
Hardisty, Canada 104 C6
Hardoi, India 69 F9
Hardwar = Haridwar, India 68 E8
Hardwick, U.S.A. 111 B12
Hardy, Pen., Chile 128 H3
Hare B., Canada 103 B8
Hareid, Norway 9 E12
Haren, Germany 24 C3
Harer, Ethiopia 81 F5
Harerge □, Ethiopia 81 F5
Hareto, Ethiopia 81 F4
Harfleur, France 18 C7
Hargeisa, Somali Rep. 74 F3
Harghita □, Romania 43 D10
Harghita, Munții, Romania 43 D10
Hargshamn, Sweden 10 D12
Hari →, Indonesia 62 E2
Haria, Canary Is. 37 E6
Haridwar, India 68 E8
Harim, Jabal al, Oman 71 E8
Haringhata →, Bangla. 67 J16
Harīrūd →, Asia 66 A2
Härjedalen, Sweden 10 B7
Harlan, Iowa, U.S.A. 112 E7
Harlan, Ky., U.S.A. 109 G4
Hârlău, Romania 43 C11
Harlech, U.K. 12 E3
Harlem, U.S.A. 114 B9
Hårlev, Denmark 11 J6
Harlingen, Neths. 17 A5
Harlingen, U.S.A. 113 M6
Harlow, U.K. 13 F8
Harlowton, U.S.A. 114 C9
Harmancık, Turkey 39 B11
Harmånger, Sweden 10 C11
Harmil, Eritrea 81 D5
Harnai, Pakistan 68 D2
Harney Basin, U.S.A. 114 E4
Harney L., U.S.A. 114 E4
Harney Peak, U.S.A. 112 D3
Härnön, Sweden 10 B12
Härnösand, Sweden 10 B11
Haro, Spain 32 C2
Haroldswick, U.K. 14 A8
Harp L., Canada 103 A7
Harper, Liberia 82 E3
Harplinge, Sweden 11 H6
Harr, Mauritania 82 B2
Harrai, India 69 H8
Harrand, Pakistan 68 E4
Ḥarrat Khaybar, Si. Arabia 80 B5
Ḥarrat Nawāṣīf, Si. Arabia 80 C5
Harricana →, Canada 102 B4
Harriman, U.S.A. 109 H3
Harrington Harbour, Canada 103 B8
Harris, U.K. 14 D2
Harris, Sd. of, U.K. 14 D1
Harris L., Australia 95 E2
Harris Pt., Canada 110 C2
Harrisburg, Ill., U.S.A. 113 G10
Harrisburg, Nebr., U.S.A. 112 E3
Harrisburg, Pa., U.S.A. 110 F8
Harrismith, S. Africa 89 D4
Harrison, Ark., U.S.A. 113 G8
Harrison, Maine, U.S.A. 111 B14
Harrison, Nebr., U.S.A. 112 D3
Harrison, C., Canada 103 B8
Harrison L., Canada 104 D4
Harrisonburg, U.S.A. 108 F6
Harrisonville, U.S.A. 112 F7
Harriston, Canada 110 C4
Harrisville, Mich., U.S.A. 110 B1
Harrisville, N.Y., U.S.A. 111 B9
Harrisville, Pa., U.S.A. 110 E5
Harrodsburg, U.S.A. 108 G3
Harrogate, U.K. 12 C6
Harrow, U.K. 13 F7
Harrowsmith, Canada 111 B8
Harry S. Truman Reservoir, U.S.A. 112 F7
Harsefeld, Germany 24 B5
Harsewinkel, Germany 24 D4
Harsīn, Iran 70 C5
Hârșova, Romania 43 F12
Harstad, Norway 8 B17
Harsud, India 68 H7
Hart, U.S.A. 108 D2
Hart, L., Australia 95 E2
Hartbees →, S. Africa 88 D3
Hartberg, Austria 26 D8
Hartford, Conn., U.S.A. 111 E12
Hartford, Ky., U.S.A. 108 G2
Hartford, S. Dak., U.S.A. 112 D6
Hartford, Wis., U.S.A. 112 D10
Hartford City, U.S.A. 108 E3
Hartland, Canada 103 C6
Hartland Pt., U.K. 13 F3
Hartlepool, U.K. 12 C6
Hartlepool □, U.K. 12 C6
Hartley Bay, Canada 104 C3
Hartmannberge, Namibia 88 B1
Hartney, Canada 105 D8
Hârtop, Moldova 43 D13
Harts →, S. Africa 88 D3
Hartselle, U.S.A. 109 H2
Hartshorne, U.S.A. 113 H7
Hartstown, U.S.A. 110 E4
Hartsville, U.S.A. 109 H5
Hartswater, S. Africa 88 D3
Hartwell, U.S.A. 109 H4
Harunabad, Pakistan 68 E5
Harvand, Iran 71 D7
Harvey, Australia 93 F2
Harvey, Ill., U.S.A. 108 E2
Harvey, N. Dak., U.S.A. 112 B5
Harwich, U.K. 13 F9
Haryana □, India 68 E7
Haryn →, Belarus 47 F4
Harz, Germany 24 D6
Harzgerode, Germany 24 D7
Hasa □, Si. Arabia 71 E6
Hasaheisa, Sudan 81 E3
Ḥasanābād, Iran 71 C7
Hasdo →, India 69 J10
Haselünne, Germany 24 C3
Hashimoto, Japan 55 G7
Hashtjerd, Iran 71 C6
Haskell, U.S.A. 113 J5
Hasköy, Turkey 41 E10
Haslach, Germany 25 G4
Hasle, Denmark 11 J8
Haslemere, U.K. 13 F7
Haslev, Denmark 11 J5
Hasparren, France 20 E2
Hassa, Turkey 72 D7
Hassela, Sweden 10 B10
Hasselt, Belgium 17 D5
Hassfurt, Germany 25 E6
Hassi Messaoud, Algeria 78 B7
Hässleholm, Sweden 11 H7
Hassloch, Germany 25 F4
Hästholmen, Sweden 11 F8
Hastings, N.Z. 91 H6
Hastings, U.K. 13 G8
Hastings, Mich., U.S.A. 108 D3
Hastings, Minn., U.S.A. 112 C8
Hastings, Nebr., U.S.A. 112 E5
Hastings Ra., Australia 95 E5
Hästveda, Sweden 11 H7
Hat Yai, Thailand 65 J3
Hatanbulag = Ergel, Mongolia 56 C5
Hatay = Antalya, Turkey 72 D4
Hatch, U.S.A. 115 K10
Hatchet L., Canada 105 B8
Hațeg, Romania 42 E7
Hateruma-Shima, Japan 55 M1
Hatfield P.O., Australia 95 E3
Hatgal, Mongolia 60 A5
Hathras, India 68 F8
Hatia, Bangla. 67 H17
Ḥāṭibah, Ra's, Si. Arabia 80 C4
Hato Mayor, Dom. Rep. 121 C6
Hatta, India 69 G8
Hattah, Australia 95 E3
Hatteras, C., U.S.A. 109 H8
Hattiesburg, U.S.A. 113 K10
Hatvan, Hungary 42 C4
Hau Bon = Cheo Reo, Vietnam 62 B3
Hau Duc, Vietnam 64 E7
Haugesund, Norway 9 G11
Haukipudas, Finland 8 D21
Haultain →, Canada 105 B7
Hauraki G., N.Z. 91 G5
Hausruck, Austria 26 C6
Haut Atlas, Morocco 78 B4
Haut-Rhin □, France 19 E14
Haut-Zaïre = Orientale □, Dem. Rep. of the Congo 86 B2
Haute-Corse □, France 21 F13
Haute-Garonne □, France 20 E5
Haute-Loire □, France 20 C7
Haute-Marne □, France 19 D12
Haute-Normandie □, France 18 C7
Haute-Saône □, France 19 E13
Haute-Savoie □, France 21 C10
Haute-Vienne □, France 20 C5
Hautes-Alpes □, France 21 D10
Hautes Fagnes = Hohe Venn, Belgium 17 D6
Hautes-Pyrénées □, France 20 F4
Hauteville-Lompnès, France 21 C9
Hautmont, France 19 B10
Hauts-de-Seine □, France 19 D9
Hauts Plateaux, Algeria 76 C4
Hauzenberg, Germany 25 G9
Havana = La Habana, Cuba 120 B3
Havana, U.S.A. 112 E9
Havant, U.K. 13 G7
Havârna, Romania 43 B11
Havasu, L., U.S.A. 117 L12
Havdhem, Sweden 11 G12
Havel →, Germany 24 C8
Havelian, Pakistan 68 B5
Havelock, Canada 102 D4
Havelock, N.Z. 91 J4
Havelock, U.S.A. 109 H7
Haverfordwest, U.K. 13 F3
Haverhill, U.S.A. 111 D13
Haverstraw, U.S.A. 111 E11
Håverud, Sweden 11 F6
Havirga, Mongolia 56 B7
Havířov, Czech. 27 B11
Havlíčkův Brod, Czech Rep. 26 B8
Havneby, Denmark 11 J2
Havran, Turkey 39 B9
Havre, U.S.A. 114 B9
Havre-Aubert, Canada 103 C7
Havre-St.-Pierre, Canada 103 B7
Havsa, Turkey 41 E10
Havza, Turkey 72 B6
Haw →, U.S.A. 109 H6
Hawaii □, U.S.A. 106 H16
Hawaii I., Pac. Oc. 106 J17
Hawaiian Is., Pac. Oc. 106 H17
Hawaiian Ridge, Pac. Oc. 97 E11
Hawarden, U.S.A. 112 D6
Hawea, L., N.Z. 91 L2
Hawera, N.Z. 91 H5
Hawick, U.K. 14 F6
Hawk Junction, Canada 102 C3
Hawke B., N.Z. 91 H6
Hawker, Australia 95 E2
Hawkesbury, Canada 102 C5
Hawkesbury I., Canada 104 C3
Hawkesbury Pt., Australia 94 A1
Hawkinsville, U.S.A. 109 J4
Hawley, Minn., U.S.A. 112 B6
Hawley, Pa., U.S.A. 111 E9
Ḥawrān, W. →, Iraq 70 C4
Hawsh Müssá, Lebanon 75 B4
Hawthorne, U.S.A. 114 G4
Hay, Australia 95 E3
Hay →, Australia 94 C2
Hay →, Canada 104 A5
Hay, C., Australia 92 B4
Hay I., Canada 110 B4
Hay L., Canada 104 B5
Hay-on-Wye, U.K. 13 E4
Hay River, Canada 104 A5
Hay Springs, U.S.A. 112 D3
Haya = Tehoru, Indonesia 63 E7
Hayachine-San, Japan 54 E10
Hayange, France 19 C13
Haydarlı, Turkey 39 C12
Hayden, U.S.A. 114 F10
Haydon, Australia 94 B3
Hayes, U.S.A. 112 C4
Hayes →, Canada 102 A1
Hayes Creek, Australia 92 B5
Hayle, U.K. 13 G2
Hayling I., U.K. 13 G7
Haymana, Turkey 72 C5
Hayrabolu, Turkey 41 E11
Hays, Canada 104 C6
Hays, U.S.A. 112 F5
Haysyn, Ukraine 47 H5
Hayvoron, Ukraine 47 H5
Hayward, Calif., U.S.A. 116 H4
Hayward, Wis., U.S.A. 112 B9
Haywards Heath, U.K. 13 G7
Hazafon □, Israel 75 C4
Hazārān, Kūh-e, Iran 71 D8
Hazard, U.S.A. 108 G4
Hazaribag, India 69 H11
Hazaribag Road, India 69 G11
Hazebrouck, France 19 B9
Hazelton, Canada 104 B3
Hazelton, U.S.A. 112 B4
Hazen, U.S.A. 112 B4
Hazlehurst, Ga., U.S.A. 109 K4
Hazlehurst, Miss., U.S.A. 113 K9
Hazlet, U.S.A. 111 F10
Hazleton, U.S.A. 111 F9
Hazlett, L., Australia 92 D4
Hazro, Turkey 70 B4
He Xian, Anhui, China 59 B12
He Xian, Guangxi Zhuangzu, China 59 E8
Head of Bight, Australia 93 F5
Headlands, Zimbabwe 87 F3
Healdsburg, U.S.A. 116 G4
Healdton, U.S.A. 113 H6
Healesville, Australia 95 F4
Heany Junction, Zimbabwe 89 C4
Heard I., Ind. Oc. 3 G13
Hearne, U.S.A. 113 K6
Hearst, Canada 102 C3
Heart →, U.S.A. 112 B4
Heart's Content, Canada 103 C9
Heath Pt., Canada 103 C7
Heavener, U.S.A. 113 H7
Hebbronville, U.S.A. 113 M5
Hebei □, China 56 E9
Hebel, Australia 95 D4
Heber, U.S.A. 117 N11
Heber City, U.S.A. 114 F8
Heber Springs, U.S.A. 113 H9
Hebert, Canada 105 C7
Hebgen L., U.S.A. 114 D8
Hebi, China 56 G8
Hebrides, U.K. 6 D4
Hebron = Al Khalīl, West Bank 75 D4
Hebron, Canada 101 C13
Hebron, N. Dak., U.S.A. 112 B3
Hebron, Nebr., U.S.A. 112 E6
Heby, Sweden 10 E10
Hecate Str., Canada 104 C2
Heceta I., U.S.A. 104 B2
Hechi, China 58 E7
Hechingen, Germany 25 G4
Hechuan, China 58 B6
Hecla, U.S.A. 112 C5
Hecla I., Canada 105 C9
Hédé, France 18 D5
Hede, Sweden 10 B7
Hedemora, Sweden 10 D9
Hedensted, Denmark 11 J3
Hedesunda, Sweden 10 D10
Heerde, Neths. 17 B6
Heerenveen, Neths. 17 B5
Heerhugowaard, Neths. 17 B4
Heerlen, Neths. 17 D5
Ḥefa, Israel 75 C4
Ḥefa □, Israel 75 C4
Hefei, China 59 B11
Hefeng, China 59 C8
Hegalig, Sudan 81 E3
Hegang, China 60 B8
Heiban, Sudan 81 E3
Heichengzhen, China 56 F4
Heide, Germany 24 A5
Heidelberg, Germany 25 F4
Heidelberg, S. Africa 88 E3
Heidenau, Germany 24 E9
Heidenheim, Germany 25 G6
Heijing, China 58 E3
Heilbad Heiligenstadt, Germany 24 D6
Heilbron, S. Africa 89 D4
Heilbronn, Germany 25 F5
Heiligenblut, Austria 26 D5
Heiligenhafen, Germany 24 A6
Heilongjiang □, China 60 B7
Heilunkiang = Heilongjiang □, China 60 B7
Heimaey, Iceland 8 E3
Heinola, Finland 9 F22
Heinsberg, Germany 24 D2
Heinze Is., Burma 67 M20
Heishan, China 57 D12
Heishui, Liaoning, China 57 C10
Heishui, Sichuan, China 58 A4
Hejaz = Ḥijāz □, Si. Arabia 70 E3
Hejian, China 56 E9
Hejiang, China 58 C5
Hejin, China 56 G6
Hekimhan, Turkey 70 B3
Hekla, Iceland 8 E4
Hekou, Guangdong, China 59 F9
Hekou, Yunnan, China 58 F4
Hel, Poland 44 D5
Helagsfjället, Sweden 10 B6
Helan Shan, China 56 E3
Helechosa, Spain 35 F6
Helen Atoll, Pac. Oc. 63 D8
Helena, Ark., U.S.A. 113 H9
Helena, Mont., U.S.A. 114 C7
Helendale, U.S.A. 117 L9
Helensburgh, U.K. 14 E4
Helensville, N.Z. 91 G5
Helenvale, Australia 94 B4
Helgasjön, Sweden 11 H8
Helgeland, Norway 8 C15
Helgoland, Germany 24 A3
Heligoland = Helgoland, Germany 24 A3
Heligoland B. = Deutsche Bucht, Germany 24 A4
Heliopolis, Egypt 80 H7
Hella, Iceland 8 E3
Hellertown, U.S.A. 111 F9
Hellespont = Çanakkale Boğazı, Turkey 41 F10
Hellevoetsluis, Neths. 17 C4
Hellín, Spain 33 G3
Helmand □, Afghan. 66 D4
Helmand →, Afghan. 66 D2
Helme →, Germany 24 D7
Helmeringhausen, Namibia 88 D2
Helmond, Neths. 17 C5
Helmsdale, U.K. 14 C5
Helmsdale →, U.K. 14 C5
Helmstedt, Germany 24 C7
Helong, China 57 C15
Helper, U.S.A. 114 G8
Helsingborg, Sweden 11 H6
Helsinge, Denmark 11 H6
Helsingfors = Helsinki, Finland 9 F21
Helsingør, Denmark 11 H6
Helsinki, Finland 9 F21
Helska, Mierzeja, Poland 44 D5
Helston, U.K. 13 G2
Helvellyn, U.K. 12 C4
Helwân, Egypt 80 J7
Hemel Hempstead, U.K. 13 F7
Hemet, U.S.A. 117 M10
Hemingford, U.S.A. 112 D3
Hemmingford, Canada 111 A11
Hempstead, U.S.A. 113 K6
Hemse, Sweden 11 G12
Hemsön, Sweden 10 B12
Henån, Sweden 11 F5
Henan □, China 56 H8
Henares →, Spain 34 E7
Henashi-Misaki, Japan 54 D9
Hendaye, France 20 E2
Hendek, Turkey 72 B4
Henderson, Argentina 126 D3
Henderson, Ky., U.S.A. 108 G2
Henderson, N.C., U.S.A. 109 G6
Henderson, Nev., U.S.A. 117 J12
Henderson, Tenn., U.S.A. 109 H1
Henderson, Tex., U.S.A. 113 J7
Hendersonville, N.C., U.S.A. 109 H4
Hendersonville, Tenn., U.S.A. 109 G2
Hendījān, Iran 71 D6
Hendorābī, Iran 71 E7
Heng Jiang, China 58 C5
Heng Xian, China 58 F7
Hengcheng, China 56 E4
Hëngchun, Taiwan 59 F13
Hengdaohezi, China 57 B15
Hengelo, Neths. 17 B6
Hengfeng, China 59 C10
Hengshan, Hunan, China 59 D9
Hengshan, Shaanxi, China 56 F5
Hengshui, China 56 F8
Hengyang, Hunan, China 59 D9
Hengyang, Hunan, China 59 D9
Henichesk, Ukraine 47 J8
Hénin-Beaumont, France 19 B9
Henlopen, C., U.S.A. 108 F8
Hennan, Sweden 10 B9
Hennebont, France 18 E3
Hennenman, S. Africa 88 D4
Hennessey, U.S.A. 113 G6
Hennigsdorf, Germany 24 C9
Henrietta, U.S.A. 113 J5
Henrietta, Ostrov = Genriyetty, Ostrov, Russia 51 B16
Henrietta Maria, C., Canada 102 A3
Henry, U.S.A. 112 E10
Henryetta, U.S.A. 113 H7
Henryville, Canada 111 A11
Hensall, Canada 110 C3
Henstedt-Ulzburg, Germany 24 B6
Hentiesbaai, Namibia 88 C1
Hentiyn Nuruu, Mongolia 60 B5
Henty, Australia 95 F4
Henzada, Burma 67 L19
Hephaestia, Greece 39 B7
Heping, China 59 E10
Heppner, U.S.A. 114 D4
Hepu, China 58 G7
Hepworth, Canada 110 B3
Heqing, China 58 D3
Hequ, China 56 E6
Héraðsflói, Iceland 8 D6
Héraðsvötn →, Iceland 8 D4
Herald Cays, Australia 94 B4
Herāt, Afghan. 66 B3
Herāt □, Afghan. 66 B3
Hérault □, France 20 E7

Hérault →, France 20 E7
Herbault, France 18 E8
Herbert →, Australia 94 B4
Herberton, Australia 94 B4
Herbertsdale, S. Africa 88 E3
Herbignac, France 18 E4
Herborn, Germany 24 E4
Herby, Poland 45 H5
Herceg-Novi, Montenegro, Yug. 40 D2
Herchmer, Canada 105 B10
Herðubreið, Iceland 8 D5
Hereford, U.K. 13 E5
Hereford, U.S.A. 113 H3
Herefordshire □, U.K. 13 E5
Hereke, Turkey 41 F13
Herencia, Spain 35 F7
Herentals, Belgium 17 C4
Herford, Germany 24 C4
Héricourt, France 19 E13
Herington, U.S.A. 112 F6
Herisau, Switz. 25 H5
Hérisson, France 19 F9
Herkimer, U.S.A. 111 D10
Herlong, U.S.A. 116 E6
Herm, U.K. 13 H5
Hermann, U.S.A. 112 F9
Hermannsburg, Australia 92 D5
Hermannsburg, Germany 24 C6
Hermanus, S. Africa 88 E2
Herment, France 20 C6
Hermidale, Australia 95 E4
Hermiston, U.S.A. 114 D4
Hermitage, N.Z. 91 K3
Hermite, I., Chile 128 H3
Hermon, U.S.A. 111 B9
Hermon, Mt. = Shaykh, J. ash, Lebanon 75 B4
Hermosillo, Mexico 118 B2
Hernád →, Hungary 42 C6
Hernandarias, Paraguay 127 B5
Hernandez, U.S.A. 116 J6
Hernando, Argentina 126 C3
Hernando, U.S.A. 113 H10
Hernani, Spain 32 B3
Herndon, U.S.A. 110 F8
Herne, Germany 17 C7
Herne Bay, U.K. 13 F9
Herning, Denmark 11 H2
Heroica = Caborca, Mexico 118 A2
Heroica Nogales = Nogales, Mexico 118 A2
Heron Bay, Canada 102 C2
Herradura, Pta. de la, Canary Is. 37 F5
Herreid, U.S.A. 112 C4
Herrenberg, Germany 25 G4
Herrera, Spain 35 H6
Herrera de Alcántara, Spain 35 F3
Herrera de Pisuerga, Spain 34 C6
Herrera del Duque, Spain 35 F5
Herrestad, Sweden 11 F5
Herrin, U.S.A. 113 G10
Herriot, Canada 105 B8
Herrljunga, Sweden 11 F7
Hersbruck, Germany 25 F7
Hershey, U.S.A. 111 F8
Hersonissos, Greece 36 D7
Herstal, Belgium 17 D5
Hertford, U.K. 13 F7
Hertfordshire □, U.K. 13 F7
's-Hertogenbosch, Neths. 17 C5
Hertzogville, S. Africa 88 D4
Hervás, Spain 34 E5
Hervey B., Australia 94 C5
Herzberg, Brandenburg, Germany 24 D9
Herzberg, Niedersachsen, Germany 24 D6
Herzliyya, Israel 75 C3
Herzogenburg, Austria 26 C8
Ḩeşār, Fārs, Iran 71 D6
Ḩeşār, Markazī, Iran 71 C6
Hesdin, France 19 B9
Heshan, China 58 F7
Heshui, China 56 G5
Heshun, China 56 F7
Hesperia, U.S.A. 117 L9
Hesse = Hessen □, Germany 24 E4
Hessen □, Germany 24 E4
Hestra, Sweden 11 G7
Hetch Hetchy Aqueduct, U.S.A. 116 H5
Hettinger, U.S.A. 112 C3
Hettstedt, Germany 24 D7
Heuvelton, U.S.A. 111 B9
Heves, Hungary 42 C5
Heves □, Hungary 42 C5
Hewitt, U.S.A. 113 K6
Hexham, U.K. 12 C5
Hexi, Yunnan, China 58 E4
Hexi, Zhejiang, China 59 D12
Hexigten Qi, China 57 C9
Ḩeydarābād, Iran 71 D7
Heysham, U.K. 12 C5
Heyuan, China 59 F10
Heywood, Australia 95 F3
Heze, China 56 G8
Hezhang, China 58 D5
Hi Vista, U.S.A. 117 L9
Hialeah, U.S.A. 109 N5
Hiawatha, U.S.A. 112 F7
Hibbing, U.S.A. 112 B8
Hibbs B., Australia 94 G4
Hibernia Reef, Australia 92 B3
Hickman, U.S.A. 113 G10
Hickory, U.S.A. 109 H5
Hicks, Pt., Australia 95 F4
Hicks L., Canada 105 A9
Hicksville, U.S.A. 111 F11
Hida, Romania 43 C8
Hida-Gawa →, Japan 55 G8
Hida-Sammyaku, Japan 55 F8
Hidaka-Sammyaku, Japan 54 C11
Hidalgo, Mexico 119 C5
Hidalgo □, Mexico 119 C5
Hidalgo, Presa M., Mexico 118 B3
Hidalgo, Pta. del, Canary Is. 37 F3
Hidalgo del Parral, Mexico 118 B3
Hiddensee, Germany 24 A9
Hieflau, Austria 26 D7
Hiendelaencina, Spain 32 D2
Hierro, Canary Is. 37 G1
Higashiajima-San, Japan 54 F10
Higashiōsaka, Japan 55 G7
Higgins, U.S.A. 113 G4
Higgins Corner, U.S.A. 116 F5
High Atlas = Haut Atlas, Morocco 78 B4
High Bridge, U.S.A. 111 F10
High Level, Canada 104 B5
High Point, U.S.A. 109 H6
High Prairie, Canada 104 B5
High River, Canada 104 C6
High Tatra = Tatry, Slovak Rep. 27 B13
High Veld, Africa 76 J6
High Wycombe, U.K. 13 F7
Highland □, U.K. 14 D4
Highland Park, U.S.A. 108 D2
Highmore, U.S.A. 112 C5
Highrock L., Man., Canada 105 B8
Highrock L., Sask., Canada 105 B7
Higüey, Dom. Rep. 121 C6
Hihya, Egypt 80 H7
Hiiumaa, Estonia 9 G20
Híjar, Spain 32 D4
Ḩijāz □, Si. Arabia 70 E3
Hijo = Tagum, Phil. 61 H6
Hikari, Japan 55 H5
Hikmak, Ras el, Egypt 80 A2
Hiko, U.S.A. 116 H11
Hikone, Japan 55 G8
Hikurangi, N.Z. 91 F5
Hikurangi, Mt., N.Z. 91 H6
Hildburghausen, Germany 24 E6
Hildesheim, Germany 24 C5
Hill →, Australia 93 F2
Hill City, Idaho, U.S.A. 114 E6
Hill City, Kans., U.S.A. 112 F5
Hill City, S. Dak., U.S.A. 112 D3
Hill Island L., Canada 105 A7
Hillared, Sweden 11 G7
Hillcrest Center, U.S.A. 117 K8
Hillegom, Neths. 17 B4
Hillerød, Denmark 11 J6
Hillerstorp, Sweden 11 G7
Hillsboro, Kans., U.S.A. 112 F6
Hillsboro, N. Dak., U.S.A. 112 B6
Hillsboro, N.H., U.S.A. 111 C13
Hillsboro, Ohio, U.S.A. 108 F4
Hillsboro, Oreg., U.S.A. 116 E4
Hillsboro, Tex., U.S.A. 113 J6
Hillsborough, Grenada 121 D7
Hillsdale, Mich., U.S.A. 108 E3
Hillsdale, N.Y., U.S.A. 111 D11
Hillsport, Canada 102 C2
Hillston, Australia 95 E4
Hilo, U.S.A. 106 J17
Hilton, U.S.A. 110 C7
Hilton Head Island, U.S.A. 109 J5
Hilvan, Turkey 73 D8
Hilversum, Neths. 17 B5
Himachal Pradesh □, India 68 D7
Himalaya, Asia 69 E11
Himamaylan, Phil. 61 F5
Himara, Albania 40 F3
Himatnagar, India 66 H8
Himeji, Japan 55 G7
Himi, Japan 55 F8
Himmerland, Denmark 11 H3
Ḩimş, Syria 75 A5
Ḩimş □, Syria 75 A6
Hinche, Haiti 121 C5
Hinchinbrook I., Australia 94 B4
Hinckley, U.K. 13 E6
Hinckley, U.S.A. 112 B8
Hindaun, India 68 F7
Hindmarsh, L., Australia 95 F3
Hindsholm, Denmark 11 J4
Hindu Bagh, Pakistan 68 D2
Hindu Kush, Asia 66 B7
Hindubagh, Pakistan 66 D5
Hindupur, India 66 N10
Hines Creek, Canada 104 B5
Hinesville, U.S.A. 109 K5
Hinganghat, India 66 J11
Hingham, U.S.A. 114 B8
Hingir, India 69 J10
Hingoli, India 66 K10
Hinigaran, Phil. 61 F5
Hinis, Turkey 73 C9
Hinna = Imi, Ethiopia 81 F5
Hinna, Nigeria 83 C7
Hinnerup, Denmark 11 H4
Hinnøya, Norway 8 B16
Hinojosa del Duque, Spain 35 G5
Hinsdale, U.S.A. 111 D12
Hinterrhein →, Switz. 25 J5
Hinton, Canada 104 C5
Hinton, U.S.A. 108 G5
Hınzır Burnu, Turkey 72 D6
Hirado, Japan 55 H4
Hirakud Dam, India 67 J13
Hiran →, India 69 H8
Hirapur, India 69 G8
Hiratsuka, Japan 55 G9
Hirfanlı Baraji, Turkey 72 C5
Hiroo, Japan 54 C11
Hirosaki, Japan 54 D10
Hiroshima, Japan 55 G6
Hiroshima □, Japan 55 G6
Hirson, France 19 C11
Hirtshals, Denmark 11 G3
Hisar, India 68 E6
Hisarcık, Turkey 39 B11
Hisaria, Bulgaria 41 D8
Hisb →, Iraq 70 D5
Ḩismá, Si. Arabia 70 D3
Hispaniola, W. Indies 121 C5
Hīt, Iraq 70 C4
Hita, Japan 55 H5
Hitachi, Japan 55 F10
Hitchin, U.K. 13 F7
Hitoyoshi, Japan 55 H5
Hitra, Norway 8 E13
Hitzacker, Germany 24 B7
Hixon, Canada 104 C4
Ḩiyyon, N. →, Israel 75 E4
Hjalmar L., Canada 105 A7
Hjälmaren, Sweden 10 E9
Hjältevad, Sweden 11 G9
Hjo, Sweden 11 F8
Hjørring, Denmark 11 G3
Hjortkvarn, Sweden 11 F9
Hlinsko, Czech Rep. 26 B8
Hlobane, S. Africa 89 D5
Hlohovec, Slovak Rep. 27 C10
Hlučín, Czech Rep. 27 B11
Hluhluwe, S. Africa 89 D5
Hlukhiv, Ukraine 47 G7
Hlyboka, Ukraine 47 H3
Hlybokaye, Belarus 46 E4
Hnúšt'a, Slovak Rep. 27 C12
Ho, Ghana 83 D5
Ho Chi Minh City = Phanh Bho Ho Chi Minh, Vietnam 65 G6
Ho Thuong, Vietnam 64 C5
Hoa Binh, Vietnam 58 G5
Hoa Da, Vietnam 65 G7
Hoa Hiep, Vietnam 65 G5
Hoai Nhon, Vietnam 64 E7
Hoang Lien Son, Vietnam 58 F4
Hoanib →, Namibia 88 B2
Hoare B., Canada 101 B13
Hoarusib →, Namibia 88 B2
Hobart, Australia 94 G4
Hobart, U.S.A. 113 H5
Hobbs, U.S.A. 113 J3
Hobbs Coast, Antarctica 5 D14
Hobe Sound, U.S.A. 109 M5
Hoboken, U.S.A. 111 F10
Hobro, Denmark 11 H3
Hoburgen, Sweden 11 H12
Hocalar, Turkey 39 C11
Hochfeld, Namibia 88 C2
Hochschwab, Austria 26 D8
Höchstadt, Germany 25 F6
Hockenheim, Germany 25 F4
Hodaka-Dake, Japan 55 F8
Hodgeville, Canada 105 C7
Hodgson, Canada 105 C9
Hódmezővásárhely, Hungary 42 D5
Hodna, Chott el, Algeria 78 A6
Hodonín, Czech Rep. 27 C10
Hoeamdong, N. Korea 57 C16
Hœdic, Î. de, France 18 E4
Hoek van Holland, Neths. 17 C4
Hoengsŏng, S. Korea 57 F14
Hoeryong, N. Korea 57 C15
Hoeyang, N. Korea 57 E14
Hof, Germany 25 E7
Hofgeismar, Germany 24 D5
Hofheim, Germany 25 E4
Hofmeyr, S. Africa 88 E4
Höfn, Iceland 8 D6
Hofors, Sweden 10 D10
Hofsjökull, Iceland 8 D4
Hōfu, Japan 55 G5
Hogan Group, Australia 95 F4
Höganäs, Sweden 11 H6
Hogarth, Mt., Australia 94 C2
Hoggar = Ahaggar, Algeria 78 D7
Högsäter, Sweden 11 F6
Högsby, Sweden 11 G10
Högsjö, Sweden 10 E9
Hogsty Reef, Bahamas 121 B5
Hoh →, U.S.A. 116 C2
Hohe Acht, Germany 25 E3
Hohe Tauern, Austria 26 D5
Hohe Venn, Belgium 17 D6
Hohenau, Austria 27 C9
Hohenems, Austria 26 D2
Hohenloher Ebene, Germany 25 F5
Hohenwald, U.S.A. 109 H2
Hohenwestedt, Germany 24 A5
Hoher Rhön = Rhön, Germany 24 E5
Hohhot, China 56 D6
Hóhlakas, Greece 36 D9
Hohoe, Ghana 83 D5
Hoi An, Vietnam 64 E7
Hoi Xuan, Vietnam 58 G5
Hoisington, U.S.A. 112 F5
Højer, Denmark 11 K2
Hōjō, Japan 55 H6
Hok, Sweden 11 G8
Hökensås, Sweden 11 G8
Hökerum, Sweden 11 G7
Hokianga Harbour, N.Z. 91 F4
Hokitika, N.Z. 91 K3
Hokkaidō □, Japan 54 C11
Hol-Hol, Djibouti 81 E5
Hola Pristan, Ukraine 47 J7
Holbæk, Denmark 11 J5
Holbrook, Australia 95 F4
Holbrook, U.S.A. 115 J8
Holden, U.S.A. 114 G7
Holdenville, U.S.A. 113 H6
Holdrege, U.S.A. 112 E5
Holešov, Czech Rep. 27 B10
Holguín, Cuba 120 B4
Holíč, Slovak Rep. 27 C10
Holice, Czech Rep. 26 A8
Höljes, Sweden 10 D6
Hollabrunn, Austria 26 C9
Hollams Bird I., Namibia 88 C1
Holland, Mich., U.S.A. 108 D2
Holland, N.Y., U.S.A. 110 D6
Hollandale, U.S.A. 113 J9
Hollandia = Jayapura, Indonesia 63 E10
Holley, U.S.A. 110 C6
Hollfeld, Germany 25 F7
Hollidaysburg, U.S.A. 110 F6
Hollis, U.S.A. 113 H5
Hollister, Calif., U.S.A. 116 J5
Hollister, Idaho, U.S.A. 114 E6
Höllviken, Sweden 11 J6
Holly Hill, U.S.A. 109 L5
Holly Springs, U.S.A. 113 H10
Hollywood, Calif., U.S.A. 106 D3
Hollywood, Fla., U.S.A. 109 N5
Holman, Canada 100 A8
Hólmavík, Iceland 8 D3
Holmen, U.S.A. 112 D9
Holmes Reefs, Australia 94 B4
Holmsjö, Sweden 11 H9
Holmsjön, Västernorrland, Sweden 10 B10
Holmsjön, Västernorrland, Sweden 10 B9
Holmsland Klit, Denmark 11 J2
Holmsund, Sweden 8 E19
Holod, Romania 42 D7
Holroyd →, Australia 94 A3
Holstebro, Denmark 11 H2
Holsworthy, U.K. 13 G3
Holton, Canada 103 B8
Holton, U.S.A. 112 F7
Holtville, U.S.A. 117 N11
Holwerd, Neths. 17 A5
Holy I., Angl., U.K. 12 D3
Holy I., Northumb., U.K. 12 B6
Holyhead, U.K. 12 D3
Holyoke, Colo., U.S.A. 112 E3
Holyoke, Mass., U.S.A. 111 D12
Holyrood, Canada 103 C9
Holzkirchen, Germany 25 H7
Holzminden, Germany 24 D5
Homa Bay, Kenya 86 C3
Homalin, Burma 67 G19
Homand, Iran 71 C8
Homathko →, Canada 104 C4
Homberg, Germany 24 D5
Hombori, Mali 83 B4
Homburg, Germany 25 F3
Home B., Canada 101 B13
Home Hill, Australia 94 B4
Homedale, U.S.A. 114 E5
Homer, Alaska, U.S.A. 100 C4
Homer, La., U.S.A. 113 J8
Homer City, U.S.A. 110 F5
Homestead, Australia 94 C4
Homestead, U.S.A. 109 N5
Homewood, U.S.A. 116 F6
Homoine, Mozam. 89 C6
Homoljske Planina, Serbia, Yug. 40 B5
Homorod, Romania 43 D10
Homs = Ḩimş, Syria 75 A5
Homyel, Belarus 47 F6
Hon Chong, Vietnam 65 G5
Hon Me, Vietnam 64 C5
Honan = Henan □, China 56 H8
Honaz, Turkey 39 D11
Honbetsu, Japan 54 C11
Honcut, U.S.A. 116 F5
Honda Bay, Phil. 61 G3
Hondarribia, Spain 32 B3
Hondeklipbaai, S. Africa 88 E2
Hondo, Japan 55 H5
Hondo, U.S.A. 113 L5
Hondo →, Belize 119 D7
Honduras ■, Cent. Amer. 120 D2
Honduras, G. de, Caribbean 120 C2
Hønefoss, Norway 9 F14
Honesdale, U.S.A. 111 E9
Honey L., U.S.A. 116 E6
Honfleur, France 18 C7
Høng, Denmark 11 J5
Hong →, Vietnam 58 F5
Hong Gai, Vietnam 58 G6
Hong He →, China 56 H8
Hong Hu, China 59 C9
Hong Kong □, China 59 F10
Hong'an, China 59 B10
Hongch'ŏn, S. Korea 57 F14
Honghai Wan, China 59 F10
Honghe, China 58 F4
Honghu, China 59 C9
Hongjiang, China 58 D7
Hongliu He →, China 56 F5
Hongor, Mongolia 56 B7
Hongsa, Laos 64 C3
Hongshui He →, China 58 F7
Hongsŏng, S. Korea 57 F14
Hongtong, China 56 F6
Honguedo, Détroit d', Canada 103 C7
Hongwon, N. Korea 57 E14
Hongya, China 58 C4
Hongyuan, China 58 A4
Hongze Hu, China 57 H10
Honiara, Solomon Is. 96 H7
Honiton, U.K. 13 G4
Honjō, Japan 54 E10
Honkorâb, Ras, Egypt 80 C4
Honningsvåg, Norway 8 A21
Hönö, Sweden 11 G5
Honolulu, U.S.A. 106 H16
Honshū, Japan 55 G9
Hontoria del Pinar, Spain 32 D1
Hood, Mt., U.S.A. 114 D3
Hood, Pt., Australia 93 F2
Hood River, U.S.A. 114 D3
Hoodsport, U.S.A. 116 C3
Hooge, Germany 24 A4
Hoogeveen, Neths. 17 B6
Hoogezand-Sappemeer, Neths. 17 A6
Hooghly = Hugli →, India 69 J13
Hooghly-Chinsura = Chunchura, India 69 H13
Hook Hd., Ireland 15 D5
Hook I., Australia 94 C4
Hook of Holland = Hoek van Holland, Neths. 17 C4
Hooker, U.S.A. 113 G4
Hooker Creek, Australia 92 C5
Hoonah, U.S.A. 104 B1
Hooper Bay, U.S.A. 100 B3
Hoopeston, U.S.A. 108 E2
Hoopstad, S. Africa 88 D4
Höör, Sweden 11 J7
Hoorn, Neths. 17 B5
Hoover, U.S.A. 109 J2
Hoover Dam, U.S.A. 117 K12
Hooversville, U.S.A. 110 F6
Hop Bottom, U.S.A. 111 E9
Hopa, Turkey 73 B9
Hope, Canada 104 D4
Hope, Ariz., U.S.A. 117 M13
Hope, Ark., U.S.A. 113 J8
Hope, L., S. Austral., Australia 95 D2
Hope, L., W. Austral., Australia 93 F3
Hope I., Canada 110 B4
Hope Town, Bahamas 120 A4
Hopedale, Canada 103 A7
Hopedale, U.S.A. 111 D13
Hopefield, S. Africa 88 E2
Hopei = Hebei □, China 56 E9
Hopelchén, Mexico 119 D7
Hopetoun, Vic., Australia 95 F3
Hopetoun, W. Austral., Australia 93 F3
Hopetown, S. Africa 88 D3
Hopevale, Australia 94 B4
Hopewell, U.S.A. 108 G7
Hopfgarten, Austria 26 D5
Hopkins, L., Australia 92 D4
Hopkinsville, U.S.A. 109 G2
Hopland, U.S.A. 116 G3
Hoquiam, U.S.A. 116 D3
Horasan, Turkey 73 B10
Horažďovice, Czech Rep. 26 B6
Horb, Germany 25 G4
Hörby, Sweden 11 J7
Horcajo de Santiago, Spain 32 F1
Horden Hills, Australia 92 D5
Horezu, Romania 43 E8
Horgen, Switz. 25 H4
Horgoš, Serbia, Yug. 42 D4
Hořice, Czech Rep. 26 A8
Horinger, China 56 D6
Horki, Belarus 46 E6
Horlick Mts., Antarctica 5 E15
Horlivka, Ukraine 47 H10
Hormak, Iran 71 D9
Hormoz, Iran 71 E7
Hormoz, Jaz.-ye, Iran 71 E8
Hormozgān □, Iran 71 E8
Hormuz, Kūh-e, Iran 71 E7
Hormuz, Str. of, The Gulf 71 E8
Horn, Austria 26 C8
Horn, Iceland 8 C2
Horn, Sweden 11 G9
Horn →, Canada 104 A5
Horn, Cape = Hornos, C. de, Chile 122 J4
Horn Head, Ireland 15 A3
Horn I., Australia 94 A3
Horn Mts., Canada 104 A5
Hornachuelos, Spain 35 H5
Hornavan, Sweden 8 C17
Hornbeck, U.S.A. 113 K8
Hornbrook, U.S.A. 114 F2
Hornburg, Germany 24 C6
Horncastle, U.K. 12 D7
Horndal, Sweden 10 D10
Hornell, U.S.A. 110 D7
Hornell L., Canada 104 A5
Hornepayne, Canada 102 C3
Horní Planá, Czech Rep. 26 C7
Hornings Mills, Canada 110 B4
Hornitos, U.S.A. 116 H6
Hornos, C. de, Chile 122 J4
Hornoy-le-Bourg, France 19 C8
Hornsea, U.K. 12 D7
Hornslandet, Sweden 10 C11
Hörnum, Germany 24 A4
Horobetsu, Japan 54 C10
Horodenka, Ukraine 47 H3
Horodnya, Ukraine 47 G6
Horodok, Khmelnytskyy, Ukraine 47 H4
Horodok, Lviv, Ukraine 47 H2
Horodyshche, Ukraine 47 H6
Horokhiv, Ukraine 47 G3
Horovice, Czech Rep. 26 B6
Horqin Youyi Qianqi, China 57 A12
Horqueta, Paraguay 126 A4
Horred, Sweden 11 G6
Horse Creek, U.S.A. 112 E3
Horse Is., Canada 103 B8
Horsefly L., Canada 104 C4
Horseheads, U.S.A. 110 D8
Horsens, Denmark 11 J3
Horsham, Australia 95 F3
Horsham, U.K. 13 F7
Horšovský Týn, Czech Rep. 26 B5
Horten, Norway 9 G14

Hortobágy →, Hungary ... 42 C6
Horton, U.S.A. 112 F7
Horton →, Canada 100 B7
Horwood L., Canada ... 102 C3
Hosaina, Ethiopia 81 F4
Hose, Gunung-Gunung,
   Malaysia 62 D4
Ḥoseynābād, Khuzestān, Iran 71 C6
Ḥoseynābād, Kordestān, Iran 70 C5
Hoshangabad, India 68 H7
Hoshiarpur, India 68 D6
Hospet, India 66 M10
Hoste, I., Chile 128 H3
Hostens, France 20 D3
Hot, Thailand 64 C2
Hot Creek Range, U.S.A. .. 114 G6
Hot Springs, Ark., U.S.A. .. 113 H8
Hot Springs, S. Dak., U.S.A. 112 D3
Hotagen, Sweden 8 E16
Hotan, China 60 C2
Hotan →, China 60 C3
Hotazel, S. Africa 88 D3
Hotchkiss, U.S.A. 115 G10
Hotham, C., Australia ... 92 B5
Hoting, Sweden 8 D17
Hotolishti, Albania 40 E4
Hotte, Massif de la, Haiti 121 C5
Hottentotsbaai, Namibia .. 88 D1
Houat, Î. de, France 18 E4
Houdan, France 19 D8
Houei Sai, Laos 58 G3
Houeillès, France 20 D4
Houffalize, Belgium 17 D5
Houghton, Mich., U.S.A. .. 112 B10
Houghton, N.Y., U.S.A. .. 110 D6
Houghton L., U.S.A. 108 C3
Houhora Heads, N.Z. 91 F4
Houlton, U.S.A. 109 B12
Houma, U.S.A. 113 L9
Houndé, Burkina Faso .. 82 C4
Hourtin, France 20 C2
Hourtin-Carcans, Étang d',
   France 20 C2
Housatonic →, U.S.A. .. 111 E11
Houston, Canada 104 C3
Houston, Mo., U.S.A. ... 113 G9
Houston, Tex., U.S.A. .. 113 L7
Hout →, S. Africa 89 C4
Houtkraal, S. Africa 88 E3
Houtman Abrolhos,
   Australia 93 E1
Hovd, Mongolia 60 B4
Hove, U.K. 13 G7
Hoveyzeh, Iran 71 D6
Hovmantorp, Sweden ... 11 H9
Hövsgöl, Mongolia 56 C5
Hövsgöl Nuur, Mongolia .. 60 A5
Hovsta, Sweden 10 E9
Howakil, Eritrea 81 D5
Howar, Wadi →, Sudan .. 81 D2
Howard, Australia 95 D5
Howard, Pa., U.S.A. ... 110 F7
Howard, S. Dak., U.S.A. .. 112 C6
Howe, U.S.A. 114 E7
Howe, C., Australia 95 F5
Howe I., Canada 111 B8
Howell, U.S.A. 108 D4
Howick, Canada 111 A11
Howick, S. Africa 89 D5
Howick Group, Australia .. 94 A4
Howitt, L., Australia ... 95 D2
Howland I., Pac. Oc. 96 G10
Howrah = Haora, India .. 69 H13
Howth Hd., Ireland 15 C5
Höxter, Germany 24 D5
Hoy, U.K. 14 C5
Hoya, Germany 24 C5
Høyanger, Norway 9 F12
Hoyerswerda, Germany .. 24 D10
Hoylake, U.K. 12 D4
Hoyos, Spain 34 E4
Hpa-an = Pa-an, Burma .. 67 L20
Hpungan Pass, Burma ... 67 F20
Hradec Králové, Czech Rep. 26 A8
Hrádek, Czech Rep. 27 C9
Hranice, Czech Rep. 27 B10
Hrazdan, Armenia 49 K7
Hrebenka, Ukraine 47 G7
Hrodna, Belarus 46 F2
Hrodzyanka, Belarus ... 46 F5
Hron →, Slovak Rep. ... 27 D11
Hrubieszów, Poland 45 H10
Hrubý Jeseník, Czech Rep. 27 A10
Hrvatska = Croatia ■,
   Europe 29 C13
Hrymayliv, Ukraine 47 H4
Hsenwi, Burma 67 H20
Hsiamen = Xiamen, China 59 E12
Hsian = Xi'an, China ... 56 G5
Hsinchu, Taiwan 59 E13
Hsinhailien = Lianyungang,
   China 57 G10
Hsinying, Taiwan 59 F13
Hsopket, Burma 58 F2
Hsüchou = Xuzhou, China 57 G9
Hu Xian, China 56 G5
Hua Hin, Thailand 64 F2
Hua Xian, Henan, China 56 G8
Hua Xian, Shaanxi, China 56 G5
Hua'an, China 59 E11
Huab →, Namibia 88 B2
Huachinera, Mexico ... 118 A3
Huacho, Peru 124 F3
Huade, China 56 D7
Huadu, China 59 F9
Huai He →, China 59 A12
Huai Yot, Thailand 65 J2
Huai'an, Hebei, China .. 56 D8
Huai'an, Jiangsu, China .. 57 H10
Huaibei, China 56 G9

Huaibin, China 59 A10
Huaide = Gongzhuling,
   China 57 C13
Huaidezhen, China 57 C13
Huaihua, China 58 D7
Huaiji, China 59 F9
Huainan, China 59 A11
Huaining, China 59 B11
Huairen, China 56 E7
Huairou, China 56 D9
Huaiyang, China 56 H8
Huaiyin, China 57 H10
Huaiyuan, Anhui, China .. 57 H9
Huaiyuan,
   Guangxi Zhuangzu, China 58 E7
Huajianzi, China 57 D13
Huajuapan de Leon, Mexico 119 D5
Hualapai Peak, U.S.A. .. 115 J7
Hualien, Taiwan 59 E13
Huallaga →, Peru 124 E3
Huambo, Angola 85 G3
Huan Jiang →, China .. 56 G5
Huan Xian, China 56 F4
Huancabamba, Peru ... 124 E3
Huancane, Peru 124 G5
Huancavelica, Peru 124 F3
Huancayo, Peru 124 F3
Huanchaca, Bolivia 124 H5
Huang Hai = Yellow Sea,
   China 57 G12
Huang He →, China ... 57 F10
Huang Xian, China 57 F11
Huangchuan, China 59 A10
Huanggang, China 59 B10
Huangguoshu, China ... 58 E5
Huangling, China 56 G5
Huanglong, China 56 G5
Huanglongtan, China .. 59 A8
Huangmei, China 59 B10
Huangpi, China 59 B10
Huangping, China 58 D6
Huangshan, China 59 C12
Huangshi, China 59 B10
Huangsongdian, China .. 57 C14
Huangyan, China 59 C13
Huangyangsi, China ... 59 D8
Huaning, China 58 E4
Huanjiang, China 58 E7
Huantai, China 57 F9
Huánuco, Peru 124 E3
Huaping, China 58 D3
Huaraz, Peru 124 E3
Huarmey, Peru 124 F3
Huarong, China 59 C9
Huascarán, Peru 122 D3
Huasco, Chile 126 B1
Huasco →, Chile 126 B1
Huasna, U.S.A. 117 K6
Huatabampo, Mexico .. 118 B3
Huauchinango, Mexico .. 119 C5
Huautla de Jiménez, Mexico 119 D5
Huaxi, China 58 D6
Huay Namota, Mexico .. 118 C4
Huayin, China 56 G6
Huayuan, China 58 C7
Huayun, China 58 B6
Huazhou, China 59 G8
Hubbard, Ohio, U.S.A. .. 110 E4
Hubbard, Tex., U.S.A. .. 113 K6
Hubbart Pt., Canada ... 105 B10
Hubei □, China 59 B9
Hubli, India 66 M9
Huch'ang, N. Korea 57 D14
Hucknall, U.K. 12 D6
Huddersfield, U.K. 12 D6
Hude, Germany 24 B4
Hudi, Sudan 80 D3
Hudiksvall, Sweden ... 10 C11
Hudson, Canada 102 B1
Hudson, Mass., U.S.A. .. 111 D13
Hudson, N.Y., U.S.A. .. 111 D11
Hudson, Wis., U.S.A. .. 112 C8
Hudson, Wyo., U.S.A. .. 114 E9
Hudson →, U.S.A. 111 F10
Hudson Bay, N.W.T.,
   Canada 101 C11
Hudson Bay, Sask., Canada 105 C8
Hudson Falls, U.S.A. .. 111 C11
Hudson Mts., Antarctica .. 5 D16
Hudson Str., Canada ... 101 B13
Hudson's Hope, Canada .. 104 B4
Hue, Vietnam 64 D6
Huebra →, Spain 34 D4
Huedin, Romania 42 D8
Huehuetenango, Guatemala 120 C1
Huejúcar, Mexico 118 C4
Huélamo, Spain 32 E3
Huelgoat, France 18 D3
Huelma, Spain 35 H7
Huelva, Spain 35 H4
Huelva □, Spain 35 H4
Huelva →, Spain 35 H5
Huentelauquén, Chile .. 126 C1
Huércal-Overa, Spain .. 33 H3
Huerta, Sa. de la, Argentina 126 C2
Huertas, C. de las, Spain 33 G4
Huerva →, Spain 32 D4
Huesca, Spain 32 C4
Huesca □, Spain 32 C5
Huéscar, Spain 33 H2
Huetamo, Mexico 118 D4
Huete, Spain 32 E2
Hugh →, Australia ... 94 D1
Hughenden, Australia .. 94 C3
Hughes, Australia 93 F4
Hughes →, Canada ... 105 B9
Hughesville, U.S.A. ... 111 E8
Hugli →, India 69 J13
Hugo, Colo., U.S.A. .. 112 F3
Hugo, Okla., U.S.A. ... 113 H7
Hugoton, U.S.A. 113 G4
Hui Xian = Huixian, China 56 G7

Hui Xian, China 56 H4
Hui'an, China 59 E12
Hui'anbu, China 56 F4
Huichang, China 59 E10
Huichapán, Mexico ... 119 C5
Huidong, Guangdong, China 59 F10
Huidong, Sichuan, China .. 58 D4
Huifa He →, China ... 57 C14
Huila, Nevado del, Colombia 124 C3
Huilai, China 59 F11
Huili, China 58 D4
Huimin, China 57 F9
Huinan, China 57 C14
Huinca Renancó, Argentina 126 C3
Huining, China 56 G3
Huinong, China 56 E4
Huisache, Mexico 118 C4
Huishui, China 58 D6
Huisne →, France 18 E7
Huiting, China 56 G9
Huitong, China 58 D7
Huixian, China 56 G7
Huixtla, Mexico 119 D6
Huize, China 58 D4
Huizhou, China 59 F10
Hukawng Valley, Burma .. 67 F20
Hukou, China 59 C11
Hukuntsi, Botswana ... 88 C3
Huld = Ulaanjirem,
   Mongolia 56 B3
Hulin He →, China ... 57 B12
Hull = Kingston upon Hull,
   U.K. 12 D7
Hull, Canada 102 C4
Hull →, U.K. 12 D7
Hulst, Neths. 17 C4
Hultsfred, Sweden 11 G9
Hulun Nur, China 60 B6
Hulyaypole, Ukraine .. 47 J9
Humahuaca, Argentina .. 126 A2
Humaitá, Brazil 124 E6
Humaitá, Paraguay ... 126 B4
Humansdorp, S. Africa .. 88 E3
Humara, J., Sudan 81 D3
Humbe, Angola 88 B1
Humber →, U.K. 12 D7
Humboldt, Canada 105 C7
Humboldt, Iowa, U.S.A. .. 112 D7
Humboldt, Tenn., U.S.A. .. 113 H10
Humboldt →, U.S.A. .. 114 F4
Humboldt Gletscher,
   Greenland 4 B4
Hume, U.S.A. 116 J8
Hume, L., Australia ... 95 F4
Humenné, Slovak Rep. .. 27 C14
Hummelsta, Sweden ... 10 E10
Humphreys, Mt., U.S.A. .. 116 H8
Humphreys Peak, U.S.A. .. 115 J8
Humpolec, Czech Rep. .. 26 B8
Humptulips, U.S.A. 116 C3
Hūn, Libya 79 C9
Hun Jiang →, China .. 57 D13
Húnaflói, Iceland 8 D3
Hunan □, China 59 D9
Hunchun, China 57 C16
Hundested, Denmark .. 11 J5
Hundewali, Pakistan .. 68 D5
Hundred Mile House,
   Canada 104 C4
Hunedoara, Romania .. 42 E7
Hunedoara □, Romania .. 42 E7
Hünfeld, Germany 24 E5
Hung Yen, Vietnam ... 58 G6
Hungary ■, Europe ... 27 D12
Hungary, Plain of, Europe .. 6 F10
Hungerford, Australia .. 95 D3
Hungnam, N. Korea ... 57 E14
Hungt'ou Hsü, Taiwan .. 59 F13
Huni Valley, Ghana ... 82 D4
Hunneberg, Sweden ... 11 F6
Hunnebostrand, Sweden .. 11 F5
Hunsberge, Namibia .. 88 D2
Hunsrück, Germany ... 25 F3
Hunstanton, U.K. 12 E8
Hunte →, Germany ... 24 B4
Hunter, U.S.A. 111 D10
Hunter I., Australia ... 94 G3
Hunter I., Canada 104 C3
Hunter Ra., Australia .. 95 E5
Hunters Road, Zimbabwe .. 87 F2
Hunterville, N.Z. 91 H5
Huntingburg, U.S.A. .. 108 F2
Huntingdon, Canada .. 102 C5
Huntingdon, U.K. 13 E7
Huntingdon, U.S.A. ... 110 F6
Huntington, Ind., U.S.A. .. 108 E3
Huntington, Oreg., U.S.A. .. 114 D5
Huntington, Utah, U.S.A. .. 114 G8
Huntington, W. Va., U.S.A. 108 F4
Huntington Beach, U.S.A. .. 117 M9
Huntington Station, U.S.A. 111 F11
Huntly, N.Z. 91 G5
Huntly, U.K. 14 D6
Huntsville, Canada ... 102 C4
Huntsville, Ala., U.S.A. .. 109 H2
Huntsville, Tex., U.S.A. .. 113 K7
Hunyani →, Zimbabwe .. 87 F3
Hunyuan, China 56 E7
Hunza →, India 69 B6
Huo Xian = Huozhou,
   China 56 F6
Huo Hoa, Vietnam 64 D6
Huong Khe, Vietnam .. 64 C5
Huonville, Australia .. 94 G4
Huoqiu, China 59 A11
Huoshan, Anhui, China .. 59 A12
Huoshan, Anhui, China .. 59 B11
Huoshao Dao = Lü-Tao,
   Taiwan 59 F13
Huozhou, China 56 F6

Hupeh = Hubei □, China .. 59 B9
Ḥūr, Iran 71 D8
Hurbanovo, Slovak Rep. .. 27 D11
Hurd, C., Canada 110 A3
Hure Qi, China 57 C11
Hurezani, Romania ... 43 F8
Hurghada, Egypt 80 B3
Hurley, N. Mex., U.S.A. .. 115 K9
Hurley, Wis., U.S.A. ... 112 B9
Huron, Calif., U.S.A. .. 116 J6
Huron, Ohio, U.S.A. ... 110 E2
Huron, S. Dak., U.S.A. .. 112 C5
Huron, L., U.S.A. 110 B2
Hurricane, U.S.A. 115 H7
Hurso, Ethiopia 81 F5
Hurunui →, N.Z. 91 K4
Hurup, Denmark 11 H2
Húsavík, Iceland 8 C5
Huși, Romania 43 D13
Huskvarna, Sweden ... 11 G8
Hustadvika, Norway ... 8 E12
Hustontown, U.S.A. .. 110 F6
Hustopeče, Czech Rep. .. 27 C9
Husum, Germany 24 A5
Husum, Sweden 10 A13
Hutchinson, Kans., U.S.A. 113 F6
Hutchinson, Minn., U.S.A. 112 C7
Hutte Sauvage, L. de la,
   Canada 103 A7
Hüttenberg, Austria ... 26 E7
Hutton, Mt., Australia .. 95 D4
Huwun, Ethiopia 81 G5
Huy, Belgium 17 D5
Huzhou, China 59 B13
Hvalpsund, Denmark .. 11 H3
Hvammstangi, Iceland .. 8 D3
Hvar, Croatia 29 E13
Hvarski Kanal, Croatia .. 29 E13
Hvítá →, Iceland 8 D3
Hwachŏn-chŏsuji, S. Korea 57 E14
Hwang Ho = Huang He →,
   China 57 F10
Hwange, Zimbabwe ... 87 F2
Hwange Nat. Park,
   Zimbabwe 88 B4
Hyannis, Mass., U.S.A. .. 108 E10
Hyannis, Nebr., U.S.A. .. 112 E4
Hyargas Nuur, Mongolia .. 60 B4
Hybo, Sweden 10 C10
Hydaburg, U.S.A. 104 B2
Hyde Park, U.S.A. 111 E11
Hyden, Australia 93 F2
Hyder, U.S.A. 104 B2
Hyderabad, India 66 L11
Hyderabad, Pakistan .. 68 G3
Hyères, France 21 E10
Hyères, Îs. d', France .. 21 F10
Hyesan, N. Korea 57 D15
Hyland →, Canada ... 104 B3
Hyltebruk, Sweden ... 11 H7
Hymia, India 69 C8
Hyndman Peak, U.S.A. .. 114 E6
Hyōgo □, Japan 55 G7
Hyrum, U.S.A. 114 F8
Hysham, U.S.A. 114 C10
Hythe, U.K. 13 F9
Hyūga, Japan 55 H5
Hyvinge = Hyvinkää,
   Finland 9 F21
Hyvinkää, Finland 9 F21

I

I-n-Gall, Niger 83 B6
I-n-Oudad, Algeria 83 A5
I-n-Ouzzal, Algeria ... 83 A5
I-n-Tadreft, Niger 83 B6
Iablanița, Romania ... 42 F7
Iaco →, Brazil 124 E5
Iacobeni, Romania ... 43 C10
Iakora, Madag. 89 C8
Ialomița □, Romania .. 43 F12
Ialomița →, Romania .. 43 F12
Ialoveni, Moldova 43 D13
Ialpug →, Moldova ... 43 E13
Ianca, Romania 43 E12
Iara, Romania 43 D8
Iarda, Ethiopia 81 E4
Iargara, Moldova 43 D13
Iași, Romania 43 C12
Iași □, Romania 43 C12
Iasmos, Greece 41 E9
Ib →, India 69 J10
Iba, Phil. 61 D3
Ibadan, Nigeria 83 D5
Ibagué, Colombia 124 C3
Iballja, Albania 40 D4
Ibănești, Botoșani, Romania 43 B11
Ibănești, Mureș, Romania .. 43 D9
Ibar →, Serbia, Yug. .. 40 C4
Ibaraki □, Japan 55 F10
Ibarra, Ecuador 124 C3
Ibba, Sudan 81 G2
Ibba, Bahr el →, Sudan .. 81 F2
Ibbenbüren, Germany .. 24 C3
Ibembo,
   Dem. Rep. of the Congo .. 86 B1
Ibera, L., Argentina ... 126 B4
Iberian Peninsula, Europe .. 6 H5
Iberville, Canada 102 C5
Iberville, Lac d', Canada .. 102 A5
Ibi, Nigeria 83 D6
Ibiá, Brazil 125 G9
Ibicuí →, Brazil 127 B4
Ibicuy, Argentina 126 C4
Ibioapaba, Sa. da, Brazil .. 125 D10
Ibiza = Eivissa, Spain .. 37 C7

Íblei, Monti, Italy 31 E7
Ibo, Mozam. 87 E5
Ibonma, Indonesia 63 E8
Ibotirama, Brazil 125 F10
Ibrāhīm →, Lebanon .. 75 A4
'Ibrī, Oman 71 F8
Ibriktepe, Turkey 41 E10
Ibshawâi, Egypt 80 J7
Ibu, Indonesia 63 D7
Ibusuki, Japan 55 J5
Ica, Peru 124 F3
Iça →, Brazil 124 D5
Içana, Brazil 124 C4
Içana →, Brazil 124 C5
İçel = Mersin, Turkey .. 70 D2
Iceland ■, Europe 8 D4
Ich'ang = Yichang, China 59 B8
Ichchapuram, India .. 67 K14
Ichhawar, India 68 H7
Ichihara, Japan 55 G10
Ichikawa, Japan 55 G9
Ichilo →, Bolivia 124 G6
Ichinohe, Japan 54 D10
Ichinomiya, Japan 55 G8
Ichinoseki, Japan 54 E10
Ichnya, Ukraine 47 G7
Ichŏn, S. Korea 57 F14
Icod, Canary Is. 37 F3
Ida Grove, U.S.A. 112 D7
Idabel, U.S.A. 113 J7
Idaga Hamus, Ethiopia .. 81 E4
Idah, Nigeria 83 D6
Idaho □, U.S.A. 114 D7
Idaho City, U.S.A. 114 E6
Idaho Falls, U.S.A. ... 114 E7
Idanha-a-Nova, Portugal .. 34 F3
Idar-Oberstein, Germany .. 25 F3
Idfû, Egypt 80 C3
Ídhi Óros, Greece 36 D6
Ídhra, Greece 38 D5
Idi, Indonesia 62 C1
Idiofa,
   Dem. Rep. of the Congo .. 84 E3
Idkerberget, Sweden .. 10 D9
Idku, Bahra el, Egypt .. 80 H7
Idlib, Syria 70 C3
Idre, Sweden 10 C6
Idria, U.S.A. 116 J6
Idrija, Slovenia 29 C11
Idritsa, Russia 46 D5
Idutywa, S. Africa 89 E4
Ieper, Belgium 17 D2
Ierápetra, Greece 36 E7
Ierissós, Greece 40 F7
Ierissoú Kólpos, Greece .. 40 F7
Iernut, Romania 43 D9
Iesi, Italy 29 E10
Iésolo, Italy 29 C9
Ifach, Peñón de, Spain .. 33 G5
Ifakara, Tanzania 84 F7
'Ifāl, W. al →, Si. Arabia 70 D2
Ifanadiana, Madag. ... 89 C8
Ife, Nigeria 83 D5
Iférouâne, Niger 83 B6
Iffley, Australia 94 B3
Ifni, Morocco 78 C3
Ifon, Nigeria 83 D6
Iforas, Adrar des, Mali .. 83 B5
Ifould, L., Australia .. 93 F5
Iganga, Uganda 86 B3
Igarapava, Brazil 125 H9
Igarka, Russia 50 C9
Igatimi, Paraguay 127 A4
Igbetti, Nigeria 83 D5
Igbo-Ora, Nigeria 83 D5
Igboho, Nigeria 83 D5
Igbor, Nigeria 83 D6
Iğdır, Turkey 73 C11
Igelfors, Sweden 11 F9
Iggesund, Sweden 10 C11
Iglésias, Italy 30 C1
Igloolik, Canada 101 B11
Igluligaarjuk, Canada .. 101 B10
'Igma, Gebel el, Egypt .. 80 B3
Ignace, Canada 102 C1
İğneada, Turkey 41 E11
İğneada Burnu, Turkey .. 41 E12
Igoumenítsa, Greece .. 38 B2
Igra, Russia 48 B11
Iguaçu →, Brazil 127 B5
Iguaçu, Cat. del, Brazil .. 127 B5
Iguaçu Falls = Iguaçu, Cat.
   del, Brazil 127 B5
Iguala, Mexico 119 D5
Igualada, Spain 32 D6
Iguassu = Iguaçu →, Brazil 127 B5
Iguatu, Brazil 125 E11
Iharana, Madag. 89 A9
Ihbulag, Mongolia ... 56 C4
Iheya-Shima, Japan .. 55 L3
Ihiala, Nigeria 83 D6
Ihosy, Madag. 89 C8
Ihotry, Farihy, Madag. .. 89 C7
Ihugh, Nigeria 83 D6
Ii, Finland 8 D21
Ii-Shima, Japan 55 L3
Iida, Japan 55 G8
Iijoki →, Finland 8 D21
Iisalmi, Finland 8 E22
Iiyama, Japan 55 F9
Iizuka, Japan 55 H5
Ijebu-Igbo, Nigeria .. 83 D5
Ijebu-Ode, Nigeria ... 83 D5
IJmuiden, Neths. 17 B4
IJssel →, Neths. 17 B5
IJsselmeer, Neths. ... 17 B5
Ijuí, Brazil 127 B5
Ijuí →, Brazil 127 B4
Ikalamavony, Madag. .. 89 C8
Ikale, Nigeria 83 D6
Ikaluktutiak, Canada .. 100 B9

Ikang, *Nigeria* 83 E6
Ikara, *Nigeria* 83 C6
Ikare, *Nigeria* 83 D6
Ikaría, *Greece* 39 D8
Ikast, *Denmark* 11 H3
Ikeda, *Japan* 55 G6
Ikeja, *Nigeria* 83 D5
Ikela,
Dem. Rep. of the Congo . 84 E4
Ikerre-Ekiti, *Nigeria* 83 D6
Ikhtiman, *Bulgaria* 40 D7
Iki, *Japan* 55 H4
Ikimba L., *Tanzania* 86 C3
İkire, *Nigeria* 83 D5
İkizdere, *Turkey* 73 B9
Ikom, *Nigeria* 83 D6
Ikongo, *Madag.* 89 C8
Ikopa →, *Madag.* 89 B8
Ikot Ekpene, *Nigeria* 83 D6
Ikungu, *Tanzania* 86 C3
Ikurun, *Nigeria* 83 D5
Ila, *Nigeria* 83 D5
Ilagan, *Phil.* 61 C4
Ilaka, *Madag.* 89 B8
Īlām, *Iran* 70 C5
Ilam, *Nepal* 69 F12
Ilam □, *Iran* 70 C5
Ilan, *Taiwan* 59 E13
Ilanskiy, *Russia* 51 D10
Ilaro, *Nigeria* 83 D5
Ilatane, *Niger* 83 B5
Iława, *Poland* 44 E6
Ile-à-la-Crosse, *Canada* 105 B7
Ile-à-la-Crosse, Lac, *Canada* 105 B7
Île-de-France □, *France* 19 D9
Ileanda, *Romania* 43 C8
Ilebo,
Dem. Rep. of the Congo . 84 E4
Ilek, *Russia* 50 D6
Ilero, *Nigeria* 83 D5
Ilesha, *Kwara, Nigeria* 83 D5
Ilesha, *Oyo, Nigeria* 83 D5
Ilford, *Canada* 105 B9
Ilfracombe, *Australia* 94 C3
Ilfracombe, *U.K.* 13 F3
Ilgaz, *Turkey* 72 B5
Ilgaz Dağları, *Turkey* 72 B5
Ilgın, *Turkey* 72 C4
Ílhavo, *Portugal* 34 E2
Ilhéus, *Brazil* 125 F11
Ili →, *Kazakstan* 50 E8
Ilia, *Romania* 42 E7
Ilia □, *Greece* 38 D3
Iliamna L., *U.S.A.* 100 C4
Iliç, *Turkey* 73 C8
Ilıca, *Turkey* 39 B9
Ilichevsk, *Azerbaijan* 73 C11
Iligan, *Phil.* 61 G6
Iligan Bay, *Phil.* 61 G6
Ilíki, L., *Greece* 38 C5
Ilin I., *Phil.* 61 E4
Iliodhrómia, *Greece* 38 B5
Ilion, *U.S.A.* 111 D9
Ilirska-Bistrica, *Slovenia* . . . 29 C11
Ilkeston, *U.K.* 12 E6
Ilkley, *U.K.* 12 D6
Illampu = Ancohuma,
Nevada, *Bolivia* 122 E4
Illana B., *Phil.* 61 H5
Illapel, *Chile* 126 C1
Ille-et-Vilaine □, *France* . . . 18 D5
Ille-sur-Têt, *France* 20 F6
Illéla, *Niger* 83 C6
Iller →, *Germany* 25 G5
Illertissen, *Germany* 25 G6
Illescas, *Spain* 34 E7
Illetas, *Spain* 37 B9
Illichivsk, *Ukraine* 47 J6
Illiers-Combray, *France* 18 D8
Illimani, Nevado, *Bolivia* . . 124 G5
Illinois □, *U.S.A.* 112 E10
Illinois →, *U.S.A.* 107 C8
Illium = Troy, *Turkey* 39 B8
Illizi, *Algeria* 78 C7
Illkirch-Graffenstaden,
France 19 D14
Illoqqortoormiit, *Greenland* 4 B6
Íllora, *Spain* 35 H7
Ilm →, *Germany* 24 D7
Ilmajoki, *Finland* 9 E20
Ilmen, Ozero, *Russia* 46 C6
Ilmenau, *Germany* 24 E6
Ilo, *Peru* 124 G4
Ilobu, *Nigeria* 83 D5
Iloilo, *Phil.* 61 F5
Ilora, *Nigeria* 83 D5
Ilorin, *Nigeria* 83 D5
Ilovatka, *Russia* 48 E7
Ilovlya, *Russia* 49 F7
Ilovlya →, *Russia* 49 F7
Iłowa, *Poland* 45 G2
Ilubabor □, *Ethiopia* 81 F4
Ilva Mică, *Romania* 43 C9
Ilwaco, *U.S.A.* 116 D2
Ilwaki, *Indonesia* 63 F7
Ilyichevsk = Illichivsk,
Ukraine 47 J6
Iłża, *Poland* 45 G8
Iłzanka →, *Poland* 45 G8
Imabari, *Japan* 55 G6
İmaloto →, *Madag.* 89 C8
İmamoğlu, *Turkey* 72 D6
Imandra, Ozero, *Russia* 50 C4
Imanombo, *Madag.* 89 C8
Imari, *Japan* 55 H4
Imasa, *Sudan* 80 D4
Imathía □, *Greece* 40 F6
Imatra, *Finland* 46 B5
Imbil, *Australia* 95 D5
Iménas, *Mali* 83 B5
imeni 26 Bakinskikh
Komissarov = Neftçala,
Azerbaijan 71 B6
imeni 26 Bakinskikh
Komissarov, *Turkmenistan* 71 B7
Imeri, Serra, *Brazil* 124 C5
Imerimandroso, *Madag.* . . . 89 B8
Imi, *Ethiopia* 81 F5
Imishly = Imişli, *Azerbaijan* 49 L9
Imişli, *Azerbaijan* 49 L9
Imlay, *U.S.A.* 114 F4
Imlay City, *U.S.A.* 110 D1
Immaseri, *Sudan* 81 D2
Immenstadt, *Germany* 25 H6
Immingham, *U.K.* 12 D7
Immokalee, *U.S.A.* 109 M5
Imo □, *Nigeria* 83 D6
Imo →, *Nigeria* 83 E6
Ímola, *Italy* 29 D8
Imotski, *Croatia* 29 E14
Imperatriz, *Brazil* 125 E9
Impéria, *Italy* 28 E5
Imperial, *Canada* 105 C7
Imperial, *Calif., U.S.A.* 117 N11
Imperial, *Nebr., U.S.A.* 112 E4
Imperial Beach, *U.S.A.* 117 N9
Imperial Dam, *U.S.A.* 117 N12
Imperial Reservoir, *U.S.A.* . 117 N12
Imperial Valley, *U.S.A.* 117 N11
Imperieuse Reef, *Australia* . 92 C2
Impfondo, *Congo* 84 D3
Imphal, *India* 67 G18
Imphy, *France* 19 F10
Imranlı, *Turkey* 73 C8
İmroz = Gökçeada, *Turkey* 41 F9
İmroz, *Turkey* 41 F9
Imst, *Austria* 26 D3
Imuris, *Mexico* 118 A2
Imuruan B., *Phil.* 63 B5
In Akhmed, *Mali* 83 B4
In-Aleï, *Mali* 82 B4
In Delimane, *Mali* 83 B5
In-Guezzam, *Niger* 83 B6
In Koufi, *Mali* 83 B5
In Salah, *Algeria* 78 C6
In Tallak, *Mali* 83 B5
In Tebezas, *Mali* 83 B5
Ina, *Japan* 55 G8
Inangahua Junction, *N.Z.* . . 91 J3
Inanwatan, *Indonesia* 63 E8
Iñapari, *Peru* 124 F5
Inari, *Finland* 8 B22
Inarijärvi, *Finland* 8 B22
Inawashiro-Ko, *Japan* 54 F10
Inca, *Spain* 37 B9
Inca de Oro, *Chile* 126 B2
Incaguasi, *Chile* 126 B1
İnce Burun, *Turkey* 72 A6
İncekum Burnu, *Turkey* . . . 72 D5
İncesu, *Turkey* 70 B2
Inch'ŏn, *S. Korea* 57 F14
İncio = Cruz de Incio, *Spain* 34 C3
İncirliova, *Turkey* 39 D9
Incline Village, *U.S.A.* 114 G4
Incomáti →, *Mozam.* 89 D5
Inda Silase, *Ethiopia* 81 E4
Indal, *Sweden* 10 B11
Indalsälven →, *Sweden* 10 B11
Indaw, *Burma* 67 G20
Indbir, *Ethiopia* 81 F4
Independence, *Calif., U.S.A.* 116 J8
Independence, *Iowa, U.S.A.* 112 D9
Independence, *Kans., U.S.A.* 113 G7
Independence, *Ky., U.S.A.* . 108 F3
Independence, *Mo., U.S.A.* 112 F7
Independence Fjord,
Greenland 4 A6
Independence Mts., *U.S.A.* . 114 F5
Independenţa, *Romania* 43 E12
Index, *U.S.A.* 116 C5
India ■, *Asia* 66 K11
Indian →, *U.S.A.* 109 M5
Indian Cabins, *Canada* 104 B5
Indian Harbour, *Canada* . . . 103 B8
Indian Head, *Canada* 105 C8
Indian Lake, *U.S.A.* 111 C10
Indian Ocean 52 K11
Indian Springs, *U.S.A.* 117 J11
Indiana, *U.S.A.* 110 F5
Indiana □, *U.S.A.* 108 F3
Indianapolis, *U.S.A.* 108 F2
Indianola, *Iowa, U.S.A.* . . . 112 E8
Indianola, *Miss., U.S.A.* . . . 113 J9
Indigirka →, *Russia* 51 B15
Indija, *Serbia, Yug.* 42 E5
Indio, *U.S.A.* 117 M10
Indo-China, *Asia* 52 H14
Indonesia ■, *Asia* 62 F5
Indore, *India* 68 H6
Indramayu, *Indonesia* 63 G13
Indravati →, *India* 67 K12
Indre □, *France* 19 F8
Indre →, *France* 18 E7
Indre-et-Loire □, *France* . . . 18 E7
Indulkana, *Australia* 95 D1
Indus →, *Pakistan* 68 G2
Indus, Mouth of the,
Pakistan 68 H3
İnebolu, *Turkey* 72 B5
İnecik, *Turkey* 41 F11
İnegöl, *Turkey* 41 F13
Ineu, *Romania* 42 D6
Infantes = Villanueva de los
Infantes, *Spain* 35 G7
Infiernillo, Presa del, *Mexico* 118 D4
Infiesto, *Spain* 34 B5
Ingelstad, *Sweden* 11 H8
Ingenio, *Canary Is.* 37 G4
Ingenio Santa Ana,
Argentina 126 B2
Ingersoll, *Canada* 102 D3
Ingham, *Australia* 94 B4
Ingleborough, *U.K.* 12 C5
Inglewood, *Queens.*,
Australia 95 D5
Inglewood, *Vic., Australia* . . 95 F3
Inglewood, *N.Z.* 91 H5
Inglewood, *U.S.A.* 117 M8
Ingólfshöfði, *Iceland* 8 E5
Ingolstadt, *Germany* 25 G7
Ingomar, *U.S.A.* 114 C10
Ingonish, *Canada* 103 C7
Ingore, *Guinea-Biss.* 82 C1
Ingraj Bazar, *India* 69 G13
Ingrid Christensen Coast,
Antarctica 5 C6
Ingul → = Inhul →,
Ukraine 47 J7
Ingulec = Inhulec, *Ukraine* . 47 J7
Ingulets → = Inhulets →,
Ukraine 47 J7
Inguri → = Enguri →,
Georgia 49 J5
Ingushetia □, *Russia* 49 J7
Ingwavuma, *S. Africa* 89 D5
Inhaca, *Mozam.* 89 D5
Inhafenga, *Mozam.* 89 C5
Inhambane, *Mozam.* 89 C6
Inhambane □, *Mozam.* 89 C5
Inhaminga, *Mozam.* 87 F4
Inharrime, *Mozam.* 89 C6
Inharrime →, *Mozam.* 89 C6
Inhisar, *Turkey* 39 A12
Inhul →, *Ukraine* 47 J7
Inhulec, *Ukraine* 47 J7
Inhulets →, *Ukraine* 47 J7
Iniesta, *Spain* 33 F3
Ining = Yining, *China* 50 E9
Inírida →, *Colombia* 124 C5
Inishbofin, *Ireland* 15 C1
Inisheer, *Ireland* 15 C2
Inishfree B., *Ireland* 15 A3
Inishkea North, *Ireland* 15 B1
Inishkea South, *Ireland* 15 B1
Inishmaan, *Ireland* 15 C2
Inishmore, *Ireland* 15 C2
Inishowen Pen., *Ireland* 15 A4
Inishshark, *Ireland* 15 C1
Inishturk, *Ireland* 15 C1
Inishvickillane, *Ireland* 15 D1
Injibara, *Ethiopia* 81 E4
Injune, *Australia* 95 D4
Inklin →, *Canada* 104 B2
Inle L., *Burma* 67 J20
Inlet, *U.S.A.* 111 C10
Inn →, *Austria* 26 C6
Innamincka, *Australia* 95 D3
Inner Hebrides, *U.K.* 14 E2
Inner Mongolia = Nei
Mongol Zizhiqu □, *China* 56 D7
Inner Sound, *U.K.* 14 D3
Innerkip, *Canada* 110 C4
Innetalling I., *Canada* 102 A4
Innisfail, *Australia* 94 B4
Innisfail, *Canada* 104 C6
In'no-shima, *Japan* 55 G6
Innsbruck, *Austria* 26 D4
Innviertel, *Austria* 26 C6
Inny →, *Ireland* 15 C4
Inongo,
Dem. Rep. of the Congo . 84 E3
İnönü, *Turkey* 39 B12
Inoucdjouac = Inukjuak,
Canada 101 C12
Inowrocław, *Poland* 45 F5
Inpundong, *N. Korea* 57 D14
Inscription, C., *Australia* . . . 93 E1
Insein, *Burma* 67 L20
Insjön, *Sweden* 10 D9
Ińsko, *Poland* 44 E2
Însurăţei, *Romania* 43 F12
Inta, *Russia* 50 C6
Intendente Alvear, *Argentina* 126 D3
Intepe, *Turkey* 39 A8
Interlaken, *Switz.* 25 J3
Interlaken, *U.S.A.* 111 D8
International Falls, *U.S.A.* . 112 A8
Intiyaco, *Argentina* 126 B3
Întorsura Buzăului, *Romania* 43 E11
Inukjuak, *Canada* 101 C12
Inútil, B., *Chile* 128 G2
Inuvik, *Canada* 100 B6
Inveraray, *U.K.* 14 E3
Inverbervie, *U.K.* 14 E6
Invercargill, *N.Z.* 91 M2
Inverclyde □, *U.K.* 14 F4
Inverell, *Australia* 95 D5
Invergordon, *U.K.* 14 D4
Inverloch, *Australia* 95 F4
Invermere, *Canada* 104 C5
Inverness, *Canada* 103 C7
Inverness, *U.K.* 14 D4
Inverness, *U.S.A.* 109 L4
Inverurie, *U.K.* 14 D6
Investigator Group, *Australia* 95 E1
Investigator Str., *Australia* . 95 F2
Inya, *Russia* 50 D9
Inyanga, *Zimbabwe* 87 F3
Inyangani, *Zimbabwe* 87 F3
Inyantue, *Zimbabwe* 88 B4
Inyo Mts., *U.S.A.* 116 J9
Inyokern, *U.S.A.* 117 K9
Inza, *Russia* 48 D8
Inzhavino, *Russia* 48 D6
Iō-Jima, *Japan* 55 J5
Ioánnina, *Greece* 38 B2
Ioánnina □, *Greece* 38 B2
Iola, *U.S.A.* 113 G7
Ion Corvin, *Romania* 43 F12
Iona, *U.K.* 14 E2
Ione, *U.S.A.* 116 G6
Ionia, *U.S.A.* 108 D3
Ionian Is. = Iónioi Nísoi,
Greece 38 C2
Ionian Sea, *Medit. S.* 6 H9
Iónioi Nísoi, *Greece* 38 C2
Iónioi Nísoi □, *Greece* 38 C2
Íos, *Greece* 39 E7
Iowa □, *U.S.A.* 112 D8
Iowa →, *U.S.A.* 112 E9
Iowa City, *U.S.A.* 112 E9
Iowa Falls, *U.S.A.* 112 D8
Iowa Park, *U.S.A.* 113 J5
Ipala, *Tanzania* 86 C3
Ipameri, *Brazil* 125 G9
Ipáti, *Greece* 38 C4
Ipatinga, *Brazil* 125 G10
Ipatovo, *Russia* 49 H6
Ipel' →, *Europe* 27 D11
Ipiales, *Colombia* 124 C3
Ipin = Yibin, *China* 58 C5
Ípiros □, *Greece* 38 B2
Ipixuna, *Brazil* 124 E4
Ipoh, *Malaysia* 65 K3
Ippy, *C.A.R.* 84 C4
Ipsala, *Turkey* 41 F10
Ipsárion, Óros, *Greece* 41 F8
Ipswich, *Australia* 95 D5
Ipswich, *U.K.* 13 E9
Ipswich, *Mass., U.S.A.* 111 D14
Ipswich, *S. Dak., U.S.A.* . . 112 C5
Ipu, *Brazil* 125 D10
Iqaluit, *Canada* 101 B13
Iquique, *Chile* 124 H4
Iquitos, *Peru* 124 D4
Irabu-Jima, *Japan* 55 M2
Iracoubo, *Fr. Guiana* 125 B8
Īrafshān, *Iran* 71 E9
Irahuan, *Phil.* 61 G3
Iráklia, *Kikládhes, Greece* . . 39 E7
Iráklia, *Sérrai, Greece* 40 E7
Iráklion, *Greece* 36 D7
Iráklion □, *Greece* 36 D7
Irala, *Paraguay* 127 B5
Iran ■, *Asia* 71 C7
Iran, Gunung-Gunung,
Malaysia 62 D4
Iran, Plateau of, *Asia* 52 F9
Iran Ra. = Iran, Gunung-
Gunung, *Malaysia* 62 D4
Īrānshahr, *Iran* 71 E9
Irapuato, *Mexico* 118 C4
Iraq ■, *Asia* 70 C5
Irati, *Brazil* 127 B5
Irbes saurums, *Latvia* 44 A9
Irbid, *Jordan* 75 C4
Irbid □, *Jordan* 75 C5
Iregua →, *Spain* 32 C7
Ireland ■, *Europe* 15 C4
Irele, *Nigeria* 83 D6
Irgiz, Bolshaya →, *Russia* . 48 D9
Irhyangdong, *N. Korea* 57 D15
Iri, *S. Korea* 57 G14
Irian Jaya □, *Indonesia* 63 E9
Irié, *Guinea* 82 D3
Iriga, *Phil.* 61 E5
Iringa, *Tanzania* 86 D4
Iringa □, *Tanzania* 86 D4
Iriomote-Jima, *Japan* 55 M1
Iriona, *Honduras* 120 C2
Iriri →, *Brazil* 125 D8
Irish Republic ■, *Europe* . . 15 C3
Irish Sea, *U.K.* 12 D3
Irkutsk, *Russia* 51 D11
Irlığanlı, *Turkey* 39 D11
Irma, *Canada* 105 C6
Irō-Zaki, *Japan* 55 G9
Iroise, Mer d', *France* 18 D2
Iron Baron, *Australia* 95 E2
Iron Gate = Portile de Fier,
Europe 42 F7
Iron Knob, *Australia* 95 E2
Iron Mountain, *U.S.A.* 108 C1
Iron River, *U.S.A.* 112 B10
Irondequoit, *U.S.A.* 110 C7
Ironton, *Mo., U.S.A.* 113 G9
Ironton, *Ohio, U.S.A.* 108 F4
Ironwood, *U.S.A.* 112 B9
Iroquois, *Canada* 111 B9
Iroquois Falls, *Canada* 102 C3
Irosin, *Phil.* 61 E6
Irpin, *Ukraine* 47 G6
Irrara Cr. →, *Australia* 95 D4
Irrawaddy □, *Burma* 67 L19
Irrawaddy →, *Burma* 67 M19
Irricana, *Canada* 104 C6
Irsina, *Italy* 31 B9
Irtysh →, *Russia* 50 C7
Irumu,
Dem. Rep. of the Congo . 86 B2
Irún, *Spain* 32 B3
Irunea = Pamplona, *Spain* . 32 C3
Irurzun, *Spain* 32 C3
Irvine, *Canada* 105 D6
Irvine, *U.K.* 14 F4
Irvine, *Calif., U.S.A.* 117 M9
Irvine, *Ky., U.S.A.* 108 G4
Irvinestown, *U.K.* 15 B4
Irving, *U.S.A.* 113 J6
Irvona, *U.S.A.* 110 F6
Irwin →, *Australia* 93 E1
Irymple, *Australia* 95 E3
Is, Jebel, *Sudan* 80 C4
Is-sur-Tille, *France* 19 E12
Isa, *Nigeria* 83 C6
Isa Khel, *Pakistan* 68 C4
Isaac →, *Australia* 94 C4
Isabel, *U.S.A.* 112 C4
Isabela, *Phil.* 61 H5
Isabela, I., *Mexico* 118 C3
Isabelia, Cord., *Nic.* 120 D2
Isabella Ra., *Australia* 92 D3
Isaccea, *Romania* 43 E13
Ísafjarðardjúp, *Iceland* 8 C2
Ísafjörður, *Iceland* 8 C2
Isagarh, *India* 68 G7
Isahaya, *Japan* 55 H5
Isaka, *Tanzania* 86 C3
Isakly, *Russia* 48 C10
Işalniţa, *Romania* 43 F8
Isan →, *India* 69 F9
Isana = Içana →, *Brazil* . . 124 C5
Isanlu Makutu, *Nigeria* 83 D6
Isar →, *Germany* 25 G8
Isarco →, *Italy* 29 B8
Ísari, *Greece* 38 D3
Íscar, *Spain* 34 D6
Iscehisar, *Turkey* 39 C12
Íschia, *Italy* 30 B6
Isdell →, *Australia* 92 C3
Ise, *Japan* 55 G8
Ise-Wan, *Japan* 55 G8
Isefjord, *Denmark* 11 J5
Isel →, *Austria* 26 E5
Iseo, *Italy* 28 C7
Iseo, L. d', *Italy* 28 C7
Iseramagazi, *Tanzania* 86 C3
Isère □, *France* 21 C9
Isère →, *France* 21 D8
Iserlohn, *Germany* 24 D3
Isérnia, *Italy* 31 A7
Iseyin, *Nigeria* 83 D5
Isfahan = Eşfahān, *Iran* 71 C6
Ishigaki-Shima, *Japan* 55 M2
Ishikari-Gawa →, *Japan* . . . 54 C10
Ishikari-Sammyaku, *Japan* . . 54 C11
Ishikari-Wan, *Japan* 54 C10
Ishikawa □, *Japan* 55 F8
Ishim, *Russia* 50 D7
Ishim →, *Russia* 50 D8
Ishinomaki, *Japan* 54 E10
Ishioka, *Japan* 55 F10
Ishkuman, *Pakistan* 69 A5
Ishmi, *Albania* 40 E3
Ishpeming, *U.S.A.* 108 B2
Isigny-sur-Mer, *France* 18 C5
Isıklar Dağı, *Turkey* 41 F11
Işıklı, *Turkey* 39 C11
Isil Kul, *Russia* 50 D8
Ísili, *Italy* 30 C2
Isiolo, *Kenya* 86 B4
Isiro,
Dem. Rep. of the Congo . 86 B2
Isisford, *Australia* 94 C3
İskenderun, *Turkey* 70 B3
İskenderun Körfezi, *Turkey* 72 D6
İskilip, *Turkey* 72 B6
Iskŭr →, *Bulgaria* 41 C8
Iskŭr, Yazovir, *Bulgaria* . . . 40 D7
Iskut →, *Canada* 104 B2
Isla →, *U.K.* 14 E5
Isla Cristina, *Spain* 35 H3
Isla Vista, *U.S.A.* 117 L7
İslâhiye, *Turkey* 72 D7
Islam Headworks, *Pakistan* . 68 E5
Islamabad, *Pakistan* 68 C5
Islamgarh, *Pakistan* 68 F4
Islamkot, *Pakistan* 68 G4
Islampur, *India* 69 G11
Island L., *Canada* 105 C10
Island Lagoon, *Australia* . . . 95 E2
Island Pond, *U.S.A.* 111 B13
Islands, B. of, *Canada* 103 C8
Islay, *U.K.* 14 F2
Isle →, *France* 20 D3
Isle aux Morts, *Canada* 103 C8
Isle of Wight □, *U.K.* 13 G6
Isle Royale, *U.S.A.* 112 B10
Isle Royale National Park,
U.S.A. 112 B10
Isleton, *U.S.A.* 116 G5
Ismail = Izmayil, *Ukraine* . . 47 K5
Ismâ'ilîya, *Egypt* 80 H8
Ismaning, *Germany* 25 G7
Isna, *Egypt* 80 B3
Isoanala, *Madag.* 89 C8
Isogstalo, *India* 69 B8
Ísola del Liri, *Italy* 29 G10
Ísola della Scala, *Italy* 28 C7
Ísola di Capo Rizzuto, *Italy* 31 D10
Isparta, *Turkey* 39 D12
Isperikh, *Bulgaria* 41 C10
Íspica, *Italy* 31 F7
Israel ■, *Asia* 75 D3
Isratu, *Eritrea* 81 D4
Issia, *Ivory C.* 82 D3
Issoire, *France* 20 C7
Issoudun, *France* 19 F8
Issyk-Kul, Ozero = Ysyk-
Köl, Ozero, *Kyrgyzstan* . . 50 E8
Ist, *Croatia* 29 D11
Istállós-kő, *Hungary* 42 B5
İstanbul, *Turkey* 41 E12
İstanbul □, *Turkey* 41 E12
İstanbul Boğazı, *Turkey* 41 E13
Istiaía, *Greece* 38 C5
Istok, *Kosovo, Yug.* 40 D4
Istokpoga, L., *U.S.A.* 109 M5
Istra, *Croatia* 29 C10
Istres, *France* 21 E8
Istria = Istra, *Croatia* 29 C10
Itá, *Paraguay* 126 B4
Itaberaba, *Brazil* 125 F10
Itabira, *Brazil* 125 G10
Itabirito, *Brazil* 127 A7
Itabuna, *Brazil* 125 F11
Itacaunas →, *Brazil* 125 E9
Itacoatiara, *Brazil* 124 D7
Itaipú, Reprêsa de, *Brazil* . . 127 B5
Itaituba, *Brazil* 125 D7
Itajaí, *Brazil* 127 B6
Itajubá, *Brazil* 127 A6

Itaka, *Tanzania* 87 D3
Italy ■, *Europe* 7 G8
Itamaraju, *Brazil* 125 G11
Itampolo, *Madag.* 89 C7
Itandrano, *Madag.* 89 C8
Itapecuru-Mirim, *Brazil* 125 D10
Itaperuna, *Brazil* 127 A7
Itapetininga, *Brazil* 127 A6
Itapeva, *Brazil* 127 A6
Itapicuru →, *Bahia, Brazil* 125 F11
Itapicuru →, *Maranhão, Brazil* 125 D10
Itapipoca, *Brazil* 125 D11
Itapuá □, *Paraguay* 127 B4
Itaquari, *Brazil* 127 A7
Itaquí, *Brazil* 126 B4
Itararé, *Brazil* 127 A6
Itarsi, *India* 68 H7
Itatí, *Argentina* 126 B4
Itbayat, *Phil.* 61 A4
Itchen →, *U.K.* 13 G6
Itéa, *Greece* 38 C4
Itezhi Tezhi, L., *Zambia* 87 F2
Ithaca = Itháki, *Greece* 38 C2
Ithaca, *U.S.A.* 111 D8
Itháki, *Greece* 38 C2
Itiquira →, *Brazil* 125 G7
Ito, *Japan* 55 G9
Ito Aba I., *S. China Sea* 62 B4
Itoigawa, *Japan* 55 F8
Iton →, *France* 18 C8
Itonamas →, *Bolivia* 124 F6
Itri, *Italy* 30 A6
Itsa, *Egypt* 80 J7
Ittiri, *Italy* 30 B1
Itu, *Brazil* 127 A6
Itu, *Nigeria* 83 D6
Ituiutaba, *Brazil* 125 G9
Itumbiara, *Brazil* 125 G9
Ituna, *Canada* 105 C8
Itunge Port, *Tanzania* 87 D3
Iturbe, *Argentina* 126 A2
Ituri →, *Dem. Rep. of the Congo* 86 B2
Iturup, Ostrov, *Russia* 51 E15
Ituxi →, *Brazil* 124 E6
Ituyuro →, *Argentina* 126 A3
Itzehoe, *Germany* 24 B5
Ivahona, *Madag.* 89 C8
Ivaí →, *Brazil* 127 A5
Ivalo, *Finland* 8 B22
Ivalojoki →, *Finland* 8 B22
Ivanava, *Belarus* 47 F3
Ivančice, *Czech Rep.* 27 B9
Ivăneşti, *Romania* 43 D12
Ivangorod, *Russia* 46 C5
Ivanhoe, *Australia* 95 E3
Ivanhoe, *Calif., U.S.A.* 116 J7
Ivanhoe, *Minn., U.S.A.* 112 C6
Ivanić Grad, *Croatia* 29 C13
Ivanjica, *Serbia, Yug.* 40 C4
Ivanjska, *Bos.-H.* 42 F2
Ivankoyskoye Vdkhr., *Russia* 46 D9
Ivano-Frankivsk, *Ukraine* 47 H3
Ivano-Frankovsk = Ivano-Frankivsk, *Ukraine* 47 H3
Ivanovo = Ivanava, *Belarus* 47 F3
Ivanovo, *Russia* 46 D11
Ivanšćica, *Croatia* 29 B13
Ivato, *Madag.* 89 C8
Ivatsevichy, *Belarus* 47 F3
Ivaylovgrad, *Bulgaria* 41 E10
Ivinheima →, *Brazil* 127 A5
Ivinhema, *Brazil* 127 A5
Ivohibe, *Madag.* 89 C8
Ivory Coast, *W. Afr.* 82 E4
Ivory Coast ■, *Africa* 82 D4
Ivösjön, *Sweden* 11 H8
Ivrea, *Italy* 28 C4
Ivrindi, *Turkey* 39 B9
Ivujivik, *Canada* 101 B12
Ivybridge, *U.K.* 13 G4
Iwaizumi, *Japan* 54 E10
Iwaki, *Japan* 55 F10
Iwakuni, *Japan* 55 G6
Iwamizawa, *Japan* 54 C10
Iwanai, *Japan* 54 C10
Iwata, *Japan* 55 G8
Iwate □, *Japan* 54 E10
Iwate-San, *Japan* 54 E10
Iwo, *Nigeria* 83 D5
Iwonicz-Zdrój, *Poland* 45 J8
Ixiamas, *Bolivia* 124 F5
Ixopo, *S. Africa* 89 E5
Ixtepec, *Mexico* 119 D5
Ixtlán del Río, *Mexico* 118 C4
Iyal Bakhit, *Sudan* 81 E2
Iyo, *Japan* 55 H6
Izabal, L. de, *Guatemala* 120 C2
Izamal, *Mexico* 119 C7
Izberbash, *Russia* 49 J8
Izbica, *Poland* 45 H10
Izbica Kujawska, *Poland* 45 F5
Izbiceni, *Romania* 43 G9
Izena-Shima, *Japan* 55 L3
Izgrev, *Bulgaria* 41 C10
Izhevsk, *Russia* 50 D6
Izmayil, *Ukraine* 47 K5
İzmir, *Turkey* 39 C9
İzmir □, *Turkey* 39 C9
İzmir Körfezi, *Turkey* 39 C8
İzmit = Kocaeli, *Turkey* 41 F13
Iznájar, *Spain* 35 H6
Iznalloz, *Spain* 35 H7
İznik, *Turkey* 72 B3
İznik Gölü, *Turkey* 41 F13
Izobil'nyy, *Russia* 49 H5
Izola, *Slovenia* 29 C10
Izra, *Syria* 75 C5
Iztochni Rodopi, *Bulgaria* 41 E9
Izu-Shotō, *Japan* 55 G10
Izúcar de Matamoros, *Mexico* 119 D5
Izumi-sano, *Japan* 55 G7
Izumo, *Japan* 55 G6
Izyaslav, *Ukraine* 47 G4
Izyum, *Ukraine* 47 H9

J

Jaba, *Ethiopia* 81 F4
Jabal al Awliyā, *Sudan* 81 D3
Jabal at Tā'ir, *Eritrea* 81 D5
Jabalón →, *Spain* 35 G6
Jabalpur, *India* 69 H8
Jabbūl, *Syria* 70 B3
Jabiru, *Australia* 92 B5
Jablah, *Syria* 70 C3
Jablanac, *Croatia* 29 D11
Jablanica, *Bos.-H.* 42 G2
Jablonec nad Nisou, *Czech Rep.* 26 A8
Jablonica, *Slovak Rep.* 27 C10
Jabłonowo Pomorskie, *Poland* 44 E6
Jablunkov, *Czech Rep.* 27 B11
Jaboatão, *Brazil* 125 E11
Jaboticabal, *Brazil* 127 A6
Jabukovac, *Serbia, Yug.* 40 B6
Jaca, *Spain* 32 C4
Jacareí, *Brazil* 127 A6
Jacarèzinho, *Brazil* 127 A6
Jackman, *U.S.A.* 109 C10
Jacksboro, *U.S.A.* 113 J5
Jackson, *Ala., U.S.A.* 109 K2
Jackson, *Calif., U.S.A.* 116 G6
Jackson, *Ky., U.S.A.* 108 G4
Jackson, *Mich., U.S.A.* 108 D3
Jackson, *Minn., U.S.A.* 112 D7
Jackson, *Miss., U.S.A.* 113 J9
Jackson, *Mo., U.S.A.* 113 G10
Jackson, *N.H., U.S.A.* 111 B13
Jackson, *Ohio, U.S.A.* 108 F4
Jackson, *Tenn., U.S.A.* 109 H1
Jackson, *Wyo., U.S.A.* 114 E8
Jackson B., *N.Z.* 91 K2
Jackson L., *U.S.A.* 114 E8
Jacksons, *N.Z.* 91 K3
Jackson's Arm, *Canada* 103 C8
Jacksonville, *Ala., U.S.A.* 109 J3
Jacksonville, *Ark., U.S.A.* 113 H8
Jacksonville, *Calif., U.S.A.* 116 H6
Jacksonville, *Fla., U.S.A.* 109 K5
Jacksonville, *Ill., U.S.A.* 112 F9
Jacksonville, *N.C., U.S.A.* 109 H7
Jacksonville, *Tex., U.S.A.* 113 K7
Jacksonville Beach, *U.S.A.* 109 K5
Jacmel, *Haiti* 121 C5
Jacob Lake, *U.S.A.* 115 H7
Jacobabad, *Pakistan* 68 E3
Jacobina, *Brazil* 125 F10
Jacques Cartier, Dét. de, *Canada* 103 C7
Jacques-Cartier, Mt., *Canada* 103 C6
Jacques Cartier, Parc Prov., *Canada* 103 C5
Jacqueville, *Ivory C.* 82 D4
Jacuí →, *Brazil* 127 C5
Jacumba, *U.S.A.* 117 N10
Jacundá →, *Brazil* 125 D8
Jade, *Germany* 24 B4
Jadebusen, *Germany* 24 B4
Jadotville = Likasi, *Dem. Rep. of the Congo* 87 E2
Jadovnik, *Serbia, Yug.* 40 C3
Jadraque, *Spain* 32 E2
Jaén, *Peru* 124 E3
Jaén, *Spain* 35 H7
Jaén □, *Spain* 35 H7
Jafarabad, *India* 68 J4
Jaffa = Tel Aviv-Yafo, *Israel* 75 C3
Jaffa, C., *Australia* 95 F2
Jaffna, *Sri Lanka* 66 Q12
Jaffrey, *U.S.A.* 111 D12
Jagadhri, *India* 68 D7
Jagadishpur, *India* 69 G11
Jagdalpur, *India* 67 K13
Jagersfontein, *S. Africa* 88 D4
Jaghīn →, *Iran* 71 E8
Jagodina, *Serbia, Yug.* 40 B5
Jagraon, *India* 66 D9
Jagst →, *Germany* 25 F5
Jagtial, *India* 66 K11
Jaguariaíva, *Brazil* 127 A6
Jaguaribe →, *Brazil* 125 D11
Jagüey Grande, *Cuba* 120 B3
Jahanabad, *India* 69 G11
Jahazpur, *India* 68 G6
Jahrom, *Iran* 71 D7
Jaijon, *India* 68 D7
Jailolo, *Indonesia* 63 D7
Jailolo, Selat, *Indonesia* 63 D7
Jaipur, *India* 68 F6
Jais, *India* 69 F9
Jaisalmer, *India* 68 F4
Jaisinghnagar, *India* 69 H8
Jaitaran, *India* 68 F5
Jaithari, *India* 69 H8
Jājarm, *Iran* 71 B8
Jajce, *Bos.-H.* 42 F2
Jakam →, *India* 68 H6
Jakarta, *Indonesia* 63 G12
Jakhal, *India* 68 E6
Jakhau, *India* 68 H3
Jakobstad = Pietarsaari, *Finland* 8 E20
Jakupica, *Macedonia* 40 E5
Jal, *U.S.A.* 113 J3
Jalalabad, *Afghan.* 68 B4
Jalalabad, *India* 69 F8
Jalalpur Jattan, *Pakistan* 68 C6
Jalama, *U.S.A.* 117 L6
Jalapa, *Guatemala* 120 D2
Jalapa Enríquez, *Mexico* 119 D5
Jalasjärvi, *Finland* 9 E20
Jalaun, *India* 69 F8
Jaldhaka →, *Bangla.* 69 F13
Jalesar, *India* 68 F8
Jaleswar, *Nepal* 69 F11
Jalgaon, *Maharashtra, India* 66 J10
Jalgaon, *Maharashtra, India* 66 J9
Jalībah, *Iraq* 70 D5
Jalingo, *Nigeria* 83 D7
Jalisco □, *Mexico* 118 D4
Jalkot, *Pakistan* 69 B5
Jallas →, *Spain* 34 C1
Jalna, *India* 66 K9
Jalón →, *Spain* 32 D3
Jalor, *India* 68 G5
Jalpa, *Mexico* 118 C4
Jalpaiguri, *India* 67 F16
Jaluit I., *Marshall Is.* 96 G8
Jalūlā, *Iraq* 70 C5
Jamaari, *Nigeria* 83 C6
Jamaica ■, *W. Indies* 120 C4
Jamalpur, *Bangla.* 67 G16
Jamalpur, *India* 69 G12
Jamalpurganj, *India* 69 H13
Jamanxim →, *Brazil* 125 D7
Jambi, *Indonesia* 62 E2
Jambi □, *Indonesia* 62 E2
Jambusar, *India* 68 H5
James →, *S. Dak., U.S.A.* 112 D6
James →, *Va., U.S.A.* 108 G7
James B., *Canada* 102 B3
James Ranges, *Australia* 92 D5
James Ross I., *Antarctica* 5 C18
Jamesabad, *Pakistan* 68 G3
Jamestown, *Australia* 95 E2
Jamestown, *S. Africa* 88 E4
Jamestown, *N. Dak., U.S.A.* 112 B5
Jamestown, *N.Y., U.S.A.* 110 D5
Jamestown, *Pa., U.S.A.* 110 E4
Jamīlābād, *Iran* 71 C6
Jamiltepec, *Mexico* 119 D5
Jamira →, *India* 69 J13
Jämjö, *Sweden* 11 H9
Jamkhandi, *India* 66 L9
Jammerbugt, *Denmark* 11 G3
Jammu, *India* 68 C6
Jammu & Kashmir □, *India* 69 B7
Jamnagar, *India* 68 H4
Jamni →, *India* 69 G8
Jampur, *Pakistan* 68 E4
Jamrud, *Pakistan* 68 C4
Jämsä, *Finland* 9 F21
Jamshedpur, *India* 69 H12
Jamtara, *India* 69 H12
Jämtland, *Sweden* 8 E15
Jämtlands län □, *Sweden* 10 B7
Jan L., *Canada* 105 C8
Jan Mayen, *Arctic* 4 B7
Janakkala, *Finland* 9 F21
Janaúba, *Brazil* 125 G10
Jand, *Pakistan* 68 C5
Jandaq, *Iran* 71 C7
Jandia, *Canary Is.* 37 F5
Jandia, Pta. de, *Canary Is.* 37 F5
Jandola, *Pakistan* 68 C4
Jandowae, *Australia* 95 D5
Jándula →, *Spain* 35 G6
Janesville, *U.S.A.* 112 D10
Janga, *Ghana* 83 C4
Jangamo, *Mozam.* 89 C6
Janghai, *India* 69 G10
Janikowo, *Poland* 45 F5
Janīn, *West Bank* 75 C4
Janinà = Ioánnina □, *Greece* 38 B2
Janja, *Bos.-H.* 42 F4
Janjevo, *Kosovo, Yug.* 40 D5
Janjgir, *India* 69 J10
Janjina, *Croatia* 29 F14
Janjina, *Madag.* 89 C8
Janos, *Mexico* 118 A3
Jánoshalma, *Hungary* 42 D4
Jánosháza, *Hungary* 42 C2
Jánossomorja, *Hungary* 42 C2
Janów, *Poland* 45 H6
Janów Lubelski, *Poland* 45 H9
Janów Podlaski, *Poland* 45 F10
Janowiec Wielkopolski, *Poland* 45 F4
Januária, *Brazil* 125 G10
Janub Dârfûr □, *Sudan* 81 E2
Janub Kordofân □, *Sudan* 81 E3
Janubio, *Canary Is.* 37 F6
Janville, *France* 19 D8
Janzé, *France* 18 E5
Jaora, *India* 68 H6
Japan ■, *Asia* 55 G8
Japan, Sea of, *Asia* 54 E7
Japan Trench, *Pac. Oc.* 52 F18
Japen = Yapen, *Indonesia* 63 E9
Japla, *India* 69 G11
Japurá →, *Brazil* 122 D4
Jaquarão, *Brazil* 127 C5
Jaqué, *Panama* 120 E4
Jarābulus, *Syria* 70 B3
Jaraicejo, *Spain* 35 F5
Jaraíz de la Vera, *Spain* 34 E5
Jarama →, *Spain* 34 E7
Jaramānah, *Syria* 72 F7
Jarandilla, *Spain* 34 E5
Jaranwala, *Pakistan* 68 D5
Jarash, *Jordan* 75 C4
Järbo, *Sweden* 10 D10
Jardim, *Brazil* 126 A4
Jardín →, *Spain* 33 G2
Jardines de la Reina, Arch. de los, *Cuba* 120 B4
Jargalang, *China* 57 C12
Jargalant = Hovd, *Mongolia* 60 B4
Jari →, *Brazil* 125 D8
Jarīr, W. al →, *Si. Arabia* 70 E4
Järlåsa, *Sweden* 10 E11
Jarmen, *Germany* 24 B9
Järna, *Kopparberg, Sweden* 10 D8
Järna, *Stockholm, Sweden* 10 E11
Jarnac, *France* 20 C3
Jarny, *France* 19 C12
Jarocin, *Poland* 45 G4
Jaroměř, *Czech Rep.* 26 A8
Jarosław, *Poland* 45 H9
Järpås, *Sweden* 11 F6
Järpen, *Sweden* 10 A7
Jarrahdale, *Australia* 93 F2
Jarrahi →, *Iran* 71 D6
Jarres, Plaine des, *Laos* 64 C4
Jarso, *Ethiopia* 81 F4
Jartai, *China* 56 E3
Jarud Qi, *China* 57 B11
Järvenpää, *Finland* 9 F21
Jarvis, *Canada* 110 D4
Jarvis I., *Pac. Oc.* 97 H12
Jarvorník, *Czech Rep.* 27 A10
Järvsö, *Sweden* 10 C10
Jarwa, *India* 69 F10
Jaša Tomić, *Serbia, Yug.* 42 E5
Jasdan, *India* 68 H4
Jashpurnagar, *India* 69 H11
Jasidih, *India* 69 G12
Jasień, *Poland* 45 G2
Jāsimīyah, *Iraq* 70 C5
Jasin, *Malaysia* 65 L4
Jāsk, *Iran* 71 E8
Jasło, *Poland* 45 J8
Jasmund, *Germany* 24 A9
Jaso, *India* 69 G9
Jasper, *Alta., Canada* 104 C5
Jasper, *Ont., Canada* 111 B9
Jasper, *Ala., U.S.A.* 109 J2
Jasper, *Fla., U.S.A.* 109 K4
Jasper, *Ind., U.S.A.* 108 F2
Jasper, *Tex., U.S.A.* 113 K8
Jasper Nat. Park, *Canada* 104 C5
Jasrasar, *India* 68 F5
Jastarnia, *Poland* 44 D5
Jastrebarsko, *Croatia* 29 C12
Jastrowie, *Poland* 44 E3
Jastrzębie Zdrój, *Poland* 45 J5
Jász-Nagykun-Szolnok □, *Hungary* 42 C5
Jászapáti, *Hungary* 42 C5
Jászárokszállás, *Hungary* 42 C4
Jászberény, *Hungary* 42 C4
Jászkisér, *Hungary* 42 C5
Jászladány, *Hungary* 42 C5
Jataí, *Brazil* 125 G8
Jati, *Pakistan* 68 G3
Jatibarang, *Indonesia* 63 G13
Jatinegara, *Indonesia* 63 G12
Játiva = Xátiva, *Spain* 33 G4
Jättendal, *Sweden* 10 C11
Jaú, *Brazil* 127 A6
Jauja, *Peru* 124 F3
Jaunpur, *India* 69 G10
Java = Jawa, *Indonesia* 63 G14
Java Barat □, *Indonesia* 63 G12
Java Sea, *Indonesia* 62 E3
Java Tengah □, *Indonesia* 63 G14
Java Timur □, *Indonesia* 63 G15
Java Trench, *Ind. Oc.* 62 F3
Javalambre, Sa. de, *Spain* 32 E4
Jávea, *Spain* 33 G5
Javhlant = Uliastay, *Mongolia* 60 B4
Jawa, *Indonesia* 63 G14
Jawad, *India* 68 G6
Jawor, *Poland* 45 G3
Jaworzno, *Poland* 45 H6
Jaworzyna Śląska, *Poland* 45 H3
Jay Peak, *U.S.A.* 111 B12
Jaya, Puncak, *Indonesia* 63 E9
Jayanti, *India* 67 F16
Jayapura, *Indonesia* 63 E10
Jayawijaya, Pegunungan, *Indonesia* 63 E9
Jaynagar, *India* 67 F15
Jayrūd, *Syria* 70 C3
Jayton, *U.S.A.* 113 J4
Jāz Mūrīān, Hāmūn-e, *Iran* 71 E8
Jazīreh-ye Shīf, *Iran* 71 D6
Jazminal, *Mexico* 118 C4
Jazzīn, *Lebanon* 75 B4
Jean, *U.S.A.* 117 K11
Jean Marie River, *Canada* 104 A4
Jean Rabel, *Haiti* 121 C5
Jeanerette, *U.S.A.* 113 L9
Jeanette, Ostrov = Zhannetty, Ostrov, *Russia* 51 B16
Jeannette, *U.S.A.* 110 F5
Jebāl Bārez, Kūh-e, *Iran* 71 D8
Jebba, *Nigeria* 83 D5
Jebel, Bahr el →, *Sudan* 81 F3
Jebel Dud, *Sudan* 81 E3
Jebel Qerri, *Sudan* 81 D3
Jedburgh, *U.K.* 14 F6
Jedda = Jiddah, *Si. Arabia* 74 C2
Jeddore L., *Canada* 103 C8
Jedlicze, *Poland* 45 J8
Jędrzejów, *Poland* 45 H7
Jedwabne, *Poland* 45 E9
Jeetzel →, *Germany* 24 B7
Jefferson, *Iowa, U.S.A.* 112 D7
Jefferson, *Ohio, U.S.A.* 110 E4
Jefferson, *Tex., U.S.A.* 113 J7
Jefferson, Mt., *Nev., U.S.A.* 114 G5
Jefferson, Mt., *Oreg., U.S.A.* 114 D3
Jefferson City, *Mo., U.S.A.* 112 F8
Jefferson City, *Tenn., U.S.A.* 109 G4
Jeffersontown, *U.S.A.* 108 F3
Jeffersonville, *U.S.A.* 108 F3
Jeffrey City, *U.S.A.* 114 E10
Jega, *Nigeria* 83 C5
Jēkabpils, *Latvia* 9 H21
Jekyll I., *U.S.A.* 109 K5
Jelcz-Laskowice, *Poland* 45 G4
Jelenia Góra, *Poland* 45 H2
Jelgava, *Latvia* 9 H20
Jelgava □, *Latvia* 44 B10
Jelica, *Serbia, Yug.* 40 C4
Jelli, *Sudan* 81 F3
Jelšava, *Slovak Rep.* 27 C13
Jemaja, *Indonesia* 65 L5
Jemaluang, *Malaysia* 65 L4
Jember, *Indonesia* 63 H15
Jembongan, *Malaysia* 62 C5
Jena, *Germany* 24 E7
Jena, *U.S.A.* 113 K8
Jenbach, *Austria* 26 D4
Jenkins, *U.S.A.* 108 G4
Jenner, *U.S.A.* 116 G3
Jennings, *U.S.A.* 113 K8
Jepara, *Indonesia* 63 G14
Jeparit, *Australia* 95 F3
Jequié, *Brazil* 125 F10
Jequitinhonha, *Brazil* 125 G10
Jequitinhonha →, *Brazil* 125 G11
Jerantut, *Malaysia* 65 L4
Jérémie, *Haiti* 121 C5
Jerez, Punta, *Mexico* 119 C5
Jerez de García Salinas, *Mexico* 118 C4
Jerez de la Frontera, *Spain* 35 J4
Jerez de los Caballeros, *Spain* 35 G4
Jericho = El Arīḥā, *West Bank* 75 D4
Jericho, *Australia* 94 C4
Jerichow, *Germany* 24 C8
Jerilderie, *Australia* 95 F4
Jermyn, *U.S.A.* 111 E9
Jerome, *U.S.A.* 114 E6
Jerramungup, *Australia* 93 F2
Jersey, *U.K.* 13 H5
Jersey City, *U.S.A.* 111 F10
Jersey Shore, *U.S.A.* 110 E7
Jerseyville, *U.S.A.* 112 F9
Jerusalem, *Israel* 75 D4
Jervis B., *Australia* 95 F5
Jervis Inlet, *Canada* 104 C4
Jerzu, *Italy* 30 C2
Jesenice, *Slovenia* 29 B11
Jeseník, *Czech Rep.* 27 A10
Jesenké, *Slovak Rep.* 27 C13
Jesselton = Kota Kinabalu, *Malaysia* 62 C5
Jessnitz, *Germany* 24 D8
Jessore, *Bangla.* 67 H16
Jesup, *U.S.A.* 109 K5
Jesús Carranza, *Mexico* 119 D5
Jesús María, *Argentina* 126 C3
Jetmore, *U.S.A.* 113 F5
Jetpur, *India* 68 J4
Jeumont, *France* 19 B11
Jevnaker, *Norway* 9 F14
Jewett, *U.S.A.* 110 F3
Jewett City, *U.S.A.* 111 E13
Jeyḩūnābād, *Iran* 71 C6
Jeypore, *India* 67 K13
Jeziorak, Jezioro, *Poland* 44 E6
Jeziorany, *Poland* 44 E7
Jeziorka →, *Poland* 45 F8
Jha Jha, *India* 69 G12
Jhabua, *India* 68 H6
Jhajjar, *India* 68 E7
Jhal, *Pakistan* 68 E2
Jhal Jhao, *Pakistan* 66 F4
Jhalawar, *India* 68 G7
Jhalida, *India* 69 H11
Jhalrapatan, *India* 68 G7
Jhang Maghiana, *Pakistan* 68 D5
Jhansi, *India* 69 G8
Jhargram, *India* 69 H12
Jharia, *India* 69 H12
Jharsuguda, *India* 67 J14
Jhelum, *Pakistan* 68 C5
Jhelum →, *Pakistan* 68 D5
Jhilmilli, *India* 69 H10
Jhudo, *Pakistan* 68 G3
Jhunjhunu, *India* 68 E6
Ji-Paraná, *Brazil* 124 F6
Ji Xian, *Hebei, China* 56 F8
Ji Xian, *Henan, China* 56 G8
Ji Xian, *Shanxi, China* 56 F6
Jia Xian, *Henan, China* 56 H7
Jia Xian, *Shaanxi, China* 56 E6
Jiading, *China* 59 B13
Jiahe, *China* 59 E9
Jialing Jiang →, *China* 58 C6
Jiamusi, *China* 60 B8
Ji'an, *Jiangxi, China* 59 D10
Ji'an, *Jilin, China* 57 D14
Jianchang, *China* 57 D11
Jianchangying, *China* 57 D10
Jianchuan, *China* 58 D2
Jiande, *China* 59 C12
Jiang'an, *China* 58 C5
Jiangbei, *China* 58 C6
Jiangcheng, *China* 58 F3
Jiangchuan, *China* 58 E4
Jiangdi, *China* 58 D4
Jiangdu, *China* 59 A12
Jiange, *China* 58 A5
Jianghua, *China* 59 E8
Jiangjin, *China* 58 C6
Jiangkou, *China* 58 D7
Jiangle, *China* 59 D11
Jiangling, *China* 59 B9

Jiangmen, *China* 59 F9
Jiangning, *China* 59 B12
Jiangshan, *China* 59 C12
Jiangsu □, *China* 57 H11
Jiangxi □, *China* 59 D11
Jiangyan, *China* 59 A13
Jiangyin, *China* 59 B13
Jiangyong, *China* 59 E8
Jiangyou, *China* 58 B5
Jianhe, *China* 58 D7
Jianli, *China* 59 C9
Jianning, *China* 59 D11
Jian'ou, *China* 59 D12
Jianshi, *China* 58 B7
Jianshui, *China* 58 F4
Jianyang, *Fujian, China* 59 D12
Jianyang, *Sichuan, China* 58 B5
Jiao Xian = Jiaozhou, *China* 57 F11
Jiaohe, *Hebei, China* 56 E9
Jiaohe, *Jilin, China* 57 C14
Jiaojiang, *China* 59 C13
Jiaoling, *China* 59 E11
Jiaozhou, *China* 57 F11
Jiaozhou Wan, *China* 57 F11
Jiaozuo, *China* 56 G7
Jiashan, *China* 59 B13
Jiawang, *China* 57 G9
Jiaxiang, *China* 56 G9
Jiaxing, *China* 59 B13
Jiayi = Chiai, *Taiwan* 59 F13
Jiayu, *China* 59 C9
Jibiya, *Nigeria* 83 C6
Jibou, *Romania* 43 C8
Jibuti = Djibouti ■, *Africa* 81 E5
Jicarón, I., *Panama* 120 E3
Jičín, *Czech Rep.* 26 A8
Jiddah, *Si. Arabia* 74 C2
Jido, *India* 67 E19
Jieshou, *China* 56 H8
Jiexiu, *China* 56 F6
Jieyang, *China* 59 F11
Jigawa □, *Nigeria* 83 C6
Jiggalong, *Australia* 92 D3
Jigni, *India* 69 G8
Jihlava, *Czech Rep.* 26 B8
Jihlava →, *Czech Rep.* 27 C9
Jihočeský □, *Czech Rep.* 26 B7
Jihomoravský □, *Czech Rep.* 27 B9
Jijiga, *Ethiopia* 74 F3
Jikamshi, *Nigeria* 83 C6
Jikau, *Sudan* 81 F3
Jilin, *China* 57 C14
Jilin □, *China* 57 C14
Jiloca →, *Spain* 32 D3
Jilong = Chilung, *Taiwan* 59 E13
Jim Thorpe, *U.S.A.* 111 F9
Jima, *Ethiopia* 81 F4
Jimbolia, *Romania* 42 E5
Jimena de la Frontera, *Spain* 35 J5
Jiménez, *Mexico* 118 B4
Jimo, *China* 57 F11
Jin Jiang →, *China* 59 C10
Jin Xian = Jinzhou, *China* 56 E8
Jin Xian, *China* 57 E11
Jinan, *China* 56 F9
Jincheng, *China* 56 G7
Jinchuan, *China* 58 B4
Jind, *India* 68 E7
Jindabyne, *Australia* 95 F4
Jindřichův Hradec, *Czech Rep.* 26 B8
Jing He →, *China* 56 G5
Jing Shan, *China* 59 B8
Jing Xian, *China* 59 B12
Jing'an, *China* 59 C10
Jingbian, *China* 56 F5
Jingchuan, *China* 56 G4
Jingde, *China* 59 B12
Jingdezhen, *China* 59 C11
Jingdong, *China* 58 E3
Jinggangshan, *China* 59 D10
Jinggu, *China* 58 F3
Jinghai, *China* 56 E9
Jinghong, *China* 58 G3
Jingjiang, *China* 59 A13
Jingle, *China* 56 E6
Jingmen, *China* 59 B9
Jingning, *China* 56 G3
Jingpo Hu, *China* 57 C15
Jingshan, *China* 59 B9
Jingtai, *China* 56 F3
Jingxi, *China* 58 F6
Jingxing, *China* 56 E8
Jingyang, *China* 56 G5
Jingyu, *China* 57 C14
Jingyuan, *China* 56 F3
Jingzhou, *China* 58 D7
Jingziguan, *China* 56 H6
Jinhua, *China* 59 C12
Jining, *Nei Mongol Zizhiqu, China* 56 D7
Jining, *Shandong, China* 56 G9
Jinja, *Uganda* 86 B3
Jinjang, *Malaysia* 65 L3
Jinji, *China* 56 F4
Jinjiang, *Fujian, China* 59 E12
Jinjiang, *Yunnan, China* 58 D3
Jinjie, *China* 58 F6
Jinjini, *Ghana* 82 D4
Jinkou, *China* 59 B10
Jinkouhe, *China* 58 C4
Jinmen Dao, *China* 59 E12
Jinnah Barrage, *Pakistan* 66 C7
Jinning, *China* 58 E4
Jinotega, *Nic.* 120 D2
Jinotepe, *Nic.* 120 D2
Jinping, *Guizhou, China* 58 D7
Jinping, *Yunnan, China* 58 F4
Jinsha, *China* 58 D6
Jinsha Jiang →, *China* 58 C5
Jinshan, *China* 59 B13
Jinshi, *China* 59 C8
Jintan, *China* 59 B12
Jinxi, *Jiangxi, China* 59 D11
Jinxi, *Liaoning, China* 57 D11
Jinxian, *China* 59 C11
Jinxiang, *China* 56 G9
Jinyang, *China* 58 D4
Jinyun, *China* 59 C13
Jinzhai, *China* 59 B10
Jinzhou, *Hebei, China* 56 E8
Jinzhou, *Liaoning, China* 57 D11
Jiparaná →, *Brazil* 124 E6
Jipijapa, *Ecuador* 124 D2
Jiquilpan, *Mexico* 118 D4
Jishan, *China* 56 G6
Jishou, *China* 58 C7
Jishui, *China* 59 D10
Jisr ash Shughūr, *Syria* 70 C3
Jitarning, *Australia* 93 F2
Jitra, *Malaysia* 65 J3
Jiu →, *Romania* 43 G8
Jiudengkou, *China* 56 E4
Jiujiang, *Guangdong, China* 59 F9
Jiujiang, *Jiangxi, China* 59 C10
Jiuling Shan, *China* 59 C10
Jiulong, *China* 58 C3
Jiutai, *China* 57 B13
Jiuxiangcheng, *China* 56 H8
Jiuxincheng, *China* 56 E8
Jiuyuhang, *China* 59 B12
Jixi, *Anhui, China* 59 B12
Jixi, *Heilongjiang, China* 57 B16
Jiyang, *China* 57 F9
Jiyuan, *China* 56 G7
Jīzān, *Si. Arabia* 74 D3
Jize, *China* 56 F8
Jizera →, *Czech Rep.* 26 A7
Jizl, W. →, *Si. Arabia* 80 B4
Jizl, Wādī al, *Si. Arabia* 70 E3
Jizō-Zaki, *Japan* 55 G6
Jizzakh, *Uzbekistan* 50 E7
Joaçaba, *Brazil* 127 B5
Joal Fadiout, *Senegal* 82 C1
João Pessoa, *Brazil* 125 E12
Joaquín V. González, *Argentina* 126 B3
Jobat, *India* 68 H6
Jobourg, Nez de, *France* 18 C5
Jódar, *Spain* 35 H7
Jodhpur, *India* 68 F5
Jodiya, *India* 68 H4
Jōetsu, *Japan* 55 F9
Jœuf, *France* 19 C12
Jofane, *Mozam.* 89 C5
Jogbani, *India* 69 F12
Jõgeva, *Estonia* 9 G22
Jogjakarta = Yogyakarta, *Indonesia* 63 G14
Johannesburg, *S. Africa* 89 D4
Johannesburg, *U.S.A.* 117 K9
Johansfors, *Sweden* 11 H9
Johilla →, *India* 69 H9
John Day, *U.S.A.* 114 D4
John Day →, *U.S.A.* 114 D3
John D'Or Prairie, *Canada* 104 B5
John H. Kerr Reservoir, *U.S.A.* 109 G6
John o' Groats, *U.K.* 14 C5
Johnnie, *U.S.A.* 117 J10
John's Ra., *Australia* 94 C1
Johnson, *Kans., U.S.A.* 113 G4
Johnson, *Vt., U.S.A.* 111 B12
Johnson City, *N.Y., U.S.A.* 111 D9
Johnson City, *Tenn., U.S.A.* 109 G4
Johnson City, *Tex., U.S.A.* 113 K5
Johnsonburg, *U.S.A.* 110 E6
Johnsondale, *U.S.A.* 117 K8
Johnson's Crossing, *Canada* 104 A2
Johnston, L., *Australia* 93 F3
Johnston Falls = Mambilima Falls, *Zambia* 87 E2
Johnston I., *Pac. Oc.* 97 F11
Johnstone Str., *Canada* 104 C3
Johnstown, *N.Y., U.S.A.* 111 C10
Johnstown, *Ohio, U.S.A.* 110 F2
Johnstown, *Pa., U.S.A.* 110 F6
Johor Baharu, *Malaysia* 65 M4
Jõhvi, *Estonia* 9 G22
Joigny, *France* 19 E10
Joinville, *Brazil* 127 B6
Joinville, *France* 19 D12
Joinville I., *Antarctica* 5 C18
Jojutla, *Mexico* 119 D5
Jokkmokk, *Sweden* 8 C18
Jökulsá á Bru →, *Iceland* 8 D6
Jökulsá á Fjöllum →, *Iceland* 8 C5
Jolfā, *Āzarbājān-e Sharqī, Iran* 70 B5
Jolfā, *Eşfahan, Iran* 71 C6
Joliet, *U.S.A.* 108 E1
Joliette, *Canada* 102 C5
Jolo, *Phil.* 61 J4
Jolon, *U.S.A.* 116 K5
Jomalig I., *Phil.* 61 D5
Jombang, *Indonesia* 63 G15
Jomda, *China* 58 B2
Jonava, *Lithuania* 9 J21
Jones Sound, *Canada* 4 B3
Jonesboro, *Ark., U.S.A.* 113 H9
Jonesboro, *La., U.S.A.* 113 J8
Jong →, *S. Leone* 82 D2
Jonglei, *Sudan* 81 F3
Jonglei □, *Sudan* 81 F3
Joniškis, *Lithuania* 9 H20
Jönköping, *Sweden* 11 G8
Jönköpings län □, *Sweden* 11 G8
Jonquière, *Canada* 103 C5
Jonsered, *Sweden* 11 G6
Jonzac, *France* 20 C3
Joplin, *U.S.A.* 113 G7
Jora, *India* 68 F6
Jordan, *Mont., U.S.A.* 114 C10
Jordan, *N.Y., U.S.A.* 111 C8
Jordan ■, *Asia* 75 E5
Jordan →, *Asia* 75 D4
Jordan Valley, *U.S.A.* 114 E5
Jordanów, *Poland* 45 J6
Jorhat, *India* 67 F19
Jörn, *Sweden* 8 D19
Jorong, *Indonesia* 62 E4
Jørpeland, *Norway* 9 G11
Jorquera →, *Chile* 126 B2
Jos, *Nigeria* 83 D6
Jos Plateau, *Nigeria* 83 D6
Jošanička Banja, *Serbia, Yug.* 40 C4
José Batlle y Ordóñez, *Uruguay* 127 C4
Joseni, *Romania* 43 D10
Joseph, L., *Nfld., Canada* 103 B6
Joseph, L., *Ont., Canada* 110 A5
Joseph Bonaparte G., *Australia* 92 B4
Joshinath, *India* 69 D8
Joshua Tree, *U.S.A.* 117 L10
Joshua Tree National Park, *U.S.A.* 117 M10
Josselin, *France* 18 E4
Jostedalsbreen, *Norway* 9 F12
Jotunheimen, *Norway* 9 F13
Joubertberge, *Namibia* 88 B1
Joué-lès-Tours, *France* 18 E7
Jourdanton, *U.S.A.* 113 L5
Joutseno, *Finland* 46 B5
Jovellanos, *Cuba* 120 B3
Joyeuse, *France* 21 D8
Józefów, *Lubelskie, Poland* 45 H10
Józefów, *Mazowieckie, Poland* 45 F8
Ju Xian, *China* 57 F10
Juan Aldama, *Mexico* 118 C4
Juan Bautista Alberdi, *Argentina* 126 C3
Juan de Fuca Str., *Canada* 116 B3
Juan de Nova, *Ind. Oc.* 89 B7
Juan Fernández, Arch. de, *Pac. Oc.* 122 G2
Juan José Castelli, *Argentina* 126 B3
Juan L. Lacaze, *Uruguay* 126 C4
Juankoski, *Finland* 8 E23
Juárez, *Argentina* 126 D4
Juárez, *Mexico* 117 N11
Juárez, Sierra de, *Mexico* 118 A1
Juàzeiro, *Brazil* 125 E10
Juàzeiro do Norte, *Brazil* 125 E11
Juba, *Sudan* 81 G3
Jubayl, *Lebanon* 75 A4
Jubbah, *Si. Arabia* 70 D4
Jubbal, *India* 68 D7
Jubbulpore = Jabalpur, *India* 69 H8
Jübek, *Germany* 24 A5
Jubga, *Russia* 49 H4
Jubilee L., *Australia* 93 E4
Juby, C., *Morocco* 78 C3
Júcar = Xúquer →, *Spain* 33 F4
Júcaro, *Cuba* 120 B4
Juchitán, *Mexico* 119 D5
Judaea = Har Yehuda, *Israel* 75 D3
Judenburg, *Austria* 26 D7
Judith →, *U.S.A.* 114 C9
Judith, Pt., *U.S.A.* 111 E13
Judith Gap, *U.S.A.* 114 C9
Juelsminde, *Denmark* 11 J4
Jugoslavia = Yugoslavia ■, *Europe* 40 C4
Juigalpa, *Nic.* 120 D2
Juillac, *France* 20 C5
Juist, *Germany* 24 B2
Juiz de Fora, *Brazil* 127 A7
Jujuy □, *Argentina* 126 A2
Julesburg, *U.S.A.* 112 E3
Juli, *Peru* 124 G5
Julia Cr. →, *Australia* 94 C3
Julia Creek, *Australia* 94 C3
Juliaca, *Peru* 124 G4
Julian, *U.S.A.* 117 M10
Julian Alps = Julijske Alpe, *Slovenia* 29 B11
Julian L., *Canada* 102 B4
Julianatop, *Surinam* 125 C7
Julianehåb = Qaqortoq, *Greenland* 4 C5
Jülich, *Germany* 24 E2
Julijske Alpe, *Slovenia* 29 B11
Julimes, *Mexico* 118 B3
Jullundur, *India* 68 D6
Julu, *China* 56 F8
Jumbo, *Zimbabwe* 87 F3
Jumbo Pk., *U.S.A.* 117 J12
Jumentos Cays, *Bahamas* 120 B4
Jumilla, *Spain* 33 G3
Jumla, *Nepal* 69 E10
Jumna = Yamuna →, *India* 69 G9
Junagadh, *India* 68 J4
Junction, *Tex., U.S.A.* 113 K5
Junction, *Utah, U.S.A.* 115 G7
Junction B., *Australia* 94 A1
Junction City, *Kans., U.S.A.* 112 F6
Junction City, *Oreg., U.S.A.* 114 D2
Junction Pt., *Australia* 94 A1
Jundah, *Australia* 94 C3
Jundiaí, *Brazil* 127 A6
Juneau, *U.S.A.* 104 B2
Junee, *Australia* 95 E4
Jungfrau, *Switz.* 25 J3
Junggar Pendi, *China* 60 B3
Jungshahi, *Pakistan* 68 G2
Juniata →, *U.S.A.* 110 F7
Junín, *Argentina* 126 C3
Junín de los Andes, *Argentina* 128 D2
Jūniyah, *Lebanon* 75 B4
Junlian, *China* 58 C5
Juntas, *Chile* 126 B2
Juntura, *U.S.A.* 114 E4
Jur, Nahr el →, *Sudan* 81 F2
Jura = Jura, Mts. du, *Europe* 19 F13
Jura = Schwäbische Alb, *Germany* 25 G5
Jura, *U.K.* 14 F3
Jura □, *France* 19 F12
Jura □, *Switz.* 25 H3
Jūra →, *Lithuania* 44 C9
Jura, Mts. du, *Europe* 19 F13
Jura, Sd. of, *U.K.* 14 F3
Jurbarkas, *Lithuania* 9 J20
Jurien, *Australia* 93 F2
Jurilovca, *Romania* 43 F13
Jūrmala, *Latvia* 9 H20
Jurong, *China* 59 B12
Juruá →, *Brazil* 122 D4
Juruena, *Brazil* 124 F7
Juruena →, *Brazil* 124 E7
Juruti, *Brazil* 125 D7
Jussey, *France* 19 E12
Justo Daract, *Argentina* 126 C2
Jutaí →, *Brazil* 124 D5
Jüterbog, *Germany* 24 D9
Juticalpa, *Honduras* 120 D2
Jutland = Jylland, *Denmark* 11 H3
Juventud, I. de la, *Cuba* 120 B3
Juvigny-sous-Andaine, *France* 18 D6
Juwain, *Afghan.* 66 D2
Jūy Zar, *Iran* 70 C5
Juye, *China* 56 G9
Juzennecourt, *France* 19 D11
Jvari, *Georgia* 49 J6
Jwaneng, *Botswana* 85 J4
Jyderup, *Denmark* 11 J5
Jylland, *Denmark* 11 H3
Jyväskylä, *Finland* 9 E21

K

K2, *Pakistan* 69 B7
Ka →, *Nigeria* 83 C5
Kaap Plateau, *S. Africa* 88 D3
Kaapkruis, *Namibia* 88 C1
Kaapstad = Cape Town, *S. Africa* 88 E2
Kaba, *Guinea* 82 C2
Kabaena, *Indonesia* 63 F6
Kabala, *S. Leone* 82 D2
Kabale, *Uganda* 86 C3
Kabalo, *Dem. Rep. of the Congo* 86 D2
Kabambare, *Dem. Rep. of the Congo* 86 C2
Kabango, *Dem. Rep. of the Congo* 87 D2
Kabanjahe, *Indonesia* 62 D1
Kabankalan, *Phil.* 61 G5
Kabara, *Mali* 82 B4
Kabardinka, *Russia* 47 K10
Kabardino-Balkar Republic = Kabardino-Balkaria □, *Russia* 49 J6
Kabardino-Balkaria □, *Russia* 49 J6
Kabarega Falls = Murchison Falls, *Uganda* 86 B3
Kabasalan, *Phil.* 61 H5
Kabba, *Nigeria* 83 D6
Kabetogama, *U.S.A.* 112 A8
Kabi, *Niger* 83 C7
Kabin Buri, *Thailand* 64 F3
Kabinakagami L., *Canada* 102 C3
Kabinda, *Dem. Rep. of the Congo* 84 F4
Kabna, *Sudan* 80 D3
Kabompo, *Zambia* 87 E1
Kabompo →, *Zambia* 85 G4
Kabondo, *Dem. Rep. of the Congo* 87 D2
Kabongo, *Dem. Rep. of the Congo* 86 D2
Kabot, *Guinea* 82 C2
Kabou, *Togo* 83 D5
Kabr, *Sudan* 81 E2
Kabūd Gonbad, *Iran* 71 B8
Kabugao, *Phil.* 61 B4
Kābul, *Afghan.* 68 B3
Kābul □, *Afghan.* 66 B6
Kabul →, *Pakistan* 68 C5
Kabunga, *Dem. Rep. of the Congo* 86 C2
Kaburuang, *Indonesia* 63 D7
Kabushiya, *Sudan* 81 D3
Kabwe, *Zambia* 87 E2
Kačanik, *Kosovo, Yug.* 40 D5
Kačerginė, *Lithuania* 44 D10
Kachchh, Gulf of, *India* 68 H3
Kachchh, Rann of, *India* 68 H4
Kachchhidhana, *India* 69 J8
Kachebera, *Zambia* 87 E3
Kachia, *Nigeria* 83 D6
Kachikau, *Botswana* 88 B3
Kachin □, *Burma* 58 D1
Kachira, L., *Uganda* 86 C3
Kachiry, *Kazakstan* 50 D8
Kachisi, *Ethiopia* 81 F4
Kachnara, *India* 68 H6
Kachot, *Cambodia* 65 G4
Kaçkar, *Turkey* 73 B9
Kadan, *Czech Rep.* 26 A6
Kadan Kyun, *Burma* 64 F2
Kadanai →, *Afghan.* 68 D1
Kadarkút, *Hungary* 42 D2
Kade, *Ghana* 83 D4
Kadi, *India* 68 H5
Kadina, *Australia* 95 E2
Kadınhanı, *Turkey* 72 C5
Kadiolo, *Mali* 82 C3
Kadipur, *India* 69 F10
Kadirli, *Turkey* 70 B3
Kadiyevka = Stakhanov, *Ukraine* 47 H10
Kadodo, *Sudan* 81 E2
Kadoka, *U.S.A.* 112 D4
Kadom, *Russia* 48 C6
Kadoma, *Zimbabwe* 87 F2
Kâdugli, *Sudan* 81 E2
Kaduna, *Nigeria* 83 C6
Kaduna □, *Nigeria* 83 C6
Kaduy, *Russia* 46 C9
Kaédi, *Mauritania* 82 B2
Kaélé, *Cameroon* 83 C7
Kaeng Khoï, *Thailand* 64 E3
Kaesŏng, *N. Korea* 57 F14
Kāf, *Si. Arabia* 70 D3
Kafan = Kapan, *Armenia* 70 B5
Kafanchan, *Nigeria* 83 D6
Kafareti, *Nigeria* 83 C7
Kaffrine, *Senegal* 82 C1
Kafin, *Nigeria* 83 D6
Kafin Madaki, *Nigeria* 83 C6
Kafinda, *Zambia* 87 E3
Kafirévs, Ákra, *Greece* 38 C6
Kafr el Battikh, *Egypt* 80 H7
Kafr el Dauwâr, *Egypt* 80 H7
Kafr el Sheikh, *Egypt* 80 H7
Kafue, *Zambia* 87 F2
Kafue →, *Zambia* 85 H5
Kafue Flats, *Zambia* 87 F2
Kafue Nat. Park, *Zambia* 87 F2
Kafulwe, *Zambia* 87 D2
Kaga, *Afghan.* 68 B4
Kaga Bandoro, *C.A.R.* 84 C3
Kagan, *Uzbekistan* 50 F7
Kagarko, *Nigeria* 83 D6
Kagawa □, *Japan* 55 G7
Kagera □, *Tanzania* 86 C3
Kagera →, *Uganda* 86 C3
Kağızman, *Turkey* 70 B4
Kagmar, *Sudan* 81 E3
Kagoshima, *Japan* 55 J5
Kagoshima □, *Japan* 55 J5
Kagul = Cahul, *Moldova* 43 E13
Kahak, *Iran* 71 B6
Kahama, *Tanzania* 86 C3
Kahan, *Pakistan* 68 E3
Kahang, *Malaysia* 65 L4
Kahayan →, *Indonesia* 62 E4
Kahe, *Tanzania* 86 C4
Kahnūj, *Iran* 71 E8
Kahoka, *U.S.A.* 112 E9
Kahoolawe, *U.S.A.* 106 H16
Kahramanmaraş, *Turkey* 70 B3
Kâhta, *Turkey* 73 D8
Kahuta, *Pakistan* 68 C5
Kai, Kepulauan, *Indonesia* 63 F8
Kai Besar, *Indonesia* 63 F8
Kai Is. = Kai, Kepulauan, *Indonesia* 63 F8
Kai Kecil, *Indonesia* 63 F8
Kai Xian, *China* 58 B7
Kaiama, *Nigeria* 83 D5
Kaiapoi, *N.Z.* 91 K4
Kaieteur Falls, *Guyana* 124 B7
Kaifeng, *China* 56 G8
Kaihua, *China* 59 C12
Kaijiang, *China* 58 B6
Kaikohe, *N.Z.* 91 F4
Kaikoura, *N.Z.* 91 K4
Kaikoura Ra., *N.Z.* 91 J4
Kailahun, *S. Leone* 82 D2
Kaili, *China* 58 D6
Kailu, *China* 57 C11
Kailua Kona, *U.S.A.* 106 J17
Kaimana, *Indonesia* 63 E8
Kaimanawa Mts., *N.Z.* 91 H5
Kaimganj, *India* 69 F8
Kaimur Hills, *India* 69 G10
Kainab →, *Namibia* 88 D2
Kaingaroa Forest, *N.Z.* 91 H6
Kainji Dam, *Nigeria* 83 D5
Kainji Res., *Nigeria* 83 C5
Kainuu, *Finland* 8 D23
Kaipara Harbour, *N.Z.* 91 G5
Kaiping, *China* 59 F9
Kaipokok B., *Canada* 103 B8
Kaira, *India* 68 H5
Kairana, *India* 68 E7
Kaironi, *Indonesia* 63 E8
Kairouan, *Tunisia* 79 A8
Kaiserslautern, *Germany* 25 F3
Kaiserstuhl, *Germany* 25 G3
Kaitaia, *N.Z.* 91 F4
Kaitangata, *N.Z.* 91 M2
Kaithal, *India* 68 E7
Kaitu →, *Pakistan* 68 C4
Kaiwi Channel, *U.S.A.* 106 H16
Kaiyang, *China* 58 D6
Kaiyuan, *Liaoning, China* 57 C13
Kaiyuan, *Yunnan, China* 58 F4
Kajaani, *Finland* 8 D22
Kajabbi, *Australia* 94 C3
Kajana = Kajaani, *Finland* 8 D22
Kajang, *Malaysia* 65 L3
Kajaran, *Armenia* 73 C12
Kajiado, *Kenya* 86 C4
Kajo Kaji, *Sudan* 81 G3
Kajuru, *Nigeria* 83 C6
Kaka, *Sudan* 81 E3
Kakabeka Falls, *Canada* 102 C2
Kakadu Nat. Park, *Australia* 92 B5
Kakamas, *S. Africa* 88 D3
Kakamega, *Kenya* 86 B3

Kakanj, *Bos.-H.* 42 F3
Kakanui Mts., *N.Z.* 91 L3
Kakata, *Liberia* 82 D2
Kakdwip, *India* 69 J13
Kake, *Japan* 55 G6
Kake, *U.S.A.* 104 B2
Kakegawa, *Japan* 55 G9
Kakeroma-Jima, *Japan* 55 K4
Kakhib, *Russia* 49 J8
Kakhovka, *Ukraine* 47 J7
Kakhovske Vdskh., *Ukraine* 47 J7
Kakinada, *India* 67 L13
Kakisa →, *Canada* 104 A5
Kakisa L., *Canada* 104 A5
Kakogawa, *Japan* 55 G7
Kakwa →, *Canada* 104 C5
Kāl Gūsheh, *Iran* 71 D8
Kal Safīd, *Iran* 70 C5
Kala, *Nigeria* 83 C7
Kalaallit Nunaat = Greenland ■, *N. Amer.* 4 C5
Kalabagh, *Pakistan* 68 C4
Kalabahi, *Indonesia* 63 F6
Kalabáka, *Greece* 38 B3
Kalabana, *Mali* 82 C3
Kalach, *Russia* 48 E5
Kalach na Donu, *Russia* 49 F6
Kaladan →, *Burma* 67 J18
Kaladar, *Canada* 102 D4
Kalahari, *Africa* 88 C3
Kalahari Gemsbok Nat. Park, *S. Africa* 88 D3
Kalajoki, *Finland* 8 D20
Kālak, *Iran* 71 E8
Kalakamati, *Botswana* 89 C4
Kalakan, *Russia* 51 D12
K'alak'unlun Shank'ou = Karakoram Pass, *Pakistan* 69 B7
Kalam, *Pakistan* 69 B5
Kalama, *Dem. Rep. of the Congo* 86 C2
Kalama, *U.S.A.* 116 E4
Kalámai, *Greece* 38 D4
Kalamariá, *Greece* 40 F6
Kalamata = Kalámai, *Greece* 38 D4
Kalamazoo, *U.S.A.* 108 D3
Kalamazoo →, *U.S.A.* 108 D2
Kalambo Falls, *Tanzania* 87 D3
Kálamos, *Attikí, Greece* 38 C5
Kálamos, *Iónioi Nísoi, Greece* 38 C2
Kalan, *Turkey* 70 B3
Kalankalan, *Guinea* 82 C3
Kalannie, *Australia* 93 F2
Kalāntarī, *Iran* 71 C7
Kalao, *Indonesia* 63 F6
Kalaotoa, *Indonesia* 63 F6
Kälarne, *Sweden* 10 B10
Kalasin, *Thailand* 64 D4
Kalat, *Pakistan* 66 E5
Kalāteh, *Iran* 71 B7
Kalāteh-ye Ganj, *Iran* 71 E8
Kálathos, *Greece* 39 E10
Kalaus →, *Russia* 49 H7
Kalávrita, *Greece* 38 C4
Kalbarri, *Australia* 93 E1
Kale, *Antalya, Turkey* 39 E12
Kale, *Denizli, Turkey* 39 D10
Kalecik, *Turkey* 72 B5
Kalegauk Kyun, *Burma* 67 M20
Kalehe, *Dem. Rep. of the Congo* 86 C2
Kalema, *Tanzania* 86 C3
Kalemie, *Dem. Rep. of the Congo* 86 D2
Kalety, *Poland* 45 H5
Kalewa, *Burma* 67 H19
Kaleybar, *Iran* 70 B5
Kalgan = Zhangjiakou, *China* 56 D8
Kalgoorlie-Boulder, *Australia* 93 F3
Kali →, *India* 69 F8
Kali Sindh →, *India* 68 G6
Kaliakra, Nos, *Bulgaria* 41 C12
Kalianda, *Indonesia* 62 F3
Kalibo, *Phil.* 61 F5
Kalima, *Dem. Rep. of the Congo* 86 C2
Kalimantan □, *Indonesia* 62 E4
Kalimantan Barat □, *Indonesia* 62 E4
Kalimantan Selatan □, *Indonesia* 62 E5
Kalimantan Tengah □, *Indonesia* 62 E4
Kalimantan Timur □, *Indonesia* 62 D5
Kálimnos, *Greece* 39 D8
Kalimpong, *India* 69 F13
Kalinin = Tver, *Russia* 46 D8
Kaliningrad, *Russia* 9 J19
Kalininsk, *Russia* 48 E7
Kalinkavichy, *Belarus* 47 F5
Kalinkovichi = Kalinkavichy, *Belarus* 47 F5
Kalinovik, *Bos.-H.* 40 C2
Kalipetrovo, *Bulgaria* 41 B11
Kaliro, *Uganda* 86 B3
Kalirrákhi, *Greece* 41 F8
Kalispell, *U.S.A.* 114 B6
Kalisz, *Poland* 45 G5
Kalisz Pomorski, *Poland* 45 E2
Kaliua, *Tanzania* 86 D3
Kalívia Thorikoú, *Greece* 38 D5
Kalix, *Sweden* 8 D20
Kalix →, *Sweden* 8 D20
Kalka, *India* 68 D7
Kalkan, *Turkey* 39 E11
Kalkarindji, *Australia* 92 C5
Kalkaska, *U.S.A.* 108 C3
Kalkfeld, *Namibia* 88 C2
Kalkfontein, *Botswana* 88 C3
Kalkım, *Turkey* 39 B9
Kalkrand, *Namibia* 88 C2
Kållandsö, *Sweden* 11 F7
Kallavesi, *Finland* 8 E22
Källby, *Sweden* 11 F7
Kållered, *Sweden* 11 G6
Kallimasiá, *Greece* 39 C8
Kallinge, *Sweden* 11 H9
Kallithéa, *Greece* 38 D5
Kallmeti, *Albania* 40 E3
Kalloní, *Greece* 39 B8
Kallonís, Kólpos, *Greece* 39 B8
Kallsjön, *Sweden* 8 E15
Kalmalo, *Nigeria* 83 C6
Kalmar, *Sweden* 11 H10
Kalmar län □, *Sweden* 11 G10
Kalmar sund, *Sweden* 11 H10
Kalmyk Republic = Kalmykia □, *Russia* 49 G8
Kalmykia □, *Russia* 49 G8
Kalmykovo, *Kazakstan* 50 E6
Kalna, *India* 69 H13
Kalnai, *India* 69 H10
Kalocsa, *Hungary* 42 D4
Kalofer, *Bulgaria* 41 D8
Kalokhorio, *Cyprus* 36 E12
Kaloko, *Dem. Rep. of the Congo* 86 D2
Kalol, *Gujarat, India* 68 H5
Kalol, *Gujarat, India* 68 H5
Kalolímnos, *Greece* 39 D9
Kalomo, *Zambia* 87 F2
Kalonerón, *Greece* 38 D3
Kalpi, *India* 69 F8
Kaltern = Caldaro, *Italy* 29 B8
Kaltungo, *Nigeria* 83 D7
Kalu, *Pakistan* 68 G2
Kaluga, *Russia* 46 E9
Kalulushi, *Zambia* 87 E2
Kalundborg, *Denmark* 11 J5
Kalush, *Ukraine* 47 H3
Kałuszyn, *Poland* 45 F8
Kalutara, *Sri Lanka* 66 R12
Kalvarija, *Lithuania* 44 D10
Kalyazin, *Russia* 46 D9
Kam →, *Nigeria* 83 D7
Kama, *Dem. Rep. of the Congo* 86 C2
Kama →, *Russia* 6 D16
Kamachumu, *Tanzania* 86 C3
Kamaishi, *Japan* 54 E10
Kamalia, *Pakistan* 68 D5
Kaman, *India* 68 F6
Kaman, *Turkey* 72 C5
Kamanjab, *Namibia* 88 B2
Kamapanda, *Zambia* 87 E1
Kamaran, *Yemen* 74 D3
Kamativi, *Zimbabwe* 88 B4
Kamba, *Nigeria* 83 C5
Kambalda, *Australia* 93 F3
Kambar, *Pakistan* 68 F3
Kambia, *S. Leone* 82 D2
Kambolé, *Togo* 83 D5
Kambolé, *Zambia* 87 D3
Kambos, *Cyprus* 36 D11
Kambove, *Dem. Rep. of the Congo* 87 E2
Kamchatka, Poluostrov, *Russia* 51 D16
Kamchatka Pen. = Kamchatka, Poluostrov, *Russia* 51 D16
Kamchiya →, *Bulgaria* 41 C11
Kamen, *Russia* 50 D9
Kamen-Rybolov, *Russia* 54 B6
Kamenica, *Serbia, Yug.* 40 C6
Kamenica, *Serbia, Yug.* 40 B3
Kamenice nad Lipou, *Czech Rep.* 26 B8
Kamenjak, Rt., *Croatia* 29 D10
Kamenka = Kaminka, *Ukraine* 47 H7
Kamenka, *Kazakstan* 48 E10
Kamenka, *Penza, Russia* 48 D6
Kamenka, *Voronezh, Russia* 47 G10
Kamenka Bugskaya = Kamyanka-Buzka, *Ukraine* 47 G3
Kamenka Dneprovskaya = Kamyanka-Dniprovska, *Ukraine* 47 J8
Kamennomostskiy, *Russia* 49 H5
Kameno, *Bulgaria* 41 D11
Kamenolomini, *Russia* 49 G5
Kamensk-Shakhtinskiy, *Russia* 49 F5
Kamensk Uralskiy, *Russia* 50 D7
Kamenskiy, *Russia* 48 E7
Kamenskoye, *Russia* 51 C17
Kamenyak, *Bulgaria* 41 C10
Kamenz, *Germany* 24 D10
Kameoka, *Japan* 55 G7
Kami, *Albania* 40 D4
Kamiah, *U.S.A.* 114 C5
Kamień Krajeński, *Poland* 44 E4
Kamień Pomorski, *Poland* 44 E1
Kamienna →, *Poland* 45 G8
Kamienna Góra, *Poland* 45 H3
Kamieńsk, *Poland* 45 G6
Kamieskroon, *S. Africa* 88 E2
Kamilukuak, L., *Canada* 105 A8
Kamin-Kashyrskyy, *Ukraine* 47 G3
Kamina, *Dem. Rep. of the Congo* 87 D2
Kaminak L., *Canada* 105 A10
Kaministiquia, *Canada* 102 C1
Kaminka, *Ukraine* 47 H7
Kaminoyama, *Japan* 54 E10
Kamiros, *Greece* 36 C9
Kamituga, *Dem. Rep. of the Congo* 86 C2
Kamla →, *India* 69 G12
Kamloops, *Canada* 104 C4
Kamnik, *Slovenia* 29 B11
Kamo, *Armenia* 49 K7
Kamo, *Japan* 54 F9
Kamoke, *Pakistan* 68 C6
Kamp →, *Austria* 26 C8
Kampala, *Uganda* 86 B3
Kampang Chhnang, *Cambodia* 65 F5
Kampar, *Malaysia* 65 K3
Kampar →, *Indonesia* 62 D2
Kampen, *Neths.* 17 B5
Kampene, *Dem. Rep. of the Congo* 84 E5
Kamphaeng Phet, *Thailand* 64 D2
Kampolombo, L., *Zambia* 87 E2
Kampong Saom, *Cambodia* 65 G4
Kampong Saom, Chaak, *Cambodia* 65 G4
Kampong To, *Thailand* 65 J3
Kampot, *Cambodia* 65 G5
Kampti, *Burkina Faso* 82 C4
Kampuchea = Cambodia ■, *Asia* 64 F5
Kampung Air Putih, *Malaysia* 65 K4
Kampung Jerangau, *Malaysia* 65 K4
Kampung Raja, *Malaysia* 65 K4
Kampungbaru = Tolitoli, *Indonesia* 63 D6
Kamrau, Teluk, *Indonesia* 63 E8
Kamsack, *Canada* 105 C8
Kamsai, *Guinea* 82 C2
Kamskoye Ustye, *Russia* 48 C9
Kamuchawie L., *Canada* 105 B8
Kamuela, *U.S.A.* 106 H17
Kamui-Misaki, *Japan* 54 C10
Kamyanets-Podilskyy, *Ukraine* 47 H4
Kamyanka-Buzka, *Ukraine* 47 G3
Kamyanka-Dniprovska, *Ukraine* 47 J8
Kāmyārān, *Iran* 70 C5
Kamyshin, *Russia* 48 E7
Kamyzyak, *Russia* 49 G9
Kan, *Sudan* 81 F3
Kanaaupscow, *Canada* 102 B4
Kanaaupscow →, *Canada* 101 C12
Kanab, *U.S.A.* 115 H7
Kanab →, *U.S.A.* 115 H7
Kanagi, *Japan* 54 D10
Kanairiktok →, *Canada* 103 A7
Kanália, *Greece* 38 B4
Kananga, *Dem. Rep. of the Congo* 84 F4
Kanash, *Russia* 48 C8
Kanaskat, *U.S.A.* 116 C5
Kanastraíon, Ákra = Paliourion, Ákra, *Greece* 40 G7
Kanawha →, *U.S.A.* 108 F4
Kanazawa, *Japan* 55 F8
Kanchanaburi, *Thailand* 64 E2
Kanchenjunga, *Nepal* 69 F13
Kanchipuram, *India* 66 N11
Kańczuga, *Poland* 45 J9
Kandaghat, *India* 68 D7
Kandahar = Qandahār, *Afghan.* 66 D4
Kandalaksha, *Russia* 50 C4
Kandalu, *Afghan.* 66 E3
Kandangan, *Indonesia* 62 E5
Kandanghaur, *Indonesia* 63 G13
Kandanos, *Greece* 36 D5
Kandava, *Latvia* 44 A9
Kandhíla, *Greece* 38 D4
Kandhkot, *Pakistan* 68 E3
Kandhla, *India* 68 E7
Kandi, *Benin* 83 C5
Kandi, *India* 69 H13
Kandiaro, *Pakistan* 68 F3
Kandıra, *Turkey* 72 B4
Kandla, *India* 68 H4
Kandos, *Australia* 95 E4
Kandreho, *Madag.* 89 B8
Kandy, *Sri Lanka* 66 R12
Kane, *U.S.A.* 110 E6
Kane Basin, *Greenland* 4 B4
Kanel, *Senegal* 82 B2
Kaneohe, *U.S.A.* 106 H16
Kanevskaya, *Russia* 49 G4
Kanfanar, *Croatia* 29 C10
Kang, *Botswana* 88 C3
Kangaba, *Mali* 82 C3
Kangal, *Turkey* 72 C7
Kangān, *Fārs, Iran* 71 E7
Kangān, *Hormozgān, Iran* 71 E8
Kangar, *Malaysia* 65 J3
Kangaré, *Mali* 82 C3
Kangaroo I., *Australia* 95 F2
Kangaroo Mts., *Australia* 94 C3
Kangasala, *Finland* 9 F21
Kangāvar, *Iran* 71 C6
Kangding, *China* 58 B3
Kangdong, *N. Korea* 57 E14
Kangean, Kepulauan, *Indonesia* 62 F5
Kangean Is. = Kangean, Kepulauan, *Indonesia* 62 F5
Kangen →, *Sudan* 81 F3
Kanggye, *N. Korea* 57 D14
Kanggyŏng, *S. Korea* 57 F14
Kanghwa, *S. Korea* 57 F14
Kangikajik, *Greenland* 4 B6
Kangiqsualujjuaq, *Canada* 101 C13
Kangiqsujuaq, *Canada* 101 B12
Kangirsuk, *Canada* 101 B13
Kangnŭng, *S. Korea* 57 F15
Kangping, *China* 57 C12
Kangra, *India* 68 C7
Kangto, *India* 67 F18
Kanhar →, *India* 69 G10
Kani, *Ivory C.* 82 D3
Kaniama, *Dem. Rep. of the Congo* 86 D1
Kaniapiskau = Caniapiscau →, *Canada* 103 A6
Kaniapiskau, Res. = Caniapiscau Rés. de, *Canada* 103 B6
Kanin, Poluostrov, *Russia* 50 C5
Kanin Nos, Mys, *Russia* 50 C5
Kanin Pen. = Kanin, Poluostrov, *Russia* 50 C5
Kanina, *Albania* 40 F3
Kaniva, *Australia* 95 F3
Kanjiža, *Serbia, Yug.* 42 D5
Kanjut Sar, *Pakistan* 69 A6
Kankaanpää, *Finland* 9 F20
Kankakee, *U.S.A.* 108 E2
Kankakee →, *U.S.A.* 108 E1
Kankan, *Guinea* 82 C3
Kankendy = Xankändi, *Azerbaijan* 70 B5
Kanker, *India* 67 J12
Kankossa, *Mauritania* 82 B2
Kankroli, *India* 68 G5
Kannapolis, *U.S.A.* 109 H5
Kannauj, *India* 69 F8
Kannod, *India* 66 H10
Kano, *Nigeria* 83 C6
Kano □, *Nigeria* 83 C6
Kan'onji, *Japan* 55 G6
Kanoroba, *Ivory C.* 82 D3
Kanowit, *Malaysia* 62 D4
Kanoya, *Japan* 55 J5
Kanpetlet, *Burma* 67 J18
Kanpur, *India* 69 F9
Kansas □, *U.S.A.* 112 F6
Kansas →, *U.S.A.* 112 F7
Kansas City, *Kans., U.S.A.* 112 F7
Kansas City, *Mo., U.S.A.* 112 F7
Kansenia, *Dem. Rep. of the Congo* 87 E2
Kansk, *Russia* 51 D10
Kansŏng, *S. Korea* 57 E15
Kansu = Gansu □, *China* 56 G3
Kantaphor, *India* 68 H7
Kantchari, *Burkina Faso* 83 C5
Kantché, *Niger* 83 C6
Kanté, *Togo* 83 D5
Kantemirovka, *Russia* 47 H10
Kantharalak, *Thailand* 64 E5
Kantli →, *India* 68 E6
Kantō □, *Japan* 55 F9
Kantō-Sanchi, *Japan* 55 G9
Kanturk, *Ireland* 15 D3
Kanuma, *Japan* 55 F9
Kanus, *Namibia* 88 D2
Kanye, *Botswana* 88 C4
Kanzenze, *Dem. Rep. of the Congo* 87 E2
Kanzi, Ras, *Tanzania* 86 D4
Kaohsiung, *Taiwan* 59 F13
Kaokoveld, *Namibia* 88 B1
Kaolack, *Senegal* 82 C1
Kaoshan, *China* 57 B13
Kapaa, *U.S.A.* 106 G15
Kapadvanj, *India* 68 H5
Kapaklı, *Turkey* 41 E11
Kapan, *Armenia* 70 B5
Kapanga, *Dem. Rep. of the Congo* 84 F4
Kapchagai = Qapshaghay, *Kazakstan* 50 E8
Kapela = Velika Kapela, *Croatia* 29 C12
Kapéllo, Ákra, *Greece* 38 E5
Kapema, *Dem. Rep. of the Congo* 87 E2
Kapfenberg, *Austria* 26 D8
Kapı Dağı, *Turkey* 41 F11
Kapiri Mposhi, *Zambia* 87 E2
Kapiskau →, *Canada* 102 B3
Kapit, *Malaysia* 62 D4
Kapiti I., *N.Z.* 91 J5
Kaplan, *U.S.A.* 113 K8
Kaplice, *Czech Rep.* 26 C7
Kapoe, *Thailand* 65 H2
Kapoeta, *Sudan* 81 G3
Kápolnásnyék, *Hungary* 42 C3
Kapos →, *Hungary* 42 D3
Kaposvár, *Hungary* 42 D2
Kapowsin, *U.S.A.* 116 D4
Kappeln, *Germany* 24 A5
Kappelshamn, *Sweden* 11 G12
Kapps, *Namibia* 88 C2
Kaprije, *Croatia* 29 E12
Kapsan, *N. Korea* 57 D15
Kapsukas = Marijampolė, *Lithuania* 9 J20
Kapuas →, *Indonesia* 62 E3
Kapuas Hulu, Pegunungan, *Malaysia* 62 D4
Kapuas Hulu Ra. = Kapuas Hulu, Pegunungan, *Malaysia* 62 D4
Kapulo, *Dem. Rep. of the Congo* 87 D2
Kapunda, *Australia* 95 E2
Kapuni, *N.Z.* 91 H5
Kapurthala, *India* 68 D6
Kapuskasing, *Canada* 102 C3
Kapuskasing →, *Canada* 102 C3
Kapustin Yar, *Russia* 49 F7
Kaputar, *Australia* 95 E5
Kaputir, *Kenya* 86 B4
Kapuvár, *Hungary* 42 C2
Kara, *Russia* 50 C7
Karā, W. →, *Si. Arabia* 80 C5
Kara Ada, *Turkey* 39 E9
Kara Bogaz Gol, Zaliv = Garabogazköl Aylagy, *Turkmenistan* 50 E6
Kara Burun, *Turkey* 39 E9
Kara Kalpak Republic = Karakalpakstan □, *Uzbekistan* 50 E6
Kara Kum, *Turkmenistan* 50 F6
Kara Sea, *Russia* 50 B7
Karaadilli, *Turkey* 39 C12
Karabiğa, *Turkey* 41 F11
Karabük, *Turkey* 72 B5
Karaburun, *Turkey* 39 C8
Karaburuni, *Albania* 40 F3
Karabutak = Qarabutaq, *Kazakstan* 50 E7
Karacabey, *Turkey* 41 F12
Karacakılavuz, *Turkey* 41 E11
Karacaköy, *Turkey* 41 E12
Karacasu, *Turkey* 39 D10
Karachala = Qaraçala, *Azerbaijan* 49 L9
Karachayevsk, *Russia* 49 J5
Karachev, *Russia* 47 F8
Karachey-Cherkessia □, *Russia* 49 J5
Karachi, *Pakistan* 68 G2
Karad, *India* 66 L9
Karadirek, *Turkey* 39 C12
Karaga, *Ghana* 83 D4
Karaganda = Qaraghandy, *Kazakstan* 50 E8
Karagayly, *Kazakstan* 50 E8
Karaginskiy, Ostrov, *Russia* 51 D17
Karagola Road, *India* 69 G12
Karagüney Dağları, *Turkey* 72 B6
Karahallı, *Turkey* 39 C11
Karaikal, *India* 66 P11
Karaikkudi, *India* 66 P11
Karaisali, *Turkey* 72 D6
Karaj, *Iran* 71 C6
Karak, *Malaysia* 65 L4
Karakalpakstan □, *Uzbekistan* 50 E6
Karakelong, *Indonesia* 63 D7
Karakitang, *Indonesia* 63 D7
Karaklis = Vanadzor, *Armenia* 49 K7
Karakoçan, *Turkey* 73 C9
Karakoram Pass, *Pakistan* 69 B7
Karakoram Ra., *Pakistan* 69 B7
Karakurt, *Turkey* 73 B10
Karakuwisa, *Namibia* 88 B2
Karalon, *Russia* 51 D12
Karama, *Jordan* 75 D4
Karaman, *Balıkesir, Turkey* 39 B9
Karaman, *Konya, Turkey* 70 B2
Karamanlı, *Turkey* 39 D11
Karamay, *China* 60 B3
Karambu, *Indonesia* 62 E5
Karamea Bight, *N.Z.* 91 J3
Karamnasa →, *India* 69 G10
Karamürsel, *Turkey* 41 F13
Karand, *Iran* 70 C5
Karangana, *Mali* 82 C3
Karanganyar, *Indonesia* 63 G13
Karanjia, *India* 69 J11
Karankasso, *Burkina Faso* 82 C4
Karaova, *Turkey* 39 D9
Karapınar, *Turkey* 72 D5
Karasburg, *Namibia* 88 D2
Karasino, *Russia* 50 C9
Karasjok, *Norway* 8 B21
Karasu, *Turkey* 72 B4
Karasu →, *Turkey* 39 E12
Karasuk, *Russia* 50 D8
Karasuyama, *Japan* 55 F10
Karataş, *Adana, Turkey* 72 D6
Karataş, *Manisa, Turkey* 39 C10
Karataş Burnu, *Turkey* 72 D6
Karatau = Qarataū, *Kazakstan* 50 E8
Karatau, Khrebet, *Kazakstan* 50 E7
Karatoprak, *Turkey* 39 D9
Karatsu, *Japan* 55 H5
Karaul, *Russia* 50 B9
Karauli, *India* 68 F7
Karavastasë, L. e, *Albania* 40 F3
Karávi, *Greece* 38 E5
Karavostasi, *Cyprus* 36 D11
Karawang, *Indonesia* 63 G12
Karawanken, *Europe* 26 E7
Karayazı, *Turkey* 73 C10
Karazhal, *Kazakstan* 50 E8
Karbalā', *Iraq* 70 C5
Kårböle, *Sweden* 10 C9
Karcag, *Hungary* 42 C5
Karcha →, *Pakistan* 69 B7
Karchana, *India* 69 G9
Karczew, *Poland* 45 F8
Kardam, *Bulgaria* 41 C12
Kardeljovo = Ploče, *Croatia* 29 E14
Kardhámila, *Greece* 39 C8
Kardhamíli, *Greece* 38 E4
Kardhítsa, *Greece* 38 B3
Kardhítsa □, *Greece* 38 B3
Kärdla, *Estonia* 9 G20
Kareeberge, *S. Africa* 88 E3
Kareha →, *India* 69 G12
Kareima, *Sudan* 80 D3
Karelia □, *Russia* 50 C4
Karelian Republic = Karelia □, *Russia* 50 C4
Karera, *India* 68 G8
Kārevāndar, *Iran* 71 E9
Kargasok, *Russia* 50 D9
Kargat, *Russia* 50 D9
Kargı, *Turkey* 72 B6
Kargil, *India* 69 B7
Kargopol, *Russia* 46 B10
Kargowa, *Poland* 45 F2

Karguéri, *Niger* 83 C7
Karhal, *India* 69 F8
Kariá, *Greece* 38 C2
Kariaí, *Greece* 41 F8
Karīān, *Iran* 71 E8
Karianga, *Madag.* 89 C8
Kariba, *Zimbabwe* 87 F2
Kariba, L., *Zimbabwe* 87 F2
Kariba Dam, *Zimbabwe* 87 F2
Kariba Gorge, *Zambia* 87 F2
Karibib, *Namibia* 88 C2
Karimata, Kepulauan, *Indonesia* 62 E3
Karimata, Selat, *Indonesia* 62 E3
Karimata Is. = Karimata, Kepulauan, *Indonesia* 62 E3
Karimnagar, *India* 66 K11
Karimunjawa, Kepulauan, *Indonesia* 62 F4
Karin, *Somali Rep.* 74 E4
Káristos, *Greece* 38 C6
Karīt, *Iran* 71 C8
Kariya, *Japan* 55 G8
Kariyangwe, *Zimbabwe* 89 B4
Karjala, *Finland* 46 A5
Karkaralinsk = Qarqaraly, *Kazakstan* 50 E8
Karkheh →, *Iran* 70 D5
Karkinitska Zatoka, *Ukraine* 47 K7
Karkinitskiy Zaliv = Karkinitska Zatoka, *Ukraine* 47 K7
Karkur Tohl, *Egypt* 80 C2
Karl Liebknecht, *Russia* 47 G8
Karl-Marx-Stadt = Chemnitz, *Germany* 24 E8
Karlholmsbruk, *Sweden* 10 D11
Karlino, *Poland* 44 D2
Karlivka, *Ukraine* 47 H8
Karlobag, *Croatia* 29 D12
Karlovac, *Croatia* 29 C12
Karlovka = Karlivka, *Ukraine* 47 H8
Karlovo, *Bulgaria* 41 D8
Karlovy Vary, *Czech Rep.* 26 A5
Karlsbad = Karlovy Vary, *Czech Rep.* 26 A5
Karlsborg, *Sweden* 11 F8
Karlshamn, *Sweden* 11 H8
Karlskoga, *Sweden* 10 E8
Karlskrona, *Sweden* 11 H9
Karlsruhe, *Germany* 25 F4
Karlstad, *Sweden* 10 E7
Karlstad, *U.S.A.* 112 A6
Karlstadt, *Germany* 25 F5
Karma, *Niger* 83 C5
Karmėlava, *Lithuania* 44 D11
Karmi'el, *Israel* 75 C4
Karnak, *Egypt* 79 C12
Karnal, *India* 68 E7
Karnali →, *Nepal* 69 E9
Karnaphuli Res., *Bangla.* 67 H18
Karnaprayag, *India* 69 D8
Karnataka □, *India* 66 N10
Karnes City, *U.S.A.* 113 L6
Karnische Alpen, *Europe* 26 E6
Karnobat, *Bulgaria* 41 D10
Kärnten □, *Austria* 26 E6
Karo, *Mali* 82 C4
Karoi, *Zimbabwe* 87 F2
Karonga, *Malawi* 87 D3
Karoonda, *Australia* 95 F2
Karor, *Pakistan* 68 D4
Karora, *Sudan* 80 D4
Káros, *Greece* 39 E7
Karounga, *Mali* 82 B3
Karousádhes, *Greece* 38 B1
Karpacz, *Poland* 45 H2
Karpasia □, *Cyprus* 36 D13
Kárpathos, *Greece* 39 F9
Kárpathos, Stenón, *Greece* 39 F9
Karpenísion, *Greece* 38 C3
Karpuz Burnu = Apostolos Andreas, C., *Cyprus* 36 D13
Karpuzlu, *Turkey* 39 D9
Karratha, *Australia* 92 D2
Kars, *Turkey* 73 B10
Karsakpay, *Kazakstan* 50 E7
Karsha, *Kazakstan* 48 F10
Karshi = Qarshi, *Uzbekistan* 50 F7
Karsiyang, *India* 69 F13
Karsog, *India* 68 D7
Karst = Kras, *Croatia* 29 C10
Kartal, *Turkey* 41 F13
Kartál Óros, *Greece* 41 E9
Kartaly, *Russia* 50 D7
Kartapur, *India* 68 D6
Karthaus, *U.S.A.* 110 E6
Kartuzy, *Poland* 44 D5
Karufa, *Indonesia* 63 E8
Karumba, *Australia* 94 B3
Karumo, *Tanzania* 86 C3
Karumwa, *Tanzania* 86 C3
Kārūn →, *Iran* 71 D6
Karungu, *Kenya* 86 C3
Karup, *Denmark* 11 H3
Karviná, *Czech Rep.* 27 B11
Karwan →, *India* 68 F8
Karwar, *India* 66 M9
Karwi, *India* 69 G9
Kaş, *Turkey* 39 E11
Kasaba, *Turkey* 39 E11
Kasache, *Malawi* 87 E3
Kasai →, *Dem. Rep. of the Congo* 84 E3
Kasaï-Oriental □, *Dem. Rep. of the Congo* 86 D1
Kasaji, *Dem. Rep. of the Congo* 87 E1
Kasama, *Zambia* 87 E3
Kasan-dong, *N. Korea* 57 D14
Kasane, *Namibia* 88 B3
Kasanga, *Tanzania* 87 D3
Kasar, Ras, *Sudan* 80 D4
Kasaragod, *India* 66 N9
Kasba L., *Canada* 105 A8
Kāseh Garān, *Iran* 70 C5
Kasempa, *Zambia* 87 E2
Kasenga, *Dem. Rep. of the Congo* 87 E2
Kasese, *Uganda* 86 B3
Kasewa, *Zambia* 87 E2
Kasganj, *India* 69 F8
Kashabowie, *Canada* 102 C1
Kashaf, *Iran* 71 C9
Kāshān, *Iran* 71 C6
Kashechewan, *Canada* 102 B3
Kashi, *China* 60 C2
Kashimbo, *Dem. Rep. of the Congo* 87 E2
Kashin, *Russia* 46 D9
Kashipur, *India* 69 E8
Kashira, *Russia* 46 E10
Kashiwazaki, *Japan* 55 F9
Kashk-e Kohneh, *Afghan.* 66 B3
Kashkū'īyeh, *Iran* 71 D7
Kāshmar, *Iran* 71 C8
Kashmir, *Asia* 69 C7
Kashmor, *Pakistan* 68 E3
Kashpirovka, *Russia* 48 D9
Kashun Noerh = Gaxun Nur, *China* 60 B5
Kasiari, *India* 69 H12
Kasimov, *Russia* 48 C5
Kasinge, *Dem. Rep. of the Congo* 86 D2
Kasiruta, *Indonesia* 63 E7
Kaskaskia →, *U.S.A.* 112 G10
Kaskattama →, *Canada* 105 B10
Kaskinen, *Finland* 9 E19
Kaslo, *Canada* 104 D5
Kasmere L., *Canada* 105 B8
Kasongo, *Dem. Rep. of the Congo* 86 C2
Kasongo Lunda, *Dem. Rep. of the Congo* 84 F3
Kásos, *Greece* 39 F8
Kásos, Stenón, *Greece* 39 F8
Kaspi, *Georgia* 49 K7
Kaspichan, *Bulgaria* 41 C11
Kaspiysk, *Russia* 49 J8
Kaspiyskiy, *Russia* 49 H8
Kassab ed Doleib, *Sudan* 81 E3
Kassaba, *Egypt* 80 C2
Kassalâ, *Sudan* 81 D4
Kassalâ □, *Sudan* 81 D4
Kassándra, *Greece* 40 F7
Kassándrinon, *Greece* 40 F7
Kassel, *Germany* 24 D5
Kassinger, *Sudan* 80 D3
Kassiópi, *Greece* 36 A3
Kasson, *U.S.A.* 112 C8
Kastamonu, *Turkey* 72 B5
Kastav, *Croatia* 29 C11
Kastélli, *Greece* 36 D5
Kastéllion, *Greece* 36 D7
Kastellórizon = Megiste, *Greece* 39 E11
Kástellos, *Greece* 39 E9
Kastellou, Ákra, *Greece* 39 F9
Kasterlee, *Belgium* 17 C4
Kastlösa, *Sweden* 11 H10
Kastóri, *Greece* 38 D4
Kastoría, *Greece* 40 F5
Kastoría □, *Greece* 40 F5
Kastorías, Límni, *Greece* 40 F5
Kastornoye, *Russia* 47 G10
Kastós, *Greece* 38 C2
Kastrosikiá, *Greece* 38 B2
Kastsyukovichy, *Belarus* 46 F7
Kasulu, *Tanzania* 86 C3
Kasumi, *Japan* 55 G7
Kasumkent, *Russia* 49 K9
Kasungu, *Malawi* 87 E3
Kasur, *Pakistan* 68 D6
Kataba, *Zambia* 87 F2
Katagum, *Nigeria* 83 C7
Katahdin, Mt., *U.S.A.* 109 C11
Katako Kombe, *Dem. Rep. of the Congo* 86 C1
Katákolon, *Greece* 38 D3
Katale, *Tanzania* 86 C3
Katanda, *Katanga, Dem. Rep. of the Congo* 86 D1
Katanda, *Nord-Kivu, Dem. Rep. of the Congo* 86 C2
Katanga □, *Dem. Rep. of the Congo* 86 D2
Katangi, *India* 66 J11
Katanning, *Australia* 93 F2
Katastári, *Greece* 38 D2
Katavi Swamp, *Tanzania* 86 D3
Kateríni, *Greece* 40 F6
Katghora, *India* 69 H10
Katha, *Burma* 67 G20
Katherîna, Gebel, *Egypt* 70 D2
Katherine, *Australia* 92 B5
Katherine Gorge, *Australia* 92 B5
Kathi, *India* 68 J6
Kathiawar, *India* 68 H4
Kathikas, *Cyprus* 36 E11
Kathua, *India* 68 C6
Kati, *Mali* 82 C3
Katihar, *India* 69 G12
Katima Mulilo, *Zambia* 88 B3
Katimbira, *Malawi* 87 E3
Katingan = Mendawai →, *Indonesia* 62 E4
Katiola, *Ivory C.* 82 D3
Katlanovo, *Macedonia* 40 E5
Katmandu, *Nepal* 69 F11
Katni, *India* 69 H9
Kato Akhaïa, *Greece* 38 C3
Káto Arkhánai, *Greece* 36 D7
Káto Khorió, *Greece* 36 D7
Kato Pyrgos, *Cyprus* 36 D11
Káto Stavros, *Greece* 40 F7
Katokhí, *Greece* 38 C3
Katompe, *Dem. Rep. of the Congo* 86 D2
Katonga →, *Uganda* 86 B3
Katoomba, *Australia* 95 E5
Katoúna, *Greece* 38 C3
Katowice, *Poland* 45 H6
Katrancı Dağı, *Turkey* 39 D12
Katrine, L., *U.K.* 14 E4
Katrineholm, *Sweden* 11 E10
Katsepe, *Madag.* 89 B8
Katsina, *Nigeria* 83 C6
Katsina □, *Nigeria* 83 C6
Katsina Ala, *Nigeria* 83 D6
Katsina Ala →, *Nigeria* 83 D6
Katsumoto, *Japan* 55 H4
Katsuura, *Japan* 55 G10
Katsuyama, *Japan* 55 F8
Kattaviá, *Greece* 36 D9
Kattegat, *Denmark* 11 H5
Katthammarsvik, *Sweden* 11 G12
Katul, J., *Sudan* 81 E2
Katumba, *Dem. Rep. of the Congo* 86 D2
Katungu, *Kenya* 86 C5
Katwa, *India* 69 H13
Katwijk, *Neths.* 17 B4
Kąty Wrocławskie, *Poland* 45 G3
Kauai, *U.S.A.* 106 H15
Kauai Channel, *U.S.A.* 106 H15
Kaub, *Germany* 25 E3
Kaufbeuren, *Germany* 25 H6
Kaufman, *U.S.A.* 113 J6
Kauhajoki, *Finland* 9 E20
Kaukauna, *U.S.A.* 108 C1
Kaukauveld, *Namibia* 88 C3
Kaunakakai, *U.S.A.* 106 H16
Kaunas, *Lithuania* 9 J20
Kaunia, *Bangla.* 69 G13
Kaunos, *Turkey* 39 E10
Kaura Namoda, *Nigeria* 83 C6
Kauru, *Nigeria* 83 C6
Kautokeino, *Norway* 8 B20
Kauwapur, *India* 69 F10
Kavacha, *Russia* 51 C17
Kavadarci, *Macedonia* 40 E6
Kavaja, *Albania* 40 E3
Kavak, *Turkey* 72 B7
Kavak Dağı, *Turkey* 39 D10
Kavaklı, *Turkey* 41 E11
Kavaklıdere, *Turkey* 39 D10
Kavalerovo, *Russia* 54 B7
Kavali, *India* 66 M12
Kavála, *Greece* 41 F8
Kavála □, *Greece* 41 E8
Kavála Kólpos, *Greece* 41 F8
Kavār, *Iran* 71 D7
Kavarna, *Bulgaria* 41 C12
Kavi, *India* 68 H5
Kavimba, *Botswana* 88 B3
Kavīr, Dasht-e, *Iran* 71 C7
Kavkaz, *Russia* 47 K9
Kävlinge, *Sweden* 11 J7
Kavos, *Greece* 36 B4
Kavoúsi, *Greece* 39 F7
Kaw, *Fr. Guiana* 125 C8
Kawa, *Sudan* 81 E3
Kawagama L., *Canada* 110 A6
Kawagoe, *Japan* 55 G9
Kawaguchi, *Japan* 55 G9
Kawaihae, *U.S.A.* 106 H17
Kawambwa, *Zambia* 87 D2
Kawanoe, *Japan* 55 G6
Kawardha, *India* 69 J9
Kawasaki, *Japan* 55 G9
Kawasi, *Indonesia* 63 E7
Kawerau, *N.Z.* 91 H6
Kawhia Harbour, *N.Z.* 91 H5
Kawio, Kepulauan, *Indonesia* 63 D7
Kawnro, *Burma* 67 H21
Kawthaung, *Burma* 65 H2
Kawthoolei = Kawthule □, *Burma* 67 L20
Kawthule □, *Burma* 67 L20
Kaxholmen, *Sweden* 11 G8
Kaya, *Burkina Faso* 83 C4
Kayah □, *Burma* 67 K20
Kayalıköy Barajı, *Turkey* 41 E11
Kayan →, *Indonesia* 62 D5
Kaycee, *U.S.A.* 114 E10
Kayeli, *Indonesia* 63 E7
Kayenta, *U.S.A.* 115 H8
Kayes, *Mali* 82 C2
Kayı, *Turkey* 39 B12
Kayima, *S. Leone* 82 D2
Kayin = Kawthule □, *Burma* 67 L20
Kaymakçı, *Turkey* 39 C10
Kayoa, *Indonesia* 63 D7
Kayomba, *Zambia* 87 E1
Kaysatskoye, *Russia* 48 F8
Kayseri, *Turkey* 70 B2
Kaysville, *U.S.A.* 114 F8
Kaz Dağı, *Turkey* 39 B8
Kazachye, *Russia* 51 B14
Kazakstan ■, *Asia* 50 E7
Kazan, *Russia* 48 C9
Kazan →, *Canada* 105 A9
Kazan-Rettō, *Pac. Oc.* 96 E6
Kazanlŭk, *Bulgaria* 41 D9
Kazanskaya, *Russia* 48 F5
Kazatin = Kozyatyn, *Ukraine* 47 H5
Kazaure, *Nigeria* 83 C6
Kazbek, *Russia* 49 J7
Kāzerūn, *Iran* 71 D6
Kazi Magomed = Qazimämmäd, *Azerbaijan* 49 K9
Kazimierz Dolny, *Poland* 45 G8
Kazimierza Wielka, *Poland* 45 H7
Kazincbarcika, *Hungary* 42 B5
Kazlų Rūda, *Lithuania* 44 D10
Kaztalovka, *Kazakstan* 48 F9
Kazuno, *Japan* 54 D10
Kazym →, *Russia* 50 C7
Kcynia, *Poland* 45 F4
Ké-Macina, *Mali* 82 C3
Kéa, *Greece* 38 D6
Keady, *U.K.* 15 B5
Kearney, *U.S.A.* 112 E5
Kearny, *U.S.A.* 115 K8
Kearsarge, Mt., *U.S.A.* 111 C13
Keban, *Turkey* 73 C8
Keban Baraji, *Turkey* 70 B3
Kebbi □, *Nigeria* 83 C5
Kébi, *Ivory C.* 82 D3
Kebnekaise, *Sweden* 8 C18
Kebri Dehar, *Ethiopia* 74 F3
Kebumen, *Indonesia* 63 G13
Kecel, *Hungary* 42 D4
Kechika →, *Canada* 104 B3
Keçiborlu, *Turkey* 39 D12
Kecskemét, *Hungary* 42 D4
Kedada, *Ethiopia* 81 F4
Kėdainiai, *Lithuania* 9 J21
Kedarnath, *India* 69 D8
Kedgwick, *Canada* 103 C6
Kédhros Óros, *Greece* 36 D6
Kediri, *Indonesia* 63 G15
Kedjebi, *Ghana* 83 D5
Kédougou, *Senegal* 82 C2
Kędzierzyn-Koźle, *Poland* 45 H5
Keeler, *U.S.A.* 116 J9
Keeley L., *Canada* 105 C7
Keeling Is. = Cocos Is., *Ind. Oc.* 96 J1
Keelung = Chilung, *Taiwan* 59 E13
Keene, *Canada* 110 B6
Keene, *Calif., U.S.A.* 117 K8
Keene, *N.H., U.S.A.* 111 D12
Keene, *N.Y., U.S.A.* 111 B11
Keeper Hill, *Ireland* 15 D3
Keer-Weer, C., *Australia* 94 A3
Keeseville, *U.S.A.* 111 B11
Keetmanshoop, *Namibia* 88 D2
Keewatin, *Canada* 105 D10
Keewatin →, *Canada* 105 B8
Kefa □, *Ethiopia* 81 F4
Kefallinía, *Greece* 38 C2
Kefallinía □, *Greece* 38 C2
Kéfalos, *Greece* 39 E8
Kefamenanu, *Indonesia* 63 F6
Kefar Sava, *Israel* 75 C3
Keffi, *Nigeria* 83 D6
Keffin Hausa, *Nigeria* 83 C6
Keflavík, *Iceland* 8 D2
Keftya, *Ethiopia* 81 E4
Keg River, *Canada* 104 B5
Kegaska, *Canada* 103 B7
Keheili, *Sudan* 80 D3
Kehl, *Germany* 25 G3
Keighley, *U.K.* 12 D6
Keila, *Estonia* 9 G21
Keimoes, *S. Africa* 88 D3
Keita, *Niger* 83 C6
Keitele, *Finland* 8 E22
Keith, *Australia* 95 F3
Keith, *U.K.* 14 D6
Keizer, *U.S.A.* 114 D2
Kejimkujik Nat. Park, *Canada* 103 D6
Kejser Franz Joseph Fd., *Greenland* 4 B6
Kekri, *India* 68 G6
Kelam, *Ethiopia* 81 G4
Kelamet, *Eritrea* 81 D4
Kelan, *China* 56 E6
Kelang, *Malaysia* 65 L3
Kelantan →, *Malaysia* 65 J4
Këlcyra, *Albania* 40 F4
Kelekçi, *Turkey* 39 D11
Keles, *Turkey* 41 G13
Keleti-főcsatorna, *Hungary* 42 C6
Kelheim, *Germany* 25 G7
Kelkit, *Turkey* 73 B8
Kelkit →, *Turkey* 72 B7
Kellerberrin, *Australia* 93 F2
Kellett, C., *Canada* 4 B1
Kelleys I., *U.S.A.* 110 E2
Kellogg, *U.S.A.* 114 C5
Kells = Ceanannus Mor, *Ireland* 15 C5
Kelmė, *Lithuania* 44 C9
Kelokedhara, *Cyprus* 36 E11
Kelowna, *Canada* 104 D5
Kelseyville, *U.S.A.* 116 G4
Kelso, *N.Z.* 91 L2
Kelso, *U.K.* 14 F6
Kelso, *U.S.A.* 116 D4
Keluang, *Malaysia* 65 L4
Kelvington, *Canada* 105 C8
Kem, *Russia* 50 C4
Kema, *Indonesia* 63 D7
Kemah, *Turkey* 70 B3
Kemaliye, *Erzincan, Turkey* 73 C8
Kemaliye, *Manisa, Turkey* 39 C10
Kemalpaşa, *Turkey* 39 C9
Kemaman, *Malaysia* 62 D2
Kemano, *Canada* 104 C3
Kemasik, *Malaysia* 65 K4
Kembolcha, *Ethiopia* 81 E4
Kemer, *Antalya, Turkey* 39 E12
Kemer, *Burdur, Turkey* 39 D12
Kemer, *Muğla, Turkey* 39 E11
Kemer Barajı, *Turkey* 39 D10
Kemerovo, *Russia* 50 D9
Kemi, *Finland* 8 D21
Kemi älv = Kemijoki →, *Finland* 8 D21
Kemijärvi, *Finland* 8 C22
Kemijoki →, *Finland* 8 D21
Kemmerer, *U.S.A.* 114 F8
Kemmuna = Comino, *Malta* 36 C1
Kemp, L., *U.S.A.* 113 J5
Kemp Land, *Antarctica* 5 C5
Kempsey, *Australia* 95 E5
Kempt, L., *Canada* 102 C5
Kempten, *Germany* 25 H6
Kempton, *Australia* 94 G4
Kemptville, *Canada* 102 D4
Ken →, *India* 69 G9
Kenai, *U.S.A.* 100 B4
Kendai, *India* 69 H10
Kendal, *Indonesia* 63 G14
Kendal, *U.K.* 12 C5
Kendall, *Australia* 95 E5
Kendall, *U.S.A.* 109 N5
Kendall →, *Australia* 94 A3
Kendallville, *U.S.A.* 108 E3
Kendari, *Indonesia* 63 E6
Kendawangan, *Indonesia* 62 E4
Kende, *Nigeria* 83 C5
Kendrapara, *India* 67 J15
Këndrevicës, Maja e, *Albania* 40 F3
Kendrew, *S. Africa* 88 E3
Kene Thao, *Laos* 64 D3
Kenedy, *U.S.A.* 113 L6
Kenema, *S. Leone* 82 D2
Keng Kok, *Laos* 64 D5
Keng Tawng, *Burma* 67 J21
Keng Tung, *Burma* 58 G2
Kengeja, *Tanzania* 86 D4
Kenhardt, *S. Africa* 88 D3
Kéniéba, *Mali* 82 C2
Kenitra, *Morocco* 78 B4
Kenli, *China* 57 F10
Kenmare, *Ireland* 15 E2
Kenmare, *U.S.A.* 112 A3
Kenmare River, *Ireland* 15 E2
Kennebago Lake, *U.S.A.* 111 A14
Kennebec, *U.S.A.* 112 D5
Kennebec →, *U.S.A.* 109 D11
Kennebunk, *U.S.A.* 111 C14
Kennedy, *Zimbabwe* 88 B4
Kennedy Ra., *Australia* 93 D2
Kennedy Taungdeik, *Burma* 67 H18
Kenner, *U.S.A.* 113 L9
Kennet →, *U.K.* 13 F7
Kenneth Ra., *Australia* 93 D2
Kennett, *U.S.A.* 113 G9
Kennewick, *U.S.A.* 114 C4
Kenogami →, *Canada* 102 B3
Kenora, *Canada* 105 D10
Kenosha, *U.S.A.* 108 D2
Kensington, *Canada* 103 C7
Kent, *Ohio, U.S.A.* 110 E3
Kent, *Tex., U.S.A.* 113 K2
Kent, *Wash., U.S.A.* 116 C4
Kent □, *U.K.* 13 F8
Kent Group, *Australia* 94 F4
Kent Pen., *Canada* 100 B9
Kentau, *Kazakstan* 50 E7
Kentland, *U.S.A.* 108 E2
Kenton, *U.S.A.* 108 E4
Kentucky □, *U.S.A.* 108 G3
Kentucky →, *U.S.A.* 108 F3
Kentucky L., *U.S.A.* 109 G2
Kentville, *Canada* 103 C7
Kentwood, *U.S.A.* 113 K9
Kenya ■, *Africa* 86 B4
Kenya, Mt., *Kenya* 86 C4
Keo Neua, Deo, *Vietnam* 64 C5
Keokuk, *U.S.A.* 112 E9
Keonjhargarh, *India* 69 J11
Kep, *Cambodia* 65 G5
Kep, *Vietnam* 64 B6
Kepez, *Turkey* 41 F10
Kepi, *Indonesia* 63 F9
Kępice, *Poland* 44 D3
Kępno, *Poland* 45 G4
Kepsut, *Turkey* 39 B10
Kerala □, *India* 66 P10
Kerama-Rettō, *Japan* 55 L3
Keran, *Pakistan* 69 B5
Kerang, *Australia* 95 F3
Keranyo, *Ethiopia* 81 F4
Kerao →, *Sudan* 81 E3
Keratéa, *Greece* 38 D5
Keraudren, C., *Australia* 92 C2
Kerava, *Finland* 9 F21
Kerch, *Ukraine* 47 K9
Kerchenskiy Proliv, *Black Sea* 47 K9
Kerchoual, *Mali* 83 B5
Kerempe Burnu, *Turkey* 72 A5
Keren, *Eritrea* 81 D4
Kerewan, *Gambia* 82 C1
Kerguelen, *Ind. Oc.* 3 G13
Keri, *Greece* 38 D2
Keri Kera, *Sudan* 81 E3
Kericho, *Kenya* 86 C4
Kerinci, *Indonesia* 62 E2
Kerki, *Turkmenistan* 50 F7
Kerkinítis, Límni, *Greece* 40 E7
Kérkira, *Greece* 36 A3
Kérkira □, *Greece* 38 B1
Kerkrade, *Neths.* 17 D6
Kerma, *Sudan* 80 D3
Kermadec Is., *Pac. Oc.* 96 L10
Kermadec Trench, *Pac. Oc.* 96 L10
Kermān, *Iran* 71 D8
Kerman, *U.S.A.* 116 J6
Kermān □, *Iran* 71 D8
Kermān, Bīābān-e, *Iran* 71 D8
Kermānshāh = Bākhtarān, *Iran* 70 C5
Kermen, *Bulgaria* 41 D10

Kermit, *U.S.A.* 113 K3
Kern →, *U.S.A.* 117 K7
Kernhof, *Austria* 26 D8
Kernville, *U.S.A.* 117 K8
Keroh, *Malaysia* 65 K3
Kérou, *Benin* 83 C5
Kérouane, *Guinea* 82 D3
Kerpen, *Germany* 24 E2
Kerrera, *U.K.* 14 E3
Kerrobert, *Canada* 105 C7
Kerrville, *U.S.A.* 113 K5
Kerry □, *Ireland* 15 D2
Kerry Hd., *Ireland* 15 D2
Kersa, *Ethiopia* 81 F5
Kerulen →, *Asia* 60 B6
Kerzaz, *Algeria* 78 C5
Kesagami →, *Canada* 102 B4
Kesagami L., *Canada* 102 B3
Keşan, *Turkey* 41 F10
Kesennuma, *Japan* 54 E10
Keshit, *Iran* 71 D8
Keşiş Dağ, *Turkey* 73 C8
Keskin, *Turkey* 72 C5
Kestell, *S. Africa* 89 D4
Kestenga, *Russia* 50 C4
Keswick, *U.K.* 12 C4
Keszthely, *Hungary* 42 D2
Ket →, *Russia* 50 D9
Keta, *Ghana* 83 D5
Keta Lagoon, *Ghana* 83 D5
Ketapang, *Indonesia* 62 E4
Ketchikan, *U.S.A.* 104 B2
Ketchum, *U.S.A.* 114 E6
Kete Krachi, *Ghana* 83 D4
Ketef, Khalîg Umm el, *Egypt* 70 F2
Keti Bandar, *Pakistan* 68 G2
Kétou, *Benin* 83 D5
Ketri, *India* 68 E6
Kętrzyn, *Poland* 44 D8
Kettering, *U.K.* 13 E7
Kettering, *U.S.A.* 108 F3
Kettle →, *Canada* 105 B11
Kettle Falls, *U.S.A.* 114 B4
Kettle Pt., *Canada* 110 C2
Kettleman City, *U.S.A.* 116 J7
Kęty, *Poland* 45 J6
Keuka L., *U.S.A.* 110 D7
Keuruu, *Finland* 9 E21
Kevelaer, *Germany* 24 D2
Kewanee, *U.S.A.* 112 E10
Kewaunee, *U.S.A.* 108 C2
Keweenaw B., *U.S.A.* 108 B1
Keweenaw Pen., *U.S.A.* 108 B2
Keweenaw Pt., *U.S.A.* 108 B2
Key Largo, *U.S.A.* 109 N5
Key West, *U.S.A.* 107 F10
Keyala, *Sudan* 81 G3
Keynsham, *U.K.* 13 F5
Keyser, *U.S.A.* 108 F6
Kezhma, *Russia* 51 D11
Kezi, *Zimbabwe* 89 C4
Kežmarok, *Slovak Rep.* 27 B13
Khabarovsk, *Russia* 51 E14
Khabr, *Iran* 71 D8
Khābūr →, *Syria* 70 C4
Khachmas = Xaçmaz, *Azerbaijan* 49 K9
Khachrod, *India* 68 H6
Khadari, W. el →, *Sudan* 81 E2
Khadro, *Pakistan* 68 F3
Khadyzhensk, *Russia* 49 H4
Khadzhilyangar, *India* 69 B8
Khaga, *India* 69 G9
Khagaria, *India* 69 G12
Khaipur, *Pakistan* 68 E5
Khair, *India* 68 F7
Khairabad, *India* 69 F9
Khairagarh, *India* 69 J9
Khairpur, *Pakistan* 68 F3
Khairpur Nathan Shah, *Pakistan* 68 F2
Khairwara, *India* 68 H5
Khaisor →, *Pakistan* 68 D3
Khajuri Kach, *Pakistan* 68 C3
Khakassia □, *Russia* 50 D9
Khakhea, *Botswana* 88 C3
Khalafābād, *Iran* 71 D6
Khalilabad, *India* 69 F10
Khalīlī, *Iran* 71 E7
Khalkhāl, *Iran* 71 B6
Khálki, *Dhodhekánisos, Greece* 39 E9
Khálki, *Thessalía, Greece* 38 B4
Khalkidhikí □, *Greece* 40 F7
Khalkís, *Greece* 38 C5
Khalmer-Sede = Tazovskiy, *Russia* 50 C8
Khalmer Yu, *Russia* 50 C7
Khalūf, *Oman* 74 C6
Kham Keut, *Laos* 64 C5
Khamaria, *India* 69 H9
Khambhaliya, *India* 68 H3
Khambhat, *India* 68 H5
Khambhat, G. of, *India* 66 J8
Khamilonísion, *Greece* 39 F8
Khamīr, *Iran* 71 E7
Khamir, *Yemen* 74 D3
Khamsa, *Egypt* 75 E1
Khan →, *Namibia* 88 C2
Khān Abū Shāmat, *Syria* 75 B5
Khān Azād, *Iraq* 70 C5
Khān Mujiddah, *Iraq* 70 C4
Khān Shaykhūn, *Syria* 70 C3
Khān Yūnis, *Gaza Strip* 75 D3
Khanai, *Pakistan* 68 D2
Khānaqīn, *Iraq* 70 C5
Khānbāghī, *Iran* 71 B7
Khandrá, *Greece* 39 F8
Khandwa, *India* 66 J10
Khandyga, *Russia* 51 C14
Khāneh, *Iran* 70 B5
Khanewal, *Pakistan* 68 D4
Khangah Dogran, *Pakistan* 68 D5
Khanh Duong, *Vietnam* 64 F7
Khaniá, *Greece* 36 D6
Khaniá □, *Greece* 36 D6
Khaniadhana, *India* 68 G8
Khaníon, Kólpos, *Greece* 36 D5
Khanka, L., *Asia* 51 E14
Khankendy = Xankändi, *Azerbaijan* 70 B5
Khanna, *India* 68 D7
Khanozai, *Pakistan* 68 D2
Khanpur, *Pakistan* 68 E4
Khanty-Mansiysk, *Russia* 50 C7
Khapalu, *Pakistan* 69 B7
Khapcheranga, *Russia* 51 E12
Kharabali, *Russia* 49 G8
Kharaghoda, *India* 68 H4
Kharagpur, *India* 69 H12
Khárakas, *Greece* 36 D7
Kharan Kalat, *Pakistan* 66 E4
Kharānaq, *Iran* 71 C7
Kharda, *India* 66 K9
Khardung La, *India* 69 B7
Khârga, El Wâhât-el, *Egypt* 80 B3
Khargon, *India* 66 J9
Khari →, *India* 68 G6
Kharian, *Pakistan* 68 C5
Kharit, Wadi el →, *Egypt* 80 C3
Khārk, Jazīreh-ye, *Iran* 71 D6
Kharkiv, *Ukraine* 47 H9
Kharkov = Kharkiv, *Ukraine* 47 H9
Kharmanli, *Bulgaria* 41 E9
Kharovsk, *Russia* 46 C11
Kharsawangarh, *India* 69 H11
Kharta, *Turkey* 72 B3
Khartoum = El Khartûm, *Sudan* 81 D3
Khasan, *Russia* 54 C5
Khasavyurt, *Russia* 49 J8
Khāsh, *Iran* 66 E2
Khashm el Girba, *Sudan* 81 E4
Khashum, *Sudan* 81 E2
Khashuri, *Georgia* 49 J6
Khaskovo, *Bulgaria* 41 E9
Khaskovo □, *Bulgaria* 41 E9
Khatanga, *Russia* 51 B11
Khatanga →, *Russia* 51 B11
Khatauli, *India* 68 E7
Khatra, *India* 69 H12
Khātūnābād, *Iran* 71 D7
Khatyrka, *Russia* 51 C18
Khavda, *India* 68 H3
Khaybar, Harrat, *Si. Arabia* 70 E4
Khayelitsha, *S. Africa* 85 L3
Khāzimiyah, *Iraq* 70 C4
Khazzān Jabal al Awliyā, *Sudan* 81 D3
Khe Bo, *Vietnam* 64 C5
Khe Long, *Vietnam* 64 B5
Khed Brahma, *India* 66 G8
Khekra, *India* 68 E7
Khemarak Phouminville, *Cambodia* 65 G4
Khemisset, *Morocco* 78 B4
Khemmarat, *Thailand* 64 D5
Khenāmān, *Iran* 71 D8
Khenchela, *Algeria* 78 A7
Khersān →, *Iran* 71 D6
Khérson, *Greece* 40 E6
Kherson, *Ukraine* 47 J7
Khersónisos Akrotíri, *Greece* 36 D6
Kheta →, *Russia* 51 B11
Khewari, *Pakistan* 68 F3
Khilchipur, *India* 68 G7
Khiliomódhion, *Greece* 38 D4
Khilok, *Russia* 51 D12
Khimki, *Russia* 46 E9
Khíos, *Greece* 39 C8
Khíos □, *Greece* 39 C8
Khirsadoh, *India* 69 H8
Khiuma = Hiiumaa, *Estonia* 9 G20
Khiva, *Uzbekistan* 50 E7
Khīyāv, *Iran* 70 B5
Khlebarovo, *Bulgaria* 41 C10
Khlong Khlung, *Thailand* 64 D2
Khmelnik, *Ukraine* 47 H4
Khmelnitskiy = Khmelnytskyy, *Ukraine* 47 H4
Khmelnytskyy, *Ukraine* 47 H4
Khmer Rep. = Cambodia ■, *Asia* 64 F5
Khoai, Hon, *Vietnam* 65 H5
Khodoriv, *Ukraine* 47 H3
Khodzent = Khudzhand, *Tajikistan* 50 E7
Khojak Pass, *Afghan.* 68 D2
Khok Kloi, *Thailand* 65 H2
Khok Pho, *Thailand* 65 J3
Kholm, *Russia* 46 D6
Kholmsk, *Russia* 51 E15
Khomas Hochland, *Namibia* 88 C2
Khombole, *Senegal* 82 C1
Khomeyn, *Iran* 71 C6
Khomeynī Shahr, *Iran* 71 C6
Khomodino, *Botswana* 88 C3
Khon Kaen, *Thailand* 64 D4
Khong →, *Cambodia* 64 F5
Khong Sedone, *Laos* 64 E5
Khonuu, *Russia* 51 C15
Khoper →, *Russia* 48 F6
Khor el 'Atash, *Sudan* 81 E3
Khóra, *Greece* 38 D3
Khóra Sfakíon, *Greece* 36 D6
Khorāsān □, *Iran* 71 C8
Khorat = Nakhon Ratchasima, *Thailand* 64 E4
Khorat, Cao Nguyen, *Thailand* 64 E4
Khorixas, *Namibia* 88 C1
Khorol, *Ukraine* 47 H7
Khorramābād, *Khorāsān, Iran* 71 C8
Khorramābād, *Lorestān, Iran* 71 C6
Khorrāmshahr, *Iran* 71 D6
Khorugh, *Tajikistan* 50 F8
Khosravī, *Iran* 71 D6
Khosrowābād, *Khuzestān, Iran* 71 D6
Khosrowābād, *Kordestān, Iran* 70 C5
Khost, *Pakistan* 68 D2
Khosūyeh, *Iran* 71 D7
Khotyn, *Ukraine* 47 H4
Khouribga, *Morocco* 78 B4
Khowai, *Bangla.* 67 G17
Khowst, *Afghan.* 68 C3
Khoyniki, *Belarus* 47 G5
Khrami →, *Georgia* 49 K7
Khrenovoye, *Russia* 48 E5
Khrisoúpolis, *Greece* 41 F8
Khristianá, *Greece* 39 E7
Khrysokhou B., *Cyprus* 36 D11
Khtapodhiá, *Greece* 39 D7
Khu Khan, *Thailand* 64 E5
Khudzhand, *Tajikistan* 50 E7
Khuff, *Si. Arabia* 70 E5
Khūgīānī, *Afghan.* 68 D1
Khuis, *Botswana* 88 D3
Khuiyala, *India* 68 F4
Khujner, *India* 68 H7
Khulna, *Bangla.* 67 H16
Khulna □, *Bangla.* 67 H16
Khulo, *Georgia* 49 K6
Khumago, *Botswana* 88 C3
Khūnsorkh, *Iran* 71 E8
Khunti, *India* 69 H11
Khūr, *Iran* 71 C8
Khurai, *India* 68 G8
Khurayş, *Si. Arabia* 71 E6
Khureit, *Sudan* 81 E2
Khurīyā Murīyā, Jazā 'ir, *Oman* 74 D6
Khurja, *India* 68 E7
Khūrmāl, *Iraq* 70 C5
Khurr, Wādī al, *Iraq* 70 C4
Khūsf, *Iran* 71 C8
Khush, *Afghan.* 66 C3
Khushab, *Pakistan* 68 C5
Khust, *Ukraine* 47 H2
Khuzdar, *Pakistan* 68 F2
Khūzestān □, *Iran* 71 D6
Khvāf, *Iran* 71 C9
Khvājeh, *Iran* 70 B5
Khvalynsk, *Russia* 48 D9
Khvānsār, *Iran* 71 D7
Khvatovka, *Russia* 48 D8
Khvor, *Iran* 71 C7
Khvorgū, *Iran* 71 E8
Khvormūj, *Iran* 71 D6
Khvoy, *Iran* 70 B5
Khvoynaya, *Russia* 46 C8
Khyber Pass, *Afghan.* 68 B4
Kiabukwa, *Dem. Rep. of the Congo* 87 D1
Kiama, *Australia* 95 E5
Kiamba, *Phil.* 61 H6
Kiambi, *Dem. Rep. of the Congo* 86 D2
Kiambu, *Kenya* 86 C4
Kiangara, *Madag.* 89 B8
Kiangsi = Jiangxi □, *China* 59 D11
Kiangsu = Jiangsu □, *China* 57 H11
Kiáton, *Greece* 38 C4
Kibæk, *Denmark* 11 H2
Kibanga Port, *Uganda* 86 B3
Kibara, *Tanzania* 86 C3
Kibare, Mts., *Dem. Rep. of the Congo* 86 D2
Kibombo, *Dem. Rep. of the Congo* 86 C2
Kibondo, *Tanzania* 86 C3
Kibre Mengist, *Ethiopia* 81 F4
Kibumbu, *Burundi* 86 C2
Kibungo, *Rwanda* 86 C3
Kibuye, *Burundi* 86 C2
Kibuye, *Rwanda* 86 C2
Kibwesa, *Tanzania* 86 D2
Kibwezi, *Kenya* 86 C4
Kicasalih, *Turkey* 41 E10
Kičevo, *Macedonia* 40 E4
Kichha, *India* 69 E8
Kichha →, *India* 69 E8
Kicking Horse Pass, *Canada* 104 C5
Kidal, *Mali* 83 B5
Kidderminster, *U.K.* 13 E5
Kidete, *Tanzania* 86 D4
Kidira, *Senegal* 82 C2
Kidnappers, C., *N.Z.* 91 H6
Kidsgrove, *U.K.* 12 D5
Kidston, *Australia* 94 B3
Kidugallo, *Tanzania* 86 D4
Kiel, *Germany* 24 A6
Kiel Canal = Nord-Ostsee-Kanal, *Germany* 24 A5
Kielce, *Poland* 45 H7
Kielder Water, *U.K.* 12 B5
Kieler Bucht, *Germany* 24 A6
Kiembara, *Burkina Faso* 82 C4
Kien Binh, *Vietnam* 65 H5
Kien Tan, *Vietnam* 65 G5
Kienge, *Dem. Rep. of the Congo* 87 E2
Kiessé, *Niger* 83 C5
Kiev = Kyyiv, *Ukraine* 47 G6
Kifaya, *Guinea* 82 C2
Kiffa, *Mauritania* 82 B2
Kifisiá, *Greece* 38 C5
Kifissós →, *Greece* 38 C5
Kifrī, *Iraq* 70 C5
Kigali, *Rwanda* 86 C3
Kigarama, *Tanzania* 86 C3
Kigelle, *Sudan* 81 F3
Kigoma □, *Tanzania* 86 D3
Kigoma-Ujiji, *Tanzania* 86 C2
Kigomasha, Ras, *Tanzania* 86 C4
Kığzı, *Turkey* 70 B4
Kihei, *U.S.A.* 106 H16
Kihnu, *Estonia* 9 G21
Kii-Sanchi, *Japan* 55 G8
Kii-Suidō, *Japan* 55 H7
Kikaiga-Shima, *Japan* 55 K4
Kikinda, *Serbia, Yug.* 42 E5
Kikládhes, *Greece* 38 E6
Kikládhes □, *Greece* 38 D6
Kikwit, *Dem. Rep. of the Congo* 84 E3
Kil, *Sweden* 10 E7
Kilafors, *Sweden* 10 C10
Kilar, *India* 68 C7
Kilauea, *U.S.A.* 106 J14
Kilauea Crater, *U.S.A.* 106 J17
Kilbrannan Sd., *U.K.* 14 F3
Kilchu, *N. Korea* 57 D15
Kilcoy, *Australia* 95 D5
Kildare, *Ireland* 15 C5
Kildare □, *Ireland* 15 C5
Kileikli, *Sudan* 81 E2
Kilfinnane, *Ireland* 15 D3
Kilgore, *U.S.A.* 113 J7
Kilibo, *Benin* 83 D5
Kilifi, *Kenya* 86 C4
Kilimanjaro, *Tanzania* 86 C4
Kilimanjaro □, *Tanzania* 86 C4
Kilimli, *Turkey* 72 B4
Kilindini, *Kenya* 86 C4
Kilis, *Turkey* 70 B3
Kiliya, *Ukraine* 47 K5
Kilkee, *Ireland* 15 D2
Kilkeel, *U.K.* 15 B5
Kilkenny, *Ireland* 15 D4
Kilkenny □, *Ireland* 15 D4
Kilkieran B., *Ireland* 15 C2
Kilkís, *Greece* 40 F6
Kilkís □, *Greece* 40 E6
Killala, *Ireland* 15 B2
Killala B., *Ireland* 15 B2
Killaloe, *Ireland* 15 D3
Killaloe Sta., *Canada* 110 A7
Killarney, *Australia* 95 D5
Killarney, *Canada* 105 D9
Killarney, *Ireland* 15 D2
Killary Harbour, *Ireland* 15 C2
Killdeer, *U.S.A.* 112 B3
Killeberg, *Sweden* 11 H8
Killeen, *U.S.A.* 113 K6
Killin, *U.K.* 14 E4
Killíni, *Ilía, Greece* 38 D3
Killíni, *Korinthía, Greece* 38 D4
Killorglin, *Ireland* 15 D2
Killybegs, *Ireland* 15 B3
Kilmarnock, *U.K.* 14 F4
Kilmez, *Russia* 48 B10
Kilmez →, *Russia* 48 B10
Kilmore, *Australia* 95 F3
Kilondo, *Tanzania* 87 D3
Kilosa, *Tanzania* 86 D4
Kilrush, *Ireland* 15 D2
Kilwa Kisiwani, *Tanzania* 87 D4
Kilwa Kivinje, *Tanzania* 87 D4
Kilwa Masoko, *Tanzania* 87 D4
Kilwinning, *U.K.* 14 F4
Kim, *U.S.A.* 113 G3
Kim →, *Cameroon* 83 D7
Kimaam, *Indonesia* 63 F9
Kimamba, *Tanzania* 86 D4
Kimba, *Australia* 95 E2
Kimball, *Nebr., U.S.A.* 112 E3
Kimball, *S. Dak., U.S.A.* 112 D5
Kimberley, *Australia* 92 C4
Kimberley, *Canada* 104 D5
Kimberley, *S. Africa* 88 D3
Kimberly, *U.S.A.* 114 E6
Kimch'aek, *N. Korea* 57 D15
Kimch'ŏn, *S. Korea* 57 F15
Kími, *Greece* 38 C6
Kimje, *S. Korea* 57 G14
Kimmirut, *Canada* 101 B13
Kímolos, *Greece* 38 E6
Kimovsk, *Moskva, Russia* 46 E9
Kimovsk, *Tula, Russia* 46 E10
Kimparana, *Mali* 82 C4
Kimpese, *Dem. Rep. of the Congo* 84 F2
Kimry, *Russia* 46 D9
Kimstad, *Sweden* 11 F9
Kinabalu, Gunong, *Malaysia* 62 C5
Kínaros, *Greece* 39 E8
Kinaskan L., *Canada* 104 B2
Kinbasket L., *Canada* 104 C5
Kincardine, *Canada* 102 D3
Kincolith, *Canada* 104 B3
Kinda, *Dem. Rep. of the Congo* 87 D2
Kindberg, *Austria* 26 D8
Kinde, *U.S.A.* 110 C2
Kinder Scout, *U.K.* 12 D6
Kindersley, *Canada* 105 C7
Kindia, *Guinea* 82 D2
Kindu, *Dem. Rep. of the Congo* 86 C2
Kinel, *Russia* 48 D10
Kineshma, *Russia* 48 B6
Kinesi, *Tanzania* 86 C3
King, L., *Australia* 93 F2
King, Mt., *Australia* 94 D4
King City, *U.S.A.* 116 J5
King Cr. →, *Australia* 94 C2
King Edward →, *Australia* 92 B4
King Frederick VI Land = Kong Frederik VI Kyst, *Greenland* 4 C5
King George B., *Falk. Is.* 128 G4
King George I., *Antarctica* 5 C18
King George Is., *Canada* 101 C11
King I. = Kadan Kyun, *Burma* 64 F2
King I., *Australia* 94 F3
King I., *Canada* 104 C3
King Leopold Ranges, *Australia* 92 C4
King of Prussia, *U.S.A.* 111 F9
King Sd., *Australia* 92 C3
King William I., *Canada* 100 B10
King William's Town, *S. Africa* 88 E4
Kingaroy, *Australia* 95 D5
Kingfisher, *U.S.A.* 113 H6
Kingirbān, *Iraq* 70 C5
Kingisepp = Kuressaare, *Estonia* 9 G20
Kingisepp, *Russia* 46 C5
Kingman, *Ariz., U.S.A.* 117 K12
Kingman, *Kans., U.S.A.* 113 G5
Kingoonya, *Australia* 95 E2
Kingri, *Pakistan* 68 D3
Kings →, *U.S.A.* 116 J7
Kings Canyon National Park, *U.S.A.* 116 J8
King's Lynn, *U.K.* 12 E8
Kings Mountain, *U.S.A.* 109 H5
Kings Park, *U.S.A.* 111 F11
King's Peak, *U.S.A.* 114 F8
Kingsbridge, *U.K.* 13 G4
Kingsburg, *U.S.A.* 116 J7
Kingscote, *Australia* 95 F2
Kingscourt, *Ireland* 15 C5
Kingsford, *U.S.A.* 108 C1
Kingsland, *U.S.A.* 109 K5
Kingsley, *U.S.A.* 112 D7
Kingsport, *U.S.A.* 109 G4
Kingston, *Canada* 102 D4
Kingston, *Jamaica* 120 C4
Kingston, *N.Z.* 91 L2
Kingston, *N.H., U.S.A.* 111 D13
Kingston, *N.Y., U.S.A.* 111 E11
Kingston, *Pa., U.S.A.* 111 E9
Kingston, *R.I., U.S.A.* 111 E13
Kingston Pk., *U.S.A.* 117 K11
Kingston South East, *Australia* 95 F2
Kingston upon Hull, *U.K.* 12 D7
Kingston upon Hull □, *U.K.* 12 D7
Kingston-upon-Thames, *U.K.* 13 F7
Kingstown, *St. Vincent* 121 D7
Kingstree, *U.S.A.* 109 J6
Kingsville, *Canada* 102 D3
Kingsville, *U.S.A.* 113 M6
Kingussie, *U.K.* 14 D4
Kingwood, *U.S.A.* 113 K7
Kınık, *Antalya, Turkey* 39 E11
Kınık, *İzmir, Turkey* 39 B9
Kinistino, *Canada* 105 C7
Kinkala, *Congo* 84 E2
Kinki □, *Japan* 55 H8
Kinleith, *N.Z.* 91 H5
Kinmount, *Canada* 110 B6
Kinna, *Sweden* 11 G6
Kinnairds Hd., *U.K.* 14 D6
Kinnared, *Sweden* 11 G7
Kinnarodden, *Norway* 6 A11
Kinnarp, *Sweden* 11 F7
Kinneviken, *Sweden* 11 F7
Kino, *Mexico* 118 B2
Kinoje →, *Canada* 102 B3
Kinomoto, *Japan* 55 G8
Kinoni, *Uganda* 86 C3
Kinoosao, *Canada* 105 B8
Kinross, *U.K.* 14 E5
Kinsale, *Ireland* 15 E3
Kinsale, Old Hd. of, *Ireland* 15 E3
Kinsha = Chang Jiang →, *China* 59 B13
Kinshasa, *Dem. Rep. of the Congo* 84 E3
Kinsley, *U.S.A.* 113 G5
Kinsman, *U.S.A.* 110 E4
Kinston, *U.S.A.* 109 H7
Kintampo, *Ghana* 83 D4
Kintore Ra., *Australia* 92 D4
Kintyre, *U.K.* 14 F3
Kintyre, Mull of, *U.K.* 14 F3
Kinushseo →, *Canada* 102 A3
Kinuso, *Canada* 104 B5
Kinyangiri, *Tanzania* 86 C3
Kinyeti, *Sudan* 81 G3
Kinzig →, *Germany* 25 G3
Kinzua, *U.S.A.* 110 E6
Kinzua Dam, *U.S.A.* 110 E6
Kióni, *Greece* 38 C2
Kiosk, *Canada* 102 C4
Kiowa, *Kans., U.S.A.* 113 G5
Kiowa, *Okla., U.S.A.* 113 H7
Kipahigan L., *Canada* 105 B8
Kipanga, *Tanzania* 86 D4
Kiparissía, *Greece* 38 D3
Kiparissiakós Kólpos, *Greece* 38 D3
Kipawa, L., *Canada* 102 C4
Kipembawe, *Tanzania* 86 D3
Kipengere Ra., *Tanzania* 87 D3
Kipili, *Tanzania* 86 D3
Kipini, *Kenya* 86 C5
Kipling, *Canada* 105 C8
Kippure, *Ireland* 15 C5
Kipushi, *Dem. Rep. of the Congo* 87 E2
Kirane, *Mali* 82 B2
Kiranomena, *Madag.* 89 B8
Kiraz, *Turkey* 39 C10
Kirazlı, *Turkey* 41 F10
Kirchhain, *Germany* 24 E4
Kirchheim, *Germany* 25 G5
Kirchheimbolanden, *Germany* 25 F3

Kirchschlag, *Austria* 27 D9
Kireç, *Turkey* 39 B10
Kirensk, *Russia* 51 D11
Kirghizia = Kyrgyzstan ■, *Asia* 50 E8
Kirghizstan = Kyrgyzstan ■, *Asia* 50 E8
Kiribati ■, *Pac. Oc.* 96 H10
Kırıkhan, *Turkey* 72 D7
Kırıkkale, *Turkey* 72 C5
Kirillov, *Russia* 46 C10
Kirin = Jilin, *China* 57 C14
Kirishi, *Russia* 46 C7
Kiritimati, *Kiribati* 97 G12
Kırka, *Turkey* 39 B12
Kırkağaç, *Turkey* 39 B9
Kirkby, *U.K.* 12 D5
Kirkby Lonsdale, *U.K.* 12 C5
Kirkcaldy, *U.K.* 14 E5
Kirkcudbright, *U.K.* 14 G4
Kirkee, *India* 66 K8
Kirkenes, *Norway* 8 B23
Kirkfield, *Canada* 110 B6
Kirkjubæjarklaustur, *Iceland* 8 E4
Kirkkonummi, *Finland* 9 F21
Kirkland Lake, *Canada* 102 C3
Kırklareli, *Turkey* 41 E11
Kırklareli □, *Turkey* 41 E11
Kirksville, *U.S.A.* 112 E8
Kirkūk, *Iraq* 70 C5
Kirkwall, *U.K.* 14 C6
Kirkwood, *S. Africa* 88 E4
Kirn, *Germany* 25 F3
Kirov, *Kaluga, Russia* 46 E8
Kirov, *Kirov, Russia* 50 D5
Kirovabad = Gäncä, *Azerbaijan* 49 K8
Kirovakan = Vanadzor, *Armenia* 49 K7
Kirovograd = Kirovohrad, *Ukraine* 47 H7
Kirovohrad, *Ukraine* 47 H7
Kirovsk = Babadayhan, *Turkmenistan* 50 F7
Kirovskiy, *Astrakhan, Russia* 49 H9
Kirovskiy, *Kamchatka, Russia* 51 D16
Kirovskiy, *Primorsk, Russia* 54 B6
Kirriemuir, *U.K.* 14 E5
Kirsanov, *Russia* 48 D6
Kırşehir, *Turkey* 70 B2
Kirtachi, *Niger* 83 C5
Kirthar Range, *Pakistan* 68 F2
Kirtland, *U.S.A.* 115 H9
Kiruna, *Sweden* 8 C19
Kirundu, *Dem. Rep. of the Congo* 86 C2
Kirya, *Russia* 48 C8
Kiryū, *Japan* 55 F9
Kisa, *Sweden* 11 G9
Kisaga, *Tanzania* 86 C3
Kisalaya, *Nic.* 120 D3
Kisalföld, *Hungary* 42 C2
Kisámou, Kólpos, *Greece* 36 D5
Kisanga, *Dem. Rep. of the Congo* 86 B2
Kisangani, *Dem. Rep. of the Congo* 86 B2
Kisar, *Indonesia* 63 F7
Kisarawe, *Tanzania* 86 D4
Kisarazu, *Japan* 55 G9
Kisbér, *Hungary* 42 C3
Kishanganga →, *Pakistan* 69 B5
Kishanganj, *India* 69 F13
Kishangarh, *Raj., India* 68 F6
Kishangarh, *Raj., India* 68 F4
Kishi, *Nigeria* 83 D5
Kishinev = Chişinău, *Moldova* 43 C13
Kishiwada, *Japan* 55 G7
Kishtwar, *India* 69 C6
Kisielice, *Poland* 44 E6
Kisii, *Kenya* 86 C3
Kisiju, *Tanzania* 86 D4
Kisir, *Turkey* 73 B10
Kisizi, *Uganda* 86 C2
Kiskomárom = Zalakomár, *Hungary* 42 D2
Kiskörei-víztároló, *Hungary* 42 C5
Kiskőrös, *Hungary* 42 D4
Kiskundorozsma, *Hungary* 42 D5
Kiskunfélegyháza, *Hungary* 42 D4
Kiskunhalas, *Hungary* 42 D4
Kiskunmajsa, *Hungary* 42 D4
Kislovodsk, *Russia* 49 J6
Kismayu = Chisimaio, *Somali Rep.* 77 G8
Kiso-Gawa →, *Japan* 55 G8
Kiso-Sammyaku, *Japan* 55 G8
Kisofukushima, *Japan* 55 G8
Kisoro, *Uganda* 86 C2
Kissidougou, *Guinea* 82 D2
Kissimmee, *U.S.A.* 109 L5
Kissimmee →, *U.S.A.* 109 M5
Kississing L., *Canada* 105 B8
Kissónerga, *Cyprus* 36 E11
Kissu, J., *Sudan* 80 C2
Kistanje, *Croatia* 29 E12
Kisújszállás, *Hungary* 42 C5
Kisumu, *Kenya* 86 C3
Kisvárda, *Hungary* 42 B7
Kiswani, *Tanzania* 86 C4
Kiswere, *Tanzania* 87 D4
Kit Carson, *U.S.A.* 112 F3
Kita, *Mali* 82 C3
Kitaibaraki, *Japan* 55 F10
Kitakami, *Japan* 54 E10
Kitakami-Gawa →, *Japan* 54 E10
Kitakami-Sammyaku, *Japan* 54 E10
Kitakata, *Japan* 54 F9
Kitakyūshū, *Japan* 55 H5
Kitale, *Kenya* 86 B4
Kitami, *Japan* 54 C11
Kitami-Sammyaku, *Japan* 54 B11
Kitangiri, L., *Tanzania* 86 C3
Kitaya, *Tanzania* 87 E5
Kitchener, *Canada* 102 D3
Kitee, *Finland* 46 A6
Kitega = Gitega, *Burundi* 86 C2
Kitengo, *Dem. Rep. of the Congo* 86 D1
Kitgum, *Uganda* 86 B3
Kíthira, *Greece* 38 E5
Kíthnos, *Greece* 38 D6
Kiti, *Cyprus* 36 E12
Kiti, C., *Cyprus* 36 E12
Kitimat, *Canada* 104 C3
Kitinen →, *Finland* 8 C22
Kitiyab, *Sudan* 81 D3
Kítros, *Greece* 40 F6
Kitsuki, *Japan* 55 H5
Kittakittaooloo, L., *Australia* 95 D2
Kittanning, *U.S.A.* 110 F5
Kittatinny Mts., *U.S.A.* 111 F10
Kittery, *U.S.A.* 109 D10
Kittilä, *Finland* 8 C21
Kitui, *Kenya* 86 C4
Kitwanga, *Canada* 104 B3
Kitwe, *Zambia* 87 E2
Kitzbühel, *Austria* 26 D5
Kitzbühler Alpen, *Austria* 26 D5
Kitzingen, *Germany* 25 F6
Kivarli, *India* 68 G5
Kivertsi, *Ukraine* 47 G3
Kividhes, *Cyprus* 36 E11
Kivik, *Sweden* 11 J8
Kivotós, *Greece* 40 F5
Kivu, L., *Dem. Rep. of the Congo* 86 C2
Kiyev = Kyyiv, *Ukraine* 47 G6
Kiyevskoye Vdkhr. = Kyyivske Vdskh., *Ukraine* 47 G6
Kıyıköy, *Turkey* 41 E12
Kiziguru, *Rwanda* 86 C3
Kızıl Adalar, *Turkey* 41 F13
Kızıl Irmak →, *Turkey* 72 B6
Kizil Jilga, *India* 69 B8
Kizil Yurt, *Russia* 49 J8
Kızılcabölük, *Turkey* 39 D11
Kızılcadağ, *Turkey* 39 D11
Kızılcahamam, *Turkey* 72 B5
Kızılhisar, *Turkey* 72 D3
Kızılırmak, *Turkey* 72 B5
Kızılkaya, *Turkey* 39 D12
Kızılören, *Turkey* 39 C12
Kızıltepe, *Turkey* 70 B4
Kizimkazi, *Tanzania* 86 D4
Kizlyar, *Russia* 49 J8
Kizyl-Arvat = Gyzylarbat, *Turkmenistan* 50 F6
Kjellerup, *Denmark* 11 H3
Kjölur, *Iceland* 8 D4
Kladanj, *Bos.-H.* 42 F3
Kladnica, *Serbia, Yug.* 40 C4
Kladno, *Czech Rep.* 26 A7
Kladovo, *Serbia, Yug.* 40 B6
Klaeng, *Thailand* 64 F3
Klagenfurt, *Austria* 26 E7
Klaipėda, *Lithuania* 9 J19
Klaipėda □, *Lithuania* 44 C8
Klaksvík, *Færoe Is.* 8 E9
Klamath →, *U.S.A.* 114 F1
Klamath Falls, *U.S.A.* 114 E3
Klamath Mts., *U.S.A.* 114 F2
Klamono, *Indonesia* 63 E8
Klanjec, *Croatia* 29 B12
Klappan →, *Canada* 104 B3
Klarälven →, *Sweden* 10 E7
Klässbol, *Sweden* 10 E6
Klatovy, *Czech Rep.* 26 B6
Klawer, *S. Africa* 88 E2
Klazienaveen, *Neths.* 17 B6
Klé, *Mali* 82 C3
Klecko, *Poland* 45 F4
Kleczew, *Poland* 45 F5
Kleena Kleene, *Canada* 104 C4
Klein-Karas, *Namibia* 88 D2
Klekovača, *Bos.-H.* 29 D13
Klenoec, *Macedonia* 40 E4
Klenovec, *Slovak Rep.* 27 C12
Klerksdorp, *S. Africa* 88 D4
Kleszczele, *Poland* 45 F10
Kletnya, *Russia* 46 F7
Kletsk = Klyetsk, *Belarus* 47 F4
Kletskiy, *Russia* 49 F6
Kleve, *Germany* 24 D2
Klickitat, *U.S.A.* 114 D3
Klickitat →, *U.S.A.* 116 E5
Klidhes, *Cyprus* 36 D13
Klimovichi, *Belarus* 46 F6
Klin, *Russia* 46 D9
Klina, *Kosovo, Yug.* 40 D4
Klinaklini →, *Canada* 104 C3
Klintehamn, *Sweden* 11 G12
Klintsy, *Russia* 47 F7
Klip →, *S. Africa* 89 D4
Klipdale, *S. Africa* 88 E2
Klippan, *Sweden* 11 H7
Klipplaat, *S. Africa* 88 E3
Klisura, *Bulgaria* 41 D8
Kljajićevo, *Serbia, Yug.* 42 E4
Ključ, *Bos.-H.* 29 D13
Kłobuck, *Poland* 45 H5
Klockestrand, *Sweden* 10 B11
Kłodawa, *Poland* 45 F5
Kłodzko, *Poland* 45 H3
Klosi, *Albania* 40 E4
Klosterneuburg, *Austria* 27 C9
Klosters, *Switz.* 25 J5
Klötze, *Germany* 24 C7
Klouto, *Togo* 83 D5
Kluane L., *Canada* 100 B6
Kluane Nat. Park, *Canada* 104 A1
Kluczbork, *Poland* 45 H5
Klukwan, *U.S.A.* 104 B1
Klyetsk, *Belarus* 47 F4
Klyuchevskaya, Gora, *Russia* 51 D17
Knäred, *Sweden* 11 H7
Knaresborough, *U.K.* 12 C6
Knee L., *Man., Canada* 102 A1
Knee L., *Sask., Canada* 105 B7
Knezha, *Bulgaria* 41 C8
Knić, *Serbia, Yug.* 40 C4
Knight Inlet, *Canada* 104 C3
Knighton, *U.K.* 13 E4
Knights Ferry, *U.S.A.* 116 H6
Knights Landing, *U.S.A.* 116 G5
Knin, *Croatia* 29 D13
Knislinge, *Sweden* 11 H8
Knittelfeld, *Austria* 26 D7
Knivsta, *Sweden* 10 E11
Knjaževac, *Serbia, Yug.* 40 C6
Knob, C., *Australia* 93 F2
Knock, *Ireland* 15 C3
Knockmealdown Mts., *Ireland* 15 D4
Knokke-Heist, *Belgium* 17 C3
Knossós, *Greece* 36 D7
Knowlton, *Canada* 111 A12
Knox, *U.S.A.* 108 E2
Knox Coast, *Antarctica* 5 C8
Knoxville, *Iowa, U.S.A.* 112 E8
Knoxville, *Pa., U.S.A.* 110 E7
Knoxville, *Tenn., U.S.A.* 109 H4
Knysna, *S. Africa* 88 E3
Knyszyn, *Poland* 44 E9
Ko Kha, *Thailand* 64 C2
Koartac = Quaqtaq, *Canada* 101 B13
Koba, *Indonesia* 63 F8
Kobarid, *Slovenia* 29 B10
Kobayashi, *Japan* 55 J5
Kobdo = Hovd, *Mongolia* 60 B4
Kōbe, *Japan* 55 G7
Kobelyaky, *Ukraine* 47 H8
København, *Denmark* 11 J6
Københavns Amtskommune □, *Denmark* 11 J6
Kobenni, *Mauritania* 82 B3
Kōbi-Sho, *Japan* 55 M1
Koblenz, *Germany* 25 E3
Kobo, *Ethiopia* 81 E4
Kobryn, *Belarus* 47 F3
Kobuleti, *Georgia* 49 K5
Kobylin, *Poland* 45 G4
Kobyłka, *Poland* 45 F8
Kobylkino, *Russia* 48 C6
Koca →, *Turkey* 41 F11
Kocabaş, *Turkey* 39 D11
Kocaeli, *Turkey* 41 F13
Kocaeli □, *Turkey* 41 F13
Kočane, *Serbia, Yug.* 40 C5
Kočani, *Macedonia* 40 E6
Koçarlı, *Turkey* 39 D9
Koceljevo, *Serbia, Yug.* 40 B3
Kočevje, *Slovenia* 29 C11
Koch Bihar, *India* 67 F16
Kochang, *S. Korea* 57 G14
Kochas, *India* 69 G10
Kocher →, *Germany* 25 F5
Kōchi, *Japan* 55 H6
Kōchi □, *Japan* 55 H6
Kochiu = Gejiu, *China* 58 F4
Kock, *Poland* 45 G9
Kodarma, *India* 69 G11
Kode, *Sweden* 11 G5
Kodiak, *U.S.A.* 100 C4
Kodiak I., *U.S.A.* 100 C4
Kodinar, *India* 68 J4
Kodok, *Sudan* 81 F3
Kodori →, *Georgia* 49 J5
Koedoesberge, *S. Africa* 88 E3
Koes, *Namibia* 88 D2
Kofçaz, *Turkey* 41 E11
Koffiefontein, *S. Africa* 88 D4
Kofiau, *Indonesia* 63 E7
Köflach, *Austria* 26 D8
Koforidua, *Ghana* 83 D4
Kōfu, *Japan* 55 G9
Koga, *Japan* 55 F9
Kogaluk →, *Canada* 103 A7
Køge, *Denmark* 11 J6
Køge Bugt, *Denmark* 11 J6
Kogi □, *Nigeria* 83 D6
Kogin Baba, *Nigeria* 83 D7
Koh-i-Bābā, *Afghan.* 66 B5
Koh-i-Khurd, *Afghan.* 68 C1
Koh-i-Maran, *Pakistan* 68 E2
Kohat, *Pakistan* 68 C4
Kohima, *India* 67 G19
Kohkīlūyeh va Būyer Aḥmadi □, *Iran* 71 D6
Kohler Ra., *Antarctica* 5 D15
Kohlu, *Pakistan* 68 E3
Kohtla-Järve, *Estonia* 9 G22
Koillismaa, *Finland* 8 D23
Koin-dong, *N. Korea* 57 D14
Koinare, *Bulgaria* 41 C8
Koindu, *S. Leone* 82 D2
Kojetín, *Czech Rep.* 27 B10
Kojō, *N. Korea* 57 E14
Kojonup, *Australia* 93 F2
Kojūr, *Iran* 71 B6
Koka, *Sudan* 80 C3
Kokand = Qŭqon, *Uzbekistan* 50 E8
Kokas, *Indonesia* 63 E8
Kokava, *Slovak Rep.* 27 C12
Kokchetav = Kökshetaū, *Kazakstan* 50 D7
Kokemäenjoki →, *Finland* 9 F19
Kokhma, *Russia* 48 B5
Koki, *Senegal* 82 B1
Kokkola, *Finland* 8 E20
Koko, *Nigeria* 83 C5
Koko Kyunzu, *Burma* 67 M18
Kokolopozo, *Ivory C.* 82 D3
Kokomo, *U.S.A.* 108 E2
Kokoro, *Niger* 83 C5
Koksan, *N. Korea* 57 E14
Kökshetaū, *Kazakstan* 50 D7
Koksoak →, *Canada* 101 C13
Kokstad, *S. Africa* 89 E4
Kokubu, *Japan* 55 J5
Kola, *Indonesia* 63 F8
Kola Pen. = Kolskiy Poluostrov, *Russia* 50 C4
Kolachi →, *Pakistan* 68 F2
Kolahoi, *India* 69 B6
Kolahun, *Liberia* 82 D2
Kolaka, *Indonesia* 63 E6
Kolar, *India* 66 N11
Kolar Gold Fields, *India* 66 N11
Kolaras, *India* 68 G6
Kolari, *Finland* 8 C20
Kolárovo, *Slovak Rep.* 27 D10
Kolašin, *Montenegro, Yug.* 40 D3
Kolayat, *India* 66 F8
Kolbäck, *Sweden* 10 E10
Kolbäcksån →, *Sweden* 10 E10
Kolbermoor, *Germany* 25 H8
Kolbuszowa, *Poland* 45 H8
Kolchugino = Leninsk-Kuznetskiy, *Russia* 50 D9
Kolchugino, *Russia* 46 D10
Kolda, *Senegal* 82 C2
Koldegi, *Sudan* 81 E3
Kolding, *Denmark* 11 J3
Kolepom = Dolak, Pulau, *Indonesia* 63 F9
Kolguyev, Ostrov, *Russia* 50 C5
Kolhapur, *India* 66 L9
Kolia, *Ivory C.* 82 D3
Kolín, *Czech Rep.* 26 A8
Kolind, *Denmark* 11 H4
Kolkas rags, *Latvia* 9 H20
Kölleda, *Germany* 24 D7
Kollum, *Neths.* 17 A6
Kolmanskop, *Namibia* 88 D2
Köln, *Germany* 24 E2
Kolno, *Poland* 44 E8
Koło, *Poland* 45 F5
Kołobrzeg, *Poland* 44 D2
Kolokani, *Mali* 82 C3
Koloko, *Burkina Faso* 82 C3
Kololo, *Ethiopia* 81 F5
Kolomna, *Russia* 46 E10
Kolomyya, *Ukraine* 47 H3
Kolondiéba, *Mali* 82 C3
Kolonodale, *Indonesia* 63 E6
Kolonowskie, *Poland* 45 H5
Kolosib, *India* 67 G18
Kolpashevo, *Russia* 50 D9
Kolpino, *Russia* 46 C6
Kolpny, *Russia* 47 F9
Kolskiy Poluostrov, *Russia* 50 C4
Kolsva, *Sweden* 10 E9
Kolubara →, *Serbia, Yug.* 40 B4
Koluszki, *Poland* 45 G6
Kolwezi, *Dem. Rep. of the Congo* 87 E2
Kolyma →, *Russia* 51 C17
Kolymskoye Nagorye, *Russia* 51 C16
Kôm Hamâda, *Egypt* 80 H7
Kôm Ombo, *Egypt* 80 C3
Komadugu Gana →, *Nigeria* 83 C7
Komandorskiye Is. = Komandorskiye Ostrova, *Russia* 51 D17
Komandorskiye Ostrova, *Russia* 51 D17
Komárno, *Slovak Rep.* 27 D11
Komárom, *Hungary* 42 C3
Komárom-Esztergom □, *Hungary* 42 C3
Komatipoort, *S. Africa* 89 D5
Komatou Yialou, *Cyprus* 36 D13
Komatsu, *Japan* 55 F8
Komatsujima, *Japan* 55 H7
Kombissiri, *Burkina Faso* 83 C4
Kombori, *Burkina Faso* 82 C4
Kombóti, *Greece* 38 B3
Komen, *Slovenia* 29 C10
Komenda, *Ghana* 83 D4
Komi □, *Russia* 50 C6
Komiža, *Croatia* 29 E13
Komló, *Hungary* 42 D3
Kommunarsk = Alchevsk, *Ukraine* 47 H10
Kommunizma, Pik, *Tajikistan* 50 F8
Komodo, *Indonesia* 63 F5
Komoé →, *Ivory C.* 82 D4
Komoran, Pulau, *Indonesia* 63 F9
Komoro, *Japan* 55 F9
Komotini, *Greece* 41 E9
Komovi, *Montenegro, Yug.* 40 D3
Kompasberg, *S. Africa* 88 E3
Kompong Bang, *Cambodia* 65 F5
Kompong Cham, *Cambodia* 65 F5
Kompong Chhnang = Kampang Chhnang, *Cambodia* 65 F5
Kompong Chikreng, *Cambodia* 64 F5
Kompong Kleang, *Cambodia* 64 F5
Kompong Luong, *Cambodia* 65 G5
Kompong Pranak, *Cambodia* 64 F5
Kompong Som = Kampong Saom, *Cambodia* 65 G4
Kompong Som, Chhung = Kampong Saom, Chaak, *Cambodia* 65 G4
Kompong Speu, *Cambodia* 65 G5
Kompong Sralao, *Cambodia* 64 E5
Kompong Thom, *Cambodia* 64 F5
Kompong Trabeck, *Cambodia* 64 F5
Kompong Trabeck, *Cambodia* 65 G5
Kompong Trach, *Cambodia* 65 G5
Kompong Tralach, *Cambodia* 65 G5
Komrat = Comrat, *Moldova* 43 D13
Komsberg, *S. Africa* 88 E3
Komsomolets, Ostrov, *Russia* 51 A10
Komsomolsk, *Amur, Russia* 51 D14
Komsomolsk, *Ivanovo, Russia* 46 D11
Komsomolskiy, *Russia* 48 C7
Kömür Burnu, *Turkey* 39 C8
Kon Tum, *Vietnam* 64 E7
Kon Tum, Plateau du, *Vietnam* 64 E7
Kona, *Mali* 82 C4
Konakovo, *Russia* 46 D9
Konarhā □, *Afghan.* 66 B7
Konārī, *Iran* 71 D6
Konch, *India* 69 G8
Konde, *Tanzania* 86 C4
Kondiá, *Greece* 39 B7
Kondinin, *Australia* 93 F2
Kondoa, *Tanzania* 86 C4
Kondókali, *Greece* 36 A3
Kondopaga, *Russia* 46 A8
Kondratyevo, *Russia* 51 D10
Kondrovo, *Russia* 46 E8
Konduga, *Nigeria* 83 C7
Köneürgench, *Turkmenistan* 50 E6
Konevo, *Russia* 46 A10
Kong = Khong →, *Cambodia* 64 F5
Kong, *Ivory C.* 82 D4
Kong, Koh, *Cambodia* 65 G4
Kong Christian IX Land, *Greenland* 4 C6
Kong Christian X Land, *Greenland* 4 B6
Kong Frederik IX Land, *Greenland* 4 C5
Kong Frederik VI Kyst, *Greenland* 4 C5
Kong Frederik VIII Land, *Greenland* 4 B6
Kong Oscar Fjord, *Greenland* 4 B6
Kongeå →, *Denmark* 11 J2
Kongerslev, *Denmark* 11 H4
Kongju, *S. Korea* 57 F14
Konglu, *Burma* 67 F20
Kongola, *Namibia* 88 B3
Kongolo, *Kasai-Or., Dem. Rep. of the Congo* 86 D1
Kongolo, *Katanga, Dem. Rep. of the Congo* 86 D2
Kongor, *Sudan* 81 F3
Kongoussi, *Burkina Faso* 83 C4
Kongsberg, *Norway* 9 G13
Kongsvinger, *Norway* 9 F15
Kongwa, *Tanzania* 86 D4
Koni, *Dem. Rep. of the Congo* 87 E2
Koni, Mts., *Dem. Rep. of the Congo* 87 E2
Koniakari, *Mali* 82 C2
Koniecpol, *Poland* 45 H6
Königs Wusterhausen, *Germany* 24 C9
Königsberg = Kaliningrad, *Russia* 9 J19
Königsbrunn, *Germany* 25 G6
Königslutter, *Germany* 24 C6
Konin, *Poland* 45 F5
Konispoli, *Albania* 40 G4
Kónitsa, *Greece* 38 A2
Konjic, *Bos.-H.* 42 G2
Konkiep, *Namibia* 88 D2
Konkouré →, *Guinea* 82 D2
Könnern, *Germany* 24 D7
Kono, *S. Leone* 82 D2
Konongo, *Ghana* 83 D4
Konosha, *Russia* 46 B11
Kōnosu, *Japan* 55 F9
Konotop, *Ukraine* 47 G7
Konsankoro, *Guinea* 82 D3
Końskie, *Poland* 45 G7
Konstancin-Jeziorna, *Poland* 45 F8
Konstantinovka = Kostyantynivka, *Ukraine* 47 H9
Konstantinovsk, *Russia* 49 G5
Konstantynów Łódźki, *Poland* 45 G6
Konstanz, *Germany* 25 H5
Kont, *Iran* 71 E9
Kontagora, *Nigeria* 83 C6
Kontcha, *Cameroon* 83 D7
Konya, *Turkey* 70 B2
Konya Ovası, *Turkey* 72 C5
Konz, *Germany* 25 F2
Konza, *Kenya* 86 C4
Koocanusa, L., *Canada* 114 B6
Kookynie, *Australia* 93 E3
Koolyanobbing, *Australia* 93 F2
Koonibba, *Australia* 95 E1
Koorawatha, *Australia* 95 E4
Koorda, *Australia* 93 F2
Kooskia, *U.S.A.* 114 C6
Kootenay →, *U.S.A.* 104 D5
Kootenay L., *Canada* 104 D5
Kootenay Nat. Park, *Canada* 104 C5
Kootjieskolk, *S. Africa* 88 E3
Kopanovka, *Russia* 49 G8
Kopaonik, *Yugoslavia* 40 C4
Kópavogur, *Iceland* 8 D3
Koper, *Slovenia* 29 C10
Kopervik, *Norway* 9 G11

Kulpawn

Kopet Dagh, *Asia* 71 B8
Kopi, *Australia* 95 E2
Köping, *Sweden* 10 E10
Köpingsvik, *Sweden* 11 H10
Kopište, *Croatia* 29 F13
Kopliku, *Albania* 40 D3
Köpmanholmen, *Sweden* 10 A12
Kopparberg, *Sweden* 10 E9
Kopparbergs län □, *Sweden* 10 C8
Koppeh Dāgh = Kopet Dagh, *Asia* 71 B8
Koppies, *S. Africa* 89 D4
Koppom, *Sweden* 10 E6
Koprivlen, *Bulgaria* 40 E7
Koprivnica, *Croatia* 29 B13
Kopřivnice, *Czech Rep.* 27 B11
Koprivshtitsa, *Bulgaria* 41 D8
Köprübaşı, *Turkey* 39 C10
Kopychyntsi, *Ukraine* 47 H3
Korab, *Macedonia* 40 E4
Korakiána, *Greece* 36 A3
Koral, *India* 68 J5
Korarou, L., *Mali* 82 B4
Korba, *India* 69 H10
Korbach, *Germany* 24 D4
Korbu, G., *Malaysia* 65 K3
Korça, *Albania* 40 F4
Korce = Korça, *Albania* 40 F4
Korčula, *Croatia* 29 F13
Korčulanski Kanal, *Croatia* 29 E13
Kord Kūy, *Iran* 71 B7
Kord Sheykh, *Iran* 71 D7
Kordestān □, *Iran* 70 C5
Kordofân, *Sudan* 79 F11
Koré Mayroua, *Niger* 83 C5
Korea, North ■, *Asia* 57 E14
Korea, South ■, *Asia* 57 G15
Korea Bay, *Korea* 57 E13
Korea Strait, *Asia* 57 H15
Korem, *Ethiopia* 81 E4
Korenevo, *Russia* 47 G8
Korenovsk, *Russia* 49 H4
Korets, *Ukraine* 47 G4
Korfantów, *Poland* 45 H4
Korgan, *Turkey* 72 B7
Korgus, *Sudan* 80 D3
Korhogo, *Ivory C.* 82 D3
Koribundu, *S. Leone* 82 D2
Korienzé, *Mali* 82 B4
Korinthía □, *Greece* 38 D4
Korinthiakós Kólpos, *Greece* 38 C4
Kórinthos, *Greece* 38 D4
Korioumé, *Mali* 82 B4
Koríssa, Límni, *Greece* 36 B3
Kōriyama, *Japan* 54 F10
Korkuteli, *Turkey* 39 D12
Kormakiti, C., *Cyprus* 36 D11
Körmend, *Hungary* 42 C1
Kornat, *Croatia* 29 E12
Korneshty = Corneşti, *Moldova* 43 C13
Korneuburg, *Austria* 27 C9
Kórnik, *Poland* 45 F4
Koro, *Fiji* 91 C8
Koro, *Ivory C.* 82 D3
Koro, *Mali* 82 C4
Koro Sea, *Fiji* 91 C9
Korocha, *Russia* 47 G9
Köroğlu Dağları, *Turkey* 72 B5
Korogwe, *Tanzania* 86 D4
Koronadal, *Phil.* 61 H6
Koróni, *Greece* 38 E3
Korónia, Límni, *Greece* 40 F7
Koronís, *Greece* 39 D7
Koronowo, *Poland* 45 E4
Koror, *Palau* 63 C8
Körös →, *Hungary* 42 D5
Köröstarcsa, *Hungary* 42 D6
Korosten, *Ukraine* 47 G5
Korostyshev, *Ukraine* 47 G5
Korotoyak, *Russia* 47 G10
Korraraika, Helodranon' i, *Madag.* 89 B7
Korsakov, *Russia* 51 E15
Korsberga, *Sweden* 11 G9
Korshunovo, *Russia* 51 D12
Korsør, *Denmark* 11 J5
Korsun Shevchenkovskiy, *Ukraine* 47 H6
Korsze, *Poland* 44 D8
Korti, *Sudan* 80 D3
Kortrijk, *Belgium* 17 D3
Korucu, *Turkey* 39 B9
Korwai, *India* 68 G8
Koryakskoye Nagorye, *Russia* 51 C18
Koryŏng, *S. Korea* 57 G15
Koryukovka, *Ukraine* 47 G7
Kos, *Greece* 39 E9
Kosa, *Ethiopia* 81 F4
Kosaya Gora, *Russia* 46 E9
Kościan, *Poland* 45 F3
Kościerzyna, *Poland* 44 D4
Kosciusko, *U.S.A.* 113 J10
Kosciuszko, Mt., *Australia* 95 F4
Kösély →, *Hungary* 42 C6
Kosha, *Sudan* 80 C3
Koshava, *Bulgaria* 40 B7
K'oshih = Kashi, *China* 60 C2
Koshiki-Rettō, *Japan* 55 J4
Kosi, *India* 68 F7
Kosi →, *India* 69 E8
Košice, *Slovak Rep.* 27 C14
Košický □, *Slovak Rep.* 27 C14
Kosjerić, *Serbia, Yug.* 40 B3
Köşk, *Turkey* 39 D10
Koskhinoú, *Greece* 36 C10
Koslan, *Russia* 50 C5
Kosŏng, *N. Korea* 57 E15
Kosovo □, *Yugoslavia* 40 D4
Kosovo Polje, *Kosovo, Yug.* 40 D5
Kosovska Kamenica, *Kosovo, Yug.* 40 D5
Kosovska Mitrovica, *Kosovo, Yug.* 40 D4
Kossou, L. de, *Ivory C.* 82 D3
Kosta, *Sweden* 11 H9
Kostajnica, *Croatia* 29 C13
Kostanjevica, *Slovenia* 29 C12
Kostenets, *Bulgaria* 40 D7
Koster, *S. Africa* 88 D4
Kôstî, *Sudan* 81 E3
Kostinbrod, *Bulgaria* 40 D7
Kostolac, *Serbia, Yug.* 40 B5
Kostopil, *Ukraine* 47 G4
Kostroma, *Russia* 46 D11
Kostromskoye Vdkhr., *Russia* 46 D11
Kostrzyn, *Lubuskie, Poland* 45 F1
Kostrzyn, *Wielkopolskie, Poland* 45 F4
Kostyantynivka, *Ukraine* 47 H9
Kostyukovichi = Kastsyukovichy, *Belarus* 46 F7
Koszalin, *Poland* 44 D3
Kőszeg, *Hungary* 42 C1
Kot Addu, *Pakistan* 68 D4
Kot Kapura, *India* 68 D6
Kot Moman, *Pakistan* 68 C5
Kot Sultan, *Pakistan* 68 D4
Kota, *India* 68 G6
Kota Baharu, *Malaysia* 65 J4
Kota Barrage, *India* 68 G6
Kota Belud, *Malaysia* 62 C5
Kota Kinabalu, *Malaysia* 62 C5
Kota Kubu Baharu, *Malaysia* 65 L3
Kota Tinggi, *Malaysia* 65 M4
Kotaagung, *Indonesia* 62 F2
Kotabaru, *Indonesia* 62 E5
Kotabumi, *Indonesia* 62 E2
Kotamobagu, *Indonesia* 63 D6
Kotcho L., *Canada* 104 B4
Kotdwara, *India* 69 E8
Kotel, *Bulgaria* 41 D10
Kotelnich, *Russia* 48 A9
Kotelnikovo, *Russia* 49 G6
Kotelnyy, Ostrov, *Russia* 51 B14
Kothari →, *India* 68 G6
Köthen, *Germany* 24 D7
Kothi, *Mad. P., India* 69 H10
Kothi, *Mad. P., India* 69 G9
Kotiro, *Pakistan* 68 F2
Kotka, *Finland* 9 F22
Kotlas, *Russia* 50 C5
Kotlenska Planina, *Bulgaria* 41 D10
Kotli, *Pakistan* 68 C5
Kotma, *India* 69 H9
Kotmul, *Pakistan* 69 B6
Koton-Karifi, *Nigeria* 83 D6
Kotonkoro, *Nigeria* 83 C6
Kotor, *Montenegro, Yug.* 40 D2
Kotor Varoš, *Bos.-H.* 42 F2
Kotoriba, *Croatia* 29 B13
Kotovo, *Russia* 48 E7
Kotovsk, *Russia* 48 D5
Kotovsk, *Ukraine* 47 J5
Kotputli, *India* 68 F7
Kotri, *Pakistan* 68 G3
Kótronas, *Greece* 38 E4
Kötschach-Mauthen, *Austria* 26 E6
Kottayam, *India* 66 Q10
Kotturu, *India* 66 M10
Kotuy →, *Russia* 51 B11
Kotzebue, *U.S.A.* 100 B3
Koudougou, *Burkina Faso* 82 C4
Koufonísi, *Greece* 36 E8
Koufonísia, *Greece* 39 E7
Kougaberge, *S. Africa* 88 E3
Kouibli, *Ivory C.* 82 D3
Kouilou →, *Congo* 84 E2
Koula Moutou, *Gabon* 84 E2
Koulen = Kulen, *Cambodia* 64 F5
Koulikoro, *Mali* 82 C3
Kouloúra, *Greece* 36 A3
Koúm-bournoú, Ákra, *Greece* 36 C10
Koumala, *Australia* 94 C4
Koumankou, *Mali* 82 C3
Koumbia, *Burkina Faso* 82 C4
Koumbia, *Guinea* 82 C2
Koumboum, *Guinea* 82 C2
Koumpenntoum, *Senegal* 82 C2
Koumra, *Chad* 79 G9
Koun-Fao, *Ivory C.* 82 D4
Koundara, *Guinea* 82 C2
Koundian, *Guinea* 82 C3
Koungheul, *Senegal* 82 C2
Kounradskiy, *Kazakstan* 50 E8
Kountze, *U.S.A.* 113 K7
Koupéla, *Burkina Faso* 83 C4
Kourémalé, *Mali* 82 C3
Kouris →, *Cyprus* 36 E11
Kourou, *Fr. Guiana* 125 B8
Kourouba, *Mali* 82 C2
Kouroukoto, *Mali* 82 C2
Kourouma, *Burkina Faso* 82 C4
Kourouninkoto, *Mali* 82 C3
Kouroussa, *Guinea* 82 C3
Koussanar, *Senegal* 82 C2
Koussané, *Mali* 82 C2
Koussane, *Senegal* 82 C2
Kousseri, *Cameroon* 79 F8
Koutiala, *Mali* 82 C3
Kouto, *Ivory C.* 82 D3
Kouvé, *Togo* 83 D5
Kouvola, *Finland* 9 F22
Kovačica, *Serbia, Yug.* 42 E5
Kovel, *Ukraine* 47 G3
Kovin, *Serbia, Yug.* 42 F5
Kovrov, *Russia* 48 B5
Kowal, *Poland* 45 F6
Kowalewo Pomorskie, *Poland* 45 E5
Kowanyama, *Australia* 94 B3
Kowloon, *H.K.* 59 F10
Kowŏn, *N. Korea* 57 E14
Köyceğiz, *Turkey* 39 E10
Köyceğiz Gölü, *Turkey* 39 E10
Koyulhisar, *Turkey* 72 B7
Koyunyeri, *Turkey* 41 F10
Koza, *Japan* 55 L3
Kozak, *Turkey* 39 B9
Kozan, *Turkey* 70 B2
Kozáni, *Greece* 40 F5
Kozáni □, *Greece* 40 F5
Kozara, *Bos.-H.* 29 D14
Kozarac, *Bos.-H.* 29 D13
Kozelets, *Ukraine* 47 G6
Kozelsk, *Russia* 46 E8
Kozhikode = Calicut, *India* 66 P9
Koziegłowy, *Poland* 45 H6
Kozienice, *Poland* 45 G8
Kozje, *Slovenia* 29 B12
Kozloduy, *Bulgaria* 40 C7
Kozlovets, *Bulgaria* 41 C9
Kozlovka, *Russia* 48 C9
Kozlu, *Turkey* 72 B4
Kozluk, *Turkey* 73 C9
Koźmin, *Poland* 45 G4
Kozmodemyansk, *Russia* 48 B8
Kożuchów, *Poland* 45 G2
Kozyatyn, *Ukraine* 47 H5
Kpabia, *Ghana* 83 D4
Kpalimé, *Togo* 83 D5
Kpandae, *Ghana* 83 D4
Kpessi, *Togo* 83 D5
Kra, Isthmus of = Kra, Kho Khot, *Thailand* 65 G2
Kra, Kho Khot, *Thailand* 65 G2
Kra Buri, *Thailand* 65 G2
Kraai →, *S. Africa* 88 E4
Krabi, *Thailand* 65 H2
Kracheh, *Cambodia* 64 F6
Kragan, *Indonesia* 63 G14
Kragerø, *Norway* 9 G13
Kragujevac, *Serbia, Yug.* 40 B4
Krajenka, *Poland* 45 E3
Krajina, *Bos.-H.* 29 D13
Krakatau = Rakata, Pulau, *Indonesia* 62 F3
Krakatoa = Rakata, Pulau, *Indonesia* 62 F3
Krakor, *Cambodia* 64 F5
Kraków, *Poland* 45 H6
Kralanh, *Cambodia* 64 F4
Králíky, *Czech Rep.* 27 A9
Kraljevo, *Serbia, Yug.* 40 C4
Královský Chlmec, *Slovak Rep.* 27 C14
Kralupy nad Vltavou, *Czech Rep.* 26 A7
Kramatorsk, *Ukraine* 47 H9
Kramfors, *Sweden* 10 B11
Kraniá, *Greece* 40 G5
Kranía Elassónas, *Greece* 38 B4
Kranídhion, *Greece* 38 D5
Kranj, *Slovenia* 29 B11
Kranjska Gora, *Slovenia* 29 B10
Krankskop, *S. Africa* 89 D5
Krapina, *Croatia* 29 B12
Krapina →, *Croatia* 29 C12
Krapkowice, *Poland* 45 H4
Kras, *Croatia* 29 C10
Kraskino, *Russia* 51 E14
Krāslava, *Latvia* 46 E4
Kraslice, *Czech Rep.* 26 A5
Krasnaya Gorbatka, *Russia* 48 C5
Krasnaya Polyana, *Russia* 49 J5
Kraśnik, *Poland* 45 H9
Krasnoarmeisk, *Ukraine* 47 H9
Krasnoarmeysk, *Russia* 48 E7
Krasnoarmeyskiy, *Russia* 49 G6
Krasnobrod, *Poland* 45 H10
Krasnodar, *Russia* 49 H4
Krasnodon, *Ukraine* 47 H10
Krasnogorskiy, *Russia* 48 B9
Krasnograd = Krasnohrad, *Ukraine* 47 H8
Krasnogvardeyskoye, *Russia* 49 H5
Krasnogvardyesk, *Ukraine* 47 K8
Krasnohrad, *Ukraine* 47 H8
Krasnokutsk, *Ukraine* 47 G8
Krasnolesnyy, *Russia* 47 G10
Krasnoperekopsk, *Ukraine* 47 J7
Krasnorechenskiy, *Russia* 54 B7
Krasnoselkup, *Russia* 50 C9
Krasnoslobodsk, *Mordvinia, Russia* 48 C6
Krasnoslobodsk, *Volgograd, Russia* 49 F7
Krasnoturinsk, *Russia* 50 D7
Krasnovodsk = Türkmenbashi, *Turkmenistan* 50 E6
Krasnoyarsk, *Russia* 51 D10
Krasnoye = Krasnyy, *Russia* 46 E6
Krasnozavodsk, *Russia* 46 D10
Krasny Sulin, *Russia* 47 J11
Krasnystaw, *Poland* 45 H10
Krasnyy, *Russia* 46 E6
Krasnyy Kholm, *Russia* 46 C9
Krasnyy Kut, *Russia* 48 E8
Krasnyy Liman, *Ukraine* 47 H9
Krasnyy Luch, *Ukraine* 47 H10
Krasnyy Profintern, *Russia* 46 D11
Krasnyy Yar, *Astrakhan, Russia* 49 G9
Krasnyy Yar, *Samara, Russia* 48 D10
Krasnyy Yar, *Volgograd, Russia* 48 E7
Krasnyye Baki, *Russia* 48 B7
Krasnyyoskolske Vdskh., *Ukraine* 47 H9
Kraszna →, *Hungary* 42 B7
Kratie = Kracheh, *Cambodia* 64 F6
Kratovo, *Macedonia* 40 D6
Krau, *Indonesia* 63 E10
Kravanh, Chuor Phnum, *Cambodia* 65 G4
Krefeld, *Germany* 24 D2
Krémaston, Límni, *Greece* 38 C3
Kremen, *Croatia* 29 D12
Kremenchug = Kremenchuk, *Ukraine* 47 H7
Kremenchuk, *Ukraine* 47 H7
Kremenchuksk Vdskh., *Ukraine* 47 H7
Kremenets, *Ukraine* 47 G3
Kremennaya, *Ukraine* 47 H10
Kremges = Svitlovodsk, *Ukraine* 47 H7
Kremmen, *Germany* 24 C9
Kremmling, *U.S.A.* 114 F10
Kremnica, *Slovak Rep.* 27 C11
Krems, *Austria* 26 C8
Kremsmünster, *Austria* 26 C7
Kretinga, *Lithuania* 9 J19
Krettsy, *Russia* 46 C7
Kreuzberg, *Germany* 25 E5
Kreuztal, *Germany* 24 E4
Kría Vrísi, *Greece* 40 F6
Kribi, *Cameroon* 83 E6
Krichem, *Bulgaria* 41 D8
Krichev = Krychaw, *Belarus* 46 F6
Krim, *Slovenia* 29 C11
Kriós, Ákra, *Greece* 36 D5
Krishna →, *India* 67 M12
Krishnanagar, *India* 69 H13
Kristdala, *Sweden* 11 G10
Kristiansand, *Norway* 9 G13
Kristianstad, *Sweden* 11 H8
Kristiansund, *Norway* 8 E12
Kristiinankaupunki, *Finland* 9 E19
Kristinehamn, *Sweden* 10 E8
Kristinestad = Kristiinankaupunki, *Finland* 9 E19
Kríti, *Greece* 36 D7
Kritsá, *Greece* 36 D7
Kriva →, *Macedonia* 40 D5
Kriva Palanka, *Macedonia* 40 D6
Krivaja →, *Bos.-H.* 42 F3
Krivelj, *Serbia, Yug.* 40 B6
Krivoy Rog = Kryvyy Rih, *Ukraine* 47 J7
Križevci, *Croatia* 29 B13
Krk, *Croatia* 29 C11
Krka →, *Slovenia* 29 C12
Krkonoše, *Czech Rep.* 26 A8
Krnov, *Czech Rep.* 27 A10
Krobia, *Poland* 45 G3
Krokeaí, *Greece* 38 E4
Krokek, *Sweden* 11 F10
Krokodil →, *Mozam.* 89 D5
Krokom, *Sweden* 10 A8
Krokowa, *Poland* 44 D5
Krolevets, *Ukraine* 47 G7
Kroměříž, *Czech Rep.* 27 B10
Krompachy, *Slovak Rep.* 27 C13
Kromy, *Russia* 47 F8
Kronach, *Germany* 25 E7
Krong Kaoh Kong, *Cambodia* 62 B2
Kronobergs län □, *Sweden* 11 H8
Kronprins Olav Kyst, *Antarctica* 5 C5
Kronshtadt, *Russia* 46 C5
Kroonstad, *S. Africa* 88 D4
Kröpelin, *Germany* 24 A7
Kropotkin, *Russia* 49 H5
Kropp, *Germany* 24 A5
Krosna, *Lithuania* 44 D10
Krośniewice, *Poland* 45 F6
Krosno, *Poland* 45 J8
Krosno Odrzańskie, *Poland* 45 F2
Krotoszyn, *Poland* 45 G4
Krotovka, *Russia* 48 D10
Kroussón, *Greece* 36 D6
Krraba, *Albania* 40 E3
Krško, *Slovenia* 29 C12
Krstača, *Serbia, Yug.* 40 D4
Kruger Nat. Park, *S. Africa* 89 C5
Krugersdorp, *S. Africa* 89 D4
Kruisfontein, *S. Africa* 88 E3
Kruja, *Albania* 40 E3
Krulevshchina = Krulyewshchyna, *Belarus* 46 E4
Krulyewshchyna, *Belarus* 46 E4
Kruma, *Albania* 40 D4
Krumbach, *Germany* 25 G6
Krumovgrad, *Bulgaria* 41 E9
Krung Thep = Bangkok, *Thailand* 64 F3
Krupanj, *Serbia, Yug.* 40 B3
Krupina, *Slovak Rep.* 27 C12
Krupinica →, *Slovak Rep.* 27 C11
Krupki, *Belarus* 46 E5
Kruševac, *Serbia, Yug.* 40 C5
Kruševo, *Macedonia* 40 E5
Kruszwica, *Poland* 45 F5
Krychaw, *Belarus* 46 F6
Krymsk, *Russia* 47 K10
Krymskiy Poluostrov = Krymskyy Pivostriv, *Ukraine* 47 K8
Krymskyy Pivostriv, *Ukraine* 47 K8
Krynica, *Poland* 45 J7
Krynica Morska, *Poland* 44 D6
Krynki, *Poland* 45 E10
Kryvyy Rih, *Ukraine* 47 J7
Krzepice, *Poland* 45 H5
Krzeszów, *Poland* 45 H9
Krzna →, *Poland* 45 F10
Krzywiń, *Poland* 45 G3
Krzyż Wielkopolski, *Poland* 45 F2
Ksar el Kebir, *Morocco* 78 B4
Ksar es Souk = Ar Rachidiya, *Morocco* 78 B5
Książ Wielkopolski, *Poland* 45 F4
Kstovo, *Russia* 48 B7
Ku, W. el →, *Sudan* 81 E2
Kuala Belait, *Malaysia* 62 D4
Kuala Berang, *Malaysia* 65 K4
Kuala Dungun = Dungun, *Malaysia* 65 K4
Kuala Kangsar, *Malaysia* 65 K3
Kuala Kelawang, *Malaysia* 65 L4
Kuala Kerai, *Malaysia* 65 K4
Kuala Lipis, *Malaysia* 65 K4
Kuala Lumpur, *Malaysia* 65 L3
Kuala Nerang, *Malaysia* 65 J3
Kuala Pilah, *Malaysia* 65 L4
Kuala Rompin, *Malaysia* 65 L4
Kuala Selangor, *Malaysia* 65 L3
Kuala Sepetang, *Malaysia* 65 K3
Kuala Terengganu, *Malaysia* 65 K4
Kualajelai, *Indonesia* 62 E4
Kualakapuas, *Indonesia* 62 E4
Kualakurun, *Indonesia* 62 E4
Kualapembuang, *Indonesia* 62 E4
Kualasimpang, *Indonesia* 62 D1
Kuancheng, *China* 57 D10
Kuandang, *Indonesia* 63 D6
Kuandian, *China* 57 D13
Kuangchou = Guangzhou, *China* 59 F9
Kuanshan, *Taiwan* 59 F13
Kuantan, *Malaysia* 65 L4
Kuba = Quba, *Azerbaijan* 49 K9
Kuban →, *Russia* 47 K9
Kubenskoye, Ozero, *Russia* 46 C10
Kubokawa, *Japan* 55 H6
Kubrat, *Bulgaria* 41 C10
Kučevo, *Serbia, Yug.* 40 B5
Kucha Gompa, *India* 69 B7
Kuchaman, *India* 68 F6
Kuchenspitze, *Austria* 26 D3
Kuchinda, *India* 69 J11
Kuching, *Malaysia* 62 D4
Kuchino-eruba-Jima, *Japan* 55 J5
Kuchino-Shima, *Japan* 55 K4
Kuchinotsu, *Japan* 55 H5
Kuchl, *Austria* 26 D6
Kucing = Kuching, *Malaysia* 62 D4
Kuçovë, *Albania* 40 F3
Küçükbahçe, *Turkey* 39 C8
Küçükköy, *Turkey* 39 B8
Küçükkuyu, *Turkey* 39 B8
Küçükmenderes →, *Turkey* 39 D9
Kud →, *Pakistan* 68 F2
Kuda, *India* 66 H7
Kudat, *Malaysia* 62 C5
Kudirkos Naumiestis, *Lithuania* 44 D9
Kudowa-Zdrój, *Poland* 45 H3
Kudus, *Indonesia* 63 G14
Kudymkar, *Russia* 50 D6
Kueiyang = Guiyang, *China* 58 D6
Kufra Oasis = Al Kufrah, *Libya* 79 D10
Kufstein, *Austria* 26 D5
Kugluktuk, *Canada* 100 B8
Kugong I., *Canada* 102 A4
Kūhak, *Iran* 66 F3
Kuhan, *Pakistan* 68 E2
Kūhbonān, *Iran* 71 D8
Kūhestak, *Iran* 71 E8
Kuhin, *Iran* 71 B6
Kūhīrī, *Iran* 71 E9
Kuhnsdorf, *Austria* 26 E7
Kūhpāyeh, *Eşfahan, Iran* 71 C7
Kūhpāyeh, *Kermān, Iran* 71 D8
Kūhrān, Kūh-e, *Iran* 71 E8
Kui Buri, *Thailand* 65 F2
Kuiseb →, *Namibia* 88 B2
Kuito, *Angola* 85 G3
Kuiu I., *U.S.A.* 104 B2
Kujang, *N. Korea* 57 E14
Kujawsko-Pomorskie □, *Poland* 44 E5
Kuji, *Japan* 54 D10
Kujū-San, *Japan* 55 H5
Kukavica, *Serbia, Yug.* 40 D5
Kukawa, *Nigeria* 83 C7
Kukësi, *Albania* 40 D4
Kukmor, *Russia* 48 B10
Kukup, *Malaysia* 65 M4
Kukvidze, *Russia* 48 E6
Kula, *Bulgaria* 40 C6
Kula, *Serbia, Yug.* 42 E4
Kula, *Turkey* 39 C10
Kulachi, *Pakistan* 68 D4
Kulai, *Malaysia* 65 M4
Kulal, Mt., *Kenya* 86 B4
Kulaly, Ostrov, *Kazakstan* 49 H10
Kulasekarappattinam, *India* 66 Q11
Kulautuva, *Lithuania* 44 D10
Kuldīga, *Latvia* 9 H19
Kuldīga □, *Latvia* 44 B8
Kuldja = Yining, *China* 50 E9
Kuldu, *Sudan* 81 E2
Kulebaki, *Russia* 48 C6
Kulen, *Cambodia* 64 F5
Kulen Vakuf, *Bos.-H.* 29 D13
Kulgam, *India* 69 C6
Kulgera, *Australia* 94 D1
Kulim, *Malaysia* 65 K3
Kulin, *Australia* 93 F2
Kullen, *Sweden* 11 H6
Kulmbach, *Germany* 25 E7
Kŭlob, *Tajikistan* 50 F7
Kulp, *Turkey* 73 C9
Kulpawn →, *Ghana* 83 D4

Kulsary, *Kazakstan* 50 E6
Kulti, *India* 69 H12
Kulu, *India* 68 D7
Kulu, *Turkey* 72 C5
Kulumbura, *Australia* 92 B4
Kulunda, *Russia* 50 D8
Kulungar, *Afghan.* 68 C3
Külvand, *Iran* 71 D7
Kulwin, *Australia* 95 F3
Kulyab = Kŭlob, *Tajikistan* 50 F7
Kuma →, *Russia* 49 H8
Kumafşarı, *Turkey* 39 D11
Kumaganum, *Nigeria* 83 C7
Kumagaya, *Japan* 55 F9
Kumai, *Indonesia* 62 E4
Kumalar Dağı, *Turkey* 39 C12
Kumamba, Kepulauan, *Indonesia* 63 E9
Kumamoto, *Japan* 55 H5
Kumamoto □, *Japan* 55 H5
Kumanovo, *Macedonia* 40 D5
Kumara, *N.Z.* 91 K3
Kumarina, *Australia* 93 D2
Kumasi, *Ghana* 82 D4
Kumayri = Gyumri, *Armenia* 49 K6
Kumba, *Cameroon* 83 E6
Kumbağ, *Turkey* 41 F11
Kumbakonam, *India* 66 P11
Kumbarilla, *Australia* 95 D5
Kumbhraj, *India* 68 G7
Kumbia, *Australia* 95 D5
Kumbo, *Cameroon* 83 D7
Kŭmch'ŏn, *N. Korea* 57 E14
Kumdok, *India* 69 C8
Kume-Shima, *Japan* 55 L3
Kumeny, *Russia* 48 A9
Kumharsain, *India* 68 D7
Kŭmhwa, *S. Korea* 57 E14
Kumi, *Uganda* 86 B3
Kumkale, *Turkey* 41 G10
Kumla, *Sweden* 10 E9
Kumluca, *Turkey* 39 E12
Kummerower See, *Germany* 24 B8
Kumo, *Nigeria* 83 C7
Kumon Bum, *Burma* 67 F20
Kumylzhenskaya, *Russia* 48 F6
Kunágota, *Hungary* 42 D6
Kunashir, Ostrov, *Russia* 51 E15
Kunda, *Estonia* 9 G22
Kunda, *India* 69 G9
Kundar →, *Pakistan* 68 D3
Kundian, *Pakistan* 68 C4
Kundla, *India* 68 J4
Kunga →, *Bangla.* 69 J13
Kungälv, *Sweden* 11 G5
Kunghit I., *Canada* 104 C2
Kungrad = Qŭnghirot, *Uzbekistan* 50 E6
Kungsängen, *Sweden* 10 E11
Kungsbacka, *Sweden* 11 G6
Kungsgården, *Sweden* 10 D10
Kungshamn, *Sweden* 11 F5
Kungsör, *Sweden* 10 E10
Kungur, *Russia* 50 D6
Kunhar →, *Pakistan* 69 B5
Kunhegyes, *Hungary* 42 C5
Kuningan, *Indonesia* 63 G13
Kunlong, *Burma* 58 F2
Kunlun Shan, *Asia* 60 C3
Kunmadaras, *Hungary* 42 C5
Kunming, *China* 58 E4
Kunów, *Poland* 45 H8
Kunsan, *S. Korea* 57 G14
Kunshan, *China* 59 B13
Kunszentmárton, *Hungary* 42 D5
Kunszentmiklós, *Hungary* 42 C4
Kuntaur, *Senegal* 82 C2
Kununurra, *Australia* 92 C4
Kunwari →, *India* 69 F8
Kunya-Urgench = Köneürgench, *Turkmenistan* 50 E6
Künzelsau, *Germany* 25 F5
Kuopio, *Finland* 8 E22
Kupa →, *Croatia* 29 C13
Kupang, *Indonesia* 63 F6
Kupreanof I., *U.S.A.* 104 B2
Kupres, *Bos.-H.* 42 G2
Kupyansk, *Ukraine* 47 H9
Kupyansk-Uzlovoi, *Ukraine* 47 H9
Kuqa, *China* 60 B3
Kür →, *Azerbaijan* 73 C13
Kür Dili, *Azerbaijan* 71 B6
Kura = Kür →, *Azerbaijan* 73 C13
Kuranda, *Australia* 94 B4
Kuranga, *India* 68 H3
Kurashiki, *Japan* 55 G6
Kurayoshi, *Japan* 55 G6
Kürdämir, *Azerbaijan* 49 K9
Kurdistan, *Asia* 73 D10
Kŭrdzhali, *Bulgaria* 41 E9
Kure, *Japan* 55 G6
Küre, *Turkey* 72 B5
Küre Dağları, *Turkey* 72 B6
Kuressaare, *Estonia* 9 G20
Kurgan, *Russia* 50 D7
Kurganinsk, *Russia* 49 H5
Kurgannaya = Kurganinsk, *Russia* 49 H5
Kuri, *India* 68 F4
Kuria Maria Is. = Khurīyā Murīyā, Jazā 'ir, *Oman* 74 D6
Kuridala, *Australia* 94 C3
Kurigram, *Bangla.* 67 G16
Kurikka, *Finland* 9 E20
Kuril Is. = Kurilskiye Ostrova, *Russia* 51 E15
Kuril Trench, *Pac. Oc.* 52 E19
Kurilsk, *Russia* 51 E15
Kurilskiye Ostrova, *Russia* 51 E15
Kurino, *Japan* 55 J5
Kurinskaya Kosa = Kür Dili, *Azerbaijan* 71 B6
Kurkur, *Egypt* 80 C3
Kurlovskiy, *Russia* 48 C5
Kurmuk, *Sudan* 81 E3
Kurnool, *India* 66 M11
Kuro-Shima, *Kagoshima, Japan* 55 J4
Kuro-Shima, *Okinawa, Japan* 55 M2
Kuror, J., *Sudan* 80 C3
Kurow, *N.Z.* 91 L3
Kurów, *Poland* 45 G9
Kurram →, *Pakistan* 68 C4
Kurri Kurri, *Australia* 95 E5
Kurrimine, *Australia* 94 B4
Kursavka, *Russia* 49 H6
Kuršėnai, *Lithuania* 44 B9
Kurshskiy Zaliv, *Russia* 9 J19
Kursk, *Russia* 47 G9
Kuršumlija, *Serbia, Yug.* 40 C5
Kuršumlijska Banja, *Serbia, Yug.* 40 C5
Kurşunlu, *Bursa, Turkey* 41 F13
Kurşunlu, *Çankırı, Turkey* 72 B5
Kurtalan, *Turkey* 73 D9
Kurtbey, *Turkey* 41 E10
Kuru, *Sudan* 81 F2
Kuru, Bahr el →, *Sudan* 81 F2
Kurucaşile, *Turkey* 72 B5
Kuruçay, *Turkey* 70 B3
Kuruktag, *China* 60 B3
Kuruman, *S. Africa* 88 D3
Kuruman →, *S. Africa* 88 D3
Kurume, *Japan* 55 H5
Kurun →, *Sudan* 81 F3
Kurunegala, *Sri Lanka* 66 R12
Kurya, *Russia* 50 C6
Kus Gölü, *Turkey* 41 F11
Kuşadası, *Turkey* 72 D2
Kuşadası Körfezi, *Turkey* 39 D8
Kusatsu, *Japan* 55 F9
Kusawa L., *Canada* 104 A1
Kusel, *Germany* 25 F3
Kushaka, *Nigeria* 83 C6
Kushalgarh, *India* 68 H6
Kushchevskaya, *Russia* 49 G4
Kusheriki, *Nigeria* 83 C6
Kushikino, *Japan* 55 J5
Kushima, *Japan* 55 J5
Kushimoto, *Japan* 55 H7
Kushiro, *Japan* 54 C12
Kushiro-Gawa →, *Japan* 54 C12
Kūshk, *Iran* 71 D8
Kushka = Gushgy, *Turkmenistan* 50 F7
Kūshkī, *Iran* 70 C5
Kushol, *India* 69 C7
Kushtia, *Bangla.* 67 H16
Kushum →, *Kazakstan* 48 F10
Kuskokwim B., *U.S.A.* 100 C3
Kusmi, *India* 69 H10
Kussharo-Ko, *Japan* 54 C12
Kustanay = Qostanay, *Kazakstan* 50 D7
Kut, Ko, *Thailand* 65 G4
Kütahya, *Turkey* 39 B12
Kütahya □, *Turkey* 39 B11
Kutaisi, *Georgia* 49 J6
Kutaraja = Banda Aceh, *Indonesia* 62 C1
Kutch, Gulf of = Kachchh, Gulf of, *India* 68 H3
Kutch, Rann of = Kachchh, Rann of, *India* 68 H4
Kutina, *Croatia* 29 C13
Kutiyana, *India* 68 J4
Kutjevo, *Croatia* 42 E2
Kutkashen, *Azerbaijan* 49 K8
Kutná Hora, *Czech Rep.* 26 B8
Kutno, *Poland* 45 F6
Kutse, *Botswana* 88 C3
Kutu, *Dem. Rep. of the Congo* 84 E3
Kutum, *Sudan* 81 E1
Kúty, *Slovak Rep.* 27 C10
Kuujjuaq, *Canada* 101 C13
Kuujjuarapik, *Canada* 102 A4
Kuŭp-tong, *N. Korea* 57 D14
Kuusamo, *Finland* 8 D23
Kuusankoski, *Finland* 9 F22
Kuvshinovo, *Russia* 46 D8
Kuwait = Al Kuwayt, *Kuwait* 70 D5
Kuwait ■, *Asia* 70 D5
Kuwana, *Japan* 55 G8
Kuwana →, *India* 69 F10
Kuybyshev = Samara, *Russia* 48 D10
Kuybyshev, *Russia* 50 D8
Kuybyshevo, *Ukraine* 47 J9
Kuybyshevskoye Vdkhr., *Russia* 48 C9
Kuye He →, *China* 56 E6
Küyeh, *Iran* 70 B5
Küysanjaq, *Iraq* 70 B5
Kuyucak, *Turkey* 39 D10
Kuyumba, *Russia* 51 C10
Kuzey Anadolu Dağları, *Turkey* 72 B7
Kuzmin, *Serbia, Yug.* 42 E4
Kuznetsk, *Russia* 48 D8
Kuzomen, *Russia* 50 C4
Kvænangen, *Norway* 8 A19
Kværndrup, *Denmark* 11 J4
Kvaløy, *Norway* 8 B18
Kvänum, *Sweden* 11 F7
Kvareli = Qvareli, *Georgia* 49 K7
Kvarner, *Croatia* 29 D11
Kvarnerič, *Croatia* 29 D11
Kvicksund, *Sweden* 10 E10
Kvillsfors, *Sweden* 11 G9
Kvismare kanal, *Sweden* 10 E9
Kvissleby, *Sweden* 10 B11
Kwa-Nobuhle, *S. Africa* 85 L5
Kwabhaca, *S. Africa* 89 E4
Kwakhanai, *Botswana* 88 C3
Kwakoegron, *Surinam* 125 B7
Kwale, *Kenya* 86 C4
Kwale, *Nigeria* 83 D6
KwaMashu, *S. Africa* 89 D5
Kwando →, *Africa* 88 B3
Kwangdaeri, *N. Korea* 57 D14
Kwangju, *S. Korea* 57 G14
Kwango →, *Dem. Rep. of the Congo* 77 G5
Kwangsi-Chuang = Guangxi Zhuangzu Zizhiqu □, *China* 58 F7
Kwangtung = Guangdong □, *China* 59 F9
Kwara □, *Nigeria* 83 D6
Kwataboahegan →, *Canada* 102 B3
Kwatisore, *Indonesia* 63 E8
KwaZulu Natal □, *S. Africa* 89 D5
Kweichow = Guizhou □, *China* 58 D6
Kwekwe, *Zimbabwe* 87 F2
Kwidzyn, *Poland* 44 E5
Kwiha, *Ethiopia* 81 E4
Kwinana New Town, *Australia* 93 F2
Kwisa →, *Poland* 45 G2
Kwoka, *Indonesia* 63 E8
Kwolla, *Nigeria* 83 D6
Kyabra Cr. →, *Australia* 95 D3
Kyabram, *Australia* 95 F4
Kyaikto, *Burma* 64 D1
Kyakhta, *Russia* 51 D11
Kyancutta, *Australia* 95 E2
Kyangin, *Burma* 67 K19
Kyaukpadaung, *Burma* 67 J19
Kyaukpyu, *Burma* 67 K18
Kyaukse, *Burma* 67 J20
Kybartai, *Lithuania* 44 D9
Kyburz, *U.S.A.* 116 G6
Kyelang, *India* 68 C7
Kyenjojo, *Uganda* 86 B3
Kyjov, *Czech Rep.* 27 B10
Kyle, *Canada* 105 C7
Kyle Dam, *Zimbabwe* 87 G3
Kyle of Lochalsh, *U.K.* 14 D3
Kyll →, *Germany* 25 F2
Kyllburg, *Germany* 25 E2
Kymijoki →, *Finland* 9 F22
Kyneton, *Australia* 95 F3
Kynuna, *Australia* 94 C3
Kyō-ga-Saki, *Japan* 55 G7
Kyoga, L., *Uganda* 86 B3
Kyogle, *Australia* 95 D5
Kyom →, *Sudan* 81 F2
Kyongju, *S. Korea* 57 G15
Kyongpyaw, *Burma* 67 L19
Kyŏngsŏng, *N. Korea* 57 D15
Kyōto, *Japan* 55 G7
Kyōto □, *Japan* 55 G7
Kyparissovouno, *Cyprus* 36 D12
Kyperounda, *Cyprus* 36 E11
Kyrenia, *Cyprus* 36 D12
Kyrgyzstan ■, *Asia* 50 E8
Kyritz, *Germany* 24 C8
Kyrkhult, *Sweden* 11 H8
Kyrönjoki →, *Finland* 8 E19
Kystatyam, *Russia* 51 C13
Kysucké Nové Mesto, *Slovak Rep.* 27 B11
Kythréa, *Cyprus* 36 D12
Kyunhla, *Burma* 67 H19
Kyuquot Sound, *Canada* 104 D3
Kyurdamir = Kürdämir, *Azerbaijan* 49 K9
Kyūshū, *Japan* 55 H5
Kyūshū □, *Japan* 55 H5
Kyūshū-Sanchi, *Japan* 55 H5
Kyustendil, *Bulgaria* 40 D6
Kyusyur, *Russia* 51 B13
Kyyiv, *Ukraine* 47 G6
Kyyivske Vdskh., *Ukraine* 47 G6
Kyzyl, *Russia* 51 D10
Kyzyl Kum, *Uzbekistan* 50 E7
Kyzyl-Kyya, *Kyrgyzstan* 50 E8
Kyzyl-Orda = Qyzylorda, *Kazakstan* 50 E7

L

La Albuera, *Spain* 35 G4
La Alcarria, *Spain* 32 E2
La Almarcha, *Spain* 32 F2
La Almunia de Doña Godina, *Spain* 32 D3
La Asunción, *Venezuela* 124 A6
La Baie, *Canada* 103 C5
La Banda, *Argentina* 126 B3
La Bañeza, *Spain* 34 C5
La Barca, *Mexico* 118 C4
La Barge, *U.S.A.* 114 E8
La Bastide-Puylaurent, *France* 20 D7
La Baule-Escoubiac, *France* 18 E4
La Belle, *U.S.A.* 109 M5
La Biche →, *Canada* 104 B4
La Biche, L., *Canada* 104 C6
La Bisbal d'Empordà, *Spain* 32 D8
La Bomba, *Mexico* 118 A1
La Bresse, *France* 19 D13
La Bureba, *Spain* 34 C7
La Calera, *Chile* 126 C1
La Campiña, *Spain* 35 H6
La Canal = Sa Canal, *Spain* 37 C7
La Cañiza = A Cañiza, *Spain* 34 C2
La Canourgue, *France* 20 D7
La Capelle, *France* 19 C10
La Carlota, *Argentina* 126 C3
La Carlota, *Phil.* 61 F5
La Carlota, *Spain* 35 H6
La Carolina, *Spain* 35 G7
La Cavalerie, *France* 20 D7
La Ceiba, *Honduras* 120 C2
La Chaise-Dieu, *France* 20 C7
La Chapelle d'Angillon, *France* 19 E9
La Chapelle-St-Luc, *France* 19 D11
La Chapelle-sur-Erdre, *France* 18 E5
La Charité-sur-Loire, *France* 19 E10
La Chartre-sur-le-Loir, *France* 18 E7
La Châtaigneraie, *France* 20 B3
La Châtre, *France* 19 F9
La Chaux-de-Fonds, *Switz.* 25 H2
La Chorrera, *Panama* 120 E4
La Ciotat, *France* 21 E9
La Clayette, *France* 19 F11
La Cocha, *Argentina* 126 B2
La Concepción = Ri-Aba, *Eq. Guin.* 83 E6
La Concepción, *Panama* 120 E3
La Concordia, *Mexico* 119 D6
La Coruña = A Coruña, *Spain* 34 B2
La Coruña □, *Spain* 34 B2
La Côte-St-André, *France* 21 C9
La Courtine-le-Trucq, *France* 20 C6
La Crau, *Bouches-du-Rhône, France* 21 E8
La Crau, *Var, France* 21 E10
La Crescent, *U.S.A.* 112 D9
La Crete, *Canada* 104 B5
La Crosse, *Kans., U.S.A.* 112 F5
La Crosse, *Wis., U.S.A.* 112 D9
La Cruz, *Costa Rica* 120 D2
La Cruz, *Mexico* 118 C3
La Désirade, *Guadeloupe* 121 C7
La Escondida, *Mexico* 118 C5
La Esmeralda, *Paraguay* 126 A3
La Esperanza, *Cuba* 120 B3
La Esperanza, *Honduras* 120 D2
La Estrada = A Estrada, *Spain* 34 C2
La Faouët, *France* 18 D3
La Fayette, *U.S.A.* 109 H3
La Fé, *Cuba* 120 B3
La Fère, *France* 19 C10
La Ferté-Bernard, *France* 18 D7
La Ferté-Gaucher, *France* 19 D10
La Ferté-Macé, *France* 18 D6
La Ferté-St-Aubin, *France* 19 E8
La Ferté-sous-Jouarre, *France* 19 D10
La Ferté-Vidame, *France* 18 D7
La Flèche, *France* 18 E6
La Follette, *U.S.A.* 109 G3
La Fregeneda, *Spain* 34 E4
La Fuente de San Esteban, *Spain* 34 E4
La Gacilly, *France* 18 E4
La Gineta, *Spain* 33 F2
La Grand-Combe, *France* 21 D8
La Grande, *U.S.A.* 114 D4
La Grande →, *Canada* 102 B5
La Grande Deux, Rés., *Canada* 102 B4
La Grande-Motte, *France* 21 E8
La Grande Quatre, Rés., *Canada* 102 B5
La Grande Trois, Rés., *Canada* 102 B4
La Grange, *Calif., U.S.A.* 116 H6
La Grange, *Ga., U.S.A.* 109 J3
La Grange, *Ky., U.S.A.* 108 F3
La Grange, *Tex., U.S.A.* 113 L6
La Grave, *France* 21 C10
La Guaira, *Venezuela* 124 A5
La Guardia = A Guarda, *Spain* 34 D2
La Gudiña = A Gudiña, *Spain* 34 C3
La Guerche-de-Bretagne, *France* 18 E5
La Guerche-sur-l'Aubois, *France* 19 F9
La Habana, *Cuba* 120 B3
La Haye-du-Puits, *France* 18 C5
La Horra, *Spain* 34 D7
La Independencia, *Mexico* 119 D6
La Isabela, *Dom. Rep.* 121 C5
La Jonquera, *Spain* 32 C7
La Junta, *U.S.A.* 113 F3
La Laguna, *Canary Is.* 37 F3
La Libertad, *Guatemala* 120 C1
La Libertad, *Mexico* 118 B2
La Ligua, *Chile* 126 C1
La Línea de la Concepción, *Spain* 35 J5
La Loche, *Canada* 105 B7
La Londe-les-Maures, *France* 21 E10
La Lora, *Spain* 34 C7
La Loupe, *France* 18 D8
La Louvière, *Belgium* 17 D4
La Machine, *France* 19 F10
La Maddalena, *Italy* 30 A2
La Malbaie, *Canada* 103 C5
La Mancha, *Spain* 33 F2
La Mariña, *Spain* 34 B3
La Martre, L., *Canada* 104 A5
La Mesa, *U.S.A.* 117 N9
La Misión, *Mexico* 118 A1
La Mothe-Achard, *France* 18 F5
La Motte, *France* 21 D10
La Motte-Chalançon, *France* 21 D9
La Motte-Servolex, *France* 21 C9
La Moure, *U.S.A.* 112 B5
La Muela, *Spain* 32 D3
La Mure, *France* 21 D9
La Negra, *Chile* 126 A1
La Oliva, *Canary Is.* 37 F6
La Orotava, *Canary Is.* 37 F3
La Oroya, *Peru* 124
La Pacaudière, *France* 19 F10
La Palma, *Canary Is.* 37 F2
La Palma, *Panama* 120 E4
La Palma del Condado, *Spain* 35 H4
La Paloma, *Chile* 126 C1
La Pampa □, *Argentina* 126 D2
La Paragua, *Venezuela* 124 B6
La Paz, *Entre Ríos, Argentina* 126 C4
La Paz, *San Luis, Argentina* 126 C2
La Paz, *Bolivia* 124 G5
La Paz, *Honduras* 120 D2
La Paz, *Mexico* 118 C2
La Paz, *Phil.* 61 D4
La Paz Centro, *Nic.* 120 D2
La Pedrera, *Colombia* 124 D5
La Pérade, *Canada* 103 C5
La Perouse Str., *Asia* 54 B11
La Pesca, *Mexico* 119 C5
La Piedad, *Mexico* 118 C4
La Pine, *U.S.A.* 114 E3
La Plata, *Argentina* 126 D4
La Pobla de Lillet, *Spain* 32 C6
La Pocatière, *Canada* 103 C5
La Pola de Gordón, *Spain* 34 C5
La Porta, *France* 21 F13
La Porte, *Ind., U.S.A.* 108 E2
La Porte, *Tex., U.S.A.* 113 L7
La Presanella, *Italy* 28 B7
La Puebla = Sa Pobla, *Spain* 32 F8
La Puebla de Cazalla, *Spain* 35 H5
La Puebla de los Infantes, *Spain* 35 H5
La Puebla de Montalbán, *Spain* 34 F6
La Puebla del Río, *Spain* 35 H4
La Puerta de Segura, *Spain* 35 G8
La Purísima, *Mexico* 118 B2
La Push, *U.S.A.* 116 C2
La Quiaca, *Argentina* 126 A2
La Réole, *France* 20 D3
La Restinga, *Canary Is.* 37 G2
La Rioja, *Argentina* 126 B2
La Rioja □, *Argentina* 126 B2
La Rioja □, *Spain* 32 C2
La Robla, *Spain* 34 C5
La Roche-Bernard, *France* 18 E4
La Roche-Canillac, *France* 20 C5
La Roche-en-Ardenne, *Belgium* 17 D5
La Roche-sur-Foron, *France* 19 F13
La Roche-sur-Yon, *France* 18 F5
La Rochefoucauld, *France* 20 C4
La Rochelle, *France* 20 B2
La Roda, *Spain* 33 F2
La Roda de Andalucía, *Spain* 35 H6
La Romana, *Dom. Rep.* 121 C6
La Ronge, *Canada* 105 B7
La Rumorosa, *Mexico* 117 N10
La Sabina = Sa Savina, *Spain* 37 C7
La Sagra, *Spain* 33 H2
La Salle, *U.S.A.* 112 E10
La Sanabria, *Spain* 34 C4
La Santa, *Canary Is.* 37 E6
La Sarre, *Canada* 102 C4
La Scie, *Canada* 103 C8
La Selva, *Spain* 32 C7
La Selva Beach, *U.S.A.* 116 J5
La Selva del Camp, *Spain* 32 D6
La Serena, *Chile* 126 B1
La Serena, *Spain* 35 G5
La Seu d'Urgell, *Spain* 32 C6
La Seyne-sur-Mer, *France* 21 E9
La Sila, *Italy* 31 C9
La Solana, *Spain* 35 G7
La Soufrière, *St. Vincent* 121 D7
La Souterraine, *France* 19 F8
La Spézia, *Italy* 28 D6
La Suze-sur-Sarthe, *France* 18 E7
La Tagua, *Colombia* 124 C4
La Teste, *France* 20 D2
La Tortuga, *Venezuela* 121 D6
La Tour-du-Pin, *France* 21 C9
La Tranche-sur-Mer, *France* 18 F5
La Tremblade, *France* 20 C2
La Tuque, *Canada* 102 C5
La Unión, *Chile* 128 E2
La Unión, *El Salv.* 120 D2
La Unión, *Mexico* 118 D4
La Unión, *Spain* 33 H4
La Urbana, *Venezuela* 124 B5
La Vall d'Uixó, *Spain* 32 F4
La Vecilla de Curveño, *Spain* 34 C5
La Vega, *Dom. Rep.* 121 C5
La Vela de Coro, *Venezuela* 124 A5
La Veleta, *Spain* 35 H7
La Venta, *Mexico* 119 D6
La Ventura, *Mexico* 118 C4
La Voulte-sur-Rhône, *France* 21 D8
Laa an der Thaya, *Austria* 27 C9
Laaber, Grosse →, *Germany* 25 G8
Laage, *Germany* 24 B8
Laatzen, *Germany* 24 C5
Laba →, *Russia* 49 H4
Labason, *Phil.* 61 G5
Labastide-Murat, *France* 20 D5
Labastide-Rouairoux, *France* 20 E6
Labbézenga, *Mali* 83 B5

Labe = Elbe →, *Europe* 24 B4
Labé, *Guinea* 82 C2
Laberge, L., *Canada* 104 A1
Labin, *Croatia* 29 C11
Labinsk, *Russia* 49 H5
Labis, *Malaysia* 65 L4
Łabiszyn, *Poland* 45 F4
Labo, *Phil.* 61 D5
Laboe, *Germany* 24 A6
Laborec →, *Slovak Rep.* 27 C14
Labouheyre, *France* 20 D3
Laboulaye, *Argentina* 126 C3
Labrador, *Canada* 103 B7
Labrador City, *Canada* 103 B6
Labrador Sea, *Atl. Oc.* 101 C14
Lábrea, *Brazil* 124 E6
Labrède, *France* 20 D3
Labruguière, *France* 20 E6
Labuan, *Malaysia* 62 C5
Labuan, Pulau, *Malaysia* 62 C5
Labuha, *Indonesia* 63 E7
Labuhan, *Indonesia* 63 G11
Labuhanbajo, *Indonesia* 63 F6
Labuk, Telok, *Malaysia* 62 C5
Labyrinth, L., *Australia* 95 E2
Labytnangi, *Russia* 50 C7
Laç, *Albania* 40 E3
Lac Bouchette, *Canada* 103 C5
Lac Édouard, *Canada* 102 C5
Lac La Biche, *Canada* 104 C6
Lac la Martre = Wha Ti, *Canada* 100 B8
Lac La Ronge Prov. Park, *Canada* 105 B7
Lac-Mégantic, *Canada* 103 C5
Lac Seul, Res., *Canada* 102 B1
Lac Thien, *Vietnam* 64 F7
Lacanau, *France* 20 D2
Lacanau, Étang de, *France* 20 D2
Lacantúm →, *Mexico* 119 D6
Lacara →, *Spain* 35 G4
Lacaune, *France* 20 E6
Lacaune, Mts. de, *France* 20 E6
Laccadive Is. = Lakshadweep Is., *Ind. Oc.* 52 H11
Lacepede B., *Australia* 95 F2
Lacepede Is., *Australia* 92 C3
Lacerdónia, *Mozam.* 87 F4
Lacey, *U.S.A.* 116 C4
Lachhmangarh, *India* 68 F6
Lachi, *Pakistan* 68 C4
Lachine, *Canada* 102 C5
Lachlan →, *Australia* 95 E3
Lachute, *Canada* 102 C5
Lackawanna, *U.S.A.* 110 D6
Lackawaxen, *U.S.A.* 111 E10
Lacolle, *Canada* 111 A11
Lacombe, *Canada* 104 C6
Lacona, *U.S.A.* 111 C8
Láconi, *Italy* 30 C2
Laconia, *U.S.A.* 111 C13
Lacq, *France* 20 E3
Ladakh Ra., *India* 69 C8
Lądek-Zdrój, *Poland* 45 H3
Ládhon →, *Greece* 38 D3
Ladik, *Turkey* 72 B6
Ladismith, *S. Africa* 88 E3
Ladíspoli, *Italy* 29 G9
Lādīz, *Iran* 71 D9
Ladnun, *India* 68 F6
Ladoga, L. = Ladozhskoye Ozero, *Russia* 46 B6
Ladozhskoye Ozero, *Russia* 46 B6
Lady Elliott I., *Australia* 94 C5
Lady Grey, *S. Africa* 88 E4
Ladybrand, *S. Africa* 88 D4
Ladysmith, *Canada* 104 D4
Ladysmith, *S. Africa* 89 D4
Ladysmith, *U.S.A.* 112 C9
Lae, *Papua N. G.* 96 H6
Laem Ngop, *Thailand* 65 F4
Laem Pho, *Thailand* 65 J3
Læsø, *Denmark* 11 G5
Læsø Rende, *Denmark* 11 G4
Lafayette, *Colo., U.S.A.* 112 F2
Lafayette, *Ind., U.S.A.* 108 E2
Lafayette, *La., U.S.A.* 113 K9
Lafayette, *Tenn., U.S.A.* 109 G2
Laferte →, *Canada* 104 A5
Lafia, *Nigeria* 83 D6
Lafiagi, *Nigeria* 83 D6
Lafleche, *Canada* 105 D7
Lafon, *Sudan* 81 F3
Lagan, *Sweden* 11 H7
Lagan →, *Sweden* 11 H6
Lagan →, *U.K.* 15 B6
Lagarfljót →, *Iceland* 8 D6
Lage, *Germany* 24 D4
Lågen →, *Oppland, Norway* 9 F14
Lågen →, *Vestfold, Norway* 9 G14
Lägerdorf, *Germany* 24 B5
Laghouat, *Algeria* 78 B6
Lagnieu, *France* 21 C9
Lagny-sur-Marne, *France* 19 D9
Lago, *Italy* 31 C9
Lagôa, *Portugal* 35 H2
Lagoa Vermelha, *Brazil* 127 B5
Lagoaça, *Portugal* 34 D4
Lagodekhi, *Georgia* 49 K8
Lagónegro, *Italy* 31 B8
Lagonoy G., *Phil.* 61 E5
Lagos, *Nigeria* 83 D5
Lagos, *Portugal* 35 H2
Lagos □, *Nigeria* 83 D5
Lagos de Moreno, *Mexico* 118 C4
Lagrange, *Australia* 92 C3
Lagrange B., *Australia* 92 C3
Laguardia, *Spain* 32 C2
Laguépie, *France* 20 D5
Laguna, *Brazil* 127 B6
Laguna, *U.S.A.* 115 J10
Laguna Beach, *U.S.A.* 117 M9
Laguna de Duera, *Spain* 34 D6
Laguna Limpia, *Argentina* 126 B4
Laguna Madre, *U.S.A.* 119 B5
Lagunas, *Chile* 126 A2
Lagunas, *Peru* 124 E3
Lahad Datu, *Malaysia* 63 C5
Lahad Datu, Teluk, *Malaysia* 63 D5
Lahan Sai, *Thailand* 64 E4
Lahanam, *Laos* 64 D5
Lahar, *India* 69 F8
Laharpur, *India* 69 F9
Lahat, *Indonesia* 62 E2
Lahewa, *Indonesia* 62 D1
Lāhījān, *Iran* 71 B6
Lahn →, *Germany* 25 E3
Lahnstein, *Germany* 25 E3
Laholm, *Sweden* 11 H7
Laholmsbukten, *Sweden* 11 H6
Lahore, *Pakistan* 68 D6
Lahr, *Germany* 25 G3
Lahri, *Pakistan* 68 E3
Lahti, *Finland* 9 F21
Lahtis = Lahti, *Finland* 9 F21
Laï, *Chad* 79 G9
Lai Chau, *Vietnam* 58 F4
Lai'an, *China* 59 A12
Laibin, *China* 58 F7
Laifeng, *China* 58 C7
L'Aigle, *France* 18 D7
Laignes, *France* 19 E11
L'Aiguillon-sur-Mer, *France* 20 B2
Laila = Laylá, *Si. Arabia* 74 C4
Laingsburg, *S. Africa* 88 E3
Lainio älv →, *Sweden* 8 C20
Lairg, *U.K.* 14 C4
Laishui, *China* 56 E8
Laissac, *France* 20 D6
Láives, *Italy* 29 B8
Laiwu, *China* 57 F9
Laixi, *China* 57 F11
Laiyang, *China* 57 F11
Laiyuan, *China* 56 E8
Laizhou, *China* 57 F10
Laizhou Wan, *China* 57 F10
Laja →, *Mexico* 118 C4
Lajere, *Nigeria* 83 C7
Lajes, *Brazil* 127 B5
Lajkovac, *Serbia, Yug.* 40 B4
Lajosmizse, *Hungary* 42 C4
Lak Sao, *Laos* 64 C5
Lakaband, *Pakistan* 68 D3
Lakamané, *Mali* 82 C3
Lake Alpine, *U.S.A.* 116 G7
Lake Andes, *U.S.A.* 112 D5
Lake Arthur, *U.S.A.* 113 K8
Lake Cargelligo, *Australia* 95 E4
Lake Charles, *U.S.A.* 113 K8
Lake City, *Colo., U.S.A.* 115 G10
Lake City, *Fla., U.S.A.* 109 K4
Lake City, *Mich., U.S.A.* 108 C3
Lake City, *Minn., U.S.A.* 112 C8
Lake City, *Pa., U.S.A.* 110 D4
Lake City, *S.C., U.S.A.* 109 J6
Lake Cowichan, *Canada* 104 D4
Lake District, *U.K.* 12 C4
Lake Elsinore, *U.S.A.* 117 M9
Lake George, *U.S.A.* 111 C11
Lake Grace, *Australia* 93 F2
Lake Harbour = Kimmirut, *Canada* 101 B13
Lake Havasu City, *U.S.A.* 117 L12
Lake Hughes, *U.S.A.* 117 L8
Lake Isabella, *U.S.A.* 117 K8
Lake Jackson, *U.S.A.* 113 L7
Lake Junction, *U.S.A.* 114 D8
Lake King, *Australia* 93 F2
Lake Lenore, *Canada* 105 C8
Lake Louise, *Canada* 104 C5
Lake Mead National Recreation Area, *U.S.A.* 117 K12
Lake Mills, *U.S.A.* 112 D8
Lake Placid, *U.S.A.* 111 B11
Lake Pleasant, *U.S.A.* 111 C10
Lake Providence, *U.S.A.* 113 J9
Lake St. Peter, *Canada* 110 A6
Lake Superior Prov. Park, *Canada* 102 C3
Lake Village, *U.S.A.* 113 J9
Lake Wales, *U.S.A.* 109 M5
Lake Worth, *U.S.A.* 109 M5
Lakefield, *Canada* 102 D4
Lakehurst, *U.S.A.* 111 F10
Lakeland, *Australia* 94 B3
Lakeland, *U.S.A.* 109 M5
Lakemba, *Fiji* 91 D9
Lakeport, *Calif., U.S.A.* 116 F4
Lakeport, *Mich., U.S.A.* 110 C2
Lakes Entrance, *Australia* 95 F4
Lakeside, *Ariz., U.S.A.* 115 J9
Lakeside, *Calif., U.S.A.* 117 N10
Lakeside, *Nebr., U.S.A.* 112 D3
Lakeside, *Ohio, U.S.A.* 110 E2
Lakeview, *U.S.A.* 114 E3
Lakeville, *U.S.A.* 112 C8
Lakewood, *Colo., U.S.A.* 112 F2
Lakewood, *N.J., U.S.A.* 111 F10
Lakewood, *N.Y., U.S.A.* 110 D5
Lakewood, *Ohio, U.S.A.* 110 E3
Lakewood, *Wash., U.S.A.* 116 C4
Lakha, *India* 68 F4
Lakhaniá, *Greece* 36 D9
Lakhimpur, *India* 69 F9
Lakhnadon, *India* 69 H8
Lakhonpheng, *Laos* 64 E5
Lakhpat, *India* 68 H3
Läki, *Azerbaijan* 49 K8
Lakin, *U.S.A.* 113 G4
Lakitusaki →, *Canada* 102 B3
Lakki, *Pakistan* 68 C4
Lákkoi, *Greece* 36 D5
Lakonía □, *Greece* 38 E4
Lakonikós Kólpos, *Greece* 38 E4
Lakor, *Indonesia* 63 F7
Lakota, *Ivory C.* 82 D3
Lakota, *U.S.A.* 112 A5
Laksar, *India* 68 E8
Laksefjorden, *Norway* 8 A22
Lakselv, *Norway* 8 A21
Lakshadweep Is., *Ind. Oc.* 52 H11
Lakshmanpur, *India* 69 H10
Lakshmikantapur, *India* 69 H13
Lala Ghat, *India* 67 G18
Lala Musa, *Pakistan* 68 C5
Lalago, *Tanzania* 86 C3
Lalapanzi, *Zimbabwe* 87 F3
Lalapaşa, *Turkey* 41 E10
Lalbenque, *France* 20 D5
L'Albufera, *Spain* 33 F4
Lalganj, *India* 69 G11
Lalgola, *India* 69 G13
Lālī, *Iran* 71 C6
Lalibela, *Ethiopia* 81 E4
Lalin, *China* 57 B14
Lalín, *Spain* 34 C2
Lalin He →, *China* 57 B13
Lalinde, *France* 20 D4
Lalitapur = Patan, *Nepal* 67 F14
Lalitpur, *India* 69 G8
Lalkua, *India* 69 E8
Lalsot, *India* 68 F7
Lam, *Vietnam* 64 B6
Lam Pao Res., *Thailand* 64 D4
Lama Kara, *Togo* 83 D5
Lamaing, *Burma* 67 M20
Lamar, *Colo., U.S.A.* 112 F3
Lamar, *Mo., U.S.A.* 113 G7
Lamas, *Peru* 124 E3
Lamastre, *France* 21 D8
Lambach, *Austria* 26 C6
Lamballe, *France* 18 D4
Lambaréné, *Gabon* 84 E2
Lambasa, *Fiji* 91 C8
Lambay I., *Ireland* 15 C5
Lambert Glacier, *Antarctica* 5 D6
Lambert's Bay, *S. Africa* 88 E2
Lambesc, *France* 21 E9
Lambeth, *Canada* 110 D3
Lambi Kyun, *Burma* 65 G2
Lámbia, *Greece* 38 D3
Lambomakondro, *Madag.* 89 C7
Lambro →, *Italy* 28 C6
Lame, *Nigeria* 83 C6
Lame Deer, *U.S.A.* 114 D10
Lamego, *Portugal* 34 D3
Lamèque, *Canada* 103 C7
Lameroo, *Australia* 95 F3
Lamesa, *U.S.A.* 113 J4
Lamía, *Greece* 38 C4
Lamitan, *Phil.* 61 H5
Lammermuir Hills, *U.K.* 14 F6
Lammhult, *Sweden* 11 G8
Lamoille →, *U.S.A.* 111 B11
Lamon B., *Phil.* 61 D5
Lamont, *Canada* 104 C6
Lamont, *Calif., U.S.A.* 117 K8
Lamont, *Wyo., U.S.A.* 114 E10
Lamotte-Beuvron, *France* 19 E9
Lampa, *Peru* 124 G4
Lampang, *Thailand* 64 C2
Lampasas, *U.S.A.* 113 K5
Lampazos de Naranjo, *Mexico* 118 B4
Lampertheim, *Germany* 25 F4
Lampeter, *U.K.* 13 E3
Lampman, *Canada* 105 D8
Lamprechtshausen, *Austria* 26 D5
Lampung □, *Indonesia* 62 F2
Lamta, *India* 69 H9
Lamu, *Kenya* 86 C5
Lamy, *U.S.A.* 115 J11
Lan Xian, *China* 56 E6
Lan Yu = Hungt'ou Hsü, *Taiwan* 59 F13
Lanai, *U.S.A.* 106 H16
Lanak La, *India* 69 B8
Lanak'o Shank'ou = Lanak La, *India* 69 B8
Lanao, L., *Phil.* 61 H6
Lanark, *Canada* 111 A8
Lanark, *U.K.* 14 F5
Lancang, *China* 58 F2
Lancang Jiang →, *China* 58 G3
Lancashire □, *U.K.* 12 D5
Lancaster, *Canada* 111 A10
Lancaster, *U.K.* 12 C5
Lancaster, *Calif., U.S.A.* 117 L8
Lancaster, *Ky., U.S.A.* 108 G3
Lancaster, *N.H., U.S.A.* 111 B13
Lancaster, *N.Y., U.S.A.* 110 D6
Lancaster, *Ohio, U.S.A.* 108 F4
Lancaster, *Pa., U.S.A.* 111 F8
Lancaster, *S.C., U.S.A.* 109 H5
Lancaster, *Wis., U.S.A.* 112 D9
Lancaster Sd., *Canada* 101 A11
Lancelin, *Australia* 93 F2
Lanchow = Lanzhou, *China* 56 F2
Lanciano, *Italy* 29 F11
Lancun, *China* 57 F11
Łańcut, *Poland* 45 H9
Landau, *Bayern, Germany* 25 G8
Landau, *Rhld-Pfz., Germany* 25 F4
Landeck, *Austria* 26 D3
Lander, *U.S.A.* 114 E9
Lander →, *Australia* 92 D5
Landerneau, *France* 18 D2
Landeryd, *Sweden* 11 G7
Landes, *France* 20 D2
Landes □, *France* 20 E3
Landete, *Spain* 32 F3
Landi Kotal, *Pakistan* 68 B4
Landisburg, *U.S.A.* 110 F7
Landivisiau, *France* 18 D2
Landquart, *Switz.* 25 J5
Landrecies, *France* 19 B10
Land's End, *U.K.* 13 G2
Landsberg, *Germany* 25 G6
Landsborough Cr. →, *Australia* 94 C3
Landsbro, *Sweden* 11 G8
Landshut, *Germany* 25 G8
Landskrona, *Sweden* 11 J6
Landstuhl, *Germany* 25 F3
Landvetter, *Sweden* 11 G6
Lanesboro, *U.S.A.* 111 E9
Lanester, *France* 18 E3
Lanett, *U.S.A.* 109 J3
Lang Qua, *Vietnam* 64 A5
Lang Shan, *China* 56 D4
Lang Son, *Vietnam* 58 G6
Lang Suan, *Thailand* 65 H2
Langå, *Denmark* 11 H3
La'nga Co, *China* 67 D12
Lángadhás, *Greece* 40 F7
Langádhia, *Greece* 38 D4
Långan →, *Sweden* 10 A8
Langano, L., *Ethiopia* 81 F4
Langar, *Iran* 71 C9
Langara I., *Canada* 104 C2
Långås, *Sweden* 11 H6
Langdai, *China* 58 D5
Langdon, *U.S.A.* 112 A5
Långe Jan = Ölands södra udde, *Sweden* 11 H10
Langeac, *France* 20 C7
Langeais, *France* 18 E7
Langeb Baraka →, *Sudan* 80 D4
Langeberg, *S. Africa* 88 E3
Langeberge, *S. Africa* 88 D3
Langeland, *Denmark* 11 K4
Langelands Bælt, *Denmark* 11 K4
Langen, *Hessen, Germany* 25 F4
Langen, *Niedersachsen, Germany* 24 B4
Langenburg, *Canada* 105 C8
Langeneß, *Germany* 24 A4
Langenlois, *Austria* 26 C8
Langeoog, *Germany* 24 B3
Langeskov, *Denmark* 11 J4
Länghem, *Sweden* 11 G7
Langhirano, *Italy* 28 D7
Langholm, *U.K.* 14 F5
Langjökull, *Iceland* 8 D3
Langkawi, Pulau, *Malaysia* 65 J2
Langklip, *S. Africa* 88 D3
Langkon, *Malaysia* 62 C5
Langlade, *St- P. & M.* 103 C8
Langley, *Canada* 116 A4
Langnau, *Switz.* 25 J3
Langogne, *France* 20 D7
Langon, *France* 20 D3
Langøya, *Norway* 8 B16
Langreo, *Spain* 34 B5
Langres, *France* 19 E12
Langres, Plateau de, *France* 19 E12
Langsa, *Indonesia* 62 D1
Långsele, *Sweden* 10 A11
Långshyttan, *Sweden* 10 D10
Langtry, *U.S.A.* 113 L4
Langu, *Thailand* 65 J2
Languedoc, *France* 20 E7
Languedoc-Roussillon □, *France* 20 E6
Langxi, *China* 59 B12
Langxiangzhen, *China* 56 E9
Langzhong, *China* 58 B5
Lanigan, *Canada* 105 C7
Lankao, *China* 56 G8
Länkäran, *Azerbaijan* 71 B6
Lanmeur, *France* 18 D3
Lannemezan, *France* 20 E4
Lannilis, *France* 18 D2
Lannion, *France* 18 D3
L'Annonciation, *Canada* 102 C5
Lanouaille, *France* 20 C5
Lanping, *China* 58 D2
Lansdale, *U.S.A.* 111 F9
Lansdowne, *Australia* 95 E5
Lansdowne, *Canada* 111 B8
Lansdowne, *India* 69 E8
Lansdowne House, *Canada* 102 B2
L'Anse, *Mich., U.S.A.* 108 B1
L'Anse, *Mich., U.S.A.* 112 B10
L'Anse au Loup, *Canada* 103 B8
L'Anse aux Meadows, *Canada* 103 B8
Lansford, *U.S.A.* 111 F9
Lanshan, *China* 59 E9
Lansing, *U.S.A.* 108 D3
Lanslebourg-Mont-Cenis, *France* 21 C10
Lanta Yai, Ko, *Thailand* 65 J2
Lantewa, *Nigeria* 83 C7
Lantian, *China* 56 G5
Lanus, *Argentina* 126 C4
Lanusei, *Italy* 30 C2
Lanuza, *Phil.* 61 G7
Lanxi, *China* 59 C12
Lanzarote, *Canary Is.* 37 F6
Lanzhou, *China* 56 F2
Lanzo Torinese, *Italy* 28 C4
Lao →, *Italy* 31 C8
Lao Bao, *Laos* 64 D6
Lao Cai, *Vietnam* 58 F4
Laoag, *Phil.* 61 B4
Laoang, *Phil.* 61 E6
Laoha He →, *China* 57 C11
Laohekou, *China* 59 A8
Laois □, *Ireland* 15 D4
Laon, *France* 19 C10
Laona, *U.S.A.* 108 C1
Laos ■, *Asia* 64 D5
Lapa, *Brazil* 127 B6
Lapai, *Nigeria* 83 D6
Lapalisse, *France* 19 F10
Lapeer, *U.S.A.* 108 D4
Lapeyrade, *France* 20 D3
Lapithos, *Cyprus* 36 D12
Lapland = Lappland, *Europe* 8 B21
Laporte, *U.S.A.* 111 E8
Lapovo, *Serbia, Yug.* 40 B5
Lappeenranta, *Finland* 9 F23
Lappland, *Europe* 8 B21
Laprida, *Argentina* 126 D3
Lapseki, *Turkey* 41 F10
Laptev Sea, *Russia* 51 B13
Lapua, *Finland* 8 E20
Lăpuş →, *Romania* 43 C8
Lapuş, Munţii, *Romania* 43 C8
Lăpuşna, *Moldova* 43 D13
Łapy, *Poland* 45 F9
Laqiya Arba'in, *Sudan* 80 C2
Laqiya Umran, *Sudan* 80 D2
L'Áquila, *Italy* 29 F10
Lār, *Āzarbājān-e Sharqī, Iran* 70 B5
Lār, *Fārs, Iran* 71 E7
Larabanga, *Ghana* 82 D4
Laragne-Montéglin, *France* 21 D9
Laramie, *U.S.A.* 112 E2
Laramie →, *U.S.A.* 114 F11
Laramie Mts., *U.S.A.* 112 E2
Laranjeiras do Sul, *Brazil* 127 B5
Larantuka, *Indonesia* 63 F6
Larat, *Indonesia* 63 F8
L'Arbresle, *France* 21 C8
Lärbro, *Sweden* 11 G12
Larde, *Mozam.* 87 F4
Larder Lake, *Canada* 102 C4
Lardhos, Ákra = Líndhos, Ákra, *Greece* 36 C10
Lardhos, Órmos, *Greece* 36 C10
Laredo, *Spain* 34 B7
Laredo, *U.S.A.* 113 M5
Laredo Sd., *Canada* 104 C3
Largentière, *France* 21 D8
L'Argentière-la-Bessée, *France* 21 D10
Largo, *U.S.A.* 109 M4
Largs, *U.K.* 14 F4
Lari, *Italy* 28 E7
Lariang, *Indonesia* 63 E5
Larimore, *U.S.A.* 112 B6
Lārīn, *Iran* 71 C7
Larino, *Italy* 29 G11
Lárisa, *Greece* 38 B4
Lárisa □, *Greece* 38 B4
Larkana, *Pakistan* 68 F3
Larnaca, *Cyprus* 36 E12
Larnaca Bay, *Cyprus* 36 E12
Larne, *U.K.* 15 B6
Larned, *U.S.A.* 112 F5
Laroquebrou, *France* 20 D6
Larose, *U.S.A.* 113 L9
Larrimah, *Australia* 92 C5
Larsen Ice Shelf, *Antarctica* 5 C17
Laruns, *France* 20 F3
Larvik, *Norway* 9 G14
Larzac, Causse du, *France* 20 E7
Las Alpujarras, *Spain* 33 J1
Las Animas, *U.S.A.* 112 F3
Las Anod, *Somali Rep.* 74 F4
Las Arenas, *Spain* 34 B6
Las Aves, Is., *W. Indies* 121 C7
Las Brenãs, *Argentina* 126 B3
Las Cabezas de San Juan, *Spain* 35 J5
Las Cejas, *Argentina* 128 B4
Las Chimeneas, *Mexico* 117 N10
Las Cruces, *U.S.A.* 115 K10
Las Flores, *Argentina* 126 D4
Las Heras, *Argentina* 126 C2
Las Lajas, *Argentina* 128 D2
Las Lomitas, *Argentina* 126 A3
Las Marismas, *Spain* 35 H4
Las Minas, *Spain* 33 G3
Las Navas de la Concepción, *Spain* 35 H5
Las Navas del Marqués, *Spain* 34 E6
Las Palmas, *Argentina* 126 B4
Las Palmas, *Canary Is.* 37 F4
Las Palmas →, *Mexico* 117 N10
Las Pedroñas, *Spain* 33 F2
Las Piedras, *Uruguay* 127 C4
Las Pipinas, *Argentina* 126 D4
Las Plumas, *Argentina* 128 E3
Las Rosas, *Argentina* 126 C3
Las Rozas, *Spain* 34 E7
Las Tablas, *Panama* 120 E3
Las Termas, *Argentina* 126 B3
Las Toscas, *Argentina* 126 B4
Las Truchas, *Mexico* 118 D4
Las Varillas, *Argentina* 126 C3
Las Vegas, *N. Mex., U.S.A.* 115 J11
Las Vegas, *Nev., U.S.A.* 117 J11
Lasarte, *Spain* 32 B2
Lascano, *Uruguay* 127 C5
Lashburn, *Canada* 105 C7
Lashio, *Burma* 67 H20
Lashkar, *India* 68 F8
Łasin, *Poland* 44 E6
Lasíthi, *Greece* 36 D7
Lasíthi □, *Greece* 36 D7
Lāsjerd, *Iran* 71 C7
Lask, *Poland* 45 G6
Łaskarzew, *Poland* 45 G8
Laško, *Slovenia* 29 B12
Lassay-les-Châteaux, *France* 18 D6
Lassen Pk., *U.S.A.* 114 F3
Lassen Volcanic National Park, *U.S.A.* 114 F3
Last Mountain L., *Canada* 105 C7
Lastchance Cr. →, *U.S.A.* 116 E5

Lastoursville, *Gabon* 84 E2
Lastovo, *Croatia* 29 F13
Lastovski Kanal, *Croatia* 29 F14
Lat Yao, *Thailand* 64 E2
Latacunga, *Ecuador* 124 D3
Latakia = Al Lādhiqīyah, *Syria* 70 C2
Latchford, *Canada* 102 C4
Latehar, *India* 69 H11
Laterza, *Italy* 31 B9
Latham, *Australia* 93 E2
Lathen, *Germany* 24 C3
Lathi, *India* 68 F4
Lathrop Wells, *U.S.A.* 117 J10
Latiano, *Italy* 31 B10
Latina, *Italy* 30 A5
Latisana, *Italy* 29 C10
Latium = Lazio □, *Italy* 29 F9
Laton, *U.S.A.* 116 J7
Latorytsya →, *Slovak Rep.* 27 C14
Latouche Treville, C., *Australia* 92 C3
Latrobe, *Australia* 94 G4
Latrobe, *U.S.A.* 110 F5
Latrónico, *Italy* 31 B9
Latvia ■, *Europe* 9 H20
Lau, *Nigeria* 83 D7
Lau Group, *Fiji* 91 C9
Lauchhammer, *Germany* 24 D9
Lauda-Königshofen, *Germany* 25 F5
Lauenburg, *Germany* 24 B6
Lauf, *Germany* 25 F7
Laughlin, *U.S.A.* 115 J6
Laujar de Andarax, *Spain* 33 H2
Laukaa, *Finland* 9 E21
Launceston, *Australia* 94 G4
Launceston, *U.K.* 13 G3
Laune →, *Ireland* 15 D2
Launglon Bok, *Burma* 64 F1
Laupheim, *Germany* 25 G5
Laura, *Australia* 94 B3
Laureana di Borrello, *Italy* 31 D9
Laurel, *Miss., U.S.A.* 113 K10
Laurel, *Mont., U.S.A.* 114 D9
Laurencekirk, *U.K.* 14 E6
Laurens, *U.S.A.* 109 H4
Laurentian Plateau, *Canada* 103 B6
Lauria, *Italy* 31 B8
Laurie L., *Canada* 105 B8
Laurinburg, *U.S.A.* 109 H6
Laurium, *U.S.A.* 108 B1
Lausanne, *Switz.* 25 J2
Laut, *Indonesia* 65 K6
Laut, Pulau, *Indonesia* 62 E5
Laut Kecil, Kepulauan, *Indonesia* 62 E5
Lauterbach, *Germany* 24 E5
Lauterecken, *Germany* 25 F3
Lautoka, *Fiji* 91 C7
Lauzès, *France* 20 D5
Lavagh More, *Ireland* 15 B3
Lavagna, *Italy* 28 D6
Laval, *France* 18 D6
Lavalle, *Argentina* 126 B2
Lavant Station, *Canada* 111 A8
Lāvar Meydān, *Iran* 71 D7
Lávara, *Greece* 41 E10
Lavardac, *France* 20 D4
Lavaur, *France* 20 E5
Lavelanet, *France* 20 F5
Lavello, *Italy* 31 A8
Laverton, *Australia* 93 E3
Lavis, *Italy* 28 B8
Lávkos, *Greece* 38 B5
Lavos, *Portugal* 34 E2
Lavradio, *Portugal* 35 G1
Lavras, *Brazil* 127 A7
Lavre, *Portugal* 35 G2
Lávrion, *Greece* 38 D6
Lávris, *Greece* 36 D6
Lavumisa, *Swaziland* 89 D5
Lawas, *Malaysia* 62 D5
Lawele, *Indonesia* 63 F6
Lawng Pit, *Burma* 67 G20
Lawqah, *Si. Arabia* 70 D4
Lawra, *Ghana* 82 C4
Lawrence, *N.Z.* 91 L2
Lawrence, *Kans., U.S.A.* 112 F7
Lawrence, *Mass., U.S.A.* 111 D13
Lawrenceburg, *Ind., U.S.A.* 108 F3
Lawrenceburg, *Tenn., U.S.A.* 109 H2
Lawrenceville, *Ga., U.S.A.* 109 J4
Lawrenceville, *Pa., U.S.A.* 110 E7
Laws, *U.S.A.* 116 H8
Lawton, *U.S.A.* 113 H5
Lawu, *Indonesia* 63 G14
Lawz, J. al, *Si. Arabia* 80 B4
Laxå, *Sweden* 11 F8
Laxford, L., *U.K.* 14 C3
Laxou, *France* 19 D13
Lay →, *France* 20 B2
Laylá, *Si. Arabia* 74 C4
Laylān, *Iraq* 70 C5
Layon →, *France* 18 E6
Layton, *U.S.A.* 114 F7
Laytonville, *U.S.A.* 114 G2
Lazarevac, *Serbia, Yug.* 40 B4
Lazarevskoye, *Russia* 49 J4
Lazarivo, *Madag.* 89 C8
Lazdijai, *Lithuania* 44 D10
Lazio □, *Italy* 29 F9
Lazo, *Moldova* 43 C13
Lazo, *Russia* 54 C6
Le Beausset, *France* 21 E9
Le Blanc, *France* 20 B5
Le Bleymard, *France* 20 D7
Le Bourgneuf-la-Fôret, *France* 18 D6
Le Bugue, *France* 20 D4
Le Canourgue = La Canourgue, *France* 20 D7
Le Cateau Cambrésis, *France* 19 B10
Le Caylar, *France* 20 E7
Le Chambon-Feugerolles, *France* 21 C8
Le Châtelet, *France* 19 F9
Le Chesne, *France* 19 C11
Le Cheylard, *France* 21 D8
Le Conquet, *France* 18 D2
Le Creusot, *France* 19 F11
Le Croisic, *France* 18 E4
Le Donjon, *France* 19 F10
Le Dorat, *France* 20 B5
Le François, *Martinique* 121 D7
Le Grand-Lucé, *France* 18 E7
Le Grand-Pressigny, *France* 18 F7
Le Grand-Quevilly, *France* 18 C8
Le Havre, *France* 18 C7
Le Lavandou, *France* 21 E10
Le Lion-d'Angers, *France* 18 E6
Le Louroux-Béconnais, *France* 18 E6
Le Luc, *France* 21 E10
Le Lude, *France* 18 E7
Le Mans, *France* 18 E7
Le Mars, *U.S.A.* 112 D6
Le Mayet-de-Montagne, *France* 19 F10
Le Mêle-sur-Sarthe, *France* 18 D7
Le Monastier-sur-Gazeille, *France* 20 D7
Le Monêtier-les-Bains, *France* 21 D10
Le Mont-Dore, *France* 20 C6
Le Mont-St-Michel, *France* 18 D5
Le Moule, *Guadeloupe* 121 C7
Le Muy, *France* 21 E10
Le Palais, *France* 18 E3
Le Perthus, *France* 20 F6
Le Puy-en-Velay, *France* 20 C7
Le Sueur, *U.S.A.* 112 C8
Le Teil, *France* 21 D8
Le Teilleul, *France* 18 D6
Le Theil, *France* 18 D7
Le Thillot, *France* 19 E13
Le Thuy, *Vietnam* 64 D6
Le Touquet-Paris-Plage, *France* 19 B8
Le Tréport, *France* 18 B8
Le Val-d'Ajol, *France* 19 E13
Le Verdon-sur-Mer, *France* 20 C2
Le Vigan, *France* 20 E7
Lea →, *U.K.* 13 F8
Leach, *Cambodia* 65 F4
Lead, *U.S.A.* 112 C3
Leader, *Canada* 105 C7
Leadville, *U.S.A.* 115 G10
Leaf →, *U.S.A.* 113 K10
Leaf Rapids, *Canada* 105 B9
Leamington, *Canada* 102 D3
Leamington, *U.S.A.* 114 G7
Leamington Spa = Royal Leamington Spa, *U.K.* 13 E6
Le'an, *China* 59 D10
Leandro Norte Alem, *Argentina* 127 B4
Leane, L., *Ireland* 15 D2
Learmonth, *Australia* 92 D1
Leask, *Canada* 105 C7
Leatherhead, *U.K.* 13 F7
Leavenworth, *Kans., U.S.A.* 112 F7
Leavenworth, *Wash., U.S.A.* 114 C3
Łeba, *Poland* 44 D4
Łeba →, *Poland* 44 D4
Lebach, *Germany* 25 F2
Lebak, *Phil.* 61 H6
Lebam, *U.S.A.* 116 D3
Lebane, *Serbia, Yug.* 40 D5
Lebanon, *Ind., U.S.A.* 108 E2
Lebanon, *Kans., U.S.A.* 112 F5
Lebanon, *Ky., U.S.A.* 108 G3
Lebanon, *Mo., U.S.A.* 113 G8
Lebanon, *N.H., U.S.A.* 111 C12
Lebanon, *Oreg., U.S.A.* 114 D2
Lebanon, *Pa., U.S.A.* 111 F8
Lebanon, *Tenn., U.S.A.* 109 G2
Lebanon ■, *Asia* 75 B5
Lebec, *U.S.A.* 117 L8
Lebedyan, *Russia* 47 F10
Lebedyn, *Ukraine* 47 G8
Lebel-sur-Quévillon, *Canada* 102 C4
Lebomboberge, *S. Africa* 89 C5
Lębork, *Poland* 44 D4
Lebrija, *Spain* 35 J4
Łebsko, Jezioro, *Poland* 44 D4
Lebu, *Chile* 126 D1
Leca da Palmeira, *Portugal* 34 D2
Lecce, *Italy* 31 B11
Lecco, *Italy* 28 C6
Lecco, L. di, *Italy* 28 C6
Lécera, *Spain* 32 D4
Lech, *Austria* 26 D3
Lech →, *Germany* 25 G6
Lechang, *China* 59 E9
Lechtaler Alpen, *Austria* 26 D3
Lecontes Mills, *U.S.A.* 110 E6
Lectoure, *France* 20 E4
Łęczna, *Poland* 45 G9
Łęczyca, *Poland* 45 F6
Ledesma, *Spain* 34 D5
Ledong, *China* 64 C7
Leduc, *Canada* 104 C6
Lee, *U.S.A.* 111 D11
Lee →, *Ireland* 15 E3
Lee Vining, *U.S.A.* 116 H7
Leech L., *U.S.A.* 112 B7
Leechburg, *U.S.A.* 110 F5
Leeds, *U.K.* 12 D6
Leeds, *U.S.A.* 109 J2
Leek, *Neths.* 17 A6
Leek, *U.K.* 12 D5
Leeman, *Australia* 93 E1
Leeper, *U.S.A.* 110 E5
Leer, *Germany* 24 B3
Leesburg, *U.S.A.* 109 L5
Leesville, *U.S.A.* 113 K8
Leeton, *Australia* 95 E4
Leetonia, *U.S.A.* 110 F4
Leeu Gamka, *S. Africa* 88 E3
Leeuwarden, *Neths.* 17 A5
Leeuwin, C., *Australia* 93 F2
Leeward Is., *Atl. Oc.* 121 C7
Lefka, *Cyprus* 36 D11
Lefkoniko, *Cyprus* 36 D12
Lefroy, *Canada* 110 B5
Lefroy, L., *Australia* 93 F3
Łeg →, *Poland* 45 H8
Leganés, *Spain* 34 E7
Legazpi, *Phil.* 61 E5
Lège, *France* 20 D2
Lege Hida, *Ethiopia* 81 F5
Legendre I., *Australia* 92 D2
Leghorn = Livorno, *Italy* 28 E7
Legionowo, *Poland* 45 F7
Legnago, *Italy* 29 C8
Legnano, *Italy* 28 C5
Legnica, *Poland* 45 G3
Legrad, *Croatia* 29 B13
Leh, *India* 69 B7
Lehigh Acres, *U.S.A.* 109 M5
Lehighton, *U.S.A.* 111 F9
Lehliu, *Romania* 43 F11
Leho, *Sudan* 81 F3
Lehrte, *Germany* 24 C5
Lehututu, *Botswana* 88 C3
Lei Shui →, *China* 59 D9
Leiah, *Pakistan* 68 D4
Leibnitz, *Austria* 26 E8
Leibo, *China* 58 C4
Leicester, *U.K.* 13 E6
Leicester City □, *U.K.* 13 E6
Leicestershire □, *U.K.* 13 E6
Leichhardt →, *Australia* 94 B2
Leichhardt Ra., *Australia* 94 C4
Leiden, *Neths.* 17 B4
Leie →, *Belgium* 17 C3
Leifers = Láives, *Italy* 29 B8
Leigh Creek, *Australia* 95 E2
Leimen, *Germany* 25 F4
Leine →, *Germany* 24 C5
Leinefelde, *Germany* 24 D6
Leinster, *Australia* 93 E3
Leinster □, *Ireland* 15 C4
Leinster, Mt., *Ireland* 15 D5
Leipalingis, *Lithuania* 44 D10
Leipzig, *Germany* 24 D8
Leiria, *Portugal* 34 F2
Leiria □, *Portugal* 34 F2
Leirvik, *Norway* 9 G11
Leishan, *China* 58 D7
Leisler, Mt., *Australia* 92 D4
Leith, *U.K.* 14 F5
Leith Hill, *U.K.* 13 F7
Leitha →, *Europe* 27 D10
Leitrim, *Ireland* 15 B3
Leitrim □, *Ireland* 15 B4
Leitza, *Spain* 32 B3
Leiyang, *China* 59 D9
Leizhou, *China* 59 G8
Leizhou Bandao, *China* 58 G7
Leizhou Wan, *China* 59 G8
Lek →, *Neths.* 17 C4
Leka, *Norway* 8 D14
Lekáni, *Greece* 41 E8
Lekbibaj, *Albania* 40 D3
Lekeitio, *Spain* 32 B2
Lekhainá, *Greece* 38 D3
Lekoui, *Burkina Faso* 82 C4
Leksand, *Sweden* 10 D9
Lékva Óros, *Greece* 36 D6
Leland, *Mich., U.S.A.* 108 C3
Leland, *Miss., U.S.A.* 113 J9
Lelång, *Sweden* 10 E6
Leleque, *Argentina* 128 E2
Lelystad, *Neths.* 17 B5
Lem, *Denmark* 11 H2
Lema, *Nigeria* 83 C5
Lema Shilindi, *Ethiopia* 81 G5
Léman, L., *Europe* 19 F13
Lemera, *Dem. Rep. of the Congo* 86 C2
Lemery, *Phil.* 61 E4
Lemhi Ra., *U.S.A.* 114 D7
Lemmer, *Neths.* 17 B5
Lemmon, *U.S.A.* 112 C3
Lemon Grove, *U.S.A.* 117 N9
Lemoore, *U.S.A.* 116 J7
Lempdes, *France* 20 C7
Lemvig, *Denmark* 11 H2
Lena →, *Russia* 51 B13
Lenart, *Slovenia* 29 B12
Lenartovce, *Slovak Rep.* 27 C13
Lencloître, *France* 18 F7
Léndas, *Greece* 36 E6
Lendava, *Slovenia* 29 B13
Lendeh, *Iran* 71 D6
Lendinara, *Italy* 29 C8
Lengerich, *Germany* 24 C3
Lenggong, *Malaysia* 65 K3
Lenggries, *Germany* 25 H7
Lengshuijiang, *China* 59 D8
Lengshuitan, *China* 59 D8
Lengua de Vaca, Pta., *Chile* 126 C1
Lengyeltóti, *Hungary* 42 D2
Lenhovda, *Sweden* 11 G9
Lenina, Kanal →, *Russia* 49 J7
Leninabad = Khudzhand, *Tajikistan* 50 E7
Leninakan = Gyumri, *Armenia* 49 K6
Leningrad = Sankt-Peterburg, *Russia* 46 C6
Lenino, *Ukraine* 47 K8
Leninogorsk, *Kazakstan* 50 D9
Leninsk, *Russia* 49 F7
Leninsk-Kuznetskiy, *Russia* 50 D9
Leninskoye, *Russia* 48 A8
Lenk, *Switz.* 25 J3
Lenkoran = Länkäran, *Azerbaijan* 71 B6
Lenmalu, *Indonesia* 63 E8
Lenne →, *Germany* 24 D3
Lennestadt, *Germany* 24 D4
Lennox, *U.S.A.* 112 D6
Lennoxville, *Canada* 111 A13
Leno, *Italy* 28 C7
Lenoir, *U.S.A.* 109 H5
Lenoir City, *U.S.A.* 109 H3
Lenore L., *Canada* 105 C8
Lenox, *U.S.A.* 111 D11
Lens, *France* 19 B9
Lensahn, *Germany* 24 A6
Lensk, *Russia* 51 C12
Lentekhi, *Georgia* 49 J6
Lenti, *Hungary* 42 D1
Lentini, *Italy* 31 E8
Lenwood, *U.S.A.* 117 L9
Lenya, *Burma* 62 B1
Lenzen, *Germany* 24 B7
Léo, *Burkina Faso* 82 C4
Leoben, *Austria* 26 D8
Leodhas = Lewis, *U.K.* 14 C2
Leola, *U.S.A.* 112 C5
Leominster, *U.K.* 13 E5
Leominster, *U.S.A.* 111 D13
Léon, *France* 20 E2
León, *Mexico* 118 C4
León, *Nic.* 120 D2
León, *Spain* 34 C5
Leon, *U.S.A.* 112 E8
León □, *Spain* 34 C5
Leon →, *U.S.A.* 113 K6
León, Montes de, *Spain* 34 C4
Leonardtown, *U.S.A.* 108 F7
Leonardville, *Namibia* 88 C2
Leonberg, *Germany* 25 G5
Leonding, *Austria* 26 C7
Leonessa, *Italy* 29 F9
Leonforte, *Italy* 31 E7
Leongatha, *Australia* 95 F4
Leonídhion, *Greece* 38 D4
Leonora, *Australia* 93 E3
Léopold II, Lac = Mai-Ndombe, L., *Dem. Rep. of the Congo* 84 E3
Leopoldina, *Brazil* 127 A7
Leopoldsburg, *Belgium* 17 C5
Léopoldville = Kinshasa, *Dem. Rep. of the Congo* 84 E3
Leoti, *U.S.A.* 112 F4
Leova, *Moldova* 43 D13
Leoville, *Canada* 105 C7
Lepe, *Spain* 35 H3
Lepel = Lyepyel, *Belarus* 46 E5
Lepenoú, *Greece* 38 C3
Leping, *China* 59 C11
Lépo, L. do, *Angola* 88 B2
Lepontine, Alpi, *Italy* 28 B5
Leppävirta, *Finland* 9 E22
Lepsény, *Hungary* 42 D3
Lequeitio = Lekeitio, *Spain* 32 B2
Lercara Friddi, *Italy* 30 E6
Lerdo, *Mexico* 118 B4
Léré, *Chad* 83 D7
Léré, *Mali* 82 B4
Lere, *Bauchi, Nigeria* 83 D6
Lere, *Kaduna, Nigeria* 83 C6
Leribe, *Lesotho* 89 D4
Lérici, *Italy* 28 D6
Lérida = Lleida, *Spain* 32 D5
Lérins, Îs. de, *France* 21 E11
Lerma, *Spain* 34 C7
Léros, *Greece* 39 D8
Lérouville, *France* 19 D12
Lerum, *Sweden* 11 G6
Lerwick, *U.K.* 14 A7
Leş, *Romania* 42 D6
Les Abrets, *France* 21 C9
Les Andelys, *France* 18 C8
Les Borges Blanques, *Spain* 32 D5
Les Cayes, *Haiti* 121 C5
Les Essarts, *France* 18 F5
Les Herbiers, *France* 18 F5
Les Minquiers, Plateau des, *Chan. Is.* 18 D4
Les Pieux, *France* 18 C5
Les Ponts-de-Cé, *France* 18 E6
Les Riceys, *France* 19 E11
Les Sables-d'Olonne, *France* 20 B2
Les Vans, *France* 21 D8
Lesbos = Lésvos, *Greece* 39 B8
L'Escala, *Spain* 32 C8
Leshan, *China* 58 C4
Lésina, *Italy* 29 G12
Lésina, L. di, *Italy* 29 G12
Lesjöfors, *Sweden* 10 E8
Lesko, *Poland* 45 J9
Leskov I., *Antarctica* 5 B1
Leskovac, *Serbia, Yug.* 40 C5
Leskoviku, *Albania* 40 F4
Leśna, *Poland* 45 G2
Lesneven, *France* 18 D2
Leśnica, *Poland* 45 H5
Lešnica, *Serbia, Yug.* 40 B3
Lesnoye, *Russia* 46 C8
Lesopilnoye, *Russia* 54 A7
Lesotho ■, *Africa* 89 D4
Lesozavodsk, *Russia* 51 E14
Lesparre-Médoc, *France* 20 C3
Lessay, *France* 18 C5
Lesse →, *Belgium* 17 D4
Lessebo, *Sweden* 11 H9
Lesser Antilles, *W. Indies* 121 D7
Lesser Slave L., *Canada* 104 B5
Lesser Sunda Is., *Indonesia* 63 F6
Lessines, *Belgium* 17 D3
Lester, *U.S.A.* 116 C5
Lestock, *Canada* 105 C8
Lesuer I., *Australia* 92 B4
Lésvos, *Greece* 39 B8
Leszno, *Poland* 45 G3
Letaba, *S. Africa* 89 C5
Letälven, *Sweden* 10 E8
Létavértes, *Hungary* 42 C6
Letchworth, *U.K.* 13 F7
Letea, Ostrov, *Romania* 43 E14
Lethbridge, *Canada* 104 D6
Lethem, *Guyana* 124 C7
Leti, Kepulauan, *Indonesia* 63 F7
Leti Is. = Leti, Kepulauan, *Indonesia* 63 F7
Letiahau →, *Botswana* 88 C3
Leticia, *Colombia* 124 D5
Leting, *China* 57 E10
Letjiesbos, *S. Africa* 88 E3
Letlhakane, *Botswana* 88 C4
Letlhakeng, *Botswana* 88 C3
Letong, *Indonesia* 62 D3
Letpadan, *Burma* 67 L19
Letpan, *Burma* 67 K19
Letsôk-aw Kyun, *Burma* 65 G2
Letterkenny, *Ireland* 15 B4
Leu, *Romania* 43 F9
Leucadia, *U.S.A.* 117 M9
Leucate, *France* 20 F7
Leucate, Étang de, *France* 20 F7
Leuk, *Switz.* 25 J3
Leuşeni, *Moldova* 43 D13
Leuser, G., *Indonesia* 62 D1
Leutkirch, *Germany* 25 H6
Leuven, *Belgium* 17 D4
Leuze-en-Hainaut, *Belgium* 17 D3
Lev Tolstoy, *Russia* 46 F10
Levádhia, *Greece* 38 C4
Levanger, *Norway* 8 E14
Levani, *Albania* 40 F3
Levant, Î. du, *France* 21 E10
Lévanto, *Italy* 28 D6
Lévanzo, *Italy* 30 D5
Levelland, *U.S.A.* 113 J3
Leven, *U.K.* 14 E6
Leven, L., *U.K.* 14 E5
Leven, Toraka, *Madag.* 89 A8
Leveque C., *Australia* 92 C3
Leverano, *Italy* 31 B10
Leverkusen, *Germany* 24 D3
Levice, *Slovak Rep.* 27 C11
Lévico Terme, *Italy* 29 C8
Levie, *France* 21 G13
Levier, *France* 19 F13
Levin, *N.Z.* 91 J5
Lévis, *Canada* 103 C5
Levis, L., *Canada* 104 A5
Levítha, *Greece* 39 D8
Levittown, *N.Y., U.S.A.* 111 F11
Levittown, *Pa., U.S.A.* 111 F10
Levka, *Bulgaria* 41 E10
Levkás, *Greece* 38 C2
Levkás □, *Greece* 38 C2
Levkímmi, *Greece* 36 B4
Levkímmi, Ákra, *Greece* 36 B4
Levkôsia = Nicosia, *Cyprus* 36 D12
Levoča, *Slovak Rep.* 27 B13
Levroux, *France* 19 F8
Levski, *Bulgaria* 41 C9
Levskigrad = Karlovo, *Bulgaria* 41 D8
Lewes, *U.K.* 13 G8
Lewes, *U.S.A.* 108 F8
Lewin Brzeski, *Poland* 45 H4
Lewis, *U.K.* 14 C2
Lewis →, *U.S.A.* 116 E4
Lewis, Butt of, *U.K.* 14 C2
Lewis Ra., *Australia* 92 D4
Lewis Range, *U.S.A.* 114 C7
Lewis Run, *U.S.A.* 110 E6
Lewisburg, *Pa., U.S.A.* 110 F8
Lewisburg, *Tenn., U.S.A.* 109 H2
Lewisburg, *W. Va., U.S.A.* 108 G5
Lewisporte, *Canada* 103 C8
Lewiston, *Idaho, U.S.A.* 114 C5
Lewiston, *Maine, U.S.A.* 109 C11
Lewiston, *N.Y., U.S.A.* 110 C5
Lewistown, *Mont., U.S.A.* 114 C9
Lewistown, *Pa., U.S.A.* 110 F7
Lexington, *Ill., U.S.A.* 112 E10
Lexington, *Ky., U.S.A.* 108 F3
Lexington, *Mich., U.S.A.* 110 C2
Lexington, *Mo., U.S.A.* 112 F8
Lexington, *N.C., U.S.A.* 109 H5
Lexington, *N.Y., U.S.A.* 111 D10
Lexington, *Nebr., U.S.A.* 112 E5
Lexington, *Ohio, U.S.A.* 110 F2
Lexington, *Tenn., U.S.A.* 109 H1
Lexington, *Va., U.S.A.* 108 G6
Lexington Park, *U.S.A.* 108 F7
Leyburn, *U.K.* 12 C6
Leye, *China* 58 E6
Leyland, *U.K.* 12 D5
Leyre →, *France* 20 D2
Leyte □, *Phil.* 61 F6
Leyte Gulf, *Phil.* 61 F6
Leżajsk, *Poland* 45 H9
Lezay, *France* 20 B3
Lezha, *Albania* 40 E3
Lezhi, *China* 58 B5
Lézignan-Corbières, *France* 20 E6
Lezoux, *France* 20 C7
Lgov, *Russia* 47 G8
Lhasa, *China* 60 D4
Lhazê, *China* 60 D3
Lhokkruet, *Indonesia* 62 D1

Lhokseumawe, Indonesia 62 C1
L'Hospitalet de Llobregat, Spain 32 D7
Lhuntsi Dzong, India 67 F17
Li, Thailand 64 D2
Li Shui →, China 59 C9
Li Xian, Gansu, China 56 G3
Li Xian, Hebei, China 56 E8
Li Xian, Hunan, China 59 C8
Liádhoi, Greece 39 E8
Liancheng, China 59 E11
Lianga, Phil. 61 G7
Liangcheng, Nei Mongol Zizhiqu, China 56 D7
Liangcheng, Shandong, China 57 G10
Liangdang, China 56 H4
Lianghe, China 58 E2
Lianghekou, China 58 C7
Liangping, China 58 B6
Liangpran, Indonesia 62 D4
Lianhua, China 59 D9
Lianjiang, Fujian, China 59 D12
Lianjiang, Guangdong, China 59 G8
Lianping, China 59 E10
Lianshan, China 59 E9
Lianshanguan, China 57 D12
Lianshui, China 57 H10
Lianyuan, China 59 D8
Lianyungang, China 57 G10
Lianzhou, China 59 E9
Liao He →, China 57 D11
Liaocheng, China 56 F8
Liaodong Bandao, China 57 E12
Liaodong Wan, China 57 D11
Liaoning □, China 57 D12
Liaoyang, China 57 D12
Liaoyuan, China 57 C13
Liaozhong, China 57 D12
Liapádhes, Greece 38 B1
Liard →, Canada 104 A4
Liard River, Canada 104 B3
Liari, Pakistan 68 G2
Libau = Liepāja, Latvia 9 H19
Libby, U.S.A. 114 B6
Libenge, Dem. Rep. of the Congo 84 D3
Liberal, U.S.A. 113 G4
Liberec, Czech Rep. 26 A8
Liberia, Costa Rica 120 D2
Liberia ■, W. Afr. 82 D3
Liberty, Mo., U.S.A. 112 F7
Liberty, N.Y., U.S.A. 111 E10
Liberty, Pa., U.S.A. 110 E7
Liberty, Tex., U.S.A. 113 K7
Libiąż, Poland 45 H6
Lîbîya, Sahrâ', Africa 79 C10
Libo, China 58 E6
Libobo, Tanjung, Indonesia 63 E7
Libode, S. Africa 89 E4
Libohava, Albania 40 F4
Libourne, France 20 D3
Libramont, Belgium 17 E5
Librazhdi, Albania 40 E4
Libreville, Gabon 84 D1
Libya ■, N. Afr. 79 C9
Libyan Desert = Lîbîya, Sahrâ', Africa 79 C10
Libyan Plateau = Ed-Déffa, Egypt 80 A2
Licantén, Chile 126 D1
Licata, Italy 30 E6
Lice, Turkey 73 C9
Licheng, China 56 F7
Lichfield, U.K. 13 E6
Lichinga, Mozam. 87 E4
Lichtenburg, S. Africa 88 D4
Lichtenfels, Germany 25 E7
Lichuan, Hubei, China 58 B7
Lichuan, Jiangxi, China 59 D11
Licking →, U.S.A. 108 F3
Licosa, Punta, Italy 31 B7
Lida, Belarus 9 K21
Liden, Sweden 10 B10
Lidhoríkion, Greece 38 C4
Lidhult, Sweden 11 H7
Lidköping, Sweden 11 F7
Lido, Italy 29 C9
Lido, Niger 83 C5
Lido di Roma = Óstia, Lido di, Italy 29 G9
Lidzbark, Poland 45 E6
Lidzbark Warmiński, Poland 44 D7
Liebenwalde, Germany 24 C9
Lieberose, Germany 24 D10
Liebig, Mt., Australia 92 D5
Liebling, Romania 42 E6
Liechtenstein ■, Europe 25 H5
Liège, Belgium 17 D5
Liège □, Belgium 17 D5
Liegnitz = Legnica, Poland 45 G3
Lienart, Dem. Rep. of the Congo 86 B2
Lienyünchiangshih = Lianyungang, China 57 G10
Lienz, Austria 26 E5
Liepāja, Latvia 9 H19
Liepāja □, Latvia 44 B8
Liepājas ezers, Latvia 44 B8
Lier, Belgium 17 C4
Liernais, France 19 E11
Liești, Romania 43 E12
Liévin, France 19 B9
Lièvre →, Canada 102 C4
Liezen, Austria 26 D7
Liffey →, Ireland 15 C5
Lifford, Ireland 15 B4
Liffré, France 18 D5
Lifudzin, Russia 54 B7
Ligao, Phil. 61 E5
Lightning Ridge, Australia 95 D4
Lignano Sabbiadoro, Italy 29 C10
Ligny-en-Barrois, France 19 D12
Ligonier, U.S.A. 110 F5
Ligoúrion, Greece 38 D5
Ligueil, France 18 E7
Liguria □, Italy 28 D5
Ligurian Sea, Medit. S. 6 G7
Lihou Reefs and Cays, Australia 94 B5
Lihue, U.S.A. 106 H15
Lijiang, China 58 D3
Likasi, Dem. Rep. of the Congo 87 E2
Likenäs, Sweden 10 D8
Likhoslavl, Russia 46 D8
Likhovskoy, Russia 47 H11
Likoma I., Malawi 87 E3
Likumburu, Tanzania 87 D4
L'Île-Bouchard, France 18 E7
L'Île-Rousse, France 21 F12
Liling, China 59 D9
Lilla Edet, Sweden 11 F6
Lille, France 19 B10
Lille Bælt, Denmark 11 J3
Lillebonne, France 18 C7
Lillehammer, Norway 9 F14
Lillesand, Norway 9 G13
Lillhärdal, Sweden 10 C8
Lillian Pt., Australia 93 E4
Lillo, Spain 34 F7
Lillooet, Canada 104 C4
Lillooet →, Canada 104 D4
Lilongwe, Malawi 87 E3
Liloy, Phil. 63 C6
Lim →, Bos.-H. 40 C3
Lima, Indonesia 63 E7
Lima, Peru 124 F3
Lima, Mont., U.S.A. 114 D7
Lima, Ohio, U.S.A. 108 E3
Lima →, Portugal 34 D2
Liman, Indonesia 63 G14
Liman, Russia 49 H8
Limanowa, Poland 45 J7
Limassol, Cyprus 36 E12
Limavady, U.K. 15 A5
Limay →, Argentina 128 D3
Limay Mahuida, Argentina 126 D2
Limbach-Oberfrohna, Germany 24 E8
Limbang, Brunei 62 D5
Limbara, Mte., Italy 30 B2
Limbaži, Latvia 9 H21
Limbdi, India 68 H4
Limbe, Cameroon 83 E6
Limburg, Germany 25 E4
Limburg □, Belgium 17 C5
Limburg □, Neths. 17 C5
Limedsforsen, Sweden 10 D7
Limeira, Brazil 127 A6
Limenária, Greece 41 F8
Limerick, Ireland 15 D3
Limerick, U.S.A. 111 C14
Limerick □, Ireland 15 D3
Limestone, U.S.A. 110 D6
Limestone →, Canada 105 B10
Limfjorden, Denmark 11 H3
Limia = Lima →, Portugal 34 D2
Limín Khersonísou, Greece 39 F7
Limingen, Norway 8 D15
Limmared, Sweden 11 G7
Limmen Bight, Australia 94 A2
Limmen Bight →, Australia 94 B2
Límni, Greece 38 C5
Límnos, Greece 39 B7
Limoges, Canada 111 A9
Limoges, France 20 C5
Limón, Costa Rica 120 E3
Limon, U.S.A. 112 F3
Limone Piemonte, Italy 28 D4
Limousin, France 20 C5
Limousin, Plateaux du, France 20 C5
Limoux, France 20 E6
Limpopo →, Africa 89 D5
Limuru, Kenya 86 C4
Lin Xian, China 56 F6
Lin'an, China 59 B12
Linapacan I., Phil. 61 F3
Linapacan Str., Phil. 61 F3
Linares, Chile 126 D1
Linares, Mexico 119 C5
Linares, Spain 35 G7
Linaro, Capo, Italy 29 F8
Línas Mte., Italy 30 C1
Lincang, China 58 F3
Lincheng, China 56 F8
Linchuan, China 59 D11
Lincoln, Argentina 126 C3
Lincoln, N.Z. 91 K4
Lincoln, U.K. 12 D7
Lincoln, Calif., U.S.A. 116 G5
Lincoln, Ill., U.S.A. 112 E10
Lincoln, Kans., U.S.A. 112 F5
Lincoln, Maine, U.S.A. 109 C11
Lincoln, N.H., U.S.A. 111 B13
Lincoln, N. Mex., U.S.A. 115 K11
Lincoln, Nebr., U.S.A. 112 E6
Lincoln City, U.S.A. 114 D1
Lincoln Hav = Lincoln Sea, Arctic 4 A5
Lincoln Sea, Arctic 4 A5
Lincolnshire □, U.K. 12 D7
Lincolnshire Wolds, U.K. 12 D7
Lincolnton, U.S.A. 109 H5
L'Incudine, France 21 G13
Lind, U.S.A. 114 C4
Linda, U.S.A. 116 F5
Lindau, Germany 25 H5
Linden, Guyana 124 B7
Linden, Ala., U.S.A. 109 J2
Linden, Calif., U.S.A. 116 G5
Linden, Tex., U.S.A. 113 J7
Lindenhurst, U.S.A. 111 F11
Lindesberg, Sweden 10 E9
Lindesnes, Norway 9 H12
Líndhos, Greece 36 C10
Líndhos, Ákra, Greece 36 C10
Lindi, Tanzania 87 D4
Lindi □, Tanzania 87 D4
Lindi →, Dem. Rep. of the Congo 86 B2
Lindö, Sweden 11 F10
Lindome, Sweden 11 G6
Lindoso, Portugal 34 D2
Lindow, Germany 24 C8
Lindsay, Canada 102 D4
Lindsay, Calif., U.S.A. 116 J7
Lindsay, Okla., U.S.A. 113 H6
Lindsborg, U.S.A. 112 F6
Lindsdal, Sweden 11 H10
Linesville, U.S.A. 110 E4
Linfen, China 56 F6
Ling Xian, Hunan, China 59 D9
Ling Xian, Shandong, China 56 F9
Lingao, China 64 C7
Lingayen, Phil. 63 A6
Lingayen G., Phil. 61 C4
Lingbi, China 57 H9
Lingbo, Sweden 10 C10
Lingchuan, Guangxi Zhuangzu, China 59 E8
Lingchuan, Shanxi, China 56 G7
Lingen, Germany 24 C3
Lingga, Indonesia 62 E2
Lingga, Kepulauan, Indonesia 62 E2
Lingga Arch. = Lingga, Kepulauan, Indonesia 62 E2
Linghem, Sweden 11 F9
Lingle, U.S.A. 112 D2
Lingqiu, China 56 E8
Lingshan, China 58 F7
Lingshi, China 56 F6
Lingshou, China 56 E8
Lingshui, China 64 C8
Lingtai, China 56 G4
Linguère, Senegal 82 B1
Lingui, China 59 E8
Lingwu, China 56 E4
Lingyuan, China 57 D10
Lingyun, China 58 E6
Linhai, China 59 C13
Linhares, Brazil 125 G10
Linhe, China 56 D4
Linjiang, China 57 D14
Linköping, Sweden 11 F9
Linkou, China 57 B16
Linli, China 59 C8
Linnhe, L., U.K. 14 E3
Linqi, China 56 G7
Linqing, China 56 F8
Linqu, China 57 F10
Linru, China 56 G7
Lins, Brazil 127 A6
Linshui, China 58 B6
Linta →, Madag. 89 D7
Linth →, Switz. 25 H5
Linthal, Switz. 25 J5
Linton, Ind., U.S.A. 108 F2
Linton, N. Dak., U.S.A. 112 B4
Lintong, China 56 G5
Linwood, Canada 110 C4
Linwu, China 59 E9
Linxi, China 57 C10
Linxia, China 60 C5
Linxiang, China 59 C9
Linyanti →, Africa 88 B4
Linyi, China 57 G10
Linz, Austria 26 C7
Linz, Germany 24 E3
Linzhenzhen, China 56 F5
Linzi, China 57 F10
Lion, G. du, France 20 E7
Lionárisso, Cyprus 36 D13
Lioni, Italy 31 B8
Lions, G. of = Lion, G. du, France 20 E7
Lion's Den, Zimbabwe 87 F3
Lion's Head, Canada 110 B3
Liozno = Lyozna, Belarus 46 E6
Lipa, Phil. 61 E4
Lipali, Mozam. 87 F4
Lipany, Slovak Rep. 27 B13
Lípari, Italy 31 D7
Lípari, I., Italy 31 D7
Lípari, Is. = Eólie, Ís., Italy 31 D7
Lipcani, Moldova 43 B11
Lipetsk, Russia 47 F10
Lipiany, Poland 45 E1
Liping, China 58 D7
Lipkany = Lipcani, Moldova 43 B11
Lipljan, Kosovo, Yug. 40 D5
Lipník nad Bečvou, Czech Rep. 27 B10
Lipno, Poland 45 F6
Lipova, Romania 42 D6
Lipovcy Manzovka, Russia 54 B6
Lipovets, Ukraine 47 H5
Lippe →, Germany 24 D2
Lippstadt, Germany 24 D4
Lipscomb, U.S.A. 113 G4
Lipsk, Poland 44 E10
Lipsko, Poland 45 G8
Lipsói, Greece 39 D8
Liptovský Hrádok, Slovak Rep. 27 B12
Liptovský Mikuláš, Slovak Rep. 27 B12
Liptrap C., Australia 95 F4
Lipu, China 59 E8
Lira, Uganda 86 B3
Liri →, Italy 30 A6
Liria = Llíria, Spain 33 F4
Lisala, Dem. Rep. of the Congo 84 D4
Lisboa, Portugal 35 G1
Lisboa □, Portugal 35 F1
Lisbon = Lisboa, Portugal 35 G1
Lisbon, N. Dak., U.S.A. 112 B6
Lisbon, N.H., U.S.A. 111 B13
Lisbon, Ohio, U.S.A. 110 F4
Lisbon Falls, U.S.A. 109 D10
Lisburn, U.K. 15 B5
Liscannor B., Ireland 15 D2
Liscia →, Italy 30 A2
Lishe Jiang →, China 58 E3
Lishi, China 56 F6
Lishu, China 57 C13
Lishui, Jiangsu, China 59 B12
Lishui, Zhejiang, China 59 C12
Lisianski I., Pac. Oc. 96 E10
Lisichansk = Lysychansk, Ukraine 47 H10
Lisieux, France 18 C7
Liski, Russia 47 G10
L'Isle-Jourdain, Gers, France 20 E5
L'Isle-Jourdain, Vienne, France 20 B4
L'Isle-sur-la-Sorgue, France 21 E9
Lisle-sur-Tarn, France 20 E5
Lismore, Australia 95 D5
Lismore, Ireland 15 D4
Lista, Norway 9 G12
Lister, Mt., Antarctica 5 D11
Liston, Australia 95 D5
Listowel, Canada 102 D3
Listowel, Ireland 15 D2
Lit, Sweden 10 A8
Lit-et-Mixe, France 20 D2
Litang, Guangxi Zhuangzu, China 58 F7
Litang, Sichuan, China 58 B3
Litang Qu →, China 58 C3
Litani →, Lebanon 75 B4
Litchfield, Calif., U.S.A. 116 E6
Litchfield, Conn., U.S.A. 111 E11
Litchfield, Ill., U.S.A. 112 F10
Litchfield, Minn., U.S.A. 112 C7
Liteni, Romania 43 C11
Lithgow, Australia 95 E5
Líthinon, Ákra, Greece 36 E6
Lithuania ■, Europe 9 J20
Litija, Slovenia 29 B11
Lititz, U.S.A. 111 F8
Litókhoron, Greece 40 F6
Litoměřice, Czech Rep. 26 A7
Litomyšl, Czech Rep. 27 B9
Litschau, Austria 26 C8
Little Abaco I., Bahamas 120 A4
Little Barrier I., N.Z. 91 G5
Little Belt Mts., U.S.A. 114 C8
Little Blue →, U.S.A. 112 F6
Little Buffalo →, Canada 104 A6
Little Cayman, I., Cayman Is. 120 C3
Little Churchill →, Canada 105 B9
Little Colorado →, U.S.A. 115 H8
Little Current, Canada 102 C3
Little Current →, Canada 102 B3
Little Falls, Minn., U.S.A. 112 C7
Little Falls, N.Y., U.S.A. 111 C10
Little Fork →, U.S.A. 112 A8
Little Grand Rapids, Canada 105 C9
Little Humboldt →, U.S.A. 114 F5
Little Inagua I., Bahamas 121 B5
Little Karoo, S. Africa 88 E3
Little Lake, U.S.A. 117 K9
Little Laut Is. = Laut Kecil, Kepulauan, Indonesia 62 E5
Little-Mecatina = Petit-Mécatina →, Canada 103 B8
Little Minch, U.K. 14 D2
Little Missouri →, U.S.A. 112 B3
Little Ouse →, U.K. 13 E9
Little Rann, India 68 H4
Little Red →, U.S.A. 113 H9
Little River, N.Z. 91 K4
Little Rock, U.S.A. 113 H8
Little Ruaha →, Tanzania 86 D4
Little Sable Pt., U.S.A. 108 D2
Little Scarcies →, S. Leone 82 D2
Little Sioux →, U.S.A. 112 E6
Little Smoky →, Canada 104 C5
Little Snake →, U.S.A. 114 F9
Little Valley, U.S.A. 110 D6
Little Wabash →, U.S.A. 108 G1
Little White →, U.S.A. 112 D4
Littlefield, U.S.A. 113 J3
Littlehampton, U.K. 13 G7
Littleton, U.S.A. 111 B13
Litvinov, Czech Rep. 26 A6
Liu He →, China 57 D11
Liu Jiang →, China 58 F7
Liuba, China 56 H4
Liucheng, China 58 E7
Liugou, China 57 D10
Liuhe, China 57 C13
Liuheng Dao, China 59 C14
Liujiang, China 58 E7
Liukang Tenggaja = Sabalana, Kepulauan, Indonesia 63 F5
Liuli, Tanzania 87 E3
Liuwa Plain, Zambia 85 G4
Liuyang, China 59 C9
Liuzhou, China 58 E7
Liuzhuang, China 57 H11
Livada, Romania 42 C8
Livadherón, Greece 40 F5
Livadhia, Cyprus 36 E12
Livádhion, Greece 38 A4
Livarot, France 18 D7
Live Oak, Calif., U.S.A. 116 F5
Live Oak, Fla., U.S.A. 109 K4
Liveras, Cyprus 36 D11
Livermore, U.S.A. 116 H5
Livermore, Mt., U.S.A. 113 K2
Livermore Falls, U.S.A. 109 C11
Liverpool, Canada 103 D7
Liverpool, U.K. 12 D4
Liverpool, U.S.A. 111 C8
Liverpool Bay, U.K. 12 D4
Liverpool Plains, Australia 95 E5
Liverpool Ra., Australia 95 E5
Livigno, Italy 28 B7
Livingston, Guatemala 120 C2
Livingston, U.K. 14 F5
Livingston, Ala., U.S.A. 109 J1
Livingston, Calif., U.S.A. 116 H6
Livingston, Mont., U.S.A. 114 D8
Livingston, S.C., U.S.A. 109 J5
Livingston, Tenn., U.S.A. 109 G3
Livingston, Tex., U.S.A. 113 K7
Livingston, L., U.S.A. 113 K7
Livingston Manor, U.S.A. 111 E10
Livingstone, Zambia 87 F2
Livingstone Mts., Tanzania 87 D3
Livingstonia, Malawi 87 E3
Livno, Bos.-H. 42 G2
Livny, Russia 47 F9
Livonia, Mich., U.S.A. 108 D4
Livonia, N.Y., U.S.A. 110 D7
Livorno, Italy 28 E7
Livramento, Brazil 127 C4
Livron-sur-Drôme, France 21 D8
Liwale, Tanzania 87 D4
Liwiec →, Poland 45 F8
Lixi, China 58 D3
Lixian, China 58 B4
Lixoúrion, Greece 38 C2
Liyang, China 59 B12
Lizard I., Australia 94 A4
Lizard Pt., U.K. 13 H2
Lizzano, Italy 31 B10
Ljig, Serbia, Yug. 40 B4
Ljubija, Bos.-H. 29 D13
Ljubinje, Bos.-H. 40 D2
Ljubljana, Slovenia 29 B11
Ljubno, Slovenia 29 B11
Ljubovija, Serbia, Yug. 40 B3
Ljugarn, Sweden 11 G12
Ljung, Sweden 11 G7
Ljungan →, Sweden 10 B11
Ljungaverk, Sweden 10 B10
Ljungby, Sweden 9 H15
Ljungbyholm, Sweden 11 H10
Ljungdalen, Sweden 10 B6
Ljungsbro, Sweden 11 F9
Ljungskile, Sweden 11 F5
Ljusdal, Sweden 10 C10
Ljusfallshammar, Sweden 11 F9
Ljusnan →, Sweden 10 C11
Ljusne, Sweden 10 C11
Ljutomer, Slovenia 29 B13
Llagostera, Spain 32 D7
Llancanelo, Salina, Argentina 126 D2
Llandeilo, U.K. 13 F4
Llandovery, U.K. 13 F4
Llandrindod Wells, U.K. 13 E4
Llandudno, U.K. 12 D4
Llanelli, U.K. 13 F3
Llanes, Spain 34 B6
Llangollen, U.K. 12 E4
Llanidloes, U.K. 13 E4
Llano, U.S.A. 113 K5
Llano →, U.S.A. 113 K5
Llano Estacado, U.S.A. 113 J3
Llanos, S. Amer. 122 C3
Llanquihue, L., Chile 128 E1
Llanwrtyd Wells, U.K. 13 E4
Llebeig, C. des, Spain 37 B9
Lleida, Spain 32 D5
Lleida □, Spain 32 C6
Llentrisca, C., Spain 37 C7
Llera, Mexico 119 C5
Llerena, Spain 35 G5
Lleyn Peninsula, U.K. 12 E3
Llico, Chile 126 C1
Llíria, Spain 33 F4
Llobregat →, Spain 32 D7
Llodio, Spain 32 B2
Lloret de Mar, Spain 32 D7
Lloyd B., Australia 94 A3
Lloyd L., Canada 105 B7
Lloydminster, Canada 105 C7
Llucena del Cid, Spain 32 E4
Llucmajor, Spain 37 B9
Llullaillaco, Volcán, S. Amer. 126 A2
Lo →, Vietnam 64 B5
Loa, U.S.A. 115 G8
Loa →, Chile 126 A1
Loaita I., S. China Sea 62 B4
Loange →, Dem. Rep. of the Congo 84 E4
Loano, Italy 28 D5
Lobatse, Botswana 88 D4
Löbau, Germany 24 D10
Lobenstein, Germany 24 E7
Lobería, Argentina 126 D4
Löberöd, Sweden 11 J7
Łobez, Poland 44 E2
Lobito, Angola 85 G2
Lobo →, Ivory C. 82 D3
Lobos, Argentina 126 D4
Lobos, I., Mexico 118 B2
Lobos, I. de, Canary Is. 37 F6
Łobżenica, Poland 45 E4
Loc Binh, Vietnam 64 B6
Loc Ninh, Vietnam 65 G6
Locarno, Switz. 25 J4
Loch Baghasdail = Lochboisdale, U.K. 14 D1

Loch Garman = Wexford, Ireland 15 D5
Loch Nam Madadh = Lochmaddy, U.K. 14 D1
Lochaber, U.K. 14 E3
Locharbriggs, U.K. 14 F5
Lochboisdale, U.K. 14 D1
Loche, L. La, Canada 105 B7
Lochem, Neths. 17 B6
Loches, France 18 E7
Lochgilphead, U.K. 14 E3
Lochinver, U.K. 14 C3
Lochmaddy, U.K. 14 D1
Lochnagar, Australia 94 C4
Lochnagar, U.K. 14 E5
Łochów, Poland 45 F8
Lochy, L., U.K. 14 E4
Lock, Australia 95 E2
Lock Haven, U.S.A. 110 E7
Lockeford, U.S.A. 116 G5
Lockeport, Canada 103 D6
Lockerbie, U.K. 14 F5
Lockhart, Australia 95 F4
Lockhart, U.S.A. 113 L6
Lockhart, L., Australia 93 F2
Lockhart River, Australia 94 A3
Lockney, U.S.A. 113 H4
Lockport, U.S.A. 110 C6
Locminé, France 18 E4
Locri, Italy 31 D9
Locronan, France 18 D2
Lod, Israel 75 D3
Lodeinoye Pole, Russia 46 B7
Lodève, France 20 E7
Lodge Bay, Canada 103 B8
Lodge Grass, U.S.A. 114 D10
Lodgepole Cr. →, U.S.A. 112 E2
Lodhran, Pakistan 68 E4
Lodi, Italy 28 C6
Lodi, Calif., U.S.A. 116 G5
Lodi, Ohio, U.S.A. 110 E3
Lodja, Dem. Rep. of the Congo 86 C1
Lodosa, Spain 32 C2
Lödöse, Sweden 11 F6
Lodwar, Kenya 86 B4
Łódź, Poland 45 G6
Łódzkie □, Poland 45 G6
Loei, Thailand 64 D3
Loengo, Dem. Rep. of the Congo 86 C2
Loeriesfontein, S. Africa 88 E2
Lofa →, Liberia 83 D2
Lofer, Austria 26 D5
Lofoten, Norway 8 B15
Lofsdalen, Sweden 10 B7
Lofsen →, Sweden 10 B7
Loftahammar, Sweden 11 G10
Loga, Niger 83 C5
Logan, Iowa, U.S.A. 112 E7
Logan, Ohio, U.S.A. 108 F4
Logan, Utah, U.S.A. 114 F8
Logan, W. Va., U.S.A. 108 G5
Logan, Mt., Canada 100 B5
Logandale, U.S.A. 117 J12
Logansport, Ind., U.S.A. 108 E2
Logansport, La., U.S.A. 113 K8
Logirim, Sudan 81 G3
Logo, Sudan 81 F3
Logone →, Chad 79 F9
Logroño, Spain 32 C2
Logrosán, Spain 35 F5
Løgstør, Denmark 11 H3
Løgumkloster, Denmark 11 J2
Lohals, Denmark 11 J4
Lohardaga, India 69 H11
Loharia, India 68 H6
Loharu, India 68 E6
Lohja, Finland 9 F21
Löhne, Germany 24 C4
Lohr, Germany 25 F5
Lohri Wah →, Pakistan 68 F2
Loi-kaw, Burma 67 K20
Loimaa, Finland 9 F20
Loir →, France 18 E6
Loir-et-Cher □, France 18 E8
Loire □, France 21 C8
Loire →, France 18 E4
Loire-Atlantique □, France 18 E5
Loiret □, France 19 E9
Loitz, Germany 24 B9
Loja, Ecuador 124 D3
Loja, Spain 35 H6
Loji = Kawasi, Indonesia 63 E7
Løjt Kirkeby, Denmark 11 J3
Lojung, China 58 E7
Loka, Sudan 81 G3
Lokandu, Dem. Rep. of the Congo 86 C2
Lokeren, Belgium 17 C3
Lokgwabe, Botswana 88 C3
Lokhvitsa, Ukraine 47 G7
Lokichokio, Kenya 86 B3
Lokitaung, Kenya 86 B4
Lokkan tekojärvi, Finland 8 C22
Løkken, Denmark 11 G3
Loknya, Russia 46 D6
Loko, Nigeria 83 D6
Lokoja, Nigeria 83 D6
Lokot, Russia 47 F8
Lol →, Sudan 81 F2
Lola, Guinea 82 D3
Lola, Mt., U.S.A. 116 F6
Lolibai, Gebel, Sudan 81 G3
Lolimi, Sudan 81 G3
Loliondo, Tanzania 86 C4
Lolland, Denmark 11 K5
Lollar, Germany 24 E4
Lolo, U.S.A. 114 C6
Lolodorf, Cameroon 83 E7
Lom, Bulgaria 40 C7
Lom →, Bulgaria 40 C7
Lom Kao, Thailand 64 D3
Lom Sak, Thailand 64 D3
Loma, U.S.A. 114 C8
Loma Linda, U.S.A. 117 L9
Lomami →, Dem. Rep. of the Congo 86 B1
Lomas de Zamóra, Argentina 126 C4
Lombadina, Australia 92 C3
Lombárdia □, Italy 28 C6
Lombardy = Lombárdia □, Italy 28 C6
Lombez, France 20 E4
Lomblen, Indonesia 63 F6
Lombok, Indonesia 62 F5
Lomé, Togo 83 D5
Lomela, Dem. Rep. of the Congo 84 E4
Lomela →, Dem. Rep. of the Congo 84 E4
Lomianki, Poland 45 F7
Lomma, Sweden 11 J7
Lommel, Belgium 17 C5
Lomond, Canada 104 C6
Lomond, L., U.K. 14 E4
Lomphat, Cambodia 64 F6
Lompobatang, Indonesia 63 F5
Lompoc, U.S.A. 117 L6
Łomża, Poland 45 E9
Loncoche, Chile 128 D2
Londa, India 66 M9
Londiani, Kenya 86 C4
Londinières, France 18 C8
London, Canada 102 D3
London, U.K. 13 F7
London, Ky., U.S.A. 108 G3
London, Ohio, U.S.A. 108 F4
London, Greater □, U.K. 13 F7
Londonderry, U.K. 15 B4
Londonderry □, U.K. 15 B4
Londonderry, C., Australia 92 B4
Londonderry, I., Chile 128 H2
Londres, Argentina 128 B3
Londrina, Brazil 127 A5
Lone Pine, U.S.A. 116 J8
Lonely Mine, Zimbabwe 89 B4
Long B., U.S.A. 109 J6
Long Beach, Calif., U.S.A. 117 M8
Long Beach, N.Y., U.S.A. 111 F11
Long Beach, Wash., U.S.A. 116 D2
Long Branch, U.S.A. 111 F11
Long Creek, U.S.A. 114 D4
Long Eaton, U.K. 12 E6
Long I., Australia 94 C4
Long I., Bahamas 121 B4
Long I., Canada 102 B4
Long I., Ireland 15 E2
Long I., U.S.A. 111 F11
Long Island Sd., U.S.A. 111 E12
Long L., Canada 102 C2
Long Lake, U.S.A. 111 C10
Long Point B., Canada 110 D4
Long Prairie →, U.S.A. 112 C7
Long Pt., Canada 110 D4
Long Range Mts., Canada 103 C8
Long Reef, Australia 92 B4
Long Spruce, Canada 105 B10
Long Str. = Longa, Proliv, Russia 4 C16
Long Thanh, Vietnam 65 G6
Long Xian, China 56 G4
Long Xuyen, Vietnam 65 G5
Longá, Greece 38 E3
Longa, Proliv, Russia 4 C16
Long'an, China 58 F6
Longarone, Italy 29 B9
Longbenton, U.K. 12 B6
Longboat Key, U.S.A. 109 M4
Longchang, China 58 C5
Longchi, China 58 C4
Longchuan, Guangdong, China 59 E10
Longchuan, Yunnan, China 58 E1
Longde, China 56 G4
Longeau, France 19 E12
Longford, Australia 94 G4
Longford, Ireland 15 C4
Longford □, Ireland 15 C4
Longguan, China 56 D8
Longhai, China 59 E11
Longhua, China 57 D9
Longhui, China 59 D8
Longido, Tanzania 86 C4
Longiram, Indonesia 62 E5
Longkou, Jiangxi, China 59 D10
Longkou, Shandong, China 57 F11
Longlac, Canada 102 C2
Longli, China 58 D6
Longlin, China 58 E5
Longling, China 58 E2
Longmeadow, U.S.A. 111 D12
Longmen, China 59 F10
Longming, China 58 F6
Longmont, U.S.A. 112 E2
Longnan, China 59 E10
Longnawan, Indonesia 62 D4
Longobucco, Italy 31 C9
Longquan, China 59 C12
Longreach, Australia 94 C3
Longshan, China 58 C7
Longsheng, China 59 E8
Longué-Jumelles, France 18 E6
Longueau, France 19 C9
Longueuil, Canada 111 A11
Longuyon, France 19 C12
Longvic, France 19 E12
Longview, Tex., U.S.A. 113 J7
Longview, Wash., U.S.A. 116 D4
Longwy, France 19 C12
Longxi, China 56 G3
Longyan, China 59 E11
Longyou, China 59 C12
Longzhou, China 58 F6
Lonigo, Italy 29 C8
Löningen, Germany 24 C3
Lonja →, Croatia 29 C13
Lonoke, U.S.A. 113 H9
Lonquimay, Chile 128 D2
Lons-le-Saunier, France 19 F12
Lönsboda, Sweden 11 H8
Looe, U.K. 13 G3
Lookout, C., Canada 102 A3
Lookout, C., U.S.A. 109 H7
Loolmalasin, Tanzania 86 C4
Loon →, Alta., Canada 104 B5
Loon →, Man., Canada 105 B8
Loon Lake, Canada 105 C7
Loongana, Australia 93 F4
Loop Hd., Ireland 15 D2
Lop Buri, Thailand 64 E3
Lop Nor = Lop Nur, China 60 B4
Lop Nur, China 60 B4
Lopare, Bos.-H. 42 F3
Lopatin, Russia 49 J8
Lopatina, Gora, Russia 51 D15
Lopaye, Sudan 81 F3
Lopez, Phil. 61 E5
Lopez, U.S.A. 111 E8
Lopez, C., Gabon 84 E1
Lopphavet, Norway 8 A19
Lora →, Afghan. 66 D4
Lora, Hamun-i-, Pakistan 66 E4
Lora Cr. →, Australia 95 D2
Lora del Río, Spain 35 H5
Lorain, U.S.A. 110 E2
Loralai, Pakistan 68 D3
Lorca, Spain 33 H3
Lord Howe I., Pac. Oc. 96 L7
Lord Howe Ridge, Pac. Oc. 96 L8
Lordsburg, U.S.A. 115 K9
Lorestan □, Iran 71 C6
Loreto, Brazil 125 E9
Loreto, Italy 29 E10
Loreto, Mexico 118 B2
Lorgues, France 21 E10
Lorhosso, Burkina Faso 82 C4
Lorient, France 18 E3
Lőrinci, Hungary 42 C4
Lormi, India 69 H9
Lorn, U.K. 14 E3
Lorn, Firth of, U.K. 14 E3
Lorne, Australia 95 F3
Loronyo, Sudan 81 G3
Lorovouno, Cyprus 36 D11
Lörrach, Germany 25 H3
Lorraine □, France 19 D13
Los, Sweden 10 C9
Los, Îles de, Guinea 82 D2
Los Alamos, Calif., U.S.A. 117 L6
Los Alamos, N. Mex., U.S.A. 115 J10
Los Altos, U.S.A. 116 H4
Los Andes, Chile 126 C1
Los Angeles, Chile 126 D1
Los Angeles, U.S.A. 117 M8
Los Angeles, Bahia de, Mexico 118 B2
Los Angeles Aqueduct, U.S.A. 117 K9
Los Banos, U.S.A. 116 H6
Los Barrios, Spain 35 J5
Los Blancos, Argentina 126 A3
Los Chiles, Costa Rica 120 D3
Los Corrales de Buelna, Spain 34 B6
Los Cristianos, Canary Is. 37 F3
Los Gallardos, Spain 33 H3
Los Gatos, U.S.A. 116 H5
Los Hermanos Is., Venezuela 121 D7
Los Islotes, Canary Is. 37 E6
Los Llanos de Aridane, Canary Is. 37 F2
Los Loros, Chile 126 B1
Los Lunas, U.S.A. 115 J10
Los Mochis, Mexico 118 B3
Los Monegros, Spain 32 D4
Los Nietos, Spain 33 H4
Los Olivos, U.S.A. 117 L6
Los Palacios, Cuba 120 B3
Los Palacios y Villafranca, Spain 35 H5
Los Reyes, Mexico 118 D4
Los Roques Is., Venezuela 121 D6
Los Santos de Maimona, Spain 35 G4
Los Teques, Venezuela 124 A5
Los Testigos, Is., Venezuela 124 A6
Los Vilos, Chile 126 C1
Los Yébenes, Spain 35 F7
Łosice, Poland 45 F9
Loskop Dam, S. Africa 89 D4
Løsning, Denmark 11 J3
Lossiemouth, U.K. 14 D5
Lostwithiel, U.K. 13 G3
Lot □, France 20 D5
Lot →, France 20 D4
Lot-et-Garonne □, France 20 D4
Lota, Chile 126 D1
Lotagipi Swamp, Sudan 81 G3
Loţfābād, Iran 71 B8
Lothair, S. Africa 89 D5
Lotorp, Sweden 11 F9
Lötschbergtunnel, Switz. 25 J3
Löttorp, Sweden 11 G11
Lotung, Taiwan 59 E13
Loubomo, Congo 84 E2
Loudéac, France 18 D4
Loudi, China 59 D8
Loudonville, U.S.A. 110 F2
Loudun, France 18 E7
Loue →, France 19 E12
Louga, Senegal 82 B1
Loughborough, U.K. 12 E6
Loughrea, Ireland 15 C3
Loughros More B., Ireland 15 B3
Louhans, France 19 F12
Louis Trichardt, S. Africa 89 C4
Louis XIV, Pte., Canada 102 B4
Louisa, U.S.A. 108 F4
Louisbourg, Canada 103 C8
Louise I., Canada 104 C2
Louiseville, Canada 102 C5
Louisiade Arch., Papua N. G. 96 J7
Louisiana, U.S.A. 112 F9
Louisiana □, U.S.A. 113 K9
Louisville, Ky., U.S.A. 108 F3
Louisville, Miss., U.S.A. 113 J10
Louisville, Ohio, U.S.A. 110 F3
Loulay, France 20 B3
Loulé, Portugal 35 H3
Louny, Czech Rep. 26 A6
Loup City, U.S.A. 112 E5
Loups Marins, Lacs des, Canada 102 A5
Lourdes, France 20 E3
Lourenço-Marques = Maputo, Mozam. 89 D5
Lourinhã, Portugal 35 F1
Lousã, Portugal 34 E2
Louta, Burkina Faso 82 C4
Louth, Australia 95 E4
Louth, Ireland 15 C5
Louth, U.K. 12 D7
Louth □, Ireland 15 C5
Loutrá Aidhipsoú, Greece 38 C5
Loutráki, Greece 38 D4
Louvain = Leuven, Belgium 17 D4
Louviers, France 18 C8
Louwsburg, S. Africa 89 D5
Lovat →, Russia 46 C6
Lovćen, Montenegro, Yug. 40 D2
Lovech, Bulgaria 41 C8
Lovech □, Bulgaria 41 C8
Loveland, U.S.A. 112 E2
Lovell, U.S.A. 114 D9
Lovelock, U.S.A. 114 F4
Lóvere, Italy 28 C7
Lövestad, Sweden 11 J7
Loviisa, Finland 9 F22
Loving, U.S.A. 113 J2
Lovington, U.S.A. 113 J3
Lovisa = Loviisa, Finland 9 F22
Lovosice, Czech Rep. 26 A7
Lovran, Croatia 29 C11
Lovrin, Romania 42 E5
Lövstabruk, Sweden 10 D11
Lövstabukten, Sweden 10 D11
Low, L., Canada 102 B4
Low Pt., Australia 93 F4
Low Tatra = Nízké Tatry, Slovak Rep. 27 C12
Lowa, Dem. Rep. of the Congo 86 C2
Lowa →, Dem. Rep. of the Congo 86 C2
Lowell, U.S.A. 111 D13
Lowellville, U.S.A. 110 E4
Löwen →, Namibia 88 D2
Lower Alkali L., U.S.A. 114 F3
Lower Arrow L., Canada 104 D5
Lower Austria = Niederösterreich □, Austria 26 C8
Lower California = Baja California, Mexico 118 A1
Lower Hutt, N.Z. 91 J5
Lower Lake, U.S.A. 116 G4
Lower Manitou L., Canada 105 D10
Lower Post, Canada 104 B3
Lower Red L., U.S.A. 112 B7
Lower Saxony = Niedersachsen □, Germany 24 C4
Lower Tunguska = Tunguska, Nizhnyaya →, Russia 51 C9
Lowestoft, U.K. 13 E9
Łowicz, Poland 45 F6
Lowville, U.S.A. 111 C9
Loxton, Australia 95 E3
Loxton, S. Africa 88 E3
Loyalton, U.S.A. 116 F6
Loyalty Is. = Loyauté, Is., N. Cal. 96 K8
Loyang = Luoyang, China 56 G7
Loyauté, Is., N. Cal. 96 K8
Loyev = Loyew, Belarus 47 G6
Loyew, Belarus 47 G6
Loyoro, Uganda 86 B3
Lož, Slovenia 29 C11
Lozère □, France 20 D7
Loznica, Serbia, Yug. 40 B3
Lozova, Ukraine 47 H9
Lü Shan, China 59 C11
Lü-Tao, Taiwan 59 F13
Luachimo, Angola 84 F4
Luajan →, India 69 G11
Lualaba →, Dem. Rep. of the Congo 86 B2
Luampa, Zambia 87 F1
Lu'an, China 59 B11
Luan Chau, Vietnam 58 G4
Luan He →, China 57 E10
Luan Xian, China 57 E10
Luancheng, Guangxi Zhuangzu, China 58 F7
Luancheng, Hebei, China 56 F8
Luanco, Spain 34 B5
Luanda, Angola 84 F2
Luang, Thale, Thailand 65 J3
Luang Prabang, Laos 58 H4
Luangwa, Zambia 87 F3
Luangwa →, Zambia 87 E3
Luangwa Valley, Zambia 87 E3
Luanne, China 57 D9
Luanping, China 57 D9
Luanshya, Zambia 87 E2
Luapula □, Zambia 87 E2
Luapula →, Africa 87 D2
Luarca, Spain 34 B4
Luashi, Dem. Rep. of the Congo 87 E1
Luau, Angola 84 G4
Lubaczów, Poland 45 H10
Lubań, Poland 45 G2
Lubana, Ozero = Lubānas Ezers, Latvia 9 H22
Lubānas Ezers, Latvia 9 H22
Lubang, Phil. 61 E4
Lubang Is., Phil. 63 B6
Lubartów, Poland 45 G9
Lubawa, Poland 44 E6
Lübbecke, Germany 24 C4
Lübben, Germany 24 D9
Lübbenau, Germany 24 D9
Lubbock, U.S.A. 113 J4
Lübeck, Germany 24 B6
Lübecker Bucht, Germany 24 A6
Lubefu, Dem. Rep. of the Congo 86 C1
Lubefu →, Dem. Rep. of the Congo 86 C1
Lubelskie □, Poland 45 G9
Lubero = Luofu, Dem. Rep. of the Congo 86 C2
Lubersac, France 20 C5
Lubicon L., Canada 104 B5
Lubień Kujawski, Poland 45 F6
Lubilash →, Dem. Rep. of the Congo 84 F4
Lubin, Poland 45 G3
Lublin, Poland 45 G9
Lubliniec, Poland 45 H5
Lubnān, Jabal, Lebanon 75 B4
Lubniewice, Poland 45 F2
Lubny, Ukraine 47 G7
Lubomierz, Poland 45 G2
Luboń, Poland 45 F3
Lubongola, Dem. Rep. of the Congo 86 C2
L'ubotín, Slovak Rep. 27 B13
Lubraniec, Poland 45 F5
Lubsko, Poland 45 G1
Lübtheen, Germany 24 B7
Lubuagan, Phil. 61 C4
Lubudi, Dem. Rep. of the Congo 84 F5
Lubudi →, Dem. Rep. of the Congo 87 D2
Lubuklinggau, Indonesia 62 E2
Lubuksikaping, Indonesia 62 D2
Lubumbashi, Dem. Rep. of the Congo 87 E2
Lubunda, Dem. Rep. of the Congo 86 D2
Lubungu, Zambia 87 E2
Lubuskie □, Poland 45 F2
Lubutu, Dem. Rep. of the Congo 86 C2
Luc An Chau, Vietnam 64 A5
Luc-en-Diois, France 21 D9
Lucan, Canada 110 C3
Lucania, Mt., Canada 100 B5
Lucas Channel, Canada 110 A3
Lucban, Phil. 61 D4
Lucca, Italy 28 E7
Lucé, France 18 D8
Luce Bay, U.K. 14 G4
Lucea, Jamaica 120 C4
Lucedale, U.S.A. 109 K1
Lucena, Phil. 61 E4
Lucena, Spain 35 H6
Lučenec, Slovak Rep. 27 C12
Lucera, Italy 31 A8
Lucerne = Luzern, Switz. 25 H4
Lucerne, U.S.A. 116 F4
Lucerne Valley, U.S.A. 117 L10
Lucero, Mexico 118 A3
Luchena →, Spain 33 H3
Lucheng, China 56 F7
Lucheringo →, Mozam. 87 E4
Lüchow, Germany 24 C7
Luchuan, China 59 F8
Lucia, U.S.A. 116 J5
Lucinda, Australia 94 B4
Lucindale, Australia 95 F3
Luckau, Germany 24 D9
Luckenwalde, Germany 24 C9
Luckhoff, S. Africa 88 D3
Lucknow, Canada 110 C3
Lucknow, India 69 F9
Luçon, France 20 B2
Lüda = Dalian, China 57 E11
Luda Kamchiya →, Bulgaria 41 C11
Ludbreg, Croatia 29 B13
Lüdenscheid, Germany 24 D3
Lüderitz, Namibia 88 D2
Lüderitzbaai, Namibia 88 D2
Ludhiana, India 68 D6
Ludian, China 58 D4
Luding Qiao, China 58 C4
Lüdinghausen, Germany 24 D3
Ludington, U.S.A. 108 D2
Ludlow, U.K. 13 E5
Ludlow, Calif., U.S.A. 117 L10
Ludlow, Pa., U.S.A. 110 E6
Ludlow, Vt., U.S.A. 111 C12
Ludus, Romania 43 D9
Ludvika, Sweden 10 D9
Ludwigsburg, Germany 25 G5
Ludwigsfelde, Germany 24 C9
Ludwigshafen, Germany 25 F4
Ludwigslust, Germany 24 B7

Ludza, *Latvia* 46 D4
Lueki, *Dem. Rep. of the Congo* 86 C2
Luena, *Dem. Rep. of the Congo* 87 D2
Luena, *Zambia* 87 E3
Lüeyang, *China* 56 H4
Lufeng, *Guangdong, China* 59 F10
Lufeng, *Yunnan, China* 58 E4
Lufira →, *Dem. Rep. of the Congo* 87 D2
Lufkin, *U.S.A.* 113 K7
Lufupa, *Dem. Rep. of the Congo* 87 E1
Luga, *Russia* 46 C5
Luga →, *Russia* 46 C5
Lugano, *Switz.* 25 J4
Lugano, L. di, *Switz.* 28 C6
Lugansk = Luhansk, *Ukraine* 47 H10
Lugard's Falls, *Kenya* 86 C4
Lugela, *Mozam.* 87 F4
Lugenda →, *Mozam.* 87 E4
Lugh Ganana, *Somali Rep.* 74 G3
Lugnaquilla, *Ireland* 15 D5
Lugo, *Italy* 29 D8
Lugo, *Spain* 34 B3
Lugo □, *Spain* 34 C3
Lugoj, *Romania* 42 E6
Lugovoy, *Kazakstan* 50 E8
Luhansk, *Ukraine* 47 H10
Luhe, *China* 59 A12
Luhe →, *Germany* 24 B6
Luhuo, *China* 58 B3
Luiana, *Angola* 88 B3
Luimneach = Limerick, *Ireland* 15 D3
Luing, *U.K.* 14 E3
Luino, *Italy* 28 C5
Luís Correia, *Brazil* 125 D10
Luitpold Coast, *Antarctica* 5 D1
Luiza, *Dem. Rep. of the Congo* 84 F4
Luizi, *Dem. Rep. of the Congo* 86 D2
Luján, *Argentina* 126 C4
Lujiang, *China* 59 B11
Lukang, *Taiwan* 59 E13
Lukanga Swamp, *Zambia* 87 E2
Lukavac, *Bos.-H.* 42 F3
Lukenie →, *Dem. Rep. of the Congo* 84 E3
Lukhisaral, *India* 69 G12
Lŭki, *Bulgaria* 41 E8
Lukolela, *Dem. Rep. of the Congo* 86 D1
Lukosi, *Zimbabwe* 87 F2
Lukovë, *Albania* 40 G3
Lukovit, *Bulgaria* 41 C8
Łuków, *Poland* 45 G9
Lukoyanov, *Russia* 48 C7
Lule älv →, *Sweden* 8 D19
Luleå, *Sweden* 8 D20
Lüleburgaz, *Turkey* 41 E11
Luliang, *China* 58 E4
Luling, *U.S.A.* 113 L6
Lulong, *China* 57 E10
Lulonga →, *Dem. Rep. of the Congo* 84 D3
Lulua →, *Dem. Rep. of the Congo* 84 E4
Luluabourg = Kananga, *Dem. Rep. of the Congo* 84 F4
Lumajang, *Indonesia* 63 H15
Lumbala N'guimbo, *Angola* 85 G4
Lumberton, *U.S.A.* 109 H6
Lumbwa, *Kenya* 86 C4
Lumsden, *Canada* 105 C8
Lumsden, *N.Z.* 91 L2
Lumut, *Malaysia* 65 K3
Lumut, Tanjung, *Indonesia* 62 E3
Luna, *India* 68 H3
Lunan, *China* 58 E4
Lunavada, *India* 68 H5
Lunca, *Romania* 43 C10
Lunca Corbului, *Romania* 43 F9
Lund, *Sweden* 11 J7
Lundazi, *Zambia* 87 E3
Lunderskov, *Denmark* 11 J3
Lundi →, *Zimbabwe* 87 G3
Lundu, *Malaysia* 62 D3
Lundy, *U.K.* 13 F3
Lune →, *U.K.* 12 C5
Lüneburg, *Germany* 24 B6
Lüneburg Heath = Lüneburger Heide, *Germany* 24 B6
Lüneburger Heide, *Germany* 24 B6
Lunel, *France* 21 E8
Lünen, *Germany* 24 D3
Lunenburg, *Canada* 103 D7
Lunéville, *France* 19 D13
Lunga →, *Zambia* 87 E2
Lungi Airport, *S. Leone* 82 D2
Lunglei, *India* 67 H18
Luni, *India* 68 G5
Luni →, *India* 68 G4
Luninets = Luninyets, *Belarus* 47 F4
Luning, *U.S.A.* 114 G4
Lunino, *Russia* 48 D7
Luninyets, *Belarus* 47 F4
Lunkaransar, *India* 68 E5
Lunsemfwa →, *Zambia* 87 E3
Lunsemfwa Falls, *Zambia* 87 E2
Luo He →, *China* 56 G6
Luocheng, *China* 58 E7
Luochuan, *China* 56 G5
Luoci, *China* 58 E4
Luodian, *China* 58 E6
Luoding, *China* 59 F8
Luofu, *Dem. Rep. of the Congo* 86 C2
Luohe, *China* 56 H8
Luojiang, *China* 58 B5
Luonan, *China* 56 G6
Luoning, *China* 56 G6
Luoshan, *China* 59 A10
Luotian, *China* 59 B10
Luoxiao Shan, *China* 59 D10
Luoyang, *China* 56 G7
Luoyuan, *China* 59 D12
Luozigou, *China* 57 C16
Lupanshui, *China* 58 D5
Lupeni, *Romania* 43 E8
Lupilichi, *Mozam.* 87 E4
Łupków, *Poland* 45 J9
Lupoing, *China* 58 E5
Luquan, *China* 58 E4
Luque, *Paraguay* 126 B4
Lúras, *Italy* 30 B2
Luray, *U.S.A.* 108 F6
Lure, *France* 19 E13
Lurgan, *U.K.* 15 B5
Lusaka, *Zambia* 87 F2
Lusambo, *Dem. Rep. of the Congo* 86 C1
Lusangaye, *Dem. Rep. of the Congo* 86 C2
Luseland, *Canada* 105 C7
Lushan, *Henan, China* 56 H7
Lushan, *Sichuan, China* 58 B4
Lushi, *China* 56 G6
Lushnja, *Albania* 40 F3
Lushoto, *Tanzania* 86 C4
Lushui, *China* 58 E2
Lüshun, *China* 57 E11
Lusignan, *France* 20 B4
Lusigny-sur-Barse, *France* 19 D11
Lusk, *U.S.A.* 112 D2
Lussac-les-Châteaux, *France* 20 B4
Lustenau, *Austria* 26 D2
Lūt, Dasht-e, *Iran* 71 D8
Luta = Dalian, *China* 57 E11
Lutherstadt Wittenberg, *Germany* 24 D8
Luton, *U.K.* 13 F7
Luton □, *U.K.* 13 F7
Lutselke, *Canada* 105 A6
Lutsk, *Ukraine* 47 G3
Lützow Holmbukta, *Antarctica* 5 C4
Lutzputs, *S. Africa* 88 D3
Luverne, *Ala., U.S.A.* 109 K2
Luverne, *Minn., U.S.A.* 112 D6
Luvua, *Dem. Rep. of the Congo* 87 D2
Luvua →, *Dem. Rep. of the Congo* 86 D2
Luvuvhu →, *S. Africa* 89 C5
Luwegu →, *Tanzania* 87 D4
Luwuk, *Indonesia* 63 E6
Luxembourg, *Lux.* 17 E6
Luxembourg □, *Belgium* 17 E5
Luxembourg ■, *Europe* 7 F7
Luxeuil-les-Bains, *France* 19 E13
Luxi, *Hunan, China* 59 C8
Luxi, *Yunnan, China* 58 E4
Luxi, *Yunnan, China* 58 E2
Luxor = El Uqsur, *Egypt* 80 B3
Luy-de-Béarn →, *France* 20 E3
Luy-de-France →, *France* 20 E3
Luyi, *China* 56 H8
Luz-St-Sauveur, *France* 20 F4
Luzern, *Switz.* 25 H4
Luzern □, *Switz.* 25 H3
Luzhai, *China* 58 E7
Luzhi, *China* 58 D5
Luzhou, *China* 58 C5
Luziânia, *Brazil* 125 G9
Lužnice →, *Czech Rep.* 26 B7
Luzon, *Phil.* 61 D4
Luzy, *France* 19 F10
Luzzi, *Italy* 31 C9
Lviv, *Ukraine* 47 H3
Lvov = Lviv, *Ukraine* 47 H3
Lwówek, *Poland* 45 F3
Lwówek Śląski, *Poland* 45 G2
Lyakhavichy, *Belarus* 47 F4
Lyakhovskiye, Ostrova, *Russia* 51 B15
Lyaki = Läki, *Azerbaijan* 49 K8
Lyal I., *Canada* 110 B3
Lyallpur = Faisalabad, *Pakistan* 68 D5
Lyaskovets, *Bulgaria* 41 C9
Lybster, *U.K.* 14 C5
Lycaonia, *Turkey* 72 D5
Lychen, *Germany* 24 B9
Lychkova, *Russia* 46 D7
Lycia, *Turkey* 39 E11
Lyckebyån →, *Sweden* 11 H9
Lycksele, *Sweden* 8 D18
Lycosura, *Greece* 38 D4
Lydda = Lod, *Israel* 75 D3
Lydenburg, *S. Africa* 89 D5
Lydia, *Turkey* 39 C10
Łydynia →, *Poland* 45 F7
Lyell, *N.Z.* 91 J4
Lyell I., *Canada* 104 C2
Lyepyel, *Belarus* 46 E5
Lygnern, *Sweden* 11 G6
Lykens, *U.S.A.* 111 F8
Lyman, *U.S.A.* 114 F8
Lyme B., *U.K.* 13 G4
Lyme Regis, *U.K.* 13 G5
Lymington, *U.K.* 13 G6
Łyna →, *Poland* 9 J19
Lynchburg, *U.S.A.* 108 G6
Lynd →, *Australia* 94 B3
Lynd Ra., *Australia* 95 D4
Lynden, *Canada* 110 C4
Lynden, *U.S.A.* 116 B4
Lyndhurst, *Australia* 95 E2
Lyndon →, *Australia* 93 D1
Lyndonville, *N.Y., U.S.A.* 110 C6
Lyndonville, *Vt., U.S.A.* 111 B12
Lyngen, *Norway* 8 B19
Lynher Reef, *Australia* 92 C3
Lynn, *U.S.A.* 111 D14
Lynn Lake, *Canada* 105 B8
Lynnwood, *U.S.A.* 116 C4
Lynton, *U.K.* 13 F4
Lyntupy, *Belarus* 9 J22
Lynx L., *Canada* 105 A7
Lyon, *France* 21 C8
Lyonnais, *France* 21 C8
Lyons = Lyon, *France* 21 C8
Lyons, *Ga., U.S.A.* 109 J4
Lyons, *Kans., U.S.A.* 112 F5
Lyons, *N.Y., U.S.A.* 110 C8
Lyons →, *Australia* 93 E2
Lyons Falls, *U.S.A.* 111 C9
Lyozna, *Belarus* 46 E6
Lys = Leie →, *Belgium* 17 C3
Lysá nad Labem, *Czech Rep.* 26 A7
Lysekil, *Sweden* 11 F5
Lyskovo, *Russia* 48 B7
Lystrup, *Denmark* 11 H4
Lysvik, *Sweden* 10 D7
Lysychansk, *Ukraine* 47 H10
Lytham St. Anne's, *U.K.* 12 D4
Lyttelton, *N.Z.* 91 K4
Lytton, *Canada* 104 C4
Lyuban, *Russia* 46 C6
Lyubertsy, *Russia* 46 E9
Lyubim, *Russia* 46 C11
Lyubimets, *Bulgaria* 41 E10
Lyuboml, *Ukraine* 47 G3
Lyubotyn, *Ukraine* 47 H8
Lyubytino, *Russia* 46 C7
Lyudinovo, *Russia* 46 F8

M

M.R. Gomez, Presa, *Mexico* 119 B5
Ma →, *Vietnam* 58 H5
Ma'adaba, *Jordan* 75 E4
Maamba, *Zambia* 88 B4
Ma'ān, *Jordan* 75 E4
Ma'ān □, *Jordan* 75 F5
Maanselkä, *Finland* 8 C23
Ma'anshan, *China* 59 B12
Maarianhamina, *Finland* 9 F18
Ma'arrat an Nu'mān, *Syria* 70 C3
Maas →, *Neths.* 17 C4
Maaseik, *Belgium* 17 C5
Maasin, *Phil.* 63 B6
Maastricht, *Neths.* 17 D5
Maave, *Mozam.* 89 C5
Mababe Depression, *Botswana* 88 B3
Mabalane, *Mozam.* 89 C5
Mabel L., *Canada* 104 C5
Mabenge, *Dem. Rep. of the Congo* 86 B1
Maberly, *Canada* 111 B8
Mabian, *China* 58 C4
Mabil, *Ethiopia* 81 E4
Mablethorpe, *U.K.* 12 D8
Mably, *France* 19 F11
Maboma, *Dem. Rep. of the Congo* 86 B2
Mabonto, *S. Leone* 82 D2
Mabrouk, *Mali* 83 B4
Mac Bac, *Vietnam* 65 H6
Macachín, *Argentina* 126 D3
Macaé, *Brazil* 127 A7
Macael, *Spain* 33 H2
McAlester, *U.S.A.* 113 H7
McAllen, *U.S.A.* 113 M5
MacAlpine L., *Canada* 100 B9
Macamic, *Canada* 102 C4
Macao = Macau, *Asia* 59 F9
Macão, *Portugal* 35 F3
Macapá, *Brazil* 125 C8
McArthur →, *Australia* 94 B2
McArthur, Port, *Australia* 94 B2
Macau, *Brazil* 125 E11
Macau, *Asia* 59 F9
McBride, *Canada* 104 C4
McCall, *U.S.A.* 114 D5
McCamey, *U.S.A.* 113 K3
McCammon, *U.S.A.* 114 E7
McCauley I., *Canada* 104 C2
McCleary, *U.S.A.* 116 C3
Macclenny, *U.S.A.* 109 K4
Macclesfield, *U.K.* 12 D5
M'Clintock Chan., *Canada* 100 A9
McClintock Ra., *Australia* 92 C4
McCloud, *U.S.A.* 114 F2
McCluer I., *Australia* 92 B5
McClure, *U.S.A.* 110 F7
McClure, L., *U.S.A.* 116 H6
M'Clure Str., *Canada* 4 B2
McClusky, *U.S.A.* 112 B4
McComb, *U.S.A.* 113 K9
McConaughy, L., *U.S.A.* 112 E4
McCook, *U.S.A.* 112 E4
McCreary, *Canada* 105 C9
McCullough Mt., *U.S.A.* 117 K11
McCusker →, *Canada* 105 B7
McDame, *Canada* 104 B3
McDermitt, *U.S.A.* 114 F5
McDonald, *U.S.A.* 110 F4
Macdonald, L., *Australia* 92 D4
McDonald Is., *Ind. Oc.* 3 G13
MacDonnell Ranges, *Australia* 92 D5
MacDowell L., *Canada* 102 B1
Macduff, *U.K.* 14 D6
Maceda, *Spain* 34 C3
Macedonia, *U.S.A.* 110 E3
Macedonia ■, *Europe* 40 E5
Maceió, *Brazil* 125 E11
Maceira, *Portugal* 34 F2
Macenta, *Guinea* 82 D3
Macerata, *Italy* 29 E10
McFarland, *U.S.A.* 117 K7
McFarlane →, *Canada* 105 B7
Macfarlane, L., *Australia* 95 E2
McGehee, *U.S.A.* 113 J9
McGill, *U.S.A.* 114 G6
Macgillycuddy's Reeks, *Ireland* 15 E2
McGraw, *U.S.A.* 111 D8
McGregor, *U.S.A.* 112 D9
McGregor Ra., *Australia* 95 D3
Mach, *Pakistan* 66 E5
Māch Kowr, *Iran* 71 E9
Machado = Jiparaná →, *Brazil* 124 E6
Machagai, *Argentina* 126 B3
Machakos, *Kenya* 86 C4
Machala, *Ecuador* 124 D3
Machanga, *Mozam.* 89 C6
Machattie, L., *Australia* 94 C2
Machault, *France* 19 C11
Machava, *Mozam.* 89 D5
Machece, *Mozam.* 87 F4
Machecoul, *France* 18 F5
Macheke, *Zimbabwe* 89 B5
Macheng, *China* 59 B10
Machero, *Spain* 35 F6
Machhu →, *India* 68 H4
Machias, *Maine, U.S.A.* 109 C12
Machias, *N.Y., U.S.A.* 110 D6
Machichi →, *Canada* 105 B10
Machico, *Madeira* 37 D3
Machilipatnam, *India* 67 L12
Machiques, *Venezuela* 124 A4
Machupicchu, *Peru* 124 F4
Machynlleth, *U.K.* 13 E4
Macia, *Mozam.* 89 D5
Maciejowice, *Poland* 45 G8
McIlwraith Ra., *Australia* 94 A3
Măcin, *Romania* 43 E13
Macina, *Mali* 82 C4
McInnes L., *Canada* 105 C10
McIntosh, *U.S.A.* 112 C4
McIntosh L., *Canada* 105 B8
Macintosh Ra., *Australia* 93 E4
Macintyre →, *Australia* 95 D5
Macizo Galaico, *Spain* 34 C3
Mackay, *Australia* 94 C4
Mackay, *U.S.A.* 114 E7
MacKay →, *Canada* 104 B6
Mackay, L., *Australia* 92 D4
McKay Ra., *Australia* 92 D3
McKeesport, *U.S.A.* 110 F5
McKellar, *Canada* 110 A5
McKenna, *U.S.A.* 116 D4
Mackenzie, *Canada* 104 B4
McKenzie, *U.S.A.* 109 G1
Mackenzie →, *Australia* 94 C4
Mackenzie →, *Canada* 100 B6
McKenzie →, *U.S.A.* 114 D2
Mackenzie Bay, *Canada* 4 B1
Mackenzie City = Linden, *Guyana* 124 B7
Mackenzie Mts., *Canada* 100 B6
Mackinaw City, *U.S.A.* 108 C3
McKinlay, *Australia* 94 C3
McKinlay →, *Australia* 94 C3
McKinley, Mt., *U.S.A.* 100 B4
McKinley Sea, *Arctic* 4 A7
McKinney, *U.S.A.* 113 J6
Mackinnon Road, *Kenya* 86 C4
McKittrick, *U.S.A.* 117 K7
Macklin, *Canada* 105 C7
Macksville, *Australia* 95 E5
McLaughlin, *U.S.A.* 112 C4
Maclean, *Australia* 95 D5
McLean, *U.S.A.* 113 H4
McLeansboro, *U.S.A.* 112 F10
Maclear, *S. Africa* 89 E4
Macleay →, *Australia* 95 E5
McLennan, *Canada* 104 B5
McLeod →, *Canada* 104 C5
MacLeod, B., *Canada* 105 A7
McLeod, L., *Australia* 93 D1
MacLeod Lake, *Canada* 104 C4
McLoughlin, Mt., *U.S.A.* 114 E2
McMechen, *U.S.A.* 110 G4
McMinnville, *Oreg., U.S.A.* 114 D2
McMinnville, *Tenn., U.S.A.* 109 H3
McMurdo Sd., *Antarctica* 5 D11
McMurray = Fort McMurray, *Canada* 104 B6
McMurray, *U.S.A.* 116 B4
Macodoene, *Mozam.* 89 C6
Macomb, *U.S.A.* 112 E9
Macomer, *Italy* 30 B1
Mâcon, *France* 19 F11
Macon, *Ga., U.S.A.* 109 J4
Macon, *Miss., U.S.A.* 109 J1
Macon, *Mo., U.S.A.* 112 F8
Macossa, *Mozam.* 87 F3
Macoun L., *Canada* 105 B8
Macovane, *Mozam.* 89 C6
McPherson, *U.S.A.* 112 F6
McPherson Pk., *U.S.A.* 117 L7
McPherson Ra., *Australia* 95 D5
Macquarie →, *Australia* 95 E4
Macquarie Harbour, *Australia* 94 G4
Macquarie Is., *Pac. Oc.* 96 N7
MacRobertson Land, *Antarctica* 5 D6
Macroom, *Ireland* 15 E3
MacTier, *Canada* 110 A5
Macubela, *Mozam.* 87 F4
Macugnaga, *Italy* 28 C4
Macuiza, *Mozam.* 87 F3
Macusani, *Peru* 124 F4
Macuse, *Mozam.* 87 F4
Macuspana, *Mexico* 119 D6
Macusse, *Angola* 88 B3
Mada →, *Nigeria* 83 D6
Madadeni, *S. Africa* 89 D5
Madagali, *Nigeria* 83 C7
Madagascar ■, *Africa* 89 C8
Madā'in Sālih, *Si. Arabia* 70 E3
Madama, *Niger* 79 D8
Madame I., *Canada* 103 C7
Madan, *Bulgaria* 41 E8
Madaoua, *Niger* 83 C6
Madara, *Nigeria* 83 C7
Madaripur, *Bangla.* 67 H17
Madauk, *Burma* 67 L20
Madawaska, *Canada* 110 A7
Madawaska →, *Canada* 102 C4
Madaya, *Burma* 67 H20
Madbar, *Sudan* 81 F3
Maddalena, *Italy* 30 A2
Maddaloni, *Italy* 31 A7
Madeira, *Atl. Oc.* 37 D3
Madeira →, *Brazil* 122 D5
Madeleine, Îs. de la, *Canada* 103 C7
Maden, *Turkey* 73 C8
Madera, *Mexico* 118 B3
Madera, *Calif., U.S.A.* 116 J6
Madera, *Pa., U.S.A.* 110 F6
Madha, *India* 66 L9
Madhavpur, *India* 68 J3
Madhepura, *India* 69 F12
Madhubani, *India* 69 F12
Madhupur, *India* 69 G12
Madhya Pradesh □, *India* 68 J8
Madian, *China* 59 A11
Madidi →, *Bolivia* 124 F5
Madikeri, *India* 66 N9
Madill, *U.S.A.* 113 H6
Madimba, *Dem. Rep. of the Congo* 84 E3
Ma'din, *Syria* 70 C3
Madina, *Mali* 82 C3
Madinani, *Ivory C.* 82 D3
Madingou, *Congo* 84 E2
Madirovalo, *Madag.* 89 B8
Madison, *Calif., U.S.A.* 116 G5
Madison, *Fla., U.S.A.* 109 K4
Madison, *Ind., U.S.A.* 108 F3
Madison, *Nebr., U.S.A.* 112 E6
Madison, *Ohio, U.S.A.* 110 E3
Madison, *S. Dak., U.S.A.* 112 D6
Madison, *Wis., U.S.A.* 112 D10
Madison →, *U.S.A.* 114 D8
Madison Heights, *U.S.A.* 108 G6
Madisonville, *Ky., U.S.A.* 108 G2
Madisonville, *Tex., U.S.A.* 113 K7
Madista, *Botswana* 88 C4
Madiun, *Indonesia* 63 G14
Madoc, *Canada* 110 B7
Madol, *Sudan* 81 F2
Madon →, *France* 19 D13
Madona, *Latvia* 9 H22
Madonie, *Italy* 30 E6
Madonna di Campíglio, *Italy* 28 B7
Madra Dağı, *Turkey* 39 B9
Madrakah, Ra's al, *Oman* 74 D6
Madras = Chennai, *India* 66 N12
Madras = Tamil Nadu □, *India* 66 P10
Madras, *U.S.A.* 114 D3
Madre, L., *Mexico* 119 C5
Madre, Laguna, *U.S.A.* 113 M6
Madre, Sierra, *Phil.* 61 C5
Madre de Dios →, *Bolivia* 122 E4
Madre de Dios, I., *Chile* 122 J3
Madre del Sur, Sierra, *Mexico* 119 D5
Madre Occidental, Sierra, *Mexico* 118 B3
Madre Oriental, Sierra, *Mexico* 118 C5
Madri, *India* 68 G5
Madrid, *Spain* 34 E7
Madrid, *U.S.A.* 111 B9
Madrid □, *Spain* 34 E7
Madridejos, *Spain* 35 F7
Madrigal de las Altas Torres, *Spain* 34 D6
Madrona, Sierra, *Spain* 35 G6
Madroñera, *Spain* 35 F5
Madu, *Sudan* 81 E2
Madura, *Australia* 93 F4
Madura, *Indonesia* 63 G15
Madura, Selat, *Indonesia* 63 G15
Madurai, *India* 66 Q11
Madurantakam, *India* 66 N11
Madzhalis, *Russia* 49 J8
Mae Chan, *Thailand* 64 B2
Mae Hong Son, *Thailand* 64 C2
Mae Khlong →, *Thailand* 64 F3
Mae Phrik, *Thailand* 64 D2
Mae Ramat, *Thailand* 64 D2
Mae Rim, *Thailand* 64 C2
Mae Sot, *Thailand* 64 D2
Mae Suai, *Thailand* 58 H2
Mae Tha, *Thailand* 64 C2
Maebashi, *Japan* 55 F9
Maella, *Spain* 32 D5
Maesteg, *U.K.* 13 F4
Maestra, Sierra, *Cuba* 120 B4
Maevatanana, *Madag.* 89 B8
Mafeking = Mafikeng, *S. Africa* 88 D4
Mafeking, *Canada* 105 C8
Maféré, *Ivory C.* 82 D4
Mafeteng, *Lesotho* 88 D4
Maffra, *Australia* 95 F4

Mafia I., *Tanzania* 86 D4
Mafikeng, *S. Africa* 88 D4
Mafra, *Brazil* 127 B6
Mafra, *Portugal* 35 G1
Mafungabusi Plateau, *Zimbabwe* 87 F2
Magadan, *Russia* 51 D16
Magadi, *Kenya* 86 C4
Magadi, L., *Kenya* 86 C4
Magaliesburg, *S. Africa* 89 D4
Magallanes, Estrecho de, *Chile* 122 J3
Magaluf, *Spain* 33 F7
Magangué, *Colombia* 124 B4
Magaria, *Niger* 83 C6
Magburaka, *S. Leone* 82 D2
Magdalen Is. = Madeleine, Îs. de la, *Canada* 103 C7
Magdalena, *Argentina* 126 D4
Magdalena, *Bolivia* 124 F6
Magdalena, *Mexico* 118 A2
Magdalena, *U.S.A.* 115 J10
Magdalena →, *Colombia* 122 B3
Magdalena →, *Mexico* 118 A2
Magdalena, B., *Mexico* 118 C2
Magdalena, Llano de la, *Mexico* 118 C2
Magdeburg, *Germany* 24 C7
Magdelaine Cays, *Australia* 94 B5
Magdub, *Sudan* 81 E2
Magee, *U.S.A.* 113 K10
Magelang, *Indonesia* 63 G14
Magellan's Str. = Magallanes, Estrecho de, *Chile* 122 J3
Magenta, *Italy* 28 C5
Magenta, L., *Australia* 93 F2
Magerøya, *Norway* 8 A21
Maggia →, *Switz.* 25 J4
Maggiorasca, Mte., *Italy* 28 D6
Maggiore, Lago, *Italy* 28 C5
Maghâgha, *Egypt* 80 B3
Maghama, *Mauritania* 82 B2
Magherafelt, *U.K.* 15 B5
Maghreb, *N. Afr.* 78 B5
Magione, *Italy* 29 E9
Magistralnyy, *Russia* 51 D11
Maglaj, *Bos.-H.* 42 F3
Magliano in Toscana, *Italy* 29 F8
Máglie, *Italy* 31 B11
Magnac-Laval, *France* 20 B5
Magnetic Pole (North) = North Magnetic Pole, *Canada* 4 B2
Magnetic Pole (South) = South Magnetic Pole, *Antarctica* 5 C9
Magnisía □, *Greece* 38 B5
Magnitogorsk, *Russia* 50 D6
Magnolia, *Ark., U.S.A.* 113 J8
Magnolia, *Miss., U.S.A.* 113 K9
Magny-en-Vexin, *France* 19 C8
Magog, *Canada* 103 C5
Magoro, *Uganda* 86 B3
Magosa = Famagusta, *Cyprus* 36 D12
Magouládhes, *Greece* 36 A3
Magoye, *Zambia* 87 F2
Magozal, *Mexico* 119 C5
Magpie, L., *Canada* 103 B7
Magrath, *Canada* 104 D6
Magre →, *Spain* 33 F4
Magrur, *Sudan* 81 E3
Magrur, Wadi →, *Sudan* 81 D2
Magta Lahjar, *Mauritania* 82 B2
Maguan, *China* 58 F5
Maguarinho, C., *Brazil* 125 D9
Magude, *Mozam.* 89 D5
Mağusa = Famagusta, *Cyprus* 36 D12
Maguse L., *Canada* 105 A9
Maguse Pt., *Canada* 105 A10
Magvana, *India* 68 H3
Magwe, *Burma* 67 J19
Magwe, *Sudan* 81 G3
Maha Sarakham, *Thailand* 64 D4
Mahābād, *Iran* 70 B5
Mahabharat Lekh, *Nepal* 69 E10
Mahabo, *Madag.* 89 C7
Mahadeo Hills, *India* 69 H8
Mahaffey, *U.S.A.* 110 F6
Mahagi, *Dem. Rep. of the Congo* 86 B3
Mahajamba →, *Madag.* 89 B8
Mahajamba, Helodranon' i, *Madag.* 89 B8
Mahajan, *India* 68 E5
Mahajanga, *Madag.* 89 B8
Mahajanga □, *Madag.* 89 B8
Mahajilo →, *Madag.* 89 B8
Mahakam →, *Indonesia* 62 E5
Mahalapye, *Botswana* 88 C4
Maḥallāt, *Iran* 71 C6
Māhān, *Iran* 71 D8
Mahan →, *India* 69 H10
Mahanadi →, *India* 67 J15
Mahananda →, *India* 69 G12
Mahanoro, *Madag.* 89 B8
Mahanoy City, *U.S.A.* 111 F8
Maharashtra □, *India* 66 J9
Mahari Mts., *Tanzania* 86 D3
Mahasham, W. →, *Egypt* 75 E3
Mahasoa, *Madag.* 89 C8
Mahasolo, *Madag.* 89 B8
Mahattat ash Shīdīyah, *Jordan* 75 F4
Mahattat 'Unayzah, *Jordan* 75 E4
Mahavavy →, *Madag.* 89 B8
Mahaxay, *Laos* 64 D5
Mahbubnagar, *India* 66 L10
Maḥḍah, *Oman* 71 E7
Mahdia, *Tunisia* 79 A8
Mahe, *India* 69 C8
Mahendragarh, *India* 68 E7
Mahenge, *Tanzania* 87 D4
Maheno, *N.Z.* 91 L3
Mahesana, *India* 68 H5
Maheshwar, *India* 68 H6
Mahgawan, *India* 69 F8
Mahi →, *India* 68 H5
Mahia Pen., *N.Z.* 91 H6
Mahilyow, *Belarus* 46 F6
Mahmiya, *Sudan* 81 D3
Mahmud Kot, *Pakistan* 68 D4
Mahmudia, *Romania* 43 E14
Mahmudiye, *Turkey* 39 B12
Mahmutbey, *Turkey* 41 E12
Mahnomen, *U.S.A.* 112 B7
Mahoba, *India* 69 G8
Mahón = Maó, *Spain* 37 B11
Mahone Bay, *Canada* 103 D7
Mahopac, *U.S.A.* 111 E11
Mahuta, *Nigeria* 83 C5
Mahuva, *India* 68 J4
Mahya Daği, *Turkey* 41 E11
Mai-Ndombe, L., *Dem. Rep. of the Congo* 84 E3
Mai-Sai, *Thailand* 58 G2
Maia, *Portugal* 34 D2
Maia, *Spain* 32 B3
Maials, *Spain* 32 D5
Maîche, *France* 19 E13
Maicurú →, *Brazil* 125 D8
Máida, *Italy* 31 D9
Maidan Khula, *Afghan.* 68 C3
Maidenhead, *U.K.* 13 F7
Maidstone, *Canada* 105 C7
Maidstone, *U.K.* 13 F8
Maiduguri, *Nigeria* 83 C7
Măieruş, *Romania* 43 E10
Maigatari, *Nigeria* 83 C6
Maignelay Montigny, *France* 19 C9
Maigo, *Phil.* 61 G5
Maigudo, *Ethiopia* 81 F4
Maihar, *India* 69 G9
Maijdi, *Bangla.* 67 H17
Maikala Ra., *India* 67 J12
Mailani, *India* 69 E9
Maillezais, *France* 20 B3
Mailsi, *Pakistan* 68 E5
Main →, *Germany* 25 F4
Main →, *U.K.* 15 B5
Mainburg, *Germany* 25 G7
Maine, *France* 18 D6
Maine □, *U.S.A.* 109 C11
Maine →, *Ireland* 15 D2
Maine-et-Loire □, *France* 18 E6
Maïne-Soroa, *Niger* 83 C7
Maingkwan, *Burma* 67 F20
Mainit, L., *Phil.* 61 G6
Mainland, *Orkney, U.K.* 14 C5
Mainland, *Shet., U.K.* 14 A7
Mainoru, *Australia* 94 A1
Mainpuri, *India* 69 F8
Maintal, *Germany* 25 E4
Maintenon, *France* 19 D8
Maintirano, *Madag.* 89 B7
Mainz, *Germany* 25 E4
Maipú, *Argentina* 126 D4
Maiquetía, *Venezuela* 124 A5
Máira →, *Italy* 28 D4
Mairabari, *India* 67 F18
Maisí, *Cuba* 121 B5
Maisí, Pta. de, *Cuba* 121 B5
Maitland, *N.S.W., Australia* 95 E5
Maitland, *S. Austral., Australia* 95 E2
Maitland →, *Canada* 110 C3
Maiyema, *Nigeria* 83 C5
Maiyuan, *China* 59 E11
Maiz, Is. del, *Nic.* 120 D3
Maizuru, *Japan* 55 G7
Majalengka, *Indonesia* 63 G13
Majene, *Indonesia* 63 E5
Majevica, *Bos.-H.* 42 F3
Maji, *Ethiopia* 81 F4
Majiang, *China* 58 D6
Majorca = Mallorca, *Spain* 37 B10
Maka, *Senegal* 82 C2
Makaha, *Zimbabwe* 89 B5
Makak, *Cameroon* 83 E7
Makalamabedi, *Botswana* 88 C3
Makale, *Indonesia* 63 E5
Makamba, *Burundi* 86 C2
Makari, *Cameroon* 83 C7
Makarikari = Makgadikgadi Salt Pans, *Botswana* 88 C4
Makarovo, *Russia* 51 D11
Makarska, *Croatia* 29 E14
Makaryev, *Russia* 48 B6
Makasar = Ujung Pandang, *Indonesia* 63 F5
Makasar, Selat, *Indonesia* 63 E5
Makasar, Str. of = Makasar, Selat, *Indonesia* 63 E5
Makat, *Kazakstan* 50 E6
Makedonija = Macedonia ■, *Europe* 40 E5
Makena, *U.S.A.* 106 H16
Makeni, *S. Leone* 82 D2
Makeyevka = Makiyivka, *Ukraine* 47 H9
Makgadikgadi Salt Pans, *Botswana* 88 C4
Makhachkala, *Russia* 49 J8
Makharadze = Ozurgeti, *Georgia* 49 K5
Makhmūr, *Iraq* 70 C4
Makian, *Indonesia* 63 D7
Makindu, *Kenya* 86 C4
Makinsk, *Kazakstan* 50 D8
Makiyivka, *Ukraine* 47 H9
Makkah, *Si. Arabia* 74 C2
Makkovik, *Canada* 103 A8
Makó, *Hungary* 42 D5
Mako, *Senegal* 82 C2
Makokou, *Gabon* 84 D2
Makongo, *Dem. Rep. of the Congo* 86 B2
Makoro, *Dem. Rep. of the Congo* 86 B2
Maków Mazowiecki, *Poland* 45 F8
Maków Podhalański, *Poland* 45 J6
Makrá, *Greece* 39 E7
Makrai, *India* 66 H10
Makran Coast Range, *Pakistan* 66 G4
Makrana, *India* 68 F6
Mákri, *Greece* 41 F9
Makriyialos, *Greece* 36 D7
Mākū, *Iran* 70 B5
Makunda, *Botswana* 88 C3
Makung, *Taiwan* 59 F12
Makurazaki, *Japan* 55 J5
Makurdi, *Nigeria* 83 D6
Makūyeh, *Iran* 71 D7
Makwassie, *S. Africa* 88 D4
Makwiro, *Zimbabwe* 89 B5
Mâl, *Mauritania* 82 B2
Mal B., *Ireland* 15 D2
Mala, Pta., *Panama* 120 E3
Mala Belozërka, *Ukraine* 47 J8
Mala Kapela, *Croatia* 29 D12
Mała Panew →, *Poland* 45 H4
Mala Vyska, *Ukraine* 47 H6
Malabang, *Phil.* 61 H6
Malabar Coast, *India* 66 P9
Malabo = Rey Malabo, *Eq. Guin.* 83 E6
Malabon, *Phil.* 61 D4
Malabu, *Nigeria* 83 D7
Malacca, Str. of, *Indonesia* 65 L3
Malacky, *Slovak Rep.* 27 C10
Malad City, *U.S.A.* 114 E7
Maladeta, *Spain* 32 C5
Maladzyechna, *Belarus* 46 E4
Málaga, *Spain* 35 J6
Málaga □, *Spain* 35 J6
Malagarasi, *Tanzania* 86 D3
Malagarasi →, *Tanzania* 86 D2
Malagasy Rep. = Madagascar ■, *Africa* 89 C8
Malagón, *Spain* 35 F7
Malagón →, *Spain* 35 H3
Malahide, *Ireland* 15 C5
Malaimbandy, *Madag.* 89 C8
Malakâl, *Sudan* 81 F3
Malakand, *Pakistan* 68 B4
Malakwal, *Pakistan* 68 C5
Malamala, *Indonesia* 63 E6
Malanda, *Australia* 94 B4
Malang, *Indonesia* 63 G15
Malangen, *Norway* 8 B18
Malanje, *Angola* 84 F3
Mälaren, *Sweden* 10 E11
Malargüe, *Argentina* 126 D2
Malartic, *Canada* 102 C4
Malaryta, *Belarus* 47 G3
Malatya, *Turkey* 70 B3
Malawi ■, *Africa* 87 E3
Malawi, L. = Nyasa, L., *Africa* 87 E3
Malay Pen., *Asia* 65 J3
Malaya Belozërka = Mala Belozërka, *Ukraine* 47 J8
Malaya Vishera, *Russia* 46 C7
Malaya Viska = Mala Vyska, *Ukraine* 47 H6
Malaybalay, *Phil.* 61 G6
Malāyer, *Iran* 71 C6
Malaysia ■, *Asia* 65 K4
Malazgirt, *Turkey* 70 B4
Malbaza, *Niger* 83 C6
Malbon, *Australia* 94 C3
Malbooma, *Australia* 95 E1
Malbork, *Poland* 44 D6
Malcésine, *Italy* 28 C7
Malchin, *Germany* 24 B8
Malchow, *Germany* 24 B8
Malcolm, *Australia* 93 E3
Malcolm, Pt., *Australia* 93 F3
Malczyce, *Poland* 45 G3
Maldah, *India* 69 G13
Maldegem, *Belgium* 17 C3
Malden, *Mass., U.S.A.* 111 D13
Malden, *Mo., U.S.A.* 113 G10
Malden I., *Kiribati* 97 H12
Maldives ■, *Ind. Oc.* 52 J11
Maldonado, *Uruguay* 127 C5
Maldonado, Punta, *Mexico* 119 D5
Malè, *Italy* 28 B7
Malé, *Maldives* 53 J11
Malé Karpaty, *Slovak Rep.* 27 C10
Maléa, Ákra, *Greece* 38 E5
Malegaon, *India* 66 J9
Malei, *Mozam.* 87 F4
Malek, *Sudan* 81 F3
Malek Kandī, *Iran* 70 B5
Malela, *Dem. Rep. of the Congo* 86 C2
Malema, *Mozam.* 87 E4
Máleme, *Greece* 36 D5
Maleny, *Australia* 95 D5
Målerås, *Sweden* 11 H9
Malerkotla, *India* 68 D6
Máles, *Greece* 36 D7
Malesherbes, *France* 19 D9
Maleshevska Planina, *Europe* 40 E7
Malesína, *Greece* 38 C5
Malestroit, *France* 18 E4
Malfa, *Italy* 31 D7
Malgobek, *Russia* 49 J7
Malgomaj, *Sweden* 8 D17
Malgrat = Malgrat de Mar, *Spain* 32 D7
Malgrat de Mar, *Spain* 32 D7
Malha, *Sudan* 81 D2
Malhargarh, *India* 68 G6
Malheur →, *U.S.A.* 114 D5
Malheur L., *U.S.A.* 114 E4
Mali, *Guinea* 82 C2
Mali ■, *Africa* 82 B4
Mali →, *Burma* 67 G20
Mali Kanal, *Serbia, Yug.* 42 E4
Mali Kyun, *Burma* 64 F2
Malibu, *U.S.A.* 117 L8
Maliku, *Indonesia* 63 E6
Malili, *Indonesia* 63 E6
Målilla, *Sweden* 11 G9
Malimba, Mts., *Dem. Rep. of the Congo* 86 D2
Malin Hd., *Ireland* 15 A4
Malin Pen., *Ireland* 15 A4
Malindi, *Kenya* 86 C5
Malines = Mechelen, *Belgium* 17 C4
Malino, *Indonesia* 63 D6
Malinyi, *Tanzania* 87 D4
Malipo, *China* 58 F5
Maliqi, *Albania* 40 F4
Malita, *Phil.* 63 C7
Maliwun, *Burma* 62 B1
Maliya, *India* 68 H4
Maljenik, *Serbia, Yug.* 40 C5
Malkara, *Turkey* 41 F10
Małkinia Górna, *Poland* 45 F9
Malko Tŭrnovo, *Bulgaria* 41 E11
Mallacoota Inlet, *Australia* 95 F4
Mallaig, *U.K.* 14 D3
Mallaoua, *Niger* 83 C6
Mallawan, *India* 69 F9
Mallawi, *Egypt* 80 B3
Mallemort, *France* 21 E9
Málles Venosta, *Italy* 28 B7
Mállia, *Greece* 36 D7
Mallión, Kólpos, *Greece* 36 D7
Mallorca, *Spain* 37 B10
Mallorytown, *Canada* 111 B9
Mallow, *Ireland* 15 D3
Malmbäck, *Sweden* 11 G8
Malmberget, *Sweden* 8 C19
Malmédy, *Belgium* 17 D6
Malmesbury, *S. Africa* 88 E2
Malmköping, *Sweden* 10 E10
Malmö, *Sweden* 11 J6
Malmslätt, *Sweden* 11 F9
Malmyzh, *Russia* 48 B10
Malnaş, *Romania* 43 D10
Malo Konare, *Bulgaria* 41 D8
Maloarkhangelsk, *Russia* 47 F9
Malolos, *Phil.* 63 B6
Malombe L., *Malawi* 87 E4
Małomice, *Poland* 45 G2
Malomir, *Bulgaria* 41 D10
Malone, *U.S.A.* 111 B10
Malong, *China* 58 E4
Małopolskie □, *Poland* 45 J7
Malorad, *Bulgaria* 40 C7
Måløy, *Norway* 9 F11
Maloyaroslovets, *Russia* 46 E9
Malpartida, *Spain* 35 F4
Malpaso, *Canary Is.* 37 G1
Malpelo, I. de, *Colombia* 124 C2
Malpica de Bergantiños, *Spain* 34 B2
Malpur, *India* 68 H5
Malpura, *India* 68 F6
Mals = Málles Venosta, *Italy* 28 B7
Malta, *Idaho, U.S.A.* 114 E7
Malta, *Mont., U.S.A.* 114 B10
Malta ■, *Europe* 36 D2
Maltahöhe, *Namibia* 88 C2
Maltepe, *Turkey* 41 F13
Malton, *Canada* 110 C5
Malton, *U.K.* 12 C7
Maluku, *Indonesia* 63 E7
Maluku □, *Indonesia* 63 E7
Maluku Sea = Molucca Sea, *Indonesia* 63 E6
Malumfashi, *Nigeria* 83 C6
Malung, *Sweden* 10 D7
Malungsfors, *Sweden* 10 D7
Maluwe, *Ghana* 82 D4
Malvan, *India* 66 L8
Malvern, *U.S.A.* 113 H8
Malvern Hills, *U.K.* 13 E5
Malvinas, Is. = Falkland Is. □, *Atl. Oc.* 128 G5
Malý Dunaj →, *Slovak Rep.* 27 D11
Malya, *Tanzania* 86 C3
Malyn, *Ukraine* 47 G5
Malyy Lyakhovskiy, Ostrov, *Russia* 51 B15
Mama, *Russia* 51 D12
Mamadysh, *Russia* 48 C10
Mamanguape, *Brazil* 125 E11
Mamarr Mitlā, *Egypt* 75 E1
Mamasa, *Indonesia* 63 E5
Mambasa, *Dem. Rep. of the Congo* 86 B2
Mamberamo →, *Indonesia* 63 E9
Mambilima Falls, *Zambia* 87 E2
Mambirima, *Dem. Rep. of the Congo* 87 E2
Mambo, *Tanzania* 86 C4
Mambrui, *Kenya* 86 C5
Mamburao, *Phil.* 61 E4
Mameigwess L., *Canada* 102 B2
Mamers, *France* 18 D7
Mamfé, *Cameroon* 83 D6
Mammoth, *U.S.A.* 115 K8
Mammoth Cave National Park, *U.S.A.* 108 G3
Mamoré →, *Bolivia* 122 E4
Mamou, *Guinea* 82 C2
Mampatá, *Guinea-Biss.* 82 C2
Mampikony, *Madag.* 89 B8
Mampong, *Ghana* 83 D4
Mamry, Jezioro, *Poland* 44 D8
Mamuju, *Indonesia* 63 E5
Mamuno, *Botswana* 88 C3
Mamuras, *Albania* 40 E3
Man, *Ivory C.* 82 D3
Man, I. of, *U.K.* 12 C3
Man-Bazar, *India* 69 H12
Man Na, *Burma* 67 H20
Mana →, *Fr. Guiana* 125 B8
Manaar, G. of = Mannar, G. of, *Asia* 66 Q11
Manacapuru, *Brazil* 124 D6
Manacor, *Spain* 37 B10
Manado, *Indonesia* 63 D6
Managua, *Nic.* 120 D2
Managua, L. de, *Nic.* 120 D2
Manakara, *Madag.* 89 C8
Manali, *India* 68 C7
Manama = Al Manāmah, *Bahrain* 71 E6
Manambao →, *Madag.* 89 B7
Manambato, *Madag.* 89 A8
Manambolo →, *Madag.* 89 B7
Manambolosy, *Madag.* 89 B8
Mananara, *Madag.* 89 B8
Mananara →, *Madag.* 89 C8
Mananjary, *Madag.* 89 C8
Manankoro, *Mali* 82 C3
Manantenina, *Madag.* 89 C8
Manaos = Manaus, *Brazil* 124 D7
Manapire →, *Venezuela* 124 B5
Manapouri, *N.Z.* 91 L1
Manapouri, L., *N.Z.* 91 L1
Manaqil, *Sudan* 81 E3
Manār, Jabal, *Yemen* 74 E3
Manaravolo, *Madag.* 89 C8
Manas, *China* 60 B3
Manas →, *India* 67 F17
Manaslu, *Nepal* 69 E11
Manasquan, *U.S.A.* 111 F10
Manassa, *U.S.A.* 115 H11
Manaung, *Burma* 67 K18
Manaus, *Brazil* 124 D7
Manavgat, *Turkey* 72 D4
Manawan L., *Canada* 105 B8
Manay, *Phil.* 61 H7
Manbij, *Syria* 70 B3
Mancha Real, *Spain* 35 H7
Manche □, *France* 18 C5
Manchegorsk, *Russia* 50 C4
Manchester, *U.K.* 12 D5
Manchester, *Calif., U.S.A.* 116 G3
Manchester, *Conn., U.S.A.* 111 E12
Manchester, *Ga., U.S.A.* 109 J3
Manchester, *Iowa, U.S.A.* 112 D9
Manchester, *Ky., U.S.A.* 108 G4
Manchester, *N.H., U.S.A.* 111 D13
Manchester, *N.Y., U.S.A.* 110 D7
Manchester, *Pa., U.S.A.* 111 F8
Manchester, *Tenn., U.S.A.* 109 H2
Manchester, *Vt., U.S.A.* 111 C11
Manchester L., *Canada* 105 A7
Manchhar L., *Pakistan* 68 F2
Manchuria = Dongbei, *China* 57 D13
Manchurian Plain, *China* 52 E16
Manciano, *Italy* 29 F8
Mancifa, *Ethiopia* 81 F5
Mand →, *India* 69 J10
Mand →, *Iran* 71 D7
Manda, *Chunya, Tanzania* 86 D3
Manda, *Ludewe, Tanzania* 87 E3
Mandabé, *Madag.* 89 C7
Mandaguari, *Brazil* 127 A5
Mandah = Töhöm, *Mongolia* 56 B5
Mandal, *Norway* 9 G12
Mandala, Puncak, *Indonesia* 63 E10
Mandalay, *Burma* 67 J20
Mandale = Mandalay, *Burma* 67 J20
Mandalgarh, *India* 68 G6
Mandalgovi, *Mongolia* 56 B4
Mandalī, *Iraq* 70 C5
Mandan, *U.S.A.* 112 B4
Mandaon, *Phil.* 61 E5
Mandar, Teluk, *Indonesia* 63 E5
Mándas, *Italy* 30 C2
Mandaue, *Phil.* 61 F5
Mandelieu-la-Napoule, *France* 21 E10
Mandera, *Kenya* 86 B5
Mandi, *India* 68 D7
Mandi Dabwali, *India* 68 E6
Mandiana, *Guinea* 82 C3
Mandimba, *Mozam.* 87 E4
Mandioli, *Indonesia* 63 E7
Mandla, *India* 69 H9
Mandø, *Denmark* 11 J2
Mandorah, *Australia* 92 B5
Mandoto, *Madag.* 89 B8
Mandoúdhion, *Greece* 38 C5
Mándra, *Greece* 38 C5
Mandra, *Pakistan* 68 C5
Mandrákhi, *Greece* 39 E9
Mandrare →, *Madag.* 89 D8
Mandritsara, *Madag.* 89 B8
Mandronarivo, *Madag.* 89 C8
Mandsaur, *India* 68 G6
Mandurah, *Australia* 93 F2
Mandúria, *Italy* 31 B10
Mandvi, *India* 68 H3
Mandya, *India* 66 N10
Mandzai, *Pakistan* 68 D2
Mané, *Burkina Faso* 83 C4
Maneh, *Iran* 71 B8
Manenggouba, Mts., *Cameroon* 83 E6

Manera, *Madag.* 89 C7
Manérbio, *Italy* 28 C7
Maneroo Cr. →, *Australia* 94 C3
Manfalût, *Egypt* 80 B3
Manfredónia, *Italy* 29 G12
Manfredónia, G. di, *Italy* 29 G13
Manga, *Burkina Faso* 83 C4
Manga, *Niger* 83 C7
Mangabeiras, Chapada das, *Brazil* 125 F9
Mangalia, *Romania* 43 G13
Mangalore, *India* 66 N9
Mangan, *India* 69 F13
Mangaung, *S. Africa* 85 K5
Mangawan, *India* 69 G9
Mangaweka, *N.Z.* 91 H5
Manggar, *Indonesia* 62 E3
Manggawitu, *Indonesia* 63 E8
Mangindrano, *Madag.* 89 A8
Mangkalihat, Tanjung, *Indonesia* 63 D5
Mangla, *Pakistan* 68 C5
Mangla Dam, *Pakistan* 69 C5
Manglaur, *India* 68 E7
Mangnai, *China* 60 C4
Mango, *Togo* 83 C5
Mangoche, *Malawi* 87 E4
Mangoky →, *Madag.* 89 C7
Mangole, *Indonesia* 63 E6
Mangombe, *Dem. Rep. of the Congo* 86 C2
Mangonui, *N.Z.* 91 F4
Mangoro →, *Madag.* 89 B8
Mangrol, *Mad. P., India* 68 J4
Mangrol, *Raj., India* 68 G6
Mangualde, *Portugal* 34 E3
Mangueira, L. da, *Brazil* 127 C5
Mangum, *U.S.A.* 113 H5
Mangyshlak Poluostrov, *Kazakstan* 50 E6
Manhattan, *U.S.A.* 112 F6
Manhiça, *Mozam.* 89 D5
Mania →, *Madag.* 89 B8
Maniago, *Italy* 29 B9
Manica, *Mozam.* 89 B5
Manica □, *Mozam.* 89 B5
Manicaland □, *Zimbabwe* 87 F3
Manicoré, *Brazil* 124 E6
Manicouagan →, *Canada* 103 C6
Manicouagan, Rés., *Canada* 103 B6
Maniema □, *Dem. Rep. of the Congo* 86 C2
Manīfah, *Si. Arabia* 71 E6
Manifold, C., *Australia* 94 C5
Maniganggo, *China* 58 B2
Manigotagan, *Canada* 105 C9
Manigotagan →, *Canada* 105 C9
Manihari, *India* 69 G12
Manihiki, *Cook Is.* 97 J11
Manika, Plateau de la, *Dem. Rep. of the Congo* 87 E2
Manikpur, *India* 69 G9
Manila, *Phil.* 61 D4
Manila, *U.S.A.* 114 F9
Manila B., *Phil.* 61 D4
Manilla, *Australia* 95 E5
Manimpé, *Mali* 82 C3
Maningrida, *Australia* 94 A1
Maninian, *Ivory C.* 82 C3
Manipur □, *India* 67 G19
Manipur →, *Burma* 67 H19
Manisa, *Turkey* 39 C9
Manisa □, *Turkey* 39 C9
Manistee, *U.S.A.* 108 C2
Manistee →, *U.S.A.* 108 C2
Manistique, *U.S.A.* 108 C2
Manito L., *Canada* 105 C7
Manitoba □, *Canada* 105 B9
Manitoba, L., *Canada* 105 C9
Manitou, *Canada* 105 D9
Manitou, L., *Canada* 103 B6
Manitou Is., *U.S.A.* 108 C3
Manitou Springs, *U.S.A.* 112 F2
Manitoulin I., *Canada* 102 C3
Manitouwadge, *Canada* 102 C2
Manitowoc, *U.S.A.* 108 C2
Manizales, *Colombia* 124 B3
Manja, *Madag.* 89 C7
Manjacaze, *Mozam.* 89 C5
Manjakandriana, *Madag.* 89 B8
Manjhand, *Pakistan* 68 G3
Manjil, *Iran* 71 B6
Manjimup, *Australia* 93 F2
Manjra →, *India* 66 K10
Mankato, *Kans., U.S.A.* 112 F5
Mankato, *Minn., U.S.A.* 112 C8
Mankayane, *Swaziland* 89 D5
Mankera, *Pakistan* 68 D4
Mankim, *Cameroon* 83 D7
Mankono, *Ivory C.* 82 D3
Mankota, *Canada* 105 D7
Manlay = Üydzin, *Mongolia* 56 B4
Manlleu, *Spain* 32 C7
Manmad, *India* 66 J9
Mann Ranges, *Australia* 93 E5
Manna, *Indonesia* 62 E2
Mannahill, *Australia* 95 E3
Mannar, *Sri Lanka* 66 Q11
Mannar, G. of, *Asia* 66 Q11
Mannar I., *Sri Lanka* 66 Q11
Mannheim, *Germany* 25 F4
Manning, *Canada* 104 B5
Manning, *Oreg., U.S.A.* 116 E3
Manning, *S.C., U.S.A.* 109 J5
Manning Prov. Park, *Canada* 104 D4
Mannu →, *Italy* 30 C2
Mannu, C., *Italy* 30 B1
Mannum, *Australia* 95 E2
Mano, *S. Leone* 82 D2
Mano →, *Liberia* 82 D2
Mano River, *Liberia* 82 D2
Manoharpur, *India* 69 H11
Manokwari, *Indonesia* 63 E8
Manolás, *Greece* 38 C3
Manombo, *Madag.* 89 C7
Manono, *Dem. Rep. of the Congo* 86 D2
Manoppello, *Italy* 29 F11
Manosque, *France* 21 E9
Manotick, *Canada* 111 A9
Manouane →, *Canada* 103 C5
Manouane, L., *Canada* 103 B5
Manp'o, *N. Korea* 57 D14
Manpojin = Manp'o, *N. Korea* 57 D14
Manpur, *Mad. P., India* 68 H6
Manpur, *Mad. P., India* 69 H10
Manresa, *Spain* 32 D6
Mansa, *Gujarat, India* 68 H5
Mansa, *Punjab, India* 68 E6
Mansa, *Zambia* 87 E2
Månsåsen, *Sweden* 10 A8
Mansehra, *Pakistan* 68 B5
Mansel I., *Canada* 101 B11
Mansfield, *Australia* 95 F4
Mansfield, *U.K.* 12 D6
Mansfield, *La., U.S.A.* 113 J8
Mansfield, *Mass., U.S.A.* 111 D13
Mansfield, *Ohio, U.S.A.* 110 F2
Mansfield, *Pa., U.S.A.* 110 E7
Mansfield, Mt., *U.S.A.* 111 B12
Mansilla de las Mulas, *Spain* 34 C5
Mansle, *France* 20 C4
Mansoa, *Guinea-Biss.* 82 C1
Manson Creek, *Canada* 104 B4
Manta, *Ecuador* 124 D2
Mantalingajan, Mt., *Phil.* 61 G2
Mantare, *Tanzania* 86 C3
Manteca, *U.S.A.* 116 H5
Manteo, *U.S.A.* 109 H8
Mantes-la-Jolie, *France* 19 D8
Manthani, *India* 66 K11
Manti, *U.S.A.* 114 G8
Mantiqueira, Serra da, *Brazil* 127 A7
Manton, *U.S.A.* 108 C3
Mantorp, *Sweden* 11 F9
Mántova, *Italy* 28 C7
Mänttä, *Finland* 9 E21
Mantua = Mántova, *Italy* 28 C7
Manturovo, *Russia* 48 A7
Manu, *Peru* 124 F4
Manu →, *Peru* 124 F4
Manua Is., *Amer. Samoa* 91 B14
Manuel Alves →, *Brazil* 125 F9
Manui, *Indonesia* 63 E6
Manuripi →, *Bolivia* 124 F5
Many, *U.S.A.* 113 K8
Manyara, L., *Tanzania* 86 C4
Manyas, *Turkey* 41 F11
Manych →, *Russia* 49 G5
Manych-Gudilo, Ozero, *Russia* 49 G6
Manyonga →, *Tanzania* 86 C3
Manyoni, *Tanzania* 86 D3
Manzai, *Pakistan* 68 C4
Manzala, Bahra el, *Egypt* 80 H7
Manzanares, *Spain* 35 F7
Manzaneda, *Spain* 34 C3
Manzanillo, *Cuba* 120 B4
Manzanillo, *Mexico* 118 D4
Manzanillo, Pta., *Panama* 120 E4
Manzano Mts., *U.S.A.* 115 J10
Manzarīyeh, *Iran* 71 C6
Manzhouli, *China* 60 B6
Manzini, *Swaziland* 89 D5
Mao, *Chad* 79 F9
Maó, *Spain* 37 B11
Maoke, Pegunungan, *Indonesia* 63 E9
Maolin, *China* 57 C12
Maoming, *China* 59 G8
Maopi T'ou, *China* 59 G13
Maouri, Dallol →, *Niger* 83 C5
Maoxian, *China* 58 B4
Maoxing, *China* 57 B13
Mapam Yumco, *China* 60 C3
Mapastepec, *Mexico* 119 D6
Mapia, Kepulauan, *Indonesia* 63 D8
Mapimí, *Mexico* 118 B4
Mapimí, Bolsón de, *Mexico* 118 B4
Maping, *China* 59 B9
Mapinga, *Tanzania* 86 D4
Mapinhane, *Mozam.* 89 C6
Maple Creek, *Canada* 105 D7
Maple Valley, *U.S.A.* 116 C4
Mapleton, *U.S.A.* 114 D2
Mapuera →, *Brazil* 124 D7
Mapulanguene, *Mozam.* 89 C5
Maputo, *Mozam.* 89 D5
Maputo □, *Mozam.* 89 D5
Maputo, B. de, *Mozam.* 89 D5
Maqiaohe, *China* 57 B16
Maqnā, *Si. Arabia* 70 D2
Maqueda, *Spain* 34 E6
Maquela do Zombo, *Angola* 84 F3
Maquinchao, *Argentina* 128 E3
Maquoketa, *U.S.A.* 112 D9
Mar, Serra do, *Brazil* 127 B6
Mar Chiquita, L., *Argentina* 126 C3
Mar del Plata, *Argentina* 126 D4
Mar Menor, *Spain* 33 H4
Mara, *Tanzania* 86 C3
Mara □, *Tanzania* 86 C3
Maraã, *Brazil* 124 D5
Marabá, *Brazil* 125 E9
Maracá, I. de, *Brazil* 125 C8
Maracaibo, *Venezuela* 124 A4
Maracaibo, L. de, *Venezuela* 122 C3
Maracaju, *Brazil* 127 A4
Maracay, *Venezuela* 124 A5
Maracena, *Spain* 35 H7
Maradi, *Niger* 83 C6
Marāgheh, *Iran* 70 B5
Marāh, *Si. Arabia* 70 E5
Marajó, I. de, *Brazil* 122 D6
Marākand, *Iran* 70 B5
Maralal, *Kenya* 86 B4
Maralinga, *Australia* 93 F5
Maramaraereğlisi, *Turkey* 41 F11
Marampa, *S. Leone* 82 D2
Maramureş □, *Romania* 43 C9
Maran, *Malaysia* 65 L4
Marana, *U.S.A.* 115 K8
Maranboy, *Australia* 92 B5
Maranchón, *Spain* 32 D2
Marand, *Iran* 70 B5
Marang, *Malaysia* 65 K4
Maranguape, *Brazil* 125 D11
Maranhão = São Luís, *Brazil* 125 D10
Maranhão □, *Brazil* 125 E9
Marano, L. di, *Italy* 29 C10
Maranoa →, *Australia* 95 D4
Marañón →, *Peru* 122 D3
Marão, *Mozam.* 89 C5
Maraş = Kahramanmaraş, *Turkey* 70 B3
Mărăşeşti, *Romania* 43 E12
Maratea, *Italy* 31 C8
Marateca, *Portugal* 35 G2
Marathasa □, *Cyprus* 36 E11
Marathókambos, *Greece* 39 D8
Marathon, *Australia* 94 C3
Marathon, *Canada* 102 C2
Marathón, *Greece* 38 C5
Marathon, *N.Y., U.S.A.* 111 D8
Marathon, *N.Y., U.S.A.* 111 D8
Marathon, *Tex., U.S.A.* 113 K3
Marathóvouno, *Cyprus* 36 D12
Maratua, *Indonesia* 63 D5
Maravatío, *Mexico* 118 D4
Marawi City, *Phil.* 61 G6
Marāwih, *U.A.E.* 71 E7
Marbella, *Spain* 35 J6
Marble Bar, *Australia* 92 D2
Marble Falls, *U.S.A.* 113 K5
Marblehead, *U.S.A.* 111 D14
Marburg, *Germany* 24 E4
Marcal →, *Hungary* 42 C2
Marcali, *Hungary* 42 D2
Marcaria, *Italy* 28 C7
Mărcăuţi, *Moldova* 43 B12
March, *U.K.* 13 E8
Marche, *France* 20 B5
Marche □, *Italy* 29 E10
Marche-en-Famenne, *Belgium* 17 D5
Marchena, *Spain* 35 H5
Marches = Marche □, *Italy* 29 E10
Marciana Marina, *Italy* 28 F7
Marcianise, *Italy* 31 A7
Marcigny, *France* 19 F11
Marcillat-en-Combraille, *France* 19 F9
Marck, *France* 19 B8
Marckolsheim, *France* 19 D14
Marco, *U.S.A.* 109 N5
Marcos Juárez, *Argentina* 126 C3
Mărculeşti, *Moldova* 43 C13
Marcus I. = Minami-Tori-Shima, *Pac. Oc.* 96 E7
Marcus Necker Ridge, *Pac. Oc.* 96 F9
Marcy, Mt., *U.S.A.* 111 B11
Mardan, *Pakistan* 68 B5
Mardin, *Turkey* 70 B4
Mårdsjön, *Sweden* 10 A9
Marécchia →, *Italy* 29 D9
Maree, L., *U.K.* 14 D3
Mareeba, *Australia* 94 B4
Mareetsane, *S. Africa* 88 D4
Maremma, *Italy* 29 F8
Maréna, *Mali* 82 C2
Maréna, *Mali* 82 C3
Marengo, *U.S.A.* 112 E8
Marennes, *France* 20 C2
Marenyi, *Kenya* 86 C4
Marerano, *Madag.* 89 C7
Marettimo, *Italy* 30 E5
Mareuil, *France* 20 C4
Marfa, *U.S.A.* 113 K2
Marfa Pt., *Malta* 36 D1
Marganets = Marhanets, *Ukraine* 47 J8
Margaret →, *Australia* 92 C4
Margaret Bay, *Canada* 104 C3
Margaret L., *Canada* 104 B5
Margaret River, *Australia* 93 F2
Margarita, I. de, *Venezuela* 122 B4
Margarítion, *Greece* 38 B2
Margaritovo, *Russia* 54 C7
Margate, *S. Africa* 89 E5
Margate, *U.K.* 13 F9
Margeride, Mts. de la, *France* 20 D7
Margherita di Savóia, *Italy* 31 A9
Marghita, *Romania* 42 C7
Margonin, *Poland* 45 F4
Margosatubig, *Phil.* 61 H5
Mārgow, Dasht-e, *Afghan.* 66 D3
Marguerite, *Canada* 104 C4
Marhanets, *Ukraine* 47 J8
Mari El □, *Russia* 48 B8
Mari Indus, *Pakistan* 68 C4
Mari Republic = Mari El □, *Russia* 48 B8
María, Sa. de, *Spain* 33 H2
María Elena, *Chile* 126 A2
María Grande, *Argentina* 126 C4
Maria I., *N. Terr., Australia* 94 A2
Maria I., *Tas., Australia* 94 G4
Maria van Diemen, C., *N.Z.* 91 F4
Mariager, *Denmark* 11 H3
Mariager Fjord, *Denmark* 11 H4
Mariakani, *Kenya* 86 C4
Marian, *Australia* 94 C4
Marian L., *Canada* 104 A5
Mariana Trench, *Pac. Oc.* 52 H18
Marianao, *Cuba* 120 B3
Marianna, *Ark., U.S.A.* 113 H9
Marianna, *Fla., U.S.A.* 109 K3
Mariannelund, *Sweden* 11 G9
Mariánské Lázně, *Czech Rep.* 26 B5
Marias →, *U.S.A.* 114 C8
Mariato, Punta, *Panama* 120 E3
Mariazell, *Austria* 26 D8
Maribo, *Denmark* 11 K5
Maribor, *Slovenia* 29 B12
Marico →, *Africa* 88 C4
Maricopa, *Ariz., U.S.A.* 115 K7
Maricopa, *Calif., U.S.A.* 117 K7
Marīdī, *Sudan* 81 G2
Maridi, Wadi →, *Sudan* 81 F2
Marié →, *Brazil* 124 D5
Marie Byrd Land, *Antarctica* 5 D14
Marie-Galante, *Guadeloupe* 121 C7
Mariecourt = Kangiqsujuaq, *Canada* 101 B12
Mariefred, *Sweden* 10 E11
Marieholm, *Sweden* 11 J7
Mariembourg, *Belgium* 17 D4
Marienbad = Mariánské Lázně, *Czech Rep.* 26 B5
Marienberg, *Germany* 24 E9
Mariental, *Namibia* 88 C2
Marienville, *U.S.A.* 110 E5
Mariestad, *Sweden* 11 F7
Marietta, *Ga., U.S.A.* 109 J3
Marietta, *Ohio, U.S.A.* 108 F5
Marieville, *Canada* 111 A11
Mariga →, *Nigeria* 83 C6
Marignane, *France* 21 E9
Marihatag, *Phil.* 61 G7
Mariinsk, *Russia* 50 D9
Mariinskiy Posad, *Russia* 48 B8
Marijampolė, *Lithuania* 9 J20
Marijampolės □, *Lithuania* 44 D10
Marília, *Brazil* 127 A6
Marín, *Spain* 34 C2
Marina, *U.S.A.* 116 J5
Marinduque, *Phil.* 63 B6
Marine City, *U.S.A.* 110 D2
Marineo, *Italy* 30 E6
Marinette, *U.S.A.* 108 C2
Maringá, *Brazil* 127 A5
Marinha Grande, *Portugal* 34 F2
Marino, *Italy* 29 G9
Marion, *Ala., U.S.A.* 109 J2
Marion, *Ill., U.S.A.* 113 G10
Marion, *Ind., U.S.A.* 108 E3
Marion, *Iowa, U.S.A.* 112 D9
Marion, *Kans., U.S.A.* 112 F6
Marion, *N.C., U.S.A.* 109 H5
Marion, *Ohio, U.S.A.* 108 E4
Marion, *S.C., U.S.A.* 109 H6
Marion, *Va., U.S.A.* 109 G5
Marion, L., *U.S.A.* 109 J5
Mariposa, *U.S.A.* 116 H7
Mariscal Estigarribia, *Paraguay* 126 A3
Maritime Alps = Maritimes, Alpes, *Europe* 21 D11
Maritimes, Alpes, *Europe* 21 D11
Maritsa = Évros →, *Bulgaria* 72 B2
Maritsá, *Greece* 36 C10
Mariupol, *Ukraine* 47 J9
Marīvān, *Iran* 70 C5
Marj 'Uyûn, *Lebanon* 75 B4
Marka, *Si. Arabia* 80 D5
Markam, *China* 58 C2
Markaryd, *Sweden* 11 H7
Markazī □, *Iran* 71 C6
Markdale, *Canada* 110 B4
Marked Tree, *U.S.A.* 113 H9
Markelsdorfer Huk, *Germany* 24 A7
Market Drayton, *U.K.* 12 E5
Market Harborough, *U.K.* 13 E7
Market Rasen, *U.K.* 12 D7
Markham, *Canada* 110 C5
Markham, Mt., *Antarctica* 5 E11
Marki, *Poland* 45 F8
Markkleeberg, *Germany* 24 D8
Markleeville, *U.S.A.* 116 G7
Markoupoulon, *Greece* 38 D5
Markovac, *Serbia, Yug.* 40 B5
Markovo, *Russia* 51 C17
Markoye, *Burkina Faso* 83 C5
Marks, *Russia* 48 E8
Marksville, *U.S.A.* 113 K8
Markt Schwaben, *Germany* 25 G7
Marktoberdorf, *Germany* 25 H6
Marktredwitz, *Germany* 25 E8
Marl, *Germany* 24 D3
Marla, *Australia* 95 D1
Marlbank, *Canada* 110 B7
Marlboro, *Mass., U.S.A.* 111 D13
Marlboro, *N.Y., U.S.A.* 111 E11
Marlborough, *Australia* 94 C4
Marlborough, *U.K.* 13 F6
Marlborough Downs, *U.K.* 13 F6
Marle, *France* 19 C10
Marlin, *U.S.A.* 113 K6
Marlow, *Germany* 24 A8
Marlow, *U.S.A.* 113 H6
Marmagao, *India* 66 M8
Marmande, *France* 20 D4
Marmara, *Turkey* 41 F11
Marmara, Sea of = Marmara Denizi, *Turkey* 41 F12
Marmara Denizi, *Turkey* 41 F12
Marmara Gölü, *Turkey* 39 C10
Marmaris, *Turkey* 39 E10
Marmaris Limanı, *Turkey* 39 E10
Marmion, Mt., *Australia* 93 E2
Marmion L., *Canada* 102 C1
Marmolada, Mte., *Italy* 29 B8
Marmolejo, *Spain* 35 G6
Marmora, *Canada* 102 D4
Mármora, La, *Italy* 30 C2
Marnay, *France* 19 E12
Marne, *Germany* 24 B5
Marne □, *France* 19 D11
Marne →, *France* 19 D9
Marneuli, *Georgia* 49 K7
Maroala, *Madag.* 89 B8
Maroantsetra, *Madag.* 89 B8
Maroelaboom, *Namibia* 88 B2
Marofandilia, *Madag.* 89 C7
Marolambo, *Madag.* 89 C8
Maromandia, *Madag.* 89 A8
Marondera, *Zimbabwe* 87 F3
Maroni →, *Fr. Guiana* 125 B8
Marónia, *Greece* 41 F9
Maronne →, *France* 20 C5
Maroochydore, *Australia* 95 D5
Maroona, *Australia* 95 F3
Maros →, *Hungary* 42 D5
Marosakoa, *Madag.* 89 B8
Maroseranana, *Madag.* 89 B8
Maróstica, *Italy* 29 C8
Marotandrano, *Madag.* 89 B8
Marotaolano, *Madag.* 89 A8
Maroua, *Cameroon* 83 C7
Marovato, *Madag.* 89 B8
Marovoay, *Madag.* 89 B8
Marquard, *S. Africa* 88 D4
Marquesas Is. = Marquises, Is., *Pac. Oc.* 97 H14
Marquette, *U.S.A.* 108 B2
Marquise, *France* 19 B8
Marquises, Is., *Pac. Oc.* 97 H14
Marra, Djebel, *Sudan* 79 F10
Marra, Gebel, *Sudan* 81 F2
Marracuene, *Mozam.* 89 D5
Marradi, *Italy* 29 D8
Marrakech, *Morocco* 78 B4
Marratxi, *Spain* 32 F7
Marrawah, *Australia* 94 G3
Marree, *Australia* 95 D2
Marrero, *U.S.A.* 113 L9
Marrimane, *Mozam.* 89 C5
Marromeu, *Mozam.* 89 B6
Marroquí, Punta, *Spain* 35 K5
Marrowie Cr. →, *Australia* 95 E4
Marrubane, *Mozam.* 87 F4
Marrúbiu, *Italy* 30 C1
Marrupa, *Mozam.* 87 E4
Mars Hill, *U.S.A.* 109 B12
Marsa Alam, *Egypt* 80 B3
Marsá Matrûh, *Egypt* 80 A2
Marsa Sha'b, *Sudan* 80 C4
Marsabit, *Kenya* 86 B4
Marsala, *Italy* 30 E5
Marsalforn, *Malta* 36 C1
Mârşani, *Romania* 43 F9
Marsberg, *Germany* 24 D4
Marsciano, *Italy* 29 F9
Marsden, *Australia* 95 E4
Marseillan, *France* 20 E7
Marseille, *France* 21 E9
Marseilles = Marseille, *France* 21 E9
Marsh I., *U.S.A.* 113 L9
Marshall, *Liberia* 82 D2
Marshall, *Ark., U.S.A.* 113 H8
Marshall, *Mich., U.S.A.* 108 D3
Marshall, *Minn., U.S.A.* 112 C7
Marshall, *Mo., U.S.A.* 112 F8
Marshall, *Tex., U.S.A.* 113 J7
Marshall →, *Australia* 94 C2
Marshall Is. ■, *Pac. Oc.* 96 G9
Marshalltown, *U.S.A.* 112 D8
Marshbrook, *Zimbabwe* 89 B5
Marshfield, *Mo., U.S.A.* 113 G8
Marshfield, *Vt., U.S.A.* 111 B12
Marshfield, *Wis., U.S.A.* 112 C9
Marshūn, *Iran* 71 B6
Marsico Nuovo, *Italy* 31 B8
Märsta, *Sweden* 10 E11
Marstal, *Denmark* 11 K4
Marstrand, *Sweden* 11 G5
Mart, *U.S.A.* 113 K6
Marta →, *Italy* 29 F8
Martaban, *Burma* 67 L20
Martaban, G. of, *Burma* 67 L20
Martano, *Italy* 31 B11
Martapura, *Kalimantan, Indonesia* 62 E4
Martapura, *Sumatera, Indonesia* 62 E2
Marte, *Nigeria* 83 C7
Martel, *France* 20 D5
Martelange, *Belgium* 17 E5
Martellago, *Italy* 29 C9
Martés, Sierra, *Spain* 33 F4
Martfű, *Hungary* 42 C5
Martha's Vineyard, *U.S.A.* 111 E14
Martigné-Ferchaud, *France* 18 E5
Martigny, *Switz.* 25 J3
Martigues, *France* 21 E9
Martin, *Slovak Rep.* 27 B11
Martin, *S. Dak., U.S.A.* 112 D4
Martin, *Tenn., U.S.A.* 113 G10
Martín →, *Spain* 32 D4
Martin L., *U.S.A.* 109 J3
Martina Franca, *Italy* 31 B10
Martinborough, *N.Z.* 91 J5
Martinez, *Calif., U.S.A.* 116 G4
Martinez, *Ga., U.S.A.* 109 J4
Martinique ■, *W. Indies* 121 D7
Martinique Passage, *W. Indies* 121 C7
Martínon, *Greece* 38 C5

Martinópolis, *Brazil* 127 A5
Martins Ferry, *U.S.A.* 110 F4
Martinsberg, *Austria* 26 C8
Martinsburg, *Pa., U.S.A.* 110 F6
Martinsburg, *W. Va., U.S.A.* 108 F7
Martinsicuro, *Italy* 29 F10
Martinsville, *Ind., U.S.A.* 108 F2
Martinsville, *Va., U.S.A.* 109 G6
Marton, *N.Z.* 91 J5
Martorell, *Spain* 32 D6
Martos, *Spain* 35 H7
Martuni, *Armenia* 49 K7
Maru, *Nigeria* 83 C6
Marudi, *Malaysia* 62 D4
Ma'ruf, *Afghan.* 66 D5
Marugame, *Japan* 55 G6
Marunga, *Angola* 88 B3
Marungu, Mts., *Dem. Rep. of the Congo* 86 D3
Marv Dasht, *Iran* 71 D7
Marvast, *Iran* 71 D7
Marvejols, *France* 20 D7
Marvel Loch, *Australia* 93 F2
Marwar, *India* 68 G5
Mary, *Turkmenistan* 50 F7
Maryborough = Port Laoise, *Ireland* 15 C4
Maryborough, *Queens., Australia* 95 D5
Maryborough, *Vic., Australia* 95 F3
Maryfield, *Canada* 105 D8
Maryland □, *U.S.A.* 108 F7
Maryland Junction, *Zimbabwe* 87 F3
Maryport, *U.K.* 12 C4
Mary's Harbour, *Canada* 103 B8
Marystown, *Canada* 103 C8
Marysville, *Canada* 104 D5
Marysville, *Calif., U.S.A.* 116 F5
Marysville, *Kans., U.S.A.* 112 F6
Marysville, *Mich., U.S.A.* 110 D2
Marysville, *Ohio, U.S.A.* 108 E4
Marysville, *Wash., U.S.A.* 116 B4
Maryville, *Mo., U.S.A.* 112 E7
Maryville, *Tenn., U.S.A.* 109 H4
Marzūq, *Libya* 79 C8
Masahunga, *Tanzania* 86 C3
Masai Steppe, *Tanzania* 86 C4
Masaka, *Uganda* 86 C3
Masalembo, Kepulauan, *Indonesia* 62 F4
Masalima, Kepulauan, *Indonesia* 62 F5
Masallı, *Azerbaijan* 73 C13
Masamba, *Indonesia* 63 E6
Masan, *S. Korea* 57 G15
Masandam, Ra's, *Oman* 71 E8
Masasi, *Tanzania* 87 E4
Masaya, *Nic.* 120 D2
Masba, *Nigeria* 83 C7
Masbate, *Phil.* 61 E5
Máscali, *Italy* 31 E8
Mascara, *Algeria* 78 A6
Mascota, *Mexico* 118 C4
Masela, *Indonesia* 63 F7
Maseru, *Lesotho* 88 D4
Mashaba, *Zimbabwe* 87 G3
Mashābih, *Si. Arabia* 70 E3
Mashan, *China* 58 F7
Mashar, *Sudan* 81 F2
Mashegu, *Nigeria* 83 D6
Masherbrum, *Pakistan* 69 B7
Mashhad, *Iran* 71 B8
Mashi, *Nigeria* 83 C6
Mashīz, *Iran* 71 D8
Mashkel, Hamun-i, *Pakistan* 66 E3
Mashki Chāh, *Pakistan* 66 E3
Mashonaland, *Zimbabwe* 85 H6
Mashonaland Central □, *Zimbabwe* 89 B5
Mashonaland East □, *Zimbabwe* 89 B5
Mashonaland West □, *Zimbabwe* 89 B4
Mashrakh, *India* 69 F11
Mashtaga = Maştağa, *Azerbaijan* 49 K10
Masindi, *Uganda* 86 B3
Masindi Port, *Uganda* 86 B3
Maşīrah, *Oman* 74 C6
Maşīrah, Khalīj, *Oman* 74 C6
Masisi, *Dem. Rep. of the Congo* 86 C2
Masjed Soleyman, *Iran* 71 D6
Mask, L., *Ireland* 15 C2
Maskin, *Oman* 71 F8
Maslen Nos, *Bulgaria* 41 D11
Maslinica, *Croatia* 29 E13
Masnou = El Masnou, *Spain* 32 D7
Masoala, Tanjon' i, *Madag.* 89 B9
Masoarivo, *Madag.* 89 B7
Masohi = Amahai, *Indonesia* 63 E7
Masomeloka, *Madag.* 89 C8
Mason, *Nev., U.S.A.* 116 G7
Mason, *Tex., U.S.A.* 113 K5
Mason City, *U.S.A.* 112 D8
Maspalomas, *Canary Is.* 37 G4
Maspalomas, Pta., *Canary Is.* 37 G4
Masqat, *Oman* 74 C6
Massa, *Italy* 28 D7
Massa Maríttima, *Italy* 28 E7
Massachusetts □, *U.S.A.* 111 D13
Massachusetts B., *U.S.A.* 111 D14
Massafra, *Italy* 31 B10
Massakory, *Chad* 79 F9
Massanella, *Spain* 37 B9
Massangena, *Mozam.* 89 C5
Massango, *Angola* 84 F3
Massat, *France* 20 F5
Massawa = Mitsiwa, *Eritrea* 81 D4
Massena, *U.S.A.* 111 B10
Massénya, *Chad* 79 F9
Masset, *Canada* 104 C2
Masseube, *France* 20 E4
Massiac, *France* 20 C7
Massif Central, *France* 20 D7
Massigui, *Mali* 82 C3
Massillon, *U.S.A.* 110 F3
Massinga, *Mozam.* 89 C6
Massingir, *Mozam.* 89 C5
Mässlingen, *Sweden* 10 B6
Masson, *Canada* 111 A9
Masson I., *Antarctica* 5 C7
Maştağa, *Azerbaijan* 49 K10
Mastanli = Momchilgrad, *Bulgaria* 41 E9
Masterton, *N.Z.* 91 J5
Mastic, *U.S.A.* 111 F12
Mástikho, Ákra, *Greece* 39 C8
Mastuj, *Pakistan* 69 A5
Mastung, *Pakistan* 66 E5
Mastūrah, *Si. Arabia* 80 C4
Masty, *Belarus* 46 F3
Masuda, *Japan* 55 G5
Masvingo, *Zimbabwe* 87 G3
Masvingo □, *Zimbabwe* 87 G3
Maşyāf, *Syria* 70 C3
Maszewo, *Poland* 44 E2
Matabeleland, *Zimbabwe* 85 H5
Matabeleland North □, *Zimbabwe* 87 F2
Matabeleland South □, *Zimbabwe* 87 G2
Matachel →, *Spain* 35 G4
Matachewan, *Canada* 102 C3
Matadi, *Dem. Rep. of the Congo* 84 F2
Matagalpa, *Nic.* 120 D2
Matagami, *Canada* 102 C4
Matagami, L., *Canada* 102 C4
Matagorda B., *U.S.A.* 113 L6
Matagorda I., *U.S.A.* 113 L6
Matak, *Indonesia* 65 L6
Mátala, *Greece* 36 E6
Matam, *Senegal* 82 B2
Matameye, *Niger* 83 C6
Matamoros, *Campeche, Mexico* 119 D6
Matamoros, *Coahuila, Mexico* 118 B4
Matamoros, *Tamaulipas, Mexico* 119 B5
Ma'ṭan as Sarra, *Libya* 79 D10
Matandu →, *Tanzania* 87 D3
Matane, *Canada* 103 C6
Matang, *China* 58 F5
Matankari, *Niger* 83 C5
Matanomadh, *India* 68 H3
Matanzas, *Cuba* 120 B3
Matapa, *Botswana* 88 C3
Matapan, C. = Taínaron, Ákra, *Greece* 38 E4
Matapédia, *Canada* 103 C6
Matara, *Sri Lanka* 66 S12
Mataram, *Indonesia* 62 F5
Matarani, *Peru* 124 G4
Mataranka, *Australia* 92 B5
Matarma, Râs, *Egypt* 75 E1
Mataró, *Spain* 32 D7
Matarraña →, *Spain* 32 D5
Mataruška Banja, *Serbia, Yug.* 40 C4
Matatiele, *S. Africa* 89 E4
Mataura, *N.Z.* 91 M2
Matehuala, *Mexico* 118 C4
Mateke Hills, *Zimbabwe* 87 G3
Matera, *Italy* 31 B9
Matese, Monti del, *Italy* 31 A7
Mátészalka, *Hungary* 42 C7
Matetsi, *Zimbabwe* 87 F2
Matfors, *Sweden* 10 B11
Matha, *France* 20 C3
Mathis, *U.S.A.* 113 L6
Mathráki, *Greece* 36 A3
Mathura, *India* 68 F7
Mati, *Phil.* 61 H7
Mati →, *Albania* 40 E3
Matiakoali, *Burkina Faso* 83 C5
Matiali, *India* 69 F13
Matías Romero, *Mexico* 119 D5
Matibane, *Mozam.* 87 E5
Matima, *Botswana* 88 C3
Matiri Ra., *N.Z.* 91 J4
Matjiesfontein, *S. Africa* 88 E3
Matla →, *India* 69 J13
Matlamanyane, *Botswana* 88 B4
Matli, *Pakistan* 68 G3
Matlock, *U.K.* 12 D6
Matna, *Sudan* 81 E4
Mato Grosso □, *Brazil* 125 F8
Mato Grosso, Planalto do, *Brazil* 122 E5
Mato Grosso do Sul □, *Brazil* 125 G8
Matochkin Shar, *Russia* 50 B6
Matopo Hills, *Zimbabwe* 87 G2
Matopos, *Zimbabwe* 87 G2
Matosinhos, *Portugal* 34 D2
Matour, *France* 19 F11
Maṭraḥ, *Oman* 74 C6
Matroosberg, *S. Africa* 88 E2
Matsena, *Nigeria* 83 C7
Matsesta, *Russia* 49 J4
Matsu Tao, *Taiwan* 59 E13
Matsue, *Japan* 55 G6
Matsumae, *Japan* 54 D10
Matsumoto, *Japan* 55 F9
Matsusaka, *Japan* 55 G8
Matsutō, *Japan* 55 F8
Matsuura, *Japan* 55 H4
Matsuyama, *Japan* 55 H6
Mattagami →, *Canada* 102 B3
Mattancheri, *India* 66 Q10
Mattawa, *Canada* 102 C4
Matterhorn, *Switz.* 25 K3
Mattersburg, *Austria* 27 D9
Matthew Town, *Bahamas* 121 B5
Matthew's Ridge, *Guyana* 124 B6
Mattice, *Canada* 102 C3
Mattituck, *U.S.A.* 111 F12
Mattoon, *U.S.A.* 108 F1
Matuba, *Mozam.* 89 C5
Matucana, *Peru* 124 F3
Matūn = Khowst, *Afghan.* 68 C3
Maturín, *Venezuela* 124 B6
Matveyev Kurgan, *Russia* 47 J10
Matxitxako, C., *Spain* 32 B2
Mau, *Mad. P., India* 69 F8
Mau, *Ut. P., India* 69 G10
Mau, *Ut. P., India* 69 G9
Mau Escarpment, *Kenya* 86 C4
Mau Ranipur, *India* 69 G8
Maubeuge, *France* 19 B10
Maubourguet, *France* 20 E4
Maud, Pt., *Australia* 92 D1
Maude, *Australia* 95 E3
Maudin Sun, *Burma* 67 M19
Maués, *Brazil* 124 D7
Mauganj, *India* 67 G12
Maughold Hd., *U.K.* 12 C3
Mauguio, *France* 20 E7
Maui, *U.S.A.* 106 H16
Maulamyaing = Moulmein, *Burma* 67 L20
Maule □, *Chile* 126 D1
Mauléon-Licharre, *France* 20 E3
Maumee, *U.S.A.* 108 E4
Maumee →, *U.S.A.* 108 E4
Maumere, *Indonesia* 63 F6
Maumusson, Pertuis de, *France* 20 C2
Maun, *Botswana* 88 C3
Mauna Kea, *U.S.A.* 106 J17
Mauna Loa, *U.S.A.* 106 J17
Maungmagan Is., *Burma* 64 E1
Maungmagan Kyunzu, *Burma* 67 N20
Maupin, *U.S.A.* 114 D3
Maure-de-Bretagne, *France* 18 E5
Maurepas, L., *U.S.A.* 113 K9
Maures, *France* 21 E10
Mauriac, *France* 20 C6
Maurice, L., *Australia* 93 E5
Mauricie, Parc Nat. de la, *Canada* 102 C5
Maurienne, *France* 21 C10
Mauritania ■, *Africa* 78 E3
Mauritius ■, *Ind. Oc.* 77 J9
Mauron, *France* 18 D4
Maurs, *France* 20 D6
Mauston, *U.S.A.* 112 D9
Mauterndorf, *Austria* 26 D6
Mauthen, *Austria* 26 E6
Mauvezin, *France* 20 E4
Mauzé-sur-le-Mignon, *France* 20 B3
Mavli, *India* 68 G5
Mavrova, *Albania* 40 F3
Mavuradonha Mts., *Zimbabwe* 87 F3
Mawa, *Dem. Rep. of the Congo* 86 B2
Mawai, *India* 69 H9
Mawana, *India* 68 E7
Mawand, *Pakistan* 68 E3
Mawk Mai, *Burma* 67 J20
Mawlaik, *Burma* 67 H19
Mawlamyine = Moulmein, *Burma* 67 L20
Mawqaq, *Si. Arabia* 70 E4
Mawson Coast, *Antarctica* 5 C6
Max, *U.S.A.* 112 B4
Maxcanú, *Mexico* 119 C6
Maxesibeni, *S. Africa* 89 E4
Maxhamish L., *Canada* 104 B4
Maxixe, *Mozam.* 89 C6
Maxville, *Canada* 111 A10
Maxwell, *U.S.A.* 116 F4
Maxwelton, *Australia* 94 C3
May, C., *U.S.A.* 108 F8
May Pen, *Jamaica* 120 C4
Maya →, *Russia* 51 D14
Maya Mts., *Belize* 119 D7
Mayaguana, *Bahamas* 121 B5
Mayagüez, *Puerto Rico* 121 C6
Mayahi, *Niger* 83 C6
Mayals = Maials, *Spain* 32 D5
Mayāmey, *Iran* 71 B7
Mayang, *China* 58 D7
Mayanup, *Australia* 93 F2
Mayapan, *Mexico* 119 C7
Mayarí, *Cuba* 121 B4
Maybell, *U.S.A.* 114 F9
Maybole, *U.K.* 14 F4
Maychew, *Ethiopia* 81 E4
Maydān, *Iraq* 70 C5
Maydena, *Australia* 94 G4
Mayen, *Germany* 25 E3
Mayenne, *France* 18 D6
Mayenne □, *France* 18 D6
Mayenne →, *France* 18 E6
Mayer, *U.S.A.* 115 J7
Mayerthorpe, *Canada* 104 C5
Mayfield, *Ky., U.S.A.* 109 G1
Mayfield, *N.Y., U.S.A.* 111 C10
Mayhill, *U.S.A.* 115 K11
Maykop, *Russia* 49 H5
Maymyo, *Burma* 64 A1
Maynard, *Mass., U.S.A.* 111 D13
Maynard, *Wash., U.S.A.* 116 C4
Maynard Hills, *Australia* 93 E2
Mayne →, *Australia* 94 C3
Maynooth, *Ireland* 15 C5
Mayo, *Canada* 100 B6
Mayo □, *Ireland* 15 C2
Mayo Daga, *Nigeria* 83 D7
Mayo Faran, *Nigeria* 83 D7
Mayon Volcano, *Phil.* 61 E5
Mayor I., *N.Z.* 91 G6
Mayorga, *Spain* 34 C5
Mayotte, *Ind. Oc.* 85 G9
Mayraira Pt., *Phil.* 61 B4
Mayskiy, *Russia* 49 J7
Maysville, *U.S.A.* 108 F4
Mayu, *Indonesia* 63 D7
Mayville, *N. Dak., U.S.A.* 112 B6
Mayville, *N.Y., U.S.A.* 110 D5
Mayya, *Russia* 51 C14
Mazabuka, *Zambia* 87 F2
Mazagán = El Jadida, *Morocco* 78 B4
Mazagão, *Brazil* 125 D8
Mazamet, *France* 20 E6
Mazán, *Peru* 124 D4
Māzandarān □, *Iran* 71 B7
Mazapil, *Mexico* 118 C4
Mazara del Vallo, *Italy* 30 E5
Mazarrón, *Spain* 33 H3
Mazarrón, G. de, *Spain* 33 H3
Mazaruni →, *Guyana* 124 B7
Mazatán, *Mexico* 118 B2
Mazatenango, *Guatemala* 120 D1
Mazatlán, *Mexico* 118 C3
Mažeikiai, *Lithuania* 9 H20
Māzhān, *Iran* 71 C8
Mazīnān, *Iran* 71 B8
Mazoe, *Mozam.* 87 F3
Mazoe →, *Mozam.* 87 F3
Mazowe, *Zimbabwe* 87 F3
Mazowieckie □, *Poland* 45 F8
Mazrûb, *Sudan* 81 E2
Mazu Dao, *China* 59 D12
Mazurian Lakes = Mazurski, Pojezierze, *Poland* 44 E7
Mazurski, Pojezierze, *Poland* 44 E7
Mazyr, *Belarus* 47 F5
Mbaba, *Senegal* 82 C1
Mbabane, *Swaziland* 89 D5
Mbagne, *Mauritania* 82 B2
M'bahiakro, *Ivory C.* 82 D4
Mbaïki, *C.A.R.* 84 D3
Mbala, *Zambia* 87 D3
Mbalabala, *Zimbabwe* 89 C4
Mbale, *Uganda* 86 B3
Mbalmayo, *Cameroon* 83 E7
Mbam →, *Cameroon* 83 E7
Mbamba Bay, *Tanzania* 87 E3
Mbandaka, *Dem. Rep. of the Congo* 84 D3
Mbanga, *Cameroon* 83 E6
Mbanza Congo, *Angola* 84 F2
Mbanza Ngungu, *Dem. Rep. of the Congo* 84 F2
Mbarara, *Uganda* 86 C3
Mbashe →, *S. Africa* 89 E4
Mbatto, *Ivory C.* 82 D4
Mbenkuru →, *Tanzania* 87 D4
Mberengwa, *Zimbabwe* 87 G2
Mberengwa, Mt., *Zimbabwe* 87 G2
Mberubu, *Nigeria* 83 D6
Mbesuma, *Zambia* 87 E3
Mbeya, *Tanzania* 87 D3
Mbeya □, *Tanzania* 86 D3
M'bili, *Sudan* 81 F2
Mbinga, *Tanzania* 87 E4
Mbini □, *Eq. Guin.* 84 D2
Mboki, *C.A.R.* 81 F2
M'bonge, *Cameroon* 83 E6
Mboro, *Senegal* 82 B1
M'boukou Res., *Cameroon* 83 D7
Mboune, *Senegal* 82 C2
Mbour, *Senegal* 82 C1
Mbout, *Mauritania* 82 B2
Mbuji-Mayi, *Dem. Rep. of the Congo* 86 D1
Mbulu, *Tanzania* 86 C4
Mburucuyá, *Argentina* 126 B4
Mchinja, *Tanzania* 87 D4
Mchinji, *Malawi* 87 E3
Mdantsane, *S. Africa* 85 L5
Mead, L., *U.S.A.* 117 J12
Meade, *U.S.A.* 113 G4
Meadow Lake, *Canada* 105 C7
Meadow Lake Prov. Park, *Canada* 105 C7
Meadow Valley Wash →, *U.S.A.* 117 J12
Meadville, *U.S.A.* 110 E4
Meaford, *Canada* 102 D3
Mealhada, *Portugal* 34 E2
Mealy Mts., *Canada* 103 B8
Meander River, *Canada* 104 B5
Meares, C., *U.S.A.* 114 D2
Mearim →, *Brazil* 125 D10
Meath □, *Ireland* 15 C5
Meath Park, *Canada* 105 C7
Meaulne, *France* 19 F9
Meaux, *France* 19 D9
Mebechi-Gawa →, *Japan* 54 D10
Mecanhelas, *Mozam.* 87 F4
Mecca = Makkah, *Si. Arabia* 74 C2
Mecca, *U.S.A.* 117 M10
Mechanicsburg, *U.S.A.* 110 F8
Mechanicville, *U.S.A.* 111 D11
Mechara, *Ethiopia* 81 F5
Mechelen, *Belgium* 17 C4
Mecheria, *Algeria* 78 B5
Mechernich, *Germany* 24 E2
Mechetinskaya, *Russia* 49 G5
Mecidiye, *Turkey* 41 F10
Mecitözü, *Turkey* 72 B6
Mecklenburg-Vorpommern □, *Germany* 24 B8
Mecklenburger Bucht, *Germany* 24 A7
Meconta, *Mozam.* 87 E4
Mecsek, *Hungary* 42 D3
Meda, *Portugal* 34 E3
Medan, *Indonesia* 62 D1
Medanosa, Pta., *Argentina* 128 F3
Mede, *Italy* 28 C5
Médéa, *Algeria* 78 A6
Mededa, *Bos.-H.* 42 G4
Medellín, *Colombia* 124 B3
Medelpad, *Sweden* 10 B10
Medemblik, *Neths.* 17 B5
Mederdra, *Mauritania* 82 B1
Medford, *Mass., U.S.A.* 111 D13
Medford, *Oreg., U.S.A.* 114 E2
Medford, *Wis., U.S.A.* 112 C9
Medgidia, *Romania* 43 F13
Medi, *Sudan* 81 F3
Media Agua, *Argentina* 126 C2
Media Luna, *Argentina* 126 C2
Medianeira, *Brazil* 127 B5
Mediaş, *Romania* 43 D9
Medicina, *Italy* 29 D8
Medicine Bow, *U.S.A.* 114 F10
Medicine Bow Pk., *U.S.A.* 114 F10
Medicine Bow Ra., *U.S.A.* 114 F10
Medicine Hat, *Canada* 105 D6
Medicine Lake, *U.S.A.* 112 A2
Medicine Lodge, *U.S.A.* 113 G5
Medina = Al Madīnah, *Si. Arabia* 70 E3
Medina, *N. Dak., U.S.A.* 112 B5
Medina, *N.Y., U.S.A.* 110 C6
Medina, *Ohio, U.S.A.* 110 E3
Medina →, *U.S.A.* 113 L5
Medina de Pomar, *Spain* 34 C7
Medina de Ríoseco, *Spain* 34 D5
Medina del Campo, *Spain* 34 D6
Medina L., *U.S.A.* 113 L5
Medina Sidonia, *Spain* 35 J5
Medinaceli, *Spain* 32 D2
Medinipur, *India* 69 H12
Mediterranean Sea, *Europe* 6 H7
Médoc, *France* 20 C3
Medulin, *Croatia* 29 D10
Medveđa, *Serbia, Yug.* 40 D5
Medvedevo, *Russia* 48 B8
Medveditsa →, *Tver, Russia* 46 D9
Medveditsa →, *Volgograd, Russia* 48 F6
Medvedok, *Russia* 48 B10
Medvezhi, Ostrava, *Russia* 51 B17
Medvezhyegorsk, *Russia* 50 C4
Medway →, *U.K.* 13 F8
Medway Towns □, *U.K.* 13 F8
Medzev, *Slovak Rep.* 27 C13
Medzilaborce, *Slovak Rep.* 27 B14
Medžitlija, *Macedonia* 40 F5
Meekatharra, *Australia* 93 E2
Meeker, *U.S.A.* 114 F10
Meelpaeg Res., *Canada* 103 C8
Meersburg, *Germany* 25 H5
Meerut, *India* 68 E7
Meeteetse, *U.S.A.* 114 D9
Mega, *Ethiopia* 81 G4
Megálo Khorío, *Greece* 39 E9
Megálo Petalí, *Greece* 38 D6
Megalópolis, *Greece* 38 D4
Meganísi, *Greece* 38 C2
Mégara, *Greece* 38 D5
Megasini, *India* 69 J12
Megdhova →, *Greece* 38 B3
Megève, *France* 21 C10
Meghalaya □, *India* 67 G17
Meghezez, *Ethiopia* 81 F4
Mégiscane, L., *Canada* 102 C4
Megiste, *Greece* 39 E11
Megra, *Russia* 46 B9
Mehadia, *Romania* 42 F7
Meharry, Mt., *Australia* 92 D2
Mehedeby, *Sweden* 10 D11
Mehedinţi □, *Romania* 42 F7
Meheisa, *Sudan* 80 D3
Mehlville, *U.S.A.* 112 F9
Mehndawal, *India* 69 F10
Mehr Jān, *Iran* 71 C7
Mehrābād, *Iran* 70 B5
Mehrān, *Iran* 70 C5
Mehrīz, *Iran* 71 D7
Mehun-sur-Yèvre, *France* 19 E9
Mei Jiang →, *China* 59 E11
Mei Xian, *China* 56 G4
Meicheng, *China* 59 C12
Meichengzhen, *China* 59 C8
Meichuan, *China* 59 B10
Meigu, *China* 58 C4
Meiktila, *Burma* 67 J19
Meinerzhagen, *Germany* 24 D3
Meiningen, *Germany* 24 E6
Meira, Serra de, *Spain* 34 B3
Meiringen, *Switz.* 25 J4
Meishan, *China* 58 B4
Meissen, *Germany* 24 D9
Meissner, *Germany* 24 D5
Meitan, *China* 58 D6
Meizhou, *China* 59 E11
Meja, *India* 69 G10
Mejillones, *Chile* 126 A1
Mekdela, *Ethiopia* 81 E4
Mekele, *Ethiopia* 81 E4
Mekhtar, *Pakistan* 66 D6
Meknès, *Morocco* 78 B4
Meko, *Nigeria* 83 D5
Mekong →, *Asia* 65 H6
Mekongga, *Indonesia* 63 E6
Mekrou →, *Benin* 83 C5
Mekvari = Kür →, *Azerbaijan* 73 C13
Mel, *Italy* 29 B9
Melagiri Hills, *India* 66 N10
Melaka, *Malaysia* 65 L4
Melalap, *Malaysia* 62 C5

Mélambes, *Greece* 36 D6
Melanesia, *Pac. Oc.* 96 H7
Melbourne, *Australia* 95 F4
Melbourne, *U.S.A.* 109 L5
Melchor Múzquiz, *Mexico* 118 B4
Melchor Ocampo, *Mexico* 118 C4
Méldola, *Italy* 29 D9
Meldorf, *Germany* 24 A5
Melegnano, *Italy* 28 C6
Melenci, *Serbia, Yug.* 42 E5
Melenki, *Russia* 48 C5
Mélèzes →, *Qué., Canada* 101 C12
Mélèzes →, *Qué., Canada* 102 A5
Melfi, *Italy* 31 B8
Melfort, *Canada* 105 C8
Melfort, *Zimbabwe* 87 F3
Melgaço, *Portugal* 34 C2
Melgar de Fernamental, *Spain* 34 C6
Melhus, *Norway* 8 E14
Melide, *Spain* 34 C2
Meligalá, *Greece* 38 D3
Melilla, *N. Afr.* 78 A5
Melilli, *Italy* 31 E8
Melipilla, *Chile* 126 C1
Mélissa, Ákra, *Greece* 36 D6
Mélissa Óros, *Greece* 39 D8
Melita, *Canada* 105 D8
Mélito di Porto Salvo, *Italy* 31 E8
Melitopol, *Ukraine* 47 J8
Melk, *Austria* 26 C8
Mellan Fryken, *Sweden* 10 E7
Mellansel, *Sweden* 8 E18
Mellbystrand, *Sweden* 11 H6
Melle, *France* 20 B3
Melle, *Germany* 24 C4
Mellen, *U.S.A.* 112 B9
Mellerud, *Sweden* 11 F6
Mellette, *U.S.A.* 112 C5
Mellid = Melide, *Spain* 34 C2
Mellieha, *Malta* 36 D1
Mellit, *Sudan* 81 E2
Mellrichstadt, *Germany* 24 E6
Melnik, *Bulgaria* 40 E7
Mělník, *Czech Rep.* 26 A7
Melo, *Uruguay* 127 C5
Melolo, *Indonesia* 63 F6
Melouprey, *Cambodia* 64 F5
Melrose, *Australia* 95 E4
Melrose, *U.K.* 14 F6
Melrose, *Minn., U.S.A.* 112 C7
Melrose, *N. Mex., U.S.A.* 113 H3
Melstone, *U.S.A.* 114 C10
Melsungen, *Germany* 24 D5
Melton Mowbray, *U.K.* 12 E7
Melun, *France* 19 D9
Melut, *Sudan* 81 E3
Melville, *Canada* 105 C8
Melville, C., *Australia* 94 A3
Melville, L., *Canada* 103 B8
Melville B., *Australia* 94 A2
Melville I., *Australia* 92 B5
Melville I., *Canada* 4 B2
Melville Pen., *Canada* 101 B11
Mélykút, *Hungary* 42 D4
Memaliaj, *Albania* 40 F3
Memba, *Mozam.* 87 E5
Memboro, *Indonesia* 63 F5
Membrilla, *Spain* 35 G7
Memel = Klaìpėda, *Lithuania* 9 J19
Memel, *S. Africa* 89 D4
Memmingen, *Germany* 25 H6
Mempawah, *Indonesia* 62 D3
Memphis, *Egypt* 80 J7
Memphis, *Mich., U.S.A.* 110 D2
Memphis, *Tenn., U.S.A.* 113 H10
Memphis, *Tex., U.S.A.* 113 H4
Memphremagog, L., *U.S.A.* 111 B12
Mena, *Ukraine* 47 G7
Mena, *U.S.A.* 113 H7
Mena →, *Ethiopia* 81 F5
Menai Strait, *U.K.* 12 D3
Ménaka, *Mali* 83 B5
Menan = Chao Phraya →, *Thailand* 64 F3
Menarandra →, *Madag.* 89 D7
Menard, *U.S.A.* 113 K5
Menawashei, *Sudan* 81 E1
Mendawai →, *Indonesia* 62 E4
Mende, *France* 20 D7
Mendebo, *Ethiopia* 81 F4
Menden, *Germany* 24 D3
Menderes, *Turkey* 39 C9
Mendez, *Mexico* 119 B5
Mendhar, *India* 69 C6
Mendi, *Ethiopia* 81 F4
Mendip Hills, *U.K.* 13 F5
Mendocino, *U.S.A.* 114 G2
Mendocino, C., *U.S.A.* 114 F1
Mendooran, *Australia* 95 E4
Mendota, *Calif., U.S.A.* 116 J6
Mendota, *Ill., U.S.A.* 112 E10
Mendoza, *Argentina* 126 C2
Mendoza □, *Argentina* 126 C2
Mene Grande, *Venezuela* 124 B4
Menemen, *Turkey* 39 C9
Menen, *Belgium* 17 D3
Menfi, *Italy* 30 E5
Mengdingjie, *China* 58 F2
Mengeš, *Slovenia* 29 B11
Menggala, *Indonesia* 62 E3
Menghai, *China* 58 G3
Mengíbar, *Spain* 35 H7
Mengjin, *China* 56 G7
Mengla, *China* 58 G3
Menglian, *China* 58 F2
Mengshan, *China* 59 E8
Mengyin, *China* 57 G9
Mengzhe, *China* 58 F3
Mengzi, *China* 58 F4
Menihek, *Canada* 103 B6
Menihek L., *Canada* 103 B6
Menin = Menen, *Belgium* 17 D3
Menindee, *Australia* 95 E3
Menindee L., *Australia* 95 E3
Meningie, *Australia* 95 F2
Menlo Park, *U.S.A.* 116 H4
Menominee, *U.S.A.* 108 C2
Menominee →, *U.S.A.* 108 C2
Menomonie, *U.S.A.* 112 C9
Menongue, *Angola* 85 G3
Menorca, *Spain* 37 B11
Mentakab, *Malaysia* 65 L4
Mentawai, Kepulauan, *Indonesia* 62 E1
Menton, *France* 21 E11
Mentor, *U.S.A.* 110 E3
Menzies, *Australia* 93 E3
Meob B., *Namibia* 88 B2
Me'ona, *Israel* 75 B4
Meoqui, *Mexico* 118 B3
Mepaco, *Mozam.* 87 F3
Meppel, *Neths.* 17 B6
Meppen, *Germany* 24 C3
Mequinenza, *Spain* 32 D5
Mequinenza, Embalse de, *Spain* 32 D5
Mer, *France* 18 E8
Merabéllou, Kólpos, *Greece* 36 D7
Merak, *Indonesia* 63 F12
Meramangye, L., *Australia* 93 E5
Meran = Merano, *Italy* 29 B8
Merano, *Italy* 29 B8
Merate, *Italy* 28 C6
Merauke, *Indonesia* 63 F10
Merbein, *Australia* 95 E3
Merca, *Somali Rep.* 74 G3
Mercato Saraceno, *Italy* 29 E9
Merced, *U.S.A.* 116 H6
Merced →, *U.S.A.* 116 H6
Merced Pk., *U.S.A.* 116 H7
Mercedes, *Buenos Aires, Argentina* 126 C4
Mercedes, *Corrientes, Argentina* 126 B4
Mercedes, *San Luis, Argentina* 126 C2
Mercedes, *Uruguay* 126 C4
Mercedes, *U.S.A.* 113 M6
Merceditas, *Chile* 126 B1
Mercer, *N.Z.* 91 G5
Mercer, *U.S.A.* 110 E4
Mercer Island, *U.S.A.* 116 C4
Mercury, *U.S.A.* 117 J11
Mercy C., *Canada* 101 B13
Merdrignac, *France* 18 D4
Mere, *U.K.* 13 F5
Meredith, C., *Falk. Is.* 128 G4
Meredith, L., *U.S.A.* 113 H4
Merefa, *Ukraine* 47 H9
Merei, *Romania* 43 E11
Merga = Nukheila, *Sudan* 80 D2
Mergui, *Burma* 64 F2
Mergui Arch. = Myeik Kyunzu, *Burma* 65 G1
Meriç, *Turkey* 41 E10
Meriç →, *Turkey* 41 F10
Mérida, *Mexico* 119 C7
Mérida, *Spain* 35 G4
Mérida, *Venezuela* 124 B4
Mérida, Cord. de, *Venezuela* 122 C3
Meriden, *U.K.* 13 E6
Meriden, *U.S.A.* 111 E12
Meridian, *Calif., U.S.A.* 116 F5
Meridian, *Idaho, U.S.A.* 114 E5
Meridian, *Miss., U.S.A.* 109 J1
Mérignac, *France* 20 D3
Merimbula, *Australia* 95 F4
Mérinaghène, *Senegal* 82 B1
Merinda, *Australia* 94 C4
Mering, *Germany* 25 G6
Meringa, *Nigeria* 83 C7
Meringur, *Australia* 95 E3
Merir, *Pac. Oc.* 63 D8
Merirumã, *Brazil* 125 C8
Merkel, *U.S.A.* 113 J5
Mermaid Reef, *Australia* 92 C2
Merowe, *Sudan* 80 D3
Merredin, *Australia* 93 F2
Merrick, *U.K.* 14 F4
Merrickville, *Canada* 111 B9
Merrill, *Oreg., U.S.A.* 114 E3
Merrill, *Wis., U.S.A.* 112 C10
Merrimack →, *U.S.A.* 111 D14
Merriman, *U.S.A.* 112 D4
Merritt, *Canada* 104 C4
Merritt Island, *U.S.A.* 109 L5
Merriwa, *Australia* 95 E5
Merry I., *Canada* 102 A4
Merryville, *U.S.A.* 113 K8
Mersa Fatma, *Eritrea* 81 E5
Mersch, *Lux.* 17 E6
Merse →, *Italy* 29 E8
Mersea I., *U.K.* 13 F8
Merseburg, *Germany* 24 D7
Mersey →, *U.K.* 12 D4
Merseyside □, *U.K.* 12 D4
Mersin, *Turkey* 70 B2
Mersing, *Malaysia* 65 L4
Merta, *India* 68 F6
Merta Road, *India* 68 F5
Merthyr Tydfil, *U.K.* 13 F4
Merthyr Tydfil □, *U.K.* 13 F4
Mértola, *Portugal* 35 H3
Mertzon, *U.S.A.* 113 K4
Méru, *France* 19 C9
Meru, *Kenya* 86 B4
Meru, *Tanzania* 86 C4
Merville, *France* 19 B9
Méry-sur-Seine, *France* 19 D10
Merzifon, *Turkey* 72 B6
Merzig, *Germany* 25 F2
Mesa, *U.S.A.* 115 K8
Mesa Verde National Park, *U.S.A.* 115 H9
Mesagne, *Italy* 31 B10
Mesanagrós, *Greece* 36 C9
Mesaoría □, *Cyprus* 36 D12
Mesarás, Kólpos, *Greece* 36 D6
Meschede, *Germany* 24 D4
Mescit, *Turkey* 73 B9
Mesfinto, *Ethiopia* 81 E4
Mesgouez, L., *Canada* 102 B5
Meshchovsk, *Russia* 46 E8
Meshed = Mashhad, *Iran* 71 B8
Meshoppen, *U.S.A.* 111 E8
Meshra er Req, *Sudan* 81 F2
Mesilinka →, *Canada* 104 B4
Mesilla, *U.S.A.* 115 K10
Meslay-du-Maine, *France* 18 E6
Mesocco, *Switz.* 25 J5
Mesolóngion, *Greece* 38 C3
Mesopotamia = Al Jazirah, *Iraq* 70 C5
Mesopotamia, *U.S.A.* 110 E4
Mesopótamon, *Greece* 38 B2
Mesoraca, *Italy* 31 C9
Mésou Volímais = Volímai, *Greece* 38 D2
Mesquite, *U.S.A.* 115 H6
Messac, *France* 18 E5
Messad, *Algeria* 78 B6
Messalo →, *Mozam.* 87 E4
Méssaména, *Cameroon* 83 E7
Messeue, *Greece* 38 D3
Messina, *Italy* 31 D8
Messina, *S. Africa* 89 C5
Messina, Str. di, *Italy* 31 D8
Messíni, *Greece* 38 D4
Messinía □, *Greece* 38 D3
Messiniakós Kólpos, *Greece* 38 E4
Messkirch, *Germany* 25 H5
Messonghi, *Greece* 36 B3
Mesta →, *Bulgaria* 40 E7
Mestá, Ákra, *Greece* 39 C7
Mestanza, *Spain* 35 G6
Mestre, *Italy* 29 C9
Mesudiye, *Turkey* 72 B7
Meta →, *S. Amer.* 122 C4
Meta Incognita Peninsula, *Canada* 101 B13
Metabetchouan, *Canada* 103 C5
Metairie, *U.S.A.* 113 L9
Metalici, Munţii, *Romania* 42 D7
Metaline Falls, *U.S.A.* 114 B5
Metallifere, Colline, *Italy* 28 E8
Metán, *Argentina* 126 B3
Metangula, *Mozam.* 87 E3
Metauro →, *Italy* 29 E10
Metema, *Ethiopia* 81 E4
Metengobalame, *Mozam.* 87 E3
Méthana, *Greece* 38 D5
Methóni, *Greece* 38 E3
Methven, *N.Z.* 91 K3
Metil, *Mozam.* 87 F4
Metkovets, *Bulgaria* 40 C7
Metković, *Croatia* 29 E14
Metlakatla, *U.S.A.* 100 C6
Metlika, *Slovenia* 29 C12
Metropolis, *U.S.A.* 113 G10
Métsovon, *Greece* 38 B3
Mettur Dam, *India* 66 P10
Metu, *Ethiopia* 81 F4
Metz, *France* 19 C13
Metzingen, *Germany* 25 G5
Meulaboh, *Indonesia* 62 D1
Meung-sur-Loire, *France* 19 E8
Meureudu, *Indonesia* 62 C1
Meurthe →, *France* 19 D13
Meurthe-et-Moselle □, *France* 19 D13
Meuse □, *France* 19 C12
Meuse →, *Europe* 17 D5
Meuselwitz, *Germany* 24 D8
Mexia, *U.S.A.* 113 K6
Mexiana, I., *Brazil* 125 D9
Mexicali, *Mexico* 117 N11
Mexican Plateau, *Mexico* 98 G9
Mexican Water, *U.S.A.* 115 H9
México, *Mexico* 119 D5
Mexico, *Maine, U.S.A.* 111 B14
Mexico, *Mo., U.S.A.* 112 F9
Mexico, *N.Y., U.S.A.* 111 C8
México □, *Mexico* 119 D5
Mexico ■, *Cent. Amer.* 118 C4
Mexico, G. of, *Cent. Amer.* 119 C7
Mexico B., *U.S.A.* 111 C8
Meydān-e Naftūn, *Iran* 71 D6
Meydani, Ra's-e, *Iran* 71 E8
Meyenburg, *Germany* 24 B8
Meymac, *France* 20 C6
Meymaneh, *Afghan.* 66 B4
Meyrueis, *France* 20 D7
Meyssac, *France* 20 C5
Meyzieu, *France* 21 C8
Mezdra, *Bulgaria* 40 C7
Mèze, *France* 20 E7
Mezen, *Russia* 50 C5
Mezen →, *Russia* 50 C5
Mézenc, Mt., *France* 21 D8
Mezeş, Munţii, *Romania* 42 C8
Mezha →, *Russia* 46 E6
Mezhdurechenskiy, *Russia* 50 D7
Mézidon-Canon, *France* 18 C6
Mézières-en-Brenne, *France* 20 B5
Mézilhac, *France* 21 D8
Mézin, *France* 20 D4
Mezöberény, *Hungary* 42 D6
Mezőfalva, *Hungary* 42 D3
Mezőhegyes, *Hungary* 42 D5
Mezőkövácsháza, *Hungary* 42 D5
Mezőkövesd, *Hungary* 42 C5
Mézos, *France* 20 D2
Mezőtúr, *Hungary* 42 C5
Mezquital, *Mexico* 118 C4
Mezzolombardo, *Italy* 28 B8
Mfolozi →, *S. Africa* 89 D5
Mgeta, *Tanzania* 87 D4
Mglin, *Russia* 47 F7
Mhlaba Hills, *Zimbabwe* 87 F3
Mhow, *India* 68 H6
Miahuatlán, *Mexico* 119 D5
Miajadas, *Spain* 35 F5
Miami, *Fla., U.S.A.* 109 N5
Miami, *Okla., U.S.A.* 113 G7
Miami, *Tex., U.S.A.* 113 H4
Miami Beach, *U.S.A.* 109 N5
Mian Xian, *China* 56 H4
Mianchi, *China* 56 G6
Mīāndarreh, *Iran* 71 C7
Mīāndowāb, *Iran* 70 B5
Miandrivazo, *Madag.* 89 B8
Mīāneh, *Iran* 70 B5
Mianning, *China* 58 C4
Mianwali, *Pakistan* 68 C4
Mianyang, *China* 58 B5
Mianzhu, *China* 58 B5
Miaoli, *Taiwan* 59 E13
Miarinarivo, *Antananarivo, Madag.* 89 B8
Miarinarivo, *Toamasina, Madag.* 89 B8
Miariravaratra, *Madag.* 89 C8
Miass, *Russia* 50 D7
Miasteczko Krajeńskie, *Poland* 45 E4
Miastko, *Poland* 44 E3
Mica, *S. Africa* 89 C5
Micăsasa, *Romania* 43 D9
Michalovce, *Slovak Rep.* 27 C14
Michigan □, *U.S.A.* 108 C3
Michigan, L., *U.S.A.* 108 D2
Michigan City, *U.S.A.* 108 E2
Michika, *Nigeria* 83 C7
Michipicoten I., *Canada* 102 C2
Michoacan □, *Mexico* 118 D4
Michurin, *Bulgaria* 41 D11
Michurinsk, *Russia* 48 D5
Mico, Pta., *Nic.* 120 D3
Micronesia, *Pac. Oc.* 96 G7
Micronesia, Federated States of ■, *Pac. Oc.* 96 G7
Midai, *Indonesia* 65 L6
Midale, *Canada* 105 D8
Middelburg, *Neths.* 17 C3
Middelburg, *Eastern Cape, S. Africa* 88 E4
Middelburg, *Mpumalanga, S. Africa* 89 D4
Middelfart, *Denmark* 11 J3
Middelpos, *S. Africa* 88 E3
Middelwit, *S. Africa* 88 C4
Middle Alkali L., *U.S.A.* 114 F3
Middle Bass I., *U.S.A.* 110 E2
Middle East, *Asia* 52 F7
Middle Fork Feather →, *U.S.A.* 116 F5
Middle I., *Australia* 93 F3
Middle Loup →, *U.S.A.* 112 E5
Middle Sackville, *Canada* 103 D7
Middleboro, *U.S.A.* 111 E14
Middleburg, *Fla., U.S.A.* 109 K5
Middleburg, *N.Y., U.S.A.* 111 D10
Middleburg, *Pa., U.S.A.* 110 F7
Middlebury, *U.S.A.* 111 B11
Middlemount, *Australia* 94 C4
Middleport, *N.Y., U.S.A.* 110 C6
Middleport, *Ohio, U.S.A.* 108 F4
Middlesboro, *U.S.A.* 109 G4
Middlesbrough, *U.K.* 12 C6
Middlesbrough □, *U.K.* 12 C6
Middlesex, *Belize* 120 C2
Middlesex, *N.J., U.S.A.* 111 F10
Middlesex, *N.Y., U.S.A.* 110 D7
Middleton, *Australia* 94 C3
Middleton, *Canada* 103 D6
Middleton Cr. →, *Australia* 94 C3
Middletown, *U.K.* 15 B5
Middletown, *Calif., U.S.A.* 116 G4
Middletown, *Conn., U.S.A.* 111 E12
Middletown, *N.Y., U.S.A.* 111 E10
Middletown, *Ohio, U.S.A.* 108 F3
Middletown, *Pa., U.S.A.* 111 F8
Midhurst, *U.K.* 13 G7
Midī, *Yemen* 81 D5
Midi, Canal du →, *France* 20 E5
Midi d'Ossau, Pic du, *France* 20 F3
Midi-Pyrénées □, *France* 20 E5
Midland, *Canada* 102 D4
Midland, *Calif., U.S.A.* 117 M12
Midland, *Mich., U.S.A.* 108 D3
Midland, *Pa., U.S.A.* 110 F4
Midland, *Tex., U.S.A.* 113 K3
Midlands □, *Zimbabwe* 87 F2
Midleton, *Ireland* 15 E3
Midlothian, *U.S.A.* 113 J6
Midlothian □, *U.K.* 14 F5
Midongy, Tangorombohitr' i, *Madag.* 89 C8
Midongy Atsimo, *Madag.* 89 C8
Midou →, *France* 20 E3
Midouze →, *France* 20 E3
Midsayap, *Phil.* 61 H6
Midu, *China* 58 E3
Midway Is., *Pac. Oc.* 96 E10
Midway Wells, *U.S.A.* 117 N11
Midwest, *U.S.A.* 107 B9
Midwest, *Wyo., U.S.A.* 114 E10
Midwest City, *U.S.A.* 113 H6
Midyat, *Turkey* 70 B4
Midžor, *Bulgaria* 40 C6
Mie □, *Japan* 55 G8
Miechów, *Poland* 45 H7
Miedwie, Jezioro, *Poland* 45 E1
Międzybórz, *Poland* 45 G4
Międzychód, *Poland* 45 F2
Międzylesie, *Poland* 45 H3
Międzyrzec Podlaski, *Poland* 45 G9
Międzyrzecz, *Poland* 45 F2
Międzyzdroje, *Poland* 44 E1
Miejska Górka, *Poland* 45 G3
Miélan, *France* 20 E4
Mielec, *Poland* 45 H8
Mienga, *Angola* 88 B2
Miercurea-Ciuc, *Romania* 43 D10
Miercurea Sibiului, *Romania* 43 E8
Mieres, *Spain* 34 B5
Mieroszów, *Poland* 45 H3
Mieso, *Ethiopia* 81 F5
Mieszkowice, *Poland* 45 F1
Mifflintown, *U.S.A.* 110 F7
Mifraz Ḥefa, *Israel* 75 C4
Migennes, *France* 19 E10
Migliarino, *Italy* 29 D8
Miguel Alemán, Presa, *Mexico* 119 D5
Miguelturra, *Spain* 35 G7
Mihăileni, *Romania* 43 C11
Mihăileşti, *Romania* 43 F10
Mihailovca, *Moldova* 43 D13
Mihalgazi, *Turkey* 39 A12
Mihaliççık, *Turkey* 72 C4
Mihara, *Japan* 55 G6
Miheşu de Cîmpie, *Romania* 43 D9
Mijas, *Spain* 35 J6
Mikese, *Tanzania* 86 D4
Mikha-Tskhakaya = Senaki, *Georgia* 49 J6
Mikhailovka = Mykhaylivka, *Ukraine* 47 J8
Mikhaylov, *Russia* 46 E10
Mikhaylovgrad = Montana, *Bulgaria* 40 C7
Mikhaylovka, *Russia* 48 E6
Mikhnevo, *Russia* 46 E9
Mikínai, *Greece* 38 D4
Mikkeli, *Finland* 9 F22
Mikkwa →, *Canada* 104 B6
Mikniya, *Sudan* 81 D3
Mikołajki, *Poland* 44 E8
Míkonos, *Greece* 39 D7
Míkrí Préspa, Límni, *Greece* 40 F5
Míkrón Dhérion, *Greece* 41 E10
Mikstat, *Poland* 45 G4
Mikulov, *Czech Rep.* 27 C9
Mikumi, *Tanzania* 86 D4
Milaca, *U.S.A.* 112 C8
Milagro, *Ecuador* 124 D3
Milagros, *Phil.* 61 E5
Milan = Milano, *Italy* 28 C6
Milan, *Mo., U.S.A.* 112 E8
Milan, *Tenn., U.S.A.* 109 H1
Milang, *Australia* 95 F2
Milange, *Mozam.* 87 F4
Milano, *Italy* 28 C6
Milanoa, *Madag.* 89 A8
Milâs, *Turkey* 39 D9
Mílatos, *Greece* 36 D7
Milazzo, *Italy* 31 D8
Milbank, *U.S.A.* 112 C6
Milbanke Sd., *Canada* 104 C3
Milden, *Canada* 105 C7
Mildenhall, *U.K.* 13 E8
Mildmay, *Canada* 110 B3
Mildura, *Australia* 95 E3
Mile, *China* 58 E4
Miléai, *Greece* 38 B5
Miles, *Australia* 95 D5
Miles City, *U.S.A.* 112 B2
Mileşti, *Moldova* 43 C13
Milestone, *Canada* 105 D8
Mileto, *Italy* 31 D9
Miletto, Mte., *Italy* 31 A7
Miletus, *Turkey* 39 D9
Milevsko, *Czech Rep.* 26 B7
Milford, *Calif., U.S.A.* 116 E6
Milford, *Conn., U.S.A.* 111 E11
Milford, *Del., U.S.A.* 108 F8
Milford, *Mass., U.S.A.* 111 D13
Milford, *N.H., U.S.A.* 111 D13
Milford, *Pa., U.S.A.* 111 E10
Milford, *Utah, U.S.A.* 115 G7
Milford Haven, *U.K.* 13 F2
Milford Sd., *N.Z.* 91 L1
Milḥ, Baḥr al, *Iraq* 70 C4
Milicz, *Poland* 45 G4
Milikapiti, *Australia* 92 B5
Miling, *Australia* 93 F2
Militello in Val di Catánia, *Italy* 31 E7
Milk →, *U.S.A.* 114 B10
Milk, Wadi el →, *Sudan* 80 D3
Milk River, *Canada* 104 D6
Mill I., *Antarctica* 5 C8
Mill Valley, *U.S.A.* 116 H4
Millárs →, *Spain* 32 F4
Millau, *France* 20 D7
Millbridge, *Canada* 110 B7
Millbrook, *Canada* 110 B6
Millbrook, *U.S.A.* 111 E11
Mille Lacs, L. des, *Canada* 102 C1
Mille Lacs L., *U.S.A.* 112 B8
Milledgeville, *U.S.A.* 109 J4
Millen, *U.S.A.* 109 J5
Miller, *U.S.A.* 112 C5
Millerovo, *Russia* 49 F5
Millersburg, *Ohio, U.S.A.* 110 F3
Millersburg, *Pa., U.S.A.* 110 F8
Millerton, *U.S.A.* 111 E11
Millerton L., *U.S.A.* 116 J7
Millevaches, Plateau de, *France* 20 C6
Millheim, *U.S.A.* 110 F7
Millicent, *Australia* 95 F3

Millington, U.S.A. 113 H10
Millinocket, U.S.A. 109 C11
Millmerran, Australia 95 D5
Millom, U.K. 12 C4
Mills L., Canada 104 A5
Millsboro, U.S.A. 110 G5
Milltown Malbay, Ireland 15 D2
Millville, N.J., U.S.A. 108 F8
Millville, Pa., U.S.A. 111 E8
Millwood L., U.S.A. 113 J8
Milna, Croatia 29 E13
Milne →, Australia 94 C2
Milo, U.S.A. 109 C11
Mílos, Greece 38 E6
Miłosław, Poland 45 F4
Milot, Albania 40 E3
Milparinka, Australia 95 D3
Miltenberg, Germany 25 F5
Milton, N.S., Canada 103 D7
Milton, Ont., Canada 110 C5
Milton, N.Z. 91 M2
Milton, Calif., U.S.A. 116 G6
Milton, Fla., U.S.A. 109 K2
Milton, Pa., U.S.A. 110 F8
Milton, Vt., U.S.A. 111 B11
Milton-Freewater, U.S.A. 114 D4
Milton Keynes, U.K. 13 E7
Milton Keynes □, U.K. 13 E7
Miluo, China 59 C9
Milverton, Canada 110 C4
Milwaukee, U.S.A. 108 D2
Milwaukee Deep, Atl. Oc. 121 C6
Milwaukie, U.S.A. 116 E4
Mim, Ghana 82 D4
Mimizan, France 20 D2
Mimoň, Czech Rep. 26 A7
Min Jiang →, Fujian, China 59 E12
Min Jiang →, Sichuan, China 58 C5
Min Xian, China 56 G3
Mina Pirquitas, Argentina 126 A2
Mīnā Su'ud, Si. Arabia 71 D6
Mīnā'al Aḩmadī, Kuwait 71 D6
Minago →, Canada 105 C9
Minaki, Canada 105 D10
Minamata, Japan 55 H5
Minami-Tori-Shima, Pac. Oc. 96 E7
Minas, Uruguay 127 C4
Minas, Sierra de las, Guatemala 120 C2
Minas Basin, Canada 103 C7
Minas de Rio Tinto = Minas de Riotinto, Spain 35 H4
Minas de Riotinto, Spain 35 H4
Minas Gerais □, Brazil 125 G9
Minatitlán, Mexico 119 D6
Minbu, Burma 67 J19
Minchinabad, Pakistan 68 D5
Mincio →, Italy 28 C7
Minčol, Slovak Rep. 27 B13
Mindanao, Phil. 61 H6
Mindanao Sea = Bohol Sea, Phil. 63 C6
Mindanao Trench, Pac. Oc. 61 F7
Mindel →, Germany 25 G6
Mindelheim, Germany 25 G6
Minden, Canada 110 B6
Minden, Germany 24 C4
Minden, La., U.S.A. 113 J8
Minden, Nev., U.S.A. 116 G7
Mindiptana, Indonesia 63 F10
Mindoro, Phil. 61 E4
Mindoro Str., Phil. 61 E4
Mine, Japan 55 G5
Minehead, U.K. 13 F4
Mineola, N.Y., U.S.A. 111 F11
Mineola, Tex., U.S.A. 113 J7
Mineral King, U.S.A. 116 J8
Mineral Wells, U.S.A. 113 J5
Mineralnyye Vody, Russia 49 H6
Minersville, U.S.A. 111 F8
Minerva, U.S.A. 110 F3
Minervino Murge, Italy 31 A9
Minetto, U.S.A. 111 C8
Mingäçevir, Azerbaijan 49 K8
Mingäçevir Su Anbarı, Azerbaijan 49 K8
Mingan, Canada 103 B7
Mingechaur = Mingäçevir, Azerbaijan 49 K8
Mingechaurskoye Vdkhr. = Mingäçevir Su Anbarı, Azerbaijan 49 K8
Mingela, Australia 94 B4
Mingenew, Australia 93 E2
Mingera Cr. →, Australia 94 C2
Minggang, China 59 A10
Mingguang, China 59 A11
Mingin, Burma 67 H19
Mingir, Moldova 43 D13
Minglanilla, Spain 33 F3
Minglun, China 58 E7
Mingo Junction, U.S.A. 110 F4
Mingorria, Spain 34 E6
Mingshan, China 58 B4
Mingxi, China 59 D11
Mingyuegue, China 57 C15
Minho = Miño →, Spain 34 D2
Minhou, China 59 E12
Minićevo, Serbia, Yug. 42 G7
Minidoka, U.S.A. 114 E7
Minigwal, L., Australia 93 E3
Minilya →, Australia 93 D1
Minilya Roadhouse, Australia 93 D1
Minipi L., Canada 103 B7
Mink L., Canada 104 A5
Minkammen, Sudan 81 F3
Minna, Nigeria 83 D6
Minneapolis, Kans., U.S.A. 112 F6
Minneapolis, Minn., U.S.A. 112 C8
Minnedosa, Canada 105 C9
Minnesota □, U.S.A. 112 B8
Minnesota →, U.S.A. 112 C8
Minnewaukan, U.S.A. 112 A5
Minnipa, Australia 95 E2
Minnitaki L., Canada 102 C1
Mino, Japan 55 G8
Miño, Spain 34 B2
Miño →, Spain 34 D2
Minoa, Greece 39 F7
Minorca = Menorca, Spain 37 B11
Minot, U.S.A. 112 A4
Minqin, China 56 E2
Minqing, China 59 D12
Minsen, Germany 24 B3
Minsk, Belarus 46 F4
Mińsk Mazowiecki, Poland 45 F8
Mintabie, Australia 95 D1
Mintaka Pass, Pakistan 69 A6
Minteke Daban = Mintaka Pass, Pakistan 69 A6
Minto, Canada 103 C6
Minto, L., Canada 102 A5
Minton, Canada 105 D8
Minturn, U.S.A. 114 G10
Minturno, Italy 30 A6
Minûf, Egypt 80 H7
Minusinsk, Russia 51 D10
Minutang, India 67 E20
Minya el Qamh, Egypt 80 H7
Mionica, Bos.-H. 42 F3
Mionica, Serbia, Yug. 40 B4
Miquelon, Canada 102 C4
Miquelon, St- P. & M. 103 C8
Mir, Niger 83 C7
Mīr Kūh, Iran 71 E8
Mīr Shahdād, Iran 71 E8
Mira, Italy 29 C9
Mira, Portugal 34 E2
Mira →, Portugal 35 H2
Mira por vos Cay, Bahamas 121 B5
Mirabella Eclano, Italy 31 A7
Miraj, India 66 L9
Miram Shah, Pakistan 68 C4
Miramar, Argentina 126 D4
Miramar, Mozam. 89 C6
Miramas, France 21 E8
Mirambeau, France 20 C3
Miramichi, Canada 103 C6
Miramichi B., Canada 103 C7
Miramont-de-Guyenne, France 20 D4
Miranda, Brazil 125 H7
Miranda →, Brazil 124 G7
Miranda de Ebro, Spain 32 C2
Miranda do Corvo, Portugal 34 E2
Miranda do Douro, Portugal 34 D4
Mirande, France 20 E4
Mirandela, Portugal 34 D3
Mirándola, Italy 28 D8
Mirandópolis, Brazil 127 A5
Mirango, Malawi 87 E3
Mirano, Italy 29 C9
Miras, Albania 40 F4
Mirassol, Brazil 127 A6
Mirbāţ, Oman 74 D5
Mirear, Egypt 80 C4
Mirebeau, Côte-d'Or, France 19 E12
Mirebeau, Vienne, France 18 F7
Mirecourt, France 19 D13
Mirgorod = Myrhorod, Ukraine 47 H7
Miri, Malaysia 62 D4
Miriam Vale, Australia 94 C5
Miribel, France 19 G11
Mirim, L., S. Amer. 127 C5
Mirnyy, Russia 51 C12
Miroč, Serbia, Yug. 40 B6
Mirokhan, Pakistan 68 F3
Mirond L., Canada 105 B8
Mirosławiec, Poland 44 E3
Mirpur, Pakistan 69 C5
Mirpur Batoro, Pakistan 68 G3
Mirpur Bibiwari, Pakistan 68 E2
Mirpur Khas, Pakistan 68 G3
Mirpur Sakro, Pakistan 68 G2
Mirria, Niger 83 C6
Mirsk, Poland 45 H2
Mirtağ, Turkey 70 B4
Miryang, S. Korea 57 G15
Mirzaani, Georgia 49 K8
Mirzapur, India 69 G10
Mirzapur-cum-Vindhyachal = Mirzapur, India 69 G10
Misantla, Mexico 119 D5
Misawa, Japan 54 D10
Miscou I., Canada 103 C7
Mish'āb, Ra's al, Si. Arabia 71 D6
Mishan, China 60 B8
Mishawaka, U.S.A. 108 E2
Mishbih, Gebel, Egypt 80 C3
Mishima, Japan 55 G9
Misión, Mexico 117 N10
Misiones □, Argentina 127 B5
Misiones □, Paraguay 126 B4
Miskah, Si. Arabia 70 E4
Miskitos, Cayos, Nic. 120 D3
Miskolc, Hungary 42 B5
Misoke, Dem. Rep. of the Congo 86 C2
Misool, Indonesia 63 E8
Misrātah, Libya 79 B9
Missanabie, Canada 102 C3
Missinaibi →, Canada 102 B3
Missinaibi L., Canada 102 C3
Mission, Canada 104 D4
Mission, S. Dak., U.S.A. 112 D4
Mission, Tex., U.S.A. 113 M5
Mission Beach, Australia 94 B4
Mission Viejo, U.S.A. 117 M9
Missirah, Senegal 82 C1
Missisa L., Canada 102 B2
Missisicabi →, Canada 102 B4
Mississagi →, Canada 102 C3
Mississauga, Canada 110 C5
Mississippi □, U.S.A. 113 J10
Mississippi →, U.S.A. 113 L10
Mississippi L., Canada 111 A8
Mississippi River Delta, U.S.A. 113 L9
Mississippi Sd., U.S.A. 113 K10
Missoula, U.S.A. 114 C7
Missouri □, U.S.A. 112 F8
Missouri →, U.S.A. 112 F9
Missouri City, U.S.A. 113 L7
Missouri Valley, U.S.A. 112 E7
Mist, U.S.A. 116 E3
Mistassibi →, Canada 103 B5
Mistassini, Canada 103 C5
Mistassini →, Canada 103 C5
Mistassini, L., Canada 102 B5
Mistastin L., Canada 103 A7
Mistelbach, Austria 27 C9
Misterbianco, Italy 31 E8
Mistinibi, L., Canada 103 A7
Mistretta, Italy 31 E7
Misty L., Canada 105 B8
Misurata = Misrātah, Libya 79 B9
Mît Ghamr, Egypt 80 H7
Mitatib, Sudan 81 D4
Mitchell, Australia 95 D4
Mitchell, Canada 110 C3
Mitchell, Nebr., U.S.A. 112 E3
Mitchell, Oreg., U.S.A. 114 D3
Mitchell, S. Dak., U.S.A. 112 D6
Mitchell →, Australia 94 B3
Mitchell, Mt., U.S.A. 109 H4
Mitchell Ranges, Australia 94 A2
Mitchelstown, Ireland 15 D3
Mitha Tiwana, Pakistan 68 C5
Mithi, Pakistan 68 G3
Míthimna, Greece 39 B8
Mithrao, Pakistan 68 F3
Mitilíni, Greece 39 B8
Mitilinoí, Greece 39 D8
Mito, Japan 55 F10
Mitrofanovka, Russia 47 H10
Mitrovica = Kosovska Mitrovica, Kosovo, Yug. 40 D4
Mitsinjo, Madag. 89 B8
Mitsiwa, Eritrea 81 D4
Mitsiwa Channel, Eritrea 81 D5
Mitsukaidō, Japan 55 F9
Mittagong, Australia 95 E5
Mittelberg, Austria 26 D3
Mittelfranken □, Germany 25 F6
Mittellandkanal →, Germany 24 C4
Mittenwalde, Germany 24 C9
Mittersill, Austria 26 D5
Mitterteich, Germany 25 F8
Mittweida, Germany 24 E8
Mitú, Colombia 124 C4
Mitumba, Tanzania 86 D3
Mitumba, Mts., Dem. Rep. of the Congo 86 D2
Mitwaba, Dem. Rep. of the Congo 87 D2
Mityana, Uganda 86 B3
Mixteco →, Mexico 119 D5
Miyagi □, Japan 54 E10
Miyâh, W. el →, Egypt 80 C3
Miyah, W. el →, Syria 70 C3
Miyake-Jima, Japan 55 G9
Miyako, Japan 54 E10
Miyako-Jima, Japan 55 M2
Miyako-Rettō, Japan 55 M2
Miyakonojō, Japan 55 J5
Miyani, India 68 J3
Miyanoura-Dake, Japan 55 J5
Miyazaki, Japan 55 J5
Miyazaki □, Japan 55 H5
Miyazu, Japan 55 G7
Miyet, Bahr el = Dead Sea, Asia 75 D4
Miyi, China 58 D4
Miyoshi, Japan 55 G6
Miyun, China 56 D9
Miyun Shuiku, China 57 D9
Mizan Teferi, Ethiopia 81 F4
Mizdah, Libya 79 B8
Mizen Hd., Cork, Ireland 15 E2
Mizen Hd., Wick., Ireland 15 D5
Mizhi, China 56 F6
Mizil, Romania 43 F11
Mizoram □, India 67 H18
Mizpe Ramon, Israel 75 E3
Mizusawa, Japan 54 E10
Mjällby, Sweden 11 H8
Mjöbäck, Sweden 11 G6
Mjölby, Sweden 11 F9
Mjörn, Sweden 11 G6
Mjøsa, Norway 9 F14
Mkata, Tanzania 86 D4
Mkokotoni, Tanzania 86 D4
Mkomazi, Tanzania 86 C4
Mkomazi →, S. Africa 89 E5
Mkulwe, Tanzania 87 D3
Mkumbi, Ras, Tanzania 86 D4
Mkushi, Zambia 87 E2
Mkushi River, Zambia 87 E2
Mkuze, S. Africa 89 D5
Mladá Boleslav, Czech Rep. 26 A7
Mladenovac, Serbia, Yug. 40 B4
Mlala Hills, Tanzania 86 D3
Mlange = Mulanje, Malawi 87 F4
Mlanje, Pic, Malawi 85 H7
Mlava →, Serbia, Yug. 40 B5
Mława, Poland 45 E7
Mlinište, Bos.-H. 29 D13
Mljet, Croatia 29 F14
Mljetski Kanal, Croatia 29 F14
Młynary, Poland 44 D6
Mmabatho, S. Africa 88 D4
Mme, Cameroon 83 D7
Mnichovo Hradiště, Czech Rep. 26 A7
Mo i Rana, Norway 8 C16
Moa, Cuba 121 B4
Moa, Indonesia 63 F7
Moa →, S. Leone 82 D2
Moab, U.S.A. 115 G9
Moala, Fiji 91 D8
Moama, Australia 95 F3
Moamba, Mozam. 89 D5
Moapa, U.S.A. 117 J12
Moate, Ireland 15 C4
Moba, Dem. Rep. of the Congo 86 D2
Mobārakābād, Iran 71 D7
Mobaye, C.A.R. 84 D4
Mobayi, Dem. Rep. of the Congo 84 D4
Moberley Lake, Canada 104 B4
Moberly, U.S.A. 112 F8
Mobile, U.S.A. 109 K1
Mobile B., U.S.A. 109 K2
Mobridge, U.S.A. 112 C4
Mobutu Sese Seko, L. = Albert L., Africa 86 B3
Moc Chau, Vietnam 64 B5
Moc Hoa, Vietnam 65 G5
Mocabe Kasari, Dem. Rep. of the Congo 87 D2
Moçambique, Mozam. 87 F5
Moçâmedes = Namibe, Angola 85 H2
Mocanaqua, U.S.A. 111 E8
Mochudi, Botswana 88 C4
Mocimboa da Praia, Mozam. 87 E5
Mociu, Romania 43 D9
Möckeln, Sweden 11 H8
Mockfjärd, Sweden 10 D8
Moclips, U.S.A. 116 C2
Mocoa, Colombia 124 C3
Mococa, Brazil 127 A6
Mocorito, Mexico 118 B3
Moctezuma, Mexico 118 B3
Moctezuma →, Mexico 119 C5
Mocuba, Mozam. 87 F4
Mocúzari, Presa, Mexico 118 B3
Modane, France 21 C10
Modasa, India 68 H5
Modder →, S. Africa 88 D3
Modderrivier, S. Africa 88 D3
Módena, Italy 28 D7
Modena, U.S.A. 115 H7
Modesto, U.S.A. 116 H6
Módica, Italy 31 F7
Mödling, Austria 27 C9
Modo, Sudan 81 F3
Modra, Slovak Rep. 27 C10
Modriča, Bos.-H. 42 F3
Moe, Australia 95 F4
Moebase, Mozam. 87 F4
Moëlan-sur-Mer, France 18 E3
Moengo, Surinam 125 B8
Moffat, U.K. 14 F5
Moga, India 68 D6
Mogadishu = Muqdisho, Somali Rep. 74 G4
Mogador = Essaouira, Morocco 78 B4
Mogadouro, Portugal 34 D4
Mogalakwena →, S. Africa 89 C4
Mogami-Gawa →, Japan 54 E10
Mogán, Canary Is. 37 G4
Mogaung, Burma 67 G20
Mogente = Moixent, Spain 33 G4
Mogho, Ethiopia 81 G5
Mogi das Cruzes, Brazil 127 A6
Mogi-Guaçu →, Brazil 127 A6
Mogi-Mirim, Brazil 127 A6
Mogielnica, Poland 45 G7
Mogige, Ethiopia 81 F4
Mogilev = Mahilyow, Belarus 46 F6
Mogilev-Podilskiy = Mohyliv-Podilskyy, Ukraine 47 H4
Mogilno, Poland 45 F4
Mogincual, Mozam. 87 F5
Mogliano Véneto, Italy 29 C9
Mogocha, Russia 51 D12
Mogok, Burma 67 H20
Mogollon Rim, U.S.A. 115 J8
Mógoro, Italy 30 C1
Mograt, Sudan 80 D3
Moguer, Spain 35 H4
Mogumber, Australia 93 F2
Mohács, Hungary 42 E3
Mohales Hoek, Lesotho 88 E4
Mohall, U.S.A. 112 A4
Moḩammadābād, Iran 71 B8
Mohammedia, Morocco 78 B4
Mohana →, India 69 G11
Mohanlalganj, India 69 F9
Mohave, L., U.S.A. 117 K12
Mohawk →, U.S.A. 111 D11
Moheda, Sweden 11 G8
Mohenjodaro, Pakistan 68 F3
Mohicanville Reservoir, U.S.A. 110 F3
Möhne →, Germany 24 D3
Mohoro, Tanzania 86 D4
Mohyliv-Podilskyy, Ukraine 47 H4
Moia, Sudan 81 F2
Moidart, L., U.K. 14 E3
Moineşti, Romania 43 D11
Moira →, Canada 110 B7
Moirans, France 21 C9
Moirans-en-Montagne, France 19 F12
Moíres, Greece 36 D6
Mõisaküla, Estonia 9 G21
Moisie, Canada 103 B6
Moisie →, Canada 103 B6
Moissac, France 20 D5
Moita, Portugal 35 G2
Moixent, Spain 33 G4
Möja, Sweden 10 E12
Mojácar, Spain 33 H3
Mojados, Spain 34 D6
Mojave, U.S.A. 117 K8
Mojave Desert, U.S.A. 117 L10
Mojiang, China 58 F3
Mojjo →, Ethiopia 81 F5
Mojkovac, Montenegro, Yug. 40 D3
Mojo, Bolivia 126 A2
Mojo, Ethiopia 81 F4
Mojokerto, Indonesia 63 G15
Mokai, N.Z. 91 H5
Mokambo, Dem. Rep. of the Congo 87 E2
Mokameh, India 69 G11
Mokelumne →, U.S.A. 116 G5
Mokelumne Hill, U.S.A. 116 G6
Mokhós, Greece 36 D7
Mokhotlong, Lesotho 89 D4
Möklinta, Sweden 10 D10
Mokokchung, India 67 F19
Mokolo, Cameroon 83 C7
Mokolo →, S. Africa 89 C4
Mokp'o, S. Korea 57 G14
Mokra Gora, Yugoslavia 40 D4
Mokronog, Slovenia 29 C12
Moksha →, Russia 48 C6
Mokshan, Russia 48 D7
Mokwa, Nigeria 83 D6
Mol, Belgium 17 C5
Mola di Bari, Italy 31 A10
Molale, Ethiopia 81 E4
Moláoi, Greece 38 E4
Molara, Italy 30 B2
Molat, Croatia 29 D11
Molchanovo, Russia 50 D9
Mold, U.K. 12 D4
Moldava nad Bodvou, Slovak Rep. 27 C14
Moldavia = Moldova ■, Europe 43 C13
Moldavia, Romania 43 D12
Molde, Norway 8 E12
Moldova ■, Europe 43 C13
Moldova Nouă, Romania 42 F6
Moldoveana, Vf., Romania 43 E9
Moldoviţa, Romania 43 C10
Mole →, U.K. 13 F7
Mole Creek, Australia 94 G4
Molepolole, Botswana 88 C4
Molfetta, Italy 31 A9
Molina de Aragón, Spain 32 E3
Molina de Segura, Spain 33 G3
Moline, U.S.A. 112 E9
Molinella, Italy 29 D8
Molinos, Argentina 126 B2
Moliro, Dem. Rep. of the Congo 86 D3
Moliterno, Italy 31 B8
Molkom, Sweden 10 E7
Mölle, Sweden 11 H6
Molledo, Spain 34 B6
Mollendo, Peru 124 G4
Mollerin, L., Australia 93 F2
Mollerussa, Spain 32 D5
Mollina, Spain 35 H6
Mölln, Germany 24 B6
Mölltorp, Sweden 11 F8
Mölnlycke, Sweden 11 G6
Molochansk, Ukraine 47 J8
Molochnoye, Ozero, Ukraine 47 J8
Molodechno = Maladzyechna, Belarus 46 E4
Molokai, U.S.A. 106 H16
Molong, Australia 95 E4
Molopo →, Africa 88 D3
Mólos, Greece 38 C4
Molotov = Perm, Russia 50 D6
Molsheim, France 19 D14
Molson L., Canada 105 C9
Molteno, S. Africa 88 E4
Molu, Indonesia 63 F8
Molucca Sea, Indonesia 63 E6
Moluccas = Maluku, Indonesia 63 E7
Moma, Dem. Rep. of the Congo 86 C1
Moma, Mozam. 87 F4
Mombasa, Kenya 86 C4
Mombetsu, Japan 54 B11
Mombuey, Spain 34 C4
Momchilgrad, Bulgaria 41 E9
Momi, Dem. Rep. of the Congo 86 C2
Mompós, Colombia 124 B4
Møn, Denmark 11 K6
Mon →, Burma 67 J19
Mona, Canal de la, W. Indies 121 C6
Mona, Isla, Puerto Rico 121 C6
Mona, Pta., Costa Rica 120 E3
Monaca, U.S.A. 110 F4
Monaco ■, Europe 21 E11
Monadhliath Mts., U.K. 14 D4
Monadnock, Mt., U.S.A. 111 D12
Monaghan, Ireland 15 B5
Monaghan □, Ireland 15 B5
Monahans, U.S.A. 113 K3
Monapo, Mozam. 87 E5
Monar, L., U.K. 14 D3
Monarch Mt., Canada 104 C3
Monashee Mts., Canada 104 C5
Monasterevin, Ireland 15 C4

Monastir = Bitola, *Macedonia* 40 E5
Moncada, *Phil.* 61 D4
Moncalieri, *Italy* 28 D4
Moncalvo, *Italy* 28 C5
Moncão, *Portugal* 34 C2
Moncarapacho, *Portugal* 35 H3
Moncayo, Sierra del, *Spain* 32 D3
Mönchengladbach, *Germany* 24 D2
Monchique, *Portugal* 35 H2
Moncks Corner, *U.S.A.* 109 J5
Monclova, *Mexico* 118 B4
Moncontour, *France* 18 D4
Moncton, *Canada* 103 C7
Mondariz, *Spain* 34 C2
Mondego →, *Portugal* 34 E2
Mondego, C., *Portugal* 34 E2
Mondeodo, *Indonesia* 63 E6
Mondeville, *France* 18 C6
Mondolfo, *Italy* 29 E10
Mondoñedo, *Spain* 34 B3
Mondovì, *Italy* 28 D4
Mondragon, *Phil.* 61 E6
Mondragone, *Italy* 30 A6
Mondrain I., *Australia* 93 F3
Monemvasía, *Greece* 38 E5
Monessen, *U.S.A.* 110 F5
Monesterio, *Spain* 35 G4
Monestier-de-Clermont, *France* 21 D9
Monett, *U.S.A.* 113 G8
Moneymore, *U.K.* 15 B5
Monfalcone, *Italy* 29 C10
Monflanquin, *France* 20 D4
Monforte, *Portugal* 35 F3
Monforte de Lemos, *Spain* 34 C3
Mong Hsu, *Burma* 58 G2
Mong Kung, *Burma* 67 J20
Mong Nai, *Burma* 67 J20
Mong Pawk, *Burma* 67 H21
Mong Ping, *Burma* 58 G2
Mong Ton, *Burma* 67 J21
Mong Wa, *Burma* 67 J22
Mong Yai, *Burma* 67 H21
Mongalla, *Sudan* 81 F3
Mongers, L., *Australia* 93 E2
Monghyr = Munger, *India* 69 G12
Mongibello = Etna, *Italy* 31 E7
Mongo, *Chad* 79 F9
Mongo →, *S. Leone* 82 D2
Mongolia ■, *Asia* 51 E10
Mongonu, *Nigeria* 83 C7
Mongu, *Zambia* 85 H4
Môngua, *Angola* 88 B2
Monifieth, *U.K.* 14 E6
Monistrol-sur-Loire, *France* 21 C8
Monkey Bay, *Malawi* 87 E4
Monkey Mia, *Australia* 93 E1
Monkey River, *Belize* 119 D7
Mońki, *Poland* 44 E9
Monkoto, *Dem. Rep. of the Congo* 84 E4
Monkton, *Canada* 110 C3
Monmouth, *U.K.* 13 F5
Monmouth, *Ill., U.S.A.* 112 E9
Monmouth, *Oreg., U.S.A.* 114 D2
Monmouthshire □, *U.K.* 13 F5
Mono L., *U.S.A.* 116 H7
Monolith, *U.S.A.* 117 K8
Monólithos, *Greece* 36 C9
Monongahela, *U.S.A.* 110 F5
Monópoli, *Italy* 31 B10
Monor, *Hungary* 42 C4
Monóvar, *Spain* 33 G4
Monreal del Campo, *Spain* 32 E3
Monreale, *Italy* 30 D6
Monroe, *Ga., U.S.A.* 109 J4
Monroe, *La., U.S.A.* 113 J8
Monroe, *Mich., U.S.A.* 108 E4
Monroe, *N.C., U.S.A.* 109 H5
Monroe, *N.Y., U.S.A.* 111 E10
Monroe, *Utah, U.S.A.* 115 G7
Monroe, *Wash., U.S.A.* 116 C5
Monroe, *Wis., U.S.A.* 112 D10
Monroe City, *U.S.A.* 112 F9
Monroeton, *U.S.A.* 111 E8
Monroeville, *Ala., U.S.A.* 109 K2
Monroeville, *Pa., U.S.A.* 110 F5
Monrovia, *Liberia* 82 D2
Mons, *Belgium* 17 D3
Møns Klint, *Denmark* 11 K6
Monsaraz, *Portugal* 35 G3
Monse, *Indonesia* 63 E6
Monségur, *France* 20 D4
Monsélice, *Italy* 29 C8
Mönsterås, *Sweden* 11 G10
Mont Cenis, Col du, *France* 21 C10
Mont-de-Marsan, *France* 20 E3
Mont-Joli, *Canada* 103 C6
Mont-Laurier, *Canada* 102 C4
Mont-Louis, *Canada* 103 C6
Mont-roig del Camp, *Spain* 32 D5
Mont-St-Michel, Le = Le Mont-St-Michel, *France* 18 D5
Mont Tremblant, Parc Recr. du, *Canada* 102 C5
Montabaur, *Germany* 24 E3
Montagnac, *France* 20 E7
Montagnana, *Italy* 29 C8
Montagu, *S. Africa* 88 E3
Montagu I., *Antarctica* 5 B1
Montague, *Canada* 103 C7
Montague, I., *Mexico* 118 A2
Montague Ra., *Australia* 93 E2
Montague Sd., *Australia* 92 B4
Montaigu, *France* 18 F5
Montalbán, *Spain* 32 E4
Montalbano Iónico, *Italy* 31 B9
Montalbo, *Spain* 32 F2
Montalcino, *Italy* 29 E8
Montalegre, *Portugal* 34 D3
Montalto, *Italy* 31 D8
Montalto di Castro, *Italy* 29 F8
Montalto Uffugo, *Italy* 31 C9
Montalvo, *U.S.A.* 117 L7
Montamarta, *Spain* 34 D5
Montana, *Bulgaria* 40 C7
Montaña, *Peru* 124 E4
Montana □, *Bulgaria* 40 C7
Montana □, *U.S.A.* 114 C9
Montaña Clara, I., *Canary Is.* 37 E6
Montánchez, *Spain* 35 F4
Montargil, *Portugal* 35 F2
Montargis, *France* 19 E9
Montauban, *France* 20 D5
Montauk, *U.S.A.* 111 E13
Montauk Pt., *U.S.A.* 111 E13
Montbard, *France* 19 E11
Montbarrey, *France* 19 E12
Montbéliard, *France* 19 E13
Montblanc, *Spain* 32 D6
Montbrison, *France* 21 C8
Montcalm, Pic de, *France* 20 F5
Montceau-les-Mines, *France* 19 F11
Montcenis, *France* 21 B8
Montclair, *U.S.A.* 111 F10
Montcornet, *France* 19 C11
Montcuq, *France* 20 D5
Montdidier, *France* 19 C9
Monte Albán, *Mexico* 119 D5
Monte Alegre, *Brazil* 125 D8
Monte Azul, *Brazil* 125 G10
Monte Bello Is., *Australia* 92 D2
Monte-Carlo, *Monaco* 21 E11
Monte Caseros, *Argentina* 126 C4
Monte Comán, *Argentina* 126 C2
Monte Cristi, *Dom. Rep.* 121 C5
Monte Lindo →, *Paraguay* 126 A4
Monte Patria, *Chile* 126 C1
Monte Quemado, *Argentina* 126 B3
Monte Redondo, *Portugal* 34 F2
Monte Rio, *U.S.A.* 116 G4
Monte San Giovanni Campano, *Italy* 30 A6
Monte San Savino, *Italy* 29 E8
Monte Sant' Ángelo, *Italy* 29 G12
Monte Santu, C. di, *Italy* 30 B2
Monte Vista, *U.S.A.* 115 H10
Monteagudo, *Argentina* 127 B5
Montealegre del Castillo, *Spain* 33 G3
Montebello, *Canada* 102 C5
Montebello Iónico, *Italy* 31 E8
Montebelluna, *Italy* 29 C9
Montebourg, *France* 18 C5
Montecastrilli, *Italy* 29 F9
Montecatini Terme, *Italy* 28 E7
Montecito, *U.S.A.* 117 L7
Montecristo, *Italy* 28 F7
Montefalco, *Italy* 29 F9
Montefiascone, *Italy* 29 F9
Montefrío, *Spain* 35 H7
Montegiórgio, *Italy* 29 E10
Montego Bay, *Jamaica* 120 C4
Montehermoso, *Spain* 34 E4
Montejicar, *Spain* 35 H7
Montélimar, *France* 21 D8
Montella, *Italy* 31 B8
Montellano, *Spain* 35 J5
Montello, *U.S.A.* 112 D10
Montemor-o-Novo, *Portugal* 35 G2
Montemor-o-Velho, *Portugal* 34 E2
Montemorelos, *Mexico* 119 B5
Montendre, *France* 20 C3
Montenegro, *Brazil* 127 B5
Montenegro □, *Yugoslavia* 40 D3
Montenero di Bisáccia, *Italy* 29 G11
Montepuez, *Mozam.* 87 E4
Montepuez →, *Mozam.* 87 E5
Montepulciano, *Italy* 29 E8
Montereale, *Italy* 29 F10
Montereau-Faut-Yonne, *France* 19 D9
Monterey, *U.S.A.* 116 J5
Monterey B., *U.S.A.* 116 J5
Montería, *Colombia* 124 B3
Monteros, *Argentina* 126 B2
Monterotondo, *Italy* 29 F9
Monterrey, *Mexico* 118 B4
Montes Claros, *Brazil* 125 G10
Montesano, *U.S.A.* 116 D3
Montesano sulla Marcellana, *Italy* 31 B8
Montesárchio, *Italy* 31 A7
Montescaglioso, *Italy* 31 B9
Montesilvano, *Italy* 29 F11
Montevarchi, *Italy* 29 E8
Montevideo, *Uruguay* 127 C4
Montevideo, *U.S.A.* 112 C7
Montezuma, *U.S.A.* 112 E8
Montfaucon, *France* 18 E5
Montfaucon-d'Argonne, *France* 19 C12
Montfaucon-en-Velay, *France* 21 C8
Montfort, *France* 18 D5
Montfort-le-Gesnois, *France* 18 D7
Montgenèvre, *France* 21 D10
Montgomery = Sahiwal, *Pakistan* 68 D5
Montgomery, *U.K.* 13 E4
Montgomery, *Ala., U.S.A.* 109 J2
Montgomery, *Pa., U.S.A.* 110 E8
Montgomery, *W. Va., U.S.A.* 108 F5
Montgomery City, *U.S.A.* 112 F9
Montguyon, *France* 20 C3
Monthermé, *France* 19 C11
Monthey, *Switz.* 25 J2
Monthois, *France* 19 C11
Monti, *Italy* 30 B2
Monticelli d'Ongina, *Italy* 28 C6
Monticello, *Ark., U.S.A.* 113 J9
Monticello, *Fla., U.S.A.* 109 K4
Monticello, *Ind., U.S.A.* 108 E2
Monticello, *Iowa, U.S.A.* 112 D9
Monticello, *Ky., U.S.A.* 109 G3
Monticello, *Minn., U.S.A.* 112 C8
Monticello, *Miss., U.S.A.* 113 K9
Monticello, *N.Y., U.S.A.* 111 E10
Monticello, *Utah, U.S.A.* 115 H9
Montichiari, *Italy* 28 C7
Montier-en-Der, *France* 19 D11
Montignac, *France* 20 C5
Montigny-les-Metz, *France* 19 C13
Montigny-sur-Aube, *France* 19 E11
Montijo, *Portugal* 35 G2
Montijo, *Spain* 35 G4
Montilla, *Spain* 35 H6
Montivilliers, *France* 18 C7
Montluçon, *France* 19 F9
Montmagny, *Canada* 103 C5
Montmarault, *France* 19 F9
Montmartre, *Canada* 105 C8
Montmédy, *France* 19 C12
Montmélian, *France* 21 C10
Montmirail, *France* 19 D10
Montmoreau-St-Cybard, *France* 20 C4
Montmorillon, *France* 20 B4
Montmort-Lucy, *France* 19 D10
Monto, *Australia* 94 C5
Montoire-sur-le-Loir, *France* 18 E7
Montório al Vomano, *Italy* 29 F10
Montoro, *Spain* 35 G6
Montour Falls, *U.S.A.* 110 D8
Montoursville, *U.S.A.* 110 E8
Montpelier, *Idaho, U.S.A.* 114 E8
Montpelier, *Vt., U.S.A.* 111 B12
Montpellier, *France* 20 E7
Montpezat-de-Quercy, *France* 20 D5
Montpon-Ménestérol, *France* 20 D4
Montréal, *Canada* 102 C5
Montréal, *Aude, France* 20 E6
Montréal, *Gers, France* 20 E4
Montreal →, *Canada* 102 C3
Montreal L., *Canada* 105 C7
Montreal Lake, *Canada* 105 C7
Montredon-Labessonnié, *France* 20 E6
Montrésor, *France* 18 E8
Montret, *France* 19 F12
Montreuil, *Pas-de-Calais, France* 19 B8
Montreuil, *Seine-St-Denis, France* 19 D9
Montreuil-Bellay, *France* 18 E6
Montreux, *Switz.* 25 J2
Montrevel-en-Bresse, *France* 19 F12
Montrichard, *France* 18 E8
Montrose, *U.K.* 14 E6
Montrose, *Colo., U.S.A.* 115 G10
Montrose, *Pa., U.S.A.* 111 E9
Monts, Pte. des, *Canada* 103 C6
Montsalvy, *France* 20 D6
Montsant, Serra de, *Spain* 32 D6
Montsauche-les-Settons, *France* 19 E11
Montsec, Serra del, *Spain* 32 C5
Montserrat, *Spain* 32 D6
Montserrat ■, *W. Indies* 121 C7
Montuenga, *Spain* 34 D6
Montuiri, *Spain* 37 B9
Monywa, *Burma* 67 H19
Monza, *Italy* 28 C6
Monze, *Zambia* 87 F2
Monze, C., *Pakistan* 68 G2
Monzón, *Spain* 32 D5
Mooers, *U.S.A.* 111 B11
Mooi →, *S. Africa* 89 D5
Mooi River, *S. Africa* 89 D4
Moonah →, *Australia* 94 C2
Moonda, L., *Australia* 94 D3
Moonie, *Australia* 95 D5
Moonie →, *Australia* 95 D4
Moonta, *Australia* 95 E2
Moora, *Australia* 93 F2
Moorcroft, *U.S.A.* 112 C2
Moore →, *Australia* 93 F2
Moore, L., *Australia* 93 E2
Moore Park, *Australia* 94 C5
Moore Reefs, *Australia* 94 B4
Moorefield, *U.S.A.* 108 F6
Moores Res., *U.S.A.* 111 B13
Moorfoot Hills, *U.K.* 14 F5
Moorhead, *U.S.A.* 112 B6
Moormerland, *Germany* 24 B3
Moorpark, *U.S.A.* 117 L8
Moorreesburg, *S. Africa* 88 E2
Moosburg, *Germany* 25 G7
Moose →, *Canada* 102 B3
Moose →, *U.S.A.* 111 C9
Moose Creek, *Canada* 111 A10
Moose Factory, *Canada* 102 B3
Moose Jaw, *Canada* 105 C7
Moose Jaw →, *Canada* 105 C7
Moose Lake, *Canada* 105 C8
Moose Lake, *U.S.A.* 112 B8
Moose Mountain Prov. Park, *Canada* 105 D8
Moosehead L., *U.S.A.* 109 C11
Mooselookmeguntic L., *U.S.A.* 109 C10
Moosilauke, Mt., *U.S.A.* 111 B13
Moosomin, *Canada* 105 C8
Moosonee, *Canada* 102 B3
Moosup, *U.S.A.* 111 E13
Mopane, *S. Africa* 89 C4
Mopeia Velha, *Mozam.* 87 F4
Mopipi, *Botswana* 88 C3
Mopoi, *C.A.R.* 86 A2
Mopti, *Mali* 82 C4
Moqatta, *Sudan* 81 E4
Moqor, *Afghan.* 68 C2
Moquegua, *Peru* 124 G4
Mór, *Hungary* 42 C3
Mora, *Cameroon* 83 C7
Móra, *Portugal* 35 G2
Mora, *Spain* 35 F7
Mora, *Sweden* 10 C8
Mora, *Minn., U.S.A.* 112 C8
Mora, *N. Mex., U.S.A.* 115 J11
Mora →, *U.S.A.* 113 H2
Mora de Ebro = Mòra d'Ebre, *Spain* 32 D5
Mora de Rubielos, *Spain* 32 E4
Mòra d'Ebre, *Spain* 32 D5
Mòra la Nova, *Spain* 32 D5
Morača →, *Montenegro, Yug.* 40 D3
Moradabad, *India* 69 E8
Morafenobe, *Madag.* 89 B7
Morąg, *Poland* 44 E6
Moral de Calatrava, *Spain* 35 G7
Moraleja, *Spain* 34 E4
Moramanga, *Madag.* 89 B8
Moran, *Kans., U.S.A.* 113 G7
Moran, *Wyo., U.S.A.* 114 E8
Moranbah, *Australia* 94 C4
Morano Cálabro, *Italy* 31 C9
Morant Cays, *Jamaica* 120 C4
Morant Pt., *Jamaica* 120 C4
Morar, *India* 68 F8
Morar, L., *U.K.* 14 E3
Moratalla, *Spain* 33 G3
Moratuwa, *Sri Lanka* 66 R11
Morava →, *Slovak Rep.* 27 C9
Moravia, *U.S.A.* 111 D8
Moravian Hts. = Českomoravská Vrchovina, *Czech Rep.* 26 B8
Moravica →, *Serbia, Yug.* 40 C4
Moraviţa, *Romania* 42 E6
Moravská Třebová, *Czech Rep.* 27 B9
Moravské Budějovice, *Czech Rep.* 26 B8
Morawa, *Australia* 93 E2
Morawhanna, *Guyana* 124 B7
Moray □, *U.K.* 14 D5
Moray Firth, *U.K.* 14 D5
Morbach, *Germany* 25 F3
Morbegno, *Italy* 28 B6
Morbi, *India* 68 H4
Morbihan □, *France* 18 E4
Mörbylånga, *Sweden* 11 H10
Morcenx, *France* 20 D3
Morcone, *Italy* 31 A7
Mordelles, *France* 18 D5
Morden, *Canada* 105 D9
Mordoğan, *Turkey* 39 C8
Mordovian Republic = Mordvinia □, *Russia* 48 C7
Mordovo, *Russia* 48 D5
Mordvinia □, *Russia* 48 C7
Mordy, *Poland* 45 F9
Morea, *Greece* 6 H10
Moreau →, *U.S.A.* 112 C4
Morecambe, *U.K.* 12 C5
Morecambe B., *U.K.* 12 C5
Moree, *Australia* 95 D4
Morehead, *U.S.A.* 108 F4
Morehead City, *U.S.A.* 109 H7
Morel →, *India* 68 F7
Morelia, *Mexico* 118 D4
Morella, *Australia* 94 C3
Morella, *Spain* 32 E4
Morelos, *Mexico* 118 B3
Morelos □, *Mexico* 119 D5
Morena, *India* 68 F8
Morena, Sierra, *Spain* 35 G7
Moreni, *Romania* 43 F10
Moreno Valley, *U.S.A.* 117 M10
Moresby I., *Canada* 104 C2
Morestel, *France* 21 C9
Moreton I., *Australia* 95 D5
Moreuil, *France* 19 C9
Morey, *Spain* 37 B10
Morez, *France* 19 F13
Morgan, *U.S.A.* 114 F8
Morgan City, *U.S.A.* 113 L9
Morgan Hill, *U.S.A.* 116 H5
Morganfield, *U.S.A.* 108 G2
Morganton, *U.S.A.* 109 H5
Morgantown, *U.S.A.* 108 F6
Morgenzon, *S. Africa* 89 D4
Morges, *Switz.* 25 J2
Morghak, *Iran* 71 D8
Morgongåva, *Sweden* 10 E10
Morhange, *France* 19 D13
Morhar →, *India* 69 G11
Mori, *Italy* 28 C7
Moriarty, *U.S.A.* 115 J10
Moribaya, *Guinea* 82 D3
Morice L., *Canada* 104 C3
Moriki, *Nigeria* 83 C6
Morinville, *Canada* 104 C6
Morioka, *Japan* 54 E10
Moris, *Mexico* 118 B3
Morlaàs, *France* 20 E3
Morlaix, *France* 18 D3
Mörlunda, *Sweden* 11 G9
Mormanno, *Italy* 31 C8
Mormant, *France* 19 D9
Mornington, *Australia* 95 F4
Mornington, I., *Chile* 128 F1
Mornington I., *Australia* 94 B2
Mórnos →, *Greece* 38 C3
Moro, *Pakistan* 68 F2
Moro, *Sudan* 81 E3
Moro →, *Pakistan* 68 E2
Moro G., *Phil.* 61 H5
Morocco ■, *N. Afr.* 78 B4
Morogoro, *Tanzania* 86 D4
Morogoro □, *Tanzania* 86 D4
Moroleón, *Mexico* 118 C4
Morombe, *Madag.* 89 C7
Moron, *Argentina* 126 C4
Morón, *Cuba* 120 B4
Morón de Almazán, *Spain* 32 D2
Morón de la Frontera, *Spain* 35 H5
Morona →, *Peru* 124 D3
Morondava, *Madag.* 89 C7
Morondo, *Ivory C.* 82 D3
Morongo Valley, *U.S.A.* 117 L10
Moroni, *Comoros Is.* 77 H8
Moroni, *U.S.A.* 114 G8
Moronou, *Ivory C.* 82 D4
Morotai, *Indonesia* 63 D7
Moroto, *Uganda* 86 B3
Moroto Summit, *Kenya* 86 B3
Morozov, *Bulgaria* 41 D9
Morozovsk, *Russia* 49 F5
Morpeth, *U.K.* 12 B6
Morphou, *Cyprus* 36 D11
Morphou Bay, *Cyprus* 36 D11
Morrilton, *U.S.A.* 113 H8
Morrinhos, *Brazil* 125 G9
Morrinsville, *N.Z.* 91 G5
Morris, *Canada* 105 D9
Morris, *Ill., U.S.A.* 112 E10
Morris, *Minn., U.S.A.* 112 C7
Morris, *N.Y., U.S.A.* 111 D9
Morris, *Pa., U.S.A.* 110 E7
Morris, Mt., *Australia* 93 E5
Morrisburg, *Canada* 111 B9
Morristown, *Ariz., U.S.A.* 115 K7
Morristown, *N.J., U.S.A.* 111 F10
Morristown, *N.Y., U.S.A.* 111 B9
Morristown, *Tenn., U.S.A.* 109 G4
Morrisville, *N.Y., U.S.A.* 111 D9
Morrisville, *Pa., U.S.A.* 111 F10
Morrisville, *Vt., U.S.A.* 111 B12
Morro, Pta., *Chile* 126 B1
Morro Bay, *U.S.A.* 116 K6
Morro del Jable, *Canary Is.* 37 F5
Morro Jable, Pta. de, *Canary Is.* 37 F5
Morrosquillo, G. de, *Colombia* 120 E4
Mörrum, *Sweden* 11 H8
Morrumbene, *Mozam.* 89 C6
Mörrumsån →, *Sweden* 11 H8
Mors, *Denmark* 11 H2
Morshansk, *Russia* 48 D5
Mörsil, *Sweden* 10 A7
Mortagne →, *France* 19 D13
Mortagne-au-Perche, *France* 18 D7
Mortagne-sur-Gironde, *France* 20 C3
Mortagne-sur-Sèvre, *France* 18 F6
Mortain, *France* 18 D6
Mortara, *Italy* 28 C5
Morteau, *France* 19 E13
Morteros, *Argentina* 126 C3
Mortlach, *Canada* 105 C7
Mortlake, *Australia* 95 F3
Morton, *Tex., U.S.A.* 113 J3
Morton, *Wash., U.S.A.* 116 D4
Morundah, *Australia* 95 E4
Moruya, *Australia* 95 F5
Morvan, *France* 19 E11
Morven, *Australia* 95 D4
Morvern, *U.K.* 14 E3
Morwell, *Australia* 95 F4
Moryń, *Poland* 45 F1
Morzine, *France* 19 F13
Mosalsk, *Russia* 46 E8
Mosbach, *Germany* 25 F5
Mošćenice, *Croatia* 29 C11
Mosciano Sant' Ángelo, *Italy* 29 F10
Moscos Is. = Maungmagan Is., *Burma* 64 E1
Moscow = Moskva, *Russia* 46 E9
Moscow, *Idaho, U.S.A.* 114 C5
Moscow, *Pa., U.S.A.* 111 E9
Mosel →, *Europe* 19 B14
Moselle = Mosel →, *Europe* 19 B14
Moselle □, *France* 19 D13
Moses Lake, *U.S.A.* 114 C4
Mosgiel, *N.Z.* 91 L3
Moshaweng →, *S. Africa* 88 D3
Moshi, *Tanzania* 86 C4
Moshupa, *Botswana* 88 C4
Mosina, *Poland* 45 F3
Mosjøen, *Norway* 8 D15
Moskenesøya, *Norway* 8 C15
Moskenstraumen, *Norway* 8 C15
Moskva, *Russia* 46 E9
Moskva →, *Russia* 46 E10
Moslavačka Gora, *Croatia* 29 C13
Mosomane, *Botswana* 88 C4
Moson-magyaróvár, *Hungary* 42 C2
Mošorin, *Serbia, Yug.* 42 E5
Mospino, *Ukraine* 47 J9
Mosquera, *Colombia* 124 C3
Mosquero, *U.S.A.* 113 H3
Mosqueruela, *Spain* 32 E4
Mosquitia, *Honduras* 120 C3
Mosquito Coast = Mosquitia, *Honduras* 120 C3
Mosquito Creek L., *U.S.A.* 110 E4
Mosquito L., *Canada* 105 A8
Mosquitos, G. de los, *Panama* 120 E3
Moss, *Norway* 9 G14
Moss Vale, *Australia* 95 E5
Mossbank, *Canada* 105 D7
Mossburn, *N.Z.* 91 L2
Mosselbaai, *S. Africa* 88 E3

Mossendjo, *Congo* 84 E2
Mossgiel, *Australia* 95 E3
Mossingen, *Germany* 25 G5
Mossman, *Australia* 94 B4
Mossoró, *Brazil* 125 E11
Mossuril, *Mozam.* 87 E5
Most, *Czech Rep.* 26 A6
Mosta, *Malta* 36 D1
Moşţafáābād, *Iran* 71 C7
Mostaganem, *Algeria* 78 A6
Mostar, *Bos.-H.* 42 G2
Mostardas, *Brazil* 127 C5
Mostiska = Mostyska, *Ukraine* 47 H2
Móstoles, *Spain* 34 E7
Mosty = Masty, *Belarus* 46 F3
Mostyska, *Ukraine* 47 H2
Mosul = Al Mawşil, *Iraq* 70 B4
Mosŭlpo, *S. Korea* 57 H14
Mota, *Ethiopia* 81 E4
Mota del Cuervo, *Spain* 33 F2
Mota del Marqués, *Spain* 34 D5
Motagua →, *Guatemala* 120 C2
Motala, *Sweden* 11 F9
Motaze, *Mozam.* 89 C5
Moţca, *Romania* 43 C11
Moth, *India* 69 G8
Motherwell, *U.K.* 14 F5
Motihari, *India* 69 F11
Motilla del Palancar, *Spain* 33 F3
Motnik, *Slovenia* 29 B11
Motovun, *Croatia* 29 C10
Motozintla de Mendoza, *Mexico* 119 D6
Motril, *Spain* 35 J7
Motru, *Romania* 42 F7
Motru →, *Romania* 43 F8
Mott, *U.S.A.* 112 B3
Móttola, *Italy* 31 B10
Motueka, *N.Z.* 91 J4
Motueka →, *N.Z.* 91 J4
Motul, *Mexico* 119 C7
Mouchalagane →, *Canada* 103 B6
Moúdhros, *Greece* 39 B7
Mouding, *China* 58 E3
Moudjeria, *Mauritania* 82 B2
Moudon, *Switz.* 25 J2
Mouila, *Gabon* 84 E2
Moulamein, *Australia* 95 F3
Moulianá, *Greece* 36 D7
Moulins, *France* 19 F10
Moulmein, *Burma* 67 L20
Moulouya, O. →, *Morocco* 78 B5
Moultrie, *U.S.A.* 109 K4
Moultrie, L., *U.S.A.* 109 J5
Mound City, *Mo., U.S.A.* 112 E7
Mound City, *S. Dak., U.S.A.* 112 C4
Moúnda, Ákra, *Greece* 38 C2
Moundou, *Chad* 79 G9
Moundsville, *U.S.A.* 110 G4
Moung, *Cambodia* 64 F4
Mount Airy, *U.S.A.* 109 G5
Mount Albert, *Canada* 110 B5
Mount Barker, *S. Austral., Australia* 95 F2
Mount Barker, *W. Austral., Australia* 93 F2
Mount Beauty, *Australia* 95 F4
Mount Brydges, *Canada* 110 D3
Mount Burr, *Australia* 95 F3
Mount Carmel, *Ill., U.S.A.* 108 F2
Mount Carmel, *Pa., U.S.A.* 111 F8
Mount Charleston, *U.S.A.* 117 J11
Mount Clemens, *U.S.A.* 110 D2
Mount Coolon, *Australia* 94 C4
Mount Darwin, *Zimbabwe* 87 F3
Mount Desert I., *U.S.A.* 109 C11
Mount Dora, *U.S.A.* 109 L5
Mount Edziza Prov. Park, *Canada* 104 B2
Mount Fletcher, *S. Africa* 89 E4
Mount Forest, *Canada* 102 D3
Mount Gambier, *Australia* 95 F3
Mount Garnet, *Australia* 94 B4
Mount Holly, *U.S.A.* 111 G10
Mount Holly Springs, *U.S.A.* 110 F7
Mount Hope, *N.S.W., Australia* 95 E4
Mount Hope, *S. Austral., Australia* 95 E2
Mount Isa, *Australia* 94 C2
Mount Jewett, *U.S.A.* 110 E6
Mount Kisco, *U.S.A.* 111 E11
Mount Laguna, *U.S.A.* 117 N10
Mount Larcom, *Australia* 94 C5
Mount Lofty Ra., *Australia* 95 E2
Mount Magnet, *Australia* 93 E2
Mount Maunganui, *N.Z.* 91 G6
Mount Molloy, *Australia* 94 B4
Mount Morgan, *Australia* 94 C5
Mount Morris, *U.S.A.* 110 D7
Mount Pearl, *Canada* 103 C9
Mount Penn, *U.S.A.* 111 F9
Mount Perry, *Australia* 95 D5
Mount Pleasant, *Iowa, U.S.A.* 112 E9
Mount Pleasant, *Mich., U.S.A.* 108 D3
Mount Pleasant, *Pa., U.S.A.* 110 F5
Mount Pleasant, *S.C., U.S.A.* 109 J6
Mount Pleasant, *Tenn., U.S.A.* 109 H2
Mount Pleasant, *Tex., U.S.A.* 113 J7
Mount Pleasant, *Utah, U.S.A.* 114 G8
Mount Pocono, *U.S.A.* 111 E9
Mount Rainier Nat. Park, *U.S.A.* 116 D5
Mount Revelstoke Nat. Park, *Canada* 104 C5
Mount Robson Prov. Park, *Canada* 104 C5
Mount Selinda, *Zimbabwe* 89 C5
Mount Shasta, *U.S.A.* 114 F2
Mount Signal, *U.S.A.* 117 N11
Mount Sterling, *Ill., U.S.A.* 112 F9
Mount Sterling, *Ky., U.S.A.* 108 F4
Mount Surprise, *Australia* 94 B3
Mount Union, *U.S.A.* 110 F7
Mount Upton, *U.S.A.* 111 D9
Mount Vernon, *Ill., U.S.A.* 108 F1
Mount Vernon, *Ind., U.S.A.* 112 F10
Mount Vernon, *N.Y., U.S.A.* 111 F11
Mount Vernon, *Ohio, U.S.A.* 110 F2
Mount Vernon, *Wash., U.S.A.* 116 B4
Mountain Ash, *U.K.* 13 F4
Mountain Center, *U.S.A.* 117 M10
Mountain City, *Nev., U.S.A.* 114 F6
Mountain City, *Tenn., U.S.A.* 109 G5
Mountain Dale, *U.S.A.* 111 E10
Mountain Grove, *U.S.A.* 113 G8
Mountain Home, *Ark., U.S.A.* 113 G8
Mountain Home, *Idaho, U.S.A.* 114 E6
Mountain Iron, *U.S.A.* 112 B8
Mountain Pass, *U.S.A.* 117 K11
Mountain View, *Ark., U.S.A.* 113 H8
Mountain View, *Calif., U.S.A.* 116 H4
Mountain View, *Hawaii, U.S.A.* 106 J17
Mountainair, *U.S.A.* 115 J10
Mountlake Terrace, *U.S.A.* 116 C4
Mountmellick, *Ireland* 15 C4
Mountrath, *Ireland* 15 D4
Moura, *Australia* 94 C4
Moura, *Brazil* 124 D6
Moura, *Portugal* 35 G3
Mourão, *Portugal* 35 G3
Mourdi, Dépression du, *Chad* 79 E10
Mourdiah, *Mali* 82 C3
Mourenx-Ville-Nouvelle, *France* 20 E3
Mouri, *Ghana* 83 D4
Mourilyan, *Australia* 94 B4
Mourmelon-le-Grand, *France* 19 C11
Mourne →, *U.K.* 15 B4
Mourne Mts., *U.K.* 15 B5
Mourniaí, *Greece* 36 D6
Mournies = Mourniaí, *Greece* 36 D6
Mouscron, *Belgium* 17 D3
Moussoro, *Chad* 79 F9
Mouthe, *France* 19 F13
Moutier, *Switz.* 25 H3
Moûtiers, *France* 21 C10
Moutohara, *N.Z.* 91 H6
Moutong, *Indonesia* 63 D6
Mouy, *France* 19 C9
Mouzáki, *Greece* 38 B3
Mouzon, *France* 19 C12
Movas, *Mexico* 118 B3
Moville, *Ireland* 15 A4
Mowandjum, *Australia* 92 C3
Moy →, *Ireland* 15 B2
Moyale, *Kenya* 81 G4
Moyamba, *S. Leone* 82 D2
Moyen Atlas, *Morocco* 78 B4
Moyne, L. le, *Canada* 103 A6
Moyo, *Indonesia* 62 F5
Moyobamba, *Peru* 124 E3
Moyyero →, *Russia* 51 C11
Moyynty, *Kazakstan* 50 E8
Mozambique = Moçambique, *Mozam.* 87 F5
Mozambique ■, *Africa* 87 F4
Mozambique Chan., *Africa* 89 B7
Mozdok, *Russia* 49 J7
Mozdūrān, *Iran* 71 B9
Mozhaysk, *Russia* 46 E9
Mozhga, *Russia* 48 B11
Mozhnābād, *Iran* 71 C9
Mozirje, *Slovenia* 29 B11
Mozyr = Mazyr, *Belarus* 47 F5
Mpanda, *Tanzania* 86 D3
Mpésoba, *Mali* 82 C3
Mphoengs, *Zimbabwe* 89 C4
Mpika, *Zambia* 87 E3
Mpulungu, *Zambia* 87 D3
Mpumalanga, *S. Africa* 89 D5
Mpumalanga □, *S. Africa* 89 B5
Mpwapwa, *Tanzania* 86 D4
Mqanduli, *S. Africa* 89 E4
Mqinvartsveri = Kazbek, *Russia* 49 J7
Mrągowo, *Poland* 44 E8
Mramor, *Serbia, Yug.* 40 C5
Mrkonjić Grad, *Bos.-H.* 42 F2
Mrkopalj, *Croatia* 29 C11
Mrocza, *Poland* 45 E4
Msambansovu, *Zimbabwe* 87 F3
M'sila →, *Algeria* 78 A6
Msoro, *Zambia* 87 E3
Msta →, *Russia* 46 C6
Mstislavl = Mstsislaw, *Belarus* 46 E6
Mstsislaw, *Belarus* 46 E6
Mszana Dolna, *Poland* 45 J7
Mszczonów, *Poland* 45 G7
Mtama, *Tanzania* 87 E4
Mtamvuna →, *S. Africa* 89 E5
Mtilikwe →, *Zimbabwe* 87 G3
Mtsensk, *Russia* 46 F9
Mtskheta, *Georgia* 49 K7
Mtubatuba, *S. Africa* 89 D5
Mtwalume, *S. Africa* 89 E5
Mtwara-Mikindani, *Tanzania* 87 E5
Mu Gia, Deo, *Vietnam* 64 D5
Mu Us Shamo, *China* 56 E5
Muang Chiang Rai = Chiang Rai, *Thailand* 58 H2
Muang Khong, *Laos* 64 E5
Muang Lamphun, *Thailand* 64 C2
Muang Pak Beng, *Laos* 58 H3
Muar, *Malaysia* 65 L4
Muarabungo, *Indonesia* 62 E2
Muaraenim, *Indonesia* 62 E2
Muarajuloi, *Indonesia* 62 E4
Muarakaman, *Indonesia* 62 E5
Muaratebo, *Indonesia* 62 E2
Muaratembesi, *Indonesia* 62 E2
Muaratewe, *Indonesia* 62 E4
Mubarakpur, *India* 69 F10
Mubarraz = Al Mubarraz, *Si. Arabia* 71 E6
Mubende, *Uganda* 86 B3
Mubi, *Nigeria* 83 C7
Mubur, Pulau, *Indonesia* 65 L6
Mucajaí →, *Brazil* 124 C6
Muchachos, Roque de los, *Canary Is.* 37 F2
Mücheln, *Germany* 24 D7
Muchinga Mts., *Zambia* 87 E3
Muchkapskiy, *Russia* 48 E6
Muchuan, *China* 58 C5
Muck, *U.K.* 14 E2
Muckadilla, *Australia* 95 D4
Mucur, *Turkey* 72 C6
Mucuri, *Brazil* 125 G11
Mucusso, *Angola* 88 B3
Muda, *Canary Is.* 37 F6
Mudanjiang, *China* 57 B15
Mudanya, *Turkey* 41 F12
Muddy Cr. →, *U.S.A.* 115 H8
Mudgee, *Australia* 95 E4
Mudjatik →, *Canada* 105 B7
Mudurnu, *Turkey* 72 B4
Muecate, *Mozam.* 87 E4
Mueda, *Mozam.* 87 E4
Mueller Ra., *Australia* 92 C4
Muende, *Mozam.* 87 E3
Muerto, Mar, *Mexico* 119 D6
Mufu Shan, *China* 59 C10
Mufulira, *Zambia* 87 E2
Mufumbiro Range, *Africa* 86 C2
Mugardos, *Spain* 34 B2
Muge →, *Portugal* 35 F2
Múggia, *Italy* 29 C10
Mughal Sarai, *India* 69 G10
Mughayrā', *Si. Arabia* 70 D3
Mugi, *Japan* 55 H7
Mugia = Muxía, *Spain* 34 B1
Mugila, Mts., *Dem. Rep. of the Congo* 86 D2
Muğla, *Turkey* 39 D10
Muğla □, *Turkey* 39 D10
Muglad, *Sudan* 81 E2
Müglizh, *Bulgaria* 41 D9
Mugu, *Nepal* 69 E10
Muhammad, Ras, *Egypt* 70 E2
Muhammad Qol, *Sudan* 80 C4
Muhammadabad, *India* 69 F10
Muhesi →, *Tanzania* 86 D4
Mühlacker, *Germany* 25 G4
Mühldorf, *Germany* 25 G8
Mühlhausen, *Germany* 24 D6
Mühlig Hofmann fjell, *Antarctica* 5 D3
Mühlviertel, *Austria* 26 C7
Muhos, *Finland* 8 D22
Muhu, *Estonia* 9 G20
Muhutwe, *Tanzania* 86 C3
Muine Bheag, *Ireland* 15 D5
Muir, L., *Australia* 93 F2
Mukacheve, *Ukraine* 47 H2
Mukachevo = Mukacheve, *Ukraine* 47 H2
Mukah, *Malaysia* 62 D4
Mukandwara, *India* 68 G6
Mukawwa, Geziret, *Egypt* 80 C4
Mukawwar, *Sudan* 80 C4
Mukdahan, *Thailand* 64 D5
Mukden = Shenyang, *China* 57 D12
Mukerian, *India* 68 D6
Mukhtolovo, *Russia* 48 C6
Mukhtuya = Lensk, *Russia* 51 C12
Mukinbudin, *Australia* 93 F2
Mukishi, *Dem. Rep. of the Congo* 87 D1
Mukomuko, *Indonesia* 62 E2
Mukomwenze, *Dem. Rep. of the Congo* 86 D2
Muktsar, *India* 68 D6
Mukur = Moqor, *Afghan.* 68 C2
Mukutawa →, *Canada* 105 C9
Mukwela, *Zambia* 87 F2
Mula, *Spain* 33 G3
Mula →, *Pakistan* 68 F2
Mulange, *Dem. Rep. of the Congo* 86 C2
Mulanje, *Malawi* 87 F4
Mulchén, *Chile* 126 D1
Mulde →, *Germany* 24 D8
Mule Creek Junction, *U.S.A.* 112 D2
Muleba, *Tanzania* 86 C3
Mulejé, *Mexico* 118 B2
Muleshoe, *U.S.A.* 113 H3
Muletta, Gara, *Ethiopia* 81 F5
Mulgrave, *Canada* 103 C7
Mulhacén, *Spain* 35 H7
Mülheim, *Germany* 24 D2
Mulhouse, *France* 19 E14
Muli, *China* 58 D3
Muling, *China* 57 B16
Mull, *U.K.* 14 E3
Mull, Sound of, *U.K.* 14 E3
Mullaittivu, *Sri Lanka* 66 Q12
Mullen, *U.S.A.* 112 D4
Mullens, *U.S.A.* 108 G5
Muller, Pegunungan, *Indonesia* 62 D4
Mullet Pen., *Ireland* 15 B1
Mullewa, *Australia* 93 E2
Müllheim, *Germany* 25 H3
Mulligan →, *Australia* 94 D2
Mullingar, *Ireland* 15 C4
Mullins, *U.S.A.* 109 H6
Mullsjö, *Sweden* 11 G7
Mullumbimby, *Australia* 95 D5
Mulobezi, *Zambia* 87 F2
Mulroy B., *Ireland* 15 A4
Multan, *Pakistan* 68 D4
Mulumbe, Mts., *Dem. Rep. of the Congo* 87 D2
Mulungushi Dam, *Zambia* 87 E2
Mulvane, *U.S.A.* 113 G6
Mulwad, *Sudan* 80 D3
Mumbai, *India* 66 K8
Mumbwa, *Zambia* 87 F2
Mumra, *Russia* 49 H8
Mun →, *Thailand* 64 E5
Muna, *Indonesia* 63 F6
Munabao, *India* 68 G4
Munamagi, *Estonia* 9 H22
Münchberg, *Germany* 25 E7
Müncheberg, *Germany* 24 C10
München, *Germany* 25 G7
Munchen-Gladbach = Mönchengladbach, *Germany* 24 D2
Muncho Lake, *Canada* 104 B3
Munch'ŏn, *N. Korea* 57 E14
Muncie, *U.S.A.* 108 E3
Muncoonie, L., *Australia* 94 D2
Mundabbera, *Australia* 95 D5
Munday, *U.S.A.* 113 J5
Münden, *Germany* 24 D5
Mundiwindi, *Australia* 92 D3
Mundo →, *Spain* 33 G2
Mundo Novo, *Brazil* 125 F10
Mundra, *India* 68 H3
Mundrabilla, *Australia* 93 F4
Munera, *Spain* 33 F2
Mungallala, *Australia* 95 D4
Mungallala Cr. →, *Australia* 95 D4
Mungana, *Australia* 94 B3
Mungaoli, *India* 68 G8
Mungari, *Mozam.* 87 F3
Mungbere, *Dem. Rep. of the Congo* 86 B2
Mungeli, *India* 69 H9
Munger, *India* 69 G12
Munich = München, *Germany* 25 G7
Munising, *U.S.A.* 108 B2
Munka-Ljungby, *Sweden* 11 H6
Munkebo, *Denmark* 11 J4
Munkedal, *Sweden* 11 F5
Munkfors, *Sweden* 10 E7
Munku-Sardyk, *Russia* 51 D11
Münnerstadt, *Germany* 25 E6
Muñoz Gamero, Pen., *Chile* 128 G2
Munroe L., *Canada* 105 B9
Munsan, *S. Korea* 57 F14
Munster, *France* 19 D14
Munster, *Niedersachsen, Germany* 24 C6
Münster, *Nordrhein-Westfalen, Germany* 24 D3
Munster □, *Ireland* 15 D3
Muntadgin, *Australia* 93 F2
Muntele Mare, Vf., *Romania* 43 D8
Muntok, *Indonesia* 62 E3
Munyama, *Zambia* 87 F2
Munzur Dağları, *Turkey* 73 C8
Muong Beng, *Laos* 58 G3
Muong Boum, *Vietnam* 58 F4
Muong Et, *Laos* 64 B5
Muong Hai, *Laos* 58 G3
Muong Hiem, *Laos* 64 B4
Muong Houn, *Laos* 58 G3
Muong Hung, *Vietnam* 58 G4
Muong Kau, *Laos* 64 E5
Muong Khao, *Laos* 64 C4
Muong Khoua, *Laos* 58 G4
Muong Liep, *Laos* 64 C3
Muong May, *Laos* 64 E6
Muong Ngeun, *Laos* 58 G3
Muong Ngoi, *Laos* 58 G4
Muong Nhie, *Vietnam* 58 F4
Muong Nong, *Laos* 64 D6
Muong Ou Tay, *Laos* 58 F3
Muong Oua, *Laos* 64 C3
Muong Peun, *Laos* 58 G4
Muong Phalane, *Laos* 64 D5
Muong Phieng, *Laos* 64 C3
Muong Phine, *Laos* 64 D6
Muong Sai, *Laos* 58 G3
Muong Saiapoun, *Laos* 64 C3
Muong Sen, *Vietnam* 64 C5
Muong Sing, *Laos* 58 G3
Muong Son, *Laos* 58 G4
Muong Soui, *Laos* 64 C4
Muong Va, *Laos* 58 G4
Muong Xia, *Vietnam* 64 B5
Muonio, *Finland* 8 C20
Muonionjoki →, *Finland* 8 C20
Muping, *China* 57 F11
Mupoi, *Sudan* 81 F2
Muqaddam, Wadi →, *Sudan* 80 D3
Muqdisho, *Somali Rep.* 74 G4
Mur →, *Austria* 27 E9
Mur-de-Bretagne, *France* 18 D4
Muradiye, *Manisa, Turkey* 39 C9
Muradiye, *Van, Turkey* 73 C10
Murakami, *Japan* 54 E9
Murallón, Cerro, *Chile* 128 F2
Muranda, *Rwanda* 86 C2
Murang'a, *Kenya* 86 C4
Murashi, *Russia* 50 D5
Murat, *France* 20 C6
Murat →, *Turkey* 73 C9
Murat Dağı, *Turkey* 39 C11
Muratlı, *Turkey* 41 E11
Murato, *France* 21 F13
Murau, *Austria* 26 D7
Muravera, *Italy* 30 C2
Murayama, *Japan* 54 E10
Murban, *U.A.E.* 71 F7
Murça, *Portugal* 34 D3
Murchison →, *Australia* 93 E1
Murchison, Mt., *Antarctica* 5 D11
Murchison Falls, *Uganda* 86 B3
Murchison Ra., *Australia* 94 C1
Murchison Rapids, *Malawi* 87 F3
Murcia, *Spain* 33 G3
Murcia □, *Spain* 33 H3
Murdo, *U.S.A.* 112 D4
Murdoch Pt., *Australia* 94 A3
Mürefte, *Turkey* 41 F11
Mureş □, *Romania* 43 D9
Mureş →, *Romania* 42 D5
Mureşul = Mureş →, *Romania* 42 D5
Muret, *France* 20 E5
Murewa, *Zimbabwe* 89 B5
Murfreesboro, *N.C., U.S.A.* 109 G7
Murfreesboro, *Tenn., U.S.A.* 109 H2
Murgab = Murghob, *Tajikistan* 50 F8
Murgab →, *Turkmenistan* 71 B9
Murgenella, *Australia* 92 B5
Murgeni, *Romania* 43 D13
Murgha Kibzai, *Pakistan* 68 D3
Murghob, *Tajikistan* 50 F8
Murgon, *Australia* 95 D5
Muri, *India* 69 H11
Muria, *Indonesia* 63 G14
Muriaé, *Brazil* 127 A7
Murias de Paredes, *Spain* 34 C4
Muriel Mine, *Zimbabwe* 87 F3
Müritz, *Germany* 24 B8
Murka, *Kenya* 86 C4
Murliganj, *India* 69 G12
Murmansk, *Russia* 50 C4
Murnau, *Germany* 25 H7
Muro, *France* 21 F12
Muro, *Spain* 37 B10
Muro, C. de, *France* 21 G12
Muro de Alcoy, *Spain* 33 G4
Muro Lucano, *Italy* 31 B8
Murom, *Russia* 48 C6
Muroran, *Japan* 54 C10
Muros, *Spain* 34 C1
Muros y de Noya, Ría de, *Spain* 34 C1
Muroto, *Japan* 55 H7
Muroto-Misaki, *Japan* 55 H7
Murowana Goślina, *Poland* 45 F3
Murphy, *U.S.A.* 114 E5
Murphys, *U.S.A.* 116 G6
Murrat, *Sudan* 80 D2
Murrat Wells, *Sudan* 80 C3
Murray, *Ky., U.S.A.* 109 G1
Murray, *Utah, U.S.A.* 114 F8
Murray →, *Australia* 95 F2
Murray, L., *U.S.A.* 109 H5
Murray Bridge, *Australia* 95 F2
Murray Harbour, *Canada* 103 C7
Murraysburg, *S. Africa* 88 E3
Murree, *Pakistan* 68 C5
Murrieta, *U.S.A.* 117 M9
Murro di Porco, Capo, *Italy* 31 F8
Murrumbidgee →, *Australia* 95 E3
Murrumburrah, *Australia* 95 E4
Murrurundi, *Australia* 95 E5
Murshid, *Sudan* 80 C3
Murshidabad, *India* 69 G13
Murska Sobota, *Slovenia* 29 B13
Murtle L., *Canada* 104 C5
Murtoa, *Australia* 95 F3
Murtosa, *Portugal* 34 E2
Murungu, *Tanzania* 86 C3
Mururoa, *Pac. Oc.* 97 K14
Murwara, *India* 69 H9
Murwillumbah, *Australia* 95 D5
Mürz →, *Austria* 26 D8
Mürzzuschlag, *Austria* 26 D8
Muş, *Turkey* 70 B4
Mûsa, Gebel, *Egypt* 70 D2
Musa Khel, *Pakistan* 68 D3
Mūsā Qal'eh, *Afghan.* 66 C4
Musaffargarh, *Pakistan* 66 D7
Musafirkhana, *India* 69 F9
Musala, *Bulgaria* 40 D7
Musala, *Indonesia* 62 D1
Musan, *N. Korea* 57 C15
Musangu, *Dem. Rep. of the Congo* 87 E1
Musasa, *Tanzania* 86 C3
Musay'īd, *Qatar* 71 E6
Muscat = Masqat, *Oman* 74 C6
Muscat & Oman = Oman ■, *Asia* 74 C6
Muscatine, *U.S.A.* 112 E9
Musgrave Harbour, *Canada* 103 C9
Musgrave Ranges, *Australia* 93 E5
Mushie, *Dem. Rep. of the Congo* 84 E3
Mushin, *Nigeria* 83 D5

Musi →, *Indonesia* 62 E2
Muskeg →, *Canada* 104 A4
Muskegon, *U.S.A.* 108 D2
Muskegon →, *U.S.A.* 108 D2
Muskegon Heights, *U.S.A.* 108 D2
Muskogee, *U.S.A.* 113 H7
Muskoka, L., *Canada* 110 B5
Muskwa →, *Canada* 104 B4
Muslīmiyah, *Syria* 70 B3
Musmar, *Sudan* 80 D4
Musofu, *Zambia* 87 E2
Musoma, *Tanzania* 86 C3
Musquaro, L., *Canada* 103 B7
Musquodoboit Harbour, *Canada* 103 D7
Musselburgh, *U.K.* 14 F5
Musselshell →, *U.S.A.* 114 C10
Mussidan, *France* 20 C4
Mussomeli, *Italy* 30 E6
Mussoorie, *India* 68 D8
Mussuco, *Angola* 88 B2
Mustafakemalpaşa, *Turkey* 41 F12
Mustang, *Nepal* 69 E10
Musters, L., *Argentina* 128 F3
Musudan, *N. Korea* 57 D15
Muswellbrook, *Australia* 95 E5
Muszyna, *Poland* 45 J7
Mût, *Egypt* 80 B2
Mut, *Turkey* 70 B2
Mutanda, *Mozam.* 89 C5
Mutanda, *Zambia* 87 E2
Mutare, *Zimbabwe* 87 F3
Muting, *Indonesia* 63 F10
Mutoko, *Zimbabwe* 89 B5
Mutoray, *Russia* 51 C11
Mutshatsha, *Dem. Rep. of the Congo* 87 E1
Mutsu, *Japan* 54 D10
Mutsu-Wan, *Japan* 54 D10
Muttaburra, *Australia* 94 C3
Muttalip, *Turkey* 39 B12
Mutton I., *Ireland* 15 D2
Mutuáli, *Mozam.* 87 E4
Mutum Biyu, *Nigeria* 83 D7
Muweilih, *Egypt* 75 E3
Muxía, *Spain* 34 B1
Muy Muy, *Nic.* 120 D2
Muyinga, *Burundi* 86 C3
Muynak, *Uzbekistan* 50 E6
Muzaffarabad, *Pakistan* 69 B5
Muzaffargarh, *Pakistan* 68 D4
Muzaffarnagar, *India* 68 E7
Muzaffarpur, *India* 69 F11
Muzafirpur, *Pakistan* 68 D3
Muzhi, *Russia* 50 C7
Muzillac, *France* 18 E4
Muzūra, *Egypt* 80 J7
Mvôlô, *Sudan* 81 F2
Mvuma, *Zimbabwe* 87 F3
Mvurwi, *Zimbabwe* 87 F3
Mwadui, *Tanzania* 86 C3
Mwambo, *Tanzania* 87 E5
Mwandi, *Zambia* 87 F1
Mwanza, *Dem. Rep. of the Congo* 86 D2
Mwanza, *Tanzania* 86 C3
Mwanza, *Zambia* 87 F1
Mwanza □, *Tanzania* 86 C3
Mwaya, *Tanzania* 87 D3
Mweelrea, *Ireland* 15 C2
Mweka, *Dem. Rep. of the Congo* 84 E4
Mwenezi, *Zimbabwe* 87 G3
Mwenezi →, *Mozam.* 87 G3
Mwenga, *Dem. Rep. of the Congo* 86 C2
Mweru, L., *Zambia* 87 D2
Mweza Range, *Zimbabwe* 87 G3
Mwilambwe, *Dem. Rep. of the Congo* 86 D2
Mwimbi, *Tanzania* 87 D3
Mwinilunga, *Zambia* 87 E1
My Tho, *Vietnam* 65 G6
Myajlar, *India* 68 F4
Myanaung, *Burma* 67 K19
Myanmar = Burma ■, *Asia* 67 J20
Myaungmya, *Burma* 67 L19
Myeik Kyunzu, *Burma* 65 G1
Myers Chuck, *U.S.A.* 104 B2
Myerstown, *U.S.A.* 111 F8
Myingyan, *Burma* 67 J19
Myitkyina, *Burma* 67 G20
Myjava, *Slovak Rep.* 27 C10
Mykhaylivka, *Ukraine* 47 J8
Mykines, *Færoe Is.* 8 E9
Mykolayiv, *Ukraine* 47 J7
Mymensingh, *Bangla.* 67 G17
Mynydd Du, *U.K.* 13 F4
Mýrdalsjökull, *Iceland* 8 E4
Myrhorod, *Ukraine* 47 H7
Myrtle Beach, *U.S.A.* 109 J6
Myrtle Creek, *U.S.A.* 114 E2
Myrtle Point, *U.S.A.* 114 E1
Myrtou, *Cyprus* 36 D12
Mysia, *Turkey* 41 G11
Myślenice, *Poland* 45 J6
Myślibórz, *Poland* 45 F1
Mysłowice, *Poland* 45 H6
Mysore = Karnataka □, *India* 66 N10
Mysore, *India* 66 N10
Mystic, *U.S.A.* 111 E13
Myszków, *Poland* 45 H6
Myszyniec, *Poland* 44 E8
Mytishchi, *Russia* 46 E9
Mývatn, *Iceland* 8 D5
Mže →, *Czech Rep.* 26 B6
Mzimba, *Malawi* 87 E3
Mzimkulu →, *S. Africa* 89 E5
Mzimvubu →, *S. Africa* 89 E4
Mzuzu, *Malawi* 87 E3

N

Na Hearadh = Harris, *U.K.* 14 D2
Na Noi, *Thailand* 64 C3
Na Phao, *Laos* 64 D5
Na Sam, *Vietnam* 58 F6
Na San, *Vietnam* 64 B5
Naab →, *Germany* 25 F8
Na'am, *Sudan* 81 F2
Na'am →, *Sudan* 81 F2
Naantali, *Finland* 9 F19
Naas, *Ireland* 15 C5
Nababeep, *S. Africa* 88 D2
Nabadwip = Navadwip, *India* 69 H13
Nabari, *Japan* 55 G8
Nabawa, *Australia* 93 E1
Nabberu, L., *Australia* 93 E3
Nabburg, *Germany* 25 F8
Naberezhnyye Chelny, *Russia* 48 C11
Nabeul, *Tunisia* 79 A8
Nabha, *India* 68 D7
Nabīd, *Iran* 71 D8
Nabire, *Indonesia* 63 E9
Nabisar, *Pakistan* 68 G3
Nabisipi →, *Canada* 103 B7
Nabiswera, *Uganda* 86 B3
Nablus = Nābulus, *West Bank* 75 C4
Naboomspruit, *S. Africa* 89 C4
Nabou, *Burkina Faso* 82 C4
Nabua, *Phil.* 61 E5
Nābulus, *West Bank* 75 C4
Nacala, *Mozam.* 87 E5
Nacala-Velha, *Mozam.* 87 E5
Nacaome, *Honduras* 120 D2
Nacaroa, *Mozam.* 87 E4
Naches, *U.S.A.* 114 C3
Naches →, *U.S.A.* 116 D6
Nachicapau, L., *Canada* 103 A6
Nachingwea, *Tanzania* 87 E4
Nachna, *India* 68 F4
Náchod, *Czech Rep.* 26 A9
Nacimiento L., *U.S.A.* 116 K6
Naco, *Mexico* 118 A3
Nacogdoches, *U.S.A.* 113 K7
Nácori Chico, *Mexico* 118 B3
Nacozari, *Mexico* 118 A3
Nadi, *Sudan* 80 D3
Nadiad, *India* 68 H5
Nădlac, *Romania* 42 D5
Nador, *Morocco* 78 B5
Nadur, *Malta* 36 C1
Nadūshan, *Iran* 71 C7
Nadvirna, *Ukraine* 47 H3
Nadvornaya = Nadvirna, *Ukraine* 47 H3
Nadym, *Russia* 50 C8
Nadym →, *Russia* 50 C8
Nærbø, *Norway* 9 G11
Næstved, *Denmark* 11 J5
Nafada, *Nigeria* 83 C7
Naft-e Safīd, *Iran* 71 D6
Naftshahr, *Iran* 70 C5
Nafud Desert = An Nafūd, *Si. Arabia* 70 D4
Nag Hammâdi, *Egypt* 80 B3
Naga, *Phil.* 61 E5
Nagahama, *Japan* 55 G8
Nagai, *Japan* 54 E10
Nagaland □, *India* 67 G19
Nagano, *Japan* 55 F9
Nagano □, *Japan* 55 F9
Nagaoka, *Japan* 55 F9
Nagappattinam, *India* 66 P11
Nagar →, *Bangla.* 69 G13
Nagar Parkar, *Pakistan* 68 G4
Nagasaki, *Japan* 55 H4
Nagasaki □, *Japan* 55 H4
Nagato, *Japan* 55 G5
Nagaur, *India* 68 F5
Nagda, *India* 68 H6
Nagercoil, *India* 66 Q10
Nagina, *India* 69 E8
Nagīneh, *Iran* 71 C8
Nagir, *Pakistan* 69 A6
Naglarby, *Sweden* 10 D9
Nagod, *India* 69 G9
Nagold, *Germany* 25 G4
Nagold →, *Germany* 25 G4
Nagoorin, *Australia* 94 C5
Nagorno-Karabakh, *Azerbaijan* 70 B5
Nagornyy, *Russia* 51 D13
Nagoya, *Japan* 55 G8
Nagpur, *India* 66 J11
Nagua, *Dom. Rep.* 121 C6
Nagyatád, *Hungary* 42 D2
Nagyecsed, *Hungary* 42 C7
Nagykálló, *Hungary* 42 C6
Nagykanizsa, *Hungary* 42 D2
Nagykáta, *Hungary* 42 C4
Nagykőrös, *Hungary* 42 C4
Naha, *Japan* 55 L3
Nahan, *India* 68 D7
Nahanni Butte, *Canada* 104 A4
Nahanni Nat. Park, *Canada* 104 A4
Nahargarh, *Mad. P., India* 68 G6
Nahargarh, *Raj., India* 68 G7
Nahariyya, *Israel* 70 C2
Nahāvand, *Iran* 71 C6
Nahe →, *Germany* 25 F3
Nahîya, W. →, *Egypt* 80 B3
Naicá, *Mexico* 118 B3
Naicam, *Canada* 105 C8
Naikoon Prov. Park, *Canada* 104 C2
Naila, *Germany* 25 E7
Naimisharanya, *India* 69 F9
Nain, *Canada* 103 A7
Nā'īn, *Iran* 71 C7
Naini Tal, *India* 69 E8
Nainpur, *India* 66 H12
Naintré, *France* 18 F7
Nainwa, *India* 68 G6
Naipu, *Romania* 43 F10
Nairn, *U.K.* 14 D5
Nairobi, *Kenya* 86 C4
Naissaar, *Estonia* 9 G21
Naita, Mt., *Ethiopia* 81 F4
Naivasha, *Kenya* 86 C4
Naivasha, L., *Kenya* 86 C4
Najac, *France* 20 D5
Najafābād, *Iran* 71 C6
Najd, *Si. Arabia* 74 B3
Nájera, *Spain* 32 C2
Najerilla →, *Spain* 32 C2
Najibabad, *India* 68 E8
Najin, *N. Korea* 57 C16
Najmah, *Si. Arabia* 71 E6
Naju, *S. Korea* 57 G14
Nakadōri-Shima, *Japan* 55 H4
Nakalagba, *Dem. Rep. of the Congo* 86 B2
Nakaminato, *Japan* 55 F10
Nakamura, *Japan* 55 H6
Nakano, *Japan* 55 F9
Nakano-Shima, *Japan* 55 K4
Nakashibetsu, *Japan* 54 C12
Nakfa, *Eritrea* 81 D4
Nakhfar al Buşayyah, *Iraq* 70 D5
Nakhichevan = Naxçıvan, *Azerbaijan* 70 B5
Nakhichevan Republic = Naxçıvan □, *Azerbaijan* 50 F5
Nakhl, *Egypt* 75 F2
Nakhl-e Taqī, *Iran* 71 E7
Nakhodka, *Russia* 51 E14
Nakhon Nayok, *Thailand* 64 E3
Nakhon Pathom, *Thailand* 64 F3
Nakhon Phanom, *Thailand* 64 D5
Nakhon Ratchasima, *Thailand* 64 E4
Nakhon Sawan, *Thailand* 64 E3
Nakhon Si Thammarat, *Thailand* 65 H3
Nakhon Thai, *Thailand* 64 D3
Nakhtarana, *India* 68 H3
Nakina, *Canada* 102 B2
Nakło nad Notecią, *Poland* 45 E4
Nako, *Burkina Faso* 82 C4
Nakodar, *India* 68 D6
Nakskov, *Denmark* 11 K5
Naktong →, *S. Korea* 57 G15
Nakuru, *Kenya* 86 C4
Nakuru, L., *Kenya* 86 C4
Nakusp, *Canada* 104 C5
Nal, *Pakistan* 68 F2
Nal →, *Pakistan* 68 G1
Nalázi, *Mozam.* 89 C5
Nalchik, *Russia* 49 J6
Nałęczów, *Poland* 45 G9
Nalerigu, *Ghana* 83 C4
Nalgonda, *India* 66 L11
Nalhati, *India* 69 G12
Naliya, *India* 68 H3
Nallamalai Hills, *India* 66 M11
Nallıhan, *Turkey* 72 B4
Nalón →, *Spain* 34 B4
Nam Can, *Vietnam* 65 H5
Nam-ch'on, *N. Korea* 57 E14
Nam Co, *China* 60 C4
Nam Dinh, *Vietnam* 58 G6
Nam Du, Hon, *Vietnam* 65 H5
Nam Ngum Dam, *Laos* 64 C4
Nam-Phan = Cochin China, *Vietnam* 65 G6
Nam Phong, *Thailand* 64 D4
Nam Tha, *Laos* 58 G3
Nam Tok, *Thailand* 64 E2
Namacunde, *Angola* 88 B2
Namacurra, *Mozam.* 89 B6
Namak, Daryācheh-ye, *Iran* 71 C7
Namak, Kavir-e, *Iran* 71 C8
Namakzār, Daryācheh-ye, *Iran* 71 C9
Namaland, *Namibia* 88 C2
Namangan, *Uzbekistan* 50 E8
Namapa, *Mozam.* 87 E4
Namaqualand, *S. Africa* 88 E2
Namasagali, *Uganda* 86 B3
Namber, *Indonesia* 63 E8
Nambour, *Australia* 95 D5
Nambucca Heads, *Australia* 95 E5
Namche Bazar, *Nepal* 69 F12
Namchonjŏm = Nam-ch'on, *N. Korea* 57 E14
Namecunda, *Mozam.* 87 E4
Nameponda, *Mozam.* 87 F4
Náměšť nad Oslavou, *Czech Rep.* 27 B9
Námestovo, *Slovak Rep.* 27 B12
Nametil, *Mozam.* 87 F4
Namew L., *Canada* 105 C8
Namgia, *India* 69 D8
Namhkam, *Burma* 58 E1
Namib Desert = Namibwoestyn, *Namibia* 88 C2
Namibe, *Angola* 85 H2
Namibe □, *Angola* 88 B1
Namibia ■, *Africa* 88 C2
Namibwoestyn, *Namibia* 88 C2
Namīn, *Iran* 73 C13
Namlea, *Indonesia* 63 E7
Namoi →, *Australia* 95 E4
Nampa, *U.S.A.* 114 E5
Nampala, *Mali* 82 B3
Namp'o, *N. Korea* 57 E13
Nampō-Shotō, *Japan* 55 J10
Nampula, *Mozam.* 87 F4
Namrole, *Indonesia* 63 E7
Namse Shankou, *China* 67 E13
Namsen →, *Norway* 8 D14
Namsos, *Norway* 8 D14
Namtsy, *Russia* 51 C13
Namtu, *Burma* 67 H20
Namtumbo, *Tanzania* 87 E4
Namu, *Canada* 104 C3
Namur, *Belgium* 17 D4
Namur □, *Belgium* 17 D4
Namutoni, *Namibia* 88 B2
Namwala, *Zambia* 87 F2
Namwŏn, *S. Korea* 57 G14
Namysłów, *Poland* 45 G4
Nan, *Thailand* 64 C3
Nan →, *Thailand* 64 E3
Nan-ch'ang = Nanchang, *China* 59 C10
Nan Ling, *China* 59 E8
Nan Xian, *China* 59 C9
Nana, *Romania* 43 F11
Nana Kru, *Liberia* 82 E3
Nanaimo, *Canada* 104 D4
Nanam, *N. Korea* 57 D15
Nanan, *China* 59 E12
Nanango, *Australia* 95 D5
Nan'ao, *China* 59 F11
Nanao, *Japan* 55 F8
Nanbu, *China* 58 B6
Nanchang, *Jiangxi, China* 59 C10
Nanchang, *Kiangsi, China* 59 C10
Nancheng, *China* 59 D11
Nanching = Nanjing, *China* 59 A12
Nanchong, *China* 58 B6
Nanchuan, *China* 58 C6
Nancy, *France* 19 D13
Nanda Devi, *India* 69 D8
Nanda Kot, *India* 69 D9
Nandan, *China* 58 E6
Nandan, *Japan* 55 G7
Nanded, *India* 66 K10
Nandewar Ra., *Australia* 95 E5
Nandi, *Fiji* 91 C7
Nandigram, *India* 69 H12
Nandurbar, *India* 66 J9
Nandyal, *India* 66 M11
Nanfeng, *Guangdong, China* 59 F8
Nanfeng, *Jiangxi, China* 59 D11
Nanga-Eboko, *Cameroon* 83 E7
Nanga Parbat, *Pakistan* 69 B6
Nangade, *Mozam.* 87 E4
Nangapinoh, *Indonesia* 62 E4
Nangarhār □, *Afghan.* 66 B7
Nangatayap, *Indonesia* 62 E4
Nangeya Mts., *Uganda* 86 B3
Nangis, *France* 19 D10
Nangong, *China* 56 F8
Nanhua, *China* 58 E3
Nanhuang, *China* 57 F11
Nanhui, *China* 59 B13
Nanjeko, *Zambia* 87 F1
Nanji Shan, *China* 59 D13
Nanjian, *China* 58 E3
Nanjiang, *China* 58 A6
Nanjing, *Fujian, China* 59 E11
Nanjing, *Jiangsu, China* 59 A12
Nanjirinji, *Tanzania* 87 D4
Nankana Sahib, *Pakistan* 68 D5
Nankang, *China* 59 E10
Nanking = Nanjing, *China* 59 A12
Nankoku, *Japan* 55 H6
Nanling, *China* 59 B12
Nanning, *China* 58 F7
Nannup, *Australia* 93 F2
Nanpan Jiang →, *China* 58 E6
Nanpara, *India* 69 F9
Nanpi, *China* 56 E9
Nanping, *Fujian, China* 59 D12
Nanping, *Henan, China* 59 C9
Nanri Dao, *China* 59 E12
Nanripe, *Mozam.* 87 E4
Nansei-Shotō = Ryūkyū-rettō, *Japan* 55 M3
Nansen Sd., *Canada* 4 A3
Nanshan I., *S. China Sea* 62 B5
Nansio, *Tanzania* 86 C3
Nant, *France* 20 D7
Nanterre, *France* 19 D9
Nantes, *France* 18 E5
Nantiat, *France* 20 B5
Nanticoke, *U.S.A.* 111 E8
Nanton, *Canada* 104 C6
Nantong, *China* 59 A13
Nantou, *Taiwan* 59 F13
Nantua, *France* 19 F12
Nantucket I., *U.S.A.* 108 E10
Nantwich, *U.K.* 12 D5
Nanty Glo, *U.S.A.* 110 F6
Nanuque, *Brazil* 125 G10
Nanusa, Kepulauan, *Indonesia* 63 D7
Nanutarra Roadhouse, *Australia* 92 D2
Nanxi, *China* 58 C5
Nanxiong, *China* 59 E10
Nanyang, *China* 56 H7
Nanyi Hu, *China* 59 B12
Nanyuan, *China* 56 E9
Nanyuki, *Kenya* 86 B4
Nanzhang, *China* 59 B8
Nao, C. de la, *Spain* 33 G5
Naococane, L., *Canada* 103 B5
Náousa, *Imathía, Greece* 40 F6
Náousa, *Kikládhes, Greece* 39 D7
Naozhou Dao, *China* 59 G8
Napa, *U.S.A.* 116 G4
Napa →, *U.S.A.* 116 G4
Napanee, *Canada* 102 D4
Napanoch, *U.S.A.* 111 E10
Nape, *Laos* 64 C5
Nape Pass = Keo Neua, Deo, *Vietnam* 64 C5
Napier, *N.Z.* 91 H6
Napier Broome B., *Australia* 92 B4
Napier Pen., *Australia* 94 A2
Napierville, *Canada* 111 A11
Naples = Nápoli, *Italy* 31 B7
Naples, *U.S.A.* 109 M5
Napo, *China* 58 F5
Napo →, *Peru* 122 D3
Napoleon, *N. Dak., U.S.A.* 112 B5
Napoleon, *Ohio, U.S.A.* 108 E3
Nápoli, *Italy* 31 B7
Nápoli, G. di, *Italy* 31 B7
Napopo, *Dem. Rep. of the Congo* 86 B2
Naqâda, *Egypt* 80 B3
Naqadeh, *Iran* 73 D11
Naqb, Ra's an, *Jordan* 75 F4
Naqqāsh, *Iran* 71 C6
Nara, *Japan* 55 G7
Nara, *Mali* 82 B3
Nara □, *Japan* 55 G8
Nara Canal, *Pakistan* 68 G3
Nara Visa, *U.S.A.* 113 H3
Naracoorte, *Australia* 95 F3
Naradhan, *Australia* 95 E4
Naraini, *India* 69 G9
Narasapur, *India* 67 L12
Narathiwat, *Thailand* 65 J3
Narayanganj, *Bangla.* 67 H17
Narayanpet, *India* 66 L10
Narbonne, *France* 20 E7
Narcea →, *Spain* 34 B4
Nardīn, *Iran* 71 B7
Nardò, *Italy* 31 B11
Narembeen, *Australia* 93 F2
Narendranagar, *India* 68 D8
Nares Str., *Arctic* 98 A13
Naretha, *Australia* 93 F3
Narew →, *Poland* 45 F7
Nari →, *Pakistan* 68 F2
Narin, *Afghan.* 66 A6
Narindra, Helodranon' i, *Madag.* 89 A8
Narita, *Japan* 55 G10
Närke, *Sweden* 10 E8
Narmada →, *India* 68 J5
Narman, *Turkey* 73 B9
Narmland, *Sweden* 9 F15
Narnaul, *India* 68 E7
Narni, *Italy* 29 F9
Naro, *Ghana* 82 C4
Naro Fominsk, *Russia* 46 E9
Narodnaya, *Russia* 6 B17
Narok, *Kenya* 86 C4
Narón, *Spain* 34 B2
Narooma, *Australia* 95 F5
Narowal, *Pakistan* 68 C6
Narrabri, *Australia* 95 E4
Narran →, *Australia* 95 D4
Narrandera, *Australia* 95 E4
Narrogin, *Australia* 93 F2
Narromine, *Australia* 95 E4
Narrow Hills Prov. Park, *Canada* 105 C8
Narsimhapur, *India* 69 H8
Narsinghgarh, *India* 68 H7
Nartes, L. e, *Albania* 40 F3
Nartkala, *Russia* 49 J6
Naruto, *Japan* 55 G7
Narva, *Estonia* 46 C5
Narva →, *Russia* 9 G22
Narvik, *Norway* 8 B17
Narvskoye Vdkhr., *Russia* 46 C5
Narwana, *India* 68 E7
Naryan-Mar, *Russia* 50 C6
Narym, *Russia* 50 D9
Naryn, *Kyrgyzstan* 50 E8
Nasa, *Norway* 8 C16
Nasarawa, *Nigeria* 83 D6
Năsăud, *Romania* 43 C9
Naseby, *N.Z.* 91 L3
Naselle, *U.S.A.* 116 D3
Naser, Buheirat en, *Egypt* 80 C3
Nashua, *Mont., U.S.A.* 114 B10
Nashua, *N.H., U.S.A.* 111 D13
Nashville, *Ark., U.S.A.* 113 J8
Nashville, *Ga., U.S.A.* 109 K4
Nashville, *Tenn., U.S.A.* 109 G2
Našice, *Croatia* 42 E3
Nasielsk, *Poland* 45 F7
Nasik, *India* 66 K8
Nasipit, *Phil.* 61 G6
Nasir, *Sudan* 81 F3
Nasirabad, *India* 68 F6
Nasirabad, *Pakistan* 68 E3
Naskaupi →, *Canada* 103 B7
Naso, *Italy* 31 D7
Naşrābād, *Iran* 71 C6
Naşriān-e Pā'īn, *Iran* 70 C5
Nass →, *Canada* 104 C3
Nassarawa □, *Nigeria* 83 D6
Nassau, *Bahamas* 120 A4
Nassau, *U.S.A.* 111 D11
Nassau, B., *Chile* 128 H3
Nasser, L. = Naser, Buheirat en, *Egypt* 80 C3
Nasser City = Kôm Ombo, *Egypt* 80 C3
Nassian, *Ivory C.* 82 D4
Nässjö, *Sweden* 11 G8
Nastapoka →, *Canada* 102 A4
Nastapoka, Is., *Canada* 102 A4
Nasugbu, *Phil.* 61 D4
Näsum, *Sweden* 11 H8
Näsviken, *Sweden* 10 C10
Nata, *Botswana* 88 C4
Nata →, *Botswana* 88 C4
Natal, *Brazil* 125 E11
Natal, *Indonesia* 62 D1
Natal, *S. Africa* 85 K6
Natalinci, *Serbia, Yug.* 42 F5

Naţanz, *Iran* 71 C6
Natashquan, *Canada* 103 B7
Natashquan →, *Canada* 103 B7
Natchez, *U.S.A.* 113 K9
Natchitoches, *U.S.A.* 113 K8
Nathalia, *Australia* 95 F4
Nathdwara, *India* 68 G5
Nati, Pta., *Spain* 37 A10
Natimuk, *Australia* 95 F3
Nation →, *Canada* 104 B4
National City, *U.S.A.* 117 N9
Natitingou, *Benin* 83 C5
Natividad, I., *Mexico* 118 B1
Natkyizin, *Burma* 64 E1
Natron, L., *Tanzania* 86 C4
Natrona Heights, *U.S.A.* 110 F5
Natrûn, W. el →, *Egypt* 80 H7
Nättraby, *Sweden* 11 H9
Natukanaoka Pan, *Namibia* 88 B2
Natuna Besar, Kepulauan, *Indonesia* 65 L7
Natuna Is. = Natuna Besar, Kepulauan, *Indonesia* 65 L7
Natuna Selatan, Kepulauan, *Indonesia* 65 L7
Natural Bridge, *U.S.A.* 111 B9
Naturaliste, C., *Australia* 94 G4
Nau Qala, *Afghan.* 68 B3
Naucelle, *France* 20 D6
Nauders, *Austria* 26 E3
Nauen, *Germany* 24 C8
Naugatuck, *U.S.A.* 111 E11
Naujoji Akmenė, *Lithuania* 44 B9
Naumburg, *Germany* 24 D7
Nā'ūr at Tunayb, *Jordan* 75 D4
Nauru ■, *Pac. Oc.* 96 H8
Naushahra = Nowshera, *Pakistan* 66 C8
Naushahro, *Pakistan* 68 F3
Naushon I., *U.S.A.* 111 E14
Nauta, *Peru* 124 D4
Nautanwa, *India* 67 F13
Nautla, *Mexico* 119 C5
Nava, *Mexico* 118 B4
Nava, *Spain* 34 B5
Nava del Rey, *Spain* 34 D5
Navadwip, *India* 69 H13
Navahermosa, *Spain* 35 F6
Navahrudak, *Belarus* 46 F3
Navajo Reservoir, *U.S.A.* 115 H10
Navalcarnero, *Spain* 34 E6
Navalmoral de la Mata, *Spain* 34 F5
Navalvillar de Pela, *Spain* 35 F5
Navan = An Uaimh, *Ireland* 15 C5
Navapolatsk, *Belarus* 46 E5
Navarino, I., *Chile* 128 H3
Navarra □, *Spain* 32 C3
Navarre, *U.S.A.* 110 F3
Navarro →, *U.S.A.* 116 F3
Navas de San Juan, *Spain* 35 G7
Navasota, *U.S.A.* 113 K6
Navassa I., *W. Indies* 121 C5
Nävekvarn, *Sweden* 11 F10
Naver →, *U.K.* 14 C4
Navia, *Spain* 34 B4
Navia →, *Spain* 34 B4
Navia de Suarna, *Spain* 34 C3
Navibandar, *India* 68 J3
Navidad, *Chile* 126 C1
Naviraí, *Brazil* 127 A5
Navlakhi, *India* 68 H4
Navlya, *Russia* 47 F8
Năvodari, *Romania* 43 F13
Navoi = Nawoiy, *Uzbekistan* 50 E7
Navojoa, *Mexico* 118 B3
Navolato, *Mexico* 118 C3
Návpaktos, *Greece* 38 C3
Návplion, *Greece* 38 D4
Navrongo, *Ghana* 83 C4
Navsari, *India* 66 J8
Nawa Kot, *Pakistan* 68 E4
Nawab Khan, *Pakistan* 68 D3
Nawabganj, *Ut. P., India* 69 F9
Nawabganj, *Ut. P., India* 69 E8
Nawabshah, *Pakistan* 68 F3
Nawada, *India* 69 G11
Nawakot, *Nepal* 69 F11
Nawalgarh, *India* 68 F6
Nawanshahr, *India* 69 C6
Nawar, Dasht-i-, *Afghan.* 68 C3
Nawi, *Sudan* 80 D3
Nawoiy, *Uzbekistan* 50 E7
Naxçıvan, *Azerbaijan* 70 B5
Naxçıvan □, *Azerbaijan* 50 F5
Náxos, *Greece* 39 D7
Nay, *France* 20 E3
Nay, Mui, *Vietnam* 62 B3
Nāy Band, *Būshehr, Iran* 71 E7
Nāy Band, *Khorāsān, Iran* 71 C8
Nayakhan, *Russia* 51 C16
Nayarit □, *Mexico* 118 C4
Nayé, *Senegal* 82 C2
Nayong, *China* 58 D5
Nayoro, *Japan* 54 B11
Nayyāl, W. →, *Si. Arabia* 70 D3
Nazaré, *Brazil* 125 F11
Nazaré, *Portugal* 35 F1
Nazareth = Nazerat, *Israel* 75 C4
Nazareth, *U.S.A.* 111 F9
Nazas, *Mexico* 118 B4
Nazas →, *Mexico* 118 B4
Nazca, *Peru* 124 F4
Naze, The, *U.K.* 13 F9
Nazerat, *Israel* 75 C4
Nāzīk, *Iran* 70 B5
Nazilli, *Turkey* 39 D10
Nazir Hat, *Bangla.* 67 H17
Nazko, *Canada* 104 C4
Nazko →, *Canada* 104 C4
Nazret, *Ethiopia* 81 F4
Nazwá, *Oman* 74 C6
Nchanga, *Zambia* 87 E2
Ncheu, *Malawi* 87 E3
Ndala, *Tanzania* 86 C3
Ndalatando, *Angola* 84 F2
Ndali, *Benin* 83 D5
Ndareda, *Tanzania* 86 C4
Ndélé, *C.A.R.* 84 C4
Ndikiniméki, *Cameroon* 83 E7
N'Dioum, *Senegal* 82 B2
Ndjamena, *Chad* 79 F8
Ndola, *Zambia* 87 E2
Ndoto Mts., *Kenya* 86 B4
Nduguti, *Tanzania* 86 C3
Néa Alikarnassós, *Greece* 39 F7
Néa Ankhíalos, *Greece* 38 B4
Néa Epídhavros, *Greece* 38 D5
Néa Flippiás, *Greece* 38 B2
Néa Ionia, *Greece* 38 B4
Néa Kallikrátia, *Greece* 40 F7
Néa Mákri, *Greece* 38 C5
Néa Moudhaniá, *Greece* 40 F7
Néa Péramos, *Attikí, Greece* 38 C5
Néa Péramos, *Kaválla, Greece* 41 F8
Néa Víssi, *Greece* 41 E10
Néa Zíkhna, *Greece* 40 E7
Neagh, Lough, *U.K.* 15 B5
Neah Bay, *U.S.A.* 116 B2
Neale, L., *Australia* 92 D5
Neamţ □, *Romania* 43 C11
Neápolis, *Kozáni, Greece* 40 F5
Neápolis, *Kríti, Greece* 36 D7
Neápolis, *Lakonía, Greece* 38 E5
Near Is., *U.S.A.* 100 C1
Neath, *U.K.* 13 F4
Neath Port Talbot □, *U.K.* 13 F4
Nebbou, *Burkina Faso* 83 C4
Nebelat el Hagana, *Sudan* 81 E2
Nebine Cr. →, *Australia* 95 D4
Nebitdag, *Turkmenistan* 50 F6
Nebo, *Australia* 94 C4
Nebolchy, *Russia* 46 C7
Nebraska □, *U.S.A.* 112 E5
Nebraska City, *U.S.A.* 112 E7
Nébrodi, Monti, *Italy* 31 E7
Necedah, *U.S.A.* 112 C9
Nechako →, *Canada* 104 C4
Neches →, *U.S.A.* 113 L8
Neckar →, *Germany* 25 F4
Necochea, *Argentina* 126 D4
Neda, *Spain* 34 B2
Nedelino, *Bulgaria* 41 E9
Nedelišće, *Croatia* 29 B13
Nédha →, *Greece* 38 D3
Needles, *Canada* 104 D5
Needles, *U.S.A.* 117 L12
Needles, The, *U.K.* 13 G6
Ñeembucú □, *Paraguay* 126 B4
Neemuch = Nimach, *India* 68 G6
Neenah, *U.S.A.* 108 C1
Neepawa, *Canada* 105 C9
Neftçala, *Azerbaijan* 71 B6
Neftegorsk, *Russia* 49 H4
Neftekumsk, *Russia* 49 H7
Nefyn, *U.K.* 12 E3
Négala, *Mali* 82 C3
Negapatam = Nagappattinam, *India* 66 P11
Negaunee, *U.S.A.* 108 B2
Negele, *Ethiopia* 81 F4
Negev Desert = Hanegev, *Israel* 75 E4
Negoiul, Vf., *Romania* 43 E9
Negombo, *Sri Lanka* 66 R11
Negotin, *Serbia, Yug.* 40 B6
Negotino, *Macedonia* 40 E6
Negra, Peña, *Spain* 34 C4
Negra, Pta., *Peru* 122 D2
Negrais, C. = Maudin Sun, *Burma* 67 M19
Negreşti, *Romania* 43 D12
Negreşti-Oaş, *Romania* 43 C8
Negril, *Jamaica* 120 C4
Negro →, *Argentina* 122 H4
Negro →, *Brazil* 122 D4
Negro →, *Uruguay* 127 C4
Negros, *Phil.* 61 G5
Negru Vodă, *Romania* 43 G13
Neguac, *Canada* 103 C6
Nehalem →, *U.S.A.* 116 E3
Nehāvand, *Iran* 71 C6
Nehbandān, *Iran* 71 D9
Nehoiu, *Romania* 43 E11
Nei Mongol Zizhiqu □, *China* 56 D7
Neijiang, *China* 58 C5
Neillsville, *U.S.A.* 112 C9
Neilton, *U.S.A.* 114 C2
Neiqiu, *China* 56 F8
Neiva, *Colombia* 124 C3
Neixiang, *China* 56 H6
Nejanilini L., *Canada* 105 B9
Nejd = Najd, *Si. Arabia* 74 B3
Nejo, *Ethiopia* 81 F4
Nekā, *Iran* 71 B7
Nekemte, *Ethiopia* 81 F4
Nêkheb, *Egypt* 80 B3
Neksø, *Denmark* 11 J9
Nelas, *Portugal* 34 E3
Nelia, *Australia* 94 C3
Nelidovo, *Russia* 46 D7
Neligh, *U.S.A.* 112 D5
Nelkan, *Russia* 51 D14
Nellore, *India* 66 M11
Nelson, *Canada* 104 D5
Nelson, *N.Z.* 91 J4
Nelson, *U.K.* 12 D5
Nelson, *Ariz., U.S.A.* 115 J7
Nelson, *Nev., U.S.A.* 117 K12
Nelson →, *Canada* 105 C9
Nelson, C., *Australia* 95 F3
Nelson, Estrecho, *Chile* 128 G2
Nelson Bay, *Australia* 95 E5
Nelson Forks, *Canada* 104 B4
Nelson House, *Canada* 105 B9
Nelson L., *Canada* 105 B8
Nelspoort, *S. Africa* 88 E3
Nelspruit, *S. Africa* 89 D5
Néma, *Mauritania* 82 B3
Neman, *Russia* 9 J20
Neman →, *Lithuania* 9 J20
Neméa, *Greece* 38 D4
Nemeiben L., *Canada* 105 B7
Nemërçkës, Mal, *Albania* 40 F4
Nemira, Vf., *Romania* 43 D11
Némiscau, *Canada* 102 B4
Némiscau, L., *Canada* 102 B4
Nemours, *France* 19 D9
Nemšová, *Slovak Rep.* 27 C11
Nemunas = Neman →, *Lithuania* 9 J20
Nemuro, *Japan* 54 C12
Nemuro-Kaikyō, *Japan* 54 C12
Nen Jiang →, *China* 57 B13
Nenagh, *Ireland* 15 D3
Nenasi, *Malaysia* 65 L4
Nene →, *U.K.* 13 E8
Nénita, *Greece* 39 C8
Nenjiang, *China* 60 B7
Neno, *Malawi* 87 F3
Neodesha, *U.S.A.* 113 G7
Neokhórion, *Aitolía kai Akarnanía, Greece* 38 C3
Neokhórion, *Árta, Greece* 38 B2
Néon Karlovásion, *Greece* 39 D8
Néon Petrítsi, *Greece* 40 E7
Neosho, *U.S.A.* 113 G7
Neosho →, *U.S.A.* 113 H7
Nepal ■, *Asia* 69 F11
Nepalganj, *Nepal* 69 E9
Nepalganj Road, *India* 69 E9
Nephi, *U.S.A.* 114 G8
Nephin, *Ireland* 15 B2
Nepi, *Italy* 29 F9
Nepomuk, *Czech Rep.* 26 B6
Neptune, *U.S.A.* 111 F10
Nera →, *Italy* 29 F9
Nera →, *Romania* 42 F6
Nérac, *France* 20 D4
Nerang, *Australia* 95 D5
Neratovice, *Czech Rep.* 26 A7
Nerchinsk, *Russia* 51 D12
Nereju, *Romania* 43 E11
Nerekhta, *Russia* 46 D11
Néret, L., *Canada* 103 B5
Neretvanski Kanal, *Croatia* 29 E14
Neringa, *Lithuania* 9 J19
Nerja, *Spain* 35 J7
Nerl →, *Russia* 46 D11
Nerpio, *Spain* 33 G2
Nerva, *Spain* 35 H4
Nervi, *Italy* 28 D6
Neryungri, *Russia* 51 D13
Nescopeck, *U.S.A.* 111 E8
Nesebŭr, *Bulgaria* 41 D11
Ness, L., *U.K.* 14 D4
Ness City, *U.S.A.* 112 F5
Nesterov, *Poland* 47 G2
Nestórion, *Greece* 40 F5
Néstos →, *Greece* 41 E8
Nesvady, *Slovak Rep.* 27 D11
Nesvizh = Nyasvizh, *Belarus* 47 F4
Netanya, *Israel* 75 C3
Netarhat, *India* 69 H11
Nete →, *Belgium* 17 C4
Netherdale, *Australia* 94 C4
Netherlands ■, *Europe* 17 C5
Netherlands Antilles ■, *W. Indies* 124 A5
Neto →, *Italy* 31 C10
Netrang, *India* 68 J5
Nettancourt, *France* 19 D11
Nettetal, *Germany* 24 D2
Nettilling L., *Canada* 101 B12
Nettuno, *Italy* 30 A5
Netzahualcoyotl, Presa, *Mexico* 119 D6
Neu-Isenburg, *Germany* 25 E4
Neu-Ulm, *Germany* 25 G6
Neubrandenburg, *Germany* 24 B9
Neubukow, *Germany* 24 A7
Neuburg, *Germany* 25 G7
Neuchâtel, *Switz.* 25 J2
Neuchâtel □, *Switz.* 25 J2
Neuchâtel, Lac de, *Switz.* 25 J2
Neudau, *Austria* 26 D9
Neuenhagen, *Germany* 24 C9
Neuenhaus, *Germany* 24 C2
Neuf-Brisach, *France* 19 D14
Neufahrn, *Bayern, Germany* 25 G8
Neufahrn, *Bayern, Germany* 25 G7
Neufchâteau, *Belgium* 17 E5
Neufchâteau, *France* 19 D12
Neufchâtel-en-Bray, *France* 18 C8
Neufchâtel-sur-Aisne, *France* 19 C11
Neuhaus, *Germany* 24 B6
Neuillé-Pont-Pierre, *France* 18 E7
Neuilly-St-Front, *France* 19 C10
Neukalen, *Germany* 24 B8
Neumarkt, *Germany* 25 F7
Neumünster, *Germany* 24 A5
Neung-sur-Beuvron, *France* 19 E8
Neunkirchen, *Austria* 26 D9
Neunkirchen, *Germany* 25 F3
Neuquén, *Argentina* 128 D3
Neuquén □, *Argentina* 126 D2
Neuruppin, *Germany* 24 C8
Neusäss, *Germany* 25 G6
Neuse →, *U.S.A.* 109 H7
Neusiedl, *Austria* 27 D9
Neusiedler See, *Austria* 27 D9
Neuss, *Germany* 24 D2
Neussargues-Moissac, *France* 20 C7
Neustadt, *Bayern, Germany* 25 F8
Neustadt, *Bayern, Germany* 25 G7
Neustadt, *Bayern, Germany* 25 F6
Neustadt, *Bayern, Germany* 25 E7
Neustadt, *Brandenburg, Germany* 24 C8
Neustadt, *Hessen, Germany* 24 E5
Neustadt, *Niedersachsen, Germany* 24 C5
Neustadt, *Rhld-Pfz., Germany* 25 F4
Neustadt, *Sachsen, Germany* 24 D10
Neustadt, *Schleswig-Holstein, Germany* 24 A6
Neustadt, *Thüringen, Germany* 24 E7
Neustrelitz, *Germany* 24 B9
Neuvic, *France* 20 C6
Neuville-sur-Saône, *France* 21 C8
Neuvy-le-Roi, *France* 18 E7
Neuvy-St-Sépulchre, *France* 19 F8
Neuvy-sur-Barangeon, *France* 19 E9
Neuwerk, *Germany* 24 B4
Neuwied, *Germany* 24 E3
Neva →, *Russia* 46 C6
Nevada, *Iowa, U.S.A.* 112 D8
Nevada, *Mo., U.S.A.* 113 G7
Nevada □, *U.S.A.* 114 G5
Nevada, Sierra, *Spain* 35 H7
Nevada, Sierra, *U.S.A.* 114 G3
Nevada City, *U.S.A.* 116 F6
Nevado, Cerro, *Argentina* 126 D2
Nevel, *Russia* 46 D5
Nevers, *France* 19 F10
Nevertire, *Australia* 95 E4
Nevesinje, *Bos.-H.* 40 C2
Neville, *Canada* 105 D7
Nevinnomyssk, *Russia* 49 H6
Nevis, *W. Indies* 121 C7
Nevrokop = Gotse Delchev, *Bulgaria* 40 E7
Nevşehir, *Turkey* 70 B2
New →, *U.S.A.* 108 F5
New Aiyansh, *Canada* 104 B3
New Albany, *Ind., U.S.A.* 108 F3
New Albany, *Miss., U.S.A.* 113 H10
New Albany, *Pa., U.S.A.* 111 E8
New Amsterdam, *Guyana* 124 B7
New Angledool, *Australia* 95 D4
New Baltimore, *U.S.A.* 110 D2
New Bedford, *U.S.A.* 111 E14
New Berlin, *N.Y., U.S.A.* 111 D9
New Berlin, *Pa., U.S.A.* 110 F8
New Bern, *U.S.A.* 109 H7
New Bethlehem, *U.S.A.* 110 F5
New Bloomfield, *U.S.A.* 110 F7
New Boston, *U.S.A.* 113 J7
New Braunfels, *U.S.A.* 113 L5
New Brighton, *N.Z.* 91 K4
New Brighton, *U.S.A.* 110 F4
New Britain, *Papua N. G.* 96 H7
New Britain, *U.S.A.* 111 E12
New Brunswick, *U.S.A.* 111 F10
New Brunswick □, *Canada* 103 C6
New Bussa, *Nigeria* 83 D5
New Caledonia ■, *Pac. Oc.* 96 K8
New Castile = Castilla-La Mancha □, *Spain* 6 H5
New Castle, *Ind., U.S.A.* 108 F3
New Castle, *Pa., U.S.A.* 110 F4
New City, *U.S.A.* 111 E11
New Concord, *U.S.A.* 110 G3
New Cumberland, *U.S.A.* 110 F4
New Cuyama, *U.S.A.* 117 L7
New Delhi, *India* 68 E7
New Denver, *Canada* 104 D5
New Don Pedro Reservoir, *U.S.A.* 116 H6
New England, *U.S.A.* 112 B3
New England Ra., *Australia* 95 E5
New Forest, *U.K.* 13 G6
New Galloway, *U.K.* 14 F4
New Glasgow, *Canada* 103 C7
New Guinea, *Oceania* 52 K17
New Hamburg, *Canada* 110 C4
New Hampshire □, *U.S.A.* 111 C13
New Hampton, *U.S.A.* 112 D8
New Hanover, *S. Africa* 89 D5
New Hartford, *U.S.A.* 111 C9
New Haven, *Conn., U.S.A.* 111 E12
New Haven, *Mich., U.S.A.* 110 D2
New Hazelton, *Canada* 104 B3
New Hebrides = Vanuatu ■, *Pac. Oc.* 96 J8
New Holland, *U.S.A.* 111 F8
New Iberia, *U.S.A.* 113 K9
New Ireland, *Papua N. G.* 96 H7
New Jersey □, *U.S.A.* 108 E8
New Kensington, *U.S.A.* 110 F5
New Lexington, *U.S.A.* 108 F4
New Liskeard, *Canada* 102 C4
New London, *Conn., U.S.A.* 111 E12
New London, *Ohio, U.S.A.* 110 E2
New London, *Wis., U.S.A.* 112 C10
New Madrid, *U.S.A.* 113 G10
New Martinsville, *U.S.A.* 108 F5
New Meadows, *U.S.A.* 114 D5
New Melones L., *U.S.A.* 116 H6
New Mexico □, *U.S.A.* 115 J10
New Milford, *Conn., U.S.A.* 111 E11
New Milford, *Pa., U.S.A.* 111 E9
New Norcia, *Australia* 93 F2
New Norfolk, *Australia* 94 G4
New Orleans, *U.S.A.* 113 L9
New Philadelphia, *U.S.A.* 110 F3
New Plymouth, *N.Z.* 91 H5
New Plymouth, *U.S.A.* 114 E5
New Port Richey, *U.S.A.* 109 L4
New Providence, *Bahamas* 120 A4
New Quay, *U.K.* 13 E3
New Radnor, *U.K.* 13 E4
New Richmond, *Canada* 103 C6
New Richmond, *U.S.A.* 112 C8
New Roads, *U.S.A.* 113 K9
New Rochelle, *U.S.A.* 111 F11
New Rockford, *U.S.A.* 112 B5
New Romney, *U.K.* 13 G8
New Ross, *Ireland* 15 D5
New Salem, *U.S.A.* 112 B4
New Scone, *U.K.* 14 E5
New Siberian I. = Novaya Sibir, Ostrov, *Russia* 51 B16
New Siberian Is. = Novosibirskiye Ostrova, *Russia* 51 B15
New Smyrna Beach, *U.S.A.* 109 L5
New South Wales □, *Australia* 95 E4
New Town, *U.S.A.* 112 B3
New Tredegar, *U.K.* 13 F4
New Ulm, *U.S.A.* 112 C7
New Waterford, *Canada* 103 C7
New Westminster, *Canada* 116 A4
New York, *U.S.A.* 111 F11
New York □, *U.S.A.* 111 D9
New York Mts., *U.S.A.* 115 J6
New Zealand ■, *Oceania* 91 J6
Newaj →, *India* 68 G7
Newala, *Tanzania* 87 E4
Newark, *Del., U.S.A.* 108 F8
Newark, *N.J., U.S.A.* 111 F10
Newark, *N.Y., U.S.A.* 110 C7
Newark, *Ohio, U.S.A.* 110 F2
Newark-on-Trent, *U.K.* 12 D7
Newark Valley, *U.S.A.* 111 D8
Newberg, *U.S.A.* 114 D2
Newberry, *Mich., U.S.A.* 108 B3
Newberry, *S.C., U.S.A.* 109 H5
Newberry Springs, *U.S.A.* 117 L10
Newboro L., *Canada* 111 B8
Newbridge = Droichead Nua, *Ireland* 15 C5
Newburgh, *Canada* 110 B8
Newburgh, *U.S.A.* 111 E10
Newbury, *U.K.* 13 F6
Newbury, *N.H., U.S.A.* 111 B12
Newbury, *Vt., U.S.A.* 111 B12
Newburyport, *U.S.A.* 109 D10
Newcastle, *Australia* 95 E5
Newcastle, *N.B., Canada* 103 C6
Newcastle, *Ont., Canada* 102 D4
Newcastle, *S. Africa* 89 D4
Newcastle, *U.K.* 15 B6
Newcastle, *Calif., U.S.A.* 116 G5
Newcastle, *Wyo., U.S.A.* 112 D2
Newcastle Emlyn, *U.K.* 13 E3
Newcastle Ra., *Australia* 92 C5
Newcastle-under-Lyme, *U.K.* 12 D5
Newcastle-upon-Tyne, *U.K.* 12 C6
Newcastle Waters, *Australia* 94 B1
Newcastle West, *Ireland* 15 D2
Newcomb, *U.S.A.* 111 C10
Newcomerstown, *U.S.A.* 110 F3
Newdegate, *Australia* 93 F2
Newell, *Australia* 94 B4
Newell, *U.S.A.* 112 C3
Newfane, *U.S.A.* 110 C6
Newfield, *U.S.A.* 111 D8
Newfound L., *U.S.A.* 111 C13
Newfoundland, *N. Amer.* 98 E14
Newfoundland, *U.S.A.* 111 E9
Newfoundland □, *Canada* 103 B8
Newhall, *U.S.A.* 117 L8
Newhaven, *U.K.* 13 G8
Newkirk, *U.S.A.* 113 G6
Newlyn, *U.K.* 13 G2
Newman, *Australia* 92 D2
Newman, *U.S.A.* 116 H5
Newmarket, *Canada* 110 B5
Newmarket, *Ireland* 15 D2
Newmarket, *U.K.* 13 E8
Newmarket, *N.H., U.S.A.* 111 C14
Newmarket, *N.H., U.S.A.* 111 C14
Newnan, *U.S.A.* 109 J3
Newport, *Ireland* 15 C2
Newport, *I. of W., U.K.* 13 G6
Newport, *Newp., U.K.* 13 F5
Newport, *Ark., U.S.A.* 113 H9
Newport, *Ky., U.S.A.* 108 F3
Newport, *N.H., U.S.A.* 111 C12
Newport, *N.Y., U.S.A.* 111 C9
Newport, *Oreg., U.S.A.* 114 D1
Newport, *Pa., U.S.A.* 110 F7
Newport, *R.I., U.S.A.* 111 E13
Newport, *Tenn., U.S.A.* 109 H4
Newport, *Vt., U.S.A.* 111 B12
Newport, *Wash., U.S.A.* 114 B5
Newport □, *U.K.* 13 F4
Newport Beach, *U.S.A.* 117 M9
Newport News, *U.S.A.* 108 G7
Newport Pagnell, *U.K.* 13 E7
Newquay, *U.K.* 13 G2
Newry, *U.K.* 15 B5
Newton, *Ill., U.S.A.* 112 F10
Newton, *Iowa, U.S.A.* 112 E8
Newton, *Kans., U.S.A.* 113 F6
Newton, *Mass., U.S.A.* 111 D13
Newton, *Miss., U.S.A.* 113 J10
Newton, *N.C., U.S.A.* 109 H5
Newton, *N.J., U.S.A.* 111 E10
Newton, *Tex., U.S.A.* 113 K8
Newton Abbot, *U.K.* 13 G4
Newton Aycliffe, *U.K.* 12 C6
Newton Falls, *U.S.A.* 110 E4
Newton Stewart, *U.K.* 14 G4
Newtonmore, *U.K.* 14 D4
Newtown, *U.K.* 13 E4
Newtownabbey, *U.K.* 15 B6

Newtownards, *U.K.* 15 B6
Newtownbarry = Bunclody, *Ireland* 15 D5
Newtownstewart, *U.K.* 15 B4
Newville, *U.S.A.* 110 F7
Nexon, *France* 20 C5
Neya, *Russia* 48 A6
Neyrīz, *Iran* 71 D7
Neyshābūr, *Iran* 71 B8
Nezhin = Nizhyn, *Ukraine* 47 G6
Nezperce, *U.S.A.* 114 C5
Ngabang, *Indonesia* 62 D3
Ngabordamlu, Tanjung, *Indonesia* 63 F8
N'Gage, *Angola* 84 F3
Ngala, *Nigeria* 83 C7
Ngambé, *Cameroon* 83 D7
Ngambé, *Cameroon* 83 D7
Ngami Depression, *Botswana* 88 C3
Ngamo, *Zimbabwe* 87 F2
Ngangala, *Sudan* 81 G3
Nganglong Kangri, *China* 67 C12
Ngao, *Thailand* 64 C2
Ngaoundéré, *Cameroon* 84 C2
Ngapara, *N.Z.* 91 L3
Ngara, *Tanzania* 86 C3
Ngawi, *Indonesia* 63 G14
Nghia Lo, *Vietnam* 58 G5
Ngoboli, *Sudan* 81 G3
Ngoma, *Malawi* 87 E3
Ngomahura, *Zimbabwe* 87 G3
Ngomba, *Tanzania* 87 D3
Ngop, *Sudan* 81 F3
Ngoring Hu, *China* 60 C4
Ngorkou, *Mali* 82 B4
Ngorongoro, *Tanzania* 86 C4
Ngozi, *Burundi* 86 C2
Ngudu, *Tanzania* 86 C3
Nguigmi, *Niger* 79 F8
Nguila, *Cameroon* 83 E7
Nguiu, *Australia* 92 B5
Ngukurr, *Australia* 94 A1
Ngulu Atoll, *Pac. Oc.* 63 C9
Ngunga, *Tanzania* 86 C3
Nguru, *Nigeria* 83 C7
Nguru Mts., *Tanzania* 86 D4
Nguyen Binh, *Vietnam* 58 F5
Nha Trang, *Vietnam* 65 F7
Nhacoongo, *Mozam.* 89 C6
Nhamaabué, *Mozam.* 87 F4
Nhamundá →, *Brazil* 125 D7
Nhangulaze, L., *Mozam.* 89 C5
Nhill, *Australia* 95 F3
Nho Quan, *Vietnam* 58 G5
Nhulunbuy, *Australia* 94 A2
Nia-nia, *Dem. Rep. of the Congo* 86 B2
Niafounké, *Mali* 82 B4
Niagara Falls, *Canada* 102 D4
Niagara Falls, *U.S.A.* 110 C6
Niagara-on-the-Lake, *Canada* 110 C5
Niah, *Malaysia* 62 D4
Niamey, *Niger* 83 C5
Niandan-Koro, *Guinea* 82 C3
Nianforando, *Guinea* 82 D2
Niangara, *Dem. Rep. of the Congo* 86 B2
Niangbo, *Ivory C.* 82 D3
Niangoloko, *Burkina Faso* 82 C4
Niantic, *U.S.A.* 111 E12
Niaro, *Sudan* 81 E3
Nias, *Indonesia* 62 D1
Niassa □, *Mozam.* 87 E4
Nibāk, *Si. Arabia* 71 E7
Nibe, *Denmark* 11 H3
Nicaragua ■, *Cent. Amer.* 120 D2
Nicaragua, L. de, *Nic.* 120 D2
Nicastro, *Italy* 31 D9
Nice, *France* 21 E11
Niceville, *U.S.A.* 109 K2
Nichicun, L., *Canada* 103 B5
Nichinan, *Japan* 55 J5
Nicholás, Canal, *W. Indies* 120 B3
Nicholasville, *U.S.A.* 108 G3
Nichols, *U.S.A.* 111 D8
Nicholson, *Australia* 92 C4
Nicholson, *U.S.A.* 111 E9
Nicholson →, *Australia* 94 B2
Nicholson L., *Canada* 105 A8
Nicholson Ra., *Australia* 93 E2
Nicholville, *U.S.A.* 111 B10
Nicobar Is., *Ind. Oc.* 52 J13
Nicola, *Canada* 104 C4
Nicolls Town, *Bahamas* 120 A4
Nicopolis, *Greece* 38 B2
Nicosia, *Cyprus* 36 D12
Nicosia, *Italy* 31 E7
Nicótera, *Italy* 31 D8
Nicoya, *Costa Rica* 120 D2
Nicoya, G. de, *Costa Rica* 120 E3
Nicoya, Pen. de, *Costa Rica* 120 E2
Nidd →, *U.K.* 12 D6
Nidda, *Germany* 25 E5
Nidda →, *Germany* 25 E4
Nidwalden □, *Switz.* 25 J4
Nidzica, *Poland* 45 E7
Niebüll, *Germany* 24 A4
Nied →, *Germany* 19 C13
Niederaula, *Germany* 24 E5
Niederbayern □, *Germany* 25 G8
Niederbronn-les-Bains, *France* 19 D14
Niedere Tauern, *Austria* 26 D7
Niederlausitz, *Germany* 24 D9
Niederösterreich □, *Austria* 26 C8
Niedersachsen □, *Germany* 24 C4
Niekerkshoop, *S. Africa* 88 D3
Niellé, *Ivory C.* 82 C3
Niemba, *Dem. Rep. of the Congo* 86 D2
Niemen = Neman →, *Lithuania* 9 J20
Niemodlin, *Poland* 45 H4
Nienburg, *Germany* 24 C5
Niepołomice, *Poland* 45 H7
Niers →, *Germany* 24 D1
Niesky, *Germany* 24 D10
Nieszawa, *Poland* 45 F5
Nieu Bethesda, *S. Africa* 88 E3
Nieuw Amsterdam, *Surinam* 125 B7
Nieuw Nickerie, *Surinam* 125 B7
Nieuwoudtville, *S. Africa* 88 E2
Nieuwpoort, *Belgium* 17 C2
Nieves, Pico de las, *Canary Is.* 37 G4
Nièvre □, *France* 19 E10
Niga, *Mali* 82 C3
Niğde, *Turkey* 70 B2
Nigel, *S. Africa* 89 D4
Niger □, *Nigeria* 83 D6
Niger ■, *W. Afr.* 83 B7
Niger →, *W. Afr.* 83 D6
Niger Delta, *Africa* 83 E6
Nigeria ■, *W. Afr.* 83 D6
Nighasin, *India* 69 E9
Nightcaps, *N.Z.* 91 L2
Nigríta, *Greece* 40 F7
Nii-Jima, *Japan* 55 G9
Niigata, *Japan* 54 F9
Niigata □, *Japan* 55 F9
Niihama, *Japan* 55 H6
Niihau, *U.S.A.* 106 H14
Niimi, *Japan* 55 G6
Niitsu, *Japan* 54 F9
Nijar, *Spain* 33 J2
Nijil, *Jordan* 75 E4
Nijkerk, *Neths.* 17 B5
Nijmegen, *Neths.* 17 C5
Nijverdal, *Neths.* 17 B6
Nīk Pey, *Iran* 71 B6
Nike, *Nigeria* 83 D6
Nikiniki, *Indonesia* 63 F6
Nikísiani, *Greece* 41 F8
Nikítas, *Greece* 40 F7
Nikki, *Benin* 83 D5
Nikkō, *Japan* 55 F9
Nikolayev = Mykolayiv, *Ukraine* 47 J7
Nikolayevsk, *Russia* 48 E7
Nikolayevsk-na-Amur, *Russia* 51 D15
Nikolsk, *Russia* 48 D8
Nikolskoye, *Russia* 51 D17
Nikopol, *Bulgaria* 41 C8
Nikopol, *Ukraine* 47 J8
Niksar, *Turkey* 72 B7
Nīkshahr, *Iran* 71 E9
Nikšić, *Montenegro, Yug.* 40 D2
Nîl, Nahr en →, *Africa* 80 H7
Nîl el Abyad →, *Sudan* 81 D3
Nîl el Azraq →, *Sudan* 81 D3
Nila, *Indonesia* 63 F7
Niland, *U.S.A.* 117 M11
Nile = Nîl, Nahr en →, *Africa* 80 H7
Niles, *Mich., U.S.A.* 108 E2
Niles, *Ohio, U.S.A.* 110 E4
Nilüfer →, *Turkey* 41 F12
Nim Ka Thana, *India* 68 F6
Nimach, *India* 68 G6
Nimbahera, *India* 68 G6
Nîmes, *France* 21 E8
Nimfaíon, Ákra = Pínnes, Ákra, *Greece* 41 F8
Nimmitabel, *Australia* 95 F4
Nimule, *Sudan* 81 G3
Nin, *Croatia* 29 D12
Nīnawá, *Iraq* 70 B4
Nindigully, *Australia* 95 D4
Nineveh = Nīnawá, *Iraq* 70 B4
Ning Xian, *China* 56 G4
Ning'an, *China* 57 B15
Ningbo, *China* 59 C13
Ningcheng, *China* 57 D10
Ningde, *China* 59 D12
Ningdu, *China* 59 D10
Ninggang, *China* 59 D9
Ningguo, *China* 59 B12
Ninghai, *China* 59 C13
Ninghua, *China* 59 D11
Ningi, *Nigeria* 83 C6
Ningjin, *China* 56 F8
Ningjing Shan, *China* 58 C2
Ninglang, *China* 58 D3
Ningling, *China* 56 G8
Ningming, *China* 58 F6
Ningnan, *China* 58 D4
Ningpo = Ningbo, *China* 59 C13
Ningqiang, *China* 56 H4
Ningshan, *China* 56 H5
Ningsia Hui A.R. = Ningxia Huizu Zizhiqu □, *China* 56 F4
Ningwu, *China* 56 E7
Ningxia Huizu Zizhiqu □, *China* 56 F4
Ningxiang, *China* 59 C9
Ningyang, *China* 56 G9
Ningyuan, *China* 59 E8
Ninh Binh, *Vietnam* 58 G5
Ninh Giang, *Vietnam* 64 B6
Ninh Hoa, *Vietnam* 64 F7
Ninh Ma, *Vietnam* 64 F7
Ninove, *Belgium* 17 D4
Nioaque, *Brazil* 127 A4
Niobrara, *U.S.A.* 112 D6
Niobrara →, *U.S.A.* 112 D6
Niono, *Mali* 82 C3
Nionsamoridougou, *Guinea* 82 D3
Nioro du Rip, *Senegal* 82 C1
Nioro du Sahel, *Mali* 82 B3
Niort, *France* 20 B3
Nipawin, *Canada* 105 C8
Nipfjället, *Sweden* 10 C6
Nipigon, *Canada* 102 C2
Nipigon, L., *Canada* 102 C2
Nipishish L., *Canada* 103 B7
Nipissing, L., *Canada* 102 C4
Nipomo, *U.S.A.* 117 K6
Nipton, *U.S.A.* 117 K11
Niquelândia, *Brazil* 125 F9
Nīr, *Iran* 70 B5
Nirasaki, *Japan* 55 G9
Nirmal, *India* 66 K11
Nirmali, *India* 69 F12
Niš, *Serbia, Yug.* 40 C5
Nisa, *Portugal* 35 F3
Nişāb, *Si. Arabia* 70 D5
Nişāb, *Yemen* 74 E4
Nišava →, *Serbia, Yug.* 40 C5
Niscemi, *Italy* 31 E7
Nishinomiya, *Japan* 55 G7
Nishino'omote, *Japan* 55 J5
Nishiwaki, *Japan* 55 G7
Nísíros, *Greece* 39 E9
Niška Banja, *Serbia, Yug.* 40 C6
Niskibi →, *Canada* 102 A2
Nisko, *Poland* 45 H9
Nisporeni, *Moldova* 43 C13
Nisqually →, *U.S.A.* 116 C4
Nissáki, *Greece* 36 A3
Nissan →, *Sweden* 11 H6
Nissum Bredning, *Denmark* 11 H2
Nissum Fjord, *Denmark* 11 H2
Nistru = Dnister →, *Europe* 47 J6
Nisutlin →, *Canada* 104 A2
Nitchequon, *Canada* 103 B5
Niterói, *Brazil* 127 A7
Nith →, *Canada* 110 C4
Nith →, *U.K.* 14 F5
Nitra, *Slovak Rep.* 27 C11
Nitra →, *Slovak Rep.* 27 D11
Nitriansky □, *Slovak Rep.* 27 C11
Nittenau, *Germany* 25 F8
Niuafo'ou, *Tonga* 91 B11
Niue, *Cook Is.* 97 J11
Niulan Jiang →, *China* 58 D4
Niut, *Indonesia* 62 D4
Niutou Shan, *China* 59 C13
Niuzhuang, *China* 57 D12
Nivala, *Finland* 8 E21
Nivelles, *Belgium* 17 D4
Nivernais, *France* 19 E10
Niwas, *India* 69 H9
Nixon, *U.S.A.* 113 L6
Nizamabad, *India* 66 K11
Nizamghat, *India* 67 E19
Nizhne Kolymsk, *Russia* 51 C17
Nizhnegorskiy = Nyzhnohirskyy, *Ukraine* 47 K8
Nizhnekamsk, *Russia* 48 C10
Nizhneudinsk, *Russia* 51 D10
Nizhnevartovsk, *Russia* 50 C8
Nizhniy Chir, *Russia* 49 F6
Nizhniy Lomov, *Russia* 48 D6
Nizhniy Novgorod, *Russia* 48 B7
Nizhniy Tagil, *Russia* 50 D6
Nizhyn, *Ukraine* 47 G6
Nizina Mazowiecka, *Poland* 45 F8
Nizip, *Turkey* 70 B3
Nízké Tatry, *Slovak Rep.* 27 C12
Nízký Jeseník, *Czech Rep.* 27 B10
Nizza Monferrato, *Italy* 28 D5
Njakwa, *Malawi* 87 E3
Njanji, *Zambia* 87 E3
Njegoš, *Montenegro, Yug.* 40 D2
Njinjo, *Tanzania* 87 D4
Njombe, *Tanzania* 87 D3
Njombe →, *Tanzania* 86 D4
Njurundabommen, *Sweden* 10 B11
Nkambe, *Cameroon* 83 D7
Nkana, *Zambia* 87 E2
Nkandla, *S. Africa* 89 D5
Nkawkaw, *Ghana* 83 D4
Nkayi, *Zimbabwe* 87 F2
Nkhotakota, *Malawi* 87 E3
Nkongsamba, *Cameroon* 83 E6
Nkurenkuru, *Namibia* 88 B2
Nkwanta, *Ghana* 82 D4
Nmai →, *Burma* 58 F2
Noakhali = Maijdi, *Bangla.* 67 H17
Nobel, *Canada* 110 A4
Nobeoka, *Japan* 55 H5
Noblejas, *Spain* 34 F7
Noblesville, *U.S.A.* 108 E3
Noce →, *Italy* 28 B8
Nocera Inferiore, *Italy* 31 B7
Nocera Umbra, *Italy* 29 E9
Noci, *Italy* 31 B10
Nocona, *U.S.A.* 113 J6
Nocrich, *Romania* 43 E9
Noda, *Japan* 55 G9
Nogales, *Mexico* 118 A2
Nogales, *U.S.A.* 115 L8
Nogaro, *France* 20 E3
Nogat →, *Poland* 44 D6
Nōgata, *Japan* 55 H5
Nogent, *France* 19 D12
Nogent-le-Rotrou, *France* 18 D7
Nogent-sur-Seine, *France* 19 D10
Noggerup, *Australia* 93 F2
Noginsk, *Moskva, Russia* 46 E10
Noginsk, *Tunguska, Russia* 51 C10
Nogoa →, *Australia* 94 C4
Nogoyá, *Argentina* 126 C4
Nógrád □, *Hungary* 42 C4
Noguera Pallaresa →, *Spain* 32 D5
Noguera Ribagorzana →, *Spain* 32 D5
Nohar, *India* 68 E6
Nohfelden, *Germany* 25 F3
Nohta, *India* 69 H8
Noia, *Spain* 34 C2
Noire, Montagne, *France* 20 E6
Noire, Mt., *France* 18 D3
Noirétable, *France* 20 C7
Noirmoutier, Î. de, *France* 18 F4
Noirmoutier-en-l'Île, *France* 18 F4
Nojane, *Botswana* 88 C3
Nojima-Zaki, *Japan* 55 G9
Nok Kundi, *Pakistan* 66 E3
Nokaneng, *Botswana* 88 B3
Nokia, *Finland* 9 F20
Nokomis, *Canada* 105 C8
Nokomis L., *Canada* 105 B8
Nol, *Sweden* 11 G6
Nola, *C.A.R.* 84 D3
Nola, *Italy* 31 B7
Nolay, *France* 19 F11
Noli, C. di, *Italy* 28 D5
Nolinsk, *Russia* 48 B9
Noma Omuramba →, *Namibia* 88 B3
Nombre de Dios, *Panama* 120 E4
Nome, *U.S.A.* 100 B3
Nomo-Zaki, *Japan* 55 H4
Nonacho L., *Canada* 105 A7
Nonancourt, *France* 18 D8
Nonda, *Australia* 94 C3
None, *Italy* 28 D4
Nong Chang, *Thailand* 64 E2
Nong Het, *Laos* 64 C4
Nong Khai, *Thailand* 64 D4
Nong'an, *China* 57 B13
Nongoma, *S. Africa* 89 D5
Nonoava, *Mexico* 118 B3
Nonoava →, *Mexico* 118 B3
Nonthaburi, *Thailand* 64 F3
Nontron, *France* 20 C4
Nonza, *France* 21 F13
Noonamah, *Australia* 92 B5
Noord Brabant □, *Neths.* 17 C5
Noord Holland □, *Neths.* 17 B4
Noordbeveland, *Neths.* 17 C3
Noordoostpolder, *Neths.* 17 B5
Noordwijk, *Neths.* 17 B4
Nootka I., *Canada* 104 D3
Nopiming Prov. Park, *Canada* 105 C9
Nora, *Eritrea* 81 D5
Nora, *Sweden* 10 E9
Noralee, *Canada* 104 C3
Noranda = Rouyn-Noranda, *Canada* 102 C4
Norberg, *Sweden* 10 D9
Nórcia, *Italy* 29 F10
Norco, *U.S.A.* 117 M9
Nord □, *France* 19 B10
Nord-Kivu □, *Dem. Rep. of the Congo* 86 C2
Nord-Ostsee-Kanal, *Germany* 24 A5
Nord-Pas-de-Calais □, *France* 19 B9
Nordaustlandet, *Svalbard* 4 B9
Nordborg, *Denmark* 11 J3
Nordby, *Denmark* 11 J2
Norddeich, *Germany* 24 B3
Nordegg, *Canada* 104 C5
Norden, *Germany* 24 B3
Nordenham, *Germany* 24 B4
Norderney, *Germany* 24 B3
Norderstedt, *Germany* 24 B6
Nordfjord, *Norway* 9 F11
Nordfriesische Inseln, *Germany* 24 A4
Nordhausen, *Germany* 24 D6
Nordhorn, *Germany* 24 C3
Norðoyar, *Færoe Is.* 8 E9
Nordingrå, *Sweden* 10 B12
Nordjyllands Amtskommune □, *Denmark* 11 G4
Nordkapp, *Norway* 8 A21
Nordkapp, *Svalbard* 4 A9
Nordkinn = Kinnarodden, *Norway* 6 A11
Nordkinn-halvøya, *Norway* 8 A22
Nördlingen, *Germany* 25 G6
Nordrhein-Westfalen □, *Germany* 24 D3
Nordstrand, *Germany* 24 A4
Nordvik, *Russia* 51 B12
Nore →, *Ireland* 15 D4
Norfolk, *Nebr., U.S.A.* 112 D6
Norfolk, *Va., U.S.A.* 108 G7
Norfolk □, *U.K.* 13 E8
Norfolk I., *Pac. Oc.* 96 K8
Norfork L., *U.S.A.* 113 G8
Norilsk, *Russia* 51 C9
Norma, Mt., *Australia* 94 C3
Normal, *U.S.A.* 112 E10
Norman, *U.S.A.* 113 H6
Norman →, *Australia* 94 B3
Norman Wells, *Canada* 100 B7
Normanby →, *Australia* 94 A3
Normandin, *Canada* 102 C5
Normanhurst, Mt., *Australia* 93 E3
Normanton, *Australia* 94 B3
Normétal, *Canada* 102 C4
Norquay, *Canada* 105 C8
Norquinco, *Argentina* 128 E2
Norra Dellen, *Sweden* 10 C10
Norra Ulvön, *Sweden* 10 A12
Norrahammar, *Sweden* 11 G8
Norrbotten □, *Sweden* 8 C19
Nørre Åby, *Denmark* 11 J3
Nørre Alslev, *Denmark* 11 K5
Nørresundby, *Denmark* 11 G3
Norrhult, *Sweden* 11 G9
Norris Point, *Canada* 103 C8
Norristown, *U.S.A.* 111 F9
Norrköping, *Sweden* 11 F10
Norrland, *Sweden* 9 E16
Norrsundet, *Sweden* 10 D11
Norrtälje, *Sweden* 10 E12
Norseman, *Australia* 93 F3
Norsk, *Russia* 51 D14
Norte, Pta. del, *Canary Is.* 37 G2
Norte, Serra do, *Brazil* 124
North, C., *Canada* 103 C7
North Adams, *U.S.A.* 111 D11
North Arm, *Canada* 104 A5
North Augusta, *U.S.A.* 109 J5
North Ayrshire □, *U.K.* 14 F4
North Bass I., *U.S.A.* 110 E2
North Battleford, *Canada* 105 C7
North Bay, *Canada* 102 C4
North Belcher Is., *Canada* 102 A4
North Bend, *Oreg., U.S.A.* 114 E1
North Bend, *Pa., U.S.A.* 110 E7
North Bend, *Wash., U.S.A.* 116 C5
North Bennington, *U.S.A.* 111 D11
North Berwick, *U.K.* 14 E6
North Berwick, *U.S.A.* 111 C14
North C., *Canada* 103 C7
North C., *N.Z.* 91 F4
North Canadian →, *U.S.A.* 113 H7
North Canton, *U.S.A.* 110 F3
North Cape = Nordkapp, *Norway* 8 A21
North Cape = Nordkapp, *Svalbard* 4 A9
North Caribou L., *Canada* 102 B1
North Carolina □, *U.S.A.* 109 H6
North Cascades National Park, *U.S.A.* 114 B3
North Channel, *Canada* 102 C3
North Channel, *U.K.* 14 F3
North Charleston, *U.S.A.* 109 J6
North Chicago, *U.S.A.* 108 D2
North Creek, *U.S.A.* 111 C11
North Dakota □, *U.S.A.* 112 B5
North Downs, *U.K.* 13 F8
North East, *U.S.A.* 110 D5
North East Frontier Agency = Arunachal Pradesh □, *India* 67 F19
North East Lincolnshire □, *U.K.* 12 D7
North Eastern □, *Kenya* 86 B5
North Esk →, *U.K.* 14 E6
North European Plain, *Europe* 6 E10
North Foreland, *U.K.* 13 F9
North Fork, *U.S.A.* 116 H7
North Fork American →, *U.S.A.* 116 G5
North Fork Feather →, *U.S.A.* 116 F5
North Fork Grand →, *U.S.A.* 112 C3
North Fork Red →, *U.S.A.* 113 H5
North Frisian Is. = Nordfriesische Inseln, *Germany* 24 A4
North Gower, *Canada* 111 A9
North Hd., *Australia* 93 F1
North Henik L., *Canada* 105 A9
North Highlands, *U.S.A.* 116 G5
North Horr, *Kenya* 86 B4
North I., *Kenya* 86 B4
North I., *N.Z.* 91 H5
North Kingsville, *U.S.A.* 110 E4
North Knife →, *Canada* 105 B10
North Koel →, *India* 69 G10
North Korea ■, *Asia* 57 E14
North Lakhimpur, *India* 67 F19
North Lanarkshire □, *U.K.* 14 F5
North Las Vegas, *U.S.A.* 117 J11
North Lincolnshire □, *U.K.* 12 D7
North Little Rock, *U.S.A.* 113 H8
North Loup →, *U.S.A.* 112 E5
North Magnetic Pole, *Canada* 4 B2
North Minch, *U.K.* 14 C3
North Moose L., *Canada* 105 C8
North Myrtle Beach, *U.S.A.* 109 J6
North Nahanni →, *Canada* 104 A4
North Olmsted, *U.S.A.* 110 E3
North Ossetia □, *Russia* 49 J7
North Pagai, I. = Pagai Utara, Pulau, *Indonesia* 62 E2
North Palisade, *U.S.A.* 116 H8
North Platte, *U.S.A.* 112 E4
North Platte →, *U.S.A.* 112 E4
North Pole, *Arctic* 4 A
North Portal, *Canada* 105 D8
North Powder, *U.S.A.* 114 D5
North Pt., *U.S.A.* 110 A1
North Rhine Westphalia = Nordrhein-Westfalen □, *Germany* 24 D3
North River, *Canada* 103 B8
North Ronaldsay, *U.K.* 14 B6
North Saskatchewan →, *Canada* 105 C7
North Sea, *Europe* 6 D6
North Seal →, *Canada* 105 B9
North Somerset □, *U.K.* 13 F5
North Sporades = Vóriai Sporádhes, *Greece* 38 B5
North Sydney, *Canada* 103 C7
North Syracuse, *U.S.A.* 111 C8
North Taranaki Bight, *N.Z.* 91 H5
North Thompson →, *Canada* 104 C4
North Tonawanda, *U.S.A.* 110 C6
North Troy, *U.S.A.* 111 B12
North Truchas Pk., *U.S.A.* 115 J11
North Twin I., *Canada* 102 B4
North Tyne →, *U.K.* 12 B5
North Uist, *U.K.* 14 D1
North Vancouver, *Canada* 104 D4
North Vernon, *U.S.A.* 108 F3

North Wabasca L., Canada 104 B6
North Walsham, U.K. 12 E9
North-West □, S. Africa 88 D4
North West C., Australia 92 D1
North West Christmas I. Ridge, Pac. Oc. 97 G11
North West Frontier □, Pakistan 68 C4
North West Highlands, U.K. 14 D4
North West River, Canada 103 B7
North Western □, Zambia 87 E2
North Wildwood, U.S.A. 108 F8
North York Moors, U.K. 12 C7
North Yorkshire □, U.K. 12 C6
Northallerton, U.K. 12 C6
Northam, Australia 93 F2
Northam, S. Africa 88 C4
Northampton, Australia 93 E1
Northampton, U.K. 13 E7
Northampton, Mass., U.S.A. 111 D12
Northampton, Pa., U.S.A. 111 F9
Northamptonshire □, U.K. 13 E7
Northbridge, U.S.A. 111 D13
Northcliffe, Australia 93 F2
Northeast Providence Chan., W. Indies 120 A4
Northeim, Germany 24 D6
Northern □, Ghana 83 D4
Northern □, Malawi 87 E3
Northern □, Uganda 86 B3
Northern □, Zambia 87 E3
Northern Cape □, S. Africa 88 D3
Northern Circars, India 67 L13
Northern Indian L., Canada 105 B9
Northern Ireland □, U.K. 15 B5
Northern Light L., Canada 102 C1
Northern Marianas ■, Pac. Oc. 96 F6
Northern Province □, S. Leone 82 D2
Northern Province □, S. Africa 89 C4
Northern Territory □, Australia 92 D5
Northfield, Minn., U.S.A. 112 C8
Northfield, Vt., U.S.A. 111 B12
Northland □, N.Z. 91 F4
Northome, U.S.A. 112 B7
Northport, Ala., U.S.A. 109 J2
Northport, Wash., U.S.A. 114 B5
Northumberland □, U.K. 12 B6
Northumberland, C., Australia 95 F3
Northumberland Is., Australia 94 C4
Northumberland Str., Canada 103 C7
Northville, U.S.A. 111 C10
Northwest Providence Channel, W. Indies 120 A4
Northwest Territories □, Canada 100 B9
Northwood, Iowa, U.S.A. 112 D8
Northwood, N. Dak., U.S.A. 112 B6
Norton, U.S.A. 112 F5
Norton, Zimbabwe 87 F3
Norton Sd., U.S.A. 100 B3
Nortorf, Germany 24 A5
Norwalk, Calif., U.S.A. 117 M8
Norwalk, Conn., U.S.A. 111 E11
Norwalk, Iowa, U.S.A. 112 E8
Norwalk, Ohio, U.S.A. 110 E2
Norway, Maine, U.S.A. 109 C10
Norway, Mich., U.S.A. 108 C2
Norway ■, Europe 8 E14
Norway House, Canada 105 C9
Norwegian Sea, Atl. Oc. 4 C8
Norwich, Canada 110 D4
Norwich, U.K. 13 E9
Norwich, Conn., U.S.A. 111 E12
Norwich, N.Y., U.S.A. 111 D9
Norwood, Canada 110 B7
Norwood, U.S.A. 111 B10
Noshiro, Japan 54 D10
Nosivka, Ukraine 47 G6
Nosovka = Nosivka, Ukraine 47 G6
Noşratābād, Iran 71 D8
Noss Hd., U.K. 14 C5
Nossebro, Sweden 11 F6
Nossob →, S. Africa 88 D3
Nossombougou, Mali 82 C3
Nosy Barren, Madag. 85 H8
Nosy Be, Madag. 85 G9
Nosy Boraha, Madag. 89 B8
Nosy Lava, Madag. 89 A8
Nosy Varika, Madag. 89 C8
Noteć →, Poland 45 F2
Notikewin →, Canada 104 B5
Notios Evvoïkos Kólpos, Greece 38 C5
Noto, Italy 31 F8
Noto, G. di, Italy 31 F8
Notodden, Norway 9 G13
Notre Dame B., Canada 103 C8
Notre Dame de Koartac = Quaqtaq, Canada 101 B13
Notre-Dame-des-Bois, Canada 111 A13
Notre Dame d'Ivugivic = Ivujivik, Canada 101 B12
Notre-Dame-du-Nord, Canada 102 C4
Notsé, Togo 83 D5
Nottawasaga B., Canada 110 B4
Nottaway →, Canada 102 B4
Nottingham, U.K. 12 E6
Nottingham, City of □, U.K. 12 E6
Nottingham I., Canada 101 B12
Nottinghamshire □, U.K. 12 D6
Nottoway →, U.S.A. 108 G7
Notwane →, Botswana 88 C4
Nouâdhibou, Mauritania 78 D2
Nouâdhibou, Ras, Mauritania 78 D2
Nouakchott, Mauritania 82 B1
Nouâmghâr, Mauritania 82 B1
Nouméa, N. Cal. 96 K8
Nouna, Burkina Faso 82 C4
Noupoort, S. Africa 88 E3
Nouveau Comptoir = Wemindji, Canada 102 B4
Nouvelle-Amsterdam, I., Ind. Oc. 3 F13
Nouvelle-Calédonie = New Caledonia ■, Pac. Oc. 96 K8
Nouzonville, France 19 C11
Nová Baňa, Slovak Rep. 27 C11
Nová Bystřice, Czech Rep. 26 B8
Nova Casa Nova, Brazil 125 E10
Nova Esperança, Brazil 127 A5
Nova Friburgo, Brazil 127 A7
Nova Gaia = Cambundi-Catembo, Angola 84 G3
Nova Gorica, Slovenia 29 C10
Nova Gradiška, Croatia 42 E2
Nova Iguaçu, Brazil 127 A7
Nova Iorque, Brazil 125 E10
Nova Kakhovka, Ukraine 47 J7
Nova Lamego, Guinea-Biss. 82 C2
Nova Lima, Brazil 127 A7
Nova Lisboa = Huambo, Angola 85 G3
Nova Lusitânia, Mozam. 87 F3
Nova Mambone, Mozam. 89 C6
Nova Odesa, Ukraine 47 J6
Nová Paka, Czech Rep. 26 A8
Nova Pavova, Serbia, Yug. 42 F5
Nova Scotia □, Canada 103 C7
Nova Siri, Italy 31 B9
Nova Sofala, Mozam. 89 C5
Nova Varoš, Serbia, Yug. 40 C3
Nova Venécia, Brazil 125 G10
Nova Zagora, Bulgaria 41 D10
Novaci, Macedonia 40 E5
Novaci, Romania 43 E8
Novaféltria, Italy 29 E9
Novaleksandrovskaya = Novoaleksandrovsk, Russia 49 H5
Novannenskiy = Novoannenskiy, Russia 48 E6
Novar, Canada 110 A5
Novara, Italy 28 C5
Novato, U.S.A. 116 G4
Novaya Kakhovka = Nova Kakhovka, Ukraine 47 J7
Novaya Kazanka, Kazakstan 49 F9
Novaya Ladoga, Russia 46 B7
Novaya Lyalya, Russia 50 D7
Novaya Sibir, Ostrov, Russia 51 B16
Novaya Zemlya, Russia 50 B6
Nové Město, Slovak Rep. 27 C10
Nové Město na Moravě, Czech Rep. 26 B9
Nové Město nad Metují, Czech Rep. 27 A9
Nové Zámky, Slovak Rep. 27 C11
Novelda, Spain 33 G4
Novellara, Italy 28 D7
Noventa Vicentina, Italy 29 C8
Novgorod, Russia 46 C6
Novgorod-Severskiy = Novhorod-Siverskyy, Ukraine 47 G7
Novhorod-Siverskyy, Ukraine 47 G7
Novi Bečej, Serbia, Yug. 42 E5
Novi Iskar, Bulgaria 40 D7
Novi Kneževac, Serbia, Yug. 42 D5
Novi Lígure, Italy 28 D5
Novi Pazar, Bulgaria 41 C11
Novi Pazar, Serbia, Yug. 40 C4
Novi Sad, Serbia, Yug. 42 E4
Novi Slankamen, Serbia, Yug. 42 E5
Novi Travnik, Bos.-H. 42 F2
Novi Vinodolski, Croatia 29 C11
Novigrad, Istra, Croatia 29 C10
Novigrad, Zadar, Croatia 29 D12
Novigradsko More, Croatia 29 D12
Nôvo Hamburgo, Brazil 127 B5
Novo Mesto, Slovenia 29 C12
Novo Miloševo, Serbia, Yug. 42 E5
Novo Remanso, Brazil 125 E10
Novoaleksandrovsk, Russia 49 H5
Novoannenskiy, Russia 48 E6
Novoataysk, Russia 50 D9
Novoazovsk, Ukraine 47 J10
Novocheboksarsk, Russia 48 B8
Novocherkassk, Russia 49 G5
Novodevichye, Russia 48 D9
Novogrudok = Navahrudak, Belarus 46 F3
Novohrad-Volynskyy, Ukraine 47 G4
Novokachalinsk, Russia 54 B6
Novokazalinsk = Zhangaqazaly, Kazakstan 50 E7
Novokhopersk, Russia 48 E5
Novokuybyshevsk, Russia 48 D9
Novokuznetsk, Russia 50 D9
Novomirgorod, Ukraine 47 H6
Novomoskovsk, Russia 46 E10
Novomoskovsk, Ukraine 47 H8
Novopolotsk = Navapolatsk, Belarus 46 E5
Novorossiysk, Russia 47 K9
Novorybnoye, Russia 51 B11
Novorzhev, Russia 46 D5
Novosej, Albania 40 E4
Novoselytsya, Ukraine 47 H4
Novoshakhtinsk, Russia 47 J10
Novosibirsk, Russia 50 D9
Novosibirskiye Ostrova, Russia 51 B15
Novosil, Russia 47 F9
Novosokolniki, Russia 46 D6
Novotitarovskaya, Russia 49 H4
Novotroitsk, Russia 50 D6
Novoukrayinka, Ukraine 47 H6
Novouljanovsk, Russia 48 C9
Novouzensk, Russia 48 E9
Novovolynsk, Ukraine 47 G3
Novovoronezhskiy, Russia 47 G10
Novozybkov, Russia 47 F6
Novska, Croatia 29 C14
Novy Urengoy, Russia 50 C8
Nový Bor, Czech Rep. 26 A7
Novy Bug = Novyy Buh, Ukraine 47 J7
Nový Bydžov, Czech Rep. 26 A8
Novy Dwór Mazowiecki, Poland 45 F7
Nový Jičín, Czech Rep. 27 B11
Novyy Afon, Georgia 49 J5
Novyy Buh, Ukraine 47 J7
Novyy Oskol, Russia 47 G9
Novyy Port, Russia 50 C8
Now Shahr, Iran 71 B6
Nowa Deba, Poland 45 H8
Nowa Ruda, Poland 45 H3
Nowa Sarzyna, Poland 45 H9
Nowa Sól, Poland 45 G2
Nowata, U.S.A. 113 G7
Nowbarān, Iran 71 C6
Nowe, Poland 44 E5
Nowe Miasteczko, Poland 45 G2
Nowe Miasto, Poland 45 G7
Nowe Miasto Lubawskie, Poland 44 E6
Nowe Skalmierzyce, Poland 45 G4
Nowe Warpno, Poland 44 E1
Nowghāb, Iran 71 C8
Nowgong, Assam, India 67 F18
Nowgong, Mad. P., India 69 G8
Nowogard, Poland 44 E2
Nowogród, Poland 45 E8
Nowogród Bobrzanski, Poland 45 G2
Nowogrodziec, Poland 45 G2
Nowra-Bomaderry, Australia 95 E5
Nowshera, Pakistan 66 C8
Nowy Dwór Gdański, Poland 44 D6
Nowy Sącz, Poland 45 J7
Nowy Staw, Poland 44 D6
Nowy Targ, Poland 45 J7
Nowy Tomyśl, Poland 45 F3
Nowy Wiśnicz, Poland 45 J7
Noxen, U.S.A. 111 E8
Noxon, U.S.A. 114 C6
Noyabr'sk, Russia 50 C8
Noyant, France 18 E7
Noyers, France 19 E10
Noyon, France 19 C9
Noyon, Mongolia 56 C2
Nozay, France 18 E5
Nqutu, S. Africa 89 D5
Nsanje, Malawi 87 F4
Nsawam, Ghana 83 D4
Nsomba, Zambia 87 E2
Nsukka, Nigeria 83 D6
Ntui, Cameroon 83 E7
Nu Jiang →, China 58 E2
Nu Shan, China 58 E2
Nuba Mts. = Nubah, Jibalan, Sudan 81 E3
Nubah, Jibalan, Sudan 81 E3
Nubia, Africa 76 D7
Nubian Desert = Nûbîya, Es Sahrâ en, Sudan 80 C3
Nûbîya, Es Sahrâ en, Sudan 80 C3
Nubledo, Spain 34 B5
Nuboai, Indonesia 63 E9
Nubra →, India 69 B7
Nucet, Romania 42 D7
Nueces →, U.S.A. 113 M6
Nueltin L., Canada 105 A9
Nueva Asunción □, Paraguay 126 A3
Nueva Carteya, Spain 35 H6
Nueva Gerona, Cuba 120 B3
Nueva Palmira, Uruguay 126 C4
Nueva Rosita, Mexico 118 B4
Nueva San Salvador, El Salv. 120 D2
Nueva Tabarca, Spain 33 G4
Nuéve de Julio, Argentina 126 D3
Nuevitas, Cuba 120 B4
Nuevo, G., Argentina 128 E4
Nuevo Casas Grandes, Mexico 118 A3
Nuevo Guerrero, Mexico 119 B5
Nuevo Laredo, Mexico 119 B5
Nuevo León □, Mexico 118 C5
Nuevo Rocafuerte, Ecuador 124 D3
Nugget Pt., N.Z. 91 M2
Nugrus, Gebel, Egypt 80 C3
Nuhaka, N.Z. 91 H6
Nuits-St-Georges, France 19 E11
Nukey Bluff, Australia 95 E2
Nukheila, Sudan 80 D2
Nukhuyb, Iraq 70 C4
Nuku'alofa, Tonga 91 E12
Nukus, Uzbekistan 50 E6
Nules, Spain 32 F4
Nullagine, Australia 92 D3
Nullagine →, Australia 92 D3
Nullarbor, Australia 93 F5
Nullarbor Plain, Australia 93 F4
Numalla, L., Australia 95 D3
Numan, Nigeria 83 D7
Numata, Japan 55 F9
Numatinna →, Sudan 81 F2
Numazu, Japan 55 G9
Numbulwar, Australia 94 A2
Numfoor, Indonesia 63 E8
Numurkah, Australia 95 F4
Nunaksaluk I., Canada 103 A7
Nunap Isua, Greenland 4 D5
Nunavut □, Canada 101 B11
Nunda, U.S.A. 110 D7
Nungarin, Australia 93 F2
Nungo, Mozam. 87 E4
Nungwe, Tanzania 86 C3
Nunivak I., U.S.A. 100 B3
Nunkun, India 69 C7
Núoro, Italy 30 B2
Nūrābād, Iran 71 E8
Nure →, Italy 28 C6
Nuremberg = Nürnberg, Germany 25 F7
Nuri, Mexico 118 B3
Nuriootpa, Australia 95 E2
Nurlat, Russia 48 C10
Nurmes, Finland 8 E23
Nürnberg, Germany 25 F7
Nurpur, Pakistan 68 D4
Nurra, La, Italy 30 B1
Nurran, L. = Terewah, L., Australia 95 D4
Nurrari Lakes, Australia 93 E5
Nurri, Italy 30 C2
Nürtingen, Germany 25 G5
Nurzec →, Poland 45 F9
Nus, Italy 28 C4
Nusa Barung, Indonesia 63 H15
Nusa Kambangan, Indonesia 63 G13
Nusa Tenggara Barat □, Indonesia 62 F5
Nusa Tenggara Timur □, Indonesia 63 F6
Nusaybin, Turkey 73 D9
Nushki, Pakistan 68 E2
Nuuk, Greenland 101 B14
Nuwakot, Nepal 69 E10
Nuweiba', Egypt 70 D2
Nuwerus, S. Africa 88 E2
Nuweveldberge, S. Africa 88 E3
Nuyts, C., Australia 93 F5
Nuyts, Pt., Australia 93 G2
Nuyts Arch., Australia 95 E1
Nxau-Nxau, Botswana 88 B3
Nyaake, Liberia 82 E3
Nyabing, Australia 93 F2
Nyack, U.S.A. 111 E11
Nyagan, Russia 50 C7
Nyahanga, Tanzania 86 C3
Nyahua, Tanzania 86 D3
Nyahururu, Kenya 86 B4
Nyainqentanglha Shan, China 60 C4
Nyakanazi, Tanzania 86 C3
Nyakrom, Ghana 83 D4
Nyâlâ, Sudan 81 E1
Nyamandhlovu, Zimbabwe 87 F2
Nyambiti, Tanzania 86 C3
Nyamlell, Sudan 81 F2
Nyamwaga, Tanzania 86 C3
Nyandekwa, Tanzania 86 C3
Nyanding →, Sudan 81 F3
Nyandoma, Russia 46 B11
Nyangana, Namibia 88 B3
Nyanguge, Tanzania 86 C3
Nyankpala, Ghana 83 D4
Nyanza, Rwanda 86 C2
Nyanza □, Kenya 86 C3
Nyanza-Lac, Burundi 86 C2
Nyaponges, Sudan 81 F3
Nyasa, L., Africa 87 E3
Nyasvizh, Belarus 47 F4
Nyazura, Zimbabwe 87 F3
Nyazwidzi →, Zimbabwe 87 G3
Nyborg, Denmark 11 J4
Nybro, Sweden 11 H9
Nyda, Russia 50 C8
Nyeri, Kenya 86 C4
Nyerol, Sudan 81 F3
Nyhammar, Sweden 10 D8
Nyinahin, Ghana 82 D4
Nyíradony, Hungary 42 C6
Nyírbátor, Hungary 42 C7
Nyíregyháza, Hungary 42 C6
Nykøbing, Storstrøm, Denmark 11 K5
Nykøbing, Vestsjælland, Denmark 11 J5
Nykøbing, Viborg, Denmark 11 H2
Nyköping, Sweden 11 F11
Nykroppa, Sweden 10 E8
Nykvarn, Sweden 10 E11
Nyland, Sweden 10 A11
Nylstroom, S. Africa 89 C4
Nymagee, Australia 95 E4
Nymburk, Czech Rep. 26 A8
Nynäshamn, Sweden 11 F11
Nyngan, Australia 95 E4
Nyoma Rap, India 69 C8
Nyoman = Neman →, Lithuania 9 J20
Nyon, Switz. 25 J2
Nyong →, Cameroon 83 E6
Nyons, France 21 D9
Nyou, Burkina Faso 83 C4
Nýrsko, Czech Rep. 26 B6
Nysa, Poland 45 H4
Nysa →, Europe 24 C10
Nysa Kłodzka →, Poland 45 H4
Nysäter, Sweden 10 E6
Nyssa, U.S.A. 114 E5
Nysted, Denmark 11 K5
Nyunzu, Dem. Rep. of the Congo 86 D2
Nyurba, Russia 51 C12
Nyzhnohirskyy, Ukraine 47 K8
Nzébéla, Guinea 82 D3
Nzega, Tanzania 86 C3
Nzérékoré, Guinea 82 D3
Nzeto, Angola 84 F2
Nzilo, Chutes de, Dem. Rep. of the Congo 87 E2
Nzo →, Ivory C. 82 D3
Nzubuka, Tanzania 86 C3

O

O Barco, Spain 34 C4
O Carballiño, Spain 34 C2
O Corgo, Spain 34 C3
O Pino, Spain 34 C2
O Porriño, Spain 34 C2
Ō-Shima, Japan 55 G9
Oa, Mull of, U.K. 14 F2
Oacoma, U.S.A. 112 D5
Oahe, L., U.S.A. 112 C4
Oahe Dam, U.S.A. 112 C4
Oahu, U.S.A. 106 H16
Oak Harbor, U.S.A. 116 B4
Oak Hill, U.S.A. 108 G5
Oak Ridge, U.S.A. 109 G3
Oak View, U.S.A. 117 L7
Oakan-Dake, Japan 54 C12
Oakdale, Calif., U.S.A. 116 H6
Oakdale, La., U.S.A. 113 K8
Oakes, U.S.A. 112 B5
Oakesdale, U.S.A. 114 C5
Oakey, Australia 95 D5
Oakfield, U.S.A. 110 C6
Oakham, U.K. 13 E7
Oakhurst, U.S.A. 116 H7
Oakland, U.S.A. 116 H4
Oakley, Idaho, U.S.A. 114 E7
Oakley, Kans., U.S.A. 112 F4
Oakover →, Australia 92 D3
Oakridge, U.S.A. 114 E2
Oakville, Canada 110 C5
Oakville, U.S.A. 116 D3
Oamaru, N.Z. 91 L3
Oancea, Romania 43 E12
Oasis, Calif., U.S.A. 117 M10
Oasis, Nev., U.S.A. 116 H9
Oates Land, Antarctica 5 C11
Oatlands, Australia 94 G4
Oatman, U.S.A. 117 K12
Oaxaca, Mexico 119 D5
Oaxaca □, Mexico 119 D5
Ob →, Russia 50 C7
Oba, Canada 102 C3
Obala, Cameroon 83 E7
Obama, Japan 55 G7
Oban, Nigeria 83 D6
Oban, U.K. 14 E3
Obbia, Somali Rep. 74 F4
Obera, Argentina 127 B4
Oberammergau, Germany 25 H7
Oberasbach, Germany 25 F6
Oberbayern □, Germany 25 G7
Oberdrauburg, Austria 26 E5
Oberfranken □, Germany 25 E7
Oberhausen, Germany 24 D2
Oberkirch, Germany 25 G4
Oberlausitz, Germany 24 D10
Oberlin, Kans., U.S.A. 112 F4
Oberlin, La., U.S.A. 113 K8
Oberlin, Ohio, U.S.A. 110 E2
Obernai, France 19 D14
Oberndorf, Germany 25 G4
Oberon, Australia 95 E4
Oberösterreich □, Austria 26 C7
Oberpfalz □, Germany 25 F8
Oberpfälzer Wald, Germany 25 F8
Oberstdorf, Germany 25 H6
Oberursel, Germany 25 E4
Oberwart, Austria 27 D9
Obi, Kepulauan, Indonesia 63 E7
Obi Is. = Obi, Kepulauan, Indonesia 63 E7
Obiaruku, Nigeria 83 D6
Óbidos, Brazil 125 D7
Óbidos, Portugal 35 F1
Obihiro, Japan 54 C11
Obilatu, Indonesia 63 E7
Obilnoye, Russia 49 G7
Obing, Germany 25 G8
Objat, France 20 C5
Obluchye, Russia 51 E14
Obninsk, Russia 46 E9
Obo, C.A.R. 86 A2
Oboa, Mt., Uganda 86 B3
Obock, Djibouti 81 E5
Oborniki, Poland 45 F3
Oborniki Śląskie, Poland 45 G3
Oboyan, Russia 47 G9
Obozerskaya = Obozerskiy, Russia 50 C5
Obozerskiy, Russia 50 C5
Obrenovac, Serbia, Yug. 40 B4
Obrovac, Croatia 29 D12
Obruk, Turkey 72 C5
Obrzycko, Poland 45 F3
Observatory Inlet, Canada 104 B3
Obshchi Syrt, Russia 6 E16
Obskaya Guba, Russia 50 C8
Obuasi, Ghana 83 D4
Obubra, Nigeria 83 D6
Obudu, Nigeria 83 D6
Obwalden □, Switz. 25 J4
Obzor, Bulgaria 41 D11
Ocala, U.S.A. 109 L4
Ocampo, Chihuahua, Mexico 118 B3
Ocampo, Tamaulipas, Mexico 119 C5
Ocaña, Spain 34 F7
Ocanomowoc, U.S.A. 112 D10

Occidental, Cordillera, *Colombia* 122 C3
Ocean City, *Md., U.S.A.* 108 F8
Ocean City, *N.J., U.S.A.* 108 F8
Ocean City, *Wash., U.S.A.* 116 C2
Ocean Falls, *Canada* 104 C3
Ocean I. = Banaba, *Kiribati* 96 H8
Ocean Park, *U.S.A.* 116 D2
Oceano, *U.S.A.* 117 K6
Oceanport, *U.S.A.* 111 F10
Oceanside, *U.S.A.* 117 M9
Ochagavía, *Spain* 32 C3
Ochakiv, *Ukraine* 47 J6
Ochamchira, *Georgia* 49 J5
Ochil Hills, *U.K.* 14 E5
Ochsenfurt, *Germany* 25 F6
Ochsenhausen, *Germany* 25 G5
Ocilla, *U.S.A.* 109 K4
Ockelbo, *Sweden* 10 D10
Ocmulgee →, *U.S.A.* 109 K4
Ocna Mureş, *Romania* 43 D8
Ocna Sibiului, *Romania* 43 E9
Ocnele Mari, *Romania* 43 E9
Ocniţa, *Moldova* 43 B12
Oconee →, *U.S.A.* 109 K4
Oconto, *U.S.A.* 108 C2
Oconto Falls, *U.S.A.* 108 C1
Ocosingo, *Mexico* 119 D6
Ocotal, *Nic.* 120 D2
Ocotlán, *Mexico* 118 C4
Ocotlán de Morelos, *Mexico* 119 D5
Ocreza →, *Portugal* 35 F3
Öcsa, *Hungary* 42 C4
Octeville, *France* 18 C5
Oda, *Ghana* 83 D4
Ōda, *Japan* 55 G6
Oda, J., *Sudan* 80 C4
Ódáðahraun, *Iceland* 8 D5
Ödåkra, *Sweden* 11 H6
Odate, *Japan* 54 D10
Odawara, *Japan* 55 G9
Odda, *Norway* 9 F12
Odder, *Denmark* 11 J4
Odei →, *Canada* 105 B9
Odemira, *Portugal* 35 H2
Ödemiş, *Turkey* 39 C9
Odendaalsrus, *S. Africa* 88 D4
Odensbacken, *Sweden* 10 E9
Odense, *Denmark* 11 J4
Odenwald, *Germany* 25 F5
Oder →, *Europe* 24 B10
Oder-Havel Kanal, *Germany* 24 C10
Oderzo, *Italy* 29 C9
Odesa, *Ukraine* 47 J6
Ödeshög, *Sweden* 11 F8
Odessa = Odesa, *Ukraine* 47 J6
Odessa, *Canada* 111 B8
Odessa, *Tex., U.S.A.* 113 K3
Odessa, *Wash., U.S.A.* 114 C4
Odiakwe, *Botswana* 88 C4
Odiel →, *Spain* 35 H4
Odienné, *Ivory C.* 82 D3
Odintsovo, *Russia* 46 E9
Odiongan, *Phil.* 61 E4
Odobeşti, *Romania* 43 E12
Odolanów, *Poland* 45 G4
O'Donnell, *U.S.A.* 113 J4
Odorheiu Secuiesc, *Romania* 43 D10
Odoyevo, *Russia* 46 F9
Odra = Oder →, *Europe* 24 B10
Odra →, *Spain* 34 C6
Odžaci, *Serbia, Yug.* 42 E4
Odžak, *Bos.-H.* 42 E3
Odzi, *Zimbabwe* 89 B5
Odzi →, *Zimbabwe* 89 B5
Oebisfelde, *Germany* 24 C6
Oeiras, *Brazil* 125 E10
Oeiras, *Portugal* 35 G1
Oelrichs, *U.S.A.* 112 D3
Oelsnitz, *Germany* 25 E8
Oelwein, *U.S.A.* 112 D9
Oenpelli, *Australia* 92 B5
Oetz, *Austria* 26 D3
Of, *Turkey* 73 B9
Ofanto →, *Italy* 31 A9
Offa, *Nigeria* 83 D5
Offaly □, *Ireland* 15 C4
Offenbach, *Germany* 25 E4
Offenburg, *Germany* 25 G3
Offida, *Italy* 29 F10
Ofidhousa, *Greece* 39 E8
Ofotfjorden, *Norway* 8 B17
Ōfunato, *Japan* 54 E10
Oga, *Japan* 54 E9
Oga-Hantō, *Japan* 54 E9
Ogaden, *Ethiopia* 74 F3
Ōgaki, *Japan* 55 G8
Ogallala, *U.S.A.* 112 E4
Ogasawara Gunto, *Pac. Oc.* 52 G18
Ogbomosho, *Nigeria* 83 D5
Ogden, *U.S.A.* 114 F7
Ogdensburg, *U.S.A.* 111 B9
Ogeechee →, *U.S.A.* 109 K5
Ogilby, *U.S.A.* 117 N12
Oglio →, *Italy* 28 C7
Ogmore, *Australia* 94 C4
Ognon →, *France* 19 E12
Ogoja, *Nigeria* 83 D6
Ogoki, *Canada* 102 B2
Ogoki →, *Canada* 102 B2
Ogoki L., *Canada* 102 B2
Ogoki Res., *Canada* 102 B2
Ogooué →, *Gabon* 84 E1
Ogosta →, *Bulgaria* 40 C7
Ogowe = Ogooué →, *Gabon* 84 E1
Ogr = Sharafa, *Sudan* 81 E2
Ograźden, *Macedonia* 40 E6
Ogre, *Latvia* 9 H21
Ogrein, *Sudan* 80 D3
Ogulin, *Croatia* 29 C12
Ogun □, *Nigeria* 83 D5
Ogurchinskiy, Ostrov, *Turkmenistan* 71 B7
Oguta, *Nigeria* 83 D6
Ogwashi-Uku, *Nigeria* 83 D6
Ogwe, *Nigeria* 83 E6
Ohai, *N.Z.* 91 L2
Ohakune, *N.Z.* 91 H5
Ohata, *Japan* 54 D10
Ohau, L., *N.Z.* 91 L2
Ohio □, *U.S.A.* 110 F2
Ohio →, *U.S.A.* 108 G1
Ohře →, *Czech Rep.* 26 A7
Ohre →, *Germany* 24 C7
Ohrid, *Macedonia* 40 E4
Ohridsko Jezero, *Macedonia* 40 E4
Ohrigstad, *S. Africa* 89 C5
Öhringen, *Germany* 25 F5
Oi Qu, *China* 58 C2
Oiapoque, *Brazil* 125
Oikou, *China* 57 E9
Oil City, *U.S.A.* 110 E5
Oil Springs, *Canada* 110 D2
Oildale, *U.S.A.* 117 K7
Oinousa, *Greece* 39 C8
Oise □, *France* 19 C9
Oise →, *France* 19 C9
Ōita, *Japan* 55 H5
Ōita □, *Japan* 55 H5
Oiticica, *Brazil* 125 E10
Ojacaliente, *Mexico* 118 C4
Ojai, *U.S.A.* 117 L7
Ojinaga, *Mexico* 118 B4
Ojiya, *Japan* 55 F9
Ojos del Salado, Cerro, *Argentina* 126 B2
Oka →, *Russia* 48 B7
Okaba, *Indonesia* 63 F9
Okahandja, *Namibia* 88 C2
Okahukura, *N.Z.* 91 H5
Okanagan L., *Canada* 104 D5
Okanogan, *U.S.A.* 114 B4
Okanogan →, *U.S.A.* 114 B4
Okány, *Hungary* 42 D6
Okaputa, *Namibia* 88 C2
Okara, *Pakistan* 68 D5
Okarito, *N.Z.* 91 K3
Okaukuejo, *Namibia* 88 B2
Okavango Swamps, *Botswana* 88 B3
Okaya, *Japan* 55 F9
Okayama, *Japan* 55 G6
Okayama □, *Japan* 55 G6
Okazaki, *Japan* 55 G8
Oke-Iho, *Nigeria* 83 D5
Okeechobee, *U.S.A.* 109 M5
Okeechobee, L., *U.S.A.* 109 M5
Okefenokee Swamp, *U.S.A.* 109 K4
Okehampton, *U.K.* 13 G4
Okene, *Nigeria* 83 D6
Oker →, *Germany* 24 C6
Okha, *India* 68 H3
Okha, *Russia* 51 D15
Ókhi Óros, *Greece* 38 C6
Okhotsk, *Russia* 51 D15
Okhotsk, Sea of, *Asia* 51 D15
Okhotskiy Perevoz, *Russia* 51 C14
Okhtyrka, *Ukraine* 47 G8
Oki-Shotō, *Japan* 55 F6
Okiep, *S. Africa* 88 D2
Okigwi, *Nigeria* 83 D6
Okija, *Nigeria* 83 D6
Okinawa □, *Japan* 55 L4
Okinawa-Guntō, *Japan* 55 L4
Okinawa-Jima, *Japan* 55 L4
Okino-erabu-Shima, *Japan* 55 L4
Okitipupa, *Nigeria* 83 D5
Oklahoma □, *U.S.A.* 113 H6
Oklahoma City, *U.S.A.* 113 H6
Okmulgee, *U.S.A.* 113 H7
Oknitsa = Ocniţa, *Moldova* 43 B12
Oko, W. →, *Sudan* 80 C4
Okolo, *Uganda* 86 B3
Okolona, *U.S.A.* 113 J10
Okombahe, *Namibia* 88 C2
Okonek, *Poland* 44 E3
Okotoks, *Canada* 104 C6
Okrika, *Nigeria* 83 E6
Oksibil, *Indonesia* 63 E10
Oktabrsk = Oktyabrsk, *Kazakstan* 50 E6
Oktyabrsk, *Kazakstan* 50 E6
Oktyabrsk, *Russia* 48 D9
Oktyabrskiy = Aktsyabrski, *Belarus* 47 F5
Oktyabrskiy, *Russia* 49 G5
Oktyabrskoy Revolyutsii, Ostrov, *Russia* 51 B10
Oktyabrskoye = Zhovtneve, *Ukraine* 47 J7
Okulovka, *Russia* 46 C7
Okuru, *N.Z.* 91 K2
Okushiri-Tō, *Japan* 54 C9
Okuta, *Nigeria* 83 D5
Okwa →, *Botswana* 88 C3
Ola, *U.S.A.* 113 H8
Ólafsfjörður, *Iceland* 8 C4
Ólafsvík, *Iceland* 8 D2
Olaine, *Latvia* 44 B10
Olancha, *U.S.A.* 117 J8
Olancha Pk., *U.S.A.* 117 J8
Olanchito, *Honduras* 120 C2
Öland, *Sweden* 11 H10
Ölands norra udde, *Sweden* 11 G11
Ölands södra udde, *Sweden* 11 H10
Olargues, *France* 20 E6
Olary, *Australia* 95 E3
Olascoaga, *Argentina* 126 D3
Olathe, *U.S.A.* 112 F7
Olavarría, *Argentina* 126 D3
Oława, *Poland* 45 H4
Olbernhau, *Germany* 24 E9
Ólbia, *Italy* 30 B2
Ólbia, G. di, *Italy* 30 B2
Olching, *Germany* 25 G7
Olcott, *U.S.A.* 110 C6
Old Bahama Chan. = Bahama, Canal Viejo de, *W. Indies* 120 B4
Old Baldy Pk. = San Antonio, Mt., *U.S.A.* 117 L9
Old Castile = Castilla y Leon □, *Spain* 34 D6
Old Crow, *Canada* 100 B6
Old Dale, *U.S.A.* 117 L11
Old Dongola, *Sudan* 80 D3
Old Forge, *N.Y., U.S.A.* 111 C10
Old Forge, *Pa., U.S.A.* 111 E9
Old Perlican, *Canada* 103 C9
Old Shinyanga, *Tanzania* 86 C3
Old Speck Mt., *U.S.A.* 111 B14
Old Town, *U.S.A.* 109 C11
Old Washington, *U.S.A.* 110 F3
Old Wives L., *Canada* 105 C7
Oldbury, *U.K.* 13 F5
Oldcastle, *Ireland* 15 C4
Oldeani, *Tanzania* 86 C4
Oldenburg, *Niedersachsen, Germany* 24 B4
Oldenburg, *Schleswig-Holstein, Germany* 24 A6
Oldenzaal, *Neths.* 17 B6
Oldham, *U.K.* 12 D5
Oldman →, *Canada* 104 D6
Oldmeldrum, *U.K.* 14 D6
Olds, *Canada* 104 C6
Oldziyt, *Mongolia* 56 B5
Olean, *U.S.A.* 110 D6
Olecko, *Poland* 44 D9
Oléggio, *Italy* 28 C5
Oleiros, *Portugal* 34 F3
Oleiros, *Spain* 34 B2
Olekma →, *Russia* 51 C13
Olekminsk, *Russia* 51 C13
Oleksandriya, *Kirovohrad, Ukraine* 47 H7
Oleksandriya, *Rivne, Ukraine* 47 G4
Oleksandrovka, *Ukraine* 47 H7
Olema, *U.S.A.* 116 G4
Olenek, *Russia* 51 C12
Olenek →, *Russia* 51 B13
Olenino, *Russia* 46 D7
Oléron, Î. d', *France* 20 C2
Oleśnica, *Poland* 45 G4
Olesno, *Poland* 45 H5
Olevsk, *Ukraine* 47 G4
Olga, *Russia* 51 E14
Olga, L., *Canada* 102 C4
Olga, Mt., *Australia* 93 E5
Ølgod, *Denmark* 11 J2
Olhão, *Portugal* 35 H3
Olib, *Croatia* 29 D11
Oliena, *Italy* 30 B2
Oliete, *Spain* 32 D4
Olifants →, *Africa* 89 C5
Olifants →, *Namibia* 88 C2
Olifantshoek, *S. Africa* 88 D3
Ólimbos, *Greece* 39 F9
Ólimbos, Óros, *Greece* 40 F6
Olímpia, *Brazil* 127 A6
Olinda, *Brazil* 125 E12
Olite, *Spain* 32 C3
Oliva, *Argentina* 126 C3
Oliva, *Spain* 33 G4
Oliva, Punta del, *Spain* 34 B5
Oliva de la Frontera, *Spain* 35 G4
Olivares, *Spain* 32 F2
Olivehurst, *U.S.A.* 116 F5
Oliveira de Azeméis, *Portugal* 34 E2
Oliveira do Douro, *Portugal* 34 D2
Olivenza, *Spain* 35 G3
Oliver, *Canada* 104 D5
Oliver L., *Canada* 105 B8
Olivet, *France* 19 E8
Olkhovka, *Russia* 48 F7
Olkusz, *Poland* 45 H6
Ollagüe, *Chile* 126 A2
Olmedo, *Spain* 34 D6
Olmeto, *France* 21 G12
Olney, *Ill., U.S.A.* 108 F1
Olney, *Tex., U.S.A.* 113 J5
Olofström, *Sweden* 11 H8
Oloma, *Cameroon* 83 E7
Olomane →, *Canada* 103 B7
Olomouc, *Czech Rep.* 27 B10
Olonets, *Russia* 46 B7
Olongapo, *Phil.* 61 D4
Olonne-sur-Mer, *France* 20 B2
Oloron, Gave d' →, *France* 20 E2
Oloron-Ste-Marie, *France* 20 E3
Olot, *Spain* 32 C7
Olovo, *Bos.-H.* 42 F3
Olovyannaya, *Russia* 51 D12
Oloy →, *Russia* 51 C16
Olsberg, *Germany* 24 D4
Olshammar, *Sweden* 11 F8
Olshanka, *Ukraine* 47 H6
Olshany, *Ukraine* 47 G8
Olsztyn, *Poland* 44 E7
Olsztynek, *Poland* 44 E7
Olt □, *Romania* 43 F9
Olt →, *Romania* 43 G9
Olten, *Switz.* 25 H3
Olteniţa, *Romania* 43 F11
Olton, *U.S.A.* 113 H3
Oltu, *Turkey* 73 B9
Oluanpi, *Taiwan* 59 G13
Olula del Rio, *Spain* 33 H2
Olur, *Turkey* 73 B10
Olutanga, *Phil.* 61 H5
Olvega, *Spain* 32 D2
Olvera, *Spain* 35 J5
Olymbos, *Cyprus* 36 D12
Olympia, *Greece* 38 D3
Olympia, *U.S.A.* 116 D4
Olympic Dam, *Australia* 95 E2
Olympic Mts., *U.S.A.* 116 C3
Olympic Nat. Park, *U.S.A.* 116 C3
Olympus, *Cyprus* 36 E11
Olympus, Mt. = Ólimbos, Óros, *Greece* 40 F6
Olympus, Mt. = Uludağ, *Turkey* 41 F13
Olympus, Mt., *U.S.A.* 116 C3
Olyphant, *U.S.A.* 111 E9
Om →, *Russia* 50 D8
Om Hajer, *Eritrea* 81 E4
Om Koi, *Thailand* 64 D2
Ōma, *Japan* 54 D10
Ōmachi, *Japan* 55 F8
Omae-Zaki, *Japan* 55 G9
Ōmagari, *Japan* 54 E10
Omagh, *U.K.* 15 B4
Omagh □, *U.K.* 15 B4
Omaha, *U.S.A.* 112 E7
Omak, *U.S.A.* 114 B4
Omalos, *Greece* 36 D5
Oman ■, *Asia* 74 C6
Oman, G. of, *Asia* 71 E8
Omaruru, *Namibia* 88 C2
Omaruru →, *Namibia* 88 C1
Omate, *Peru* 124 G4
Ombai, Selat, *Indonesia* 63 F6
Omboué, *Gabon* 84 E1
Ombrone →, *Italy* 28 F8
Omdurmân, *Sudan* 81 D3
Omegna, *Italy* 28 C5
Omemee, *Canada* 110 B6
Omeo, *Australia* 95 F4
Omeonga, *Dem. Rep. of the Congo* 86 C1
Ometepe, I. de, *Nic.* 120 D2
Ometepec, *Mexico* 119 D5
Ominato, *Japan* 54 D10
Omineca →, *Canada* 104 B4
Omiš, *Croatia* 29 E13
Omišalj, *Croatia* 29 C11
Omitara, *Namibia* 88 C2
Ōmiya, *Japan* 55 G9
Omme Å →, *Denmark* 11 J2
Ommen, *Neths.* 17 B6
Ömnögovĭ □, *Mongolia* 56 C3
Omo →, *Ethiopia* 81 F4
Omodeo, L., *Italy* 30 B1
Omodhos, *Cyprus* 36 E11
Omoko, *Nigeria* 83 D6
Omolon →, *Russia* 51 C16
Omono-Gawa →, *Japan* 54 E10
Omsk, *Russia* 50 D8
Omsukchan, *Russia* 51 C16
Ōmu, *Japan* 54 B11
Omul, Vf., *Romania* 43 E10
Omulew →, *Poland* 45 E8
Ōmura, *Japan* 55 H4
Omuramba Omatako →, *Namibia* 88 B2
Omuramba Ovambo →, *Namibia* 88 B2
Omurtag, *Bulgaria* 41 C10
Ōmuta, *Japan* 55 H5
Oña, *Spain* 34 C7
Onaga, *U.S.A.* 112 F6
Onalaska, *U.S.A.* 112 D9
Onancock, *U.S.A.* 108 G8
Onang, *Indonesia* 63 E5
Onaping L., *Canada* 102 C3
Oñati, *Spain* 32 B2
Onavas, *Mexico* 118 B3
Onawa, *U.S.A.* 112 D6
Oncócua, *Angola* 88 B1
Onda, *Spain* 32 F4
Ondaejin, *N. Korea* 57 D15
Ondangua, *Namibia* 88 B2
Ondarroa, *Spain* 32 B2
Ondava →, *Slovak Rep.* 27 C14
Ondjiva, *Angola* 88 B2
Ondo, *Nigeria* 83 D5
Ondo □, *Nigeria* 83 D6
Öndörshil, *Mongolia* 56 B5
Öndverðarnes, *Iceland* 8 D1
One Tree, *Australia* 95 E3
Onega, *Russia* 50 C4
Onega →, *Russia* 6 C13
Onega, L. = Onezhskoye Ozero, *Russia* 46 B8
Onehunga, *N.Z.* 91 G5
Oneida, *U.S.A.* 111 C9
Oneida L., *U.S.A.* 111 C9
O'Neill, *U.S.A.* 112 D5
Onekotan, Ostrov, *Russia* 51 E16
Onema, *Dem. Rep. of the Congo* 86 C1
Oneonta, *U.S.A.* 111 D9
Oneşti, *Romania* 43 D11
Onezhskoye Ozero, *Russia* 46 B8
Ongarue, *N.Z.* 91 H5
Ongers →, *S. Africa* 88 E3
Ongerup, *Australia* 93 F2
Ongjin, *N. Korea* 57 F13
Ongkharak, *Thailand* 64 E3
Ongniud Qi, *China* 57 C10
Ongoka, *Dem. Rep. of the Congo* 86 C2
Ongole, *India* 66 M12
Ongon = Havirga, *Mongolia* 56 B7
Oni, *Georgia* 49 J6
Onida, *U.S.A.* 112 C4
Onilahy →, *Madag.* 89 C7
Onitsha, *Nigeria* 83 D6
Onoda, *Japan* 55 G5
Onpyŏng-ni, *S. Korea* 57 H14
Ons, I. de, *Spain* 34 C2
Onslow, *Australia* 92 D2
Onslow B., *U.S.A.* 109 H7
Ontake-San, *Japan* 55 G8
Ontario, *Calif., U.S.A.* 117 L9
Ontario, *Oreg., U.S.A.* 114 D5
Ontario □, *Canada* 102 B2
Ontario, L., *N. Amer.* 102 D4
Ontinyent, *Spain* 33 G4
Ontonagon, *U.S.A.* 112 B10
Ontur, *Spain* 33 G3
Onyx, *U.S.A.* 117 K8
Oodnadatta, *Australia* 95 D2
Ooldea, *Australia* 93 F5
Oombulgurri, *Australia* 92 C4
Oorindi, *Australia* 94 C3
Oost-Vlaanderen □, *Belgium* 17 C3
Oostende, *Belgium* 17 C2
Oosterhout, *Neths.* 17 C4
Oosterschelde →, *Neths.* 17 C4
Oosterwolde, *Neths.* 17 B6
Ootacamund = Udagamandalam, *India* 66 P10
Ootsa L., *Canada* 104 C3
Opaka, *Bulgaria* 41 C10
Opala, *Dem. Rep. of the Congo* 86 C1
Opalenica, *Poland* 45 F3
Opan, *Bulgaria* 41 D9
Opanake, *Sri Lanka* 66 R12
Opasatika, *Canada* 102 C3
Opasquia Prov. Park, *Canada* 102 B1
Opatija, *Croatia* 29 C11
Opatów, *Poland* 45 H8
Opava, *Czech Rep.* 27 B10
Opelika, *U.S.A.* 109 J3
Opelousas, *U.S.A.* 113 K8
Opémisca, L., *Canada* 102 C5
Opheim, *U.S.A.* 114 B10
Ophthalmia Ra., *Australia* 92 D2
Opi, *Nigeria* 83 D6
Opinaca →, *Canada* 102 B4
Opinaca, Rés., *Canada* 102 B4
Opinnagau →, *Canada* 102 B3
Opiscoteo, L., *Canada* 103 B6
Opobo, *Nigeria* 83 E6
Opochka, *Russia* 46 D5
Opoczno, *Poland* 45 G7
Opol, *Phil.* 61 G6
Opole, *Poland* 45 H4
Opole Lubelskie, *Poland* 45 G8
Opolskie □, *Poland* 45 H5
Oponono L., *Namibia* 88 B2
Oporto = Porto, *Portugal* 34 D2
Opotiki, *N.Z.* 91 H6
Opp, *U.S.A.* 109 K2
Oppdal, *Norway* 9 E13
Óppido Mamertina, *Italy* 31 D8
Opportunity, *U.S.A.* 114 C5
Oprişor, *Romania* 42 F8
Oprtalj, *Croatia* 29 C10
Opua, *N.Z.* 91 F5
Opunake, *N.Z.* 91 H4
Opuwo, *Namibia* 88 B1
Opuzen, *Croatia* 29 E14
Ora, *Cyprus* 36 E12
Oracle, *U.S.A.* 115 K8
Oradea, *Romania* 42 C6
Öræfajökull, *Iceland* 8 D5
Orahovac, *Kosovo, Yug.* 40 D4
Orahovica, *Croatia* 42 E2
Orai, *India* 69 G8
Oraison, *France* 21 E9
Oral = Zhayyq →, *Kazakstan* 50 E6
Oral, *Kazakstan* 48 E10
Oran, *Algeria* 78 A5
Orange, *Australia* 95 E4
Orange, *France* 21 D8
Orange, *Calif., U.S.A.* 117 M9
Orange, *Mass., U.S.A.* 111 D12
Orange, *Tex., U.S.A.* 113 K8
Orange, *Va., U.S.A.* 108 F6
Orange →, *S. Africa* 88 D2
Orange, C., *Brazil* 122 C5
Orange Cove, *U.S.A.* 116 J7
Orange Free State = Free State □, *S. Africa* 88 D4
Orange Grove, *U.S.A.* 113 M6
Orange Walk, *Belize* 119 D7
Orangeburg, *U.S.A.* 109 J5
Orangeville, *Canada* 102 D3
Orango, *Guinea-Biss.* 82 C1
Orani, *Phil.* 61 D4
Oranienburg, *Germany* 24 C9
Oranje = Orange →, *S. Africa* 88 D2
Oranje Vrystaat = Free State □, *S. Africa* 88 D4
Oranjemund, *Namibia* 88 D2
Oranjerivier, *S. Africa* 88 D3
Orapa, *Botswana* 85 J5
Orarak, *Sudan* 81 F3
Oras, *Phil.* 61 E6
Orašje, *Bos.-H.* 42 E3
Orăştie, *Romania* 43 E8
Oraşul Stalin = Braşov, *Romania* 43 E10
Orava →, *Slovak Rep.* 27 B12
Orava, Vodna nádriž, *Slovak Rep.* 27 B12
Oraviţa, *Romania* 42 E6
Orb →, *France* 20 E7
Orba →, *Italy* 28 D5
Ørbæk, *Denmark* 11 J4
Orbe, *Switz.* 25 J2
Orbec, *France* 18 C7
Orbetello, *Italy* 29 F8
Órbigo →, *Spain* 34 C5
Orbisonia, *U.S.A.* 110 F7

Orbost, *Australia* 95 F4
Örbyhus, *Sweden* 10 D11
Orcas I., *U.S.A.* 116 B4
Orce, *Spain* 33 H2
Orce →, *Spain* 33 H2
Orchard City, *U.S.A.* 115 G10
Orchies, *France* 19 B10
Orchila, I., *Venezuela* 121 D6
Órcia →, *Italy* 29 F8
Orco →, *Italy* 28 C4
Orcutt, *U.S.A.* 117 L6
Ord, *U.S.A.* 112 E5
Ord →, *Australia* 92 C4
Ord, Mt., *Australia* 92 C4
Ordenes = Ordes, *Spain* 34 B2
Orderville, *U.S.A.* 115 H7
Ordes, *Spain* 34 B2
Ording = St-Peter-Ording, *Germany* 24 A4
Ordos = Mu Us Shamo, *China* 56 E5
Ordu, *Turkey* 72 B7
Ordubad, *Azerbaijan* 73 C12
Orduña, *Álava, Spain* 32 C2
Orduña, *Granada, Spain* 35 H7
Ordway, *U.S.A.* 112 F3
Ordzhonikidze = Vladikavkaz, *Russia* 49 J7
Ordzhonikidze, *Ukraine* 47 J8
Ore, *Dem. Rep. of the Congo* 86 B2
Ore Mts. = Erzgebirge, *Germany* 24 E8
Orebić, *Croatia* 29 F14
Örebro, *Sweden* 10 E9
Örebro län □, *Sweden* 10 E8
Oregon, *U.S.A.* 112 D10
Oregon □, *U.S.A.* 114 E3
Oregon City, *U.S.A.* 116 E4
Öregrund, *Sweden* 10 D12
Öregrundsgrepen, *Sweden* 10 D12
Orekhov = Orikhiv, *Ukraine* 47 J8
Orekhovo-Zuyevo, *Russia* 46 E10
Orel, *Russia* 47 F9
Orel →, *Ukraine* 47 H8
Orellana, *Spain* 35 F5
Orellana, Canal de, *Spain* 35 F5
Orellana, Embalse de, *Spain* 35 F5
Orem, *U.S.A.* 114 F8
Ören, *Turkey* 39 D9
Orenburg, *Russia* 50 D6
Örencik, *Turkey* 39 B11
Orense = Ourense, *Spain* 34 C3
Orense □, *Spain* 34 C3
Orepuki, *N.Z.* 91 M1
Orestiás, *Greece* 41 E10
Orestos Pereyra, *Mexico* 118 B3
Øresund, *Europe* 11 J6
Orford Ness, *U.K.* 13 E9
Orgañà = Organyà, *Spain* 32 C6
Organos, Pta. de los, *Canary Is.* 37 F2
Organyà, *Spain* 32 C6
Orgaz, *Spain* 35 F7
Orgeyev = Orhei, *Moldova* 43 C13
Orhaneli, *Turkey* 41 G12
Orhaneli →, *Turkey* 41 G12
Orhangazi, *Turkey* 41 F13
Orhei, *Moldova* 43 C13
Orhon Gol →, *Mongolia* 60 A5
Ória, *Italy* 31 B10
Oriental, Cordillera, *Colombia* 122 C3
Orientale □, *Dem. Rep. of the Congo* 86 B2
Oriente, *Argentina* 126 D3
Orihuela, *Spain* 33 G4
Orihuela del Tremedal, *Spain* 32 E3
Orikhiv, *Ukraine* 47 J8
Oriku, *Albania* 40 F3
Orillia, *Canada* 102 D4
Orinoco →, *Venezuela* 122 C4
Orion, *Canada* 105 D6
Oriskany, *U.S.A.* 111 C9
Orissa □, *India* 67 K14
Orissaare, *Estonia* 9 G20
Oristano, *Italy* 30 C1
Oristano, G. di, *Italy* 30 C1
Orizaba, *Mexico* 119 D5
Orizare, *Bulgaria* 41 D11
Orjen, *Bos.-H.* 40 D2
Orjiva, *Spain* 35 J7
Orkanger, *Norway* 8 E13
Örkelljunga, *Sweden* 11 H7
Örken, *Sweden* 11 G9
Örkény, *Hungary* 42 C4
Orkla →, *Norway* 8 E13
Orkney, *S. Africa* 88 D4
Orkney □, *U.K.* 14 B5
Orkney Is., *U.K.* 14 B6
Orland, *U.S.A.* 116 F4
Orlando, *U.S.A.* 109 L5
Orlando, C. d', *Italy* 31 D7
Orléanais, *France* 19 E9
Orléans, *France* 19 E8
Orleans, *U.S.A.* 111 B12
Orléans, I. d', *Canada* 103 C5
Orlice →, *Czech Rep.* 26 A8
Orlov, *Slovak Rep.* 27 B13
Orlov Gay, *Russia* 48 E9
Orlová, *Czech Rep.* 27 B11
Orlovat, *Serbia, Yug.* 42 E5
Ormara, *Pakistan* 66 G4
Ormea, *Italy* 28 D4
Ormília, *Greece* 40 F7
Ormoc, *Phil.* 61 F6
Ormond, *N.Z.* 91 H6
Ormond Beach, *U.S.A.* 109 L5
Ormož, *Slovenia* 29 B13
Ormskirk, *U.K.* 12 D5
Ormstown, *Canada* 111 A11
Ornans, *France* 19 E13
Orne □, *France* 18 D7
Orne →, *France* 18 C6
Orneta, *Poland* 44 D7
Ornö, *Sweden* 10 E12
Örnsköldsvik, *Sweden* 10 A12
Oro, *N. Korea* 57 D14
Oro →, *Mexico* 118 B3
Oro Grande, *U.S.A.* 117 L9
Oro Valley, *U.S.A.* 115 K8
Orobie, Alpi, *Italy* 28 B6
Orocué, *Colombia* 124 C4
Orodara, *Burkina Faso* 82 C4
Orodo, *Nigeria* 83 D6
Orofino, *U.S.A.* 114 C5
Orol Dengizi = Aral Sea, *Asia* 50 E7
Oromocto, *Canada* 103 C6
Oron, *Nigeria* 83 E6
Orono, *Canada* 110 C6
Orono, *U.S.A.* 109 C11
Oronsay, *U.K.* 14 E2
Oropesa, *Spain* 34 F5
Oroquieta, *Phil.* 61 G5
Orosei, *Italy* 30 B2
Orosei, G. di, *Italy* 30 B2
Orosháza, *Hungary* 42 D5
Oroszlány, *Hungary* 42 C3
Orotukan, *Russia* 51 C16
Oroville, *Calif., U.S.A.* 116 F5
Oroville, *Wash., U.S.A.* 114 B4
Oroville, L., *U.S.A.* 116 F5
Orrefors, *Sweden* 11 H9
Orroroo, *Australia* 95 E2
Orrviken, *Sweden* 10 A8
Orrville, *U.S.A.* 110 F3
Orsa, *Sweden* 10 C8
Orsara di Púglia, *Italy* 31 A8
Orsasjön, *Sweden* 10 C8
Orsha, *Belarus* 46 E6
Örsjö, *Sweden* 11 H9
Orsk, *Russia* 50 D6
Orşova, *Romania* 42 F7
Ørsted, *Denmark* 11 H4
Örsundsbro, *Sweden* 10 E11
Orta, L. d', *Italy* 28 C5
Orta Nova, *Italy* 31 A8
Ortaca, *Turkey* 39 E10
Ortakent, *Turkey* 39 D9
Ortaklar, *Turkey* 39 D9
Ortaköy, *Çorum, Turkey* 72 B6
Ortaköy, *Niğde, Turkey* 72 C6
Orte, *Italy* 29 F9
Ortegal, C., *Spain* 34 B3
Orthez, *France* 20 E3
Ortigueira, *Spain* 34 B3
Orting, *U.S.A.* 116 C4
Ortisei, *Italy* 29 B8
Ortles, *Italy* 28 B7
Ortón →, *Bolivia* 124 F5
Ortona, *Italy* 29 F11
Ortonville, *U.S.A.* 112 C6
Orūmīyeh, *Iran* 70 B5
Orūmīyeh, Daryācheh-ye, *Iran* 70 B5
Orune, *Italy* 30 B2
Oruro, *Bolivia* 124 G5
Orust, *Sweden* 11 F5
Oruzgān □, *Afghan.* 66 C5
Orvault, *France* 18 E5
Orvieto, *Italy* 29 F9
Orwell, *N.Y., U.S.A.* 111 C9
Orwell, *Ohio, U.S.A.* 110 E4
Orwell →, *U.K.* 13 F9
Orwigsburg, *U.S.A.* 111 F8
Oryakhovo, *Bulgaria* 40 C7
Orzinuovi, *Italy* 28 C6
Orzyc →, *Poland* 45 F8
Orzysz, *Poland* 44 E8
Osa →, *Poland* 44 E5
Osa, Pen. de, *Costa Rica* 120 E3
Osage, *U.S.A.* 112 D8
Osage →, *U.S.A.* 112 F9
Osage City, *U.S.A.* 112 F7
Ōsaka, *Japan* 55 G7
Osan, *S. Korea* 57 F14
Osawatomie, *U.S.A.* 112 F7
Osborne, *U.S.A.* 112 F5
Osby, *Sweden* 11 H7
Osceola, *Ark., U.S.A.* 113 H10
Osceola, *Iowa, U.S.A.* 112 E8
Oschatz, *Germany* 24 D9
Oschersleben, *Germany* 24 C7
Óschiri, *Italy* 30 B2
Oscoda, *U.S.A.* 110 B1
Osečina, *Serbia, Yug.* 40 B3
Ösel = Saaremaa, *Estonia* 9 G20
Osery, *Russia* 46 E10
Osgoode, *Canada* 111 A9
Osh, *Kyrgyzstan* 50 E8
Oshakati, *Namibia* 85 H3
Oshawa, *Canada* 102 D4
Oshigambo, *Namibia* 88 B2
Oshkosh, *Nebr., U.S.A.* 112 E3
Oshkosh, *Wis., U.S.A.* 112 C10
Oshmyany = Ashmyany, *Belarus* 9 J21
Oshnovīyeh, *Iran* 70 B5
Oshogbo, *Nigeria* 83 D5
Oshtorīnān, *Iran* 71 C6
Oshwe, *Dem. Rep. of the Congo* 84 E3
Osi, *Nigeria* 83 D6
Osieczna, *Poland* 45 G3
Osijek, *Croatia* 42 E3
Ósilo, *Italy* 30 B1
Ósimo, *Italy* 29 E10
Osintorf, *Belarus* 46 E6
Osipenko = Berdyansk, *Ukraine* 47 J9
Osipovichi = Asipovichy, *Belarus* 46 F5
Osiyan, *India* 68 F5
Osizweni, *S. Africa* 89 D5
Oskaloosa, *U.S.A.* 112 E8
Oskarshamn, *Sweden* 11 G10
Oskarström, *Sweden* 11 H6
Oskélanéo, *Canada* 102 C4
Öskemen, *Kazakstan* 50 E9
Oskol →, *Ukraine* 47 H9
Oslo, *Norway* 9 G14
Oslob, *Phil.* 61 G5
Oslofjorden, *Norway* 9 G14
Osmanabad, *India* 66 K10
Osmancık, *Turkey* 72 B6
Osmaniye, *Turkey* 70 B3
Osmanlı, *Turkey* 41 E10
Ösmo, *Sweden* 10 F11
Osnabrück, *Germany* 24 C4
Ośno Lubuskie, *Poland* 45 F1
Osoblaha, *Czech Rep.* 27 A10
Osogovska Planina, *Macedonia* 40 D6
Osor, *Italy* 29 D11
Osorio, *Brazil* 127 B5
Osorno, *Chile* 128 E2
Osorno, *Spain* 34 C6
Osoyoos, *Canada* 104 D5
Osøyro, *Norway* 9 F11
Ospika →, *Canada* 104 B4
Osprey Reef, *Australia* 94 A4
Oss, *Neths.* 17 C5
Ossa, Mt., *Australia* 94 G4
Óssa, Óros, *Greece* 38 B4
Ossa de Montiel, *Spain* 33 G2
Ossabaw I., *U.S.A.* 109 K5
Osse →, *France* 20 D4
Osse →, *Nigeria* 83 D6
Ossi, *Italy* 30 B1
Ossining, *U.S.A.* 111 E11
Ossipee, *U.S.A.* 111 C13
Ossokmanuan L., *Canada* 103 B7
Ossora, *Russia* 51 D17
Ostashkov, *Russia* 46 D7
Östavall, *Sweden* 10 B9
Oste →, *Germany* 24 B5
Ostend = Oostende, *Belgium* 17 C2
Oster, *Ukraine* 47 G6
Osterburg, *Germany* 24 C7
Osterburg, *U.S.A.* 110 F6
Osterburken, *Germany* 25 F5
Österbybruk, *Sweden* 10 D11
Österbymo, *Sweden* 11 G9
Österdalälven, *Sweden* 10 C7
Østerdalen, *Norway* 9 F14
Österfärnebo, *Sweden* 10 D10
Österforse, *Sweden* 10 A11
Östergötlands län □, *Sweden* 11 F9
Osterholz-Scharmbeck, *Germany* 24 B4
Østerild, *Denmark* 11 G2
Osterode, *Germany* 24 D6
Östersund, *Sweden* 10 A8
Östervåla, *Sweden* 10 D11
Ostfriesische Inseln, *Germany* 24 B3
Ostfriesland, *Germany* 24 B3
Östhammar, *Sweden* 10 D12
Óstia, Lido di, *Italy* 29 G9
Ostíglia, *Italy* 29 C8
Östmark, *Sweden* 10 D6
Östra Husby, *Sweden* 11 F10
Ostrava, *Czech Rep.* 27 B11
Ostróda, *Poland* 44 E6
Ostrogozhsk, *Russia* 47 G10
Ostroh, *Ukraine* 47 G4
Ostrołęka, *Poland* 45 E8
Ostrov, *Bulgaria* 41 C8
Ostrov, *Czech Rep.* 26 A5
Ostrov, *Romania* 43 F12
Ostrov, *Russia* 46 D5
Ostrów Lubelski, *Poland* 45 G9
Ostrów Mazowiecka, *Poland* 45 F8
Ostrów Wielkopolski, *Poland* 45 G4
Ostrowiec-Świętokrzyski, *Poland* 45 H8
Ostrožac, *Bos.-H.* 42 G2
Ostrzeszów, *Poland* 45 G4
Ostseebad Kühlungsborn, *Germany* 24 A7
Osttirol □, *Austria* 26 E5
Ostuni, *Italy* 31 B10
Osŭm →, *Bulgaria* 41 C8
Osumi →, *Albania* 40 F4
Ōsumi-Kaikyō, *Japan* 55 J5
Ōsumi-Shotō, *Japan* 55 J5
Osun □, *Nigeria* 83 D5
Osuna, *Spain* 35 H5
Oswegatchie →, *U.S.A.* 111 B9
Oswego, *U.S.A.* 111 C8
Oswego →, *U.S.A.* 111 C8
Oswestry, *U.K.* 12 E4
Oświęcim, *Poland* 45 H6
Otaci, *Moldova* 43 B12
Otago □, *N.Z.* 91 L2
Otago Harbour, *N.Z.* 91 L3
Ōtake, *Japan* 55 G6
Otaki, *N.Z.* 91 J5
Otaru, *Japan* 54 C10
Otaru-Wan = Ishikari-Wan, *Japan* 54 C10
Otava →, *Czech Rep.* 26 B7
Otavalo, *Ecuador* 124 C3
Otavi, *Namibia* 88 B2
Otchinjau, *Angola* 88 B1
Otelec, *Romania* 42 E5
Otelnuk L., *Canada* 103 A6
Oţelu Roşu, *Romania* 42 E7
Otero de Rey = Outeiro de Rei, *Spain* 34 B3
Othello, *U.S.A.* 114 C4
Othonoí, *Greece* 38 B1
Óthris, Óros, *Greece* 38 B4
Otira Gorge, *N.Z.* 91 K3
Otjiwarongo, *Namibia* 88 C2
Otmuchów, *Poland* 45 H4
Otočac, *Croatia* 29 D12
Otoineppu, *Japan* 54 B11
Otok, *Croatia* 29 E13
Otorohanga, *N.Z.* 91 H5
Otoskwin →, *Canada* 102 B2
Otra →, *Norway* 9 G13
Otradnyy, *Russia* 48 D10
Otranto, *Italy* 31 B11
Otranto, C. d', *Italy* 31 B11
Otranto, Str. of, *Italy* 31 B11
Otrokovice, *Czech Rep.* 27 B10
Otse, *S. Africa* 88 D4
Ōtsu, *Japan* 55 G7
Ōtsuki, *Japan* 55 G9
Ottawa = Outaouais →, *Canada* 102 C5
Ottawa, *Canada* 102 C4
Ottawa, *Ill., U.S.A.* 112 E10
Ottawa, *Kans., U.S.A.* 112 F7
Ottawa Is., *Canada* 101 C11
Ottélé, *Cameroon* 83 E7
Ottensheim, *Austria* 26 C7
Otter Cr. →, *U.S.A.* 111 B11
Otter L., *Canada* 105 B8
Otterndorf, *Germany* 24 B4
Otterup, *Denmark* 11 J4
Otterville, *Canada* 110 D4
Ottery St. Mary, *U.K.* 13 G4
Otto Beit Bridge, *Zimbabwe* 87 F2
Ottosdal, *S. Africa* 88 D4
Ottumwa, *U.S.A.* 112 E8
Otu, *Nigeria* 83 D5
Otukpa, *Nigeria* 83 D6
Oturkpo, *Nigeria* 83 D6
Otway, B., *Chile* 128 G2
Otway, C., *Australia* 95 F3
Otwock, *Poland* 45 F8
Ötztaler Ache →, *Austria* 26 D3
Ötztaler Alpen, *Austria* 26 E3
Ou →, *Laos* 64 B4
Ou Neua, *Laos* 58 F3
Ou-Sammyaku, *Japan* 54 E10
Ouachita →, *U.S.A.* 113 K9
Ouachita, L., *U.S.A.* 113 H8
Ouachita Mts., *U.S.A.* 113 H7
Ouagadougou, *Burkina Faso* 83 C4
Ouahigouya, *Burkina Faso* 82 C4
Ouahran = Oran, *Algeria* 78 A5
Oualâta, *Mauritania* 82 B3
Ouallam, *Niger* 83 C5
Ouallene, *Algeria* 78 D6
Ouargaye, *Burkina Faso* 83 C5
Ouargla, *Algeria* 78 B7
Ouarkoye, *Burkina Faso* 82 C4
Ouarzazate, *Morocco* 78 B4
Ouassouas, *Mali* 83 B5
Ouatagouna, *Mali* 83 B5
Oubangi →, *Dem. Rep. of the Congo* 84 E3
Ouche →, *France* 19 E12
Ouddorp, *Neths.* 17 C3
Oude Rijn →, *Neths.* 17 B4
Oudeïka, *Mali* 83 B4
Oudenaarde, *Belgium* 17 D3
Oudon →, *France* 18 E6
Oudtshoorn, *S. Africa* 88 E3
Ouellé, *Ivory C.* 82 D4
Ouémé →, *Benin* 83 D5
Ouessa, *Burkina Faso* 82 C4
Ouessant, Î. d', *France* 18 D1
Ouesso, *Congo* 84 D3
Ouest, Pte. de l', *Canada* 103 C7
Ouezzane, *Morocco* 78 B4
Ougarou, *Burkina Faso* 83 C5
Oughterard, *Ireland* 15 C2
Ouidah, *Benin* 83 D5
Ouidi, *Niger* 83 C7
Ouistreham, *France* 18 C6
Oujda, *Morocco* 78 B5
Oujeft, *Mauritania* 82 A2
Oulainen, *Finland* 8 D21
Ould Yenjé, *Mauritania* 82 B2
Oullins, *France* 21 C8
Oulu, *Finland* 8 D21
Oulujärvi, *Finland* 8 D22
Oulujoki →, *Finland* 8 D21
Oulx, *Italy* 28 C3
Oum Chalouba, *Chad* 79 E10
Oum Hadjer, *Chad* 79 F9
Oumé, *Ivory C.* 82 D3
Ounasjoki →, *Finland* 8 C21
Ounguati, *Namibia* 88 C2
Ounianga Sérir, *Chad* 79 E10
Our →, *Lux.* 17 E6
Ouranópolis, *Greece* 40 F7
Ourârene, *Niger* 83 B6
Ouray, *U.S.A.* 115 G10
Ourcq →, *France* 19 C10
Ourense, *Spain* 34 C3
Ouricuri, *Brazil* 125 E10
Ourinhos, *Brazil* 127 A6
Ourique, *Portugal* 35 H2
Ouro Fino, *Brazil* 127 A6
Ouro-Ndia, *Mali* 82 B4
Ouro Prêto, *Brazil* 127 A7
Ouro Sogui, *Senegal* 82 B2
Oursi, *Burkina Faso* 83 C4
Ourthe →, *Belgium* 17 D5
Ouse →, *E. Susx., U.K.* 13 G8
Ouse →, *N. Yorks., U.K.* 12 D7
Oust, *France* 20 F5
Oust →, *France* 18 E4
Outaouais →, *Canada* 102 C5
Outardes →, *Canada* 103 C6
Outeiro de Rei, *Spain* 34 B3
Outer Hebrides, *U.K.* 14 D1
Outes = Serra de Outes, *Spain* 34 C2
Outjo, *Namibia* 88 C2
Outlook, *Canada* 105 C7
Outokumpu, *Finland* 8 E23
Outreau, *France* 19 B8
Ouvèze →, *France* 21 E8
Ouyen, *Australia* 95 F3
Ouzouer-le-Marché, *France* 19 E8
Ovada, *Italy* 28 D5
Ovalau, *Fiji* 91 C8
Ovalle, *Chile* 126 C1
Ovamboland, *Namibia* 88 B2
Ovar, *Portugal* 34 E2
Overath, *Germany* 24 E3
Overflakkee, *Neths.* 17 C4
Overijssel □, *Neths.* 17 B6
Overland Park, *U.S.A.* 112 F7
Overton, *U.S.A.* 117 J12
Övertorneå, *Sweden* 8 C20
Överum, *Sweden* 11 F10
Ovid, *U.S.A.* 111 D8
Ovidiopol, *Ukraine* 47 J6
Ovidiu, *Romania* 43 F13
Oviedo, *Spain* 34 B5
Oviksfjällen, *Sweden* 10 A7
Oviši, *Latvia* 9 H19
Ovoot, *Mongolia* 56 B7
Övör Hangay □, *Mongolia* 56 B2
Ovoro, *Nigeria* 83 D6
Øvre Årdal, *Norway* 9 F12
Övre Fryken, *Sweden* 10 E7
Ovruch, *Ukraine* 47 G5
Owaka, *N.Z.* 91 M2
Owambo = Ovamboland, *Namibia* 88 B2
Owasco L., *U.S.A.* 111 D8
Owase, *Japan* 55 G8
Owatonna, *U.S.A.* 112 C8
Owbeh, *Afghan.* 66 B3
Owego, *U.S.A.* 111 D8
Owen Falls Dam, *Uganda* 86 B3
Owen Sound, *Canada* 102 D3
Owens →, *U.S.A.* 116 J9
Owens L., *U.S.A.* 117 J9
Owensboro, *U.S.A.* 108 G2
Owerri, *Nigeria* 83 D6
Owl →, *Canada* 105 B10
Owo, *Nigeria* 83 D6
Owosso, *U.S.A.* 108 D3
Owyhee, *U.S.A.* 114 F5
Owyhee →, *U.S.A.* 114 E5
Owyhee, L., *U.S.A.* 114 E5
Ox Mts. = Slieve Gamph, *Ireland* 15 B3
Öxarfjörður, *Iceland* 8 C5
Oxbow, *Canada* 105 D8
Oxelösund, *Sweden* 11 F11
Oxford, *N.Z.* 91 K4
Oxford, *U.K.* 13 F6
Oxford, *Mass., U.S.A.* 111 D13
Oxford, *Miss., U.S.A.* 113 H10
Oxford, *N.C., U.S.A.* 109 G6
Oxford, *N.Y., U.S.A.* 111 D9
Oxford, *Ohio, U.S.A.* 108 F3
Oxford L., *Canada* 105 C9
Oxfordshire □, *U.K.* 13 F6
Oxía, *Greece* 38 C3
Oxie, *Sweden* 11 J7
Oxílithos, *Greece* 38 C6
Oxnard, *U.S.A.* 117 L7
Oxsjövålen, *Sweden* 10 B7
Oxus = Amudarya →, *Uzbekistan* 50 E6
Oya, *Malaysia* 62 D4
Oyama, *Japan* 55 F9
Oyem, *Gabon* 84 D2
Oyen, *Canada* 105 C6
Oykel →, *U.K.* 14 D4
Oymyakon, *Russia* 51 C15
Oyo, *Nigeria* 83 D5
Oyo □, *Nigeria* 83 D5
Oyonnax, *France* 19 F12
Oyster Bay, *U.S.A.* 111 F11
Ōyūbari, *Japan* 54 C11
Özalp, *Turkey* 73 C10
Ozamiz, *Phil.* 61 G5
Ozark, *Ala., U.S.A.* 109 K3
Ozark, *Ark., U.S.A.* 113 H8
Ozark, *Mo., U.S.A.* 113 G8
Ozark Plateau, *U.S.A.* 113 G9
Ozarks, L. of the, *U.S.A.* 112 F8
Ożarów, *Poland* 45 H8
Ózd, *Hungary* 42 B5
Ozernoye, *Russia* 48 E10
Ozette L., *U.S.A.* 116 B2
Ozieri, *Italy* 30 B2
Ozimek, *Poland* 45 H5
Ozinki, *Russia* 48 E9
Ozona, *U.S.A.* 113 K4
Ozorków, *Poland* 45 G6
Ozren, *Bos.-H.* 42 G3
Ozuluama, *Mexico* 119 C5
Ozun, *Romania* 43 E10
Ozurgeti, *Georgia* 49 K5

P

Pa, *Burkina Faso* 82 C4
Pa-an, *Burma* 67 L20
Pa Mong Dam, *Thailand* 64 D4
Pa Sak →, *Thailand* 62 B2
Paamiut, *Greenland* 4 C5
Paar →, *Germany* 25 G7
Paarl, *S. Africa* 88 E2
Paauilo, *U.S.A.* 106 H17
Pab Hills, *Pakistan* 68 F2
Pabbay, *U.K.* 14 D1

Pabianice, Poland 45 G6
Pabna, Bangla. 67 G16
Pabo, Uganda 86 B3
Pacaja →, Brazil 125 D8
Pacaraima, Sa., S. Amer. 122 C4
Pacasmayo, Peru 124 E3
Paceco, Italy 30 E5
Pachhar, India 68 G7
Pachino, Italy 31 F8
Pachitea →, Peru 124 E4
Pachmarhi, India 69 H8
Pachpadra, India 66 G8
Pachuca, Mexico 119 C5
Pacific, Canada 104 C3
Pacific-Antarctic Ridge, Pac. Oc. 97 M16
Pacific Grove, U.S.A. 116 J5
Pacific Ocean, Pac. Oc. 97 G14
Pacific Rim Nat. Park, Canada 116 B2
Pacifica, U.S.A. 116 H4
Pacitan, Indonesia 63 H14
Packwood, U.S.A. 116 D5
Pacov, Czech Rep. 26 B8
Pacy-sur-Eure, France 18 C8
Padaido, Kepulauan, Indonesia 63 E9
Padang, Indonesia 62 E2
Padang Endau, Malaysia 65 L4
Padangpanjang, Indonesia 62 E2
Padangsidempuan, Indonesia 62 D1
Padborg, Denmark 11 K3
Paddle Prairie, Canada 104 B5
Paddockwood, Canada 105 C7
Paderborn, Germany 24 D4
Padeş, Vf., Romania 42 E7
Padina, Romania 43 F12
Padma, India 69 G11
Pádova, Italy 29 C8
Padra, India 68 H5
Padrauna, India 69 F10
Padre I., U.S.A. 113 M6
Padrón, Spain 34 C2
Padstow, U.K. 13 G3
Padua = Pádova, Italy 29 C8
Paducah, Ky., U.S.A. 108 G1
Paducah, Tex., U.S.A. 113 H4
Padul, Spain 35 H7
Paengnyŏng-do, S. Korea 57 F13
Paeroa, N.Z. 91 G5
Paesana, Italy 28 D4
Pafúri, Mozam. 89 C5
Pag, Croatia 29 D12
Paga, Ghana 83 C4
Pagadian, Phil. 61 H5
Pagai Selatan, Pulau, Indonesia 62 E2
Pagai Utara, Pulau, Indonesia 62 E2
Pagalu = Annobón, Atl. Oc. 77 G4
Pagara, India 69 G9
Pagastikós Kólpos, Greece 38 B5
Pagatan, Indonesia 62 E5
Page, U.S.A. 115 H8
Pagėgiai, Lithuania 44 C8
Pago Pago, Amer. Samoa 91 B13
Pagosa Springs, U.S.A. 115 H10
Pagwa River, Canada 102 B2
Pahala, U.S.A. 106 J17
Pahang →, Malaysia 65 L4
Pahiatua, N.Z. 91 J5
Pahokee, U.S.A. 109 M5
Pahrump, U.S.A. 117 J11
Pahute Mesa, U.S.A. 116 H10
Pai, Thailand 64 C2
Paia, U.S.A. 106 H16
Paicines, U.S.A. 116 J5
Paide, Estonia 9 G21
Paignton, U.K. 13 G4
Paiho, Taiwan 59 F13
Päijänne, Finland 9 F21
Pailani, India 69 G9
Pailin, Cambodia 64 F4
Paimpol, France 18 D3
Painan, Indonesia 62 E2
Painesville, U.S.A. 110 E3
Paint Hills = Wemindji, Canada 102 B4
Paint L., Canada 105 B9
Painted Desert, U.S.A. 115 J8
Paintsville, U.S.A. 108 G4
País Vasco □, Spain 32 C2
Paisley, Canada 110 B3
Paisley, U.K. 14 F4
Paisley, U.S.A. 114 E3
Paita, Peru 124 E2
Paiva →, Portugal 34 D2
Paizhou, China 59 B9
Pajares, Spain 34 B5
Pajares, Puerto de, Spain 34 C5
Pajęczno, Poland 45 G5
Pak Lay, Laos 64 C3
Pak Phanang, Thailand 65 H3
Pak Sane, Laos 64 C4
Pak Song, Laos 64 E6
Pak Suong, Laos 58 H4
Pakaur, India 69 G12
Pakenham, Canada 111 A8
Pákhnes, Greece 36 D6
Pakhuis, S. Africa 88 E2
Pakistan ■, Asia 68 E4
Pakkading, Laos 64 C4
Pakokku, Burma 67 J19
Pakość, Poland 45 F5
Pakowki L., Canada 105 D6
Pakpattan, Pakistan 68 D5
Pakrac, Croatia 42 E2
Pakruojis, Lithuania 44 C10
Paks, Hungary 42 D3
Paktīā □, Afghan. 66 C6
Pakwach, Uganda 86 B3
Pakxe, Laos 64 E5
Pal Lahara, India 69 J11
Pala, Chad 79 G9
Pala, Dem. Rep. of the Congo 86 D2
Pala, U.S.A. 117 M9
Palabek, Uganda 86 B3
Palacios, U.S.A. 113 L6
Palafrugell, Spain 32 D8
Palagiano, Italy 31 B10
Palagonía, Italy 31 E7
Palagruža, Croatia 29 F13
Palaiókastron, Greece 36 D8
Palaiokhóra, Greece 36 D5
Pálairos, Greece 38 C2
Palaiseau, France 19 D9
Palam, India 66 K10
Palamás, Greece 38 B4
Palamós, Spain 32 D8
Palampur, India 68 C7
Palamut, Turkey 39 C9
Palana, Australia 94 F4
Palana, Russia 51 D16
Palanan, Phil. 61 C5
Palanan Pt., Phil. 61 C5
Palandri, Pakistan 69 C5
Palanga, Lithuania 9 J19
Palangkaraya, Indonesia 62 E4
Palani Hills, India 66 P10
Palanpur, India 68 G5
Palapye, Botswana 88 C4
Palas, Pakistan 69 B5
Palas de Rei, Spain 34 C3
Palashi, India 69 H13
Palasponga, India 69 J11
Palatka, Russia 51 C16
Palatka, U.S.A. 109 L5
Palau, Italy 30 A2
Palau ■, Pac. Oc. 63 C8
Palauk, Burma 64 F2
Palawan, Phil. 61 G3
Palayankottai, India 66 Q10
Palazzo, Pte., France 21 F12
Palazzo San Gervásio, Italy 31 B8
Palazzolo Acréide, Italy 31 E7
Paldiski, Estonia 9 G21
Pale, Bos.-H. 42 G3
Paleleh, Indonesia 63 D6
Palembang, Indonesia 62 E2
Palencia, Spain 34 C6
Palencia □, Spain 34 C6
Palenque, Mexico 119 D6
Paleokastrítsa, Greece 36 A3
Paleometokho, Cyprus 36 D12
Palermo, Italy 30 D6
Palermo, U.S.A. 114 G3
Palestina, Chile 128 A3
Palestine, Asia 75 D4
Palestine, U.S.A. 113 K7
Palestrina, Italy 29 G9
Paletwa, Burma 67 J18
Palghat, India 66 P10
Palgrave, Mt., Australia 92 D2
Pali, India 68 G5
Palikir, Micronesia 96 G7
Palinuro, Italy 31 B8
Palinuro, C., Italy 31 B8
Palioúrion, Ákra, Greece 40 G7
Palisades Reservoir, U.S.A. 114 E8
Paliseul, Belgium 17 E5
Palitana, India 68 J4
Palizada, Mexico 119 D6
Palk Bay, Asia 66 Q11
Palk Strait, Asia 66 Q11
Palkānah, Iraq 70 C5
Palkot, India 69 H11
Palla Road = Dinokwe, Botswana 88 C4
Pallanza = Verbánia, Italy 28 C5
Pallarenda, Australia 94 B4
Pallasovka, Russia 48 E8
Pallës, Bishti i, Albania 40 E3
Pallinup →, Australia 93 F2
Pallisa, Uganda 86 B3
Pallu, India 68 E6
Palm Bay, U.S.A. 109 L5
Palm Beach, U.S.A. 109 M6
Palm Coast, U.S.A. 109 L5
Palm Desert, U.S.A. 117 M10
Palm Is., Australia 94 B4
Palm Springs, U.S.A. 117 M10
Palma, Mozam. 87 E5
Palma, B. de, Spain 37 B9
Palma de Mallorca, Spain 37 B9
Palma del Río, Spain 35 H5
Palma di Montechiaro, Italy 30 E6
Palma Soriano, Cuba 120 B4
Palmares, Brazil 125 E11
Palmarola, Italy 30 B5
Palmas, Brazil 127 B5
Palmas, C., Liberia 82 E3
Pálmas, G. di, Italy 30 D1
Palmdale, U.S.A. 117 L8
Palmeira das Missões, Brazil 127 B5
Palmeira dos Índios, Brazil 125 E11
Palmela, Portugal 35 G2
Palmer, U.S.A. 100 B5
Palmer →, Australia 94 B3
Palmer Arch., Antarctica 5 C17
Palmer Lake, U.S.A. 112 F2
Palmer Land, Antarctica 5 D18
Palmerston, Canada 110 C4
Palmerston, N.Z. 91 L3
Palmerston North, N.Z. 91 J5
Palmerton, U.S.A. 111 F9
Palmetto, U.S.A. 109 M4
Palmi, Italy 31 D8
Palmira, Argentina 126 C2
Palmira, Colombia 124 C3
Palmyra = Tudmur, Syria 70 C3
Palmyra, Mo., U.S.A. 112 F9
Palmyra, N.J., U.S.A. 111 F9
Palmyra, N.Y., U.S.A. 110 C7
Palmyra, Pa., U.S.A. 111 F8
Palmyra Is., Pac. Oc. 97 G11
Palo Alto, U.S.A. 116 H4
Palo Verde, U.S.A. 117 M12
Paloich, Sudan 81 E3
Palompon, Phil. 61 F6
Palopo, Indonesia 63 E6
Palos, C. de, Spain 33 H4
Palos de la Frontera, Spain 35 H4
Palos Verdes, U.S.A. 117 M8
Palos Verdes, Pt., U.S.A. 117 M8
Pålsboda, Sweden 10 E9
Palu, Indonesia 63 E5
Palu, Turkey 70 B3
Paluke, Liberia 82 D3
Paluzza, Italy 29 B10
Palwal, India 68 E7
Pama, Burkina Faso 83 C5
Pamanukan, Indonesia 63 G12
Pamiers, France 20 E5
Pamir, Tajikistan 50 F8
Pamlico →, U.S.A. 109 H7
Pamlico Sd., U.S.A. 109 H8
Pampa, U.S.A. 113 H4
Pampa de las Salinas, Argentina 126 C2
Pampanua, Indonesia 63 E6
Pampas, Argentina 126 D3
Pampas, Peru 124 F4
Pamphylia, Turkey 72 D4
Pamplona, Colombia 124 B4
Pamplona, Spain 32 C3
Pampoenpoort, S. Africa 88 E3
Pamukçu, Turkey 39 B9
Pamukkale, Turkey 39 D11
Pan Xian, China 58 E5
Pana, U.S.A. 112 F10
Panabo, Phil. 61 H6
Panaca, U.S.A. 115 H6
Panagyurishte, Bulgaria 41 D8
Panaitan, Indonesia 63 G11
Panaji, India 66 M8
Panamá, Panama 120 E4
Panama ■, Cent. Amer. 120 E4
Panamá, G. de, Panama 120 E4
Panama Canal, Panama 120 E4
Panama City, U.S.A. 109 K3
Panamint Range, U.S.A. 117 J9
Panamint Springs, U.S.A. 117 J9
Panão, Peru 124 E3
Panaon I., Phil. 61 F6
Panare, Thailand 65 J3
Panarea, Italy 31 D8
Panaro →, Italy 29 D8
Panay, Phil. 61 F5
Panay, G., Phil. 63 B6
Pančevo, Serbia, Yug. 42 F5
Panch'iao, Taiwan 59 E13
Panciu, Romania 43 E12
Pancorbo, Desfiladero, Spain 34 C7
Pâncota, Romania 42 D6
Panda, Mozam. 89 C5
Pandan, Antique, Phil. 61 F5
Pandan, Catanduanes, Phil. 61 D6
Pandegelang, Indonesia 63 G12
Pandhana, India 68 J7
Pandharpur, India 66 L9
Pando, Uruguay 127 C4
Pando, L. = Hope, L., Australia 95 D2
Pandokrátor, Greece 36 A3
Pandora, Costa Rica 120 E3
Pandrup, Denmark 11 G3
Panevėžys, Lithuania 9 J21
Panfilov, Kazakstan 50 E8
Panfilovo, Russia 48 E6
Pang-Long, Burma 67 H21
Pang-Yang, Burma 67 H21
Panga, Dem. Rep. of the Congo 86 B2
Pangaíon Óros, Greece 41 F8
Pangalanes, Canal des = Ampangalana, Lakandranon', Madag. 89 C8
Pangani, Tanzania 86 D4
Pangani →, Tanzania 86 D4
Pangfou = Bengbu, China 57 H9
Pangil, Dem. Rep. of the Congo 86 C2
Pangkah, Tanjung, Indonesia 63 G15
Pangkajene, Indonesia 63 E5
Pangkalanbrandan, Indonesia 62 D1
Pangkalanbuun, Indonesia 62 E4
Pangkalpinang, Indonesia 62 E3
Pangnirtung, Canada 101 B13
Pangong Tso, India 68 B8
Panguitch, U.S.A. 115 H7
Pangutaran Group, Phil. 61 H4
Panhandle, U.S.A. 113 H4
Pani Mines, India 68 H5
Pania-Mutombo, Dem. Rep. of the Congo 86 D1
Panikota I., India 68 J4
Panipat, India 68 E7
Panjal Range, India 68 C7
Panjang, Hon, Vietnam 65 H4
Panjgur, Pakistan 66 F4
Panjim = Panaji, India 66 M8
Panjin, China 57 D12
Panjinad Barrage, Pakistan 66 E7
Panjnad →, Pakistan 68 E4
Panjwai, Afghan. 68 D1
Pankshin, Nigeria 83 D6
Panmunjŏm, N. Korea 57 F14
Panna, India 69 G9
Panna Hills, India 69 G9
Pannawonica, Australia 92 D2
Pano Akil, Pakistan 68 F3
Pano Lefkara, Cyprus 36 E12
Pano Panayia, Cyprus 36 E11
Panorama, Brazil 127 A5
Pánormon, Greece 36 D6
Pansemal, India 68 J6
Panshan = Panjin, China 57 D12
Panshi, China 57 C14
Pantanal, Brazil 124 H7
Pantar, Indonesia 63 F6
Pante Macassar, Indonesia 63 F6
Pantelleria, Italy 30 F4
Pantón, Spain 34 C3
Pánuco, Mexico 119 C5
Panyam, Nigeria 83 D6
Panyu, China 59 F9
Panzhihua, China 58 D3
Páola, Italy 31 C9
Paola, Malta 36 D2
Paola, U.S.A. 112 F7
Paonia, U.S.A. 115 G10
Paoting = Baoding, China 56 E8
Paot'ou = Baotou, China 56 D6
Paoua, C.A.R. 84 C3
Pápa, Hungary 42 C2
Papa Stour, U.K. 14 A7
Papa Westray, U.K. 14 B6
Papagayo →, Mexico 119 D5
Papagayo, G. de, Costa Rica 120 D2
Papakura, N.Z. 91 G5
Papantla, Mexico 119 C5
Papar, Malaysia 62 C5
Pápas, Ákra, Greece 38 C3
Papeete, Tahiti 97 J13
Papenburg, Germany 24 B3
Paphlagonia, Turkey 72 B5
Paphos, Cyprus 36 E11
Papien Chiang = Da →, Vietnam 58 G5
Papigochic →, Mexico 118 B3
Paposo, Chile 126 B1
Papoutsa, Cyprus 36 E12
Papua New Guinea ■, Oceania 96 H6
Papudo, Chile 126 C1
Papuk, Croatia 42 E2
Papun, Burma 67 K20
Papunya, Australia 92 D5
Pará = Belém, Brazil 125 D9
Pará □, Brazil 125 D8
Paraburdoo, Australia 92 D2
Paracale, Phil. 61 D5
Paracatu, Brazil 125 G9
Paracel Is., S. China Sea 62 A4
Parachilna, Australia 95 E2
Parachinar, Pakistan 68 C4
Paraćin, Serbia, Yug. 40 C5
Paradas, Spain 35 H5
Paradela, Spain 34 C3
Paradhísi, Greece 36 C10
Paradip, India 67 J15
Paradise, Calif., U.S.A. 116 F5
Paradise, Nev., U.S.A. 117 J11
Paradise →, Canada 103 B8
Paradise Hill, Canada 105 C7
Paradise River, Canada 103 B8
Paradise Valley, U.S.A. 114 F5
Parado, Indonesia 63 F5
Paragould, U.S.A. 113 G9
Paragua →, Venezuela 124 B6
Paraguaçu →, Brazil 125 F11
Paraguaçu Paulista, Brazil 127 A5
Paraguaná, Pen. de, Venezuela 124 A5
Paraguarí, Paraguay 126 B4
Paraguarí □, Paraguay 126 B4
Paraguay ■, S. Amer. 126 A4
Paraguay →, Paraguay 126 B4
Paraíba = João Pessoa, Brazil 125 E12
Paraíba □, Brazil 125 E11
Paraíba do Sul →, Brazil 127 A7
Parainen, Finland 9 F20
Paraiso, Mexico 119 D6
Parak, Iran 71 E7
Parakhino Paddubye, Russia 46 C7
Parakou, Benin 83 D5
Paralimni, Cyprus 36 D12
Parálion-Astrous, Greece 38 D4
Paramaribo, Surinam 125 B7
Paramithiá, Greece 38 B2
Paramushir, Ostrov, Russia 51 D16
Paran →, Israel 75 E4
Paraná, Argentina 126 C3
Paranã, Brazil 125 F9
Paraná □, Brazil 127 A5
Paraná →, Argentina 126 C4
Paranaguá, Brazil 127 B6
Paranaíba, Brazil 125 G8
Paranaíba →, Brazil 125 H8
Paranapanema →, Brazil 127 A5
Paranapiacaba, Serra do, Brazil 127 A6
Paranas, Phil. 61 F6
Paranavaí, Brazil 127 A5
Parang, Maguindanao, Phil. 63 C6
Parang, Sulu, Phil. 61 J4
Parângul Mare, Vf., Romania 43 E8
Parapóla, Greece 38 E5
Paraspóri, Ákra, Greece 39 F9
Paray-le-Monial, France 19 F11
Parbati →, Mad. P., India 68 G7
Parbati →, Raj., India 68 F7
Parbhani, India 66 K10
Parchim, Germany 24 B7
Parczew, Poland 45 G9
Pardes Hanna-Karkur, Israel 75 C3
Pardilla, Spain 34 D7
Pardo →, Bahia, Brazil 125 G11
Pardo →, Mato Grosso, Brazil 127 A5
Pardubice, Czech Rep. 26 A8
Pare, Indonesia 63 G15
Pare Mts., Tanzania 86 C4
Parecis, Serra dos, Brazil 124 F7
Paredes de Nava, Spain 34 C6
Paren, Russia 51 C17
Parent, Canada 102 C5
Parent, L., Canada 102 C4
Parentis-en-Born, France 20 D2
Parepare, Indonesia 63 E5
Parfino, Russia 46 D6
Párga, Greece 38 B2
Pargo, Pta. do, Madeira 37 D2
Pariaguán, Venezuela 124 B6
Paricutín, Cerro, Mexico 118 D4
Parigi, Indonesia 63 E6
Parika, Guyana 124 B7
Parikkala, Finland 46 B5
Parima, Serra, Brazil 124 C6
Parinari, Peru 124 D4
Pariñas, Pta., S. Amer. 122 D2
Parincea, Romania 43 D12
Parintins, Brazil 125 D7
Pariparit Kyun, Burma 67 M18
Paris, Canada 110 C4
Paris, France 19 D9
Paris, Idaho, U.S.A. 114 E8
Paris, Ky., U.S.A. 108 F3
Paris, Tenn., U.S.A. 109 G1
Paris, Tex., U.S.A. 113 J7
Paris, Ville de □, France 19 D9
Parish, U.S.A. 111 C8
Parishville, U.S.A. 111 B10
Park, U.S.A. 116 B4
Park City, U.S.A. 113 G6
Park Falls, U.S.A. 112 C9
Park Head, Canada 110 B3
Park Hills, U.S.A. 113 G9
Park Range, U.S.A. 114 G10
Park Rapids, U.S.A. 112 B7
Park River, U.S.A. 112 A6
Park Rynie, S. Africa 89 E5
Parkā Bandar, Iran 71 E8
Parkano, Finland 9 E20
Parker, Ariz., U.S.A. 117 L12
Parker, Pa., U.S.A. 110 E5
Parker Dam, U.S.A. 117 L12
Parkersburg, U.S.A. 108 F5
Parkes, Australia 95 E4
Parkfield, U.S.A. 116 K6
Parkhill, Canada 110 C3
Parkland, U.S.A. 116 C4
Parkston, U.S.A. 112 D6
Parksville, Canada 104 D4
Parla, Spain 34 E7
Pârliţa, Moldova 43 C12
Parma, Italy 28 D7
Parma, Idaho, U.S.A. 114 E5
Parma, Ohio, U.S.A. 110 E3
Parma →, Italy 28 D7
Parnaguá, Brazil 125 F10
Parnaíba, Brazil 125 D10
Parnaíba →, Brazil 122 D6
Parnassós, Greece 38 C4
Párnis, Greece 38 C5
Párnon Óros, Greece 38 D4
Pärnu, Estonia 9 G21
Paroo →, Australia 95 E3
Páros, Greece 39 D7
Parowan, U.S.A. 115 H7
Parpaillon, France 21 D10
Parral, Chile 126 D1
Parras, Mexico 118 B4
Parrett →, U.K. 13 F4
Parris I., U.S.A. 109 J5
Parrsboro, Canada 103 C7
Parry I., Canada 110 A4
Parry Is., Canada 4 B2
Parry Sound, Canada 102 C4
Parsberg, Germany 25 F7
Parsęta →, Poland 44 D2
Parsnip →, Canada 104 B4
Parsons, U.S.A. 113 G7
Parsons Ra., Australia 94 A2
Partanna, Italy 30 E5
Parthenay, France 18 F6
Partinico, Italy 30 D6
Partizánske, Slovak Rep. 27 C11
Partridge I., Canada 102 A2
Paru →, Brazil 125 D8
Parvān □, Afghan. 66 B6
Parvatipuram, India 67 K13
Parvatsar, India 68 F6
Påryd, Sweden 11 H9
Parys, S. Africa 88 D4
Pas, Pta. des, Spain 37 C7
Pas-de-Calais □, France 19 B9
Pasada, Spain 34 B5
Pasadena, Canada 103 C8
Pasadena, Calif., U.S.A. 117 L8
Pasadena, Tex., U.S.A. 113 L7
Pasaje →, Argentina 126 B3
Paşalimanı, Turkey 41 F11
Pasay, Phil. 61 D4
Pascagoula, U.S.A. 113 K10
Pascagoula →, U.S.A. 113 K10
Paşcani, Romania 43 C11
Pasco, U.S.A. 114 C4
Pasco, Cerro de, Peru 124 F3
Pasco I., Australia 92 D2
Pascoag, U.S.A. 111 E13
Pascua, I. de, Pac. Oc. 97 K17
Pasewalk, Germany 24 B9
Pasfield L., Canada 105 B7
Pasha →, Russia 46 B7
Pashiwari, Pakistan 69 B6
Pashmakli = Smolyan, Bulgaria 41 E8
Pasinler, Turkey 73 C9
Pasir Mas, Malaysia 65 J4
Pasir Putih, Malaysia 65 K4
Pasirian, Indonesia 63 H15

Pasirkuning, *Indonesia* 62 E2
Påskallavik, *Sweden* 11 G10
Paskūh, *Iran* 71 E9
Pasłęk, *Poland* 44 D6
Pasłęka →, *Poland* 44 D6
Pasley, C., *Australia* 93 F3
Pašman, *Croatia* 29 E12
Pasni, *Pakistan* 66 G3
Paso Cantinela, *Mexico* 117 N11
Paso de Indios, *Argentina* 128 E3
Paso de los Libres, *Argentina* 126 B4
Paso de los Toros, *Uruguay* 126 C4
Paso Robles, *U.S.A.* 115 J3
Paspébiac, *Canada* 103 C6
Pasrur, *Pakistan* 68 C6
Passage West, *Ireland* 15 E3
Passaic, *U.S.A.* 111 F10
Passau, *Germany* 25 G9
Passero, C., *Italy* 31 F8
Passo Fundo, *Brazil* 127 B5
Passos, *Brazil* 125 H9
Passow, *Germany* 24 B10
Passy, *France* 21 C10
Pastavy, *Belarus* 9 J22
Pastaza →, *Peru* 124 D3
Pasto, *Colombia* 124 C3
Pastrana, *Spain* 32 E2
Pasuruan, *Indonesia* 63 G15
Pasym, *Poland* 44 E7
Pásztó, *Hungary* 42 C4
Patagonia, *Argentina* 122 H4
Patagonia, *U.S.A.* 115 L8
Patambar, *Iran* 71 D9
Patan, *Gujarat, India* 66 H8
Patan, *Maharashtra, India* 68 H5
Patan, *Nepal* 67 F14
Patani, *Indonesia* 63 D7
Pătârlagele, *Romania* 43 E11
Pataudi, *India* 68 E7
Patchewollock, *Australia* 95 F3
Patchogue, *U.S.A.* 111 F11
Patea, *N.Z.* 91 H5
Pategi, *Nigeria* 83 D6
Patensie, *S. Africa* 88 E3
Paterna, *Spain* 33 F4
Paternion, *Austria* 26 E6
Paternò, *Italy* 31 E7
Pateros, *U.S.A.* 114 B4
Paterson, *U.S.A.* 111 F10
Paterson Ra., *Australia* 92 D3
Pathankot, *India* 68 C6
Pathfinder Reservoir, *U.S.A.* 114 E10
Pathiu, *Thailand* 65 G2
Pathum Thani, *Thailand* 64 E3
Pati, *Indonesia* 63 G14
Patía →, *Colombia* 124 C3
Patiala, *Punjab, India* 68 D7
Patiala, *Ut. P., India* 69 F8
Patine Kouka, *Senegal* 82 C2
Patitírion, *Greece* 38 B5
Patkai Bum, *India* 67 F19
Pátmos, *Greece* 39 D8
Patna, *India* 69 G11
Patnos, *Turkey* 73 C10
Pato Branco, *Brazil* 127 B5
Patonga, *Uganda* 86 B3
Patos, *Brazil* 125 E11
Patos, L. dos, *Brazil* 127 C5
Patos, Río de los →, *Argentina* 126 C2
Patos de Minas, *Brazil* 125 G9
Patosi, *Albania* 40 F3
Patquía, *Argentina* 126 C2
Pátrai, *Greece* 38 C3
Pátraikós Kólpos, *Greece* 38 C3
Patras = Pátrai, *Greece* 38 C3
Patrocínio, *Brazil* 125 G9
Patta, *Kenya* 86 C5
Pattada, *Italy* 30 B2
Pattani, *Thailand* 65 J3
Pattaya, *Thailand* 62 B2
Patten, *U.S.A.* 109 C11
Patterson, *Calif., U.S.A.* 116 H5
Patterson, *La., U.S.A.* 113 L9
Patterson, Mt., *U.S.A.* 116 G7
Patti, *Punjab, India* 68 D6
Patti, *Ut. P., India* 69 G10
Patti, *Italy* 31 D7
Pattoki, *Pakistan* 68 D5
Patton, *U.S.A.* 110 F6
Patuakhali, *Bangla.* 67 H17
Patuanak, *Canada* 105 B7
Patuca →, *Honduras* 120 C3
Patuca, Punta, *Honduras* 120 C3
Pătulele, *Romania* 42 F7
Pátzcuaro, *Mexico* 118 D4
Pau, *France* 20 E3
Pau, Gave de →, *France* 20 E2
Pauillac, *France* 20 C3
Pauk, *Burma* 67 J19
Paul I., *Canada* 103 A7
Paul Smiths, *U.S.A.* 111 B10
Paulatuk, *Canada* 100 B7
Paulhan, *France* 20 E7
Paulis = Isiro, *Dem. Rep. of the Congo* 86 B2
Paulistana, *Brazil* 125 E10
Paulo Afonso, *Brazil* 125 E11
Paulpietersburg, *S. Africa* 89 D5
Pauls Valley, *U.S.A.* 113 H6
Pauma Valley, *U.S.A.* 117 M10
Pauri, *India* 69 D8
Pāveh, *Iran* 70 C5
Pavelets, *Russia* 46 F10
Pavia, *Italy* 28 C6
Pavilion, *U.S.A.* 110 D6
Pavilly, *France* 18 C7
Pāvilosta, *Latvia* 9 H19
Pavlikeni, *Bulgaria* 41 C9
Pavlodar, *Kazakstan* 50 D8
Pavlograd = Pavlohrad, *Ukraine* 47 H8
Pavlohrad, *Ukraine* 47 H8
Pavlovo, *Russia* 48 C6
Pavlovsk, *Russia* 48 E5
Pavlovskaya, *Russia* 49 G4
Pavlovskiy-Posad, *Russia* 46 E10
Pavullo nel Frignano, *Italy* 28 D7
Pawayan, *India* 69 E9
Pawhuska, *U.S.A.* 113 G6
Pawling, *U.S.A.* 111 E11
Pawnee, *U.S.A.* 113 G6
Pawnee City, *U.S.A.* 112 E6
Pawtucket, *U.S.A.* 111 E13
Paximádhia, *Greece* 36 E6
Paxoí, *Greece* 38 B2
Paxton, *Ill., U.S.A.* 108 E1
Paxton, *Nebr., U.S.A.* 112 E4
Payakumbuh, *Indonesia* 62 E2
Payerne, *Switz.* 25 J2
Payette, *U.S.A.* 114 D5
Paymogo, *Spain* 35 H3
Payne Bay = Kangirsuk, *Canada* 101 B13
Payne L., *Canada* 101 C12
Paynes Find, *Australia* 93 E2
Paynesville, *Liberia* 82 D2
Paynesville, *U.S.A.* 112 C7
Pays de la Loire □, *France* 18 E6
Paysandú, *Uruguay* 126 C4
Payson, *U.S.A.* 115 J8
Paz →, *Guatemala* 120 D1
Paz, B. la, *Mexico* 118 C2
Pāzanān, *Iran* 71 D6
Pazar, *Turkey* 73 B9
Pazarcık, *Turkey* 72 D7
Pazardzhik, *Bulgaria* 41 D8
Pazarköy, *Turkey* 39 B9
Pazarlar, *Turkey* 39 C11
Pazaryeri, *Turkey* 39 B11
Pazaryolu, *Turkey* 73 B9
Pazin, *Croatia* 29 C10
Pčinja →, *Macedonia* 40 E5
Pe Ell, *U.S.A.* 116 D3
Peabody, *U.S.A.* 111 D14
Peace →, *Canada* 104 B6
Peace Point, *Canada* 104 B6
Peace River, *Canada* 104 B5
Peach Springs, *U.S.A.* 115 J7
Peachland, *Canada* 104 D5
Peachtree City, *U.S.A.* 109 J3
Peak, The = Kinder Scout, *U.K.* 12 D6
Peak District, *U.K.* 12 D6
Peak Hill, *N.S.W., Australia* 95 E4
Peak Hill, *W. Austral., Australia* 93 E2
Peak Ra., *Australia* 94 C4
Peake Cr. →, *Australia* 95 D2
Peal de Becerro, *Spain* 35 H7
Peale, Mt., *U.S.A.* 115 G9
Pearblossom, *U.S.A.* 117 L9
Pearl →, *U.S.A.* 113 K10
Pearl City, *U.S.A.* 106 H16
Pearl Harbor, *U.S.A.* 106 H16
Pearl River, *U.S.A.* 111 E10
Pearsall, *U.S.A.* 113 L5
Peary Land, *Greenland* 4 A6
Pease →, *U.S.A.* 113 H5
Peawanuck, *Canada* 101 C11
Pebane, *Mozam.* 87 F4
Pebas, *Peru* 124 D4
Pebble Beach, *U.S.A.* 116 J5
Peć, *Kosovo, Yug.* 40 D4
Pécciolí, *Italy* 28 E7
Pechea, *Romania* 43 E12
Pechenga, *Russia* 50 C4
Pechenizhyn, *Ukraine* 47 H3
Pechiguera, Pta., *Canary Is.* 37 F6
Pechnezhskoye Vdkhr., *Ukraine* 47 G9
Pechora, *Russia* 50 C6
Pechora →, *Russia* 50 C6
Pechorskaya Guba, *Russia* 50 C6
Pecica, *Romania* 42 D6
Pecka, *Serbia, Yug.* 40 B3
Pécora, C., *Italy* 30 C1
Pečory, *Russia* 9 H22
Pecos, *U.S.A.* 113 K3
Pecos →, *U.S.A.* 113 L3
Pécs, *Hungary* 42 D3
Pedder, L., *Australia* 94 G4
Peddie, *S. Africa* 89 E4
Pédernales, *Dom. Rep.* 121 C5
Pedieos →, *Cyprus* 36 D12
Pedirka, *Australia* 95 D2
Pedra Azul, *Brazil* 125 G10
Pedreguer, *Spain* 33 G5
Pedreiras, *Brazil* 125 D10
Pedro Afonso, *Brazil* 125 E9
Pedro Cays, *Jamaica* 120 C4
Pedro de Valdivia, *Chile* 126 A2
Pedro Juan Caballero, *Paraguay* 127 A4
Pedro Muñoz, *Spain* 35 F8
Pedrógão Grande, *Portugal* 34 F2
Pee Dee →, *U.S.A.* 109 J6
Peebinga, *Australia* 95 E3
Peebles, *U.K.* 14 F5
Peekskill, *U.S.A.* 111 E11
Peel, *U.K.* 12 C3
Peel →, *Australia* 95 E5
Peel →, *Canada* 100 B6
Peel Sound, *Canada* 100 A10
Peene →, *Germany* 24 A9
Peera Peera Poolanna L., *Australia* 95 D2
Peerless Lake, *Canada* 104 B6
Peers, *Canada* 104 C5
Pegasus Bay, *N.Z.* 91 K4
Peggau, *Austria* 26 D8
Pegnitz, *Germany* 25 F7
Pegnitz →, *Germany* 25 F6
Pego, *Spain* 33 G4
Pegu, *Burma* 67 L20
Pegu Yoma, *Burma* 67 K20
Pehčevo, *Macedonia* 40 E6
Pehlivanköy, *Turkey* 41 E10
Pehuajó, *Argentina* 126 D3
Pei Xian = Pizhou, *China* 56 G9
Peine, *Chile* 126 A2
Peine, *Germany* 24 C6
Peip'ing = Beijing, *China* 56 E9
Peipus, L. = Chudskoye, Ozero, *Russia* 9 G22
Peissenberg, *Germany* 25 H7
Peitz, *Germany* 24 D10
Peixe, *Brazil* 125 F9
Peixe →, *Brazil* 125 H8
Pek →, *Serbia, Yug.* 40 B5
Pekalongan, *Indonesia* 63 G13
Pekan, *Malaysia* 65 L4
Pekanbaru, *Indonesia* 62 D2
Pekang, *Taiwan* 59 F13
Pekin, *U.S.A.* 112 E10
Peking = Beijing, *China* 56 E9
Péla, *Guinea* 82 D3
Pelabuhan Kelang, *Malaysia* 65 L3
Pelabuhan Ratu, Teluk, *Indonesia* 63 G12
Pelabuhanratu, *Indonesia* 63 G12
Pélagos, *Greece* 38 B6
Pelaihari, *Indonesia* 62 E4
Pelat, Mt., *France* 21 D10
Pełczyce, *Poland* 45 E2
Peleaga, Vf., *Romania* 42 E7
Pelée, Mt., *Martinique* 121 D7
Pelee, Pt., *Canada* 102 D3
Pelee I., *Canada* 102 D3
Pelekech, *Kenya* 86 B4
Peleng, *Indonesia* 63 E6
Pélézi, *Ivory C.* 82 D3
Pelhřimov, *Czech Rep.* 26 B8
Pelican, *U.S.A.* 104 B1
Pelican L., *Canada* 105 C8
Pelican Narrows, *Canada* 105 B8
Pelješac, *Croatia* 29 F14
Pelkosenniemi, *Finland* 8 C22
Pella, *Greece* 40 F6
Pella, *S. Africa* 88 D2
Pella, *U.S.A.* 112 E8
Péllа □, *Greece* 40 F6
Pello, *Finland* 8 C21
Pellworm, *Germany* 24 A4
Pelly →, *Canada* 100 B6
Pelly Bay, *Canada* 101 B11
Peloponnese = Pelopónnisos □, *Greece* 38 D4
Pelopónnisos □, *Greece* 38 D4
Peloritani, Monti, *Italy* 31 D8
Pelorus Sd., *N.Z.* 91 J4
Pelotas, *Brazil* 127 C5
Pelotas →, *Brazil* 127 B5
Pelovo, *Bulgaria* 41 C8
Pelplin, *Poland* 44 E5
Pelvoux, Massif du, *France* 21 D10
Pemalang, *Indonesia* 63 G13
Pemanggil, Pulau, *Malaysia* 65 L5
Pematangsiantar, *Indonesia* 62 D1
Pemba, *Mozam.* 87 E5
Pemba, *Zambia* 87 F2
Pemba Channel, *Tanzania* 86 D4
Pemba I., *Tanzania* 86 D4
Pemberton, *Australia* 93 F2
Pemberton, *Canada* 104 C4
Pembina, *U.S.A.* 112 A6
Pembroke, *Canada* 102 C4
Pembroke, *U.K.* 13 F3
Pembrokeshire □, *U.K.* 13 F3
Pen-y-Ghent, *U.K.* 12 C5
Peña, Sierra de la, *Spain* 32 C4
Peña de Francia, Sierra de la, *Spain* 34 E4
Penafiel, *Portugal* 34 D2
Peñafiel, *Spain* 34 D6
Peñaflor, *Spain* 35 H5
Peñalara, *Spain* 34 E7
Penamacôr, *Portugal* 34 E3
Penang = Pinang, *Malaysia* 65 K3
Penápolis, *Brazil* 127 A6
Peñaranda de Bracamonte, *Spain* 34 E5
Peñarroya, *Spain* 32 E4
Peñarroya-Pueblonuevo, *Spain* 35 G5
Penarth, *U.K.* 13 F4
Peñas, C. de, *Spain* 34 B5
Penas, G. de, *Chile* 122 H3
Peñas de San Pedro, *Spain* 33 G3
Peñas del Chache, *Canary Is.* 37 E6
Peñausende, *Spain* 34 D5
Pench'i = Benxi, *China* 57 D12
Pend Oreille →, *U.S.A.* 114 B5
Pend Oreille, L., *U.S.A.* 114 C5
Pendálofon, *Greece* 40 F5
Pendembu, *Eastern, S. Leone* 82 D2
Pendembu, *Northern, S. Leone* 82 D2
Pender B., *Australia* 92 C3
Pendik, *Turkey* 41 F13
Pendjari →, *Benin* 83 C5
Pendleton, *U.S.A.* 114 D4
Pendra, *India* 69 H9
Penedo, *Brazil* 125 F11
Penetanguishene, *Canada* 102 D4
Penfield, *U.S.A.* 110 E6
Pengalengan, *Indonesia* 63 G12
Penge, *Kasai-Or., Dem. Rep. of the Congo* 86 D1
Penge, *Sud-Kivu, Dem. Rep. of the Congo* 86 C2
Penghu, *Taiwan* 59 F12
Penglai, *China* 57 F11
Pengshan, *China* 58 B4
Pengshui, *China* 58 C7
Penguin, *Australia* 94 G4
Pengxi, *China* 58 B5
Pengze, *China* 59 C11
Penhalonga, *Zimbabwe* 87 F3
Peniche, *Portugal* 35 F1
Penicuik, *U.K.* 14 F5
Penida, *Indonesia* 62 F5
Peninnes, Alpes = Pennine, Alpi, *Alps* 25 J3
Peninsular Malaysia □, *Malaysia* 65 L4
Peñíscola, *Spain* 32 E5
Penitente, Serra do, *Brazil* 125 E9
Penkridge, *U.K.* 12 E5
Penmarch, *France* 18 E2
Penmarch, Pte. de, *France* 18 E2
Penn Hills, *U.S.A.* 110 F5
Penn Yan, *U.S.A.* 110 D7
Penna, Punta della, *Italy* 29 F11
Pennant, *Canada* 105 C7
Penne, *Italy* 29 F10
Penner →, *India* 66 M12
Pennine, Alpi, *Alps* 25 J3
Pennines, *U.K.* 12 C5
Pennington, *U.S.A.* 116 F5
Pennington →, *Nigeria* 83 E6
Pennino, Mte., *Italy* 29 E9
Pennsburg, *U.S.A.* 111 F9
Pennsylvania □, *U.S.A.* 108 E7
Penny, *Canada* 104 C4
Peno, *Russia* 46 D7
Penobscot →, *U.S.A.* 109 C11
Penobscot B., *U.S.A.* 109 C11
Penola, *Australia* 95 F3
Penong, *Australia* 93 F5
Penonomé, *Panama* 120 E3
Penrith, *Australia* 95 E5
Penrith, *U.K.* 12 C5
Penryn, *U.K.* 13 G2
Pensacola, *U.S.A.* 109 K2
Pensacola Mts., *Antarctica* 5 E1
Pense, *Canada* 105 C8
Penshurst, *Australia* 95 F3
Penticton, *Canada* 104 D5
Pentland, *Australia* 94 C4
Pentland Firth, *U.K.* 14 C5
Pentland Hills, *U.K.* 14 F5
Penza, *Russia* 48 D7
Penzance, *U.K.* 13 G2
Penzberg, *Germany* 25 H7
Penzhino, *Russia* 51 C17
Penzhinskaya Guba, *Russia* 51 C17
Penzhou, *China* 58 B4
Penzlin, *Germany* 24 B9
Peoria, *Ariz., U.S.A.* 115 K7
Peoria, *Ill., U.S.A.* 112 E10
Pepacton Reservoir, *U.S.A.* 111 D10
Pepani →, *S. Africa* 88 D3
Pepel, *S. Leone* 82 D2
Peqini, *Albania* 40 E3
Pera Hd., *Australia* 94 A3
Perabumulih, *Indonesia* 62 E2
Perak →, *Malaysia* 65 K3
Perakhóra, *Greece* 38 C4
Perales de Alfambra, *Spain* 32 E4
Perales del Puerto, *Spain* 34 E4
Pérama, *Kérkira, Greece* 36 A3
Pérama, *Kríti, Greece* 36 D6
Peräpohjola, *Finland* 8 C22
Perast, *Montenegro, Yug.* 40 D2
Percé, *Canada* 103 C7
Perche, *France* 18 D8
Perchtoldsdorf, *Austria* 27 C9
Percival Lakes, *Australia* 92 D4
Percy, *France* 18 D5
Percy Is., *Australia* 94 C5
Perdido, Mte., *Spain* 32 C5
Perdu, Mt. = Perdido, Mte., *Spain* 32 C5
Pereira, *Colombia* 124 C3
Perelazovskiy, *Russia* 49 F6
Perenjori, *Australia* 93 E2
Peresecina, *Moldova* 43 C13
Pereslavl-Zalesskiy, *Russia* 46 D10
Peretu, *Romania* 43 F10
Pereyaslav-Khmelnytskyy, *Ukraine* 47 G6
Pérez, I., *Mexico* 119 C7
Perg, *Austria* 26 C7
Pergamino, *Argentina* 126 C3
Pergau →, *Malaysia* 65 K3
Pérgine Valsugana, *Italy* 29 B8
Pérgola, *Italy* 29 E9
Perham, *U.S.A.* 112 B7
Perhentian, Kepulauan, *Malaysia* 62 C2
Periam, *Romania* 42 D5
Péribonca →, *Canada* 103 C5
Péribonca, L., *Canada* 103 B5
Perico, *Argentina* 126 A2
Pericos, *Mexico* 118 B3
Périers, *France* 18 C5
Périgord, *France* 20 D4
Périgueux, *France* 20 C4
Perijá, Sierra de, *Colombia* 124 B4
Peristéra, *Greece* 38 B5
Peristerona →, *Cyprus* 36 D12
Perito Moreno, *Argentina* 128 F2
Perivol = Dragovishtitsa, *Bulgaria* 40 D6
Perkasie, *U.S.A.* 111 F9
Perković, *Croatia* 29 E13
Perlas, Arch. de las, *Panama* 120 E4
Perlas, Punta de, *Nic.* 120 D3
Perleberg, *Germany* 24 B7
Perlez, *Serbia, Yug.* 42 E5
Perm, *Russia* 50 D6
Përmeti, *Albania* 40 F4
Pernambuco = Recife, *Brazil* 125 E12
Pernambuco □, *Brazil* 125 E11
Pernatty Lagoon, *Australia* 95 E2
Pernik, *Bulgaria* 40 D7
Peron Is., *Australia* 92 B5
Peron Pen., *Australia* 93 E1
Péronne, *France* 19 C9
Perosa Argentina, *Italy* 28 D4
Perow, *Canada* 104 C3
Perpendicular Pt., *Australia* 95 E5
Perpignan, *France* 20 F6
Perris, *U.S.A.* 117 M9
Perros-Guirec, *France* 18 D3
Perry, *Fla., U.S.A.* 109 K4
Perry, *Ga., U.S.A.* 109 J4
Perry, *Iowa, U.S.A.* 112 E7
Perry, *Okla., U.S.A.* 113 G6
Perryton, *U.S.A.* 113 G4
Perryville, *U.S.A.* 113 G10
Persan, *France* 19 C9
Persberg, *Sweden* 10 E8
Perşembe, *Turkey* 72 B7
Persepolis, *Iran* 71 D7
Pershotravensk, *Ukraine* 47 G4
Persia = Iran ■, *Asia* 71 C7
Persian Gulf = Gulf, The, *Asia* 71 E6
Perstorp, *Sweden* 11 H7
Pertek, *Turkey* 73 C8
Perth, *Australia* 93 F2
Perth, *Canada* 102 D4
Perth, *U.K.* 14 E5
Perth & Kinross □, *U.K.* 14 E5
Perth Amboy, *U.S.A.* 111 F10
Perth-Andover, *Canada* 103 C6
Pertuis, *France* 21 E9
Pertusato, C., *France* 21 G13
Peru, *Ind., U.S.A.* 108 E2
Peru, *N.Y., U.S.A.* 111 B11
Peru ■, *S. Amer.* 124 D4
Peru-Chile Trench, *Pac. Oc.* 124 G3
Perúgia, *Italy* 29 E9
Perušić, *Croatia* 29 D12
Pervomaysk, *Russia* 48 C6
Pervomaysk, *Ukraine* 47 H6
Pervouralsk, *Russia* 50 D6
Pésaro, *Italy* 29 E9
Pescadores = Penghu, *Taiwan* 59 F12
Pescara, *Italy* 29 F11
Pescara →, *Italy* 29 F11
Peschanokopskoye, *Russia* 49 G5
Péscia, *Italy* 28 E7
Pescina, *Italy* 29 F10
Peshawar, *Pakistan* 68 B4
Peshkopi, *Albania* 40 E4
Peshtera, *Bulgaria* 41 D8
Peshtigo, *U.S.A.* 108 C2
Peski, *Russia* 48 E6
Pêso da Régua, *Portugal* 34 D3
Pesqueira, *Brazil* 125 E11
Pessac, *France* 20 D3
Pest □, *Hungary* 42 C4
Pestovo, *Russia* 46 C8
Pestravka, *Russia* 48 D9
Péta, *Greece* 38 B3
Petah Tiqwa, *Israel* 75 C3
Petalídhion, *Greece* 38 E3
Petaling Jaya, *Malaysia* 65 L3
Petaloudhes, *Greece* 36 C10
Petaluma, *U.S.A.* 116 G4
Pétange, *Lux.* 17 E5
Petaro, *Pakistan* 68 G3
Petatlán, *Mexico* 118 D4
Petauke, *Zambia* 87 E3
Petawawa, *Canada* 102 C4
Petén Itzá, L., *Guatemala* 120 C2
Peter I.s Øy, *Antarctica* 5 C16
Peter Pond L., *Canada* 105 B7
Peterbell, *Canada* 102 C3
Peterborough, *Australia* 95 E2
Peterborough, *Canada* 102 D4
Peterborough, *U.K.* 13 E7
Peterborough, *U.S.A.* 111 D13
Peterborough □, *U.K.* 13 E7
Peterculter, *U.K.* 14 D6
Peterhead, *U.K.* 14 D7
Peterlee, *U.K.* 12 C6
Petermann Bjerg, *Greenland* 98 B17
Petermann Ranges, *Australia* 92 E5
Petersburg, *Alaska, U.S.A.* 100 C6
Petersburg, *Pa., U.S.A.* 110 F6
Petersburg, *Va., U.S.A.* 108 G7
Petersburg, *W. Va., U.S.A.* 108 F6
Petersfield, *U.K.* 13 F7
Petershagen, *Germany* 24 C4
Petília Policastro, *Italy* 31 C9
Petit Goâve, *Haiti* 121 C5
Petit Jardin, *Canada* 103 C8
Petit Lac Manicouagan, *Canada* 103 B6
Petit-Mécatina →, *Canada* 103 B8
Petit-Mécatina, I. du, *Canada* 103 B8
Petit Saint Bernard, Col du, *Italy* 21 C10
Petitcodiac, *Canada* 103 C6
Petite Baleine →, *Canada* 102 A4
Petite Saguenay, *Canada* 103 C5
Petitot →, *Canada* 104 A4
Petitsikapau L., *Canada* 103 B6
Petlad, *India* 68 H5
Peto, *Mexico* 119 C7
Petone, *N.Z.* 91 J5
Petorca, *Chile* 126 C1
Petoskey, *U.S.A.* 108 C3
Petra, *Jordan* 75 E4
Petra, *Spain* 37 B10
Petra, Ostrova, *Russia* 4 B13
Petra Velikogo, Zaliv, *Russia* 54 C6

Plessisville

Petrel = Petrer, *Spain* 33 G4
Petrella, Monte, *Italy* 30 A6
Petrer, *Spain* 33 G4
Petreto-Bicchisano, *France* 21 G12
Petrich, *Bulgaria* 40 E7
Petrified Forest National Park, *U.S.A.* 115 J9
Petrijanec, *Croatia* 29 B13
Petrikov = Pyetrikaw, *Belarus* 47 F5
Petrila, *Romania* 43 E8
Petrinja, *Croatia* 29 C13
Petrodvorets, *Russia* 46 C5
Petrograd = Sankt-Peterburg, *Russia* 46 C6
Petrolândia, *Brazil* 125 E11
Petrolia, *Canada* 102 D3
Petrolina, *Brazil* 125 E10
Petropavl, *Kazakstan* 50 D7
Petropavlovsk = Petropavl, *Kazakstan* 50 D7
Petropavlovsk-Kamchatskiy, *Russia* 51 D16
Petropavlovskiy = Akhtubinsk, *Russia* 49 F8
Petrópolis, *Brazil* 127 A7
Petroşani, *Romania* 43 E8
Petrova Gora, *Croatia* 29 C12
Petrovac, *Montenegro, Yug.* 40 D2
Petrovac, *Serbia, Yug.* 40 B5
Petrovaradin, *Serbia, Yug.* 42 E4
Petrovsk, *Russia* 48 D7
Petrovsk-Zabaykalskiy, *Russia* 51 D11
Petrovskaya, *Russia* 47 K9
Petrovskoye = Svetlograd, *Russia* 49 H6
Petrozavodsk, *Russia* 46 B8
Petrus Steyn, *S. Africa* 89 D4
Petrusburg, *S. Africa* 88 D4
Petzeck, *Austria* 26 E5
Peumo, *Chile* 126 C1
Peureulak, *Indonesia* 62 D1
Pevek, *Russia* 51 C18
Peveragno, *Italy* 28 D4
Peyrehorade, *France* 20 E2
Peyruis, *France* 21 D9
Pézenas, *France* 20 E7
Pezinok, *Slovak Rep.* 27 C10
Pfaffenhofen, *Germany* 25 G7
Pfarrkirchen, *Germany* 25 G8
Pfeffenhausen, *Germany* 25 G7
Pforzheim, *Germany* 25 G4
Pfullendorf, *Germany* 25 H5
Pfungstadt, *Germany* 25 F4
Phagwara, *India* 66 D9
Phaistós, *Greece* 36 D6
Phala, *Botswana* 88 C4
Phalera = Phulera, *India* 68 F6
Phalodi, *India* 68 F5
Phalsbourg, *France* 19 D14
Phan, *Thailand* 64 C2
Phan Rang, *Vietnam* 65 G7
Phan Ri = Hoa Da, *Vietnam* 65 G7
Phan Thiet, *Vietnam* 65 G7
Phanae, *Greece* 39 C7
Phanat Nikhom, *Thailand* 64 F3
Phangan, Ko, *Thailand* 65 H3
Phangnga, *Thailand* 65 H2
Phanh Bho Ho Chi Minh, *Vietnam* 65 G6
Phanom Sarakham, *Thailand* 64 F3
Phaphund, *India* 69 F8
Pharenda, *India* 69 F10
Pharr, *U.S.A.* 113 M5
Phatthalung, *Thailand* 65 J3
Phayao, *Thailand* 64 C2
Phelps, *U.S.A.* 110 D7
Phelps L., *Canada* 105 B8
Phenix City, *U.S.A.* 109 J3
Phet Buri, *Thailand* 64 F2
Phetchabun, *Thailand* 64 D3
Phetchabun, Thiu Khao, *Thailand* 64 E3
Phetchaburi = Phet Buri, *Thailand* 64 F2
Phi Phi, Ko, *Thailand* 65 J2
Phiafay, *Laos* 64 E6
Phibun Mangsahan, *Thailand* 64 E5
Phichai, *Thailand* 64 D3
Phichit, *Thailand* 64 D3
Philadelphia, *Miss., U.S.A.* 113 J10
Philadelphia, *N.Y., U.S.A.* 111 B9
Philadelphia, *Pa., U.S.A.* 111 G9
Philip, *U.S.A.* 112 C4
Philippeville, *Belgium* 17 D4
Philippi, *Greece* 41 E8
Philippi, *U.S.A.* 108 F5
Philippi L., *Australia* 94 C2
Philippines ■, *Asia* 61 F5
Philippolis, *S. Africa* 88 E4
Philippopolis = Plovdiv, *Bulgaria* 41 D8
Philipsburg, *Canada* 111 A11
Philipsburg, *Mont., U.S.A.* 114 C7
Philipsburg, *Pa., U.S.A.* 110 F6
Philipstown = Daingean, *Ireland* 15 C4
Philipstown, *S. Africa* 88 E3
Phillip I., *Australia* 95 F4
Phillips, *U.S.A.* 112 C9
Phillipsburg, *Kans., U.S.A.* 112 F5
Phillipsburg, *N.J., U.S.A.* 111 F9
Philmont, *U.S.A.* 111 D11
Philomath, *U.S.A.* 114 D2
Phimai, *Thailand* 64 E4
Phitsanulok, *Thailand* 64 D3
Phnom Dangrek, *Thailand* 62 B2
Phnom Penh, *Cambodia* 65 G5
Phnum Penh = Phnom Penh, *Cambodia* 65 G5
Phoenicia, *U.S.A.* 111 D10
Phoenix, *Ariz., U.S.A.* 115 K7
Phoenix, *N.Y., U.S.A.* 111 C8
Phoenix Is., *Kiribati* 96 H10
Phoenixville, *U.S.A.* 111 F9
Phon, *Thailand* 64 E4
Phon Tiou, *Laos* 64 D5
Phong →, *Thailand* 64 D4
Phong Saly, *Laos* 58 G4
Phong Tho, *Vietnam* 64 A4
Phonhong, *Laos* 64 C4
Phonum, *Thailand* 65 H2
Phosphate Hill, *Australia* 94 C2
Photharam, *Thailand* 64 F2
Phra Nakhon Si Ayutthaya, *Thailand* 64 E3
Phra Thong, Ko, *Thailand* 65 H2
Phrae, *Thailand* 64 C3
Phrom Phiram, *Thailand* 64 D3
Phrygia, *Turkey* 72 C4
Phu Dien, *Vietnam* 64 C5
Phu Loi, *Laos* 64 B4
Phu Ly, *Vietnam* 58 G5
Phu Quoc, Dao, *Vietnam* 65 G4
Phu Tho, *Vietnam* 58 G5
Phuc Yen, *Vietnam* 58 G5
Phuket, *Thailand* 65 J2
Phuket, Ko, *Thailand* 65 J2
Phul, *India* 68 D6
Phulad, *India* 68 G5
Phulchari, *Bangla.* 69 G13
Phulera, *India* 68 F6
Phulpur, *India* 69 G10
Phun Phin, *Thailand* 65 H2
Piacenza, *Italy* 28 C6
Pian Cr. →, *Australia* 95 E4
Piana, *France* 21 F12
Pianella, *Italy* 29 F11
Pianosa, *Puglia, Italy* 29 F12
Pianosa, *Toscana, Italy* 28 F7
Piapot, *Canada* 105 D7
Pias, *Portugal* 35 G3
Piaseczno, *Poland* 45 F8
Piaski, *Poland* 45 G9
Piastów, *Poland* 45 F7
Piatra, *Romania* 43 G10
Piatra Neamţ, *Romania* 43 D11
Piatra Olt, *Romania* 43 F9
Piauí □, *Brazil* 125 E10
Piauí →, *Brazil* 125 E10
Piave →, *Italy* 29 C9
Piazza Ármerina, *Italy* 31 E7
Pibor →, *Sudan* 81 F3
Pibor Post, *Sudan* 81 F3
Picardie, *France* 19 C10
Picardie, Plaine de, *France* 19 C9
Picardy = Picardie, *France* 19 C10
Picayune, *U.S.A.* 113 K10
Picerno, *Italy* 31 B8
Pichhor, *India* 69 G8
Pichilemu, *Chile* 126 C1
Pichor, *India* 68 G8
Pickerel L., *Canada* 102 C1
Pickering, *U.K.* 12 C7
Pickering, Vale of, *U.K.* 12 C7
Pickle Lake, *Canada* 102 B1
Pickwick L., *U.S.A.* 109 H1
Pico Truncado, *Argentina* 128 F3
Picos, *Brazil* 125 E10
Picton, *Australia* 95 E5
Picton, *Canada* 102 D4
Picton, *N.Z.* 91 J5
Pictou, *Canada* 103 C7
Picture Butte, *Canada* 104 D6
Picún Leufú, *Argentina* 128 D3
Pidurutalagala, *Sri Lanka* 66 R12
Piechowice, *Poland* 45 H2
Piedmont = Piemonte □, *Italy* 28 D5
Piedmont, *Ala., U.S.A.* 109 J3
Piedmont, *S.C., U.S.A.* 107 D10
Piedmonte Matese, *Italy* 31 A7
Piedra →, *Spain* 32 D3
Piedrabuena, *Spain* 35 G6
Piedrahita, *Spain* 34 E5
Piedralaves, *Spain* 34 E6
Piedras Blancas, *Spain* 34 B5
Piedras Negras, *Mexico* 118 B4
Piekary Śląskie, *Poland* 45 H5
Pieksämäki, *Finland* 9 E22
Piemonte □, *Italy* 28 D5
Pienaarsrivier, *S. Africa* 89 D4
Pieniężno, *Poland* 44 D7
Pieńsk, *Poland* 45 G2
Piercefield, *U.S.A.* 111 B10
Pierceland, *Canada* 105 C7
Piería □, *Greece* 40 F6
Pierpont, *U.S.A.* 110 E4
Pierre, *U.S.A.* 112 C4
Pierre-Buffière, *France* 20 C5
Pierre-de-Bresse, *France* 19 F12
Pierrefontaine-les-Varans, *France* 19 E13
Pierrefort, *France* 20 D6
Pierrelatte, *France* 21 D8
Piešťany, *Slovak Rep.* 27 C10
Piesting →, *Austria* 27 C9
Pieszyce, *Poland* 45 H3
Piet Retief, *S. Africa* 89 D5
Pietarsaari, *Finland* 8 E20
Pietermaritzburg, *S. Africa* 89 D5
Pietersburg, *S. Africa* 89 C4
Pietragalla, *Italy* 31 B8
Pietrasanta, *Italy* 28 E7
Pietroşiţa, *Romania* 43 E10
Pietrosul, Vf., *Maramureş, Romania* 43 C9
Pietrosul, Vf., *Suceava, Romania* 43 C10
Pieve di Cadore, *Italy* 29 B9
Pieve di Teco, *Italy* 28 D4
Pievepélago, *Italy* 28 D7
Pigadhítsa, *Greece* 40 G5
Pigeon L., *Canada* 110 B6
Piggott, *U.S.A.* 113 G9
Pigna, *Italy* 28 E4
Pigüe, *Argentina* 126 D3
Pihani, *India* 69 F9
Pihlajavesi, *Finland* 9 F23
Pijijiapan, *Mexico* 119 D6
Pikalevo, *Russia* 46 C8
Pikangikum Berens, *Canada* 105 C10
Pikes Peak, *U.S.A.* 112 F2
Piketberg, *S. Africa* 88 E2
Pikeville, *U.S.A.* 108 G4
Pikou, *China* 57 E12
Pikwitonei, *Canada* 105 B9
Piła, *Poland* 45 E3
Pila, *Spain* 33 G3
Pilaía, *Greece* 40 F6
Pilani, *India* 68 E6
Pilar, *Paraguay* 126 B4
Pilar de la Horadada, *Spain* 33 H4
Pilawa, *Poland* 45 G8
Pilaya →, *Bolivia* 124 H6
Pilbara, *Australia* 92 D2
Pilcomayo →, *Paraguay* 126 B4
Pilgrim's Rest, *S. Africa* 89 C5
Pilgrimstad, *Sweden* 10 B9
Píli, *Greece* 39 E9
Pilibhit, *India* 69 E8
Pilica →, *Poland* 45 G8
Pilion, *Greece* 38 B5
Pilis, *Hungary* 42 C4
Pilisvörösvár, *Hungary* 42 C3
Pilkhawa, *India* 68 E7
Pilliga, *Australia* 95 E4
Pílos, *Greece* 38 E3
Pilot Mound, *Canada* 105 D9
Pilot Point, *U.S.A.* 113 J6
Pilot Rock, *U.S.A.* 114 D4
Pilsen = Plzeň, *Czech Rep.* 26 B6
Pilštanj, *Slovenia* 29 B12
Piltene, *Latvia* 44 A8
Pilzno, *Poland* 45 J8
Pima, *U.S.A.* 115 K9
Pimba, *Australia* 95 E2
Pimenta Bueno, *Brazil* 124 F6
Pimentel, *Peru* 124 E3
Pina de Ebro, *Spain* 32 D4
Pinamalayan, *Phil.* 61 E4
Pinang, *Malaysia* 65 K3
Pinar, C. des, *Spain* 37 B10
Pinar del Río, *Cuba* 120 B3
Pınarbaşı, *Çanakkale, Turkey* 39 B8
Pınarbaşı, *Kayseri, Turkey* 72 C7
Pınarhisar, *Turkey* 41 E11
Pinatubo, Mt., *Phil.* 61 D3
Pincehely, *Hungary* 42 D3
Pinchang, *China* 58 B6
Pincher Creek, *Canada* 104 D6
Pinchi L., *Canada* 104 C4
Pinckneyville, *U.S.A.* 112 F10
Pińczów, *Poland* 45 H7
Pindar, *Australia* 93 E2
Pindi Gheb, *Pakistan* 68 C5
Pindiga, *Nigeria* 83 D7
Pindos Óros, *Greece* 38 B3
Pindus Mts. = Pindos Óros, *Greece* 38 B3
Pine →, *B.C., Canada* 104 B4
Pine →, *Sask., Canada* 105 B7
Pine, C., *Canada* 103 C9
Pine Bluff, *U.S.A.* 113 H9
Pine Bluffs, *U.S.A.* 112 E2
Pine City, *U.S.A.* 112 C8
Pine Cr. →, *U.S.A.* 110 E7
Pine Creek, *Australia* 92 B5
Pine Falls, *Canada* 105 C9
Pine Flat Res., *U.S.A.* 116 J7
Pine Grove, *U.S.A.* 111 F8
Pine Pass, *Canada* 104 B4
Pine Point, *Canada* 104 A6
Pine Ridge, *U.S.A.* 112 D3
Pine River, *Canada* 105 C8
Pine River, *U.S.A.* 112 B7
Pine Valley, *U.S.A.* 117 N10
Pinecrest, *U.S.A.* 116 G6
Pineda de Mar, *Spain* 32 D7
Pinedale, *Calif., U.S.A.* 116 J7
Pinedale, *Wyo., U.S.A.* 114 E9
Pinega →, *Russia* 50 C5
Pinehill, *Australia* 94 C4
Pinehouse L., *Canada* 105 B7
Pineimuta →, *Canada* 102 B1
Pinerolo, *Italy* 28 D4
Pineto, *Italy* 29 F11
Pinetop, *U.S.A.* 115 J9
Pinetown, *S. Africa* 89 D5
Pineville, *U.S.A.* 113 K8
Piney, *France* 19 D11
Ping →, *Thailand* 64 E3
Pingaring, *Australia* 93 F2
Pingba, *China* 58 D6
Pingbian, *China* 58 F4
Pingchuan, *China* 58 D3
Pingding, *China* 56 F7
Pingdingshan, *China* 56 H7
Pingdong, *Taiwan* 59 F13
Pingdu, *China* 57 F10
Pingelly, *Australia* 93 F2
Pingguo, *China* 58 F6
Pinghe, *China* 59 E11
Pinghu, *China* 59 B13
Pingjiang, *China* 59 C9
Pingle, *China* 59 E8
Pingli, *China* 58 A7
Pingliang, *China* 56 G4
Pinglu, *China* 56 E7
Pingluo, *China* 56 E4
Pingnan, *Fujian, China* 59 D12
Pingnan, *Guangxi Zhuangzu, China* 59 F8
Pingquan, *China* 57 D10
Pingrup, *Australia* 93 F2
Pingshan, *China* 58 C5
Pingtan, *China* 59 E12
Pingtang, *China* 58 E6
P'ingtung, *Taiwan* 59 F13
Pingwu, *China* 56 H3
Pingxiang, *Guangxi Zhuangzu, China* 58 F6
Pingxiang, *Jiangxi, China* 59 D9
Pingyao, *China* 56 F7
Pingyi, *China* 57 G9
Pingyin, *China* 56 F9
Pingyuan, *Guangdong, China* 59 E10
Pingyuan, *Shandong, China* 56 F9
Pingyuanjie, *China* 58 F4
Pinhal, *Brazil* 127 A6
Pinhal Novo, *Portugal* 35 G2
Pinheiro, *Brazil* 125 D9
Pinheiro Machado, *Brazil* 127 C5
Pinhel, *Portugal* 34 E3
Pini, *Indonesia* 62 D1
Piniós →, *Ilía, Greece* 38 D3
Piniós →, *Tríkkala, Greece* 38 B4
Pinjarra, *Australia* 93 F2
Pink Mountain, *Canada* 104 B4
Pinkafeld, *Austria* 27 D9
Pinnacles, *U.S.A.* 116 J5
Pinnaroo, *Australia* 95 F3
Pinneberg, *Germany* 24 B5
Pínnes, Ákra, *Greece* 41 F8
Pinon Hills, *U.S.A.* 117 L9
Pinos, *Mexico* 118 C4
Pinos, Mt., *U.S.A.* 117 L7
Pinos Pt., *U.S.A.* 115 H3
Pinos Puente, *Spain* 35 H7
Pinotepa Nacional, *Mexico* 119 D5
Pinrang, *Indonesia* 63 E5
Pins, Pte. aux, *Canada* 110 D3
Pinsk, *Belarus* 47 F4
Pintados, *Chile* 124 H5
Pinyang, *China* 59 D13
Pinyug, *Russia* 50 C5
Pioche, *U.S.A.* 115 H6
Piombino, *Italy* 28 F7
Piombino, Canale di, *Italy* 28 F7
Pioner, Ostrov, *Russia* 51 B10
Pionki, *Poland* 45 G8
Piorini, L., *Brazil* 124 D6
Piotrków Trybunalski, *Poland* 45 G6
Piove di Sacco, *Italy* 29 C9
Pīp, *Iran* 71 E9
Pipar, *India* 68 F5
Pipar Road, *India* 68 F5
Piparia, *Mad. P., India* 68 H8
Piparia, *Mad. P., India* 68 J7
Pipéri, *Greece* 38 B6
Pipestone, *U.S.A.* 112 D6
Pipestone →, *Canada* 102 B2
Pipestone Cr. →, *Canada* 105 D8
Piplan, *Pakistan* 68 C4
Piploda, *India* 68 H6
Pipmuacan, Rés., *Canada* 103 C5
Pippingarra, *Australia* 92 D2
Pipriac, *France* 18 E5
Piqua, *U.S.A.* 108 E3
Piquiri →, *Brazil* 127 A5
Pīr Sohrāb, *Iran* 71 E9
Pira, *Benin* 83 D5
Piracicaba, *Brazil* 127 A6
Piracuruca, *Brazil* 125 D10
Piræus = Piraiévs, *Greece* 38 D5
Piraiévs, *Greece* 38 D5
Pirajuí, *Brazil* 127 A6
Piram I., *India* 68 J5
Piran, *Slovenia* 29 C10
Pirané, *Argentina* 126 B4
Pirano = Piran, *Slovenia* 29 C10
Pirapora, *Brazil* 125 G10
Pirawa, *India* 68 G7
Pirdop, *Bulgaria* 41 D8
Pírgos, *Ilía, Greece* 38 D3
Pírgos, *Kríti, Greece* 39 F7
Pirgovo, *Bulgaria* 41 C9
Piribebuy, *Paraguay* 126 B4
Pirimapun, *Indonesia* 63 F9
Pirin Planina, *Bulgaria* 40 E7
Pírineos = Pyrénées, *Europe* 20 F4
Piripiri, *Brazil* 125 D10
Pirmasens, *Germany* 25 F3
Pirna, *Germany* 24 E9
Pirot, *Serbia, Yug.* 40 C6
Piru, *Indonesia* 63 E7
Piru, *U.S.A.* 117 L8
Piryatin = Pyryatyn, *Ukraine* 47 G7
Piryí, *Greece* 39 C7
Pisa, *Italy* 28 E7
Pisa →, *Poland* 45 E8
Pisagne, *Italy* 28 C7
Pisagua, *Chile* 124 G4
Pisarovina, *Croatia* 29 C12
Pisco, *Peru* 124 F3
Piscu, *Romania* 43 E12
Písek, *Czech Rep.* 26 B7
Pishan, *China* 60 C2
Pīshīn, *Iran* 71 E9
Pishin, *Pakistan* 68 D2
Pishin Lora →, *Pakistan* 68 E1
Pisidia, *Turkey* 72 D4
Pising, *Indonesia* 63 F6
Pismo Beach, *U.S.A.* 117 K6
Piso, L., *Liberia* 82 D2
Pissila, *Burkina Faso* 83 C4
Pissis, Cerro, *Argentina* 126 B2
Pissos, *France* 20 D3
Pissouri, *Cyprus* 36 E11
Pisticci, *Italy* 31 B9
Pistóia, *Italy* 28 E7
Pistol B., *Canada* 105 A10
Pisuerga →, *Spain* 34 D6
Pisz, *Poland* 44 E8
Pit →, *U.S.A.* 114 F2
Pita, *Guinea* 82 C2
Pitarpunga, L., *Australia* 95 E3
Pitcairn I., *Pac. Oc.* 97 K14
Pite älv →, *Sweden* 8 D19
Piteå, *Sweden* 8 D19
Piterka, *Russia* 48 E8
Piteşti, *Romania* 43 F9
Pithapuram, *India* 67 L13
Pithara, *Australia* 93 F2
Píthion, *Greece* 41 E10
Pithiviers, *France* 19 D9
Pithoragarh, *India* 69 E9
Pithoro, *Pakistan* 68 G3
Pitigliano, *Italy* 29 F8
Pitkyaranta, *Russia* 46 B6
Pitlochry, *U.K.* 14 E5
Pitsilia □, *Cyprus* 36 E12
Pitt I., *Canada* 104 C3
Pittsburg, *Calif., U.S.A.* 116 G5
Pittsburg, *Kans., U.S.A.* 113 G7
Pittsburg, *Tex., U.S.A.* 113 J7
Pittsburgh, *U.S.A.* 110 F5
Pittsfield, *Ill., U.S.A.* 112 F9
Pittsfield, *Maine, U.S.A.* 109 C11
Pittsfield, *Mass., U.S.A.* 111 D11
Pittsfield, *N.H., U.S.A.* 111 C13
Pittston, *U.S.A.* 111 E9
Pittsworth, *Australia* 95 D5
Pituri →, *Australia* 94 C2
Piura, *Peru* 124 E2
Piva →, *Montenegro, Yug.* 40 C2
Piwniczna, *Poland* 45 J7
Pixley, *U.S.A.* 116 K7
Piyai, *Greece* 38 B3
Pizarra, *Spain* 35 J6
Pizhou, *China* 56 G9
Pizzo, *Italy* 31 D9
Placentia, *Canada* 103 C9
Placentia B., *Canada* 103 C9
Placer, *Masbate, Phil.* 61 F5
Placer, *Surigao N., Phil.* 61 G6
Placerville, *U.S.A.* 116 G6
Placetas, *Cuba* 120 B4
Plačkovica, *Macedonia* 40 E6
Plainfield, *N.J., U.S.A.* 111 F10
Plainfield, *Ohio, U.S.A.* 110 F3
Plainfield, *Vt., U.S.A.* 111 B12
Plains, *Mont., U.S.A.* 114 C6
Plains, *Tex., U.S.A.* 113 J3
Plainview, *Nebr., U.S.A.* 112 D6
Plainview, *Tex., U.S.A.* 113 H4
Plainwell, *U.S.A.* 108 D3
Plaisance, *France* 20 E4
Plaistow, *U.S.A.* 111 D13
Pláka, *Greece* 39 B7
Pláka, Ákra, *Greece* 36 D8
Plakenska Planina, *Macedonia* 40 E5
Planá, *Czech Rep.* 26 B5
Plana Cays, *Bahamas* 121 B5
Planada, *U.S.A.* 116 H6
Plancoët, *France* 18 D4
Plandište, *Serbia, Yug.* 42 E6
Plano, *U.S.A.* 113 J6
Plant City, *U.S.A.* 109 M4
Plaquemine, *U.S.A.* 113 K9
Plasencia, *Spain* 34 E4
Plaški, *Croatia* 29 C12
Plaster City, *U.S.A.* 117 N11
Plaster Rock, *Canada* 103 C6
Plastun, *Russia* 54 B8
Plasy, *Czech Rep.* 26 B6
Plata, Río de la, *S. Amer.* 126 C4
Plátani →, *Italy* 30 E6
Plátanos, *Greece* 36 D5
Plateau □, *Nigeria* 83 D6
Platí, Ákra, *Greece* 41 F8
Platte, *U.S.A.* 112 D5
Platte →, *Mo., U.S.A.* 112 F7
Platte →, *Nebr., U.S.A.* 112 E7
Platteville, *U.S.A.* 112 D9
Plattling, *Germany* 25 G8
Plattsburgh, *U.S.A.* 111 B11
Plattsmouth, *U.S.A.* 112 E7
Plau, *Germany* 24 B8
Plauen, *Germany* 24 E8
Plauer See, *Germany* 24 B8
Plav, *Montenegro, Yug.* 40 D3
Plavinas, *Latvia* 9 H21
Plavnica, *Montenegro, Yug.* 40 D3
Plavno, *Croatia* 29 D13
Plavsk, *Russia* 46 F9
Playa Blanca, *Canary Is.* 37 F6
Playa Blanca Sur, *Canary Is.* 37 F6
Playa de las Americas, *Canary Is.* 37 F3
Playa de Mogán, *Canary Is.* 37 G4
Playa del Inglés, *Canary Is.* 37 G4
Playa Esmerelda, *Canary Is.* 37 F5
Playgreen L., *Canada* 105 C9
Pleasant Bay, *Canada* 103 C7
Pleasant Hill, *U.S.A.* 116 H4
Pleasant Mount, *U.S.A.* 111 E9
Pleasanton, *Calif., U.S.A.* 116 H5
Pleasanton, *Tex., U.S.A.* 113 L5
Pleasantville, *N.J., U.S.A.* 108 F8
Pleasantville, *Pa., U.S.A.* 110 E5
Pléaux, *France* 20 C6
Plei Ku, *Vietnam* 64 F7
Plélan-le-Grand, *France* 18 D4
Pléneuf-Val-André, *France* 18 D4
Pleniţa, *Romania* 43 F8
Plenty →, *Australia* 94 C2
Plenty, B. of, *N.Z.* 91 G6
Plentywood, *U.S.A.* 112 A2
Plérin, *France* 18 D4
Plessisville, *Canada* 103 C5

Plestin-les-Grèves, *France* 18 D3
Pleszew, *Poland* 45 G4
Pleternica, *Croatia* 42 E2
Plétipi, L., *Canada* 103 B5
Pleven, *Bulgaria* 41 C8
Plevlja, *Montenegro, Yug.* 40 C3
Plevna, *Canada* 110 B8
Plješevica, *Croatia* 29 D12
Ploaghe, *Italy* 30 B1
Plo'ana, *Slovak Rep.* 27 C12
Ploče, *Croatia* 29 E14
Płock, *Poland* 45 F6
Plöckenpass, *Italy* 29 B9
Plöckenstein, *Germany* 25 G9
Ploemeur, *France* 18 E3
Ploërmel, *France* 18 E4
Ploieşti, *Romania* 43 F11
Plomárion, *Greece* 39 C8
Plombières-les-Bains, *France* 19 E13
Plomin, *Croatia* 29 C11
Plön, *Germany* 24 A6
Plonge, Lac la, *Canada* 105 B7
Płońsk, *Poland* 45 F7
Plopeni, *Romania* 43 E10
Plopişului, Munţii, *Romania* 42 C7
Płoty, *Poland* 44 E2
Plouaret, *France* 18 D3
Plouay, *France* 18 E3
Ploučnice →, *Czech Rep.* 26 A7
Ploudalmézeau, *France* 18 D2
Plouescat, *France* 18 D2
Plougasnou, *France* 18 D3
Plougastel-Daoulas, *France* 18 D2
Plouguerneau, *France* 18 D2
Plouha, *France* 18 D4
Plouhinec, *France* 18 E2
Plovdiv, *Bulgaria* 41 D8
Plovdiv □, *Bulgaria* 41 D8
Plum, *U.S.A.* 110 F5
Plum I., *U.S.A.* 111 E12
Plumas, *U.S.A.* 116 F7
Plummer, *U.S.A.* 114 C5
Plumtree, *Zimbabwe* 87 G2
Plungė, *Lithuania* 9 J19
Pluvigner, *France* 18 E3
Plymouth, *U.K.* 13 G3
Plymouth, *Calif., U.S.A.* 116 G6
Plymouth, *Ind., U.S.A.* 108 E2
Plymouth, *Mass., U.S.A.* 111 E14
Plymouth, *N.C., U.S.A.* 109 H7
Plymouth, *N.H., U.S.A.* 111 C13
Plymouth, *Pa., U.S.A.* 111 E9
Plymouth, *Wis., U.S.A.* 108 D2
Plynlimon = Pumlumon Fawr, *U.K.* 13 E4
Plyusa, *Russia* 46 C5
Plyusa →, *Russia* 46 C5
Plyussa = Plyusa, *Russia* 46 C5
Plyussa → = Plyusa →, *Russia* 46 C5
Plzeň, *Czech Rep.* 26 B6
Pniewy, *Poland* 45 F3
Pô, *Burkina Faso* 83 C4
Po →, *Italy* 29 D9
Po, Foci del, *Italy* 29 D9
Po Hai = Bo Hai, *China* 57 E10
Pobé, *Benin* 83 D5
Pobé, *Burkina Faso* 83 C4
Pobeda, *Russia* 51 C15
Pobedy, Pik, *Kyrgyzstan* 50 E8
Pobiedziska, *Poland* 45 F4
Pobla de Segur, *Spain* 32 C5
Pobladura del Valle, *Spain* 34 C5
Pobra de Trives, *Spain* 34 C3
Pocahontas, *Ark., U.S.A.* 113 G9
Pocahontas, *Iowa, U.S.A.* 112 D7
Pocatello, *U.S.A.* 114 E7
Počátky, *Czech Rep.* 26 B8
Pochep, *Russia* 47 F7
Pochinki, *Russia* 48 C7
Pochinok, *Russia* 46 E7
Pöchlarn, *Austria* 26 C8
Pochutla, *Mexico* 119 D5
Pocito Casas, *Mexico* 118 B2
Pocking, *Germany* 25 G9
Pocomoke City, *U.S.A.* 108 F8
Poços de Caldas, *Brazil* 127 A6
Podbořany, *Czech Rep.* 26 A6
Poddębice, *Poland* 45 G5
Poděbrady, *Czech Rep.* 26 A8
Podensac, *France* 20 D3
Podenzano, *Italy* 28 D6
Podgorač, *Croatia* 42 E3
Podgorica, *Montenegro, Yug.* 40 D3
Podgorie, *Albania* 40 F4
Podilska Vysochyna, *Ukraine* 47 H4
Podkarpackie □, *Poland* 45 H9
Podkova, *Bulgaria* 41 E9
Podlapača, *Croatia* 29 D12
Podlaskie □, *Poland* 45 E10
Podoleni, *Romania* 43 D11
Podolínec, *Slovak Rep.* 27 B13
Podolsk, *Russia* 46 E9
Podor, *Senegal* 82 B1
Podporozhye, *Russia* 46 B8
Podu Iloaiei, *Romania* 43 C12
Podu Turcului, *Romania* 43 D12
Podujevo, *Kosovo, Yug.* 40 D5
Poel, *Germany* 24 B6
Pofadder, *S. Africa* 88 D2
Poggiardo, *Italy* 31 B11
Poggibonsi, *Italy* 28 E8
Póggio Mirteto, *Italy* 29 F9
Pogoanele, *Romania* 43 F12
Pogorzela, *Poland* 45 G4
Pogradeci, *Albania* 40 F4
Pogranitšnyi, *Russia* 54 B5
Poh, *Indonesia* 63 E6
P'ohang, *S. Korea* 57 F15
Pohjanmaa, *Finland* 8 E20
Pohnpei, *Micronesia* 96 G7
Pohorelá, *Slovak Rep.* 27 C13
Pohořelice, *Czech Rep.* 27 C9
Pohorje, *Slovenia* 29 B12
Pohri, *India* 68 G6
Poiana Mare, *Romania* 42 G8
Poiana Ruscăi, Munţii, *Romania* 42 E7
Poiana Stampei, *Romania* 43 C10
Poinsett, C., *Antarctica* 5 C8
Point Arena, *U.S.A.* 116 G3
Point Baker, *U.S.A.* 104 B2
Point Edward, *Canada* 102 D3
Point Hope, *U.S.A.* 100 B3
Point L., *Canada* 100 B8
Point Pedro, *Sri Lanka* 66 Q12
Point Pleasant, *N.J., U.S.A.* 111 F10
Point Pleasant, *W. Va., U.S.A.* 108 F4
Pointe-à-Pitre, *Guadeloupe* 121 C7
Pointe-Claire, *Canada* 111 A11
Pointe-Gatineau, *Canada* 111 A9
Pointe-Noire, *Congo* 84 E2
Poio, *Spain* 34 C2
Poirino, *Italy* 28 D4
Poisonbush Ra., *Australia* 92 D3
Poissonnier Pt., *Australia* 92 C2
Poitiers, *France* 18 F7
Poitou, *France* 20 B3
Poitou-Charentes □, *France* 20 B4
Poix-de-Picardie, *France* 19 C8
Poix-Terron, *France* 19 C11
Pojoaque, *U.S.A.* 115 J11
Pokaran, *India* 66 F7
Pokataroo, *Australia* 95 D4
Pokhara, *Nepal* 69 E10
Pokhvistnevo, *Russia* 48 D11
Poko, *Dem. Rep. of the Congo* 86 B2
Poko, *Sudan* 81 F3
Pokrov, *Russia* 46 E10
Pokrovsk = Engels, *Russia* 48 E8
Pokrovsk, *Russia* 51 C13
Pokrovskoye, *Russia* 47 J10
Pola = Pula, *Croatia* 29 D10
Pola, *Russia* 46 D7
Pola de Allande, *Spain* 34 B4
Pola de Lena, *Spain* 34 B5
Pola de Siero, *Spain* 34 B5
Pola de Somiedo, *Spain* 34 B4
Polacca, *U.S.A.* 115 J8
Polan, *Iran* 71 E9
Poland ■, *Europe* 45 G3
Polanica-Zdrój, *Poland* 45 H3
Połaniec, *Poland* 45 H8
Polanów, *Poland* 44 D3
Polar Bear Prov. Park, *Canada* 102 A2
Polatlı, *Turkey* 72 C5
Polatsk, *Belarus* 46 E5
Polcura, *Chile* 126 D1
Połczyn-Zdrój, *Poland* 44 E3
Polessk, *Russia* 9 J19
Polesye = Pripet Marshes, *Europe* 47 F5
Polgar, *Hungary* 42 C6
Pŏlgyo-ri, *S. Korea* 57 G14
Poli, *Cameroon* 83 C7
Políaigos, *Greece* 38 E6
Policastro, G. di, *Italy* 31 C8
Police, *Poland* 44 E1
Polička, *Czech Rep.* 27 B9
Policoro, *Italy* 31 B9
Polignano a Mare, *Italy* 31 A9
Poligny, *France* 19 F12
Políkhnitas, *Greece* 39 B8
Polillo Is., *Phil.* 61 D4
Polillo Strait, *Phil.* 61 D4
Polis, *Cyprus* 36 D11
Polístena, *Italy* 31 D9
Políyiros, *Greece* 40 F7
Polk, *U.S.A.* 110 E5
Polkowice, *Poland* 45 G3
Polla, *Italy* 31 B8
Pollachi, *India* 66 P10
Pollença, *Spain* 37 B10
Pollença, B. de, *Spain* 37 B10
Póllica, *Italy* 31 B8
Pollino, Mte., *Italy* 31 C9
Polna, *Russia* 46 C5
Polnovat, *Russia* 50 C7
Pology, *Ukraine* 47 J9
Polonne, *Ukraine* 47 G4
Polonnoye = Polonne, *Ukraine* 47 G4
Polski Trŭmbesh, *Bulgaria* 41 C9
Polsko Kosovo, *Bulgaria* 41 C9
Polson, *U.S.A.* 114 C6
Poltár, *Slovak Rep.* 27 C12
Poltava, *Ukraine* 47 H8
Põltsamaa, *Estonia* 9 G21
Polunochnoye, *Russia* 50 C7
Põlva, *Estonia* 9 G22
Polynesia, *Pac. Oc.* 97 J11
Polynésie française = French Polynesia ■, *Pac. Oc.* 97 K13
Pomarance, *Italy* 28 E7
Pomaro, *Mexico* 118 D4
Pombal, *Portugal* 34 F2
Pómbia, *Greece* 36 E6
Pomene, *Mozam.* 89 C6
Pomeroy, *Ohio, U.S.A.* 108 F4
Pomeroy, *Wash., U.S.A.* 114 C5
Pomézia, *Italy* 30 A5
Pomichna, *Ukraine* 47 H6
Pomona, *Australia* 95 D5
Pomona, *U.S.A.* 117 L9
Pomorie, *Bulgaria* 41 D11
Pomorskie □, *Poland* 44 D5
Pomorskie, Pojezierze, *Poland* 44 E3
Pomos, *Cyprus* 36 D11
Pomos, C., *Cyprus* 36 D11
Pompano Beach, *U.S.A.* 109 M5
Pompeí, *Italy* 31 B7
Pompey, *France* 19 D13
Pompeys Pillar, *U.S.A.* 114 D10
Pompton Lakes, *U.S.A.* 111 F10
Ponape = Pohnpei, *Micronesia* 96 G7
Ponask L., *Canada* 102 B1
Ponca, *U.S.A.* 112 D6
Ponca City, *U.S.A.* 113 G6
Ponce, *Puerto Rico* 121 C6
Ponchatoula, *U.S.A.* 113 K9
Poncheville, L., *Canada* 102 B4
Pond, *U.S.A.* 117 K7
Pond Inlet, *Canada* 101 A12
Pondicherry, *India* 66 P11
Ponds, I. of, *Canada* 103 B8
Ponferrada, *Spain* 34 C4
Pongo, Wadi →, *Sudan* 81 F2
Poniatowa, *Poland* 45 G9
Poniec, *Poland* 45 G3
Ponikva, *Slovenia* 29 B12
Ponnani, *India* 66 P9
Ponnyadaung, *Burma* 67 J19
Ponoka, *Canada* 104 C6
Ponorogo, *Indonesia* 63 G14
Pons = Ponts, *Spain* 32 D6
Pons, *France* 20 C3
Ponsul →, *Portugal* 34 F3
Pont-à-Mousson, *France* 19 D13
Pont-Audemer, *France* 18 C7
Pont-Aven, *France* 18 E3
Pont Canavese, *Italy* 28 C4
Pont-d'Ain, *France* 19 F12
Pont-de-Roide, *France* 19 E13
Pont-de-Salars, *France* 20 D6
Pont-de-Vaux, *France* 19 F11
Pont-de-Veyle, *France* 19 F11
Pont-du-Château, *France* 19 G10
Pont-l'Abbé, *France* 18 E2
Pont-l'Évêque, *France* 18 C7
Pont-St-Esprit, *France* 21 D8
Pont-St-Martin, *Italy* 28 C4
Pont-Ste-Maxence, *France* 19 C9
Pont-sur-Yonne, *France* 19 D10
Ponta do Sol, *Madeira* 37 D2
Ponta Grossa, *Brazil* 127 B5
Ponta Pora, *Brazil* 127 A4
Pontacq, *France* 20 E3
Pontailler-sur-Saône, *France* 19 E12
Pontarlier, *France* 19 F13
Pontassieve, *Italy* 29 E8
Pontaumur, *France* 20 C6
Pontcharra, *France* 21 C10
Pontchartrain L., *U.S.A.* 113 K10
Pontchâteau, *France* 18 E4
Ponte da Barca, *Portugal* 34 D2
Ponte de Sor, *Portugal* 35 F2
Ponte dell'Ólio, *Italy* 28 D6
Ponte di Legno, *Italy* 28 B7
Ponte do Lima, *Portugal* 34 D2
Ponte do Pungué, *Mozam.* 87 F3
Ponte-Leccia, *France* 21 F13
Ponte nelle Alpi, *Italy* 29 B9
Ponte Nova, *Brazil* 127 A7
Ponteareas, *Spain* 34 C2
Pontebba, *Italy* 29 B10
Ponteceso, *Spain* 34 B2
Pontecorvo, *Italy* 30 A6
Pontedeume, *Spain* 34 B2
Ponteix, *Canada* 105 D7
Pontevedra, *Spain* 34 C2
Pontevedra □, *Spain* 34 C2
Pontevedra, R. de →, *Spain* 34 C2
Pontevico, *Italy* 28 C7
Pontiac, *Ill., U.S.A.* 112 E10
Pontiac, *Mich., U.S.A.* 108 D4
Pontian Kecil, *Malaysia* 65 M4
Pontianak, *Indonesia* 62 E3
Pontine Is. = Ponziane, Ísole, *Italy* 30 B5
Pontine Mts. = Kuzey Anadolu Dağları, *Turkey* 72 B7
Pontínia, *Italy* 30 A6
Pontivy, *France* 18 D4
Pontoise, *France* 19 C9
Ponton →, *Canada* 104 B5
Pontorson, *France* 18 D5
Pontrémoli, *Italy* 28 D6
Pontrieux, *France* 18 D3
Ponts, *Spain* 32 D6
Pontypool, *Canada* 110 B6
Pontypool, *U.K.* 13 F4
Ponza, *Italy* 30 B5
Ponziane, Ísole, *Italy* 30 B5
Poochera, *Australia* 95 E1
Poole, *U.K.* 13 G6
Poole □, *U.K.* 13 G6
Poona = Pune, *India* 66 K8
Pooncarie, *Australia* 95 E3
Poopelloe L., *Australia* 95 E3
Poopó, L. de, *Bolivia* 122 E4
Popayán, *Colombia* 124 C3
Poperinge, *Belgium* 17 D2
Popilta L., *Australia* 95 E3
Popina, *Bulgaria* 41 B10
Popio L., *Australia* 95 E3
Poplar, *U.S.A.* 112 A2
Poplar →, *Canada* 105 C9
Poplar Bluff, *U.S.A.* 113 G9
Poplarville, *U.S.A.* 113 K10
Popocatépetl, Volcán, *Mexico* 119 D5
Popokabaka, *Dem. Rep. of the Congo* 84 F3
Pópoli, *Italy* 29 F10
Popovača, *Croatia* 29 C13
Popovo, *Bulgaria* 41 C10
Poppberg, *Germany* 25 F7
Poppi, *Italy* 29 E8
Poprad, *Slovak Rep.* 27 B13
Poprad →, *Slovak Rep.* 27 B13
Porali →, *Pakistan* 68 G2
Porbandar, *India* 66 J6
Porcher I., *Canada* 104 C2
Porcuna, *Spain* 35 H6
Porcupine →, *Canada* 105 B8
Porcupine →, *U.S.A.* 100 B5
Pordenone, *Italy* 29 C9
Pordim, *Bulgaria* 41 C8
Poreč, *Croatia* 29 C10
Poretskoye, *Russia* 48 C8
Pori, *Finland* 9 F19
Porí, *Greece* 38 F5
Porkhov, *Russia* 46 D5
Porlamar, *Venezuela* 124 A6
Porlezza, *Italy* 28 B6
Porma →, *Spain* 34 C5
Pornic, *France* 18 E4
Poronaysk, *Russia* 51 E15
Póros, *Greece* 38 D5
Poroshiri-Dake, *Japan* 54 C11
Poroszló, *Hungary* 42 C5
Poroto Mts., *Tanzania* 87 D3
Porpoise B., *Antarctica* 5 C9
Porquerolles, Î. de, *France* 21 F10
Porrentruy, *Switz.* 25 H3
Porreres, *Spain* 37 B10
Porsangen, *Norway* 8 A21
Porsgrunn, *Norway* 9 G13
Port Alberni, *Canada* 104 D4
Port Alfred, *S. Africa* 88 E4
Port Alice, *Canada* 104 C3
Port Allegany, *U.S.A.* 110 E6
Port Allen, *U.S.A.* 113 K9
Port Alma, *Australia* 94 C5
Port Angeles, *U.S.A.* 116 B3
Port Antonio, *Jamaica* 120 C4
Port Aransas, *U.S.A.* 113 M6
Port Arthur = Lüshun, *China* 57 E11
Port Arthur, *Australia* 94 G4
Port Arthur, *U.S.A.* 113 L8
Port au Choix, *Canada* 103 B8
Port au Port B., *Canada* 103 C8
Port-au-Prince, *Haiti* 121 C5
Port Augusta, *Australia* 95 E2
Port Austin, *U.S.A.* 110 B2
Port Bell, *Uganda* 86 B3
Port Bergé Vaovao, *Madag.* 89 B8
Port Blandford, *Canada* 103 C9
Port-Bouët, *Ivory C.* 82 D4
Port Bradshaw, *Australia* 94 A2
Port Broughton, *Australia* 95 E2
Port Burwell, *Canada* 110 D4
Port Campbell, *Australia* 95 F3
Port Canning, *India* 69 H13
Port-Cartier, *Canada* 103 B6
Port Chalmers, *N.Z.* 91 L3
Port Charlotte, *U.S.A.* 109 M4
Port Chester, *U.S.A.* 111 F11
Port Clements, *Canada* 104 C2
Port Clinton, *U.S.A.* 108 E4
Port Colborne, *Canada* 102 D4
Port Coquitlam, *Canada* 104 D4
Port Credit, *Canada* 110 C5
Port Curtis, *Australia* 94 C5
Port d'Alcúdia, *Spain* 37 B10
Port Dalhousie, *Canada* 110 C5
Port Darwin, *Australia* 92 B5
Port Darwin, *Falk. Is.* 128 G5
Port Davey, *Australia* 94 G4
Port-de-Bouc, *France* 21 E8
Port-de-Paix, *Haiti* 121 C5
Port de Pollença, *Spain* 37 B10
Port de Sóller, *Spain* 37 B9
Port Dickson, *Malaysia* 65 L3
Port Douglas, *Australia* 94 B4
Port Dover, *Canada* 110 D4
Port Edward, *Canada* 104 C2
Port Elgin, *Canada* 102 D3
Port Elizabeth, *S. Africa* 88 E4
Port Ellen, *U.K.* 14 F2
Port-en-Bessin, *France* 18 C6
Port Erin, *U.K.* 12 C3
Port Essington, *Australia* 92 B5
Port Etienne = Nouâdhibou, *Mauritania* 78 D2
Port Ewen, *U.S.A.* 111 E11
Port Fairy, *Australia* 95 F3
Port Fouâd = Bûr Fuad, *Egypt* 80 H8
Port Gamble, *U.S.A.* 116 C4
Port-Gentil, *Gabon* 84 E1
Port Germein, *Australia* 95 E2
Port Gibson, *U.S.A.* 113 K9
Port Glasgow, *U.K.* 14 F4
Port Harcourt, *Nigeria* 83 E6
Port Hardy, *Canada* 104 C3
Port Harrison = Inukjuak, *Canada* 101 C12
Port Hawkesbury, *Canada* 103 C7
Port Hedland, *Australia* 92 D2
Port Henry, *U.S.A.* 111 B11
Port Hood, *Canada* 103 C7
Port Hope, *Canada* 102 D4
Port Hope, *U.S.A.* 110 C2
Port Hope Simpson, *Canada* 103 B8
Port Hueneme, *U.S.A.* 117 L7
Port Huron, *U.S.A.* 110 D2
Port Iliç, *Azerbaijan* 73 C13
Port Jefferson, *U.S.A.* 111 F11
Port Jervis, *U.S.A.* 111 E10
Port-Joinville, *France* 18 F4
Port Katon, *Russia* 47 J10
Port Kelang = Pelabuhan Kelang, *Malaysia* 65 L3
Port Kenny, *Australia* 95 E1
Port-la-Nouvelle, *France* 20 E7
Port Lairge = Waterford, *Ireland* 15 D4
Port Laoise, *Ireland* 15 C4
Port Lavaca, *U.S.A.* 113 L6
Port Leyden, *U.S.A.* 111 C9
Port Lincoln, *Australia* 95 E2
Port Loko, *S. Leone* 82 D2
Port Louis, *France* 18 E3
Port Louis, *Mauritius* 77 H9
Port Lyautey = Kenitra, *Morocco* 78 B4
Port MacDonnell, *Australia* 95 F3
Port McNeill, *Canada* 104 C3
Port Macquarie, *Australia* 95 E5
Port Maria, *Jamaica* 120 C4
Port Matilda, *U.S.A.* 110 F6
Port Mellon, *Canada* 104 D4
Port-Menier, *Canada* 103 C7
Port Moody, *Canada* 116 A4
Port Morant, *Jamaica* 120 C4
Port Moresby, *Papua N. G.* 96 H6
Port Musgrave, *Australia* 94 A3
Port-Navalo, *France* 18 E4
Port Neches, *U.S.A.* 113 L8
Port Nolloth, *S. Africa* 88 D2
Port Nouveau-Québec = Kangiqsualujjuaq, *Canada* 101 C13
Port of Spain, *Trin. & Tob.* 121 D7
Port Orange, *U.S.A.* 109 L5
Port Orchard, *U.S.A.* 116 C4
Port Orford, *U.S.A.* 114 E1
Port Pegasus, *N.Z.* 91 M1
Port Perry, *Canada* 102 D4
Port Phillip B., *Australia* 95 F3
Port Pirie, *Australia* 95 E2
Port Radium = Echo Bay, *Canada* 100 B8
Port Renfrew, *Canada* 104 D4
Port Roper, *Australia* 94 A2
Port Rowan, *Canada* 110 D4
Port Safaga = Bûr Safâga, *Egypt* 70 E2
Port Said = Bûr Sa'îd, *Egypt* 80 H8
Port St. Joe, *U.S.A.* 109 L3
Port St. Johns = Umzimvubu, *S. Africa* 89 E4
Port-St-Louis-du-Rhône, *France* 21 E8
Port St. Lucie, *U.S.A.* 109 M5
Port-Ste-Marie, *France* 20 D4
Port Sanilac, *U.S.A.* 110 C2
Port Severn, *Canada* 110 B5
Port Shepstone, *S. Africa* 89 E5
Port Simpson, *Canada* 104 C2
Port Stanley = Stanley, *Falk. Is.* 128 G5
Port Stanley, *Canada* 102 D3
Port Sudan = Bûr Sûdân, *Sudan* 80 D4
Port Sulphur, *U.S.A.* 113 L10
Port-sur-Saône, *France* 19 E13
Port Talbot, *U.K.* 13 F4
Port Taufîq = Bûr Taufiq, *Egypt* 80 J8
Port Townsend, *U.S.A.* 116 B4
Port-Vendres, *France* 20 F7
Port Vila, *Vanuatu* 96 J8
Port Wakefield, *Australia* 95 E2
Port Washington, *U.S.A.* 108 D2
Port Weld = Kuala Sepetang, *Malaysia* 65 K3
Portadown, *U.K.* 15 B5
Portaferry, *U.K.* 15 B6
Portage, *Pa., U.S.A.* 110 F6
Portage, *Wis., U.S.A.* 112 D10
Portage La Prairie, *Canada* 105 D9
Portageville, *U.S.A.* 113 G10
Portalegre, *Portugal* 35 F3
Portalegre □, *Portugal* 35 F3
Portales, *U.S.A.* 113 H3
Portarlington, *Ireland* 15 C4
Portbou, *Spain* 32 C8
Portel, *Portugal* 35 G3
Porter L., *N.W.T., Canada* 105 A7
Porter L., *Sask., Canada* 105 B7
Porterville, *S. Africa* 88 E2
Porterville, *U.S.A.* 116 J8
Portes-lès-Valence, *France* 21 D8
Porthcawl, *U.K.* 13 F4
Porthill, *U.S.A.* 114 B5
Porthmadog, *U.K.* 12 E3
Portile de Fier, *Europe* 42 F7
Portimão, *Portugal* 35 H2
Portishead, *U.K.* 13 F5
Portiţei, Gura, *Romania* 43 F14
Portknockie, *U.K.* 14 D6
Portland, *N.S.W., Australia* 95 E5
Portland, *Vic., Australia* 95 F3
Portland, *Canada* 111 B8
Portland, *Conn., U.S.A.* 111 E12
Portland, *Maine, U.S.A.* 101 D12
Portland, *Mich., U.S.A.* 108 D3
Portland, *Oreg., U.S.A.* 116 E4
Portland, *Pa., U.S.A.* 111 F9
Portland, *Tex., U.S.A.* 113 M6
Portland, I. of, *U.K.* 13 G5
Portland B., *Australia* 95 F3
Portland Bill, *U.K.* 13 G5
Portland Canal, *U.S.A.* 104 B2
Portmadoc = Porthmadog, *U.K.* 12 E3
Porto, *France* 21 F12
Porto, *Portugal* 34 D2
Porto □, *Portugal* 34 D2
Porto, G. de, *France* 21 F12
Pôrto Alegre, *Brazil* 127 C5
Porto Amboim = Gunza, *Angola* 84 G2
Porto Azzurro, *Italy* 28 F7
Porto Cristo, *Spain* 37 B10
Pôrto de Móz, *Brazil* 125 D8
Porto Empédocle, *Italy* 30 E6
Pôrto Esperança, *Brazil* 124 G7

Pôrto Franco, *Brazil* 125 E9
Pórto Lágos, *Greece* 41 E9
Porto Mendes, *Brazil* 127 A5
Porto Moniz, *Madeira* 37 D2
Pôrto Murtinho, *Brazil* 124 H7
Pôrto Nacional, *Brazil* 125 F9
Porto-Novo, *Benin* 83 D5
Porto Petro, *Spain* 37 B10
Porto San Giórgio, *Italy* 29 E10
Porto Sant' Elpídio, *Italy* 29 E10
Porto Santo, *Madeira* 78 B2
Porto Santo Stéfano, *Italy* 28 F8
Pôrto São José, *Brazil* 127 A5
Pôrto Seguro, *Brazil* 125 G11
Porto Tolle, *Italy* 29 D9
Porto Tórres, *Italy* 30 B1
Pôrto União, *Brazil* 127 B5
Pôrto Válter, *Brazil* 124 E4
Porto-Vecchio, *France* 21 G13
Pôrto Velho, *Brazil* 124 E6
Portobelo, *Panama* 120 E4
Portoferráio, *Italy* 28 F7
Portogruaro, *Italy* 29 C9
Portola, *U.S.A.* 116 F6
Portomaggiore, *Italy* 29 D8
Portoscuso, *Italy* 30 C1
Portovénere, *Italy* 28 D6
Portoviejo, *Ecuador* 124 D2
Portpatrick, *U.K.* 14 G3
Portree, *U.K.* 14 D2
Portrush, *U.K.* 15 A5
Portsmouth, *Domin.* 121 C7
Portsmouth, *U.K.* 13 G6
Portsmouth, *N.H., U.S.A.* 109 D10
Portsmouth, *Ohio, U.S.A.* 108 F4
Portsmouth, *R.I., U.S.A.* 111 E13
Portsmouth, *Va., U.S.A.* 108 G7
Portsmouth □, *U.K.* 13 G6
Portsoy, *U.K.* 14 D6
Portstewart, *U.K.* 15 A5
Porttipahtan tekojärvi, *Finland* 8 B22
Portugal ■, *Europe* 34 F3
Portugalete, *Spain* 32 B1
Portumna, *Ireland* 15 C3
Portville, *U.S.A.* 110 D6
Porvenir, *Chile* 128 G2
Porvoo, *Finland* 9 F21
Porzuna, *Spain* 35 F6
Posada, *Italy* 30 B2
Posada →, *Italy* 30 B2
Posadas, *Argentina* 127 B4
Posadas, *Spain* 35 H5
Poschiavo, *Switz.* 25 J6
Posets, *Spain* 32 C5
Poshan = Boshan, *China* 57 F9
Posht-e-Badam, *Iran* 71 C7
Posídhion, Ákra, *Greece* 40 G7
Posidium, *Greece* 39 F9
Poso, *Indonesia* 63 E6
Posong, *S. Korea* 57 G14
Posse, *Brazil* 125 F9
Possession I., *Antarctica* 5 D11
Pössneck, *Germany* 24 E7
Possum Kingdom L., *U.S.A.* 113 J5
Post, *U.S.A.* 113 J4
Post Falls, *U.S.A.* 114 C5
Postavy = Pastavy, *Belarus* 9 J22
Poste-de-la-Baleine = Kuujjuarapik, *Canada* 102 A4
Postmasburg, *S. Africa* 88 D3
Postojna, *Slovenia* 29 C11
Poston, *U.S.A.* 117 M12
Postville, *Canada* 103 B8
Potamós, *Andikíthira, Greece* 38 F5
Potamós, *Kíthira, Greece* 38 E4
Potchefstroom, *S. Africa* 88 D4
Potcoava, *Romania* 43 F9
Poteau, *U.S.A.* 113 H7
Poteet, *U.S.A.* 113 L5
Potenza, *Italy* 31 B8
Potenza →, *Italy* 29 E10
Potenza Picena, *Italy* 29 E10
Poteriteri, L., *N.Z.* 91 M1
Potgietersrus, *S. Africa* 89 C4
Poti, *Georgia* 49 J5
Potiskum, *Nigeria* 83 C7
Potlogi, *Romania* 43 F10
Potomac →, *U.S.A.* 108 G7
Potosí, *Bolivia* 124 G5
Potosi Mt., *U.S.A.* 117 K11
Pototan, *Phil.* 61 F5
Potrerillos, *Chile* 126 B2
Potsdam, *Germany* 24 C9
Potsdam, *U.S.A.* 111 B10
Pottenstein, *Germany* 25 F7
Pottersville, *U.S.A.* 111 C11
Pottery Hill = Abu Ballas, *Egypt* 80 C2
Pottstown, *U.S.A.* 111 F9
Pottsville, *U.S.A.* 111 F8
Pottuvil, *Sri Lanka* 66 R12
P'otzu, *Taiwan* 59 F13
Pouancé, *France* 18 E5
Pouce Coupé, *Canada* 104 B4
Poughkeepsie, *U.S.A.* 111 E11
Pouilly-sur-Loire, *France* 19 E9
Poulaphouca Res., *Ireland* 15 C5
Poulsbo, *U.S.A.* 116 C4
Poultney, *U.S.A.* 111 C11
Poulton-le-Fylde, *U.K.* 12 D5
Pouso Alegre, *Brazil* 127 A6
Pout, *Senegal* 82 C1
Pouthisat, *Cambodia* 64 F4
Pouzauges, *France* 18 F6
Pova de Sta. Iria, *Portugal* 35 G1
Považská Bystrica, *Slovak Rep.* 27 B11
Poverty B., *N.Z.* 91 H7
Povlen, *Serbia, Yug.* 40 B3
Póvoa de Lanhosa, *Portugal* 34 D2
Póvoa de Varzim, *Portugal* 34 D2
Povorino, *Russia* 48 E6
Povungnituk = Puvirnituq, *Canada* 101 B12
Powassan, *Canada* 102 C4
Poway, *U.S.A.* 117 N9
Powder →, *U.S.A.* 112 B2
Powder River, *U.S.A.* 114 E10
Powell, *U.S.A.* 114 D9
Powell, L., *U.S.A.* 115 H8
Powell River, *Canada* 104 D4
Powers, *U.S.A.* 108 C2
Powys □, *U.K.* 13 E4
Poyang Hu, *China* 59 C11
Poyarkovo, *Russia* 51 E13
Poysdorf, *Austria* 27 C9
Poza de la Sal, *Spain* 34 C7
Poza Rica, *Mexico* 119 C5
Pozanti, *Turkey* 72 D6
Požarevac, *Serbia, Yug.* 40 B5
Pozazal, Puerto, *Spain* 34 C6
Požega, *Croatia* 42 E2
Požega, *Serbia, Yug.* 40 C4
Poznań, *Poland* 45 F3
Pozo, *U.S.A.* 117 K6
Pozo Alcón, *Spain* 35 H8
Pozo Almonte, *Chile* 124 H5
Pozo Colorado, *Paraguay* 126 A4
Pozoblanco, *Spain* 35 G6
Pozzallo, *Italy* 31 F7
Pozzomaggiore, *Italy* 30 B1
Pozzuoli, *Italy* 31 B7
Pra →, *Ghana* 83 D4
Prabuty, *Poland* 44 E6
Prača, *Bos.-H.* 42 G3
Prachatice, *Czech Rep.* 26 B6
Prachin Buri, *Thailand* 64 E3
Prachuap Khiri Khan, *Thailand* 65 G2
Pradelles, *France* 20 D7
Prades, *France* 20 F6
Prado, *Brazil* 125 G11
Prado del Rey, *Spain* 35 J5
Præstø, *Denmark* 11 J6
Pragersko, *Slovenia* 29 B12
Prague = Praha, *Czech Rep.* 26 A7
Praha, *Czech Rep.* 26 A7
Prahecq, *France* 20 B3
Prahova □, *Romania* 43 E10
Prahova →, *Romania* 43 F10
Prahovo, *Serbia, Yug.* 40 B6
Praia, *C. Verde Is.* 77 E1
Práia a Mare, *Italy* 31 C8
Praid, *Romania* 43 D10
Prainha, *Amazonas, Brazil* 124 E6
Prainha, *Pará, Brazil* 125 D8
Prairie, *Australia* 94 C3
Prairie City, *U.S.A.* 114 D4
Prairie Dog Town Fork →, *U.S.A.* 113 H5
Prairie du Chien, *U.S.A.* 112 D9
Prairies, L. of the, *Canada* 105 C8
Pramánda, *Greece* 38 B3
Prampram, *Ghana* 83 D5
Pran Buri, *Thailand* 64 F2
Prang, *Ghana* 83 D4
Prapat, *Indonesia* 62 D1
Prasonísi, Ákra, *Greece* 36 D9
Prästmon, *Sweden* 10 A11
Praszka, *Poland* 45 G5
Prata, *Brazil* 125 G9
Pratabpur, *India* 69 H10
Pratapgarh, *Raj., India* 68 G6
Pratapgarh, *Ut. P., India* 69 G9
Prato, *Italy* 28 E8
Prátola Peligna, *Italy* 29 F10
Prats-de-Mollo-la-Preste, *France* 20 F6
Pratt, *U.S.A.* 113 G5
Prattville, *U.S.A.* 109 J2
Pravdinsk, *Russia* 48 B6
Pravets, *Bulgaria* 40 D7
Pravia, *Spain* 34 B4
Praya, *Indonesia* 62 F5
Pré-en-Pail, *France* 18 D6
Precordillera, *Argentina* 126 C2
Predáppio, *Italy* 29 D8
Predazzo, *Italy* 29 B8
Predeal, *Romania* 43 E10
Predejane, *Serbia, Yug.* 40 D6
Preeceville, *Canada* 105 C8
Preetz, *Germany* 24 A6
Pregrada, *Croatia* 29 B12
Preiļi, *Latvia* 9 H22
Preko, *Croatia* 29 D12
Prelog, *Croatia* 29 B13
Prémery, *France* 19 E10
Premià de Mar, *Spain* 32 D7
Premont, *U.S.A.* 113 M5
Premuda, *Croatia* 29 D11
Prenjasi, *Albania* 40 E4
Prentice, *U.S.A.* 112 C9
Prenzlau, *Germany* 24 B9
Preobrazheniye, *Russia* 54 C6
Preparis North Channel, *Ind. Oc.* 67 M18
Preparis South Channel, *Ind. Oc.* 67 M18
Přerov, *Czech Rep.* 27 B10
Prescott, *Canada* 102 D4
Prescott, *Ariz., U.S.A.* 115 J7
Prescott, *Ark., U.S.A.* 113 J8
Prescott Valley, *U.S.A.* 115 J7
Preservation Inlet, *N.Z.* 91 M1
Preševo, *Serbia, Yug.* 40 D5
Presho, *U.S.A.* 112 D4
Presicce, *Italy* 31 C11
Presidencia de la Plaza, *Argentina* 126 B4
Presidencia Roque Saenz Peña, *Argentina* 126 B3
Presidente Epitácio, *Brazil* 125 H8
Presidente Hayes □, *Paraguay* 126 A4
Presidente Prudente, *Brazil* 127 A5
Presidio, *Mexico* 118 B4
Presidio, *U.S.A.* 113 L2
Preslav, *Bulgaria* 41 C10
Preslavska Planina, *Bulgaria* 41 C10
Prešov, *Slovak Rep.* 27 B14
Prešovský □, *Slovak Rep.* 27 B13
Prespa, *Bulgaria* 41 E8
Prespa, L. = Prespansko Jezero, *Macedonia* 40 F5
Prespansko Jezero, *Macedonia* 40 F5
Presque I., *U.S.A.* 110 D4
Presque Isle, *U.S.A.* 109 B12
Prestatyn, *U.K.* 12 D4
Prestea, *Ghana* 82 D4
Presteigne, *U.K.* 13 E5
Přeštice, *Czech Rep.* 26 B6
Preston, *Canada* 110 C4
Preston, *U.K.* 12 D5
Preston, *Idaho, U.S.A.* 114 E8
Preston, *Minn., U.S.A.* 112 D8
Preston, C., *Australia* 92 D2
Prestonburg, *U.S.A.* 108 G4
Prestwick, *U.K.* 14 F4
Pretoria, *S. Africa* 89 D4
Preuilly-sur-Claise, *France* 18 F7
Préveza, *Greece* 38 C2
Préveza □, *Greece* 38 B2
Prey Veng, *Cambodia* 65 G5
Priazovskoye, *Ukraine* 47 J8
Pribilof Is., *U.S.A.* 100 C2
Priboj, *Serbia, Yug.* 40 C3
Příbram, *Czech Rep.* 26 B7
Price, *U.S.A.* 114 G8
Price I., *Canada* 104 C3
Prichard, *U.S.A.* 109 K1
Priego, *Spain* 32 E2
Priego de Córdoba, *Spain* 35 H6
Priekule, *Latvia* 9 H19
Prien, *Germany* 25 H8
Prienai, *Lithuania* 9 J20
Prieska, *S. Africa* 88 D3
Priest L., *U.S.A.* 114 B5
Priest River, *U.S.A.* 114 B5
Priest Valley, *U.S.A.* 116 J6
Prievidza, *Slovak Rep.* 27 C11
Prignitz, *Germany* 24 B7
Prijedor, *Bos.-H.* 29 D13
Prijepolje, *Serbia, Yug.* 40 C3
Prikaspiyskaya Nizmennost = Caspian Depression, *Eurasia* 49 G9
Prikro, *Ivory C.* 82 D4
Prikubanskaya Nizmennost, *Russia* 49 H4
Prilep, *Macedonia* 40 E5
Priluki = Pryluky, *Ukraine* 47 G7
Prime Seal I., *Australia* 94 G4
Primorsk, *Russia* 46 B5
Primorsko, *Bulgaria* 41 D11
Primorsko-Akhtarsk, *Russia* 47 J10
Primorskoye, *Ukraine* 47 J9
Primrose L., *Canada* 105 C7
Prince Albert, *Canada* 105 C7
Prince Albert, *S. Africa* 88 E3
Prince Albert Mts., *Antarctica* 5 D11
Prince Albert Nat. Park, *Canada* 105 C7
Prince Albert Pen., *Canada* 100 A8
Prince Albert Sd., *Canada* 100 A8
Prince Alfred, C., *Canada* 4 B1
Prince Charles I., *Canada* 101 B12
Prince Charles Mts., *Antarctica* 5 D6
Prince Edward I. □, *Canada* 103 C7
Prince Edward Is., *Ind. Oc.* 3 G11
Prince Edward Pt., *Canada* 110 C8
Prince George, *Canada* 104 C4
Prince of Wales, C., *U.S.A.* 98 C3
Prince of Wales I., *Australia* 94 A3
Prince of Wales I., *Canada* 100 A10
Prince of Wales I., *U.S.A.* 100 C6
Prince Patrick I., *Canada* 4 B2
Prince Regent Inlet, *Canada* 4 B3
Prince Rupert, *Canada* 104 C2
Princess Charlotte B., *Australia* 94 A3
Princess May Ranges, *Australia* 92 C4
Princess Royal I., *Canada* 104 C3
Princeton, *Canada* 104 D4
Princeton, *Calif., U.S.A.* 116 F4
Princeton, *Ill., U.S.A.* 112 E10
Princeton, *Ind., U.S.A.* 108 F2
Princeton, *Ky., U.S.A.* 108 G2
Princeton, *Mo., U.S.A.* 112 E8
Princeton, *N.J., U.S.A.* 111 F10
Princeton, *W. Va., U.S.A.* 108 G5
Principe, I. de, *Atl. Oc.* 76 F4
Principe da Beira, *Brazil* 124 F6
Prineville, *U.S.A.* 114 D3
Prins Harald Kyst, *Antarctica* 5 D4
Prinsesse Astrid Kyst, *Antarctica* 5 D3
Prinsesse Ragnhild Kyst, *Antarctica* 5 D4
Prinzapolca, *Nic.* 120 D3
Prior, C., *Spain* 34 B2
Priozersk, *Russia* 46 B6
Pripet = Prypyat →, *Europe* 47 G6
Pripet Marshes, *Europe* 47 F5
Pripyat Marshes = Pripet Marshes, *Europe* 47 F5
Pripyats = Prypyat →, *Europe* 47 G6
Prislop, Pasul, *Romania* 43 C9
Pristen, *Russia* 47 G9
Priština, *Kosovo, Yug.* 40 D5
Pritzwalk, *Germany* 24 B8
Privas, *France* 21 D8
Priverno, *Italy* 30 A6
Privolzhsk, *Russia* 48 B5
Privolzhskaya Vozvyshennost, *Russia* 48 E7
Privolzhskiy, *Russia* 48 E8
Privolzhye, *Russia* 48 D9
Priyutnoye, *Russia* 49 G6
Prizren, *Kosovo, Yug.* 40 D4
Prizzi, *Italy* 30 E6
Prnjavor, *Bos.-H.* 42 F2
Probolinggo, *Indonesia* 63 G15
Prochowice, *Poland* 45 G3
Proctor, *U.S.A.* 111 C11
Proddatur, *India* 66 M11
Prodhromos, *Cyprus* 36 E11
Proença-a-Nova, *Portugal* 34 F3
Profítis Ilías, *Greece* 36 C9
Profondeville, *Belgium* 17 D4
Progreso, *Coahuila, Mexico* 118 B4
Progreso, *Yucatán, Mexico* 119 C7
Prokhladnyy, *Russia* 49 J7
Prokletije, *Albania* 40 D3
Prokopyevsk, *Russia* 50 D9
Prokuplje, *Serbia, Yug.* 40 C5
Proletarsk, *Russia* 49 G5
Proletarskaya = Proletarsk, *Russia* 49 G5
Prome = Pyè, *Burma* 67 K19
Prophet →, *Canada* 104 B4
Prophet River, *Canada* 104 B4
Propriá, *Brazil* 125 F11
Propriano, *France* 21 G12
Proserpine, *Australia* 94 C4
Prosna →, *Poland* 45 F4
Prospect, *U.S.A.* 111 C9
Prosser, *U.S.A.* 114 C4
Prostějov, *Czech Rep.* 27 B10
Prostki, *Poland* 44 E9
Proston, *Australia* 95 D5
Proszowice, *Poland* 45 H7
Próti, *Greece* 38 D3
Provadiya, *Bulgaria* 41 C11
Provence, *France* 21 E9
Provence-Alpes-Côte d'Azur □, *France* 21 D10
Providence, *Ky., U.S.A.* 108 G2
Providence, *R.I., U.S.A.* 111 E13
Providence Bay, *Canada* 102 C3
Providence Mts., *U.S.A.* 117 K11
Providencia, I. de, *Colombia* 120 D3
Provideniya, *Russia* 51 C19
Provins, *France* 19 D10
Provo, *U.S.A.* 114 F8
Provost, *Canada* 105 C6
Prozor, *Bos.-H.* 42 G2
Prudhoe Bay, *U.S.A.* 100 A5
Prudhoe I., *Australia* 94 C4
Prud'homme, *Canada* 105 C7
Prudnik, *Poland* 45 H4
Prüm, *Germany* 25 E2
Prundu, *Romania* 43 F11
Pruszcz Gdański, *Poland* 44 D5
Pruszków, *Poland* 45 F7
Prut →, *Romania* 43 E13
Pruzhany, *Belarus* 47 F3
Prvič, *Croatia* 29 D11
Prydz B., *Antarctica* 5 C6
Pryluky, *Ukraine* 47 G7
Pryor, *U.S.A.* 113 G7
Prypyat →, *Europe* 47 G6
Przasnysz, *Poland* 45 E7
Przedbórz, *Poland* 45 G6
Przedecz, *Poland* 45 F5
Przemków, *Poland* 45 G2
Przemyśl, *Poland* 45 J9
Przeworsk, *Poland* 45 H9
Przewóz, *Poland* 45 G1
Przhevalsk, *Kyrgyzstan* 50 E8
Przysucha, *Poland* 45 G7
Psakhná, *Greece* 38 C5
Psará, *Greece* 39 C7
Psathoúra, *Greece* 38 B6
Psel →, *Ukraine* 47 H7
Pserimos, *Greece* 39 E9
Psíra, *Greece* 36 D7
Pskov, *Russia* 46 D5
Pskovskoye, Ozero, *Russia* 9 H22
Psunj, *Croatia* 42 E2
Pteleón, *Greece* 38 B4
Ptich = Ptsich →, *Belarus* 47 F5
Ptolemaís, *Greece* 40 F5
Ptsich →, *Belarus* 47 F5
Ptuj, *Slovenia* 29 B12
Ptujska Gora, *Slovenia* 29 B12
Pu Xian, *China* 56 F6
Pua, *Thailand* 64 C3
Puán, *Argentina* 126 D3
Pu'an, *China* 58 E5
Puan, *S. Korea* 57 G14
Pubei, *China* 58 F7
Pucallpa, *Peru* 124 E4
Pucheng, *China* 59 D12
Pucheni, *Romania* 43 E10
Puchheim, *Germany* 25 G7
Púchov, *Slovak Rep.* 27 B11
Pucioasa, *Romania* 43 E10
Pučišća, *Croatia* 29 E13
Puck, *Poland* 44 D5
Pucka, Zatoka, *Poland* 44 D5
Puçol, *Spain* 33 F4
Pudasjärvi, *Finland* 8 D22
Puding, *China* 58 D5
Pudozh, *Russia* 46 B9
Pudukkottai, *India* 66 P11
Puebla, *Mexico* 119 D5
Puebla □, *Mexico* 119 D5
Puebla de Alcocer, *Spain* 35 G5
Puebla de Don Fadrique, *Spain* 33 H2
Puebla de Don Rodrigo, *Spain* 35 F6
Puebla de Guzmán, *Spain* 35 H3
Puebla de la Calzada, *Spain* 35 G4
Puebla de Sanabria, *Spain* 34 C4
Puebla de Trives = Pobra de Trives, *Spain* 34 C3
Pueblo, *U.S.A.* 112 F2
Pueblo Hundido, *Chile* 126 B1
Puelches, *Argentina* 126 D2
Puelén, *Argentina* 126 D2
Puente Alto, *Chile* 126 C1
Puente-Genil, *Spain* 35 H6
Puente la Reina, *Spain* 32 C3
Puenteareas = Ponteareas, *Spain* 34 C2
Puentedeume = Pontedeume, *Spain* 34 B2
Puentes de Garcia Rodriguez = As Pontes de García Rodríquez, *Spain* 34 B3
Pu'er, *China* 58 F3
Puerco →, *U.S.A.* 115 J10
Puerto, *Canary Is.* 37 F2
Puerto Aisén, *Chile* 128 F2
Puerto Ángel, *Mexico* 119 D5
Puerto Arista, *Mexico* 119 D6
Puerto Armuelles, *Panama* 120 E3
Puerto Ayacucho, *Venezuela* 124 B5
Puerto Barrios, *Guatemala* 120 C2
Puerto Bermejo, *Argentina* 126 B4
Puerto Bermúdez, *Peru* 124 F4
Puerto Bolívar, *Ecuador* 124 D3
Puerto Cabello, *Venezuela* 124 A5
Puerto Cabezas, *Nic.* 120 D3
Puerto Cabo Gracias á Dios, *Nic.* 120 D3
Puerto Carreño, *Colombia* 124 B5
Puerto Castilla, *Honduras* 120 C2
Puerto Chicama, *Peru* 124 E3
Puerto Coig, *Argentina* 128 G3
Puerto Cortés, *Costa Rica* 120 E3
Puerto Cortés, *Honduras* 120 C2
Puerto Cumarebo, *Venezuela* 124 A5
Puerto de Alcudia = Port d'Alcúdia, *Spain* 37 B10
Puerto de Andraitx, *Spain* 37 B9
Puerto de Cabrera, *Spain* 37 B9
Puerto de Gran Tarajal, *Canary Is.* 37 F5
Puerto de la Cruz, *Canary Is.* 37 F3
Puerto de Mazarrón, *Spain* 33 H3
Puerto de Pozo Negro, *Canary Is.* 37 F6
Puerto de Sóller = Port de Sóller, *Spain* 37 B9
Puerto de Somosierra, *Spain* 34 D7
Puerto del Carmen, *Canary Is.* 37 F6
Puerto del Rosario, *Canary Is.* 37 F6
Puerto Deseado, *Argentina* 128 F3
Puerto Escondido, *Mexico* 119 D5
Puerto Heath, *Bolivia* 124 F5
Puerto Inírida, *Colombia* 124 C5
Puerto Juárez, *Mexico* 119 C7
Puerto La Cruz, *Venezuela* 124 A6
Puerto Leguízamo, *Colombia* 124 D4
Puerto Limón, *Colombia* 124 C4
Puerto Lobos, *Argentina* 128 E3
Puerto Lumbreras, *Spain* 33 H3
Puerto Madryn, *Argentina* 128 E3
Puerto Maldonado, *Peru* 124 F5
Puerto Manotí, *Cuba* 120 B4
Puerto Mazarrón = Puerto de Mazarrón, *Spain* 33 H3
Puerto Montt, *Chile* 128 E2
Puerto Morazán, *Nic.* 120 D2
Puerto Morelos, *Mexico* 119 C7
Puerto Natales, *Chile* 128 G2
Puerto Padre, *Cuba* 120 B4
Puerto Páez, *Venezuela* 124 B5
Puerto Peñasco, *Mexico* 118 A2
Puerto Pinasco, *Paraguay* 126 A4
Puerto Plata, *Dom. Rep.* 121 C5
Puerto Pollensa = Port de Pollença, *Spain* 37 B10
Puerto Princesa, *Phil.* 61 G3
Puerto Quepos, *Costa Rica* 120 E3
Puerto Real, *Spain* 35 J4
Puerto Rico, *Canary Is.* 37 G4
Puerto Rico ■, *W. Indies* 121 C6
Puerto Rico Trench, *Atl. Oc.* 121 C6
Puerto San Julián, *Argentina* 128 F3
Puerto Sastre, *Paraguay* 126 A4
Puerto Serrano, *Spain* 35 J5
Puerto Suárez, *Bolivia* 124 G7
Puerto Vallarta, *Mexico* 118 C3
Puerto Wilches, *Colombia* 124 B4
Puertollano, *Spain* 35 G6
Pueyrredón, L., *Argentina* 128 F2
Puffin I., *Ireland* 15 E1
Pugachev, *Russia* 48 D9
Pugal, *India* 68 E5
Puge, *China* 58 D4
Puge, *Tanzania* 86 C3
Puget Sound, *U.S.A.* 114 C2
Puget-Théniers, *France* 21 E10
Púglia □, *Italy* 31 A9
Pugŏdong, *N. Korea* 57 C16
Pugu, *Tanzania* 86 D4
Pūgūnzī, *Iran* 71 E8
Pui, *Romania* 42 E8
Puieşti, *Romania* 43 D12
Puig Major, *Spain* 37 B9
Puigcerdà, *Spain* 32 C6
Puigmal, *Spain* 32 C7
Puigpunyent, *Spain* 37 B9
Puijiang, *China* 58 B4

Puisaye, Collines de la, *France* 19 E10
Puiseaux, *France* 19 D9
Pujehun, *S. Leone* 82 D2
Pujiang, *China* 59 C12
Pujols, *France* 20 D3
Pujon-chŏsuji, *N. Korea* 57 D14
Puka, *Albania* 40 D3
Pukaki L., *N.Z.* 91 L3
Pukapuka, *Cook Is.* 97 J11
Pukaskwa Nat. Park, *Canada* 102 C2
Pukatawagan, *Canada* 105 B8
Pukchin, *N. Korea* 57 D13
Pukch'ŏng, *N. Korea* 57 D15
Pukekohe, *N.Z.* 91 G5
Pukhrayan, *India* 69 F8
Pukou, *China* 59 A12
Pula, *Croatia* 29 D10
Pula, *Italy* 30 C1
Pulacayo, *Bolivia* 124 H5
Pulandian, *China* 57 E11
Pularumpi, *Australia* 92 B5
Pulaski, *N.Y., U.S.A.* 111 C8
Pulaski, *Tenn., U.S.A.* 109 H2
Pulaski, *Va., U.S.A.* 108 G5
Pulau →, *Indonesia* 63 F9
Puławy, *Poland* 45 G8
Pulga, *U.S.A.* 116 F5
Pulicat L., *India* 66 N12
Pullman, *U.S.A.* 114 C5
Pulo-Anna, *Pac. Oc.* 63 D8
Pulog, Mt., *Phil.* 61 C4
Pułtusk, *Poland* 45 F8
Pülümür, *Turkey* 73 C8
Pumlumon Fawr, *U.K.* 13 E4
Puná, I., *Ecuador* 124 D2
Punakha, *Bhutan* 67 F16
Punasar, *India* 68 F5
Punata, *Bolivia* 124 G5
Punch, *India* 69 C6
Punch →, *Pakistan* 68 C5
Punda Maria, *S. Africa* 89 C5
Pune, *India* 66 K8
P'ungsan, *N. Korea* 57 D15
Pungue, Ponte de, *Mozam.* 87 F3
Puning, *China* 59 F11
Punjab □, *India* 68 D7
Punjab □, *Pakistan* 68 E6
Puno, *Peru* 124 G4
Punpun →, *India* 69 G11
Punta Alta, *Argentina* 128 D4
Punta Arenas, *Chile* 128 G2
Punta de Díaz, *Chile* 126 B1
Punta Gorda, *Belize* 119 D7
Punta Gorda, *U.S.A.* 109 M5
Punta Prieta, *Mexico* 118 B2
Punta Prima, *Spain* 37 B11
Punta Umbría, *Spain* 35 H4
Puntarenas, *Costa Rica* 120 E3
Punto Fijo, *Venezuela* 124 A4
Punxsatawney, *U.S.A.* 110 F6
Puqi, *China* 59 C9
Puquio, *Peru* 124 F4
Pur →, *Russia* 50 C8
Purace, Vol., *Colombia* 124 C3
Puračić, *Bos.-H.* 42 F3
Puralia = Puruliya, *India* 69 H12
Puranpur, *India* 69 E9
Purbeck, Isle of, *U.K.* 13 G6
Purcell, *U.S.A.* 113 H6
Purcell Mts., *Canada* 104 D5
Puri, *India* 67 K14
Purmerend, *Neths.* 17 B4
Purnia, *India* 69 G12
Pursat = Pouthisat, *Cambodia* 64 F4
Purukcahu, *Indonesia* 62 E4
Puruliya, *India* 69 H12
Purus →, *Brazil* 122 D4
Puruvesi, *Finland* 46 B5
Purvis, *U.S.A.* 113 K10
Pŭrvomay, *Bulgaria* 41 D9
Purwa, *India* 69 F9
Purwakarta, *Indonesia* 63 G12
Purwodadi, *Indonesia* 63 G14
Purwokerto, *Indonesia* 63 G13
Puryŏng, *N. Korea* 57 C15
Pusa, *India* 69 G11
Pusan, *S. Korea* 57 G15
Pushkin, *Russia* 46 C6
Pushkino, *Moskva, Russia* 46 D9
Pushkino, *Saratov, Russia* 48 E8
Püspökladány, *Hungary* 42 C6
Pustoshka, *Russia* 46 D5
Puszczykowo, *Poland* 45 F3
Putahow L., *Canada* 105 B8
Putao, *Burma* 67 F20
Putaruru, *N.Z.* 91 H5
Putbus, *Germany* 24 A9
Puthein Myit →, *Burma* 67 M19
Putian, *China* 59 E12
Putignano, *Italy* 31 B10
Puting, Tanjung, *Indonesia* 62 E4
Putlitz, *Germany* 24 B8
Putna, *Romania* 43 C10
Putna →, *Romania* 43 E12
Putnam, *U.S.A.* 111 E13
Putnok, *Hungary* 42 B5
Putorana, Gory, *Russia* 51 C10
Puttalam, *Sri Lanka* 66 Q11
Puttgarden, *Germany* 24 A7
Püttlingen, *Germany* 25 F2
Putumayo →, *S. Amer.* 122 D4
Putuo, *China* 59 C14
Putussibau, *Indonesia* 62 D4
Puvirnituq, *Canada* 101 B12
Puy-de-Dôme, *France* 20 C6
Puy-de-Dôme □, *France* 20 C7
Puy-l'Évêque, *France* 20 D5
Puyallup, *U.S.A.* 116 C4
Puyang, *China* 56 G8
Puylaurens, *France* 20 E6
Pūzeh Rīg, *Iran* 71 E8
Pwani □, *Tanzania* 86 D4
Pweto, *Dem. Rep. of the Congo* 87 D2
Pwllheli, *U.K.* 12 E3
Pyana →, *Russia* 48 C8
Pyapon, *Burma* 67 L19
Pyasina →, *Russia* 51 B9
Pyatigorsk, *Russia* 49 H6
Pyatykhatky, *Ukraine* 47 H7
Pydna, *Greece* 40 F6
Pyè, *Burma* 67 K19
Pyetrikaw, *Belarus* 47 F5
Pyhäjoki, *Finland* 8 D21
Pyinmana, *Burma* 67 K20
Pyla, C., *Cyprus* 36 E12
Pymatuning Reservoir, *U.S.A.* 110 E4
Pyŏktong, *N. Korea* 57 D13
Pyŏnggang, *N. Korea* 57 E14
P'yŏngt'aek, *S. Korea* 57 F14
P'yŏngyang, *N. Korea* 57 E13
Pyote, *U.S.A.* 113 K3
Pyramid L., *U.S.A.* 114 G4
Pyramid Pk., *U.S.A.* 117 J10
Pyramids, *Egypt* 80 J7
Pyrénées, *Europe* 20 F4
Pyrénées-Atlantiques □, *France* 20 E3
Pyrénées-Orientales □, *France* 20 F6
Pyryatyn, *Ukraine* 47 G7
Pyrzyce, *Poland* 45 E1
Pyskowice, *Poland* 45 H5
Pytalovo, *Russia* 46 D4
Pyu, *Burma* 67 K20
Pyzdry, *Poland* 45 F4

Q

Qaanaaq, *Greenland* 4 B4
Qabirri →, *Azerbaijan* 49 K8
Qachasnek, *S. Africa* 89 E4
Qa'el Jafr, *Jordan* 75 E5
Qa'emābād, *Iran* 71 D9
Qā'emshahr, *Iran* 71 B7
Qagan Nur, *China* 56 C8
Qahar Youyi Zhongqi, *China* 56 D7
Qahremānshahr = Bākhtarān, *Iran* 70 C5
Qaidam Pendi, *China* 60 C4
Qajarīyeh, *Iran* 71 D6
Qala, Ras il, *Malta* 36 C1
Qala-i-Jadid = Spīn Búldak, *Afghan.* 68 D2
Qala Viala, *Pakistan* 68 D2
Qala Yangi, *Afghan.* 68 B2
Qal'at al Akhḍar, *Si. Arabia* 70 E3
Qal'at Dīzah, *Iraq* 70 B5
Qal'at Ṣaliḥ, *Iraq* 70 D5
Qal'at Sukkar, *Iraq* 70 D5
Qal'eh Shaharak, *Afghan.* 66 B4
Qalyûb, *Egypt* 80 H7
Qamdo, *China* 58 B1
Qamruddin Karez, *Pakistan* 68 D3
Qandahār, *Afghan.* 66 D4
Qandahār □, *Afghan.* 66 D4
Qapān, *Iran* 71 B7
Qapshaghay, *Kazakstan* 50 E8
Qaqortoq, *Greenland* 4 C5
Qâra, *Egypt* 80 B2
Qara Qash →, *India* 69 B8
Qarabutaq, *Kazakstan* 50 E7
Qaraçala, *Azerbaijan* 49 L9
Qaraghandy, *Kazakstan* 50 E8
Qārah, *Si. Arabia* 70 D4
Qarataū, *Kazakstan* 50 E8
Qardud, *Sudan* 81 E2
Qareh →, *Iran* 70 B5
Qareh Tekān, *Iran* 71 B6
Qarqan He →, *China* 60 C3
Qarqaraly, *Kazakstan* 50 E8
Qarrasa, *Sudan* 81 E3
Qarshi, *Uzbekistan* 50 F7
Qartabā, *Lebanon* 75 A4
Qaryat al Gharab, *Iraq* 70 D5
Qaryat al 'Ulyā, *Si. Arabia* 70 E5
Qasr 'Amra, *Jordan* 70 D3
Qaṣr-e Qand, *Iran* 71 E9
Qasr Farâfra, *Egypt* 80 B2
Qatanā, *Syria* 75 B5
Qatar ■, *Asia* 71 E6
Qatlīsh, *Iran* 71 B8
Qattâra, *Egypt* 80 A2
Qattâra, Munkhafed el, *Egypt* 80 B2
Qattâra Depression = Qattâra, Munkhafed el, *Egypt* 80 B2
Qawām al Ḥamzah, *Iraq* 70 D5
Qāyen, *Iran* 71 C8
Qazaqstan = Kazakstan ■, *Asia* 50 E7
Qazimämmäd, *Azerbaijan* 49 K9
Qazvin, *Iran* 71 B6
Qeissan, *Sudan* 81 E3
Qena, *Egypt* 80 B3
Qena, W. →, *Egypt* 80 B3
Qeqertarsuaq, *Greenland* 4 C5
Qeqertarsuaq, *Greenland* 4 C5
Qeshlāq, *Iran* 70 C5
Qeshm, *Iran* 71 E8
Qeys, *Iran* 71 E7
Qezel Owzen →, *Iran* 71 B6
Qezi'ot, *Israel* 75 E3
Qi Xian, *China* 56 G8
Qian Gorlos, *China* 57 B13
Qian Xian, *China* 56 G5
Qiancheng, *China* 58 D7
Qianjiang, *Guangxi Zhuangzu, China* 58 F7
Qianjiang, *Hubei, China* 59 B9
Qianjiang, *Sichuan, China* 58 C7
Qianshan, *China* 59 B11
Qianwei, *China* 58 C4
Qianxi, *China* 58 D6
Qianyang, *Hunan, China* 59 D8
Qianyang, *Shaanxi, China* 56 G4
Qianyang, *Zhejiang, China* 59 B12
Qiaojia, *China* 58 D4
Qibā', *Si. Arabia* 70 E5
Qichun, *China* 59 B10
Qidong, *Hunan, China* 59 D9
Qidong, *Jiangsu, China* 59 B13
Qijiang, *China* 58 C6
Qikiqtarjuaq, *Canada* 101 B13
Qila Safed, *Pakistan* 66 E2
Qila Saifullāh, *Pakistan* 68 D3
Qilian Shan, *China* 60 C4
Qimen, *China* 59 C11
Qin He →, *China* 56 G7
Qin Jiang →, *Guangxi Zhuangzu, China* 58 F7
Qin Jiang →, *Jiangxi, China* 59 D10
Qin Ling = Qinling Shandi, *China* 56 H5
Qin'an, *China* 56 G3
Qing Xian, *China* 56 E9
Qingcheng, *China* 57 F9
Qingdao, *China* 57 F11
Qingfeng, *China* 56 G8
Qinghai □, *China* 60 C4
Qinghai Hu, *China* 60 C5
Qinghecheng, *China* 57 D13
Qinghemen, *China* 57 D11
Qingjian, *China* 56 F6
Qingjiang = Huaiyin, *China* 57 H10
Qingliu, *China* 59 D11
Qinglong, *China* 58 E5
Qingping, *China* 58 D6
Qingpu, *China* 59 B13
Qingshui, *China* 56 G4
Qingshuihe, *China* 56 E6
Qingtian, *China* 59 C13
Qingtongxia Shuiku, *China* 56 F3
Qingxi, *China* 58 D7
Qingxu, *China* 56 F7
Qingyang, *Anhui, China* 59 B11
Qingyang, *Gansu, China* 56 F4
Qingyi Jiang →, *China* 58 C4
Qingyuan, *Guangdong, China* 59 F9
Qingyuan, *Liaoning, China* 57 C13
Qingyuan, *Zhejiang, China* 59 D12
Qingyun, *China* 57 F9
Qingzhen, *China* 58 D6
Qinhuangdao, *China* 57 E10
Qinling Shandi, *China* 56 H5
Qinshui, *China* 56 G7
Qinyang = Jiyuan, *China* 56 G7
Qinyuan, *China* 56 F7
Qinzhou, *China* 58 G7
Qionghai, *China* 64 C8
Qionglai, *China* 58 B4
Qionglai Shan, *China* 58 B4
Qiongzhou Haixia, *China* 64 B8
Qiqihar, *China* 51 E13
Qiraîya, W. →, *Egypt* 75 E3
Qiryat Ata, *Israel* 75 C4
Qiryat Gat, *Israel* 75 D3
Qiryat Mal'akhi, *Israel* 75 D3
Qiryat Shemona, *Israel* 75 B4
Qiryat Yam, *Israel* 75 C4
Qishan, *China* 56 G4
Qitai, *China* 60 B3
Qiubei, *China* 58 E5
Qixia, *China* 57 F11
Qiyang, *China* 59 D8
Qızılağac Körfäzi, *Azerbaijan* 71 B6
Qojūr, *Iran* 70 B5
Qom, *Iran* 71 C6
Qomolangma Feng = Everest, Mt., *Nepal* 69 E12
Qomsheh, *Iran* 71 D6
Qorveh, *Iran* 73 E12
Qostanay, *Kazakstan* 50 D7
Qotūr, *Iran* 73 C11
Qu Jiang →, *China* 58 B6
Qu Xian, *China* 58 B6
Quabbin Reservoir, *U.S.A.* 111 D12
Quairading, *Australia* 93 F2
Quakenbrück, *Germany* 24 C3
Quakertown, *U.S.A.* 111 F9
Qualicum Beach, *Canada* 104 D4
Quambatook, *Australia* 95 F3
Quambone, *Australia* 95 E4
Quamby, *Australia* 94 C3
Quan Long = Ca Mau, *Vietnam* 65 H5
Quanah, *U.S.A.* 113 H5
Quang Ngai, *Vietnam* 64 E7
Quang Tri, *Vietnam* 64 D6
Quang Yen, *Vietnam* 58 G6
Quannan, *China* 59 E10
Quantock Hills, *U.K.* 13 F4
Quanzhou, *Fujian, China* 59 E12
Quanzhou, *Guangxi Zhuangzu, China* 59 E8
Qu'Appelle, *Canada* 105 C8
Quaqtaq, *Canada* 101 B13
Quaraí, *Brazil* 126 C4
Quarré-les-Tombes, *France* 19 E11
Quarteira, *Portugal* 35 H2
Quartu Sant'Elena, *Italy* 30 C2
Quartzsite, *U.S.A.* 117 M12
Quatsino Sd., *Canada* 104 C3
Quba, *Azerbaijan* 49 K9
Qūchān, *Iran* 71 B8
Queanbeyan, *Australia* 95 F4
Québec, *Canada* 103 C5
Québec □, *Canada* 103 C6
Quedlinburg, *Germany* 24 D7
Queen Alexandra Ra., *Antarctica* 5 E11
Queen Charlotte City, *Canada* 104 C2
Queen Charlotte Is., *Canada* 104 C2
Queen Charlotte Sd., *Canada* 104 C3
Queen Charlotte Strait, *Canada* 104 C3
Queen Elizabeth Is., *Canada* 98 B10
Queen Elizabeth Nat. Park, *Uganda* 86 C3
Queen Mary Land, *Antarctica* 5 D7
Queen Maud G., *Canada* 100 B9
Queen Maud Land, *Antarctica* 5 D3
Queen Maud Mts., *Antarctica* 5 E13
Queens Chan., *Australia* 92 C4
Queenscliff, *Australia* 95 F3
Queensland □, *Australia* 94 C3
Queenstown, *Australia* 94 G4
Queenstown, *N.Z.* 91 L2
Queenstown, *S. Africa* 88 E4
Queets, *U.S.A.* 116 C2
Queguay Grande →, *Uruguay* 126 C4
Queimadas, *Brazil* 125 F11
Quelimane, *Mozam.* 87 F4
Quellón, *Chile* 128 E2
Quelpart = Cheju do, *S. Korea* 57 H14
Queluz, *Portugal* 35 G1
Quemado, *N. Mex., U.S.A.* 115 J9
Quemado, *Tex., U.S.A.* 113 L4
Quemoy = Chinmen, *Taiwan* 59 E13
Quemú-Quemú, *Argentina* 126 D3
Quequén, *Argentina* 126 D4
Querétaro, *Mexico* 118 C4
Querétaro □, *Mexico* 118 C5
Querfurt, *Germany* 24 D7
Quérigut, *France* 20 F6
Querqueville, *France* 18 C5
Quesada, *Spain* 35 H7
Queshan, *China* 56 H8
Quesnel, *Canada* 104 C4
Quesnel →, *Canada* 104 C4
Quesnel L., *Canada* 104 C4
Questa, *U.S.A.* 115 H11
Questembert, *France* 18 E4
Quetico Prov. Park, *Canada* 102 C1
Quetta, *Pakistan* 68 D2
Quezaltenango, *Guatemala* 120 D1
Quezon City, *Phil.* 61 D4
Qufār, *Si. Arabia* 70 E4
Qui Nhon, *Vietnam* 64 F7
Quibaxe, *Angola* 84 F2
Quibdo, *Colombia* 124 B3
Quiberon, *France* 18 E3
Quiberon, Presqu'île de, *France* 18 E3
Quickborn, *Germany* 24 B5
Quiet L., *Canada* 104 A2
Quiindy, *Paraguay* 126 B4
Quila, *Mexico* 118 C3
Quilán, C., *Chile* 128 E2
Quilcene, *U.S.A.* 116 C4
Quilimarí, *Chile* 126 C1
Quilino, *Argentina* 126 C3
Quill Lakes, *Canada* 105 C8
Quillabamba, *Peru* 124 F4
Quillagua, *Chile* 126 A2
Quillaicillo, *Chile* 126 C1
Quillan, *France* 20 F6
Quillota, *Chile* 126 C1
Quilmes, *Argentina* 126 C4
Quilon, *India* 66 Q10
Quilpie, *Australia* 95 D3
Quilpué, *Chile* 126 C1
Quilua, *Mozam.* 87 F4
Quimilí, *Argentina* 126 B3
Quimper, *France* 18 E2
Quimperlé, *France* 18 E3
Quinault →, *U.S.A.* 116 C2
Quincy, *Calif., U.S.A.* 116 F6
Quincy, *Fla., U.S.A.* 109 K3
Quincy, *Ill., U.S.A.* 112 F9
Quincy, *Mass., U.S.A.* 111 D14
Quincy, *Wash., U.S.A.* 114 C4
Quines, *Argentina* 126 C2
Quinga, *Mozam.* 87 F5
Quingey, *France* 19 E12
Quinns Rocks, *Australia* 93 F2
Quintana de la Serena, *Spain* 35 G5
Quintana Roo □, *Mexico* 119 D7
Quintanar de la Orden, *Spain* 35 F7
Quintanar de la Sierra, *Spain* 32 D2
Quintanar del Rey, *Spain* 33 F3
Quintero, *Chile* 126 C1
Quintin, *France* 18 D4
Quinto, *Spain* 32 D4
Quípar →, *Spain* 33 G3
Quirihue, *Chile* 126 D1
Quirindi, *Australia* 95 E5
Quirinópolis, *Brazil* 125 G8
Quiroga, *Spain* 34 C3
Quissac, *France* 21 E8
Quissanga, *Mozam.* 87 E5
Quissico, *Mozam.* 89 C5
Quitilipi, *Argentina* 126 B3
Quitman, *U.S.A.* 109 K4
Quito, *Ecuador* 124 D3
Quixadá, *Brazil* 125 D11
Quixaxe, *Mozam.* 87 F5
Qujing, *China* 58 E4
Qul'ân, Jazâ'ir, *Egypt* 70 E2
Qumbu, *S. Africa* 89 E4
Quneitra, *Syria* 75 B4
Qŭnghirot, *Uzbekistan* 50 E6
Qu'nyido, *China* 58 B2
Quoin I., *Australia* 92 B4
Quoin Pt., *S. Africa* 88 E2
Quorn, *Australia* 95 E2
Qŭqon, *Uzbekistan* 50 E8
Qurein, *Sudan* 81 E3
Qurnat as Sawdā', *Lebanon* 75 A5
Qûs, *Egypt* 80 B3
Qusar, *Azerbaijan* 49 K9
Quṣaybā', *Si. Arabia* 70 E4
Qusaybah, *Iraq* 70 C4
Quseir, *Egypt* 70 E2
Qūshchī, *Iran* 70 B5
Quthing, *Lesotho* 89 E4
Qūṭīābād, *Iran* 71 C6
Quwo, *China* 56 G6
Quyang, *China* 56 E8
Quynh Nhai, *Vietnam* 64 B4
Quyon, *Canada* 111 A8
Quzhou, *China* 59 C12
Quzi, *China* 56 F4
Qvareli, *Georgia* 49 K7
Qytet Stalin = Kuçovë, *Albania* 40 F3
Qyzylorda, *Kazakstan* 50 E7

R

Ra, Ko, *Thailand* 65 H2
Raab, *Austria* 26 C6
Raahe, *Finland* 8 D21
Raalte, *Neths.* 17 B6
Raasay, *U.K.* 14 D2
Raasay, Sd. of, *U.K.* 14 D2
Rab, *Croatia* 29 D11
Raba, *Indonesia* 63 F5
Rába →, *Hungary* 42 C2
Raba →, *Poland* 45 H7
Rabaçal →, *Portugal* 34 D3
Rabah, *Nigeria* 83 C6
Rabai, *Kenya* 86 C4
Rabak, *Sudan* 81 E3
Rabastens, *France* 20 E5
Rabastens-de-Bigorre, *France* 20 E4
Rabat, *Malta* 36 D1
Rabat, *Morocco* 78 B4
Rabaul, *Papua N. G.* 96 H7
Rābigh, *Si. Arabia* 74 C2
Rabka, *Poland* 45 J6
Râbniţa, *Moldova* 43 C14
Rābor, *Iran* 71 D8
Rača, *Serbia, Yug.* 40 B4
Răcăciuni, *Romania* 43 D11
Răcăşdia, *Romania* 42 F6
Racconigi, *Italy* 28 D4
Race, C., *Canada* 103 C9
Rach Gia, *Vietnam* 65 G5
Rachid, *Mauritania* 82 B2
Raciąż, *Poland* 45 F7
Racibórz, *Poland* 45 H5
Racine, *U.S.A.* 108 D2
Rackerby, *U.S.A.* 116 F5
Radama, Nosy, *Madag.* 89 A8
Radama, Saikanosy, *Madag.* 89 A8
Radan, *Serbia, Yug.* 40 D5
Rădăuţi, *Romania* 43 C10
Rădăuţi-Prut, *Romania* 43 B11
Radbuza →, *Czech Rep.* 26 B6
Radcliff, *U.S.A.* 108 G3
Radebeul, *Germany* 24 D9
Radeburg, *Germany* 24 D9
Radeče, *Slovenia* 29 B12
Radekhiv, *Ukraine* 47 G3
Radekhov = Radekhiv, *Ukraine* 47 G3
Radenthein, *Austria* 26 E6
Radew →, *Poland* 44 D2
Radford, *U.S.A.* 108 G5
Radhanpur, *India* 68 H4
Radhwa, Jabal, *Si. Arabia* 70 E3
Radika →, *Macedonia* 40 E4
Radisson, *Qué., Canada* 102 B4
Radisson, *Sask., Canada* 105 C7
Radium Hot Springs, *Canada* 104 C5
Radlje ob Dravi, *Slovenia* 29 B12
Radnevo, *Bulgaria* 41 D9
Radnice, *Czech Rep.* 26 B6
Radnor Forest, *U.K.* 13 E4
Radolfzell, *Germany* 25 H4
Radom, *Poland* 45 G8
Radomir, *Bulgaria* 40 D6
Radomka →, *Poland* 45 G8
Radomsko, *Poland* 45 G6
Radomyshl, *Ukraine* 47 G5
Radomyśl Wielki, *Poland* 45 H8
Radoszyce, *Poland* 45 G7
Radoviš, *Macedonia* 40 E6
Radovljica, *Slovenia* 29 B11
Radstadt, *Austria* 26 D6
Radstock, C., *Australia* 95 E1
Răducăneni, *Romania* 43 D12
Raduša, *Macedonia* 40 D5
Radviliškis, *Lithuania* 9 J20
Radville, *Canada* 105 D8
Raḍwá, J., *Si. Arabia* 80 C4
Radymno, *Poland* 45 J9
Radzanów, *Poland* 45 F7
Radziejów, *Poland* 45 F5
Radzyń Chełmiński, *Poland* 44 E5
Radzyń Podlaski, *Poland* 45 G9
Rae, *Canada* 104 A5
Rae Bareli, *India* 69 F9
Rae Isthmus, *Canada* 101 B11
Raeren, *Belgium* 17 D6

Revillagigedo, Is. de

Raeside, L., *Australia* 93 E3
Raetihi, *N.Z.* 91 H5
Rafaela, *Argentina* 126 C3
Rafah, *Gaza Strip* 75 D3
Rafai, *C.A.R.* 86 B1
Raffadali, *Italy* 30 E6
Raffili, *Sudan* 81 F2
Rafḩā, *Si. Arabia* 70 D4
Rafsanjān, *Iran* 71 D8
Raft Pt., *Australia* 92 C3
Râgâ, *Sudan* 81 F2
Raga →, *Sudan* 81 F2
Ragachow, *Belarus* 47 F6
Ragag, *Sudan* 81 E1
Ragama, *Sri Lanka* 66 R11
Ragged, Mt., *Australia* 93 F3
Raghunathpalli, *India* 69 H11
Raghunathpur, *India* 69 H12
Raglan, *N.Z.* 91 G5
Ragusa, *Italy* 31 F7
Raha, *Indonesia* 63 E6
Rahad, Nahr ed →, *Sudan* 81 E3
Rahaeng = Tak, *Thailand* 64 D2
Rahatgarh, *India* 69 H8
Rahden, *Germany* 24 C4
Raheita, *Eritrea* 81 E5
Raḩīmah, *Si. Arabia* 71 E6
Rahimyar Khan, *Pakistan* 68 E4
Rāhjerd, *Iran* 71 C6
Rahon, *India* 68 D7
Raichur, *India* 66 L10
Raiganj, *India* 69 G13
Raigarh, *India* 67 J13
Raijua, *Indonesia* 63 F6
Raikot, *India* 68 D6
Railton, *Australia* 94 G4
Rainbow Lake, *Canada* 104 B5
Rainier, *U.S.A.* 116 D4
Rainier, Mt., *U.S.A.* 116 D5
Rainy L., *Canada* 105 D10
Rainy River, *Canada* 105 D10
Raippaluoto, *Finland* 8 E19
Raipur, *India* 67 J12
Ra'is, *Si. Arabia* 80 C4
Raisen, *India* 68 H8
Raisio, *Finland* 9 F20
Raj Nandgaon, *India* 67 J12
Raj Nilgiri, *India* 69 J12
Raja, Ujung, *Indonesia* 62 D1
Raja Ampat, Kepulauan, *Indonesia* 63 E7
Rajahmundry, *India* 67 L12
Rajang →, *Malaysia* 62 D4
Rajanpur, *Pakistan* 68 E4
Rajapalaiyam, *India* 66 Q10
Rajasthan □, *India* 68 F5
Rajasthan Canal, *India* 68 F5
Rajauri, *India* 69 C6
Rajgarh, *Mad. P., India* 68 G7
Rajgarh, *Raj., India* 68 F7
Rajgarh, *Raj., India* 68 E6
Rajgir, *India* 69 G11
Rajgród, *Poland* 44 E9
Rajkot, *India* 68 H4
Rajmahal Hills, *India* 69 G12
Rajpipla, *India* 66 J8
Rajpur, *India* 68 H6
Rajpura, *India* 68 D7
Rajshahi, *Bangla.* 67 G16
Rajshahi □, *Bangla.* 69 G13
Rajula, *India* 68 J4
Rakaia, *N.Z.* 91 K4
Rakaia →, *N.Z.* 91 K4
Rakan, Ra's, *Qatar* 71 E6
Rakaposhi, *Pakistan* 69 A6
Rakata, Pulau, *Indonesia* 62 F3
Rakhiv, *Ukraine* 47 H3
Rakhni, *Pakistan* 68 D3
Rakhni →, *Pakistan* 68 E3
Rakitnoye, *Russia* 54 B7
Rakitovo, *Bulgaria* 41 E8
Rakoniewice, *Poland* 45 F3
Rakops, *Botswana* 88 C3
Rakovica, *Croatia* 29 D12
Rakovník, *Czech Rep.* 26 A6
Rakovski, *Bulgaria* 41 D8
Rakvere, *Estonia* 9 G22
Raleigh, *U.S.A.* 109 H6
Raleigh B., *U.S.A.* 107 D11
Ralja, *Serbia, Yug.* 40 B4
Ralls, *U.S.A.* 113 J4
Ralston, *U.S.A.* 110 E8
Ram →, *Canada* 104 A4
Rām Allāh, *West Bank* 75 D4
Ram Hd., *Australia* 95 F4
Rama, *Nic.* 120 D3
Ramacca, *Italy* 31 E7
Ramakona, *India* 69 J8
Ramales de la Victoria, *Spain* 34 B7
Raman, *Thailand* 65 J3
Ramanathapuram, *India* 66 Q11
Ramanetaka, B. de, *Madag.* 89 A8
Ramanujganj, *India* 69 H10
Ramat Gan, *Israel* 75 C3
Ramatlhabama, *S. Africa* 88 D4
Ramban, *India* 69 C6
Rambervillers, *France* 19 D13
Rambipuji, *Indonesia* 63 H15
Rambouillet, *France* 19 D8
Ramechhap, *Nepal* 69 F12
Ramenskoye, *Russia* 46 E10
Ramganga →, *India* 69 F8
Ramgarh, *Bihar, India* 69 H11
Ramgarh, *Raj., India* 68 F6
Ramgarh, *Raj., India* 68 F4
Rāmhormoz, *Iran* 71 D6
Ramīān, *Iran* 71 B7
Ramingining, *Australia* 94 A2
Ramla, *Israel* 75 D3
Ramlu, *Eritrea* 81 E5
Râmna →, *Romania* 43 E12
Ramnad = Ramanathapuram, *India* 66 Q11
Ramnagar, *Jammu & Kashmir, India* 69 C6
Ramnagar, *Ut. P., India* 69 E8
Ramnäs, *Sweden* 10 E10
Râmnicu Sărat, *Romania* 43 E12
Râmnicu Vâlcea, *Romania* 43 E9
Ramon, *Russia* 47 G10
Ramona, *U.S.A.* 117 M10
Ramonville-St-Agne, *France* 20 E5
Ramore, *Canada* 102 C3
Ramos →, *Nigeria* 83 D6
Ramotswa, *Botswana* 88 C4
Rampur, *H.P., India* 68 D7
Rampur, *Mad. P., India* 68 H5
Rampur, *Ut. P., India* 69 E8
Rampur Hat, *India* 69 G12
Rampura, *India* 68 G6
Ramrama Tola, *India* 69 J8
Ramree I. = Ramree Kyun, *Burma* 67 K19
Ramree Kyun, *Burma* 67 K19
Rāmsar, *Iran* 71 B6
Ramsey, *U.K.* 12 C3
Ramsey, *U.S.A.* 111 E10
Ramsey L., *Canada* 102 C3
Ramsgate, *U.K.* 13 F9
Ramsjö, *Sweden* 10 B9
Ramstein, *Germany* 25 F3
Ramtek, *India* 66 J11
Ramvik, *Sweden* 10 B11
Rana Pratap Sagar Dam, *India* 68 G6
Ranaghat, *India* 69 H13
Ranahu, *Pakistan* 68 G3
Ranau, *Malaysia* 62 C5
Rancagua, *Chile* 126 C1
Rance →, *France* 18 D5
Rancheria →, *Canada* 104 A3
Ranchester, *U.S.A.* 114 D10
Ranchi, *India* 69 H11
Rancho Cucamonga, *U.S.A.* 117 L9
Randalstown, *U.K.* 15 B5
Randan, *France* 19 F10
Randazzo, *Italy* 31 E7
Randers, *Denmark* 11 H4
Randers Fjord, *Denmark* 11 H4
Randfontein, *S. Africa* 89 D4
Randle, *U.S.A.* 116 D5
Randolph, *Mass., U.S.A.* 111 D13
Randolph, *N.Y., U.S.A.* 110 D6
Randolph, *Utah, U.S.A.* 114 F8
Randolph, *Vt., U.S.A.* 111 C12
Randsburg, *U.S.A.* 117 K9
Råne älv →, *Sweden* 8 D20
Rangae, *Thailand* 65 J3
Rangaunu B., *N.Z.* 91 F4
Rangeley, *U.S.A.* 111 B14
Rangeley L., *U.S.A.* 111 B14
Rangely, *U.S.A.* 114 F9
Ranger, *U.S.A.* 113 J5
Rangia, *India* 67 F17
Rangiora, *N.Z.* 91 K4
Rangitaiki →, *N.Z.* 91 G6
Rangitata →, *N.Z.* 91 K3
Rangkasbitung, *Indonesia* 63 G12
Rangon →, *Burma* 67 L20
Rangoon, *Burma* 67 L20
Rangpur, *Bangla.* 67 G16
Rangsit, *Thailand* 64 F3
Ranibennur, *India* 66 M9
Raniganj, *Ut. P., India* 69 F9
Raniganj, *W. Bengal, India* 67 H15
Ranikhet, *India* 69 E8
Raniwara, *India* 66 G8
Rāniyah, *Iraq* 70 B5
Ranka, *India* 69 H10
Ranken →, *Australia* 94 C2
Rankin, *U.S.A.* 113 K4
Rankin Inlet, *Canada* 100 B10
Rankins Springs, *Australia* 95 E4
Rankweil, *Austria* 26 D2
Rannoch, L., *U.K.* 14 E4
Rannoch Moor, *U.K.* 14 E4
Ranobe, Helodranon' i, *Madag.* 89 C7
Ranohira, *Madag.* 89 C8
Ranomafana, *Toamasina, Madag.* 89 B8
Ranomafana, *Toliara, Madag.* 89 C8
Ranomena, *Madag.* 89 C8
Ranong, *Thailand* 65 H2
Ranotsara Nord, *Madag.* 89 C8
Rānsa, *Iran* 71 C6
Ransiki, *Indonesia* 63 E8
Rantabe, *Madag.* 89 B8
Rantauprapat, *Indonesia* 62 D1
Rantemario, *Indonesia* 63 E5
Rantoul, *U.S.A.* 108 E1
Ranum, *Denmark* 11 H3
Ranyah, W. →, *Si. Arabia* 80 C5
Raon l'Étape, *France* 19 D13
Raoping, *China* 59 F11
Raoyang, *China* 56 E8
Rapa, *Pac. Oc.* 97 K13
Rapallo, *Italy* 28 D6
Rapar, *India* 68 H4
Rāpch, *Iran* 71 E8
Raper, C., *Canada* 101 B13
Rapid City, *U.S.A.* 112 D3
Rapid River, *U.S.A.* 108 C2
Rapla, *Estonia* 9 G21
Rapti →, *India* 69 F10
Rapu Rapu I., *Phil.* 61 E6
Raqaba ez Zarqa →, *Sudan* 81 F2
Raquette →, *U.S.A.* 111 B10
Raquette Lake, *U.S.A.* 111 C10
Rarotonga, *Cook Is.* 97 K12
Ra's al 'Ayn, *Syria* 70 B4
Ra's al Khaymah, *U.A.E.* 71 E7
Râs el Mâ, *Mali* 82 B4
Ras Ghârib, *Egypt* 80 B3
Ras Mallap, *Egypt* 80 B3
Râs Timirist, *Mauritania* 82 B1
Rasca, Pta. de la, *Canary Is.* 37 G3
Râşcani, *Moldova* 43 C12
Raseiniai, *Lithuania* 9 J20
Rashad, *Sudan* 81 E3
Rashîd, *Egypt* 80 H7
Rashîd, Masabb, *Egypt* 80 H7
Rashmi, *India* 68 G6
Rasht, *Iran* 71 B6
Rasi Salai, *Thailand* 64 E5
Raška, *Serbia, Yug.* 40 C4
Râsnov, *Romania* 43 E10
Rason L., *Australia* 93 E3
Raşova, *Romania* 43 F12
Rasovo, *Bulgaria* 40 C7
Rasra, *India* 69 G10
Rasskazovo, *Russia* 48 D5
Rast, *Romania* 43 G8
Rastatt, *Germany* 25 G4
Rastede, *Germany* 24 B4
Răstoliţa, *Romania* 43 D9
Rasul, *Pakistan* 68 C5
Raszków, *Poland* 45 G4
Rat Buri, *Thailand* 64 F2
Rat Islands, *U.S.A.* 100 C1
Rat L., *Canada* 105 B9
Ratangarh, *India* 68 E6
Rätansbyn, *Sweden* 10 B8
Raţāwī, *Iraq* 70 D5
Ratcatchers L., *Australia* 95 E3
Rath, *India* 69 G8
Rath Luirc, *Ireland* 15 D3
Rathdrum, *Ireland* 15 D5
Rathenow, *Germany* 24 C8
Rathkeale, *Ireland* 15 D3
Rathlin I., *U.K.* 15 A5
Rathmelton, *Ireland* 15 A4
Ratibor = Racibórz, *Poland* 45 H5
Rätikon, *Austria* 26 D2
Ratingen, *Germany* 24 D2
Ratlam, *India* 68 H6
Ratnagiri, *India* 66 L8
Ratodero, *Pakistan* 68 F3
Raton, *U.S.A.* 113 G2
Rattaphum, *Thailand* 65 J3
Ratten, *Austria* 26 D8
Rattray Hd., *U.K.* 14 D7
Rättvik, *Sweden* 10 D9
Ratz, Mt., *Canada* 104 B2
Ratzeburg, *Germany* 24 B6
Raub, *Malaysia* 65 L3
Rauch, *Argentina* 126 D4
Raudales de Malpaso, *Mexico* 119 D6
Raufarhöfn, *Iceland* 8 C6
Raufoss, *Norway* 9 F14
Raukumara Ra., *N.Z.* 91 H6
Rauma, *Finland* 9 F19
Raurkela, *India* 69 H11
Rausu-Dake, *Japan* 54 B12
Răut →, *Moldova* 43 C14
Rava-Ruska, *Poland* 47 G2
Rava Russkaya = Rava-Ruska, *Poland* 47 G2
Ravalli, *U.S.A.* 114 C6
Ravānsar, *Iran* 70 C5
Ravanusa, *Italy* 30 E6
Rāvar, *Iran* 71 D8
Ravena, *U.S.A.* 111 D11
Ravenna, *Italy* 29 D9
Ravenna, *Nebr., U.S.A.* 112 E5
Ravenna, *Ohio, U.S.A.* 110 E3
Ravensburg, *Germany* 25 H5
Ravenshoe, *Australia* 94 B4
Ravensthorpe, *Australia* 93 F3
Ravenswood, *Australia* 94 C4
Ravenswood, *U.S.A.* 108 F5
Ravi →, *Pakistan* 68 D4
Ravna Gora, *Croatia* 29 C11
Ravna Reka, *Serbia, Yug.* 40 B5
Ravne na Koroškem, *Slovenia* 29 B11
Rawa Mazowiecka, *Poland* 45 G7
Rawalpindi, *Pakistan* 68 C5
Rawāndūz, *Iraq* 70 B5
Rawang, *Malaysia* 65 L3
Rawene, *N.Z.* 91 F4
Rawicz, *Poland* 45 G3
Rawka →, *Poland* 45 F7
Rawlinna, *Australia* 93 F4
Rawlins, *U.S.A.* 114 F10
Rawlinson Ra., *Australia* 93 D4
Rawson, *Argentina* 128 E3
Raxaul, *India* 69 F11
Ray, *U.S.A.* 112 A3
Ray, C., *Canada* 103 C8
Rayadurg, *India* 66 M10
Rayagada, *India* 67 K13
Raychikhinsk, *Russia* 51 E13
Rāyen, *Iran* 71 D8
Rayleigh, *U.K.* 13 F8
Raymond, *Canada* 104 D6
Raymond, *Calif., U.S.A.* 116 H7
Raymond, *N.H., U.S.A.* 111 C13
Raymond, *Wash., U.S.A.* 116 D3
Raymond Terrace, *Australia* 95 E5
Raymondville, *U.S.A.* 113 M6
Raymore, *Canada* 105 C8
Rayón, *Mexico* 118 B2
Rayong, *Thailand* 64 F3
Rayville, *U.S.A.* 113 J9
Raz, Pte. du, *France* 18 D2
Razan, *Iran* 71 C6
Ražana, *Serbia, Yug.* 40 B3
Ražanj, *Serbia, Yug.* 40 C5
Razdelna, *Bulgaria* 41 C11
Razdel'naya = Rozdilna, *Ukraine* 47 J6
Razdolnoye, *Russia* 54 C5
Razdolnoye, *Ukraine* 47 K7
Razeh, *Iran* 71 C6
Razgrad, *Bulgaria* 41 C10
Razim, Lacul, *Romania* 43 F14
Razlog, *Bulgaria* 40 E7
Razmak, *Pakistan* 68 C3
Ré, Î. de, *France* 20 B2
Reading, *U.K.* 13 F7
Reading, *U.S.A.* 111 F9
Reading □, *U.K.* 13 F7
Realicó, *Argentina* 126 D3
Réalmont, *France* 20 E6
Ream, *Cambodia* 65 G4
Reata, *Mexico* 118 B4
Reay Forest, *U.K.* 14 C4
Rebais, *France* 19 D10
Rebi, *Indonesia* 63 F8
Rebiana, *Libya* 79 D10
Rebun-Tō, *Japan* 54 B10
Recanati, *Italy* 29 E10
Recaş, *Romania* 42 E6
Recco, *Italy* 28 D6
Recherche, Arch. of the, *Australia* 93 F3
Rechna Doab, *Pakistan* 68 D5
Rechytsa, *Belarus* 47 F6
Recife, *Brazil* 125 E12
Recklinghausen, *Germany* 17 C7
Reconquista, *Argentina* 126 B4
Recreo, *Argentina* 126 B2
Recz, *Poland* 45 E2
Red →, *La., U.S.A.* 113 K9
Red →, *N. Dak., U.S.A.* 100 C10
Red Bank, *U.S.A.* 111 F10
Red Bay, *Canada* 103 B8
Red Bluff, *U.S.A.* 114 F2
Red Bluff L., *U.S.A.* 113 K3
Red Cliffs, *Australia* 95 E3
Red Cloud, *U.S.A.* 112 E5
Red Creek, *U.S.A.* 111 C8
Red Deer, *Canada* 104 C6
Red Deer →, *Alta., Canada* 105 C7
Red Deer →, *Man., Canada* 105 C8
Red Deer L., *Canada* 105 C8
Red Hook, *U.S.A.* 111 E11
Red Indian L., *Canada* 103 C8
Red L., *Canada* 105 C10
Red Lake, *Canada* 105 C10
Red Lake Falls, *U.S.A.* 112 B6
Red Lake Road, *Canada* 105 C10
Red Lodge, *U.S.A.* 114 D9
Red Mountain, *U.S.A.* 117 K9
Red Oak, *U.S.A.* 112 E7
Red Rock, *Canada* 102 C2
Red Rock, L., *U.S.A.* 112 E8
Red Rocks Pt., *Australia* 93 F4
Red Sea, *Asia* 74 C2
Red Slate Mt., *U.S.A.* 116 H8
Red Sucker L., *Canada* 102 B1
Red Tower Pass = Turnu Roşu, P., *Romania* 43 E9
Red Wing, *U.S.A.* 112 C8
Reda, *Poland* 44 D5
Redang, *Malaysia* 62 C2
Redange, *Lux.* 17 E5
Redcar, *U.K.* 12 C6
Redcar & Cleveland □, *U.K.* 12 C7
Redcliff, *Canada* 105 C6
Redcliffe, *Australia* 95 D5
Redcliffe, Mt., *Australia* 93 E3
Reddersburg, *S. Africa* 88 D4
Redding, *U.S.A.* 114 F2
Redditch, *U.K.* 13 E6
Redfield, *U.S.A.* 112 C5
Redford, *U.S.A.* 111 B11
Redkino, *Russia* 46 D9
Redlands, *U.S.A.* 117 M9
Redmond, *Oreg., U.S.A.* 114 D3
Redmond, *Wash., U.S.A.* 116 C4
Redon, *France* 18 E4
Redonda, *Antigua* 121 C7
Redondela, *Spain* 34 C2
Redondo, *Portugal* 35 G3
Redondo Beach, *U.S.A.* 117 M8
Redruth, *U.K.* 13 G2
Redvers, *Canada* 105 D8
Redwater, *Canada* 104 C6
Redwood, *U.S.A.* 111 B9
Redwood City, *U.S.A.* 116 H4
Redwood Falls, *U.S.A.* 112 C7
Redwood National Park, *U.S.A.* 114 F1
Ree, L., *Ireland* 15 C3
Reed, L., *Canada* 105 C8
Reed City, *U.S.A.* 108 D3
Reedley, *U.S.A.* 116 J7
Reedsburg, *U.S.A.* 112 D9
Reedsport, *U.S.A.* 114 E1
Reedsville, *U.S.A.* 110 F7
Reefton, *N.Z.* 91 K3
Rees, *Germany* 24 D2
Reese →, *U.S.A.* 114 F5
Refahiye, *Turkey* 73 C8
Reftele, *Sweden* 11 G7
Refugio, *U.S.A.* 113 L6
Rega →, *Poland* 44 D2
Regalbuto, *Italy* 31 E7
Regen, *Germany* 25 G9
Regen →, *Germany* 25 F8
Regensburg, *Germany* 25 F8
Regenstauf, *Germany* 25 F8
Reggello, *Italy* 29 E8
Réggio di Calábria, *Italy* 31 D8
Réggio nell'Emília, *Italy* 28 D7
Reghin, *Romania* 43 D9
Regina, *Canada* 105 C8
Regina Beach, *Canada* 105 C8
Registro, *Brazil* 127 A6
Reguengos de Monsaraz, *Portugal* 35 G3
Rehar →, *India* 69 H10
Rehli, *India* 69 H8
Rehoboth, *Namibia* 88 C2
Rehovot, *Israel* 75 D3
Reichenbach, *Germany* 24 E8
Reid, *Australia* 93 F4
Reidsville, *U.S.A.* 109 G6
Reigate, *U.K.* 13 F7
Reillo, *Spain* 32 F3
Reims, *France* 19 C11
Reina Adelaida, Arch., *Chile* 128 G2
Reinbek, *Germany* 24 B6
Reindeer →, *Canada* 105 B8
Reindeer I., *Canada* 105 C9
Reindeer L., *Canada* 105 B8
Reinga, C., *N.Z.* 91 F4
Reinosa, *Spain* 34 B6
Reitz, *S. Africa* 89 D4
Reivilo, *S. Africa* 88 D3
Rejaf, *Sudan* 81 G3
Rejmyre, *Sweden* 11 F9
Rejowiec Fabryczny, *Poland* 45 G10
Reka →, *Slovenia* 29 C11
Rekovac, *Serbia, Yug.* 40 C5
Reliance, *Canada* 105 A7
Rémalard, *France* 18 D7
Remarkable, Mt., *Australia* 95 E2
Rembang, *Indonesia* 63 G14
Remedios, *Panama* 120 E3
Remeshk, *Iran* 71 E8
Remetea, *Romania* 43 D10
Remich, *Lux.* 17 E6
Remiremont, *France* 19 D13
Remo, *Ethiopia* 81 F5
Remontnoye, *Russia* 49 G6
Remoulins, *France* 21 E8
Remscheid, *Germany* 17 C7
Ren Xian, *China* 56 F8
Rende, *Italy* 31 C9
Rendína, *Greece* 38 B3
Rendsburg, *Germany* 24 A5
Renfrew, *Canada* 102 C4
Renfrewshire □, *U.K.* 14 F4
Rengat, *Indonesia* 62 E2
Rengo, *Chile* 126 C1
Renhua, *China* 59 E9
Renhuai, *China* 58 D6
Reni, *Ukraine* 47 K5
Renk, *Sudan* 81 E3
Renmark, *Australia* 95 E3
Rennell Sd., *Canada* 104 C2
Renner Springs, *Australia* 94 B1
Rennes, *France* 18 D5
Rennie L., *Canada* 105 A7
Reno, *U.S.A.* 116 F7
Reno →, *Italy* 29 D9
Renovo, *U.S.A.* 110 E7
Renqiu, *China* 56 E9
Rens, *Denmark* 11 K3
Renshou, *China* 58 C5
Rensselaer, *Ind., U.S.A.* 108 E2
Rensselaer, *N.Y., U.S.A.* 111 D11
Rentería, *Spain* 32 B3
Renton, *U.S.A.* 116 C4
Réo, *Burkina Faso* 82 C4
Reocín, *Spain* 34 B6
Reotipur, *India* 69 G10
Répcelak, *Hungary* 42 C2
Republic, *Mo., U.S.A.* 113 G8
Republic, *Wash., U.S.A.* 114 B4
Republican →, *U.S.A.* 112 F6
Repulse Bay, *Canada* 101 B11
Requena, *Peru* 124 E4
Requena, *Spain* 33 F3
Réquista, *France* 20 D6
Reşadiye = Datça, *Turkey* 39 E9
Reşadiye, *Turkey* 72 B7
Reşadiye Yarımadası, *Turkey* 39 E9
Resavica, *Serbia, Yug.* 40 B5
Resen, *Macedonia* 40 E5
Reserve, *U.S.A.* 115 K9
Resht = Rasht, *Iran* 71 B6
Resistencia, *Argentina* 126 B4
Reşiţa, *Romania* 42 E6
Resko, *Poland* 44 E2
Resolution I., *Canada* 101 B13
Resolution I., *N.Z.* 91 L1
Ressano Garcia, *Mozam.* 89 D5
Reston, *Canada* 105 D8
Reszel, *Poland* 44 D8
Retalhuleu, *Guatemala* 120 D1
Retenue, L. de, *Dem. Rep. of the Congo* 87 E2
Retezat, Munţii, *Romania* 42 E8
Retford, *U.K.* 12 D7
Rethel, *France* 19 C11
Rethem, *Germany* 24 C5
Réthímnon, *Greece* 36 D6
Réthímnon □, *Greece* 36 D6
Reti, *Pakistan* 68 E3
Retiche, Alpi, *Switz.* 25 J6
Retiers, *France* 18 E5
Retortillo, *Spain* 34 E4
Retournac, *France* 21 C8
Rétság, *Hungary* 42 C4
Réunion ■, *Ind. Oc.* 77 J9
Reus, *Spain* 32 D6
Reuterstadt Stavenhagen, *Germany* 24 B8
Reutlingen, *Germany* 25 G5
Reutte, *Austria* 26 D3
Reval = Tallinn, *Estonia* 9 G21
Revel, *France* 20 E6
Revelganj, *India* 69 G11
Revelstoke, *Canada* 104 C5
Reventazón, *Peru* 124 E2
Revigny-sur-Ornain, *France* 19 D11
Revillagigedo, Is. de, *Pac. Oc.* 118 D2

Revin, France 19 C11
Revúca, Slovak Rep. 27 C13
Revuè →, Mozam. 87 F3
Rewa, India 69 G9
Rewari, India 68 E7
Rexburg, U.S.A. 114 E8
Rey, Iran 71 C6
Rey, I. del, Panama 120 E4
Rey, Rio del →, Nigeria 83 E6
Rey Malabo, Eq. Guin. 83 E6
Reyðarfjörður, Iceland 8 D6
Reyes, Pt., U.S.A. 116 H3
Reyhanlı, Turkey 72 D7
Reykjahlið, Iceland 8 D5
Reykjanes, Iceland 8 E2
Reykjavík, Iceland 8 D3
Reynolds Ra., Australia 92 D5
Reynoldsville, U.S.A. 110 E6
Reynosa, Mexico 119 B5
Rēzekne, Latvia 9 H22
Rezina, Moldova 43 C13
Rezovo, Bulgaria 41 D12
Rezvān, Iran 71 E8
Rgotina, Serbia, Yug. 40 B6
Rhamnus, Greece 38 C6
Rhayader, U.K. 13 E4
Rheda-Wiedenbrück, Germany 24 D4
Rhede, Germany 24 D2
Rhein →, Europe 17 C6
Rhein-Main-Donau-Kanal, Germany 25 F7
Rheinbach, Germany 24 E2
Rheine, Germany 24 C3
Rheinfelden, Germany 25 H3
Rheinhessen-Pfalz □, Germany 25 F3
Rheinland-Pfalz □, Germany 25 E2
Rheinsberg, Germany 24 B8
Rhin = Rhein →, Europe 17 C6
Rhine = Rhein →, Europe 17 C6
Rhinebeck, U.S.A. 111 E11
Rhineland-Palatinate = Rheinland-Pfalz □, Germany 25 E2
Rhinelander, U.S.A. 112 C10
Rhinns Pt., U.K. 14 F2
Rhino Camp, Uganda 86 B3
Rhir, Cap, Morocco 78 B4
Rho, Italy 28 C6
Rhode Island □, U.S.A. 111 E13
Rhodes = Ródhos, Greece 36 C10
Rhodesia = Zimbabwe ■, Africa 87 F3
Rhodope Mts. = Rhodopi Planina, Bulgaria 41 E8
Rhodopi Planina, Bulgaria 41 E8
Rhön, Germany 24 E5
Rhondda, U.K. 13 F4
Rhondda Cynon Taff □, U.K. 13 F4
Rhône □, France 21 C8
Rhône →, France 21 E8
Rhône-Alpes □, France 21 C9
Rhum, U.K. 14 E2
Rhyl, U.K. 12 D4
Ri-Aba, Eq. Guin. 83 E6
Riachão, Brazil 125 E9
Riangnom, Sudan 81 F3
Riaño, Spain 34 C6
Rians, France 21 E9
Riansáres →, Spain 35 F7
Riasi, India 69 C6
Riau □, Indonesia 62 D2
Riau, Kepulauan, Indonesia 62 D2
Riau Arch. = Riau, Kepulauan, Indonesia 62 D2
Riaza, Spain 34 D7
Riaza →, Spain 34 D7
Riba de Saelices, Spain 32 E2
Riba-Roja de Turia, Spain 33 F4
Ribadavia, Spain 34 C2
Ribadeo, Spain 34 B3
Ribadesella, Spain 34 B5
Ribado, Nigeria 83 D7
Ribao, Cameroon 83 D7
Ribas = Ribes de Freser, Spain 32 C7
Ribas do Rio Pardo, Brazil 125 H8
Ribble →, U.K. 12 D5
Ribe, Denmark 11 J2
Ribe Amtskommune □, Denmark 11 J2
Ribeauvillé, France 19 D14
Ribécourt-Dreslincourt, France 19 C9
Ribeira = Santa Uxía, Spain 34 C2
Ribeira Brava, Madeira 37 D2
Ribeirão Prêto, Brazil 127 A6
Ribemont, France 19 C10
Ribera, Italy 30 E6
Ribérac, France 20 C4
Riberalta, Bolivia 124 F5
Ribes de Freser, Spain 32 C7
Ribnica, Slovenia 29 C11
Ribnitz-Damgarten, Germany 24 A8
Ričany, Czech Rep. 26 B7
Riccarton, N.Z. 91 K4
Ríccia, Italy 31 A7
Riccione, Italy 29 E9
Rice, U.S.A. 117 L12
Rice L., Canada 110 B6
Rice Lake, U.S.A. 112 C9
Rich, C., Canada 110 B4
Richard Toll, Senegal 82 B1
Richards Bay, S. Africa 89 D5
Richardson →, Canada 105 B6
Richardson Lakes, U.S.A. 108 C10
Richardson Springs, U.S.A. 116 F5
Riche, C., Australia 93 F2
Richelieu, France 18 E7
Richey, U.S.A. 112 B2
Richfield, U.S.A. 115 G8
Richfield Springs, U.S.A. 111 D10
Richford, U.S.A. 111 B12
Richibucto, Canada 103 C7
Richland, Ga., U.S.A. 109 J3
Richland, Wash., U.S.A. 114 C4
Richland Center, U.S.A. 112 D9
Richlands, U.S.A. 108 G5
Richmond, Australia 94 C3
Richmond, N.Z. 91 J4
Richmond, U.K. 12 C6
Richmond, Calif., U.S.A. 116 H4
Richmond, Ind., U.S.A. 108 F3
Richmond, Ky., U.S.A. 108 G3
Richmond, Mich., U.S.A. 110 D2
Richmond, Mo., U.S.A. 112 F8
Richmond, Tex., U.S.A. 113 L7
Richmond, Utah, U.S.A. 114 F8
Richmond, Va., U.S.A. 108 G7
Richmond, Vt., U.S.A. 111 B12
Richmond Hill, Canada 110 C5
Richmond Ra., Australia 95 D5
Richwood, U.S.A. 108 F5
Ricla, Spain 32 D3
Ridder = Leninogorsk, Kazakstan 50 D9
Riddlesburg, U.S.A. 110 F6
Ridgecrest, U.S.A. 117 K9
Ridgefield, Conn., U.S.A. 111 E11
Ridgefield, Wash., U.S.A. 116 E4
Ridgeland, U.S.A. 109 J5
Ridgetown, Canada 102 D3
Ridgewood, U.S.A. 111 F10
Ridgway, U.S.A. 110 E6
Riding Mountain Nat. Park, Canada 105 C9
Ridley, Mt., Australia 93 F3
Riebeek-Oos, S. Africa 88 E4
Ried, Austria 26 C6
Riedlingen, Germany 25 G5
Riedstadt, Germany 25 F4
Rienza →, Italy 29 B8
Riesa, Germany 24 D9
Riesi, Italy 31 E7
Riet →, S. Africa 88 D3
Rietavas, Lithuania 44 C8
Rietbron, S. Africa 88 E3
Rietfontein, Namibia 88 C3
Rieti, Italy 29 F9
Rieupeyroux, France 20 D6
Riez, France 21 E10
Riffe L., U.S.A. 116 D4
Rifle, U.S.A. 114 G10
Rift Valley □, Kenya 86 B4
Rīga, Latvia 9 H21
Riga, G. of, Latvia 9 H20
Rigacikun, Nigeria 83 C6
Rīgān, Iran 71 D8
Rīgas Jūras Līcis = Riga, G. of, Latvia 9 H20
Rigaud, Canada 111 A10
Rigby, U.S.A. 114 E8
Rīgestān □, Afghan. 66 D4
Riggins, U.S.A. 114 D5
Rignac, France 20 D6
Rigolet, Canada 103 B8
Rihand Dam, India 69 G10
Riihimäki, Finland 9 F21
Riiser-Larsen-halvøya, Antarctica 5 C4
Rijau, Nigeria 83 C6
Rijeka, Croatia 29 C11
Rijeka Crnojevića, Montenegro, Yug. 40 D3
Rijssen, Neths. 17 B6
Rike, Ethiopia 81 E4
Rikuzentakada, Japan 54 E10
Rila, Bulgaria 40 D7
Rila Planina, Bulgaria 40 D7
Riley, U.S.A. 114 E4
Rima →, Nigeria 83 C6
Rimah, Wadi ar →, Si. Arabia 70 E4
Rimavská Sobota, Slovak Rep. 27 C13
Rimbey, Canada 104 C6
Rimbo, Sweden 10 E12
Rimersburg, U.S.A. 110 E5
Rimforsa, Sweden 11 F9
Rimi, Nigeria 83 C6
Rímini, Italy 29 D9
Rimouski, Canada 103 C6
Rimrock, U.S.A. 116 D5
Rinca, Indonesia 63 F5
Rincón de la Victoria, Spain 35 J6
Rincón de Romos, Mexico 118 C4
Rinconada, Argentina 126 A2
Rind →, India 69 G9
Ringarum, Sweden 11 F10
Ringas, India 68 F6
Ringe, Denmark 11 J4
Ringim, Nigeria 83 C6
Ringkøbing, Denmark 11 H2
Ringkøbing Amtskommune □, Denmark 11 H2
Ringkøbing Fjord, Denmark 11 H2
Ringsjön, Sweden 11 J7
Ringsted, Denmark 11 J5
Ringvassøy, Norway 8 B18
Ringwood, U.S.A. 111 E10
Rinía, Greece 39 D7
Rinjani, Indonesia 62 F5
Rinteln, Germany 24 C5
Río, Punta del, Spain 33 J2
Rio Branco, Brazil 124 E5
Río Branco, Uruguay 127 C5
Río Bravo del Norte →, Mexico 119 B5
Rio Brilhante, Brazil 127 A5
Rio Claro, Brazil 127 A6
Rio Claro, Trin. & Tob. 121 D7
Río Colorado, Argentina 128 D4
Río Cuarto, Argentina 126 C3
Rio das Pedras, Mozam. 89 C6
Rio de Janeiro, Brazil 127 A7
Rio de Janeiro □, Brazil 127 A7
Rio do Sul, Brazil 127 B6
Río Gallegos, Argentina 128 G3
Rio Grande = Grande, Rio →, U.S.A. 113 N6
Río Grande, Argentina 128 G3
Rio Grande, Brazil 127 C5
Río Grande, Mexico 118 C4
Río Grande, Nic. 120 D3
Rio Grande City, U.S.A. 113 M5
Río Grande de Santiago →, Mexico 118 C3
Rio Grande do Norte □, Brazil 125 E11
Rio Grande do Sul □, Brazil 127 C5
Río Hato, Panama 120 E3
Río Lagartos, Mexico 119 C7
Rio Largo, Brazil 125 E11
Rio Maior, Portugal 35 F2
Rio Marina, Italy 28 F7
Río Mulatos, Bolivia 124 G5
Río Muni = Mbini □, Eq. Guin. 84 D2
Rio Negro, Brazil 127 B6
Rio Pardo, Brazil 127 C5
Rio Rancho, U.S.A. 115 J10
Río Segundo, Argentina 126 C3
Río Tercero, Argentina 126 C3
Rio Tinto, Portugal 34 D2
Rio Verde, Brazil 125 G8
Río Verde, Mexico 119 C5
Rio Vista, U.S.A. 116 G5
Ríobamba, Ecuador 124 D3
Ríohacha, Colombia 124 A4
Riom, France 20 C7
Riom-ès-Montagnes, France 20 C6
Rion-des-Landes, France 20 E3
Rionero in Vúlture, Italy 31 B8
Rioni →, Georgia 49 J5
Riós, Spain 34 D3
Ríosucio, Colombia 124 B3
Riou L., Canada 105 B7
Rioz, France 19 E13
Ripatransone, Italy 29 F10
Ripley, Canada 110 B3
Ripley, Calif., U.S.A. 117 M12
Ripley, N.Y., U.S.A. 110 D5
Ripley, Tenn., U.S.A. 113 H10
Ripley, W. Va., U.S.A. 108 F5
Ripoll, Spain 32 C7
Ripon, U.K. 12 C6
Ripon, Calif., U.S.A. 116 H5
Ripon, Wis., U.S.A. 108 D1
Riposto, Italy 31 E8
Risan, Montenegro, Yug. 40 D2
Riscle, France 20 E3
Rishā', W. ar →, Si. Arabia 70 E5
Rishiri-Tō, Japan 54 B10
Rishon le Ziyyon, Israel 75 D3
Risle →, France 18 C7
Rison, U.S.A. 113 J8
Risør, Norway 9 G13
Rita Blanca Cr. →, U.S.A. 113 H3
Riti, Nigeria 83 D6
Ritter, Mt., U.S.A. 116 H7
Rittman, U.S.A. 110 F3
Ritzville, U.S.A. 114 C4
Riva del Garda, Italy 28 C7
Riva Lígure, Italy 28 E4
Rivadavia, Buenos Aires, Argentina 126 D3
Rivadavia, Mendoza, Argentina 126 C2
Rivadavia, Salta, Argentina 126 A3
Rivadavia, Chile 126 B1
Rivarolo Canavese, Italy 28 C4
Rivas, Nic. 120 D2
Rive-de-Gier, France 21 C8
River Cess, Liberia 82 D3
River Jordan, Canada 116 B2
Rivera, Argentina 126 D3
Rivera, Uruguay 127 C4
Riverbank, U.S.A. 116 H6
Riverdale, U.S.A. 116 J7
Riverhead, U.S.A. 111 F12
Riverhurst, Canada 105 C7
Rivers, Canada 105 C8
Rivers □, Nigeria 83 E6
Rivers Inlet, Canada 104 C3
Riversdale, S. Africa 88 E3
Riverside, U.S.A. 117 M9
Riverton, Australia 95 E2
Riverton, Canada 105 C9
Riverton, N.Z. 91 M2
Riverton, U.S.A. 114 E9
Riverton Heights, U.S.A. 116 C4
Rives, France 21 C9
Rivesaltes, France 20 F6
Riviera, U.S.A. 117 K12
Riviera di Levante, Italy 28 D6
Riviera di Ponente, Italy 28 D5
Rivière-au-Renard, Canada 103 C7
Rivière-du-Loup, Canada 103 C6
Rivière-Pentecôte, Canada 103 C6
Rivière-Pilote, Martinique 121 D7
Rivière St. Paul, Canada 103 B8
Rivne, Ukraine 47 G4
Rívoli, Italy 28 C4
Rivoli B., Australia 95 F3
Rixheim, France 19 E14
Riyadh = Ar Riyāḍ, Si. Arabia 70 E5
Rize, Turkey 73 B9
Rizhao, China 57 G10
Rizokarpaso, Cyprus 36 D13
Rizzuto, C., Italy 31 D10
Rjukan, Norway 9 G13
Ro, Greece 39 E11
Roa, Spain 34 D7
Road Town, Virgin Is. 121 C7
Roan Plateau, U.S.A. 114 G9
Roanne, France 19 F11
Roanoke, Ala., U.S.A. 109 J3
Roanoke, Va., U.S.A. 108 G6
Roanoke →, U.S.A. 109 H7
Roanoke I., U.S.A. 109 H8
Roanoke Rapids, U.S.A. 109 G7
Roatán, Honduras 120 C2
Robāt Sang, Iran 71 C8
Robbins I., Australia 94 G4
Róbbio, Italy 28 C5
Robe, Australia 95 F2
Robe →, Australia 92 D2
Röbel, Germany 24 B8
Robert Lee, U.S.A. 113 K4
Robertsdale, U.S.A. 110 F6
Robertsganj, India 69 G10
Robertson, S. Africa 88 E2
Robertson I., Antarctica 5 C18
Robertson Ra., Australia 92 D3
Robertsport, Liberia 82 D2
Robertstown, Australia 95 E2
Roberval, Canada 103 C5
Robeson Chan., Greenland 4 A4
Robesonia, U.S.A. 111 F8
Robi, Ethiopia 81 F4
Robinson, U.S.A. 108 F2
Robinson →, Australia 94 B2
Robinson Ra., Australia 93 E2
Robinvale, Australia 95 E3
Robledo, Spain 33 G2
Roblin, Canada 105 C8
Roboré, Bolivia 124 G7
Robson, Canada 104 D5
Robson, Mt., Canada 104 C5
Robstown, U.S.A. 113 M6
Roca, C. da, Portugal 35 G1
Roca Partida, I., Mexico 118 D2
Rocamadour, France 20 D5
Rocas, I., Brazil 125 D12
Rocca San Casciano, Italy 29 D8
Roccadáspide, Italy 31 B8
Roccastrada, Italy 29 F8
Roccella Iónica, Italy 31 D9
Rocha, Uruguay 127 C5
Rochdale, U.K. 12 D5
Rochechouart, France 20 C4
Rochefort, Belgium 17 D5
Rochefort, France 20 C3
Rochefort-en-Terre, France 18 E4
Rochelle, U.S.A. 112 E10
Rocher River, Canada 104 A6
Rocheservière, France 18 F5
Rochester, U.K. 13 F8
Rochester, Ind., U.S.A. 108 E2
Rochester, Minn., U.S.A. 112 C8
Rochester, N.H., U.S.A. 111 C14
Rochester, N.Y., U.S.A. 110 C7
Rociu, Romania 43 F10
Rock →, Canada 104 A3
Rock Creek, U.S.A. 110 E4
Rock Falls, U.S.A. 112 E10
Rock Hill, U.S.A. 109 H5
Rock Island, U.S.A. 112 E9
Rock Rapids, U.S.A. 112 D6
Rock Sound, Bahamas 120 B4
Rock Springs, Mont., U.S.A. 114 C10
Rock Springs, Wyo., U.S.A. 114 F9
Rock Valley, U.S.A. 112 D6
Rockall, Atl. Oc. 6 D3
Rockdale, Tex., U.S.A. 113 K6
Rockdale, Wash., U.S.A. 116 C5
Rockefeller Plateau, Antarctica 5 E14
Rockford, U.S.A. 112 D10
Rockglen, Canada 105 D7
Rockhampton, Australia 94 C5
Rockingham, Australia 93 F2
Rockingham, U.S.A. 109 H6
Rockingham B., Australia 94 B4
Rocklake, U.S.A. 112 A5
Rockland, Canada 111 A9
Rockland, Idaho, U.S.A. 114 E7
Rockland, Maine, U.S.A. 109 C11
Rockland, Mich., U.S.A. 112 B10
Rocklin, U.S.A. 116 G5
Rockport, Mass., U.S.A. 111 D14
Rockport, Mo., U.S.A. 112 E7
Rockport, Tex., U.S.A. 113 L6
Rocksprings, U.S.A. 113 K4
Rockville, Conn., U.S.A. 111 E12
Rockville, Md., U.S.A. 108 F7
Rockwall, U.S.A. 113 J6
Rockwell City, U.S.A. 112 D7
Rockwood, Canada 110 C4
Rockwood, Maine, U.S.A. 109 C11
Rockwood, Tenn., U.S.A. 109 H3
Rocky Ford, U.S.A. 112 F3
Rocky Gully, Australia 93 F2
Rocky Harbour, Canada 103 C8
Rocky Island L., Canada 102 C3
Rocky Lane, Canada 104 B5
Rocky Mount, U.S.A. 109 H7
Rocky Mountain House, Canada 104 C6
Rocky Mountain National Park, U.S.A. 114 F11
Rocky Mts., N. Amer. 114 G10
Rocky Point, Namibia 88 B2
Rocroi, France 19 C11
Rod, Pakistan 66 E3
Rødby, Denmark 11 K5
Rødbyhavn, Denmark 11 K5
Roddickton, Canada 103 B8
Rødding, Denmark 11 J3
Rödeby, Sweden 11 H9
Rødekro, Denmark 11 J3
Rodenkirchen, Germany 24 B4
Rodez, France 20 D6
Rodholívas, Greece 40 F7
Rodhópi □, Greece 41 E9
Rodhopoú, Greece 36 D5
Ródhos, Greece 36 C10
Rodi Gargánico, Italy 29 G12
Rodna, Romania 43 C9
Rodnei, Munţii, Romania 43 C9
Rodney, Canada 110 D3
Rodney, C., N.Z. 91 G5
Rodniki, Russia 48 B5
Rodonit, Kepi i, Albania 40 E3
Rodriguez, Ind. Oc. 3 E13
Roe →, U.K. 15 A5
Roebling, U.S.A. 111 F10
Roebourne, Australia 92 D2
Roebuck B., Australia 92 C3
Roermond, Neths. 17 C6
Roes Welcome Sd., Canada 101 B11
Roeselare, Belgium 17 D3
Rogachev = Ragachow, Belarus 47 F6
Rogačica, Serbia, Yug. 40 B3
Rogagua, L., Bolivia 124 F5
Rogaška Slatina, Slovenia 29 B12
Rogatec, Slovenia 29 B12
Rogatica, Bos.-H. 42 G4
Rogatyn, Ukraine 47 H3
Rogdhia, Greece 36 D7
Rogers, U.S.A. 113 G7
Rogers City, U.S.A. 108 C4
Rogersville, Canada 103 C6
Roggan →, Canada 102 B4
Roggan L., Canada 102 B4
Roggeveldberge, S. Africa 88 E3
Roggiano Gravina, Italy 31 C9
Rogliano, France 21 F13
Rogliano, Italy 31 C9
Rogoaguado, L., Bolivia 124 F5
Rogoźno, Poland 45 F3
Rogue →, U.S.A. 114 E1
Rohan, France 18 D4
Róhda, Greece 36 A3
Rohnert Park, U.S.A. 116 G4
Rohri, Pakistan 68 F3
Rohri Canal, Pakistan 68 F3
Rohtak, India 68 E7
Roi Et, Thailand 64 D4
Roja, Latvia 9 H20
Rojas, Argentina 126 C3
Rojişte, Romania 43 F8
Rojo, C., Mexico 119 C5
Rokan →, Indonesia 62 D2
Rokel →, S. Leone 82 D2
Rokiškis, Lithuania 9 J21
Rokitno, Russia 47 G8
Rokycany, Czech Rep. 26 B6
Rolândia, Brazil 127 A5
Rolla, U.S.A. 113 G9
Rolleston, Australia 94 C4
Rollingstone, Australia 94 B4
Rom, Sudan 81 F3
Roma, Australia 95 D4
Roma, Italy 29 G9
Roma, Sweden 11 G12
Roma, U.S.A. 113 M5
Romain C., U.S.A. 109 J6
Romaine, Canada 103 B7
Romaine →, Canada 103 B7
Roman, Bulgaria 40 C7
Roman, Romania 43 D11
Roman-Kosh, Gora, Ukraine 47 K8
Romanche →, France 21 C9
Romang, Indonesia 63 F7
Români, Egypt 75 E1
Romania ■, Europe 43 D10
Romanija, Bos.-H. 42 G3
Romano, Cayo, Cuba 120 B4
Romanovka = Basarabeasca, Moldova 43 D13
Romans-sur-Isère, France 21 C9
Romanshorn, Switz. 25 H5
Rombari, Sudan 81 G3
Romblon, Phil. 61 E5
Rome = Roma, Italy 29 G9
Rome, Ga., U.S.A. 109 H3
Rome, N.Y., U.S.A. 111 C9
Rome, Pa., U.S.A. 111 E8
Rometta, Italy 31 D8
Romilly-sur-Seine, France 19 D10
Romney, U.S.A. 108 F6
Romney Marsh, U.K. 13 F8
Romny, Ukraine 47 G7
Rømø, Denmark 11 J2
Romodan, Ukraine 47 G7
Romodanovo, Russia 48 C7
Romont, Switz. 25 J2
Romorantin-Lanthenay, France 19 E8
Romsdalen, Norway 9 E12
Romsey, U.K. 13 G6
Ron, Vietnam 64 D6
Rona, U.K. 14 D3
Ronan, U.S.A. 114 C6
Roncador, Cayos, Caribbean 120 D3
Roncador, Serra do, Brazil 125 F8
Ronciglione, Italy 29 F9
Ronco →, Italy 29 D9
Ronda, Spain 35 J5
Ronda, Serranía de, Spain 35 J5
Rondane, Norway 9 F13
Rondônia □, Brazil 124 F6
Rondonópolis, Brazil 125 G8
Rong, Koh, Cambodia 65 G4
Rong Jiang →, China 58 E7
Rong Xian, Guangxi Zhuangzu, China 59 F8
Rong Xian, Sichuan, China 58 C5

Rong'an, *China* 58 E7
Rongchang, *China* 58 C5
Ronge, L. la, *Canada* 105 B7
Rongjiang, *China* 58 E7
Rongshui, *China* 58 E7
Rønne, *Denmark* 11 J8
Ronne Ice Shelf, *Antarctica* 5 D18
Ronneby, *Sweden* 11 H9
Ronnebyån →, *Sweden* 11 H9
Rönneshytta, *Sweden* 11 F9
Ronsard, C., *Australia* 93 D1
Ronse, *Belgium* 17 D3
Roodepoort, *S. Africa* 89 D4
Roof Butte, *U.S.A.* 115 H9
Rooiboklaagte →, *Namibia* 88 C3
Roorkee, *India* 68 E7
Roosendaal, *Neths.* 17 C4
Roosevelt, *U.S.A.* 114 F8
Roosevelt →, *Brazil* 122 D4
Roosevelt, Mt., *Canada* 104 B3
Roosevelt I., *Antarctica* 5 D12
Ropczyce, *Poland* 45 H8
Roper →, *Australia* 94 A2
Roper Bar, *Australia* 94 A1
Roque Pérez, *Argentina* 126 D4
Roquefort, *France* 20 D3
Roquemaure, *France* 21 D8
Roquetas de Mar, *Spain* 33 J2
Roquetes, *Spain* 32 E5
Roquevaire, *France* 21 E9
Roraima □, *Brazil* 124 C6
Roraima, Mt., *Venezuela* 122 C4
Røros, *Norway* 9 E14
Rorschach, *Switz.* 25 H5
Rosa, *Zambia* 87 D3
Rosa, L., *Bahamas* 121 B5
Rosa, Monte, *Italy* 28 C4
Rosal de la Frontera, *Spain* 35 H3
Rosalia, *U.S.A.* 114 C5
Rosamond, *U.S.A.* 117 L8
Rosans, *France* 21 D9
Rosario, *Argentina* 126 C3
Rosário, *Brazil* 125 D10
Rosario, *Baja Calif., Mexico* 118 B1
Rosario, *Sinaloa, Mexico* 118 C3
Rosario, *Paraguay* 126 A4
Rosario de la Frontera, *Argentina* 126 B3
Rosario de Lerma, *Argentina* 126 A2
Rosario del Tala, *Argentina* 126 C4
Rosário do Sul, *Brazil* 127 C5
Rosarito, *Mexico* 117 N9
Rosarno, *Italy* 31 D8
Rosas = Roses, *Spain* 32 C8
Roscoe, *U.S.A.* 111 E10
Roscoff, *France* 18 D3
Roscommon, *Ireland* 15 C3
Roscommon □, *Ireland* 15 C3
Roscrea, *Ireland* 15 D4
Rose →, *Australia* 94 A2
Rose Blanche, *Canada* 103 C8
Rose Pt., *Canada* 104 C2
Rose Valley, *Canada* 105 C8
Roseau, *Domin.* 121 C7
Roseau, *U.S.A.* 112 A7
Rosebery, *Australia* 94 G4
Rosebud, *S. Dak., U.S.A.* 112 D4
Rosebud, *Tex., U.S.A.* 113 K6
Roseburg, *U.S.A.* 114 E2
Rosedale, *U.S.A.* 113 J9
Roseland, *U.S.A.* 116 G4
Rosemary, *Canada* 104 C6
Rosenberg, *U.S.A.* 113 L7
Rosendaël, *France* 19 A9
Rosenheim, *Germany* 25 H8
Roses, *Spain* 32 C8
Roses, G. de, *Spain* 32 C8
Roseto degli Abruzzi, *Italy* 29 F11
Rosetown, *Canada* 105 C7
Rosetta = Rashîd, *Egypt* 80 H7
Roseville, *Calif., U.S.A.* 116 G5
Roseville, *Mich., U.S.A.* 110 D2
Rosewood, *Australia* 95 D5
Roshkhvär, *Iran* 71 C8
Rosières-en-Santerre, *France* 19 C9
Rosignano Maríttimo, *Italy* 28 E7
Rosignol, *Guyana* 124 B7
Roşiori de Vede, *Romania* 43 F10
Rositsa, *Bulgaria* 41 C11
Rositsa →, *Bulgaria* 41 C9
Roskilde, *Denmark* 11 J6
Roskilde Amtskommune □, *Denmark* 11 J6
Roskovec, *Albania* 40 F3
Roslavl, *Russia* 46 F7
Rosmaninhal, *Portugal* 34 F3
Rosmead, *S. Africa* 88 E4
Røsnæs, *Denmark* 11 J4
Rosolini, *Italy* 31 F7
Rosporden, *France* 18 E3
Ross, *Australia* 94 G4
Ross, *N.Z.* 91 K3
Ross Béthio, *Mauritania* 82 B1
Ross I., *Antarctica* 5 D11
Ross Ice Shelf, *Antarctica* 5 E12
Ross L., *U.S.A.* 114 B3
Ross-on-Wye, *U.K.* 13 F5
Ross River, *Australia* 94 C1
Ross River, *Canada* 104 A2
Ross Sea, *Antarctica* 5 D11
Rossall Pt., *U.K.* 12 D4
Rossan Pt., *Ireland* 15 B3
Rossano, *Italy* 31 C9
Rossburn, *Canada* 105 C8
Rosseau, *Canada* 110 A5
Rosseau L., *Canada* 110 A5
Rosses, The, *Ireland* 15 A3
Rossignol, L., *Canada* 102 B5
Rossignol Res., *Canada* 103 D6
Rossland, *Canada* 104 D5
Rosslare, *Ireland* 15 D5
Rosslau, *Germany* 24 D8
Rosso, *Mauritania* 82 B1
Rosso, C., *France* 21 F12
Rossosh, *Russia* 47 G10
Røssvatnet, *Norway* 8 D16
Røst, *Norway* 8 C15
Rosthern, *Canada* 105 C7
Rostock, *Germany* 24 A8
Rostov, *Don, Russia* 47 J10
Rostov, *Yaroslavl, Russia* 46 D10
Rostrenen, *France* 18 D3
Roswell, *Ga., U.S.A.* 109 H3
Roswell, *N. Mex., U.S.A.* 113 J2
Rota, *Spain* 35 J4
Rotan, *U.S.A.* 113 J4
Rotenburg, *Hessen, Germany* 24 E5
Rotenburg, *Niedersachsen, Germany* 24 B5
Roth, *Germany* 25 F7
Rothaargebirge, *Germany* 24 D4
Rothenburg ob der Tauber, *Germany* 25 F6
Rother →, *U.K.* 13 G8
Rotherham, *U.K.* 12 D6
Rothes, *U.K.* 14 D5
Rothesay, *Canada* 103 C6
Rothesay, *U.K.* 14 F3
Roti, *Indonesia* 63 F6
Rotja, Pta., *Spain* 33 G6
Roto, *Australia* 95 E4
Rotoroa, L., *N.Z.* 91 J4
Rotorua, *N.Z.* 91 H6
Rotorua, L., *N.Z.* 91 H6
Rott →, *Germany* 25 G9
Rottenburg, *Germany* 25 G4
Rottenmann, *Austria* 26 D7
Rotterdam, *Neths.* 17 C4
Rotterdam, *U.S.A.* 111 D10
Rottne, *Sweden* 11 G8
Rottnest I., *Australia* 93 F2
Rottumeroog, *Neths.* 17 A6
Rottweil, *Germany* 25 G4
Rotuma, *Fiji* 96 J9
Roubaix, *France* 19 B10
Roudnice nad Labem, *Czech Rep.* 26 A7
Rouen, *France* 18 C8
Rouergue, *France* 20 D5
Rouillac, *France* 20 C3
Rouleau, *Canada* 105 C8
Round Mountain, *U.S.A.* 114 G5
Round Mt., *Australia* 95 E5
Round Rock, *U.S.A.* 113 K6
Roundup, *U.S.A.* 114 C9
Rousay, *U.K.* 14 B5
Rouses Point, *U.S.A.* 111 B11
Rouseville, *U.S.A.* 110 E5
Roussillon, *Isère, France* 21 C8
Roussillon, *Pyrénées-Or., France* 20 F6
Rouxville, *S. Africa* 88 E4
Rouyn-Noranda, *Canada* 102 C4
Rovaniemi, *Finland* 8 C21
Rovato, *Italy* 28 C7
Rovenki, *Ukraine* 47 H10
Rovereto, *Italy* 28 C8
Rovigo, *Italy* 29 C8
Rovinj, *Croatia* 29 C10
Rovno = Rivne, *Ukraine* 47 G4
Rovnoye, *Russia* 48 E8
Rovuma = Ruvuma →, *Tanzania* 87 E5
Row'ān, *Iran* 71 C6
Rowena, *Australia* 95 D4
Rowley Shoals, *Australia* 92 C2
Roxa, *Guinea-Biss.* 82 C1
Roxas, *Capiz, Phil.* 61 F5
Roxas, *Isabela, Phil.* 61 C4
Roxas, *Mind. Or., Phil.* 61 E4
Roxboro, *U.S.A.* 109 G6
Roxburgh, *N.Z.* 91 L2
Roxbury, *U.S.A.* 110 F7
Roxen, *Sweden* 11 F9
Roy, *Mont., U.S.A.* 114 C9
Roy, *N. Mex., U.S.A.* 113 H2
Roy, *Utah, U.S.A.* 114 F7
Royal Canal, *Ireland* 15 C4
Royal Leamington Spa, *U.K.* 13 E6
Royal Tunbridge Wells, *U.K.* 13 F8
Royan, *France* 20 C2
Roye, *France* 19 C9
Royston, *U.K.* 13 E7
Rožaj, *Montenegro, Yug.* 40 D4
Różan, *Poland* 45 F8
Rozay-en-Brie, *France* 19 D9
Rozdilna, *Ukraine* 47 J6
Rozhyshche, *Ukraine* 47 G3
Rožmitál pod Třemšínem, *Czech Rep.* 26 B6
Rožňava, *Slovak Rep.* 27 C13
Rozogi, *Poland* 44 E8
Rozoy-sur-Serre, *France* 19 C11
Rozzano, *Italy* 28 C6
Rrësheni, *Albania* 40 E3
Rrogozhino, *Albania* 40 E3
Rtanj, *Serbia, Yug.* 40 C5
Rtishchevo, *Russia* 48 D6
Rúa = A Rúa, *Spain* 34 C3
Ruacaná, *Angola* 88 B1
Ruahine Ra., *N.Z.* 91 H6
Ruapehu, *N.Z.* 91 H5
Ruapuke I., *N.Z.* 91 M2
Ruâq, W. →, *Egypt* 75 F2
Rub' al Khālī, *Si. Arabia* 74 D4
Rubeho Mts., *Tanzania* 86 D4
Rubezhnoye = Rubizhne, *Ukraine* 47 H10
Rubh a' Mhail, *U.K.* 14 F2
Rubha Hunish, *U.K.* 14 D2
Rubha Robhanais = Lewis, Butt of, *U.K.* 14 C2
Rubi, *Spain* 32 D7
Rubicon →, *U.S.A.* 116 G5
Rubicone →, *Italy* 29 D9
Rubik, *Albania* 40 E3
Rubino, *Ivory C.* 82 D4
Rubio, *Venezuela* 124 B4
Rubizhne, *Ukraine* 47 H10
Rubtsovsk, *Russia* 50 D9
Ruby L., *U.S.A.* 114 F6
Ruby Mts., *U.S.A.* 114 F6
Rubyvale, *Australia* 94 C4
Rucheng, *China* 59 E9
Ruciane-Nida, *Poland* 44 E8
Rūd Sar, *Iran* 71 B6
Ruda, *Sweden* 11 G10
Ruda Śląska, *Poland* 45 H5
Rudall, *Australia* 95 E2
Rudall →, *Australia* 92 D3
Rüdersdorf, *Germany* 24 C9
Rudewa, *Tanzania* 87 E3
Rudkøbing, *Denmark* 11 K4
Rudna, *Poland* 45 G3
Rudnik, *Bulgaria* 41 D11
Rudnik, *Poland* 45 H9
Rudnik, *Serbia, Yug.* 40 B4
Rudnya, *Russia* 46 E6
Rudnyy, *Kazakstan* 50 D7
Rudo, *Bos.-H.* 42 G4
Rudolfa, Ostrov, *Russia* 50 A6
Rudolstadt, *Germany* 24 E7
Rudong, *China* 59 A13
Rudozem, *Bulgaria* 41 E8
Rudyard, *U.S.A.* 108 B3
Rue, *France* 19 B8
Rufa'a, *Sudan* 81 E3
Rufiji →, *Tanzania* 86 D4
Rufino, *Argentina* 126 C3
Rufisque, *Senegal* 82 C1
Rufunsa, *Zambia* 87 F2
Rugao, *China* 59 A13
Rugby, *U.K.* 13 E6
Rugby, *U.S.A.* 112 A5
Rügen, *Germany* 24 A9
Rugles, *France* 18 D7
Ruhengeri, *Rwanda* 86 C2
Ruhla, *Germany* 24 E6
Ruhland, *Germany* 24 D9
Ruhnu, *Estonia* 9 H20
Ruhr →, *Germany* 24 D2
Ruhuhu →, *Tanzania* 87 E3
Rui'an, *China* 59 D13
Ruichang, *China* 59 C10
Ruidoso, *U.S.A.* 115 K11
Ruijin, *China* 59 E10
Ruili, *China* 58 E1
Ruivo, Pico, *Madeira* 37 D3
Ruj, *Bulgaria* 40 D6
Rujen, *Macedonia* 40 D6
Rujm Tal'at al Jamā'ah, *Jordan* 75 E4
Ruk, *Pakistan* 68 F3
Rukhla, *Pakistan* 68 C4
Ruki →, *Dem. Rep. of the Congo* 84 E3
Rukwa □, *Tanzania* 86 D3
Rukwa, L., *Tanzania* 86 D3
Rulhieres, C., *Australia* 92 B4
Rum = Rhum, *U.K.* 14 E2
Rum Cay, *Bahamas* 121 B5
Rum Jungle, *Australia* 92 B5
Ruma, *Serbia, Yug.* 42 E4
Rumāḩ, *Si. Arabia* 70 E5
Rumania = Romania ■, *Europe* 43 D10
Rumaylah, *Iraq* 70 D5
Rumbêk, *Sudan* 81 F2
Rumburk, *Czech Rep.* 26 A7
Rumford, *U.S.A.* 109 C10
Rumia, *Poland* 44 D5
Rumilly, *France* 21 C9
Rumoi, *Japan* 54 C10
Rumonge, *Burundi* 86 C2
Rumson, *U.S.A.* 111 F11
Rumuruti, *Kenya* 86 B4
Runan, *China* 56 H8
Runanga, *N.Z.* 91 K3
Runaway, C., *N.Z.* 91 G6
Runcorn, *U.K.* 12 D5
Rundu, *Namibia* 88 B2
Rungwa, *Tanzania* 86 D3
Rungwa →, *Tanzania* 86 D3
Rungwe, *Tanzania* 87 D3
Rungwe, Mt., *Tanzania* 84 F6
Runka, *Nigeria* 83 C6
Runn, *Sweden* 10 D9
Runton Ra., *Australia* 92 D3
Ruokolahti, *Finland* 46 B5
Ruoqiang, *China* 60 C3
Rupa, *India* 67 F18
Rupar, *India* 68 D7
Rupat, *Indonesia* 62 D2
Rupea, *Romania* 43 D10
Rupen →, *India* 68 H4
Rupert, *U.S.A.* 114 E7
Rupert →, *Canada* 102 B4
Rupert B., *Canada* 102 B4
Rupert House = Waskaganish, *Canada* 102 B4
Rupsa, *India* 69 J12
Rur →, *Germany* 24 D1
Rurrenabaque, *Bolivia* 124 F5
Rus →, *Spain* 33 F2
Rusambo, *Zimbabwe* 87 F3
Rusape, *Zimbabwe* 87 F3
Ruschuk = Ruse, *Bulgaria* 41 C9
Ruse, *Bulgaria* 41 C9
Ruse □, *Bulgaria* 41 C10
Ruşeţu, *Romania* 43 F12
Rush, *Ireland* 15 C5
Rushan, *China* 57 F11
Rushden, *U.K.* 13 E7
Rushmore, Mt., *U.S.A.* 112 D3
Rushville, *Ill., U.S.A.* 112 E9
Rushville, *Ind., U.S.A.* 108 F3
Rushville, *Nebr., U.S.A.* 112 D3
Russas, *Brazil* 125 D11
Russell, *Canada* 105 C8
Russell, *Kans., U.S.A.* 112 F5
Russell, *N.Y., U.S.A.* 111 B9
Russell, *Pa., U.S.A.* 110 E5
Russell L., *Man., Canada* 105 B8
Russell L., *N.W.T., Canada* 104 A5
Russellkonda, *India* 67 K14
Russellville, *Ala., U.S.A.* 109 H2
Russellville, *Ark., U.S.A.* 113 H8
Russellville, *Ky., U.S.A.* 109 G2
Rüsselsheim, *Germany* 25 F4
Russi, *Italy* 29 D9
Russia ■, *Eurasia* 51 C11
Russian →, *U.S.A.* 116 G3
Russkoye Ustie, *Russia* 4 B15
Rust, *Austria* 27 D9
Rustam, *Pakistan* 68 B5
Rustam Shahr, *Pakistan* 68 F2
Rustavi, *Georgia* 49 K7
Rustenburg, *S. Africa* 88 D4
Ruston, *U.S.A.* 113 J8
Rutana, *Burundi* 86 C3
Rute, *Spain* 35 H6
Ruteng, *Indonesia* 63 F6
Ruth, *U.S.A.* 110 C2
Rutherford, *U.S.A.* 116 G4
Rutland, *U.S.A.* 111 C12
Rutland □, *U.K.* 13 E7
Rutland Water, *U.K.* 13 E7
Rutledge →, *Canada* 105 A6
Rutledge L., *Canada* 105 A6
Rutqa, W. →, *Syria* 73 E9
Rutshuru, *Dem. Rep. of the Congo* 86 C2
Ruvo di Púglia, *Italy* 31 A9
Ruvu, *Tanzania* 86 D4
Ruvu →, *Tanzania* 86 D4
Ruvuma □, *Tanzania* 87 E4
Ruvuma →, *Tanzania* 87 E5
Ruwais, *U.A.E.* 71 E7
Ruwenzori, *Africa* 86 B2
Ruya →, *Zimbabwe* 89 B5
Ruyigi, *Burundi* 86 C3
Ruyuan, *China* 59 E9
Ruzayevka, *Russia* 48 C7
Rŭzhevo Konare, *Bulgaria* 41 D8
Ružomberok, *Slovak Rep.* 27 B12
Rwanda ■, *Africa* 86 C3
Ryakhovo, *Bulgaria* 41 C10
Ryan, L., *U.K.* 14 G3
Ryazan, *Russia* 46 E10
Ryazhsk, *Russia* 46 F11
Rybache = Rybachye, *Kazakstan* 50 E9
Rybachye, *Kazakstan* 50 E9
Rybinsk, *Russia* 46 C10
Rybinskoye Vdkhr., *Russia* 46 C10
Rybnik, *Poland* 45 H5
Rybnitsa = Râbniţa, *Moldova* 43 C14
Rybnoye, *Russia* 46 E10
Rychnov nad Kněžnou, *Czech Rep.* 27 A9
Rychwał, *Poland* 45 F5
Rycroft, *Canada* 104 B5
Ryd, *Sweden* 11 H8
Rydaholm, *Sweden* 11 H8
Ryde, *U.K.* 13 G6
Ryderwood, *U.S.A.* 116 D3
Rydzyna, *Poland* 45 G3
Rye, *U.K.* 13 G8
Rye →, *U.K.* 12 C7
Rye Bay, *U.K.* 13 G8
Rye Patch Reservoir, *U.S.A.* 114 F4
Ryegate, *U.S.A.* 114 C9
Ryki, *Poland* 45 G8
Ryley, *Canada* 104 C6
Rylsk, *Russia* 47 G8
Rylstone, *Australia* 95 E4
Rymanów, *Poland* 45 J8
Ryn, *Poland* 44 E8
Ryn Peski, *Kazakstan* 49 G9
Ryōtsu, *Japan* 54 E9
Rypin, *Poland* 45 E6
Ryssby, *Sweden* 11 H8
Ryūgasaki, *Japan* 55 G10
Ryūkyū Is. = Ryūkyū-rettō, *Japan* 55 M3
Ryūkyū-rettō, *Japan* 55 M3
Rzepin, *Poland* 45 F1
Rzeszów, *Poland* 45 H8
Rzhev, *Russia* 46 D8

S

Sa, *Thailand* 64 C3
Sa Canal, *Spain* 37 C7
Sa Conillera, *Spain* 37 C7
Sa Dec, *Vietnam* 65 G5
Sa Dragonera, *Spain* 37 B9
Sa Mesquida, *Spain* 37 B11
Sa Pobla, *Spain* 32 F8
Sa Savina, *Spain* 37 C7
Sa'ādatābād, *Fārs, Iran* 71 D7
Sa'ādatābād, *Hormozgān, Iran* 71 D7
Sa'ādatābād, *Kermān, Iran* 71 D7
Saale →, *Germany* 24 D7
Saaler Bodden, *Germany* 24 A8
Saalfeld, *Germany* 24 E7
Saalfelden, *Austria* 26 D5
Saane →, *Switz.* 25 H3
Saar →, *Europe* 17 E6
Saarbrücken, *Germany* 25 F2
Saarburg, *Germany* 25 F2
Saaremaa, *Estonia* 9 G20
Saarijärvi, *Finland* 9 E21
Saariselkä, *Finland* 8 B23
Saarland □, *Germany* 25 F2
Saarlouis, *Germany* 25 F2
Sab 'Ābar, *Syria* 70 C3
Saba, *W. Indies* 121 C7
Šabac, *Serbia, Yug.* 40 B3
Sabadell, *Spain* 32 D7
Sabah □, *Malaysia* 62 C5
Sabak Bernam, *Malaysia* 65 L3
Sabalān, Kūhhā-ye, *Iran* 70 B5
Sabalana, Kepulauan, *Indonesia* 63 F5
Sábana de la Mar, *Dom. Rep.* 121 C6
Sábanalarga, *Colombia* 124 A4
Sabang, *Indonesia* 62 C1
Săbăoani, *Romania* 43 C11
Sabará, *Brazil* 125 G10
Sabarmati →, *India* 68 H5
Sabattis, *U.S.A.* 111 B10
Sabáudia, *Italy* 30 A6
Saberania, *Indonesia* 63 E9
Sabhah, *Libya* 79 C8
Sabi →, *India* 68 E7
Sabidana, J., *Sudan* 80 D4
Sabie, *S. Africa* 89 D5
Sabinal, *Mexico* 118 A3
Sabinal, *U.S.A.* 113 L5
Sabiñánigo, *Spain* 32 C4
Sabinar, Punta del, *Spain* 33 J2
Sabinas, *Mexico* 118 B4
Sabinas →, *Mexico* 118 B4
Sabinas Hidalgo, *Mexico* 118 B4
Sabine →, *U.S.A.* 113 L8
Sabine L., *U.S.A.* 113 L8
Sabine Pass, *U.S.A.* 113 L8
Sabinov, *Slovak Rep.* 27 B14
Sabinsville, *U.S.A.* 110 E7
Sabirabad, *Azerbaijan* 49 K9
Sabkhet el Bardawîl, *Egypt* 75 D2
Sablayan, *Phil.* 61 E4
Sable, *Canada* 103 A6
Sable, C., *Canada* 103 D6
Sable, C., *U.S.A.* 107 E10
Sable I., *Canada* 103 D8
Sablé-sur-Sarthe, *France* 18 E6
Sabonkafi, *Niger* 83 C6
Sabor →, *Portugal* 34 D3
Sabou, *Burkina Faso* 82 C4
Sabres, *France* 20 D3
Sabrina Coast, *Antarctica* 5 C9
Sabugal, *Portugal* 34 E3
Sabulubbek, *Indonesia* 62 E1
Sabuncu, *Turkey* 39 B12
Sabzevār, *Iran* 71 B8
Sabzvārān, *Iran* 71 D8
Sac City, *U.S.A.* 112 D7
Sacedón, *Spain* 32 E2
Săcele, *Romania* 43 E10
Sachigo →, *Canada* 102 A2
Sachigo, L., *Canada* 102 B1
Sachkhere, *Georgia* 49 J6
Sachsen □, *Germany* 24 E9
Sachsen-Anhalt □, *Germany* 24 D7
Sacile, *Italy* 29 C9
Sackets Harbor, *U.S.A.* 111 C8
Sackville, *Canada* 103 C7
Saco, *Maine, U.S.A.* 109 D10
Saco, *Mont., U.S.A.* 114 B10
Sacramento, *U.S.A.* 116 G5
Sacramento →, *U.S.A.* 116 G5
Sacramento Mts., *U.S.A.* 115 K11
Sacramento Valley, *U.S.A.* 116 G5
Sacratif, C., *Spain* 35 J7
Săcueni, *Romania* 42 C7
Sada, *Spain* 34 B2
Sada-Misaki, *Japan* 55 H6
Sádaba, *Spain* 32 C3
Sadabad, *India* 68 F8
Sadani, *Tanzania* 86 D4
Sadao, *Thailand* 65 J3
Sadd el Aali, *Egypt* 80 C3
Saddle Mt., *U.S.A.* 116 E3
Sade, *Nigeria* 83 C7
Sadimi, *Dem. Rep. of the Congo* 87 D1
Sadiola, *Mali* 82 C2
Sa'dīyah, Hawr as, *Iraq* 73 F12
Sado, *Japan* 54 F9
Sado →, *Portugal* 35 G2
Sadon, *Burma* 67 G20
Sadon, *Russia* 49 J6
Sadra, *India* 68 H5
Sadri, *India* 68 G5
Sæby, *Denmark* 11 G4
Saegertown, *U.S.A.* 110 E4
Saelices, *Spain* 32 F2
Safaalan, *Turkey* 41 E12
Safaga, *Egypt* 80 B3
Şafājah, *Si. Arabia* 70 E3
Šafárikovo = Tornal'a, *Slovak Rep.* 27 C13
Säffle, *Sweden* 10 E6
Safford, *U.S.A.* 115 K9
Saffron Walden, *U.K.* 13 E8
Safi, *Morocco* 78 B4
Şafīābād, *Iran* 71 B8
Safīd Dasht, *Iran* 71 C6
Safīd Kūh, *Afghan.* 66 B3
Safīd Rūd →, *Iran* 71 B6
Safipur, *India* 69 F9
Safonovo, *Russia* 46 E7
Safranbolu, *Turkey* 72 B5
Saft Rashîn, *Egypt* 80 J7
Safwān, *Iraq* 70 D5
Sag Harbor, *U.S.A.* 111 F12
Saga, *Japan* 55 H5

Saga □, *Japan* 55 H5
Sagae, *Japan* 54 E10
Sagala, *Mali* 82 C3
Sagamore, *U.S.A.* 110 F5
Sagar, *Karnataka, India* 66 M9
Sagar, *Mad. P., India* 69 H8
Sagara, L., *Tanzania* 86 D3
Sagay, *Phil.* 61 F5
Saginaw, *U.S.A.* 108 D4
Saginaw →, *U.S.A.* 108 D4
Saginaw B., *U.S.A.* 108 D4
Sagleipie, *Liberia* 82 D3
Saglouc = Salluit, *Canada* 101 B12
Sagŏ-ri, *S. Korea* 57 G14
Sagone, *France* 21 F12
Sagone, G. de, *France* 21 F12
Sagres, *Portugal* 35 J2
Sagua la Grande, *Cuba* 120 B3
Saguache, *U.S.A.* 115 G10
Saguaro Nat. Park, *U.S.A.* 115 K8
Saguenay →, *Canada* 103 C5
Sagunt, *Spain* 32 F4
Sagunto = Sagunt, *Spain* 32 F4
Sagwara, *India* 68 H6
Sahaba, *Sudan* 80 D3
Sahagún, *Spain* 34 C5
Saḩam al Jawlān, *Syria* 75 C4
Sahamandrevo, *Madag.* 89 C8
Sahand, Kūh-e, *Iran* 70 B5
Sahara, *Africa* 78 D6
Saharan Atlas = Saharien, Atlas, *Algeria* 78 B6
Saharanpur, *India* 68 E7
Saharien, Atlas, *Algeria* 78 B6
Saharsa, *India* 69 G12
Sahasinaka, *Madag.* 89 C8
Sahaswan, *India* 69 E8
Sahel, *Africa* 78 E5
Sahel, Canal du, *Mali* 82 C3
Sahibganj, *India* 69 G12
Sāḩilīyah, *Iraq* 70 C4
Sahiwal, *Pakistan* 68 D5
Şahneh, *Iran* 70 C5
Sahuaripa, *Mexico* 118 B3
Sahuarita, *U.S.A.* 115 L8
Sahuayo, *Mexico* 118 C4
Šahy, *Slovak Rep.* 27 C11
Sai →, *India* 69 G10
Sai Buri, *Thailand* 65 J3
Sa'id Bundâs, *Sudan* 81 F1
Sa'īdābād, *Kermān, Iran* 71 D7
Sa'īdābād, *Semnān, Iran* 71 B7
Sa'īdīyeh, *Iran* 71 B6
Saidpur, *Bangla.* 67 G16
Saidpur, *India* 69 G10
Saidu, *Pakistan* 69 B5
Saignes, *France* 20 C6
Saigon = Phanh Bho Ho Chi Minh, *Vietnam* 65 G6
Saijō, *Japan* 55 H6
Saikanosy Masoala, *Madag.* 89 B9
Saikhoa Ghat, *India* 67 F19
Saiki, *Japan* 55 H5
Sailana, *India* 68 H6
Saillans, *France* 21 D9
Sailolof, *Indonesia* 63 E8
Saimaa, *Finland* 9 F23
Saimbeyli, *Turkey* 72 D7
Şa'in Dezh, *Iran* 70 B5
St. Abb's Head, *U.K.* 14 F6
St-Affrique, *France* 20 E6
St-Agrève, *France* 21 C8
St-Aignan, *France* 18 E8
St. Alban's, *Canada* 103 C8
St. Albans, *U.K.* 13 F7
St. Albans, *Vt., U.S.A.* 111 B11
St. Albans, *W. Va., U.S.A.* 108 F5
St. Alban's Head, *U.K.* 13 G5
St. Albert, *Canada* 104 C6
St-Amand-en-Puisaye, *France* 19 E10
St-Amand-les-Eaux, *France* 19 B10
St-Amand-Montrond, *France* 19 F9
St-Amarin, *France* 19 E14
St-Amour, *France* 19 F12
St-André-de-Cubzac, *France* 20 D3
St-André-les-Alpes, *France* 21 E10
St. Andrew's, *Canada* 103 C8
St. Andrews, *U.K.* 14 E6
St-Anicet, *Canada* 111 A10
St. Ann B., *Canada* 103 C7
St. Ann's Bay, *Jamaica* 120 C4
St. Anthony, *Canada* 103 B8
St. Anthony, *U.S.A.* 114 E8
St. Antoine, *Canada* 103 C7
St-Antonin-Noble-Val, *France* 20 D5
St. Arnaud, *Australia* 95 F3
St-Astier, *France* 20 C4
St-Aubin-du-Cormier, *France* 18 D5
St-Augustin →, *Canada* 103 B8
St-Augustin-Saguenay, *Canada* 103 B8
St. Augustine, *U.S.A.* 109 L5
St-Aulaye, *France* 20 C4
St. Austell, *U.K.* 13 G3
St-Avold, *France* 19 C13
St. Barbe, *Canada* 103 B8
St-Barthélemy, *W. Indies* 121 C7
St-Béat, *France* 20 F4
St. Bees Hd., *U.K.* 12 C4
St-Benoît-du-Sault, *France* 20 B5
St-Bonnet, *France* 21 D10
St-Brévin-les-Pins, *France* 18 E4
St-Brice-en-Coglès, *France* 18 D5
St. Bride's, *Canada* 103 C9
St. Brides B., *U.K.* 13 F2
St-Brieuc, *France* 18 D4
St-Calais, *France* 18 E7
St-Cast-le-Guildo, *France* 18 D4
St. Catharines, *Canada* 102 D4
St. Catherines I., *U.S.A.* 109 K5
St. Catherine's Pt., *U.K.* 13 G6
St-Céré, *France* 20 D5
St-Cergue, *Switz.* 25 J2
St-Cernin, *France* 20 C6
St-Chamond, *France* 21 C8
St. Charles, *Ill., U.S.A.* 108 E1
St. Charles, *Mo., U.S.A.* 112 F9
St. Charles, *Va., U.S.A.* 108 F7
St-Chély-d'Apcher, *France* 20 D7
St-Chinian, *France* 20 E6
St. Christopher-Nevis = St. Kitts & Nevis ■, *W. Indies* 121 C7
St-Ciers-sur-Gironde, *France* 20 C3
St. Clair, *Mich., U.S.A.* 110 D2
St. Clair, *Pa., U.S.A.* 111 F8
St. Clair →, *U.S.A.* 110 D2
St. Clair, L., *Canada* 102 D3
St. Clair, L., *U.S.A.* 110 D2
St. Clairsville, *U.S.A.* 110 F4
St-Claud, *France* 20 C4
St. Claude, *Canada* 105 D9
St-Claude, *France* 19 F12
St-Clet, *Canada* 111 A10
St. Cloud, *Fla., U.S.A.* 109 L5
St. Cloud, *Minn., U.S.A.* 112 C7
St. Cricq, C., *Australia* 93 E1
St. Croix, *Virgin Is.* 121 C7
St. Croix →, *U.S.A.* 112 C8
St. Croix Falls, *U.S.A.* 112 C8
St-Cyprien, *France* 20 F7
St-Cyr-sur-Mer, *France* 21 E9
St. David's, *Canada* 103 C8
St. David's, *U.K.* 13 F2
St. David's Head, *U.K.* 13 F2
St-Denis, *France* 19 D9
St-Dié, *France* 19 D13
St-Dizier, *France* 19 D11
St-Égrève, *France* 21 C9
St. Elias, Mt., *U.S.A.* 100 B5
St. Elias Mts., *Canada* 104 A1
St. Elias Mts., *U.S.A.* 100 C6
St-Eloy-les-Mines, *France* 19 F9
St-Émilion, *France* 20 D3
St-Étienne, *France* 21 C8
St-Étienne-de-Tinée, *France* 21 D10
St-Étienne-du-Rouvray, *France* 18 C8
St. Eugène, *Canada* 111 A10
St. Eustatius, *W. Indies* 121 C7
St-Fargeau, *France* 19 E10
St-Félicien, *Canada* 102 C5
St-Florent, *France* 21 F13
St-Florent, G. de, *France* 21 F13
St-Florent-sur-Cher, *France* 19 F9
St-Florentin, *France* 19 E10
St-Flour, *France* 20 C7
St. Francis, *U.S.A.* 112 F4
St. Francis →, *U.S.A.* 113 H9
St. Francis, C., *S. Africa* 88 E3
St. Francisville, *U.S.A.* 113 K9
St-François, L., *Canada* 111 A10
St-Fulgent, *France* 18 F5
St-Gabriel, *Canada* 102 C5
St. Gallen = Sankt Gallen, *Switz.* 25 H5
St-Galmier, *France* 19 G11
St-Gaudens, *France* 20 E4
St-Gaultier, *France* 18 F8
St-Gengoux-le-National, *France* 19 F11
St-Geniez-d'Olt, *France* 20 D6
St. George, *Australia* 95 D4
St. George, *Canada* 103 C6
St. George, *S.C., U.S.A.* 109 J5
St. George, *Utah, U.S.A.* 115 H7
St. George, C., *Canada* 103 C8
St. George, C., *U.S.A.* 109 L3
St. George Ra., *Australia* 92 C4
St. George's, *Canada* 103 C8
St-Georges, *Canada* 103 C5
St. George's, *Grenada* 121 D7
St. George's B., *Canada* 103 C8
St. Georges Basin, *N.S.W., Australia* 95 F5
St. Georges Basin, *W. Austral., Australia* 92 C4
St. George's Channel, *Europe* 15 E6
St. Georges Hd., *Australia* 95 F5
St-Georges-lès-Baillargeaux, *France* 20 B4
St-Germain-de-Calberte, *France* 20 D7
St-Germain-en-Laye, *France* 19 D9
St-Germain-Lembron, *France* 20 C7
St-Gervais-d'Auvergne, *France* 19 F9
St-Gervais-les-Bains, *France* 21 C10
St-Gildas, Pte. de, *France* 18 E4
St-Gilles, *France* 21 E8
St-Girons, *Ariège, France* 20 F5
St-Girons, *Landes, France* 20 E2
St. Gotthard P. = San Gottardo, P. del, *Switz.* 25 J4
St. Helena, *U.S.A.* 114 G2
St. Helena ■, *Atl. Oc.* 76 H3
St. Helena, Mt., *U.S.A.* 116 G4
St. Helena B., *S. Africa* 88 E2
St. Helens, *Australia* 94 G4
St. Helens, *U.K.* 12 D5
St. Helens, *U.S.A.* 116 E4
St. Helens, Mt., *U.S.A.* 116 D4
St. Helier, *U.K.* 13 H5
St-Herblain, *France* 18 E5
St-Hilaire-du-Harcouët, *France* 18 D5
St-Hippolyte, *France* 19 E13
St-Hippolyte-du-Fort, *France* 20 E7
St-Honoré-les-Bains, *France* 19 F10
St-Hubert, *Belgium* 17 D5
St-Hyacinthe, *Canada* 102 C5
St. Ignace, *U.S.A.* 108 C3
St. Ignace I., *Canada* 102 C2
St. Ignatius, *U.S.A.* 114 C6
St-Imier, *Switz.* 25 H2
St. Ives, *U.K.* 13 G2
St-James, *France* 18 D5
St. James, *U.S.A.* 112 D7
St-Jean →, *Canada* 103 B7
St-Jean, L., *Canada* 103 C5
St-Jean-d'Angély, *France* 20 C3
St-Jean-de-Braye, *France* 19 E8
St-Jean-de-Luz, *France* 20 E2
St-Jean-de-Maurienne, *France* 21 C10
St-Jean-de-Monts, *France* 18 F4
St-Jean-du-Gard, *France* 20 D7
St-Jean-en-Royans, *France* 21 C9
St-Jean-Pied-de-Port, *France* 20 E2
St-Jean-Port-Joli, *Canada* 103 C5
St-Jean-sur-Richelieu, *Canada* 102 C5
St-Jérôme, *Canada* 102 C5
St. John, *Canada* 103 C6
St. John, *U.S.A.* 113 G5
St. John →, *Liberia* 82 D2
St. John →, *U.S.A.* 109 C12
St. John, C., *Canada* 103 C8
St. John's, *Antigua* 121 C7
St. John's, *Canada* 103 C9
St. Johns, *Ariz., U.S.A.* 115 J9
St. Johns, *Mich., U.S.A.* 108 D3
St. Johns →, *U.S.A.* 109 K5
St. John's Pt., *Ireland* 15 B3
St. Johnsbury, *U.S.A.* 111 B12
St. Johnsville, *U.S.A.* 111 D10
St. Joseph, *La., U.S.A.* 113 K9
St. Joseph, *Mo., U.S.A.* 112 F7
St. Joseph →, *U.S.A.* 108 D2
St. Joseph, I., *Canada* 102 C3
St. Joseph, L., *Canada* 102 B1
St-Jovite, *Canada* 102 C5
St-Juéry, *France* 20 E6
St-Julien-Chapteuil, *France* 21 C8
St-Julien-de-Vouvantes, *France* 18 E5
St-Julien-en-Genevois, *France* 19 F13
St-Junien, *France* 20 C4
St-Just-en-Chaussée, *France* 19 C9
St-Just-en-Chevalet, *France* 20 C7
St. Kilda, *N.Z.* 91 L3
St. Kitts & Nevis ■, *W. Indies* 121 C7
St. Laurent, *Canada* 105 C9
St-Laurent-de-la-Salanque, *France* 20 F6
St-Laurent-du-Pont, *France* 21 C9
St-Laurent-en-Grandvaux, *France* 19 F12
St-Laurent-et-Benon, *France* 20 C3
St. Lawrence, *Australia* 94 C4
St. Lawrence, *Canada* 103 C8
St. Lawrence →, *Canada* 103 C6
St. Lawrence, Gulf of, *Canada* 103 C7
St. Lawrence I., *U.S.A.* 100 B3
St. Leonard, *Canada* 103 C6
St-Léonard-de-Noblat, *France* 20 C5
St. Lewis →, *Canada* 103 B8
St-Lô, *France* 18 C5
St-Louis, *France* 19 E14
St. Louis, *Senegal* 82 B1
St. Louis, *U.S.A.* 112 F9
St. Louis →, *U.S.A.* 112 B8
St-Loup-sur-Semouse, *France* 19 E13
St. Lucia ■, *W. Indies* 121 D7
St. Lucia, L., *S. Africa* 89 D5
St. Lucia Channel, *W. Indies* 121 D7
St. Maarten, *W. Indies* 121 C7
St. Magnus B., *U.K.* 14 A7
St-Maixent-l'École, *France* 20 B3
St-Malo, *France* 18 D4
St-Malo, G. de, *France* 18 D4
St-Mandrier-sur-Mer, *France* 21 E9
St-Marc, *Haiti* 121 C5
St-Marcellin, *France* 21 C9
St-Marcouf, Îs., *France* 18 C5
St. Maries, *U.S.A.* 114 C5
St-Martin, *W. Indies* 121 C7
St. Martin, L., *Canada* 105 C9
St-Martin-de-Crau, *France* 21 E8
St-Martin-de-Ré, *France* 20 B2
St-Martin-d'Hères, *France* 21 C9
St-Martin-Vésubie, *France* 21 D11
St-Martory, *France* 20 E4
St. Mary Pk., *Australia* 95 E2
St. Marys, *Australia* 94 G4
St. Marys, *Canada* 110 C3
St. Mary's, *Corn., U.K.* 13 H1
St. Mary's, *Orkney, U.K.* 14 C6
St. Marys, *Ga., U.S.A.* 109 K5
St. Marys, *Pa., U.S.A.* 110 E6
St. Mary's, C., *Canada* 103 C9
St. Mary's B., *Canada* 103 C9
St. Marys Bay, *Canada* 103 D6
St-Mathieu, Pte., *France* 18 D2
St. Matthew I., *U.S.A.* 100 B2
St. Matthews, I. = Zadetkyi Kyun, *Burma* 65 G1
St-Maurice →, *Canada* 102 C5
St-Maximin-la-Ste-Baume, *France* 21 E9
St-Médard-en-Jalles, *France* 20 D3
St-Méen-le-Grand, *France* 18 D4
St-Mihiel, *France* 19 D12
St. Moritz, *Switz.* 25 J5
St-Nazaire, *France* 18 E4
St. Neots, *U.K.* 13 E7
St-Nicolas-de-Port, *France* 19 D13
St-Niklaas, *Belgium* 17 C4
St-Omer, *France* 19 B9
St-Palais-sur-Mer, *France* 20 C2
St-Pamphile, *Canada* 103 C6
St-Pardoux-la-Rivière, *France* 20 C4
St. Pascal, *Canada* 103 C6
St. Paul, *Canada* 104 C6
St-Paul, *France* 21 D10
St. Paul, *Minn., U.S.A.* 112 C8
St. Paul, *Nebr., U.S.A.* 112 E5
St-Paul →, *Canada* 103 B8
St. Paul →, *Liberia* 82 D2
St. Paul, I., *Ind. Oc.* 3 F13
St-Paul-de-Fenouillet, *France* 20 F6
St. Paul I., *Canada* 103 C7
St-Paul-lès-Dax, *France* 20 E2
St-Péray, *France* 21 D8
St. Peter, *U.S.A.* 112 C8
St-Peter-Ording, *Germany* 24 A4
St. Peter Port, *U.K.* 13 H5
St. Peters, *N.S., Canada* 103 C7
St. Peters, *P.E.I., Canada* 103 C7
St. Petersburg = Sankt-Peterburg, *Russia* 46 C6
St. Petersburg, *U.S.A.* 109 M4
St-Philbert-de-Grand-Lieu, *France* 18 E5
St-Pie, *Canada* 111 A12
St-Pierre, *St- P. & M.* 103 C8
St-Pierre, L., *Canada* 102 C5
St-Pierre-d'Oléron, *France* 20 C2
St-Pierre-en-Port, *France* 18 C7
St-Pierre et Miquelon □, *St- P. & M.* 103 C8
St-Pierre-le-Moûtier, *France* 19 F10
St-Pierre-sur-Dives, *France* 18 C6
St-Pol-de-Léon, *France* 18 D3
St-Pol-sur-Mer, *France* 19 A9
St-Pol-sur-Ternoise, *France* 19 B9
St-Pons, *France* 20 E6
St-Pourçain-sur-Sioule, *France* 19 F10
St-Priest, *France* 21 C8
St-Quay-Portrieux, *France* 18 D4
St. Quentin, *Canada* 103 C6
St-Quentin, *France* 19 C10
St-Rambert-d'Albon, *France* 21 C8
St-Raphaël, *France* 21 E10
St. Regis, *U.S.A.* 114 C6
St-Renan, *France* 18 D2
St-Saëns, *France* 18 C8
St-Savin, *France* 20 B4
St-Savinien, *France* 20 C3
St. Sebastien, Tanjon' i, *Madag.* 89 A8
St-Seine-l'Abbaye, *France* 19 E11
St-Sernin-sur-Rance, *France* 20 E6
St-Sever, *France* 20 E3
St-Siméon, *Canada* 103 C6
St. Simons I., *U.S.A.* 109 K5
St. Simons Island, *U.S.A.* 109 K5
St. Stephen, *Canada* 103 C6
St-Sulpice, *France* 20 E5
St-Sulpice-Laurière, *France* 20 B5
St-Sulpice-les-Feuilles, *France* 20 B5
St-Syprien = St-Cyprien, *France* 20 F7
St-Thégonnec, *France* 18 D3
St. Thomas, *Canada* 102 D3
St. Thomas I., *Virgin Is.* 121 C7
St-Tite, *Canada* 102 C5
St-Tropez, *France* 21 E10
St. Troud = St. Truiden, *Belgium* 17 D5
St. Truiden, *Belgium* 17 D5
St-Vaast-la-Hougue, *France* 18 C5
St-Valery-en-Caux, *France* 18 C7
St-Valéry-sur-Somme, *France* 19 B8
St-Vallier, *France* 19 F11
St-Vallier-de-Thiey, *France* 21 E10
St-Varent, *France* 18 F6
St-Vaury, *France* 20 B5
St. Vincent, *Italy* 28 C4
St. Vincent, G., *Australia* 95 F2
St. Vincent & the Grenadines ■, *W. Indies* 121 D7
St-Vincent-de-Tyrosse, *France* 20 E2
St. Vincent Passage, *W. Indies* 121 D7
St-Vith, *Belgium* 17 D6
St-Vivien-de-Médoc, *France* 20 C2
St. Walburg, *Canada* 105 C7
St-Yrieix-la-Perche, *France* 20 C5
Ste-Adresse, *France* 18 C7
Ste-Agathe-des-Monts, *Canada* 102 C5
Ste-Anne, L., *Canada* 103 B6
Ste-Anne-des-Monts, *Canada* 103 C6
Ste-Croix, *Switz.* 25 J2
Ste-Enimie, *France* 20 D7
Ste-Foy-la-Grande, *France* 20 D4
Ste. Genevieve, *U.S.A.* 112 G9
Ste-Hermine, *France* 20 B2
Ste-Livrade-sur-Lot, *France* 20 D4
Ste-Marguerite →, *Canada* 103 B6
Ste-Marie, *Martinique* 121 D7
Ste-Marie-aux-Mines, *France* 19 D14
Ste-Marie de la Madeleine, *Canada* 103 C5
Ste-Maure-de-Touraine, *France* 18 E7
Ste-Maxime, *France* 21 E10
Ste-Menehould, *France* 19 C11
Ste-Mère-Église, *France* 18 C5
Ste-Rose, *Guadeloupe* 121 C7
Ste. Rose du Lac, *Canada* 105 C9
Ste-Savine, *France* 19 D11
Ste-Sigolène, *France* 21 C8
Saintes, *France* 20 C3
Saintes, I. des, *Guadeloupe* 121 C7
Stes-Maries-de-la-Mer, *France* 21 E8
Saintfield, *U.K.* 15 B6
Saintonge, *France* 20 C3
Saipan, *Pac. Oc.* 96 F6
Sairang, *India* 67 H18
Sairecábur, Cerro, *Bolivia* 126 A2
Saitama □, *Japan* 55 F9
Saiteli = Kadınhanı, *Turkey* 72 C5
Saiţi, *Moldova* 43 D14
Saiyid, *Pakistan* 68 C5
Sajama, *Bolivia* 124 G5
Sajan, *Serbia, Yug.* 42 E5
Sajó →, *Hungary* 42 C6
Sajószentpéter, *Hungary* 42 B5
Sajum, *India* 69 C8
Sak →, *S. Africa* 88 E3
Sakaba, *Nigeria* 83 C6
Sakai, *Japan* 55 G7
Sakaide, *Japan* 55 G6
Sakaiminato, *Japan* 55 G6
Sakākah, *Si. Arabia* 70 D4
Sakakawea, L., *U.S.A.* 112 B4
Sakami →, *Canada* 102 B4
Sakami, L., *Canada* 102 B4
Sâkâne, 'Erg i-n, *Mali* 83 A4
Sakania, *Dem. Rep. of the Congo* 87 E2
Sakaraha, *Madag.* 89 C7
Sakarya, *Turkey* 72 B4
Sakarya →, *Turkey* 72 B4
Sakashima-Guntō, *Japan* 55 M2
Sakassou, *Ivory C.* 82 D3
Sakata, *Japan* 54 E9
Sakchu, *N. Korea* 57 D13
Sakeny →, *Madag.* 89 C8
Sakété, *Benin* 83 D5
Sakha □, *Russia* 51 C13
Sakhalin, *Russia* 51 D15
Sakhalinskiy Zaliv, *Russia* 51 D15
Şaki, *Azerbaijan* 49 K8
Šakiai, *Lithuania* 9 J20
Sakon Nakhon, *Thailand* 64 D5
Sakrand, *Pakistan* 68 F3
Sakri, *India* 69 F12
Sakrivier, *S. Africa* 88 E3
Sakskøbing, *Denmark* 11 K5
Sakti, *India* 69 H10
Sakuma, *Japan* 55 G8
Sakurai, *Japan* 55 G7
Saky, *Ukraine* 47 K7
Sal →, *Russia* 49 G5
Sala, *Eritrea* 81 D4
Šal'a, *Slovak Rep.* 27 C10
Sala, *Sweden* 10 E10
Sala →, *Eritrea* 81 D4
Sala Consilina, *Italy* 31 B8
Sala-y-Gómez, *Pac. Oc.* 97 K17
Salaberry-de-Valleyfield, *Canada* 102 C5
Saladas, *Argentina* 126 B4
Saladillo, *Argentina* 126 D4
Salado →, *Buenos Aires, Argentina* 126 D4
Salado →, *La Pampa, Argentina* 128 D3
Salado →, *Santa Fe, Argentina* 126 C3
Salado →, *Mexico* 113 M5
Salaga, *Ghana* 83 D4
Sālah, *Syria* 75 C5
Sălaj □, *Romania* 42 C8
Sálakhos, *Greece* 36 C9
Salala, *Liberia* 82 D2
Salala, *Sudan* 80 C4
Salālah, *Oman* 74 D5
Salamanca, *Chile* 126 C1
Salamanca, *Spain* 34 E5
Salamanca, *U.S.A.* 110 D6
Salamanca □, *Spain* 34 E5
Salāmatābād, *Iran* 70 C5
Salamis, *Cyprus* 36 D12
Salamís, *Greece* 38 D5
Salar de Atacama, *Chile* 126 A2
Salar de Uyuni, *Bolivia* 124 H5
Sălard, *Romania* 42 C7
Salas, *Spain* 34 B4
Salas de los Infantes, *Spain* 34 C7
Salatiga, *Indonesia* 63 G14
Salaverry, *Peru* 124 E3
Salawati, *Indonesia* 63 E8
Salaya, *India* 68 H3
Salayar, *Indonesia* 63 F6
Salazar →, *Spain* 32 C3
Salbris, *France* 19 E9
Salcia, *Romania* 43 G9
Sălciua, *Romania* 43 D8
Salcombe, *U.K.* 13 G4
Saldaña, *Spain* 34 C6
Saldanha, *S. Africa* 88 E2
Saldanha B., *S. Africa* 88 E2
Saldus, *Latvia* 9 H20
Saldus □, *Latvia* 44 B9
Sale, *Australia* 95 F4
Sale, *Italy* 28 D5
Salé, *Morocco* 78 B4
Sale, *U.K.* 12 D5
Salekhard, *Russia* 50 C7
Salem, *India* 66 P11
Salem, *Ill., U.S.A.* 108 F1
Salem, *Ind., U.S.A.* 108 F2
Salem, *Mass., U.S.A.* 111 D14
Salem, *Mo., U.S.A.* 113 G9
Salem, *N.H., U.S.A.* 111 D13
Salem, *N.J., U.S.A.* 108 F8
Salem, *N.Y., U.S.A.* 111 C11
Salem, *Ohio, U.S.A.* 110 F4
Salem, *Oreg., U.S.A.* 114 D2
Salem, *S. Dak., U.S.A.* 112 D6
Salem, *Va., U.S.A.* 108 G5
Salemi, *Italy* 30 E5

Sälen, *Sweden* 10 C7
Salernes, *France* 21 E10
Salerno, *Italy* 31 B7
Salerno, G. di, *Italy* 31 B7
Salford, *U.K.* 12 D5
Salgir →, *Ukraine* 47 K8
Salgótarján, *Hungary* 42 B4
Salgueiro, *Brazil* 125 E11
Salibabu, *Indonesia* 63 D7
Salida, *U.S.A.* 106 C5
Salies-de-Béarn, *France* 20 E3
Salihli, *Turkey* 72 C3
Salihorsk, *Belarus* 47 F4
Salima, *Malawi* 85 G6
Salina, *Italy* 31 D7
Salina, *Kans., U.S.A.* 112 F6
Salina, *Utah, U.S.A.* 115 G8
Salina Cruz, *Mexico* 119 D5
Salinas, *Brazil* 125 G10
Salinas, *Chile* 126 A2
Salinas, *Ecuador* 124 D2
Salinas, *U.S.A.* 116 J5
Salinas →, *Guatemala* 119 D6
Salinas →, *U.S.A.* 116 J5
Salinas, B. de, *Nic.* 120 D2
Salinas, Pampa de las, *Argentina* 126 C2
Salinas Ambargasta, *Argentina* 126 B3
Salinas de Hidalgo, *Mexico* 118 C4
Salinas Grandes, *Argentina* 126 C3
Saline →, *Ark., U.S.A.* 113 J8
Saline →, *Kans., U.S.A.* 112 F6
Salines, *Spain* 37 B10
Salines, C. de ses, *Spain* 37 B10
Salinópolis, *Brazil* 125 D9
Salins-les-Bains, *France* 19 F12
Salir, *Portugal* 35 H2
Salisbury = Harare, *Zimbabwe* 87 F3
Salisbury, *U.K.* 13 F6
Salisbury, *Md., U.S.A.* 108 F8
Salisbury, *N.C., U.S.A.* 109 H5
Salisbury I., *Canada* 101 B12
Salisbury Plain, *U.K.* 13 F6
Săliște, *Romania* 43 E8
Salka, *Nigeria* 83 C5
Şalkhad, *Syria* 75 C5
Salla, *Finland* 8 C23
Sallanches, *France* 21 C10
Sallent, *Spain* 32 D6
Salles, *France* 20 D3
Salles-Curan, *France* 20 D6
Salling, *Denmark* 11 H2
Salliq, *Canada* 101 B11
Sallisaw, *U.S.A.* 113 H7
Sallom Junction, *Sudan* 80 D4
Salluit, *Canada* 101 B12
Salmās, *Iran* 70 B5
Salmerón, *Spain* 32 E2
Salmo, *Canada* 104 D5
Salmon, *U.S.A.* 114 D7
Salmon →, *Canada* 104 C4
Salmon →, *U.S.A.* 114 D5
Salmon Arm, *Canada* 104 C5
Salmon Gums, *Australia* 93 F3
Salmon River Mts., *U.S.A.* 114 D6
Salo, *Finland* 9 F20
Salò, *Italy* 28 C7
Salobreña, *Spain* 35 J7
Salome, *U.S.A.* 117 M13
Salon, *India* 69 F9
Salon-de-Provence, *France* 21 E9
Salonica = Thessaloníki, *Greece* 40 F6
Salonta, *Romania* 42 D6
Salor →, *Spain* 35 F3
Salou, *Spain* 32 D6
Salou, C. de, *Spain* 32 D6
Saloum →, *Senegal* 82 C1
Salpausselkä, *Finland* 9 F22
Salsacate, *Argentina* 126 C2
Salses, *France* 20 F6
Salsk, *Russia* 49 G5
Salso →, *Italy* 30 E6
Salsomaggiore Terme, *Italy* 28 D6
Salt, *Spain* 32 D7
Salt →, *Canada* 104 B6
Salt →, *U.S.A.* 115 K7
Salt Lake City, *U.S.A.* 114 F8
Salt Range, *Pakistan* 68 C5
Salta, *Argentina* 126 A2
Salta □, *Argentina* 126 A2
Saltara, *Italy* 29 E9
Saltash, *U.K.* 13 G3
Saltburn by the Sea, *U.K.* 12 C7
Saltcoats, *U.K.* 14 F4
Saltee Is., *Ireland* 15 D5
Saltfjellet, *Norway* 8 C16
Saltfjorden, *Norway* 8 C16
Saltholm, *Denmark* 11 J6
Saltillo, *Mexico* 118 B4
Salto, *Argentina* 126 C3
Salto, *Uruguay* 126 C4
Salto del Guaíra, *Paraguay* 127 A5
Salton City, *U.S.A.* 117 M11
Salton Sea, *U.S.A.* 117 M11
Saltpond, *Ghana* 83 D4
Saltsburg, *U.S.A.* 110 F5
Saltsjöbaden, *Sweden* 10 E12
Saluda →, *U.S.A.* 109 J5
Salûm, *Egypt* 80 A2
Salûm, Khâlig el, *Egypt* 80 A2
Salur, *India* 67 K13
Saluzzo, *Italy* 28 D4
Salvador, *Brazil* 125 F11
Salvador, *Canada* 105 C7
Salvador, L., *U.S.A.* 113 L9
Salvaterra de Magos, *Portugal* 35 F2
Sálvora, I. de, *Spain* 34 C2
Salween →, *Burma* 67 L20
Salyan, *Azerbaijan* 50 F5
Salza →, *Austria* 26 D7
Salzach →, *Austria* 26 C5
Salzburg, *Austria* 26 D6
Salzburg □, *Austria* 26 D6
Salzgitter, *Germany* 24 C6
Salzkotten, *Germany* 24 D4
Salzwedel, *Germany* 24 C7
Sam, *India* 68 F4
Sam Neua, *Laos* 58 G5
Sam Ngao, *Thailand* 64 D2
Sam Rayburn Reservoir, *U.S.A.* 113 K7
Sam Son, *Vietnam* 64 C5
Sam Teu, *Laos* 64 C5
Sama de Langreo = Langreo, *Spain* 34 B5
Samagaltay, *Russia* 51 D10
Samales Group, *Phil.* 61 J4
Samâlût, *Egypt* 80 B3
Samana, *India* 68 D7
Samaná □, *Dom. Rep.* 121 C6
Samana Cay, *Bahamas* 121 B5
Samandağı, *Turkey* 72 D6
Samandıra, *Turkey* 41 F13
Samanga, *Tanzania* 87 D4
Samangwa, *Dem. Rep. of the Congo* 86 C1
Samani, *Japan* 54 C11
Samanli Dağları, *Turkey* 41 F13
Samar, *Phil.* 61 F6
Samara, *Russia* 48 D10
Samara →, *Russia* 48 D10
Samara →, *Ukraine* 47 H8
Samaria = Shōmrōn, *West Bank* 75 C4
Samariá, *Greece* 36 D5
Samarinda, *Indonesia* 62 E5
Samarkand = Samarqand, *Uzbekistan* 50 F7
Samarqand, *Uzbekistan* 50 F7
Sāmarrā, *Iraq* 70 C4
Samastipur, *India* 69 G11
Şamaxi, *Azerbaijan* 49 K9
Samba, *Dem. Rep. of the Congo* 86 C2
Samba, *India* 69 C6
Sambalpur, *India* 67 J14
Sambar, Tanjung, *Indonesia* 62 E4
Sambas, *Indonesia* 62 D3
Sambava, *Madag.* 89 A9
Sambawizi, *Zimbabwe* 87 F2
Sambhal, *India* 69 E8
Sambhar, *India* 68 F6
Sambhar L., *India* 68 F6
Sambiase, *Italy* 31 D9
Sambir, *Ukraine* 47 H2
Sambor, *Cambodia* 64 F6
Samborombón, B., *Argentina* 126 D4
Sambuca di Sicília, *Italy* 30 E6
Samch'ŏk, *S. Korea* 57 F15
Samch'onp'o, *S. Korea* 57 G15
Same, *Tanzania* 86 C4
Samer, *France* 19 B8
Samfya, *Zambia* 87 E2
Sámi, *Greece* 38 C2
Şämkir, *Azerbaijan* 49 K8
Şamlı, *Turkey* 39 B9
Samnah, *Si. Arabia* 70 E3
Samo Alto, *Chile* 126 C1
Samoa = Western Samoa ■, *Pac. Oc.* 91 B13
Samobor, *Croatia* 29 C12
Samoëns, *France* 19 F13
Samokov, *Bulgaria* 40 D7
Šamorín, *Slovak Rep.* 27 C10
Samorogouan, *Burkina Faso* 82 C4
Sámos, *Greece* 39 D8
Samoš, *Serbia, Yug.* 42 E5
Samos, *Spain* 34 C3
Sámos □, *Greece* 39 D8
Samothráki = Mathráki, *Greece* 36 A3
Samothráki, *Greece* 41 F9
Samothráki, *Évros, Greece* 41 F9
Samoylovka, *Russia* 48 E6
Sampa, *Ghana* 82 D4
Sampacho, *Argentina* 126 C3
Sampang, *Indonesia* 63 G15
Samper de Calanda, *Spain* 32 D4
Sampéyre, *Italy* 28 D4
Sampit, *Indonesia* 62 E4
Sampit, Teluk, *Indonesia* 62 E4
Samrong, *Cambodia* 64 E4
Samrong, *Thailand* 64 E3
Samsø, *Denmark* 11 J4
Samsø Bælt, *Denmark* 11 J4
Samsun, *Turkey* 72 B7
Samtredia, *Georgia* 49 J6
Samui, Ko, *Thailand* 65 H3
Samur →, *Russia* 49 K9
Samurskiy Khrebet, *Russia* 49 K8
Samusole, *Dem. Rep. of the Congo* 87 E1
Samut Prakan, *Thailand* 64 F3
Samut Songkhram →, *Thailand* 62 B1
Samwari, *Pakistan* 68 E2
San, *Mali* 82 C4
San →, *Cambodia* 64 F5
San →, *Poland* 45 H8
San Adrián, *Spain* 32 C3
San Adrián, C. de, *Spain* 34 B2
San Agustin, C., *Phil.* 61 H7
San Agustín de Valle Fértil, *Argentina* 126 C2
San Ambrosio, *Pac. Oc.* 122 F3
San Andreas, *U.S.A.* 116 G6
San Andres, *Phil.* 61 E6
San Andrés, I. de, *Caribbean* 120 D3
San Andrês del Rabanedo, *Spain* 34 C5
San Andres Mts., *U.S.A.* 115 K10
San Andrés Tuxtla, *Mexico* 119 D5
San Angelo, *U.S.A.* 113 K4
San Anselmo, *U.S.A.* 116 H4
San Antonio, *Belize* 119 D7
San Antonio, *Chile* 126 C1
San Antonio, *Phil.* 61 D4
San Antonio, *N. Mex., U.S.A.* 115 K10
San Antonio, *Tex., U.S.A.* 113 L5
San Antonio →, *U.S.A.* 113 L6
San Antonio, C., *Argentina* 126 D4
San Antonio, C., *Cuba* 120 B3
San Antonio, C. de, *Spain* 33 G5
San Antonio, Mt., *U.S.A.* 117 L9
San Antonio de los Baños, *Cuba* 120 B3
San Antonio de los Cobres, *Argentina* 126 A2
San Antonio Oeste, *Argentina* 128 E4
San Arcángelo, *Italy* 31 B9
San Ardo, *U.S.A.* 116 J6
San Augustín, *Canary Is.* 37 G4
San Augustine, *U.S.A.* 113 K7
San Bartolomé, *Canary Is.* 37 F6
San Bartolomé de Tirajana, *Canary Is.* 37 G4
San Bartolomeo in Galdo, *Italy* 31 A8
San Benedetto del Tronto, *Italy* 29 F10
San Benedetto Po, *Italy* 28 C7
San Benedicto, I., *Mexico* 118 D2
San Benito, *U.S.A.* 113 M6
San Benito →, *U.S.A.* 116 J5
San Benito Mt., *U.S.A.* 116 J6
San Bernardino, *U.S.A.* 117 L9
San Bernardino Mts., *U.S.A.* 117 L10
San Bernardino Str., *Phil.* 61 E6
San Bernardo, *Chile* 126 C1
San Bernardo, I. de, *Colombia* 124 B3
San Blas, *Mexico* 118 B3
San Blas, Arch. de, *Panama* 120 E4
San Blas, C., *U.S.A.* 109 L3
San Bonifacio, *Italy* 29 C8
San Borja, *Bolivia* 124 F5
San Buenaventura, *Mexico* 118 B4
San Carlos = Butuku-Luba, *Eq. Guin.* 83 E6
San Carlos = Sant Carles, *Spain* 37 B8
San Carlos, *Argentina* 126 C2
San Carlos, *Chile* 126 D1
San Carlos, *Baja Calif. S., Mexico* 118 C2
San Carlos, *Coahuila, Mexico* 118 B4
San Carlos, *Nic.* 120 D3
San Carlos, *Neg. Occ., Phil.* 61 F5
San Carlos, *Pangasinan, Phil.* 61 D4
San Carlos, *Uruguay* 127 C5
San Carlos, *U.S.A.* 115 K8
San Carlos, *Venezuela* 124 B5
San Carlos de Bariloche, *Argentina* 128 E2
San Carlos de Bolívar, *Argentina* 128 D4
San Carlos de la Rápita = Sant Carles de la Ràpita, *Spain* 32 E5
San Carlos del Zulia, *Venezuela* 124 B4
San Carlos L., *U.S.A.* 115 K8
San Cataldo, *Italy* 30 E6
San Celoni = Sant Celoni, *Spain* 32 D7
San Clemente, *Chile* 126 D1
San Clemente, *Spain* 33 F2
San Clemente, *U.S.A.* 117 M9
San Clemente I., *U.S.A.* 117 N8
San Cristóbal = Es Migjorn Gran, *Spain* 37 B11
San Cristóbal, *Argentina* 126 C3
San Cristóbal, *Dom. Rep.* 121 C5
San Cristóbal, *Venezuela* 124 B4
San Cristóbal de la Casas, *Mexico* 119 D6
San Damiano d'Asti, *Italy* 28 D5
San Daniele del Friuli, *Italy* 29 B10
San Diego, *Calif., U.S.A.* 117 N9
San Diego, *Tex., U.S.A.* 113 M5
San Diego, C., *Argentina* 128 G3
San Diego de la Unión, *Mexico* 118 C4
San Dimitri, Ras, *Malta* 36 C1
San Donà di Piave, *Italy* 29 C9
San Estanislao, *Paraguay* 126 A4
San Esteban de Gormaz, *Spain* 32 D1
San Felice Circeo, *Italy* 30 A6
San Felice sul Panaro, *Italy* 29 D8
San Felipe, *Chile* 126 C1
San Felipe, *Mexico* 118 A2
San Felipe, *Venezuela* 124 A5
San Felipe →, *U.S.A.* 117 M11
San Félix, *Chile* 126 B1
San Félix, *Pac. Oc.* 122 F2
San Fernando = Sant Ferran, *Spain* 37 C7
San Fernando, *Chile* 126 C1
San Fernando, *Baja Calif., Mexico* 118 B1
San Fernando, *Tamaulipas, Mexico* 119 C5
San Fernando, *La Union, Phil.* 61 C4
San Fernando, *Pampanga, Phil.* 61 D4
San Fernando, *Spain* 35 J4
San Fernando, *Trin. & Tob.* 121 D7
San Fernando, *U.S.A.* 117 L8
San Fernando de Apure, *Venezuela* 124 B5
San Fernando de Atabapo, *Venezuela* 124 C5
San Fernando di Púglia, *Italy* 31 A9
San Francisco, *Argentina* 126 C3
San Francisco, *U.S.A.* 116 H4
San Francisco →, *U.S.A.* 115 K9
San Francisco, Paso de, *S. Amer.* 126 B2
San Francisco de Macorís, *Dom. Rep.* 121 C5
San Francisco del Monte de Oro, *Argentina* 126 C2
San Francisco del Oro, *Mexico* 118 B3
San Francisco Javier = Sant Francesc de Formentera, *Spain* 37 C7
San Francisco Solano, Pta., *Colombia* 122 C3
San Fratello, *Italy* 31 D7
San Gabriel, *Chile* 126 C1
San Gabriel Mts., *U.S.A.* 117 L9
San Gavino Monreale, *Italy* 30 C1
San Gimignano, *Italy* 28 E8
San Giórgio di Nogaro, *Italy* 29 C10
San Giórgio Iónico, *Italy* 31 B10
San Giovanni Bianco, *Italy* 28 C6
San Giovanni in Fiore, *Italy* 31 C9
San Giovanni in Persiceto, *Italy* 29 D8
San Giovanni Rotondo, *Italy* 29 G12
San Giovanni Valdarno, *Italy* 29 E8
San Giuliano Terme, *Italy* 28 E7
San Gorgonio Mt., *U.S.A.* 117 L10
San Gottardo, P. del, *Switz.* 25 J4
San Gregorio, *Uruguay* 127 C4
San Gregorio, *U.S.A.* 116 H4
San Guiseppe Jato, *Italy* 30 E6
San Ignacio, *Belize* 119 D7
San Ignacio, *Bolivia* 124 G6
San Ignacio, *Mexico* 118 B2
San Ignacio, *Paraguay* 120 C2
San Ignacio, L., *Mexico* 118 B2
San Ildefonso, C., *Phil.* 61 C5
San Isidro, *Argentina* 126 C4
San Isidro, *Phil.* 61 H7
San Jacinto, *U.S.A.* 117 M10
San Jaime = Sant Jaume, *Spain* 37 B11
San Javier, *Misiones, Argentina* 127 B4
San Javier, *Santa Fe, Argentina* 126 C4
San Javier, *Bolivia* 124 G6
San Javier, *Chile* 126 D1
San Javier, *Spain* 33 H4
San Jeronimo Taviche, *Mexico* 119 D5
San Joaquin, *U.S.A.* 116 J6
San Joaquin →, *U.S.A.* 116 G5
San Joaquin Valley, *U.S.A.* 116 J6
San Jon, *U.S.A.* 113 H3
San Jordi = Sant Jordi, *Spain* 37 B9
San Jorge, *Argentina* 126 C3
San Jorge, *Spain* 37 C7
San Jorge, B. de, *Mexico* 118 A2
San Jorge, G., *Argentina* 128 F3
San Jorge, G. of, *Argentina* 122 H4
San José = San Josep, *Spain* 37 C7
San José, *Costa Rica* 120 E3
San José, *Guatemala* 120 D1
San José, *Mexico* 118 C2
San Jose, *Mind. Occ., Phil.* 61 E4
San Jose, *Nueva Ecija, Phil.* 61 D4
San Jose, *U.S.A.* 116 H5
San Jose →, *U.S.A.* 115 J10
San Jose de Buenavista, *Phil.* 63 B6
San José de Chiquitos, *Bolivia* 124 G6
San José de Feliciano, *Argentina* 126 C4
San José de Jáchal, *Argentina* 126 C2
San José de Mayo, *Uruguay* 126 C4
San José del Cabo, *Mexico* 118 C3
San José del Guaviare, *Colombia* 124 C4
San Josep, *Spain* 37 C7
San Juan, *Argentina* 126 C2
San Juan, *Mexico* 118 C4
San Juan, *Phil.* 61 F6
San Juan, *Puerto Rico* 121 C6
San Juan □, *Argentina* 126 C2
San Juan □, *Dom. Rep.* 121 C5
San Juan →, *Argentina* 126 C2
San Juan →, *Nic.* 120 D3
San Juan →, *U.S.A.* 115 H8
San Juan Bautista = Sant Joan Baptista, *Spain* 37 B8
San Juan Bautista, *Paraguay* 126 B4
San Juan Bautista, *U.S.A.* 116 J5
San Juan Bautista Valle Nacional, *Mexico* 119 D5
San Juan Capistrano, *U.S.A.* 117 M9
San Juan Cr. →, *U.S.A.* 116 J5
San Juan de Alicante, *Spain* 33 G4
San Juan de Guadalupe, *Mexico* 118 C4
San Juan de la Costa, *Mexico* 118 C2
San Juan de los Morros, *Venezuela* 124 B5
San Juan del Norte, *Nic.* 120 D3
San Juan del Norte, B. de, *Nic.* 120 D3
San Juan del Río, *Mexico* 119 C5
San Juan del Sur, *Nic.* 120 D2
San Juan I., *U.S.A.* 116 B3
San Juan Mts., *U.S.A.* 115 H10
San Just, Sierra de, *Spain* 32 E4
San Justo, *Argentina* 126 C3
San Kamphaeng, *Thailand* 64 C2
San Lázaro, C., *Mexico* 118 C2
San Lázaro, Sa., *Mexico* 118 C3
San Leandro, *U.S.A.* 116 H4
San Leonardo de Yagüe, *Spain* 32 D1
San Lorenzo = Sant Llorenç des Cardassar, *Spain* 37 B10
San Lorenzo, *Argentina* 126 C3
San Lorenzo, *Ecuador* 124 C3
San Lorenzo, *Paraguay* 126 B4
San Lorenzo →, *Mexico* 118 C3
San Lorenzo, I., *Mexico* 118 B2
San Lorenzo, Mte., *Argentina* 128 F2
San Lorenzo de la Parrilla, *Spain* 32 F2
San Lorenzo de Morunys = Sant Llorenç de Morunys, *Spain* 32 C6
San Lucas, *Bolivia* 124 H5
San Lucas, *Baja Calif. S., Mexico* 118 C3
San Lucas, *Baja Calif. S., Mexico* 118 B2
San Lucas, *U.S.A.* 116 J5
San Lucas, C., *Mexico* 118 C3
San Lúcido, *Italy* 31 C9
San Luis, *Argentina* 126 C2
San Luis, *Cuba* 120 B3
San Luis, *Guatemala* 120 C2
San Luis, *Ariz., U.S.A.* 115 K6
San Luis, *Colo., U.S.A.* 115 H11
San Luis □, *Argentina* 126 C2
San Luis, I., *Mexico* 118 B2
San Luis, Sierra de, *Argentina* 126 C2
San Luis de la Paz, *Mexico* 118 C4
San Luis Obispo, *U.S.A.* 117 K6
San Luis Potosí, *Mexico* 118 C4
San Luis Potosí □, *Mexico* 118 C4
San Luis Reservoir, *U.S.A.* 116 H5
San Luis Río Colorado, *Mexico* 118 A2
San Manuel, *U.S.A.* 115 K8
San Marco, C., *Italy* 30 C1
San Marco Argentano, *Italy* 31 C9
San Marco in Lámis, *Italy* 29 G12
San Marcos, *Guatemala* 120 D1
San Marcos, *Mexico* 118 B2
San Marcos, *Calif., U.S.A.* 117 M9
San Marcos, *Tex., U.S.A.* 113 L6
San Marino, *San Marino* 29 E9
San Marino ■, *Europe* 29 E9
San Martín, *Argentina* 126 C2
San Martín →, *Bolivia* 124 F6
San Martín, L., *Argentina* 128 F2
San Martín de la Vega, *Spain* 34 E7
San Martin de los Andes, *Argentina* 128 E2
San Martín de Valdeiglesias, *Spain* 34 E6
San Mateo = Sant Mateu, *Baleares, Spain* 37 B7
San Mateo = Sant Mateu, *Valencia, Spain* 32 E5
San Mateo, *Phil.* 61 C4
San Mateo, *U.S.A.* 116 H4
San Matías, *Bolivia* 124 G7
San Matías, G., *Argentina* 122 H4
San Miguel = Sant Miquel, *Spain* 37 B7
San Miguel, *El Salv.* 120 D2
San Miguel, *Panama* 120 E4
San Miguel, *U.S.A.* 116 K6
San Miguel →, *Bolivia* 124 F6
San Miguel de Tucumán, *Argentina* 126 B2
San Miguel del Monte, *Argentina* 126 D4
San Miguel I., *U.S.A.* 117 L6
San Miniato, *Italy* 28 E7
San Nicolás, *Canary Is.* 37 G4
San Nicolas, *Phil.* 61 B4
San Nicolás de los Arroyas, *Argentina* 126 C3
San Nicolas I., *U.S.A.* 117 M7
San Onofre, *U.S.A.* 117 M9
San Pablo, *Bolivia* 126 A2
San Pablo, *Phil.* 61 D4
San Pablo, *U.S.A.* 116 H4
San Páolo di Civitate, *Italy* 29 G12
San Pedro, *Buenos Aires, Argentina* 126 C4
San Pedro, *Misiones, Argentina* 127 B5
San Pedro, *Chile* 126 C1
San Pédro, *Ivory C.* 82 E3
San Pedro, *Mexico* 118 C2
San Pedro □, *Paraguay* 126 A4
San Pedro →, *Chihuahua, Mexico* 118 B3
San Pedro →, *Nayarit, Mexico* 118 C3
San Pedro →, *U.S.A.* 115 K8
San Pedro, Pta., *Chile* 126 B1
San Pedro, Sierra de, *Spain* 35 F4
San Pedro Channel, *U.S.A.* 117 M8
San Pedro de Atacama, *Chile* 126 A2
San Pedro de Jujuy, *Argentina* 126 A3
San Pedro de las Colonias, *Mexico* 118 B4

San Pedro de Macorís,
  Dom. Rep. 121 C6
San Pedro del Norte, *Nic.* .. 120 D3
San Pedro del Pinatar, *Spain* 33 H4
San Pedro del Paraná,
  Paraguay 126 B4
San Pedro Mártir, Sierra,
  Mexico 118 A1
San Pedro Mixtepec, *Mexico* 119 D5
San Pedro Ocampo =
  Melchor Ocampo, *Mexico* 118 C4
San Pedro Sula, *Honduras* . 120 C1
San Pietro, *Italy* 30 C1
San Pietro Vernótico, *Italy* 31 B11
San Quintín, *Mexico* 118 A1
San Rafael, *Argentina* 126 C2
San Rafael, *Calif., U.S.A.* . 115 H4
San Rafael, *N. Mex., U.S.A.* 115 J10
San Rafael Mt., *U.S.A.* 117 L7
San Rafael Mts., *U.S.A.* ... 117 L7
San Ramón de la Nueva
  Orán, *Argentina* 126 A3
San Remo, *Italy* 28 E4
San Roque, *Argentina* 126 B4
San Roque, *Spain* 35 J5
San Rosendo, *Chile* 126 D1
San Saba, *U.S.A.* 113 K5
San Salvador, *El Salv.* 120 D2
San Salvador, *Spain* 37 B10
San Salvador de Jujuy,
  Argentina 126 A3
San Salvador I., *Bahamas* .. 121 B5
San Salvo, *Italy* 29 F11
San Sebastián = Donostia-
  San Sebastián, *Spain* ... 32 B3
San Sebastián, *Argentina* .. 128 G3
San Sebastian de la Gomera,
  Canary Is. 37 F2
San Serra = Son Serra,
  Spain 37 B9
San Serverino Marche, *Italy* 29 E10
San Severo, *Italy* 29 G12
San Simeon, *U.S.A.* 116 K5
San Simon, *U.S.A.* 115 K9
San Stéfano di Cadore, *Italy* 29 B9
San Stino di Livenza, *Italy* . 29 C9
San Telmo = Sant Telm,
  Spain 37 B9
San Telmo, *Mexico* 118 A1
San Tiburcio, *Mexico* 118 C4
San Valentin, Mte., *Chile* .. 122 H3
San Vicente de Alcántara,
  Spain 35 F3
San Vicente de la Barquera,
  Spain 34 B6
San Vicente del Raspeig,
  Spain 33 G4
San Vincenzo, *Italy* 28 E7
San Vito, *Costa Rica* 120 E3
San Vito, *Italy* 30 C2
San Vito, C., *Italy* 30 D5
San Vito al Tagliamento,
  Italy 29 C9
San Vito Chietino, *Italy* ... 29 F11
San Vito dei Normanni, *Italy* 31 B10
Sana', *Yemen* 74 D3
Sana →, *Bos.-H.* 29 C13
Sanaba, *Burkina Faso* 82 C4
Şanäfir, *Si. Arabia* 80 B3
Sanaga →, *Cameroon* 83 E6
Sanaloa, Presa, *Mexico* ... 118 C3
Sanana, *Indonesia* 63 E7
Sanand, *India* 68 H5
Sanandaj, *Iran* 70 C5
Sanandita, *Bolivia* 126 A3
Sanary-sur-Mer, *France* ... 21 E9
Sanawad, *India* 68 H7
Sancellas = Sencelles, *Spain* 37 B9
Sancergues, *France* 19 E9
Sancerre, *France* 19 E9
Sancerrois, Collines du,
  France 19 E9
Sancha He →, *China* 58 D6
Sanchahe, *China* 57 B14
Sánchez, *Dom. Rep.* 121 C6
Sanchor, *India* 68 G4
Sancoins, *France* 19 F9
Sancti Spíritus, *Cuba* 120 B4
Sancy, Puy de, *France* 20 C6
Sand →, *S. Africa* 89 C5
Sand Hills, *U.S.A.* 112 D4
Sand Springs, *U.S.A.* 113 G6
Sanda, *Japan* 55 G7
Sandakan, *Malaysia* 62 C5
Sandan = Sambor,
  Cambodia 64 F6
Sandanski, *Bulgaria* 40 E7
Sandaré, *Mali* 82 C2
Sandared, *Sweden* 11 G6
Sandarne, *Sweden* 10 C11
Sanday, *U.K.* 14 B6
Sandefjord, *Norway* 9 G14
Sanders, *U.S.A.* 115 J9
Sanderson, *U.S.A.* 113 K3
Sandersville, *U.S.A.* 109 J4
Sandfire Roadhouse,
  Australia 92 C3
Sandfly L., *Canada* 105 B7
Sandfontein, *Namibia* 88 C2
Sandhammaren, C., *Sweden* 11 J8
Sandía, *Peru* 124 F5
Sandıklı, *Turkey* 39 C12
Sandila, *India* 69 F9
Sandnes, *Norway* 9 G11
Sandnessjøen, *Norway* 8 C15
Sandoa,
  Dem. Rep. of the Congo . 84 F4
Sandomierz, *Poland* 45 H8
Sândominic, *Romania* 43 D10
Sandover →, *Australia* 94 C2
Sandoway, *Burma* 67 K19

Sandoy, *Færoe Is.* 8 F9
Sandpoint, *U.S.A.* 114 B5
Sandray, *U.K.* 14 E1
Sandringham, *U.K.* 12 E8
Sandstone, *Australia* 93 E2
Sandu, *China* 58 E6
Sandusky, *Mich., U.S.A.* .. 110 C2
Sandusky, *Ohio, U.S.A.* .. 110 E2
Sandvig, *Sweden* 11 J8
Sandviken, *Sweden* 10 D10
Sandwich, C., *Australia* ... 94 B4
Sandwich B., *Canada* 103 B8
Sandwich B., *Namibia* 88 C1
Sandwip Chan., *Bangla.* .. 67 H17
Sandy, *Oreg., U.S.A.* 116 E4
Sandy, *Pa., U.S.A.* 110 E6
Sandy, *Utah, U.S.A.* 114 F8
Sandy Bay, *Canada* 105 B8
Sandy Bight, *Australia* 93 F3
Sandy C., *Queens., Australia* 94 C5
Sandy C., *Tas., Australia* .. 94 G3
Sandy Cay, *Bahamas* 121 B4
Sandy Cr. →, *U.S.A.* 114 F9
Sandy L., *Canada* 102 B1
Sandy Lake, *Canada* 102 B1
Sandy Valley, *U.S.A.* 117 K11
Sanford, *Fla., U.S.A.* 109 L5
Sanford, *Maine, U.S.A.* ... 109 D10
Sanford, *N.C., U.S.A.* 109 H6
Sanford →, *Australia* 93 E2
Sanford, Mt., *U.S.A.* 100 B5
Sang-i-Masha, *Afghan.* ... 68 C2
Sanga, *Mozam.* 87 E4
Sanga →, *Congo* 84 E3
Sangamner, *India* 66 K9
Sangar, *Afghan.* 68 C1
Sangar, *Russia* 51 C13
Sangar Sarai, *Afghan.* 68 B4
Sangaredi, *Guinea* 82 C2
Sangarh →, *Pakistan* 68 D4
Sangasso, *Mali* 82 C3
Sangatte, *France* 19 B8
Sangay, *Ecuador* 124 D3
Sange,
  Dem. Rep. of the Congo . 86 D2
Sangeang, *Indonesia* 63 F5
Sângeorz-Bǎi, *Romania* ... 43 C9
Sanger, *U.S.A.* 116 J7
Sângera, *Moldova* 43 D13
Sangerhausen, *Germany* .. 24 D7
Sanggan He →, *China* 56 E9
Sanggau, *Indonesia* 62 D4
Sanghar, *Pakistan* 68 F3
Sangihe, Kepulauan,
  Indonesia 63 D7
Sangihe, Pulau, *Indonesia* . 63 D7
Sangju, *S. Korea* 57 F15
Sangkapura, *Indonesia* 62 F4
Sangkhla, *Thailand* 64 E2
Sangkulirang, *Indonesia* ... 62 D5
Sangla, *Pakistan* 68 D5
Sangli, *India* 66 L9
Sangmélima, *Cameroon* ... 83 E7
Sangod, *India* 68 G7
Sangre de Cristo Mts.,
  U.S.A. 113 G2
Sangro →, *Italy* 29 F11
Sangrur, *India* 68 D6
Sangudo, *Canada* 104 C6
Sangue →, *Brazil* 124 F7
Sangüesa, *Spain* 32 C3
Sanguinaires, Îs., *France* .. 21 G12
Sangzhi, *China* 59 C8
Sanhala, *Ivory C.* 82 C3
Sanibel, *U.S.A.* 109 M4
Sanirajak, *Canada* 101 B11
Sanjawi, *Pakistan* 68 D3
Sanje, *Uganda* 86 C3
Sanjiang, *China* 58 E7
Sanjo, *Japan* 54 F9
Sankh →, *India* 69 H11
Sankt Andrä, *Austria* 26 E7
Sankt Augustin, *Germany* . 24 E3
Sankt Blasien, *Germany* ... 25 H4
Sankt Gallen, *Switz.* 25 H5
Sankt Gallen □, *Switz.* 25 H5
Sankt Goar, *Germany* 25 E3
Sankt Ingbert, *Germany* ... 25 F3
Sankt Johann im Pongau,
  Austria 26 D6
Sankt Johann in Tirol,
  Austria 26 D5
Sankt-Peterburg, *Russia* .. 46 C6
Sankt Pölten, *Austria* 26 C8
Sankt Ulrich = Ortisei, *Italy* 29 B8
Sankt Valentin, *Austria* ... 26 C7
Sankt Veit an der Glan,
  Austria 26 E7
Sankt Wendel, *Germany* .. 25 F3
Sankt Wolfgang, *Austria* .. 26 D6
Sankuru →,
  Dem. Rep. of the Congo . 84 E4
Sanliurfa, *Turkey* 70 B3
Sanlúcar de Barrameda,
  Spain 35 J4
Sanluri, *Italy* 30 C1
Sânmartin, *Romania* 43 D10
Sanmen, *China* 59 C13
Sanmenxia, *China* 56 G6
Sanming, *China* 59 D11
Sannaspos, *S. Africa* 88 D4
Sannicandro Gargánico, *Italy* 29 G12
Sânnicolau Mare, *Romania* . 42 D5
Sannieshof, *S. Africa* 88 D4
Sannīn, J., *Lebanon* 75 B4
Sanniquellie, *Liberia* 82 D3
Sannūr, W. →, *Egypt* 80 B3
Sanok, *Poland* 45 J9
Sanquhar, *U.K.* 14 F5
Sansanding, *Mali* 82 C3
Sansepolcro, *Italy* 29 E9

Sansha, *China* 59 D13
Sanshui, *China* 59 F9
Sanski Most, *Bos.-H.* 29 D13
Sansui, *China* 58 D7
Sant Antoni Abat, *Spain* ... 37 C7
Sant Boi de Llobregat, *Spain* 32 D7
Sant Carles, *Spain* 37 B8
Sant Carles de la Ràpita,
  Spain 32 E5
Sant Celoni, *Spain* 32 D7
Sant Feliu de Guíxols, *Spain* 32 D8
Sant Feliu de Llobregat,
  Spain 32 D7
Sant Ferran, *Spain* 37 C7
Sant Francesc de
  Formentera, *Spain* 37 C7
Sant Jaume, *Spain* 37 B11
Sant Joan Baptista, *Spain* .. 37 B8
Sant Jordi, *Spain* 37 B9
Sant Jordi, G. de, *Spain* ... 32 E6
Sant Llorenç de Morunys,
  Spain 32 C6
Sant Llorenç des Cardassar,
  Spain 37 B10
Sant Mateu, *Baleares, Spain* 37 B7
Sant Mateu, *Valencia, Spain* 32 E5
Sant Miquel, *Spain* 37 B7
Sant Telm, *Spain* 37 B9
Sant' Ágata Militello, *Italy* .. 31 D7
Santa Agnés, *Spain* 37 B7
Santa Ana, *Bolivia* 124 F5
Santa Ana, *El Salv.* 120 D2
Santa Ana, *Mexico* 118 A2
Santa Ana, *U.S.A.* 117 M9
Sant' Ángelo Lodigiano, *Italy* 28 C6
Sant' Antíoco, *Italy* 30 C1
Santa Bárbara, *Chile* 126 D1
Santa Bárbara, *Honduras* .. 120 D2
Santa Bárbara, *Mexico* 118 B3
Santa Bárbara, *Spain* 32 E5
Santa Barbara, *U.S.A.* 117 L7
Santa Bárbara, Mt., *Spain* . 33 H2
Santa Barbara Channel,
  U.S.A. 117 L7
Santa Barbara I., *U.S.A.* ... 117 M7
Santa Catalina, Gulf of,
  U.S.A. 117 N9
Santa Catalina, I., *Mexico* . 118 B2
Santa Catalina I., *U.S.A.* .. 117 M8
Santa Catarina □, *Brazil* .. 127 B6
Santa Catarina, I. de, *Brazil* 127 B6
Santa Caterina di Pittinuri,
  Italy 30 B1
Santa Caterina Villarmosa,
  Italy 31 E7
Santa Cecília, *Brazil* 127 B5
Santa Clara, *Cuba* 120 B4
Santa Clara, *Calif., U.S.A.* . 116 H5
Santa Clara, *Utah, U.S.A.* . 115 H7
Santa Clara, El Golfo de,
  Mexico 118 A2
Santa Clara de Olimar,
  Uruguay 127 C5
Santa Clarita, *U.S.A.* 117 L8
Santa Clotilde, *Peru* 124 D4
Santa Coloma de Farners,
  Spain 32 D7
Santa Coloma de Gramenet,
  Spain 32 D7
Santa Comba, *Spain* 34 B2
Santa Croce Camerina, *Italy* 31 F7
Santa Croce di Magliano,
  Italy 29 G11
Santa Cruz, *Argentina* 128 G3
Santa Cruz, *Bolivia* 124 G6
Santa Cruz, *Chile* 126 C1
Santa Cruz, *Costa Rica* ... 120 D2
Santa Cruz, *Madeira* 37 D3
Santa Cruz, *Phil.* 61 D4
Santa Cruz, *U.S.A.* 116 J4
Santa Cruz →, *U.S.A.* 115 K8
Santa Cruz →, *Argentina* .. 128 G3
Santa Cruz de la Palma,
  Canary Is. 37 F2
Santa Cruz de Mudela, *Spain* 35 G7
Santa Cruz de Tenerife,
  Canary Is. 37 F3
Santa Cruz del Norte, *Cuba* 120 B3
Santa Cruz del Retamar,
  Spain 34 E6
Santa Cruz del Sur, *Cuba* .. 120 B4
Santa Cruz do Rio Pardo,
  Brazil 127 A6
Santa Cruz do Sul, *Brazil* .. 127 B5
Santa Cruz I., *U.S.A.* 117 M7
Santa Cruz Is., *Solomon Is.* 96 J8
Santa Domingo, Cay,
  Bahamas 120 B4
Sant' Egídio alla Vibrata,
  Italy 29 F10
Santa Elena, *Argentina* 126 C4
Santa Elena, C., *Costa Rica* 120 D2
Sant' Eufémia, G. di, *Italy* .. 31 D9
Santa Eulàlia des Riu, *Spain* 37 C8
Santa Fe, *Argentina* 126 C3
Santa Fe, *Spain* 35 H7
Santa Fe, *U.S.A.* 115 J11
Santa Fé □, *Argentina* 126 C3
Santa Fé do Sul, *Brazil* 125 H8
Santa Filomena, *Brazil* 125 E9
Santa Fiora, *Italy* 29 F8
Santa Gertrudis, *Spain* 37 C7
Santa Giustina, *Italy* 29 B9
Santa Inês, *Brazil* 125 F11
Santa Inés, *Spain* 35 G5
Santa Inés, I., *Chile* 122 J3
Santa Isabel = Rey Malabo,
  Eq. Guin. 83 E6
Santa Isabel, *Argentina* ... 126 D2
Santa Isabel, Pico, *Eq. Guin.* 83 E6
Santa Isabel do Morro,
  Brazil 125 F8

Santa Lucía, *Corrientes,*
  Argentina 126 B4
Santa Lucía, *San Juan,*
  Argentina 126 C2
Santa Lucia, *Spain* 33 H4
Santa Lucia, *Uruguay* 126 C4
Santa Lucia Range, *U.S.A.* . 116 K5
Santa Magdalena, I., *Mexico* 118 C2
Santa Margarita, *Argentina* . 126 D3
Santa Margarita, *Spain* 37 B10
Santa Margarita, *U.S.A.* ... 116 K6
Santa Margarita →, *U.S.A.* 117 M9
Santa Margarita, I., *Mexico* 118 C2
Santa Margherita, *Italy* 30 D1
Santa Margherita Ligure,
  Italy 28 D6
Santa María, *Argentina* 126 B2
Santa Maria, *Brazil* 127 B5
Santa Maria, *Phil.* 61 C4
Santa Maria, *U.S.A.* 117 L6
Santa María →, *Mexico* ... 118 A3
Santa María, B. de, *Mexico* 118 B3
Santa Maria, C. de, *Portugal* 35 J3
Santa Maria Cápua Vétere,
  Italy 31 A7
Santa Maria da Feira,
  Portugal 34 E2
Santa Maria da Vitória,
  Brazil 125 F10
Santa Maria del Camí, *Spain* 37 B9
Santa Maria di Léuca, C.,
  Italy 31 C11
Santa María la Real de
  Nieva, *Spain* 34 D6
Santa Marinella, *Italy* 29 F8
Santa Marta, *Colombia* 124 A4
Santa Marta, Sierra Nevada
  de, *Colombia* 122 B3
Santa Marta de Tormes,
  Spain 34 E5
Santa Marta Grande, C.,
  Brazil 127 B6
Santa Marta Ortigueira, Ría
  de, *Spain* 34 B3
Santa Maura = Levkás,
  Greece 38 C2
Santa Monica, *U.S.A.* 117 M8
Santa Olalla, *Huelva, Spain* 35 H4
Santa Olalla, *Toledo, Spain* 34 E6
Santa Paula, *U.S.A.* 117 L7
Santa Pola, *Spain* 33 G4
Santa Ponsa, *Spain* 37 B9
Santa Rita, *U.S.A.* 115 K10
Santa Rosa, *La Pampa,*
  Argentina 126 D3
Santa Rosa, *San Luis,*
  Argentina 126 C2
Santa Rosa, *Brazil* 127 B5
Santa Rosa, *Calif., U.S.A.* . 116 G4
Santa Rosa, *N. Mex., U.S.A.* 113 H2
Santa Rosa de Copán,
  Honduras 120 D2
Santa Rosa de Río Primero,
  Argentina 126 C3
Santa Rosa del Sara, *Bolivia* 124 G6
Santa Rosa I., *U.S.A.* 117 M6
Santa Rosa Range, *U.S.A.* . 114 F5
Santa Rosalía, *Mexico* 118 B2
Santa Sylvina, *Argentina* .. 126 B3
Santa Tecla = Nueva San
  Salvador, *El Salv.* 120 D2
Santa Teresa, *Argentina* ... 126 C3
Santa Teresa, *Australia* 94 C1
Santa Teresa, *Mexico* 119 B5
Santa Teresa di Riva, *Italy* . 31 E8
Santa Teresa Gallura, *Italy* . 30 A2
Santa Uxía, *Spain* 34 C2
Santa Vitória do Palmar,
  Brazil 127 C5
Santa Ynez →, *U.S.A.* 117 L6
Santa Ynez Mts., *U.S.A.* .. 117 L6
Santa Ysabel, *U.S.A.* 117 M10
Santadi, *Italy* 30 C1
Santaella, *Spain* 35 H6
Santai, *China* 58 B5
Santana, *Madeira* 37 D3
Sântana, *Romania* 42 D6
Santana, Coxilha de, *Brazil* 127 C4
Santana do Livramento,
  Brazil 127 C4
Santander, *Spain* 34 B7
Santander Jiménez, *Mexico* . 119 C5
Santanyí, *Spain* 37 B10
Santaquin, *U.S.A.* 114 G8
Santarcángelo di Romagna,
  Italy 29 D9
Santarém, *Brazil* 125 D8
Santarém, *Portugal* 35 F2
Santarém □, *Portugal* 35 F2
Santaren Channel, *W. Indies* 120 B4
Santee, *U.S.A.* 109 J6
Santee →, *U.S.A.* 109 J6
Santéramo in Colle, *Italy* ... 31 B9
Santerno →, *Italy* 29 D8
Santhià, *Italy* 28 C5
Santiago, *Brazil* 127 B5
Santiago, *Chile* 126 C1
Santiago, *Panama* 120 E3
Santiago, *Phil.* 61 C4
Santiago □, *Chile* 126 C1
Santiago →, *Mexico* 98 G3
Santiago →, *Peru* 124 D3
Santiago, Punta de,
  Eq. Guin. 83 E6
Santiago de Compostela,
  Spain 34 C2
Santiago de Cuba, *Cuba* ... 120 C4
Santiago de los Cabelleros,
  Dom. Rep. 121 C5
Santiago del Estero,
  Argentina 126 B3

Santiago del Estero □,
  Argentina 126 B3
Santiago del Teide,
  Canary Is. 37 F3
Santiago do Cacém, *Portugal* 35 G2
Santiago Ixcuintla, *Mexico* . 118 C3
Santiago Papasquiaro,
  Mexico 118 C3
Santiaguillo, L. de, *Mexico* . 118 C4
Santiguila, *Mali* 82 C3
Santillana, *Spain* 34 B6
Santisteban del Puerto, *Spain* 35 G7
Santo Amaro, *Brazil* 125 F11
Santo Anastácio, *Brazil* 127 A6
Santo André, *Brazil* 127 A6
Santo Ângelo, *Brazil* 127 B5
Santo Antônio do Içá, *Brazil* 124 D5
Santo Antônio do Leverger,
  Brazil 125 G7
Santo Domingo, *Dom. Rep.* 121 C6
Santo Domingo, *Baja Calif.,*
  Mexico 118 A1
Santo Domingo,
  Baja Calif. S., Mexico ... 118 B2
Santo Domingo, *Nic.* 120 D3
Santo Domingo de la
  Calzada, *Spain* 32 C2
Santo Domingo de los
  Colorados, *Ecuador* 124 D3
Santo Domingo Pueblo,
  U.S.A. 115 J10
Santo Stéfano di Camastro,
  Italy 31 D7
Santo Tirso, *Portugal* 34 D2
Santo Tomás, *Mexico* 118 A1
Santo Tomás, *Peru* 124 F4
Santo Tomé, *Argentina* 127 B4
Santo Tomé de Guayana =
  Ciudad Guayana,
  Venezuela 124 B6
Santomera, *Spain* 33 G3
Santoña, *Spain* 34 B7
Santoríni = Thíra, *Greece* .. 39 E7
Santos, *Brazil* 127 A6
Santos, Sierra de los, *Spain* 35 G5
Santos Dumont, *Brazil* 127 A7
Sanwer, *India* 68 H6
Sanxenxo, *Spain* 34 C2
Sanyuan, *China* 56 G5
São Bartolomeu de Messines,
  Portugal 35 H2
São Bernardo do Campo,
  Brazil 127 A6
São Borja, *Brazil* 127 B4
São Brás de Alportel,
  Portugal 35 H3
São Carlos, *Brazil* 127 A6
São Cristóvão, *Brazil* 125 F11
São Domingos, *Brazil* 125 F9
São Domingos, *Guinea-Biss.* 82 C1
São Francisco, *Brazil* 125 G10
São Francisco →, *Brazil* ... 122 E7
São Francisco do Sul, *Brazil* 127 B6
São Gabriel, *Brazil* 127 C5
São Gonçalo, *Brazil* 127 A7
Sao Hill, *Tanzania* 87 D4
São João, *Brazil* 82 C1
São João da Boa Vista,
  Brazil 127 A6
São João da Madeira,
  Portugal 34 E2
São João da Pesqueira,
  Portugal 34 D3
São João del Rei, *Brazil* ... 127 A7
São João do Araguaia, *Brazil* 125 E9
São João do Piauí, *Brazil* .. 125 E10
São Joaquim, *Brazil* 127 B6
São Jorge, Pta. de, *Madeira* 37 D3
São José do Norte, *Brazil* .. 127 B5
São José do Rio Prêto,
  Brazil 127 A6
São José dos Campos, *Brazil* 127 A6
São Leopoldo, *Brazil* 127 B5
São Lourenço, *Brazil* 127 A6
São Lourenço →, *Brazil* ... 125 G7
São Lourenço, Pta. de,
  Madeira 37 D3
São Lourenço do Sul, *Brazil* 127 C5
São Luís, *Brazil* 125 D10
São Luís Gonzaga, *Brazil* .. 127 B5
São Marcos →, *Brazil* 125 G9
São Marcos, B. de, *Brazil* .. 125 D10
São Martinho da Cortiça,
  Portugal 34 E2
São Mateus, *Brazil* 125 G11
São Mateus do Sul, *Brazil* .. 127 B5
São Miguel do Oeste, *Brazil* 127 B5
São Paulo, *Brazil* 127 A6
São Paulo □, *Brazil* 127 A6
São Paulo, I., *Atl. Oc.* 2 D8
São Paulo de Olivença,
  Brazil 124 D5
São Pedro do Sul, *Portugal* . 34 E2
São Roque, *Madeira* 37 D3
São Roque, C. de, *Brazil* ... 122 D7
São Sebastião, I. de, *Brazil* . 127 A6
São Sebastião do Paraíso,
  Brazil 127 A6
São Teotónio, *Portugal* 35 H2
São Tomé, *Atl. Oc.* 76 F4
São Tomé, C. de, *Brazil* ... 127 A7
São Tomé & Principe ■,
  Africa 77 F4
São Vicente, *Brazil* 127 A6
São Vicente, *Madeira* 37 D2
São Vicente, C. de, *Portugal* 35 H1
Saona, I., *Dom. Rep.* 121 C6
Saône →, *France* 19 G11
Saône-et-Loire □, *France* .. 19 F11
Saonek, *Indonesia* 63 E8

Sápai, *Greece* 41 E9
Sapanca, *Turkey* 72 B4
Saparua, *Indonesia* 63 E7
Sapele, *Nigeria* 83 D6
Sapelo I., *U.S.A.* 109 K5
Şaphane, *Turkey* 39 B11
Sapiéntza, *Greece* 38 E3
Sapone, *Burkina Faso* 83 C4
Saposoa, *Peru* 124 E3
Sapouy, *Burkina Faso* 83 C4
Sapozhok, *Russia* 48 D5
Sapphire, *Australia* 94 C4
Sappho, *U.S.A.* 116 B2
Sapporo, *Japan* 54 C10
Sapri, *Italy* 31 B8
Sapulpa, *U.S.A.* 113 H6
Saqqez, *Iran* 70 B5
Sar Dasht, *Iran* 71 C6
Sar Gachīneh, *Iran* 71 D6
Sar Planina, *Macedonia* 40 E4
Sara, *Burkina Faso* 82 C4
Sara, *Phil.* 61 F5
Sara Buri = Saraburi, *Thailand* 64 E3
Sarāb, *Iran* 70 B5
Sarabadi, *Iraq* 70 C5
Saraburi, *Thailand* 64 E3
Sarada →, *India* 67 F12
Saradiya, *India* 68 J4
Saraféré, *Mali* 82 B4
Saragossa = Zaragoza, *Spain* 32 D4
Saraguro, *Ecuador* 124 D3
Sarai Naurang, *Pakistan* 68 C4
Saraikela, *India* 69 H11
Saraiu, *Romania* 43 F13
Sarajevo, *Bos.-H.* 42 G3
Sarakhs, *Turkmenistan* 71 B9
Saran, Gunung, *Indonesia* 62 E4
Saranac L., *U.S.A.* 111 B10
Saranac Lake, *U.S.A.* 111 B10
Saranda, *Tanzania* 86 D3
Sarandë, *Albania* 40 G3
Sarandí del Yi, *Uruguay* 127 C4
Sarandí Grande, *Uruguay* 126 C4
Sarangani B., *Phil.* 61 J6
Sarangani Is., *Phil.* 61 J6
Sarangarh, *India* 67 J13
Saransk, *Russia* 48 C7
Sarapul, *Russia* 50 D6
Sarasota, *U.S.A.* 109 M4
Saratoga, *Calif., U.S.A.* 116 H4
Saratoga, *Wyo., U.S.A.* 114 F10
Saratoga Springs, *U.S.A.* 111 C11
Saratok, *Malaysia* 62 D4
Saratov, *Russia* 48 E7
Saravane, *Laos* 64 E6
Sarawak □, *Malaysia* 62 D4
Saray, *Tekirdağ, Turkey* 41 E11
Saray, *Van, Turkey* 73 C11
Saraya, *Guinea* 82 C2
Saraya, *Senegal* 82 C2
Saraycık, *Turkey* 39 B11
Sarayköy, *Turkey* 39 D10
Saraylar, *Turkey* 41 F11
Sarayönü, *Turkey* 72 C5
Sarbāz, *Iran* 71 E9
Sarbīsheh, *Iran* 71 C8
Sárbogárd, *Hungary* 42 D3
Sarca →, *Italy* 28 C7
Sarcelles, *France* 19 D9
Sarda = Sarada →, *India* 67 F12
Sardarshahr, *India* 68 E6
Sardegna □, *Italy* 30 B1
Sardhana, *India* 68 E7
Sardina, Pta., *Canary Is.* 37 F4
Sardinia = Sardegna □, *Italy* 30 B1
Sardis, *Turkey* 39 C10
Sārdūīyeh = Dar Mazār, *Iran* 71 D8
S'Arenal, *Spain* 37 B9
Sarentino, *Italy* 29 B8
Saréyamou, *Mali* 82 B4
Sargasso Sea, *Atl. Oc.* 97 D20
Sargodha, *Pakistan* 68 C5
Sarh, *Chad* 79 G9
Sarhala, *Ivory C.* 82 D3
Sārī, *Iran* 71 B7
Sari d'Orcino, *France* 21 F12
Sária, *Greece* 39 F9
Saria, *India* 69 J10
Sariab, *Pakistan* 68 D2
Sarıbeyler, *Turkey* 39 B9
Sarıgöl, *Turkey* 72 C3
Sarikamiş, *Turkey* 73 B10
Sarıkaya, *Turkey* 72 C6
Sarikei, *Malaysia* 62 D4
Sarıköy, *Turkey* 41 F11
Sarila, *India* 69 G8
Sarina, *Australia* 94 C4
Sariñena, *Spain* 32 D4
Sarita, *U.S.A.* 113 M6
Sariwŏn, *N. Korea* 57 E13
Sariyar Baraji, *Turkey* 72 B4
Sarıyer, *Turkey* 41 E13
Sarju →, *India* 69 F9
Sark, *U.K.* 13 H5
Sarkad, *Hungary* 42 D6
Sarkari Tala, *India* 68 F4
Şarkışla, *Turkey* 72 C7
Şarköy, *Turkey* 41 F11
Sarlat-la-Canéda, *France* 20 D5
Sărmăşag, *Romania* 42 C7
Sărmaşu, *Romania* 43 D9
Sarmi, *Indonesia* 63 E9
Sarmiento, *Argentina* 128 F3
Sarmizegetusa, *Romania* 42 E7
Särna, *Sweden* 10 C7
Sarnano, *Italy* 29 E10
Sarnen, *Switz.* 25 J4
Sarnia, *Canada* 102 D3
Sarno, *Italy* 31 B7
Sarnthein = Sarentino, *Italy* 29 B8
Särö, *Sweden* 11 G5
Sarolangun, *Indonesia* 62 E2
Saronikós Kólpos, *Greece* 38 D5
Saronno, *Italy* 28 C6
Saros Körfezi, *Turkey* 41 F10
Sárospatak, *Hungary* 42 B6
Sarpsborg, *Norway* 9 G14
Sarracín, *Spain* 34 C7
Sarralbe, *France* 19 D14
Sarre = Saar →, *Europe* 17 E6
Sarre, *Italy* 28 C4
Sarre-Union, *France* 19 D14
Sarrebourg, *France* 19 D14
Sarreguemines, *France* 19 C14
Sarria, *Spain* 34 C3
Sarrión, *Spain* 32 E4
Sarro, *Mali* 82 C3
Sarstedt, *Germany* 24 C5
Sartène, *France* 21 G12
Sarthe □, *France* 18 D7
Sarthe →, *France* 18 E6
Sartilly, *France* 18 D5
Saruhanlı, *Turkey* 39 C9
Sărulești, *Romania* 43 F11
Saruna →, *Pakistan* 68 F2
Sárvár, *Hungary* 42 C1
Sarvar, *India* 68 F6
Sarvestān, *Iran* 71 D7
Särvfjället, *Sweden* 10 B7
Sárviz →, *Hungary* 42 D3
Sary-Tash, *Kyrgyzstan* 50 F8
Sarych, Mys, *Ukraine* 47 K7
Saryshagan, *Kazakstan* 50 E8
Sarzana, *Italy* 28 D6
Sarzeau, *France* 18 E4
Sasan Gir, *India* 68 J4
Sasaram, *India* 69 G11
Sasebo, *Japan* 55 H4
Saser, *India* 69 B7
Saskatchewan □, *Canada* 105 C7
Saskatchewan →, *Canada* 105 C8
Saskatoon, *Canada* 105 C7
Saskylakh, *Russia* 51 B12
Sasolburg, *S. Africa* 89 D4
Sasovo, *Russia* 48 C5
Sassandra, *Ivory C.* 82 E3
Sassandra →, *Ivory C.* 82 E3
Sássari, *Italy* 30 B1
Sassnitz, *Germany* 24 A9
Sasso Marconi, *Italy* 29 D8
Sassocorvaro, *Italy* 29 E9
Sassoferrato, *Italy* 29 E9
Sasstown, *Liberia* 82 E3
Sassuolo, *Italy* 28 D7
Sástago, *Spain* 32 D4
Sasumua Dam, *Kenya* 86 C4
Sasyk, Ozero, *Ukraine* 47 K5
Sata-Misaki, *Japan* 55 J5
Satadougou, *Mali* 82 C2
Satakunta, *Finland* 9 F20
Satama-Soukoura, *Ivory C.* 82 D4
Satara, *India* 66 L8
Satara, *S. Africa* 89 C5
Satbarwa, *India* 69 H11
Såtenäs, *Sweden* 11 F6
Säter, *Sweden* 10 D9
Satevó, *Mexico* 118 B3
Satilla →, *U.S.A.* 109 K5
Satmala Hills, *India* 66 J9
Satna, *India* 69 G9
Šator, *Bos.-H.* 29 D13
Sátoraljaújhely, *Hungary* 42 B6
Satpura Ra., *India* 66 J10
Satrup, *Germany* 24 A5
Satsuna-Shotō, *Japan* 55 K5
Sattahip, *Thailand* 64 F3
Satu Mare, *Romania* 42 C7
Satu Mare □, *Romania* 42 C8
Satui, *Indonesia* 62 E5
Satun, *Thailand* 65 J3
Saturnina →, *Brazil* 124 F7
Sauce, *Argentina* 126 C4
Sauceda, *Mexico* 118 B4
Saucillo, *Mexico* 118 B3
Sauda, *Norway* 9 G12
Sauðarkrókur, *Iceland* 8 D4
Saudi Arabia ■, *Asia* 74 B3
Saugeen →, *Canada* 110 B3
Saugerties, *U.S.A.* 111 D11
Saugues, *France* 20 D7
Saugus, *U.S.A.* 117 L8
Saujon, *France* 20 C3
Sauk Centre, *U.S.A.* 112 C7
Sauk Rapids, *U.S.A.* 112 C7
Saulgau, *Germany* 25 G5
Saulieu, *France* 19 E11
Sault, *France* 21 D9
Sault Ste. Marie, *Canada* 102 C3
Sault Ste. Marie, *U.S.A.* 101 D11
Saumlaki, *Indonesia* 63 F8
Saumur, *France* 18 E6
Saunders C., *N.Z.* 91 L3
Saunders I., *Antarctica* 5 B1
Saunders Point, *Australia* 93 E4
Sauri, *Nigeria* 83 C6
Saurimo, *Angola* 84 F4
Sausalito, *U.S.A.* 116 H4
Sauveterre-de-Béarn, *France* 20 E3
Sauzé-Vaussais, *France* 20 B4
Savá, *Honduras* 120 C2
Sava, *Italy* 31 B10
Sava →, *Serbia, Yug.* 42 F5
Savage, *U.S.A.* 112 B2
Savage I. = Niue, *Cook Is.* 97 J11
Savage River, *Australia* 94 G4
Savai'i, *W. Samoa* 91 A12
Savalou, *Benin* 83 D5
Savane, *Mozam.* 87 F4
Savanna, *U.S.A.* 112 D9
Savanna-la-Mar, *Jamaica* 120 C4
Savannah, *Ga., U.S.A.* 109 J5
Savannah, *Mo., U.S.A.* 112 F7
Savannah, *Tenn., U.S.A.* 109 H1
Savannah →, *U.S.A.* 109 J5
Savannakhet, *Laos* 64 D5
Savant L., *Canada* 102 B1
Savant Lake, *Canada* 102 B1
Savanur, *India* 66 M9
Săvârşin, *Romania* 42 D7
Savaştepe, *Turkey* 39 B9
Savé, *Benin* 83 D5
Save →, *France* 20 E5
Save →, *Mozam.* 89 C5
Sāveh, *Iran* 71 C6
Savelugu, *Ghana* 83 D4
Savenay, *France* 18 E5
Săveni, *Romania* 43 C11
Saverdun, *France* 20 E5
Saverne, *France* 19 D14
Savigliano, *Italy* 28 D4
Savigny-sur-Braye, *France* 18 E7
Sávio →, *Italy* 29 D9
Šavnik, *Montenegro, Yug.* 40 D3
Savo, *Finland* 8 E22
Savoie □, *France* 21 C10
Savona, *Italy* 28 D5
Savona, *U.S.A.* 110 D7
Savonlinna, *Finland* 46 B5
Savoy = Savoie □, *France* 21 C10
Şavşat, *Turkey* 73 B10
Sävsjö, *Sweden* 11 G8
Savur, *Turkey* 70 B4
Sawahlunto, *Indonesia* 62 E2
Sawai, *Indonesia* 63 E7
Sawai Madhopur, *India* 68 G7
Sawang Daen Din, *Thailand* 64 D4
Sawankhalok, *Thailand* 64 D2
Sawara, *Japan* 55 G10
Sawatch Range, *U.S.A.* 115 G10
Sawel Mt., *U.K.* 15 B4
Sawi, *Thailand* 65 G2
Sawla, *Ghana* 82 D4
Sawmills, *Zimbabwe* 87 F2
Sawtooth Range, *U.S.A.* 114 E6
Sawu, *Indonesia* 63 F6
Sawu Sea, *Indonesia* 63 F6
Saxby →, *Australia* 94 B3
Saxmundham, *U.K.* 13 E9
Saxony = Sachsen □, *Germany* 24 E9
Saxony, Lower = Niedersachsen □, *Germany* 24 C4
Saxton, *U.S.A.* 110 F6
Say, *Mali* 82 C4
Say, *Niger* 83 C5
Saya, *Nigeria* 83 D5
Sayabec, *Canada* 103 C6
Sayaboury, *Laos* 64 C3
Sayán, *Peru* 124 F3
Sayan, Vostochnyy, *Russia* 51 D10
Sayan, Zapadnyy, *Russia* 51 D10
Saydā, *Lebanon* 75 B4
Sayhandulaan = Oldziyt, *Mongolia* 56 B5
Sayhūt, *Yemen* 74 D5
Saykhin, *Kazakstan* 49 F8
Saynshand, *Mongolia* 56 B6
Sayre, *Okla., U.S.A.* 113 H5
Sayre, *Pa., U.S.A.* 111 E8
Sayreville, *U.S.A.* 111 F10
Sayula, *Mexico* 118 D4
Sayward, *Canada* 104 C3
Sazanit, *Albania* 40 F3
Sázava →, *Czech Rep.* 26 B7
Sazin, *Pakistan* 69 B5
Sazlika →, *Bulgaria* 41 E9
Scaër, *France* 18 D3
Scafell Pike, *U.K.* 12 C4
Scalea, *Italy* 31 C8
Scalloway, *U.K.* 14 A7
Scalpay, *U.K.* 14 D3
Scandia, *Canada* 104 C6
Scandiano, *Italy* 28 D7
Scandicci, *Italy* 29 E8
Scandinavia, *Europe* 6 C8
Scansano, *Italy* 29 F8
Scapa Flow, *U.K.* 14 C5
Scappoose, *U.S.A.* 116 E4
Scarámia, Capo, *Italy* 31 F7
Scarba, *U.K.* 14 E3
Scarborough, *Trin. & Tob.* 121 D7
Scarborough, *U.K.* 12 C7
Scariff I., *Ireland* 15 E1
Scarp, *U.K.* 14 C1
Scebeli, Wabi →, *Somali Rep.* 74 G3
Šćedro, *Croatia* 29 E13
Schaal See, *Germany* 24 B6
Schaffhausen, *Switz.* 25 H4
Schagen, *Neths.* 17 B4
Schaghticoke, *U.S.A.* 111 D11
Schärding, *Austria* 26 C6
Scharhörn, *Germany* 24 B4
Scheessel, *Germany* 24 B5
Schefferville, *Canada* 103 B6
Scheibbs, *Austria* 26 C8
Schelde →, *Belgium* 17 C4
Schell Creek Ra., *U.S.A.* 114 G6
Schellsburg, *U.S.A.* 110 F6
Schenectady, *U.S.A.* 111 D11
Schenevus, *U.S.A.* 111 D10
Scherfede, *Germany* 24 D5
Schesslitz, *Germany* 25 F7
Schiedam, *Neths.* 17 C4
Schiermonnikoog, *Neths.* 17 A6
Schiltigheim, *France* 19 D14
Schio, *Italy* 29 C8
Schladming, *Austria* 26 D6
Schlanders = Silandro, *Italy* 28 B7
Schlei →, *Germany* 24 A5
Schleiden, *Germany* 24 E2
Schleiz, *Germany* 24 E7
Schleswig, *Germany* 24 A5
Schleswig-Holstein □, *Germany* 24 A5
Schlüchtern, *Germany* 25 E5
Schmalkalden, *Germany* 24 E6
Schmölln, *Germany* 24 E8
Schneeberg, *Austria* 26 D8
Schneeberg, *Germany* 24 E8
Schneverdingen, *Germany* 24 B5
Schoharie, *U.S.A.* 111 D10
Schoharie →, *U.S.A.* 111 D10
Scholls, *U.S.A.* 116 E4
Schönberg, *Mecklenburg-Vorpommern, Germany* 24 B6
Schönberg, *Schleswig-Holstein, Germany* 24 A6
Schönebeck, *Germany* 24 C7
Schongau, *Germany* 25 H6
Schöningen, *Germany* 24 C6
Schopfheim, *Germany* 25 H3
Schorndorf, *Germany* 25 G5
Schortens, *Germany* 24 B3
Schouten I., *Australia* 94 G4
Schouten Is. = Supiori, *Indonesia* 63 E9
Schouwen, *Neths.* 17 C3
Schramberg, *Germany* 25 G4
Schrankogel, *Austria* 26 D4
Schreiber, *Canada* 102 C2
Schrems, *Austria* 26 C8
Schrobenhausen, *Germany* 25 G7
Schroffenstein, *Namibia* 88 D2
Schroon Lake, *U.S.A.* 111 C11
Schruns, *Austria* 26 D2
Schuler, *Canada* 105 C6
Schumacher, *Canada* 102 C3
Schurz, *U.S.A.* 114 G4
Schuyler, *U.S.A.* 112 E6
Schuylerville, *U.S.A.* 111 C11
Schuylkill →, *U.S.A.* 111 G9
Schuylkill Haven, *U.S.A.* 111 F8
Schwabach, *Germany* 25 F7
Schwaben □, *Germany* 25 G6
Schwäbisch Gmünd, *Germany* 25 G5
Schwäbisch Hall, *Germany* 25 F5
Schwäbische Alb, *Germany* 25 G5
Schwabmünchen, *Germany* 25 G6
Schwalmstadt, *Germany* 24 E5
Schwandorf, *Germany* 25 F8
Schwaner, Pegunungan, *Indonesia* 62 E4
Schwanewede, *Germany* 24 B4
Schwarmstedt, *Germany* 24 C5
Schwarze Elster →, *Germany* 24 D8
Schwarzenberg, *Germany* 24 E8
Schwarzrand, *Namibia* 88 D2
Schwarzwald, *Germany* 25 G4
Schwaz, *Austria* 26 D4
Schwechat, *Austria* 27 C9
Schwedt, *Germany* 24 B10
Schweinfurt, *Germany* 25 E6
Schweizer-Reneke, *S. Africa* 88 D4
Schwenningen = Villingen-Schwenningen, *Germany* 25 G4
Schwerin, *Germany* 24 B7
Schweriner See, *Germany* 24 B7
Schwetzingen, *Germany* 25 F4
Schwyz, *Switz.* 25 H4
Schwyz □, *Switz.* 25 H4
Sciacca, *Italy* 30 E6
Scicli, *Italy* 31 F7
Scilla, *Italy* 31 D8
Scilly, Isles of, *U.K.* 13 H1
Ścinawa, *Poland* 45 G3
Scione, *Greece* 40 G7
Scioto →, *U.S.A.* 108 F4
Scituate, *U.S.A.* 111 D14
Scobey, *U.S.A.* 112 A2
Scone, *Australia* 95 E5
Scordia, *Italy* 31 E7
Scoresbysund = Illoqqortoormiit, *Greenland* 4 B6
Scorniceşti, *Romania* 43 F9
Scotia, *Calif., U.S.A.* 114 F1
Scotia, *N.Y., U.S.A.* 111 D11
Scotia Sea, *Antarctica* 5 B18
Scotland, *Canada* 110 C4
Scotland □, *U.K.* 14 E5
Scott, C., *Australia* 92 B4
Scott City, *U.S.A.* 112 F4
Scott Glacier, *Antarctica* 5 C8
Scott I., *Antarctica* 5 C11
Scott Is., *Canada* 104 C3
Scott L., *Canada* 105 B7
Scott Reef, *Australia* 92 B3
Scottburgh, *S. Africa* 89 E5
Scottdale, *U.S.A.* 110 F5
Scottish Borders □, *U.K.* 14 F6
Scottsbluff, *U.S.A.* 112 E3
Scottsboro, *U.S.A.* 109 H3
Scottsburg, *U.S.A.* 108 F3
Scottsdale, *Australia* 94 G4
Scottsdale, *U.S.A.* 115 K7
Scottsville, *Ky., U.S.A.* 109 G2
Scottsville, *N.Y., U.S.A.* 110 C7
Scottville, *U.S.A.* 108 D2
Scranton, *U.S.A.* 111 E9
Scugog, L., *Canada* 110 B6
Sculeni, *Moldova* 43 C12
Scunthorpe, *U.K.* 12 D7
Scuol Schuls, *Switz.* 25 J6
Scutari = Üsküdar, *Turkey* 41 F13
Seabrook, L., *Australia* 93 F2
Seaford, *U.K.* 13 G8
Seaford, *U.S.A.* 108 F8
Seaforth, *Australia* 94 C4
Seaforth, *Canada* 110 C3
Seaforth, L., *U.K.* 14 D2
Seagraves, *U.S.A.* 113 J3
Seaham, *U.K.* 12 C6
Seal →, *Canada* 105 B10
Seal L., *Canada* 103 B7
Sealy, *U.S.A.* 113 L6
Searchlight, *U.S.A.* 117 K12
Searcy, *U.S.A.* 113 H9
Searles L., *U.S.A.* 117 K9
Seascale, *U.K.* 12 C4
Seaside, *Calif., U.S.A.* 116 J5
Seaside, *Oreg., U.S.A.* 116 E3
Seaspray, *Australia* 95 F4
Seattle, *U.S.A.* 116 C4
Seaview Ra., *Australia* 94 B4
Sebago L., *U.S.A.* 111 C14
Sebago Lake, *U.S.A.* 111 C14
Sebastián Vizcaíno, B., *Mexico* 118 B2
Sebastopol = Sevastopol, *Ukraine* 47 K7
Sebastopol, *U.S.A.* 116 G4
Sebba, *Burkina Faso* 83 C5
Sebderat, *Eritrea* 81 D4
Sébékoro, *Mali* 82 C3
Seben, *Turkey* 72 B4
Sebeş, *Romania* 43 E8
Sebeşului, Munţii, *Romania* 43 E8
Sebewaing, *U.S.A.* 108 D4
Sebezh, *Russia* 46 D5
Sebha = Sabhah, *Libya* 79 C8
Sébi, *Mali* 82 B4
Şebinkarahisar, *Turkey* 73 B8
Sebiş, *Romania* 42 D7
Sebnitz, *Germany* 24 E10
Sebring, *Fla., U.S.A.* 109 M5
Sebring, *Ohio, U.S.A.* 110 F3
Sebringville, *Canada* 110 C3
Sebta = Ceuta, *N. Afr.* 78 A4
Sebuku, *Indonesia* 62 E5
Sebuku, Teluk, *Malaysia* 62 D5
Sečanj, *Serbia, Yug.* 42 E5
Secchia →, *Italy* 28 C8
Sechelt, *Canada* 104 D4
Sechura, Desierto de, *Peru* 124 E2
Seclin, *France* 19 B10
Secondigny, *France* 18 F6
Sečovce, *Slovak Rep.* 27 C14
Secretary I., *N.Z.* 91 L1
Secunderabad, *India* 66 L11
Security-Widefield, *U.S.A.* 112 F2
Sedalia, *U.S.A.* 112 F8
Sedan, *France* 19 C11
Sedan, *U.S.A.* 113 G6
Sedano, *Spain* 34 C7
Seddon, *N.Z.* 91 J5
Seddonville, *N.Z.* 91 J4
Sedé Boqér, *Israel* 75 E3
Sedeh, *Fārs, Iran* 71 D7
Sedeh, *Khorāsān, Iran* 71 C8
Séderon, *France* 21 D9
Sederot, *Israel* 75 D3
Sédhiou, *Senegal* 82 C1
Sedico, *Italy* 29 B9
Sedlčany, *Czech Rep.* 26 B7
Sedley, *Canada* 105 C8
Sedona, *U.S.A.* 115 J8
Sedova, Pik, *Russia* 50 B6
Sedro Woolley, *U.S.A.* 116 B4
Šeduva, *Lithuania* 44 C10
Sędziszów, *Poland* 45 H7
Sędziszów Małapolski, *Poland* 45 H8
Seebad Ahlbeck, *Germany* 24 B10
Seefeld in Tirol, *Austria* 26 D4
Seehausen, *Germany* 24 C7
Seeheim, *Namibia* 88 D2
Seeheim-Jugenheim, *Germany* 25 F4
Seeis, *Namibia* 88 C2
Seekoei →, *S. Africa* 88 E4
Seeley's Bay, *Canada* 111 B8
Seelow, *Germany* 24 C10
Sées, *France* 18 D7
Seesen, *Germany* 24 D6
Seevetal, *Germany* 24 B6
Sefadu, *S. Leone* 82 D2
Seferihisar, *Turkey* 39 C8
Séfeto, *Mali* 82 C3
Sefwi Bekwai, *Ghana* 82 D4
Segamat, *Malaysia* 65 L4
Şegarcea, *Romania* 43 F8
Ségbana, *Benin* 83 C5
Segbwema, *S. Leone* 82 D2
Seget, *Indonesia* 63 E8
Segonzac, *France* 20 C3
Segorbe, *Spain* 32 F4
Ségou, *Mali* 82 C3
Segovia = Coco →, *Cent. Amer.* 120 D3
Segovia, *Spain* 34 E6
Segovia □, *Spain* 34 E6
Segré, *France* 18 E6
Segre →, *Spain* 32 D5
Séguéla, *Ivory C.* 82 D3
Séguénéga, *Burkina Faso* 83 C4
Seguin, *U.S.A.* 113 L6
Segundo →, *Argentina* 126 C3
Segura →, *Spain* 33 G4
Segura, Sierra de, *Spain* 33 G2
Seh Konj, Kūh-e, *Iran* 71 D8
Seh Qal'eh, *Iran* 71 C8
Sehitwa, *Botswana* 88 C3
Sehore, *India* 68 H7
Sehwan, *Pakistan* 68 F2
Şeica Mare, *Romania* 43 D9
Seil, *U.K.* 14 E3
Seiland, *Norway* 8 A20

Seilhac, *France* 20 C5
Seiling, *U.S.A.* 113 G5
Seille →, *Moselle, France* 19 C13
Seille →, *Saône-et-Loire, France* 19 F11
Sein, Î. de, *France* 18 D2
Seinäjoki, *Finland* 9 E20
Seine →, *France* 18 C7
Seine, B. de la, *France* 18 C6
Seine-et-Marne □, *France* 19 D10
Seine-Maritime □, *France* 18 C7
Seine-St-Denis □, *France* 19 D9
Seini, *Romania* 43 C8
Seirijai, *Lithuania* 44 D10
Sejerø, *Denmark* 11 J5
Sejerø Bugt, *Denmark* 11 J5
Sejny, *Poland* 44 D10
Seka, *Ethiopia* 81 F4
Sekayu, *Indonesia* 62 E2
Seke, *Tanzania* 86 C3
Sekenke, *Tanzania* 86 C3
Seki, *Turkey* 39 E11
Sekondi-Takoradi, *Ghana* 82 E4
Sekota, *Ethiopia* 81 E4
Seksna, *Russia* 46 C10
Sekuma, *Botswana* 88 C3
Selah, *U.S.A.* 114 C3
Selama, *Malaysia* 65 K3
Selárgius, *Italy* 30 C2
Selaru, *Indonesia* 63 F8
Selb, *Germany* 25 E8
Selby, *U.K.* 12 D6
Selby, *U.S.A.* 112 C4
Selca, *Croatia* 29 E13
Selçuk, *Turkey* 39 D9
Selden, *U.S.A.* 112 F4
Sele →, *Italy* 31 B7
Selebi-Pikwe, *Botswana* 89 C4
Selemdzha →, *Russia* 51 D13
Selendi, *Manisa, Turkey* 39 C10
Selendi, *Manisa, Turkey* 39 C9
Selenga = Selenge Mörön →, *Asia* 60 A5
Selenge Mörön →, *Asia* 60 A5
Selenica, *Albania* 40 F3
Selenter See, *Germany* 24 A6
Sélestat, *France* 19 D14
Seletan, Tanjung, *Indonesia* 62 E4
Selevac, *Serbia, Yug.* 40 B4
Sélibabi, *Mauritania* 82 B2
Seliger, Ozero, *Russia* 46 D7
Seligman, *U.S.A.* 115 J7
Şelim, *Turkey* 73 B10
Selîma, El Wâhât el, *Sudan* 80 C2
Selimiye, *Turkey* 39 D9
Selinda Spillway →, *Botswana* 88 B3
Selinoús, *Greece* 38 D3
Selinsgrove, *U.S.A.* 110 F8
Selizharovo, *Russia* 46 D7
Selkirk, *Canada* 105 C9
Selkirk, *U.K.* 14 F6
Selkirk I., *Canada* 105 C9
Selkirk Mts., *Canada* 100 C8
Sellama, *Sudan* 81 E2
Selliá, *Greece* 36 D6
Sellières, *France* 19 F12
Sells, *U.S.A.* 115 L8
Sellye, *Hungary* 42 E2
Selma, *Ala., U.S.A.* 109 J2
Selma, *Calif., U.S.A.* 116 J7
Selma, *N.C., U.S.A.* 109 H6
Selmer, *U.S.A.* 109 H1
Selongey, *France* 19 E12
Selowandoma Falls, *Zimbabwe* 87 G3
Selpele, *Indonesia* 63 E8
Selsey Bill, *U.K.* 13 G7
Seltso, *Russia* 46 F8
Seltz, *France* 19 D15
Selu, *Indonesia* 63 F8
Sélune →, *France* 18 D5
Selva = La Selva del Camp, *Spain* 32 D6
Selva, *Argentina* 126 B3
Selvas, *Brazil* 122 D4
Selwyn L., *Canada* 105 B8
Selwyn Mts., *Canada* 100 B6
Selwyn Ra., *Australia* 94 C3
Semani →, *Albania* 40 F3
Semarang, *Indonesia* 63 G14
Sembabule, *Uganda* 86 C3
Şemdinli, *Turkey* 73 D11
Sémé, *Senegal* 82 B2
Semeih, *Sudan* 81 E3
Semenov, *Russia* 48 B7
Semenovka, *Chernihiv, Ukraine* 47 F7
Semenovka, *Kremenchuk, Ukraine* 47 H7
Semeru, *Indonesia* 63 H15
Semey, *Kazakstan* 50 D9
Semikarakorskiy, *Russia* 49 G5
Semiluki, *Russia* 47 G10
Seminoe Reservoir, *U.S.A.* 114 F10
Seminole, *Okla., U.S.A.* 113 H6
Seminole, *Tex., U.S.A.* 113 J3
Seminole Draw →, *U.S.A.* 113 J3
Semipalatinsk = Semey, *Kazakstan* 50 D9
Semirara Is., *Phil.* 61 F4
Semitau, *Indonesia* 62 D4
Semiyarka, *Kazakstan* 50 D8
Semiyarskoye = Semiyarka, *Kazakstan* 50 D8
Semmering P., *Austria* 26 D8
Semnān, *Iran* 71 C7
Semnān □, *Iran* 71 C7
Semporna, *Malaysia* 63 D5
Semuda, *Indonesia* 62 E4
Semur-en-Auxois, *France* 19 E11
Sen →, *Cambodia* 62 B3
Senā, *Iran* 71 D6
Sena, *Mozam.* 87 F4
Sena Madureira, *Brazil* 124 E5
Senador Pompeu, *Brazil* 125 E11
Senaki, *Georgia* 49 J6
Senanga, *Zambia* 88 B3
Senatobia, *U.S.A.* 113 H10
Sencelles, *Spain* 37 B9
Sendafa, *Ethiopia* 81 F4
Sendai, *Kagoshima, Japan* 55 J5
Sendai, *Miyagi, Japan* 54 E10
Sendai-Wan, *Japan* 54 E10
Senden, *Bayern, Germany* 25 G6
Senden, *Nordrhein-Westfalen, Germany* 24 D3
Sendhwa, *India* 68 J6
Sene →, *Ghana* 83 D4
Senec, *Slovak Rep.* 27 C10
Seneca, *U.S.A.* 109 H4
Seneca Falls, *U.S.A.* 111 D8
Seneca L., *U.S.A.* 110 D8
Senecaville L., *U.S.A.* 110 G3
Senegal ■, *W. Afr.* 82 C2
Sénégal →, *W. Afr.* 82 B1
Senegambia, *Africa* 76 E2
Senekal, *S. Africa* 89 D4
Senftenberg, *Germany* 24 D10
Senga Hill, *Zambia* 87 D3
Senge Khambab = Indus →, *Pakistan* 68 G2
Sengiley, *Russia* 48 D9
Sengua →, *Zimbabwe* 87 F2
Senhor-do-Bonfim, *Brazil* 125 F10
Senica, *Slovak Rep.* 27 C10
Senigállia, *Italy* 29 E10
Senio →, *Italy* 29 D9
Senirkent, *Turkey* 39 C12
Senise, *Italy* 31 B9
Senj, *Croatia* 29 D11
Senja, *Norway* 8 B17
Senkaku-Shotō, *Japan* 55 L1
Senlis, *France* 19 C9
Senmonorom, *Cambodia* 64 F6
Sennâr, *Sudan* 81 E3
Sennar □, *Sudan* 81 E3
Senneterre, *Canada* 102 C4
Senno, *Belarus* 46 E5
Sénnori, *Italy* 30 B1
Seno, *Laos* 64 D5
Senonches, *France* 18 D8
Senorbì, *Italy* 30 C2
Senožeče, *Slovenia* 29 C11
Sens, *France* 19 D10
Senta, *Serbia, Yug.* 42 E5
Sentani, *Indonesia* 63 E10
Sentery, *Dem. Rep. of the Congo* 86 D2
Sentinel, *U.S.A.* 115 K7
Šentjur, *Slovenia* 29 B12
Senya Beraku, *Ghana* 83 D4
Seo de Urgel = La Seu d'Urgell, *Spain* 32 C6
Seohara, *India* 69 E8
Seonath →, *India* 69 J10
Seondha, *India* 69 F8
Seoni, *India* 69 H8
Seoni Malwa, *India* 68 H8
Seoul = Sŏul, *S. Korea* 57 F14
Sepīdān, *Iran* 71 D7
Sepo-ri, *N. Korea* 57 E14
Sępólno Krajeńskie, *Poland* 44 E4
Sepone, *Laos* 64 D6
Sępopol, *Poland* 44 D8
Sept-Îles, *Canada* 103 B6
Septemvri, *Bulgaria* 41 D8
Sepúlveda, *Spain* 34 D7
Sequeros, *Spain* 34 E4
Sequim, *U.S.A.* 116 B3
Sequoia National Park, *U.S.A.* 116 J8
Serafimovich, *Russia* 48 F6
Seraing, *Belgium* 17 D5
Seraja, *Indonesia* 65 L7
Serakhis →, *Cyprus* 36 D11
Seram, *Indonesia* 63 E7
Seram Sea, *Indonesia* 63 E7
Seranantsara, *Madag.* 89 B8
Serang, *Indonesia* 63 G12
Serasan, *Indonesia* 65 L7
Seravezza, *Italy* 28 E7
Şerbettar, *Turkey* 41 E10
Serbia □, *Yugoslavia* 40 C5
Şercaia, *Romania* 43 E10
Serdo, *Ethiopia* 81 E5
Serdobsk, *Russia* 48 D7
Sered', *Slovak Rep.* 27 C10
Seredka, *Russia* 46 C5
Şereflikoçhisar, *Turkey* 72 C5
Seregno, *Italy* 28 C6
Seremban, *Malaysia* 65 L3
Serengeti Plain, *Tanzania* 86 C4
Serenje, *Zambia* 87 E3
Sereth = Siret →, *Romania* 43 E12
Sergach, *Russia* 48 C7
Sergen, *Turkey* 41 E11
Sergino, *Russia* 50 C7
Sergipe □, *Brazil* 125 F11
Sergiyev Posad, *Russia* 46 D10
Seria, *Brunei* 62 D4
Serian, *Malaysia* 62 D4
Seriate, *Italy* 28 C6
Seribu, Kepulauan, *Indonesia* 62 F3
Sérifontaine, *France* 19 C8
Sérifos, *Greece* 38 D6
Sérignan, *France* 20 E7
Sérigny →, *Canada* 103 A6
Serik, *Turkey* 72 D4
Seringapatam Reef, *Australia* 92 B3
Serinhisar, *Turkey* 39 D11
Sermaize-les-Bains, *France* 19 D11
Sermata, *Indonesia* 63 F7
Sérmide, *Italy* 29 D8
Sernovodsk, *Russia* 48 D10
Sernur, *Russia* 48 B9
Serock, *Poland* 45 F8
Serón, *Spain* 33 H2
Seròs, *Spain* 32 D5
Serov, *Russia* 50 D7
Serowe, *Botswana* 88 C4
Serpa, *Portugal* 35 H3
Serpeddí, Punta, *Italy* 30 C2
Serpentara, *Italy* 30 C2
Serpentine Lakes, *Australia* 93 E4
Serpis →, *Spain* 33 G4
Serpukhov, *Russia* 46 E9
Serra de Outes, *Spain* 34 C2
Serra do Navio, *Brazil* 125 C8
Serra San Bruno, *Italy* 31 D9
Serradilla, *Spain* 34 F4
Sérrai, *Greece* 40 E7
Sérrai □, *Greece* 40 E7
Serramanna, *Italy* 30 C1
Serravalle Scrívia, *Italy* 28 D5
Serre-Ponçon, L. de, *France* 21 D10
Serres, *France* 21 D9
Serrezuela, *Argentina* 126 C2
Serrinha, *Brazil* 125 F11
Sersale, *Italy* 31 C9
Sertã, *Portugal* 34 F2
Sertanópolis, *Brazil* 127 A5
Sêrtar, *China* 58 A3
Serua, *Indonesia* 63 F8
Serui, *Indonesia* 63 E9
Serule, *Botswana* 88 C4
Sérvia, *Greece* 40 F6
Serzedelo, *Portugal* 34 D2
Sese Is., *Uganda* 86 C3
Sesepe, *Indonesia* 63 E7
Sesfontein, *Namibia* 88 B1
Sesheke, *Zambia* 88 B3
Sésia →, *Italy* 28 C5
Sesimbra, *Portugal* 35 G1
S'Espalmador, *Spain* 37 C7
S'Espardell, *Spain* 37 C7
Sessa Aurunca, *Italy* 30 A6
S'Estanyol, *Spain* 37 B9
Sestao, *Spain* 32 B2
Sesto Calende, *Italy* 28 C5
Sesto San Giovanni, *Italy* 28 C6
Sestri Levante, *Italy* 28 D6
Sestriere, *Italy* 28 D3
Sestroretsk, *Russia* 46 B6
Sestrunj, *Croatia* 29 D11
Sestu, *Italy* 30 C2
Setana, *Japan* 54 C9
Sète, *France* 20 E7
Sete Lagôas, *Brazil* 125 G10
Sétif, *Algeria* 78 A7
Seto, *Japan* 55 G8
Setonaikai, *Japan* 55 G6
Settat, *Morocco* 78 B4
Séttimo Torinese, *Italy* 28 C4
Setting L., *Canada* 105 C9
Settle, *U.K.* 12 C5
Settlement Pt., *Bahamas* 109 M6
Settlers, *S. Africa* 89 C4
Setúbal, *Portugal* 35 G2
Setúbal □, *Portugal* 35 G2
Setúbal, B. de, *Portugal* 35 G2
Seugne →, *France* 20 C3
Seul, Lac, *Canada* 100 C10
Seurre, *France* 19 F12
Sevan, *Armenia* 49 K7
Sevan, Ozero = Sevana Lich, *Armenia* 49 K7
Sevana Lich, *Armenia* 49 K7
Sevastopol, *Ukraine* 47 K7
Seven Sisters, *Canada* 104 C3
Sever →, *Spain* 35 F3
Sévérac-le-Château, *France* 20 D7
Severn →, *Canada* 102 A2
Severn →, *U.K.* 13 F5
Severn L., *Canada* 102 B1
Severnaya Zemlya, *Russia* 51 B10
Severo-Kurilsk, *Russia* 51 D16
Severo-Yeniseyskiy, *Russia* 51 C10
Severočeský □, *Czech Rep.* 26 A7
Severodonetsk = Syeverodonetsk, *Ukraine* 47 H10
Severodvinsk, *Russia* 50 C4
Severomoravský □, *Czech Rep.* 27 B10
Sevier, *U.S.A.* 115 G7
Sevier →, *U.S.A.* 115 G7
Sevier Desert, *U.S.A.* 114 G7
Sevier L., *U.S.A.* 114 G7
Sevilla, *Spain* 35 H5
Sevilla □, *Spain* 35 H5
Seville = Sevilla, *Spain* 35 H5
Sevlievo, *Bulgaria* 41 C9
Sevnica, *Slovenia* 29 B12
Sèvre-Nantaise →, *France* 18 E5
Sèvre-Niortaise →, *France* 20 B3
Sevsk, *Russia* 47 F8
Sewa →, *S. Leone* 82 D2
Sewani, *India* 68 E6
Seward, *Alaska, U.S.A.* 100 B5
Seward, *Nebr., U.S.A.* 112 E6
Seward, *Pa., U.S.A.* 110 F5
Seward Peninsula, *U.S.A.* 100 B3
Sewell, *Chile* 126 C1
Sewer, *Indonesia* 63 F8
Sewickley, *U.S.A.* 110 F4
Sexsmith, *Canada* 104 B5
Seychelles ■, *Ind. Oc.* 52 K9
Seyðisfjörður, *Iceland* 8 D6
Seydişehir, *Turkey* 72 D4
Seydvān, *Iran* 70 B5
Seyhan →, *Turkey* 70 B2
Seyhan Barajı, *Turkey* 72 D6
Seyitgazi, *Turkey* 39 B12
Seyitömer, *Turkey* 39 B11
Seym →, *Ukraine* 47 G7
Seymen, *Turkey* 41 E11
Seymour, *Australia* 95 F4
Seymour, *S. Africa* 89 E4
Seymour, *Conn., U.S.A.* 111 E11
Seymour, *Ind., U.S.A.* 108 F3
Seymour, *Tex., U.S.A.* 113 J5
Seyne, *France* 21 D10
Seyssel, *France* 21 C9
Sežana, *Slovenia* 29 C10
Sézanne, *France* 19 D10
Sezze, *Italy* 30 A6
Sfântu Gheorghe, *Covasna, Romania* 43 E10
Sfântu Gheorghe, *Tulcea, Romania* 43 F14
Sfântu Gheorghe, Braţul →, *Romania* 43 F14
Sfax, *Tunisia* 79 B8
Sha Xi →, *China* 59 D12
Sha Xian, *China* 59 D11
Shaanxi □, *China* 56 G5
Shaba = Katanga □, *Dem. Rep. of the Congo* 86 D2
Shabla, *Bulgaria* 41 C12
Shabogamo L., *Canada* 103 B6
Shabunda, *Dem. Rep. of the Congo* 86 C2
Shache, *China* 60 C2
Shackleton Ice Shelf, *Antarctica* 5 C8
Shackleton Inlet, *Antarctica* 5 E11
Shādegān, *Iran* 71 D6
Shadi, *China* 59 D10
Shadi, *India* 69 C7
Shadrinsk, *Russia* 50 D7
Shadyside, *U.S.A.* 110 G4
Shaffa, *Nigeria* 83 C7
Shafter, *U.S.A.* 117 K7
Shaftesbury, *U.K.* 13 F5
Shagamu, *Nigeria* 83 D5
Shagram, *Pakistan* 69 A5
Shah Alizai, *Pakistan* 68 E2
Shah Bunder, *Pakistan* 68 G2
Shahabad, *Punjab, India* 68 D7
Shahabad, *Raj., India* 68 G7
Shahabad, *Ut. P., India* 69 F8
Shahadpur, *Pakistan* 68 G3
Shahba, *Syria* 75 C5
Shahdād, *Iran* 71 D8
Shahdād, Namakzār-e, *Iran* 71 D8
Shahdadkot, *Pakistan* 68 F2
Shahdol, *India* 69 H9
Shahe, *China* 56 F8
Shahganj, *India* 69 F10
Shahgarh, *India* 66 F6
Shahjahanpur, *India* 69 F8
Shahpur, *India* 68 H7
Shahpur, *Baluchistan, Pakistan* 68 E3
Shahpur, *Punjab, Pakistan* 68 C5
Shahpur Chakar, *Pakistan* 68 F3
Shahpura, *Mad. P., India* 69 H9
Shahpura, *Raj., India* 68 G6
Shahr-e Bābak, *Iran* 71 D7
Shahr-e Kord, *Iran* 71 C6
Shāhrakht, *Iran* 71 C9
Shahrig, *Pakistan* 68 D2
Shahukou, *China* 56 D7
Shaikhabad, *Afghan.* 68 B3
Shajapur, *India* 68 H7
Shakargarh, *Pakistan* 68 C6
Shakawe, *Botswana* 88 B3
Shaker Heights, *U.S.A.* 110 E3
Shakhty, *Russia* 49 G5
Shakhunya, *Russia* 48 B8
Shaki, *Nigeria* 83 D5
Shâkir, *Egypt* 80 B3
Shala, L., *Ethiopia* 81 F4
Shali, *Russia* 49 J7
Shallow Lake, *Canada* 110 B3
Shalqar, *Kazakstan* 50 E6
Shalskiy, *Russia* 46 B8
Shaluli Shan, *China* 58 B2
Shām, *Iran* 71 E8
Shām, Bādiyat ash, *Asia* 70 C3
Shamâl Bahr el Ghazal □, *Sudan* 81 F2
Shamâl Dârfûr □, *Sudan* 81 E2
Shamâl Kordofân □, *Sudan* 81 E3
Shamattawa, *Canada* 102 A1
Shamattawa →, *Canada* 102 A2
Shambe, *Sudan* 81 F3
Shambu, *Ethiopia* 81 F4
Shamīl, *Iran* 71 E8
Shamkhor = Şämkir, *Azerbaijan* 49 K8
Shāmkūh, *Iran* 71 C8
Shamli, *India* 68 E7
Shammar, Jabal, *Si. Arabia* 70 E4
Shamo = Gobi, *Asia* 56 C6
Shamo, L., *Ethiopia* 81 F4
Shamokin, *U.S.A.* 111 F8
Shamrock, *U.S.A.* 113 H4
Shamva, *Zimbabwe* 87 F3
Shan □, *Burma* 67 J21
Shan Xian, *China* 56 G9
Shanan →, *Ethiopia* 81 F5
Shanchengzhen, *China* 57 C13
Shāndak, *Iran* 71 D9
Shandon, *U.S.A.* 116 K6
Shandong □, *China* 57 G10
Shandong Bandao, *China* 57 F11
Shang Xian = Shangzhou, *China* 56 H5
Shanga, *Nigeria* 78 F6
Shangalowe, *Dem. Rep. of the Congo* 87 E2
Shangani, *Zimbabwe* 89 B4
Shangani →, *Zimbabwe* 87 F2
Shangbancheng, *China* 57 D10
Shangcheng, *China* 59 B10
Shangchuan Dao, *China* 59 G9
Shangdu, *China* 56 D7
Shanggao, *China* 59 C10
Shanghai, *China* 59 B13
Shanghai □, *China* 59 B13
Shanghai Shi □, *China* 59 B13
Shanghang, *China* 59 E11
Shanghe, *China* 57 F9
Shanglin, *China* 58 F7
Shangnan, *China* 56 H6
Shangqiu, *China* 56 G8
Shangrao, *China* 59 C11
Shangshui, *China* 56 H8
Shangsi, *China* 58 F6
Shangyou, *China* 59 E10
Shangyu, *China* 59 B13
Shangzhi, *China* 57 B14
Shangzhou, *China* 56 H5
Shanhetun, *China* 57 B14
Shani, *Nigeria* 83 C7
Shannon, *N.Z.* 91 J5
Shannon →, *Ireland* 15 D2
Shannon, Mouth of the, *Ireland* 15 D2
Shannon Airport, *Ireland* 15 D3
Shansi = Shanxi □, *China* 56 F7
Shantar, Ostrov Bolshoy, *Russia* 51 D14
Shantipur, *India* 69 H13
Shantou, *China* 59 F11
Shantung = Shandong □, *China* 57 G10
Shanwei, *China* 59 F10
Shanxi □, *China* 56 F7
Shanyang, *China* 56 H5
Shanyin, *China* 56 E7
Shaodong, *China* 59 D8
Shaoguan, *China* 59 E9
Shaoshan, *China* 59 D9
Shaowu, *China* 59 D11
Shaoxing, *China* 59 C13
Shaoyang, *Hunan, China* 59 D8
Shaoyang, *Hunan, China* 59 D8
Shap, *U.K.* 12 C5
Shapinsay, *U.K.* 14 B6
Shaqq el Gi'eifer →, *Sudan* 81 D2
Shaqra', *Si. Arabia* 70 E5
Shaqrā', *Yemen* 74 E4
Sharafa, *Sudan* 81 E2
Sharafkhāneh, *Iran* 70 B5
Sharbot Lake, *Canada* 111 B8
Shari, *Japan* 54 C12
Sharjah = Ash Shāriqah, *U.A.E.* 71 E7
Shark B., *Australia* 93 E1
Sharm el Sheikh, *Egypt* 80 B3
Sharon, *Mass., U.S.A.* 111 D13
Sharon, *Pa., U.S.A.* 110 E4
Sharon Springs, *Kans., U.S.A.* 112 F4
Sharon Springs, *N.Y., U.S.A.* 111 D10
Sharp Pt., *Australia* 94 A3
Sharpe L., *Canada* 102 B1
Sharpsville, *U.S.A.* 110 E4
Sharq el Istiwa'iya □, *Sudan* 81 G3
Sharya, *Russia* 48 A7
Shasha, *Ethiopia* 81 F4
Shashemene, *Ethiopia* 81 F4
Shashi, *Botswana* 89 C4
Shashi, *China* 59 B9
Shashi →, *Africa* 87 G2
Shasta, Mt., *U.S.A.* 114 F2
Shasta L., *U.S.A.* 114 F2
Shatawi, *Sudan* 81 E3
Shatsk, *Russia* 48 C5
Shatt al'Arab →, *Iraq* 71 D6
Shatura, *Russia* 46 E10
Shaumyani = Shulaveri, *Georgia* 49 K7
Shaunavon, *Canada* 105 D7
Shaver L., *U.S.A.* 116 H7
Shaw →, *Australia* 92 D2
Shaw I., *Australia* 94 C4
Shawanaga, *Canada* 110 A4
Shawangunk Mts., *U.S.A.* 111 E10
Shawano, *U.S.A.* 108 C1
Shawinigan, *Canada* 102 C5
Shawnee, *U.S.A.* 113 H6
Shay Gap, *Australia* 92 D3
Shayang, *China* 59 B9
Shaybārā, *Si. Arabia* 70 E3
Shayib el Banat, Gebel, *Egypt* 80 B3
Shaykh, J. ash, *Lebanon* 75 B4
Shaykh Miskīn, *Syria* 75 C5
Shaykh Sa'īd, *Iraq* 70 C5
Shchekino, *Russia* 46 E9
Shcherbakov = Rybinsk, *Russia* 46 C10
Shchigry, *Russia* 47 G9
Shchors, *Ukraine* 47 G6
Shchuchinsk, *Kazakstan* 50 D8
She Xian, *Anhui, China* 59 C12
She Xian, *Hebei, China* 56 F7
Shebekino, *Russia* 47 G9
Shebele = Scebeli, Wabi →, *Somali Rep.* 74 G3
Sheboygan, *U.S.A.* 108 D2
Shebshi Mts., *Nigeria* 83 D7
Shediac, *Canada* 103 C7
Sheelin, L., *Ireland* 15 C4
Sheep Haven, *Ireland* 15 A4
Sheerness, *U.K.* 13 F8
Sheet Harbour, *Canada* 103 D7
Sheffield, *U.K.* 12 D6
Sheffield, *Ala., U.S.A.* 109 H2
Sheffield, *Mass., U.S.A.* 111 D11

Sheffield, *Pa., U.S.A.* 110 E5
Shehojele, *Ethiopia* 81 E4
Shehong, *China* 58 B5
Sheikh Idris, *Sudan* 81 E3
Sheikhpura, *India* 69 G11
Shek Hasan, *Ethiopia* 81 E4
Shekhupura, *Pakistan* 68 D5
Sheki = Şaki, *Azerbaijan* 49 K8
Shelburne, *N.S., Canada* 103 D6
Shelburne, *Ont., Canada* 102 D3
Shelburne, *U.S.A.* 111 B11
Shelburne B., *Australia* 94 A3
Shelburne Falls, *U.S.A.* 111 D12
Shelby, *Mich., U.S.A.* 108 D2
Shelby, *Miss., U.S.A.* 113 J9
Shelby, *Mont., U.S.A.* 114 B8
Shelby, *N.C., U.S.A.* 109 H5
Shelby, *Ohio, U.S.A.* 110 F2
Shelbyville, *Ill., U.S.A.* 112 F10
Shelbyville, *Ind., U.S.A.* 108 F3
Shelbyville, *Ky., U.S.A.* 108 F3
Shelbyville, *Tenn., U.S.A.* 109 H2
Sheldon, *U.S.A.* 112 D7
Sheldrake, *Canada* 103 B7
Shelengo, K. →, *Sudan* 81 E2
Shelikhova, Zaliv, *Russia* 51 D16
Shell Lakes, *Australia* 93 E4
Shellbrook, *Canada* 105 C7
Shellharbour, *Australia* 95 E5
Shelon →, *Russia* 46 C6
Shelter I, *U.S.A.* 111 E12
Shelton, *Conn., U.S.A.* 111 E11
Shelton, *Wash., U.S.A.* 116 C3
Shemakha = Şamaxi, *Azerbaijan* 49 K9
Shemsi, *Sudan* 80 D2
Shen Xian, *China* 56 F8
Shenandoah, *Iowa, U.S.A.* 112 E7
Shenandoah, *Pa., U.S.A.* 111 F8
Shenandoah, *Va., U.S.A.* 108 F6
Shenandoah →, *U.S.A.* 108 F7
Shenandoah National Park, *U.S.A.* 108 F6
Shenchi, *China* 56 E7
Shendam, *Nigeria* 83 D6
Shendî, *Sudan* 81 D3
Shenge, *S. Leone* 82 D2
Shengfang, *China* 56 E9
Shëngjergji, *Albania* 40 E4
Shëngjin, *Albania* 40 E3
Shengzhou, *China* 59 C13
Shenjingzi, *China* 57 B13
Shenmëria, *Albania* 40 D4
Shenmu, *China* 56 E6
Shennongjia, *China* 59 B8
Shenqiu, *China* 56 H8
Shenqiucheng, *China* 56 H8
Shensi = Shaanxi □, *China* 56 G5
Shenyang, *China* 57 D12
Shenzhen, *China* 59 F10
Sheo, *India* 68 F4
Sheopur Kalan, *India* 66 G10
Shepetivka, *Ukraine* 47 G4
Shepetovka = Shepetivka, *Ukraine* 47 G4
Shepparton, *Australia* 95 F4
Sheppey, I. of, *U.K.* 13 F8
Shepton Mallet, *U.K.* 13 F5
Sheqi, *China* 56 H7
Sher Qila, *Pakistan* 69 A6
Sherab, *Sudan* 81 E1
Sherborne, *U.K.* 13 G5
Sherbro →, *S. Leone* 82 D2
Sherbro I., *S. Leone* 82 D2
Sherbrooke, *N.S., Canada* 103 C7
Sherbrooke, *Qué., Canada* 103 C5
Sherburne, *U.S.A.* 111 D9
Shereik, *Sudan* 80 D3
Shergarh, *India* 68 F5
Sherghati, *India* 69 G11
Sheridan, *Ark., U.S.A.* 113 H8
Sheridan, *Wyo., U.S.A.* 114 D10
Sheringham, *U.K.* 12 E9
Sherkin I., *Ireland* 15 E2
Sherkot, *India* 69 E8
Sherman, *U.S.A.* 113 J6
Sherpur, *India* 69 G10
Sherridon, *Canada* 105 B8
Sherwood Forest, *U.K.* 12 D6
Sherwood Park, *Canada* 104 C6
Sheslay →, *Canada* 104 B2
Shethanei L., *Canada* 105 B9
Shetland □, *U.K.* 14 A7
Shetland Is., *U.K.* 14 A7
Shetrunji →, *India* 68 J5
Shewa □, *Ethiopia* 81 F4
Shewa Gimira, *Ethiopia* 81 F4
Sheyenne →, *U.S.A.* 112 B6
Shibām, *Yemen* 74 D4
Shibata, *Japan* 54 F9
Shibecha, *Japan* 54 C12
Shibetsu, *Japan* 54 B11
Shibîn el Kôm, *Egypt* 80 H7
Shibîn el Qanâtir, *Egypt* 80 H7
Shibing, *China* 58 D7
Shibogama L., *Canada* 102 B2
Shibushi, *Japan* 55 J5
Shicheng, *China* 59 D11
Shickshinny, *U.S.A.* 111 E8
Shickshock Mts. = Chic-Chocs, Mts., *Canada* 103 C6
Shidao, *China* 57 F12
Shidian, *China* 58 E2
Shido, *Japan* 55 G7
Shiel, L., *U.K.* 14 E3
Shield, C., *Australia* 94 A2
Shifang, *China* 58 B5
Shiga □, *Japan* 55 G8
Shigu, *China* 58 D2
Shiguaigou, *China* 56 D6
Shihchiachuangi = Shijiazhuang, *China* 56 E8
Shijaku, *Albania* 40 E3
Shijiazhuang, *China* 56 E8
Shijiu Hu, *China* 59 B12
Shikarpur, *India* 68 E8
Shikarpur, *Pakistan* 68 F3
Shikohabad, *India* 69 F8
Shikoku □, *Japan* 55 H6
Shikoku-Sanchi, *Japan* 55 H6
Shiliguri, *India* 67 F16
Shilka, *Russia* 51 D12
Shilka →, *Russia* 51 D13
Shillelagh, *Ireland* 15 D5
Shillington, *U.S.A.* 111 F9
Shillong, *India* 67 G17
Shilo, *West Bank* 75 C4
Shilong, *China* 59 F9
Shilou, *China* 56 F6
Shilovo, *Russia* 48 C5
Shimabara, *Japan* 55 H5
Shimada, *Japan* 55 G9
Shimane □, *Japan* 55 G6
Shimanovsk, *Russia* 51 D13
Shimen, *China* 59 C8
Shimenjie, *China* 59 C11
Shimian, *China* 58 C4
Shimizu, *Japan* 55 G9
Shimodate, *Japan* 55 F9
Shimoga, *India* 66 N9
Shimoni, *Kenya* 86 C4
Shimonoseki, *Japan* 55 H5
Shimpuru Rapids, *Angola* 88 B2
Shimsk, *Russia* 46 C6
Shin, L., *U.K.* 14 C4
Shinan, *China* 58 F7
Shinano-Gawa →, *Japan* 55 F9
Shināş, *Oman* 71 E8
Shīndand, *Afghan.* 66 C3
Shinglehouse, *U.S.A.* 110 E6
Shingū, *Japan* 55 H7
Shingwidzi, *S. Africa* 89 C5
Shinjō, *Japan* 54 E10
Shinkafe, *Nigeria* 83 C6
Shinshār, *Syria* 75 A5
Shinyanga, *Tanzania* 86 C3
Shinyanga □, *Tanzania* 86 C3
Shio-no-Misaki, *Japan* 55 H7
Shiogama, *Japan* 54 E10
Shiojiri, *Japan* 55 F8
Shipchenski Prokhod, *Bulgaria* 41 D9
Shiping, *China* 58 F4
Shipki La, *India* 66 D11
Shippegan, *Canada* 103 C7
Shippensburg, *U.S.A.* 110 F7
Shippenville, *U.S.A.* 110 E5
Shiprock, *U.S.A.* 115 H9
Shiqian, *China* 58 D7
Shiqma, N. →, *Israel* 75 D3
Shiquan, *China* 56 H5
Shiquan He = Indus →, *Pakistan* 68 G2
Shīr Kūh, *Iran* 71 D7
Shiragami-Misaki, *Japan* 54 D10
Shirakawa, *Fukushima, Japan* 55 F10
Shirakawa, *Gifu, Japan* 55 F8
Shirane-San, *Gumma, Japan* 55 F9
Shirane-San, *Yamanashi, Japan* 55 G9
Shiraoi, *Japan* 54 C10
Shīrāz, *Iran* 71 D7
Shirbīn, *Egypt* 80 H7
Shire →, *Africa* 87 F4
Shiretoko-Misaki, *Japan* 54 B12
Shirinab →, *Pakistan* 68 D2
Shiriya-Zaki, *Japan* 54 D10
Shiroishi, *Japan* 54 F10
Shīrvān, *Iran* 71 B8
Shirwa, L. = Chilwa, L., *Malawi* 87 F4
Shishi, *China* 59 E12
Shishou, *China* 59 C9
Shitai, *China* 59 B11
Shivpuri, *India* 68 G7
Shixian, *China* 57 C15
Shixing, *China* 59 E10
Shiyan, *China* 59 A8
Shiyata, *Egypt* 80 B2
Shizhu, *China* 58 C7
Shizong, *China* 58 E5
Shizuishan, *China* 56 E4
Shizuoka, *Japan* 55 G9
Shizuoka □, *Japan* 55 G9
Shklov = Shklow, *Belarus* 46 E6
Shklow, *Belarus* 46 E6
Shkoder = Shkodra, *Albania* 40 D3
Shkodra, *Albania* 40 D3
Shkumbini →, *Albania* 40 E3
Shmidta, Ostrov, *Russia* 51 A10
Shō-Gawa →, *Japan* 55 F8
Shoal L., *Canada* 105 D9
Shoal Lake, *Canada* 105 C8
Shōdo-Shima, *Japan* 55 G7
Sholapur = Solapur, *India* 66 L9
Shologontsy, *Russia* 51 C12
Shōmrōn, *West Bank* 75 C4
Shoreham by Sea, *U.K.* 13 G7
Shori →, *Pakistan* 68 E3
Shorkot Road, *Pakistan* 68 D5
Shoshone, *Calif., U.S.A.* 117 K10
Shoshone, *Idaho, U.S.A.* 114 E6
Shoshone L., *U.S.A.* 114 D8
Shoshone Mts., *U.S.A.* 114 G5
Shoshong, *Botswana* 88 C4
Shoshoni, *U.S.A.* 114 E9
Shostka, *Ukraine* 47 G7
Shou Xian, *China* 59 A11
Shouchang, *China* 59 C12
Shouguang, *China* 57 F10
Shouning, *China* 59 D12
Shouyang, *China* 56 F7
Show Low, *U.S.A.* 115 J9
Shpola, *Ukraine* 47 H6
Shreveport, *U.S.A.* 113 J8
Shrewsbury, *U.K.* 13 E5
Shri Mohangarh, *India* 68 F4
Shrirampur, *India* 69 H13
Shropshire □, *U.K.* 13 E5
Shu, *Kazakstan* 50 E8
Shu →, *Kazakstan* 52 E10
Shuangbai, *China* 58 E3
Shuangcheng, *China* 57 B14
Shuangfeng, *China* 59 D9
Shuanggou, *China* 57 G9
Shuangjiang, *China* 58 F2
Shuangliao, *China* 57 C12
Shuangshanzi, *China* 57 D10
Shuangyang, *China* 57 C13
Shuangyashan, *China* 60 B8
Shubra Khit, *Egypt* 80 H7
Shucheng, *China* 59 B11
Shugozero, *Russia* 46 C8
Shuguri Falls, *Tanzania* 87 D4
Shuiji, *China* 59 D12
Shuiye, *China* 56 F8
Shujalpur, *India* 68 H7
Shukpa Kunzang, *India* 69 B8
Shulan, *China* 57 B14
Shulaveri, *Georgia* 49 K7
Shule, *China* 60 C2
Shumagin Is., *U.S.A.* 100 C4
Shumen, *Bulgaria* 41 C10
Shumerlya, *Russia* 48 C8
Shumikha, *Russia* 50 D7
Shunchang, *China* 59 D11
Shunde, *China* 59 F9
Shungay, *Kazakstan* 49 F8
Shuo Xian = Shuozhou, *China* 56 E7
Shuozhou, *China* 56 E7
Shūr →, *Fārs, Iran* 71 D7
Shūr →, *Kermān, Iran* 71 D8
Shūr →, *Yazd, Iran* 71 D7
Shūr Āb, *Iran* 71 C6
Shūr Gaz, *Iran* 71 D8
Shūrāb, *Iran* 71 C8
Shūrjestān, *Iran* 71 D7
Shurugwi, *Zimbabwe* 87 F3
Shūsf, *Iran* 71 D9
Shūsh, *Iran* 73 F13
Shūshtar, *Iran* 71 D6
Shuswap L., *Canada* 104 C5
Shuya, *Russia* 48 B5
Shuyang, *China* 57 G10
Shūzū, *Iran* 71 D7
Shwebo, *Burma* 67 H19
Shwegu, *Burma* 67 G20
Shweli →, *Burma* 67 H20
Shymkent, *Kazakstan* 50 E7
Shyok, *India* 69 B8
Shyok →, *Pakistan* 69 B6
Si Chon, *Thailand* 65 H2
Si Kiang = Xi Jiang →, *China* 59 F9
Si-ngan = Xi'an, *China* 56 G5
Si Prachan, *Thailand* 64 E3
Si Racha, *Thailand* 64 F3
Si Xian, *China* 57 H9
Siahaf →, *Pakistan* 68 E3
Siahan Range, *Pakistan* 66 F4
Siaksriindrapura, *Indonesia* 62 D2
Sialkot, *Pakistan* 68 C6
Siam = Thailand ■, *Asia* 64 E4
Sian = Xi'an, *China* 56 G5
Sianów, *Poland* 44 D3
Siantan, *Indonesia* 62 D3
Sīāreh, *Iran* 71 D9
Siargao I., *Phil.* 61 G7
Siari, *Pakistan* 69 B7
Siasi, *Phil.* 63 C6
Siasi I., *Phil.* 61 J4
Siátista, *Greece* 40 F5
Siau, *Indonesia* 63 D7
Šiauliai, *Lithuania* 9 J20
Šiauliai □, *Lithuania* 44 C10
Siazan = Siyäzän, *Azerbaijan* 49 K9
Sibâi, Gebel el, *Egypt* 70 E2
Sibayi, L., *S. Africa* 89 D5
Sibdu, *Sudan* 81 E2
Šibenik, *Croatia* 29 E12
Siberia, *Russia* 4 D13
Siberut, *Indonesia* 62 E1
Sibi, *Pakistan* 68 E2
Sibil = Oksibil, *Indonesia* 63 E10
Sibiti, *Congo* 84 E2
Sibiu, *Romania* 43 E9
Sibiu □, *Romania* 43 E9
Sibley, *U.S.A.* 112 D7
Sibolga, *Indonesia* 62 D1
Sibsagar, *India* 67 F19
Sibu, *Malaysia* 62 D4
Sibuco, *Phil.* 61 H5
Sibuguey B., *Phil.* 61 H5
Sibut, *C.A.R.* 84 C3
Sibutu, *Phil.* 63 D5
Sibutu Group, *Phil.* 61 J3
Sibutu Passage, *E. Indies* 63 D5
Sibuyan I., *Phil.* 61 E5
Sibuyan Sea, *Phil.* 61 E5
Sic, *Romania* 43 D8
Sicamous, *Canada* 104 C5
Siccus →, *Australia* 95 E2
Sichuan □, *China* 58 B5
Sichuan Pendi, *China* 58 B5
Sicilia, *Italy* 31 E7
Sicilia □, *Italy* 31 E7
Sicily = Sicilia, *Italy* 31 E7
Sicuani, *Peru* 124 F4
Šid, *Serbia, Yug.* 42 E4
Sidamo □, *Ethiopia* 81 G4
Sidaouet, *Niger* 83 B6
Sidári, *Greece* 36 A3
Siddhapur, *India* 68 H5
Siddipet, *India* 66 K11
Sidensjö, *Sweden* 10 A12
Sidéradougou, *Burkina Faso* 82 C4
Siderno, *Italy* 31 D9
Sidhauli, *India* 69 F9
Sídheros, Ákra, *Greece* 36 D8
Sidhi, *India* 69 G9
Sidhirókastron, *Greece* 40 E7
Sîdi Abd el Rahmân, *Egypt* 80 A2
Sîdi Barrâni, *Egypt* 80 A2
Sidi-bel-Abbès, *Algeria* 78 A5
Sidi Haneish, *Egypt* 80 A2
Sidi Omar, *Egypt* 80 A1
Sidlaw Hills, *U.K.* 14 E5
Sidley, Mt., *Antarctica* 5 D14
Sidmouth, *U.K.* 13 G4
Sidmouth, C., *Australia* 94 A3
Sidney, *Canada* 104 D4
Sidney, *Mont., U.S.A.* 112 B2
Sidney, *N.Y., U.S.A.* 111 D9
Sidney, *Nebr., U.S.A.* 112 E3
Sidney, *Ohio, U.S.A.* 108 E3
Sidney Lanier L., *U.S.A.* 109 H4
Sido, *Mali* 82 C3
Sidoarjo, *Indonesia* 63 G15
Sidon = Saydā, *Lebanon* 75 B4
Sidra, G. of = Surt, Khalīj, *Libya* 79 B9
Siedlce, *Poland* 45 F9
Sieg →, *Germany* 24 E3
Siegburg, *Germany* 24 E3
Siegen, *Germany* 24 E4
Siem Pang, *Cambodia* 64 E6
Siem Reap = Siemreab, *Cambodia* 64 F4
Siemiatycze, *Poland* 45 F9
Siemreab, *Cambodia* 64 F4
Siena, *Italy* 29 E8
Sieniawa, *Poland* 45 H9
Sieradz, *Poland* 45 G5
Sieraków, *Poland* 45 F3
Sierck-les-Bains, *France* 19 C13
Sierning, *Austria* 26 C7
Sierpc, *Poland* 45 F6
Sierra Blanca, *U.S.A.* 115 L11
Sierra Blanca Peak, *U.S.A.* 115 K11
Sierra City, *U.S.A.* 116 F6
Sierra Colorada, *Argentina* 128 E3
Sierra de Yeguas, *Spain* 35 H6
Sierra Gorda, *Chile* 126 A2
Sierra Leone ■, *W. Afr.* 82 D2
Sierra Madre, *Mexico* 119 D6
Sierra Mojada, *Mexico* 118 B4
Sierra Nevada, *U.S.A.* 116 H8
Sierra Vista, *U.S.A.* 115 L8
Sierraville, *U.S.A.* 116 F6
Sierre, *Switz.* 25 J3
Sifani, *Ethiopia* 81 E5
Sifié, *Ivory C.* 82 D3
Sífnos, *Greece* 38 E6
Sifton, *Canada* 105 C8
Sifton Pass, *Canada* 104 B3
Sigean, *France* 20 E6
Sighetu-Marmaţiei, *Romania* 43 C8
Sighişoara, *Romania* 43 D9
Sigli, *Indonesia* 62 C1
Siglufjörður, *Iceland* 8 C4
Sigmaringen, *Germany* 25 G5
Signa, *Italy* 28 E8
Signakhi = Tsnori, *Georgia* 49 K7
Signal, *U.S.A.* 117 L13
Signal Pk., *U.S.A.* 117 M12
Signy-l'Abbaye, *France* 19 C11
Sigsig, *Ecuador* 124 D3
Sigüenza, *Spain* 32 D2
Siguiri, *Guinea* 82 C3
Sigulda, *Latvia* 9 H21
Sihanoukville = Kampong Saom, *Cambodia* 65 G4
Sihora, *India* 69 H9
Sihui, *China* 59 F9
Siikajoki →, *Finland* 8 D21
Siilinjärvi, *Finland* 8 E22
Siirt, *Turkey* 73 D9
Sijarira Ra., *Zimbabwe* 87 F2
Sika, *India* 68 H3
Sikao, *Thailand* 65 J2
Sikar, *India* 68 F6
Sikasso, *Mali* 82 C3
Sikeston, *U.S.A.* 113 G10
Sikhote Alin, Khrebet, *Russia* 51 E14
Sikhote Alin Ra. = Sikhote Alin, Khrebet, *Russia* 51 E14
Sikiá., *Greece* 40 F7
Síkinos, *Greece* 39 E7
Sikkani Chief →, *Canada* 104 B4
Sikkim □, *India* 67 F16
Siklós, *Hungary* 42 E3
Sikotu-Ko, *Japan* 54 C10
Sil →, *Spain* 34 C3
Silacayoapan, *Mexico* 119 D5
Šilalė, *Lithuania* 44 C9
Silandro, *Italy* 28 B7
Silawad, *India* 68 J6
Silay, *Phil.* 61 F5
Silba, *Croatia* 29 D11
Silchar, *India* 67 G18
Şile, *Turkey* 41 E13
Siler City, *U.S.A.* 109 H6
Silgarhi Doti, *Nepal* 69 E9
Silghat, *India* 67 F18
Sili, *Burkina Faso* 82 C4
Silifke, *Turkey* 70 B2
Siliguri = Shiliguri, *India* 67 F16
Siling Co, *China* 60 C3
Silistea Nouă, *Romania* 43 F10
Silistra, *Bulgaria* 41 B11
Silivri, *Turkey* 41 E12
Siljan, *Sweden* 10 D8
Siljansnäs, *Sweden* 10 D8
Silkeborg, *Denmark* 11 H3
Silkwood, *Australia* 94 B4
Silla, *Spain* 33 F4
Sillajhuay, Cordillera, *Chile* 124 G5
Sillamäe, *Estonia* 9 G22
Sillé-le-Guillaume, *France* 18 D6
Silleda, *Spain* 34 C2
Silloth, *U.K.* 12 C4
Sílo, *Greece* 41 E9
Siloam Springs, *U.S.A.* 113 G7
Silopi, *Turkey* 73 D10
Silsbee, *U.S.A.* 113 K7
Šiluko, *Nigeria* 83 D6
Šilutė, *Lithuania* 9 J19
Silva Porto = Kuito, *Angola* 85 G3
Silvan, *Turkey* 73 C9
Silvani, *India* 69 H8
Silver City, *U.S.A.* 115 K9
Silver Cr. →, *U.S.A.* 114 E4
Silver Creek, *U.S.A.* 110 D5
Silver L., *U.S.A.* 116 G6
Silver Lake, *Calif., U.S.A.* 117 K10
Silver Lake, *Oreg., U.S.A.* 114 E3
Silverdalen, *Sweden* 11 G9
Silverton, *Colo., U.S.A.* 115 H10
Silverton, *Tex., U.S.A.* 113 H4
Silves, *Portugal* 35 H2
Silvi Marina, *Italy* 29 F11
Silvies →, *U.S.A.* 114 E4
Silvrettahorn, *Switz.* 28 B7
Silwa Bahari, *Egypt* 80 C3
Silz, *Austria* 26 D3
Simaltala, *India* 69 G12
Simanggang = Bandar Sri Aman, *Malaysia* 62 D4
Simao, *China* 58 F3
Simard, L., *Canada* 102 C4
Şimareh →, *Iran* 73 F12
Simav, *Turkey* 39 B10
Simav →, *Turkey* 41 F12
Simav Dağları, *Turkey* 39 B10
Simba, *Tanzania* 86 C4
Simbach, *Germany* 25 G9
Simbirsk, *Russia* 48 C9
Simbo, *Tanzania* 86 C2
Simcoe, *Canada* 102 D3
Simcoe, L., *Canada* 102 D4
Simdega, *India* 69 H11
Simeonovgrad, *Bulgaria* 41 D9
Simeria, *Romania* 42 E8
Simeto →, *Italy* 31 E8
Simeulue, *Indonesia* 62 D1
Simferopol, *Ukraine* 47 K8
Sími, *Greece* 39 E9
Simi Valley, *U.S.A.* 117 L8
Simikot, *Nepal* 69 E9
Simitli, *Bulgaria* 40 E7
Simla, *India* 68 D7
Simlångsdalen, *Sweden* 11 H7
Şimleu-Silvaniei, *Romania* 42 C7
Simmern, *Germany* 25 F3
Simmie, *Canada* 105 D7
Simmler, *U.S.A.* 117 K7
Simnas, *Lithuania* 44 D10
Simojoki →, *Finland* 8 D21
Simojovel, *Mexico* 119 D6
Simonette →, *Canada* 104 B5
Simonstown, *S. Africa* 88 E2
Simontornya, *Hungary* 42 D3
Simplonpass, *Switz.* 25 J4
Simplontunnel, *Switz.* 25 J4
Simpson Desert, *Australia* 94 D2
Simpson Pen., *Canada* 101 B11
Simpungdong, *N. Korea* 57 D15
Simrishamn, *Sweden* 11 J8
Simsbury, *U.S.A.* 111 E12
Simushir, Ostrov, *Russia* 51 E16
Sin Cowe I., *S. China Sea* 62 C4
Sinabang, *Indonesia* 62 D1
Sinadogo, *Somali Rep.* 74 F4
Sinai = Es Sînâ', *Egypt* 75 F3
Sinai, Mt. = Mûsa, Gebel, *Egypt* 70 D2
Sinai Peninsula, *Egypt* 75 F3
Sinaia, *Romania* 43 E10
Sinaloa □, *Mexico* 118 C3
Sinaloa de Leyva, *Mexico* 118 B3
Sinalunga, *Italy* 29 E8
Sinan, *China* 58 D7
Sînandrei, *Romania* 42 E6
Sinarádhes, *Greece* 36 A3
Sincan, *Turkey* 72 B5
Sincanlı, *Turkey* 39 C12
Sincelejo, *Colombia* 124 B3
Sinch'ang, *N. Korea* 57 D15
Sinchang-ni, *N. Korea* 57 E14
Sinclair, *U.S.A.* 114 F10
Sinclair Mills, *Canada* 104 C4
Sinclair's B., *U.K.* 14 C5
Sinclairville, *U.S.A.* 110 D5
Sincorá, Serra do, *Brazil* 125 F10
Sind, *Pakistan* 68 G3
Sind □, *Pakistan* 68 G3
Sind →, *Jammu & Kashmir, India* 69 B6
Sind →, *Mad. P., India* 69 F8
Sind Sagar Doab, *Pakistan* 68 D4
Sindal, *Denmark* 11 G4
Sindangan, *Phil.* 61 G5
Sindangbarang, *Indonesia* 63 G12
Sinde, *Zambia* 87 F2
Sindelfingen, *Germany* 25 G4
Sındırgı, *Turkey* 39 B10
Sindou, *Burkina Faso* 82 C3
Sindri, *India* 69 H12
Sine →, *Senegal* 82 C1
Sinegorskiy, *Russia* 49 G5

Sinekli, *Turkey* 41 E12
Sinelnikovo = Synelnykove, *Ukraine* 47 H8
Sinendé, *Benin* 83 C5
Sines, *Portugal* 35 H2
Sines, C. de, *Portugal* 35 H2
Sineu, *Spain* 37 B10
Sinfra, *Ivory C.* 82 D3
Sing Buri, *Thailand* 64 E3
Singa, *Sudan* 81 E3
Singapore ■, *Asia* 65 M4
Singapore, Straits of, *Asia* 65 M5
Singaraja, *Indonesia* 62 F5
Singen, *Germany* 25 H4
Singida, *Tanzania* 86 C3
Singida □, *Tanzania* 86 D3
Singitikós Kólpos, *Greece* 40 F7
Singkaling Hkamti, *Burma* 67 G19
Singkang, *Indonesia* 63 E6
Singkawang, *Indonesia* 62 D3
Singkep, *Indonesia* 62 E2
Singleton, *Australia* 95 E5
Singleton, Mt., *N. Terr., Australia* 92 D5
Singleton, Mt., *W. Austral., Australia* 93 E2
Singö, *Sweden* 10 D12
Singoli, *India* 68 G6
Singora = Songkhla, *Thailand* 65 J3
Singosan, *N. Korea* 57 E14
Sinhung, *N. Korea* 57 D14
Sînî □, *Egypt* 75 F3
Siniátsikon, Óros, *Greece* 40 F5
Siniscóla, *Italy* 30 B2
Sinj, *Croatia* 29 E13
Sinjai, *Indonesia* 63 F6
Sinjajevina, *Montenegro, Yug.* 40 D3
Sinjār, *Iraq* 70 B4
Sinkat, *Sudan* 80 D4
Sinkiang Uighur = Xinjiang Uygur Zizhiqu □, *China* 60 B3
Sinmak, *N. Korea* 57 E14
Sinnai, *Italy* 30 C2
Sinnamary, *Fr. Guiana* 125 B8
Sinni →, *Italy* 31 B9
Sinnuris, *Egypt* 80 J7
Sinoie, Lacul, *Romania* 43 F13
Sinop, *Turkey* 72 A6
Sinor, *India* 68 J5
Sinp'o, *N. Korea* 57 E15
Sinsheim, *Germany* 25 F4
Sinsk, *Russia* 51 C13
Sintang, *Indonesia* 62 D4
Sinton, *U.S.A.* 113 L6
Sintra, *Portugal* 35 G1
Sinŭiju, *N. Korea* 57 D13
Sinyukha →, *Ukraine* 47 H6
Sinzig, *Germany* 24 E3
Sio →, *Hungary* 42 D3
Siocon, *Phil.* 61 H5
Siófok, *Hungary* 42 D3
Sioma, *Zambia* 88 B3
Sion, *Switz.* 25 J3
Sion Mills, *U.K.* 15 B4
Sioux City, *U.S.A.* 112 D6
Sioux Falls, *U.S.A.* 112 D6
Sioux Lookout, *Canada* 102 B1
Sioux Narrows, *Canada* 105 D10
Sipalay, *Phil.* 61 G5
Šipan, *Croatia* 40 D1
Siping, *China* 57 C13
Sipiwesk L., *Canada* 105 B9
Šipovo, *Bos.-H.* 42 F2
Sipra →, *India* 68 H6
Sipura, *Indonesia* 62 E1
Siquia →, *Nic.* 120 D3
Siquijor, *Phil.* 61 G5
Siquirres, *Costa Rica* 120 D3
Şīr Banī Yās, *U.A.E.* 71 E7
Sir Edward Pellew Group, *Australia* 94 B2
Sir Graham Moore Is., *Australia* 92 B4
Sir James MacBrien, Mt., *Canada* 100 B7
Sira →, *Norway* 9 G12
Siracusa, *Italy* 31 E8
Sirajganj, *Bangla.* 69 G13
Sirakoro, *Mali* 82 C3
Şiran, *Turkey* 73 B8
Sirasso, *Ivory C.* 82 D3
Sirathu, *India* 69 G9
Sīrdān, *Iran* 71 B6
Sirdaryo = Syrdarya →, *Kazakstan* 50 E7
Sire, *Ethiopia* 81 F4
Siren, *U.S.A.* 112 C8
Sirer, *Spain* 37 C7
Siret, *Romania* 43 C11
Siret →, *Romania* 43 E12
Sirghāyā, *Syria* 75 B5
Şiria, *Romania* 42 D6
Sirino, Mte., *Italy* 31 B8
Sirmaur, *India* 69 G9
Sírna, *Greece* 39 E8
Şirnak, *Turkey* 73 D10
Sirohi, *India* 68 G5
Sironj, *India* 68 G7
Síros, *Greece* 38 D6
Sirretta Pk., *U.S.A.* 117 K8
Sīrrī, *Iran* 71 E7
Sirsa, *India* 68 E6
Sirsa →, *India* 69 F8
Siruela, *Spain* 35 G5
Sisak, *Croatia* 29 C13
Sisaket, *Thailand* 64 E5
Sisante, *Spain* 33 F2
Sisargas, Is., *Spain* 34 B2
Sishen, *S. Africa* 88 D3
Sishui, *Henan, China* 56 G7
Sishui, *Shandong, China* 57 G9
Sisipuk L., *Canada* 105 B8
Sisophon, *Cambodia* 64 F4
Sisseton, *U.S.A.* 112 C6
Sissonne, *France* 19 C10
Sīstān, *Asia* 71 D9
Sīstān, Daryācheh-ye, *Iran* 66 D2
Sīstān va Balūchestān □, *Iran* 71 E9
Sisteron, *France* 21 D9
Sisters, *U.S.A.* 114 D3
Siswa Bazar, *India* 69 F10
Sitakili, *Mali* 82 C2
Sitamarhi, *India* 69 F11
Sitampiky, *Madag.* 89 B8
Sitapur, *India* 69 F9
Siteki, *Swaziland* 89 D5
Sitges, *Spain* 32 D6
Sithoniá, *Greece* 40 F7
Sitía, *Greece* 36 D8
Sitka, *U.S.A.* 104 B1
Sitoti, *Botswana* 88 C3
Sitra, *Egypt* 80 B2
Sittang Myit →, *Burma* 67 L20
Sittard, *Neths.* 17 C5
Sittensen, *Germany* 24 B5
Sittingbourne, *U.K.* 13 F8
Sittona, *Eritrea* 81 E4
Sittoung = Sittang Myit →, *Burma* 67 L20
Sittwe, *Burma* 67 J18
Situbondo, *Indonesia* 63 G16
Siuna, *Nic.* 120 D3
Siuri, *India* 69 H12
Siutghiol, Lacul, *Romania* 43 F13
Sīvand, *Iran* 71 D7
Sivas, *Turkey* 70 B3
Sivaslı, *Turkey* 39 C11
Siverek, *Turkey* 70 B3
Sivrihisar, *Turkey* 72 C4
Sîwa, *Egypt* 80 B2
Sîwa, El Wâhât es, *Egypt* 80 B2
Siwa Oasis, *Egypt* 76 D6
Siwalik Range, *Nepal* 69 F10
Siwan, *India* 69 F11
Siwana, *India* 68 G5
Siximilebridge, *Ireland* 15 D3
Sixth Cataract, *Sudan* 81 D3
Siyâl, Jazâ'ir, *Egypt* 80 C4
Siyäzän, *Azerbaijan* 49 K9
Siziwang Qi, *China* 56 D6
Sjælland, *Denmark* 11 J5
Sjællands Odde, *Denmark* 11 J5
Sjenica, *Serbia, Yug.* 40 C3
Sjöbo, *Sweden* 11 J7
Sjötofta, *Sweden* 11 G7
Sjötorp, *Sweden* 11 F8
Sjumen = Shumen, *Bulgaria* 41 C10
Sjuntorp, *Sweden* 11 F6
Skadarsko Jezero, *Montenegro, Yug.* 40 D3
Skadovsk, *Ukraine* 47 J7
Skælskør, *Denmark* 11 J5
Skærbæk, *Denmark* 11 J2
Skaftafell, *Iceland* 8 D5
Skagafjörður, *Iceland* 8 D4
Skagastølstindane, *Norway* 9 F12
Skagaströnd, *Iceland* 8 D3
Skagen, *Denmark* 11 G4
Skagern, *Sweden* 11 F8
Skagerrak, *Denmark* 11 G2
Skagit →, *U.S.A.* 116 B4
Skagway, *U.S.A.* 100 C6
Skala-Podilska, *Ukraine* 47 H4
Skala Podolskaya = Skala-Podilska, *Ukraine* 47 H4
Skalat, *Ukraine* 47 H3
Skalbmierz, *Poland* 45 H7
Skälderviken, *Sweden* 11 H6
Skalica, *Slovak Rep.* 27 C10
Skallingen, *Denmark* 11 J2
Skalni Dol = Kamenyak, *Bulgaria* 41 C10
Skanderborg, *Denmark* 11 H3
Skåne, *Sweden* 11 J7
Skåne län □, *Sweden* 11 H7
Skaneateles, *U.S.A.* 111 D8
Skaneateles L., *U.S.A.* 111 D8
Skänninge, *Sweden* 11 F9
Skanör med Falsterbo, *Sweden* 11 J6
Skantzoúra, *Greece* 38 B6
Skara, *Sweden* 11 F7
Skaraborgs län □, *Sweden* 11 F7
Skärblacka, *Sweden* 11 F9
Skardu, *Pakistan* 69 B6
Skåre, *Sweden* 10 E7
Skärhamn, *Sweden* 11 G5
Skarszewy, *Poland* 44 D5
Skaryszew, *Poland* 45 G8
Skarżysko-Kamienna, *Poland* 45 G7
Skattkärr, *Sweden* 10 E7
Skattungbyn, *Sweden* 10 C8
Skawina, *Poland* 45 J6
Skebobruk, *Sweden* 10 E12
Skeena →, *Canada* 104 C2
Skeena Mts., *Canada* 104 B3
Skegness, *U.K.* 12 D8
Skeldon, *Guyana* 124 B7
Skeleton Coast Park, *Namibia* 88 C1
Skellefte älv →, *Sweden* 8 D19
Skellefteå, *Sweden* 8 D19
Skelleftehamn, *Sweden* 8 D19
Skender Vakuf, *Bos.-H.* 42 F2
Skerries, The, *U.K.* 12 D3
Skhíza, *Greece* 38 E3
Skhoinoúsa, *Greece* 39 E7
Ski, *Norway* 9 G14
Skíathos, *Greece* 38 B5
Skibbereen, *Ireland* 15 E2
Skiddaw, *U.K.* 12 C4
Skidegate, *Canada* 104 C2
Skídhra, *Greece* 40 F6
Skien, *Norway* 9 G13
Skierniewice, *Poland* 45 G7
Skikda, *Algeria* 78 A7
Skillingaryd, *Sweden* 11 G8
Skillinge, *Sweden* 11 J8
Skilloura, *Cyprus* 36 D12
Skinári, Ákra, *Greece* 38 D2
Skinnskatteberg, *Sweden* 10 E9
Skipton, *U.K.* 12 D5
Skirmish Pt., *Australia* 94 A1
Skiropoúla, *Greece* 38 C6
Skíros, *Greece* 38 C6
Skivarp, *Sweden* 11 J7
Skive, *Denmark* 11 H3
Skjálfandafljót →, *Iceland* 8 D5
Skjálfandi, *Iceland* 8 C5
Skjern, *Denmark* 11 J2
Skoczów, *Poland* 45 J5
Škofja Loka, *Slovenia* 29 B11
Skoghall, *Sweden* 10 E7
Skogstorp, *Sweden* 10 E10
Skoki, *Poland* 45 F4
Skole, *Ukraine* 47 H2
Skópelos, *Greece* 38 B5
Skopí, *Greece* 36 D8
Skopin, *Russia* 46 F10
Skopje, *Macedonia* 40 D5
Skórcz, *Poland* 44 E5
Skørping, *Denmark* 11 H3
Skövde, *Sweden* 11 F7
Skovorodino, *Russia* 51 D13
Skowhegan, *U.S.A.* 109 C11
Skradin, *Croatia* 29 E12
Skrea, *Sweden* 11 H6
Skrunda, *Latvia* 44 B9
Skrwa →, *Poland* 45 F6
Skull, *Ireland* 15 E2
Skultorp, *Sweden* 11 F7
Skultuna, *Sweden* 10 E10
Skunk →, *U.S.A.* 112 E9
Skuodas, *Lithuania* 9 H19
Skurup, *Sweden* 11 J7
Skutskär, *Sweden* 10 D11
Skvyra, *Ukraine* 47 H5
Skwierzyna, *Poland* 45 F2
Skye, *U.K.* 14 D2
Skykomish, *U.S.A.* 114 C3
Skyros = Skíros, *Greece* 38 C6
Skyttorp, *Sweden* 10 D11
Slættaratindur, *Færoe Is.* 8 E9
Slagelse, *Denmark* 11 J5
Slamet, *Indonesia* 63 G13
Slaney →, *Ireland* 15 D5
Slangberge, *S. Africa* 88 E3
Slănic, *Romania* 43 E10
Slano, *Croatia* 40 D1
Slantsy, *Russia* 46 C5
Slaný, *Czech Rep.* 26 A7
Śląskie □, *Poland* 45 H6
Slätbaken, *Sweden* 11 F10
Slate Is., *Canada* 102 C2
Slatina, *Croatia* 42 E2
Slatina, *Romania* 43 F9
Slatina Timiş, *Romania* 42 E7
Slatington, *U.S.A.* 111 F9
Slaton, *U.S.A.* 113 J4
Slave →, *Canada* 104 A6
Slave Coast, *W. Afr.* 83 D5
Slave Lake, *Canada* 104 B6
Slave Pt., *Canada* 104 A5
Slavgorod, *Russia* 50 D8
Slavinja, *Serbia, Yug.* 40 C6
Slavkov u Brna, *Czech Rep.* 27 B9
Slavonija, *Europe* 42 E2
Slavonski Brod, *Croatia* 42 E3
Slavuta, *Ukraine* 47 G4
Slavyanka, *Russia* 54 C5
Slavyanovo, *Bulgaria* 41 C8
Slavyansk = Slovyansk, *Ukraine* 47 H9
Slavyansk-na-Kubani, *Russia* 47 K10
Sława, *Poland* 45 G3
Slawharad, *Belarus* 46 F6
Sławno, *Poland* 44 D3
Sławoborze, *Poland* 44 E2
Sleaford, *U.K.* 12 D7
Sleaford B., *Australia* 95 E2
Sleat, Sd. of, *U.K.* 14 D3
Sleeper Is., *Canada* 101 C11
Sleepy Eye, *U.S.A.* 112 C7
Slemon L., *Canada* 104 A5
Ślesin, *Poland* 45 F5
Slide Mt., *U.S.A.* 111 E10
Slidell, *U.S.A.* 113 K10
Sliema, *Malta* 36 D2
Slieve Aughty, *Ireland* 15 C3
Slieve Bloom, *Ireland* 15 C4
Slieve Donard, *U.K.* 15 B6
Slieve Gamph, *Ireland* 15 B3
Slieve Gullion, *U.K.* 15 B5
Slieve Mish, *Ireland* 15 D2
Slievenamon, *Ireland* 15 D4
Sligeach = Sligo, *Ireland* 15 B3
Sligo, *Ireland* 15 B3
Sligo, *U.S.A.* 110 E5
Sligo □, *Ireland* 15 B3
Sligo B., *Ireland* 15 B3
Slippery Rock, *U.S.A.* 110 E4
Slite, *Sweden* 11 G12
Sliven, *Bulgaria* 41 D10
Slivnitsa, *Bulgaria* 40 D7
Sljeme, *Croatia* 29 C12
Sloan, *U.S.A.* 117 K11
Sloansville, *U.S.A.* 111 D10
Slobozia, *Moldova* 43 D14
Slobozia, *Argeş, Romania* 43 F10
Slobozia, *Ialomiţa, Romania* 43 F12
Slocan, *Canada* 104 D5
Słomniki, *Poland* 45 H7
Slonim, *Belarus* 47 F3
Slough, *U.K.* 13 F7
Slough □, *U.K.* 13 F7
Sloughhouse, *U.S.A.* 116 G5
Slovak Rep. ■, *Europe* 27 C13
Slovakia = Slovak Rep. ■, *Europe* 27 C13
Slovakian Ore Mts. = Slovenské Rudohorie, *Slovak Rep.* 27 C12
Slovenia ■, *Europe* 29 C11
Slovenija = Slovenia ■, *Europe* 29 C11
Slovenj Gradec, *Slovenia* 29 B12
Slovenska Bistrica, *Slovenia* 29 B12
Slovenske Konjice, *Slovenia* 29 B12
Slovenské Rudohorie, *Slovak Rep.* 27 C12
Slovyansk, *Ukraine* 47 H9
Słubice, *Poland* 45 F1
Sluch →, *Ukraine* 47 G4
Sluis, *Neths.* 17 C3
Slŭnchev Bryag, *Bulgaria* 41 D11
Slunj, *Croatia* 29 C12
Słupca, *Poland* 45 F4
Słupia →, *Poland* 44 D3
Słupsk, *Poland* 44 D4
Slurry, *S. Africa* 88 D4
Slutsk, *Belarus* 47 F4
Slyne Hd., *Ireland* 15 C1
Slyudyanka, *Russia* 51 D11
Småland, *Sweden* 11 G9
Smålandsfarvandet, *Denmark* 11 J5
Smålandsstenar, *Sweden* 11 G7
Smalltree L., *Canada* 105 A8
Smallwood Res., *Canada* 103 B7
Smara, *Morocco* 78 B4
Smarhon, *Belarus* 46 E4
Smarje, *Slovenia* 29 B12
Smartt Syndicate Dam, *S. Africa* 88 E3
Smartville, *U.S.A.* 116 F5
Smeaton, *Canada* 105 C8
Smedby, *Sweden* 11 H10
Smederevo, *Serbia, Yug.* 40 B4
Smederevska Palanka, *Serbia, Yug.* 40 B4
Smedjebacken, *Sweden* 10 D9
Smela = Smila, *Ukraine* 47 H6
Smerwick Harbour, *Ireland* 15 D1
Smethport, *U.S.A.* 110 E6
Smidovich, *Russia* 51 E14
Śmigiel, *Poland* 45 F3
Smila, *Ukraine* 47 H6
Smilyan, *Bulgaria* 41 E8
Smith, *Canada* 104 B6
Smith Center, *U.S.A.* 112 F5
Smith Sund, *Greenland* 4 B4
Smithburne →, *Australia* 94 B3
Smithers, *Canada* 104 C3
Smithfield, *S. Africa* 89 E4
Smithfield, *N.C., U.S.A.* 109 H6
Smithfield, *Utah, U.S.A.* 114 F8
Smiths Falls, *Canada* 102 D4
Smithton, *Australia* 94 G4
Smithville, *Canada* 110 C5
Smithville, *U.S.A.* 113 K6
Smoky →, *Canada* 104 B5
Smoky Bay, *Australia* 95 E1
Smoky Hill →, *U.S.A.* 112 F6
Smoky Hills, *U.S.A.* 112 F5
Smoky Lake, *Canada* 104 C6
Smøla, *Norway* 8 E13
Smolensk, *Russia* 46 E7
Smolikas, Óros, *Greece* 40 F4
Smolník, *Slovak Rep.* 27 C13
Smolyan, *Bulgaria* 41 E8
Smooth Rock Falls, *Canada* 102 C3
Smoothstone L., *Canada* 105 C7
Smorgon = Smarhon, *Belarus* 46 E4
Smulţi, *Romania* 43 E12
Smyadovo, *Bulgaria* 41 C11
Smygehamn, *Sweden* 11 J7
Smyrna = İzmir, *Turkey* 39 C9
Smyrna, *U.S.A.* 108 F8
Snæfell, *Iceland* 8 D6
Snaefell, *U.K.* 12 C3
Snæfellsjökull, *Iceland* 8 D2
Snake →, *U.S.A.* 114 C4
Snake I., *Australia* 95 F4
Snake Range, *U.S.A.* 114 G6
Snake River Plain, *U.S.A.* 114 E7
Snasahögarna, *Sweden* 10 A6
Snåsavatnet, *Norway* 8 D14
Snedsted, *Denmark* 11 H2
Sneek, *Neths.* 17 A5
Sneeuberge, *S. Africa* 88 E3
Snejbjerg, *Denmark* 11 H2
Snelling, *U.S.A.* 116 H6
Snezhnoye, *Ukraine* 47 J10
Sneżnik, *Slovenia* 29 C11
Śniadowo, *Poland* 45 E8
Śniardwy, Jezioro, *Poland* 44 E8
Śnieżka, *Europe* 26 A8
Snigirevka = Snihurivka, *Ukraine* 47 J7
Snihurivka, *Ukraine* 47 J7
Snina, *Slovak Rep.* 27 C15
Snizort, L., *U.K.* 14 D2
Snøhetta, *Norway* 9 E13
Snohomish, *U.S.A.* 116 C4
Snoul, *Cambodia* 65 F6
Snow Hill, *U.S.A.* 108 F8
Snow Lake, *Canada* 105 C8
Snow Mt., *Calif., U.S.A.* 116 F4
Snow Mt., *Maine, U.S.A.* 111 A14
Snow Shoe, *U.S.A.* 110 E7
Snowbird L., *Canada* 105 A8
Snowdon, *U.K.* 12 D3
Snowdrift →, *Canada* 105 A6
Snowflake, *U.S.A.* 115 J8
Snowshoe Pk., *U.S.A.* 114 B6
Snowtown, *Australia* 95 E2
Snowville, *U.S.A.* 114 F7
Snowy →, *Australia* 95 F4
Snowy Mt., *U.S.A.* 111 C10
Snowy Mts., *Australia* 95 F4
Snug Corner, *Bahamas* 121 B5
Snyatyn, *Ukraine* 47 H3
Snyder, *Okla., U.S.A.* 113 H5
Snyder, *Tex., U.S.A.* 113 J4
Soahanina, *Madag.* 89 B7
Soalala, *Madag.* 89 B8
Soaloka, *Madag.* 89 B8
Soamanonga, *Madag.* 89 C7
Soan →, *Pakistan* 68 C4
Soanierana-Ivongo, *Madag.* 89 B8
Soanindraniny, *Madag.* 89 B8
Şoarş, *Romania* 43 E9
Soavina, *Madag.* 89 C8
Soavinandriana, *Madag.* 89 B8
Soba, *Nigeria* 83 C6
Sobat, Nahr →, *Sudan* 81 F3
Soběslav, *Czech Rep.* 26 B7
Sobhapur, *India* 68 H8
Sobinka, *Russia* 46 E11
Sobótka, *Poland* 45 H3
Sobra, *Croatia* 29 F14
Sobradinho, Reprêsa de, *Brazil* 125 E10
Sobral, *Brazil* 125 D10
Sobrance, *Slovak Rep.* 27 C15
Sobreira Formosa, *Portugal* 34 F3
Soc Giang, *Vietnam* 58 F6
Soc Trang, *Vietnam* 65 H5
Soča →, *Europe* 26 E6
Socastee, *U.S.A.* 109 J6
Sochaczew, *Poland* 45 F7
Soch'e = Shache, *China* 60 C2
Sochi, *Russia* 49 J4
Société, Is. de la, *Pac. Oc.* 97 J12
Society Is. = Société, Is. de la, *Pac. Oc.* 97 J12
Socompa, Portezuelo de, *Chile* 126 A2
Socorro, *N. Mex., U.S.A.* 115 J10
Socorro, *Tex., U.S.A.* 115 L10
Socorro, I., *Mexico* 118 D2
Socotra, *Ind. Oc.* 74 E5
Socovos, *Spain* 33 G3
Socuéllamos, *Spain* 33 F2
Soda L., *U.S.A.* 115 J5
Soda Plains, *India* 69 B8
Soda Springs, *U.S.A.* 114 E8
Sodankylä, *Finland* 8 C22
Soddy-Daisy, *U.S.A.* 109 H3
Söderala, *Sweden* 10 C10
Söderbärke, *Sweden* 10 D9
Söderfors, *Sweden* 10 D11
Söderhamn, *Sweden* 10 C11
Söderköping, *Sweden* 11 F10
Södermanland, *Sweden* 9 G17
Södermanlands län □, *Sweden* 10 E10
Södertälje, *Sweden* 10 E11
Sodiri, *Sudan* 81 E2
Sodo, *Ethiopia* 81 F4
Södra Dellen, *Sweden* 10 C10
Södra Finnskoga, *Sweden* 10 D6
Södra Sandby, *Sweden* 11 J7
Södra Ulvön, *Sweden* 10 B12
Södra Vi, *Sweden* 11 G9
Sodražica, *Slovenia* 29 C11
Sodus, *U.S.A.* 110 C7
Soekmekaar, *S. Africa* 89 C4
Soest, *Germany* 24 D4
Soest, *Neths.* 17 B5
Sofádhes, *Greece* 38 B4
Sofala □, *Mozam.* 89 B5
Sofara, *Mali* 82 C4
Sofia = Sofiya, *Bulgaria* 40 D7
Sofia →, *Madag.* 89 B8
Sofiever, *Ukraine* 47 H7
Sofikón, *Greece* 38 D5
Sofiya, *Bulgaria* 40 D7
Sofiya □, *Bulgaria* 40 D7
Sōfu-Gan, *Japan* 55 K10
Sogakofe, *Ghana* 83 D5
Sogamoso, *Colombia* 124 B4
Sogār, *Iran* 71 E8
Sögel, *Germany* 24 C3
Sogndalsfjøra, *Norway* 9 F12
Søgne, *Norway* 9 G12
Sognefjorden, *Norway* 9 F11
Söğüt, *Bilecik, Turkey* 39 A12
Söğüt, *Burdur, Turkey* 39 D11
Söğüt Dağı, *Turkey* 39 D11
Söğütköy, *Turkey* 39 E10
Sögwipo, *S. Korea* 57 H14
Soh, *Iran* 71 C6
Sohâg, *Egypt* 80 B3
Sohagpur, *India* 68 H8
Sŏhori, *N. Korea* 57 D15
Soignies, *Belgium* 17 D4
Soin, *Burkina Faso* 82 C4
Soira, *Eritrea* 81 E4
Soissons, *France* 19 C10
Sōja, *Japan* 55 G6
Sojat, *India* 68 G5
Sok →, *Russia* 48 D10
Sokal, *Ukraine* 47 G3
Söke, *Turkey* 39 D9
Sokelo, *Dem. Rep. of the Congo* 87 D1
Sokhós, *Greece* 40 F7
Sokhumi, *Georgia* 49 J5
Soko Banja, *Serbia, Yug.* 40 C5
Sokodé, *Togo* 83 D5
Sokol, *Russia* 46 C11

Sokolac, *Bos.-H.* 42 G3
Sokółka, *Poland* 44 E10
Sokolo, *Mali* 82 C3
Sokolo, *Mali* 82 C3
Sokolov, *Czech Rep.* 26 A5
Sokołów Małpolski, *Poland* 45 H9
Sokołów Podlaski, *Poland* 45 F9
Sokoły, *Poland* 45 F9
Sokoto, *Nigeria* 83 C6
Sokoto □, *Nigeria* 83 C6
Sokoto →, *Nigeria* 83 C5
Sol Iletsk, *Russia* 50 D6
Sola →, *Poland* 45 H6
Solai, *Kenya* 86 B4
Solan, *India* 68 D7
Solano, *Phil.* 61 C4
Solapur, *India* 66 L9
Solca, *Romania* 43 C10
Solda Gölü, *Turkey* 39 D11
Soldăneşti, *Moldova* 43 C13
Soldotna, *U.S.A.* 100 B4
Soléa □, *Cyprus* 36 D12
Solec Kujawski, *Poland* 45 E5
Soledad, *Colombia* 124 A4
Soledad, *U.S.A.* 116 J5
Soledad, *Venezuela* 124 B6
Solent, The, *U.K.* 13 G6
Solenzara, *France* 21 G13
Solesmes, *France* 19 B10
Solfonn, *Norway* 9 F12
Solhan, *Turkey* 70 B4
Soligorsk = Salihorsk, *Belarus* 47 F4
Solihull, *U.K.* 13 E6
Solikamsk, *Russia* 50 D6
Solila, *Madag.* 89 C8
Solimões = Amazonas →, *S. Amer.* 122 D5
Solin, *Croatia* 29 E13
Solingen, *Germany* 24 D3
Sollebrunn, *Sweden* 11 F6
Sollefteå, *Sweden* 10 A11
Sollentuna, *Sweden* 10 E11
Sóller, *Spain* 37 B9
Sollerön, *Sweden* 10 D8
Solling, *Germany* 24 D5
Solnechnogorsk, *Russia* 46 D9
Solo →, *Indonesia* 63 G15
Solofra, *Italy* 31 B7
Sologne, *France* 19 E8
Solok, *Indonesia* 62 E2
Sololá, *Guatemala* 120 D1
Solomon, N. Fork →, *U.S.A.* 112 F5
Solomon, S. Fork →, *U.S.A.* 112 F5
Solomon Is. ■, *Pac. Oc.* 96 H7
Solon, *China* 60 B7
Solon Springs, *U.S.A.* 112 B9
Solor, *Indonesia* 63 F6
Solotcha, *Russia* 46 E10
Solothurn, *Switz.* 25 H3
Solothurn □, *Switz.* 25 H3
Solsona, *Spain* 32 C6
Solt, *Hungary* 42 D4
Šolta, *Croatia* 29 E13
Solṭānābād, *Khorāsān, Iran* 71 C8
Solṭānābād, *Khorāsān, Iran* 71 B8
Soltau, *Germany* 24 C5
Soltsy, *Russia* 46 C6
Solunska Glava, *Macedonia* 40 E5
Solvang, *U.S.A.* 117 L6
Solvay, *U.S.A.* 111 C8
Sölvesborg, *Sweden* 11 H8
Solway Firth, *U.K.* 12 C4
Solwezi, *Zambia* 87 E2
Sōma, *Japan* 54 F10
Soma, *Turkey* 39 B9
Somabhula, *Zimbabwe* 89 B4
Somali Pen., *Africa* 76 F8
Somali Rep. ■, *Africa* 74 F4
Somalia = Somali Rep. ■, *Africa* 74 F4
Sombernon, *France* 19 E11
Sombor, *Serbia, Yug.* 42 E4
Sombra, *Canada* 110 D2
Sombrerete, *Mexico* 118 C4
Sombrero, *Anguilla* 121 C7
Şomcuta Mare, *Romania* 43 C8
Somdari, *India* 68 G5
Somers, *U.S.A.* 114 B6
Somerset, *Ky., U.S.A.* 108 G3
Somerset, *Mass., U.S.A.* 111 E13
Somerset, *Pa., U.S.A.* 110 F5
Somerset □, *U.K.* 13 F5
Somerset East, *S. Africa* 88 E4
Somerset I., *Canada* 100 A10
Somerset West, *S. Africa* 88 E2
Somersworth, *U.S.A.* 111 C14
Somerton, *U.S.A.* 115 K6
Somerville, *U.S.A.* 111 F10
Someş →, *Romania* 42 C7
Someşul Mare →, *Romania* 43 C8
Somme □, *France* 19 C9
Somme →, *France* 19 B8
Somme, B. de la, *France* 18 B8
Sommen, *Jönköping, Sweden* 11 F8
Sommen, *Östergötland, Sweden* 11 F9
Sommepy-Tahure, *France* 19 C11
Sömmerda, *Germany* 24 D7
Sommesous, *France* 19 D11
Sommières, *France* 21 E8
Somnath, *India* 68 J4
Somogy □, *Hungary* 42 D2
Somogyszob, *Hungary* 42 D2
Somoto, *Nic.* 120 D2
Sompolno, *Poland* 45 F5
Somport, Puerto de, *Spain* 32 C4
Son →, *India* 69 G11
Son Ha, *Vietnam* 64 E7
Son Hoa, *Vietnam* 64 F7
Son La, *Vietnam* 58 G4
Son Serra, *Spain* 37 B10
Son Servera, *Spain* 32 F8
Son Tay, *Vietnam* 58 G5
Soná, *Panama* 120 E3
Sonamarg, *India* 69 B6
Sonamukhi, *India* 69 H12
Sonar →, *India* 69 G8
Sŏnch'ŏn, *N. Korea* 57 E13
Sondags →, *S. Africa* 88 E4
Sóndalo, *Italy* 28 B7
Sondar, *India* 69 C6
Sønder Felding, *Denmark* 11 J2
Sønder Omme, *Denmark* 11 J2
Sønderborg, *Denmark* 11 K3
Sønderjyllands Amtskommune □, *Denmark* 11 J3
Sondershausen, *Germany* 24 D6
Sóndrio, *Italy* 28 B6
Sone, *Mozam.* 87 F3
Sonepur, *India* 67 J13
Song, *Nigeria* 83 D7
Song, *Thailand* 64 C3
Song Cau, *Vietnam* 64 F7
Song Xian, *China* 56 G7
Songch'ŏn, *N. Korea* 57 E14
Songea, *Tanzania* 87 E4
Songeons, *France* 19 C8
Songhua Hu, *China* 57 C14
Songhua Jiang →, *China* 60 B8
Songjiang, *China* 59 B13
Songjin, *N. Korea* 57 D15
Songjŏng-ni, *S. Korea* 57 G14
Songkan, *China* 58 C6
Songkhla, *Thailand* 65 J3
Songming, *China* 58 E4
Songnim, *N. Korea* 57 E13
Songo, *Mozam.* 85 H6
Songo, *Sudan* 79 G10
Songpan, *China* 58 A4
Songtao, *China* 58 C7
Songwe, *Dem. Rep. of the Congo* 86 C2
Songwe →, *Africa* 87 D3
Songxi, *China* 59 D12
Songzi, *China* 59 B8
Sonhat, *India* 69 H10
Sonid Youqi, *China* 56 C7
Sonipat, *India* 68 E7
Sonkach, *India* 68 H7
Sonkovo, *Russia* 46 D9
Sonmiani, *Pakistan* 68 G2
Sonmiani B., *Pakistan* 68 G2
Sonnino, *Italy* 30 A6
Sono →, *Brazil* 125 E9
Sonoma, *U.S.A.* 116 G4
Sonora, *Calif., U.S.A.* 116 H6
Sonora, *Tex., U.S.A.* 113 K4
Sonora □, *Mexico* 118 B2
Sonora →, *Mexico* 118 B2
Sonoran Desert, *U.S.A.* 117 L12
Sonoyta, *Mexico* 118 A2
Sonqor, *Iran* 73 E12
Sŏnsan, *S. Korea* 57 F15
Sonseca, *Spain* 35 F7
Sonsonate, *El Salv.* 120 D2
Sonsorol Is., *Pac. Oc.* 63 C8
Sonstorp, *Sweden* 11 F9
Sonthofen, *Germany* 25 H6
Soochow = Suzhou, *China* 59 B13
Sooke, *Canada* 116 B3
Sop Hao, *Laos* 58 G5
Sop Prap, *Thailand* 64 D2
Sopelana, *Spain* 32 B2
Sopi, *Indonesia* 63 D7
Sopo, Nahr →, *Sudan* 81 F2
Sopot, *Bulgaria* 41 D8
Sopot, *Poland* 44 D5
Sopot, *Serbia, Yug.* 40 B4
Sopotnica, *Macedonia* 40 E5
Sopron, *Hungary* 42 C1
Sopur, *India* 69 B6
Sør-Rondane, *Antarctica* 5 D4
Sora, *Italy* 29 G10
Sorah, *Pakistan* 68 F3
Soråker, *Sweden* 10 B11
Sorano, *Italy* 29 F8
Soraon, *India* 69 G9
Sorbas, *Spain* 33 H2
Sörbygden, *Sweden* 10 B10
Sore, *France* 20 D3
Sorel, *Canada* 102 C5
Soresina, *Italy* 28 C6
Sörforsa, *Sweden* 10 C10
Sórgono, *Italy* 30 B2
Sorgues, *France* 21 D8
Sorgun, *Turkey* 72 C6
Soria, *Spain* 32 D2
Soria □, *Spain* 32 D2
Soriano, *Uruguay* 126 C4
Soriano nel Cimino, *Italy* 29 F9
Sorkh, Kuh-e, *Iran* 71 C8
Sorø, *Denmark* 11 J5
Soro, *Guinea* 82 C3
Soroca, *Moldova* 43 B13
Sorocaba, *Brazil* 127 A6
Soroki = Soroca, *Moldova* 43 B13
Sorol Atoll, *Pac. Oc.* 63 C10
Sorong, *Indonesia* 63 E8
Soroní, *Greece* 36 C10
Soroti, *Uganda* 86 B3
Sørøya, *Norway* 8 A20
Sørøysundet, *Norway* 8 A20
Sorraia →, *Portugal* 35 G2
Sorrell, *Australia* 94 G4
Sorrento, *Italy* 31 B7
Sorsele, *Sweden* 8 D17
Sörsjön, *Sweden* 10 C7
Sorso, *Italy* 30 B1
Sorsogon, *Phil.* 61 E6
Sortavala, *Russia* 46 B6
Sortino, *Italy* 31 E8
Sortland, *Norway* 8 B16
Sorvizhi, *Russia* 48 B9
Sos = Sos del Rey Católico, *Spain* 32 C3
Sos del Rey Católico, *Spain* 32 C3
Sŏsan, *S. Korea* 57 F14
Soscumica, L., *Canada* 102 B4
Sösdala, *Sweden* 11 H7
Sosna →, *Russia* 47 F10
Sosnovka, *Kirov, Russia* 48 B10
Sosnovka, *Tambov, Russia* 48 D5
Sosnovyy Bor, *Russia* 46 C5
Sosnowiec, *Poland* 45 H6
Sospel, *France* 21 E11
Sossus Vlei, *Namibia* 88 C2
Šoštanj, *Slovenia* 29 B12
Sŏsura, *N. Korea* 57 C16
Sot →, *India* 69 F8
Sotkamo, *Finland* 8 D23
Soto del Barco, *Spain* 34 B4
Soto la Marina →, *Mexico* 119 C5
Soto y Amío, *Spain* 34 C5
Sotrondio, *Spain* 34 B5
Sotuta, *Mexico* 119 C7
Souanké, *Congo* 84 D2
Soubré, *Ivory C.* 82 D3
Souderton, *U.S.A.* 111 F9
Soúdha, *Greece* 36 D6
Soúdhas, Kólpos, *Greece* 36 D6
Souflíon, *Greece* 41 E10
Soufrière, *St. Lucia* 121 D7
Souillac, *France* 20 D5
Souilly, *France* 19 C12
Soukhouma, *Laos* 64 E5
Sŏul, *S. Korea* 57 F14
Soulac-sur-Mer, *France* 20 C2
Soulougou, *Burkina Faso* 83 C5
Soultz-sous-Forêts, *France* 19 D14
Sound, The = Øresund, *Europe* 11 J6
Sound, The, *U.K.* 13 G3
Soúnion, Ákra, *Greece* 38 D6
Sources, Mt. aux, *Lesotho* 89 D4
Soure, *Brazil* 125 D9
Soure, *Portugal* 34 E2
Souris, *Man., Canada* 105 D8
Souris, *P.E.I., Canada* 103 C7
Souris →, *Canada* 112 A5
Sourou →, *Africa* 82 C4
Soúrpi, *Greece* 38 B4
Sousa, *Brazil* 125 E11
Sousel, *Portugal* 35 G3
Sousse, *Tunisia* 79 A8
Soustons, *France* 20 E2
Sout →, *S. Africa* 88 E2
South Africa ■, *Africa* 88 E3
South America 122 E5
South Atlantic Ocean 122 H7
South Aulatsivik I., *Canada* 103 A7
South Australia □, *Australia* 95 E2
South Ayrshire □, *U.K.* 14 F4
South Baldy, *U.S.A.* 115 J10
South Bass I., *U.S.A.* 110 E2
South Bend, *Ind., U.S.A.* 108 E2
South Bend, *Wash., U.S.A.* 116 D3
South Boston, *U.S.A.* 109 G6
South Branch, *Canada* 103 C8
South Brook, *Canada* 103 C8
South Carolina □, *U.S.A.* 109 J5
South Charleston, *U.S.A.* 108 F5
South China Sea, *Asia* 62 C4
South Dakota □, *U.S.A.* 112 C5
South Deerfield, *U.S.A.* 111 D12
South Downs, *U.K.* 13 G7
South East C., *Australia* 94 G4
South East Is., *Australia* 93 F3
South Esk →, *U.K.* 14 E6
South Foreland, *U.K.* 13 F9
South Fork American →, *U.S.A.* 116 G5
South Fork Feather →, *U.S.A.* 116 F5
South Fork Grand →, *U.S.A.* 112 C3
South Fork Republican →, *U.S.A.* 112 E4
South Georgia, *Antarctica* 122 J7
South Gloucestershire □, *U.K.* 13 F5
South Hadley, *U.S.A.* 111 D12
South Haven, *U.S.A.* 108 D2
South Henik, L., *Canada* 105 A9
South Honshu Ridge, *Pac. Oc.* 96 E6
South Horr, *Kenya* 86 B4
South I., *Kenya* 86 B4
South I., *N.Z.* 91 L3
South Indian Lake, *Canada* 105 B9
South Invercargill, *N.Z.* 91 M2
South Knife →, *Canada* 105 B10
South Koel →, *India* 69 H11
South Korea ■, *Asia* 57 G15
South Lake Tahoe, *U.S.A.* 116 G6
South Lanarkshire □, *U.K.* 14 F5
South Loup →, *U.S.A.* 112 E5
South Magnetic Pole, *Antarctica* 5 C9
South Milwaukee, *U.S.A.* 108 D2
South Molton, *U.K.* 13 F4
South Moose L., *Canada* 105 C8
South Nahanni →, *Canada* 104 A4
South Nation →, *Canada* 111 A9
South Natuna Is. = Natuna Selatan, Kepulauan, *Indonesia* 65 L7
South Negril Pt., *Jamaica* 120 C4
South Orkney Is., *Antarctica* 5 C18
South Ossetia □, *Georgia* 49 J7
South Pagai, I. = Pagai Selatan, Pulau, *Indonesia* 62 E2
South Paris, *U.S.A.* 111 B14
South Pittsburg, *U.S.A.* 109 H3
South Platte →, *U.S.A.* 112 E4
South Pole, *Antarctica* 5 E
South Porcupine, *Canada* 102 C3
South Portland, *U.S.A.* 109 D10
South Pt., *U.S.A.* 110 B1
South River, *Canada* 102 C4
South River, *U.S.A.* 111 F10
South Ronaldsay, *U.K.* 14 C6
South Sandwich Is., *Antarctica* 5 B1
South Saskatchewan →, *Canada* 105 C7
South Seal →, *Canada* 105 B9
South Shetland Is., *Antarctica* 5 C18
South Shields, *U.K.* 12 C6
South Sioux City, *U.S.A.* 112 D6
South Taranaki Bight, *N.Z.* 91 H5
South Thompson →, *Canada* 104 C4
South Twin I., *Canada* 102 B4
South Tyne →, *U.K.* 12 C5
South Uist, *U.K.* 14 D1
South West Africa = Namibia ■, *Africa* 88 C2
South West C., *Australia* 94 G4
South West Rocks, *Australia* 95 E5
South Williamsport, *U.S.A.* 110 E8
South Yorkshire □, *U.K.* 12 D6
Southampton, *Canada* 102 D3
Southampton, *U.K.* 13 G6
Southampton, *U.S.A.* 111 F12
Southampton □, *U.K.* 13 G6
Southampton I., *Canada* 101 B11
Southaven, *U.S.A.* 113 H9
Southbank, *Canada* 104 C3
Southbridge, *N.Z.* 91 K4
Southbridge, *U.S.A.* 111 D12
Southend, *Canada* 105 B8
Southend-on-Sea, *U.K.* 13 F8
Southend-on-Sea □, *U.K.* 13 F8
Southern □, *Malawi* 87 F4
Southern □, *S. Leone* 82 D2
Southern □, *Uganda* 86 C3
Southern □, *Zambia* 87 F2
Southern Alps, *N.Z.* 91 K3
Southern Cross, *Australia* 93 F2
Southern Indian L., *Canada* 105 B9
Southern Ocean, *Antarctica* 5 C6
Southern Pines, *U.S.A.* 109 H6
Southern Uplands, *U.K.* 14 F5
Southington, *U.S.A.* 111 E12
Southold, *U.S.A.* 111 E12
Southport, *Australia* 95 D5
Southport, *U.K.* 12 D4
Southport, *Fla., U.S.A.* 109 K3
Southport, *N.Y., U.S.A.* 110 D8
Southwest C., *N.Z.* 91 M1
Southwold, *U.K.* 13 E9
Soutpansberg, *S. Africa* 89 C4
Souvigny, *France* 19 F10
Sovata, *Romania* 43 D10
Soverato, *Italy* 31 D9
Sovetsk, *Kaliningd., Russia* 9 J19
Sovetsk, *Kirov, Russia* 48 B9
Sovetskaya Gavan = Vanino, *Russia* 51 E15
Sovicille, *Italy* 29 E8
Soweto, *S. Africa* 89 D4
Sōya-Kaikyō = La Perouse Str., *Asia* 54 B11
Sōya-Misaki, *Japan* 54 B10
Soyaux, *France* 20 C4
Sozh →, *Belarus* 47 F6
Sozopol, *Bulgaria* 41 D11
Spa, *Belgium* 17 D5
Spain ■, *Europe* 7 H5
Spalding, *Australia* 95 E2
Spalding, *U.K.* 12 E7
Spangler, *U.S.A.* 110 F6
Spanish, *Canada* 102 C3
Spanish Fork, *U.S.A.* 114 F8
Spanish Town, *Jamaica* 120 C4
Sparks, *U.S.A.* 116 F7
Sparreholm, *Sweden* 10 E10
Sparta = Spárti, *Greece* 38 D4
Sparta, *Mich., U.S.A.* 108 D3
Sparta, *N.J., U.S.A.* 111 E10
Sparta, *Wis., U.S.A.* 112 D9
Spartanburg, *U.S.A.* 109 H5
Spartansburg, *U.S.A.* 110 E5
Spárti, *Greece* 38 D4
Spartivento, C., *Calabria, Italy* 31 E9
Spartivento, C., *Sard., Italy* 30 D1
Sparwood, *Canada* 104 D6
Spas-Demensk, *Russia* 46 E7
Spas-Klepiki, *Russia* 46 E11
Spassk Dalniy, *Russia* 51 E14
Spassk-Ryazanskiy, *Russia* 46 E11
Spátha, Ákra, *Greece* 36 D5
Spatsizi →, *Canada* 104 B3
Spatsizi Plateau Wilderness Park, *Canada* 104 B3
Spean →, *U.K.* 14 E4
Spearfish, *U.S.A.* 112 C3
Spearman, *U.S.A.* 113 G4
Speculator, *U.S.A.* 111 C10
Speia, *Moldova* 43 D14
Speightstown, *Barbados* 121 D8
Speke Gulf, *Tanzania* 86 C3
Spello, *Italy* 29 F9
Spencer, *Idaho, U.S.A.* 114 D7
Spencer, *Iowa, U.S.A.* 112 D7
Spencer, *N.Y., U.S.A.* 111 D8
Spencer, *Nebr., U.S.A.* 112 D5
Spencer, C., *Australia* 95 F2
Spencer B., *Namibia* 88 D1
Spencer G., *Australia* 95 E2
Spencerville, *Canada* 111 B9
Spences Bridge, *Canada* 104 C4
Spennymoor, *U.K.* 12 C6
Spenser Mts., *N.Z.* 91 K4
Spentrup, *Denmark* 11 H4
Sperkhiós →, *Greece* 38 C4
Sperrin Mts., *U.K.* 15 B5
Spessart, *Germany* 25 F5
Spétsai, *Greece* 38 D5
Spey →, *U.K.* 14 D5
Speyer, *Germany* 25 F4
Spezand, *Pakistan* 68 E2
Spezzano Albanese, *Italy* 31 C9
Spiekeroog, *Germany* 24 B3
Spiez, *Switz.* 25 J3
Spíli, *Greece* 36 D6
Spilimbergo, *Italy* 29 B9
Spīn Búldak, *Afghan.* 68 D2
Spinalónga, *Greece* 36 D7
Spinazzola, *Italy* 31 B9
Spineni, *Romania* 43 F9
Spirit Lake, *U.S.A.* 116 D4
Spirit River, *Canada* 104 B5
Spiritwood, *Canada* 105 C7
Spišská Nová Ves, *Slovak Rep.* 27 C13
Spišské Podhradie, *Slovak Rep.* 27 B13
Spital, *Austria* 26 D7
Spithead, *U.K.* 13 G6
Spittal an der Drau, *Austria* 26 E6
Spitzbergen = Svalbard, *Arctic* 4 B8
Spjelkavik, *Norway* 9 E12
Split, *Croatia* 29 E13
Split L., *Canada* 105 B9
Split Lake, *Canada* 105 B9
Splitski Kanal, *Croatia* 29 E13
Splügenpass, *Switz.* 25 J5
Spofford, *U.S.A.* 113 L4
Spokane, *U.S.A.* 114 C5
Spoleto, *Italy* 29 F9
Spooner, *U.S.A.* 112 C9
Sporyy Navolok, Mys, *Russia* 50 B7
Sprague, *U.S.A.* 114 C5
Spratly I., *S. China Sea* 62 C4
Spratly Is., *S. China Sea* 62 C4
Spray, *U.S.A.* 114 D4
Spreča →, *Bos.-H.* 42 F3
Spree →, *Germany* 24 C9
Spreewald, *Germany* 24 D9
Spremberg, *Germany* 24 D10
Sprengisandur, *Iceland* 8 D5
Spring City, *U.S.A.* 111 F9
Spring Creek, *U.S.A.* 114 F6
Spring Garden, *U.S.A.* 116 F6
Spring Hill, *U.S.A.* 109 L4
Spring Mts., *U.S.A.* 115 H6
Spring Valley, *U.S.A.* 117 N10
Springbok, *S. Africa* 88 D2
Springboro, *U.S.A.* 110 E4
Springdale, *Canada* 103 C8
Springdale, *U.S.A.* 113 G7
Springe, *Germany* 24 C5
Springer, *U.S.A.* 113 G2
Springerville, *U.S.A.* 115 J9
Springfield, *Canada* 110 D4
Springfield, *N.Z.* 91 K3
Springfield, *Colo., U.S.A.* 113 G3
Springfield, *Ill., U.S.A.* 112 F10
Springfield, *Mass., U.S.A.* 111 D12
Springfield, *Mo., U.S.A.* 113 G8
Springfield, *Ohio, U.S.A.* 108 F4
Springfield, *Oreg., U.S.A.* 114 D2
Springfield, *Tenn., U.S.A.* 109 G2
Springfield, *Vt., U.S.A.* 111 C12
Springfontein, *S. Africa* 88 E4
Springhill, *Canada* 103 C7
Springhill, *U.S.A.* 113 J8
Springhouse, *Canada* 104 C4
Springs, *S. Africa* 89 D4
Springsure, *Australia* 94 C4
Springvale, *U.S.A.* 111 C14
Springville, *Calif., U.S.A.* 116 J8
Springville, *N.Y., U.S.A.* 110 D6
Springville, *Utah, U.S.A.* 114 F8
Springwater, *U.S.A.* 110 D7
Spruce-Creek, *U.S.A.* 110 F6
Spruce Mt., *U.S.A.* 111 B12
Spur, *U.S.A.* 113 J4
Spurn Hd., *U.K.* 12 D8
Spuž, *Montenegro, Yug.* 40 D3
Spuzzum, *Canada* 104 D4
Squam L., *U.S.A.* 111 C13
Squamish, *Canada* 104 D4
Square Islands, *Canada* 103 B8
Squillace, G. di, *Italy* 31 D9
Squinzano, *Italy* 31 B11
Squires, Mt., *Australia* 93 E4
Srbac, *Bos.-H.* 42 E2
Srbica, *Kosovo, Yug.* 40 D4
Srbija = Serbia □, *Yugoslavia* 40 C5
Srbobran, *Serbia, Yug.* 42 E4
Sre Ambel, *Cambodia* 65 G4
Sre Khtum, *Cambodia* 65 F6
Sre Umbell = Sre Ambel, *Cambodia* 65 G4
Srebrenica, *Bos.-H.* 42 F4
Sredinny Ra. = Sredinnyy Khrebet, *Russia* 51 D16
Sredinnyy Khrebet, *Russia* 51 D16
Središče, *Slovenia* 29 B13
Sredna Gora, *Bulgaria* 41 D8
Srednekolymsk, *Russia* 51 C16
Sredni Rodopi, *Bulgaria* 41 E8
Srednogorie, *Bulgaria* 41 D8
Śrem, *Poland* 45 F4

Sremska Mitrovica, *Serbia, Yug.* 42 F4
Sremski Karlovci, *Serbia, Yug.* 42 E4
Srepok →, *Cambodia* 64 F6
Sretensk, *Russia* 51 D12
Sri Lanka ■, *Asia* 66 R12
Srikakulam, *India* 67 K13
Srinagar, *India* 69 B6
Środa Śląska, *Poland* 45 G3
Środa Wielkopolski, *Poland* 45 F4
Srpska Crnja, *Serbia, Yug.* 42 E5
Srpski Itebej, *Serbia, Yug.* 42 E5
Staaten →, *Australia* 94 B3
Staberhuk, *Germany* 24 A7
Stade, *Germany* 24 B5
Stadskanaal, *Neths.* 17 A6
Stadtallendorf, *Germany* 24 E5
Stadthagen, *Germany* 24 C5
Stadtlohn, *Germany* 24 D2
Stadtroda, *Germany* 24 E7
Staffa, *U.K.* 14 E2
Staffanstorp, *Sweden* 11 J7
Stafford, *U.K.* 12 E5
Stafford, *U.S.A.* 113 G5
Stafford Springs, *U.S.A.* 111 E12
Staffordshire □, *U.K.* 12 E5
Stagnone, *Italy* 30 E5
Staines, *U.K.* 13 F7
Stainz, *Austria* 26 E8
Stakhanov, *Ukraine* 47 H10
Stalać, *Serbia, Yug.* 40 C5
Stalingrad = Volgograd, *Russia* 49 F7
Staliniri = Tskhinvali, *Georgia* 49 J7
Stalino = Donetsk, *Ukraine* 47 J9
Stalinogorsk = Novomoskovsk, *Russia* 46 E10
Stalis, *Greece* 36 D7
Stallarholmen, *Sweden* 10 E11
Ställdalen, *Sweden* 10 E8
Stalowa Wola, *Poland* 45 H9
Stalybridge, *U.K.* 12 D5
Stamford, *Australia* 94 C3
Stamford, *U.K.* 13 E7
Stamford, *Conn., U.S.A.* 111 E11
Stamford, *N.Y., U.S.A.* 111 D10
Stamford, *Tex., U.S.A.* 113 J5
Stampriet, *Namibia* 88 C2
Stamps, *U.S.A.* 113 J8
Stančevo = Kalipetrovo, *Bulgaria* 41 B11
Standerton, *S. Africa* 89 D4
Standish, *U.S.A.* 108 D4
Stanford, *S. Africa* 88 E2
Stanford, *U.S.A.* 114 C8
Stånga, *Sweden* 11 G12
Stanger, *S. Africa* 89 D5
Stanišić, *Serbia, Yug.* 42 E4
Stanislaus →, *U.S.A.* 116 H5
Stanislav = Ivano-Frankivsk, *Ukraine* 47 H3
Stanisławów, *Poland* 45 F8
Stanley, *Australia* 94 G4
Stanley, *Canada* 105 B8
Stanley, *Falk. Is.* 128 G5
Stanley, *U.K.* 12 C6
Stanley, *Idaho, U.S.A.* 114 D6
Stanley, *N. Dak., U.S.A.* 112 A3
Stanley, *N.Y., U.S.A.* 110 D7
Stanovoy Khrebet, *Russia* 51 D13
Stanovoy Ra. = Stanovoy Khrebet, *Russia* 51 D13
Stansmore Ra., *Australia* 92 D4
Stanthorpe, *Australia* 95 D5
Stanton, *U.S.A.* 113 J4
Stanwood, *U.S.A.* 116 B4
Staples, *U.S.A.* 112 B7
Stąporków, *Poland* 45 G7
Star City, *Canada* 105 C8
Star Lake, *U.S.A.* 111 B9
Stará L'ubovňa, *Slovak Rep.* 27 B13
Stara Moravica, *Serbia, Yug.* 42 E4
Stara Pazova, *Serbia, Yug.* 42 F5
Stara Planina, *Bulgaria* 40 C7
Stará Turá, *Slovak Rep.* 27 C10
Stara Zagora, *Bulgaria* 41 D9
Starachowice, *Poland* 45 G8
Staraya Russa, *Russia* 46 D6
Starbuck I., *Kiribati* 97 H12
Starchiojd, *Romania* 43 E11
Stargard Szczeciński, *Poland* 44 E2
Stari Bar, *Montenegro, Yug.* 40 D3
Stari Trg, *Slovenia* 29 C12
Staritsa, *Russia* 46 D8
Starke, *U.S.A.* 109 L4
Starnberg, *Germany* 25 H7
Starnberger See, *Germany* 25 H7
Starobilsk, *Ukraine* 47 H10
Starodub, *Russia* 47 F7
Starogard Gdański, *Poland* 44 E5
Starokonstantinov = Starokonstyantyniv, *Ukraine* 47 H4
Starokonstyantyniv, *Ukraine* 47 H4
Starominskaya, *Russia* 47 J10
Staroshcherbinovskaya, *Russia* 47 J10
Start Pt., *U.K.* 13 G4
Stary Sącz, *Poland* 45 J7
Staryy Biryuzyak, *Russia* 49 H8
Staryy Chartoriysk, *Ukraine* 47 G3
Staryy Krym, *Ukraine* 47 K8
Staryy Oskol, *Russia* 47 G9
Stassfurt, *Germany* 24 D7
Staszów, *Poland* 45 H8
State College, *U.S.A.* 110 F7
Stateline, *U.S.A.* 116 G7
Staten, I. = Estados, I. de Los, *Argentina* 122 J4
Staten I., *U.S.A.* 111 F10
Statesboro, *U.S.A.* 109 J5
Statesville, *U.S.A.* 109 H5
Stauffer, *U.S.A.* 117 L7
Staunton, *Ill., U.S.A.* 112 F10
Staunton, *Va., U.S.A.* 108 F6
Stavanger, *Norway* 9 G11
Staveley, *N.Z.* 91 K3
Stavelot, *Belgium* 17 D5
Stavern, *Norway* 9 G14
Stavoren, *Neths.* 17 B5
Stavropol, *Russia* 49 H6
Stavros, *Cyprus* 36 D11
Stavrós, *Greece* 36 D6
Stavrós, Ákra, *Greece* 36 D6
Stavroúpolis, *Greece* 41 E8
Stawell, *Australia* 95 F3
Stawell →, *Australia* 94 C3
Stawiski, *Poland* 44 E9
Stawiszyn, *Poland* 45 G5
Stayner, *Canada* 110 B4
Stayton, *U.S.A.* 114 D2
Steamboat Springs, *U.S.A.* 114 F10
Stebleva, *Albania* 40 E4
Steele, *U.S.A.* 112 B5
Steelton, *U.S.A.* 110 F8
Steen River, *Canada* 104 B5
Steenkool = Bintuni, *Indonesia* 63 E8
Steens Mt., *U.S.A.* 114 E4
Steenwijk, *Neths.* 17 B6
Steep Pt., *Australia* 93 E1
Steep Rock, *Canada* 105 C9
Ştefan Vodă, *Moldova* 43 D14
Ştefăneşti, *Romania* 43 C12
Stefanie L. = Chew Bahir, *Ethiopia* 81 G4
Stefansson Bay, *Antarctica* 5 C5
Stege, *Denmark* 11 K6
Ştei, *Romania* 42 D7
Steiermark □, *Austria* 26 D8
Steigerwald, *Germany* 25 F6
Steilacoom, *U.S.A.* 116 C4
Steilrandberge, *Namibia* 88 B1
Steinbach, *Canada* 105 D9
Steinfurt, *Germany* 24 C3
Steinhausen, *Namibia* 88 C2
Steinheim, *Germany* 24 D5
Steinhuder Meer, *Germany* 24 C5
Steinkjer, *Norway* 8 D14
Steinkopf, *S. Africa* 88 D2
Stellarton, *Canada* 103 C7
Stellenbosch, *S. Africa* 88 E2
Stelvio, Paso dello, *Italy* 28 B7
Stenay, *France* 19 C12
Stendal, *Germany* 24 C7
Stende, *Latvia* 44 A9
Stenhamra, *Sweden* 10 E11
Stenstorp, *Sweden* 11 F7
Stenungsund, *Sweden* 11 F5
Steornabhaigh = Stornoway, *U.K.* 14 C2
Stepanakert = Xankändi, *Azerbaijan* 70 B5
Stepanavan, *Armenia* 49 K7
Stephens Creek, *Australia* 95 E3
Stephens I., *Canada* 104 C2
Stephens L., *Canada* 105 B9
Stephenville, *Canada* 103 C8
Stephenville, *U.S.A.* 113 J5
Stepnica, *Poland* 44 E1
Stepnoi = Elista, *Russia* 49 G7
Steppe, *Asia* 52 D9
Stereá Ellas □, *Greece* 38 C4
Sterkstroom, *S. Africa* 88 E4
Sterling, *Colo., U.S.A.* 112 E3
Sterling, *Ill., U.S.A.* 112 E10
Sterling, *Kans., U.S.A.* 112 F5
Sterling City, *U.S.A.* 113 K4
Sterling Heights, *U.S.A.* 108 D4
Sterling Run, *U.S.A.* 110 E6
Sterlitamak, *Russia* 50 D6
Sternberg, *Germany* 24 B7
Šternberk, *Czech Rep.* 27 B10
Stérnes, *Greece* 36 D6
Sterzing = Vipiteno, *Italy* 29 B8
Stettin = Szczecin, *Poland* 44 E1
Stettiner Haff, *Germany* 24 B10
Stettler, *Canada* 104 C6
Steubenville, *U.S.A.* 110 F4
Stevenage, *U.K.* 13 F7
Stevens Point, *U.S.A.* 112 C10
Stevenson, *U.S.A.* 116 E5
Stevenson L., *Canada* 105 C9
Stevensville, *U.S.A.* 114 C6
Stevns Klint, *Denmark* 11 J6
Stewart, *B.C., Canada* 104 B3
Stewart, *N.W.T., Canada* 100 B6
Stewart, *U.S.A.* 116 F7
Stewart, C., *Australia* 94 A1
Stewart, I., *Chile* 128 G2
Stewart I., *N.Z.* 91 M1
Stewarts Point, *U.S.A.* 116 G3
Stewartville, *U.S.A.* 112 D8
Stewiacke, *Canada* 103 C7
Steynsburg, *S. Africa* 88 E4
Steyr, *Austria* 26 C7
Steyr →, *Austria* 26 C7
Steytlerville, *S. Africa* 88 E3
Stia, *Italy* 29 E8
Stigler, *U.S.A.* 113 H7
Stigliano, *Italy* 31 B9
Stigtomta, *Sweden* 11 F10
Stikine →, *Canada* 104 B2
Stilfontein, *S. Africa* 88 D4
Stílis, *Greece* 38 C4
Stillwater, *N.Z.* 91 K3
Stillwater, *Minn., U.S.A.* 112 C8
Stillwater, *N.Y., U.S.A.* 111 D11
Stillwater, *Okla., U.S.A.* 113 G6
Stillwater Range, *U.S.A.* 114 G4
Stillwater Reservoir, *U.S.A.* 111 C9
Stilo, Pta., *Italy* 31 D9
Stilwell, *U.S.A.* 113 H7
Štip, *Macedonia* 40 E6
Stíra, *Greece* 38 C6
Stirling, *Canada* 110 B7
Stirling, *U.K.* 14 E5
Stirling □, *U.K.* 14 E4
Stirling Ra., *Australia* 93 F2
Stittsville, *Canada* 111 A9
Stjernøya, *Norway* 8 A20
Stjørdalshalsen, *Norway* 8 E14
Stockach, *Germany* 25 H5
Stockaryd, *Sweden* 11 G8
Stockerau, *Austria* 27 C9
Stockholm, *Sweden* 10 E12
Stockholms län □, *Sweden* 10 E12
Stockport, *U.K.* 12 D5
Stocksbridge, *U.K.* 12 D6
Stockton, *Calif., U.S.A.* 116 H5
Stockton, *Kans., U.S.A.* 112 F5
Stockton, *Mo., U.S.A.* 113 G8
Stockton-on-Tees, *U.K.* 12 C6
Stockton-on-Tees □, *U.K.* 12 C6
Stockton Plateau, *U.S.A.* 113 K3
Stoczek Łukowski, *Poland* 45 G8
Stöde, *Sweden* 10 B10
Stoeng Treng, *Cambodia* 64 F5
Stoer, Pt. of, *U.K.* 14 C3
Stogovo, *Macedonia* 40 E4
Stoholm, *Denmark* 11 H3
Stoke-on-Trent, *U.K.* 12 D5
Stoke-on-Trent □, *U.K.* 12 D5
Stokes Pt., *Australia* 94 G3
Stokes Ra., *Australia* 92 C5
Stokksnes, *Iceland* 8 D6
Stokmarknes, *Norway* 8 B16
Stolac, *Bos.-H.* 40 C1
Stolberg, *Germany* 24 E2
Stolbovoy, Ostrov, *Russia* 51 D17
Stolbtsy = Stowbtsy, *Belarus* 46 F4
Stolin, *Belarus* 47 G4
Stöllet, *Sweden* 10 D7
Stolnici, *Romania* 43 F9
Stomíon, *Greece* 36 D5
Ston, *Croatia* 29 F14
Stone, *U.K.* 12 E5
Stoneboro, *U.S.A.* 110 E4
Stonehaven, *U.K.* 14 E6
Stonehenge, *Australia* 94 C3
Stonehenge, *U.K.* 13 F6
Stonewall, *Canada* 105 C9
Stony L., *Man., Canada* 105 B9
Stony L., *Ont., Canada* 110 B6
Stony Point, *U.S.A.* 111 E11
Stony Pt., *U.S.A.* 111 C8
Stony Rapids, *Canada* 105 B7
Stony Tunguska = Tunguska, Podkamennaya →, *Russia* 51 C10
Stonyford, *U.S.A.* 116 F4
Stopnica, *Poland* 45 H7
Storå, *Sweden* 10 E9
Storå →, *Denmark* 11 H2
Stora Gla, *Sweden* 10 E6
Stora Le, *Sweden* 10 E5
Stora Lulevatten, *Sweden* 8 C18
Storavan, *Sweden* 8 D18
Stord, *Norway* 9 G11
Store Bælt, *Denmark* 11 J4
Store Heddinge, *Denmark* 11 J6
Storebro, *Sweden* 11 G9
Storfors, *Sweden* 10 E8
Storlien, *Sweden* 10 A6
Storm B., *Australia* 94 G4
Storm Lake, *U.S.A.* 112 D7
Stormberge, *S. Africa* 88 E4
Stormsrivier, *S. Africa* 88 E3
Stornoway, *U.K.* 14 C2
Storo, *Italy* 28 C7
Storozhinets = Storozhynets, *Ukraine* 47 H3
Storozhynets, *Ukraine* 47 H3
Storrs, *U.S.A.* 111 E12
Storsjön, *Gävleborg, Sweden* 10 D10
Storsjön, *Jämtland, Sweden* 10 B7
Storsjön, *Jämtland, Sweden* 10 A8
Storstrøms Amtskommune □, *Denmark* 11 J5
Storuman, *Sweden* 8 D17
Storuman, sjö, *Sweden* 8 D17
Storvätteshågna, *Sweden* 10 B6
Storvik, *Sweden* 10 D10
Storvreta, *Sweden* 10 E11
Stouffville, *Canada* 110 C5
Stoughton, *Canada* 105 D8
Stour →, *Dorset, U.K.* 13 G6
Stour →, *Kent, U.K.* 13 F9
Stour →, *Suffolk, U.K.* 13 F9
Stourbridge, *U.K.* 13 E5
Stout L., *Canada* 105 C10
Stove Pipe Wells Village, *U.S.A.* 117 J9
Støvring, *Denmark* 11 H3
Stow, *U.S.A.* 110 E3
Stowbtsy, *Belarus* 46 F4
Stowmarket, *U.K.* 13 E9
Strabane, *U.K.* 15 B4
Stracin, *Macedonia* 40 D6
Stradella, *Italy* 28 C6
Strahan, *Australia* 94 G4
Strajitsa, *Bulgaria* 41 C9
Strakonice, *Czech Rep.* 26 B6
Straldzha, *Bulgaria* 41 D10
Stralsund, *Germany* 24 A9
Strand, *S. Africa* 88 E2
Stranda, *Møre og Romsdal, Norway* 9 E12
Stranda, *Nord-Trøndelag, Norway* 8 E14
Strandby, *Denmark* 11 G4
Strangford L., *U.K.* 15 B6
Strängnäs, *Sweden* 10 E11
Stranraer, *U.K.* 14 G3
Strasbourg, *Canada* 105 C8
Strasbourg, *France* 19 D14
Strasburg, *Germany* 24 B9
Străşeni, *Moldova* 43 C13
Stråssa, *Sweden* 10 E9
Stratford, *Canada* 102 D3
Stratford, *N.Z.* 91 H5
Stratford, *Calif., U.S.A.* 116 J7
Stratford, *Conn., U.S.A.* 111 E11
Stratford, *Tex., U.S.A.* 113 G3
Stratford-upon-Avon, *U.K.* 13 E6
Strath Spey, *U.K.* 14 D5
Strathalbyn, *Australia* 95 F2
Strathaven, *U.K.* 14 F4
Strathcona Prov. Park, *Canada* 104 D3
Strathmore, *Canada* 104 C6
Strathmore, *U.K.* 14 E5
Strathmore, *U.S.A.* 116 J7
Strathnaver, *Canada* 104 C4
Strathpeffer, *U.K.* 14 D4
Strathroy, *Canada* 102 D3
Strathy Pt., *U.K.* 14 C4
Strattanville, *U.S.A.* 110 E5
Stratton, *U.S.A.* 111 A14
Stratton Mt., *U.S.A.* 111 C12
Straubing, *Germany* 25 G8
Straumnes, *Iceland* 8 C2
Strausberg, *Germany* 24 C9
Strawberry →, *U.S.A.* 114 F8
Strážnice, *Czech Rep.* 27 C10
Streaky B., *Australia* 95 E1
Streaky Bay, *Australia* 95 E1
Streator, *U.S.A.* 112 E10
Středočeský □, *Czech Rep.* 26 B7
Streetsboro, *U.S.A.* 110 E3
Streetsville, *Canada* 110 C5
Strehaia, *Romania* 43 F8
Strelcha, *Bulgaria* 41 D8
Strelka, *Russia* 51 D10
Streng →, *Cambodia* 64 F4
Stresa, *Italy* 28 C5
Streymoy, *Færoe Is.* 8 E9
Strezhevoy, *Russia* 50 C8
Stříbro, *Czech Rep.* 26 A6
Strimón →, *Greece* 40 F7
Strimonikós Kólpos, *Greece* 40 F7
Strofádhes, *Greece* 38 D3
Stroma, *U.K.* 14 C5
Strómboli, *Italy* 31 D8
Stromeferry, *U.K.* 14 D3
Stromness, *U.K.* 14 C5
Strömsbruk, *Sweden* 10 C11
Stromsburg, *U.S.A.* 112 E6
Strömsnäsbruk, *Sweden* 11 H7
Strömstad, *Sweden* 11 F5
Strömsund, *Sweden* 8 E16
Strongilí, *Greece* 39 E11
Stróngoli, *Italy* 31 C10
Strongsville, *U.S.A.* 110 E3
Stronie Ślaskie, *Poland* 45 H3
Stronsay, *U.K.* 14 B6
Stropkov, *Slovak Rep.* 27 B14
Stroud, *U.K.* 13 F5
Stroud Road, *Australia* 95 E5
Stroudsburg, *U.S.A.* 111 F9
Stroumbi, *Cyprus* 36 E11
Struer, *Denmark* 11 H2
Struga, *Macedonia* 40 E4
Strugi Krasnyye, *Russia* 46 C5
Strumica, *Macedonia* 40 E6
Strumica →, *Europe* 40 E7
Struthers, *Canada* 102 C2
Struthers, *U.S.A.* 110 E4
Stryama, *Bulgaria* 41 D8
Stryker, *U.S.A.* 114 B6
Stryków, *Poland* 45 G6
Stryy, *Ukraine* 47 H2
Strzegom, *Poland* 45 H3
Strzelce Krajeńskie, *Poland* 45 F2
Strzelce Opolskie, *Poland* 45 H5
Strzelecki Cr. →, *Australia* 95 D2
Strzelin, *Poland* 45 H4
Strzelno, *Poland* 45 F5
Strzybnica, *Poland* 45 H5
Strzyżów, *Poland* 45 J8
Stuart, *Fla., U.S.A.* 109 M5
Stuart, *Nebr., U.S.A.* 112 D5
Stuart →, *Canada* 104 C4
Stuart Bluff Ra., *Australia* 92 D5
Stuart L., *Canada* 104 C4
Stuart Ra., *Australia* 95 D1
Stubbekøbing, *Denmark* 11 K6
Stuben, *Austria* 26 D3
Studen Kladenets, Yazovir, *Bulgaria* 41 E9
Studenka, *Czech Rep.* 27 B11
Stugun, *Sweden* 10 A9
Stuhr, *Germany* 24 B4
Stull L., *Canada* 102 B1
Stung Treng = Stoeng Treng, *Cambodia* 64 F5
Stupart →, *Canada* 102 A1
Stupava, *Slovak Rep.* 27 C10
Stupino, *Russia* 46 E10
Sturgeon B., *Canada* 105 C9
Sturgeon Bay, *U.S.A.* 108 C2
Sturgeon Falls, *Canada* 102 C4
Sturgeon L., *Alta., Canada* 104 B5
Sturgeon L., *Ont., Canada* 102 C1
Sturgeon L., *Ont., Canada* 110 B6
Sturgis, *Canada* 105 C8
Sturgis, *Mich., U.S.A.* 108 E3
Sturgis, *S. Dak., U.S.A.* 112 C3
Šturkö, *Sweden* 11 H9
Štúrovo, *Slovak Rep.* 27 D11
Sturt Cr. →, *Australia* 92 C4
Stutterheim, *S. Africa* 88 E4
Stuttgart, *Germany* 25 G5
Stuttgart, *U.S.A.* 113 H9
Stuyvesant, *U.S.A.* 111 D11
Stykkishólmur, *Iceland* 8 D2
Styria = Steiermark □, *Austria* 26 D8
Styrsö, *Sweden* 11 G5
Su Xian = Suzhou, *China* 56 H9
Suakin, *Sudan* 80 D4
Suan, *N. Korea* 57 E14
Suaqui, *Mexico* 118 B3
Suar, *India* 69 E8
Subang, *Indonesia* 63 G12
Subansiri →, *India* 67 F18
Subarnarekha →, *India* 69 H12
Subayhah, *Si. Arabia* 70 D3
Subcetate, *Romania* 42 E8
Subi, *Indonesia* 65 L7
Subiaco, *Italy* 29 G10
Subotica, *Serbia, Yug.* 42 D4
Suca, *Ethiopia* 81 F4
Suceava, *Romania* 43 C11
Suceava □, *Romania* 43 C10
Suceava →, *Romania* 43 C11
Sucha-Beskidzka, *Poland* 45 J6
Suchań, *Poland* 45 E2
Suchan, *Russia* 54 C6
Suchedniów, *Poland* 45 G7
Suchitoto, *El Salv.* 120 D2
Suchou = Suzhou, *China* 59 B13
Süchow = Xuzhou, *China* 57 G9
Suchowola, *Poland* 44 E10
Suck →, *Ireland* 15 C3
Sucre, *Bolivia* 124 G5
Sućuraj, *Croatia* 29 E14
Sucuriú →, *Brazil* 125 H8
Sud, Pte. du, *Canada* 103 C7
Sud-Kivu □, *Dem. Rep. of the Congo* 86 C2
Sud-Ouest, Pte. du, *Canada* 103 C7
Suda →, *Russia* 46 C9
Sudak, *Ukraine* 47 K8
Sudan, *U.S.A.* 113 H3
Sudan ■, *Africa* 81 E3
Sudbury, *Canada* 102 C3
Sudbury, *U.K.* 13 E8
Sûdd, *Sudan* 81 F3
Süderbrarup, *Germany* 24 A5
Süderlügum, *Germany* 24 A4
Süderoogsand, *Germany* 24 A4
Sudeten Mts. = Sudety, *Europe* 27 A9
Sudety, *Europe* 27 A9
Suðuroy, *Færoe Is.* 8 F9
Sudi, *Tanzania* 87 E4
Sudirman, Pegunungan, *Indonesia* 63 E9
Sudiţi, *Romania* 43 F12
Sudogda, *Russia* 48 C5
Sudr, *Egypt* 80 B3
Sudzha, *Russia* 47 G8
Sue →, *Sudan* 81 F2
Sueca, *Spain* 33 F4
Süedinenie, *Bulgaria* 41 D8
Suemez I., *U.S.A.* 104 B2
Suez = El Suweis, *Egypt* 80 J8
Suez, G. of = Suweis, Khalîg el, *Egypt* 80 J8
Suez Canal = Suweis, Qanâ es, *Egypt* 80 H8
Suffield, *Canada* 104 C6
Suffolk, *U.S.A.* 108 G7
Suffolk □, *U.K.* 13 E9
Şugag, *Romania* 43 E8
Sugargrove, *U.S.A.* 110 E5
Sugarive →, *India* 69 F12
Suğla Gölü, *Turkey* 72 D5
Sugluk = Salluit, *Canada* 101 B12
Suhaia, Lacul, *Romania* 43 G10
Şuḩār, *Oman* 71 E8
Sühbaatar □, *Mongolia* 56 B8
Suhl, *Germany* 24 E6
Şuhut, *Turkey* 39 C12
Sui, *Pakistan* 68 E3
Sui Xian, *China* 56 G8
Šuica, *Bos.-H.* 42 G2
Suichang, *China* 59 C12
Suichuan, *China* 59 D10
Suide, *China* 56 F6
Suifenhe, *China* 57 B16
Suihua, *China* 60 B7
Suijiang, *China* 58 C4
Suining, *Hunan, China* 59 D8
Suining, *Jiangsu, China* 57 H9
Suining, *Sichuan, China* 58 B5
Suiping, *China* 56 H7
Suippes, *France* 19 C11
Suir →, *Ireland* 15 D4
Suisun City, *U.S.A.* 116 G4
Suixi, *China* 59 G8
Suiyang, *Guizhou, China* 58 D6
Suiyang, *Heilongjiang, China* 57 B16
Suizhong, *China* 57 D11
Suizhou, *China* 59 B9
Sujangarh, *India* 68 F6
Sukabumi, *Indonesia* 63 G12
Sukadana, *Indonesia* 62 E3
Sukagawa, *Japan* 55 F10
Sukaraja, *Indonesia* 62 E4
Sukarnapura = Jayapura, *Indonesia* 63 E10
Sukch'ŏn, *N. Korea* 57 E13
Sukhindol, *Bulgaria* 41 C9
Sukhinichi, *Russia* 46 E8
Sukhona →, *Russia* 50 D4
Sukhothai, *Thailand* 64 D2
Sukhumi = Sokhumi, *Georgia* 49 J5
Sukkur, *Pakistan* 68 F3
Sukkur Barrage, *Pakistan* 68 F3

Sukovo, *Serbia, Yug.* 40 C6
Sukri →, *India* 68 G4
Sukumo, *Japan* 55 H6
Sukunka →, *Canada* 104 B4
Sula →, *Ukraine* 47 H7
Sula, Kepulauan, *Indonesia* 63 E7
Sulaco →, *Honduras* 120 C2
Sulaiman Range, *Pakistan* 68 D3
Sulak →, *Russia* 49 J8
Sūlār, *Iran* 71 D6
Sulawesi Sea = Celebes Sea, *Indonesia* 63 D6
Sulawesi Selatan □, *Indonesia* 63 E6
Sulawesi Utara □, *Indonesia* 63 D6
Sulechów, *Poland* 45 F2
Sulęcin, *Poland* 45 F2
Sulejów, *Poland* 45 G6
Sulejówek, *Poland* 45 F8
Süleymanlı, *Turkey* 39 C9
Sulima, *S. Leone* 82 D2
Sulina, *Romania* 43 E14
Sulina, Braţul →, *Romania* 43 E14
Sulingen, *Germany* 24 C4
Suliţa, *Romania* 43 C11
Sulitjelma, *Norway* 8 C17
Sułkowice, *Poland* 45 J6
Sullana, *Peru* 124 D2
Süller, *Turkey* 39 C11
Sullivan, *Ill., U.S.A.* 112 F10
Sullivan, *Ind., U.S.A.* 108 F2
Sullivan, *Mo., U.S.A.* 112 F9
Sullivan Bay, *Canada* 104 C3
Sullivan I. = Lambi Kyun, *Burma* 65 G2
Sully-sur-Loire, *France* 19 E9
Sulmierzyce, *Poland* 45 G4
Sulmona, *Italy* 29 F10
Süloğlu, *Turkey* 41 E10
Sulphur, *La., U.S.A.* 113 K8
Sulphur, *Okla., U.S.A.* 113 H6
Sulphur Pt., *Canada* 104 A6
Sulphur Springs, *U.S.A.* 113 J7
Sultan, *Canada* 102 C3
Sultan, *U.S.A.* 116 C5
Sultan Dağları, *Turkey* 72 C4
Sultanhisar, *Turkey* 39 D10
Sultaniça, *Turkey* 41 F10
Sultaniye, *Turkey* 41 F12
Sultanpur, *Mad. P., India* 68 H8
Sultanpur, *Punjab, India* 68 D6
Sultanpur, *Ut. P., India* 69 F10
Sulu Arch., *Phil.* 61 J4
Sulu Sea, *E. Indies* 61 G4
Sülüklü, *Turkey* 72 C5
Sululta, *Ethiopia* 81 F4
Suluova, *Turkey* 72 B6
Suluq, *Libya* 79 B10
Sulzbach, *Germany* 25 F3
Sulzbach-Rosenberg, *Germany* 25 F7
Sulzberger Ice Shelf, *Antarctica* 5 D10
Sumalata, *Indonesia* 63 D6
Sumampa, *Argentina* 126 B3
Sumatera □, *Indonesia* 62 D2
Sumatera Barat □, *Indonesia* 62 E2
Sumatera Utara □, *Indonesia* 62 D1
Sumatra = Sumatera □, *Indonesia* 62 D2
Sumba, *Indonesia* 63 F5
Sumba, Selat, *Indonesia* 63 F5
Sumbawa, *Indonesia* 62 F5
Sumbawa Besar, *Indonesia* 62 F5
Sumbawanga □, *Tanzania* 84 F6
Sumbe, *Angola* 84 G2
Sumburgh Hd., *U.K.* 14 B7
Sumdeo, *India* 69 D8
Sumdo, *India* 69 B8
Sumedang, *Indonesia* 63 G12
Sümeg, *Hungary* 42 D2
Sumeih, *Sudan* 81 F2
Šumen = Shumen, *Bulgaria* 41 C10
Sumenep, *Indonesia* 63 G15
Sumgait = Sumqayıt, *Azerbaijan* 49 K9
Summer L., *U.S.A.* 114 E3
Summerland, *Canada* 104 D5
Summerside, *Canada* 103 C7
Summersville, *U.S.A.* 108 F5
Summerville, *Ga., U.S.A.* 109 H3
Summerville, *S.C., U.S.A.* 109 J5
Summit Lake, *Canada* 104 C4
Summit Peak, *U.S.A.* 115 H10
Sumner, *Iowa, U.S.A.* 112 D8
Sumner, *Wash., U.S.A.* 116 C4
Sumoto, *Japan* 55 G7
Šumperk, *Czech Rep.* 27 B9
Sumqayıt, *Azerbaijan* 49 K9
Sumter, *U.S.A.* 109 J5
Sumy, *Ukraine* 47 G8
Sun City, *Ariz., U.S.A.* 115 K7
Sun City, *Calif., U.S.A.* 117 M9
Sun City Center, *U.S.A.* 109 M4
Sun Lakes, *U.S.A.* 115 K8
Sun Valley, *U.S.A.* 114 E6
Sunagawa, *Japan* 54 C10
Sunan, *N. Korea* 57 E13
Sunart, L., *U.K.* 14 E3
Sunburst, *U.S.A.* 114 B8
Sunbury, *Australia* 95 F3
Sunbury, *U.S.A.* 111 F8
Sunchales, *Argentina* 126 C3
Suncho Corral, *Argentina* 126 B3
Sunch'ŏn, *S. Korea* 57 G14
Suncook, *U.S.A.* 111 C13
Sunda, Selat, *Indonesia* 62 F3
Sunda Is., *Indonesia* 52 K14
Sunda Str. = Sunda, Selat, *Indonesia* 62 F3
Sundance, *Canada* 105 B10
Sundance, *U.S.A.* 112 C2
Sundar Nagar, *India* 68 D7
Sundarbans, The, *Asia* 67 J16
Sundargarh, *India* 67 H14
Sundays = Sondags →, *S. Africa* 88 E4
Sunderland, *Canada* 110 B5
Sunderland, *U.K.* 12 C6
Sundre, *Canada* 104 C6
Sunds, *Denmark* 11 H3
Sundsvall, *Sweden* 10 B11
Sundsvallsbukten, *Sweden* 10 B11
Sung Hei, *Vietnam* 65 G6
Sungai Kolok, *Thailand* 65 J3
Sungai Lembing, *Malaysia* 65 L4
Sungai Petani, *Malaysia* 65 K3
Sungaigerong, *Indonesia* 62 E2
Sungailiat, *Indonesia* 62 E3
Sungaipenuh, *Indonesia* 62 E2
Sungari = Songhua Jiang →, *China* 60 B8
Sunghua Chiang = Songhua Jiang →, *China* 60 B8
Sungikai, *Sudan* 81 E2
Sungurlu, *Turkey* 72 B6
Sunja, *Croatia* 29 C13
Sunland Park, *U.S.A.* 115 L10
Sunnansjö, *Sweden* 10 D8
Sunndalsøra, *Norway* 9 E13
Sunne, *Sweden* 10 E7
Sunnemo, *Sweden* 10 E7
Sunnyside, *U.S.A.* 114 C3
Sunnyvale, *U.S.A.* 116 H4
Suntar, *Russia* 51 C12
Sunyani, *Ghana* 82 D4
Suomenselkä, *Finland* 8 E21
Suomussalmi, *Finland* 8 D23
Suoyarvi, *Russia* 46 A7
Supai, *U.S.A.* 115 H7
Supaul, *India* 69 F12
Superior, *Ariz., U.S.A.* 115 K8
Superior, *Mont., U.S.A.* 114 C6
Superior, *Nebr., U.S.A.* 112 E5
Superior, *Wis., U.S.A.* 112 B8
Superior, L., *N. Amer.* 102 C2
Supetar, *Croatia* 29 E13
Suphan Buri, *Thailand* 64 E3
Suphan Dağı, *Turkey* 70 B4
Supiori, *Indonesia* 63 E9
Supraśl, *Poland* 45 E10
Supraśl →, *Poland* 45 E9
Supung Shuiku, *China* 57 D13
Sūq Suwayq, *Si. Arabia* 70 E3
Suqian, *China* 57 H10
Sūr, *Lebanon* 75 B4
Sūr, *Oman* 74 C6
Sur, Pt., *U.S.A.* 116 J5
Sura →, *Russia* 48 C8
Surab, *Pakistan* 68 E2
Surabaja = Surabaya, *Indonesia* 63 G15
Surabaya, *Indonesia* 63 G15
Surahammar, *Sweden* 10 E10
Suraia, *Romania* 43 E12
Surakarta, *Indonesia* 63 G14
Surakhany, *Azerbaijan* 49 K10
Šurany, *Slovak Rep.* 27 C11
Surat, *Australia* 95 D4
Surat, *India* 66 J8
Surat Thani, *Thailand* 65 H2
Suratgarh, *India* 68 E5
Suraż, *Poland* 45 F9
Surazh, *Belarus* 46 E6
Surazh, *Russia* 47 F7
Surduc, *Romania* 43 C8
Surduc Pasul, *Romania* 43 E8
Surdulica, *Serbia, Yug.* 40 D6
Surendranagar, *India* 68 H4
Surf, *U.S.A.* 117 L6
Surgères, *France* 20 B3
Surgut, *Russia* 50 C8
Sùria, *Spain* 32 D6
Suriapet, *India* 66 L11
Surigao, *Phil.* 61 G6
Surigao Strait, *Phil.* 61 F6
Surin, *Thailand* 64 E4
Surin Nua, Ko, *Thailand* 65 H1
Surinam ■, *S. Amer.* 125 C7
Suriname = Surinam ■, *S. Amer.* 125 C7
Suriname →, *Surinam* 125 B7
Sūrmaq, *Iran* 71 D7
Sürmene, *Turkey* 73 B9
Surovikino, *Russia* 49 F6
Surrey □, *U.K.* 13 F7
Sursand, *India* 69 F11
Sursar →, *India* 69 F12
Sursee, *Switz.* 25 H4
Sursk, *Russia* 48 D7
Surskoye, *Russia* 48 C8
Surt, *Libya* 79 B9
Surt, Khalīj, *Libya* 79 B9
Surtanahu, *Pakistan* 68 F4
Surte, *Sweden* 11 G6
Surtsey, *Iceland* 8 E3
Sürüç, *Turkey* 73 D8
Suruga-Wan, *Japan* 55 G9
Susa, *Italy* 28 C4
Susā →, *Denmark* 11 J5
Sušac, *Croatia* 29 F13
Susak, *Croatia* 29 D11
Susaki, *Japan* 55 H6
Süsangerd, *Iran* 71 D6
Susanville, *U.S.A.* 114 F3
Susch, *Switz.* 25 J6
Suşehri, *Turkey* 73 B8
Sušice, *Czech Rep.* 26 B6
Susleni, *Moldova* 43 C13
Susner, *India* 68 H7
Susong, *China* 59 B11
Susquehanna, *U.S.A.* 111 E9
Susquehanna →, *U.S.A.* 111 G8
Susques, *Argentina* 126 A2
Sussex, *Canada* 103 C6
Sussex, *U.S.A.* 111 E10
Sussex, E. □, *U.K.* 13 G8
Sussex, W. □, *U.K.* 13 G7
Sustut →, *Canada* 104 B3
Susuman, *Russia* 51 C15
Susunu, *Indonesia* 63 E8
Susurluk, *Turkey* 39 B10
Susuz, *Turkey* 73 B10
Susz, *Poland* 44 E6
Sütçüler, *Turkey* 72 D4
Şuţeşti, *Romania* 43 E12
Sutherland, *S. Africa* 88 E3
Sutherland, *U.S.A.* 112 E4
Sutherland Falls, *N.Z.* 91 L1
Sutherlin, *U.S.A.* 114 E2
Suthri, *India* 68 H3
Sutlej →, *Pakistan* 68 E4
Sutter, *U.S.A.* 116 F5
Sutter Creek, *U.S.A.* 116 G6
Sutton, *Canada* 111 A12
Sutton, *Nebr., U.S.A.* 112 E6
Sutton, *W. Va., U.S.A.* 108 F5
Sutton →, *Canada* 102 A3
Sutton Coldfield, *U.K.* 13 E6
Sutton in Ashfield, *U.K.* 12 D6
Sutton L., *Canada* 102 B3
Suttor →, *Australia* 94 C4
Suttsu, *Japan* 54 C10
Suva, *Fiji* 91 D8
Suva Gora, *Macedonia* 40 E5
Suva Planina, *Serbia, Yug.* 40 C6
Suva Reka, *Kosovo, Yug.* 40 D4
Suvorov, *Russia* 46 E9
Suvorov Is. = Suwarrow Is., *Cook Is.* 97 J11
Suvorovo, *Bulgaria* 41 C11
Suwałki, *Poland* 44 D9
Suwannaphum, *Thailand* 64 E4
Suwannee →, *U.S.A.* 109 L4
Suwanose-Jima, *Japan* 55 K4
Suwarrow Is., *Cook Is.* 97 J11
Suwayq aş Şuqban, *Iraq* 70 D5
Suweis, Khalîg el, *Egypt* 80 J8
Suweis, Qanâ es, *Egypt* 80 H8
Suwŏn, *S. Korea* 57 F14
Suzdal, *Russia* 46 D11
Suzhou, *Anhui, China* 56 H9
Suzhou, *Jiangsu, China* 59 B13
Suzu, *Japan* 55 F8
Suzu-Misaki, *Japan* 55 F8
Suzuka, *Japan* 55 G8
Suzzara, *Italy* 28 D7
Svalbard, *Arctic* 4 B8
Svalöv, *Sweden* 11 J7
Svaneke, *Denmark* 11 J9
Svängsta, *Sweden* 11 H8
Svanskog, *Sweden* 10 E6
Svappavaara, *Sweden* 8 C19
Svärdsjö, *Sweden* 10 D9
Svartå, *Sweden* 10 E8
Svartisen, *Norway* 8 C15
Svartvik, *Sweden* 10 B11
Svatove, *Ukraine* 47 H10
Svatovo = Svatove, *Ukraine* 47 H10
Svay Chek, *Cambodia* 64 F4
Svay Rieng, *Cambodia* 65 G5
Svealand □, *Sweden* 10 D9
Svedala, *Sweden* 11 J7
Sveg, *Sweden* 10 B8
Svendborg, *Denmark* 11 J4
Svenljunga, *Sweden* 11 G7
Svenstavik, *Sweden* 10 B8
Svenstrup, *Denmark* 11 H3
Sverdlovsk = Yekaterinburg, *Russia* 50 D7
Sverdlovsk, *Ukraine* 47 H10
Sverdrup Is., *Canada* 4 B3
Svetac, *Croatia* 29 E12
Sveti Nikola, Prokhad, *Europe* 40 C6
Sveti Nikole, *Macedonia* 40 E5
Sveti Rok, *Croatia* 29 D12
Svetlaya, *Russia* 54 A9
Svetlogorsk = Svyetlahorsk, *Belarus* 47 F5
Svetlograd, *Russia* 49 H6
Svetlovodsk = Svitlovodsk, *Ukraine* 47 H7
Svidník, *Slovak Rep.* 27 B14
Svilaja Planina, *Croatia* 29 E13
Svilajnac, *Serbia, Yug.* 40 B5
Svilengrad, *Bulgaria* 41 E10
Svir →, *Russia* 46 B7
Sviritsa, *Russia* 46 B7
Svishtov, *Bulgaria* 41 C9
Svislach, *Belarus* 47 F3
Svitava →, *Czech Rep.* 27 B9
Svitavy, *Czech Rep.* 27 B9
Svitlovodsk, *Ukraine* 47 H7
Svobodnyy, *Russia* 51 D13
Svoge, *Bulgaria* 40 D7
Svolvær, *Norway* 8 B16
Svratka →, *Czech Rep.* 27 B9
Svrljig, *Serbia, Yug.* 40 C6
Svyetlahorsk, *Belarus* 47 F5
Swabian Alps = Schwäbische Alb, *Germany* 25 G5
Swainsboro, *U.S.A.* 109 J4
Swakop →, *Namibia* 88 C2
Swakopmund, *Namibia* 88 C1
Swale →, *U.K.* 12 C6
Swan →, *Australia* 93 F2
Swan →, *Canada* 105 C8
Swan Hill, *Australia* 95 F3
Swan Hills, *Canada* 104 C5
Swan Is., *W. Indies* 120 C3
Swan L., *Canada* 105 C8
Swan Peak, *U.S.A.* 114 C7
Swan Ra., *U.S.A.* 114 C7
Swan Reach, *Australia* 95 E2
Swan River, *Canada* 105 C8
Swanage, *U.K.* 13 G6
Swansea, *Australia* 94 G4
Swansea, *Canada* 110 C5
Swansea, *U.K.* 13 F4
Swansea □, *U.K.* 13 F3
Swar →, *Pakistan* 69 B5
Swartberge, *S. Africa* 88 E3
Swartmodder, *S. Africa* 88 D3
Swartnossob →, *Namibia* 88 C2
Swartruggens, *S. Africa* 88 D4
Swarzędz, *Poland* 45 F4
Swastika, *Canada* 102 C3
Swatow = Shantou, *China* 59 F11
Swaziland ■, *Africa* 89 D5
Sweden ■, *Europe* 9 G16
Swedru, *Ghana* 83 D4
Sweet Home, *U.S.A.* 114 D2
Sweetgrass, *U.S.A.* 114 B8
Sweetwater, *Nev., U.S.A.* 116 G7
Sweetwater, *Tenn., U.S.A.* 109 H3
Sweetwater, *Tex., U.S.A.* 113 J4
Sweetwater →, *U.S.A.* 114 E10
Swellendam, *S. Africa* 88 E3
Świder →, *Poland* 45 F8
Świdnica, *Poland* 45 H3
Świdnik, *Poland* 45 G9
Świdwin, *Poland* 44 E2
Świebodzice, *Poland* 45 H3
Świebodzin, *Poland* 45 F2
Świecie, *Poland* 44 E5
Świerzawa, *Poland* 45 G2
Świętokrzyskie □, *Poland* 45 H7
Świętokrzyskie, Góry, *Poland* 45 H7
Swift Current, *Canada* 105 C7
Swiftcurrent →, *Canada* 105 C7
Swilly, L., *Ireland* 15 A4
Swindon, *U.K.* 13 F6
Swindon □, *U.K.* 13 F6
Swinemünde = Świnoujście, *Poland* 44 E1
Swinford, *Ireland* 15 C3
Świnoujście, *Poland* 44 E1
Switzerland ■, *Europe* 25 J4
Swords, *Ireland* 15 C5
Swoyerville, *U.S.A.* 111 E9
Syasstroy, *Russia* 46 B7
Sychevka, *Russia* 46 E8
Syców, *Poland* 45 G4
Sydenham →, *Canada* 110 D2
Sydney, *Australia* 95 E5
Sydney, *Canada* 103 C7
Sydney L., *Canada* 105 C10
Sydney Mines, *Canada* 103 C7
Sydprøven = Alluitsup Paa, *Greenland* 4 C5
Sydra, G. of = Surt, Khalīj, *Libya* 79 B9
Syeverodonetsk, *Ukraine* 47 H10
Syke, *Germany* 24 C4
Sykesville, *U.S.A.* 110 E6
Syktyvkar, *Russia* 50 C6
Sylacauga, *U.S.A.* 109 J2
Sylarna, *Sweden* 8 E15
Sylhet, *Bangla.* 67 G17
Sylt, *Germany* 24 A4
Sylvan Beach, *U.S.A.* 111 C9
Sylvan Lake, *Canada* 104 C6
Sylvania, *U.S.A.* 109 J5
Sylvester, *U.S.A.* 109 K4
Sym, *Russia* 50 C9
Symón, *Mexico* 118 C4
Synelnykove, *Ukraine* 47 H8
Synnott Ra., *Australia* 92 C4
Syracuse, *Kans., U.S.A.* 113 G4
Syracuse, *N.Y., U.S.A.* 111 C8
Syracuse, *Nebr., U.S.A.* 112 E6
Syrdarya →, *Kazakstan* 50 E7
Syria ■, *Asia* 70 C3
Syrian Desert = Shām, Bādiyat ash, *Asia* 70 C3
Sysslebäck, *Sweden* 10 D6
Syzran, *Russia* 48 D9
Szabolcs-Szatmár-Bereg □, *Hungary* 42 B6
Szadek, *Poland* 45 G5
Szamocin, *Poland* 45 E4
Szamos →, *Hungary* 42 B7
Szamotuły, *Poland* 45 F3
Száraz →, *Hungary* 42 D6
Szarvas, *Hungary* 42 D5
Százhalombatta, *Hungary* 42 C3
Szczawnica, *Poland* 45 J7
Szczebrzeszyn, *Poland* 45 H9
Szczecin, *Poland* 44 E1
Szczecinek, *Poland* 44 E3
Szczeciński, Zalew = Stettiner Haff, *Germany* 24 B10
Szczekociny, *Poland* 45 H6
Szczucin, *Poland* 45 H8
Szczuczyn, *Poland* 44 E9
Szczyrk, *Poland* 45 J6
Szczytna, *Poland* 45 H3
Szczytno, *Poland* 44 E7
Szechwan = Sichuan □, *China* 58 B5
Szécsény, *Hungary* 42 B4
Szeged, *Hungary* 42 D5
Szeghalom, *Hungary* 42 C6
Székesfehérvár, *Hungary* 42 C3
Szekszárd, *Hungary* 42 D3
Szendrő, *Hungary* 42 B5
Szentendre, *Hungary* 42 C4
Szentes, *Hungary* 42 D5
Szentgotthárd, *Hungary* 42 D1
Szentlőrinc, *Hungary* 42 D3
Szerencs, *Hungary* 42 B6
Szigetszentmiklós, *Hungary* 42 C4
Szigetvár, *Hungary* 42 D2
Szikszó, *Hungary* 42 B5
Szklarska Poreba, *Poland* 45 H2
Szkwa →, *Poland* 45 E8
Szlichtyngowa, *Poland* 45 G3
Szob, *Hungary* 42 C3
Szolnok, *Hungary* 42 C5
Szombathely, *Hungary* 42 C1
Szprotawa, *Poland* 45 G2
Sztum, *Poland* 44 E6
Sztutowo, *Poland* 44 D6
Szubin, *Poland* 45 E4
Szydłowiec, *Poland* 45 G7
Szypliszki, *Poland* 44 D10

T

Ta Khli Khok, *Thailand* 64 E3
Ta Lai, *Vietnam* 65 G6
Tab, *Hungary* 42 D3
Tabacal, *Argentina* 126 A3
Tabaco, *Phil.* 61 E5
Tabagné, *Ivory C.* 82 D4
Ţābah, *Si. Arabia* 70 E4
Tabankort, *Niger* 83 B5
Ţabas, *Khorāsān, Iran* 71 C9
Ţabas, *Khorāsān, Iran* 71 C8
Tabasará, Serranía de, *Panama* 120 E3
Tabasco □, *Mexico* 119 D6
Tabāsīn, *Iran* 71 D8
Tabatinga, Serra da, *Brazil* 125 F10
Taber, *Canada* 104 D6
Taberg, *Sweden* 11 G8
Taberg, *U.S.A.* 111 C9
Tabla, *Niger* 83 C5
Tablas I., *Phil.* 61 E5
Tablas Strait, *Phil.* 61 E4
Table B. = Tafelbaai, *S. Africa* 88 E2
Table B., *Canada* 103 B8
Table Mt., *S. Africa* 88 E2
Table Rock L., *U.S.A.* 113 G8
Tabletop, Mt., *Australia* 94 C4
Tábor, *Czech Rep.* 26 B7
Tabora, *Tanzania* 86 D3
Tabora □, *Tanzania* 86 D3
Tabou, *Ivory C.* 82 E3
Tabrīz, *Iran* 70 B5
Tabuaeran, *Pac. Oc.* 97 G12
Tabuenca, *Spain* 32 D3
Tabūk, *Si. Arabia* 70 D3
Täby, *Sweden* 10 E12
Tacámbaro de Codallos, *Mexico* 118 D4
Tacheng, *China* 60 B3
Tach'i, *Taiwan* 59 E13
Tachia, *Taiwan* 59 E13
Tach'ing Shan = Daqing Shan, *China* 56 D6
Tachov, *Czech Rep.* 26 B5
Tácina →, *Italy* 31 D9
Tacloban, *Phil.* 61 F6
Tacna, *Peru* 124 G4
Tacoma, *U.S.A.* 116 C4
Tacuarembó, *Uruguay* 127 C4
Tademaït, Plateau du, *Algeria* 78 C6
Tadio, L., *Ivory C.* 82 D3
Tadjoura, *Djibouti* 81 E5
Tadjoura, Golfe de, *Djibouti* 81 E5
Tadmor, *N.Z.* 91 J4
Tadoule, L., *Canada* 105 B9
Tadoussac, *Canada* 103 C6
Tadzhikistan = Tajikistan ■, *Asia* 50 F8
Taechŏn-ni, *S. Korea* 57 F14
Taegu, *S. Korea* 57 G15
Taegwan, *N. Korea* 57 D13
Taejŏn, *S. Korea* 57 F14
Tafalla, *Spain* 32 C3
Tafar, *Sudan* 81 F2
Tafelbaai, *S. Africa* 88 E2
Tafermaar, *Indonesia* 63 F8
Tafí Viejo, *Argentina* 126 B2
Tafīhān, *Iran* 71 D7
Tafiré, *Ivory C.* 82 D3
Tafo, *Ghana* 83 D4
Tafresh, *Iran* 71 C6
Taft, *Iran* 71 D7
Taft, *Phil.* 61 F6
Taft, *U.S.A.* 117 K7
Taftān, Kūh-e, *Iran* 71 D9
Taga Dzong, *Bhutan* 67 F16
Taganrog, *Russia* 47 J10
Taganrogskiy Zaliv, *Russia* 47 J10
Tagânt, *Mauritania* 82 B2
Tagatay, *Phil.* 61 D4
Tagbilaran, *Phil.* 61 G5
Tàggia, *Italy* 28 E4
Tagish, *Canada* 104 A2
Tagish L., *Canada* 104 A2
Tagliacozzo, *Italy* 29 F10
Tagliamento →, *Italy* 29 C10
Táglio di Po, *Italy* 29 D9
Tago, *Phil.* 61 G7
Tagomago, *Spain* 37 B8
Tagourăret, *Mauritania* 82 B3
Taguatinga, *Brazil* 125 F10
Tagudin, *Phil.* 61 C4
Tagum, *Phil.* 61 H6
Tagus = Tejo →, *Europe* 35 F2
Tahakopa, *N.Z.* 91 M2
Tahan, Gunong, *Malaysia* 65 K4
Tahat, *Algeria* 78 D7
Tāherī, *Iran* 71 E7
Tahiti, *Pac. Oc.* 97 J13
Tahlequah, *U.S.A.* 113 H7

Tahoe, L., *U.S.A.* 116 G6
Tahoe City, *U.S.A.* 116 F6
Tahoka, *U.S.A.* 113 J4
Taholah, *U.S.A.* 116 C2
Tahoua, *Niger* 83 C6
Tahrūd, *Iran* 71 D8
Tahsis, *Canada* 104 D3
Tahta, *Egypt* 80 B3
Tahtaköprü, *Turkey* 41 G13
Tahtalı Dağları, *Turkey* 72 C7
Tahulandang, *Indonesia* 63 D7
Tahuna, *Indonesia* 63 D7
Taï, *Ivory C.* 82 D3
Tai Hu, *China* 59 B12
Tai Shan, *China* 57 F9
Tai'an, *China* 57 F9
Taibei = T'aipei, *Taiwan* 59 E13
Taibique, *Canary Is.* 37 G2
Taibus Qi, *China* 56 D8
Taicang, *China* 59 B13
T'aichung, *Taiwan* 59 E13
Taieri →, *N.Z.* 91 M3
Taigu, *China* 56 F7
Taihang Shan, *China* 56 G7
Taihape, *N.Z.* 91 H5
Taihe, *Anhui, China* 56 H8
Taihe, *Jiangxi, China* 59 D10
Taihu, *China* 59 B11
Taijiang, *China* 58 D7
Taikang, *China* 56 G8
Tailem Bend, *Australia* 95 F2
Tailfingen, *Germany* 25 G5
Tailuko, *Taiwan* 59 E13
Taimyr Peninsula = Taymyr, Poluostrov, *Russia* 51 B11
Tain, *U.K.* 14 D4
T'ainan, *Taiwan* 59 F13
Taínaron, Ákra, *Greece* 38 E4
Taining, *China* 59 D11
T'aipei, *Taiwan* 59 E13
Taiping, *China* 59 B12
Taiping, *Malaysia* 65 K3
Taipingzhen, *China* 56 H6
Tairbeart = Tarbert, *U.K.* 14 D2
Taishan, *China* 59 F9
Taishun, *China* 59 D12
Taita Hills, *Kenya* 86 C4
Taitao, Pen. de, *Chile* 122 H3
T'aitung, *Taiwan* 59 F13
Taivalkoski, *Finland* 8 D23
Taiwan ■, *Asia* 59 F13
Taiwan Strait, *Asia* 59 E12
Taixing, *China* 59 A13
Taiyara, *Sudan* 81 E3
Taïyetos Óros, *Greece* 38 D4
Taiyiba, *Israel* 75 C4
Taiyuan, *China* 56 F7
Taizhong = T'aichung, *Taiwan* 59 E13
Taizhou, *China* 59 A12
Taizhou Liedao, *China* 59 C13
Ta'izz, *Yemen* 74 E3
Tājābād, *Iran* 71 D7
Tajikistan ■, *Asia* 50 F8
Tajima, *Japan* 55 F9
Tajo = Tejo →, *Europe* 35 F2
Tajrīsh, *Iran* 71 C6
Tak, *Thailand* 64 D2
Takāb, *Iran* 70 B5
Takachiho, *Japan* 55 H5
Takachu, *Botswana* 88 C3
Takada, *Japan* 55 F9
Takahagi, *Japan* 55 F10
Takaka, *N.Z.* 91 J4
Takamatsu, *Japan* 55 G7
Takaoka, *Japan* 55 F8
Takapuna, *N.Z.* 91 G5
Takasaki, *Japan* 55 F9
Takatsuki, *Japan* 55 G7
Takaungu, *Kenya* 86 C4
Takayama, *Japan* 55 F8
Take-Shima, *Japan* 55 J5
Takefu, *Japan* 55 G8
Takengon, *Indonesia* 62 D1
Takeo, *Japan* 55 H5
Tåkern, *Sweden* 11 F8
Tākestān, *Iran* 71 C6
Taketa, *Japan* 55 H5
Takev, *Cambodia* 65 G5
Takh, *India* 69 C7
Takht-Sulaiman, *Pakistan* 68 D3
Takikawa, *Japan* 54 C10
Takla L., *Canada* 104 B3
Takla Landing, *Canada* 104 B3
Takla Makan = Taklamakan Shamo, *China* 52 F12
Taklamakan Shamo, *China* 52 F12
Taku →, *Canada* 104 B2
Takum, *Nigeria* 83 D6
Tal Halāl, *Iran* 71 D7
Tala, *Uruguay* 127 C4
Talachyn, *Belarus* 46 E5
Talacogan, *Phil.* 61 G6
Talagang, *Pakistan* 68 C5
Talagante, *Chile* 126 C1
Talak, *Niger* 83 B6
Talamanca, Cordillera de, *Cent. Amer.* 120 E3
Talant, *France* 19 E11
Talara, *Peru* 124 D2
Talas, *Kyrgyzstan* 50 E8
Talas, *Turkey* 72 C6
Talâta, *Egypt* 75 E1
Talata Mafara, *Nigeria* 83 C6
Talaud, Kepulauan, *Indonesia* 63 D7
Talaud Is. = Talaud, Kepulauan, *Indonesia* 63 D7
Talavera de la Reina, *Spain* 34 F6
Talavera la Real, *Spain* 35 G4
Talayan, *Phil.* 61 H6
Talayuela, *Spain* 34 F5
Talbandh, *India* 69 H12
Talbert, Sillon de, *France* 18 D3
Talbot, C., *Australia* 92 B4
Talbragar →, *Australia* 95 E4
Talca, *Chile* 126 D1
Talcahuano, *Chile* 126 D1
Talcher, *India* 67 J14
Talcho, *Niger* 83 C5
Taldy Kurgan = Taldyqorghan, *Kazakstan* 50 E8
Taldyqorghan, *Kazakstan* 50 E8
Tālesh, *Iran* 71 B6
Tālesh, Kūhhā-ye, *Iran* 71 B6
Talguharai, *Sudan* 80 D4
Tali Post, *Sudan* 81 F3
Taliabu, *Indonesia* 63 E6
Talibon, *Phil.* 63 B6
Talibong, Ko, *Thailand* 65 J2
Talihina, *U.S.A.* 113 H7
Talisayan, *Phil.* 61 G6
Taliwang, *Indonesia* 62 F5
Tall 'Afar, *Iraq* 70 B4
Tall Kalakh, *Syria* 75 A5
Talla, *Egypt* 80 B3
Talladega, *U.S.A.* 109 J2
Tallahassee, *U.S.A.* 109 K3
Tallangatta, *Australia* 95 F4
Tallard, *France* 21 D10
Tällberg, *Sweden* 10 D9
Tallering Pk., *Australia* 93 E2
Talli, *Pakistan* 68 E3
Tallinn, *Estonia* 9 G21
Tallmadge, *U.S.A.* 110 E3
Tallulah, *U.S.A.* 113 J9
Tălmaciu, *Romania* 43 E9
Talmont-St-Hilaire, *France* 20 B2
Talne, *Ukraine* 47 H6
Talnoye = Talne, *Ukraine* 47 H6
Talodi, *Sudan* 81 E3
Talovaya, *Russia* 48 E5
Taloyoak, *Canada* 100 B10
Talpa de Allende, *Mexico* 118 C4
Talsi, *Latvia* 9 H20
Talsi □, *Latvia* 44 A9
Taltal, *Chile* 126 B1
Taltson →, *Canada* 104 A6
Talwood, *Australia* 95 D4
Talyawalka →, *Australia* 95 E3
Tam Chau, *Vietnam* 65 G5
Tam Ky, *Vietnam* 64 E7
Tam Quan, *Vietnam* 64 E7
Tama, *U.S.A.* 112 E8
Tamale, *Ghana* 83 D4
Taman, *Russia* 47 K9
Tamani, *Mali* 82 C3
Tamano, *Japan* 55 G6
Tamanrasset, *Algeria* 78 D7
Tamaqua, *U.S.A.* 111 F9
Tamar →, *U.K.* 13 G3
Tamarinda, *Spain* 37 B10
Tamarite de Litera, *Spain* 32 D5
Tamashima, *Japan* 55 G6
Tamási, *Hungary* 42 D3
Tamaské, *Niger* 83 C6
Tamaulipas □, *Mexico* 119 C5
Tamaulipas, Sierra de, *Mexico* 119 C5
Tamazula, *Mexico* 118 C3
Tamazunchale, *Mexico* 119 C5
Tamba-Dabatou, *Guinea* 82 C2
Tambacounda, *Senegal* 82 C2
Tambelan, Kepulauan, *Indonesia* 62 D3
Tambellup, *Australia* 93 F2
Tambo, *Australia* 94 C4
Tambo de Mora, *Peru* 124 F3
Tambohorano, *Madag.* 89 B7
Tambora, *Indonesia* 62 F5
Tambov, *Russia* 48 D5
Tambre →, *Spain* 34 C2
Tambuku, *Indonesia* 63 G15
Tamburâ, *Sudan* 81 F2
Tâmchekket, *Mauritania* 82 B2
Tâmega →, *Portugal* 34 D2
Tamenglong, *India* 67 G18
Tamgué, Massif du, *Guinea* 82 C2
Tamiahua, L. de, *Mexico* 119 C5
Tamil Nadu □, *India* 66 P10
Tamis →, *Serbia, Yug.* 42 F5
Tamluk, *India* 69 H12
Tammerfors = Tampere, *Finland* 9 F20
Tammisaari, *Finland* 9 F20
Tämnaren, *Sweden* 10 D11
Tamo Abu, Pegunungan, *Malaysia* 62 D5
Tampa, *U.S.A.* 109 M4
Tampa B., *U.S.A.* 109 M4
Tampere, *Finland* 9 F20
Tampico, *Mexico* 119 C5
Tampin, *Malaysia* 65 L4
Tamsweg, *Austria* 26 D6
Tamu, *Burma* 67 G19
Tamuja →, *Spain* 35 F4
Tamworth, *Australia* 95 E5
Tamworth, *Canada* 110 B8
Tamworth, *U.K.* 13 E6
Tamyang, *S. Korea* 57 G14
Tan An, *Vietnam* 65 G6
Tan-Tan, *Morocco* 78 C3
Tana →, *Kenya* 86 C5
Tana →, *Norway* 8 A23
Tana, L., *Ethiopia* 81 E4
Tana River, *Kenya* 86 C4
Tanabe, *Japan* 55 H7
Tanafjorden, *Norway* 8 A23
Tanaga, Pta., *Canary Is.* 37 G1
Tanahbala, *Indonesia* 62 E1
Tanahgrogot, *Indonesia* 62 E5
Tanahjampea, *Indonesia* 63 F6
Tanahmasa, *Indonesia* 62 E1
Tanahmerah, *Indonesia* 63 F10
Tanakpur, *India* 69 E9
Tanakura, *Japan* 55 F10
Tanami, *Australia* 92 C4
Tanami Desert, *Australia* 92 C5
Tanana →, *U.S.A.* 100 B4
Tananarive = Antananarivo, *Madag.* 89 B8
Tánaro →, *Italy* 28 D5
Tancheng, *China* 57 G10
Tanch'ŏn, *N. Korea* 57 D15
Tanda, *Ut. P., India* 69 F10
Tanda, *Ut. P., India* 69 E8
Tanda, *Ivory C.* 82 D4
Tandag, *Phil.* 61 G7
Tandaia, *Tanzania* 87 D3
Tăndărei, *Romania* 43 F12
Tandaué, *Angola* 88 B2
Tandil, *Argentina* 126 D4
Tandil, Sa. del, *Argentina* 126 D4
Tandlianwala, *Pakistan* 68 D5
Tando Adam, *Pakistan* 68 G3
Tando Allahyar, *Pakistan* 68 G3
Tando Bago, *Pakistan* 68 G3
Tando Mohommed Khan, *Pakistan* 68 G3
Tandou L., *Australia* 95 E3
Tandragee, *U.K.* 15 B5
Tandsjöborg, *Sweden* 10 C8
Tane-ga-Shima, *Japan* 55 J5
Taneatua, *N.Z.* 91 H6
Tanen Tong Dan, *Burma* 64 D2
Tanew →, *Poland* 45 H9
Tanezrouft, *Algeria* 78 D6
Tang, Koh, *Cambodia* 65 G4
Tang, Ra's-e, *Iran* 71 E8
Tang Krasang, *Cambodia* 64 F5
Tanga, *Tanzania* 86 D4
Tanga □, *Tanzania* 86 D4
Tanganyika, L., *Africa* 86 D3
Tangaza, *Nigeria* 83 C5
Tanger = Tangier, *Morocco* 78 A4
Tangerang, *Indonesia* 63 G12
Tangerhütte, *Germany* 24 C7
Tangermünde, *Germany* 24 C7
Tanggu, *China* 57 E9
Tanggula Shan, *China* 60 C4
Tanghe, *China* 56 H7
Tangier, *Morocco* 78 A4
Tangorin, *Australia* 94 C3
Tangorombohitr'i Makay, *Madag.* 89 C8
Tangshan, *China* 57 E10
Tangtou, *China* 57 G10
Tanguiéta, *Benin* 83 C5
Tangxi, *China* 59 C12
Tangyan He →, *China* 58 C7
Tanimbar, Kepulauan, *Indonesia* 63 F8
Tanimbar Is. = Tanimbar, Kepulauan, *Indonesia* 63 F8
Taninthari = Tenasserim □, *Burma* 64 F2
Tanjay, *Phil.* 61 G5
Tanjong Malim, *Malaysia* 65 L3
Tanjore = Thanjavur, *India* 66 P11
Tanjung, *Indonesia* 62 E5
Tanjungbalai, *Indonesia* 62 D1
Tanjungbatu, *Indonesia* 62 D5
Tanjungkarang Telukbetung, *Indonesia* 62 F3
Tanjungpandan, *Indonesia* 62 E3
Tanjungpinang, *Indonesia* 62 D2
Tanjungredeb, *Indonesia* 62 D5
Tanjungselor, *Indonesia* 62 D5
Tank, *Pakistan* 68 C4
Tankhala, *India* 68 J5
Tännäs, *Sweden* 10 B6
Tannersville, *U.S.A.* 111 E9
Tannis Bugt, *Denmark* 11 G4
Tannu-Ola, *Russia* 51 D10
Tannum Sands, *Australia* 94 C5
Tano →, *Ghana* 82 D4
Tanon Str., *Phil.* 61 F5
Tanout, *Niger* 83 C6
Tanshui, *Taiwan* 59 E13
Tansilla, *Burkina Faso* 82 C4
Tanta, *Egypt* 80 H7
Tantoyuca, *Mexico* 119 C5
Tantung = Dandong, *China* 57 D13
Tanumshede, *Sweden* 11 F5
Tanunda, *Australia* 95 E2
Tanus, *France* 20 D6
Tanzania ■, *Africa* 86 D3
Tanzilla →, *Canada* 104 B2
Tao, Ko, *Thailand* 65 G2
Tao'an = Taonan, *China* 57 B12
Tao'er He →, *China* 57 B13
Taohua Dao, *China* 59 C14
Taolanaro, *Madag.* 89 D8
Taole, *China* 56 E4
Taonan, *China* 57 B12
Taormina, *Italy* 31 E8
Taos, *U.S.A.* 115 H11
Taoudenni, *Mali* 78 D5
Taoyuan, *China* 59 C8
T'aoyüan, *Taiwan* 59 E13
Tapa, *Estonia* 9 G21
Tapa Shan = Daba Shan, *China* 58 B7
Tapachula, *Mexico* 119 E6
Tapah, *Malaysia* 65 K3
Tapajós →, *Brazil* 122 D5
Tapaktuan, *Indonesia* 62 D1
Tapanahoni →, *Surinam* 125 C8
Tapanui, *N.Z.* 91 L2
Tapauá →, *Brazil* 124 E6
Tapes, *Brazil* 127 C5
Tapeta, *Liberia* 82 D3
Taphan Hin, *Thailand* 64 D3
Tapia de Casariego, *Spain* 34 B4
Tapirapecó, Serra, *Venezuela* 124 C6
Tapolca, *Hungary* 42 D2
Tapuaenuku, Mt., *N.Z.* 91 K4
Tapul Group, *Phil.* 61 J4
Tapurucuará, *Brazil* 124 D5
Ţaqţaq, *Iraq* 70 C5
Taquara, *Brazil* 127 B5
Taquari →, *Brazil* 124 G7
Tara, *Australia* 95 D5
Tara, *Canada* 110 B3
Tara, *Russia* 50 D8
Tara, *Zambia* 87 F2
Tara →, *Montenegro, Yug.* 40 C2
Taraba □, *Nigeria* 83 D7
Taraba →, *Nigeria* 83 D7
Tarabagatay, Khrebet, *Kazakstan* 50 E9
Tarābulus, *Lebanon* 75 A4
Tarābulus, *Libya* 79 B8
Taraclia, *Moldova* 43 D14
Taraclia, *Moldova* 43 E13
Taradehi, *India* 69 H8
Tarajalejo, *Canary Is.* 37 F5
Tarakan, *Indonesia* 62 D5
Tarakit, Mt., *Kenya* 86 B4
Tarama-Jima, *Japan* 55 M2
Taran, Mys, *Russia* 9 J18
Taranagar, *India* 68 E6
Taranaki □, *N.Z.* 91 H5
Tarancón, *Spain* 32 E1
Taranga Hill, *India* 66 H8
Taransay, *U.K.* 14 D1
Táranto, *Italy* 31 B10
Táranto, G. di, *Italy* 31 B10
Tarapacá, *Colombia* 124 D5
Tarapacá □, *Chile* 126 A2
Tarapoto, *Peru* 124 E3
Tarare, *France* 21 C8
Tararua Ra., *N.Z.* 91 J5
Tarascon, *France* 21 E8
Tarascon-sur-Ariège, *France* 20 F5
Tarashcha, *Ukraine* 47 H6
Tarauacá, *Brazil* 124 E4
Tarauacá →, *Brazil* 124 E5
Taravo →, *France* 21 G12
Tarawa, *Kiribati* 96 G9
Tarawera, *N.Z.* 91 H6
Tarawera L., *N.Z.* 91 H6
Tarazona, *Spain* 32 D3
Tarazona de la Mancha, *Spain* 33 F3
Tarbat Ness, *U.K.* 14 D5
Tarbela Dam, *Pakistan* 68 B5
Tarbert, *Arg. & Bute, U.K.* 14 F3
Tarbert, *W. Isles, U.K.* 14 D2
Tarbes, *France* 20 E4
Tarboro, *U.S.A.* 109 H7
Tărcău, Munţii, *Romania* 43 D11
Tarcento, *Italy* 29 B10
Tarcoola, *Australia* 95 E1
Tarcoon, *Australia* 95 E4
Tardets-Sorholus, *France* 20 E3
Tardoire →, *France* 20 C4
Taree, *Australia* 95 E5
Tarfa, W. el →, *Egypt* 80 B3
Tarfaya, *Morocco* 78 C3
Târgovişte, *Romania* 43 F10
Târgu Bujor, *Romania* 43 E12
Târgu Cărbuneşti, *Romania* 43 F8
Târgu Frumos, *Romania* 43 C12
Târgu-Jiu, *Romania* 43 E8
Târgu Lăpuş, *Romania* 43 C8
Târgu Mureş, *Romania* 43 D9
Târgu Neamţ, *Romania* 43 C11
Târgu Ocna, *Romania* 43 D11
Târgu Secuiesc, *Romania* 43 E11
Târguşor, *Romania* 43 F13
Tărhăus, Vf., *Romania* 43 D11
Ţarif, *U.A.E.* 71 E7
Tarifa, *Spain* 35 J5
Tarija, *Bolivia* 126 A3
Tarija □, *Bolivia* 126 A3
Tariku →, *Indonesia* 63 E9
Tarim Basin = Tarim Pendi, *China* 60 C3
Tarim He →, *China* 60 C3
Tarim Pendi, *China* 60 C3
Taritatu →, *Indonesia* 63 E9
Tarka →, *S. Africa* 88 E4
Tarkastad, *S. Africa* 88 E4
Tarkhankut, Mys, *Ukraine* 47 K7
Tarko Sale, *Russia* 50 C8
Tarkwa, *Ghana* 82 D4
Tarlac, *Phil.* 61 D4
Tarm, *Denmark* 11 J2
Tarma, *Peru* 124 F3
Tarn □, *France* 20 E6
Tarn →, *France* 20 D5
Tarn-et-Garonne □, *France* 20 D5
Tarna →, *Hungary* 42 C4
Târnava Mare →, *Romania* 43 D8
Târnava Mică →, *Romania* 43 D8
Tărnăveni, *Romania* 43 D9
Tarnica, *Poland* 45 J9
Tarnobrzeg, *Poland* 45 H8
Tarnogród, *Poland* 45 H9
Tarnos, *France* 20 E2
Târnova, *Moldova* 43 B12
Târnova, *Romania* 42 E6
Tarnów, *Poland* 45 H8
Tarnowskie Góry, *Poland* 45 H5
Tärnsjö, *Sweden* 10 D10
Táro →, *Italy* 28 C7
Ţārom, *Iran* 71 D7
Taroom, *Australia* 95 D4
Taroudannt, *Morocco* 78 B4
Tarp, *Germany* 24 A5
Tarpon Springs, *U.S.A.* 109 L4
Tarquínia, *Italy* 29 F8
Tarragona, *Spain* 32 D6
Tarragona □, *Spain* 32 D6
Tarraleah, *Australia* 94 G4
Tarrasa = Terrassa, *Spain* 32 D7
Tàrrega, *Spain* 32 D6
Tarrytown, *U.S.A.* 111 E11
Târs, *Denmark* 11 G4
Tarshiha = Me'ona, *Israel* 75 B4
Tarso Emissi, *Chad* 79 D9
Tarsus, *Turkey* 70 B2
Tartagal, *Argentina* 126 A3
Tärtär, *Azerbaijan* 49 K8
Tärtär →, *Azerbaijan* 49 K8
Tartas, *France* 20 E3
Tartu, *Estonia* 9 G22
Ţarţūs, *Syria* 70 C2
Tarumizu, *Japan* 55 J5
Tarussa, *Russia* 46 E9
Tarutao, Ko, *Thailand* 65 J2
Tarutung, *Indonesia* 62 D1
Tarvísio, *Italy* 29 B10
Taseko →, *Canada* 104 C4
Tash-Kömür, *Kyrgyzstan* 50 E8
Tash-Kumyr = Tash-Kömür, *Kyrgyzstan* 50 E8
Tashauz = Dashhowuz, *Turkmenistan* 50 E6
Tashi Chho Dzong = Thimphu, *Bhutan* 67 F16
Ţashk, Daryācheh-ye, *Iran* 71 D7
Tashkent = Toshkent, *Uzbekistan* 50 E7
Tashtagol, *Russia* 50 D9
Tasiilaq, *Greenland* 4 C6
Tasikmalaya, *Indonesia* 63 G13
Tåsinge, *Denmark* 11 J4
Tåsjön, *Sweden* 8 D16
Taskan, *Russia* 51 C16
Tasker, *Niger* 83 C7
Taşköprü, *Turkey* 72 B6
Taşlâc, *Moldova* 43 C14
Tasman B., *N.Z.* 91 J4
Tasman Mts., *N.Z.* 91 J4
Tasman Pen., *Australia* 94 G4
Tasman Sea, *Pac. Oc.* 96 L8
Tasmania □, *Australia* 94 G4
Tăşnad, *Romania* 42 C7
Tassili n'Ajjer, *Algeria* 78 C7
Tassili Tin-Rerhoh, *Algeria* 83 A5
Tata, *Hungary* 42 C3
Tatabánya, *Hungary* 42 C3
Tatahouine, *Tunisia* 79 B8
Tatar Republic = Tatarstan □, *Russia* 48 C10
Tatarbunary, *Ukraine* 47 K5
Tatarsk, *Russia* 50 D8
Tatarstan □, *Russia* 48 C10
Tateyama, *Japan* 55 G9
Tathlina L., *Canada* 104 A5
Tathra, *Australia* 95 F4
Tati →, *India* 66 J8
Tatinnai L., *Canada* 105 A9
Tatla L., *Canada* 104 C4
Tatlısu, *Turkey* 41 F11
Tatnam, C., *Canada* 105 B10
Tatra = Tatry, *Slovak Rep.* 27 B13
Tatry, *Slovak Rep.* 27 B13
Tatshenshini →, *Canada* 104 B1
Tatsuno, *Japan* 55 G7
Tatta, *Pakistan* 68 G2
Tatuī, *Brazil* 127 A6
Tatum, *U.S.A.* 113 J3
Tat'ung = Datong, *China* 56 D7
Tatvan, *Turkey* 70 B4
Taubaté, *Brazil* 127 A6
Tauberbischofsheim, *Germany* 25 F5
Taucha, *Germany* 24 D8
Tauern-tunnel, *Austria* 26 D6
Taufikia, *Sudan* 81 F3
Taulé, *France* 18 D3
Taumarunui, *N.Z.* 91 H5
Taumaturgo, *Brazil* 124 E4
Taung, *S. Africa* 88 D3
Taungdwingyi, *Burma* 67 J19
Taunggyi, *Burma* 67 J20
Taungup, *Burma* 67 K19
Taungup Pass, *Burma* 67 K19
Taungup Taunggya, *Burma* 67 K18
Taunsa, *Pakistan* 68 D4
Taunsa Barrage, *Pakistan* 68 D4
Taunton, *U.K.* 13 F4
Taunton, *U.S.A.* 111 E13
Taunus, *Germany* 25 E4
Taupo, *N.Z.* 91 H6
Taupo, L., *N.Z.* 91 H5
Tauragė, *Lithuania* 9 J20
Tauragė □, *Lithuania* 44 C9
Tauranga, *N.Z.* 91 G6
Tauranga Harb., *N.Z.* 91 G6
Taureau, Rés., *Canada* 102 C5
Taurianova, *Italy* 31 D9
Taurus Mts. = Toros Dağları, *Turkey* 70 B2
Tauste, *Spain* 32 D3
Tauz = Tovuz, *Azerbaijan* 49 K7
Tavas, *Turkey* 39 D11
Tavda, *Russia* 50 D7
Tavda →, *Russia* 50 D7
Tavernes de la Valldigna, *Spain* 33 F4
Taveta, *Tanzania* 86 C4
Taveuni, *Fiji* 91 C9
Taviano, *Italy* 31 C11
Tavignano →, *France* 21 F13
Tavira, *Portugal* 35 H3
Tavistock, *Canada* 110 C4
Tavistock, *U.K.* 13 G3
Tavolara, *Italy* 30 B2
Távora →, *Portugal* 34 D3
Tavoy = Dawei, *Burma* 64 E2
Tavşanlı, *Turkey* 39 B11

Thornhill

Taw →, *U.K.* 13 F3
Tawa →, *India* 68 H8
Tawas City, *U.S.A.* 108 C4
Tawau, *Malaysia* 62 D5
Taweisha, *Sudan* 81 E2
Tawitawi, *Phil.* 63 B6
Tawu, *Taiwan* 59 F13
Taxco de Alarcón, *Mexico* 119 D5
Taxila, *Pakistan* 68 C5
Tay →, *U.K.* 14 E5
Tay, Firth of, *U.K.* 14 E5
Tay, L., *Australia* 93 F3
Tay, L., *U.K.* 14 E4
Tay Ninh, *Vietnam* 65 G6
Tayabamba, *Peru* 124 E3
Tayabas Bay, *Phil.* 61 E4
Taylakova, *Russia* 50 D8
Taylakovy = Taylakova, *Russia* 50 D8
Taylor, *Canada* 104 B4
Taylor, *Nebr., U.S.A.* 112 E5
Taylor, *Pa., U.S.A.* 111 E9
Taylor, *Tex., U.S.A.* 113 K6
Taylor, Mt., *U.S.A.* 115 J10
Taylorville, *U.S.A.* 112 F10
Taymā, *Si. Arabia* 70 E3
Taymyr, Oz., *Russia* 51 B11
Taymyr, Poluostrov, *Russia* 51 B11
Tayport, *U.K.* 14 E6
Tayshet, *Russia* 51 D10
Taytay, *Phil.* 61 F3
Taz →, *Russia* 50 C8
Taza, *Morocco* 78 B5
Tāzah Khurmātū, *Iraq* 70 C5
Tazawa-Ko, *Japan* 54 E10
Tazin, *Canada* 105 B7
Tazin L., *Canada* 105 B7
Tazovskiy, *Russia* 50 C8
Tbilisi, *Georgia* 49 K7
Tchad = Chad ■, *Africa* 79 E9
Tchad, L., *Chad* 79 F8
Tchaourou, *Benin* 83 D5
Tch'eng-tou = Chengdu, *China* 58 B5
Tchentlo L., *Canada* 104 B4
Tchetti, *Benin* 83 D5
Tchibanga, *Gabon* 84 E2
Tchien, *Liberia* 82 D3
Tchin Tabaraden, *Niger* 83 B6
Tch'ong-k'ing = Chongqing, *China* 58 C6
Tczew, *Poland* 44 D5
Te Anau, L., *N.Z.* 91 L1
Te Aroha, *N.Z.* 91 G5
Te Awamutu, *N.Z.* 91 H5
Te Kuiti, *N.Z.* 91 H5
Te-n-Dghâmcha, Sebkhet, *Mauritania* 82 B1
Te Puke, *N.Z.* 91 G6
Te Waewae B., *N.Z.* 91 M1
Teaca, *Romania* 43 D9
Teague, *U.S.A.* 113 K6
Teano, *Italy* 31 A7
Teapa, *Mexico* 119 D6
Teba, *Spain* 35 J6
Tebakang, *Malaysia* 62 D4
Teberda, *Russia* 49 J5
Tébessa, *Algeria* 78 A7
Tebicuary →, *Paraguay* 126 B4
Tebingtinggi, *Indonesia* 62 D1
Tebintingii, *Indonesia* 62 E2
Tebulos, *Georgia* 49 J7
Tecate, *Mexico* 117 N10
Tecer Dağları, *Turkey* 72 C7
Tech →, *France* 20 F7
Techiman, *Ghana* 82 D4
Techirghiol, *Romania* 43 F13
Tecka, *Argentina* 128 E2
Tecomán, *Mexico* 118 D4
Tecopa, *U.S.A.* 117 K10
Tecoripa, *Mexico* 118 B3
Tecuala, *Mexico* 118 C3
Tecuci, *Romania* 43 E12
Tecumseh, *Canada* 110 D2
Tecumseh, *Mich., U.S.A.* 108 D4
Tecumseh, *Okla., U.S.A.* 113 H6
Tedzhen = Tejen, *Turkmenistan* 50 F7
Tees →, *U.K.* 12 C6
Tees B., *U.K.* 12 C6
Teeswater, *Canada* 110 C3
Tefé, *Brazil* 124 D6
Tefenni, *Turkey* 39 D11
Tegal, *Indonesia* 63 G13
Tegernsee, *Germany* 25 H7
Teggiano, *Italy* 31 B8
Tegid, L. = Bala, L., *U.K.* 12 E4
Tegina, *Nigeria* 83 C6
Tegucigalpa, *Honduras* 120 D2
Teguidda i-n-Tessoum, *Niger* 83 B6
Tehachapi, *U.S.A.* 117 K8
Tehachapi Mts., *U.S.A.* 117 L8
Tehamiyam, *Sudan* 80 D4
Tehilla, *Sudan* 80 D4
Téhini, *Ivory C.* 82 D4
Tehoru, *Indonesia* 63 E7
Tehrān, *Iran* 71 C6
Tehri, *India* 69 D8
Tehuacán, *Mexico* 119 D5
Tehuantepec, *Mexico* 119 D5
Tehuantepec, G. de, *Mexico* 119 D5
Tehuantepec, Istmo de, *Mexico* 119 D6
Teide, *Canary Is.* 37 F3
Teifi →, *U.K.* 13 E3
Teign →, *U.K.* 13 G4
Teignmouth, *U.K.* 13 G4
Teiuş, *Romania* 43 D8
Teixeira Pinto, *Guinea-Biss.* 82 C1
Tejam, *India* 69 E9
Tejen, *Turkmenistan* 50 F7
Tejen →, *Turkmenistan* 71 B9
Tejo →, *Europe* 35 F2
Tejon Pass, *U.S.A.* 117 L8
Tekamah, *U.S.A.* 112 E6
Tekapo, L., *N.Z.* 91 K3
Tekax, *Mexico* 119 C7
Teke, *Turkey* 41 E13
Tekeli, *Kazakstan* 50 E8
Tekeze →, *Ethiopia* 81 E4
Tekija, *Serbia, Yug.* 40 B6
Tekirdağ, *Turkey* 41 F11
Tekirdağ □, *Turkey* 41 E11
Tekirova, *Turkey* 39 E12
Tekkali, *India* 67 K14
Tekke, *Turkey* 72 B7
Tekman, *Turkey* 73 C9
Tekoa, *U.S.A.* 114 C5
Tel Aviv-Yafo, *Israel* 75 C3
Tel Lakhish, *Israel* 75 D3
Tel Megiddo, *Israel* 75 C4
Tela, *Honduras* 120 C2
Telanaipura = Jambi, *Indonesia* 62 E2
Telavi, *Georgia* 49 J7
Telč, *Czech Rep.* 26 B8
Telciu, *Romania* 43 C9
Telde, *Canary Is.* 37 G4
Telegraph Creek, *Canada* 104 B2
Telekhany = Tsyelyakhany, *Belarus* 47 F3
Telemark, *Norway* 9 G12
Telén, *Argentina* 126 D2
Teleneşti, *Moldova* 43 C13
Teleng, *Iran* 71 E9
Teleño, *Spain* 34 C4
Teleorman □, *Romania* 43 G10
Teleorman →, *Romania* 43 G10
Teles Pires →, *Brazil* 122 D5
Telescope Pk., *U.S.A.* 117 J9
Teletaye, *Mali* 83 B5
Telfer Mine, *Australia* 92 C3
Telford, *U.K.* 13 E5
Telford and Wrekin □, *U.K.* 12 E5
Telfs, *Austria* 26 D4
Télimélé, *Guinea* 82 C2
Teljo, J., *Sudan* 81 E2
Telkwa, *Canada* 104 C3
Tell City, *U.S.A.* 108 G2
Tellicherry, *India* 66 P9
Telluride, *U.S.A.* 115 H10
Teloloapán, *Mexico* 119 D5
Telpos Iz, *Russia* 6 C17
Telsen, *Argentina* 128 E3
Telšiai, *Lithuania* 9 H20
Telšiai □, *Lithuania* 44 C9
Teltow, *Germany* 24 C9
Teluk Anson = Teluk Intan, *Malaysia* 65 K3
Teluk Betung = Tanjungkarang Telukbetung, *Indonesia* 62 F3
Teluk Intan, *Malaysia* 65 K3
Telukbutun, *Indonesia* 65 K7
Telukdalem, *Indonesia* 62 D1
Tema, *Ghana* 83 D5
Temax, *Mexico* 119 C7
Temba, *S. Africa* 89 D4
Tembagapura, *Indonesia* 63 E9
Tembe, *Dem. Rep. of the Congo* 86 C2
Tembleque, *Spain* 34 F7
Temblor Range, *U.S.A.* 117 K7
Teme →, *U.K.* 13 E5
Temecula, *U.S.A.* 117 M9
Temerloh, *Malaysia* 62 D2
Teminabuan, *Indonesia* 63 E8
Temir, *Kazakstan* 50 E6
Temirtau, *Kazakstan* 50 D8
Temirtau, *Russia* 50 D9
Témiscamie →, *Canada* 103 B5
Témiscaming, *Canada* 102 C4
Témiscamingue, L., *Canada* 102 C4
Temnikov, *Russia* 48 C6
Temo →, *Italy* 30 B1
Temosachic, *Mexico* 118 B3
Tempe, *U.S.A.* 115 K8
Témpio Pausánia, *Italy* 30 B2
Tempiute, *U.S.A.* 116 H11
Temple, *U.S.A.* 113 K6
Temple B., *Australia* 94 A3
Templemore, *Ireland* 15 D4
Templeton, *U.S.A.* 116 K6
Templeton →, *Australia* 94 C2
Templin, *Germany* 24 B9
Tempoal, *Mexico* 119 C5
Temryuk, *Russia* 47 K9
Temska →, *Serbia, Yug.* 40 C6
Temuco, *Chile* 128 D2
Temuka, *N.Z.* 91 L3
Tenabo, *Mexico* 119 C6
Tenaha, *U.S.A.* 113 K7
Tenakee Springs, *U.S.A.* 104 B1
Tenali, *India* 66 L12
Tenancingo, *Mexico* 119 D5
Tenango, *Mexico* 119 D5
Tenasserim, *Burma* 65 F2
Tenasserim □, *Burma* 64 F2
Tenby, *U.K.* 13 F3
Tenda, Colle di, *France* 21 D11
Tendaho, *Ethiopia* 81 E5
Tende, *France* 21 D11
Tendelti, *Sudan* 81 E3
Tendrovskaya Kosa, *Ukraine* 47 J6
Tendukhera, *India* 69 H8
Teneida, *Egypt* 80 B2
Tenenkou, *Mali* 82 C4
Ténéré, *Niger* 83 B7
Tenerife, *Canary Is.* 37 F3
Tenerife, Pico, *Canary Is.* 37 G1
Teng Xian, *Guangxi Zhuangzu, China* 59 F8
Teng Xian, *Shandong, China* 57 G9
Tengah □, *Indonesia* 63 E6
Tengah, Kepulauan, *Indonesia* 62 F5
Tengchong, *China* 58 E2
Tengchowfu = Penglai, *China* 57 F11
Tenggara □, *Indonesia* 63 E6
Tenggarong, *Indonesia* 62 E5
Tenggol, Pulau, *Malaysia* 65 K4
Tengiz, Ozero, *Kazakstan* 50 D7
Tenhult, *Sweden* 11 G8
Tenino, *U.S.A.* 116 D4
Tenkasi, *India* 66 Q10
Tenke, *Katanga, Dem. Rep. of the Congo* 87 E2
Tenke, *Katanga, Dem. Rep. of the Congo* 87 E2
Tenkodogo, *Burkina Faso* 83 C4
Tenna →, *Italy* 29 E10
Tennant Creek, *Australia* 94 B1
Tennessee □, *U.S.A.* 109 H2
Tennessee →, *U.S.A.* 108 G1
Teno, Pta. de, *Canary Is.* 37 F3
Tenom, *Malaysia* 62 C5
Tenosique, *Mexico* 119 D6
Tenryū-Gawa →, *Japan* 55 G8
Tenterden, *U.K.* 13 F8
Tenterfield, *Australia* 95 D5
Teo, *Spain* 34 C2
Teófilo Otoni, *Brazil* 125 G10
Tepa, *Indonesia* 63 F7
Tepalcatepec →, *Mexico* 118 D4
Tepecik, *Bursa, Turkey* 41 F12
Tepecik, *Kütahya, Turkey* 39 B11
Tepehuanes, *Mexico* 118 B3
Tepelena, *Albania* 40 F4
Tepetongo, *Mexico* 118 C4
Tepic, *Mexico* 118 C4
Teplá, *Czech Rep.* 26 B5
Teplice, *Czech Rep.* 26 A6
Tepoca, C., *Mexico* 118 A2
Tequila, *Mexico* 118 C4
Ter →, *Spain* 32 C8
Ter Apel, *Neths.* 17 B7
Téra, *Niger* 83 C5
Tera →, *Spain* 34 D5
Teraina, *Kiribati* 97 G11
Terakeka, *Sudan* 81 F3
Téramo, *Italy* 29 F10
Terang, *Australia* 95 F3
Terazit, Massif de, *Niger* 83 A6
Tercan, *Turkey* 73 C9
Tercero →, *Argentina* 126 C3
Terebovlya, *Ukraine* 47 H3
Teregova, *Romania* 42 E7
Tereida, *Sudan* 81 E3
Terek →, *Russia* 49 J8
Tereshka →, *Russia* 48 E8
Teresina, *Brazil* 125 E10
Terespol, *Poland* 45 F10
Terewah, L., *Australia* 95 D4
Terges →, *Portugal* 35 H3
Tergnier, *France* 19 C10
Teridgerie Cr. →, *Australia* 95 E4
Terlizzi, *Italy* 31 A9
Terme, *Turkey* 72 B7
Termez = Termiz, *Uzbekistan* 50 F7
Términi Imerese, *Italy* 30 E6
Términos, L. de, *Mexico* 119 D6
Termiz, *Uzbekistan* 50 F7
Térmoli, *Italy* 29 F12
Ternate, *Indonesia* 63 D7
Terneuzen, *Neths.* 17 C3
Terney, *Russia* 51 E14
Terni, *Italy* 29 F9
Ternitz, *Austria* 26 D9
Ternopil, *Ukraine* 47 H3
Ternopol = Ternopil, *Ukraine* 47 H3
Terowie, *Australia* 95 E2
Terpní, *Greece* 40 F7
Terra Bella, *U.S.A.* 117 K7
Terra Nova Nat. Park, *Canada* 103 C9
Terrace, *Canada* 104 C3
Terrace Bay, *Canada* 102 C2
Terracina, *Italy* 30 A6
Terralba, *Italy* 30 C1
Terranova = Ólbia, *Italy* 30 B2
Terrasini, *Italy* 30 D6
Terrassa, *Spain* 32 D7
Terrasson-la-Villedieu, *France* 20 C5
Terre Haute, *U.S.A.* 108 F2
Terrebonne B., *U.S.A.* 113 L9
Terrell, *U.S.A.* 113 J6
Terrenceville, *Canada* 103 C9
Terry, *U.S.A.* 112 B2
Terryville, *U.S.A.* 111 E11
Terschelling, *Neths.* 17 A5
Tersko-Kumskiy Kanal →, *Russia* 49 H7
Tertenía, *Italy* 30 C2
Terter → = Tärtär →, *Azerbaijan* 49 K8
Teruel, *Spain* 32 E3
Teruel □, *Spain* 32 E4
Tervel, *Bulgaria* 41 C11
Tervola, *Finland* 8 C21
Teryaweyna L., *Australia* 95 E3
Tešanj, *Bos.-H.* 42 F3
Teseney, *Eritrea* 81 D4
Tesha →, *Russia* 48 C6
Teshio, *Japan* 54 B10
Teshio-Gawa →, *Japan* 54 B10
Tešica, *Serbia, Yug.* 40 C5
Tesiyn Gol →, *Mongolia* 60 A4
Teslić, *Bos.-H.* 42 F2
Teslin, *Canada* 104 A2
Teslin →, *Canada* 104 A2
Teslin L., *Canada* 104 A2
Tessalit, *Mali* 83 A5
Tessaoua, *Niger* 83 C6
Tessin, *Germany* 24 A8
Tessit, *Mali* 83 B5
Test →, *U.K.* 13 G6
Testa del Gargano, *Italy* 29 G13
Testigos, Is. Las, *Venezuela* 121 D7
Tét, *Hungary* 42 C2
Têt →, *France* 20 F7
Tetachuck L., *Canada* 104 C3
Tetas, Pta., *Chile* 126 A1
Tete, *Mozam.* 87 F3
Tete □, *Mozam.* 87 F3
Teterev →, *Ukraine* 47 G6
Teterow, *Germany* 24 B8
Teteven, *Bulgaria* 41 D8
Tethul →, *Canada* 104 A6
Tetiyev, *Ukraine* 47 H5
Teton →, *U.S.A.* 114 C8
Tétouan, *Morocco* 78 A4
Tetovo, *Macedonia* 40 D4
Tetyushi, *Russia* 48 C9
Teuco →, *Argentina* 126 B3
Teulada, *Italy* 30 D1
Teulon, *Canada* 105 C9
Teun, *Indonesia* 63 F7
Teutoburger Wald, *Germany* 24 C4
Tevere →, *Italy* 29 G9
Teverya, *Israel* 75 C4
Teviot →, *U.K.* 14 F6
Tewantin, *Australia* 95 D5
Tewkesbury, *U.K.* 13 F5
Texada I., *Canada* 104 D4
Texarkana, *Ark., U.S.A.* 113 J8
Texarkana, *Tex., U.S.A.* 113 J7
Texas, *Australia* 95 D5
Texas □, *U.S.A.* 113 K5
Texas City, *U.S.A.* 113 L7
Texel, *Neths.* 17 A4
Texline, *U.S.A.* 113 G3
Texoma, L., *U.S.A.* 113 J6
Teykovo, *Russia* 46 D11
Teza →, *Russia* 48 B5
Tezin, *Afghan.* 68 B3
Teziutlán, *Mexico* 119 D5
Tezpur, *India* 67 F18
Tezzeron L., *Canada* 104 C4
Tha-anne →, *Canada* 105 A10
Tha Deua, *Laos* 64 D4
Tha Deua, *Laos* 64 C3
Tha Pla, *Thailand* 64 D3
Tha Rua, *Thailand* 64 E3
Tha Sala, *Thailand* 65 H2
Tha Song Yang, *Thailand* 64 D1
Thaba Putsoa, *Lesotho* 89 D4
Thabana Ntlenyana, *Lesotho* 89 D4
Thabazimbi, *S. Africa* 89 C4
Thādiq, *Si. Arabia* 70 E5
Thai Binh, *Vietnam* 58 G6
Thai Muang, *Thailand* 65 H2
Thai Nguyen, *Vietnam* 58 G5
Thailand ■, *Asia* 64 E4
Thailand, G. of, *Asia* 65 G3
Thakhek, *Laos* 64 D5
Thal, *Pakistan* 68 C4
Thal Desert, *Pakistan* 68 D4
Thala La, *Burma* 67 E20
Thalabarivat, *Cambodia* 64 F5
Thallon, *Australia* 95 D4
Thalwil, *Switz.* 25 H4
Thames, *N.Z.* 91 G5
Thames →, *Canada* 102 D3
Thames →, *U.K.* 13 F8
Thames →, *U.S.A.* 111 E12
Thames Estuary, *U.K.* 13 F8
Thamesford, *Canada* 110 C4
Thamesville, *Canada* 110 D3
Than, *India* 68 H4
Than Uyen, *Vietnam* 64 B4
Thana Gazi, *India* 68 F7
Thandla, *India* 68 H6
Thane, *India* 66 K8
Thanesar, *India* 68 D7
Thanet, I. of, *U.K.* 13 F9
Thangool, *Australia* 94 C5
Thanh Hoa, *Vietnam* 64 C5
Thanh Hung, *Vietnam* 65 H5
Thanh Pho Ho Chi Minh = Phanh Bho Ho Chi Minh, *Vietnam* 65 G6
Thanh Thuy, *Vietnam* 64 A5
Thanjavur, *India* 66 P11
Thann, *France* 19 E14
Thano Bula Khan, *Pakistan* 68 G2
Thaolinta L., *Canada* 105 A9
Thaon-les-Vosges, *France* 19 D13
Thap Sakae, *Thailand* 65 G2
Thap Than, *Thailand* 64 E2
Thar Desert, *India* 68 F5
Tharad, *India* 68 G4
Thargomindah, *Australia* 95 D3
Tharrawaddy, *Burma* 67 L19
Tharthār, Mileh, *Iraq* 70 C4
Tharthār, W. ath →, *Iraq* 70 C4
Thasopoúla, *Greece* 41 F8
Thásos, *Greece* 41 F8
That Khe, *Vietnam* 58 F6
Thatcher, *Ariz., U.S.A.* 115 K9
Thatcher, *Colo., U.S.A.* 113 G2
Thaton, *Burma* 67 L20
Thau, Bassin de, *France* 20 E7
Thaungdut, *Burma* 67 G19
Thayer, *U.S.A.* 113 G9
Thayetmyo, *Burma* 67 K19
Thazi, *Burma* 67 J20
The Alberga →, *Australia* 95 D2
The Bight, *Bahamas* 121 B4
The Coorong, *Australia* 95 F2
The Dalles, *U.S.A.* 114 D3
The English Company's Is., *Australia* 94 A2
The Frome →, *Australia* 95 D2
The Great Divide = Great Dividing Ra., *Australia* 94 C4
The Hague = 's-Gravenhage, *Neths.* 17 B4
The Hamilton →, *Australia* 95 D2
The Macumba →, *Australia* 95 D2
The Neales →, *Australia* 95 D2
The Officer →, *Australia* 93 E5
The Pas, *Canada* 105 C8
The Range, *Zimbabwe* 87 F3
The Rock, *Australia* 95 F4
The Salt L., *Australia* 95 E3
The Sandheads, *India* 69 J13
The Stevenson →, *Australia* 95 D2
The Warburton →, *Australia* 95 D2
The Woodlands, *U.S.A.* 113 K7
Thebes = Thívai, *Greece* 38 C5
Thebes, *Egypt* 80 B3
Thedford, *Canada* 110 C3
Thedford, *U.S.A.* 112 E4
Theebine, *Australia* 95 D5
Thekulthili L., *Canada* 105 A7
Thelon →, *Canada* 105 A8
Thénezay, *France* 18 F6
Thenon, *France* 20 C5
Theodore, *Australia* 94 C5
Theodore, *Canada* 105 C8
Theodore, *U.S.A.* 109 K1
Theodore Roosevelt National Memorial Park, *U.S.A.* 112 B3
Theodore Roosevelt Res., *U.S.A.* 115 K8
Thepha, *Thailand* 65 J3
Thérain →, *France* 19 C9
Theresa, *U.S.A.* 111 B9
Thermaïkós Kólpos, *Greece* 40 F6
Thermí, *Greece* 39 B8
Thermopolis, *U.S.A.* 114 E9
Thermopylae P., *Greece* 38 C4
Thesprotía □, *Greece* 38 B2
Thessalía □, *Greece* 38 B4
Thessalon, *Canada* 102 C3
Thessaloníki, *Greece* 40 F6
Thessaloníki □, *Greece* 40 F7
Thessaloniki, Gulf of = Thermaïkós Kólpos, *Greece* 40 F6
Thessaly = Thessalía □, *Greece* 38 B4
Thetford, *U.K.* 13 E8
Thetford Mines, *Canada* 103 C5
Theun →, *Laos* 64 C5
Theunissen, *S. Africa* 88 D4
Thevenard, *Australia* 95 E1
Thiámis →, *Greece* 38 B2
Thiberville, *France* 18 C7
Thibodaux, *U.S.A.* 113 L9
Thicket Portage, *Canada* 105 B9
Thief River Falls, *U.S.A.* 112 A6
Thiel Mts., *Antarctica* 5 E16
Thiene, *Italy* 29 C8
Thiérache, *France* 19 C10
Thiers, *France* 20 C7
Thiès, *Senegal* 82 C1
Thiesi, *Italy* 30 B1
Thiet, *Sudan* 81 F2
Thika, *Kenya* 86 C4
Thikombia, *Fiji* 91 B9
Thille-Boubacar, *Senegal* 82 B1
Thimphu, *Bhutan* 67 F16
þingvallavatn, *Iceland* 8 D3
Thionville, *France* 19 C13
Thíra, *Greece* 39 E7
Thirasía, *Greece* 39 E7
Third Cataract, *Sudan* 80 D3
Thirsk, *U.K.* 12 C6
Thisted, *Denmark* 11 H2
Thistle I., *Australia* 95 F2
Thívai, *Greece* 38 C5
Thiviers, *France* 20 C4
Thizy, *France* 19 F11
þjórsá →, *Iceland* 8 E3
Thlewiaza →, *Man., Canada* 105 B8
Thlewiaza →, *N.W.T., Canada* 105 A10
Thmar Puok, *Cambodia* 64 F4
Tho Vinh, *Vietnam* 64 C5
Thoa →, *Canada* 105 A7
Thoen, *Thailand* 64 D2
Thoeng, *Thailand* 64 C3
Thohoyandou, *S. Africa* 85 J6
Tholdi, *Pakistan* 69 B7
Thomas, *U.S.A.* 113 H5
Thomas, L., *Australia* 95 D2
Thomaston, *U.S.A.* 109 J3
Thomasville, *Ala., U.S.A.* 109 K2
Thomasville, *Ga., U.S.A.* 109 K4
Thomasville, *N.C., U.S.A.* 109 H5
Thompson, *Canada* 105 B9
Thompson, *U.S.A.* 111 E9
Thompson →, *Canada* 104 C4
Thompson →, *U.S.A.* 112 F8
Thompson Falls, *U.S.A.* 114 C6
Thompson Pk., *U.S.A.* 114 F2
Thompson Springs, *U.S.A.* 115 G9
Thompsontown, *U.S.A.* 110 F7
Thomson, *U.S.A.* 109 J4
Thomson →, *Australia* 94 C3
Thomson's Falls = Nyahururu, *Kenya* 86 B4
Thônes, *France* 21 C10
Thonon-les-Bains, *France* 19 F13
Thorez, *Ukraine* 47 H10
þórisvatn, *Iceland* 8 D4
Thornaby on Tees, *U.K.* 12 C6
Thornbury, *Canada* 110 B4
Thorne, *U.K.* 12 D7
Thornhill, *Canada* 104 C3

Thorold, *Canada* 110 C5
Þórshöfn, *Iceland* 8 C6
Thouarcé, *France* 18 E6
Thouars, *France* 18 F6
Thouet →, *France* 18 E6
Thouin, C., *Australia* 92 D2
Thousand Oaks, *U.S.A.* 117 L8
Thrace, *Turkey* 41 F10
Thrakikón Pélagos, *Greece* 41 F8
Three Forks, *U.S.A.* 114 D8
Three Gorges Dam, *China* 59 B8
Three Hills, *Canada* 104 C6
Three Hummock I., *Australia* 94 G3
Three Points, C., *Ghana* 82 E4
Three Rivers, *Calif., U.S.A.* 116 J8
Three Rivers, *Tex., U.S.A.* 113 L5
Three Sisters, *U.S.A.* 114 D3
Three Springs, *Australia* 93 E2
Throssell, L., *Australia* 93 E3
Throssell Ra., *Australia* 92 D3
Thuan Hoa, *Vietnam* 65 H5
Thubun Lakes, *Canada* 105 A6
Thueyts, *France* 21 D8
Thuin, *Belgium* 17 D4
Thuir, *France* 20 F6
Thule = Qaanaaq, *Greenland* 4 B4
Thun, *Switz.* 25 J3
Thunder B., *U.S.A.* 110 B1
Thunder Bay, *Canada* 102 C2
Thunersee, *Switz.* 25 J3
Thung Song, *Thailand* 65 H2
Thunkar, *Bhutan* 67 F17
Thuong Tra, *Vietnam* 64 D6
Thur →, *Switz.* 25 H5
Thurgau □, *Switz.* 25 H5
Thüringen □, *Germany* 24 D6
Thüringer Wald, *Germany* 24 E6
Thurles, *Ireland* 15 D4
Thurn P., *Austria* 26 D5
Thurrock □, *U.K.* 13 F8
Thursday I., *Australia* 94 A3
Thurso, *Canada* 102 C4
Thurso, *U.K.* 14 C5
Thurso →, *U.K.* 14 C5
Thurston I., *Antarctica* 5 D16
Thury-Harcourt, *France* 18 D6
Thutade L., *Canada* 104 B3
Thy, *Denmark* 11 H2
Thyborøn, *Denmark* 11 H2
Thyolo, *Malawi* 87 F4
Thysville = Mbanza Ngungu, *Dem. Rep. of the Congo* 84 F2
Ti-n-Amzi →, *Niger* 83 B5
Ti-n-Barraouene, O. →, *Africa* 83 B5
Ti-n-Zaouatène, *Algeria* 83 B5
Ti Tree, *Australia* 94 C1
Tiadiaye, *Senegal* 82 C1
Tian Shan, *Asia* 60 B3
Tianchang, *China* 59 A12
Tiandeng, *China* 58 F6
Tiandong, *China* 58 F6
Tian'e, *China* 58 E6
Tianhe, *China* 58 E7
Tianjin, *China* 57 E9
Tiankoura, *Burkina Faso* 82 C4
Tianlin, *China* 58 E6
Tianmen, *China* 59 B9
Tianquan, *China* 58 B4
Tianshui, *China* 56 G3
Tiantai, *China* 59 C13
Tianyang, *China* 58 F6
Tianzhen, *China* 56 D8
Tianzhu, *China* 58 D7
Tianzhuangtai, *China* 57 D12
Tiaret, *Algeria* 78 A6
Tiassalé, *Ivory C.* 82 D4
Tibagi, *Brazil* 127 A5
Tibagi →, *Brazil* 127 A5
Tibati, *Cameroon* 83 D7
Tibe, *Ethiopia* 81 F4
Tiber = Tevere →, *Italy* 29 G9
Tiberias = Teverya, *Israel* 75 C4
Tiberias, L. = Yam Kinneret, *Israel* 75 C4
Tibesti, *Chad* 79 D9
Tibet = Xizang Zizhiqu □, *China* 60 C3
Tibet, Plateau of, *Asia* 52 F12
Tibiao, *Phil.* 61 F5
Tibiri, *Niger* 83 C6
Țibleș, Vf., *Romania* 43 C9
Țibleșului, Munții, *Romania* 43 C9
Tibnī, *Syria* 70 C3
Tibooburra, *Australia* 95 D3
Tibro, *Sweden* 11 F8
Tiburón, I., *Mexico* 118 B2
Ticao I., *Phil.* 61 E5
Tîchît, *Mauritania* 82 B3
Ticho, *Ethiopia* 81 F4
Ticino □, *Switz.* 25 J4
Ticino →, *Italy* 25 K5
Ticleni, *Romania* 43 F8
Ticonderoga, *U.S.A.* 111 C11
Ticul, *Mexico* 119 C7
Tidaholm, *Sweden* 11 F7
Tidan, *Sweden* 11 F8
Tiddim, *Burma* 67 H18
Tidioute, *U.S.A.* 110 E5
Tidjikja, *Mauritania* 82 B2
Tidore, *Indonesia* 63 D7
Tiébissou, *Ivory C.* 82 D3
Tiel, *Neths.* 17 C5
Tiel, *Senegal* 82 C1
Tieling, *China* 57 C12
Tielt, *Belgium* 17 C3
Tien Shan = Tian Shan, *Asia* 60 B3
Tien-tsin = Tianjin, *China* 57 E9
Tien Yen, *Vietnam* 64 B6
T'ienching = Tianjin, *China* 57 E9
Tienen, *Belgium* 17 D4
Tiénigbé, *Ivory C.* 82 D3
Tientsin = Tianjin, *China* 57 E9
Tieri, *Australia* 94 C4
Tierp, *Sweden* 10 D11
Tierra Amarilla, *Chile* 126 B1
Tierra Amarilla, *U.S.A.* 115 H10
Tierra Colorada, *Mexico* 119 D5
Tierra de Barros, *Spain* 35 G4
Tierra de Campos, *Spain* 34 C6
Tierra del Fuego, I. Gr. de, *Argentina* 122 J4
Tiétar →, *Spain* 34 F4
Tieté →, *Brazil* 127 A5
Tiffin, *U.S.A.* 108 E4
Tiflis = Tbilisi, *Georgia* 49 K7
Tifton, *U.S.A.* 109 K4
Tifu, *Indonesia* 63 E7
Tighina, *Moldova* 43 D14
Tigil, *Russia* 51 D16
Tignish, *Canada* 103 C7
Tigray □, *Ethiopia* 81 E4
Tigre →, *Peru* 124 D4
Tigre →, *Venezuela* 124 B6
Tigris = Dijlah, Nahr →, *Asia* 70 D5
Tigveni, *Romania* 43 E9
Tigyaing, *Burma* 67 H20
Tîh, Gebel el, *Egypt* 80 B3
Tijara, *India* 68 F7
Tijuana, *Mexico* 117 N9
Tikal, *Guatemala* 120 C2
Tikamgarh, *India* 69 G8
Tikaré, *Burkina Faso* 83 C4
Tikhoretsk, *Russia* 49 H5
Tikhvin, *Russia* 46 C7
Tiko, *Cameroon* 83 E6
Tikrīt, *Iraq* 70 C4
Tiksi, *Russia* 51 B13
Tilamuta, *Indonesia* 63 D6
Tilburg, *Neths.* 17 C5
Tilbury, *Canada* 102 D3
Tilbury, *U.K.* 13 F8
Tilcara, *Argentina* 126 A2
Tilden, *U.S.A.* 112 D6
Tilemses, *Niger* 83 B5
Tilemsi, Vallée du, *Mali* 83 B5
Tilhar, *India* 69 F8
Tilichiki, *Russia* 51 C17
Tílissos, *Greece* 36 D7
Till →, *U.K.* 12 B5
Tillabéri, *Niger* 83 C5
Tillamook, *U.S.A.* 114 D2
Tillberga, *Sweden* 10 E10
Tillia, *Niger* 83 B5
Tillsonburg, *Canada* 102 D3
Tillyeria □, *Cyprus* 36 D11
Tilogne, *Senegal* 82 B2
Tílos, *Greece* 39 E9
Tilpa, *Australia* 95 E3
Tilsit = Sovetsk, *Russia* 9 J19
Tilt →, *U.K.* 14 E5
Tilton, *U.S.A.* 111 C13
Tiltonsville, *U.S.A.* 110 F4
Tim, *Denmark* 11 H2
Timagami, L., *Canada* 102 C3
Timaru, *N.Z.* 91 L3
Timashevo, *Russia* 48 D10
Timashevsk, *Russia* 49 H4
Timau, *Kenya* 86 B4
Timbákion, *Greece* 36 D6
Timbedgha, *Mauritania* 82 B3
Timber Creek, *Australia* 92 C5
Timber Lake, *U.S.A.* 112 C4
Timber Mt., *U.S.A.* 116 H10
Timbo, *Guinea* 82 C2
Timbo, *Liberia* 82 D3
Timbuktu = Tombouctou, *Mali* 82 B4
Timeiaouine, *Algeria* 83 A5
Timétrine, Mts., *Mali* 83 B4
Timfi Óros, *Greece* 38 B2
Timfristós, Óros, *Greece* 38 C3
Timi, *Cyprus* 36 E11
Tîmia, *Niger* 83 B6
Timimoun, *Algeria* 78 C6
Timiș = Tamis →, *Serbia, Yug.* 42 F5
Timiș □, *Romania* 42 E6
Timișoara, *Romania* 42 E6
Timmersdala, *Sweden* 11 F7
Timmins, *Canada* 102 C3
Timok →, *Serbia, Yug.* 40 B6
Timor, *Indonesia* 63 F7
Timor Sea, *Ind. Oc.* 92 B4
Timor Timur □, *Indonesia* 63 F7
Timrå, *Sweden* 10 B11
Tin Can Bay, *Australia* 95 D5
Tin Ethisane, *Mali* 83 B4
Tin Gornai, *Mali* 83 B4
Tin Mt., *U.S.A.* 116 J9
Tina →, *S. Africa* 89 E4
Tîna, Khalîg el, *Egypt* 80 A3
Tinaca Pt., *Phil.* 61 J6
Tinajo, *Canary Is.* 37 E6
Tinca, *Romania* 42 D6
Tindal, *Australia* 92 B5
Tindouf, *Algeria* 78 C4
Tinée →, *France* 21 E11
Tineo, *Spain* 34 B4
Ting Jiang →, *China* 59 E11
Tinggi, Pulau, *Malaysia* 65 L5
Tinglev, *Denmark* 11 K3
Tingo Maria, *Peru* 124 E3
Tingrela, *Ivory C.* 82 C3
Tingsryd, *Sweden* 11 H9
Tingstäde, *Sweden* 11 G12
Tinh Bien, *Vietnam* 65 G5
Tinnevelly = Tirunelveli, *India* 66 Q10
Tinogasta, *Argentina* 126 B2
Tínos, *Greece* 39 D7
Tiñoso, C., *Spain* 33 H3
Tinpahar, *India* 69 G12
Tintina, *Argentina* 126 B3
Tintinara, *Australia* 95 F3
Tintioulé, *Guinea* 82 C3
Tinto →, *Spain* 35 H4
Tioga, *N. Dak., U.S.A.* 112 A3
Tioga, *Pa., U.S.A.* 110 E7
Tioman, Pulau, *Malaysia* 65 L5
Tione di Trento, *Italy* 28 B7
Tionesta, *U.S.A.* 110 E5
Tior, *Sudan* 81 F3
Tipongpani, *India* 67 F19
Tipperary, *Ireland* 15 D3
Tipperary □, *Ireland* 15 D4
Tipton, *Calif., U.S.A.* 116 J7
Tipton, *Iowa, U.S.A.* 112 E9
Tipton Mt., *U.S.A.* 117 K12
Tiptonville, *U.S.A.* 113 G10
Tīrān, *Iran* 71 C6
Tīrān, *Si. Arabia* 80 B3
Tirana, *Albania* 40 E3
Tiranë = Tirana, *Albania* 40 E3
Tirano, *Italy* 28 B7
Tiraspol, *Moldova* 43 D14
Tirdout, *Mali* 83 B4
Tire, *Turkey* 39 C9
Tirebolu, *Turkey* 73 B8
Tiree, *U.K.* 14 E2
Tiree, Passage of, *U.K.* 14 E2
Tîrgoviște = Târgoviște, *Romania* 43 F10
Tîrgu-Jiu = Târgu-Jiu, *Romania* 43 E8
Tîrgu Mureș = Târgu Mureș, *Romania* 43 D9
Tirich Mir, *Pakistan* 66 A7
Tiriolo, *Italy* 31 D9
Tiriro, *Guinea* 82 C3
Tírnavos, *Greece* 38 B4
Tirodi, *India* 66 J11
Tirol □, *Austria* 26 D3
Tirschenreuth, *Germany* 25 F8
Tirso →, *Italy* 30 C1
Tirstrup, *Denmark* 11 H4
Tiruchchirappalli, *India* 66 P11
Tirunelveli, *India* 66 Q10
Tirupati, *India* 66 N11
Tiruppur, *India* 66 P10
Tiruvannamalai, *India* 66 N11
Tisa, *India* 68 C7
Tisa →, *Serbia, Yug.* 42 E5
Tisdale, *Canada* 105 C8
Tishomingo, *U.S.A.* 113 H6
Tisjön, *Sweden* 10 D7
Tisnaren, *Sweden* 11 F9
Tišnov, *Czech Rep.* 27 B9
Tisovec, *Slovak Rep.* 27 C12
Tisza = Tisa →, *Serbia, Yug.* 42 E5
Tiszaföldvár, *Hungary* 42 D5
Tiszafüred, *Hungary* 42 C5
Tiszalök, *Hungary* 42 B6
Tiszavasvári, *Hungary* 42 C6
Tit-Ary, *Russia* 51 B13
Titaguas, *Spain* 32 F3
Titao, *Burkina Faso* 83 C4
Titel, *Serbia, Yug.* 42 E5
Tithwal, *Pakistan* 69 B5
Titicaca, L., *S. Amer.* 122 E4
Titisee, *Germany* 25 H4
Titiwa, *Nigeria* 83 C7
Tito, *Italy* 31 B8
Titograd = Podgorica, *Montenegro, Yug.* 40 D3
Titova Korenica, *Croatia* 29 D12
Titu, *Romania* 43 F10
Titule, *Dem. Rep. of the Congo* 86 B2
Titusville, *Fla., U.S.A.* 109 L5
Titusville, *Pa., U.S.A.* 110 E5
Tivaouane, *Senegal* 82 C1
Tivat, *Montenegro, Yug.* 40 D2
Tiverton, *U.K.* 13 G4
Tívoli, *Italy* 29 G9
Tiyo, *Eritrea* 81 E5
Tizi-Ouzou, *Algeria* 78 A6
Tizimín, *Mexico* 119 C7
Tjæreborg, *Denmark* 11 J2
Tjällmo, *Sweden* 11 F9
Tjeggelvas, *Sweden* 8 C17
Tjirebon = Cirebon, *Indonesia* 63 G13
Tjörn, *Sweden* 11 F5
Tkibuli = Tqibuli, *Georgia* 49 J6
Tkvarcheli = Tqvarcheli, *Georgia* 49 J5
Tlacotalpan, *Mexico* 119 D5
Tlahualilo, *Mexico* 118 B4
Tlaquepaque, *Mexico* 118 C4
Tlaxcala, *Mexico* 119 D5
Tlaxcala □, *Mexico* 119 D5
Tlaxiaco, *Mexico* 119 D5
Tlemcen, *Algeria* 78 B5
Tłuszcz, *Poland* 45 F8
Tlyarata, *Russia* 49 J8
To Bong, *Vietnam* 64 F7
Toad →, *Canada* 104 B4
Toad River, *Canada* 104 B3
Toamasina, *Madag.* 89 B8
Toamasina □, *Madag.* 89 B8
Toay, *Argentina* 126 D3
Toba, *China* 58 B1
Toba, *Japan* 55 G8
Toba, Danau, *Indonesia* 62 D1
Toba Kakar, *Pakistan* 68 D3
Toba Tek Singh, *Pakistan* 68 D5
Tobago, *W. Indies* 121 D7
Tobarra, *Spain* 33 G3
Tobelo, *Indonesia* 63 D7
Tobermory, *Canada* 102 C3
Tobermory, *U.K.* 14 E2
Tobi, *Pac. Oc.* 63 D8
Tobin, *U.S.A.* 116 F5
Tobin, L., *Australia* 92 D4
Tobin L., *Canada* 105 C8
Toblach = Dobbiaco, *Italy* 29 B9
Toboali, *Indonesia* 62 E3
Tobol →, *Russia* 50 D7
Toboli, *Indonesia* 63 E6
Tobolsk, *Russia* 50 D7
Tobor, *Senegal* 82 C1
Tobruk = Tubruq, *Libya* 79 B10
Tobyhanna, *U.S.A.* 111 E9
Tobyl = Tobol →, *Russia* 50 D7
Tocantinópolis, *Brazil* 125 E9
Tocantins □, *Brazil* 125 F9
Tocantins →, *Brazil* 122 D6
Toccoa, *U.S.A.* 109 H4
Toce →, *Italy* 28 C5
Tochi →, *Pakistan* 68 C4
Tochigi, *Japan* 55 F9
Tochigi □, *Japan* 55 F9
Tocina, *Spain* 35 H5
Töcksfors, *Sweden* 10 E5
Toconao, *Chile* 126 A2
Tocopilla, *Chile* 126 A1
Tocumwal, *Australia* 95 F4
Tocuyo →, *Venezuela* 124 A5
Todd →, *Australia* 94 C2
Todeli, *Indonesia* 63 E6
Todenyang, *Kenya* 86 B4
Todgarh, *India* 68 G5
Todi, *Italy* 29 F9
Todos os Santos, B. de, *Brazil* 125 F11
Todos Santos, *Mexico* 118 C2
Todtnau, *Germany* 25 H3
Toe Hd., *U.K.* 14 D1
Toecé, *Burkina Faso* 83 C4
Tofield, *Canada* 104 C6
Tofino, *Canada* 104 D3
Tofua, *Tonga* 91 D11
Tōgane, *Japan* 55 G10
Togba, *Mauritania* 82 B2
Togian, Kepulauan, *Indonesia* 63 E6
Togliatti, *Russia* 48 D9
Togo ■, *W. Afr.* 83 D5
Togtoh, *China* 56 D6
Tohma →, *Turkey* 72 C7
Tōhoku □, *Japan* 54 E10
Töhöm, *Mongolia* 56 B5
Toinya, *Sudan* 81 F2
Toiyabe Range, *U.S.A.* 114 G5
Tojikiston = Tajikistan ■, *Asia* 50 F8
Tojo, *Indonesia* 63 E6
Tōjō, *Japan* 55 G6
Tok, *U.S.A.* 100 B5
Tok-do, *Japan* 55 F5
Tokachi-Dake, *Japan* 54 C11
Tokachi-Gawa →, *Japan* 54 C11
Tokaj, *Hungary* 42 B6
Tokala, *Indonesia* 63 E6
Tōkamachi, *Japan* 55 F9
Tokanui, *N.Z.* 91 M2
Tokar, *Sudan* 80 D4
Tokara-Rettō, *Japan* 55 K4
Tokarahi, *N.Z.* 91 L3
Tokashiki-Shima, *Japan* 55 L3
Tokat, *Turkey* 72 B7
Tŏkch'ŏn, *N. Korea* 57 E14
Tokeland, *U.S.A.* 116 D3
Tokelau Is., *Pac. Oc.* 96 H10
Tokmak, *Kyrgyzstan* 50 E8
Tokmak, *Ukraine* 47 J8
Toko Ra., *Australia* 94 C2
Tokoro-Gawa →, *Japan* 54 B12
Tokuno-Shima, *Japan* 55 L4
Tokushima, *Japan* 55 G7
Tokushima □, *Japan* 55 H7
Tokuyama, *Japan* 55 G5
Tōkyō, *Japan* 55 G9
Tolaga Bay, *N.Z.* 91 H7
Tolbukhin = Dobrich, *Bulgaria* 41 C11
Toledo, *Brazil* 127 A5
Toledo, *Spain* 34 F6
Toledo, *Ohio, U.S.A.* 108 E4
Toledo, *Oreg., U.S.A.* 114 D2
Toledo, *Wash., U.S.A.* 114 C2
Toledo, Montes de, *Spain* 35 F6
Toledo Bend Reservoir, *U.S.A.* 113 K8
Tolentino, *Italy* 29 E10
Tolfa, *Italy* 29 F8
Tolga, *Australia* 94 B4
Toliara, *Madag.* 89 C7
Toliara □, *Madag.* 89 C8
Tolima, *Colombia* 124 C3
Tolitoli, *Indonesia* 63 D6
Tolkmicko, *Poland* 44 D6
Tollarp, *Sweden* 11 J7
Tollensesee, *Germany* 24 B9
Tollhouse, *U.S.A.* 116 H7
Tolmachevo, *Russia* 46 C5
Tolmezzo, *Italy* 29 B10
Tolmin, *Slovenia* 29 B10
Tolna, *Hungary* 42 D3
Tolna □, *Hungary* 42 D3
Tolo, Teluk, *Indonesia* 63 E6
Tolochin = Talachyn, *Belarus* 46 E5
Tolosa, *Spain* 32 B2
Tolox, *Spain* 35 J6
Toluca, *Mexico* 119 D5
Tom Burke, *S. Africa* 89 C4
Tom Price, *Australia* 92 D2
Toma, *Burkina Faso* 82 C4
Tomah, *U.S.A.* 112 D9
Tomahawk, *U.S.A.* 112 C10
Tomai, *Moldova* 43 D13
Tomakomai, *Japan* 54 C10
Tomales, *U.S.A.* 116 G4
Tomales B., *U.S.A.* 116 G3
Tomar, *Portugal* 35 F2
Tómaros, Óros, *Greece* 38 B2
Tomarza, *Turkey* 72 C6
Tomaszów Lubelski, *Poland* 45 H10
Tomaszów Mazowiecki, *Poland* 45 G7
Tomatlán, *Mexico* 118 D3
Tombadonkéa, *Guinea* 82 C2
Tombador, Serra do, *Brazil* 124 F7
Tombe, *Sudan* 81 F3
Tombigbee →, *U.S.A.* 109 K2
Tombouctou, *Mali* 82 B4
Tombstone, *U.S.A.* 115 L8
Tombua, *Angola* 88 B1
Tomé, *Chile* 126 D1
Tomelilla, *Sweden* 11 J7
Tomelloso, *Spain* 35 F7
Tomini, *Indonesia* 63 D6
Tomini, Teluk, *Indonesia* 63 E6
Tominian, *Mali* 82 C4
Tomiño, *Spain* 34 D2
Tomintoul, *U.K.* 14 D5
Tomislavgrad, *Bos.-H.* 42 G2
Tomkinson Ranges, *Australia* 93 E4
Tommot, *Russia* 51 D13
Tomnop Ta Suos, *Cambodia* 65 G5
Tomo →, *Colombia* 124 B5
Toms Place, *U.S.A.* 116 H8
Toms River, *U.S.A.* 111 G10
Tomsk, *Russia* 50 D9
Tomtabacken, *Sweden* 11 G8
Tona, *Spain* 32 D7
Tonalá, *Mexico* 119 D6
Tonale, Passo del, *Italy* 28 B7
Tonantins, *Brazil* 124 D5
Tonasket, *U.S.A.* 114 B4
Tonawanda, *U.S.A.* 110 D6
Tonbridge, *U.K.* 13 F8
Tondano, *Indonesia* 63 D6
Tondela, *Portugal* 34 E2
Tønder, *Denmark* 11 K2
Tondi Kiwindi, *Niger* 83 C5
Tondibi, *Mali* 83 B4
Tondoro, *Namibia* 88 B2
Tone →, *Australia* 93 F2
Tone-Gawa →, *Japan* 55 F9
Tonekābon, *Iran* 71 B6
Tong Xian, *China* 56 E9
Tongâ, *Sudan* 81 F3
Tonga ■, *Pac. Oc.* 91 D11
Tonga Trench, *Pac. Oc.* 96 J10
Tongaat, *S. Africa* 89 D5
Tong'an, *China* 59 E12
Tongareva, *Cook Is.* 97 H12
Tongatapu, *Tonga* 91 E12
Tongbai, *China* 59 A9
Tongcheng, *Anhui, China* 59 B11
Tongcheng, *Hubei, China* 59 C9
Tongchŏn-ni, *N. Korea* 57 E14
Tongchuan, *China* 56 G5
Tongdao, *China* 58 D7
Tongeren, *Belgium* 17 D5
Tonggu, *China* 59 C10
Tongguan, *China* 56 G6
Tonghai, *China* 58 E4
Tonghua, *China* 57 D13
Tongjiang, *China* 58 B6
Tongjosŏn Man, *N. Korea* 57 E15
Tongking, G. of, *Asia* 64 B7
Tongking, G. of = Tongkin, G. of, *Asia* 64 B7
Tongliang, *China* 58 C6
Tongliao, *China* 57 C12
Tongling, *China* 59 B11
Tonglu, *China* 59 C12
Tongnae, *S. Korea* 57 G15
Tongnan = Anyue, *China* 58 B5
Tongobory, *Madag.* 89 C7
Tongoy, *Chile* 126 C1
Tongren, *China* 58 D7
Tongres = Tongeren, *Belgium* 17 D5
Tongsa Dzong, *Bhutan* 67 F17
Tongue, *U.K.* 14 C4
Tongue →, *U.S.A.* 112 B2
Tongwei, *China* 56 G3
Tongxiang, *China* 59 B13
Tongxin, *China* 56 F3
Tongyang, *N. Korea* 57 E14
Tongyu, *China* 57 B12
Tongzi, *China* 58 C6
Tonj, *Sudan* 81 F2
Tonj →, *Sudan* 81 F2
Tonk, *India* 68 F6
Tonkawa, *U.S.A.* 113 G6
Tonkin = Bac Phan, *Vietnam* 64 B5
Tonle Sap, *Cambodia* 64 F4
Tonnay-Charente, *France* 20 C3
Tonneins, *France* 20 D4
Tonnerre, *France* 19 E10
Tönning, *Germany* 24 A4
Tono, *Japan* 54 E10
Tonopah, *U.S.A.* 115 G5
Tonosí, *Panama* 120 E3
Tons →, *Haryana, India* 68 D7
Tons →, *Ut. P., India* 69 F10
Tønsberg, *Norway* 9 G14
Tonya, *Turkey* 73 B8
Toobanna, *Australia* 94 B4
Toodyay, *Australia* 93 F2
Tooele, *U.S.A.* 114 F7
Toompine, *Australia* 95 D3
Toora, *Australia* 95 F4
Toora-Khem, *Russia* 51 D10
Toowoomba, *Australia* 95 D5

Top Springs, Australia 92 C5
Topalu, Romania 43 F13
Topaz, U.S.A. 116 G7
Topeka, U.S.A. 112 F7
Topl'a →, Slovak Rep. 27 C14
Topley, Canada 104 C3
Toplica →, Serbia, Yug. 40 C5
Toplița, Romania 43 D10
Topocalma, Pta., Chile 126 C1
Topock, U.S.A. 117 L12
Topola, Serbia, Yug. 40 B4
Topolčani, Macedonia 40 E5
Topoľčany, Slovak Rep. 27 C11
Topolnitsa →, Bulgaria 41 D8
Topolobampo, Mexico 118 B3
Topoloveni, Romania 43 F10
Topolovgrad, Bulgaria 41 D10
Topolvățu Mare, Romania 42 E6
Toppenish, U.S.A. 114 C3
Topraisar, Romania 43 F13
Topusko, Croatia 29 C12
Torà, Spain 32 D6
Tora Kit, Sudan 81 E3
Toraka Vestale, Madag. 89 B7
Torata, Peru 124 G4
Torbalı, Turkey 39 C9
Torbat-e Heydārīyeh, Iran 71 C8
Torbat-e Jām, Iran 71 C9
Torbay, Canada 103 C9
Torbay □, U.K. 13 G4
Torbjörntorp, Sweden 11 F7
Tordesillas, Spain 34 D6
Töreboda, Sweden 11 F8
Torekov, Sweden 11 H6
Torellò, Spain 32 C7
Toreno, Spain 34 C4
Torfaen □, U.K. 13 F4
Torgau, Germany 24 D8
Torgelow, Germany 24 B10
Torhamn, Sweden 11 H9
Torhout, Belgium 17 C3
Tori, Ethiopia 81 F3
Tori-Shima, Japan 55 J10
Torigni-sur-Vire, France 18 C6
Torija, Spain 32 E1
Torin, Mexico 118 B2
Torino, Italy 28 C4
Torit, Sudan 81 G3
Torkamān, Iran 70 B5
Torkovichi, Russia 46 C6
Tormac, Romania 42 E6
Tormes →, Spain 34 D4
Tornado Mt., Canada 104 D6
Tornal'a, Slovak Rep. 27 C13
Torne älv →, Sweden 8 D21
Torneå = Tornio, Finland 8 D21
Torneträsk, Sweden 8 B18
Tornio, Finland 8 D21
Tornionjoki →, Finland 8 D21
Tornquist, Argentina 126 D3
Toro, Baleares, Spain 37 B11
Toro, Zamora, Spain 34 D5
Torö, Sweden 11 F11
Toro, Cerro del, Chile 126 B2
Toro Pk., U.S.A. 117 M10
Törökszentmiklós, Hungary 42 C5
Toronĩos Kólpos, Greece 40 F7
Toronto, Canada 102 D4
Toronto, U.S.A. 110 F4
Toropets, Russia 46 D6
Tororo, Uganda 86 B3
Toros Dağları, Turkey 70 B2
Torpa, India 69 H11
Torquay, Australia 95 F3
Torquay, U.K. 13 G4
Torquemada, Spain 34 C6
Torrance, U.S.A. 117 M8
Torrão, Portugal 35 G2
Torre Annunziata, Italy 31 B7
Torre de Moncorvo, Portugal 34 D3
Torre del Campo, Spain 35 H7
Torre del Greco, Italy 31 B7
Torre del Mar, Spain 35 J6
Torre-Pacheco, Spain 33 H4
Torre Péllice, Italy 28 D4
Torreblanca, Spain 32 E5
Torrecampo, Spain 35 G6
Torrecilla en Cameros, Spain 32 C2
Torredembarra, Spain 32 D6
Torredonjimeno, Spain 35 H7
Torrejón de Ardoz, Spain 34 E7
Torrejoncillo, Spain 34 F4
Torrelaguna, Spain 34 E7
Torrelavega, Spain 34 B6
Torremaggiore, Italy 29 G12
Torremolinos, Spain 35 J6
Torrens, L., Australia 95 E2
Torrens Cr. →, Australia 94 C4
Torrens Creek, Australia 94 C4
Torrent, Spain 33 F4
Torrenueva, Spain 35 G7
Torreón, Mexico 118 B4
Torreperogil, Spain 35 G7
Torres, Brazil 127 B5
Torres, Mexico 118 B2
Torres Novas, Portugal 35 F2
Torres Strait, Australia 96 H6
Torres Vedras, Portugal 35 F1
Torrevieja, Spain 33 H4
Torrey, U.S.A. 115 G8
Torridge →, U.K. 13 G3
Torridon, L., U.K. 14 D3
Torrijos, Spain 34 F6
Tørring, Denmark 11 J3
Torrington, Conn., U.S.A. 111 E11
Torrington, Wyo., U.S.A. 112 D2
Torroella de Montgrì, Spain 32 C8
Torrox, Spain 35 J7
Torsås, Sweden 11 H9
Torsby, Sweden 10 D6
Torshälla, Sweden 10 E10
Tórshavn, Færoe Is. 8 E9
Torslanda, Sweden 11 G5
Torsö, Sweden 11 F7
Tortola, Virgin Is. 121 C7
Tórtoles de Esgueva, Spain 34 D6
Tortolì, Italy 30 C2
Tortona, Italy 28 D5
Tortorici, Italy 31 D7
Tortosa, Spain 32 E5
Tortosa, C., Spain 32 E5
Tortosendo, Portugal 34 E3
Tortue, I. de la, Haiti 121 B5
Tortum, Turkey 73 B9
Ţorūd, Iran 71 C7
Torul, Turkey 73 B8
Toruń, Poland 45 E5
Tory I., Ireland 15 A3
Torysa →, Slovak Rep. 27 C14
Torzhok, Russia 46 D8
Torzym, Poland 45 F2
Tosa, Japan 55 H6
Tosa-Shimizu, Japan 55 H6
Tosa-Wan, Japan 55 H6
Toscana □, Italy 28 E8
Toscano, Arcipelago, Italy 28 F7
Toshkent, Uzbekistan 50 E7
Tosno, Russia 46 C6
Tossa de Mar, Spain 32 D7
Tösse, Sweden 11 F6
Tostado, Argentina 126 B3
Tostedt, Germany 24 B5
Tostón, Pta. de, Canary Is. 37 F5
Tosu, Japan 55 H5
Tosya, Turkey 72 B6
Toszek, Poland 45 H5
Totana, Spain 33 H3
Totebo, Sweden 11 G10
Toteng, Botswana 88 C3
Tôtes, France 18 C8
Tótkomlós, Hungary 42 D5
Totma, Russia 50 C5
Totnes, U.K. 13 G4
Totness, Surinam 125 B7
Toto, Nigeria 83 D6
Totonicapán, Guatemala 120 D1
Totten Glacier, Antarctica 5 C8
Tottenham, Australia 95 E4
Tottenham, Canada 110 B5
Tottori, Japan 55 G7
Tottori □, Japan 55 G7
Touaret, Niger 83 A6
Touba, Ivory C. 82 D3
Touba, Senegal 82 C1
Toubkal, Djebel, Morocco 78 B4
Toucy, France 19 E10
Tougan, Burkina Faso 82 C4
Touggourt, Algeria 78 B7
Tougouri, Burkina Faso 83 C4
Tougué, Guinea 82 C2
Toukoto, Mali 82 C3
Toul, France 19 D12
Toulepleu, Ivory C. 82 D3
Toulon, France 21 E9
Toulouse, France 20 E5
Toummo, Niger 79 D8
Toumodi, Ivory C. 82 D3
Tounan, Taiwan 59 F13
Toungo, Nigeria 83 D7
Toungoo, Burma 67 K20
Touques →, France 18 C7
Touraine, France 18 E7
Tourane = Da Nang, Vietnam 64 D7
Tourcoing, France 19 B10
Touriñán, C., Spain 34 B1
Tournai, Belgium 17 D3
Tournan-en-Brie, France 19 D9
Tournay, France 20 E4
Tournon-St-Martin, France 18 F7
Tournon-sur-Rhône, France 21 C8
Tournus, France 19 F11
Tours, France 18 E7
Tousidé, Pic, Chad 79 D9
Toussora, Mt., C.A.R. 84 C4
Touws →, S. Africa 88 E3
Touwsrivier, S. Africa 88 E3
Tovarkovskiy, Russia 46 F10
Tovuz, Azerbaijan 49 K7
Towada, Japan 54 D10
Towada-Ko, Japan 54 D10
Towanda, U.S.A. 111 E8
Towang, India 67 F17
Tower, U.S.A. 112 B8
Towerhill Cr. →, Australia 94 C3
Towner, U.S.A. 112 A4
Townsend, U.S.A. 114 C8
Townshend I., Australia 94 C5
Townsville, Australia 94 B4
Towson, U.S.A. 108 F7
Towuti, Danau, Indonesia 63 E6
Toya-Ko, Japan 54 C10
Toyama, Japan 55 F8
Toyama □, Japan 55 F8
Toyama-Wan, Japan 55 F8
Toyohashi, Japan 55 G8
Toyokawa, Japan 55 G8
Toyonaka, Japan 55 G7
Toyooka, Japan 55 G7
Toyota, Japan 55 G8
Tozeur, Tunisia 78 B7
Tqibuli, Georgia 49 J6
Tqvarcheli, Georgia 49 J5
Trá Li = Tralee, Ireland 15 D2
Tra On, Vietnam 65 H5
Trabancos →, Spain 34 D5
Traben-Trarbach, Germany 25 F3
Trabzon, Turkey 73 B8
Tracadie, Canada 103 C7
Tracy, Calif., U.S.A. 116 H5
Tracy, Minn., U.S.A. 112 C7
Tradate, Italy 28 C5
Trade Town, Liberia 82 D3
Trafalgar, C., Spain 35 J4
Traian, Brăila, Romania 43 E12
Traian, Tulcea, Romania 43 E13
Trail, Canada 104 D5
Trainor L., Canada 104 A4
Trákhonas, Cyprus 36 D12
Tralee, Ireland 15 D2
Tralee B., Ireland 15 D2
Tramore, Ireland 15 D4
Tramore B., Ireland 15 D4
Tran Ninh, Cao Nguyen, Laos 64 C4
Tranås, Sweden 11 F8
Tranbjerg, Denmark 11 H4
Trancas, Argentina 126 B2
Trancoso, Portugal 34 E3
Tranebjerg, Denmark 11 J4
Tranemo, Sweden 11 G7
Trang, Thailand 65 J2
Trangahy, Madag. 89 B7
Trangan, Indonesia 63 F8
Trangie, Australia 95 E4
Trångsviken, Sweden 10 A7
Trani, Italy 31 A9
Tranoroa, Madag. 89 C8
Tranqueras, Uruguay 127 C4
Transantarctic Mts., Antarctica 5 E12
Transilvania, Romania 43 D9
Transilvanian Alps = Carpații Meridionali, Romania 43 E9
Transtrand, Sweden 10 C7
Transtrandsfjällen, Sweden 10 C6
Transvaal, S. Africa 85 K5
Transylvania = Transilvania, Romania 43 D9
Trápani, Italy 30 D5
Trapper Pk., U.S.A. 114 D6
Traralgon, Australia 95 F4
Trarza, Mauritania 82 B2
Trasacco, Italy 29 G10
Trăscău, Munții, Romania 43 D8
Trasimeno, L., Italy 29 E9
Träslövsläge, Sweden 11 G6
Trasvase Tajo-Segura, Canal de, Spain 32 E2
Trat, Thailand 65 F4
Tratani →, Pakistan 68 E3
Traun, Austria 26 C7
Traunreut, Germany 25 H8
Traunsee, Austria 26 D6
Traunstein, Germany 25 H8
Travellers L., Australia 95 E3
Travemünde, Germany 24 B6
Travers, Mt., N.Z. 91 K4
Traverse City, U.S.A. 108 C3
Travis, L., U.S.A. 113 K5
Travnik, Bos.-H. 42 F2
Trbovlje, Slovenia 29 B12
Trébbia →, Italy 28 C6
Trebel →, Germany 24 B9
Trébeurden, France 18 D3
Třebíč, Czech Rep. 26 B8
Trebinje, Bos.-H. 40 D2
Trebisacce, Italy 31 C9
Trebišnjica →, Bos.-H. 40 D2
Trebišov, Slovak Rep. 27 C14
Trebižat →, Bos.-H. 29 E14
Trebnje, Slovenia 29 C12
Třeboň, Czech Rep. 26 B7
Trebonne, Australia 94 B4
Trebujena, Spain 35 J4
Trecate, Italy 28 C5
Tregaron, U.K. 13 E4
Tregnago, Italy 29 C8
Tregrosse Is., Australia 94 B5
Tréguier, France 18 D3
Trégunc, France 18 E3
Treherne, Canada 105 D9
Tréia, Italy 29 E10
Treignac, France 20 C5
Treinta y Tres, Uruguay 127 C5
Treis-karden, Germany 25 E3
Treklyano, Bulgaria 40 D6
Trelawney, Zimbabwe 89 B5
Trélazé, France 18 E6
Trelew, Argentina 128 E3
Trélissac, France 20 C4
Trelleborg, Sweden 11 J7
Tremadog Bay, U.K. 12 E3
Trémiti, Italy 29 F12
Tremonton, U.S.A. 114 F7
Tremp, Spain 32 C5
Trenche →, Canada 102 C5
Trenčiansky □, Slovak Rep. 27 C11
Trenčín, Slovak Rep. 27 C11
Trenggalek, Indonesia 63 H14
Trenque Lauquen, Argentina 126 D3
Trent →, Canada 110 B7
Trent →, U.K. 12 D7
Trentino-Alto Adige □, Italy 29 B8
Trento, Italy 28 B8
Trenton, Canada 102 D4
Trenton, Mo., U.S.A. 112 E8
Trenton, N.J., U.S.A. 111 F10
Trenton, Nebr., U.S.A. 112 E4
Trepassey, Canada 103 C9
Trepuzzi, Italy 31 B11
Tres Arroyos, Argentina 126 D3
Três Corações, Brazil 127 A6
Três Lagoas, Brazil 125 H8
Tres Lomas, Argentina 126 D3
Tres Marías, Islas, Mexico 118 C3
Tres Montes, C., Chile 128 F1
Tres Pinos, U.S.A. 116 J5
Três Pontas, Brazil 127 A6
Tres Puentes, Chile 126 B1
Tres Puntas, C., Argentina 128 F3
Três Rios, Brazil 127 A7
Tres Valles, Mexico 119 D5
Tresco, U.K. 13 H1
Treska →, Macedonia 40 E5
Treskavica, Bos.-H. 42 G3
Trespaderne, Spain 34 C7
Trets, France 21 E9
Treuchtlingen, Germany 25 G6
Treuenbrietzen, Germany 24 C8
Trevi, Italy 29 F9
Trevíglio, Italy 28 C6
Trevinca, Peña, Spain 34 C4
Treviso, Italy 29 C9
Trévoux, France 21 C8
Trgovište, Serbia, Yug. 40 D6
Triabunna, Australia 94 G4
Triánda, Greece 36 C10
Triangle, Zimbabwe 89 C5
Triaucourt-en-Argonne, France 19 D12
Tribsees, Germany 24 A8
Tribulation, C., Australia 94 B4
Tribune, U.S.A. 112 F4
Tricárico, Italy 31 B9
Tricase, Italy 31 C11
Trichinopoly = Tiruchchirappalli, India 66 P11
Trichur, India 66 P10
Trida, Australia 95 E4
Trier, Germany 25 F2
Trieste, Italy 29 C10
Trieste, G. di, Italy 29 C10
Trieux →, France 18 D3
Triggiano, Italy 31 A9
Triglav, Slovenia 29 B10
Trigno →, Italy 29 F11
Trigueros, Spain 35 H4
Tríkeri, Greece 38 B5
Trikhonis, Límni, Greece 38 C3
Tríkkala, Greece 38 B3
Tríkkala □, Greece 38 B3
Trikomo, Cyprus 36 D12
Trikora, Puncak, Indonesia 63 E9
Trilj, Croatia 29 E13
Trillo, Spain 32 E2
Trim, Ireland 15 C5
Trincomalee, Sri Lanka 66 Q12
Trindade, Brazil 125 G9
Trindade, I., Atl. Oc. 2 F8
Třinec, Czech Rep. 27 B11
Trinidad, Bolivia 124 F6
Trinidad, Cuba 120 B4
Trinidad, Uruguay 126 C4
Trinidad, U.S.A. 113 G2
Trinidad, W. Indies 121 D7
Trinidad →, Mexico 119 D5
Trinidad & Tobago ■, W. Indies 121 D7
Trinitápoli, Italy 31 A9
Trinity, Canada 103 C9
Trinity, U.S.A. 113 K7
Trinity →, Calif., U.S.A. 114 F2
Trinity →, Tex., U.S.A. 113 L7
Trinity B., Canada 103 C9
Trinity Is., U.S.A. 100 C4
Trinity Range, U.S.A. 114 F4
Trinkitat, Sudan 80 D4
Trino, Italy 28 C5
Trinway, U.S.A. 110 F2
Trionto, C., Italy 31 C9
Triora, Italy 28 D4
Tripoli = Tarābulus, Lebanon 75 A4
Tripoli = Tarābulus, Libya 79 B8
Trípolis, Greece 38 D4
Tripolitania, Libya 76 C5
Tripolitania, N. Afr. 79 B8
Tripura □, India 67 H18
Tripylos, Cyprus 36 E11
Trischen, Germany 24 A4
Tristan da Cunha, Atl. Oc. 77 K2
Trisul, India 69 D8
Trivandrum, India 66 Q10
Trivento, Italy 29 G11
Trnava, Slovak Rep. 27 C10
Trnavský □, Slovak Rep. 27 C10
Troarn, France 18 C6
Trochu, Canada 104 C6
Trodely I., Canada 102 B4
Troezen, Greece 38 D5
Trogir, Croatia 29 E13
Troglav, Croatia 29 E13
Tróia, Italy 31 A8
Troilus, L., Canada 102 B5
Troina, Italy 31 E7
Trois-Pistoles, Canada 103 C6
Trois-Rivières, Canada 102 C5
Troisdorf, Germany 24 E3
Troitsk, Russia 50 D7
Troitsko Pechorsk, Russia 50 C6
Trölladyngja, Iceland 8 D5
Trollhättan, Sweden 11 F6
Trollheimen, Norway 8 E13
Trombetas →, Brazil 125 D7
Tromsø, Norway 8 B18
Trona, U.S.A. 117 K9
Tronador, Mte., Argentina 128 E2
Trøndelag, Norway 8 D14
Trondheim, Norway 8 E14
Trondheimsfjorden, Norway 8 E14
Trönninge, Sweden 11 H6
Tronto →, Italy 29 F10
Troodos, Cyprus 36 E11
Troon, U.K. 14 F4
Tropea, Italy 31 D8
Tropic, U.S.A. 115 H7
Tropoja, Albania 40 D4
Trosa, Sweden 11 F11
Trostan, U.K. 15 A5
Trostberg, Germany 25 G8
Trostyanets, Ukraine 47 G8
Trout →, Canada 104 A5
Trout L., N.W.T., Canada 104 A4
Trout L., Ont., Canada 105 C10
Trout Lake, Canada 104 B6
Trout Lake, U.S.A. 116 E5
Trout River, Canada 103 C8
Trout Run, U.S.A. 110 E7
Trouville-sur-Mer, France 18 C7
Trowbridge, U.K. 13 F5
Troy, Turkey 39 B8
Troy, Ala., U.S.A. 109 K3
Troy, Kans., U.S.A. 112 F7
Troy, Mo., U.S.A. 112 F9
Troy, Mont., U.S.A. 114 B6
Troy, N.Y., U.S.A. 111 D11
Troy, Ohio, U.S.A. 108 E3
Troy, Pa., U.S.A. 111 E8
Troyan, Bulgaria 41 D8
Troyes, France 19 D11
Trpanj, Croatia 29 E14
Trstenik, Serbia, Yug. 40 C5
Trubchevsk, Russia 47 F7
Truchas Peak, U.S.A. 113 H2
Trucial States = United Arab Emirates ■, Asia 71 F7
Truckee, U.S.A. 116 F6
Trudfront, Russia 49 H8
Trudovoye, Russia 54 C6
Trujillo, Honduras 120 C2
Trujillo, Peru 124 E3
Trujillo, Spain 35 F5
Trujillo, U.S.A. 113 H2
Trujillo, Venezuela 124 B4
Truk, Micronesia 96 G7
Trumann, U.S.A. 113 H9
Trumansburg, U.S.A. 111 D8
Trumbull, Mt., U.S.A. 115 H7
Trŭn, Bulgaria 40 D6
Trun, France 18 D7
Trundle, Australia 95 E4
Trung-Phan = Annam, Vietnam 64 E7
Truro, Canada 103 C7
Truro, U.K. 13 G2
Truskavets, Ukraine 47 H2
Trŭstenik, Bulgaria 41 C8
Trustrup, Denmark 11 H4
Trutch, Canada 104 B4
Truth or Consequences, U.S.A. 115 K10
Trutnov, Czech Rep. 26 A8
Truxton, U.S.A. 111 D8
Truyère →, France 20 D6
Tryavna, Bulgaria 41 D9
Tryonville, U.S.A. 110 E5
Trzcianka, Poland 45 E3
Trzciel, Poland 45 F2
Trzcińsko Zdrój, Poland 45 F1
Trzebiatów, Poland 44 D2
Trzebiez, Poland 44 E1
Trzebnica, Poland 45 G4
Trzemeszno, Poland 45 F4
Tržič, Slovenia 29 B11
Tsagan Aman, Russia 49 G8
Tsamandás, Greece 38 B2
Tsandi, Namibia 88 B1
Tsaratanana, Madag. 89 B8
Tsaratanana, Mt. de, Madag. 89 A8
Tsarevo = Michurin, Bulgaria 41 D11
Tsarevo, Bulgaria 41 D9
Tsaritsáni, Greece 38 B4
Tsau, Botswana 88 C3
Tsebrykove, Ukraine 47 J6
Tselinograd = Astana, Kazakstan 50 D8
Tses, Namibia 88 D2
Tsetserleg, Mongolia 60 B5
Tsévié, Togo 83 D5
Tshabong, Botswana 88 D3
Tshane, Botswana 88 C3
Tshela, Dem. Rep. of the Congo 84 E2
Tshesebe, Botswana 89 C4
Tshibeke, Dem. Rep. of the Congo 86 C2
Tshibinda, Dem. Rep. of the Congo 86 C2
Tshikapa, Dem. Rep. of the Congo 84 F4
Tshilenge, Dem. Rep. of the Congo 86 D1
Tshinsenda, Dem. Rep. of the Congo 87 E2
Tshofa, Dem. Rep. of the Congo 86 D2
Tshwane, Botswana 88 C3
Tsigara, Botswana 88 C4
Tsihombe, Madag. 89 D8
Tsiigehtchic, Canada 100 B6
Tsimlyansk, Russia 49 G6
Tsimlyansk Res. = Tsimlyanskoye Vdkhr., Russia 49 F6
Tsimlyanskoye Vdkhr., Russia 49 F6
Tsinan = Jinan, China 56 F9
Tsineng, S. Africa 88 D3
Tsínga, Greece 41 E8
Tsinghai = Qinghai □, China 60 C4
Tsingtao = Qingdao, China 57 F11
Tsinjoarivo, Madag. 89 B8
Tsinjomitondraka, Madag. 89 B8
Tsiroanomandidy, Madag. 89 B8
Tsiteli-Tsqaro, Georgia 49 K8
Tsitondroina, Madag. 89 C8
Tsivilsk, Russia 48 C8
Tsivory, Madag. 89 C8
Tskhinvali, Georgia 49 J7
Tsna →, Russia 48 C6
Tsnori, Georgia 49 K7
Tso Moriri, L., India 69 C8

Tsobis, *Namibia* 88 B2
Tsodilo Hill, *Botswana* 88 B3
Tsogttsetsiy = Baruunsuu, *Mongolia* 56 C3
Tsolo, *S. Africa* 89 E4
Tsomo, *S. Africa* 89 E4
Tsu, *Japan* 55 G8
Tsu L., *Canada* 104 A6
Tsuchiura, *Japan* 55 F10
Tsuen Wan, *H.K.* 59 F10
Tsugaru-Kaikyō, *Japan* 54 D10
Tsumeb, *Namibia* 88 B2
Tsumis, *Namibia* 88 C2
Tsuruga, *Japan* 55 G8
Tsurugi-San, *Japan* 55 H7
Tsuruoka, *Japan* 54 E9
Tsushima, *Gifu, Japan* 55 G8
Tsushima, *Nagasaki, Japan* 55 G4
Tsuyama, *Japan* 55 G7
Tsvetkovo, *Ukraine* 47 H6
Tsyelyakhany, *Belarus* 47 F3
Tua →, *Portugal* 34 D3
Tual, *Indonesia* 63 F8
Tuam, *Ireland* 15 C3
Tuamotu Arch. = Tuamotu Is., *Pac. Oc.* 97 J13
Tuamotu Is., *Pac. Oc.* 97 J13
Tuamotu Ridge, *Pac. Oc.* 97 K14
Tuanfeng, *China* 59 B10
Tuanxi, *China* 58 D6
Tuao, *Phil.* 61 C4
Tuapse, *Russia* 49 H4
Tuatapere, *N.Z.* 91 M1
Tuba City, *U.S.A.* 115 H8
Tuban, *Indonesia* 63 G15
Tubani, *Botswana* 88 C3
Tubarão, *Brazil* 127 B6
Tūbās, *West Bank* 75 C4
Tubas →, *Namibia* 88 C2
Tübingen, *Germany* 25 G5
Tubruq, *Libya* 79 B10
Tubuai Is., *Pac. Oc.* 97 K13
Tuc Trung, *Vietnam* 65 G6
Tucacas, *Venezuela* 124 A5
T'uch'ang, *Taiwan* 59 E13
Tuchodi →, *Canada* 104 B4
Tuchola, *Poland* 44 E4
Tuchów, *Poland* 45 J8
Tuckanarra, *Australia* 93 E2
Tucson, *U.S.A.* 115 K8
Tucumán □, *Argentina* 126 B2
Tucumcari, *U.S.A.* 113 H3
Tucupita, *Venezuela* 124 B6
Tucuruí, *Brazil* 125 D9
Tucuruí, Reprêsa de, *Brazil* 125 D9
Tuczno, *Poland* 45 E3
Tudela, *Spain* 32 C3
Tudmur, *Syria* 70 C3
Tudor, L., *Canada* 103 A6
Tudora, *Romania* 43 C11
Tuella →, *Portugal* 34 D3
Tugela →, *S. Africa* 89 D5
Tuguegarao, *Phil.* 61 C4
Tugur, *Russia* 51 D14
Tui, *Spain* 34 C2
Tuineje, *Canary Is.* 37 F5
Tukangbesi, Kepulauan, *Indonesia* 63 F6
Tukarak I., *Canada* 102 A4
Tukayyid, *Iraq* 70 D5
Tûkh, *Egypt* 80 H7
Tukobo, *Ghana* 82 D4
Tuktoyaktuk, *Canada* 100 B6
Tukums, *Latvia* 9 H20
Tukums □, *Latvia* 44 B10
Tukuyu, *Tanzania* 87 D3
Tula, *Hidalgo, Mexico* 119 C5
Tula, *Tamaulipas, Mexico* 119 C5
Tula, *Nigeria* 83 D7
Tula, *Russia* 46 E9
Tulancingo, *Mexico* 119 C5
Tulare, *Serbia, Yug.* 40 D5
Tulare, *U.S.A.* 116 J7
Tulare Lake Bed, *U.S.A.* 116 K7
Tularosa, *U.S.A.* 115 K10
Tulbagh, *S. Africa* 88 E2
Tulcán, *Ecuador* 124 C3
Tulcea, *Romania* 43 E13
Tulcea □, *Romania* 43 E13
Tulchyn, *Ukraine* 47 H5
Tūleh, *Iran* 71 C7
Tulemalu L., *Canada* 105 A9
Tulgheş, *Romania* 43 D10
Tuli, *Zimbabwe* 87 G2
Tulia, *U.S.A.* 113 H4
Tuliszków, *Poland* 45 F5
Tulita, *Canada* 100 B7
Ṭūlkarm, *West Bank* 75 C4
Tulla, *Ireland* 15 D3
Tullahoma, *U.S.A.* 109 H2
Tullamore, *Australia* 95 E4
Tullamore, *Ireland* 15 C4
Tulle, *France* 20 C5
Tulln, *Austria* 26 C9
Tullow, *Ireland* 15 D5
Tullus, *Sudan* 81 E1
Tully, *Australia* 94 B4
Tully, *U.S.A.* 111 D8
Tulnici, *Romania* 43 E11
Tulovo, *Bulgaria* 41 D9
Tulsa, *U.S.A.* 113 G7
Tulsequah, *Canada* 104 B2
Tulu Milki, *Ethiopia* 81 F4
Tulu Welel, *Ethiopia* 81 F3
Tulua, *Colombia* 124 C3
Tulucești, *Romania* 43 E13
Tulun, *Russia* 51 D11
Tulungagung, *Indonesia* 63 H14
Tuma, *Russia* 46 E11
Tuma →, *Nic.* 120 D3
Tumaco, *Colombia* 124 C3
Tumatumari, *Guyana* 124 B7
Tumba, *Sweden* 10 E11
Tumba, L., *Dem. Rep. of the Congo* 84 E3
Tumbarumba, *Australia* 95 F4
Tumbaya, *Argentina* 126 A2
Tumbes, *Peru* 124 D2
Tumbur, *Sudan* 81 G3
Tumbwe, *Dem. Rep. of the Congo* 87 E2
Tumby Bay, *Australia* 95 E2
Tumd Youqi, *China* 56 D6
Tumen, *China* 57 C15
Tumen Jiang →, *China* 57 C16
Tumeremo, *Venezuela* 124 B6
Tumkur, *India* 66 N10
Tump, *Pakistan* 66 F3
Tumpat, *Malaysia* 65 J4
Tumu, *Ghana* 82 C4
Tumucumaque, Serra, *Brazil* 122 C5
Tumut, *Australia* 95 F4
Tumwater, *U.S.A.* 116 C4
Tuna, *India* 68 H4
Tunadal, *Sweden* 10 B11
Tunas de Zaza, *Cuba* 120 B4
Tunbridge Wells = Royal Tunbridge Wells, *U.K.* 13 F8
Tunçbilek, *Turkey* 39 B11
Tunceli, *Turkey* 73 C8
Tuncurry-Forster, *Australia* 95 E5
Tundla, *India* 68 F8
Tundubai, *Sudan* 80 D2
Tunduru, *Tanzania* 87 E4
Tundzha →, *Bulgaria* 41 E10
Tunga Pass, *India* 67 E19
Tungabhadra →, *India* 66 M11
Tungaru, *Sudan* 81 E3
Tungla, *Nic.* 120 D3
Tungsha Tao, *Taiwan* 59 G11
Tungshih, *Taiwan* 59 E13
Tungsten, *Canada* 104 A3
Tunguska, Nizhnyaya →, *Russia* 51 C9
Tunguska, Podkamennaya →, *Russia* 51 C10
Tunica, *U.S.A.* 113 H9
Tunis, *Tunisia* 79 A8
Tunisia ■, *Africa* 79 A7
Tunja, *Colombia* 124 B4
Tunkhannock, *U.S.A.* 111 E9
Tunliu, *China* 56 F7
Tunnsjøen, *Norway* 8 D15
Tunø, *Denmark* 11 J4
Tunungayualok I., *Canada* 103 A7
Tunuyán, *Argentina* 126 C2
Tunuyán →, *Argentina* 126 C2
Tuo Jiang →, *China* 58 C5
Tuolumne, *U.S.A.* 116 H6
Tuolumne →, *U.S.A.* 116 H5
Tūp Āghāj, *Iran* 70 B5
Tupã, *Brazil* 127 A5
Tupelo, *U.S.A.* 109 H1
Tupik, *Russia* 46 E7
Tupinambaranas, *Brazil* 124 D7
Tupiza, *Bolivia* 126 A2
Tupižnica, *Serbia, Yug.* 40 C6
Tupman, *U.S.A.* 117 K7
Tupper, *Canada* 104 B4
Tupper Lake, *U.S.A.* 111 B10
Tupungato, Cerro, *S. Amer.* 126 C2
Tuquan, *China* 57 B11
Túquerres, *Colombia* 124 C3
Tura, *Russia* 51 C11
Turabah, *Si. Arabia* 70 D4
Turabah, *Si. Arabia* 80 C5
Tūrān, *Iran* 71 C8
Turan, *Russia* 51 D10
Ṭurayf, *Si. Arabia* 70 D3
Turbacz, *Poland* 45 J7
Turbe, *Bos.-H.* 42 F2
Turčianske Teplice, *Slovak Rep.* 27 C11
Turcoaia, *Romania* 43 E13
Turda, *Romania* 43 D8
Turek, *Poland* 45 F5
Turen, *Venezuela* 124 B5
Turfan = Turpan, *China* 60 B3
Turfan Depression = Turpan Hami, *China* 52 E12
Turgeon →, *Canada* 102 C4
Tŭrgovishte, *Bulgaria* 41 C10
Turgut, *Turkey* 39 D10
Turgutlu, *Turkey* 39 C9
Turgwe →, *Zimbabwe* 89 C5
Turhal, *Turkey* 72 B7
Turia →, *Spain* 33 F4
Turiaçu, *Brazil* 125 D9
Turiaçu →, *Brazil* 125 D9
Turiec →, *Slovak Rep.* 27 B11
Turin = Torino, *Italy* 28 C4
Turkana, L., *Africa* 86 B4
Türkeli, *Turkey* 41 F11
Turkestan = Türkistan, *Kazakstan* 50 E7
Túrkeve, *Hungary* 42 C5
Turkey ■, *Eurasia* 72 C7
Turkey Creek, *Australia* 92 C4
Turki, *Russia* 48 D6
Türkistan, *Kazakstan* 50 E7
Türkmenbashi, *Turkmenistan* 50 E6
Turkmenistan ■, *Asia* 50 F6
Türkmenli, *Turkey* 39 B8
Türkoğlu, *Turkey* 72 D7
Turks & Caicos Is. ■, *W. Indies* 121 B5
Turks Island Passage, *W. Indies* 121 B5
Turku, *Finland* 9 F20
Turkwel →, *Kenya* 86 B4
Turlock, *U.S.A.* 116 H6
Turnagain →, *Canada* 104 B3
Turnagain, C., *N.Z.* 91 J6
Turneffe Is., *Belize* 119 D7
Turner, *U.S.A.* 114 B9
Turner Pt., *Australia* 94 A1
Turner Valley, *Canada* 104 C6
Turners Falls, *U.S.A.* 111 D12
Turnhout, *Belgium* 17 C4
Türnitz, *Austria* 26 D8
Turnor L., *Canada* 105 B7
Turnov, *Czech Rep.* 26 A8
Tŭrnovo = Veliko Tŭrnovo, *Bulgaria* 41 C9
Turnu Măgurele, *Romania* 43 G9
Turnu Roşu, P., *Romania* 43 E9
Turobin, *Poland* 45 H9
Turpan, *China* 60 B3
Turpan Hami, *China* 52 E12
Turrës, Kalaja e, *Albania* 40 E3
Turriff, *U.K.* 14 D6
Tursāq, *Iraq* 70 C5
Tursi, *Italy* 31 B9
Turtle Head I., *Australia* 94 A3
Turtle Is., *S. Leone* 82 D2
Turtle L., *Canada* 105 C7
Turtle Lake, *U.S.A.* 112 B4
Turtleford, *Canada* 105 C7
Turukhansk, *Russia* 51 C9
Turzovka, *Slovak Rep.* 27 B11
Tuscaloosa, *U.S.A.* 109 J2
Tuscánia, *Italy* 29 F8
Tuscany = Toscana □, *Italy* 28 E8
Tuscarawas →, *U.S.A.* 110 F3
Tuscarora Mt., *U.S.A.* 110 F7
Tuscola, *Ill., U.S.A.* 108 F1
Tuscola, *Tex., U.S.A.* 113 J5
Tuscumbia, *U.S.A.* 109 H2
Tuskegee, *U.S.A.* 109 J3
Tustin, *U.S.A.* 117 M9
Tuszyn, *Poland* 45 G6
Tutak, *Turkey* 73 C10
Tutayev, *Russia* 46 D10
Tuticorin, *India* 66 Q11
Tutin, *Serbia, Yug.* 40 D4
Tutóia, *Brazil* 125 D10
Tutong, *Brunei* 62 D4
Tutova →, *Romania* 43 D12
Tutrakan, *Bulgaria* 41 B10
Tuttle Creek L., *U.S.A.* 112 F6
Tuttlingen, *Germany* 25 H4
Tutuala, *Indonesia* 63 F7
Tutuila, *Amer. Samoa* 91 B13
Tutume, *Botswana* 85 J5
Tutun, *Egypt* 80 J7
Tututepec, *Mexico* 119 D5
Tuva □, *Russia* 51 D10
Tuvalu ■, *Pac. Oc.* 96 H9
Tuxer Alpen, *Austria* 26 D4
Tuxpan, *Mexico* 119 C5
Tuxtla Gutiérrez, *Mexico* 119 D6
Tuy = Tui, *Spain* 34 C2
Tuy An, *Vietnam* 64 F7
Tuy Duc, *Vietnam* 65 F6
Tuy Hoa, *Vietnam* 64 F7
Tuy Phong, *Vietnam* 65 G7
Tuya L., *Canada* 104 B2
Tuyen Hoa, *Vietnam* 64 D6
Tuyen Quang, *Vietnam* 58 G5
Tūysarkān, *Iran* 71 C6
Tuz Gölü, *Turkey* 72 C5
Ṭūz Khurmātū, *Iraq* 70 C5
Tuzi, *Montenegro, Yug.* 40 D3
Tuzla, *Bos.-H.* 42 F3
Tuzlov →, *Russia* 47 J10
Tuzluca, *Turkey* 73 B10
Tvååker, *Sweden* 11 G6
Tvardiţa, *Moldova* 43 D13
Tver, *Russia* 46 D8
Tvrdošin, *Slovak Rep.* 27 B12
Tvrdošovce, *Slovak Rep.* 27 C11
Tvŭrditsa, *Bulgaria* 41 D9
Twain, *U.S.A.* 116 E5
Twain Harte, *U.S.A.* 116 G6
Twardogóra, *Poland* 45 G4
Tweed, *Canada* 110 B7
Tweed →, *U.K.* 14 F6
Tweed Heads, *Australia* 95 D5
Tweedsmuir Prov. Park, *Canada* 104 C3
Twentynine Palms, *U.S.A.* 117 L10
Twillingate, *Canada* 103 C9
Twin Bridges, *U.S.A.* 114 D7
Twin Falls, *Canada* 103 B7
Twin Falls, *U.S.A.* 114 E6
Twin Valley, *U.S.A.* 112 B6
Twinsburg, *U.S.A.* 110 E3
Twistringen, *Germany* 24 C4
Twitchell Reservoir, *U.S.A.* 117 L6
Two Harbors, *U.S.A.* 112 B9
Two Hills, *Canada* 104 C6
Two Rivers, *U.S.A.* 108 C2
Two Rocks, *Australia* 93 F2
Twofold B., *Australia* 95 F4
Tyachiv, *Ukraine* 47 H2
Tychy, *Poland* 45 H5
Tyczyn, *Poland* 45 J9
Tykocin, *Poland* 45 E9
Tyler, *Minn., U.S.A.* 112 C6
Tyler, *Tex., U.S.A.* 113 J7
Tyligul →, *Ukraine* 47 J6
Týn nad Vltavou, *Czech Rep.* 26 B7
Tynda, *Russia* 51 D13
Tyndall, *U.S.A.* 112 D6
Tyne →, *U.K.* 12 C6
Tyne & Wear □, *U.K.* 12 B6
Týnec nad Sázavou, *Czech Rep.* 26 B7
Tynemouth, *U.K.* 12 B6
Tyre = Sūr, *Lebanon* 75 B4
Tyrifjorden, *Norway* 9 F14
Tyringe, *Sweden* 11 H7
Tyrnyauz, *Russia* 49 J6
Tyrol = Tirol □, *Austria* 26 D3
Tyrone, *U.S.A.* 110 F6
Tyrone □, *U.K.* 15 B4
Tyrrell →, *Australia* 95 F3
Tyrrell, L., *Australia* 95 F3
Tyrrell L., *Canada* 105 A7
Tyrrhenian Sea, *Medit. S.* 6 G8
Tysfjorden, *Norway* 8 B17
Tystberga, *Sweden* 11 F11
Tytuvėnai, *Lithuania* 44 C10
Tyub Karagan, Mys, *Kazakstan* 49 H10
Tyuleni, Ostrova, *Kazakstan* 49 H10
Tyuleniy, *Russia* 49 H8
Tyuleniy, Mys, *Azerbaijan* 49 K10
Tyumen, *Russia* 50 D7
Tywi →, *U.K.* 13 F3
Tywyn, *U.K.* 13 E3
Tzaneen, *S. Africa* 89 C5
Tzermiádhes, *Greece* 36 D7
Tzoumérka, Óros, *Greece* 38 B3
Tzukong = Zigong, *China* 58 C5

U

U Taphao, *Thailand* 64 F3
U.S.A. = United States of America ■, *N. Amer.* 106 C7
Uatumã →, *Brazil* 124 D7
Uaupés, *Brazil* 124 D5
Uaupés →, *Brazil* 124 C5
Uaxactún, *Guatemala* 120 C2
Ub, *Serbia, Yug.* 40 B4
Ubá, *Brazil* 127 A7
Uba, *Nigeria* 83 C7
Ubaitaba, *Brazil* 125 F11
Ubangi = Oubangi →, *Dem. Rep. of the Congo* 84 E3
Ubauro, *Pakistan* 68 E3
Ubaye →, *France* 21 D10
Ubayyiḍ, W. al →, *Iraq* 70 C4
Ube, *Japan* 55 H5
Úbeda, *Spain* 35 G7
Uberaba, *Brazil* 125 G9
Uberlândia, *Brazil* 125 G9
Überlingen, *Germany* 25 H5
Ubiaja, *Nigeria* 83 D6
Ubolratna Res., *Thailand* 64 D4
Ubombo, *S. Africa* 89 D5
Ubon Ratchathani, *Thailand* 64 E5
Ubondo, *Dem. Rep. of the Congo* 86 C2
Ubort →, *Belarus* 47 F5
Ubrique, *Spain* 35 J5
Ubundu, *Dem. Rep. of the Congo* 86 C2
Ucayali →, *Peru* 122 D3
Uchab, *Namibia* 88 B2
Uchiura-Wan, *Japan* 54 C10
Uchquduq, *Uzbekistan* 50 E7
Uchte, *Germany* 24 C4
Uchur →, *Russia* 51 D14
Uckermark, *Germany* 24 B9
Ucluelet, *Canada* 104 D3
Uda →, *Russia* 51 D14
Udagamandalam, *India* 66 P10
Udainagar, *India* 68 H7
Udaipur, *India* 68 G5
Udaipur Garhi, *Nepal* 69 F12
Udala, *India* 69 J12
Udbina, *Croatia* 29 D12
Uddeholm, *Sweden* 10 D7
Uddevalla, *Sweden* 11 F5
Uddjaur, *Sweden* 8 D17
Uden, *Neths.* 17 C5
Udgir, *India* 66 K10
Udhampur, *India* 69 C6
Udi, *Nigeria* 83 D6
Údine, *Italy* 29 B10
Udmurtia □, *Russia* 50 D6
Udon Thani, *Thailand* 64 D4
Udupi, *India* 66 N9
Udvoy Balkan, *Bulgaria* 41 D10
Udzungwa Range, *Tanzania* 87 D4
Ueckermünde, *Germany* 24 B10
Ueda, *Japan* 55 F9
Uedineniya, Os., *Russia* 4 B12
Uele →, *Dem. Rep. of the Congo* 84 D4
Uelen, *Russia* 51 C19
Uelzen, *Germany* 24 C6
Uetersen, *Germany* 24 B5
Uetze, *Germany* 24 C6
Ufa, *Russia* 50 D6
Uffenheim, *Germany* 25 F6
Ugab →, *Namibia* 88 C1
Ugalla →, *Tanzania* 86 D3
Uganda ■, *Africa* 86 B3
Ugento, *Italy* 31 C11
Ugep, *Nigeria* 83 D6
Ughelli, *Nigeria* 83 D6
Ugie, *S. Africa* 89 E4
Ugíjar, *Spain* 35 J7
Ugine, *France* 21 C10
Uglegorsk, *Russia* 51 E15
Uglich, *Russia* 46 D10
Ugljan, *Croatia* 29 D12
Ugljane, *Croatia* 29 E13
Ugra →, *Russia* 46 E9
Uğurchin, *Bulgaria* 41 C8
Uh →, *Slovak Rep.* 27 C15
Uherské Hradiště, *Czech Rep.* 27 B10
Uherský Brod, *Czech Rep.* 27 B10
Úhlava →, *Czech Rep.* 26 B6
Uhlenhorst, *Namibia* 88 C2
Uhrichsville, *U.S.A.* 110 F3
Uibhist a Deas = South Uist, *U.K.* 14 D1
Uibhist a Tuath = North Uist, *U.K.* 14 D1
Uig, *U.K.* 14 D2
Uíge, *Angola* 84 F2
Uijŏngbu, *S. Korea* 57 F14
Ŭiju, *N. Korea* 57 D13
Uinta Mts., *U.S.A.* 114 F8
Uis, *Namibia* 88 B2
Uitenhage, *S. Africa* 88 E4
Uithuizen, *Neths.* 17 A6
Ujazd, *Poland* 45 H5
Újfehértó, *Hungary* 42 C6
Ujh →, *India* 68 C6
Ujhani, *India* 69 F8
Uji-guntō, *Japan* 55 J4
Ujjain, *India* 68 H6
Ujście, *Poland* 45 E3
Újszász, *Hungary* 42 C5
Ujung Pandang, *Indonesia* 63 F5
Uka, *Russia* 51 D17
Ukara I., *Tanzania* 86 C3
Uke-Shima, *Japan* 55 K4
Ukerewe I., *Tanzania* 86 C3
Ukholovo, *Russia* 48 D5
Ukhrul, *India* 67 G19
Ukhta, *Russia* 50 C6
Ukiah, *U.S.A.* 116 F3
Ukki Fort, *India* 69 C7
Ukmergė, *Lithuania* 9 J21
Ukraine ■, *Europe* 47 H7
Ukwi, *Botswana* 88 C3
Ulaan-Uul, *Mongolia* 56 B6
Ulaanbaatar, *Mongolia* 51 E11
Ulaangom, *Mongolia* 60 A4
Ulaanjirem, *Mongolia* 56 B3
Ulamba, *Dem. Rep. of the Congo* 87 D1
Ulan Bator = Ulaanbaatar, *Mongolia* 51 E11
Ulan Erge, *Russia* 49 G7
Ulan Khol, *Russia* 49 H8
Ulan Ude, *Russia* 51 D11
Ulanów, *Poland* 45 H9
Ulaş, *Sivas, Turkey* 72 C7
Ulaş, *Tekirdağ, Turkey* 41 E11
Ulaya, *Morogoro, Tanzania* 86 D4
Ulaya, *Tabora, Tanzania* 86 C3
Ulcinj, *Montenegro, Yug.* 40 E3
Ulco, *S. Africa* 88 D3
Ulefoss, *Norway* 9 G13
Ulëza, *Albania* 40 E3
Ulfborg, *Denmark* 11 H2
Ulhasnagar, *India* 66 K8
Uliastay, *Mongolia* 60 B4
Ulithi Atoll, *Pac. Oc.* 63 B9
Uljma, *Serbia, Yug.* 42 E6
Ulla →, *Spain* 34 C2
Ulladulla, *Australia* 95 F5
Ullapool, *U.K.* 14 D3
Ullared, *Sweden* 11 G6
Ulldecona, *Spain* 32 E5
Ullswater, *U.K.* 12 C5
Ullŭng-do, *S. Korea* 55 F5
Ulm, *Germany* 25 G5
Ulmarra, *Australia* 95 D5
Ulmeni, *Buzău, Romania* 43 E11
Ulmeni, *Maramureş, Romania* 43 C8
Ulonguè, *Mozam.* 87 E3
Ulricehamn, *Sweden* 11 G7
Ulrika, *Sweden* 11 F9
Ulsan, *S. Korea* 57 G15
Ulsta, *U.K.* 14 A7
Ulster □, *U.K.* 15 B5
Ulstrem, *Bulgaria* 41 D10
Ulubat Gölü, *Turkey* 41 F12
Ulubey, *Turkey* 39 C11
Uluborlu, *Turkey* 39 C12
Uluçinar, *Turkey* 72 D6
Uludağ, *Turkey* 41 F13
Uludere, *Turkey* 73 D10
Uluguru Mts., *Tanzania* 86 D4
Ulukışla, *Turkey* 72 D6
Ulungur He →, *China* 60 B3
Uluru = Ayers Rock, *Australia* 93 E5
Uluru Nat. Park, *Australia* 93 E5
Ulutau, *Kazakstan* 50 E7
Ulva, *U.K.* 14 E2
Ulverston, *U.K.* 12 C4
Ulverstone, *Australia* 94 G4
Ulya, *Russia* 51 D15
Ulyanovsk = Simbirsk, *Russia* 48 C9
Ulyasutay = Uliastay, *Mongolia* 60 B4
Ulysses, *U.S.A.* 113 G4
Umag, *Croatia* 29 C10
Umala, *Bolivia* 124 G5
Uman, *Ukraine* 47 H6
Umaria, *India* 67 H12
Umarkot, *Pakistan* 66 G6
Umarpada, *India* 68 J5
Umatilla, *U.S.A.* 114 D4
Umbagog L., *U.S.A.* 111 B13
Umbakumba, *Australia* 94 A2
Umbértide, *Italy* 29 E9
Umbrella Mts., *N.Z.* 91 L2
Umbria □, *Italy* 29 F9
Ume älv →, *Sweden* 8 E19
Umeå, *Sweden* 8 E19
Umera, *Indonesia* 63 E7
Umfuli →, *Zimbabwe* 87 F2
Umgusa, *Zimbabwe* 87 F2
Umim Urūmah, *Si. Arabia* 80 B4

Umka, Serbia, Yug. 40 B4
Umkomaas, S. Africa 89 E5
Umlazi, S. Africa 85 L6
Umm ad Daraj, J., Jordan 75 C4
Umm al Qaywayn, U.A.E. 71 E7
Umm al Qittayn, Jordan 75 C5
Umm Arda, Sudan 81 D3
Umm Bāb, Qatar 71 E6
Umm Badr, Sudan 81 E2
Umm Baiyud, Sudan 81 E3
Umm Bel, Sudan 81 E2
Umm Birkah, Si. Arabia 80 B4
Umm Boim, Sudan 81 E2
Umm Dam, Sudan 81 E3
Umm Debi, Sudan 81 E3
Umm Dubban, Sudan 81 D3
Umm el Fahm, Israel 75 C4
Umm Gafala, Sudan 81 E2
Umm Gimala, Sudan 81 E2
Umm Inderaba, Sudan 80 D3
Umm Keddada, Sudan 81 E2
Umm Koweika, Sudan 81 E3
Umm Lajj, Si. Arabia 70 E3
Umm Merwa, Sudan 80 D3
Umm Qantur, Sudan 81 E3
Umm Qurein, Sudan 81 F2
Umm Ruwaba, Sudan 81 E3
Umm Saiyala, Sudan 81 E3
Umm Shanqa, Sudan 81 E2
Umm Shutur, Sudan 81 F3
Umm Sidr, Sudan 81 E2
Umm Zehetir, Egypt 80 J8
Umnak I., U.S.A. 100 C3
Umniati →, Zimbabwe 87 F2
Umpqua →, U.S.A. 114 E1
Umreth, India 68 H5
Umtata, S. Africa 89 E4
Umuahia, Nigeria 83 D6
Umuarama, Brazil 127 A5
Umurbey, Turkey 41 F10
Umvukwe Ra., Zimbabwe 87 F3
Umzimvubu, S. Africa 89 E4
Umzingwane →, Zimbabwe 87 G2
Umzinto, S. Africa 89 E5
Una, India 68 J4
Una →, Bos.-H. 29 D13
Unac →, Bos.-H. 29 D13
Unadilla, U.S.A. 111 D9
Unalakleet, U.S.A. 100 B3
Unalaska, U.S.A. 100 C3
Unalaska I., U.S.A. 100 C3
'Unayzah, Si. Arabia 70 E4
'Unāzah, J., Asia 70 C3
Uncastillo, Spain 32 C3
Uncía, Bolivia 124 G5
Uncompahgre Peak, U.S.A. 115 G10
Uncompahgre Plateau, U.S.A. 115 G9
Unden, Sweden 11 F8
Underbool, Australia 95 F3
Undersaker, Sweden 10 A7
Unecha, Russia 47 F7
Ungarie, Australia 95 E4
Ungarra, Australia 95 E2
Ungava, Pén. d', Canada 101 C12
Ungava B., Canada 101 C13
Ungeny = Ungheni, Moldova 43 C12
Unggi, N. Korea 57 C16
Ungheni, Moldova 43 C12
Unguala →, Ethiopia 81 F5
Ungwatiri, Sudan 81 D4
Uni, Russia 48 B10
União da Vitória, Brazil 127 B5
Uničov, Czech Rep. 27 B10
Uniejów, Poland 45 G5
Unije, Croatia 29 D11
Unimak I., U.S.A. 100 C3
Union, Miss., U.S.A. 113 J10
Union, Mo., U.S.A. 112 F9
Union, S.C., U.S.A. 109 H5
Union City, Calif., U.S.A. 116 H4
Union City, N.J., U.S.A. 111 F10
Union City, Pa., U.S.A. 110 E5
Union City, Tenn., U.S.A. 113 G10
Union Gap, U.S.A. 114 C3
Union Springs, U.S.A. 109 J3
Uniondale, S. Africa 88 E3
Uniontown, U.S.A. 108 F6
Unionville, U.S.A. 112 E8
Unirea, Romania 43 F12
United Arab Emirates ■, Asia 71 F7
United Kingdom ■, Europe 7 E5
United States of America ■, N. Amer. 106 C7
Unity, Canada 105 C7
Universales, Mtes., Spain 32 E3
University Park, U.S.A. 115 K10
Unjha, India 68 H5
Unna, Germany 24 D3
Unnao, India 69 F9
Uno, Ilha, Guinea-Biss. 82 C1
Unst, U.K. 14 A8
Unstrut →, Germany 24 D7
Unterfranken □, Germany 25 F5
Unterschleissheim, Germany 25 G7
Unuk →, Canada 104 B2
Ünye, Turkey 72 B7
Unzha, Russia 48 A7
Unzha →, Russia 48 B6
Uozu, Japan 55 F8
Upata, Venezuela 124 B6
Upemba, L., Dem. Rep. of the Congo 87 D2
Upernavik, Greenland 4 B5
Upington, S. Africa 88 D3
Upleta, India 68 J4
Upolu, W. Samoa 91 A13
Upper □, Ghana 83 C4
Upper Alkali L., U.S.A. 114 F3
Upper Arrow L., Canada 104 C5
Upper Austria = Oberösterreich □, Austria 26 C7
Upper Foster L., Canada 105 B7
Upper Hutt, N.Z. 91 J5
Upper Klamath L., U.S.A. 114 E3
Upper Lake, U.S.A. 116 F4
Upper Musquodoboit, Canada 103 C7
Upper Red L., U.S.A. 112 A7
Upper Sandusky, U.S.A. 108 E4
Upper Volta = Burkina Faso ■, Africa 82 C4
Upphärad, Sweden 11 F6
Uppland, Sweden 10 E11
Upplands-Väsby, Sweden 10 E11
Uppsala, Sweden 10 E11
Uppsala län □, Sweden 10 D11
Upshi, India 69 C7
Upstart, C., Australia 94 B4
Upton, U.S.A. 112 C2
Ur, Iraq 70 D5
Urad Qianqi, China 56 D5
Urakawa, Japan 54 C11
Ural = Zhayyq →, Kazakstan 50 E6
Ural, Australia 95 E4
Ural Mts. = Uralskie Gory, Eurasia 50 D6
Uralla, Australia 95 E5
Uralsk = Oral, Kazakstan 48 E10
Uralskie Gory, Eurasia 50 D6
Urambo, Tanzania 86 D3
Urana, Australia 95 F4
Urandangi, Australia 94 C2
Uranium City, Canada 105 B7
Uraricoera →, Brazil 124 C6
Urawa, Japan 55 G9
Uray, Russia 50 C7
'Uray'irah, Si. Arabia 71 E6
Urbana, Ill., U.S.A. 108 E1
Urbana, Ohio, U.S.A. 108 E4
Urbánia, Italy 29 E9
Urbel →, Spain 34 C7
Urbino, Italy 29 E9
Urbión, Picos de, Spain 32 C2
Urcos, Peru 124 F4
Urdinarrain, Argentina 126 C4
Urdos, France 20 F3
Urdzhar, Kazakstan 50 E9
Ure →, U.K. 12 C6
Uren, Russia 48 B7
Ures, Mexico 118 B2
Urfa = Sanliurfa, Turkey 70 B3
Urganch, Uzbekistan 50 E7
Urgench = Urganch, Uzbekistan 50 E7
Ürgüp, Turkey 70 B2
Uri, India 69 B6
Uri □, Switz. 25 J4
Uribia, Colombia 124 A4
Uricani, Romania 42 E8
Uriondo, Bolivia 126 A3
Urique, Mexico 118 B3
Urique →, Mexico 118 B3
Urk, Neths. 17 B5
Urla, Turkey 39 C8
Urlați, Romania 43 F11
Urmia = Orūmīyeh, Iran 70 B5
Urmia, L. = Orūmīyeh, Daryācheh-ye, Iran 70 B5
Uroševac, Kosovo, Yug. 40 D5
Urshult, Sweden 11 H8
Uruaçu, Brazil 125 F9
Uruapan, Mexico 118 D4
Urubamba →, Peru 124 F4
Uruçara, Brazil 124 D7
Uruçuí, Brazil 125 E10
Uruguai →, Brazil 127 B5
Uruguaiana, Brazil 126 B4
Uruguay ■, S. Amer. 126 C4
Uruguay →, S. Amer. 126 C4
Urumchi = Ürümqi, China 50 E9
Ürümqi, China 50 E9
Urup →, Russia 49 H5
Urup, Ostrov, Russia 51 E16
Uryupinsk, Russia 48 E5
Urzhum, Russia 48 B9
Urziceni, Romania 43 F11
Usa →, Russia 50 C6
Uşak, Turkey 39 C11
Uşak □, Turkey 39 C11
Usakos, Namibia 88 C2
Ušće, Serbia, Yug. 40 C4
Usedom, Germany 24 B10
Useless Loop, Australia 93 E1
'Usfān, Si. Arabia 80 C4
Ush-Tobe, Kazakstan 50 E8
Ushakova, Ostrov, Russia 4 A12
Ushant = Ouessant, Î. d', France 18 D1
Ushashi, Tanzania 86 C3
Ushat, Sudan 81 F2
'Ushayrah, Si. Arabia 80 C5
Ushibuka, Japan 55 H5
Ushuaia, Argentina 128 G3
Ushumun, Russia 51 D13
Usk, Canada 104 C3
Usk →, U.K. 13 F5
Uska, India 69 F10
Üsküdar, Turkey 41 F13
Uslar, Germany 24 D5
Usman, Russia 47 F10
Usoke, Tanzania 86 D3
Usolye Sibirskoye, Russia 51 D11
Usoro, Nigeria 83 D6
Uspallata, P. de, Argentina 126 C2
Uspenskiy, Kazakstan 50 E8
Ussel, France 20 C6
Usson-du-Poitou, France 20 B4
Ussuri →, Asia 54 A7
Ussuriysk, Russia 51 E14
Ussurka, Russia 54 B6
Ust-Aldan = Batamay, Russia 51 C13
Ust-Amginskoye = Khandyga, Russia 51 C14
Ust-Bolsheretsk, Russia 51 D16
Ust-Buzulukskaya, Russia 48 E6
Ust-Chaun, Russia 51 C18
Ust-Donetskiy, Russia 49 G5
Ust-Ilimpeya = Yukta, Russia 51 C11
Ust-Ilimsk, Russia 51 D11
Ust-Ishim, Russia 50 D8
Ust-Kamchatsk, Russia 51 D17
Ust-Kamenogorsk = Öskemen, Kazakstan 50 E9
Ust-Khayryuzovo, Russia 51 D16
Ust-Kut, Russia 51 D11
Ust-Kuyga, Russia 51 B14
Ust-Labinsk, Russia 49 H4
Ust-Luga, Russia 46 C5
Ust-Maya, Russia 51 C14
Ust-Mil, Russia 51 D14
Ust-Nera, Russia 51 C15
Ust-Nyukzha, Russia 51 D13
Ust-Olenek, Russia 51 B12
Ust-Omchug, Russia 51 C15
Ust-Port, Russia 50 C9
Ust-Tsilma, Russia 50 C6
Ust Urt = Ustyurt Plateau, Asia 50 E6
Ustaritz, France 20 E2
Uster, Switz. 25 H4
Ústí nad Labem, Czech Rep. 26 A7
Ústí nad Orlicí, Czech Rep. 27 B9
Ústica, Italy 30 D6
Ustinov = Izhevsk, Russia 50 D6
Ustka, Poland 44 D3
Ustroń, Poland 45 J5
Ustrzyki Dolne, Poland 45 J9
Ustyurt Plateau, Asia 50 E6
Ustyuzhna, Russia 46 C9
Usu, China 60 B3
Usuki, Japan 55 H5
Usulután, El Salv. 120 D2
Usumacinta →, Mexico 119 D6
Usumbura = Bujumbura, Burundi 86 C2
Usure, Tanzania 86 C3
Usutuo →, Mozam. 89 D5
Uta, Indonesia 63 E9
Utah □, U.S.A. 114 G8
Utah L., U.S.A. 114 F8
Utansjö, Sweden 10 B11
Utarni, India 68 F4
Utatlan, Guatemala 120 C1
Ute Creek →, U.S.A. 113 H3
Utebo, Spain 32 D3
Utena, Lithuania 9 J21
Utete, Tanzania 86 D4
Uthai Thani, Thailand 64 E3
Uthal, Pakistan 68 G2
Utiariti, Brazil 124 F7
Utica, N.Y., U.S.A. 111 C9
Utica, Ohio, U.S.A. 110 F2
Utiel, Spain 33 F3
Utikuma L., Canada 104 B5
Utö, Sweden 10 F12
Utopia, Australia 94 C1
Utraula, India 69 F10
Utrecht, Neths. 17 B5
Utrecht, S. Africa 89 D5
Utrecht □, Neths. 17 B5
Utrera, Spain 35 H5
Utsjoki, Finland 8 B22
Utsunomiya, Japan 55 F9
Uttar Pradesh □, India 69 F9
Uttaradit, Thailand 64 D3
Uttoxeter, U.K. 12 E6
Uummannarsuaq = Nunap Isua, Greenland 4 D5
Uusikaarlepyy, Finland 8 E20
Uusikaupunki, Finland 9 F19
Uva, Russia 48 B11
Uvac →, Serbia, Yug. 40 C3
Uvalde, U.S.A. 113 L5
Uvarovo, Russia 48 E6
Uvat, Russia 50 D7
Uvinza, Tanzania 86 D3
Uvira, Dem. Rep. of the Congo 86 C2
Uvs Nuur, Mongolia 60 A4
'Uwairidh, Harrat al, Si. Arabia 70 E3
Uwajima, Japan 55 H6
Uweinat, Jebel, Sudan 80 C1
Uxbridge, Canada 110 B5
Uxin Qi, China 56 E5
Uxmal, Mexico 119 C7
Üydzin, Mongolia 56 B4
Uyo, Nigeria 83 D6
Üyüklü Tepe, Turkey 39 D9
Uyûn Mûsa, Egypt 75 F1
Uyuni, Bolivia 124 H5
Uzbekistan ■, Asia 50 E7
Uzen, Bolshoi →, Kazakstan 49 F9
Uzen, Mal →, Kazakstan 49 F9
Uzerche, France 20 C5
Uzès, France 21 D8
Uzh →, Ukraine 47 G6
Uzhgorod = Uzhhorod, Ukraine 47 H2
Uzhhorod, Ukraine 47 H2
Užice, Serbia, Yug. 40 C3
Uzlovaya, Russia 46 F10
Üzümlü, Turkey 39 E11
Uzunköprü, Turkey 41 E10
Uzunkuyu, Turkey 39 C8

V

Vaal →, S. Africa 88 D3
Vaal Dam, S. Africa 89 D4
Vaalwater, S. Africa 89 C4
Vaasa, Finland 8 E19
Vabre, France 20 E6
Vác, Hungary 42 C4
Vacaria, Brazil 127 B5
Vacaville, U.S.A. 116 G5
Vaccarès, Étang de, France 21 E8
Vach = Vakh →, Russia 50 C8
Vache, Î. à, Haiti 121 C5
Väckelsång, Sweden 11 H8
Väddö, Sweden 10 D12
Väderstad, Sweden 11 F8
Vadnagar, India 68 H5
Vado Lígure, Italy 28 D5
Vadodara, India 68 H5
Vadsø, Norway 8 A23
Vadstena, Sweden 11 F8
Vaduz, Liech. 25 H5
Værøy, Norway 8 C15
Vágar, Færoe Is. 8 E9
Vaggeryd, Sweden 11 G8
Vagney, France 19 D13
Vagnhärad, Sweden 11 F11
Vagos, Portugal 34 E2
Vågsfjorden, Norway 8 B17
Váh →, Slovak Rep. 27 D11
Vahsel B., Antarctica 5 D1
Vái, Greece 36 D8
Vaigach, Russia 50 B6
Vaiges, France 18 D6
Vaihingen, Germany 25 G4
Vail, U.S.A. 106 C5
Vailly-sur-Aisne, France 19 C10
Vaisali →, India 69 F8
Vaison-la-Romaine, France 21 D9
Vakarel, Bulgaria 40 D7
Vakfikebir, Turkey 73 B8
Vakh →, Russia 50 C8
Vakhtan, Russia 48 B8
Vál, Hungary 42 C3
Val-de-Marne □, France 19 D9
Val-d'Isère, France 21 C10
Val-d'Oise □, France 19 C9
Val-d'Or, Canada 102 C4
Val Marie, Canada 105 D7
Valaam, Russia 46 B6
Valadares, Portugal 34 D2
Valahia, Romania 43 F9
Valais □, Switz. 25 J3
Valais, Alpes du, Switz. 25 J3
Valandovo, Macedonia 40 E6
Valašské Meziříčí, Czech Rep. 27 B10
Valáxa, Greece 38 C6
Vålberg, Sweden 10 E7
Valbo, Sweden 10 D10
Valbondione, Italy 28 B7
Vălcani, Romania 42 D5
Vâlcea □, Romania 43 F9
Valcheta, Argentina 128 E3
Valdagno, Italy 29 C8
Valdahon, France 19 E13
Valday, Russia 46 D7
Valdayskaya Vozvyshennost, Russia 46 D7
Valdeazogues →, Spain 35 G6
Valdecañas, Embalse de, Spain 34 F5
Valdemarsvik, Sweden 11 F10
Valdemoro, Spain 34 E7
Valdepeñas, Spain 35 G7
Valderaduey →, Spain 34 D5
Valdérice, Italy 30 D5
Valderrobres, Spain 32 E5
Valdés, Pen., Argentina 122 H4
Valdez, U.S.A. 100 B5
Valdivia, Chile 128 D2
Valdobbiádene, Italy 29 C8
Valdosta, U.S.A. 109 K4
Valdoviño, Spain 34 B2
Valdres, Norway 9 F13
Vale, Georgia 49 K6
Vale, U.S.A. 114 E5
Vale of Glamorgan □, U.K. 13 F4
Valea lui Mihai, Romania 42 C7
Valea Mărului, Romania 43 E12
Valemount, Canada 104 C5
Valença, Brazil 125 F11
Valença, Portugal 34 C2
Valença do Piauí, Brazil 125 E10
Valençay, France 19 E8
Valence = Valence d'Agen, France 20 D4
Valence, France 21 D8
Valence d'Agen, France 20 D4
Valencia, Spain 33 F4
Valencia, U.S.A. 115 J10
Valencia, Venezuela 124 A5
Valencia □, Spain 33 F4
Valencia, G. de, Spain 33 F5
Valencia de Alcántara, Spain 35 F3
Valencia de Don Juan, Spain 34 C5
Valencia I., Ireland 15 E1
Valenciennes, France 19 B10
Văleni, Romania 43 F9
Vălenii de Munte, Romania 43 E11
Valensole, France 21 E9
Valentigney, France 19 E13
Valentim, Sa. do, Brazil 125 E10
Valentin, Russia 54 C7
Valentine, U.S.A. 113 K2
Valenza, Italy 28 C5
Valera, Venezuela 124 B4
Valga, Estonia 9 H22
Valguarnera Caropepe, Italy 31 E7
Valier, U.S.A. 114 B7
Valinco, G. de, France 21 G12
Valjevo, Serbia, Yug. 40 B3
Valka, Latvia 9 H21
Valkeakoski, Finland 9 F20
Valkenswaard, Neths. 17 C5
Vall de Uxó = La Vall d'Uixó, Spain 32 F4
Valla, Sweden 10 E10
Valladolid, Mexico 119 C7
Valladolid, Spain 34 D6
Valladolid □, Spain 34 D6
Vallata, Italy 31 A8
Valldemossa, Spain 37 B9
Valle d'Aosta □, Italy 28 C4
Valle de Arán, Spain 32 C5
Valle de la Pascua, Venezuela 124 B5
Valle de las Palmas, Mexico 117 N10
Valle de Santiago, Mexico 118 C4
Valle de Suchil, Mexico 118 C4
Valle de Zaragoza, Mexico 118 B3
Valle Fértil, Sierra del, Argentina 126 C2
Valle Hermoso, Mexico 119 B5
Valledupar, Colombia 124 A4
Vallehermoso, Canary Is. 37 F2
Vallejo, U.S.A. 116 G4
Vallenar, Chile 126 B1
Vallentuna, Sweden 10 E12
Valleraugue, France 20 D7
Vallet, France 18 E5
Valletta, Malta 36 D2
Valley Center, U.S.A. 117 M9
Valley City, U.S.A. 112 B6
Valley Falls, Oreg., U.S.A. 114 E3
Valley Falls, R.I., U.S.A. 111 E13
Valley Springs, U.S.A. 116 G6
Valley View, U.S.A. 111 F8
Valley Wells, U.S.A. 117 K11
Valleyview, Canada 104 B5
Valli di Comácchio, Italy 29 D9
Vallimanca, Arroyo, Argentina 126 D4
Vallo della Lucánia, Italy 31 B8
Vallon-Pont-d'Arc, France 21 D8
Vallorbe, Switz. 25 J2
Valls, Spain 32 D6
Valmaseda = Balmaseda, Spain 32 B1
Valmiera, Latvia 9 H21
Valnera, Spain 34 B7
Valognes, France 18 C5
Valona = Vlóra, Albania 40 F3
Valongo, Portugal 34 D2
Valozhyn, Belarus 46 E4
Valpaços, Portugal 34 D3
Valparaíso, Chile 126 C1
Valparaíso, Mexico 118 C4
Valparaiso, U.S.A. 108 E2
Valparaíso □, Chile 126 C1
Valpovo, Croatia 42 E3
Valréas, France 21 D9
Vals, Switz. 25 J5
Vals →, S. Africa 88 D4
Vals, Tanjung, Indonesia 63 F9
Vals-les-Bains, France 21 D8
Valsad, India 66 J8
Valtellina, Italy 28 B6
Valuyki, Russia 47 G10
Valverde, Canary Is. 37 G2
Valverde del Camino, Spain 35 H4
Valverde del Fresno, Spain 34 E4
Vama, Romania 43 C10
Vamdrup, Denmark 11 J3
Våmhus, Sweden 10 C8
Vammala, Finland 9 F20
Vámos, Greece 36 D6
Van, Turkey 70 B4
Van, L. = Van Gölü, Turkey 70 B4
Van Alstyne, U.S.A. 113 J6
Van Blommestein Meer, Surinam 125 C7
Van Buren, Canada 103 C6
Van Buren, Ark., U.S.A. 113 H7
Van Buren, Maine, U.S.A. 109 B11
Van Buren, Mo., U.S.A. 113 G9
Van Canh, Vietnam 64 F7
Van Diemen, C., N. Terr., Australia 92 B5
Van Diemen, C., Queens., Australia 94 B2
Van Diemen G., Australia 92 B5
Van Gölü, Turkey 70 B4
Van Horn, U.S.A. 113 K2
Van Ninh, Vietnam 64 F7
Van Rees, Pegunungan, Indonesia 63 E9
Van Wert, U.S.A. 108 E3
Van Yen, Vietnam 58 G5
Vanadzor, Armenia 49 K7
Vanavara, Russia 51 C11
Vancouver, Canada 104 D4
Vancouver, U.S.A. 116 E4
Vancouver, C., Australia 93 G2
Vancouver I., Canada 104 D3
Vandalia, Ill., U.S.A. 112 F10
Vandalia, Mo., U.S.A. 112 F9
Vandenburg, U.S.A. 117 L6
Vanderbijlpark, S. Africa 89 D4
Vandergrift, U.S.A. 110 F5
Vanderhoof, Canada 104 C4
Vanderkloof Dam, S. Africa 88 E3
Vanderlin I., Australia 94 B2
Vänern, Sweden 11 F7
Vänersborg, Sweden 11 F6
Vang Vieng, Laos 64 C4
Vanga, Kenya 86 C4
Vangaindrano, Madag. 89 C8
Vanguard, Canada 105 D7
Vanino, Russia 51 E15
Vânju Mare, Romania 42 F7

Vanna, *Norway* 8 A18
Vännäs, *Sweden* 8 E18
Vannes, *France* 18 E4
Vanoise, *France* 21 C10
Vanrhynsdorp, *S. Africa* 88 E2
Vansbro, *Sweden* 10 D8
Vansittart B., *Australia* 92 B4
Vantaa, *Finland* 9 F21
Vanua Levu, *Fiji* 91 C8
Vanua Mbalavu, *Fiji* 91 C9
Vanuatu ■, *Pac. Oc.* 96 J8
Vanwyksvlei, *S. Africa* 88 E3
Vanzylsrus, *S. Africa* 88 D3
Vapnyarka, *Ukraine* 47 H5
Var □, *France* 21 E10
Var →, *France* 21 E11
Vara, *Sweden* 11 F6
Varades, *France* 18 E5
Varáita →, *Italy* 28 D4
Varallo, *Italy* 28 C5
Varanasi, *India* 69 G10
Varanger-halvøya, *Norway* 8 A23
Varangerfjorden, *Norway* 8 A23
Varano, Lago di, *Italy* 29 G12
Varaždin, *Croatia* 29 B13
Varazze, *Italy* 28 D5
Varberg, *Sweden* 11 G6
Vardar = Axiós →, *Greece* 40 F6
Varde, *Denmark* 11 J2
Varde Å →, *Denmark* 11 J2
Vardø, *Norway* 8 A24
Varel, *Germany* 24 B4
Varella, Mui, *Vietnam* 64 F7
Varėna, *Lithuania* 9 J21
Varennes-sur-Allier, *France* 19 F10
Varennes-Vauzelles, *France* 19 E10
Vareš, *Bos.-H.* 42 F3
Varese, *Italy* 28 C5
Vârfurile, *Romania* 42 D7
Vårgårda, *Sweden* 11 F6
Varginha, *Brazil* 127 A6
Vargön, *Sweden* 11 F6
Varillas, *Chile* 126 A1
Varkaus, *Finland* 9 E22
Värmdölandet, *Sweden* 10 E12
Värmeln, *Sweden* 10 E6
Värmlands Bro, *Sweden* 10 E7
Värmlands län □, *Sweden* 10 E6
Varna, *Bulgaria* 41 C11
Varna □, *Bulgaria* 41 C11
Värnamo, *Sweden* 11 G8
Varnsdorf, *Czech Rep.* 26 A7
Várpalota, *Hungary* 42 C3
Vars, *Canada* 111 A9
Vars, *France* 21 D10
Varto, *Turkey* 73 C9
Varvarin, *Serbia, Yug.* 40 C5
Varysburg, *U.S.A.* 110 D6
Varzaneh, *Iran* 71 C7
Varzi, *Italy* 28 D6
Varzo, *Italy* 28 B5
Varzy, *France* 19 E10
Vas □, *Hungary* 42 C1
Vasa Barris →, *Brazil* 125 F11
Vásárosnamény, *Hungary* 42 B7
Vascão →, *Portugal* 35 H3
Vaşcău, *Romania* 42 D7
Vascongadas = País Vasco □, *Spain* 32 C2
Vasht = Khāsh, *Iran* 66 E2
Vasilevichi, *Belarus* 47 F5
Vasilikón, *Greece* 38 C5
Vasilkov = Vasylkiv, *Ukraine* 47 G6
Vaslui, *Romania* 43 D12
Vaslui □, *Romania* 43 D12
Väsman, *Sweden* 10 D9
Vassar, *Canada* 105 D9
Vassar, *U.S.A.* 108 D4
Västerås, *Sweden* 10 E10
Västerbotten, *Sweden* 8 D18
Västerdalälven →, *Sweden* 10 D8
Västergötland, *Sweden* 11 F7
Västerhaninge, *Sweden* 10 E12
Västervik, *Sweden* 11 G10
Västmanland, *Sweden* 9 G16
Västmanlands län □, *Sweden* 10 E10
Vasto, *Italy* 29 F11
Vasvár, *Hungary* 42 C1
Vasylkiv, *Ukraine* 47 G6
Vatan, *France* 19 E8
Vatersay, *U.K.* 14 E1
Váthia, *Greece* 38 E4
Vatican City ■, *Europe* 29 G9
Vaticano, C., *Italy* 31 D8
Vatili, *Cyprus* 36 D12
Vatin, *Serbia, Yug.* 42 E6
Vatnajökull, *Iceland* 8 D5
Vatoa, *Fiji* 91 D9
Vatólakkos, *Greece* 36 D5
Vatoloha, *Madag.* 89 B8
Vatomandry, *Madag.* 89 B8
Vatra-Dornei, *Romania* 43 C10
Vatrak →, *India* 68 H5
Vättern, *Sweden* 11 F8
Vaucluse □, *France* 21 E9
Vaucouleurs, *France* 19 D12
Vaud □, *Switz.* 25 J2
Vaughn, *Mont., U.S.A.* 114 C8
Vaughn, *N. Mex., U.S.A.* 115 J11
Vaujours L., *Canada* 102 A5
Vaupés = Uaupés →, *Brazil* 124 C5
Vaupes □, *Colombia* 124 C4
Vauvert, *France* 21 E8
Vauxhall, *Canada* 104 C6
Vav, *India* 68 G4
Vavatenina, *Madag.* 89 B8
Vava'u, *Tonga* 91 D12
Vavoua, *Ivory C.* 82 D3
Vawkavysk, *Belarus* 47 F3
Vaxholm, *Sweden* 10 E12
Växjö, *Sweden* 11 H8
Våxtorp, *Sweden* 11 H7
Vaygach, Ostrov, *Russia* 50 C6
Váyia, *Greece* 38 C5
Váyia, Ákra, *Greece* 36 C10
Vechelde, *Germany* 24 C6
Vechta, *Germany* 24 C4
Vechte →, *Neths.* 17 B6
Vecsés, *Hungary* 42 C4
Veddige, *Sweden* 11 G6
Vedea →, *Romania* 43 G10
Vedia, *Argentina* 126 C3
Vedum, *Sweden* 11 F7
Veendam, *Neths.* 17 A6
Veenendaal, *Neths.* 17 B5
Vefsna →, *Norway* 8 D15
Vega, *Norway* 8 D14
Vega, *U.S.A.* 113 H3
Vegadeo, *Spain* 34 B3
Vegorrítis, Límni, *Greece* 40 F5
Vegreville, *Canada* 104 C6
Veinge, *Sweden* 11 H7
Veisiejai, *Lithuania* 44 D10
Vejbystrand, *Sweden* 11 H6
Vejen, *Denmark* 11 J3
Vejer de la Frontera, *Spain* 35 J5
Vejle, *Denmark* 11 J3
Vejle Amtskommune □, *Denmark* 11 J3
Vejle Fjord, *Denmark* 11 J3
Vela Luka, *Croatia* 29 F13
Velas, C., *Costa Rica* 120 D2
Velasco, Sierra de, *Argentina* 126 B2
Velay, Mts. du, *France* 20 D7
Velbert, *Germany* 24 D3
Velddrif, *S. Africa* 88 E2
Velebit Planina, *Croatia* 29 D12
Velebitski Kanal, *Croatia* 29 D11
Veleka →, *Bulgaria* 41 D11
Velencei-tó, *Hungary* 42 C3
Velenje, *Slovenia* 29 B12
Veles, *Macedonia* 40 E5
Velestínon, *Greece* 38 B4
Vélez-Málaga, *Spain* 35 J6
Vélez Rubio, *Spain* 33 H2
Velhas →, *Brazil* 125 G10
Velika, *Croatia* 42 E2
Velika Gorica, *Croatia* 29 C13
Velika Kapela, *Croatia* 29 C12
Velika Kladuša, *Bos.-H.* 29 C12
Velika Kruša, *Kosovo, Yug.* 40 D4
Velika Morava →, *Serbia, Yug.* 40 B5
Velika Plana, *Serbia, Yug.* 40 B5
Velikaya →, *Russia* 46 D5
Velikaya Kema, *Russia* 54 B8
Velikaya Lepetikha, *Ukraine* 47 J7
Veliké Kapušany, *Slovak Rep.* 27 C15
Velike Lašče, *Slovenia* 29 C11
Veliki Jastrebac, *Serbia, Yug.* 40 C5
Veliki Kanal, *Serbia, Yug.* 42 E4
Veliki Popović, *Serbia, Yug.* 40 B5
Velikiye Luki, *Russia* 46 D6
Veliko Gradište, *Serbia, Yug.* 40 B5
Veliko Tŭrnovo, *Bulgaria* 41 C9
Velikonda Range, *India* 66 M11
Vélingara, *Senegal* 82 C2
Vélingara, *Senegal* 82 B2
Velingrad, *Bulgaria* 40 D7
Velino, Mte., *Italy* 29 F10
Velizh, *Russia* 46 E6
Velké Karlovice, *Czech Rep.* 27 B11
Velké Meziříčí, *Czech Rep.* 26 B9
Vel'ký Javorník, *Slovak Rep.* 27 B11
Vel'ký Krtíš, *Slovak Rep.* 27 C12
Vel'ký Meder, *Slovak Rep.* 27 D10
Vel'ký Tribeč, *Slovak Rep.* 27 C11
Velletri, *Italy* 30 A5
Vellinge, *Sweden* 11 J6
Vellmar, *Germany* 24 D5
Vellore, *India* 66 N11
Velsk, *Russia* 46 B11
Velten, *Germany* 24 C9
Velva, *U.S.A.* 112 A4
Velvendós, *Greece* 40 F6
Vemb, *Denmark* 11 H2
Vemdalen, *Sweden* 10 B7
Ven, *Sweden* 11 J6
Venaco, *France* 21 F13
Venado Tuerto, *Argentina* 126 C3
Venafro, *Italy* 31 A7
Venarey-les-Laumes, *France* 19 E11
Venaría, *Italy* 28 C4
Venčane, *Serbia, Yug.* 40 B4
Vence, *France* 21 E11
Vendas Novas, *Portugal* 35 G2
Vendée □, *France* 18 F5
Vendée →, *France* 18 F5
Vendéen, Bocage, *France* 20 B2
Vendeuvre-sur-Barse, *France* 19 D11
Vendôme, *France* 18 E8
Vendrell = El Vendrell, *Spain* 32 D6
Vendsyssel, *Denmark* 11 G4
Venelles, *France* 21 E9
Véneta, L., *Italy* 29 C9
Véneto □, *Italy* 29 C9
Venev, *Russia* 46 E10
Venézia, *Italy* 29 C9
Venézia, G. di, *Italy* 29 C10
Venezuela ■, *S. Amer.* 124 B5
Venezuela, G. de, *Venezuela* 122 B3
Vengurla, *India* 66 M8
Venice = Venézia, *Italy* 29 C9
Venice, *U.S.A.* 109 M4
Vénissieux, *France* 21 C8
Venjansjön, *Sweden* 10 D8
Venkatapuram, *India* 67 K12
Venlo, *Neths.* 17 C6
Vennesla, *Norway* 9 G12
Venosa, *Italy* 31 B8
Venray, *Neths.* 17 C6
Venta, *Lithuania* 44 B9
Venta →, *Latvia* 44 A8
Venta de Baños, *Spain* 34 D6
Venta de Cardeña = Cardeña, *Spain* 35 G6
Ventana, Punta de la, *Mexico* 118 C3
Ventana, Sa. de la, *Argentina* 126 D3
Ventersburg, *S. Africa* 88 D4
Venterstad, *S. Africa* 88 E4
Ventimíglia, *Italy* 28 E4
Ventnor, *U.K.* 13 G6
Ventotène, *Italy* 30 B6
Ventoux, Mt., *France* 21 D9
Ventspils, *Latvia* 9 H19
Ventspils □, *Latvia* 44 A8
Ventuarí →, *Venezuela* 124 C5
Ventucopa, *U.S.A.* 117 L7
Ventura, *U.S.A.* 117 L7
Venus B., *Australia* 95 F4
Vera, *Argentina* 126 B3
Vera, *Spain* 33 H3
Veracruz, *Mexico* 119 D5
Veracruz □, *Mexico* 119 D5
Veraval, *India* 68 J4
Verbánia, *Italy* 28 C5
Verbicaro, *Italy* 31 C8
Verbier, *Switz.* 25 J3
Vercelli, *Italy* 28 C5
Verchovchevo, *Ukraine* 47 H8
Verdalsøra, *Norway* 8 E14
Verde →, *Argentina* 128 E3
Verde →, *Goiás, Brazil* 125 G8
Verde →, *Mato Grosso do Sul, Brazil* 125 H8
Verde →, *Chihuahua, Mexico* 118 B3
Verde →, *Oaxaca, Mexico* 119 D5
Verde →, *Veracruz, Mexico* 118 C4
Verde →, *Paraguay* 126 A4
Verde →, *U.S.A.* 106 D4
Verde, Cay, *Bahamas* 120 B4
Verde Island Pass, *Phil.* 61 E4
Verden, *Germany* 24 C5
Verdhikoúsa, *Greece* 38 B3
Verdi, *U.S.A.* 116 F7
Verdon →, *France* 21 E9
Verdun, *France* 19 C12
Verdun-sur-le-Doubs, *France* 19 F12
Vereeniging, *S. Africa* 89 D4
Verga, C., *Guinea* 82 C2
Vergara, *Uruguay* 127 C5
Vergato, *Italy* 28 D8
Vergemont Cr. →, *Australia* 94 C3
Vergennes, *U.S.A.* 111 B11
Vergt, *France* 20 C4
Verín, *Spain* 34 D3
Verkhnedvinsk = Vyerkhnyadzvinsk, *Belarus* 46 E4
Verkhnevilyuysk, *Russia* 51 C13
Verkhniy Baskunchak, *Russia* 49 F8
Verkhovye, *Russia* 47 F9
Verkhoyansk, *Russia* 51 C14
Verkhoyansk Ra. = Verkhoyanskiy Khrebet, *Russia* 51 C13
Verkhoyanskiy Khrebet, *Russia* 51 C13
Vermenton, *France* 19 E10
Vermilion, *Canada* 105 C6
Vermilion, *U.S.A.* 110 E2
Vermilion →, *Alta., Canada* 105 C6
Vermilion →, *Qué., Canada* 102 C5
Vermilion, B., *U.S.A.* 113 L9
Vermilion Bay, *Canada* 105 D10
Vermilion L., *U.S.A.* 112 B8
Vermillion, *U.S.A.* 112 D6
Vermont □, *U.S.A.* 111 C12
Vermosh, *Albania* 40 D3
Vernal, *U.S.A.* 114 F9
Vernalis, *U.S.A.* 116 H5
Vernazza, *Italy* 28 D6
Verner, *Canada* 102 C3
Verneuil-sur-Avre, *France* 18 D7
Verneukpan, *S. Africa* 88 E3
Vernier, *Switz.* 25 J2
Vérnio, *Italy* 28 D8
Vernon, *Canada* 104 C5
Vernon, *France* 18 C8
Vernon, *U.S.A.* 113 H5
Vernonia, *U.S.A.* 116 E3
Vernouillet, *France* 18 D8
Vero Beach, *U.S.A.* 109 M5
Véroia, *Greece* 40 F6
Véroli, *Italy* 29 G10
Verona, *Canada* 111 B8
Verona, *Italy* 28 C7
Verona, *U.S.A.* 112 D10
Verrès, *Italy* 28 C4
Versailles, *France* 19 D9
Versmold, *Germany* 24 C4
Vert, C., *Senegal* 82 C1
Vertou, *France* 18 E5
Vertus, *France* 19 D11
Verulam, *S. Africa* 89 D5
Verviers, *Belgium* 17 D5
Vervins, *France* 19 C10
Veržej, *Slovenia* 29 B13
Verzy, *France* 19 C11
Vescovato, *France* 21 F13
Veselí nad Lužnicí, *Czech Rep.* 26 B7
Veselie, *Bulgaria* 41 D11
Veselovskoye Vdkhr., *Russia* 49 G5
Veshenskaya, *Russia* 48 F5
Vesle →, *France* 19 C10
Vesoul, *France* 19 E13
Vessigebro, *Sweden* 11 H6
Vesterålen, *Norway* 8 B16
Vestfjorden, *Norway* 8 C15
Vestmannaeyjar, *Iceland* 8 E3
Vestsjællands Amtskommune □, *Denmark* 11 J5
Vestspitsbergen, *Svalbard* 4 B8
Vestvågøy, *Norway* 8 B15
Vesuvio, *Italy* 31 B7
Vesuvius, Mt. = Vesuvio, *Italy* 31 B7
Vesyegonsk, *Russia* 46 C9
Veszprém, *Hungary* 42 C2
Veszprém □, *Hungary* 42 C2
Vésztő, *Hungary* 42 D6
Vetlanda, *Sweden* 11 G9
Vetluga, *Russia* 48 B7
Vetlugu →, *Russia* 48 B8
Vetluzhskiy, *Kostroma, Russia* 48 A7
Vetluzhskiy, *Nizhniy Novgorod, Russia* 48 B7
Vetovo, *Bulgaria* 41 C10
Vetralla, *Italy* 29 F9
Vetren, *Bulgaria* 41 D8
Vettore, Mte., *Italy* 29 F10
Veurne, *Belgium* 17 C2
Veveno →, *Sudan* 81 F3
Vevey, *Switz.* 25 J2
Vévi, *Greece* 40 F5
Veynes, *France* 21 D9
Veys, *Iran* 71 D6
Vézelay, *France* 19 E10
Vézelise, *France* 19 D13
Vézère →, *France* 20 D4
Vezhen, *Bulgaria* 41 D8
Vezirköprü, *Turkey* 72 B6
Vezzani, *France* 21 F13
Vi Thanh, *Vietnam* 65 H5
Viacha, *Bolivia* 124 G5
Viadana, *Italy* 28 D7
Viamão, *Brazil* 127 C5
Viana, *Brazil* 125 D10
Viana, *Spain* 32 C2
Viana do Alentejo, *Portugal* 35 G3
Viana do Bolo, *Spain* 34 C3
Viana do Castelo, *Portugal* 34 D2
Viana do Castelo □, *Portugal* 34 D2
Vianden, *Lux.* 17 E6
Vianópolis, *Brazil* 125 G9
Viar →, *Spain* 35 H5
Viaréggio, *Italy* 28 E7
Viaur →, *France* 20 D5
Vibble, *Sweden* 11 G12
Vibo Valéntia, *Italy* 31 D9
Viborg, *Denmark* 11 H3
Viborg Amtskommune □, *Denmark* 11 H3
Vibraye, *France* 18 D7
Vic, *Spain* 32 D7
Vic, Étang de, *France* 20 E7
Vic-en-Bigorre, *France* 20 E4
Vic-Fézensac, *France* 20 E4
Vic-le-Comte, *France* 19 G10
Vic-sur-Cère, *France* 20 D6
Vícar, *Spain* 33 J2
Vicenza, *Italy* 29 C8
Vich = Vic, *Spain* 32 D7
Vichada →, *Colombia* 124 C5
Vichuga, *Russia* 48 B5
Vichy, *France* 19 F10
Vicksburg, *Ariz., U.S.A.* 117 M13
Vicksburg, *Miss., U.S.A.* 113 J9
Vico, *France* 21 F12
Vico, L. di, *Italy* 29 F9
Vico del Gargano, *Italy* 29 G12
Vicovu de Sus, *Romania* 43 C10
Victor, *India* 68 J4
Victor, *U.S.A.* 110 D7
Victor Harbor, *Australia* 95 F2
Victoria = Labuan, *Malaysia* 62 C5
Victoria, *Argentina* 126 C3
Victoria, *Canada* 104 D4
Victoria, *Chile* 128 D2
Victoria, *Guinea* 82 C2
Victoria, *Malta* 36 C1
Victoria, *Phil.* 61 D4
Victoria, *Romania* 43 E9
Victoria, *Kans., U.S.A.* 112 F5
Victoria, *Tex., U.S.A.* 113 L6
Victoria □, *Australia* 95 F3
Victoria →, *Australia* 92 C4
Victoria, Grand L., *Canada* 102 C4
Victoria, L., *Africa* 86 C3
Victoria, L., *Australia* 95 E3
Victoria Beach, *Canada* 105 C9
Victoria de Durango = Durango, *Mexico* 118 C4
Victoria de las Tunas, *Cuba* 120 B4
Victoria Falls, *Zimbabwe* 87 F2
Victoria Harbour, *Canada* 110 B5
Victoria I., *Canada* 100 A8
Victoria L., *Canada* 103 C8
Victoria Ld., *Antarctica* 5 D11
Victoria Nile →, *Uganda* 86 B3
Victoria River, *Australia* 92 C5
Victoria Str., *Canada* 100 B9
Victoria Taungdeik, *Burma* 67 J18
Victoria West, *S. Africa* 88 E3
Victorias, *Phil.* 61 F5
Victoriaville, *Canada* 103 C5
Victorica, *Argentina* 126 D2
Victorville, *U.S.A.* 117 L9
Vicuña, *Chile* 126 C1
Vicuña Mackenna, *Argentina* 126 C3
Vidal, *U.S.A.* 117 L12
Vidal Junction, *U.S.A.* 117 L12
Vidalia, *U.S.A.* 109 J4
Vidauban, *France* 21 E10
Videbæk, *Denmark* 11 H2
Videle, *Romania* 43 F10
Vídho, *Greece* 36 A3
Vidigueira, *Portugal* 35 G3
Vidin, *Bulgaria* 40 C6
Vidio, C., *Spain* 34 B4
Vidisha, *India* 68 H7
Vidra, *Romania* 43 E11
Viduša, *Bos.-H.* 40 D2
Vidzy, *Belarus* 9 J22
Viechtach, *Germany* 25 F8
Viedma, *Argentina* 128 E4
Viedma, L., *Argentina* 128 F2
Vieira do Minho, *Portugal* 34 D2
Vielha, *Spain* 32 C5
Viella = Vielha, *Spain* 32 C5
Vielsalm, *Belgium* 17 D5
Vienenburg, *Germany* 24 D6
Vieng Pou Kha, *Laos* 58 G3
Vienna = Wien, *Austria* 27 C9
Vienna, *Ill., U.S.A.* 113 G10
Vienna, *Mo., U.S.A.* 112 F9
Vienne, *France* 21 C8
Vienne □, *France* 20 B4
Vienne →, *France* 18 E7
Vientiane, *Laos* 64 D4
Vientos, Paso de los, *Caribbean* 121 C5
Viernheim, *Germany* 25 F4
Viersen, *Germany* 24 D2
Vierwaldstättersee, *Switz.* 25 J4
Vierzon, *France* 19 E9
Vieste, *Italy* 29 G13
Vietnam ■, *Asia* 64 C6
Vieux-Boucau-les-Bains, *France* 20 E2
Vif, *France* 21 C9
Vigan, *Phil.* 61 C4
Vigévano, *Italy* 28 C5
Vigia, *Brazil* 125 D9
Vigía Chico, *Mexico* 119 D7
Víglas, Ákra, *Greece* 36 D9
Vignemale, *France* 20 F3
Vigneulles-lès-Hattonchâtel, *France* 19 D12
Vignola, *Italy* 28 D8
Vigo, *Spain* 34 C2
Vigo, Ría de, *Spain* 34 C2
Vigsø Bugt, *Denmark* 11 G2
Vihiers, *France* 18 E6
Vihowa, *Pakistan* 68 D4
Vihowa →, *Pakistan* 68 D4
Vijayawada, *India* 67 L12
Vík, *Iceland* 8 E4
Vika, *Sweden* 10 D8
Vikarbyn, *Sweden* 10 D9
Vikeke, *Indonesia* 63 F7
Viken, *Skåne, Sweden* 11 H6
Viken, *Skaraborg, Sweden* 11 F8
Viking, *Canada* 104 C6
Vikmanshyttan, *Sweden* 10 D9
Vikna, *Norway* 8 D14
Vila da Maganja, *Mozam.* 87 F4
Vila de João Belo = Xai-Xai, *Mozam.* 89 D5
Vila de Rei, *Portugal* 34 F2
Vila do Bispo, *Portugal* 35 H2
Vila do Conde, *Portugal* 34 D2
Vila Franca de Xira, *Portugal* 35 G2
Vila Gamito, *Mozam.* 87 E3
Vila Gomes da Costa, *Mozam.* 89 C5
Vila Machado, *Mozam.* 87 F3
Vila Mouzinho, *Mozam.* 87 E3
Vila Nova de Famalicão, *Portugal* 34 D2
Vila Nova de Fos Côa, *Portugal* 34 D3
Vila Nova de Foscôa = Vila Nova de Fos Côa, *Portugal* 34 D3
Vila Nova de Gaia, *Portugal* 34 D2
Vila Nova de Ourém, *Portugal* 34 F2
Vila Pouca de Aguiar, *Portugal* 34 D3
Vila Real, *Portugal* 34 D3
Vila Real □, *Portugal* 34 D3
Vila-real de los Infantes, *Spain* 32 F4
Vila Real de Santo António, *Portugal* 35 H3
Vila Vasco da Gama, *Mozam.* 87 E3
Vila Velha, *Brazil* 127 A7
Vila Viçosa, *Portugal* 35 G3
Vilafranca del Maestrat, *Spain* 32 E4
Vilafranca del Penedès, *Spain* 32 D6
Vilagarcía de Arousa, *Spain* 34 C2
Vilaine →, *France* 18 E4
Vilanandro, Tanjona, *Madag.* 89 B7
Vilanculos, *Mozam.* 89 C6
Vilanova de Castelló, *Spain* 33 F4
Vilanova i la Geltrú, *Spain* 32 D6
Vilar Formosa, *Portugal* 34 E4
Vilaseca, *Spain* 32 D6
Vilaseca-Salou = Vilaseca, *Spain* 32 D6
Vilbjerg, *Denmark* 11 H2
Vilches, *Spain* 35 G7
Vileyka, *Belarus* 46 E4
Vilhelmina, *Sweden* 8 D17
Vilhena, *Brazil* 124 F6
Viliga, *Russia* 51 C16
Viliya →, *Lithuania* 9 J21

Viljandi, *Estonia* 9 G21
Vilkaviškis, *Lithuania* 44 D10
Vilkija, *Lithuania* 44 C10
Vilkitskogo, Proliv, *Russia* 51 B11
Vilkovo = Vylkove, *Ukraine* 47 K5
Villa Abecia, *Bolivia* 126 A2
Villa Ahumada, *Mexico* 118 A3
Villa Ana, *Argentina* 126 B4
Villa Ángela, *Argentina* 126 B3
Villa Bella, *Bolivia* 124 F5
Villa Bens = Tarfaya, *Morocco* 78 C3
Villa Cañás, *Argentina* 126 C3
Villa Cisneros = Dakhla, *W. Sahara* 78 D2
Villa Colón, *Argentina* 126 C2
Villa Constitución, *Argentina* 126 C3
Villa de María, *Argentina* 126 B3
Villa del Rio, *Spain* 35 H6
Villa Dolores, *Argentina* 126 C2
Villa Frontera, *Mexico* 118 B4
Villa Guillermina, *Argentina* 126 B4
Villa Hayes, *Paraguay* 126 B4
Villa Iris, *Argentina* 126 D3
Villa Juárez, *Mexico* 118 B4
Villa María, *Argentina* 126 C3
Villa Mazán, *Argentina* 126 B2
Villa Minozzo, *Italy* 28 D7
Villa Montes, *Bolivia* 126 A3
Villa Ocampo, *Argentina* 126 B4
Villa Ocampo, *Mexico* 118 B3
Villa Ojo de Agua, *Argentina* 126 B3
Villa San Giovanni, *Italy* 31 D8
Villa San José, *Argentina* 126 C4
Villa San Martín, *Argentina* 126 B3
Villa Santina, *Italy* 29 B9
Villa Unión, *Mexico* 118 C3
Villablino, *Spain* 34 C4
Villacarlos, *Spain* 37 B11
Villacarriedo, *Spain* 34 B7
Villacarrillo, *Spain* 35 G7
Villacastín, *Spain* 34 E6
Villach, *Austria* 26 E6
Villacidro, *Italy* 30 C1
Villada, *Spain* 34 C6
Villadiego, *Spain* 34 C6
Villadóssola, *Italy* 28 B5
Villafeliche, *Spain* 32 D3
Villafranca, *Spain* 32 C3
Villafranca de los Barros, *Spain* 35 G4
Villafranca de los Caballeros, *Baleares, Spain* 37 B10
Villafranca de los Caballeros, *Toledo, Spain* 35 F7
Villafranca del Cid = Vilafranca del Maestrat, *Spain* 32 E4
Villafranca del Panadés = Vilafranca del Penedès, *Spain* 32 D6
Villafranca di Verona, *Italy* 28 C7
Villafranca Tirrena, *Italy* 31 D8
Villagrán, *Mexico* 119 C5
Villaguay, *Argentina* 126 C4
Villaharta, *Spain* 35 G6
Villahermosa, *Mexico* 119 D6
Villahermosa, *Spain* 33 G2
Villaines-la-Juhel, *France* 18 D6
Villajoyosa, *Spain* 33 G4
Villalba, *Spain* 34 B3
Villalba de Guardo, *Spain* 34 C6
Villalón de Campos, *Spain* 34 C5
Villalpando, *Spain* 34 D5
Villaluenga, *Spain* 34 E7
Villamanán, *Spain* 34 C5
Villamartín, *Spain* 35 J5
Villamayor de Santiago, *Spain* 32 F2
Villamblard, *France* 20 C4
Villanova Monteleone, *Italy* 30 B1
Villanueva, *U.S.A.* 113 H2
Villanueva de Castellón = Vilanova de Castelló, *Spain* 33 F4
Villanueva de Córdoba, *Spain* 35 G6
Villanueva de la Fuente, *Spain* 33 G2
Villanueva de la Serena, *Spain* 35 G5
Villanueva de la Sierra, *Spain* 34 E4
Villanueva de los Castillejos, *Spain* 35 H3
Villanueva de los Infantes, *Spain* 35 G7
Villanueva del Arzobispo, *Spain* 33 G2
Villanueva del Fresno, *Spain* 35 G3
Villanueva y Geltrú = Vilanova i la Geltrú, *Spain* 32 D6
Villaputzu, *Italy* 30 C2
Villaquilambre, *Spain* 34 C5
Villar del Arzobispo, *Spain* 32 F4
Villar del Rey, *Spain* 35 F4
Villard-de-Lans, *France* 21 C9
Villarramiel, *Spain* 34 C6
Villarreal = Vila-real de los Infantes, *Spain* 32 F4
Villarrica, *Chile* 128 D2
Villarrica, *Paraguay* 126 B4
Villarrobledo, *Spain* 33 F2
Villarroya de la Sierra, *Spain* 32 D3
Villarrubia de los Ojos, *Spain* 35 F7
Villars-les-Dombes, *France* 19 F12
Villasayas, *Spain* 32 D2
Villaseca de los Gamitos = Villaseco de los Gamitos, *Spain* 34 D4
Villaseco de los Gamitos, *Spain* 34 D4
Villasimíus, *Italy* 30 C2
Villastar, *Spain* 32 E3
Villatobas, *Spain* 34 F7
Villavicencio, *Argentina* 126 C2
Villavicencio, *Colombia* 124 C4
Villaviciosa, *Spain* 34 B5
Villazón, *Bolivia* 126 A2
Ville-Marie, *Canada* 102 C4
Ville Platte, *U.S.A.* 113 K8
Villedieu-les-Poêles, *France* 18 D5
Villefort, *France* 20 D7
Villefranche-de-Lauragais, *France* 20 E5
Villefranche-de-Rouergue, *France* 20 D6
Villefranche-du-Périgord, *France* 20 D5
Villefranche-sur-Saône, *France* 21 C8
Villel, *Spain* 32 E3
Villemur-sur-Tarn, *France* 20 E5
Villena, *Spain* 33 G4
Villenauxe-la-Grande, *France* 19 D10
Villenave-d'Ornon, *France* 20 D3
Villeneuve-d'Ascq, *France* 19 B10
Villeneuve-l'Archevêque, *France* 19 D10
Villeneuve-lès-Avignon, *France* 21 E8
Villeneuve-sur-Allier, *France* 19 F10
Villeneuve-sur-Lot, *France* 20 D4
Villeneuve-sur-Yonne, *France* 19 D10
Villeréal, *France* 20 D4
Villers-Bocage, *France* 18 C6
Villers-Cotterêts, *France* 19 C10
Villers-sur-Mer, *France* 18 C6
Villersexel, *France* 19 E13
Villerupt, *France* 19 C12
Villeurbanne, *France* 21 C8
Villiers, *S. Africa* 89 D4
Villingen-Schwenningen, *Germany* 25 G4
Vilna, *Canada* 104 C6
Vilnius, *Lithuania* 9 J21
Vils, *Austria* 26 D3
Vils →, *Bayern, Germany* 25 G9
Vils →, *Bayern, Germany* 25 F7
Vilsbiburg, *Germany* 25 G8
Vilshofen, *Germany* 25 G9
Vilusi, *Montenegro, Yug.* 40 D2
Vilvoorde, *Belgium* 17 D4
Vilyuy →, *Russia* 51 C13
Vilyuysk, *Russia* 51 C13
Vimianzo, *Spain* 34 B1
Vimioso, *Portugal* 34 D4
Vimmerby, *Sweden* 11 G9
Vimoutiers, *France* 18 D7
Vimperk, *Czech Rep.* 26 B6
Viña del Mar, *Chile* 126 C1
Vinarós, *Spain* 32 E5
Vincennes, *U.S.A.* 108 F2
Vincent, *U.S.A.* 117 L8
Vinchina, *Argentina* 126 B2
Vindelälven →, *Sweden* 8 E18
Vindeln, *Sweden* 8 D18
Vinderup, *Denmark* 11 H2
Vindhya Ra., *India* 68 H7
Vineland, *U.S.A.* 108 F8
Vineuil, *France* 18
Vinga, *Romania* 42 D6
Vingåker, *Sweden* 10 E9
Vinh, *Vietnam* 64 C5
Vinh Linh, *Vietnam* 64 D6
Vinh Long, *Vietnam* 65 G5
Vinh Yen, *Vietnam* 58 G5
Vinhais, *Portugal* 34 D3
Vinica, *Croatia* 29 B13
Vinica, *Macedonia* 40 E6
Vinica, *Slovenia* 29 C12
Vinita, *U.S.A.* 113 G7
Vinkovci, *Croatia* 42 E3
Vinnitsa = Vinnytsya, *Ukraine* 47 H5
Vinnytsya, *Ukraine* 47 H5
Vinslöv, *Sweden* 11 H7
Vintjärn, *Sweden* 10 D10
Vinton, *Calif., U.S.A.* 116 F6
Vinton, *Iowa, U.S.A.* 112 D8
Vinton, *La., U.S.A.* 113 K8
Vințu de Jos, *Romania* 43 D8
Viöl, *Germany* 24 A5
Vipava, *Slovenia* 29 C10
Vipiteno, *Italy* 29 B8
Vir, *Croatia* 29 D12
Virac, *Phil.* 61 E6
Virachei, *Cambodia* 64 F6
Virago Sd., *Canada* 104 C2
Viramgam, *India* 68 H5
Viranşehir, *Turkey* 70 B3
Virawah, *Pakistan* 68 G4
Virbalis, *Lithuania* 44 D9
Virden, *Canada* 105 D8
Vire, *France* 18 D6
Vire →, *France* 18 C5
Vírgenes, C., *Argentina* 128 G3
Virgin →, *U.S.A.* 115 H6
Virgin Gorda, *Virgin Is.* 121 C7
Virgin Is. (British) ■, *W. Indies* 121 C7
Virgin Is. (U.S.) ■, *W. Indies* 121 C7
Virginia, *S. Africa* 88 D4
Virginia, *U.S.A.* 112 B8
Virginia □, *U.S.A.* 108 G7
Virginia Beach, *U.S.A.* 108 G8
Virginia City, *Mont., U.S.A.* 114 D8
Virginia City, *Nev., U.S.A.* 116 F7
Virginia Falls, *Canada* 104 A3
Virginiatown, *Canada* 102 C4
Virje, *Croatia* 29 B13
Viroqua, *U.S.A.* 112 D9
Virovitica, *Croatia* 42 E2
Virpazar, *Montenegro, Yug.* 40 D3
Virpur, *India* 68 J4
Virserum, *Sweden* 11 G9
Virton, *Belgium* 17 E5
Virudunagar, *India* 66 Q10
Vis, *Croatia* 29 E13
Visalia, *U.S.A.* 116 J7
Visayan Sea, *Phil.* 61 F5
Visby, *Sweden* 11 G12
Viscount Melville Sd., *Canada* 4 B2
Visé, *Belgium* 17 D5
Višegrad, *Bos.-H.* 42 G4
Viseu, *Brazil* 125 D9
Viseu, *Portugal* 34 E3
Viseu □, *Portugal* 34 E3
Vişeu de Sus, *Romania* 43 C9
Vishakhapatnam, *India* 67 L13
Vişina, *Romania* 43 G9
Vişineşti, *Moldova* 43 D13
Visingsö, *Sweden* 11 F8
Viskafors, *Sweden* 11 G6
Viskan →, *Sweden* 11 G6
Viški Kanal, *Croatia* 29 E13
Vislanda, *Sweden* 11 H8
Visnagar, *India* 68 H5
Višnja Gora, *Slovenia* 29 C11
Viso, Mte., *Italy* 28 D4
Viso del Marqués, *Spain* 35 G7
Visoko, *Bos.-H.* 42 G3
Visokoi I., *Antarctica* 5 B1
Visp, *Switz.* 25 J3
Vissefjärda, *Sweden* 11 H9
Visselhövede, *Germany* 24 C5
Vissenbjerg, *Denmark* 11 J4
Vista, *U.S.A.* 117 M9
Vistonikos, Ormos = Vistonís, Límni, *Greece* 41 E9
Vistonís, Límni, *Greece* 41 E9
Vistula = Wisła →, *Poland* 44 D5
Vit →, *Bulgaria* 41 C8
Vitanje, *Slovenia* 29 B12
Vitebsk = Vitsyebsk, *Belarus* 46 E6
Viterbo, *Italy* 29 F9
Vitez, *Bos.-H.* 42 F2
Viti Levu, *Fiji* 91 C7
Vitigudino, *Spain* 34 D4
Vitim, *Russia* 51 D12
Vitim →, *Russia* 51 D12
Vitina, *Bos.-H.* 29 E14
Vitína, *Greece* 38 D4
Vítkov, *Czech Rep.* 27 B10
Vitória, *Brazil* 125 H10
Vitória da Conquista, *Brazil* 125 F10
Vitória de São Antão, *Brazil* 125 E11
Vitoria-Gasteiz, *Spain* 32 C2
Vitré, *France* 18 D5
Vitry-le-François, *France* 19 D11
Vitry-sur-Seine, *France* 19 D9
Vitsand, *Sweden* 10 D7
Vitsi, Óros, *Greece* 40 F5
Vitsyebsk, *Belarus* 46 E6
Vittaryd, *Sweden* 11 H7
Vitteaux, *France* 19 E11
Vittel, *France* 19 D12
Vittória, *Italy* 31 F7
Vittório Véneto, *Italy* 29 C9
Vittsjö, *Sweden* 11 H7
Viveiro, *Spain* 34 B3
Vivian, *U.S.A.* 113 J8
Viviers, *France* 21 D8
Vivonne, *France* 20 B4
Vizcaíno, Desierto de, *Mexico* 118 B2
Vizcaíno, Sierra, *Mexico* 118 B2
Vizcaya □, *Spain* 32 B2
Vize, *Turkey* 41 E11
Vizianagaram, *India* 67 K13
Vizille, *France* 21 C9
Viziñada, *Croatia* 29 C10
Viziru, *Romania* 43 E12
Vizzini, *Italy* 31 E7
Vjosa →, *Albania* 40 F3
Vlaardingen, *Neths.* 17 C4
Vlădeasa, Vf., *Romania* 42 D7
Vladičin Han, *Serbia, Yug.* 40 D6
Vladikavkaz, *Russia* 49 J7
Vladimir, *Russia* 46 D11
Vladimir Volynskiy = Volodymyr-Volynskyy, *Ukraine* 47 G3
Vladimirci, *Serbia, Yug.* 40 B3
Vladimirovac, *Serbia, Yug.* 42 E5
Vladimirovka, *Russia* 49 F8
Vladimirovo, *Bulgaria* 40 C7
Vladimorvka, *Kazakstan* 48 E10
Vladislavovka, *Ukraine* 47 K8
Vladivostok, *Russia* 51 E14
Vlăhiţa, *Romania* 43 D10
Vlakhiótis, *Greece* 38 E4
Vlasenica, *Bos.-H.* 42 F3
Vlašić, *Bos.-H.* 42 F2
Vlašim, *Czech Rep.* 26 B7
Vlasinsko Jezero, *Serbia, Yug.* 40 D6
Vlasotince, *Serbia, Yug.* 40 D6
Vlieland, *Neths.* 17 A4
Vlissingen, *Neths.* 17 C3
Vlóra, *Albania* 40 F3
Vlorës, Gjiri i, *Albania* 40 F3
Vltava →, *Czech Rep.* 26 A7
Vo Dat, *Vietnam* 65 G6
Vobarno, *Italy* 28 C7
Voćin, *Croatia* 42 E2
Vöcklabruck, *Austria* 26 C6
Vodice, *Croatia* 29 E12
Vodňany, *Czech Rep.* 26 B7
Vodnjan, *Croatia* 29 D10
Voe, *U.K.* 14 A7
Vogel Pk., *Nigeria* 83 D7
Vogelkop = Doberai, Jazirah, *Indonesia* 63 E8
Vogelsberg, *Germany* 24 E5
Voghera, *Italy* 28 D6
Vohibinany, *Madag.* 89 B8
Vohilava, *Madag.* 89 C8
Vohimarina = Iharana, *Madag.* 89 A9
Vohimena, Tanjon' i, *Madag.* 89 D8
Vohipeno, *Madag.* 89 C8
Voi, *Kenya* 86 C4
Void-Vacon, *France* 19 D12
Voineşti, *Iaşi, Romania* 43 C12
Voineşti, *Prahova, Romania* 43 E10
Voíotía □, *Greece* 38 C5
Voiron, *France* 21 C9
Voisey B., *Canada* 103 A7
Voitsberg, *Austria* 26 D8
Vojens, *Denmark* 11 J3
Vojmsjön, *Sweden* 8 D17
Vojnić, *Croatia* 29 C12
Vojnik, *Italy* 29 B12
Vojvodina □, *Serbia, Yug.* 42 E5
Vokhtoga, *Russia* 46 C11
Volary, *Czech Rep.* 26 C6
Volborg, *U.S.A.* 112 C2
Volcano Is. = Kazan-Rettō, *Pac. Oc.* 96 E6
Volchansk = Vovchansk, *Ukraine* 47 G9
Volchya →, *Ukraine* 47 H8
Volda, *Norway* 9 E12
Volga, *Russia* 46 C10
Volga →, *Russia* 49 G9
Volga Hts. = Privolzhskaya Vozvyshennost, *Russia* 48 E7
Volgo-Baltiyskiy Kanal, *Russia* 46 B9
Volgo-Donskoy Kanal, *Russia* 49 F7
Volgodonsk, *Russia* 49 G6
Volgograd, *Russia* 49 F7
Volgogradskoye Vdkhr., *Russia* 48 E8
Volgorechensk, *Russia* 48 B5
Volímai, *Greece* 38 D2
Volintiri, *Moldova* 43 D14
Volissós, *Greece* 39 C7
Volkach, *Germany* 25 F6
Völkermarkt, *Austria* 26 E7
Volkhov, *Russia* 46 C7
Volkhov →, *Russia* 46 B7
Völklingen, *Germany* 25 F2
Volkovysk = Vawkavysk, *Belarus* 47 F3
Volksrust, *S. Africa* 89 D4
Volnansk, *Ukraine* 47 H8
Volnovakha, *Ukraine* 47 J9
Volochanka, *Russia* 51 B10
Volodarsk, *Russia* 48 B6
Volodymyr-Volynskyy, *Ukraine* 47 G3
Vologda, *Russia* 46 C10
Volokolamsk, *Russia* 46 D8
Volokonovka, *Russia* 47 G9
Vólos, *Greece* 38 B4
Volosovo, *Russia* 46 C5
Volovets, *Ukraine* 47 H2
Volovo, *Russia* 46 F10
Volozhin = Valozhyn, *Belarus* 46 E4
Volsk, *Russia* 48 D8
Volta □, *Ghana* 83 D5
Volta →, *Ghana* 83 D5
Volta, L., *Ghana* 83 D5
Volta Blanche = White Volta →, *Ghana* 83 D4
Volta Redonda, *Brazil* 127 A7
Voltaire, C., *Australia* 92 B4
Volterra, *Italy* 28 E7
Voltri, *Italy* 28 D5
Volturno →, *Italy* 30 A6
Vólvi, L., *Greece* 40 F7
Volyně, *Czech Rep.* 26 B6
Volzhsk, *Russia* 48 C9
Volzhskiy, *Russia* 49 F7
Vondrozo, *Madag.* 89 C8
Vónitsa, *Greece* 38 C2
Vopnafjörður, *Iceland* 8 D6
Vorarlberg □, *Austria* 26 D2
Vóras Óros, *Greece* 40 F5
Vorbasse, *Denmark* 11 J3
Vorchdorf, *Austria* 26 C6
Vorderrhein →, *Switz.* 25 J5
Vordingborg, *Denmark* 11 J5
Vorë, *Albania* 40 E3
Voreppe, *France* 21 C9
Vóriai Sporádhes, *Greece* 38 B5
Vórios Aiyaíon □, *Greece* 39 C7
Vórios Evvoïkos Kólpos, *Greece* 38 C5
Vorkuta, *Russia* 50 C7
Vormsi, *Estonia* 9 G20
Vorona →, *Russia* 48 E6
Voronezh, *Russia* 47 G10
Voronezh, *Ukraine* 47 G7
Voronezh →, *Russia* 47 G10
Vorontsovo-Aleksandrovskoye = Zelenokumsk, *Russia* 49 H6
Voroshilovgrad = Luhansk, *Ukraine* 47 H10
Voroshilovsk = Alchevsk, *Ukraine* 47 H10
Vórroi, *Greece* 38 F6
Vorskla →, *Ukraine* 47 H8
Võrts Järv, *Estonia* 9 G22
Võru, *Estonia* 9 H22
Vosges, *France* 19 D14
Vosges □, *France* 19 D13
Voskopoja, *Albania* 40 F4
Voskresensk, *Russia* 46 E10
Voskresenskoye, *Russia* 48 B7
Voss, *Norway* 9 F12
Vostok I., *Kiribati* 97 J12
Votice, *Czech Rep.* 26 B7
Votsuri-Shima, *Japan* 55 M1
Vouga →, *Portugal* 34 E2
Vouillé, *France* 18 F7
Voúxa, Ákra, *Greece* 36 D5
Vouzela, *Portugal* 34 E2
Vouziers, *France* 19 C11
Vovchansk, *Ukraine* 47 G9
Vozhe, Ozero, *Russia* 46 B10
Vozhega, *Russia* 46 B11
Voznesensk, *Ukraine* 47 J6
Voznesenye, *Russia* 46 B8
Vrå, *Denmark* 11 G3
Vráble, *Slovak Rep.* 27 C11
Vračevšnica, *Serbia, Yug.* 40 B4
Vrakhnéïka, *Greece* 38 C3
Vrancea □, *Romania* 43 E11
Vrancei, Munţii, *Romania* 43 E11
Vrangelya, Ostrov, *Russia* 51 B19
Vranica, *Bos.-H.* 42 G2
Vranje, *Serbia, Yug.* 40 D5
Vranjska Banja, *Serbia, Yug.* 40 D6
Vranov nad Topl'ou, *Slovak Rep.* 27 C14
Vransko, *Slovenia* 29 B11
Vransko Jezero, *Croatia* 29 E12
Vrapčište, *Macedonia* 40 E4
Vratsa, *Bulgaria* 40 C7
Vrbas, *Serbia, Yug.* 42 E4
Vrbas →, *Bos.-H.* 42 E2
Vrbnik, *Croatia* 29 C11
Vrbovec, *Croatia* 29 C13
Vrbovsko, *Croatia* 29 C12
Vrchlabí, *Czech Rep.* 26 A8
Vrede, *S. Africa* 89 D4
Vredefort, *S. Africa* 88 D4
Vreden, *Germany* 24 C2
Vredenburg, *S. Africa* 88 E2
Vredendal, *S. Africa* 88 E2
Vretstorp, *Sweden* 10 E8
Vrgorac, *Croatia* 29 E14
Vrhnika, *Slovenia* 29 C11
Vridi, *Ivory C.* 82 D4
Vrigstad, *Sweden* 11 G8
Vrindavan, *India* 68 F7
Vríses, *Greece* 36 D6
Vrnograč, *Bos.-H.* 29 C12
Vrondádhes, *Greece* 39 C8
Vrpolje, *Croatia* 42 E3
Vršac, *Serbia, Yug.* 42 E6
Vrsacki Kanal, *Serbia, Yug.* 42 E5
Vrútky, *Slovak Rep.* 27 B11
Vryburg, *S. Africa* 88 D3
Vryheid, *S. Africa* 89 D5
Vsetín, *Czech Rep.* 27 B11
Vu Liet, *Vietnam* 64 C5
Vŭcha →, *Bulgaria* 41 D8
Vučitrn, *Kosovo, Yug.* 40 D4
Vukovar, *Croatia* 42 E3
Vulcan, *Canada* 104 C6
Vulcan, *Romania* 43 E8
Vulcaneşti, *Moldova* 43 E13
Vulcano, *Italy* 31 D7
Vŭlchedruma, *Bulgaria* 40 C7
Vulkaneshty = Vulcaneşti, *Moldova* 43 E13
Vunduzi →, *Mozam.* 87 F3
Vung Tau, *Vietnam* 65 G6
Vŭrbitsa, *Bulgaria* 41 D10
Vurshets, *Bulgaria* 40 C7
Vutcani, *Romania* 43 D12
Vuya, *Sudan* 81 F2
Vyartsilya, *Russia* 46 A6
Vyatka = Kirov, *Russia* 50 D5
Vyatka →, *Russia* 48 C10
Vyatskiye Polyany, *Russia* 48 B10
Vyazemskiy, *Russia* 51 E14
Vyazma, *Russia* 46 E8
Vyazniki, *Russia* 48 B6
Vyborg, *Russia* 46 B5
Vychegda →, *Russia* 50 C5
Vychodné Beskydy, *Europe* 27 B15
Východočeský □, *Czech Rep.* 26 E8
Vyerkhnyadzvinsk, *Belarus* 46 E4
Vyksa, *Russia* 48 C6
Vylkove, *Ukraine* 47 K5
Vynohradiv, *Ukraine* 47 H2
Vyrnwy, L., *U.K.* 12 E4
Vyshniy Volochek, *Russia* 46 D8
Vyshzha = imeni 26 Bakinskikh Komissarov, *Turkmenistan* 71 B7
Vyškov, *Czech Rep.* 27 B9
Vysoké Mýto, *Czech Rep.* 27 B9
Vysokovsk, *Russia* 46 D9
Vyšší Brod, *Czech Rep.* 26 C7
Vytegra, *Russia* 46 B9

W

W.A.C. Bennett Dam, *Canada* 104 B4
Wa, *Ghana* 82 C4
Waal →, *Neths.* 17 C5
Waalwijk, *Neths.* 17 C5
Waat, *Sudan* 81 F3
Wabana, *Canada* 103 C9
Wabasca →, *Canada* 104 B5
Wabasca-Desmarais, *Canada* 104 B6

Wabash, *U.S.A.* 108 E3
Wabash →, *U.S.A.* 108 G1
Wabi →, *Ethiopia* 81 F5
Wabigoon L., *Canada* 105 D10
Wabowden, *Canada* 105 C9
Wąbrzeźno, *Poland* 45 E5
Wabu Hu, *China* 59 A11
Wabuk Pt., *Canada* 102 A2
Wabush, *Canada* 103 B6
Wąchock, *Poland* 45 G8
Wächtersbach, *Germany* 25 E5
Waco, *U.S.A.* 113 K6
Waconichi, L., *Canada* 102 B5
Wad Ban Naqa, *Sudan* 81 D3
Wad Banda, *Sudan* 81 E2
Wad el Haddad, *Sudan* 81 E3
Wad en Nau, *Sudan* 81 E3
Wad Hamid, *Sudan* 81 D3
Wad Medanî, *Sudan* 81 E3
Wad Thana, *Pakistan* 68 F2
Wadai, *Africa* 76 E5
Wadayama, *Japan* 55 G7
Waddeneilanden, *Neths.* 17 A5
Waddenzee, *Neths.* 17 A5
Waddington, *U.S.A.* 111 B9
Waddington, Mt., *Canada* 104 C3
Waddy Pt., *Australia* 95 C5
Wadebridge, *U.K.* 13 G3
Wadena, *Canada* 105 C8
Wadena, *U.S.A.* 112 B7
Wädenswil, *Switz.* 25 H4
Wadern, *Germany* 25 F2
Wadeye, *Australia* 92 B4
Wadhams, *Canada* 104 C3
Wādī as Sīr, *Jordan* 75 D4
Wadi Gemâl, *Egypt* 80 C4
Wadi Halfa, *Sudan* 80 C3
Wadian, *China* 59 A9
Wadlew, *Poland* 45 G6
Wadowice, *Poland* 45 J6
Wadsworth, *Nev., U.S.A.* 114 G4
Wadsworth, *Ohio, U.S.A.* 110 E3
Waegwan, *S. Korea* 57 G15
Wafangdian, *China* 57 E11
Wafrah, *Si. Arabia* 70 D5
Wageningen, *Neths.* 17 C5
Wager B., *Canada* 101 B11
Wagga Wagga, *Australia* 95 F4
Waghete, *Indonesia* 63 E9
Wagin, *Australia* 93 F2
Wagner, *U.S.A.* 112 D5
Wagon Mound, *U.S.A.* 113 G2
Wagoner, *U.S.A.* 113 H7
Wągrowiec, *Poland* 45 F4
Wah, *Pakistan* 68 C5
Wahai, *Indonesia* 63 E7
Wahiawa, *U.S.A.* 106 H15
Wâḥid, *Egypt* 75 E1
Wahnai, *Afghan.* 68 C1
Wahni, *Ethiopia* 81 E4
Wahoo, *U.S.A.* 112 E6
Wahpeton, *U.S.A.* 112 B6
Wai, Koh, *Cambodia* 65 H4
Waiau →, *N.Z.* 91 K4
Waibeem, *Indonesia* 63 E8
Waiblingen, *Germany* 25 G5
Waidhofen an der Thaya, *Austria* 26 C8
Waidhofen an der Ybbs, *Austria* 26 D7
Waigeo, *Indonesia* 63 E8
Waihi, *N.Z.* 91 G5
Waihou →, *N.Z.* 91 G5
Waika, *Dem. Rep. of the Congo* 86 C2
Waikabubak, *Indonesia* 63 F5
Waikari, *N.Z.* 91 K4
Waikato →, *N.Z.* 91 G5
Waikerie, *Australia* 95 E3
Waikokopu, *N.Z.* 91 H6
Waikouaiti, *N.Z.* 91 L3
Wailuku, *U.S.A.* 106 H16
Waimakariri →, *N.Z.* 91 K4
Waimate, *N.Z.* 91 L3
Wainganga →, *India* 66 K11
Waingapu, *Indonesia* 63 F6
Waini →, *Guyana* 124 B7
Wainwright, *Canada* 105 C6
Waiouru, *N.Z.* 91 H5
Waipara, *N.Z.* 91 K4
Waipawa, *N.Z.* 91 H6
Waipiro, *N.Z.* 91 H7
Waipu, *N.Z.* 91 F5
Waipukurau, *N.Z.* 91 J6
Wairakei, *N.Z.* 91 H6
Wairarapa, L., *N.Z.* 91 J5
Wairoa, *N.Z.* 91 H6
Waitaki →, *N.Z.* 91 L3
Waitara, *N.Z.* 91 H5
Waitsburg, *U.S.A.* 114 C5
Waiuku, *N.Z.* 91 G5
Wajima, *Japan* 55 F8
Wajir, *Kenya* 86 B5
Waka, *Ethiopia* 81 F4
Wakasa, *Japan* 55 G7
Wakasa-Wan, *Japan* 55 G7
Wakatipu, L., *N.Z.* 91 L2
Wakaw, *Canada* 105 C7
Wakayama, *Japan* 55 G7
Wakayama □, *Japan* 55 H7
Wake Forest, *U.S.A.* 109 H6
Wake I., *Pac. Oc.* 96 F8
WaKeeney, *U.S.A.* 112 F5
Wakefield, *N.Z.* 91 J4
Wakefield, *U.K.* 12 D6
Wakefield, *Mass., U.S.A.* 111 D13
Wakefield, *Mich., U.S.A.* 112 B10
Wakema, *Burma* 67 L19
Wakkanai, *Japan* 54 B10
Wakkerstroom, *S. Africa* 89 D5
Wakool, *Australia* 95 F3
Wakool →, *Australia* 95 F3
Wakre, *Indonesia* 63 E8
Wakuach, L., *Canada* 103 A6
Walamba, *Zambia* 87 E2
Wałbrzych, *Poland* 45 H3
Walbury Hill, *U.K.* 13 F6
Walcha, *Australia* 95 E5
Walcheren, *Neths.* 17 C3
Walcott, *U.S.A.* 114 F10
Wałcz, *Poland* 45 E3
Waldbröl, *Germany* 24 E3
Waldburg Ra., *Australia* 93 D2
Waldeck, *Germany* 24 D5
Walden, *Colo., U.S.A.* 114 F10
Walden, *N.Y., U.S.A.* 111 E10
Waldkirch, *Germany* 25 G3
Waldkirchen, *Germany* 25 G9
Waldkraiburg, *Germany* 25 G8
Waldport, *U.S.A.* 114 D1
Waldron, *U.S.A.* 113 H7
Waldviertel, *Austria* 26 C8
Walebing, *Australia* 93 F2
Walembele, *Ghana* 82 C4
Walensee, *Switz.* 25 H5
Wales □, *U.K.* 13 E3
Walewale, *Ghana* 83 C4
Walgett, *Australia* 95 E4
Walgreen Coast, *Antarctica* 5 D15
Walker, *U.S.A.* 112 B7
Walker, L., *Canada* 103 B6
Walker L., *Canada* 105 C9
Walker L., *U.S.A.* 114 G4
Walkerston, *Australia* 94 C4
Walkerton, *Canada* 102 D3
Wall, *U.S.A.* 112 D3
Walla Walla, *U.S.A.* 114 C4
Wallace, *Idaho, U.S.A.* 114 C6
Wallace, *N.C., U.S.A.* 109 H7
Wallaceburg, *Canada* 102 D3
Wallachia = Valahia, *Romania* 43 F9
Wallal, *Australia* 95 D4
Wallam Cr. →, *Australia* 95 D4
Wallambin, L., *Australia* 93 F2
Wallan, *Australia* 95 F3
Wallangarra, *Australia* 95 D5
Wallaroo, *Australia* 95 E2
Walldürn, *Germany* 25 F5
Wallenhorst, *Germany* 24 C4
Wallenpaupack, L., *U.S.A.* 111 E9
Wallingford, *U.S.A.* 111 E12
Wallis & Futuna, Is., *Pac. Oc.* 96 J10
Wallowa, *U.S.A.* 114 D5
Wallowa Mts., *U.S.A.* 114 D5
Walls, *U.K.* 14 A7
Wallula, *U.S.A.* 114 C4
Wallumbilla, *Australia* 95 D4
Walmsley, L., *Canada* 105 A7
Walney, I. of, *U.K.* 12 C4
Walnut Creek, *U.S.A.* 116 H4
Walnut Ridge, *U.S.A.* 113 G9
Walpole, *Australia* 93 F2
Walpole, *U.S.A.* 111 D13
Wals, *Austria* 26 D5
Walsall, *U.K.* 13 E6
Walsenburg, *U.S.A.* 113 G2
Walsh, *U.S.A.* 113 G3
Walsh →, *Australia* 94 B3
Walsrode, *Germany* 24 C5
Walterboro, *U.S.A.* 109 J5
Walters, *U.S.A.* 113 H5
Waltershausen, *Germany* 24 E6
Waltham, *U.S.A.* 111 D13
Waltman, *U.S.A.* 114 E10
Walton, *U.S.A.* 111 D9
Walton-on-the-Naze, *U.K.* 13 F9
Walvis Bay, *Namibia* 88 C1
Walvisbaai = Walvis Bay, *Namibia* 88 C1
Wamba, *Dem. Rep. of the Congo* 86 B2
Wamba, *Kenya* 86 B4
Wamba, *Nigeria* 83 D6
Wamego, *U.S.A.* 112 F6
Wamena, *Indonesia* 63 E9
Wamsutter, *U.S.A.* 114 F9
Wamulan, *Indonesia* 63 E7
Wan Xian, *China* 56 E8
Wana, *Pakistan* 68 C3
Wanaaring, *Australia* 95 D3
Wanaka, *N.Z.* 91 L2
Wanaka L., *N.Z.* 91 L2
Wan'an, *China* 59 D10
Wanapitei L., *Canada* 102 C3
Wandel Sea = McKinley Sea, *Arctic* 4 A7
Wandérama, *Ivory C.* 82 D4
Wanderer, *Zimbabwe* 87 F3
Wandhari, *Pakistan* 68 F2
Wanding, *China* 58 E2
Wandoan, *Australia* 95 D4
Wanfu, *China* 57 D12
Wang →, *Thailand* 64 D2
Wang Kai, *Sudan* 81 F2
Wang Noi, *Thailand* 64 E3
Wang Saphung, *Thailand* 64 D3
Wang Thong, *Thailand* 64 D3
Wanga, *Dem. Rep. of the Congo* 86 B2
Wangal, *Indonesia* 63 F8
Wanganella, *Australia* 95 F3
Wanganui, *N.Z.* 91 H5
Wangaratta, *Australia* 95 F4
Wangary, *Australia* 95 E2
Wangcang, *China* 58 A6
Wangcheng, *China* 59 C9
Wangdu, *China* 56 E8
Wangen, *Germany* 25 H5
Wangerooge, *Germany* 24 B3
Wangi, *Kenya* 86 C5
Wangiwangi, *Indonesia* 63 F6
Wangjiang, *China* 59 B11
Wangmo, *China* 58 E6
Wangolodougou, *Ivory C.* 82 D3
Wangqing, *China* 57 C15
Wankaner, *India* 68 H4
Wanless, *Canada* 105 C8
Wannian, *China* 59 C11
Wanning, *Taiwan* 64 C8
Wanon Niwat, *Thailand* 64 D4
Wanquan, *China* 56 D8
Wanrong, *China* 56 G6
Wanshan, *China* 58 D7
Wanshengchang, *China* 58 C6
Wantage, *U.K.* 13 F6
Wanyuan, *China* 58 A7
Wanzai, *China* 59 C10
Wapakoneta, *U.S.A.* 108 E3
Wapato, *U.S.A.* 114 C3
Wapawekka L., *Canada* 105 C8
Wapikopa L., *Canada* 102 B2
Wapiti →, *Canada* 104 B5
Wappingers Falls, *U.S.A.* 111 E11
Wapsipinicon →, *U.S.A.* 112 E9
Warab □, *Sudan* 81 F2
Warangal, *India* 66 L11
Waraseoni, *India* 69 J9
Waratah, *Australia* 94 G4
Waratah B., *Australia* 95 F4
Warburg, *Germany* 24 D5
Warburton, *Vic., Australia* 95 F4
Warburton, *W. Austral., Australia* 93 E4
Warburton Ra., *Australia* 93 E4
Ward, *N.Z.* 91 J5
Ward →, *Australia* 95 D4
Ward Mt., *U.S.A.* 116 H8
Warden, *S. Africa* 89 D4
Wardha, *India* 66 J11
Wardha →, *India* 66 K11
Ware, *Canada* 104 B3
Ware, *U.S.A.* 111 D12
Waregem, *Belgium* 17 D3
Wareham, *U.S.A.* 111 E14
Waremme, *Belgium* 17 D5
Waren, *Germany* 24 B8
Warendorf, *Germany* 24 D4
Warialda, *Australia* 95 D5
Wariap, *Indonesia* 63 E8
Warin Chamrap, *Thailand* 64 E5
Warka, *Poland* 45 G8
Warkopi, *Indonesia* 63 E8
Warm Springs, *U.S.A.* 115 G5
Warman, *Canada* 105 C7
Warmbad, *Namibia* 88 D2
Warmbad, *S. Africa* 89 C4
Warmińsko-Mazurskie □, *Poland* 44 D8
Warminster, *U.K.* 13 F5
Warminster, *U.S.A.* 111 F9
Warnemünde, *Germany* 24 A8
Warner Mts., *U.S.A.* 114 F3
Warner Robins, *U.S.A.* 109 J4
Warnow →, *Germany* 24 A8
Waroona, *Australia* 93 F2
Warracknabeal, *Australia* 95 F3
Warragul, *Australia* 95 F4
Warrego →, *Australia* 95 E4
Warrego Ra., *Australia* 94 C4
Warren, *Australia* 95 E4
Warren, *Ark., U.S.A.* 113 J8
Warren, *Mich., U.S.A.* 108 D4
Warren, *Minn., U.S.A.* 112 A6
Warren, *Ohio, U.S.A.* 110 E4
Warren, *Pa., U.S.A.* 110 E5
Warrenpoint, *U.K.* 15 B5
Warrensburg, *Mo., U.S.A.* 112 F8
Warrensburg, *N.Y., U.S.A.* 111 C11
Warrenton, *S. Africa* 88 D3
Warrenton, *U.S.A.* 116 D3
Warri, *Nigeria* 83 D6
Warrina, *Australia* 95 D2
Warrington, *U.K.* 12 D5
Warrington, *U.S.A.* 109 K2
Warrington □, *U.K.* 12 D5
Warrnambool, *Australia* 95 F3
Warroad, *U.S.A.* 112 A7
Warruwi, *Australia* 94 A1
Warsa, *Indonesia* 63 E9
Warsak Dam, *Pakistan* 68 B4
Warsaw = Warszawa, *Poland* 45 F8
Warsaw, *Ind., U.S.A.* 108 E3
Warsaw, *N.Y., U.S.A.* 110 D6
Warsaw, *Ohio, U.S.A.* 110 F3
Warstein, *Germany* 24 D4
Warszawa, *Poland* 45 F8
Warta, *Poland* 45 G5
Warta →, *Poland* 45 F1
Warthe = Warta →, *Poland* 45 F1
Waru, *Indonesia* 63 E8
Warwick, *Australia* 95 D5
Warwick, *U.K.* 13 E6
Warwick, *N.Y., U.S.A.* 111 E10
Warwick, *R.I., U.S.A.* 111 E13
Warwickshire □, *U.K.* 13 E6
Wasaga Beach, *Canada* 110 B4
Wasagaming, *Canada* 105 C9
Wasatch Ra., *U.S.A.* 114 F8
Wasbank, *S. Africa* 89 D5
Wasco, *Calif., U.S.A.* 117 K7
Wasco, *Oreg., U.S.A.* 114 D3
Wase, *Nigeria* 83 D6
Waseca, *U.S.A.* 112 C8
Wasekamio L., *Canada* 105 B7
Wash, The, *U.K.* 12 E8
Washago, *Canada* 110 B5
Washburn, *N. Dak., U.S.A.* 112 B4
Washburn, *Wis., U.S.A.* 112 B9
Washim, *India* 66 J10
Washington, *U.K.* 12 C6
Washington, *D.C., U.S.A.* 108 F7
Washington, *Ga., U.S.A.* 109 J4
Washington, *Ind., U.S.A.* 108 F2
Washington, *Iowa, U.S.A.* 112 E9
Washington, *Mo., U.S.A.* 112 F9
Washington, *N.C., U.S.A.* 109 H7
Washington, *N.J., U.S.A.* 111 F10
Washington, *Pa., U.S.A.* 110 F4
Washington, *Utah, U.S.A.* 115 H7
Washington □, *U.S.A.* 114 C3
Washington, Mt., *U.S.A.* 111 B13
Washington Court House, *U.S.A.* 108 F4
Washington I., *U.S.A.* 108 C2
Washougal, *U.S.A.* 116 E4
Wasian, *Indonesia* 63 E8
Wasilków, *Poland* 45 E10
Wasilla, *U.S.A.* 100 B5
Wasior, *Indonesia* 63 E8
Waskaganish, *Canada* 102 B4
Waskaiowaka, L., *Canada* 105 B9
Waskesiu Lake, *Canada* 105 C7
Wasserburg, *Germany* 25 G8
Wasserkuppe, *Germany* 24 E5
Wassy, *France* 19 D11
Waswanipi, *Canada* 102 C4
Waswanipi, L., *Canada* 102 C4
Watampone, *Indonesia* 63 E6
Water Park Pt., *Australia* 94 C5
Water Valley, *U.S.A.* 113 H10
Waterberge, *S. Africa* 89 C4
Waterbury, *Conn., U.S.A.* 111 E11
Waterbury, *Vt., U.S.A.* 111 B12
Waterbury L., *Canada* 105 B8
Waterdown, *Canada* 110 C5
Waterford, *Canada* 110 D4
Waterford, *Ireland* 15 D4
Waterford, *Calif., U.S.A.* 116 H6
Waterford, *Pa., U.S.A.* 110 E5
Waterford □, *Ireland* 15 D4
Waterford Harbour, *Ireland* 15 D5
Waterhen L., *Canada* 105 C9
Waterloo, *Belgium* 17 D4
Waterloo, *Ont., Canada* 102 D3
Waterloo, *Qué., Canada* 111 A12
Waterloo, *S. Leone* 82 D2
Waterloo, *Ill., U.S.A.* 112 F9
Waterloo, *Iowa, U.S.A.* 112 D8
Waterloo, *N.Y., U.S.A.* 110 D8
Watersmeet, *U.S.A.* 112 B10
Waterton Lakes Nat. Park, *U.S.A.* 114 B7
Watertown, *Conn., U.S.A.* 111 E11
Watertown, *N.Y., U.S.A.* 111 C9
Watertown, *S. Dak., U.S.A.* 112 C6
Watertown, *Wis., U.S.A.* 112 D10
Waterval-Boven, *S. Africa* 89 D5
Waterville, *Canada* 111 A13
Waterville, *Maine, U.S.A.* 109 C11
Waterville, *N.Y., U.S.A.* 111 D9
Waterville, *Pa., U.S.A.* 110 E7
Waterville, *Wash., U.S.A.* 114 C3
Watervliet, *U.S.A.* 111 D11
Wates, *Indonesia* 63 G14
Watford, *Canada* 110 D3
Watford, *U.K.* 13 F7
Watford City, *U.S.A.* 112 B3
Wathaman →, *Canada* 105 B8
Wathaman L., *Canada* 105 B8
Watheroo, *Australia* 93 F2
Wating, *China* 56 G4
Watkins Glen, *U.S.A.* 110 D8
Watling I. = San Salvador I., *Bahamas* 121 B5
Watonga, *U.S.A.* 113 H5
Watrous, *Canada* 105 C7
Watrous, *U.S.A.* 113 H2
Watsa, *Dem. Rep. of the Congo* 86 B2
Watseka, *U.S.A.* 108 E2
Watson, *Australia* 93 F5
Watson, *Canada* 105 C8
Watson Lake, *Canada* 104 A3
Watsontown, *U.S.A.* 110 E8
Watsonville, *U.S.A.* 116 J5
Wattiwarriganna Cr. →, *Australia* 95 D2
Wattwil, *Switz.* 25 H5
Watuata = Batuata, *Indonesia* 63 F6
Watubela, Kepulauan, *Indonesia* 63 E8
Watubela Is. = Watubela, Kepulauan, *Indonesia* 63 E8
Wau, *Sudan* 77 F6
Waubamik, *Canada* 110 A4
Waubay, *U.S.A.* 112 C6
Wauchope, *N.S.W., Australia* 95 E5
Wauchope, *N. Terr., Australia* 94 C1
Waukarlycarly, L., *Australia* 92 D3
Waukegan, *U.S.A.* 108 D2
Waukesha, *U.S.A.* 108 D1
Waukon, *U.S.A.* 112 D9
Waupaca, *U.S.A.* 112 C10
Waupun, *U.S.A.* 112 D10
Waurika, *U.S.A.* 113 H6
Wausau, *U.S.A.* 112 C10
Wautoma, *U.S.A.* 112 C10
Wauwatosa, *U.S.A.* 108 D2
Waveney →, *U.K.* 13 E9
Waverley, *N.Z.* 91 H5
Waverly, *Iowa, U.S.A.* 112 D8
Waverly, *N.Y., U.S.A.* 111 E8
Wavre, *Belgium* 17 D4
Wâw, *Sudan* 81 F2
Wāw al Kabīr, *Libya* 79 C9
Wawa, *Canada* 102 C3
Wawa, *Nigeria* 83 D5
Wawa, *Sudan* 80 C3
Wawanesa, *Canada* 105 D9
Wawona, *U.S.A.* 116 H7
Waxahachie, *U.S.A.* 113 J6
Way, L., *Australia* 93 E3
Waycross, *U.S.A.* 109 K4
Wayi, *Sudan* 81 F3
Wayland, *U.S.A.* 110 D7
Wayne, *Nebr., U.S.A.* 112 D6
Wayne, *W. Va., U.S.A.* 108 F4
Waynesboro, *Ga., U.S.A.* 109 J4
Waynesboro, *Miss., U.S.A.* 109 K1
Waynesboro, *Pa., U.S.A.* 108 F7
Waynesboro, *Va., U.S.A.* 108 F6
Waynesburg, *U.S.A.* 108 F5
Waynesville, *U.S.A.* 109 H4
Waynoka, *U.S.A.* 113 G5
Wazirabad, *Pakistan* 68 C6
Wda →, *Poland* 44 E5
We, *Indonesia* 62 C1
Weald, The, *U.K.* 13 F8
Wear →, *U.K.* 12 C6
Weatherford, *Okla., U.S.A.* 113 H5
Weatherford, *Tex., U.S.A.* 113 J6
Weaverville, *U.S.A.* 114 F2
Webb City, *U.S.A.* 113 G7
Webequie, *Canada* 102 B2
Webo = Nyaake, *Liberia* 82 E3
Webster, *Mass., U.S.A.* 111 D13
Webster, *N.Y., U.S.A.* 110 C7
Webster, *S. Dak., U.S.A.* 112 C6
Webster City, *U.S.A.* 112 D8
Webster Springs, *U.S.A.* 108 F5
Weda, *Indonesia* 63 D7
Weda, Teluk, *Indonesia* 63 D7
Weddell I., *Falk. Is.* 128 G4
Weddell Sea, *Antarctica* 5 D1
Wedderburn, *Australia* 95 F3
Wedel, *Germany* 24 B5
Wedemark, *Germany* 24 C5
Wedgeport, *Canada* 103 D6
Wedza, *Zimbabwe* 87 F3
Wee Waa, *Australia* 95 E4
Weed, *U.S.A.* 114 F2
Weed Heights, *U.S.A.* 116 G7
Weedsport, *U.S.A.* 111 C8
Weedville, *U.S.A.* 110 E6
Weenen, *S. Africa* 89 D5
Weener, *Germany* 24 B3
Weert, *Neths.* 17 C5
Węgierska-Górka, *Poland* 45 J6
Węgliniec, *Poland* 45 G2
Węgorzewo, *Poland* 44 D8
Węgorzyno, *Poland* 44 E2
Węgrów, *Poland* 45 F9
Wehda □, *Sudan* 81 F3
Wei He →, *Hebei, China* 56 F8
Wei He →, *Shaanxi, China* 56 G6
Weichang, *China* 57 D9
Weichuan, *China* 56 G7
Weida, *Germany* 24 E8
Weiden, *Germany* 25 F8
Weifang, *China* 57 F10
Weihai, *China* 57 F12
Weil, *Germany* 25 H3
Weilburg, *Germany* 24 E4
Weilheim, *Germany* 25 H7
Weimar, *Germany* 24 E7
Weinan, *China* 56 G5
Weingarten, *Germany* 25 F4
Weinheim, *Germany* 25 F4
Weining, *China* 58 D5
Weipa, *Australia* 94 A3
Weir →, *Australia* 95 D4
Weir →, *Canada* 105 B10
Weir River, *Canada* 105 B10
Weirton, *U.S.A.* 110 F4
Weiser, *U.S.A.* 114 D5
Weishan, *Shandong, China* 57 G9
Weishan, *Yunnan, China* 58 E3
Weissenburg, *Germany* 25 F6
Weissenfels, *Germany* 24 D7
Weisswasser, *Germany* 24 D10
Wéitra, *Austria* 26 C7
Weixi, *China* 58 D2
Weixin, *China* 58 D5
Weiyuan, *China* 56 G3
Weiz, *Austria* 26 D8
Weizhou Dao, *China* 58 G7
Wejherowo, *Poland* 44 D5
Wekusko L., *Canada* 105 C9
Welch, *U.S.A.* 108 G5
Weldya, *Ethiopia* 81 E4
Welega □, *Ethiopia* 81 F3
Welkite, *Ethiopia* 81 F4
Welkom, *S. Africa* 88 D4
Welland, *Canada* 102 D4
Welland →, *U.K.* 13 E7
Wellesley Is., *Australia* 94 B2
Wellingborough, *U.K.* 13 E7
Wellington, *Australia* 95 E4
Wellington, *Canada* 110 C7
Wellington, *N.Z.* 91 J5
Wellington, *S. Africa* 88 E2
Wellington, *Somst., U.K.* 13 G4
Wellington, *Telford & Wrekin, U.K.* 13 E5
Wellington, *Colo., U.S.A.* 112 E2
Wellington, *Kans., U.S.A.* 113 G6
Wellington, *Nev., U.S.A.* 116 G7
Wellington, *Ohio, U.S.A.* 110 E2
Wellington, *Tex., U.S.A.* 113 H4
Wellington, I., *Chile* 122 H3
Wellington, L., *Australia* 95 F4
Wells, *U.K.* 13 F5
Wells, *Maine, U.S.A.* 111 C14
Wells, *N.Y., U.S.A.* 111 C10
Wells, *Nev., U.S.A.* 114 F6
Wells, L., *Australia* 93 E3
Wells, Mt., *Australia* 92 C4
Wells Gray Prov. Park, *Canada* 104 C4

Wells-next-the-Sea, *U.K.* 12 E8
Wells River, *U.S.A.* 111 B12
Wellsboro, *U.S.A.* 110 E7
Wellsburg, *U.S.A.* 110 F4
Wellsville, *N.Y., U.S.A.* 110 D7
Wellsville, *Ohio, U.S.A.* 110 F4
Wellsville, *Utah, U.S.A.* 114 F8
Wellton, *U.S.A.* 115 K6
Welmel, Wabi →, *Ethiopia* 81 F5
Welo □, *Ethiopia* 81 E4
Wels, *Austria* 26 C7
Welshpool, *U.K.* 13 E4
Welwyn Garden City, *U.K.* 13 F7
Wem, *U.K.* 12 E5
Wembere →, *Tanzania* 86 C3
Wemindji, *Canada* 102 B4
Wen Xian, *China* 56 G7
Wenatchee, *U.S.A.* 114 C3
Wenchang, *China* 64 C8
Wencheng, *China* 59 D13
Wenchi, *Ghana* 82 D4
Wenchow = Wenzhou, *China* 59 D13
Wenchuan, *China* 58 B4
Wenden, *U.S.A.* 117 M13
Wendeng, *China* 57 F12
Wendesi, *Indonesia* 63 E8
Wendo, *Ethiopia* 81 F4
Wendover, *U.S.A.* 114 F6
Weng'an, *China* 58 D6
Wengcheng, *China* 59 E9
Wengyuan, *China* 59 E10
Wenjiang, *China* 58 B4
Wenling, *China* 59 C13
Wenlock →, *Australia* 94 A3
Wenshan, *China* 58 F5
Wenshang, *China* 56 G9
Wenshui, *Guizhou, China* 58 C6
Wenshui, *Shanxi, China* 56 F7
Wensleydale, *U.K.* 12 C6
Wensu, *China* 60 B3
Wensum →, *U.K.* 12 E8
Wentworth, *Australia* 95 E3
Wentzel L., *Canada* 104 B6
Wenut, *Indonesia* 63 E8
Wenxi, *China* 56 G6
Wenxian, *China* 56 H3
Wenzhou, *China* 59 D13
Weott, *U.S.A.* 114 F2
Wepener, *S. Africa* 88 D4
Werda, *Botswana* 88 D3
Werdau, *Germany* 24 E8
Werder, *Germany* 24 C8
Werdohl, *Germany* 24 D3
Wereilu, *Ethiopia* 81 E4
Weri, *Indonesia* 63 E8
Werneck, *Germany* 25 F6
Wernigerode, *Germany* 24 D6
Werra →, *Germany* 24 D5
Werrimull, *Australia* 95 E3
Werris Creek, *Australia* 95 E5
Wertach →, *Germany* 25 G6
Wertheim, *Germany* 25 F5
Wertingen, *Germany* 25 G6
Wesel, *Germany* 24 D2
Weser →, *Germany* 24 B4
Weser-Ems □, *Germany* 24 C3
Weserbergland, *Germany* 24 C5
Wesiri, *Indonesia* 63 F7
Weslemkoon L., *Canada* 110 A7
Wesleyville, *Canada* 103 C9
Wesleyville, *U.S.A.* 110 D4
Wessel, C., *Australia* 94 A2
Wessel Is., *Australia* 94 A2
Wesselburen, *Germany* 24 A4
Wessington Springs, *U.S.A.* 112 C5
West, *U.S.A.* 113 K6
West →, *U.S.A.* 111 D12
West Baines →, *Australia* 92 C4
West Bank □, *Asia* 75 C4
West Bend, *U.S.A.* 108 D1
West Bengal □, *India* 69 H13
West Berkshire □, *U.K.* 13 F6
West Beskids = Západné Beskydy, *Europe* 27 B12
West Branch, *U.S.A.* 108 C3
West Branch Susquehanna →, *U.S.A.* 111 F8
West Bromwich, *U.K.* 13 E6
West Burra, *U.K.* 14 A7
West Canada Cr. →, *U.S.A.* 111 C10
West Cape Howe, *Australia* 93 G2
West Chazy, *U.S.A.* 111 B11
West Chester, *U.S.A.* 111 G9
West Columbia, *U.S.A.* 113 L7
West Covina, *U.S.A.* 117 L9
West Des Moines, *U.S.A.* 112 E8
West Dunbartonshire □, *U.K.* 14 F4
West End, *Bahamas* 120 A4
West Falkland, *Falk. Is.* 122 J4
West Fargo, *U.S.A.* 112 B6
West Farmington, *U.S.A.* 110 E4
West Fjord = Vestfjorden, *Norway* 8 C15
West Fork Trinity →, *U.S.A.* 113 J6
West Frankfort, *U.S.A.* 112 G10
West Hartford, *U.S.A.* 111 E12
West Haven, *U.S.A.* 111 E12
West Hazleton, *U.S.A.* 111 F9
West Helena, *U.S.A.* 113 H9
West Hurley, *U.S.A.* 111 E10
West Ice Shelf, *Antarctica* 5 C7
West Indies, *Cent. Amer.* 121 D7
West Jordan, *U.S.A.* 114 F8
West Lorne, *Canada* 110 D3
West Lothian □, *U.K.* 14 F5
West Lunga →, *Zambia* 87 E1
West Memphis, *U.S.A.* 113 H9
West Midlands □, *U.K.* 13 E6
West Mifflin, *U.S.A.* 110 F5
West Milton, *U.S.A.* 110 E8
West Monroe, *U.S.A.* 113 J8
West Newton, *U.S.A.* 110 F5
West Nicholson, *Zimbabwe* 87 G2
West Palm Beach, *U.S.A.* 109 M5
West Plains, *U.S.A.* 113 G9
West Point, *N.Y., U.S.A.* 111 E11
West Point, *Nebr., U.S.A.* 112 E6
West Point, *Va., U.S.A.* 108 G7
West Pt. = Ouest, Pte. de l', *Canada* 103 C7
West Pt., *Australia* 95 F2
West Road →, *Canada* 104 C4
West Rutland, *U.S.A.* 111 C11
West Schelde = Westerschelde →, *Neths.* 17 C3
West Seneca, *U.S.A.* 110 D6
West Siberian Plain, *Russia* 52 C11
West Sussex □, *U.K.* 13 G7
West-Terschelling, *Neths.* 17 A5
West Valley City, *U.S.A.* 114 F8
West Virginia □, *U.S.A.* 108 F5
West-Vlaanderen □, *Belgium* 17 D2
West Walker →, *U.S.A.* 116 G7
West Wyalong, *Australia* 95 E4
West Yellowstone, *U.S.A.* 114 D8
West Yorkshire □, *U.K.* 12 D6
Westall Pt., *Australia* 95 E1
Westbrook, *U.S.A.* 109 D10
Westbury, *Australia* 94 G4
Westby, *U.S.A.* 112 A2
Westend, *U.S.A.* 117 K9
Westerland, *Germany* 9 J13
Westerly, *U.S.A.* 111 E13
Western □, *Ghana* 82 D4
Western □, *Kenya* 86 B3
Western □, *S. Leone* 82 D2
Western □, *Uganda* 86 B3
Western □, *Zambia* 87 F1
Western Australia □, *Australia* 93 E2
Western Cape □, *S. Africa* 88 E3
Western Dvina = Daugava →, *Latvia* 9 H21
Western Ghats, *India* 66 N9
Western Isles □, *U.K.* 14 D1
Western Sahara ■, *Africa* 78 D3
Western Samoa ■, *Pac. Oc.* 91 B13
Westernport, *U.S.A.* 108 F6
Westerschelde →, *Neths.* 17 C3
Westerstede, *Germany* 24 B3
Westerwald, *Germany* 24 E3
Westfield, *Mass., U.S.A.* 111 D12
Westfield, *N.Y., U.S.A.* 110 D5
Westfield, *Pa., U.S.A.* 110 E7
Westhill, *U.K.* 14 D6
Westhope, *U.S.A.* 112 A4
Westland Bight, *N.Z.* 91 K3
Westlock, *Canada* 104 C6
Westmar, *Australia* 95 D4
Westmeath □, *Ireland* 15 C4
Westminster, *U.S.A.* 108 F7
Westmont, *U.S.A.* 110 F6
Westmorland, *U.S.A.* 117 M11
Weston, *Oreg., U.S.A.* 114 D4
Weston, *W. Va., U.S.A.* 108 F5
Weston I., *Canada* 102 B4
Weston-super-Mare, *U.K.* 13 F5
Westover, *U.S.A.* 110 F6
Westport, *Canada* 111 B8
Westport, *Ireland* 15 C2
Westport, *N.Z.* 91 J3
Westport, *N.Y., U.S.A.* 111 B11
Westport, *Oreg., U.S.A.* 116 D3
Westport, *Wash., U.S.A.* 116 D2
Westray, *Canada* 105 C8
Westray, *U.K.* 14 B5
Westree, *Canada* 102 C3
Westville, *U.S.A.* 116 F6
Westwood, *U.S.A.* 114 F3
Wetar, *Indonesia* 63 F7
Wetaskiwin, *Canada* 104 C6
Wete, *Tanzania* 84 F7
Wetherby, *U.K.* 12 D6
Wethersfield, *U.S.A.* 111 E12
Wetteren, *Belgium* 17 D3
Wetzlar, *Germany* 24 E4
Wewoka, *U.S.A.* 113 H6
Wexford, *Ireland* 15 D5
Wexford □, *Ireland* 15 D5
Wexford Harbour, *Ireland* 15 D5
Weyburn, *Canada* 105 D8
Weyer Markt, *Austria* 26 D7
Weyhe, *Germany* 24 C4
Weyib →, *Ethiopia* 81 F5
Weymouth, *Canada* 103 D6
Weymouth, *U.K.* 13 G5
Weymouth, *U.S.A.* 111 D14
Weymouth, C., *Australia* 94 A3
Wha Ti, *Canada* 100 B8
Whakatane, *N.Z.* 91 G6
Whale →, *Canada* 103 A6
Whale Cove, *Canada* 105 A10
Whales, B. of, *Antarctica* 5 D12
Whalsay, *U.K.* 14 A8
Whangamomona, *N.Z.* 91 H5
Whangarei, *N.Z.* 91 F5
Whangarei Harb., *N.Z.* 91 F5
Wharfe →, *U.K.* 12 D6
Wharfedale, *U.K.* 12 C5
Wharton, *N.J., U.S.A.* 111 F10
Wharton, *Pa., U.S.A.* 110 E6
Wharton, *Tex., U.S.A.* 113 L6
Wheatland, *Calif., U.S.A.* 116 F5
Wheatland, *Wyo., U.S.A.* 112 D2
Wheatley, *Canada* 110 D2
Wheaton, *Md., U.S.A.* 108 F7
Wheaton, *Minn., U.S.A.* 112 C6
Wheelbarrow Pk., *U.S.A.* 116 H10
Wheeler, *Oreg., U.S.A.* 114 D2
Wheeler, *Tex., U.S.A.* 113 H4
Wheeler →, *Canada* 103 A6
Wheeler L., *U.S.A.* 109 H2
Wheeler Pk., *N. Mex., U.S.A.* 115 H11
Wheeler Pk., *Nev., U.S.A.* 115 G6
Wheeler Ridge, *U.S.A.* 117 L8
Wheeling, *U.S.A.* 110 F4
Whernside, *U.K.* 12 C5
Whiskey Jack L., *Canada* 105 B8
Whistleduck Cr. →, *Australia* 94 C2
Whistler, *Canada* 104 C4
Whitby, *Canada* 110 C6
Whitby, *U.K.* 12 C7
White →, *Ark., U.S.A.* 113 J9
White →, *Ind., U.S.A.* 108 F2
White →, *S. Dak., U.S.A.* 112 D5
White →, *Tex., U.S.A.* 113 J4
White →, *Utah, U.S.A.* 114 F9
White →, *Vt., U.S.A.* 111 C12
White →, *Wash., U.S.A.* 116 C4
White, L., *Australia* 92 D4
White B., *Canada* 103 C8
White Bird, *U.S.A.* 114 D5
White Butte, *U.S.A.* 112 B3
White City, *U.S.A.* 114 E2
White Cliffs, *Australia* 95 E3
White Hall, *U.S.A.* 112 F9
White Haven, *U.S.A.* 111 E9
White Horse, Vale of, *U.K.* 13 F6
White I., *N.Z.* 91 G6
White L., *Canada* 111 A8
White L., *U.S.A.* 113 L8
White Mountain Peak, *U.S.A.* 115 G4
White Mts., *Calif., U.S.A.* 116 H8
White Mts., *N.H., U.S.A.* 111 B13
White Nile = Nîl el Abyad →, *Sudan* 81 D3
White Nile Dam = Khazzān Jabal al Awliyā, *Sudan* 81 D3
White Otter L., *Canada* 102 C1
White Pass, *U.S.A.* 116 D5
White Plains, *U.S.A.* 111 E11
White River, *Canada* 102 C2
White River, *S. Africa* 89 D5
White River, *U.S.A.* 112 D4
White Rock, *Canada* 116 A4
White Russia = Belarus ■, *Europe* 46 F4
White Sea = Beloye More, *Russia* 50 C4
White Sulphur Springs, *Mont., U.S.A.* 114 C8
White Sulphur Springs, *W. Va., U.S.A.* 108 G5
White Swan, *U.S.A.* 116 D6
White Volta →, *Ghana* 83 D4
Whitecliffs, *N.Z.* 91 K3
Whitecourt, *Canada* 104 C5
Whiteface Mt., *U.S.A.* 111 B11
Whitefield, *U.S.A.* 111 B13
Whitefish, *U.S.A.* 114 B6
Whitefish L., *Canada* 105 A7
Whitefish Point, *U.S.A.* 108 B3
Whitegull, L., *Canada* 103 A7
Whitehall, *Mich., U.S.A.* 108 D2
Whitehall, *Mont., U.S.A.* 114 D7
Whitehall, *N.Y., U.S.A.* 111 C11
Whitehall, *Wis., U.S.A.* 112 C9
Whitehaven, *U.K.* 12 C4
Whitehorse, *Canada* 104 A1
Whitemark, *Australia* 94 G4
Whiteplains, *Liberia* 82 D2
Whiteriver, *U.S.A.* 115 K9
Whitesand →, *Canada* 104 A5
Whitesands, *S. Africa* 88 E3
Whitesboro, *N.Y., U.S.A.* 111 C9
Whitesboro, *Tex., U.S.A.* 113 J6
Whiteshell Prov. Park, *Canada* 105 D9
Whitesville, *U.S.A.* 110 D7
Whiteville, *U.S.A.* 109 H6
Whitewater, *U.S.A.* 108 D1
Whitewater Baldy, *U.S.A.* 115 K9
Whitewater L., *Canada* 102 B2
Whitewood, *Australia* 94 C3
Whitewood, *Canada* 105 C8
Whithorn, *U.K.* 14 G4
Whitianga, *N.Z.* 91 G5
Whitman, *U.S.A.* 111 D14
Whitney, *Canada* 102 C4
Whitney, Mt., *U.S.A.* 116 J8
Whitney Point, *U.S.A.* 111 D9
Whitstable, *U.K.* 13 F9
Whitsunday I., *Australia* 94 C4
Whittier, *U.S.A.* 117 M8
Whittlesea, *Australia* 95 F4
Wholdaia L., *Canada* 105 A8
Whyalla, *Australia* 95 E2
Wiarton, *Canada* 102 D3
Wiawso, *Ghana* 82 D4
Wiay, *U.K.* 14 D1
Wiązów, *Poland* 45 H4
Wibaux, *U.S.A.* 112 B2
Wichian Buri, *Thailand* 64 E3
Wichita, *U.S.A.* 113 G6
Wichita Falls, *U.S.A.* 113 J5
Wick, *U.K.* 14 C5
Wicked Pt., *Canada* 110 C7
Wickenburg, *U.S.A.* 115 K7
Wickepin, *Australia* 93 F2
Wickham, *Australia* 92 D2
Wickham, C., *Australia* 94 F3
Wickliffe, *U.S.A.* 110 E3
Wicklow, *Ireland* 15 D5
Wicklow □, *Ireland* 15 D5
Wicklow Hd., *Ireland* 15 D6
Wicklow Mts., *Ireland* 15 C5
Widawa, *Poland* 45 G5
Widawka →, *Poland* 45 G5
Widgeegoara Cr. →, *Australia* 95 D4
Widgiemooltha, *Australia* 93 F3
Widnes, *U.K.* 12 D5
Więcbork, *Poland* 45 E4
Wiehl, *Germany* 24 E3
Wiek, *Germany* 24 A9
Wielbark, *Poland* 44 E7
Wieleń, *Poland* 45 F3
Wielichowo, *Poland* 45 F3
Wieliczka, *Poland* 45 J7
Wielkopolskie □, *Poland* 45 F4
Wieluń, *Poland* 45 G5
Wien, *Austria* 27 C9
Wiener Neustadt, *Austria* 27 D9
Wieprz →, *Poland* 45 G8
Wieprza →, *Poland* 44 D3
Wieruszów, *Poland* 45 G5
Wiesbaden, *Germany* 25 E4
Wiesental, *Germany* 25 F4
Wiesloch, *Germany* 25 F4
Wiesmoor, *Germany* 24 B3
Wieżyca, *Poland* 44 D5
Wigan, *U.K.* 12 D5
Wiggins, *Colo., U.S.A.* 112 E2
Wiggins, *Miss., U.S.A.* 113 K10
Wight, I. of □, *U.K.* 13 G6
Wigry, Jezioro, *Poland* 44 D10
Wigston, *U.K.* 13 E6
Wigton, *U.K.* 12 C4
Wigtown, *U.K.* 14 G4
Wigtown B., *U.K.* 14 G4
Wil, *Switz.* 25 H5
Wilamowice, *Poland* 45 J6
Wilber, *U.S.A.* 112 E6
Wilberforce, *Canada* 110 A6
Wilberforce, C., *Australia* 94 A2
Wilburton, *U.S.A.* 113 H7
Wilcannia, *Australia* 95 E3
Wilcox, *U.S.A.* 110 E6
Wildbad, *Germany* 25 G4
Wildeshausen, *Germany* 24 C4
Wildon, *Austria* 26 E8
Wildrose, *U.S.A.* 117 J9
Wildspitze, *Austria* 26 E3
Wilga →, *Poland* 45 G8
Wilge →, *S. Africa* 89 D4
Wilhelm II Coast, *Antarctica* 5 C7
Wilhelmsburg, *Austria* 26 C8
Wilhelmshaven, *Germany* 24 B4
Wilhelmstal, *Namibia* 88 C2
Wilkes-Barre, *U.S.A.* 111 E9
Wilkie, *Canada* 105 C7
Wilkinsburg, *U.S.A.* 110 F5
Wilkinson Lakes, *Australia* 93 E5
Willandra Creek →, *Australia* 95 E4
Willapa B., *U.S.A.* 114 C2
Willapa Hills, *U.S.A.* 116 D3
Willard, *N.Y., U.S.A.* 110 D8
Willard, *Ohio, U.S.A.* 110 E2
Willcox, *U.S.A.* 115 K9
Willemstad, *Neth. Ant.* 121 D6
Willet, *U.S.A.* 111 D9
William →, *Canada* 105 B7
William 'Bill' Dannely Res., *U.S.A.* 109 J2
William Creek, *Australia* 95 D2
Williams, *Australia* 93 F2
Williams, *Ariz., U.S.A.* 115 J7
Williams, *Calif., U.S.A.* 116 F4
Williams Harbour, *Canada* 103 B8
Williams Lake, *Canada* 104 C4
Williamsburg, *Ky., U.S.A.* 109 G3
Williamsburg, *Pa., U.S.A.* 110 F6
Williamsburg, *Va., U.S.A.* 108 G7
Williamson, *N.Y., U.S.A.* 110 C7
Williamson, *W. Va., U.S.A.* 108 G4
Williamsport, *U.S.A.* 110 E7
Williamston, *U.S.A.* 109 H7
Williamstown, *Australia* 95 F3
Williamstown, *Ky., U.S.A.* 108 F3
Williamstown, *Mass., U.S.A.* 111 D11
Williamstown, *N.Y., U.S.A.* 111 C9
Willimantic, *U.S.A.* 111 E12
Willingboro, *U.S.A.* 108 E8
Willis Group, *Australia* 94 B5
Williston, *S. Africa* 88 E3
Williston, *Fla., U.S.A.* 109 L4
Williston, *N. Dak., U.S.A.* 112 A3
Williston L., *Canada* 104 B4
Willits, *U.S.A.* 114 G2
Willmar, *U.S.A.* 112 C7
Willoughby, *U.S.A.* 110 E3
Willow Bunch, *Canada* 105 D7
Willow L., *Canada* 104 A5
Willow Wall, The, *China* 57 C12
Willowick, *U.S.A.* 110 E3
Willowlake →, *Canada* 104 A4
Willowmore, *S. Africa* 88 E3
Willows, *U.S.A.* 116 F4
Willowvale = Gatyana, *S. Africa* 89 E4
Wills, L., *Australia* 92 D4
Wills Cr. →, *Australia* 94 C3
Willsboro, *U.S.A.* 111 B11
Willunga, *Australia* 95 F2
Wilmette, *U.S.A.* 108 D2
Wilmington, *Australia* 95 E2
Wilmington, *Del., U.S.A.* 108 F8
Wilmington, *N.C., U.S.A.* 109 H7
Wilmington, *Ohio, U.S.A.* 108 F4
Wilmington, *Vt., U.S.A.* 111 D12
Wilmslow, *U.K.* 12 D5
Wilpena →, *Australia* 95 E2
Wilsall, *U.S.A.* 114 D8
Wilson, *N.C., U.S.A.* 109 H7
Wilson, *N.Y., U.S.A.* 110 C6
Wilson, *Pa., U.S.A.* 111 F9
Wilson →, *Australia* 92 C4
Wilson Bluff, *Australia* 93 F4
Wilson Inlet, *Australia* 93 G2
Wilsons Promontory, *Australia* 95 F4
Wilster, *Germany* 24 B5
Wilton, *U.S.A.* 112 B4
Wilton →, *Australia* 94 A1
Wiltshire □, *U.K.* 13 F6
Wiltz, *Lux.* 17 E5
Wiluna, *Australia* 93 E3
Wimborne Minster, *U.K.* 13 G6
Wimereux, *France* 19 B8
Wimmera →, *Australia* 95 F3
Winam G., *Kenya* 86 C3
Winburg, *S. Africa* 88 D4
Winchendon, *U.S.A.* 111 D12
Winchester, *U.K.* 13 F6
Winchester, *Conn., U.S.A.* 111 E11
Winchester, *Idaho, U.S.A.* 114 C5
Winchester, *Ind., U.S.A.* 108 E3
Winchester, *Ky., U.S.A.* 108 G3
Winchester, *N.H., U.S.A.* 111 D12
Winchester, *Nev., U.S.A.* 117 J11
Winchester, *Tenn., U.S.A.* 109 H2
Winchester, *Va., U.S.A.* 108 F6
Wind →, *U.S.A.* 114 E9
Wind River Range, *U.S.A.* 114 E9
Windau = Ventspils, *Latvia* 9 H19
Windber, *U.S.A.* 110 F6
Winder, *U.S.A.* 109 J4
Windermere, *U.K.* 12 C5
Windhoek, *Namibia* 88 C2
Windischgarsten, *Austria* 26 D7
Windom, *U.S.A.* 112 D7
Windorah, *Australia* 94 D3
Window Rock, *U.S.A.* 115 J9
Windrush →, *U.K.* 13 F6
Windsor, *Australia* 95 E5
Windsor, *N.S., Canada* 103 D7
Windsor, *Ont., Canada* 102 D3
Windsor, *U.K.* 13 F7
Windsor, *Colo., U.S.A.* 112 E2
Windsor, *Conn., U.S.A.* 111 E12
Windsor, *Mo., U.S.A.* 112 F8
Windsor, *N.Y., U.S.A.* 111 D9
Windsor, *Vt., U.S.A.* 111 C12
Windsor & Maidenhead □, *U.K.* 13 F7
Windsorton, *S. Africa* 88 D3
Windward Is., *W. Indies* 121 D7
Windward Passage = Vientos, Paso de los, *Caribbean* 121 C5
Winefred L., *Canada* 105 B6
Winejok, *Sudan* 81 F2
Winfield, *U.S.A.* 113 G6
Wingate Mts., *Australia* 92 B5
Wingham, *Australia* 95 E5
Wingham, *Canada* 102 D3
Winisk, *Canada* 102 A2
Winisk →, *Canada* 102 A2
Winisk L., *Canada* 102 B2
Wink, *U.S.A.* 113 K3
Winkler, *Canada* 105 D9
Winklern, *Austria* 26 E5
Winlock, *U.S.A.* 116 D4
Winneba, *Ghana* 83 D4
Winnebago, L., *U.S.A.* 108 D1
Winnecke Cr. →, *Australia* 92 C5
Winnemucca, *U.S.A.* 114 F5
Winnemucca L., *U.S.A.* 114 F4
Winnett, *U.S.A.* 114 C9
Winnfield, *U.S.A.* 113 K8
Winnibigoshish, L., *U.S.A.* 112 B7
Winnipeg, *Canada* 105 D9
Winnipeg →, *Canada* 105 C9
Winnipeg, L., *Canada* 105 C9
Winnipeg Beach, *Canada* 105 C9
Winnipegosis, *Canada* 105 C9
Winnipegosis L., *Canada* 105 C9
Winnipesaukee, L., *U.S.A.* 111 C13
Winnisquam L., *U.S.A.* 111 C13
Winnsboro, *La., U.S.A.* 113 J9
Winnsboro, *S.C., U.S.A.* 109 H5
Winnsboro, *Tex., U.S.A.* 113 J7
Winokapau, L., *Canada* 103 B7
Winona, *Minn., U.S.A.* 112 C9
Winona, *Miss., U.S.A.* 113 J10
Winooski, *U.S.A.* 111 B11
Winooski →, *U.S.A.* 111 B11
Winschoten, *Neths.* 17 A7
Winsen, *Germany* 24 B6
Winsford, *U.K.* 12 D5
Winslow, *Ariz., U.S.A.* 115 J8
Winslow, *Wash., U.S.A.* 116 C4
Winsted, *U.S.A.* 111 E11
Winston-Salem, *U.S.A.* 109 G5
Winter Garden, *U.S.A.* 109 L5
Winter Haven, *U.S.A.* 109 M5
Winter Park, *U.S.A.* 109 L5
Winterberg, *Germany* 24 D4
Winterhaven, *U.S.A.* 117 N12
Winters, *U.S.A.* 116 G5
Wintersville, *U.S.A.* 110 F4
Winterswijk, *Neths.* 17 C6
Winterthur, *Switz.* 25 H4
Winthrop, *U.S.A.* 114 B3
Winton, *Australia* 94 C3
Winton, *N.Z.* 91 M2
Wipper →, *Germany* 24 D7
Wirrulla, *Australia* 95 E1
Wisbech, *U.K.* 13 E8
Wisconsin □, *U.S.A.* 112 C10
Wisconsin →, *U.S.A.* 112 D9
Wisconsin Rapids, *U.S.A.* 112 C10
Wisdom, *U.S.A.* 114 D7
Wishaw, *U.K.* 14 F5
Wishek, *U.S.A.* 112 B5
Wisła, *Poland* 45 J5
Wisła →, *Poland* 44 D5
Wisłok →, *Poland* 45 H9

Wisłoka →, *Poland* 45 H8
Wismar, *Germany* 24 B7
Wisner, *U.S.A.* 112 E6
Wissant, *France* 19 B8
Wissembourg, *France* 19 C14
Wisznice, *Poland* 45 G10
Witbank, *S. Africa* 89 D4
Witdraai, *S. Africa* 88 D3
Witham, *U.K.* 13 F8
Witham →, *U.K.* 12 E7
Withernsea, *U.K.* 12 D8
Witkowo, *Poland* 45 F4
Witney, *U.K.* 13 F6
Witnica, *Poland* 45 F1
Witnossob →, *Namibia* 88 D3
Wittdün, *Germany* 24 A4
Witten, *Germany* 24 D3
Wittenberge, *Germany* 24 B7
Wittenburg, *Germany* 24 B7
Wittenheim, *France* 19 E14
Wittenoom, *Australia* 92 D2
Wittingen, *Germany* 24 C6
Wittlich, *Germany* 25 F2
Wittmund, *Germany* 24 B3
Wittow, *Germany* 24 A9
Wittstock, *Germany* 24 B8
Witvlei, *Namibia* 88 C2
Witzenhausen, *Germany* 24 D5
Wkra →, *Poland* 45 F7
Władysławowo, *Poland* 44 D5
Wleń, *Poland* 45 G2
Wlingi, *Indonesia* 63 H15
Włocławek, *Poland* 45 F6
Włodawa, *Poland* 45 G10
Włoszczowa, *Poland* 45 H6
Woburn, *U.S.A.* 111 D13
Wodian, *China* 56 H7
Wodzisław Śląski, *Poland* 45 H5
Wœrth, *France* 19 D14
Woinbogoin, *China* 58 A2
Woippy, *France* 19 C13
Wojcieszow, *Poland* 45 H2
Wokam, *Indonesia* 63 F8
Woking, *U.K.* 13 F7
Wokingham □, *U.K.* 13 F7
Wolbrom, *Poland* 45 H6
Wołczyn, *Poland* 45 G5
Woldegk, *Germany* 24 B9
Wolf →, *Canada* 104 A2
Wolf Creek, *U.S.A.* 114 C7
Wolf L., *Canada* 104 A2
Wolf Point, *U.S.A.* 112 A2
Wolfe I., *Canada* 102 D4
Wolfeboro, *U.S.A.* 111 C13
Wolfen, *Germany* 24 D8
Wolfenbüttel, *Germany* 24 C6
Wolfratshausen, *Germany* 25 H7
Wolfsberg, *Austria* 26 E7
Wolfsburg, *Germany* 24 C6
Wolgast, *Germany* 24 A9
Wolhusen, *Switz.* 25 H4
Wolin, *Poland* 44 E1
Wollaston, Is., *Chile* 128 H3
Wollaston L., *Canada* 105 B8
Wollaston Lake, *Canada* 105 B8
Wollaston Pen., *Canada* 100 B8
Wollongong, *Australia* 95 E5
Wolmaransstad, *S. Africa* 88 D4
Wolmirstedt, *Germany* 24 C7
Wołomin, *Poland* 45 F8
Wołów, *Poland* 45 G3
Wolseley, *S. Africa* 88 E2
Wolsey, *U.S.A.* 112 C5
Wolstenholme, C., *Canada* 98 C12
Wolsztyn, *Poland* 45 F3
Wolvega, *Neths.* 17 B6
Wolverhampton, *U.K.* 13 E5
Wondai, *Australia* 95 D5
Wongalarroo L., *Australia* 95 E3
Wongan Hills, *Australia* 93 F2
Wŏnju, *S. Korea* 57 F14
Wonosari, *Indonesia* 63 G14
Wonosobo, *Indonesia* 63 G13
Wonowon, *Canada* 104 B4
Wŏnsan, *N. Korea* 57 E14
Wonthaggi, *Australia* 95 F4
Wood Buffalo Nat. Park, *Canada* 104 B6
Wood Is., *Australia* 92 C3
Wood L., *Canada* 105 B8
Woodah I., *Australia* 94 A2
Woodbourne, *U.S.A.* 111 E10
Woodbridge, *Canada* 110 C5
Woodbridge, *U.K.* 13 E9
Woodburn, *U.S.A.* 114 D2
Woodenbong, *Australia* 95 D5
Woodend, *Australia* 95 F3
Woodford, *Australia* 95 D5
Woodfords, *U.S.A.* 116 G7
Woodlake, *U.S.A.* 116 J7
Woodland, *Calif., U.S.A.* 116 G5
Woodland, *Maine, U.S.A.* 109 C12
Woodland, *Pa., U.S.A.* 110 F6
Woodland, *Wash., U.S.A.* 116 E4
Woodland Caribou Prov. Park, *Canada* 105 C10
Woodridge, *Canada* 105 D9
Woodroffe, Mt., *Australia* 93 E5
Woods, L., *Australia* 94 B1
Woods, L. of the, *Canada* 105 D10
Woodside, *Australia* 95 F4
Woodstock, *Australia* 94 B4
Woodstock, *N.B., Canada* 103 C6
Woodstock, *Ont., Canada* 102 D3
Woodstock, *U.K.* 13 F6
Woodstock, *Ill., U.S.A.* 112 D10
Woodstock, *Vt., U.S.A.* 111 C12
Woodsville, *U.S.A.* 111 B13
Woodville, *N.Z.* 91 J5
Woodville, *Miss., U.S.A.* 113 K9
Woodville, *Tex., U.S.A.* 113 K7
Woodward, *U.S.A.* 113 G5
Woody, *U.S.A.* 117 K8
Woody →, *Canada* 105 C8
Woolamai, C., *Australia* 95 F4
Wooler, *U.K.* 12 B5
Woolgoolga, *Australia* 95 E5
Woomera, *Australia* 95 E2
Woonsocket, *R.I., U.S.A.* 111 E13
Woonsocket, *S. Dak., U.S.A.* 112 C5
Wooramel →, *Australia* 93 E1
Wooramel Roadhouse, *Australia* 93 E1
Wooster, *U.S.A.* 110 F3
Worcester, *S. Africa* 88 E2
Worcester, *U.K.* 13 E5
Worcester, *Mass., U.S.A.* 111 D13
Worcester, *N.Y., U.S.A.* 111 D10
Worcestershire □, *U.K.* 13 E5
Wörgl, *Austria* 26 D5
Workington, *U.K.* 12 C4
Worksop, *U.K.* 12 D6
Workum, *Neths.* 17 B5
Worland, *U.S.A.* 114 D10
Wormhout, *France* 19 B9
Worms, *Germany* 25 F4
Worsley, *Canada* 104 B5
Wörth, *Germany* 25 F8
Wortham, *U.S.A.* 113 K6
Wörther See, *Austria* 26 E7
Worthing, *U.K.* 13 G7
Worthington, *Minn., U.S.A.* 112 D7
Worthington, *Pa., U.S.A.* 110 F5
Wosi, *Indonesia* 63 E7
Wou-han = Wuhan, *China* 59 B10
Wousi = Wuxi, *China* 59 B13
Wowoni, *Indonesia* 63 E6
Wrangel I. = Vrangelya, Ostrov, *Russia* 51 B19
Wrangell, *U.S.A.* 104 B2
Wrangell Mts., *U.S.A.* 100 B5
Wrath, C., *U.K.* 14 C3
Wray, *U.S.A.* 112 E3
Wrekin, The, *U.K.* 13 E5
Wrens, *U.S.A.* 109 J4
Wrexham, *U.K.* 12 D4
Wrexham □, *U.K.* 12 D5
Wriezen, *Germany* 24 C10
Wright = Paranas, *Phil.* 61 F6
Wright, *U.S.A.* 112 D2
Wright Pt., *Canada* 110 C3
Wrightson Mt., *U.S.A.* 115 L8
Wrightwood, *U.S.A.* 117 L9
Wrigley, *Canada* 100 B7
Wrocław, *Poland* 45 G4
Wronki, *Poland* 45 F3
Września, *Poland* 45 F4
Wschowa, *Poland* 45 G3
Wu Jiang →, *China* 58 C6
Wu'an, *China* 56 F8
Wubin, *Australia* 93 F2
Wubu, *China* 56 F6
Wuchang, *China* 57 B14
Wucheng, *China* 56 F9
Wuchuan, *Guangdong, China* 59 G8
Wuchuan, *Guizhou, China* 58 C7
Wuchuan, *Nei Mongol Zizhiqu, China* 56 D6
Wudi, *China* 57 F9
Wuding, *China* 58 E4
Wuding He →, *China* 56 F6
Wudinna, *Australia* 95 E2
Wudu, *China* 56 H3
Wufeng, *China* 59 B8
Wugang, *China* 59 D8
Wugong Shan, *China* 59 D9
Wuhan, *China* 59 B10
Wuhe, *China* 57 H9
Wuhsi = Wuxi, *China* 59 B13
Wuhu, *China* 59 B12
Wujiang, *China* 59 B13
Wukari, *Nigeria* 83 D6
Wulajie, *China* 57 B14
Wulanbulang, *China* 56 D6
Wular L., *India* 69 B6
Wulehe, *Ghana* 83 D5
Wulian, *China* 57 G10
Wuliang Shan, *China* 58 E3
Wuliaru, *Indonesia* 63 F8
Wuling Shan, *China* 58 C7
Wulong, *China* 58 C6
Wulumuchi = Ürümqi, *China* 50 E9
Wum, *Cameroon* 83 D7
Wuming, *China* 58 F7
Wun Rog, *Sudan* 81 F2
Wundowie, *Australia* 93 F2
Wuning, *China* 59 C10
Wunnummin L., *Canada* 102 B2
Wunsiedel, *Germany* 25 E8
Wunstorf, *Germany* 24 C5
Wuntho, *Burma* 67 H19
Wuping, *China* 59 E11
Wuppertal, *Germany* 24 D3
Wuppertal, *S. Africa* 88 E2
Wuqing, *China* 57 E9
Wurtsboro, *U.S.A.* 111 E10
Würzburg, *Germany* 25 F5
Wurzen, *Germany* 24 D8
Wushan, *China* 56 G3
Wushishi, *Nigeria* 83 D6
Wusuli Jiang = Ussuri →, *Asia* 54 A7
Wutach →, *Germany* 25 H4
Wutai, *China* 56 E7
Wuting = Huimin, *China* 57 F9
Wutong, *China* 59 E8
Wutonghaolai, *China* 57 C11
Wutongqiao, *China* 58 C4
Wuwei, *Anhui, China* 59 B11
Wuwei, *Gansu, China* 60 C5
Wuxi, *Jiangsu, China* 59 B13
Wuxi, *Sichuan, China* 58 B7
Wuxiang, *China* 56 F7
Wuxuan, *China* 58 F7
Wuxue, *China* 59 C10
Wuyang, *China* 56 H7
Wuyi, *Hebei, China* 56 F8
Wuyi, *Zhejiang, China* 59 C12
Wuyi Shan, *China* 59 D11
Wuyishan, *China* 59 D12
Wuyo, *Nigeria* 83 C7
Wuyuan, *Jiangxi, China* 59 C11
Wuyuan, *Nei Mongol Zizhiqu, China* 56 D5
Wuzhai, *China* 56 E6
Wuzhi Shan, *China* 64 C7
Wuzhong, *China* 56 E4
Wuzhou, *China* 59 F8
Wyaaba Cr. →, *Australia* 94 B3
Wyalkatchem, *Australia* 93 F2
Wyalusing, *U.S.A.* 111 E8
Wyandotte, *U.S.A.* 108 D4
Wyandra, *Australia* 95 D4
Wyangala Res., *Australia* 95 E4
Wyara, L., *Australia* 95 D3
Wycheproof, *Australia* 95 F3
Wye →, *U.K.* 13 F5
Wyemandoo, *Australia* 93 E2
Wyk, *Germany* 24 A4
Wymondham, *U.K.* 13 E9
Wymore, *U.S.A.* 112 E6
Wyndham, *Australia* 92 C4
Wyndham, *N.Z.* 91 M2
Wynne, *U.S.A.* 113 H9
Wynyard, *Australia* 94 G4
Wynyard, *Canada* 105 C8
Wyola L., *Australia* 93 E5
Wyoming, *Canada* 110 D2
Wyoming □, *U.S.A.* 114 E10
Wyomissing, *U.S.A.* 111 F9
Wyong, *Australia* 95 E5
Wyrzysk, *Poland* 45 E4
Wyśmierzyce, *Poland* 45 G7
Wysoka, *Poland* 45 E4
Wysokie, *Poland* 45 H9
Wysokie Mazowieckie, *Poland* 45 F9
Wyszków, *Poland* 45 F8
Wyszogród, *Poland* 45 F7
Wytheville, *U.S.A.* 108 G5
Wyżyna Małopolska, *Poland* 45 H7

X

Xaçmaz, *Azerbaijan* 49 K9
Xai-Xai, *Mozam.* 89 D5
Xainza, *China* 60 C3
Xangongo, *Angola* 88 B2
Xankändi, *Azerbaijan* 70 B5
Xanlar, *Azerbaijan* 49 K8
Xanten, *Germany* 24 D2
Xánthi, *Greece* 41 E8
Xánthi □, *Greece* 41 E8
Xanthos, *Turkey* 39 E11
Xanxerê, *Brazil* 127 B5
Xapuri, *Brazil* 124 F5
Xar Moron He →, *China* 57 C11
Xarrë, *Albania* 40 G4
Xátiva, *Spain* 33 G4
Xau, L., *Botswana* 88 C3
Xavantina, *Brazil* 127 A5
Xenia, *U.S.A.* 108 F4
Xeropotamos →, *Cyprus* 36 E11
Xertigny, *France* 19 D13
Xhora, *S. Africa* 89 E4
Xhumo, *Botswana* 88 C3
Xi Jiang →, *China* 59 F9
Xi Xian, *Henan, China* 59 A10
Xi Xian, *Shanxi, China* 56 F6
Xia Xian, *China* 56 G6
Xiachengzi, *China* 57 B16
Xiachuan Dao, *China* 59 G9
Xiaguan, *China* 58 E3
Xiajiang, *China* 59 D10
Xiajin, *China* 56 F9
Xiamen, *China* 59 E12
Xi'an, *China* 56 G5
Xian Xian, *China* 56 E9
Xianfeng, *China* 58 C7
Xiang Jiang →, *China* 59 C9
Xiangcheng, *Henan, China* 56 H8
Xiangcheng, *Henan, China* 56 H7
Xiangcheng, *Sichuan, China* 58 C2
Xiangdu, *China* 58 F6
Xiangfan, *China* 59 A9
Xianggang = Hong Kong □, *China* 59 F10
Xianghuang Qi, *China* 56 C7
Xiangning, *China* 56 G6
Xiangquan, *China* 56 F7
Xiangquan He = Sutlej →, *Pakistan* 68 E4
Xiangshan, *China* 59 C13
Xiangshui, *China* 57 G10
Xiangtan, *China* 59 D9
Xiangxiang, *China* 59 D9
Xiangyin, *China* 59 C9
Xiangyun, *China* 58 E3
Xiangzhou, *China* 58 F7
Xianju, *China* 59 C13
Xianning, *China* 59 C10
Xianshui He →, *China* 58 B3
Xiantao, *China* 59 B9
Xianyang, *China* 56 G5
Xianyou, *China* 59 E12
Xiao Hinggan Ling, *China* 60 B7
Xiao Xian, *China* 56 G9
Xiaofeng, *China* 59 B12
Xiaogan, *China* 59 B9
Xiaojin, *China* 58 B4
Xiaolan, *China* 59 F9
Xiaoshan, *China* 59 B13
Xiaoyi, *China* 56 F6
Xiapu, *China* 59 D12
Xiawa, *China* 57 C11
Xiayi, *China* 56 G9
Xichang, *China* 58 D4
Xichong, *China* 58 B5
Xichou, *China* 58 E5
Xichuan, *China* 56 H6
Xide, *China* 58 C4
Xiemahe, *China* 59 B8
Xieng Khouang, *Laos* 64 C4
Xifei He →, *China* 56 H9
Xifeng, *Gansu, China* 56 G4
Xifeng, *Guizhou, China* 58 D6
Xifeng, *Liaoning, China* 57 C13
Xifengzhen = Xifeng, *China* 56 G4
Xigazê, *China* 60 D3
Xihe, *China* 56 G3
Xihua, *China* 56 H8
Xilaganí, *Greece* 41 F9
Xiliao He →, *China* 57 C12
Xilin, *China* 58 E5
Xilókastron, *Greece* 38 C4
Xime, *Guinea-Biss.* 82 C2
Ximeng, *China* 58 F2
Xin Jiang →, *China* 59 C11
Xin Xian = Xinzhou, *China* 56 E7
Xinavane, *Mozam.* 89 D5
Xinbin, *China* 57 D13
Xincai, *China* 59 A10
Xinchang, *China* 59 C13
Xincheng, *Guangxi Zhuangzu, China* 58 E7
Xincheng, *Jiangxi, China* 59 D10
Xindu, *China* 58 B5
Xinfeng, *Guangdong, China* 59 E10
Xinfeng, *Jiangxi, China* 59 D11
Xinfeng, *Jiangxi, China* 59 E10
Xinfengjiang Skuiku, *China* 59 F10
Xing Xian, *China* 56 E6
Xing'an, *Guangxi Zhuangzu, China* 59 E8
Xingan, *Jiangxi, China* 59 D10
Xingcheng, *China* 57 D11
Xingguo, *China* 59 D10
Xinghe, *China* 56 D7
Xinghua, *China* 57 H10
Xinghua Wan, *China* 59 E12
Xinglong, *China* 57 D9
Xingning, *China* 59 E10
Xingping, *China* 56 G5
Xingren, *China* 58 E5
Xingshan, *China* 59 B8
Xingtai, *China* 56 F8
Xingu →, *Brazil* 122 D5
Xingwen, *China* 58 C5
Xingyang, *China* 56 G7
Xinhe, *China* 56 F8
Xinhua, *China* 59 D8
Xinhuang, *China* 58 D7
Xinhui, *China* 59 F9
Xining, *China* 60 C5
Xinjian, *China* 59 C10
Xinjiang, *China* 56 G6
Xinjiang Uygur Zizhiqu □, *China* 60 B3
Xinjie, *China* 58 D3
Xinjin = Pulandian, *China* 57 E11
Xinjin, *China* 58 B4
Xinkai He →, *China* 57 C12
Xinle, *China* 56 E8
Xinlitun, *China* 57 D12
Xinlong, *China* 58 B3
Xinmin, *China* 57 D12
Xinning, *China* 59 D8
Xinping, *China* 58 E3
Xinshao, *China* 59 D8
Xintai, *China* 57 G9
Xintian, *China* 59 E9
Xinxian, *China* 59 B10
Xinxiang, *China* 56 G7
Xinxing, *China* 59 F9
Xinyang, *China* 59 A10
Xinye, *China* 59 A9
Xinyi, *China* 59 F8
Xinyu, *China* 59 D10
Xinzhan, *China* 57 C14
Xinzheng, *China* 56 G7
Xinzhou, *Hubei, China* 59 B10
Xinzhou, *Shanxi, China* 56 E7
Xinzo de Limia, *Spain* 34 C3
Xiong Xian, *China* 56 E9
Xiongyuecheng, *China* 57 D12
Xiping, *Henan, China* 56 H8
Xiping, *Henan, China* 56 H6
Xiping, *Zhejiang, China* 59 C12
Xique-Xique, *Brazil* 125 F10
Xisha Qundao = Paracel Is., *S. China Sea* 62 A4
Xishui, *Guizhou, China* 58 C6
Xishui, *Hubei, China* 59 B10
Xitole, *Guinea-Biss.* 82 C2
Xiu Shui →, *China* 59 C10
Xiuning, *China* 59 C12
Xiuren, *China* 59 E8
Xiushan, *China* 58 C7
Xiushui, *China* 59 C10
Xiuwen, *China* 58 D6
Xiuyan, *China* 57 D12
Xixabangma Feng, *China* 67 E14
Xixia, *China* 56 H6
Xixiang, *China* 56 H4
Xiyang, *China* 56 F7
Xizang Zizhiqu □, *China* 60 C3
Xlendi, *Malta* 36 C1
Xu Jiang →, *China* 59 D11
Xuan Loc, *Vietnam* 65 G6
Xuan'en, *China* 58 C7
Xuanhan, *China* 58 B6
Xuanhua, *China* 56 D8
Xuanwei, *China* 58 C5
Xuanzhou, *China* 59 B12
Xuchang, *China* 56 G7
Xudat, *Azerbaijan* 49 K9
Xuefeng Shan, *China* 59 D8
Xuejiaping, *China* 59 B8
Xun Jiang →, *China* 59 F8
Xun Xian, *China* 56 G8
Xundian, *China* 58 E4
Xunwu, *China* 59 E10
Xunyang, *China* 56 H5
Xunyi, *China* 56 G5
Xupu, *China* 59 D8
Xúquer →, *Spain* 33 F4
Xushui, *China* 56 E8
Xuwen, *China* 59 G8
Xuyen Moc, *Vietnam* 65 G6
Xuyong, *China* 58 C5
Xuzhou, *China* 57 G9
Xylophagou, *Cyprus* 36 E12

Y

Ya Xian, *China* 64 C7
Yaamba, *Australia* 94 C5
Ya'an, *China* 58 C4
Yaapeet, *Australia* 95 F3
Yabassi, *Cameroon* 83 E6
Yabelo, *Ethiopia* 81 G4
Yablanitsa, *Bulgaria* 41 C8
Yablonovy Ra. = Yablonovyy Khrebet, *Russia* 51 D12
Yablonovyy Khrebet, *Russia* 51 D12
Yabrai Shan, *China* 56 E2
Yabrūd, *Syria* 75 B5
Yacheng, *China* 64 C7
Yacuiba, *Bolivia* 126 A3
Yacuma →, *Bolivia* 124 F5
Yadgir, *India* 66 L10
Yadkin →, *U.S.A.* 109 H5
Yadrin, *Russia* 48 C8
Yaeyama-Rettō, *Japan* 55 M1
Yagaba, *Ghana* 83 C4
Yağcılar, *Turkey* 39 B10
Yagodnoye, *Russia* 51 C15
Yahila, *Dem. Rep. of the Congo* 86 B1
Yahk, *Canada* 104 D5
Yahotyn, *Ukraine* 47 G6
Yahuma, *Dem. Rep. of the Congo* 84 D4
Yahyalı, *Turkey* 72 C6
Yaita, *Japan* 55 F9
Yaiza, *Canary Is.* 37 F6
Yajiang, *China* 58 B3
Yajua, *Nigeria* 83 C7
Yakima, *U.S.A.* 114 C3
Yakima →, *U.S.A.* 114 C3
Yako, *Burkina Faso* 82 C4
Yakobi I., *U.S.A.* 104 B1
Yakoruda, *Bulgaria* 40 D7
Yakovlevka, *Russia* 54 B6
Yaku-Shima, *Japan* 55 J5
Yakumo, *Japan* 54 C10
Yakutat, *U.S.A.* 100 C6
Yakutia = Sakha □, *Russia* 51 C13
Yakutsk, *Russia* 51 C13
Yala, *Thailand* 65 J3
Yale, *U.S.A.* 110 C2
Yalgoo, *Australia* 93 E2
Yalinga, *C.A.R.* 84 C4
Yalkubul, Punta, *Mexico* 119 C7
Yalleroi, *Australia* 94 C4
Yalobusha →, *U.S.A.* 113 J9
Yalong Jiang →, *China* 58 D3
Yalova, *Turkey* 41 F13
Yalta, *Ukraine* 47 K8
Yalu Jiang →, *China* 57 E13
Yalvaç, *Turkey* 72 C4
Yam Ha Melah = Dead Sea, *Asia* 75 D4
Yam Kinneret, *Israel* 75 C4
Yamada, *Japan* 55 H5
Yamagata, *Japan* 54 E10
Yamagata □, *Japan* 54 E10
Yamaguchi, *Japan* 55 G5
Yamaguchi □, *Japan* 55 G5
Yamal, Poluostrov, *Russia* 50 B8
Yamal Pen. = Yamal, Poluostrov, *Russia* 50 B8
Yamanashi □, *Japan* 55 G9
Yamba, *Australia* 95 D5
Yambarran Ra., *Australia* 92 C5
Yambéring, *Guinea* 82 C2
Yâmbiô, *Sudan* 81 G2
Yambol, *Bulgaria* 41 D10
Yamdena, *Indonesia* 63 F8
Yame, *Japan* 55 H5
Yamethin, *Burma* 67 J20
Yamma-Yamma, L., *Australia* 95 D3
Yamoussoukro, *Ivory C.* 82 D3
Yampa →, *U.S.A.* 114 F9
Yampi Sd., *Australia* 92 C3
Yampil, *Moldova* 47 H5
Yampol = Yampil, *Moldova* 47 H5
Yamrat, *Nigeria* 83 C6
Yamrukchal = Botev, *Bulgaria* 41 D8

Yamuna →, *India* 69 G9
Yamunanagar, *India* 68 D7
Yamzho Yumco, *China* 60 D4
Yan, *Nigeria* 83 C7
Yana →, *Russia* 51 B14
Yanagawa, *Japan* 55 H5
Yanai, *Japan* 55 H6
Yan'an, *China* 56 F5
Yanbian, *China* 58 D3
Yanbu 'al Baḩr, *Si. Arabia* 70 F3
Yanchang, *China* 56 F6
Yancheng, *Henan, China* 56 H8
Yancheng, *Jiangsu, China* 57 H11
Yanchep Beach, *Australia* 93 F2
Yanchi, *China* 56 F4
Yanchuan, *China* 56 F6
Yanco, *Australia* 95 E4
Yanco Cr. →, *Australia* 95 F4
Yandoon, *Burma* 67 L19
Yanfeng, *China* 58 E3
Yanfolila, *Mali* 82 C3
Yang Xian, *China* 56 H4
Yang-Yang, *Senegal* 82 B1
Yangambi, *Dem. Rep. of the Congo* 86 B1
Yangbi, *China* 58 E2
Yangcheng, *China* 56 G7
Yangch'ü = Taiyuan, *China* 56 F7
Yangchun, *China* 59 F8
Yanggao, *China* 56 D7
Yanggu, *China* 56 F8
Yangjiang, *China* 59 G8
Yangliuqing, *China* 57 E9
Yangon = Rangoon, *Burma* 67 L20
Yangping, *China* 59 B8
Yangpingguan, *China* 56 H4
Yangquan, *China* 56 F7
Yangshan, *China* 59 E9
Yangshuo, *China* 59 E8
Yangtse = Chang Jiang →, *China* 59 B13
Yangtze Kiang = Chang Jiang →, *China* 59 B13
Yangxin, *China* 59 C10
Yangyang, *S. Korea* 57 E15
Yangyuan, *China* 56 D8
Yangzhong, *China* 59 A12
Yangzhou, *China* 59 A12
Yanhe, *China* 58 C7
Yanji, *China* 57 C15
Yanjin, *China* 58 C5
Yanjing, *China* 58 C2
Yankton, *U.S.A.* 112 D6
Yanonge, *Dem. Rep. of the Congo* 86 B1
Yanqi, *China* 60 B3
Yanqing, *China* 56 D8
Yanshan, *Hebei, China* 57 E9
Yanshan, *Jiangxi, China* 59 C11
Yanshan, *Yunnan, China* 58 F5
Yanshou, *China* 57 B15
Yantabulla, *Australia* 95 D4
Yantai, *China* 57 F11
Yanting, *China* 58 B5
Yantra →, *Bulgaria* 41 C9
Yanwa, *China* 58 D2
Yanyuan, *China* 58 D3
Yanzhou, *China* 56 G9
Yao Xian, *China* 56 G5
Yao Yai, Ko, *Thailand* 65 J2
Yao'an, *China* 58 E3
Yaodu, *China* 58 A5
Yaoundé, *Cameroon* 83 E7
Yaowan, *China* 57 G10
Yap I., *Pac. Oc.* 96 G5
Yapen, *Indonesia* 63 E9
Yapen, Selat, *Indonesia* 63 E9
Yapero, *Indonesia* 63 E9
Yappar →, *Australia* 94 B3
Yaqui →, *Mexico* 118 B2
Yar-Sale, *Russia* 50 C8
Yaraka, *Australia* 94 C3
Yaransk, *Russia* 48 B8
Yarbasan, *Turkey* 39 C10
Yardımcı Burnu, *Turkey* 39 E12
Yare →, *U.K.* 13 E9
Yaremcha, *Ukraine* 47 H3
Yarensk, *Russia* 50 C5
Yarfa, *Si. Arabia* 80 C4
Yarí →, *Colombia* 124 D4
Yarkand = Shache, *China* 60 C2
Yarker, *Canada* 111 B8
Yarkhun →, *Pakistan* 69 A5
Yarmouth, *Canada* 103 D6
Yarmūk →, *Syria* 75 C4
Yaroslavl, *Russia* 46 D10
Yarqa, W. →, *Egypt* 75 F2
Yarra Yarra Lakes, *Australia* 93 E2
Yarram, *Australia* 95 F4
Yarraman, *Australia* 95 D5
Yarras, *Australia* 95 E5
Yartsevo, *Sib., Russia* 51 C10
Yartsevo, *Smolensk, Russia* 46 E7
Yarumal, *Colombia* 124 B3
Yasawa Group, *Fiji* 91 C7
Yaselda, *Belarus* 47 F4
Yashi, *Nigeria* 83 C6
Yashikera, *Nigeria* 83 D5
Yashkul, *Russia* 49 G7
Yasin, *Pakistan* 69 A5
Yasinovataya, *Ukraine* 47 H9
Yasinski, L., *Canada* 102 B4
Yasinya, *Ukraine* 47 H3
Yasothon, *Thailand* 64 E5
Yass, *Australia* 95 E4
Yatağan, *Turkey* 39 D10
Yatakala, *Niger* 83 C5
Yates Center, *U.S.A.* 113 G7
Yathkyed L., *Canada* 105 A9
Yatsushiro, *Japan* 55 H5
Yatta Plateau, *Kenya* 86 C4
Yavari →, *Peru* 124 D4
Yávaros, *Mexico* 118 B3
Yavatmal, *India* 66 J11
Yavne, *Israel* 75 D3
Yavoriv, *Ukraine* 47 H2
Yavorov = Yavoriv, *Ukraine* 47 H2
Yavuzeli, *Turkey* 72 D7
Yawatahama, *Japan* 55 H6
Yawri B., *S. Leone* 82 D2
Yaxi, *China* 58 D6
Yazd, *Iran* 71 D7
Yazd □, *Iran* 71 D7
Yazd-e Khvāst, *Iran* 71 D7
Yazıköy, *Turkey* 39 E9
Yazman, *Pakistan* 68 E4
Yazoo →, *U.S.A.* 113 J9
Yazoo City, *U.S.A.* 113 J9
Ybbs, *Austria* 26 C8
Yding Skovhøj, *Denmark* 11 J3
Ye Xian = Laizhou, *China* 57 F10
Ye Xian, *China* 56 H7
Yebyu, *Burma* 64 E2
Yechŏn, *S. Korea* 57 F15
Yecla, *Spain* 33 G3
Yécora, *Mexico* 118 B3
Yedintsy = Edineţ, *Moldova* 43 B12
Yedseram →, *Nigeria* 83 C7
Yefremov, *Russia* 46 F10
Yeghegnadzor, *Armenia* 73 C11
Yegorlyk →, *Russia* 49 G5
Yegorlykskaya, *Russia* 49 G5
Yegoryevsk, *Russia* 46 E10
Yegros, *Paraguay* 126 B4
Yehuda, Midbar, *Israel* 75 D4
Yei, *Sudan* 81 G3
Yei, Nahr →, *Sudan* 81 F3
Yejmiadzin, *Armenia* 49 K7
Yekaterinburg, *Russia* 50 D7
Yekaterinodar = Krasnodar, *Russia* 49 H4
Yelabuga, *Russia* 48 C11
Yelan, *Russia* 48 E6
Yelarbon, *Australia* 95 D5
Yelatma, *Russia* 48 C5
Yelets, *Russia* 47 F10
Yélimané, *Mali* 82 B2
Yelizavetgrad = Kirovohrad, *Ukraine* 47 H7
Yell, *U.K.* 14 A7
Yell Sd., *U.K.* 14 A7
Yellow Sea, *China* 57 G12
Yellowhead Pass, *Canada* 104 C5
Yellowknife, *Canada* 104 A6
Yellowknife →, *Canada* 104 A6
Yellowstone →, *U.S.A.* 112 B3
Yellowstone L., *U.S.A.* 114 D8
Yellowstone National Park, *U.S.A.* 114 D9
Yelnya, *Russia* 46 E7
Yelsk, *Belarus* 47 G5
Yelwa, *Nigeria* 83 C5
Yemen ■, *Asia* 74 E3
Yen Bai, *Vietnam* 58 G5
Yenagoa, *Nigeria* 83 E6
Yenakiyeve, *Ukraine* 47 H10
Yenakiyevo = Yenakiyeve, *Ukraine* 47 H10
Yenangyaung, *Burma* 67 J19
Yenbo = Yanbu 'al Baḩr, *Si. Arabia* 70 F3
Yenda, *Australia* 95 E4
Yende Millimou, *Guinea* 82 D2
Yendéré, *Burkina Faso* 82 C4
Yendi, *Ghana* 83 D4
Yéni, *Niger* 83 C5
Yenice, *Ankara, Turkey* 72 C5
Yenice, *Aydın, Turkey* 39 D10
Yenice, *Çanakkale, Turkey* 39 B9
Yenice, *Edirne, Turkey* 41 F10
Yenice →, *Turkey* 72 D6
Yenifoça, *Turkey* 39 C8
Yenihisar, *Turkey* 39 D9
Yeniköy, *Bursa, Turkey* 41 F13
Yeniköy, *Çanakkale, Turkey* 39 B8
Yeniköy, *Kütahya, Turkey* 39 C11
Yenipazar, *Turkey* 39 D10
Yenisaía, *Greece* 41 E8
Yenişehir, *Turkey* 41 F13
Yenisey →, *Russia* 50 B9
Yeniseysk, *Russia* 51 D10
Yeniseyskiy Zaliv, *Russia* 50 B9
Yennádhi, *Greece* 36 C9
Yenne, *France* 21 C9
Yenotayevka, *Russia* 49 G8
Yenyuka, *Russia* 51 D13
Yeo →, *U.K.* 13 G5
Yeo, L., *Australia* 93 E3
Yeo I., *Canada* 110 A3
Yeola, *India* 66 J9
Yeoryioúpolis, *Greece* 36 D6
Yeovil, *U.K.* 13 G5
Yepes, *Spain* 34 F7
Yeppoon, *Australia* 94 C5
Yeráki, *Greece* 38 D4
Yerbent, *Turkmenistan* 50 F6
Yerbogachen, *Russia* 51 C11
Yerevan, *Armenia* 49 K7
Yerington, *U.S.A.* 114 G4
Yerkesik, *Turkey* 39 D10
Yerköy, *Turkey* 72 C6
Yermak, *Kazakstan* 50 D8
Yermo, *U.S.A.* 117 L10
Yerólakkos, *Cyprus* 36 D12
Yeropol, *Russia* 51 C17
Yeropótamos →, *Greece* 36 D6
Yeroskipos, *Cyprus* 36 E11
Yershov, *Russia* 48 E9
Yerushalayim = Jerusalem, *Israel* 75 D4
Yerville, *France* 18 C7
Yes Tor, *U.K.* 13 G4
Yesan, *S. Korea* 57 F14
Yeşilhisar, *Turkey* 72 C6
Yeşilırmak →, *Turkey* 72 B7
Yeşilkent, *Turkey* 72 D7
Yeşilköy, *Turkey* 41 F12
Yeşilova, *Turkey* 39 D11
Yeşilyurt, *Manisa, Turkey* 39 C10
Yeşilyurt, *Muğla, Turkey* 39 D10
Yesnogorsk, *Russia* 46 E9
Yeso, *U.S.A.* 113 H2
Yessentuki, *Russia* 49 H6
Yessey, *Russia* 51 C11
Yeste, *Spain* 33 G2
Yetman, *Australia* 95 D5
Yeu, Î. d', *France* 18 F4
Yevlakh = Yevlax, *Azerbaijan* 49 K8
Yevlax, *Azerbaijan* 49 K8
Yevpatoriya, *Ukraine* 47 K7
Yeya →, *Russia* 47 J10
Yeysk, *Russia* 47 J10
Yezd = Yazd, *Iran* 71 D7
Yezerishche, *Belarus* 46 E5
Yhati, *Paraguay* 126 B4
Yhú, *Paraguay* 127 B4
Yi →, *Uruguay* 126 C4
Yi 'Allaq, G., *Egypt* 75 E2
Yi He →, *China* 57 G10
Yi Xian, *Anhui, China* 59 C11
Yi Xian, *Hebei, China* 56 E8
Yi Xian, *Liaoning, China* 57 D11
Yialí, *Greece* 39 E9
Yialiás →, *Cyprus* 36 D12
Yi'allaq, G., *Egypt* 80 A3
Yialousa, *Cyprus* 36 D13
Yiáltra, *Greece* 38 C4
Yianisádhes, *Greece* 36 D8
Yiannitsa, *Greece* 40 F6
Yibin, *China* 58 C5
Yichang, *China* 59 B8
Yicheng, *Henan, China* 59 B9
Yicheng, *Shanxi, China* 56 G6
Yichuan, *China* 56 F6
Yichun, *Heilongjiang, China* 60 B7
Yichun, *Jiangxi, China* 59 D10
Yidu, *China* 57 F10
Yidun, *China* 58 B2
Yifag, *Ethiopia* 81 E4
Yifeng, *China* 59 C10
Yihuang, *China* 59 D11
Yijun, *China* 56 G5
Yıldız Dağları, *Turkey* 41 E11
Yıldızeli, *Turkey* 72 C7
Yiliang, *Yunnan, China* 58 D5
Yiliang, *Yunnan, China* 58 E4
Yilong, *China* 58 B6
Yimen, *China* 58 E4
Yimianpo, *China* 57 B15
Yinchuan, *China* 56 E4
Yindarlgooda, L., *Australia* 93 F3
Ying He →, *China* 56 H9
Ying Xian, *China* 56 E7
Yingcheng, *China* 59 B9
Yingde, *China* 59 E9
Yingjiang, *China* 58 E1
Yingjing, *China* 58 C4
Yingkou, *China* 57 D12
Yingshan, *Henan, China* 59 B9
Yingshan, *Hubei, China* 59 B10
Yingshan, *Sichuan, China* 58 B6
Yingshang, *China* 59 A11
Yingtan, *China* 59 C11
Yining, *China* 50 E9
Yinjiang, *China* 58 C7
Yinmabin, *Burma* 67 H19
Yiofiros →, *Greece* 36 D7
Yioúra, *Nótios Aiyaíon, Greece* 38 D6
Yioúra, *Thessalía, Greece* 38 B6
Yipinglang, *China* 58 E3
Yirba Muda, *Ethiopia* 81 F4
Yirga Alem, *Ethiopia* 81 F4
Yirol, *Sudan* 81 F3
Yirrkala, *Australia* 94 A2
Yishan, *China* 58 E7
Yishui, *China* 57 G10
Yíthion, *Greece* 38 E4
Yitiaoshan, *China* 56 F3
Yitong, *China* 57 C13
Yiwu, *China* 59 C13
Yixing, *China* 59 B12
Yiyang, *Henan, China* 56 G7
Yiyang, *Hunan, China* 59 C9
Yiyang, *Jiangxi, China* 59 C11
Yizhang, *China* 59 E9
Yizheng, *China* 59 A12
Yli-Kitka, *Finland* 8 C23
Ylitornio, *Finland* 8 C20
Ylivieska, *Finland* 8 D21
Yngaren, *Sweden* 11 F10
Yoakum, *U.S.A.* 113 L6
Yobe □, *Nigeria* 83 C7
Yog Pt., *Phil.* 63 B6
Yogan, *Togo* 83 D5
Yoğuntaş, *Turkey* 41 E11
Yogyakarta, *Indonesia* 63 G14
Yoho Nat. Park, *Canada* 104 C5
Yojoa, L. de, *Honduras* 120 D2
Yŏju, *S. Korea* 57 F14
Yokadouma, *Cameroon* 84 D2
Yokkaichi, *Japan* 55 G8
Yoko, *Cameroon* 83 D7
Yokohama, *Japan* 55 G9
Yokosuka, *Japan* 55 G9
Yokote, *Japan* 54 E10
Yola, *Nigeria* 83 D7
Yolaina, Cordillera de, *Nic.* 120 D3
Yoloten, *Turkmenistan* 71 B9
Yom →, *Thailand* 62 A2
Yonago, *Japan* 55 G6
Yonaguni-Jima, *Japan* 55 M1
Yŏnan, *N. Korea* 57 F14
Yonezawa, *Japan* 54 F10
Yong Peng, *Malaysia* 65 L4
Yong Sata, *Thailand* 65 J2
Yongamp'o, *N. Korea* 57 E13
Yong'an, *China* 59 E11
Yongcheng, *China* 56 H9
Yŏngch'ŏn, *S. Korea* 57 G15
Yongchuan, *China* 58 C5
Yongchun, *China* 59 E12
Yongde, *China* 58 E2
Yongdeng, *China* 56 F2
Yongding, *China* 59 E11
Yŏngdŏk, *S. Korea* 57 F15
Yŏngdŭngpo, *S. Korea* 57 F14
Yongfeng, *China* 59 D10
Yongfu, *China* 58 E7
Yonghe, *China* 56 F6
Yŏnghŭng, *N. Korea* 57 E14
Yongji, *China* 56 G6
Yongjia, *China* 59 C13
Yŏngju, *S. Korea* 57 F15
Yongkang, *Yunnan, China* 58 E2
Yongkang, *Zhejiang, China* 59 C13
Yongnian, *China* 56 F8
Yongning, *Guangxi Zhuangzu, China* 58 F7
Yongning, *Ningxia Huizu, China* 56 E4
Yongping, *China* 58 E2
Yongqing, *China* 56 E9
Yongren, *China* 58 D3
Yongshan, *China* 58 C4
Yongsheng, *China* 58 D3
Yongshun, *China* 58 C7
Yongtai, *China* 59 E12
Yŏngwŏl, *S. Korea* 57 F15
Yongxin = Jinggangshan, *China* 59 D10
Yongxing, *China* 59 D9
Yongxiu, *China* 59 C10
Yongzhou, *China* 59 D8
Yonibana, *S. Leone* 82 D2
Yonkers, *U.S.A.* 111 F11
Yonne □, *France* 19 E10
Yonne →, *France* 19 D9
York, *Australia* 93 F2
York, *U.K.* 12 D6
York, *Ala., U.S.A.* 113 J10
York, *Nebr., U.S.A.* 112 E6
York, *Pa., U.S.A.* 108 F7
York, C., *Australia* 94 A3
York, City of □, *U.K.* 12 D6
York, Kap, *Greenland* 4 B4
York, Vale of, *U.K.* 12 C6
York Haven, *U.S.A.* 110 F8
York Sd., *Australia* 92 C4
Yorke Pen., *Australia* 95 E2
Yorketown, *Australia* 95 F2
Yorkshire Wolds, *U.K.* 12 C7
Yorkton, *Canada* 105 C8
Yorkville, *U.S.A.* 116 G3
Yoro, *Honduras* 120 C2
Yoron-Jima, *Japan* 55 L4
Yorosso, *Mali* 82 C4
Yos Sudarso, Pulau = Dolak, Pulau, *Indonesia* 63 F9
Yosemite National Park, *U.S.A.* 116 H7
Yosemite Village, *U.S.A.* 116 H7
Yoshkar Ola, *Russia* 48 B8
Yŏsu, *S. Korea* 57 G14
Yotvata, *Israel* 75 F4
You Jiang →, *China* 58 F6
You Xian, *China* 59 D9
Youbou, *Canada* 116 B2
Youghal, *Ireland* 15 E4
Youghal B., *Ireland* 15 E4
Youkounkoun, *Guinea* 82 C2
Young, *Australia* 95 E4
Young, *Canada* 105 C7
Young, *Uruguay* 126 C4
Younghusband, L., *Australia* 95 E2
Younghusband Pen., *Australia* 95 F2
Youngstown, *Canada* 105 C6
Youngstown, *N.Y., U.S.A.* 110 C5
Youngstown, *Ohio, U.S.A.* 110 E4
Youngsville, *U.S.A.* 110 E5
Youngwood, *U.S.A.* 110 F5
Youxi, *China* 59 D12
Youyang, *China* 58 C7
Youyu, *China* 56 D7
Yozgat, *Turkey* 72 C6
Ypané →, *Paraguay* 126 A4
Yport, *France* 18 C7
Ypres = Ieper, *Belgium* 17 D2
Yreka, *U.S.A.* 114 F2
Yssingeaux, *France* 21 C8
Ystad, *Sweden* 11 J7
Ysyk-Köl, Ozero, *Kyrgyzstan* 50 E8
Ythan →, *U.K.* 14 D7
Ytterhogdal, *Sweden* 10 B8
Ytyk Kyuyel, *Russia* 51 C14
Yu Jiang →, *China* 58 F7
Yu Xian = Yuzhou, *China* 56 G7
Yu Xian, *Hebei, China* 56 E8
Yu Xian, *Shanxi, China* 56 E7
Yuan Jiang →, *Hunan, China* 59 C8
Yuan Jiang →, *Yunnan, China* 58 F4
Yuan'an, *China* 59 B8
Yuanjiang, *Hunan, China* 59 C9
Yuanjiang, *Yunnan, China* 58 F4
Yüanli, *Taiwan* 59 E13
Yüanlin, *Taiwan* 59 F13
Yuanling, *China* 59 C8
Yuanmou, *China* 58 E3
Yuanqu, *China* 56 G6
Yuanyang, *Henan, China* 56 G7
Yuanyang, *Yunnan, China* 58 F4
Yuba →, *U.S.A.* 116 F5
Yuba City, *U.S.A.* 116 F5
Yūbari, *Japan* 54 C10
Yubdo, *Ethiopia* 81 F4
Yūbetsu, *Japan* 54 B11
Yubo, *Sudan* 81 F2
Yucatán □, *Mexico* 119 C7
Yucatán, Canal de, *Caribbean* 120 B2
Yucatán, Península de, *Mexico* 98 H11
Yucatán Basin, *Cent. Amer.* 98 H11
Yucatan Str. = Yucatán, Canal de, *Caribbean* 120 B2
Yucca, *U.S.A.* 117 L12
Yucca Valley, *U.S.A.* 117 L10
Yucheng, *China* 56 F9
Yuci, *China* 56 F7
Yudu, *China* 59 E10
Yuechi, *China* 58 B6
Yuendumu, *Australia* 92 D5
Yueqing, *China* 59 C13
Yueqing Wan, *China* 59 D13
Yuexi, *Anhui, China* 59 B11
Yuexi, *Sichuan, China* 58 C4
Yueyang, *China* 59 C9
Yugan, *China* 59 C11
Yugoslavia ■, *Europe* 40 C4
Yuhuan, *China* 59 C13
Yuhuan Dao, *China* 59 C13
Yujiang, *China* 59 C11
Yukhnov, *Russia* 46 E8
Yukon →, *U.S.A.* 100 B3
Yukon Territory □, *Canada* 100 B6
Yüksekova, *Turkey* 73 D11
Yukta, *Russia* 51 C11
Yukuhashi, *Japan* 55 H5
Yulara, *Australia* 93 E5
Yule →, *Australia* 92 D2
Yuleba, *Australia* 95 D4
Yuli, *Nigeria* 83 D7
Yuli, *Taiwan* 59 F13
Yulin, *Guangxi Zhuangzu, China* 59 F8
Yülin, *Hainan, China* 65 C7
Yulin, *Shaanxi, China* 56 E5
Yuma, *Ariz., U.S.A.* 117 N12
Yuma, *Colo., U.S.A.* 112 E3
Yuma, B. de, *Dom. Rep.* 121 C6
Yumbe, *Uganda* 86 B3
Yumbi, *Dem. Rep. of the Congo* 86 C2
Yumen, *China* 60 C4
Yumurtalık, *Turkey* 72 D6
Yun Gui Gaoyuan, *China* 58 E3
Yun Ho →, *China* 57 E9
Yun Ling, *China* 58 D2
Yun Xian, *Hubei, China* 58 A8
Yun Xian, *Yunnan, China* 58 E3
Yuna, *Australia* 93 E2
Yunak, *Turkey* 72 C4
Yunan, *China* 59 F8
Yuncheng, *Henan, China* 56 G8
Yuncheng, *Shanxi, China* 56 G6
Yunfu, *China* 59 F9
Yungas, *Bolivia* 124 G5
Yungay, *Chile* 126 D1
Yunhe, *China* 59 C12
Yunkai Dashan, *China* 59 F8
Yunlin, *Taiwan* 59 F13
Yunlong, *China* 58 E2
Yunmeng, *China* 59 B9
Yunnan □, *China* 58 E4
Yunquera de Henares, *Spain* 32 E1
Yunt Dağı, *Turkey* 39 C9
Yunta, *Australia* 95 E2
Yunxi, *China* 56 H6
Yunxiao, *China* 59 F11
Yuping, *China* 58 D7
Yupyongdong, *N. Korea* 57 D15
Yuqing, *China* 58 D6
Yurga, *Russia* 50 D9
Yurimaguas, *Peru* 124 E3
Yuryev-Polskiy, *Russia* 46 D10
Yuryevets, *Russia* 48 B6
Yuryung Kaya, *Russia* 51 B12
Yuscarán, *Honduras* 120 D2
Yushan, *China* 59 C12
Yushanzhen, *China* 58 C7
Yushe, *China* 56 F7
Yushu, *Jilin, China* 57 B14
Yushu, *Qinghai, China* 60 C4
Yusufeli, *Turkey* 73 B9
Yutai, *China* 56 G9
Yutian, *China* 57 E9
Yuxarı Qarabağ = Nagorno-Karabakh, *Azerbaijan* 70 B5
Yuxi, *China* 58 E4
Yuyao, *China* 59 B13
Yuzawa, *Japan* 54 E10
Yuzha, *Russia* 48 B6
Yuzhno-Sakhalinsk, *Russia* 51 E15
Yuzhou, *China* 56 G7
Yvelines □, *France* 19 D8
Yverdon-les-Bains, *Switz.* 25 J2
Yvetot, *France* 18 C7
Yzeure, *France* 19 F10

Z

Zaanstad, *Neths.* 17 B4
Zāb al Kabīr →, *Iraq* 70 C4
Zāb aş Şagīr →, *Iraq* 70 C4
Žabalj, *Serbia, Yug.* 42 E5
Žabari, *Serbia, Yug.* 40 B5
Zabarjad, *Egypt* 80 C4

Zabaykalsk, *Russia* 51 E12
Zabki, *Poland* 45 F8
Ząbkowice Śląskie, *Poland* 45 H3
Žabljak, *Montenegro, Yug.* 40 C3
Zabłudów, *Poland* 45 F9
Żabno, *Poland* 45 H7
Zābol, *Iran* 71 D9
Zābolī, *Iran* 71 E9
Zabré, *Burkina Faso* 83 C4
Zábřeh, *Czech Rep.* 27 B9
Zabrze, *Poland* 45 H5
Zabzuga, *Ghana* 83 D5
Zacapa, *Guatemala* 120 D2
Zacapu, *Mexico* 118 D4
Zacatecas, *Mexico* 118 C4
Zacatecas □, *Mexico* 118 C4
Zacatecoluca, *El Salv.* 120 D2
Zachary, *U.S.A.* 113 K9
Zachodnio-Pomorskie □, *Poland* 44 E2
Zacoalco, *Mexico* 118 C4
Zacualtipán, *Mexico* 119 C5
Zadar, *Croatia* 29 D12
Zadawa, *Nigeria* 83 C7
Zadetkyi Kyun, *Burma* 65 G1
Zadonsk, *Russia* 47 F10
Zafarqand, *Iran* 71 C7
Zafora, *Greece* 39 E8
Zafra, *Spain* 35 G4
Żagań, *Poland* 45 G2
Zagaoua, *Chad* 79 E10
Žagarė, *Lithuania* 44 B10
Zagazig, *Egypt* 80 H7
Zāgheh, *Iran* 71 C6
Zaglivérion, *Greece* 40 F7
Zagnanado, *Benin* 83 D5
Zagorá, *Greece* 38 B5
Zagorje, *Slovenia* 29 B11
Zagórów, *Poland* 45 F4
Zagorsk = Sergiyev Posad, *Russia* 46 D10
Zagórz, *Poland* 45 J9
Zagreb, *Croatia* 29 C12
Zāgros, Kūhhā-ye, *Iran* 71 C6
Zagros Mts. = Zāgros, Kūhhā-ye, *Iran* 71 C6
Žagubica, *Serbia, Yug.* 40 B5
Zaguinaso, *Ivory C.* 82 C3
Zagyva →, *Hungary* 42 C5
Zāhedān, *Fārs, Iran* 71 D7
Zāhedān, *Sīstān va Balūchestān, Iran* 71 D9
Zahlah, *Lebanon* 75 B4
Zahna, *Germany* 24 D8
Záhony, *Hungary* 42 B7
Zainsk, *Russia* 48 C11
Zaïre = Congo →, *Africa* 84 F2
Zaječar, *Serbia, Yug.* 40 C6
Zaka, *Zimbabwe* 89 C5
Zakamensk, *Russia* 51 D11
Zakataly = Zaqatala, *Azerbaijan* 49 K8
Zakháro, *Greece* 38 D3
Zakhodnaya Dzvina = Daugava →, *Latvia* 9 H21
Zākhū, *Iraq* 70 B4
Zákinthos, *Greece* 38 D2
Zákinthos □, *Greece* 38 D2
Zakopane, *Poland* 45 J6
Zakroczym, *Poland* 45 F7
Zákros, *Greece* 36 D8
Zala, *Ethiopia* 81 F4
Zala □, *Hungary* 42 D1
Zala →, *Hungary* 42 D2
Zalaegerszeg, *Hungary* 42 D1
Zalakomár, *Hungary* 42 D2
Zalalövő, *Hungary* 42 D1
Zalamea de la Serena, *Spain* 35 G5
Zalamea la Real, *Spain* 35 H4
Zalău, *Romania* 42 C8
Žalec, *Slovenia* 29 B12
Zaleshchiki = Zalishchyky, *Ukraine* 47 H3
Zalew Wiślany, *Poland* 44 D6
Zalewo, *Poland* 44 E6
Zalingei, *Sudan* 79 F10
Zalishchyky, *Ukraine* 47 H3
Zama L., *Canada* 104 B5
Zambeke, *Dem. Rep. of the Congo* 86 B2
Zambeze →, *Africa* 87 F4
Zambezi = Zambeze →, *Africa* 87 F4
Zambezi, *Zambia* 85 G4
Zambezia □, *Mozam.* 87 F4
Zambia ■, *Africa* 87 F2
Zamboanga, *Phil.* 61 H5
Zambrów, *Poland* 45 F9
Zametchino, *Russia* 48 D6
Zamfara □, *Nigeria* 83 C6
Zamfara →, *Nigeria* 83 C5
Zamora, *Mexico* 118 D4
Zamora, *Spain* 34 D5
Zamora □, *Spain* 34 D5
Zamość, *Poland* 45 H10
Zamtang, *China* 58 A3
Zan, *Ghana* 83 D4
Záncara →, *Spain* 33 F1
Zandvoort, *Neths.* 17 B4
Zanesville, *U.S.A.* 110 G2
Zangābād, *Iran* 70 B5
Zangue →, *Mozam.* 87 F4
Zanjān, *Iran* 71 B6
Zanjān □, *Iran* 71 B6
Zanjān →, *Iran* 71 B6
Zannone, *Italy* 30 B6
Zante = Zákinthos, *Greece* 38 D2
Zanthus, *Australia* 93 F3
Zanzibar, *Tanzania* 86 D4
Zaouiet El-Kala = Bordj Omar Driss, *Algeria* 78 C7
Zaouiet Reggane, *Algeria* 78 C6
Zaoyang, *China* 59 A9
Zaozhuang, *China* 57 G9
Zap Suyu = Zāb al Kabīr →, *Iraq* 70 C4
Zapadna Morava →, *Serbia, Yug.* 40 C5
Zapadnaya Dvina = Daugava →, *Latvia* 9 H21
Zapadnaya Dvina, *Russia* 46 D7
Západné Beskydy, *Europe* 27 B12
Zapadni Rodopi, *Bulgaria* 40 E7
Západočeský □, *Czech Rep.* 26 B6
Zapala, *Argentina* 128 D2
Zapaleri, Cerro, *Bolivia* 126 A2
Zapata, *U.S.A.* 113 M5
Zapatón →, *Spain* 35 F4
Zaporizhzhya, *Ukraine* 47 J8
Zaporozhye = Zaporizhzhya, *Ukraine* 47 J8
Zaqatala, *Azerbaijan* 49 K8
Zara, *Turkey* 70 B3
Zaragoza, *Coahuila, Mexico* 118 B4
Zaragoza, *Nuevo León, Mexico* 119 C5
Zaragoza, *Spain* 32 D4
Zaragoza □, *Spain* 32 D4
Zarand, *Kermān, Iran* 71 D8
Zarand, *Markazī, Iran* 71 C6
Zărandului, Munţii, *Romania* 42 D7
Zaranj, *Afghan.* 66 D2
Zarasai, *Lithuania* 9 J22
Zarate, *Argentina* 126 C4
Zarautz, *Spain* 32 B2
Zaraysk, *Russia* 46 E10
Zard, Kūh-e, *Iran* 71 C6
Zāreh, *Iran* 71 C6
Zari, *Nigeria* 83 C7
Zaria, *Nigeria* 83 C6
Żarki, *Poland* 45 H6
Zárkon, *Greece* 38 B4
Zarneh, *Iran* 70 C5
Zărneşti, *Romania* 43 E10
Zarós, *Greece* 36 D6
Żarów, *Poland* 45 H3
Zarqā', Nahr az →, *Jordan* 75 C4
Zarrīn, *Iran* 71 C7
Zaruma, *Ecuador* 124 D3
Żary, *Poland* 45 G2
Zarza de Granadilla, *Spain* 34 E4
Zarzis, *Tunisia* 79 B8
Zas, *Spain* 34 B2
Zaskar →, *India* 69 B7
Zaskar Mts., *India* 69 C7
Zastron, *S. Africa* 88 E4
Žatec, *Czech Rep.* 26 A6
Zaterechnyy, *Russia* 49 H7
Zator, *Poland* 45 J6
Zavala, *Bos.-H.* 40 D1
Zavāreh, *Iran* 71 C7
Zave, *Zimbabwe* 89 B5
Zavetnoye, *Russia* 49 G6
Zavidovići, *Bos.-H.* 42 F3
Zavitinsk, *Russia* 51 D13
Zavodovski, I., *Antarctica* 5 B1
Zavolzhsk, *Russia* 48 B6
Zavolzhye, *Russia* 48 B6
Zawadzkie, *Poland* 45 H5
Zawichost, *Poland* 45 H8
Zawidów, *Poland* 45 G2
Zawiercie, *Poland* 45 H6
Zāwiyat al Baydā = Al Baydā, *Libya* 79 B10
Zâwyet Shammas, *Egypt* 80 A2
Zâwyet Um el Rakham, *Egypt* 80 A2
Zâwyet Ungeîla, *Egypt* 80 A2
Zāyā, *Iraq* 70 C5
Zāyandeh →, *Iran* 71 C7
Zaysan, *Kazakstan* 50 E9
Zaysan, Oz., *Kazakstan* 50 E9
Zayü, *China* 58 C1
Zazafotsy, *Madag.* 89 C8
Zázrivá, *Slovak Rep.* 27 B12
Zbarazh, *Ukraine* 47 H3
Zbąszyń, *Poland* 45 F2
Zbąszynek, *Poland* 45 F2
Zblewo, *Poland* 44 E5
Žďár nad Sázavov, *Czech Rep.* 26 B8
Zdolbuniv, *Ukraine* 47 G4
Ždrelo, *Serbia, Yug.* 40 B5
Zduńska Wola, *Poland* 45 G5
Zduny, *Poland* 45 G4
Zeballos, *Canada* 104 D3
Zebediela, *S. Africa* 89 C4
Zebila, *Ghana* 83 C4
Zeebrugge, *Belgium* 17 C3
Zeehan, *Australia* 94 G4
Zeeland □, *Neths.* 17 C3
Zeerust, *S. Africa* 88 D4
Zefat, *Israel* 75 C4
Zege, *Ethiopia* 81 E4
Zeggerene, Iracher, *Mali* 83 B5
Zégoua, *Mali* 82 C3
Zehdenick, *Germany* 24 C9
Zeil, Mt., *Australia* 92 D5
Zeila, *Somali Rep.* 74 E3
Zeist, *Neths.* 17 B5
Zeitz, *Germany* 24 D8
Żelechów, *Poland* 45 G8
Zelengora, *Bos.-H.* 40 C2
Zelenodolsk, *Russia* 48 C9
Zelenogorsk, *Russia* 46 B5
Zelenograd, *Russia* 46 D9
Zelenogradsk, *Russia* 9 J19
Zelenokumsk, *Russia* 49 H6
Železná Ruda, *Czech Rep.* 26 B6
Železnik, *Serbia, Yug.* 40 B4
Zelienople, *U.S.A.* 110 F4
Želiezovce, *Slovak Rep.* 27 C11
Zelina, *Croatia* 29 C13
Zell, *Baden-W., Germany* 25 H3
Zell, *Rhld-Pfz., Germany* 25 E3
Zell am See, *Austria* 26 D5
Zella-Mehlis, *Germany* 24 E6
Zelów, *Poland* 45 G6
Zeltweg, *Austria* 26 D7
Zémio, *C.A.R.* 86 A2
Zempléni-hegység, *Hungary* 42 B6
Zemplínska šírava, *Slovak Rep.* 27 C15
Zemun, *Serbia, Yug.* 40 B4
Zengbé, *Cameroon* 83 D7
Zengcheng, *China* 59 F9
Zenica, *Bos.-H.* 42 F2
Žepče, *Bos.-H.* 42 F3
Zeraf, Bahr ez →, *Sudan* 81 F3
Zerbst, *Germany* 24 D8
Żerków, *Poland* 45 F4
Zermatt, *Switz.* 25 J3
Zernez, *Switz.* 25 J6
Zernograd, *Russia* 49 G5
Zerqani, *Albania* 40 E4
Zestaponi, *Georgia* 49 J6
Zetel, *Germany* 24 B3
Zeulenroda, *Germany* 24 E7
Zeven, *Germany* 24 B5
Zevenaar, *Neths.* 17 C6
Zévio, *Italy* 28 C8
Zeya, *Russia* 51 D13
Zeya →, *Russia* 51 D13
Zeytinbaği, *Turkey* 41 F12
Zeytindağ, *Turkey* 39 C9
Zghartā, *Lebanon* 75 A4
Zgierz, *Poland* 45 G6
Zgorzelec, *Poland* 45 G2
Zgurița, *Moldova* 43 B13
Zhabinka, *Belarus* 47 F3
Zhailma, *Kazakstan* 50 D7
Zhambyl, *Kazakstan* 50 E8
Zhangaly, *Kazakstan* 49 G10
Zhangaqazaly, *Kazakstan* 50 E7
Zhangbei, *China* 56 D8
Zhangguangcai Ling, *China* 57 B15
Zhangjiakou, *China* 56 D8
Zhangping, *China* 59 E11
Zhangpu, *China* 59 E11
Zhangshu, *China* 59 C10
Zhangwu, *China* 57 C12
Zhangye, *China* 60 C5
Zhangzhou, *China* 59 E11
Zhanhua, *China* 57 F10
Zhanjiang, *China* 59 G8
Zhannetty, Ostrov, *Russia* 51 B16
Zhanyi, *China* 58 E4
Zhanyu, *China* 57 B12
Zhao Xian, *China* 56 F8
Zhao'an, *China* 59 F11
Zhaocheng, *China* 56 F6
Zhaojue, *China* 58 C4
Zhaoping, *China* 59 E8
Zhaoqing, *China* 59 F9
Zhaotong, *China* 58 D4
Zhaoyuan, *Heilongjiang, China* 57 B13
Zhaoyuan, *Shandong, China* 57 F11
Zharkovskiy, *Russia* 46 E7
Zhashkiv, *Ukraine* 47 H6
Zhashui, *China* 56 H5
Zhayyq →, *Kazakstan* 50 E6
Zhdanov = Mariupol, *Ukraine* 47 J9
Zhecheng, *China* 56 G8
Zhegao, *China* 59 B11
Zhejiang □, *China* 59 C13
Zheleznogorsk, *Russia* 47 F8
Zheleznogorsk-Ilimskiy, *Russia* 51 D11
Zheltyye Vody = Zhovti Vody, *Ukraine* 47 H7
Zhen'an, *China* 56 H5
Zhenba, *China* 58 A6
Zhenfeng, *China* 58 E5
Zheng'an, *China* 58 C6
Zhengding, *China* 56 E8
Zhenghe, *China* 59 D12
Zhengyang, *China* 59 A10
Zhengyangguan, *China* 59 A11
Zhengzhou, *China* 56 G7
Zhenhai, *China* 59 C13
Zhenjiang, *China* 59 A12
Zhenkang, *China* 58 F2
Zhenlai, *China* 57 B12
Zhenning, *China* 58 D5
Zhenping, *Henan, China* 56 H7
Zhenping, *Shaanxi, China* 58 B7
Zhenxiong, *China* 58 D5
Zhenyuan, *Gansu, China* 56 G4
Zhenyuan, *Guizhou, China* 58 D7
Zherdevka, *Russia* 48 E5
Zherong, *China* 59 D12
Zhetiqara, *Kazakstan* 50 D7
Zhezqazghan, *Kazakstan* 50 E7
Zhicheng, *China* 59 B8
Zhidan, *China* 56 F5
Zhigansk, *Russia* 51 C13
Zhigulevsk, *Russia* 48 D9
Zhijiang, *Hubei, China* 59 B8
Zhijiang, *Hunan, China* 58 D7
Zhijin, *China* 58 D5
Zhilinda, *Russia* 51 C12
Zhirnovsk, *Russia* 48 E7
Zhitomir = Zhytomyr, *Ukraine* 47 G5
Zhizdra, *Russia* 46 F8
Zhlobin, *Belarus* 47 F6
Zhmerinka = Zhmerynka, *Ukraine* 47 H5
Zhmerynka, *Ukraine* 47 H5
Zhob, *Pakistan* 68 D3
Zhob →, *Pakistan* 68 C3
Zhodino = Zhodzina, *Belarus* 46 E5
Zhodzina, *Belarus* 46 E5
Zhokhova, Ostrov, *Russia* 51 B16
Zhongdian, *China* 58 D2
Zhongdong, *China* 58 F6
Zhongdu, *China* 58 E7
Zhongning, *China* 56 F3
Zhongshan, *Guangdong, China* 59 F9
Zhongshan, *Guangxi Zhuangzu, China* 59 E8
Zhongtiao Shan, *China* 56 G6
Zhongwei, *China* 56 F3
Zhongxiang, *China* 59 B9
Zhongyang, *China* 56 F6
Zhoucun, *China* 57 F9
Zhouning, *China* 59 D12
Zhoushan, *China* 59 B14
Zhoushan Dao, *China* 59 C14
Zhouzhi, *China* 56 G5
Zhovti Vody, *Ukraine* 47 H7
Zhovtneve, *Ukraine* 47 J7
Zhovtnevoye = Zhovtneve, *Ukraine* 47 J7
Zhu Jiang →, *China* 59 F9
Zhuanghe, *China* 57 E12
Zhucheng, *China* 57 G10
Zhugqu, *China* 56 H3
Zhuhai, *China* 59 F9
Zhuji, *China* 59 C13
Zhukovka, *Russia* 46 F7
Zhumadian, *China* 56 H8
Zhuo Xian = Zhuozhou, *China* 56 E8
Zhuolu, *China* 56 D8
Zhuozhou, *China* 56 E8
Zhuozi, *China* 56 D7
Zhushan, *China* 59 A8
Zhuxi, *China* 58 A7
Zhuzhou, *China* 59 D9
Zhytomyr, *Ukraine* 47 G5
Zi Shui →, *China* 59 C9
Žiar nad Hronom, *Slovak Rep.* 27 C11
Zīārān, *Iran* 71 B6
Ziarat, *Pakistan* 68 D2
Zibo, *China* 57 F10
Zichang, *China* 56 F5
Zidarovo, *Bulgaria* 41 D11
Ziębice, *Poland* 45 H4
Zielona Góra, *Poland* 45 G2
Zierikzee, *Neths.* 17 C3
Ziesar, *Germany* 24 C8
Zifta, *Egypt* 80 H7
Zigey, *Chad* 79 F9
Zigong, *China* 58 C5
Ziguinchor, *Senegal* 82 C1
Zihuatanejo, *Mexico* 118 D4
Zijin, *China* 59 F10
Zile, *Turkey* 72 B6
Žilina, *Slovak Rep.* 27 B11
Žilinský □, *Slovak Rep.* 27 B12
Zillah, *Libya* 79 C9
Zillertaler Alpen, *Austria* 26 D4
Zima, *Russia* 51 D11
Zimapán, *Mexico* 119 C5
Zimba, *Zambia* 87 F2
Zimbabwe, *Zimbabwe* 87 G3
Zimbabwe ■, *Africa* 87 F3
Zimi, *S. Leone* 82 D2
Zimnicea, *Romania* 43 G10
Zimovniki, *Russia* 49 G6
Zinder, *Niger* 83 C6
Zinga, *Tanzania* 87 D4
Zingst, *Germany* 24 A8
Ziniaré, *Burkina Faso* 83 C4
Zinnowitz, *Germany* 24 A9
Zion National Park, *U.S.A.* 115 H7
Zirbitzkogel, *Austria* 26 D7
Zirc, *Hungary* 42 C2
Žiri, *Slovenia* 29 B11
Žirje, *Croatia* 29 E12
Zirl, *Austria* 26 D4
Zirndorf, *Germany* 25 F6
Ziros, *Greece* 36 D8
Zisterdorf, *Austria* 27 C9
Zitácuaro, *Mexico* 118 D4
Žitava →, *Slovak Rep.* 27 C11
Žitište, *Serbia, Yug.* 42 E5
Zitong, *China* 58 B5
Zítsa, *Greece* 38 B2
Zittau, *Germany* 24 E10
Zitundo, *Mozam.* 89 D5
Živinice, *Bos.-H.* 42 F3
Ziway, L., *Ethiopia* 81 F4
Zixi, *China* 59 D11
Zixing, *China* 59 E9
Ziyang, *Shaanxi, China* 56 H5
Ziyang, *Sichuan, China* 58 B5
Ziyuan, *China* 59 D8
Ziyun, *China* 58 E6
Zizhong, *China* 58 C5
Zlarin, *Croatia* 29 E12
Zlatar, *Croatia* 29 B13
Zlatar, *Serbia, Yug.* 40 C3
Zlataritsa, *Bulgaria* 41 C9
Zlaté Moravce, *Slovak Rep.* 27 C11
Zlatibor, *Serbia, Yug.* 40 C3
Zlatitsa, *Bulgaria* 41 D8
Zlatna, *Romania* 43 D8
Zlatna Panega, *Bulgaria* 41 C8
Zlatni Pyasŭtsi, *Bulgaria* 41 C12
Zlatograd, *Bulgaria* 41 E9
Zlatoust, *Russia* 50 D6
Zletovo, *Macedonia* 40 E6
Zlín, *Czech Rep.* 27 B10
Złocieniec, *Poland* 44 E3
Złoczew, *Poland* 45 G5
Zlot, *Serbia, Yug.* 40 B5
Złotoryja, *Poland* 45 G2
Złotów, *Poland* 44 E4
Zmeinogorsk, *Kazakstan* 50 D9
Żmigród, *Poland* 45 G3
Zmiyev, *Ukraine* 47 H9
Znamenka = Znamyanka, *Ukraine* 47 H7
Znamyanka, *Ukraine* 47 H7
Żnin, *Poland* 45 F4
Znojmo, *Czech Rep.* 26 C9
Zobeyrī, *Iran* 70 C5
Zobia, *Dem. Rep. of the Congo* 86 B2
Zoetermeer, *Neths.* 17 B4
Zogang, *China* 58 C1
Zogno, *Italy* 28 C6
Zogqên, *China* 58 A2
Zolochev = Zolochiv, *Ukraine* 47 H3
Zolochiv, *Ukraine* 47 H3
Zolotonosha, *Ukraine* 47 H7
Zomba, *Malawi* 87 F4
Zongo, *Dem. Rep. of the Congo* 84 D3
Zonguldak, *Turkey* 72 B4
Zongyang, *China* 59 B11
Zonqor Pt., *Malta* 36 D2
Zonza, *France* 21 G13
Zorgo, *Burkina Faso* 83 C4
Zorita, *Spain* 35 F5
Zorleni, *Romania* 43 D12
Zornitsa, *Bulgaria* 41 D10
Zorritos, *Peru* 124 D2
Żory, *Poland* 45 H5
Zorzor, *Liberia* 82 D3
Zossen, *Germany* 24 C9
Zou Xiang, *China* 56 G9
Zouan-Hounien, *Ivory C.* 82 D3
Zouar, *Chad* 79 D9
Zouérate = Zouîrât, *Mauritania* 78 D3
Zouîrât, *Mauritania* 78 D3
Zourika, *Niger* 83 B6
Zourma, *Burkina Faso* 83 C4
Zoushan Dao, *China* 59 B14
Zoutkamp, *Neths.* 17 A6
Zrenjanin, *Serbia, Yug.* 42 E5
Zuarungu, *Ghana* 83 C4
Zuba, *Nigeria* 83 D6
Zubayr, *Yemen* 81 D5
Zubtsov, *Russia* 46 D8
Zuénoula, *Ivory C.* 82 D3
Zuera, *Spain* 32 D4
Zufār, *Oman* 74 D5
Zug □, *Switz.* 25 H4
Zugdidi, *Georgia* 49 J5
Zugersee, *Switz.* 25 H4
Zugspitze, *Germany* 25 H6
Zuid-Holland □, *Neths.* 17 C4
Zuidbeveland, *Neths.* 17 C3
Zuidhorn, *Neths.* 17 A6
Zújar, *Spain* 35 H8
Zújar →, *Spain* 35 G5
Żukowo, *Poland* 44 D5
Zula, *Eritrea* 81 D4
Zülpich, *Germany* 24 E2
Zumaia, *Spain* 32 B2
Zumárraga, *Spain* 32 B2
Zumbo, *Mozam.* 87 F3
Zummo, *Nigeria* 83 D7
Zumpango, *Mexico* 119 D5
Zungeru, *Nigeria* 83 D6
Zunhua, *China* 57 D9
Zuni, *U.S.A.* 115 J9
Zunyi, *China* 58 D6
Zuo Jiang →, *China* 58 F6
Zuozhou, *China* 58 F6
Županja, *Croatia* 42 E3
Žur, *Kosovo, Yug.* 40 D4
Zurbātīyah, *Iraq* 70 C5
Zürich, *Switz.* 25 H4
Zürich □, *Switz.* 25 H4
Zürichsee, *Switz.* 25 H4
Zuromin, *Poland* 45 E6
Žut, *Croatia* 29 E12
Zutphen, *Neths.* 17 B6
Zuwārah, *Libya* 79 B8
Zūzan, *Iran* 71 C8
Žužemberk, *Slovenia* 29 C11
Zvenigorodka = Zvenyhorodka, *Ukraine* 47 H6
Zvenyhorodka, *Ukraine* 47 H6
Zverinogolovskoye, *Russia* 50 D7
Zvezdets, *Bulgaria* 41 D11
Zvishavane, *Zimbabwe* 87 G3
Zvolen, *Slovak Rep.* 27 C12
Zvonce, *Serbia, Yug.* 40 D6
Zvornik, *Bos.-H.* 42 F4
Zwedru = Tchien, *Liberia* 82 D3
Zweibrücken, *Germany* 25 F3
Zwenkau, *Germany* 24 D8
Zwettl, *Austria* 26 C8
Zwickau, *Germany* 24 E8
Zwierzyniec, *Poland* 45 H9
Zwiesel, *Germany* 25 F9
Zwoleń, *Poland* 45 G8
Zwolle, *Neths.* 17 B6
Zwolle, *U.S.A.* 113 K8
Zychlin, *Poland* 45 F6
Żyrardów, *Poland* 45 F7
Zyryan, *Kazakstan* 50 E9
Zyryanka, *Russia* 51 C16
Zyryanovsk = Zyryan, *Kazakstan* 50 E9
Żywiec, *Poland* 45 J6
Zyyi, *Cyprus* 36 E12

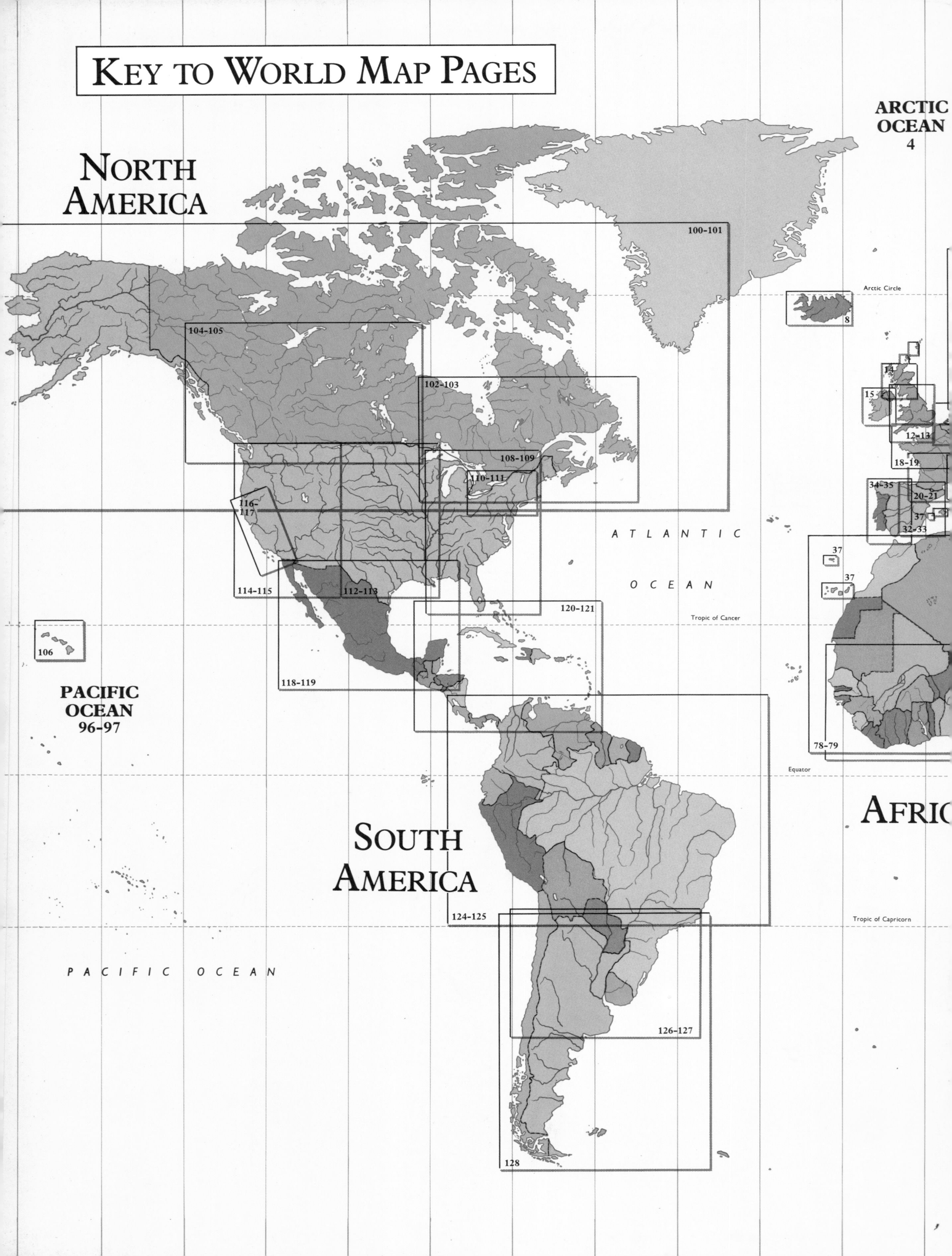

KEY TO WORLD MAP PAGES

NORTH AMERICA

ARCTIC OCEAN 4

Arctic Circle

PACIFIC OCEAN 96-97

106

100-101

104-105

102-103

108-109

110-111

116-117

114-115

112-113

120-121

118-119

8

14

15

12-13

18-19

34-35

20-21

37

32-33

37

37

78-79

ATLANTIC

OCEAN

Tropic of Cancer

Equator

SOUTH AMERICA

124-125

Tropic of Capricorn

126-127

AFRICA

PACIFIC OCEAN

128